LAW AND PUBLIC EDUCATION

CONTEMPORARY
LEGAL EDUCATION SERIES

LAW SCHOOL ADVISORY BOARD

CO-CHAIRS

Howard P. Fink
*Isadore and Ida Topper Professor
  of Law*
*The Ohio State University
College of Law*

Stephen A. Saltzburg
*Howrey Professor of Trial Advocacy,
  Litigation and Professional
  Responsibility*
*George Washington University
National Law Center*

MEMBERS

Charles B. Craver
*Leroy S. Merrifield Research Professor
  of Law*
*George Washington University
National Law Center*

Jane C. Ginsburg
*Morton L. Janklow Professor of
  Literary and Artistic
  Property Law*
Columbia University School of Law

Edward J. Imwinkelried
Professor of Law
*University of California at Davis
School of Law*

Daniel R. Mandelker
Howard A. Stamper Professor of Law
*Washington University
School of Law*

Mark V. Tushnet
Professor of Law
*Georgetown University
National Law Center*

Law and Public Education

CASES AND MATERIALS

Third Edition

STEPHEN R. GOLDSTEIN
Edward Silver Professor of Civil Procedure
Hebrew University of Jerusalem

E. GORDON GEE
President and Professor of Law
The Ohio State University

PHILIP T.K. DANIEL
Associate Professor, Educational Administration
Adjunct Professor of Law
The Ohio State University

MICHIE
Law Publishers
CHARLOTTESVILLE, VIRGINIA

COPYRIGHT © 1995
BY
MICHIE
A Division of Reed Elsevier Inc.

Library of Congress Catalog Card No. 95-81090
ISBN 1-55834-272-9

Printed in the United States of America
All rights reserved.

2000 Reprint

To Gert, Marcie, and Richard
— Professor Goldstein

To Constance and Rebekah
— President Gee

To Vesta, Asegai, and Thamret
— Professor Daniel

Preface

All three branches of government, legislative, executive, and judicial, play a significant role in shaping and influencing the enterprise of American public education. Certainly, since the decision in *Brown v. Board of Education*, the federal government has reformed educational policy, and much decision-making undertaken by local and state school officials has been litigated in the courts. This third edition of *Law and Public Education* represents the authors' efforts to keep pace with the changes in education and the dynamic impact the law has had on this transformation of authority. The changes have been substantial since the publication of the second edition in 1980 and, as a result, much of the current edition represents a rewriting of materials and the introduction of the most recent case law.

In focusing on the institution of public education, an education law course divides the law vertically and therefore intersects horizontal slices of the law, particularly administrative and constitutional law. *Law and Public Education* can thus serve as an advanced course of study in these areas, enabling students to develop further their analytical and critical skills by focusing on the application of general administrative and constitutional law principles to the particular institution of public education, and, it is hoped, providing occasions for them to rethink such principles in light of this analysis. The book can be used additionally as an introduction to these general areas of the law for students who have not yet been exposed to the horizontal courses. In view of the dynamic development of the challenging field of law, we offer this book to students, lawyers, educators, and others concerned with public education for study and analysis as an end in itself.

Although primarily a legal work, the book also contains historical, pedagogical, economic, and other social science literature as required to understand and analyze the subject matter. Three themes pervade these materials. The first concerns the decision-making process and the proper allocation of decision-making power among those who compete for it. The other two themes relate to the substance of the decisions made by this process: the conflicts involved in a liberal, democratic society seeking to inculcate values in its young; and the tensions that pervade a nation and an educational system torn between values of national unity, secularism and universalism on the one hand and the desire to preserve pluralism and enhance sectarian and parochial subgroup cultures and values on the other.

The cases and other materials in this book have generally been included in fuller versions than in many other casebooks, as we believe it important for the student to deal with the complexities, ambiguities, and nuances of meaning that can only be experienced when the cases are edited with a slight hand. Where substantive material has been removed from cases or other materials, the deletions are indicated. Citations and footnotes contained in cases and materials have, however, been eliminated without indication. Where such footnotes have been included, they retain their original numbers, enclosed in brackets. The editors' footnotes are indicated by asterisks. Some clearly typographical errors in cases or other materials have been corrected without indication.

The first edition of this book was written by Professor Goldstein while teaching at the University of Pennsylvania Law School. The following former students provided valuable research assistance in developing the first edition: Rita L. Bernstein, Ellen Josephson, Linda Lipton, Roderick R. McKelvie, Helen M. Pomerantz, Sherri E. Raiken, Stephen A. Saltzburg, Stephen J. Shapiro, and Diana J. Simon.

President Gee, who assumed major responsibility for the second edition of the book, would like to thank Jeanne Bryan, a former student at the J. Reuben Clark Law School, Brigham Young University, and Susan Marks, a former student at the West Virginia University College of Law, who acted as research assistants.

Professor Daniel and President Gee, who authored the third edition, extend appreciation for research assistance to Patrick Pauken, J.D., a Ph.D. student in both law and educational administration at The Ohio State University. They also thank Suzanne Cupp, Angela Doerschlag, Marianne L. Johnson, and Dina M. Minton for their contributions toward preparing the manuscript for publication.

Stephen R. Goldstein
E. Gordon Gee
Philip T.K. Daniel

Jerusalem, Israel
Columbus, Ohio

November, 1995

Summary Table of Contents

	Page
Preface	vii
Table of Contents	xiii
Table of Cases	1519

PART ONE

HISTORY, STRUCTURE, AND CURRICULUM

CHAPTER 1. HISTORY AND STRUCTURE OF AMERICAN PUBLIC
    EDUCATION 3
    A. Introduction 3
    B. Historical Development of American Education 5
    C. Current Structure of Public Education 11

CHAPTER 2. UNIVERSAL AND COMPULSORY EDUCATION 15
    A. Right of Universal Education 15
    B. Residence and Citizenship Requirements — Limitations
       on the Universal Right 24
    C. Compulsory Education 61

CHAPTER 3. CURRICULUM 89
    A. State and Local Control of Curriculum 89
    B. Constitutional Limitations on State and Local Control 91
    C. Parent Control of Curriculum 121
    D. Teacher Control of Curriculum 136

PART TWO

STUDENTS' RIGHTS AND RESPONSIBILITIES

CHAPTER 4. STUDENT CLASSIFICATION BY SEX, AGE, AND RACE 153
    A. Student Classification By Sex 153
    B. Student Classification By Age 215
    C. Student Classification By Race 222

CHAPTER 5. SCHOOL CONTROL OF STUDENT CONDUCT 249
    A. Student Conduct and School Authority 249
    B. Marriage, Motherhood, Pregnancy, and the Student 282
    C. Schools and Law Enforcement 296

CHAPTER 6. SCHOOL CONTROL OF STUDENT EXPRESSION 307
    A. Political and Other Student Expression 307
    B. Student Publications and Other School-Sponsored
       Student Activities 342

CHAPTER 7. PROCEDURAL PROBLEMS IN ENFORCING STUDENT CONDUCT AND STATUS RULES ... 381
A. Vagueness and the Need for Pre-existing Rules ... 381
B. Right to an Administrative Hearing ... 397
C. Search and Seizure ... 431

CHAPTER 8. SANCTIONS FOR BREACHES OF RULES ... 497
A. Suspensions and Expulsions ... 497
B. Corporal Punishment ... 526
C. Academic Sanctions ... 550

PART THREE
TEACHERS' RIGHTS AND RESPONSIBILITIES

CHAPTER 9. TEACHERS AND THE EMPLOYMENT RELATIONSHIP ... 563
A. Teacher Collective Bargaining ... 563
B. Hiring and Discharge ... 608

CHAPTER 10. THE TEACHER AS CITIZEN ... 701
A. School Control Over Teacher Expression ... 701
B. School Control of Teacher Conduct ... 755

PART FOUR
EQUAL EDUCATIONAL OPPORTUNITY

CHAPTER 11. RACIAL SEGREGATION IN THE PUBLIC SCHOOLS ... 771

CHAPTER 12. ABILITY GROUPING AND BILINGUAL EDUCATION ... 907
A. Ability Grouping and Tracking ... 907
B. Bilingual Education ... 953

CHAPTER 13. THE EDUCATION OF EXCEPTIONAL CHILDREN ... 977
A. Eligibility ... 979
B. Free Appropriate Public Education ... 988
C. Individualized Education Program ... 1003
D. Extended School Year Programs ... 1016
E. Least Restrictive Environment ... 1026
F. Related Services ... 1045
G. Idea and the Establishment Clause ... 1052
H. The "Stay-Put" Provision ... 1057
I. Remedies ... 1070
J. The Americans with Disabilities Act ... 1082
K. Gifted and Talented Students ... 1086

	Page
CHAPTER 14. FINANCING PUBLIC EDUCATION	1095

PART FIVE

CHURCH-STATE RELATIONS

CHAPTER 15. THE RELIGION CLAUSES AND PUBLIC EDUCATION 1185
    A. Religion and the Public School Curriculum 1185
    B. Released Time for Religious Instruction 1228
    C. Religious Objections to Public School Activities 1237

CHAPTER 16. ALTERNATIVES TO PUBLIC EDUCATION 1275
    A. Financing Private Schools for Public Benefit 1277
    B. Private Schools: Government Action and Racial Segregation 1334
    C. Educational Choice 1363

PART SIX

TORTS

CHAPTER 17. SUPERVISION AND TORT LIABILITY 1407
    A. Negligence and Strict Liability 1409
    B. Defenses to Negligence and Strict Liability 1444
    C. Tort Immunity 1470
    D. Defamation 1492

Index 1533

Table of Contents

	Page
Preface	vii
Summary Table of Contents	ix
Table of Cases	1519

PART ONE

HISTORY, STRUCTURE, AND CURRICULUM

CHAPTER 1. HISTORY AND STRUCTURE OF AMERICAN PUBLIC EDUCATION	3
A. Introduction	3
B. Historical Development of American Education	5
Massachusetts (Colony) Laws and Statutes ("Old Deluder Satan Act")	5
Colonial Records of the State of Georgia, compiled and published under authority of the Legislature by Candler	6
Jefferson, Notes on Virginia, in 4 Works of Thomas Jefferson (Jefferson's Explanation of his "Bill for the More General Diffusion of Knowledge")	6
Jefferson's Letter to Burwell in Padover, The Complete Jefferson	9
C. Current Structure of Public Education	11
1. The School District	11
2. The State Education Agency and Intermediate Units	12
3. The Fiscal Structure of Public Education	13
4. The Federal Government and Educational Policy	14
CHAPTER 2. UNIVERSAL AND COMPULSORY EDUCATION	15
A. Right of Universal Education	15
1. Foundations of the Right in Gaining an Understanding of the Present Structure of American Education	15
2. Expanding Boundaries of the Right — Educational Accountability	17
B.M. v. State of Montana	19
B. Residence and Citizenship Requirements — Limitations on the Universal Right	24
Plyler v. Doe	24
Orozco v. Sobol	36
Harrison v. Sobol	42
Lampkin v. District of Columbia	47
McCain v. Koch	55
C. Compulsory Education	61
Pierce v. Society of Sisters of the Holy Names of Jesus and Mary	61
Same v. Hill Military Academy	61
Wisconsin v. Yoder	65

	Page
CHAPTER 3. CURRICULUM	89
A. State and Local Control of Curriculum	89
1. State Prescribed Offerings	90
2. Board Policy, Curriculum Guides, and Lesson Plans	90
B. Constitutional Limitations on State and Local Control	91
Meyer v. State of Nebraska	91
Epperson v. Arkansas	96
Board of Education, Island Trees Union Free School District No. 26 v. Pico	103
Virgil v. School Board of Columbia County, Florida	116
C. Parent Control of Curriculum	121
State ex rel. Kelley v. Ferguson	121
Mozert v. Hawkins County Board of Education	124
D. Teacher Control of Curriculum	136
Parducci v. Rutland	136
Fowler v. Board of Education of Lincoln County, Kentucky	141

PART TWO

STUDENTS' RIGHTS AND RESPONSIBILITIES

CHAPTER 4. STUDENT CLASSIFICATION BY SEX, AGE, AND RACE	153
A. Student Classification By Sex	153
1. Academic Opportunities	153
Newberg v. Board of Public Education	153
Cannon v. University of Chicago	158
Sharif v. New York State Education Department	164
Garrett v. Board of Education of School District of City of Detroit	177
2. Athletics	187
Yellow Springs Exempted Village School District v. Ohio High School Athletic Association	187
Israel v. West Virginia Secondary Schools Activities Commission	202
3. Remedies	207
Franklin v. Gwinnett County Public Schools	207
B. Student Classification By Age	215
Arkansas Activities Association v. Meyer	215
C. Student Classification By Race	222
Regents of the University of California v. Bakke	224
Podberesky v. Kirwan	241
CHAPTER 5. SCHOOL CONTROL OF STUDENT CONDUCT	249
A. Student Conduct and School Authority	249
Flory v. Smith	249
Board of Education of Rogers, Arkansas v. McCluskey	253
Smith v. School City of Hobart	256

TABLE OF CONTENTS

	Page
Olesen v. Board of Education of School District No. 228	265
Harper v. Edgewood Board of Education	272
Fricke v. Lynch	275
B. Marriage, Motherhood, Pregnancy, and the Student	282
Street v. Cobb County School District	282
Pfeiffer v. Marion Center Area School District	287
C. Schools and Law Enforcement	296
Salazar v. Luty	296
Mitchell v. Board of Trustees of Oxford Municipal Separate School District	300

CHAPTER 6. SCHOOL CONTROL OF STUDENT EXPRESSION ... 307
  A. Political and Other Student Expression ... 307
    Tinker v. Des Moines Independent Community School District ... 307
    Frain v. Baron ... 319
    Bethel School District No. 403 v. Fraser ... 326
    Pyle v. South Hadley School Committee ... 332
    Boyd v. Board of Directors of McGehee School District No. 17 ... 334
    Crosby v. Holsinger ... 339
  B. Student Publications and Other School-Sponsored Student Activities ... 342
    Hazelwood School District v. Kuhlmeier ... 342
    Golub, *Tinker* to *Fraser* to *Hazelwood* — Supreme Court's Double Play Combination Defeats High School Students' Rally for First Amendment Rights: *Hazelwood School Dist. v. Kuhlmeier* ... 347
    Planned Parenthood of Southern Nevada, Inc. v. Clark County School District ... 352
    Duran v. Nitsche ... 362
    Poling v. Murphy ... 369
    Bartlett, The Closing of the School House Gates: Increasing Restrictions on the Public School Student's Exercise of Speech and Expression ... 376

CHAPTER 7. PROCEDURAL PROBLEMS IN ENFORCING STUDENT CONDUCT AND STATUS RULES ... 381
  A. Vagueness and the Need for Pre-existing Rules ... 381
    Soglin v. Kauffman ... 381
    Esteban v. Central Missouri State College ... 384
    Wiemerslage v. Maine Township High School District 207 ... 392
  B. Right to an Administrative Hearing ... 397
    1. Due Process Requirements ... 397
    Dixon v. Alabama State Board of Education ... 397
    Goss v. Lopez ... 405
    Gonzales v. McEuen ... 416

	Page
2. Liability of School Authorities for Failure to Provide Procedural Protections	425
Wood v. Strickland	425
C. Search and Seizure	431
New Jersey v. T.L.O.	432
1. Reasonable Suspicion	442
Edwards v. Rees	442
Cales v. Howell Public Schools	444
2. Individualized Suspicion	450
Webb v. McCullough	450
Burnham v. West	455
3. Locker Searches	463
Commonwealth v. Carey	463
4. Automobile Searches	466
State of Washington v. Slattery	466
5. "Sniff Searches"	469
Horton v. Goose Creek Independent School District	469
6. Strip Searches	477
Williams v. Ellington	477
7. Student Drug Testing	487
Schaill v. Tippecanoe County School Corporation	487

CHAPTER 8. SANCTIONS FOR BREACHES OF RULES 497
  A. Suspensions and Expulsions 497
      Daniel and Coriell, Suspension and Expulsion in America's Public
        Schools: Has Unfairness Resulted From a Narrowing of
        Due Process? 498
      1. Suspension 500
          Pollnow v. Glennon 500
          Smith v. Little Rock School District 505
      2. Expulsion 510
          Newsome v. Batavia Local School District 510
          Draper v. Columbus Public Schools 515
          Hawkins v. Coleman 520
  B. Corporal Punishment 526
      Ingraham v. Wright 526
      Garcia v. Miera 537
      Fee v. Herndon 543
  C. Academic Sanctions 550
      Slocum v. Holton Board of Education 550
      New Braunfels Independent School District v. Armke 554
      Katzman v. Cumberland Valley School District 556

TABLE OF CONTENTS

PART THREE

TEACHERS' RIGHTS AND RESPONSIBILITIES

	Page
CHAPTER 9. TEACHERS AND THE EMPLOYMENT RELATIONSHIP	563
A. Teacher Collective Bargaining	563
1. The "Right" to Bargain Collectively	563
Jersey Shore Area School District v. Jersey Shore Education Association	564
Texas State Teachers Association v. Garland Independent School District	571
2. Statutory Protections and Public Sector Bargaining	577
Abood v. Detroit Board of Education	577
Chicago Teachers Union, Local No. 1, AFT, AFL-CIO v. Hudson	589
Davis v. Henry	596
Babin, *Davis v. Henry*: One More Piece to the Public Employee Strike Rights Puzzle	604
B. Hiring and Discharge	608
1. Age	608
Geller v. Markham	608
2. Race	616
Wygant v. Jackson Board of Education	617
Krueth v. Independent School District No. 38, Red Lake, Minnesota	632
3. Citizenship	642
Ambach v. Norwick	642
4. Gender	646
Meritor Savings Bank, F.S.B. v. Vinson	648
Yatvin v. Madison Metropolitan School District	662
5. Religion	668
Ansonia Board of Education v. Philbrook	668
6. Disability	674
School Board of Nassau County, Florida v. Arline	674
Chalk v. United States District Court Central District of California	679
7. Due Process	687
Board of Regents v. Roth	687
Perry v. Sindermann	692
CHAPTER 10. THE TEACHER AS CITIZEN	701
A. School Control Over Teacher Expression	701
Pickering v. Board of Education	701
Mt. Healthy City School Board of Education v. Doyle	709
Connick v. Myers	716
Miles v. Denver Public Schools	727
Levin v. Harleston	739

	Page
B. School Control of Teacher Conduct	755
1. Outside the School	755
Keyishian v. Board of Regents	755
2. Inside the Classroom	764
Bradley v. Pittsburgh Board of Education	765

PART FOUR

EQUAL EDUCATIONAL OPPORTUNITY

CHAPTER 11. RACIAL SEGREGATION IN THE PUBLIC SCHOOLS	771
Brown v. Board of Education	771
Green v. County School Board	777
Swann v. Charlotte-Mecklenburg Board of Education	784
Keyes v. School District No. 1	797
Milliken v. Bradley	810
Dayton Board of Education v. Brinkman	818
Columbus Board of Education v. Penick	824
Board of Education of Oklahoma City Public Schools v. Dowell	852
Freeman v. Pitts	868
Dayton, Desegregation: Is the Court Preparing to Say It is Finished?	900
CHAPTER 12. ABILITY GROUPING AND BILINGUAL EDUCATION	907
A. Ability Grouping and Tracking	907
Hobson v. Hansen	907
McNeal v. Tate County School District	928
Quarles v. Oxford Municipal Separate School District	931
Larry P. v. Riles	939
Parents in Action on Special Education (PASE) v. Hannon	946
B. Bilingual Education	953
Lau v. Nichols	954
Castaneda v. Pickard	958
Martin Luther King Jr. Elementary School Children v. Ann Arbor School District	971
CHAPTER 13. THE EDUCATION OF EXCEPTIONAL CHILDREN	977
A. Eligibility	979
Timothy W. v. Rochester, New Hampshire School District	979
B. Free Appropriate Public Education	988
Board of Education of Hendrick Hudson Central School District v. Rowley	988
Polk v. Central Susquehanna Intermediate Unit 16	995
C. Individualized Education Program	1003
Doe v. Defendant I	1003

	Page
Lascari v. Board of Education of Ramapo Indian Hills Regional High School District	1008
D. Extended School Year Programs	1016
Cordrey v. Euckert	1016
E. Least Restrictive Environment	1026
Daniel R.R. v. State Board of Education	1026
Sacramento City Unified School District Board of Education v. Holland	1035
F. Related Services	1045
Irving Independent School District v. Tatro	1045
G. Idea and the Establishment Clause	1052
Zobrest v. Catalina Foothills School District	1052
H. The "Stay-Put" Provision	1057
Honig v. Doe	1057
Metropolitan School District of Wayne Township, Marion County, Indiana v. Davila	1064
I. Remedies	1070
School Committee of the Town of Burlington, Massachusetts v. Department of Education of Massachusetts	1070
John and Kathryn G. v. Board of Education of Mount Vernon Public Schools	1077
J. The Americans with Disabilities Act	1082
Wenkert, The Americans with Disabilities Act and Its Impact on Public Education	1082
K. Gifted and Talented Students	1086
Centennial School District v. Commonwealth Department of Education	1086
CHAPTER 14. FINANCING PUBLIC EDUCATION	1095
San Antonio Independent School District v. Rodriguez	1096
Robinson v. Cahill	1108
Stubbs, After *Rodriguez*: Recent Developments in School Finance Reform	1115
Abbott v. Burke	1118
Helena Elementary School District No. 1 v. State of Montana	1138
Edgewood Independent School District v. Kirby	1147
Rose v. Council for Better Education, Inc.	1155
Thro, The Role of Language of the State Education Clauses in School Finance Litigation	1175

PART FIVE

CHURCH-STATE RELATIONS

	Page
CHAPTER 15. THE RELIGION CLAUSES AND PUBLIC EDUCATION	1185
A. Religion and the Public School Curriculum	1185
1. Bible Reading and Prayer	1185
School District of Abington Township v. Schempp	1185
Wallace v. Jaffree	1191
2. General Restraints	1207
Lee v. Weisman	1207
Jones v. Clear Creek Independent School District	1217
B. Released Time for Religious Instruction	1228
McCollum v. Board of Education	1228
Zorach v. Clauson	1230
C. Religious Objections to Public School Activities	1237
Smith v. Board of School Commissioners of Mobile County	1237
West Virginia State Board of Education v. Barnette	1246
Aguilar v. Felton	1251
Board of Education of Kiryas Joel Village School District v. Grumet	1255
CHAPTER 16. ALTERNATIVES TO PUBLIC EDUCATION	1275
Mawdsley, Emerging Legal Issues in Nonpublic Education	1275
A. Financing Private Schools for Public Benefit	1277
1. Textbooks, Transportation and Other Special Services	1277
Everson v. Board of Education	1277
Wolman v. Walter	1284
2. Payment for Personnel Salaries, Tuition, and Other Tax Benefits	1300
Lemon v. Kurtzman	1300
Tilton v. Richardson	1308
Committee for Public Education v. Nyquist	1316
Mueller v. Allen	1325
B. Private Schools: Government Action and Racial Segregation	1334
Runyon v. McCrary	1334
Bob Jones University v. United States	1341
Allen v. Wright	1349
C. Educational Choice	1363
1. Public School Problems and Choice Proposals	1363
Jencks, Is the Public School Obsolete?	1363
Friedman, Capitalism and Freedom	1369
Tancredo, The Case for Vouchers	1375

	Page
Daniel, A Comprehensive Analysis of Educational Choice: Can the Polemic of Legal Problems be Overcome?	1378
2. Parental Choice	1389
Teachers, Inc. v. Smith	1389

PART SIX

TORTS

	Page
CHAPTER 17. SUPERVISION AND TORT LIABILITY	1407
A. Negligence and Strict Liability	1409
Roberts v. Robertson County Board of Education	1409
Levie, III v. Orleans Parish School Board	1420
Eisel v. Board of Education of Montgomery County	1423
Brownell v. Los Angeles Unified School District	1432
Mirand v. New York	1439
B. Defenses to Negligence and Strict Liability	1444
Hurlburt v. Noxon	1444
Brazell v. Board of Education of Niskayuna Public Schools	1449
Jarreau v. Orleans Parish School Board	1452
Arbegast v. Board of Education of South New Berlin Central School	1457
Goplerud, Liability of Schools and Coaches: The Current Status of Sovereign Immunity and Assumption of the Risk	1463
C. Tort Immunity	1470
Stoneking v. Bradford Area School District	1470
Valente, Liability for Teacher's Sexual Misconduct With Students — Closing and Opening Vistas	1479
Doe v. Escambia County School Board	1483
Parker v. Wynn	1485
Burns v. Board of Education of Stamford	1487
D. Defamation	1492
Brewer v. Rogers	1492
Freier v. Independent School District No. 197	1498
Kelley v. Bonney	1505
Index	1533

PART ONE

HISTORY, STRUCTURE, AND CURRICULUM

Chapter 1
HISTORY AND STRUCTURE OF AMERICAN PUBLIC EDUCATION

A. INTRODUCTION

The central concern of this book is with the legal problems involved in government-supported education below the college level. While this primarily means public education, elementary and secondary, Chapter 2 discusses compulsory education as applied to both public and private schools and Chapter 16 explores in cursory fashion some of the problems involved in government support of private schools as alternatives to the public school system. Legal issues involving colleges are also discussed where such discussion may be relevant to exposing and exploring arguably similar issues involving elementary and secondary education.

In exploring the law and public education, the book focuses primarily on the allocation of decision-making power over public education among competing groups and individuals, *e.g.*, school boards, school administrators, teachers, students, parents, community leaders, federal and state administrative agencies, legislators, and courts, and the institutional structuring of educational decision-making power.

The legal power of various individuals and groups to control educational decision-making is a central issue in the interface of law and education. Decision-making by bodies charged with the administration of public education is one of the most significant areas of law in terms of its effects on the lives of individuals and groups in American society. Although figures do not tell the whole story, they do illuminate at least part of the enormous significance of educational decision-making in American society.

The latest available figures show that in the United States a total of 37,150,456 students attend public schools, of which 26,459,776 are in elementary and intermediate schools and 10,690,680 in high schools. Moreover, there are 2,431,000 teachers engaged in public education and we as a nation spend in excess of $250 billion annually to support public elementary and secondary education in some 16,661 school districts.*

Intimately connected with the issue of who wields educational decision-making power is the issue of what kind of power can be exerted through the educational

---

*The preceding figures as to students are contained in *School Enrollment — Social and Economic Characteristics of Students*, U.S. Dep't of Commerce, Bureau of Statistics, 10 (1992). The figures for teachers, the annual budget, and the numbers of school districts and schools are from the *Digest of Educational Statistics*, National Ctr. for Educ. Statistics, U.S. Dep't of Educ., 149 (1992).

structure. For example, how much power can and has society given the educational establishment to inculcate values in the next generation? How much is the educational structure designed to foster assimilationism and nationalism norms as opposed to fostering pluralism and subgroup autonomy norms? These questions go to the heart of the American societal structure.

In attempting to grapple with the varied and complex problems presented by the United States public education system, legislators and judges frequently seek guidance from the historical foundations of the present system. Their search of America's past may be of quite a cursory nature, but its effect on the approaches ultimately chosen to resolve current policy questions is important for the student of education law to note.

This chapter contains the first American statute concerning public education, a law making it a crime to teach Black and American Indian slaves, two excerpts from the writings of Thomas Jefferson, a brief outline of American education history, and a description of the current governmental structure of our public education bureaucracy. These readings highlight some of the premises of American educational policy makers and should present you with an idea of the individuals and groups — parents, teachers, administrators, students, communities, legislatures, courts, etc., who compete for educational decision-making power and whose interests determine the structure and direction of the United States public school system.

As you read this and subsequent chapters, reflect on the questions suggested by the readings that follow:

1. What is the nature of education? Is it a process concerned only with the development of cognitive skills and techniques of problem solving, or is it also a mechanism through which the present generation attempts to inculcate future generations with its traditions — morality, customs and modes of thought, political, social and economic beliefs? Does not a society require some transmission of values and traditions? Is such a process of transmission inevitable? Indeed, is the choice not to inculcate values a form of inculcation?

2. If our schools do not attempt to transmit society's values, will some other institution do so? Is this a role which is required to be filled by some institution? Should the answer depend upon the ability of institutions to perform this role? Will this vary with the receptivity of the young at different political, economic, and social time periods?

3. If there is to be a transmission of traditions in the classroom, what are the respective roles of the state, the local school board or superintendent, the principal, the teacher, and the parent in determining what and how the traditions are to be transmitted? Do students have an affirmative part in this process?

4. Are the traditions and values discussed above national, state, local, community or familial? What is the place of sectarian or parochial (racial, ethnic, or religious) traditions in American education? What is the place of universal, secular and national traditions in our schools? Are the schools to be used as an integrative societal device to further a more homogeneous society? Are the

schools also to be used to achieve egalitarian values? What do we mean by egalitarian in this context — equal attainment by all students, meritocratic reward based on equal access to resources producing unequal attainment, or something else? Do goals either of equality or national integration posit norms of all children equally benefitting from the educational structure, of equal resources being expended on each child, of racial, ethnic, religious, or social class-integrated education?

5. How has American education historically addressed these questions? Are the historic answers valid today for all parts of the public school system? For some? For none? Can we ignore the historic answers in working with today's educational structure?

B. HISTORICAL DEVELOPMENT OF AMERICAN EDUCATION

Massachusetts (Colony) Laws and Statutes, ch. 88, (1647) ("Old Deluder Satan Act")

Sec. 1. It being one chief project of Satan to keep men from the knowledge of the scripture, as in former times keeping them in unknown tongues so in these latter times by persuading from the use of tongues, that so at least the true sense and meaning of the original might be clouded and corrupted with false glosses of deceivers; to the end that learning may not be buried in the graves of our forefathers, in church and commonwealth, the Lord assisting our endeavors;

It is therefore ordered by this court and authority thereof, that every township within this jurisdiction, after the Lord hath increased them to the number of fifty householders, shall then forthwith appoint one within their towns to teach all such children as shall resort to him to write and read, whose wages shall be paid either by the parents or masters of such children, or by the inhabitants in general, by way of supply, as the major part of those that order the prudentials of the town shall appoint; provided that those who send their children be not oppressed by paying much more than they can have them taught for in other towns.

Sec. 2. And it is further ordered, that where any town shall increase to the number of one hundred families or householders, they shall set up a grammar school, the master thereof being able to instruct youth so far as they may be fitted for the university; and if any town neglect the performance hereof above one year, then every such town shall pay five pounds per annum to the next such school, till they shall perform this order.

Sec. 3. Forasmuch as it greatly concerns the welfare of this country, that the youth thereof be educated, not only in good literature, but in sound doctrine:

This court doth therefore commend it to the serious consideration and special care of our overseers of the college, and the selectmen in the several towns, not to admit or suffer any such to be continued in the office or place of teaching, educating, or instructing youth or children in the college or schools, that have manifested themselves unsound in the faith, or scandalous in their lives, and have not given satisfaction according to the rules of Christ.

Colonial Records of the State of Georgia, compiled and published under authority of the Legislature by Allen D. Candler, Vol. 18 (1904-1910), pp. 108-09, 136.

[B]e it Enacted ... that all Negroes, Indians, Mulatos (*sic*) or Mestizos who now are or shall hereafter be in this Province and all their issue and offspring born or to be born shall be and they are hereby declared to be and remain for ever hereafter absolute slaves and shall follow the condition of the mother and shall be deemed in law to be chattels personal in the hands of their owners and possessors and their executors, administrators and assigns....

....

And whereas the having of slaves taught to write or suffering them to be employed in writing may be attended with great Inconveniencys (*sic*), be it therefore enacted by the authority [of the state of Georgia], that all and every person and persons whatsoever who shall hereafter teach or cause any slave or slaves to be taught to write or shall use or employ any slave or slaves as a scribe in any manner of writing whatsoever hereafter taught to write, every such person and persons shall for every such offense forfeit the sum of fifteen pounds sterling.

Jefferson, Notes On Virginia, in Four Works of Thomas Jefferson (Federal Edition 1904), pp. 60-65 (Jefferson's Explanation of his "Bill for the More General Diffusion of Knowledge")

Another object of the revisal is, to diffuse knowledge more generally through the mass of the people. This bill proposes to lay off every country into small districts of five or six miles square, called hundreds and in each of them to establish a school for teaching reading, writing, and arithmetic. The tutor to be supported by the hundred, and every person in it entitled to send their children three years gratis, and as much longer as they please, paying for it. These schools to be under a visitor who is annually to chuse the boy of best genius in the school, of those whose parents are too poor to give them further education, and to send him forward to one of the grammar schools, of which twenty are proposed to be erected in different parts of the country, for teaching Greek, Latin, geography, and the higher branches of numerical arithmetic. Of the boys thus sent in any one year, trial is to be made at the grammar schools one or two years, and the best genius of the whole selected, and continued six years, and the residue dismissed. By this means twenty of the best geniuses will be raked from the rubbish annually, and be instructed, at the public expence, so far as the grammar schools go. At the end of six years instruction, one half are to be discontinued (from among whom the grammar schools will probably be supplied with future masters); and the other half, who are to be chosen for the superiority of their parts and disposition, are to be sent and continued three years in the study of such sciences as they shall chuse, at William and Mary college, the plan of which is proposed to be enlarged, as will be hereafter explained, and extended to all the useful sciences. The ultimate result of the whole scheme of education would be the teaching all the children of the State reading, writing, and common arithmetic; turning out ten annually, of superior genius, well taught in Greek, Latin, geography, and the higher branches of arithmetic; turning out ten others annually, of still superior parts, who, to those branches of learning, shall have added such of the sciences as their genius shall have them led to; the furnishing to the wealthier part of the people convenient schools at which their children may be educated at their own expence. — The general objects of this law are to provide an education adapted to the years, to the capacity, and the condition of every one, and directed to their freedom and happiness. Specific details were not proper for the law. These must be the business of the visitors entrusted with its execution. The first stage of this education being the schools of the hundreds, wherein the great mass of the people will receive their instruction, the principal foundations of future order will be laid here. Instead, therefore, of putting the Bible and Testament into the hands of the children at an age when their judgments are not sufficiently matured for religious inquiries, their memories may here be stored with the most useful facts from Grecian, Roman, European, and American history. The first elements of morality too may be instilled into their minds; such as, when further developed as their judgments advance in strength, may teach them how to work out their own greatest happiness, by shewing them that it does not depend on the condition of life in which chance has placed them, but is always the result of a good conscience, good health, occupation, and freedom in all just pursuits. — Those whom either the wealth of their parents or the adoption of the state shall destine to higher degrees of learning, will go on to the grammar schools, which constitute the next stage, there to be instructed in the languages. The learning Greek and Latin, I am told, is going into disuse in Europe. I know not what their manners and occupations may call for: but it would be very ill-judged in us to follow their example in this instance. There is a certain period of life, say from eight to fifteen or sixteen years of age, when the mind like the body is not yet firm enough for laborious and close operations. If applied to such, it falls an early victim to premature exertion; exhibiting, indeed, at first, in these young and tender subjects, the flattering appearance of their being men while they are yet children, but ending in reducing them to be children when they should be men. The memory is then most susceptible and tenacious of impressions; and the learning of languages being chiefly a work of memory, it seems precisely fitted to the powers of this period, which is long enough too for acquiring the most useful languages, antient and modern. I do not pretend that language is science. It is only an instrument for the attainment of science. But that time is not lost which is employed in providing tools for future operation: more especially as in this case the books put into the hands of the youth for this purpose may be such as will at the same time impress their minds with useful facts and good principles. If this period be suffered to pass in idleness, the mind becomes lethargic and impotent, as would the body it inhabits if unexercised during the same time. The sympathy between body and mind during their rise, progress and decline, is too strict and obvious to endanger our being misled while we reason from the one to the other. — As soon as they are of sufficient age, it is supposed they will be sent on from the grammar schools to the university, which constitutes our third and last stage, there to study those sciences which may be adapted to their views. — By that part of our plan which prescribes the selection of the youths of genius from among the classes of the poor, we hope to avail the state of those talents which nature has shown as liberally among the poor as the rich, but which perish without use, if not sought for and cultivated. — But of all the views of this law none is more important, none more legitimate, than that of rendering the people the safe, as they are the ultimate, guardians of their own liberty. For this purpose the reading in the first stage, where they will receive their whole education, is proposed, as has been said, to be chiefly historical. History, by apprising them of the past, will enable them to judge of the future; it will avail them of the experience of other times and other nations; it will qualify them as judges of the actions and designs of men; it will enable them to know ambition under every disguise it may assume; and knowing it, to defeat its views. In every government on earth is some trace of human weakness, some germ of corruption and degeneracy, which cunning will discover, and wickedness insensibly open, cultivate and improve. Every government degenerates when trusted to the rulers of the people alone. The people themselves therefore are its only safe depositories. And to render even them safe, their minds must be improved to a certain degree. This indeed is not all that is necessary, though it be essentially necessary. An amendment of our constitution must here come in aid of the public education. The influence over government must be shared among all the people. If every individual which composes their mass participates of the ultimate authority, the government will be safe; because the corrupting the whole mass will exceed any private resources of wealth; and public ones cannot be provided but by levies on the people. In this case every man would have to pay his own price. The government of Great Britain has been corrupted, because but one man in ten has a right to vote for members of parliament. The sellers of the government, therefore, get nine-tenths of their price clear. It has been thought that corruption is restrained by confining the right of suffrage to a few of the wealthier of the people: but it would be more effectually restrained by an extension of that right to such members as would bid defiance to the means of corruption.

B. HISTORICAL DEVELOPMENT OF AMERICAN EDUCATION

Jefferson's Letter to N. Burwell in K. Padover, The Complete Jefferson (1943), p. 1085 (Jefferson's idea about education for girls in the year 1818).

[Education for girls should be that which] might enable them, when they become mothers, to educate their own daughters, and even to direct the course for sons, should their fathers be lost, or incapable or inattentive.

Although, as with other institutions, the origins and development of American public education are not free from doubt and controversy, the following is a brief sketch of the broad outline of this development.

The early English settlers in the colonies brought with them a heritage of English education that was centered around family, community and church. All three of these educated primarily through natural, informal processes of socializing the young into the world of their elders. The role of formal schooling was quite limited and markedly utilitarian in training people for assumed social roles. It was almost exclusively supported by private funds. The entire system was predicated on the belief that the society consisted of an integrated, unified, and essentially static culture, whose main functions were conducted by interconnected vehicles of family, local community, and church.

This societal view, however, was seriously changed by the move to the New World with the resultant breakdown in the traditional English family life. Professor Bailyn, in his book, Education in the Forming of American Society 22-23 (Norton Pub. ed. 1970), attributes this to the following factors:

> a. The strange, forbidding nature of the wilderness and its new problems which the older generation had no greater expertise than the younger in confronting, and indeed, the younger, not shackled by past experiences, may have even been in a better position to confront.
>
> b. Parental prestige humbled by manual labor, by food scarcity, and by the need to subdivide large households;
>
> c. The economic independence presented by abundant land so that young adults could leave the family and stand on their own.

The breakdown in the role of the family produced legislation in all colonies requiring children to obey parents and providing sanctions for disobedience. It also produced education laws of which the Massachusetts Statute of 1647, quoted above, was the first and paradigm. Note the need for formal, community supported education for the basic moral end of avoiding Satan and the cultural end of preventing learning from being "buried in the graves of our forefathers." Other significant factors in colonial education included a growth in the bargaining power of apprentices due to the open land and labor shortage which resulted in greater requirements for masters to see to the nonvocational education of their apprentices by placing them in schools, and the increased development of sectarian schools as churches turned to education as a means of obtaining and retaining adherents to replace the former means of legal coercion or pressures from a close knit community. Finally, as Jefferson's statement indicates, there was the growing pressure of democratic government as a postulate for universal education, at least of a minimum level. Note, however, that the legacy of slavery and discrimination continued in that several states, especially those in the south, had no public schooling for African-Americans until well into the 20th century. For further discussion of the colonial period in American education, *see* B. Bailyn, *supra* and L.A. Cremin, American Education: The Colonial Experience, 1607-1783 (1970). *See also* J.D. Anderson, The Education of Blacks in the South: 1860-1935 (1988) and P. T.K. Daniel, A History of Discrimination Against Students in Chicago Secondary Schools, 20 History of Education Quarterly 147 (1980).

Although the colonial period produced the beginning of the American system of public education and following the Revolution a number of states incorporated public education provisions in their constitutions, it was not until the 1820s that the movement for "common schools" began. The "common school," *i.e.*, a school funded by public money and controlled by public authorities which is attended by all children, rich and poor, has been termed the "uniquely American contribution" to the idea of public education. *See* M. Mayer, The Schools, p. 39 (1963). Prior to the development of common schools under the leadership of Horace Mann, first Secretary of the Massachusetts State Board of Education, the publicly supported schools had been mainly of poor quality and for poor children, with the wealthy going to the better private schools. The dream of the common school movement was that the public schools would be of the highest quality and attended by all children who chose, or whose parents chose for them, to attend school.

The common school was still voluntary, however, with the majority of American children not attending any school until schooling became compulsory. Massachusetts in 1852 was the first state to adopt a compulsory school law. It was not until the late nineteenth century and the early twentieth century that compulsory education became universal in the United States.

For some additional information concerning the history and structure of public education, *see* the following recent publications: J. Spring, American Education, (1994); G. Willis, et al., The American Curriculum: A Documentary History (1992); C. Kaestle, Pillars of the Republic (1983); D. Ravitch, The Troubled Crusade (1983); L. Cremin, American Education: The National Experience (1980); D. Tyack, The One Best System; A History of American Urban Education (1974).

In recent years American public education has been under attack from many quarters and a good part of this book is concerned with the legal ramifications of such attacks. A sampling of some of the more provocative works, not already cited in this chapter, include: J. Spring, The American School: 1642-1993 (1994); J. Kozol, Savage Inequalities (1991); J. Rury, Education and Women's

Work: Female Schooling and the Division of Labor in Urban America (1991); S. De Castell et al. (eds.), Literacy, Society and Schooling: A Reader (1986); D. Nasaw, Schooled to Order: A Social History of Public Schooling in the U.S. (1980); S. Bowles and H. Gintis, Schooling in Capitalist America (1976).

C. CURRENT STRUCTURE OF PUBLIC EDUCATION

There are approximately 59,258 elementary and 20,120 secondary public schools. There are also 5,278 "alternative schools" designed essentially for disabled students, students with discipline problems or other traits that are sometimes better served in less traditional settings. These 83,656 institutions are organized into 16,661 school districts. The organization and control of the public school systems under the various state education codes is generally vested in a three-tiered administrative structure. There is also federal government involvement.

1. THE SCHOOL DISTRICT

Forming the base of the structure is the local school district, the most numerous unit of local government. It has quasi-corporate powers, is controlled by a governing board, in the majority of cases has taxing power, and may or may not employ a superintendent. Some states, such as Nebraska and Illinois, are divided into more than a thousand districts. Hawaii, on the other hand, has only one. As an instrumentality of the state, the local district implements state policy. However, the opportunity for local school board control of the management and operations of the schools is great, as its statutory grant of power usually states that the function of the board in providing a public education is "to do anything not inconsistent with this act."

Approximately 90 percent of all local school board members are elected. However, in districts with populations over 500,000, more than half of all board members are appointed. *See generally* P. First & H. Walberg (eds.), School Boards: Changing Local Control (1992). Except in the larger cities board members are not paid. The board's functions are essentially policy oriented. They oversee the implementation of state decisions and determine the local educational budget, programs, salaries, facility requirements, etc. The line, however, between the policy-determining functions of the laymen board members and the administrative duties of their chief executives, the superintendents, is often somewhat less than precise. In any case, as chief executive officer, the local superintendent is charged with the responsibility for the efficient management and effective organization and administration of the district schools. The local school district also acts as a taxing unit. Currently, on a national basis approximately 44.1 percent of the expenditures for public education are raised through local taxation.

2. THE STATE EDUCATION AGENCY AND INTERMEDIATE UNITS

The major components of the state education agency or department of education are: (1) the state board of education, (2) the chief state school officer, and (3) the state department of education staff. Forty-nine states, all except Wisconsin, have a state board of education. The average board has seven members. They are appointed by the governor in 34 states, directly elected in nine, and either elected by local school districts or appointed by the legislature in the rest. The chief state school officer, usually the Superintendent of Public Instruction or Commissioner of Education, is appointed by the state board of education in 24 states, directly elected in 21, and appointed by the governor in the other five.

Most state boards, in addition to exercising general control over the elementary and secondary schools of the state, formulate educational policies for the state, recommend needed legislation, develop a state education budget, and appoint staff members to the department. Unlike the local boards, the state board of education is not a taxing authority, and therefore must depend on the legislature for funds to operate the department of education, the professional arm of the state agency. The department's administrative organization properly reflects the various areas of decision-making at the state level. The responsibilities of the state agency can be separated into five basic areas.

First, it is responsible for the state educational program. That is, it defines the scope of the enterprise, certain minimum standards, and often the course of study. Second, it is responsible for state schools such as special schools for orphans or the disabled, community colleges and often the state universities. In a number of states, however, there are multiple boards to meet these specialized needs. Third, it exercises certification control over personnel at all levels in the system. Fourth, it exercises some control over local school facilities, including establishment of plant standards, and approval of plans, specifications and sites. Finally, the state agency must oversee the distribution of funds to local schools. In most states, the financial controls imposed on the school districts — limitations upon a district's borrowing capacity, tax rate restrictions, required budget presentations, and even state assessment practices — are stipulated by the legislature. Therefore, while the state agency supervises the allocation of funds, it rarely exercises any extensive discretionary power. Approximately 47.3 percent of the money for public education on a national basis derives from statewide sources.

Twenty-seven states have a three-echelon structure with an office or agency in an intermediate position between the state department of education and the local districts. The units are governed in 14 states by an elected board, and in 11 states by an elected county superintendent. South Carolina has appointed boards and New Jersey has appointed superintendents.

The status of these intermediate units has long been a source of controversy in educational administration circles. Their duties are relatively vague. In Illinois,

C. CURRENT STRUCTURE OF PUBLIC EDUCATION

for example, the county superintendent's responsibilities include "to inspect and survey all public schools under his or her supervision," Ill. St. Ch. 105 Sec. 5/3-14.21 (1994); "exercise supervision and control over all schools," Ill. St. Ch. 105 Sec. 5/3-14.2 (1994); "to labor in every practical way to elevate the standards of teaching and to improve the condition of the common schools of his county," Ill. St. Ch. 105 Sec. 5/3-14.9 (1994). In practice the intermediate units have taken on the role of resource personnel. They offer curricular, management, and purchasing services. Their greatest impact has been in coordinating and supplementing the efforts of the smaller districts.

3. THE FISCAL STRUCTURE OF PUBLIC EDUCATION

All levels of government contribute to public school financing. Approximately 44.1 percent of school revenues comes from local sources, 47.3 percent from the states, and 6.2 percent from the federal government. Moreover, approximately 2.5 percent of the financial support of public education emanates from private sources. For the most part these are in-kind gifts to school districts from private industry for such items as computers and other equipment. The real property tax provides almost all locally raised school revenues. The tax, attacked by some as an unfair measure of ability to pay, has failed to generate sufficient income to adequately meet increasing costs of school finance, particularly in cities where the tax base has diminished or failed to keep pace with other rising costs. Furthermore, variations in the per-pupil amount of assessed valuation among the districts of the states have contributed to inequalities of "educational opportunity." *See* Chapter 14, *infra*, for a discussion of judicial responses to tax-generated inequalities.

State aid to education has addressed these problems. Originally, state aid took the form of flat grants, its major purpose being to supplement generally inadequate local resources. More recently, recognition of the differing abilities of local school districts to raise adequate funds has led to various attempts to equalize, at least at some minimal level, the educational opportunities of all the students within a given state. Some states require that all districts assess a certain mill levy. If that tax does not generate sufficient revenue to meet a minimum or foundation level of financing, usually based on a predetermined dollar amount per student, the state subsidizes the district to the minimum amount. Some other states have open-end, or shared-cost, equalization plans. Those states determine the individual district's ability to pay, based on the amount of assessed property value per student in the district, and assign the district responsibility for a percentage of school revenue. The state then matches all local monies raised.

Federal government participation in school funding includes subsidy to the school lunch program and impact aid to districts which contain federal tax exempt lands, an important source of financial relief in the western states. In recent years, federal aid has increased significantly, often taking the form of categorical aid with attached conditions, alleviating in some measure the increasing financial pressures on state and local governments, but raising the specter of unwanted federal control.

For a wide-ranging discussion of the history and present structure of public school finance, *see* R. Johns, E. Morphet, K. Alexander, The Economics and Financing of Education (1983).

4. THE FEDERAL GOVERNMENT AND EDUCATIONAL POLICY

Early in the history of the United States a system of shared governance was established with virtual control of education eventually falling under the aegis of the states. While the United States Congress is not directly empowered to enact legislation regulating education, all forms of government must adhere to the dictates of the U.S. Constitution, especially those amendments prohibiting discrimination. Hence, the federal government has promulgated legislation that has a direct bearing on educational policy.

Federal directives now influence school practices in employment, curriculum, extra-curricular activities and discipline. Under Title VI of the Civil Rights Act of 1964, Title VII of the Act as amended in 1972, Title IX of the Education Amendments of 1972, Section 504 of the Rehabilitation Act of 1973, the Education for All Handicapped Children's Act of 1975 (renamed the Individuals with Disabilities Education Act in 1990) and the Americans with Disabilities Act of 1990, all federally assisted education systems, *i.e.*, all public school districts, must comply or face possible legal action and loss of funding.

The direction of education, then, has been made subject to the taxing and spending power of the Congress with approximately 500 federal programs in the area of education administered through federal agencies. For fiscal year 1993, $68.4 billion was spent by these agencies for K-12 public schools, higher education institutions and private schools. Of this figure, $30.7 billion or 45% came from the U.S. Office of Education. Significant amounts also came from the Department of Health and Human Services ($11.3 billion), the Department of Agriculture ($8.3 billion), the Department of Defense ($4.0 billion), the Department of Labor ($3.9 billion) and the Department of Energy ($2.8 billion).

Chapter 2
UNIVERSAL AND COMPULSORY EDUCATION

A. RIGHT OF UNIVERSAL EDUCATION

1. FOUNDATIONS OF THE RIGHT IN GAINING AN UNDERSTANDING OF THE PRESENT STRUCTURE OF AMERICAN EDUCATION

> Today, education is perhaps the most important function of state and local governments. Compulsory school attendance laws and the great expenditures for education both demonstrate our recognition of the importance of education to our democratic society. It is required in the performance of our most basic public responsibilities, even service in the armed forces. It is the very foundation of good citizenship. Today it is a principal instrument in awakening the child to cultural values, in preparing him for later professional training, and in helping him to adjust normally to his environment. In these days, it is doubtful that any child may reasonably be expected to succeed in life if he is denied the opportunity of an education. Such an opportunity, where the state has undertaken to provide it, is a right which must be made available to all on equal terms. *Brown v. Board of Education*, 347 U.S. 483, 493 (1954).

It is important to recognize that all states have developed a norm of universal right to education. The most obvious illustration of this norm is the existence of compulsory attendance laws in all states. Mississippi was the last state to mandate compulsory education. Legislation in 1987 requires children to attend public or private school until they are fourteen. (*see* Miss. Code Ann. § 37-13-91 (1990)). This legislation restored compulsory education, which was repealed in the 1950s, apparently in response to school desegregation fears.

In addition to these compulsory attendance laws there are state constitutional and legislative provisions that provide for universal public education. Virtually every one of these provisions authorizes the legislature to establish and maintain a system of free public education. A number of these provisions explicitly state that these free public schools shall be open to all children in the state.... Finally, pursuant to these constitutional mandates, state legislatures have established public schools which, in accordance with statutes, are usually open to all resident children between certain ages, with only narrowly drawn exceptions, *e.g.*, N.Y. Educ. Law § 3202 (1970 and Supp. 1978):

> A person over five and under twenty-one years of age is entitled to attend the public schools maintained in the district or city in which such person resides without the payment of tuition.

As indicated by the New York statute, the ages during which a child *may* go to school are much more inclusive than those during which he/she *must* go to school. In most states the compulsory attendance requirement is from seven to sixteen. The permissive age normally begins at age six and extends to age 21. Thus, the norm of universal public education is broader than the compulsory education mandate, including within its bounds all students who have a positive legal right to attend school.

As stated by the California Supreme Court in *Ward v. Flood*, 48 Cal. 36, 50, 17 Am. R. 405, 410 (1874):

> The advantage or benefit thereby vouchsafed to each child, of attending public school is therefore, one derived and secured to it under the highest sanction of positive law. It is therefore, a right — a legal right — as distinctively so as the vested right in property owned is a legal right, and as such is protected, and entitled to be protected by all the guarantees by which other legal rights are protected and secured to the possessor.

A judicially enforceable legal right to education may not, however, flow directly from the state constitution. For example, in *State ex rel. Shineman v. Board of Educ.*, 152 Neb. 644, 42 N.W.2d 168 (1950), plaintiffs brought a mandamus action seeking to compel a local school board to provide instruction for five-year-olds. The Nebraska Constitution provides:

> The legislature shall provide for the free instruction in the common schools of this state of all persons between the ages of five and twenty-one years. Art. VII, § 6.

The state supreme court found the provision directed to the legislature and therefore not self-executing; it is not complete in itself and could not become operative without the aid of supportive or enabling legislation.

Much of the legislation passed to maintain these systems of free public education and the litigation that results from them deal with school finance. Is there a fundamental right to public school education? *See San Antonio Indep. Sch. Dist. v. Rodriguez*, 411 U.S. 1 (1973), in which the Supreme Court held that wealth is not a suspect class in the context of scrutinizing educational disparities under the equal protection clause of the fourteenth amendment and, as such, differential funding of school districts in the same state is not unconstitutional. While supporting the significance of education to individual citizens and society, the Court ruled that education was neither an explicitly, nor implicitly, protected right under the Constitution. Federal court rulings, notwithstanding, the issue of education as a right protected in the states has continued unabated since *Rodriguez*. *See* Chapter 14 for a rendering of the case law in school finance equity issues. In *Robinson v. Cahill*, 62 N.J. 473, 306 A.2d 65 (1973), decided eleven days after the decision in *Rodriguez*, the New Jersey Supreme Court held the method of financing schools in that state, based in part on local taxation, violated the New Jersey constitutional provision requiring the legislature to

A. RIGHT OF UNIVERSAL EDUCATION

"provide for the maintenance and support of a thorough and efficient system of free public schools for the instruction of all children in this state between the ages of five and eighteen years" in that it resulted in grossly different expenditure levels among school districts in the state. Like *Rodriguez*, however, the court refused to hold that education is a fundamental right. (*See also Abbott v. Burke*, 575 A.2d 359 (N.J. 1990), another New Jersey case that held similarly.)

Despite not finding a fundamental right to education, the courts have recognized education as an important function of state and local government. In quoting *Brown v. Board of Educ.*, as above, the *Rodriguez* court stated that "what was said there in the context of racial discrimination has lost none of its vitality with the passage of time," 411 U.S. 1, 29 (1973). "Nothing this Court holds today in any way detracts from our historical dedication to public education." *Id.* at 30. Whether it is segregated school systems in the 1950's with *Brown* or inadequate and inequitable funding programs decades later with *Cahill*, *Abbott*, and *Rodriguez*, the right to education heads the list as one of the most important school issues.

For discussions on the right to education under both state and federal constitutions, *see* Hubsch, *The Emerging Right to Education under State Constitutional Law*, 65 Temple L. Rev. 1325 (1992) and Walsh, *Education as a Fundamental Right under the United States Constitution*, 29 Willamette L. Rev. 279 (1993).

2. EXPANDING BOUNDARIES OF THE RIGHT — EDUCATIONAL ACCOUNTABILITY

In *Peter W. v. San Francisco Unified Sch. Dist.*, 60 Cal. App. 3d 814, 131 Cal. Rptr. 854 (1976), the plaintiff, a high school graduate, brought a tort action against public authorities who operated and administered the public school system in which he had been "inadequately" educated. After spending twelve years in the school district, the student could read only at a fifth grade level. His alleged injury was "permanent disability and inability to gain meaningful employment." *Id.* at 818. The court ruled that the plaintiff had failed to state a cause of action for negligence and noted two distinct public policy considerations dictating against imposition of a duty of care:

> 1. "[T]he achievement of literacy in the schools, or its failure, [is] influenced by a host of factors which affect the pupil subjectively, from outside the formal teaching process, and beyond the control of its ministers. They may be physical, neurological, emotional, cultural, environmental; they may be present but not perceived, recognized but not identified." *Id.* at 824.
>
> 2. "To hold [schools] to an actionable 'duty of care,' in the discharge of their academic functions, would expose them to tort claims — real or imagined — of disaffected students and parents in countless numbers.... The

ultimate consequences, in terms of public time and money, would burden them — and society — beyond calculation." *Id.* at 824.

Courts have decided similarly in cases brought at the higher education level. In *Ross v. Creighton Univ.*, 740 F. Supp. 1319 (N.D. Ill. 1990), a former basketball player complained that the university rendered inadequate instructional aid relating to reading problems and that emotional distress resulted from this. The court ruled against the tort claims of educational malpractice and negligent infliction of emotional distress. In its holding, the court spoke of judicial deference to education decisions involving instruction and admission indicating that the athlete did not criticize the quality of instruction, but instead questioned, because of his disadvantaged academic background, whether he should have ever been admitted to the university and, if so, whether the institution had a duty to educate him and not just support him as an athlete. The court responded by reiterating judicial deference to education decisions:

> It must be remembered that education is a service rendered on an immensely greater scale than other professional services. If every failed student could seek tort damages against any teacher, administrator and school he feels may have shortchanged him at some point in his education, the courts could be deluged and shut down. *Id.* at 1328.
>
> ....
>
> To allow [the student] to recover ... would ... endanger the admissions prospects of thousands of marginal students, as schools scrambled to factor into their admissions calculations whether a potentially "negligent factor" now could cost unforeseeable tort damages later. The Court should not and will not craft a new tort for [this student]. *Id.* at 1330.

The *Ross* decision was affirmed by the Seventh Circuit Court of Appeals in 1992. *See Ross v. Creighton Univ.*, 957 F.2d 410 (7th Cir. 1992).

Can "educational malpractice" be compared with medical malpractice? That question was raised by the dissent in *Donohue v. Copiague Sch. Dist.*, 64 App. Div. 2d 29, 407 N.Y.S.2d 874 (1978), *aff'd*, 47 N.Y.2d 440 (1979), a case in which the school had neglected to test a student whose performance fell within statutory guidelines for "under-achievement" and to prescribe an appropriate course of study: "[T]he negligence alleged in the case at bar is not unlike that of a doctor who, although confronted with a cancerous condition, fails to pursue medically accepted procedures to (1) diagnose the specific condition and (2) treat the condition, and instead allows the patient to suffer the inevitable consequences of the disease." *Id.* at 44. The majority, however, refused to recognize "educational malpractice" as a cause of action. Given the issue raised in dissent, how might the majority have distinguished it from medical malpractice?

Court opinions also indicate that various other theories of educational liability may succeed. Again, in *Peter W.*, the plaintiff's second count alleged intentional or negligent misrepresentation to the plaintiff's parent that the plaintiff was performing at or near grade level in basic academic skills such as reading and writing. Although the court refused to recognize the possibility of stating a cause of action for negligent misrepresentation, it held that a cause of action for intentional misrepresentation could be stated, if facts were pleaded showing the requisite element of reliance. What questions does this raise as to the school's responsibility in reporting student progress to parents? Is the teacher who will fail no one, or whose curve is skewed toward "A's" and "B's," liable for negligent or intentional misrepresentation if a child is discovered not to be performing at the level indicated by the teacher?

Another theory of liability was recognized in *Pierce v. Board of Educ.*, 44 Ill. App. 3d 324, 358 N.E.2d 67 (1976), where an appellate court in Illinois reversed a motion to dismiss. In that case, parents of the minor-plaintiff had notified the school that family physicians had recommended the boy be transferred into special education or learning disabilities classes. The school neither transferred the boy nor undertook its own testing. The court held that the school's nonfeasance could amount to an "intentional breach of duty" and that the board could be liable for the minor's resultant emotional injuries. *Id.* at 69. Can this case be distinguished from *Peter W.*? Is the court's characterization of the breach as "intentional" a sufficient explanation?

For further discussion of the issue of education malpractice, *see* John Collis, Educational Malpractice (Michie, 1990), detailing reported and unreported cases in this area as well as other references regarding the subject matter. *See also* Brown and Cannon, *Educational Malpractice Actions: A Remedy for What Ails Our Schools?*, 78 Educ. L. Rep. 643 (1993); Jurenas, *Will Educational Malpractice Be Revived?*, 74 Educ. L. Rep. 449 (1992); Culhane, *Reinvigorating Educational Malpractice Claims: A Representative Focus*, 67 Wash. L. Rev. 349 (1992); Davis, *Examining Educational Malpractice Jurisprudence: Should a Cause of Action Be Created for Student-Athletes?*, 69 Denv. U. L. Rev. 57 (1992).

B.M. v. STATE OF MONTANA

Supreme Court of Montana
200 Mont. 58, 649 P.2d 425 (1982)

SHEA, JUSTICE:

B.M., a minor, through her foster mother, appeals from summary judgment.... The child's claim for damages arises from her placement in a special education program when she was six years old.

The child's complaint alleged that the State was negligent in placing her in such a program and that the alleged misplacement violated her constitutional rights of due process and equal protection....

The child's foster mother contends here that the trial court erred in ruling that the State was immune from negligence actions arising from the administration of special education programs in public schools. She further argues that the trial court erred in holding that the State owes no legal duty of care toward students who are negligently misplaced in special education programs. We reverse the trial court and hold that the State is not protected by immunity and that the State has a duty to use due care in placing students in special education programs. The question of whether the State breached that duty of care and whether the breach was the cause of any injury raise material questions of fact for which a trial is necessary. We further hold, however, that the trial court properly dismissed the claims that the child's due process and equal protection rights were violated. No facts were alleged sufficient to allege a constitutional violation.

The child was born in 1967 and at nine months of age was placed in the foster home of Fred and Leona Burger. While in kindergarten in Nashua, Montana, she displayed learning difficulties, apparently the result of a speech problem. In January 1973, upon the recommendation of Superintendent of Schools Sam Gramlich, and with the consent of her foster father, the child was tested by psychologist William Jones of the Eastern Montana Regional Mental Health Center.

As a result of this testing, Jones recommended that the child either repeat her year in kindergarten or receive special educational help. The school officials decided that state funds would be sought for a special education program for first graders, including the child.

An application and plan were submitted to the office of the Superintendent of Public Instruction outlining the needs of the children for special help. On the application, the child was classified as "educable mentally retarded (EMR)." To be eligible under State policy for EMR status, absent sufficient written justification, a student must have an individual learning aptitude score of 50 to 75. (Special Education Handbook; Program Procedures and Guidelines for Children and Youth With Learning Handicaps, § III, B, February 1973 (Handbook).) The child's overall IQ was determined to be 76.

The State superintendent approved the application and the program was started in September 1973. The program intended for this "primary educable class" was a "team-teaching situation." The four children in the program were to attend the regular first grade classroom, but their special education teacher was also to give them the special help and support needed "without segregating and labeling them." Of the four children in this program, only the child involved here was not mentally retarded.

... After five weeks, the child and the other three EMR students in the special program were found to be easily distracted and were moved to the "resource room" for their morning classes. This constituted approximately 40 percent of their daily classroom time, the rest of the day being spent as before. While in the resource room, the newly hired teacher taught the children with the same materials, but at a slower pace. The foster parents were not told of this change in the program.

The foster mother learned that the child was in the segregated classroom only after the child had been attending classes there for nine weeks. The foster mother

A. RIGHT OF UNIVERSAL EDUCATION

immediately removed the child from the program and the school officials then abruptly terminated the program. It was during this nine week period that the foster mother claims she witnessed a dramatic worsening in the child's behavior. For example, the child refused to dress herself and refused to eat properly. The foster mother then filed suit as a result of this alleged misplacement of the child in the segregated classroom for the mentally retarded.

Sovereign Immunity

The trial court held the State's acts were not subject to judicial review because they were discretionary. The Montana Constitution (Art. II, § 18), abolishes sovereign immunity except in situations where the legislature, by a two-thirds vote, enacts contrary legislation. Section 2-9-102, MCA, enacted to give meaning to this constitutional provision provides: "Every governmental entity is subject to liability for its torts and those of its employees acting within the scope of their employment or duties whether arising out of a governmental or proprietary function except as specifically provided by the legislature ..."

The legislature has not enacted legislation to limit the liability of the school boards in the administration of special education programs....

Despite these clear constitutional and statutory provisions, and the failure of the legislature to enact laws expanding immunity to the situation involved here, the State argues that public policy prohibits a holding that the State can be held liable for negligent administration of a special education program. Not only do we not see any public policy requirements in support of such an argument, in the absence of a clear statutory declaration granting immunity, it is our duty to permit rather than to deny an action for negligence.

Duty of Care

We have no difficulty in finding a duty of care owed to special education students. The general tenor of education for all citizens in Montana is stated in Art. X § 1, 1972 Mont. Const.: "It is the goal of the people to establish a system of education which will develop the full educational potential of each person. Equality of educational opportunity is guaranteed to each person of the state." ...

... [S]ection 20-7-402, MCA, provides that school districts "shall comply" with policies recommended by the State Superintendent of Public Instruction in administering special education programs. The Superintendent's office, under this statutory mandate has published a "Special Education Handbook" which outlines for individual school districts, the procedures and guidelines to be followed in administering special education programs.

In addition, section 20-7-401, MCA, sets up a special class of students for which special education programs are provided. The child clearly falls within this class. The complaint here is that the school district failed to follow the statutory and regulatory policies governing the placement of students in the special education program.

The school authorities owed the child a duty of reasonable care in testing her and placing her in an appropriate special education program. Whether that duty was breached here, and assuming a breach, whether the child was injured by the breach of duty, are questions not before this Court. Nor were those issues placed before the trial court in the motion for summary judgment. We therefore reverse the trial court's order and remand for further proceedings.

....

---

1. In *B.M.*, the state supreme court found possible liability for misplacing a child in a segregated class for the mentally disabled, as there were program guidelines prohibiting such segregation. Citing state statutory and regulatory policies governing the placement of students in special education programs, the court found that a duty of reasonable care existed. Additionally, the court stated that this duty was not superseded by a public policy favoring immunity of school authorities absent legislative or constitutional immunity. However, the court did not reach the issue of whether the duty owed by school authorities to students was breached or, if it was, whether it resulted in injury to the plaintiff. As this case involved violations of mandatory state statutes, can it be argued that it should be limited to its holding in that the court's finding was restricted to that class of cases alleging student misplacement in special education programs, as opposed to those alleging inadequate or incompetent instruction? Is *B.M.* really a malpractice case or merely a failure to follow the guidelines of state law?

2. *B.M.* is the only case to date where a court has accepted the concept of educational malpractice. Most courts adjudging this issue have followed the holding in *Peter W. See* for example, *Helbig v. City of New York*, 597 N.Y.S.2d 585 (1993), "no cause of action exists for educational malpractice"; *Poe v. Hamilton*, 56 Ohio App. 3d 137, 565 N.E.2d 887 (1990), "public policy precluded cause of action for educational malpractice"; *DeRosa v. City of New York*, 132 A.D.2d 592, 517 N.Y.S.2d 754 (1987), "educational malpractice [is] not a cognizable cause of action"; *Torres v. Little Flower Children's Servs.*, 64 N.Y.2d 119, 474 N.E.2d 223, 485 N.Y.S.2d 15 (1984), *cert. denied*, 474 U.S. 864 (1985), "educational malpractice action by functionally illiterate plaintiff ... was barred for public policy reasons"; *Doe v. Board of Educ. of Montgomery County*, 295 Md. 67, 453 A.2d 814, "complaint ... alleging negligent evaluation and placement of learning disabled student failed to state cause of action"; *D.S.W. v. Fairbanks North Star Borough Sch. Dist.*, 628 P.2d 554 (1981), "actions for damages could not be maintained against school district for negligent classification, placement or teaching of students suffering from dyslexia."

These courts have all refused to recognize a claim of educational malpractice. *Donohue* represents the position best, stating that accepting such a complaint would constitute unwarranted judicial intrusion on the administrative responsibilities of school officials. *Donohue, supra*, 47 N.Y.2d 440, 443. Are the concerns of these courts misplaced? Are not the courts already intruding on the decision making of school administrators in areas like desegregation, school finance, personnel practices, and discipline? Why make an exception for the tort of malpractice?

3. The cases cited up until now all relate to educational malpractice vis-à-vis public schools. What of such a cause of action in private school? In *Squires v. Sierra Nevada Educ. Found., Inc.*, 107 Nev. 902, 823 P.2d 256 (1991), parents of an elementary school child sued a private school alleging educational malpractice, misrepresentation, and breach of contract. The child was sent to this school because of reading difficulties and because school personnel advised the parents that they could diagnose and remediate any difficulty. Proof was brought at trial that the student's reading skills worsened at the school and that these additional deficiencies were caused by inappropriate instruction. The appeals court held a cause of action in contract could be claimed in that school personnel failed to live up to a promise to provide individualized reading instruction and adequate diagnostic and remedial services. Similarly, the court held for the plaintiffs as to misrepresentation in that school officials sent progress reports home which they either negligently or knowingly misrepresented stating that the student was having no academic difficulties. Indicating that the plaintiffs successfully brought claims in the above causes of action, the court declined to address the justiciability of the educational malpractice allegation. Note that the possibility of a misrepresentation claim was first proposed in *Peter W.* where the court seemed to suggest that if such a cause of action had been properly pleaded, it might have survived judicial scrutiny. *Peter W. v. San Francisco Unified Sch. Dist.*, 60 Cal. App. 3d 814, 827, 131 Cal. Rptr. 854, 862 (1976).

Malpractice was taken up by another court for allegations against a private school. In *Rich v. Kentucky Country Day Sch., Inc.*, 793 S.W.2d 832 (Ky. Ct. App. 1990), plaintiffs claimed personal injury when school officials reacted to a diagnosis of Attention Deficit Disorder on the part of a student by expressing instead that the student was lazy and indulged too much in social activities. The court ruled in favor of the school by, on the one hand, distinguishing *B.M.*, in that the present case was not a failure to comply with a statutory requirement, and on the other hand, analogizing to *Donohue*, stating that to entertain an educational malpractice cause of action "would require the courts not merely to make judgments as to the validity of broad educational policies ... but, more importantly, to sit in review of the day-to-day implementation of these policies." *Id.* at 836. The court went on to say that it would not micromanage educational decisions made in the context of either public or private schools. Does the court in *Rich* give a rationale for why it makes no distinction between public and private schools as regards the claim of educational malpractice? Should there be such a distinction?

B. RESIDENCE AND CITIZENSHIP REQUIREMENTS — LIMITATIONS ON THE UNIVERSAL RIGHT

PLYLER v. DOE

Supreme Court of the United States
457 U.S. 202 (1982)

JUSTICE BRENNAN delivered the opinion of the Court:

The question presented by these cases is whether, consistent with the Equal Protection Clause of the Fourteenth Amendment, Texas may deny to undocumented school-age children the free public education that it provides to children who are citizens of the United States or legally admitted aliens.

I

Since the late 19th century, the United States has restricted immigration into this country. Unsanctioned entry into the United States is a crime, 8 U.S.C. § 1325, and those who have entered unlawfully are subject to deportation, 8 U.S.C. §§ 1251, 1252 (1976 ed. and Supp.IV). But despite the existence of these legal restrictions, a substantial number of persons have succeeded in unlawfully entering the United States, and now live within various States, including the State of Texas.

In May 1975, the Texas Legislature revised its education laws to withhold from local school districts any state funds for the education of children who were not "legally admitted" into the United States. The 1975 revision also authorized local school districts to deny enrollment in their public schools to children not "legally admitted" to the country. Tex.Educ.Code Ann. § 21.031 (Vernon Supp. 1981).[1] [This] case involve[s] constitutional challenges to those provisions.

This is a class action, filed in the United States District Court for the Eastern District of Texas in September 1977, on behalf of certain school-age children of Mexican origin residing in Smith County, Tex., who could not establish that they

---

[1] That section provides, in pertinent part:

(a) All children who are citizens of the United States or legally admitted aliens and who are over the age of five years and under the age of 21 years on the first day of September of any scholastic year shall be entitled to the benefits of the Available School Fund for that year. (b) Every child in this state who is a citizen of the United States or a legally admitted alien and who is over the age of five years and not over the age of 21 years on the first day of September of the year in which admission is sought shall be permitted to attend the public free schools of the district in which he resides or in which his parent, guardian, or the person having lawful control of him resides at the time he applies for admission. (c) The board of trustees of any public free school district of this state shall admit into the public free schools of the district free of tuition all persons who are either citizens of the United States or legally admitted aliens and who are over five and not over 21 years of age at the beginning of the scholastic year if such person or his parent, guardian or person having lawful control resides within the school district.

B. RESIDENCE AND CITIZENSHIP REQUIREMENTS

had been legally admitted into the United States. The action complained of the exclusion of plaintiff children from the public schools of the Tyler Independent School District.... After certifying a class consisting of all undocumented school-age children of Mexican origin residing within the School District, the District Court preliminarily enjoined defendants from denying a free education to members of the plaintiff class. In December 1977, the court conducted an extensive hearing on plaintiffs' motion for permanent injunctive relief.

....

A

Sheer incapability or lax enforcement of the laws barring entry into this country, coupled with the failure to establish an effective bar to the employment of undocumented aliens, has resulted in the creation of a substantial "shadow population" of illegal migrants — numbering in the millions — within our borders. This situation raises the specter of a permanent caste of undocumented resident aliens, encouraged by some to remain here as a source of cheap labor, but nevertheless denied the benefits that our society makes available to citizens and lawful residents. The existence of such an underclass presents most difficult problems for a Nation that prides itself on adherence to principles of equality under law.[19]

The children who are plaintiffs in these cases are special members of this underclass. Persuasive arguments support the view that a State may withhold its beneficence from those whose very presence within the United States is the product of their own unlawful conduct. These arguments do not apply with the same force to classifications imposing disabilities on the minor children of such illegal entrants. At the least, those who elect to enter our territory by stealth and in violation of our law should be prepared to bear the consequences, including, but not limited to, deportation. But the children of those illegal entrants are not comparably situated. Their "parents have the ability to conform their conduct to societal norms," and presumably the ability to remove themselves from the State's jurisdiction; but the children who are plaintiffs in these cases "can affect

---

[19]We reject the claim that "illegal aliens" are a "suspect class." No case in which we have attempted to define a suspect class, ... has addressed the status of persons unlawfully in our country. Unlike most of the classifications that we have recognized as suspect, entry into this class, by virtue of entry into this country, is the product of voluntary action. Indeed, entry into the class is itself a crime. In addition, it could hardly be suggested that undocumented status is a "constitutional irrelevancy." With respect to the actions of the Federal Government, alienage classifications may be intimately related to the conduct of foreign policy, to the federal prerogative to control access to the United States, and to the plenary federal power to determine who has sufficiently manifested his allegiance to become a citizen of the Nation. No State may independently exercise a like power. But if the Federal Government has by uniform rule prescribed what it believes to be appropriate standards for the treatment of an alien subclass, the States may, of course, follow the federal direction. See *DeCanas v. Bica*, 424 U.S. 351 (1976).

neither their parents' conduct nor their own status." *Trimble v. Gordon*, 430 U.S. 762, 770 (1977). Even if the State found it expedient to control the conduct of adults by acting against their children, legislation directing the onus of a parent's misconduct against his children does not comport with fundamental conceptions of justice....

Of course, undocumented status is not irrelevant to any proper legislative goal. Nor is undocumented status an absolutely immutable characteristic since it is the product of conscious, indeed unlawful, action. But § 21.031 is directed against children, and imposes its discriminatory burden on the basis of a legal characteristic over which children can have little control. It is thus difficult to conceive of a rational justification for penalizing these children for their presence within the United States. Yet that appears to be precisely the effect of § 21.031.

Public education is not a "right" granted to individuals by the Constitution. *San Antonio Independent School Dist. v. Rodriguez*, 411 U.S. 1, 35 (1973). But neither is it merely some governmental "benefit" indistinguishable from other forms of social welfare legislation. Both the importance of education in maintaining our basic institutions, and the lasting impact of its deprivation on the life of the child, mark the distinction. The "American people have always regarded education and [the] acquisition of knowledge as matters of supreme importance." *Meyer v. Nebraska*, 262 U.S. 390, 400, (1923). We have recognized "the public schools as a most vital civic institution for the preservation of a democratic system of government," *Abington School District v. Schempp*, 374 U.S. 203, 230 (1963) (BRENNAN, J., concurring), and as the primary vehicle for transmitting "the values on which our society rests." *Ambach v. Norwick*, 441 U.S. 68, 76, (1979). "[A]s ... pointed out early in our history, ... some degree of education is necessary to prepare citizens to participate effectively and intelligently in our open political system if we are to preserve freedom and independence." *Wisconsin v. Yoder*, 406 U.S. 205, 221, (1972). And these historic "perceptions of the public schools as inculcating fundamental values necessary to the maintenance of a democratic political system have been confirmed by the observations of social scientists." *Ambach v. Norwick, supra*, 441 U.S. at 77. In addition, education provides the basic tools by which individuals might lead economically productive lives to the benefit of us all. In sum, education has a fundamental role in maintaining the fabric of our society. We cannot ignore the significant social costs borne by our Nation when select groups are denied the means to absorb the values and skills upon which our social order rests.

In addition to the pivotal role of education in sustaining our political and cultural heritage, denial of education to some isolated group of children poses an affront to one of the goals of the Equal Protection Clause: the abolition of governmental barriers presenting unreasonable obstacles to advancement on the basis of individual merit. Paradoxically, by depriving the children of any disfavored group of an education, we foreclose the means by which that group might raise the level of esteem in which it is held by the majority. But more

B. RESIDENCE AND CITIZENSHIP REQUIREMENTS

directly, "education prepares individuals to be self-reliant and self-sufficient participants in society" *Wisconsin v. Yoder, supra,* 406 U.S. at 221. Illiteracy is an enduring disability. The inability to read and write will handicap the individual deprived of a basic education each and every day of his life. The inestimable toll of that deprivation on the social, economic, intellectual, and psychological well-being of the individual, and the obstacle it poses to individual achievement, make it most difficult to reconcile the cost or the principle of a status-based denial of basic education with the framework of equality embodied in the Equal Protection Clause....

B

These well-settled principles allow us to determine the proper level of deference to be afforded § 21.031. Undocumented aliens cannot be treated as a suspect class because their presence in this country in violation of federal law is not a "constitutional irrelevancy." Nor is education a fundamental right; a State need not justify by compelling necessity every variation in the manner in which education is provided to its population. *See San Antonio Independent School Distr. v. Rodriguez, supra,* at 28-39. But more is involved in these cases than the abstract question whether § 21.031 discriminates against a suspect class, or whether education is a fundamental right. Section 21.031 imposes a lifetime hardship on a discrete class of children not accountable for their disabling status. The stigma of illiteracy will mark them for the rest of their lives. By denying these children a basic education, we deny them the ability to live within the structure of our civic institutions, and foreclose any realistic possibility that they will contribute in even the smallest way to the progress of our Nation. In determining the rationality of § 21.031, we may appropriately take into account its costs to the Nation and to the innocent children who are its victims. In light of these countervailing costs, the discrimination contained in § 21.031 can hardly be considered rational unless it furthers some substantial goal of the State.

....

IV

It is the State's principal argument, and apparently the view of the dissenting Justices, that the undocumented status of these children *vel non* establishes a sufficient rational basis for denying them benefits that a State might choose to afford other residents. The State notes that while other aliens are admitted "on an equality of legal privileges with all citizens under non-discriminatory laws," *Takahashi v. Fish & Game Comm'n,* 334 U.S. 410, 420, (1948), the asserted right of these children to an education can claim no implicit congressional imprimatur. Indeed, in the State's view, Congress' apparent disapproval of the presence of these children within the United States, and the evasion of the federal regulatory program that is the mark of undocumented status, provide authority for its decision to impose upon them special disabilities. Faced with an equal protection challenge respecting the treatment of aliens, we agree that the courts must be attentive to congressional policy; the exercise of congressional power might well affect the State's prerogatives to afford differential treatment to a particular class of aliens. But we are unable to find in the congressional immigration scheme any statement of policy that might weigh significantly in arriving at an equal protection balance concerning the State's authority to deprive these children of an education.

....

As we recognized in *DeCanas v. Bica*, 424 U.S. 351, (1976), the States do have some authority to act with respect to illegal aliens, at least where such action mirrors federal objectives and furthers a legitimate state goal. In *DeCanas*, the State's program reflected Congress' intention to bar from employment all aliens except those possessing a grant of permission to work in this country. *Id.* at 361. In contrast, there is no indication that the disability imposed by § 21.031 corresponds to any identifiable congressional policy. The State does not claim that the conservation of state educational resources was ever a congressional concern in restricting immigration. More importantly, the classification reflected in § 21.031 does not operate harmoniously within the federal program.

To be sure, like all persons who have entered the United States unlawfully, these children are subject to deportation. 8 U.S.C. §§ 1251, 1252 (1976 ed. and Supp.IV). But there is no assurance that a child subject to deportation will ever be deported. An illegal entrant might be granted federal permission to continue to reside in this country, or even to become a citizen. *See, e.g.*, 8 U.S.C. §§ 1252, 1253(h), 1254 (1976 ed. and Supp.IV). In light of the discretionary federal power to grant relief from deportation, a State cannot realistically determine that any particular undocumented child will in fact be deported until after deportation proceedings have been completed. It would of course be most difficult for the State to justify a denial of education to a child enjoying an inchoate federal permission to remain.

We are reluctant to impute to Congress the intention to withhold from these children, for so long as they are present in this country through no fault of their own, access to a basic education. In other contexts, undocumented status, coupled with some articulable federal policy, might enhance state authority with respect to the treatment of undocumented aliens. But in the area of special constitutional sensitivity presented by these cases, and in the absence of any contrary indication fairly discernible in the present legislative record, we perceive no national policy that supports the State in denying these children an elementary education. The State may borrow the federal classification. But to justify its use as a criterion for its own discriminatory policy, the State must demonstrate that the classification is reasonably adapted to "the purposes for which the state desires to use it." *Oyama v. California*, 332 U.S. 633, 664-665, (1948) (MURPHY, J., concurring). We therefore turn to the state objectives that are said to support § 21.031.

B. RESIDENCE AND CITIZENSHIP REQUIREMENTS

V

Appellants argue that the classification at issue furthers an interest in the "preservation of the state's limited resources for the education of its lawful residents." Of course, a concern for the preservation of resources standing alone can hardly justify the classification used in allocating those resources. *Graham v. Richardson*, 403 U.S. 365, 374-375, (1971). The State must do more than justify its classification with a concise expression of an intention to discriminate. Apart from the asserted state prerogative to act against undocumented children solely on the basis of their undocumented status — an asserted prerogative that carries only minimal force in the circumstances of these cases — we discern three colorable state interests that might support § 21.031.

First, appellants appear to suggest that the State may seek to protect itself from an influx of illegal immigrants. While a State might have an interest in mitigating the potentially harsh economic effects of sudden shifts in population, § 21.031 hardly offers an effective method of dealing with an urgent demographic or economic problem. There is no evidence in the record suggesting that illegal entrants impose any significant burden on the State's economy. To the contrary, the available evidence suggests that illegal aliens underutilize public services, while contributing their labor to the local economy and tax money to the state fisc. The dominant incentive for illegal entry into the State of Texas is the availability of employment; few if any illegal immigrants come to this country, or presumably to the State of Texas, in order to avail themselves of a free education. Thus, even making the doubtful assumption that the net impact of illegal aliens on the economy of the State is negative, we think it clear that "[c]harging tuition to the undocumented children constitutes a ludicrously ineffectual attempt to stem the tide of illegal immigration," at least when compared with the alternative of prohibiting the employment of illegal aliens.

Second, while it is apparent that a State may "not ... reduce expenditures for education by barring [some arbitrarily chosen class of] children from its schools," *Shapiro v. Thompson*, 394 U.S. 618, 633, (1969), appellants suggest that undocumented children are appropriately singled out for exclusion because of the special burdens they impose on the State's ability to provide high-quality public education. But the record in no way supports the claim that exclusion of undocumented children is likely to improve the overall quality of education in the State.... Of course, even if improvement in the quality of education were a likely result of barring some number of children from the schools of the State, the State must support its selection of this group as the appropriate target for exclusion. In terms of educational cost and need, however, undocumented children are "basically indistinguishable" from legally resident alien children.

Finally, appellants suggest that undocumented children are appropriately singled out because their unlawful presence within the United States renders them less likely than other children to remain within the boundaries of the State, and to put their education to productive social or political use within the State. Even assuming that such an interest is legitimate, it is an interest that is most difficult to quantify. The State has no assurance that any child, citizen or not, will employ the education provided by the State within the confines of the State's borders. In any event, the record is clear that many of the undocumented children disabled by this classification will remain in this country indefinitely, and that some will become lawful residents or citizens of the United States. It is difficult to understand precisely what the State hopes to achieve by promoting the creation and perpetuation of a subclass of illiterates within our boundaries, surely adding to the problems and costs of unemployment, welfare, and crime. It is thus clear that whatever savings might be achieved by denying these children an education, they are wholly insubstantial in light of the costs involved to these children, the State, and the Nation.

VI

If the State is to deny a discrete group of innocent children the free public education that it offers to other children residing within its borders, that denial must be justified by a showing that it furthers some substantial state interest. No such showing was made here. Accordingly, the judgment of the Court of Appeals in each of these cases is

Affirmed.

[JUSTICES MARSHALL, BLACKMUN and POWELL each filed concurring opinions.]

....

CHIEF JUSTICE BURGER, with whom JUSTICE WHITE, JUSTICE REHNQUIST, and JUSTICE O'CONNOR join, dissenting:

Were it our business to set the Nation's social policy, I would agree without hesitation that it is senseless for an enlightened society to deprive any children — including illegal aliens — of an elementary education. I fully agree that it would be folly — and wrong — to tolerate creation of a segment of society made up of illiterate persons, many having a limited or no command of our language. However, the Constitution does not constitute us as "Platonic Guardians" nor does it vest in this Court the authority to strike down laws because they do not meet our standards of desirable social policy, "wisdom," or "common sense."

... We trespass on the assigned function of the political branches under our structure of limited and separated powers when we assume a policy-making role as the Court does today.

The Court makes no attempt to disguise that it is acting to make up for Congress' lack of "effective leadership" in dealing with the serious national problems caused by the influx of uncountable millions of illegal aliens across our borders.... The failure of enforcement of the immigration laws over more than a decade and the inherent difficulty and expense of sealing our vast borders have combined to create a grave socioeconomic dilemma. It is a dilemma that has not yet even been fully assessed, let alone addressed. However, it is not the function

B. RESIDENCE AND CITIZENSHIP REQUIREMENTS

of the Judiciary to provide "effective leadership" simply because the political branches of government fail to do so.

The Court's holding today manifests the justly criticized judicial tendency to attempt speedy and wholesale formulation of "remedies" for the failures — or simply the laggard pace — of the political processes of our system of government. The Court employs, and in my view abuses, the Fourteenth Amendment in an effort to become an omnipotent and omniscient problem solver. That the motives for doing so are noble and compassionate does not alter the fact that the Court distorts our constitutional function to make amends for the defaults of others.

I

In a sense, the Court's opinion rests on such unique confluence of theories and rationale that it will likely stand for little beyond the results in these particular cases. Yet the extent to which the Court departs from principled constitutional adjudication is nonetheless disturbing.

I have no quarrel with the conclusion that the Equal Protection Clause of the Fourteenth Amendment applies to aliens who, after their illegal entry into this country, are indeed physically "within the jurisdiction" of a state. However, as the Court concedes, this "only begins the inquiry." The Equal Protection Clause does not mandate identical treatment of different categories of persons.

The dispositive issue ... simply put, is whether, for purposes of allocating its finite resources, a state has a legitimate reason to differentiate between persons who are lawfully within the state and those who are unlawfully there. The distinction the State of Texas has drawn — based not only upon its own legitimate interests but on classifications established by the Federal Government in its immigration laws and policies — is not unconstitutional.

A

The Court acknowledges that, except in those cases when state classifications disadvantage a "suspect class" or impinge upon a "fundamental right," the Equal Protection Clause permits a state "substantial latitude" in distinguishing between different groups of persons. Moreover, the Court expressly — and correctly — rejects any suggestion that illegal aliens are a suspect class, or that education is a fundamental right. Yet by patching together bits and pieces of what might be termed quasi-suspect-class and quasi-fundamental-rights analysis, the Court spins out a theory custom-tailored to the facts of these cases.

....

... The fact that the distinction is drawn in legislation affecting access to public education — as opposed to legislation allocating other important governmental benefits, such as public assistance, health care, or housing — cannot make a difference in the level of scrutiny applied.

B

Once it is conceded — as the Court does — that illegal aliens are not a suspect class, and that education is not a fundamental right, our inquiry should focus on and be limited to whether the legislative classification at issue bears a rational relationship to a legitimate state purpose.

The State contends primarily that § 21.031 serves to prevent undue depletion of its limited revenues available for education, and to preserve the fiscal integrity of the State's school-financing system against an ever-increasing flood of illegal aliens — aliens over whose entry or continued presence it has no control. Of course such fiscal concerns alone could not justify discrimination against a suspect class or an arbitrary and irrational denial of benefits to a particular group of persons. Yet I assume no Member of this Court would argue that prudent conservation of finite state revenues is per se an illegitimate goal....

Without laboring what will undoubtedly seem obvious to many, it simply is not "irrational" for a state to conclude that it does not have the same responsibility to provide benefits for persons whose very presence in the state and this country is illegal as it does to provide for persons lawfully present. By definition, illegal aliens have no right whatever to be here, and the state may reasonably, and constitutionally, elect not to provide them with governmental services at the expense of those who are lawfully in the state....

....

II

The Constitution does not provide a cure for every social ill, nor does it vest judges with a mandate to try to remedy every social problem.

Congress, "vested by the Constitution with the responsibility of protecting our borders and legislating with respect to aliens," bears primary responsibility for addressing the problems occasioned by the millions of illegal aliens flooding across our southern border. Similarly, it is for Congress, and not this Court, to assess the "social costs borne by our Nation when select groups are denied the means to absorb the values and skills upon which our social order rests." While the "specter of a permanent caste" of illegal Mexican residents of the United States is indeed a disturbing one, it is for the political branches to solve. I find it difficult to believe that Congress would long tolerate such a self-destructive result — that it would fail to deport these illegal alien families or to provide for the education of their children. Yet instead of allowing the political processes to run their course — albeit with some delay — the Court seeks to do Congress' job for it, compensating for congressional inaction. It is not unreasonable to think that this encourages the political branches to pass their problems to the Judiciary.

The solution to this seemingly intractable problem is to defer to the political processes, unpalatable as that may be to some.

B. RESIDENCE AND CITIZENSHIP REQUIREMENTS

1. In *Plyler*, the children of undocumented aliens challenged a state law that prevented their being admitted and educated in the local school districts. In response to this equal protection claim, the Supreme Court affirmed its ruling in *San Antonio Indep. Sch. Dist. v. Rodriguez*, 411 U.S. 1, 35 (1973) (*See* Chapter 14), that education has no explicit or implicit mention in the Constitution as a fundamental right and that children of nondocumented workers cannot be treated as a suspect class. The Court's analysis did not cease at these conclusions, however. Specifically, "more is involved in [this] case[] than the abstract question whether ... [the state law] discriminates against a suspect class, or whether education is a fundamental right." *Plyler*, at 223. Justice William Brennan, speaking for the majority, allowed that the absence of a suspect classification and fundamental rights status notwithstanding, the law in question "imposes a lifetime hardship on a discrete class of children not accountable for their disabling status." *Id*. Hence, the state statute was declared unconstitutional. What is the constitutional foundation for such a ruling? Is it possible for the Court to apply heightened scrutiny to education claims where there is no finding of an "immutable" class of persons and without a judicial determination that education is a fundamental right? If not heightened scrutiny, what was the appropriate level of judicial analysis here?

2. Consider the following passage from Lawrence Tribe's text, American Constitutional Law, at 1551-52:*

> The *Plyler* majority was constrained by the Court's decision in [*Rodriguez*] from declaring public education to be a right guaranteed by the Constitution, but the majority [also] made it clear that public education was not just another governmental benefit either. Public education might not be a "fundamental right," but it plays a "fundamental role in maintaining the fabric of our society." [*Plyler*] at 220. Writing for the *Plyler* majority, Justice Brennan then mated this not-quite-fundamental right with this not-quite suspect class to produce a hybrid equal protection test: in order to be considered rational the [state] education law would have to further a "substantial" state interest.

Tribe's comments incorporate Chief Justice Burger's dissent in *Plyler* which described the majority's holding as "patching together bits and pieces of what might be termed quasi-suspect-class and quasi-fundamental-rights analysis." *Plyler*, at 244. If the Burger and Tribe statements are an accurate description of Court actions here, does this mean that future cases about rights in education could receive heightened scrutiny without the finding of a fundamental right or suspect class?

---

*Copyright © 1988 by Foundation Press, Inc. Reprinted with permission.

3. For a response to and an analysis of *Plyler* written shortly after the Supreme Court's decision, *see* Hull, *Undocumented Alien Children and Free Public Education: An Analysis of* Plyler v. Doe, 44 U. Pitt. L. Rev. 409 (1983).

4. The "Platonic Guardians" statement by Justice Burger in his dissent raises an interesting point. How important is judicial restraint compared to avoiding the creation of a "segment of society made up of illiterate persons, many having limited or no command of our language?" *Plyler*, at 242. Burger criticizes the Court for its tendency to attempt speedy and wholesale formulation of "remedies" for the failures (the "laggard pace") of the political processes of American government.

Judicial restraint is a positive notion. It is important for the courts not to overstep judicial limits; it is equally important to keep a check on the other branches of government. However, judicial activism may also be necessary, especially when the wheels of the legislative process are so slow as to effectively deprive children of an education. Is *Plyler* a case where the latter theory outweighed the former because of governmental inertia?

5. *Plyler*, of course, is not the only case where the Supreme Court has addressed the constitutionality of education rights. In *Meyer v. Nebraska*, 262 U.S. 390 (1923) (*see* Chapter 3), the court noted that "[t]he American people have always regarded education and the acquisition of knowledge as matters of supreme importance which should be diligently promoted." *Id.* at 400. In *Meyer*, a teacher had been convicted of violating a state statute forbidding the teaching of a foreign language to school children. The Court held the statute unconstitutional as it violated parents' liberty under the due process clause. *Id.* at 401, 403. *Meyer* was extended two years later in *Pierce v. Society of Sisters of the Holy Names of Jesus and Mary*, 268 U.S. 510 (1925) (*see* Part C, this chapter) where the Court enjoined enforcement of a state statute requiring parents to enroll their children only in the state's public schools. Declaring the statute as an unreasonable infringement on parents' liberty interests, the Court invalidated the law, indicating that "[t]he child is not the mere creature of the state; those who nurture him and direct his destiny have the right, coupled with the ... duty, to ... prepare him for additional obligations." *Id.* at 535. *Meyer* and *Pierce* are still considered good law, surviving more now to support a right against government intrusion in the pursuit of knowledge and information. *See* Lawrence Tribe, American Constitutional Law (2d ed. 1988).

6. Decades later the Equal Protection Clause was used by plaintiffs in an attempt to establish education as a right protected by the Constitution. In *San Antonio Indep. Sch. Dist. v. Rodriguez*, cited in note 1 *supra*, minority children challenged state law, complaining that state financing of education was inequitable in that poor communities received fewer dollars to provide education than wealthier communities, and this caused a vast difference in academic offerings. *Rodriquez*, at 4. To pursue the challenge, the Court required the plaintiffs to prove that state law either infringed a fundamental right or had a negative effect upon them as a suspect class. Even recognizing the need of every

B. RESIDENCE AND CITIZENSHIP REQUIREMENTS

citizen for an education, the Court determined that there is no explicit or implicit guarantee of education in the Constitution and hence, education is not a fundamental right. The Court did not rest here, however, in its comments about the fundamentality of education. In *dicta*, the court stated that under other circumstances, such as when children are denied the basics of education, it might find there is a duty on the part of the state to provide minimal skills. However, this issue was not reached as there was no showing of an absolute denial of education to the children. Does this mean that under the circumstances stated by the Court, *i.e.*, an absolute denial of education, there could be a finding of a constitutional right to education?

7. There have been cases subsequent to *Plyler* where the Supreme Court has entertained the question of education as a fundamental right. Note that *Plyler's* holding serves as a pivotal judicial response even with cases that do not concern citizenship issues. In *Papasan v. Allain*, 478 U.S. 265 (1986), children and local school officials in Northern Mississippi challenged that state's distribution of public land funds. The complaint charged that allocation of these funds resulted in a disparity between rich and poor school districts and thus denied plaintiffs the minimally adequate education guaranteed by the state constitution. *Id.* at 274. The plaintiffs argued that the disparity violated the equal protection clause as students were denied a right to minimally adequate education. *Id.* at 285. The Court explained ultimately that the plaintiffs had alleged no facts in support of the claim that they in fact had been deprived of an education since it was not unconstitutional, as decided in *Rodriguez*, for there to be funding disparities between poor and wealthy school districts. *Id.* at 286. *Papasan*, however, still did not settle the question as to whether education is a fundamental right:

> As *Rodriguez* and *Plyler* indicate, this Court has not yet definitively settled the questions whether a minimally adequate education is a fundamental right and whether a statute alleged to discriminatorily infringe that right should be accorded heightened equal protection review. *Id.* at 285.

8. The Supreme Court also addresses the issue of education as a fundamental right in *Kadrmas v. Dickinson Pub. Schs.*, 487 U.S. 450 (1988). A public school student claimed a denial of equal protection based on a state statute that charged a bus fee to persons who lived a certain distance from the nearest school. The state statute permitted some school districts to charge such a fee on their own administrative authority, but permitted the fee for other districts only upon the approval of voters. The Kadrmases lived in a district where administrators made the decision and contended that the fee difference authorization resulted in an equal protection violation; specifically, the user fee charged deprived those who could not afford it minimum access to education and the statute warranting such fees should be subject to the heightened scrutiny standard of judicial review used in *Plyler*. *Kadrmas,* at 455.

The Court declined to uphold the plaintiff's claim distinguishing this case from *Plyler* and further, indicating that the *Plyler* decision was somewhat of an anomaly. The Court stated that a heightened level of review was limited to "cases that involved discriminatory classifications based on sex or illegitimacy." *Id.* at 459. And while agreeing that such a judicial level of scrutiny had been used in *Plyler*, the Court explained that its holding in that case had not been extended beyond the "unique circumstances" that provoked its "unique confluence of theories and rationales." *Id.*

Further distinguishing the facts of *Plyler*, the Court observed that no children were being denied a benefit because of the illegal actions of parents. Here, in fact, the child was denied travel to a school simply because her parents declined to pay a user bus fee charged to all other parents in the area. The Court was disinclined to support the claim that the fee "promoted the creation and perpetuation of a sub-class of illiterates within our boundaries, surely adding to the problems and costs of unemployment, welfare, and crime."*Id.* The Court determined that a heightened level of scrutiny was not the proper assessment standard as the state law did not discriminate against a suspect class, as wealth is not to be considered, and that the statute did not interfere with a fundamental right, as education has not attained such a status in the courts. *Id.* at 465. The Court then concluded no violation had occurred since plaintiffs had not demonstrated that the state's actions were arbitrary or irrational. *Id.* Are the facts of *Kadrmas* really as close to that of *Plyler* as the Court describes? Isn't there more of an analogy to *Rodriguez* and its "wealth classification" principle? Does *Kadrmas* extend the Court's previous ambivalence about a right to education seen in *Rodriguez, Plyler,* and *Papasan,* or does it sound a death knell to future cases in this area?

OROZCO v. SOBOL

United States District Court
674 F. Supp. 125 (S.D.N.Y. 1987)

GOETTEL, DISTRICT JUDGE:

This case is an outgrowth of the myriad of problems confronting our society due to homelessness in America. The immediate issue before this court is deciding the appropriateness of granting a preliminary injunction directing either the Yonkers or Mount Vernon School District to admit a seven-year-old homeless child into their school system....

I. *Facts*

Plaintiff, Sixta Orozco, a United States citizen, was born on November 29, 1980 in Puerto Rico. Plaintiff and her mother, Margarita Arroyo, left Puerto Rico several years ago and lived for a period of time in Mount Vernon, New York. At some point, they returned to Puerto Rico, and plaintiff attended first grade at a public school in San Lorenzo.

In May of 1987, for personal reasons, Ms. Arroyo again left Puerto Rico. She and her daughter returned to New York, ... Ms. Arroyo applied for public

B. RESIDENCE AND CITIZENSHIP REQUIREMENTS

assistance with the Westchester County Department of Social Services ("DSS"). Her case was accepted, and DSS immediately provided the family with emergency housing at the Trade Winds Motel in Yonkers, New York. The family remains at that location.

Despite the fact that the family, at least temporarily, resides in Yonkers, Ms. Arroyo claims contacts with Mount Vernon and hopes to find permanent residence there. Consequently, she sought to enroll her daughter in the Mount Vernon school system. In August, she contacted the central offices of the Mount Vernon Board of Education. Ms. Arroyo maintains that unnamed employees of the Mount Vernon Board advised her that plaintiff could enroll at the Hamilton Elementary School in Mount Vernon. On September 9, Ms. Arroyo went to the Hamilton School to register her daughter for classes, but apparently was told that plaintiff could not be registered since the family resided in Yonkers, not Mount Vernon. Ms Arroyo returned to the central offices of the Mount Vernon Board, and this time was directed to contact the Yonkers Board of Education.

It appears that no "hearing," however minimal, was held and that no written notice was provided to Ms. Arroyo explaining the basis of the decision and her options. Those options include the right to appeal the local decision to the State commissioner of education pursuant to N.Y.Educ.Law § 310 (McKinney 1969 & Supp.1987) ("section 310"). On the other hand, Ms. Arroyo must have understood that the reason for Mount Vernon's decision was that DSS was sheltering her and her child in Yonkers and not in Mount Vernon.

On September 10, Ms. Arroyo contacted the Yonkers Board of Education. An unnamed employee of the Board apparently advised her that, because the family did not permanently reside in Yonkers, plaintiff could not be enrolled in the Yonkers school system. She did not make a more formal application and no hearing or notice was provided to Ms. Arroyo.

A caseworker for the DSS then contacted defendants Joseph Williams, Attendance Officer for the Mount Vernon School District, and Jerry Frank, Court Liaison Officer for the Yonkers School District. Each advised the caseworker that the plaintiff belonged in the other's school system.

At that point, rather than filing an appeal with the commissioner of education pursuant to section 310, plaintiff ... filed a complaint with this court on September 22 under 42 U.S.C. § 1983, alleging various violations of her fourteenth amendment rights to due process of law and equal protection under the law. Plaintiff immediately moved for a temporary restraining order and preliminary injunction (1) directing that Mount Vernon school officials temporarily enroll plaintiff in the Mount Vernon school system and (2) directing that the commissioner of education hold a hearing on plaintiff's case and render a decision as to which school district, Mount Vernon or Yonkers, should officially enroll plaintiff.

On September 24, we granted a temporary restraining order directing that plaintiff immediately be registered in the Yonkers school system. That order was extended by stipulation of the parties, and so ordered by this court, until

November 20, the date set for oral argument on the present motion. On November 20, we ordered that plaintiff be allowed to remain in the Yonkers school system pending our decision on the motion, which was agreed to by the Yonkers School District. We now consider plaintiff's request for a preliminary injunction and, for the reasons that follow, grant a preliminary injunction extending plaintiff's enrollment in the Yonkers school system until the merits of this case are decided, but deny plaintiff's request for injunctive relief against the State commissioner of education.

II. *Discussion*

The standards for injunctive relief in this circuit are well established. Plaintiff must show "(a) irreparable harm and (b) either (1) likelihood of success on the merits or (2) sufficiently serious questions going to the merits to make them a fair ground for litigation and a balance of hardships tipping decidedly toward the party requesting the preliminary relief." *Jackson Dairy, Inc. v. H.P. Hood & Sons, Inc.*, 596 F.2d 70, 72 (2d Cir.1979) (*per curiam*).

There can be no doubt that plaintiff could suffer irreparable harm if she is denied attendance at a New York public school. "[I]nterruption of a child's schooling[,] causing a hiatus not only in the student's education but also in the other social and psychological development processes that take place during the child's schooling, raises, a strong possibility of irreparable injury." *Ross v. Disare*, 500 F.Supp. 928, 934 (S.D.N.Y.1977). We agree with plaintiff's counsel that this possibility is heightened even further when, as here, the child is likely to receive little or no home instruction. Public schooling will provide this plaintiff with a crucial and desperately-needed foundation. Among other things, the plaintiff is not fluent in English, which is a substantial handicap to immigrants and Puerto Ricans. The educational and social maturity she loses, forfeited as a result of forces well beyond her control, could constitute irreparable harm under any reading of that terminology.

It is in satisfying the second prong of the *Jackson Dairy* test whereby plaintiff seeks to send this court into uncharted and potentially hostile waters. Although this court will not shirk its duty and responsibility to protect individual rights, we have determined it best to tread warily in this case. As the Supreme Court wisely cautioned: "...By and large, public education in our Nation is committed to the control of state and local authorities. Courts do not and cannot intervene in the resolution of conflicts which arise in the daily operation of school systems and which do not directly and sharply implicate basic constitutional values." *Epperson v. Arkansas*, 393 U.S. 97, 104, (1968).

... [T]he crux of the merits center on alleged violations of the Due Process Clause of the fourteenth amendment.

In determining "whether due process requirements apply in the first place, we must look ... to the nature of the interest at stake." *Board of Regents v. Roth*, 408 U.S. 564, 570-71 (1972). Here, the New York Constitution expressly directs that "[t]he legislature shall provide for the maintenance and support of a system

B. RESIDENCE AND CITIZENSHIP REQUIREMENTS

of free common schools, wherein all of the children of this state may be educated." N.Y. Const. art. XI, § 1. Although there is considerable debate in this case as to what constitutes plaintiff's legal residence, there can be no doubt that, as an eligible recipient of public assistance from the Westchester County DSS, plaintiff actually resides in New York and is a child of this State. As such, she is entitled to a free public education under the New York Constitution, a property right that can not be abridged or extinguished without plaintiff first being accorded the protections afforded by due process. Indeed, none of the defendants contest this fact....

Having determined that plaintiff is entitled to due process protection, we are left with the more difficult questions in this case of how much process is due and who must provide it. Although, at this stage, we need not definitively resolve these issues, we must, at a minimum, satisfy ourselves as to the sufficient seriousness of these questions, and balance the relevant hardships, if injunctive relief is to issue against any or all of the defendants.

The Local School Districts

....

... [P]laintiff does not have an unfettered right to a tuition-free education at any public school in New York. Indeed, if that were so, local school districts would have to provide notice and hearing to any prospective student seeking admission, for whatever reasons, to a given school. Instead, plaintiff's right is limited by a residency requirement embodied in N.Y.Educ.Law § 3202(1) (McKinney 1981), which provides in pertinent part: "A person over five and under twenty-one years of age who has not received a high school diploma is entitled to attend the public schools maintained in the district in which such person resides without the payment of tuition." The question, therefore, is squarely presented. What type of hearing should be conducted, and by whom, in settling an inter-district dispute over establishing plaintiff's residency under N.Y.Educ.Law § 3202?

....

No guidelines exist to aid school districts in settling these disputes; neither the State legislature nor the State Department of Education has acted to fill this void. Local school districts are left to fend for themselves on an ad hoc basis, leaving aggrieved students and their families with the responsibility of appealing to the commissioner of education pursuant to N.Y.Educ. Law § 310, *supra* note 2. Of course, if those same students and families are not apprised of this appellate right, one is left wondering how it can be exercised.

The failure of legislative and/or regulatory leadership on this issue is at the center of this action. Perhaps in this age when legislators won't legislate and regulators won't regulate, preferring instead to spend their time carping at Federal judges who ultimately must step into the breach to protect individual rights from the capriciousness of ad hoc decision making, one should not be surprised at this state of affairs. On the other hand, it sadly leaves the goal of judicial restraint as a forgotten dream as we are forced to devote our energies full time to safeguarding constitutionally-protected rights from being sucked up in the vacuum of legislative and regulatory dereliction.

This court is all too directly and keenly aware of the thorny policy choices this case, and others like it, present. We also recognize that legislative haste can make political waste; but plaintiff and the hundreds (or thousands) like her do not have the luxury of waiting for that slumbering giant in Albany to work its will. Although we can not and need not say with certainty at this stage that a hearing is the constitutionally-mandated solution, nor do we need now resolve who has the initial responsibility for holding such a hearing, these certainly are sufficiently serious questions going to the merits, and the hardships tip so very decidedly in plaintiff's favor, that preliminary injunctive relief against one of the local school districts is warranted. Although *Takeall v. Ambach*, 609 F.Supp. 81 (S.D.N.Y. 1985) appears to have involved a student who ... was already within the school districts control before his dismissal, the applicability of *Takeall* (which required a local school district to provide notice and hearing before excluding a student on grounds of non-residency) to the instant case is a serious question going to the merits. At this stage, however, without the benefit of a full hearing on the merits, we decline to direct a local school district(s) to provide plaintiff with notice and hearing on the residency question.

In the interim, until the merits are reached, a preliminary determination permitting plaintiff to attend school must be made. This case is unlike *Matter of Richards*, 25 Ed.Dep't Rep. 38 (July 17, 1985), which addressed residency in the context of students who were established New York residents and already members of a school district and then became homeless. Likewise, traditional legal concepts used to establish legal domicile — physical presence coupled with an intent to remain indefinitely — are unavailing since, whatever the family's intent, Westchester County DSS largely will control the locus of plaintiff's residence. When we granted the temporary restraining order in this case, we believed it more likely that plaintiff would be able to establish residency for school attendance purposes in Yonkers, rather than Mount Vernon. We continue to adhere to that view. As noted, regardless of her desire to live in Mount Vernon, Ms. Arroyo's situation is controlled largely by the DSS and where they place her. We believe, therefore, that in this case the DSS placement should operate presumptively as plaintiff's legal residence. Accordingly, we grant a preliminary injunction, but against the Yonkers, and not the Mount Vernon, School District. We direct the Yonkers School District to continue to educate plaintiff tuition-free, as long as the family continues to live under current or similar conditions in Yonkers, until the merits of this case are decided.

The Commissioner of Education

Plaintiff next seeks a preliminary injunction against the State commissioner of education, initially on the ground that the section 310 appeals procedure is far too complex. burdensome, and time-consuming to satisfy any reasonable standard of

B. RESIDENCE AND CITIZENSHIP REQUIREMENTS

due process. Plaintiff, however, has not availed herself of the section 310 process; she instead filed a section 1983 claim with this court....

We recognize that plaintiff must clear many hurdles to sustain an action in Federal court, and we suspect that her counsel has not initiated a section 310 appeal in an attempt to sidestep altogether one such hurdle — mootness. Had plaintiff initiated a section 310 appeal when this case was filed (September 22), a decision from the commissioner would surely have by now been rendered — no matter how flawed or imperfect the process — thereby potentially mooting plaintiff's claim against the State. *Cf.* M. Schwartz & J. Kirklin, Section 1983 Litigation: Claims, Defenses, and Fees § 13.5 (1986) (discussing mootness and "capable of repetition, yet evading review" exception).

Given the fact that our earlier grant of injunctive relief protects plaintiff from whatever irreparable harm may attach pending review of this case on its merits, and mindful of our need to tread warily, *Epperson*, 393 U.S. at 104, (cited in full *supra*), we think the balance of hardships weighs heavily against this request. This is particularly so when a grant of injunctive relief may have the effect of scuttling an administrative plan that has not yet been tested by this plaintiff. When regulators do regulate, we should avoid interposing our will without concrete evidence of the regulation's constitutional failings.

Apparently in recognition of this potential weakness, and in furtherance of the broader agenda clearly afoot here, plaintiff's counsel sought at oral argument on the instant motion to shift the focus of the injunctive claim against the State. Plaintiff now asks that we direct the commissioner, and not the local school districts, to hold the initial hearing in a potential inter-district dispute — this despite the fact that the complaint itself makes clear that plaintiff seeks declaratory injunctive relief against the State for failure to establish an adequate mechanism to review residency determinations after initial hearings by local school districts. Again, we hasten to emphasize that our earlier grant of injunctive relief against the Yonkers School District protects the plaintiff from further harm pending a decision on the merits. Given that fact, and for policy reasons previously highlighted, we are especially reluctant, on a request for a preliminary injunction, to effectively construct via judicial caveat a new regulatory scheme to deal with these issues.

Conclusion

For all of the foregoing reasons:

(1) preliminary injunctive relief against the Yonkers School District is granted, and the District is directed to continue plaintiff's education, as long as the family continues to live under current or similar conditions in Yonkers, until the merits of this case are decided; and

(2) Plaintiff's request for preliminary injunctive relief against the State commissioner of education is denied.

HARRISON v. SOBOL

United States District Court
705 F. Supp. 870 (S.D.N.Y. 1988)

BRIEANT, CHIEF JUDGE:

This is an action brought by a homeless woman on behalf of herself and her two children pursuant to 42 U.S.C. § 1983 against the Peekskill School District ("the District"), two of its officers, Rose Norelli, a Registration Officer, and Donald Rickett, Superintendent of Schools, both as officers of the District and individually, and the New York State Commissioner of Education, Thomas Sobol ("Commissioner"), both in his official capacity and individually, for the wrongful exclusion of her children from the District. Plaintiff claims that the procedures for terminating a pupil's education for nonresidence violate the due process clause of the 14th amendment, and that defendant Commissioner has failed to provide a meaningful opportunity for homeless children attending school to contest termination of their education by a local school board at a hearing.

....

Background

Plaintiff and her children have been homeless since May, 1986 as a result of a fire in their former apartment in Lake Mohegan, New York. They moved to a Mahopac motel after having moved to Florida, and then to various residences in the Southern District. Plaintiff's children lived briefly with their father, a Peekskill resident, and, beginning in July 1987, were registered in the Peekskill School District. On October 9, 1987, the children were required to move from their father's residence by his landlord, and moved back with their mother in the Mahopac motel. Neither the motel nor the Lake Mohegan premises are located within the Peekskill School District.

On October 21, 1987, defendant Rose Norelli, a registration officer with the District, notified plaintiff by telephone that her children were no longer eligible to be enrolled in the District, and should instead be enrolled in Mahopac schools, unless their mother found an apartment in Peekskill. Plaintiff alleges that she was told that her children would not be admitted to the Peekskill schools after November 2, 1987, and that she received no written notice providing factual and legal grounds for the exclusion, or informing her of her right to a hearing and to a decision by the Commissioner pursuant to § 301 of the New York Education Law, or to state court review pursuant to New York C.P.L.R. art. 78.

Mahopac school officials allegedly said that the children should be in Peekskill schools, and refused to admit them to Mahopac schools. Due to this useless bureaucratic tangle, the children were out of school for four to five days, from November 2 to November 9, and neither district profited from the per capita aid due from the state for the plaintiff's children's attendance.

On November 4, 1987, Plaintiff moved for a preliminary injunction against the defendants, seeking to have her children readmitted to the Peekskill schools. The

B. RESIDENCE AND CITIZENSHIP REQUIREMENTS

motion was withdrawn without prejudice on April 13, 1988 because of Peekskill's agreement, made on the record in court on November 9, 1987, to readmit plaintiff's children voluntarily and to continue to educate them pending further order of this Court or plaintiff's voluntary enrollment of her children in another school district.

....

Equitable Relief

Plaintiffs seek a declaratory judgment pursuant to 28 U.S.C. § 2201 that defendants violated their right to due process of law, as well as a permanent injunction pursuant to Fed.R.Civ.P. 65 enjoining defendants from excluding plaintiffs from the Peekskill public schools on the ground of alleged nonresidence, without notice and an opportunity for a hearing.

Due process analysis makes the relevant threshold inquiry whether the plaintiff has a "legitimate claim of entitlement" to a benefit that is grounded in state law, thereby warranting due process analysis. *Goldberg v. Kelly*, 397 U.S. 254, (1969). A school-age child in New York "is entitled to attend the public schools maintained in the district in which [the child] resides without the payment of tuition." N.Y.Ed.L. § 3203. The New York Commissioner of Education has held that, for school residency purposes, "homeless" children temporarily housed in motels are entitled under § 3202 of the New York Education Law to continue to attend their home school districts. *Matter of Richards*, 25 Ed.Dep't Rep. 38 (July 17, 1985).

Plaintiff's children were clearly denied the right to education to which they are entitled under New York law, without due process.... The District in its answer stated that whenever a student in the District is considered a "nonresident," a written notice is forwarded to the student, which states that the individual can appeal to the Commissioner. Defendant has admitted that, in this case, no written notice was given, but merely an oral directive. The procedures alleged by defendants Rickett and Norelli to exist concerning suspension or expulsion of students for nonresidence were not followed in this case.

On July 8, 1988, however, a new regulation proposed by the Commissioner and approved by the Board of Regents, 8 N.Y.C.R.R. § 100.2(x), went into effect. Under the new regulation, parents of displaced homeless children are able to designate either the school district in which the child resided at the time he or she became homeless or the school district in which the child is temporarily living as the district in which their children will attend school. Also adopted and effective on July 8, 1988 was a regulation requiring districts which deny admission to a child based on nonresidence to provide written notification to the parents and an "opportunity to submit information concerning the child's right to attend school in the district." 8 N.Y.C.R.R. § 100.2(y).

In light of the adoption of these new regulations for the education of homeless children, plaintiffs' claims for equitable relief in the form of a declaratory judgment and permanent injunction are moot. Moreover, following the commencement of this action, the District readmitted plaintiff's children to its schools and obligated itself to continue plaintiff's children in school there. Thereafter, in September 1988, plaintiff's children were voluntarily enrolled in the Lakeland School District. Accordingly, plaintiff's motion for summary judgment as to declaratory and injunctive relief is denied as moot.

While an exception to the general rule for determining mootness has been recognized in some cases where the conduct "originally complained of is 'capable of repetition, yet evading review,'" *Honig v. Doe*, 484 U.S. 305 (1988), the exception only applies if there is a "reasonable expectation that the same complaining party would be subjected to the same action again." *Murphy v. Hunt*, 455 U.S. 478, 482 (1982). The exception is not applicable here because of the new regulations, which would prevent a recurrence. If now denied enrollment in a district, plaintiff would be notified of any procedures for review within the district, she would be afforded "the opportunity to submit information concerning the child's right to attend school in the district," and she would receive a written notice of the basis for the determination and her right to a § 310 appeal to the Commissioner. 8 N.Y.C.R.R. § 100.2(y).

....

Plaintiff also seeks a declaratory judgment against the Commissioner on the ground that the section 310 appeals procedure is far too complex, burdensome, and time-consuming to satisfy any reasonable standard of due process. She alleges that the Commissioner has failed "to establish a meaningful opportunity to review local school officials' termination of education," thereby denying the children due process. Complaint, ¶ 44. Plaintiff, however, has not availed herself of the Sec. 310 process; she instead filed a sec. 1983 claim with this Court. This claim against the Commissioner, therefore, is based on speculation and is not ripe for adjudication. *United Public Workers v. Mitchell*, 330 U.S. 75, 89-91 (1947).

Plaintiff lacks standing to sue the Commissioner on this ground. Plaintiff has not suffered actual injury as a result of a sec. 310 appeal since one has not yet been initiated.... Consequently, a case or controversy has not been presented to the Court on the sec. 310 issue. U.S. Const. art. III, sec. 2.

Defenses

A. *Venue*

Venue is proper in the Southern District under 28 U.S.C. sec. 1392, even though the Commissioner is located in the Northern District....

....

B. *Abstention*

The Commissioner alleges that *Pullman* or *Burford* abstention is appropriate. Under *Railroad Commission of Texas v. Pullman Co.*, 312 U.S. 496 (1941), abstention is appropriate where the "dispute concerns a controlling issue of state

B. RESIDENCE AND CITIZENSHIP REQUIREMENTS

law that is unclear and the resolution of which could avoid the constitutional issue presented...." *Catlin v. Ambach*, F.2d 588, 589 (2nd Cir.1987).

Plaintiffs have not raised an "as applied" equal protection claim that could be resolved by construction of a state statute. No state law or regulation required the notice and hearing to which plaintiffs claim they were entitled when they were determined to be nonresidents. The case presents a question of what due process is required when a pupil's education is terminated for nonresidence, which is a question of federal constitutional law. Because there is no unclear issue of state law, the case presents solely a question of procedural due process under the Constitution, and the Court should not abstain under *Pullman*.

The Commissioner also alleges that abstention is appropriate under *Burford v. Sun Oil Co.*, 319 U.S. 315 (1943). The standard for invoking the *Burford* doctrine requires that three criteria be met: "(1) the order, regulation, or provision attacked in federal court relates to a sophisticated state regulatory scheme involving complex subject matter of a special state interest in which judicial review of administrative decisions by state courts is considered an integral part of that scheme because it promotes uniformity by minimizing the potential for multiple inconsistent adjudications and helps assure that the tribunal of choice possesses a certain degree of expertise in the complex subject matter involved; (2) the exercise of jurisdiction by the federal court threatens to disrupt the state's regulatory scheme; and (3) the action brought in federal court largely involves issues of state law." *Long Island Lighting Co. v. Cuomo*, 666 F.Supp. 370, 399 (N.D.N.Y. 1987).

Because these three requirements have not been met, this Court should not abstain pursuant to *Burford*. Plaintiff does not seek to invalidate a complex state regulatory scheme, the predominant issue is the constitutional due process to be afforded to students being expelled from school for nonresidence, and thus, this action does not involve predominantly issues of state law.

C. *Immunity*

Commissioner Sobol has moved to dismiss the claim against him in its entirety, claiming immunity from suit in his official capacity.

The Legislature has charged the State Education Department "with the general management and supervision of all public schools and all of the educational work of the state." N.Y.Ed.L. § 101. The head of the Education Department is the state Board of Regents. *Id.*; N.Y. Const., Art. 11, § 2. The Board of Regents appoints the Commissioner of Education. N.Y.Ed.L. § 101. The Commissioner "enforce[s] all general and special laws relating to the educational system of the state and execute[s] all educational policies determined upon by the Board of Regents," and has "general supervision over all schools." N.Y.Ed.L. § 305(2).

The 11th amendment bars suit in federal court against a state official in his official capacity where the claim is that the official violated state law in carrying out his duties, and the relief sought would operate against the state. *See Pennhurst State School & Hosp. v. Halderman*, 465 U.S. 89 (1984). Where a suit challenges the constitutionality of a state official's actions, however, the 11th amendment does not require dismissal. Rather, the 11th amendment operates to preclude certain forms of relief, particularly damages, against the state. *See id.* at 98, *Edelman v. Jordan*, 415 U.S. 651 (1974).

However, an official with administrative responsibility who has actual or constructive knowledge of, or who condones, a pervasive custom or practice of local districts under his administrative supervision to deny constitutional rights will be liable in damages. *McCann v. Coughlin*, 698 F.2d 112, 124-25 (2d Cir.1983). In *Duchesne v. Sugarman*, 566 F.2d 817 (2d Cir.1987), the Court of Appeals held that state and local officials may be liable for damages if their official policies or practices lead to due process violations, and it makes no difference whether the violations occur as a result of their action or inaction. *Id.* at 832. If the Commissioner has "actual or constructive notice" of deficient procedures, this is "an adequate basis for liability pursuant to sec. 1983." *McCann v. Coughlin*, 698 F.2d at 125.

In this case, the complaint alleges that the Commissioner violated plaintiffs' right to due process by establishing a custom of approving local school district reliance on informal oral notice of residency determinations. A question of federal constitutional law is raised. The Commissioner's counsel was apprised on November 4, 1987 that the children were not in school, but no action was taken to direct the District to allow plaintiffs to continue in attendance while the residence dispute was resolved. At the time, there was no statute or regulations of the Commissioner requiring any written notice before termination of a pupil's education. Thus, the Commissioner is not entitled to immunity and will be accountable in damages for the lack of procedural due process afforded the plaintiffs. The Commissioner is not protected from liability by legislative, judicial, or qualified immunity.

Damages

The requests for declaratory and injunctive relief by plaintiffs are rendered moot by the intervening regulations which were promulgated by the Board of Regents and the Commissioner, and the subsequent enrollment of the children in the Lakeland School District. Thus, the only remaining dispute is whether plaintiff's children were damaged, and to what extent, by their lack of school attendance for four or five days.

Nominal damages of $1.00 may be recovered for a constitutional violation in a sec. 1983 case, and will carry with them reasonable legal fees. *Mindich Developers, Inc. v. Hunziker*, 622 F.Supp. 1513, 1517 (S.D.N.Y.1985). Under the rule of *Carey v. Piphus*, 435 U.S. 247, 266 (1978), plaintiffs in suits under sec. 1983 who are deprived of procedural due process may recover nominal damages without proof of actual injury. Plaintiffs have established that the actions of the defendants denied them due process. There is no proof of actual damage flowing from an absence from school no longer than that which often follows from the common cold. Accordingly, plaintiffs are entitled to nominal damages of $1.00, from all defendants, jointly and severally.

Plaintiffs allege that because defendants knew, or should have known when they denied education to the plaintiff's children that they were required under the due process clause to provide adequate notice of their proposed action, and an opportunity for a hearing and decision prior to the termination, they are therefore liable for punitive damages pursuant to 42 U.S.C. sec. 1983. Plaintiffs also allege that defendant Commissioner knew or should have known that his rules and procedures failed to provide homeless children in New York State and their parents notice and the opportunity for a meaningful hearing on their exclusion from school based on nonresidence, and therefore he is liable for punitive damages.

Here, the plaintiffs were totally excluded from school. The violation of their rights was obvious and unnecessary. The actual damages, however, are trivial, and wilfulness as well as motive are entirely lacking. Thus, punitive damages are unwarranted.

....

The entry of final judgment is deferred.

LAMPKIN v. DISTRICT OF COLUMBIA

United States District Court, District of Columbia
60 USLW 2807 (D.D.C 1992) (Not Reported in F. Supp.)

LAMBERTH, DISTRICT JUDGE:

This matter comes before the court upon plaintiffs' motion for preliminary injunction and defendants' motion to dismiss pursuant to Federal Rule of Civil Procedure 12(b)(6). Plaintiffs in this matter are ten homeless parents (who are bringing this action on behalf of their children) and the National Law Center on Homelessness and Poverty. Defendants are the District of Columbia, Sharon Pratt Kelly in her official capacity as Mayor of the District of Columbia, the District of Columbia Public Schools, and Dr. Franklin L. Smith in his official capacity as the Superintendent of the District of Columbia public school system.

Plaintiffs bring this action for declaratory and injunctive relief pursuant to section 1983 of the Civil Rights Act, 42 U.S.C. § 1983 (1981 and supp.1991) ("section 1983"). Plaintiffs contend that defendants have denied plaintiffs' rights under Title VI of the Stewart B. McKinney Homeless Assistance Act, 42 U.S.C. §§ 11421-11432 (Supp.1991). For the following reasons, plaintiffs' motion for preliminary injunction shall be denied and defendants' motion to dismiss shall be granted.

I. *Facts*

In 1987, Congress passed the Stewart B. McKinney Homeless Assistance Act. 42 U.S.C. §§ 11421-11432 (Supp.1991) ("McKinney Act" or "the Act"). The Act is based upon Congress' policy that state educational systems shall assure that homeless children have equal access to free education. Title VI, Part B of the Act, entitled Education for Homeless Children and Youth, is basically a grant statute. It authorizes the Secretary of Education to grant federal funds to states so that these states can carry out the activities that are described in subsections (c), (d) and (e) of section 11432. *Id.* at § 11432(a). In the present case, the District of Columbia[3] received $50,000 pursuant to the Act. *See id.* at § 11432(b).

Pursuant to subsection (c) of section 11432, these funds are to be used to, among other things: carry out the policies of the Act; provide such services and activities to homeless children and youths to enable them to enroll in, attend and achieve in school; carry out the state plan (discussed *infra*); and to develop and implement programs for school personnel to heighten awareness of the specific problems that surround the education of homeless children and youth. *Id.* at § 11432(c). The relevant portions of subsection (d) state that the Coordinator of Education of Homeless Children and Youth shall facilitate coordination between various state agencies and shall develop relationships between various educational programs and providers to "improve the provision of comprehensive services to homeless children and homeless youths and the families of such children and youths." *Id.* at § 11432(d)(4), (5).

Most of plaintiffs' claims are based upon defendants' alleged failure to comply with subsection (e). This subsection, entitled "State Plan," states that "[e]ach State shall adopt a plan to provide for the education of each homeless child or homeless youth within the State...." *Id.* at § 11432(e)(1). Among other things, each state plan must authorize the state educational agency to make the necessary determinations under this section and address the various problems that stand in the way of educating homeless children. *See id.* at § 11432(e)(1)(A)-(I).

Subsection (e) also provides in relevant part that:

> (2) Each plan adopted under this subsection shall assure, to the extent practicable under requirements relating to education established by State law, that local educational agencies within the State shall comply with the requirements of paragraphs (3) through (9). (3)(A) The local educational agency of each homeless child and each homeless youth shall either — (i) continue the child's or youth's education in the school of origin — (I) for the remainder of the academic year; or (II) in any case in which a family member becomes homeless between academic years, for the following academic year; or (ii) enroll the child or youth in any school that nonhomeless students who live in the attendance area in which the child or youth is actually living are eligible to attend; whichever is in the child's best interest or the youth's best interest. (B) In determining the best interests of the child or youth for purposes of making a school assignment under subparagraph

---

[3] The District of Columbia is considered a "state" for the purposes of Title VI of the McKinney Act. *See* 42 U.S.C. § 1142(d).

B. RESIDENCE AND CITIZENSHIP REQUIREMENTS 49

(A), consideration shall be given to a request made by a parent regarding school selection.

....

(5) Each homeless child shall be provided services comparable to services offered to other students in the school selected according to the provisions of paragraph (3), including transportation services, educational services for which the child meets the eligibility criteria, such as compensatory educational programs for the disadvantaged, and the educational programs for the handicapped and for students with limited English proficiency; programs for vocational education; programs for the gifted and talented; and school meal programs. (7) Each local educational agency serving homeless children or youth that receives assistance under this subchapter shall coordinate with local social services agencies, and other agencies or programs providing services to such children or youth an[d] their families. (9) Each State and local educational agency shall review and revise any policies that may act as barriers to the enrollment of homeless children and youth in schools selected in accordance with paragraph (3). In reviewing and revising such policies, consideration shall be given to issues concerning transportation, requirements of immunization, residency, birth certificates, school records, or other documentation, and guardianship. Special attention shall be given to ensuring the enrollment and attendance of homeless children and youths who are not currently attending school. *Id.* at § 11432(e).

Also relevant to this case is section 11432(f) of the Act. This section provides that "[n]o State may receive a grant under this section unless the State educational agency submits an application to the Secretary at such time, in such manner, and containing or accompanied by such information as the Secretary may reasonably require." *Id.* at § 11432(f). *See also id.* at § 11433(d)(1) (which provides that "[a] local educational agency that desires to receive a grant under this section shall submit an application to the State educational agency at such time, in such manner, and containing or accompanied by such information as the State agency may reasonably require according to the guidelines issued by the Secretary"). The application must include: (A) a description of the services and programs for which assistance is sought and the problems sought to be addressed through the provisions of such services and programs; (B) assurances that the applicant complies with or will use requested funds to come into compliance with paragraphs (3) through (9) of section 11432(e) of this title; (C) an assurance that assistance under the grant will supplement and not supplant funds used before the award of the grant for purposes of providing services to homeless children and homeless youth. (D) a description of policies and procedures that the agency will implement to ensure that activities carried out by the agency will not isolate or stigmatize homeless children or homeless youth. *Id.* at § 11933(d)(1).

The final provision of the Act which is relevant to this case is section 11434. This section imposes various duties upon the Secretary of Education. This provision states, in relevant part, that: [i]n reviewing the State plans submitted by the State educational agencies under section 11432(e) of this title, the Secretary shall evaluate whether State laws, policies, and practices described in such plans adequately address the problems of homeless children and homeless youth relating to access to education and placement as described in such plans. *Id.* at §11434(b)(1).

Plaintiffs assert that defendants have failed to comply with Title VI of the McKinney Act in that defendants have: (1) failed to implement a best interest standard in placing homeless children in schools; (2) failed to ensure transportation to and from the school that is in the best interest of homeless children to attend; (3) failed to coordinate social services and public education for homeless children, and to ensure access to comparable educational services and school meal programs; and (4) failed to provide access to free, appropriate public education for homeless children.

In addition to their section 1983 claims under the McKinney Act, plaintiffs allege that defendants violated their rights to equal protection under the Fifth Amendment to the United States Constitution. Plaintiffs state that although they are similarly situated to handicapped children in their need for transportation assistance, defendants provide transportation assistance to handicapped children and not to homeless children.

Defendants oppose plaintiffs' motion for preliminary injunction on the ground that plaintiffs are not entitled to injunctive relief. Further, in their motion to dismiss, defendants assert that plaintiffs have failed to state a claim upon which relief can be granted because plaintiffs do not have a private right of action under the McKinney Act for the relief sought and because [they] have failed to adequately plead an equal protection claim.

II. *Analysis*

A. *Legal Standard*

Pursuant to the Federal Rules of Civil Procedure, the court may dismiss plaintiffs' claims for failure to state a claim upon which relief may be granted. Fed.R.Civ.P. 12(b)(6). For the purposes of this motion, the court shall accept all of plaintiffs' allegations as true.

B. *Section 1983*

42 U.S.C. § 1983 provides a federal remedy for "the deprivation of any rights, privileges, or immunities secured by the Constitution and federal laws." Section 1983 is available as a remedy for violations of federal statutes as well as for constitutional violations. *See Maine v. Thiboutot*, 448 U.S. 1 (1980). Prior to the United States Supreme Court's ruling in *Suter v. Artist M.*, ___ U.S. ___, 112 S.Ct. 1260 (1992), the Court had developed a two-part line of inquiry for

B. RESIDENCE AND CITIZENSHIP REQUIREMENTS

determining whether section 1983 provides a remedy for a statutory violation. First, since section 1983 speaks in terms of "rights, privileges or immunities," not violations of federal law, the court must determine whether plaintiff asserted a violation of a federal right. *Golden State Transit Corp. v. City of Los Angeles*, 493 U.S. 103, 106 (1989)....

Second, should the court find that plaintiffs have asserted a federal right, section 1983 provides a remedial cause of action "unless the state actor demonstrates by express provision or other specific evidence from the statute itself that Congress intended to foreclose such private enforcement." *Wright*, 479 U.S. at 418.... The Court rarely finds that a remedial scheme established by Congress is sufficient to displace the remedy that is provided by § 1983.[4] *See Wilder*, 110 S.Ct. at 2523.

The availability of an administrative mechanism is not necessarily seen by the Court as sufficient to show that Congress intended to foreclose a section 1983 remedy. Rather, a private right of action under section 1983 is foreclosed "only when the statute itself creates a remedial scheme that is 'sufficiently comprehensive ... to demonstrate congressional intent to preclude the remedy of suits under § 1983.'" *Wilder v. Virginia Hospital Ass'n.*, 496 U.S. 498, 1990) (quoting *Sea Clammers*, 453 U.S. 1, 20 (1981)).

Moreover, the Court has also held that the generalized authority to cut off federal funds is "insufficient to indicate a congressional intention to foreclose § 1983 remedies." *Wright*, 479 U.S. at 428 (cites omitted)....

In *Suter*, which is factually similar to the present case, the Court broke from this line of inquiry. *See Suter*, 112 S.Ct. at 1376 (BLACKMUN, J., dissenting). The issue presented in *Suter* was whether section 1983 permits private individuals the right to enforce the Adoption Assistance and Child Welfare Act of 1980, 42 U.S.C. §§ 620-28, 670-79a ("Adoption Act"). The Adoption Act established a federal reimbursement program for various expenses incurred by states in administering foster care and adoption services. *Suter*, 112 S.Ct. at 1363....

In order to participate in the reimbursement program, the Adoption Act required that states submit a plan to the Secretary of Health and Human Services for approval by the Secretary. The Adoption Act listed 16 qualifications that state plans must contain in order to gain the Secretary's approval. One of the requisite features was that "reasonable efforts will be made [by the state agency] (A) prior to the placement of a child in foster care, to prevent or eliminate the need for removal of the child from his home, and (B) to make it possible for the child to return to his home." *Id.* (quoting 42 U.S.C. § 671(a)(15)).

Respondents in *Suter* filed a class-action suit seeking declaratory and injunctive relief under the Adoption Act. Respondents claimed that the state agency, in

---

[4] In *Wilder*, the Court noted that it has found that Congress's remedial scheme was sufficient to displace section 1983 only on two occasions.... [*Middlesex County Sewage Authority v. National Sea Clammers Ass'n*, 453 U.S.1 (1981)]; *Smith v. Robinson*, 468 U.S. 992, 1009 (1984).

violation of the Adoption Act, "failed to make reasonable efforts to prevent removal of children from their homes and to facilitate reunification of families where removal had occurred." *Id*....

The Supreme Court ... held that the Adoption Act does not confer an enforceable right of action based on section 1983. *Suter*, 112 S.Ct. at 1365. The Court held that the fact that the language of 42 U.S.C. § 671(a)(15) is mandatory in its terms does not alone create a right that is enforceable under section 1983. Rather, the Court considered exactly what the Act required the states to do. *Id.* at 1367. The Court then held that the Adoption Act only required that states have their plans approved by the Secretary, meaning that their plans must contain the 16 features that are required by the statute. *Id.* The Court then recognized that Illinois' state plan was approved by the Secretary. *Id.* The Court distinguished the Adoption Act from the statute in *Wilder*, a case in which the Court found created an enforceable right, because the statute in *Wilder* actually required that states adopt reasonable and adequate rates. *Id.* at 1368.

Title VI of the McKinney Act, Part B, closely resembles the Adoption Act in *Suter* in two ways. First, like the Adoption Act, portions of the McKinney Act are mandatory in their terms. For example, 42 U.S.C. § 11432(e)(3)(A) provides that the local educational agency

> shall either — continue the child's or youth's education in the school of origin ... or ... enroll the child or youth in any school that nonhomeless students who live in the attendance area in which the child or youth is actually living are eligible to attend; whichever is in the child's best interest or in the youth's best interest.

According to *Suter*, however, such mandatory language alone does not create a right of action under § 1983. Rather, the court must determine exactly what the McKinney Act requires defendants to do.

The second similarity between the McKinney Act and the Adoption Act is the fact that both statutes only require states to submit plans or applications to be approved by the federal government. Title VI of the McKinney Act authorizes the Secretary of Education to grant federal funds to state educational agencies so that these agencies may carry out the activities that are authorized in subsections (c), (d) and (e) of section 11432. 42 U.S.C. § 11432(a), (b). One of these activities is preparing and carrying out a state plan which must comply with the requirements that are set forth in subsection (e). *Id.* at § 11432(d), (e). The state plan is designed to assure that local agencies comply with the provisions that are set forth in § 11432(e)(3) through (9), the sections which contain the mandatory language that plaintiffs point to in claiming that the Act creates a private right of action. *Id.* at § 11432(e)(2).

Section 11432(f) of the McKinney Act provides that no state may receive grants under the Act unless it submits a proper application to the Secretary of Education. Such an application must, among other things, assure that the applicant will use its federal funds to come into compliance with the requirements

B. RESIDENCE AND CITIZENSHIP REQUIREMENTS

of section 11432(e)(3)-(9). The final piece of this statutory framework is provided by section 11434. This section requires the Secretary of Education to assure that the State educational agencies' applications are proper in order for it to grant federal funds under this statute.

Thus, much like the Adoption Act in *Suter*, the McKinney Act does not confer an enforceable right upon plaintiffs. Rather, the only requirement that the Act imposes upon states is the duty to submit a proper application if the state wishes to receive federal funding to educate homeless children. *See id.* at § 11432(f); § 11433(d). The only enforceable duty that the Act may impose is upon the Secretary of Education. The Secretary must comply with section 11434 and review state plans as well as state laws, policies and practices to assure that the states adequately address the problems of educating homeless children before the Secretary may grant federal funds to each state. *See id.* at §§ 11434(b)(1).

Accordingly, like in *Suter*, the mandatory language that is cited by plaintiffs in section 11432(e)(3)-(9) does not create an enforceable right under section 1983. Rather, this language merely sets forth the criteria that the Secretary must consider when deciding whether a state's application is proper. *See id.* at § 11434(b)(1). It is then up to the Secretary to determine whether the states' applications are adequate and whether the states deserve a federal grant. *See id.* Consequently, the court shall grant defendants' motion to dismiss plaintiffs' section 1983 claims because plaintiffs have failed to state a claim upon which relief can be granted.[8]

C. *Implied Right of Action*

In *Suter*, after finding that the Adoption Act did not create an enforceable right of action under section 1983, the Court briefly addressed whether the Adoption Act contained an implied right of action. The Court applied the familiar test from *Cort v. Ash*, 422 U.S. 66 (1975), and held that the Adoption Act did not. In the present case, plaintiffs' statutory claims are based solely upon section 1983 and not directly under the McKinney Act. Thus the court need not address whether the McKinney Act creates an implied right of action. Even if the court were to address this issue, however, the court would conclude that the McKinney Act does not contain an implied right of action.

. . . .

In addition, granting an implied right of action in this case would be inconsistent with the McKinney Act's overall statutory scheme. When read in its entirety, it is evident that the Act is designed to provide federal assistance to those states that choose to provide these programs to help educate homeless children. These grants are made only if the states submit a proper application and

---

[8]Since the court shall grant defendants' motion to dismiss on the ground that plaintiffs do not have a right of action under section 1983, the court need not pass on whether defendants have actually complied with the McKinney Act.

the decision to grant federal funds is left to the Secretary upon his review of the states' applications, laws and policies. Thus, according to the letter of the Act, the remedy for a state's failure to comply with its state plan lies with the Secretary of Education, not with parties like plaintiffs. To find an implied right of action in this case would be the equivalent of the judiciary rewriting the statute.

D. *Equal Protection*

The court shall also dismiss plaintiffs' equal protection claim.... In the present case, both parties agree that education is not a fundamental right and that no suspect classes are involved. *See Kadrmas v. Dickenson Public Schools*, 487 U.S. 451, 457-58 (1988). Thus, both parties recognize that rational basis scrutiny is appropriate for evaluating this claim.

Plaintiffs assert that defendants have violated their equal protection rights because defendants refuse to provide homeless children with necessary transportation assistance to and from school but defendants do provide transportation assistance to mentally and physically handicapped children. Defendants do treat homeless children differently than handicapped children for the purposes of providing transportation assistance to and from school. The court cannot find, however, that this disparate treatment violates plaintiffs' rights to equal protection under the Fifth and Fourteenth Amendments.

Defendants are required to provide transportation assistance to handicapped children under the Education for All Handicapped Children Act, 20 U.S.C. §§ 1400 *et seq*....

Defendants have a rational basis for treating handicapped children differently than homeless children for the purposes of providing transportation assistance to and from school. Handicapped children, because of their disability, are by definition less able to travel to school than non-disabled children. Plaintiffs have failed to show that homeless children, by virtue of their homelessness alone, are physically or mentally less capable of travelling to school than nonhomeless children.

Order

...For the reasons stated in the court's memorandum opinion of this date, it is hereby ORDERED that

    1. Defendants' motion to dismiss is GRANTED.
    2. Plaintiffs' motion for preliminary injunction is DENIED as moot.
    3. This case stands DISMISSED WITH PREJUDICE.

B. RESIDENCE AND CITIZENSHIP REQUIREMENTS

McCAIN v. KOCH
Supreme Court, Appellate Division
117 A.D.2d 198, 502 N.Y.S.2d 720 (1986)

ROSENBERGER, JUSTICE:

On these consolidated appeals we are called upon to consider whether homeless families with children are entitled to emergency shelter under the guarantees of equal protection of the New York State Constitution, the federal Constitution, and the State Plan for Emergency Assistance to Families with Needy Children. The issues arise in the context of appeals and cross-appeals from four orders entered by Special Term, New York County, in *Yvonne McCain v. Koch* and from an order entered in *Matter of Sharon Fulton v. Krauskopf*.

Statutory Framework and Factual Background

Under the New York Social Services Laws, policy and rule-making authority are concentrated in the State Department of Social Services (State DSS).... Primary responsibility for providing assistance and care, and for day-to-day administration of the manifold public assistance programs devolves upon the local social services departments.

New York participates in the federally funded program for Aid to Families With Dependent Children (AFDC). In conjunction with the AFDC program, New York has elected to participate in the program for Emergency Assistance to Needy Families with Children (EAF). Additional emergency and short-term aid are available under state-funded public assistance programs such as Home Relief (HR) and Emergency Assistance to Adults. Social Services Law §§ 157, 300. The State DSS monitors the local services departments, and when it discovers a failure to adhere to binding policies, directives, state regulations, or federal regulations in the AFDC and EAF programs, it may withhold or deny state reimbursement or require corrective action. Social Services Law § 20, 45 CFR 206.10(a)(12).

The City Department of Social Services (City DSS) operates Income Maintenance Centers (IMCs) which administer, *inter alia*, the AFDC, EAF and HR programs for client-recipients on a daily basis, and place families who have requested emergency shelter. The City DSS operates an Emergency Assistance Unit (EAU) in each borough except Staten Island. Families who seek emergency shelter during a weekend, or who have not received referrals to temporary housing from an IMC at the end of the business day, are referred to an EAU for placement. The City DSS attempts to locate hotel accommodations for homeless families. It provides shelter allowances for such accommodations for six months, and thereafter, for so long as the client seeks permanent housing. It receives state reimbursement for these payments for six months and thereafter, unless the average length of stay in such accommodations exceeds six months. 18 NYCRR 352.3(f). More recently the City DSS has sought space for clients in three family shelters operated by non-profit sponsors under contract with the City.

....

McCain v. Koch

Plaintiff Yvonne McCain and members of thirteen other homeless families with children commenced an action against the City, the State and City Commissioners of Social Services, and various city officials charged with the administration of programs to assist homeless families....

....

In their amended complaint, plaintiffs .... request a declaration that defendants' failures to provide eligible homeless families with (1) safe, suitable, and adequate emergency housing; (2) relocation benefits; (3) school transportation allowances, and, (4) notice and a hearing prior to termination of emergency shelter, violate the federal and state constitutions, statutes, and regulations. Plaintiffs pray for an injunction requiring defendants, *inter alia*, to provide the aforementioned benefits ...

Matter of Fulton v. Krauskopf

Petitioners Sharon Fulton and four other members of homeless families, including petitioner Yvonne McCain, commenced an Article 78 proceeding seeking class certification and a preliminary injunction requiring respondent Commissioners of the State and City DSS to provide emergency housing within the area where their minor children attend school or to provide transportation allowances based on actual costs for children and their parents where necessary. Their petition alleges that the City DSS has failed to comply with state policy concerning school transportation allowances and that its refusal to provide such allowances deprives their children of their right to a free education.

....

Decision at Special Term *in* Matter of Fulton v. Krauskopf

By decision ... and order entered June 29, 1984, in *Matter of Sharon Fulton v. Krauskopf*, Special Term (GREENFIELD, J.) issued a preliminary injunction directing respondents, the State and City Commissioners of DSS, to provide an allowance for actual school transportation costs on an individualized basis to homeless children and their parents. Special Term held that the $18 weekly travel allowance provided to parents as a matter of City policy was inadequate. JUSTICE GREENFIELD granted class certification, holding that the numerical requirement was met by the estimated number of 2,500 families affected and, additionally, that the matter would be decided most appropriately pursuant to generally applicable principles. It denied the respondents' cross-motion to dismiss, and ruled that the matter was not moot because of its "ongoing nature, and the lack of adequate general provision." Thereafter, respondents' application for leave to

B. RESIDENCE AND CITIZENSHIP REQUIREMENTS

appeal to this court was granted, and the appeal was consolidated with the appeals pending in *McCain v. Koch*....

....

Matter of Sharon Fulton v. Koch

... Section 62 of the Social Services Law places primary responsibility upon the local social services agencies for the delivery of services and assistance to needy families. *See Matter of Toia v. Regan*, 54 A.D.2d 46, 50, 387 N.Y.S.2d 309 (4th Dept., 1976), *affd.* 40 N.Y.2d 837, 387 N.Y.S.2d 832, 356 N.E.2d 276 (1976). The State DSS, in contrast, is responsible for supervision and reimbursement for the various state-funded programs of public assistance. Only the City DSS is the relevant party here, because it alone is accountable for the direct payment of actual transportation expenses incurred by or for relocation of homeless families. Contrary to the contention of the City DSS, this controversy is not moot. The City's failure, either to rehouse families in the area of their children's schools, or provide an adequate transportation allowance to cover the expense of commuting to school for children until they receive a transportation pass as well as for the parents of children too young to travel alone, presents an ongoing problem of public importance which is properly entertainable. *Matter of Jones v. Berman, supra* 37 N.Y.2d at 57, 371 N.Y.S.2d 422, 332 N.E.2d 303.

Under Article 11, Section 1 of the New York State Constitution and Article 65 of the Education Law, the State must provide free education to all children over age five. Compulsory attendance on a full-time basis is required, with exceptions not here relevant. Education Law § 3205(1). Section 3209 of the Education Law squarely places responsibility upon public welfare officials in local social services districts to provide indigent children with suitable clothing, shoes, books, food and other necessaries to enable them to attend school. *See also* Social Services Law § 397(1)(c). Funds for school transportation are a necessity under the meaning of these provisions. In our view, these statutes clearly obligate City DSS to provide actual transportation expenses, both for children until they obtain transportation passes from the Board of Education, and for the parents of young children who must be accompanied to school.

We agree with Special Term that the recently adopted City DSS policy of providing a flat travel allowance of $18 per week for parents is inadequate. In many instances the parents of children who reside in emergency shelters must travel through more than one fare zone each day. It makes no provision for children until their receipt of a transportation pass from the Board of Education. A flat grant forces these families to make an impossible choice between adequate nourishment and education. This policy is unconstitutional in that it deprives indigent children of the right to free education and amounts to a refusal to aid needy children. *See Tucker v. Toia, supra*, 43 N.Y.2d at 8, 400 N.Y.S.2d 728, 371 N.E.2d 449.

Contrary to respondents' contentions, Social Services Law § 350-j and its implementing regulation, 18 NYCRR § 372.4(d), also mandate the payment of transportation allowances for eligible families residing in emergency shelter. The State Commissioner's interpretation of the Section 350-j and 18 NYCRR § 372.4(d) as only authorizing benefits on a case-by-case basis cannot be sustained since it is irrational and unreasonable. As the EAF program concededly authorizes the subject benefits for eligible families in emergency situations, these benefits should be administered, like the emergency shelter benefits to which they relate, on a mandatory basis. 42 U.S.C. § 602(a)(1). *See Quern v. Mandley, supra,* 436 U.S. at 741-42. The State Commissioner's argument that ad hoc determinations distinct from the initial EAF eligibility determination are necessary is not persuasive. Homeless families who have met the test of eligibility for emergency shelter under the EAF program are automatically entitled to a transportation allowance if they have been relocated at a distance from their former communities and their children's schools. Special Term only recognized and declared petitioners' substantive right to reimbursement for actual transportation expenses. The court neither usurped the municipal respondents' adjudicatory authority nor bypassed the eligibility criteria for the EAF program.

....

Order of the Supreme Court, New York County (GREENFIELD, J.), ... in *Matter of Sharon Fulton v. Koch, et al.*, which granted petitioners' motion for class certification and a preliminary injunction to the extent of directing respondent State and City Commissioners of Social Services to provide the parent of each school-age child who needs accompaniment to and from school, a transportation allowance, and to provide each such child with such an allowance until the Board of Education provides such child with a transportation pass and denied respondents' cross-motions to dismiss the proceeding, should be modified, on the law, the motion for class certification should be denied, the cross-motion of the respondent State Commissioner to dismiss the petition should be granted and the proceeding should be dismissed against him, and, as so modified, should otherwise be affirmed, without costs.

....

All concur.

---

1. The very witty Judge Goettel in *Orozco* makes a point about judicial activism, just as Justice Rehnquist did in his *Plyler* dissent:

Perhaps in this age when legislators won't legislate and regulators won't regulate, preferring instead to spend their time carping at Federal judges who ultimately must step into the breach to protect individual rights from the capriciousness of ad hoc decision making, one should not be surprised at this state of affairs. On the other hand, it sadly leaves the goal of judicial restraint as a forgotten dream as we are forced to devote our energies full

B. RESIDENCE AND CITIZENSHIP REQUIREMENTS

time to safeguarding constitutionally-protected rights from being sucked up in the vacuum of legislative and regulatory dereliction.

Is judicial restraint a valid excuse? Did the dissent in *Plyler* have other hidden reasons for criticizing the majority decision?

Note that both the Courts in *Plyler* and *Orozco* recognized what their assigned tasks are as Courts, but also noticed the importance of providing educational opportunities to groups of people who may not have received them as quickly and efficiently through other means.

2. Both *Orozco* and *Harrison* cite to *United Pub. Workers v. Mitchell*, 330 U.S. 75 (1947), with respect to the plaintiffs' claims that the section 310 appeals process is "too complex, burdensome, and time-consuming" to satisfy due process. *Orozco*, at 131; *Harrison*, at 875. Interestingly enough, both plaintiffs never availed themselves of this process (going instead with a section 1983 claim) and therefore would not know (or it would be hard to show) just how burdensome the procedure is. As a consequence, both section 301 claims were dismissed for lack of standing.

3. *Lampkin* appears to indicate a shift of direction in cases dealing with the education of homeless children. In the other two such cases presented here (*Orozco* and *Harrison*), much care was taken in granting plaintiffs relief. In *Lampkin*, however, plaintiffs' action was dismissed for failure to state a claim upon which relief could be granted. The court noted that the mandatory language in the McKinney Act did not create an enforceable right under section 1983; it merely told the Secretary of Education what to consider when reviewing applications for federal funding for education for the homeless.

4. Both *Orozco* and *Harrison* were filed following the enactment of the McKinney Homeless Assistance Act, Pub. L. No. 100-77, § 103(a), 101 Stat. 482 (1987). *Orozco*, like *Lampkin*, was a section 1983 action filed with violations of the McKinney Act in mind. But, in an age of continuing concern and support for the homeless, *Lampkin* was decided against the plaintiffs. What is the difference between *Lampkin* and these other cases? How much of a role does the 1992 *Suter* case, cited in *Lampkin*, play?

5. Should punitive damages have been awarded in *Harrison*? The court emphasized the new regulations which required written notice and an opportunity to be heard regarding the child's right to attend school in the district which denied admission. 8 NYCRR § 100.2(x-y). Surely the defendants knew about these and the N.Y. Educ. L. §§ 3202-03.

6. "The New York Commissioner of Education has held that, for school residency purposes, 'homeless' children temporarily housed in motels are entitled under § 3202 of the New York Education Law to continue to attend their home school districts." *Matter of Richards*, 25 Educ. Dep't Rep. 38 (July 17, 1985). *Harrison* at 874.

What does the Commissioner mean by the phrase "*home* school districts"? Does this apply only to families who *become* homeless after living in a home in the district? Does it apply to the district in which the motel is located? How does this affect the Harrison family? Is this 1985 decision in *Richards* consistent with *Orozco*, a 1987 decision? What are the "home" districts in *Orozco* and *Harrison*?

7. Camilla M. Cochrane, in an article for the *University of Miami Law Review* notes that in cases argued prior to the passage of the McKinney Act — *Delgado*, for example — the issue concerned residency requirements. "The right to education was never in question." *The Homeless School-Age Child: Can Educational Rights Meet Educational Needs*, 45 U. Miami L. Rev. 537, 546 (1990-1991).*

Another concern of Cochrane's was that the McKinney Act did not provide sanctions for noncompliance. This leaves the rights derived from the McKinney Act extremely dependent on the initiative of individual states to implement the provisions of the Act. *Id*. at 541.

8. Are handicapped children and homeless children comparable? Cochrane thinks they are, and suggests that litigants use special education jurisprudence to "provide teeth for the McKinney Act." *Id*. at 566.

For example, according to Cochrane:

> Section 504 of the Rehabilitation Act could provide a vehicle for homeless handicapped children to assert claims for substantial denials of educational opportunity. A state's failure to develop and implement state plan requirements related to breaking down barriers to educational access — as in a failure to provide transportation — would be grounds for a claim. *Id*. at 561.

Under the broad interpretation of 504, "handicapped individuals" include those who have a physical or mental impairment which substantially limits one or more of their major life activities, have a record of such impairment, or are regarded as having such an impairment. Insofar as their conditions impair their ability to learn, homeless children may be able to assert claims under 504. Cochrane at 557.

9. Patricia First and G. Robb Cooper compare homeless children to children of illegal aliens and migrants. *Access to Education by Homeless Children*, 53 Educ. L. Rep. 757 (1989). In *Plyler v. Doe*, presented earlier in this chapter, the Supreme Court ruled that the children of illegal aliens were entitled to access to public education under the aegis of the equal protection clause of the Fourteenth Amendment and that all children are subject to the laws of the state.

Applying *Plyler* to homeless children, First and Robb concluded that since every state has established a system of free public education and every homeless

---

*Reprinted with permission of the University of Miami Law Review, which holds copyright on this article.

child in the United States is a person within the jurisdiction of some state, then every homeless child is entitled to access to a system of public education.

How does this conclusion hold up against the many remarks that the *Plyler* decision was explicitly narrow?

10. What about alternative school programs for the homeless? Examples include schools conducted in homeless shelters, and mobile schools. Would these violate the McKinney Act? They seem to, since one of the Act's primary goals is to enroll homeless children in regular public schools. Integration of homeless children with the non-homeless is key, with the assurance that the children are not isolated and stigmatized. However, what are some of the advantages of alternative school programs for the homeless? More children may be reached. With more attention paid to the needs of these children, there may be a greater possibility for success. Some may say that the current state of affairs in public school systems is poor enough that non-homeless children are not even getting the proper education. *See* Masters, *Opening the Schoolhouse Gate to Homeless Children*, 1991 U. Chi. Legal F. 335 (1991).

C. COMPULSORY EDUCATION

PIERCE v. SOCIETY OF SISTERS OF THE HOLY NAMES OF JESUS AND MARY
SAME v. HILL MILITARY ACADEMY

Supreme Court of the United States
268 U.S. 510 (1925)

MR. JUSTICE MCREYNOLDS delivered the opinion of the Court:

These appeals are from decrees, based upon undenied allegations, which granted preliminary orders restraining appellants from threatening or attempting to enforce the Compulsory Education Act adopted November 7, 1922 (Laws Or. 1923, p. 9), under the initiative provision of her Constitution by the voters of Oregon. Judicial Code, § 266 (Comp.St. § 1243). They present the same points of law; there are no controverted questions of fact. Rights said to be guaranteed by the federal Constitution were specially set up, and appropriate prayers asked for their protection.

The challenged Act, effective September 1, 1926, requires every parent, guardian or other person having control or charge or custody of a child between 8 and 16 years to send him "to a public school for the period of time a public school shall be held during the current year" in the district where the child resides; and failure so to do is declared a misdemeanor. There are exemptions — not specially important here — for children who are not normal, or who have completed the eighth grade, or who reside at considerable distances from any public school, or whose parents or guardians hold special permits from the county superintendent. The manifest purpose is to compel general attendance at public schools by normal children, between 8 and 16, who have not completed the eighth grade. And without doubt enforcement of the statute would seriously impair, perhaps destroy, the profitable features of appellees' business and greatly diminish the value of their property.

Appellee, the Society of Sisters, is an Oregon corporation, organized in 1880, with power to care for orphans, educate and instruct the youth, establish and maintain academies or schools, and acquire necessary real and personal property. It has long devoted its property and effort to the secular and religious education and care of children, and has acquired the valuable good will of many parents and guardians. It conducts interdependent primary and high schools and junior colleges, and maintains orphanages for the custody and control of children between 8 and 16. In its primary schools many children between those ages are taught the subjects usually pursued in Oregon public schools during the first eight years. Systematic religious instruction and moral training according to the tenets of the Roman Catholic Church are also regularly provided. All courses of study, both temporal and religious, contemplate continuity of training under appellee's charge; the primary schools are essential to the system and the most profitable. It owns valuable buildings, especially constructed and equipped for school purposes. The business is remunerative — the annual income from primary schools exceeds $30,000 — and the successful conduct of this requires long-time contracts with teachers and parents. The Compulsory Education Act of 1922 has already caused the withdrawal from its schools of children who would otherwise continue, and their income has steadily declined. The appellants, public officers, have proclaimed their purpose strictly to enforce the statute.

After setting out the above facts, the Society's bill alleges that the enactment conflicts with the right of parents to choose schools where their children will receive appropriate mental and religious training, the right of the child to influence the parents' choice of a school, the right of schools and teachers therein to engage in a useful business or profession, and is accordingly repugnant to the Constitution and void. And, further, that unless enforcement of the measure is enjoined the corporation's business and property will suffer irreparable injury.

Appellee, Hill Military Academy, is a private corporation organized in 1908 under the laws of Oregon, engaged in owning, operating and conducting for profit an elementary, college preparatory and military training school for boys between the ages of 5 and 21 years. The average attendance is 100, and the annual fees received for each student amount to some $800. The elementary department is divided into eight grades, as in the public schools; the college preparatory department has four grades, similar to those of the public high schools; the courses of study conform to the requirements of the State Board of Education. Military instruction and training are also given, under the supervision of an Army officer. It owns considerable real and personal property, some useful only for school purposes. The business and incident good will are very valuable. In order to conduct its affairs, long-time contracts must be made for supplies, equipment, teachers and pupils. Appellants, law officers of the State and County, have publicly announced that the Act of November 7, 1922, is valid and have

C. COMPULSORY EDUCATION

declared their intention to enforce it. By reason of the statute and threat of enforcement appellee's business is being destroyed and its property depreciated; parents and guardians are refusing to make contracts for the future instruction of their sons, and some are being withdrawn.

The Academy's bill states the foregoing facts and then alleges that the challenged Act contravenes the corporation's rights guaranteed by the Fourteenth Amendment and that unless appellants are restrained from proclaiming its validity and threatening to enforce it, irreparable injury will result. The prayer is for an appropriate injunction.

No answer was interposed in either cause, and after proper notices they were heard by three judges (Judicial Code § 266 [Comp. St. § 1243]) on motions for preliminary injunctions upon the specifically alleged facts. The court ruled that the Fourteenth Amendment guaranteed appellees against the deprivation of their property without due process of law consequent upon the unlawful interference by appellants with the free choice of patrons, present and prospective. It declared the right to conduct schools was property and that parents and guardians, as a part of their liberty, might direct the education of children by selecting reputable teachers and places. Also, that these schools were not unfit or harmful to the public, and that enforcement of the challenged statute would unlawfully deprive them of patronage and thereby destroy their owners' business and property. Finally, that the threats to enforce the Act would continue to cause irreparable injury; and the suits were not premature.

No question is raised concerning the power of the State reasonably to regulate all schools, to inspect, supervise and examine them, their teachers and pupils; to require that all children of proper age attend some school, that teachers shall be of good moral character and patriotic disposition, that certain studies plainly essential to good citizenship must be taught, and that nothing be taught which is manifestly inimical to the public welfare.

The inevitable practical result of enforcing the Act under consideration would be destruction of appellees' primary schools, and perhaps all other private primary schools for normal children within the State of Oregon. These parties are engaged in a kind of undertaking not inherently harmful, but long regarded as useful and meritorious. Certainly there is nothing in the present records to indicate that they have failed to discharge their obligations to patrons, students or the State. And there are no peculiar circumstances or present emergencies which demand extraordinary measures relative to primary education.

Under the doctrine of *Meyer v. Nebraska*, 262 U.S. 390, we think it entirely plain that the Act of 1922 unreasonably interferes with the liberty of parents and guardians to direct the upbringing and education of children under their control. As often heretofore pointed out, rights guaranteed by the Constitution may not be abridged by legislation which has no reasonable relation to some purpose within the competency of the State. The fundamental theory of liberty upon which all governments in this Union repose excludes any general power of the State to standardize its children by forcing them to accept instruction from public teachers only. The child is not the mere creature of the State; those who nurture him and direct his destiny have the right, coupled with the high duty, to recognize and prepare him for additional obligations.

....

The suits were not premature. The injury to appellees was present and very real, not a mere possibility in the remote future. If no relief had been possible prior to the effective date of the Act, the injury would have become irreparable. Prevention of impending injury by unlawful action is a well-recognized function of courts of equity.

The decrees below are

Affirmed.

....

---

1. In *Pierce*, the Court relied heavily on the "doctrine of *Meyer v. Nebraska*," which appears in Chapter 3. Justice McReynolds was also the author of *Meyer*, in which the Court reversed the conviction of a private school teacher under a Nebraska statute making it a crime to teach any language other than English or any other subject in a language other than English to students who have not finished eighth grade. The Court held that the Fourteenth Amendment right to be free from deprivation of liberty without due process of law protected the right of the teacher to teach a language, German in this case, and the right of the parents so to engage him.

Both cases, *Pierce* and *Meyer*, are best understood when placed in historical perspective. At the time they were decided, they were consistent with the generally prevailing judicial skepticism regarding any government interference with the rights of citizens. *Pierce* and *Meyer* are both couched in the same substantive due process language which characterized the now discredited cases, such as *Lochner v. New York*, 198 U.S. 45 (1905), declaring state attempts to regulate the economy invalid.

2. Should either *Pierce* or *Meyer* still be good law? For example, is the Fourteenth Amendment violated by a state decision to compel every person of a certain age to attend public school, based on the state's view that only then will the school serve its function as a "melting pot"? If the answer to this is that such action is unconstitutional, does that answer change if the state's purpose is to compel integration by preventing whites from starting private schools to avoid the thrust of *Brown v. Board of Educ.*, 347 U.S. 483 (1954)?

3. On the other hand, what of the argument that *Pierce* and *Meyer* represent decisions protecting generally the privacy of the family unit, particularly, the right of parents to control the education and lifestyle of their children? Note that in *Griswold v. Connecticut*, 381 U.S. 479 (1965), (where the Connecticut statute banning the use of contraceptives was held to be unconstitutional), both the majority opinion of Justice Douglas and the concurring opinion of Justice Goldberg cite *Pierce* and *Meyer* with approval.

The majority opinion states:

> By *Pierce v. Society of Sisters, supra*, the right to educate one's children as one chooses is made applicable to the States by force of the First and Fourteenth Amendments. By *Meyer v. Nebraska, supra*, the same dignity is given the right to study the German language in a private school. 381 U.S. at 482.

See also Roe v. Wade, 410 U.S. 113, 152-55, 170 (1973) and *Wisconsin v. Yoder*, which follows these notes.

If this is so, what does this right mean as to the issues of public funding of private schools, curriculum choice, school control over student conduct, community control, and, indeed, compulsory education itself? How does this right fare when it conflicts with the "rights" of the general community, the students, the teachers and administrators, and, indeed, of other parents?

4. If the statute in *Pierce* were rewritten to exempt private and religion-affiliated schools which conform to the requirements of the State board of education, would it survive a constitutional challenge?

5. Does the statute in *Pierce*, and the Court's opinion, allow for home schooling?

The questions in this note will be treated throughout the materials in this book.

WISCONSIN v. YODER

Supreme Court of the United States
406 U.S. 205 (1972)

MR. CHIEF JUSTICE BURGER delivered the opinion of the Court:

On petition of the State of Wisconsin, we granted the writ in this case to review a decision of the Wisconsin Supreme Court holding that respondents' convictions for violating the State's compulsory school attendance law were invalid under the Free Exercise Clause of the First Amendment to the United States Constitution made applicable to the State by the Fourteenth Amendment. For the reasons hereafter stated we affirm the judgment of the Supreme Court of Wisconsin.

Respondents Jonas Yoder and Adin Yutzy are members of the Old Order Amish Religion, and respondent Wallace Miller is a member of the Conservative Amish Mennonite Church. They and their families are residents of Green County, Wisconsin. Wisconsin's compulsory school attendance law required them to cause their children to attend public or private school until reaching age 16 but the respondents declined to send their children, ages 14 and 15, to public school after they completed the eighth grade. The children were not enrolled in any private school, or within any recognized exception to the compulsory-attendance law,[2] and they are conceded to be subject to the Wisconsin statute.

On complaint of the school district administrator for the public schools, respondents were charged, tried, and convicted of violating the compulsory-attendance law in Green County Court and were fined the sum of $5.00 each. Respondents defended on the ground that the application of the compulsory-attendance law violated their rights under the First and Fourteenth Amendments. The trial testimony showed that respondents believed, in accordance with the tenets of Old Order Amish communities generally, that their children's attendance at high school, public or private, was contrary to the Amish religion and way of life. They believed that by sending their children to high school, they would not only expose themselves to the danger of the censure of the church community, but, as found by the county court, also endanger their own salvation and that of their children. The State stipulated that respondents' religious beliefs were sincere.

In support of their position, respondents presented as expert witnesses scholars on religion and education whose testimony is uncontradicted. They expressed their opinions on the relationship of the Amish belief concerning school attendance to the more general tenets of their religion, and described the impact that compulsory high school attendance could have on the continued survival of Amish communities as they exist in the United States today. The history of the Amish sect was given in some detail, beginning with the Swiss Anabaptists of the 16th century who rejected institutionalized churches and sought to return to the

---

[2]Wis.Stat. § 118.15 (1969) provides in pertinent part:

118.15 Compulsory school attendance

(1)(a) Unless the child has a legal excuse or has graduated from high school, any person having under his control a child who is between the ages of 7 and 16 years shall cause such child to attend school regularly during the full period and hours, religious holidays excepted, that the public or private school in which such child should be enrolled is in session until the end of the school term, quarter or semester of the school year in which he becomes 16 years of age.

(3) This section does not apply to any child who is not in proper physical or mental condition to attend school, to any child exempted for good cause by the school board of the district in which the child resides or to any child who has completed the full 4-year high school course. The certificate of a reputable physician in general practice shall be sufficient proof that a child is unable to attend school.

(4) Instruction during the required period elsewhere than at school may be substituted for school attendance. Such instruction must be approved by the state superintendent as substantially equivalent to instruction given to children of like ages in the public or private schools where such children reside.

(5) Whoever violates this section ... may be fined not less than $5 nor more than $50 or imprisoned not more than 3 months or both.

Section 118.15(1)(b) requires attendance to age 18 in a school district containing a "vocational, technical and adult education school," but this section is concededly inapplicable in this case, for there is no such school in the district involved.

C. COMPULSORY EDUCATION

early, simple, Christian life de-emphasizing material success, rejecting the competitive spirit, and seeking to insulate themselves from the modern world. As a result of their common heritage, Old Order Amish communities today are characterized by a fundamental belief that salvation requires life in a church community separate and apart from the world and worldly influence. This concept of life aloof from the world and its values is central to their faith.

....

Formal high school education beyond the eighth grade is contrary to Amish beliefs, not only because it places Amish children in an environment hostile to Amish beliefs with increasing emphasis on competition in class work and sports and with pressure to conform to the styles, manners, and ways of the peer group, but also because it takes them away from their community, physically and emotionally, during the crucial and formative adolescent period of life....

The Amish do not object to elementary education through the first eight grades as a general proposition because they agree that their children must have basic skills in the "three R's" in order to read the Bible, to be good farmers and citizens, and to be able to deal with non-Amish people when necessary in the course of daily affairs. They view such a basic education as acceptable because it does not significantly expose their children to worldly values or interfere with their development in the Amish community during the crucial adolescent period. While Amish accept compulsory elementary education generally, wherever possible they have established their own elementary schools in many respects like the small local schools of the past. In the Amish belief higher learning tends to develop values they reject as influences that alienate man from God.

....

I

There is no doubt as to the power of a State, having a high responsibility for education of its citizens, to impose reasonable regulations for the control and duration of basic education. *See, e.g., Pierce v. Society of Sisters*, 268 U.S. 510, 534 (1925). Providing public schools ranks at the very apex of the function of a State. Yet even this paramount responsibility was, in *Pierce*, made to yield to the right of parents to provide an equivalent education in a privately operated system. There the Court held that Oregon's statute compelling attendance in a public school from age eight to age 16 unreasonably interfered with the interest of parents in directing the rearing of their offspring, including their education in church-operated schools. As that case suggests, the values of parental direction of the religious upbringing and education of their children in their early and formative years have a high place in our society. *See also Ginsberg v. New York*, 390 U.S. 629, 639 (1968); *Meyer v. Nebraska*, 262 U.S. 390 (1923); *cf. Rowan v. Post Office Dept.*, 397 U.S. 728 (1970). Thus, a State's interest in universal education, however highly we rank it, is not totally free from a balancing process when it impinges on fundamental rights and interests, such as those specifically protected by the Free Exercise Clause of the First Amendment, and the traditional interest of parents with respect to the religious upbringing of their children so long as they, in the words of *Pierce*, "prepare [them] for additional obligations." 268 U.S. at 535.

It follows that in order for Wisconsin to compel school attendance beyond the eighth grade against a claim that such attendance interferes with the practice of a legitimate religious belief, it must appear either that the State does not deny the free exercise of religious belief by its requirement, or that there is a state interest of sufficient magnitude to override the interest claiming protection under the Free Exercise Clause....

....

II

We come then to the quality of the claims of the respondents concerning the alleged encroachment of Wisconsin's compulsory school-attendance statute on their rights and the rights of their children to the free exercise of the religious beliefs they and their forbears have adhered to for almost three centuries. In evaluating those claims we must be careful to determine whether the Amish religious faith and their mode of life are, as they claim, inseparable and interdependent. A way of life, however virtuous and admirable, may not be interposed as a barrier to reasonable state regulation of education if it is based on purely secular considerations; to have the protection of the Religion Clauses, the claims must be rooted in religious belief. Although a determination of what is a "religious" belief or practice entitled to constitutional protection may present a most delicate question, the very concept of ordered liberty precludes allowing every person to make his own standards on matters of conduct in which society as a whole has important interests. Thus, if the Amish asserted their claims because of their subjective evaluation and rejection of the contemporary secular values accepted by the majority, much as Thoreau rejected the social values of his time and isolated himself at Walden Pond, their claims would not rest on a religious basis. Thoreau's choice was philosophical and personal rather than religious, and such belief does not rise to the demands of the Religion Clauses.

Giving no weight to such secular considerations, however, we see that the record in this case abundantly supports the claim that the traditional way of life of the Amish is not merely a matter of personal preference, but one of deep religious conviction, shared by an organized group, and intimately related to daily living. That the Old Order Amish daily life and religious practice stem from their faith is shown by the fact that it is in response to their literal interpretation of the Biblical injunction from the Epistle of Paul to the Romans, "be not conformed to this world...." This command is fundamental to the Amish faith. Moreover, for the Old Order Amish, religion is not simply a matter of theocratic belief. As the expert witnesses explained, the Old Order Amish religion pervades and determines virtually their entire way of life, regulating it with the detail of the Talmudic diet through the strictly enforced rules of the church community.

C. COMPULSORY EDUCATION

The record shows that the respondents' religious beliefs and attitude toward life, family, and home have remained constant — perhaps some would say static — in a period of unparalleled progress in human knowledge generally and great changes in education. The respondents freely concede, and indeed assert as an article of faith, that their religious beliefs and what we would today call "life style" have not altered in fundamentals for centuries. Their way of life in a church-oriented community, separated from the outside world and "worldly" influences, their attachment to nature and the soil, is a way inherently simple and uncomplicated, albeit difficult to preserve against the pressures to conform. Their rejection of telephones, automobiles, radios, and television, their mode of dress, of speech, their habits of manual work do indeed set them apart from much of contemporary society; these customs are both symbolic and practical.

As the society around the Amish has become more populous, urban, industrialized, and complex, particularly in this century, government regulation of human affairs has correspondingly become more detailed and pervasive. The Amish mode of life has thus come into conflict increasingly with requirements of contemporary society exerting a hydraulic insistence on conformity to majoritarian standards. So long as compulsory education laws were confined to eight grades of elementary basic education imparted in a nearby rural schoolhouse, with a large proportion of students of the Amish faith, the Old Order Amish had little basis to fear that school attendance would expose their children to the worldly influence they reject. But modern compulsory secondary education in rural areas is now largely carried on in a consolidated school, often remote from the student's home and alien to his daily home life. As the record so strongly shows, the values and programs of the modern secondary school are in sharp conflict with the fundamental mode of life mandated by the Amish religion; modern laws requiring compulsory secondary education have accordingly engendered great concern and conflict. The conclusion is inescapable that secondary schooling, by exposing Amish children to worldly influences in terms of attitudes, goals, and values contrary to beliefs, and by substantially interfering with the religious development of the Amish child and his integration into the way of life of the Amish faith community at the crucial adolescent stage of development, contravenes the basic religious tenets and practice of the Amish faith, both as to the parent and the child.

The impact of the compulsory-attendance law on respondents' practice of the Amish religion is not only severe, but inescapable, for the Wisconsin law affirmatively compels them, under threat of criminal sanction, to perform acts undeniably at odds with fundamental tenets of their religious beliefs. *See Braunfeld v. Brown*, 366 U.S. 599, 605 (1961). Nor is the impact of the compulsoryattendance law confined to grave interference with important Amish religious tenets from a subjective point of view. It carries with it precisely the kind of objective danger to the free exercise of religion that the First Amendment was designed to prevent. As the record shows, compulsory school attendance to age 16 for Amish children carries with it a very real threat of undermining the

Amish community and religious practice as they exist today; they must either abandon belief and be assimilated into society at large, or be forced to migrate to some other and more tolerant region.[9]

In sum, the unchallenged testimony of acknowledged experts in education and religious history, almost 300 years of consistent practice, and strong evidence of a sustained faith pervading and regulating respondents' entire mode of life support the claim that enforcement of the State's requirement of compulsory formal education after the eighth grade would gravely endanger if not destroy the free exercise of respondents' religious beliefs.

III

Neither the findings of the trial court nor the Amish claims as to the nature of their faith are challenged in this Court by the State of Wisconsin. Its position is that the State's interest in universal compulsory formal secondary education to age 16 is so great that it is paramount to the undisputed claims of respondents that their mode of preparing their youth for Amish life, after the traditional elementary education, is an essential part of their religious belief and practice. Nor does the State undertake to meet the claim that the Amish mode of life and education is inseparable from and a part of the basic tenets of their religion — indeed, as much a part of their religious beliefs and practices as baptism, the confessional, or a sabbath may be for others.

Wisconsin concedes that under the Religion Clauses religious beliefs are absolutely free from the State's control, but it argues that "actions," even though religiously grounded, are outside the protection of the First Amendment. But our decisions have rejected the idea that religiously grounded conduct is always outside the protection of the Free Exercise Clause....

Nor can this case be disposed of on the grounds that Wisconsin's requirement for school attendance to age 16 applies uniformly to all citizens of the State and does not, on its face, discriminate against religions or a particular religion, or that it is motivated by legitimate secular concerns. A regulation neutral on its face may, in its application, nonetheless offend the constitutional requirement for governmental neutrality if it unduly burdens the free exercise of religion....

We turn, then, to the State's broader contention that its interest in its system of compulsory education is so compelling that even the established religious practices of the Amish must give way. Where fundamental claims of religious freedom are at stake, however, we cannot accept such a sweeping claim; despite its admitted validity in the generality of cases, we must searchingly examine the interests that the State seeks to promote by its requirement for compulsory

---

[9]Some States have developed working arrangements with the Amish regarding high school attendance. However, the danger to the continued existence of an ancient religious faith cannot be ignored simply because of the assumption that its adherents will continue to be able, at considerable sacrifice, to relocate in some more tolerant State or country or work out accommodations under threat of criminal prosecution....

C. COMPULSORY EDUCATION

education to age 16, and the impediment to those objectives that would flow from recognizing the claimed Amish exemption.

The State advances two primary arguments in support of its system of compulsory education. It notes, as Thomas Jefferson pointed out early in our history, that some degree of education is necessary to prepare citizens to participate effectively and intelligently in our open political system if we are to preserve freedom and independence. Further, education prepares individuals to be self-reliant and self-sufficient participants in society. We accept these propositions.

However, the evidence adduced by the Amish in this case is persuasively to the effect that an additional one or two years of formal high school [education] for Amish children in place of their long-established program of informal vocational education would do little to serve those interests. Respondents' experts testified at trial, without challenge, that the value of all education must be assessed in terms of its capacity to prepare the child for life. It is one thing to say that compulsory education for a year or two beyond the eighth grade may be necessary when its goal is the preparation of the child for life in modern society as the majority live, but it is quite another if the goal of education be viewed as the preparation of the child for life in the separated agrarian community that is the keystone of the Amish faith.

The State attacks respondents' position as one fostering "ignorance" from which the child must be protected by the State. No one can question the State's duty to protect children from ignorance but this argument does not square with the facts disclosed in the record. Whatever their idiosyncrasies as seen by the majority, this record strongly shows that the Amish community has been a highly successful social unit within our society, even if apart from the conventional "mainstream." Its members are productive and very law-abiding members of society; they reject public welfare in any of its usual modern forms. The Congress itself recognized their selfsufficiency by authorizing exemption of such groups as the Amish from the obligation to pay social security taxes.

It is neither fair nor correct to suggest that the Amish are opposed to education beyond the eighth grade level. What this record shows is that they are opposed to conventional formal education of the type provided by a certified high school because it comes at the child's crucial adolescent period of religious development. Dr. Donald Erickson, for example, testified that their system of learning-by-doing was an "ideal system" of education in terms of preparing Amish children for life as adults in the Amish community, and that "I would be inclined to say they do a better job in this than most of the rest of us do." As he put it, "These people aren't purporting to be learned people, and it seems to me the self-sufficiency of the community is the best evidence I can point to — whatever is being done seems to function well."

We must not forget that in the Middle Ages important values of the civilization of the Western World were preserved by members of religious orders who isolated themselves from all worldly influences against great obstacles. There can be no assumption that today's majority is "right" and the Amish and others like them are "wrong." A way of life that is odd or even erratic but interferes with no rights or interests of others is not to be condemned because it is different.

The State, however, supports its interest in providing an additional one or two years of compulsory high school education to Amish children because of the possibility that some such children will choose to leave the Amish community, and that if this occurs they will be ill-equipped for life. The State argues that if Amish children leave their church they should not be in the position of making their way in the world without the education available in the one or two additional years the State requires. However, on this record, that argument is highly speculative. There is no specific evidence of the loss of Amish adherents by attrition, nor is there any showing that upon leaving the Amish community Amish children, with their practical agricultural training and habits of industry and self-reliance, would become burdens on society because of educational shortcomings. Indeed, this argument of the State appears to rest primarily on the State's mistaken assumption, already noted, that the Amish do not provide any education for their children beyond the eighth grade, but allow them to grow in "ignorance." To the contrary, not only do the Amish accept the necessity for formal schooling through the eighth grade level, but continue to provide what has been characterized by the undisputed testimony of expert educators as an "ideal" vocational education for their children in the adolescent years.

There is nothing in this record to suggest that the Amish qualities of reliability, self-reliance, and dedication to work would fail to find ready markets in today's society. Absent some contrary evidence supporting the State's position, we are unwilling to assume that persons possessing such valuable vocational skills and habits are doomed to become burdens on society should they determine to leave the Amish faith, nor is there any basis in the record to warrant a finding that an additional one or two years of formal school education beyond the eighth grade would serve to eliminate any such problem that might exist.

Insofar as the State's claim rests on the view that a brief additional period of formal education is imperative to enable the Amish to participate effectively and intelligently in our democratic process, it must fall. The Amish alternative to formal secondary school education has enabled them to function effectively in their day-to-day life under self-imposed limitations on relations with the world, and to survive and prosper in contemporary society as a separate, sharply identifiable and highly self-sufficient community for more than 200 years in this country. In itself this is strong evidence that they are capable of fulfilling the social and political responsibilities of citizenship without compelled attendance beyond the eighth grade at the price of jeopardizing their free exercise of religious belief. When Thomas Jefferson emphasized the need for education as a bulwark of a free people against tyranny, there is nothing to indicate he had in mind compulsory education through any fixed age beyond a basic education. Indeed, the Amish communities singularly parallel and reflect many of the virtues of Jefferson's ideal of the "sturdy yeoman" who would form the basis of what

C. COMPULSORY EDUCATION

he considered as the ideal of a democratic society. Even their idiosyncratic separateness exemplifies the diversity we profess to admire and encourage.

The requirement for compulsory education beyond the eighth grade is a relatively recent development in our history. Less than 60 years ago, the educational requirements of almost all of the States were satisfied by completion of the elementary grades, at least where the child was regularly and lawfully employed. The independence and successful social functioning of the Amish community for a period approaching almost three centuries and more than 200 years in this country are strong evidence that there is at best a speculative gain, in terms of meeting the duties of citizenship, from an additional one or two years of compulsory formal education. Against this background it would require a more particularized showing from the State on this point to justify the severe interference with religious freedom such additional compulsory attendance would entail.

We should also note that compulsory education and child labor laws find their historical origin in common humanitarian instincts, and that the age limits of both laws have been coordinated to achieve their related objectives. In the context of this case, such considerations, if anything, support rather than detract from respondents' position. The origins of the requirement for school attendance to age 16, an age falling after the completion of elementary school but before completion of high school, are not entirely clear. But to some extent such laws reflected the movement to prohibit most child labor under age 16 that culminated in the provisions of the Federal Fair Labor Standards Act of 1938. It is true, then, that the 16-year child labor age limit may to some degree derive from a contemporary impression that children should be in school until that age. But at the same time, it cannot be denied that, conversely, the 16-year education limit reflects, in substantial measure, the concern that children under that age not be employed under conditions hazardous to their health, or in work that should be performed by adults.

The requirement of compulsory schooling to age 16 must therefore be viewed as aimed not merely at providing educational opportunities for children, but as an alternative to the equally undesirable consequence of unhealthful child labor displacing adult workers, or, on the other hand, forced idleness. The two kinds of statutes — compulsory school attendance and child labor laws — tend to keep children of certain ages off the labor market and in school; this regimen in turn provides opportunity to prepare for a livelihood of a higher order than that which children could pursue without education and protects their health in adolescence.

In these terms, Wisconsin's interest in compelling the school attendance of Amish children to age 16 emerges as somewhat less substantial than requiring such attendance for children generally. For, while agricultural employment is not totally outside the legitimate concerns of the child labor laws, employment of children under parental guidance and on the family farm from age 14 to age 16 is an ancient tradition that lies at the periphery of the objectives of such laws. There is no intimation that the Amish employment of their children on family farms is in any way deleterious to their health or that Amish parents exploit children at tender years. Any such inference would be contrary to the record before us. Moreover, employment of Amish children on the family farm does not present the undesirable economic aspects of eliminating jobs that might otherwise be held by adults.

IV

Finally, the State, on authority of *Prince v. Massachusetts*, argues that a decision exempting Amish children from the State's requirement fails to recognize the substantive right of the Amish child to a secondary education, and fails to give due regard to the power of the State as *parens patriae* to extend the benefit of secondary education to children regardless of the wishes of their parents. Taken at its broadest sweep, the Court's language in *Prince*, might be read to give support to the State's position. However, the Court was not confronted in *Prince* with a situation comparable to that of the Amish as revealed in this record; this is shown by the Court's severe characterization of the evils that it thought the legislature could legitimately associate with child labor, even when performed in the company of an adult. 321 U.S. at 169-70. The Court later took great care to confine *Prince* to a narrow scope in *Sherbert v. Verner*, when it stated:

> "On the other hand, the Court has rejected challenges under the Free Exercise Clause to governmental regulation of certain overt acts prompted by religious beliefs or principles, for 'even when the action is in accord with one's religious convictions, [it] is not totally free from legislative restrictions.' *Braunfeld v. Brown*, 366 U.S. 599, 603. The conduct or actions so regulated have invariably posed some substantial threat to public safety, peace or order. *See, e.g., Reynolds v. United States*, 98 U.S. 145; *Jacobson v. Massachusetts*, 197 U.S. 11; *Prince v. Massachusetts*, 321 U.S. 158...." 374 U.S. at 402-03.

This case, of course, is not one in which any harm to the physical or mental health of the child or to the public safety, peace, order, or welfare has been demonstrated or may be properly inferred. The record is to the contrary, and any reliance on that theory would find no support in the evidence.

Contrary to the suggestion of the dissenting opinion of MR. JUSTICE DOUGLAS, our holding today in no degree depends on the assertion of the religious interest of the child as contrasted with that of the parents. It is the parents who are subject to prosecution here for failing to cause their children to attend school, and it is their right of free exercise, not that of their children, that must determine Wisconsin's power to impose criminal penalties on the parent. The dissent argues that a child who expresses a desire to attend public high school in conflict with the wishes of his parents should not be prevented from doing so. There is no reason for the Court to consider that point since it is not an issue in the case. The children are not parties to this litigation. The State has at no point

C. COMPULSORY EDUCATION

tried this case on the theory that respondents were preventing their children from attending school against their expressed desires, and indeed the record is to the contrary. The State's position from the outset has been that it is empowered to apply its compulsory-attendance law to Amish parents in the same manner as to other parents — that is, without regard to the wishes of the child. That is the claim we reject today.

Our holding in no way determines the proper resolution of possible competing interests of parents, children, and the State in an appropriate state court proceeding in which the power of the State is asserted on the theory that Amish parents are preventing their minor children from attending high school despite their expressed desires to the contrary. Recognition of the claim of the State in such a proceeding would, of course, call into question traditional concepts of parental control over the religious upbringing and education of their minor children recognized in this Court's past decisions. It is clear that such an intrusion by a State into family decisions in the area of religious training would give rise to grave questions of religious freedom comparable to those raised here and those presented in *Pierce v. Society of Sisters*, 268 U.S. 510 (1925). On this record we neither reach nor decide those issues.

The State's argument proceeds without reliance on any actual conflict between the wishes of parents and children. It appears to rest on the potential that exemption of Amish parents from the requirements of the compulsory-education law might allow some parents to act contrary to the best interests of their children by foreclosing their opportunity to make an intelligent choice between the Amish way of life and that of the outside world. The same argument could, of course, be made with respect to all church schools short of college. There is nothing in the record or in the ordinary course of human experience to suggest that non-Amish parents generally consult with children of ages 14-16 if they are placed in a church school of the parents' faith.

Indeed it seems clear that if the State is empowered, as *parens patriae*, to "save" a child from himself or his Amish parents by requiring an additional two years of compulsory formal high school education, the State will in large measure influence, if not determine, the religious future of the child. Even more markedly than in *Prince*, therefore, this case involves the fundamental interest of parents, as contrasted with that of the State, to guide the religious future and education of their children. The history and culture of Western civilization reflect a strong tradition of parental concern for the nurture and upbringing of their children. This primary role of the parents in the upbringing of their children is now established beyond debate as an enduring American tradition. If not the first, perhaps the most significant statements of the Court in this area are found in *Pierce v. Society of Sisters*, in which the Court observed:

> Under the doctrine of *Meyer v. Nebraska*, 262 U.S. 390, we think it entirely plain that the Act of 1922 unreasonably interferes with the liberty of parents and guardians to direct the upbringing and education of children

under their control. As often heretofore pointed out, rights guaranteed by the Constitution may not be abridged by legislation which has no reasonable relation to some purpose within the competency of the State. The fundamental theory of liberty upon which all governments in this Union repose excludes any general power of the State to standardize its children by forcing them to accept instruction from public teachers only. The child is not the mere creature of the State; those who nurture him and direct his destiny have the right, coupled with the high duty, to recognize and prepare him for additional obligations. 268 U.S. at 534-35.

The duty to prepare the child for "additional obligations," referred to by the Court, must be read to include the inculcation of moral standards, religious beliefs, and elements of good citizenship. *Pierce*, of course, recognized that where nothing more than the general interest of the parent in the nurture and education of his children is involved, it is beyond dispute that the State acts "reasonably" and constitutionally in requiring education to age 16 in some public or private school meeting the standards prescribed by the State.

However read, the Court's holding in *Pierce* stands as a charter of the rights of parents to direct the religious upbringing of their children. And, when the interests of parenthood are combined with a free exercise claim of the nature revealed by this record, more than merely a "reasonable relation to some purpose within the competency of the State" is required to sustain the validity of the State's requirement under the First Amendment. To be sure, the power of the parent, even when linked to a free exercise claim, may be subject to limitation under *Prince* if it appears that parental decisions will jeopardize the health or safety of the child, or have a potential for significant social burdens. But in this case, the Amish have introduced persuasive evidence undermining the arguments the State has advanced to support its claims in terms of the welfare of the child and society as a whole. The record strongly indicates that accommodating the religious objections of the Amish by forgoing one, or at most two, additional years of compulsory education will not impair the physical or mental health of the child, or result in an inability to be self-supporting or to discharge the duties and responsibilities of citizenship, or in any other way materially detract from the welfare of society.

In the face of our consistent emphasis on the central values underlying the Religion Clauses in our constitutional scheme of government, we cannot accept a *parens patriae* claim of such all-encompassing scope and with such sweeping potential for broad and unforeseeable application as that urged by the State.

V

For the reasons stated we hold, with the Supreme Court of Wisconsin, that the First and Fourteenth Amendments prevent the State from compelling respondents

C. COMPULSORY EDUCATION

to cause their children to attend formal high school to age 16.[22] Our disposition of this case, however, in no way alters our recognition of the obvious facts that courts are not school boards or legislatures, and are ill-equipped to determine the "necessity" of discrete aspects of a State's program of compulsory education. This should suggest that courts must move with great circumspection in performing the sensitive and delicate task of weighing a State's legitimate social concern when faced with religious claims for exemption from generally applicable educational requirements. It cannot be overemphasized that we are not dealing with a way of life and mode of education by a group claiming to have recently discovered some "progressive" or more enlightened process for rearing children for modern life.

Aided by a history of three centuries as an identifiable religious sect and a long history as a successful and self-sufficient segment of American society, the Amish in this case have convincingly demonstrated the sincerity of their religious beliefs, the interrelationship of belief with their mode of life, the vital role that belief and daily conduct play in the continued survival of Old Order Amish communities and their religious organization, and the hazards presented by the State's enforcement of a statute generally valid as to others. Beyond this, they have carried the even more difficult burden of demonstrating the adequacy of their alternative mode of continuing informal vocational education in terms of precisely those overall interests that the State advances in support of its program of compulsory high school education. In light of this convincing showing, one that probably few other religious groups or sects could make, and weighing the minimal difference between what the State would require and what the Amish already accept, it was incumbent on the State to show with more particularity how its admittedly strong interest in compulsory education would be adversely affected by granting an exemption to the Amish. *Sherbert v. Verner, supra.*

Nothing we hold is intended to undermine the general applicability of the State's compulsory school-attendance statutes or to limit the power of the State to promulgate reasonable standards that, while not impairing the free exercise of

---

[22]What we have said should meet the suggestion that the decision of the Wisconsin Supreme Court recognizing an exemption for the Amish from the State's system of compulsory education constituted an impermissible establishment of religion. In *Walz v. Tax Commission*, the Court saw the three main concerns against which the Establishment Clause sought to protect as "sponsorship, financial support, and active involvement of the sovereign in religious activity." 397 U.S. 664, 668 (1970). Accommodating the religious beliefs of the Amish can hardly be characterized as sponsorship or active involvement. The purpose and effect of such an exemption are not to support, favor, advance, or assist the Amish, but to allow their centuries-old religious society, here long before the advent of any compulsory education, to survive free from the heavy impediment compliance with the Wisconsin compulsory-education law would impose. Such an accommodation "reflects nothing more than the governmental obligation of neutrality in the face of religious differences, and does not represent that involvement of religious with secular institutions which it is the object of the Establishment Clause to forestall." *Sherbert v. Verner*, 374 U.S. 398, 409 (1963).

religion, provide for continuing agricultural vocational education under parental and church guidance by the Old Order Amish or others similarly situated. The States have had a long history of amicable and effective relationships with church-sponsored schools, and there is no basis for assuming that, in this related context, reasonable standards cannot be established concerning the content of the continuing vocational education of Amish children under parental guidance, provided always that state regulations are not inconsistent with what we have said in this opinion.

Affirmed.

....

MR. JUSTICE WHITE, with whom MR. JUSTICE BRENNAN and MR. JUSTICE STEWART join, concurring:

Cases such as this one inevitably call for a delicate balancing of important but conflicting interests. I join the opinion and judgment of the Court because I cannot say that the State's interest in requiring two more years of compulsory education in the ninth and tenth grades outweighs the importance of the concededly sincere Amish religious practice to the survival of that sect.

This would be a very different case for me if respondents' claim were that their religion forbade their children from attending any school at any time and from complying in any way with the educational standards set by the State. Since the Amish children are permitted to acquire the basic tools of literacy to survive in modern society by attending grades one through eight and since the deviation from the State's compulsory education law is relatively slight, I conclude that respondents' claim must prevail, largely because "religious freedom — the freedom to believe and to practice strange and, it may be, foreign creeds — has classically been one of the highest values of our society." *Braunfeld v. Brown*, 366 U.S. 599, 612 (1961) (Brennan, J., concurring and dissenting).

The importance of the state interest asserted here cannot be denigrated, however:

> Today, education is perhaps the most important function of state and local governments. Compulsory school attendance laws and the great expenditures for education both demonstrate our recognition of the importance of education to our democratic society. It is required in the performance of our most basic public responsibilities, even service in the armed forces. It is the very foundation of good citizenship. Today it is a principal instrument in awakening the child to cultural values, in preparing him for later professional training, and in helping him to adjust normally to his environment. *Brown v. Board of Educ.*, 347 U.S. 483, 493 (1954).

As recently as last Term, the Court re-emphasized the legitimacy of the State's concern for enforcing minimal educational standards, *Lemon v. Kurtzman*, 403 U.S. 602, 613 (1971). *Pierce v. Society of Sisters*, 268 U.S. 510 (1925), lends no support to the contention that parents may replace state educational requirements with their own idiosyncratic views of what knowledge a child needs to be a productive and happy member of society; in *Pierce*, both the parochial and military schools were in compliance with all the educational standards which the State had set, and the Court held simply that while a State may posit such standards, it may not pre-empt the educational process by requiring children to attend public schools. In the present case, the State is not concerned with the maintenance of an educational system as an end in itself, it is rather attempting to nurture and develop the human potential of its children, whether Amish or non-Amish: to expand their knowledge, broaden their sensibilities, kindle their imagination, foster a spirit of free inquiry, and increase their human understanding and tolerance. It is possible that most Amish children will wish to continue living the rural life of their parents, in which case their training at home will adequately equip them for their future role. Others, however, may wish to become nuclear physicists, ballet dancers, computer programmers, or historians, and for these occupations, formal training will be necessary. There is evidence in the record that many children desert the Amish faith when they come of age. A State has a legitimate interest not only in seeking to develop the latent talents of its children but in seeking to prepare them for the life style which they may later choose or at least to provide them with an option other than the life they have led in the past. In the circumstances of this case, although the question is close, I am unable to say that the State has demonstrated that Amish children who leave school in the eighth grade will be intellectually stultified or unable to acquire new academic skills later. The statutory minimum school attendance age set by the State is, after all, only 16.

Decision in cases such as this and the administration of an exemption for Old Order Amish from the State's compulsory school attendance laws will inevitably involve the kind of close and perhaps repeated scrutiny of religious practices, as exemplified in today's opinion, which the Court has heretofore been anxious to avoid. But such entanglement does not create a forbidden establishment of religion where it is essential to implement free exercise values threatened by an otherwise neutral program instituted to foster some permissible, nonreligious state objective. I join the Court because the sincerity of the Amish religious policy here is uncontested, because the potential adverse impact of the state requirement is great and because the State's valid interest in education has already been largely satisfied by the eight years the children have already spent in school.

MR. JUSTICE DOUGLAS, dissenting in part:

I

I agree with the Court that the religious scruples of the Amish are opposed to the education of their children beyond the grade schools, yet I disagree with the Court's conclusion that the matter is within the dispensation of parents alone. The Court's analysis assumes that the only interests at stake in the case are those of the Amish parents on the one hand, and those of the State on the other. The difficulty with this approach is that, despite the Court's claim, the parents are seeking to vindicate not only their own free exercise claims, but also those of their high-school-age children.

It is argued that the right of the Amish children to religious freedom is not presented by the facts of the case, as the issue before the Court involves only the Amish parents' religious freedom to defy a state criminal statute imposing upon them an affirmative duty to cause their children to attend high school.

First, respondents' motion to dismiss in the trial court expressly asserts, not only the religious liberty of the adults, but also that of the children, as a defense to the prosecutions. It is, of course, beyond question that the parents have standing as defendants in a criminal prosecution to assert the religious interests of their children as a defense. Although the lower courts and a majority of this Court assume an identity of interest between parent and child, it is clear that they have treated the religious interest of the child as a factor in the analysis.

Second, it is essential to reach the question to decide the case, not only because the question was squarely raised in the motion to dismiss, but also because no analysis of religious-liberty claims can take place in a vacuum. If the parents in this case are allowed a religious exemption, the inevitable effect is to impose the parents' notions of religious duty upon their children. Where the child is mature enough to express potentially conflicting desires, it would be an invasion of the child's rights to permit such an imposition without canvassing his views. As in *Prince v. Massachusetts*, 321 U.S. 158, it is an imposition resulting from this very litigation. As the child has no other effective forum, it is in this litigation that his rights should be considered. And, if an Amish child desires to attend high school, and is mature enough to have that desire respected, the State may well be able to override the parents' religiously motivated objections.

Religion is an individual experience. It is not necessary, nor even appropriate, for every Amish child to express his views on the subject in a prosecution of a single adult. Crucial, however, are the views of the child whose parent is the subject of the suit. Frieda Yoder has in fact testified that her own religious views are opposed to high-school education. I therefore join the judgment of the Court as to respondent Jonas Yoder. But Frieda Yoder's views may not be those of Vernon Yutzy or Barbara Miller. I must dissent, therefore, as to respondents Adin Yutzy and Wallace Miller as their motion to dismiss also raised the question of their children's religious liberty.

II

This issue has never been squarely presented before today. Our opinions are full of talk about the power of the parents over the child's education. *See Pierce v. Society of Sisters*, 268 U.S. 510; *Meyer v. Nebraska*, 262 U.S. 390. And we have in the past analyzed similar conflicts between parent and State with little regard for the views of the child. *See Prince v. Massachusetts*, *supra*. Recent

C. COMPULSORY EDUCATION

cases, however, have clearly held that the children themselves have constitutionally protectable interests.

These children are "persons" within the meaning of the Bill of Rights. We have so held over and over again....

....

On this important and vital matter of education, I think the children should be entitled to be heard. While the parents, absent dissent, normally speak for the entire family, the education of the child is a matter on which the child will often have decided views. He may want to be a pianist or an astronaut or an oceanographer. To do so he will have to break from the Amish tradition.[2]

It is the future of the student, not the future of the parents, that is imperiled by today's decision. If a parent keeps his child out of school beyond the grade school, then the child will be forever barred from entry into the new and amazing world of diversity that we have today. The child may decide that that is the preferred course, or he may rebel. It is the student's judgment, not his parents', that is essential if we are to give full meaning to what we have said about the Bill of Rights and of the right of students to be masters of their own destiny. If he is harnessed to the Amish way of life by those in authority over him and if his education is truncated, his entire life may be stunted and deformed. The child, therefore, should be given an opportunity to be heard before the State gives the exemption which we honor today.

The views of the two children in question were not canvassed by the Wisconsin courts. The matter should be explicitly reserved so that new hearings can be held on remand of the case.

....

---

1. One lawyer-educator, in an article which preceded the Court's decision, commented:

> Running through the discussions of political and economic reasons for compulsory education, and appearing in the *Yoder* testimony, is the notion that the state has a compelling interest in socializing children — in doing what it can to cast them into a behavioral mold acceptable to the majority. The issue of socialization is the most complex and troublesome one in the case. The Amish challenge to our right to prescribe and teach acceptable values ought to make us think twice about the validity of the old notion that

---

[2] A significant number of Amish children do leave the Old Order. Professor Hostetler notes that "[t]he loss of members is very limited in some Amish districts and considerable in others." J. Hostetler, *Amish Society* 226 (1968). In one Pennsylvania church, he observed a defection rate of 30%. *Ibid.* Rates up to 50% have been reported by others. Casad, *Compulsory High School Attendance and the Old Order Amish: A Commentary on State v. Garber*, 16 Kan. L. Rev. 423, 434 n.51 (1968).

society can be improved by means of schooling. Arons, *Compulsory Education: The Plain People Resist*, Saturday Review, January 15, 1972, at 56.

Is this the "old notion" set forth in the 1647 Massachusetts "Old Deluder Satan Act", Chapter 1, *supra*, and developed further in the common-school movement? In what sense do compulsory attendance laws facilitate society's response to community needs? The Court draws a crucial distinction between basic and secondary education. How valid is the dichotomy? Does it go to a basic difference in the content of what is taught, a cumulative effect of exposure to a relatively homogeneous educational offering, a change in the nature of the educational institution, or the age of students? Does it provide a valid framework in which to analyze the issue raised by the Amish? Chief Justice Burger suggests the distinction rests on the educational offering. Once a child has learned basic reading, writing, and elementary mathematics, the traits, skills, and attitudes needed to perform the adult role of an Amish farmer or housewife are best learned through example and "doing" rather than in a classroom. Is this an appropriate issue for a court to decide? Has not the legislature decided just the contrary?

2. Professor Kurland has argued that in stating the twin aims of education in *Yoder*, preparation for effective and intelligent participation in the American political system and preparation for self-reliance and self-sufficiency in the American society, the court ignored the use of the public school system as a means of integrating a large community in disregard of *Brown v. Board of Educ.* Kurland, *The Supreme Court, Compulsory Education, and the First Amendment's Religion Clauses*, 75 W. Va. L. Rev. 213 (1973). Do you agree? Is the *Yoder* rationale inconsistent with that of *Brown*? Should the community integration aspects of public education prevail over the Amish concern to protect themselves from such integration in order to preserve their group integrity? Does the Constitution choose between the aims of autonomy and integration? Consider *Pierce* again in this regard. Is *Yoder* a predicate for a right of community control or for government funding of parochial schools? We will also deal with these issues again at length in Chapters 11, 15 and 16.

3. Consider also the treatment of the importance of education in *Yoder*, as compared with the language of *Brown* quoted by Justice White. Is such language consistent with the Court's statement in *Yoder* that "[t]his case, of course, is not one in which any harm to the physical or mental health of the child or to the public safety, peace, order, or welfare, has been demonstrated or may be properly inferred"? Note that *Prince v. Massachusetts*, 321 U.S. 158 (1944), distinguished by the court in *Yoder*, involved the sale of religious literature by minors in public places under adult supervision. Do you agree that such action is more harmful to the physical or mental health of a child than exclusion from secondary school?

C. COMPULSORY EDUCATION

4. Consider the emphasis in the opinion on the fact that the objection to the compulsory school laws was religiously based. Why did the Court choose to base its decision on these grounds rather than the due process "liberty" grounds of *Meyer* and *Pierce*? What is the operative effect of the different grounds? Should parental objections to state control of children's education be given greater credence when the objections are religiously based rather than based solely on a parent's desire to control the upbringing of his child? What of a secularly based parental desire to control the religious education of their children? Is this protected by *Yoder*? We will consider these questions again in the next chapter on curriculum determination.

In addition, the Court places a good deal of emphasis on the unique status of the Amish. Why? In this regard you might be interested in the case *In re Jension*, involving the contempt conviction of a woman who refused jury service based on her strict adherence to the Biblical injunction: "Judge not, that you will not be judged." In the first decision by the Minnesota Supreme Court, 265 Minn. 96, 120 N.W.2d 515 (1963), the conviction was upheld over First Amendment objection on the ground of the paramount and essential interest of the state in securing jurors. On appeal to the United States Supreme Court, 375 U.S. 14 (1963), the judgment was vacated and the case remanded for reconsideration "in the light of *Sherbert v. Verner*, 374 U.S. 398 (1963)," the case holding that a state could not deny unemployment benefits to a Sabbatarian on grounds that she was "unavailable" for work since she refused to work on Saturday. On remand, the Minnesota Supreme Court reversed the conviction on First Amendment grounds, holding:

> In the absence of a present or prospective showing that the effectiveness of the jury system will be seriously jeopardized by excusing from duty jurors whose religious convictions prohibit them from serving such persons shall hereafter be exempt. 267 Minn. 136, 125 N.W.2d 588, 589 (1963).

Is there then a general principle that the state interest necessary to override First Amendment objections to compelled action be based not on generalities of need but on the specific need for the particular group involved to perform the action? If so, what is the relationship of this principle to *Yoder*?

Does the fact that the Amish are a small sect also affect the argument that the *Yoder* result does not produce an unconstitutional establishment of religion? *See* Kurland, *supra* note 2, at 82. Generally, are you satisfied that an exemption from compulsory schooling in order to enable the Amish to inculcate their sectarian values and lifestyle in their young does not represent an establishment of religion? Is such an exemption different from government funding of an Amish school in order to achieve the same result? Compare the discussion on aid to non-public schools in Chapter 16 *infra*. Is the establishment argument in *Yoder* persuasively settled by the statement in footnote [22] that the exemption is not affirmative support to the Amish but a neutral removal of the "impediment" of governmentally compelled education? If so, does the same argument apply to government aid to parochial schools, given compulsory education laws, the practical need for education in our society (some of which need has, at least arguably, been furthered by governmental action) and the heavy tax burden on all citizens required to support the public schools?

5. In *Commonwealth v. Bey*, 166 Pa. Super. 136, 70 A.2d 693 (1950), Moslem parents were prosecuted under the Pennsylvania compulsory attendance laws for refusing to send their children to school on Fridays, the sacred day of that religion. The court, in upholding their conviction, found:

> ... [S]ince the parent may avail himself of other schools, including parochial or denominational schools, the statute does not interfere with or impinge upon the religious freedom of parents or the guarantees of either the Federal or State constitution.

And held:

> Having exercised the option provided by the statute and elected to send their children to the public schools, appellants are bound to perform all the requirements of the compulsory attendance provisions. They cannot send their children to the public schools upon condition that they shall be excused on Fridays.

Is this still good law after *Yoder*? The court suggests the alternative of a parochial school. Yet, what of those religious groups that cannot afford to run their own schools? Also, is it mere coincidence that the public schools are closed on Saturdays and Sundays? On the other hand, the public schools would seem to be able to require Friday attendance if to do otherwise would seriously interfere with the education of the other students. What if this were not true, however, and non-attendance only interfered with the education of Bey? Should the school still have the right to compel his attendance on Fridays? At an extreme, nonattendance on Fridays might so diminish Bey's education that the minimum education required by compulsory school laws may not be met. But is that the sole issue involved? Is it valid for the state to declare that a parent cannot avail himself of the facilities of a public school and then deny that institution the power to perform the function for which it was created — a function that includes providing education in excess of the bare minimum required by compulsory schooling? Or does such a principle create too great a restriction on parental control, particularly on those parents who lack realistic alternatives to the public school system?

6. The emphasis in the *Bey* and *Yoder* decisions is on the rights of religious groups or rights of parents to control their children's education. What about the argument raised by Justice Douglas that the courts should look to the rights of the child? *In re Gault*, 387 U.S. 1 (1967), cited by Justice Douglas, involved a juvenile delinquency proceeding and the due process rights of a minor. In holding a minor entitled to comprehensive due process rights including notice, counsel,

C. COMPULSORY EDUCATION

cross examination, and the privilege against self incrimination, the Court set out a traditional view of a child's rights in this situation:

> The right of the state, as *parens patriae*, to deny to the child procedural rights available to his elders was elaborated by the assertion that a child, unlike an adult, has a right "not to liberty but to custody." He can be made to attorn to his parents, to go to school, etc. If his parents default in effectively performing their custodial functions — that is, if the child is "delinquent" — the state may intervene. In doing so, it does not deprive the child of any rights, because he has none. It merely provides the "custody" to which the child is entitled. On this basis, proceedings involving juveniles were described as "civil" not "criminal" and therefore not subject to the requirements which restrict the state when it seeks to deprive a person of his liberty. 387 U.S. at 17.

This view that the child cannot be denied liberty because he has none, can be contrasted with the approach suggested by the Court in *Lippincott v. Lippincott*, 97 N.J. Eq. 517, 128 A. 254 (1925):

> ... [T]he touchstone of our jurisprudence in matters dealing with the custody and control of infants is the welfare and happiness of the infant, not the filial affections naturally arising from parental or family relationship.
>
> ....
>
> Thus, it has been quite generally held that even the natural right of the father to the custody of his child cannot be treated as an absolute property right, but rather as a trust reposed in the father by the state, as *parens patriae* for the welfare of the infant. 97 N.J. Eq. 519, 128 A. 255.

See also Armstrong v. Manzo, 380 U.S. 545 (1965), where the Court held that failure to give a father notice of the pending adoption of his daughter deprived him of his rights (presumably property) without due process of law.

The above cases raise the question of what is the correct view of the child-parent-state relationship. In the compulsory education area, the majority in *Yoder* would have the religious beliefs of the parents prevail over the state, at least, in the absence of a contrary belief of the child. Justice Douglas would apparently have the belief of the child prevail over either the parents or the state. Note that he would do this even though he states that if a child's education is terminated, "his entire life may be stunted and deformed." If this is so, should even the child's choice not to go to school prevail over that of the state? What would Justice Douglas do if the child were too young for Justice Douglas to recognize the validity of his choice? Do you agree with Justice Douglas as to the maturity of the students involved in *Yoder*? More generally, should the state in *Yoder* be viewed as an outside force impinging on the rights of the parent, or child, or family unit, or rather as an alternate decision maker to the parents in making a decision for one who cannot do it for himself — the child? How does Chief Justice Burger view the situation? How does Justice Douglas view it?

Are the religious and educational views of children, as they relate to (and perhaps differ from) the views of their parents, appropriate concerns for the Court? Or are they properly left to the privacy of the home?

The dissent of Justice Douglas has been widely quoted by children's rights advocates because of Douglas' concern for the rights of the child when the child's judgment differs from that of his parents. For a response to issues Douglas raises, *see* Hafen, *Children's Liberation and the New Egalitarianism: Some Reservations About Abandoning Youth to Their "Rights,"* 1976 B.Y.U. L. Rev. 605.

7. Is the State's interest in an educated society diminished by the fact that the Amish are not actually a part of mainstream society? Or does it simply lose on balance?

8. "[T]o have the protection of the Religion Clauses, the claims must be rooted in religious belief." *Yoder*, at 215. How firmly must these claims be rooted? How widespread must they be? Has *Yoder* opened up the floor for *many* home schooling claims from parents claiming religious freedom? Does the religious belief have to have three centuries of history? How easy would it be for courts to label these and similar beliefs "philosophical," like Thoreau, rather than "religious," like the Amish, in order to defeat a claim?

9. The Court stated that wherever possible, the Amish have established their own elementary schools, although accepting compulsory education through the eighth grade. *Yoder*, at 212. Would these schools be subject to review and monitoring by the State to determine if they are meeting the requirements of the standard elementary education? *See Yoder*, at 236. *See also Pierce v. Society of Sisters*, 268 U.S. 510 (1925).

10. The Court seems to congratulate the Amish on a job well done — the Amish have managed, with two fewer years of required schooling, to build and maintain self-sufficient societies. Is this case an invitation for other religious groups to separate from society? What about cult compounds like the one maintained by the Branch Davidians in Waco, Texas?

11. According to Justice White's concurrence, the respondents' deviation from the compulsory education law is "slight." How many years away from the 16-year-old requirement would *not* be slight?

12. The United States Supreme Court recently upheld the denial of unemployment benefits to two discharged employees who ingested peyote, a hallucinogenic drug considered a controlled substance under an Oregon criminal statute. It was the employees' claim that they took the drug for sacramental purposes at a ceremony of their Native American Church, and that they are entitled to unemployment compensation as a matter of free exercise of religion. *Employment Division, Dep't of Human Resources of Oregon v. Smith*, 110 S. Ct. 1595 (1989).

Has *Yoder* been reversed by *Smith*? The *Yoder* court placed great emphasis on the Amish sincerity of religious belief by the faith-driven daily life. Blackmun's dissent in *Smith* said that the peyote plant embodied the deity of the Native

American Church and that eating it was an act of communion; that their sincerity was never at issue. *Id.* at 1622. The majority, however, did not consider sincerity, stating that courts are not permitted "to determine the place of a particular belief in a religion or the plausibility of a religious claim." *Id.* at 1604.

Under *Yoder*, once a claimant produced a burden to a sincerely-held religious belief, the burden shifted to the State to produce a compelling governmental interest. *Yoder*, at 227. It may be said that *Smith* abolished the compelling interest test in cases where the free exercise clause is the sole defense. If this is the case, is *Yoder* effectively overruled, or merely restricted to education cases where the rights of parents are asserted together with a free exercise claim?

See Mawdsley, *Has Wisconsin v. Yoder Been Reversed? Analysis of Employment Division v. Smith*, 63 Educ. L. Rep. 11 (1990).

Chapter 3
CURRICULUM

A. STATE AND LOCAL CONTROL OF CURRICULUM
1. STATE PRESCRIBED OFFERINGS

State school codes reflect both the differences in states' economic and physical conditions and the time at which they were drawn. The most common provisions, aside from those requiring compulsory attendance and prescribing the length of the school day and term, are those requiring that course materials be presented in English with English textbooks. Beyond this, there is no typical formula for a prescribed curriculum. School codes vary greatly in length, detail, and emphasis. They prescribe such unusual and unrelated subject matter as the accomplishments of Leif Erickson, 122 Ill. Rev. Stat. § 27-19; the political and economic contributions of women, Cal. Reorganized Educ. Code § 37226 (West); emphasis on the worth of kindness to all living creatures, Wash. Rev. Code Ann. § 28A.05.010; and instruction in cooperative marketing and consumers' cooperatives, Wis. Stat. Ann. § 40.46(8). Methodology is rarely, if ever, discussed in the codes, although Pennsylvania does require that all courses of study be adapted to the age of the pupils, 24 Pa. Stat. Ann. § 15-1512; California has provisions for intensive reading programs for underachievers, Cal. Reorganized Educ. Code § 54101 (West); and Massachusetts recently established a program of transitional bilingual education for children of limited English-speaking ability, Mass. Gen. Laws Ann. ch. 71A, § 2 (West).

Iowa and Massachusetts have the most interesting and flexible approaches. Massachusetts provides that in all schools of at least 150 pupils, if twenty parents request in writing that a course be taught and an enrollment of twenty can be secured, the course must be taught. Mass. Gen. Laws Ann. ch. 71, § 13 (West). The Iowa code provides that at the regular election, voters have the power to "determine upon additional branches that shall be taught." 12 Iowa Code Ann. § 278.1. Are such statutes wise?

Without statutes like those found in Massachusetts and Iowa, no court has held that parents have a right to compel the teaching of a given course. However, recent court decisions have required special programs for non-English-speaking students, and cases guaranteeing mentally retarded children a right to education have accorded parents the opportunity to challenge not only the placement of their children in special programs but also the adequacy of the particular curriculum made available in these programs. See particularly the cases and statutes discussed in Chapters 12 and 13.

Should parents of children without special educational problems be treated differently from parents of children with such problems in terms of their desire to have a particular course offered to their child?

2. BOARD POLICY, CURRICULUM GUIDES, AND LESSON PLANS

Though the code provisions for a prescribed curriculum may vary greatly, the process of curriculum determination in each of the states is relatively uniform. For example, the Maryland Code specifically provides that schools offer instruction in health, safety, drug, and physical education. They must also provide for daily patriotic exercises and silent meditation, as well as a minimum of ten fire drills a year. The legislature has established a State Board of Education to carry the provisions of the code into effect and "determine the educational policies of the State." 7 Md. Ann. Code 77, § 6. The Board exercises general control and supervision over the public schools and educational interests of the state.

An example of this generalized control over the schools' curriculum is Bylaw 720, § 3, subsec. 4, adopted by the Maryland State Board of Education. It provides:

> It is the responsibility of the local school system to provide a comprehensive program of family life and sex education in every elementary and secondary school for all students as an integral part of the curriculum including a planned and sequential program of health education.

In Maryland it is the duty of the county board of education and its executive officer, the county superintendent, to see that the State Board's bylaws and policies are carried into effect, as well as to adopt county policy, rules, and regulations. The county superintendent must prepare curriculum guides, specific courses of study, resource material, and teaching aids. He is also responsible for recommending the purchase and distribution of textbooks, materials, and supplies. The county board then prescribes the curriculum guides and courses of study, and supplies copies to teachers and interested parents. Therefore, under the above bylaw, the Superintendent of Baltimore County and his Director of Curriculum and Instructional Services prepared and presented to the County Board of Education a guide to a sixth-grade program in family life and human development entitled The Development of Self. The guide presents an integrated philosophy for the subject matter, an overview and set of objectives for the sixth-grade offering, the unit plan, and lesson plan suggestions with material, teaching suggestions, and references.

Once a generalized curriculum has been prescribed at the city or county level, the individual teacher organizes the material for presentation to his class. Often, as in New York City, the administration will require that he file lesson plans with the principal a few weeks before he intends to implement them.

B. CONSTITUTIONAL LIMITATIONS ON STATE AND LOCAL CONTROL

MEYER v. STATE OF NEBRASKA

Supreme Court of the United States
262 U.S. 390 (1923)

MR. JUSTICE MCREYNOLDS delivered the opinion of the Court:

Plaintiff in error was tried and convicted in the district court for Hamilton County, Nebraska, under an information which charged that on May 25, 1920, while an instructor in Zion Parochial School he unlawfully taught the subject of reading in the German language to Raymond Parpart, a child of 10 years, who had not attained and successfully passed the eighth grade. The information is based upon "An act relating to the teaching of foreign languages in the state of Nebraska," approved April 9, 1919 (Laws 1919, c. 249), which follows:

> Sec. 1. No person, individually or as a teacher, shall, in any private, denominational, parochial or public school, teach any subject to any person in any language other than the English language.
>
> Sec. 2. Languages, other than the English language, may be taught as languages only after a pupil shall have attained and successfully passed the eighth grade as evidenced by a certificate of graduation issued by the county superintendent of the county in which the child resides.
>
> Sec. 3. Any person who violates any of the provisions of this act shall be deemed guilty of a misdemeanor and upon conviction, shall be subject to a fine of not less than twenty-five dollars ($25), nor more than one hundred dollars ($100), or be confined in the county jail for any period not exceeding thirty days for each offense.
>
> Sec. 4. Whereas, an emergency exists, this act shall be in force from and after its passage and approval.

The Supreme Court of the state affirmed the judgment of conviction. It declared the offense charged and established was "the direct and intentional teaching of the German language as a distinct subject to a child who had not passed the eighth grade," in the parochial school maintained by Zion Evangelical Lutheran Congregation, a collection of Biblical stories being used therefor. And it held that the statute forbidding this did not conflict with the Fourteenth Amendment, but was a valid exercise of the police power. The following excerpts from the opinion sufficiently indicate the reasons advanced to support the conclusion:

> The salutary purpose of the statute is clear. The Legislature had seen the baneful effects of permitting foreigners, who had taken residence in this country, to rear and educate their children in the language of their native land. The result of that condition was found to be inimical to our own safety. To allow the children of foreigners, who had emigrated here, to be

taught from early childhood the language of the country of their parents was to rear them with that language as their mother tongue. It was to educate them so that they must always think in that language, and, as a consequence, naturally inculcate in them the ideas and sentiments foreign to the best interests of this country. The statute, therefore, was intended not only to require that the education of all children be conducted in the English language, but that, until they had grown into that language and until it had become a part of them, they should not in the schools be taught any other language. The obvious purpose of this statute was that the English language should be and become the mother tongue of all children reared in this state. The enactment of such a statute comes reasonably within the police power of the state.

It is suggested that the law is an unwarranted restriction, in that it applies to all citizens of the state and arbitrarily interferes with the rights of citizens who are not of foreign ancestry, and prevents them, without reason, from having their children taught foreign languages in school. That argument is not well taken, for it assumes that every citizen finds himself restrained by the statute. The hours which a child is able to devote to study in the confinement of school are limited. It must have ample time for exercise or play. Its daily capacity for learning is comparatively small. A selection of subjects for its education, therefore, from among the many that might be taught, is obviously necessary. The Legislature no doubt had in mind the practical operation of the law. The law affects few citizens, except those of foreign lineage. Other citizens, in their selection of studies, except perhaps in rare instances, have never deemed it of importance to teach their children foreign languages before such children have reached the eighth grade. In the legislative mind, the salutary effect of the statute no doubt outweighed the restriction upon the citizens generally, which, it appears, was a restriction of no real consequence.

The problem for our determination is whether the statute as construed and applied unreasonably infringes the liberty guaranteed to the plaintiff in error by the Fourteenth Amendment: "No state ... shall deprive any person of life, liberty or property without due process of law."

While this court has not attempted to define with exactness the liberty thus guaranteed, the term has received much consideration and some of the included things have been definitely stated. Without doubt, it denotes not merely freedom from bodily restraint but also the right of the individual to contract, to engage in any of the common occupations of life, to acquire useful knowledge, to marry, establish a home and bring up children, to worship God according to the dictates of his own conscience, and generally to enjoy those privileges long recognized at common law as essential to the orderly pursuit of happiness by free men. The established doctrine is that this liberty may not be interfered with, under the guise of protecting the public interest, by legislative action which is arbitrary or

B. CONSTITUTIONAL LIMITATIONS ON STATE AND LOCAL CONTROL

without reasonable relation to some purpose within the competency of the state to effect. Determination by the Legislature of what constitutes proper exercise of police power is not final or conclusive but is subject to supervision by the courts.

The American people have always regarded education and acquisition of knowledge as matters of supreme importance which should be diligently promoted. The Ordinance of 1787 declares: "Religion, morality and knowledge being necessary to good government and the happiness of mankind, schools and the means of education shall forever be encouraged."

Corresponding to the right of control, it is the natural duty of the parent to give his children education suitable to their station in life; and nearly all the states, including Nebraska, enforce this obligation by compulsory laws.

Practically, education of the young is only possible in schools conducted by especially qualified persons who devote themselves thereto. The calling always has been regarded as useful and honorable, essential, indeed, to the public welfare. Mere knowledge of the German language cannot reasonably be regarded as harmful. Heretofore it has been commonly looked upon as helpful and desirable. Plaintiff in error taught this language in school as part of his occupation. His right thus to teach and the right of parents to engage him so to instruct their children, we think, are within the liberty of the amendment.

The challenged statute forbids the teaching in school of any subject except in English; also the teaching of any other language until the pupil has attained and successfully passed the eighth grade, which is not usually accomplished before the age of twelve. The Supreme Court of the state has held that "the so-called ancient or dead languages" are not "within the spirit or the purpose of the act." Latin, Greek, Hebrew are not proscribed; but German, French, Spanish, Italian, and every other alien speech are within the ban. Evidently the Legislature has attempted materially to interfere with the calling of modern language teachers, with the opportunities of pupils to acquire knowledge, and with the power of parents to control the education of their own.

It is said the purpose of the legislation was to promote civic development by inhibiting training and education of the immature in foreign tongues and ideals before they could learn English and acquire American ideals, and "that the English language should be and become the mother tongue of all children reared in this state." It is also affirmed that the foreign born population is very large, that certain communities commonly use foreign words, follow foreign leaders, move in a foreign atmosphere, and that the children are thereby hindered from becoming citizens of the most useful type and the public safety is imperiled.

That the state may do much, go very far, indeed, in order to improve the quality of its citizens, physically, mentally and morally, is clear; but the individual has certain fundamental rights which must be respected. The protection of the Constitution extends to all, to those who speak other languages as well as to those born with English on the tongue. Perhaps it would be highly advantageous if all had ready understanding of our ordinary speech, but this cannot be coerced by methods which conflict with the Constitution — a desirable end cannot be promoted by prohibited means.

....

The desire of the Legislature to foster a homogenous people with American ideals prepared readily to understand current discussions of civic matters is easy to appreciate. Unfortunate experiences during the late war and aversion toward every character of truculent adversaries were certainly enough to quicken that aspiration. But the means adopted, we think, exceed the limitations upon the power of the state and conflict with rights assured to plaintiff in error. The interference is plain enough and no adequate reason therefor in time of peace and domestic tranquility has been shown.

The power of the state to compel attendance at some school and to make reasonable regulations for all schools, including a requirement that they shall give instructions in English, is not questioned. Nor has challenge been made of the state's power to prescribe a curriculum for institutions which it supports. Those matters are not within the present controversy. Our concern is with the prohibition approved by the Supreme Court. *Adams v. Tanner*, 244 U.S. 594 (1916), pointed out that mere abuse incident to an occupation ordinarily useful is not enough to justify its abolition, although regulation may be entirely proper. No emergency has arisen which renders knowledge by a child of some language other than English so clearly harmful as to justify its inhibition with the consequent infringement of rights long freely enjoyed. We are constrained to conclude that the statute as applied is arbitrary and without reasonable relation to any end within the competency of the state.

As the statute undertakes to interfere only with teaching which involves a modern language, leaving complete freedom as to other matters, there seems no adequate foundation for the suggestion that the purpose was to protect the child's health by limiting his mental activities. It is well known that proficiency in a foreign language seldom comes to one not instructed at an early age, and experience shows that this is not injurious to the health, morals or understanding of the ordinary child.

The judgment of the court below must be reversed and the cause remanded for further proceedings not inconsistent with this opinion.

Reversed.

MR. JUSTICE HOLMES and MR. JUSTICE SUTHERLAND, dissent:

[Opinion following companion case, *Bartels v. Iowa*, 262 U.S. 404 (1923).]

MR. JUSTICE HOLMES: We all agree, I take it, that it is desirable that all the citizens of the United States should speak a common tongue, and therefore that the end aimed at by the statute is a lawful and proper one. The only question is whether the means adopted deprive teachers of the liberty secured to them by the Fourteenth Amendment. It is with hesitation and unwillingness that I differ from my brethren with regard to a law like this but I cannot bring my mind to believe that in some circumstances, and circumstances existing it is said in Nebraska, the

B. CONSTITUTIONAL LIMITATIONS ON STATE AND LOCAL CONTROL 95

statute might not be regarded as a reasonable or even necessary method of reaching the desired result. The part of the act with which we are concerned deals with the teaching of young children. Youth is the time when familiarity with a language is established and if there are sections in the State where a child would hear only Polish or French or German spoken at home, I am not prepared to say that it is unreasonable to provide that in his early years he shall hear and speak only English at school. But if it is reasonable it is not an undue restriction of the liberty either of teacher or scholar. No one would doubt that a teacher might be forbidden to teach many things, and the only criterion of his liberty under the Constitution that I can think of is "whether considering the end in view, the statute passes the bounds of reason and assumes the character of a merely arbitrary fiat." I think I appreciate the objection to the law but it appears to me to present a question upon which men reasonably might differ and therefore I am unable to say that the Constitution of the United States prevents the experiment being tried.

---

1. Note that *Meyer* arises out of a criminal prosecution of a teacher. In the first part of his opinion, Justice McReynolds speaks of the liberty guaranteed to an individual (presumably referring to the defendant teacher), but he quickly jumps to a discussion of the duties and concomitant rights of parents in supplying an education for their young. The decision seems to rely on three distinct freedoms: freedom to pursue one's calling; freedom of students to acquire knowledge; and the freedom of parents to control their children's education. Apparently, the Court *sub silentio* gives a teacher standing to assert the rights of children and parents.

What is the relationship of these three rights in *Meyer*? Do the student and parental rights set forth in *Meyer* suggest the right of these groups to curriculum control? Does the case offer any guidance as to the proper result if assertion of the teacher's right conflicts with the desires of parents and/or students? *See West Virginia State Bd. of Educ. v. Barnette*, 319 U.S. 624 (1943), presented in Chapter 15, in which the Court enjoined enforcement of a West Virginia State Board of Education resolution requiring all public school pupils to salute the flag after students of the Jehovah's Witness faith claimed the regulation was invalid under the Due Process and Equal Protection Clauses of the Fourteenth Amendment.

2. In considering the rationale of *Meyer*, review the discussion of *Pierce* in Chapter 2. Should *Meyer* continue to be "good law" after the demise of substantive due process in economic regulation decisions?

3. Again considering the implication of *Meyer* to teachers, what is the significance of the fact in *Meyer* that the defendant taught in a private, parochial school? Is a public school district free to fire a teacher who injects material into his courses which the district has previously ordered him not to teach? Is a legislature free to restrict what may be taught in the public schools of its state?

EPPERSON v. ARKANSAS

Supreme Court of the United States
393 U.S. 97 (1969)

MR. JUSTICE FORTAS delivered the opinion of the Court:

I

This appeal challenges the constitutionality of the "anti-evolution" statute which the State of Arkansas adopted in 1928 to prohibit the teaching in its public schools and universities of the theory that man evolved from other species of life. The statute was a product of the upsurge of "fundamentalist" religious fervor of the twenties. The Arkansas statute was an adaptation of the famous Tennessee "monkey law" which that State adopted in 1925. The constitutionality of the Tennessee law was upheld by the Tennessee Supreme Court in the celebrated Scopes case in 1927.

The Arkansas law makes it unlawful for a teacher in any state-supported school or university "to teach the theory or doctrine that mankind ascended or descended from a lower order of animals," or "to adopt or use in any such institution a textbook that teaches" this theory. Violation is a misdemeanor and subjects the violator to dismissal from his position.

The present case concerns the teaching of biology in a high school in Little Rock. According to the testimony, until the events here in litigation, the official textbook furnished for the high school biology course "did not have a section on the Darwinian Theory." Then, for the academic year 1965-1966, the school administration, on recommendation of the teachers of biology in the school system, adopted and prescribed a textbook which contained a chapter setting forth "the theory about the origin ... of man from a lower form of animal."

Susan Epperson, a young woman who graduated from Arkansas' school system and then obtained her master's degree in zoology at the University of Illinois, was employed by the Little Rock school system in the fall of 1964 to teach 10th grade biology at Central High School. At the start of the next academic year, 1965, she was confronted by the new textbook (which one surmises from the record was not unwelcome to her). She faced at least a literal dilemma because she was supposed to use the new textbook for classroom instruction and presumably to teach the statutorily condemned chapter; but to do so would be a criminal offense and subject her to dismissal.

She instituted the present action in the Chancery Court of the State, seeking a declaration that the Arkansas statute is void and enjoining the State and the defendant officials of the Little Rock school system from dismissing her for violation of the statute's provisions. H.H. Blanchard, a parent of children attending the public schools, intervened in support of the action.

B. CONSTITUTIONAL LIMITATIONS ON STATE AND LOCAL CONTROL

The Chancery Court, in an opinion by Chancellor Murray O. Reed, held that the statute violated the Fourteenth Amendment to the United States Constitution. The court noted that this Amendment encompasses the prohibitions upon state interference with freedom of speech and thought which are contained in the First Amendment. Accordingly, it held that the challenged statute is unconstitutional because, in violation of the First Amendment, it "tends to hinder the quest for knowledge, restrict the freedom to learn, and restrain the freedom to teach." In this perspective, the Act, it held, was an unconstitutional and void restraint upon the freedom of speech guaranteed by the Constitution.

On appeal, the Supreme Court of Arkansas reversed. Its two-sentence opinion ... sustained the statute as an exercise of the State's power to specify the curriculum in public schools. It did not address itself to the competing constitutional considerations.

Appeal was duly prosecuted to this Court under 28 U.S.C. § 1257(2). Only Arkansas, Mississippi, and Tennessee have such "anti-evolution" or "monkey" laws on their books. There is no record of any prosecutions in Arkansas under its statute. It is possible that the statute is presently more of a curiosity than a vital fact of life in these States. Nevertheless, the present case was brought, the appeal as of right is properly here, and it is our duty to decide the issues presented.

II

At the outset, it is urged upon us that the challenged statute is vague and uncertain and therefore within the condemnation of the Due Process Clause of the Fourteenth Amendment. The contention that the Act is vague and uncertain is supported by language in the brief opinion of Arkansas' Supreme Court. That court, perhaps reflecting the discomfort which the statute's quixotic prohibition necessarily engenders in the modern mind, stated that it "expresses no opinion" as to whether the Act prohibits "explanation" of the theory of evolution or merely forbids "teaching that the theory is true." Regardless of this uncertainty, the court held that the statute is constitutional.

On the other hand, counsel for the State, in oral argument in this Court, candidly stated that, despite the State Supreme Court's equivocation, Arkansas would interpret the statute "to mean that to make a student aware of the theory ... just to teach that there was such a theory" would be grounds for dismissal and for prosecution under the statute; and he said "that the Supreme Court of Arkansas' opinion should be interpreted in that manner." He said "If Mrs. Epperson would tell her students that 'Here is Darwin's theory, that man ascended or descended from a lower form of being,' then I think she would be under this statute liable for prosecution."

In any event, we do not rest our decision upon the asserted vagueness of the statute. On either interpretation of its language, Arkansas' statute cannot stand. It is of no moment whether the law is deemed to prohibit mention of Darwin's theory, or to forbid any or all of the infinite varieties of communication embraced within the term "teaching." Under either interpretation, the law must be stricken because of its conflict with the constitutional prohibition of state laws respecting an establishment of religion or prohibiting the free exercise thereof. The overriding fact is that Arkansas' law selects from the body of knowledge a particular segment which it proscribes for the sole reason that it is deemed to conflict with a particular religious doctrine; that is, with a particular interpretation of the Book of Genesis by a particular religious group.

III

The antecedents of today's decision are many and unmistakable. They are rooted in the foundation soil of our Nation. They are fundamental to freedom.

Government in our democracy, state and national, must be neutral in matters of religious theory, doctrine, and practice. It may not be hostile to any religion or to the advocacy of no-religion; and it may not aid, foster, or promote one religion or religious theory against another or even against the militant opposite. The First Amendment mandates governmental neutrality between religion and religion, and between religion and nonreligion.

As early as 1872, this Court said: "The law knows no heresy, and is committed to the support of no dogma, the establishment of no sect." *Watson v. Jones*, 13 Wall. 679, 728. This has been the interpretation of the great First Amendment which this Court has applied in the many and subtle problems which the ferment of our national life has presented for decision within the Amendment's broad command.

Judicial interposition in the operation of the public school system of the Nation raises problems requiring care and restraint. Our courts, however, have not failed to apply the First Amendment's mandate in our educational system where essential to safeguard the fundamental values of freedom of speech and inquiry and of belief. By and large, public education in our Nation is committed to the control of state and local authorities. Courts do not and cannot intervene in the resolution of conflicts which arise in the daily operation of school systems and which do not directly and sharply implicate basic constitutional values. On the other hand, "The vigilant protection of constitutional freedoms is nowhere more vital than in the community of American schools," *Shelton v. Tucker*, 364 U.S. 479 (1960), and this Court will be alert against invasions of academic freedom, *Barenblatt v. United States*, 360 U.S. 109 (1959). As this Court said in *Keyishian v. Board of Regents*, the First Amendment "does not tolerate laws that cast a pall of orthodoxy over the classroom." 385 U.S. 589, 603 (1967).

The earliest cases in this Court on the subject of the impact of constitutional guarantees upon the classroom were decided before the Court expressly applied the specific prohibitions of the First Amendment to the States. But as early as 1923, the Court did not hesitate to condemn under the Due Process Clause "arbitrary" restrictions upon the freedom of teachers to teach and of students to learn. In that year, the Court, in an opinion by Justice McReynolds, held unconstitutional an Act of the State of Nebraska making it a crime to teach any subject in any language other than English to pupils who had not passed the eighth grade. The State's purpose in enacting the law was to promote civic cohesiveness by encouraging the learning of English and to combat the "baneful effect" of permitting foreigners to rear and educate their children in the language of the parents' native land. The Court recognized these purposes, and it acknowledged the State's power to prescribe the school curriculum, but it held that these were not adequate to support the restriction upon the liberty of teacher and pupil. The challenged statute, it held, unconstitutionally interfered with the right of the individuals, guaranteed by the Due Process Clause, to engage in any of the common occupations of life and to acquire useful knowledge. *Meyer v. State of Nebraska*, 262 U.S. 390 (1923). *See also Bartels v. State of Iowa*, 262 U.S. 404 (1923).

For purposes of the present case, we need not re-enter the difficult terrain which the Court, in 1923, traversed without apparent misgivings.... Today's problem is capable of resolution in the narrower terms of the First Amendment's prohibition of laws respecting an establishment of religion or prohibiting the free exercise thereof.

There is and can be no doubt that the First Amendment does not permit the State to require that teaching and learning must be tailored to the principles or prohibitions of any religious sect or dogma. In *Everson v. Board of Education*, this Court, in upholding a state law to provide free bus service to school children, including those attending parochial schools, said: "Neither [a State nor the Federal Government] can pass laws which aid one religion, aid all religions, or prefer one religion, or prefer one religion over another." 330 U.S. 1, 15 (1947).

... While study of religions and of the Bible from a literary and historic viewpoint, presented objectively as part of a secular program of education, need not collide with the First Amendment's prohibition, the State may not adopt programs or practices in its public schools or colleges which "aid or oppose" any religion. *Abington School District v. Schempp*, 374 U.S. [203,] 225. This prohibition is absolute. It forbids alike the preference of a religious doctrine or the prohibition of theory which is deemed antagonistic to a particular dogma....

These precedents inevitably determine the result in the present case. The State's undoubted right to prescribe the curriculum for its public schools does not carry with it the right to prohibit, on pain of criminal penalty, the teaching of a scientific theory or doctrine where that prohibition is based upon reasons that violate the First Amendment. It is much too late to argue that the State may impose upon the teachers in its schools any conditions that it chooses, however restrictive they may be of constitutional guarantees. *Keyishian v. Board of Regents*, 385 U.S. 589 (1967).

In the present case, there can be no doubt that Arkansas has sought to prevent its teachers from discussing the theory of evolution because it is contrary to the belief of some that the Book of Genesis must be the exclusive source of doctrine as to the origin of man. No suggestion has been made that Arkansas' law may be justified by considerations of state policy other than the religious views of some of its citizens. It is clear that fundamentalist sectarian conviction was and is the law's reason for existence. Its antecedent, Tennessee's "monkey law," candidly stated its purpose: to make it unlawful "to teach any theory that denies the story of the Divine Creation of man, as taught in the Bible, and to teach instead, that man has descended from a lower order of animals." Perhaps the sensational publicity attended upon the Scopes trial induced Arkansas to adopt less explicit language. It eliminated Tennessee's reference to "the story of the Divine Creation of man" as taught in the Bible, but there is no doubt that the motivation for the law was the same: to suppress the teaching of a theory which, it was thought, "denied" the divine creation of man.

... Plainly, the law is contrary to the mandate of the First, and in violation of the Fourteenth, Amendment to the Constitution.

The judgment of the Supreme Court of Arkansas is reversed.

MR. JUSTICE BLACK, concurring:

....

It is plain that a state law prohibiting all teaching of human development or biology is constitutionally quite different from a law that compels a teacher to teach as true only one theory of a given doctrine. It would be difficult to make a First Amendment case out of a state law eliminating the subject of higher mathematics, or astronomy, or biology from its curriculum. And for all the Supreme Court of Arkansas has said, this particular Act may prohibit that and nothing else. This Court, however, treats the Arkansas Act as though it made it a misdemeanor to teach or to use a book that teaches that evolution is true. But it is not for this Court to arrogate to itself the power to determine the scope of Arkansas statutes. Since the highest court of Arkansas has deliberately refused to give its statute that meaning, we should not presume to do so.

It seems to me that in this situation the statute is too vague for us to strike it down on any ground but that: vagueness. Under this statute as construed by the Arkansas Supreme Court, a teacher cannot know whether he is forbidden to mention Darwin's theory at all or only free to discuss it as long as he refrains from contending that it is true.

....

The Court, not content to strike down this Arkansas Act on the unchallengeable ground of its plain vagueness, chooses rather to invalidate it as a violation of the Establishment of Religion Clause of the First Amendment. I would not decide this case on such a sweeping ground....

MR. JUSTICE STEWART, concurring in the result:

The States are most assuredly free "to choose their own curriculums for their own schools." A State is entirely free, for example, to decide that the only foreign language to be taught in its public school system shall be Spanish. But would a State be constitutionally free to punish a teacher for letting his students know that other languages are also spoken in the world? I think not.

B. CONSTITUTIONAL LIMITATIONS ON STATE AND LOCAL CONTROL

It is one thing for a State to determine that "the subject of higher mathematics, or astronomy, or biology" shall or shall not be included in its public school curriculum. It is quite another thing for a State to make it a criminal offense for a public school teacher so much as to mention the very existence of an entire system of respected human thought. That kind of criminal law, I think, would clearly impinge upon the guarantees of free communication contained in the First Amendment, and made applicable to the States by the Fourteenth.

The Arkansas Supreme Court has said that the statute before us may or may not be just such a law. The result, as Mr. Justice Black points out, is that "a teacher cannot know whether he is forbidden to mention Darwin's theory at all." Since I believe that no State could constitutionally forbid a teacher "to mention Darwin's theory at all," and since Arkansas may, or may not, have done just that, I conclude that the statute before us is so vague as to be invalid under the Fourteenth Amendment. *See Cramp v. Board of Pub. Instruction*, 368 U.S. 278.

---

1. Justice Fortas states that whether the statute is interpreted as prohibiting the teaching of the existence of the theory of evolution or merely the teaching that evolution is true, the result of the case will be the same. In spite of stating that this distinction will not affect the result, he bases his opinion not on freedom of speech and thought, as did the trial court, but on religious freedom. If the prohibition only limits teaching the truth of the doctrine, how does the statute violate the establishment or free exercise clause? How could the government be more neutral? Indeed, assuming that the statute even precludes the teaching of evolution completely, is the state not being neutral, if the law at the same time prohibits the teaching of Genesis; if the law prohibits completely the teaching of any theory concerning the origin of man? Would such an explicit prohibition satisfy the Court in *Epperson*? Is such a hypothetical situation different than what Arkansas did in *Epperson*?

Although he chooses only to raise the issue, rather than to rely on it, Justice Fortas considers the freedom to teach discussed in *Meyer*. Is Justice Fortas correct in applying the rationale of *Meyer*, which was based on a private school teacher's prerogatives, to *Epperson*, where a public school curriculum was under challenge? Consider in this regard Justice Stewart's statement in his concurrence that a state is free to decide that the only foreign language to be taught in its public school system shall be Spanish. Justice Stewart must therefore either be distinguishing between public or private schools or explicitly repudiating *Meyer*, mustn't he? If the state is running public schools, need not some state official determine what is or is not taught? If this is so, then what is unconstitutional about having the legislature do it? Do individual teachers have a constitutional right to be the primary decider of what they teach? Alternatively, do they have a constitutional right to be free of arbitrary restrictions on what they teach? Would this second, more limited position support the result in *Epperson*?

Is there a difference between a legislature telling teachers not to teach evolution and telling them not to teach that there are those who believe that there may be innate differences in intelligence among racial groups? Is any of this different than hiring a teacher to teach history and firing him because he teaches mathematics; hiring one to teach American literature and firing him because he teaches British literature?

2. Does a person who is qualified to teach biology have a right to be hired to do so by a school district that does not choose to include biology in its curriculum? Does a teacher already on a school's staff teaching another subject have a right to teach biology if the school board does not want to have biology taught? Does it make a difference whether such a teacher seeks to teach biology in lieu of, or in addition to, the courses he was hired to teach?

3. Is the situation different if a teacher is hired to teach biology but told not to teach anything about the origins of man? Can the answer to the validity of this prohibition be based on some notion of the general meaning of "biology" external to the school board decisions in this hypothetical case?

Compare carefully the following two cases:

(a) A school board syllabus for a large urban school district's sex education course states that the teachers of this course are not to teach anything about birth control and "[i]f any pupils ask questions concerning birth control or contraceptives, they should be told to consult their parents, religious adviser and family physician for advice. *No specific answers to these questions should be given by teachers.*" (Emphasis in the original.) Can the school district validly fire a teacher for violating this directive by initiating the teaching of birth control, or by responding to student questions about birth control? Does it matter whether the teacher answered such questions during, or after, class hours? Is it relevant that some religious denominations oppose birth control, while others do not? *See Mercer v. Michigan*, 379 F. Supp. 580 (E.D. Mich. 1974), *aff'd mem.*, 419 U.S. 1081 (1974).

(b) A school board in a racially heterogeneous area directs that no teacher shall make known to his or her students the existence of theories of possible genetic differences in intelligence among racial groups. The board's decision was made after discussing the fact that these theories are topics of great controversy in the academic community and that reputable scholars disagree on the validity of the theories. Consequently, the board concluded that discussion of such theories in high school would be too likely to cause racial confrontations. May a teacher constitutionally be fired for violating this directive?

4. Both of the preceding hypothetical cases involve the firing of a teacher rather than the criminal penalty involved in *Epperson*. Does this distinguish the hypotheticals from *Epperson*? How significant was the fact of the criminal

B. CONSTITUTIONAL LIMITATIONS ON STATE AND LOCAL CONTROL 103

penalty in the majority opinion in *Epperson*, in Justice Black's or Justice Stewart's opinion?

5. The preceding two hypotheticals also involved school board determinations rather than a legislative decision as in *Epperson*. What, if any, is the significance of that fact? Are state legislatures more, or less, constitutionally restricted in determining curriculum than are school boards?

6. What if a state enacted the following statute?

> § 1. Any biology textbook used for teaching in the public schools, which expresses an opinion of, or relates a theory about origins or creation of man and his world shall be prohibited from being used as a textbook in such system unless it specifically states that it is a theory as to the origin and creation of man and his world and is not represented to be scientific fact. Any textbook so used in the public education system which expresses an opinion or relates to a theory or theories shall give in the same textbook and under the same subject commensurate attention to, and an equal amount of emphasis on, the origins and creation of man and his world as the same is recorded in other theories, including, but not limited to, the Genesis account in the Bible.

A similar statute was promulgated by the state of Louisiana. Specifically, teachers were forbidden from teaching "evolution science" in public schools unless accompanied by a balanced treatment of "creation science." The state supreme court had held that the state legislature had absolute authority over education and, as such, the "balanced treatment" order was upheld. The United States Supreme Court in *Edwards v. Aguillard*, 482 U.S. 578 (1987), differed, however, finding that the Establishment Clause of the First Amendment was violated in that the purpose of the statute was a religious one. The Court ruled that the legislation skewed science as a curriculum toward an impermissible religious view. The curriculum either totally eliminated the scientific theory of creation as an area of study or commanded the presentation of a religious fundamentalist position, masquerading as a science, alongside that of evolution.

BOARD OF EDUCATION, ISLAND TREES UNION FREE SCHOOL DISTRICT NO. 26 v. PICO

United States Supreme Court
457 U.S. 853 (1982)

JUSTICE BRENNAN announced the judgment of the Court and delivered an opinion, in which JUSTICE MARSHALL and JUSTICE STEVENS joined, and in which JUSTICE BLACKMUN joined except for Part II-A-(1):

The principal question presented is whether the First Amendment imposes limitations upon the exercise by a local school board of its discretion to remove library books from high school and junior high school libraries.

I

Petitioners are the Board of Education of the Island Trees Union Free School District No. 26, in New York.... Respondents ... were students at the High School ... and a student at the Junior High School.

In September 1975, [members of the board] attended a conference sponsored by Parents of New York United (PONYU), a politically conservative organization of parents concerned about education legislation in the State of New York. At the conference these petitioners obtained lists of books described ... as "objectionable," [and] as "improper fare for school students." It was later determined that the High School library contained nine of the listed books, and that another listed book was in the Junior High School library. In February 1976, at a meeting with the Superintendent of Schools and the Principals of the High School and Junior High School, the Board gave an "unofficial direction" that the listed books be removed from the library shelves and delivered to the Board's office, so that Board members could read them. When this directive was carried out, it became publicized, and the Board issued a press release justifying its actions. It characterized the removed books as "anti-American, anti-Christian, anti-Sem[i]tic, and just plain filthy," and concluded that "[i]t is our duty, our moral obligation, to protect the children in our schools from this moral danger as surely as from physical and medical dangers."

A short time later, the Board appointed a "Book Review Committee," consisting of four Island Trees parents and four members of the Island Trees schools staff, to read the listed books and to recommend to the Board whether the books should be retained, taking into account the books' "educational suitability," "good taste," "relevance," and "appropriateness to age and grade level." In July, the Committee made its final report to the Board, recommending that five of the listed books be retained and that two others be removed from the school libraries. As for the remaining four books, the Committee could not agree on two, took no position on one, and recommended that the last book be made available to students only with parental approval. The Board substantially rejected the Committee's report later that month, deciding that only one book should be returned to the High School library without restriction, that another should be made available subject to parental approval, but that the remaining nine books should "be removed from elementary and secondary libraries and [from] use in the curriculum." *Id.* at 391. The Board gave no reasons for rejecting the recommendations of the Committee that it had appointed.

Respondents reacted to the Board's decision by bringing the present action under 42 U.S.C. § 1983 in the United States District Court for the Eastern District of New York. They alleged that petitioners had "ordered the removal of the books from school libraries and proscribed their use in the curriculum because particular passages in the books offended their social, political and moral tastes and not because the books, taken as a whole, were lacking in educational value."

B. CONSTITUTIONAL LIMITATIONS ON STATE AND LOCAL CONTROL

Respondents claimed that the Board's actions denied them their rights under the First Amendment. They asked the court for a declaration that the Board's actions were unconstitutional, and for preliminary and permanent injunctive relief ordering the Board to return the nine books to the school libraries and to refrain from interfering with the use of those nine books in the schools' curricula. *Id.* at 5-6.

....

II

We emphasize at the outset the limited nature of the substantive question presented by the case before us. Our precedents have long recognized certain constitutional limits upon the power of the State to control even the curriculum and classroom. For example, *Meyer v. Nebraska*, 262 U.S. 390 (1923), struck down a state law that forbade the teaching of modern foreign languages in public and private schools, and *Epperson v. Arkansas*, 393 U.S. 97 (1968), declared unconstitutional a state law that prohibited the teaching of the Darwinian theory of evolution in any state-supported school. But the current action does not require us to re-enter this difficult terrain, which *Meyer* and *Epperson* traversed without apparent misgiving. For as this case is presented to us, it does not involve textbooks, or indeed any books that Island Trees students would be required to read. Respondents do not seek in this Court to impose limitations upon their school Board's discretion to prescribe the curricula of the Island Tree schools. On the contrary, the only books at issue in this case are library books, books that by their nature are optional rather than required reading. Our adjudication of the present case thus does not intrude into the classroom, or into the compulsory courses taught there. Furthermore, even as to library books, the action before us does not involve acquisition of books. Respondents have not sought to compel their school Board to add to the school library shelves any books that students desire to read. Rather, the only action challenged in this case is the removal from school libraries of books originally placed there by the school authorities, or without objection from them.

The substantive question before us is still further constrained by the procedural posture of this case. Petitioners were granted summary judgment by the District Court. The Court of Appeals reversed that judgment, and remanded the action for a trial on the merits of respondents' claims. We can reverse the judgment of the Court of Appeals, and grant petitioners' request for reinstatement of the summary judgment in their favor, only if we determine that "there is no genuine issue as to any material fact," and that petitioners are "entitled to a judgment as a matter of law." Fed. Rule Civ. Proc. 56(c)....

In sum, the issue before us in this case is a narrow one, both substantively and procedurally. It may best be restated as two distinct questions. First, does the First Amendment impose any limitations upon the discretion of petitioners to remove library books from the Island Trees High School and Junior High School? Second, if so, do the affidavits and other evidentiary materials before the

District Court, construed most favorably to respondents, raise a genuine issue of fact whether petitioners might have exceeded those limitations? If we must answer either of these questions in the negative, then we must reverse the judgment of the Court of Appeals and reinstate the District Court's summary judgment for petitioners. If we answer both questions in the affirmative, then we must affirm the judgment below. We examine these questions in turn.

A

(1)

The Court has long recognized that local school boards have broad discretion in the management of school affairs. *See, e.g., Meyer v. Nebraska, supra* at 402; *Pierce v. Society of Sisters*, 268 U.S. 510, 534 (1925). *Epperson v. Arkansas, supra*, 393 U.S. at 104, reaffirmed that, by and large, "public education in our Nation is committed to the control of state and local authorities," and that federal courts should not ordinarily "intervene in the resolution of conflicts which arise in the daily operation of school systems." *Tinker v. Des Moines School Dist.*, 393 U.S. 503, 507 (1969), noted that we have "repeatedly emphasized ... the comprehensive authority of the States and of school officials ... to prescribe and control conduct in the schools." We have also acknowledged that public schools are vitally important "in the preparation of individuals for participation as citizens," and as vehicles for "inculcating fundamental values necessary to the maintenance of a democratic political system." *Ambach v. Norwick*, 441 U.S. 68, 76-77 (1979). We are therefore in full agreement with petitioners that local school boards must be permitted "to establish and apply their curriculum in such a way as to transmit community values," and that "there is a legitimate and substantial community interest in promoting respect for authority and traditional values be they social, moral, or political."

At the same time, however, we have necessarily recognized that the discretion of the States and local school boards in matters of education must be exercised in a manner that comports with the transcendent imperatives of the First Amendment. In *West Virginia Board of Education v. Barnette*, 319 U.S. 624 (1943), we held that under the First Amendment a student in a public school could not be compelled to salute the flag. We reasoned:

> "Boards of Education ... have, of course, important, delicate, and highly discretionary functions, but none that they may not perform within the limits of the Bill of Rights. That they are educating the young for citizenship is reason for scrupulous protection of Constitutional freedoms of the individual, if we are not to strangle the free mind at its source and teach youth to discount important principles of our government as mere platitudes." *Id.* at 637.

... In sum, students do not "shed their constitutional rights to freedom of speech or expression at the schoolhouse gate," [*Tinker v. Des Moines School*

Dist., 393 U.S. 503,] at 506, and therefore local school boards must discharge their "important, delicate, and highly discretionary functions" within the limits and constraints of the First Amendment.

....

Of course, courts should not "intervene in the resolution of conflicts which arise in the daily operation of school systems" unless "basic constitutional values" are "directly and sharply implicate[d]" in those conflicts. *Epperson v. Arkansas*, 393 U.S. at 104. But we think that the First Amendment rights of students may be directly and sharply implicated by the removal of books from the shelves of a school library. Our precedents have focused "not only on the role of the First Amendment in fostering individual self-expression but also on its role in affording the public access to discussion, debate, and the dissemination of information and ideas." *First National Bank of Boston v. Bellotti*, 435 U.S. 765, 783 (1978). And we have recognized that "the State may not, consistently with the spirit of the First Amendment, contract the spectrum of available knowledge." *Griswold v. Connecticut*, 381 U.S. 479, 482 (1965). In keeping with this principle, we have held that in a variety of contexts "the Constitution protects the right to receive information and ideas." *Stanley v. Georgia*, 394 U.S. 557, 564 (1969); *see Kleindienst v. Mandel*, 408 U.S. 753, 762-763 (1972) (citing cases). This right is an inherent corollary of the rights of free speech and press that are explicitly guaranteed by the Constitution, in two senses. First, the right to receive ideas follows ineluctably from the sender's First Amendment right to send them: "The right of freedom of speech and press ... embraces the right to distribute literature, and necessarily protects the right to receive it." *Martin v. Struthers*, 319 U.S. 141, 143 (1943)....

More importantly, the right to receive ideas is a necessary predicate to the recipient's meaningful exercise of his own rights of speech, press, and political freedom. Madison admonished us: "A popular Government, without popular information, or the means of acquiring it, is but a Prologue to a Farce or a Tragedy; or, perhaps both. Knowledge will forever govern ignorance: And a people who mean to be their own Governors, must arm themselves with the power which knowledge gives." 9 Writings of James Madison 103 (G. Hunt ed. 1910).

....

In sum, just as access to ideas makes it possible for citizens generally to exercise their rights of free speech and press in a meaningful manner, such access prepares students for active and effective participation in the pluralistic, often contentious society in which they will soon be adult members. Of course all First Amendment rights accorded to students must be construed "in light of the special characteristics of the school environment." *Tinker v. Des Moines School Dist.*, 393 U.S. at 506. But the special characteristics of the school library make that environment especially appropriate for the recognition of the First Amendment rights of students.

A school library, no less than any other public library, is "a place dedicated to quiet, to knowledge, and to beauty." *Brown v. Louisiana*, 383 U.S. 131, 142 (1966) (opinion of Fortas, J.). *Keyishian v. Board of Regents*, 385 U.S. 589, (1967), observed that "'students must always remain free to inquire, to study and to evaluate, to gain new maturity and understanding.'" The school library is the principal locus of such freedom.

Petitioners emphasize the inculcative function of secondary education, and argue that they must be allowed unfettered discretion to "transmit community values" through the Island Trees schools. But that sweeping claim overlooks the unique role of the school library. It appears from the record that use of the Island Trees school libraries is completely voluntary on the part of students. Their selection of books from these libraries is entirely a matter of free choice; the libraries afford them an opportunity at self-education and individual enrichment that is wholly optional. Petitioners might well defend their claim of absolute discretion in matters of curriculum by reliance upon their duty to inculcate community values. But we think that petitioners' reliance upon that duty is misplaced where, as here, they attempt to extend their claim of absolute discretion beyond the compulsory environment of the classroom, into the school library and the regime of voluntary inquiry that there holds sway.

(2)

In rejecting petitioners' claim of absolute discretion to remove books from their school libraries, we do not deny that local school boards have a substantial legitimate role to play in the determination of school library content. We thus must turn to the question of the extent to which the First Amendment places limitations upon the discretion of petitioners to remove books from the libraries....

....

... Petitioners rightly possess significant discretion to determine the content of their school libraries. But that discretion may not be exercised in a narrowly partisan or political manner. If a Democratic school board, motivated by party affiliation, ordered the removal of all books written by or in favor of Republicans, few would doubt that the order violated the constitutional rights of the students denied access to those books. The same conclusion would surely apply if an all-white school board, motivated by racial animus, decided to remove all books authored by blacks or advocating racial equality and integration. Our Constitution does not permit the official suppression of ideas. Thus whether petitioners' removal of books from their school libraries denied respondents access to ideas with which petitioners disagreed, and if this intent was the decisive factor in petitioners' decision, then petitioners have exercised their discretion in violation of the Constitution. To permit such intentions to control official actions would be to encourage the precise sort of officially prescribed orthodoxy unequivocally condemned in *Barnette*. On the other hand, respondents implicitly concede that an unconstitutional motivation that would not be demonstrated if it were shown that petitioners had decided to remove the books at issue because those books were pervasively vulgar. And again, respondents concede that if it were demonstrated that the removal decision was based solely upon the "educational suitability" of the books in question, then their removal would be "perfectly permissible." *Id.* at 53. In other words, in respondents' view such motivations, if decisive of petitioners' actions, would not carry danger of an official suppression of ideas, and thus would not violate respondents' First Amendment rights.

As noted earlier, nothing in our decision today affects in any way the discretion of a local school board to choose books to add to the libraries of their schools. Because we are concerned in this case with the suppression of ideas, our holding today affects only the discretion to remove books. In brief, we hold that local school boards may not remove books from school library shelves simply because they dislike the ideas contained in those books and seek by their removal to "prescribe what shall be orthodox in politics, nationalism, religion, or other matters of opinion." *West Virginia Board of Education v. Barnette*, 319 U.S. at 642. Such purposes stand inescapably by our precedents.

B

[JUSTICE BRENNAN found a genuine issue of material fact in whether the books were removed due to the ideas contained therein or for lack of educational suitability. BRENNAN agreed with the Court of Appeals' reversal of summary judgment.]

Affirmed.

JUSTICE BLACKMUN, concurring in part and concurring in the judgment:

While I agree with much in today's plurality opinion, and while I accept the standard laid down by the plurality to guide proceedings on remand, I write separately because I have a somewhat different perspective on the nature of the First Amendment right involved.

....

To my mind, this case presents a particularly complex problem because it involves two competing principles of constitutional stature. On the one hand, ... local education officials may attempt "to promote civic virtues," *Ambach v. Norwick*, 441 U.S. and to "awake[n] the child to cultural values." *Brown v. Board of Education*, 347 U.S. 483, 393 (1954). Indeed, the Constitution presupposes the existence of an informed citizenry prepared to participate in governmental affairs, and these democratic principles obviously are constitutionally incorporated into the structure of our government. It therefore seems entirely appropriate that the State use "public schools [to] ... inculcat[e] fundamental values necessary to the maintenance of a democratic political system." *Ambach v. Norwick*, 441 U.S. at 77.

On the other hand, as the plurality demonstrates, it is beyond dispute that schools and school boards must operate within the confines of the First Amendment....

....

In my view, then, the principle involved here is both narrower and more basic than the "right to receive information" identified by the plurality. I do not suggest that the State has any affirmative obligation to provide students with information or ideas, something that may well be associated with a "right to receive." And I do not believe, as the plurality suggests, that the right at issue here is somehow associated with the peculiar nature of the school library; if schools may be used to inculcate ideas, surely libraries may play a role in that process. Instead, I suggest that certain forms of state discrimination between ideas are improper. In particular, our precedents command the conclusion that the State may not act to deny access to an idea simply because state officials disapprove of that idea for partisan or political reasons.

....

CHIEF JUSTICE BURGER, with whom JUSTICE POWELL, JUSTICE REHNQUIST, and JUSTICE O'CONNOR join, dissenting:

....

It is true that where there is a willing distributor of materials, the government may not impose unreasonable obstacles to dissemination by the third party. And where the speaker desires to express certain ideas, the government may not impose unreasonable restraints. It does not follow, however, that a school board must affirmatively aid the speaker in his communication with the recipient. In short the plurality suggests today that if a writer has something to say, the government through its schools must be the courier. None of the cases cited by the plurality establish this broad-based proposition.

....

... If, as we have held, schools may legitimately be used as vehicles for "inculcating fundamental values necessary to the maintenance of a democratic political system," *Ambach v. Norwick*, 441 U.S. 68, 77 (1979), school authorities must have broad discretion to fulfill that obligation. Presumably all activity within a primary or secondary school involves the conveyance of information and at least an implied approval of the worth of that information. How are "fundamental values" to be inculcated except by having school boards make content-based decisions about the appropriateness of retaining materials in the school library and curriculum? In order to fulfill its function, an elected student board must express its views on the subjects which are taught to its students. In doing so those elected officials express the views of their community; they may err, of course, and the voters may remove them. It is a startling erosion of the very ideas of democratic government to have this Court arrogate to itself the power the plurality asserts today.

B. CONSTITUTIONAL LIMITATIONS ON STATE AND LOCAL CONTROL

JUSTICE REHNQUIST, with whom THE CHIEF JUSTICE and JUSTICE POWELL join, dissenting:

Addressing only those aspects of the constitutional question which must be decided to determine whether or not the District Court was correct in granting summary judgment, I conclude that it was. I agree fully with the views expressed by THE CHIEF JUSTICE, and concur in his opinion. I disagree with JUSTICE BRENNAN's opinion because it is largely hypothetical in character, failing to take account of the facts as admitted by the parties pursuant to local rules of the District Court for the Eastern District of New York, and because it is analytically unsound and internally inconsistent.

I

A

....

... Petitioners did not, for the reasons stated hereafter, run afoul of the First and Fourteenth Amendments by removing these particular books from the library in the manner in which they did. I would save for another day — feeling quite confident that that day will not arrive — the extreme examples posed in JUSTICE BRENNAN's opinion.

B

Considerable light is shed on the correct resolution of the constitutional question in this case by examining the role played by petitioners. Had petitioners been the members of a town council, I suppose all would agree that, absent a good deal more than is present in this record, they could not have prohibited the sale of these books by private booksellers within the municipality. But we have also recognized that the government may act in other capacities than as sovereign, and when it does the First Amendment may speak with a different voice:

> [I]t cannot be gainsaid that the State has interests as an employer in regulating the speech of its employees that differ significantly from those it possesses in connection with regulation of the speech of the citizenry in general. The problem in any case is to arrive at a balance between the interests of the teacher, as a citizen, in commenting upon matters of concern and the interest of the State, as an employer, in promoting the efficiency of the public services it performs through its employees. *Pickering v. Board of Education*, 391 U.S. 563, 568 (1968).

By the same token, expressive conduct which may not be prohibited by the State as sovereign may be proscribed by the State as property owner: "The State, no less than a private owner of property, has power to preserve the property under its control for the use to which it is lawfully dedicated." *Adderley v.*

Florida, 385 U.S. 39, 47 (1966) (upholding state prohibition of expressive conduct on certain state property).

With these differentiated roles of government in mind, it is helpful to assess the role of government as educator, as compared with the role of government as sovereign. When it acts as an educator, at least at the elementary and secondary school level, the government is engaged in inculcating social values and knowledge in relatively impressionable young people. Obviously there are innumerable decisions to be made as to what courses should be taught, what books should be purchased, or what teachers should be employed. In every one of these areas the members of a school board will act on the basis of their own personal or moral values, will attempt to mirror those of the community, or will abdicate the making of such decisions to so-called "experts." ... In the very course of administering the many-faceted operations of a school district, the mere decision to purchase some books will necessarily preclude the possibility of purchasing others. The decision to teach a particular subject may preclude the possibility of teaching another subject. A decision to replace a teacher because of ineffectiveness may by implication be seen as a disparagement of the subject matter taught. In each of these instances, however, the book or the exposure to the subject matter may be acquired elsewhere. The managers of the school district are not proscribing it as to the citizenry in general, but are simply determining that it will not be included in the curriculum or school library. In short, actions by the government as educator do not raise the same First Amendment concerns as actions by the government as sovereign.

II

JUSTICE BRENNAN would hold that the First Amendment gives high school and junior high school students a "right to receive ideas" in the school....

....

Despite JUSTICE BRENNAN's suggestion to the contrary, this Court has never held that the First Amendment grants junior high school and high school students a right of access to certain information in school.... Our past decisions are ... unlike this case where the removed books are readily available to students and non-students at the corner bookstore or the public library.

B

There are even greater reasons for rejecting JUSTICE BRENNAN's analysis, however, than the significant fact that we have never adopted it in the past. "The importance of public schools in the preparation of individuals for participation as citizens, and in the preservation of the values on which our society rests, has long been recognized by our decisions." *Ambach v. Norwick*, 441 U.S. 68, 76 (1979). Public schools fulfill the vital role of teaching students the basic skills necessary to function in our society, and of "inculcating fundamental values necessary to the maintenance of a democratic political system." *Id*. at 77. The idea that such students have a right of access, in the school, to information other than that thought by their educators to be necessary is contrary to the very nature of an inculcative education.

Education consists of the selective presentation and explanation of ideas. The effective acquisition of knowledge depends upon an orderly exposure to relevant information. Nowhere is this more true than in elementary and secondary schools, where, unlike the broad-ranging inquiry available to university students, the courses taught are those thought most relevant to the young students' individual development. Of necessity, elementary and secondary educators must separate the relevant from the irrelevant, the appropriate from the inappropriate. Determining what information not to present to the students is often as important as identifying relevant material. This winnowing process necessarily leaves much information to be discovered by students at another time or in another place, and is fundamentally inconsistent with any constitutionally required eclecticism in public education.

....

As already mentioned, elementary and secondary schools are inculcative in nature. The libraries of such schools serve as supplements to this inculcative role. Unlike university or public libraries, elementary and secondary school libraries are not designed for freewheeling inquiry; they are tailored, as the public school curriculum is tailored, to the teaching of basic skills and ideas. Thus, JUSTICE BRENNAN cannot rely upon the nature of school libraries to escape the fact that the First Amendment right to receive information simply has no application to the one public institution which, by its very nature, is a place for the selective conveyance of ideas.

After all else is said, however, the most obvious reason that petitioners' removal of the books did not violate respondents' right to receive information is the ready availability of the books elsewhere. Students are not denied books by their removal from a school library. The books may be borrowed from a public library, read at a university library, purchased at a bookstore, or loaned by a friend. The government as educator does not seek to reach beyond the confines of the school. Indeed, following the removal from the school library of the books at issue in this case, the local public library put all nine books on display for public inspection. Their contents were fully accessible to any inquisitive student.

C

JUSTICE BRENNAN's own discomfort with the idea that students have a right to receive information from their elementary or secondary schools is demonstrated by the artificial limitations which he places upon the right — limitations which are supported neither by logic nor authority and which are inconsistent with the right itself. The attempt to confine the right to the library is one such limitation, the fallacies of which have already been demonstrated.

As a second limitation, JUSTICE BRENNAN distinguishes the act of removing a previously acquired book from the act of refusing to acquire the book in the first place: "[N]othing in our decision today affects in any way the discretion of a local school board to choose books to add to the libraries of their schools. [O]ur holding today affects only the discretion to remove books." If JUSTICE BRENNAN truly has found a "right to receive ideas," however, this distinction between acquisition and removal makes little sense. The failure of a library to acquire a book denies access to its contents just as effectively as does the removal of the book from the library's shelf. As a result of either action the book cannot be found in the "principal locus" of freedom discovered by JUSTICE BRENNAN.

....

The final limitation placed by JUSTICE BRENNAN upon his newly discovered right is a motive requirement: the First Amendment is violated only "[i]f petitioners intended by their removal decision to deny respondents access to ideas with which petitioners disagreed." But bad motives and good motives alike deny access to the books removed. If JUSTICE BRENNAN truly recognizes a constitutional right to receive information, it is difficult to see why the reason for the denial makes any difference. Of course JUSTICE BRENNAN's view is that intent matters because the First Amendment does not tolerate an officially prescribed orthodoxy. But this reasoning mixes First Amendment apples and oranges. The right to receive information differs from the right to be free from an officially prescribed orthodoxy. Not every educational denial of access to information casts a pall of orthodoxy over the classroom.

It is difficult to tell from JUSTICE BRENNAN's opinion just what motives he would consider constitutionally impermissible. I had thought that the First Amendment proscribes content-based restrictions on the marketplace of ideas. JUSTICE BRENNAN concludes, however, that a removal decision based solely upon the "educational suitability" of a book or upon its perceived vulgarity is "'perfectly permissible.'" But such determinations are based as much on the content of the book as determinations that the book espouses pernicious political views.

Moreover, JUSTICE BRENNAN's motive test is difficult to square with his distinction between acquisition and removal. If a school board's removal of books might be motivated by a desire to promote favored political or religious views, there is no reason that its acquisition policy might not also be so motivated. And yet the "pall of orthodoxy" cast by a carefully executed book-acquisition program apparently would not violate the First Amendment under JUSTICE BRENNAN's view.

D

Intertwined as a basis for JUSTICE BRENNAN's opinion, along with the "right to receive information," is the statement that "[o]ur Constitution does not permit the official suppression of ideas." ...

....

In the case before us the petitioners may in one sense be said to have "suppressed" the "ideas" of vulgarity and profanity, but that is hardly an apt description of what was done. They ordered the removal of books containing vulgarity and profanity, but they did not attempt to preclude discussion about the themes of the books or the books themselves. Such a decision, on respondents' version of the facts in this case, is sufficiently related to "educational suitability" to pass muster under the First Amendment.

E

....

... With respect to the education of children in elementary and secondary schools, the school board may properly determine in many cases that a particular book, a particular course, or even a particular area of knowledge is not educationally suitable for inclusion within the body of knowledge which the school seeks to impart. Without more, this is not a condemnation of the book or the course; it is only a determination akin to that referred to by the Court in *Village of Euclid v. Ambler Realty Co.*, 272 U.S. 365, 388 (1926): "A nuisance may be merely a right thing in the wrong place, like a pig in the parlor instead of the barnyard."

III

Accepting as true respondents' assertion that petitioners acted on the basis of their own "personal values, morals and tastes," I find the actions taken in this case hard to distinguish from the myriad choices made by school boards in the routine supervision of elementary and secondary schools. "Courts do not and cannot intervene in the resolution of conflicts which arise in the daily operation of school systems and which do not directly and sharply implicate basic constitutional values." *Epperson v. Arkansas*, 393 U.S. 97, 104 (1968). In this case respondents' rights of free speech and expression were not infringed, and by respondents' own admission no ideas were "suppressed." I would leave to another day the harder cases.

....

---

1. There are seven different opinions in this case. A plurality agreed that a school board may not "remove books from school library shelves simply because they dislike the ideas contained in those books and seek by their removal to 'prescribe what shall be orthodox in politics, nationalism, religion or other matters of opinion'" (p. 109 of this text). However, only three justices agreed that public school students have a right to receive information. Does this mean that the decision is likely to have less impact on the discretionary powers of school boards? Does this also mean that, absent a majority decision here, the Supreme Court has not recognized a public school student's right to receive information?

2. Justice Brennan, in his opinion, distinguished between the school board's claim of absolute discretion in matters of curriculum and its hegemony over items in the school library. Inasmuch as the school library still falls under the aegis of the school, why is this distinction so important? In light of the decision in *Hazelwood v. Kuhlmeier, supra* Chapter 6, what is the true weight of *Pico*?

3. Justice Blackmun, in his concurring opinion, declined to recognize the right to receive ideas. He instead found that, since schools could inculcate ideas, libraries would play a role in that process. What, then, was his objection to the activity of the school board? Under Blackmun's position, are boards so restricted that they must be required to demonstrate a proper motive for removing library books? If so, must this be examined under a First Amendment analysis?

4. Just prior to the *Pico* decision a federal district court in Maine held against a school board's banning of a book from the library for its "objectionable language where the ban extended to mere possession of the book anywhere on school property." *Sheck v. Baileyville Sch. Comm.*, 530 F. Supp. 679 (D. Maine 1982).

In *Roberts v. Madigan*, 702 F. Supp. 1505 (D. Colo. 1989), a district court held that the Establishment Clause does not require that religious books like the Bible be removed from school libraries. The court ruled that such books may remain as long as no one sect is favored and their presence demonstrates no preference for religious works in general.

VIRGIL v. SCHOOL BOARD OF COLUMBIA COUNTY, FLORIDA

United States Court of Appeals
862 F.2d 1517 (11th Cir. 1989)

ANDERSON, CIRCUIT JUDGE:

This case presents the question of whether the first amendment prevents a school board from removing a previously approved textbook from an elective high school class because of objections to the material's vulgarity and sexual explicitness. We conclude that a school board may, without contravening constitutional limits, take such action where, as here, its methods are "reasonably related to legitimate pedagogical concerns." Accordingly, we affirm the judgment of the district court.

I. *Facts*

The essential facts were stipulated by the parties to this dispute. Since about 1975 the educational curriculum at Columbia High School has included a course entitled "Humanities to 1500" offered as part of a two-semester survey of Western thought, art and literature. In 1985 the school designed the course for eleventh- and twelfth-grade students and prescribed as a textbook Volume I of The Humanities: Cultural Roots and Continuities. This book contained both required and optional readings for the course.

Among the selections included in Volume I of Humanities which were neither required nor assigned are English translations of Lysistrata, written by the Greek dramatist Aristophanes in approximately 411 B.C., and The Miller's Tale, written by the English poet Geoffrey Chaucer around 1380-1390 A.D. During the fall semester of the 1985-86 school year, a portion of Lysistrata was read aloud in class during a session of the Humanities course.

In the spring of 1986, after the first semester had ended, the Reverend and Mrs. Fritz M. Fountain, the parents of a student who had taken the class in the fall of 1985, filed a formal complaint concerning Volume I of Humanities with the School Board of Columbia County. The Fountains also submitted a Request for Examination of School Media. Their objections centered upon Lysistrata and The Miller's Tale.

In response to this parental complaint, the School Board on April 8, 1986, adopted a Policy on Challenged State Adopted Textbooks to address any complaints regarding books in use in the curriculum. Pursuant to the new policy, the School Board appointed an advisory committee to review Volume I of Humanities. Upon examination, the committee recommended that the textbook be retained in the curriculum, but that Lysistrata and The Miller's Tale not be assigned as required reading.

At its April 22, 1986, meeting the School Board considered the advisory committee's report. Silas Pittman, Superintendent of the Columbia County School System, offered his disagreement with the committee's conclusion, and recommended that the two disputed selections be deleted from Volume I or that use of the book in the curriculum be terminated. Adopting the latter proposal, the School Board voted to discontinue any future use of Volume I in the curriculum.

Pursuant to the Board decision, Volume I of Humanities was placed in locked storage and has been kept there ever since. Volume II was used as the course textbook for the rest of the second semester of the 1985-86 academic year, as well as for both semesters of the Humanities course during the 1986-87 term. Since the Board's removal decision, both Volumes I and II have been available in the school library for student use, along with other adaptations and translations of Lysistrata and The Miller's Tale.

... [P]arents of students at Columbia High School filed an action against the School Board and the Superintendent seeking an injunction against the textbook removal and a declaration that such action violated their first amendment rights. Cross-motions for summary judgment were filed by defendants-appellees, on June 22, 1987, and by plaintiffs-appellants, on July 27, 1987. On August 24, 1987, the defendants-appellees filed a response to plaintiffs-appellants' motion. Hearings were held in the district court on September 10 and December 16, 1987. On January 29, 1988, the district court denied the plaintiffs-appellants' motion and granted the defendants-appellees' motion for summary judgment.

The district court found that the two principal factors giving rise to the School Board's decision were "the sexuality in the two selections" and their "excessively vulgar ... language and subject matter." 677 F. Supp. at 1552. In the court's view, the other reasons stipulated by the Board members "simply amplify why they believed that vulgar and sexually explicit materials could properly be removed from the curriculum." *Id.* The court acknowledged that "the School

Board's decision reflects its own restrictive views of the appropriate values to which Columbia High School students should be exposed," *Id.*, and expressed the difficulty it had in "apprehend[ing] the harm which could conceivably be caused to a group of eleventh- and twelfth-grade students by exposure to Aristophanes and Chaucer." *Id.* Nonetheless, the court held that the deferential standard recently established in *Hazelwood School District v. Kuhlmeier*, ___ U.S. ___, 108 S. Ct. 562 (1988), had been met, as the removal decision was "reasonably related" to the "legitimate pedagogical concern" of denying students access to "potentially sensitive topics" such as sexuality. 677 F. Supp. at 1553-54.

... [P]laintiffs-appellants filed notice of appeal to this court.

II. *Discussion*

....

In matters pertaining to the curriculum, educators have been accorded greater control over expression than they may enjoy in other spheres of activity. *See Hazelwood School District v. Kuhlmeier*, ___ U.S. ___, ___, 108 S. Ct. 562, 568-70 (1988) (upholding restriction of expression in school-sponsored student newspaper or in other activities which "may fairly be characterized as part of the school curriculum"). *See also Board of Education v. Pico*, 457 U.S. 853, 869 (1982) (plurality opinion) (indicating that broad school board discretion in matters of curriculum may be defended by reliance upon school board's duty to inculcate community values)....

Still, courts ... have failed to achieve a consensus on the degree of discretion to be accorded school boards to restrict access to curricular materials....

The most direct guidance from the Supreme Court is found in the recent case of *Hazelwood School District v. Kuhlmeier*, ___ U.S. ___, 108 S. Ct. 562, 98 (1988). In *Hazelwood* the Court upheld the authority of a high school principal to excise two pages from a school-sponsored student newspaper on the grounds that articles concerning teenage pregnancy and divorce were inappropriate for the level of maturity of the intended readers, the privacy interests of the articles' subjects were insufficiently protected, and the controversial views contained therein might erroneously be attributed to the school. *Hazelwood* established a relatively lenient test for regulation of expression which "may fairly be characterized as part of the school curriculum." Such regulation is permissible so long as it is "reasonably related to legitimate pedagogical concerns." ___ U.S. at ___, 108 S.Ct. at 570-71.

In applying that test the Supreme Court identified one such legitimate concern which is relevant to this case: "a school must be able to take into account the emotional maturity of the intended audience in determining whether to disseminate student speech on potentially sensitive topics ... [*e.g.*] the particulars of teenage sexual activity." *Id.* at 570. *See also Bethel School District v. Fraser*, 478 U.S. 675, 683 (1986) (recognizing interest in protecting minors from exposure to "sexually explicit" speech and "vulgar" or "offensive" spoken language); *Pico*, 457 U.S. at 871 (plurality opinion) (removal of books from library would be permissible if decision were based on determination that books were "pervasively vulgar" or not "educational[ly] suitab[le]"); *Id.* at 880 (Blackmun, J., concurring in part and concurring in judgment) (removal permissible if motivated by concern that material "contains offensive language ... or because it is psychologically or intellectually inappropriate for the age group").

In applying the *Hazelwood* standard to the instant case, two considerations are particularly significant. First, we conclude that the Board decisions at issue were curricular decisions. The materials removed were part of the textbook used in a regularly scheduled course of study in the school. Plaintiffs argue that this particular course was an elective course, and not a required course. However, common sense indicates that the overall curriculum offered by a school includes not only the core curriculum (*i.e.*, required courses) but also such additional, elective courses of study that school officials design and offer. Each student is expected to select from the several elective courses which school officials deem appropriate in order to fashion a curriculum tailored to his individual needs.

. . . .

Plaintiffs further point out that the materials removed in this case not only were part of an elective course, but were optional, not required readings. For the reasons just mentioned, we conclude that the optional readings removed in this case were part of the school curriculum. Just as elective courses are designed by school officials to supplement required courses, optional readings in a particular class are carefully selected by the teacher as relevant and appropriate to supplement required readings in order to further the educational goals of the course. This is especially true in the instant circumstances, where the optional readings were included within the text itself, and thus had to accompany the student every time the text was taken home. Such materials would obviously carry the imprimatur of school approval.

The second consideration that is significant in applying the *Hazelwood* standard to this case is the fact that the motivation for the Board's removal of the readings has been stipulated to be related to the explicit sexuality and excessively vulgar language in the selections. It is clear from *Hazelwood* and other cases that this is a legitimate concern. School officials can "take into account the emotional maturity of the intended audience in determining ... [the appropriateness of] potentially sensitive topics" such as sex and vulgarity. *Hazelwood*, ___ U.S. at ___, 108 S. Ct. at 570.

Since the stipulated motivation of the School Board relates to legitimate concerns, we need only determine whether the Board action was reasonably related thereto. It is of course true, as plaintiffs so forcefully point out, that Lysistrata and The Miller's Tale are widely acclaimed masterpieces of Western literature. However, after careful consideration, we cannot conclude that the school board's actions were not reasonably related to its legitimate concerns regarding the appropriateness (for this high school audience) of the sexuality and vulgarity in these works. Notwithstanding their status as literary classics, Lysistrata and The Miller's Tale contain passages of exceptional sexual explicitness, as numerous commentators have noted. In assessing the reasonableness of the Board's action, we also take into consideration the fact that most of the high school students involved ranged in age from fifteen to just over eighteen, and a substantial number had not yet reached the age of majority. We also note that the disputed materials have not been banned from the school. The Humanities textbook and other adaptations of Lysistrata and The Miller's Tale are available in the school library. No student or teacher is prohibited from assigning or reading these works or discussing the themes contained therein in class or on school property. *Cf. Sheck v. Baileyville School Committee*, 530 F. Supp. 679 (D. Maine 1982).... Under all the circumstances of this case, we cannot conclude that the Board's action was not reasonably related to the stated legitimate concern.

We decide today only that the Board's removal of these works from the curriculum did not violate the Constitution. Of course, we do not endorse the Board's decision. Like the district court, we seriously question how young persons just below the age of majority can be harmed by these masterpieces of Western literature. However, having concluded that there is no constitutional violation, our role is not to second guess the wisdom of the Board's action.

The judgment of the district court is

Affirmed.

---

1. Can the *Virgil* decision be distinguished from that in *Pico, supra,* because the school board removed books from a course instead of the library? If a student has a right to receive information in the library, as was the case here, why not in the classroom?

2. "The Humanities textbook and adaptations of Lysistrata and The Miller's Tale are available in the school library. No student is prohibited from assigning or reading these works or discussing the themes contained therein in class or on school property." Does this excerpt from the *Virgil* opinion effectively circumvent the Board's decision (which the court ultimately upholds)? If teachers are free to assign readings from the disputed works and discuss the themes in them, has the Board's ban from the school curriculum been compromised? Would a teacher be permitted to assign any of the readings that Justice Powell found so appalling in *Pico*?

3. In another curricular case, *Roberts v. Madigan*, 702 F. Supp 1505 (D. Colo. 1989), *aff'd*, 921 F.2d 1047 (10th Cir. 1990), a teacher challenged the school officials' request to cease reading the Bible in class and that he remove two religious books from his class library. Holding in favor of the school, the court stated that the school officials acted properly in removing the books in that the school's purpose was to promote religious neutrality and to insulate students from undue exposure to the teacher's chosen religion.

In *McCarthy v. Fletcher*, 207 Cal. App. 3d 130, 254 Cal. Rptr. 714 (1989), students challenged the removal of Grendel, by J. Gardner, and One Hundred Years of Solitude, by G. Garcia Marquez. The court, in considering the evidence, determined that the school board's motivation was to advance a certain religious theology. The court held that the board could not remove books because it disagreed with their ideas.

C. PARENT CONTROL OF CURRICULUM

STATE EX REL. KELLEY v. FERGUSON
Supreme Court of Nebraska
95 Neb. 63, 144 N.W. 1039 (1914)

FAWCETT, J.

....

The issue presented by the pleadings and decided by the district court is clean-cut and raises the single question: Can the parent of a child in a city graded school decide the question as to whether or not such child shall be required to carry any particular study which has been prescribed by the board of education; or does the power to make such decision rest entirely in such board? Or, to state it another way, has the parent a right to make a reasonable selection from the prescribed studies for his child to pursue, and, upon having done so, must this selection be respected by the board of education? If the parent has such right, the judgment in this case must be affirmed, for we do not think a case could be presented where a selection made by a parent would more clearly be a reasonable selection than the one attempted to be made in this case. The relator's child was a girl 12 years of age. She was in the sixth grade. The study which the relator directed her not to take was that of cooking, which is required under the subject of domestic science. The other studies which she was required to take and was taking were reading, spelling, arithmetic, geography, general lessons, drawing and writing. The testimony of the father is that at the time the disagreement arose the daughter was studying music, which required not less than two hours a day. If the relator desired to have his daughter study music, he had the unquestionable right to have her do so, and if he thought that the taking of lessons in music, in addition to the studies she was taking in school, as above set out, was all she was able to carry, then, if he had a right to make a selection at all, it must be conceded that it was reasonable for him to select the lesson in domestic science, which took substantially one-tenth of her entire school time, as the lesson to be dropped, in order that she might continue her music. It is contended that this selection was not made by the relator in good faith, but was made because of the fact that the school authorities declined to permit his daughter, at the close of the cooking lesson at the Capitol school, to which the class were taken in a body by the teacher from the Saratoga school, to return to her home on the Seventeenth street car line, instead of requiring her to return with the entire class to the Saratoga school and to be there dismissed. We do not think this fact, even if it were the cause which finally impelled relator to make his attempted selection, is very material. The important question to the school board and to parents generally is that of the right of a parent to make a reasonable selection from the prescribed studies for his child to pursue.

The question is not a new one. It was considered and decided by this court in *State ex rel. Sheibley v. School Dist.*, 31 Neb. 552. In that case the father expressed a desire to have his daughter study grammar instead of rhetoric. His wish was respected and the change made. Subsequently he objected to her studying grammar and demanded that she be excused from continuing the study. When asked what reason he had for not wanting his daughter to pursue the study, he informed the board "that said study was not taught in said school as he had been instructed when he went to school." That was the only reason he would offer for not wanting his daughter to pursue the study. Under his direction the daughter refused to pursue the study, and as a result of such refusal she was expelled. An original application for mandamus was made in this court and the writ awarded. The syllabus holds: "The school trustees of a high school have authority to classify and grade the scholars in the district and cause them to be taught in such departments as they may deem expedient; they may also prescribe the courses of study and textbooks for the use of the school, and such reasonable rules and regulations as they may think needful. They may also require prompt attendance, respectful deportment, and diligence in study. The parent, however, has a right to make a reasonable selection from the prescribed studies for his child to pursue, and this selection must be respected by the trustees, as the right of the parent in that regard is superior to that of the trustees and the teachers."...

Now, who is to determine what studies she shall pursue in school; a teacher, who has a mere temporary interest in her welfare, or her father, who may reasonably be supposed to be desirous of pursuing such course as will best promote the happiness of his child? The father certainly possesses superior opportunities of knowing the physical and mental capabilities of his child. It may be apparent that all the prescribed course of studies is more than the strength of the child can undergo; or he may be desirous, as is frequently the case, that his child, while attending school, should also take lessons in music, painting, etc., from private teachers. This he has a right to do. The right of the parent, therefore, to determine what studies his child shall pursue is paramount to that of the trustees or teacher. Schools are provided by the public in which prescribed branches are taught, which are free to all within the district between certain ages. But no pupil attending the school can be compelled to study any prescribed branch against the protest of the parent that the child shall not study such branch, and any rule or regulation that requires the pupil to continue such studies is arbitrary and unreasonable. There is no good reason why the failure of one or more pupils to study one or more prescribed branches should result disastrously to the proper discipline, efficiency, and well-being of the school. Such pupils are

C. PARENT CONTROL OF CURRICULUM

not idle, but merely devoting their attention to other branches; and so long as the failure of the students, thus excepted, to study all the branches of the prescribed course does not prejudice the equal rights of other students, there is no cause for complaint.

... The public school is one of the main bulwarks of our nation, and we would not knowingly do anything to undermine it; but we should be careful to avoid permitting our love for this noble institution to cause us to regard it as "all in all" and destroy both the God-given and constitutional right of a parent to have some voice in the bringing up and education of his children. We believe in the doctrine of the greatest good to the greatest number, and that the welfare of the individual must give way to the welfare of society in general. The whole current of modern thought and agitation is "onward." The people are beginning to realize as never before that, if we continue to jog along in the ruts our fathers before us have made, little will be accomplished in the way of national and social improvement. The state is more and more taking hold of the private affairs of individuals and requiring that they conduct their business affairs honestly and with due regard for the public good. All this is commendable and must receive the sanction of every good citizen, but, in this age of agitation, such as the world has never known before, we want to be careful lest we carry the doctrine of governmental paternalism too far, for, after all is said and done, the prime factor in our scheme of government is the American home.

Our public schools should receive the earnest and conscientious support of every citizen. To that end the school authorities should be upheld in their control and regulation of our school system; but their power and authority should not be unlimited. They should exercise their authority over and their desire to further the best interests of their scholars, with a due regard for the desires and inborn solicitude of the parents of such children. They should not too jealously assert or attempt to defend their supposed prerogatives. If a reasonable request is made by a parent, it should be heeded.

In the present case, we think it was not unreasonable for the relator to request that his little girl be permitted, at the close of the cooking lessons on Friday afternoons, to be dismissed and permitted to return to her home by a car line which would require a walk of but one block, instead of being taken by the teacher a mile and a quarter and there dismissed, where she would be compelled to take a car line which would impose upon her a walk of nine blocks, a distance of nearly three-quarters of a mile. We are unable to see how the granting of this request could in any manner have embarrassed the school authorities or have caused any break in the discipline of the school. Had this slight request been granted, this controversy might never have arisen. In addition to this, if the relator desired that his little girl should take music lessons from a private instructor and devote an hour or two a day to that study, in lieu of the modern lesson of cooking in the public school, we are unable to see how excusing her from that lesson could have interfered with the discipline of the school. However that may be, this court has expressly decided that the parent has a right to make such selection....

The judgment of the district court is therefore affirmed.

....

---

1. Does the reasoning of the majority in *Ferguson* distinguish what might be termed the "core of an education" from the more peripheral academic courses? If so, how do you view *State ex rel. Sheibley v. School Dist.*, discussed in *Ferguson*, in which a father successfully objected to his daughter's studying grammar? Perhaps even grammar is peripheral, and the *Ferguson* court would decide differently if reading, writing, or arithmetic were the subject in question, on the ground that these subjects are required "to promote a common interest and the efficiency of the school." If, however, history, spelling, geography, etc. are to be treated differently than the three "R's," the court must be saying that the school can function without instructing all students in these subjects and also that the child will not be irreparably injured by this gap in his education. Assuming this thinking underlies these distinctions, is there any way to justify compulsory education beyond learning the three "R's"? What of a subject like sex education, which is peripheral in an academic sense but in which there may be strong public interests such as health or avoidance of illegitimacy? Is the result in *Ferguson* consistent with compulsory education discussed in Chapter 2? Are they consistent with the teacher's rights cases discussed later in this chapter?

2. If the theory of the cases which uphold a parent's right to excuse his child from attending certain classes is, in part at least, that the schools have not totally supplanted the parent's common-law right and duty to educate his children, why are parents denied the right to compel that certain courses be taught, especially if the course is to be elective, rather than compulsory?

MOZERT v. HAWKINS COUNTY BOARD OF EDUCATION

United States Court of Appeals
827 F.2d 1058 (6th Cir. 1987)

LIVELY, CHIEF JUDGE.

....

I

A

Early in 1983 the Hawkins County, Tennessee Board of Education adopted the Holt, Rinehart and Winston basic reading series (the Holt series) for use in grades 1-8 of the public schools of the county. In grades 1-4, reading is not taught as a separate subject at a designated time in the school day. Instead, the teachers in these grades use the reading texts throughout the day in conjunction

C. PARENT CONTROL OF CURRICULUM

with other subjects. In grades 5-8, reading is taught as a separate subject at a designated time in each class. However, the schools maintain an integrated curriculum which requires that ideas appearing in the reading programs reoccur in other courses. By statute public schools in Tennessee are required to include "character education" in their curricula. The purpose of this requirement is "to help each student develop positive values and to improve student conduct as students learn to act in harmony with their positive values and learn to become good citizens in their school, community, and society." Tennessee Code Annotated (TCA) 49-6-1007 (1986 Supp.).

....

The plaintiff Vicki Frost is the mother of four children, three of whom were students in Hawkins County public schools in 1983. At the beginning of the 1983-84 school year Mrs. Frost read a story in a daughter's sixth grade reader that involved mental telepathy. Mrs. Frost, who describes herself as a "born again Christian," has a religious objection to any teaching about mental telepathy. Reading further, she found additional themes in the reader to which she had religious objections. After discussing her objections with other parents, Mrs. Frost talked with the principal of Church Hill Middle School and obtained an agreement for an alternative reading program for students whose parents objected to the assigned Holt reader. The students who elected the alternative program left their classrooms during the reading sessions and worked on assignments from an older textbook series in available office or library areas. Other students in two elementary schools were excused from reading the Holt books.

B

In November 1983 the Hawkins County School Board voted unanimously to eliminate all alternative reading programs and require every student in the public schools to attend classes using the Holt series. Thereafter the plaintiff students refused to read the Holt series or attend reading classes where the series was being used. The children of several of the plaintiffs were suspended for brief periods for this refusal. Most of the plaintiff students were ultimately taught at home, or attended religious schools, or transferred to public schools outside Hawkins County. One student returned to school because his family was unable to afford alternate schooling. Even after the board's order, two students were allowed some accommodation, in that the teacher either excused them from reading the Holt stories, or specifically noted on worksheets that the student was not required to believe the stories.

On December 2, 1983, the plaintiffs, consisting of seven families — 14 parents and 17 children — filed this action pursuant to 42 U.S.C. § 1983. In their complaint the plaintiffs asserted that they have sincere religious beliefs which are contrary to the values taught or inculcated by the reading textbooks and that it is a violation of the religious beliefs and convictions of the plaintiff students to be required to read the books and a violation of the religious beliefs of the plaintiff parents to permit their children to read the books. The plaintiffs sought to hold the defendants liable because "forcing the student-plaintiffs to read school books which teach or inculcate values in violation of their religious beliefs and convictions is a clear violation of their rights to the free exercise of religion protected by the First and Fourteenth Amendments to the United States Constitution."

....

II

....

B

Vicki Frost was the first witness for the plaintiffs and she presented the most complete explanation of the plaintiffs' position. The plaintiffs do not belong to a single church or denomination, but all consider themselves born again Christians. Mrs. Frost testified that the word of God as found in the Christian Bible "is the totality of my beliefs." There was evidence that other members of their churches, and even their pastors, do not agree with their position in this case.

Mrs. Frost testified that she had spent more than 200 hours reviewing the Holt series and had found numerous passages that offended her religious beliefs. She stated that the offending materials fell into seventeen categories which she listed. These ranged from such familiar concerns of fundamentalist Christians as evolution and "secular humanism" to less familiar themes such as "futuristic supernaturalism," pacifism, magic and false views of death.

In her lengthy testimony Mrs. Frost identified passages from stories and poems used in the Holt series that fell into each category. Illustrative is her first category, futuristic supernaturalism, which she defined as teaching "Man As God." Passages that she found offensive described Leonardo da Vinci as the human with a creative mind that "came closest to the divine touch." Similarly, she felt that a passage entitled "Seeing Beneath the Surface" related to an occult theme, by describing the use of imagination as a vehicle for seeing things not discernible through our physical eyes. She interpreted a poem, "Look at Anything," as presenting the idea that by using imagination a child can become part of anything and thus understand it better. Mrs. Frost testified that it is an "occult practice" for children to use imagination beyond the limitation of scriptural authority. She testified that the story that alerted her to the problem with the reading series fell into the category of futuristic supernaturalism. Entitled "A Visit to Mars," the story portrays thought transfer and telepathy in such a way that "it could be considered a scientific concept," according to this witness. This theme appears in the testimony of several witnesses, *i.e.*, the materials objected to "could" be interpreted in a manner repugnant to their religious beliefs.

Mrs. Frost described objectionable passages from other categories in much the same way. Describing evolution as a teaching that there is no God, she identified 24 passages that she considered to have evolution as a theme. She admitted that the textbooks contained a disclaimer that evolution is a theory, not a proven scientific fact. Nevertheless, she felt that references to evolution were so pervasive and presented in such a factual manner as to render the disclaimer meaningless. After describing her objection to passages that encourage children to make moral judgments about whether it is right or wrong to kill animals, the witness stated, "I thought they would be learning to read, to have good English and grammar, and to be able to do other subject work." Asked by plaintiffs' attorney to define her objection to the textbooks, Mrs. Frost replied:

> Very basically, I object to the Holt, Rhinehart [sic] Winston series as a whole, what the message is as a whole. There are some contents which are objectionable by themselves, but my most withstanding [sic] objection would be to the series as a whole.

....

C

The district court held that the plaintiffs' free exercise rights have been burdened because their "religious beliefs compel them to refrain from exposure to the Holt series," and the defendant school board "has effectively required that the student plaintiffs either read the offensive texts or give up their free public education." *Mozert v. Hawkins County Public Schools*, 647 F. Supp. 1194, 1200 (E.D. Tenn. 1986)....

The district court went on to find that the state had a compelling interest "in the education of its young," 647 F. Supp. at 1200, but that it had erred in choosing "to further its legitimate and overriding interest in public education by mandating the use of a single basic reading series," *Id.* at 1201, in the face of the plaintiffs' religious objections. The court concluded that the proof at trial demonstrated that the defendants could accommodate the plaintiffs without material and substantial disruption to the educational process by permitting the objecting students to "opt out of the school district's reading program," *Id.* at 1203, and meet the reading requirements by home schooling....

The court entered an injunction prohibiting the defendants "from requiring the student-plaintiffs to read from the Holt series," and ordering the defendants to excuse the student plaintiffs from their classrooms "[d]uring the normal reading period" and to provide them with suitable space in the library or elsewhere for a study hall. [*Id.*] at 1203....

III

A

The first question to be decided is whether a governmental requirement that a person be exposed to ideas he or she finds objectionable on religious grounds constitutes a burden on the free exercise of that person's religion as forbidden by the First Amendment. This is precisely the way the superintendent of the Hawkins County schools framed the issue in an affidavit filed early in this litigation. In his affidavit the superintendent set forth the school system's interest in a uniformity of reading texts. The affidavit also countered the claims of the plaintiffs that the schools were inculcating values and religious doctrines contrary to their religious beliefs, stating:

> Without expressing an opinion as to the plaintiffs' religious beliefs, I am of the opinion that plaintiffs misunderstand the fact that exposure to something does not constitute teaching, indoctrination, opposition or promotion of the things exposed. While it is true that these textbooks expose the student to varying values and religious backgrounds, neither the textbooks nor the teachers teach, indoctrinate, oppose or promote any particular value or religion.

....

It is also clear that exposure to objectionable material is what the plaintiffs objected to albeit they emphasize the repeated nature of the exposure. The complaint mentioned only the textbooks that the students were required to read. It did not seek relief from any method of teaching the material and did not mention the teachers' editions. The plaintiffs did not produce a single student or teacher to testify that any student was ever required to affirm his or her belief or disbelief in any idea or practice mentioned in the various stories and passages contained in the Holt series. However, the plaintiffs appeared to assume that materials clearly presented as poetry, fiction and even "make-believe" in the Holt series were presented as facts which the students were required to believe. Nothing in the record supports this assumption.

... Proof that an objecting student was required to participate beyond reading and discussing assigned materials, or was disciplined for disputing assigned materials, might well implicate the Free Exercise Clause because the element of compulsion would then be present. But this was not the case either as pled or proved. The record leaves no doubt that the district court correctly viewed this case as one involving exposure to repugnant ideas and themes as presented by the Holt series.

Vicki Frost testified that an occasional reference to role reversal, pacifism, rebellion against parents, one-world government and other objectionable concepts would be acceptable, but she felt it was the repeated references to such subjects that created the burden. The district court suggested that it was a matter of balance. *Id.* at 1199, apparently believing that a reading series that presented ideas with which the plaintiffs agree in juxtaposition to those with which they disagree would pass constitutional muster. While balanced textbooks are certainly desirable, there would be serious difficulties with trying to cure the omissions in the Holt series, as plaintiffs and their expert witnesses view the texts.

However, the plaintiffs' own testimony casts serious doubt on their claim that a more balanced presentation would satisfy their religious views. Mrs. Frost testified that it would be acceptable for the schools to teach her children about other philosophies and religions, but if the practices of other religions were described in detail, or if the philosophy was "profound" in that it expressed a world view that deeply undermined her religious beliefs, then her children "would have to be instructed to [the] error [of the other philosophy]." It is clear that to the plaintiffs there is but one acceptable view — the Biblical view, as they interpret the Bible. Furthermore, the plaintiffs view every human situation and decision, whether related to personal belief and conduct or to public policy and programs, from a theological or religious perspective. Mrs. Frost testified that many political issues have theological roots and that there would be "no way" certain themes could be presented without violating her religious beliefs. She identified such themes as evolution, false supernaturalism, feminism, telepathy and magic as matters that could not be presented in any way without offending her beliefs. The only way to avoid conflict with the plaintiffs' beliefs in these sensitive areas would be to eliminate all references to the subjects so identified. However, the Supreme Court has clearly held that it violates the Establishment Clause to tailor a public school's curriculum to satisfy the principles or prohibitions of any religion. *Epperson v. Arkansas*, 393 U.S. 97, 106 (1968).

....

B

....

... The requirement that students read the assigned materials and attend reading classes, in the absence of a showing that this participation entailed affirmation or denial of a religious belief, or performance or non-performance of a religious exercise or practice, does not place an unconstitutional burden on the students' free exercise of religion.

C

... [T]he plaintiffs, in this court, have relied particularly upon three Supreme Court decisions. We find them all distinguishable.

The issue in *Torcaso v. Watkins*, 367 U.S. 488 (1961), was whether a state could deny public office to a person solely because of the person's refusal to declare a belief in God. Quoting from its earlier decision in *Everson v. Board of Education*, 330 U.S. 1, 15 (1947), the Court stated:

> We repeat and reaffirm that neither a State nor the Federal Government can constitutionally force a person "to profess a belief or disbelief in any religion." *Id.* at 495.

Since there was no evidence that the plaintiff students were ever required to profess or deny a religious belief the issue in *Torcaso* simply is not presented by the instant case.

Board of Education v. Barnette, 319 U.S. 624 (1943), grew out of a school board rule that required all schools to make a salute to the flag and a pledge of allegiance a regular part of their daily program. All teachers and students were required to participate in the exercise and refusal to engage in the salute was considered an act of insubordination which could lead to expulsion and possible delinquency charges for being unlawfully absent. The plaintiff was a Jehovah's Witness who considered the flag an "image" which the Bible forbids worshiping in any way. JUSTICE JACKSON, writing for the Court, stated:

> Here, ... we are dealing with a compulsion of students to declare a belief. They are not merely made acquainted with the flag salute so that they may be informed as to what it is or even what it means. *Id.* at 631....

....

It is clear that governmental compulsion either to do or refrain from doing an act forbidden or required by one's religion, or to affirm or disavow a belief forbidden or required by one's religion, is the evil prohibited by the Free Exercise Clause. In *Abington School District v. Schempp*, 374 U.S. 203, 223 (1963), the Court described the Free Exercise Clause as follows:

> Its purpose is to secure religious liberty in the individual by prohibiting any invasions thereof by civil authority. Hence it is necessary in a free exercise case for one to show the coercive effect of the enactment as it operates against him in the practice of his religion. The distinction between the two clauses is apparent — a violation of the Free Exercise Clause is predicated on coercion while the Establishment Clause violation need not be so attended.

The plaintiffs appear to contend that the element of compulsion was supplied by the requirement of class participation in the reading exercises. As we have pointed out earlier, there is no proof in the record that any plaintiff student was required to engage in role play, make up magic chants, read aloud or engage in the activity of haggling. In fact, the Director of Education for the State of Tennessee testified that most teachers do not adhere to the suggestions in the teachers' manuals and a teacher for 11 years in the Hawkins County system stated that she looks at the lesson plans in the teachers' editions, but "does her

C. PARENT CONTROL OF CURRICULUM

own thing." Being exposed to other students performing these acts might be offensive to the plaintiffs, but it does not constitute the compulsion described in the Supreme Court cases, where the objector was required to affirm or deny a religious belief or engage or refrain from engaging in a practice contrary to sincerely held religious beliefs.

D

The third Supreme Court decision relied upon by the plaintiffs is the only one that might be read to support the proposition that requiring mere exposure to materials that offend one's religious beliefs creates an unconstitutional burden on the free exercise of religion. *Wisconsin v. Yoder*, 406 U.S. 205 (1972). However, *Yoder* rested on such a singular set of facts that we do not believe it can be held to announce a general rule that exposure without compulsion to act, believe, affirm or deny creates an unconstitutional burden. The plaintiff parents in *Yoder* were Old Order Amish and members of the Conservative Amish Mennonite Church, who objected to their children being required to attend either public or private schools beyond the eighth grade. Wisconsin school attendance law required them to cause their children to attend school until they reached the age of 16. Unlike the plaintiffs in the present case, the parents in *Yoder* did not want their children to attend any high school or be exposed to any part of a high school curriculum. The Old Order Amish and the Conservative Amish Mennonites separate themselves from the world and avoid assimilation into society, and attempt to shield their children from all worldly influences. The Supreme Court found from the record that —

> [C]ompulsory school attendance to age 16 for Amish children carries with it a very real threat to undermining the Amish community and religious practice as they exist today; they must either abandon belief and be assimilated into society at large, or be forced to migrate to some other and more tolerant region. *Id.* at 218.

As if to emphasize the narrowness of its holding because of the unique 300 year history of the Old Amish Order, the Court wrote:

> It is one thing to say that compulsory education for a year or two beyond the eighth grade may be necessary when its goal is the preparation of the child for life in modern society as the majority live, but it is quite another if the goal of education be viewed as the preparation of the child for life in the separated agrarian community that is the keystone of the Amish faith. *Id.* at 222.

This statement points up dramatically the difference between *Yoder* and the present case. The parents in *Yoder* were required to send their children to some school that prepared them for life in the outside world, or face official sanctions. The parents in the present case want their children to acquire all the skills required to live in modern society. They also want to have them excused from exposure to some ideas they find offensive. Tennessee offers two options to accommodate this latter desire. The plaintiff parents can either send their children to church schools or private schools, as many of them have done, or teach them at home....

Yoder was decided in large part on the impossibility of reconciling the goals of public education with the religious requirement of the Amish that their children be prepared for life in a separated community. As the Court noted, the requirement of school attendance to age 16 posed a "very real threat of undermining the Amish community and religious practice as they exist today....'' 406 U.S. at 218. No such threat exists in the present case, and Tennessee's school attendance laws offer several options to those parents who want their children to have the benefit of an education which prepares for life in the modern world without being exposed to ideas which offend their religious beliefs.

....

IV

....

The judgment of the district court granting injunctive relief and damages is reversed, and the case is remanded with directions to dismiss the complaint. No costs are allowed. The parties will bear their own costs on appeal.

....

---

1. *Mozert* and the other cases discussed in this section pit the rights of parents against the interests of the school board as to the control of the curriculum. What of the rights of students? *Tinker v. Des Moines Indep. Community Sch. Dist.*, 393 U.S. 503 (1969), described public school students as "persons under our Constitution possessed of fundamental rights which the states must respect." Recall though in *Meyer v. Nebraska, supra,* where the Supreme Court described the rights of parents as "control[ling] the education of their children" and "the natural duty of the parent to give his children education suitable to their station in life...." Hence, is there a "tug of war" of competing interests that includes parents, schools, and children? In the cases herein, who speaks for the students? Do parents or school officials have total hegemony over the lives of students? Justice Douglas in his partial dissent in *Wisconsin v. Yoder*, 406 U.S. 205, 245 (1972) responds with the following:

> [I]t is the student's judgment, not his parents', that is essential if we are to give full meaning to what we have said about the Bill of Rights and of the right of students to be masters of their own destiny.

2. *Mozert* is a case indicating that students need not be exempted from the study of certain materials or subjects unless parents' free exercise rights of religion are burdened. At what point do such burdens accrue as regards student

C. PARENT CONTROL OF CURRICULUM

participation? By simply having to read the information or to be tested on it? The court allows that one threshold area rests with indoctrination, i.e., school board interests cease at the point where curriculum materials result in such influence. Who makes this judgment? And if one of the major reasons for having public schools in the United States is values inculcation, wouldn't this involve indoctrination in some form?

3. Recall that one of the teachers in *Mozert* said that the students were not required to believe the stories they read in the Holt readers. Does this work to relieve the tension of religious differences between school, books, and the children who have to read the books? Does it depend on the age of the student?

The court finds that the parents objected to student exposure to the Holt, Rinehart and Winston series. Can it be assumed that parents fear that this exposure will ultimately have an adverse effect on the religious views of their children? Are the plaintiffs' children young enough to think that they are required to believe what they read in the series? Is this a part of the plaintiffs' claim? The court says no.

Do you agree with the court on this issue? Is it possible that teaching of such values could be more implicit and constitute a valid claim for the plaintiffs?

> Proof that an objecting student was required to participate beyond reading and discussing assigned materials, or was disciplined for disputing assigned readings, might well implicate the Free Exercise Clause because the element of compulsion would then be present. But this was not the case pled or proved.

By this statement, is the court deliberately avoiding what likely was the true claim of the plaintiffs? Or was it properly limiting the claim to what was pled and proved?

Think of a case you have read in this text whose decision you disagree with. Imagine yourself in a class where the instructor required you to not only study it, but to adopt it as your principle point of view on the subject. Could you do so comfortably? If not, this may be because you have reached a level of maturity at which you can form independent opinions confidently. Can the same be said for school children exposed to alleged offensive books? Is it a fair justification of the holding in *Mozert* to say that the parents who disagree with the books used at the school can simply enroll their children in private schools or teach them at home?

4. The court mentioned that ministers and other churchgoers disagreed with plaintiffs' position in this case. Did this have an effect on the decision in the case? Should it influence a judge's decision?

5. Two recent cases involved the reading series Impressions and constitutional challenges by parents of students alleging violations of the Establishment and Free Exercise Clauses. In both cases, summary judgments were entered for the defendant school systems. *See Brown v. Woodland Joint Unified Sch. Dist.*, 1992

WL 361696 (E.D. Cal. 1992); and *Fleischfresser v. Directors of Sch. Dist. 200,* 15 F.3d 680 (7th Cir. 1994). The court in *Brown* stated the following:

> While the court is not unsympathetic to plaintiffs' concerns, there is no constitutional basis for the court to order that the activities in question be excluded from the classroom simply because isolated instances of those activities may happen to coincide or harmonize with the tenets of two relatively obscure religions. *Brown,* at 16.

The plaintiffs claimed that portions of the books in the series endorsed and sponsored witchcraft and neopaganism. How "obscure" do the religions have to be and how isolated do the related activities have to be in order for the school to prevail on summary judgment?

The Court in *Fleischfresser,* 15 F.3d at 686, 688-89, held:

> In the context of this balance between the parents' rights and the directors' discretion, courts have held a number of activities to be violations of the Establishment Clause. These include: 1) inviting clergy to offer invocation and benediction prayers at formal graduation ceremonies for high schools and middle schools, *Lee v. Weisman,* 112 S. Ct. 2649; 2) daily readings from the Bible, *Abington Sch. Dist.,* 374 U.S. 203; 3) daily recitation of the Lord's Prayer, *Id.*; 4) distributing Gideon Bibles to fifth grade public school students, *Berger,* 982 F.2d 1160; 5) posting the Ten Commandments in every classroom, *Stone v. Graham,* 449 U.S. 39; 6) requiring the teaching of evolution science with creation science or not at all, *Edwards,* 482 U.S. 578; 7) beginning school assemblies with prayer, *Collins,* 644 F.2d 759; and 8) teaching a Transcendental Meditation course that includes a ceremony involving offerings to a deity, *Malnak v. Yogi,* 592 F.2d 197 (3d Cir., 1979). Courts have not been inclined to find a violation of the First Amendment, however, with respect to the use of certain books in a public school curriculum. These cases deal with novels, textbooks, and reading series, including the Impressions Reading Series at issue in the instant case.... Moreover, even the Bible itself may be used in public schools to teach literary and historical lessons. *Abington Sch. Dist.,* 374 U.S. at 225....
>
> ....
>
> In this case, the parents have not alleged that the purpose of using the series is exclusively religious. But even if they had, there is a clear secular purpose. As we noted above, public school curricula traditionally rely on fantasy and "make-believe" to hold a student's attention to develop reading skills and to instill a sense of creativity and imagination. That this particular series relies on witches and goblins in a few stories to develop the children's minds fits the norm. As a result, we hold that the directors' use of the series has a secular purpose.

C. PARENT CONTROL OF CURRICULUM

... [W]e are concerned, of course, with the effect on the elementary school students of using the Impressions Reading Series. Further, in evaluating the primary effect of the use of the series, we must focus on the entire series, not simply the passages the parents find offensive because to "[f]ocus exclusively on the religious component of any activity would inevitably lead to its invalidation." *Id.* at 679-80.

The stories which the parents contend are offensive are a relatively small minority when compared with the series as a whole. Further, the series is also comprised of some stories, also in a small minority, which presumably are consistent with the parents' Catholic and Protestant beliefs, including "The Best Christmas Pageant Ever," "How Six Found Christmas," and "The Twelve Days of Christmas." But, it is not enough that certain stories in the series strike the parents as reflecting the religions of Neo-Paganism or Witchcraft, or reference Christian holidays. The Establishment Clause is not violated because government action "happens to coincide or harmonize with the tenets of some or all religions." *Harris v. McRae*, 448 U.S. 297, 319 (1980) (citing *McGowan v. Maryland*, 366 U.S. 420, 442 (1961)). In this case, the primary or principle effect of the use of the reading series at issue is not to endorse these religions, but simply to educate the children by improving their reading skills and to develop imagination and creativity. Any religious references are secondary, if not trivial....

The parents also claim that because a curriculum review committee reviewed the series before it was purchased, the directors became entangled with religion. This claim is without merit. School boards have broad discretion in determining curricula in their schools. Surely, the mere exercise of this discretion cannot constitute excessive entanglement with religion. Further, there is no allegation that the publisher of the reading series is a religious organization or that the directors are in some way dealing with a particular religious organization. Nothing, then, supports a claim that the use of this reading series constitutes excessive entanglement with religion.

6. Should the public schools make an effort to accommodate religious differences among students with modifications of lessons if overhaul of the textbooks used does not occur or is not feasible? In *Grove v. Mead Sch. Dist. No. 354*, 753 F.2d 1528 (9th Cir. 1985), the school exercised such an accommodation and was upheld in this activity by the Ninth Circuit:

The burden on Grove's [plaintiff's] free exercise of religion was minimal. Cassie [Grove] was assigned an alternate book as soon as she and Grove objected to The Learning Tree.... The state interest in providing well-rounded public education would be critically impeded by accommodation of [all of] Grove's wishes. If we are to eliminate everything that is objectionable to any of [the religious bodies existing in the United States] or inconsistent with any of their doctrines, we will leave public education in shreds. *Id.* at 1533.

7. Should public school music groups be permitted to learn and perform religious music? Should school choirs be restricted from singing and playing the "Hallelujah Chorus" from Handel's The Messiah during the Christmas season? How does the interest in the students' learning music or the history of that music (with its religious influence) stack up with constitutional complaints?

8. In a case similar to *Mozert*, a district court entered an order forbidding the use of forty-four textbooks in such subjects as home economics and history on the ground that they promoted "secular humanism" in violation of the Establishment Clause. In *Smith v. Board of Sch. Comm'rs of Ala.*, 827 F.2d 684 (11th Cir. 1987), a federal appeals court reversed. "Even assuming that secular humanism is a religion for purposes of the Establishment Clause," the challenged books did not convey a message of state approval of religion, did not disapprove of other religions, and essentially had the primary effect that was neutral on religious content. *See* Chapter 15 for a full discussion of this case.

D. TEACHER CONTROL OF CURRICULUM

PARDUCCI v. RUTLAND

United States District Court
316 F. Supp. 352 (M.D. Ala. 1970)

Order

JOHNSON, CHIEF JUDGE: — Plaintiff was dismissed from her position as a high school teacher in the Montgomery public schools for assigning a certain short story to her junior (eleventh grade) English classes. In her complaint ... plaintiff alleges that defendants, in ordering her dismissal, violated her First Amendment right to academic freedom and her Fourteenth Amendment right to due process of law.... The defendants are the members of the Montgomery County Board of Education, the Superintendent of Schools of the county, the Associate Superintendent, and the Principal of plaintiff's high school....

....

On April 21, 1970, plaintiff assigned as outside reading to her junior English classes a story, entitled "Welcome to the Monkey House." The story, a comic satire, was selected by plaintiff to give her students a better understanding of one particular genre of western literature — the short story. The story's author, Kurt Vonnegut, Jr., is a prominent contemporary writer who has published numerous short stories and novels, including The Cat's Cradle and a recent best seller, Slaughter-House Five.

The following morning, plaintiff was called to Principal Rutland's office for a conference with him and the Associate Superintendent of the school system. Both men expressed their displeasure with the content of the story, which they described as "literary garbage," and with the "philosophy" of the story, which

D. TEACHER CONTROL OF CURRICULUM

they construed as condoning, if not encouraging, "the killing off of elderly people and free sex."[1] They also expressed concern over the fact that three of plaintiff's students had asked to be excused from the assignment and that several disgruntled parents had called the school to complain. They then admonished plaintiff not to teach the story in any of her classes.

Plaintiff retorted that she was bewildered by their interpretation of and attitude toward the story, that she still considered it to be a good literary work, and that, while not meaning to cause any trouble, she felt that she had a professional obligation to teach the story. The Associate Superintendent then warned plaintiff that he would have to report this incident to the Superintendent who might very well order her dismissal. Plaintiff, who by this time had become very emotionally upset, responded to this threat by tendering her resignation.

... [D]efendants agreed at the hearing to allow plaintiff to withdraw her resignation and to accord plaintiff a hearing before the Montgomery County Board of Education on the question of dismissal.... [T]he School Board notified plaintiff that she had been dismissed from her job for assigning materials which had a "disruptive" effect on the school and for refusing "the counselling and advice of the school principal." The School Board also advised the plaintiff that one of the bases for her dismissal was "insubordination" by reason of a statement that she made to the Principal and Associate Superintendent that "regardless of their counselling" she "would continue to teach the eleventh grade English class at the Jeff Davis High School by the use of whatever material" she wanted "and in whatever manner" she thought best.

....

I

Plaintiff asserts in her complaint that her dismissal for assigning "Welcome to the Monkey House" violated her First Amendment right to academic freedom.

That teachers are entitled to First Amendment freedoms is an issue no longer in dispute. "It can hardly be argued that either students or teachers shed their constitutional rights to freedom of speech or expression at the schoolhouse gate." *Tinker v. Des Moines Independent Community School District*, 393 U.S. 503, 506 (1969); *see Pickering v. Board of Education*, 391 U.S. 563, 568 (1968). These constitutional protections are unaffected by the presence or absence of tenure under state law. *McLaughlin v. Tilendis*, 398 F.2d 287 (7th Cir. 1968); *Johnson v. Branch*, 364 F.2d 177 (4th Cir. 1966), *cert. denied*, 385 U.S. 1003 (1967).

Although academic freedom is not one of the enumerated rights of the First Amendment, the Supreme Court has on numerous occasions emphasized that the right to teach, to inquire, to evaluate and to study is fundamental to a democratic society. In holding a New York loyalty oath statute unconstitutionally vague, the

---

[1] Both Mr. Rutland and Mr. Garrett later testified that neither of them was much of a reader, had any special expertise in the field of literature, or had ever taught an English course.

Court stressed the need to expose students to a robust exchange of ideas in the classroom:

> Our nation is deeply committed to safeguarding academic freedom, which is of transcendent value to all of us and not merely to the teachers concerned. That freedom is therefore a special concern of the First Amendment, which does not tolerate laws that cast a pall of orthodoxy over the classroom.... The classroom is peculiarly the "marketplace of ideas."[4]

Furthermore, the safeguards of the First Amendment will quickly be brought into play to protect the right of academic freedom because any unwarranted invasion of this right will tend to have a chilling effect on the exercise of the right by other teachers. *Cf. Wieman v. Updegraff*, 344 U.S. at 194, 195 (FRANKFURTER, J., concurring); *Pickering v. Board of Education, supra* 391 U.S. at 574.

The right to academic freedom, however, like all other constitutional rights, is not absolute and must be balanced against the competing interests of society. This Court is keenly aware of the state's vital interest in protecting the impressionable minds of its young people from any form of extreme propagandism in the classroom.

> A teacher works in a sensitive area in a schoolroom. There he shapes the attitudes of young minds towards the society in which they live. In this, the state has a vital concern.[5]

....

Thus, the first question to be answered is whether "Welcome to the Monkey House" is inappropriate reading for high school juniors. While the story contains several vulgar terms and a reference to an involuntary act of sexual intercourse, the Court, having read the story very carefully, can find nothing that would render it obscene either under the standards of *Roth v. United States*, or under the stricter standards for minors as set forth in *Ginsberg v. New York*.

The slang words are contained in two short rhymes which are less ribald than those found in many of Shakespeare's plays. The reference in the story to an act of sexual intercourse is no more descriptive than the rape scene in Pope's "Rape of the Lock." As for the theme of the story, the Court notes that the anthology in which the story was published was reviewed by several of the popular national weekly magazines, none of which found the subject matter of any of the stories to be offensive. It appears to the Court, moreover, that the author, rather than advocating the "killing off of old people," satirizes the practice to symbolize the increasing depersonalization of man in society.

---

[4]Keyishian v. Board of Regents, 385 U.S. 589, 603 (1967).
[5]Shelton v. Tucker, 364 U.S. 479 (1960).

D. TEACHER CONTROL OF CURRICULUM

The Court's finding as to the appropriateness of the story for high school students is confirmed by the reaction of the students themselves. Rather than there being a threatened or actual substantial disruption to the educational processes of the school, the evidence reflects that the assigning of the story was greeted with apathy by most of the students. Only three of plaintiff's students asked to be excused from the assignment. On this question of whether there was a material and substantial threat of disruption, the Principal testified at the School Board hearing that there was no indication that any of plaintiff's other 87 students were planning to disrupt the normal routine of the school. This Court now specifically finds and concludes that the conduct for which plaintiff was dismissed was not such that "would materially and substantially interfere with" reasonable requirements of discipline in the school.

....

Since the defendants have failed to show either that the assignment was inappropriate reading for high school juniors, or that it created a significant disruption to the educational processes of this school, this Court concludes that plaintiff's dismissal constituted an unwarranted invasion of her First Amendment right to academic freedom.

II

Plaintiff also alleges that she was denied "the right to use the short story in question as extra reading without a clear and concise written standard to determine which books are obscene."

The record shows that prior to plaintiff's dismissal, there was no written or announced policy at Jefferson Davis High School governing the selection and assignment of outside materials. One of the defendants testified at the School Board hearing that the selection of outside readings was a matter determined solely by the good taste and good judgment of the individual teacher. The only question before this Court on this point, therefore, is whether plaintiff was entitled, under the Due Process Clause, to prior notice that the conduct for which she was punished was prohibited.

Our laws in this country have long recognized that no person should be punished for conduct unless such conduct has been proscribed in clear and precise terms. *See Connally v. General Constr. Co.*, 269 U.S. 385, 391 (1926). When the conduct being punished involves First Amendment rights, as is the case here, the standards for judging permissible vagueness will be even more strictly applied.

In the case now before the Court, we are concerned not merely with vague standards, but with the total absence of standards. When a teacher is forced to speculate as to what conduct is permissible and what conduct is proscribed, he is apt to be overly cautious and reserved in the classroom. Such a reluctance on the part of the teacher to investigate and experiment with new and different ideas is anathema to the entire concept of academic freedom.

This Court is well aware of the fact that "school officials should be given wide discretion in administering their schools" and that "courts should be reluctant to interfere with or place limits on that discretion." Such legal platitudes should not, however, be allowed to become euphemisms for "infringement upon" and "deprivations of" constitutional rights. However wide the discretion of school officials, such discretion cannot be exercised so as to arbitrarily deprive teachers of their First Amendment rights. *See Johnson v. Branch, supra*, 364 F.2d at 180. This Court cannot, on the facts of this case, find any substantial interest of the schools to be served by giving defendants unfettered discretion to decide how the First Amendment rights of teachers are to be exercised. *Cf. Niemotko v. Maryland*, 340 U.S. 268 (1951).

. . . .

III

The English Department at Jefferson Davis High School publishes "English Reading Lists" for the benefit of its teachers and students. Each list (the lists are compiled separately for each grade) contains the names of approximately twenty-five recommended works.

One of the recommended novels on the "Junior English Reading List" is J.D. Salinger's Catcher in The Rye. This novel, while undisputedly a classic in American literature, contains far more offensive and descriptive language than that found in plaintiff's assigned story. The "Senior English Reading List" contains a number of works, such as Huxley's Brave New World and Orwell's 1984 which have highly provocative and sophisticated themes. Furthermore, the school library contains a number of books with controversial words and philosophies.

This situation illustrates how easily arbitrary discrimination can occur when public officials are given unfettered discretion to decide what books should be taught and what books should be banned. While not questioning either the motives or good faith of the defendants, this Court finds their inconsistency to be not only enigmatic but also grossly unfair.

With these several basic constitutional principles in mind it inevitably follows that the defendants in this case cannot justify the dismissal of this plaintiff under the guise of insubordination. The facts are clear that plaintiff's "insubordination" was not insubordination in any sense and was not, in reality, a reason for the School Board's action. *Dickey v. Alabama State Board of Education*, 273 F. Supp. 613 (D.C.).

In accordance with the foregoing, it is the order, judgment and decree of this Court that the plaintiff be reinstated as a teacher for the duration of her contract, with the same rights and privileges which attached to her status prior to her illegal suspension.

D. TEACHER CONTROL OF CURRICULUM

FOWLER v. BOARD OF EDUCATION OF LINCOLN COUNTY, KENTUCKY

United States Court of Appeals
819 F.2d 657 (6th Cir. 1987)

MILBURN, CIRCUIT JUDGE:

....

I

Plaintiff Jacqueline Fowler was a tenured teacher employed by the Lincoln County, Kentucky, school system for fourteen years. She was discharged in July, 1984 for insubordination and conduct unbecoming a teacher. The basis for this action was that she had an "R" rated movie, Pink Floyd — The Wall, shown to her high school students on the last day of the 1983-84 school year. The students in Fowler's classes were in grades nine through eleven and were of the ages fourteen through seventeen.

The day on which the movie was shown, May 31, 1984, was a noninstructional day used by teachers for completing grade cards. A group of students requested that Fowler allow the movie to be shown while she was completing the grade cards. Fowler was unfamiliar with the movie and asked the students whether it was appropriate for viewing at school. Charles Bailey, age fifteen, who had seen the movie on prior occasions, indicated that the movie had "one bad place in it."

Fowler rented the video tape at a video store in Danville, Kentucky. The clerk who rented the "R" rated tape to Fowler told her that there was some nudity in the movie during a song called "Young Lust" and warned that she might wish to delete that section. However, Fowler did not preview the movie before having it shown to her morning class because the store did not have a tape compatible with her own VCR and because she did not have time to make other arrangements to preview the movie.

When Fowler had the movie shown on the morning of May 31, 1984, she instructed Charles Bailey, the fifteen-year-old student who had seen the movie, to edit out any parts that were unsuitable for viewing at school. He did so by attempting to cover the 25" screen with an 8½" by 11" letter-sized file folder.

There is conflicting testimony as to whether, or how much, nudity was seen by the students. At the administrative hearing, several students testified that they saw no nudity. One student testified that she saw "glimpses" of nudity, but "nothing really offending." Assistant Principal Michael Candler, who observed the movie during part of the afternoon showing, testified that Charles Bailey's editing attempt was not sufficient to preclude the students from seeing the nudity. On cross-examination, Charles Bailey testified that Mrs. Fowler told him to open the file folder while editing after Candler entered the room. It is undisputed that the audio portion of the movie, which contained enough offensive language to mandate an automatic "R" rating under motion picture industry standards, was played through the entire movie.

There is also conflicting testimony regarding the amount of sexual innuendo existing in the "unedited" version of the film. Because some parts of the film are animated, they are susceptible to varying interpretations. One particularly controversial segment of scenes is animated in which flowers appear on the screen, are transformed into the shape of male and female sex organs and then engage in an act of intercourse. This segment of the film was shown in the morning session. Other segments involving a violent rape, nudity, a suggestion of oral sex, and a naked woman and naked man in bed engaging in foreplay and intercourse were also shown in the morning.[1]

Once again, there is conflicting testimony concerning the effectiveness of the editing attempt. Moreover, there is testimony supporting the fact that more editing was done in the afternoon showing than in the morning showing.

In addition to the sexual aspects of the movie, there is a great deal of violence. One scene involves a bloody battlefield. Another shows police brutality. Another shows the protagonist cutting his chest with a razor. Another scene shows children being fed into a giant sausage machine.

On the afternoon of May 31, 1984, Principal Jack Portwood asked Fowler to give him the video tape, and she did so. After the movie was viewed by the superintendent and members of the Lincoln County Board of Education, proceedings were instituted to terminate Fowler's contract.

Plaintiff Fowler received her termination notice on or about June 19, 1984. The notice advised her that a hearing would be held on July 10, 1984, and she subsequently advised the board of her intention to appear at the hearing and contest the charges.

On July 10, 1984, plaintiff Fowler appeared with counsel at the administrative hearing. She testified that, despite the fact that she had never seen the movie before having it shown to her students, and despite the fact that she was posting grades on report cards and left the room several times while the movie was being shown, she believed it had significant value. She believed the movie portrayed the dangers of alienation between people and of repressive educational systems. She testified that she would show an edited version of the movie again if given the opportunity to explain it. She stated that she did not at any time discuss the movie with her students because she did not have enough time.

---

[1] The district court found that the movie "contains a very limited amount of material which is sexually suggestive," that the movie does not contain "any 'simulation' of a sexual act," and that "any scenes involving nudity or suggestive conduct were edited from the view of students" during both showings. District Court Opinion at 6. We have viewed the film in conjunction with Fowler's testimony concerning the portions of the film which were edited during the two showings, and we conclude that the district court's findings in this regard are clearly erroneous. Similarly, his finding that Fowler formed an opinion regarding the significance of the film during the morning showing is clearly erroneous. It is undisputed that Fowler left the room several times while the movie was being shown, and that she was posting grades during the time she was present in the classroom....

D. TEACHER CONTROL OF CURRICULUM

The board viewed the movie once in its entirety and once as it had been edited in the classroom. The board then retired into executive session. Following this executive session, the board returned to open session and voted unanimously to terminate plaintiff's employment for insubordination and conduct unbecoming a teacher.

Following her termination, plaintiff Fowler initiated her action in the district court alleging that her First and Fourteenth Amendment rights were violated by her discharge, and that the Kentucky statutes forming the basis for her discharge were unconstitutionally vague or overbroad. She also alleged that the factual findings made in support of her discharge were not supported by substantial evidence.

....

The district court concluded that Fowler's conduct was protected by the First Amendment, and that she was discharged for exercising her constitutionally protected rights....

....

II

A

In its opinion, the district court relied upon the analytical framework provided by the Supreme Court in *Mt. Healthy City School District Board of Education v. Doyle*, 429 U.S. 274 (1977). Under the *Mt. Healthy* standard, a public employee establishes a *prima facie* case of a constitutional violation if she shows that she was engaged in protected activity, and that such activity was a substantial or motivating factor in the decision to terminate her employment. *Id.* at 287. In order to defend itself against such a claim, the government must establish by a preponderance of the evidence that the decision to terminate would have been made in the absence of the exercise of the constitutionally protected right. *Id.*

In the present case, it is undisputed that plaintiff's employment was terminated because she had the "R" rated movie shown to her students and because she said she would do it again. Consequently, the focus of our inquiry is whether Fowler's conduct was constitutionally protected.

The Supreme Court has consistently recognized the importance of the exercise of First Amendment rights in the context of public schools.

> First Amendment rights, applied in light of the special characteristics of the school environment, are available to teachers and students. It can hardly be argued that either students or teachers shed their constitutional rights to freedom of speech or expression at the schoolhouse gate. This has been the unmistakable holding of this Court for almost 50 years. *Tinker v. Des Moines Independent Community School District*, 393 U.S. 503, 506 (1969)....

Among the "special circumstances" which must be considered in defining the scope of First Amendment protection inside the classroom is the "inculcat[ion of] fundamental values necessary to the maintenance of a democratic political system." *Bethel School District No. 403 v. Fraser*, 106 S. Ct. 3159, 3164 (1986) (quoting *Ambach v. Norwick*, 441 U.S. 68, 76-77, (1979)).

....

The single most important element of this inculcative process is the teacher. "Consciously or otherwise, teachers ... demonstrate the appropriate form of civil discourse and political expression by their conduct and deportment in and out of class. Inescapably, like parents, they are role models." *Fraser*, 106 S. Ct. at 3165....

The accommodation of these sometimes conflicting fundamental values has caused great tension, particularly when the conflict arises within the classroom. *See, e.g., Martin v. Parrish*, 805 F.2d 583 (5th Cir. 1986); *Zykan v. Warsaw Community School Corp.*, 631 F.2d 1300 (7th Cir. 1980); *Russo v. Central School District No. 1*, 469 F.2d 623 (2d Cir. 1972), *cert. denied*, 411 U.S. 932 (1973); *James v. Board of Education*, 461 F.2d 566 (2d Cir.), *cert. denied*, 409 U.S. 1042 (1972)....

In the present case the district court concluded that Mrs. Fowler was entitled to the protection of the First Amendment while acting as a teacher. That a teacher does have First Amendment protection under certain circumstances cannot be denied. *See Tinker*, 393 U.S. at 506. Likewise, a motion picture is a form of expression which may be entitled to the protection of the First Amendment. *Joseph Burstyn, Inc. v. Wilson*, 343 U.S. 495, 501-02 (1952).

However, I conclude that Fowler's conduct in having the movie shown under the circumstances present here did not constitute expression protected by the First Amendment. It is undisputed that Fowler was discharged for the showing of the movie, Pink Floyd — The Wall. Such conduct, under the circumstances involved, clearly is not "speech" in the traditional sense of the expression of ideas through use of the spoken or written word.

....

[N]ot every form of conduct is protected by the First Amendment right of free speech.

> To determine whether [plaintiff's] conduct is entitled to first amendment protection, "the nature of [plaintiff's] activity, combined with the factual context and environment in which it was undertaken" must be considered. *Spence v. Washington*, 418 U.S. 405, 409-10 (1974). If [plaintiff] shows "[a]n intent to convey a particularized message ... and in the surrounding circumstances the likelihood was great that the message would be understood by those who viewed it," *Id.* at 410-11, the activity falls within the scope of the first and fourteenth amendments. *Monroe v. State Court of Fulton County*, 739 F.2d 568, 571 (11th Cir.1984).

D. TEACHER CONTROL OF CURRICULUM   145

In the present case, it is undisputed that Fowler did not see the movie before she had it shown to her class on the morning of May 31, 1984, a noninstructional day.... It is also undisputed that she left the room on several occasions while the film was being shown. Under circumstances such as these, I cannot conclude that Fowler possessed "[a]n intent to convey a particularized message" to her students. *Spence*, 418 U.S. at 410. The mere fact that at some point she may have developed an approval of the content of the movie is not, standing alone, a sufficient basis for the conclusion that her conduct in having the movie shown was a form of expression entitled to protection under the First Amendment.

....

Moreover, the surrounding circumstances in the present case indicate that there was little likelihood "that the message would be understood by those who viewed it." *Spence*, 418 U.S. at 411. As we have noted, the "R" rated movie was shown on a noninstructional day to students in Fowler's classes in grades nine through eleven who were of ages ranging from fourteen through seventeen. Furthermore, Fowler never at any time made an attempt to explain any message that the students might derive from viewing the movie.

Thus, this case is distinguishable from those in which the Supreme Court has afforded First Amendment protection in cases involving expressive conduct. In *Spence*, the undisputed facts established that the appellant hung a United States flag with a peace symbol affixed to it because he "wanted people to know that [he] thought America stood for peace." 418 U.S. at 409....

Because the intent to express was coupled with a great likelihood that the message would be understood, the Court concluded that the conduct was entitled to protection under the First Amendment.

Similarly, in *Tinker*, the uncontroverted evidence showed that the students who wore the black armbands were engaged in an expression of opposition to the Vietnam war, which the Court concluded was akin to "pure speech." 393 U.S. at 505-08. And in *Barnette*, the court recognized that a flag salute is a form of communicative conduct which implicates the First Amendment. 319 U.S. at 632.

The cases just discussed demonstrate that conduct is protected by the First Amendment only when it is expressive or communicative in nature. In the present case, because plaintiff's conduct in having the movie shown cannot be considered expressive or communicative, under the circumstances presented, the protection of the First Amendment is not implicated.

B

Plaintiff argues that Ky. Rev. Stat. § 161.790(1)(b), which proscribes "conduct unbecoming a teacher," is unconstitutionally vague as applied to her because the statute failed to give notice that her conduct would result in discipline. We find this argument to be without merit.

The vagueness doctrine requires that a statute proscribing certain conduct must be drafted "with sufficient definiteness that ordinary people can understand what conduct is prohibited and in a manner that does not encourage arbitrary and discriminatory enforcement." *Kolender v. Lawson*, 461 U.S. 352, 357 (1983); *Grayned v. City of Rockford*, 408 U.S. 104, 108-09 (1972); *511 Detroit Street, Inc. v. Kelley*, 807 F.2d 1293, 1295 (6th Cir. 1986).

....

"[I]t is not feasible or necessary for the Government to spell out in detail all that conduct which will result in retaliation. The most conscientious of codes that define prohibited conduct of employees includes 'catchall' clauses prohibiting employee 'misconduct,' 'immorality,' or 'conduct unbecoming.'" *Arnett [v. Kennedy]*, 416 U.S. [134,] 161 [(1974)] (quoting *Meehan v. Macy*, 392 F.2d 822, 835 (D.C. Cir. 1968), *modified*, 425 F.2d 469 (D.C. Cir.), *aff'd en banc*, 425 F.2d 472 (D.C. Cir. 1969)).

....

In the present case, plaintiff Fowler had a fifteen-year-old student show a controversial, highly suggestive and somewhat sexually explicit movie to a group of high school students aged fourteen to seventeen. She did not preview the movie, despite the fact that she had been warned that portions were unsuitable for viewing in this context. She made no attempt at any time to explain the meaning of the movie or to use it as an educational tool. Rather, she had it shown for the purpose of keeping her students occupied during a noninstructional day while she was involved in posting grades on report cards. We conclude that the statute proscribing "conduct unbecoming a teacher" gave her adequate notice that such conduct would subject her to discipline. Accordingly, we conclude that the statute is not unconstitutionally vague as applied to Fowler's conduct.

C

Finally, we must determine whether plaintiff's conduct constituted "conduct unbecoming a teacher" within the meaning of Ky. Rev. Stat. § 161.790(1)(b)....

....

In the present case, we conclude that plaintiff's conduct, although not illegal, constituted serious misconduct. Moreover, there was a direct connection between this misconduct and Fowler's work as a teacher. She introduced a controversial and sexually explicit movie into a classroom of adolescents without preview, preparation or discussion. In the process, she abdicated her function as an educator. Her having the movie shown under the circumstances involved demonstrates a blatant lack of judgment. Having considered the entire record, including the viewing of the movie, which we describe as gross and bizarre and containing material completely unsuitable for viewing by a classroom of students aged fourteen to seventeen, we conclude that such conduct falls within the concept of conduct unbecoming a teacher under Kentucky law.

....

III

Accordingly, for the reasons stated, the judgment of the district court is **VACATED**, and this cause is **DISMISSED**.

D. TEACHER CONTROL OF CURRICULUM

....

MERRITT, CIRCUIT JUDGE, dissenting:

Federal judges and local school boards do not make good movie critics or good censors of movie content. What one judge sees as "gross and bizarre," another may find, as did District Judge Scott Reed below, mild and not very "sexually suggestive."

The movie here seems to me to present a message similar to that expounded by Dr. Spock: abuse of sex and drugs as well as various forms of mental instability and anti-social conduct are associated with an overly authoritarian society. The message is that unloving, overly rigid and authoritarian parents, teachers, judges and officials create disturbed individuals and societies. This lack of love is the figurative "wall" shown in the movie.

But whatever the meaning of the movie, however good or bad it may be, my main concern is that the holdings of both JUDGE MILBURN and JUDGE PECK are in error. JUDGE MILBURN makes a distinction between "academic freedom" and showing a movie in class....

... JUDGE MILBURN states further that "plaintiff's conduct in having the movie shown cannot be considered expressive or communicative...." *Id.* at p. 664.

Purely expressive works — songs, movies and books of entertainment value only — are protected by the First Amendment just like works of moral philosophy....

In fact, Mrs. Fowler was not discharged because she entertained her students: she was discharged because the school board did not like the content of the movie. Mrs. Fowler proved at trial, as Judge Milburn says at page 660 of his opinion, that she was discharged because the board members regarded the movie as "immoral, antieducation, antifamily, antijudiciary, and antipolice." There is no support for the proposition — nor does the school board argue — that a teacher's academic freedom or a student's right to hear may be abridged simply because a school board dislikes the content of the protected speech. Furthermore, since this was a "free day" for the students, no departure from a board-mandated curriculum occurred. It is obvious, therefore, that Mrs. Fowler's discharge was prompted by the content of the movie.

Assuming that the school board could have properly discharged Mrs. Fowler for poor judgment and lack of remorse in showing an "R-rated" movie which had short scenes depicting nudity and sexual foreplay, but not for the other reasons given, this case must be decided under the "mixed-motive" analysis of *Mt. Healthy City School Dist. Bd. of Educ. v. Doyle*, 429 U.S. 274 (1977). Where a plaintiff can show that her constitutionally-protected conduct was a "substantial" or "motivating" factor in the discharge decision, the employer must prove "by a preponderance of the evidence that it would have reached the same decision as to ... re-employment even in the absence of the protected conduct." *Mt. Healthy*, 429 U.S. at 287.

Although Judge Peck's opinion concedes that "the school board clearly expressed displeasure with the anti-establishment focus of the film," he argues nonetheless that the board's "objections to the 'immoral' content of the film were intertwined with constitutionally permissible objections to the film's above mentioned vulgarity and unsuitability for the student age group...." I do not believe an argument based on intertwining can be used to suppress protected speech; vulgarity should not be allowed to subsume that which is protected.

....

---

1. For a similar case, *see Krizek v. Board of Educ. of Cicero-Stickney Twp. High Sch. Dist. No. 201*, 713 F. Supp. 1131 (N.D. Ill. 1989). In *Krizek*, a teacher's contract was not renewed after she showed the R-rated movie "About Last Night" in class. The district court denied a motion for preliminary injunction.

2. Judge Merritt makes a point in his dissent that the courts are not movie critics and may not declare what films mean. Nor may school boards call "The Wall" immoral and fire a teacher for that reason alone. Whereas there may have been no mandated curriculum for that day, should Fowler have attempted to justify showing the movie by encouraging and participating in a discussion of the film's themes with the class? Would this have changed the minds of any of the authorities? Or was Fowler's dismissal based solely on the "review" of school officials and this court? Does Judge Merritt merely agree with the district court's "review" of the movie?

3. How do the religious views of the teachers stack up to the government's concerns and interests about curriculum? In *Palmer v. Board of Educ. of City of Chicago*, 603 F.2d 1271 (7th Cir. 1979), the court said that although a teacher has a right to his or her own religious views and practices, there is a compelling state interest in the choice of and adherence to a suitable curriculum for the benefit of young citizens and society. A teacher may not disregard prescribed curriculum merely because adherence thereto may conflict with his or her own religious beliefs. The curriculum in *Palmer* involved participating in the Pledge of Allegiance, singing patriotic songs, and celebrating certain holidays.

4. May a teacher *supplement* the curriculum with additional, potentially controversial readings and survive a challenge to that supplement on First Amendment grounds? In *Kirkland v. Northside Indep. Sch. Dist.*, 890 F.2d 794 (5th Cir. 1989), the court held that the teacher's supplemental reading list did not present a "matter of public concern." The speech, if protected as a matter of public concern, must be expressed by the teacher in his capacity as a citizen, not as an employee of the school district. In *Kirkland*, the court also noted that the school had a special policy for adopting and amending curriculum. In the Northside District, parents, administrators, and elected officials also have a legitimate role in developing curriculum.

D. TEACHER CONTROL OF CURRICULUM

In another case holding that a teacher's First Amendment rights do not permit him to vary the curriculum, the Seventh Circuit affirmed the dismissal of a claim that a teacher in the public school district is allowed to teach a nonevolutionary theory of creation in the classroom. *Webster v. New Lenox Sch. Dist. No. 122*, 917 F.2d 1004 (7th Cir. 1990).

PART TWO

STUDENTS' RIGHTS AND RESPONSIBILITIES

Chapter 4
STUDENT CLASSIFICATION BY SEX, AGE, AND RACE

A. STUDENT CLASSIFICATION BY SEX

1. ACADEMIC OPPORTUNITIES

NEWBERG v. BOARD OF PUBLIC EDUCATION
26 D. & C.3d 682 (1983)

MARUTANI, J.

Preliminary Statement

Before this court is a class-action proceeding by three female students whose applications for admission to Central High School, an all-male public institution in Philadelphia, had been rejected solely on the basis of the applicants' sex. Plaintiffs challenge such sex-based rejections as being violative of their rights in derogation of the provisions of the amendment of May 18, 1971 — the so-called "Equal Rights Amendment" — to the Constitution of the Commonwealth of Pennsylvania, as well as Article I, Sections 1 and 26 of the same Constitution, and the "equal protection" provision of the Fourteenth Amendment. Plaintiffs seek a declaration holding defendants' policy to be unconstitutional and therefore seek to enjoin defendants from excluding female students from admission to Central High School on the basis of their sex alone.

. . . .

Discussion

. . . .

Vorchheimer v. School District of Philadelphia, 532 F.2d 880 (3rd Cir. 1976):

The federal proceeding in *Vorchheimer* involved the same two schools presently before this court and the question of the constitutionality of separate, gender-based schooling. The matter was heard in May of 1975, in a non-jury proceeding before the HONORABLE CLARENCE C. NEWCOMER of the United States District Court for the Eastern District of Pennsylvania. The trial court declined to accept pendant jurisdiction over plaintiff's claim under Pennsylvania's Equal Rights Amendment "since standards governing the applicability of this amendment in the educational field have not been clearly established by the state courts."[96] However, applying the test of "fair and substantial relationship," the court found a denial to plaintiff of equal protection under the Fourteenth Amendment.

On appeal to the Third Circuit Court of Appeals, the majority reversed — with CIRCUIT JUDGE JOHN J. GIBBONS dissenting. Regarding the applicable standard of review, the Third Circuit majority concluded: "We need not decide whether this case requires application of the rational or substantial relationships tests because, using either, the result is the same." 432 F. 2d at 888.... [T]his decision of the Third Circuit Court of Appeals was affirmed by an equally divided Supreme Court: 430 U.S. 703 (1977).

Res Judicata and Collateral Estoppel:

Pointing to *Vorchheimer*, defendants in the present proceedings contend that the doctrine of *res judicata* bars plaintiffs from litigating their equal protection claim....

....

Initially, we find that the *Vorchheimer* plaintiff's counsel's representation of plaintiff's cause was materially inadequate. In that proceeding, counsel: (a) propounded one set of interrogatories, consisting of three pages, and limited to seven questions probing superficial areas; (b) deposed only one witness, Matthew W. Constanzo, then-superintendent of schools; (c) presented testimony of only four witnesses: student-plaintiff Vorchheimer; an expert on education; a student from Central High to testify on the history of Central High; and a rebuttal witness, primarily on the validity of a study, additionally on two questions and answers from Superintendent Constanzo's depositions; and (d) offered thirteen exhibits. The *Vorchheimer* court data was not provided with many relevant available data, or was provided with only tentative and incomplete facts and evidence. This becomes readily apparent when compared to the facts and evidence presented in the instant proceeding, not all of which have been reduced to findings of fact set forth hereinbefore. Specifically, incomplete or no evidence was presented as to the following facts: Girls High students attend classes at Central High (thus undermining the conclusion that "adolescents may study more effectively in single-sex schools"); Central High graduates (who have passed all major subjects above ninth grade) are awarded Bachelor of Arts degrees, whereas Girls High graduates receive high school diplomas; there are 2.7 times more Ph.D.,'s and 1.5 times more teachers with 21 years (or more) of teaching experience at Central High; Central High's campus is almost three times larger; Central High's library not only contains 50,000 volumes (a fact brought out in *Vorchheimer*) but Girls High's library contains almost 50 percent fewer volumes at 26,300; the library room and setting at Central High are appreciably more aesthetic; Central High has more instructional equipment, including a separate

---

[96]400 F. Supp. at 333....

A. STUDENT CLASSIFICATION BY SEX

computer room; both Central High and Girls High offer courses, as well as some club activities, that are not available at the other; additional prerequisites for AP [Advanced Placement] Chemistry and AP Physics are imposed upon Girls High students but not Central High students; Girls High students almost invariably score lower than Central High students in testing on the Preliminary Scholastic Aptitude Test/National Merit Scholarship Qualifying Test as well as on the Scholastic Aptitude Test (SAT); whereas 91.8 percent of Central High students are accepted into college, four percent less or 87.8 percent of Girls High students are so accepted; Central High students were beneficiaries (at least in 1979) of 1.2 million dollars in college scholarships, whereas Girls High students were beneficiaries of less than half that sum at one-half million dollars; the option of "contract gym," while available to Central High students, is not granted to Girls High students; while students attending Central High have been beneficiaries of some $382,145 over a 12-year period from the Barnwell Foundation, students at Girls High are excluded therefrom, the latter group engaging in annual magazine subscription sales to gain funding.

These facts were either overlooked entirely by counsel in *Vorchheimer* or, at best, touched upon only superficially and partially. Plaintiff's counsel in *Vorchheimer* failed to meet the basic standards for adequate representation which require that counsel be "qualified, experienced, and generally able to conduct the ... litigation...." *Wetzel v. Liberty Mutual Insurance Company*, 508 F.2d 239, 247 (3d Circ. 1975). Particularly where "rights of numerous persons not before the Court are at stake," counsel in a class action is expected to protect these rights "with greater vigor and thoroughness, both factually and legally" than would otherwise be required. *Johnson v. Shreveport Garment Company*, 422 F.Supp. 526, 535 (W.D. La. 1976). This vigorous standard applies to "preparation of pleadings, pretrial motions, discovery, [and] the trial itself, including the presentation of evidence...." *Id.* at 534-35.

....

While we do not question that there indeed are "educators who regard education in a single-sex school as a natural and reasonable educational approach," such a concession is meaningless without background information concerning the educators, their qualifications, sources and analyses — as well as those holding opposing views....

The foregoing litany of inadequate representation compels the conclusion that *res judicata* may not operate to restrict the present plaintiffs' equal protection claim. Because of these same inadequacies, plaintiffs here are not bound by the findings in *Vorchheimer*, which findings were based upon the paucity of evidence made available to the court, relating to comparability of the two schools.

....

Equal Protection of the Laws:

The findings of fact in this proceeding ... establish that the two schools, and in particular the educational opportunities provided, are materially unequal.

Indeed, the evidence would indicate that students at Girls High have received, and unless appropriate remedial steps are taken, will continue to receive, disparate schooling — as ultimately reflected over the years in their comparative performances in the academic testings as well as their different percentages of acceptances into colleges and universities.

Applying the substantial relationship test, we conclude that: first, there is absent an "important governmental objective" to be served by maintaining these separate, single-gender public schools; second, that the means employed are not "substantially related" to the vague, unsubstantiated theory of single-gender schooling. Indeed, the very actions of the defendants in permitting Girls High students to take courses at Central High and allowing Central High students to regularly utilize the tennis courts and basketball courts at Girls High, "fatally undermine[] [the] claim that women [or men] ... are adversely affected by the presence of men [or women]."

....

---

1. One year following the County Court decision in *Newberg*, the Superior Court of Pennsylvania denied a petition for leave to intervene and quashed an appeal to the lower court holding. *Newberg v. Board of Pub. Educ.*, 330 Pa. Super. 65, 478 A.2d 1352 (1984). The Superior Court held that students and graduates of the single-sex schools, which had participated in the trial court as *amici curiae*, had no standing to appeal the final decree. "'Except where the right of appeal is enlarged by statute, any party who is aggrieved by an appealable order ... may appeal therefrom.' Pa.R.A.P. 501. Accordingly, an appeal by one who was not a party to a proceeding in the trial court must be quashed." *Id.* at 68.

The Superior Court also held that petition for leave to intervene which was not filed until after the final adjudication was not timely and was, therefore, properly denied.

2. *Newberg*, a state court case, distinguished itself from *Vorchheimer v. School Dist. of Phila.*, 532 F. 2d 889 (3rd Cir. 1976), *aff'd by an equally divided court*, 430 U.S. 703 (1977). The *Vorchheimer* court decided that state legislation on the issue of single-sex schools was at best ambiguous and that, inasmuch as access was the concern of the plaintiff, there was no Fourteenth Amendment Equal Protection violation since the facilities at each of the schools were somewhat synonymous. Seven years later, based on similar data about facilities, the *Newberg* court held just the opposite. What rules of law distinguish the two cases? Is it possible that the difference in the decisions rests only on what the *Newberg* court described as inadequate representation by legal counsel for the plaintiff? Given the *Newberg* decision, is *Vorchheimer* still good law? Does *Newberg* subject all past decisions to new review? What do the two cases together say about *res judicata*? For legal malpractice?

A. STUDENT CLASSIFICATION BY SEX

3. Did the court work too hard to get the result arrived at? What does "materially unequal" mean in the context of this case? For example, the court mentioned that Central High has attracted many celebrities (mostly political) to their "Hall of Fame Dinners," while there is no similar list for Girls High. Is this (and other discoveries like it) important to the determination of equal protection? Should the case have been decided in line with *Vorchheimer*?

4. The *Vorchheimer* court noted that there was sufficient evidence to establish that a legitimate educational policy may be served by utilizing single-sex high schools. How strong is the theory that adolescents are able to study more effectively in the single-sex schools? Is it strong enough to allow the continuance of single-sex public schools, as in *Vorchheimer*? The county trial court in *Newberg* heard testimony from Michael Contompasis, graduate of, former teacher, and then current headmaster at Boston Latin School, a historically all-male school. Hearing testimony against the theory of single-sex schooling, the court found:

. . . .

The Boston Latin School (Boston Latin) in Boston, Massachusetts, is the oldest public school in the United States, having been founded in 1635. It, too, is a "magnet" or special admission school in that it draws its students from throughout the city, and admission is based upon academic performance and qualifying test scores. It also is primarily a college preparatory school, with a student population of 2,250. It differs from Central High in two principal respects: although from 1635 it was an all-male school, in 1972 it became coeducational so that today approximately half of its students are female; it has students from grades seven through 12 as compared to Central High's (and Girls High's) ninth through 12th grades.

Prior to 1972, just as Philadelphia had its Girls High, Boston had its counterpart known as "Girls Latin School" with a student population of approximately 1,500. In 1972, Girls Latin School also became coeducational.

Michael Contompasis, the Headmaster of Boston Latin, dispelled, seriatim, the various negative consequences predicted by theorists advocating retention of single-gender schooling. His testimony is to be evaluated, as based not only upon empirical data but also upon his background and experience: first, himself a student who graduated from Boston Latin when the school was all-male; next, a teacher at Boston Latin for eight years (1968-1976) spanning the period when the school changed from all-male to coeducational; and, third, currently as Headmaster, since 1977.

Specifically, Mr. Contompasis testified that since the school has become coeducational (after 337 years of being an all-male institution): (a) there has been no regression in quality of academic programs, academic achievement, school spirit, atmosphere of learning or dedication on the part of the students; (b) indeed, "increased ... involvement" in activities has occurred, with both male and female students being elected as class presidents, achieving valedictorian status, staffing the yearbook, etc.; and (c) a "higher degree of respect for students of opposite sexes [*sic*]" has been achieved. The verity of this experience is to be evaluated by the time-span of ten years of coeducational experience and by the age-span covering students from 12 years of age through 17 (seventh through 12th grades). Beyond all this, there was an additional change which may be deemed significant: before Boston Latin became coeducational, its teaching and supportive staff was all male (except for the school nurse and women who worked in the cafeteria), and currently the staff at Boston Latin consists of 35-40 percent females, including department heads.

This court finds this empirical data to be compelling in contrast to the tentative predictions and opinions of theorists. It would be obdurate folly to evaluate the evidence otherwise.

For a discussion of related claims at Boston Latin, *see Bray v. Lee*, 337 F. Supp. 934 (D. Mass. 1972).

CANNON v. UNIVERSITY OF CHICAGO

Supreme Court of the United States
441 U.S. 677 (1979)

MR. JUSTICE STEVENS delivered the opinion of the Court:

Petitioner's complaints allege that her applications for admission to medical school were denied by the respondents because she is a woman.[1] Accepting the truth of those allegations for the purpose of its decision, the Court of Appeals held that petitioner has no right of action against respondents that may be asserted in a federal court. 559 F.2d 1063. We granted certiorari to review that holding, 441 U.S. 677.

Only two facts alleged in the complaints are relevant to our decision. First, petitioner was excluded from participation in the respondents' medical education programs because of her sex. Second, these education programs were receiving federal financial assistance at the time of her exclusion. These facts, admitted *arguendo* by respondents' motion to dismiss the complaints, establish a violation

---

[1] Each of petitioner's two complaints names as defendant a private university — the University of Chicago and Northwestern University — and various officials of the medical school operated by that university. In addition, both complaints name the Secretary and the Region V director of the Department of Health, Education, and Welfare. Although all of these defendants prevailed below, and are respondents here, the federal defendants have taken a position that basically accords with the position advanced by petitioner.... Unless otherwise clear in context, all references to respondents in this opinion will refer to the private defendants named in petitioner's complaints.

A. STUDENT CLASSIFICATION BY SEX

of § 901(a) of Title IX of the Education Amendments of 1972 (hereinafter "Title IX"). That section, in relevant part, provides:

> No person in the United States shall, on the basis of sex, be excluded from participation in, be denied the benefits of, or be subjected to discrimination under any education program or activity receiving Federal financial assistance....

The statute does not, however, expressly authorize a private right of action by a person injured by a violation of § 901. For that reason, and because it concluded that no private remedy should be inferred, the District Court granted the respondents' motions to dismiss. 406 F. Supp. 1257, 1259.

The Court of Appeals agreed that the statute did not contain an implied private remedy. Noting that § 902 of the Act establishes a procedure for the termination of federal financial support for institutions violating § 901, the Court of Appeals concluded that Congress intended that remedy to be the exclusive means of enforcement. It recognized that the statute was patterned after Title VI of the Civil Rights Act of 1964 (hereinafter "Title VI"), but rejected petitioners' argument that Title VI included an implied private cause of action. 559 F.2d at 1071-75.

....

The Court of Appeals quite properly devoted careful attention to this question of statutory construction. As our recent cases — particularly *Cort v. Ash*, 422 U.S. 66 — demonstrate, the fact that a federal statute has been violated and some person harmed does not automatically give rise to a private cause of action in favor of that person. Instead, before concluding that Congress intended to make a remedy available to a special class of litigants, a court must carefully analyze the four factors that *Cort* identifies as indicative of such an intent. Our review of those factors persuades us, however, that the Court of Appeals reached the wrong conclusion and that petitioner does have a statutory right to pursue her claim that respondents rejected her application on the basis of her sex. After commenting on each of the four factors, we shall explain why they are not overcome by respondents' countervailing arguments.

I

First, the threshold question under *Cort* is whether the statute was enacted for the benefit of a special class of which the plaintiff is a member. That question is answered by looking to the language of the statute itself....

....

... [T]here would be far less reason to infer a private remedy in favor of individual persons if Congress, instead of drafting Title IX with an unmistakable focus on the benefited class, had written it simply as a ban on discriminatory conduct by recipients of federal funds or as a prohibition against the disbursement of public funds to educational institutions engaged in discriminatory practices.

Unquestionably, therefore, the first of the four factors identified in *Cort* favors the implication of a private cause of action. Title IX explicitly confers a benefit on persons discriminated against on the basis of sex, and petitioner is clearly a member of that class for whose special benefit the statute was enacted.

Second, the *Cort* analysis requires consideration of legislative history. We must recognize, however, that the legislative history of a statute that does not expressly create or deny a private remedy will typically be equally silent or ambiguous on the question. Therefore, in situations such as the present one "in which it is clear that federal law has granted a class of persons certain rights, it is not necessary to show an intention to *create* a private cause of action, although an explicit purpose to *deny* such cause of action would be controlling." *Cort*, *supra*, 422 U.S. at 82 (emphasis in original). But this is not the typical case. Far from evidencing any purpose to *deny* a private cause of action, the history of Title IX rather plainly indicates that Congress intended to create such a remedy.

Title IX was patterned after Title VI of the Civil Rights Act of 1964. Except for the substitution of the word "sex" in Title IX to replace the words "race, color, or national origin" in Title VI, the two statutes use identical language to describe the benefited class. Both statutes provide the same administrative mechanism for terminating federal financial support for institutions engaged in prohibited discrimination. Neither statute expressly mentions a private remedy for the person excluded from participation in a federally funded program. The drafters of Title IX explicitly assumed that it would be interpreted and applied as Title VI had been during the preceding eight years.

In 1972 when Title IX was enacted, the critical language in Title VI had already been construed as creating a private remedy.... It is always appropriate to assume that our elected representatives, like other citizens, know the law; in this case, because of their repeated references to Title VI and its modes of enforcement, we are especially justified in presuming both that those representatives were aware of the prior interpretation of Title VI and that that interpretation reflects their intent with respect to Title IX.

....

It is not, however, necessary to rely on these presumptions. The package of statutes of which Title IX is one part also contains a provision whose language and history demonstrate that Congress itself understood Title VI, and thus its companion, Title IX, as creating a private remedy. Section 718 of the Education Amendments authorizes federal courts to award fees to the prevailing parties, other than the United States, in private actions brought against local educational agencies, States, state agencies, and the United States to enforce Title VI in the context of elementary and secondary education. The language of this provision explicitly presumes the availability of private suits to enforce Title VI in the education context. For many such suits, no express cause of action was then available; hence Congress must have assumed that one could be implied under Title VI itself. That assumption was made explicit during the debates on § 718. It was also aired during the debates on other provisions in the Education

A. STUDENT CLASSIFICATION BY SEX

Amendments of 1972 and on Title IX itself, and is consistent with the Executive Branch's apparent understanding of Title VI at the time.

Finally, the very persistence — before 1972 and since, among judges and executive officials, as well as among litigants and their counsel, and even implicit in decisions of this Court — of the assumption that both Title VI and Title IX created a private right of action for the victims of illegal discrimination and the absence of legislative action to change that assumption provide further evidence that Congress at least acquiesces in, and apparently affirms, that assumption.... We have no doubt that Congress intended to create Title IX remedies comparable to those available under Title VI and that it understood Title VI as authorizing an implied private cause of action for victims of the prohibited discrimination.

Third, under *Cort*, a private remedy should not be implied if it would frustrate the underlying purpose of the legislative scheme. On the other hand, when that remedy is necessary or at least helpful to the accomplishment of the statutory purpose, the Court is decidedly receptive to its implication under the statute.

Title IX, like its model Title VI, sought to accomplish two related, but nevertheless somewhat different, objectives. First, Congress wanted to avoid the use of federal resources to support discriminatory practices; second, it wanted to provide individual citizens effective protection against those practices. Both of these purposes were repeatedly identified in the debates on the two statutes.

The first purpose is generally served by the statutory procedure for the termination of federal financial support for institutions engaged in discriminatory practices. That remedy is, however, severe and often may not provide an appropriate means of accomplishing the second purpose if merely an isolated violation has occurred. In that situation, the violation might be remedied more efficiently by an order requiring an institution to accept an applicant who had been improperly excluded. Moreover, in that kind of situation it makes little sense to impose on an individual, whose only interest is in obtaining a benefit for herself, or on HEW, the burden of demonstrating that an institution's practices are so pervasively discriminatory that a complete cut-off of federal funding is appropriate. The award of individual relief to a private litigant who has prosecuted her own suit is not only sensible but is fully consistent with — and in some cases even necessary to — the orderly enforcement of the statute.

The Department of Health, Education, and Welfare, which is charged with the responsibility for administering Title IX, perceives no inconsistency between the private remedy and the public remedy. On the contrary, the agency takes the unequivocal position that the individual remedy will provide effective assistance to achieving the statutory purposes.... The agency's position is unquestionably correct.

Fourth, the final inquiry suggested by *Cort* is whether implying a federal remedy is inappropriate because the subject matter involves an area basically of concern to the States. No such problem is raised by a prohibition against invidious discrimination of any sort, including that on the basis of sex.... Moreover, it is the expenditure of federal funds that provides the justification for this particular statutory prohibition. There can be no question but that this aspect of the *Cort* analysis supports the implication of a private federal remedy.

In sum, there is no need in this case to weigh the four *Cort* factors; all of them support the same result. Not only the words and history of Title IX, but also its subject matter and underlying purposes, counsel implication of a cause of action in favor of private victims of discrimination.

II

Respondents' principal argument against implying a cause of action under Title IX is that it is unwise to subject admissions decisions of universities to judicial scrutiny at the behest of disappointed applicants on a case-by-case basis. They argue that this kind of litigation is burdensome and inevitably will have an adverse effect on the independence of members of university committees.

This argument is not original to this litigation. It was forcefully advanced in both 1964 and 1972 by the congressional opponents of Title VI and Title IX, and squarely rejected by the congressional majorities that passed the two statutes. In short, respondents' principal contention is not a legal argument at all; it addresses a policy issue that Congress has already resolved.

... Nothing but speculation supports the argument that university administrators will be so concerned about the risk of litigation that they will fail to discharge their important responsibilities in an independent and professional manner.

III

Respondents advance two other arguments that deserve brief mention. Starting from the premise that Title IX and Title VI should receive the same construction, respondents argue (1) that a comparison of Title VI with other titles of the Civil Rights Act of 1964 demonstrates that Congress created express private remedies whenever it found them desirable; and (2) that certain excerpts from the legislative history of Title VI foreclose the implication of a private remedy.

Even if these arguments were persuasive with respect to Congress' understanding in 1964 when it passed Title VI, they would not overcome the fact that in 1972 when it passed Title IX, Congress was under the impression that Title VI could be enforced by a private action and that Title IX would be similarly enforceable....

The fact that other provisions of a complex statutory scheme create express remedies has not been accepted as a sufficient reason for refusing to imply an otherwise appropriate remedy under a separate section. *See, e.g., J.I. Case Co. v. Borak; Wyandotte Transportation Co. v. United States.* Rather, the Court has generally avoided this type of "excursion into extrapolation of legislative intent," *Cort v. Ash, supra,* 422 U.S. at 82 n.14, unless there is other, more convincing, evidence that Congress meant to exclude the remedy. *See National Railroad Passenger Corp. v. National Assn. of Railroad Passengers,* 414 U.S. at 458-61.

With one set of exceptions, the excerpts from the legislative history cited by respondents as contrary to implication of a private remedy under Title VI, were all concerned with a procedure for terminating federal funding. None of them evidences any hostility toward an implied private remedy to terminate the offending discrimination....

The only excerpt relied upon by respondent that deals precisely with the question whether the victim of discrimination has a private remedy under Title VI was a comment by Senator Keating. In it, he expressed disappointment at the administration's failure to include his suggestion for an express remedy in its final proposed bill. Our analysis of the legislative history convinces us, however, that neither the administration's decision not to incorporate that suggestion expressly in its bill, nor Senator Keating's response to that decision, is indicative of a rejection of a private right of action against recipients of federal funds. Instead, the former appears to have been a compromise aimed at protecting individual rights without subjecting the Government to suits, while the latter is merely one Senator's isolated expression of a preference for an express private remedy. In short, neither is inconsistent with the implication of such a remedy. Nor is there any other indication in the legislative history that any Member of Congress voted in favor of the statute in reliance on an understanding that Title VI did not include a private remedy.

IV

When Congress intends private litigants to have a cause of action to support their statutory rights, the far better course is for it to specify as much when it creates those rights. But the Court has long recognized that under certain limited circumstances the failure of Congress to do so is not inconsistent with an intent on its part to have such a remedy available to the persons benefited by its legislation. Title IX presents the atypical situation in which all of the circumstances that the Court has previously identified as supportive of an implied remedy are present. We therefore conclude that petitioner may maintain her lawsuit, despite the absence of any express authorization for it in the statute.

The judgment of the Court of Appeals is reversed and the case is remanded for further proceedings consistent with this opinion.

---

1. Prior to the Supreme Court's decision in *Cannon*, the courts were split as to whether an implied private right of action was appropriate under Title IX. For contrasting policy considerations, *see Alexander v. Yale Univ.*, 459 F. Supp. 1 (D. Conn. 1977), recognizing a private right of action, and *Cannon v. University of Chicago*, 559 F.2d 1063 (7th Cir. 1976), concluding that a private remedy should not be inferred. *See also* Comment, *Private Rights of Action Under Title IX*, 13 Harv. C.R.-C.L. L. Rev. 425 (1978) and Note, *Implied Right of Action to Enforce Civil Rights: The Case for a Sympathetic View*, 87 Yale L. J. 1378 (1978).

2. Justice White argued in his dissent that the majority had misread the legislative history when they found that Congress had intended to create a private right of action for either Title VI or Title IX. He argued that Title VI and Title IX prescribed enforcement by termination of funds and that the private right of action, existing contemporaneously with the Title VI remedy, derived from 42 U.S.C. 1983, which provided a private remedy "for deprivations under color of state law of any rights 'secured by the Constitution and laws.'" *Cannon*, at 723. He maintained, however, that "Congress did not intend to create a private remedy for discrimination practiced not under color of state law but by private parties and institutions." *Id*.

Under *Cannon*, what kinds of liabilities will private schools assume upon receipt of federal funds? What resources do private schools have to meet those liabilities? How do these factors bear on the majority's determination that the adverse effect of any burdensome litigation on the independence of university committees is merely speculative? Is the speculative burden greater for a private than for a public school?

3. Justice White reversed his opposition to the existence of a private right of action under Title IX in 1992 when he rendered the opinion of a unanimous Supreme Court in *Franklin v. Gwinnett County Schs.*, 112 S. Ct. 1028 (1992). In *Franklin* a former secondary school student brought a Title IX action seeking damages for alleged intentional gender-based discrimination in connection with sexual harassment and abuse by a coach-teacher. Citing Congressional legislation in the post-*Cannon* period consisting of Civil Rights Remedies Equalization Amendment of 1986, 42 U.S.C. Sec. 2000d-7 (1988) and the Civil Rights Restoration Act of 1987, Pub. L. No. 100-259, 102 Stat. 28, Justice White ruled that in addition to a private right of action under Title IX, there was also an implied right to recover damages for intentional statutory violations. (*See* this chapter for the *Gwinnett Schools* case).

SHARIF v. NEW YORK STATE EDUCATION DEPARTMENT

United States District Court
709 F. Supp. 345 (S.D.N.Y. 1989)

WALKER, DISTRICT JUDGE:

This case raises the important question of whether New York State denies female students an equal opportunity to receive prestigious state merit scholarships by its sole reliance upon the Scholastic Aptitude Test ("SAT") to determine eligibility. To the Court's knowledge, this is the first case where female students are seeking to use the federal civil rights statute prohibiting sex discrimination in federally-funded educational programs to challenge a state's reliance on standardized tests. This case also presents a legal issue of first impression: whether discrimination under Title IX can be established by proof of disparate impact without proof of intent to discriminate.

A. STUDENT CLASSIFICATION BY SEX

After careful consideration, this Court finds that defendants are discriminating against female plaintiffs and their putative class in violation of Title IX and the equal protection clause of the U.S. Constitution. For the reasons set forth below, this Court enjoins the State Education Department and its Commissioner from awarding the merit scholarships at issue solely on the basis of the SAT.

I. *The Present Action*

In November, 1988, plaintiffs — ten high school students, individually and behalf of all others similarly situated, and two organizational plaintiffs[1] — brought an action for declaratory and injunctive relief against the State Education Department ("SED") and Commissioner of Education Thomas Sobol, in his official capacity, alleging that New York's exclusive reliance on the SAT to award Empire and Regents scholarships discriminates against female students in violation of the equal protection clause of the Fourteenth Amendments to the U.S. Constitution, Title IX of the Education Amendments of 1972, 20 U.S.C. §§ 1681 *et seq.*, as amended by the Civil Rights Restoration Act of 1987, Pub.L. 100-259, and the regulations pursuant to Title IX, 34 CFR Part 106. Plaintiff's proposed class is composed of "all female high school seniors in New York State who are or will be applicants for Regents College Scholarships and Empire State Scholarships of Excellence."

In essence, plaintiffs contend that the SED's reliance upon the SAT disproportionately impacts female students without advancing the legislature's purpose of recognizing and awarding superior high school achievement. Plaintiffs argue: "(1) the SAT was not designed to measure academic performance and achievement, and cannot appropriately be put to that use, (2) but even if it did, the SAT discriminates against female applicants for scholarships, because it underpredicts academic performance for females as compared to males."

. . . .

II. *Background*

A. *Evolution of New York State Scholarship Awards*

. . . .

3. *Reliance Upon SATs and GPAs: The 1987 Experiment*

In response to allegations that the SED's practice of relying solely upon the SAT in awarding Regents and Empire State Scholarships discriminated against females who consistently scored below males, the Board of Regents asked the Governor and legislature for $100,000 to develop a new scholarship achievement examination. The legislature declined to fund a special examination but, instead, amended the Education Law to require that the awards be based upon in part

---

[1] The students bring the suit by their parents and next friends. The organizational plaintiffs are the Girls Clubs of America and National Organization for Women.

upon the student's grade point average ("GPA") as a measure of high school achievement. Senator Kenneth Lavalle, introducing the legislation, explained that the "statute intended to correct a gross inequity that pervaded the New York educational system caused by awarding of Regents College Scholarships and Empire State Scholarships of Excellence based solely on the results of a nationally administered standardized examination." The SED specified in its announcement of the new legislation to high school principals that the law was changed "[i]n order to provide for a better balance of male and female winners." P.App. I, Ex. 10.

The new legislation, for the first time, expressly stated that awards are to be based on a measure of "high school performance." Act approved and effective Aug. 7, 1987, ch. 837, 1987 N.Y. Laws §§ 1, 2. In doing so, the legislature altered the criteria for scholarship eligibility — on a one-year, experimental basis — to require the SED Commissioner to base awards on a formula which at least includes a measure of high school performance, and which may include nationally established competitive examinations. The amendment also required the Commissioner to "complete a statistical review of the gender, racial and ethnic composition of students awarded such scholarships within sixty days of the announcement of such scholarship award." Id. The legislation included a sunset provision that provided that the amendment would automatically lapse after one year if it were not affirmatively extended.

In May 1987, the SED examined possible measures of high school performance that could be used to select scholarship winners equitably.... The possibility of using class rank as a measure of high school performance was dropped for three reasons: (1) it is not used by all schools; (2) it adversely affects students in highly selective schools; (3) it cannot be used to compare students from schools of difference size.

The SED also found drawbacks to the use of grade point averages. Because of the volume of scholarship applications it receives yearly, approximately 100,000, the SED would be unable to individually evaluate the GPA information submitted for each candidate as is done by college admission committees. Also, the SED concluded that it was difficult to convert grade point average information to a common scale....

Despite comparability difficulties, the SED chose to use GPAs as the best available measure of high school achievement. In awarding the Regents and Empire Scholarships for the 1988 graduates, the SED gave equal weight to students' SAT scores and GPAs, as the measure of high school performance. The SED, however, did not issue specific instructions to schools as to how grades should be reported. As a result, some schools reported weighted grades, taking into account course difficulty, while others reported students' grades as they appeared on their transcripts. Such inconsistent reporting practices touched off a controversy among school administrators who accused each other of cheating in weighting and reporting grades.

A. STUDENT CLASSIFICATION BY SEX

In 1988, under the procedure using a combination of grades and SATs weighted equally women received substantially more Regents and Empire Scholarships than in all prior years in which the SAT had been the sole criterion. In both 1987 and 1988, young women comprised approximately 54 percent of the applicant pool for the scholarship, yet the results in 1988 when grades and SATs were used were markedly different. The results are summarized as follows:

	Winners of Empire State Scholarships of Excellence		Winners of Regents College Scholarships	
	Males	Females	Males	Females
1988	62	38	51	49
1987	72	28	57	43

... [A]lthough use of GPA information reduced the disparity between the number of males and females receiving Scholarships, Commissioner Sobol recommended that the practice be discontinued, as soon as a new scholarship exam was developed, because: (1) use of GPA information put an increased burden on school staff; (2) use of GPA did not provide an equitable way to compare students from different schools; and (3) use of GPA would encourage students to avoid more challenging courses in order to obtain better grades for Scholarship purposes. Sobol requested funds for a new scholarship exam but also recommended that, until a separate Regents Scholarship examination could be established, GPAs continue to be used in conjunction with SAT scores.

Despite Commissioner Sobol's recommendation, the legislature allowed to lapse the eligibility calculation "based on a formula which includes high school performance and which may include nationally competitive examinations."... In September, 1989, the SED determined that it would award Regents and Empire Scholarships to 1989 high school graduates on the basis of SAT scores alone. It is the SED's sole reliance on SAT scores for 1989 graduates that plaintiffs complain denies them equal protection under the fourteenth amendment to the U.S. Constitution and violates Title IX of the Education Amendments of 1972.

B. *Use of the SAT for Merit Scholarship Awards*

1. *ETS Recommendations and States' Practice*

The Educational Testing Service ("ETS") developed the SAT in order to predict academic performance in college. The ability of the SAT to serve this purpose has been statistically "validated." It is undisputed, however, that the SAT predicts the success of students differently for males and females.... The SAT has never been validated as a measure of past high school performance....

Both the ETS and the College Board, which administers the SAT, specifically advise against exclusive reliance upon the SAT, even for the purpose for which the SAT has been validated — predicting future college performance. Instead, ETS researchers recommend that college admissions counselors use a combination of high school grades and test scores because this combination provides the highest median correlation with freshman grades. Additionally, the National Association of College Admission Counselors' ("NACAC") Code of Ethics requires member institutions to refrain from using minimum test scores as the sole criterion for admission, to use test scores in conjunction with other data such as school record and recommendations, and to refrain from using tests in any manner that may discriminate against students. Thus, many colleges refrain from using test scores exclusively to decide admissions questions.

Notwithstanding ETS and NACAC guidelines recommending against using the SAT as the sole basis on which to award scholarships or offer admissions, the SED adopted such a policy in 1974. New York State is one of only two states in the nation to rely solely on SAT scores for the award of state-sponsored merit scholarships instead of factoring in other measurements, such as grade point average or high school rank....

2. *SAT as Measure of High School Performance*

Both the Empire and Regents Scholarships are intended to reward past academic achievement of high school students, and to encourage those students who have demonstrated such achievement to pursue their educations in New York State. It is undisputed, however, that the SAT was developed and validated to serve a different purpose — predicting performance in college.

....

Notwithstanding the absence of validation studies, it is the SED's current position that the SAT provides a good measure of high school performance because it "measures skills and knowledge primarily developed in school." The SED does not dispute that the SAT does not measure performance in all high school courses, but claims merely that the SAT partially tracks high school English and Math courses and thus tests achievement. The SED concedes that the SAT does not measure achievement in other subject matters such as science, social studies, and foreign languages. Moreover, the SED concedes that overall GPAs are a better measure of high school performance than SATs.

3. *Statistical Impact on Men and Women Statewide*

Males have outscored females on the verbal portion of the SAT since 1972, with an average score differential of at least 10 points since 1981. Males have also consistently outscored females on the mathematics portion, with an average differential of at least 40 points since 1967. In 1988, for example, girls scored 56 points lower than boys on the test. The probability that these score differentials happened by chance is approximately about one in a billion and the probability that the result could consistently be so different is essentially zero.

Statisticians have attempted to explain the score differentials between males and females by removing the effect of "neutral" variables, such as ethnicity, socioeducational status (parental education), high school classes, and proposed college major. However, under the most conservative studies presented in evidence, even after removing the effect of these factors, at least a 30 point combined differential remains unexplained.

As a result of the State's practice of basing scholarship awards solely upon SAT scores, males have consistently received substantially more scholarships than females. In 1987 for example, males were 47 percent of the scholarship competitors, but received 72 percent of the Empire State Scholarships and 57 percent of the Regents Scholarships. For Empire State Scholarships, these results represent 15.8 standard deviations from the mean; for Regents Scholarships, the difference represents 31.7 standard deviations. In other words, the probability that the Empire Scholarship results would occur by chance is less than one in a billion, and the probability of the Regents Scholarship results would occur by chance is even less.

III. *Discussion*

....

B. *The Preliminary Injunction*

The standard for reviewing a request for a preliminary injunction is well established. In this circuit, a preliminary injunction can be granted if plaintiff shows irreparable injury, combined with either a probability of success on the merits, or a fair ground for litigation and a balance of the hardships in his favor. *The Video Trip Corporation v. Lightning Video, Inc.*, 866 F.2d 50, 52 (2d Cir.1989), citing *Wainwright Securities, Inc. v. Wall Street Transcript Corp.*, 558 F.2d 91, 94 (2d Cir.1977), *cert. denied*, 434 U.S. 1014 (1987).

....

1. *Irreparable Harm*

Plaintiffs have demonstrated that if the SED is not enjoined from its current practices, they will suffer irreparable harm. Defendants do not dispute that Regents and Empire State scholarships are prestigious awards, and that students benefit from receiving such awards. Rather, they merely argue that Regents scholarships are worth less than Empire scholarships, and because it is unlikely that any of the named plaintiffs would receive Empire awards, plaintiffs have not shown irreparable harm. This is defendants' standing argument that was dismissed above....

"When an alleged deprivation of a constitutional right is involved, most courts hold that no further showing of irreparable injury is necessary." *Mitchell v. Cuomo*, 748 F.2d 804, 806 (2d Cir.1984). Plaintiffs here go further than merely alleging deprivation of a constitutional right — they document the harm that would result if the SED continued its practice of reliance upon the SAT. Thus, plaintiffs clearly have demonstrated "irreparable harm."

2. Likelihood of Success on Merits

a. *Title IX*

Plaintiffs invoke the protections provided by Title IX, which prohibits sex discrimination in federally-funded educational programs. Plaintiffs do not claim that defendants have intentionally discriminated against them based on their sex. Rather, they claim that defendants' practice of sole reliance upon SAT scores to award prestigious state scholarships disparately impacts female students. To this Court's knowledge, this is the first disparate impact case challenging educational testing practices under Title IX.

Neither the Supreme Court nor any court in the Second Circuit has determined whether intent must be shown in Title IX cases. This Court, however, is not without substantial guidance. Recognizing that "Title IX was patterned after Title VI of the Civil Rights Act of 1964," *Grove City College v. Bell*, 465 U.S. 555, 566 (1984) courts examining Title IX questions have looked to the substantial body of law developed under Title VI, 42 U.S.C. § 2000d, which prohibits race discrimination in federally-funded programs, and Title VII, 42 U.S.C. § 2000e, which prohibits discrimination in employment. *See, e.g., Mabry v. State Board of Community Colleges and Occupational Education*, 813 F.2d 311, 317 (10th Cir.), *cert. denied*, ___ U.S. ___, 108 S.Ct. 148 (1987); *Haffer v. Temple University*, 678 F.Supp. 517, 539 (E.D.Pa.1987).

In *Guardians Association v. Civil Service Commission*, 463 U.S. 582 (1983), the Supreme Court held that a violation of Title VI itself requires proof of discriminatory intent. However, a majority also agreed that proof of discriminatory effect suffices to establish liability when a suit is brought to enforce the regulations promulgated under Title VI, rather than statute itself. *See also Alexander v. Choate*, 469 U.S. 287, 293-294 (1985); *Latinos Unidos de Chelsea v. Secretary of Housing*, 799 F.2d 774, 785 n. 20 (1st Cir.1986).

Plaintiffs' amended complaint explicitly alleges both violations of Title IX and its implementing regulations. This Court finds no persuasive reason not to apply Title VI's substantive standards to the present Title IX suit. Under analogous circumstances, one district court reasoned: The Title IX regulations, like the Title VI regulations at issue in *Guardians*, do not explicitly impose an intent requirement. As there is no reason that a Title IX plaintiff should have a higher burden of proof than a Title VI plaintiff, *see, e.g., Cannon v. University of Chicago*, 441 U.S. 677 (1979) (interpretation of Title IX dependent upon interpretation of Title VI) ..., I hold that plaintiffs need not prove discriminatory intent to succeed on their claim. *Haffer*, 678 F.Supp. at 539-40.

The Title IX implementing regulations, like the regulations promulgated under Title VI, to which Title IX is frequently compared, are consistent with this interpretation of the comprehensive reach of the statute. Several Title IX regulations specifically prohibit facially neutral policies. For example, the provision governing admissions procedures, 34 CFR § 106.21(b)(2), prohibits a recipient from administer[ing] or operat[ing] any test or other criteria for

A. STUDENT CLASSIFICATION BY SEX

admission which has a disproportionately adverse effect on persons on the basis of sex unless the use of such test or criterion is shown to predict validly success in the education program or activity in question and alternative tests or criteria which do not have such a disproportionate adverse effect are shown to be unavailable. *See also* 34 C.F.R. §§ 106.22, 106.23(b), 106.34(d), 106.37(b), 106.52, and 106.53.(b).

Based upon a reading of the Title IX regulations, as well as the decisions that apply them, the Court finds that Title IX regulations, like the Title VI regulations at issue in *Guardians*, prohibit testing practices with a discriminatory effect on one sex. Consequently, plaintiffs need not prove intentional discrimination.

In Title VII testing cases, the Supreme Court developed a three-pronged formulation to analyze disparate impact claims. Under this scheme, plaintiffs first must show that a facially neutral practice has a disproportionate effect. After such a showing, the burden shifts to defendants to prove a substantial legitimate justification — a "business necessity" — for its practice. The plaintiff then may ultimately prevail by offering either an equally effective alternative practice which has a less of a discriminatory impact, or proof that the legitimate practices are a pretext for discrimination. *Connecticut v. Teal*, 457 U.S. 440 (1982); *Albemarle Paper Co. v. Moody*, 422 U.S. 405 (1975); *McDonnell Douglas Corp. v. Green*, 411 U.S. 792 (1973); *Griggs v. Duke Power Co.*, 401 U.S. 424 (1971); *Sheehan v. Purolator*, 839 F.2d 99, 104 (2d Cir.1988).

In educational testing cases, instead of requiring defendants to demonstrate a "business necessity," courts have required defendants to show an "educational necessity." For example, the Eleventh Circuit, in *Georgia State Conf. of Branches of NAACP v. State of Georgia*, 775 F.2d 1403 (11th Cir.1985), held that defendants had a burden of proving that their practices in question bore "a manifest demonstrable relationship to classroom education." *Id.* at 1418. *See also Board of Education v. Harris*, 444 U.S. 130, 151 (1979) ("educational necessity" analogous to "business necessity").

Applying the Title VII formulations to this Title IX case as modified to take into account "educational necessity," this Court finds that plaintiffs have demonstrated a likelihood of success on the merits. Plaintiffs have met their burden of establishing a *prima facie* case through persuasive statistical evidence and credible expert testimony that the composition of scholarship winners tilted decidedly toward males and could not have occurred by a random distribution. Defendants have failed to attack plaintiffs' evidence of statewide disparate impact but have instead focused in an ad hoc fashion on individual schools and counties. In a case alleging statewide discrimination, such a focus does not rebut plaintiffs' statewide *prima facie* case.

Plaintiffs, moreover, have established that the probability, absent discriminatory causes, that women would consistently score 60 points less on the SAT than men is nearly zero. Defendants concede that at least half of this differential cannot be explained away by "neutral" variables. Based upon the totality of evidence, then, this Court finds that plaintiffs have demonstrated that the State's practice of sole reliance upon the SAT disparately impacts young women.

Thus, to prevail, defendants must show a manifest relationship between use of the SAT and recognition and award of academic achievement in high school. The Court finds that defendants have failed to show even a reasonable relationship between their practice and their conceded purpose. The SAT was not designed to measure achievement in high school and was never validated for that purpose. Instead, in arguing that the SAT somehow measures high school performance, defendants rely upon anecdotal evidence that the SAT partially tracks what is generally learned in high school Math and English courses. This argument is meritless.

Plaintiffs have offered substantial evidence that the SATs do not mirror high school Math and English classes....

Moreover, even if SATs provided a partial measurement of what is learned in high school Math and English, these two courses constitute only 20 percent of a high school student's studies. The SAT fails to provide any measure of what a student learns in foreign language, science, and social studies courses. Moreover, there can be no serious claim that a test given on one single morning can take into account a student's diligence, creativity and social development and work habits in that student's environment — all part of high school achievement. After a careful review of the evidence, this Court concludes that SAT scores capture a student's academic achievement no more than a student's yearbook photograph captures the full range of her experiences in high school.

Plaintiffs have offered an alternative to sole reliance upon the SAT: a combination of GPAs and SATs. The SED's use of this alternative in 1988 sharply reduced the disparate impact against females caused by the use of the SAT alone. A significantly greater number of female students received scholarships in 1988 than in each prior year in which the SED relied solely upon the SAT. Defendants concede that females had a greater opportunity to receive scholarships under the combination system. Defendants also concede that grades are the best measure of high school achievement within the walls of a single school. Instead, they argue that since there is a disparity among schools and their grading systems it is both unfair and impossible to use grades as part of the scholarship eligibility determination. Defendants plan instead to develop a statewide achievement test. While this Court does not dispute the apparent advantages of a statewide achievement test — if indeed a valid test can be developed — it does not agree that pending the implication of such a test, use of grades would be either unfair or infeasible.

While a combination system — using both GPAs and SATs — is not a perfect alternative, it is the best alternative presently available. The SED is concerned that students in academically superior high schools not be disadvantaged by the use of GPAs. This concern is addressed by the combination system because in effect grades would be weighted by SATs. The SAT component which cannot properly itself measure achievement serves to balance the grade component that does. In this way, the SED's concern that use of grades alone will deprive good students in superior high schools of scholarships is ameliorated. Also, as a testing expert explained at the hearing, few students will be displaced if a combination system is used:

> What happens when you add GPA in with the SAT is you eliminate people who had sufficiently high SATs but low grade point averages. And they get replaced by people with slightly lower SATs who have higher — very high grade point averages. So the movement of individuals is not really all that severe, it's ... really just taking scholarships away from the high SAT performers who did not actually achieve in high school...

More importantly, the combination system would be "fair" in the larger sense of the word, because it would better advance the state's goal of awarding high school performance and would better provide all students — not just male students or students from selective schools — with an equal opportunity to compete for prestigious state scholarships.

....

The SED cannot justify its discriminatory practice because any alternative would be more difficult to administer. All states giving merit scholarships awards, with the exception of New York and Massachusetts, use GPAs, without concern for either administrative difficulties, grade inflation or the comparability of grades. Any administrative difficulties that the SED experienced in 1988, when it used a combination system, were attributable to the SED's own failure to implement and clarify specific guidelines for the collections of grades, and to provide any enforcement mechanisms to guard against cheating.... The Court notes ... that to verify accuracy, the SED could follow the practice of many states and require school administrators to submit a signed certificate of accuracy.

Faced with a conflict between the SED's administrative concerns on the one hand, and the risk of substantial discriminatory harm to plaintiffs on the other, the Court has little difficulty in concluding that the balance of hardships tips decidedly in plaintiffs' favor. *See Mitchell v. Cuomo*, 748 F.2d 804, 808 (2d Cir.1984). The Court finds that plaintiffs have offered a feasible alternative to sole reliance upon SATs. Accordingly, the Court finds that plaintiffs have demonstrated a likelihood of success on the merits of their Title IX claim and, thus, a preliminary injunction is warranted.

b. *Equal Protection*

Alternatively, a preliminary injunction is warranted because plaintiffs also have established a likelihood that they will succeed on their equal protection claim. The classification of scholarship applicants solely on the basis of SAT scores violates the equal protection clause of the Fourteenth Amendment because this method is not rationally related to the state's goal of rewarding students who have demonstrated academic achievement.

Under the lowest standard of equal protection review — the "rational relationship standard" — "[t]he State may not rely on a classification whose relationship to an asserted goal is so attenuated as to render the distinction arbitrary or irrational." *City of Cleburne v. Cleburne Living Center*, 473 U.S. 432, 446 (1985). Although considerable deference is given to the decisions of legislators and state administrators under the rational basis test, the test "is not a toothless one." *Baccus v. Karger*, 692 F.Supp. 290, 298 (S.D.N.Y.1988) (invalidating New York bar rule that required applicants for bar admission to have commenced the study of law after their 18th birthday), citing *Schweiker v. Wilson*, 450 U.S. 221, 234, (1980)....

For the reasons stated above, the SED's use of the SAT as a proxy for high school achievement is too unrelated to the legislative purpose of awarding academic achievement in high school to survive even the most minimal scrutiny. The evidence is clear that females score significantly below males on the SAT while they perform equally or slightly better than males in high school. Therefore, the SED's use of the SAT as the sole criterion for awarding Regents and Empire Scholarships discriminates against females and, since such a practice is not rationally related to the legislative purpose, it unconstitutionally denies young women equal protection of the laws and must be enjoined on that ground as well.

IV. *Conclusion*

Defendants' practice of relying solely upon SAT scores in awarding Regents and Empire Scholarships deprives young women of the opportunity to compete equally for these prestigious scholarships in violation of both Title IX and the Constitution's equal protection clause. Defendants are hereby ordered to discontinue such discriminatory practices and, instead, to award Regents and Empire Scholarships in a manner that more accurately measures students' high school achievement. For the present year, the best available alternative is a combination of grades and SATs. The SAT component is justified, not as a measure of achievement, but to weight the GPA component. The Court, however, does not limit the SED's discretion to develop other alternatives in the future, including a statewide achievement test.

So Ordered.

....

---

1. There is continuing criticism of standardized tests as projectors of academic ability. *See, e.g.*, Linda Darling-Hammond and Ann Lieberman, *The Shortcomings of Standardized Tests*, *The Chronicle of Higher Education*, B2 (January 29, 1992) (arguing that such tests "are inappropriate for many of the purposes they are expected to serve"); Jennifer Wallace, *Ready or Not — Can a Test Tell?*, 11

State Education Leader, 16 (Spring, 1992) (stating that "readiness tests" should be used only for instructional practices and not placement as such tests tend to segregate children); Thomas Toch and Betsy Wagner, *Schools for Scandal*, U.S. News and World Report, 6 (April 27, 1992) (finding "widespread cheating on standardized tests").

2. Given the existence of National Merit and Achievement Scholarships awarded for outstanding performance on the PSAT and SAT, are New York's scholarships redundant? Would it be better, despite the cost, to return to the old scholarship program with a different exam or altered criteria, giving other students an opportunity to successfully compete? Note that of the states giving merit scholarships, only New York and Massachusetts use the aptitude test. *Sharif*, at 345, 363.

3. *Sharif* makes an important reference to an expansion of the scope of Title IX with the passage of the Civil Rights Restoration Act, cited in note 3 following *Cannon*. Title IX, which provides that no person shall, on the basis of sex be excluded from the benefits of, or be subjected to discrimination under any education program or activity receiving any federal assistance, now applies institution-wide. The new Act directly reverses *Grove City College v. Bell*, 465 U.S. 555 (1984), which limited the coverage of Title IX to specific programs or activities that actually receive federal funds. *Sharif*, at 345, 360.

4. For a discussion of issues presented in *Sharif* and similar cases, *see* Connor and Vargyas, *The Legal Implication of Gender Bias in Standardized Testing*, 7 Berkeley Women's L.J. 13. Can the statements about bias in standardized testing be made with respect to such testing and ethnic minorities?

5. Consider the following from a case note written shortly after *Sharif* was decided:

> ... [B]y extending the impact analysis applied in employment and federal-funding cases to education cases, *Sharif* significantly eased the evidentiary burden of Title IX plaintiffs, and thus provided greater protection against *sex* discrimination. The Supreme Court's recent decision in *Wards Cove Packing Co. v. Atonio*,[7] which stiffened plaintiffs' evidentiary burden in Title VII disparate-impact cases, however, raises doubts about the protection established by *Sharif*.
>
> ....
>
> *Sharif* significantly expanded Title IX. Although the case extends disparate-impact analysis for the first time to the educational-testing context, the use of impact analysis in Title IX cases is doctrinally sound. To hold otherwise would create arbitrary and overly formalistic distinctions between Title IX and the two statutes that provide its analytic foundation. Moreover, one court has already permitted disparate-impact analysis in Title IX employment cases. To employ a different analysis in education cases would

---

[7] 109 S. Ct. 2115 (1989).

create inconsistency in Title IX enforcement mechanisms and present a baseless distinction between sex discrimination in employment and sex discrimination in education. After the Supreme Court's decision ... in *Wards Cove Packing Co. v. Atonio*, however the efficacy of a Title IX disparate-impact claim is uncertain. Nevertheless, although Sharif relied on the more lenient standard articulated in *Griggs*, its prohibition against the sole use of SAT scores to award scholarships should be upheld even under the more rigorous *Wards Cove* standards.

Wards Cove's restricted definition of what constitutes sufficient statistical evidence to establish prima facie disparate impact does not jeopardize *Sharif*'s result. Unlike the *Wards Cove* plaintiffs, the *Sharif* plaintiffs presented statistics pertaining specifically to the relevant group — the men and women taking the SAT — not a general comparison of the number of female scholarship recipients to the number of male recipients. Thus, *Sharif*'s statistical evidence would be persuasive even under *Wards Cove*.

Similarly, although *Sharif* required defendants to prove a "necessity" for using the SAT, rather than a mere "legitimate purpose" that *Wards Cove* allows, future courts could still determine that no legitimate purpose exists for using the SAT — an aptitude test — as an achievement test. Moreover, even if defendants can show a legitimate purpose, plaintiffs may still respond with a less discriminatory alternative. For instance, averaging scores from several standardized tests, employing customized tests, or using *Sharif*'s GPA/SAT standard are all alternatives that could reduce disparity significantly without reducing accuracy. A multidimensional standard that tests a wide variety of skills will likely measure high school achievement more accurately than a single test such as the SAT. Although the *Wards Cove* Court deemed the additional cost of such alternatives relevant in determining the "effectiveness" of alternative approaches, the Court did not suggest that administrative burdens be dispositive. When important interests are at stake, courts generally do not weigh administrative costs heavily in proposing remedies or evaluation defenses.

The disparate-impact analysis adopted in *Sharif* redresses bias in standardized testing more effectively than would an intent standard. Test bias will more likely result from the test makers' possible subconscious prejudices than from an intent to skew the content of the test. In such cases, proving intent to *discriminate* would be an extremely difficult, if not unintentional, systematic discrimination as well as intentional, individualized discrimination. By invalidating tests that disadvantage women, disparate-impact analysis rejects the false assumption that test results reflect actual difference between female and male intellects, and prevents the inequities that result when disproportionate numbers of female students are denied equal access to educational programs. Society has a fundamental commitment to provide nondiscriminatory access to educational opportunities. Allocating such opportunities by means of a test that *discriminates* against women undermines that principle. By adopting disparate-impact analysis, *Sharif* properly created a stronger, more proactive role for Title IX in preventing the denial of educational opportunities to traditionally disadvantaged groups.

Civil Rights — Disparate-Impact Doctrine — Court Prohibits Awarding Scholarships on the Basis of Standardized Tests that Discriminatorily Impact Women. Sharif v. New York State Education Department, 709 F. Supp. 345 (S.D.N.Y. 1989), 103 Harv. L. Rev. 806 (1990).* The author discusses *Ward's Cove Packing Co. v. Atonio*, 109 S. Ct. 2115 (1989), a case about employment discrimination of ethnic minorities in Alaska based on "disparate impact." The author postulates that *Sharif* would have been decided the same even after *Ward's Cove*. Is the author convincing in this argument? How much weight would disparate impact court decisions in the employment sphere have on those involving education? Could *Franklin v. Gwinnett County Schs.*, mentioned in the notes following *Cannon*, and presented later in this chapter, provide any answers?

GARRETT v. BOARD OF EDUCATION OF SCHOOL DISTRICT OF CITY OF DETROIT

United States District Court
775 F. Supp. 1004 (E.D. Mich. 1991)

WOODS, DISTRICT JUDGE:

Plaintiffs filed this suit on Monday, August 5, 1991, alleging the defendant Board of Education of the School District of the City of Detroit ("Board") violated the Fourteenth Amendment to the United States Constitution, Article 1, § 2 of the Michigan Constitution, Title IX, the Equal Educational Opportunities Act, Michigan's Elliott-Larsen Act and Michigan's School Code through the establishment of male-only academies. Plaintiffs are girls enrolled in Detroit public schools and their parents. Plaintiff Nancy Doe is a Detroit resident with daughters aged 11, 6, and 5, all of whom will attend Detroit public schools this fall. Defendant Board of Education for the School District of the City of Detroit controls, manages and administers the public schools for the city pursuant to Mich.Comp.Laws Ann.§ 380.401 *et seq.* (West 1988).

On August 5, 1991, plaintiffs moved this Court to issue a temporary restraining order to enjoin the Board from taking any further steps to implement the male academies. This motion was denied; the Court set an expedited hearing date for the resolution of plaintiffs' motion for preliminary injunction. The Court heard oral argument August 15, 1991, and issued its opinion from the bench. This written opinion supplements the bench order.

---

*Copyright © 1990 by the Harvard Law Review Association. Reprinted with permission.

I

Three male academies ("Academies") are scheduled to open on August 26, 1991. The Academies will serve approximately 250 boys in preschool through fifth grade. Grades six through eight will be phased in over the next few years. The Academies offer special programs including a class entitled "Rites of Passage", an Afrocentric (Pluralistic) curriculum, futuristic lessons in preparation for 21st century careers, an emphasis on male responsibility, mentors, Saturday classes, individualized counseling, extended classroom hours, and student uniforms.

Plaintiffs contend that these special offerings (1) do not require a uniquely male atmosphere to succeed; and (2) address issues that face all children and adolescents, including females. Plaintiffs further charge that despite the stated goal of the Academies to address the high unemployment rates, school dropout levels and homicide among urban males, the Academies do not target "at-risk" males; rather, they serve a mix of boys from all achievement levels.

II

The Sixth Circuit requires the Court to consider four factors in deciding a motion for injunctive relief: (1) the likelihood of plaintiffs' success on the merits; (2) whether the injunction will save the plaintiffs from irreparable injury; (3) whether the harm to plaintiffs if relief is not granted outweighs the harm to others if relief is granted; and (4) whether the public interest would best be served by the issuing of the injunction. *In Re DeLorean Motor Co.*, 755 F.2d 1223, 1228 (6th Cir.1985). The Court will address each in turn.

A. *Likelihood of Success*

Plaintiffs allege in their complaint that the defendant has deliberately chosen to disregard the rights of girls in the public school system, despite the specific advice of state governmental authorities and the federal policy requiring equal educational opportunities without regard to sex. Each of the laws allegedly violated by defendant Board is discussed below.

1. *Federal and State Constitutions*

Gender-based classifications implicate the protection afforded by the Equal Protection Clause of the Fourteenth Amendment to the United States Constitution as well as the corresponding provision of the Michigan Constitution, Article 1, Section 2. The Equal Protection Clause of the Michigan Constitution, Article 1, § 2, provides protection against discrimination equal to or greater than the protection provided by the federal Constitution. *Doe v. Dep't of Social Services*, 187 Mich.App. 493, 512-19, 468 N.W.2d 862 (1991). Because plaintiffs offer no additional arguments based on the greater protection offered by the Michigan Constitution, the analysis is combined for the sake of brevity.

A. STUDENT CLASSIFICATION BY SEX

In *Mississippi v. Hogan*, 458 U.S. 718, 724 (1982), the Supreme Court held that exclusion of an individual from a publicly-funded school because of his or her sex violates the Equal Protection Clause of the Fourteenth Amendment, unless the defendant can show the sex-based "classification serves 'important governmental objectives and that the discriminatory means employed'" are "substantially related to the achievement of those objectives." *Hogan*, 458 U.S. at 724 (quoting *Wengler v. Druggist Mutual Ins. Co.*, 446 U.S. 142, 150 (1980)).

Plaintiffs maintain the Board cannot meet this standard because the Board's policy of excluding girls inappropriately relies on gender as a proxy for "at-risk" students. The Academies were developed in response to the crisis facing African-American males manifested by high homicide, unemployment, and drop-out rates. While these statistics underscore a compelling need, they fall short of demonstrating that excluding girls is substantially related to the achievement of the Board's objectives. The Board has proffered no evidence that the presence of girls in the classroom bears a substantial relationship to the difficulties facing urban males.

Accordingly, plaintiffs conclude that the male academies improperly use gender as a "proxy for other, more germane bases of classification," *Craig v. Boren*, 429 U.S. 190, 198 (1976), in this instance, for "at risk" students. Specifically, the gender specific data presented in defense of the Academies ignores the fact that all children in the Detroit public schools face significant obstacles to success. In fact, in its resolution establishing the Academies, the Board acknowledged an "equally urgent and unique crisis facing ... female students." Urban girls drop out of school, suffer loss of self esteem and become involved in criminal activity. Ignoring the plight of urban females institutionalizes inequality and perpetuates the myth that females are doing well in the current system. Accordingly, plaintiffs contend there is no adequate justification for the Academies' exclusive focus on boys. *See Craig v. Boren*, 429 U.S. 190, 204 (1976).

Plaintiffs also assert that the special curriculum proposed for the Academies suggests a false dichotomy between the roles and responsibilities of boys and girls. For example, the Rites of Passage curriculum teaches that "men need a vision and a plan for living," "men master their emotions," and "men acquire skills and knowledge to overcome life's obstacles." These issues confront all adolescents and are not rites peculiarly male. Therefore, they are insufficient to justify gender-based classification.

Defendant responds that the validity of the objective of the male academies distinguishes the instant matter from the program found unconstitutional in *Hogan*, wherein the Supreme Court addressed the single sex admissions policy of the Mississippi University for Women School of Nursing. In *Hogan*, the State attempted to justify the policy by proving it compensated for historical discrimination against women. The Court rejected this argument. In contrast, the defendant here argues it has confirmed the present delivery of education has resulted in substantially lower achievement levels for males than for females and that the Academies are the solution to this problem. The primary rationale for the Academies is simply that co-educational programs aimed at improving male performance have failed.

The Court is wary of accepting such a rationale. Although co-educational programs have failed, there is no showing that it is the co-educational factor that results in failure. Even more dangerous is the prospect that should the male academies proceed and succeed, success would be equated with the absence of girls rather than any of the educational factors that more probably caused the outcome.

Defendant argues that just because females also face academic performance problems does not weaken the importance of their objective in opening the male academies. Further, the Board states it has recognized the difficulties faced by urban females and developed alternative programs housed in single sex schools that specifically address the needs of females, such as pregnancy-related programs. The Court does not find fault with this argument; the objective of the male academies is important; but, the degree of importance does not eliminate the defendant's burden of showing that the second prong of the *Hogan* test is met.

Defendant argues in the alternative that the second prong, "substantially related" is satisfied for three reasons. First, the establishment of male academies is critical to expeditiously determine what curriculum and training programs will work to keep urban males out of the City's morgues and prisons. Second, the Board has already reviewed smaller scale experimental programs at two schools that specifically addressed the special needs of urban males and found them successful in improving the overall academic and behavioral aspects of the urban males' life style. Third, the Board knows that current co-ed programs do not work. Consequently, the Board finds that research supports the establishment of an experimental school with a specialized curriculum to address the special needs of urban males.

None of these findings meet the defendant's burden of showing how the exclusion of females from the Academies is necessary to combat unemployment, dropout and homicide rates among urban males. There is no evidence that the educational system is failing urban males because females attend schools with males. In fact, the educational system is also failing females. Thus, the Court concludes the application of the second prong of the *Hogan* test to the facts at hand, makes it likely that the plaintiffs will succeed on a constitutional argument.

2. *Title IX*

Plaintiffs also argue that the Academies violate Title IX of the Education Act Amendments of 1972, 20 U.S.C. § 1681 *et seq.*, (1990), and its implementing regulations, 24 C.F.R. 106, *et seq.*, (1990). Title IX prohibits those educational programs receiving federal funds from treating students unequally on the basis of sex. The regulations implementing Title IX provide that students may not be

A. STUDENT CLASSIFICATION BY SEX

given "different aid, benefits, or services" because of their sex. 34 C.F.R. § 106.31(b)(2). In addition, the regulations prohibit recipients of federal financial assistance from providing any course or otherwise carrying out any of its educational programs on the basis of sex, or from requiring or refusing participation therein by any students on such basis. 34 C.F.R. § 106.36. The regulations also list the exceptions; that is, the types of classes which may be single sex. See 24 C.F.R. § 106.34(c), (e), and (f). Because the Academies do not fall within the listed exceptions, plaintiffs conclude that they violate Title IX.

Defendant argues the plaintiffs cannot succeed on this theory because Title IX (1) excludes from coverage, admission plans in kindergarten through grade twelve; and (2) its legislative history recognized the need for continued experimentation with unique methods of education, such as the Academies.

Regarding admission plans, 20 U.S.C. § 1681(a)(1) provides as follows: "Classes of Educational Institutions Subject to Prohibition. In regard to admissions to educational institutions, this section shall apply only to institutions of vocational education, professional education, and graduate higher education, and to public institutions of undergraduate higher education". This section would allow for the selection of prospective students on the basis of sex. Therefore, defendant concludes, all things being equal, a school could be created that would admit students of only one sex. Defendant's argument is flawed. The Court views this exemption for admissions as applicable primarily to historically pre-existing single sex schools; it is not viewed as authorization to establish new single sex schools. No case has ever upheld the existence of a sex-segregated public school that has the effect of favoring one sex over another. The interplay of the Constitution and other statutes, as well as the legislative history, diminishes the persuasiveness of this argument.

The Court examines defendant's second argument, that congressional intent allows for experimentation with single sex educational options noting exceptions for military academies, social fraternities, and youth service organizations. An additional exemption is made for any public institution of undergraduate higher education that "traditionally and continually from its establishment has had a policy of admitting only students of one sex." Accordingly, the statute recognizes the value of single sex public schools and did not intend to preclude experimental programs designed as such.

Plaintiffs' claims, however, do not rest solely on the denial of admission; rather, they rely on Title IX to protect their right to the same benefits and services. Undoubtedly, plaintiffs desire access to the programs offered at the Academies. Defendant, by way of the affidavit of Arthur M. Carter, Interim Deputy Superintendent of the Board, states that the educational programs are no different from the individualized instruction and benefits offered in other schools throughout the system. It is unclear, however, whether all of the course offerings available at the Academies can be had at any one school and from the evidence before the Court it appears this is not the case.

Additionally, defendant argues that the Secretary of Education has promulgated regulations under Title IX that allow the Board of Education to establish the male academies. 24 C.F.R.§ 106.3 provides in relevant part:

> [I]f ... a recipient has discriminated against persons on the basis of sex ... recipient shall take such remedial action as the Assistant Secretary deems necessary to overcome the effects of such discrimination. (b) In the absence of finding of discrimination on the basis of sex ...recipient may take affirmative action to overcome the effects of conditions which resulted in limited participation therein by persons of a particular sex.

The Board has reviewed the evidence and determined that conditions have resulted in limited participation of urban males in educational programs and activities. Therefore, even in the absence of a specific finding of discrimination by the Assistant Secretary of Education, the Board maintains that the regulations do not prohibit the action it has taken.

Despite the Board's stance, the Office of Civil Rights of the Department of Education, ("OCR"), the federal governmental authority charged with administrative enforcement of Title IX, has opined that all male public elementary and secondary school programs violate Title IX. Also, the Michigan State Department of Education notified defendant that the male academies violated Title IX. At this stage in the litigation, this Court defers to the opinion of the OCR. Therefore, plaintiffs have met their burden of showing the likelihood of success on this cause of action.

3. *Equal Educational Opportunities Act*

The Equal Educational Opportunities Act, ("EEOA"), 20 U.S.C.§ 1701, *et seq.*, (1990), prohibits a student assignment to a school other than a neighborhood school if reassignment "results in a greater degree of segregation of students on the basis of ... sex ... among the schools of such agency than would result if such students were assigned to the school closest to his or her place of residence within the school district of such agency providing the appropriate grade level and type of education for such student." 20 U.S.C.§ 1703 (1990). This act was passed to eliminate the vestiges of dual school assignments based on racial discrimination and no mention of single sex schools ever occurred in the Senate and House debates.

The only reported decision considering the issue of sex segregation under the EEOA, *United States v. Hinds County School Bd.*, 560 F.2d 619 (5th Cir.1977), held that the sex-segregated schools violated the EEOA. The Fifth Circuit Court of Appeals concluded that the EEOA expressly "prohibits ... sex-segregated student assignment," even if there is some educational purpose in implementing the system. *Id.* at 625. Plaintiffs cite this case in support of their position that the Academies violate the EEOA.

Defendant distinguishes this case factually. In *Hinds*, the school district was comprised of four schools, all of which segregated children by sex. Furthermore,

A. STUDENT CLASSIFICATION BY SEX

the School District there argued that the assignments should be permanent. In the case at bar, the Academies are experimental in nature; the charter authorizes a three-year existence. Also, there are 251 schools in the Detroit district; the Academies number 3. Finally, the defendant argues that a female academy will be established "soon."

Defendant also argues that the EEOA section cited by plaintiffs is inapplicable as it deals with "the assignment" by an educational agency whereas students are not assigned to any school by the Board. Rather, the students at the Academies are volunteers.

Plaintiff responds to these arguments as follows: the EEOA does not make exceptions for "separate but equal" programs....

Because the only applicable case is so easily distinguished, the Court finds the plaintiffs have not demonstrated probability of success sufficient to meet their burden as to this cause of action.

4. *Michigan's Elliott-Larsen Act*

The Elliott-Larsen Act, Mich.Comp.Laws Ann. §§ 37.2102(a), 37.2302(a), 37.2402, (West 1985), provides that "full and equal utilization" of and benefit from educational institutions and facilities and public accommodations shall not be denied on the basis of an individual's sex. In 1986, the Michigan Supreme Court held that "when evaluating whether a classification by gender amounts to impermissible sex discrimination under Section 302(a) of the Civil Rights Act, Art. 1, § 2 of the Michigan Constitution, or under the Equal Protection Clause of the Fourteenth Amendment of the United States Constitution, the standard to be applied is the same." *Civil Rights Dept. v. Waterford*, 425 Mich. 173, 190, 387 N.W.2d 821 (1986)....

....

Because the Court has already determined that the plaintiffs will likely succeed on the merits of their constitutional claim it logically concludes success is also likely on the ground that the Academies violate the Elliott-Larsen Civil Rights Act.

5. *Michigan School Code*

Section 380.1146 of the Michigan State School Code of 1976 ("Code") provides in full: A separate school or department shall not be kept for a person on account of race, color, or sex. This section shall not be construed to prevent grading of schools according to the intellectual progress of the pupil to be taught in separate places as may be deemed expedient. (Mich.Comp.Laws Ann. § 380.1146 (West 1988).

This provision is a limitation on the power of local school boards to establish schools and attendance areas within the district. *See Hiers v. Brownell*, 376 Mich. 225, 235, 136 N.W.2d 10 (1965). It incorporates a private right of action to enforce its requirements. *See Mason v. Board of Education*, 6 Mich.App. 364,

370 n. 6, 149 N.W.2d 239 (1967) (private suit brought to enforce the Code of 1955, the predecessor statute to MCLA § 380.1146).

The Code of 1976 added sex as a prohibited classification but in all other respects was a recodification of prior law. The prior law prohibited the establishment of a school excluding students based on a suspect classification. Accordingly, plaintiffs assert that the Board's policy of establishing male academies and excluding girls from those Academies violates the Code.

Defendant concedes that the Code prohibits the establishment of a separate school on the basis of sex, but argues it does not prohibit separate alternative educational programs tailored to the needs of students at risk. The Board also maintains that the male academies are not separate schools.

Defendant argues that the Academies are not intended and do not have the effect of existing as separate schools that disadvantage students or deny them equal educational benefits because of sex. Rather, they are designed to obtain information in an experimental setting and the knowledge generated from this experiment will be used to benefit all students, male and female. Defendant asserts that the purpose of the male academies is not to separate or ban female students, thus, it is not the activity the legislature intended to prohibit by enactment of § 380.1146. Mich.Comp.Laws Ann.§ 380.1146 (West 1988).

....

The Board notes the Academies do not specifically prohibit attendance by females. This argument cannot save the Board. The name, "Male Academies," in and of itself, as well as the descriptive literature, clearly excludes females from real participation in the program. Although the Board states the Male Academies are not intended or designed to be discriminatory single-sex programs in one breath, in the next it asserts that the program is designed to gather data to determine what type of curriculum and teacher training programs are necessary to alleviate the disparate impact of the current educational system on urban males. The Board cannot have it both ways. The Code explicitly bans sex segregation and explicitly states exceptions to this rule. Plaintiffs are, therefore, likely to succeed with their claim on this cause of action.

The Court, convinced that plaintiffs have met their burden on the first factor necessary for injunctive relief, turns to the second factor.

B. *Irreparable Harm*

Plaintiffs argue they will suffer serious, irreparable and immediate harm unless injunctive relief is granted. An injury is irreparable only if it cannot be undone through monetary remedies. *Ohio v. Nuclear Regulatory Comm'n*, 812 F.2d 288, 290 (6th Cir.1987).

....

Such an irreparable injury may also be found here. The fact that plaintiffs may continue in the regular school system does not eliminate or render harmless the denial of their rights to equal opportunity under the Equal Protection Clause. *See Deerfield Medical Center v. Deerfield Beach*, 661 F.2d 328, 338 (5th Cir.1981).

The *Deerfield* court goes on to state that loss of First Amendment rights for even minimal periods of time constitutes irreparable injury justifying the grant of a preliminary injunction. *Id*. This analysis is also applicable to the Fourteenth Amendment rights at stake here.

The Board hints that an academy for girls is in the works. This intimation about establishing a girls' academy does not alleviate the injury. Later attempts to equalize opportunities to girls will not compensate for the plaintiffs' lost opportunities to learn, gain self-esteem and be trained for a successful future....

C. *Harm to Others If the Stay is Granted*

....

... [T]he Court must consider whether the Board has any valid interest in opening the male academies in light of the finding that plaintiffs are likely to succeed on the merits of this case. Relying on the reasoning used by the Sixth Circuit in *Ohio v. Nuclear Regulatory Comm'n*, this Court finds no substantial harm would result from preventing the operation of an unconstitutional school.

D. *Public Interest*

Plaintiffs argue that the public interest is better served by preventing the opening of an unconstitutional educational facility. Defendant argues the Academies seek a bona fide public good to the detriment of no one. Defendant further contends that the creation of the Academies is substantially related to the important governmental interest of the Detroit Public Schools in obtaining information directed toward meeting the special educational needs of inner-city males. This "pilot setting" affords the public schools the opportunity to evaluate the effectiveness of various curricula and other programs in meeting the educational needs of males.

This Court views the purpose for which the Academies came into being as an important one. It acknowledges the status of urban males as an "endangered species." The purpose, however, is insufficient to override the rights of females to equal opportunities.

Now, therefore, this Court GRANTS plaintiffs' motion for preliminary injunction.

So ordered.

---

1. Would establishing a similar academy for girls have solved the problem here or have Detroit and other big city school systems learned from the experience in *Newberg*, presented earlier in this chapter?

2. *See* Vergon, *Male Academies for At-Risk Urban Youth: Legal and Policy lessons from the Detroit Experience*, 79 Educ. L. Rep. 351 (1993). The Detroit Board of Education is not alone in its attempts to climb out of the dilemma that big-city public education seems to be in. School districts and community groups in Baltimore, Los Angeles, Milwaukee, Minneapolis, New York and Washington, D.C. have considered similar schools. Given the current state of affairs in large cities, is a school for at-risk urban males worth a try, despite the critics? What alternatives exist in education that would solve the unique problems of urban males identified in the case?

3. Vergon says that a focus on more than schools is necessary. He also urges a look at males and females. 79 Educ. L. Rep. 51. "[A] more comprehensive youth policy and more coordinated approach will be required." *Id.* *

4. Daniel Gardenswartz, in an article for the *Emory Law Journal*, noted that Detroit originally planned on a "point system" to determine if a child is at risk and eligible to enroll in the special school. *Public Education: An Inner-City Crisis! Single-Sex Schools: An Inner-City Answer?*, 42 Emory L.J. 591 (1993). Under the plan, each student was to be given points based on the following variables: citizenship, days absent, single parent status, mother's highest grade of school completed, grade-point average and amount of time retained in grade. *Id.* Would the creation of a point system have saved this case? Are the variables too broad? Broad enough?

5. The case cites to *Mississippi Univ. for Women v. Hogan*, 478 U.S. 718 (1982) for the legal principle that 'exclusion of an individual from a publicly-funded school because of his or her sex violates the Equal Protection Clause of the Fourteenth Amendment unless the defendant can show the sex-based "classification serves important government objectives and that the discriminatory means employed are substantially related to the achievement of those objectives."' *Id.* at 1006. The *Garrett* court then goes on to acknowledge that urban males are an '"endangered species."' *Id.* at 1014. Is it beyond cavil to say that elimination of an important part of the country's human population from the "endangered species list" is an important government objective and that all-male academies might help to eliminate their slaughter since no other education program has come close?

6. The controversy surrounding single-sex education has affected higher education, as well. Most recently, this battle was played out on the campuses of historically all-male, state-supported military colleges. *See United States v. Commonwealth of Virginia*, 44 F.3d 1229 (4th Cir. 1995). (Although the state could sponsor single-gender education — at Virginia Military Institute — without violating the equal protection clause, it could only do so if it provided comparable education to women in the form of leadership training at an all-women's college); *Faulkner v. Jones*, 51 F.3d 440 (4th Cir. 1995). (State's support of a male-only military college — the Citadel — violated the equal protection rights of female student-applicants, and defendants were ordered to admit female applicants, despite the state's claim that it would establish a female-only college).

---

*Copyright © 1993 by West Publishing Company. Reprinted with permission.

A. STUDENT CLASSIFICATION BY SEX

2. ATHLETICS

YELLOW SPRINGS EXEMPTED VILLAGE SCHOOL DISTRICT v. OHIO HIGH SCHOOL ATHLETIC ASSOCIATION

United States Court of Appeals
647 F.2d 651 (6th Cir. 1981)

CORNELIA G. KENNEDY, CIRCUIT JUDGE:

....

Yellow Springs is a very small school district composed of 950 students, 220 of whom were in the middle school, at the time suit was filed. The school district determined that at the middle school level mixed-sex athletic teams have educational advantages and thus tried to emphasize coeducational activities in general. This decision was based on the school district's observation that girls and boys at this level have essentially the same athletic skills. However, Yellow Springs was unable to offer a coed basketball team, because the rules of the OHSAA [Ohio High School Athletics Association] prohibit coed teams in interscholastic contact sports, and basketball is defined as a contact sport. This practice was called into question when in the fall of 1974 two Yellow Springs middle school girls tried out for and made the boys' basketball team. They were not permitted to participate since if Yellow Springs attempted to field girl team members it would be prohibited by the OHSAA from participating in interscholastic competition. The school district then attempted to set up a girls' team; however, there were no other girls' teams against which it could play that year. It has since fielded a girls' team. Yellow Springs also attempted by a referendum of member schools of the OHSAA to change the rule to permit coed teams within an individual school's discretion but was unsuccessful. Fearing that compliance with the OHSAA rule violated federal law and might render it ineligible for federal funds, Yellow Springs filed this suit.

The OHSAA is a voluntary unincorporated association to which virtually all senior high schools (defined as schools which have seventh grade students and above) in Ohio belong.... The OHSAA organizes competitions, sets up schedules, arranges places to play tournament games (including school facilities), and provides injury insurance. It also prescribes uniform rules of play and has the power to sanction schools which violate them. Schools belong as individuals, and both state-accredited private and public schools may be members. The overwhelming majority of members, approximately 90% from 1972 to 1976, are public schools.

In order to be a member of the OHSAA, a school must be accredited by the State Board of Education. Membership in the OHSAA is a virtual necessity, since the State Board does not provide any interscholastic athletic programs although it has the authority to do so. Considering the importance of athletics to a well-rounded education, it is evident that individual schools or school districts would be required to find a replacement for the OHSAA's activities if the OHSAA did not exist.... Individual schools may vote on and approve rules and regulations of the OHSAA and may also be expelled from membership if they do not comply. School budgets provide funding for training and travel to OHSAA meets, and the OHSAA returns some money to schools if it operates with a surplus in a particular year. Most of the OHSAA's budget of approximately one million dollars is generated through tournaments, many of which are held on school or public property. Local school board members have an interest in and have participated voluntarily in governing the OHSAA.

....

The District Judge found that the OHSAA's activities constituted state action. He found that the OHSAA was dependent on the use of public facilities for its operating revenue and noted the involvement of public officials in OHSAA decision-making. The trial judge found that public schools predominated in its membership. Finally, the District Judge found significant the OHSAA's ability to sanction state schools for noncompliance with its rules, a role which permitted "a technically non-governmental entity to dictate terms to a state entity." For example, its rules have provided that the school administrator must assume the financial responsibility for interscholastic athletics and may not delegate the responsibility to other members of the staff except under certain conditions.

The rules even regulate school participation in non-OHSAA meets. The judge concluded that the OHSAA functioned as an instrumentality of the state and as an agent of the schools. The OHSAA's character as a semi-official in its activities and its symbiotic relationship with the state lead to the conclusion that the trial judge correctly found state action.

....

This Court has dealt more specifically with state board of education liability in discrimination cases since the trial judge wrote his opinion. In *Penick v. Columbus Board of Education*, 583 F.2d 787 (6th Cir. 1978), *aff'd*, 443 U.S. 449 (1979), although the District Judge had found intentional support for segregation in a state board's failure to take action to end the segregation, this Court found it necessary to remand for more detailed fact-finding on the following specific issues: (1) the state board's knowledge of intentional practices by the local board; (2) the state board's failure to protest or restrain the local board; (3) the state board's continuing support of the local board in the face of such knowledge; (4) the motivation of the state board in failing to investigate; and (5) the effect of findings under (1) through (4). *Id.* at 818; accord, *Reed v. Rhodes*, 607 F.2d 714, 718 (6th Cir. 1979), *cert. denied*, 445 U.S. 935 (1980). We conclude that under the teachings of *Penick* and *Reed* we must remand. These questions cannot be answered on the present record. It is questionable whether they can be resolved on a motion for summary judgment. We do not dismiss the state defendants but remand to permit the plaintiffs to show upon further proceedings that there was "intentional support of the local board(s) in pursuing (discriminatory) practices," *Id.* at 718, and that they seek relief that the state can provide.

A. STUDENT CLASSIFICATION BY SEX

The rules of the OHSAA apply to both senior high schools and junior high schools, with some special rules pertaining only to junior high students. On July 1, 1975, Part I of the rules, which applies to all students, provided: "Boys teams must be composed of boys only IN ALL CONTACT SPORTS. (Football, wrestling, ice hockey, soccer, basketball, and baseball)" Rule I, § 2. A footnote to the rule stated that it was intended to comply with decisions of this Circuit. After it was brought to the Association's attention that its rules might also not comply with Title IX, they were redrafted and reissued on July 1, 1976, for the sole articulated purpose of complying with Title IX. The boys and girls sections were combined, and several other significant changes were made, including the following: "In all contact sports (Football, Wrestling, Ice Hockey and Basketball) team members shall be boys only. Girls may play on a boys team in non-contact sports, if there is no girls team or if the overall opportunities for interscholastic competition is (sic) limited for girls." Rule I, § 6.

Teams of the opposite sex shall not compete against each other in any interscholastic athletic contests. Rule I, § 7.

The OHSAA argues that the changes brought their rules into compliance with Title IX and its regulations. The relevant regulation is 45 C.F.R. § 86.41:

> (a) General. No person shall, on the basis of sex, be excluded from participation in, be denied the benefits of, be treated differently from another person or otherwise be discriminated against in any interscholastic athletics offered by a recipient, and no recipient shall provide any such athletics separately on such basis.
>
> (b) Separate teams. Notwithstanding the requirements of paragraph (a) of this section, a recipient may operate or sponsor separate teams for members of each sex where selection for such teams is based upon competitive skill or the activity involved is a contact sport. However, where a recipient operates or sponsors a team in a particular sport for members of one sex but operates or sponsors no such team for members of the other sex, and athletic opportunities for members of that sex have previously been limited, members of the excluded sex must be allowed to try-out for the team offered unless the sport involved is a contact sport.
>
> (c) Equal opportunity. A recipient which operates or sponsors interscholastic athletics shall provide equal athletic opportunity for members of both sexes. In determining whether equal opportunities are available the Director will consider, among other factors: (1) Whether the selection of sports and levels of competition effectively accommodate the interests and abilities of members of both sexes.

A reading of the regulation discloses that Title IX requires measures to be taken which will provide equal athletic opportunity. Thus the entire regulation must be interpreted in light of that requirement. The first way this may be achieved is by providing coeducational sports. The regulation additionally permits separate teams in sports which require competitive selection but also requires measures to be taken to ensure equality for the excluded sex, including where necessary an opportunity to try out for the team. It also provides for separate teams in defined contact sports but does not clearly prohibit try-outs for a position on such a team by the excluded sex.

In its motion for summary judgment, Yellow Springs asked only that the District Court declare Rule I, § 6 of the OHSAA to be null and void and unenforceable. The motion did not request a declaration that the Title IX regulation was unconstitutional. Indeed the complaint and plaintiffs' reply to defendants' motion to dismiss or for a more definite statement assert that the OHSAA rule violates the regulation.... Yellow Springs argued that the OHSAA rule was mandatory and prohibitory, in that it prevents its member schools from adopting the many means Title IX offers for achieving compliance. The OHSAA replied in its motion for summary judgment: "Section 86.41(b) permits separate teams for contact sports, but that is not a requirement. It is strictly permissive because much more is considered in the question of 'equal athletic opportunity for members of both sexes.'" The parties are thus in basic agreement that the regulations under Title IX do not proscribe girls' competing on the same team with boys in contact sports but instead provide for a permissive approach as long as the goal of equal athletic opportunity is achieved. The only issue then is whether the OHSAA may, without unlawful discrimination, frame its rules in a manner which limits recipients to providing only single-sex teams in contact sports and eliminates options which may be necessary for achieving the goal of equal educational opportunities. All the parties agree that the OHSAA rules must comply with 45 C.F.R. § 86.41(b), (c).

The trial judge assumed without examination that the OHSAA rule and the Title IX regulation were identical and proceeded immediately to consider the constitutionality of the regulation, ultimately holding it unconstitutional as a violation of substantive due process. However, they are not identical, and a careful inquiry discloses that the rules of the OHSAA do not comply with the regulation. Although the rules provide that girls may play on the boy's team in non-contact sports in language that tracks the regulation, the OHSAA rule for contact sports has been interpreted and applied to prohibit girls from participating on a boys' team in any contact sport at all levels under its jurisdiction. It conflicts in this regard with Title IX, which is purposely permissive and flexible on this point, rather than mandatory. *See* Note, *Sex Discrimination and Intercollegiate Athletics: Putting Some Muscle on Title IX*, 88 Yale L.J. 1254, 1269-72 (1979). The rule violates Title IX in that the recipient is provided no mechanism for achieving equal athletic opportunity. The rule thus operates to take away the discretion Title IX mandates be given recipient schools to determine how best to provide equal athletic opportunity and in some instances, such as here, may even prevent them from doing so. Insofar as the OHSAA rules are more restrictive than 45 C.F.R. § 86.41 and operate to prevent compliance with Title IX, they should be enjoined.

The OHSAA might ask why, if Title IX grants a measure of discretion to recipients, that discretion may not be further delegated to the OHSAA to determine how best to implement Title IX. The simple answer is that the focus of both Title IX and the regulations is on "recipients." It is federal aid to "recipients" that will be cut off if Title IX is not complied with. "Recipients" bear ultimate responsibility for providing an equal educational opportunity. The OHSAA is not a "recipient," and does not bear the burden of non-compliance, so may not adopt a rule which limits the ability of recipients to furnish girls the same athletic opportunities it provides for boys. The OHSAA has not claimed that it attempted to frame rules with an eye to achieving the goal of universally applicable equal athletic opportunity. Thus, based on this record, we conclude that the determination as to compliance with Title IX must be made by individual schools, not the OHSAA.

There was testimony in this case that at the middle school level students of both sexes are of approximately the same skill level and size, with much greater differences appearing within sexes than between them. *See National Organization For Women v. Little League Baseball, Inc.*, 127 N.J.Super. 522, 318 A.2d 33 (1974). In the case before the court, in which the girls were physically able to play as equals, in which the school sought to promote coed activities generally, and in which a girls' team had no opportunity for equal competition for lack of girls' teams at other schools, coeducational teams can further the goals of Title IX. At other schools or at other levels where there are greater average physical differences between sexes this same goal may be better achieved with separate teams. Congress passed Title IX in the face of longstanding sexual stereotypes that led educational institutions to make arbitrary distinctions. Thus, an overriding purpose of the statute was to determine the nature of equality for men and women in contexts in which their differences are particularly relevant. *Note, supra*, 88 Yale L.J. at 1263; *see Hoover v. Meiklejohn*, 430 F.Supp. 164, 166 (D.Colo.1977) (dealing with the physical differences between males and females). We merely observe that such differences may not be presumed to exist where they do not in fact exist to serve as a basis for a broad, gender-based difference in treatment. *Craig v. Boren*, 429 U.S. 190, 204 (1976).

To hold that a recipient of federal aid may let girls at the middle school level compete on the same team with boys, if this furthers the goal of equal athletic opportunity, is not to hold that all teams must be coeducational at all levels or to imply that Title IX's regulation must be held unconstitutional for expressly permitting separate teams. In Title IX, Congress struck a balance between the needs of the individual athlete and the group and determined that for purposes of the statute equality is to be measured by the opportunities offered to the group, *Note, supra*, 88 Yale L.J. at 1265, not by the makeup of any individual team. It may have once been that requiring the superior female athlete to play on the girls' or women's team was to remove all possibility of developing her skills to the highest level attainable. However, with the advent of Title IX, it may be that required participation on the female team is not always unequal treatment.

Indeed, with more attention being paid to women's sports in general and with a nearer approach to equality as provided in 45 C.F.R. § 86.41(c), the opportunities for the outstanding female athlete to excel are enhanced. Separate teams may to a large extent aid in this equalization not only because they provide more opportunities but also because they make monitoring of the opportunities provided easier.

Our understanding of what constitutes unconstitutional discrimination on the basis of sex has become more sophisticated through the years as a result of repeated scrutiny by the courts. The Supreme Court has now clearly held that in most cases of alleged sex discrimination it is equal protection which provides the standard for judicial scrutiny, *Craig v. Boren*, 429 U.S. at 197, not due process. A regulation that discriminates may not be upheld where sex is not a legitimate, accurate proxy for existing differences. *Id.* at 204. Once a law is found to make a distinction on the basis of sex, the burden shifts to the defendants to prove the rule bears a fair and substantial relationship to an important state objective. *See e.g., id.* at 197-204. However, in order to measure equal opportunity, present relevant differences cannot be ignored. When males and females are not in fact similarly situated and when the law is blind to those differences, there may be as much a denial of equality as when a difference is created which does not exist. *See Caban v. Mohammed*, 441 U.S. 380, 398 (1979) (Stewart, J., dissenting). When considering the constitutionality of Title IX and its regulations, a blanket requirement of one team at each age level might result in male dominance of all teams and cause a return to pre-Title IX conditions, a result completely at variance with the statute's purpose. *Cf. United Steelworkers of America v. Weber*, 443 U.S. 193, 202 (1979). It is desirable to maximize the opportunities for individual women, but a requirement that boys play only on boys' teams while girls may compete either with the boys or in an all-girls' program (as they wish) might have a similar undesirable effect on the fledgling women's athletic programs; women's athletics may be significantly harmed if the best female competition is lost to the boys' program.

Although the District Judge held § 86.41 unconstitutional, no party urged that position and no evidence was offered on that issue. The appellees do not ask for such a declaration here. The Department of Health, Education, and Welfare, which promulgated the regulation, is not a party to this lawsuit. The District Court suggested some arguments for and against its constitutionality. However, that discussion was not necessary to the question before it, and we believe it inappropriate for this court to make any ruling on the matter at this time on a motion for summary judgment. The issue can only be properly resolved upon a complete record and a full presentation of all views....

Accordingly, for the reasons stated above, we reverse the judgment of the District Court which held that 45 C.F.R. § 86.41 is unconstitutional. Appellees are entitled, however, to an injunction enjoining the OHSAA from enforcing Association Rule I § 6. We remand to the District Court for further proceedings consistent with this opinion....

A. STUDENT CLASSIFICATION BY SEX

NATHANIEL R. JONES, Circuit Judge, concurring in part and dissenting in part:

In my view, the constitutionality of OHSAA Rule 1, § 6 denying the Yellow Springs school district the opportunity to allow its female middle school students to play on the presently all-male interscholastic basketball team is plainly raised and must be decided.... I would hold that OHSAA Rule 1, § 6 violates the equal protection clause of the Fifth and Fourteenth Amendments.

I. *Summary Judgment*

Contrary to the majority opinion, I read the parties' summary judgment motions as raising and arguing the constitutionality of OHSAA Rule 1, § 6.... Plaintiffs assert that the OHSAA's enforcement of Part I, Rule 1, § 6 has forced or is forcing them to violate both the Constitution and laws of the United States by requiring them to deny equal educational opportunities to female students solely because of the students' sex. As such, the enforcement of the rules and regulations of the O.H.S.A.A. conflicts with the Constitution and laws of the United States....

In its cross motion for summary judgment, OHSAA argued first that its regulation comported with the Title IX regulations. Then OHSAA contended that "Part I, Rule 1, of the OHSAA rules and regulations does not deny to plaintiffs and students Fourteenth Amendment rights." OHSAA argued that the equal protection clause permits the separate classification of females in contact sports, since it bears a rational relationship to a legitimate government objective....

....

Despite their recognition of the Constitutional issue, the defendants presented no evidence to demonstrate the substantial relationship between the OHSAA rule and important and substantial government objectives. Because the stipulated facts established plaintiffs' prima facie case of discrimination, to avoid or defeat summary judgment, the defendants had to produce evidence to contradict plaintiffs' prima facie case or to establish a defense. *Smith v. Hudson*, 600 F.2d 60, 65 (6th Cir. 1979). Defendants did neither, but instead sought summary judgment on the basis of the stipulation of facts. Defendants' failure to introduce any evidence as to the purpose of the OHSAA rule has left the record barren of any justification for it. Consequently, summary judgment in favor of plaintiffs on the constitutional issue was plainly proper, if the constitutional question must be reached.

II. *Title IX and its Regulations*

....

A. § 86.41

The initial inquiry is whether the application of OHSAA Rule 1, § 6 to prohibit the two Morgan Middle School girls from playing on the varsity basketball team contravened 45 C.F.R. § 86.41. The short answer is that Yellow Springs' compliance with the OHSAA rule did not violate § 86.41, because this regulation did not become effective until July 21, 1975. 45 C.F.R. § 86.1. Therefore, in November, 1974, when Morgan Middle School forbade the two female athletes from playing on the boys' basketball team, and in January 1975, when it formed a separate girls' basketball team, § 86.41 had no effect. This denial provides the sole actual and concrete controversy before the court. Consequently, the lawfulness of Rule 1, § 6 at that time must be judged against Title IX and, if necessary, the Constitution.

B. *Title IX*

Title IX prohibits discrimination on the basis of sex in any educational programs receiving federal funds, except for stated exemptions.... Morgan Middle School, as a recipient of federal funds which are used in part to finance its interscholastic athletic program, must comply with Title IX.

Congress did not expressly exempt contact sports programs from the prohibition of Title IX. Nevertheless, I conclude that Congress did not intend to proscribe separate sex teams in contact sports.... Congress included many exceptions to the general prohibition against discrimination on the basis of sex in educational programs. Thus, Congress never intended a total ban on sex classifications in educational programs. Instead, Congress recognized the value or legacy of sex classifications in certain limited contexts.

The legislative history on the application of Title IX to athletic programs is scanty. However, the intent of Congress not to prohibit separate teams in contact sports does appear. Senator Bayh, the sponsor of the amendment to include the prohibition against sex discrimination, stated, in response to a series of clarifying questions asked by Senator Dominick, that his amendment would not require the "desegregation of football fields." 117 Cong.Rec.S. 30407 (August 6, 1971).... The 1974 amendment to Title IX, which expressly authorizes a consideration of differences between female and male intercollegiate athletic programs, bolsters this reading of Congressional intent. Pub.L.No.93-380, § 844, 88 Stat. 612 (1974).

Congress' inaction in modifying the Title IX regulations lends further support to my conclusion.... The proposed regulations implementing Title IX were published shortly before the 1974 amendment. These regulations permitted separate sex teams when the team members were selected by competitive skill. The 1974 amendment did not overturn HEW's interpretation of Title IX. Similarly, the 1976 amendments to Title IX did not modify the final HEW regulations, which permitted separate sex teams in contact sports. Nor has Congress acted at any time since then to change HEW's interpretation of Title IX. Therefore, Title IX does not prohibit the exclusion of female athletes from male interscholastic teams in contact sports. Consequently, OHSAA Rule 1, § 6 is consistent with Title IX.

Finding no violation of Title IX or its regulations, I must address the constitutionality of OHSAA Rule 1, § 6.

A. STUDENT CLASSIFICATION BY SEX

III. *Fourteenth Amendment and the OHSAA Rule*

....

C. *Equal Protection*

The constitutional question in this case has two parts. First, did the OHSAA rule violate the Fourteenth Amendment in the autumn of 1974 when it deprived Yellow Springs of the opportunity to allow two female middle school athletes to play on the interscholastic basketball team? Second, if so, did the creation of a separate but equal basketball team for the female athletes provide a sufficient remedy for the constitutional violation?

The OHSAA rule must foster an important government objective and be substantially related to that objective in order to withstand scrutiny under the equal protection clause. *Orr v. Orr*, 440 U.S. 268 (1979); *Craig v. Boren*, 429 U.S. 190 (1976). The rule is presumed to be valid. *Robinson v. Board of Regents of Eastern Kentucky University*, 475 F.2d 707 (6th Cir. 1973), *cert. denied*, 416 U.S. 982 (1974). However, the rule may not be premised on archaic stereotypes or generalizations about the role of women. Defendants contend that the rule fulfills two important goals: protecting the safety of female athletes and promoting the full participation of females in sports.

....

Two district courts in this Circuit have addressed the question of female participation on "male teams" in contact sports. In *Carnes v. Tennessee Secondary School Athletic Ass'n*, 415 F.Supp. 569 (E.D.Tenn.1976), a preliminary injunction issued against the enforcement of a rule prohibiting high school women from playing varsity baseball. The Association's rationale of safety was held to be insubstantial, as men highly prone to injury could play. A second justification of protecting female sports teams from male intrusion was found not applicable, because the high school did not have a women's baseball team. Questioning the reasonableness of classifying baseball as a contact sport, the district judge assumed that the sexes could be separate for contact sports.

In *Clinton v. Nagy*, 411 F.Supp. 1396 (N.D.Ohio 1974), the district court granted a temporary restraining order against a rule of the Cleveland Brown's Muny Football League which prohibited girls from playing. The district judge emphasized that defendants had not presented any evidence showing that the plaintiff herself was physically incapable of playing football against boys.

Other district courts have considered the issue at hand in a very thoughtful fashion. In *Leffel v. Wisconsin Interscholastic Ass'n*, 444 F.Supp. 1117 (E.D.Wis.1978), the district court held unconstitutional an Association rule prohibiting coed teams in high school. The high school did not have separate female teams in baseball and tennis. There was a separate female swimming team. The district court held that female athletes must be allowed to compete for positions on the varsity team where there is no separate female team. The district court declared that a school cannot absolutely deny females the opportunity to compete in contact sports when males have that opportunity. Finding that the plaintiffs did not allege that defendants intentionally imposed different levels of competition between male and female teams in the same sport, the district court also ruled that plaintiffs' claim did not raise the issue of different levels of competition. Further, the district court held that plaintiffs' demand for relief was satisfied by separate female programs providing comparable facilities. Therefore, it did not address the issue of whether the maintaining of separate female teams violates the equal protection clause.

In *Hoover v. Meiklejohn*, 430 F.Supp. 164 (D.Colo.1977), the district court struck down a Colorado High School Activities Association rule which prohibited high school women from participating in soccer, a contact sport. The state justification of safety was discredited because physical criteria for playing had not been established for men. The district court also noted that the range of different physical ability among individuals of both sexes was greater than the average difference between the sexes. The district court called the rule simply "patronizing protection" for women. However, the district court, in discussing a remedy, determined that a "separate but equal" female program in soccer would suffice. It distinguished *Brown v. Board of Education*, 347 U.S. 483 (1954), stating that confining the female athletes to separate programs would not stigmatize them....

. . . .

As noted earlier, the defendants proffer two government objectives for the OHSAA rule: protecting the safety of female athletes and promoting the full participation of women in sports. I assume that these objectives are legitimate and important. However, the means chosen to implement these goals, the OHSAA rule, is not substantially related to them. As discussed above, the courts have strongly and uniformly rejected both justifications where a separate female team has not been provided. OHSAA has not offered any evidence in support of its justifications.

The safety rationale is not persuasive. Though not all females may have the skills, strength, and stamina to compete with males in contact sports, some females, like the two middle school girls in Yellow Springs, do have the physical ability....

The second objective of promoting the full participation of women in sports is patently not served when female athletes are denied any opportunity to play basketball. In the context of an opportunity to play on a separate female team, this objective actually contains three arguments. The first argument is that allowing the top female athletes to play on the "male team" would significantly harm the female athletic program. The second contention is that, if females are permitted to play on male teams, then males must be allowed to play on female teams. The result, it is argued, would be male dominance in female sports programs, denying women any opportunity to compete in interscholastic sports. The third argument is that schools will cut back on female athletic programs by fielding just one "open team" in each sport.

A. STUDENT CLASSIFICATION BY SEX

Defendants' arguments are not supported at all in the record. Their first argument rests on sheer speculation. Plaintiffs could as easily contend that the participation of top female athletes with men will enhance the reputation and glamour of female athletics and encourage more women to participate. Plaintiffs might say that, though a team may lose its top player, the overall effect on the program would be positive, by calling attention to the abilities of female athletes and consequently raising fan interest and funding. Of course, neither speculation is accepted as fact.

Similarly the record does not support a finding that enjoining enforcement of the OHSAA rule will result in male domination of female sports programs. No court has adopted the Association's reasoning. One district court has opined, relying on *Califano v. Webster*, 430 U.S. 313 (1977), that separate and exclusive female teams are constitutionally permissible, so that women would have the choice of competing on an "open team" or a single-sex female team. *Gomes v. Rhode Island Interscholastic League*, 469 F.Supp. 659 (D.R.I.), *vacated and dismissed as moot at the time of appeal*, 604 F.2d 733 (1st Cir. 1979). Of course, I do not express an opinion on the right of male athletes to play on female teams, since this issue is not in controversy. My discussion is aimed only at illustrating the large extent to which the defendants' second justification rests on speculation.

The record indicates that Yellow Springs is fully committed to developing a sports program for its female athletes. Not a shred of evidence suggests that Yellow Springs would use a ruling permitting mixed sex teams to cut back on its program for female athletes....

I would hold that the defendants have not demonstrated that the OHSAA rule is substantially related to either proffered government objective. Therefore, the two female basketball players were entitled under the equal protection clause to play on the "male" interscholastic basketball team in November, 1974, when Morgan Middle School did not have a female interscholastic basketball team. The OHSAA rule violated the Constitution by prohibiting Yellow Springs from affording these players that opportunity.

Yellow Springs formed a female interscholastic basketball team in January, 1975. Consequently, the question of whether organizing this separate team was an adequate remedy for the constitutional violation arises....

The defendants' justifications for their rule requiring separate teams in contact sports are totally unsupported in the record. Therefore, to reach my conclusion that the "separate but equal" basketball program at Morgan Middle School contravenes the equal protection clause, I only need to find a constitutional harm in offering separate sports programs.

Two district courts have expressed in dicta or assumed the conclusion that "separate but equal" programs are constitutionally sufficient. In *Leffel v. Wisconsin Interscholastic Ass'n, supra*, the district court held that plaintiffs must allege that defendants intentionally imposed different levels of competition on the male and female teams in order to state a claim. In *Hoover v. Meiklejohn, supra*, the district court distinguished *Brown v. Board of Education, supra*, and declared that female athletes would not suffer a stigma by being restricted to separate teams. I decline to follow the reasoning or assumed result of either district court.

In my view, the question is whether or not separate teams will provide female athletes with an equal opportunity to compete in sports. The focus must be placed on the quality of the competitive experience. The indisputable fact is the quality of competition among some male interscholastic teams is higher than among some female interscholastic teams. The two female basketball players at Morgan Middle School decided that they could best develop their skills by playing on the "boys team." By requiring separate male and female teams, the defendants have imposed a lower level of competition upon female athletes. Though many female athletes will gain a very beneficial experience in competing on a separate female team against other female teams, in our case the female athletes will not be sufficiently challenged by the lower level of competition. Top female athletes need to compete on the best interscholastic team in order to achieve their peak performance. When female athletes are denied this opportunity by being restricted to a lower level of competition, equal opportunity is not provided. *See Commonwealth v. Pennsylvania Interscholastic Athletic Ass'n*, 18 Pa.Cmwlth. 45, 334 A.2d 839, 842 (1975) (decided according to Pennsylvania Constitution). The equal protection clause demands that female athletes not be denied the opportunity to play on the best interscholastic team simply because of their sex. An individualized determination of a female athlete's ability is required.

Contrary to *Hoover*, I believe a stigma may attach when qualified female athletes are not allowed to compete on teams with male athletes solely because they are female. The separation could characterize female athletes as less able, less aggressive, and more fragile[,] in a word, inferior to male athletes. This characterization would be the sort of archaic and harmful stereotype which the equal protection clause forbids.

....

Equal participation in sports by female athletes would be a major step in overcoming the outmoded notions of female roles still prevalent in our society. I cannot overlook the impact of education and athletics as "a principal instrument in awakening the child to cultural values, in preparing him (or her) for later professional training, and in helping him (or her) to adjust normally to his (or her) environment." *Id.* at 493. Sex discrimination in sports is debilitating to the individual athlete whose development and career is stunted and to women as a whole who labor under the burden of traditional notions of their role in society.

Therefore, I would hold that restricting the female athletes to a "separate but equal" basketball program at Morgan Middle School transgresses their constitutional right to an equal opportunity to participate in sports. Further, I would hold that defendants have completely failed to demonstrate that the separation or classification required by the OHSAA rule is substantially related to an important government objective.

A. STUDENT CLASSIFICATION BY SEX

IV. *Title IX Regulations*

....

Given my resolution of the constitutional question, it is not necessary to address the question of any conflict arising later in time between the Title IX regulations and the OHSAA rule on contact sports. However, I do concur with the majority's reasoning and conclusion that the mandatory separation required by the OHSAA rule does conflict with the permissive rule stated in the Title IX regulation....

....

---

1. The *Yellow Springs* District Court and Court of Appeals dissents raise and reject two governmental interests that might be asserted in support of the Association rule — an interest in protecting children from injury and an interest in maximizing female athletic opportunities by removing them from competition with males presumed to be more athletically proficient. Are there other significant governmental interests? What about the issue of sexual propriety? Is it outside the sphere of governmental protection? Would the court then prohibit sexually-segregated dressing facilities? If not, then at what point and on what grounds would it draw a line? What of the interests of families who want their children to participate in athletics but have moral objections to the physical intimacies that co-ed contact sports may foster?

2. Is the issue of bodily contact the only difference between basketball and tennis? What is the significance, if any, of the fact that singles tennis is not a sport that requires coordinated team play? Would an objection that a girl's participation in baseball or basketball adversely affects team morale be a valid basis for denying her right to try to make the team?

3. A variety of rulings have issued on the question of female participation in contact sports with males. Many of these are considered in the dissenting opinion. *See Clinton v. Nagy*, 411 F. Supp. 1396 (N.D. Ohio 1974) (court ruled that a twelve-year-old girl showed substantial likelihood of success on merits of her claim that city's regulation which prevented her from playing football did not bear a reasonable relationship to any legitimate state purpose and that the football association should be enjoined from enforcing such regulations in the absence of any evidence that the girl did not possess qualifications and physical ability required of male members to participate in football league or evidence that she was more susceptible to injury than male members of the league): *Commonwealth v. Pennsylvania Interscholastic Athletic Ass'n*, 18 Pa. Commw. 389, 334 A.2d 839 (Pa. Commw. 1975) (a bylaw of the State Interscholastic Athletic Association that would not allow girls to compete or practice against boys in any athletic contest was held unconstitutional); *Darrin v. Gould*, 85 Wash. 2d 859, 450 P.2d 882 (1975) (the court ruled that a school district could not constitutionally deny fully qualified high school students permission to play on high school football teams in interscholastic competition solely on the ground that the students were girls); *Carnes v. Tennessee Secondary Sch. Athletic Ass'n*, 415 F. Supp. 568 (E.D. Tenn 1976) (it was held that an injunction would lie to inhibit enforcement of an athletic association rule prohibiting mixed participation competition in contact sports, including baseball, as to a female student who wished to participate in baseball programs where there was a likelihood that female students would prevail on merits of claim that invalidity of rule and where the denial of a preliminary injunction would result in irreparable harm to this female student whose last opportunity to play high school baseball was drawing to an end); *Hoover v. Meiklejohn*, 430 F. Supp. 164 (D. Colo. 1977) (the court held that a complete denial of any opportunity to play interscholastic soccer was a violation of a female student's right to equal protection; but that the school district had the option to discontinue soccer, fielding separate teams for male and female with substantially equal support and substantially comparable programs, or permitting both sexes to compete on the same team). But see *Cape v. Tennessee Secondary School Athletic Ass'n*, 563 F.2d 793 (6th Cir. 1977), where the court ruled that an athletic association's split-court rules for girls basketball promulgated and enforced by public school officials, which were different by distinct difference in physical characteristics and capabilities between the sexes and therefore did not violate Equal Protection Clause of the Federal Constitution. If it is not unconstitutional for an athletic association to develop different rules for all-girl teams and for all-boys teams based upon differences in physical characteristics, then why is it unconstitutional to prevent them from playing in mixed-team contact sport competition?

4. Consider *Force v. Pierce City R-VI Sch. Dist.*, 570 F. Supp. 1020 (W.D. Mo. 1983). The district court held for plaintiff, a thirteen-year-old girl who wished to play on the high school football team. The court found no substantial relationship between the blanket prohibition against female participation and Title IX, high school activities association rules and regulations, and asserted objectives if maximizing female participation in athletics, maintaining athletic educational programs which are as safe for participants as possible, or administrative ease.

5. Several courts have considered the question of whether separate girls' and boys' teams are truly equal if the girls are required to play by different rules. In *Dodson v. Arkansas Athletic Ass'n*, 468 F. Supp. 394 (E.D. Ark. W.D. 1979), a female junior high school student challenged the constitutionality of the rules for girls' junior and senior high school basketball developed by the Association for statewide use. She argued the rules, which included provisions for "half court" rather than "full court" play, were so lacking in justification and so injurious to girls as to deprive them of the equal protection of the laws. The court agreed, noting: "Those (girls) whose ambition it is to play basketball in college, perhaps even on scholarship, are at a marked disadvantage. College basketball is full-court, for women as well as men. For that matter, almost no one plays half-court anymore. Most Arkansas private schools play full-court for boys and girls. International competition is full-court. Every state except Arkansas, Iowa, Oklahoma, and Tennessee is full-court in secondary school. (Texas was apparently in the process of changing when this case was tried. It seems now to play full-court.) If an Arkansas girl wishes to compete on a college team, she must overcome substantial obstacles. Most of her opposition will have played full-court in high school. The lack of training and conditioning, the psychological barrier of the center line, which she has been schooled not to cross, and, in the case of guards, the lack of shooting experience — all these factors make the Arkansas girl less able to compete. The disadvantage is 'tremendous.' It takes about a year for a half-court girl with talent to adjust to the difference in games. Even the University of Arkansas does most of its recruiting out of state, for just this reason. 'The primary basketball player will be from outside of the state of Arkansas, which will be a disadvantage to those young girls who are in this state going to high school.'" *Id.* at 396-97.

The *Dodson* court rejected as unpersuasive the reasoning advanced by courts in two similar cases: *Jones v. Oklahoma Secondary Sch. Activities Ass'n*, 453 F. Supp. 150 (W.D. Okla. 1977), in which the court held allegations of reduced opportunity to compete in amateur, professional and olympic basketball and of reduced opportunity for a college basketball scholarship did not rise to the level of equal protection deprivations and *Cape v. Tennessee Secondary School Athletic Ass'n*, 563 F.2d 793 (6th Cir. 1977), in which the court held different rules were justified by distinct differences in physical characteristics and capabilities between the sexes.

6. Is it proper to exclude a girl from a boys' team in order to promote the development of girls' athletics so as better to maintain girls' teams for those girls' who cannot compete with the boys? Does this present the problem of grouping people not to promote their own interests, but the interest of others? If so, is that a permissible basis for grouping? If not, what is the problem? Does the problem exist, if we do not begin with boy athletes and girl athletes but just with athletes, of various levels of ability? On the other hand, does the Constitution force a disregard of differences between boy and girl tennis players?

Note that in *Bucha v. Illinois High Sch. Ass'n*, 351 F. Supp. 69 (N.D. Ill. 1972), the court assumed that if girls were allowed to be on boys' teams, boys could no longer be excluded from girls' teams. Is that assumption correct? If so, is the result desirable? If not, how do we resolve the problem? Consider the case of a boy who does not make the boys' tennis team but is better than some of the girls on the girls' team. Can he be precluded from the girls' team? Does the answer depend on whether or not girls are allowed to compete for the boys' team?

To challenge your reactions to the preceding questions, compare a situation in an integrated high school where the varsity basketball team turns out to be made up of players all of one race. Could the school, in order to provide opportunities for the members of the race who did not make the varsity team, provide for a second team made up of only members of such race? Is this similar to separate girls' teams? What of separate teams based on low weight (such as is common in football and crew), where heavier players are excluded? Could a high school provide a special basketball team limited to students under six feet tall who could not make the regular team?

7. Which do you think would better serve athletics for women at all levels: separate teams and leagues, or coeducational teams? What factors need to be considered in answering this? What are the advantages and disadvantages of each alternative? The *Yellow Springs* majority mentions that women's athletics may suffer (and does) in either case, though the dissent feels this may be sheer speculation.

Does the existence of coeducational teams make it more difficult for girls to play sports in school? If so, can this be considered "equal"? Will schools that do not have separate teams have to lower try-out criteria to get equal involvement?

8. Note that *Yellow Springs* represents one of perhaps few cases where a school district sues to allow girls to play on boys' teams.

ISRAEL v. WEST VIRGINIA SECONDARY SCHOOLS ACTIVITIES COMMISSION

Supreme Court of Appeals
182 W. Va. 454, 388 S.E.2d 480 (1989)

MILLER, JUSTICE:

....

[Erin] Israel has a great deal of experience playing baseball. She began playing baseball at the age of six in the local park and recreation league where she learned the basic fundamentals of the game. At the age of nine, Ms. Israel progressed into the Little League system. Her Little League coach testified that Ms. Israel's skills were always above average. He stated that "[s]he was very aggressive, understood the game, its concepts, and its technique." While playing Little League, Ms. Israel was nominated for every all-star team. At the age of thirteen, she became the first female to ever play on a Pony League team in Pleasants County. When Ms. Israel was a freshman at St. Marys High School, and expressed a desire to play on the all-male baseball team, the high school baseball coach told her he had no objections to her playing for him and promised to give her a fair tryout. In February, 1984, Ms. Israel tried out for the all-male high school baseball team. She was prohibited from playing on the team because of a regulation promulgated by the Secondary Schools Activities Commission (SSAC).

The Board of Education of the County of Pleasants (Board) is a member of the SSAC. The SSAC is a nonprofit organization created by W.Va.Code, 18-2-25 (1967), which authorizes county boards of education to delegate their supervisory authority over interscholastic athletic events and band activities to the SSAC. It

A. STUDENT CLASSIFICATION BY SEX

is not disputed that every county board of education in West Virginia has delegated this responsibility and authority to the SSAC. In the exercise of its delegated authority, the SSAC adopted Rule No. 3.9, which provides:

> If a school maintains separate teams in the same or related sports (example: baseball or softball) for girls and boys during the school year, regardless of the sports season, girls may not participate on boys' teams and boys may not participate on girls' teams. However, should a school not maintain separate teams in the same or related sports for boys and girls, then boys and girls may participate on the same team except in contact sports such as football and wrestling.

Shortly after Ms. Israel tried out to play on the baseball team, she was informed by St. Marys' assistant principal that she was ineligible to play on the baseball team because St. Marys had a girls' softball team. The assistant principal explained that if the school allowed Ms. Israel to play baseball, it would be in violation of Rule 3.9 and would be barred from playing in state tournaments. After numerous futile efforts to have the rule changed through the internal mechanisms provided by the SSAC, Ms. Israel filed a complaint with the Human Rights Commission (Commission).

The Commission issued Ms. Israel a right-to-sue letter, and she filed this action against the SSAC and the Board on April 18, 1986, in the Circuit Court of Pleasants County. The circuit court exonerated the Board, finding that it had made a good-faith effort to have the SSAC change the rule and that if the Board had ignored Rule 3.9, it would have been subject to severe sanctions by the SSAC. Ms. Israel does not appeal this ruling. She does appeal the circuit court's decision that the SSAC rule was valid.

I

Mootness

Initially, the SSAC argues that because Ms. Israel has graduated from high school, her claims for injunctive and declaratory relief are now moot....

However, we, along with most courts, have tempered the inflexibility of mootness jurisprudence in recent years....

... [F]irst, we take note that West Virginia's climate and early-June graduation combine to make the spring high school baseball season a brief affair. It is quite unlikely, if not impossible, that a fully litigated case on this issue could reach us before becoming "moot." That the issue is capable of repetition is self-evident. Moreover, deciding the validity of SSAC Rule 3.9 will have sufficient collateral consequences that our decision on the issue will not be a vain exercise. Finally, this question "undisputably involves a most vital public function — education of our youth. Because it is foreseeable that it will arise again, we find the question remains justiciable for future guidance." *White by White v. Linkinoggor*, 176 W.Va. 410, 412, 344 S.E.2d 633, 635 (1986). (Citations omitted).

II

Equal Protection

Equal protection of the law is implicated when a classification treats similarly situated persons in a disadvantageous manner. *Reed v. Reed*, 404 U.S. 71, 75 (1971). The claimed discrimination must be a product of state action[4] as distinguished from a purely private activity. *See Burton v. Wilmington Parking Auth.*, 365 U.S. 715 (1961).

A

Fourteenth Amendment Equal Protection

....

Under the United States Constitution, a gender-based discrimination is subject to a level of scrutiny somewhere between the traditional equal protection analysis and the highest level of scrutiny utilized for suspect classes. The intermediate level of scrutiny as applied to gender-based discrimination was stated in *Craig v. Boren*, 429 U.S. 190, 197 (1976): "[C]lassifications by gender must serve important governmental objectives and must be substantially related to achievement of those objectives" in order to withstand an equal protection challenge.

Under the middle-tier analysis for gender-based discrimination claims, courts have recognized that it is constitutionally permissible under certain circumstances for public schools to maintain separate sports teams for males and females so long as they are substantially equivalent. This result has been justified by one or more of the following reasons: (1) there are physical and psychological differences between males and females; (2) the maintenance of separate teams promotes athletic opportunities for women; and, as a corollary to (2), (3) if there were not separate teams, men might dominate in certain sports....

While courts have recognized the concept of substantial equivalency in the area of interscholastic sports, this does not mean that mere superficial equivalency will be found constitutional under equal protection principles....

From the record in this case, we find that the games of baseball and softball are not substantially equivalent. There is, of course, a superficial similarity between the games because both utilize a similar format. However, when the rules are analyzed, there is a substantial disparity in the equipment used and in the skill level required. The difference begins with the size of the ball and its delivery, and differences continue throughout. The softball is larger and must be thrown underhand, which forecloses the different types of pitching that can be accomplished in the overhand throw of a baseball.

---

[4]Every court that has considered the question whether associations like the SSAC are state actors have found that those organizations are so intertwined with the state that their acts constitute state action....

A. STUDENT CLASSIFICATION BY SEX

There are ten players on the softball team and nine on a baseball team. The distance between the bases in softball is sixty feet, while in baseball it is ninety feet. The pitcher's mound is elevated in baseball and is not in softball. The distance from the pitcher's mound to home plate is sixty feet in baseball and only forty feet in softball. In baseball, a bat of forty-two inches is permitted, while in softball the maximum length is thirty-four inches.

Moreover, the skill level is much more demanding in baseball because the game is played at a more vigorous pace. There are more intangible rewards available if one can make the baseball team. For a skilled player, such as the record demonstrates Ms. Israel to be, it would be deeply frustrating to be told she could not try out for the baseball team, not because she did not possess the necessary skills, but only because she was female. The entire thrust of the equal protection doctrine is to avoid this type of artificial distinction based solely on gender.

We agree with the SSAC that by providing a softball team for females, it was promoting more athletic opportunities for females. However, this purpose does not satisfy the equal protection mandate requiring substantial equivalency. We do not believe that by permitting females to try out for the boys' baseball team, a mass exodus from the girls' softball team will result. There are obvious practical considerations that will forestall such a result. Gender does not provide an automatic admission to play on a boys' baseball team. The team is selected from those who apply and possess the requisite skill to make the team. What we deal with in this case is an opportunity to have a chance to try out for the team. Aside from the baseball-softball dichotomy, other athletic events ordinarily operate on the same rules such that the substantial equivalency issue would be unlikely to arise.

B

State Equal Protection

. . . .

... [W]e adopt the analysis used by the United States Supreme Court and other state courts. We therefore hold that a gender-based classification challenged as denying equal protection under Article III, Section 10 of our constitution can be upheld only if the classification serves an important governmental objective and is substantially related to the achievement of that objective.... It is apparent that the two tests are substantially equivalent. For this reason, we do not view the new gender-based equal protection rule to provide any less protection.

We have previously discussed in Section II(A), *supra*, the equal protection standard under the federal constitution and found the SSAC rule to be unconstitutional. For these same reasons, Rule 3.9 also violates our state equal protection constitutional standard.

III

The West Virginia Human Rights Act

....

B

Interscholastic Athletics

This is the first occasion that we have had to consider admission to tryout for an athletic team under our Human Rights Act. There are no applicable regulations. Elsewhere courts have referred to their state human rights acts, but have decided the issue on constitutional equal protection or equal rights grounds. *See Petrie v. Illinois High School Ass'n*, 75 Ill.App.3d 980, 31 Ill.Dec. 653, 394 N.E.2d 855 (1979); *Darrin v. Gould*, 85 Wash.2d 859, 540 P.2d 882 (1975).

....

We have in Part II(A), *supra*, analyzed and applied equal protection principles and found that the regulation, as it relates to the games of baseball and softball, fails to meet the substantially equivalent standard. Since this same standard applies under our Human Rights Act, we need not repeat the analysis here.

....

Reversed and remanded.

---

1. The *Israel* court made no mention of whether baseball is considered a "contact sport" in West Virginia, as the *Yellow Springs* court did with respect to baseball in Ohio. *Yellow Springs v. OHSAA*, 647 F.2d 651, 654 (6th Cir. 1981). OHSAA Rule I, § 2, held, thus, that school baseball teams would not be coeducational. The West Virginia Supreme Court in *Israel* did not consider Title IX at all, or its regulation 86.41(b) which permits separate teams for contact sports. Why? Is SSAC not receiving federal funds? Did this court measure the defendant's policies against the Fourteenth Amendment only? Would an analysis under Title IX change the result here?

See also Leffel v. Wisconsin Interscholastic Athletic Ass'n, 444 F. Supp. 1117, 1120-21 (E.D. Wis. 1978). In *Leffel*, the court held unconstitutional a school athletic association rule prohibiting coeducational teams in high school. Since the high school did not have separate female teams for baseball and tennis, females were allowed to compete for positions on the currently all-male varsity teams. This holding extends to contact sports, as well. The court in *Leffel* also chose not to apply Title IX, declining to address the defendant's argument that Title IX permits different treatment of boys and girls with respect to contact sports. The court opted to decide the case under the Fourteenth Amendment.

2. Regulation 86.41(b) permits separate teams for members of each sex where selection for such teams is based on competitive skills or the activity involved is a contact sport. What is the intention of this regulation? Are there any women's "contact" sports that do not have a direct male counterpart?

Should baseball be considered a "contact" sport? Or has it been given this designation simply because it is a traditionally male sport?

3. The Ohio High School Athletics Association, as its name implies, applies to school sports teams throughout the state of Ohio, as it did in *Yellow Springs*. What about the West Virginia Secondary Schools Activities Commission? Is the West Virginia Commission applicable to activities other than sports — for example, men's and women's glee clubs?

For an example at the college level, *see Iron Arrow Honor Society v. Heckler*, 464 U.S. 67 (1983). An all-male honorary organization brought action challenging a regulation which would ban its group from campus. Should groups like the Iron Arrow Honor Society be compelled to admit women?

3. REMEDIES

FRANKLIN v. GWINNETT COUNTY PUBLIC SCHOOLS

Supreme Court of the United States
112 S. Ct. 1028 (1992)

....

JUSTICE WHITE delivered the opinion of the Court:

This case presents the question whether the implied right of action under Title IX of the Education Amendments of 1972, 20 U.S.C. §§ 1681-88 (Title IX),[1] which this Court recognized in *Cannon v. University of Chicago*, 441 U.S. 677 (1979), supports a claim for monetary damages.

I

Petitioner Christine Franklin was a student at North Gwinnett High School in Gwinnett County, Georgia, between September 1985 and August 1989. Respondent Gwinnett County School District operates the high school and receives federal funds. According to the complaint filed on December 29, 1988 in the United States District Court for the Northern District of Georgia, Franklin was subjected to continual sexual harassment beginning in the autumn of her tenth grade year (1986).... Among other allegations, Franklin avers that [Andrew] Hill engaged her in sexually-oriented conversations in which he asked about her sexual experiences with her boyfriend and whether she would consider having sexual intercourse with an older man, that Hill forcibly kissed her on the mouth in the school parking lot, that he telephoned her at her home and asked if she would meet him socially, and that, on three occasions in her junior year,

---

[1] This statute provides in pertinent part that "No person in the United States shall, on the basis of sex, be excluded from participation in, be denied the benefits of, or be subjected to discrimination under any education program or activity receiving Federal financial assistance." 20 U.S.C. § 1681(a).

Hill interrupted a class, requested that the teacher excuse Franklin, and took her to a private office where he subjected her to coercive intercourse. The complaint further alleges that though they became aware of and investigated Hill's sexual harassment of Franklin and other female students, teachers and administrators took no action to halt it and discouraged Franklin from pressing charges against Hill. On April 14, 1988, Hill resigned on the condition that all matters pending against him be dropped. The school thereupon closed its investigation.

In this action, the District Court dismissed the complaint on the ground that Title IX does not authorize an award of damages. The Court of Appeals affirmed. *Franklin v. Gwinnett Cty. Public Schools*, 911 F.2d 617 (CA11 1990)....

....

II

In *Cannon v. University of Chicago*, 441 U.S. 677 (1979), the Court held that Title IX is enforceable through an implied right of action. We have no occasion here to reconsider that decision. Rather, in this case we must decide what remedies are available in a suit brought pursuant to this implied right. As we have often stated, the question of what remedies are available under a statute that provides a private right of action is "analytically distinct" from the issue of whether such a right exists in the first place. *Davis v. Passman*, 442 U.S. 228, 239 (1979). Thus, although we examine the text and history of a statute to determine whether Congress intended to create a right of action, *Touche Ross & Co. v. Redington*, 442 U.S. 560, 575-76 (1979), we presume the availability of all appropriate remedies unless Congress has expressly indicated otherwise. *Davis, supra*, 442 U.S. at 246-47. This principle has deep roots in our jurisprudence.

A

"[W]here legal rights have been invaded, and a federal statute provides for a general right to sue for such invasion, federal courts may use any available remedy to make good the wrong done." *Bell v. Hood*, 327 U.S. 678, 684 (1946). The Court explained this longstanding rule as jurisdictional, and upheld the exercise of the federal courts' power to award appropriate relief so long as a cause of action existed under the Constitution or laws of the United States. *Ibid*.

....

That a statute does not authorize the remedy at issue "in so many words is no more significant than the fact that it does not in terms authorize execution to issue on a judgment." ...

The United States contends that the traditional presumption in favor of all appropriate relief was abandoned by the Court in *Davis v. Passman*, 442 U.S. 228 (1979), and that the *Bell v. Hood* rule was limited to actions claiming constitutional violations. The United States quotes language in Davis to the effect that "the question of who may enforce a statutory right is fundamentally different from the question of who may enforce a right that is protected by the Constitution." *Davis*, 442 U.S. at 241. The Government's position, however, mirrors the very misunderstanding over the difference between a cause of action and the relief afforded under it that sparked the confusion we attempted to clarify in *Davis*. Whether Congress may limit the class of persons who have a right of action under Title IX is irrelevant to the issue in this lawsuit. To reiterate, "the question whether a litigant has a 'cause of action' is analytically distinct and prior to the question of what relief, if any, a litigant may be entitled to receive." *Id.* at 239. *Davis*, therefore, did nothing to interrupt the long line of cases in which the Court has held that if a right of action exists to enforce a federal right and Congress is silent on the question of remedies, a federal court may order any appropriate relief. *See id.* at 247, n. 26 (contrasting *Brown v. General Services Administration*, 425 U.S. 820.

Contrary to arguments by respondents and the United States that *Guardians Assn. v. Civil Service Comm'n of New York City*, 463 U.S. 582 (1983), eroded this traditional presumption, that case in fact supports it. Though the multiple opinions in *Guardians* suggest the difficulty of inferring the common ground among the Justices in that case, a clear majority expressed the view that damages were available under Title VI in an action seeking remedies for an intentional violation, and no Justice challenged the traditional presumption in favor of a federal court's power to award appropriate relief in a cognizable cause of action. *See Guardians*, 463 U.S. at 595.... The correctness of this inference was made clear the following Term when the Court unanimously held that the 1978 amendment to § 504 of the Rehabilitation Act of 1973 — which had expressly incorporated the "remedies, procedures, and rights set forth in title VI" (29 U.S.C. § 794a(a)(2)) — authorizes an award of backpay. In *Darrone*, the Court observed that a majority in *Guardians* had "agreed that retroactive relief is available to private plaintiffs for all discrimination...that is actionable under Title VI." 465 U.S. at 630. The general rule, therefore, is that absent clear direction to the contrary by Congress, the federal courts have the power to award any appropriate relief in a cognizable cause of action brought pursuant to a federal statute.

III

We now address whether Congress intended to limit application of this general principle in the enforcement of Title IX....

... [I]n the years before and after Congress enacted this statute, the Court "follow[ed] a common-law tradition [and] regarded the denial of a remedy as the exception rather than the rule." ... [I]n *Cannon*, the majority upheld an implied right of action in part because in the decade immediately preceding enactment of Title IX in 1972, this Court had found implied rights of action in six cases.... Wholly apart from the wisdom of the *Cannon* holding, therefore, the same contextual approach used to justify an implied right of action more than amply demonstrates the lack of any legislative intent to abandon the traditional presumption in favor of all available remedies.

In the years after the announcement of *Cannon*, on the other hand, a more traditional method of statutory analysis is possible, because Congress was legislating with full cognizance of that decision. Our reading of the two amendments to Title IX enacted after *Cannon* leads us to conclude that Congress did not intend to limit the remedies available in a suit brought under Title IX. In the Civil Rights Remedies Equalization Amendment of 1986, 42 U.S.C. § 2000d-7, Congress abrogated the States' Eleventh Amendment immunity under Title IX, Title VI, § 504 of the Rehabilitation Act of 1973, and the Age Discrimination Act of 1975. This statute cannot be read except as a validation of Cannon's holding. A subsection of the 1986 law provides that in a suit against a State, "remedies (including remedies both at law and in equity) are available for such a violation to the same extent as such remedies are available for such a violation in the suit against any public or private entity other than a State." 42 U.S.C. § 2000d-7(a)(2). While it is true that this savings clause says nothing about the nature of those other available remedies, ... absent any contrary indication in the text or history of the statute, we presume Congress enacted this statute with the prevailing traditional rule in mind.

In addition to the Civil Rights Remedies Equalization Amendment of 1986, Congress also enacted the Civil Rights Restoration Act of 1987, Pub.L. 100-259, 102 Stat. 28 (1988). Without in any way altering the existing rights of action and the corresponding remedies permissible under Title IX, Title VI, § 504 of the Rehabilitation Act, and the Age Discrimination Act, Congress broadened the coverage of these antidiscrimination provisions in this legislation. In seeking to correct what it considered to be an unacceptable decision on our part in *Grove City College v. Bell*, 465 U.S. 555 (1984), Congress made no effort to restrict the right of action recognized in Cannon and ratified in the 1986 Act or to alter the traditional presumption in favor of any appropriate relief for violation of a federal right. We cannot say, therefore, that Congress has limited the remedies available to a complainant in a suit brought under Title IX.

IV

Respondents and the United States nevertheless suggest three reasons why we should not apply the traditional presumption in favor of appropriate relief in this case.

A

First, respondents argue that an award of damages violates separation of powers principles because it unduly expands the federal courts' power into a sphere properly reserved to the Executive and Legislative Branches. In making this argument, respondents misconceive the difference between a cause of action and a remedy. Unlike the finding of a cause of action, which authorizes a court to hear a case or controversy, the discretion to award appropriate relief involves no such increase in judicial power. *See generally* Note, *Federal Jurisdiction in Suits for Damages Under Statutes Not Affording Such Remedy*, 48 Colum.L.Rev. 1090, 1094-1095 (1948). Federal courts cannot reach out to award remedies when the Constitution or laws of the United States do not support a cause of action. Indeed, properly understood, respondents' position invites us to abdicate our historic judicial authority to award appropriate relief in cases brought in our court system. It is well to recall that such authority historically has been thought necessary to provide an important safeguard against abuses of legislative and executive power, *see Kendall v. United States*, 37 U.S. (12 Pet.) 524 (1838), as well as to insure an independent judiciary. *See generally* Katz, *The Jurisprudence of Remedies: Constitutional Legality and the Law of Torts in Bell v. Hood*, 117 U.Pa.L.Rev. 1, 16-17 (1968). Moreover, selective abdication of the sort advocated here would harm separation of powers principles in another way, by giving judges the power to render inutile causes of action authorized by Congress through a decision that no remedy is available.

B

Next, ...respondents and the United States contend that the normal presumption in favor of all appropriate remedies should not apply because Title IX was enacted pursuant to Congress's Spending Clause power. In *Pennhurst State School and Hospital v. Halderman*, 451 U.S. 1, 28-29 (1981), the Court observed that remedies were limited under such Spending Clause statutes when the alleged violation was unintentional. Respondents and the United States maintain that this presumption should apply equally to intentional violations. We disagree. The point of not permitting monetary damages for an unintentional violation is that the receiving entity of federal funds lacks notice that it will be liable for a monetary award. *See id.* at 17. This notice problem does not arise in a case such as this, in which intentional discrimination is alleged. Unquestionably, Title IX placed on the Gwinnett County Schools the duty not to discriminate on the basis of sex, and "when a supervisor sexually harasses a subordinate because of the subordinate's sex, that supervisor 'discriminate[s]' on the basis of sex." *Meritor Savings Bank, FSB v. Vinson*, 477 U.S. 57, 64 (1986). We believe the same rule should apply when a teacher sexually harasses and abuses a student. Congress surely did not intend for federal monies to be expended to support the intentional actions it sought by statute to proscribe....

C

Finally, the United States asserts that the remedies permissible under Title IX should nevertheless be limited to backpay and prospective relief. In addition to diverging from our traditional approach to deciding what remedies are available for violation of a federal right, this position conflicts with sound logic. First, both remedies are equitable in nature, and it is axiomatic that a court should determine the adequacy of a remedy in law before resorting to equitable relief. Under the ordinary convention, the proper inquiry would be whether monetary damages provided an adequate remedy, and if not, whether equitable relief would be appropriate. *Whitehead v. Shattuck*, 138 U.S. 146 (1891). Moreover, in this case the equitable remedies suggested by respondent and the Federal Government are clearly inadequate. Backpay does nothing for petitioner, because she was a student when the alleged discrimination occurred. Similarly, because Hill — the person she claims subjected her to sexual harassment — no longer teaches at the school and she herself no longer attends a school in the Gwinnett system, prospective relief accords her no remedy at all. The government's answer that administrative action helps other similarly-situated students in effect acknowledges that its approach would leave petitioner remediless.

V

In sum, we conclude that a damages remedy is available for an action brought to enforce Title IX. The judgment of the Court of Appeals, therefore, is reversed and the case is remanded for further proceedings consistent with this opinion.

So ordered.

JUSTICE SCALIA, with whom THE CHIEF JUSTICE and JUSTICE THOMAS join, concurring in the judgment:

The substantive right at issue here is one that Congress did not expressly create, but that this Court found to be "implied." *See Cannon v. University of Chicago*, 441 U.S. 677 (1979). Quite obviously, the search for what was Congress's remedial intent as to a right whose very existence Congress did not expressly acknowledge is unlikely to succeed....

. . . .

In my view, when rights of action are judicially "implied," categorical limitations upon their remedial scope may be judicially implied as well. *Cf. Cort v. Ash*, 422 U.S. 66, 84-85, 26. Although we have abandoned the expansive rights-creating approach exemplified by *Cannon, see Touche Ross & Co. v. Redington*, 442 U.S. 560, 575-76 (1979); *Transamerica Mortgage Advisors, Inc. v. Lewis*, 444 U.S. 11, 18, 23-24 (1979) — and perhaps ought to abandon the notion of implied causes of action entirely, *see Thompson v. Thompson*, 484 U.S. 174, 191 (1988) (SCALIA, J., concurring in judgment) — causes of action that came into existence under the ancien regime should be limited by the same logic that gave them birth. To require, with respect to a right that is not consciously and intentionally created, that any limitation of remedies must be express, is to provide, in effect, that the most questionable of private rights will also be the most expansively remediable. As the United States puts it, "[w]hatever the merits of 'implying' rights of action may be, there is no justification for treating [congressional] silence as the equivalent of the broadest imaginable grant of remedial authority."

I nonetheless agree with the Court's disposition of this case. Because of legislation enacted subsequent to *Cannon*, it is too late in the day to address whether a judicially implied exclusion of damages under Title IX would be appropriate. The Civil Rights Remedies Equalization Amendment of 1986, 42 U.S.C. § 2000d-7(a)(2), must be read, in my view, not only "as a validation of Cannon's holding," *ante*, at 1036, but also as an implicit acknowledgment that damages are available.... I therefore concur in the judgment.

---

1. The unanimous decision in *Franklin* has the potential for great impact upon cases of gender discrimination, particularly those involving Title IX, 20 U.S.C. Sec. 1687 (1988) violations. The Supreme Court indicated in its ruling that two congressional enactments following its holding in *Cannon v. University of Chicago*, the Civil Rights Remedies Equalization Amendment of 1986, 42 U.S.C. Sec. 2000d-7 (1988) and the Civil Rights Restoration Act, Pub. L. No. 100-259, 102 Stat. 28, demonstrated that Congress intended to provide the full range of remedies to victims of gender discrimination. The said impact is broad, especially with the passage of the Restoration Act, for Title IX applies to all educational programs and activities conducted by recipients of federal funding whether or not the particular program or activity was the center of discrimination. 20 U.S.C. Sec. 1687, note 1687 and note 1688. Moreover, Title IX regulations, 34 C.F.R. Sec. 106 *et seq.* (1988) prohibit gender discrimination in public schools and colleges and universities in such areas as curricular offerings, Sec. 106.46; extracurricular offerings, *Id.*; athletics, Sec. 106.41; health benefits, Sec. 106.39; employment, Secs. 106.51-106.61; testing, Sec. 106.53; and financial aid, Sec. 106.37. There is also prohibition of discrimination based on pregnancy and family or marital status where students would be treated differently based on gender, Sec. 106.40.

2. In the area of intercollegiate athletics, *Franklin* is already playing an important role in Title IX litigation. *See, e.g., Roberts v. Colorado State Univ.*, 998 F.2d 824 (10th Cir. 1993) (women's softball team reinstated as its discontinuance violated Title IX and *Franklin*'s private cause of action against gender discrimination); *Cohen v. Brown Univ.*, 991 F.2d 888 (1st Cir. 1993) (restoration of women's gymnastics and volleyball teams to full varsity status based on a violation of Title IX and *Franklin*); *Favia v. Indiana Univ. of Pa.*, 812 F. Supp. 578 (W.D. Pa. 1993) (restoration of women's gymnastics and field hockey teams based on a violation of Title IX and *Franklin*).

3. *Franklin* established relief for federal statutes other than Title IX because civil rights laws are interpreted consistently and are modeled upon one another. Also, the Court in this case specifically cited certain other statutes that were collectively affected by the Civil Rights Remedies Equalization Act. *Franklin*, at 1036. This means that *Franklin* could be used as a foundation for a damages remedy for Title VI of the Civil Rights Act of 1964, 42 U.S.C. Sec. 2000d (1988), prohibiting discrimination based on race and national origin; Section 504 of the Rehabilitation Act of 1973, 29 U.S.C. Sec. 794 (1988) (prohibiting discrimination based on handicap; and the Age Discrimination Act, 42 U.S.C.

Sec. 6101 (1988 and Supp. III 1991). In fact, the case has been relied on in suits involving violations of Section 504. *See, e.g., McGregor v. Louisiana State Univ. Bd. of Supvrs.*, 1992 WL 189489 (E.D. La.); *Doe v. District of Columbia*, 796 F. Supp. 559 (D.D.C. 1992) and *Tanberg v. Weld County Sheriff*, 787 F. Supp. 970 (D. Colo. 1992).

4. The *Franklin* Court's reading of Title IX also has the potential for employment related gender discrimination in that it offers advantages not found in Title VII, 42 U.S.C. Sec. 2000e *et seq.*, (1972 and Supp. III 1991). In Title VII the plaintiff has a duty to first exhaust administrative remedies; no such requirement exists with Title IX. Also, Title VII, under the Civil Rights Act of 1991, sets a sliding scale cap, based on the number of employees of the defendant, on the amount of damages to be collected in a gender suit, *Equal Employment Opportunity Commission Decision No. 915.002*, July 14, 1992, (1992 WL 189089) at 3. Title IX does not have a damage limit. This could cause movement from Title VII to Title IX in gender employment discrimination that occurs in the education context.

5. *Franklin* applies to Title IX violations that are intentional. *Franklin*, 112 S. Ct. at 1035. This does not mean that monetary damages will accrue in each case, however. In fact, Title IX is quite clear that enforcement action by a federal agency cannot take place until after notice of a violation is given and a determination is made that compliance cannot be accomplished voluntarily. *See* 20 U.S.C. Sec. 1687 (1988). But if intent is required, will education institutions be able to defend on an absence of notice? Couldn't it be argued that after years of discrimination against female athletic programs that universities had not only constructive notice, but actual notice? Consider, *e.g.*, the 1992 gender equity study of the National Collegiate Athletic Association where women were found to represent over 50% of the college age population, but totaled less then one-third of those in athletics. The study also found that over time women athletics gained only 30% of the athletic scholarships and 20% of the total university funds supporting athletic programs. In addition, many coaches of women's teams are men, women coaches earn far less than their male counterparts, and women are more likely than men to hold part-time coaching positions. *See* NCAA Gender-Equity Study, The NCAA (1992).

6. What of violations of gender discrimination under Title IX are unintentional? Should educational institutions still be held to a damages remedy? In fact, the *Franklin* Court did not address the availability of damages in such cases and, therefore, the application of Title IX and *Franklin* here remains unsettled. Note that at least one lower court has found Title IX to apply even with discrimination based on result, rather than intent. *See Sharif v. New York State Educ. Dep't*, 709 F. Supp. 345 (S.D.N.Y 1989), in this chapter.

7. The Supreme Court in *Franklin* overturned the Eleventh Circuit which had held that compensatory relief is not available under Title IX. *See Franklin v. Gwinnett County Pub. Schs.*, 911 F.2d 617, 622 (11th Cir. 1990); this of course suggests that the remedy sought by Franklin was limited to compensatory damages. The Supreme Court did not state in its decision what specific damages were available, but assumed "the availability of all appropriate remedies ..." *Franklin*, 112 S. Ct. at 1032, and indicated that a court "could offer any appropriate relief." *Id.,* at 1034. Does the decision provide any standard to aid courts in determining appropriate remedies? Do the court's statements here suggest that punitive damages may be considered appropriate relief in a successful Title IX suit? Punitive damages, an additional sum over and above compensation for demonstrated loss, may be awarded to a plaintiff when defendants engage in acts that are willful, wanton or attached to some violent act. *See* Prosser et al., Torts: Cases and Materials 528-29 (8th ed. 1988). Note, therefore, that an award of punitive damages does not even need to meet the "intent" test outlined in *Franklin*; "extremely reckless" acts are often enough to satisfy such relief. Could it be argued that the sexual acts committed by the coach-teacher in *Franklin* were willful, wanton and violent? Could it also be argued that because the school district had notice of these acts and discouraged the student from pressing charges that they were wanton or reckless and, in fact, ratified the teacher's actions? Would this be enough to subject schools in such cases to these kinds of damages? What of a case of intercollegiate athletics where female students allege that the elimination of certain sports was intentionally done to deter female participation and, hence, caused intentional infliction of emotional distress? Could institutional liability be found if school officials have no notice of offending conduct by school personnel? What if the school had no direct information about civil rights violations, but was exposed to rumor or innuendo?

B. STUDENT CLASSIFICATION BY AGE

ARKANSAS ACTIVITIES ASSOCIATION v. MEYER

Supreme Court of Arkansas
805 S.W.2d 58, 304 Ark. 718 (1991)

BROWN, JUSTICE:

This dispute involves the power of the courts to interfere with the rules of a voluntary regulatory agency, the Arkansas Activities Association ("AAA"), which is established and supported by local junior and senior high school systems. More specifically, the case involves the AAA's appeal from an adverse chancery court decision denying the application of its age rule to appellee Shane William Meyer and enjoining the AAA from prohibiting Meyer's participation in interscholastic activities including athletics.

The facts are not contested by the parties. In September of 1980 the AAA, which has 495 public and private junior and senior high schools as its members, adopted an age rule for interscholastic events:

> B. Senior High. A senior high student whose 19th birthday is on or before October 1, may not participate in an interscholastic event.

NOTE: Grandfather Clause. This rule may be waived for a senior high school student who is ineligible by the above rule due to events that occurred before adoption (September 1980). He may participate until the day he is 20 years old, if normal progression has occurred since 1980 and upon approval of the AAA Executive Director.

Meyer is a student at Highland High School, which is located in Ash Flat. Highland High is an AAA member. Meyer was born on July 10, 1971, and was age nineteen at the beginning of his senior year and as of October 1, 1990, which disqualified him from interscholastic events under the AAA age rule. Meyer runs afoul of the age rule because although he entered public schools before September 1980 (the operative date for the grandfather clause under the rule), he repeated the fifth grade in academic year 1983-84. This repetition was not the decision of the school administration but was instead at his mother's request. Meyer's mother was not aware of the AAA age rule in 1983, and the AAA took no steps to inform parents of elementary students of the rule at that time.

Meyer was notified about the age rule during his junior year in high school, and on February 28, 1990, he petitioned the AAA Executive Director, Lamar Cole, for a hardship exception to the rule. The petition was denied, and the AAA Executive Committee affirmed that decision on March 15, 1990. Meyer then filed a petition for injunctive relief against the AAA in chancery court. After a full hearing on his petition, the chancellor, on July 2, 1990, permanently enjoined the AAA from halting Meyer's participation in interscholastic activities for the 1990-91 school year and further permanently enjoined the AAA from requiring the school to forfeit any AAA regulated activity in which Meyer participated. In a letter opinion which accompanied the chancellor's order, he found that the age rule itself was rational based on safety considerations but then went on to make additional findings relative to the grandfather clause:

> ....
>
> b. It does not appear to this court that the AAA was rational in making an exception to the rule grandfathering students in who would otherwise be ineligible after the adoption date of said rule.
> c. Since the rule was adopted to protect students and an exception was made to the rule grandfathering students in until their 20th birthday regardless of their size, mental status, or athletic ability as long as normal school progression had occurred, each case should be determined with the safety and fairness of other students in mind.
> d. Shane Meyer was held back in the 5th grade by his parents, not the school, therefore, he should have passed on to the 6th grade.
> e. Shane Meyer has progressed normally since being involved in activities under the AAA rules and regulations.
> f. Shane Meyer's mental or physical ability does not present an unfair or unsafe condition to other students should he be permitted to participate under the grandfather exception.

B. STUDENT CLASSIFICATION BY AGE

We disagree with the chancery court's analysis of the grandfather clause, and we reverse the chancellor's order and vacate the permanent injunction.

The AAA first raises the argument that the courts are powerless to interfere in the affairs of voluntary organizations....

Appellee Meyer, nonetheless, contested the grandfather clause of the AAA age rule on a variety of constitutional grounds including arbitrariness and capriciousness, denial of due process, deprivation of pursuit of happiness and enjoyment of life, and violation of equal protection of the laws. The constitutional issues raised easily place the matter within the narrow criteria where judicial review is appropriate.

A threshold question is whether the allegations of constitutional deprivation involve state action. Here, we are concerned with a voluntary association; while it is not a state agency, the association has significant contacts and relationships with the public schools of this state. For example, the AAA membership consists of the superintendents and principals of the 495 member schools who are responsible for adopting the rules which regulate interscholastic activities at those schools. Under such circumstances state action has been found to exist.... We hold that it exists in this case due to the close and symbiotic relationship between the AAA and the Arkansas public school system.

The AAA argues that Meyer's right to participate in interscholastic events is more a privilege than a constitutional right. While that may be, the distinction between rights and privileges, where governmental benefits are concerned, has been largely discarded by the United States Supreme Court. *See Graham v. Richardson*, 403 U.S. 365 (1971). Be that as it may, there is clearly no constitutional right to play sports or engage in other school activities.... It legitimately falls within the purview of a voluntary association like the AAA, acting in conjunction with the schools, to regulate such activities. However, to the extent that rules are adopted by the AAA they must satisfy constitutional principles as applied and may not impinge on due process or equal protection rights. A student has the right to have his or her request to participate in student athletics reviewed under rules that are constitutional. Here, Meyer's assertion is the AAA's grandfather clause fails to pass constitutional muster as applied to his situation.

The crux of this case, then, is whether a rational basis exists for the grandfather clause under the age rule. Neither party contests the age rule itself or the policy rationale supporting the rule. But Meyer contends the grandfather clause unfairly discriminates against him and in favor of nineteen-year-olds who did normally progress through school after September 1980, and, therefore, it violates the Equal Protection Clause of the state and federal constitutions. Both Meyer and the AAA agree that the test for determining whether the classification between students normally progressing and those who do not under the grandfather exception is whether the exception bears a rational relationship to a legitimate state interest.

In a situation bearing striking similarities to the present case, the Fifth Circuit Court of Appeals refused to find that a distinction drawn by a high school athletic association between repeating a grade voluntarily and a mandatory repetition due to academic failure was either inherently suspect or an encroachment of a fundamental right under the Equal Protection Clause. *Mitchell v. Louisiana High School Ass'n*, 430 F.2d 1155 (5th Cir. 1970). There, the issue was whether three students who had voluntarily repeated a grade lost their fourth year of eligibility to play sports in high school. The association rule was clear in saying that the three students who voluntarily repeated did lose their eligibility. But the rule also provided that it did not apply to students repeating a grade due to academic failure.

The three students contested the rule, specifically the classification between academic failure and voluntary repetition. The court found that the classification was grounded in and related to a legitimate state interest which was "to minimize the hazard of having usual high school athletes competing with older, more skilled players." 430 F.2d at 1158. More specifically, the court said that the repetition of a grade due to academic failure was less likely to be influenced by athletic considerations than voluntary repetition.

The Mitchell case offers substantial guidance in this case. Here, too, there is a legitimate state interest sustaining the AAA rule — the safety of the younger players. There is, further, a legitimate interest in permitting students already in the school system as of September 1980 to play until age twenty, if they normally progress from grade to grade. Failure to progress normally due to a voluntary repetition of a grade could be used as a subterfuge to enable older students to engage in activities like sports during their senior year.

It is true that the grandfather clause allows students already in school as of September 1980 to play sports until age twenty, if they satisfy the "normal progression" requirement. This seemingly undermines the purpose of the rule in that it permits nineteen-year-olds to engage in interscholastic sports with all of the implied safety risks. At the same time the grandfather exception is grounded in legitimate public policy. To have changed the rules in September 1980 and thereby denied to existing students who started school late the right to engage in certain school activities would have been a deprivation of their rights without notice. The rights of such existing students who were older than their classmates as of September 1980 must also be protected against any arbitrary severance of their rights occasioned by the new rule.

We have continuously upheld the legitimacy of grandfather clauses and the policy behind them. *See, e.g., Kittler v. State*, 304 Ark. 344, 802 S.W.2d 925 (1991). Legislators have the right to make distinctions in their enactments between existing rights and conditions and those that may come into existence in the future, when there is a rational basis for that distinction. *Valley Bank v. State*, 115 N.H. 151, 335 A.2d 652 (1975). We hold that a rational relationship to a legitimate state interest exists for the grandfather clause in the AAA age rule, that is, that existing students in September 1980 not be penalized by the

B. STUDENT CLASSIFICATION BY AGE

adoption of a new rule so long as they progress normally through school from that date forward. Meyer, ironically, argues that the grandfather clause is invalid on constitutional grounds. But without the grandfather clause, he has no recourse for a hardship exception, since he was clearly nineteen and ineligible for 1990-91 activities under the rule itself.

The grandfather exception to the AAA age rule is uniformly applied by the association in that all students "grandfathered in" must satisfy the normal progression requirement as of September 1980. Meyer failed to do so and because of that is rendered ineligible. In addition to uniform application the exception has a legitimate reason for its genesis as discussed above. Under these circumstances we find no grounds for a finding of arbitrary or capricious behavior on the part of the AAA.

It is true that Mrs. Meyer was not aware of the AAA age rule in 1983, when she held her son back to repeat the fifth grade, and it is further true that the AAA did not advise parents of elementary students of the age rule at that time. But that information was available to her had she sought it out from the school administration or the AAA. She did not, and this leads to a harsh result for her son. We hold, however, that the lack of notice to Mrs. Meyer in 1983 does not rise to the magnitude of a constitutional deprivation of due process of law under either the state or federal constitutions. *See Mitchell v. Louisiana High School Ass'n, supra* (failure to give notice of an association rule was not a violation of due process under the federal constitution).

Finally, we cannot agree that Meyer normally progressed through school after September 1980, when he repeated the fifth grade in 1983-84. This simply is not normal progression. The fact that he did so at his mother's behest rather than the school's is not a persuasive argument. The safety policy set out in the age rule is clearly jeopardized by a repetition of grades, regardless of the reason for that repetition.

We hold today that the court clearly erred in finding no rational basis for the age rule's grandfather clause and further erred in concluding that Meyer progressed normally through school after September 1980. The permanent injunction is therefore vacated and this case is dismissed.

Reversed.

GLAZE, J., concurs.

---

1. Does the decision in this case, in effect, penalize education-minded parents? The student's mother, not aware of the athletic association rule, voluntarily held her son back in fifth grade, likely due to academics or social maturity and not to athletics. Should such decisions, though not made by the school, be permitted to haunt students and well-intentioned parents?

2. The decision in *Meyer* is not an isolated one. An Alabama court held that a high school student was age-ineligible for football in his senior year as his parents had voluntarily held him back in eighth grade. An athletic association rule stated that "a pupil becomes ineligible when he has attended any junior or senior high school eight semesters after completing the eighth grade or entering the ninth grade.... [W]hen an eighth grade student establishes eligibility for a succeeding year, he shall be classified in the ninth grade." *Alabama High Sch. Athletic Ass'n v. Medders*, 456 So. 2d 284, 285 (Ala. 1982). The rule was promulgated for the purpose of preventing "redshirting" of students. This, in turn, would prevent older and more experienced players from dominating a contact sport and alleviate some pressure on the part of school personnel as regards the health, safety and welfare of students.

But see *Florida High Sch. Activities Ass'n v. Bryant*, 313 So. 2d 57 (Fla. App. 1975), where the court said that a showing of extreme hardship — prior problems as a juvenile delinquent — was enough to waive a four-year athletics eligibility rule. The court stated that the sport of basketball was an important part of the student's life, providing the impetus for general scholastic and social development and rehabilitation.

Could this mean that if the parents in *Meyer* and *Medders* had been less concerned about their children's academic progress and permitted them to develop delinquent behaviors that there could have been a more favorable court ruling?

3. *Meyer* is a case of a student who is age-ineligible for an extracurricular activity. Parents and educators have also had conflict over the placement of a student in the most appropriate grade so as to maximize intellectual potential. This happens most with students who are labeled "gifted" and claim "age discrimination" if not permitted to enter an advanced program or who are prevented by school personnel from skipping a grade. *See, e.g., Ackerman v. Rubin*, 35 Misc. 2d 707, 231 N.Y.S.2d 112 (1962), where a New York state court decided that school personnel and not parents are in the best position to decide if a student is intellectually and socially mature enough to function at a grade level much higher than called for by his chronological age.

4. Consider the following hypothetical:

> The school officials decide that a child should skip sixth grade. He is an exceptionally bright boy, they argue, and for him to take sixth-grade work would be a waste of his and the teacher's time. Indeed, he might cause disciplinary problems by moving only into the sixth grade, for he will be so bored with his studies that he will be very likely to misbehave and to disrupt class. Only by skipping sixth grade and going on to seventh will he attain his full educational development. The boy's parents object. They admit that their son is bright, but they also know that he is socially immature; in their opinion, to put him in the seventh grade would cause him to suffer a serious social maladjustment. They do not want him to be a maladjusted genius even

B. STUDENT CLASSIFICATION BY AGE

if he has the capacity to be one. They are adamant in refusing to let him skip the sixth grade.

How does the parents' view, based on their intimate knowledge of and concern for their son's personality and social development, weigh against the school officials' view, when buttressed by their professional skills and their informed observation of the boy's scholastic ability, performance, and behavior? Would it help to determine whether the problem pertains mostly to the child's out-of-school well-being or mostly to his in-school well-being? Or is the problem so inextricably involved in both aspects of his life that neither is clearly paramount? Should the child's own position on the issue be given any weight?

In considering the role of parents in the age classification situation, note the growing extensive parental involvement in the process of classifying a child as disabled, discussed in Chapter 13.

5. Gifted students face many issues other than age discrimination. For example, in *Bennett v. City Sch. Dist. of New Rochelle*, 114 A.D. 58, 497 N.Y.S.2d 72 (N.Y. App. Div. 1985), parents filed suit to compel the school district to admit their daughter to its gifted program. The district had limited spots for the full-time gifted program and implemented a lottery to determine which students would be admitted. The parents claimed a state statute required admission of all such students who qualified. N.Y. Education Law, Article 90.

The court held that Article 90 was an enabling act, authorizing the New York State Education Department to assist school districts in meeting the educational needs of its gifted population. It further held that the act only requires a school district that receives State aid for the education of gifted students to use those funds for that purpose. *Id.* at 63, 497 N.Y.S.2d at 76.

Plaintiffs' claim was denied. The court found that the district had the discretion to employ a lottery to select the program's full-time participants. The affected student in *Bennett* was offered a spot in the modified, half-day program. The lottery was held to be rationally related to the school district's goal of improving the educational system and was neither arbitrary nor capricious in violation of equal protection. *Id.* at 66-68, 497 N.Y.S.2d at 77-79.

For further discussion of this and related issues, *see* Marquardt and Karnes, *The Courts and Gifted Education*, 50 Educ. L. Rep. 9 (1989) and Zirkel, *The Law Concerning Public Education of Gifted Students*, 34 Educ. L. Rep. 353 (1986).

6. Of course age discrimination against public school students is not limited to those labeled as "gifted," Congress, recognizing that states were unilaterally dismissing or excluding "handicapped" students from schools promulgated the Individuals with Disabilities Education Act (IDEA), 20 U.S.C. Sec. 1400 *et seq.* (1988). IDEA's eligibility requirements have an age provision:

> [A] free appropriate public education will be available for all children with disabilities between the ages ... of three and twenty-one ... except that, with respect to children with disabilities aged three to five and aged eighteen to

twenty-one, inclusive, the requirements of this clause shall not be applied in any State if the application of such requirements would be inconsistent with State law or practice, or the order of any court, respecting public education within the age groups of the state. 20 U.S.C. 1412 (2)(B)....

What if a disabled student argues that her academic problems continue even though she has graduated high school? This was the case in *O'Donniley v. Metropolitan Pub. Schs.*, 1990 WL 183938 (6th Cir. (Tenn.)), where the student alleged that IDEA was violated because the education provided from the time the student entered third grade was inappropriate in that she had failed a number of classes, had to repeat the sixth grade and, in high school, performed very poorly on the ACT. Ultimately, the student did pass the state proficiency test and finished high school with her peers. The Sixth Circuit considered all of these factors as very important to the "Eligibility Clause" of IDEA since education provided for non-disabled students beyond the age of eighteen must also be provided for handicapped students. *Id.* at 4 (citing 20 U.S.C. Sec. 1412 (2)(B)). However, the court also noted that consistent with IDEA, once "a handicapped student appropriately graduates from high school, the obligations of the school board cease." *Id.* at 4.

What, though, if a student has not graduated and state law provides for education beyond the age limits stated in IDEA? In *Board of Educ. v. West Virginia Human Rights Comm'n*, 385 S.E.2d 637 (W. Va. 1989), disabled students argued that they were due an education to age 24 which was in fact consistent with state law. The court agreed, reasoning that states, of course, may not supplant a federal statute; they may, however, exceed it. West Virginia's state regulations explicitly provided education for disabled students beyond the age limits of IDEA, and state law was said to be applicable in this situation.

May states change age limits to eliminate disabled students whom they feel would not benefit from further education? *See Evans v. Tuttle*, 613 N.E.2d 854 (Ind. Ct. App. 1993), where state officials sought to change state law that heretofore had extended education to disabled students to age 19 or 21 depending upon severity of the disability. The state promulgated new rules whereby a "State Conference Committee" would determine whether further education was warranted beyond the age of eighteen based on the student's education needs. The court ruled that such a change would be a violation of IDEA as education of a disabled student is not optional for those school districts receiving federal funds and that school districts cannot unilaterally exclude disabled children of a certain age "on the ground that they are uneducable." *Id.* at 860.

C. STUDENT CLASSIFICATION BY RACE

The Supreme Court has given little specific guidance regarding the issue of racial classification. The historic struggle to remove the stigmatization, prejudice, and lack of opportunity associated with segregation has led the Court to issue

C. STUDENT CLASSIFICATION BY RACE

various integration orders, to be addressed in Chapter 11. These orders have been, in some respects, a mandate to do away with classification based on race.

In the 1970's, concern arose concerning other remedies used by courts and institutions to hasten the integration of minorities into society through preferential treatment plans. These plans generally required racially-based classifications under which minorities were given limited advantages, sometimes to the exclusion of other equally or better qualified individuals outside the recognized minorities.

The question raised, then, was whether classifications based on race were or were not legitimate, and if legitimate, under what circumstances. The Supreme Court has addressed this issue in *Regents of the Univ. of California v. Bakke*.

Bakke, an applicant for admission to the medical school of the University of California at Davis, was rejected in 1973 and 1974. At the time of his applications, Davis had two admission programs through which the entering class of one hundred was selected — the regular program and a special program. Sixteen of the hundred first-year slots were reserved for admittees under the special program, which was open only to members of minority groups found to be economically and/or educationally disadvantaged. In both years special applicants with significantly lower scores than Bakke's were admitted. He alleged that the special admissions program operated to exclude him on the basis of race in violation of the Equal Protection Clause of the Fourteenth Amendment, a provision of the California Constitution, and § 601 of Title VI of the Civil Rights Act of 1964, which provides that no person shall be excluded from participating in any program receiving federal financial assistance because of his race. Davis cross-claimed for a declaration that its special admissions program was lawful. The trial court found that the special program operated as a racial quota, because minority applicants in that program were rated only against one another, and 16 places in the class of 100 were reserved for them. Declaring that petitioner could not take race into account in making admissions decisions, the program was held to violate the Federal and State Constitutions and Title VI. Bakke's admission was not ordered, however, for lack of proof that he would have been admitted but for the special program. The California Supreme Court, applying a strict-scrutiny standard, concluded that the special admissions program was not the least intrusive means of achieving the goals of the admittedly compelling state interests of integrating the medical profession and increasing the number of doctors willing to serve minority patients. Without passing on the state constitutional or federal statutory grounds, that court held that petitioner's special admissions program violated the Equal Protection Clause. Since Davis could not satisfy its burden of demonstrating that Bakke, absent the special program, would not have been admitted, the court ordered his admission to Davis.

Two specific issues were addressed when the case went before the Supreme Court. The broader issue, whether race can be taken into account as a factor in admissions decisions, is discussed in Chapter 11. The narrower issue, the legitimacy of a classification based on race, *i.e.*, of racial quotas per se, was decided by the swing vote of Justice Powell, whose opinion follows.

REGENTS OF THE UNIVERSITY OF CALIFORNIA v. BAKKE

Supreme Court of the United States
438 U.S. 265 (1978)

MR. JUSTICE POWELL announced the judgment of the Court:

....

I

The Medical School of the University of California at Davis opened in 1968 with an entering class of 50 students. In 1971, the size of the entering class was increased to 100 students, a level at which it remains. No admissions program for disadvantaged or minority students existed when the school opened, and the first class contained three Asians but no blacks, no Mexican-Americans, and no American Indians. Over the next two years, the faculty devised a special admissions program to increase the representation of "disadvantaged" students in each medical school class. The special program consisted of a separate admissions system operating in coordination with the regular admissions process.

Under the regular admissions procedure, a candidate could submit his application to the Medical School beginning in July of the year preceding the academic year for which admission was sought.... Because of the large number of applications, the admissions committee screened each one to select candidates for further consideration. Candidates whose overall undergraduate grade point averages fell below 2.5 on a scale of 4.0 were summarily rejected.... About one out of six applicants was invited for a personal interview.... Following the interviews, each candidate was rated on a scale of 1 to 100 by his interviewers and four other members of the admissions committee. The rating embraced the interviewers' summaries, the candidate's overall grade point average, grade point average in science courses, scores on the Medical College Admissions Test (MCAT), letters of recommendation, extracurricular activities, and other biographical data.... The ratings were added together to arrive at each candidate's "benchmark" score. Since five committee members rated each candidate in 1973, a perfect score was a 500; in 1974, six members rated each candidate, so that a perfect score was 600. The full committee then reviewed the file and scores of each applicant and made offers of admission on a "rolling" basis. The chairman was responsible for placing names on the waiting list. They were not placed in strict numerical order; instead, the chairman had discretion to include persons with "special skills."...

The special admissions program operated with a separate committee, a majority of whom were members of minority groups.... On the 1973 application form, candidates were asked to indicate whether they wished to be considered as "economically and/or educationally disadvantaged" applicants; on the 1974 form

C. STUDENT CLASSIFICATION BY RACE

the question was whether they wished to be considered as members of a "minority group," which the Medical School apparently viewed as "Blacks," "Chicanos," "Asians," and "American Indians."... If these questions were answered affirmatively, the application was forwarded to the special admissions committee. No formal definition of "disadvantaged" was ever produced, ... but the chairman of the special committee screened each application to see whether it reflected economic or educational deprivation. Having passed this initial hurdle, the applications then were rated by the special committee in a fashion similar to that used by the general admissions committee, except that special candidates did not have to meet the 2.5 grade point average cutoff applied to regular applicants. About one-fifth of the total number of special applicants were invited for interviews in 1973 and 1974. Following each interview, the special committee assigned each special applicant a benchmark score. The special committee then presented its top choices to the general admissions committee. The latter did not rate or compare the special candidates against the general applicants, ... but could reject recommended special candidates for failure to meet course requirements or other specific deficiencies.... The special committee continued to recommend special applicants until a number prescribed by faculty vote were admitted. While the overall class size was still 50, the prescribed number was 8; in 1973 and 1974, when the class size had doubled to 100, the prescribed number of special admissions also doubled, to 16....

From the year of the increase in class size — 1971 — through 1974, the special program resulted in the admission of 21 black students, 30 Mexican-Americans, and 12 Asians, for a total of 63 minority students. Over the same period, the regular admissions program produced 1 black, 6 Mexican-Americans, and 37 Asians, for a total of 44 minority students. Although disadvantaged whites applied to the special program in large numbers, ... none received an offer of admission through that process. Indeed, in 1974, at least, the special committee explicitly considered only "disadvantaged" special applicants who were members of one of the designated minority groups....

Allan Bakke is a white male who applied to the Davis Medical School in both 1973 and 1974. In both years Bakke's application was considered under the general admissions program, and he received an interview. His 1973 interview was with Dr. Theodore C. West, who considered Bakke "a very desirable applicant to [the] medical school."... Despite a strong benchmark score of 468 out of 500, Bakke was rejected. His application had come late in the year, and no applicants in the general admissions process with scores below 470 were accepted after Bakke's application was completed.... There were four special admissions slots unfilled at that time, however, for which Bakke was not considered. After his 1973 rejection, Bakke wrote to Dr. George H. Lowrey, Associate Dean and Chairman of the Admissions Committee, protesting that the special admissions program operated as a racial and ethnic quota....

Bakke's 1974 application was completed early in the year.... His student interviewer gave him an overall rating of 94, finding him "friendly, well tempered, conscientious and delightful to speak with."... His faculty interviewer was, by coincidence, the same Dr. Lowrey to whom he had written in protest of the special admissions program. Dr. Lowrey found Bakke "rather limited in his approach" to the problems of the medical profession and found disturbing Bakke's "very definite opinions which were based more on his personal viewpoints than upon a study of the total problem."... Dr. Lowrey gave Bakke the lowest of his six ratings, an 86; his total was 549 out of 600.... Again, Bakke's application was rejected. In neither year did the chairman of the admissions committee, Dr. Lowrey, exercise his discretion to place Bakke on the waiting list.... In both years, applicants were admitted under the special program with grade point averages, MCAT scores, and benchmark scores significantly lower than Bakke's.

After the second rejection, Bakke filed the instant suit in the Superior Court of California. He sought mandatory, injunctive, and declaratory relief compelling his admission to the Medical School. He alleged that the Medical School's special admissions program operated to exclude him from the school on the basis of his race, in violation of his rights under the Equal Protection Clause of the Fourteenth Amendment, Art. I, § 21, of the California Constitution, and § 601 of Title VI of the Civil Rights Act of 1964, 78 Stat. 252, 42 U.S.C. § 2000d. The University cross-complained for a declaration that its special admissions program was lawful. The trial court found that the special program operated as a racial quota, because minority applicants in the special program were rated only against one another, ... and 16 places in the class of 100 were reserved for them.... Declaring that the University could not take race into account in making admissions decisions, the trial court held the challenged program violative of the Federal Constitution, the state constitution, and Title VI. The court refused to order Bakke's admission, however, holding that he had failed to carry his burden of proving that he would have been admitted but for the existence of the special program.

Bakke appealed from the portion of the trial court judgment denying him admission, and the University appealed from the decision that its special admissions program was unlawful and the order enjoining it from considering race in the processing of applications. The Supreme Court of California transferred the case directly from the trial court, "because of the importance of the issues involved." The California court accepted the findings of the trial court with respect to the University's program. Because the special admissions program involved a racial classification, the Supreme Court held itself bound to apply strict scrutiny. *Id.* at 49, 553 P.2d at 1162-63. It then turned to the goals the University presented as justifying the special program. Although the court agreed that the goals of integrating the medical profession and increasing the number of physicians willing to serve members of minority groups were compelling state interests, *id.* at 53, 553 P.2d at 1165, it concluded that the special admissions program was not the least intrusive means of achieving those goals. Without passing on the state constitutional or the federal statutory grounds cited in the

C. STUDENT CLASSIFICATION BY RACE

trial court's judgment, the California court held that the Equal Protection Clause of the Fourteenth Amendment required that "no applicant may be rejected because of his race, in favor of another who is less qualified, as measured by standards applied without regard to race." *Id.* at 55, 553 P.2d at 1166.

Turning to Bakke's appeal, the court ruled that since Bakke had established that the University had discriminated against him on the basis of his race, the burden of proof shifted to the University to demonstrate that he would not have been admitted even in the absence of the special admissions program. *Id.* at 63-64, 553 P.2d at 1172. The court analogized Bakke's situation to that of a plaintiff under Title VII of the Civil Rights Act of 1964, 42 U.S.C. §§ 2000e-17 (1970 ed., Supp. V). On this basis, the court initially ordered a remand for the purpose of determining whether, under the newly allocated burden of proof, Bakke would have been admitted to either the 1973 or the 1974 entering class in the absence of the special admissions program. App. A to Application for Stay 48. In its petition for rehearing below, however, the University conceded its inability to carry that burden. App. B to Application for Stay A19-A20. The California court thereupon amended its opinion to direct that the trial court enter judgment ordering Bakke's admission to the Medical School. That order was stayed pending review in this Court. We granted *certiorari* to consider the important constitutional issue.

II

[Section II addresses the applicability of Title VI. For purposes of this case, the Court assumed that the respondent had a private right of action under Title VI. The Court then held that Title VI must be read to proscribe only those racial classifications that would violate the Equal Protection Clause or the Fifth Amendment.]

III

A

Petitioner does not deny that decisions based on race or ethnic origin by faculties and administrations of state universities are reviewable under the Fourteenth Amendment. For his part, respondent does not argue that all racial or ethnic classifications are per se invalid. The parties do disagree as to the level of judicial scrutiny to be applied to the special admissions program. Petitioner argues that the court below erred in applying strict scrutiny, as this inexact term has been applied in our cases. That level of review, petitioner asserts, should be reserved for classifications that disadvantage "discrete and insular minorities." Respondent, on the other hand, contends that the California court correctly rejected the notion that the degree of judicial scrutiny accorded a particular racial or ethnic classification hinges upon membership in a discrete and insular minority and duly recognized that the "rights established [by the Fourteenth Amendment] are personal rights."

En route to this crucial battle over the scope of judicial review, the parties fight a sharp preliminary action over the proper characterization of the special admissions program. Petitioner prefers to view it as establishing a "goal" of minority representation in the Medical School. Respondent, echoing the courts below, labels it a racial quota.

This semantic distinction is beside the point: The special admissions program is undeniably a classification based on race and ethnic background. To the extent that there existed a pool of at least minimally qualified minority applicants to fill the 16 special admissions seats, white applicants could compete only for 84 seats in the entering class, rather than the 100 open to minority applicants. Whether this limitation is described as a quota or a goal, it is a line drawn on the basis of race and ethnic status.

The guarantees of the Fourteenth Amendment extend to all persons. Its language is explicit: "No State shall ... deny to any person within its jurisdiction the equal protection of the laws." It is settled beyond question that the "rights created by the first section of the Fourteenth Amendment are, by its terms, guaranteed to the individual. The rights established are personal rights." The guarantee of equal protection cannot mean one thing when applied to one individual and something else when applied to a person of another color. If both are not accorded the same protection, then it is not equal.

Nevertheless, petitioner argues that the court below erred in applying strict scrutiny to the special admissions program because white males, such as respondent, are not a "discrete and insular minority" requiring extraordinary protection from the majoritarian political process. This rationale, however, has never been invoked in our decisions as a prerequisite to subjecting racial or ethnic distinctions to strict scrutiny. Nor has this Court held that discreteness and insularity constitute necessary preconditions to a holding that a particular classification is invidious. These characteristics may be relevant in deciding whether or not to add new types of classifications to the list of "suspect" categories or whether a particular classification survives close examination. Racial and ethnic classifications, however, are subject to stringent examination without regard to these additional characteristics. We declared as much in the first cases explicitly to recognize racial distinctions as suspect:

> Distinctions between citizens solely because of their ancestry are by their very nature odious to a free people whose institutions are founded upon the doctrine of equality.
>
> [A]ll legal restrictions which curtail the civil rights of a single racial group are immediately suspect. That is not to say that all such restrictions are unconstitutional. It is to say that courts must subject them to the most rigid scrutiny.

The Court has never questioned the validity of those pronouncements. Racial and ethnic distinctions of any sort are inherently suspect and thus call for the most exacting judicial examination.

C. STUDENT CLASSIFICATION BY RACE 229

B

....

... [B]ecause the landmark decisions in this area arose in response to the continued exclusion of Negroes from the mainstream of American society, they could be characterized as involving discrimination by the "majority" white race against the Negro minority. But they need not be read as depending upon that characterization for their results. It suffices to say that "[o]ver the years, this Court has consistently repudiated '[d]istinctions between citizens solely because of their ancestry' as being 'odious to a free people whose institutions are founded upon the doctrine of equality.'" *Loving v. Virginia*, 388 U.S. 1, 11 (1967), quoting *Hirabayashi*, 320 U.S. at 100.

Petitioner urges us to adopt for the first time a more restrictive view of the Equal Protection Clause and hold that discrimination against members of the white "majority" cannot be suspect if its purpose can be characterized as "benign."[34] The clock of our liberties, however, cannot be turned back to 1868. It is far too late to argue that the guarantee of equal protection to all persons permits the recognition of special wards entitled to a degree of protection greater than that accorded others. "The Fourteenth Amendment is not directed solely against discrimination due to a 'two-class theory' — that is, based upon differences between 'white' and Negro."

Once the artificial line of a "two-class theory" of the Fourteenth Amendment is put aside, the difficulties entailed in varying the level of judicial review according to a perceived "preferred" status of a particular racial or ethnic minority are intractable. The concepts of "majority" and "minority" necessarily reflect temporary arrangements and political judgments. As observed above, the white "majority" itself is composed of various minority groups, most of which

---

[34]In the view of MR. JUSTICE BRENNAN, MR. JUSTICE WHITE, MR. JUSTICE MARSHALL, and MR. JUSTICE BLACKMUN, the pliable notion of "stigma" is the crucial element in analyzing racial classifications. *See, e.g., post*, at 361, 362. The Equal Protection Clause is not framed in terms of "stigma." Certainly the word has no clearly defined constitutional meaning. It reflects a subjective judgment that is standardless. All state-imposed classifications that rearrange burdens and benefits on the basis of race are likely to be viewed with deep resentment by the individuals burdened. The denial to innocent persons of equal rights and opportunities may outrage those so deprived and therefore may be perceived as invidious. These individuals are likely to find little comfort in the notion that the deprivation they are asked to endure is merely the price of membership in the dominant majority and that its imposition is inspired by the supposedly benign purpose of aiding others. One should not lightly dismiss the inherent unfairness of, and the perception of mistreatment that accompanies, a system of allocating benefits and privileges on the basis of skin color and ethnic origin. Moreover, MR. JUSTICE BRENNAN, MR. JUSTICE WHITE, MR. JUSTICE MARSHALL, and MR. JUSTICE BLACKMUN offer no principle for deciding whether preferential classifications reflect a benign remedial purpose or a malevolent stigmatic classification, since they are willing in this case to accept mere *post hoc* declarations by an isolated state entity — a medical school faculty — unadorned by particularized findings of past discrimination, to establish such a remedial purpose.

can lay claim to a history of prior discrimination at the hands of the State and private individuals. Not all of these groups can receive preferential treatment and corresponding judicial tolerance of distinctions drawn in terms of race and nationality, for then the only "majority" left would be a new minority of white Anglo-Saxon Protestants. There is no principled basis for deciding which groups would merit "heightened judicial solicitude" and which would not.[36] ...

....

If it is the individual who is entitled to judicial protection against classifications based upon his racial or ethnic background because such distinctions impinge upon personal rights, rather than the individual only because of his membership in a particular group, then constitutional standards may be applied consistently. Political judgments regarding the necessity for the particular classification may be weighed in the constitutional balance, but the standard of justification will remain constant. This is as it should be, since those political judgments are the product of rough compromise struck by contending groups within the democratic process. When they touch upon an individual's race or ethnic background, he is entitled to a judicial determination that the burden he is asked to bear on that basis is precisely tailored to serve a compelling governmental interest. The Constitution guarantees that right to every person regardless of his background.

---

[36] As I am in agreement with the view that race may be taken into account as a factor in an admissions program, I agree with my Brothers BRENNAN, WHITE, MARSHALL, and BLACKMUN that the portion of the judgment that would proscribe all consideration of race must be reversed. *See* Part V, *infra*. But I disagree with much that is said in their opinion.

They would require as a justification for a program such as petitioner's, only two findings: (i) that there has been some form of discrimination against the preferred minority groups by "society at large," *post*, at 369 (it being conceded that petitioner had no history of discrimination), and (ii) that "there is reason to believe" that the disparate impact sought to be rectified by the program is the "product" of such discrimination:

> If it was reasonable to conclude — as we hold that it was — that the failure of minorities to qualify for admission at Davis under regular procedures was due principally to the effects of past discrimination, then there is a reasonable likelihood that, but for pervasive racial discrimination, respondent would have failed to qualify for admission even in the absence of Davis' special admissions program. *Post*, at 365-66.

The breadth of this hypothesis is unprecedented in our constitutional system. The first step is easily taken. No one denies the regrettable fact there has been societal discrimination in this country against various racial and ethnic groups. The second step, however, involves a speculative leap: but for this discrimination by society at large, Bakke "would have failed to qualify for admission" because Negro applicants — nothing is said about Asians, *cf.*, *e.g.*, *post*, at 374 n.57 — would have made better scores. Not one word in the record supports this conclusion, and the authors of the opinion offer no standard for courts to use in applying such a presumption of causation to other racial or ethnic classifications....

C

Petitioner contends that on several occasions this Court has approved preferential classifications without applying the most exacting scrutiny. Most of the cases upon which petitioner relies are drawn from three areas: school desegregation, employment discrimination, and sex discrimination. Each of the cases cited presented a situation materially different from the facts of this case.

The school desegregation cases are inapposite. Each involved remedies for clearly determined constitutional violations. Racial classifications thus were designed as remedies for the vindication of constitutional entitlement. Moreover, the scope of the remedies was not permitted to exceed the extent of the violations. Here, there was no judicial determination of constitutional violation as a predicate for the formulation of a remedial classification.

The employment discrimination cases also do not advance petitioner's cause. For example, in *Franks v. Bowman Transportation Co.*, 424 U.S. 747 (1976), we approved a retroactive award of seniority to a class of Negro truck drivers who had been the victims of discrimination — not just by society at large, but by the respondent in that case. While this relief imposed some burdens on other employees, it was held necessary "'to make [the victims] whole for injuries suffered on account of unlawful employment discrimination.'" The Courts of Appeals have fashioned various types of racial preferences as remedies for constitutional or statutory violations resulting in identified, race-based injuries to individuals held entitled to the preference. *E.g., Bridgeport Guardians, Inc. v. Bridgeport Civil Service Commission*, 482 F.2d 1333 (CA2 1973); *Carter v. Gallagher*, 452 F.2d 315 (CA8 1972), modified on rehearing *en banc, id.* at 327. Such preferences also have been upheld where a legislative or administrative body charged with the responsibility made determinations of past discrimination by the industries affected, and fashioned remedies deemed appropriate to rectify the discrimination. *E.g., Contractors Association of Eastern Pennsylvania v. Secretary of Labor*, 442 F.2d 159 (CA3), *cert. denied*, 404 U.S. 854 (1971); *Associated General Contractors of Massachusetts, Inc. v. Altshuler*, 490 F.2d 9 (CA1 1973), *cert. denied*, 416 U.S. 957 (1974); *cf. Katzenbach v. Morgan*, 384 U.S. 641 (1966). But we have never approved preferential classifications in the absence of proved constitutional or statutory violations.

Nor is petitioner's view as to the applicable standard supported by the fact that gender-based classifications are not subjected to this level of scrutiny. *E.g., Califano v. Webster*, 430 U.S. 313, 316-17 (1977); *Craig v. Boren*, 429 U.S. 190, 211 (1976) (POWELL, J., concurring). Gender-based distinctions are less likely to create the analytical and practical problems present in preferential programs premised on racial or ethnic criteria. With respect to gender there are only two possible classifications. The incidence of the burdens imposed by preferential classifications is clear. There are no rival groups which can claim that they, too, are entitled to preferential treatment. Classwide questions as to the group suffering previous injury and groups which fairly can be burdened are relatively manageable for reviewing courts. The resolution of these same questions in the context of racial and ethnic preferences presents far more complex and intractable problems than gender-based classifications. More importantly, the perception of racial classifications as inherently odious stems from a lengthy and tragic history that gender-based classifications do not share. In sum, the Court has never viewed such classification as inherently suspect or as comparable to racial or ethnic classifications for the purpose of equal protection analysis.

....

IV

We have held that in "order to justify the use of a suspect classification, a State must show that its purpose or interest is both constitutionally permissible and substantial, and that its use of the classification is 'necessary ... to the accomplishment' of its purpose or the safeguarding of its interest." The special admissions program purports to serve the purposes of: (i) "reducing the historic deficit of traditionally disfavored minorities in medical schools and in the medical profession," Brief for Petitioner 32; (ii) countering the effects of societal discrimination; (iii) increasing the number of physicians who will practice in communities currently underserved; and (iv) obtaining the educational benefits that flow from an ethnically diverse student body. It is necessary to decide which, if any, of these purposes is substantial enough to support the use of a suspect classification.

A

If petitioner's purpose is to assure within its student body some specified percentage of a particular group merely because of its race or ethnic origin, such a preferential purpose must be rejected not as insubstantial but as facially invalid. Preferring members of any one group for no reason other than race or ethnic origin is discrimination for its own sake. This the Constitution forbids.

B

The State certainly has a legitimate and substantial interest in ameliorating, or eliminating where feasible, the disabling effects of identified discrimination. The line of school desegregation cases, commencing with *Brown*, attests to the importance of this state goal and the commitment of the judiciary to affirm all lawful means toward its attainment. In the school cases, the States were required by court order to redress the wrongs worked by specific instances of racial discrimination. That goal was far more focused than the remedying of the effects of "societal discrimination," an amorphous concept of injury that may be ageless in its reach into the past.

We have never approved a classification that aids persons perceived as members of relatively victimized groups at the expense of other innocent individuals in the absence of judicial, legislative, or administrative findings of constitutional or statutory violations. After such findings have been made, the governmental interest in preferring members of the injured groups at the expense of others is substantial, since the legal rights of the victims must be vindicated. In such a case, the extent of the injury and the consequent remedy will have been judicially, legislatively, or administratively defined. Also, the remedial action usually remains subject to continuing oversight to assure that it will work the least harm possible to other innocent persons competing for the benefit. Without such findings of constitutional or statutory violations, it cannot be said that the government has any greater interest in helping one individual than in refraining from harming another. Thus, the government has no compelling justification for inflicting such harm.

Petitioner does not purport to have made, and is in no position to make, such findings. Its broad mission is education, not the formulation of any legislative policy or the adjudication of particular claims of illegality. For reasons similar to those stated in Part III of this opinion, isolated segments of our vast governmental structures are not competent to make those decisions, at least in the absence of legislative mandates and legislatively determined criteria. Before relying upon these sorts of findings in establishing a racial classification, a governmental body must have the authority and capability to establish, in the record, that the classification is responsive to identified discrimination. Lacking this capability, petitioner has not carried its burden of justification on this issue.

Hence, the purpose of helping certain groups whom the faculty of the Davis Medical School perceived as victims of "societal discrimination" does not justify a classification that imposes disadvantages upon persons like respondent, who bear no responsibility for whatever harm the beneficiaries of the special admissions program are thought to have suffered. To hold otherwise would be to convert a remedy heretofore reserved for violations of legal rights into a privilege that all institutions throughout the Nation could grant at their pleasure to whatever groups are perceived as victims of societal discrimination. That is a step we have never approved.

C

Petitioner identifies, as another purpose of its program, improving the delivery of health-care services to communities currently underserved. It may be assumed that in some situations a State's interest in facilitating the health care of its citizens is sufficiently compelling to support the use of a suspect classification. But there is virtually no evidence in the record indicating that petitioner's special admissions program is either needed or geared to promote that goal....

Petitioner simply has not carried its burden of demonstrating that it must prefer members of particular ethnic groups over all other individuals in order to promote better health-care delivery to deprived citizens. Indeed, petitioner has not shown that its preferential classification is likely to have any significant effect on the problem.

D

The fourth goal asserted by petitioner is the attainment of a diverse student body. This clearly is a constitutionally permissible goal for an institution of higher education. Academic freedom, though not a specifically enumerated constitutional right, long has been viewed as a special concern of the First Amendment. The freedom of a university to make its own judgments as to education includes the selection of its student body....

....

The atmosphere of "speculation, experiment and creation" — so essential to the quality of higher education — is widely believed to be promoted by a diverse student body. As the Court noted in *Keyishian*, it is not too much to say that the "nation's future depends upon leaders trained through wide exposure" to the ideas and mores of students as diverse as this Nation of many peoples.

Thus, in arguing that its universities must be accorded the right to select those students who will contribute the most to the "robust exchange of ideas," petitioner invokes a countervailing constitutional interest, that of the First Amendment. In this light, petitioner must be viewed as seeking to achieve a goal that is of paramount importance in the fulfillment of its mission.

It may be argued that there is greater force to these views at the undergraduate level than in a medical school where the training is centered primarily on professional competency. But even at the graduate level, our tradition and experience lend support to the view that the contribution of diversity is substantial. In *Sweatt v. Painter*, 339 U.S. at 634, the Court made a similar point with specific reference to legal education:

> The law school, the proving ground for legal learning and practice, cannot be effective in isolation from the individuals and institutions with which the law interacts. Few students and no one who has practiced law would choose to study in an academic vacuum, removed from the interplay of ideas and the exchange of views with which the law is concerned.

Physicians serve a heterogeneous population. An otherwise qualified medical student with a particular background — whether it be ethnic, geographic, culturally advantaged or disadvantaged — may bring to a professional school of medicine experiences, outlooks, and ideas that enrich the training of its student body and better equip its graduates to render with understanding their vital service to humanity.

Ethnic diversity, however, is only one element in a range of factors a university properly may consider in attaining the goal of a heterogeneous student body. Although a university must have wide discretion in making the sensitive judgments as to who should be admitted, constitutional limitations protecting individual rights may not be disregarded. Respondent urges — and the courts below have held — that petitioner's dual admissions program is a racial classification that impermissibly infringes his rights under the Fourteenth

Amendment. As the interest of diversity is compelling in the context of a university's admissions program, the question remains whether the program's racial classification is necessary to promote this interest.

V

A

It may be assumed that the reservation of a specified number of seats in each class for individuals from the preferred ethnic groups would contribute to the attainment of considerable ethnic diversity in the student body. But petitioner's argument that this is the only effective means of serving the interest of diversity is seriously flawed. In a most fundamental sense the argument misconceives the nature of the state interest that would justify consideration of race or ethnic background. It is not an interest in simple ethnic diversity, in which a specified percentage of the student body is in effect guaranteed to be members of selected ethnic groups, with the remaining percentage an undifferentiated aggregation of students. The diversity that furthers a compelling state interest encompasses a far broader array of qualifications and characteristics of which racial or ethnic origin is but a single though important element. Petitioner's special admissions program, focused *solely* on ethnic diversity, would hinder rather than further attainment of genuine diversity.

Nor would the state interest in genuine diversity be served by expanding petitioner's two-track system into a multitrack program with a prescribed number of seats set aside for each identifiable category of applicants. Indeed, it is inconceivable that a university would thus pursue the logic of petitioner's two-track program to the illogical end of insulating each category of applicants with certain desired qualifications from competition with all other applicants.

The experience of other university admissions programs, which take race into account in achieving the educational diversity valued by the First Amendment, demonstrates that the assignment of a fixed number of places to a minority group is not a necessary means toward that end. An illuminating example is found in the Harvard College program:

> In recent years Harvard College has expanded the concept of diversity to include students from disadvantaged economic, racial and ethnic groups. Harvard College now recruits not only Californians or Louisianans but also blacks and Chicanos and other minority students....
>
> In practice, this new definition of diversity has meant that race has been a factor in some admission decisions. When the Committee on Admissions reviews the large middle group of applicants who are "admissible" and deemed capable of doing good work in their courses, the race of an applicant may tip the balance in his favor just as geographic origin or a life spent on a farm may tip the balance in other candidates' cases. A farm boy from Idaho can bring something to Harvard College that a Bostonian cannot

offer. Similarly, a black student can usually bring something that a white person cannot offer.... [*See* Appendix hereto.]

In Harvard college admissions the Committee has not set target-quotas for the number of blacks, or of musicians, football players, physicists or Californians to be admitted in a given year.... But that awareness [of the necessity of including more than a token number of black students] does not mean that the Committee sets a minimum number of blacks or of people from west of the Mississippi who are to be admitted. It means only that in choosing among thousands of applicants who are not only "admissible" academically but have other strong qualities, the Committee, with a number of criteria in mind, pays some attention to distribution among many types and categories of students.

In such an admissions program, race or ethnic background may be deemed a "plus" in a particular applicant's file, yet it does not insulate the individual from comparison with all other candidates for the available seats. The file of a particular black applicant may be examined for his potential contribution to diversity without the factor of race being decisive when compared, for example, with that of an applicant identified as an Italian-American if the latter is thought to exhibit qualities more likely to promote beneficial educational pluralism. Such qualities could include exceptional personal talents, unique work or service experience, leadership potential, maturity, demonstrated compassion, a history of overcoming disadvantage, ability to communicate with the poor, or other qualifications deemed important. In short, an admissions program operated in this way is flexible enough to consider all pertinent elements of diversity in light of the particular qualifications of each applicant, and to place them on the same footing for consideration, although not necessarily according them the same weight. Indeed, the weight attributed to a particular quality may vary from year to year depending upon the "mix" both of the student body and the applicants for the incoming class.

This kind of program treats each applicant as an individual in the admissions process. The applicant who loses out on the last available seat to another candidate receiving a "plus" on the basis of ethnic background will not have been foreclosed from all consideration for that seat simply because he was not the right color or had the wrong surname. It would mean only that his combined qualifications, which may have included similar nonobjective factors, did not outweigh those of the other applicant. His qualifications would have been weighed fairly and competitively, and he would have no basis to complain of unequal treatment under the Fourteenth Amendment.

It has been suggested that an admissions program which considers race only as one factor is simply a subtle and more sophisticated — but no less effective — means of according racial preference than the Davis program. A facial intent to discriminate, however, is evident in petitioner's preference program and not denied in this case. No such facial infirmity exists in an admissions program where race or ethnic background is simply one element — to be weighed fairly against other elements — in the selection process. "A boundary line," as MR. JUSTICE FRANKFURTER remarked in another connection, "is none the worse for being narrow." *McLeod v. Dilworth,* 322 U.S. 327, 329 (1944). And a court would not assume that a university, professing to employ a facially nondiscriminatory admissions policy, would operate it as a cover for the functional equivalent of a quota system. In short, good faith would be presumed in the absence of a showing to the contrary in the manner permitted by our cases.

B

In summary, it is evident that the Davis special admissions program involves the use of an explicit racial classification never before countenanced by this Court. It tells applicants who are not Negro, Asian, or Chicano that they are totally excluded from a specific percentage of the seats in an entering class. No matter how strong their qualifications, quantitative and extracurricular, including their own potential for contribution to educational diversity, they are never afforded the chance to compete with applicants from the preferred groups for the special admissions seats. At the same time, the preferred applicants have the opportunity to compete for every seat in the class.

The fatal flaw in petitioner's preferential program is its disregard of individual rights as guaranteed by the Fourteenth Amendment. *Shelley v. Kraemer,* 334 U.S. at 22. Such rights are not absolute. But when a State's distribution of benefits or imposition of burdens hinges on ancestry or the color of a person's skin or ancestry, that individual is entitled to a demonstration that the challenged classification is necessary to promote a substantial state interest. Petitioner has failed to carry this burden. For this reason, that portion of the California court's judgment holding petitioner's special admissions program invalid under the Fourteenth Amendment must be affirmed.

C

In enjoining petitioner from ever considering the race of any applicant, however, the courts below failed to recognize that the State has a substantial interest that legitimately may be served by a properly devised admissions program involving the competitive consideration of race and ethnic origin. For this reason, so much of the California court's judgment as enjoins petitioner from any consideration of the race of any applicant must be reversed.

VI

With respect to respondent's entitlement to an injunction directing his admission to the Medical School, petitioner has conceded that it could not carry its burden of proving that, but for the existence of its unlawful special admissions program, respondent still would not have been admitted. Hence, respondent is entitled to the injunction, and that portion of the judgment must be affirmed.

1. The excerpts above are from the opinion of Justice Powell, in part of which four justices (Stevens, Burger, Stewart, and Rehnquist) concurred and in part of which the other four justices (Brennan, White, Marshall, and Blackmun) concurred. The Stevens group restricted themselves to determining whether the decision of the California Supreme Court, ordering Bakke's admission to Davis medical school, should be affirmed or reversed. Concurring with Justice Powell on this point, the Stevens group constituted the majority affirming the order. They contended, however, that Justice Powell's consideration of the possible uses of race in other admissions programs was inappropriate, finding that this broader issue was not before the Court.

Justice Brennan's group concurred with Justice Powell as to the permissibility of certain race-conscious admissions programs. They dissented, however, to the judgment that the Davis program did not fall within the category of constitutionally permissible race-conscious programs.

2. Many commentators have noted that the *Bakke* decision lacks clarity as precedent due to the various opinions and the fragmented rationale underlying the majority holdings. Consider the following summary of the possible implications of the opinion:

> *Bakke* settles so little that it is virtually useless as a precedent. The Court invalidated Davis's Program, which both Justice Powell and the Stevens group referred to as an exclusionary system, and except for another program virtually identical to it, *Bakke* would not be controlling. Even another program virtually identical to Davis's might be upheld by the Court because Justice Powell indicated that he might favor such a program if appropriate judicial, legislative or administrative efforts have been made to justify such a program as a remedy for past racial discrimination.
>
> Many possible admissions systems might pass muster. For example, Justice Powell was the only Justice expressly to condemn Davis's two-track system of admissions — one for minorities and the other for nonminorities. So long as no one was excluded on racial grounds, Mr. Justice Stevens's group would not find a two-track system objectionable, and Mr. Justice Brennan's group did not. Justice Powell's approach permits extremely broad discretionary powers to be vested in admission authorities. The Stevens group was silent on the use of race in a flexible, discretionary program, while the Brennan group presumably would permit it. Thus, no Justice spoke against the use of race within a flexible and discretionary admissions program. Courts have a long history of deferring to decisions made by administrative officers so long as it is clear that the discretion has been vested in that officer. Although the permissible range of discretion might be less when race is a decision factor, it appears a majority of the Court would permit the use of informed administrative judgment rather than insist on rigidly articulated standards to control that judgment.

C. STUDENT CLASSIFICATION BY RACE

There are potentially many programs that *Bakke* would permit. One example will suffice. Suppose Davis's Medical School sets a target range for its admission committee of somewhere between 10 to 25 minority students in order to insure diversity in its first-year entering class of 100. The admissions process is unitary now in the sense that there is only one admission committee. It has been given vast discretionary powers. It considers every application; selecting students on the basis of a set of criteria that includes predicted academic performance and a variety of other criteria linked to a student's potential for contributing to the medical school and to the profession. Criteria indicating potential contribution to school or the profession are similar but not identical to Mr. Justice Powell's criteria showing genuine diversity; *e.g.*, exceptional personal talents, unique work or service experience, leadership potential, ability to communicate with average people, and demonstrated compassion. The admission committee considers race only after assessing an applicant's potential contribution and predicted performance.

This example does not use *Bakke*'s two-track system of admissions. It allows every applicant to compete with every other applicant for every available place. Thus, Justice Powell's concerns are allayed. He would allow race to function as a "plus", as it does in the example. This example also differs from *Bakke*'s quota in that it gives the committee a range to work within, allowing individual comparative assessments to be made of all applicants. The example is like *Bakke* in that it is possible for a racial "plus" awarded to an applicant later to prove decisive in the admission decision. Nevertheless, judged by the *dicta* in *Bakke*, this program is one that might be upheld by five Justices of the Supreme Court. Morris, *The Bakke Decision: Implications for Admissions*, [1979] Contemporary Legal Issues in Education 100-01.

3. The following language from the Brennan opinion indicates the position of the dissent on the specific question of racial quotas:

Finally, Davis's special admissions program cannot be said to violate the Constitution simply because it has set aside a predetermined number of places for qualified minority applicants rather than using minority status as a positive factor to be considered in evaluating the applications of disadvantaged minority applicants. For purposes of constitutional adjudication, there is no difference between the two approaches. In any admissions program which accords special consideration to disadvantaged racial minorities, a determination of the degree of preference to be given is unavoidable, and any given preference that results in the exclusion of a white candidate is no more or less constitutionally acceptable than a program such as that at Davis. Furthermore, the extent of the preference inevitably depends on how many minority applicants the particular school is seeking to admit in any particular year so long as the number of qualified minority applicants exceeds that number. There is no sensible, and certainly no constitutional, distinction between, for example, adding a set number of points to the admissions rating of disadvantaged minority applicants as an expression of the preference with the expectation that this will result in the admission of an approximately determined number of qualified minority applicants and setting a fixed number of places for such applicants as was done here. *Bakke*, at 378.

Is there a fundamental difference in the assumptions made here when compared with those made by Justice Powell? Consider again this sentence from his opinion: "And a court would not assume that a university, professing to employ a facially non-discriminatory admissions policy, would operate it as a cover for the functional equivalent of a quota system." *Id.* at 318.

4. The conflict of divergent opinions in *Bakke* has caused at least one district court to call the decision into question as providing no guidance in race-based cases. In *Peters v. Moses*, 613 F. Supp. 1328 (W.D. Va. 1985), where whites claimed that actions of county board members prevented them from running for school board seats, the court found the dissent in *Fullilove v. Klutznick*, 438 U.S. 448 (1980) to be insightful.

5. *Bakke* is limited in its approach as regards racial discrimination in that it cites to Title VI, 42 U.S.C. Sec. 2000d-1. The *Bakke* court found Title VI's reach limited to acts of intentional discrimination. What is a plaintiff's redress if the discrimination is unintentional or occurs by way of impact or result of some institutional rule or regulation? This concern was addressed in *Knight v. State of Alabama*, 787 F. Supp. 1030 (N.D. Ala. 1991), where African-American students alleged that the use of ACT scores, the predominant white composition of the various boards of trustees of the state's colleges, and prior de jure segregation all contributed to racial discrimination. In holding partly for the students, the court recognized the limits of the *Bakke* decision and cited to *Guardians Ass'n v. Civil Service Comm'n, N.Y.C.*, 463 U.S. 582 (1983), which in fact went beyond *Bakke* and held that proof of discriminatory impact may suffice under Title VI even though unintentional racial discrimination is not proscribed under the statute.

6. *Bakke* has inspired a great deal of legal research, much of it filled with what Adolphus Williams characterizes as "uncertainty, anguish, bitterness and even hostility." *See* Williams, *A Critical Analysis of the Bakke Case*, 16 S.U. L. Rev. 129 (1989).* To survey Williams criticism *see* Bistline, *Preferential Admissions Policies and Single-Minority Scholarships: The Legal Implications of Race-Preference in Education*, 97 Dick. L. Rev. 283 (1993); Foster, *Difference and Equality: A Critical Assessment of the Concept of "Diversity,"* 1993 Wis. L. Rev. 105 (1993); Fetzer, *'Reverse Discrimination': The Political Use of*

---

*Copyright © 1989 by Southern University Law Review. Reprinted with permission.

Language, 17 T. Marshall L. Rev. 293 (1992); Powell, *Racial Realism or Racial Despair?*, 24 Conn. L. Rev. 533 (1992); Grunewald, *Contemporary Challenges to Judging: History, Politics, Values, Quotas, Politics and Judicial Statesmanship: The Civil Rights Act of 1991 and Powell's* Bakke, 49 Wash. & Lee L. Rev. 53 (1992); Stokes & Pachman, *Are Race-Based Scholarships Illegal?*, 69 Educ. L. Rep. 663 (1992); Spector, *Minority Scholarships: A New Battle in the War on Affirmative Action*, 77 Iowa L. Rev. 307 (1991).

7. Although white males may be most likely to bring so-called "reverse discrimination" cases, this is not always the situation. In *Henson v. University of Arkansas*, 519 F.2d 576 (8th Cir. 1975), a white female brought action against the University of Arkansas School of Law and alleged that the law school's "affirmative action" policies with regard to admission of minority students deprived her of equal protection of the law inasmuch as she was denied admission to the school while minority students with lesser academic qualifications were admitted. The Court of Appeals affirmed the trial court's dismissal of the action, finding that the student would not have been admitted even in absence of the school's minority preference admission system. What if she would have been admitted? Does the fact that Henson would have been rejected for admission anyway change the constitutionality of the preferential admission programs? Should plaintiffs find other rejected applicants and file as a class?

8. Is there such a thing as "reverse" discrimination? Does it have any legal validity? Reread Section of Title VI. 42 U.S.C. Sec. 2000e-2. Do social, political, and legislative history here affect the meaning of Title VI, necessitating terms like "reverse discrimination"?

PODBERESKY v. KIRWAN

United States Court of Appeals
956 F.2d 52 (4th Cir. 1992)

RESTANI, JUDGE:

Appellant, Daniel J. Podberesky, appeals from a grant of summary judgment entered on May 15, 1991. 764 F.Supp. 364. Appellees are the president of the University of Maryland at College Park ("UMCP") and UMCP itself, which maintains a race-based scholarship program from which appellant was excluded. Appellant sued for injunctive, declaratory and compensatory relief alleging violations of his rights under the Fourteenth Amendment and 42 U.S.C. §§ 1981, 1983 and 2000d *et seq*.

Background

Appellant is a nineteen year old Hispanic male who was admitted to UMCP in the fall of 1989. As an applicant to UMCP, appellant had an excellent academic record: his Scholastic Aptitude Test score was 1340, out of a possible 1600; his grade point average as calculated by his high school was over 4.0 (as calculated by UMCP, his grade point average was 3.56); and he actively participated in several extracurricular activities.

Along with his application to UMCP, appellant requested that he be considered for an academic scholarship.[1] UMCP maintains several scholarship programs, one of which is the Benjamin Banneker Scholarship Program ("Banneker Program" or "Banneker Scholarship"), a scholarship program not based on need, under which a minimum of twenty scholarships are awarded each year. UMCP established the Banneker Program in 1978; however, for the first decade of its existence it was limited in scope. Originally, the program provided two-year scholarships with stipends of $1,000 per year. In approximately 1985, the program was expanded to four-year scholarships. In 1988, the amount of the scholarship was increased to full in-state tuition or out-of-state tuition, plus room, board and mandatory fees, worth in excess of $33,500 over the four years.

At the time appellant applied for the Banneker Scholarship, the minimum requirements for further consideration under the Banneker Program were a 900 Scholastic Achievement Test score and a 3.0 grade point average. Only students of African-American heritage are considered for the Banneker Scholarship. Appellant's credentials exceeded those required for further consideration under the Banneker Program; nevertheless, appellant was not considered for this scholarship because he was not of African-American heritage.

The Banneker Program was intended as a partial remedy for past discriminatory action by the State of Maryland. For many years the State of Maryland maintained a system of higher education consisting of separate racially-segregated institutions. After *Brown v. Board of Education*, 347 U.S. 483 (1954), Congress enacted Title VI of the Civil Rights Act of 1964 which forbids federal fund recipients from discriminating in any manner on the basis of race, color, or national origin. 42 U.S.C.§ 2000d *et seq.* (1964). In 1969, the Office for Civil Rights ("OCR") of the Department of Health, Education, and Welfare (now the Department of Education) notified Maryland that its higher education system was still segregated in violation of Title VI. If OCR is unable to obtain compliance with Title VI, it is authorized to initiate formal administrative proceedings against the offending institution. OCR has never initiated formal proceedings against UMCP.

Between 1969 and 1974, Maryland submitted three desegregation plans to OCR. After rejecting the first two, OCR accepted the third plan in 1974. In 1975, the Acting Director of OCR informed the state that it was still in violation of Title VI. In 1978, OCR published new guidelines which set forth criteria required for preparation of acceptable plans for post secondary public education.

In 1980, Maryland adopted the Equal Educational Opportunity Plan for 1980-1985 ("1980-85 Plan"), in which it attempted to meet the requirements of

---

[1]It should be noted that the race-based classification at issue relates to a non-need-based scholarship program voluntarily established by appellee....

C. STUDENT CLASSIFICATION BY RACE

the 1978 guidelines. The 1980-85 Plan contained many goals, one of which was a freshmen class at UMCP that included between ten to twelve percent black students by the year 1985. The Banneker Program was not mentioned in this plan. In May 1985, UMCP specifically mentioned the Banneker Program to OCR when it submitted a "Black Undergraduate Recruitment Program." In June 1985, the State adopted the Plan to Assure Equal Post Secondary Educational Opportunity 1985-89 ("1985-89 Plan"). In this plan, Maryland established a goal of fourteen percent black freshmen at UMCP by the year 1989. No mention was made of the Banneker Program.

In its comments to the 1985-89 Plan, OCR noted that UMCP presented "a detailed discussion of recruitment measures which include listings of recruitment tools, outreach strategies, on-campus programs, summer programs, activities to attract prospective black applicants, recruitment visitors and follow-up procedures." OCR, however, did not directly acknowledge the Banneker Program. In 1987, UMCP submitted a revised "Black Undergraduate Recruitment Program" in which it listed the Banneker Program as an example of the expanded merit-based financial aid for minority students.

OCR is currently visiting public institutions of post secondary education to determine the progress made under the 1985-89 Plan. Maryland states that it will continue to follow the goals set forth in the 1985-89 Plan until a new one is developed. Accordingly, UMCP plans to continue offering the Banneker scholarships to black freshmen.

Discussion

We review a decision granting summary judgment *de novo*.

The trial court correctly found that the Banneker Program should be examined in light of the equal protection clause of the Fourteenth Amendment and subjected to a strict scrutiny test. To survive strict scrutiny, as the trial judge noted, an affirmative action plan must serve "a compelling governmental interest" and be "narrowly tailored to the achievement of that goal." *Wygant v. Jackson Bd. of Educ.*, 476 U.S. 267, 274 (POWELL, J.) (1986).

In *Wygant*, the Supreme Court held that "societal discrimination" was a concept too amorphous in nature to supply the justification for a race-conscious classification. *Id.* at 276 (plurality opinion). Because of the danger of stigmatic harm, classifications based on race, understandably, must be reserved for remedial settings. *City of Richmond v. J.A. Croson Co.*, 488 U.S. 469, 493-94 (1989).

At issue in *Croson* was a plan adopted by the City of Richmond requiring general contractors who were awarded city construction contracts to subcontract at least thirty percent of the total dollar amount of each contract to a "Minority Business Enterprise," a business at least fifty-one percent owned and controlled by individuals of certain specified racial and ethnic minorities. The Court found that the city had failed to demonstrate a compelling governmental interest which justified the plan. *Id.* at 505. Finding it significant that the city was unable to point to any identified discrimination in the Richmond construction industry, the Court rejected Richmond's claim that past societal discrimination could justify racial set-asides. *Id.* at 505-06. The Court emphasized that Richmond must have a "strong basis in evidence for its conclusion that remedial action ... [is] necessary."

Classification based upon race must be justified by specific judicial, legislative, or administrative findings of past discrimination. *Id.* 488 U.S. at 497 (quoting *University of California Regents v. Bakke*, 438 U.S. 265, 307 (1978)). It is the state that must show the existence of prior discrimination, and a strong evidentiary basis for concluding that remedial action is necessary.

The district court stated that "[t]he question ... [is] whether UMCP has demonstrated with sufficient particularity that it has a history of racial discrimination which can justify the Banneker Program's existence." In answering this question, the court found OCR's administrative "findings" concerning the noncompliance of Maryland with Title VI demonstrated past discrimination. The court rejected appellant's view that a formal court or administrative agency finding of noncompliance was necessary in order to satisfy the evidentiary standard in *Croson*, 488 U.S. 469, finding that *Croson*'s "strong basis in evidence" was satisfied in this case.

Once a court has determined that a state has proceeded upon strong evidence of discrimination in other than the immediate past, the inquiry into the legitimacy of a race-based classification turns to the state's basis for finding continuing effects of such past discrimination. In Bakke, a case involving explicit racial classifications in the admissions process of a graduate school, the Supreme Court stated that "[t]he State certainly has a legitimate and substantial interest in ameliorating, or eliminating where feasible, the disabling effects of identified discrimination." *Bakke*, 438 U.S. at 307. By focusing the inquiry on the present-day effects, the Court limited the race-based action to redressing the present continuing manifestations of past discrimination. In *Wygant*, the Court continued to emphasize that the legitimate objective behind such affirmative action policies is to remedy "the present effects of past discrimination."

In *Croson*, the Court stated that "if the city could show that it had essentially become a "passive participant" in a system of racial exclusion practiced by elements of the local construction industry, we think it clear that the city could take affirmative steps to dismantle such a system." *Croson*, 488 U.S. at 492. Thus, *Croson* indicates that race-based action may be legitimate governmental action if it is designed to "dismantle" or remedy discriminatory aspects of a system. The Court obviously intended that for a program to withstand scrutiny, there must be some discriminatory effect which could be the subject of present remediation.

Although it recognized that the program could not withstand scrutiny unless the state could cite present effects of past discrimination, the district court wavered at this point. The court began its analysis of present effects by observing that there was "some evidence" that there were no present effects of past Title

VI violations at UMCP. Specifically, the court noted that in 1989, UMCP exceeded its goal for recruiting black freshmen, and nearly met its goal for retention of black undergraduates. The record before this court indicates that during the academic years 1989 and 1990, more than fifteen percent of the incoming freshmen class was black.

Moreover, the court observed that the President of UMCP testified that, with regard to admission and financial aid, UMCP had not discriminated against blacks for many years. Although the President of UMCP referred to the "lingering effects of historic discrimination" in his deposition, he did not explain what he meant. As indicated in *Croson*, general societal harm is insufficient.

The district court concluded that the effects of longstanding discrimination were so pervasive that it was "premature to find that there are no present effects of past discrimination at the institution." Later, the district court referred to the "now-dormant specter of past discrimination." Based upon this language, it appears that the district court, although recognizing the need to identify some present effect of past discrimination, failed to make a specific finding of such present effect. Rather, it merely found that it would be prudent to keep the race-exclusionary scholarship in place at least until OCR concluded its investigation of UMCP. While this might be perceived as fair to UMCP, it does not satisfy constitutional standards. As indicated earlier, in order to justify a race-based remedy in a case where identifiable discrimination occurred a number of years in the past, a finding of such past discrimination is not sufficient. There must be some present effect of this past discrimination that the program is designed to redress.

Conclusion

. . . .

Judgment for appellees must be based on facts which show that vestiges of past discrimination existed, which made the 1988-90 form of the Banneker Program a legitimate, constitutional remedy on or about the time appellant was denied the opportunity to compete for the scholarship. Accordingly, we hereby reverse the grant of summary judgment and remand this action to the district court for a determination as to the present effects of past discrimination at UMCP. Should no further evidence be available upon remand, summary judgment for appellant would be appropriate.

Reversed and Remanded.

---

1. An interesting angle on discrimination is presented in *Podberesky*. Usually, programs which are aimed at broadening student diversity are applicable to all traditional minority students — African Americans, Native Americans, Hispanics, Asian Americans, or any other non-white group. In *Podberesky*, a civil rights claim was filed by a Hispanic student challenging a scholarship program for black students. Will the university be required to broaden the Banneker Scholarship to include Hispanics (and other students of color) or will it have to consider separate awards for each group. Which solution is better for university "diversity?" Are "diversity" and equal protection too different to coexist?

2. Consider the following excerpt from Andrea Bistline's article: *Preferential Admissions Policies and Single-Minority Scholarships: The Legal Implications of Race-Preference in Higher Education*, 97 Dick. L. Rev. 283 (1993):*

....

Preferential admissions policies are admittedly discriminatory, but they have been declared constitutional as a form of "benign discrimination," in that they benefit rather than burden particular minorities. However, this is often viewed instead as "reverse discrimination" and a way of "punishing" present majority students for acts of discrimination committed by their predecessors years ago. Such policies have been justified not only as a method of compensation for past discrimination, but also as a way of insuring racial balance and remedying minority under-representation....

....

... Many scholarship donors, for whatever purpose, choose to place restrictions on exactly what type of student will receive their donated funds. If such restrictions are racially-based, the Fourteenth Amendment is necessarily implicated. Such restrictive scholarship programs, while perhaps as wide spread, have not received the attention, or faced the challenges that minority-based admissions programs have....

....

Today, racially restrictive scholarship programs are evaluated under a two-prong test for affirmative action plans set down by the Supreme Court in 1989 in the case *City of Richmond v. J.A. Croson Co.* In that case, which involved an employment situation, the Court held that such plans must be justified by a compelling governmental interest and also that they must be narrowly tailored to remedy the effects of prior discrimination.

....

Podberesky v. Kirwan is just another case in a long line of cases involving race discrimination in education, and yet it is very different. The Court must now decide not only the validity and viability of the two-prong *Croson* strict scrutiny test as applied to affirmative action programs in general, but also as applied to affirmative action programs that discriminate against other minorities. If remnants of past discrimination are still visible on today's campuses, and if special programs are still necessary to ensure minorities a place in the higher education setting, then it seems only logical that they be applied even-handedly to all minorities. It is not only blacks, but Hispanics as well, who have suffered the effects of race discrimination. If

---

*Copyright © 1993 by Dickinson Law Review. Reprinted with permission.

one minority group is entitled to special treatment under these circumstances, common sense dictates that other minority groups in the same situation are entitled to it as well.

Such preferential policies in both admissions and scholarship administration have been in effect for many years, however, and it is possible that their purpose has been served. Discrimination in these areas is a thing of the past, and continued special treatment of minorities, rather than fostering goodwill, is creating tension and strife on many campuses. It is time to take a hard look at affirmative action policies, to determine their purpose in the educational setting of today, and to decide if their effects, in many cases, may be detrimental. *Podberesky v. Kirwan* may provide the vehicle for the Supreme Court to make just such a determination.

Do you agree with Bistline? How do you think the Supreme Court would hold if it hears this case or one like it?

3. Should state institutions be allowed to maintain separate scholarships for women? One court in Delaware said yes, considering such a scholarship benign discrimination. *See Trustees of Univ. of Delaware v. Gebelein*, 420 A.2d 1191 (Del. Ch. 1980). Would "benign" discrimination ever favor white males?

Chapter 5
SCHOOL CONTROL OF STUDENT CONDUCT

The topic of pupil control by the school system considered in this and the next three chapters can be broken down into three general categories:

1. the power to make the substantive rules to which the pupils must conform;
2. the procedures utilized for putting sanctions into effect; and
3. the types of sanctions imposed for violation of substantive rules.

These categories will be discussed in order, with this and the following chapter concentrating on the power to make substantive rules. The next chapter focuses on expressive conduct relating to schools while this chapter deals with other types of student conduct and status.

It must be borne in mind that the three categories stated above are often closely related. Usually the type of rule will itself limit the form of enforcement to be employed: *e.g.*, one would not expect a rule against wearing gang paraphernalia to be enforced by a reduction of the offender's grade in English. Also, as some of the following cases indicate, the procedure and the type of enforcement method employed by the school personnel may significantly influence the decision of the court as to the validity of the substantive rule.

Yet the issues may be analyzed separately. The validity of a substantive rule does not mean that the procedural requirements are irrelevant. It is clear that the validity of both the substantive rule and the procedure followed does not mean that the sanction employed for the violation is necessarily valid or required.

A. STUDENT CONDUCT AND SCHOOL AUTHORITY

FLORY v. SMITH
Supreme Court of Appeals of Virginia
145 Va. 164, 134 S.E. 360 (1926)

CAMPBELL, J. The object of this suit is to test the legality of a rule promulgated by the school board of Gloucester county. This rule is as follows:

> Student Regulation. — Leaving the campus between the hours of 9 a.m. and 3:35 p.m. is strictly prohibited, unless students are accompanied by a teacher.

The appellees, husband and wife, who are residents of the town of Gloucester Court House, at the opening of the 1925-26 session of the public school, entered their two children, Nellie Shackelford Smith, age 11, and Charles S. Smith, III, age 9, in the Botetourt school, situated in the town.

It was the desire of the appellees that their children be relieved of the restriction placed upon them by the rule stated, *supra*, and that the children be permitted to eat their midday meal, either in the home, situated about a mile distant from the school, or to eat same with their father at the hotel in the town.

The special privilege was denied by the principal of the school. Thereupon the children of appellees absented themselves from the campus, in violation of the rule, in order to take their midday meal with their father. This they continued to do until the 29th day of September, when, because of the infraction of the rule in this regard, Charles S. Smith, III, was suspended from school and Nellie S. Smith was withdrawn as a pupil therefrom.

....

At common law the education of the child by the state was unknown. In Virginia, the idea that the welfare of the state could be advanced by the education of the masses was first advanced by Mr. Jefferson. As early as 1779, Mr. Jefferson, at the request of the General Assembly, proposed an act whereby every county should be divided into wards and districts, and a sufficient tax be levied to maintain, not elementary schools only, but academies, colleges, and a university. In 1796 this law was enacted, but with a proviso that destroyed its efficiency. This proviso left it to the county courts to determine whether the act should go into effect in their respective counties. The county courts refused to incur the burden of taxation imposed by the act, so the scheme was not put into effect in any county.

In 1810 what was called the "literary fund" was formed, and the revenue derived therefrom was devoted to the educating of the "poor children." By slow stages education of the masses progressed. In 1869 there was written into the Constitution of the state the provision that the General Assembly should provide by law a uniform system of public free schools. Minor's Inst. vol. 1, p. 417. A similar provision is contained in the present Constitution, section 129 providing that "the General Assembly shall establish and maintain an efficient system of public free schools throughout the state."

The statutory enactments pertinent to the instant case are found in sections 632, 659, 660, 666 and 691 of the Code, and in the Acts of 1920 and 1922.

Formerly it was confided to the district school board to make rules for the government of the schools, but the Act of 1922 (Acts 1922, c. 423), when it abolished the district school board, conferred upon the county school board the power to make local regulations for the conduct of the schools and for the proper discipline of students. This power, however, was to be exercised in connection with, and not paramount to, the general provisions of the Code relative to the operation of the public schools. Pursuant to this legislative grant of authority, the county school board made the regulation complained of.

While the Constitution of the state provides in mandatory terms that the Legislature shall establish and maintain public free schools, there is neither mandate nor inhibition in the provisions as to the regulation thereof. The Legislature, therefore, has the power to enact any legislation in regard to the

A. STUDENT CONDUCT AND SCHOOL AUTHORITY

conduct, control, and regulation of the public free schools, which does not deny to the citizen the constitutional right to enjoy life and liberty, to pursue happiness and to acquire property.

In the conduct of the public schools it is essential that power be vested in some legalized agency in order to maintain discipline and promote efficiency. In considering the exercise of this power, the courts are not concerned with the wisdom or unwisdom of the act done. The only concern of the court is the reasonableness of the regulation promulgated. To hold otherwise would be to substitute judicial opinion for the legislative will.

In *Spedden v. Board of Education*, 74 W.Va. 181, 81 S.E. 725, 52 L.R.A. (N.S.) 163, the court said:

> The law commits the government and conduct of the school, in general, to the discretion of the board of education of the district, and places it beyond that of the patrons. Let the results be good or bad, there is no remedy, so long as the board acts within the limits of its legal power and authority. If it employs such teachers as the law authorizes it to employ, the patrons cannot interfere by injunction or otherwise, merely because it might have found others more competent or satisfactory. The same rule applies to all other things left to its discretion. *County Court v. Armstrong*, 34 W. Va. 326, 12 S.E. 488; *County Court v. Boreman*, 34 W. Va. 87, 11 S.E. 747.

This same principle is recognized in *Stone v. Fritts*, 169 Ind. 361, 82 N.E. 792, 15 L.R.A. (n.s.) 1147, 14 Ann. Cas. 295; *Pickler v. Board of Educ.*, 149 N.C. 221, 62 S.E. 902; and *In re Rebenack*, 62 Mo. App. 8.

While appellees allege in their bill "that it is their right to select and provide the best and most suitable food for the nourishment of their children, and to select the mode and manner by which such food shall be received by their children, to the end that their children may be best nourished and their physical development may be best promoted," it is nowhere alleged that the physical condition of the children is such that results detrimental to their physical well-being will follow if the right alleged is denied.

While it may be argued with force that a warm meal at midday is preferable to a cold lunch, it is not conclusive that the latter is destructive of health. It is a matter of common knowledge that in the towns and rural sections the vast majority of school children partake of a cold lunch at midday. In the larger cities, where paternalism is further advanced, children are encouraged to partake of hot food furnished them for a consideration.

Considering the regulation from the viewpoint afforded us by the bill of complaint, the demurrer and answer, we are unable to say that the regulation is an unreasonable one....

For the reasons stated, the decree of the circuit court [which had enjoined the enforcement of the rule against the plaintiff] must be reversed, and this court will enter a decree dismissing the bill of complaint.

Reversed.

---

1. Decisions reaching results similar to those in *Flory* include *Richardson v. Braham*, 125 Neb. 142, 249 N.W. 557 (1933); *Casey County Bd. of Educ. v. Luster*, 282 S.W.2d 333 (Ky. Ct. App. 1955); and *Fitzpatrick v. Board of Educ.*, 54 Misc. 2d 1085, 284 N.Y.S.2d 590 (Sup. Ct. 1967). *But see Hailey v. Brooks*, 191 S.W. 781 (Tex. Civ. App. 1916). Note, however, that there really are two questions involved in the *Flory* case. The first is whether the school authorities have the power to adopt rules in this area. The second, assuming the power, is whether the adopted rule and its accompanying sanction are reasonable.

It is in regard to this latter question that the court's deference to education administrators would seem appropriate. It is not at all clear, though, that deference to education administrators is warranted on the first question, *i.e.*, the question of whether or not the regulated subject is in their bailiwick. Acceptance of reasonable judgments of education administrators must mean that there has been an initial judgment made that the primary interest involved is that of the educational structure. Where, if any place, was this determination made in the preceding case? Did the school make it? Did the court make it? Did the legislature make it?

Many schools today have "open lunch" policies, allowing some or all of their students to leave school grounds. However, the schools that do not give such privileges may have good reason, *i.e.*, the health, safety and welfare of students or the imposed supervisory duty placed on schools and school officials. For example, *see Maness v. City of New York*, 607 N.Y.S.2d 325, (N.Y. App. Div. 1994). In *Maness*, a thirteen-year-old child was shot to death in the vicinity of his school during lunch hour. The main issue in the case was whether the school had met its duty of supervision to its students. For similar cases, *see* Chapter 17.

2. The statutory delegation of power to school boards is invariably framed in broad terms giving control of the management of schools to the board. One might argue that these statutes are invalid as delegations of legislative power to school boards without adequate standards. For discussions of the delegation argument, *see* R. Stewart, *Beyond the Delegation Doctrine*, 36 Am. U. L. Rev. 323 (1987), and D. Schoenbrod, *The Delegation Doctrine: Could the Court Give It Substance?*, 83 Mich. L. Rev. 1223 (1985).

There is also another aspect of the delegation doctrine. The classic delegation doctrine is premised on the theory that certain policy decisions in our society had to be made by the legislature and that the legislature could not avoid this responsibility by passing the problem on to administrators. This doctrine in its absolute formulation may have minimal validity today. *See, e.g., Industrial*

A. STUDENT CONDUCT AND SCHOOL AUTHORITY

Union Dep't v. American Petr. Inst., 448 U.S. 607 (1980); *Morrison v. Olson*, 487 U.S. 654 (1988); and *Mistretta v. United States*, 488 U.S. 361 (1989). *See also Bowsher v. Snyar*, 478 U.S. 714 (1986). Yet the underlying assumption that our societal and governmental structures assume that certain areas of conduct, if regulated at all by government, should be regulated at the legislative level, still has a great deal of validity.

It is against the background of this structure that the statutory delegation of power to school boards should be viewed. When looked at this way, it seems evident that general grants of power to school boards should be construed only to allow them to make reasonable decisions in areas where the primary consideration involved is education. If the legislature intends to delegate broader powers over general social policies to school boards, it must say so explicitly.

In order to analyze school administrative actions from this delegation perspective, it is necessary to determine the extent of the educational function which the legislature has entrusted to school authorities.

3. Suppose that a school district today were to promulgate a rule similar to that in *Flory*. Even with the school's broad power, would the rule be reasonable?

4. Isn't this case about *more* than a hot lunch? Why did the school board of Gloucester County establish this rule? It can safely be stated that a school which makes a similar rule has in mind factors other than adequate provision of food at lunch. What are some of these factors? Would these factors make the rule more reasonable and the parents more accepting of it?

Consider a rule which keeps students on the premises the entire day except at lunch times. Is such a rule reasonable? Is it contrary to the spirit of *Flory*?

BOARD OF EDUCATION OF ROGERS, ARKANSAS v. McCLUSKEY

Supreme Court of the United States
458 U.S. 966 (1982)

PER CURIAM.

Respondent, a 10th-grade student in the Rogers, Ark. School District, left school ... after the first period without permission, and, with four other students, consumed alcohol and became intoxicated. When he returned to school ... to go on a band trip, he was notified that he was suspended from school. His parents were notified ... that their son had been suspended pending a hearing before the Rogers School Board.... At the hearing before the Board, none of the five students denied that they had been drinking, and the Board voted to expel all five for the remainder of the semester.

Respondent immediately sought injunctive relief under 42 U.S.C. § 1983 (1976 ed., Supp.IV), and the case was heard by the United States District Court for the Western District of Arkansas.... The District Court decided that the School Board had violated respondent's right to substantive due process, and ordered that he be granted credit for the semester during which he was suspended and that all references to his suspension be expunged from his school records.

The District Court's action was based on its interpretation of the School Board's rules and its conclusions concerning which rules the Board invoked in suspending respondent. There is no doubt that the Board had the authority to suspend respondent under §§ 9 and 10 of its written Policies on Pupil Suspension. Section 9 provides that the Board may suspend or expel any student "for good cause." Section 10 defines "good cause," and provides that it includes "sale, use or possession of alcoholic beverages or illegal drugs." Thus it was clearly within the Board's discretion to suspend a student for becoming intoxicated.

The District Court decided that the Board had acted under § 11 of its rules, which provides for mandatory suspension when it applies. Section 11 provides:

> For the protection of other pupils in the school grades 9-12, the school board shall expel for the remainder of the semester with loss of credit for the semester's work any pupil whenever it has been established to the satisfaction of the board, or the superintendent, or the principal, or his assistant in charge, that the pupil has on school premises or at school sponsored activities (including trips) used, sold, been under the influence of, or been in possession of narcotics or other hallucinogenics, drugs, or controlled substances classified as such by Act 590 of 1971, as amended.

There was conflicting testimony concerning which section the Board had invoked. The letters sent to respondent's parents informing them of the suspension and the hearing cited both § 10 and § 11. Adams, a Board member and a lawyer, testified that he based his motion to expel McCluskey on § 10 because he had doubts about the applicability of § 11. The Chairman of the Board testified that the Board had suspended students under § 11 for alcohol offenses for the past five years.

The District Court found as a matter of fact that the Board acted under § 11 when it suspended respondent. It then went on to decide that § 11 did not apply to alcohol. Section 11 applies to "narcotics or other hallucinogenics, drugs, or controlled substances classified as such by Act 590 of 1971, as amended." Act 590, Ark.Stat. Ann. § 82- 2602(e) (Supp.1981), specifically exempts alcohol from its coverage; therefore, alcohol is not a "controlled substance." Nor is it a "narcotic or other hallucinogenic." The District Court also concluded that alcohol is not a "drug." While technically alcohol is a drug, the District Court noted, it is not considered a drug in common parlance. For this reason, the District Court concluded, the Board had acted unreasonably by suspending respondent under § 11. It held that the Board violated substantive due process by suspending him under the mandatory terms of § 11, even though the Board had discretion to suspend him under § 10.

A divided Court of Appeals for the Eighth Circuit affirmed. 662 F.2d 1263 (1981). It reviewed the District Court's conclusion that the Board acted under § 11 rather than § 10 under the clearly-erroneous standard of Federal Rule of Civil Procedure 52(a), and held that the District Court's conclusion passed muster. It also affirmed the District Court's holding that § 11 cannot reasonably be interpreted to apply to alcohol because "the express terms of section 11 apply only to 'drugs' and expressly exempt alcohol." 662 F.2d at 1267. For this reason, the Court of Appeals concluded, *Wood v. Strickland*, 420 U.S. 308 (1975), was distinguishable. There this Court had stated that "§ 1983 does not extend the right to relitigate in federal court evidentiary questions arising in school disciplinary proceedings or the proper construction of school regulations." *Id.* at 326. Although this Court had plainly stated that federal courts were not authorized to construe school regulations, the Court of Appeals concluded that *Wood v. Strickland* was distinguishable because the school board in that case had construed its regulations reasonably, while here the Board had construed its regulations unreasonably. 662 F.2d at 1267....

. . . .

The Court of Appeals and the District Court plainly erred in distinguishing *Wood v. Strickland* on the ground that the Board's interpretation of § 11 in this case was unreasonable while the school board's construction of "alcoholic beverage" in *Wood v. Strickland* was reasonable. A case may be hypothesized in which a school board's interpretation of its rules is so extreme as to be a violation of due process, but this is surely not that case. The Board's interpretation of § 11 is reasonable. Contrary to the Court of Appeals, alcohol is not expressly exempted from the coverage of § 11. Section 11 covers "controlled substances classified as such by Act 590," and Act 590 expressly exempts alcohol from its coverage. Therefore, alcohol is not a "controlled substance" under § 11. But § 11 also covers "drugs," and, as the District Court conceded, alcohol is a "drug." Moreover, § 11 mandates suspension of students under the influence of drugs while on school premises. Section 10, which gives the Board discretion to suspend students for drug use, is not limited in its application to drug use on school premises. It is reasonable to conclude that the regulations require suspension for any drug use, including use of alcohol, on school premises, while permitting suspension for drug use off school premises.

In any case, even if the District Court's and the Court of Appeals' views of § 11 struck us as clearly preferable to the Board's — which they do not — the Board's interpretation of its regulations controls under *Wood v. Strickland*. The Chairman of the Board testified that the Board had interpreted § 11 as requiring the suspension of students found intoxicated on school grounds for a number of years prior to respondent's suspension, and it is undisputed that the Board had the authority to suspend students for that reason. We conclude that the District Court and the Court of Appeals plainly erred in replacing the Board's construction of § 11 with their own notions under the facts of this case. Accordingly, the petition for *certiorari* is granted, and the judgment of the Court of Appeals is

Reversed.

SMITH v. SCHOOL CITY OF HOBART
United States District Court
811 F. Supp. 391 (N.D. Indiana 1993)

LOZANO, DISTRICT JUDGE:

....

... [S]mith was a senior class student at Hobart Senior High School in Hobart, Indiana [who], with two other girls, left their fifth period class to go to their Medical Biology Class located at a medical center. On the way, the girls stopped at one of the other girls' homes and drank beer. After admitting to drinking the alcoholic beverage, Smith was suspended for five (5) days. The School reduced Smith's grades twenty percent (20%) in each class for the semester. The student handbook provides that knowingly possessing or consuming alcoholic beverages or intoxicants of any kind subjects a student to suspension and/or expulsion. The handbook also provides for a grade reduction of four percent (4%) of the student's grade for the nine-week grading period for each class missed each day during suspension.

Smith alleges that her constitutional right to substantive due process was violated by the reduction of her grades during her suspension. Smith claims that the School's reduction of her grades was arbitrary, capricious, and excessive based on her actions and seeks damages and attorney's fees pursuant to 42 U.S.C. §§ 1983 and 1988.

....

Before diving into the murky waters of substantive due process, it is necessary to first note that school discipline is not an area in which courts lay claim to any expertise, nor should consider lightly. As so aptly stated by Judge Mills:

> School discipline is an area which courts enter with great hesitation and reluctance — and rightly so. School officials are trained and paid to determine what form of punishment best addresses a particular student's transgression. They are in a far better position than is a black-robed judge to decide what to do with a disobedient child at school. They can best determine, for instance, whether a suspension or an after-school detention will be more effective in correcting a student's behavior. Because of their expertise and their closest situation — and because we do not want them to fear court challenges to their every act — school officials are given wide discretion in their disciplinary actions. *Donaldson v. Board of Educ.*, 98 Ill.App.3d 438, 424 N.E.2d 737, 738 (1981).

With this in mind, the School acknowledges that students do have constitutional rights, but contends that a public high school grade reduction for consuming alcohol during school hours does not violate a student's right to substantive due process under 42 U.S.C. § 1983. The School relies on *Wood v. Strickland*, 420 U.S. 308, 214 (1975), in support of its argument....

A. STUDENT CONDUCT AND SCHOOL AUTHORITY

[In that case, it was stated] "It is not the role of the federal courts to set aside decisions of school administrators which the court may view as lacking a basis in wisdom or compassion...." *Id.* at 326.

But at issue in this case is not whether it is proper for a court to substitute its judgment for that of a school administrator. Rather, at issue is whether the School's rule is constitutional. Students do not "'shed their constitutional rights' at the school house door." *Goss v. Lopez*, 419 U.S. 565, 574 (1975). The due process clause forbids arbitrary deprivations of liberty. *Id.* "Where a person's good name, reputation, honor, or integrity is at stake because of the what the government is doing to him," the minimal requirements of the due process clause must be satisfied. *Id.* In *Goss v. Lopez*, the United States Supreme Court held that students have procedural due process rights to notice and a hearing before suspension. *Id.* at 579. In *Goss*, "[s]chool authorities ... suspended appellees from school for periods of up to 10 days based on charges of misconduct. If sustained and recorded, those charges could seriously damage the students' standing with their fellow pupils and their teachers as well as interfere with later opportunities for higher education and employment." *Id.* at 574-75. It is thus clear that a student's academic record has importance not only as to the student's high school or grade school standing, but also affects the student's ability to enter the college of his choice, obtain postgraduate degrees, and eventually affects the student's chances of obtaining a job. Academic records are also routinely examined when applying to the military or other government jobs.

The School's rules regarding suspensions are as follows:

> All absences except those set forth in the previous section, Excused Absence, shall be considered unexcused absences.
> 1. Students will be permitted to make up work missed during such absences
> 2. Unexcused absences are, but not limited to, the following:
>   a. Suspensions "out-of-school"
>   b. Truancy
> 3. Unexcused Absences Due to Disciplinary Suspension(s)
>   a. Students who receive an "in-school" suspension will be permitted to make up classroom work while in suspension, but will suffer grade deduction. Failure to do make-up work will result in a loss of learning for the day(s) of suspension.
>   b. Students who receive an "out-of-school" suspension will be permitted to make up their class work for the day(s) of suspension, and will suffer grade deduction.
> 4. All unexcused absences, except truancy, will be assessed a 1% grade deduction for each class missed during the week of the incident.
> ....
> In-School Suspension
> 1. Students will attend school but in a special room during the school day.

2. The student will do work assigned by the classroom teacher and have no other privileges such as library passes, convocations or other extra-curricular activities.
3. The detention room will be supervised.
4. There will be a 2% grade deduction for the 9-weeks grading period.

Out-of School Suspension
1. Students will have the opportunity to make up work in the time designated by the teacher.
2. Student must forfeit all school activities during the period of suspension.
3. Student will suffer a 4% grade deduction for each class missed during the time of suspension, to be deducted for the 9-weeks grading period.

Classroom Discipline
1. Students may be suspended from classroom for various reasons. Before doing so, teachers should make out a referral slip and conferences should be set up with parents and/or a counselor and administrator.
2. If a student is suspended from a class, the teacher must provide class work for the student to work on while in suspension.
3. Grade deduction while in suspension is 2% per each day in that status.

Smith claims that the School violated her substantive due process rights when it reduced her grades by twenty percent (20%) for the nine-week grading period. She argues that the use of academic sanctions for nonacademic misconduct constitutes arbitrary and capricious action, as the penalty was not rationally related to the misconduct and not rationally related to the disciplinary purpose. Moreover, Smith avers that the School's imposition of both a suspension and grade reduction amounted to excessive double punishment. Although it is not patently clear, it appears that Smith's grades were reduced by four percent (4%) for each class missed during the time of her suspension, a total of five days, because she was punished with out-of-school suspension, as opposed to in-school suspension.

Conversely, the School argues that a rational relationship between the grade reduction and the use of alcohol during school hours exists, namely "it is that the use of alcohol during school hours, as occurred here, affects adversely the academic accomplishment of the student user." In support of its position, the School cites *Knight v. Board of Educ.*, 38 Ill.App.3d 603, 348 N.E.2d 299 (1976). In *Knight*, the plaintiff, a senior in high school, did not attend classes for two days. The school administration did not excuse the absences. On the days the plaintiff was absent, the school district had in force the following regulation: "Under an unexcused absence, makeup work shall be done without credit and grades shall be lowered by one letter grade per class." As a result of this policy, the plaintiff's grades were lowered two letter grades per class for the final

A. STUDENT CONDUCT AND SCHOOL AUTHORITY

quarter of the year. The plaintiff filed suit, requesting a writ of mandamus to have his grades recomputed for the quarter without consideration being given to the absences, that the old grades be ordered expunged, that the policies set forth in the rule be declared void, and that all the defendants be enjoined from enforcing the rule. *Id.*

The *Knight* court recognized that students do have substantive due process rights, and stated that the test for a deprivation of such rights is "to weigh the severity of the punitive effect of the sanction against the severity of the conduct sanctioned." *Id.* at 303. In applying this test, the court held that:

> ... [W]e do not find the reduction in plaintiff's grades by one letter grade for a period of one quarter of the year in three subjects in consequence of two days of truancy to be so harsh as to deprive him of substantive due process. We note that any damage to plaintiff was somewhat remote. He was admitted the next year to a junior college, the only school to which he sought admission and later dropped out.

However, the *Knight* court did not pass on whether the school regulation was a violation of the plaintiff's substantive due process rights as the rule had been rescinded before appeal. *Id.* Accordingly, the *Knight* court was only evaluating the severity of the punishment imposed upon the plaintiff in this case, and not the validity of the rule itself....

In this case, the plaintiff's quarterly grades were reduced; the record is clear that the reduction of the quarterly grades adversely affected the final grade. The final grade constitutes a record that purports to measure academic attainment. We should take judicial notice of the fact that prospective employers as well as institutions of higher learning concern themselves with true academic achievement.

I would reverse the judgment of the circuit court of Livingston County and remand this case with directions to enter a judgment declaring the rule invalid.

It is also important to note that the majority in *Knight* sustained the student's grade reduction because it found that the teachers retained the discretion to decide whether or not to lower the student's grade one letter grade per class due to an unexcused absence despite the mandatory language of the rule. Although it did not have to decide the constitutionality of the rule, the court stated, "[w]here a grade is dispensed by a teacher within the teacher's subjective discretion, we can see no justification for court intervention." *Id.* If a rule provided for a grade reduction without a subjective determination of a teacher, the Court opined that, "[u]nder these circumstances a grading procedure could be used that would be so palpable as to justify court intervention." Thus, the *Knight* court intimated that the rule before it may be invalid, even if its application was not unduly harsh.

....

In Indiana, a school corporation is administered by a "governing body" which means any institution charged by law with the responsibility of administering the affairs of a school corporation. Ind.Code Ann. § 20-8.1-1-2 (West 1984). The school corporation delegated the following authority:

....

(b) Subject to the limitations in section 3 of this chapter, each principal may take any action concerning his school or any school activity within his jurisdiction which is reasonably necessary to carry out or prevent interference with an educational function or school purposes. Such action may include establishing written rules and standards to govern student conduct. Similarly, the superintendent, or his administrative staff with his approval, may take any action with respect to all schools within the superintendent's jurisdiction which is reasonably necessary to carry out or prevent interference with an educational function or school purposes.

(c) The governing body may make written rules and establish written standards concerning student conduct which are reasonably necessary to carry out, or to prevent interference with carrying out, an educational function or school purpose.

....

(g) The governing body may make such other delegations of rulemaking, disciplinary, and other authority as are reasonably necessary in carrying out the school purposes of the school corporation.

Clearly, the emphasis in Indiana is on the reasonableness of the school's regulations, which is in accord with this Court's standard of review for said regulations and rules....

While the issue of reducing a student's grades as punishment for nonacademic conduct is not well-settled in this country, or Indiana for that matter, a general consensus can be reached as to what a student's grades should represent. A student's grade or credit should reflect the student's academic performance or achievement, including participation in class, and presence in class. Reducing grades unrelated to academic conduct results in a skewed and inaccurate reflection of a student's academic performance.

....

[Therefore], this Court must find that the rule in question is unreasonable and arbitrary on its face. The parties stipulated that "the grade reductions were not imposed for lack of effort of academics, but were imposed as part of the disciplinary action to discourage the consumption of alcohol during school hours." By the School's own admission, the sanctions were imposed on Smith as a disciplinary measure and not imposed due to a lack of effort in academics. The School claims that the use of alcohol during school hours adversely affects academic achievement of the student user. Put this way, any type of misconduct would adversely affect a student's academic accomplishments, including skipping school, not paying attention in class, causing disruption, etc.

A. STUDENT CONDUCT AND SCHOOL AUTHORITY

Based on the record before the Court, the Court finds that the School has not advanced a reasonable relationship between the use of alcohol during school hours, and the 4% reduction in grades for each day suspended for said alcohol use. Moreover, the policy is arbitrary because the grade of the student who missed class that day for serving suspension or other reasons was reduced by 4%, but the student who was in class and not serving suspension did not have 4% of his grade determined that day. To warrant an academic sanction, a student's misconduct must be directly related to the student's academic performance, and there is no indication in this record that such is the case.... As noted above, a student's grades should be a reflection of the student's academic performance, which are determined by the teacher based on a number of factors, including test scores, class participation, and attendance. The rule at hand gives the teacher no discretion in whether to deduct a student's grade for their suspension, which may lead to arbitrary results in practice, that is, disproportionate punishment for an incident. Such is the case here, and the Court further finds that the punishment imposed on Smith, out-of-class suspension plus a 20% grade reduction in each class, was excessive and disproportionate to her violation of the School's rules.

....

---

1. As noted, *Flory v. Smith, supra,* connotes a two-part test to determine the circumstances under which school officials have hegemony over the conduct of students: 1) whether school authorities have the power to adopt certain rules of conduct in the first place and 2) assuming such power, whether the rules and accompanying sanctions are reasonable. That school boards have such power was consummated in *Wood v. Strickland,* 420 U.S. 308 (1975), as seen in Chapter 7 of this book, and that case was relied on by the majority opinions in both *McCluskey* and *Smith.* Similar to these two latter cases, *Wood* concerned secondary school students expelled for violating their school's policy against the possession or consumption of alcohol at school or school-related activities. The students added malt liquor to punch served to students at a school function. After punishment by school officials ensued, the students brought a cause of action under 42 U.S.C. 1983 claiming a denial of their Fourteenth Amendment right to due process. The district court directed a verdict for school officials, reasoning that such persons are immune from suit absent malice or ill-will. The Eighth Circuit Court of Appeals reversed the decision and, based on its interpretation of school board regulations, found official violation of the students' substantive due process rights. The Supreme Court then vacated the Court of Appeals decision by stating the following:

> It is not the role of the federal courts to set aside decisions of school administrators which the court may view as lacking a basis in wisdom or compassion. Public school students do have substantive and procedural

rights while at school ... But, Section 1983 does not extend the right to relitigate in federal court evidentiary questions arising in school disciplinary proceedings or the proper construction of school regulations. The system of public education that has evolved in this Nation relies necessarily upon the discretion and judgment of school administrators and school board members and Section 1983 was not intended to be a vehicle for federal court correction of errors in the exercise of that discretion which do not rise to the level of violations of specific constitutional guarantees. *Id.* at 326.

2. Why is it important to sustain school board authority in cases like *McCluskey*? See *Katchak v. Glasgow Indep. Sch. Sys.*, 690 F. Supp. 580 (W.D. Kentucky 1988) (Injunctive relief improper in alcohol-related suspension case in light of public interest in cultivating a learning environment by maintaining proper discipline in the public schools).

Similar interests in creating a safe atmosphere have prompted courts to deny due process claims in cases involving weapons. See *Mitchell v. Board of Trustees of Oxford Separate Sch. Dist.*, 625 F.2d 660 (5th Cir. 1980), *infra*; *McClain v. Lafayette County Bd. of Educ.*, 673 F.2d 106 (5th Cir. 1982).

3. All states have developed codes which require school boards to make reasonable regulations relative to the governance of schools. *Smith* lists a code of student conduct typical of many states. The following excerpts from Ohio Revised Code, Title 33, Section 3313.20 (Page's Ohio Revised Code Annotated, 1993) are characteristic of state statutes vesting school boards with the power and discretion to manage schools and regulate the activities of students:

> (A) The board of education shall make any rules that are necessary for its government and the government of its employees, pupils of its schools, and all persons entering upon its grounds or premises.
>
> (1) A school board may interpret its rule providing for suspension for being "under the influence" to include any ingestion of alcohol. It is not necessary for the student to manifest being under the influence.

[The reader should note here that the mixture of alcohol and students has made for rules and case law in many states, Ohio being no exception. See, *e.g.*, *Rohraugh v. Elida Bd. of Educ.*, 63 Ohio App. 3d 685, 579 N.E.2d 782 (Ohio Ct. App. 1990) ("board of education acted within its discretion in interpreting school policy prohibiting student from being 'under the influence' of alcohol ... while under school jurisdiction.")]

> (15) In determining whether a proposed rule is reasonable, boards of education must take into account the extent the rule invades the privacy and dignity of the student.
>
> (23) The elected board of education of a city school district is the administrative agency (possessing certain quasi-legislative and quasi-judicial duties) charged with the responsibility of management,

control and government of the city school district and may adopt reasonable rules and regulations therefor.

(26) A board of education has that power and only that power to make rules and regulations over student conduct and status which are directly related to its function of educating the pupils in its charge; there must be a reasonable relationship between the rule and the furtherance of a valid educational purpose.

4. The holding in *Wood*, that courts may not supplant educators' discretion based on reasonable rules rightly falling under school board ambit, was clearly followed in *McCluskey*. But that case carries a caveat; to wit: "A case may be hypothesized in which a school board's interpretation of its rules is so extreme as to be a violation of due process...." *McCluskey*, 458 U.S. at 970. This suggests that school officials do not have unfettered discretion in matters of school discipline. But is such discretion so broad that it can only be countered by students in very exceptional circumstances as is suggested by the *McCluskey* decision? What, if anything, would motivate a court to substitute its interpretation of school rules in an ordinary or commonplace disciplinary dispute?

5. *Smith v. School City of Hobart* provides some insight into when a court might overrule a school board decision concerning student discipline. Recall that *Smith*, too, is a case about a breach of school rules through abuse of alcohol. Part of the penalty, however, dealt with the reduction of grades, which inspired the student to claim a violation of substantive due process. The court decided in the student's favor, finding the school rule arbitrary and unreasonable as there was no rational relationship between the use of alcohol during school hours and the reduction of grades. The court went on to say that in order for such a relationship to be established, "a student's misconduct must be directly related to the student's academic performance." *Smith*, 811 F. Supp. at 399. Is this ruling truly based on the kind of unconstitutional and exceptional behavior of school administrators as envisioned in *Wood* and *McCluskey*? Is the *Smith* court declaring that reduction of grades as a penalty for ingesting alcohol (an issue under the school's police power of protecting the health, safety and welfare of students) is beyond the ambit of the school board?

6. While it may be argued that little symbiosis can be found between disciplinary misconduct and academic penalties, *Smith* spells of no precedent. In fact, state courts are divided on the issue of disciplinary infractions and academic sanction. *See, e.g., Katzman v. Cumberland Valley Sch. Dist.*, 84 Pa. Commnw. 474, 479 A.2d 671 (1984) (reduction of grades and exclusion from National Honorary Society represents illegal application of school board discretion for student accused of drinking wine while on a school field trip); *Hamer v. Board of Educ.*, 66 Ill. App. 3d, 383 N.E.2d 231 (1978), (grade reduction for unexcused absences has no reasonable relationship to disciplinary objective being sought). *But see Slocum v. Holton Bd. of Educ.*, 171 Mich. App. 92, 429 N.W.2d 607 (1988) (unexcused absences are appropriate factors to be considered in grading a student's academic performance); *New Braunfels Indep. Sch. Dist. v. Armke*, 658 S.W.2d 330 (Tex. App. 1983) (no specific constitutional guarantee of due process rights for student under *Wood v. Strickland* for being suspended for alcohol consumption and thereby missing school exams); *Donaldson v. Board of Educ.*, 98 Ill. App. 3d 438, 424 N.E.2d 737 (1981) (no denial of due process rights to student suspended for fighting and missing school exams).

7. The *Smith* court implies in its decision that a school rule with more teacher discretion as to the reduction of grades might meet constitutional muster. This presumably means that more of the human element would make for less disproportionate punishment. Couldn't the opposite be true, *i.e.*, might not teachers be just as prone to misuse such power against students? Moreover, where does the court get the foundation for suggesting that teacher judgments should be given more weight than that which has been legislatively placed in the hands of school board members?

8. Note that the combination of academics and discipline does not represent the only means by which a court will intervene and overturn a school board decision. Moreover, *Robinson v. Oak Park and River Forest High Sch.*, 571 N.E.2d 931 (Ill. App. Ct. 1991), represents a case where the "exceptional circumstances" condition found in *McCluskey* has no application. In *Robinson*, two high school students sought an injunction restraining the board of education from expelling them. The expulsion was the result of a fight that occurred after the school day and away from school property. Neither student had recorded misconduct or behavioral problems prior to this incident. Based on the facts of the case, one of the expelled students had attempted to break up the fight, and the other student only struck a blow in self defense. At a school board meeting both students were expelled for the remainder of the school year or what amounted to six months of time out of school.

In analyzing the propriety of the school board decision, the court reviewed state law as grounds for expulsions and determined that such punishment could only be administered if student activity "might reasonably lead school authorities to forecast substantial disruption or material interference with school activities or which is a substantial disruption or material interference with school activities...." *Id.* at 933. The court determined that there was no evidence that the students would substantially disrupt or materially interfere with school activity. The court then held that the expulsion, which amounted to six months for a random incident and off the grounds of the school, was an abuse of discretion by the school board. The court agreed that school boards have broad discretion in the area of student discipline, but allowed that such discretion is not unlimited. The court then formulated a test for determining when boards of education engage in an abuse of discretion vis-à-vis the discipline of students:

1. the egregiousness of the student's conduct;
2. the history or record of the student's past conduct;

A. STUDENT CONDUCT AND SCHOOL AUTHORITY 265

3. the likelihood that such conduct will affect the delivery of educa- tional services to other children;
4. severity of the punishment; and
5. the interest of the child. *Id.* at 935.

9. Courts have also found an abuse of discretion in cases of racial discrimination. In *Sherpell v. Humnoke Sch. Dist. No. 5*, 619 F. Supp. 670 (E.D. Ark. 1985), *appeal dismissed*, 814 F.2d 538 (8th Cir. 1985), a federal district court found that school rules were vague and allowed teachers too much discretion in the administration of punishment. This unfortunate combination of vagueness and discretion resulted in African-American students being disciplined for actions for which white students were not. The court ordered that "uniform and objective guidelines be established to eliminate the opportunity to administer discipline on an uneven handed basis." *Id.* at 677.

10. School district authority as to discipline may also be overridden by a court in circumstances where children are in need of special services. The case of *In the Matter of P.J.*, 575 N.E.2d 22 (Ind. Ct. App. 1991), is illustrative. A high school student was suspended from school for violating rules against the consumption of alcohol. Thereafter, the school board also issued a notice of expulsion which the student appealed. At the hearing it was revealed that the student had informed a school counselor that she had been a victim of sexual molestation. (Though not specifically stated, the facts hinted that a family member committed this abuse.) Although school officials were aware of the crimes against the student, none of the counselor's testimony was considered in the decision to expel. In viewing the student's appeal, the court allowed that school boards generally have authority over student discipline and courts are not free to override reasonable decisions. However, in circumstances where children are in need of special services to address emotional or physical trauma, manifested in a violation of school rules, courts may set aside school punishment and offer injunctive relief.

OLESEN v. BOARD OF EDUCATION OF SCHOOL DISTRICT NO. 228

United States District Court
676 F. Supp. 820 (N.D. Ill. 1987)

PLUNKETT, DISTRICT JUDGE:

This case is about a boy, a school board and a rule. The boy is the plaintiff Darryl Olesen, Jr., a senior at Bremen High School in Midlothian, Illinois. The school board is the Board of Education of School District No. 228 which is responsible for the operation of four high schools including Bremen. The Board's rule forbids all gang activities at the schools, including the wearing of gang symbols, jewelry and emblems. The wearing of earrings by male students is included in that ban.

Darryl Olesen wishes to wear an earring to Bremen because he believes it expresses his individuality and may be attractive to the young women in his school. He has worn his earring to school on several occasions, each time with identical results — he has been suspended. Olesen now challenges the constitutionality of the school rule claiming that it violates his right of free speech and expression under the First Amendment and his right to equal protection under the Fourteenth Amendment. (The ban does not, on its face, forbid earrings on girls.) Olesen seeks an injunction against the enforcement of the school policy and an expungement from his school records of all disciplinary action taken against him under the school rule.

....

The Boy

Darryl Olesen is in his fourth but not his final year at Bremen. He began high school with considerable promise. His preadmission test showed him to be bright and he was placed in several advanced courses in his freshman year. At the end of that year his grades, with few exceptions, were good and his attendance consistent. His next two and a half years have witnessed a steady erosion of his earlier promise. He now misses more classes than he attends and fails more courses than he passes. He has attended meetings of the Simon City Royals, a large gang of youths with members at Bremen. He claims not to be affiliated with that gang, but his protest is difficult to accept. The Simon City Royals, like other gangs, advertise their presence at the school with symbols and emblems including a cross, a pitchfork and a six-pointed star. Olesen's "favorite" earring has a cross appended to it. He disavows any connection between that earring and the Simon City Royals and we will give him the benefit of the doubt. We will accept that his earring is solely an effort to express his own individuality. He does not credibly claim that it makes any other statement.

The School Board

School Board No. 228, like other school boards, has been forced to meet a gang problem in its schools. Between 1981 and 1985 the Board discovered that: (a) students had been intimidated by gang members both in and around the schools; (b) gang members were attempting to recruit new members in the school buildings; (c) many students were afraid of gang members and often reluctant to come to school; (d) acts of violence occurred on school grounds which resulted from warring factions in competing gangs.

The Board sought the assistance of the local police, parents and other school boards who had more experience with the problem. The Board concluded that it needed a comprehensive policy which would prevent gangs from operating in its schools. In 1984 it enacted a gang policy which it applied to all high school students in its district.

A. STUDENT CONDUCT AND SCHOOL AUTHORITY

The Rule

The Board's policy banned the wearing or display of any gang symbol, any act or speech showing gang affiliation and any conduct in furtherance of gang activity.[*] The Board policy did not specifically ban the wearing of earrings. The Board recognized, however, that each school might effectuate the gang policy in different ways. The administration at Bremen concluded that many of the male students at that school wear earrings to demonstrate their gang affiliation. Accordingly, Bremen's handbook of rules for students not only contained the Board's anti-gang policy, but also a specific prohibition against the wearing of earrings by male students. The earring prohibition is contained in the student dress code section because the Bremen administration believes that the students were more likely to read the dress code.

The Board's gang policy has been successful. Both the Principal and the Dean of Students at Bremen testified that gang activities, once threatening to pervade the school, have been brought under control.

The Law and the Federal Court

The Board of Education of School District No. 228 is elected by the citizens of that district to oversee the operation of its high schools. That Board has the responsibility to teach not only English and History, but the role of young men and women in our democratic society. Students learn to think and to question. But students are also expected to learn the rules which govern their behavior not only in school but in society. They are taught that they have individual rights and that those rights must be balanced with the rights of others. The direction and

---

[*] Policy of the Board of Education of School District No. 228, Cook County, Illinois Prohibiting Gangs and Gang Activities (Adopted on 4-24-84) This Board of Education feels that the presence of gangs and gang activities can cause a substantial disruption of or material interferences with school and school activities. A "gang" as defined in this policy is any group of two or more persons whose purposes include the commission of illegal acts. By this policy, the Board of Education acts to prohibit existence of gangs and gang activities as follows:

No student on or about school property or at any school activity:

1. Shall wear, possess, use, distribute, display or sell any clothing, jewelry, emblem, badge, symbol, sign or other things which are evidence of membership or affiliation in any gang
2. Shall commit any act or omission, or use any speech, either verbal or non-verbal (gestures, hand-shakes, etc.) showing membership or affiliation in a gang
3. Shall use any speech or commit any act or omission in furtherance of the interests of any gang or gang activity, including, but not limited to:
   a. soliciting others for membership in any gangs
   b. requesting any person to pay protection or otherwise intimidating or threatening any person
   c. committing any other illegal act or other violation of school district policies
   d. inciting other students to act with physical violence upon any other person.

manner of this instruction rests with the Board, not the federal court. *See Bethel Dist. No. 403 v. Fraser,* [478] U.S. [675], 106 S.Ct. 3159 (1986).

Olesen claims that the school's anti-gang policy which includes a prohibition against males wearing earrings violates his right of free speech and expression. We disagree.... Olesen's only message is one of his "individuality." In order to send that message, he is willing to violate school rules designed to protect him and his fellow students. We find that his "message" is not within the protected scope of the First Amendment. *See, e.g., Fowler v. Board of Education of Lincoln County, Kentucky,* 819 F.2d 657 (6th Cir.1987).

.... In the hair length cases, the Board was unable to articulate a rational basis for its rule. [*See Breen v. Kahl,* 419 F.2d 1034 (1969); *Crews v. Cloncs,* 432 F.2d 1259 (1970).] Here, by contrast, the Board has convincingly enunciated a rationale directly related to the safety and well-being of its students — curtailment of gang activities. Further, the stricture involved here requires only that the student not wear his earring during school hours and on school grounds. *Breen* and *Crews* struck down regulations which dictated the students' appearance both in and out of school. We find that the Board's gang policy is rational and does not unconstitutionally curtail a student's freedom to choose his own appearance. *See Kelley v. Johnson,* 425 U.S. 238 (1976).

As mentioned earlier, Olesen has also mounted an assault against the policy on the grounds of equal protection — the school forbids earrings on boys, but not on girls. That argument need not detain us for long. Olesen must show that the gender-based classification does not substantially relate to a legitimate government objective. *O'Connor v. Board of Education of School District No. 23,* 645 F.2d 578 (7th Cir.1981). Olesen has failed to do so. The Board members and Bremen's administrators have recognized that the wearing of earrings by males generally connote gang membership. While girls may be gang members, they symbolize their affiliation in other ways — ways that are also prohibited by the school policy. We find no unconstitutional gender-based discrimination here.

....

---

1. School officials and their attorneys must review the court decisions which have hegemony over their school districts. This is because there may be different decisions of courts even within the same circuit. For example, the Seventh Circuit Court of Appeals in *Breen v. Kahl,* 419 F.2d 1034 (1969), struck down restrictions on the length of male students' hair, establishing a "sphere of personal liberty." The *Olesen* court distinguished its facts from *Breen* on two grounds: 1) hair length requirements, unlike dress codes, affect the student day and night and 2) the school district in *Breen* was unable to articulate a rational basis for its policy, whereas the school district in *Olesen* instituted the policy to protect the health, safety and welfare of other students.

A. STUDENT CONDUCT AND SCHOOL AUTHORITY

The decisions in the cases appropriately categorize the limits of court reasoning as regards the internal affairs of school free expression regulations. Courts will, of course, support school officials in the quest to maintain a good academic environment. Hence, a dress code that controls attire that has the potential for causing school disruptions stands a better chance of being declared constitutional. However, the courts also recognize the other side of the continuum supporting a student's right to wear clothing that would not cause school disruption. *See Tinker v. Des Moines Indep. Sch. Dist.*, 393 U.S. 503 (1969).

2. Many more cases involving student expression based on hair length have been decided by federal courts than those regarding dress codes related to student conduct. Issues of student expression, particularly as regards hair length are in Chapter 6. For research on the divergent court applications toward hair length and dress codes *see* Bartlett, *Hair and Dress Codes Revisited*, 33 Educ. L. Rep. 7 (1986).

3. Courts have typically distinguished between codes regulating hair styles and those determining attire. In *Wallace v. Ford*, 346 F. Supp. 156 (E.D. Ark. 1972), for example, a federal district court ruled that a greater level of court scrutiny should be undertaken when considering cases of hair length over cases involving clothing. Hair, the court reasoned, was another part of the body, while clothing could be changed at will. A court of appeals rendered a similar decision in *Richards v. Thurston*, 424 F.2d. 1281 (1st Cir. 1970), noting that school officials have more power to promulgate dress codes than to command hair cuts.

4. The holding in *Olesen* suggests that the impetus behind its decision to uphold the school's dress code is gang-related violence; specifically, the courts desire to promote schools as safe havens for learning rather than places of fear, intimidation and violence. This means that such codes will be upheld by the courts against First Amendment claims if school districts can document that the learning environment is threatened or the rights of other students are being infringed. But is student dress really the cause of the problem here? Should the right to wear clothing be suppressed or should school officials seek to tackle the root cause of the problem — the gangs themselves? Is there any empirical evidence that dress codes inhibit gang activity in schools? *See* Murphy, *Restricting Gang Clothing in Public Schools: Does a Dress Code Violate a Student's Right of Free Expression?*, 64 Cal. L. Rev. 1321 (1991), stating that there is no nexus between the codes and gang activity. *Id.* at 1329.

Consider the following excerpt from a recent article concerning regulations of gang-related clothing in the schools:

> One aspect of gang-related activity of great interest to school administrators is the type of clothing worn by many students/gang members. Although the psychology behind wearing gang clothing is an involved issue of its own, it is generally accepted that students' primary reason for wearing gang clothing is to show gang affiliation. It is debatable what messages gang

members are conveying, either consciously or subconsciously, and the response to the gang regalia by other students, gang-connected or not, is even more uncertain. However, there is little debate that gangs are empowered by being able to readily identify a co-gang member by his or her gang clothing or symbol.

With the increase in violence, school boards and administrators throughout the country are struggling with ways to curb gang activity. Efforts have included increased surveillance by police, locking doors during school hours, installing metal detectors at school entrances, canceling after-school activities and athletics, and imposing restrictions on gang-related clothing and hairstyles. Many of these remedies require considerable expense and, in a time of declining revenues for schools, most of these efforts are thereby impractical or impossible. In 1988 New York City spent $62 million on school security with larger budgets anticipated in subsequent years. From a purely economic standpoint, attempting to limit the growth of gang activity via restrictions placed on gang clothing is a viable option. The form of clothing restrictions ranges from mandates against "any gang affiliated clothing" to dress codes that articulate exactly what can and can not be worn, to policy memoranda distributed to students, parents, and teachers addressing the potential implications of wearing gang-related clothing.

For example, on August 29, 1991, the Oakland, California Board of Education postponed until a later date its decision on a controversial dress code. As proposed, the dress code would prohibit the wearing of gang colors and hairstyles, certain sports jackets and other items that have been identified as gang-related. It also would encourage the wearing of uniforms and discourage students from attending school in expensive jewelry and clothing. Although California state law prohibits mandatory attire in its public schools, 15 of Oakland's public schools have adopted uniforms which are worn voluntarily.

It is not too surprising that clothing and hair restrictions are being met with some adversity. After Northglenn High School in Denver, Colorado announced a new dress code that bans all hats or caps of any style, do-rags, headbands, and bandannas, any clothing bearing professional sports insignia, or any clothing that looks intimidating or dangerous, the students staged demonstrations and the media came alive with editorials from angered parents who claimed their child's constitutional rights were being violated. It is worth noting that at the time of this writing, only one court had directly addressed the gang clothing issue. [*Olesen v. Board of Educ.*, 676 F. Supp. 820 N.D. Ill. (1987)]

From a lay person's perspective, the parents' assertion seems rather simple and straightforward. From a legal perspective, two issues are pending: first, whether schools can or should restrict gang clothing, and second, how to restrict gang clothing without infringing upon the constitutional rights of the students.

N. Denise Burke, *Restricting Gang Clothing in the Public Schools*, 80 Educ. L. Rep. 513 (1993).*

5. Is the right to govern one's appearance strong enough to overcome a school's reasons for implementing a dress code? Consider Maloney, *Constitutional Problems Surrounding the implementation of "Anti-Gang" Regulations in the Public Schools*, 75 Marq. L. Rev. 179 (1991). In his article, Maloney briefly discusses approaches taken by schools. Some jurisdictions deny the existence of a right; others find a limited right noting (as in *Olesen*) a message of individuality is not protected under the First Amendment. According to Maloney, the bottom line approach is as follows:**

> The approach applied often seems based upon the nature of the underlying regulations and the challenge brought against it. However, as a general rule, the state has no great burden when attempting to prescribe certain clothing and hairstyles for the student body as long as the regulation in question meets a basic test of "reasonableness". This results primarily from the assumption that "anti-gang" dress codes foster safety in the school (*i.e.*, a compelling state interest), unlike the dress codes of the 1960 and 1970 cases, which addressed general concerns of school decorum.

If dress code restrictions were to be struck down in favor of a right to govern one's own appearance, then what is the justification? What is the source of this right? Maloney lists seven possible sources:

(1) First Amendment right of free expression;
(2) Ninth Amendment rights retained by the people;
(3) Fourteenth Amendment right of privacy;
(4) Fourteenth Amendment right to due process;
(5) Fourteenth Amendment right of equal protection;
(6) Right to be let alone;
(7) "No Reasonableness" arguments (the reasonableness test merely fails). Maloney at 181-82.

6. As mentioned in note 3 above, there is some feeling that school dress codes like the kind upheld in *Olesen* only divert attention away from the societal problem with gang activity. There is also the criticism that such codes contain an inherent racial bias against African-American and other students of color. *See* Murphy, at 1356, *supra* note 4. Those in favor of such codes agree that there is a disproportionate impact on non-white students, but this is warranted as such students make up the majority of the gangs. Murphy, at 1358. Others in favor

---

*Reprinted with permission. Copyright © 1993 by West Publishing Company.
**Copyright © 1991 by The Marquette Law Review. Reprinted with permission.

of the codes go so far as to suggest a lessening of constitutional protection for students of color in that many live in neighborhoods of high crime and poverty; this, as the reasoning goes, means a probable lack of parental supervision. Hence, one way to solve the problem is to permit school officials to bypass the First and Fourteenth Amendments when formulating policies for student conduct in "crime-ridden and poverty-stricken neighborhoods." *See* Rabkin, *Racial Progress and Constitutional Roadblocks*, 34 Wm. & Mary L. Rev. 75, 86 (1992). Is it possible that this sort of racial bias serves as a contributor to the formation of dress codes such as the one found in *Olesen*? What safeguards should school boards develop that would effectively respond to this outcome?

HARPER v. EDGEWOOD BOARD OF EDUCATION
United States District Court
655 F. Supp. 1353 (S.D. Ohio 1987)

CARL B. RUBIN, CHIEF JUDGE:

This matter is before the Court on motions for summary judgment by defendants Edgewood Board of Education, Dr. Roger Compton, Gene Smith, Dr. John Burly, M. Phillip Stroup, Jean Hanselman, Stephen Hester, Edith Pate and Kenneth Ziegler (hereinafter the "Edgewood defendants") and by defendants Miami University and Clyde E. Banks Jr. Plaintiffs, Warren Harper and his sister Florence Harper, brought this action alleging violations of and conspiracy to violate plaintiffs' rights under the First and Fourteenth Amendments to the United States Constitution, because they were not permitted to attend the Edgewood High School Prom dressed in clothing of the opposite sex. . . .

On the evening of May 18, 1985, Warren and Florence Harper arrived at Miami University in Oxford, Ohio to attend the Edgewood High School Junior-Senior Prom. Warren Harper was a senior at Edgewood High School at that time and had purchased tickets for the prom in advance. Warren Harper arrived at the prom attired as a woman, wearing earrings, stockings, high heels, a dress and a fur cape. Florence Harper wore a black tuxedo and men's shoes.

Upon plaintiffs' arrival, Gene Smith, the high school principal, asked to speak with Mr. Harper and directed him to an area separated from the corridor by glass doors. There, Mr. Smith and Roger Compton, the school superintendent asked Mr. Harper to change his clothes. Mr. Harper refused, and plaintiffs took their leave from Mr. Smith and Mr. Compton and entered the ballroom. Shortly thereafter, at the request of the Edgewood School officials, a Miami University police officer escorted plaintiffs from the prom.

Plaintiffs allege that defendants' actions deprived them of their constitutional rights in violation of 42 U.S.C. §§ 1981, 1983 and 1985....

. . . .

... [T]he Court will address the parties legal arguments as to each of plaintiffs' claims separately.

A. *42 U.S.C. § 1981*

....

42 U.S.C. § 1981 provides: All persons within the jurisdiction of the United States shall have the same right in every state and territory to make and enforce contracts, to sue, be parties, give evidence and to the full and equal benefit of all laws and proceedings for the security of persons and property as is enjoyed by white citizens, and shall be subject to like punishment, pains, penalties, taxes, licenses, and exactions of every kind and to no other.

It is well settled that section 1981 applies to race discrimination. *Runyon v. McCrary*, 427 U.S. 160 (1976); *Givan v. Greyhound Lines, Inc.*, 616 F.Supp. 1223 (S.D.Ohio 1985). Plaintiffs are white and do not allege that defendants discriminated against them based on their race. Therefore, defendants' motions for summary judgment on plaintiffs' section 1981 claims are granted and such claims are hereby dismissed.

B. *42 U.S.C. § 1983*

Plaintiffs allege that defendants violated their constitutional rights under the First Amendment and the Due Process and Equal Protection Clauses of the Fourteenth Amendment in violation of 42 U.S.C. § 1983.

The Supreme Court has held that "First Amendment rights, applied in light of the special characteristics of the school environment, are available to teachers and students." *Tinker v. Des Moines School District*, 393 U.S. 503 (1969). The Court added, however, that school officials have "comprehensive authority" subject to constitutional safeguards, "to prescribe and control conduct in the school." Citing *Tinker*, the United States Court of Appeals for the Sixth Circuit has upheld school grooming codes regarding hair length as reasonably related to "the maintenance of discipline, promotion of safety ... and the furtherance of valid educational purposes, including the teaching of grooming, discipline and etiquette." *Gfell v. Rickelman*, 441 F.2d 444 (6th Cir.1971)....

In the present case, the school board's dress regulations are reasonably related to the valid educational purposes of teaching community values and maintaining school discipline. Therefore, the school officials did not violate any rights plaintiffs might have under the First Amendment by prohibiting them from attending the Junior-Senior Prom dressed as members of the opposite sex.

Plaintiffs also claim that defendants deprived plaintiffs of their liberty without due process of law by falsely arresting and imprisoning them, and by removing them from the prom. In *Parratt v. Taylor*, 451 U.S. 527 (1981), the United States Supreme Court held that an action under section 1983 for deprivation of property without due process does not lie where the state provides an adequate postdeprivation remedy for the alleged tort. In *Wilson v. Beebe*, 770 F.2d 578 (6th Cir.1985) the Sixth Circuit extended that rationale to limit section 1983 actions where liberty interests are involved. Clearly, Ohio common law provides a remedy for false arrest and/or false imprisonment if such claims can be proved.

Moreover, plaintiffs have failed even to plead the inadequacy of state processes. Therefore, plaintiffs have no cause of action under section 1983 against the Edgewood defendants, Officer Banks or Miami University for deprivation of liberty without due process....

Plaintiffs final claim under section 1983 is that the Edgewood defendants violated plaintiffs' rights under the Equal Protection Clause of the Fourteenth Amendment because defendants allowed female students to wear dresses and male students to wear tuxedos to the prom but did not allow Warren Harper to wear a dress or Florence Harper to wear a tuxedo to this event. This claim must also fail. The school dress code does not differentiate based on sex. The dress code requires all students to dress in conformity with the accepted standards of the community. In upholding a regulation concerning the length of hair for male students only, the Sixth Circuit noted that "such regulations and regulations which deal generally with dress and the like are a part of the disciplinary process which is necessary in maintaining a balance as between the rights of individual students and the rights of the whole in the functioning of schools." *Gfell*, 441 F.2d at 446, quoting *Ferrell v. Dallas Independent School System*, 392 F.2d 697, 703 (5th Cir.), *cert. denied*, 393 U.S. 856 (1968)....

C. *42 U.S.C. § 1985*

Plaintiffs allege that the Edgewood defendants, Officer Banks and Miami University conspired to interfere with plaintiffs' civil rights. 42 U.S.C. § 1985(3) prohibits any conspiracy to deny a plaintiff equal protection, where a coconspirator injures the plaintiff while acting to further the conspiracy. In *Griffin v. Breckenridge*, 403 U.S. 88, 102-03 1798, (1971), the United States Supreme Court held that "[t]he language requiring intent to deprive of equal protection, or equal privileges and immunities, means that there must be some racial, or perhaps otherwise class based invidiously discriminatory animus behind the conspiracy action." Neither homosexuals, nor transvestites, nor those in sympathy with them are a "class" within the meaning of § 1985(3). *DeSantis v. Pacific Telephone & Telegraph Company, Inc.*, 608 F.2d 327 (9th Cir.1979). Moreover, this Court has held that the school officials actions in implementing the school dress code did not deny plaintiffs equal protection of the law. Therefore, defendants are entitled to summary judgment on plaintiffs section 1985 claim.

III. *Conclusion*

Finding no infringement of plaintiffs' constitutional rights, the Court reiterates the statement of the Court of Appeals for the Sixth Circuit that "the responsibility for maintaining proper standards of decorum and discipline and a wholesome academic environment ... is not vested in the federal courts, but in the principal and faculty of the school...." *Jackson v. Dorrier*, 424 F.2d 218-19 (6th Cir. 1970).

A. STUDENT CONDUCT AND SCHOOL AUTHORITY

For the foregoing reasons, defendants' motions for summary judgment on claims under 42 U.S.C. §§ 1981, 1983 and 1985 are granted and such claims are hereby dismissed. Furthermore, no federal claim survives, the Court declines to exercise jurisdiction over plaintiffs' claims under state law, and such claims are hereby dismissed.

....

FRICKE v. LYNCH
United States District Court
491 F. Supp. 381 (D.R.I. 1980)

PETTINE, CHIEF JUDGE:

Most of the time, a young man's choice of a date for the senior prom is of no great interest to anyone other than the student, his companion, and, perhaps, a few of their classmates. But in Aaron Fricke's case, the school authorities actively disapprove of his choice, the other students are upset, the community is abuzz, and out-of-state newspapers consider the matter newsworthy. All this fuss arises because Aaron Fricke's intended escort is another young man. Claiming that the school's refusal to allow him to bring a male escort violates his first and fourteenth amendment rights, Fricke seeks a preliminary injunction ordering the school officials to allow him to attend with a male escort.

Two days of testimony have revealed the following facts. The senior reception at Cumberland High School is a formal dinner-dance sponsored and run by the senior class. It is held shortly before graduation but is not a part of the graduation ceremonies. This year the students have decided to hold the dance at the Pleasant Valley Country Club in Sutton, Massachusetts on Friday, May 30. All seniors except those on suspension are eligible to attend the dance; no one is required to go. All students who attend must bring an escort, although their dates need not be seniors or even Cumberland High School students. Each student is asked the name of his date at the time he buys the tickets.

The principal testified that school dances are chaperoned by him, two assistant principals, and one or two class advisers. They are sometimes joined by other teachers who volunteer to help chaperone; such teachers are not paid. Often these teachers will drop in for part of the dance. Additionally, police officers are on duty at the dance. Usually two officers attend; last year three plainclothes officers were at the junior prom.

The seeds of the present conflict were planted a year ago when Paul Guilbert, then a junior at Cumberland High School, sought permission to bring a male escort to the junior prom. The principal, Richard Lynch (the defendant here), denied the request, fearing that student reaction could lead to a disruption at the dance and possibly to physical harm to Guilbert....

This year, during or after an assembly in April in which senior class events were discussed, Aaron Fricke, a senior at Cumberland High School, decided that he wanted to attend the senior reception with a male companion. Aaron considers himself a homosexual, and has never dated girls, although he does socialize with female friends. He has never taken a girl to a school dance. Until this April, he had not "come out of the closet" by publicly acknowledging his sexual orientation.

Aaron asked principal Lynch for permission to bring a male escort, which Lynch denied. A week later (during vacation), Aaron asked Paul Guilbert who now lives in New York to be his escort (if allowed), and Paul accepted. Aaron met again with Lynch, at which time they discussed Aaron's commitment to homosexuality; Aaron indicated that although it was possible he might someday be bisexual, at the present he is exclusively homosexual and could not conscientiously date girls. Lynch gave Aaron written reasons for his action; his prime concern was the fear that a disruption would occur and Aaron or, especially, Paul would be hurt. He indicated in court that he would allow Aaron to bring a male escort if there were no threat of violence.

After Aaron filed suit in this Court, an event reported by the Rhode Island and Boston papers, a student shoved and, the next day, punched Aaron. The unprovoked, surprise assault necessitated five stitches under Aaron's right eye. The assailant was suspended for nine days. After this, Aaron was given a special parking space closer to the school doors and has been provided with an escort (principal or assistant principal) between classes. No further incidents have occurred.

This necessarily brief account does not convey the obvious concern and good faith Lynch has displayed in his handling of the matter. Lynch sincerely believes that there is a significant possibility that some students will attempt to injure Aaron and Paul if they attend the dance. Moreover, Lynch's actions in school have displayed a concern for Aaron's safety while at school. Perhaps one cannot be at all sure a totally different approach by Lynch might have kept the matter from reaching its present proportions, but I am convinced that Lynch's actions have stemmed in significant part from a concern for disruption.

Aaron contends that the school's action violates his first amendment right of association, his first amendment right to free speech, and his fourteenth amendment right to equal protection of the laws. (The equal protection claim is a "hybrid" one that he has been treated differently than others because of the content of his communication.)

The starting point in my analysis of Aaron's first amendment free speech claim must be, of course, to determine whether the action he proposes to take has a "communicative content sufficient to bring it within the ambit of the first amendment." *Gay Students Organization v. Bonner*, 509 F.2d 652 (1st Cir. 1974) (hereinafter *Bonner*).... This normally difficult task is made somewhat easier here, however, by the precedent set in *Bonner, supra*. In that case, the University of New Hampshire prohibited the Gay Students' Organization (GSO) from holding dances and other social events. The first circuit explicitly rejected the idea that traditional first amendment rights of expression were not involved. 509 F.2d at 660. The Court found that not only did discussion and exchange of ideas take place at informal social functions, *Id.* at 660-61, but also that:

A. STUDENT CONDUCT AND SCHOOL AUTHORITY

"beyond the specific communications at such events is the basic 'message' GSO seeks to convey that homosexuals exist, that they feel repressed by existing laws and attitudes, that they wish to emerge from their isolation, and that public understanding of their attitudes and problems is desirable for society." *Id.* at 661. Here too the proposed activity has significant expressive content. Aaron testified that he wants to go because he feels he has a right to attend and participate just like all the other students and that it would be dishonest to his own sexual identity to take a girl to the dance. He went on to acknowledge that he feels his attendance would have a certain political element and would be a statement for equal rights and human rights. Admittedly, his explanation of his "message" was hesitant and not nearly as articulate as Judge Coffin's restatement of the GSO's message, cited above. Nevertheless, I believe Aaron's testimony that he is sincerely although perhaps not irrevocably committed to a homosexual orientation and that attending the dance with another young man would be a political statement....

Accordingly, the school's action must be judged by the standards articulated in *United States v. O'Brien*, 391 U.S. 367 (1968), and applied in *Bonner*: (1) was the regulation within the constitutional power of the government; (2) did it further an important or substantial governmental interest; (3) was the governmental interest unrelated to the suppression of free expression; and (4) was the incidental restriction on alleged first amendment freedoms no greater than essential to the furtherance of that interest? *Bonner* at 662.

I need not dwell on the first two *O'Brien* requirements: the school unquestionably has an important interest in student safety and has the power to regulate students' conduct to ensure safety. As to the suppression of free expression, Lynch's testimony indicated that his personal views on homosexuality did not affect his decision, and that but for the threat of violence he would let the two young men go together. Thus the government's interest here is not in squelching a particular message because it objects to its content as such. On the other hand, the school's interest is in suppressing certain speech activity because of the reaction its message may engender. Surely this is still suppression of free expression.

It is also clear that the school's action fails to meet the last criterion set out in *O'Brien*, the requirement that the government employ the "least restrictive alternative" before curtailing speech. The plaintiff argues, and I agree, that the school can take appropriate security measures to control the risk of harm.... Although Lynch did not say that any additional security measures would be adequate, from the testimony I find that significant measures could be taken and would in all probability critically reduce the likelihood of any disturbance.... The measures taken already, especially the escort system, have been highly effective in preventing any further problems at school. Appropriate security measures coupled with a firm, clearly communicated attitude by the administration that any disturbance will not be tolerated appear to be a realistic, and less restrictive, alternative to prohibiting Aaron from attending the dance with the date of his choice.

The analysis so far has been along traditional first amendment lines, making no real allowance for the fact that this case arises in a high school setting. The most difficult problem this controversy presents is how this setting should affect the result. *Tinker v. Des Moines Independent Community School District*, 393 U.S. 503 (1969), makes clear that high school students do not "shed their constitutional rights to freedom of speech or expression at the schoolhouse gate." *Id.* at 506. As the *Tinker* Court stated: But, in our system, undifferentiated fear or apprehension of disturbance is not enough to overcome the right to freedom of expression. Any departure from absolute regimentation may cause trouble. Any variation from the majority's opinion may inspire fear. Any word spoken, in class, in the lunchroom, or on the campus, that deviates from the views of another person may start an argument or cause a disturbance. But our Constitution says we must take this risk; and our history says that it is this sort of hazardous freedom this kind of openness that is the basis of our national strength and of the independence and vigor of Americans who grow up and live in this relatively permissive, often disputatious, society. In order for the State in the person of school officials to justify prohibition of a particular expression of opinion, it must be able to show that its action was caused by something more than a mere desire to avoid the discomfort and unpleasantness that always accompany an unpopular viewpoint. Certainly where there is no finding and no showing that engaging in the forbidden conduct would "materially and substantially interfere with the requirements of appropriate discipline in the operation of the school," the prohibition cannot be sustained. *Burnside v. Byars* (363 F.2d 744).... *Tinker* at 508-09....

Tinker did, however, indicate that there are limits on first amendment rights within the school: A student's rights, therefore, do not embrace merely the classroom hours.... [C]onduct by the student, in class or out of it, which for any reason whether it stems from time, place or type of behavior materially disrupts classwork or involves substantial disorder or invasion of the rights of others is, of course, not immunized by the constitutional guarantee of freedom of speech. *Cf. Blackwell v. Issaquena County Board of Education*, 363 F.2d 749 (C.A. 5th Cir. 1966). *Tinker* at 513.

It seems to me that here, not unlike in *Tinker*, the school administrators were acting on "an undifferentiated fear or apprehension of disturbance." True, Aaron was punched and then security measures were taken, but since that incident he has not been threatened with violence nor has he been attacked. There has been no disruption at the school; classes have not been cancelled, suspended, or interrupted. In short, while the defendants have perhaps shown more of a basis for fear of harm than in *Tinker*, they have failed to make a "showing" that Aaron's conduct would "materially and substantially interfere" with school discipline. *See Tinker* at 509. However, even if the Court assumes that there is justifiable fear and that Aaron's peaceful speech leads, or may lead, to a violent

A. STUDENT CONDUCT AND SCHOOL AUTHORITY 279

reaction from others, the question remains: may the school prohibit the speech, or must it protect the speaker?

....

After considerable thought and research, I have concluded that even a legitimate interest in school discipline does not outweigh a student's right to peacefully express his views in an appropriate time, place, and manner. To rule otherwise would completely subvert free speech in the schools by granting other students a "heckler's veto," allowing them to decide through prohibited and violent methods what speech will be heard. The first amendment does not tolerate mob rule by unruly school children.... In such a context, the school does have an obligation to take reasonable measures to protect and foster free speech, not to stand helpless before unauthorized student violence.

....

The present case is so difficult because the Court is keenly sensitive to the testimony regarding the concerns of a possible disturbance, and of physical harm to Aaron or Paul. However, I am convinced that meaningful security measures are possible, and the first amendment requires that such steps be taken to protect rather than to stifle free expression. Some may feel that Aaron's attendance at the reception and the message he will thereby convey is trivial compared to other social debates, but to engage in this kind of a weighing in process is to make the content-based evaluation forbidden by the first amendment.

....

Because the free speech claim is dispositive, I find it unnecessary to reach the plaintiff's right of association argument or to deal at length with his equal protection claim. I find that the plaintiff has established a probability of success on the merits and has shown irreparable harm; accordingly his request for a preliminary injunction is hereby granted.

....

---

1. Do dress codes, in general, "differentiate based on sex?" *Harper*, 655 F. Supp. 1353, 1356. Is it possible for a dress code that restricts hair length and earrings for men, but not for women, to not differentiate based on sex? Would a female student have been able to wear *one* cross earring in Olesen's school without similar disciplinary action? Would *Harper* have been decided differently if only Florence (the sister) had arrived in clothing generally worn by the opposite sex?

2. The student in *Fricke* prevailed because his appearance at the prom with another male was considered a "political statement" under the First Amendment. Is this consistent with other cases involving students' First Amendment rights? (*See* Chapter 6.) Aside from the end result in this case, would Fricke be pleased with the reasoning? Was the decision in this case a reflection of the times, *i.e.*, were the public views toward homosexuality in 1980 such that a gay couple at a high school prom could be considered nothing but political? If this is true, would *Fricke* be decided differently today?

3. In light of a case like *Fricke*, does the result in *Harper* seem fair? Could the actions of Warren and Florence Harper in dressing up in prom clothes of the opposite sex be considered a political statement protected by the First Amendment? Which expressive conduct, that of Harper or of Fricke, do you think is "more" political? Perhaps the Harpers were attempting to show the school how overexaggerated high school proms can be. Under reasoning similar to that in *Fricke*, would this have worked in favor of the Harpers?

4. Consider the following voter initiative to amend the Colorado State Constitution (which passed by a vote of 53% to 47% in 1993):

> Neither the State of Colorado, through any of its branches or departments, nor any of its agencies, political subdivisions, municipalities or *school districts*, shall enact, adopt or enforce any statute, regulation, ordinance or policy whereby homosexual, lesbian or bisexual orientation, conduct, practices or relationships shall constitute or otherwise be the basis of, or entitle any person or class of persons to have or to claim any discrimination. (authors' emphasis) *Evans v. Romer*, 1993 WL 518586 (Colo. Dist. Ct.) at 1.

What is the possible impact of such an amendment on the decision making of school administrators as to the expressive conduct of students such as those found in *Fricke* and *Harper*? Would the decision in *Fricke* have been rendered differently had the case arisen in a Colorado state court?

The proposed amendment was declared unconstitutional by the Supreme Court of Colorado in *Evans v. Romer*, 854 P.2d 1270 (Colo. 1993). The court held that: "... [T]he equal protection clause of the United States Constitution protects the fundamental right to participate equally in the political process, and that any legislation or state constitutional amendment which infringes on this right by "fencing out" an independently identifiable class of persons must be subject to strict judicial scrutiny." *Id.* at 1282.

The decision in *Romer* suggests some similarity to that of *Fricke* as to a denial of the fundamental right to participate in the political process or to make a political statement. However, the court in *Romer* stated that the voter initiative had to be examined under the rubric of strict scrutiny. Did the district court use the same test in *Fricke*?

The courts send mixed signals relative to the tests to be used for gay or lesbian activity. For example, recently a federal district and circuit court applied the rational basis test to resolve whether gays and lesbians should be excluded from the military. In each case, unlike *Romer*, no fundamental right was involved. *See Steffan v. Aspin*, 1993 WL 465530 (D.C. Cir.) and *Dahl v. Secretary of U.S. Navy*, 830 F. Supp. 1319 (E.D. Cal. 1993). Both cases found no rational basis for excluding gays and lesbians from military service. Note, however, that the court in *Steffan* distinguished its decision from that in *Bowers v. Hardwick*, 478

U.S. 186 (1986) (described in Note 6 below) in that *Steffan* was a case of sexual orientation and *Bowers* was one of conduct. The question of whether government can discriminate on the basis of orientation was not definitively answered in *Steffan*.

5. Should gays/lesbians be considered a suspect class? This has been a recent argument of some legal commentators. *See, e.g.,* Niblock, *Anti-Gay Initiatives: A Call for Heightened Judicial Scrutiny,* 41 UCLA L. Rev. 153 (1993); Culverhouse and Lewis, *Homosexuality as a Suspect Class,* 34 S. Tex. L. Rev. 205 (1993); Ackerman, *Beyond Carolene Products,* 98 Harv. L. Rev. 713 (1985). Also, at least one court has argued that the "strict scrutiny" standard should be applied to complaints of discrimination based on sexual orientation. *See Watkins v. United States Army,* 847 F.2d 1329 (9th Cir. 1988). By and large, however, courts have not held gay/lesbian orientation or conduct to fall under the protection of suspect classification. For a rendition of additional cases involving the military or other defense-related agencies and appeals for suspect class status *see Webster v. Doe,* 486 U.S. 592 (1988); *High Tech Gays v. Defense Indus. Sec. Clearance Office,* 895 F.2d 563 (9th Cir. 1990); *Ben-Shalom v. Marsh,* 881 F.2d 454 (7th Cir. 1989); *Dubbs v. Central Intelligence Agency,* 866 F.2d 1114 (9th Cir. 1989); *Dronenburg v. Zeck,* 741 F.2d 1388 (D.C. Cir. 1984); *Steffan v. Cheney,* 780 F. Supp. 1 (D.D.C. 1991).

See also Narogon v. Wharton, 737 F.2d 1403 (5th Cir. 1984) in which a graduate student filed suit under Fourteenth Amendment protection claiming that she had been denied teaching duties due to her sexual orientation. The court found evidence sufficient enough to hold that the lesbian orientation of the student was not a motivating factor in the decision of the university to change her assignment. Actually, so ruled the court, the change in assignment was prompted by considerations much more compelling than her particular sexual preference. What compelling interest did the university have?

What is the status of gay and lesbian student groups on college campuses? How do they fare in equal protection claims? Results are mixed. *See* Note, *Increasing the Speed: Diversity, Campus Speech Codes and the Pursuit of Truth,* 67 S. Cal. L. Rev. 407 (1994); Cain, *Symposium on Sexual Orientation and the Law: Litigating for Lesbian and Gay Rights: A Legal History,* 79 Va. L. Rev. 1551 (1993); Note, *Constitutional Limits on Anti-Gay Rights Initiatives,* 106 Harv. L. Rev. 1905 (1993).

6. To date the United States Supreme Court has not recognized sexual orientation as a suspect classification. The argument was perhaps most fully developed in *Bowers v. Hardwick,* 478 U.S. 186 (1986) where the court ruled that the Constitution does not guarantee a right to engage in homosexual sodomy. The ruling in *Bowers,* as noted, has been used in other federal courts to reject the use of heightened scrutiny for discrimination against gays and lesbians. *See, e.g., Padula v. Webster,* 822 F.2d 97, 103 (D.C. Cir. 1987), "if the [*Bowers*] Court was unwilling to object to state laws that criminalize behavior that defines the class, it is hardly open to a lower court to conclude that state sponsored discrimination against the class is invidious." *See also Ben-Shalom v. Marsh*, cited above, where the Seventh Circuit, relying on the decision in *Bowers* held that "homosexuals do not constitute a suspect or quasi-suspect class entitled to greater than rational basis scrutiny for equal protection purposes." *Id.* at 464.

7. Justice White rendered the majority decision in *Bowers*, reasoning that the right to engage in gay/lesbian activity was not "implicit in the concept of ordered liberty, such that 'neither liberty nor justice would exist if [it] were sacrificed.'" *Bowers*, at 191-92 (quoting *Palko v. Connecticut*, 302 U.S. 319, 325-26 (1937)). This distinction from other such cases that have been found to be "implicit in the concept of ordered liberty" enables the Court to find no platform for strict scrutiny. *See Roe v. Wade*, 410 U.S. 113 (1973) "Right of personal privacy or a guarantee of certain areas or zones of privacy does exist under the Constitution, and only personal rights that can be deemed fundamental or implicit in the concept of ordered liberty are included in this guarantee of personal privacy...." *Roe*, at 115. However, Justice Blackmun (who delivered the majority opinion in *Roe*) dissented in *Bowers*, reasoning that the Court must approach the conduct issue in a broader and more basic fashion: "[T]his case is about 'the most comprehensive of rights and the right most valued by civilized men,' namely, 'the right to be let alone.'" *Bowers*, at 199 (Blackmun, J., dissenting) (quoting *Olmstead v. United States*, 277 U.S. 438, 478 (1928) (Brandeis, J., dissenting)). Why didn't Blackmun see a right of privacy in *Roe* as the "right to be let alone?" Is it possible that the Supreme Court would not follow such reasoning? *See* Justice Stewart's concurring opinion in *Roe*: "'[T]he protection of a person's right to privacy — his right to be *let alone* [authors' emphasis] by other people — is like the protection of his property and his very life, left largely to the law of the individual States.'" *Roe*, at 168 (Stewart, J., concurring) (quoting *Katz v. United States*, 389 U.S. 347, 350-51 (1967)). Could this also be the reason that the students in neither *Fricke* nor *Harper* brought such a cause of action?

B. MARRIAGE, MOTHERHOOD, PREGNANCY, AND THE STUDENT

STREET v. COBB COUNTY SCHOOL DISTRICT

United States District Court
520 F. Supp. 1170 (N.D. Ga. 1981)

ORINDA D. EVANS, DISTRICT JUDGE:

This matter is before the Court on Plaintiff's Motion for a Preliminary Injunction to enjoin the Cobb County School District from preventing her participation in the day school program at South Cobb High School. An evidentiary hearing was held on July 31, 1981. On August 25, 1981, the Court entered an Order granting Plaintiff's Motion. The following findings of fact and conclusions of law are entered in support of that Order.

B. MARRIAGE, MOTHERHOOD, PREGNANCY, AND THE STUDENT

The basic facts, most of which are undisputed, are found to be as follows: Plaintiff is a seventeen year old who has attended South Cobb High School for the past two years. Until late April, 1981, she lived with her mother and stepfather, who reside in the South Cobb High School District; thereafter, she moved to an apartment to live with her eighteen year old boyfriend and then to her boyfriend's parents' home (also in the South Cobb High School District) where she and her boyfriend presently live.

On May 15, 1981, the high school learned of Plaintiff's living arrangements. She was called to the principal's office and informed that she could no longer attend South Cobb High School because the school district's policies were interpreted to permit only "resident students" to attend. A "resident student" is defined in the school board's policies as "a student who resides with his parents or in the event of divorce, with the custodial parent and/or legal guardian within the Cobb County School District."

. . . .

Plaintiff seeks preliminary and permanent injunctive relief to permit her to now proceed to commence and complete her senior year at the high school.

The School District's position is two-fold: first, it says Plaintiff does not fit the definition of "resident student" and therefore she cannot attend.... Secondly, the School District contends that because of Plaintiff's unconventional living arrangements, her presence in the school population might be a bad influence on impressionable students. The School District points out that it has an adult education program which is available to Plaintiff and that it is not seeking to totally deny her an education.

The evidence at the hearing showed that the School District does permit married students under the age of eighteen who are living apart from their parents to attend the day school program. Also, the School District permits unwed pregnant students to continue in the day school program, provided such students live with a parent or guardian.

. . . .

Plaintiff testified that she had traditionally made B's and C's in high school. However, in the spring quarter of 1981, her grades were D's and F's. Plaintiff nonetheless states a definite desire to return to South Cobb High this fall. She considers the adult education program inferior to the day school program.

. . . .

For reasons that will be discussed hereinafter, the Court believes the central finding to be made by the Court is whether or not Plaintiff is an emancipated or unemancipated minor. This finding is important both to the Court's analysis of her substantive claim and also to Plaintiff's entitlement to maintain this lawsuit in her own name. If Plaintiff is an unemancipated minor, she may not maintain this suit on her own but rather suit would have to be maintained by her guardian, in this case, her mother. If her mother were not to find the maintenance of the suit in the daughter's interest, that might very well terminate the litigation.

In Georgia, an unemancipated minor is subject to the power of his or her parent or guardian. An emancipated minor is not. *See* Ga.Code Ann. § 74-108. There are several ways for a minor to become emancipated. First, marriage emancipates. *See McGregor v. McGregor*, 237 Ga. 57, 226 S.E.2d 591 (1976). Additionally, emancipation may be shown by one of the grounds set out in Ga.Code Ann. § 74-108. Section 74-108 provides, in part, that parental power may be lost by: (1) Voluntary contract, releasing the right to a third person. (2) Consenting to the adoption of the child by a third person. (3) Failure to provide necessaries for the child, or abandonment of the child. (4) Consent to the child's receiving the proceeds of his own labor, which consent shall be revocable at any time. (5) Consent to the marriage of the child, who thus assumes inconsistent responsibilities. (6) Cruel treatment of the child.

Looking at the totality of circumstances involved here, the Court finds, not without some hesitation, that Plaintiff is an emancipated minor. She has been living away from home for four months and has evidenced no intent to return. Since November 1980, she has worked and furnished her own income, which income has neither been requested by nor received by her mother. Although her mother has made it clear she wants her daughter to come home, she has also stated she will consent to her daughter's marriage. Finally, Plaintiff is only eight months away from the age of majority.

The Court now looks to see what implications Plaintiff's status as an emancipated minor has for the outcome of this case. She brings this action under 42 U.S.C. § 1983, which proscribes the deprivation of federally guaranteed rights under color of state law. The Cobb County School District is, of course, an arm of the State. The federally guaranteed right involved, according to Plaintiff, is the equal protection guaranteed by the Fourteenth Amendment of the United States Constitution. Her argument is that the School District does not treat emancipated minors equally, because the School District permits married minors to attend the day school program, but not single emancipated minors.

The initial step in equal protection analysis is to determine the nature of the interest affected or classification involved. *Dunn v. Blumstein*, 405 U.S. 330 (1972). When a state rule is attacked as violating the equal protection clause it must be examined against one of two constitutional tests. Where the state rule impinges upon a fundamental right or creates a classification which is based upon inherently suspect criteria, the required standard of review is that of strict scrutiny. Under strict scrutiny it must be shown that the classification furthers a compelling state interest and that the means chosen to effectuate that purpose is the least restrictive alternative available. *San Antonio School District v. Rodriquez*, 411 U.S. 1 (1972). Where no fundamental right is infringed upon or no suspect class is present, the appropriate constitutional test is rational relationship. Under "rational relationship" the classification must be examined to determine whether it is rationally related to a legitimate state purpose. *San Antonio, supra*; *Eisentadt v. Baird*, 405 U.S. 438 (1972).

B. MARRIAGE, MOTHERHOOD, PREGNANCY, AND THE STUDENT

The Supreme Court has held that the right to an education is not a "fundamental" right. *San Antonio, supra.* No suspect classification is involved. Therefore, the test to be applied is the "rational relationship" test.

Is a School District policy which permits a married minor, but not an emancipated single minor to attend school rationally related to a legitimate state purpose? Put another way, is there a rational basis for distinguishing between the two groups? The Court has no difficulty concluding that the School District's stated purpose for the rule does not support the distinction. The School District has contended that it needs access to a parent or guardian who has control over the child when same is required in connection with academic or deportment matters involving the student. In the case of a married minor, the testimony was that the school would simply deal with the student, not his or her spouse. It would seem to the Court that the same situation is presented as to an emancipated minor, who in the Court's view is not apt to be any more or less mature than a married student similarly situated.

This then leaves for the Court's consideration, the School District's alternate position, namely, that it desires to exclude from the school population those who may set an undesirable example for impressionable students. The Fifth Circuit has held that a teacher's aide who has borne a child out of wedlock may not be excluded from employment for that reason alone. *Andrews v. Drew Municipal Separate School District,* 507 F.2d 611 (5th Cir. 1975). The court's reasoning, in part, was that students were not apt to "... seek out knowledge of the personal and private family lifestyles of teachers...." *Id.* at 617. The Court is not certain that the same rationale would apply to the facts presented here, but the Court finds it unnecessary to resolve that issue. This is because the School District permits pregnant students to attend the day school program. Thus, assuming the School District may legally enforce policies calculated to foster morality in personal living arrangements, the Court can see no rational basis for excluding someone in Plaintiff's situation, but not excluding a pregnant student. In other words, the School District's stated alternate reason fails equal protection analysis too.

In summary, the Court finds that the School District's policy as applied to Plaintiff is in violation of the Equal Protection Clause of the Fourteenth Amendment of the United States Constitution. For that reason, it cannot be enforced against her so as to exclude her from the School District's day school program.

---

1. Would the result in this case be different if the student's parents lived *outside* the school district or could not be located?

2. Which do you think is more impressionable and influential on students — unwed pregnancy or emancipation of minors under the circumstances in *Street*? If earlier courts had allowed schools to exclude unwed pregnant students and to enroll them in evening classes, would the court in *Street* have been compelled to find in favor of the school?

3. What about when a school *teacher* is the unwed mother? *See Dayton Christian Schs. v. Ohio Civil Rights Comm'n*, 766 F.2d 932 (6th Cir. 1985); *Vigars v. Valley Christian Center of Dublin, California*, 805 F. Supp. 802 (N.D. Calif. 1992). Most of these cases deal with out-of-wedlock pregnancy resulting from sexual intercourse. For a case involving out-of-wedlock pregnancy resulting from artificial insemination, *see Cameron v. Board of Educ. of the Hillsboro, Ohio, City Sch. Dist.*, 795 F. Supp. 228 (S.D. Ohio 1991).

4. Should an unmarried teacher be forced to take a leave of absence when it is discovered that she is pregnant? *See Ponton v. Newport News Sch. Bd.*, 632 F. Supp. 1056 (E.D. Va. 1986). *See also Chambers v. Omaha Girls Club*, 834 F.2d 697 (8th Cir. 1988), in which an unmarried pregnant woman was fired under the club's "negative role model" policy. The court held that the role model rule was a bona fide occupational qualification.

5. To highlight how important continued educational opportunity might be for unwed teenage mothers, read the following poem, written by a high school teacher, published in *Showcase '89* The Columbus Public Schools (1989):*

Children at Risk
They are both seventeen
she, in years
he, in months.
She has grown
matured
aged
far beyond
the chronological.
Raising him
as well as herself
she struggles.
He cries
in the night
she echoes
the sound
is pitiful.
She wants
her mother, too.
The alarm comes too soon
and she is off
to the sitter
the school

---

*Copyright © 1989 by Terry Monnett. Reprinted with permission.

> the job
> then back to him.
> How could she hold
> so much love
> for a mistake?
> They are both tired
> children
> in need of love
> desperate
> dependent.

PFEIFFER v. MARION CENTER AREA SCHOOL DISTRICT

United States Court of Appeals,
917 F.2d 779 (3d Cir. 1990)

ALDISERT, CIRCUIT JUDGE:

The major question for decision in this appeal by an unsuccessful plaintiff in a gender discrimination case is whether, based on the testimony admitted into evidence, the district court erred in concluding that there was no violation of Title IX of the Education Amendments of 1972, 20 U.S.C. §§ 1681, *et seq.*, when Arlene Pfeiffer was dismissed as a member of a high school chapter of the National Honor Society. The district court found as a fact that she was dismissed because of premarital sexual activity and not because of gender discrimination. Applying the appropriate standard of review, we hold that the finding was not clearly erroneous and accordingly affirm this determination of the court.

We are troubled, however, with an evidentiary ruling that excluded the testimony of a male student member of the school's chapter of the National Honor Society. We remand, therefore, for the limited purpose of admitting the proffered testimony. We hold that this testimony has the potential of being relevant to whether there was discriminatory intent by members of the faculty council when they met on November 9, 1983, and unanimously voted by secret ballot to dismiss Pfeiffer from the high school chapter. By our action we do not suggest that the admission of this evidence would, in and of itself, produce a different result from that previously reached by the trial court. We hold merely that the district court in reaching a fresh decision should consider this evidence along with all the other evidence previously adduced.

Should the trial court find that the dismissal was not motivated by a discriminatory intent that violates Title IX, then it would be appropriate to enter again judgment for the appellees. Should liability be determined, however, we conclude that the district court should consider the possibility of compensatory damages.

II

The appellant, Arlene Pfeiffer, was a member of the class of 1984 at the Marion Center Area High School in Marion, Indiana County, Pennsylvania. She was a good student who earned high grades and participated in a wide variety of school organizations, including serving as president of the student council. Based on her record, she was elected to her high school's chapter of the National Honor Society (NHS) in 1981. The society had a local chapter in existence at the school from approximately 1975 until 1986. The local chapter was governed by a faculty council composed of Robert L. Stewart, the principal of the high school, and Theda Lightcap, Jane Smith, Judith Skubis, and George Krivonick, all teachers at the Marion Center Area High School.

During the spring of 1983, Pfeiffer, who was unmarried, discovered that she was pregnant. She informed her school guidance counselor and principal and indicated that she wanted to rear her child but that she also wanted to finish high school. Principal Stewart told her that he saw no problem in her plan to continue school and graduate.

The handbook for the National Honor Society requires that students be selected for membership on the basis of scholarship, service, leadership and character. The constitution of the local chapter followed that of the national organization, requiring admission and maintenance be based on the same qualities. The high school had a selection procedure which followed the national organization's instructions, in which these qualities were assessed by teachers. To be admitted into the NHS, a student was rated by at least five teachers. In the instructions under the heading "Leadership" one of the qualities to be assessed was whether the student exerted the type of leadership which directly influences others for good conduct. Another quality to be assessed under the heading "Character" was whether the student upholds principles of morality and ethics.

Upon learning of Pfeiffer's pregnancy, Judith Skubis, a teacher and member of the faculty council, brought the matter to the attention of the other council members in the spring of 1983. That fall, when school resumed, the council scheduled a meeting for November 4, 1983, and Pfeiffer was invited to attend. The council members explained to her that her NHS membership was in question because premarital sex appeared to be contrary to the qualities of leadership and character essential for membership. When asked if her sexual activity leading to her pregnancy had been voluntary, the plaintiff answered in the affirmative. The council deferred further action.

On November 8, 1983, Pfeiffer's father, Delmont Pfeiffer, telephoned Principal Stewart requesting a prompt decision because an induction ceremony for seniors was scheduled for the next day and Arlene wanted to attend. The council met on the morning of November 9, 1983, and by secret ballot unanimously voted to dismiss her from the NHS chapter....

On November 30, 1983, the council met with her parents, who requested that the subject be placed on the agenda of the school board meeting scheduled for

December 12, 1983. Pfeiffer and her parents appeared at the meeting with counsel. The board requested that the matter be discussed privately, but Pfeiffer and her parents insisted that the issue be discussed publicly.

At the discussion, the board was asked to review the decision of the faculty council. On December 19, 1983, the board and the council met to consider the matter further and on January 16, 1984, the school board adopted a resolution unanimously affirming the action of the faculty council.

....

III

Arlene Pfeiffer filed suit alleging discrimination in her dismissal from the local chapter of the NHS, seeking an injunction that she be reinstated in the chapter, that the records of the school district be corrected to show that she remains in good standing in the society, that a procedure for dismissal be ordered that is not discriminatory, that the NHS be prohibited from disseminating information about her dismissal and that she be awarded compensatory and punitive damages.

Injunctive relief and damages were requested under Title IX of the Education Amendments of 1972, 20 U.S.C. §§ 1681, *et seq.*, and its implementing regulations. The complaint included claims of gender discrimination pursuant to 42 U.S.C. § 1983 and 1985 and included state law claims under the Pennsylvania Human Relations Act (PHRA), 43 P.S. 955(i)(1) (Purdon's Supp.1988), and the Pennsylvania Equal Rights Amendment, Commonwealth Constitution art. 1, § 28.

....

IV

At the onset of the case, the question arose whether Title IX applied because the School District did not receive federal funds for the operation of its chapter of the NHS, while it did receive federal funds for its school lunch program. Under the holding of *Grove City College v. Bell*, 465 U.S. 555 (1984), the district court denied Pfeiffer her Title IX claim. While the case was pending, Congress passed the Civil Rights Restoration Act of 1987, part of which amended Title IX to circumvent the Supreme Court's decision in *Grove City*. By an Opinion and Order of August 17, 1989, the district court ruled that the Restoration Act made the School District subject to Title IX, but that Pfeiffer's constitutional claims were subsumed within the Title IX claim. In addition, the court held that the state law claims would be considered during trial.

....

Testimony was presented that a pregnant female student had resigned from the NHS chapter after an admission of engaging in premarital sex 10 to 12 years earlier. She apparently had been given the choice of resignation or dismissal by the faculty council. No male member of the chapter has ever been dismissed for premarital sexual activity. The appellant offered to introduce testimony by a former student who was a male member of the chapter, that two years after Pfeiffer's dismissal, while a senior at the high school he impregnated his girlfriend and that he was not dismissed from the chapter. The district court excluded the evidence.

After considering the admitted evidence, the district court made a factual finding that the plaintiff was not dismissed for her pregnancy but because the faculty council concluded that she had failed to uphold the standards of the National Honor Society by engaging in premarital sexual intercourse.

V

Title IX of the Education Amendment of 1972 provides, in part, as follows:

> No person in the United States shall, on the basis of sex, be excluded from participation in, be denied the benefits of, or be subjected to discrimination under any education program or activity receiving Federal financial assistance. 20 U.S.C. § 1681(a). Regulations promulgated pursuant to Title IX specifically apply its prohibition against gender discrimination to discrimination on the basis of pregnancy, parental status, and marital status. Pursuant to 34 C.F.R. § 106.40 (1980), A recipient shall not apply any rule concerning a student's actual or potential parental, family, or marital status which treats students differently on the basis of sex.
>
> ....
>
> (b)(1) A recipient shall not discriminate against any student or exclude any student from its education program or activity, including any class or extracurricular activity, on the basis of such student's pregnancy, childbirth, false pregnancy, termination of pregnancy or recovery therefrom unless the student requests voluntarily to participate in a separate portion of the program or activity of the recipient.

The district court held that the faculty council and the school board did not violate Title IX or the regulations because the plaintiff was not dismissed from the NHS because of her pregnancy but because the faculty council considered premarital sex as setting an example inconsistent with the objectives and standards of [leadership and character].... This is a finding of fact, and it may not be disturbed unless clearly erroneous.

VI

In *Wort v. Vierling*, No. 82-3169, slip op. (C.D.Ill. Sept. 4, 1984), aff'd on other grounds, 778 F.2d 1233 (7th Cir.1985), the court held that a school district's dismissal of a pregnant student from the National Honor Society was a violation both of Title IX and the equal protection clause of the fourteenth amendment. In *Wort*, the court concluded that "[p]laintiff was dismissed from the NHS because of her pregnancy or the acts leading up to her pregnancy." *Id.* slip. op. at 4.

In reaching that decision, the court in *Wort* declined to distinguish the sexual conduct from the resulting pregnancy. But the district court here did make this distinction. It specifically found that Pfeiffer was dismissed not because she was

B. MARRIAGE, MOTHERHOOD, PREGNANCY, AND THE STUDENT

pregnant but because she had engaged in premarital sexual activity. This is an important distinction between the two cases. Regulation of conduct of unmarried high school student members is within the realm of authority of the National Honor Society given its emphasis on leadership and character.

In any event, the appellant's entire argument before us rests upon her allegation that she was dismissed from the chapter because of her condition of pregnancy. Unfortunately for her theory, however, the district court found that the plaintiff was not dismissed for her pregnancy but because the council thought she had failed to uphold the standards already discussed.... As a finding of fact, this holding may not be disturbed unless clearly erroneous. We do not believe that it is erroneous. Supporting this finding is the stated reason given by the council for her dismissal: Failure to uphold the standards of leadership and character required for admission and maintenance of membership. Moreover, the finding is supported by the testimony of the faculty council members before the district court, each of whom testified at trial. Each faculty council member specifically denied that his or her dismissal vote was based anywhere on Pfeiffer's sex, on her pregnancy, or on her failure to marry after she had engaged in premarital sexual activity.

This factual finding is bolstered by the district court's reasoning that [f]aced with the task of educating hundreds of young people, and with constant demand by the public that the schools instill attributes of good character as part of the educational process, the Council and the Board can scarcely be criticized for taking the action which was taken. Indeed, the Supreme Court has given us express guidance in matters relating to student conduct in public schools:

> The process of educating our youth for citizenship in public schools is not confined to books, the curriculum, and the civics class; schools must teach by example the shared values of a civilized social order. Consciously or otherwise, teachers — and indeed the older students — demonstrate the appropriate form of ... conduct and deportment in and out of class. Inescapably, like parents, they are role models. The schools, as instruments of the state, may determine that the essential lessons of civil, mature conduct cannot be conveyed in a school that tolerates lewd, indecent, or offensive speech and conduct.... *Bethel School Dist. No. 403 v. Fraser*, 478 U.S. 675, 683 (1986).

VII

More difficult, however, is appellant's contention that the district court abused its discretion in excluding the proffered testimony of a former student, a male member of the Marion Center Area High School chapter of the NHS. At trial, the following colloquy took place:

THE COURT: Do you want to make an offer?
MR. RUBIN: Yes, your Honor. What we intend to prove with [the proffered testimony] is that he was in fact a student in the Marion Center

Area High School and was a member of the National Honor Society in the same year that Arlene was a senior. He was a sophomore and was also a member during that year and was knowledgeable as to the events regarding Arlene's dismissal. Further we would like to offer that, during his senior year two years later, with the same faculty council sitting on the National Honor Society, that he in fact got married, had a child, shortly thereafter getting married, and he had informed his teacher and other members of the Marion Center community that he was the father and that he got married because his fiance had gotten pregnant. Additionally, we would be able to show through evidence that a document of the Marion Center Area School District called biographies has two entries into it showing that this boy was known generally in the high school community by the nickname daddy, and that he made the comment at his 15th year reunion he will be able to celebrate his wedding anniversary and child's birth. The point of putting this individual on is that he can testify that nobody ever approached him about his conduct with regard to premarital sexual activity, that nobody ever approached him from the National Honor Society concerning this. There is evidence through depositions that they have stated on numerous occasions if they were aware of any situation dealing with a male, that they would in fact consider that in the same light that they had considered Arlene.

We find this evidence can possibly be relevant to the state of mind of the faculty council on November 3, 1983, and whether the council and the board's explanation for their actions was pretextual when they dismissed Pfeiffer. The proffered testimony is relevant to the issue of intentional discrimination at the time Pfeiffer was dismissed. We, therefore, disagree with the district court's exclusion of it on the grounds that the events in the proffer post-dated by some years the November 1983 action of the council.

... [W]e believe that the evidence has the potential of being relevant to whether the council members followed a double standard in evaluating premarital sexual activities of NHS chapter members. Under these circumstances, to exclude it was not consistent with sound exercise of discretion.

....

What is important to the ultimate determination is what information was communicated to the council members. Lacking such communication, the testimony may not even be relevant. Moreover, even if the district court finds that the council did know of the male student's premarital sexual activity and did nothing about it, this by itself does not require the district court to make automatic findings one way or another. By remanding, we only instruct the district court to consider the proffered testimony for what it may be worth.

VIII

....

A

There is also a serious question as to what monetary damages, if any, could be available to the appellant, should the district court determine that she was discriminated against in violation of Title IX. Her dismissal from the NHS did not affect her status or record as a student. She graduated with honors and with her class. She did not apply for, or lose, any collegiate scholarships or awards because of her dismissal from the NHS. She elected not to attend college for reasons having nothing to do with her dismissal and was not denied a job because she was dismissed from the NHS. To the extent that Pfeiffer's dismissal became public knowledge, that knowledge resulted from her own actions and those of her parents, including appearances on several national and local television programs. She has admitted that she knows of no one who holds her in disrepute because of her dismissal from the NHS.

B

Assuming, without deciding, that some monetary damages could be calculated, ... it becomes necessary to meet the vexing problem of whether monetary damages are available for breach of Title IX. The district court concluded that Pfeiffer was not entitled to compensatory damages under Title IX because victims of discrimination are entitled to declaratory and injunctive relief alone. It relied upon the reasoning of the Court of Appeals for the Seventh Circuit in *Cannon v. University of Health Sciences/The Chicago Medical School*, 710 F.2d 351 (7th Cir.1983); *Lieberman v. University of Chicago*, 660 F.2d 1185 (7th Cir.1981), *cert. denied*, 456 U.S. 937 (1982), and *Bougher v. University of Pittsburgh*, 713 F.Supp. 139 (W.D.Pa.), *aff'd* on other grounds, 882 F.2d 74 (3d Cir.1989).

....

Ultimately two theories of statutory construction oppose each other in this inquiry. On one side exists the principle that when a statute expressly provides a particular remedy, it is improper to imply the existence of other remedies. *Lieberman*, 660 F.2d at 1187 n. 4 (citing *Transamerica Mortgage Advisors, Inc. v. Lewis*, 444 U.S. 11 (1979)).... On the other side is the precept that the existence of a statutory right implies the existence of all necessary and appropriate remedies. *Lieberman*, 660 F.2d at 1187 n. 4; *see also Bell v. Hood*, 327 U.S. 678, 684 (1946) ("where federally protected rights have been invaded, it has been the rule from the beginning that courts will be alert to adjust their remedies so as to grant the necessary relief"); ....

In *Cannon* [*v. University of Chicago*, 441 U.S. 677 (1979)], the Supreme Court indicated that Congress intended to create remedies in Title IX comparable to those available under Title VI. We thus look to guidance from the Supreme Court in cases involving Title IX and its statutory predecessor, Title VI. In

Guardians Ass'n v. Civil Service Comm'n of N.Y. City, 463 U.S. 582 (1983), a majority of the Court found that compensatory relief based on past violations of conditions regulating use of federal funds is available for Title VI violations when intentional discrimination is present. *Id.* at 602-03; *see also* 463 U.S. at 606-07, (WHITE, J., announcing judgment of the Court, joined by REHNQUIST, J.); *Id.* at 610- 11, (POWELL, J., concurring, joined by BURGER, C.J., and REHNQUIST J.); *Id.* at 615, (O'CONNOR, J., concurring). Tracking this analysis to a Title IX claim, we now conclude, not without some difficulty, that compensatory relief is available for certain Title IX violations and that this is one of them.

....

D

Neither the Supreme Court nor this court has decided specifically whether intent is a necessary element of a Title IX claim. However, recognizing that "Title IX was patterned after Title VI of the Civil Rights Act of 1964," *Grove City College v. Bell*, 465 U.S. 555 (1984), we believe that the standard adopted for Title VI actions in *Guardians Ass'n* should be required in Title IX cases....

In *Guardians*, the "threshold issue before the Court [was] whether ... private plaintiffs ... need to prove discriminatory intent to establish a violation of Title VI ... and administrative implementing regulations promulgated thereunder." *Id.* 463 U.S. at 584. A majority of the Court agreed that a violation of the statute itself requires proof of discriminatory intent....

... [T]he gravamen of Pfeiffer's complaint is that she was intentionally discriminated against in violation of Title IX and its implementing regulations.... Because an intentional violation has been alleged, we find it unnecessary to enter into the quagmire created by the Supreme Court's fragmented opinions in *Guardians Ass'n*.... We find it sufficient to allow a remedy of compensatory damages when a plaintiff alleges and then establishes discriminatory intent.

....

XI

The judgment of the district court will be affirmed in part and vacated and remanded in part.

---

1. *Pfeiffer* served as a center-piece in the Supreme Court's struggle to determine whether plaintiffs bringing causes of action for gender discrimination under Title IX could obtain compensatory relief. A split of authority existed between the Seventh and Eleventh Circuits and the Third Circuit on this issue. In *Lieberman v. University of Chicago*, 660 F.2d 1185 (7th Cir. 1981), the Seventh Circuit held that Title IX cases were governed by Spending Clause legislation and as such, Congress must state unambiguously its desires about remedies against recipients of federal funds. The court reasoned that a damages remedy by Congress, rather than the courts, would give institutions notice and guidance about Title IX liability. Given this reasoning, the court then held that compensatory relief was not available as Congress had not been so explicit.

The Eleventh Circuit in *Franklin v. Gwinnett Schs.*, 911 F.2d 617 (11th Cir. 1990), also held that compensatory relief was not an appropriate remedy under Title IX. Relying on *Drayden v. Needville Indep. Sch. Dist.*, 642 F.2d 129 (5th Cir. 1981), which held that compensatory relief was not available under Title VI for racial discrimination, the court found no such relief under Title IX since Congress had patterned one statute on the other using nearly identical language to define the benefit class and provided for similar termination of federal funds to institutions which so discriminated.

The Third Circuit in *Pfeiffer*, unlike the other two circuits, found in *Guardians Ass'n v. Civil Serv. Comm'n*, 463 U.S. 582 (1983), that the Supreme Court recognized the availability of compensatory damages for intentional discrimination. Recall that Pfeiffer alleged that the school district intentionally discriminated against her for becoming pregnant by dismissal from the National Honor Society. By offering a damage remedy, the Third Circuit became the first court of appeals to find a right to compensatory damages under Title IX.

The Supreme Court settled the conflict by rendering its decision in *Franklin v. Gwinnett Schs.*, 112 S. Ct. 1028 (1992), sanctioning the decision in *Pfeiffer*. (*See* Chapter 4). The *Franklin* majority allowed that the silence of Congress on the issue of private remedy did not result in the conclusion that the legislature intended that there be no such remedy. The Court, instead, reasoned that in the absence of Congressional intent to the contrary, federal courts may award appropriate relief in a cause of action governed by a federal statute.

2. The student in *Pfeiffer* alleged intentional discrimination complaining that male members of the National Honor Society who impregnated female students did not suffer club dismissal. What if the discriminatory policy of the school board had been declared unintentional by the Third Circuit; would the decision have been the same?

3. The *Pfeiffer* court relied on *Guardians*, cited in Note 1 above, which denied compensatory damages to black and hispanic police officers who had brought a Title VI racial discrimination suit against the City of New York. In *Guardians* there is no majority decision as six opinions were filed including three different concurring opinions. Noting the ambiguity of the Court, the Eleventh Circuit in *Franklin* held that *Guardians* "leaves open the question whether compensatory damages for intentional discrimination may be sought." *Franklin*, at 621. Where, then, does the Third Circuit find its basis for a damage remedy in *Pfeiffer*?

4. Where does the *Pfeiffer* decision leave boards of education and administrators in the promulgation of rules for sexual activity? Are school systems strictly liable for policies that are found to be discriminatory because of the inherent vulnerability of students? Does the court articulate any standards or guidance for determining how students sexual proclivities may be contained?

5. *Wort v. Vierling*, cited and discussed by the court, held that the plaintiff was dismissed from the National Honor Society "because of her pregnancy," while *Pfeiffer* struck down a challenge by a student which was based on discrimination due to the pregnancy alone. The *Pfeiffer* court made a distinction between the pregnancy and the acts leading up to it, while *Wort* did not. Are these two cases reconcilable? Do the two different results indicate that discrimination based on whether a student has engaged in premarital sex resulting in no pregnancy is allowed, while discrimination based on pregnancy is not?

6. If the district court distinguished between premarital sex and pregnancy when it decided against Pfeiffer, how convincing are its reasons for excluding the testimony of the former male student who had engaged in premarital sex and had not been dismissed from the National Honor Society? Does this testimony make Pfeiffer's claim — that she was dismissed due to pregnancy — more viable?

7. The decision in *Pfeiffer* turned on whether a constitutional right to equal protection had been violated. What if the decision to remove a student from an activity was based on the regulations established for that activity? *See Elliot v. Rice*, No. 83-CV-316 (CP, Greene, 5-23-83), where a pregnant student's dismissal from the National Honor Society was upheld because an organization handbook provided for removal if members flagrantly disregarded organizational standards.

C. SCHOOLS AND LAW ENFORCEMENT

SALAZAR v. LUTY
United States District Court
761 F. Supp. 45 (S.D. Tex. 1991)

HUGHES, DISTRICT JUDGE:

1. *Introduction*

An off-duty police officer working for a Texas public school assisted in detecting a student's violation of the school's drug policy. The student was not prosecuted criminally, but he was disciplined by the school. The process afforded the student was constitutionally adequate. The student will take nothing by his suit.

2. *Parties*

A. The plaintiff is James Salazar, who was a student at Pasadena Independent School District's South Houston High School.

B. The defendants are numerous trustees, administrators, and employees of the Pasadena Independent School District.

3. *Chronology, 1984*

September 13: Carter (assistant principal) and Pierson (security guard) took Thomas Watson, a student, out of class and asked him about packages of

C. SCHOOLS AND LAW ENFORCEMENT

marijuana that were found in his student locker. Watson said that he had bought it from James Salazar at school on September 10. Watson made a written statement.

September 19: Carter took Salazar out of his first class and brought him to his office. Carter, Pierson, and a Pasadena police officer, Will Kelly, interrogated Salazar for 30-40 minutes. After the interrogation, Carter suspended Salazar for violating the district's drug policy.

September 21: Barber (principal) gave Salazar a hearing. Salazar left the hearing when the decision was announced to refuse him readmittance. Later that day, Bondy (assistant superintendent) rescinded the suspension until Barber held a second hearing.

September 24: Salazar was readmitted to school at the Pasadena School's Community Guidance Center, a disciplinary facility used by the school district. His parents received notice that he was indefinitely suspended.

September 27: Barber held a second hearing. Salazar chose not to testify. Barber suspended Salazar for the rest of the year.

October 1: Salazar appealed.

October 2: Bondy overruled the suspension, and he instructed Barber to reassign Salazar to the Guidance Center for 60 days.

October 3: Barber and Carter sent Salazar's parents notice of the 60-day suspension. Salazar stopped attending school.

October 4: Salazar appealed the 60-day suspension to Meyer (superintendent), who affirmed it.

October 10 & 17: The school board held a hearing on Salazar. The board decreased the suspension to 30 days in the Guidance Center.

October 22: Salazar returned to regular classes. He was given credit for 30 days at the Guidance Center, under the two-for-one rule for good behavior; he spent three days on suspension and 12 days at the Guidance Center.

4. *14th Amendment*

In a public school's disciplinary proceeding, the United States Constitution requires that before a student may be suspended the school district must observe the procedural safeguards. The process that is due a student, at a minimum, is: A. The student must be informed of the accusation against him; B. The student must be informed of the factual basis for the charge; and C. The student must have an opportunity to tell his side of the story to an official, who is not directly involved in the incident and who can dispassionately evaluate the proposed guilt and punishment. *Goss v. Lopez*, 419 U.S. 565 (1975).

In this instance, Salazar had a prompt hearing, with the opportunity to appeal the decision at each level. Indeed, he took those opportunities. He had the chance to introduce witnesses and documents, examine witnesses, and argue. The district and the officials afforded Salazar all the process that he is due under the fourteenth amendment. Even though the district met its duty under the specifics of the court-adopted rule, a careful examination of the whole incident and the disciplinary response gives no sense of abuse of authority or phoney hearings. The requirement that the district, like all governments, carry out its responsibilities with procedural regularity was met.

5. *Texas law*

Under the Texas statutes, a student may not be denied the privileges of his home campus unless the board of trustees determines that the student's presence presents a continuing danger of physical harm to him or to others. Texas Education Act § 21.301 (1984). The standard for using the statute requires that: A. The district's rule must be rationally related to the objective harm sought to be avoided; B. The process for enforcing the rule must be adequately cross-checked with safeguards; and C. Substantial evidence must support the decision of the school board.

The district's rule allowing suspension for selling drugs at school is rational because the presence of illegal drugs is manifestly a source of probable physical harm to students and staff. Even if the marijuana were arguably not intrinsically harmful, the behavior associated with black market dealings in drugs is closely involved with physical harm. The school was not enforcing some silly hair length dispute.

The process is adequate because there were all of the hearings and verifications already discussed. It was also adequate in the sense that there was an effort by the school to limit the damage to Salazar while protecting the other students by isolating him in a "special" school facility. Some limited, temporary measure was needed until the board's permanent decision could be made. Also, substantial evidence supported both the initial administrative decision to discipline Salazar and the final board decision that Salazar violated the school drug policy.

6. *State actors and other rights*

This case involves a school disciplinary proceeding. It is not a criminal case. Criminal charges were never filed against Salazar. The presence of Jim Kelly, who was an off-duty city police officer, does not convert this education administration problem into a criminal prosecution. The effect of his presence and acts in a criminal case are not a question for this case.

Kelly was a state actor against whom all the constitutional restrictions on the use of governmental power apply. Although he was working a second job as a school security officer, he was hired because of his ability to use his governmental association as an additional weapon against the troubles he found at school. As a security agent of the public school, he would be a state actor in any event, even if he had come from Brinks.

Salazar claims the school violated his right to be free from: A. Unreasonable searches and seizures under the fourth amendment to the United States Constitution; B. Custodial interrogation and self-incrimination under the fifth amendment; and C. The right to counsel under the sixth amendment. Each of

C. SCHOOLS AND LAW ENFORCEMENT

these rights applies almost only to criminal prosecutions, so there is no violation of the restrictions on the government in the proceeding at school.

7. *The Texas Constitution*

The Texas Constitution guarantees rights independently of the protections to individuals afforded by the Federal Constitution. The Texas Constitution has a provision parallel to the due process clause. It is the law of the land clause, which is evocative of Magna Carta's *lex terre*. Although they have an independent source and independent content, Salazar's claims under the 4th, 5th, 6th, and 14th amendments are roughly analogous to his claims under the Texas Constitution's article I, sections 9, 10, and 19. Salazar's position implicates none of the protections under the Texas Constitution; he has no claims under the state's defense of liberty that he was the object of an abuse of governmental power.

8. *Conclusion*

Salazar will take nothing from the district or from the people he sued. The district met its duty to Salazar with the full range of hearings to which he was entitled under the procedural regularity clauses of both the United States and Texas Constitutions.

---

1. The *Salazar* court noted that South Houston High School, in the Pasadena Independent School District, employed off-duty police officers to assist in detecting violations of the school's drug policy. Is a school allowed to use *undercover* officers to meet this goal? In *Gordon v. Warren Consol. Bd. of Educ.*, 706 F.2d 778 (6th Cir. 1983), the Sixth Circuit held that placement of such officers in the classrooms was not a chilling of First Amendment rights where the surveillance did not disrupt classroom activities or education, though the investigation focused on classes involving students and teachers with "liberal sociopolitical" views.

2. What happens when a school's drug policy and associated punishment interferes with its provision of special education services? In *School Bd. of the County of Prince William, Virginia v. Malone*, 662 F. Supp. 978 (E.D. Va. 1984), the court held that expulsion of a handicapped child for distributing drugs was not appropriate under the Education for All Handicapped Children Act (renamed as the Individuals with Disabilities Education Act). Two reasons were given for this result: (1) no alternative punishment was considered; and (2) the behavior was caused by his handicapping condition. For a detailed discussion on special education issues *see* Chapter 13.

3. Should schools engage in activities such as investigation and interrogation of students without imposing sanctions in response to, for example, a police request to investigate drug use by its students off campus? Is the fact that there are differences in procedural standards between school discipline and juvenile courts relevant to either or both of the above questions? Is it appropriate for the school to act in regard to drug use off campus in order to protect the students by deterring the police from acting?

4. Traditionally, the campus of colleges and universities has been regarded as a sanctuary from police and other local government officials who have been less concerned with enforcing many of the general criminal laws on campus, because they were confident that the college officials, with the use of campus security guards and sanctions like suspension or expulsion, would handle their own problems. It has been suggested that the increasing resort by students to courts in disputes with universities might jeopardize this traditional relationship. Perhaps, however, the sanctuary concept violates a notion of equal protection of the laws or, more accurately, equal application of the laws. Should there be a sanctuary for campuses but not for company towns? When the same crimes have been committed can the state make the determination that it will preserve the sanctuary in those schools that have better resources to handle the student misbehavior while using its own resources for students who do not attend such schools? If the theory is that the college will punish in lieu of the state, why is a private employer different from the college? If the sanctuary theory is justifiable as to universities, should it apply to elementary or secondary schools?

5. Is the effectiveness of school investigative procedures or sanctions relevant to these issues? Should the school's abilities be compared with that of the police or juvenile courts in terms of effectiveness? Is there a value in not increasing the incidence of adversarial confrontations between schools and students, even where the purpose is to protect the students from "worse" adversaries?

6. Should the "benefit of the doubt" approach be taken by the schools when deciding on punishment for violations of the school's drug policy? For instance, if the student possesses redeeming qualities such as good grades and otherwise good leadership and character, should mitigating factors play a role in deciding what punishment to grant? *See Cross v. Princeton City Sch. Dist. Bd. of Educ.*, 49 Ohio Misc. 2d 1, 550 N.E.2d 219 (1989).

7. For another due process case dealing with drug possession in the school setting, also holding in favor of the school, *see Brewer v. Austin Indep. Sch. Dist.*, 779 F.2d 260 (5th Cir. 1985).

MITCHELL v. BOARD OF TRUSTEES OF OXFORD MUNICIPAL SEPARATE SCHOOL DISTRICT

United States Court of Appeals
625 F.2d 660 (5th Cir. 1980)

KRAVITCH, CIRCUIT JUDGE:

Dennis Mitchell and Leon Coleman, together with their mothers as next friends, brought this action for injunctive and declaratory relief and for damages against the Oxford Municipal Separate School District (hereafter the School

C. SCHOOLS AND LAW ENFORCEMENT

Board) and its members. The plaintiffs alleged that their substantive due process rights were violated by application of a School Board policy which mandates the automatic expulsion of "(a)ny student who brings a knife or any other object which would be classified as a weapon to school...." Final judgment was entered for the defendants. We affirm.

A detailed explanation of the facts is not necessary. Both plaintiffs admitted violating the rule against bringing knives or other weapons to school. Mitchell is 16 years old and actually threatened another student with a knife. Coleman is 12 years old and asserted that he found the knife he brought to school on the school bus. While at school he showed the knife to at least two of his classmates; one of the classmates testified Coleman threatened to cut him if he reported the incident.

Both students were expelled for the remainder of the semester, after hearings before the School Board at which only two factual issues were addressed: whether the student was in possession of a knife at school and whether he knew there was a School Board policy which prohibited students from bringing knives to school.

The legal issue in the case as advanced by the plaintiffs is whether, as a matter of substantive due process, a student is guaranteed some discretion by the School Board in fixing the punishment for violation of a rule. The plaintiffs argue they have such a right; we disagree.

The policy as issued by the School Board states:

> It is the policy of the Oxford Municipal Separate School District Board of Trustees that no knives are to be brought to school by any student. Any student who brings a knife or any other object which would be classified as a weapon to school or on the school grounds with him shall be immediately expelled from school for the remainder of the semester with no grades and credits being given.

Although by its terms the policy is mandatory, based on the reasoning in *Fisher v. Burkburnett Independent School District*, 419 F.Supp. 1200 (N.D.Tex.1976), the district court held that the School Board has inherent authority to ignore the mandatory language and impose a lesser punishment. The court went on to hold that the punishment imposed here was not so excessive that it lacks a rational relationship to a legitimate educational purpose.

The plaintiffs argue that the district court was wrong in concluding that the rule is not mandatory and, when properly viewed as mandatory, the rule is unconstitutional. We are not completely comfortable with the conclusion that the School Board has inherent authority to ignore its own rule. The rule as written is mandatory and we will consider it as such.

As revealed in reported court cases, school rules for disciplining students fall into one of two categories. On one side are rules which provide that the punishment must fit the misbehavior and be tailored to the pupil's age, intelligence and personal history. In the other category are rules which decree consistency in the punishment of certain misbehavior in all pupils. If the broken rule is in the first category, then the disciplinarian will consider such factors as whether the child has engaged in the same misbehavior before, how well the child understood that his behavior would be unacceptable, and what circumstances surrounded the misconduct. For example, schools which use corporal punishment tend to tailor it to the child rather than setting down fixed rules such as: "Misbehavior A will be punished by a spanking." *See, e.g., Ingraham v. Wright*, 430 U.S. 651 (1977)....

In the other category are mandatory rules which represent the administration's response to certain articulable and well-defined problems. These rules tell the students that if misbehavior A occurs, punishment B will follow. *See, e.g., Wood v. Strickland*, 420 U.S. 308 (1975) (the use or possession of intoxicating beverages at school shall be punished by suspension for the balance of the semester); *Caldwell v. Cannady*, 340 F.Supp. 835 (N.D.Tex.1972) (school altered a rule which gave the school board discretion to expel a student who uses, sells or possesses a dangerous drug to a rule which required expulsion in such cases).

The School Board in Oxford has adopted a rule in the latter category to insure the safety of students. Undeniably, the School Board has the right, power, and duty to make and enforce a rule against bringing weapons to school. To satisfy that responsibility, the Board responded with a rule which is consistent and simple to apply.

We have discovered no circuit court cases and few district court cases in which the validity of a rule which mandated a certain punishment for violation of a certain rule was directly at issue.

In *Caldwell v. Cannady*, 340 F.Supp. 835 (N.D.Tex.1972), the plaintiffs levied a substantive due process challenge against a school board policy which required the expulsion from school of any student who sells, uses or possesses any dangerous drug or narcotic. The mandatory expulsion rule had superseded a prior discretionary expulsion rule. The district court upheld the mandatory rule as a "reasonable exercise of the power vested in [the] local school board." 340 F.Supp. at 838.

In *Fisher v. Burkburnett Independent School District*, 419 F.Supp. 1200 (N.D.Tex.1976), the plaintiff had been expelled from school because of drug abuse. The district court held that despite the mandatory language of the policy violated, the school board had had a hearing on the correctness of the punishment and thus there was no procedural due process violation. The district court also rejected a claim that the punishment was so disproportionately harsh compared to the misbehavior that it constituted a violation of substantive due process.

These district courts protected from constitutional challenges rules which resulted in virtually no discretion in the disciplinarian. Once a violation was found, a punishment mandated by the rule followed. Appellants argue, however, that *Lee v. Macon County Board of Education*, 490 F.2d 458 (5th Cir. 1974), requires a different result here.

C. SCHOOLS AND LAW ENFORCEMENT

In *Lee*, the plaintiffs were permanently expelled from school for a series of misbehavior. A board member testified in district court that the Board's policy is to grant expulsion upon recommendation of the principal. The district court held that the permanent expulsion from school was not an arbitrary punishment and that there was sufficient evidence before the Board of Education to support the determination that the children were guilty of the infractions charged.

The Fifth Circuit reversed stating: "Formalistic acceptance or ratification of the principal's request or recommendation as to the scope of punishment, without independent Board consideration of what, under all the circumstances, the penalty should be, is less than full due process. Appropriate punishment is for the Board to determine, in the exercise of its independent judgment." *Id.* 490 F.2d at 460.

Appellants argue that *Lee* constitutionally requires the Board to exercise discretion before expelling a child. We do not read Lee so broadly. Rather, the discretion *Lee* mandates was exercised; it was exercised when the Board adopted the rule setting expulsion as the punishment for bringing a knife to school. That the Board exercised its discretion to opt for consistency of punishment rather than a tailoring of punishment to the child, simply does not implicate the due process clause of the Constitution.

This court has consistently stated that school disciplinary matters are best resolved in the local community and within the school system. *Lee v. Macon County Board of Education*, 490 F.2d 458, 460 (5th Cir. 1974), citing *Stevenson v. Board of Education of Wheeler County*, 426 F.2d 1154 (5th Cir.), *cert. denied*, 400 U.S. 957 (1970); *Wood v. Alamo Heights Indep. School District*, 433 F.2d 355 (5th Cir. 1970). If the plaintiffs believe the rule mandating expulsion for the bringing of weapons to school is too harsh, their remedy is to persuade the School Board to change it.

The School Board is under an obligation to educate the children of Oxford County. The Board is also under an obligation to provide a safe environment for the children so they can learn. Unfortunately, violence in the schools is increasingly becoming a way of life. This School Board has responded to that problem by making a strict rule, and punishing violations with one of the most severe weapons in its arsenal of punishments. Because the rule and the punishment for violating the rule clearly are rationally related to the goal of providing a safe environment in which children can learn, it comports with substantive due process.

---

1. The facts of *Mitchell* only add to the prevalent view that the nation's schools are becoming increasingly violent; hence, more severe disciplinary measures are being called for. The news accounts tell the story. For example, the following headline appeared in the daily newspaper of Ohio's largest city. "FBI: Violent Crime by Youth up 25% in Decade." A news article went on to explain that William Sessions, then FBI director, stated that a rising wave of murders, rapes and assaults is pervading the schools. *See The Columbus Dispatch*, Aug. 30, 1992, at 1A.

2. Other commentators have written that weapons-related crimes perpetrated by school children are increasing at an alarming rate. In a recent national crime survey conducted by the Department of Justice over a six-month period, approximately one-half million American children reported experiencing one or more violent crimes while at school. About 1.5 million students reported being the victims of property crimes. And nearly 2 million children said they had been victimized at least once at school. Twenty-two percent of children in the study reported that they feared they might be attacked at school, and nearly one-half million said they had actually taken a weapon to school for protection. *See* Beci, *School Violence: Protecting Our Children and the Fourth Amendment*, 41 Catholic U. L. Rev. 817, 820 (1992), citing Bastian and Taylor, U.S. Dep't of Justice, *School Crime: A National Crime Victimization Survey Report* (NCJ — 131645) (1991).

3. Interestingly, it is state legislatures, more than school officials, that have responded most forcefully in the promulgation of school-violence related rules. Some state legislatures, for example have enacted statutes requiring school officials to adhere to stringent incident reporting procedures when violent activities occur in school. To illustrate, Connecticut requires that each local school board of education must file an annual report with the state board of education indicating the number of threats and physical assaults made by students upon teachers and other school personnel and the number of assaults that involved dangerous weapons by students against other students. Conn. Gen. Stat. Ann. Secs. 10-233g(a). Other states require this information to be reported to law enforcement agencies, Tenn. Code Ann. Sec. 4906-4301 (1955-92). Still other states have enacted "Gun-Free School Zone" statutes which will cause any violator of the statute to be guilty of a felony if the firearm was discharged or brandished near a school. *See* Va. Code Ann. Secs. 18.2-280, 18.2-282, 18.2-308.1; Cal. Penal Code Secs. 626.9, 626.10.

4. Some states have taken a very severe look at violence in the school promulgating statutes that permit school boards to order the permanent exclusion of students caught with weapons or contraband on school grounds or at school functions. The sponsor of such a bill in Ohio stated that the intent "... is aimed at those individuals who really pose a threat to the staff and our students." Testimony of State Representative Donald Czarcinski on House Bill 154. "Student Crime Is Targeted" *The Columbus Dispatch*, April 3, 1993 at A1. *See* Ohio Rev. Code Sec. 3313.662.

5. The United States Congress has responded to citizen concerns about violence in the schools by amending the Elementary and Secondary Schools Act with the *Gun-Free Schools Act of 1994*, Pub. L. 103-22, Title X. Part B, 108 Stat. 270 [20 U.S.C.A. Secs. 2701, 3351, 3381-86] (1994). Under the Act, states must promulgate laws requiring the expulsion of students, for not less than one year, if it is determined that such students have brought guns into school.

C. SCHOOLS AND LAW ENFORCEMENT

Moreover, states must also develop policies requiring that students be referred to the criminal justice system or to the juvenile justice system if they bring a gun or other dangerous weapon into school. States failing to procure such policies run the risk of losing federal funds designated for education purposes.

The new amendments carry provisions for disabled students as well. The "stay-put" provision found in *Honing v. Doe*, 484 U.S. 305 (1988), stipulating no indefinite suspensions, has been modified by the amendments to require that disabled students committing such infractions receive education services in an "alternative education placement" for up to 45 days during the pendency of due process hearings. The Supreme Court decision in *Honing* had limited such suspensions to 10 days. *See* Chapter 13 for more on discipline and disabled students.

6. What has been the approach in the courts as regards the rights of students accused of dangerous activities in the schools? In *Tinker v. Des Moines Indep. Community Sch. Dist.*, 393 U.S. 503 (1969), the Supreme Court found that students can exercise constitutional rights so long as their activities do not "materially and substantially interfere with the requirement of appropriate discipline in the operation of the school." *Id.* at 515. This position did not hold however, as the Court in *New Jersey v. T.L.O.*, 469 U.S. 325 (1985), held that "... the constitutional rights of students in public school are not automatically coexistensive with the rights of adults of other settings." as quoted in *Bethel School Dist No. 403 v. Fraser*, 478 U.S. 675, 682 (1986). Would the above statutes and cases permit *Mitchell* to be decided differently? Could the students in *Mitchell* have received a greater punishment had the case been heard 10 years later? Should incidents like the ones cited in *Mitchell* be treated like that described in the Czarcinski testimony or should schools use the approach of conflict resolution? Should the official response simply be one of removing students accused of violent acts from schools?

Chapter 6
SCHOOL CONTROL OF STUDENT EXPRESSION

A. POLITICAL AND OTHER STUDENT EXPRESSION

School administrators, as representatives of the states, are required to accord students their First Amendment rights to freedom of speech. They are simultaneously charged with the duty to maintain order in the schools. The potential conflict between those responsibilities, although present in society generally, is increased in the school environment, where children and adolescents may respond impulsively. The following cases detail judicial determinations of some questions generated by the conflict. All of the cases attempt to strike a balance between the two responsibilities. Where on the spectrum this balance lies often changes from case to case, and the direction the balancing point travels along this spectrum often changes from era to era.

TINKER v. DES MOINES INDEPENDENT COMMUNITY SCHOOL DISTRICT

Supreme Court of the United States
393 U.S. 503 (1969)

JUSTICE FORTAS delivered the opinion of the Court:

Petitioner John F. Tinker, 15 years old, and petitioner Christopher Eckhardt, 16 years old, attended high schools in Des Moines. Petitioner Mary Beth Tinker, John's sister, was a 13-year-old student in junior high school.

In December 1965, a group of adults and students in Des Moines, Iowa, held a meeting at the Eckhardt home. The group determined to publicize their objections to the hostilities in Vietnam and their support for a truce by wearing black armbands during the holiday season and by fasting on December 16 and New Year's Eve. Petitioners and their parents had previously engaged in similar activities, and they decided to participate in the program.

The principals of the Des Moines schools became aware of the plan to wear armbands. On December 14, 1965, they met and adopted a policy that any student wearing an armband to school would be asked to remove it, and if he refused he would be suspended until he returned without the armband. Petitioners were aware of the regulation that the school authorities adopted.

On December 16, Mary Beth and Christopher wore black armbands to their schools. John Tinker wore his armband the next day. They were all sent home and suspended from school until they would come back without their armbands. They did not return to school until after the planned period for wearing armbands had expired — that is, until after New Year's Day.

This complaint was filed in the United States District Court by petitioners, through their fathers, under § 1983 of Title 42 of the United States Code.... The court referred to but expressly declined to follow the Fifth Circuit's holding in a similar case that prohibition of the wearing of symbols like the armbands cannot be sustained unless it "materially and substantially interfere[s] with the requirements of appropriate discipline in the operation of the school." *Burnside v. Byars*, 363 F.2d 744, 749 (1966).

On appeal, the Court of Appeals for the Eighth Circuit considered the case en banc. The court was equally divided, and the District Court's decision was accordingly affirmed, without opinion.... We granted certiorari.

I

First Amendment rights, applied in light of the special characteristics of the school environment, are available to teachers and students. It can hardly be argued that either students or teachers shed their constitutional rights to freedom of speech or expression at the schoolhouse gate. This has been the unmistakable holding of this Court for almost 50 years. In *Meyer v. Nebraska* and *Bartels v. Iowa*, this Court, in opinions by Mr. Justice McReynolds, held that the Due Process Clause of the Fourteenth Amendment prevents States from forbidding the teaching of a foreign language to young students. Statutes to this effect, the Court held, unconstitutionally interfere with the liberty of teacher, student, and parent.

In *West Virginia State Board of Education v. Barnette*, this Court held that under the First Amendment, the student in public school may not be compelled to salute the flag. Speaking through Mr. Justice Jackson, the Court said:

> The Fourteenth Amendment, as now applied to the States, protects the citizen against the State itself and all of its creatures — Boards of Education not excepted. These have, of course, important, delicate, and highly discretionary functions, but none that they may not perform within the limits of the Bill of Rights. That they are educating the young for citizenship is reason for scrupulous protection of Constitutional freedoms of the individual, if we are not to strangle the free mind at its source and teach youth to discount important principles of our government as mere platitudes. 319 U.S. at 637.

On the other hand, the Court has repeatedly emphasized the need for affirming the comprehensive authority of the States and of school authorities, consistent with fundamental constitutional safeguards, to prescribe and control conduct in the schools. *See Epperson v. Arkansas*, 393 U.S. at 104; *Meyer v. Nebraska*, 262 U.S. at 402. Our problem lies in the area where students in the exercise of First Amendment rights collide with the rules of the school authorities.

II

The problem presented by the present case does not relate to regulation of the length of skirts or the type of clothing, to hair style or deportment.... It does not

A. POLITICAL AND OTHER STUDENT EXPRESSION

concern aggressive, disruptive action or even group demonstrations. Our problem involves direct, primary First Amendment rights akin to "pure speech."

The school officials banned and sought to punish petitioners for a silent, passive, expression of opinion, unaccompanied by any disorder or disturbance on the part of petitioners. There is here no evidence whatever of petitioners' interference, actual or nascent, with the school's work or of collision with the rights of other students to be secure and to be let alone. Accordingly, this case does not concern speech or action that intrudes upon the work of the school or the rights of other students.

Only a few of the 18,000 students in the school system wore the black armbands. Only five students were suspended for wearing them. There is no indication that the work of the school or any class was disrupted. Outside the classrooms, a few students made hostile remarks to the children wearing armbands, but there were no threats or acts of violence on school premises.

The District Court concluded that the action of the school authorities was reasonable because it was based upon their fear of a disturbance from the wearing of the armbands. But, in our system, undifferentiated fear or apprehension of disturbance is not enough to overcome the right to freedom of expression. Any departure from absolute regimentation may cause trouble. Any variation from the majority's opinion may inspire fear. Any word spoken, in class, in the lunchroom or on the campus, that deviates from the views of another person, may start an argument or cause a disturbance. But our Constitution says we must take this risk, ... and our history says that it is this sort of hazardous freedom — this kind of openness — that is the basis of our national strength and of the independence and vigor of Americans who grow up and live in this relatively permissive, often disputatious society.

In order for the State in the person of school officials to justify prohibition of a particular expression of opinion, it must be able to show that its action was caused by something more than a mere desire to avoid the discomfort and unpleasantness that always accompany an unpopular viewpoint. Certainly where there is no finding and no showing that the exercise of the forbidden right would "materially and substantially interfere with the requirements of appropriate discipline in the operation of the school," the prohibition cannot be sustained. *Burnside v. Byars, supra,* 363 F.2d at 749.

In the present case, the District Court made no such finding, and our independent examination of the record fails to yield evidence that the school authorities had reason to anticipate that the wearing of the armbands would substantially interfere with the work of the school or impinge upon the rights of other students. Even an official memorandum prepared after the suspension that listed the reasons for the ban on wearing the armbands made no reference to the anticipation of such disruption.

On the contrary, the action of the school authorities appears to have been based upon an urgent wish to avoid the controversy which might result from the expression, even by the silent symbol of armbands, of opposition to this Nation's part in the conflagration in Vietnam. It is revealing, in this respect, that the meeting at which the school principals decided to issue the contested regulation was called in response to a student's statement to the journalism teacher in one of the schools that he wanted to write an article on Vietnam and have it published in the school paper. (The student was dissuaded.)

It is also relevant that the school authorities did not purport to prohibit the wearing of all symbols of political or controversial significance. The record shows that students in some of the schools wore buttons relating to national political campaigns, and some even wore the Iron Cross, traditionally a symbol of Nazism. The order prohibiting the wearing of armbands did not extend to these. Instead, a particular symbol — black armbands worn to exhibit opposition to this Nation's involvement in Vietnam — was singled out for prohibition. Clearly, the prohibition of expression of one particular opinion, at least without evidence that it is necessary to avoid material and substantial interference with school work or discipline, is not constitutionally permissible.

In our system, state-operated schools may not be enclaves of totalitarianism. School officials do not possess absolute authority over their students. Students in school as well as out of school are "persons" under our Constitution. They are possessed of fundamental rights which the State must respect, just as they themselves must respect their obligations to the State. In our system, students may not be regarded as closed-circuit recipients of only that which the State chooses to communicate. They may not be confined to the expression of those sentiments that are officially approved. In the absence of a specific showing of constitutionally valid reasons to regulate their speech, students are entitled to freedom of expression of their views. As Judge Gewin, speaking for the Fifth Circuit said, school officials cannot suppress "expressions of feelings with which they do not wish to contend." *Burnside v. Byars*, *supra*, 363 F.2d at 749.

In *Meyer v. Nebraska*, *supra*, 262 U.S. at 402, Justice McReynolds expressed this Nation's repudiation of the principle that a State might so conduct its schools as to "foster a homogeneous people." He said:

> In order to submerge the individual and develop ideal citizens, Sparta assembled the males at seven into barracks and intrusted their subsequent education and training to official guardians. Although such measures have been deliberately approved by men of great genius, their ideas touching the relation between individual and State were wholly different from those upon which our institutions rest; and it hardly will be affirmed that any Legislature could impose such restrictions upon the people of a state without doing violence to both letter and spirit of the Constitution.

A. POLITICAL AND OTHER STUDENT EXPRESSION

This principle has been repeated by this Court on numerous occasions during the intervening years. In *Keyishian v. Board of Regents*, 385 U.S. 589, 603, Mr. Justice Brennan, speaking for the Court, said:

> The vigilant protection of constitutional freedom is nowhere more vital than in the community of American schools. [*Shelton v. Tucker*, 364 U.S. 479, 487]. The classroom is peculiarly the "marketplace of ideas." The Nation's future depends upon leaders trained through wide exposure to that robust exchange of ideas which discover truth "out of a multitude of tongues, [rather] than through any kind of authoritative selection."

The principle of these cases is not confined to the supervised and ordained discussion which takes place in the classroom. The principal use to which the schools are dedicated is to accommodate students during prescribed hours for the purpose of certain types of activities. Among those activities is personal intercommunication among the students. This is not only an inevitable part of the process of attending school. It is also an important part of the educational process. A student's rights therefore, do not embrace merely the classroom hours. When he is in the cafeteria, or on the playing field, or on the campus during the authorized hours, he may express his opinions, even on controversial subjects like the conflict in Vietnam, if he does so "[without] materially and substantially interfering with ... appropriate discipline in the operation of the school" and without colliding with the rights of others. *Burnside v. Byars, supra*, 363 F.2d at 749. But conduct by the student, in class or out of it, which for any reason — whether it stems from time, place, or type of behavior — materially disrupts classwork or involves substantial disorder or invasion of the rights of others is, of course, not immunized by the constitutional guaranty of freedom of speech. *Cf. Blackwell v. Issaquena County Bd. of Educ.*, 363 F.2d 749 (C.A. 5th Cir., 1966).

Under our Constitution, free speech is not a right that is given only to be so circumscribed that it exists in principle but not in fact. Freedom of expression would not truly exist if the right could be exercised only in an area that a benevolent government has provided as a safe haven for crackpots. The Constitution says that Congress (and the States) may not abridge the right to free speech. This provision means what it says. We properly read it to permit reasonable regulation of speech-connected activities in carefully restricted circumstances. But we do not confine the permissible exercise of First Amendment rights to a telephone booth or the four corners of a pamphlet, or to supervised and ordained discussion in a school classroom.

If a regulation were adopted by school officials forbidding discussion of the Vietnam conflict, or the expression by any student of opposition to it anywhere on school property except as part of a prescribed classroom exercise, it would be obvious that the regulation would violate the constitutional rights of students, at least if it could not be justified by a showing that the students' activities would materially and substantially disrupt the work and discipline of the school. *Cf.*

Hammond v. South Carolina State College, 272 F. Supp. 947 (D.C.D.S.C.1967) (orderly protest meeting on state college campus); *Dickey v. Alabama State Bd. of Educ.*, 273 F. Supp. 613 (D.C.M.D. Ala. 1967) (expulsion of student editor of college newspaper). In the circumstances of the present case, the prohibition of the silent, passive "witness of the armbands," as one of the children called it, is no less offensive to the constitution's guarantees.

As we have discussed, the record does not demonstrate any facts which might reasonably have led school authorities to forecast substantial disruption of or material interference with school activities, and no disturbances or disorders on the school premises in fact occurred. These petitioners merely went about their ordained rounds in school. Their deviation consisted only in wearing on their sleeve a band of black cloth, not more than two inches wide. They wore it to exhibit their disapproval of the Vietnam hostilities and their advocacy of a truce, to make their views known, and by their example, to influence others to adopt them. They neither interrupted school activities nor sought to intrude in the school affairs or the lives of others. They caused discussion outside of the classrooms, but no interference with work and no disorder. In the circumstances, our Constitution does not permit officials of the State to deny their form of expression.

We express no opinion as to the form of relief which should be granted, this being a matter for the lower courts to determine. We reverse and remand for further proceedings consistent with this opinion.

Reversed and remanded.

---

1. Consider the following comment, written one year after the *Tinker* decision:

> First, there is a growing recognition that students cannot be regarded as merely passive vessels into which education is poured, but must, at least to a limited extent, be regarded as active participants in the educational process. To oversimplify, education can be divided, for analytical purposes, into two models: prescriptive and analytic. In the prescriptive model, information and accepted truths are furnished to a theoretically passive, absorbent student. The teacher's role is to convey these truths rather than to create new wisdom. Both teacher and student appear almost as automatons. Analytic education, however, signifies the examination of data and values in a way that involves the student and teacher as active participants in the search for truth. While these polar models represent only a theoretical paradigm that can never exist in pure form, we have traditionally conceived of pre-college public education as essentially prescriptive, and college and post-graduate studies as analytic.
>
> Now, however, one senses that the courts, along with the rest of society, see these lines (which were never clearly drawn to begin with) becoming

A. POLITICAL AND OTHER STUDENT EXPRESSION 313

more and more blurred. With greater numbers of people going to college today than ever before, with more and more college remedial programs available for the poor and disadvantaged, and with the creation of new institutions such as junior and community colleges, many colleges may be moving somewhat from the analytic model, once envisioned as the ideal for higher education, toward the prescriptive secondary school model.

Paradoxically, and more important from the point of view of student "rights," a strong movement exists at the moment to make high schools more analytic. Many high school students today are intellectually more mature than their college counterparts of a generation ago. The influences of television and other mass media on the perspectives of even our very young children are pervasive. Possessed of heretofore unparalleled training and maturity, today's high school student may be dissatisfied with the traditional mode of public education.

Sympathetic concern for student unhappiness, as well as impatience with a primarily prescriptive model of high school education, finds judicial expression in cases like *Tinker v. Des Moines Independent Community School District*. As Mr. Justice Fortas stated for the Court:

> In our system, students may not be regarded as closed-circuit recipients of only that which the State chooses to communicate. They may not be confined to the expression of those sentiments that are officially approved.

Goldstein, *Reflections on Developing Trends in the Law of Student Rights*, 118 U. Pa. L. Rev. 612, 614-15 (1970).*

Now consider the following, written 20 years after *Tinker*:

> Imagine the following scenario taking place in a school classroom. A history teacher asks her students, "What is George Washington famous for?" One student responds, "He was the first president of the United States," and after a pause adds, "and he owned slaves." Assume further that the school's intended curricular message, as represented in its textbook, is to identify George Washington as our nation's first president. The prescribed textbook does not mention that George Washington owned slaves. The teacher responds to the student's remarks by saying, "Yes, it's important to know that George Washington was our first president. But it is also true that he owned slaves. Let's assess George Washington's significance in light of his ownership of slaves among his other attributes and accomplishments."
>
> What is the extent of school authorities' power to object to or restrict the student's contribution of the fact that Washington owned slaves? Is the student's right to make this remark defensible under either the Constitution

---

*Reprinted by permission of the University of Pennsylvania Law Review and Fred B. Rothman & Co.

or educational policy? How should the teacher have responded to the slave-ownership part of the student's answer? Should the teacher have "corrected" the student by reasserting the school's official lesson, as stated in its textbook? Should the teacher have ignored the student's comment? Could the school reprimand the teacher for promoting the view that Washington owned slaves? Could the school in any other way limit the student's expression regarding Washington's slave ownership? What are the constitutional and policy implications of the effect on students' civic development resulting from school programs that either encourage or discourage student speech diverging from the school's officially established curriculum?

How courts and education policymakers address these questions depends on their perception of the education function of the schools, which is also known as "the work of the schools." The first amendment is implicated when school authorities restrict or suppress speech that they believe to be educationally inappropriate or incompatible with this work. However, the Supreme Court has recently granted schools broad powers to limit student speech otherwise protected by the first amendment when such speech interferes with the schools' educational function.[6] School authorities can, according to their view of the work of the schools, restrict student speech to shape educational practices, but such restrictions may retard students' development of the knowledge and skills fundamental to personal growth and to effective political, economic, and social participation in society. The interaction between the schools' curriculum and student expression in American precollege education has been characterized by tension between polar views of the function of schools: one to socialize young people in the ideas and values deemed essential to enable them to participate in our democratic society ("inculcation of values"), the other to expose young people to a variety of ideas and values that they learn and evaluate on the basis of their own developing knowledge, experience, and judgment ("marketplace of ideas").

. . . .

The notion of the school as a marketplace of ideas has been largely unpersuasive in the area of student expression, and courts have generally limited its application to postsecondary education.[16] The marketplace

---

[6]*See, e.g., Hazelwood Sch. Dist. v. Kuhlmeier*, 484 U.S. 260, 273 (1988) (school can censor student-written articles in high school newspaper if such action is reasonably related to legitimate pedagogical concerns.) ...

[16]*See, e.g., Bender v. Williamsport Area Sch. Dist.*, 741 F.2d 538, 547-59 (3d Cir. 1984) (although colleges may be marketplaces of ideas and hence open forums for their students, high school expression is more circumscribed), *vacated*, 475 U.S. 534 (1986) (lack of standing); *see also* Goldstein, [*The Asserted Constitutional Right of Public School Teachers to Determine What They Teach*, 124 U. Pa. L. Rev. 1293] at 1341-43 (Marketplace-of-ideas paradigm generally

model allows students to exercise their constitutional freedoms, a practice that necessarily restrains the state from imposing its official dogma. But such restraint on the power of school authorities does not comport with the Court's current willingness to grant schools power to restrict student expression.

... Educational policy and constitutional rules would be more properly fashioned according to an alternative "conceptual-development" model. This model views the educational mission of schools to be development of students' knowledge in conjunction with their cognitive capacities. The notion of conceptual development draws from both the inculcation and marketplace models as well as from longstanding educational practice, democratic educational theory, and recent developments in cognitive psychology.

....

Three general principles of cognitive and conceptual development reveal both that the inculcative model has limits and that the learning process is essential to effective education. First, students are not "empty vessels" waiting passively to be filled by the school's lessons. Rather, they come to the learning process with a base of knowledge and values as well as some cognitive structures already in place. Second, the building of cognitive structures, although greatly influenced by schooling, is ultimately a function of the learner, not the school. Knowledge is not simply inculcated or instilled directly by instruction but is assimilated or accommodated by the learner, who should not be viewed as merely a recipient of information but rather as a "constructor of meaning." Third, both the building and reformulation of cognitive structures are substantially enhanced by the learner's expression of ideas.

....

In the inculcative model, instructional ideas are prescribed, developed, and validated in terms of the curriculum. The Supreme Court adopts this view when it describes inculcative teaching as a one-way transmission from teacher to student. Student communication is qualitatively limited to recitation of the school's relatively concrete curricular message. This model attributes little value to student expression:

> Throughout the school year, the teacher, after attempting to convey to the students the required version of a particular subject, tests them to see if they have learned the material properly. Answers conforming to the

---

pertains to higher education, while value inculcation has traditionally been viewed as the role of precollege education). The most recent Supreme Court cases have ignored marketplace rationales. *See, e.g., Hazelwood Sch. Dist. v. Kuhlmeier*, 484 U.S. 260 (1988); *Bethel Sch. Dist. No. 403 v. Fraser*, 478 U.S. 675 (1986).

view taught in the class get high marks, while inconsistent views may get low marks.

Little or no value is accorded to student-generated ideas that diverge from the highly prescriptive curriculum, which establishes a concrete set of desired facts and norms. Student knowledge of these facts and norms is the primary end of instruction. Under the *Fraser/Kuhlmeier* approach, schools may "disassociate" themselves from and express disapproval of divergent views by either suppressing or punishing speech.

In contrast, the conceptual-development model views the curriculum in terms of the origination, development, and assessment of ideas that accommodate both the school's curricular messages and the students' contributions. The school's voice is not the only one heard — while the school establishes curricular goals and objectives, these goals contemplate student input into their specific formulation. The students' role in the learning process is to examine the curricular propositions as much as it is to recite them, and throughout this process students are invited to contribute their own ideas. The classroom is characterized by student-teacher interaction, a give and take, that produces the dynamic nature of quality education. Ideas are both announced and interchanged — they proceed not only from teacher to student but also from student to teacher and student to student. In addition to the recitation of facts, students are involved in other intellectual processes such as application, analysis, synthesis, and evaluation.

....

... Current court deference standards, based on the inculcative model of education, are insufficient to provide adequate protection to speech that is educationally valuable although distinct from the school's message....

....

The courts should take a fresh look at education. They will find that the conceptual-development model of education is consistent with and supportive of first amendment values and student attainment of civic competence and that they need to establish a new strategy for evaluating student-speech cases. First, courts should understand the work of the schools in cognitive rather than inculcative terms. Next, courts should examine with closer scrutiny the compatibility of schools' avowed educational objectives with the student speech that school authorities seek to suppress. Finally, courts should accord less weight to the prescriptive power of the schools and more weight to the value of student speech.

The constitutional rules determining the limits of school curricular authority over student expression inevitably shape both the values to be learned by students and the processes under which these values are learned. The power of the law in American society is such that legal rules often attain normative force beyond their purely legal force. That is, the fact that the law says one can legally act in a certain manner does not mean that one should. In particular, the fact that the United States Supreme Court will broadly defer to school authorities' decisions on the appropriateness of student speech in matters of curriculum does not mean that educators should restrict student speech with which they disagree in form or content. Even if the courts do not come to understand the work of the schools under a conceptual-development theory and fail to establish protections for student expression consistent with this theory and democratic education, school authorities can nevertheless abide by standards that accommodate conceptual development and encourage education consistent with the exercise of free expression in a democracy.

An understanding of schooling in cognitive terms does not preclude inculcation. Rather, the school maintains both its socialization function and its power to prescribe the curriculum; even under conceptual-development theory, students still have to demonstrate that they have learned that George Washington was our first president. The Article looks beyond inculcative education, however, and maintains that student speech offering nondisruptive and noninjurious additions or alternatives to the school's preferred messages, such as a student comment that "George Washington owned slaves," should be tolerated by school authorities as consistent with the school's educational mission. Moreover, student speech that diverges from curricular norms should be encouraged to the extent that such speech contributes to cognitive progress in learning. Assessment of the relevance, worth, correctness, or any other qualities of speech and its relationship to the curriculum should be the function of the teacher in the classroom. The teacher who responds to a student's comment that "George Washington owned slaves" by developing her students' capacities to assess both the validity of that comment and Washington's presidency in light of it is teaching in a manner that ought to be applauded.

Richard L. Roe, *Valuing Student Speech: The Work of the Schools as Conceptual Development*, 79 Cal. L. Rev. 1269 (October 1991).*

2. If the Goldstein comment is correct, is *Tinker* correct? In other words, is *Tinker* a proper use of judicial power if ultimately it rests on pedagogical judgments? Does the First Amendment itself contain pedagogical judgments? If so, what are they and how are they derived? If not, is the Court still justified in making pedagogical judgments because those they make are so clearly correct as to be beyond reasoned debate? Or, perhaps, do First Amendment considerations override, and make irrelevant, pedagogical judgments in this area? We will return to the issue of pedagogical judgments in our coverage of *Hazelwood v. Kuhlmeier* and related cases.

---

*Copyright © 1991 by Professor Richard L. Roe and the California Law Review, Inc. Reprinted with permission.

3. There has been much discussion lately regarding the Courts' recent treatment and application (or lack thereof) of *Tinker*. Many critics feel that *Tinker*'s holding has been watered down or ignored by subsequent rulings, mainly during the past decade. Note, however, that limitations on the holding in *Tinker* started early after the 1969 decision.

Although reversing a dismissal originally granted to the school officials and remanding for further proceedings, the Seventh Circuit in *Scoville v. Board of Educ. of Joliet Twp. High Sch. Dist. 204*, 425 F.2d 10 (7th Cir. 1970), *cert. denied* 400 U.S. 826 (1970), recognized that states and school officials have the authority to prescribe and control conduct in schools through reasonable rules consistent with the fundamental constitutional safeguards outlined in *Tinker*. Where these rules infringe upon freedom of expression, the officials have the burden of showing justification. The plaintiffs were students, staff members of "Grass High," an underground publication containing poetry, essays, movie and music reviews, and critical editorials. The publication was labeled as "inappropriate and indecent," and the plaintiffs were expelled. Despite the acknowledgment of school authority, the court sided with the students.

The Sixth Circuit sided with the school officials in *Guzick v. Drebus*, 431 F.2d 594 (6th Cir. 1970), *cert. denied*, 401 U.S. 948 (1971). The school had a longstanding rule forbidding all wearing of buttons, badges, scarves and other means whereby the wearers identify themselves as supporters of a cause or bearing messages unrelated to their education. The Sixth Circuit upheld this rule. Regulations such as the button rule are constitutional if they are reasonably related to the prevention of disruptive conduct.

> We must be aware in these contentious times that America's classrooms and their environs will lose their usefulness as places in which to educate our young people if pupils come to school wearing the badges of their respective disagreements and provoking confrontations with their fellows and their teachers.

Is *Guzick* consistent with *Tinker*? Note that the trial court found that the particular buttons involved would not themselves be disruptive. It did, however, find that other buttons rendering different messages might be, and that the process banning some buttons and allowing others would be difficult, if not impossible, to administer. But the distinction between permissible and impermissible is usually required by the First Amendment. Does the school situation in *Guzick* allow for such a deviation from the requirement? If not, does *Guzick* expose a basic problem with the usual First Amendment analysis? If *Guzick* is understood to permit the prohibition of some buttons and the display of others, its holding is clearly in conflict with that of *Tinker*:

> It is ... relevant that the school authorities did not purport to prohibit the wearing of all symbols of political or controversial significance. The record shows that students in some of the schools wore buttons relating to national

A. POLITICAL AND OTHER STUDENT EXPRESSION

political campaigns, and some even wore the Iron Cross, traditionally a symbol of Nazism. The order prohibiting the wearing of armbands did not extend to these. *Tinker*, 393 U.S. at 510.

4. Note the *Tinker* Court's reliance on *Meyer v. Nebraska*. Can you explain why the opinion does not refer to the fact that *Meyer* involved a private school? Is that fact relevant to the case as precedent in *Tinker*?

FRAIN v. BARON
United States District Court
307 F. Supp. 27 (E.D.N.Y. 1969)

JUDD, DISTRICT JUDGE:

These civil rights actions are significant because they pit popular ideas of patriotism and the authority of school administrators against students' rights of free expression. The particular controversy is minor, involving the refusal of three students to leave their "homerooms" during the daily Pledge of Allegiance, as a condition for exercising their undoubted constitutional right not to participate in the Pledge. The resulting collision is serious, because it involves suspension from school as one alternative, and a court injunction against the school authorities as the other.

The facts and legal authorities must be reviewed in the light of the principle that:

> It is now beyond dispute that the constitution goes to school with the student and that the state may not interfere with the student's enjoyment of its presence. Denno, *Mary Beth Tinker Takes the Constitution to School*, 38 Fordham L. Rev. (1969) 35, 56.

Facts

....

The Commissioner of Education is required by statute to prepare a program for a daily salute and pledge of allegiance to the flag. Education Law § 802, McKinney's Consol. Laws, c. 16, subd. 1. The By-Laws of the New York City Board of Education require a salute to the flag only once a week (Sec. 90, subd. 31), but a Circular from the Superintendent of Schools in 1963 directed that "at the commencement of each school day, the Pledge of Allegiance to the Flag be followed by the singing in unison of a patriotic song."

The purpose of the ceremony is to encourage patriotism and loyalty to democratic institutions.

Plaintiffs Mary Frain and Susan Keller are twelve-year-old white girls attending Junior High School 217Q, in an accelerated class which does three years' work in two years.

Plaintiff Raymond Miller is a black boy, a senior at Jamaica High School.

All three plaintiffs refused to recite the Pledge of Allegiance, because of a belief that the words "with liberty and justice for all" are not true in America today. One is an atheist, who also objected to the words "under God."

They refused to stand during the Pledge, because that would constitute participation in what they considered a lie. They also refused to leave the room, and stand in the hall outside their homerooms until the conclusion of the ceremony, because they considered exclusion from the room to be a punishment for their exercise of constitutional rights.

It does not appear whether any plaintiff joined in the required patriotic song, or whether they were required to stay in the hall during the singing as well as the Pledge.

Plaintiff Miller was required to submit to the Assistant Principal for Guidance a written statement of his reasons for not saluting. His typewritten statement, in one page, expresses the belief that "America is perhaps the greatest country in the world," but that it must undergo certain basic changes, and provide true equality, freedom and justice for all, end oppression of minorities, and give black people a greater opportunity to advance. He concluded that "[a]s for the pledge: I believe it is untrue ('Liberty and justice for all') and I refuse to swear to a lie."

Mary Frain and Susan Keller are the remnant of a larger group who previously sat in silence during the Pledge of Allegiance. The others, after being summoned to the Principal's office to discuss their conduct, accepted one of the alternatives, of standing silently or going outside their classrooms during the Pledge. The papers do not show what supervision, if any, is provided in the halls while the non-participating students are excluded from class.

The policy of requiring a non-participating student to leave the area in which the flag salute is taking place was adopted by the Superintendent of Schools in March, 1969, in granting a petition from a student at Jamaica High School to be excused from taking part. The Superintendent stated:

> This decision is based on rulings by the United States Supreme Court and more recently by a Trial Examiner designated by the Board of Education, that both pupils and teachers have a right, as a matter of conscience, to refuse to salute the flag and recite the Pledge of Allegiance. I believe that no pupil should be permitted to sit during such a ceremony, since to do so might create disorder.

Raymond Miller asserts that he was nevertheless permitted to remain seated from March to October, when the publicity about the Frain suit called attention to the matter. Defendants assert that he stood silently during this time, and was not observed to remain seated until October 17, 1969, when his conduct resulted in suspension. This minor dispute of fact does not require decision at this time.

Between October 10, when the Frain and Miller girls were returned to school under this court's temporary restraining order, and November 10, when the City's reply papers were submitted, fifty other students in Junior High School

A. POLITICAL AND OTHER STUDENT EXPRESSION

217Q have also sat silently during the Pledge of Allegiance, on one or more occasions. There is no showing that this has caused any disorder.

For two months in 1967 a teacher in Far Rockaway High School remained seated during the Pledge of Allegiance and did not recite the Pledge. A special Trial Examiner for the Board of Education, in ruling on charges against the teacher, found that his conduct did not cause disorder in the classroom. *Matter of Superintendent of Schools v. Jacobs.*

The principal of Jamaica High School asserts in an affidavit filed in this case that permitting a student to remain seated during the Pledge could be "a real and present threat to the maintenance of discipline" and would be "pedagogically fool-hardy." Other school administrators echo these words. For the purpose of the pending motions, these conclusory assertions are insufficient to support a finding of serious harm to defendants from the granting of an injunction.

. . . .

Legal Authorities

The thrust of recent decisions of the Supreme Court and lower federal courts has been toward increasing judicial concern with the clash between student expression and school authorities. This increasing concern has been accompanied by a shift in focus, well illustrated by comparing the Supreme Court's decision in *West Virginia State Bd. of Educ. v. Barnette*, 319 U.S. 624 (1943), overruling *Minersville School Dist. v. Gobitis*, 310 U.S. 586 (1940), with the recent decision in *Tinker v. Des Moines Independent Community School Dist.*, 393 U.S. 503 (1969). The original concern with limitation of the state's power to compel a student to act contrary to his beliefs has shifted to a concern for affirmative protection of the student's right to express his beliefs. The present case is novel in that the context, school patriotic exercises, is one in which courts have previously intervened to limit participation, while these plaintiffs are urging not only a right of non-participation but a right of silent protest by remaining seated.

Barnette established the right of students to refrain from participation in a legislatively mandated flag ceremony. Rejecting compulsory participation as a proper vehicle for instilling patriotism, MR. JUSTICE JACKSON stated (319 U.S. at 642):

> If there is any fixed star in our constitutional constellation, it is that no official, high or petty, can prescribe what shall be orthodox in politics, nationalism, religion, or other matters of opinion or force citizens to confess by word or act their faith therein.

Of pertinence to the present case, the opinion recognized that "The freedom asserted by these appellees does not bring them into collision with rights asserted by any other individual." 319 U.S. at 630. JUSTICE JACKSON also foreshadowed the present case by commenting that "liberty and justice for all," unless accepted merely as an ideal, "might to some seem an overstatement." 319 U.S. at 634, n. 14.

Under the authority of Barnette, a federal district court held that a refusal to stand during the singing of the National Anthem did not justify exclusion from school. *Sheldon v. Fannin*, 221 F. Supp. 766 (D. Ariz. 1963). However, *Barnette*, standing alone, might not be decisive of the present case. While MR. JUSTICE JACKSON's opinion expressly disclaimed reliance on the religious beliefs of the plaintiffs, who were Jehovah's Witnesses, two of the six majority justices concurred on that basis. The plaintiffs in *Sheldon* were also Jehovah's Witnesses. In addition, neither *Barnette* nor *Sheldon* involved the alternative to participation of waiting outside the room; the choice was participation or exclusion from school.

The Supreme Court's decision in *Tinker* makes it unnecessary to explore further the differences between *Barnette* and the present case. *Tinker* held that public school students could not be suspended for wearing black arm-bands to protest American involvement in Vietnam, a form of silent expression in the classroom. While *Tinker* did not involve a refusal to participate in patriotic exercises in school, the Supreme Court did not tie its opinion to a particular set of facts, but enunciated a rule of general applicability. MR. JUSTICE FORTAS stated (393 U.S. 509):

> In order for the State in the person of school officials to justify prohibition of a particular expression of opinion, it must be able to show that its action was caused by something more than a mere desire to avoid the discomfort and unpleasantness that always accompany an unpopular viewpoint. Certainly where there is no finding and no showing that the exercise of the forbidden right would "*materially and substantially interfere with the requirements of appropriate discipline* in the operation of the school," the prohibition cannot be sustained. *Burnside v. Byars, supra*, 363 F.2d at 749. (Emphasis supplied.)

....

Tinker thus places on the school authorities the burden of justifying a particular restriction on student expression. The student is free to select his form of expression, so long as he does not materially infringe the rights of other students or disrupt school activities.

....

Respondent advances no persuasive reason why the approach of *Tinker* should not be used here. Accordingly, it is not incumbent upon plaintiffs to convince the court that the offered alternative of leaving the room during the Pledge of Allegiance constituted punishment. Rather, respondent must convince the court that the particular expression of protest chosen by plaintiffs, remaining seated, materially infringed the rights of other students or caused disruption.

Supreme Court decisions involving the exercise of First Amendment rights in non-school contexts support plaintiffs' position here. In *Brown v. Louisiana*, 383 U.S. 131 (1966), involving a sit-in in a segregated public library, the court stated that the right of free speech is not confined to verbal expression but includes

A. POLITICAL AND OTHER STUDENT EXPRESSION

"the right in a peaceable and orderly manner to protest by silent and reproachful presence, *in a place where the protestant has every right to be.*" (Emphasis added.) In *Street v. New York*, 394 U.S. 576 (1969), Mr. Justice Harlan, one of the dissenters in *Tinker*, stated that the First Amendment provides "freedom to express publicly one's opinions about our flag, including those opinions which are defiant or contemptuous."

The draft-card burning case on which the City relies (*United States v. Miller*, 367 F.2d 72 (2d Cir. 1966)) is not comparable. Destruction of even trivial property is more than free speech. Of some similarity to the present case is a recent decision in another Circuit sustaining a mild penalty for a spectator's refusal to stand at the beginning of a court session. *United States ex rel. Robson v. Malone*, 412 F.2d 848 (7th Cir. 1969). The decision is not binding here and, in any event, is distinguished by the fact that a spectator's attendance in the courtroom is voluntary, while attendance in a public high school is compulsory.

Fear of disorder, which the City cites to justify its policy, has been ruled out as a ground for limiting peaceful exercise of First Amendment rights. *Edwards v. South Carolina*, 372 U.S. 229 (1963). The Supreme Court dealt with this argument again in *Tinker*, saying (393 U.S. at 508):

> The District Court concluded that the action of the school authorities was reasonable because it was based upon their fear of a disturbance from the wearing of the armbands. But, in our system, undifferentiated fear or apprehension of disturbance is not enough to overcome the right to freedom of expression. Any departure from absolute regimentation may cause trouble. Any variation from the majority's opinion may inspire fear. Any word spoken, in class, in the lunchroom, or on the campus, that deviates from the views of another person, may start an argument or cause a disturbance. But our Constitution says we must take this risk....

Pedagogical opinions, or appeals to courtesy, are also inadequate grounds for coercive responses to First Amendment expressions.

Certainly, the fact that others have joined the plaintiffs in sitting out the Pledge is no justification for impeding plaintiffs' protests. The First Amendment protects successful dissent as well as ineffective protests.

This does not mean that the court has created an open season for students to defy authority. The same panel of the same court which upheld the wearing of "freedom buttons" in *Burnside, supra*, 363 F.2d 744, also held that the right to wear the buttons was forfeited where the button-wearers harassed other students and created a disturbance. *Blackwell v. Issaquena County Bd. of Educ.*, 363 F.2d 749 (5th Cir. 1966).

President Harold C. Martin of Union College recently called attention to the emotions which are aroused by a case like this:

> The refusal of some religious sects today to swear an oath of allegiance to the flag infuriates many citizens who find themselves unable to consent to a set of principles different from the one they hold. The Meaning of "Law and Order," 74 Case & Comment 45, at 46, Nov.-Dec., 1969.

The policy of the New York City Board of Education is a sincere attempt to prevent disorders which may develop as the reaction of infuriated members of the majority to the silent dissent expressed by plaintiffs. The flaw in the policy is that the constitution does not recognize fears of a disorderly reaction as ground for restricting peaceful expression of views. As the court said in *Tinker*:

> Freedom of expression would not truly exist if the right could be exercised only in an area that a benevolent government has provided as a safe haven for crackpots. (393 U.S. at 513).

Preliminary Injunction

On the basis of the facts and legal authorities, the court is satisfied that plaintiffs have a strong possibility of ultimate success on the merits, that the grant of a preliminary injunction will cause no appreciable harm to defendants, and that denial of an injunction would be prejudicial to plaintiffs.

New rules adopted by the Board of Education since the argument of these motions would limit the Board's power of suspension, but do not affect the court's jurisdiction of this action.

It is therefore ordered

. . . .

(4) That defendants be enjoined during the pendency of this action from excluding plaintiffs from their classrooms during the Pledge of Allegiance, or from treating any student who refuses for reasons of conscience to participate in the Pledge in any different way from those who participate.

---

1. Is the court correct in *Frain* in stating that the plaintiffs were urging an affirmative right of protest which was based on *Tinker* and not *Barnette*? If so, is the provision of an affirmative right of protest a constitutional requirement under *Tinker*?

2. Compare *Goetz v. Ansell*, 477 F.2d 636 (2d Cir. 1973), which reaches the same result as *Frain* on the theory that having to stand is a compelled act of patriotism and having to leave the room may reasonably be viewed by some as punishment for refusing to salute the flag. For this latter point the court cites only Justice Brennan's concurrence in *Schempp*, 374 U.S. 203 (1963). Is such a citation sufficient to show punishment in a flag salute case?

A. POLITICAL AND OTHER STUDENT EXPRESSION

3. "Not many symbols stir the emotions of the American public as does the American flag. Whether in politics, protests, or pedagogy, the use or abuse of the flag calls upon strong and deep-seated feelings.... Long before newspaper front pages carried pictures of protestors burning flags, perhaps even before presidential candidates wrestled in the folds of the flag, the American flag found a place in American public schools." Bartlett, *The Pledge of Allegiance in the Public Schools on the 200th Anniversary of the Bill of Rights*, 67 Educ. L. Rep. 867 (1991).*

The fifty-year-old ruling in *Barnette*, used in both the *Tinker* and *Frain* decisions, remains clear and unequivocal. Students may not be compelled to participate in flag salutes if doing so conflicts with free exercise of religion and speech rights protected by the First Amendment. However, the Supreme Court never told us what "an objecting student is to do while classmates participate in the pledge." *Id.*

4. In *Frain*, the principal testified that it would be a "threat to the maintenance of discipline" and "pedagogically foolhardy" to allow a student to remain seated during the classroom's recitation of the Pledge.

Two decades later, an Illinois Federal District Court considered pedagogical concerns when deciding a similar case. *Sherman v. Community Consol. Sch. Dist.*, 758 F. Supp. 1244 (N.D. Ill. 1991). In upholding the state's mandate requiring Pledge recitation, the court recognized that instilling patriotic values in elementary school children has a legitimate secular legislative purpose which neither advances nor inhibits religion. *Id.* at 1247. Of course, as a compromise to allowing such a mandate to be a part of the school's curriculum, the school must allow students to remain seated and not participate. *Barnette*, *Tinker*, and *Frain* dictate these free religion and speech rights.

5. Bartlett offers some thoughts on the future of the Pledge in the courts:

> If a mandatory pledge is upheld, it will likely be on the basis that the pledge of allegiance is an integral part of a curricular component designed to instill patriotism and respect for the nation's symbol. It can be argued from both recent and historical precedent that the courts should leave to school officials the determination of how best to instill important national and community values [*Hazelwood* and *Gobitis*].... The current trend in student first amendment rulings may signal that the issue of compulsory participation in the pledge of allegiance again may be left to pedagogical rather than legal decision makers. 67 Educ. L. Rep. 867 (1991).

---

*Copyright © 1991 by West Publishing Company. Reprinted with permission.

BETHEL SCHOOL DISTRICT NO. 403 v. FRASER
Supreme Court of the United States
478 U.S. 675 (1986)

CHIEF JUSTICE BURGER delivered the opinion of the Court:

We granted certiorari to decide whether the First Amendment prevents a school district from disciplining a high school student for giving a lewd speech at a school assembly.

I

A

On April 26, 1983, respondent Matthew N. Fraser, a student at Bethel High School in Pierce County, Washington, delivered a speech nominating a fellow student for student elective office. Approximately 600 high school students, many of whom were 14-year-olds, attended the assembly. Students were required to attend the assembly or to report to the study hall. The assembly was part of a school-sponsored educational program in self-government. Students who elected not to attend the assembly were required to report to study hall. During the entire speech, Fraser referred to his candidate in terms of an elaborate, graphic, and explicit sexual metaphor.

Two of Fraser's teachers, with whom he discussed the contents of his speech in advance, informed him that the speech was "inappropriate and that he probably should not deliver it," and that his delivery of the speech might have "severe consequences."

During Fraser's delivery of the speech, a school counselor observed the reaction of students to the speech. Some students hooted and yelled; some by gestures graphically simulated the sexual activities pointedly alluded to in respondent's speech. Other students appeared to be bewildered and embarrassed by the speech. One teacher reported that on the day following the speech, she found it necessary to forgo a portion of the scheduled class lesson in order to discuss the speech with the class.

A Bethel High School disciplinary rule prohibiting the use of obscene language in the school provides: "Conduct which materially and substantially interferes with the educational process is prohibited, including the use of obscene, profane language or gestures." The morning after the assembly, the Assistant Principal called Fraser into her office and notified him that the school considered his speech to have been a violation of this rule. Fraser was presented with copies of five letters submitted by teachers, describing his conduct at the assembly; he was given a chance to explain his conduct, and he admitted to having given the speech described and that he deliberately used sexual innuendo in the speech. Fraser was then informed that he would be suspended for three days, and that his name would be removed from the list of candidates for graduation speaker at the school's commencement exercises.

A. POLITICAL AND OTHER STUDENT EXPRESSION

Fraser sought review of this disciplinary action through the School District's grievance procedures. The hearing officer determined that the speech given by respondent was "indecent, lewd, and offensive to the modesty and decency of many of the students and faculty in attendance at the assembly." The examiner determined that the speech fell within the ordinary meaning of "obscene," as used in the disruptive-conduct rule, and affirmed the discipline in its entirety. Fraser served two days of his suspension, and was allowed to return to school on the third day.

B

Respondent, by his father as guardian ad litem, then brought this action in the United States District Court for the Western District of Washington. Respondent alleged a violation of his First Amendment right to freedom of speech and sought both injunctive relief and monetary damages under 42 U.S.C. § 1983. The District Court held that the school's sanctions violated respondent's right to freedom of speech under the First Amendment to the United States Constitution ...

The Court of Appeals for the Ninth Circuit affirmed the judgment of the District Court ....

... [W]e reverse.

II

This Court acknowledged in *Tinker v. Des Moines Independent Community School Dist.*, 393 U.S. 503 (1969), that students do not "shed their constitutional rights to freedom of speech or expression at the schoolhouse gate." *Id.*, 393 U.S. at 506. The Court of Appeals read that case as precluding any discipline of Fraser for indecent speech and lewd conduct in the school assembly. That court appears to have proceeded on the theory that the use of lewd and obscene speech in order to make what the speaker considered to be a point in a nominating speech for a fellow student was essentially the same as the wearing of an armband in *Tinker* as a form of protest or the expression of a political position.

The marked distinction between the political "message" of the armbands in Tinker and the sexual content of respondent's speech in this case seems to have been given little weight by the Court of Appeals. In upholding the students' right to engage in a nondisruptive, passive expression of a political viewpoint in *Tinker*, this Court was careful to note that the case did "not concern speech or action that intrudes upon the work of the schools or the rights of other students." 393 U.S. at 508.

It is against this background that we turn to consider the level of First Amendment protection accorded to Fraser's utterances and actions before an official high school assembly attended by 600 students.

III

The role and purpose of the American public school system were well described by two historians, who stated: "[P]ublic education must prepare pupils for citizenship in the Republic.... It must inculcate the habits and manners of civility as values in themselves conducive to happiness and as indispensable to the practice of self-government in the community and the nation." C. Beard & M. Beard, New Basic History of the United States 228 (1968). In *Ambach v. Norwick*, 441 U.S. 68, 76-77 (1979), we echoed the essence of this statement of the objectives of public education as the "inculcat[ion of] fundamental values necessary to the maintenance of a democratic political system."

These fundamental values of "habits and manners of civility" essential to a democratic society must, of course, include tolerance of divergent political and religious views, even when the views expressed may be unpopular. But these "fundamental values" must also take into account consideration of the sensibilities of others, and, in the case of a school, the sensibilities of fellow students. The undoubted freedom to advocate unpopular and controversial views in schools and classrooms must be balanced against the society's countervailing interest in teaching students the boundaries of socially appropriate behavior. Even the most heated political discourse in a democratic society requires consideration for the personal sensibilities of the other participants and audiences.

In our Nation's legislative halls, where some of the most vigorous political debates in our society are carried on, there are rules prohibiting the use of expressions offensive to other participants in the debate.... Can it be that what is proscribed in the halls of Congress is beyond the reach of school officials to regulate?

The First Amendment guarantees wide freedom in matters of adult public discourse. A sharply divided Court upheld the right to express an antidraft viewpoint in a public place, albeit in terms highly offensive to most citizens. *See Cohen v. California*, 403 U.S. 15, (1971). It does not follow, however, that simply because the use of an offensive form of expression may not be prohibited to adults making what the speaker considers a political point, the same latitude must be permitted to children in a public school....

Surely it is a highly appropriate function of public school education to prohibit the use of vulgar and offensive terms in public discourse. Indeed, the "fundamental values necessary to the maintenance of a democratic political system" disfavor the use of terms of debate highly offensive or highly threatening to others. Nothing in the Constitution prohibits the states from insisting that certain modes of expression are inappropriate and subject to sanctions. The inculcation of these values is truly the "work of the schools." *Tinker*, 393 U.S. at 508. The determination of what manner of speech in the classroom or in school assembly is inappropriate properly rests with the school board.

The process of educating our youth for citizenship in public schools is not confined to books, the curriculum, and the civics class; schools must teach by example the shared values of a civilized social order. Consciously or otherwise, teachers — and indeed the older students — demonstrate the appropriate form of civil discourse and political expression by their conduct and deportment in and out of class. Inescapably, like parents, they are role models. The schools, as instruments of the state, may determine that the essential lessons of civil, mature conduct cannot be conveyed in a school that tolerates lewd, indecent, or offensive speech and conduct such as that indulged in by this confused boy.

The pervasive sexual innuendo in Fraser's speech was plainly offensive to both teachers and students — indeed to any mature person. By glorifying male sexuality, and in its verbal content, the speech was acutely insulting to teenage girl students. The speech could well be seriously damaging to its less mature audience, many of whom were only 14 years old and on the threshold of awareness of human sexuality. Some students were reported as bewildered by the speech and the reaction of mimicry it provoked.

This Court's First Amendment jurisprudence has acknowledged limitations on the otherwise absolute interest of the speaker in reaching an unlimited audience where the speech is sexually explicit and the audience may include children.... *Ginsberg v. New York*, 390 U.S. 629, (1968) ... *Board of Education v. Pico*, 457 U.S. 853, 871-72, (1982) (plurality opinion); *Id.* at 879-81, (BLACKMUN, J., concurring in part and in judgment); *Id.* at 918-20, (REHNQUIST, J., dissenting). These cases recognize the obvious concern on the part of parents, and school authorities acting *in loco parentis*, to protect children — especially in a captive audience — from exposure to sexually explicit, indecent, or lewd speech.

We have also recognized an interest in protecting minors from exposure to vulgar and offensive spoken language. In *FCC v. Pacifica Foundation*, 438 U.S. 726, (1978)....

We hold that petitioner School District acted entirely within its permissible authority in imposing sanctions upon Fraser in response to his offensively lewd and indecent speech. Unlike the sanctions imposed on the students wearing armbands in *Tinker*, the penalties imposed in this case were unrelated to any political viewpoint. The First Amendment does not prevent the school officials from determining that to permit a vulgar and lewd speech such as respondent's would undermine the school's basic educational mission. A high school assembly or classroom is no place for a sexually explicit monologue directed towards an unsuspecting audience of teenage students. Accordingly, it was perfectly appropriate for the school to disassociate itself to make the point to the pupils that vulgar speech and lewd conduct is wholly inconsistent with the "fundamental values" of public school education....

IV

Respondent contends that the circumstances of his suspension violated due process because he had no way of knowing that the delivery of the speech in question would subject him to disciplinary sanctions. This argument is wholly without merit.... Given the school's need to be able to impose disciplinary sanctions for a wide range of unanticipated conduct disruptive of the educational process, the school disciplinary rules need not be as detailed as a criminal code which imposes criminal sanctions....

The judgment of the Court of Appeals for the Ninth Circuit is

Reversed.

JUSTICE BLACKMUN concurs in the result.

JUSTICE BRENNAN, concurring in the judgment:

Respondent gave the following speech at a high school assembly in support of a candidate for student government office:

> I know a man who is firm — he's firm in his pants, he's firm in his shirt, his character is firm — but most ... of all, his belief in you, the students of Bethel, is firm. Jeff Kuhlman is a man who takes his point and pounds it in. If necessary, he'll take an issue and nail it to the wall. He doesn't attack things in spurts — he drives hard, pushing and pushing until finally — he succeeds. Jeff is a man who will go to the very end — even the climax, for each and every one of you. So vote for Jeff for A.S.B. vice-president — he'll never come between you and the best our high school can be.

The Court, referring to these remarks as "obscene," "vulgar," "lewd," and "offensively lewd," concludes that school officials properly punished respondent for uttering the speech. Having read the full text of respondent's remarks, I find it difficult to believe that it is the same speech the Court describes. To my mind, the most that can be said about respondent's speech — and all that need be said — is that in light of the discretion school officials have to teach high school students how to conduct civil and effective public discourse, and to prevent disruption of school educational activities, it was not unconstitutional for school officials to conclude, under the circumstances of this case, that respondent's remarks exceeded permissible limits....

The Court today reaffirms the unimpeachable proposition that students do not "'shed their constitutional rights to freedom of speech or expression at the schoolhouse gate.'" *Ante*, at 3163 (quoting *Tinker v. Des Moines Independent Community School Dist.*, 393 U.S. 503, 506 (1969)). If respondent had given the same speech outside of the school environment, he could not have been penalized simply because government officials considered his language to be inappropriate, *see Cohen v. California*, 403 U.S. 15 (1971); the Court's opinion does not suggest otherwise. Moreover, despite the Court's characterizations, the language respondent used is far removed from the very narrow class of "obscene" speech which the Court has held is not protected by the First Amendment. *Ginsberg v. New York*, 390 U.S. 629, 635 (1968); *Roth v. United States*, 354 U.S. 476, 485 (1957). It is true, however, that the State has interests in teaching high school students how to conduct civil and effective public discourse and in avoiding disruption of educational school activities. Thus, the Court holds that under certain circumstances, high school students may properly be reprimanded for

A. POLITICAL AND OTHER STUDENT EXPRESSION

giving a speech at a high school assembly which school officials conclude disrupted the school's educational mission. Respondent's speech may well have been protected had he given it in school but under different circumstances, where the school's legitimate interests in teaching and maintaining civil public discourse were less weighty.

. . . .

The authority school officials have to regulate such speech by high school students is not limitless. *See Thomas v. Board of Education, Granville Central School Dist.*, 607 F.2d 1043, 1057 (CA2 1979) (Newman, J., concurring in result) ... Under the circumstances of this case, however, I believe that school officials did not violate the First Amendment in determining that respondent should be disciplined for the disruptive language he used while addressing a high school assembly. Thus, I concur in the judgment reversing the decision of the Court of Appeals.

. . . .

Tinker delineated a standard for determining the constitutionality of regulated student speech. Under the standard, a school system could not justifiably infringe on student's First Amendment rights unless it could reasonably "... forecast substantial disruption of or material interference with school activities...." 393 U.S. 503, 514. Cases since *Tinker* demonstrate that the courts have struggled in trying to resolve the tension between the authority of public schools to inculcate values on one hand and the school's obligation to maintain a "free marketplace of ideas" and to refrain from imposing a "pall of orthodoxy" on the other. As to free speech, the Supreme Court's decision in *Bethel* enabled school officials to place a finger on the scales of justice:

> The determination of what manner of speech in the classroom or in the school assembly is inappropriate properly rests with the school board. 478 U.S. 675, 683.

Bethel, hence, elucidates the principle that while the right of students to engage in symbolic speech on matters of public concern is still protected under *Tinker*, "... the freedom to advocate unpopular and controversial views in schools ... must be balanced against society's countervailing interest in teaching students the boundaries of socially appropriate behavior." 478 U.S. 675, 681. *Bethel*, therefore, ushers in an era where student education and student expression, whether in the form of speech or appearance, may be accorded only minimal constitutional protection. For more on the impact of *Bethel*, *see* S. Slaff, *Silencing Student Speech* Bethel School District No 403 v. Fraser, 37 Am. U. L. Rev. 203 (1987); L. Salfrank, *The Fraser Balancing Test: Leaving Cohen's Jacket at the School House Gate*, 52 Mo. L. Rev. 913 (1987); and P. Graubard, *The Expanded Role of School Administrators and Governing Boards in First*

Amendment Student Speech Disputes: Bethel School District No. 403 v. Fraser, 17 Golden State U. L. Rev. 257 (1987).

PYLE v. SOUTH HADLEY SCHOOL COMMITTEE
United States District Court
824 F. Supp. 7 (D. Mass. 1993)

PONSOR, UNITED STATES MAGISTRATE JUDGE:

....

The court must decide whether the plaintiffs, two minor high school students bringing suit through their father, are entitled to temporary, immediate relief against a policy that, as applied by administrators at South Hadley High School in Massachusetts, prohibits their wearing on school premises either of two T-shirts, one offering a suggestive sexual slogan and the other bearing a slang reference to male genitalia.

Plaintiffs take the position that by barring this dress the defendants violated their right to freedom of expression guaranteed under the First Amendment.

The court's analysis begins with *Tinker v. Des Moines Indep. Comm. School Dist.*, 393 U.S. 503 (1969). In this case the court reversed a district court decision upholding an Iowa high school's prohibition against wearing black armbands as a protest against the war in Vietnam. Noting that students and teachers do not "shed their constitutional rights to freedom of speech or expression at the schoolhouse gate," the Court held that the school's action violated the plaintiff's First Amendment rights. Significantly, however, Justice Fortas observed that the "[p]roblem posed by the present case does not relate to regulations of the length of skirts or the type of clothing, to hair style, or deportment." *Id.* at 507-08....

The *Tinker* holding was refined in *Bethel School Dist. v. Fraser*. In that case the lower court had found a First Amendment violation where school authorities disciplined a high school student for presenting a speech employing sexual metaphor at a high school assembly. The Court reversed....

....

The key passage reads as follows:

> We hold that petitioner School District acted entirely within its permissible authority in imposing sanctions upon Fraser in response to his offensively lewd and indecent speech. Unlike the sanctions imposed on the students wearing armbands in *Tinker*, the penalties imposed in this case were unrelated to any political viewpoint. The First Amendment does not prevent the school officials from determining that to permit a vulgar and lewd speech such as respondent's would undermine the school's basic educational mission....

A. POLITICAL AND OTHER STUDENT EXPRESSION

At least one other court has wrestled with the issue of provocative dress. In *Broussard v. School Bd. of Norfolk*, 801 F.Supp. 1526 (E.D.Va.1992), the district court held that a school administrator's one-day suspension of a student for wearing a "Drugs Suck!" T-shirt did not violate the First Amendment. The judge concluded that the restriction was content-neutral, affecting the mode of communication and not the message itself. Plaintiffs concede that *Broussard* is on point but urge this court not to follow it.

Turning to the specifics of this case, the T-shirts in question bear the slogans: "Coed Naked Band; Do It To The Rhythm" and "See Dick Drink. See Dick Drive. See Dick Die. Don't Be A Dick."

A few preliminary concerns may be combed away. First, the defendants' goal here is not to prohibit books or class discussion regarding supposedly objectionable material or subjects....

Second, this case involves minors ranging in age from as young as twelve years old. It obviously does not address what these minors do outside school hours.

Third, the defendants' actions do not limit the content of any political or other substantive message. Except for the sexual innuendo, it is hard to discern any substance in the invocation to, "Do It To The Rhythm." As for the "Don't Be A Dick" T-shirt, plaintiffs do not, and could not, seriously suggest that the defendants are determined to suppress the message that students should not drink and drive. While perhaps not on all fours, this case bears far more resemblance to *Fraser* than *Tinker*.

Fourth, this case is not about the policy that this judge, if he were a member of the School Committee, might personally argue for. Plaintiffs' counsel forcefully contends that some T-shirts, apparently now tolerated at the high school by the defendants, offer more pungent phrases or depictions than the two at issue. Indeed, the record contains evidence that some of the administrators and teachers at South Hadley disagree, as individuals, about what dress might be preferable. As all parents know, however, line-drawing with adolescents is never simple; instances falling on one side or the other of the boundary will be forever subject to debate. The fact that the precise outline of what is acceptable may be a theme for disagreement among reasonable people does not suggest that no line may ever be drawn — much less, that the line is unconstitutional.

Fifth, the T-shirts themselves are not horribly offensive. Particularly when compared to other influences twelve-year-olds encounter in today's world, they could be seen as fairly innocuous. The defendants do not allege that this clothing will provoke instant fisticuffs or an outbreak of nausea within the student body. However, as plaintiffs for their part recognize, the First Amendment does not require that school administrators wait before acting until they confront something truly sickening.

For the defendants, the issue in its essence is the atmosphere they feel responsible for fostering at the school. On this point this court must move from the preliminaries to the center of the discussion.

Two justifications are offered for the defendants' decision: first, that the T-shirts' suggestive, and (to some) vulgar, mode of communication interferes with the school's basic educational mission, and, second, that the sexually charged messages are demeaning to women. Again, it is important to emphasize that the First Amendment does not require the court to substitute its own judgment on these issues for that of the defendants, but only to determine based on the record whether these concerns are reasonable. Placing the issue in the context of the motion for temporary restraining order, the court must decide whether the defendants' action is so lacking in legitimacy as to make the likelihood of plaintiffs' ultimate success on the merits sufficiently high to justify emergency relief.

Having read the memoranda and the extensive affidavits filed by both sides, the court has concluded that it is unlikely that the plaintiffs will prove that the defendants' actions violated the First Amendment.

....

Defendants' concerns cannot be brushed aside.... [N]o teacher or school administrator's concern about the effects of a sexually charged atmosphere on the welfare of students — and on their ability to learn — can be dismissed as trivial.

The issue on this case is not whether plaintiffs' First Amendment rights will be protected. The issue is what plaintiffs' First Amendment rights are, given the particular expression and the particular setting. If a school committee and administration decide to limit clothing with sexually provocative slogans, and diffuse somewhat an already highly charged atmosphere, in order to protect students and enhance the educational environment — even where the specific items banned may be relatively innocuous in today's world — the court is unlikely to conclude that this action violates the First Amendment.

BOYD v. BOARD OF DIRECTORS OF McGEHEE SCHOOL DISTRICT NO. 17

United States District Court, Pine Bluff Div.
612 F. Supp. 86 (E.D. Ark. 1985)

GEORGE HOWARD, JR., DISTRICT JUDGE:

This action was filed on October 7, 1983, under 42 U.S.C. § 1983 and 28 U.S.C. §§ 1343, 2201 and 2202 by Jamesina Boyd and Orlando Johnson, black students, of McGehee High School in McGehee School District No. 17, Desha County, Arkansas, by and through their parents and guardians, praying a preliminary and final injunction requiring defendants, Board of Directors of McGehee School District No. 17, Buford Conner, ... Superintendent of the McGehee School District No. 17, Robert Hardin, Carol Lucky, Breck Smith, Robert Prosser, Tyrone Broomfield, ... members of the Board of Directors of McGehee School District No. 17, and Sammy Gill, coach for the McGehee School District No. 17, to certify Jamesina Boyd, a black female high school senior, as 1983-84 McGehee High School homecoming queen instead of certifying Kristy Wynn, a white female high school senior. The plaintiffs alleged

A. POLITICAL AND OTHER STUDENT EXPRESSION

that Boyd had polled the highest number of votes — a majority — cast by members of the football team, twenty-eight votes of the fifty-four members of the team, during an election for homecoming queen, but defendant Gill had manipulated the results of the election, because of the race of Boyd, so that Wynn could serve as homecoming queen.

The Court is persuaded that the election conducted pursuant to this Court's order rendered the issue involving the selection of homecoming queen moot, and, therefore, the central issue to be resolved is whether the suspension of Johnson from the McGehee High School football team, within the context of the facts in this case, constituted an infringement of Johnson's right to freedom of expression as secured under the First and Fourteenth Amendments to the Federal Constitution....

Relevant Facts

On September 12, 1983, an election was conducted by the head football coach, Sammy Gill, for the position of High School homecoming queen for the 1983-84 school year. In accordance with the custom and practice of the McGehee High School, only members of the high school football team were eligible to participate in the election. There were fifty-four members constituting the current team consisting of twenty-eight white and twenty-six black players.

Four female high school students were nominated for the position, three whites and one black. The black nominee was Jamesina Boyd. The players were directed to indicate their choice for queen by the "show-of-hands" as each nominee's name was called. Purportedly, Boyd, the black nominee, received the highest number of votes and should have been designated queen. However, Gill directed the players to indicate their preference between the two white nominees who had polled the highest number of votes between the three white nominees in the initial vote. Wynn won the election involving the two white nominees. Gill then directed the players to vote their preference between Boyd and Wynn. This election was by secret ballot — each player indicated his preference on a slip of paper and delivered the slip to Gill. Gill took immediate possession of the slips and departed for his home without announcing the results. The following day, Gill announced that Wynn, the white nominee, had won the last election and, consequently, was the 1983-1984 McGehee High School homecoming queen.

Practically all of the black players believed that Boyd had won the election initially and that Gill had manipulated the election so that one of the white nominees could be designated queen....

On September 23, 1983, twenty-five of the twenty-six black players, in order to protest what they perceived to have been an act of racial discrimination in the selection of the queen, walked out of a pep rally during the afternoon and refused to participate in the game scheduled for that night.

On September 26, 1983, Johnson and the other twenty-four black players participating in the "boycott" of the scheduled game were suspended from participating on the football team for the remainder of the 1983-84 season....

Plaintiffs contend that the black players were suspended because of their race and as punishment for the exercise of their right of "freedom of expression." On the other hand, defendants assert that the black players were suspended because they had violated an unwritten rule maintained by Gill to the effect that any player who missed a game or football practice "without good cause" or "proper excuse" would be suspended from the team; and that the suspension was not because of race or the exercise of First Amendment rights.

On October 11, 1983, Orlando Johnson filed his motion for preliminary injunction requiring defendants to reinstate him as a player on the football team.

On October 14, 1983, this Court entered its order directing defendants to reinstate Johnson as a member of the football team immediately and afford him the same opportunities he enjoyed as a team member prior to his suspension.

On October 20, 1983, Johnson filed his motion for an order directing defendants to show cause why defendants should not be held in contempt for violating this Court's order of October 14, 1983, directing defendants to reinstate Johnson as a member of the football team....

On December 12, 1983, the Court conducted a hearing on the merits.

Decision

I. First Amendment Issue

Before addressing the issue to be resolved, the Court deems it fitting to delineate some general observations pertaining to the rights of students.... The responsibility for public education is primarily the concern of the states. The exercise of this responsibility, however, must be consistent with federal constitutional requirements.... In *Tinker v. Des Moines School District*, 393 U.S. 503 (1969), the Supreme Court observed:

> First Amendment rights, applied in light of the special characteristics of the school environment, are available to teachers and students. It can hardly be argued that either students or teachers shed their constitutional rights to freedom of speech or expression at the schoolhouse gate. This has been the unmistakable holding of this Court for almost 50 years....
>
> ....
>
> In order for ... school officials to justify prohibition of a particular expression of opinion, it must be able to show that its action was caused by something more than a mere desire to avoid the discomfort and unpleasantness that always accompany an unpopular viewpoint. Certainly where there is no finding and no showing that engaging in the forbidden conduct would 'materially and substantially interfere with the requirements of appropriate discipline in the operation of the school,' the prohibition cannot be sustained.
>
> ....
>
> ... [A] student's rights, therefore, do not embrace merely the classroom hours. When he is in the cafeteria, or on the playing field, or on the campus

A. POLITICAL AND OTHER STUDENT EXPRESSION

during the authorized hours, he may express his opinions, even on controversial subjects....

After carefully scrutinizing the evidence contained in this record, the black members of the McGehee High School football team who took part in the demonstration had reasonable grounds to believe that Coach Gill had purposely manipulated the election to preclude Boyd from serving as homecoming queen because of her race and color. This conclusion is predicated on the following findings:

1. During the 1975-76 school term, a black female contestant for homecoming queen was prevented from serving as queen, although she had polled more votes than the white nominees, because Gill felt that "McGehee High School was not ready for a black homecoming queen."

....

2. As head coach, Gill personally created and fostered a racial atmosphere in the athletic department of the McGehee High School. Gill often referred to black players as "niggers" and specifically referred to Johnson as his "little black nigger from Chicago." Gill admitted that he had used the racial slur.

3. The failure of Gill to announce immediately the results of the election between Boyd and Wynn; and the purported disappearance of the ballots, which prevented the players from inspecting the ballots, created a strong suspicion of manipulation of the election by Gill.

While it is well settled that public education in our country is the responsibility of school administrators and courts are reluctant to intervene in conflicts which develop in the day to day operation of a school system, this does not mean either that free expression, as enunciated under the Federal Constitution, must exist in a vacuum as opposed to a living reality on the school campus, or that school officials, as agents of the state, may stifle free expression, whether by written or unwritten policies, where, as here, the expression does not "materially and substantially interfere with the requirement of appropriate discipline in the operation of the school" and the rights of others. *Burnside v. Byars*, 363 F.2d 744 (5th Cir.1966).

It is clear from this record that 49% of the fifty-four member football team cherished the opportunity and honor, and to this end strove conscientiously to hasten the day, when the school's first black homecoming queen could be elected.... The black players believed that they had achieved that goal in the 1983 election, but only to have their hopes frustrated and the long sought after goal nullified by Coach Gill. Their first act to rectify what was perceived as racism in its truest form was to confer with Coach Gill. Without success, the black players and their parents sought help from the Board of Directors. The Board assuming a posture of what the black players perceived as a hands off approach to the problem, the black players were left without any recourse other than what Americans, from the very inception of this Republic, regard as fundamental and basic in a democracy, namely, "freedom of expression," when peaceful and in good order, to communicate views on questions of group interest. First, the black players walked out of the pep rally and, secondly, refused to participate in a scheduled game. This action was without any substantial intrusion of the work and discipline of the school. Johnson has met the burden of establishing that his conduct was constitutionally protected and that his action was the motivating factor in Coach Gill's act in suspending him from the football team, in effect permanently. Coach Gill has not demonstrated that he would have suspended Johnson from the team in the absence of the protected conduct. Nor is the Court persuaded that Coach Gill's unwritten policy that a player is automatically suspended who, "without good cause" or "proper excuse", misses a practice session or fails to participate in a scheduled game takes precedent over a student's right of free expression in the context of the factual setting of this case. Moreover, such a policy, which is purely subjective and depends upon the idiosyncrasies of the head football coach can neither frustrate nor chill the First Amendment rights of students. There are no standards to determine "without good cause" or "proper excuse", objectively. Peaceful protest by students in the factual backdrop of this controversy may not be contingent upon the uncontrolled will of the head coach.

Defendants argue that what is involved here is not "pure speech" — communication of ideas — but a form of protest which is comparable to picketing. But the Court hastens to emphasize that the Supreme Court has made it crystal clear that picketing and parading do constitute methods of expression warranting First Amendment protection. *Shuttlesworth v. Birmingham*, 394 U.S. 147, 152; *Cox v. Louisiana*, 379 U.S. 536.

Given the fact that it has been the custom and practice of the Board of Directors of the McGehee School District to delegate to the head football coach the responsibility to supervise the selection of the homecoming queen each year and the proof further demonstrates that the board members did not personally participate in the suspension of Johnson, the Court holds that only Coach Gill may be held accountable to Johnson and Mason for the deprivation of their First Amendment rights under this Section 1983 action.

II. *Procedural Due Process of Law*

The question here for resolution is whether Johnson was entitled to procedural due process — notice of the charge against him and an opportunity to present his side of controversy — before Coach Gill suspended Johnson from the football team for the remainder of the term.

... Johnson's continued status as a member of the McGehee High School football team during his last year was very important to Johnson's development educationally and economically in the future. Thus, Johnson's privilege of participating in interscholastic athletics must be deemed a property interest protected by the due process clause of the Fourteenth Amendment....

Absent any clear urgency for acting prior to a hearing, Johnson was constitutionally entitled to procedural due process before Coach Gill could

A. POLITICAL AND OTHER STUDENT EXPRESSION

suspend him from the McGehee High School football team for the rest of the season. *See Strickland v. Inlow,* 485 F.2d 186 (8th Cir. 1973). There were no urgent circumstances confronting Coach Gill, the educational process or other students at the time. It is clear from the evidence that the "boycott" was not disruptive in any way. Of course, it goes without saying where there exists a clear urgency, procedural due process is afforded by granting a hearing within a reasonable time after the fact — the suspension. The Court is persuaded that Johnson has stated a cause of action under Title 42 U.S.C. § 1983 against Coach Gill, but not against the other defendants.

III. *Contempt*

Johnson's motion for an order of the Court citing Gill for contempt of this Court's Order of November 14, 1983, directing the reinstatement of Johnson as a member of the football team and sanctions are denied....

....

CROSBY v. HOLSINGER
United States Court of Appeals
852 F.2d 801 (4th Cir. 1988)

ERVIN, CIRCUIT JUDGE:

This is the second appearance of "Johnny Reb" in this court. Johnny Reb, the former cartoon symbol of the Fairfax High School Rebels, was eliminated by defendant-appellee Harry Holsinger, the school's principal, after he received complaints from black students and parents. Students protested his decision in a number of ways before filing this action. The district court initially dismissed it as frivolous, but we reversed. 816 F.2d 162 (4th Cir.1987). At trial, the court granted a directed verdict for Holsinger as to the broad "censorship" claim, and the jury returned a verdict for him on plaintiff-appellant Cheryl Crosby's narrower "protest restriction" claim. We affirm.

Holsinger acted to remove the symbol based on complaints that it offended black students and a suggestion by the school's Minority Achievement Task Force. He then allowed the students to choose a new symbol which was to be unrelated to the Confederacy.

After the elimination of Johnny Reb, the students protested by holding rallies at school, mounting a petition drive, attending a school board meeting, and displaying blue ribbons. Except for a single incident involving Crosby, Holsinger did nothing to interfere with these protests. In the one instance, he initially stopped Crosby from posting notices on school bulletin boards of the school board meeting before allowing it the next day. This incident is the basis of Crosby's individual claim.

While students do not "shed their constitutional rights to freedom of speech or expression at the schoolhouse gate," *Tinker v. Des Moines Independent Community School Dist.*, 393 U.S. 503, 506, (1969), school officials need not sponsor or promote all student speech. *See Hazelwood School Dist. v. Kuhlmeier*, ___ U.S. ___, ___, (1988); *Bethel School Dist. No. 403 v. Fraser*, 478 U.S. 675, 681, (1986).[1] This is particularly true for anything that the public "might reasonably perceive to bear the imprimatur of the school." *Kuhlmeier*, ___ U.S. at ___, 108. There is a difference between tolerating student speech and affirmatively promoting it. *Id*.

A school mascot or symbol bears the stamp of approval of the school itself. Therefore, school authorities are free to disassociate the school from such a symbol because of educational concerns. Here, Principal Holsinger received complaints that Johnny Reb offended blacks and limited their participation in school activities, so he eliminated the symbol based on legitimate concerns. Except to make the rough threshold judgment that this decision has an educational component, we will not interfere, and it is clear that educational concerns prompted Holsinger's decision.[2]

Turning to Crosby's individual claim based on the one day delay in posting notices for the school board meeting, we must uphold the jury's verdict if "there was evidence upon which the jury could reasonably return a verdict for him." *Mays v. Pioneer Lumber Corp.*, 502 F.2d 106, 107 (4th Cir.1974), *cert. denied*, 420 U.S. 927, (1975). Here, the jury could have found that there was only a de minimis violation in the one day delay. The jury could also have decided that Holsinger acted in good faith. *See Wood v. Strickland*, 420 U.S. 308, 321-22, (1975). Because there are at least two reasonable views of the evidence to support the verdict, we will not disturb it.

Under the recent Supreme Court decisions noted above, school officials have the authority to disassociate the school from controversial speech even if it may limit student expression. Principal Holsinger was within his power to remove a school symbol that blacks found offensive.

Affirmed.

---

1. In *Smith v. St. Tammany Parish Sch. Bd.*, 316 F. Supp. 1174 (E.D. La. 1970), *aff'd*, 448 F.2d 414 (5th Cir. 1971), the District Court ordered all Confederate flags as well as other symbols of racism removed from the schools.

---

[1] Because we can decide this case under *Kuhlmeier* and *Fraser*, we assume that the students have a collective first amendment right in their school's symbol. That issue has not been decided authoritatively, and we do not reach it here.

[2] Appellants argue that Holsinger created a public forum by opening the selection process for a new symbol to outside suggestions. School facilities, however, are deemed a public forum only if opened "for indiscriminate use by the general public," while "permitting limited discourse" does not create such a forum. *Kuhlmeier*, ___ U.S. at ___. The outside input in this case is limited discourse, not indiscriminate use, so we do not apply the public forum doctrine.

A. POLITICAL AND OTHER STUDENT EXPRESSION

How much does a result like this depend upon the context of a recently integrated Southern school?

2. The school in *Crosby* eliminated the use of the "Johnny Reb" mascot. What about the use of the name "Rebels" for athletic teams where African-Americans protest it as indicating racial bias? If a school discontinues the use of confederate symbols following protests, may the student wear the discontinued symbol in an unofficial and individual capacity? *See Banks v. Muncie Community Schs.*, 433 F.2d 292 (7th Cir. 1970) (Use of Rebels, Southern Aires for a glee club, and Southern Belle for the Homecoming Queen did *not* yield evidence of discrimination against African-Americans or a denial of First Amendment rights). *See also Augustus v. School Bd.*, 507 F.2d 152 (5th Cir. 1975) (Confederate symbols seriously interfered with the operation of a unitary system. Injunction prohibiting official use by the school *and* individual use by students at school functions did not violate First Amendment.

3. Is it relevant in these cases whether or not the school authorities are acting on their own or are responding to requests of students, parents, or community members? The school board in *Tate* and the principal in *Crosby*, for example, cited student and community protests as one of the primary motives for their actions. What, if any, criteria should school administrators use in making school decisions that might affect student racial or other sensibilities when free speech is challenged?

4. Teacher Expression: Symbolic Speech v. General Expressions of Personal Liberty. In *Mississippi Emp. Sec. Comm'n v. McGlothin*, 556 So. 2d 324 (Miss. 1990), an African-American teacher was fired for insubordination for refusing to discontinue wearing a head wrap. The court ordered entitlement to unemployment benefits since her expression was protected under the First Amendment as a religious and cultural expression. The court found that her discharge was not attributable to "misconduct" under unemployment law. The key language in the opinion reads:

> More specifically, public schools have authority to promulgate and enforce reasonable dress codes for faculty, staff and students, provided only that it does not infringe rights otherwise protected and even then the schools may enforce such a code when undergirded by some compelling governmental interest reasonably related to their educational mission, so long as the least restrictive means reasonably available be employed. For example, we have no doubt a school could preclude a Native American Indian teacher from coming to school dressed as an Indian warrior, with full feathered head piece, clad in loin cloth, war painted, carrying a tomahawk or a Christian teacher emulating Adam before the Fall — as expression of his religious and cultural heritage.

This section of the opinion connotes that the court conferred special protection on religious attire, requiring that the school demonstrate a compelling governmental interest in restricting such expression. In arriving at this decision, the court was seemingly influenced by the fact that there was no board policy prohibiting head wraps and there was no evidence that the wearing of a head wrap by this teacher had any adverse impact on the classroom or the school.

See also Cooper v. Eugene Sch. Dist. No. 4J, 723 P.2d 298 (Or. 1986), which upheld a state law prohibiting public school teachers from wearing "any religious dress while engaged in the performance of duties as a teacher; *McCutheon v. Bd. of Educ. of City of Chicago*, 419 N.E. 2d 451 (1981), *cert. den.* 455 U.S. 1018 (1982), which upheld the dismissal of a teacher for, among other things, being on two occasions "scantily and indecently attired"; *East Hartford Educ. Ass'n v. Board of Educ. of East Hartford*, 562 F.2d 838 (2d Cir. 1977), which upheld a teacher dress code requiring the wearing of a necktie for men.

B. STUDENT PUBLICATIONS AND OTHER SCHOOL-SPONSORED STUDENT ACTIVITIES

How does *Tinker* hold up in cases involving school sponsored publications and other activities? The following cases demonstrate that, while the courts still recognize the existence of First Amendment rights for students in school-sponsored situations, the judiciary is granting schools and school officials much more deference. A pattern of judicial restraint enables the courts to avoid the daily operation of school systems, causing the balancing point between free speech and the maintenance of order to move toward school authority and away from students' rights.

HAZELWOOD SCHOOL DISTRICT v. KUHLMEIER
Supreme Court of the United States
484 U.S. 260 (1988)

JUSTICE WHITE delivered the opinion of the Court:
This case concerns the extent to which educators may exercise editorial control over the contents of a high school newspaper produced as part of the school's journalism curriculum.

I

Petitioners are the Hazelwood School District in St. Louis County, Missouri; various school officials; Robert Eugene Reynolds, the principal of Hazelwood East High School; and Howard Emerson, a teacher in the school district. Respondents are three former Hazelwood East students who were staff members of *Spectrum*, the school newspaper. They contend that school officials violated their First Amendment rights by deleting two pages of articles from the May 13, 1983, issue of *Spectrum*.

Spectrum was written and edited by the Journalism II class at Hazelwood East. The newspaper was published every three weeks or so during the 1982-1983 school year. More than 4,500 copies of the newspaper were distributed during that year to students, school personnel, and members of the community.

B. STUDENT PUBLICATIONS AND OTHER SCHOOL-SPONSORED ACTIVITIES

The Board of Education allocated funds from its annual budget for the printing of *Spectrum*. These funds were supplemented by proceeds from sales of the newspaper.... The other costs associated with the newspaper — such as supplies, textbooks, and a portion of the journalism teacher's salary — were borne entirely by the Board.

The Journalism II course was taught by Robert Stergos for most of the 1982-1983 academic year. Stergos left Hazelwood East to take a job in private industry on April 29, 1983, when the May 13 edition of *Spectrum* was nearing completion, and petitioner Emerson took his place as newspaper adviser for the remaining weeks of the term.

The practice at Hazelwood East during the spring 1983 semester was for the journalism teacher to submit page proofs of each *Spectrum* issue to Principal Reynolds for his review prior to publication. On May 10, Emerson delivered the proofs of the May 13 edition to Reynolds, who objected to two of the articles scheduled to appear in that edition. One of the stories described three Hazelwood East students' experiences with pregnancy; the other discussed the impact of divorce on students at the school.

Reynolds was concerned that, although the pregnancy story used false names "to keep the identity of these girls a secret," the pregnant students still might be identifiable from the text. He also believed that the article's references to sexual activity and birth control were inappropriate for some of the younger students at the school. In addition, Reynolds was concerned [with] a student identified by name in the divorce story.... He was unaware that Emerson had deleted the student's name from the final version of the article.

Reynolds believed that there was no time to make the necessary changes in the stories before the scheduled press run and that the newspaper would not appear before the end of the school year if printing were delayed to any significant extent. He concluded that his only options under the circumstances were to publish a four-page newspaper instead of the planned six-page newspaper, eliminating the two pages on which the offending stories appeared, or to publish no newspaper at all. Accordingly, he directed Emerson to withhold from publication the two pages containing the stories on pregnancy and divorce. He informed his superiors of the decision, and they concurred.

Respondents subsequently commenced this action in the United States District Court for the Eastern District of Missouri seeking a declaration that their First Amendment rights had been violated, injunctive relief, and monetary damages. After a bench trial, the District Court denied an injunction, holding that no First Amendment violation had occurred.

The District Court concluded that school officials may impose restraints on students' speech in activities that are "an integral part of the school's educational function" — including the publication of a school-sponsored newspaper by a journalism class — so long as their decision has "a substantial and reasonable basis."...

The Court of Appeals for the Eighth Circuit reversed.... The court ... concluded that *Spectrum*'s status as a public forum precluded school officials from censoring its contents except when "'necessary to avoid material and substantial interference with school work or discipline ... or the rights of others.'" (quoting *Tinker v. Des Moines Independent Community School Dist.*, 393 U.S. 503, 511, (1969)).

....

We granted certiorari, ... and we now reverse.

II

Students in the public schools do not "shed their constitutional rights to freedom of speech or expression at the schoolhouse gate." *Tinker, supra*, 393 U.S. at 506....

We have nonetheless recognized that the First Amendment rights of students in the public schools "are not automatically coextensive with the rights of adults in other settings," *Bethel School District No. 403 v. Fraser*, 478 U.S. 675, 682, (1986), and must be "applied in light of the special characteristics of the school environment." *Tinker, supra*, 393 U.S. at 506. A school need not tolerate student speech that is inconsistent with its "basic educational mission," *Fraser, supra*, 478 U.S. at 685, even though the government could not censor similar speech outside the school.... It is in this context that respondents' First Amendment claims must be considered.

A

We deal first with the question whether *Spectrum* may appropriately be characterized as a forum for public expression. The public schools do not possess all of the attributes of streets, parks, and other traditional public forums ... Hence, school facilities may be deemed to be public forums only if school authorities have "by policy or by practice" opened those facilities "for indiscriminate use by the general public," *Perry Education Assn. v. Perry Local Educators' Assn.*, 460 U.S. 37, 47, (1983), or by some segment of the public, such as student organizations. *Id.* at 46, n. 7 (citing *Widmar v. Vincent*). If the facilities have instead been reserved for other intended purposes, "communicative or otherwise," then no public forum has been created, and school officials may impose reasonable restrictions on the speech of students, teachers, and other members of the school community. 460 U.S. at 46, n. 7. "The government does not create a public forum by inaction or by permitting limited discourse, but only by intentionally opening a nontraditional forum for public discourse." *Cornelius v. NAACP Legal Defense & Educational Fund, Inc.*, 473 U.S. 788, 802, (1985).

The policy of school officials toward *Spectrum* was reflected in Hazelwood School Board Policy 348.51 ... [which] provided that "[s]chool sponsored publications are developed within the adopted curriculum and its educational implications in regular classroom activities." The Hazelwood East Curriculum Guide described the Journalism II course as a "laboratory situation in which the

B. STUDENT PUBLICATIONS AND OTHER SCHOOL-SPONSORED ACTIVITIES 345

students publish the school newspaper applying skills they have learned in Journalism I."...

School officials did not deviate in practice from their policy that production of *Spectrum* was to be part of the educational curriculum and a "regular classroom activit[y]." The District Court found that Robert Stergos, the journalism teacher during most of the 1982-1983 school year, "both had the authority to exercise and in fact exercised a great deal of control over *Spectrum*."... The District Court ... found it "clear that Mr. Stergos was the final authority with respect to almost every aspect of the production and publication of *Spectrum*, including its content." Moreover, after each *Spectrum* issue had been finally approved by Stergos or his successor, the issue still had to be reviewed by Principal Reynolds prior to publication....

The evidence relied upon by the Court of Appeals in finding *Spectrum* to be a public forum ... is equivocal at best.... Although the Statement of Policy published in the September 14, 1982, issue of *Spectrum* declared that "*Spectrum*, as a student-press publication, accepts all rights implied by the First Amendment," this statement, understood in the context of the paper's role in the school's curriculum, suggests at most that the administration will not interfere with the students' exercise of those First Amendment rights that attend the publication of a school-sponsored newspaper. It does not reflect an intent to expand those rights by converting a curricular newspaper into a public forum.... Accordingly, school officials were entitled to regulate the contents of *Spectrum* in any reasonable manner. It is this standard, rather than our decision in *Tinker*, that governs this case.

B

The question whether the First Amendment requires a school to tolerate particular student speech — the question that we addressed in *Tinker* — is different from the question whether the First Amendment requires a school affirmatively to promote particular student speech. The former question addresses educators' ability to silence a student's personal expression that happens to occur on the school premises. The latter question concerns educators' authority over school-sponsored publications, theatrical productions, and other expressive activities that students, parents, and members of the public might reasonably perceive to bear the imprimatur of the school. These activities may fairly be characterized as part of the school curriculum, whether or not they occur in a traditional classroom setting, so long as they are supervised by faculty members and designed to impart particular knowledge or skills to student participants and audiences.

Educators are entitled to exercise greater control over this second form of student expression to assure that participants learn whatever lessons the activity is designed to teach, that readers or listeners are not exposed to material that may be inappropriate for their level of maturity, and that the views of the individual speaker are not erroneously attributed to the school.... A school must be able to set high standards for the student speech that is disseminated under its auspices — standards that may be higher than those demanded by some newspaper publishers or theatrical producers in the "real" world — and may refuse to disseminate student speech that does not meet those standards. In addition, a school must be able to take into account the emotional maturity of the intended audience in determining whether to disseminate student speech on potentially sensitive topics, which might range from the existence of Santa Claus in an elementary school setting to the particulars of teenage sexual activity in a high school setting. A school must also retain the authority to refuse to sponsor student speech that might reasonably be perceived to advocate drug or alcohol use, irresponsible sex, or conduct otherwise inconsistent with "the shared values of a civilized social order," *Fraser, supra*, 478 U.S. at 683, or to associate the school with any position other than neutrality on matters of political controversy....

Accordingly, we conclude that the standard articulated in *Tinker* for determining when a school may punish student expression need not also be the standard for determining when a school may refuse to lend its name and resources to the dissemination of student expression. Instead, we hold that educators do not offend the First Amendment by exercising editorial control over the style and content of student speech in school-sponsored expressive activities so long as their actions are reasonably related to legitimate pedagogical concerns.

This standard is consistent with our oft-expressed view that the education of the Nation's youth is primarily the responsibility of parents, teachers, and state and local school officials, and not of federal judges.... It is only when the decision to censor a school-sponsored publication, theatrical production, or other vehicle of student expression has no valid educational purpose that the First Amendment is so "directly and sharply implicate[d]," *ibid.*, as to require judicial intervention to protect students' constitutional rights.

III

We also conclude that Principal Reynolds acted reasonably in requiring the deletion from the May 13 issue of *Spectrum* of the pregnancy article, the divorce article, and the remaining articles that were to appear on the same pages of the newspaper.

The initial paragraph of the pregnancy article declared that "[a]ll names have been changed to keep the identity of these girls a secret." The principal concluded that the students' anonymity was not adequately protected, however, given the other identifying information in the article and the small number of pregnant students at the school.... The article did not contain graphic accounts of sexual activity. The girls did comment in the article, however, concerning their sexual histories and their use or nonuse of birth control. It was not unreasonable for the principal to have concluded that such frank talk was inappropriate in a school-sponsored publication distributed to 14-year-old freshmen ....

The student who was quoted by name in the version of the divorce article seen by Principal Reynolds made comments sharply critical of her father. The principal could reasonably have concluded that an individual publicly identified as an inattentive parent ... was entitled to an opportunity to defend himself....

Principal Reynolds testified credibly at trial that, at the time that he reviewed the proofs of the May 13 issue during an extended telephone conversation with Emerson, he believed that there was no time to make any changes in the articles, and that the newspaper had to be printed immediately or not at all....

In sum, we cannot reject as unreasonable Principal Reynolds' conclusion that neither the pregnancy article nor the divorce article was suitable for publication in *Spectrum*. Reynolds could reasonably have concluded that the students who had written and edited these articles had not sufficiently mastered those portions of the Journalism II curriculum that pertained to the treatment of controversial issues and personal attacks, the need to protect the privacy of individuals whose most intimate concerns are to be revealed in the newspaper, and "the legal, moral, and ethical restrictions imposed upon journalists within [a] school community" that includes adolescent subjects and readers. Finally, we conclude that the principal's decision to delete two pages of *Spectrum*, rather than to delete only the offending articles or to require that they be modified, was reasonable under the circumstances as he understood them. Accordingly, no violation of First Amendment rights occurred.

The judgment of the Court of Appeals for the Eighth Circuit is therefore

Reversed.

GOLUB, *TINKER* TO *FRASER* TO *HAZELWOOD* — SUPREME COURT'S DOUBLE PLAY COMBINATION DEFEATS HIGH SCHOOL STUDENTS' RALLY FOR FIRST AMENDMENT RIGHTS: *HAZELWOOD SCHOOL DISTRICT v. KUHLMEIER,* 38 DePaul L. Rev. 487 (1989)*

....

IV. *Impact*

The obvious impact of [*Hazelwood*] is on student newspaper staff members, student authors, and readers of school sponsored newspapers. Staff members will be resigned to covering topics which reflect the viewpoint and concerns of the school authorities. The appeal of journalism courses will surely dwindle. In fact, the actual immediate reactions to the decision are probably a reliable forecast of the future of high school journalism. Within one hour after the Supreme Court's decision was announced on the radio, a high school principal censored an article on AIDS. That same day, at another high school, all student staff members quit their positions at the school sponsored newspaper, in protest of the *Hazelwood*

---

*Citations from this excerpt have been omitted. Reprinted with permission.

decision, and began working on an underground newspaper. This reaction is particularly harmful because now these student journalists will not enjoy the valuable benefit of professional guidance which the staffs of official school newspapers ordinarily receive. Because the Supreme Court failed to consider an increase in underground newspapers, the holding could in fact backfire. The majority's justifications for the broad *Hazelwood* ruling, including the need for school officials to avoid school imprimatur and remain politically neutral, will not be applicable to underground newspapers, because a high school would have no tie with producing or financing such a publication.

Readers of school sponsored newspapers will also suffer if school officials choose to exercise the broad powers the Court granted them in the decision. Students look to their peers to obtain information on the pressing issues of the day and students in restricted schools will be denied the right to receive such information through the only voice the students can officially utilize.

Most importantly, the decision will have the effect of undermining the schools' duty to inculcate democratic values and teach students about constitutional rights. It will be difficult to teach students about their constitutional rights in civics and journalism courses now that the Supreme Court has afforded students' first amendment rights such inadequate protection.

There is no doubt that many school officials across the country applauded the *Hazelwood* decision. However, the ruling could have an adverse impact on schools which afford more protection to students' first amendment rights than does the Supreme Court. Prior to *Hazelwood*, these school officials could defend their decisions to refrain from censoring student expression on the basis of the *Tinker* standard. These same officials may now be subject to pressure from the community and other school officials to censor student expression that merely comes close to conflicting with any of a multitude of "legitimate pedagogical concerns."

Moreover, the *Hazelwood* holding could be extended to public university campuses, where school sponsored newspapers have enjoyed broad press freedom. Although the majority expressly reserved comment on the appropriate standard for the university level, it is more than likely that university newspapers will eventually be subject to the same fate. Although the majority's justification that school officials have the duty to shield immature students from certain topics will not be applicable, the majority's reference to the "principal as publisher" analogy could allow courts to reason that university funding, and concerns about university endorsement of student viewpoints, justify censorship.

The *Hazelwood* decision will probably lead to confusion among the circuits. Courts faced with cases involving the suppression of student expression in school sponsored activities will now have to conduct the confusing public forum analysis. Courts will also have to grapple with the vague and broad "legitimate pedagogical concern" standard. In addition, although Justice Brennan attempted to provide guidance on the *Tinker* decision's "invasion of the rights of others" prong in his dissent, the majority, in declining to apply *Tinker*, left the lower courts in need of guidance in this area.

Finally, while the majority made it clear that specific written guidelines are not necessary before school officials exercise censorship powers over school sponsored activities, it expressly declined to rule on the question of whether such guidelines are necessary for underground newspapers. This is another area in which the lower courts need guidance, and, since there likely will be a resurgence of underground newspapers, the holding could lead to additional conflicts within and among the circuits.

V. *Conclusion*

The *Hazelwood* decision marks the third step in the Supreme Court's obliteration of students' first amendment rights. In the 1969 landmark decision of *Tinker v. Des Moines Indep. Community School Dist.*, the Court acknowledged that students are entitled to constitutional rights in school including broad rights for personal expression. [Golub cites to *New Jersey v. T.L.O.*, 469 U.S. 325 (1985), and *Bethel School Dist. No. 403 v. Fraser*, 478 U.S. 675 (1956), as the first two steps.] ...

Prior to the *Hazelwood* decision, many lower court decisions followed *Tinker* and balanced students' first amendment rights with school officials' need to maintain order and control in the schools. The *Tinker* analysis could have been applied in *Hazelwood*. Instead, the Supreme Court rejected this approach and endorsed the confusing and one-sided public forum analysis. In practice, however, the public forum analysis will be an empty formality, given the Court's broad holding.

High school students immediately felt the adverse effects of the *Hazelwood* decision. College and high school students responsible for the distribution of underground newspapers escaped the broad ruling since the Court did not comment on the application of the holding to these areas. It is more than likely, however, that when the Court has the opportunity, it will extend the *Hazelwood* standard into these areas given the Court's trend towards minimizing students' constitutional rights.

---

1. "[T]he ability of school officials to restrict student expressive activity is not completely unfettered, but after *Kuhlmeier* it is clearly broader than in the past." Horner, *Student Free Speech Rights: "The Closing of the Schoolhouse Gate" and Its Public Policy Implications*, 33 S. Tex. L. Rev. 601 (1992).* So long as the imprimatur of the school is associated with the disputed student expression, the expression is subject to regulation by school administrators. "Perhaps even more importantly, in *Kuhlmeier*, the Supreme Court recognized that at least some

---

*Copyright © 1992 by South Texas Law Review. Reprinted with permission.

restrictions can be based on the content of student expression." *Id.* As a result, newspaper staff members will be resigned to covering topics which reflect the viewpoint and concerns of school officials.

Student expression is subject to greater control in other facets of the school, as well. In *Fraser*, the speech filled with sexual innuendo was subject to discipline. Now, speech that is *not* lewd or vulgar may result in the same punishment. *See Poling v. Murphy, infra*, 872 F.2d 757 (6th Cir. 1989).

Although interpretations of *Hazelwood* are still evolving, there is a definite trend of judicial deference to school authorities in ensuring that student expression is consistent with educational objectives. The courts increasingly agree: decisions regarding student expressive activity are "best left to the locally elected school board, not to a distant, life-tenured judiciary." *Poling*, at 761.

2. A number of lower federal courts recognized that educators' decisions regarding school-sponsored activities (for example, newspapers and dramatic productions) are entitled to substantial deference, even before *Fraser* and *Hazelwood* were decided. *See, e.g., Nicholson v. Board of Educ., Torrance Unified Sch. Dist.*, 682 F.2d 858 (9th Cir. 1982); *Seyfried v. Walton*, 668 F.2d 214 (3d Cir. 1982); *Trachtman v. Anker*, 563 F.2d 512 (2d Cir. 1977), *cert. denied*, 435 U.S. 925 (1978).

3. In her article excerpted above, in response to the decision in *Hazelwood*, Golub mentions several affected (or potentially affected) parties — staff members, student authors, and readers of school-sponsored publications. She also noted that the decision would cause an increase in the volume of underground newspapers. Prior to *Hazelwood*, school-sponsored and non-sponsored student publications often were viewed similarly for First Amendment purposes. However, *Hazelwood* created a double standard. School-sponsored papers can be censored in order to achieve the school's educational goals and to protect readers from overly sensitive subjects; whereas non-school student papers enjoy greater constitutional freedom.

Do schools have any authority over underground publications? Should different rules apply to publication and distribution of underground papers? Of course, reasonable time, place, and manner restrictions can be placed on the distribution of non-school (as well as sponsored) literature; distribution can be stopped in order to prevent a disruption of the educational process. Yes, regulations regarding prior review of non-school publications may be valid, but few have passed constitutional muster. *See Bystrom v. Fridley High Sch., Indep. Sch. Dist. No. 14*, 822 F.2d 747 (8th Cir. 1987) (A school rule that prohibited publication of material that was indecent or vulgar was held permissible).

4. Recall *Scoville v. Board of Educ. of Joliet Twp.*, 425 F.2d 10 (7th Cir. 1970). *See* note 3 following *Tinker*. Plaintiffs in that case were student staff members of "Grass High," an underground newspaper. The publication was labeled "inappropriate" and "indecent," yet the students won the case. How would this case be decided if the court heard it today? Noting that *Scoville* was decided only one year following *Tinker* and given the recent Supreme Court

B. STUDENT PUBLICATIONS AND OTHER SCHOOL-SPONSORED ACTIVITIES 351

direction, a school-sponsored paper which is labeled inappropriate and indecent would most likely be halted. The fact that "Grass High" was not school-sponsored would help, but it is clear that student expression is not given the weight it used to have.

5. *Fraser* and *Hazelwood* have prompted action in state legislatures and school boards throughout the country. Shoop, *States Talk Back to the Supreme Court: "Students Should Be Heard as Well as Seen,"* 59 Educ. L. Rep. 579 (1990). Some legislators believe that schools are being oppressive and inhibiting students' ability to become responsible adults.

A bill was introduced in Ohio in 1989 which provides students enrolled in public schools the right to exercise free speech. *Id.* at 580. With this bill, Ohio joined a growing number of states that have considered legislation which will restore students' free speech rights. Some states, such as Massachusetts and California, have yet to repeal laws which predate the *Hazelwood* ruling. Horner, *supra* note 1. School boards have joined the legislatures in reaffirming their commitment to the value of a free student press. Shoop, at 583.

6. The *Hazelwood* decision also is being relied on in cases dealing with teachers' academic freedom. In *Miles v. Denver Pub. Schs.*, 944 F.2d 773 (10th Cir. 1991), the Court of Appeals declared that schools can regulate a teacher's school sponsored speech for pedagogical reasons. "[A] podium before a captive audience of public school children is decisively different from a street corner soapbox." *Id.* at 776. The teacher, during his ninth-grade government class, had made a critical comment regarding the students' values. Noting that the quality of the school had declined, he commented: "I don't think in 1967 you would have seen two students making out on the tennis court." This comment referred to a rumored incident of the previous day. The parents of the students involved complained and the teacher was put on administrative leave. Miles, the teacher, filed a First Amendment claim, but the court relied on *Hazelwood* and restricted Miles' speech based on pedagogical concerns. Additionally, his class was determined *not* to be a public forum.

For similar cases and similar results, *see Webster v. New Lenox Sch. Dist.*, 917 F.2d 1004 (7th Cir. 1990) (Teacher not allowed to teach a non-evolutionary religious theory of creation); *Krizek v. Board of Educ. of Cicero-Stickney Twp.*, 713 F. Supp. 1131 (N.D. Ill. 1989) (Upheld school board decision not to renew contract of teacher who showed R-rated film to class); and *Kirtland v. Northside Indep. Sch. Dist.*, 890 F.2d 794 (5th Cir. 1989) (Teacher's supplemental reading list for world history class was not a matter of public concern deserving First Amendment protection; teacher dismissed after refusal to follow school board's prior review policy).

7. Golub also expressed concern that the *Hazelwood* decision would extend to the college campus, where school-sponsored newspapers have enjoyed broad press freedom. Golub, at 512. *See Joyner v. Whiting*, 477 F.2d 456 (4th Cir. 1973) (Once a university establishes a school paper, it may not dictate what students print). Campus newspapers of state-supported universities are entitled

to the constitutional protections afforded the press, including freedom of expression for the editors. *Sinn v. Daily Nebraskan*, 829 F.2d 662 (1986). In *Sinn*, the decision by the editorial staff not to print roommate advertisements in which advertisers stated their homosexual orientation was a constitutionally protected editorial choice.

Perhaps reflecting Golub's concern — even before *Hazelwood* — in 1985, the Fourth Circuit held that a college president may enforce a policy prohibiting the on-campus sale of *non-school* newspapers and literature supporting socialist organizations. Student organizations may sell such literature, with prior approval from the school. *Glover v. Cole*, 762 F.2d 1197 (4th Cir. 1985).

Speeches and Campaigns. Once a state university recognizes student activity which has elements of free expression, the university can act to censor that expression only if it acts consistently with First Amendment guarantees. *Bazaar v. Fortune*, 476 F.2d 570 (1973). A speech on campus cannot be stifled by the state merely because of a potentially adverse reaction from a majority of people. *Id.* Another university, in an attempt to minimize disruptions, adopted a policy allowing election speeches and debates only within one week of the election and only allowing literature distributions for the three days before the election. This policy was upheld by the Eleventh Circuit. *Alabama Student Party v. Student Gov't Ass'n of the Univ. of Alabama*, 867 F.2d 1344 (11th Cir. 1989).

8. Are *Fraser* and *Hazelwood* reconcilable with *Tinker*? Are they distinguishable? If not, has *Tinker* been effectively overruled? Which standard applies today — the "material and substantial disruption" standard or the "pedagogical concerns" standard?

PLANNED PARENTHOOD OF SOUTHERN NEVADA, INC. v. CLARK COUNTY SCHOOL DISTRICT

United States Court of Appeals
941 F.2d 817 (9th Cir. 1991)

RYMER, CIRCUIT JUDGE:

This case raises the same concern addressed by the United States Supreme Court in *Hazelwood School District v. Kuhlmeier*, 484 U.S. 260 (1988): the extent to which educators may exercise editorial control over the contents of high school publications.

....

In this case, high school educators who permit advertisements in school-sponsored publications declined to accept advertisements for the services of Planned Parenthood in student newspapers, yearbooks and athletic programs. The schools believed publishing the advertisements might implicate their classes on sex education and put the school's imprimatur on one side of a controversial issue. The district court concluded that this is a *Hazelwood* case, and we agree.

Because both are school cases and the publications are school-sponsored, we do not write on a clean slate. *Hazelwood* instructs that we are to invest high

B. STUDENT PUBLICATIONS AND OTHER SCHOOL-SPONSORED ACTIVITIES 353

school educators with greater control over expressive activities that bear the school's imprimatur than other forms of speech or use of government facilities. Thus, in striking a balance between the schools' interests and Planned Parenthood's, we must assume that school-sponsored publications are nonpublic and that unless the schools affirmatively intend to open a forum for indiscriminate use, restrictions reasonably related to the school's mission that are imposed on the content of school-sponsored publications do not violate the first amendment.

This case raises troubling issues because few things are so fundamental as our right to speak out, student or adult, pharmacist or Planned Parenthood. It is the more so because few things are so significant to our society, or reflect such deeply held and widely divergent views crying out for expression, as family planning, sex education, birth control and teenage pregnancy.

Yet "the education of the Nation's youth is primarily the responsibility of parents, teachers, and state and local officials, and not of federal judges." *Hazelwood*, 484 U.S. at 273. We are not educators and curricular choices are not ours to make. We are not members of the Board of Education and it is not open to us as judges to decide this case as we might vote were we politicians. Our task is not to decide whether the message, or the messenger, is a menace or the messiah.

Rather, we must start with *Hazelwood* and the questions we must decide are these: Are the publications in which Planned Parenthood wishes to advertise forums for public expression? Do these school-sponsored publications bear the imprimatur of the school, such that they are within the intended purpose for which the forum is reserved? Were school officials justified in refusing to accept the Planned Parenthood advertisement?

Before *Hazelwood* the district court found Planned Parenthood's first amendment rights were infringed. In light of *Hazelwood* it reconsidered and changed its ruling. In this it acted correctly, and we affirm.

I

Planned Parenthood of Southern Nevada (Planned Parenthood) brought suit under 42 U.S.C. § 1983 against the Clark County School District (school district) seeking declaratory and injunctive relief for an alleged deprivation of its first amendment rights. Planned Parenthood claims the school district violated its rights under the first and fourteenth Amendments by refusing to accept advertisements it submitted for publication in high school newspapers, yearbooks and athletic programs.

Planned Parenthood, a nonprofit corporation affiliated with Planned Parenthood Federation of America, is a family planning program that provides clinical, educational and counseling services for matters relating to reproductive health. The Clark County School District is a local school district, comprised of fifteen high schools, created under Nevada law to control and supervise the education of all minor children within the district.

The school district authorizes its high schools to publish newspapers, yearbooks and athletic programs. Newspapers and yearbooks are published as part of the school district curriculum.... Athletic programs are not produced as part of any particular course, but are distributed by the schools at school-sponsored events to inform spectators about the competition.

Principals are allowed to decide whether to accept advertising for these publications, to establish guidelines regulating acceptable advertisements and to determine whether a proposed advertisement satisfies the guidelines, if any. All of the schools but one accept advertising.

The school district's policy with respect to advertising is reflected in a memorandum from Daniel Hussey.[1] At the time of the suit, five schools had adopted written guidelines; eight promulgated them after the suit was begun, and two remain without guidelines. The guidelines typically provide that the school reserves the right to deny advertising space to any entity that does not serve the best interests of the school, the school district and the community. A faculty member, usually the principal, must approve all advertisements prior to publication. In addition to declaring that the school will not run any ads it deems lewd, obscene or vulgar, the guidelines note that advertisements for certain products will not be accepted: X- or R-rated movies, gambling aids, tobacco products, liquor products, birth control products or information, drug paraphernalia and pornography.

The school district also has enacted regulations dealing with "controversial issues," which provide in part, "No group or individual may claim the right to present arguments for or against any issue under study directly to students or to the class without authorization." Clark County School District Regulation 6124.2. Further, by statute, Nevada regulates instruction in the human reproductive system, related communicable diseases and sexual responsibility. Nev.Rev.Stat. § 389.065 (1987). Pursuant to this statute, the school district adopted Regulation 6123 which requires that sex education only be taught by qualified teachers and nurses, using only certain approved materials.

On numerous occasions between March 1984 and August 1985, Planned Parenthood submitted advertisements for publication in school district newspapers and athletic programs. The record does not show that Planned Parenthood submitted its advertisements to any yearbooks prior to commencing this suit.

---

[1]The memo, designed to "provide guidance" to principals as to what power over advertising they possess, states in part:

> A school has an important interest in avoiding the impression that it has endorsed a viewpoint at variance with its educational program.... If a school publication does accept advertising, some categories of advertising may be excluded.... If advertising is allowed which promotes one side of a controversial issue, advertisements promoting the opposing side of a controversy should be similarly accepted.... The purpose of this memo is to provide guidance to principals as to what power over advertising in [school district] publications they possess. How their power is used is within their discretion.

B. STUDENT PUBLICATIONS AND OTHER SCHOOL-SPONSORED ACTIVITIES   355

Each ad offered routine gynecological exams, birth control methods, pregnancy testing and verification, and pregnancy counseling and referral. Most schools rejected the ad; one school continues to publish it.

Following trial on stipulated facts, the district court concluded that under *San Diego Committee Against Registration and the Draft (CARD) v. Governing Board of Grossmont Union High School District*, 790 F.2d 1471 (9th Cir.1986), the publications were limited public forums for advertisements lawfully available to high school audiences, and that without showing a compelling government interest, the school district would have to publish Planned Parenthood's advertisements to the extent they fell within the forum created. When the Supreme Court thereafter decided *Hazelwood*, the district court withdrew its order and on reconsideration found that the publications were nonpublic forums and the exclusions reasonable. Planned Parenthood appealed the district court's judgment in favor of the school district. The panel affirmed ... and we took the matter en banc.

II

The parties agree that Planned Parenthood's advertisements are protected speech under the first amendment. Therefore we must first resolve whether the school newspapers, yearbooks and athletic programs are forums for public expression....

A

Planned Parenthood seeks access to advertising space in school- sponsored publications. *Hazelwood* teaches that "school facilities may be deemed to be public forums only if school authorities have 'by policy or by practice' opened those facilities 'for indiscriminate use by the general public,' ... or by some segment of the public, such as student organizations." 484 U.S. at 267. If, on the other hand, school facilities have been reserved for other intended purposes, "communicative or otherwise," no public forum will have been created and reasonable restrictions on speech may be imposed.[5] *Id.*

In *Hazelwood*, student staff members of the school newspaper, *Spectrum*, argued that their principal violated their first amendment rights when he deleted

---

[5] ... A traditional public forum is property, such as a street or park, that has immemorially been open to the public for expressive activity. In public forums the government may enforce content-based regulations only if necessary to achieve a compelling state interest and if narrowly tailored to serve that end. *Cornelius*, 473 U.S. at 800. The government may also open property for general use by the public, or some segment of the public, as a place for expressive activity. In public forums created by government designation, content-based restrictions must meet the same standard applied in a traditional public forum. *Id.* at 800. Public property which is not a public forum either by tradition or designation is subject to a different standard. In a nonpublic forum the government "may reserve the forum for its intended purposes, communicative or otherwise, as long as the regulation on speech is reasonable and not an effort to suppress expression merely because public officials oppose the speaker's view."

two pages from the paper prior to its publication. After establishing that the first amendment claims must be considered "in light of the special characteristics of the school environment," 484 U.S. at 266 (quoting *Tinker v. Des Moines Indep. Community School Dist.*, 393 U.S. 503, 506 (1969)), the Court reiterated that "'[t]he determination of what manner of speech in the classroom or in school assembly is inappropriate properly rests with the school board,' rather than with the federal courts." 484 U.S. at 267 (quoting *Bethel School Dist. No. 403 v. Fraser*, 478 U.S. 675, 683 (1986)). It then stressed that the school's intent is the critical factor in the forum calculus. "The government does not create a public forum by inaction or by permitting limited discourse, but only by intentionally opening a nontraditional forum for public discourse." *Id.* (quoting *Cornelius*, 473 U.S. at 802).

In determining whether school officials evinced any intent to open the pages of *Spectrum* to indiscriminate use, the Court considered such factors as the paper was produced as part of the high school curriculum; students received grades and academic credit for completing the course, which a faculty member taught; the school did not deviate in practice from its policy of publishing the paper as part of the educational curriculum; the teacher exercised a great deal of control over the production and publication of the paper, and both he and the principal had to approve nearly every aspect of each issue, including its content. The Court also reviewed written policy statements of the school board and *Spectrum*. One school board policy provided, among other things, that "[s]chool sponsored student publications will not restrict free expression or diverse viewpoints within the rules of responsible journalism." *Spectrum* had also declared that the paper "accepts all rights implied by the first amendment" and noted that "[o]nly speech that 'materially and substantially interferes with the requirements of appropriate discipline' can be found unacceptable and therefore be prohibited." *Hazelwood*, 484 U.S. at 269 & n. 2.

The Court concluded that this evidence failed to demonstrate the "clear intent to create a public forum," *Id.* at 270 (quoting *Cornelius*, 473 U.S. at 802).... School officials could therefore regulate the contents of the paper "in any reasonable manner." *Hazelwood*, 484 U.S. at 270.

Looking to the factors in this case that the Court found significant in *Hazelwood* leads us to the same conclusion. The school district and its principals treated all publications similarly. Their intent is most clearly evidenced by written policies that explicitly reserve the right to control content. Their practices were not inconsistent with these policies. Pursuant to them, advertising in school-sponsored publications was subject to the same right of approval as articles in *Spectrum*. We therefore cannot conclude on the record in this case that the school district clearly intended to open its publications, including advertising space, for "indiscriminate use." Rather, like the school board in *Hazelwood*, the school district here showed an affirmative intent to retain editorial control and responsibility over all publications and advertising disseminated under the auspices of its schools.

B. STUDENT PUBLICATIONS AND OTHER SCHOOL-SPONSORED ACTIVITIES

The Hussey memorandum sets out district policy on what power principals were meant to have over advertising. It notes that newspapers and yearbooks are produced as part of the curriculum and that publications and journalism courses form an integral part of the school's educational program. It affirms that

> [a] school has an important interest in avoiding the impression that it has endorsed a viewpoint at variance with its educational program. It is not at all unlikely that an advertisement may be viewed as school endorsement of its contents. It states that there is no requirement that a high school publish either a paper or yearbook, or accept advertising, but that "[i]f a school publication does accept advertising, some categories of advertising may be excluded."

Finally, it requires that if advertising is allowed which promotes one side of a controversial issue, advertisements promoting the opposite side must be accepted. In this way, the school district conferred on school principals broad authority and discretion to limit advertising which may not serve the best interests of the school or might create the impression that the school has endorsed a viewpoint at variance with its educational program.

Consistent with this general directive, individual schools established guidelines reflecting their intent to retain control over advertising in school-sponsored publications. In addition to delineating categories of advertisements that will not be accepted, the guidelines expressly "reserve [ ] the right to deny advertising space to any business and/or individual that does not serve the best interests" of the particular school. This complements the school board's policy concerning "controversial issues," requiring objective presentation of opposing points of view. Clark County School District Regulation 6124.2. Furthermore, just as the principal and teacher in *Hazelwood* had final approval over the contents of *Spectrum*, ultimate authority over what advertisements appear in school-sponsored publications rests with the principal or his assistant. The schools' consistent policy has been to limit advertising to subjects and entities that are in the best interests of the school and to require that those seeking to advertise obtain approval from the principal.

There is no evidence that advertisements in newspapers or yearbooks were accepted for any purpose other than to enable the school to raise revenue to finance the publications, and at the same time impart journalistic management skills to students. Nor does the evidence suggest that the high schools were "motivated by an affirmative desire to provide an open forum" for advertising in athletic programs ...

Both *Hazelwood* and *Cornelius* instruct that we also examine the nature of the government property involved in determining whether the forum is public or nonpublic. *Hazelwood*, 484 U.S. at 266; *Cornelius*, 473 U.S. at 806.... High schools foster learning experiences inside and outside the classroom and serve pedagogical as well as in *locus parenti* purposes. For this reason, educators have the right to control expressive activity that students, parents and other members of the public "might reasonably perceive to bear the imprimatur of the school." *Hazelwood*, 484 U.S. at 271.

In light of the schools' policy in accepting advertising in school-sponsored publications, and their practice of retaining control and requiring prior approval, we conclude that the record fails to reveal the requisite "clear intent to create a public forum" *Hazelwood* requires. 484 U.S. at 270. Therefore, these school-sponsored newspapers, yearbooks and athletic programs, including advertisements, are not public forums.

B

Planned Parenthood argues that *Hazelwood* simply says that high school publications are not traditional public forums and that beyond that courts should follow the public forum analysis set out in *Perry*, 460 U.S. at 45-47; *Cornelius*, 473 U.S. at 800-04, and our decision in *CARD*, 790 F.2d at 1474-76. It urges that the district court erred in concluding that under *Hazelwood*, the school district had "plenary control" over the contents of its high school publications. Planned Parenthood further submits that the school district in fact created a limited forum for public advertising of goods and services that are lawfully available to high school age audiences. In support, it points to the wide variety of advertising which has been received and published and contends that it may not be discriminatorily excluded from that forum.

We agree that a high school may create a public forum or designate a forum for limited purposes. *Hazelwood* does not say otherwise, but it does constrain the analysis by requiring that courts focus on unique attributes of the school environment and recognize broadly articulated purposes for which high school facilities may properly be reserved. 484 U.S. at 270-73. We also agree that this case differs from *Hazelwood* in that Planned Parenthood is an outside entity seeking to advertise in school publications, whereas *Hazelwood* concerned students who wanted to have their articles published. It is likewise true that the schools solicited and accepted an array of advertising, including some for casinos which Planned Parenthood suggests belie the district's concern for the propriety of material for a teenage audience, and some for providers of health services to whom Planned Parenthood analogizes itself. Yet we believe these points misdirect the inquiry, which the Supreme Court has instead focused on the schools' intent....

The Court has often held that selective access to government property does not alone render it a public forum. For example, in *Perry*, even though many private groups not affiliated with the school had access to and used the internal school mail facilities, the mail system was not open for use by the general public, potential users of the system were required to secure permission from the individual principals and there was no indication that permission was granted as a matter of course. The Court concluded that the property remained a nonpublic forum subject to reasonable regulation. *Perry*, 460 U.S. at 47. In *Cornelius*, ... the Court held that "[s]uch selective access, unsupported by evidence of a

B. STUDENT PUBLICATIONS AND OTHER SCHOOL-SPONSORED ACTIVITIES 359

purposeful designation for public use, does not create a public forum." [473 U.S.] at 805....

As in *Perry* and *Cornelius*, school officials in this case require permission and approval prior to granting access to high school publications. Although Planned Parenthood contends that it was the only potential advertiser excluded from the publications, the record does not demonstrate that permission and approval to advertise are granted as a matter of course. We therefore find nothing in *Perry* or *Cornelius* to support a conclusion that allowing some outside organizations to advertise converts the school-sponsored publications into public forums.

Nor do we believe that this case is controlled by *CARD*, as Planned Parenthood urges. In *CARD*, which we decided before the Court decided *Hazelwood*, we held a student newspaper, along with its advertising spaces, to be a limited public forum. *CARD*, a nonprofit organization involved in counseling young men on alternatives to military service, sought to advertise in several school papers. Despite the fact that the papers accepted military recruitment advertisements, the school district refused to publish the ad *CARD* submitted.

Because it believed that newspapers are devoted entirely to expressive activity, and the school board's admitted policy and practice was to allow the students to discuss any topic in the newspapers and allow non-students to avail themselves of the forum as long as their speech consisted of advertisements offering goods, services or vocational opportunities to students, the *CARD* majority believed the evidence indicated an intent to create a limited public forum. *CARD*, 790 F.2d at 1476. Accordingly, it concluded that the school district could not exclude the advertisement without demonstrating a compelling reason. Alternatively, the majority held that assuming the school board was correct in its assertion that the school newspapers were a nonpublic forum, the exclusion of the proffered advertisement was unreasonable and constituted impermissible viewpoint discrimination. *Id.* at 1478.

Planned Parenthood maintains that the schools' solicitation of advertisements from outside entities puts this case squarely within *CARD* rather than *Hazelwood*, which Planned Parenthood characterizes as applying only to student expression. We are not persuaded by Planned Parenthood's argument that the nature of the speech at issue here, advertisements from an outside entity rather than student speech, places this case beyond the reach of *Hazelwood*. Although the facts of *Hazelwood* dealt with student expression, its rationale was not so limited. The Court specifically spoke in terms of "school-sponsored publications, theatrical productions, and other expressive activities," 484 U.S. at 271, and remarked on a school's ability to regulate reasonably the speech not only of students, but also "teachers, and other members of the school community." *Id.* at 269. The publication is the same and the audience is the same, whether the source for the speech is from inside the school or outside, or is paid or free. The school has the same pedagogical concerns, such as respecting audience maturity, disassociating itself from speech inconsistent with its educational mission and avoiding the appearance of endorsing views, no matter who the speaker is.

... [W]e therefore believe the Court intended that the same principles that animate educational decisions regarding the content of articles in school-sponsored publications come into play when determining what advertisements are suitable for publication in school newspapers, yearbooks and athletic programs.

... [T]o the extent our opinion in *CARD* did not give weight to the same considerations emphasized by *Hazelwood*, we can no longer rely on its analysis in determining the nature of the forum. Rather it is the Supreme Court's decision in *Hazelwood* and not our prior decision in *CARD* that provides the appropriate frame of reference. Under *Hazelwood*, in cases such as this where school facilities have not intentionally been opened to indiscriminate expressive use by the public or some segment of the public, school officials retain the authority reasonably to refuse to lend the schools' name and resources to speech disseminated under school auspices.

III

....

... [W]hen "school-sponsored" speech can fairly be characterized as part of the schools' mission, which the Court defined broadly, the first amendment affords educators "greater control" in deciding when the school will affirmatively "promote" or "lend its name and resources" to particular speech. [*Hazelwood*, 484 U.S.] at 271-72. The Court recognized that school authorities have legitimate educational interests in assuring that "participants learn whatever lessons the activity is designed to teach, that readers or listeners are not exposed to material that may be inappropriate for their level of maturity, and that the views of the individual speaker are not erroneously attributed to the school." *Id*. at 271. Moreover, the school must retain the authority to refuse to sponsor speech that might reasonably "associate the school with any position other than neutrality on matters of political controversy." *Id*. at 272.

These characteristics help define what a school is about, and we must put the decision to exclude Planned Parenthood advertisements in that context. Thus, while a publisher is not normally viewed as endorsing the contents of paid advertisements, a high school stands in a different relationship with its public ...

A school's decision not to promote or sponsor speech that is unsuitable for immature audiences, or which might place it on one side of a controversial issue, is a judgment call which *Hazelwood* reposes in the discretion of school officials and which is afforded substantial deference. We therefore conclude that controlling the content of school-sponsored publications so as to maintain the appearance of neutrality on a controversial issue is within the reserved mission of the Clark County School District.

IV

Having concluded that the advertising pages in the school district's school-sponsored publications are nonpublic forums, we now consider whether the school's justification for refusing to publish Planned Parenthood's advertisement is reasonable. *Hazelwood*, 484 U.S. at 270....

The schools' refusal to publish Planned Parenthood's advertisements was viewpoint neutral. Planned Parenthood's advertisements were rejected, and schools enacted guidelines excluding advertising that pertains to "birth control products and information," in order to maintain a position of neutrality on the sensitive and controversial issue of family planning and avoid being forced to open up their publications for advertisements on both sides of the "pro-life" — "pro-choice" debate. In addition to believing the copy and Planned Parenthood to be controversial, some principals felt that parents would object to the advertisement. The school district also viewed Planned Parenthood's advertisements as implicating its statutorily prescribed sex education curriculum and sought to avoid conflict with the state requirements regarding the manner sex education is presented to students.

... [I]n light of the nature of the school environment, educators must have the ability to consider the "emotional maturity of the intended audience" as well as the authority to refuse to "associate the school with any position other than neutrality on matters of political controversy." *Hazelwood*, 484 U.S. at 272.... "Although the avoidance of controversy is not a valid ground for restricting speech in a public forum, a nonpublic forum by definition is not dedicated to general debate or the free exchange of ideas." *Cornelius*, 473 U.S. at 811....

We therefore agree with the district court that the school district's policy of not publishing advertisements that are "controversial, offensive to some groups of persons, that cause tension and anxiety between teachers and parents, and between competing groups such as [Planned Parenthood] and pro-life forces" is a reasonable one....

Related to the school district's intent to maintain a position of neutrality on controversial issues is its desire to avoid being forced to open up school publications to organizations having views competing with those of Planned Parenthood, should it be required to publish the proffered advertisements.... The school district and individual school principals could reasonably choose to have the family planning debate take place in the classroom rather than in the advertising pages of its school-sponsored publications.

V

... Because their decision to limit access, whether wise or unwise, is reasonable and not an effort at viewpoint discrimination, the school district did not violate the first amendment in declining to publish Planned Parenthood's advertisements.

Affirmed.

DURAN v. NITSCHE

United States District Court
780 F. Supp. 1048 (E.D. Pa. 1991)

BECHTLE, CHIEF JUDGE:

Findings of Fact

1. Plaintiff Diana Duran was a fifth grade student at East Coventry Elementary School of the Owen J. Roberts School District during the 1989-1990 academic year. East Coventry Elementary is a public school in Pottstown, Pennsylvania. Plaintiff, through her parents as guardians, brings this action against one of her fifth grade teachers, her fifth-grade principal, and various school district officials.

2. Plaintiff was a student in the school's Academically Talented Program ("ATP"). The ATP class met once each week. Defendant Linda Nitsche was the teacher of plaintiff's ATP class.

3. Sometime in March of 1990, defendant Nitsche gave the ATP class an "independent study" assignment. Students were to work on the independent study project during the remainder of the school year. The assignment required each student to choose a topic for research. Defendant Nitsche and the individual student's parents were to approve the topic. Students were then required to report ... on research progress during the remainder of the year.... The research was to culminate in an oral report to be presented to defendant Nitsche and the other ATP students.

4. Students were instructed to chose a topic by filling in a blank on a form given to them by defendant Nitsche. The form stated that topics should be related to "The Power of _____." Plaintiff chose as her topic "The Power of God." The topic was approved by defendant Nitsche and by plaintiff's parents.

....

6. As part of the assignment, students were required to bring their research materials to ATP class each week so that their progress on their project could be monitored by defendant Nitsche during class time. Contrary to assignment instructions, plaintiff never brought any research materials to class.[1] Further, plaintiff was not prepared for the ATP classes to the extent such classes involved the research project. Plaintiff did not meet any of the deadlines set forth in the "timeline" established by defendant Nitsche.

7. Defendant Nitsche informed the ATP students that they could include, as one of their sources, a survey of other students' views on the particular topic that was the subject of their independent study. Plaintiff was one of several ATP students who decided to conduct such a survey.

---

[1] The exhibits submitted by plaintiff at trial include a list of the resource materials plaintiff intended to use in her oral report. The list was prepared by plaintiff sometime before the report was to be given. Defendant Nitsche, however, never saw this list....

B. STUDENT PUBLICATIONS AND OTHER SCHOOL-SPONSORED ACTIVITIES 363

8. Sometime before her oral report was to be presented, plaintiff submitted a handwritten list of proposed survey questions to defendant Nitsche for review.... At no time did defendant Nitsche grant plaintiff permission to distribute her survey form. Plaintiff photocopied the survey form on school premises, despite the fact that defendant Nitsche did not grant plaintiff permission to do so. Faculty permission is generally a prerequisite to student use of school photocopying facilities.

9. The survey forms contained five "multiple choice" type questions. After asking for a student's gender, age, and class, the survey asked:

> 4. Do you believe in God? Yes No If your answer is no, please hand in your survey now.
> 5. I believe in God's power to
> control my life
> control life and death
> forgive sin
> other

A box to be checked was placed next to each choice.

10. There was nothing on the form other than these questions and some simple instructions. Accordingly, there was nothing on the form to indicate whether the survey had been prepared by a school official or by a student.

11. The ATP students were scheduled to deliver their oral presentations on June 8, 1990. Several days before her presentation was to be given, plaintiff distributed her survey form to other students. Approximately thirty of these forms were completed and returned to plaintiff.

12. On the morning of the day on which ATP students were scheduled to give their oral presentations, plaintiff asked one of her teachers, identified by the parties only as "Mr. Latshaw," if he would distribute survey forms to five (5) student volunteers from Mr. Latshaw's class. After reviewing plaintiff's survey form, Mr. Latshaw refrained from distributing it to students; instead, he brought the survey form to the attention of the principal of the school, defendant Kenneth Swart.

13. Defendant Swart informed Mr. Latshaw that he should not distribute the survey forms. Defendant Swart then called plaintiff to his office, at which time he informed plaintiff that teachers would not be permitted to distribute the survey form to other students.... At no time did defendant Swart tell plaintiff that she was not permitted to use the results of the surveys that she had distributed herself, nor did he tell her that she was precluded from distributing more survey forms without teacher assistance.

....

15. Plaintiff's unpreparedness kept defendant Nitsche from knowing the precise nature of plaintiff's proposed report. Without such information, defendant Nitsche was concerned as to whether the report was appropriate for the fifth grade classroom setting. Based on this concern, defendant Nitsche decided to

keep plaintiff from presenting her oral report to the rest of the class. Instead, defendant Nitsche required plaintiff to present her report to defendant Nitsche in the school library, without the presence of other students.

16. Plaintiff gave her oral report to defendant Nitsche in the library....

17. Plaintiff's parents approached the school district about the incident. Both defendant Swart and defendant Nitsche responded to the plaintiff's parents by justifying their decisions in writing.

18. At all times relevant to these occurrences, the School District had no stated policy specifically governing religion in School District schools. Policy No. 6144, however, governing "Controversial Issues and the School Program," was in place at the time of the incidents now in question. Since these incidents, the School District has adopted a policy specifically relating to religion in the classroom.

Discussion

Plaintiff claims violations of her constitutional right to free speech guaranteed by the First Amendment to the United States Constitution. Plaintiff claims these violations occurred by virtue of: 1) defendant Swart's decision to preclude distribution of the survey form, and 2) defendant Nitsche's decision to require plaintiff to give her oral presentation in the library, rather than in the classroom. Plaintiff seeks a declaration of the existence of an unwarranted First Amendment violation, and an injunction prohibiting the School District from acting similarly in the future. Defendants claim that no free speech violation occurred, and that even if one did, that the First Amendment's Establishment Clause justifies any free speech intrusion under these circumstances.

....

In analyzing the Constitution's free expression clause in the public school context, the court must first determine whether the school has designated a public forum for discourse under the particular circumstances of a given case. If such a public forum does not exist, content-based[4] restrictions on speech need only be "reasonable in light of the purpose served by the forum and ... viewpoint neutral." *Cornelius v. NAACP Legal Defense and Education Fund*, 473 U.S. 788, 806 (1985). In the educational setting, the standard for determining the reasonableness of a content-based restriction on school sponsored expressive activity in a non-public forum is whether the restriction is "reasonably related to legitimate pedagogical concerns." *Hazelwood School District v. Kuhlmeier*, 484 U.S. 260 (1988). If a public forum does exist, a content-based restriction on speech must be substantially related to meeting a compelling state interest. If it

---

[4]As noted in the court's Findings of Fact, defendant Nitsche's decision to hear the report in the library was based, in large part, on her concern over whether the subject matter would be appropriate for fifth grade students. As also noted in the Findings of Fact, defendant Swart based his decision to preclude faculty distribution of the survey forms on the religious content of the survey. Accordingly, the court concludes that both decisions were "content-based."

B. STUDENT PUBLICATIONS AND OTHER SCHOOL-SPONSORED ACTIVITIES

finds a first amendment violation, the court must, in the case of restrictions on speech of a religious nature made in a public forum, also determine whether the speech at issue would violate the Establishment Clause to such an extent as to provide the school with the "compelling state interest" necessary to justify a content-based free speech limitation in a public forum.

Several factors are relevant in determining whether the state has created a designated public forum. First, the court must look to governmental intent by evaluating "the policy and practice of the government to ascertain whether it intended to designate a place not traditionally open to assembly and debate as a public forum." Second, the court must analyze the use to which the forum has been put by examining whether the forum "has been limited by well-defined standards tied to the nature and function of the forum." Third, a court may also look to the "permission procedure" related to such speech, and to whether similar speech has been permitted or disallowed in the past.

Under these standards, this court has little difficulty determining that no public forum was established by the school with respect to either the distribution of the survey forms or the oral presentation. First, there has been absolutely no evidence presented that could support a conclusion that a public forum was created for the purpose of distributing survey forms by teachers during class periods. It would seem that a somewhat unusual set of facts must be presented before a court could rule that a school established a forum for uninhibited discourse in which teachers themselves would be required to disseminate surveys for student projects that relate to other classes. Suffice it to say that no such evidence was presented in the case at hand. Certainly, there is no evidence of governmental "intent" with respect to opening a forum for such a purpose in this case, and the "well defined standards" to which teachers are typically held do not require the use of the classroom for such purposes. There is no evidence of a "permission procedure" that was in place for such a purpose.

Second, defendant Nitsche did not create a "public forum" when she permitted students to give oral presentations on their report topics in her classroom. There is no evidence of her intent to allow the use of the ATP class period as a forum for open discussion. Indeed, defendant Nitsche testified that while she respects the rights of her students to express their views under appropriate circumstances, the primary purpose of the independent study assignment was to engage the students in an introduction to research skills. The independent study was not designed to operate as a vehicle for student expression and debate.

The "permission procedure" analysis, as contemplated by *Cornelius*, further supports the conclusion that defendant Nitsche did not establish an open forum. Before topics were assigned, they were approved by defendant Nitsche and then by the students' parents. At no time were students given the impression that they would be permitted to pick any topic of their choice. Presumably, the question of granting permission to a given topic carried with it issues concerning ... whether the topic's subject matter would be appropriate for fifth grade classroom discussion. Given the age of the students, defendant Nitsche understandably retained a right of approval over topic selection so that she could evaluate these concerns. The procedure by which defendant Nitsche solicited and approved of topic choices undoubtedly falls far short of permitting the type of unrestricted, uninhibited discourse necessary to support the existence of a designated public forum.[7]

Having concluded that no public forum existed, the court turns to whether the restrictions at issue were "reasonably related to legitimate pedagogical concerns." Because the restrictions are rational regulations of activities that are school sponsored and/or curriculum related,[8] the court concludes that the restrictions are, in fact, constitutionally permissible.

As the Supreme Court has recognized, the right of school officials to regulate student expression expands when the speech at issue is made in connection with school sponsored activity:

> Educators are entitled to exercise greater control over [speech in school sponsored settings] to assure that participants learn whatever lessons the activity is designed to teach, that readers or listeners are not exposed to material that may be inappropriate for their level of maturity, and that the views of the individual speaker are not erroneously attributed to the school. *Hazelwood*, 108 S.Ct. at 570.

The *Hazelwood* Court cited several lower court decisions recognizing the heightened deference afforded school officials on decisions related to school sponsored speech. Additionally, several courts since *Hazelwood* have rejected challenges to regulations of in-school expression on the ground that the speech was school sponsored or curriculum related. *See, e.g., Poling v. Murphy*, 872 F.2d 757 (6th Cir.1989), *cert. den.*, 493 U.S. 1021 (1990); ... *Bishop v. Aronov*, 926 F.2d 1066 (11th Cir. 1991).... In contrast, restrictions on student speech that have been held unconstitutional have involved school administrations' attempts to impose limitations on expression outside of the classroom. *See, e.g., Gregoire,*

---

[7]The fact that defendant Nitsche initially approved plaintiff's topic does not change the fact that the forum remained closed.... Defendant Nitsche's later determination, based on subsequent developments, that plaintiff should not give her report to the rest of the ATP class does not change the fact that the forum was not "public;" rather, it only reflects the fact that defendant Nitsche had reached the conclusion that Diana's progress reports had not satisfied her that the report was proper for the fifth-grade classroom setting.

[8]In *Hazelwood*, the court found that a high school student newspaper was school sponsored for purposes of First Amendment forum analysis in part because of the imprimatur of school endorsement stemming from the amount of control of the newspaper retained by the faculty. Certainly, the act of requiring a teacher to distribute survey forms to fifth grade students during class time presents an even stronger imprimatur of school sponsorship than that presented in *Hazelwood*. As for the oral report, it could be said that it strains language even to call the presentation school "sponsored." Because it was part of an assignment related to an actual class, the report was, in fact, school itself.

supra; *Grace Bible Fellowship v. Maine School Administrative District*, 941 F.2d 45 (1st Cir.1991).

In addition to the fact that the speech at issue in this case arises in the context of school sponsorship, three considerations mentioned in *Hazelwood* support the constitutionality of the restrictions now at issue. The *Hazelwood* Court permitted educators to exercise greater control when, *inter alia*: 1) students would be exposed to material that is inappropriate for their particular maturity level, 2) students would be subjected to expression that could be "erroneously attributed to the school," and 3) the proposed speech is "ungrammatical, poorly written, inadequately researched, [or] biased or prejudiced...." *Hazelwood*, 108 S.Ct. at 570.

Defendant Nitsche's trial testimony demonstrates how these three factors combine in the case at hand. Defendant Nitsche testified that:

> ... [T]hrough the entire process, I had seen Diana's survey and I had also seen her list of, I think, perhaps five questions. I'm not sure exactly. I had seen no other evidence other than what the questions were, no answers, and the survey. And based on those two pieces of information, I concluded that her report would perhaps be something that my other fifth-grade students should not be a party to. I did not want to appear to support nor put down any type of religion in front of my other students.... My concern is for my other fifth-grade students in my classroom, and I did not want to promote or denigrate any type of religion in my classroom....

Each of the three *Hazelwood* concerns listed above combined to form the basis for the decisions made by defendants Nitsche and Swart. Both school officials were obviously troubled by the impact of teacher involvement with religious subject matter on students of relatively tender years. To use the language of *Hazelwood*, both defendants Nitsche and Swart felt that the material was "inappropriate for [the students'] level of maturity," because of the substantial risk that "the views of the individual speaker [would be] erroneously attributed to the school." *Hazelwood*, 108 S.Ct. at 570....

The court need not engage in an analysis of whether the defendants' assessments of their students' propensities were "right," *i.e.* whether, in fact, fifth-grade students are too young to be able to appreciate the difference between private speech and school sponsored speech. The court need only determine, as it does, that the defendants' concern was reasonable. The need for judicial restraint in evaluating matters such as these is well established....

Given that the defendants justified their decisions on the very concerns that received expressed approval by the Supreme Court in *Hazelwood*, the court concludes that the restrictions on speech in the case at hand were reasonably related to legitimate pedagogical concerns, and are therefore constitutional. Accordingly, Policy No. 6144 and the policy now in place relating to religion in the school are deemed valid to the extent that they are interpreted to permit restrictions on speech of the same nature as the restrictions imposed in this case.

In light of the court's conclusion that no free speech violation has occurred, the court need not address the defendants' alternative argument relating to a compelling state interest arising out of the constitution's Establishment Clause....

Finally, the court notes that plaintiff, both at trial and in proposed conclusions of law, has made vague, cursory references to violations of the Constitution's Equal Protection Clause. No equal protection violation has occurred....

In light of the foregoing, the court makes the following Conclusions of Law:

Conclusions of Law

1. No public forum has been created by the School District.

2. The restrictions on speech in this case were reasonably related to legitimate pedagogical concerns.

3. In both the case of the decision to preclude distribution of survey forms by teachers and in the case of the decision to require plaintiff to give her report in the library, there has been no unconstitutional restriction of plaintiff's freedom of expression.

4. There has been no violation of the Constitution's Equal Protection Clause.

5. Plaintiff is not entitled to either declaratory or injunctive relief.

---

1. The 1992 Supreme Court decision in *Lee v. Weisman*, 112 S. Ct. 2649, was arguably one of the most eagerly awaited opinions in recent history. Its effects on First Amendment rights beyond the schoolhouse gate are barely known, but are sure to be significant.

Briefly, the Supreme Court struck down the use of clergy to lead prayers in school-sponsored graduation ceremonies. The Court majority relied on its findings that the prayers took place in an activity directed by school authorities and that students were expected to attend the graduation ceremony. (*See* Chapter 15 on Church-State Relations.)

The court in *Brody* suggested that if, on remand, the District Court found that a public forum existed, it should wait for the decision in the *Weisman* opinion before conducting its inquiry into whether the speech restrictions in the consent decree may survive strict scrutiny. 957 F.2d at 1121.

While the effect of *Weisman* may be great, it is likely to have little effect on cases like *Duran*. *Weisman* involves the constitutionality of *school-imposed* prayer at graduation; this type of case involves students who wish to restrict school speech. *Duran* involves a school that wishes to restrict student speech. There is no governmentally imposed limitation on *Weisman*-type speech. A different standard applies when the school attempts to restrict student speech (First Amendment analysis) than when the school attempts to issue religious speech (Establishment Clause analysis).

2. Considerable recent litigation has focused on the distribution of religious literature by students. Although most courts have not condoned literature distribution in public schools by religious organizations, requests by students to distribute religious publications themselves have been more controversial. McCarthy, *Post-Hazelwood Developments: A Threat to Free Inquiry in Public Schools*, 81 Educ. L. Rep. 685 (1993).

Some courts have recognized that content restrictions may not be imposed on religious expression that does not represent the school. In these cases, strict scrutiny (a compelling governmental interest) is required to assess content-based portions of a policy that applies to personal student expression. *See Slotterback v. Interboro Sch. Dist.*, 766 F. Supp. 280 (E.D. Pa. 1991).

Courts, however, have upheld reasonable restrictions where such materials are distributed. School officials still have authority to maintain safe, orderly halls. *Hemry v. School Bd. of Colorado Springs Sch. Dist.*, 760 F. Supp. 856 (1991). *But see Thompson v. Waynesboro Area Sch. Dist.*, 673 F. Supp. 1379 (M.D. Pa. 1987), where the students' distribution of a religious newspaper in the hallways of a junior high was protected by the First Amendment. A limited public forum was created.

How does *Weisman* affect distribution of religious literature? According to McCarthy, under *Weisman*, student distribution of religious literature would still be allowed as long as school sponsorship is not at issue. 81 Ed. Law Rep. 685 (1993).

3. Use of the school by student religious organizations also has been the source of some controversy. Often, these cases are determined by a public forum analysis. *See Garnett v. Renton Sch. Dist.*, 874 F.2d 608 (9th Cir. 1989) (Because high school was not a limited public forum, school district's refusal to allow student religious group to meet at school prior to the school day did *not* violate the students' free speech rights). *Quappe v. Endry*, 772 F. Supp. 1004 (S.D. Ohio 1991), held similarly, but allowed the group to meet in the evenings. Allowing a meeting directly after school would violate the Establishment Clause. *See also Lamb's Chapel v. Center Moriches Union Free Sch. Dist.*, 959 F.2d 381 (2d Cir. 1992), *rev'd*, 113 S. Ct. 2141 (1993); and *Gregoire v. Centennial Sch. Dist.*, 907 F.2d 1366 (3d Cir. 1990).

POLING v. MURPHY

United States Court of Appeals
872 F.2d 757 (6th Cir. 1989)

DAVID A. NELSON, CIRCUIT JUDGE:

The main question presented in this appeal is whether the Federal Constitution gives a high school student license to make admittedly "discourteous" and "rude" remarks about his schoolmasters in the course of a speech delivered at a school-sponsored assembly.... [T]he question is a serious one, under contemporary constitutional concepts, but on the factual record before us in this case, we think the answer is fairly obvious.

As the Supreme Court held last year in *Hazelwood School District v. Kuhlmeier*, 484 U.S. 260, ____ (1988), 108 S. Ct. 562, 571, "educators do not offend the First Amendment by exercising editorial control over the style and content of student speech in school-sponsored expressive activities so long as their actions are reasonably related to legitimate pedagogical concerns." (Footnote omitted.) Civility is a legitimate pedagogical concern, in our view, and we shall affirm the summary judgment that the district court entered in favor of the defendants in this case.

I

....

In May of 1987 plaintiff Dean Poling, an honor student who was subsequently to become president of his senior class, was one of about a dozen juniors who had qualified as candidates for the Unicoi High student council presidency. It was customary for such candidates to give campaign speeches at a school assembly held shortly before the election. Except for pupils with excused absences, attendance at the assembly was mandatory for all members of the student body.

According to Mrs. Barbara Ollis, a guidance counselor who served as one of two faculty sponsors of the student council, it had long been the practice for faculty sponsors to review candidates' speeches in advance of delivery....

As instructed, Dean Poling brought his proposed speech to Mrs. Ollis for review.... The proposed speech read as follows:

> Hi, I'm Dean Poling and I'm running for president of the Student Council. It's a common practice of politicians to cut down each other. Instead of doing this, I'm going to cut down you, the audience. Why am I going to do this? Because you idiots are too darn gullible. For example, what is black and blue and wrapped in plastic? A baby in a trash bag, of course. I just made you laugh at something incredibly sick. If I can do this to you, then the administration could probably take advantage of you also. For example, have you noticed that each year there are less and less assemblies? How many of you would like at least a chance at open campus? Would you like a better chance of having the prom in Johnson City? Is there something in this school you would like changed? The administration plays tricks with your mind and they hope you won't notice. Because of the administration's iron grip, our school has been kept behind other schools like Science Hill. If you want to break this grip, vote for me for president. I can try to bring back student rights that you have missed and maybe get things that you always wanted. All you have to do is vote for me, Dean Poling! Thanks.

Mrs. Ollis ... placed a mark beside the sentence that referred to "the administration's iron grip" and told Dean, as he later attested, "change this and your speech will be okay."

B. STUDENT PUBLICATIONS AND OTHER SCHOOL-SPONSORED ACTIVITIES 371

Change it he did. As delivered at the assembly on Friday, May 8, the speech had this peroration:

> The administration plays tricks with your mind and they hope you won't notice. For example, why does Mr. Davidson stutter while he is on the intercom? He doesn't have a speech impediment. If you want to break the iron grip of this school, vote for me for president. I can try to bring back student rights that you have missed and maybe get things that you have always wanted. All you have to do is vote for me, Dean Poling.

... [T]he remark unquestionably brought down the ire of the school's principal, defendant Ellis Murphy. "I was quite upset," Mr. Murphy stated, adding that "I thought that the content of this speech was inappropriate, disruptive of school discipline, and in bad taste."

At the conclusion of the assembly, according to Dean Poling's affidavit, "Mr. Murphy told me that he did not like my speech and that it was in bad taste. I responded, 'I am sorry [you didn't like it] but it got me votes.' Mr. Murphy said it did not matter that it got me votes because it was in bad taste." Mr. Murphy's affidavit says that Dean volunteered to apologize to Mr. Davidson. This proposal met with Murphy's enthusiastic approval, and the record contains no indication that Dean failed to make the promised apology to Mr. Davidson.

Later in the morning of the assembly, Mrs. Ollis tells us in her affidavit, two of the other student candidates came to her office at different times and complained that Dean Poling had gained an unfair advantage in the election by saying what he had said about Mr. Davidson. This opinion was also expressed by the incumbent student council president, a member of the senior class. Principal Murphy, the incumbent president, and both of the faculty sponsors participated in a mid-morning conference at which "[i]t was the consensus that Dean Poling should be declared ineligible to run...." Superintendent of Schools Ron Wilcox subsequently concurred in the decision to declare Dean ineligible.

....

... [O]n the morning of the election she had the following announcement read over the school's public address system during the regular daily "announcement time:" "There are two students' names that remain on the ballot for their respective offices who are no longer candidates. These students are Beth Edens and Dean Poling. Therefore, any votes cast for Beth or Dean will not be counted."

Dean's father, who had acquiesced in the school's decision on Friday, was not at all pleased by this method of effectuating the disqualification of his son. At a tape-recorded meeting held on Tuesday, May 12, 1987, between the Polings and their lawyer and the school administrators, Mr. Poling complained that "I was told that [Dean's] name would not be on the ballot and he would not be allowed to run. Monday, his name was on the ballot. Monday, over the intercom in front of everyone, they were told that ... it would do no good to vote for Dean or in words similar to that." Mr. Poling took this as an effort "to put Dean down, to humiliate him." Notwithstanding his repeated concessions that what Dean had said about Mr. Davidson was "very discourteous" — or, as he said at another point, "very rude" — Mr. Poling concluded that "[t]here was someone out to get Dean." Dean had been told to change the speech in one particular, as Mr. Poling saw it; Dean had changed the speech in that particular, in Mr. Poling's view, and an administration that had "set out to crush Dean" then publicly humiliated him.

Mr. Poling warned the administrators that "there is a higher court than you four." Superintendent Wilcox agreed, and encouraged Mr. Poling to take the matter to the board of education if he was not happy with the decision: "[O]ur board meets Thursday night and I encourage you to come to our board of Education and I encourage you to ask them for a hearing and they will hear [it] and if we're wrong they'll overturn it."

Mr. Poling did not ask for a hearing before the board of education. Instead, a federal civil rights action was filed in Dean's name, by his parents as next friends, against the four school administrators and the board of education. The complaint alleged violations of Dean's rights under the First and Fourteenth Amendments of the United States Constitution, and it sought declaratory and injunctive relief and an award of damages in the amount of $300,000.

The defendants moved for summary judgment, supporting the motion with affidavits. The Polings filed opposing affidavits. The district court ... granted the motion for summary judgment and dismissed the action. A motion for reconsideration was overruled, and this appeal followed.

II

Did the school officials overreact in declaring Dean Poling ineligible for election? The district court recognized that possibility ("it may be that the school administration overreacted to the speech"), and for all we know there may in fact have been an overreaction. But a federal court is obviously not the ideal body to try to answer such a question.

The Unicoi County Board of Education, from which the Polings could have sought redress had they wished, presumably were acquainted with at least some of the participants in this drama. We are not. We are not steeped in the culture of the place where the events occurred, moreover, and we have no firsthand knowledge of the atmosphere of the school or of the sense of propriety of those who work and study there. We are such outsiders, indeed, that we are at a loss even to understand the full significance of Dean Poling's reference to Mr. Davidson's "stutter." (The affidavit of Mrs. Ollis says, without contradiction, that Mr. Davidson does not stutter.) It is not improbable that the local board of education would have had, or could readily have acquired, a better sense of what actually was going on in the assembly than a remote federal court could reasonably aspire to.

Our impression, for whatever it may be worth, is that this is a tale without heroes and without villains.... Dean Poling appears to be an intelligent and imaginative young man, and probably no more anarchistic than many of his teachers at his age. Like most teenagers, Dean doubtless feels embarrassment very keenly — but he may not fully have appreciated that the assistant principals of this world are sentient beings also, some of whom may even be capable of experiencing embarrassment themselves. The transcript of the May 12 meeting between the Polings and the administrators — the only part of the record in which the players speak in their own voices, rather than in words written for them by their lawyers — suggests that the administrators of the Unicoi County High School are decent, well-meaning individuals who bore Dean Poling no ill will and who had no sinister plan to humiliate him before his peers. It may well be that a more relaxed or more self-assured administration would have let the incident pass without declaring Dean ineligible, and perhaps that is what this administration ought to have done; it is not for us to say. Such a question, we believe, represents a judgment call best left to the locally elected school board, not to a distant, life-tenured judiciary. *Cf. Bethel School District No. 403 v. Fraser*, 478 U.S. 675, 683 (1986).

It is true, to be sure, that students do not "shed their constitutional rights to freedom of speech or expression at the schoolhouse gate," and "[s]chool officials do not possess absolute authority over their students." *Tinker v. Des Moines Independent Community School District*, 393 U.S. 503, 506 and 511 (1969). It also remains true, however, that the Federal Constitution does not compel "teachers, parents, and elected school officials to surrender control of the American public school system to public school students." *Fraser*, 478 U.S. at 686, quoting *Tinker*, 393 U.S. at 526, (BLACK, J., dissenting). Limitations on speech that would be unconstitutional outside the schoolhouse are not necessarily unconstitutional within it.

The Supreme Court has drawn a distinction between "personal expression that happens to occur on school premises" and expressive activities that are "sponsored" by the school and "may fairly be characterized as part of the school curriculum...." *Hazelwood*. Speech sponsored by the school is subject to "greater control" by school authorities than speech not so sponsored, because educators have a legitimate interest in assuring that participants in the sponsored activity "learn whatever lessons the activity is designed to teach...." *Id.* As long as the actions of the educators are "reasonably related to legitimate pedagogical concerns," therefore, the *Hazelwood* Court held, as we have seen, that "educators do not offend the First Amendment by exercising editorial control over the style and content of student speech in school-sponsored expressive activities...." *Id.* at 571.

Applying these concepts to the case at hand, there can be no doubt that the election and election assembly were "school-sponsored" activities within the meaning of *Hazelwood*.... School officials scheduled the assembly to be held during school hours and on school property. They made attendance compulsory for everyone. They determined the eligibility of prospective speakers. They rented the voting machines. And they vetted the speeches in advance, correcting inappropriate grammar and attempting to weed out or temper inappropriate content. There is no genuine issue as to any material fact regarding school sponsorship. The only real question, under *Hazelwood*, is whether the actions of the school officials were reasonably related to "legitimate pedagogical concerns" — and the existence or nonexistence of such a relationship, we take it, is a question of law.

The universe of legitimate pedagogical concerns is by no means confined to the academic; as the Supreme Court put it in *Fraser*, "schools must teach by example the shared values of a civilized social order." 478 U.S. at 683. Sometimes, of course, these "shared values" come in conflict with one another; independence of thought and frankness of expression occupy a high place on our scale of values, or ought to, but so too do discipline, courtesy, and respect for authority....

Local school officials, better attuned than we to the concerns of the parents/taxpayers who employ them, must obviously be accorded wide latitude in choosing which pedagogical values to emphasize, and in choosing the means through which those values are to be promoted. We may disagree with the choices, but unless they are beyond the constitutional pale we have no warrant to interfere with them....

To the administrators of the Unicoi County High School, Dean Poling's seemingly gratuitous comment on Assistant Principal Davidson was in "bad taste."... It was not irrational, to say the least, for the school authorities to take offense at a remark that was calculated to get Dean votes at the expense of the assistant principal's dignity.

The art of stating one's views without indulging in personalities and without unnecessarily hurting the feelings of others surely has a legitimate place in any high school curriculum, and we are not prepared to say that the lesson Unicoi High tried to teach Dean Poling and his captive audience was illegitimate. Neither can we say that the method by which the school sought to drive the lesson home was so extreme as to violate the Constitution....

....

It is important to bear in mind, we think, that the school officials made no attempt to compel Dean Poling to say anything he did not want to say. In the great compulsory flag salute case, *West Virginia State Board of Education v. Barnette*, 319 U.S. 624 (1943), the Supreme Court was "dealing with a compulsion of students to declare a belief." *Id.* at 631. The state in that case affirmatively "require[d] the individual to communicate by word and sign his acceptance of the political ideas [the flag] ... bespeaks." *Id.* at 633. The compulsory flag salute and pledge of allegiance "require[d] affirmation of a belief and an attitude of mind," and it seemed to MR. JUSTICE JACKSON in *Barnette*, as it seems to us here, that "involuntary affirmation could be commanded only on even more immediate and urgent grounds than silence." *Id.* at 633. A student must not be compelled to affirm a belief in the flag against his will, as *Barnette* held, but it does not follow that a student must therefore be permitted to insult his teachers against their will.

It is also important to bear in mind, again, that Dean Poling's speech — unlike the symbolic acts of John and Mary Beth Tinker in wearing black armbands to school, *see Tinker, supra,* 393 U.S. 503 (1969) — was speech sponsored by the school and disseminated under its auspices. "A school must be able to set high standards for the student speech that is disseminated under its auspices," *Hazelwood, supra,* at 570, and the Supreme Court has made it quite clear that the First Amendment standard for determining when non-sponsored student speech may be punished is a standard that need not be applied where sponsored student speech (a student newspaper, *e.g.*, or a student council election campaign) is concerned. *Id.* at 571....

III

Dean Poling's disqualification did not, as we see it, violate his due process rights under the Fourteenth Amendment....

This court has heretofore held that "[t]he privilege of participating in interscholastic athletics ... [is] outside the protection of due process." *Hamilton v. Tennessee Secondary School Athletic Association,* 552 F.2d 681, 682 (6th Cir.1976). The privilege of participating in a student council election seems no different.

We are told on appeal that it has been customary to grant a $100 college scholarship to the Unicoi High student council president. If we are entitled to make use of this information, we think it changes nothing. Dean Poling had no guarantee that he would have been elected president if not disqualified, and no guarantee that he would have received the scholarship....

We see nothing improper, moreover, in the process through which Dean's disqualification was effected. Dean was put on notice before he gave his speech that it was considered important for the president of the student council "to work in a cooperative way with the Administration." He was specifically told that his proposed reference to "the administration's iron grip" would have to be changed. Dean was far too intelligent, as the district court recognized, to suppose that a reference to "the iron grip of this school" would be made more palatable to the administration by the introduction of a discourteous reference to the assistant principal and his "stutter."

....

It is true that the administration had decided to disqualify Dean for the student council presidency before he was accorded a hearing, but Dean and his father were promptly given a two-hour audience with the principal and Mrs. Ollis on Friday afternoon, three days before the election. At least two further sessions were conducted within a day or two after the election. There is no reason to doubt that the board of education would have entertained an appeal from the administration's decision had the Polings requested one, as Superintendent Wilcox encouraged them to do. Surely the Due Process Clause would have required nothing more than this even if a deprivation of some constitutionally protected liberty or property interest had been established.

The judgment of the district court is AFFIRMED.

....

---

1. The *Poling* court claimed that its decision was consistent with that in *Crosby v. Holsinger*, 852 F.2d 801 (4th Cir. 1988). In that case, a high school principal acted to censor displays of a school symbol, "Johnny Reb," because of complaints from black students and parents that they found the symbol offensive. "If it was legitimate for the school officials in *Holsinger* to restrict student expression because it insulted a segment of the student body, it was legitimate for the school officials here to restrict speech considered insulting to the officials themselves." 872 F.2d at 763. Is this reasoning correct?

2. Both *Poling* and *Fraser* are cases involving students running for offices in student government. Both involve students who delivered controversial campaign speeches (either for themselves or for a candidate). How do these cases differ? How does the existence of *Hazelwood* separate these two seemingly close cases?

3. Consider the following comment/critique on *Poling*:

BARTLETT, THE CLOSING OF THE SCHOOL HOUSE GATES: INCREASING RESTRICTIONS ON THE PUBLIC SCHOOL STUDENT'S EXERCISE OF SPEECH AND EXPRESSION,
16 T. Marshall L. Rev. 311 (1991)*

....

This review of the majority and dissenting opinions in *Hazelwood* provides greater perspective for the Sixth Circuit decision in *Poling v. Murphy*, in that *Poling* exemplifies the specific concerns about protecting the diversity of ideas in the schools raised by the dissent in *Hazelwood*. The Sixth Circuit based its decision in *Poling* on the majority holding in *Hazelwood* and ruled that civility is a legitimate pedagogical concern; thus, the school was within its rights to punish Poling for his "rude" criticism of the school's administration. This expansion of "pedagogical concerns" is alarming because it greatly increases the ability of schools to restrict students' first amendment rights. The broader scope is even more disconcerting in that it occurs outside of a classroom. Because of the importance of this expansion, it is crucial to examine the *Hazelwood* idea of a "legitimate pedagogical concern" and subsequent interpretations of the concept.

In *Hazelwood*, the censored speech partially concerned issues related to sexuality. The district court held in part that the censorship of the article on teenage pregnancy was justified "to avoid the impression that [the school]

---

*Copyright © 1991 by The Thurgood Marshall Law Review. Reprinted with permission.

endorses the sexual norms of the subjects." In relying on the *Fraser* precedent in its review of the case, the Court emphasized "the 'vulgar,' 'lewd,' and 'plainly offensive' character of [the] speech," and asserted that the "school must retain the authority to refuse to sponsor student speech that might reasonably be perceived to advocate drug or alcohol use, irresponsible sex, or conduct otherwise inconsistent with 'the shared values of a civilized social order'." In these rulings, the legitimate pedagogical concern was related to the school's interest in limiting student exposure to developmentally inappropriate material regarding sexuality.

Lower courts appear to be interpreting the *Hazelwood* holding in this manner. The Ninth Circuit relied on *Hazelwood* to uphold a school newspaper's refusal to accept "lewd, vulgar, or obscene advertisements" submitted by a family planning organization. The Eleventh Circuit permitted a school board to remove from a curriculum a textbook deemed sexual, explicit, and vulgar on the basis of a "legitimate pedagogical concern." The judges of the Eleventh Circuit and the district court disagreed with the local school board's conclusion that high school students could be harmed by "masterpieces of western literature" such as Lysistrata by Aristophanes and The Miller's Tale by Chaucer, but concluded that *Hazelwood* provided school officials with legal authority for their actions. In a case involving a teacher showing an R-rated movie in class, the federal court for the Northern District of Illinois has held that a school has a legitimate concern "over the display of vulgarity and sexual scenes to students in a public school system." We can see that courts consider exposure to sexually explicit material a legitimate pedagogical concern.

IV. Analysis of *Poling*

Recently, the courts have determined that any new restriction on student speech, including the determination of a new legitimate pedagogical concern, must meet the test of reasonableness. In a nonpublic forum, the school "may impose content based restrictions which are 'reasonable and [are] not an effort to suppress expression merely because public officials oppose the speaker's view.' The regulations of speech must be "reasonable in light of the pedagogical purposes of the particular activity." The record in *Poling* does not contain a statement from the school of the educational purpose of the campaign speeches, but it does indicate a desire to make the election resemble elections outside the school. The court in *Poling* commented "[t]he art of stating one's views without indulging in personalities and without unnecessarily hurting the feelings of others surely has a legitimate place in any high school curriculum." This after the fact determination of purpose is contradicted by the school's actions in making the election more realistic. Real campaign speeches often contain harsh, ad hominem attacks. Poling's comments seem well within the bounds of realistic political speech. In that case, regulation of Poling's speech would not be reasonable, given the apparent pedagogical aim of the activity.

Since the school permitted remarks on the administration of the school and objected only to the specific critical content of Poling's speech, the speech fell into the category of content regulation. The regulation of speech that is in "bad taste" is content based on its face and in most situations would be scrutinized strictly by the courts. Under traditional first amendment analysis, it appears that Poling had a strong case. We must, however, take into account the special context of his remarks. School administrators have great latitude in controlling what occurs within the walls of the school building. Typically, the courts will interfere only if fundamental constitutional values are jeopardized. Still, given that students do not forfeit their free speech rights by entering the schoolhouse gate, the deference given to school officials should have its limits.

Under the new standard, for Poling's comments not to be protected, a court must decide that civility is a legitimate pedagogical concern. Given judicial concern over excessive expansion of the concept, the inclusion is dubious. Civility is a nebulous, subjective concept, changing in each cultural context. Accepting "civility" as a standard for censoring student speech would have a tremendous chilling effect. The term can easily be used to censor speech on the basis of content, for harsh criticism often appears rude to the targets of the criticism. Thus, the use of "civility" as a justification for Poling's punishment, without direct support of prior court precedents, is a remarkable expansion of the school's ability to control student speech.

The decision in *Poling* is disturbing. The court upheld the discipline of a student running for the highest student elective office who dared to run on a platform challenging the authoritarian practice of school officials. (The irony of the situation escaped both school officials and the majority judges in the Sixth Circuit opinion.) However, the *Poling* decision has greater, more lasting meaning if it indeed reflects the Supreme Court's abandonment of important precedent in the area of student rights of free speech and expression. A comparison of the language of the decisions in *Fraser* and *Hazelwood* to that in *Barnette* and *Tinker* in itself indicates a change of focus, but additional cause for concern is found in the significantly different results of the student speech cases rendered by the lower courts immediately following the *Tinker* decision and those rendered subsequent to *Fraser* and *Hazelwood*. Strong dissents in *Fraser* and *Hazelwood* also highlight the officially undeclared abandonment of student speech protection precedent.

The decision in *Poling* illustrates some of the problems created by the *Fraser* and *Hazelwood* abandonment of student speech precedent. *Barnette* warned of the need to protect the critical role model nature of public education. Dean Poling was a young American educated for citizenship, but what did he learn? It can be argued that his freedom of expression was denied by the school and that he in reality learned to "discount important principles of our government as mere platitudes." He also probably learned that school officials can in fact "prescribe what shall be orthodox in politics, nationalism, religion, or other matters of opinion...."

Tinker states that public schools should not be "enclaves of totalitarianism" in which the school determines what information the students may receive. *Tinker* shows that school official action must not be motivated solely by a desire to avoid the unpleasantness of discordant opinions. These free speech values, however, were likely lost on Dean Poling and his schoolmates. As high school students, they were provided a "realistic" campaign and election for student offices, including campaign speeches and the use of voting machines. But, the lesson they learned was not about the democratic process. When public school officials forget the importance of the positive civic lessons they model and are willing to exemplify the least desirable features of an autocratic system, courts must be willing to remind them of the importance of their role of establishing in innocent youth an appreciation, by example, for the democratic principles guaranteed by the Constitution.

Just as important, *Poling* reflects problems raised by the Supreme Court not openly admitting its departure from 50 years of precedent. The dissent in *Hazelwood* considered it "ironic" that the majority opinion began its analysis by reaffirming the proposition in *Tinker* that public school students "do not shed their constitutional rights to freedom of speech or expression at the schoolhouse gate" and then proceeded to remove much of the first amendment protection prescribed in *Tinker*. The lack of express recognition of this departure from student speech precedent by the majority on the Supreme Court can result in nothing but confusion.

School boards and administrators engaged in school policy development are left in a state of uncertainty. The Hazelwood School District had policies and practices that assured journalism students of guaranteed protection for their exercise of first amendment rights, but the district's administration was upheld when it violated its own policies. When faced with critical student speech, how are school officials to be expected to distinguish between curricular and noncurricular aspects of their programs, and legitimate and nonlegitimate pedagogical concerns? Will school officials be able to distinguish the legal subtleties of a student editorial in the school-sponsored newspaper criticizing a principal for censorship, such as the censorship that occurred in *Hazelwood*, from the legal implications of similar remarks in a newspaper published as an extracurricular activity, remarks made by students in an underground publication, remarks made in the cafeteria, or remarks made in the classroom? How will reviewing courts determine whether school official decisions to censor involve a "valid educational purpose?"

In the absence of a clear statement by the Supreme Court that it has drifted or is about to drift further away from *Tinker*, as reflected in *Poling*, attorneys are unclear as to how to advise their school and student clients. Students are also puzzling how to respond to arguably autocratic policies and practices that heretofore invited or allowed challenge under *Tinker*. Now, success of court review hinges on subjective terms such as "legitimate pedagogical concerns," regulation "in any reasonable manner," and appropriateness for student "level of maturity."

V. *Conclusion*

The Supreme Court has begun to close the schoolhouse gate on student free speech without clearly expressing how narrowly ajar it may be left open. It is no wonder that three Supreme Court justices in *Hazelwood* were left shaking their heads that landmark precedent in the area of student free speech was abandoned without being expressly overruled. It is also no wonder that the dissenting judge in *Poling* was left questioning why the majority ruling applied the constitutional test of legitimate pedagogical concerns when neither *Barnette* nor *Tinker* have been overruled and still continue to teach that the Constitution protects the political speech of public school students. In the end, it is no wonder that students and educators are left struggling to resolve the tension between student free speech rights and the state's interest in educating its children.

Chapter 7
PROCEDURAL PROBLEMS IN ENFORCING STUDENT CONDUCT AND STATUS RULES

Chapters 7 and 8 address the issue of student disciplinary practices and procedures and in doing so attempt to bring some logic and order to a frontier area of education. Many important issues are yet to be resolved, and the courts are still struggling to balance the need for wide discretion in making and enforcing rules in school operations by school authorities (the so-called *in loco parentis* standard) with the civil rights of pupils. These issues become even more important when considered in light of the growing phenomenon of violence in the schools.

There are a host of reported state and federal cases addressing some aspect of student discipline — many in conflict with each other. We have therefore attempted to choose the most important of these cases, whether arising in public schools or in institutions of higher education, in order to provide the reader with some idea of general trends as they appear to be developing. Also, in what may at first appear to be an unorthodox approach, we deal with the general issue of procedural rights available to students before turning to specific sanctions.

A. VAGUENESS AND THE NEED FOR PRE-EXISTING RULES

SOGLIN v. KAUFFMAN
United States Court of Appeals
418 F.2d 163 (7th Cir. 1969)

CUMMINGS, CIRCUIT JUDGE. This is an appeal from a declaratory judgment that disciplinary proceedings of the University of Wisconsin instituted on the basis of alleged "misconduct" are unconstitutional:

The named plaintiffs are ten students at the Madison campus of the University of Wisconsin and the Madison chapter of the Students for a Democratic Society. They brought this suit on October 16, 1967, for themselves and persons similarly situated. The defendants are various officials of the University of Wisconsin, the State of Wisconsin and the City of Madison allegedly involved in disciplinary actions on the Madison campus. The final complaint alleges the following pertinent facts:

On October 18, 1967, plaintiffs and others were protesting the presence of recruiting representatives of the Dow Chemical Corporation on the Madison campus. On the following day, the defendant Dean of Student Affairs wrote two of the plaintiffs and other "members of their class" that they were "suspended from the University pending a hearing before the Administrative Division of the Committee on Student Conduct and Appeals." The ground for the suspension was stated to be violation of Chapter 11.02 of the Laws and Regulations of the University of Wisconsin, and the students were informed that a hearing date would be set at a later time. By letter of October 21, 1967, the chairman of the Administrative Division advised them that the hearing would be held on November 2, and that they would be permitted to attend classes and write examinations in the interim.

On November 1, some of the plaintiffs, as well as other individuals, received "Amended Charges" from the chairman of the Administrative Division. These charges specifically described the offensive conduct ascribed to plaintiffs, including the denial of others' rights to job interviews with the Dow Chemical Corporation by physical obstruction of the doorways and corridors of a university building. This behavior was characterized as "misconduct," as well as violative of Chapters 11.02 and 11.15 of the University Policies on the Use of Facilities and Outside Speakers.

The complaint further alleged that some of the defendants had previously expelled two plaintiffs and another member of their class "by application of the doctrine of 'misconduct,'" and were threatening to suspend or expel others for "misconduct." This doctrine was alleged to be so vague and overbroad as to violate the rights of plaintiffs under the First and Fourteenth Amendments. The complaint requested a declaratory judgment that the defendants' misconduct doctrine on its face violated the United States Constitution and prayed for an injunction against further application of that doctrine as the basis for disciplinary proceedings.

For their part, defendants answered that the term "misconduct" "as a standard for disciplinary action by the University" did not violate any of the provisions of the federal Constitution.

The district court, in a scholarly opinion, held that the standard of misconduct alone may not serve as the foundation for the expulsion or suspension of students for any significant time. 295 F. Supp. 978.

....

Turning to the merits, defendants contend that the "misconduct" doctrine does not constitute a "standard" of conduct and that it was not employed as such. They argue that "misconduct" represents the inherent power of the University to discipline students and that this power may be exercised without the necessity of relying on a specific rule of conduct. This rationale would justify the *ad hoc* imposition of discipline without reference to any preexisting standards of conduct so long as the objectionable behavior could be called misconduct at some later date. No one disputes the power of the University to protect itself by means of disciplinary action against disruptive students. Power to punish and the rules defining the exercise of that power are not, however, identical. Power alone does not supply the standards needed to determine its application to types of behavior or specific instances of "misconduct." As Professor Fuller has observed: "The first desideratum of a system for subjecting human conduct to the governance of rules is an obvious one: there must be rules." Fuller, Law and Morality, p. 46 (2d printing, 1965). The proposition that government officers, including school administrators, must act in accord with rules in meting out discipline is so fundamental that its validity tends to be assumed by courts engaged in assessing the propriety of specific regulations. The doctrines of vagueness and overbreadth, already applied in academic contexts, presuppose the existence of rules whose coherence and boundaries may be questioned. These same considerations also dictate that the rules embodying standards of discipline be contained in properly promulgated regulations. University administrators are not immune from these requirements of due process in imposing sanctions. Consequently, in the present case, the disciplinary proceedings must fail to the extent that the defendant officials of the University of Wisconsin did not base those proceedings on the students' disregard of university standards of conduct expressed in reasonably clear and narrow rules.

Having specifically charged the students with the offense of "misconduct," the University may not now claim that misconduct was not employed as a standard. When tested as such, however, the term is clearly inadequate in view of constitutional requirements. As the Supreme Court recently remarked concerning the use of the term in a jury instruction:

> If used in a *statute* which imposed forfeitures, punishments or judgments for costs, such loose and unlimiting terms [as "misconduct" or "reprehensible conduct"] would certainly cause the statute to fail to measure up to the requirements of the Due Process Clause. *Giaccio v. Pennsylvania,* 382 U.S. 399.

The use of "misconduct" as a standard in imposing the penalties threatened here must therefore fall for vagueness. The inadequacy of the rule is apparent on its face. It contains no clues which could assist a student, an administrator or a reviewing judge in determining whether conduct not transgressing statutes is susceptible to punishment by the University as "misconduct." Since the misconduct standard is invalid on its face, it was unnecessary for the district court to make any findings with respect to plaintiffs' activities on October 18, 1967. To the extent that *Esteban v. Central Missouri State College,* 290 F. Supp. 622, 630 (W.D. Mo. 1968), affirmed, 415 F.2d 1077 (8th Cir. 1969), refuses to apply standards of vagueness and overbreadth required of universities by the Fourteenth Amendment we decline to follow it.

It is not an adequate answer to contend, as do defendants, that the particular conduct which is the object of university discipline might have violated an applicable state or local law or otherwise merited punishment. The issue here is not the character of the student behavior but the validity of the administrative sanctions. Criminal laws carry their own definitions and penalties and are not enacted to enable a university to suspend or expel the wrongdoer absent a breach of a university's own rule. Nor is "misconduct" necessarily confined to disruptive actions covered by criminal codes. The ability to punish "misconduct" *per se* affords no safeguard against the imposition of disciplinary proceedings overreaching permissible limits and penalizing activities which are free from any taint of impropriety. Hence we feel compelled to strike down the University's reliance on the doctrine of misconduct in order to ensure that "reasonable regulation of speech-connected activities [of students remains confined to] carefully restricted circumstances." *Tinker v. Des Moines School District,* 393 U.S. 503, 513.

Pursuant to appropriate rule or regulation, the University has the power to maintain order by suspension or expulsion of disruptive students. Requiring that such sanctions be administered in accord with preexisting rules does not place an unwarranted burden upon university administrations. We do not require university codes of conduct to satisfy the same rigorous standards as criminal statutes. We only hold that expulsion and prolonged suspension may not be imposed on students by a university simply on the basis of allegations of "misconduct" without reference to any preexisting rule which supplies an adequate guide. The possibility of the sweeping application of the standard of "misconduct" to protected activities does not comport with the guarantees of the First and Fourteenth Amendments. The desired end must be more narrowly achieved.

Affirmed.

ESTEBAN v. CENTRAL MISSOURI STATE COLLEGE

United States Court of Appeals
415 F.2d 1077 (8th Cir. 1969), *cert. denied,* 398 U.S. 965 (1970)

BLACKMUN, CIRCUIT JUDGE: Alfredo Esteban and Steve Craig Roberds, students at Central Missouri State College, a tax-supported institution at Warrensburg, Missouri, were suspended on March 31, 1967, for two semesters but with the right thereafter to apply for readmission. The two, by their next friends, instituted the present action for declaratory and injunctive relief. The named defendants are the College, its President, and its Board of Regents. The plaintiffs allege, primarily, first, fifth, and fourteenth amendment violations. Judge Hunter, with a detailed memorandum, denied them relief and dismissed their complaint. *Esteban v. Central Missouri State College,* 290 F. Supp. 622 (W.D. Mo. 1968). The plaintiffs appeal.

....

The disciplinary action against the plaintiffs arose out of events which took place on or adjacent to the college campus on the nights of March 29 and 30, 1967. At that time Esteban was on scholastic probation and Roberds was on disciplinary probation. Esteban also had been on disciplinary probation over a knifing incident with a fellow student, but his disciplinary probation had expired a short time before.

A. VAGUENESS AND THE NEED FOR PRE-EXISTING RULES 385

Both sides in their appellate briefs specifically adopt findings of fact made by JUDGE HUNTER with respect to these March 1967 events. Accordingly, we set forth certain of those findings here:

> ... [T]hese demonstrations took place at the intersection of the public street adjacent to the school campus and State Highway 13 and overflowed onto the sidewalks and campus. On the evening of March 29, some 350 students were present in the mass and on March 30, there were some 600 students included. As a partial result of these two mass demonstrations there was in excess of $600 damages and destruction of college property, including broken school building windows and destroyed shrubbery; eggs were thrown; the Dean of Men, Dr. Chalquist, was hanged in effigy, his "dummy" torn up and set on fire; traffic was halted and blocked, cars were rocked, and their occupants ordered out into the street. The college president directed a number of his personnel, including Dr. Meverden, to go to the scene to restore order.

Esteban Event:

> ... [T]he evening of March 29, 1967, around 11:30 p.m., he left his dormitory about the time the "disturbance" had subsided. Some of the students were proceeding along the street from the mass demonstration to their dormitories. Esteban proceeded down the sidewalk to within about 100 feet of the intersection of the scene of the mass demonstration and stayed there awhile. Dr. Meverden, a faculty member, who was seeking to disperse students standing outside their dorms, approached Esteban and asked him to go inside the dormitory. Instead of complying, Esteban asked why, and on again being requested to go in, again asked why. He told Dr. Meverden that he was not in violation of any state, county, or federal law and that he had a right to be out there. Dr. Meverden asked for his student identification card which by college regulation he was required to have in his possession at all times. Esteban said ("in rough words" according to one witness) he did not have it. Nor did he give his name. Dr. Meverden again requested him to go in the dormitory and get off the street. Esteban argued with Dr. Meverden and questioned his authority, saying there were no rules limiting the time men could stay outside the dorms. Shortly, and with the encouragement of other students present, he went into the dormitory. Dr. Meverden also went in and asked Gerald Haddock, the resident assistant of Esteban's dormitory, who Esteban was. Haddock was overheard by Esteban telling Dr. Meverden Esteban's name. Esteban, as Dr. Meverden was leaving, called Haddock a prick and a bastard and told him he "would not be around very long." According to Esteban's roommate, Esteban then angrily picked up a waste can and emptied the contents on the floor at the feet of Haddock.

Roberds Event:

....

Throughout both evenings of the mass demonstrations Roberds was present as a part of the crowd. On March 29, 1967, he arrived at the scene of the demonstration about 10:15 p.m. and returned to his dormitory about 10:45 p.m. On March 30, 1967, he arrived at the scene about 9:30 p.m. and remained until about 10:30 p.m. During the first night, while a part of the gathered crowd, he talked to students who were present in it. Roberds testified that the second evening, also while a part of the crowd at the demonstration, that "I discussed some of the things that were going on, the rocking of the cars and the dummy. At that time I mentioned my disgust with the college, and we talked, as the people I had talked to had the same feeling." He saw the dummy brought to the scene of the demonstration; saw it hung, torn up and burned by students in the crowd. He saw the cars approached by the students, saw the cars rocked, saw the attempts to take the occupants out of the cars. He returned to his dormitory after the dispersal of the gathering. He stated he was at the demonstrations each evening simply as a "spectator", not participating in any of the acts of violence or destruction. [Footnote omitted]

Both sides also adopt JUDGE HUNTER's findings as to Roberds' situation prior to the March events:

Prior to the mass demonstrations, Roberds had been placed on disciplinary probation and furnished a written statement of the terms of that probation. Dean Chalquist also orally explained those terms to him. He and Dean Chalquist conversed relative to his intention to participate in a demonstration. Roberds asked about the possible repercussions of his involvement in (future) demonstrations or disturbances. He was advised "that any action on your part which may reflect unfavorably upon either you or the institution can be considered grounds for suspension." Roberds, under date of February 5, 1967, wrote E. J. Cantrell, a Representative from his county in the Missouri Legislature, the following letter:

... [I] assure you, I do not stand alone in my disgust with this institution. From suppression of speech and expression to ridiculous, trivial regulations this college has done more to discourage democratic belief than any of the world's tyrants.

... [M]y comrades and I plan on turning this school into a Berkeley if something isn't done.

....

[Following a previous order of the federal district court, written charges were filed against Esteban and Roberds.]

A. VAGUENESS AND THE NEED FOR PRE-EXISTING RULES 387

The charge against Esteban read:

> You are hereby notified that you are charged with contributing to and participating in an unruly and unlawful mass gathering occurring on the 30th day of March, 1967, at and near Central Missouri State College in that you, the said, Alfredo Esteban, did resist efforts of one Dr. M. L. Meverden in dispersing said mass gathering, failed and refused to identify yourself to Dr. Meverden as requested and used vile and obscene language towards and threatened a resident assistant of the College at Foster-Knox Hall.

That against Roberds read:

> You are hereby notified that you are charged with contributing to and participating in an unruly and unlawful mass gathering occurring on or about the 29th and 30th days of March, 1967 at and near Central Missouri State College in that you, the said Stephen Craig Roberds, on the 5th day of February, 1967 directed correspondence to Mr. E. J. Cantrell of the Missouri Legislature evidencing your intention to participate in such mass gathering, did thereafter advise Dean Hollis Chalquist, Dean of Men, of your intention to participate in such demonstration at which time you were specifically advised that such participation would result in immediate suspension from Central Missouri State College and that you did thereafter continue to contribute to and participate in said mass gathering all of which actions were in violation of the terms and provisions of your disciplinary probation.

The college regulations in effect at the time, and to the extent pertinent, provided:

> The conduct of the individual student is an important indication of character and future usefulness in life. It is therefore important that each student maintain the highest standards of integrity, honesty and morality. All students are expected to conform to ordinary and accepted social customs and to conduct themselves at all times and in all places in a manner befitting a student of Central Missouri State College.
>
> All students that enroll at C.M.S.C. assume an obligation to abide by the rules and regulations of the college as well as all local, state and federal laws.
>
> When a breach of regulations involves a mixed group, *All Members Are Held Equally Responsible.*
>
> Conduct unbefitting a student which reflects adversely upon himself or the institution will result in disciplinary action.
>
> Mass Gatherings — Participation in mass gatherings which might be considered as unruly or unlawful will subject a student to possible immediate dismissal from the College. Only a few students intentionally get involved in mob misconduct, but many so-called "spectators" get drawn

into a fracas and by their very presence contribute to the dimensions of the problems. It should be understood that the College considers no student to be immune from due process of law enforcement when he is in violation as an individual or as a member of a crowd.

[The court first held that the plaintiffs' First Amendment Rights had not been violated and then turned to the "vagueness" issue.]

....

The regulations. These are additionally attacked for vagueness and overbreadth and hence on substantive due process grounds. Some of the loyalty oath cases are cited and it is said that the regulations' word "unlawful" is only a legal conclusion and that their references to "unruly" and "spectators" and "which might be considered" are undefined and possess no standards. The regulations are likened to city ordinances which have been struck down when they lack sufficiency of definition. It is then argued that "young people should be told clearly what is right and what is wrong, as well as the consequences of their acts." *Pickering v. Board of Educ.,* 391 U.S. 563 (1968), and other cases are cited. Finally, it is said that the regulations impinge and have a chilling effect upon first and fourteenth amendment rights.

The answers to all this, we think, are several. First, the college's regulations, per se, do not appear to us to constitute the fulcrum of the plaintiffs' discomfiture. The charges against Esteban and Roberds did not even refer to the regulations. Roberds was disciplined because he had participated in the demonstrations in the face of specific warning delivered by personal interview with the dean. This was defiance of proper college authority. Esteban was disciplined because of his refusal to comply with an appropriate request by Doctor Meverden and because of his childish behavior and obscenity toward college officials. This, too, was defiance of proper college authority. There was no confusion or unawareness in either case. The exercise of common sense was all that was required. Each plaintiff knew the situation very well, knew what he was doing, and knew the consequences. Each, we might note, had had prior disciplinary experience. Their respective protestations of young and injured innocence have a hollow ring.

Secondly, we agree with JUDGE HUNTER that it is not sound to draw an analogy between student discipline and criminal procedure, that the standard of conduct which a college seeks to impose must be one relevant to "a lawful mission, process or function of the educational institution", and that,

> Certainly the regulation concerning mass demonstrations, reasonably interpreted, and as interpreted and applied by the college in the instant case to a participant in student mass demonstrations involving unlawful conduct such as the illegal blocking of a public highway and street, and the destruction of school property, is relevant to a lawful mission of the educational institution. 290 F. Supp. at 629. [Footnote omitted]

A. VAGUENESS AND THE NEED FOR PRE-EXISTING RULES

Thirdly, we do not find the regulation at all difficult to understand and we are positive the college student, who is appropriately expected to possess some minimum intelligence, would not find it difficult. It asks for the adherence to standards of conduct which befit a student and it warns of the danger of mass involvement. We must assume Esteban and Roberds can read and that they possess some power of comprehension. Their difficulty was that they chose not to read or not to comprehend.

Fourthly, we see little basically or constitutionally wrong with flexibility and reasonable breadth, rather than meticulous specificity, in college regulations relating to conduct. Certainly these regulations are not to be compared with the criminal statute. They are codes of general conduct which those qualified and experienced in the field have characterized not as punishment but as part of the educational process itself and as preferably to be expressed in general rather than in specific terms.

We agree with those courts which have held that a school has inherent authority to maintain order and to discipline students. We further agree that a school has latitude and discretion in its formulation of rules and regulations and of general standards of conduct.

....

The appellants argue, to what exact purpose we are not sure, that attendance by a Missouri resident at a publicly supported educational institution of his state is an important right. We are not certain that it is significant whether attendance at such a college, or staying there once one has matriculated, is a right rather than a privilege. Education, of course, is vital and valuable, *Brown v. Board of Educ.,* 347 U.S. 483, 493 (1954), and remaining in college in good standing, much like reputation, is also something of value. *Dixon v. Alabama State Bd. of Educ.,* 294 F.2d 150, 157 (5 Cir. 1961), *cert. denied,* 368 U.S. 930. So, too, is one's personal freedom. But one may act so as constitutionally to lose that freedom. And one may act so as constitutionally to lose his right or privilege to attend a college.

College attendance, whether it be a right or a privilege, very definitely entails responsibility. This is fundamental. It rests upon the fact that the student is approaching maturity. His elementary and secondary education is behind him. He already knows, or should know, the basics of decent conduct, of non-violence, and of respect for the rights of others. He already knows, or should know, that destruction of property, threats to others, frightening passersby, and intrusions upon their rights of travel are unacceptable, if not illegal, and are not worthy of one who would pursue knowledge at the college level.

These plaintiffs are no longer children. While they may have been minors, they were beyond the age of 18. Their days of accomplishing ends and status by force are at an end. It was time they assumed at least the outward appearance of adulthood and of manhood. The mass denial of rights of others is irresponsible and childish. So is the defiance of proper college administrative authority ("I have the right to be here"; "I refuse to identify myself"; gutter abuse of an official; the dumping of a trash can at a resident's feet; "I plan on turning this school into a Berkeley if ..."; and being a part of the proscribed college peace-disturbing and property-destroying demonstration). One might expect this from the spoiled child of tender years. One rightly does not expect it from the college student who has had two decades of life and who, in theory, is close to being "grown up."

Let there be no misunderstanding as to our precise holding. We do not hold that any college regulation, however loosely framed, is necessarily valid. We do not hold that a school has the authority to require a student to discard any constitutional right when he matriculates. We do hold that a college has the inherent power to promulgate rules and regulations; that it has the inherent power properly to discipline; that it has power appropriately to protect itself and its property; that it may expect that its students adhere to generally accepted standards of conduct; that, as to these, flexibility and elbow room are to be preferred over specificity; that procedural due process must be afforded (as Judge Hunter by his first opinion here specifically required) by way of adequate notice, definite charge; and a hearing with opportunity to present one's own side of the case and with all necessary protective measures; that school regulations are not to be measured by the standards which prevail for the criminal law and for criminal procedure; and that the courts should interfere only where there is a clear case of constitutional infringement.

....

---

1. *Soglin* stands for the proposition that public education authority must have rules, if students are to be compelled to comport their behavior to them, and the rules must provide standards to guide student conduct. While one might derive this result from the case, does this mean that school rules, even though somewhat vague or overbroad, will always be brought into question if submitted to the courts? Would courts, for example, accept the argument raised in *Soglin* that there is some inherent authority of school officials to discipline?

This question was considered by the Fifth Circuit Court of Appeals in *Jenkins v. Louisiana Bd. of Educ.*, 506 F.2d 992 (5th Cir. 1975) where the court indicated that school disciplinary regulations did not have to be developed with the same specificity as criminal codes. Citing *Murray v. West Baton Rouge Parish Sch. Bd.*, 472 F.2d 438 (5th Cir. 1973), the court stated:

> Some degree of discretion must of necessity, be left to ... school officials to determine what forms of misbehavior should be sanctioned. Absent evidence that the broad wording in the statute is, in fact, being used to infringe on First Amendment rights ... we must assume that school officials are acting responsibly in applying the broad statutory command.

2. School rules, and their clarity or limits, have some source in the authority to promulgate them in the first place. What is the source of authority in the rules created in *Soglin*? Consider the *Esteban* case with a decision inapposite to *Soglin*. What authority did school officials have for disciplining the students? *See* page 389 of this text where the court states, "We agree with those courts which have held that a school has *inherent authority* to maintain order and to discipline students." [authors' emphasis]. Is the term "inherent authority" in and of itself vague? What is its definition as used by the court? What is the difference in official decision making between "express authority," "implied authority," "apparent authority" and "inherent authority"? Will the answer to the question differ depending on the court?

3. While the *Soglin* case informs school officials of the need to prepare rules of conduct which provide a guide for behavior, the need for specificity has been brought into question by subsequent cases. *Esteban*, for example, indicated that school rules cannot be too loose. This, however, may represent no more than a floor for college regulations. Where is the ceiling? That court also went on to say that "we see little basically or constitutionally wrong with flexibility and reasonable breadth, rather than meticulous specificity, in college regulations relating to conduct." This statement by the court suggests less judicial scrutiny on the issue of vagueness than that found in *Soglin*. Are the rules against misconduct in *Esteban* less egregious than in *Soglin* or was the "inherent power" of officials in one college greater than the other? Could it be that the court in *Esteban* simply did not adequately deal with the vagueness issue?

4. Consider the following regulation, published in a university handbook:

> Any student parade, serenade, *demonstration*, rally, and/or other meeting or gathering for *any purpose*, conducted on the campus of the institution must be *scheduled with the President or designated agent at least three (3) days in advance of the event....*
>
> *Students assembling for any meetings not authorized in accordance with the aforesaid paragraphs are subject to disciplinary action which may result in dismissal* from the institution....
>
> *All events sponsored by student organizations, groups, or individual students must be registered with the Director of Student Activities, who, in cooperation with the Vice President for Student affairs, approves activities of a wholesome nature....*

This regulation was the subject of a 1980 suit similar to that in *Esteban*. The suit was filed by Iranian students who had participated in demonstrations at Jackson State University supporting the new Iranian government under the Ayatollah Khomeni.

Compare the rule to the one in *Esteban*. Is this regulation unconstitutionally vague? Inasmuch as it was determined that the students violated the policy, the Fifth Circuit Court of Appeals held said policy unreasonable and unconstitutionally vague, emphasizing problems with the word, "wholesome." *Shamloo v.*

Mississippi State Bd. of Trustees of Institutions of Higher Learning, 620 F.2d 516 (5th Cir. 1980). Do you find this result surprising in light of the Iranian hostage crisis of the time?

5. What is the message of *Esteban*? What does this decision say about the authority of schools to promulgate such rules? "[Y]oung people should be told clearly what is right and what is wrong, as well as the consequences of their acts." What makes Central Missouri State's rule succeed and Jackson State's fail?

WIEMERSLAGE v. MAINE TOWNSHIP HIGH SCHOOL DISTRICT 207

United States District Court
824 F. Supp. 136 (N.D. Ill., E.D. 1993)

NORGLE, DISTRICT JUDGE:

....

Before the court is defendants' motion to dismiss pursuant to Rule 12(b)(6) of the Federal Rules of Civil Procedure. For reasons stated below, the motion is granted.

Facts

On September 23, 1992, after classes let out at roughly 3:05 p.m., plaintiff Kurt Wiemerslage ("Wiemerslage"), a high school freshman, exited Maine Township High School South and for a short period of time stood with a friend in an area immediately adjacent to the school that is commonly referred to as the Hamlin Gate Area, an entrance and exit area located near the fieldhouse on the east side of the school's campus. Wiemerslage stood on the public sidewalk, outside of the school property, and waited as two other students joined him. The group congregated for a brief time, discussing their immediate plans, when defendant Officer Thomas Swoboda ("Swoboda") approached them.

Swoboda, a security officer retained by defendant Maine Township High School District 207, had observed the four students on the public way. The officer, after taking their names and other information, reported this activity to the school's superintendent, indicating that the students were loitering near a garage located halfway between Hamlin Avenue and Home Avenue. He cited them for violating the school's disciplinary rule against loitering in the Hamlin Gate Area.

The Maine Township High School District 207's manual outlining disciplinary procedures states, "Students are not permitted in off-limits areas at any time. The designation of these areas will be presented to students by the school administration." In August, 1992, defendant principal Thomas J. Cachur ("principal Cachur") sent a letter to parents which stated that "the Hamlin Gate area continues to be designated as an off-limits area." The letter continued, "While students can use this area to enter or leave the school campus before and after

A. VAGUENESS AND THE NEED FOR PRE-EXISTING RULES

school, loitering is not permitted in this area. A three-day suspension will be given to any student who is present in this area." The Hamlin Gate Area was placed off limits to students because community members in the area had complained about students' lack of respect for their property and disregard for traffic safety regulations.

The next day, defendant Judy Bovenmyer ("dean Bovenmyer"), the Dean of Students at the high school, advised Wiemerslage that he was observed in violation of the loitering rule. Dean Bovenmyer informed Wiemerslage that he was to be suspended from school for three days for loitering in the Hamlin Gate Area and advised his parents of the incident, the discussion, and the suspension. Wiemerslage's parents later met with dean Bovenmyer to review the matter after receiving the notification letter from her. A second informal hearing was also conducted, this time with principal Cachur. Following the second hearing, Wiemerslage's father requested a formal hearing into the suspension and in October 1992 a formal hearing was conducted. After the formal hearing, Wiemerslage's parents were notified that the Board of Education of Maine Township High School District 207 let the suspension stand.

Wiemerslage filed a single count complaint alleging that the defendants violated his rights to free speech and assembly under the first amendment, applicable through the fourteenth amendment, and also that the school's loitering rule violates due process under the fourteenth amendment. Wiemerslage claims in conclusory fashion that the defendants' aforementioned acts violated his right to exercise freedom of speech and assembly, and that defendants collectively acted with the intent of depriving Wiemerslage of these first amendment rights. Further, Wiemerslage maintains the disciplinary rule impermissibly controls the non-academic actions of school students on a public way beyond the boundaries of school property, is unconstitutionally vague on its face and as applied to his conduct, and fails to provide any procedural guidelines assuring prompt judicial review of a suspension.

Discussion

....

Federal judicial intervention in the day to day operations of public schools is highly undesirable and requires significant restraint. Federal courts must not "intervene in the resolution of conflicts which arise in the daily operation of school systems and which do not directly and sharply implicate basic constitutional values." *Epperson v. Arkansas*, 393 U.S. 97, 104 (1968). The court will consider the complaint with these principles in mind.

The primary challenge Wiemerslage mounts against the disciplinary rule disallowing loitering in the Hamlin Gate Area is that of vagueness. The vagueness doctrine guarantees that legal prohibitions will be clearly defined. *Grayned v. City of Rockford*, 408 U.S. 104, 108 (1972). If people of common intelligence must guess at an enactment's meaning and differ as to its application, the law is unconstitutionally vague and is void. *Hynes v. Oradell*, 425 U.S. 610,

620-22 (1976). Accordingly, an enactment must define the prohibited conduct with sufficient definiteness such that an ordinary individual understands just what conduct is prohibited and must define the prohibited conduct in a manner discouraging arbitrary and discriminatory enforcement.

The court recognizes the potential vagueness of the word "loitering" and also the failure of the disciplinary rule to provide a definition that would cast the word in narrow terms. Notwithstanding these concerns, vagueness considerations do not apply equally in all situations; the degree of clarity required of an enactment depends on the nature of the enactment. Appropriately, school disciplinary regulations need not be drawn with the same precision of a criminal statute. *Linwood v. Board of Education*, 463 F.2d 763, 767 (7th Cir.), *cert. denied*, 409 U.S. 1027 (1972); *Soglin v. Kauffman*, 418 F.2d 163, 168 (7th Cir.1969); *see also Shamloo v. Mississippi State Bd. of Trustees*, 620 F.2d 516, 521-22 (5th Cir.1980). The special needs of the school system warrant a broader sweep in school regulations than might be permissible in a criminal code. Further, the management of school affairs is left largely to the discretion of school boards. *Board of Educ. v. Pico*, 457 U.S. 853, 863-64 (1982). This court, therefore, does not consider a school disciplinary policy void for vagueness merely because the meaning of a term of the policy is understood by reference to definable sources other than a school manual or the rule itself.

The disciplinary rule prohibiting loitering in the Hamlin Gate Area gives parents and students a clear and specific explanation of the prohibited conduct. The August 1992 letter makes it plain that students may pass through this area to and from school but may not pause to congregate. At a minimum, "loiter" means "to delay ... with aimless idle stops and pauses" and "to remain in an area for no obvious reason." Webster's Ninth New Collegiate Dictionary 703 (1986). It also is defined as "to linger aimlessly or as if aimlessly in or about a place," "to move in a slow, idle manner; make purposeless stops in the course of a[n] ... errand," "to waste time ...," and "to pass (time) in an idle or aimless manner...." Webster's Encyclopedic Unabridged Dictionary of the English Language 843 (1989). These simple dictionary definitions of loitering are sufficiently clear to place an average student on notice of what conduct is prohibited.

Moreover, like the ordinance in *Grayned*, the high school's loitering rule is written specifically for the school context where the prohibited conduct is easily measured against the normal activities of the school. *Grayned*, 408 U.S. at 112. It cannot be said that the school does not maintain an important interest in students' affairs during their ingress or egress to and from school property. Further, the school may properly protect the property rights of those living in the surrounding homes by exercising its power *in loco parentis* to guide student behavior in such a way as to avoid vandalism or harm to the students. Schools are saddled with a vital responsibility to transmit community values and to promote respect for authority as well as for social, moral, or political values. *Pico*, 457 U.S. at 864. The scope of school officials' management of student conduct is "comprehensive." *Tinker v. Des Moines Independent Community School Dist.*, 393 U.S. 503, 507 (1969). Moreover, the loitering rule is crafted to apply to a specified area and does not merely prevent loitering on the public streets in general. Given the particular school context of the loitering rule, the disciplinary rule gives fair notice to those to whom it is directed and clearly delineates its reach in terms of common understanding....

Wiemerslage attacks the use of the phrase "Hamlin Gate Area." Although conceding that it is common knowledge within the school population that the Hamlin Gate is the particular fence gate that is situated adjacent to the public street known as "Hamlin Avenue," Wiemerslage questions whether the area covered by the disciplinary rule extends to the fence-gate proper or for some distance beyond the fence away from the school property. The court does not find the term troubling. "Condemned to the use of words, we can never expect mathematical certainty from our language." *Id.* at 110. "[T]he fertile legal 'imagination can conjure up hypothetical cases in which the meaning of [disputed] terms will be in nice question.'" *Id.* at 110, n. 15, (quoting *American Communications Ass'n v. Douds*, 339 U.S. 382, 412 (1950)). The Supreme Court has held that term "near the courthouse" is not unconstitutionally vague, *Cox v. Louisiana*, 379 U.S. 559, 568-69 (1965).... Similarily, "Hamlin Gate Area" is not vague.

The concern that the loitering rule places unfettered discretion in the hands of school officials is tenuous. School officials are afforded broad discretion in enforcement of school codes because of the important interests and responsibilities affiliated with school administration. *Pico*, 457 U.S. at 863-64. There are no specific standards governing the exercise of the discretion granted school officials by the loitering rule, but the disciplinary enforcement. All students found lingering, idling, or lolling in the Hamlin Gate Area are subject to the rule; and like the word "near" in *Cox*, the disciplinary rule allows for proper administrative discretion in the limited control of the areas in the immediate vicinity of the school. *See Cox*, 379 U.S. at 569. The students' common understanding of the Hamlin Gate Area provides ample notice that they are not to remain in this area for any period of time longer than is necessary to enter or exit the school and proceed to their destinations.

....

Rather than a work of painstaking particularity, the language of the loitering disciplinary rule is indeed flexible and broad. But flexibility and reasonable breadth are acceptable as long as it is clear what the rule as a whole prohibits. *See Grayned*, 408 U.S. at 111. The loitering rule delineates with sufficient clarity the conduct prohibited by the school officials and thus gives fair notice to students that they are not to stand in the Hamlin Gate Area but are to proceed through it. The suspension, furthermore, was accomplished through the appropriate procedures, and Wiemerslage fails to allege a violation of his first amendment rights to free speech or assembly.

Conclusion

The court grants the defendants' motion to dismiss ....

It is so ordered.

---

1. "Interstudent communication does not interfere with what a school teaches; it enriches the school environment for the students." *Burch v. Barker*, 861 F.2d at 1159. Does this court reach a decision that creates too much of a disparity between school-sponsored and non-school-sponsored activities on school property? Is there a point at which interstudent communications interfere with the school's authority to teach?

Should schools have at least some authority in these cases? *See Bystrom v. Fridley*, 822 F.2d 747 (8th Cir. 1987), where the Eighth Circuit upheld a school's prior review guidelines for underground newspapers (the rule prohibited material that was pervasively indecent or vulgar).

In *Slotterback v. Interboro Sch. Dist.*, 766 F. Supp. 280 (E.D. Pa. 1991), the district court found a genuine issue of material fact as to whether school officials had reason to anticipate that substantial interference with the work of the school would recur if students were permitted to continue their distribution of non-school materials. However, the court went on to decide that the school regulation was overly broad and gave school officials unbridled discretion to suppress protected speech in advance. *See also Rivera v. East Otero Sch. Dist.*, 721 F. Supp. 1189 (D. Colo. 1989). (Held unlawful a ban on material that proselytizes particular religious or political belief).

2. Is the *Wiemerslage* case comparable to the underground newspaper cases cited above? Consider this question with regard to the school's authority to control students' non-academic activities. Which set of cases warrants *more* school authority? Which involves a higher potential for interference with school operation and activity? What interest did the school assert in *Wiemerslage*?

3. *Wiemerslage* references a letter sent to all parents at Maine Township High School with the following passage:

> While students can use [the Hamlin Gate] area to enter or leave the school campus before and after school, loitering is not permitted in this area. A three-day suspension will be given to any student who is present in this area. 824 F. Supp. at 138-139.

Does the second sentence breathe some life into a claim for overbreadth? If so, why was this not an element in the court's decision? Could it have been that the court believed the school rule less egregious than the student conduct? Is it that the trier of fact had already settled on a rule of conduct and found the activities of the student contrary to these standards?

4. At least one court had determined that vague or overbroad school rules may allow too much discretion on the part of school administrators and that this may result in racial discrimination. In *Sherpell v. Humnoke Sch. Dist. No. 5*, 619 F. Supp. 670 (E.D. Ark.), *appeal dismissed*, 814 F.2d 538 (8th Cir. 1985), this combination of vagueness and discretion meant that African-American students were being disciplined for behaviors white students were not being disciplined for. The court ordered that "uniform and objective guidelines be established to eliminate the opportunity to administer discipline on an uneven handed basis." *Id.* at 677.

B. RIGHT TO AN ADMINISTRATIVE HEARING

Two basic problems arise when students are confronted with potential disciplinary actions. The first is whether or at what time the law requires an administrative hearing in conjunction with a given school action; the second deals with the attributes of such a hearing. The question that pervades the development of the law in this area is whether the trend toward greater formalization, "legalization," and adversariness in school disciplinary proceedings is a good one. Is the adversary method a good system of decision-making in this context? Is it better than such other things as the use of an ombudsman, mediation, or counseling? Do the delays necessitated by the adversary process dilute the effectiveness of the punishment? These and other questions will be addressed in section 1 of the following materials.

Section 2 addresses the other side of the due process coin — what remedies are available to the student and what sanctions can be levied against teachers and administrators when administrative procedures are not followed. It is hoped that the exploration of both rights and remedies in this particularly difficult and complex area will provide the reader with a better understanding of these closely related problems.

1. DUE PROCESS REQUIREMENTS

DIXON v. ALABAMA STATE BOARD OF EDUCATION

United States Court of Appeals
294 F.2d 150 (5th Cir.), *cert. denied*, 368 U.S. 930 (1961)

RIVES, CIRCUIT JUDGE:

The question presented by the pleadings and evidence, and decisive of this appeal, is whether due process requires notice and some opportunity for hearing before students at a tax-supported college are expelled for misconduct. We answer that question in the affirmative.

The misconduct for which the students were expelled has never been definitely specified. Defendant Trenholm, the President of the College, testified that he did not know why the plaintiffs and three additional students were expelled and twenty other students were placed on probation. The notice of expulsion which

Dr. Trenholm mailed to each of the plaintiffs assigned no specific ground for expulsion, but referred in general terms to "this problem of Alabama State College."

The acts of the students considered by the State Board of Education before it ordered their expulsion are described in the opinion of the district court reported in 186 F. Supp. 945, 947, from which we quote in the margin.[3]

As shown by the findings of the district court, just quoted in footnote 3, the only demonstration which the evidence showed that *all* of the expelled students took part in was that in the lunch grill located in the basement of the Montgomery County Courthouse. The other demonstrations were found to be attended "by several if not all of the plaintiffs." We have carefully read and studied the record, and agree with the district court that the evidence does not affirmatively show that all of the plaintiffs were present at any but the one demonstration.

---

[3]"On the 25th day of February, 1960, the six plaintiffs in this case were students in good standing at the Alabama State College for Negroes in Montgomery, Alabama.... On this date, approximately twenty-nine Negro students, including these six plaintiffs, according to a prearranged plan, entered as a group a publicly owned lunch grill located in the basement of the county courthouse in Montgomery, Alabama, and asked to be served. Service was refused; the lunch-room was closed; the Negroes refused to leave; police authorities were summoned; and the Negroes were ordered outside where they remained in the corridor of the courthouse for approximately one hour. On the same date, John Patterson, as Governor of the State of Alabama and as chairman of the State Board of Education, conferred with Dr. Trenholm, a Negro educator and president of the Alabama State College, concerning this activity on the part of some of the students. Dr. Trenholm was advised by the Governor that the incident should be investigated, and that if he were in the president's position he would consider expulsion and/or other appropriate disciplinary action. On February 26, 1960, several hundred Negro students from the Alabama State College, including several if not all of these plaintiffs, staged a mass attendance at a trial being held in the Montgomery County Courthouse, involving the perjury prosecution of a fellow student. After the trial these students filed two by two from the courthouse and marched through the city approximately two miles back to the college. On February 27, 1960, several hundred Negro Students from this school, including several if not all of the plaintiffs in this case, staged mass demonstrations in Montgomery and Tuskegee, Alabama. On this same date, Dr. Trenholm advised all of the student body that these demonstrations and meetings were disrupting the orderly conduct of the business at the college and were affecting the work of other students, as well as work of the participating students. Dr. Trenholm personally warned plaintiffs Bernard Lee, Joseph Peterson and Elroy Embry, to cease these disruptive demonstrations immediately, and advised the members of the student body at the Alabama State College to behave themselves and return to their classes....

"On or about March 1, 1960, approximately six hundred students of the Alabama State College engaged in hymn singing and speech making on the steps of the State Capitol. Plaintiff Bernard Lee addressed students at this demonstration, and the demonstration was attended by several if not all of the plaintiffs. Plaintiff Bernard Lee at this time called on the students to strike and boycott the college if any students were expelled because of these demonstrations."

B. RIGHT TO AN ADMINISTRATIVE HEARING 399

Only one member of the State Board of Education assigned the demonstration attended by all of the plaintiffs as the sole basis for his vote to expel them. Mr. Harry Ayers testified:

Q. Mr. Ayers, did you vote to expel these negro students because they went to the Court House and asked to be served at the white lunch counter?
A. No, I voted because they violated a law of Alabama.
Q. What law of Alabama had they violated?
A. That separating of the races in public places of that kind.
Q. And the fact that they went up there and requested service, by violating the Alabama law, then you voted to have them expelled?
A. Yes.
Q. And that is your reason why you voted?
A. That is the reason.

The most elaborate grounds for expulsion were assigned in the testimony of Governor Patterson:

Q. There is an allegation in the complaint, Governor, that — I believe it is paragraph six, the defendants' action of expulsion was taken without regard to any valid rule or regulation concerning student conduct and merely retaliated against, punished, and sought to intimidate plaintiffs for having lawfully sought service in a publicly owned lunch room with service; is that statement true or false?
A. Well, that is not true; the action taken by the State Board of Education was — was taken to prevent — to prevent incidents happening by students at the College that would bring — bring discredit upon — upon the School and be prejudicial to the School, and the State — as I said before, the State Board of Education took — considered at the time it expelled these students several incidents, one at the Court House at the lunch room demonstration, the one the next day at the trial of this student, the marching on the steps of the State Capitol, and also this rally held at the church, where — where it was reported that — that statements were made against the administration of the School. In addition to that, the — the feeling going around in the community here due to — due to the reports of these incidents of the students, by the students, and due to reports of incidents occurring involving violence in other States, which happened prior to these things starting here in Alabama, all of these things were discussed by the State Board of Education prior to the taking of the action that they did on March 2 and as I was present and acting as Chairman, as a member of the Board, I voted to expel these students and to put these others on probation because I felt that that was what was in the best interest of the College. And the — I felt that the action should be — should be prompt and immediate, because if something — something had not been done, in my opinion, it would have resulted in violence and disorder, and that we wanted to prevent, and we felt

that we had a duty to the — to the parents of the students and to the State to require that the students behave themselves while they are attending a State College, and that is (sic) the reasons why we took the action that we did. That is all.

Superintendent of Education Stewart testified that he voted for expulsion because the students had broken rules and regulations pertaining to all of the State institutions, and, when required to be more specific, testified:

> The Court: What rule had been broken is the question, that justified the expulsion insofar as he is concerned?
> A. I think demonstrations without the consent of the president of an institution.

The testimony of other members of the Board assigned somewhat varying and differing grounds and reasons for their votes to expel the plaintiffs.

The district court found the general nature of the proceedings before the State Board of Education, the action of the Board, and the official notice of expulsion given to the students as follows:

> Investigations into this conduct were made by Dr. Trenholm, as president of the Alabama State College, the Director of Public Safety for the State of Alabama under directions of the Governor, and by the investigative staff of the Attorney General for the State of Alabama.
>
> On or about March 2, 1960, the State Board of Education met and received reports from the Governor of the State of Alabama, which reports embodied the investigations that had been made and which reports identified these six plaintiffs, together with several others, as the "ring leaders" for the group of students that had been participating in the above-recited activities. During this meeting, Dr. Trenholm, in his capacity as president of the college reported to the assembled members of the State Board of Education that the action of these students in demonstrating on the college campus and in certain downtown areas was having a disruptive influence on the work of the other students at the college and upon the orderly operation of the college in general. Dr. Trenholm further reported to the Board that, in his opinion, he as president of the college could not control future disruptions and demonstrations. There were twenty-nine of the Negro students identified as the core of the organization that was responsible for these demonstrations. This group of twenty-nine included these six plaintiffs. After hearing these reports and recommendations and upon the recommendation of the Governor as chairman of the Board, the Board voted unanimously, expelling nine students, including these six plaintiffs, and placing twenty students on probation. This action was taken by Dr. Trenholm as president of the college, acting pursuant to the instructions of the State Board of Education. Each of these plaintiffs, together with the other students expelled, was officially notified of his expulsion on March 4th or 5th, 1960.

No formal charges were placed against these students and no hearing was granted any of them prior to their expulsion. *Dixon v. Alabama State Board of Educ.* (D.C.M.D. Ala. 1960), 186 F. Supp. 945, 948-49.

The evidence clearly shows that the question for decision does not concern the sufficiency of the notice or the adequacy of the hearing, but is whether the students had a right to any notice or hearing whatever before being expelled.

. . . .

Whenever a governmental body acts so as to injure an individual, the Constitution requires that the act be consonant with due process of law. The minimum procedural requirements necessary to satisfy due process depend upon the circumstances and the interests of the parties involved. As stated by Mr. Justice Frankfurter concurring in *Joint Anti-Fascist Refugee Committee v. McGrath,* 1951, 341 U.S. 123, 163:

> Whether the *ex parte* procedure to which the petitioners were subjected duly observed "the rudiments of fair play", ... cannot ... be tested by mere generalities or sentiments abstractly appealing. The precise nature of the interest that has been adversely affected, the manner in which this was done, the reasons for doing it, the available alternatives to the procedure that was followed, the protection implicit in the office of the functionary whose conduct is challenged, the balance of hurt complained of and good accomplished — these are some of the considerations that must enter into the judicial judgment.

Just last month, a closely divided Supreme Court held in a case where the governmental power was almost absolute and the private interest was slight that no hearing was required. *Cafeteria and Restaurant Workers Union v. McElroy et al.*, 1961, 81 S.Ct. 1743. In that case, a short-order cook working for a privately operated cafeteria on the premises of the Naval Gun Factory in the City of Washington was excluded from the Gun Factory as a security risk. So, too, the due process clause does not require that an alien never admitted to this country be granted a hearing before being *excluded. United States ex rel. Knauff v. Shaughnessy,* 1950, 338 U.S. 537, 542-43. In such case the executive power as implemented by Congress to exclude aliens is absolute and not subject to the review of any court, unless expressly authorized by Congress. On the other hand, once an alien has been admitted to lawful residence in the United States and remains physically present here it has been held that, "although Congress may prescribe conditions for his expulsion and deportation, not even Congress may expel him without allowing him a fair opportunity to be heard." *Kwong Hai Chew v. Colding,* 1953, 344 U.S. 590, 597-98.

It is not enough to say, as did the district court in the present case, "The right to attend a public college or university is not in and of itself a constitutional right." 186 F. Supp. at page 950. That argument was emphatically answered by the Supreme Court in the *Cafeteria and Restaurant Workers Union* case, *supra,*

[81 S.Ct. 1748.] when it said that the question of whether "... summarily denying Rachel Brawner access to the site of her former employment violated the requirements of the Due Process Clause of the Fifth Amendment ... cannot be answered by easy assertion that, because she had no constitutional right to be there in the first place, she was not deprived of liberty or property by the Superintendent's action. 'One may not have a constitutional right to go to Bagdad, but the Government may not prohibit one from going there unless by means consonant with due process of law.'" As in that case, so here, it is necessary to consider "the nature both of the private interest which has been impaired and the governmental power which has been exercised."

The appellees urge upon us that under a provision of the Board of Education's regulations the appellants waived any right to notice and a hearing before being expelled for misconduct.

> Attendance at any college is on the basis of a mutual decision of the student's parents and of the college. Attendance at a particular college is voluntary and is different from attendance at a public school where the pupil may be required to attend a particular school which is located in the neighborhood or district in which the pupil's family may live. Just as a student may choose to withdraw from a particular college at any time for any personally determined reason, the college may also at any time decline to continue to accept responsibility for the supervision and service to any student with whom the relationship becomes unpleasant and difficult.

We do not read this provision to clearly indicate an intent on the part of the student to waive notice and a hearing before expulsion. If, however, we should so assume, it nonetheless remains true that the State cannot condition the granting of even a privilege upon the renunciation of the constitutional right to procedural due process. Only private associations have the right to obtain a waiver of notice and hearing before depriving a member of a valuable right. And even here, the right to notice and a hearing is so fundamental to the conduct of our society that the waiver must be clear and explicit. *Medical and Surgical Society of Montgomery County v. Weatherly*, 75 Ala. 248, 256-59. In the absence of such an explicit waiver, Alabama has required that even private associations must provide notice and a hearing before expulsion. In *Medical and Surgical Society of Montgomery County v. Weatherly*, *supra*, it was held that a physician could not be expelled from a medical society without notice and a hearing. In *Local Union No. 57, etc. v. Boyd*, 1944, 245 Ala. 227, 16 So. 2d 705, 711, a local union was ordered to reinstate one of its members expelled after a hearing of which he had insufficient notice.

The precise nature of the private interest involved in this case is the right to remain at a public institution of higher learning in which the plaintiffs were students in good standing. It requires no argument to demonstrate that education is vital and, indeed, basic to civilized society. Without sufficient education the plaintiffs would not be able to earn an adequate livelihood, to enjoy life to the

B. RIGHT TO AN ADMINISTRATIVE HEARING

fullest, or to fulfill as completely as possible the duties and responsibilities of good citizens.

There was no offer to prove that other colleges are open to the plaintiffs. If so, the plaintiffs would nonetheless be injured by the interruption of their course of studies in mid-term. It is most unlikely that a public college would accept a student expelled from another public college of the same state. Indeed, expulsion may well prejudice the student in completing his education at any other institution. Surely no one can question that the right to remain at the college in which the plaintiffs were students in good standing is an interest of extremely great value.

Turning then to the nature of the governmental power to expel the plaintiffs, it must be conceded, as was held by the district court, that that power is not unlimited and cannot be arbitrarily exercised. Admittedly, there must be some reasonable and constitutional ground for expulsion or the courts would have a duty to require reinstatement. The possibility of arbitrary action is not excluded by the existence of reasonable regulations. There may be arbitrary application of the rule to the facts of a particular case. Indeed, that result is well nigh inevitable when the Board hears only one side of the issue. In the disciplining of college students there are no considerations of immediate danger to the public, or of peril to the national security, which should prevent the Board from exercising at least the fundamental principles of fairness by giving the accused students notice of the charges and an opportunity to be heard in their own defense. Indeed, the example set by the Board in failing so to do, if not corrected by the courts, can well break the spirits of the expelled students and of others familiar with the injustice, and do inestimable harm to their education.

The district court, however, felt that it was governed by precedent, and stated that, "the courts have consistently upheld the validity of regulations that have the effect of reserving to the college the right to dismiss students at any time for any reason without divulging its reason other than its being for the general benefit of the institution." [186 F. Supp. 951.] With deference, we must hold that the district court has simply misinterpreted the precedents.

The language above quoted from the district court is based upon language found in 14 C.J.S. Colleges and Universities § 26, p. 1360, which, in turn, is paraphrased from *Anthony v. Syracuse University*, 224 App. Div. 487, 231 N.Y.S. 435, *reversing* 130 Misc. 2d 249, 223 N.Y.S. 796-97. (14 C.J.S. Colleges and Universities § 26, pp. 1360, 1363 note 70.) This case, however, concerns a private university and follows the well-settled rule that the relations between a student and a private university are a matter of contract. The *Anthony* case held that the plaintiffs had specifically waived their rights to notice and hearing. *See also Barker v. Bryn Mawr* (1923), 278 Pa. 121, 122 A. 220. The precedents for public colleges are collected in a recent annotation cited by the district court. 58 A.L.R.2d 903-20. We have read all of the cases cited to the point, and we agree with what the annotator himself says: "The cases involving suspension or expulsion of a student from a public college or university all involve the question whether the hearing given to the student was adequate. In every instance the sufficiency of the hearing was upheld." 58 A.L.R.2d at page 909. None held that no hearing whatsoever was required. Two cases not found in the annotation have held that some form of hearing is required. In *Commonwealth ex rel. Hill v. McCauley* (1886), 3 Pa. Co. Ct. R. 77, the court went so far as to say that an informal presentation of the charges was insufficient and that a state-supported college must grant a student a full hearing on the charges before expulsion for misconduct. In *Gleason v. University of Minnesota* (1908), 104 Minn. 359, 116 N.W. 650, on reviewing the overruling of the state's demurrer to a petition for mandamus for reinstatement, the court held that the plaintiff stated a *prima facie* case upon showing that he had been expelled without a hearing for alleged insufficiency in work and acts of insubordination against the faculty.

The appellees rely also upon *Lucy v. Adams*, D.C.N.D. Ala. 1957, 134 F. Supp. 235, where Autherine Lucy was expelled from the University of Alabama without notice or hearing. That case, however, is not in point. Autherine Lucy did not raise the issue of an absence of notice or hearing.

It was not a case denying any hearing whatsoever but one passing upon the adequacy of the hearing, which provoked from Professor Warren A. Seavey of Harvard the eloquent comment:

> At this time when many are worried about dismissal from public service, when only because of the overriding need to protect the public safety is the identity of informers kept secret, when we proudly contrast the full hearings before our courts with those in the benighted countries which have no due process protection, when many of our courts are so careful in the protection of those charged with crimes that they will not permit the use of evidence illegally obtained, our sense of justice should be outraged by denial to students of the normal safeguards. It is shocking that the officials of a state educational institution, which can function properly only if our freedoms are preserved, should not understand the elementary principles of fair play. It is equally shocking to find that a court supports them in denying to a student the protection given to a pickpocket. Seavey, *Dismissal of Students: "Due Process,"* 70 Harv. L. Rev. 1406-07.

We are confident that precedent as well as a most fundamental constitutional principle support our holding that due process requires notice and some opportunity for hearing before a student at a tax-supported college is expelled for misconduct.

For the guidance of the parties in the event of further proceedings, we state our views on the nature of the notice and hearing required by due process prior to expulsion from a state college or university. They should, we think, comply with the following standards. The notice should contain a statement of the specific charges and grounds which, if proven, would justify expulsion under the regulations of the Board of Education. The nature of the hearing should vary depending upon the circumstances of the particular case. The case before us requires something more than an informal interview with an administrative authority of the college. By its nature, a charge of misconduct, as opposed to a failure to meet the scholastic standards of the college, depends upon a collection of the facts concerning the charged misconduct, easily colored by the point of view of the witnesses. In such circumstances, a hearing which gives the Board or the administrative authorities of the college an opportunity to hear both sides in considerable detail is best suited to protect the rights of all involved. This is not to imply that a full-dress judicial hearing, with the right to cross-examine witnesses, is required. Such a hearing, with the attending publicity and disturbance of college activities, might be detrimental to the college's educational atmosphere and impractical to carry out. Nevertheless, the rudiments of an adversary proceeding may be preserved without encroaching upon the interests of the college. In the instant case, the student should be given the names of the witnesses against him and an oral or written report on the facts to which each witness testifies. He should also be given the opportunity to present to the Board, or at least to an administrative official of the college, his own defense against the charges and to produce either oral testimony or written affidavits of witnesses in his behalf. If the hearing is not before the Board directly, the results and findings of the hearing should be presented in a report open to the student's inspection. If these rudimentary elements of fair play are followed in a case of misconduct of this particular type, we feel that the requirements of due process of law will have been fulfilled.

The judgment of the district court is reversed and the cause is remanded for further proceedings consistent with this opinion.

Reversed and remanded.

GOSS v. LOPEZ

Supreme Court of the United States
419 U.S. 565 (1975)

MR. JUSTICE WHITE delivered the opinion of the Court:

This appeal by various administrators of the Columbus, Ohio, Public School System (CPSS) challenges the judgment of a three-judge federal court, declaring that appellees — various high school students in the CPSS — were denied due process of law contrary to the command of the Fourteenth Amendment in that they were temporarily suspended from their high schools without a hearing either prior to suspension or within a reasonable time thereafter, and enjoining the administrators to remove all references to such suspensions from the students' records.

I

Ohio law, Rev. Code Ann. § 3313.64 (1972), provides for free education to all children between the ages of six and 21. Section 3313.66 of the Code empowers the principal of an Ohio public school to suspend a pupil for misconduct for up to 10 days or to expel him. In either case, he must notify the student's parents within 24 hours and state the reasons for his action. A pupil who is expelled, or his parents, may appeal the decision to the Board of Education and in connection therewith shall be permitted to be heard at the board meeting. The Board may reinstate the pupil following the hearing. No similar procedure is provided in § 3313.66 or any other provision of state law for a suspended student. Aside from a regulation tracking the statute, at the time of the imposition of the suspensions in this case the CPSS itself had not issued any written procedure applicable to suspension.[1] Nor, so far as the record reflects, had any of the individual high schools involved in this case. Each, however, had formally or informally described the conduct for which suspension could be imposed.

The nine named appellees, each of whom alleged that he or she had been suspended from public high school in Columbus for up to 10 days without a hearing pursuant to § 3313.66, filed an action under 42 U.S.C. § 1983 against the Columbus Board of Education and various administrators of the CPSS. The complaint sought a declaration that § 3313.66 was unconstitutional in that it permitted public school administrators to deprive plaintiffs of their rights to an education without a hearing of any kind, in violation of the procedural due process component of the Fourteenth Amendment. It also sought to enjoin the public school officials from issuing future suspensions pursuant to § 3313.66 and to require them to remove references to the past suspensions from the records of the students in question.

. . . .

[The nine named plaintiffs were involved in a variety of student disturbances and demonstrations which arose out of a period of wide-spread student unrest in

---

[1] At the time of the events involved in this case, the only administrative regulation on this subject was § 1010.04 of the Administrative Guide of the Columbus Public Schools which provided: "Pupils may be suspended or expelled from school in accordance with the provisions of Section 3313.66 of the Revised Code." Subsequent to the events involved in this lawsuit, the Department of Pupil Personnel of the CPSS issued three memoranda relating to suspension procedures, dated August 16, 1971, February 21, 1973, and July 10, 1973, respectively. The first two are substantially similar to each other and require no factfinding hearing at any time in connection with a suspension. The third, which was apparently in effect when this case was argued, places upon the principal the obligation to "investigate" "before commencing suspension procedures"; and provides as part of the procedures that the principal shall discuss the case with the pupil, so that the pupil may "be heard with respect to the alleged offense," unless the pupil is "unavailable" for such a discussion or "unwilling" to participate in it. The suspensions involved in this case occurred, and records thereof were made, prior to the effective date of these memoranda. The District Court's judgment, including its expunction order, turns on the propriety of the procedures existing at the time the suspensions were ordered and by which they were imposed.

B. RIGHT TO AN ADMINISTRATIVE HEARING

the CPSS during February and March 1971. All of the named plaintiffs were suspended for ten days or less by various school authorities.

The evidence did not show that any of the plaintiffs were provided a hearing to determine the operative facts of their suspensions. On the basis of this evidence, a three-judge court declared that plaintiffs were denied due process of law because they were "suspended without a hearing prior to suspension or without reasonable time thereafter," and that Ohio Rev. Code Ann. Sec. 3313.66 (1972) and regulations issued pursuant thereto were unconstitutional in permitting such suspensions. It was ordered that all references to plaintiffs suspensions be removed from school files. This order was appealed to the Supreme Court by defendant school administrators.]

II

At the outset, appellants contend that because there is no constitutional right to an education at public expense, the Due Process Clause does not protect against expulsions from the public school system. This position misconceives the nature of the issue and is refuted by prior decisions. The Fourteenth Amendment forbids the State to deprive any person of life, liberty, or property without due process of law. Protected interests in property are normally "not created by the Constitution. Rather, they are created and their dimensions are defined" by an independent source such as state statutes or rules entitling the citizen to certain benefits. *Board of Regents v. Roth*, 408 U.S. 564, 577 (1972).

Accordingly, a state employee who under state law, or rules promulgated by state officials, has a legitimate claim of entitlement to continued employment absent sufficient cause for discharge may demand the procedural protections of due process. So may welfare recipients who have statutory rights to welfare as long as they maintain the specified qualifications. *Goldberg v. Kelly*, 397 U.S. 254 (1970). *Morrissey v. Brewer*, 408 U.S. 471 (1972), applied the limitations of the Due Process Clause to governmental decisions to revoke parole, although a parolee has no constitutional right to that status. In like vein was *Wolf v. McDonnell*, 418 U.S. 539 (1974), where the procedural protections of the Due Process Clause were triggered by official cancellation of a prisoner's good-time credits accumulated under state law, although those benefits were not mandated by the Constitution.

Here, on the basis of state law, appellees plainly had legitimate claims of entitlement to a public education. Ohio Rev. Code Ann. §§ 3313.48 and 3313.64 (1972 and Supp. 1973) direct local authorities to provide a free education to all residents between five and 21 years of age, and a compulsory-attendance law requires attendance for a school year of not less than 32 weeks. Ohio Rev. Code Ann. § 3321.04 (1972). It is true that § 3313.66 of the Code permits school principals to suspend students for up to 10 days; but suspensions may not be imposed without any grounds whatsoever. All of the schools had their own rules specifying the grounds for expulsion or suspension. Having chosen to extend the right to an education to people of appellees' class generally, Ohio may not withdraw that right on grounds of misconduct, absent fundamentally fair procedures to determine whether the misconduct has occurred.

Although Ohio may not be constitutionally obligated to establish and maintain a public school system, it has nevertheless done so and has required its children to attend. Those young people do not "shed their constitutional rights" at the schoolhouse door. *Tinker v. Des Moines School Dist.*, 393 U.S. 503, 506 (1969). "The Fourteenth Amendment, as now applied to the States, protects the citizen against the State itself and all of its creatures — Boards of Education not excepted." *West Virginia Board of Education v. Barnette*, 319 U.S. 624, 637 (1943). The authority possessed by the State to prescribe and enforce standards of conduct in its schools although concededly very broad, must be exercised consistently with constitutional safeguards. Among other things, the State is constrained to recognize a student's legitimate entitlement to a public education as a property interest which is protected by the Due Process Clause and which may not be taken away for misconduct without adherence to the minimum procedures required by that Clause.

The Due Process Clause also forbids arbitrary deprivations of liberty. "Where a person's good name, reputation, honor, or integrity is at stake because of what the government is doing to him," the minimal requirements of the Clause must be satisfied. *Wisconsin v. Constantineau*, 400 U.S. 433, 437 (1971); *Board of Regents v. Roth, supra,* at 573. School authorities here suspended appellees from school for periods of up to 10 days based on charges of misconduct. If sustained and recorded, those charges could seriously damage the students' standing with their fellow pupils and their teachers as well as interfere with later opportunities for higher education and employment. It is apparent that the claimed right of the State to determine unilaterally and without process whether that misconduct has occurred immediately collides with the requirements of the Constitution.

Appellants proceed to argue that even if there is a right to a public education protected by the Due Process Clause generally, the Clause comes into play only when the State subjects a student to a "severe detriment or grievous loss." The loss of 10 days, it is said, is neither severe nor grievous and the Due Process Clause is therefore of no relevance. Appellants argument is again refuted by our prior decisions; for in determining "whether due process requirements apply in the first place, we must look not to the 'weight' but to the *nature* of the interest at stake." *Board of Regents v. Roth, supra,* at 570-71. Appellees were excluded from school only temporarily, it is true, but the length and consequent severity of a deprivation, while another factor to weigh in determining the appropriate form of hearing, "is not decisive of the basic right" to a hearing of some kind. *Fuentes v. Shevin*, 407 U.S. 67, 86 (1972). The Court's view has been that as long as a property deprivation is not *de minimis,* its gravity is irrelevant to the question whether account must be taken of the Due Process Clause. A 10-day suspension from school is not *de minimis* in our view and may not be imposed in complete disregard of the Due Process Clause.

A short suspension is, of course, a far milder deprivation than expulsion. But, "education is perhaps the most important function of state and local governments," *Brown v. Board of Education*, 347 U.S. 483, 493 (1954), and the total exclusion from the educational process for more than a trivial period, and certainly if the suspension is for 10 days, is a serious event in the life of the suspended child. Neither the property interest in education benefits temporarily denied nor the liberty interest in reputation, which is also implicated, is so insubstantial that suspensions may constitutionally be imposed by any procedure the school chooses, no matter how arbitrary.[8]

III

"Once it is determined that due process applies, the question remains what process is due." *Morrissey v. Brewer*, 408 U.S. at 481.

. . . .

There are certain bench marks to guide us.... *Mullane v. Central Hanover Trust Co.*, 339 U.S. 306 (1950), a case often invoked by later opinions, said that "[m]any controversies have raged about the cryptic and abstract words of the Due Process Clause but there can be no doubt that at a minimum they require that deprivation of life, liberty or property by adjudication be preceded by notice and opportunity for hearing appropriate to the nature of the case." *Id.* at 313. "The fundamental requisite of due process of law is the opportunity to be heard," *Grannis v. Ordean*, 234 U.S. 385, 394 (1914), a right that "has little reality or worth unless one is informed that the matter is pending and can choose for himself whether to ... contest." *Mullane v. Central Hanover Trust Co.*, *supra*, at 314. At the very minimum, therefore, students facing suspension and the consequent interference with a protected property interest must be given some kind of notice and afforded some kind of hearing. "Parties whose rights are to be affected are entitled to be heard; and in order that they may enjoy that right they must first be notified." *Baldwin v. Hale*, 1 Wall. 223, 233 (1864).

It also appears from our cases that the timing and content of the notice and the nature of the hearing will depend on appropriate accommodation of the competing interests involved. The student's interest is to avoid unfair or mistaken exclusion from the educational process with all of its unfortunate consequences. The Due Process Clause will not shield him from suspensions properly imposed, but it disserves both his interest and the interest of the State if his suspension is in fact unwarranted. The concern would be mostly academic if the disciplinary process were a totally accurate, unerring process, never mistaken and never unfair. Unfortunately, that is not the case, and no one suggests that it is.

---

[8]Since the landmark decision of the Court of Appeals for the Fifth Circuit in *Dixon v. Alabama State Bd. of Education*, 294 F.2d 150, *cert. denied*, 368 U.S. 930 (1961), the lower federal courts have uniformly held the Due Process Clause applicable to decisions made by tax-supported educational institutions to remove a student from the institution long enough for the removal to be classified as an expulsion.

Disciplinarians, although proceeding in utmost good faith, frequently act on the reports and advice of others; and the controlling facts and the nature of the conduct under challenge are often disputed. The risk of error is not at all trivial, and it should be guarded against if that may be done without prohibitive cost or interference with the educational process.

The difficulty is that our schools are vast and complex. Some modicum of discipline and order is essential if the educational function is to be performed. Events calling for discipline are frequent occurrences and sometimes require immediate, effective action. Suspension is considered not only to be a necessary tool to maintain order but a valuable educational device. The prospect of imposing elaborate hearing requirements in every suspension case is viewed with great concern, and many school authorities may well prefer the untrammeled power to act unilaterally, unhampered by rules about notice and hearing. But it would be a strange disciplinary system in an educational institution if no communication was sought by the disciplinarian with the student in an effort to inform him of his dereliction and to let him tell his side of the story in order to make sure that an injustice is not done. "[F]airness can rarely be obtained by secret, one-sided determination of facts decisive of rights...." "Secrecy is not congenial to truth-seeking and self-righteousness gives too slender an assurance of rightness. No better instrument has been devised for arriving at truth than to give a person in jeopardy of serious loss notice of the case against him and opportunity to meet it." *Anti-Fascist Committee v. McGrath*, 341 U.S. at 170, 171-72 (FRANKFURTER, J., concurring).

We do not believe that school authorities must be totally free from notice and hearing requirements if their schools are to operate with acceptable efficiency. Students facing temporary suspension have interests qualifying for protection of the Due Process Clause, and due process requires, in connection with a suspension of 10 days or less, that the student be given oral or written notice of the charges against him and, if he denies them, an explanation of the evidence the authorities have and an opportunity to present his side of the story. The Clause requires at least these rudimentary precautions against unfair or mistaken findings of misconduct and arbitrary exclusion from school.

There need be no delay between the time "notice" is given and the time of the hearing. In the great majority of cases the disciplinarian may informally discuss the alleged misconduct with the student minutes after it has occurred. We hold only that, in being given an opportunity to explain his version of the facts at this discussion, the student first be told what he is accused of doing and what the basis of the accusation is. Lower courts which have addressed the question of the nature of the procedures required in short suspension cases have reached the same conclusion. *Tate v. Board of Education*, 453 F.2d 975, 979 (CA8 1972); *Vail v. Board of Education*, 354 F. Supp. 592, 603 (NH 1973). Since the hearing may occur almost immediately following the misconduct, it follows that as a general rule notice and hearing should precede removal of the student from school. We agree with the District Court, however, that there are recurring

B. RIGHT TO AN ADMINISTRATIVE HEARING

situations in which prior notice and hearing cannot be insisted upon. Students whose presence poses a continuing danger to persons or property or an ongoing threat of disrupting the academic process may be immediately removed from school. In such cases, the necessary notice and rudimentary hearing should follow as soon as practicable, as the District Court indicated.

In holding as we do, we do not believe that we have imposed procedures on school disciplinarians which are inappropriate in a classroom setting. Instead we have imposed requirements which are, if anything, less than a fair-minded school principal would impose upon himself in order to avoid unfair suspensions. Indeed, according to the testimony of the principal of Marion-Franklin High School, that school had an informal procedure, remarkably similar to that which we now require, applicable to suspensions generally but which was not followed in this case. Similarly, according to the most recent memorandum applicable to the entire CPSS school principals in the CPSS are now required by local rule to provide at least as much as the constitutional minimum which we have described.

We stop short of construing the Due Process Clause to require, countrywide, that hearings in connection with short suspensions must afford the student the opportunity to secure counsel, to confront and cross-examine witnesses supporting the charge, or to call his own witnesses to verify his version of the incident. Brief disciplinary suspensions are almost countless. To impose in each such case even truncated trial-type procedures might well overwhelm administrative facilities in many places and, by diverting resources, cost more than it would save in educational effectiveness. Moreover, further formalizing the suspension process and escalating its formality and adversary nature may not only make it too costly as a regular disciplinary tool but also destroy its effectiveness as part of the teaching process.

On the other hand, requiring effective notice and informal hearing permitting the student to give his version of the events will provide a meaningful hedge against erroneous action. At least the disciplinarian will be alerted to the existence of disputes about facts and arguments about cause and effect. He may then determine himself to summon the accuser, permit cross-examination, and allow the student to present his own witnesses. In more difficult cases, he may permit counsel. In any event, his discretion will be more informed and we think the risk of error substantially reduced.

Requiring that there be at least an informal give-and-take between student and disciplinarian, preferably prior to the suspension, will add little to the factfinding function where the disciplinarian himself has witnessed the conduct forming the basis for the charge. But things are not always as they seem to be, and the student will at least have the opportunity to characterize his conduct and put it in what he deems the proper context.

We should also make it clear that we have addressed ourselves solely to the short suspension, not exceeding 10 days. Longer suspensions or expulsions for the remainder of the school term, or permanently, may require more formal procedures. Nor do we put aside the possibility that in unusual situations, although involving only a short suspension, something more than the rudimentary procedures will be required.

IV

The District Court found each of the suspensions involved here to have occurred without a hearing, either before or after the suspension, and that each suspension was therefore invalid and the statute unconstitutional insofar as it permits such suspensions without notice or hearing. Accordingly, the judgment is

Affirmed.

---

1. The *Dixon* court held that there is a constitutional right to due process including notice and a hearing before students at public educational institutions can be dismissed for disciplinary reasons. The court invoked the "balancing test" of *Joint Anti-Fascist Refugee Committee v. McGrath*, 341 U.S. 123 (1951):

> Whether the *ex parte* procedure to which the petitioners were subjected duly observed the 'rudiments of fair play', cannot be tested by mere generalities or sentiments abstractly appealing. The precise nature of the interest that has been adversely affected, the manner in which this was done, the reasons for doing it, the available alternatives to the procedure that was followed, the protection implicit in the office of the functionary whose conduct is challenged, the balance of hurt complained of and good accomplished — these are some of the considerations that must enter into the judicial judgment. *Id.* at 155.

The court then held that the interests of students in their continued education at a public institution where they were making satisfactory progress toward a degree and in good academic standing must be weighed against the interests of the state.

The significance of *Dixon* rests with the decision to render constitutional due process protection to students at public institutions for misconduct, a right which up to that time had been, for the most part, unrecognized by other courts. The leading case for eighteen years before *Dixon* was *State ex rel. Sherman v. Hyman*, 180 Tenn. 99, 171 S.W.2d 822, *cert. denied*, 319 U.S. 748 (1943), where students at the University of Tennessee were expelled without notice or a hearing. The Supreme Court of Tennessee held that the due process clause of the Fourteenth Amendment has "no application where the governing board of a school is rightfully exercising its apparent authority to discipline students, and when acting rightfully, the governing board does not proceed to enforce any rule of conduct arbitrarily and summarily." *Id.* at 104, 171 S.W.2d at 826.

2. *Dixon* established the constitutional safeguards in broad terms requiring due process before a student could be expelled for misconduct. It was left to future courts to distill the kinds of protections available for such students. Perhaps the

B. RIGHT TO AN ADMINISTRATIVE HEARING

clearest and most refined set of procedures was rendered by the district court in *Esteban v. Central Missouri State College,* 277 F. Supp. 649 (1967):

> [Plaintiffs must receive] a written statement of the charge ... or at least 10 days' notice; a hearing before the college's president, as the one person possessing the authority to expel or suspend; advance inspection by the student of any affidavits or exhibits which the College intended to submit at the hearing; the student's right to have counsel present with him at the hearing; the right to present his version as to the charge and to make such showing by way of affidavits, exhibits, and witnesses as he desired; the right to hear the evidence against him and the right to question any witness giving advance evidence; the president's determination of the facts solely on the evidence presented at the hearing and a statement by him in writing of his findings as to guilt or innocence of the conduct charged and the disposition, if any, to be made by way of disciplinary action, and permission to each side at its own expense to make a record of the events at the hearing. *Id.* at 656.

The court held that a new hearing must be provided to the students before they could be expelled. This decision was overturned in *Esteban v. Central Missouri State College,* 415 F.2d 1077 (1969), *supra,* but the above procedures were left intact.

3. Justice Powell in his dissent joined by Chief Justice Burger, Justice Brennan and Justice Rehnquist in *Goss,* concluded that:

> [T]he decision unnecessarily opens avenues for judicial intervention in the operation of our public schools and may affect adversely the quality of education ... [The Court] justifies this unprecedented intrusion into the process of elementary and secondary education by identifying a new constitutional right: the right of a student not to be suspended for as much as a single day without notice and a due process hearing either before or promptly following the suspension.

Did *Goss* really identify a new constitutional right or did the majority merely hold that some process is due before students are deprived of ten days of education? If Powell's statement is not hyperbolic, then how is it justified with prior lower court decisions like *Dixon*.

4. What of short-term suspensions, more serious conduct than that found in *Goss* and the need for additional due process? Most courts have denied the need for adversarial type hearings for cases involving short-term suspensions. For example, in *Paredes v. Curtis,* 864 F.2d 426 (6th Cir. 1988), the Sixth Circuit rejected an argument that a suspension involving drug charges was an "unusual situation" in which *Goss* implied the necessity of a more formal process than the rudimentary process for most short-term student suspensions. The court concluded that the *Goss* ruling did not require the right to cross-examine a student informant in a situation of a short-term suspension for possession of look-alike drugs.

Also, in *Abremski v. Southeastern Sch. Dist.*, 421 A.2d 485 (1980), two students were accused of smoking marijuana on a school bus. They claimed a denial of adequate due process because they were not initially granted a formal hearing before the school's disciplinary committee. The students, after meeting with only the principal, had been suspended for ten days. In determining what procedures were required under the circumstances of the case, the court looked to *Goss* and held "that the requirements of due process are flexible. Even for a ten-day suspension, there is no federal constitutional mandate for advance notice for an adversarial hearing ... so long as some form of notice and some form of hearing ... [is] provided." *Id.* at 487. *See* similar decisions in *Greenspan v. Antin*, 423 N.Y.S.2d 197 (N.Y. App. Div. 1979, *aff'd*, 433 N.Y.S.2d 761 (N.Y. 1980), and *Hillman v. Elliott*, 436 F. Supp. 812 (W.D. Va. 1977), denying adversarial hearings for short-term suspensions.

5. *Goss* involved out-of-school suspensions of ten days or less. What of in-school suspensions as when a student is physically present in the school, but isolated from other students and not exposed to class work? Is this deprivation *de minimis* and not constitutionally protected? Is the student due notice and a hearing in instances such as these?

In *Cole v. Newton Special Mun. Separate Sch. Dist.*, 676 F. Supp. 749 (S.D. Miss. 1987), a student was suspended for misconduct. When she returned to school she was required to remain isolated from other students and excluded from her classes. The student filed a complaint claiming that this was a deprivation of right to an education warranting the notice and hearing requirements of *Goss*. The school countered that since the student was physically present in school, due process requirements were inapplicable. The district court held that the school system had misread the precepts of *Goss*. Specifically, *Goss*'s dictates are broader than absence from the school's physical premises. Instead, the ruling speaks to "total exclusion from the educational process." *Goss* at 576. Hence, under circumstances of such exclusion from education, students would be due notice and a hearing even if the suspension was for less than 10 days. "Any deprivation of a student's interest in attending school must be attended by at least minimal procedural safeguards." *Cole*, 676 F. Supp. at 751.

6. The *Goss* Court held that the "notice" requirement could be oral or written. *Goss* at 581. One problem that arose following the decision was the fact that the Court did not articulate the degree of specificity required for such notice. This has sparked differing interpretations about the adequacy of notice to a student regarding an infraction of school rules. Sometimes, for example, a student is disciplined for "violating school rules" or for "serious misconduct." Courts have found that such vague accusations fail to give a student any idea of the offense committed and the rule violated. Hence, a charge of inadequate notice could be leveled against the school. In *Mills v. Board of Educ. of the Dist. of Columbia*, 348 F. Supp. 866 (D.D.C. 1972), the district court held that notice

B. RIGHT TO AN ADMINISTRATIVE HEARING

must "state specific, clear and full reasons for the proposed action, including the specification of the alleged act upon which the disciplinary action is to be based and the reference to the regulation subsection under which such action is proposed." *Id.* at 882. In other cases, however, such specificity need not be rendered. In *Wayne County Bd. of Educ. v. Tyre*, 404 S.E.2d 809 (Ga. Ct. App. 1991), a state court held that a high school student, suspended for three days for "insubordination," was accorded minimum procedural due process, where the student was given oral notice of the charges against him shortly after the incident that gave rise to his suspension. The suspension was the result of the student stepping on a large bug while attending a band competition and the "blood and guts" of the deceased bug splattered on the instructor's clothing. After refusing to remove the bug's remains from the instructor's clothing, the student was suspended.

7. What are a student's rights to a hearing if he/she admits charges of misconduct? In instances such as these, courts often find these acts sufficient cause to deny requests for prior hearings. For example, in *Coffman v. Kuehler*, 409 F. Supp. 546 (N.D. Tex. 1976), a student was suspended for an unexcused absence. The principal had previously informed the student of the school rule to obtain permission to be admitted to class after such absences and the student deliberately ignored the rule. When accused again for an unexcused absence the student made no attempt to deny the charges or to speak in his own behalf. He was thereupon suspended. The student sued based on the absence of due process with the court concluding that whatever rights the student had were waived when he chose not to speak. *Id.* at 550.

How comfortable are you with a student's admission of misconduct giving rise to a suspension, thus obviating the need for a due process hearing? What constitutes an admission? Direct confession? Following orders? Silence? Despite possible delays and inefficiencies, should there be at least an informal hearing in every case?

8. *Goss* provides a due process procedure limited to suspensions of ten days or less. That decision relates that longer-term discipline or "unusual situations" may require more in the way of process due. Given the *dicta* in *Goss*, do students accused of serious infractions such as selling drugs, where the punishment is limited to ten days or less, have a right to, say, cross-examine students? This was the issue in *Paredes v. Curtis*, 864 F.2d 426 (6th Cir. 1988). Paredes had been accused by another student of attempting to sell "look-alike" drugs on school grounds. During a hearing on the matter, Paredes claimed that his reputation was stigmatized by the accusation, thus producing the "unusual situation" mentioned in *Goss* and this in turn necessitated the additional due process of cross-examining the witness against him. The court disagreed stating that as long as the student's punishment was ten days or under, the *Goss* principle of limited due process applied.

What if the same set of facts existed and the student had been expelled from school? Would this be an "unusual situation"? *See* the notes for *Newsome v.*

Batavia Local Sch. Dist., 842 F.2d 920 (6th Cir. 1988), following *Gonzales v. McEuen, infra.*

9. Is lack of preparation time ever a deprivation of right requiring more due process? In *Nash v. Auburn Univ.*, 812 F.2d 655 (11th Cir. 1987), in the notes following *Horowitz v. Board of Curators of the Univ. of Missouri, infra*, a four-day notice to prepare for a hearing was held *not* to deprive a student of adequate due process. What about only *one* day, as the case in *Paredes*?

10. What of parents' due process rights when children are accused of infractions in suspension cases? In *Boster v. Philpot*, 645 F. Supp. 798 (D. Kan. 1986), a federal district court was asked to decide if the parents of students were due a hearing after the students confessed to vandalizing an elementary school. In an informal hearing conducted following the incident, the principal imposed three-day suspensions on all students admitting guilt to the charges. The parents later complained that their due process rights had been violated because they did not receive a hearing before the imposition of the punishment on their children. The court held that no such rights exist for parents inasmuch as the right to a free public education belongs to school students. Further, the court decided that "[t]he public school clearly had the right to impose discipline in compliance with the children's due process rights without first seeking permission or approval from the children's parents. The parents received notice of the suspension, and they were not entitled to more." *Id.* at 808.

11. For a rendition of the due process rights of disabled children accused of disciplinary infractions, *see* Chapter 13.

12. Suppose a more serious deprivation, such as expulsion from school, were at issue. Would the minimal requirements of *Goss* be expanded? Consider particularly the language, "We stop short of construing the Due Process Clause to require, country-wide, that hearings in connection with short suspensions must afford the student the opportunity to secure counsel, to confront and cross-examine witnesses supporting the charge, or to call his own witnesses to verify his version of the incident." 419 U.S. at 583. This is, of course, an expulsion issue, as seen in the case following.

GONZALES v. McEUEN

United States District Court
435 F. Supp. 460 (C.D. Cal. 1977)

TAKASUGI, DISTRICT JUDGE:

Eleven high school students, by their next friends, have brought this action under the Civil Rights Act, 42 U.S.C. § 1983, and the Due Process Clause of the Fourteenth Amendment to the Constitution of the United States. The case stems from the suspension and expulsion of the named plaintiffs from Oxnard Union High School following a period of student unrest on campus during

October 14-15, 1976. The plaintiffs were charged with having committed certain acts which, it was alleged, led to a riot at Oxnard High School.

....

Impartiality of the Board

Plaintiffs' strongest and most serious challenge is to the impartiality of the Board. They contend that they were denied their right to an impartial hearing before an independent fact-finder. The basis for this claim is, first, overfamiliarity of the Board with the case; second, the multiple role played by defendants' counsel; and, third, the involvement of the Superintendent of the District, Mr. McEuen, with the Board of Trustees during the hearings.

No one doubts that a student charged with misconduct has a right to an impartial tribunal. There is doubt, however, as to what this means. Various situations have been identified in which experience teaches that the probability of actual bias on the part of the judge or decisionmaker is too high to be constitutionally tolerable. Bias is presumed to exist, for example, in cases in which the adjudicator has a pecuniary interest in the outcome or in which he has been the target of personal attack or criticism from the person before him. The decisionmaker may also have such prior involvement with the case so as to acquire a disqualifying bias. The question before the Court is not whether the Board was actually biased, but whether, under the circumstances, there existed probability that the decisionmaker would be tempted to decide the issues with partiality to one party or the other. It is with this view that the plaintiffs' claims must be considered.

Overfamiliarity

Much has been made of "The Red Book" which, it is claimed, contained information about the academic and disciplinary records of plaintiffs. It is alleged that the Board had access to this material from twenty to thirty days before the expulsion hearings. Depositions submitted to the court show that the members of the Board met with school officials prior to the hearings. Plaintiffs contend that this prior involvement by the Board deprived plaintiffs of the opportunity for a fair hearing. The court rejects this contention. Exposure to evidence presented in a nonadversary investigative procedure is insufficient in itself to impugn the fairness of the Board members at a later adversary hearing. *Withrow v. Larkin*, 421 U.S. 35, 47 (1975). Nor is a limited combination of investigatory and adjudicatory functions in an administrative body necessarily unfair, absent a showing of other circumstances such as malice or personal interest in the outcome. *Withrow, supra*, at 47; *Jones v. Board of Educ.*, 279 F.Supp. 190, 200 (D.C., 1968). A school board would be amiss in its duties if it did not make some inquiry to know what was going on in the district for which it is responsible. Some familiarity with the facts of the case gained by an agency in the performance of its statutory role does not disqualify a decisionmaker. *Hortonville Dist. v. Hortonville Ed. Assoc.*, 426 U.S. 482, 491 (1976).

Multiple Roles of Counsel

Turning now to the issue of the multiple roles performed by defendants' counsel, the court notes that the Board members are defendants in this pending related action and may thereby become subject to personal liability.

It is undisputed that attorneys for the District who prosecuted the charges against the plaintiffs in the expulsion proceedings, also represent the Board members in this action. Plaintiffs claim that the attorneys acted in dual roles at the expulsion hearings: as prosecutors for the Administration and as legal advisors to the Board. Counsel for defendants admit that they advised the Board prior to the hearings with respect to its obligations regarding these expulsions, but they deny that they advised the Board during the proceedings themselves.

... [S]pecial mention should be made of the fact that the Board enjoys no legal expertise and must rely heavily upon its counsel. This places defendants' attorneys in a position of intolerable prominence and influence.

It is the opinion of this court that the confidential relationship between the attorneys for the District and the members of the Board, reinforced by the advisory role played by the attorneys for the Board, created an unacceptable risk of bias. Bearing in mind also that the Board members are subject to personal liability in this action, the court concludes that bias can be presumed to exist.

Involvement of Superintendent McEuen

Superintendent McEuen sat with the Board members during the expulsion hearings; he acted as Secretary to the Board on at least one occasion. By statute, Mr. McEuen is the chief advisor to the Board. The fact remains, however, that he is also the chief of the "prosecution" team, to wit, the District.

It is clear from the record that at least on one occasion, at the joint hearing of plaintiffs, Flores, Chavez and Rodriguez, Superintendent McEuen was present with the Board for approximately forty-five minutes during its deliberations on the issue of expelling these plaintiffs. The plaintiffs contend that their due process rights were violated by this involvement of Mr. McEuen with the Board. This court agrees.

Defendants' counsel maintain that Mr. McEuen did not participate in the deliberations and did no more, perhaps, than serve cookies and coffee to the Board members. Whether he did or did not participate, his presence to some extent might operate as an inhibiting restraint upon the freedom of action and expression of the Board. Defendants argue that there is no evidence that Mr. McEuen influenced or biased the Board. Proof of subjective reasoning processes are incapable of corroboration or disproval. Plaintiffs should not be forced to rely upon the memory or sense of fairness of Superintendent McEuen or the Board as to what occurred there. Perhaps Mr. McEuen's physical presence in deliberation becomes more offensive because of the pre-hearing comments which showed something less than impartiality.

The court concludes that the process utilized by the Board was fundamentally unfair. This raises a presumption of bias. In view of the alternatives for the selection of an impartial hearing body under [the] California Education Code ... it would have been more reasonable to provide procedures that insured not only that justice was done, but also that it appeared to have been done.

....

Discussion of Individual Students

David Barrington and Charles Munden

Notice

Plaintiffs Barrington and Munden were expelled at a meeting of the Board on November 10, 1976. Neither Barrington nor Munden was present; neither was represented by either parent or counsel.

On October 29, 1976, letters had been sent to the parents advising them that the principal was recommending expulsion of the students. The letters contained a specific statement of the charges: in the case of Barrington, that he was involved in a riot at school at which time he had threatened physical violence against a teacher; in the case of Munden, that he was involved in a fight with another student, Wayne Berry. The letters contained no notice to the student or parent of the student's right to be present at the hearing, to be represented by counsel, and to present evidence. This was a clear violation of § 10608 of the California Education Code. The letters to the parents stated, "If you feel that the school does not have just cause for this recommendation, you may want to attend this meeting to present your reasons why (the students) should not be expelled."

Attorneys for Munden and Barrington, on November 19 and 20, respectively, requested that the Board set aside their expulsions on account of alleged inadequacy of the notices given to the plaintiffs. They asked for new hearings at which the plaintiffs could be present to defend themselves. The Board declined to set aside these expulsions or to admit that the notices sent to these plaintiffs were constitutionally defective. The defendants maintain that the notices sent to Barrington and Munden complied, at least, with federal due process which, it is urged, requires only a hearing and notice of the charges. They contend that since a hearing was held and there was notice to the parents of the charges against the student, the requisites of procedural due process were satisfied. The court disagrees.

The precise question concerning the content of the notice to be given in expulsion proceedings will depend on the nature of the proceeding that is required.

It is now beyond argument that due process protections apply to expulsion of students by public educational institutions. The prerogative of the educational institution to regulate student conduct, though concededly broad, must be exercised consistently with constitutional safeguards. *Goss v. Lopez, supra.* The question here is common to almost every case in which it is claimed due process has been violated: "Once it is determined that due process applies, the question remains what process is due?" *Goss, supra,* 419 U.S. at 577; *Morrissey v. Brewer,* 408 U.S. 471 at 481.

The requirements of due process are flexible and different cases may require different procedural safeguards. If the possible penalties are mild, quite informal procedures may be sufficient. More formal proceedings may be required where severe penalties may attach. *See Goss v. Lopez, supra.* Where the cutoff is between a "severe" and a "mild" penalty is not clear; what is clear is that expulsion is by far the most severe.

The Supreme Court in *Goss, supra,* held that in suspensions of ten days or less due process requires at a minimum that a student be given notice and an opportunity to be heard. The court expressly refrained from construing due process to require, in short suspension situations, an opportunity to secure counsel, to confront and cross-examine witnesses, or to call witnesses. However, the court made clear that it was addressing itself solely to the short suspension, not exceeding ten days. It recognized that longer suspensions or expulsions may require more formal procedures.

Goss clearly anticipates that where the student is faced with the severe penalty of expulsion he shall have the right to be represented by and through counsel, to present evidence on his own behalf, and to confront and cross-examine adverse witnesses.

. . . .

Notice to be adequate must communicate to the recipient the nature of the proceeding. In an expulsion hearing, the notice given to the student must include a statement not only of the specific charge, but also the basic rights to be afforded the student: to be represented by counsel, to present evidence, and to confront and cross-examine adverse witnesses. Section 10608 of the California Education Code provides, *inter alia,* for notice to the student and the parent of the specific charge, of the right to be represented by counsel, and of the right to present evidence. Federal due process requires no less.

Defendants next argue that even if the notice was defective, the court must still determine whether the plaintiffs were given a fair and impartial hearing. Defendants misapprehend the meaning of notice. It is not "fair" if the student does not know, and is not told, that he has certain rights which he may exercise at the hearing.

The court, in any event, has held that there was a presumption of bias and that plaintiffs did not have a fair and impartial hearing. In the case of plaintiffs Munden and Barrington, the unfairness inherent in the duel roles is readily apparent. Mr. Hines acted as the legal advisor to the Board during the Munden-Barrington hearing on November 10. When the request was made for new, properly noticed hearings for these two students, counsel, who advised the Board in the first proceeding, urged the Board to refuse.

The court holds that the notice given to plaintiffs Barrington and Munden was defective in that it did not adequately inform them of their constitutional rights. It follows that their expulsions were improper.

....

---

1. *Gonzales* sought to answer the question of the process due for expulsions, or suspensions longer than 10 days, left unanswered in *Goss*:

> In an expulsion hearing, the notice given to the student must include a statement not only of the specific charge, but also the basic rights to be afforded the student: to be represented by counsel, to present evidence and to confront and cross-examine adverse witnesses. *Id.* at 467.

Many of the due process protections in expulsion cases had already been decided by earlier courts. *See, e.g., Pervis v. LaMarque Indep. Sch. Dist.*, 466 F.2d 1054 (5th Cir. 1972) (students subject to expulsion must receive written notice of the charges, the intention to expel and the place, time and circumstances of the hearing, with sufficient time for the defense to be prepared); *Andrews v. Knowlton*, 509 F.2d 898 (2d Cir. 1975) (students must receive a full and fair hearing before an impartial adjudicator); *Black Coalition v. Portland Sch. Dist. No. 1*, 484 F.2d 1040 (9th Cir. 1973) (students have the right to legal counsel). In cases following *Gonzales* students were also given the opportunity to present witnesses and evidence and to cross-examine opposing witnesses (*Dillon v. Pulaski County Special Sch. Dist.*, 594 F.2d 699 (8th Cir. 1979)) and to receive a written record demonstrating that the decision to expel was based on the evidence presented at the hearings (*Cashdollar v. Northridge Local Sch. Dist. Bd. of Educ.*, No. CA-3004, 1984 WL 7430 (Ohio Ct. App. 1984)).

It should not be assumed, however, that courts as regards expulsions are in any more agreement as to the proper amount of due process than they are with suspensions. *See Lamb v. Panhandle Community Unit Sch. Dist. No. 2*, 826 F.2d 526 (7th Cir. 1987), and *Keough v. Tate County Bd. of Educ.*, 748 F.2d 1077 (5th Cir. 1987), where both courts noted that *Goss* makes no formal distinction as to when a short term suspension ends and a long term expulsion begins.

2. The edited case contains only the narrative of students Barrington and Munden. The full text also features expulsion decisions for student plaintiffs Flores (insufficient evidence offered to rebut Flores' claim of self defense to battery charge), Berry (improper admission of evidence), and Gonzales (improper admission of evidence) which were set aside, while injunctions were denied for Chavez and Rodriguez (failed claims of self defense), Allen (battery of another student), Castellanos (battery of another student and teacher) and Henderson (admitted fault).

3. *Gonzales* is also a case about the multiple roles of legal counsel in student due process hearings. While bias may be seen more when the role is that of an attorney, this is more often not the case when multiple roles are played by school personnel. *See, e.g., Gorman v. University of Rhode Island*, 837 F.2d 7 (1st Cir. 1988). A student attempted to establish that appearance of his advisor on the university board of student conduct compromised the independence of the board to such an extent that the disciplinary hearings were unfair. The court disagreed, holding that there was no bias, prejudice or deprivation of due process.

See also Newsome v. Batavia Local Sch. Dist., 842 F.2d 920 (6th Cir. 1988), where the court held that a student was not deprived of due process because of participation by the principal and superintendent in a school board expulsion hearing when those same administrators had investigated the student's participation in drug trafficking and thereafter recommended expulsion. The court ruled that the principal and superintendent "were nonvoting participants in the board's deliberation ... [and their involvement] ... was limited to participating in the board's discussion." *Id.* at 926. The court went even further, however, ruling that even if the administrators had participated in the board's decision, this would not have been a denial of due process. The court made it clear that the process due includes a "pre-expulsion hearing before a trier of fact ... not ... the right to a full-blown administrative appellate process." *Id.* at 927.

See also Brewer v. Austin Indep. Sch. Dist., 779 F.2d 260 (5th Cir. 1985), another expulsion case involving drug possession, where the court stated:

> A school administrator involved in the initiation and investigation of charges is not thereby disqualified from conducting a hearing on those charges, although the facts of an occasional case may demonstrate that a school official's involvement in an incident created a bias such as to preclude his affording the student an impartial hearing. *Id.* at 264.

What would such an occasion entail? Would it be limited to the release of secret information for which the student would not have an opportunity to rebut such as that found in *Newsome*?

4. What constitutes adequate notice for expulsions? Individual circumstances play an important role in the decision; however, the courts continue to look for at least the rudimentary requirement of *Goss* for requiring greater due process in expulsions. *Gonzales* contains an important statement quoted above. Another case, *Wood v. Strickland*, 420 U.S. 308 (1975), presented following these notes, also stipulates that adequate notice must inform the student of which school rule was broken and the time and place of hearing. In *Strickland*, two students were expelled for "spiking" the punch at an extra-curricular activity. The students admitted to the principal that they had violated school regulations prohibiting the possession or use of alcoholic beverages at school functions. Although the principal informed the students that their expulsion was subject to school board disposition, he did not tell them the time and place of the planned board meeting. The parents received no notice. At the meeting, the school board voted to expel the students for the remainder of the school year.

B. RIGHT TO AN ADMINISTRATIVE HEARING

On remand, the Eighth Circuit Court of Appeals, using *Goss*, found that the principal's actions had violated the students' right to due process, "for fundamental to that concept is adequate notice and the opportunity to be heard." *Strickland v. Inlow*, 519 F.2d 744, 746 (8th Cir. 1975). In defending their actions, the board pointed to a second meeting it held where it provided the students and their parents adequate notice of the time and place of the meeting as well as an opportunity to present evidence. The court, however, held that the second meeting was little more than a "ratification of the prior Board decision and did not cure the prior violations of due process." *Id.*

5. Must a school system follow its published procedures in cases of expulsion? This question was answered in *Darby v. Schoo*, 544 F. Supp. 428 (W.D. Mich 1982), where two students brought suit after their temporary suspension turned into an expulsion without the due process that the policy required. Following an informal hearing, requested by the students, the principal dismissed the students indefinitely pending an investigation into their infractions. The students sued, claiming that only the school board could expel based on the school system's policy governing such punishments. The court determined that the board policy did not define a length for "temporary suspensions." And because the expulsions were in fact rendered by the school principal, the court held the school administration had violated its own policy which reserved the right of expulsion to the school board.

The decision in the case stands for the proposition that school districts must set the boundaries of disciplinary regulations and a determination of those responsible for decisions about disciplinary actions. For a more comprehensive response to this critical area of school discipline, *see* Linda L. Bruin, *School Discipline: Recent Developments in Student Due Process Rights*, 68 N. Mich. B.J. 1066 (1989), and Betsy Levin, *Educating Youth for Citizenship: The Conflict Between Authority and Individual Rights in the Public School*, 95 Yale L.J. 1647 (1986).

6. Do students have a right to cross-examine witnesses at expulsion hearings? The court in *M. v. Board of Educ.*, 429 F. Supp. 288 (S.D. Ill. 1977), ruled in the affirmative where a student was expelled for violating school regulations against drugs. At a subsequent hearing the student's legal counsel was permitted to examine witnesses and to present questions to the school board. However, in *Newsome v. Batavia Local Sch. Dist.*, 842 F.2d 920 (6th Cir. 1988), the court ruled that a student facing allegations by two other students that he possessed and offered a marijuana cigarette for sale on school property was not entitled to cross-examine his student accusers or to know their identity. The court concluded that the necessity of protecting witnesses from ostracism and reprisals outweighed the value of allowing cross examination.

Note, however, that *Newsome* is more about the fundamental denial of procedural due process protection than it is about a right to cross-examine witnesses. In fact, there was overwhelming evidence that the student had been selling drugs at his school; nevertheless, the student's expulsion was overturned by the Sixth Circuit Court of Appeals as he was denied due process because school officials presented new evidence at the expulsion hearing that the student did not have an opportunity to rebut.

7. Issues of expulsion stimulate questions of constitutional protections in conjunction with that of the Fourteenth Amendment. In this age of weapons and drugs in school, students found with either or both claim a Fifth Amendment right against self-incrimination in regard to procedural due process expulsion proceedings. This was the case in *Boynton v. Casey*, 543 F. Supp. 995 (D. Maine 1982), where students were expelled for possessing marijuana on school premises. The expulsion was upheld by the court with the decision that students have no right to prior advice or the right to remain silent before questioning by school authorities. The court held that the questioning did not amount to "custodial interrogation" requiring *Miranda* warnings where school authorities were not acting at the behest of the police, but rather determining whether a student should be expelled.

The *Boynton* decision follows *Miranda* which held that only those under official police restraint, as regards a criminal investigation, may employ the Fifth Amendment privilege against self-incrimination. The right to remain silent and to have the assistance of an attorney, under *Boynton* at least, has been held not to apply when education officials question students.

For more on "custodial interrogations, the Fifth Amendment and other constitutional protections for students subject to expulsion, *see* the Search and Seizure section of this chapter, *infra*.

8. How much, if any, process is due to a student accused of an academic as opposed to a disciplinary school infraction? Early cases suggested that due to the doctrine of *in loco parentis*, courts would undertake a policy of non-intervention, believing that such matters should be handled by school officials. This usually meant that students were not entitled to a hearing for academic dismissal. *See, e.g., Foley v. Benedict*, 122 Tex. 193, 55 S.W.2d 805 (1932); *Barnard v. Inhabitants of Shelburne*, 216 Mass. 19, 102 N.E. 1095 (1913); and *Gott v. Berea College*, 156 Ky. 376, 161 S.W. 204 (1913). More recently, the United States Supreme Court has decided cases that distinguish between academic failure and disciplinary misconduct relative to notice and hearing requirements. In *Board of Curators of the Univ. of Missouri v. Horowitz*, 435 U.S. 78 (1978), the Court found it unnecessary to decide whether a medical student had been deprived of either a property right or a liberty interest. In fact, the Court declared, the student had no right to a hearing. The Court established a distinction between the "process due" in cases of academic dismissal and those involving disciplinary dismissal. School authorities are uniquely qualified to evaluate academic performance while judicial officers are not. The Court held that school personnel have the academic freedom to evaluate student performance without the interference of the courts. Due process procedures in such circumstances must be flexible as "[a] school is an academic institution, not a courtroom or administrative hearing room." *Horowitz* was followed by *Regents of Univ. of*

Michigan v. Ewing, 474 U.S. 214 (1985), another medical student case, where the Supreme Court affirmed the dichotomy between academic and disciplinary dismissal as to due process protection. For cases involving the use of academic sanctions in disciplinary cases, *see* Chapter 8 of this book.

2. LIABILITY OF SCHOOL AUTHORITIES FOR FAILURE TO PROVIDE PROCEDURAL PROTECTIONS

WOOD v. STRICKLAND
Supreme Court of the United States
420 U.S. 308 (1975)

MR. JUSTICE WHITE delivered the opinion of the Court:
Respondents Peggy Strickland and Virginia Crain brought this lawsuit against petitioners, who were members of the school board at the time in question, two school administrators, and the Special School District of Mena, Ark., purporting to assert a cause of action under 42 U.S.C. § 1983, and claiming that their federal constitutional rights to due process were infringed under color of state law by their expulsion from the Mena Public High School on the grounds of their violation of a school regulation prohibiting the use or possession of intoxicating beverages at school or school activities.

. . . .

I

The violation of the school regulation prohibiting the use or possession of intoxicating beverages at school or school activities with which respondents were charged concerned their "spiking" of the punch served at a meeting of an extracurricular school organization attended by parents and students. At the time in question, respondents were 16 years old and were in the 10th grade. The relevant facts begin with their discovery that the punch had not been prepared for the meeting as previously planned. The girls then agreed to "spike" it. Since the county in which the school is located is "dry," respondents and a third girl drove across the state border into Oklahoma and purchased two 12-ounce bottles of "Right Time," a malt liquor. They then bought six 10-ounce bottles of a soft drink, and, after having mixed the contents of the eight bottles in an empty milk carton, returned to school. Prior to the meeting, the girls experienced second thoughts about the wisdom of their prank, but by then they were caught up in the force of events and the intervention of other girls prevented them from disposing of the illicit punch. The punch was served at the meeting, without apparent effect.

Ten days later, the teacher in charge of the extracurricular group and meeting, Mrs. Curtis Powell, having heard something about the "spiking," questioned the girls about it. Although first denying any knowledge, the girls admitted their involvement after the teacher said that she would handle the punishment herself.

The next day, however, she told the girls that the incident was becoming increasingly the subject of talk in the school and that the principal, P. T. Waller, would probably hear about it. She told them that her job was in jeopardy but that she would not force them to admit to Waller what they had done. If they did not go to him then, however, she would not be able to help them if the incident became "distorted." The three girls then went to Waller and admitted their role in the affair. He suspended them from school for a maximum two-week period, subject to the decision of the school board. Waller also told them that the board would meet that night, that the girls could tell their parents about the meeting, but that the parents should not contact any members of the board.

Neither the girls nor their parents attended the school board meeting that night. Both Mrs. Powell and Waller, after making their reports concerning the incident, recommended leniency. At this point, a telephone call was received by S. L. Inlow, then the superintendent of schools, from Mrs. Powell's husband, also a teacher at the high school, who reported that he had heard that the third girl involved had been in a fight that evening at a basketball game. Inlow informed the meeting of the news, although he did not mention the name of the girl involved. Mrs. Powell and Waller then withdrew their recommendations of leniency, and the board voted to expel the girls from school for the remainder of the semester, a period of approximately three months.

The board subsequently agreed to hold another meeting on the matter, and one was held approximately two weeks after the first meeting. The girls, their parents, and their counsel attended this session. The board began with a reading of a written statement of facts as it had found them. The girls admitted mixing the malt liquor into the punch with the intent of "spiking" it, but asked the board to forego its rule punishing such violations by such substantial suspensions. Neither Mrs. Powell nor Waller was present at this meeting. The board voted not to change its policy and, as before, to expel the girls for the remainder of the semester.

II

The District Court instructed the jury that a decision for respondents had to be premised upon a finding that petitioners acted with malice in expelling them and defined "malice" as meaning "ill will against a person — a wrongful act done intentionally without just cause or excuse." 348 F. Supp. at 248. In ruling for petitioners after the jury had been unable to agree, the District Court found "as a matter of law" that there was no evidence from which malice could be inferred. *Id.* at 253.

The Court of Appeals, however, viewed both the instruction and the decision of the District Court as being erroneous. Specific intent to harm wrongfully, it held, was not a requirement for the recovery of damages. Instead, "[i]t need only be established that the defendants did not, in the light of all the circumstances, act in good faith. The test is an objective, rather than a subjective, one." 485 F.2d at 191.

B. RIGHT TO AN ADMINISTRATIVE HEARING 427

Petitioners as members of the school board assert here, as they did below, an absolute immunity from liability under § 1983 and at the very least seek to reinstate the judgment of the District Court. If they are correct and the District Court's dismissal should be sustained, we need go no further in this case. Moreover, the immunity question involves the construction of a federal statute, and our practice is to deal with possibly dispositive statutory issues before reaching questions turning on the construction of the Constitution. We essentially sustain the position of the Court of Appeals with respect to the immunity issue.

....

This Court has decided three cases dealing with the scope of the immunity protecting various types of governmental officials from liability for damages under § 1983. In *Tenney v. Brandhove*, 341 U.S. 367 (1951), the question was found to be one essentially of statutory construction. Noting that the language of § 1983 is silent with respect to immunities, the Court concluded that there was no basis for believing that Congress intended to eliminate the traditional immunity of legislators from civil liability for acts done within their sphere of legislative action. That immunity, "so well grounded in history and reason ...," 341 U.S. at 376, was absolute and consequently did not depend upon the motivations of the legislators. In *Pierson v. Ray*, 386 U.S. 547, 554 (1967), finding that "[t]he legislative record gives no clear indication that Congress meant to abolish wholesale all common-law immunities" in enacting § 1983, we concluded that the common-law doctrine of absolute judicial immunity survived. Similarly, § 1983 did not preclude application of the traditional rule that a policeman, making an arrest in good-faith and with probable cause, is not liable for damages, although the person arrested proves innocent. Consequently the Court said: "Although the matter is not entirely free from doubt, the same consideration would seem to require excusing him from liability for acting under a statute that he reasonably believed to be valid but that was later held unconstitutional, on its face or as applied." 386 U.S. at 555. Finally, last Term we held that the chief executive officer of a State, the senior and subordinate officers of the State's National Guard, and the president of a state-controlled university were not absolutely immune from liability under § 1983, but instead were entitled to immunity, under prior precedent and in light of the obvious need to avoid discouraging effective official action by public officers charged with a considerable range of responsibility and discretion, only if they acted in good faith as defined by the Court:

> ... [I]n varying scope, a qualified immunity is available to officers of the executive branch of government, the variation being dependent upon the scope of discretion and responsibilities of the office and all the circumstances as they reasonably appeared at the time of the action on which liability is sought to be based. It is the existence of reasonable grounds for the belief formed at the time and in light of all the circumstances, coupled with good-faith belief, that affords a basis for qualified immunity of executive

officers for acts performed in the course of official conduct. *Scheuer v. Rhodes*, 416 U.S. 232, 247-48 (1974).

Common-law tradition, recognized in our prior decisions, and strong public-policy reasons also lead to a construction of § 1983 extending a qualified good-faith immunity to school board members from liability for damages under that section. Although there have been differing emphases and formulations of the common-law immunity of public school officials in cases of student expulsion or suspension, state courts have generally recognized that such officers should be protected from tort liability under state law for all good faith, nonmalicious action taken to fulfill their official duties.

As the facts of this case reveal, school board members function at different times in the nature of legislators and adjudicators in the school disciplinary process. Each of these functions necessarily involves the exercise of discretion, the weighing of many factors, and the formulations of long-term policy. "Like legislators and judges, these officers are entitled to rely on traditional sources for the factual information on which they decide and act." *Scheuer v. Rhodes, supra*, at 246. As with executive officers faced with instances of civil disorder, school officials, confronted with student behavior causing or threatening disruption, also have an "obvious need for prompt action, and decisions must be made in reliance on factual information supplied by others." *Ibid.*

Liability for damages for every action which is found subsequently to have been violative of a student's constitutional rights and to have caused compensable injury would unfairly impose upon the school decisionmaker the burden of mistakes made in good faith in the course of exercising his discretion within the scope of his official duties. School board members, among other duties, must judge whether there have been violations of school regulations and, if so, the appropriate sanctions for the violations. Denying any measure of immunity in these circumstances "would contribute not to principled and fearless decision-making but to intimidation." *Pierson v. Ray, supra*, at 554. The imposition of monetary costs for mistakes which were not unreasonable in the light of all the circumstances would undoubtedly deter even the most conscientious school decisionmaker from exercising his judgment independently, forcefully, and in a manner best serving the long-term interest of the school and the students. The most capable candidates for school board positions might be deterred from seeking office if heavy burdens upon their private resources from monetary liability were a likely prospect during their tenure.

These considerations have undoubtedly played a prime role in the development by state courts of a qualified immunity protecting school officials from liability for damages in lawsuits claiming improper suspensions or expulsions. But at the same time, the judgment implicit in this common-law development is that absolute immunity would not be justified since it would not sufficiently increase the ability of school officials to exercise their discretion in a forthright manner

B. RIGHT TO AN ADMINISTRATIVE HEARING 429

to warrant the absence of a remedy for students subjected to intentional or otherwise inexcusable deprivations.

Tenney v. Brandhove, Pierson v. Ray, and *Scheuer v. Rhodes* drew upon a very similar background and were animated by a very similar judgment in construing § 1983. Absent legislative guidance, we now rely on those same sources in determining whether and to what extent school officials are immune from damage suits under § 1983. We think there must be a degree of immunity if the work of the schools is to go forward; and, however worded, the immunity must be such that public school officials understand that action taken in the good-faith fulfillment of their responsibilities and within the bounds of reason under all the circumstances will not be punished and that they need not exercise their discretion with undue timidity.

> Public officials, whether governors, mayors or police, legislators or judges, who fail to make decisions when they are needed or who do not act to implement decisions when they are made do not fully and faithfully perform the duties of their offices. Implicit in the idea that officials have some immunity — absolute or qualified — for their acts, is a recognition that they may err. The concept of immunity assumes this and goes on to assume that it is better to risk some error and possible injury from such error than not to decide or act at all. *Scheuer v. Rhodes,* 416 U.S. at 241-42.

The disagreement between the Court of Appeals and the District Court over the immunity standard in this case has been put in terms of an "objective" versus a "subjective" test of good faith. As we see it, the appropriate standard necessarily contains elements of both. The official himself must be acting sincerely and with a belief that he is doing right, but an act violating a student's constitutional rights can be no more justified by ignorance or disregard of settled, indisputable law on the part of one entrusted with supervision of students' daily lives than by the presence of actual malice. To be entitled to a special exemption from the categorical remedial language of § 1983 in a case in which his action violated a student's constitutional rights, a school board member, who has voluntarily undertaken the task of supervising the operation of the school and the activities of the students, must be held to a standard of conduct based not only on permissible intentions, but also on knowledge of the basic, unquestioned constitutional rights of his charges. Such a standard imposes neither an unfair burden upon a person assuming a responsible public office requiring a high degree of intelligence and judgment for the proper fulfillment of its duties, nor an unwarranted burden in light of the value which civil rights have in our legal system. Any lesser standard would deny much of the promise of § 1983. Therefore, in the specific context of school discipline, we hold that a school board member is not immune from liability for damages under § 1983 if he knew or reasonably should have known that the action he took within his sphere of official responsibility would violate the constitutional rights of the student affected, or if he took the action with the malicious intention to cause a deprivation of constitutional rights or other injury to the student. That is not to say that school board members are "charged with predicting the future course of constitutional law." *Pierson v. Ray*, 386 U.S. at 557. A compensatory award will be appropriate only if the school board member has acted with such an impermissible motivation or with such disregard of the student's clearly established constitutional rights that his action cannot reasonably be characterized as being in good faith.

....

[Based on the foregoing rationale, the Supreme Court vacated the judgment of the Court of Appeals and remanded for further proceedings consistent with the opinion. The concurring/dissenting opinion of MR. JUSTICE POWELL, with whom the Chief Justice, MR. JUSTICE BLACK and MR. JUSTICE REHNQUIST joined, is omitted.]

---

1. What constitutes "good faith" and what is "settled law"? Consider the ambiguities addressed by one commentator.

While, admittedly, the whole tenor of the majority opinion is that school officials, whatever their actual knowledge, are charged with the knowledge of settled constitutional principles, the majority opinion is not without ambiguity. The chief ambiguity in the majority opinion concerns the burden which a school administrator must carry to take advantage of the good-faith immunity. It is possible that an administrator is charged with knowledge of the constitutional rights of his students; actions in violation of those rights could never be in good faith. Alternatively, administrators may be allowed the good-faith immunity if their actions reflect a reasonable school administrator's knowledge of students' constitutional rights. The language which suggests that the *Wood* standard is one of imputed knowledge of constitutional rights is weakened by the phrases "reasonably should have known" and "such disregard." These phrases suggest a standard of carelessness or negligence. The distinction is not without importance. For example, a constitutional issue may have been dispositively addressed by the Supreme Court on day one, and a school official may have violated the Court's newly established rule on day three. If knowledge is imputed as a matter of law, then subsequent liability for damages under section 1983 is permissible since good-faith immunity is not available. Under a negligence interpretation of good faith, however, if the law is settled and yet it is unreasonable to conclude that a school official had a sufficient opportunity to acquaint himself with the new standard, the qualified good-faith immunity would preclude liability. Perhaps, as the dissent notes, a more likely situation is that a school official may receive inadequate legal counseling as to the state of the law. Under such circumstances, the imputed-knowledge approach would yield the opposite result unless the school official had "shopped" for favorable legal advice. Under circumstances where the defendants failed to seek legal advice and had ample opportunity to do so, the failure to abide by settled constitutional principles would deprive them of their qualified immunity under either test.

Yudof, *Liability for Constitutional Torts and the Risk-Averse Public School Official,* 49 S. Cal. L. Rev. 1322, 1331-32 (1976).

2. Perhaps the greatest significance of *Wood* lies not in its actual but in its perceived holding. Stripped of its ambiguities and sophisticated qualifications, *Wood* may stand for only one thing in the layman's mind — that teachers and school officials who mistakenly deprive students of constitutional rights may be sued. Will the prospect of possible financial liability deter some from candidacy for school board elections? How will it influence the exercise of discretion by board members, principals, and teachers? Will it lead to greater concern for democratic ideals or to greater passivity and indecisiveness?

3. *Wood* decided the question of whether school officials may be sued for damages for violations of students' constitutional rights. Consider the case where a very large damage award is sought. Suppose, for instance, that a student alleges an unconstitutional expulsion which prevented his graduation and caused the loss of a $20,000 college scholarship. May the student sue the school board members as individuals only or may he sue them in their official capacity and thereby secure district monies to satisfy any judgment in his favor? Apparently, he may sue them as a board. In *Monell v. Department of Social Services*, 436 U.S. 658 (1978), the Supreme Court held that municipalities and other local government units are "persons" that can be sued directly under 42 U.S.C. § 1983 for monetary, declaratory, or injunctive relief where alleged unconstitutional action is executed by government policy or custom. However, the Court ruled that such government entities cannot be held liable on a *respondeat superior* theory.

4. *Stickland* uses the test of "good faith" to help determine the liability of school officials for the abridgment of students' constitutional rights. The case served as the foundation in *Carey v. Piphus*, 435 U.S. 247 (1978), where the Court limited any award to compensatory damages for a proven injury. Further refinement of the test of liability was rendered in *Harlow v. Fitzgerald*, 457 U.S. 800 (1982), where liability could only be found if there was a violation of clearly established statutory or constitutional rights which a reasonable school official should have known. Finally, the Court expressly decided that school official liability must be limited to compensatory or actually proven damages and ruled out a damage claim for the potential value of a constitutional right in *Memphis Community Sch. Dist. v. Stachura*, 477 U.S. 299 (1986).

C. SEARCH AND SEIZURE

Public concern over criminal activity by students and the concomitant problems of school safety have resulted in the development of more stringent disciplinary procedures by school officials. There are greater efforts to discipline students whose conduct disrupts the education process or interferes with the rights of other students. School personnel must consult the Fourth and, to some extent, the Fifth Amendments when implementing rules and regulations relative to maintaining the security of the education environment. This means there must always be consideration given to whether students' reasonable privacy expectations have been breached. This may depend upon the kind of search conducted under the auspices of the school and the nature of the items seized. The rest of this chapter will address Fourth Amendment jurisprudence concentrating on searches of persons, lockers, automobiles and personal property.

NEW JERSEY v. T.L.O.
Supreme Court of the United States
469 U.S. 325 (1985)

JUSTICE WHITE delivered the opinion of the Court:

....

I

On March 7, 1980, a teacher at Piscataway High School in Middlesex County, N.J., discovered two girls smoking in a lavatory. One of the two girls was the respondent T.L.O., who at that time was a 14-year-old high school freshman. Because smoking in the lavatory was a violation of a school rule, the teacher took the two girls to the Principal's office, where they met with Assistant Vice Principal Theodore Choplick. In response to questioning by Mr. Choplick, T.L.O.'s companion admitted that she had violated the rule. T.L.O., however, denied that she had been smoking in the lavatory and claimed that she did not smoke at all.

Mr. Choplick asked T.L.O. to come into his private office and demanded to see her purse. Opening the purse, he found a pack of cigarettes, which he removed from the purse and held before T.L.O. as he accused her of having lied to him. As he reached into the purse for the cigarettes, Mr. Choplick also noticed a package of cigarette rolling papers. In his experience, possession of rolling papers by high school students was closely associated with the use of marijuana. Suspecting that a closer examination of the purse might yield further evidence of drug use, Mr. Choplick proceeded to search the purse thoroughly. The search revealed a small amount of marijuana, a pipe, a number of empty plastic bags, a substantial quantity of money in one-dollar bills, an index card that appeared to be a list of students who owed T.L.O. money, and two letters that implicated T.L.O. in marijuana dealing.

Mr. Choplick notified T.L.O.'s mother and the police, and turned the evidence of drug dealing over to the police. At the request of the police, T.L.O.'s mother took her daughter to police headquarters, where T.L.O. confessed that she had been selling marijuana at the high school. On the basis of the confession and the evidence seized by Mr. Choplick, the State brought delinquency charges against T.L.O. in the Juvenile and Domestic Relations Court of Middlesex County.

C. SEARCH AND SEIZURE

Contending that Mr. Choplick's search of her purse violated the Fourth Amendment, T.L.O. moved to suppress the evidence found in her purse as well as her confession, which, she argued, was tainted by the allegedly unlawful search. The Juvenile Court denied the motion to suppress. *State ex rel. T.L.O.*, 178 N.J.Super. 329, 428 A.2d 1327 (1980). Although the court concluded that the Fourth Amendment did apply to searches carried out by school officials, it held that

> [A] school official may properly conduct a search of a student's person if the official has a reasonable suspicion that a crime has been or is in the process of being committed, or reasonable cause to believe that the search is necessary to maintain school discipline or enforce school policies. *Id.*, 178 N.J.Super. at 341, 428 A.2d at 1333.

....

On appeal from the final judgment of the Juvenile Court, a divided Appellate Division affirmed the trial court's finding that there had been no Fourth Amendment violation, but vacated the adjudication of delinquency and remanded for a determination whether T.L.O. had knowingly and voluntarily waived her Fifth Amendment rights before confessing. *State ex rel. T.L.O.*, 185 N.J.Super. 279, 448 A.2d 493 (1982). T.L.O. appealed the Fourth Amendment ruling, and the Supreme Court of New Jersey reversed the judgment of the Appellate Division and ordered the suppression of the evidence found in T.L.O.'s purse. *State ex rel. T.L.O.*, 94 N.J. 331, 463 A.2d 934 (1983).

The New Jersey Supreme Court agreed with the lower courts that the Fourth Amendment applies to searches conducted by school officials. The court also rejected the State of New Jersey's argument that the exclusionary rule should not be employed to prevent the use in juvenile proceedings of evidence unlawfully seized by school officials....

....

We granted the State of New Jersey's petition for certiorari....

....

II

In determining whether the search at issue in this case violated the Fourth Amendment, we are faced initially with the question whether that Amendment's prohibition on unreasonable searches and seizures applies to searches conducted by public school officials. We hold that it does.

....

These two propositions — that the Fourth Amendment applies to the States through the Fourteenth Amendment, and that the actions of public school officials are subject to the limits placed on state action by the Fourteenth Amendment — might appear sufficient to answer the suggestion that the Fourth Amendment does not proscribe unreasonable searches by school officials. On reargument, however, the State of New Jersey has argued that the history of the Fourth

Amendment indicates that the Amendment was intended to regulate only searches and seizures carried out by law enforcement officers; accordingly, although public school officials are concededly state agents for purposes of the Fourteenth Amendment, the Fourth Amendment creates no rights enforceable against them.

... [B]ut this Court has never limited the Amendment's prohibition on unreasonable searches and seizures to operations conducted by the police. Rather, the Court has long spoken of the Fourth Amendment's strictures as restraints imposed upon "governmental action" — that is, "upon the activities of sovereign authority." *Burdeau v. McDowell*, 256 U.S. 465, 475 (1921)....

....

Notwithstanding the general applicability of the Fourth Amendment to the activities of civil authorities, a few courts have concluded that school officials are exempt from the dictates of the Fourth Amendment by virtue of the special nature of their authority over schoolchildren. *See, e.g., R.C.M. v. State*, 660 S.W.2d 552 (Tex.App.1983). Teachers and school administrators, it is said, act *in loco parentis* in their dealings with students: their authority is that of the parent, not the State, and is therefore not subject to the limits of the Fourth Amendment. *Ibid*.

Such reasoning is in tension with contemporary reality and the teachings of this Court. We have held school officials subject to the commands of the First Amendment, *see Tinker v. Des Moines Independent Community School District*, 393 U.S. 503 (1969), and the Due Process Clause of the Fourteenth Amendment, *see Goss v. Lopez*, 419 U.S. 565 (1975). If school authorities are state actors for purposes of the constitutional guarantees of freedom of expression and due process, it is difficult to understand why they should be deemed to be exercising parental rather than public authority when conducting searches of their students. More generally, the Court has recognized that "the concept of parental delegation" as a source of school authority is not entirely "consonant with compulsory education laws." *Ingraham v. Wright*, 430 U.S. 651, 662 (1977). Today's public school officials do not merely exercise authority voluntarily conferred on them by individual parents; rather, they act in furtherance of publicly mandated educational and disciplinary policies. *See, e.g.*, the opinion in *State ex rel. T.L.O.*, 94 N.J. at 343, 463 A.2d at 934, 940, describing the New Jersey statutes regulating school disciplinary policies and establishing the authority of school officials over their students. In carrying out searches and other disciplinary functions pursuant to such policies, school officials act as representatives of the State, not merely as surrogates for the parents, and they cannot claim the parents' immunity from the strictures of the Fourth Amendment.

III

To hold that the Fourth Amendment applies to searches conducted by school authorities is only to begin the inquiry into the standards governing such searches. Although the underlying command of the Fourth Amendment is always that searches and seizures be reasonable, what is reasonable depends on the

C. SEARCH AND SEIZURE

context within which a search takes place. The determination of the standard of reasonableness governing any specific class of searches requires "balancing the need to search against the invasion which the search entails." *Camara v. Municipal Court, supra,* 387 U.S. at 536-537. On one side of the balance are arrayed the individual's legitimate expectations of privacy and personal security; on the other, the government's need for effective methods to deal with breaches of public order.

. . . .

Of course, the Fourth Amendment does not protect subjective expectations of privacy that are unreasonable or otherwise "illegitimate." *See, e.g., Hudson v. Palmer,* 468 U.S. 517 (1984); *Rawlings v. Kentucky,* 448 U.S. 98 (1980). To receive the protection of the Fourth Amendment, an expectation of privacy must be one that society is "prepared to recognize as legitimate." *Hudson v. Palmer, supra,* 468 U.S. at 526. The State of New Jersey has argued that because of the pervasive supervision to which children in the schools are necessarily subject, a child has virtually no legitimate expectation of privacy in articles of personal property "unnecessarily" carried into a school. This argument has two factual premises: (1) the fundamental incompatibility of expectations of privacy with the maintenance of a sound educational environment; and (2) the minimal interest of the child in bringing any items of personal property into the school. Both premises are severely flawed.

Although this Court may take notice of the difficulty of maintaining discipline in the public schools today, the situation is not so dire that students in the schools may claim no legitimate expectations of privacy. We have recently recognized that the need to maintain order in a prison is such that prisoners retain no legitimate expectations of privacy in their cells, but it goes almost without saying that "[t]he prisoner and the schoolchild stand in wholly different circumstances, separated by the harsh facts of criminal conviction and incarceration." *Ingraham v. Wright, supra,* 430 U.S. at 669. We are not yet ready to hold that the schools and the prisons need be equated for purposes of the Fourth Amendment.

Nor does the State's suggestion that children have no legitimate need to bring personal property into the schools seem well anchored in reality. Students at a minimum must bring to school not only the supplies needed for their studies, but also keys, money, and the necessaries of personal hygiene and grooming. In addition, students may carry on their persons or in purses or wallets such nondisruptive yet highly personal items as photographs, letters, and diaries. Finally, students may have perfectly legitimate reasons to carry with them articles of property needed in connection with extracurricular or recreational activities. In short, schoolchildren may find it necessary to carry with them a variety of legitimate, noncontraband items, and there is no reason to conclude that they have necessarily waived all rights to privacy in such items merely by bringing them onto school grounds.

Against the child's interest in privacy must be set the substantial interest of teachers and administrators in maintaining discipline in the classroom and on school grounds. Maintaining order in the classroom has never been easy, but in recent years, school disorder has often taken particularly ugly forms: drug use and violent crime in the schools have become major social problems....

How, then, should we strike the balance between the schoolchild's legitimate expectations of privacy and the school's equally legitimate need to maintain an environment in which learning can take place? It is evident that the school setting requires some easing of the restrictions to which searches by public authorities are ordinarily subject. The warrant requirement, in particular, is unsuited to the school environment: requiring a teacher to obtain a warrant before searching a child suspected of an infraction of school rules (or of the criminal law) would unduly interfere with the maintenance of the swift and informal disciplinary procedures needed in the schools.... [W]e hold today that school officials need not obtain a warrant before searching a student who is under their authority.

The school setting also requires some modification of the level of suspicion of illicit activity needed to justify a search. Ordinarily, a search — even one that may permissibly be carried out without a warrant — must be based upon "probable cause" to believe that a violation of the law has occurred.... However, "probable cause" is not an irreducible requirement of a valid search. The fundamental command of the Fourth Amendment is that searches and seizures be reasonable, and although "both the concept of probable cause and the requirement of a warrant bear on the reasonableness of a search, ... in certain limited circumstances neither is required." *Almeida — Sanchez v. United States*, [413 U.S. 266, 277 (1973)]....

We join the majority of courts that have examined this issue in concluding that the accommodation of the privacy interests of schoolchildren with the substantial need of teachers and administrators for freedom to maintain order in the schools does not require strict adherence to the requirement that searches be based on probable cause to believe that the subject of the search has violated or is violating the law. Rather, the legality of a search of a student should depend simply on the reasonableness, under all the circumstances, of the search. Determining the reasonableness of any search involves a twofold inquiry: first, one must consider "whether the ... action was justified at its inception," *Terry v. Ohio*, 392 U.S. at 20; second, one must determine whether the search as actually conducted "was reasonably related in scope to the circumstances which justified the interference in the first place," *ibid*. Under ordinary circumstances, a search of a student by a teacher or other school official will be "justified at its inception" when there are reasonable grounds for suspecting that the search will turn up evidence that the student has violated or is violating either the law or the rules of the school.[8] Such a search will be permissible in its scope when the measures

---

[8]We do not decide whether individualized suspicion is an essential element of the reasonableness standard we adopt for searches by school authorities. In other contexts, however, we have held that although "some quantum of individualized suspicion is usually a prerequisite to a constitutional search or seizure[,] ... the Fourth Amendment imposes no irreducible requirement

C. SEARCH AND SEIZURE

adopted are reasonably related to the objectives of the search and not excessively intrusive in light of the age and sex of the student and the nature of the infraction.

This standard will, we trust, neither unduly burden the efforts of school authorities to maintain order in their schools nor authorize unrestrained intrusions upon the privacy of schoolchildren. By focusing attention on the question of reasonableness, the standard will spare teachers and school administrators the necessity of schooling themselves in the niceties of probable cause and permit them to regulate their conduct according to the dictates of reason and common sense. At the same time, the reasonableness standard should ensure that the interests of students will be invaded no more than is necessary to achieve the legitimate end of preserving order in the schools.

IV

There remains the question of the legality of the search in this case. We recognize that the "reasonable grounds" standard applied by the New Jersey Supreme Court in its consideration of this question is not substantially different from the standard that we have adopted today. Nonetheless, we believe that the New Jersey court's application of that standard to strike down the search of T.L.O.'s purse reflects a somewhat crabbed notion of reasonableness. Our review of the facts surrounding the search leads us to conclude that the search was in no sense unreasonable for Fourth Amendment purposes.

The incident that gave rise to this case actually involved two separate searches, with the first — the search for cigarettes — providing the suspicion that gave rise to the second — the search for marijuana. Although it is the fruits of the second search that are at issue here, the validity of the search for marijuana must depend on the reasonableness of the initial search for cigarettes, as there would have been no reason to suspect that T.L.O. possessed marijuana had the first search not taken place. Accordingly, it is to the search for cigarettes that we first turn our attention.

....

... [T]he relevance of T.L.O.'s possession of cigarettes to the question whether she had been smoking and to the credibility of her denial that she smoked supplied the necessary "nexus" between the item searched for and the infraction

---

of such suspicion." *United States v. Martinez-Fuerte*, 428 U.S. 543, 560-61 (1976). *See also Camara v. Municipal Court*, 387 U.S. 523 (1967). Exceptions to the requirement of individualized suspicion are generally appropriate only where the privacy interests implicated by a search are minimal and where "other safeguards" are available "to assure that the individual's reasonable expectation of privacy is not 'subject to the discretion of the official in the field.'" *Delaware v. Prouse*, 440 U.S. 648, 654-55 (1979). Because the search of T.L.O.'s purse was based upon an individualized suspicion that she had violated school rules, *see infra,* at 745-46, we need not consider the circumstances that might justify school authorities in conducting searches unsupported by individualized suspicion.

under investigation.... Thus, if Mr. Choplick in fact had a reasonable suspicion that T.L.O. had cigarettes in her purse, the search was justified despite the fact that the cigarettes, if found, would constitute "mere evidence" of a violation.

... A teacher had reported that T.L.O. was smoking in the lavatory. Certainly this report gave Mr. Choplick reason to suspect that T.L.O. was carrying cigarettes with her; and if she did have cigarettes, her purse was the obvious place in which to find them. Mr. Choplick's suspicion that there were cigarettes in the purse was not an "inchoate and unparticularized suspicion or 'hunch,'" rather, it was the sort of "common-sense conclusio[n] about human behavior" upon which "practical people" — including government officials — are entitled to rely. *United States v. Cortez*, 449 U.S. 411, 418 (1981). Of course, even if the teacher's report were true, T.L.O. might not have had a pack of cigarettes with her; she might have borrowed a cigarette from someone else or have been sharing a cigarette with another student. But the requirement of reasonable suspicion is not a requirement of absolute certainty: "sufficient probability, not certainty, is the touchstone of reasonableness under the Fourth Amendment...."

....

Our conclusion that Mr. Choplick's decision to open T.L.O.'s purse was reasonable brings us to the question of the further search for marijuana once the pack of cigarettes was located. The suspicion upon which the search for marijuana was founded was provided when Mr. Choplick observed a package of rolling papers in the purse as he removed the pack of cigarettes. Although T.L.O. does not dispute the reasonableness of Mr. Choplick's belief that the rolling papers indicated the presence of marijuana, she does contend that the scope of the search Mr. Choplick conducted exceeded permissible bounds when he seized and read certain letters that implicated T.L.O. in drug dealing. This argument, too, is unpersuasive. The discovery of the rolling papers concededly gave rise to a reasonable suspicion that T.L.O. was carrying marijuana as well as cigarettes in her purse. This suspicion justified further exploration of T.L.O.'s purse, which turned up more evidence of drug-related activities: a pipe, a number of plastic bags of the type commonly used to store marijuana, a small quantity of marijuana, and a fairly substantial amount of money. Under these circumstances, it was not unreasonable to extend the search to a separate zippered compartment of the purse; and when a search of that compartment revealed an index card containing a list of "people who owe me money" as well as two letters, the inference that T.L.O. was involved in marijuana trafficking was substantial enough to justify Mr. Choplick in examining the letters to determine whether they contained any further evidence. In short, we cannot conclude that the search for marijuana was unreasonable in any respect.

Because the search resulting in the discovery of the evidence of marijuana dealing by T.L.O. was reasonable, the New Jersey Supreme Court's decision to exclude that evidence from T.L.O.'s juvenile delinquency proceedings on Fourth

Amendment grounds was erroneous. Accordingly, the judgment of the Supreme Court of New Jersey is

Reversed.

---

1. The decision in *T.L.O.* represents an exception to the general rule of the Fourth Amendment that warrantless searches and seizures are *per se* unreasonable. The catch words are "warrant" and "reasonable" and each, in turn was addressed by the Supreme Court in this case. The Court, as such, does not require school officials to secure warrants in the search of students because such a responsibility would "unduly interfere with the maintenance of the swift and informal disciplinary procedures needed in the schools." *T.L.O.*, at 340. In addition, the decision does not require "probable cause," a key element in criminally-based searches by law enforcement officials. Instead, the Court requires "reasonable suspicion" or "reasonable grounds for suspecting that a search will turn up evidence that the student has violated or is violating either the law or the rules of the school." *Id.* at 342. Moreover, "[s]uch a search [is reasonable if] not excessively intrusive in light of the age and sex of the student and the nature of the infraction." *Id.* Justice Marshall, in his dissent, claims that the plurality decision carves out too broad an exception to the Fourth Amendment standards already developed. Should the Court have stood by the "probable cause" standard or is that standard too unworkable and time-consuming in a school setting?

2. Does the decision in *T.L.O* give school administrators too much discretion as regards the constitutional rights of school children? What of *T.L.O.* and other Supreme Court cases like *Hazelwood* and *Fraser* (*supra*, Chapter 6); do these cases together establish a trend that, in fact, narrows the rights of such children? Consider the following article by Rose, *"Reasonableness" — The High Court's New Standard for Cases Involving Student Rights,* 69 Phi Delta Kappan 589 (1988), on the subject:*

> The Supreme Court of the United States is applying a new legal standard in court actions involving the constitutional rights of students. The change has increased the discretion of school officials in such areas as search and seizure, student publications, and student expression. In establishing the new standard, the Court seems to be giving school officials broad latitude in structuring an environment in which students can both learn and develop "socially appropriate behavior."
>
> The cases in which the Court enunciated the new standard — although they involve different areas of student activity — all grew out of situations in which the actions of school officials were viewed by students as violations

---

*Reprinted with permission of Lowell C. Rose.

of their constitutional rights. The first case, *T.L.O. v. New Jersey* (1985), involved an assistant vice principal's search of a student's purse. The student had been accused of smoking in violation of a school rule and had denied all involvement. The search uncovered marijuana and related items that implicated the student in marijuana dealing.

The second case, *Bethel Sch. Dist. #403 v. Fraser* (1986), involved a speech by a student placing another student's name in nomination for an elective office in the high school. The student giving the speech was subsequently penalized for using sexually explicit language in violation of the school's "disruptive conduct rule."

The third case, *Hazelwood Sch. Dist. v. Kuhlmeier* (1988), grew out of a high school principal's decision to prevent the publication of two pages of a student newspaper. The decision was made because the principal felt that two articles, one on student pregnancies and the other on the effects of divorce on young people, were inappropriate.

In each of these cases, the Supreme Court held that the constitutional rights of students had not been violated and upheld the actions of the school officials. More important than the decisions, however, is the fact that in each case the Court applied a standard different from the one previously used in such cases. (The choice of standard is, in the legal arena, *crucial* to the outcome since the various sets of facts are measured against that standard.) The result of the three recent decisions is that, in judging the facts in cases involving student rights, courts at all levels will be applying a standard that seems to make court intervention less likely....

The landmark case in the area of student rights has been *Tinker v. Des Moines Indep. Community Sch. Dist.* (1969). The decision in that case established the fact that students have constitutional rights that must be protected in school. The Court did recognize that these constitutional rights were different in schools but still found that these rights could not be removed except when their exercise would "substantially interfere with the work of the school or impinge upon the rights of other students." The burden for demonstrating that the standard of "substantial interference" was met rested on school officials. By selecting this standard, and by placing the burden of proof where it did, the Court required that schools make a fairly strong evidentiary showing before abridging student rights. This was the standard that was applied by the courts from 1969 until 1985.

In the three most recent cases, however, the Supreme Court established a different standard, the key to which appears to be *reasonableness*....

....

Where then do the recent Court decisions leave school officials? The Court clearly expects school officials to exercise broad authority and seems to be placing its reliance on their judgment, requiring only that "their actions are reasonably related to legitimate pedagogical concerns." This is what might be termed, at law, a "minimum scrutiny" standard.

If one considers *T.L.O.* and the search that was involved, the highest standard the Court could have established for validating the search, and the one most often used in Fourth Amendment cases, would have been the standard of "probable cause." A middle-level standard might have required a "substantial basis" for the search. The Court chose, instead, the even lower standard of "reasonableness." By establishing this standard, the Court is placing considerable confidence in school officials. It is also placing on these officials a major part of the responsibility for maintaining a proper balance between the legitimate constitutional rights of students and the school's equally legitimate need to "maintain an environment in which learning can take place."

3. Do decisions like the one in *T.L.O.* overly influence the behavior of school administrators as to the rights of students? Consider the following statement:

Good educators don't make their decisions based on "what the law will let me do." They act responsibly on behalf of their students, using an abiding sense of justice. In fact, those most concerned with what the law will or will not let them do are often most out of touch with what is required and the[y] most often ignore student rights and mistreat children. W. Wayson, *Due Process Prevents Educators' Doing Only What They Should Not Do*, 284 in T. Jones and D. Semler, *School Law Update* (1985).*

Is this the legacy of the line of Supreme Court cases cited in the Rose article or will the "reasonableness" test actually help school officials in "maintaining an environment in which learning can take place?"

4. Although it is the fruits of the second search that are at issue here, the validity of the search for marijuana must depend on the reasonableness of the initial search for cigarettes, as there would have been no reason to suspect that T.L.O. possessed marijuana had the first search not taken place. *T.L.O.* at 344.

With a statement like this, should readers of this case be concerned about a chain of reasonable searches, one reasonable search to another, then to another and so on? Could such a chain lead inevitably to a Fourth Amendment violation? Is the "sufficient probability" threshold enough to justify further searches?

5. A teacher reported the incident to an assistant principal. How much difference does the identity of the informant make? What of a chain of informants such as when A tells B who tells C who then tells the vice principal? Would this be sufficient under *T.L.O.* to give rise to a reasonable search?

6. Prior to *T.L.O.* more than a few cases held that school officials lacked reasonable suspicion to search the property of students. *See, e.g., Cales v. Howell Pub. Schs.*, 635 F. Supp. 454 (E.D. Mich. 1985) (truant student searched for drugs, but court held that while some school rule may have been violated,

---

*Copyright © 1985 by National Organization on Legal Problems in Education. Reprinted with permission.

there was no reasonable suspicion that student had drugs; *In re William G.*, 221 Cal. Rptr. 118, 709 P.2d 1287 (Cal. 1985) (although student tried to hide a bulging calculator he was accused of stealing, court held no articulable facts, simply a mere curiosity by school officials and student was permitted to assert right of privacy); *T.A. O'B v. State*, 459 So. 2d 1106 (Fla. App. 1984) (teacher observed students with cigarettes in an off-limits area, but court held this insufficient to linkage to drug use). However, after *T.L.O.* most decisions have held in favor of school officials. *See* the cases that follow in this chapter.

7. What is *T.L.O.*'s relation to personnel in the college setting? *See O'Connor v. Ortega*, 480 U.S. 709 (1987), where the court ruled that a search of a professor's desk is governed by *T.L.O.* and the courts will apply a reasonable standard.

8. The Court in *T.L.O.* made it clear that it was not reaching four legal issues as they were not extant in the facts of the case: 1) whether students have a reasonable expectation of privacy in lockers, desks and other school property; 2) whether individualized suspicion is an essential element of the "reasonableness standard"; 3) whether the exclusionary rule is the appropriate remedy for Fourth Amendment violations by school authorities; and 4) what standard should be used when school searches involve law enforcement authorities. Consider the following cases and notes.

1. REASONABLE SUSPICION

EDWARDS v. REES
United States Court of Appeals
883 F.2d 882 (10th Cir. 1989)

SETH, CIRCUIT JUDGE:

....

In December 1985, Dale Rees, a vice principal at Farmington Junior High School in Farmington, Utah, removed Craig Edwards from the class he was attending at Davis High School. Mr. Rees took the student to a closed office where he interrogated him for twenty minutes concerning a bomb threat received earlier at Farmington Junior High. It is asserted that Mr. Rees threatened the student with felony prosecution, and questioned him in an intimidating and coercive manner. Charles Edwards, in behalf of his son, Craig Alan Edwards, filed this damages action against Mr. Rees and the School District under 42 U.S.C. § 1983, alleging that the interrogation incident constituted a denial of Craig Edwards' rights under the Fourth, Fifth, and Fourteenth Amendments to the United States Constitution. Mr. Edwards also brought pendent state law claims. In a well-reasoned memorandum opinion and order, the trial court held that Craig Edwards was not deprived of a constitutional right under § 1983.

C. SEARCH AND SEIZURE

The parties were largely in agreement in their accounts of what took place at Davis High School the day Mr. Rees interrogated Craig Edwards. The areas of doubt as to the facts were not of consequence. Appellant's case suffered, however, from the paucity of facts he presented in opposition to the motion, and in particular from an overreliance on the seriously deficient affidavit of Craig Edwards. The conclusory and unsubstantiated allegations contained in that affidavit failed to controvert the facts presented by appellees to the trial judge, who relied only on those statements in the affidavit that could have been within the personal knowledge of the affiant.

In determining what limits the Constitution places on the investigative and disciplinary activities of school authorities, the courts have always sought to accommodate both the interests protected by the Constitution and the interests in providing a safe environment conducive to education in the public schools. *New Jersey v. T.L.O.*, 469 U.S. 325, 332 n. 2 (1985). While students do not "shed their constitutional rights ... at the schoolhouse gate," *Tinker v. Des Moines Ind. Community School Dist.*, 393 U.S. 503, 506 (1969), the Supreme Court has never held that "the full panoply of constitutional rules applies with the same force and effect in the schoolhouse as it does in the enforcement of criminal laws." *T.L.O.*, 469 U.S. at 350 (POWELL, J., concurring).

Appellant argues that Mr. Rees effected an unlawful seizure of Craig Edwards under the Fourth Amendment when he took him to an office in the school building to question him about the bomb threat. Appellant argues that Craig Edwards was seized for the purposes of the Fourth Amendment because he was taken to a closed office in which he felt constrained to remain until the conclusion of the interrogation. Appellees argue that the incident did not constitute a seizure because Craig Edwards was never told he could not leave, and because Mr. Rees testified in a deposition that he would not have attempted to stop Craig Edwards had he tried to leave. For the purposes of this appeal, we assume without deciding that Mr. Rees seized Craig Edwards for the purposes of the Fourth Amendment, but we hold that any such seizure was reasonable.

In considering whether Mr. Rees' conduct constituted an unreasonable seizure, the trial court applied the standard enunciated by the Supreme Court with respect to searches by school officials in *New Jersey v. T.L.O.*, 469 U.S. 325 (1969). *T.L.O.* involved the search of a student's purse by a school official who suspected her of smoking on campus. The Court held that school officials are bound by the strictures of the Fourth Amendment, but concluded that ... "the legality of a search of a student should depend simply on the reasonableness, under all the circumstances, of the search." *Id.* at 341. The Court held that a search of a student by a school official is reasonable if it is "justified at its inception," and "reasonably related in scope to the circumstances which justified the interference in the first place." *Id.* We believe that the same considerations which moved the Supreme Court to apply a relaxed Fourth Amendment standard in cases involving school searches support applying the same standard in school seizure cases.

Mr. Rees' conduct was justified at its inception by the statements made to him by two students, both of which implicated Craig Edwards as the individual who called in the threat. Appellant did not dispute that these statements were made to Mr. Rees. The statements led Mr. Rees to believe that questioning Craig Edwards about the incident might "turn up evidence that [Craig Edwards had] violated ... either the law or the rules of the school." Given the seriousness of the suspected offense, questioning Craig Edwards in an office in the school building for twenty minutes was reasonably related in scope to determining whether he had indeed called in the bomb threat.

Appellant argues, however, that the *T.L.O.* standard is not apropos here, chiefly because Mr. Rees was a vice principal of Farmington Junior High School, while Craig Edwards was a student at Davis High School, where the interrogation took place. Appellant offers no case law, nor any persuasive justification, for drawing an artificial line between schools within a school district over which a school official may not pass for the purpose of maintaining school order. We decline to draw lines that the Davis County School District apparently has determined are unnecessary to achieve its education objectives.

....

... We ... conclude that the trial court properly granted summary judgment as to both Mr. Rees and the Davis County School District. Accordingly, the judgment of the trial court is AFFIRMED in all respects.

CALES v. HOWELL PUBLIC SCHOOLS
United States District Court
635 F. Supp. 454 (E.D. Mich. 1985)

NEWBLATT, DISTRICT JUDGE:

....

... On April 30, 1980, Plaintiff Ruth Cales was 15 years of age and a 10th grade student at Howell High School assigned to the afternoon session. On that day at a time when she was required to be in school session, she was observed by the Howell High School security guard, Joe Twohig, in the parking lot attempting to avoid detection by "ducking" behind a parked car. When confronted by Twohig and asked to identify herself, she gave a name other than her own. Plaintiff was subsequently taken to the office of Assistant Principal Daniel McCarthy where she was made to dump the contents of her purse on a desk, said contents included Howell High School "readmittance slips" which were improperly in Plaintiff's possession. Plaintiff was then instructed to turn her jean pockets inside-out, and she subsequently completely removed said jeans. Plaintiff was then required to bend over so Defendant Steinhelper could visually examine the contents of her brassiere. The basis for the "search" was the belief of Assistant Principal Daniel McCarthy that the Plaintiff was in possession of illegal drugs. During the "search" the only persons present were Plaintiff, Defendant Steinhelper, Assistant Principal, and Defendant Wise, Secretary to

C. SEARCH AND SEIZURE

Defendant McCarthy who also was an Assistant Principal. At no time was Plaintiff's person or body touched in any manner.

A. *Howell Public Schools*

The appropriate standard for determining whether this defendant can be held liable for the alleged civil rights violation in this case is found in *Monell v. Dept. of Social Services*, 436 U.S. 658 (1978). In *Monell*, the Court ruled that § 1983 liability could be imposed on a unit of local government upon a showing that: The action that is alleged to be unconstitutional implements or executes a policy statement, ordinance, regulation, or decision officially adopted and promulgated by that body's officers. Moreover, although the touchstone of the § 1983 action against a government body is an allegation that official policy is responsible for a deprivation or rights protected by the Constitution, local governments, like every other § 1983 "person," by the very terms of the statute, may be sued for constitutional deprivations visited pursuant to governmental "custom" even though such a custom has not received formal approval through the body's official decision-making channels.... *Id.* at 690-91.

Thus, in this case, plaintiff must show that the Howell Public Schools had a policy or custom concerning the strip search of students which led to the alleged violation of plaintiff's constitutional rights. The record as it now exists is insufficient to allow this Court to enter summary judgment on behalf of either party on this issue. During her deposition, Mary Steinhelper testified that the authority to search came from the Student Code of Conduct. She later indicates that she is unsure whether a written policy concerning student searches exists. Finally, she indicates that while the high school administrators discussed the issue of student searches, she did not know whether the guidelines mentioned at the time represented the policies of the Howell School System. Clearly then a genuine issue of fact remains....

B. *McCarthy and Steinhelper — Liability*

1. *Daniel McCarthy*

As noted earlier, Mr. McCarthy did not take part in the search. Instead, he directed Mary Steinhelper to conduct the search. Consequently, it is more appropriate to analyze his conduct under a supervisory liability theory. Supervisory personnel are subject to liability where evidence establishes that they authorized [or] approved ... the unconstitutional conduct of the offending officers.

2. *Mary Steinhelper*

The Supreme Court in *New Jersey v. TLO*, 469 U.S. 325 (1985) recently articulated the standard to be applied in deciding whether the search of a student by school officials violates his or her Fourth Amendment rights.

... [T]he legality of a search of a student should depend simply on the reasonableness, under all the circumstances, of the search. Determining the reasonableness of any search involves a twofold inquiry: first, one must consider "whether the ... action was justified at its inception," second, one must determine whether the search as actually conducted "was reasonably related in scope to the circumstances which justified the interference in the first place." Under ordinary circumstances, a search of a student by a teacher or other school official will be "justified at its inception" when there are reasonable grounds for suspecting that the search will turn up evidence that the student has violated or is violating either the law or the rules of the school. Such a search will be permissible in its scope when the measures adopted are reasonably related to the objectives of the search and not excessively intrusive in light of the age and sex of the student and the nature of the infraction.

The facts of the instant case create an interesting situation. As previously mentioned, defendant McCarthy ordered the search, defendant Steinhelper conducted it. Thus, if defendant McCarthy was not justified in requesting the search, both he and defendant Steinhelper are liable. If, however, the search was justified, and if the scope of the search was reasonable, neither defendant can be held liable.

In addressing the first prong of the test, the Court again refers to the stipulated facts. Plaintiff was observed ducking behind a car in the Howell High School parking lot at the time she should have been in school. When questioned by a security guard, she gave a false name. Based on this conduct, defendant McCarthy concluded that plaintiff was involved in drugs and should be searched. It is clear that plaintiff's conduct created reasonable grounds for suspecting that some school rule or law had been violated. However, it does not create a reasonable suspicion that a search would turn up evidence of drug usage. Plaintiff's conduct was clearly ambiguous. It could have indicated that she was truant, or that she was stealing hubcaps, or that she had left class to meet a boyfriend. In short, it could have signified that plaintiff had violated any of an infinite number of laws or school rules. This Court does not read *TLO* so broadly as to allow a school administrator the right to search a student because that student acts in such a way so as to create a reasonable suspicion that the student has violated some rule or law. Rather, the burden is on the administrator to establish that the student's conduct is such that it creates a reasonable suspicion that a specific rule or law has been violated and that a search could reasonably be expected to produce evidence of that violation. If the administrator fails to carry this burden, any subsequent search necessarily falls beyond the parameters of the Fourth Amendment. Because the facts here establish that the search was not reasonable at its inception, it is unnecessary to address the second prong of the *TLO* test.

C. McCarthy and Steinhelper — Immunity

In *Harlow v. Fitzgerald,* 457 U.S. 800 (1982), the Supreme Court held that:

> "... government officials performing discretionary functions generally are shielded from liability for civil damages insofar as their conduct does not violate clearly established statutory or constitutional rights of which a reasonable person would have known."

1. Daniel McCarthy

The events which served as the basis for this action occurred long before the Supreme Court's holding in *TLO*.... However, the principals underlying those decisions were clearly established at the time of this action.... It is beyond peradventure that school children do not shed their constitutional rights at the school house gate. *Tinker v. Des Moines Independent Comm. School Dist.*, 393 U.S. 503, 506 (1969). It is well recognized that school officials are subject to constitutional restraints as state officials....

The deposition of Mary Steinhelper clearly establishes that the defendants were well aware that the students were entitled to Fourth Amendment protection.... Ms. Steinhelper indicates that the necessity of having probable cause before conducting a search was discussed at length at an administrators' meeting.

Thus, there can be no question that plaintiff had a clearly established right to be free from the unreasonable searches of school administrators. The only issue that was unclear at the time was the quantum of evidence necessary to justify the search. However, it is clear that defendants knew at a minimum that reasonable cause or reasonable suspicion was necessary to justify a search by school administrators. Since the Court has already concluded that reasonable suspicion was lacking here, the Court must conclude that defendant McCarthy is not entitled to qualified immunity as a matter of law.

2. Mary Steinhelper

The applicability of qualified immunity to this defendant turns on the scope of the search rather than whether the search was justified.... As the record shows, defendant Steinhelper was instructed to search for contraband in the form of drugs. She looked in plaintiff's purse, in the pockets of plaintiff's jeans, and in plaintiff's brassiere. At no time did she touch plaintiff. Clearly the measures adopted by Ms. Steinhelper were reasonably related to the objectives of the search. Moreover, the search was not excessively intrusive given plaintiff's age (15) and the seriousness of the infraction. Consequently, the court must conclude that defendant Steinhelper is entitled to qualified immunity as a matter of law.

....

Conclusion

For the reasons set forth above, plaintiff's Motion for Partial Summary Judgment and defendants' Motion for Summary Judgment as to defendant Howell

Public Schools are *denied*. Plaintiff's Motion is granted and defendants' Motion is denied as to defendant McCarthy. Defendants' Motion is granted and plaintiff's Motion is denied as to defendant Steinhelper....

It is so ordered.

---

1. The holding in *Edwards* reiterates the test of reasonableness found in *T.L.O.*, to wit: "a search of a student by a school official is reasonable if it is 'justified at its inception,' and 'reasonably related in scope to the circumstances which justified the interference in the first place.'" *Edwards* at 884 (quoting *T.L.O.* at 341). The justification for the first prong rests in statements by student informants that the student made a bomb threat. What in this case substantiates this information as reliable? Is it simply because the student did not dispute the statements?

2. School officials in *Edwards* actually argued that the actions of the assistant principal were not a Fourth Amendment violation in that no seizure was involved. Instead the student was never told he could not leave the principal's office, and moreover, the assistant principal testified in a deposition that he would not have attempted to stop the student had he tried to leave. How convincing is this testimony? When students are taken to a school administrator's office to be questioned, is it reasonable to assume that such students know that they can leave unless told otherwise? What of the condition of "captive audience" pervading the feelings of most students who face possible discipline?

3. What of the reasonableness of student informant testimony? *See, e.g., State v. Slattery*, 787 P.2d 932 (Wash. Ct. App. 1990) *rev. denied*, 114 Wash. 2d 1015 (1990) (student told a vice principal that another student was selling marijuana in the school parking lot. The court ruled the information reliable because of vice principal's past experience with the informant); *Bahr v. Jenkins*, 539 F. Supp. 483 (E.D. Ky. 1982) (reasonable suspicion found for searching a student's purse for firecrackers when several other students accused her of possession); *People v. Singletary*, 37 N.Y.2d 310, 333 N.E.2d 369 (1975) (state court upheld a successful search and seizure of heroin conducted on the basis of a student tip that had been reliable in five other instances).

4. The court stated that Berry's denial of the drug trafficking charge was one of the factors which made the search reasonable and justified at its inception. What if the student had been silent when asked if he were drug dealing? Would failure to answer questions be good enough, with the other facts as presented here, to justify the search?

5. In *Edwards v. Rees*, the student was taken out of class and detained for twenty minutes without a constitutional violation due to his alleged bomb threat. Courts have not hesitated to find such actions by school officials to be reasonable in drug possession cases. *See Cason v. Cook*, 810 F.2d 188 (8th Cir. 1987) (student removed from classroom, detained and searched by school official and

C. SEARCH AND SEIZURE

police liaison officer); and *Martens v. District No. 220 Bd. of Educ.*, 620 F. Supp. 29 (N.D. Ill. 1985) (reasonable suspicion found due to school's persistent drug problem, and tipster successfully identified another student who possessed drugs earlier that day).

6. What of circumstances when a search is said not to have been reasonable? What of the ambiguousness of a student's actions? This was just the question entertained by the Court in *Cales v. Howell Pub. Schs.* where the court allowed that a student's "ducking behind a car" did not create a reasonable suspicion that drugs would be found. Does the decision here create a burden on administrators not found in other cases?

7. Can a student who acquiesces to a search challenge that search later as a violation of constitutional rights: *See Tarter v. Rayback*, 742 F.2d 977 (6th Cir. 1984) (fact that student acquiesced in initial search did not necessarily demonstrate the relinquishment of his right to challenge where student may have submitted only because he was afraid). In *Tarter*, the school's search was upheld due to reasonable and particularized suspicion; the search was necessary in the furtherance of maintaining school discipline and safety.

8. In *Cales*, the court stated:

> Clearly, the measures adopted by Ms. Steinhelper were reasonably related to the objectives of the search. Moreover, the search was not excessively intrusive given plaintiff's age (15) and the seriousness of the infraction. Consequently, the court must conclude that defendant Steinhelper is entitled to qualified immunity as a matter of law. *Cales* at 458.

From this statement, can we assume that the age of the student and the seriousness of the infraction dictate the scope of the search? Does this mean that reasonable suspicion has nothing to do with whether such a search should begin? If so, does this create a situation where as long as school administrators suspect a serious infraction, however unreasonable, a search as personal as this one can be conducted?

Could Steinhelper's qualified immunity also be justified by the fact that she was directed by a superior to conduct the search? Has the possibility of teachers and administrators getting away with personal searches under qualified immunity increased as a result of this case?

9. For a case with similar facts, but decided differently, *see Widener v. Frye*, 809 F. Supp. 35 (S.D. Ohio 1992). The search of a high school student was reasonable as a matter of law, where school officials detected what they believed to be the odor of marijuana emanating from the student's person, and observed that the student was acting sluggish and lethargic in a manner consistent with marijuana use. Moreover, the search was reasonable in scope in light of the student's age and seriousness of the infraction. Student was asked to remove his jeans only, in the presence of two male security guards and was never threatened or touched inappropriately.

10. There are other limits on school administrators' reasonable suspicion. The fact that a student was tardy or truant from class, that the student engaged in "furtive gestures" in attempting to hide his calculator case from view of the school principal and that student demanded a warrant, provided no reasonable basis for the school official (who lacked any prior knowledge or information relating to student's possible possession, use or sale of illegal drugs or other contraband) to search student's calculator case. *In re William G.*, 40 Cal. 3d 550, 709 P.2d 1287 (1985).

2. INDIVIDUALIZED SUSPICION

WEBB v. McCULLOUGH

United States Court of Appeals
828 F.2d 1151 (6th Cir. 1987)

BOGGS, CIRCUIT JUDGE:

Wendy Webb (Webb) was sent home early from a high school trip to Hawaii and suspended from school after a search of her hotel room revealed alleged violations of school and trip rules. She sued the school administrators for alleged violations of her Fourth and Fourteenth Amendment rights. The district court granted defendants summary judgment on all the federal claims based on the searches and suspensions, and therefore dismissed pendent state claims. We affirm the grant of summary judgment on the searches and suspensions, but remand due to the possibility that an alleged battery violated Webb's substantive due process rights.

I

Webb joined about 140 other members of the Hixson High School Band in a trip to Hawaii for a band competition in late March 1985. On March 29, Webb and her roommates were getting ready to go shopping when Appellee Thomas McCullough, the Hixson High School Principal, (McCullough), used a key to enter their hotel room without warning, in the company of Mr. Crumley, a chaperon, according to Webb. All four roommates were present, one in bra and shorts. The two men left, and Mrs. McCullough entered and told the girls to finish dressing. According to McCullough, he announced his and Crumley's presence before entering, and his wife entered first to assure that the girls were dressed. McCullough and Crumley re-entered, and according to Webb, informed the girls that the front desk had told him to search the room for alcoholic beverages. He searched the bedroom, bathroom, and Webb's suitcase, including "personal hygiene items." Neither that search nor contemporaneous searches of other students' rooms found any alcoholic beverages.

That evening, McCullough held a meeting and told students that he had reason to believe that the rules had been violated. According to Webb, McCullough told the group that anyone caught with alcohol or illegal drugs would be sent home, and anyone who violated curfew would have to come in earlier the following

C. SEARCH AND SEIZURE 451

night. The students were dismissed at approximately 10:50 p.m. and Webb and her roommates went back to their room.

As Webb and her roommates returned to their room, they saw another female student in the hall, talking to two unknown boys. The girl and the two boys then came to Webb's door and Webb and her roommates sat in the hall immediately outside the door to their room talking with them. Webb's chaperon, Mrs. Bandy, gave Webb and the roommate permission to stay there until Bandy had completed her room checks.

According to Webb, there was a phone call for her as she sat talking with the other girls and the two boys, which she entered the room to answer. One of the boys followed Webb. According to Webb, she told him he couldn't stay, and went into the hallway to ask her roommates why he was in the room. McCullough then told Webb and her roommates to go into their room. They replied that they had been given permission by their chaperon to stay there for a while.

McCullough then directed the one boy in the hall to leave and told the girls to go to their room. Webb and the roommates went into their room. According to McCullough, he entered the room and found no one else present, whereupon he left. Webb disputes this, claiming that only Bandy came in shortly thereafter to discuss the next day's schedule. Neither party states any knowledge of the other boy's whereabouts, at that point.

According to McCullough, upon being informed by one of the chaperons that some students had used an unoccupied room adjacent to, and sharing a balcony with, Webb's room the previous night, he notified a hotel security officer, who opened the room. Upon entering, McCullough saw a teenage boy on the balcony of the room. The boy jumped over a barrier between the two sections of the balcony. McCullough then re-entered Webb's room, and saw the boy jump back to the balcony outside the unoccupied room. The boy was then apprehended by the security officer. According to Webb, McCullough then re-entered the room and stated that there was a boy on the balcony. He left, and motioned for Bandy to leave. He then told the girls to pack their bags because he was sending them home on the first available flight, as a boy had been caught by the security guard. While he was doing this, one of the chaperons found a six-pack of beer and a quart of wine in the adjacent room's refrigerator.

According to the girls, they attempted to offer explanations, but McCullough wouldn't listen. McCullough stated that he found wine and beer in the next room.

According to Webb, McCullough then left, and she locked herself in the bathroom. One roommate was crying, and the other two called for McCullough to return. McCullough was quite angry when he realized Webb was in the bathroom. He tried to jimmy the bathroom door lock, but Webb would not let him in. He then slammed the door three or four times with his shoulder. The door finally gave way, knocking Webb against the wall. McCullough then thrust the door open again, and it struck Webb again, throwing her to the floor. He then grabbed Webb from the floor, threw her against the wall, and slapped her. She then broke away and ran to her roommates.

McCullough telephoned Webb's parents and informed them that she was being sent home. Early the next morning, March 30, he left Webb and her roommates at the airport. Their luggage was sent ahead, and they were left at the airport with stand-by tickets for any flight headed to any city on the mainland, with funds insufficient to buy meals. The girls were not able to obtain seats until approximately 24 hours later. Therefore, they had to spend the night at the airport. After another delay and a detour to Chicago, the girls arrived in Chattanooga at about 3:30 a.m. on April 1, about 36 hours after McCullough abandoned them at the airport in Hawaii.

On April 5, McCullough suspended Webb and the roommates, effective April 8, for violation of curfew, having a male in their room, having liquor in the next room, and trespassing into adjacent rooms of the hotel. Webb contends that Superintendent James McCullough (the Superintendent) knew and approved of the suspension. McCullough (the principal) met with Webb and her parents on April 8. According to Webb, he stated that he had suspended her because her parents had spoken with members of the Board of Education concerning his actions. A meeting with the Superintendent and McCullough followed on April 10. Webb then sought a federal injunction. On April 17, an agreement was reached between Webb's attorney and the City Attorney's office to readmit Webb to school. However, Webb was never allowed to return to band class.

On May 23, 1985, Webb and her parents filed suit against the principal, the Superintendent, the Chattanooga Public Schools, and the Chattanooga Board of Education, alleging violation of her 4th Amendment and 14th Amendment rights and 42 U.S.C. § 1983 as to the search of her room and the suspension, and violation of Tennessee statutory and common law as to the suspension, her property right in the room and food for which she had paid, battering, intentional emotional distress, and publication of false and defamatory matter. When Webb reached her majority, the parent's claim was treated as withdrawn by their counsel, and later by the district court. They do not appeal this decision. Webb is now proceeding pro se. Thereafter, the defendants moved for summary judgment.... The district court granted summary judgment and dismissed the pendent state law issues as to all defendants. This appeal is from that grant and dismissal.

II

A

There can be little doubt that principal Thomas McCullough was a representative of the Chattanooga Public Schools during the trip to Hawaii and hence acting under the color of state law.... The question therefore arises as to whether there [are] any circumstances under which it is permissible for a public school official to search the private hotel room of a student.

C. SEARCH AND SEIZURE

B

The district court answered this question in the affirmative by examining the searches under the two-part test set out in *New Jersey v. T.L.O.*, 469 U.S. 325 (1985) (hereinafter, *TLO*), which holds that "the legality of a search of a student should depend simply on the reasonableness, under all the circumstances, of the search." The first step is to determine whether the search was justified at its inception by the presence of "reasonable grounds for suspecting that the search will turn up evidence that the student violated or is violating either the law or the rules of the school." If such grounds existed, the second step renders a search "permissible in its scope when the measures adopted are reasonably related to the objectives of the search and not excessively intrusive in light of the age and sex of the student and the nature of the infraction."

....

The district court conducted an incomplete analysis of the record, and thereby incorrectly granted summary judgment. Unless there was some factor which made the search reasonable even under plaintiff's view of the circumstances, the case presented questions for the trier of fact, not for a judge ruling on a motion for summary judgment.

C

Although the district court acted correctly by applying the *TLO* analysis, it erred in limiting itself solely to the *TLO* analysis. Although McCullough was a state actor at all times during the trip, the events which led to this suit did not occur in school. The *TLO* court found that school officials' need to search is based on their interest in maintaining discipline in the classroom and on school grounds.... Even in stressing that violations of rules dealing with minor infractions could justify a search, the Court still referred to "maintenance of discipline in the schools and preservation of order in the schools." This repetitive emphasis on activity at school suggests that the deference extended in *TLO* to searches by school authorities would not apply to the search of a hotel room paid for from a student's own funds or during a non-educational or partially educational field trip than a search in school, unless some other justification is available.

In the setting in which the least process is due, the school, the Supreme Court in *TLO* found permissible the search of a purse of a student who had been observed smoking, but denied smoking. The observation provided the individualized suspicion that the Supreme Court suggested is typically necessary to justify searches. We do not decide whether individualized suspicion is an essential element of the reasonableness standard we adopt for searches by school authorities. In other contexts, however, we have held that although "some quantum of individualized suspicion is usually a prerequisite to a constitutional search or seizure[,] ... the Fourth Amendment imposes no irreducible requirement of such suspicion." Exceptions to the requirement of individualized suspicion are generally appropriate only where the privacy interests implicated by a search are minimal and where "other safeguards" are available "to assure that the individual's reasonable expectation of privacy is not 'subject to the discretion of the official in the field.'"

Thus, even if this court accepted the contention that Webb was only due as much process as is necessary for a search in school, the only statement in McCullough's affidavit supporting his motion for summary judgment was an assertion that prior to his first search of Webb's room he "was advised by several chaperons that some students may have consumed alcoholic beverages while on the trip. I was also advised that some students may have had alcohol and liquor in their rooms." This affidavit does not display particularized suspicion. The record does not reflect that the first search of Webb's room was other than random. Thus, if we look solely to the application of guidelines provided by *TLO* to the facts considered by the district court, it is possible that a jury would find that the search was unreasonable, if defended solely on McCullough's affidavit. Summary judgment based solely on *TLO* would thus be improper.

D

McCullough had a source of authority for his searches of Webb's room other than his role as Principal of Hixson High School. He also had a limited scope of *in loco parentis* authority over Webb. "A person is said to stand *in loco parentis* when he puts himself in the situation of a lawful parent by assuming the obligations incident to the parental relation[ship] without going through the formalities incident to a legal adoption."

We acknowledge that the *in loco parentis* doctrine is no longer recognized as the source of school officials' general authority over pupils. The Supreme Court has noted that *in loco parentis* is not wholly compatible with compulsory school attendance, and cannot generally cloak school officials with the immunities of parents.

....

However, *in loco parentis* retains vitality in appropriate circumstances. For instance, one who is *in loco parentis* to a child who is a member of a household acquires the immunity to negligence claims of a natural parent in many jurisdictions. The trip to Hawaii was an appropriate circumstance for the operation of *in loco parentis*. The principal was acting as both a representative of the state and *in loco parentis* in his task of searching Webb's room. As the district court stated: It must be remembered that this case arose in the context of a "spring break" trip and that the school officials present were charged with the care and safety of the plaintiffs while they were more than 5,000 miles from home. More so than in an ordinary school situation, the school officials were standing *in loco parentis*. They were faced with the difficult task of supervising the students in an unstructured environment far different from that present within the confines of the schoolhouse. In such a situation, it was incumbent upon the

C. SEARCH AND SEIZURE

school personnel to be especially vigilant and ready to deal with any violations of the conduct guidelines which had been established for the trip.

The crucial factual difference between the in-school search in *TLO* and the search during a field trip in this case permits, indeed requires, the application of the *in loco parentis* doctrine. Parental permission was required for the field trip. These factors imply several significant conclusions. First, the trip did not involve mandated education, as it was a voluntary undertaking on the part of Webb and the other band members.... This undercuts the rationale given in *TLO* for the rejection there of the *in loco parentis* doctrine.

Second, a greater range of activities occur during extracurricular activities than during school. Thus, there may be a need for a greater range of intervention by an administrator....

Third, there are many more ways for a student to be injured or to transgress school rules or laws during a non-curricular field trip than during relatively orderly school hours. To expose administrators and school districts to increased tort liability while denying them the authority necessary to lessen the likelihood of student injury would be inequitable and would probably decrease the range of extracurricular activities schools would offer....

Finally, this was a search of Webb's residence, albeit a temporary residence. Such a search simply could not occur in the course of an ordinary school day, the context to which *TLO* applies.

However, *TLO* is not wholly inapplicable. The *TLO* opinion rejected the proposition that *in loco parentis* exempted school officials from the Fourth Amendment. It then held that the Fourth Amendment required that the search be reasonable, considering all the circumstances. Thus, as *in loco parentis* survives in certain prescribed circumstances, McCullough's *in loco parentis* authority is one of the circumstances which must be considered. Although we understand Webb's alleged discomfort at being intruded upon, such embarrassment alone simply does not rise to the level of a constitutional claim, because Webb's factual allegations do not show that the searches exceeded the *in loco parentis* aspect of McCullough's hybrid authority. Thus, there is no genuine issue of material fact on the question of the reasonableness of the searches, and the district court's grant of summary judgment on the issue of the searches is affirmed.

....

BURNHAM v. WEST

United States District Court
681 F.Supp. 1160 (E.D. Va. 1987)

SPENCER, DISTRICT JUDGE:

Plaintiffs, students at Albert Hill Middle School ("AHS") suing by their next friends, have moved for summary judgment in their favor on the two remaining claims in this suit, both of which concern allegedly unconstitutional searches carried out by certain teachers at the direction of Dr. Roy A. West, principal at AHS during the time period pertinent to this case. West and the named teachers (the "AHS defendants") have moved for summary judgment in their favor as to liability for one of the searches, and as to damages and declaratory and injunctive relief. Dr. Lois Harrison-Jones, the remaining defendant and West's supervisor, has moved for summary judgment on the ground that the evidence fails to show sufficient personal involvement on her part to support a claim against her.

The facts will be stated in connection with the motion to which they pertain.

I. *Motion of Dr. Lois Harrison-Jones*

In January 1987, Harrison-Jones was made aware by at least three parents that students at AHS had been searched for "Walkmen" and radios. Harrison-Jones promptly contacted West, asked him to explain his action in ordering the search, and discussed with him both the search and the question of returning the items that had been confiscated.

All or a substantial portion of the AHS student body was subsequently searched for marijuana. When Harrison-Jones learned of the later search, she met with West to discuss his policies concerning searches. Harrison-Jones subsequently sent West a letter advising him to obtain enough information to be able to confine his searches to a narrower population in the future.

At some point in the period encompassing the above events, Harrison-Jones discussed the searches with attorneys connected with the school system.

Supervisory indifference or tacit authorization of subordinates' misconduct, if demonstrably a causative factor in a constitutional injury, is actionable under 42 U.S.C. section 1983.

... Plaintiffs contend that "[t]he basis of plaintiffs' claim against defendant Harrison-Jones is not that she failed to respond at all, but that she failed to act significantly or effectively to prevent future harm...." In essence, this amounts to saying that because an injury happened, Harrison-Jones must have acted inappropriately, which obviously begs the question of how any such act or omission caused the injury. Plaintiffs have utterly failed to show how Harrison-Jones's actual approach to the situation made further violations reasonably probable.

Plaintiffs have also failed to point to evidence of any indifference or tacit approval on Harrison-Jones's part. In support of her summary judgment motion, Harrison-Jones has shown that she promptly investigated the searches in question, inquired into West's policies concerning student searches, discussed the searches with legal counsel, and recommended to West that he narrow the scope of future searches.... Because Harrison-Jones has established the absence of a material factual dispute as to inaction on her part, and as to causation, she is entitled to summary judgment.

C. SEARCH AND SEIZURE

II. *Motion of Plaintiffs*

Facts

In December 1986, during a regular class period at AHS, West announced that he had discovered defacement of school property, and directed the teachers to search students' bookbags, pockets, and pocketbooks for magic markers. Under an AHS rule, students were not permitted to have magic markers on school property unless the magic markers were required in a particular class.

Teachers proceeded to look into bookbags and pocketbooks, and required boys to turn their pockets inside out. There is no evidence that any student was physically touched during the search.

On or about January 6, 1987, a teacher told West that she had observed several students alighting from school buses that morning carrying "Walkmen" or radios. Without making any further inquiry, West ordered a search of all students' bookbags and pocketbooks for Walkmen or similar devices.

A search was conducted pursuant to West's instructions. One teacher told his students to stand by their desks and place the items in their bookbags and purses on top of their desks. He then looked into the emptied purses. Another teacher placed her hand into a plaintiff's purse, but did not find the Walkman that was inside.

On or about February 2, 1987, a teacher reported to West that she had smelled marijuana smoke in two hallway areas near the school cafeteria. Classes were in progress at this time, and no students were in the halls. West went immediately to the hallway areas and detected a strong odor of marijuana in both.... West looked for physical evidence but found none. West then made a "random check" by walking down the hall and asking several teachers whether they had excused any students from class during the period he had determined the marijuana use had occurred....

West ordered a search of all students' pocketbooks and bookbags, and of male students' pockets. During this search, one of the plaintiffs was required to empty her purse onto a teacher's desk, exposing some tampons to the view of the teacher and nearby students. Another teacher sniffed one student's hands to determine if they smelled like marijuana. Students were required to turn their pockets inside out and place the contents on top of their desks.

Discussion

Two matters must be addressed before turning to the merits of plaintiffs' Fourth Amendment claims. First, the AHS defendants made the claim at oral argument that no Fourth Amendment "searches" occurred in this case.... School children have a reasonable expectation of privacy in personal articles carried with them inside purses or wallets. There is no rational basis to exclude bookbags from this zone of protection; certainly the *T.L.O.* Court in *New Jersey v. T.L.O.*, 469 U.S. 325 (1985) suggested no distinction in this regard. Such articles have uniformly been held to be protected by the Fourth Amendment. The occasions on which plaintiffs were required to empty their purses, bookbags, and pockets, exposing the contents to view, were "searches" within the meaning of the Fourth Amendment.

The sniffing of plaintiff Tarsha Page's hands, however, was not a "search." School children do not have a reasonable expectation of privacy in the air surrounding their persons, and school officials may sample this air for the purpose of maintaining a proper learning environment to the same extent that they would be justified in conducting a purely visual inspection. Defendants will be granted summary judgment with regard to the hand-sniff incident.

Second, the AHS defendants point out in their summary judgment motion that Forrest Burnham, the only plaintiff allegedly subjected to a magic marker search, testified at his deposition that he was not searched for magic markers. In response, plaintiffs have submitted Burnham's affidavit to the effect that he misunderstood the questions at his deposition and that he was searched for magic markers. The conflict between Burnham's deposition testimony and his affidavit poses a credibility question going to the material issue of standing. Credibility questions must be resolved by the trier of fact, not by the Court on summary judgment. Plaintiffs' summary judgment motion will therefore be denied as to the magic marker search.

"[T]he underlying command of the Fourth Amendment is always that searches and seizures be reasonable...." *T.L.O.*, 469 U.S. at 337. The searches in the case at bar were all conducted in an atmosphere devoid of individualized suspicion. The United States Supreme Court has not decided whether individualized suspicion is a necessary component of the reasonableness standard applicable to school searches, but it has strongly suggested that this question should be answered by recourse to the same reasonableness balancing analysis applied in other search cases.

Exceptions to the requirement of individualized suspicion are generally appropriate only where the privacy interests implicated by a search are minimal and where "other safeguards" are available "to assure that the individual's reasonable expectation of privacy is not 'subject to the discretion of the official in the field.'" The Fourth Amendment interest-balancing process may, in some cases, entirely preclude insistence on individualized suspicion....

In school cases, the child's interest in privacy balances against the interest in maintaining discipline in the classroom and on school grounds. A search of a "closed purse or other bag" carried on a child's person, "no less than a similar search carried out on an adult, is undoubtedly a severe violation of subjective expectations of privacy." These expectations of privacy on the part of a school child are legitimate. Equally legitimate is the school's "need to maintain an environment in which learning can take place." But school officials may not unreasonably satisfy the latter need at the expense of the child's privacy interest, because the Fourth Amendment's "prohibition on unreasonable searches and seizures applies to searches conducted by public school officials." To determine the reasonableness of the searches in this case, the Court must consider first "'whether the ... action was justified at its inception....'" Under ordinary circumstances, a search of a student by a teacher or other school official will be "justified at its inception" when there are reasonable grounds for suspecting that the search will turn up evidence that the student has violated or is violating either the law or the rules of the school.

The Walkman search was unjustified at its inception because there were no reasonable grounds to suspect that the search of any given student would turn up evidence of that student's violation of any law or school rule. At best, it would have been reasonable to suspect that some unknown members of the student body had Walkmen or radios in their possession. The marijuana search illustrates even more clearly the unjustifiable nature of the sweep searches in this case, because suspicion in this instance could not reasonably be narrowed even to the entire student body. The scent of marijuana was reported to West while the students were in class, and when he investigated the hallways for himself the scent was still strong. His cursory efforts to determine whether any student had left a classroom during the relevant time period led to no evidence that a student had been in the area. In one of the hallways was a door to the outside. The places where the scent was detected were open hallways rather than confined areas to which only certain individuals had access, and the fact that these hallways led to the cafeteria indicates that nonstudents would reasonably be expected to use them during the time in question.

While the Court readily accepts the proposition that drug abuse is a serious problem, defendants have offered no evidence concerning its prevalence at AHS. Smuggling Walkmen or radios into school is obviously a less serious problem than drug abuse, and there is likewise no evidence of its prevalence at AHS. Defendants have made no sufficient showing of exigency requiring an immediate search without particularized suspicion, while plaintiffs, on the other hand, have shown a striking paucity of investigatory measures reasonably calculated to narrow the field of suspects....

General searches have uniformly been condemned in the absence of other factors supporting reasonableness.... Under the strong majority view, the Fourth Amendment requires individualized suspicion in the mass drug testing context generally.... Finally, and most importantly, the balance this Court strikes in favor of individualized suspicion accords with the decisions that have addressed the issue in the school setting.

... [T]he AHS defendants urge this Court to adopt the rule that a school administrator's search is valid so long as he or she had reasonable cause to believe that a law or a school rule had been violated. But this rule hardly furnishes an objective alternative to individualized suspicion that might safeguard the students' privacy interest. Reasonable cause to believe — or even certainty — that a violation of rule or law has occurred is no safeguard; instead, when standing alone as in this case, it serves merely as an invitation to an impermissibly broad search.... To permit searches on a mere generalized suspicion would vitiate the principles established in *T.L.O.*, because the bare suspicion that a crime or infraction has occurred offers no protection to the legitimate expectation of privacy held by each member of the student body, an expectation that *T.L.O.* teaches must at least be weighed in the balance.

....

It might be expedient to allow a general search of students in a public school setting at the whim of the principal. Such a result might indeed enhance the principal's stated goal of increased order in the school. However, neither the Constitution nor its primary guardian — the federal judiciary — should bow to expediency. The constitutional rights of all citizens should be affirmed and protected in spite of any systemic discomfort created by mandating respect for those rights. Even though it is easier and more effective, from a school administrator's point of view, to be able to authorize general searches without the burden of individualized suspicion, this Court finds no genuine, material issue of fact as to the claimed unconstitutionality of the searches under consideration, and holds that plaintiffs are entitled to summary judgment thereon.

Except for claims arising out of the magic marker search, plaintiffs' motion for summary judgment will be granted.

III. *Motion of the AHS Defendants*

The AHS defendants have moved for summary judgment in their favor on the magic marker claims. As explained above, plaintiffs' motion on the same subject must be denied because of a credibility issue arising in discovery, and defendants' motion will be denied for the same reason. The remaining issues raised by the motion concern the relief to be granted in this case.

Qualified Immunity

The AHS defendants are entitled to summary judgment on their claim of qualified immunity. This issue "turns on the 'objective legal reasonableness' of the action ... assessed in light of the legal rules that were 'clearly established' at the time it was taken."

This Court's essential determination on the Fourth Amendment issue is that the individualized suspicion requirement of certain pre-*T.L.O.* cases considering school searches retains its vitality after *T.L.O.* This determination cannot be taken as "clearly established" for the purpose of imposing monetary damages on the defendants because the issue has not been authoritatively decided by the United States Supreme Court, the United States Court of Appeals for the Fourth Circuit, or the Supreme Court of Virginia. The *T.L.O.* Court explicitly left this issue open. While the defendants must certainly be charged with knowledge that the Fourth Amendment protects students' legitimate privacy interests, plaintiffs have not shown to the requisite level of specificity that the defendants should have known that the actions taken in this case would violate those interests....

The AHS defendants' summary judgment motion will be granted as to qualified immunity against the federal and state claims.

Punitive Damages

In the preceding section, it was determined that defendants cannot be charged with knowledge of the individualized suspicion requirement in the circumstances of this case. It follows, therefore, that no jury could reasonably award punitive damages for disregarding such a requirement. In any event, plaintiffs have not pointed to sufficient evidence of defendants' "'reckless or callous indifference" or "evil intent" to justify sending the issue to a jury.

....

IV. *Order*

For the reasons stated above, it is hereby *ordered* as follows:

Plaintiffs' motion for summary judgment is *granted* as to the "Walkman" and marijuana searches, but *denied* as to the magic marker search.

The motion of defendant Harrison-Jones for summary judgment is *granted*.

The AHS defendants' motion for summary judgment is *granted* as to the claims for compensatory and punitive damages and as to the hand-sniff incident, but *denied* as to all other matters.

---

1. The *Webb* court makes it clear that this case does not decide the question of whether "individualized suspicion is an essential element of the reasonableness standard ... [to be used] ... for searches by school authorities." *Webb* at 1156. The court then went on to find that the principal, based on his affidavit, had only a generalized suspicion of a violation of school rules by the students. Where does this leave students in their desire to pursue causes of action such as these? What of the defenses to be used by school officials?

2. The court analysis emanates from the decision in *T.L.O.* where the Supreme Court refused to decide whether individualized suspicion is an essential element of reasonable suspicion. The Court stated that individualized suspicion is generally required, but the Fourth Amendment imposes no mandate for a symbiosis of the two. As a caveat, however, the Court voiced the following:

> Exceptions to the requirement of individualized suspicion are generally appropriate only where the privacy interests implicated by a search are minimal and where "other safeguards" are available to assure that the individual's reasonable expectation of privacy is not "subject to the discretion of the officer in the field." *T.L.O.* at 342.

Subsequent Fourth Amendment cases have held that individualized suspicion is not required if there is potential harm on the part of the student or the existence of an exigency situation. *See* note 7 below.

3. The court in *Webb* circumvented the issue of individualized suspicion by concentrating on the *in loco parentis* doctrine; specifically, the surrogate parent responsibilities of school personnel are heightened when school sponsored

activities take place in a non-school setting. Given this reasoning would parents escape liability by breaking into a child's room, searching willy nilly and battering a child if they were acting under color of the state? *See Kuehn v. Renton Sch. Dist. #403*, 694 P.2d 1078 (Wash. 1985).

What of the parents' Fourth Amendment rights in a case like this; could such parents bring suit against the principal here alleging no individualized suspicion to break into a room *they* were paying for?

4. Plaintiffs in *Webb* asserted other claims as well. Although (Principal) McCullough's searches of Webb's room fall within his *in loco parentis* authority, the alleged battery does not. The blows by McCullough were not struck in a school context where the need for immediate disciplinary control was at its greatest. Hence, Webb's Fourteenth Amendment claim was not precluded by summary judgment.

The student's pendent state claims of outrageous conduct, intentional infliction of emotional distress, publishing false and defamatory matter and causing the student's record to contain false information were considered on remand since there was at least one federal issue at federal court requiring further proceedings.

5. Note that in *Webb* the girls were not technically guilty of the "beer and boys" regulation. Yet the court still ruled the search reasonable. What justifications are given for this seeming ambiguity? What was the general objective of the search?

6. A supplemental opinion to *Burnham* found that teachers who search students at the expressed direction of the principal were protected from any statutory liability by the doctrine of sovereign immunity. 681 F. Supp. 1169 (E.D. Va. 1988).

7. The *Burnham* court emphasized the absence of individualized suspicion given not only the objects of the search, but the number of students to be searched. Is the seriousness of the object being searched for more determinative a Fourth Amendment violation than the number of students? *See, e.g., Wynn v. Board of Educ.*, 508 So. 2d 1170 (Ala. 1987), where a search of two students' clothing was upheld as there were reasonable grounds for suspecting that evidence of money theft would be found; *In re Alexander B.*, 220 Cal. App. 3d 1572, 270 Cal. Rptr. 342 (1990), where the search of gang members for weapons by police acting at the behest of school officials was upheld even with no individualized suspicion, as school officials have a heightened responsibility to provide a safe and secure environment. *See also Bellnier v. Lund*, 438 F. Supp. 47 (N.D.N.Y. 1977) where strip search of all students in a fifth grade class in pursuit of alleged stolen three dollars was deemed invalid for lack of individualized suspicion as there was only slight danger relative to the intrusiveness of the search.

8. In light of the fact that the "magic marker" search in *Burnham* was not killed via summary judgment, is the court saying that the reasonableness of searches depends, in part, on the object of the search? Is this consistent with the holding in *T.L.O.*?

C. SEARCH AND SEIZURE

9. The court held that the sniffing of one student's hands was not a search. *Burnham* at 1164. *See also Martinez v. School Dist. No. 60*, 852 P.2d 1275 (Colo. Ct. App. 1992). In *Martinez*, the court held that a high school monitor's requiring students to blow into his face so that he could smell their breath did not constitute a search. However, even if it did, the search would not be considered unreasonable. *Jones v. Latexo Indep. Sch. Dist.*, 499 F. Supp. 223 (E.D. Tex. 1980), cited by *Burnham*, anticipated the result in *Martinez*. For more on "sniff" searches, *see* Section 5 in this chapter.

10. Recall *Cales*, discussed earlier in the chapter. Assistant principal conducted a strip search, but given the seriousness of the student's infraction, the search was upheld. But, weren't the principal's actions in *Burnham* "reasonably related to the objectives of the search" given the seriousness of the infraction? Why then two different results in these cases? Could it be based on individual suspicion?

3. LOCKER SEARCHES

COMMONWEALTH v. CAREY

Supreme Judicial Court of Massachusetts, Middlesex
407 Mass. 528, 554 N.E.2d 1199 (1990)

LYNCH, JUSTICE:

. . . .

At the time of the events in question, the defendant, a seventeen year old young man about six weeks shy of his eighteenth birthday, was a senior at Woburn High School. On Monday morning, March 9, 1987, two students reported to their industrial arts teacher that [Craig A.] Carey had just shown them a gun that he had brought to school in response to an altercation that occurred on the previous Friday afternoon. The teacher promptly relayed the information to assistant principal Paul Sweeney. While the teacher did not tell Sweeney the names of the students who had made the report, he assured the assistant principal that he knew them from having them in his class the past six months, and felt they were reliable.

Sweeney immediately told principal James Foley and housemaster Robert DeLuca of the possibility of a gun on school premises, and the three administrators decided on a plan of action. They determined to seek out Carey and, if they could find no evidence of a gun in his possession, to search the areas where he had been, and, if that course yielded no gun, to search Carey's locker.

While these administrators at Woburn High School had never handled a situation in which a student had brought a gun to school, the judge found that they had followed precisely the same steps on numerous prior occasions when they had a reasonable belief that a student had brought contraband to school. However, because in this instance the object of the search was either an armed student or a gun, Sweeney, DeLuca, and Foley agreed to take an extra precautionary measure — they called the police. The judge found that the police had no input into the school administrators' plan, and were notified for safety reasons.

Detective Sergeant Robert Scire of the Woburn police department arrived at the high school within ten to fifteen minutes, and he and the school administrators questioned the defendant in a school office. When a search of the defendant and his most recent whereabouts failed to disclose a gun, DeLuca searched the defendant's locker. He discovered a dungaree jacket in which he found concealed a sawed-off .22 calibre rifle, a gun sight, a black powdery substance, and a bullet. DeLuca brought the jacket and the gun to Detective Scire.

After advising the defendant of his *Miranda* rights, the officer showed Carey the jacket and the gun and asked him whether they were his. After an initial disclaimer Carey acknowledged that they were. The judge found that the defendant was alert, calm, responsive, and cooperative in his interaction with the police officer throughout this period, and that he understood and voluntarily waived his *Miranda* rights. He then denied the motion to suppress.

1. *Search of student's locker.* Any inquiry into the constitutional validity of the school officials' conduct must start with an examination whether this action constituted a search to which the Fourth Amendment to the United States Constitution is applicable. As the Commonwealth concedes, school administrators are governmental actors to whose conduct Fourth Amendment strictures apply. *New Jersey v. T.L.O.*, 469 U.S. 325, 337 (1985). But the Fourth Amendment protects a person from governmental intrusions only when a "legitimate expectation of privacy [exists] in the particular circumstances." The test is whether the defendant had a subjective expectation of privacy, and if he did, "whether society is willing to recognize that expectation as reasonable." *O'Connor v. Ortega*, 480 U.S. 709, 715 (1987).

The Commonwealth asserts that any expectation of privacy a high school student might have in a locker vis-à-vis school administrators is unreasonable, and thus the Fourth Amendment does not apply. In *New Jersey v. T.L.O.*, the Supreme Court recognized, but did not decide, the issue of a student's expectation of privacy in such circumstance....

. . . .

In the absence of such a specific finding ... we conclude that the warrantless search of the locker was ... justified under the Fourth Amendment.

In *New Jersey v. T.L.O.*, 469 U.S. 325 (1985), the United States Supreme Court held that school officials need not obtain a warrant, nor meet the standard of probable cause, in order to search a student under their authority. Rather, the Court held such a search would pass Fourth Amendment muster if it were reasonable in all the circumstances.

Concerns about school officials' vital responsibility to preserve a proper educational environment prompted the Court to adopt a reduced constitutional standard to validate student searches. "The special need for an immediate response to behavior that threatens either the safety of schoolchildren and teachers or the educational process itself justifies the Court in excepting school

C. SEARCH AND SEIZURE

searches from the warrant and probable cause requirement." The Court recognized that a school administrator's task of maintaining discipline in the school has become a more difficult one, as "in recent years, school disorder has often taken particularly ugly forms: ... violent crime[s] in the schools have become major social problems."

The search here not only clearly met such a lesser test, but the facts suggest strongly that probable cause existed as well. On Monday morning, assistant principal Sweeney was told by a teacher, whom he regarded as extremely diligent and reliable from their eighteen years of working together, that two students in his class had reported to him that the defendant had shown them a gun he had brought to school as a result of the Friday afternoon brawl. The teacher assured Sweeney that he knew the students to be reliable.

Reasonable suspicion of wrongdoing is a " 'common-sense conclusio[n] about human behavior' upon which 'practical people' — including government officials — are entitled to rely." "A student's direct statement to a person in authority, indicating personal knowledge of facts which establish that another student is engaging in illegal conduct, may provide school authorities reasonable grounds to search the second student's locker."

Neither a search of Carey nor a retrace of his steps through a cafeteria and a classroom turned up the gun the two students reported seeing. On the basis of school administrators' preexisting knowledge of the defendant's Friday afternoon brawl and the two students' eyewitness report of a gun in the defendant's hands said to be linked to the Friday altercation, together with the failure to find the gun on the person of the defendant or at his most recent whereabouts, housemaster DeLuca's search of Carey's locker was clearly based on common sense, and was reasonable both at its inception and in its scope....

We affirm the judge's denial of the defendant's motion to suppress the sawed-off rifle found within the locker.

....

So ordered.

---

1. *T.L.O.* specifically avoided a decision as to a student's privacy rights in school lockers. Most cases have been decided on whether there exists some school policy about the privacy expectation in school property "provided for the storage of school supplies." The *Carey* decision itself is one example where the privacy issue would depend on whether the school has a policy for locker searches as notification to the students would itself limit intrusion since students would be reluctant to store personal items in lockers. *See also In Interest of Dumas*, 357 Pa. Super. 294, 515 A.2d 984 (1986), a case where students have a reasonable expectation of privacy in lockers equivalent as the expectation of privacy in a purse. The court's concurring opinion stressed no indication on the part of the school for special restrictions on lockers, and school officials failed to notify students of any random searches. In *State v. Joseph T.*, 336 S.E.2d 728 (W. Va. 1985), the privacy of student lockers was upheld based on the West Virginia Board of Education handbook which provided for no student searches unless school officials found a situation so necessary as to maintain the integrity of the school environment and to protect other students. Also, in *S.C. v. State*, 583 So. 2d 188 (Miss. 1991), the Mississippi Supreme Court found an expectation of privacy in lockers under the state constitution.

2. The *Carey* decision holds that reasonable suspicion existed in that there was reliable information that the student was storing a gun. The court also stated that these same facts supported the more stringent standard of probable cause. Given the absence of a written policy concerning locker searches in this case, does this mean that the court was swayed by the gravity of the student's infraction, thus the dicta about probable cause?

3. Does a school district have a duty to periodically search student lockers absent information about a school violation? *See Clark v. Jesuit High Sch.*, 572 So. 2d 830 (La. App. 4 Cir. 1990), involving a student shot in the eye by student with a pellet pistol. The injured student filed suit claiming negligence on the part of the school for failing to routinely search lockers. The court held no responsibility for locker searches absent indication of a particularized problem.

4. When is a search of student lockers not a search? In *Horton v. Goose Creek Consol. Indep. Sch. Dist.*, 690 F.2d 470 (5th Cir., *withdrawing opinion at* 677 F.2d 471 (5th Cir.), *reh'g denied*, 693 F.2d 524 (5th Cir. 1982), *cert. denied*, 463 U.S. 1207 (1983)), the court found the use of dogs to sniff outside of student lockers not a search.

4. AUTOMOBILE SEARCHES

STATE OF WASHINGTON v. SLATTERY

Court of Appeals of Washington, Division 1
56 Wash. App. 820, 787 P.2d 932 (1990)

COLEMAN, CHIEF JUDGE:

....

On February 26, 1987, a student contacted Vice Principal Sterling Thurston in his office at Thomas Jefferson High School. The student told Thurston that Mike Slattery was selling marijuana in the parking lot. Thurston believed the information to be reliable because of his past experience with the informant and because he had received other reports that Slattery was involved with drugs.

Thurston called Slattery into his office and asked him to empty his pockets. Slattery was carrying $230 cash in small bills and a piece of paper with a telephone pager number on it. Thurston recently had learned that pagers are often used by drug dealers. Thurston then called security. A security officer searched Slattery's locker, but found nothing. When Thurston told Slattery that they would have to search his car, Slattery refused. One of the security officers told Slattery

C. SEARCH AND SEIZURE

that they would get into his car one way or another. After speaking to his mother on the telephone, Slattery gave the officials his keys.

The officials found a pager and a notebook inside the car. The notebook had names with dollar amounts written next to the names. The officials then opened the locked trunk of the car. Inside they found a locked briefcase. Slattery first said that he did not know who owned the briefcase, then said a friend owned it and that he did not know the combination. The security officers then pried open the briefcase and discovered what turned out to be 80.2 grams of marijuana. The police were called and Slattery was arrested.

Slattery was charged by information with possession with intent to deliver marijuana.... Slattery was found guilty at a trial on stipulated facts on December 16, 1987.

We first consider whether the magistrate erred when he found that the school officials had reasonable grounds to search appellant and his locker, car, and locked briefcase.

The Fourth Amendment to the United States Constitution and the Washington Constitution, article 1, section 7, protects persons from unreasonable searches and seizures. Government agents, therefore, must have a search warrant unless some other condition justifies a warrantless search.... [S]ee *State v. McKinnon*, 88 Wash.2d 75, 79, 558 P.2d 781 (1977). When, as here, school officials are acting under the authority of the State, Fourth Amendment and Constitution, article 1, section 7 protections apply....

Under the school search exception, school officials may search students if, under all the circumstances, the search is reasonable. Whether a search is reasonable depends upon the satisfaction of two criteria. First, the action must have been justified at its inception. Second, the search conducted must have been reasonably related in scope to the circumstances that justified the interference in the first place. The rationale for the school search exception is that school teachers and administrators have a substantial interest "in maintaining discipline in the classroom and on school grounds", which weighs against a child's interest in privacy.

Appellant concedes that it may have been reasonable to search him and his locker, but argues that it was unreasonable to extend the search to his car and the locked briefcase in the car. The school search exception is a limited one, appellant argues, and applies only to unintrusive searches, such as of a school locker.

....

... [T]he search in this case was reasonable. The vice principal was told that appellant, who was nearly 18 years old, was selling marijuana in the parking lot. The vice principal had reason to believe the information, based upon his past experience with the informant and reports the vice principal had received earlier from others that appellant was involved with drugs. Appellant was carrying a large amount of money in small bills and a pager number that reasonably could lead the principal to expect to find drugs in appellant's possession. Drug use was a serious, ongoing problem at the school. School officials were confronted with exigent circumstances that warranted an immediate search because Slattery or a friend could have removed his car from the school grounds.

When the school officials did not find any drugs on Slattery or in his locker, they logically went outside to search his car, which was parked in the school parking lot where the informant had said Slattery had been selling marijuana. The officials found a notebook with names and dollar amounts next to the names and a telephone pager — then the officials found a locked briefcase.

The school officials' initial search of Slattery's person was justified at its inception. They had reasonable grounds for suspecting that the search of Slattery would turn up evidence that he had violated the law. The searches of Slattery's locker, car, and briefcase were reasonably related in scope to the circumstances which justified the interference in the first place. To limit the school search exception to a search of a student's body or his locker would be anomalous in light of the rationales of *T.L.O.*....

In light of our disposition, it is not necessary for us to discuss appellant's remaining contentions.

The judgment and sentence of the trial court is

Affirmed.

FORREST AND SWANSON, JJ., concur.

....

---

1. In *State v. Slattery*, the court cites to *State v. McKinnon*, 88 Wash. 2d 75, 558 P.2d 781 (1977), a state case with a more demanding standard than that of *T.L.O.* for determining Fourth Amendment violations. Which standard is used in *Slattery*? Does it make a difference?

2. Does *T.L.O.* address the search of automobiles? *See Shamberg v. State*, 762 P.2d 488 (Alaska App. 1988), where the search of a student's automobile was upheld because *T.L.O.* recognized the school's substantial interest in maintaining discipline on school grounds.

3. What of evidence found in a student's automobile during an unreasonable search later used in a criminal trial? *See Coronado v. State*, 835 S.W.2d 636 (Tex. Crim. App. 1992), where the court ruled that such evidence will be suppressed.

4. Articles in plain view in an automobile may be searched and seized without violation of the Fourth Amendment if there was prior justification for the intrusion and the item was inadvertently seen. *Harris v. United States*, 390 U.S. 234 (1968). What about anything else found in the course of a search? *See State v. D.T.W.*, 425 So. 2d 1383 (Fla. Ct. App. 1983) (Action of a teacher aide in patrolling parking lot and discovering drug paraphernalia in open view in student's car was fully justified and reasonable and not a "search" within the

C. SEARCH AND SEIZURE

Tenth Circuits have decided similar cases. In the most recent case, *Zamora v. Pomeroy*, 639 F.2d 662 (10th Cir. 1981), the Tenth Circuit upheld the use of dogs in exploratory sniffing of lockers. Although the focus of the opinion was the due process problem presented by the school's disciplinary action, the court did consider the fourth amendment issues. Noting that the school gave notice at the beginning of each school year that lockers were subject to being opened and that the school and the student possessed the locker jointly, the court held that the school administrator's duty to maintain an educational atmosphere in the school necessitated a reasonable right of inspection, even though the inspection might infringe a student's rights under the fourth amendment. *Id.* at 670.

The Seventh Circuit reached the same result on facts similar to those presented by the GCISD program. In *Doe v. Renfrow*, 475 F.Supp. 1012 (N.D. Ind.1979), op. adopted on this issue and rev'd on another issue, 631 F.2d 91 (7th Cir.) (per curiam), *cert. denied*, 451 U.S. 1022 (1981), the school, with the assistance of the police, used dogs for general, exploratory sniffing of students. The court held that the sniff of a dog is not a search, particularly in view of the diminished expectations of privacy inherent in a public school, the school's right and duty *in loco parentis* to supervise students and maintain an educationally sound environment, and the minimal intrusion involved.

A district court in our own circuit, on the other hand, reached the opposite result, explicitly rejecting *Doe v. Renfrow. Jones v. Latexo Independent School District*, 499 F.Supp. 223, 236 (E.D.Tex.1980). The Latexo Independent School District used dogs to sniff both students and automobiles. The court granted a preliminary injunction against the sniffing. In its view, the school environment was a factor to be considered, but it did not automatically outweigh all other factors. The absence of individualized suspicion, the use of large animals trained to attack, the detection of odors outside the range of the human sense of smell, and the intrusiveness of a search of the students' persons combined to convince the judge that the sniffing of the students was not reasonable. Since the students had no access to their cars during the school day, the school's interest in the sniffing of cars was minimal, and the court concluded that the sniffing of the cars was also unreasonable.... It is against the background of this split in authority that we undertake our own analysis of the question.

The problem presented in this case is the convergence of two troubling questions. First, is the sniff of a drug-detecting dog a "search" within the purview of the fourth amendment? Second, to what extent does the fourth amendment protect students against searches by school administrators seeking to maintain a safe environment conducive to education? On each question, we find an abundance of precedent but scant guidance.

A. *The Canine Sniff as a Search*

Frequent use of drug-detecting dogs by law enforcement officials has led to a great number of cases challenging the admissibility of the fruits of a canine sniff. From these cases, one proposition is clear and universally accepted: if the police have some basis for suspecting an individual of possessing contraband, they may, consonant with the fourth amendment, use a drug-detecting dog to sniff checked luggage, shipped packages, storage lockers, trailers, or cars. While the rationales of these cases are not the same, the majority view is that the sniffing of objects by a dog is not a search. *See, e.g., United States v. Waltzer*, 682 F.2d 370 (2d Cir. 1982); *United States v. Bronstein*, 521 F.2d 459 (2d Cir. 1975), cert. denied, 424 U.S. 918 (1976); *United States v. Fulero*, 498 F.2d 748 (D.C.Cir.1974). *But see, e.g., People v. Williams*, 51 Cal.App.3d 346, 124 Cal.Rptr. 253 (1975); *cf. People v. Campbell*, 67 Ill.2d 308, 10 Ill.Dec. 340, 367 N.E.2d 949, cert. denied, 435 U.S. 942 (1978) (characterization as "search" is not significant; the question is whether the investigation is reasonable). Only the Ninth Circuit has held that the sniffing of objects is a search, though it may at times be reasonable. *United States v. Beale*, 674 F.2d 1327 (9th Cir. 1982); *United States v. Solis*, 536 F.2d 880 (9th Cir. 1976).

The decision to characterize an action as a search is in essence a conclusion about whether the fourth amendment applies at all. If an activity is not a search or seizure (assuming the activity does not violate some other constitutional or statutory provision), then the government enjoys a virtual carte blanche to do as it pleases.... We must analyze the question of whether dog sniffing is a search in terms of whether the sniffing offends reasonable expectations of privacy, *Katz v. United States*, 389 U.S. 347 (1967), and must look at the degree of intrusiveness of the challenged action to determine whether it is the type of activity that can be tolerated in a free society. *Terry v. Ohio*, 392 U.S. 1 (1968); *see also* 1 W. LaFave, *Search and Seizure* § 2.2(a), at 234 (1978).

We have already held that the sniffing by dogs of luggage checked in an airport, *United States v. Goldstein*, 635 F.2d 356 (5th Cir.), cert. denied, 452 U.S. 962 (1981), and luggage checked in a bus terminal, *United States v. Viera*, 644 F.2d 509 (5th Cir.), cert. denied, 454 U.S. 867 (1981), is not a search, reasoning that "the passenger's reasonable expectation of privacy does not extend to the airspace surrounding that luggage." 635 F.2d at 361. We noted that the appellants had released their bags to the custody of the airlines, thereby relinquishing — at least temporarily — all control over them....

The courts have in effect adopted a doctrine of "public smell" analogous to the exclusion from fourth amendment coverage of things exposed to the public "view." *Katz, supra. See also United States v. Ventresca*, 380 U.S. 102 (1965) (implicit); *United States v. Rivera*, 595 F.2d 1095, 1098-99 (5th Cir. 1979) (implicit); *see generally* 1 W. LaFave, *Search and Seizure* § 2.2(a) (1978). The courts have reasoned that if a police officer, positioned in a place where he has a right to be, is conscious of an odor, say, of marijuana, no search has occurred; the aroma emanating from the property or person is considered exposed to the public "view" and, therefore, unprotected. From this proposition the courts have concluded that the sniffing of a dog is "no different," or that the dog's olfactory sense merely "enhances" that of the police officer in the same way that a flashlight enhances the officer's sight.

We find *Goldstein* to be controlling on the question of whether the dogs' sniffing of student lockers in public hallways and automobiles parked on public parking lots was a search. The sniffs occurred while the objects were unattended and positioned in public view. Had the principal of the school wandered past the lockers and smelled the pungent aroma of marijuana wafting through the corridors, it would be difficult to contend that a search had occurred. *Goldstein* stands for the proposition that the use of the dogs' nose to ferret out the scent from inanimate objects in public places is not treated any differently. We hold accordingly that the sniffs of the lockers and cars did not constitute a search and therefore we need make no inquiry into the reasonableness of the sniffing of the lockers and automobiles.

The use of the dogs to sniff the students, however, presents an entirely different problem. After all, the fourth amendment "protects people, not places." *Katz v. United States,* 389 U.S. 347, 351 (1967). Neither *Goldstein* nor *Viera* involved sniffs of persons and therefore they are not controlling.... The Seventh Circuit is the only circuit to have held that sniffs of school children do not constitute a search. We note that there was apparently no evidence in *Renfrow* that the dogs actually touched the students, while the dogs in the GCISD program put their noses right up against the children's bodies....

The students' persons certainly are not the subject of lowered expectations of privacy. On the contrary, society recognizes the interest in the integrity of one's person, and the fourth amendment applies with its fullest vigor against any intrusion on the human body.... This seems preferable to an approach which attributes too much significance to an overly technical definition of "search," and which turns in part upon a judge-made hierarchy of legislative enactments in the criminal sphere....

The circuit courts have unanimously assumed that the use of magnetometers in airport terminals to detect concealed weapons, an activity far less intrusive than the use of large dogs to sniff the bodies of children, is a search. The Fourth Circuit originally held that the magnetometer walk-through is still a search. Indeed, that is the very purpose of the magnetometer: to search for metal and disclose its presence in areas where there is a normal expectation of privacy. *United States v. Epperson,* 454 F.2d 769, 770 (4th Cir.), *cert. denied,* 406 U.S. 947 (1972).

....

We need only look at the record in this case to see how a dog's sniffing technique — *i.e.*, sniffing around each child, putting his nose on the child and scratching and manifesting other signs of excitement in the case of an alert — is intrusive. The SAI representative explained that Doberman pinschers and German shepherds were used precisely because of the image maintained by the large dogs. Plaintiff, Heather Horton, described what happened when the dog entered the classrooms: "Well, we were in the middle of a major French exam and the dog came in and walked up and down the aisles and stopped at every desk and sniffed on each side all around the people, the feet, the parts where you keep your books under the desk." Ms. Horton went on to express her fear of the large dogs. The SAI representative testified that the dogs put their noses "up against" the persons they are investigating.

On the basis of our examination of the record which indicates the degree of personal intrusiveness involved in this type of activity, we hold that sniffing by dogs of the students' persons in the manner involved in this case is a search within the purview of the fourth amendment....

Our decision that the sniffing is a search does not, however, compel the conclusion that it is constitutionally impermissible. The fourth amendment does not prohibit all searches; it only restricts the government to "reasonable" searches. The reasonableness of the procedure turns in this case on the school environment, to be discussed in Part II.B. But the reasonableness is also governed in part by general fourth amendment principles.

A dog's sniff of a person, particularly where the dogs actually touch the person as they do in the GCISD program, may be analogous to the warrantless "stop and frisk" upheld by the Supreme Court on the basis of a suspicion that fell short of probable cause. *Terry v. Ohio*, 392 U.S. 1....

The Court in effect adopted a balancing approach whereby the intrusiveness of the search is measured against society's need for the information. Similarly, the courts have upheld the warrantless use of magnetometers in light of their minimally intrusive character as weighed against the danger of skyjacking....

B. *The Fourth Amendment in the Public Schools.*

The courts have encountered substantial difficulty in accommodating the fourth amendment to the special situation presented by the public schools, where school officials have both a right and a duty to provide a safe environment conducive to education.... As courts in most recent cases have decided, we think it beyond question that the school official, employed and paid by the state and supervising children who are, for the most part, compelled to attend, is an agent of the government and is constrained by the fourth amendment. Accord, *Bellnier v. Lund*, 438 F.Supp. 47 (N.D.N.Y.1977).

But the decision that school officials are governed by the fourth amendment does not dictate a holding that their activity in this case was unconstitutional. The basic concern of the fourth amendment is reasonableness, and reasonableness depends on the circumstances.... The public school presents special circumstances that demand ... accommodations of the usual fourth amendment requirements. When society requires large groups of students, too young to be considered capable of mature restraint in their use of illegal substances or dangerous instrumentalities, it assumes a duty to protect them from dangers posed by anti-social activities — their own and those of other students — and to provide them with an environment in which education is possible. To fulfill that duty, teachers and school administrators must have broad supervisory and disciplinary powers. At the same time, though, we must protect the fourth amendment rights of students. Indeed, constitutional rights in the schools take on a special importance....

When the school official acts in furtherance of his duty to maintain a safe environment conducive to education, the usual accommodation is to require that the school official have "reasonable cause" for his action. Although the standard is less stringent than that applicable to law enforcement officers, it requires more of the school official than good faith or minimal restraint. The Constitution does not permit good intentions to justify objectively outrageous intrusions on student privacy. Thus, though we do not question the good faith of the GCISD officials in their attempt to eradicate a serious and menacing drug and alcohol abuse problem, we cannot approve the program on that basis; we must examine its objective reasonableness.

At least one case has held that the reasonable cause standard applicable in the schools requires individualized suspicion. *Bellnier, supra.* There, a teacher had reason to believe that someone in her class of fifth graders had stolen three dollars, but had no reason to suspect any particular pupil. When a search of the coats and coatroom revealed nothing, the teacher and principal required each pupil to remove his shoes and empty his pockets. The two officials then required each student to step into the washroom and strip to his undergarments. The court held the search unconstitutional, requiring the existence of facts giving the official reasonable particularized suspicions as a predicate for a search. The result in *Bellnier* is unquestionably correct, and we find its reasoning to be equally applicable to the canine sniffing of children. The intrusion on dignity and personal security that goes with the type of canine inspection of the student's person involved in this case cannot be justified by the need to prevent abuse of drugs and alcohol when there is no individualized suspicion, and we hold it unconstitutional.

C. *The Further Searches*

The plaintiffs urge that, even if the initial sniffing of the cars and lockers by the dogs is permissible, the dogs' reactions do not give the defendant a sufficiently strong basis for suspicion to justify a further search. The district court stated that the "generalized perception of a problem of drug and alcohol abuse" along with the positive reaction of the dog give the school sufficient cause to believe that the student occupant or driver has violated school policy to justify opening the locker or car and searching it. The court did not, however, make any finding on the reliability of the dogs, and there was no evidence in the record to support such a finding. In fact, although the representative of SAI asserted that the dogs were quite reliable, he admitted that there were no comprehensive records kept of those incidents when the dogs reacted positively in the absence of contraband. On this record, then, we cannot say whether the reaction of the dogs provided adequate cause for more intrusive searches, and summary judgment is inappropriate. We remand to the district court for development of the record on that point. The standard enunciated by the district court, however, was proper: GCISD need not show that the dogs are infallible or even that they are reliable enough to give the defendant probable cause; instead, the dogs must be reasonably reliable. It will not, however, be enough to show that the dogs are reasonably reliable in indicating the presence or recent presence of contraband. If the reaction is to justify a search, it must give rise to reasonable suspicion that the search will produce something — i.e., reasonable suspicion that contraband is currently present. If the school does have reasonable cause to suspect the presence of contraband, the ease with which it can be destroyed or moved presents an exigent circumstance that excuses the warrant requirement.

....

V. *Conclusion*

We conclude that the use of dogs in dragnet sniff-searches of the students of GCISD is unconstitutional, but that the use of the dogs in similar dragnet sniffing of lockers and cars is not, and we direct the district court to grant relief by appropriate declaration and injunction. Although the use of the dogs in dragnet sniffing of lockers and cars is permissible, we must remand to the district court for the case to proceed to trial on the reliability of the dogs' reactions as the basis for further searches....

....

---

1. The *Horton* case raises more than one issue about the use of "dog sniffs" in school searches. One question is whether a search occurred at all. There has been some conflict among courts represented by *Doe v. Renfrow*, 475 F. Supp. 1012 (N.D. Ind. 1979), and *Jones v. Latexo Indep Sch. Dist.*, 499 F. Supp. 223 (E.D. Tex. 1980). The *Doe* court held that the sniffing by dogs of students was not a search, while *Latexo* held just the opposite. Further questioning must proceed from these cases however. Was there an intrusion into the person's reasonable expectation of privacy, *i.e.* was the person "sniffed" as against some personal property? If the person was sniffed, was it in close proximity or at a distance? In any case, most courts have followed the reasoning of *Latexo* that a dog sniff of a person is a search. Moreover, *Renfrow* has been roundly criticized by researchers as wrongly decided. *See* Gardner, *Sniffing for Drugs in the Classroom — Perspectives on Fourth Amendment Scope*, 74 Nw. U. L. Rev. 803 (1980); Note, *The Constitutionality of Canine Searches in the Classroom*, 71 J. Crim. L. and Criminology 39 (1980); Comment, *Search and Seizure in Public Schools: Are Our Children's Rights Going to the Dogs?*, 24 St. Louis U. L.J. 119 (1979).

2. The court in *Horton*, of course, decided that a dog sniff of students is a search. This, then, brings forth the question of whether such searches are reasonable. In deciding this question courts must determine whether individual

C. SEARCH AND SEIZURE

suspicion is present or whether mass searches were conducted. In *Horton* there were dog sniff searches of the entire student body in the absence of individualized suspicion, thus a violation of the Fourth Amendment. However, the court held no violation for canine sniffing of lockers or automobiles as they were inanimate objects in public where students had only minimal expectations of privacy. Did the court here decide whether dog sniffs of people at a distance constituted a search?

3. Do school officials conduct a "search" by sniffing the hands of random students in a search for drugs? *See Burnham v. West*, 681 F. Supp. 471 (E.D. Va. 1987), where the court ruled students have no expectation of privacy in the air surrounding their persons and school officials may sample this air in an attempt to maintain the proper learning environment.

4. *Horton* examines the cases up to 1982 considering the issue of whether dog sniffs constitute a search. The issue had not been definitively settled in that at least one circuit (the Ninth) had held that sniffing of some objects was a search. This changed with the decision in *United States v. Place*, 462 U.S. 696 (1983), when the Supreme Court ruled decisively that dog sniffs of personal property are so limited in intrusiveness that they cannot be considered a search.

6. STRIP SEARCHES

WILLIAMS v. ELLINGTON

United States Court of Appeals
936 F.2d 881 (6th Cir. 1991)

CELEBREEZE, SENIOR CIRCUIT JUDGE:

....

I

The record before us reveals that on Tuesday, January 19, 1988, Graves County High School Principal Jerald Ellington received a telephone call from a student's mother who expressed concern over a situation in which her daughter, Ginger, was confronted with drugs. Although no names were disclosed, the mother reported that a student had offered drugs to her daughter. Later that day, Ellington called Ginger into his office to learn more about the incident. Ginger reported that during typing class on the day before, she had seen Williams and another girl, Michelle, with a clear glass vial containing a white powder. Ginger also stated that the two girls placed the powder on the tips of their fingers and sniffed it. One of the girls then offered the powder to Ginger, but she refused it. Ellington asked Ginger if she had any problems with the girls, and was satisfied there was no animosity between them to provide Ginger with an ulterior motive for reporting the incident.

Ellington then spoke with Williams' typing instructor, Brenda Cobb, in whose class the alleged drug use occurred.... Ellington ... relayed Ginger's report to Cobb, prompting her to remember an incident involving Williams the previous semester. During the first semester, Cobb found a typed note under Williams' desk in which she had referred to parties involving her friends and the use of the "rich man's drug." When Cobb questioned Williams about the letter, the student passed it off as a joke, and a few months later when Cobb seemed satisfied that there was not a problem, she threw the letter in the trash.

....

Also during this same week, Michelle came to Ellington and reported that another student, Kim, and Kim's boyfriend, Steve, were inhaling a substance called "rush." "Rush" is a volatile substance that can be purchased over the counter, and while possession of "rush" is legal, inhalation of it is illegal under Kentucky law.... Coincidentally, Kim and Steve also came to Ellington and insisted that it was not them, but other students, who were using the substance. Following these reports, Ellington questioned the motives of these students in coming forward and the validity of the information.

On Friday of this same week, January 22, Ginger stopped in to see Ellington during her fifth period geometry class to report "those girls are at it again," or words to that effect, and indicated she had observed the two girls with the white powdery substance again. Ellington sent Ginger back to class and decided to act on the information before the end of fifth period. Ellington contacted Assistant Principal Maxine Easley and apprised her of the week's events. Ellington and Easley then went to the geometry class and called Williams and Michelle out into the hall. Although Ellington observed that neither student appeared disoriented or intoxicated, the two girls were taken to the administrative offices. After escorting the girls into his office and confronting them with his suspicions, Michelle produced a small brown vial from her purse that contained "rush." Michelle claimed the vial belonged to Kim, and although both girls denied possession of any drugs, Ellington wanted to search the girls' lockers because the brown vial did not match the description given by Ginger.

At that time, Assistant Principal Donald Jones, who was also aware of the week's events, went to search Williams' assigned locker. No drugs were found in this locker, nor in the locker Williams had been using to store her personal items. Likewise a search of Williams' books and purse conducted by Assistant Principal Easley produced no evidence of drugs. Finally, Ellington asked Easley to take Williams into her office and search her person, in the presence of a female secretary.[2] Inside Easley's office, Williams was asked to empty her pockets which she promptly did. Easley then asked the girl to remove her T-shirt. Although she hesitated and appeared nervous, Williams complied after

---

[2]The "search and seizure policy," in effect at the time petitioner was searched, was instituted by the Board in 1985 and states the following: 1. A pupil's person will not be searched unless there is a reasonable suspicion that the pupil is concealing evidence of an illegal act.... When a pupil's person is searched, the person conducting the search shall be the same sex as the pupil; and a witness of the same sex shall be present during the search.... Graves County High School Student Handbook, 1987-88, p. 34.

Easley repeated the request. Williams was then required to lower her blue jeans to her knees. In her deposition, Williams testified that Easley pulled on the elastic of her undergarments to see if anything would fall out, but Easley disputes this contention. The district court concluded this factual discrepancy was not material for summary judgment purposes, and as troubling as that conclusion may be, the veritable inconsistency need not be addressed in light of the rationale set forth below. Finally, Williams was told to remove her shoes and socks. Easley found no evidence of drugs as a result of this search.

William Hardy Williams, Appellant's father, lodged a complaint regarding the incident with the Graves County School Board of Education. The Board, in ratifying the conduct in question, believed there existed reasonable suspicion under the search and seizure policy to justify the actions of Defendants Ellington, Jones and Easley. Angela Williams, by her father and next friend William Hardy Williams, then instituted the present suit, pursuant to 42 U.S.C. § 1983, seeking damages and injunctive and declaratory relief.

....

II

A. *Defendants Sued in Official Capacity*

The School Board, its superintendent and members assert that as an arm of the state, the Board enjoys immunity from a 42 U.S.C. § 1983 suit under the eleventh amendment to the United States Constitution. Further, the Board contends it is immune from liability based upon *Monell v. Dept. of Social Services of New York*, 436 U.S. 658 (1978), and its progeny. We agree the Board is immune from suit according to Monell, and therefore we need not address the issue on the basis of the eleventh amendment.

In *Monell v. Dept. of Social Services of New York*, the Supreme Court held that although local governments are not absolutely immune from suits instituted under 42 U.S.C. § 1983, there are some instances where local governing bodies, or officials sued in their official capacities, may nevertheless enjoy immunity. The Court concluded that a municipality may not be held liable under § 1983 based on a theory of respondeat superior; instead, a government is responsible under § 1983 only "when execution of a government's policy or custom, whether made by its lawmakers or by those whose edicts or acts may fairly be said to represent official policy, inflicts the injury...." However, the *Monell* Court was not directly confronted with the municipal liability issue, thereby leaving for further development the "full contours" of such liability under § 1983 to "another day."

In *Pembaur v. Cincinnati*, 475 U.S. 469 (1986), the Court recognized that under the appropriate circumstances, "municipal liability may be imposed for a single decision by municipal policymakers...." *Pembaur*, 475 U.S. at 480. Therefore, although liability may be imposed for an isolated decision made by policymakers, the Court expressed a need for "some limitation ... on establishing municipal liability through policies that are not themselves unconstitutional, or the test set out in *Monell* will become a dead letter." In leaving open the question whether a municipality may be subject to liability for acts taken pursuant to a policy that is not unconstitutional, the Court stated: But where the policy relied upon is not itself unconstitutional, considerably more proof than the single incident will be necessary in every case to establish both the requisite fault on the part of the municipality, and the causal connection between the "policy" and the constitutional deprivation.

In the present case, the search and seizure policy promulgated by the Graves County School Board is a facially valid district-wide policy, allowing for the search of a pupil's person if there is a reasonable suspicion that the student is concealing evidence of an illegal activity. In fact, the exact language of this policy reiterates the criteria set forth by the Supreme Court in *New Jersey v. T.L.O.*, 469 U.S. 325 (1985); in balancing a student's privacy interests under the fourth amendment against the need for order and safety in schools, the legality of a search of a student should depend upon the reasonableness of the search, under all the circumstances.

The search, which was performed in accordance with this constitutionally valid strip search policy, was subsequently ratified by the School Board when Mr. Williams filed a grievance. Therefore, Williams' only grasp at evoking municipal liability under § 1983 is to show that this subsequent ratification is sufficient to establish the necessary causation requirements. Based on the facts, the Board believed Ellington and his colleagues were justified in conducting the search of Williams. There was no history that the policy had been repeatedly or even sporadically misapplied by school officials in the past. Consequently, the School Board cannot be held liable for the ratification of the search in question, because this single, isolated decision can hardly constitute the "moving force" behind the alleged constitutional deprivation.

B. *Defendants Sued in Individual Capacity*

Principal Ellington, Assistant Principals Jones and Easley, Superintendent Watkins and Board members Goodman, Holmes, Howard, Hughes and Wiggins contend they are qualifiedly immune from a § 1983 suit for damages asserted against them in their individual capacities. The test for qualified immunity was enunciated in *Harlow v. Fitzgerald*, 457 U.S. 800 (1982). In drawing no distinction between suits against state officials under 42 U.S.C. § 1983 and suits brought under the Constitution against federal officials, the Court held: "government officials performing discretionary functions, generally are shielded from liability for civil damages insofar as their conduct does not violate clearly established statutory or constitutional rights of which a reasonable person would have known." *Harlow*, 457 U.S. at 818, & n. 30. "[W]hether an official ... may be held personally liable for an allegedly unlawful official action generally turns on the 'objective legal reasonableness' of the action, assessed in light of the legal

C. SEARCH AND SEIZURE 481

rules that were 'clearly established' at the time it was taken." *Anderson v. Creighton*, 483 U.S. 635, 639 (1987).

....

Therefore, the appropriate question is whether Defendants believed, as reasonable officials under the same circumstances, their conduct was lawful and did not violate any constitutional rights that were clearly established at the time of the conduct at issue.

....

It is well established that students do not "shed their constitutional rights ... at the schoolhouse gate." *Tinker v. Des Moines Independent Community School District*, 393 U.S. 503, 506 (1969). *New Jersey v. T.L.O.*, supra, remains the preeminent Supreme Court case discussing fourth amendment rights of school students within the confines of the educational environment....

... [T]he Court in *T.L.O.* applied the same two-fold inquiry to determine what constitutes "reasonableness, under all the circumstances." First, the search must be "justified at its inception," and a search will meet this requirement "when there are reasonable grounds for suspecting that the search will turn up evidence that the student has violated or is violating either the law or the rules of the school." Second, the ensuing search must be reasonable in its scope, and such search will be permissible "when the measures adopted are reasonably related to the objectives of the search and not excessively intrusive in light of the age and sex of the student and the nature of the infraction."

....

... A thorough review of *T.L.O.* reveals that the Court was careful to protect a school official's right to make discretionary decisions in light of the knowledge and experience of the educator and the information presented to him or her at the time such decision was made. Like police officers, school officials need discretionary authority to function with great efficiency and speed in certain situations, so long as these decisions are consistent with certain constitutional safeguards. To question an official's every decision with the benefit of hindsight would undermine the authority necessary to ensure the safety and order of our schools. Like police officers, school officials need discretionary authority to function with great efficiency and speed in certain situations, so long as these decisions are consistent with certain constitutional safeguards.

In this case, it was not unreasonable for Principal Ellington, in light of clearly established rights at the time of the search *i.e.* *New Jersey v. T.L.O.*, to believe that the ordered searches were not a violation of Angela Williams constitutional rights. Likewise, it was not unreasonable for Assistant Principals Jones and Easley to follow Ellington's recommendation, after being fully briefed on the situation, and search Williams' locker, personal belongings and person. Consequently, subsequent ratification of the administrators' conduct by the School Board was not unwarranted in light of clearly established rights.

Ellington's decision to search Williams and her possessions for the presence of drugs was based upon the events that occurred during the week of January 17,

1988. A study of the record leads us to conclude that Ellington and the remaining Defendants were not unreasonable in suspecting, based on the information available at the time, that a search of Williams would reveal evidence of drugs or drug use. Further, Defendants were not unreasonable, in light of the item sought (a small vial containing suspected narcotics), in conducting a search so personally intrusive in nature. A student approached Ellington with information that implicated Williams and Michelle using a white powdery substance during class. Although he was satisfied the informant had no ill motive toward either girl, Ellington went to Michelle's father and Angela Williams' aunt to inform them and attempt to verify the situation.... Ellington also spoke with Ms. Cobb, the typing instructor, who noticed Michelle had appeared strange in class on the day of purported drug use.... Ms. Cobb also related the troubling event regarding Williams' typed letter referring to the "rich man's drug." A few days later, Ginger, the student who had informed Ellington of Williams' alleged drug use earlier that week, left geometry class twice so that she could see Ellington and report that the same girls were using drugs again. Finally, when the two girls were summoned for questioning in Ellington's office, Michelle quickly produced a small brown vial that contained "rush," a substance the inhalation of which is illegal.

Based on these particular facts, and in light of existing case law to guide Defendants, the search was not unreasonable at its inception. Nor was the scope of the search unreasonable, taking into account the size of the clear, glass vial that was sought and the suspected nature of the white powdery substance contained in the vial. After Williams' locker and purse were searched, it was reasonable for Ellington to suspect the girl may be concealing the contraband on her person.... Like *T.L.O.*, after Ellington's initial suspicions were raised, new evidence appeared to justify the extended level of intrusion. In questioning the girls, Ellington already possessed reasonable suspicion to believe the students were concealing evidence of illegal activity; yet Michelle's production of the vial containing "rush," a substance of which inhalation is prohibited by law, warranted further investigation.

The question of qualified immunity in cases involving the fourth amendment rights of students is predicated upon rights that are "clearly established" by the Supreme Court and courts within this circuit; however, such courts have been virtually silent in defining these rights. Based upon the rights that were "clearly established" at the time of the search in question, we grant qualified immunity to Defendants sued in their individual capacity....

....

IV

Based on the foregoing, the district court's granting of summary judgment in favor of Defendants is

Affirmed.

C. SEARCH AND SEIZURE

1. Prior to the decision in *T.L.O.*, courts uniformly invalidated strip searches. *See, e.g., Tartar v. Raybuck*, 742 F.2d 977 (6th Cir. 1984); *M.M. v. Anker*, 607 F.2d 588 (2d Cir. 1979); *Doe v. Renfrow*, 475 F. Supp. 1012 (N.D. Ind. 1979); *Bellnier v. Lund*, 438 F. Supp. 47 (N.D.N.Y. 1977). The decision in *T.L.O.* established a reasonable suspicion standard that considers the reasonableness of grounds for a search as well as the reasonableness of the scope of a search under the totality of circumstances including the age of the student and the nature of the alleged misconduct. One interpretation of the *T.L.O.* standard is that strip searches of students are not expressly prohibited.

2. In the *Anker* case, cited above, the Second Circuit even allowed that as the intrusiveness of a search intensifies, the test to apply to Fourth Amendment violations is probable cause and not reasonableness. Hence, "when a teacher conducts a highly intrusive invasion such as a strip search ..., it is reasonable to require probable cause be present." *Anker* at 589. Is the *Anker* court on target here? Even before *T.L.O.*, did courts customarily require probable cause for such searches in school settings?

3. Rossow and Stubblefield, in *Student Strip Search Upheld*, 75 Educ. L. Rep. 723 (1992), ask the following in response to the decision in *Williams*: "Has the Sixth Circuit read *T.L.O.* as a 'school safety' case and not a students rights case?" "Is the *Williams* case an aberration or is the Sixth Circuit the first to begin anticipating how the Supreme Court will look at school safety issues?" The authors find grist for their queries from the following passage in *Williams*:

> A thorough review of *T.L.O.* reveals that the Court was careful to protect a school official's right to make discretionary decisions in light of the knowledge and experience of the educator and the information presented to him or her at the time such decision was made. Like police officers, school officials need discretionary authority to function with great efficiency and speed in certain situations, so long as these decisions are consistent with certain constitutional safeguards. To question an official's every decision with the benefit of hindsight would undermine the authority necessary to ensure the safety and order of our schools. *Williams*, at 886.

Has the court misspoken here? Does it really mean to equate the discretionary authority of police officers with that of school officials in issues involving search and seizure? While *T.L.O.* did not address the standard of searches conducted by school personnel and law enforcement agencies, other courts have. *See, e.g., Cason v. Cook*, 810 F.2d 188 (8th Cir. 1987), *cert. denied*, 482 U.S. 930 (1987) (reasonable suspicion as a standard applies as police officer involved in the search did not do so at the behest of a law enforcement agency); *F.P. v. State*, 528 So. 2d 1253 (Fla. App. 1988) (when school resource officer acts in the role of a police officer, the school search exception and the search must be supported by probable cause, not reasonable suspicion).

4. The court in *Williams* stated that the factual discrepancy over whether the assistant principal actually pulled the elastic of Williams' undergarments was not

material for summary judgment purposes. But, could such action by a school official be considered unreasonable in scope or excessively intrusive despite the seriousness of the infraction? If so, could a summary judgment in favor of defendants be sustained? Consider the following from Lawrence F. Rossow and Brenda L. Stubblefield:

> Both the trial and appellate courts failed to sufficiently address the obvious. Was the strip search of the female student permissible under the *T.L.O.* standard? The scope portion of the *T.L.O.* two-prong test states that "a search will be permissible in scope when the measures adopted are reasonably related to the objectives of the search and not exclusively intrusive in light of the age and sex of the student and the nature of the inaction."
>
> The Graves County school district search and seizure policy was examined by the sixth circuit court and found to be facially valid. The policy states in part: "When a pupil's person is searched, the person conducting the search shall be of the same sex as the pupil; and a witness of the same sex shall be present during the search." The appellate court opines that
>
> > ... [T]he exact language of this policy reiterates the criteria set forth by the Supreme Court in *New Jersey v. T.L.O.*, in balancing a student's privacy interests under the fourth amendment against the need for order and safety in schools, the legality of a search of a student should depend upon the reasonableness of the search, under all the circumstances.
>
> However, ordinary language analysis shows that the school district policy does not speak entirely to the scope prong as outlined in *T.L.O.* The policy requires that the person doing the search be the same sex as the pupil and that there be a same-sex witness.
>
> The scope prong in *T.L.O.* requires that the search measure be: (1) related to the objectives of the search; and (2) not extensively intrusive in light of the student's age, sex, and nature of the infraction. The district policy speaks only to the issue of the sex of the principal parties. Indeed, the *T.L.O.* court did not speak to a witness requirement. The appellate court also erred when it cited the *T.L.O.* overall balancing concept as the court's analytical test for reasonableness. Although it is true that *T.L.O.* requires that the legality of a search of a student depend on its reasonableness under all circumstances, it also provides a two-prong test for deciding school search issues. The sixth circuit failed to use this test. Rossow and Stubblefield, *Student Strip Search Upheld:* Williams by Williams v. Ellington, 75 Educ. L. Rep. 723 (Aug. 1992).*

---

*Copyright © 1992 by West Publishing Company. Reprinted with permission.

C. SEARCH AND SEIZURE

5. Could the principal in *Williams* have legally proceeded as he did in conducting the search if he had only the informant student's statements (presuming a lack of ulterior motive)? Consider the "totality of circumstances" discussion in the case.

6. How clearly established is the law with respect to the legality of student strip searches and the grant of qualified immunity to school defendants? Consider the following note by Tamela J. White in the Northern Kentucky Law Review:

In January of 1988, public school officials in Mayfield, Kentucky conducted a strip search[1] of two fourteen-year-old girls in search of a vial of white powder.[3] The authority of public school officials in conducting searches of students' possessions and persons has been a topic of dispute in cases ranging in topic from dragnet canine sniffing for contraband to visual examinations of the belongings of an entire student population for articles such as radios and "walkmen" headsets. In fact, children have been strip searched for seemingly nominal amounts of money and for suspicion regarding the size of an anatomical part.

On the other hand, educators have placed upon them great responsibility in overseeing the safety and well-being of their charges in the hours during which the school serves as custodian. It is in school that basic societal values and ideals of discipline are cultivated. In light of the need to combat drug problems among school-aged children and the concern over rising violence at school, the issue of student searches is indeed a foreseeable one.

Somewhere in the labyrinth of seemingly insurmountable social problems, student privacy rights are said to exist. The often quoted saying "[students do not] shed their constitutional rights ... at the schoolhouse gate" is clearly being put to the test by unrestrained search policies. Privacy rights, the deepest representation of freedom, must be balanced against the special problems created by what students bring to school with them.

The legal concerns arise from interpretation of the Fourth Amendment to the United States Constitution. If the purpose of the Fourth Amendment is violated, principles of qualified immunity of state officials under 42 U.S.C. § 1983 are invoked. Thus, an otherwise emotional and controversial issue is further complicated by such legal terms as "reasonableness" and "qualified immunity." The purpose of this note is to analyze the evolutionary perspective of Fourth Amendment law as it concerns student rights.

---

[1]*See Daugherty v. Campbell*, 935 F.2d 780, 781 n.1 (6th Cir.1991) (a strip search generally refers to the inspection of an individual that is nude, without inspection of the person's body cavities); *E.Z. v. Coler*, 603 F.Supp. 1546, 1548-49 n.2 (N.D.Ill. 1985) (the terms "body search," "strip search," "visual examination," or "visual inspection are defined as the removal or rearranging of clothing or the causing of such in order to visually inspect the body of the person exposed.)

[3]*Williams by Williams v. Ellington*, 936 F.2d 881, 882-83 (6th Cir. 1991).

Cases leading to the Supreme Court opinion of *New Jersey v. T.L.O.* are presented first. Then, the *T.L.O.* opinion is presented, followed by analysis of the subsequent application of the *T.L.O.* standard by lower federal courts and state courts. Issues of qualified immunity in recent student search cases are then discussed. Finally, the decision of the Sixth Circuit in the case of *Williams by Williams v. Ellington* is presented. The note points out that in regard to student strip searches, the current state of the law is far from clearly established. Both educators and students have little guidance as to the authority of school officials in conducting intrusive searches. While the thought of strip searching an innocent child is offensive to most anyone's concept of decency, the law does nothing to shield the child nor does it provide guidelines for what constitutes an appropriate search. Tamela J. White, Note, *Williams by Williams v. Ellington: Strip Searches in Public Schools — Too Many Unanswered Questions*, 19 N. Ky. L. Rev. 513 (Spring, 1992).*

7. It cannot be argued that the issue of student strip searches is yet settled. In *State v. Mark Anthony B.*, 433 S.E.2d 41 (W. Va. 1993), a state court held that reasonable suspicion existed allowing the search of a 14-year-old eighth grader, but that a strip search for missing money was unreasonable in scope. *But see Cornfield v. Consolidated High Sch. Dist. No. 230*, 991 F.2d 1316 (7th Cir. 1993), which upheld a nude strip search of a high school student as reasonable.

8. What of a student's Fifth Amendment rights against self incrimination when a search is conducted under the auspices of the school? Courts have been fairly uniform in the answer. *See, e.g., Boynton v. Casey*, 543 F. Supp. 995 (D. Me. 1982) (a student questioned for over an hour by the principal and denied permission to leave was not subjected to a custodial interrogation under the Fourth Amendment and therefore not entitled to *Miranda* warnings or to have a parent present during questioning); *People in the Interest of P.E.A.*, 754 P.2d 383 (Colo. 1988) (*Miranda* warnings are not required when a student is questioned by a principal and school security guard without a parent or guardian present); *In re Corey L.*, 250 Cal. Rptr. 359 (Cal. Ct. App. 1988) (school officials, when questioning students about drugs, are not required to advise them of their *Miranda* rights).

---

*Copyright © 1992 by Tamela J. White, Esquire, Farrell and Farrell, Huntington, West Virginia, and the Northern Kentucky University Law Review. Reprinted with permission.

7. STUDENT DRUG TESTING

SCHAILL v. TIPPECANOE COUNTY SCHOOL CORPORATION

United States Court of Appeals
864 F.2d 1309 (7th Cir. 1988)

CUDAHY, CIRCUIT JUDGE:

In this action brought under 42 U.S.C. section 1983, plaintiffs-appellants Darcy Schaill and Shelley Johnson challenge a random urinalysis program instituted by the defendant-appellee Tippecanoe County School Corporation ("TSC"). Appellants allege that the TSC urinalysis program violates their rights under the fourth amendment and the due process clause of the fourteenth amendment. After conducting a trial on the merits of appellants' claims, the district court ruled that the TSC program was constitutional. We affirm.

I

The essential facts of this case are undisputed, and can be stated quite briefly. TSC operates Harrison and McCutcheon High Schools in Indiana. In the spring of 1986, based on information concerning possible drug use by athletes on the McCutcheon High School baseball team, the team's coach ordered sixteen team members to provide urine samples. Of the sixteen students tested, five students' tests produced positive results for the presence of marijuana. Based on these results, other reports of drug use among participants in the TSC athletic program, and their concern over the high incidence of drug abuse among high school students nationwide, the board of trustees of TSC decided to institute a random urine testing program for interscholastic athletes and cheerleaders in the TSC school system.

Under the program, all students desiring to participate in interscholastic athletics and their parent or guardian are required to sign a consent form agreeing to submit to urinalysis if chosen on a random basis. Each student selected for an athletic team is assigned a number. The athletic director and head coach of each athletic team are authorized to institute random urine tests during the athletic season. In order to select individuals to be tested, the number assigned to each athlete is placed in a box, and a single number is drawn.

The student selected for testing is accompanied by a school official of the same sex to a bathroom, where the student is provided with an empty specimen bottle. The student is then allowed to enter a lavatory stall and close the door in order to produce a sample. The student is not under direct visual observation while producing the sample; however, the water in the toilet is tinted to prevent the student from substituting water for the sample, the monitor stands outside the stall to listen for normal sounds of urination and the monitor checks the temperature of the sample by hand in order to assure its genuineness.

The chain of custody of the sample is designed to insure the accuracy and anonymity of the testing procedure. The sample is sent to a private testing laboratory, where it is initially tested for the presence of controlled substances or performance-enhancing drugs using the enzyme multiplied immunoassay technique ("EMIT"). Any sample which tests positive is then retested using the more accurate, and more expensive, gas chromatography/mass spectrometry ("GC/MS") method.

If a sample tests positive under both the EMIT and GC/MS analyses, the student and his or her parent or guardian are informed of the results. They then have the opportunity to have the remaining portion of the sample tested at a laboratory of their choice. The student and his or her parent or guardian may also present the athletic director with any evidence which suggests an innocent explanation for the positive result, such as the fact that the athlete legally takes prescription or over-the-counter medication.

Barring a satisfactory explanation, the student is then suspended from participation in a portion of the varsity competitions held during the athletic season. A first positive urinalysis test results in a suspension from 30% of the athletic contests, a second positive results in a 50% suspension, a third positive causes a suspension for a full calendar year and a fourth positive results in the student's being barred from all interscholastic athletic competitions during the remainder of the student's high school career. No other penalties are imposed, and a student may decrease the specified punishment by participating in an approved drug counselling program.

In the spring of 1987, appellants Darcy Schaill and Shelley Johnson were 15-year-old sophomores at Harrison High School. Shelley had been a member of the varsity swim team as a freshman. Both appellants attended an organizational meeting for students desiring to participate in interscholastic athletics in the fall of 1987, at which time they were first informed of the proposed implementation of the TSC urinalysis program. Both appellants were offended by the thought of having to undergo urinalysis as a condition of participation in interscholastic athletics, and both decided that they would forego the opportunity to compete in interscholastic athletics if required to sign a form consenting to random urine testing.

TSC adopted the current version of its drug testing program on August 28, 1987. Appellants had filed their complaint, which initially challenged a prior version of the program, on August 25, 1987. The district court conducted a trial on the merits of appellants' fourth amendment and due process claims on December 7 and 8, 1987. On February 1, 1988, the district court entered its memorandum opinion and order denying appellants' claims for declaratory and injunctive relief. This appeal followed.

II

As a threshold matter, we must consider whether TSC's random urine testing program involves a "search" as that term is employed in the fourth amendment. The Supreme Court has held that "[a] 'search' occurs when an expectation of privacy that society is prepared to consider reasonable is infringed." *United States v. Jacobsen*, 466 U.S. 109, 113 (1984).

C. SEARCH AND SEIZURE

There can be little doubt that a person engaging in the act of urination possesses a reasonable expectation of privacy as to that act, and as to the urine which is excreted. In our society, it is expected that urination be performed in private, that urine be disposed of in private and that the act, if mentioned at all, be described in euphemistic terms....

....

It is not clear whether, or to what extent, the TSC random urinalysis program's status as a search is affected by the fact that tests will be performed only with respect to students who have previously given their consent. The consent provided in the forms supplied to students is certainly not dispositive of the "search" issue since execution of a consent form is a prerequisite to participation in interscholastic athletics.... It is certainly relevant to the ultimate question of constitutionality, however, that the activity to which random testing is attached is participation in an extracurricular activity. Random testing is not, as we discuss later, a condition of a weightier benefit such as employment or school attendance. Nonetheless, since participation in interscholastic athletics is expressly conditioned on a student's waiver of his or her fourth amendment rights, the "voluntariness" of a student's submission to urinalysis testing does not alone dispose of the constitutional issues presented by appellants. We must therefore decide whether the searches contemplated by TSC in this case violate the fourth amendment.

III

Having determined that urine testing constitutes a "search" in the constitutional sense, we must consider what level of suspicion is required to authorize urinalysis of any particular student. Appellants first argue that individual student's urine may not be tested unless TSC officials have probable cause to believe that the particular student has consumed the drugs which the test is designed to detect, and have obtained a warrant authorizing the test from a neutral and detached judicial officer.

Determining the level of suspicion required before the government may conduct a search requires "balanc[ing] the nature and quality of the intrusion on the individual's Fourth Amendment interests against the importance of the governmental interests alleged to justify the intrusion." Unfortunately for appellants, we believe that the Supreme Court has already struck the appropriate balance in the context of school searches, and has determined that the probable cause and warrant requirements do not apply.

In *New Jersey v. T.L.O.*, 469 U.S. 325 (1985), a school official searched a student's purse, based on a reasonable suspicion that the student had been smoking on school grounds, in violation of school rules. After noting that the opening of T.L.O.'s purse was "undoubtedly a severe violation of subjective expectations of privacy," *Id.* at 338, the Court canvassed the legitimate governmental interests which were furthered by the search. The Court observed that "'[e]vents calling for discipline are frequent occurrences and sometimes require immediate, effective action,'" *Id.* at 339; further, the particular demands of the school environment required that teachers have resort to "swift and informal disciplinary procedures." *Id.* at 340. The Court therefore held that the warrant and probable cause requirements did not apply; instead, school searches should be judged under the standard of "reasonableness [ ] under all the circumstances." *Id.* at 341. The Court noted that this standard would "spare teachers and school administrators the necessity of schooling themselves in the niceties of probable cause and permit them to regulate their conduct according to the dictates of reason and common sense." *Id.* at 343.

....

... [A]ppellants suggest that the decision [in *T.L.O.* was] based solely on the need for swift, or even immediate, responses to violations of a school's or employer's rules. Appellants argue that where, as here, a search is authorized well in advance of its execution, there is no "special need" to relax the traditional warrant and probable cause requirements. *See T.L.O.*, 469 U.S. at 351 (BLACKMUN, J., concurring in the judgment). We cannot accept appellant's narrow reading of *T.L.O.* The Supreme Court's concern was not merely with the time required to establish probable cause or obtain a warrant. Instead, the Court concluded that these fourth amendment requirements, traditionally (though not exclusively) applied to law enforcement investigations, would unnecessarily intrude upon the purposes of the classroom or workplace. For example, in *T.L.O.* the Court stressed that a school official's primary mission is not to ferret out crime, but is instead to teach students in a safe and secure learning environment.... It is for this reason that the Court's holding is stated quite broadly: "'when there are reasonable grounds for suspecting that [a] search will turn up evidence that the student has violated or is violating either the law or the rules of the school,' a search of the student's person or belongings is justified." *Id.* at 350 (POWELL, J., concurring) (stating the holding of the Court). The Court's holding is in no way qualified to apply only where there is a special requirement of immediate action.

The Supreme Court has ruled that the probable cause and warrant requirements are not applicable to school searches. We therefore reject appellant's broadest attack against the TSC program.

IV

Since the probable cause and warrant requirements are not applicable to the searches involved in this case, we must consider the TSC urinalysis program under the general fourth amendment standard of reasonableness. As the Supreme Court recognized in *T.L.O.*, "[t]he fundamental command of the Fourth Amendment is that searches and seizures be reasonable, and although 'both the concept of probable cause and requirement of a warrant bear on the reasonableness of a search ... in certain limited circumstances neither is required.'" 469 U.S. at 340 (quoting *Almeida-Sanchez v. United States*, 413 U.S. 266, 277 (1973) (POWELL, J., concurring)).

C. SEARCH AND SEIZURE

In the present case, TSC plans to conduct a search not only without probable cause or a warrant, but in the absence of any individualized suspicion of drug use by the students to be tested. In these circumstances, TSC bears a heavier burden to justify its contemplated actions. In a criminal law enforcement context, the Supreme Court has been extremely hesitant to condone searches performed without any articulable basis for suspecting the particular individual of unlawful conduct. However, in several carefully defined situations, the Court has recognized that searches may be conducted in the absence of any grounds to believe that the individual searched has violated the law. The Court has stressed that "[i]n those situations in which the balance of interests precludes insistence upon 'some quantum of individualized suspicion,' other safeguards are generally relied upon to assure that the individual's reasonable expectation of privacy is not 'subject to the discretion of the officer in the field'."

....

... [S]uspicionless searches are more likely to be permissible in circumstances where an individual has diminished expectations of privacy. An individual's privacy rights vary with the context — whether the individual is at home, at work, in school or in jail, in a car or on a public sidewalk. Further, in certain pursuits, an individual's expectations of privacy are diminished by a past history of significant governmental regulation.

... [T]he governmental interests furthered by a particular search must be weighty, and generally of a nature that alternate, less intrusive means of detection would not sufficiently serve the government's ends. For example, where unlawful conduct or conditions cannot be detected through other means, a warrantless and suspicionless search may be appropriate. That alternative investigative techniques would not deter unlawful conduct to the same extent as the challenged practice may also be a relevant consideration.

The extent to which the examining officer's discretion is limited by the regulatory scheme under which searches are conducted is also an important factor. Confining the enforcement discretion of the officer in the field serves several important functions. First, if individuals are selected for a search based on clearly articulated, objective criteria, the possibility that any particular search is motivated by a desire to harass or intimidate is diminished accordingly. Further, previously enunciated selection criteria assure the individuals searched that the officer is acting in accordance with his or her lawful authority. Objective selection criteria also tend to diminish the subjective intrusiveness of a particular search — the individual is able to understand how and why he or she was selected for search, and need not fear that he or she was "singled out" for improper reasons.

... [W]hether or not the search is intended to discover evidence of criminal activity is of critical importance in assessing the validity of warrantless, suspicionless searches. A search conducted for civil or non-punitive purposes may be valid in circumstances where a search conducted as part of a criminal investigation would not be permissible.

With the foregoing principles in mind, we turn to a more detailed consideration of the urinalysis program proposed in this case.

A

In general, there is a substantial expectation of privacy in connection with the act of urination. However, the privacy considerations are somewhat mitigated on the facts before us because the provider of the urine sample enters a closed lavatory stall and the person monitoring the urination stands outside listening for the sounds appropriate to what is taking place. The invasion of privacy is therefore not nearly as severe as would be the case if the monitor were required to observe the subject in the act of urination.

We also find great significance in the fact that the drug testing program in this case is being implemented solely with regard to participants in an interscholastic athletic program. In the first place, in athletic programs in general there is a much diminished expectation of privacy and, in particular, privacy with respect to urinalysis. There is an element of "communal undress" inherent in athletic participation, which suggests reduced expectations of privacy. In addition, physical examinations are integral to almost all athletic programs....

....

... [P]articipants in interscholastic athletics are also subject to training rules, including prohibitions on smoking, drinking and drug use both on and off school premises.

Perhaps even more demonstrative of the special characteristics of athletics is the high visibility and pervasiveness of drug testing in professional and collegiate athletics in this country and in the Olympic Games. The suspension and disqualification of prominent athletes on the basis of positive urinalysis results has been the subject of intense publicity all over the world.

The combination of these factors makes it quite implausible that students competing for positions on an interscholastic athletic team would have strong expectations of privacy with respect to urine tests. We can, of course, appreciate that monitored collection and subsequent testing of urine samples may be distasteful (although plaintiffs' subjective evidence on this point was not powerful), but such procedures can hardly come as a great shock or surprise under present-day circumstances. For this reason, we believe that sports are quite distinguishable from almost any other activity. Random testing of athletes does not necessarily imply random testing of band members or the chess team.

B

Obviously, TSC's interest in the particular program at issue in this case cannot be gainsaid — in fact, the Supreme Court specifically noted in *T.L.O.* that drug use by students was one of the "particularly ugly forms" in which school disciplinary problems commonly arise in present-day America. The problem of drug use among the youth of this country continues to be severe and intractable.... In the TSC school system itself, urine tests administered to members of the McCutcheon baseball team in the spring of 1986 produced 5 positive results out of 16 students tested. The incidence of drug use revealed by this test, slightly greater than 31%, is consistent with the national and state-wide statistics. Based on this evidence, the district court found that the student athletes involved here used drugs to the same extent as students in the national profile. This is certainly not an established fact, but it is not a wholly unreasonable inference.

The harm done by drug usage by student athletes was the subject of a great deal of testimony in the district court and of findings by the trial judge. Judge Sharp found, and there was evidence to support his finding, that the use of drugs presented a particular threat to athletes and cheerleaders. Due to alterations of mood, reductions of motor coordination and changes in the perception of pain attributable to drug use, the health and safety of athletes was particularly threatened....

In addition, as Judge Sharp found, "[t]he interscholastic athletes of a public school system typically enjoy a unique identity within the school community.... The student athlete is generally viewed by the broader community with admiration and respect." Because of their high visibility and leadership roles, it is not unreasonable to single out athletes and cheerleaders for special attention with respect to drug usage....

The record also contains substantial evidence that alternative methods of investigation would not adequately serve the school's interest in detection and deterrence of drug use. While there was some disagreement between plaintiffs' and defendants' experts regarding the efficacy of trained visual observation, neurobehavioral testing, education programs or individualized suspicion urine testing, we believe that the evidence of record fully supported the district court's conclusion that the choice made by TSC was reasonable in the circumstances of this case. Among other things, random testing may be particularly effective as a deterrent....

C

As noted above, where a search is based upon general factors rather than individualized suspicion, there is an additional requirement to sustain the constitutionality of the search. The search program must incorporate adequate safeguards to assure that reasonable expectations of privacy are not "subject to the discretion of the official in the field." We believe that this important requirement is met in this case.

The TSC program specifies that athletes will be selected for testing by drawing numbers on a random basis. The officials in charge will not exercise any discretion as to who will be chosen. There are specific provisions for the manner in which the sample is to be obtained, the handling and testing of the sample by a competent laboratory, the confirmation of positive test results and the consequences of confirmed positive results. We also note that students will be fully advised of the manner in which the program will operate when they are initially asked to sign consent forms, and they will be given a copy of the TSC

Drug Program. The information provided will eliminate any element of surprise if and when a particular student is selected for testing, and the student will be able to assure him or herself that he or she has been selected for testing in a fair and impartial manner. Further, the use of published selection criteria insures that a student is not stigmatized among his or her peers due to selection for testing....

D

Finally, we note that the TSC urinalysis program has been instituted in order to enforce the rules of the athletic program and the school. The program is not intended to discover evidence of unlawful activity for use in criminal prosecution. Even in the school setting, the school board has gone to great lengths to emphasize rehabilitation over punishment, as is evidenced both by the progressive nature of the sanctions for a positive test result and by the fact that a student may reduce the length of any suspension imposed by participating in an approved drug counselling program.

E

The convergence of several important factors convinces us that the searches involved here take place in one of the relatively unusual environments in which suspicionless searches are permissible: interscholastic athletes have diminished expectations of privacy, and have voluntarily chosen to participate in an activity which subjects them to pervasive regulation of off-campus behavior; the school's interest in preserving a drug-free athletic program is substantial, and cannot adequately be furthered by less intrusive measures; the TSC program adequately limits the discretion of the officials performing the search; and the information sought is intended to be used solely for noncriminal educational and rehabilitative purposes. Based on a careful and considered weighing of these factors, we conclude that the TSC urinalysis program does not violate the Fourth Amendment.

....

Affirmed.

---

1. Which would you consider more invasive — the urinalysis as conducted in *Schaill* or the strip search as conducted in *Williams*? In 1966 the United States Supreme Court found urine tests to be "highly invasive." *Schmerber v. California*, 384 U.S. 757. *See also Odenheim v. Carlstadt-East Rutherford Regional Sch. Dist.*, 211 N.J. Super. 54, 510 A.2d 709 (1985), which held that high school requirement of urine testing invaded students' rights to due process and expectation of privacy and personal security.

2. Drug testing at the University Level. In *O'Halloran v. University of Washington*, 679 F. Supp. 997 (W.D. Wash. 1988), the court held that the NCAA's urine testing program was a "search" under the Fourth Amendment which did not unreasonably infringe upon athletes' expectation of privacy. *See also* O'Neal, *The Constitutionality of NCAA Drug Testing: A Fine Specimen for Examination,* 46 SMU L. Rev. 513 (1992).

In what may be a surprising result, the University of Colorado drug testing program did not meet the compelling state interest required to justify its existence. Students did not voluntarily sign forms consenting to the urine analysis.

3. One court has held that individualized suspicion is still required to conduct urinalysis testing. *See Brooks v. East Chambers Consol. Indep. Sch. Dist.,* 730 F. Supp. 759 (S.D. Tex. 1989). *See also* Bjorklun, *Drug Testing High School Athletes and the Fourth Amendment,* 83 Educ. L. Rep. 913 (1993).

4. In 1995, the United States Supreme Court settled whatever differences that existed between *Schaill* and *Brooks.* In *Vernonia Sch. Dist. v. Acton,* ___ U.S. ___, 115 S. Ct. 2386, 1995 WL 373274, the Supreme Court upheld a random, suspicionless urinalysis drug test imposed on the school district's athletes in grades 7 through 12. The test implemented by Vernonia School District is similar to the one upheld in *Schaill.* The majority, written by Justice Scalia, balanced the intrusion on the student's Fourth Amendment rights with the legitimate governmental interests of the school district. The Court held that, due to the school setting and the *in loco parentis* relationship between schools and children, a school may exercise a greater degree of supervision and control over students than it could over adults. Citing to *Schaill,* the Court noted the voluntary nature of the participation and the "element of communal undress inherent" in school athletics. The Court also noted that a suspicion-based drug-testing program may actually be less practicable. According to the majority, with a suspicion-based program, there are risks of arbitrary (rather than "drug-likely"), wrongful accusations, expensive lawsuits, and increased and ill-suited responsibilities on the teachers to recognize drug use among students.

Chapter 8
SANCTIONS FOR BREACHES OF RULES

As the chapters in this part have demonstrated, a consideration of the types of sanctions employed is inevitably involved in a discussion of the conduct which can be sanctioned.

There are independent issues, however, concerning the sanctions themselves, particularly suspension or expulsion, corporal punishment, and academic sanctions such as grade reduction, which are explored in this chapter. In approaching this material, consider whether types of sanctions available to schools to punish student misbehavior should affect what behavior is punished. Determine also what exactly a given sanction as applied to a specific offense is intended to achieve and what are the permissible ends that schools can seek to accomplish by attaching a given sanction to a particular offense. Should the respective roles of teachers, administrators, parents, students, courts, etc., be the same or different in regard to sanctions as they are in regard to establishing substantive conduct rules? Should sanctions vary with community norms as much as, more than, or less than substantive rules so vary?

A. SUSPENSIONS AND EXPULSIONS

Although *Goss v. Lopez* and its progeny, discussed in Chapter 7, created new procedural guidelines for the suspension or expulsion of public school students, the questions underlying the use of suspension and expulsion as sanctions in the schools remain largely unstudied and unanswered by the courts. Are schools using suspension as an inexpensive method of student control when other alternatives, such as counseling or tutoring, might prove more beneficial to the student? Do school officials discriminate against racial minorities or students with special physical or emotional problems in their use of suspension as a sanction? Is the use of suspension and expulsion ever appropriate in a society which considers education the moral, and to some extent legal, right of its children? The following material illustrates the approaches taken by some courts and scholars in attempting to answer these questions.

DANIEL & CORIELL, SUSPENSION AND EXPULSION IN AMERICA'S PUBLIC SCHOOLS: HAS UNFAIRNESS RESULTED FROM A NARROWING OF DUE PROCESS?, 13 Hamline J. Pub. L. & Pol'y 1 (Spring, 1992)*

....

III. *Legal Issues in Suspensions and Expulsions*

Each year more than 1.5 million American students miss one or more days of school because they have been suspended or expelled. The vast majority of these suspensions are not for violent or criminal acts, but rather for offenses such as smoking cigarettes or truancy. The National School Boards Association has summarized available research regarding suspension and expulsion concluding that:

> Suspended students lose valuable instruction and are likely to distrust the authority that has rejected them.
>
> Minority students are disproportionately suspended and expelled.
>
> Suspension rewards teachers and others for avoiding classroom responsibilities.
>
> Suspended students are usually the very students who most need direct instruction.
>
> Some schools forfeit funds for each suspended or expelled student, under average daily attendance formulas.

The National School Boards Association has warned that "traditional approaches — such as punishment, removing troublemakers, and similar measures — often harden delinquent behavior patterns, alienate troubled youths from the schools, and foster distrust." One author of a study on school safety testified before a congressional committee that not only are educators not unduly fettered, but also that too many students are suspended. "The real problem is the failure of schools to be clear about what their disciplinary procedures are and actually to follow those procedures."

....

In order to eliminate unfairness and improper application of school discipline, a procedure must be created that ensures both substantive and procedural due process to all students. That alone, however, is not enough. Not only must there be adequate procedures, but students must be aware of all facets of the disciplinary procedure. Even these safeguards will fail if teachers, administrators, and school boards choose to turn their heads when the administration of punishment has a racially disproportionate impact despite the due process procedural safeguards.

---

*Copyright © 1992 by the Hamline Journal of Public Law and Policy. Reprinted with permission.

A. SUSPENSIONS AND EXPULSIONS

The nation's courts must consider carefully their stance of judicial deference because the Department of Education, Office of Civil Rights statistics have shown that despite disciplinary codes ensuring procedural due process, a disproportionate number of black students are being subjected to suspensions and/or expulsions for some reason.... Perhaps the best answer we can give at this point is that where the procedural due process safeguards are present, then we must look to those who are in charge of enforcing and ensuring those safeguards for the obvious disparity. In other words, it is not enough to have procedural due process safeguards in place if school administrators are using them in a discriminatory manner.

In an imperfect society, it is not possible to construct a perfect set of rules for a society which is constantly changing. Societal values, cultural differentials, and demographics must be carefully considered and weighed. At a minimum, school disciplinary policies must be directly related to the educational program and have an educational purpose. The following guidelines suggest a starting point for policy formation, which represents what the authors feel is a fair and appropriate form of procedural due process in relation to disciplinary procedures. For educators and attorneys contemplating changes in current school policies or implementation of a new policy, there are a number of basic principles which should be considered:

* Any task force or committee developing or revising disciplinary procedures must integrate all relevant actors, *i.e.*, students, parents, community leaders, teachers, administrators, school board members, and legal counsel.
* Once formulated, the written disciplinary policies and procedures must be formally distributed to all students and their parents. Copies of the policies and procedures should be readily available in all schools.
* In its most basic form, the policy must provide notice of what conduct is prohibited.
* Rules and regulations promulgated under the policy must be written in a manner that is understandable to the average student.
* All rules must be rationally related to a valid education purpose, otherwise, they will not withstand constitutional challenges.
* Language precision is essential in order to prevent infringement on constitutionally protected activities.
* Notice of potential consequences should be specific in order to provide students with notice as to any prohibited behavior.
* Types of punishment specified in disciplinary policies must be within the express or implied statutory grant to the school district by the state legislature. This will vary among the states.
* The punishment must bear a rational relationship to the severity of the misconduct or the frequency of the misconduct occurrence.

* All disciplinary procedures should take into account factors such as racial and cultural differentials.

... In addition, the efficacy and equitableness of a disciplinary procedure is totally dependent on the impartial administration of the process. The formulation of policy cannot occur in a wholesale manner without actively involving all factions whose lives it will touch and affect.

The formulation and adoption of a disciplinary procedure cannot occur in the sterile environment of the school board's meeting place. To create any policy which governs the educational process, it is necessary to emerge from our ivory towers and face the realities of today's world. The poet, William Carlos Williams wrote, that to understand the complexities and needs of our society, we "must immerse [ourselves] in the filthy Passaic." On the other hand, an effective policy cannot be formulated in the schoolyard. The worst possible scenario is to create policy in reaction to crisis. The reactionary response to a problem of this magnitude would only worsen the crisis.

1. SUSPENSION

POLLNOW v. GLENNON
United States District Court
594 F. Supp. 220 (S.D.N.Y. 1984)

OWEN, DISTRICT JUDGE:

This is a civil rights action by Otto Pollnow and his parents against various officers of the Millbrook, New York school system including the Superintendent and the Board of Education. It is before me on cross-motions for summary judgment.

On April 22, 1981, during school vacation, Otto Pollnow, a sixteen year old student and a member of the football team at Millbrook High School, was arrested and charged with seriously assaulting and attempting to stab one Adeline Wormell, the mother of one of his high school friends. The assault occurred at Mrs. Wormell's home and left bruises on her body and arms and a cut on her nose. On April 27, upon the resumption of school, as Otto stepped off the school bus he was met by John Glennon, the school superintendent, and Raymond White, administrative assistant to Millbrook High's principal. Otto went with Glennon and White to Glennon's office where they questioned him about the alleged assault. According to Glennon's later testimony, "I said to Otto 'I understand that you were in some trouble last Wednesday.' Otto said, 'Yes.' I said, 'What happened?' Otto said that he had gone to a pot party at the Tribute Garden. He said he was smoking marijuana and he did not know it but someone laced his marijuana with Angel Dust. He said that he went over to the Wormell's home and then he went crazy. I said, 'Was anyone hurt?' He said, 'Yes, Mrs. Wormell.' He said, 'I hurt her — I hit her and hurt her.'" Glennon thereupon suspended Otto from school for five days under Education Law § 3214.

A. SUSPENSIONS AND EXPULSIONS

The next day, Glennon informed Otto's parents by letter that he had scheduled for May 1 a disciplinary hearing pursuant to New York State Education Law § 3214 to evaluate "allegations of conduct that endanger the health, safety and welfare of students." Otto and his parents came to the hearing (hereafter sometimes referred to as "the first hearing") but protested to the hearing officer that the notice of hearing did not specify the charges against Otto. They also stated that they would not participate in any hearing until the criminal charges then pending against Otto were resolved. Notwithstanding this protest, the hearing was held and the hearing officer recommended that Otto be suspended indefinitely, which recommendation Glennon adopted.

Apparently concerned with the Pollnows' claim of failure to give formal notice of the charges, Glennon set up a new hearing (hereafter sometimes called "the second hearing"), this time specifying in the notice that the hearing would investigate the assault on Mrs. Wormell. In the interim, however, the Pollnows appealed from the first hearing to the New York State Commissioner of Education requesting 1) a stay of further proceedings until the pending criminal charges were resolved, and 2) Otto's immediate reinstatement to his classes.

Having not received a response from the Commissioner by the adjourned date of the second hearing, May 26, the Pollnows and their attorney attended the hearing — held before a different hearing officer — reiterated their protest that Otto's participation in any hearing before his criminal trial was concluded would prejudice his right against self-incrimination, and departed. Once again, despite plaintiffs' refusal to participate, the hearing proceeded to a conclusion. This time additional details of the assault, including photographs of Mrs. Wormell's numerous and serious injuries, were put in evidence. On the evidence the hearing officer recommended that Otto be suspended for the balance of the 1980-1 school year and the first semester of 1981-2. Glennon adopted the recommendation and, on June 8, notified the Pollnows accordingly.

Following all of this, on June 15, 1981, the Commissioner of Education issued an "Interim Order" on the Pollnow's appeal from the first hearing. That opinion, in relevant part, reads as follows:

> Petitioners appeal from the April 27, 1981 suspension of their son from attendance at school for allegedly assaulting an individual in her home. They request an immediate order permitting the student to continue to attend classes in the Millbrook Central School District pending the outcome of the disciplinary hearing until such time as criminal proceedings regarding the alleged assault are disposed of....
>
> ....
>
> Upon a review of the papers before me, it does not appear that this student's presence in respondent's classrooms will pose a hazard to any student or faculty member, or any risk of disruption to the learning process. Consequently, the student must be allowed to attend his regular classes pending respondent's determination following a hearing. As I have held in

the past, in order to preserve his right against self-incrimination, a student may request an adjournment of a disciplinary hearing pending the disposition of criminal charges against him. Based upon my review of the facts of this case and in the interests of justice, petitioners' request for such an adjournment should be granted and continuation of the section 3214 proceeding should be stayed, pending conclusion of the criminal matter....

Both Glennon and, subsequently, the Millbrook Board of Education interpreted the Interim Order as having no effect on the second hearing — which had been completed well before June 15 — and therefore disregarded it.

Thereafter, the summer passed and, beginning in mid-August, Otto participated in high school football practice. On September 4, this participation was halted by a letter from Glennon, asserting that, as adjudicated at the May 26 hearing, Otto's suspension was still in effect. Thereafter, the Pollnows appealed to the Board of Education on the ground that, in light of the Commissioner's June 15 order, Otto's continuing suspension was improper. The Board then met and unanimously upheld the suspension.

The Pollnows thereupon appealed further to the Commissioner of Education, essentially challenging the suspension following the second hearing. On October 30, the Commissioner issued a second opinion, which, after noting that the Board of Education had interpreted his June 15 order to have had no effect on the second hearing, directed, with apparent irritation, that Otto be immediately reinstated to classroom attendance, which occurred on November 4, 1981.

In their complaint, the Pollnows allege and seek actual and punitive damages against Glennon, the members of the Millbrook Board of Education and others, all in their individual capacities, for the five-month period they claim Otto was wrongfully suspended from school. In support of this, plaintiffs assert a variety of claims, pursuant to 42 U.S.C. § 1983[.]...

....

It is well established that a student has a constitutionally protected property interest in public education, which may be taken from him only after notice and opportunity for a hearing. *Goss v. Lopez*, 419 U.S. 565, 574 (1974). To this end, New York Education Law § 3214(3)(c) provides:

> No pupil may be suspended for a period in excess of five school days unless such pupil and the person in parental relation to such pupil shall have had an opportunity for a fair hearing, upon reasonable notice, at which such pupil shall have the right of representation by counsel, with the right to question witnesses against such pupil and to present witnesses and other evidence on his behalf.

....

A number of plaintiffs' claims need but scant consideration. The first is that Otto's April 27 interrogation by Glennon was improper because Otto was not advised that he could call his parents before discussing the incident. There is,

A. SUSPENSIONS AND EXPULSIONS

however, no requirement for any sort of "Miranda" type warning in such informal, non-custodial discussions.

Plaintiffs' next claim is that charges of off-campus, non-school-related conduct are insufficient bases for suspension from school. The law is to the contrary, *see Matter of Rodriguez*, 8 Ed.Dept.Rep. 214, quoted in part in fn. 2, *supra*.

Finally, as to the Pollnow's claim of impropriety in holding a § 3214 hearing while criminal charges involving the same conduct are pending, the Courts have long held this to be permissible.

> [I]f the petitioners' contentions were carried to their logical conclusion, it would result in the absurd situation wherein a student who violated a rule or regulation short of the commission of a crime could be suspended after a hearing for a period greater than five days, while one who committed a serious crime on school property, be it assault, arson, attempted murder, etc., could not be suspended for more than five days and would be entitled to attend school until there was a disposition of the criminal charges. Such a situation cannot be condoned....

The final issue raised in the complaint is whether or not Superintendent Glennon and the members of the Millbrook Board of Education are to be subjected to a trial with all its expense and the risk of personal liability for failure to reinstate Otto upon receipt of the Commissioner's Interim Order in June[.]... It is the Pollnows' position that the June Interim Order was so clear that the failure of the school officials to immediately reinstate Otto was "in bad faith, malicious ... and in deliberate disregard of law." The school officials, on the other hand, took the position at the time and take the position today that the June order had no effect upon the second hearing, which had been conducted in accordance with established law and completely concluded by the time that Interim Order was issued, and therefore assert their absence of bad faith.

This issue is appropriately resolved by the application of the holding in *Harlow v. Fitzgerald*, 457 U.S. 800 (1982). There, at fn. 29 on p. 817, the Court communicated a concrete recognition of the problem by its quotation from Judge Gesell's concurrence in *Halperin v. Kissinger*, 196 U.S.App.D.C. 285, 307, 606 F.2d 1192, 1214 (1979), *aff'd* in pertinent part by an equally divided Court, 452 U.S. 713 (1981):

> We should not close our eyes to the fact that with increasing frequency in this jurisdiction and throughout the country plaintiffs are filing suits seeking damage awards against high government officials in their personal capacities based on alleged constitutional torts.... It is not difficult for ingenious plaintiff's counsel to create a material issue of fact on some element of the immunity defense where subtle questions of constitutional law and a decision maker's mental processes are involved.... The effect of this development upon the willingness of individuals to serve their country is obvious.

Having so observed, the Court's holding was as follows:

> [W]e conclude today that bare allegations of malice should not suffice to subject government officials either to the costs of trial or to the burdens of broad-reaching discovery. We therefore hold that government officials performing discretionary functions generally are shielded from liability for civil damages insofar as their conduct does not violate clearly established statutory or constitutional rights of which a reasonable person would have known.

See Procunier v. Navarette, 434 U.S. 555, 565 (1978); *Wood v. Strickland*, 420 U.S. [308] at 322 [(1975)].

> Reliance on the objective reasonableness of an official's conduct, as measured by reference to clearly established law, should avoid excessive disruption of government and permit the resolution of many insubstantial claims on summary judgment. On summary judgment, the judge appropriately may determine, not only the currently applicable law, but whether the law was clearly established at the time an action occurred. If the law at that time was not clearly established ... [a government official could not] fairly be said to "know" that the law forbade conduct not previously identified as unlawful.

In the light of this, the simple question, as I perceive it, is whether Glennon and the individual members of the Millbrook Board of Education are chargeable with a violation of Otto's constitutional rights by reason of their conclusion that the Commissioner's Interim Order had no effect on the second hearing upon which Otto's suspension was based. I conclude that as a matter of summary judgment they are not so chargeable. The Commissioner's Interim Order was on an appeal from the first hearing and spoke but prospectively as to staying any further hearing. The Superintendent and the Board obviously knew that the second hearing — which the order speaks of staying — had already been held and completed pursuant to established law when this order issued, *Matter of Rodriguez, supra, Matter of Manigualte*, 63 Misc.2d 765, 313 N.Y.S.2d 322 (1970). Furthermore, at the second hearing, evidence was adduced which had not been before the Commissioner when he issued his Interim Order, which was, "based on [his] review of the facts of this case and in the interest of justice." I conclude that the defendants are not, on an objective viewing of these facts, to be stripped of their qualified immunity from liability for Otto's continued suspension by their failure to give effect to an order that could be viewed as moot, even though one could also quite reasonably read the Commissioner's Interim Opinion as expressing his determination that Otto should be reinstated regardless of whether the second hearing had been held and concluded or not. *Harlow* and *Wood, supra*, require more than reasonable alternative readings before immunity is lost and personal liability attaches.

Accordingly, the defendants' motion for summary judgment is granted and plaintiffs' cross-motion for summary judgment is denied.

Submit order and judgment on notice.

---

1. *Pollnow* was affirmed in the Second Circuit Court of Appeals in 1985, 757 F.2d 496. The court held that school officials were entitled to qualified immunity from the student's civil rights claims and that it was not irrational for the officials to fail to follow the Commissioner's order from the first hearing on the ground that the first hearing was rendered moot by the second hearing.

2. Recall the quote from *Matter of Johnson* used by the court in *Pollnow*:

> [I]f the petitioners' contentions were followed to their logical conclusion, it would result in the absurd situation wherein a student who violated a rule or regulation short of the commission of a crime could be suspended after a hearing for a period of greater than five days, while one who committed a serious crime *on school property* ... could not be suspended for more than five days and would be entitled to attend school until there was a disposition of the criminal charges. *Pollnow*, 594 F. Supp. at 224 (emphasis added).

Can *Johnson* (and *Manigualte*) be used here with the same force, given that Pollnow's conduct occurred *off* the school property?

3. Due to the increase of drug use among today's young people, many schools have been given the authority to suspend or expel students for off-campus drug dealing. *See Howard v. Colonial Sch. Dist.*, 621 A.2d 362 (Del. Super. 1992) (Also held that expulsion was not racially motivated and that school did not act arbitrarily or capriciously in determining that the presence of a 17-year-old drug dealer in school was potentially harmful to the other students).

SMITH v. LITTLE ROCK SCHOOL DISTRICT

United States District Court
582 F. Supp. 159 (E.D. Ark. 1984)

ROY, DISTRICT JUDGE:

....

Plaintiff is a black male, 19 years old, and a former eleventh grade student of Parkview High School, a part of the Little Rock School District.

His complaint requests injunctive and declaratory relief under Title 42 U.S.C. § 1983. Plaintiff alleges that on January 30, 1984, he was suspended from school for the purported violation of Rule No. 5 of the Little Rock School District Student Conduct Code, which reads as follows: "Criminal offenses committed away from school which may affect the school climate."

In this action plaintiff seeks *inter alia* reinstatement in the Little Rock School District, expungement of records, credits for lost time and monetary and punitive damages. Plaintiff specifically prayed that this Court hold an immediate hearing and enter a preliminary injunction prohibiting the defendants from expelling him. A hearing was held on plaintiff's motion on March 1, 1984, and testimony was received from the plaintiff, the superintendent of the Little Rock School District, the principal of Parkview High School, the president of the Little Rock School Board, and the director of the Office of Pupil Personnel.

Among other things, the plaintiff contends that Rule 5 gives him no notice as to what acts are detrimental to the school environment; that the school has no authority over his actions when he is outside the bounds of school property. He further contends that he has only been charged with a criminal offense, not found guilty, and that the school board by punishing him is preempting the role of the courts.

At the preliminary hearing the plaintiff admitted, "Yes, I shot Herbert Johnson," and that he used his own .357 Magnum pistol which he had in his pocket. Plaintiff has been charged with murder but it was stipulated that plaintiff had not been convicted of any criminal offense nor admitted that he was guilty of any offense.

The evidence reflected that the Board of Directors of the Little Rock School District ["Board"] made the following findings of fact at a hearing held on February 21, 1984: Plaintiff Gerry Smith fired a gun which caused the death of another person; and an unsafe situation could develop at Parkview High School if plaintiff Smith is allowed to return there. Based on those findings and the evidence presented at the hearing, the Board voted to expel plaintiff Smith from school for the remainder of the semester.

The February 21st hearing before the Board was the culmination of the process afforded plaintiff Smith to challenge the recommendation of Parkview principal, Mr. R. J. Altheimer, that Smith be expelled. The process began when Mr. Altheimer contacted plaintiff's mother to schedule a meeting and to give plaintiff and his mother an opportunity to respond to the proposed expulsion. Plaintiff's mother agreed with Mr. Altheimer that plaintiff should not be enrolled in Parkview High School and declined the opportunity for a meeting. Mr. Altheimer then mailed to plaintiff's mother a notice that he was recommending expulsion and the reasons supporting the recommendation. Plaintiff appealed Mr. Altheimer's recommendation to the Office of Pupil Personnel. Following a hearing conducted by defendant Jo Evelyn Elston, at which plaintiff was represented by an attorney, the recommendation of the principal was sustained. The plaintiff appealed that determination to the Board, and the Board accorded the plaintiff a full hearing at which plaintiff was represented by counsel. The Board then voted to expel plaintiff Smith for the remainder of the semester.

When Mr. Altheimer was questioned as to the bases for his recommendation of expulsion, he testified as follows:

> As I stated earlier, Gerry has a sister at Parkview, the deceased has a brother and sister. I made the judgment for the welfare of the entire student body for any type of trouble that may develop, I am charged with the

A. SUSPENSIONS AND EXPULSIONS 507

> responsibility of making those decisions there. To maintain peace and tranquility I do know my student body very well. I have to be on the alert and look out for anything that happens in the community at any time that may be brought to the school.
>
> ....
>
> It was my feelings and my beliefs and my judgment that it would not be a wholesome environment for Gerry to be there with the brother and sister of the deceased. I did this, I took this step for Gerry's welfare and for the brother and sister of the deceased....

He also testified that Gerry had been one of the students under his supervision for a number of years and that he had been disciplined for his unruly conduct on several occasions.

All high school students in the Little Rock School District are provided copies of the Student Rights and Responsibilities Handbook. The handbook is taught to the students in English classes for the first two weeks of each school year. The handbook contains a Student Conduct Code. The Code describes the types of behavior which will result in school imposed sanctions. The Student Conduct Code applies to criminal offenses committed away from school but which may affect the school climate. That provision is not intended to limit the authority of the Board to act only in situations when a student has been convicted of a criminal offense. The Court finds reasonable the argument of school authorities that if they were forced to wait for a courtroom adjudication before taking action, the rule would be meaningless. The Student Conduct Code also warns students that "conduct not specifically mentioned might also call for disciplinary action if it is disruptive or harms others."

Other factors considered by the Board are plaintiff's disciplinary record, which was before the Board at the February 21st hearing, and showed that he had been suspended from junior high school or high school six times. These offenses included fighting, using abusive and threatening language to the principal and vice principal, and disruptive behavior in class. The fact that the person who was shot and killed by plaintiff has a brother and a sister who attend Parkview might also tend to cause a very explosive situation at the school, with a potential of harm to the plaintiff himself as well as other students at Parkview.

The president of the Board, Ms. Fay Southern, testified the above enumerated factors were carefully considered by the Board and that due process was accorded the plaintiff at the Board meeting on February 21, 1984. The transcript of the meeting was received in evidence and the Court finds it supports Ms. Southern's testimony. The testimony of Dr. Ed Kelly, superintendent of the Little Rock School District, and Ms. Jo Evelyn Elston further confirmed the careful attention given to this matter by the school officials before voting to uphold the expulsion. The Court finds this testimony to be logical and convincing.

These seem to be the main facts considered by the Board. As to the law, in *O'Rourke v. Walker* (1925), 102 Conn. 130, 128 A. 25, 41 A.L.R. 1308, the court emphasized that the true test of a teacher's right to punish a pupil for conduct off the school campus is not the time or place of the offense, but its effect upon the morale and efficiency of the school, and whether it in fact is detrimental to the good order and to the welfare of the pupils.

In *R.R. v. Board of Education* (1970), 109 N.J.Super. 337, 263 A.2d 180, a high school sophomore was suspended primarily for involvement in a stabbing incident after school hours outside the school grounds. The court held that the school authorities lawfully could suspend him for events happening outside of school hours. In reaching its decision the court stated: "The school officials can suspend or expel a student for conduct outside of school hours when it is reasonably necessary for the punished student's physical or emotional safety or for the safety and well-being of other students, teachers, or public school property."

The court, in *Wood v. Strickland*, 420 U.S. 308 (1975), defined the role of federal courts in § 1983 cases: It is not the role of the federal courts to set aside decisions of school administrators which the court may view as lacking a basis in wisdom or compassion. Public high school students do have substantive and procedural rights while at school. But § 1983 does not extend the right to relitigate in federal court evidentiary questions arising in school disciplinary proceedings or the proper construction of school regulations....

... The burden is on the plaintiff to prove the insufficiency of the evidence in support of the board's decision. *Clements v. Board of Trustees of Sheridan County School District*, 585 P.2d 197, 201 (Wyo.1978), and cases cited therein.

As to whether or not a preliminary injunction should be issued, the Court must consider the four factors enunciated in *Dataphase Systems, Inc. v. C L Systems, Inc.*, 640 F.2d 109, 114 n. 9 (8th Cir.1981).

As dictated by the mandates of the Eighth Circuit, first, the Court must consider whether the plaintiff will be irreparably harmed absent an injunction. The burden of showing irreparable harm is on the plaintiff. The Court finds that the plaintiff will not be irreparably harmed in this case if an injunction is not issued. The record indicates he has amassed enough high school credits to graduate at the end of the 1984-85 school year, if he is readmitted and attends summer school and the regular term.

Next, the Court must balance the harm plaintiff may suffer as a result of his expulsion against the serious risk to other students which would be presented by plaintiff's presence at the school. The Court finds that the risk of harm to other students and the potential for disruption of educational processes outweigh whatever harm plaintiff Smith may suffer as a result of his expulsion.

As to the probability of success on the merits, the evidence in support of defendants' position appears to outweigh that of the plaintiff's. The school board's action is based not only on the Student Code of Conduct but also upon Arkansas Statutes which establish the responsibilities of the school administrators in carrying out their duties. Ark.Stat.Ann. 80-1656 — Rules and Regulations for Orderly Operation of Schools. Nothing in this Act [§§ 80-1644 — 80-1656] shall

A. SUSPENSIONS AND EXPULSIONS

be construed to limit a local school district's power to adopt reasonable rules, regulations and policies, not inconsistent with the purposes of this Act, to insure continued orderly operation of schools, including adult education and area vocational-technical high schools, and such powers are deemed to include the right of expulsion for student participation in any activity which tends, in the opinion of the Board, to disrupt, obstruct or interfere with orderly education processes. [Acts 1969, No. 63, § 13, p. 181.] Ark.Stats.Ann. 80-1516.— Suspension of pupils — Causes — Right to appeal. The directors of any school district may suspend any person from school for immorality, refractory conduct, insubordination, infectious disease, habitual uncleanliness, or other conduct that would tend to impair the discipline of the school, or harm the other pupils, but such suspension shall not extend beyond the current term. The board of directors may authorize the teacher to suspend any pupils, subject to appeal to the board. All school board meetings entertaining such appeals shall be conducted in executive session if requested by the parent or guardian of the student, provided that after hearing all testimony and debate the school board shall conclude the executive session and reconvene in public session to vote on such appeal. In this case the suspension was for the current term.

The last factor to be considered is the public interest in the case. The Court finds that public interest in maintaining safe and productive schools is of paramount importance. The public interest would not be served if the Board were enjoined from removing the plaintiff from the classroom for the balance of this semester, under the circumstances presented in this case.

Accordingly, the Court finds that the motion for relief filed by the plaintiff must be denied. This does not mean that the Court regards lightly the plaintiff's constitutional right to secure an education in our school system — this is a very important right which should be guarded carefully.

However, the Court finds the plaintiff has failed to carry the burden of proving a preliminary injunction should be issued. Nevertheless, the Court is directing the school officials to reexamine this case at the end of a 30-day period and to submit a further report to the Court. The Court is also directing the officials to hold an immediate hearing if there is any change in circumstances which would warrant a review of the expulsion order.

An appropriate order will be entered in accordance with this memorandum opinion.

---

1. The court in *Smith* allows the suspension to take place before the criminal trial is decided. What effect do you think the result of a suspension or expulsion hearing has on a criminal trial? By being suspended or expelled and going through the associated hearing, have the students in effect gone through a "criminal" trial? In answering this and other questions, you may wish to recall that the plaintiff in *Smith* was an African-American male in a city well known for its civil and political unrest.

2. Is due process denied when a student facing criminal charges invokes the Fifth Amendment right against self incrimination at a school hearing? *See Psi Upsilon v. University of Pennsylvania*, 591 A.2d 555 (Pa. Super. 1991), a case where university fraternity members "mistakenly kidnapped and terrorized" a campus visitor and ultimately faced school disciplinary and criminal charges growing out of the same set of incidents. Upholding the tough university-imposed sanctions, the court ruled that the fraternity members could either testify and possibly implicate themselves or not testify and risk not revealing important evidence that might render a different decision by the university.

3. High school students who, after admitting their involvement in grade school vandalism, were called into the principal's office and told of their three-day suspension. This was held to be sufficient to satisfy due process rights. *Boster v. Philpot*, 645 F. Supp. 798 (D. Kan. 1986). The court also held that attending athletic games as a spectator was not a constitutionally protected right.

4. In a recent case dealing with drug possession and distribution on the school grounds, a state district court in Florida held that suspension for *admitted* possession of marijuana on campus did not violate due process, even though the student had been put on notice that the administrative hearing would involve her alleged distribution of drugs, as well as the possession. *Student Alpha ID Number Guja v. School Bd. of Volusia County*, 616 So. 2d 1011 (Fla. Ct. App. 1993).

2. EXPULSION

NEWSOME v. BATAVIA LOCAL SCHOOL DISTRICT

United States Court of Appeals
842 F.2d 920 (6th Cir. 1988)

BAILEY BROWN, SENIOR CIRCUIT JUDGE:

This is an appeal from an order of the District Court for the Southern District of Ohio denying plaintiff-appellant Arthur Newsome's motion for a temporary restraining order and a preliminary injunction and dismissing his entire case on the merits. On appeal, Newsome argues that the district court erred in holding that the procedures employed by the defendant-appellee Batavia School District in expelling him from school did not violate his right to procedural due process of law under the fourteenth amendment. The procedural defects alleged by Newsome involve the denial of his request to cross-examine the witnesses against him, the denial of his right to an impartial tribunal, and the consideration, by that tribunal, of evidence not made available to Newsome....

I

Upon filing of this complaint in the district court, Newsome was a sixteen-year-old junior at Batavia High School in Batavia, Ohio. On November 3, 1986,

A. SUSPENSIONS AND EXPULSIONS

Newsome was summoned to the office of the principal, Daniel Swart, and accused of possessing and offering a marijuana cigarette for sale on high school property. Newsome denied the charges and asked the source of the accusations. The principal then informed him that the information had been obtained through interviews with two students but refused to identify them.

On November 6, 1986, Newsome was informed by a school representative that the principal intended to suspend him for ten days based on his alleged possession and attempted sale of marijuana.

On November 10, 1986, a suspension hearing was held before Batavia School Superintendent James Fite. Newsome, his mother, Don Schlunk of the Clermont County Juvenile Court, and the principal were all present. The principal recounted the substance of the student accusations upon which Newsome's proposed suspension was based. At no time were the names of the student accusers disclosed. Apparently, at some point, the superintendent privately interviewed the two students.

The hearing was continued to November 14, 1986. At this time, Don Schlunk reported that a urinalysis which Newsome had taken was negative for drug use. A juvenile court officer then testified that there was no present need for Newsome to undergo drug counselling. She recommended that Newsome be immediately returned to school. At the conclusion of the hearing, the superintendent and principal adjourned to discuss the disposition of the case. Later that day, Newsome's mother was informed that the superintendent had decided to give Newsome a clean disciplinary record if he would accept transfer to the Live Oaks Vocational School in Milford, Ohio. Newsome declined this offer, and, on November 17, 1986, he was notified that he had been expelled from school for the remainder of the fall semester.

On November 24, 1986, the Batavia School Board met in executive session to consider Newsome's appeal of his expulsion. Newsome was represented by counsel during this hearing. The principal and superintendent led off the hearing by recounting the statements of the two accusing students. Again, they did not disclose the names of these students but affirmed their belief that the students were telling the truth. The principal stated that he did not believe the students were "out to get" Newsome and that the students were not close friends. In concluding his testimony, the superintendent stated that his decision to expel Newsome was based solely on the statements of the two student informants. Newsome's attorney requested an opportunity to cross-examine the principal and superintendent, but this request was denied by the school board. The meeting concluded with Newsome's testifying that he did not possess or offer to sell marijuana on school property. Newsome's attorney then was allowed a closing argument.

After Newsome, his mother, and his attorney were excused, the school board, together with the principal and superintendent, reviewed the evidence in the case. Upon completing their review, the school board affirmed the superintendent's decision to expel Newsome by a unanimous vote. This decision was confirmed by a letter dated December 1, 1986. The letter stated that Newsome was expelled from Batavia High School until January 21, 1987.

On December 10, 1986, Newsome filed this action in the district court. The complaint, brought under 42 U.S.C. § 1983 and the fourteenth amendment, alleged that Newsome was denied procedural due process during the school board hearing in the following respects: (1) he was denied the opportunity to cross-examine or to even know the identities of his student accusers; (2) he was denied the opportunity to cross-examine the principal and superintendent; and (3) he was denied the right to an impartial tribunal since the school board allowed the principal and superintendent to participate in its review of the superintendent's decision to expel him. Newsome's prayer for relief requested a temporary restraining order and an injunction prohibiting school officials from enforcing his expulsion, an injunction requiring the school district to implement a disciplinary process that comports with the requirements of procedural due process, an injunction requiring the school district to provide tutorial assistance to him in making up the work he missed during his expulsion, and $10,000 in compensatory damages as well as attorney's fees.

....

On December 29, 1986, the district court, 656 F.Supp. 147, pursuant to Rule 65(a)(2) of the Federal Rules of Civil Procedure, issued an order denying Newsome's motion for a temporary restraining order and a preliminary injunction and dismissing his action on the merits. It is from this order that Newsome now appeals.

....

III

... We note as a general matter that, while the Supreme Court has addressed the issue of what process is due public school students in short suspension cases, *Goss v. Lopez*, 419 U.S. 565 (1975), the Court has specifically left open the question of what process is due in long-term suspensions (suspensions exceeding ten days) and expulsion cases. In the Court's words, "Longer suspensions or expulsion for the remainder of the school term, or permanently, may require more formal procedures." *Id.* at 584.

Without the aid of Supreme Court authority directly on point, we are left with resolving the procedural due process issues presented in this appeal under the more general rubric of *Mathews v. Eldridge*, 424 U.S. 319 (1976). *Mathews* provides for a flexible, policy-oriented analysis of procedural due process issues in which three competing factors are balanced against each other. These factors are: (1) the private interest that will be affected by the official action; (2) the probable value, if any, of additional or substitute procedural safeguards; and (3) the government's interest, including the fiscal and administrative burden that the additional or substitute procedural requirements would entail. *Id.* at 334-35.

....

A. SUSPENSIONS AND EXPULSIONS

A

Newsome first contends that he was denied due process of law at the school board hearing when the board denied his request for permission to cross-examine his student accusers or to at least know their identities. We disagree.

The value of cross-examination to the discovery of truth cannot be overemphasized. As the Supreme Court stated in *Davis v. Alaska*, 415 U.S. 308, 316 (1974), "Cross-examination is the principal means by which the believability of a witness and the truth of his testimony are tested." In the instant case, allowing Newsome, through his attorney, to cross-examine his student accusers, or even merely to know their names, would have afforded Newsome the opportunity to challenge the students' credibility. For example, a prior altercation of some sort between Newsome and his accusers might have been brought to light through cross-examination or by disclosure of their identities.

The value of cross-examining student witnesses in school disciplinary cases, however, is somewhat muted by the fact that the veracity of a student account of misconduct by another student is initially assessed by a school administrator — in this case, the school principal — who has, or has available to him, a particularized knowledge of the student's trustworthiness. The school administrator generally knows firsthand (or has access to school records which disclose) the accusing student's disciplinary history, which can serve as a valuable gauge in evaluating the believability of the student's account. Additionally, the school administrator often knows, or can readily discover, whether the student witness and the accused have had an amicable relationship in the past. Consequently, the process of cross-examining the student witness may often be merely duplicative of the evaluation process undertaken by the investigating school administrator.

The value of cross-examining student witnesses in pre-expulsion proceedings must be set against the burden that such a practice would place upon school administration. Today's public schools face severe challenges in maintaining the order and discipline necessary for the impartation of knowledge. A recent study conducted by the Fullerton, California, Police Department and the California Department of Education, for instance, shows that, while schoolteachers in the 1940's listed talking, chewing gum, and running in the hallways as the primary disciplinary problems they encountered, today's schoolteachers are more concerned with drug abuse, rape, robbery, assault, burglary, arson, and bombings. Bowen, *"Getting Tough,"* TIME, Feb. 1, 1988, at 54. Indeed, in a recent Supreme Court decision involving the fourth amendment restraints on school administrators, the Court noted that "drug use and violent crime in the schools have become major social problems." *New Jersey v. T.L.O.*, 469 U.S. 325, 339 (1985) (citing 1 NIE, U.S. Dept. of Health, Education and Welfare, *Violent Schools — Safe Schools: The Safe School Study Report to the Congress* (1978)).

In this turbulent, sometimes violent, school atmosphere, it is critically important that we protect the anonymity of students who "blow the whistle" on their classmates who engage in drug trafficking and other serious offenses. Without the cloak of anonymity, students who witness criminal activity on school property will be much less likely to notify school authorities, and those who do will be faced with ostracism at best and perhaps physical reprisals. Giving due weight to the important interest a student accused of serious misconduct has in his public education, we conclude that the necessity of protecting student witnesses from ostracism and reprisal outweighs the value to the truth-determining process of allowing the accused student to cross-examine his accusers.

....

---

1. For more cases involving searches and seizures with informants, *see New Jersey v. T.L.O.*, 469 U.S. 325 (1985), and other materials in Chapter 7.

2. The court in *Newsome* also held that the accused did not have a due process right to cross-examine the school administrators, but that the administrators may not present new evidence other than at the preexpulsionary hearing, so as to allow the accused to rebut the evidence.

3. The court seems to think that a school is able to tell whether the student witness is "out to get" the accused. "Additionally, the school administrator often knows or can readily discover, whether the student witness and the accused have had an amicable relationship in the past. Consequently the process of cross-examining the student witness may often be merely duplicative of the evaluation process undertaken by the investigating school administrator." *Newsome*, 842 F.2d at 294.

How convincing is this? What is the likelihood that there is a connection between the accuser and the accused that the school administrators don't know about? Consider a situation in which the accuser and the accused do not regularly associate with one another, but the accused consistently performs better academically than the accuser. In such a case, the accuser could be "out to get" the accused with very few knowing about it. Should the court depend solely on the administrators' opinions of the students' relationships when determining the veracity of the informant's statements? Should the degree of punishment — expulsion, suspension, detention, etc. — make any difference?

4. In a drug-related expulsion case, is a school required to consider the student's "good standing" at the school? *Forrest v. School City of Hobart*, 498 N.E.2d 14 (Ind. Ct. App. 1986), answered this question in the negative, holding that the expulsion for admitted use of marijuana on school property was not grossly excessive.

5. If a suspension is changed to an expulsion after it is determined that the student would not return to school, do the due process rights change? In *Darby v. Schoo*, 544 F. Supp. 428 (W.D. Mich. 1982), the court found a violation of due process when a *short-term* suspension was changed to an expulsion. Due process was met for the short suspension, but after the change, the school is

A. SUSPENSIONS AND EXPULSIONS

required to either put a cap on the suspension and to afford the student with an additional hearing, or to end the suspension and proceed with a hearing. Failure of the school to do either of these is a violation of due process.

6. Is a school required to provide an expelled student with alternative education during the period of his expulsion? *See Board of Educ. v. School Committee of Quincy*, 415 Mass. 240, 612 N.E.2d 666 (1993) (Board of Education filed suit to require school committee to provide education for expelled students. Court held that the board does not have the statutory authority to require the committee to do so).

7. What about the status of an expelled student during the pendency of his or her hearing? *Craig v. Selma City Sch. Bd.*, 801 F. Supp. 585 (S.D. Ala. 1992), denied summary judgment for both parties and held that a genuine issue of material fact existed as to whether a school district's refusing to permit students to return during pendency of expulsion hearing to get their books violated due process. The court also held that placing the students on strict conduct probation did not violate the equal protection clause.

Should an expelled student receive credit for "time served" while he or she is out of school during pendency of an expulsion hearing? In 1989, the Second Circuit Court of Appeals said there was no violation of due process when a school does not grant such credit. *See Rosa R. v. Connelly*, 889 F.2d 435 (2d Cir. 1989).

DRAPER v. COLUMBUS PUBLIC SCHOOLS
United States District Court
760 F. Supp. 131 (S.D. Ohio 1991)

GEORGE C. SMITH, DISTRICT JUDGE:

This matter is before the Court on defendants' motion for summary judgment. In this 42 U.S.C. § 1983 case, all named defendants concede that they were acting under color of state law. Defendants also concede that plaintiff Marshall Draper suffered a deprivation of constitutionally protected liberty and property interests. Thus, the lone remaining issue is whether or not the state action in question violated Constitutional requirements for procedural due process. For the reasons detailed below, the Court finds as a matter of law that the applicable Constitutional standards were met. Accordingly, defendants' motion is GRANTED.

Facts

Plaintiff Marshall Draper was an eighth grade student at Mifflin Alternative Middle School at the time of the incident which precipitated this litigation. On October 29, 1987, Marshall allegedly threatened several other Mifflin students with a knife. This purportedly occurred just after school and just beyond the school yard, while the children were walking home.

The next day the school principal, Stephen Tankovich, heard the stories of each of the children who had been involved. After hearing Marshall Draper's story, Mr. Tankovich immediately notified Marshall's parents, Mr. and Mrs. Draper, that a hearing before a representative of the Superintendent of Columbus City Schools would be held October 30, 1987, for the purpose of determining whether or not Marshall should be expelled from Mifflin.

At the October 30 hearing, Marshall Draper was expelled from Mifflin, with the provision that he could petition the Department of Pupil Personnel of the Columbus Public Schools for reinstatement on November 25, 1987. School Superintendent Damon Asbury posted a letter notifying the Drapers of the expulsion later that day. The Drapers then appealed this decision to the Columbus City Schools Board of Education.

November 12, 1987, an appeal was heard by Appellate Hearing Officer Ellen Wristen on behalf of the Columbus City School Board. Marshall Draper was there represented by his attorney in the present action, Walter G. Brooks. Ms. Wristen recommended that Marshall Draper's expulsion be affirmed. A report detailing Ms. Wristen's recommendation was mailed to Mr. Brooks on November 25, 1987. This report was affirmed by a unanimous vote of the Columbus City School Board on December 1, 1987. Notice of the School Board's final decision was posted to Mr. Brooks on December 3, 1987.

In the meanwhile, on November 20, 1987, a letter was posted to Mr. and Mrs. Draper from the Columbus Public Schools Department of Pupil Personnel, which operates under the authority of the Superintendent of Columbus City Schools. This letter informed the Drapers that Marshall was being re-assigned to Champion Alternative Middle School. Marshall began classes at Champion on November 30, 1987. He has since completed the curriculum at Champion, and is currently in high school.

November 25, 1987, a complaint was filed by Marshall Draper and his parents in the United States Court for the Southern District of Ohio, Eastern Division. The complaint alleges the violation of Marshall's due process rights, and invokes federal jurisdiction pursuant to 42 U.S.C. § 1983. Named defendants include Columbus Public Schools, the Board of Education, Mifflin Alternative Middle School, and various personnel within these entities.

. . . .

Law and Analysis

The liberty and property interests of which Marshall Draper was deprived mirror those of the plaintiffs in *Goss v. Lopez*, 419 U.S. 565 (1975). Although there is no fundamental right to a free public education, Ohio has chosen to extend free education to a defined class of persons. Accordingly, an individual falling within that group has a property interest in a legitimate government entitlement which cannot be taken from him without due process of law. *Id.* at 574. Marshall Draper is a member of the class to which Ohio offers an education, therefore he has a property interest at stake.

A. SUSPENSIONS AND EXPULSIONS

Goss also defines a liberty interest in "a person's good name, reputation, honor, or integrity." *Id.* at 574. The permanent school record of a juvenile's suspension on charges of misconduct impairs a juvenile's reputation by lowering his esteem in the eyes of fellow pupils, teachers, and others who might afford education or employment opportunities to the child in the future. *Id.* at 574-75. Under this rationale, the expulsion of Marshall Draper clearly impacted his liberty interest in his good name.

Having determined that the Plaintiff possesses liberty and property interests in his public education, it follows that any state action tending to deprive him of these interests must comply with the due process requirements of the fourteenth amendment. This leads to the next step in our analysis, for "[o]nce it is determined that due process applies, the question remains what process is due." *Morrissey v. Brewer*, 408 U.S. 471, 481 (1972).

....

The types of notice and hearing needed to conform with constitutional due process requirements vary with the practical necessities of disparate cases. "[D]ue process is flexible and calls for such procedural protections as the particular situation demands." *[Id.]* The format required in an individual case must be arrived at by measuring both the interest of the person whose rights are at stake and the competing state interest. *Id.*

In the case at bar, Marshall Draper's interest in his reputation and his uninterrupted education must be balanced against the state interest in maintaining safe, orderly, and effective public schools. The greatest guidance in construing the constitutional requirements of due process for these competing interests is that offered by the Supreme Court in *Goss v. Lopez*, supra. Although the Court in *Goss* ruled on due process requirements for a student suspension, and the instant case deals with an expulsion, the reasoning is nonetheless particularly appropriate for application to these facts. The nature of the interests of both competing parties are essentially the same in this case as those of the parties in *Goss*. In addition, the notion that expulsion is a greater violation of the plaintiff's liberty and property interests than is suspension has been greatly mitigated in this case by the re-instatement of Marshall Draper into the Columbus Public School System after only twenty-seven days.

In *Goss*, the Court proclaims that due process requires, "for a suspension, ... the student [must] be given oral or written notice of the charges against him and, if he denies them, an explanation of the evidence the authorities have and an opportunity to present his side of the story." *Id.* at 581....

Marshall Draper was given not one, but several opportunities to be heard. First, he was allowed to present his story to Principal Tankovich in an informal hearing. Written notice was sent to the Drapers of a more formal hearing to be held before an officer of the school system superintendent the next day. The Drapers were invited to attend and be heard. The Drapers were provided by the Superintendent with a letter informing them of the results of this hearing, of their right to appeal the decision to the School Board, and of their right to counsel.

Their attorney filed the notice of appeal, took part in scheduling the hearing date, and was present at the appellate hearing. It was only after their dissatisfaction with the result of this third hearing that the Drapers filed legal action asserting a denial of due process.

The process due in order to assure rudimentary precautions against unfair or mistaken findings for a 10-day suspension, as delineated in *Goss*, is merely notification of the charges and an opportunity to contest them at an informal hearing. *Id.* In the instant case, Marshall Draper was expelled for a period specified at its inception to be 27 days (*see* 10/30/87 letter from Damon Asbury to Mr. and Mrs. Draper). For the added penalty of what amounts to 17 extra days of separation from school and the transfer of institutions, in effect, Marshall Draper was granted two formal hearings and the representation of counsel. On its face, the additional process afforded to the Drapers in this action is more than adequate to offset the stiffer punishment....

In reaching a decision in this case, this Court has been mindful of the Supreme Court's following admonition: Given the fact that there was evidence supporting the charge,

> ... [i]t is not the role of the federal courts to set aside decisions of school administrators which the court may view as lacking a basis in wisdom or compassion.... [S]tudents do have substantive and procedural rights while at school.... But § 1983 does not extend the right to relitigate in federal court evidentiary questions arising in school disciplinary proceedings.... The system of public education that has evolved in this Nation relies necessarily upon the discretion and judgment of school administrators and school board members, and § 1983 was not intended to be a vehicle for federal-court corrections of errors in the exercise of that discretion which do not rise to the level of specific constitutional guarantees. *Wood v. Strickland*, 420 U.S. 308, 326 (1975).

Conclusion

Accordingly, this Court finds that as a matter of law, the plaintiffs have failed to make a showing sufficient to establish an element essential to their case. The Drapers have not met their burden of producing evidence tending to prove that the procedural process due to Marshall under the due process clause of the 14th Amendment was denied.... Furthermore, it is the opinion of this court that the Columbus Public School System and its component branches have, in this instance, met the constitutional requirements for due process.

....

---

1. Recall the article by Daniel and Coriell presented at the beginning of this chapter. The authors open their final paragraph with the following: "The formulation and adoption of a disciplinary procedure cannot occur in the sterile

A. SUSPENSIONS AND EXPULSIONS

environment of the school board's meeting place. To create any policy which governs the educational process, it is necessary to emerge from our ivory towers and face the realities of today's world." 13 Hamline J. Pub. L. & Pol'y 1 (1992).

James W. McMasters may have done just that with his article, *Mediation: New Process for High School Disciplinary Expulsions*, 84 Nw. U. L. Rev. 736 (1990). He argues that the typical notice and opportunity to be heard are insufficient and unmeaningful today, especially with respect to expulsions in the following comment:*

I. *Introduction: Gatekeeping at the Schoolhouse*

American public high school students are not expected to leave their constitutional rights at the schoolhouse gate as they enter school each morning. *Goss v. Lopez*, the Supreme Court's primer on educational due process, made clear that this holds true in the disciplinary context. In *Goss*, the Court mandated notice and a hearing for short disciplinary suspensions. Fifteen years after *Goss*, however, the Supreme Court has yet to provide further teaching on the process due in cases involving more serious sanctions.

There is disagreement as to what procedural protections school officials should provide students who are expelled from school. Recent court decisions, for example, have not favored extensive procedural protections. One federal appellate court stated that a student expelled for the remainder of a semester on drug allegations was not entitled to cross-examine student accusers, learn their identities, or cross-examine school officials.[4] That court also approved the participation of the investigating administrators in the closed deliberations of the school board — deliberations the student and his attorney were not allowed to attend. Some states, on the other hand, statutorily mandate extensive safeguards, including a right to legal counsel, examination of records, presentation of evidence, and cross-examination of witnesses.[6]

While courts are typically quite deferential to the procedures followed by administrators, the amount of litigation on the issue in recent years suggests continuing uncertainty as to precisely what process is due students facing

---

*Reprinted by special permission of Northwestern University School of Law, *Northwestern University Law Review*, Volume 84, Issue 2, p. 736 (1990).

[4]*Newsome v. Batavia Local School Dist.*, 842 F.2d 920, 924-26 (6th Cir. 1988)

[6]*See, e.g.*, Ind. Code Ann. §§ 20-8.1-5-8 to 5-10 (West 1984); Minn. Stat. Ann. § 127.31 (West 1979); W. Va. Code § 18A-5-1a(d) (1988) (except prior review of records); *see also, e.g.*, Md. Educ. Code Ann § 7-304(c) (4) (1989) (right to counsel and appeal); Wis. Stat. Ann. § 120.13(1) (c) (West Supp. 1989) (same). *But see, e.g.*, Mass. Ann. Laws ch. 76, § 17 (Law. Co-op. 1978) (only specifying "an opportunity to be heard").

possible expulsion. Undesirable results seem inevitable: schools might provide too little due process protection, depriving students of constitutionally protected rights and generating burdensome litigation expenses if students challenge the procedures; schools might provide excessive procedural mechanisms, imposing an undue burden on themselves; or, the worst possible scenario, schools might provide a number of protections that seem sufficient but are actually ineffective or inappropriate.

Evaluating the appropriateness of the process chosen in high school expulsion cases is the principal focus of this Comment. Plaintiffs in school due process cases urge the courts to mandate trial-type procedures. Most courts, however, suggest that trial-type procedures are inappropriate and burdensome. Yet, a review of due process law suggests that expelled students do have a valid claim to increased procedural safeguards.

This Comment argues that an opportunity to be heard is not meaningful — and thus not constitutionally sufficient — for a high school student facing expulsion unless that opportunity is part of a procedure that fosters open participation by both parties. Courts and schools must recognize that an expulsion warrants more process than does a short suspension. Further, consideration of the due process issue in the school context should not be limited to traditional trial-type procedures. The developmental role of schools and the goals of the educational process make the high school context the perfect environment for carefully implemented informal dispute resolution techniques. This Comment suggests that mediation, as an intermediate step between administrator action and an expulsion hearing, would be both efficient and appropriate in the school setting. Such a procedure would protect the real interests of both student and school better than applying only the limited *Goss* procedures or granting a full-scale judicial proceeding.

. . . .

HAWKINS v. COLEMAN
United States District Court
376 F. Supp. 1330 (N.D. Tex. 1974)

HUGHES, DISTRICT JUDGE:

After two years of litigation and two appeals to the Fifth Circuit, on May 7, 1974, this Court commenced hearings on plaintiffs' plea for permanent injunctive relief. Upon a consideration of the evidence, the briefs and arguments of counsel, this Opinion has been entered.

The Original Complaint was filed on April 17, 1972, by Delbert Hawkins, by his parent and next friend Ruth Hawkins, on behalf of himself and a class of black students within the Dallas Independent School District (DISD) arising from his suspension from the DISD contesting the adoption, substance and enforcement of the DISD student suspension procedures on the grounds of race discrimination,

A. SUSPENSIONS AND EXPULSIONS 521

the denial of equal protection, and the denial of both substantive and procedural due process....

The DISD is the principal school district in Dallas County, Texas, operating during the 1973-1974 school year some 24 high schools, 24 junior high schools, and 141 elementary schools. (Pl. Ex. 1). Defendants in this cause are various persons of responsibility within the DISD.

....

The issues on this hearing are substantially the same as those in the original complaint and focus upon the student suspension procedures per se or upon the application of those procedures.

It is plaintiffs' contention that (1) the suspension procedures lack due process (2) the application of the procedures amounts to a denial of equal protection and (3) the procedures are enforced in a racially discriminatory manner.

Discussing the procedures themselves, it is defendant's contention that since the hearing on the preliminary injunction new procedures have been adopted which provide procedural due process.

....

The greater part of plaintiffs' evidence dealt with the application and enforcement of the discipline procedures. This testimony consisted of (1) DISD student suspension data (2) analysis of that data by an expert witness and (3) evaluation of the meaning of the analysis.

....

While the statistical data alone reveals there is a significant disparity in suspension and corporal punishment statistics as applied to black and white students, an expert on statistical analysis, Dr. Scott Kestler, conducted an extensive analysis by using a method termed the Chi Square formula to determine whether the frequency of suspension of black students over white students is significantly different from their racial composition. (Pl. Ex. 8).

....

His calculations resulted in the following conclusions: ...

(1) Black students *are* being suspended from school significantly more frequently than are White students.
(2) Black students *are* being suspended from elementary schools significantly more frequently than are White students.
(3) Black students *are* being suspended from junior high schools significantly more frequently than are White students.
(4) Black students *are* being suspended from senior high schools significantly more frequently than are White students.
(5) Black students receive "more-than-3-day" suspension significantly more frequently than do White students.

Dr. Kestler put into graphic form his suspension and enrollment calculation.... His conclusions confirm the statistical data furnished by DISD.

Having determined there is a significant disparity between the blacks and whites disciplined, it now becomes necessary to determine the reasons for this disproportion. An examination of suspension and corporal punishment data for the years 1972-73 and the first half of 1973-74 shows that 60% were for such offenses as truancy, class cutting, talking back to the teacher, or other non-violent conduct.

As a part of his investigation Dr. Kestler visited six schools where white students outnumber black students. It was his conclusion from his visits and his calculations that the DISD applied discipline in a racially biased manner. Dr. Kestler noted there was a substantial reliance upon non-violent "offenses" as a justification for suspension when, in fact, such conduct may be a pivotal ethnic characteristic. The primary reasons, he said, for student suspension are ones that are highly susceptible of selective perception and selective prosecution.

Dr. Kestler additionally concluded there were two possible reasons for the disproportionate student suspension and corporal punishment statistics. One reason was racial bias in the administration of the student discipline procedures and policies, a factor that Dr. Kestler said definitely existed within the DISD. The second reason was increased "suspendable conduct" on the part of black students.

Dr. Reuben McDaniel, an expert on institutional racism, concluded from his examination of Dr. Kestler's data that the DISD fit into an existing national pattern of race discrimination in that the DISD is a "white controlled institution" with "institutional racism" existing in the operation of its discipline procedures. A "white controlled institution" occurs, testified Dr. McDaniel, when a large majority of the decisions about resource distribution is made by white administrators. "Institutional racism" exists, according to Dr. McDaniel, when the standard operating procedures of an institution are prejudiced against, derogatory to, or unresponsive to the needs of a particular racial group. This is distinguished from "personal racism" which exists with a given individual and do [sic] not become involved in the administration of an institution's normal operations.

Because of the existence of racism, Dr. McDaniel concluded black students will become more frustrated as the institution continues to refuse to respond to their needs and ambitions. This frustration will be reflected either in increased passivity or increased hostility. Such hostilities will result in increased "suspendable behavior", a term used by Dr. Kestler as one of the causes for the disproportionate suspension ratios. Moreover, Dr. McDaniel concludes, in a school district in which there is institutional racism toward the Blacks conduct by black students that would not be "unusual" or "offensive" in a black environment becomes to many teachers "disruptive" or "suspendable conduct." To teachers unfamiliar with Blacks, this conduct, that is non-violent and characteristic of the black race, stands out and becomes thereby subject to selective prosecution. For example, Dr. McDaniel, himself a Black, testified that among Blacks there is substantial physical contact. To a teacher unfamiliar with the subtle nuances of this type of conduct, a touch or slap by one black student on

A. SUSPENSIONS AND EXPULSIONS

another black student may be interpreted as a hostile act when in fact it was a friendly act. Therefore, this teacher may recommend disciplinary action when it is unjustified.

In conclusion, Dr. McDaniel testified that to parents and students within the DISD based on Dr. Kestler's statistical analysis the DISD would be perceived as a racial institution.

Two parents also testified at the permanent injunction hearing. From their testimony, two facts emerge. First, the reaction anticipated by Dr. McDaniel by students to white institutional racism was manifest in the children of these parents. Mrs. Porter testified that after her daughter was transferred to a predominately white school she developed discipline problems that resulted in several suspensions, mostly for tardiness and class cutting. Mrs. Porter's second daughter, Maurine, reacted differently when assigned to a predominately white junior high school. Maurine became depressed and quiet. A third daughter, Laurene, developed a change of attitude and became very hostile toward school when she was assigned to a predominately white institution.

Mrs. Hawkins testified as to similar problems with her son, Delbert, the named plaintiff.

One of the most damaging witnesses to the defendant was Dr. Nolan Estes, superintendent of the DISD, called by the plaintiffs. Asked if he was aware of anything to which he could "attribute the high number of suspensions of Blacks over Whites", he replied, "Well, we are a White controlled institution, institutional racism, racism among individuals." Later on in his testimony he admitted again that white institutional racism existed in the Dallas Schools. In response to questioning about whether he had ever before stated this he replied that he had "before our principals' group," which was not an open public meeting.

The defendants presented no evidence to rebut the testimony of Dr. Kestler, Dr. McDaniel or Dr. Estes that racism exists with the DISD and contributes to the suspension of black students.

In order to overcome the problem of racism Dr. McDaniel testified that there was a need for the school district to be responsive to the needs of black students. Such institutions, he said, had done things on four essential levels.

> "First, they had acted in terms of institutional and structural changes. Secondly, they had reacted in terms of training of teachers and counselors. Thirdly, they reacted in terms of the training of students to deal with institutionalized racism. Fourth, they had been active in terms of their community or their environment in attempting to push programs of affirmative action."

In response to questioning by counsel for both plaintiffs and defendants he gave numerous examples of the changes that were necessary. He pointed out that institutions must hold personnel accountable for decreasing racism and the ability of teachers to deal with the situation should be a criterion for promotion and pay raises. With reference to training, he pointed out programs need to be lengthy and intensive with continuity rather than "one-shot-single-topic kind of programs." Such training, he said, must involve not only the administrator "going to a special class ..., but actual interaction while the teacher is performing his role ... in class." He emphasized the necessity of training in human relations [which] must include information which makes administrators and teachers understand their own feelings and reactions toward minority students. Also teachers should have a cultural awareness of Black people which is frequently not appreciated by Whites. One characteristic, for example, of Blacks, Dr. McDaniel mentioned, was the importance of the extended family and their practice of calling other Blacks "brother and sister" as well as "uncle and aunt", persons to whom they are not related.

At the same time that teachers are being trained in ways to decrease racism, students, he said, need to learn "to manage their way through the racist institution." Racism will not be overcome quickly and in the meantime Blacks must be taught to live in a white dominated society.

With regard to a community program, he urged that the schools be active, working with groups to develop a better understanding of community problems. The institution should not simply "mirror the community."

These programs Dr. McDaniel maintained would "resolve conflict and ease tensions within the school system."

The programs initiated by the DISD since the desegregation order and testified to by Dr. Estes, while as a whole aimed at the elimination of cultural and institutional racism over a prolonged period, do not deal with the immediate problems of DISD. Moreover, they are presented to administrative and supervisory personnel rather than to teachers.

Defendants offered no evidence to establish that any administrator is currently assigned the responsibility of implementing a remedy that will eliminate the current racial application of the suspension policies. Although Dr. Estes and other DISD administrators and officials have been aware of the problem since the compilation of the 1971-72 school year suspension statistics, no affirmative countervailing action has been taken. All of the DISD programs are "long-term" permitting the continued discrimination to exist for an indefinite period.

It is apparent that the program thus far in effect in the DISD has not worked to materially change the existing racism which, in the opinion of this Court, is the chief cause of the disproportionate number of Blacks being suspended and given corporal punishment. An improvement in the situation demands an affirmative program. Such a program should include the four levels outlined by Dr. McDaniel, as heretofore discussed.

This Court will not detail such a program as the Court has no intention of taking from the School Board or the Superintendent and other officials the running of the schools.

It should be pointed out, however, that if there is to be progress in Dallas towards removing institutional racism there must be a change in attitude of both the School Board and the officials. There has prevailed among these officials a determination to resist every effort to make the changes which have been decreed and which they should know are inevitable. The law will be followed, says the School Board, but then only after every effort has been made to resist. There has been an utter lack of leadership in developing public opinion to accept necessary changes in the school if the law is to be followed.

Cooperation on the part of the school officials with the public generally, and particularly the parents, is needed at the same time changes are made in the school system. It is the responsibility of the School Board and officials to take the lead in the development of public opinion and in obtaining cooperation.

No court can decree a change in attitude. That is something within the individual. Put briefly, there must be a real effort on the part of everyone involved to accentuate the positive while at the same time eliminating the negative effects of "white institutional racism"....

While not attempting to dictate the details of an affirmative program this Court does direct the DISD to review its present program and to put into effect an affirmative program aimed at materially lessening "white institutional racism" in the DISD.

---

1. Do you think desegregation has had an effect on the disparate treatment of minorities in school disciplinary actions? If so, is this effect positive or negative? That is, has desegregation created a more level playing field among students and school officials involved in discipline cases?

2. "It is apparent that the program thus far in effect in the DISD has not worked to materially change the existing racism which, in the opinion of this Court, is the chief cause of the disproportionate number of Blacks being suspended and given corporal punishment." *Hawkins*, at 1337. If there has been a decrease in disproportionate suspensions and expulsions after desegregation, is this statement true? Consider another statement from the *Hawkins* decision:

> No court can decree a change in attitude. That is something within the individual. Put briefly, there must be a real effort on the part of everyone involved to accentuate the positive while at the same time eliminating the negative effects of "white institutional racism." *Id.* at 1338.

3. *Hawkins* was decided before *Goss v. Lopez*. What effect does *Goss* have on this decision? In a case decided just before *Goss*, the Fifth Circuit Court of Appeals held that state officials were entitled to judgment as a matter of law because decisions on disciplinary matters should be left to the schools; but that plaintiffs' claim that they were denied equal protection failed, as well, since the claim lacked factual foundation that African American students were suspended or expelled more often than white students for similar conduct. *Sweet v. Childs*, 507 F.2d 675.

In *Long v. Thornton Twp. High Sch. Dist. 205*, 82 F.R.D. 186 (N.D. Ill. 1979), the court certified a class of students subject to suspensions and expulsions *and* a subclass of African American students allegedly subject to more severe penalties than similarly situated white students. However, the court held that the due process rights of the named plaintiff were not violated. The numbers presented in the effort to certify the class and subclass were the following: Between 1971 and 1975, there were over 7,000 suspensions ordered by the school district and between 1971 and 1977, there were 84 expulsions. The facts indicated that there were over 3,400 suspensions and 64 expulsions of African American students over the same time periods.

Tasby v. Estes, 643 F.2d 1103 (5th Cir. 1981), held similarly on the due process claims, and also held the statistics presented by the plaintiffs (parents of African American children) were insufficient to establish a prima facie case of racial discrimination, absent proof of discriminatory purpose.

B. CORPORAL PUNISHMENT

INGRAHAM v. WRIGHT

Supreme Court of the United States
430 U.S. 651 (1977)

MR. JUSTICE POWELL delivered the opinion of the Court:

This case presents questions concerning the use of corporal punishment in public schools: First, whether the paddling of students as a means of maintaining school discipline constitutes cruel and unusual punishment in violation of the Eighth Amendment; and, second, to the extent that paddling is constitutionally permissible, whether the Due Process Clause of the Fourteenth Amendment requires prior notice and an opportunity to be heard.

I

....

Petitioners' evidence may be summarized briefly. In the 1970-1971 school year many of the 237 schools in Dade County used corporal punishment as a means of maintaining discipline pursuant to Florida legislation and a local school board regulation. The statute then in effect authorized limited corporal punishment by negative inference, proscribing punishment which was "degrading or unduly severe" or which was inflicted without prior consultation with the principal or the teacher in charge of the school. The regulation, Dade County School Board Policy 5144, contained explicit directions and limitations. The authorized punishment consisted of paddling the recalcitrant student on the buttocks with a flat wooden paddle measuring less than two feet long, three to four inches wide, and about one-half inch thick. The normal punishment was limited to one to five "licks" or blows with the paddle and resulted in no apparent physical injury to the student. School authorities viewed corporal punishment as a less drastic means of discipline than suspension or expulsion. Contrary to the procedural requirements of the statute and regulation, teachers often paddled students on their own authority without first consulting the principal.

Petitioners focused on Drew Junior High School, the school in which both Ingraham and Andrews were enrolled in the fall of 1970. In an apparent reference to Drew, the District Court found that "[t]he instances of punishment which could be characterized as severe, accepting the students' testimony as credible, took place in one junior high school." The evidence, consisting mainly of the testimony of 16 students, suggests that the regime at Drew was exceptionally harsh. The testimony of Ingraham and Andrews, in support of their individual claims for damages, is illustrative. Because he was slow to respond to his teacher's instructions, Ingraham was subjected to more than 20 licks with a paddle while being held over a table in the principal's office. The paddling was so severe that he suffered a hematoma requiring medical attention and keeping him out of school for several days. Andrews was paddled several times for minor infractions. On two occasions he was struck on his arms, once depriving him of the full use of his arm for a week.

The District Court made no findings on the credibility of the students' testimony. Rather, assuming their testimony to be credible, the court found no constitutional basis for relief. With respect to count three, the class action, the court concluded that the punishment authorized and practiced generally in the county schools violated no constitutional right. With respect to counts one and two, the individual damages actions, the court concluded that while corporal punishment could in some cases violate the Eighth Amendment, in this case a jury could not lawfully find "the elements of severity, arbitrary infliction, unacceptability in terms of contemporary standards, or gross disproportion which are necessary to bring 'punishment' to the constitutional level of 'cruel and unusual punishment.'"

. . . .

We granted certiorari, limited to the questions of cruel and unusual punishment and procedural due process.

II

In addressing the scope of the Eighth Amendment's prohibition on cruel and unusual punishment, this Court has found it useful to refer to "[t]raditional common-law concepts," and to the "attitude[s] which our society has traditionally taken." So, too, in defining the requirements of procedural due process under the Fifth and Fourteenth Amendments, the Court has been attuned to what "has always been the law of the land," and to "traditional ideas of fair procedure." We therefore begin by examining the way in which our traditions and our laws have responded to the use of corporal punishment in public schools.

The use of corporal punishment in this country as a means of disciplining schoolchildren dates back to the colonial period. It has survived the transformation of primary and secondary education from the colonials' reliance on optional private arrangements to our present system of compulsory education and dependence on public schools. Despite the general abandonment of corporal punishment as a means of punishing criminal offenders, the practice continues to play a role in the public education of schoolchildren in most parts of the country. Professional and public opinion is sharply divided on the practice, and has been for more than a century. Yet we can discern no trend toward its elimination.

....

Although the early cases viewed the authority of the teacher as deriving from the parents, the concept of parental delegation has been replaced by the view — more consonant with compulsory education laws — that the State itself may impose such corporal punishment as is reasonably necessary "for the proper education of the child and for the maintenance of group discipline." 1 F. Harper & F. James, Law of Torts § 3.20, p. 292 (1956). All of the circumstances are to be taken into account in determining whether the punishment is reasonable in a particular case. Among the most important considerations are the seriousness of the offense, the attitude and past behavior of the child, the nature and severity of the punishment, the age and strength of the child, and the availability of less severe but equally effective means of discipline.

....

III

The Eighth Amendment provides: "Excessive bail shall not be required, nor excessive fines imposed, nor cruel and unusual punishments inflicted." Bail, fines, and punishment traditionally have been associated with the criminal process, and by subjecting the three to parallel limitations the text of the Amendment suggests an intention to limit the power of those entrusted with the criminal-law function of government. An examination of the history of the Amendment and the decisions of this Court construing the proscription against cruel and unusual punishment confirms that it was designed to protect those convicted of crimes. We adhere to this longstanding limitation and hold that the Eighth Amendment does not apply to the paddling of children as a means of maintaining discipline in public schools.

A

....

The Americans who adopted the language of ... the English Bill of Rights in framing their own State and Federal Constitutions ... feared the imposition of torture and other cruel punishments not only by judges acting beyond their lawful authority, but also by legislatures engaged in making the laws by which judicial authority would be measured. Indeed, the principal concern of the American Framers appears to have been with the legislative definition of crimes and punishments. But if the American provision was intended to restrain government more broadly than its English model, the subject to which it was intended to apply — the criminal process — was the same.

B. CORPORAL PUNISHMENT

C

Petitioners acknowledge that the original design of the Cruel and Unusual Punishments Clause was to limit criminal punishments, but urge nonetheless that the prohibition should be extended to ban the paddling of schoolchildren. Observing that the Framers of the Eighth Amendment could not have envisioned our present system of public and compulsory education, with its opportunities for noncriminal punishments, petitioners contend that extension of the prohibition against cruel punishments is necessary lest we afford greater protection to criminals than to schoolchildren. It would be anomalous, they say, if schoolchildren could be beaten without constitutional redress, while hardened criminals suffering the same beatings at the hands of their jailors might have a valid claim under the Eighth Amendment. Whatever force this logic may have in other settings, we find it an inadequate basis for wrenching the Eighth Amendment from its historical context and extending it to traditional disciplinary practices in the public schools.

The prisoners and the schoolchild stand in wholly different circumstances, separated by the harsh facts of criminal conviction and incarceration. The prisoner's conviction entitles the State to classify him as a "criminal," and his incarceration deprives him of the freedom "to be with family and friends and to form the other enduring attachments of normal life." Prison brutality, as the Court of Appeals observed in this case, is "part of the total punishment to which the individual is being subjected for his crime and, as such, is a proper subject for Eighth Amendment scrutiny." 525 F.2d at 915. Even so, the protection afforded by the Eighth Amendment is limited. After incarceration, only the "'unnecessary and wanton infliction of pain,'" constitutes cruel and unusual punishment forbidden by the Eighth Amendment.

The schoolchild has little need for the protection of the Eighth Amendment. Though attendance may not always be voluntary, the public school remains a open institution. Except perhaps when very young, the child is not physically restrained from leaving school during school hours; and at the end of the school day, the child is invariably free to return home. Even while at school, the child brings with him the support of family and friends and is rarely apart from teachers and other pupils who may witness and protest any instances of mistreatment.

The openness of the public school and its supervision by the community afford significant safeguards against the kinds of abuses from which the Eighth Amendment protects the prisoner. In virtually every community where corporal punishment is permitted in the schools, these safeguards are reinforced by the legal constraints of the common law. Public school teachers and administrators are privileged at common law to inflict only such corporal punishment as is reasonably necessary for the proper education and discipline of the child; any punishment going beyond the privilege may result in both civil and criminal liability. As long as the schools are open to public scrutiny, there is no reason to believe that the common-law constraints will not effectively remedy and deter excesses such as those alleged in this case.

We conclude that when public school teachers or administrators impose disciplinary corporal punishment, the Eighth Amendment is inapplicable. The pertinent constitutional question is whether the imposition is consonant with the requirements of due process.

IV

The Fourteenth Amendment prohibits any state deprivation of life, liberty, or property without due process of law. Application of this prohibition requires the familiar two-stage analysis: We must first ask whether the asserted individual interests are encompassed within the Fourteenth Amendment's protection of "life, liberty or property"; if protected interest are implicated, we then must decide what procedures constitute "due process of law." Following that analysis here, we find that corporal punishment in public schools implicates a constitutionally protected liberty interest, but we hold that the traditional common-law remedies are fully adequate to afford due process.

A

... Due process is required only when a decision of the State implicates an interest within the protection of the Fourteenth Amendment. And "to determine whether due process requirements apply in the first place, we must look not to the 'weight' but to the *nature* of the interest at stake."

....

While the contours of this historic liberty interest in the context of our federal system of government have not been defined precisely, they always have been thought to encompass freedom from bodily restraint and punishment. It is fundamental that the state cannot hold and physically punish an individual except in accordance with due process of law.

This constitutionally protected liberty interest is at stake in this case. There is, of course, a *de minimis* level of imposition with which the Constitution is not concerned. But at least where school authorities, acting under color of state law, deliberately decided to punish a child for misconduct by restraining the child and inflicting appreciable physical pain, we hold that Fourteenth Amendment liberty interests are implicated.

B

"[T]he question remains what process is due." *Morrissey v. Brewer*, 408 U.S. at 481. Were it not for the common-law privilege permitting teachers to inflict reasonable corporal punishment on children in their care, and the availability of the traditional remedies for abuse, the case for requiring advance procedural safeguards would be strong indeed. But here we deal with a punishment — paddling — within that tradition, and the question is whether the common-law remedies are adequate to afford due process.

B. CORPORAL PUNISHMENT

....

1

Because it is rooted in history, the child's liberty interest in avoiding corporal punishment while in the care of public school authorities is subject to historical limitations. Under the common law, an invasion of personal security gave rise to a right to recover damages in a subsequent judicial proceeding. But the right of recovery was qualified by the concept of justification. Thus, there could be no recovery against a teacher who gave only "moderate correction" to a child. To the extent that the force used was reasonable in light of its purpose, it was not wrongful, but rather "justifiable or lawful."

The concept that reasonable corporal punishment in school is justifiable continues to be recognized in the laws of most States. It represents "the balance struck by this country," *Poe v. Ullman*, 367 U.S. 497, 542 (1961) (HARLAN, J., dissenting), between the child's interest in personal security and the traditional view that some limited corporal punishment may be necessary in the course of a child's education. Under that longstanding accommodation of interests, there can be no deprivation of substantive rights as long as disciplinary corporal punishment is within the limits of the common-law privilege.

This is not to say that the child's interest in procedural safeguards is insubstantial. The school disciplinary process is not "a totally accurate, unerring process, never mistaken and never unfair...." *Goss v. Lopez*, 419 U.S. 565, 579-80 (1975). In any deliberate infliction of corporal punishment on a child who is restrained for that purpose, there is some risk that the intrusion on the child's liberty will be unjustified and therefore unlawful. In these circumstances the child has a strong interest in procedural safeguards that minimize the risk of wrongful punishment and provide for the resolution of disputed questions of justification.

We turn now to a consideration of the safeguards that are available under applicable Florida law.

2

Florida has continued to recognize, and indeed has strengthened by statute, the common-law right of a child not to be subjected to excessive corporal punishment in school. Under Florida law the teacher and principal of the school decide in the first instance whether corporal punishment is reasonably necessary under the circumstances in order to discipline a child who has misbehaved. But they must exercise prudence and restraint. For Florida has preserved the traditional judicial proceedings for determining whether the punishment was justified. If the punishment inflicted is later found to have been excessive — not reasonably believed at the time to be necessary for the child's discipline or training — the school authorities inflicting it may be held liable in damages to the child and, if malice is shown, they may be subject to criminal penalties.

Although students have testified in this case to specific instances of abuse, there is every reason to believe that such mistreatment is an aberration. The uncontradicted evidence suggests that corporal punishment in the Dade County schools was, "[w]ith the exception of a few cases, ... unremarkable in physical severity." Moreover, because paddlings are usually inflicted in response to conduct directly observed by teachers in their presence, the risk that a child will be paddled without cause is typically insignificant. In the ordinary case, a disciplinary paddling neither threatens seriously to violate any substantive rights nor condemns the child "to suffer grievous loss of any kind."

In those cases where severe punishment is contemplated, the available civil and criminal sanctions for abuse — considered in light of the openness of the school environment — afford significant protection against unjustified corporal punishment. Teachers and school authorities are unlikely to inflict corporal punishment unnecessarily or excessively when a possible consequence of doing so is the institution of civil or criminal proceedings against them.

It still may be argued, of course, that the child's liberty interest would be better protected if the common-law remedies were supplemented by the administrative safeguards of prior notice and a hearing. We have found frequently that some kind of prior hearing is necessary to guard against arbitrary impositions on interests protected by the Fourteenth Amendment. But where the State has preserved what "has always been the law of the land," the case for administrative safeguards is significantly less compelling.

There is a relevant analogy in the criminal law. Although the Fourth Amendment specifically proscribes "seizure" of a person without probable cause, the risk that police will act unreasonably in arresting a suspect is not thought to require an advance determination of the facts. In *United States v. Watson*, 423 U.S. 411 (1976), we reaffirmed the traditional common-law rule that police officers may make warrantless public arrests on probable cause. Although we observed that an advance determination of probable cause by a magistrate would be desirable, we declined "to transform this judicial preference into a constitutional rule when the judgment of the Nation and Congress has for so long been to authorize warrantless public arrests on probable cause...." *Id.* at 423; *see id.* at 429 (POWELL J., concurring) Despite the distinct possibility that a police officer may improperly assess the facts and thus unconstitutionally deprive an individual of liberty, we declined to depart from the traditional rule by which the officer's perception is subjected to judicial scrutiny only after the fact. There is no more reason to depart from tradition and require advance procedural safeguards for intrusions on personal security to which the Fourth Amendment does not apply.

3

But even if the need for advance procedural safeguards were clear, the question would remain whether the incremental benefit could justify the cost. Acceptance of petitioners' claims would work a transformation in the law governing corporal punishment in Florida and most other States. Given the impracticability of formulating a rule of procedural due process that varies with

B. CORPORAL PUNISHMENT

the severity of the particular imposition, the prior hearing petitioners seek would have to precede *any* paddling, however moderate or trivial.

Such a universal constitutional requirement would significantly burden the use of corporal punishment as a disciplinary measure. Hearings — even informal hearings — require time, personnel, and a diversion of attention from normal school pursuits. School authorities may well choose to abandon corporal punishment rather than incur the burdens of complying with the procedural requirements. Teachers, properly concerned with maintaining authority in the classroom, may well prefer to rely on other disciplinary measures — which they may view as less effective — rather than confront the possible disruption that prior notice and a hearing may entail. Paradoxically, such an alteration of disciplinary policy is most likely to occur in the ordinary case where the contemplated punishment is well within the common-law privilege.

Elimination or curtailment of corporal punishment would be welcomed by many as a societal advance. But when such a policy choice may result from this Court's determination of an asserted right to due process, rather than from the normal processes of community debate and legislative action, the societal costs cannot be dismissed as insubstantial. We are reviewing here a legislative judgment, rooted in history and reaffirmed in the laws of many States, that corporal punishment serves important educational interests. This judgment must be viewed in light of the disciplinary problems commonplace in the schools. As noted in *Goss v. Lopez*, 419 U.S. at 580: "Events calling for discipline are frequent occurrences and sometimes require immediate, effective action." Assessment of the need for, and the appropriate means of maintaining, school discipline is committed generally to the discretion of school authorities subject to state law. "[T]he Court has repeatedly emphasized the need for affirming the comprehensive authority of the States and of school officials, consistent with fundamental constitutional safeguards, to prescribe and control conduct in the schools." *Tinker v. Des Moines School Dist.*, 393 U.S. 503, 507 (1969).

"At some point the benefit of an additional safeguard to the individual affected ... and to society in terms of increased assurance that the action is just, may be outweighed by the cost." *Mathews v. Eldridge*, 424 U.S. at 348. We think that point has been reached in this case. In view of the low incidence of abuse, the openness of our schools, and the common-law safeguards that already exist, the risk of error that may result in violation of a schoolchild's substantive rights can only be regarded as minimal. Imposing additional administrative safeguards as a constitutional requirement might reduce that risk marginally, but would also entail a significant intrusion into an area of primary educational responsibility. We conclude that the Due Process Clause does not require notice and a hearing prior to the imposition of corporal punishment in the public schools, as that practice is authorized and limited by the common law.

V

Petitioners cannot prevail on either of the theories before us in this case. The Eighth Amendment's prohibition against cruel and unusual punishment is inapplicable to school paddlings, and the Fourteenth Amendment's requirement of procedural due process is satisfied by Florida's preservation of common-law constraints and remedies. We therefore agree with the Court of Appeals that petitioners' evidence affords no basis for injunctive relief, and that petitioners cannot recover damages on the basis of any Eighth Amendment or procedural due process violation.

[MR. JUSTICE WHITE, with whom MR. JUSTICE BRENNAN, MR. JUSTICE MARSHALL, and MR. JUSTICE STEVENS joined, dissented from the majority opinion. The dissent, after a lengthy historical analysis of the Eighth Amendment concluded that the "Constitutional prohibition is against cruel and unusual punishments; nowhere is that prohibition limited or modified by the language of the Constitution.... By holding that the Eighth Amendment protects only criminals the majority adopts the view that one is entitled to the protections afforded by the Eighth Amendment only if he is punished for acts that are sufficiently opprobrious for society to make them 'criminal.' This is a curious holding in view of the fact that the more culpable the offender the more likely it is the punishment will not be disproportionate to the offense, and consequently, the less likely it is that the punishment will be cruel and unusual. Conversely, a public school student who is spanked for à mere breach of discipline may sometimes have a strong argument that the punishment does not fit the offense, depending upon the severity of the beating, and therefore that it is cruel and unusual. Yet the majority would afford the student no protection no matter how inhumane and barbaric the punishment inflicted on him might be."]

Affirmed.

---

1. Are you clear on what is meant by the term "corporal punishment"? In this regard note the difference between the situations in *Harris v. Galilley*, 125 Pa. Super. 505, 189 A. 779 (1937), and those in *Ingraham*. The latter is a case where corporal punishment is purposefully and deliberately administered as punishment for student misbehavior. *Harris*, on the other hand, involved a principal's intervention in an ongoing situation to compel a student to immediately modify his behavior. One may imagine other cases where a teacher or principal uses physical force to break up student fights, tantrums, etc. Should such cases be treated the same as those in *Ingraham* for constitutional or other purposes? Compare the New Jersey statute which prohibits corporal punishment but states that the following acts are not corporal punishment for purposes of this prohibition: (1) quelling a disturbance which threatens physical injuries to others, (2) obtaining possession of weapons or other dangerous objects within the control

B. CORPORAL PUNISHMENT

of a student, (3) self-defense, and (4) the protection of person or property, N.J. Stat. Ann. § 18A:6-1 (1968).

2. Can "corporal punishment" be outlawed without affecting the New Jersey-type exceptions? In 1993, the Ohio General Assembly passed Senate Bill 29, which amends Ohio Rev. Code § 3319.41 to prohibit corporal punishment as a means of discipline in schools, unless the local school board adopted a resolution before September 1, 1994, permitting its use. The adoption of the resolution may not be as easy as it sounds. To allow for corporal punishment, a task force must have been appointed and a written report must have been submitted to the school board well in advance of the September 1994 deadline. This task force should have included teachers, administrators, non-certified school employees, school psychologists, members of the medical profession (pediatricians if available), and representatives of parents organizations.

If a school district prohibits the use of corporal punishment, it must adopt a discipline policy that includes alternative disciplinary measures and consider what training school employees may need to implement the policy. Some of the alternatives to corporal punishment adopted by the Columbus Public School system since abandoning corporal punishment several years ago include detention, Saturday School, student mediation, in-school suspension, and constructive special assignments.

Note that some use of force or restraint is still permitted, as necessary to quell a disturbance threatening physical injury to others, to obtain weapons or other dangerous objects on the person or within his or her control, or for purposes of self-defense or for the protection of persons or property. Ohio has adopted language similar to that in New Jersey (*See* Note 1 above). As yet, the new provision in Ohio has not been tested, but it may be that corporal punishment can be "outlawed" without affecting the New Jersey exceptions.

Think about the following comment made by Carl Hansen, Superintendent of Schools, Washington, D.C., (from *Interview: School Crisis in the Nation's Capital*, 54 U.S. News & World Report, Mar. 11, 1963, at 62):

> Now youngsters will say to a teacher: "You can't touch me. You can't lay a hand on me, or you'll lose your job." And, as long as there's a rule prohibiting corporal punishment a teacher is always fearful that if she does take a youngster by the arm and says, "sit down," or pulls him out of the room by the hand, that some parent is going to say: "You struck my child...."

Does this statement serve as a justification for the majority opinion in *Ingraham*?

3. Justice White, the author of *Goss v. Lopez*, 419 U.S. 565 (1975), dissented vigorously in *Ingraham* based partially on his majority opinion in *Goss*. Does *Ingraham* severely undermine *Goss* as Justice White would have us believe?

4. The *Goss* court found that students facing temporary suspension from school have property and liberty interests that qualify them for protection under the Due

Process Clause of the Fourteenth Amendment. The liberty interest recognized was that which arises when government action threatens injury to the student's reputation or integrity. Is not that interest as much in jeopardy when the student is subjected to physical punishment? Few safeguards are placed on keeping knowledge of such punishments private; and faculty, students, and others generally become aware of those punishments and the reasons for them. Why should the "process due" be less when the deprivation threatened is equivalent?

5. In other cases in which post-deprivation hearings have been found adequate, the interests involved have generally been in "property" rather than "liberty." Property, if wrongfully taken, can often be restored. Where the injured party is subjected to loss of a liberty interest, restoration is less likely. What is the nature of the interest at stake where physical pain is inflicted? Is a post-deprivation hearing compatible with the interest implicated? *See* Rosenberg, *Ingraham v. Wright: The Supreme Court's Whipping Boy*, 78 Colum. L. Rev. 75 (1978). *See also* Piele, *Neither Punishment Cruel Nor Due Process Due: The United States Supreme Court's Decision in* Ingraham v. Wright, 7 J. L. & Educ. 1 (1978).

6. Despite some action by state legislatures, courts following *Ingraham* continued to deny plaintiffs' claims for recovery based on alleged due process violations. *See Paul v. McGhee*, 577 F. Supp. 460 (E.D. Tenn. 1983) (constitutional rights of due process are implicated by the use of corporal punishment, but all rights were satisfied due to the availability of common law remedies at the state level); *Wise v. Pea Ridge Sch. Dist.*, 855 F.2d 560 (8th Cir. 1988) (Coach gave each of seven students two "licks" for playing dodge ball against teachers' orders. Due process rights were not violated).

7. *Wise*, cited in note 6 above, also involved a claim by a special education student with a reading disorder who was placed on in-school suspension for being tardy seven times. The court held that substantive due process rights were not violated. Should more concern be taken in disciplinary actions when they involve mentally or physically disabled students? *See* Chapter 13.

8. Even with the outcry against corporal punishment, courts continue to deny Eighth Amendment claims of cruel and unusual punishment in many discipline cases. *See Thrasher v. General Cas. Co. of Wisconsin*, 722 F. Supp. 966 (W.D. Wisconsin 1990). In *Thrasher*, a student refused to do a math problem on the chalkboard. The teacher physically moved him to speak with him, and when the student resisted, the teacher threw him against the chalkboard. The court held that the Eighth Amendment did not apply to "use of force" against the student.

In *Rhodus v. Dumiller*, 552 F. Supp. 425 (M.D. La. 1982), the court held that the Eighth Amendment did not apply to cases of corporal punishment. The teacher, without witness, struck the student eight times in the kidney area. A summary judgment was granted for the teacher, despite the fact that a school board policy limited the number of hits to three and required a witness at all implementations of corporal punishment.

9. A motion for summary judgment was denied in *Turley v. School Dist. of Kansas City, Missouri*, 713 F. Supp. 331 (W.D. Mo. 1989). The District Court

B. CORPORAL PUNISHMENT

held that factual questions existed as to whether the administration of corporal punishment amounted to a due process violation. In addition, the court held that the school district's knowledge of the teacher's past violations of the district's corporal punishment policy and its knowledge that she had previously shot and killed her husband raised factual issues as to whether the school district should be held liable for failing to adequately monitor and supervise the teacher.

10. Recall *Hawkins v. Coleman* and related materials in part A of this chapter discussing allegations of racial discrimination in suspension and expulsion cases. The same situation can arise in corporal punishment cases. In the Fifth Circuit case of *Coleman v. Franklin Parish Sch. Bd.*, 702 F.2d 74 (5th Cir. 1983), parents of an African American child who was subjected to corporal punishment stated a valid cause of action for intentional and purposeful discrimination based on race.

11. If the administration of corporal punishment does not violate the student's constitutional protection against cruel and unusual punishment, does its imposition in the face of parental objections violate the parents' rights to determine the disciplinary methods to be used with their children?

12. *Ingraham* refers to the case of *Baker v. Owen*, 395 F. Supp. 294 (M.D.N.C.), *aff'd mem.* 423 U.S. 907 (1975), where a federal district court ruled that parents do not have a right to determine whether or when school personnel can administer corporal punishment.

GARCIA v. MIERA
United States Court of Appeals
817 F.2d 650 (10th Cir. 1987)

LOGAN, CIRCUIT JUDGE:

....

Teresa Garcia, an elementary school pupil in New Mexico, by her parents and next friends, Max and Sandra Garcia, sued the defendants in their individual capacities for denying her substantive due process in violation of 42 U.S.C. § 1983 because of two beatings suffered at their hands. After considerable discovery, the defendants filed a motion for summary judgment, which the court granted.... Garcia has appealed the court's order, contending that at the time of the beatings excessive corporal punishment by school officials did violate her clearly established substantive due process rights.

In 1982 Garcia was a nine-year-old student in the third grade at the Penasco Elementary School in Penasco, New Mexico. On February 10, 1982, defendant-appellee Theresa Miera, the school principal, summoned Garcia to her office for hitting a boy who had kicked her. Miera instructed Garcia to go to her chair to be paddled. Garcia refused and told Miera that her father had said that "Mrs. Miera had better shape up."

Miera responded by calling defendant J.D. Sanchez, a teacher at the school, for assistance. Sanchez held Garcia upside down by her ankles while Miera struck Garcia with a wooden paddle. The paddle "was split right down the middle, so it was two pieces, and when it hit, it clapped [and] grabbed.'' Miera hit Garcia five times on the front of the leg between the knee and the waist. After the beating, Garcia's teacher, Ruth Dominez, ''noticed blood coming through [Garcia's] clothes,'' and, on taking Garcia to the restroom, was shocked to see a ''welt'' on Garcia's leg. The beating made a two-inch cut on her leg, that left a permanent scar. Shortly after this incident, Garcia's mother and father told Miera ''not to spank Teresa again unless we were called, to make sure it was justified, and [Miera] said okay, no problems.''

The second beating at issue occurred on May 13, 1983. Miera summoned Garcia to her office for saying that defendant Judy Mestas had been seen kissing a student's father, Denny Mersereau, on a school bus during a recent field trip and that Mestas had sent love letters to Mersereau through his son.

Miera proceeded to strike Garcia two times with the paddle on the buttocks. Garcia then refused to be hit again. Miera responded by calling defendant Edward Leyba, an administrative associate at the school. Leyba pushed Garcia toward a chair over which she was to bend and receive three additional blows. Garcia and Leyba struggled and Garcia hit her back on Miera's desk, from which she suffered back pains for several weeks. Garcia then submitted to the last three blows. The beating caused severe bruises on Garcia's buttocks, which did not stop hurting for two to three weeks. The report of the school nurse indicates that as a result of the beating Garcia's ''buttocks [were] bright red with [a] crease across both.'' Dr. Albrecht, a physician who treated Garcia, stated: ''I've done hundreds of physicals of children who have had spankings ... and I have not seen bruises on the buttocks as Teresita had, from routine spankings ... [T]hey were more extensive, deeper bruises....'' Betsy Martinez, a nurse who examined Garcia, stated that if a child had received this type of injury at home she ''would have called [the police department's] Protective Services.'' The extent and severity of Garcia's bruises is independently supported by photographs of Garcia's buttocks taken on May 13 and May 18. Throughout the May 13 incident, Garcia kept asking Miera to allow her to call her mother. The principal refused, saying that she knew the law.

....

I

We first consider whether corporal punishment of a school child, in any degree of excessiveness, can violate substantive rights under the Due Process Clause. Despite the Supreme Court's explicit disclaimer that it was deciding that issue in *Ingraham v. Wright*, 430 U.S. 651 (1977), we believe that *Ingraham* requires us to hold that, at some point, excessive corporal punishment violates the pupil's substantive due process rights.... It recognized that among the liberty interests '' 'long recognized at common law as essential to the orderly pursuit of happiness by free men' '' is the ''right to be free from, and to obtain judicial relief for, unjustified intrusions on personal security,'' including ''bodily restraint and punishment.'' *Id.* at 673-74, (quoting *Meyer v. Nebraska*, 262 U.S. 390, 399

B. CORPORAL PUNISHMENT

(1923)). "[W]here school authorities, acting under color of state law, deliberately decide to punish a child for misconduct by restraining the child and inflicting appreciable physical pain, we hold that Fourteenth Amendment liberty interests are implicated." *Id.* 430 U.S. at 674. This language plainly indicates that the infliction of corporal punishment can affect a fundamental right susceptible to substantive due process protection....

Although the *Ingraham* opinion focuses on procedural due process, it discusses the history of corporal punishment in the law and applies a balancing test between the child's interest in personal security and the traditional view that a school may need to be able to impose "limited" or "reasonable" corporal punishment: "[T]here can be no deprivation of substantive rights as long as disciplinary corporal punishment is within the limits of the common-law privilege." 430 U.S. at 676....

Although *Ingraham* makes clear that ordinary corporal punishment violates no substantive due process rights of school children, by acknowledging that corporal punishment implicates a fundamental liberty interest protected by the Due Process Clause, we believe that opinion clearly signaled that, at some degree of excessiveness or cruelty, the meting out such punishment violates the substantive due process rights of the pupil.

Indeed, such a view is compelling and the general principles underlying it have been recognized at least since *Rochin v. California*, 342 U.S. 165 (1952), when the Supreme Court held that the forcible use of a stomach pump by police officers violated the individual's rights under the Due Process Clause. The Court declared that official conduct that "shocks the conscience," force that is "brutal" or "offensive to human dignity," offends the Due Process Clause. *Id.* at 172-74[.]...

This circuit applied that notion in the context of a school, albeit one for problem children, in *Milonas v. Williams*, 691 F.2d 931 (10th Cir.1982), *cert. denied*, 460 U.S. 1069 (1983). We there affirmed the issuance of a permanent injunction against the Provo Canyon School for Boys enjoining, *inter alia,* the school's use of a practice nicknamed the "hair dance." The hair dance was a form of disciplinary action whereby a school employee would "grab one of the student's arms and clutch the boy's hair with his other hand." *Id.* at 942. Our decision in *Milonas* expressly endorsed the district court's finding that the "hair dance permitted unreasonably harsh school responses to the conduct of disturbed boys." *Id.* We rejected the argument that such physical abuse was reasonably related to the legitimate objectives of the Provo Canyon School, and concluded that the defendants' actions violated the plaintiffs' due process rights. *Id.* at 940, 942.

The Fourth Circuit in *Hall v. Tawney*, 621 F.2d 607 (4th Cir.1980), a case closely analogous to the one before us, found a substantive due process right to be free of brutal, demeaning and excessive paddling by public school officials. The only appellate decision to the contrary is the Fifth Circuit decision that the Supreme Court reviewed in *Ingraham*. See *Ingraham v. Wright*, 525 F.2d 909

(5th Cir.1976) (en banc). There a majority of the en banc court found no substantive due process right and refused "to look at each individual instance of [corporal] punishment to determine if it has been administered arbitrarily or capriciously." *Id.* at 917.

... We accept and agree with the Fourth Circuit's definition of the constitutional tort:

> [T]he right to be free of state intrusions into realms of personal privacy and bodily security through means so brutal, demeaning, and harmful as literally to shock the conscience of a court.
>
> ....
>
> As in the cognate police brutality cases, the substantive due process inquiry in school corporal punishment cases must be whether the force applied caused injury so severe, was so disproportionate to the need presented, and was so inspired by malice or sadism rather than a merely careless or unwise excess of zeal that it amounted to a brutal and inhumane abuse of official power literally shocking to the conscience. *Hall*, 621 F.2d at 613.

We believe the necessary inference from the Supreme Court's *Ingraham* decision is that excessive corporal punishment less offensive than the definition quoted above does not rise to the level of a constitutional substantive due process violation. Such lesser violations implicate only a pupil's procedural due process rights. Thus, if the state were to provide no adequate remedy to deter this lesser degree of official conduct and compensate the victim of that misconduct, we would find a violation of procedural due process.

We thus envision three categories of corporal punishment. Punishments that do not exceed the traditional common law standard of reasonableness are not actionable; punishments that exceed the common law standard without adequate state remedies violate procedural due process rights; and finally, punishments that are so grossly excessive as to be shocking to the conscience violate substantive due process rights, without regard to the adequacy of state remedies.

....

II

Concluding that grossly excessive corporal punishment may indeed constitute a violation of substantive due process rights under the governing law, we now examine whether that law was established with sufficient clarity at the time of the beating incidents at issue here.

In *Harlow v. Fitzgerald*, 457 U.S. 800 (1982), the Supreme Court significantly changed the basis for establishing the defense of qualified immunity in § 1983 actions. Under the *Harlow* test, government officials "generally are shielded from liability for civil damages insofar as their conduct does not violate clearly established statutory or constitutional rights of which a reasonable person would have known." *Id.* at 818.... Determination of qualified immunity is now to be

B. CORPORAL PUNISHMENT 541

based "on the objective reasonableness of an official's conduct, as measured by reference to clearly established law." *Harlow*, 457 U.S. at 818.

The district court in the case before us noted the split between the Fourth and Fifth Circuits on the substantive due process issue, and the Supreme Court's refusal to decide the question in *Ingraham*, and on that basis found the law was not "clearly established." It therefore found for defendants.

The Supreme Court in *Harlow* expressly declined to address the issue of what constitutes "clearly established" law. 457 U.S. at 818 n. 32. In confronting the issue of what defendants should have known about the law, lower courts have had to determine the degree of "factual correspondence between the cases establishing law and the case at hand." ... As the Third Circuit has noted:

> The Court in *Harlow* suggested that there must be some factual correlation, because an official may not be required "to anticipate subsequent legal developments" nor know that "the law forbade conduct not previously identified as unlawful." *Harlow*, 457 U.S. at 818. Some courts have required a relatively strict factual identity. Other courts have insisted that officials know and apply general legal principles in appropriate factual situations. Although officials need not "predic[t] the future course of constitutional law," *Pierson v. Ray*, 386 U.S. 547, 557 (1967), they are required to relate established law to analogous factual settings. *People of Three Mile Island v. Nuclear Regulatory Commission*, 747 F.2d 139, 144 (3d Cir.1984).

We follow the Third Circuit and adopt the second approach, "requiring some but not precise factual correspondence and demanding that officials apply general, well developed legal principles." *Id.*

Applying this standard to the instant case, we hold that, at least by the time of the second beating, the law was clearly established that excessive corporal punishment could deny substantive due process. Specifically, for the reasons stated in Part I, we find that *Milonas* was sufficiently analogous to the facts of this case to put defendants on notice as to the law of this circuit. Whether the law was clearly established at the time of the first beating is a closer question, however, because it occurred before our decision in *Milonas*.

Looking first to Supreme Court precedent, we believe that the Court's refusal in *Ingraham* to address the substantive due process claim does not, without more, mandate a conclusion that the law was not clearly established. As discussed in Part I, the concept of the substantive due process right is implicit in *Ingraham*.... Moreover, the general principles underlying *Rochin* and its progeny clearly establish that egregious deprivations of fundamental rights deny substantive due process.

We agree that a direct conflict exists between the Fourth Circuit in *Hall*, which has rejected, and the Fifth Circuit in *Ingraham*, which has upheld, the constitutionality of grossly excessive corporal punishment. But the decisions of one circuit court of appeals are not binding upon another circuit. *United States v. Carson*, 793 F.2d 1141, 1147 (10th Cir.1986)....

Despite the Fifth Circuit's position, we believe the law was clearly established before *Milonas* that some high level of force in a corporal punishment context would violate a child's substantive due process rights. We think a reasonably competent legal advisor to a school district should have realized that egregious invasions of a student's personal security would be unconstitutional. "It does not require a constitutional scholar to conclude that a nude search of a thirteen-year-old child is an invasion of constitutional rights of some magnitude." *Doe v. Renfrow*, 631 F.2d 91, 92-93 (7th Cir.1980), *cert. denied*, 451 U.S. 1022 (1981).

III

Bare allegations of brutality in the administration of corporal punishment are insufficient to survive a motion for summary judgment supported by affidavits as provided in Fed.R.Civ.P. 56.

The threshold for recovery on the constitutional tort for excessive corporal punishment is high. But the allegations with respect to the first beating, that this nine-year-old girl was held up by her ankles and hit several times with a split board of substantial size on the front of her legs until they bled — supported by evidence of a permanent scar — are sufficient. The allegations with respect to the second beating, that the punishment was severe enough to cause pain for three weeks — supported by pictures of the injured buttocks, an affidavit from an examining doctor that in his long experience he had not seen bruises like that from routine spankings, and an affidavit from an examining nurse that if a child had received this type of injury at home she would have reported it as child abuse — are also sufficient. These claims may not survive the crucible of the trial, but they overcome defendants' motion for summary judgment.

Reversed and Remanded for further proceedings consistent herewith.

---

1. As exceptional as *Garcia* may be, is it strong enough to call for an overruling of *Ingraham*? By the time the court decides whether or not the school, administrators, and teachers have crossed a constitutional line, hasn't the damage already been done? Moreover, the *Garcia* court explicitly accepts the Fourth Circuit's definition of the constitutional tort involving intrusions to personal privacy and bodily security which shock the conscience. Has *Garcia*, in effect, rejected *Ingraham*'s decisions at the Fifth Circuit and the Supreme Court?

Does the division of corporal punishment into three categories adequately reconcile *Garcia* with *Ingraham*?

2. What does it take to "shock the conscience" and to allow for a successful federal due process claim against a school? According to *Brown v. Johnson*, 710 F. Supp. 183 (E.D. Ky. 1989), seven spankings with a wooden paddle

B. CORPORAL PUNISHMENT

throughout a thirty-minute period is not enough, despite severe bruises on the child.

See also Hale v. Pringle, 562 F. Supp. 598 (M.D. Ala. 1983) (Due process clause did not require notice or a hearing due to the availability of traditional common law remedies. In addition, due process was not violated even though the corporal punishment did not occur in the principal's office before one adult witness, as required by the school board).

3. The law has recognized the constitutional tort of intrusion to personal privacy and bodily security for residents of mental institutions. In *Garrett v. Rader*, 831 F.2d 202 (10th Cir. 1987), the defendants were not entitled to qualified immunity in a wrongful death action by the mother of a patient who was unreasonably restrained by employees of a state mental institution.

FEE v. HERNDON
United States Court of Appeals
900 F.2d 804 (5th Cir. 1990)

JERRY E. SMITH, CIRCUIT JUDGE:

....

The plaintiffs commenced this action pursuant to 42 U.S.C. § 1983 against the school district and various educators, averring that the fourteenth amendment's substantive due process guarantee operates to ban excessive corporal punishment in public schools. Pendent state-law tort claims were attached to this civil rights suit to raise charges of negligence and excessive force. Indisputably, however, state remedies — both criminal and civil — are available in Texas and proscribe the excessive use of corporal punishment against students, including emotionally handicapped children. That being so, our precedents instruct that the substantive component of the due process clause, though selectively applied in other contexts, is inoperative under the facts herein presented.

We adhere to this circuit's rule that no arbitrary state action exists, by definition, where states affirmatively impose reasonable limitations upon corporal punishment and provide adequate criminal or civil remedies for departures from such laws. Accordingly, we conclude that defendants here, all of whom allegedly acted in contravention of Texas's criminal or civil laws, have not implicated federal substantive due process considerations, irrespective of the argued capriciousness of the corporal punishment imposed. Thus, federal constitutional relief is not among the plaintiffs' available remedies, and consequently we affirm.

I

Tracy Fee attended special-education classes within the defendant Dickinson Independent School District. The few relevant facts not disputed by the litigants can be reduced succinctly to the following: (1) Tracy attended sixth grade at a public school within the district; (2) he had a documented history of aggressive behavioral problems; (3) he attended special classes for emotionally handicapped children; and (4) he received corporal punishment from the school's principal after his teacher sent him to the principal's office for misbehaving in class. Excluding this narrow area of accord, the facts are dramatically at odds.

School officials downplay the extent of the student's injuries and focus upon his behavioral problems. The Fees, in contrast, portray a brutal beating of their son by the principal, Joseph Herndon, which was witnessed passively by his teacher, Suzanne Lahr. School officials admit that the principal paddled Tracy three times on the buttocks to serve as punishment for his disruptive behavior during a history class, but they insist that the punishment comported with official school policy, which provides for reasonable corporal punishment.

The defendants further profess that the use of corporal punishment by school officials was agreed to expressly by the mother through a special- education consent form. Any aggravated mental or physical injury, they maintain, was self-inflicted by Tracy, as he aggressively resisted punishment and thrashed about on the principal's floor. They also reject the assertion that Tracy's teacher, who accompanied her student to the principal's office, witnessed any use of excessive force against Tracy.

The Fees allege that Tracy's injuries first became evident to them shortly after his return from school, where he complained of pain and having been beaten by the principal. They called the sheriff's department, and a police officer took pictures of the welts and scrapes on the child's body. The sheriff's department thereafter investigated the incident, but no criminal action was instituted against any defendant.

The parents assert that their son was hospitalized as a consequence of the beating and forced to spend a total of six months in a psychiatric ward; the total cost of this medical care approached $90,000. Further, Tracy has never fully recovered, we are told, as he has displayed even more pronounced antisocial behavior since the "brutal" beating. The parents admit, however, that Tracy's emotional problems predated this paddling incident.

The Fees filed a section 1983 action against Tracy's principal and teacher, the school district, and Dickinson's superintendent and trustees. The natural persons were sued in their official and individual capacities. Suit was originally commenced in state court and subsequently was removed. The complaint raises allegations of negligence, gross negligence, and excessive force with respect to the principal and teacher. Additionally, all defendants are charged with violating the student's substantive due process rights under the fourteenth amendment.

The defendants unsuccessfully moved for summary judgment at an earlier phase of this litigation. However, the district court warned the plaintiffs at that time that section 1983 does not provide for what the state-court petition terms "responded superior" [sic] liability for the negligent acts of educators. Accordingly, the court granted the Fees an opportunity to amend the complaint so that they could present their "best case." The Fees amended their complaint but not to the district court's satisfaction: The court held that the plaintiffs'

B. CORPORAL PUNISHMENT

"conclusory allegations" once again failed to premise liability upon grounds other than respondeat superior.

The defendants renewed their motion for summary judgment, which the district court construed alternatively as a Fed.R.Civ.P. 12(b)(6) motion to dismiss for failure to state a claim. The court disposed of all claims, except the state-law excessive-force charge directed at the principal only. It thereafter declined to exercise pendent jurisdiction over this residual tort dispute and remanded that sole remaining claim.

... [The Fees] argue that the substantive component of the due process clause proscribes the abusive treatment of students, especially emotionally handicapped students, in public schools and thus affords to them a federal constitutional cause of action here.

II

B

"Paddling of recalcitrant children has long been an accepted method of promoting good behavior and instilling notions of responsibility and decorum into the mischievous heads of school children." *Ingraham v. Wright*, 525 F.2d 909, 917 (5th Cir.1976) (en banc), *aff'd*, 430 U.S. 651 (1977). This common law principle, in fact, predates the American Revolution. However, coincidently with the genesis of corporal punishment, reasonable limits traditionally have been imposed upon student discipline so as not to give teachers a license to commit state-sanctioned child abuse. Specifically, post-punishment civil or criminal remedies have targeted public school teachers who departed from the disciplinary norms defined by statute or the common law.

This dispute presents the question of whether the federal Constitution independently shields public school students from excessive discipline, irrespective of state-law safeguards. In *Ingraham*, the Supreme Court declared that twenty swats to a student, which removed him from school for days with bruises and disabled his arm for a week, did not violate procedural due process guarantees. That is, while "corporal punishment in public schools implicates a constitutionally protected liberty interest," the state may impose sufficient post-punishment safeguards to satisfy procedural due process concerns. Unfortunately, the *Ingraham* Court declined to address whether teacher discipline can be so capricious as to violate the amorphous substantive due process guarantees inherent in the fourteenth amendment.

We have stated that corporal punishment in public schools "is a deprivation of substantive due process when it is arbitrary, capricious, or wholly unrelated to the legitimate state goal of maintaining an atmosphere conducive to learning." *Woodard v. Los Fresnos Ind. School Dist.*, 732 F.2d 1243, 1246 (5th Cir.1984). Thus, reasonable corporal punishment is not at odds with the fourteenth amendment and does not constitute arbitrary state action. Consistently with this caselaw, Texas has authorized educators to impose a reasonable measure of corporal punishment upon students when necessary to maintain school discipline, and the state affords students post-punishment criminal or civil remedies if teachers are unfaithful to this obligation.

Our precedents dictate that injuries sustained incidentally to corporal punishment, irrespective of the severity of these injuries or the sensitivity of the student, do not implicate the due process clause if the forum state affords adequate post-punishment civil or criminal remedies for the student to vindicate legal transgressions. The rationale for this rule, quite simply, is that such states have provided all the process constitutionally due. Specifically, states that affirmatively proscribe and remedy mistreatment of students by educators do not, by definition, act "arbitrarily," a necessary predicate for substantive due process relief. That is to say, the Constitution is not a criminal or civil code to be invoked invariably for the crimes or torts of state educators who act in contravention of the very laws designed to thwart abusive disciplinarians.

In *Cunningham v. Beavers*, 858 F.2d 269 (5th Cir.1988), *cert. denied*, ___ U.S. ___, 109 S.Ct. 1343 (1989), a six-year-old kindergarten student received a total of five paddle swats, causing severe bruising on her buttocks. The child missed six days of school, and her injuries were deemed to be abusive by social welfare workers and her doctor. We held that no deprivation of substantive due process had occurred, because Texas provides adequate state criminal and tort remedies for any excessive punishment that may have been imposed upon the student. *Cunningham*, we conclude, is dispositive here.

In this case, the student's mother authorized the use of corporal punishment against Tracy to cure his disruptive classroom behavior. The litigants agree that the principal and the teacher attempted to discipline the child for his in-class disruptions and that official school policy tolerates only reasonable corporal punishment. Although the injuries are alleged to have been severe, the student's substantive due process guarantees have not been violated under the rationale of *Cunningham*, as Texas does not allow teachers to abuse students with impunity and provides civil and criminal relief against educators who breach statutory and common law standards of conduct. Although the sheriff's department investigated the charges raised, no criminal prosecution commenced here; however, the possibility of state-law civil relief remains.

... [W]e have avoided having student discipline, a matter of public policy, shaped by the individual predilections of federal jurists rather than by state lawmakers and local officials. We find no constitutional warrant to usurp classroom discipline where states, like Texas, have taken affirmative steps to protect their students from overzealous disciplinarians.

The plaintiffs claim, however, that the viability of a section 1983 suit should not depend upon the adequacy of state remedies available against educators and, secondly, they assert that prisoners within this circuit enjoy more constitutional protection than that afforded innocent school children. The Fees admonish this circuit for adhering to an "overly rigid" rule, one that allegedly does not contemplate egregious cases of student discipline, such as physical disfigurement

B. CORPORAL PUNISHMENT

or, as here, severe emotional injury. They underscore their displeasure with *Cunningham* and other precedent by suggesting that teachers could mutilate or torture students in the pursuit of discipline without federal constitutional relief.

We reject these emotionally charged criticisms as misplaced. The plaintiffs do not, and in fact cannot, claim that they lack adequate post-punishment remedies at the state level, under the facts as alleged in this case. The fact that they perceive federal damage recovery to be potentially more generous (Title 42 U.S.C. § 1988 authorizes prevailing parties to secure attorneys' fees from constitutional violators.) is irrelevant to our inquiry and does not make state relief inadequate.

It is an overstatement to suggest that students can suffer extreme injury at the hands of educators without recourse. Admittedly, under *Cunningham* their choice of forum may be restricted to state courts. It is important to note that the *Cunningham* rule has been crafted to operate in the narrow context of student discipline administered within the public schools of states that authorize only reasonable discipline and, further, provide post-punishment relief for departures from its law. The inquiry would differ in states that authorize neither.

The cases relied upon by the Fees to underscore our alleged inflated and inconsistent concern for prisoners are also distinguishable. These cases implicate constitutional provisions other than the fourteenth amendment, principally the fourth amendment's unreasonable-search-and-seizure provision or the eighth amendment's cruel-and-unusual-punishment clause. However, the *Ingraham* Court has expressly rejected the application of the eighth amendment to student punishment, 430 U.S. at 664 and the paddling of recalcitrant students does not constitute a fourth amendment search or seizure. None of these prisoner cases is premised upon the substantive protections afforded by the fourteenth amendment's due process clause.

The Fees' argument that their federal civil rights claim is independent in and of itself and should be decoupled from any state-law inquiry also misconstrues settled constitutional principles. Federal constitutional claims regularly turn upon state law: State law, for example, defines who shall be deemed a "final policymaker" for purposes of a section 1983 action, and it defines "property" worthy of compensation under the fifth amendment's taking clause. Further, the doctrine of substantive due process focuses expressly upon the arbitrariness of state action. Thus, to dismiss the law of the forum state as irrelevant, as the Fees would have us do, is to misapply that doctrine.

We harbor no opinion as to the severity of the student's injuries in this case. We hold only that since Texas has civil and criminal laws in place to proscribe educators from abusing their charges, and further provides adequate post-punishment relief in favor of students, no substantive due process concerns are implicated because no arbitrary state action exists. Accordingly, we affirm the dismissal of the section 1983 claims asserted against all defendants.

. . . .

Affirmed.

1. The court in *Fee* stated: "Any aggravated mental or physical injury, [the school defendants] maintain, was self-inflicted by Tracy, as he aggressively resisted punishment and thrashed about on the principal's floor." *Fee*, 900 F.2d at 806.

Is this an avoidance of school obligations to special education students? Should a school be permitted to avoid liability by claiming that a student's response to punishment and his subsequent injuries were results of a disability of which the school was aware? Is Tracy Fee's response to the punishment any different or any worse than the school officials would expect from a student with a history of severe behavioral problems? What if a non-handicapped student had reacted similarly? Would the school defendants be so quick to label the student's injuries as self-inflicted?

Recall *Wise v. Pea Ridge Sch. Dist.*, 855 F.2d 560 (8th Cir. 1988), discussed in the notes following *Ingraham*, and *see also* Chapter 13 on special education.

2. Most of the cases in this section have ruled that there is no due process violation if there are state law claims and remedies available to the plaintiff. Does the existence of state-level criminal and tort remedies give schools an undeserved excuse to inflict corporal punishment on students?

3. Regardless of whether Tracy's emotional problems predated the paddling incident, should the Dickinson School District be responsible, at least in part, for Tracy's subsequent and prolonged injuries?

4. Note that *Fee* and *Cunningham v. Beavers*, 858 F.2d 269 (5th Cir. 1988), quoted widely in *Fee*, were decided in the same circuit, as *Ingraham* was on its way to the Supreme Court. Is there any significance? The Fees seem to think so.

> The Fees admonish this circuit for adhering to an "overly rigid" rule, one that allegedly does not contemplate egregious cases of student discipline, such as physical disfigurement, or, as here, severe emotional injury. They underscore their displeasure with *Cunningham* and other precedent by suggesting that teachers could mutilate or torture students in the pursuit of discipline without federal constitutional relief." *Fee*, 900 F.2d at 809.

5. The court attempts to respond to some of the Fees' concerns with the following:

> However, it is important to note that the *Cunningham* rule has been crafted to operate in the narrow context of student discipline administered within the public schools of states that authorize only reasonable discipline and, further, provide post-punishment relief for departures from its law. *Fee*, 900 F.2d at 809.

How narrow do you think the context of *Cunningham* is? The court does not tell us how many states provide post-punishment remedies and how many do not.

6. How does a *Garcia* analysis fit in here? The court seems to rest with its "state law remedy" justification for not finding a valid federal claim. How severe were the injuries here — to the severity of which the court "harbor[ed] no opinion"? Would the facts of *Fee* "shock the conscience" of the general public? Should they shock the court?

7. *Ingraham*, *Cunningham* and *Fee*, all decided in the Fifth Circuit, insist that remedies for injuries suffered from infliction of corporal punishment are available at the state level. How are states responding? Consider the following state-level cases, one of which was decided in a Fifth Circuit state.

8. Disputes in the area of corporal punishment have focused on the actions of school personnel and the use of excessive force. A profile of causes of action feature: *Ingraham* (constitutional violation based on cruel and unusual punishment); *Crews v. McQueen*, 385 S.E.2d 712 (Ga. Ct. App. 1989) (negligence); *Osterbeck v. State*, 789 P.2d 1037 (Alaska Ct. App. 1990) (child abuse); and the subject of *Fee v. Herndon* (constitutional violations based on substantive due process).

9. It is probably a safe bet that most students who suffer corporal punishment recover physically. Should schools take this chance, though, especially when there are many more positive disciplinary measures available?

Should questions like this be answered in light of the true goals of a teacher — to educate children and prepare them for a challenging, dynamic, and diverse world? Do teachers feel they have to resort to traditional corporal punishment due to the deterioration of families today and lack of preparation that children have before school and at home?

10. Are you satisfied with the directions the courts have gone regarding corporal punishment in the schools? Do you think schools should be permitted to use corporal punishment as a disciplinary measure, despite the existence of many proven alternatives? Is corporal punishment properly a state issue? Or do you think a federal constitutional violation can and should be found before the punishment "shocks the conscience"?

When you consider the landmark cases we have discussed and will discuss thus far and in later chapters, — *Brown*, *Tinker*, *T.L.O.*, and *Goss*, for example — does *Ingraham* seem out of place? It appears that over the past four decades, the courts have managed to grant more rights and freedoms to school children, in an effort to create an atmosphere free from prejudice and undue control *and* an atmosphere conducive to learning. Is such a consideration a worthy argument to overrule *Ingraham* and disallow corporal punishment? Is this a step better suited to a legislature? State or federal? Is corporal punishment one of the last strongholds maintained by the schools? How strong is it?

C. ACADEMIC SANCTIONS

SLOCUM v. HOLTON BOARD OF EDUCATION
Court of Appeals of Michigan
171 Mich. App. 92, 429 N.W.2d 607 (1988)

PER CURIAM:

Plaintiff appeals as of right from the Muskegon Circuit Court order granting summary disposition to defendant board of education and dismissing his challenge to the board's attendance policy which permits letter grade reductions of students who, having a certain number of excused absences, fail to attend mandatory after-hours study sessions. We affirm.

Lori Ann Slocum, a tenth-grade student at Holton High School in Muskegon County, Michigan, was absent from school for five days during the first of six marking periods during the 1985-86 school year. Lori's absence was due to a concussion she received during a fall, and thus was excused.

Pursuant to the attendance policy of defendant board of education, any student with more than three days of excused absences during a marking period was required to make up the missed time at after-hours study sessions. Students failing to attend the sessions were subject to having their letter grades reduced. Apparently Lori attended only one of the five sessions she was required to attend. As a result, her first marking period grades were lowered by one full letter grade.

On May 2, 1986, Richard Slocum, individually and as next friend of Lori Ann Slocum, commenced this action in the Muskegon Circuit Court, alleging that defendant's attendance policy constituted an ultra vires act and violated Lori's right to procedural and substantive due process. On August 11, 1986, defendant responded with a motion for summary disposition pursuant to MCR 2.116(C)(8), failure to state a claim on which relief can be granted.

... The court held that the attendance policy did not violate Lori's due process rights and was not arbitrary, capricious, or an abuse of discretion. Accordingly, the defendant's motion for summary disposition was granted. An order to that effect was entered on October 6, 1986.

On appeal, plaintiff first argues, as he did below, that the board of education was without authority to adopt the attendance policy and, thus, its actions were ultra vires. We disagree.

Local school districts and officers possess only those powers which statutes expressly, or by reasonably necessary implication, grant to them. *Jurva v. Attorney General*, 419 Mich. 209, 214, 351 N.W.2d 813 (1984). In the instant case, various provisions of the School Code are relevant and require discussion. Section 1282 of the code authorizes school boards to establish and maintain the grades, schools, and departments or courses of study they deem necessary or desirable for the maintenance and improvement of public education. M.C.L. § 380.1282; M.S.A. § 15.41282. School boards are also empowered to make "reasonable regulations relative to anything necessary for the proper establish-

C. ACADEMIC SANCTIONS

ment, maintenance, management, and carrying on of the public schools of the district, including regulations relative to the conduct of pupils concerning their safety while in attendance at school or enroute to and from school." M.C.L. § 380.1300; M.S.A. 15.41300. Finally, school boards are required to assist in the enforcement of the compulsory attendance law, M.C.L. § 380.1561; M.S.A. § 15.41561.... If a school board's decision is expressly or impliedly authorized by any of the above statutory provisions, this Court cannot substitute its judgment for that of the board. Inquiry is limited to whether the board's decision — which is presumed reasonable and proper unless shown to be an abuse of discretion — was arbitrary and unreasonable.... *LaPorte v. Escanaba Area Public Schools*, 51 Mich.App. 305, 308, 214 N.W.2d 840 (1974). We believe that defendant's attendance policy is impliedly authorized by statute and is not arbitrary and unreasonable.

The precise question raised by plaintiff (*i.e.*, whether a school district may consider attendance and excused absences in determining a student's course grade) was the subject of a 1978 opinion of the Michigan Attorney General, OAG, 1977-1978, No 5414, p 738 (December 20, 1978). In holding that school officials could consider attendance in grading a student's course performance, the attorney general explained:

> The compulsory attendance law recognizes an educational value in regular attendance at school. Presence in a classroom aids in instilling concepts of self-discipline and exposes a student to group interactions with teachers and fellow students. Such presence also enables a student to hear and participate in class instruction, discussion and other related learning experiences. These and similar considerations are proper educational values which will not necessarily be fully reflected in test results.
>
> School authorities may determine that attendance, class participation and similar factors are proper educational values bearing on a student's academic achievement. *Id.*, at 739-40.

We find that explanation to be sound. An education entails more than just correctly answering questions asked on an examination. Obviously, the purpose of the compulsory attendance law is to ensure that students experience those other educational intangibles described in the attorney general's opinion. A regulation which attempts to obtain that goal certainly comports with the spirit, if not the letter, of the enabling legislation. Defendant's attendance policy properly serves to facilitate the education of our state's children — a responsibility entrusted to local school boards by the School Code.

... While defendant's policy cannot replicate the actual class time missed, it instills an incentive to attend all classes and, failing that, it provides the student with a comparable (albeit after-hours) experience. We do not believe that defendant's attendance policy — which complements, not contravenes, certain statutorily prescribed responses to truancy — is precluded by the compulsory attendance law.

Plaintiff next argues that, even assuming the School Code authorizes a school board to address truancy by means not expressly prescribed by statute, defendant's attendance policy is still ultra vires because its stated purpose is to encourage "responsibility for attendance and [promote] the proper attitude for the world of employment," not for an educational purpose. That argument merely begs the question.

"Education" is not an experience which is to be measured only from within the confines of a classroom. Plaintiff offers no authority (and we cannot envision any) standing for the proposition that preparing students for the world of employment is not a goal of education. If one of the goals of our educational system is to make students functional members of society, and employment is an integral part of that society (both assumptions being beyond serious dispute), then defendant's attendance policy cannot be faulted for attempting to achieve that goal.

As a final argument on this issue, plaintiff asserts that the attendance policy, by reducing grades and possibly leading to loss of course credit, will actually act as a disincentive to continued attendance. That argument is misplaced. Unlike the cases cited by plaintiff, the students here did not unconditionally lose course credit upon the happening of an event (*e.g.*, failure to pay a parking fine or missing a certain number of classes). In this case, a student who misses more than three class periods is given the opportunity to make up that time by attending after-hours study sessions. His or her course credits are not automatically and irreversibly forfeited. Thus, students are given the incentive to make up the missed time and to attend all future classes. Plaintiff's argument to the contrary is as misplaced as his argument that the compulsory attendance law provides a disincentive to attending classes because it requires 180 days of attendance per school year. We hold that defendant's attendance policy is not ultra vires.

Next, plaintiff argues that Lori's rights to substantive and procedural due process were violated by defendant's attendance policy.

... [I]n order for due process protections, either substantive or procedural, to come into play, there must be a recognized life or liberty interest or vested property right at stake.... Here, there was neither.

To have a property interest deserving of constitutional protection, a person must have more than an abstract need, desire, or unilateral expectation of it. There must, instead, be a legitimate claim of entitlement to it. *[Bd. of Regents of State Colleges v.] Roth*, 408 U.S. [564], 577; *Edmond v. Dep't of Corrections* (On Remand), 143 Mich.App. 527, 533, 373 N.W.2d 168 (1985). With that principle in mind, we hold that Lori did not have a vested property right in any grade higher than those actually awarded to her.

At this point, it is necessary to point out that the interest at stake here is not the right to certain grades which Lori had "earned" but which were later reduced by some action of defendant. Rather, the interest here is the right not to

C. ACADEMIC SANCTIONS

have attendance considered in determining one's grades. Phrased in those terms, it is easier to understand why there was no vested property right at stake here.

... There are many factors which may properly be considered in determining a student's course grade — attendance is one such factor. To hold that Lori had a vested property interest in higher grades would be as absurd as holding that an employee has the right to a paycheck for which she has not worked or that a consumer has the right to a product for which he has not paid. The mere potential for, or expectancy of, Lori in receiving higher grades cannot create constitutional or statutory entitlement where none theretofore existed.

As to a claimed liberty interest, that term entails more than the right to be free from arbitrary personal restraint or servitude. In its broadest sense, "liberty" means

> [t]he right of the citizen to be free in the enjoyment of all his faculties; to be free to use them in all lawful ways; to live and work where he will; to earn his livelihood by any lawful calling; and to pursue any livelihood or avocation.... In short, liberty under law extends to the full range of conduct which the individual is free to pursue, and which cannot be restricted except for a proper governmental objective. 16A AmJur2d, Constitutional Law, § 554, at 463-65.

A person is not deprived of liberty, however, simply because state action "imposes burdens, abridges freedom of action, regulates occupations, or subjects individuals to restraints in matters which affect public interests or the rights of others." *Id.*, § 555, p 467.

Plaintiff claims a protected liberty interest in Lori's good name, reputation, honor or integrity which is derived from "the recognition by state law of her right to accurately reflective academic evaluations." Again, that argument merely begs the question at hand since it presupposes that class attendance is not a proper measure of academic achievement. Assuming, as one must, that an examination cannot cover every bit of information discussed in class, it would be reasonable to hold that where two students have identical examination scores the student who had greater attendance also had greater knowledge (*i.e.*, education) of the subject. Moreover, reputation alone, apart from some more tangible interest such as employment, is not enough to invoke the due process clause of the United States Constitution. *Paul v. Davis*, 424 U.S. 693, 701 (1976). The same should be true of our state constitution, especially since the judiciary must be resistant to expanding the substantive reach of due process. *Bowers v. Hardwick*, 478 U.S. 186, 194-95 (1986).

Because Lori's interest in defendant's attendance policy did not rise to the level of a constitutionally protected liberty or property interest, our inquiry is at an end. We would note in passing that, even assuming arguendo that Lori had a protected interest, the attendance policy did not violate her right to substantive and procedural due process. The policy was rationally related to a legitimate government purpose. *Campbell v. New Milford Bd. of Ed.*, 193 Conn. 93, 475

A.2d 289 (1984).... Also, Lori had notice of the policy and an opportunity to avoid its adverse effects by attending after-hours study sessions. This satisfied the requirements of procedural due process.

Affirmed.

NEW BRAUNFELS INDEPENDENT SCHOOL DISTRICT v. ARMKE

Court of Appeals of Texas
658 S.W.2d 330 (1983)

THOMAS, JUSTICE:

Appellees, who were two high school seniors at the time this action commenced, were suspended from New Braunfels High School for three days (March 18-20, 1981) for consuming an alcoholic drink on a school-sponsored trip to Austin. In addition to the suspension, Appellant-New Braunfels Independent School District declared its intent to impose a scholastic penalty on Appellees, which would result in each student receiving zeros on all graded classwork for each day of the suspension, as well as having three grade points deducted for each day of suspension from their six-week grade averages then accruing. Appellees were granted a preliminary restraining order against imposition of the scholastic penalties, which was continued as a temporary injunction.

After a hearing, the trial court found Appellant had no regulation or policy which would authorize imposition of the proposed scholastic penalties in addition to the three-day suspensions. Because of the absence of such a regulation or policy, the court concluded: (1) the imposition of scholastic penalties in connection with Appellees' suspensions was unauthorized; (2) the practice of imposing a scholastic penalty in addition to suspension was void and unenforceable for lack of sufficient legal notice to Appellees; and (3) the practice of reducing grades for non-academic disciplinary reasons was constitutionally unreasonable and impermissible and deprived Appellees of protected property rights and substantive due process. The trial court entered a declaratory judgment in Appellees' favor and permanently enjoined Appellant from reducing their grade averages or from imposing any additional disciplinary penalty.

The pivotal question in this controversy is whether Appellant had a valid policy or regulation which would authorize imposition of the proposed scholastic penalties for each day of suspension. Appellant had formally adopted a comprehensive policy manual as well as a student handbook. The handbook, which was given to each high school student at the beginning of each school year, expressly provided that a student may be suspended from class for violating school policy relating to the use of alcoholic beverages under the facts presented. Appellees do not contest this policy, nor do they deny its violation. In the student handbook, we find the following provisions:

Unexcused absences — those absences approved by the parent for the convenience of the student but not approved by the school. The student is

C. ACADEMIC SANCTIONS

penalized three points from his six-weeks grade average for each day absent. Work may not be made up.

....

Truancy — cutting school all or part of a day without approval of either parents or school. The student is penalized three points from his six-weeks average plus being given a "0" for the day's work. In addition, the student is not permitted to make up missed work. Additional punishment can be given.

Appellees argue that Appellant could not impose grade penalties, which are to be assessed for unexcused absences and truancy, to Appellees' three-day suspensions, since the student handbook or policy manual did not provide that the days Appellees were suspended from class were to be treated as unexcused absences or truancy. Appellant contends, however, that school policy relating to use of alcohol by students, and the penalties which accompany the violation of such policy, had been repeatedly explained to Appellees and their classmates at high school assemblies. Appellant presented testimony from several high school students, including a student who had already been accepted at West Point Military Academy, and school personnel that school policy and attendant penalties relating to the use of alcohol by students had been carefully explained at school assemblies. The evidence is overwhelming that the high school students knew that, if a student was suspended for violating school policy relating to the use of alcohol, each day of suspension would be considered an unexcused absence and that the suspended student would receive a zero for all graded classwork as well as having three grade points deducted from the six-week grade average then accruing. Even though the evidence shows Appellees were present at school assemblies where school policy and accompanying grade penalties regarding the use of alcohol were clearly explained, Appellees refused to acknowledge either the explanation or existence of such policy or penalties.

School policy relating to discipline need not be in writing in order to be legally enforceable. A rule or policy may be informal and may even be oral as long as it fairly apprises the student of the conduct prohibited and the penalties attached to the prohibited conduct. *Texarkana Independent School District v. Lewis*, 470 S.W.2d 727 (Tex.Civ.App. — Texarkana 1971, no writ); Tex.Att'y Gen.Op.No. M-395 (1969). We hold Appellant had orally adopted a valid policy that a student suspended for use of alcohol could receive the scholastic penalties proposed by Appellant in this instance, and that Appellees were fairly informed of the policy, the conduct prohibited, and the range of penalties attached thereto. *Graham v. Board of Ed., Idabel Sch. Dist. No. Five*, 419 F.Supp. 1214 (E.D.Okl.1976).

We sustain Appellant's first point, which contends the trial court erred in finding that Appellant had not adopted a policy or regulation which authorized the proposed scholastic penalties for each day of Appellees' suspensions. We hold the trial court's finding in that regard is against the great weight and preponderance of the evidence. Further, the trial court's conclusion that the practice of imposing scholastic penalties in addition to suspension was void and unenforceable for lack of sufficient legal notice to Appellees is erroneous.

Appellant's third point of error contends the trial court erred in concluding that imposition of an academic penalty for non-academic disciplinary purposes is constitutionally unreasonable and impermissible because it deprived Appellees of protected property rights and substantive due process. The question of whether an academic penalty may be used as punishment for unexcused absences has been decided against the trial court's legal conclusion. "We are not prepared to say that a school district may not adopt attendance regulations which impose academic penalties for unexcused absences from school.... Regulations of an independent school district which penalize students for unexcused absences by lowering their grades are not invalid on their face." Tex.Att'y Gen.Op.No. H-398 (1974). *See also Fisher v. Burkburnett Independent School Dist.*, 419 F.Supp. 1200 (N.D.Tex.1976), wherein the court held that loss of a student's trimester grades upon expulsion for violation of the school's drug abuse policy was found not to be constitutionally excessive but was in furtherance of school disciplinary policy.

A student has a constitutionally protected property right to a public education and a liberty interest in his or her good name. *Goss v. Lopez*, 419 U.S. 565 (1975). We hold that reduction of Appellees' six-week grades by three points for each day of suspension has no adverse impact on Appellees' property rights to a public education. Furthermore, the evidence does not show that imposition of the scholastic penalties proposed will have any negative impact on the honor, reputation or name of either Appellee. The record shows that Appellees, at the time of hearing below, had already been admitted to the university of their choice and does not show that imposition of the scholastic penalties in this instance will adversely affect them in their educational, professional or personal lives in the future. Appellant's third point is sustained.

We do not reach Appellant's second point of error, as the judgment of the trial court is reversed and the permanent injunction is dissolved.

KATZMAN v. CUMBERLAND VALLEY SCHOOL DISTRICT

Commonwealth Court of Pennsylvania
84 Pa. Commw. 474, 479 A.2d 671 (1984)

BARBIERI, JUDGE:

....

The parties agree that this case is one of first impression in this Commonwealth. Simply stated, we are asked to determine the legality of the grade reduction policy as administered here by the Board.

The facts are undisputed.

On December 3, 1982, Debbie, an eleventh grade student at Cumberland Valley High School, while on a field trip to New York City with her Humanities Class, joined four other students in ordering and drinking a glass of wine in a

C. ACADEMIC SANCTIONS

restaurant. When questioned later by school authorities she admitted the incident whereupon she was suspended for five days, excluded from classes, expelled from the cheer leading squad, prohibited from taking part in school activities during the five days' suspension period and was later permanently expelled from the National Honor Society. Under the District's disciplinary policy a further penalty of grade reduction was imposed. This policy is stated as follows:

> Suspension and Expulsions ... 6240.9d Reduce grades in all classes two percentage points for each day of suspension. The grades are to be reduced during the marking period when the in-school or out of school suspension occurred. In lieu of a two percentage point reduction the student may be assigned to a supervised Saturday work program provided the parent(s) and student accept the conditions of this option.

In imposing the penalty pursuant to this "policy," she was advised that, as a consequence of this suspension, her grades in each subject for the entire second marking period would be reduced by ten points, two points for each day of suspension, but that the alternative of Saturday work in lieu of suspension would be denied her because her transgression was a violation of District's policy on "alcohol abuse." ...

....

Debbie and her parents as guardians (Appellees), before us here on appeal in a proceeding under the Local Agency Law, have from the outset raised no procedural issues, nor have they contested any of the penalties imposed except only the issue as to the propriety of the grade reductions as punishment for her disciplinary infraction. We note in this connection that Debbie was a high achieving student, ranking tenth in a class of approximately 600 pupils, and that she had no record of disciplinary problems or prior offenses of any kind. The common pleas court terming the grade reductions and other punishments imposed "harsh" and "excessive," stated, however, that the nature of the punishment would have no effect in its decision invalidating the grade reductions on the basis that the Board's "policy" was in conflict with Section 12.6(f) of the Student Rights and Responsibilities Regulations adopted by the State Board of Education, 22 Pa.Code 12.6(f), and, as we have noted, ordering that Debbie's grades as originally fixed by her teachers be reinstated.

Appellant contends here that the Board of School Directors, a local public school district such as the one in this case, has the "inherent right to determine the nature of discipline to be administered to students violating its codes of behavior," that neither Section 12.6(f) or any other provision in the Students Rights and Responsibilities Regulation contains any provision which places a limitation on the Board's "discretionary authority" to impose discipline, as in this case, for a violation of its policy with regard to alcohol. In this connection, Appellant points to Section 510 of the Public School Code of 1949, Act of March 10, 1949, P.L. 30, as amended, 24 P.S. 5-510, in which the Board of School Directors is empowered to "adopt and enforce such reasonable rules and regulations as it may deem necessary and proper, regarding the management of its school affairs and the conduct and deportment of all ... pupils attending the public schools in the District...." Appellant refers us to authorities, including decisions of this and other appellate courts of Pennsylvania which we find helpful but not controlling or sufficiently persuasive to direct our disposition. Rather, it is our conclusion that there is no specific provision in State statutes, in the regulations of the State Board of Education or in prior decisions of our courts which we have been able to find in our research that specifically deals with and serves as a determinative guide to us in reaching a decision here. As a matter of first instance, therefore, we must decide the legality of a Board policy, not specifically authorized or proscribed by statute or regulation, which authorizes penalties, affecting and reducing educational standing, for infractions that are not education related.

We are aware, of course, as Appellant points out, that under Sections 510, 1317 and 1318 of the Public School Code of 1949, a board of school directors may adopt "reasonable rules and regulations" regarding the "conduct and deportment" of pupils while under the supervision of the board and teachers; ... and that "in the absence of a gross abuse of discretion, courts will not second guess policies of the several boards of school directors," *Commonwealth v. Hall*, 309 Pa.Superior Ct. 407, 412, 455 A.2d 674, 677 (1983). Nevertheless, we cannot conclude that the Legislature in authorizing the adoption and enforcement of "reasonable rules and regulations" intended to sanction a grade reduction policy, without an optional make up program, for the kind of infraction involved here.... The trial court reasoned that the "unmistakable policy behind the regulation is that students suspended for disciplinary violations should not only be permitted to make up the work they miss, but also should receive credit for that work." We believe, however, that the policy and the penalty here goes beyond the scope of making up for time lost, such as the five days of suspension. Here, rather, although the penalty was for the five days missed, the assessed penalty downgraded achievement for a full marking period of nine weeks. Of course, for college entrance and other purposes this would result in a clear misrepresentation of the student's scholastic achievement. Misrepresentation of achievement is equally improper and, we think, illegal whether the achievement is misrepresented by upgrading or by downgrading, if either is done for reasons that are irrelevant to the achievement being graded. For example, one would hardly deem acceptable an upgrading in a mathematics course for achievement on the playing fields. In this connection, we find inapt Appellant's example of downgrading for cheating. Cheating is related to grading.

We conclude, for the reasons stated, that the Board's policy and the manner in which it was exercised in this case represent an illegal application of the Board's discretion and that, therefore, as the trial court held, the grade reduction was improper. Accordingly, we will affirm the order of the common pleas court.

C. ACADEMIC SANCTIONS

1. In *Slocum*, should more weight have been given to the school's discretion and authority to develop disciplinary policies?

2. Why was the school's action in *Slocum* upheld, while that in *Katzman* was not? Compare the nature of the students' conduct in each case. The *Slocum* court's discussion of the value of class attendance is more forceful than that in *Katzman*. Why?

3. For cases finding a due process violation for academic sanctions based on alcohol use by students, consider *Smith v. School City of Hobart*, 811 F. Supp. 391 (N.D. Ind. 1993) (*see* Chapter 5), and *Warren County Bd. of Educ. v. Wilkinson*, 500 So. 2d 455 (Miss. 1986).

In *Wilkinson*, the plaintiff won a due process case against her school which had taken away a semester of credit when it discovered that the plaintiff had taken a few sips of beer at her family residence. The court held that the plaintiff had not violated any school rule. If this were a school rule, would the plaintiff have lost?

In *Smith*, the federal district court struck down a provision which provided for a 4% reduction in grades for each day a student has been suspended for alcohol use during school hours. The court held that the policy was arbitrary and that the punishment was unrelated to the conduct. A student's grade or credit should reflect his or her academic performance or achievement. The student's misconduct must be directly related to the student's academic performance for an academic sanction such as a grade lowering to be constitutional. *See Napolitano v. Trustees of Princeton Univ.*, 186 N.J. Super. 548, 453 A.2d 263 (1982) (Withholding a college degree for one year following a conviction for plagiarism was upheld. The disciplinary committee was required to review the evidence, but was not required to engage in a full hearing to satisfy due process rights).

4. Did the school district in *Armke* provide appropriate information for fixing an academic penalty for a disciplinary infraction? Typically, there is a difference in due process procedure for academic versus disciplinary issues. *See, e.g., Board of Curators of the Univ. of Mo. v. Horowitz*, 435 U.S. 78 (1975), and *Goss v. Lopez*, 419 U.S. 565 (1975), in Chapter 7. The court here, however, provides a synthesis not seen in other cases. What rationale is presented for this new posture?

5. The *Armke* court uses *Fisher v. Burkburnett Indep. Sch. Dist.*, 419 F. Supp. 1200 (N.D. Tex. 1976), as substantiation for the position that school districts may impose academic penalties for disciplinary purposes. *Fisher*, though, is a case of inadvertent academic failure resulting from a long-term expulsion where a student simply missed taking exams. *Armke* is a decision based on academic sanction. Did the court make too far a reach in making its decision?

6. If the affected students had not yet been accepted to college, would the court have found a negative impact on their collective reputation, honor and good name? If so, would this have been enough to affirm the lower court's decision in favor of the students?

7. In what ways are *Katzman* and *Armke* distinguishable? Why was the misrepresentation of true academic achievement more significant in *Katzman* than in *Armke*?

8. Did the existence of a Saturday work program in *Katzman* dictate its legal result? By permitting students to make up all work missed and receive credit for it, do schools, in effect, condone behavior that otherwise warrants suspension?

PART THREE

TEACHERS' RIGHTS AND RESPONSIBILITIES

Chapter 9
TEACHERS AND THE EMPLOYMENT RELATIONSHIP

We now turn our focus from the major consumer of educational services — the student — to the key actor in the provision of such services — the teacher. As will be seen in the following two chapters, the view of the teacher as all wise and all powerful is indeed a romantic notion. The teacher is now confronted with increasing regulations emanating from state and local school boards and growing pressures from competing organized groups wishing to have their particular views prevail. Coupling these problems with the process of financial retrenchment presently extant in most school districts, teachers find themselves caught in a crossfire, no longer able to thoughtfully control their professional lives. The schizophrenic struggle between teachers as professionals and teachers as employees presents an ever-increasing series of legal issues, leaving a patchwork of decisions, often without clear direction.

A. TEACHER COLLECTIVE BARGAINING

1. THE "RIGHT" TO BARGAIN COLLECTIVELY

Any study of public sector unionism as it affects public schools should be prefaced with an explanation of the two oft-used legal arguments which have been employed to prevent the spread of unionism in the public sector — the concept of the sovereignty of the public employer, and its offspring, the doctrine of illegal delegation of power.

The sovereignty argument, as it developed in the United States, begins with the propositions that government has sole authority over all governmental functions and that such authority cannot be delegated to, usurped by, or shared with any other party. Thus bargaining with, or striking against, government is per se illegal because such activity challenges the sovereign's exclusive right to prescribe the conditions under which public servants work. The sovereignty argument would require that government officials unilaterally establish public employment conditions. Similarly, the "illegal delegation of powers" argument provides that statutory authority exclusively grants governmental powers to government. Since the government is both possessor and guardian of governmental power, any delegation of such power to another party is a violation of statutory authority. Therefore, since collective bargaining contemplates some sharing of authority, government participation in negotiations is per se illegal.

As public employers and public employees became increasingly concerned about employment "rights," particularly the opportunity to bargain collectively, the courts were forced, as seen in the following cases, to confront the sovereignty and delegation doctrines to determine whether they, indeed, stood as an impediment to collective action.

JERSEY SHORE AREA SCHOOL DISTRICT v. JERSEY SHORE EDUCATION ASSOCIATION

Supreme Court of Pennsylvania
519 Pa. 398, 548 A.2d 1202 (1988)

STOUT, JUSTICE:

This appeal is brought by the members of the Jersey Shore Education Association, which represents the teachers of the Jersey Shore Area School District. In it we are asked to reconcile that provision of the Public Employees Relations Act (PERA) ... which gives teachers the right to strike, with that provision of the Public School Code ... which mandates that school districts provide 180 days of pupil instruction. Specifically, PERA provides:

> If a strike by public employees occurs after the collective bargaining processes set forth in Sections 801 and 802 of Article VIII of this act have been completely utilized and exhausted, it shall not be prohibited unless or until such a strike creates a clear and present danger or threat to the health, safety or welfare of the public.

On the other hand, the Public School Code provides: "All public kindergartens, elementary and secondary schools shall be kept open each school year for at least one hundred eighty (180) days of instruction for pupils."

On September 10, 1984, after only four days of pupil instruction, the teachers struck against appellee, Jersey Shore Area School District. On October 8, 1984, the school district filed for an injunction in the Court of Common Pleas of Lycoming County, in an effort to force the teachers back to work. A hearing was held on October 10, 1984, following which the Chancellor issued an injunction ordering the teachers back to work on October 11. The Association filed for reconsideration and an additional hearing was held on October 23, 1984. The Chancellor refused to lift the injunction. The Association appealed to the Commonwealth Court, which affirmed solely on the basis of the Chancellor's finding that the school district's impending inability to schedule 180 days of instruction presented a clear and present danger to the public because of a threatened loss of state subsidies.... While we disagree with the Commonwealth Court that the threatened loss of state subsidies alone would support the issuance of an injunction, we nonetheless affirm on the record as a whole.

....

At the first hearing the superintendent for the school district testified that he had prepared a revised school calendar. Allowing for six snow days and two nonmandatory holidays, the superintendent had concluded that October 15, 1984,

A. TEACHER COLLECTIVE BARGAINING

would be the last date upon which the teachers could return to the classroom while still ensuring an educationally-sound schedule. In addition, the superintendent testified extensively as to the financial impact of the strike. He stated that the school district stood to lose $26,637.00 per day in state subsidies for each day it fell short of 180 days of instruction. At the time of the hearing the superintendent estimated that the strike had cost the school district $65,944.00 in unemployment compensation, additional salaries and other costs incidental to the strike.

With respect to the students, the superintendent stated that the strike placed the seniors at a competitive disadvantage in terms of SAT testing. Seniors also faced deadlines with respect to scholarship applications and were bereft of guidance counseling services. The longer the strike, the more deleterious its effect on the future of the seniors.

With respect to other grades, students would be at a competitive disadvantage in taking state-mandated tests to determine remedial needs. With only four days of instruction, some students could be placed in remedial courses which they would not otherwise have needed. Moreover, in the event the school district could not administer these tests due to the continuation of the strike, it would lose state funding for the remedial courses themselves.

The superintendent stated that interference with a regular pattern of study, as had occurred in this strike, results in a loss of learning capacity, which increases with the length of the interruption. In support of this hypothesis he cited test scores from a previous year showing a drop in student aptitudes following a strike.

Finally, the superintendent expressed his concern that the strike deprived eligible students of a free, hot lunch, possibly the only such meal they received, while working parents were experiencing difficulties with interim babysitting arrangements.

The school teachers presented the testimony of two experts. The first disputed the superintendent's interpretation of prior test scores insofar as their reflecting a decrease in pupil learning due to the previous strike. This expert opined that it was inappropriate to compare different student groups for such a purpose. The second expert testified that, as of the date of the hearing, the school district would actually have a net savings in salaries and benefits of $24,199.00 over the potentially lost subsidy.

Having heard this evidence, the Chancellor issued the injunction on the basis of his conclusion that all of the evidence had demonstrated the existence of a clear and present danger to the health and welfare of the community.

. . . .

Since this is an issue of first impression for this Court, we shall begin our legal analysis with a brief review of the decisions of the Commonwealth Court that have addressed it. In *Armstrong School Dist. v. Armstrong Educ. Ass'n*, 5 Pa.Commw. 378, 291 A.2d 120 (1972), Commonwealth Court grappled with the definition of "clear and present danger or threat" in analogizing it to the First

Amendment, free speech and association cases.... In reversing the issuance of an injunction, the Court stated that the disruption of routine administrative procedures and the cancellation of extracurricular activities were inconveniences inherent in a teachers' strike, inconveniences envisioned by the legislature which, if considered a "clear and present danger or threat," would virtually nullify the right to strike. In dicta the Court also stated that if a strike lasted so long as to make the 180-day calendar an impossibility, and the cessation of subsidies a possibility, it properly could be enjoined.

In *Philadelphia Fed. of Teachers v. Ross*, 8 Pa.Commw. 204, 301 A.2d 405 (1973), the Court affirmed the issuance of an injunction where the board presented evidence of sharply increased gang activity that necessitated $133,000.00 per day in increased police protection, endemic student under-achievement, possible loss of state subsidies, and the disqualification of seniors from entering college. The Court opined:

> It is neither possible nor prudent to state with precision that any one or more given circumstances surrounding a strike by school teachers will constitute a threat to the health, safety or welfare of the public. Nor do we decide that any particular number of days of lost instruction caused by a strike produces such a threat.

See also Bethel Park School Dist. v. Bethel Park Fed. of Teachers, 54 Pa.Commw. 49, 52, 420 A.2d 18, 19 (1980) (loss of state subsidies, instructional days, vocational job training, higher education and special education opportunities, counseling, social and health services, extracurricular programs and employees' work and wage opportunities constituted a clear and present danger to the community).

In *Bellefonte Area School Bd. v. The Bellefonte Area Educ. Ass'n*, 9 Pa.Commw. 210, 304 A.2d 922 (1973), the Court reversed the issuance of an injunction in concluding that the facts did not support a finding of "clear and present danger or threat." Since in that case sufficient make-up days remained to replace the thirteen strike days, therefore, the loss of state subsidies was not imminent. Moreover, the possible loss of participation in an educational quality assessment program was not deemed harmful enough to justify the injunction.... In a vigorous concurring opinion, JUDGE KRAMER inveighed in *Bellefonte*:

> All of the parties to this case and the majority opinion blithely speak of using "summer vacations" or holidays as a means of making up teachers' strike days to preserve state education subsidy funds. Not one word of concern is expressed for those school students who work on holidays and vacation days to stay in school. Not one word is utilized to protect high school seniors who must attend college summer school to gain admittance to college in the fall. Not one word is devoted to what happens if high school senior's grades are not ready for timely submission to college for the fall admission. Not one word is said because the school children are not

A. TEACHER COLLECTIVE BARGAINING

represented. They are pawns in an adult game of economics. If the teachers and the school district agree to use all legal holidays, all weekends and all vacation time to make up for the lost days of a strike, does that mean the students will have no rest? Do they have any rights?

....

More recently, in *Scanlon v. Mount Union Area Bd. of School Directors*, 51 Pa.Commw. 83, 415 A.2d 96 (1980), aff'd, 499 Pa. 215, 452 A.2d 1016 (1982), Commonwealth Court held that the scheduling of 180 days by school districts was mandatory, not discretionary, while stating in dicta that:

> We are aware that strike activity might lawfully continue for such a period as to render the provision of 180 instructional days impossible within the terms of the Code defining the school year; in that event, boards must amend their schedules to comply as fully as is possible within the applicable school year.

Finally, in *Armstrong Educ. Ass'n v. Armstrong School Dist.*, 116 Pa.Commw. 571, 542 A.2d 1047 (1988), Commonwealth Court, citing the case sub judice, affirmed the issuance of an injunction where a strike threatened to foreshorten the 180-day instructional calendar.

This brief history reflects judicial difficulty, and at times divergence, in reconciling the right to strike with the requirement of 180 instructional days. While some cases have looked at a plethora of factors, including the loss of state subsidies, others have looked only at the loss of state subsidies in determining that it per se creates a clear and present danger or threat. We do not believe that the language of PERA necessitates judicial hand-wringing or hair-pulling. We hold that the loss of state educational subsidies for failure of a school district to schedule 180 days of instruction for pupils, alone, does not constitute a "clear and present danger or threat to the health, safety or welfare of the public." In this case the school district demonstrated beyond peradventure the existence of a "clear and present danger or threat to the health, safety or welfare of the public." Without focusing on any one of the myriad economic and other facts upon which the school board relied, without weighing the interests of seniors as weightier that those of kindergartners, we conclude that, in conjunction, these factors created a school district which, although perhaps able to "make up" a day or two of instruction, could not "make up" the actual, the impending and the ever-increasing harm which was being wrought upon its students. On this record, the health and welfare of the students, who cannot and must not be treated as a category separate from the public at large, was clearly endangered and threatened.

....

LARSEN, JUSTICE, dissenting:

When the legislature granted school teachers and other public employees the right to strike in 1970, it was fully cognizant of the provisions in the Public

School Code mandating that school districts provide 180 days of pupil instruction and fully aware that such strikes could infringe upon the 180 day mandate. Nevertheless, the legislature granted that right to strike ... and restricted the possibility of intervention by the courts in providing that a strike occurring after the collective bargaining procedures of Act 195 have been utilized and exhausted "shall not be prohibited unless or until such a strike creates a clear and present danger or threat to the health, safety or welfare of the public." This legislative restriction on a court's authority to intervene by injunction against a strike is strong and explicit — a strike "shall not be prohibited" in the absence of a "clear and present danger or threat" to the public's health, safety or welfare. Surely, clear and present danger or threat to the health, safety or welfare of the community requires much more than the myriad inevitable and expected inconveniences and disruptions that are the normal consequences of any school strike, even one which impinges on the mandatory 180 days of pupil instruction of which the legislature was well aware.

In support, I adopt the opinion and analysis of the Honorable Emil E. Narick, then sitting on the Court of Common Pleas of Allegheny County, in *Bethel Park School District v. Bethel Park Federation of Teachers*, 135 Pgh.L.J. 127 (C.P.Alleg.Co.1986). In this case, Judge Narick refused to issue an injunction against a strike by school teachers despite the school board's recitation of the standard litany of ills caused by the strike, namely that state subsidies were threatened, that seniors were at a competitive disadvantage with college placement and testing, that students generally were competitively disadvantaged, that special programs were threatened, etc. Recognizing that these concerns, although serious and important, were not what was contemplated when the legislature gave courts the authority to issue an injunction only when there was a "clear and present danger or threat to the health, safety or welfare of the public," Judge Narick stated as follows:

> The disruption of routine administrative procedures, the cancellation of extracurricular activities and sports and other such difficulties are most certainly inconvenient for the public, and especially for students and their parents. But these problems are inherent in the very nature of any strike by school teachers, or any other group of public employees. If we were to say that such inconveniences, which necessarily accompany any strike by school teachers from its very inception, are proper grounds for enjoining such a strike, we would in fact be nullifying the right to strike granted to the school teachers by the legislature in Act 195, as is granted to all other public employees.
>
> ....
>
> In summary, I do not believe that where a teachers' strike prevents a school district from having 180 days of instruction in the school year with a consequence of possible loss of state subsidy, there is thereby a clear and present danger or threat to the health, safety or welfare of the public.

If the contrary is true, then it would follow that any strike which infringes upon the 180-day requirement is infected with almost presumptive invalidity, and, two, the school board is assured that its position in negotiations at the bargaining table, whether fair or unfair, will prevail if only it can hold out long enough to encroach on the 180-day requirement....

In the instant case, as in the *Bethel Park* decision, there is no evidence on the record of any clear and present danger or threat to the health, safety or welfare of the public other than evidence of the normal disruptions and inconveniences associated with any strike of public school teachers. These types of harms usually associated with a public school teachers' strike were not unknown or unimaginable when the legislature prohibited courts from interfering with such strikes unless or until a clear and present danger or threat to the public health, safety or welfare were presented, and the legislature could not have equated the former harm with the latter clear and present danger or threat. The record, therefore, falls far short of justifying the "extraordinary remedy" of injunctive relief prohibiting the continuation of the strike, and the Chancellor should be reversed.

....

PAPADAKOS, J., joins in this dissenting opinion.

ZAPPALA, JUSTICE, dissenting:

I agree with the majority that the risk of loss of state educational subsidies due to a school district's failure to schedule 180 days of instruction for pupils is not a "clear and present danger or threat to the health, safety or welfare of the public." But while the majority professes to resist any temptation to judicially legislate a 180-day limitation to the right to strike, it has in fact succumbed to that temptation. By focusing its attention on the inconveniences to the students which accompany the shortened duration of the school year caused by a teachers' strike, the majority has effectively created a per se rule that the inability to schedule 180 days of instruction constitutes a clear and present danger to the health, safety or welfare of the public.

... By sustaining the grant of a preliminary injunction on the basis that those student inconveniences demonstrate a clear and present danger to the public, the majority has insured that injunctions will issue when the duration of the strike threatens the 180 day requirement. The majority is careful to emphasize that the economic threat of the loss of state subsidies is insufficient in itself to warrant the issuance of an injunction. This distinction is of no consequence. A teachers' strike which lasts long enough to create that economic threat will always give rise as well to the student inconveniences which concern the majority.

... [I]t was the clear mandate of the Legislature that a strike by public employees "shall not be prohibited unless or until the strike creates a clear and present danger or threat to the health, safety, or welfare of the public." The public at large does not share the individualized and personalized concerns of the student population. Nor are the terms synonymous. Nevertheless, the majority superimposes student inconveniences upon public welfare. In doing so, the majority places student inconveniences in a preeminent position and relegates the teachers' right to strike to a secondary concern. This is contrary to the legislative intent.

....

Although the Legislature's inattention to student inconveniences may be perceived by some as a failure, the remedy properly rests with the Legislature. I, for one, would not judicially disrupt the balance which the Legislature sought to achieve.

---

1. Much of the evidence presented by the superintendent favoring the end of the strike was based on the well-being of the students — an important thought, indeed. Whereas the weight placed on these concerns might and should be high, the issues at stake in this case deal very directly with the teachers' well-being — *i.e.*, the right to strike. Did the Chancellor or any of the courts pay enough attention to the teachers' complaint? Could the teachers' case have been stronger?

2. It is hard to argue that the inherent inconveniences associated with a teacher strike are not detrimental to the lives of school students and parents. Several of the cases cited by the majority note such inconveniences. But how convincing is Larsen's dissent in *Jersey Shore*? Is Zappala's dissenting opinion even stronger?

3. The majority in *Jersey Shore* concluded that the school system, although it could make up a lost day or two, could not make up the actual and impending harm suffered by its students as a result of the strike. Consider the possible harm to *teachers* as a result of lost school days. Should a school system be required to pay teachers' salaries for days lost, when the system could have scheduled make-up days? *See Freidhoff v. Board of Sch. Dirs. of Conemaugh Valley Sch. Dist.*, 137 Pa. Commw. 555, 586 A.2d 1038 (1991) (Teachers were entitled to pay for 171 instructional days under Weather Emergency Act even though only 160 instructional days were scheduled, where had weather emergency not occurred the board could have scheduled 171 instructional days when it revised the schedule to compensate for an earlier teachers' strike. The Act entitled teachers to the same salary they would have received had weather emergency not occurred — salary for 171 days).

Should it make a difference whether these extra days lost are the result of the weather or a teachers' strike? The *Freidhoff* court said whether the make-up days were labeled weather days or strike days was irrelevant.

4. Judge Zappala, dissenting in *Jersey Shore*, stated his concern for teachers' right to strike and that such right should not be a secondary concern to student inconveniences. In *Reichley by Wall v. North Penn Sch. Dist.*, 626 A.2d 123 (Pa. 1993), Zappala and the Supreme Court of Pennsylvania upheld public school teachers' right to strike. The provision of the Public Employee Relations Act which allows teachers to strike was not unconstitutional, even in light of a new act which suspended strikes during period of arbitration.

TEXAS STATE TEACHERS ASSOCIATION v. GARLAND INDEPENDENT SCHOOL DISTRICT

United States Court of Appeals
777 F.2d 1046 (5th Cir. 1985)

JERRE S. WILLIAMS, CIRCUIT JUDGE:

....

Facts

TSTA [Texas State Teachers Association] is a voluntary employee organization. It sought to distribute TSTA information to teachers in GISD [Garland Independent School District] schools during school hours. TSTA also wanted to use school communication facilities — including school mailboxes, billboards, and the public address system — as mediums for the distribution of their information.

GISD policy ... totally prohibits any "employee organization" from meeting or recruiting during "school hours", and from using school communication facilities for the dissemination of information concerning employee organizations. GISD policy allows employee organizations to meet or recruit teachers on school premises before 8:00 a.m. or after 3:45 p.m. "upon request to and approval by the local principal." GISD policy also allows the distribution of literature on school premises (parking lots, hallways, and placement on teachers' desk) during non-school hours.

On January 8 and 9, 1981, TSTA representatives visited numerous GISD schools during school hours. Relying on GISD Administrative Regulation 412, the principal or assistant principal of most schools refused to permit the TSTA representatives to distribute literature or to meet with GISD teachers.

This lawsuit resulted. Appellants claimed that these GISD policies violated their First and Fourteenth Amendment rights of free speech, free association, and equal protection of the laws, and were unconstitutionally vague and overbroad. Appellants argued that these policies, as interpreted and implemented by school officials, operated to deny GISD teachers their right to discuss TSTA business even during non-class times such as the lunch hour (several GISD teachers and administrators are members of TSTA). Appellants further contended that school officials routinely granted access to school communication facilities to other commercial and civic organizations (upon approval of the principal), and that "employee organizations" were discriminatorily denied access.

Appellees denied that their policies violated the appellants' First and Fourteenth Amendment rights. They argued that the GISD schools are not a public forum, and therefore appellants have no right of access. Appellees urged that reasonable alternative means of communication were available to TSTA — *i.e.*, meeting after school hours, distributing literature on school property after school hours, or contacting teachers at school or home through the United States Postal Service. Finally, appellees contended that allowing employee organizations to use school facilities would disrupt the learning process and would be contrary to Texas Education Codes 21.904 — which requires a school district to maintain a position of neutrality with respect to employee membership in various organizations.

The parties each filed a motion for summary judgment. The district court granted appellants' motion for partial summary judgment as to Admin.Reg. 412 (4) and 5 — which permits employee organizations to use school premises for meetings during non-school hours only "upon request to and approval by the local school principal." The district court held that this rule was unconstitutionally overbroad. This holding is not appealed. As to the remainder of appellants' claims, the district court granted appellees' motion for summary judgment and denied appellants' motion. We reverse in part and affirm in part.

The Right to Communicate

In granting the GISD motion for summary judgment, the district court relied upon *Perry Education Assn. v. Perry Local Educators' Assn.*, 460 U.S. 37, 103 (1983). Under *Perry*, the "existence of a right of access to public property and the standard by which limitations upon such a right must be evaluated differ depending upon the character of the property at issue."

Perry describes the three types of forums that exist in public property for First Amendment purposes at 460 U.S. 45. (1) Public Forums: These are areas "which by long tradition or by government fiat have been devoted to assembly and debate." Examples are public streets and parks. Speech may not be suppressed for content in these forums unless the state shows a "compelling state interest" and a regulation "narrowly drawn to achieve that end." Public forums are also subject to reasonable "time, place, and manner" restrictions. (2) Limited Public Forums: These are forums which the state has voluntarily "opened for use by the public as a place for expressive activity." As long as the forum remains open, speech is protected to the same extent as in a public forum. In a limited public forum, only "similar entities" to those allowed access have a protected right of speech. (3) Non-Public Forums: This is "property which is not by tradition or designation a forum for public communication." In a non-public forum, "the state may reserve the forum for its intended purposes ... so long as the regulation on speech is reasonable and not an effort to suppress expression merely because public officials oppose the speaker's view.["]

GISD policy ... affects two different classes of communications: (1) communications instigated by outside representatives of TSTA who desire access to teachers and school communication facilities; and (2) communications among GISD teachers employed by the schools. A different analysis is relevant to each separate type of communication. Because appellants are appealing a summary judgment, we must look at the evidence in the light most favorable to them.

A. Communications of Outside TSTA Representatives

1. During school hours

Schools are not considered traditional public forums in which outside visitors may freely espouse their views. Moreover, school administrators must be given broad discretion in supervising the visitation of the school environment by persons not associated with the school. Because GISD schools are not public forums, outside TSTA representatives have no constitutional right of access. Appellants argue, however, that the school has allowed other visitors from civic and commercial groups to meet with teachers during school hours, and has therefore voluntarily created either a public forum or a limited public forum.

GISD permits selected groups of educators, textbook salesmen, and representatives of civic and charitable organizations to meet with students and faculty during non-class school hours. These meetings must concern school-sponsored or related activities and must not interfere with class time. Those persons seeking access must obtain prior permission from the school principal, and in some cases, from the Superintendent's office.... This selective visitation policy does not create a public forum in GISD schools.

In addition, outside TSTA representatives are not due any right of visitation through the doctrine of "limited public forum." Even though the school district has granted access during school hours to representatives of certain civic and commercial groups, "the constitutional right of access would in any event extend only to other entities of similar character." Under *Perry*, the visitors allowed access — educators, salesmen, and the like, discussing school-related activities — are not "similar entities" to an employee organization, such as TSTA, concerned with teacher employment practices and procedures.

... We hold that GISD policies are constitutional as applied to the visitation of the school by outside TSTA representatives during school hours.

Appellants also contend that policies of GISD constitute impermissible content discrimination in violation of the equal protection clause of the Fourteenth Amendment. Since outside representatives of TSTA have no First Amendment right of access to the school, the grant of access to other organizations does not burden a fundamental right of TSTA. Therefore, the school district's policy need only rationally further a legitimate state purpose. We find one of the justifications advanced by GISD — that of limiting contacts during the school day so that teachers may concentrate on teaching — survives the test of rationality. Therefore, we find no merit in appellant's equal protection claim as it relates to outside representatives of TSTA.

2. Use of school mail facilities

Unless it has been opened to the general public, a school mail system is not a public forum. The same is true of school billboards and the public address system so long as there are alternative channels of communications.

Appellants argue that GISD allows other commercial and civic organizations to use school communication facilities. They then contend that either a public forum or a limited public forum has been created in GISD communication facilities, to which the appellants should be granted access. Appellants assert that "employee organizations" are the only groups denied access to GISD facilities.

The evidence indicates that GISD has not created a public forum in its communication facilities. On occasion, school principals have allowed certain civic and commercial groups to distribute literature through school facilities. For example, GISD sometimes allows access to organizations such as the PTA, Little League, Boy Scouts, Junior Achievement, teacher bowling and swimming groups, and Board-approved insurance companies. Similarly, in *Perry*, certain community and civic groups — *i.e.*, the Cub scouts, YMCA, local church groups, etc. — were granted access to school mailboxes. Nevertheless, *Perry* held that "[t]his type of selective access does not transform government property into a public forum." 460 U.S. at 47.

Likewise, TSTA has no right of access under a claim of "limited public forum." No "similar entities" to TSTA — *i.e.*, other employee organizations — are granted access to GISD facilities. It is permissible to refuse to "grant employee organizations the right to use the school mails at all." In short, GISD has not created a public forum and also has not created a "limited public forum" for entities similar to employee organizations. Therefore, we hold that GISD may prevent outside representatives of "employee organizations" from using school communication facilities.

....

B. *Communications of GISD Teachers*

1. *Private Communications*

Regulations on the speech of those who teach within the schools obviously must be drawn more narrowly than regulations on the speech of outside representatives.... *Tinker v. Des Moines Independent Community School District*, 393 U.S. 503 (1969) ... held that teacher communications may be suppressed only when "the expression or its method of exercise materially and substantially interferes with the activities or discipline of the school."

The evidence indicates that school officials interpret [state regulations] as prohibiting any discussions among teachers relating to TSTA or TSTA business or relating to any teacher organization that occur on school premises during school hours, even though those discussions occur during lunch hour or other non-class time....

First, it is undisputed that school officials would prohibit GISD teachers from discussing TSTA if, in their view, such discussion amounted to "promoting" the organization. The district court found (and appellees argue on appeal) that punishment of speech "promoting" employee organizations is justified under an opinion of the Texas Attorney General. [That opinion] held that it was a violation

A. TEACHER COLLECTIVE BARGAINING

of the Texas Constitution to allow teachers to perform employee organization business on a "release time" basis. The Attorney General found that such a program was unconstitutional because it "constitutes an unconditional grant of public funds to a private organization." Appellees urge that private teacher discussions during non-class time are comparable to the "release time" program.

The "release time" program is not at all comparable to private teacher conversations even though those conversations may be proselytizing. The "release time" program provided that teachers who would otherwise be teaching would be allowed to be absent from their teaching duties for a specified number of days to work for an employee organization at the school district's expense. Here, in contrast, the issue is the right of teachers to discuss matters relating to employee organizations at times when the teachers would not otherwise be required to teach, but would be "free to talk about whatever they want," including "the Cowboy game ... [or] what they did over the weekend." To allow teachers to speak favorably of an employee organization does not constitute an unlawful "grant of public funds to [the] organization," any more than to allow teachers to speak favorably of a political party, a church, a club, or a football team during the lunch hour constitutes an unlawful grant of public funds to such an organization.

Second, there is firm evidence indicating that officials might be inclined to enforce their policies against all teacher speech mentioning TSTA that occurs on school premises during the school day whether the teacher is in the classroom or not. Appellees' evidence in response demonstrates only that there is no active monitoring of teacher conversation. This evidence does not establish that officials would refrain from enforcing violations of which they became aware. For example, there is no indication that officials would not take at least some sort of disciplinary action against a teacher whose violation of Admin.Reg. 412 was reported to officials by another teacher.

Finally, the mere fact that this policy exists is sufficient to support appellants' cause of action. Even if no officials attempt to overhear teacher conversations, conscientious teachers should be expected to obey school regulations. The regulation inhibits the speech of law abiding teachers. Thus, even without actual monitoring of conversations, the rule chills teacher speech in violation of their First Amendment rights. *See Dombrowski v. Pfister*, 380 U.S. 479.

We hold that GISD policies which purport to deny teachers the right to discuss TSTA or TSTA business during non-class time are unconstitutional. Appellees have not demonstrated that such conversations result in a "material and substantial interference with the activities or discipline of the school."

2. Use of school media facilities

The primary purpose of GISD's internal mail system is to distribute official messages between school administrators and teachers and among the teachers themselves. GISD allows teachers to communicate with each other on any subject, including purely personal matters, except for subjects relating to employee organizations.

Appellees argue that prohibiting teacher communications as they relate to "employee organizations" is proper because it preserves the neutrality mandated by the Texas Education Code. As noted above, we find no merit to that contention. Teachers who have access to school media facilities for even purely personal matters cannot be prohibited from the exercise of that right simply because their internal speech may concern "employee organizations." We therefore hold that GISD policies preventing teachers from using school mail facilities to mention "employee organizations" are unconstitutional. So also are prohibitions against the use of whatever billboard facilities may be set aside for teachers' personal messages. No "material and substantial" disruption has been shown.

Conclusion

We affirm that part of the summary judgment which upholds Administrative Regulation 412's prohibition against visitation and use of school media by outside employee organization representatives during school hours. We reverse that part of the summary judgment which upholds Administrative Regulation 412's application to private teacher conversations and use of school media facilities by teachers employed in GISD schools as those media facilities are otherwise available to teachers for their personal messages. We grant appellants' motion for partial summary judgment holding the application of the Regulation to these activities unconstitutional.

Affirmed in part; *Reversed* in part; and *Remanded* for proceedings not inconsistent with this opinion.

---

1. For further discussion on First Amendment issues as they relate to teachers, *see* Chapter 10. For similar materials on student First Amendment protections, *see Tinker v. Des Moines Independent School District*, as cited by the *Garland* Court, and the rest of Chapter 6.

2. Note that the court labels Union officials as "outside representatives" and denies them access to the school's mail and bulletin board facilities and access to the school during school hours. What about the Union's "inside representatives" — the teachers? The court held the regulations on the teachers' speech — both private and public (via the school's media facilities) — unconstitutional. Is it possible for the Union to assign various teachers throughout the school district to the task of discussing Union activities and policies during school hours by way of the media facilities, and therefore, gain "access" to the school? Does the court say anything about this?

2. STATUTORY PROTECTIONS AND PUBLIC SECTOR BARGAINING

Almost in tandem with the growing judicial protection provided public school teachers and public employees in general when engaging in union-like activities was the growth of statutory enactments addressing public sector labor relations. Wisconsin enacted the first state legislation regulating public sector employment relations in 1959. The initial act was limited in coverage to municipal employees, but it initiated a new era in public sector unionism by statutorily recognizing public employees rights to join unions and rights of unions to represent their members in collective bargaining with public employers. Few states followed Wisconsin's lead in adopting public employment labor relations acts until the late 1960's, when pressure for recognition of state and local unions increased, due, in part, to Executive Order 10988, signed by President Kennedy in 1962, which allowed federal employees limited rights to join unions and bargain collectively. At the latest count 33 states have enacted collective bargaining statutes covering all or some occupational groups; in addition four others have by stature authorized bargaining for certain groups under various restricted circumstances, and the State of Illinois has extended the right of state employees to bargain by executive order. Thus, state laws now run the gamut from prohibitions of collective bargaining to comprehensive statutes specifying coverage, bargaining units, administration, scope of bargaining, impasse procedures, grievance procedures, and unfair practices. Even among those states that have comprehensive statutes the provisions and procedures vary widely. This patchwork of state collective bargaining laws has created a condition described by one observer as a "shameful hodgepodge designed largely to frustrate unionization and collective bargaining." *National Public Employment Relations Act, 1974: Hearing on S. 3295 and S. 3294 before the Subcomm. on Labor of the Senate Comm. on Labor and Public Welfare*, 93rd Cong., 2d Sess. 78, at 173 (statement of Jerry Wurf, President, AFSCME)....

Even with the enactment of public sector labor relations laws by various states the courts have continually been drawn into the bargaining process as arbiters and interpreters of legislative intent.

ABOOD v. DETROIT BOARD OF EDUCATION

Supreme Court of the United States
431 U.S. 209 (1977)

MR. JUSTICE STEWART delivered the opinion of the court:

[A Michigan statute authorizing union representation of local governmental employees permits an "agency shop" arrangement whereby every employee represented by a union, even though not a union member, must pay to the union, as a condition of employment, a service charge equal in amount to union dues. A group of teachers filed suit in Michigan State Court against the Detroit Board of Education and the Union officials challenging the validity of the agency shop clause in a collective bargaining agreement between the Board and the Union. In essence, the complaining teachers refused to pay union dues because they were opposed to collective bargaining in the public sector, and because they believed the Union was engaged in various political and other ideological activities that these particular teachers did not approve of that were not collective bargaining activities. The Michigan Court of Appeals upheld the constitutionality of the agency-shop clause, although reversing and remanding on other grounds.]

....

II

A

Consideration of the question whether an agency shop provision in a collective-bargaining agreement covering governmental employees is, as such, constitutionally valid must begin with two cases in this Court that on their face go far towards resolving the issue. The cases are *Railway Employee's Dep't v. Hanson*, 351 U.S. 225, and *International Ass'n of Machinists v. Street*, 367 U.S. 740.

[In *Hanson*, where the court was called upon to interpret the Railway Labor Act, the court held that "the requirement for financial support of the collective-bargaining agency by all who receive the benefit of its work ... does not violate ... the First Amendment."

Street, also, represented a challenge to the constitutionality of a union shop authorized by the Railway Labor Act. In *Street*, however, the record showed that some of the employee contributions were used to finance the campaigns of candidates for various elective offices. The court ruled "that the use of compulsory Union dues for political purposes violated the Act itself."]

The holding in *Hanson*, as elaborated in *Street*, reflects familiar doctrines in the federal labor laws. The principle of exclusive union representation, which underlies the National Labor Relations Act as well as the Railway Labor Act, is a central element in the congressional structuring of industrial relations. The designation of a single representative avoids the confusion that would result from attempting to enforce two or more agreements specifying different terms and conditions of employment. It prevents inter-union rivalries from creating dissension within the work force and eliminating the advantages to the employee of collectivization. It also frees the employer from the possibility of facing conflicting demands from different unions, and permits the employer and a single union to reach agreements and settlements that are not subject to attack from rival labor organizations.

The designation of a union as exclusive representative carries with it great responsibilities. The tasks of negotiating and administering a collective-bargaining agreement and representing the interests of employees in settling disputes and processing grievances are continuing and difficult ones. They often entail expenditure of much time and money. The services of lawyers, expert negotiators, economists, and a research staff, as well as general administrative personnel,

A. TEACHER COLLECTIVE BARGAINING

may be required. Moreover, in carrying out these duties, the union is obliged "fairly and equitably to represent all employees, ... union and nonunion," within the relevant unit. A union-shop arrangement has been thought to distribute fairly the cost of these activities among those who benefit, and it counteracts the incentive that employees might otherwise have to become "free riders" — to refuse to contribute to the union while obtaining benefits of union representation that necessarily accrue to all employees.

To compel employees financially to support their collective bargaining representative has an impact upon their First Amendment interests. An employee may very well have ideological objections to a wide variety of activities undertaken by the union in its role as exclusive representative. His moral or religious views about the desirability of abortion may not square with the union's policy in negotiating a medical benefits plan. One individual might disagree with a union policy of negotiating limits on the right to strike, believing that to be the road to serfdom for the working class, while another might have economic or political objections to unionism itself. An employee might object to the union's wage policy because it violates guidelines designed to limit inflation, or might object to union's seeking a clause in the collective-bargaining agreement proscribing racial discrimination. The examples could be multiplied. To be required to help finance the union as a collective-bargaining agent might well be thought, therefore, to interfere in some way with an employee's freedom to associate for the advancement of ideas, or to refrain from doing so, as he sees fit. But the judgment clearly made in *Hanson* and *Street* is that such interference as exists is constitutionally justified by the legislative assessment of the important contribution of the union shop to the system of labor relations established by Congress. "The furtherance of the common cause leaves some leeway for the leadership of the group. As long as they act to promote the cause which justified bringing the group together, the individual cannot withdraw his financial support merely because he disagrees with the group's strategy. If that were allowed, we would be reversing the *Hanson* case, *sub silentio*."

B

The National Labor Relations Act leaves regulation of labor relations of state and local governments to the States. *See* 29 U.S.C. § 152(2). Michigan has chosen to establish for local government units a regulatory scheme which, although not identical in every respect to the NLRA or RLA, is broadly modeled after federal law. Under Michigan law employees of local government units enjoy rights parallel to those protected under federal legislation: the rights to self-organization and to bargain collectively, Mich. Comp. Laws §§ 423.209, 423.215; *see* 29 U.S.C. § 157; 45 U.S.C. § 152, Fourth; and the right to secret ballot representation elections, Mich. Comp. Laws § 423.212; *see* 29 U.S.C. § 159(e)(1); 45 U.S.C. § 152, Ninth.

Several aspects of Michigan law that mirror provisions of the Railway Labor Act are of particular importance here. A union that obtains the support of a majority of employees in the appropriate bargaining unit is designated the exclusive representative of those employees. Mich.Comp.Law § 423.211. A union so designated is under a duty of fair representation to all employees in the unit, whether or not union members. And in carrying out all of its various responsibilities, a recognized union may seek to have an agency-shop clause included in a collective-bargaining agreement. Mich.Comp.Laws § 423.210(1)(c). Indeed, the 1973 amendment to the Michigan Law was specifically designed to authorize agency shops in order that "employees in the bargaining unit ... share fairly in the financial support of their exclusive bargaining representative...." *Id.*, § 423.210(2).

The governmental interests advanced by the agency shop provision in the Michigan statute are much the same as those promoted by similar provisions in federal labor law. The confusion and conflict that could arise if rival teachers' unions, holding quite different views as to the proper class hours, class sizes, holidays, tenure provisions, and grievance procedures, each sought to obtain the employer's agreement, are no different in kind from the evils that the exclusivity rule in the Railway Labor Act was designed to avoid. The desirability of labor peace is no less important in the public sector, nor is the risk of "free riders" any smaller.

Our province is not to judge the wisdom of Michigan's decision to authorize the agency shop in public employment. Rather, it is to adjudicate the constitutionality of that decision. The same important government interests recognized in the *Hanson* and *Street* cases presumptively support the impingement upon associational freedom created by the agency-shop here at issue. Thus, insofar as the service charge is used to finance expenditures by the union for the purposes of collective bargaining, contract administration, and grievance adjustment, those two decisions of this Court appear to require validation of the agency-shop agreement before us.

While recognizing the apparent precedential weight of the *Hanson* and *Street* cases, the appellants advance two reasons why those decisions should not control decision of the present case. First, the appellants note that it is *government* employment that is involved here, thus directly implicating constitutional guarantees, in contrast to the private employment that was the subject of *Hanson* and *Street* decisions. Second, the appellants say that in the public sector collective bargaining itself is inherently "political," and that to require them to give financial support to it is to require the "ideological conformity" that the Court expressly found absent in the *Hanson* case. We find neither argument persuasive.

Because it is employment by the State that is here involved, the appellants suggest that this case is governed by a long line of decisions holding that public employment cannot be conditioned upon the surrender of First Amendment rights. But, while the actions of public employers surely constitute "state action," the union shop, as authorized by the Railway Labor Act, also was found to result from governmental action in *Hanson*. The plaintiffs' claims in *Hanson* failed, not because there was no governmental action, but because there was no

A. TEACHER COLLECTIVE BARGAINING

First Amendment violation. The appellants' reliance on the "unconstitutional conditions" doctrine is therefore misplaced.

The appellants' second argument is that in any event collective bargaining in the public sector is inherently "political" and thus requires a different result under the First and Fourteenth Amendments. This contention rests upon the important and often-noted differences in the nature of collective bargaining in the public and private sectors. A public employer, unlike his private counterpart, is not guided by the profit motive and constrained by the normal operation of the market. Municipal services are typically not priced, and where they are they tend to be regarded as in some sense "essential" and therefore are often price inelastic. Although a public employer, like a private one, will wish to keep costs down, he lacks an important discipline against agreeing to increases in labor costs that in a market system would require price increases. A public sector union is correspondently less concerned that high prices due to costly wage demands will decrease output and hence employment.

The government officials making decisions as the public "employer" are less likely to act as a cohesive unit that are managers in private industry, in part because different levels of public authority — department managers, budgetary officials, and legislative bodies — are involved, and in part because each official may respond to a distinctive political constituency. And the ease of negotiating a final agreement with the union may be severely limited to statutory restrictions, by the need for the approval of a higher executive authority or a legislative body, or by the commitment of budgetary decisions of critical importance to others.

Finally, decision making by a public employer is above all a political process. The officials who represent the public employer are ultimately responsible to the electorate, which for this purpose can be viewed as comprising three overlapping classes of voters — taxpayers, users of particular government services, and government employees. Through exercise of their political influence as part of the electorate, the employees have the opportunity to affect the decisions of government representatives who sit on the other side of the bargaining table. Whether these representatives accede to a union's demands will depend upon a blend of political ingredients, including community sentiment about unionism generally and the involved union in particular, the degree of taxpayer resistance, and the views of voters as to the importance of the service involved and the relation between the demands and the quality of service. It is surely arguable, however, that permitting public employees to unionize and a union to bargain as their exclusive representative gives the employees more influence in the decision making process than is possessed by employees similarly organized in the private sector.

The distinctive nature of public-sector bargaining has led to widespread discussion about the extent to which the law governing labor relations in the private sector provides an appropriate model. To take but one example, there has been considerable debate about the desirability of prohibiting public employee unions from striking, a step that the State of Michigan itself has taken. But although Michigan has not adopted the federal model of labor relations in every respect, it has determined that labor stability will be served by a system of exclusive representation and the permissive use of an agency shop in public employment. As already stated, there can be no principled basis for according that decision less weight in the constitutional balance than was given in *Hanson* to the congressional judgment reflected in the Railway Labor Act. The only remaining constitutional inquiry evoked by the appellants' argument, therefore, is whether a public employee has a weightier First Amendment interest than a private employee in not being compelled to contribute to the costs of exclusive union representation. We think he does not.

Public employees are not basically different from private employees; on the whole, they have the same sort of skills, the same needs, and seek the same advantages. "The uniqueness of public employment is *not in the employees* nor in the work performed; the uniqueness is in the special character of the employer." The very real differences between exclusive agent collective bargaining in the public and private sectors are not such as to work any greater infringement upon the First Amendment interests of public employees. A public employee who believes that a union representing him is urging a course that is unwise as a matter of public policy is not barred from expressing his viewpoint. Besides voting in accordance with his convictions, every public employee is largely free to express his views, in public or private orally or in writing. With some exceptions not pertinent here, public employees are free to participate in the full range of political activities open to other citizens. Indeed, just this Term we have held that the First and Fourteenth Amendments protect the right of a public school teacher to oppose, at a public school board meeting, a position advanced by the teacher's union. In so ruling we recognized that the principle of exclusivity cannot constitutionally be used to muzzle a public employee who, like any other citizen, might wish to express his view about governmental decisions concerning labor relations.

There can be no quarrel with the truism that because public employee unions attempt to influence governmental policymaking, their activities — and the views of members who disagree with them — may be properly termed political. But that characterization does not raise the ideas and beliefs of public employees onto a higher plane than the ideas and beliefs of private employees. It is no doubt true that a central purpose of the First Amendment "was to protect the free discussion of governmental affairs." But our cases have never suggested that expression about philosophical, social, artistic, economic, literary, or ethical matters — to take a nonexhaustive list of labels — is not entitled to full First Amendment protection. Union members in both the public and private sector may find that a variety of union activities conflict with their beliefs. Nothing in the First Amendment or our cases discussing its meaning makes the question whether the adjective "political" can properly be attached to those beliefs the critical constitutional inquiry.

A. TEACHER COLLECTIVE BARGAINING

The differences between public and private sector collective bargaining simply do not translate into differences in First Amendment rights. Even those commentators most acutely aware of the distinctive nature of public-sector bargaining and most seriously concerned with its policy implications agree that "[t]he union security issue in the public sector ... is fundamentally the same issue ... as in the private sector.... No special dimension results from the fact that a union represents public rather than private employees." We conclude that the Michigan Court of Appeals was correct in viewing this Court's decisions in *Hanson* and *Street* as controlling in the present case insofar as the service charges are applied to collective bargaining, contract administration, and grievance adjustment purposes.

C

Because the Michigan Court of Appeals ruled that state law "sanctions the use of nonunion members' fees for purposes other than collective bargaining," and because the complaints allege that such expenditures were made, this case presents constitutional issues not decided in *Hanson* or *Street*. Indeed, *Street* embraced an interpretation of the Railway Labor Act not without its difficulties, precisely to avoid facing the constitutional issues presented by the use of union-shop dues for political and ideological purposes unrelated to collective bargaining. Since the state court's construction of the Michigan statute is authoritative, however, we must confront those issues in this case.

Our decisions establish with unmistakable clarity that the freedom of an individual to associate for the purpose of advancing beliefs and ideas is protected by the First and Fourteenth Amendments. Equally clear is the proposition that a government may not require an individual to relinquish rights guaranteed him by the First Amendment as a condition of public employment. The appellants argue that they fall within the protection of these cases because they have been prohibited not from actively associating, but rather from refusing to associate. They specifically argue that they may constitutionally prevent the Union's spending a part of their required service fees to contribute to political candidates and to express political views unrelated to its duties as exclusive bargaining representative. We have concluded that this argument is a meritorious one.

One of the principles underlying the Court's decision in *Buckley v. Valeo*, 424 U.S. 1, was that contributing to an organization for the purpose of spreading a political message is protected by the First Amendment. Because "[m]aking a contribution ... enables like-minded persons to pool their resources in furtherance of common political goals," the Court reasoned that limitations upon the freedom to contribute "implicate fundamental First Amendment interests."

The fact that the appellants are compelled to make, rather than prohibited from making, contributions for political purposes works no less an infringement of their constitutional rights. For at the heart of the First Amendment is the notion that an individual should be free to believe as he will, and that in a free society one's beliefs should be shaped by his mind and his conscience rather than coerced by the State. And the freedom of belief is no incidental or secondary aspect of the First Amendment's protections:

> If there is any fixed star in our constitutional constellation, it is that no official, high or petty, can prescribe what shall be orthodox in politics, nationalism, religion, or other matters of opinion or force citizens to confess by word or act their faith therein.

These principles prohibit a State from compelling any individual to affirm his belief in God, or to associate with a political party as a condition of retaining public employment. They are no less applicable to the case at bar, and they thus prohibit the appellees from requiring any of the appellants to contribute to the support of an ideological cause he may oppose as a condition of holding a job as a public school teacher.

We do not hold that a union cannot constitutionally spend funds for the expression of political views, on behalf of political candidates, or towards the advancement of other ideological causes not germane to its duties as collective bargaining representative. Rather, the Constitution requires only that such expenditures be financed from charges, dues, or assessments paid by employees who do not object to advancing those ideas and who are not coerced into doing so against their will by the threat of loss of governmental employment.

There will, of course, be difficult problems in drawing lines between collective bargaining activities, for which contributions may be compelled, and ideological activities unrelated to collective bargaining, for which such compulsion is prohibited. The Court held in *Street*, as a matter of statutory construction, that a similar line must be drawn under the Railway Labor Act, but in the public sector the line may be somewhat hazier. The process of establishing a written collective-bargaining agreement prescribing the terms and conditions of public employment may require not merely concord at the bargaining table, but subsequent approval by other public authorities; related budgetary and appropriations decisions might be seen as an integral part of the bargaining process. We have no occasion in this case, however, to try to define such a dividing line. The case comes to us after a judgment on the pleadings, and there is no evidentiary record of any kind. The allegations in the complaint are general ones, and the parties have neither briefed nor argued the question of what specific union activities in the present context properly fall under the definition of collective bargaining. The lack of factual concreteness and adversary presentation to aid us in approaching the difficult line-drawing questions highlight the importance of avoiding unnecessary decision of constitutional questions. All that we decide is that the general allegations in the complaint, if proven, establish a cause of action under the First and Fourteenth Amendments.

. . . .

[The court provided an extensive discussion of the appropriate remedies available to appellants in this case. It concluded that the Michigan Court of Appeals erred in holding that appellants were entitled to no relief. The court then concluded that several remedies such as enjoining the Union from expending the service charges for ideological causes posed by appellants, or ordering a refund of a portion of such charges, in the proportions such expenditures bear to the total Union expenditures, would be available. In this case, because the Union had in the interim adopted an internal Union remedy for dissenters the court ruled there may be no need for remedial relief.]

It is so ordered.

The concurring opinions of MR. JUSTICE REHNQUIST, MR. JUSTICE POWELL, and MR. JUSTICE STEVENS are deleted.

---

1. Many school boards reserve portions of their meetings for "public participation" or "visitor recognition," allowing visitors to speak to the board directly on current school and education issues. Should teachers be allowed to participate? What if they wish to speak on employment and union matters? It has been held that a school board may not selectively exclude certain issues (employment and labor relations); nor may it prevent teachers from commenting on issues subject to grievance and consultation procedures while other visitors are allowed to address the board on such matters. *See Princeton Educ. Ass'n v. Princeton Bd. of Educ.*, 480 F. Supp. 962 (S.D. Ohio 1979).

The United States Supreme Court decided similar issues in *City of Madison Joint Sch. Dist. No. 8 v. Wisconsin Emp. Relations Comm'n*, 429 U.S. 167 (1976). Two teachers, in response to a "fair share" clause in their collective bargaining agreement, sent opposition letters to all district teachers to gather support. They presented the results of this campaign at the board of education meeting. The board reserved part of each meeting for public participation. The teachers spoke for less than three minutes. The teachers union sued the school district, citing a violation of the rule which forbids the school board from "negotiating" with any party, other than the board, on collective bargaining issues. The Supreme Court of Wisconsin affirmed a ruling in favor of the union. The United States Supreme Court reversed, holding that the teachers who spoke at the public, open meeting were doing so as citizens, and were not seeking to "negotiate" with the board.

2. A key concept to collective bargaining in the American approach is the principle of exclusivity. This principle requires that a union which obtains the support of a majority of employees in any one bargaining unit becomes the exclusive representative of these employees. The purpose of this principle is to prevent the employer from being "whip-sawed" by various unions representing employees within the larger group and it allows employees to present one unified position. As a device to facilitate effective labor management relations, the exclusivity concept has undoubtedly been successful. Yet, as seen in both *Abood* and *City of Madison* there appears to be an inherent tension between this principle of effective bargaining and individual rights of public employees. Do the rulings in *Abood* and *City of Madison* leave the principle of exclusive representation basically intact or do they create exceptions which will, in the long run, significantly change bargaining patterns as parties attempt to reconcile individual rights and union needs? In *Abood* did the majority recognize an inherent distinction between the public and private sectors or did they find little difference between public and private employees? Of what significance to public educators, both as employees and as professionals, is the *Abood* approach to similarities and difference between public and private employees?

3. In *Abood* the Court rules that public employee unions may not spend forced contributions of non-members for political or social purposes with which those non-members disagree. In the public school setting how can a line separating permissible and impermissible uses of compulsory fees be drawn so as to insure that the teacher union can effectively carry out its collective bargaining function? Is not almost any expenditure made by a teacher union arguably connected in some way to its duties as a collective bargaining representative? And, at the same time, given the nature of public sector employment, are not most activities of public sector unions "political" in nature? For example, should it be prohibited to allow a teacher union to contribute compulsory dues monies to a political candidate who has pledged to work for laws favorable to teachers and public education?

Should this rule of "non-association" as developed in *Abood* extend only to political and social activities that are objectionable, or should those with religious or moral objections to certain union actions be allowed to divert their agency shop payments from union coffers?

4. In *City of Madison* does the Court address the issue of whether or not a state can designate certain conduct as "negotiation" and thus bring that conduct within the purview of the exclusivity principle as a predicate for restraining speech? Does the following language from the opinion put some parameters around the issue of what is negotiation?

> Holmquist did not seek to bargain or offer to enter into any bargain with the board, nor does it appear that he was authorized by any other teachers to enter into any agreement on their behalf. Although his views were not consistent with those of MTI, communicating such views to the employer could not change the fact that MTI alone was authorized to negotiate and to enter into contract with the board. *Madison*, at 179.

5. One of the most recent Supreme Court decisions regarding teacher collective bargaining came in the highly divided opinion in *Lehnert v. Ferris Faculty Ass'n*, 111 S. Ct. 1950 (1991). In *Lehnert*, dissenting employees brought action against college faculty bargaining representatives claiming that collection and use of service fees in agency shop violated their First and Fourteenth Amendment rights. Justice Blackmun wrote the opinion for the Court, but was joined only by Justices Rehnquist, Stevens, and White in his entire opinion. The majority

A. TEACHER COLLECTIVE BARGAINING

opinion in *Lehnert* declared that, while a "case-by-case analysis" is warranted when "determining which activities a union constitutionally may charge to dissenting employees," several guidelines may be applied to make such determinations. *Id.* at 1959. *See also* Siemer, Lehnert v. Ferris Faculty Association: *Accounting to Financial Core Members: Much A-Dues About Nothing*, 60 Fordham L. Rev. 1057 (1992).

Under Justice Blackmun's opinion, chargeable activities must: (1) be germane to collective bargaining activity; (2) be justified by the government's vital policy interest in labor peace and avoiding "free riders"; and (3) not significantly add to the burdening of free speech that is inherent in the allowance of an agency or union shop. *Lenhert*, at 1959.

Siemer's response to the *Lehnert* decision and Blackmun's application of the facts to the new three-prong test is as follows:

> ... Applying this formula to the facts in *Lehnert*, the majority concluded that political lobbying, public relation activities, and expenses of an illegal strike were nonchargeable. On the other hand, and with little logical consistency, the Court sustained as chargeable any expenses related to conventions, strike preparation, and portions of union obligations dealing with the nonmember's occupation or industry generally.

In addition to Justice Blackmun's opinion (joined by Justices Rehnquist, Stevens, and White), Justice Marshall concurred in part and dissented in part, and Justice Scalia concurred in part in the judgement and dissented in part. Justice Scalia's opinion was joined in by Justices O'Connor and Souter, and by Justice Kennedy in part. Justice Kennedy filed a separate opinion, concurring with Justice Scalia in part, and dissenting in part. Siemer summarized the opinion in the following table.*

---

*Copyright © 1988 by Foundation Press, Inc. Reprinted with permission.

LEHNERT PRINCIPLES	MAJORITY	DISSENT
Formula Chargeable activities must: (1) Be germane to collective bargaining activity (2) Be justified by govt.'s vital policy interest in labor peace and avoiding "free riders" (3) Not significantly add to burdening of free speech	Blackmun, Rehnquist, White, Stevens, Marshall	Scalia, O'Connor, Souter, Kennedy **Formula** Chargeable activities must be incurred in performance of union's statutory duties
Chargeable Activities 1. Lobbying for contract ratification 2. Pro-rata share of chargeable activities of state and national affiliates 3. De minimis costs of career support services and information 4. Costs of sending delegates to national union conventions 5. Strike preparation costs, even for potentially illegal strike	Blackmun, Rehnquist, White, Stevens, Marshall All Blackmun, Rehnquist, White, Stevens, Marshall Blackmun, Rehnquist, White, Stevens, Marshall Blackmun, Rehnquist, White, Stevens, Marshall, Kennedy	 Scalia, O'Connor, Souter, Kennedy Scalia, O'Connor, Souter, Kennedy Scalia, O'Connor, Souter
Nonchargeable Activities 1. Political lobbying outside the context of contract ratification 2. Public relations campaign 3. Expenses of an illegal strike 4. Organization or other costs to promote unionism generally	All except Marshall All except Marshall All All except Marshall	Marshall Marshall Marshall

Note: The justice first listed wrote the relevant opinion.

A. TEACHER COLLECTIVE BARGAINING

CHICAGO TEACHERS UNION, LOCAL NO. 1, AFT, AFL-CIO v. HUDSON
Supreme Court of the United States
475 U.S. 292 (1986)

JUSTICE STEVENS delivered the opinion to the court:

In *Abood v. Detroit Board of Education*, 431 U.S. 209 (1977), "we found no constitutional barrier to an agency shop agreement between a municipality and a teacher's union insofar as the agreement required every employee in the unit to pay a service fee to defray the costs of collective bargaining, contract administration, and grievance adjustment. The union, however, could not, consistently with the Constitution, collect from dissenting employees any sums for the support of ideological causes not germane to its duties as collective-bargaining agent." The [*Abood*] case was primarily concerned with the need "to define the line between union expenditures that all employees must help defray and those that are not sufficiently related to collective bargaining to justify their being imposed on dissenters." In contrast, this case concerns the constitutionality of the procedure adopted by the Chicago Teachers Union, with the approval of the Chicago Board of Education, to draw that necessary line and to respond to nonmembers' objections to the manner in which it was drawn.

I

The Chicago Teachers Union has acted as the exclusive collective-bargaining representative of the Board's educational employees continuously since 1967. Approximately 95% of the 27,500 employees in the bargaining unit are members of the Union. Until December 1982, the Union members' dues financed the entire cost of the Union's collective bargaining and contract administration. Nonmembers received the benefits of the Union's representation without making any financial contribution to its cost.

In an attempt to solve this "free rider" problem, the Union made several proposals for a "fair share fee" clause in the labor contract. Because the Illinois School Code did not expressly authorize such a provision, the Board rejected these proposals until the Illinois General Assembly amended the School Code in 1981. In the following year, the Chicago Teachers Union and the Chicago Board of Education [pursuant to the statute] entered into an agreement requiring the Board to deduct "proportionate share payments" from the paychecks of nonmembers. The new contractual provision authorized the Union to specify the amount of the payment; it stipulated that the amount could not exceed the members' dues. The contractual provision also required the Union to indemnify the Board for all action taken to implement the new provision.

For the 1982-1983 school year, the Union determined that the "proportionate share" assessed on nonmembers was 95% of union dues. At that time, the union dues were $17.35 per month for teachers and $12.15 per month for other covered employees; the corresponding deduction from the nonmembers' checks thus amounted to $16.48 and $11.54 for each of the 10 months that dues were payable.

....

The Union also established a procedure for considering objections by nonmembers. Before the deduction was made, the nonmember could not raise any objection. After the deduction was made, a nonmember could object to the "proportionate share" figure by writing to the Union President within 30 days after the first payroll deduction. The objection then would meet a three-stage procedure. First, the Union's Executive Committee would consider the objection and notify the objector within 30 days of its decision. Second, if the objector disagreed with that decision and appealed within another 30 days, the Union's Executive Board would consider the objection. Third, if the objector continued to protest after the Executive Board decision, the Union President would select an arbitrator from a list maintained by the Illinois Board of Education. The Union would pay for the arbitration, and, if there were multiple objections, they could be consolidated. If an objection was sustained at any stage of the procedure, the remedy would be an immediate reduction in the amount of future deductions for all nonmembers and a rebate for the objector.

In October 1982, the Union formally requested the Board to begin making deductions and advised it that a hearing procedure had been established for nonmembers' objections. The Board accepted the Union's 95% determination without questioning its method of calculation and without asking to review any of the records supporting it. The Board began to deduct the fee from the paychecks of nonmembers in December 1982. The Board did not provide the nonmembers with any explanation of the calculation, or of the Union's procedures. The Union did undertake certain informational efforts. It asked its member delegates at all schools to distribute flyers, display posters, inform nonmembers of the deductions, and invite nonmembers to join the Union with an amnesty for past fines. It also described the deduction and the protest procedures in the December issue of the Union newspaper, which was distributed to nonmembers.

Three nonmembers — Annie Lee Hudson, K. Celeste Campbell, and Walter Sherrills — sent identical letters of protest to the Union stating that they believed the Union was using part of their salary for purposes unrelated to collective bargaining and demanding that the deduction be reduced. A fourth nonmember — Beverly Underwood — objected to any deduction from her paycheck. The Union's response to each of the four briefly explained how the proportionate-share fee had been calculated, described the objection procedure, enclosed a copy of the Union Implementation Plan, and concluded with the advice that "any objection you may file" would be processed in compliance with that procedure. None of the letters was referred to the Executive Committee. Only Hudson wrote a second letter; her request for detailed financial information was answered with an invitation to make an appointment for an "informational conference" at the Union's office, at which she could review the Union's financial records. The four

A. TEACHER COLLECTIVE BARGAINING

nonmembers made no further effort to invoke the Union procedures; instead, they challenged the new procedure in court.

II

In March 1983, the four nonmembers, joined by three other nonmembers who had not sent any letters, filed suit in Federal District Court, naming as defendants, the Union, its officials, the Board, and the Board members. They objected to the Union procedure for three principal reasons: it violated their First Amendment rights to freedom of expression and association; it violated their Fourteenth Amendment due process rights; and it permitted the use of their proportionate shares for impermissible purposes.

The District Court rejected the challenges....

....

The Court of Appeals was unanimous in its judgment reversing the District Court. 743 F.2d 1187 (CA7 1984). All three judges agreed that the Constitution requires the Union to follow a procedure that protects the nonmembers from being compelled to subsidize political or ideological activities not germane to the collective-bargaining process, that the Union's objection procedure was inadequate, and that any rebate which allowed the Union temporary use of money for activities that violate the nonmembers' rights was unconstitutional....

....

III

In *Abood v. Detroit Board of Education*, 431 U.S. 209 (1977), we recognized that requiring nonunion employees to support their collective-bargaining representative "has an impact upon their First Amendment interests," and may well "interfere in some way with an employee's freedom to associate for the advancement of ideas, or to refrain from doing so, as he sees fit." We nevertheless rejected the claim that it was unconstitutional for a public employer to designate a union as the exclusive collective-bargaining representative of its employees, and to require nonunion employees, as a condition of employment, to pay a fair share of the union's cost of negotiating and administering a collective-bargaining agreement. We also held, however, that nonunion employees do have a constitutional right to "prevent the Union's spending a part of their required service fees to contribute to political candidates and to express political views unrelated to its duties as exclusive bargaining representative."

The question presented in this case is whether the procedure used by the Chicago Teachers Union and approved by the Chicago Board of Education adequately protects the basic distinction drawn in *Abood*. "[T]he objective must be to devise a way of preventing compulsory subsidization of ideological activity by employees who object thereto without restricting the Union's ability to require every employee to contribute to the cost of collective-bargaining activities."

Procedural safeguards are necessary to achieve this objective for two reasons. First, although the government interest in labor peace is strong enough to support an "agency shop" notwithstanding its limited infringement on nonunion employees' constitutional rights, the fact that those rights are protected by the First Amendment requires that the procedure be carefully tailored to minimize the infringement. Second, the nonunion employee — the individual whose First Amendment rights are being affected — must have a fair opportunity to identify the impact of the governmental action on his interests and to assert a meritorious First Amendment claim.

In *Ellis v. Railway Clerks*, 466 U.S., [435,] 443 (1984), we determined that, under the Railway Labor Act, a "pure rebate approach is inadequate." We explained that, under such an approach, in which the union refunds to the nonunion employee any money to which the union was not entitled, "the union obtains an involuntary loan for purposes to which the employee objects." We noted the possibility of "readily available alternatives, such as advance reduction of dues and/or interest-bearing escrow accounts," but, for purposes of that case, it was sufficient to strike down the rebate procedure.

In this case, we must determine whether the challenged Chicago Teachers Union procedure survives First Amendment scrutiny, either because the procedure upheld by the District Court was constitutionally sufficient, or because the subsequent adoption of an escrow arrangement cured any constitutional defect. We consider these questions in turn.

IV

The procedure that was initially adopted by the Union and considered by the District Court contained three fundamental flaws. First, as in *Ellis*, a remedy which merely offers dissenters the possibility of a rebate does not avoid the risk that dissenters' funds may be used temporarily for an improper purpose. "[T]he Union should not be permitted to exact a service fee from nonmembers without first establishing a procedure which will avoid the risk that their funds will be used, even temporarily, to finance ideological activities unrelated to collective bargaining." The amount at stake for each individual dissenter does not diminish this concern. For, whatever the amount, the quality of respondents' interest in not being compelled to subsidize the propagation of political or ideological views that they oppose is clear. In *Abood*, we emphasized this point by quoting the comments of Thomas Jefferson and James Madison about the tyrannical character of forcing an individual to contribute even "three pence" for the "propagation of opinions which he disbelieves". A forced exaction followed by a rebate equal to the amount improperly expended is thus not a permissible response to the nonunion employees' objections.

Second, the "advance reduction of dues" was inadequate because it provided nonmembers with inadequate information about the basis for the proportionate share. In *Abood*, we reiterated that the nonunion employee has the burden of raising an objection, but that the union retains the burden of proof: "'Since the unions possess the facts and records from which the proportion of political to total union expenditures can reasonably be calculated, basic considerations of

A. TEACHER COLLECTIVE BARGAINING

fairness compel that they, not the individual employees, bear the burden of proving such proportion'." Basic considerations of fairness, as well as concern for the First Amendment rights at stake, also dictate that the potential objectors be given sufficient information to gauge the propriety of the union's fee. Leaving the nonunion employees in the dark about the source of the figure for the agency fee — and requiring them to object in order to receive information — does not adequately protect the careful distinctions drawn in *Abood*.

In this case, the original information given to the nonunion employees was inadequate. Instead of identifying the expenditures for collective bargaining and contract administration that had been provided for the benefit of nonmembers as well as members — and for which nonmembers as well as members can fairly be charged a fee — the Union identified the amount that it admittedly had expended for purposes that did not benefit dissenting nonmembers. An acknowledgment that nonmembers would not be required to pay any part of 5% of the Union's total annual expenditures was not an adequate disclosure of the reasons why they were required to pay their share of 95%.

Finally, the original Union procedure was also defective because it did not provide for a reasonably prompt decision by an impartial decisionmaker. Although we have not so specified in the past, we now conclude that such a requirement is necessary. The nonunion employee, whose First Amendment rights are affected by the agency shop itself and who bears the burden of objecting, is entitled to have his objections addressed in an expeditious, fair, and objective manner.

The Union's procedure does not meet this requirement. As the Seventh Circuit observed, the "most conspicuous feature of the procedure is that from start to finish it is entirely controlled by the union, which is an interested party, since it is the recipient of the agency fees paid by the dissenting employees." The initial consideration of the agency fee is made by Union officials, and the first two steps of the review procedure (the Union Executive Committee and Executive Board) consist of Union officials. The third step — review by a Union-selected arbitrator — is also inadequate because the selection represents the Union's unrestricted choice from the state list.

Thus, the original Union procedure was inadequate because it failed to minimize the risk that nonunion employees' contributions might be used for impermissible purposes, because it failed to provide adequate justification for the advance reduction of dues, and because it failed to offer a reasonably prompt decision by an impartial decisionmaker.

V

The Union has not only created an escrow of 100% of the contributions exacted from the respondents, but has also advised us that it would not object to the entry of a judgment compelling it to maintain an escrow system in the future. The Union does not contend that its escrow has made the case moot. Rather, it takes the position that because a 100% escrow completely avoids the risk that dissenters' contributions could be used improperly, it eliminates any valid constitutional objection to the procedure and thereby provides an adequate remedy in this case. We reject this argument.

Although the Union's self-imposed remedy eliminates the risk that nonunion employees' contributions may be temporarily used for impermissible purposes, the procedure remains flawed in two respects. It does not provide an adequate explanation for the advance reduction of dues, and it does not provide a reasonably prompt decision by an impartial decisionmaker. We reiterate that these characteristics are required because the agency shop itself impinges on the nonunion employees' First Amendment interests, and because the nonunion employee has the burden of objection. The appropriately justified advance reduction and the prompt, impartial decisionmaker are necessary to minimize both the impingement and the burden.

....

Thus, the Union's 100% escrow does not cure all of the problems in the original procedure. Two of the three flaws remain, and the procedure therefore continues to provide less than the Constitution requires in this context.

VI

We hold today that the constitutional requirements for the Union's collection of agency fees include an adequate explanation of the basis for the fee, a reasonably prompt opportunity to challenge the amount of the fee before an impartial decisionmaker, and an escrow for the amounts reasonably in dispute while such challenges are pending.

The determination of the appropriate remedy in this case is a matter that should be addressed in the first instance by the District Court. The Court of Appeals correctly reversed the District Court's original judgment and remanded the case for further proceedings. That judgment of reversal is affirmed, and those further proceedings should be consistent with this opinion.

It is so ordered.

....

---

1. In *Hudson*, The Chicago Teachers Union determined that only 5% of the Union dues went to activities other than collective bargaining and contract administration. Hence, it determined that 95% of the fee was the "fair share" to be paid by non-members. In 1990, the Ninth Circuit required teachers associations to reduce the amount of agency shop fees collected by the amount of its ideological expenditures before collection. In addition, the court required the union to give notice and adequate information concerning these fees before they could be deducted from employees' paychecks. *See Grunwald v. San Bernardino Teachers Ass'n*, 917 F.2d 1223 (9th Cir. 1990).

A. TEACHER COLLECTIVE BARGAINING

2. In *Lowary v. Lexington Bd. of Educ.*, 903 F.2d 422 (6th Cir. 1990), the court held, similarly to *Grunwald*, that non-union members did not have to pay that portion of union fees which were allocated to ideological activities. Teachers were entitled to recover the "nonchargeable" portion of the collected fees. The court struck down the union's collection procedures, finding that the "local union presumption" for determining the percentage of expenditures chargeable to nonmembers was unconstitutional.

3. The *Hudson* court also decided that a 100% escrow was not constitutionally required for the collection procedures to be proper. The Court reasoned that while disputes are pending, a 100% escrow would deprive the union of funds to which it is rightfully entitled. This indicates that escrow accounts are permissible. What is the notice requirement associated with the use of escrow accounts in the collection of union fees? One possible answer is found in *Jerabek v. Public Emp. Relations Bd.*, 2 Cal. App. 4th 1298, 4 Cal. Rptr. 2d 181 (1992). In that case, the court upheld a "concurrent notice with escrow" provision, in which the union collected agency fees from non-members and placed the entire amount into escrow. At no time did the union have access to these fees for political and ideological activities. This procedure was held to comply with the First and Fourteenth Amendment rights of the teachers. No advance notice was required, and the nonmembers' loss of the use of the fund in escrow did not automatically violate the First Amendment.

4. Another possible collection procedure is an "opt-out" provision. The Ninth Circuit, in *Mitchell v. Los Angeles Unified Sch. Dist.*, 963 F.2d 258 (9th Cir. 1992), upheld such a plan which gave dissenting non-union employees the opportunity to object to full agency fees without a violation of their First Amendment rights.

It is fairly clear that full agency fees may not be deducted from the paychecks of dissenting employees. What about those employees who say nothing? Is affirmative consent required before full dues may be deducted? The court in *Mitchell* held that the First Amendment does not require affirmative consent.

5. If a non-union employee asks to see the figures associated with the determination of the non-member percentage fee (*i.e.*, 95% in *Hudson*), how much detail is required? The Sixth Circuit in *Gwirtz v. Ohio Educ. Ass'n*, 887 F.2d 678 (6th Cir. 1989), held that the highest level of auditing service is not required when disclosing the "fair share" data to non-union employees.

6. *Hudson* allows non-union employees to challenge the amount of the agency fee, and requires an impartial decisionmaker for the hearing. In a related case, members of the Florida Bar Association challenged a bar rule allowing compulsory bar dues to fund political lobbying. An amended rule provided for refunds of objecting members' dues. However, the court held that the fact that the arbitration panel which hears objectors' claims is composed of bar members does not taint the arbitration proceeding. *Gibson v. Florida Bar*, 906 F.2d 624 (11th Cir. 1990).

A teachers' union plan which calls for the American Arbitration Association to arbitrate fee disputes is sufficient to provide non-union members with a fair and impartial decision maker, as required in *Hudson*. *See Andrews v. Educational Ass'n of Cheshire*, 829 F.2d 335 (2d Cir. 1987).

DAVIS v. HENRY

Supreme Court of Louisiana
555 So. 2d 457 (1990)

DIXON, CHIEF JUSTICE:

At issue is whether, under Louisiana law, teachers and other school personnel who are public employees fall within the purview of the "Little Norris-LaGuardia Act" and therefore have the right to engage in a strike in support of their demand for collective bargaining.

On October 18, 1989, approximately seven hundred fifty teachers and two hundred fifty bus drivers, cafeteria workers and janitors employed by the Terrebonne Parish School Board went on strike and began to picket school board property. Various issues concerning wages, hours and working conditions are in dispute, and a stalemate has been reached over the question of whether collective bargaining will take place. The striking employees have said they will not return to work without accommodation on this question, while the school board is apparently firm in its resolve not to recognize the employees' union, the Terrebonne Parish Association of Educators, and not to engage in collective bargaining.

Despite the fact that this strike has now lasted longer than any other in Louisiana history, the board has managed to keep the schools open, using non-striking and replacement personnel. School attendance, which normally runs at 94 to 96%, declined at the beginning of the strike to 29%, then later rose to around 63% after school officials sent parents a letter encouraging them to send their children to school. The trial court found "no meaningful instruction" was being given to a large percentage of the students who do attend. On the other hand, both the school board president and the school superintendent have testified that all statutory minimums pertaining to the delivery of education are being met. The board complains that special classes, including those for the gifted and handicapped, and drug abuse and suicide prevention programs are not being offered. They conceded they have applied for waivers so that government funding will not be revoked for lack of compliance with established requirements but assert that they will be without funds to make up the days missed due to the strike.

After a November 3, 1989 board resolution stating no punitive action would be taken if the striking employees returned to work by November 6, the union representative filed a class action suit, seeking monetary damages and an injunction prohibiting the board from firing any of the employees who are on strike. The board then filed a reconventional demand, seeking a declaratory judg-

A. TEACHER COLLECTIVE BARGAINING

ment that the strike is illegal and asking for injunctive relief, barring the employees from engaging in a concerted work stoppage, from picketing school property and from encouraging other employees to participate in the strike. In support of its request for an injunction, the board argues that public employee strikes are per se illegal and that the strike is causing irreparable injury to the district's approximately twenty-one thousand students. The employees, on the other hand, claim they are engaged in lawfully protected activity, the exercise of which the board can not enjoin.

... After a hearing in the matter, the district court denied relief to both parties, finding in the absence of statutory prohibition, the strike is legal and hence not enjoinable....

....

The court of appeal ... reversed and ordered the trial court to grant the injunctive relief sought by the board. After hearing oral argument, we summarily reversed the court of appeal's judgment ... and now issue reasons for having done so.

....

Analysis

In the early part of this century, neither public nor private employees had the right to strike in concert with their fellow workers, such actions being viewed as conspiracy and subject to criminal and civil sanctions. Today, the right to strike is generally recognized as indispensable to the system of collective bargaining and negotiation. Nevertheless, public sector strikes have been treated differently from those of the private sector. Strikes against the federal government are still treated as illegal, while strikes against state and local government have been accepted in only some jurisdictions.

With the decline of the common law rule that concerted action by employees against their employer was illegal and probably criminal, Congress attempted as early as 1914 to limit jurisdiction of the federal courts in labor disputes. Nevertheless, the courts continued to issue labor injunctions. The Norris-LaGuardia Act, enacted in 1932, "was a direct response to judicial encroachment on the national policy which favored the protection of the right of labor unions to function free of governmental interference." Since passage of that act, federal courts have been restrained in issuing injunctions by the requirement that specific findings of fact must be made before issuance of either a temporary or permanent injunction in a labor dispute.

In 1934, Louisiana enacted its own anti-injunction statute, R.S. 23:821-24, 23:841-49. Patterned after the federal statute, such state anti-injunction statutes are commonly called "Little Norris-LaGuardia Acts." Some jurisdictions specifically excluded the state and its employees from operation of their statute; hence issuance of injunctions against striking public employees in those jurisdictions is permitted upon a showing of irreparable harm. The Louisiana legislature, on the other hand, did not exclude the state, its agencies and political subdivisions when it declared public policy in regard to the freedom of laborers to organize:

> Negotiation of terms and conditions of labor should result from voluntary agreement between employer and employee. Governmental authority has permitted and encouraged employers to organize in the corporate and other forms of capital control. In dealing with such employers the individual unorganized worker is helpless to exercise actual liberty of contract and to protect his freedom of labor, and thereby to obtain acceptable terms and conditions of employment. Therefore, it is necessary that the individual workman have full freedom of association, self-organization, and designation of representatives of his own choosing, to negotiate the terms and conditions of his employment, and that he shall be free from the interference, restraint, or coercion of employers of labor, or their agents, in the designation of representatives or in self-organization or in other concerted activities for the purpose of collective bargaining or other mutual aid or protection.

This provision shows a clear legislative intent to protect all employees in the exercise of their right to engage in concerted activities.

These policy statements, favoring the freedom of employees to organize and collectively bargain with their employer, could only be effectuated if the courts' ability to interfere in labor disputes was curtailed. Thus it has been provided that no injunction shall be issued against employees engaged in concerted activities.

....

... [T]he statute provides that all persons are entitled to engage in activities, such as peaceful picketing, refusing to perform work, becoming a member of a union, assembling peaceably to organize, communicating with others in regard to a labor dispute, and encouraging others to do these acts, without fear that they are in violation of the law.

The legislature recognized that sweeping injunctive relief is "peculiarly subject to abuse in labor litigation...." Hence the court's authority to grant either temporary or permanent injunctive relief in a labor dispute is limited to situations in which it has made factual findings in six specific areas. This statute, which is the heart of the "Little Norris-LaGuardia Act," provides:

> No court shall issue a temporary or permanent injunction in any case involving or growing out of a labor dispute, as herein defined, except after hearing the testimony of witnesses in open court, with opportunity for cross-examination, in support of the allegations of a complaint made under oath, and testimony in opposition thereto, if offered, and except after findings of fact by the court to the effect:
>
> > (1) That unlawful acts have been threatened or committed and will be executed or continued unless restrained;

A. TEACHER COLLECTIVE BARGAINING

> (2) That substantial and irreparable injury to complainant's property will follow unless the relief requested is granted;
>
> (3) That as to each item of relief granted greater injury will be inflicted upon complainant by the denial thereof than will be inflicted upon the defendants by the granting thereof;
>
> (4) That no item of relief granted is relief that a court has no authority to restrain or enjoin under R.S. 23:841;
>
> (5) That complainant has no adequate remedy by ordinary legal procedure; and
>
> (6) That the public officers charged with the duty to protect complainant's property have failed or are unable to furnish adequate protection...."

By placing a heavy burden on the complainant, the drafters showed their intent to make it difficult to obtain a labor injunction in Louisiana.

The school board concedes no Louisiana statute prohibits its employees from striking but contends such strikes are illegal under the common law. An analysis of our jurisprudence demonstrates that public employees possess such a right, with an exception being made for strikes which clearly endanger the public health and safety. Only the decision in *Town of New Roads v. Dukes*, 312 So.2d 890 (La.App. 1st Cir. 1975), held to the contrary. It is this decision upon which the school board bases its argument and upon which the court of appeal relied in ruling that the Terrebonne Parish School Board is entitled to an injunction. *Dukes*, in essence, held that the failure of the "Little Norris-LaGuardia Act" to expressly include the state and its employees signifies a lack of intent that the statute apply to the state. This holding is an aberration in our law and, for reasons which follow, we find the decision was in error and is hereby overruled.

Prior to the enactment of the 1974 Constitution, it was unclear whether public employees in Louisiana were entitled to organize....

....

... [T]he new Constitution took effect on December 31, 1974. Any doubt as to whether public employees in Louisiana were free to organize was removed by this provision:

> (3) ... No rule, regulation, or practice of the [Civil Service] commission, of any agency or department, or of any official of the state or any political subdivision shall favor or discriminate against any applicant or employee because of his membership or non-membership in any private organization; but this shall not prohibit any state agency, department, or political subdivision from contracting with an employee organization with respect to wages, hours, grievances, working conditions, or other conditions of employment in a manner not inconsistent with this constitution, a civil service law, or a valid rule or regulation of a commission.

This provision establishes that, as part of the state's labor policy, public employees are protected from discrimination because of their relationship with a labor organization. Likewise, the provision makes clear that state agencies and political subdivisions are free to bargain with employee organizations. Thus, with the passage of this provision, public employees became constitutionally entitled to the same right to engage in collective bargaining as held by their counterparts in the private sector. The constitutional provision took effect shortly before *Dukes* was handed down.

Yet another policy statement involving the rights of labor was made by the legislature in 1976, with enactment of the "Right to Work" law, which provides: "It is hereby declared to be the public policy of Louisiana that all persons shall have, and shall be protected in the exercise of the right, freely and without fear of penalty or reprisal, to form, join and assist labor organizations or to refrain from any such activities."

....

Another judicial contribution to public employee law was *City of New Orleans v. Police Association of Louisiana, Teamsters Local No. 253*, 369 So.2d 188 (La.App. 4th Cir. 1979), where the court ruled that police strikes are illegal....

....

The decision in *City of New Orleans v. Police Association of Louisiana*, while holding at least some public employee strikes are illegal, demonstrates an unwillingness to uniformly deny public employees the right to strike. As the court noted, the difference between a strike by police and by museum employees is obvious. "Society can tolerate the temporary closing of a museum, but not the suspension of law."

In decisions by this court, the legality of public employee strikes has been only peripherally at issue....

... [R]ecently, two decisions involving Louisiana teacher strikes addressed other issues but, significantly, did not raise the question of the legality of the strikes. In *St. John the Baptist Parish Association of Educators v. Brown*, 465 So.2d 674 (La.1985), school board officials were faced with a group of employees seeking, as are the plaintiffs here, collective bargaining. After a forty day work stoppage, the board and its employee teachers agreed to end the strike by entering an agreement whereby the question of whether collective bargaining would take place would be submitted to the voters. When the Secretary of State refused to place a referendum to this effect on the ballot, the school employees filed suit against the state. The lower courts ordered the secretary to place the issue on the ballot and the state appealed. This court ruled that a school board has no authority, either under the statutes or the constitution, to refer a decision to the electorate, and restated the rule that a school board has "the authority, with or without popular approval, to bargain collectively with its teachers." 465 So.2d at 677-78. For our purposes, the significance of the decision lies in the fact that the legality of the strike was apparently not at issue.

Neither was the question of legality addressed in *St. John the Baptist Parish Association of Educators v. St. John the Baptist Parish School Board*, 494 So.2d 553 (La.App. 5th Cir. 1986). In that case, teachers had been involved in a strike

A. TEACHER COLLECTIVE BARGAINING

which lasted from August until late October of 1984. As part of the strike settlement agreement reached by the board and the striking employees, a promise of fair treatment and no reprisals for participation in the strike was made. The board also agreed that if post-strike reduction in force became necessary, replacement teachers hired during the strike would be laid off first, while further layoffs would be made on the basis of seniority. These provisions became part of the contract accepted by the teachers in settlement of the strike. A few months later, when layoffs became necessary, the board adopted a revised schedule of layoff priority, penalizing those who struck by awarding "super-seniority" to nonstriking employees despite its earlier commitment. The court of appeal required the board to abide by the layoff agreement incorporated into the contract it had entered in ending the strike. We again find it significant that, as with the earlier *St. John the Baptist Parish* decision, the court of appeal never suggested the strike was illegal. Instead the court summarily found the teachers, who had been on strike for nearly two months, had been "engaged in a lawful strike and work stoppage...."

As these decisions and the Constitution and statutes show, with the exception of strikes by police and the contrary holding in *Dukes*, strikes by public employees in Louisiana have customarily been treated as legal. We disagree with *Dukes'* assertion that the legislature has been silent on this question, but rather find under our law an intent to afford public employees a system of organizational rights which parallels that afforded to employees in the private sector. The specter of strike, with its attendant hardships, can provide impetus for parties to agree at the bargaining table; hence the credible threat of strike may serve to avert, rather than encourage work stoppages.

. . . .

The *Dukes* court followed the reasoning of *United States v. United Mine Workers of America*[, 330 U.S. 258 (1947)]. *U.M.W.*, decided in 1947, was a contempt proceeding against John L. Lewis and the United Mine Workers. Pursuant to his wartime powers, the President had seized the coal mines; the work terms of the miners, who until then had been private employees, was thereafter controlled by an agreement entered into by the government and Lewis, on behalf of the miners. A dispute over a wage agreement later arose. When negotiations did not produce a settlement, Lewis gave unilateral notice that he was terminating the agreement. The United States sought a declaratory judgment, alleging the notice of termination was essentially a strike notice, and asked for injunctive relief. Without notice, a temporary restraining order was issued. The miners walked out, and the United States filed a rule for contempt. The defendant miners filed a motion challenging the jurisdiction of the court, arguing the Norris-LaGuardia Act deprived the court of jurisdiction. This motion was denied and the defendants were found guilty. The Supreme Court took the case on certiorari, believing prompt settlement was in the national interest.

Justice Vinson's plurality opinion was joined by two other justices (Reed and Burton). Justices Black and Douglas joined in holding that neither the Clayton

Act nor the Norris-LaGuardia Act withdrew from the government, in a dispute with its own employees, the right to employ injunctions as a remedy, and that the district court retained jurisdiction of the case. In part, the decision was based upon the rule cited in *Dukes*, that "statutes which in general terms divest pre-existing rights or privileges will not be applied to the sovereign without express words to that effect."...

U.M.W. is relevant in this case only because the Norris-LaGuardia Act was found to be inapplicable in cases involving disputes between the United States government (the "sovereign") and its employees (mine workers in formerly private coal mines seized by the government under its wartime powers). The argument made here is that the "Little Norris-LaGuardia Act" is not applicable in a dispute between a school board and its teachers.

The two situations are completely different. Neither the school board nor the state is the "sovereign." The rule of statutory construction applied by the court in *Dukes* and in *U.M.W.* has the same origin as the doctrine of "sovereign immunity" in tort law.... The rule was long used to defeat government liability for the negligent acts of its employees, yet was widely criticized for its unjust results and irrational basis. The doctrine of sovereign immunity has been abrogated in Louisiana.

We further note the Supreme Court itself said of this rule of construction that it "... is an aid to consistent construction of statutes of the enacting sovereign when their purpose is in doubt, but it does not require that the aim of a statute fairly to be inferred be disregarded because not explicitly stated." *United States v. California*, 297 U.S. 175, 186 (1935). That statement comports with our Civil Code, which provides: "When a law is clear and unambiguous and its application does not lead to absurd consequences, the law shall be applied as written and no further interpretation may be made in search of the intent of the legislature."

....

The plain words of the statute require application of the "Little Norris-LaGuardia Act" to this dispute. The teachers are employed by the school board. There is a labor dispute between them.

> (3) The term "labor dispute" includes any controversy concerning terms or conditions of employment or concerning the association or representation of persons in negotiating, fixing, maintaining, changing, or seeking to arrange terms or conditions of employment, or concerning employment relations, or any other controversy arising out of the respective interests of employer and employee, regardless of whether or not the disputants stand in the proximate relation of employer and employee. R.S. 23:821(3).

School boards can sue and be sued. School boards can enjoin and be enjoined.

Under the terms of the "Little Norris-LaGuardia Act," the Terrebonne Parish school employees can be enjoined only in accord with R.S. 23:844. The lower courts here made no factual findings, as required under R.S. 23:844, and there have been no allegations of the type of danger to the public health and safety set out in the statute. Under the act, peaceful picketing, refusal to work, communicating with others concerning a labor dispute and encouraging others to participate in a work stoppage, acts which the court of appeal ordered enjoined, are not enjoinable.

We do not suggest in this opinion that the right to strike is unlimited or unqualified....

....

We believe such a standard is appropriate. However, in light of the Louisiana legislature's failure to establish which classes of public employees are entitled to strike, we may only proceed on a case-by-case basis. We thus reaffirm the holding in *City of New Orleans v. Police Association of Louisiana*, finding it reasonable that police strikes should be barred under all circumstances given the risk they pose to the public health and safety. We find no such threat of imminent danger in the case of a strike by school employees and, therefore, relying on the statutes, the Constitution and jurisprudence, hold the strike by employees of the Terrebonne Parish School Board is subject to the terms of the "Little Norris-LaGuardia Act."

....

---

1. Can a school board, vested with the power to employ and dismiss teachers, consistent with the Due Process clause of the Fourteenth Amendment, dismiss teachers engaged in a strike prohibited by state law? In *Hortonville Joint Dist. No. 1 v. Hortonville Educ. Assoc.*, 426 U.S. 482 (1976), discharged teachers filed suit against the school district, alleging that the notice and hearing provided them were inadequate to comply with due process requirements. The union argued that the board could not act as an impartial decision maker, as due process requires. However, the Supreme Court found that the teachers failed to show that the board members had a personal stake in the decisions. There was no record of personal animosity. The teachers attempted to show school board bias by noting that the board had negotiated with the teachers before the strike and, therefore, knew the reasons for the strike. Ultimately, the Supreme Court held that state law gave to the board the power to govern the system and their daily concerns, including the power to employ and dismiss teachers. To alter these powers as a matter of federal due process would change the balance of power in labor relations — a balance already created by the state legislature.

The Wisconsin Supreme Court remanded *Hortonville* to the Circuit Court for adjudication. The plaintiffs filed amended complaints restating equal protection and teacher qualification causes of action. The Circuit Court dismissed the equal protection claim and sustained demurrer to the teacher qualification claim. The Wisconsin Supreme Court held that the board of education did not act arbitrarily or capriciously or beyond its jurisdiction in discharging teachers who had abandoned their employment by striking. Under the circumstances of the case, the court held that the board did not deny equal protection in rehiring one striking teacher who had rejected representation of the teachers association and refusing to rehire teachers who were represented by the association. *Hortonville Educ. Ass'n v. Hortonville Joint Sch. Dist. No. 1*, 274 N.W.2d 697 (Wis. 1979).

Do you agree with this decision? Does this put teachers in a rough position of loyalty? How much can they expect from their teachers' union after decisions like this?

2. What about denial of tenure rights as a penalty for participation in a strike? Is this cruel and unusual punishment? One court has said "no." *See O'Brien v. Board of Educ. of City of New York*, 498 F. Supp. 1033 (S.D.N.Y. 1980).

3. *Hortonville* dealt with the propriety of dismissing teachers who participated in illegal strikes. Are monetary remedies allowed against teachers' associations that continue an illegal strike? At least one court has said "yes," as long as the fine is not so excessive as to constitute "ruinous punishment." *See East Brunswick Bd. of Educ. v. East Brunswick Educ. Ass'n*, 235 N.J. Super. 417, 563 A.2d 55 (1989). Such a monetary sanction is permitted to sting and to force compliance. The factors which the court considered were the Association's ability to pay and the impact the sanction would have on the organization in light of its income, status, and objectives, as well as the sanction's impact on innocent third parties.

4. In terms of the length of the strike and inconveniences to students, compare *Davis v. Henry* with *Jersey Shore*, presented and discussed earlier in the chapter.

5. Are you convinced that strikes by teachers do not threaten the operation of the government, and that some line ought to be drawn, allowing strikes by some government employees, while keeping a closer watch on those government activities and agencies which truly do affect *all* of society.

6. Consider the following excerpt regarding the decision in *Davis* and what other states have done and what they can do:

BABIN, *DAVIS v. HENRY*: ONE MORE PIECE TO THE PUBLIC EMPLOYEE STRIKE RIGHTS PUZZLE, 51 La. L. Rev. 1271 (1991)*

III. *What States Have Done*

A. *The Common Law Ban*

With public employees excluded from the federal labor system, state governments are free to decide for themselves what collective bargaining and strike rights their public employees will enjoy. Generally, the common law regarded public employee strikes as illegal "per se." This "per se" rule is simple and harsh. Any concerted activity against a public employer to stop government services for the purpose of employee self gain will be enjoined, and

---

*Copyright © 1991 by the Louisiana Law Review. Reprinted with permission.

A. TEACHER COLLECTIVE BARGAINING

violators are guilty of criminal contempt of court. Four common arguments have emerged from cases and commentary addressing why public employees should be precluded from striking.

First, a strike against the government is said to be tantamount to a denial of governmental authority. Second, the terms of public employment are deemed not to be subject to bilateral collective bargaining because they are set by the legislative body. Third, since legislative bodies are responsible for public employment decision making, allowing strikes would grant public employees excessive bargaining leverage, resulting in a distortion of the political process. Fourth, public employees provide essential services which, if interrupted by employee strikes, would endanger the public welfare.

Because of the "per se" rule's harshness, it has been met with dissension and attack. One of the earliest and most notable challenges to the common law rule and rationale was Indiana Supreme Court Chief Justice DeBruler's dissent in *Anderson Federation of Teachers v. School City of Anderson*. He questioned the "per se" rule, calling the majority opinion unjustified in holding every public employee strike to be unlawful, regardless of how non-disruptive or peaceful the strike was. Chief Justice DeBruler thought the teachers' strike at issue in *Anderson* was only minimally disruptive because the school system never had to close. He further believed that, in the interest of equalizing the bargaining power of both sides of the dispute, minor interruptions and peaceful strikes should be tolerated.

Similarly, in *Timberlane Regional School District v. Timberlane Regional Education Association*, the New Hampshire Supreme Court applied a rationale analogous to Chief Justice DeBruler's and refused to enjoin a teachers' strike. At the time of the decision, New Hampshire was a state that recognized the common law ban on public employee strikes. The court refused, however, to enjoin the strike, primarily because the school district failed to show it was suffering irreparable harm, a requirement for the extraordinary remedy of injunction. The court additionally said that to grant such a remedy to movant who had not fulfilled the requirements necessary for injunctive relief would be "detrimental to the smooth operation of the collective bargaining process...."

In *County Sanitation District No. 2 v. L.A. County Employees Association*, California judicially abolished the common law rule. The Louisiana Supreme Court employed the *County Sanitation* rationale in *Davis*. Other states, however, have steadfastly maintained the common law ban on public employee strikes. Most notably, two recent opinions rejected attempts to abolish the "per se" ban. In *Jefferson County Board of Education v. Jefferson County Education Association*, and *Martin v. Montezuma-Cortez School District RC-1*, the West Virginia Supreme Court of Appeals and the Colorado Court Of Appeals, respectively, rejected the *County Sanitation* abolition of the common law strike ban. Both courts reasoned that their states differ from California because California has a well developed public employee collective bargaining statute. In contrast, West Virginia and Colorado do not have a well developed statutory procedure for handling public employee collective bargaining matters. The courts then refused to create such a system jurisprudentially.

B. *Legislative Solutions*

Many states have realized that the judiciary is ill suited to develop a system of public employee labor law. The need for stability, peace in the work force, and some degree of predictability from the viewpoint of labor and management led many state legislatures to craft mechanisms to deal with government employees. Two general types of public employee relations statutes have been adopted.

The first type of statute prohibits public employee strikes; however, the statutes provide some alternative dispute resolution machinery. These statutes are fashioned after the federal model. Under federal law, federal employees are unable to participate in strikes against their employer. Participation in strikes against the U.S. government will quickly be enjoined and future participants held in contempt for failing to comply with the injunction. As an alternative to strikes, the federal statute provides for and protects employee organization rights, mandates collective bargaining, and provides for arbitration. The statutes employed by states using this type of employee relations system are customized variations of the federal statute, but each statutorily prohibits public employee strikes.

The second type of stature legislatively grants public employees the right to strike. Eleven states (Alaska, Hawaii, Idaho, Illinois, Minnesota, Montana, Ohio, Oregon, Pennsylvania, Vermont, and Wisconsin) currently have this system. The states that allow public sector strikes do so with the same degree of control. Either by stature or by the courts' equitable power, strikes are allowed only in some instances. The right to strike is limited to public employees whose absence from their jobs would not immediately endanger the public welfare.

....

VIII. *Proposed Legislative Resolution*

... Each state must customize any proposed public employee relation statute to comply with its own needs and its own law. Prior commentators have exhaustively covered this area and provided potential drafts of such legislation for this state. This section of this note only seeks to provide generally what an effective public labor relations statute should include.

First, the act should provide public employees with the right and impose on public employers the duty to collectively bargain. Collective bargaining puts free market competition into the labor system. It allows more valuable employees to be paid accordingly; conversely, if government can provide the service more cheaply and effectively by private contracts, then the employer should be able to refuse employee demands and seek these more reasonable alternatives.

The act should also provide protection of employee organizational activities and union membership. The right to join or refuse to join, to support or not to support employee unions should be specifically granted to public employees

A. TEACHER COLLECTIVE BARGAINING

Louisiana's Right to Work Statute. Louisiana's Right to Work Statute provides some protection; however, the statute is too ambiguous to insure such protection to the public sector. While the statute does not exclude public employees, it also does not clearly include them.

An effective public labor relations statute should also provide exactly which acts employees are allowed to use as bargaining leverage and which are prohibited. Whether the statute allows strikes by certain segments of the public employ and not others or prohibits strikes by certain segments of the public employ and not others or prohibits strikes to all employees, the statute should forthrightly define what rights are granted and to whom. A general no-strike clause, similar to the federal statute, would be preferable. The statute, by mandating collective bargaining, would eliminate the need to strike to force collective bargaining. Economic strikes should also be prohibited, and some alternative dispute resolution machinery used. The goal of a successful labor system is to provide both sides the opportunity to confer, bargain, and preferably to allow each to make fair concessions to achieve a peaceful, fair result. Employers and employees reach agreement in a bargaining process by one of two ways. Either each side grants to the other some concessions, or the economically strongest party unilaterally dictates the terms. Removal of the right to strike from the employee arsenal does eliminate the possibility for employees to win an outright economic battle; however, mandatory arbitration would reach the same result without the need for disruption of government services if the employee demands are fair and well founded.

. . . .

The most effective impasse resolution device in the absence of the right to strike would be a two-tiered system, consisting of mediation followed by arbitration if the deadlock is not broken. This system should provide that if the parties bargain to an impasse, the parties themselves can agree on an independent mediator; if they cannot agree, a mediator will be chosen for them. This first tier allows the parties to resolve their differences between themselves. If this method yields no result, the parties are then referred to an independent arbitrator. This arbitrator would act as a fact finder, and, with all the objective data he can collect, he would assimilate both parties' offers and make a recommendation binding on both of them. As an added precaution, the statute may include appellate review of the arbitrator's decision to an administrative board, commission, or court. While the possibilities of the dispute resolution mechanisms are endless, the purpose of the machinery is what is important; the quicker the parties can reach a common promise, the sooner the conflict will end.

In light of the rights guaranteed to employees under the statute, the legislation should make illegal certain "unfair labor practices" for both employers and employee organizations. Such practices are prohibited by the National Labor Relations Act and violations include: interfering with employees' free exercise of their right to organize and to choose a representative, refusal to collectively bargain, engaging in discriminatory practices against those who are members of labor organizations, and engaging in other practices that diminish the employees' rights under the act. Employee organization violations are largely the same, including: interfering with employees' rights to join or not to join employee organizations, discrimination, refusal to bargain in good faith, and participating in or calling a strike if such a strike is illegal.

Finally, the statute should provide for administrative machinery to apply and enforce the law. The federal public employee relations statute provides for establishment of the Federal Labor Relations Authority. States have established similar boards or agencies charged with the duty of carrying out the policies of the act or, to avoid duplication, have charged already existing personnel boards with the task. Other states merely have mediation or arbitration commissions. To render any employee rights granted under a public employee relations act effective, some enforcement commission or board is necessary to expeditiously handle complaints. Otherwise, the violation could only be enforced in state courts, causing delays that would make the act ineffective. For example, if an employee was fired by a parish school board for his or her membership in a labor organization, a one or two year delay in the court system would tend to diminish the act's effectiveness, since an employee may not be willing to take the chance of union participation if he faces long term unemployment.

B. HIRING AND DISCHARGE

Paralleling the development of the constitutional protections of student rights, discussed in the preceding chapters, has come the rapid expansion of constitutional protections for teachers and other school employees. Some of those protections, *i.e.*, those in the area of academic freedom, have been discussed previously. In this chapter, we discuss the constitutional protections the courts afford school faculties and staffs in the sensitive areas of hiring and discharge. For purposes of pedagogy these cases are organized according to discrete "categories" (age, race, citizenship, gender, religion, and disability) which, when relevant in the employment process, have raised judicial and legislative concerns. Finally, pertinent due process issues in the hiring and discharge of educational personnel will be discussed.

1. AGE

GELLER v. MARKHAM
United States Court of Appeals
635 F.2d 1027 (2d Cir. 1980)

MANSFIELD, CIRCUIT JUDGE:

Miriam Geller, a 55-year-old teacher, brought a class action in the District Court for the District of Connecticut under the Age Discrimination in Employment Act of 1967 (ADEA), 29 U.S.C. §§ 621, et seq., claiming that defendants-appellants violated her rights by denying her employment as a teacher because of her age. She sought damages, equitable relief (including reinstatement, pension

B. HIRING AND DISCHARGE

rights, benefits and seniority) and attorney's fees. A jury trial before Judge M. Joseph Blumenfeld resulted in an award of $15,190 damages. Following the trial, Judge Blumenfeld denied her application for equitable relief but awarded attorney's fees. From this denial she appeals. Defendants cross-appeal from the judgment against them, asserting that the court erred in its conclusions as to governing legal principles and in its instructions to the jury regarding causation.

We affirm the finding of defendants' liability, since the record reveals that defendants subjected Ms. Geller to a hiring practice with both discriminatory impact, *see Griggs v. Duke Power Co.*, 401 U.S. 424 (1971), and illegally disparate treatment, *see McDonnell Douglas Co. v. Green*, 411 U.S. 792 (1973), the principles of which may be applied in ADEA cases. We also affirm the district court's refusal to award reinstatement, but reverse its decision not to award pension benefits.

Ms. Geller applied for a position as a teacher at Bugbee School in West Hartford in late August, 1976. She was then 55 years old. She had gained considerable experience as a tenured teacher in New Jersey, where she had lived until shortly before applying for the Bugbee job, and she had done some work as a substitute teacher in the Connecticut schools. She was interviewed for a permanent position to fill a "sudden opening" in the Bugbee School on September 3, 1976, and was told to be ready to begin teaching art on September 7. Meanwhile, school officials continued to interview other candidates for the job.

Ms. Geller prepared the art room over Labor Day weekend, and taught school until September 17, when she was replaced by a 25-year-old woman who had not applied for the job until September 10. Shortly thereafter, Ms. Geller brought the present suit, alleging violations of ADEA, and pointing in particular to the "Sixth Step Policy" adopted by the West Hartford Board of Education ("Board"). This cost-cutting policy, which was derived from a statement included by the previous Bugbee School Superintendent in his budget report to the Board, read: "Except in special situations and to the extent possible, teachers needed in West Hartford next year will be recruited at levels below the sixth step of the salary schedule." The sixth step is the salary grade reached by teachers with more than five years' experience.

At trial plaintiff introduced expert statistical testimony establishing that 92.6% of Connecticut teachers between 40 and 65 years old (the protected age group under ADEA) have more than 5 years experience, while only 62% of teachers under 40 have taught more than five years. She also presented considerable evidence in the form of witnesses' testimony that individual defendants had discussed the "sixth step" policy with her, and had taken the policy into account when deciding to replace her. Defendants countered that the ratio of hirees over 40 years of age to under-40 hirees had not changed substantially since the announcement of the "sixth step" policy. From these latter statistics, which were offered not by an expert statistician but by Mr. Hedrick, a named defendant, defendants argued that the "sixth step" policy had never been applied to discriminate on the basis of age. They claimed that Ms. Geller had been replaced by a younger woman because hiring officials considered the younger woman more qualified, not because the school board was unwilling to pay a woman with her experience. Defendants also argue that even if the "sixth step" was applied, they were justified in applying it because an "experience-cost criterion" for hiring was necessary in view of declining enrollments and rising school costs.

Largely on the strength of plaintiff's expert statistical evidence, Judge Blumenfeld found that defendants' "sixth step" policy was discriminatory as a matter of law. He found the case to be governed by the line of cases regulating facially neutral employment policies which have a discriminatory impact....

After instructing the jury that the "sixth step" policy was discriminatory on the basis of age as a matter of law, Judge Blumenfeld submitted to it the question of whether this policy had been applied to Ms. Geller. First, in his oral instructions to the jury, he asked it to determine "if the decision about Mrs. Geller was made in whole or in part, because she was above the fifth step," and if the "sixth step" policy "made a difference" in the decision to replace her with the younger woman, stating:

> There could have been more than one reason for defendants' decision about (Mrs. Geller's) employment but she is nevertheless entitled to recover if one factor was her (age) and if it made a difference in determining whether she would be employed. If it did not make any difference, if it was not a reason that entered into the decision, then of course she has not proved her case. But if it did, then she has.
>
> If defendants' decision about Mrs. Geller was made in whole or in part because she was above the fifth step on the salary scale, ... Mrs. Geller is entitled to recover....

....

The jury found for Ms. Geller....

In post-trial motions plaintiffs applied for equitable relief based upon the jury's verdict, specifically requesting reinstatement, pension benefits, and attorney's fees. All of these requests except for the request for attorney's fees were denied. Plaintiff has assigned as error the denial of these requests for relief, while defendants attack Judge Blumenfeld's instructions to the jury and his ruling that the "sixth step" policy was discriminatory as a matter of law.

Discussion

....

Disparate Impact

A prima facie case of discriminatory impact may be established by showing that an employer's facially neutral practice has a disparate impact upon members of plaintiff's class, in this case teachers over 40 years of age. Such a discriminatory impact is frequently evidenced by statistics from which it may be inferred

B. HIRING AND DISCHARGE

that an employer's selection methods or employment criteria result in employment of a larger share of one group (here, teachers under 40 years of age) than of another (teachers over 40). The employer may defend by showing that the employment practice is justified by business necessity or need and is related to successful performance of the job for which the practice is used, *Griggs v. Duke Power Co.* In that event the plaintiff must be given an opportunity to show that other selection methods having less discriminatory effects would serve the employer's legitimate interest in competent performance of the job.

A prima facie case of discriminatory treatment may be made out by the plaintiff's showing:

> (i) that he belongs to a racial minority; (ii) that he applied and was qualified for a job for which the employer was seeking applicants; (iii) that, despite his qualifications, he was rejected; and (iv) that, after his rejection, the position remained open and the employer continued to seek applicants from persons of complainant's qualifications.

The burden then shifts to the employer to go forward with evidence of "some legitimate, nondiscriminatory reason for the employee's rejection," in which event the plaintiff, who has the ultimate burden, must be afforded the opportunity to demonstrate by competent evidence that the employer's presumptively valid reasons are a cover-up or pretext. *Id.* at 805. If the plaintiff succeeds in this showing the employer's articulated reason will not stand.

Turning to the present case, the plaintiff showed through an accredited expert (Dr. Alan Hunt), based on his statistical analysis of the relationship between age and years of experience for teachers in Connecticut, that 92.6% of all teachers over 40 years of age have five or more years of teaching experience, which he characterized as "very significant" statistically or about "600 times the level generally required for statistical significance." Although the significance of the 92.6% figure is somewhat weakened by evidence that over 60% of teachers under 40 also have had more than five years experience, we agree with Judge Blumenfeld's finding that the high correlation between experience and membership in the protected age group (40 to 65 years of age) would render application of the "sixth step" policy discriminatory as a matter of law, since, absent countervailing statistics, the likelihood of a person over 40 being selected under the policy would be substantially less than that of a person under 40. The purpose of the "sixth step" policy was to economize by employing less experienced teachers, which would inevitably open more teaching opportunities to younger less experienced applicants than to the older, who were more experienced.

Defendants have offered two lines of defense, both of which are unpersuasive. First they contend that, although the "sixth step" policy appears to be correlated strongly to membership in the group over 40, the policy did not in fact result in discrimination against this group since the percentage of over-40 teachers hired to fill job openings before and after the application of the policy was about the same. The uncorroborated statistics offered in support of this contention, however, were so defective as to justify the district court's refusal to give them any weight. They were prepared by a named defendant in the case, a former Personnel Director for the West Hartford schools who had no expertise as a statistician and had a direct interest in the outcome of the case. He not only failed to produce any competent evidence of the applicant pool for the periods, which is essential to a statistical determination of hiring patterns, but he employed such dubious analytical techniques as obtaining an overall percentage figure by averaging annual percentages for several different years, thus contravening the basic, well-recognized principle that such averaging by percentages produces meaningless and misleading results. Moreover it appears that there were dramatic changes in the size of the applicant pool and in the number of teachers hired in the West Hartford School District during the mid-1970's, which cast serious doubt upon the statistical significance of the defendants' evidence of allegedly unchanging hiring patterns. In 1968 and 1969, according to defendants' own figures, West Hartford hired 129 and 136 teachers, of whom 28 and 33, respectively, were above the fifth step, and 17 (13%) and 15 (8%), respectively, were over 40. In 1975 and 1976, by contrast, the District hired only 35 and 53 teachers, a substantially smaller group, of whom 7 and 10 were above the fifth step and 2 (6%) and 4 (8%), respectively, were over 40.

....

Here JUDGE BLUMENFELD rightly found that the "sixth step" policy was discriminatory on its face. From there, he apparently declined to rely on statistics either to establish as a matter of law plaintiff's position that the policy was applied or to support defendants' position that it was not applied. Absent statistics regarding any changes in the applicant pool for teaching jobs as overall hiring decreased, comparative evidence of overall hiring percentages carries little weight, since these percentages may have remained constant despite an increase or fall-off in over-40 applicants. In the face of these deficiencies in the statistical proof and the existence of testimony that the "sixth step" policy was applied in Ms. Geller's individual case, which was disputed, Judge Blumenfeld properly submitted the issue of whether it was applied to the jury, which resolved the question in her favor by finding that the "sixth step" policy was one reason for the hiring of a younger replacement.

Defendants' second line of defense, somewhat inconsistent with their contention that the "sixth step" policy was never followed, is that the policy, if applied, was supportable as a necessary cost-cutting gesture in the face of tight budgetary constraints. This cost justification must fail, however, because of the clear rule that

> a general assertion that the average cost of employing older workers as a group is higher than the average cost of employing younger workers as a group will not be recognized as a differentiation under the terms and provisions of the Act, unless one of the other statutory exceptions applies.

B. HIRING AND DISCHARGE

To classify or group employees solely on the basis of age for the purpose of comparing costs, or for any other purpose, necessarily rests on the assumption that the age factor alone may be used to justify a differentiation — an assumption plainly contrary to the terms of the Act and the purpose of Congress in enacting it. Differentials so based would serve only to perpetuate and promote the very discrimination at which the Act is directed.

... Accordingly, we conclude, that Ms. Geller established disparate impact by proving that she was subjected to a facially neutral policy disproportionately disadvantaging her as a member of a protected class.

Disparate Treatment

The record also reveals that, in addition to making out a case of disparate impact, Ms. Geller established a prima facie case of discriminatory treatment ... satisfying the oft-repeated four conditions.... At age 55 she was clearly within the protected group under ADEA. She applied for the teaching job, was concededly qualified for it, and was even hired temporarily to perform it. She was then released, and saw a younger person placed in the job for which she was concededly qualified. These undisputed facts are sufficient to place upon the defendants the burden of rebutting her prima facie case. For reasons already stated, the defenses that the "sixth step" policy was not applied to Ms. Geller and that, if applied, it was cost-justified, must be rejected....

Causation

This leads us to defendants' final contention, that the court erred in instructing the jury as to the part age must play in determining whether they violated ADEA in discharging Ms. Geller. In order to make out a case under ADEA, Ms. Geller was not required to show that age discrimination was the sole cause of her discharge. Where an employer acts out of mixed motives in discharging or refusing to hire an employee, the plaintiff must show that age was a causative or determinative factor, one that made a difference in deciding whether the plaintiff should be employed. *See Loeb v. Textron, Inc.*, 600 F.2d 1003, 1019 (1st Cir. 1979) (plaintiff must prove that age was the "'determining factor' in his discharge in the sense that 'but for' his employer's motive to discriminate against him because of age, he would not have been discharged"; *Laugeson v. Anaconda Co., supra,* 510 F.2d at 317 ("We believe it was essential for the jury to understand from the instructions that there could be more than one factor in the decision to discharge him and that he was nevertheless entitled to recover if one such factor was his age and if in fact it made a difference in determining whether he was to be retained or discharged. This is so even though the need to reduce the employee force generally was also a strong, and perhaps even more compelling reason"). *Accord Cova v. Coca Cola Bottling Co.*, 574 F.2d 958 (8th Cir. 1978).

Both parties here suggest that the *Laugeson and Cova* standard is in conflict with the *Loeb* rule. We disagree. If age discrimination was a "factor ... (which) made a difference," then the employee's fortunes would have been "different" without the discriminatory action and age discrimination was therefore a "but for" cause of the result that did take place.

In the present case Judge Blumenfeld submitted to the jury a special interrogatory which asked whether the "sixth step" guideline was "one reason" for Ms. Geller's not being hired for the permanent art teacher's position. He refused to amend the interrogatory to read "one reason that made a difference." Standing alone, this refusal to amend might entitle defendants to a retrial since the jury, absent further instructions, could have found that the "sixth step" guideline, although considered by the Board as a factor, may not have been a determinative one. However, the interrogatory followed hard on the heels of an instruction in which the jury was told that it could find liability only if Ms. Geller's age "made a difference in determining whether she would be employed" and that "(i)f it did not make any difference-then of course she has not proved her case. But if it did, then she has." We conclude that, while it would have been advisable to repeat the gist of the latter language in the interrogatory, the instructions and the interrogatory, read together, were adequate. In this context the words "a reason," as used in the interrogatory, meant a reason which made a difference and hence were sufficient. Our view is fortified by undisputed evidence, including testimony of Dr. Johnson and Messrs. Metzger and Hedrick, as well as tape recordings of conversations between Ms. Geller and the various defendants, that the "key factor" was the "sixth step" policy. The principal of the school, Dr. Johnson, testified that she "rendered an excellent service. I have nothing but praise for her."

Equitable Relief

We next turn to Ms. Geller's contention that the district court erred in denying her equitable relief beyond the damages awarded by the jury. Title 29 U.S.C. § 626(c)(1) provides, "Any person aggrieved (by an alleged violation of the ADEA) may bring a civil action in any court of competent jurisdiction for such legal or equitable relief as will effectuate the purposes of this chapter." Section 626(b) defines the available legal and equitable relief as "including without limitation judgments compelling employment, reinstatement or promotion, or enforcing the liability of amounts deemed to be unpaid minimum wages or unpaid overtime compensation under this section." The Supreme Court, defining which forms of relief were legal and which equitable so that it could determine which should be submitted to a jury, has noted that § 626

> does not specify which of the listed categories of relief are legal and which are equitable. However, since it is clear that judgments compelling "employment, reinstatement of promotion" are equitable, Congress must have meant the phrase "legal relief" to refer to judgments "enforcing ...

B. HIRING AND DISCHARGE

a case compelling the plaintiff, alleging employment discrimination, to make an initial showing of "disparate impact" of the employer's actions. This could be demonstrated by evidence that a procedure or device used in the selection or promotion of employees adversely affected a protected class of persons. If the plaintiff succeeded in proving this prima facie case, the burden shifted to the employer to prove that its hiring or promotion methods were dictated by a "business necessity" and that they were directly related to actual job performance for the particular job in question.

In 1989 the Supreme Court rendered a number of decisions that effectively overturned its decision in *Griggs*. The case attracting the most attention was *Wards Cove Packing Co. v. Atonio*, 490 U.S. 642 (1989), a decision substantially decreasing the ability of plaintiffs to prevail in disparate impact disputes. The case reduced the employer's burden with respect to "business necessity" in that the employer only needed to demonstrate that a "challenged practice serves ... legitimate employment goals [as] ... there is no requirement that the challenged practice be 'essential' or 'indispensable' to the employer's business to pass muster." *Id.* at 659. The decision also provided that no longer can plaintiffs identify a group of practices that together have a disparate impact; instead, there must be a demonstration of a causal connection between each identified discriminatory practice and the disparate impact.

In 1991 Congress responded to the decision in *Wards Cove* and other cases with passage of the Civil Rights Act, 42 U.S.C.A. Secs. 2000e-2000e-16 (West Supp. 1992), so as to restore employment discrimination laws to their original intent as reflected in the *Griggs* decision. The effort was not very successful, however, as the compromise with the Bush Administration left the Act susceptible to widely differing interpretations. This has caused at least one commentator to state that "the courts, and the Supreme Court in particular ... will likely take advantage of [ambiguous language in the Act] and follow ... doctrinal and theoretical patterns in employment discrimination cases...." Note, *The Civil Rights Act of 1991: The Business Necessity Standard*, 106 Harv. L. Rev. 896 (1993). The following cases, reflect that ambiguity.

WYGANT v. JACKSON BOARD OF EDUCATION
Supreme Court of the United States
476 U.S. 267 (1986)

JUSTICE POWELL announced the judgment of the Court and delivered an opinion in which THE CHIEF JUSTICE and JUSTICE REHNQUIST joins, and in all but Part IV of which JUSTICE O'CONNOR joins:

This case presents the question whether a school board, consistent with the Equal Protection Clause, may extend preferential protection against layoffs to some of its employees because of their race or national origin.

I

In 1972 the Jackson Board of Education, because of racial tension in the community that extended to its schools, considered adding a layoff provision to the Collective Bargaining Agreement (CBA) between the Board and the Jackson Education Association (Union) that would protect employees who were members of certain minority groups against layoffs. The Board and the Union eventually approved a new provision, Article XII of the CBA, covering layoffs. It stated:

> In the event that it becomes necessary to reduce the number of teachers through layoff from employment by the Board, teachers with the most seniority in the district shall be retained, except that at no time will there be a greater percentage of minority personnel laid off than the current percentage of minority personnel employed at the time of the layoff. In no event will the number given notice of possible layoff be greater than the number of positions to be eliminated. Each teacher so affected will be called back in reverse order for positions for which he is certificated maintaining the above minority balance.

When layoffs became necessary in 1974, it was evident that adherence to the CBA would result in the layoff of tenured nonminority teachers while minority teachers on probationary status were retained. Rather than complying with Article XII, the Board retained the tenured teachers and laid off probationary minority teachers, thus failing to maintain the percentage of minority personnel that existed at the time of the layoff. The Union, together with two minority teachers who had been laid off, brought suit in federal court, (*Jackson Education Assn. v. Board of Education (Jackson I)*), claiming that the Board's failure to adhere to the layoff provision violated the Equal Protection Clause of the Fourteenth Amendment and Title VII of the Civil Rights Act of 1964. They also urged the District Court to take pendent jurisdiction over state-law contract claims. In its answer the Board denied any prior employment discrimination and argued that the layoff provision conflicted with the Michigan Teacher Tenure Act. Following trial, the District Court sua sponte concluded that it lacked jurisdiction over the case, in part because there was insufficient evidence to support the plaintiffs' claim that the Board had engaged in discriminatory hiring practices prior to 1972, and in part because the plaintiffs had not fulfilled the jurisdictional prerequisite to a Title VII claim by filing discrimination charges with the Equal Employment Opportunity Commission. After dismissing the federal claims, the District Court declined to exercise pendent jurisdiction over the state-law contract claims.

Rather than taking an appeal, the plaintiffs instituted a suit in state court, ***Jackson Education Assn. v. Board of Education***, No. 77-011484CZ *(Jackson II)*, raising in essence the same claims that had been raised in *Jackson I*. In entering judgment for the plaintiffs, the state court found that the Board had breached its contract with the plaintiffs, and that Article XII did not violate the Michigan

B. HIRING AND DISCHARGE

Teacher Tenure Act. In rejecting the Board's argument that the layoff provision violated the Civil Rights Act of 1964, the state court found that it "ha[d] not been established that the board had discriminated against minorities in its hiring practices. The minority representation on the faculty was the result of societal racial discrimination." The state court also found that "[t]here is no history of overt past discrimination by the parties to this contract." Nevertheless, the court held that Article XII was permissible, despite its discriminatory effect on nonminority teachers, as an attempt to remedy the effects of societal discrimination.

After *Jackson II*, the Board adhered to Article XII. As a result, during the 1976-1977 and 1981-1982 school years, nonminority teachers were laid off, while minority teachers with less seniority were retained. The displaced nonminority teachers, petitioners here, brought suit in Federal District Court, alleging violations of the Equal Protection Clause, Title VII, 42 U.S.C. § 1983, and other federal and state statutes. On cross-motions for summary judgment, the District Court dismissed all of petitioners' claims. With respect to the equal protection claim, the District Court held that the racial preferences granted by the Board need not be grounded on a finding of prior discrimination. Instead, the court decided that the racial preferences were permissible under the Equal Protection Clause as an attempt to remedy societal discrimination by providing "role models" for minority schoolchildren, and upheld the constitutionality of the layoff provision.

The Court of Appeals for the Sixth Circuit affirmed, largely adopting the reasoning and language of the District Court. We granted certiorari, to resolve the important issue of the constitutionality of race-based layoffs by public employers. We now reverse.

II

Petitioners' central claim is that they were laid off because of their race in violation of the Equal Protection Clause of the Fourteenth Amendment. Decisions by faculties and administrators of public schools based on race or ethnic origin are reviewable under the Fourteenth Amendment.... "Racial and ethnic distinctions of any sort are inherently suspect and thus call for the most exacting judicial examination."

The Court has recognized that the level of scrutiny does not change merely because the challenged classification operates against a group that historically has not been subject to governmental discrimination....

In this case, Article XII of the CBA operates against whites and in favor of certain minorities, and therefore constitutes a classification based on race. "Any preference based on racial or ethnic criteria must necessarily receive a most searching examination to make sure that it does not conflict with constitutional guarantees." There are two prongs to this examination. First, any racial classification "must be justified by a compelling governmental interest." Second, the means chosen by the State to effectuate its purpose must be "narrowly tailored to the achievement of that goal." We must decide whether the layoff provision is supported by a compelling state purpose and whether the means chosen to accomplish that purpose are narrowly tailored.

III

A

The Court of Appeals, relying on the reasoning and language of the District Court's opinion, held that the Board's interest in providing minority role models for its minority students, as an attempt to alleviate the effects of societal discrimination, was sufficiently important to justify the racial classification embodied in the layoff provision. The court discerned a need for more minority faculty role models by finding that the percentage of minority teachers was less than the percentage of minority students.

This Court never has held that societal discrimination alone is sufficient to justify a racial classification. Rather, the Court has insisted upon some showing of prior discrimination by the governmental unit involved before allowing limited use of racial classifications in order to remedy such discrimination. This Court's reasoning in *Hazelwood School District v. United States*, 433 U.S. 299 (1977), illustrates that the relevant analysis in cases involving proof of discrimination by statistical disparity focuses on those disparities that demonstrate such prior governmental discrimination. In *Hazelwood* the Court concluded that, absent employment discrimination by the school board, "'nondiscriminatory hiring practices will in time result in a work force more or less representative of the racial and ethnic composition of the population in the community from which employees are hired.'"... Based on that reasoning, the Court in *Hazelwood* held that the proper comparison for determining the existence of actual discrimination by the school board was "between the racial composition of [the school's] teaching staff and the racial composition of the qualified public school teacher population in the relevant labor market." 433 U.S. at 308. *Hazelwood* demonstrates this Court's focus on prior discrimination as the justification for, and the limitation on, a State's adoption of race-based remedies.

Unlike the analysis in *Hazelwood*, the role model theory employed by the District Court has no logical stopping point. The role model theory allows the Board to engage in discriminatory hiring and layoff practices long past the point required by any legitimate remedial purpose. Indeed, by tying the required percentage of minority teachers to the percentage of minority students, it requires just the sort of year-to-year calibration [this] Court stated was unnecessary....

Moreover, because the role model theory does not necessarily bear a relationship to the harm caused by prior discriminatory hiring practices, it actually could be used to escape the obligation to remedy such practices by justifying the small percentage of black teachers by reference to the small percentage of black students. Carried to its logical extreme, the idea that black students are better off with black teachers could lead to the very system the Court rejected in *Brown v. Board of Education*, 347 U.S. 483 (1954) (*Brown I*).

B. HIRING AND DISCHARGE

Societal discrimination, without more, is too amorphous a basis for imposing a racially classified remedy. The role model theory announced by the District Court and the resultant holding typify this indefiniteness. There are numerous explanations for a disparity between the percentage of minority students and the percentage of minority faculty, many of them completely unrelated to discrimination of any kind. In fact, there is no apparent connection between the two groups. Nevertheless, the District Court combined irrelevant comparisons between these two groups with an indisputable statement that there has been societal discrimination, and upheld state action predicated upon racial classifications. No one doubts that there has been serious racial discrimination in this country. But as the basis for imposing discriminatory legal remedies that work against innocent people, societal discrimination is insufficient and over expansive. In the absence of particularized findings, a court could uphold remedies that are ageless in their reach into the past, and timeless in their ability to affect the future.

B

Respondents also now argue that their purpose in adopting the layoff provision was to remedy prior discrimination against minorities by the Jackson School District in hiring teachers. Public schools, like other public employers, operate under two interrelated constitutional duties. They are under a clear command from this Court, starting with *Brown v. Board of Education*, 349 U.S. 294 (1955) [*Brown II*], to eliminate every vestige of racial segregation and discrimination in the schools. Pursuant to that goal, race-conscious remedial action may be necessary. On the other hand, public employers, including public schools, also must act in accordance with a "core purpose of the Fourteenth Amendment" which is to "do away with all governmentally imposed discriminations based on race." ...

Evidentiary support for the conclusion that remedial action is warranted becomes crucial when the remedial program is challenged in court by nonminority employees. In this case, for example, petitioners contended at trial that the remedial program — Article XII — had the purpose and effect of instituting a racial classification that was not justified by a remedial purpose. In such a case, the trial court must make a factual determination that the employer had a strong basis in evidence for its conclusion that remedial action was necessary. The ultimate burden remains with the employees to demonstrate the unconstitutionality of an affirmative-action program. But unless such a determination is made, an appellate court reviewing a challenge by nonminority employees to remedial action cannot determine whether the race-based action is justified as a remedy for prior discrimination.

Despite the fact that Article XII has spawned years of litigation and three separate lawsuits, no such determination ever has been made. Although its litigation position was different, the Board in *Jackson I* and *Jackson II* denied the existence of prior discriminatory hiring practices. This precise issue was litigated in both those suits. Both courts concluded that any statistical disparities were the result of general societal discrimination, not of prior discrimination by the Board. The Board now contends that, given another opportunity, it could establish the existence of prior discrimination. Although this argument seems belated at this point in the proceedings, we need not consider the question since we conclude below that the layoff provision was not a legally appropriate means of achieving even a compelling purpose.

....

IV

... Under strict scrutiny the means chosen to accomplish the State's asserted purpose must be specifically and narrowly framed to accomplish that purpose. "Racial classifications are simply too pernicious to permit any but the most exact connection between justification and classification."

We have recognized, however, that in order to remedy the effects of prior discrimination, it may be necessary to take race into account. As part of this Nation's dedication to eradicating racial discrimination, innocent persons may be called upon to bear some of the burden of the remedy. "When effectuating a limited and properly tailored remedy to cure the effects of prior discrimination, such a 'sharing of the burden' by innocent parties is not impermissible." In *Fullilove* [v. *Klutznick*, 448 U.S. 448, 491 (1980)], the challenged statute required at least 10 percent of federal public works funds to be used in contracts with minority-owned business enterprises. This requirement was found to be within the remedial powers of Congress in part because the "actual 'burden' shouldered by nonminority firms is relatively light."

Significantly, none of the cases discussed above involved layoffs. Here, by contrast, the means chosen to achieve the Board's asserted purposes is that of laying off nonminority teachers with greater seniority in order to retain minority teachers with less seniority.... In cases involving valid hiring goals, the burden to be borne by innocent individuals is diffused to a considerable extent among society generally. Though hiring goals may burden some innocent individuals, they simply do not impose the same kind of injury that layoffs impose. Denial of a future employment opportunity is not as intrusive as loss of an existing job.

Many of our cases involve union seniority plans with employees who are typically heavily dependent on wages for their day-to-day living. Even a temporary layoff may have adverse financial as well as psychological effects. A worker may invest many productive years in one job and one city with the expectation of earning the stability and security of seniority. "At that point, the rights and expectations surrounding seniority make up what is probably the most valuable capital asset that the worker 'owns,' worth even more than the current equity in his home." Fallon & Weiler, *Conflicting Models of Racial Justice*, 1984 S.Ct. Rev. 1, 58. Layoffs disrupt these settled expectations in a way that general hiring goals do not.

While hiring goals impose a diffuse burden, often foreclosing only one of several opportunities, layoffs impose the entire burden of achieving racial equality on particular individuals, often resulting in serious disruption of their lives. That burden is too intrusive. We therefore hold that, as a means of accomplishing purposes that otherwise may be legitimate, the Board's layoff plan is not sufficiently narrowly tailored. Other, less intrusive means of accomplishing similar purposes — such as the adoption of hiring goals — are available. For these reasons, the Board's selection of layoffs as the means to accomplish even a valid purpose cannot satisfy the demands of the Equal Protection Clause.

V

We accordingly reverse the judgment of the Court of Appeals for the Sixth Circuit.

....

JUSTICE O'CONNOR, concurring in part and concurring in the judgment:

This case requires us to define and apply the standard required by the Equal Protection Clause when a governmental agency agrees to give preferences on the basis of race or national origin in making layoffs of employees. The specific question posed is, as Justice Marshall puts it, "whether the Constitution prohibits a union and a local school board from developing a collective-bargaining agreement that apportions layoffs between two racially determined groups as a means of preserving the effects of an affirmative hiring policy." There is no issue here of the interpretation and application of Title VII of the Civil Rights Act of 1964; accordingly, we have only the constitutional issue to resolve.

....

I subscribe to Justice Powell's formulation because it mirrors the standard we have consistently applied in examining racial classifications in other contexts.... Although Justice Powell's formulation may be viewed as more stringent than that suggested by Justices Brennan, White, Marshall, and Blackmun, the disparities between the two tests do not preclude a fair measure of consensus. In particular, as regards certain state interests commonly relied upon in formulating affirmative action programs, the distinction between a "compelling" and an "important" governmental purpose may be a negligible one. The Court is in agreement that, whatever the formulation employed, remedying past or present racial discrimination by a state actor is a sufficiently weighty state interest to warrant the remedial use of a carefully constructed affirmative action program. This remedial purpose need not be accompanied by contemporaneous findings of actual discrimination to be accepted as legitimate as long as the public actor has a firm basis for believing that remedial action is required....

It appears, then, that the true source of disagreement on the Court lies not so much in defining the state interests which may support affirmative action efforts as in defining the degree to which the means employed must "fit" the ends pursued to meet constitutional standards. Yet even here the Court has forged a degree of unanimity; it is agreed that a plan need not be limited to the remedying of specific instances of identified discrimination for it to be deemed sufficiently "narrowly tailored," or "substantially related," to the correction of prior discrimination by the state actor.

In the final analysis, the diverse formulations and the number of separate writings put forth by various Members of the Court in these difficult cases do not necessarily reflect an intractable fragmentation in opinion with respect to certain core principles. Ultimately, the Court is at least in accord in believing that a public employer, consistent with the Constitution, may undertake an affirmative action program which is designed to further a legitimate remedial purpose and which implements that purpose by means that do not impose disproportionate harm on the interests, or unnecessarily trammel the rights, of innocent individuals directly and adversely affected by a plan's racial preference.

Respondent School Board argues that the governmental purpose or goal advanced here was the School Board's desire to correct apparent prior employment discrimination against minorities while avoiding further litigation.... Among the measures the School Board and the Union eventually agreed were necessary to remedy the apparent prior discrimination was the layoff provision challenged here; they reasoned that without the layoff provision, the remedial gains made under the ongoing hiring goals contained in the collective bargaining agreement could be eviscerated by layoffs.

The District Court and the Court of Appeals did not focus on the School Board's unquestionably compelling interest in remedying its apparent prior discrimination when evaluating the constitutionality of the challenged layoff provision. Instead, both courts reasoned that the goals of remedying "societal discrimination" and providing "role models" were sufficiently important to withstand equal protection scrutiny. I agree with the plurality that a governmental agency's interest in remedying "societal" discrimination, that is, discrimination not traceable to its own actions, cannot be deemed sufficiently compelling to pass constitutional muster under strict scrutiny. I also concur in the plurality's assessment that use by the courts below of a "role model" theory to justify the conclusion that this plan had a legitimate remedial purpose was in error. Thus, in my view, the District Court and the Court of Appeals clearly erred in relying on these purposes and in failing to give greater attention to the School Board's asserted purpose of rectifying its own apparent discrimination.

....

In sum, I do not think that the layoff provision was constitutionally infirm simply because the School Board, the Commission, or a court had not made particularized findings of discrimination at the time the provision was agreed upon. But when the plan was challenged, the District Court and the Court of Appeals did not make the proper inquiry into the legitimacy of the Board's asserted remedial purpose; instead, they relied upon governmental purposes that we have deemed insufficient to withstand strict scrutiny, and therefore failed to isolate a sufficiently important governmental purpose that could support the challenged provision.

B. HIRING AND DISCHARGE

There is, however, no need to inquire whether the provision actually had a legitimate remedial purpose based on the record, such as it is, because the judgment is vulnerable on yet another ground: the courts below applied a "reasonableness" test in evaluating the relationship between the ends pursued and the means employed to achieve them that is plainly incorrect under any of the standards articulated by this Court. Nor is it necessary, in my view, to resolve the troubling questions whether any layoff provision could survive strict scrutiny or whether this particular layoff provision could, when considered without reference to the hiring goal it was intended to further, pass the onerous "narrowly tailored" requirement. Petitioners have met their burden of establishing that this layoff provision is not "narrowly tailored" to achieve its asserted remedial purpose by demonstrating that the provision is keyed to a hiring goal that itself has no relation to the remedying of employment discrimination.

Although the constitutionality of the hiring goal as such is not before us, it is impossible to evaluate the necessity of the layoff provision as a remedy for the apparent prior employment discrimination absent reference to that goal. In this case, the hiring goal that the layoff provision was designed to safeguard was tied to the percentage of minority students in the school district, not to the percentage of qualified minority teachers within the relevant labor pool. The disparity between the percentage of minorities on the teaching staff and the percentage of minorities in the student body is not probative of employment discrimination; it is only when it is established that the availability of minorities in the relevant labor pool substantially exceeded those hired that one may draw an inference of deliberate discrimination in employment. Because the layoff provision here acts to maintain levels of minority hiring that have no relation to remedying employment discrimination, it cannot be adjudged "narrowly tailored" to effectuate its asserted remedial purpose.

I therefore join in Parts I, II, III and V of the plurality's opinion, and concur in the judgment.

JUSTICE WHITE, concurring in the judgment:

The School Board's policy when layoffs are necessary is to maintain a certain proportion of minority teachers. This policy requires laying off nonminority teachers solely on the basis of their race, including teachers with seniority, and retaining other teachers solely because they are black, even though some of them are in probationary status. None of the interests asserted by the Board, singly or together, justify this racially discriminatory layoff policy and save it from the strictures of the Equal Protection Clause. Whatever the legitimacy of hiring goals or quotas may be, the discharge of white teachers to make room for blacks, none of whom has been shown to be a victim of any racial discrimination, is quite a different matter. I cannot believe that in order to integrate a work force, it would be permissible to discharge whites and hire blacks until the latter comprised a suitable percentage of the work force. None of our cases suggest that this would be permissible under the Equal Protection Clause. Indeed, our cases look quite the other way. The layoff policy in this case — laying off whites who would otherwise be retained in order to keep blacks on the job — has the same effect and is equally violative of the Equal Protection Clause. I agree with the plurality that this official policy is unconstitutional and hence concur in the judgment.

JUSTICE MARSHALL, with whom JUSTICE BRENNAN and JUSTICE BLACKMUN join, dissenting:

When this Court seeks to resolve far-ranging constitutional issues, it must be especially careful to ground its analysis firmly in the facts of the particular controversy before it. Yet in this significant case, we are hindered by a record that is informal and incomplete. Both parties now appear to realize that the record is inadequate to inform the Court's decision. Both have lodged with the Court voluminous "submissions" containing factual material that was not considered by the District Court or the Court of Appeals. Petitioners have submitted 21 separate items, predominantly statistical charts, which they assert are relevant to their claim of discrimination. Respondents have submitted public documents that tend to substantiate the facts alleged in the brief accompanying their motion for summary judgment in the District Court. These include transcripts and exhibits from two prior proceedings, in which certain questions of discrimination in the Jackson schools were litigated, *Jackson Education Assn. v. Board of Education*, No. 4-72340 (ED Mich. 1976) (*Jackson I*), and *Jackson Education Assn. v. Board of Education*, No. 77-011484CZ (Jackson Cty. Cir.Ct.1979) (*Jackson II*).

We should not acquiesce in the parties' attempt to try their case before this Court. Yet it would be just as serious a mistake simply to ignore altogether, as the plurality has done, the compelling factual setting in which this case evidently has arisen. No race-conscious provision that purports to serve a remedial purpose can be fairly assessed in a vacuum.

... Rather, the District Court should have the opportunity to develop a factual record adequate to resolve the serious issue raised by the case....

I, too, believe that layoffs are unfair. But unfairness ought not be confused with constitutional injury. Paying no heed to the true circumstances of petitioners' plight, the plurality would nullify years of negotiation and compromise designed to solve serious educational problems in the public schools of Jackson, Michigan. Because I believe that a public employer, with the full agreement of its employees, should be permitted to preserve the benefits of a legitimate and constitutional affirmative-action hiring plan even while reducing its work force, I dissent.

B. HIRING AND DISCHARGE 627

II

....

The sole question posed by this case is whether the Constitution prohibits a union and a local school board from developing a collective-bargaining agreement that apportions layoffs between two racially determined groups as a means of preserving the effects of an affirmative hiring policy, the constitutionality of which is unchallenged.

....

III

Agreement upon a means for applying the Equal Protection Clause to an affirmative-action program has eluded this Court every time the issue has come before us....

....

Despite the Court's inability to agree on a route, we have reached a common destination in sustaining affirmative action against constitutional attack. In *Bakke,* we determined that a state institution may take race into account as a factor in its decisions, 438 U.S. at 326, and in *Fullilove,* the Court upheld a congressional preference for minority contractors because the measure was legitimately designed to ameliorate the present effects of past discrimination, 448 U.S. at 520.

In this case, it should not matter which test the Court applies. What is most important, under any approach to the constitutional analysis, is that a reviewing court genuinely consider the circumstances of the provision at issue. The history and application of Article XII, assuming verification upon a proper record, demonstrate that this provision would pass constitutional muster, no matter which standard the Court should adopt.

IV

The principal state purpose supporting Article XII is the need to preserve the levels of faculty integration achieved through the affirmative hiring policy adopted in the early 1970's. Justification for the hiring policy itself is found in the turbulent history of the effort to integrate the Jackson public schools — not even mentioned in the plurality opinion — which attests to the bona fides of the Board's current employment practices.

....

Moreover, under the apparent circumstances of this case, we need not rely on any general awareness of "societal discrimination" to conclude that the Board's purpose is of sufficient importance to justify its limited remedial efforts. There are allegations that the imperative to integrate the public schools was urgent. Racially motivated violence had erupted at the schools, interfering with all educational objectives. We are told that, having found apparent violations of the law and a substantial underrepresentation of minority teachers, the state agency responsible for ensuring equality of treatment for all citizens of Michigan had instituted a settlement that required the Board to adopt affirmative hiring practices in lieu of further enforcement proceedings. That agency, participating as amicus curiae through the Attorney General of Michigan, still stands fully behind the solution that the Board and the Union adopted in Article XII, viewing it as a measure necessary to attainment of stability and educational quality in the public schools. Surely, if properly presented to the District Court, this would supply the "[e]videntiary support for the conclusion that remedial action is warranted" that the plurality purports to seek, *ante*, at 1848. Since the District Court did not permit submission of this evidentiary support, I am at a loss as to why Justice Powell so glibly rejects the obvious solution of remanding for the factfinding he appears to recognize is necessary.

Were I satisfied with the record before us, I would hold that the state purpose of preserving the integrity of a valid hiring policy — which in turn sought to achieve diversity and stability for the benefit of all students — was sufficient, in this case, to satisfy the demands of the Constitution.

V

The second part of any constitutional assessment of the disputed plan requires us to examine the means chosen to achieve the state purpose. Again, the history of Article XII, insofar as we can determine it, is the best source of assistance.

....

C

Article XII is a narrow provision because it allocates the impact of an unavoidable burden proportionately between two racial groups. It places no absolute burden or benefit on one race, and, within the confines of constant minority proportions, it preserves the hierarchy of seniority in the selection of individuals for layoff. Race is a factor, along with seniority, in determining which individuals the school system will lose; it is not alone dispositive of any individual's fate. Moreover, Article XII does not use layoff protection as a tool for increasing minority representation; achievement of that goal is entrusted to the less severe hiring policies. And Article XII is narrow in the temporal sense as well. The very bilateral process that gave rise to Article XII when its adoption was necessary will also occasion its demise when remedial measures are no longer required. Finally, Article XII modifies contractual expectations that do not themselves carry any connotation of merit or achievement; it does not interfere with the "cherished American ethic" of "[f]airness in individual competition," *Bakke*, at 319, n. 53, depriving individuals of an opportunity that they could be said to deserve. In all of these important ways, Article XII metes out the hardship of layoffs in a manner that achieves its purpose with the smallest possible deviation from established norms.

The Board's goal of preserving minority proportions could have been achieved, perhaps, in a different way. For example, if layoffs had been determined by lottery, the ultimate effect would have been retention of current racial percent-

B. HIRING AND DISCHARGE

ages. A random system, however, would place every teacher in equal jeopardy, working a much greater upheaval of the seniority hierarchy than that occasioned by Article XII; it is not at all a less restrictive means of achieving the Board's goal. Another possible approach would have been a freeze on layoffs of minority teachers. This measure, too, would have been substantially more burdensome than Article XII, not only by necessitating the layoff of a greater number of white teachers, but also by erecting an absolute distinction between the races, one to be benefited and one to be burdened, in a way that Article XII avoids. Indeed, neither petitioners nor any Justice of this Court has suggested an alternative to Article XII that would have attained the stated goal in any narrower or more equitable a fashion. Nor can I conceive of one.

. . . .

The alleged facts that I have set forth above evince, at the very least, a wealth of plausible evidence supporting the Board's position that Article XII was a legitimate and necessary response both to racial discrimination and to educational imperatives. To attempt to resolve the constitutional issue either with no historical context whatever, as the plurality has done, or on the basis of a record devoid of established facts, is to do a grave injustice not only to the Board and teachers of Jackson and to the State of Michigan, but also to individuals and governments committed to the goal of eliminating all traces of segregation throughout the country. Most of all, it does an injustice to the aspirations embodied in the Fourteenth Amendment itself. I would vacate the judgment of the Court of Appeals and remand with instructions that the case be remanded to the District Court for further proceedings consistent with the views I have expressed.

JUSTICE STEVENS, dissenting:

In my opinion, it is not necessary to find that the Board of Education has been guilty of racial discrimination in the past to support the conclusion that it has a legitimate interest in employing more black teachers in the future. Rather than analyzing a case of this kind by asking whether minority teachers have some sort of special entitlement to jobs as a remedy for sins that were committed in the past, I believe that we should first ask whether the Board's action advances the public interest in educating children for the future. If so, I believe we should consider whether that public interest, and the manner in which it is pursued, justifies any adverse effects on the disadvantaged group.

I

The Equal Protection Clause absolutely prohibits the use of race in many governmental contexts. To cite only a few: the government may not use race to decide who may serve on juries, who may use public services, who may marry, and who may be fit parents. The use of race in these situations is "utterly irrational" because it is completely unrelated to any valid public purpose;

moreover, it is particularly pernicious because it constitutes a badge of oppression that is unfaithful to the central promise of the Fourteenth Amendment.

Nevertheless, in our present society, race is not always irrelevant to sound governmental decisionmaking. To take the most obvious example, in law enforcement, if an undercover agent is needed to infiltrate a group suspected of ongoing criminal behavior — and if the members of the group are all of the same race — it would seem perfectly rational to employ an agent of that race rather than a member of a different racial class. Similarly, in a city with a recent history of racial unrest, the superintendent of police might reasonably conclude that an integrated police force could develop a better relationship with the community and thereby do a more effective job of maintaining law and order than a force composed only of white officers.

In the context of public education, it is quite obvious that a school board may reasonably conclude that an integrated faculty will be able to provide benefits to the student body that could not be provided by an all- white, or nearly all-white, faculty. For one of the most important lessons that the American public schools teach is that the diverse ethnic, cultural, and national backgrounds that have been brought together in our famous "melting pot" do not identify essential differences among the human beings that inhabit our land. It is one thing for a white child to be taught by a white teacher that color, like beauty, is only "skin deep"; it is far more convincing to experience that truth on a day-to-day basis during the routine, ongoing learning process.

In this case, the collective-bargaining agreement between the Union and the Board of Education succinctly stated a valid public purpose — "recognition of the desirability of multi-ethnic representation on the teaching faculty," and thus "a policy of actively seeking minority group personnel." Nothing in the record — not a shred of evidence — contradicts the view that the Board's attempt to employ, and to retain, more minority teachers in the Jackson public school system served this completely sound educational purpose. Thus, there was a rational and unquestionably legitimate basis for the Board's decision to enter into the collective-bargaining agreement that petitioners have challenged, even though the agreement required special efforts to recruit and retain minority teachers.

....

In this case, there can be no question about either the fairness of the procedures used to adopt the race-conscious provision, or the propriety of its breadth. As JUSTICE MARSHALL has demonstrated, the procedures for adopting this provision were scrupulously fair. The Union that represents petitioners negotiated the provision and agreed to it; the agreement was put to a vote of the membership, and overwhelmingly approved. Again, not a shred of evidence in the record suggests any procedural unfairness in the adoption of the agreement. Similarly, the provision is specifically designed to achieve its objective — retaining the minority teachers that have been specially recruited to give the Jackson schools, after a period of racial unrest, an integrated faculty. Thus, in striking contrast to the procedural inadequacy and unjustified breadth of the race-based classification in *Fullilove v. Klutznick*, 448 U.S. 448 (1980), the race-conscious layoff policy here was adopted with full participation of the disadvantaged individuals and with a narrowly circumscribed berth for the policy's operation.

Finally, we must consider the harm to petitioners. Every layoff, like every refusal to employ a qualified applicant, is a grave loss to the affected individual. However, the undisputed facts in this case demonstrate that this serious consequence to petitioners is not based on any lack of respect for their race, or on blind habit and stereotype. Rather, petitioners have been laid off for a combination of two reasons: the economic conditions that have led Jackson to lay off some teachers, and the special contractual protections intended to preserve the newly integrated character of the faculty in the Jackson schools. Thus, the same harm might occur if a number of gifted young teachers had been given special contractual protection because their specialties were in short supply and if the Jackson Board of Education faced a fiscal need for layoffs. A Board decision to grant immediate tenure to a group of experts in computer technology, an athletic coach, and a language teacher, for example, might reduce the pool of teachers eligible for layoffs during a depression and therefore have precisely the same impact as the racial preference at issue here. In either case, the harm would be generated by the combination of economic conditions and the special contractual protection given a different group of teachers — a protection that, as discussed above, was justified by a valid and extremely strong public interest.

IV

We should not lightly approve the government's use of a race-based distinction. History teaches the obvious dangers of such classifications. Our ultimate goal must, of course, be "to eliminate entirely from governmental decisionmaking such irrelevant factors as a human being's race." In this case, however, I am persuaded that the decision to include more minority teachers in the Jackson, Michigan, school system served a valid public purpose, that it was adopted with fair procedures and given a narrow breadth, that it transcends the harm to petitioners, and that it is a step toward that ultimate goal of eliminating entirely from governmental decisionmaking such irrelevant factors as a human being's race. I would therefore affirm the judgment of the Court of Appeals.

KRUETH v. INDEPENDENT SCHOOL DISTRICT NO. 38, RED LAKE, MINNESOTA

Court of Appeals of Minnesota
496 N.W.2d 829 (1993)

RANDALL, JUDGE:

....

Facts

Relators were tenured teachers in respondent school district. Ordinarily, teachers are placed on unrequested leave of absence in reverse order of seniority under Minnesota's teacher tenure act. Minn.Stat. § 125.12 (1990). Relators were placed on unrequested leave of absence while less senior American Indian teachers were retained under respondent's American Indian teacher retention policy.

....

... Minnesota Statute 126.501 permits the Board of Education in placing a teacher on unrequested leave of absence, to retain a probationary teacher or a teacher with less seniority in order to retain an American Indian teacher....

In placing any teacher or teachers on unrequested leave of absence the District may retain a probationary teacher or a teacher with less seniority in order to retain an American Indian teacher regardless of the provisions of Minnesota Statute 125.12, subdivision 4, 6a or 6b; 125.17, subd. 3 and 11, or any contract provision.

....

I

Date of Contract versus Date of Tenure

The American Indian Education Act of 1988 includes a declaration of policy which provides:

> The legislature finds that a more adequate education is needed for American Indian people in the state of Minnesota. The legislature recognizes the unique educational and culturally-related academic needs of American Indian people. The legislature also is concerned about the lack of American Indian teachers in the state. Therefore, pursuant to the policy of the state to ensure equal educational opportunity to every individual, it is the purpose of sections 126.45 to 126.55 to provide for American Indian education programs specially designed to meet these unique educational or culturally-related academic needs or both. Minn.Stat. § 126.46 (1990).

B. HIRING AND DISCHARGE

As part of this act, the legislature allowed school districts with more than ten American Indian students to retain American Indian teachers with less seniority over other teachers with more seniority. Minn.Stat. § 126.501 (1990) provides:

> This section applies to a school board of a school district in which there are at least ten American Indian children enrolled. The school board shall actively recruit teacher applicants who are American Indian from the time it is reasonably expected that a position will become available until the position is filled or September 1, whichever is earlier. Notwithstanding section 125.12, subdivision 4, 6a or 6b, 125.17, subdivisions 3 and 11 [the teacher tenure act], any other law to the contrary, or any provision of a contract entered into after May 7, 1988 to the contrary, when placing a teacher on unrequested leave of absence, the board may retain a probationary teacher or a teacher with less seniority in order to retain an American Indian teacher.

Relators argue the language limiting the application of the act to contracts entered into after May 7, 1988, means any teacher tenured before May 7, 1988, is protected from application of the act. Respondent argues the term "contract" refers to the master contract controlling the school year at issue between relators and the district. Since the master contract here was signed on December 16, 1991, (well after 1988) respondent argues it is entitled to take advantage of the spirit and the letter of section 126.501 and favor less senior American Indian teachers over more senior non-Indian teachers.

....

"A teacher who has completed a probationary period in any school district, and who has not been discharged or advised of a refusal to renew the teacher's contract ... shall have a continuing contract with such district. Thereafter, the teacher's contract shall remain in full force and effect, except as modified by mutual consent of the board and the teacher...." Minn.Stat. § 125.12, subd. 4. Thus, they argue that since tenure is a type of contract, any teacher who acquired tenure before May 7, 1988, is exempt from the American Indian preference set out in section 126.501.

Respondent argues the "contract" referred to in the statute is the master contract or the collective bargaining agreement covering the teachers for that school year. Since this master contract was entered into after May 7, 1988, the statute applies, according to respondent:

> The provision in Minn.Stat. § 126.501 which permits a school district to place more senior teachers on unrequested leaves of absence in order to retain an American Indian teacher, notwithstanding any provision of a contract entered into after May 7, 1988 refers to the collective bargaining agreement covering the teacher and not the individual contract signed by a teacher at the commencement of teaching in the district. The Board rejects the hearing officer's conclusions ... and hereby determines that it may retain

less senior American Indian teachers while placing more senior non-Indian teachers who acquired continuing contract rights prior to May 7, 1988 on unrequested leave of absence pursuant to Minn.Stat. 126.501 and the District's Indian teacher retention policy....

....

II

Constitutionality

a. *Equal protection*

Relators also argue Minn.Stat. § 126.501 violates the Equal Protection clause of the Fourteenth Amendment to the United States Constitution. Under equal protection analysis, strict scrutiny is applied to legislatively created classifications if they impermissibly limit a fundamental right or affect a suspect class. Otherwise, the legislation is subject to review under the rational basis standard. Under this standard, if the classification is rationally related to a legitimate governmental purpose, it does not violate the equal protection clause.

Strict scrutiny requires the classifications to be necessary or narrowly tailored to a compelling governmental purpose. Strict scrutiny applies to state and local government racial affirmative action cases. *Wygant v. Jackson Bd.*...

Wygant involved a preference policy for lay-offs, similar to the policy in this case, which allowed minority teachers with less seniority to be retained over non-minority teachers with more seniority. The policy applied to "those employees who are Black, American Indian, Oriental, or of Spanish descendancy." The Supreme Court held that the policy in the collective bargaining agreement, which constituted state action, violated the equal protection clause. The Court found the strict scrutiny standard applied, and that the lay-off preference was not specifically and narrowly framed to accomplish a compelling governmental interest.

There was no finding of prior discrimination, and the Court found societal discrimination was not a compelling interest. The Court rejected the "role model theory," that minority students need minority teachers as role models, as sufficient grounds for the classifications. Finally, the Court noted the distinction between lay-offs and hiring goals in their burden on innocent parties. Since less intrusive means such as hiring goals were available, the lay-off preference for minority teachers could not withstand the strict scrutiny standard.

If the strict scrutiny test is applied to this case, respondent's policy is arguably not narrowly tailored and could create a problem. *Wygant* found lay-off preferences too burdensome on innocent parties compared to less intrusive alternatives such as hiring goals. Also, there is no evidence of prior discrimination against American Indian teachers, which would require a comparison of the racial composition of the teaching staff and the racial composition of the qualified

B. HIRING AND DISCHARGE

public school teacher population in the relevant labor market. No such comparison was done in this case.

The reason *Wygant* does not control this case in favor of relators is that the policy at issue in *Wygant* did not distinguish between American Indians and the other minorities involved.

If the policy had applied only to American Indians in *Wygant*, the result likely would have been different because the Supreme Court has allowed preferences in employment for American Indians. *Morton v. Mancari*, 417 U.S. 535 (1974). *Mancari* articulates that preferences for American Indians are not racial but political when the preferences apply to members of federally recognized tribes.

As commentators have noted:

> The Supreme Court employs a mere rationality test when scrutinizing tribal classifications because such classifications are viewed as political rather than racial. Laws which give preferential employment or economic benefits to members of American Indian tribes may be upheld on this basis without consideration of whether they constitute a benign racial classification which might not otherwise survive scrutiny under the equal protection guarantee. Rotunda and Nowak, *Treatise on Constitutional Law: Substance and Procedure*, § 4.2 (2d Ed. 1992).

Wygant and *Mancari* recognize a substantive difference between American Indians and other races. American Indians who belong to a recognized tribe or sovereign entity are a race and, unlike white, black and yellow, are also part of a bona fide political class. Other races are not designated as independent political entities. A preference given to American Indians, although falling heavily on those individuals affected, is neither new nor startling in view of the policy that while race, color, and creed cannot be the basis for discrimination, membership in a political entity can be.[3]

The Court in *Mancari* recognized that a special trust relationship exists between American Indians and the federal government. That relationship allows preference to be given to American Indians in certain situations. This has been characterized as the trust doctrine, which provides "[w]hen special or preferential treatment is reasonable and rationally related to the fulfillment of the special trust obligation to Indians, it is permissible differentiation in legitimate public interest rather than prohibited racial discrimination." The trust doctrine also applies to state action. "State action for the benefit of Indians can also fall under the trust doctrine and therefore be protected from challenge under the equal protection clause or civil rights statutes."

---

[3]The State of Minnesota, like all states, routinely charges nonresidents more money than residents for exactly the same services such as state school tuition, fishing and hunting licenses, et cetera. Residents of other states (we equate a state to a "tribe" for purposes of analogy), when they come into Minnesota, are bound by our laws yet can neither vote for the lawmakers nor run for office so as to have a voice in those laws.

Intertribal Housing involved legislation which provided low cost urban housing for American Indians. The federal district court in Minnesota found the Minnesota legislature's intent to benefit American Indians clearly stated in the legislation, that the preference in urban housing for American Indians was rationally related to the government's unique obligation to American Indians, and that it therefore fell under the trust doctrine and survived an equal protection challenge. The Minnesota legislature has expressed a similar clear intent to benefit American Indians under the American Indian Education Act with "American Indian education programs specially designed to meet these unique educational or culturally-related academic needs."

Mancari found the American Indian classifications were not racial but political since they were limited to members of federally recognized tribes. The classification must be limited to members of federally recognized tribes, not just people of some American Indian ancestry, otherwise strict scrutiny would apply to limit state racial affirmative action preferences. Minn.Stat. § 126.501 applies to "American Indian teachers." An "American Indian child" is defined as "any child, living on or off a reservation, who is enrolled or eligible for enrollment in a federally recognized tribe." Thus, the reasonable implied definition of an American Indian teacher is any teacher "enrolled or eligible for enrollment in a federally recognized tribe." All the teachers retained by respondent under its policy are enrolled in an American Indian tribe.

The test to be applied to Minn.Stat. § 126.501 for equal protection analysis is the rational basis test. Under the rational basis test, the policy of retaining American Indian teachers in school districts with American Indian students is rationally related to the legislature's stated purposes of improving education for American Indian students and increasing the number of American Indian teachers through education programs designed to meet the unique educational and culturally related academic needs of American Indians.

If section 126.501 has meaning anywhere in the State of Minnesota, it has meaning in Independent School District No. 38, Red Lake, Minnesota. This school district is located entirely on the Red Lake Reservation and consists of a student population almost 100% American Indian. The spirit of the law and the intent of the legislature's designation of policy fits in this school district far stronger than school districts which primarily serve non-Indian students but happen to have at least ten American Indian students in the district. If the law applies to them, it must apply here.

The goals of the American Indian Education Act and the goals of Minnesota's strong teacher tenure laws clash at the Red Lake school district. In a nation with thousands of laws, state and federal, and overlapping jurisdictions, township, school district, city, county, state and federal, it is inevitable that worthy laws, representing worthy interest groups, will meet in an impasse. So it is here. When two rivers meet, one has to yield. The Mississippi absorbs the St. Croix and the Missouri, the Gulf absorbs the Mississippi. We find the American Indian

B. HIRING AND DISCHARGE

Education Act, with its specific section 126.501, takes precedence over general teacher tenure laws when reconciliation becomes impossible.

....

---

1. "Our Constitution is color-blind and neither knows nor tolerates classes among citizens. In respect of civil rights, all citizens are equal before the law. The humblest is the peer of the most powerful. The law regards man as man, and takes no account of his surroundings or of his color when his civil rights as guaranteed by the supreme law of the land are involved." *Plessy v. Ferguson*, 163 U.S. 537, 559 (1896) (Harlan, J. dissenting).

This oft-quoted dissent by Justice Harlan has attracted several interpretations. But as to the decisions in *Wygant* and *Krueth*, does it mean that people of color, who as a group have been historically harmed by discriminatory practices in employment, should now be the beneficiaries of affirmative action over white employees with more job seniority? As noted in the introduction to this section, the Supreme Court has not presented a bright line of decisions that would give sufficient guidance to educators and other public professionals. For example, the Court in *Regents of the Univ. of California, Davis v. Bakke*, 438 U.S. 265 (1978), indicated that affirmative action as regards the admission of students of color in colleges and universities was an amorphous concept, that it injured white students, and that the university attempt to overcome discrimination against minorities "may be ageless in its reach to the past." *Id.* at 307. The Court went on to state that some remedial measures harm innocent white persons and intimated this was true of the procedures used for admission into the medical school at the University of California at Davis. *Id.* However, another Supreme Court decision ruled that innocent parties may be called upon to bear some of the burden of past discrimination. In *Franks v. Bowman Transp. Co.*, 474 U.S. 747 (1976), Justice Brennan remarked that "a sharing of the burden of ... past discrimination is presumptively necessary — is entirely consistent with any fair characterization...." *Id.* at 777.

Another case which seemed to oppose the holding in *Bakke* countering the notion of "amorphous" remedying of societal discrimination is *Fullilove v. Klutznick*, 448 U.S. 448 (1980). *Fullilove* rebuffed a constitutional challenge to a provision of the Public Works Act of 1977 requiring that an applicant for federal contracts show ten percent participation by minority businesses. The Supreme Court supported the set asides, basing its decision on Congress' desire for affirmative action in the Act which was "directed toward deliverance of the century-old promise of equality of economic opportunity." *Id.* at 463.

2. One argument implicit in both *Wygant* and *Krueth* is that the reason whites as a group have more seniority than African-Americans, American Indians, or other people of color is because these latter groups have been prevented by years of discrimination from occupying such positions. Does the Court in *Wygant* rule that the lingering effects of this past discrimination can be remedied by affirmative action policies or that school systems must choose other remedies for redress? If affirmative action can be used, are clear boundaries drawn authorizing public employers to, in some instances, hire or retain minorities over whites?

3. The Collective Bargaining Agreement (CBA) for the Jackson School System, featured in *Wygant*, monitors the percentage of minority personnel laid off and the minority personnel employed at the time of layoff. The CBA defines minorities as people of "Black, American Indian, Oriental and Spanish" descendancy. In the area of education, especially with elementary schools, could white men be considered a minority?

4. Consider the examples rendered by Justice Stevens in Part I of his dissent in *Wygant* relative to the effect of race in government decision making. How relevant are these? Granted the Supreme Court has ruled that race may not play a role in who may marry or be fit parents; but, what, if anything, does this add to the position that the lay-off provision adopted by the school district is legally sound? Is Justice Stevens' "undercover" example at all relevant?

5. The Supreme Court in *Wygant* struck down a layoff policy that discouraged the layoff of the most experienced white teachers, but only to the extent that the percentage of minority personnel laid off would not be greater than the percentage of minority personnel employed at the time. After *Wygant*, several cases continued to discuss the validity of hiring-preference programs based on the percentages of certain groups of employees.

Decided less than a year after *Wygant*, *Craig v. Alabama State Univ.*, 804 F.2d 682 (11th Cir. 1986), involved a white applicant for an administrative position at a university whose staff was then 70% African American. The university's hiring policy granted preferences to current employees on work/study programs. Is such a program valid, or does it mask a discriminatory hiring policy favoring a particular group, due to the high percentage of that group extant in the university? The Eleventh Circuit held that the white applicant made a prima facie showing of discrimination.

A similar case construed the Arkansas Dismissal Act differently when the plaintiffs were African American. Plaintiffs filed both a class action suit and individual claims alleging race discrimination in hiring practices in a local Arkansas school system. The individual claims failed, but the case was remanded to determine the relevant labor market for black teachers. *Scoggins v. Board of Educ. of Nashville, Arkansas*, 853 F.2d 1472 (8th Cir. 1988). Is a "relevant labor market" policy the same as the program in *Wygant*, and if so, should courts arrive at the same conclusion?

What if the hiring policy were expanded to cover, not the percentage of minority personnel in the school, but such a percentage in the county? Would this pass constitutional muster if senior employees were affected? *Vaughns v. Board of Educ. of Prince George's County*, 742 F. Supp. 1275 (D. Md. 1990), held such a policy was narrowly tailored to serve a compelling interest except with respect to it seniority override goal because it was based on the percentage of

B. HIRING AND DISCHARGE

blacks in the county rather than the school system. Does this case make it possible to write a layoff policy that is constitutional and consistent with the holding in *Wygant*?

6.

The development of affirmative action plans appears to contradict the equal protection clause of the fourteenth amendment by promoting government sanctioned favoritism on the basis of race. On a literal reading of the equal protection clause, it would appear that such favoritism would be unconstitutional in any circumstance. However, because of the deep-seated discrimination prevalent in many areas of American society, the Supreme Court in numerous cases has upheld the preferential employment treatment of minorities.

In December, 1978, the South Bend, Indiana, School Board, in anticipation of possible layoffs and in fear of losing the possible gains made through recent minority hirings, adopted a contractual provision to prevent the layoff of minorities. A number of nonminority teachers who were subsequently laid off challenged this 'no minority layoff provision' as denying them equal protection under the law.

In *Britton v. South Bend Community Sch. Corp.* the Seventh Circuit held, *en banc*, that the "no minority layoff" clause was per se violation of the equal protection clause of the fourteenth amendment, and also held that an absolute preference in any affirmative action plan would unconstitutional.

Shine, Burson, Schlosser, *Britton v. South Bend Community School Corporation: Do Affirmative Action Layoff Plans that Create an Absolute Racial Preference Violate Equal Protection Per Se?*, 63 Notre Dame L. Rev. 102-22 (1988).*

Britton, on rehearing from an earlier 1985 case, 819 F.2d 766 (7th Cir.) (*en banc*), *cert. denied*, 108 S. Ct. 288 (1987), rendered an affirmative answer to the question raised in this law review article. The hiring policy, which stated that no minorities would be laid off, was upheld in the 1985 decision. 775 F.2d 795 (7th Cir. 1985). The compelling interest asserted was the equalization of the percentage of minority teachers to the percentage of minority students in order to provide role models. However, a rehearing was granted due to the intervening *Wygant* decision, the case of *Johnson v. Transportation Co.*, 107 S. Ct. 1442 (1987), and the continuing controversy in South Bend. Do you think the policy violates Fourteenth Amendment Equal Protection per se? The law review article authors argue that this decision adds little clarity to the doctrine of affirmative action and argue further that the applicability of the per se rule should be limited. Do you agree?

---

*Reprinted with permission. Copyright © 1988 by *Notre Dame Law Review*. University of Notre Dame.

7. Chapter 11 of this book considers the desegregation of students. What should be done with respect to teacher desegregation?

The Supreme Court has long held that faculty desegregation is an indispensable part of the school desegregation process. But it has never made clear the scope of permissible judicial remedies involving teachers once de jure segregation has been found. Although the Court has upheld district court orders requiring school boards to reassign existing staff so that no school is racially identifiable by the composition of its faculty, it has not decided whether federal judges can also impose remedies designed to maintain or increase the number of minority teachers in the school system as a whole.

When court-ordered desegregation moved north and west in the 1970's, district judges in several cases found that the school boards engaged in racially discriminatory hiring practices. In order to vindicate minority students' constitutional right to attend school in a system free of the effects of the past discrimination, some judges imposed permanent faculty quotas designed to create racial parity, between the school system's teaching staff and the student or general population. In addition, when faculty reductions threatened to diminish the ranks of newly hired blacks in the early 1980's, judges ordered race-based layoffs that overrode the seniority rights of white teachers. In 1986 the Supreme Court invalidated under the equal protection clause a voluntarily adopted preferential layoff policy. Nonetheless, hiring and layoff orders remain in effect in some de jure segregation cases.

Court orders mandating racially representative faculties raise difficult questions about the nature of students' rights once a school system has been found unconstitutionally segregated and about the appropriate scope of desegregation remedies. Circuit courts have answered these questions differently. Emphasizing students' right to a school system free of the vestiges of segregation, the First Circuit has upheld teacher quotas and preferential layoffs. In contrast, the Sixth Circuit has rejected permanent quotas on the ground that students have no right to a faculty with a particular racial balance, and it has disallowed race-based layoffs in part by emphasizing the seniority rights of white teachers. As more teachers challenge faculty desegregation remedies and school districts subject to such orders seek judicial determinations that they have achieved unitary status — including unitariness with respect to faculty — the need for a reasoned approach to these issues increases.

Race-Based Hiring and Layoff Remedies in School Desegregation Cases, 104 Harv. L. Rev. 1917 (1991).* *See also Lujon v. Franklin County Bd. of Educ.*, 766 F.2d 917 (6th Cir. 1985), (African American football coach at all black

---

*Copyright © 1991 by the Harvard Law Review Association. Reprinted with permission.

B. HIRING AND DISCHARGE

school was demoted after desegregation in favor of a white applicant. The court found no discrimination against the black coach.)

8. The decision in *Krueth* seeks to distinguish itself from that of *Wygant* in that the former case is said to promote "hiring goals" while the latter mandates "lay-off preferences." Is the difference here as significant as the court allows especially since in each instance members of an identifiable group receive preferential treatment over those not of that group?

Also, what of the *Krueth* court's further distinction from *Wygant* based on the fact that "there is no evidence of prior discrimination against American Indian teachers, which would require a comparison of racial composition of the teaching staff and the racial composition of the qualified public school teacher population in the relevant labor market"? *Krueth* at 836. How can such a distinction be reconciled since the American Indian Education Act of Minnesota was used to maintain sufficient numbers of American Indian teachers to coincide with a significant number (ten) of American Indian students? Wasn't this teacher/student ratio position overruled by *Wygant*?

9. *Krueth* states that its ruling is governed by that of *Morton v. Mancari*, 417 U.S. 535 (1974), a case where the Supreme Court held that American Indians with equivalent qualifications with non-Indian potential employees could receive preferential treatment in hiring decisions in jobs with the Bureau of Indian Affairs. Does *Morton* really represent a good comparison? Doesn't *Krueth*, as was the case in *Wygant*, represent a case where people of color did not have parallel seniority credentials with white employees?

Justice Blackmun in his opinion in *Morton* relates that Congress, by promulgating the Indian Reorganization Act of 1934, intended to give preference to Indians as a group with issues that related to their governance and general welfare. Does this mean that Congress took a step that could be seen as some non-white groups being more equal than others?

Justice Blackmun views the legal status of Indians as a "political group" as opposed to a "racial group" as being sui generis based on Congress' will and its effect upon hiring practices. This is, of course, the same view undertaken by the court in *Krueth*. How does each court describe why such a status would invoke the constitutional test of "rationality" over "strict scrutiny"?

10. The introduction to this section on race presumes that the courts, especially the Supreme Court, will take advantage of the ambiguous language of the Civil Rights Act of 1991 and "follow ... doctrinal and theoretical patterns in employment discrimination cases." This appears to have been the rationale for the Court's decision in *St. Mary's Honor Center v. Hicks*, 113 S. Ct. 2742 (1993). A case of disparate treatment, *Hicks*, concerned an African American correctional officer who was discharged for insubordination despite the fact that he had received good evaluations for most of his career. This changed when a mostly white supervisory staff took over the minimum security prison where he worked. Following termination, Hicks sued, alleging a Title VII violation based on race.

This case is important in that such disputes had been governed by the decision of *McDonnell Douglas Corp. v. Green*, 411 U.S. 792 (1973), and reaffirmed in *Community Affairs v. Burdine*, 450 U.S. 248 (1981). In both cases a test was enunciated that required: 1) a plaintiff to make out a prima facie case of discrimination, and if so; 2) the burden to shift to the employer to produce evidence of non-discriminatory reasons for the treatment of the plaintiff; 3) if the employer does not carry this burden the plaintiff must prevail; 4) if the employer carries the burden, the employee may then demonstrate that the employer's reason was pretextual.

The decision in *Hicks* disregards the framework of *McDonnell Douglas/Burdine* determining that a showing of pretext is insufficient to compel judgment for the plaintiff, stipulating, instead, that the burden stays with the employee until he or she can demonstrate direct evidence of discriminatory intent.

In an angry dissent Justice Souter criticized the majority opinion rendered by Justice Scalia for formulating a new requirement of direct evidence, making it almost impossible for plaintiffs to overcome. Moreover, this new decision permits the employer to lie about reasons for discriminatory dismissal since there is no longer any requirement to articulate specific reasons for dismissal actions. Does this shift of the "burden of production" from the employer to the employee effectively sound the death knell for discrimination suits under Title VII since the vast majority of plaintiffs could not satisfy many aspects of the "burden"?

3. CITIZENSHIP

Constitutional protections of the rights of student-aliens, discussed in Chapter 2, appear to be much broader than those of alien-teachers. Consider the decision below.

AMBACH v. NORWICK
Supreme Court of the United States
441 U.S. 68 (1979)

MR. JUSTICE POWELL delivered the opinion of the Court:

This case presents the question whether a State, consistently with the Equal Protection Clause of the Fourteenth Amendment, may refuse to employ as elementary and secondary school teachers aliens who are eligible for United States citizenship but who refuse to seek naturalization.

I

New York Education Law §§ 3001(3) forbids certification as a public school teacher of any person who is not a citizen of the United States, unless that person has manifested an intention to apply for citizenship. The Commissioner of Education is authorized to create exemptions from this prohibition, and has done so with respect to aliens who are not yet eligible for citizenship. Unless a teacher obtains certification, he may not work in a public elementary or secondary school in New York.

Appellee Norwick was born in Scotland and is a subject of Great Britain. She has resided in this country since 1965 and is married to a United States citizen. Appellee Dachinger is a Finnish subject who came to this country in 1966 and also is married to a United States citizen. Both Norwick and Dachinger currently meet all of the educational requirements New York has set for certification as a public school teacher, but they consistently have refused to seek citizenship in spite of their eligibility to do so. Norwick applied in 1973 for a teaching certificate covering nursery school through sixth grade, and Dachinger sought a certificate covering the same grades in 1975. Both applications were denied because of appellees' failure to meet the requirements of § 3001(3). Norwick then filed this suit seeking to enjoin the enforcement of § 3001(3), and Dachinger obtained leave to intervene as a plaintiff.

... Applying the "close judicial scrutiny" standard of *Graham v. Richardson*, 403 U.S. 365, 372 (1971), the [District] court held that § 3001(3) discriminated against aliens in violation of the Equal Protection Clause. The court believed that the statute was overbroad, because it excluded all resident aliens from all teaching jobs regardless of the subject sought to be taught, the alien's nationality, the nature of the alien's relationship to this country, and the alien's willingness to substitute some other sign of loyalty to this Nation's political values, such as an oath of allegiance. We noted probable jurisdiction over the State's appeal ... and now reverse.

II

A

The decisions of this Court regarding the permissibility of statutory classifications involving aliens have not formed an unwaivering line over the years. State regulation of the employment of aliens long has been subject to constitutional constraints. In *Yick Wo v. Hopkins*, 118 U.S. 356 (1886), the Court struck down an ordinance which was applied to prevent aliens from running laundries, and in *Truax v. Raich*, 239 U.S. 33 (1915), a law requiring at least 80% of the employees of certain businesses to be citizens was held to be an unconstitutional infringement of an alien's "right to work for a living in the common occupations of the community...." At the same time, however, the Court also has recognized a greater degree of latitude for the States when aliens were sought to be excluded from public employment. At the time *Truax* was decided, the governing doctrine permitted States to exclude aliens from various activities when the restriction pertained to "the regulation or distribution of the public domain, or of the common property or resources of the people of the State...." Hence, as part of a larger authority to forbid aliens from owning land, ... harvesting wildlife, ... or maintaining an inherently dangerous enterprise, ... States permissibly could exclude aliens from working on public construction projects, ... and, it appears, from engaging in any form of public employment at all....

Over time, the Court's decisions gradually have restricted the activities from which States are free to exclude aliens.... This process of withdrawal from the former doctrine culminated in *Graham v. Richardson*, 403 U.S. 365 (1971), which for the first time treated classifications based on alienage as "inherently suspect and subject to close judicial scrutiny." ... Applying *Graham*, this Court has held invalid statutes that prevented aliens from entering a State's classified civil service, ... practicing law, ... working as an engineer, ... and receiving state educational benefits....

Although our more recent decisions have departed substantially from the public interest doctrine of *Truax*'s day, they have not abandoned the general principle that some state functions are so bound up with the operation of the State as a governmental entity as to permit the exclusion from those functions of all persons who have not become part of the process of self-government. In *Sugarman* [*v. Dougall*, 412 U.S. 634 (1973)] we recognized that a State could, "in an appropriately defined class of positions, require citizenship as a qualification for office." We went on to observe:

> Such power inheres in the State by virtue of its obligation, already noted above, ... to preserve the basic conception of a political community." ... And this power and responsibility of the State applies, not only to the qualifications of voters, but also to persons holding state elective or important nonelective executive, legislative, and judicial positions, for officers who participate directly in the formulation, execution, or review of broad public policy perform functions that go to the heart of representative government. *Id.* at 647.

The exclusion of aliens from such governmental positions would not invite as demanding scrutiny from this Court.

....

Applying the rational basis standard, we held last Term that New York could exclude aliens from the ranks of its police force. *Foley v. Connelie*, 435 U.S. 291 (1978). Because the police function fulfilled "a most fundamental obligation of government to its constituency" and by necessity cloaked policemen with substantial discretionary powers, we viewed the police force as being one of those appropriately defined classes of positions for which a citizenship requirement could be imposed. *Id.* at 297. Accordingly, the State was required to justify its classification only "by a showing of some rational relationship between the interest sought to be protected and the limiting classification."

The rule for governmental functions, which is an exception to the general standard applicable to classifications based on alienage, rests on important principles inherent in the Constitution. The distinction between citizens and aliens, though ordinarily irrelevant to private activity, is fundamental to the definition and government of a State. The Constitution itself refers to the distinction no less than 11 times, indicating that the status of citizenship was meant to have significance in the structure of our government. The assumption of that status, whether by birth or naturalization, denotes an association with the polity which, in a democratic republic, exercises the powers of governance. The form of this association is important: an oath of allegiance or similar ceremony cannot substitute for the unequivocal legal bond citizenship represents. It is because of this special significance of citizenship that governmental entities, when exercising the functions of government, have wider latitude in limiting the participation of noncitizens.

B

In determining whether, for purposes of equal protection analysis, teaching in public schools constitutes a governmental function, we look to the role of public education and to the degree of responsibility and discretion teachers possess in fulfilling that role. Each of these considerations supports the conclusion that public school teachers may be regarded as performing a task "that go[es] to the heart of representative government."

Public education, like the police function, "fulfills a most fundamental obligation of government to its constituency." The importance of public schools in the preparation of individuals for participation as citizens, and in the preservation of the values on which our society rests, long has been recognized by our decisions:

> Today, education is perhaps the most important function of state and local governments. Compulsory school attendance laws and the great expenditures for education both demonstrate our recognition of the importance of education to our democratic society. It is required in the performance of our most basic public responsibilities, even service in the armed forces. It is the very foundation of good citizenship. Today it is a principal instrument in awakening the child to cultural values, in preparing him for later professional training, and in helping him to adjust normally to his environment. *Brown v. Board of Education*, 347 U.S. 483, 493 (1954).

. . . .

Within the public school system, teachers play a critical part in developing students' attitude toward government and understanding of the role of citizens in our society. Alone among employees of the system, teachers are in direct, day-to-day contact with students both in the classrooms and in the other varied activities of a modern school. In shaping the students' experience to achieve educational goals, teachers by necessity have wide discretion over the way the course material is communicated to students. They are responsible for presenting and explaining the subject matter in a way that is both comprehensible and inspiring. No amount of standardization of teaching materials or lesson plans can eliminate the personal qualities a teacher brings to bear in achieving these goals. Further, a teacher serves as a role model for his students, exerting a subtle but important influence over their perceptions and values. Thus, through both the presentation of course materials and the example he sets, a teacher has an opportunity to influence the attitudes of students toward government, the political process, and a citizen's social responsibilities. This influence is crucial to the continued good health of a democracy.

Furthermore, it is clear that all public school teachers, and not just those responsible for teaching the courses most directly related to government, history, and civic duties, should help fulfill the broader function of the public school system. Teachers, regardless of their specialty, may be called upon to teach other subjects, including those expressly dedicated to political and social subjects. More importantly, a State properly may regard all teachers as having an obligation to promote civic virtues and understanding in their classes, regardless of the subject taught. Certainly a State also may take account of a teacher's function as an example for students, which exists independently of particular classroom subjects. In light of the foregoing considerations, we think it clear that public school teachers come well within the "governmental function" principle recognized in *Sugarman* and *Foley*. Accordingly, the Constitution requires only that a citizenship requirement applicable to teaching in the public schools bears a rational relationship to a legitimate state interest. *See Massachusetts Board of Retirement v. Murgia,* 427 U.S. 307, 314 (1976).

III

As the legitimacy of the States's interest in furthering the educational goals outlined above is undoubted, it remains only to consider whether § 3001(3) bears a rational relationship to this interest. The restriction is carefully framed to serve its purpose, as it bars from teaching only those aliens who have demonstrated their unwillingness to obtain United States citizenship. Appellees, and aliens similarly situated, in effect have chosen to classify themselves. They prefer to retain citizenship in a foreign country with the obligations it entails of primary duty and loyalty. They have rejected the open invitation extended to qualify for eligibility to teach by applying for citizenship in this country. The people of New York, acting through their elected representatives, have made a judgment that citizenship should be a qualification for teaching the young of the State in the public schools, and § 3001(3) furthers that judgment.

4. GENDER

Most current sex-discrimination litigation concerns the application of Congressional enactments and the regulations promulgated to enforce them. Title VI of the Civil Rights Act of 1964, which prohibits discrimination in federally assisted programs on grounds of race, color, or national origin, provided a pattern for later legislation prohibiting discrimination on the basis of sex. Consider the impact of Title VII of the Civil Rights Act of 1964 and Title IX of the Education Amendments of 1972, summarized below.

B. HIRING AND DISCHARGE

Title VII

Since 1972, when Congress amended Title VII of the Civil Rights Act of 1964, adding coverage of state and local governments, including educational institutions, and increasing the power of enforcement procedures, Title VII has become one of the most important and comprehensive prohibitions yet devised against racial and sexual discrimination in public employment. The purpose of Title VII is to prevent employment practices that discriminate against individuals because of their race, color, sex, religion, or national origin. To effect the goals of Title VII, Congress created the Equal Employment Opportunity Commission (EEOC), which has the power to investigate any charges of discrimination filed with it by an aggrieved citizen. If after investigating the charges the Commission determines that there is reasonable cause to believe that the charges are true, it must attempt to conciliate the case. If the conciliation attempts prove unsuccessful, the commission, in the case of public schools, must notify the Attorney General, who may bring a civil action in federal court against the school district to seek compliance with Title VII and other affirmative relief and damages deemed necessary. If the EEOC does not find cause to believe that the school districts are involved in discriminatory practices, this does not preclude the aggrieved party from bringing a private action under Title VII in federal court.

One important exception to Title VII actions, specifically applicable to charges of sex discrimination, should be noted. This is the so-called Bona Fide Occupational Qualification (BFOQ) exception, which applies if an employer can show that a specific staff position should be occupied by a particular sex in order to be performed successfully. Courts have read this exception very narrowly, placing a heavy burden of proof on the employer. As stated in one of the leading cases addressing the problems raised by a BFOQ: "[I]n order to rely on the bona fide occupational qualification exception an employer has the burden of proving that he had reasonable cause to believe, that is, a factual basis for believing, that all or substantially all women would be unable to perform safely and efficiently the duties of the job involved." *Hodgson v. Greyhound Lines, Inc.*, 499 F.2d 859 (7th Cir. 1974). Simply stated, employers will not be able to use the BFOQ exception as a subterfuge to hire individuals according to stereotyped notions ("men are less capable of assembling intricate equipment than women") or comparative general characteristics of women ("the assumption that the turnover rate among women is higher than among men") or preferences of fellow workers, clients, or others.

Title IX

To supplement the Civil Rights Act of 1964, which has general applicability to education, Congress enacted Title IX of the Education Amendments of 1972, which is directed specifically at sex-based discrimination in education. Title IX prohibits discrimination on the basis of sex in any education program receiving federal financial assistance. [Title IX does not apply to military schools, traditionally one-sex schools, one-sex religious schools, and undergraduate admissions.] The U.S. Department of Education (D.O.E.) can enforce compliance with Title IX by threatening to suspend program funds through administrative action, or by suspending such funds if schools fail to comply substantially with the Act. D.O.E. has also issued regulations that serve as guidelines for educational institutions as they develop employment practices that comport with the purpose of Title IX. For example, the regulations forbid a program employer from discriminating against an employee or applicant because of pregnancy or related conditions, or recruiting and hiring employees solely from discriminatory sources. Also, all employees must receive equal pay and equal fringe benefits for equal work. The requirements of Title IX follow very closely those found in Title VI of the Civil Rights Act of 1964 (by Congressional design), which means that Title VI actions will have great precedential value in the development of a body of law under Title IX.

Other Causes of Action

Once considered of little importance, and perhaps outside the scope of judicial review, (*see, e.g.*, *Corne v. Bausche and Lomb*, 390 F. Supp. 161 (D.C. Ariz. 1975), vacated and remanded without opinion, 562 F. 2d 55 (9th Cir. 1977) (finding supervisor's verbal and physical sexual abuse of female co-workers "nothing more than a personal proclivity, peculiarity or the [satisfaction of] a personal urge")), this area of the law also includes causes of action under 14th Amendment due process and equal protection claims, other federal statutes such as 42 U.S.C. § 1983, common law theories of civil liability, state anti-discrimination statutes, state worker's compensation statutes and criminal statutes.

MERITOR SAVINGS BANK, F.S.B. v. VINSON
Supreme Court of the United States
477 U.S. 57 (1986)

JUSTICE REHNQUIST delivered the opinion of the Court:
This case presents important questions concerning claims of workplace "sexual harassment" brought under Title VII of the Civil Rights Act of 1964, 78 Stat. 253, as amended, 42 U.S.C. § 2000e *et seq.*

I

In 1974, respondent Mechelle Vinson met Sidney Taylor, a vice president of what is now petitioner Savings Bank (bank) and manager of one of its branch offices. When respondent asked whether she might obtain employment at the bank, Taylor gave her an application, which she completed and returned the next day; later that same day Taylor called her to say that she had been hired. With Taylor as her supervisor, respondent started as a teller-trainee, and thereafter was promoted to teller, head teller, and assistant branch manager. She worked at the same branch for four years, and it is undisputed that her advancement there was

B. HIRING AND DISCHARGE 649

based on merit alone. In September 1978, respondent notified Taylor that she was taking sick leave for an indefinite period. On November 1, 1978, the bank discharged her for excessive use of that leave.

Respondent brought this action against Taylor and the bank, claiming that during her four years at the bank she had "constantly been subjected to sexual harassment" by Taylor in violation of Title VII. She sought injunctive relief, compensatory and punitive damages against Taylor and the bank, and attorney's fees.

At the 11-day bench trial, the parties presented conflicting testimony about Taylor's behavior during respondent's employment. Respondent testified that during her probationary period as a teller-trainee, Taylor treated her in a fatherly way and made no sexual advances. Shortly thereafter, however, he invited her out to dinner and, during the course of the meal, suggested that they go to a motel to have sexual relations. At first she refused, but out of what she described as fear of losing her job she eventually agreed. According to respondent, Taylor thereafter made repeated demands upon her for sexual favors, usually at the branch, both during and after business hours; she estimated that over the next several years she had intercourse with him some 40 or 50 times. In addition, respondent testified that Taylor fondled her in front of other employees, followed her into the women's restroom when she went there alone, exposed himself to her, and even forcibly raped her on several occasions. These activities ceased after 1977, respondent stated, when she started going with a steady boyfriend.

Respondent also testified that Taylor touched and fondled other women employees of the bank, and she attempted to call witnesses to support this charge. But while some supporting testimony apparently was admitted without objection, the District Court did not allow her "to present wholesale evidence of a pattern and practice relating to sexual advances to other female employees in her case in chief, but advised her that she might well be able to present such evidence in rebuttal to the defendants' cases." Respondent did not offer such evidence in rebuttal. Finally, respondent testified that because she was afraid of Taylor she never reported his harassment to any of his supervisors and never attempted to use the bank's complaint procedure.

Taylor denied respondent's allegations of sexual activity, testifying that he never fondled her, never made suggestive remarks to her, never engaged in sexual intercourse with her, and never asked her to do so. He contended instead that respondent made her accusations in response to a business-related dispute. The bank also denied respondent's allegations and asserted that any sexual harassment by Taylor was unknown to the bank and engaged in without its consent or approval.

The District Court denied relief, but did not resolve the conflicting testimony about the existence of a sexual relationship between respondent and Taylor. It found instead that "[i]f [respondent] and Taylor did engage in an intimate or sexual relationship during the time of [respondent's] employment with [the bank], that relationship was a voluntary one having nothing to do with her continued employment at [the bank] or her advancement or promotions at that institution." The court ultimately found that respondent "was not the victim of sexual harassment and was not the victim of sexual discrimination" while employed at the bank.

....

The Court of Appeals for the District of Columbia Circuit reversed. 243 U.S.App.D.C. 323, 753 F.2d 141 (1985). Relying on its earlier holding in *Bundy v. Jackson*, 205 U.S.App.D.C. 444, 641 F.2d 934 (1981), decided after the trial in this case, the court stated that a violation of Title VII may be predicated on either of two types of sexual harassment: harassment that involves the conditioning of concrete employment benefits on sexual favors, and harassment that, while not affecting economic benefits, creates a hostile or offensive working environment....

....

... We granted certiorari, ... and now affirm ....

II

Title VII of the Civil Rights Act of 1964 makes it "an unlawful employment practice for an employer ... to discriminate against any individual with respect to his compensation, terms, conditions, or privileges of employment, because of such individual's race, color, religion, sex, or national origin." 42 U.S.C. § 2000e-2(a)(1)....

Respondent argues, and the Court of Appeals held, that unwelcome sexual advances that create an offensive or hostile working environment violate Title VII. Without question, when a supervisor sexually harasses a subordinate because of the subordinate's sex, that supervisor "discriminate[s]" on the basis of sex. Petitioner apparently does not challenge this proposition. It contends instead that in prohibiting discrimination with respect to "compensation, terms, conditions, or privileges" of employment, Congress was concerned with what petitioner describes as "tangible loss" of "an economic character," not "purely psychological aspects of the workplace environment." In support of this claim petitioner observes that in both the legislative history of Title VII and this Court's Title VII decisions, the focus has been on tangible, economic barriers erected by discrimination.

We reject petitioner's view. First, the language of Title VII is not limited to "economic" or "tangible" discrimination. The phrase "terms, conditions, or privileges of employment" evinces a congressional intent "'to strike at the entire spectrum of disparate treatment of men and women'" in employment. Petitioner has pointed to nothing in the Act to suggest that Congress contemplated the limitation urged here.

Second, in 1980 the EEOC issued *Guidelines* specifying that "sexual harassment," as there defined, is a form of sex discrimination prohibited by Title VII....

B. HIRING AND DISCHARGE 651

In defining "sexual harassment," the *Guidelines* first describe the kinds of workplace conduct that may be actionable under Title VII. These include "[u]nwelcome sexual advances, requests for sexual favors, and other verbal or physical conduct of a sexual nature." Relevant to the charges at issue in this case, the *Guidelines* provide that such sexual misconduct constitutes prohibited "sexual harassment," whether or not it is directly linked to the grant or denial of an economic *quid pro quo*, where "such conduct has the purpose or effect of unreasonably interfering with an individual's work performance or creating an intimidating, hostile, or offensive working environment."

In concluding that so-called "hostile environment" (*i.e.*, *non quid pro quo*) harassment violates Title VII, the EEOC drew upon a substantial body of judicial decisions and EEOC precedent holding that Title VII affords employees the right to work in an environment free from discriminatory intimidation, ridicule, and insult. *Rogers v. EEOC*, 454 F.2d 234 (CA5 1971), *cert. denied*, 406 U.S. 957 (1972), was apparently the first case to recognize a cause of action based upon a discriminatory work environment. In *Rogers*, the Court of Appeals for the Fifth Circuit held that a Hispanic complainant could establish a Title VII violation by demonstrating that her employer created an offensive work environment for employees by giving discriminatory service to its Hispanic clientele. The court explained that an employee's protections under Title VII extend beyond the economic aspects of employment:

> [T]he phrase "terms, conditions or privileges of employment" in [Title VII] is an expansive concept which sweeps within its protective ambit the practice of creating a working environment heavily charged with ethnic or racial discrimination.... One can readily envision working environments so heavily polluted with discrimination as to destroy completely the emotional and psychological stability of minority group workers...."

Courts applied this principle to harassment based on race, *e.g.*, *Firefighters Institute for Racial Equality v. St. Louis*, 549 F.2d 506, 514-15 (CA8), *cert. denied sub nom. Banta v. United States*, 434 U.S. 819 (1977); *Gray v. Greyhound Lines, East*, 178 U.S.App.D.C. 91, 98, 545 F.2d 169, 176 (1976), religion, *e.g.*, *Compston v. Borden, Inc.*, 424 F.Supp. 157 (SD Ohio 1976), and national origin, *e.g.*, *Cariddi v. Kansas City Chiefs Football Club*, 568 F.2d 87, 88 (CA8 1977). Nothing in Title VII suggests that a hostile environment based on discriminatory sexual harassment should not be likewise prohibited. The *Guidelines* thus appropriately drew from, and were fully consistent with, the existing case law.

Since the *Guidelines* were issued, courts have uniformly held, and we agree, that a plaintiff may establish a violation of Title VII by proving that discrimination based on sex has created a hostile or abusive work environment. As the

Court of Appeals for the Eleventh Circuit wrote in *Henson v. Dundee*, 682 F.2d 897, 902 (1982):

> Sexual harassment which creates a hostile or offensive environment for members of one sex is every bit the arbitrary barrier to sexual equality at the workplace that racial harassment is to racial equality. Surely, a requirement that a man or woman run a gauntlet of sexual abuse in return for the privilege of being allowed to work and make a living can be as demeaning and disconcerting as the harshest of racial epithets.

. . . .

Of course, as the courts in both *Rogers* and *Henson* recognized, not all workplace conduct that may be described as "harassment" affects a "term, condition, or privilege" of employment within the meaning of Title VII. *See Rogers v. EEOC, supra*, at 238 ("mere utterance of an ethnic or racial epithet which engenders offensive feelings in an employee" would not affect the conditions of employment to a sufficiently significant degree to violate Title VII); *Henson*, 682 F.2d at 904 (quoting same). For sexual harassment to be actionable, it must be sufficiently severe or pervasive "to alter the conditions of [the victim's] employment and create an abusive working environment." *Ibid.* Respondent's allegations in this case — which include not only pervasive harassment but also criminal conduct of the most serious nature — are plainly sufficient to state a claim for "hostile environment" sexual harassment.

The question remains, however, whether the District Court's ultimate finding that respondent "was not the victim of sexual harassment," effectively disposed of respondent's claim. The Court of Appeals recognized, we think correctly, that this ultimate finding was likely based on one or both of two erroneous views of the law. First, the District Court apparently believed that a claim for sexual harassment will not lie absent an economic effect on the complainant's employment.... Since it appears that the District Court made its findings without ever considering the "hostile environment" theory of sexual harassment, the Court of Appeals' decision to remand was correct.

Second, the District Court's conclusion that no actionable harassment occurred might have rested on its earlier "finding" that "[i]f [respondent] and Taylor did engage in an intimate or sexual relationship ..., that relationship was a voluntary one." But the fact that sex-related conduct was "voluntary," in the sense that the complainant was not forced to participate against her will, is not a defense to a sexual harassment suit brought under Title VII. The gravamen of any sexual harassment claim is that the alleged sexual advances were "unwelcome." 29 CFR § 1604.11(a) (1985). While the question whether particular conduct was indeed unwelcome presents difficult problems of proof and turns largely on credibility determinations committed to the trier of fact, the District Court in this case erroneously focused on the "voluntariness" of respondent's participation in the claimed sexual episodes. The correct inquiry is whether respondent by her

B. HIRING AND DISCHARGE

conduct indicated that the alleged sexual advances were unwelcome, not whether her actual participation in sexual intercourse was voluntary.

Petitioner contends that even if this case must be remanded to the District Court, the Court of Appeals erred in one of the terms of its remand. Specifically, the Court of Appeals stated that testimony about respondent's "dress and personal fantasies," which the District Court apparently admitted into evidence, "had no place in this litigation." The apparent ground for this conclusion was that respondent's voluntariness vel non in submitting to Taylor's advances was immaterial to her sexual harassment claim. While "voluntariness" in the sense of consent is not a defense to such a claim, it does not follow that a complainant's sexually provocative speech or dress is irrelevant as a matter of law in determining whether he or she found particular sexual advances unwelcome. To the contrary, such evidence is obviously relevant. The EEOC Guidelines emphasize that the trier of fact must determine the existence of sexual harassment in light of "the record as a whole" and "the totality of circumstances, such as the nature of the sexual advances and the context in which the alleged incidents occurred." 29 CFR § 1604.11(b) (1985)....

III

Although the District Court concluded that respondent had not proved a violation of Title VII, it nevertheless went on to consider the question of the bank's liability. Finding that "the bank was without notice" of Taylor's alleged conduct, and that notice to Taylor was not the equivalent of notice to the bank, the court concluded that the bank therefore could not be held liable for Taylor's alleged actions. The Court of Appeals took the opposite view, holding that an employer is strictly liable for a hostile environment created by a supervisor's sexual advances, even though the employer neither knew nor reasonably could have known of the alleged misconduct. The court held that a supervisor, whether or not he possesses the authority to hire, fire, or promote, is necessarily an "agent" of his employer for all Title VII purposes, since "even the appearance" of such authority may enable him to impose himself on his subordinates.

The parties and amici suggest several different standards for employer liability. Respondent, not surprisingly, defends the position of the Court of Appeals. Noting that Title VII's definition of "employer" includes any "agent" of the employer, she also argues that "so long as the circumstance is work-related, the supervisor is the employer and the employer is the supervisor." Notice to Taylor that the advances were unwelcome, therefore, was notice to the bank.

Petitioner argues that respondent's failure to use its established grievance procedure, or to otherwise put it on notice of the alleged misconduct, insulates petitioner from liability for Taylor's wrongdoing. A contrary rule would be unfair, petitioner argues, since in a hostile environment harassment case the employer often will have no reason to know about, or opportunity to cure, the alleged wrongdoing.

The EEOC, in its brief as amicus curiae, contends that courts formulating employer liability rules should draw from traditional agency principles. Examination of those principles has led the EEOC to the view that where a supervisor exercises the authority actually delegated to him by his employer, by making or threatening to make decisions affecting the employment status of his subordinates, such actions are properly imputed to the employer whose delegation of authority empowered the supervisor to undertake them. Thus, the courts have consistently held employers liable for the discriminatory discharges of employees by supervisory personnel, whether or not the employer knew, should have known, or approved of the supervisor's actions.

The EEOC suggests that when a sexual harassment claim rests exclusively on a "hostile environment" theory, however, the usual basis for a finding of agency will often disappear. In that case, the EEOC believes, agency principles lead to

> a rule that asks whether a victim of sexual harassment had reasonably available an avenue of complaint regarding such harassment, and, if available and utilized, whether that procedure was reasonably responsive to the employee's complaint. If the employer has an expressed policy against sexual harassment and has implemented a procedure specifically designed to resolve sexual harassment claims, and if the victim does not take advantage of that procedure, the employer should be shielded from liability absent actual knowledge of the sexually hostile environment (obtained, *e.g.*, by the filing of a charge with the EEOC or a comparable state agency). In all other cases, the employer will be liable if it has actual knowledge of the harassment or if, considering all the facts of the case, the victim in question had no reasonably available avenue for making his or her complaint known to appropriate management officials.

As respondent points out, this suggested rule is in some tension with the EEOC Guidelines, which hold an employer liable for the acts of its agents without regard to notice. 29 CFR § 1604.11(c) (1985). The Guidelines do require, however, an "examin[ation of] the circumstances of the particular employment relationship and the job [f]unctions performed by the individual in determining whether an individual acts in either a supervisory or agency capacity."

This debate over the appropriate standard for employer liability has a rather abstract quality about it given the state of the record in this case. We do not know at this stage whether Taylor made any sexual advances toward respondent at all, let alone whether those advances were unwelcome, whether they were sufficiently pervasive to constitute a condition of employment, or whether they were "so pervasive and so long continuing ... that the employer must have become conscious of [them]," *Taylor v. Jones*, 653 F.2d 1193, 1197-99 (CA8 1981) (holding employer liable for racially hostile working environment based on constructive knowledge).

We therefore decline the parties' invitation to issue a definitive rule on employer liability, but we do agree with the EEOC that Congress wanted courts

B. HIRING AND DISCHARGE

to look to agency principles for guidance in this area. While such common-law principles may not be transferable in all their particulars to Title VII, Congress' decision to define "employer" to include any "agent" of an employer, 42 U.S.C. § 2000e(b), surely evinces an intent to place some limits on the acts of employees for which employers under Title VII are to be held responsible. For this reason, we hold that the Court of Appeals erred in concluding that employers are always automatically liable for sexual harassment by their supervisors. *See generally* Restatement (Second) of Agency §§ 219-37 (1958). For the same reason, absence of notice to an employer does not necessarily insulate that employer from liability.

Finally, we reject petitioner's view that the mere existence of a grievance procedure and a policy against discrimination, coupled with respondent's failure to invoke that procedure, must insulate petitioner from liability. While those facts are plainly relevant, the situation before us demonstrates why they are not necessarily dispositive. Petitioner's general nondiscrimination policy did not address sexual harassment in particular, and thus did not alert employees to their employer's interest in correcting that form of discrimination. Moreover, the bank's grievance procedure apparently required an employee to complain first to her supervisor, in this case Taylor. Since Taylor was the alleged perpetrator, it is not altogether surprising that respondent failed to invoke the procedure and report her grievance to him. Petitioner's contention that respondent's failure should insulate it from liability might be substantially stronger if its procedures were better calculated to encourage victims of harassment to come forward.

IV

....

Accordingly, the judgment of the Court of Appeals reversing the judgment of the District Court is affirmed, and the case is remanded for further proceedings consistent with this opinion.

It is so ordered.

....

JUSTICE MARSHALL, with whom JUSTICE BRENNAN, JUSTICE BLACKMUN, and JUSTICE STEVENS join, concurring in the judgment:

I fully agree with the Court's conclusion that workplace sexual harassment is illegal, and violates Title VII. Part III of the Court's opinion, however, leaves open the circumstances in which an employer is responsible under Title VII for such conduct. Because I believe that question to be properly before us, I write separately.

The issue the Court declines to resolve is addressed in the EEOC Guidelines on Discrimination Because of Sex, which are entitled to great deference. *See Griggs v. Duke Power Co.*, 401 U.S. 424, 433-34 (1971) (EEOC Guidelines on

Employment Testing Procedures of 1966); *see also ante* at 2404. The Guidelines explain:

> Applying general Title VII principles, an employer ... is responsible for its acts and those of its agents and supervisory employees with respect to sexual harassment regardless of whether the specific acts complained of were authorized or even forbidden by the employer and regardless of whether the employer knew or should have known of their occurrence. The Commission will examine the circumstances of the particular employment relationship and the job [f]unctions performed by the individual in determining whether an individual acts in either a supervisory or agency capacity.... 29 CFR §§ 1604.11(c), (d) (1985).

The Commission, in issuing the Guidelines, explained that its rule was "in keeping with the general standard of employer liability with respect to agents and supervisory employees.... [T]he Commission and the courts have held for years that an employer is liable if a supervisor or an agent violates the Title VII, regardless of knowledge or any other mitigating factor." 45 Fed.Reg. 74676 (1980). I would adopt the standard set out by the Commission.

....

The brief filed by the Solicitor General on behalf of the United States and the EEOC in this case suggests that a different rule should apply when a supervisor's harassment "merely" results in a discriminatory work environment. The Solicitor General concedes that sexual harassment that affects tangible job benefits is an exercise of authority delegated to the supervisor by the employer, and thus gives rise to employer liability. But, departing from the EEOC Guidelines, he argues that the case of a supervisor merely creating a discriminatory work environment is different because the supervisor "is not exercising, or threatening to exercise, actual or apparent authority to make personnel decisions affecting the victim." In the latter situation, he concludes, some further notice requirement should therefore be necessary.

The Solicitor General's position is untenable. A supervisor's responsibilities do not begin and end with the power to hire, fire, and discipline employees, or with the power to recommend such actions. Rather, a supervisor is charged with the day-to-day supervision of the work environment and with ensuring a safe, productive workplace. There is no reason why abuse of the latter authority should have different consequences than abuse of the former. In both cases it is the authority vested in the supervisor by the employer that enables him to commit the wrong: it is precisely because the supervisor is understood to be clothed with the employer's authority that he is able to impose unwelcome sexual conduct on subordinates. There is therefore no justification for a special rule, to be applied only in "hostile environment" cases, that sexual harassment does not create employer liability until the employee suffering the discrimination notifies other supervisors. No such requirement appears in the statute, and no such requirement can coherently be drawn from the law of agency.

Agency principles and the goals of Title VII law make appropriate some limitation on the liability of employers for the acts of supervisors. Where, for example, a supervisor has no authority over an employee, because the two work in wholly different parts of the employer's business, it may be improper to find strict employer liability. *See* 29 CFR § 1604.11(c) (1985). Those considerations, however, do not justify the creation of a special "notice" rule in hostile environment cases.

....

I therefore reject the Solicitor General's position. I would apply in this case the same rules we apply in all other Title VII cases, and hold that sexual harassment by a supervisor of an employee under his supervision, leading to a discriminatory work environment, should be imputed to the employer for Title VII purposes regardless of whether the employee gave "notice" of the offense.

---

1. The Court in *Meritor Savings* assigns "unwelcomeness" as a critical element in employment-related sexual harassment. How does one interpret "unwelcomeness" in a victim? By conduct? *See Meritor Savings* at 68-69. By provocative speech or dress? *See Jones v. Wesco Investments*, Inc, 846 F.2d 1154 (8th Cir. 1986). What of a victim's past conduct? *See Swentek v. USAir, Inc.*, 830 F.2d 552 (4th Cir. 1987). Does a sexual harassment victim have a duty to tell an aggressor that the conduct in question is unwelcome? *See Chamberlain v. 101 Realty Co.*, 915 F.2d 777 (1st Cir. 1990), and *Wesco Investments*, this note.

2. Will previous consensual acts, such as the ones alleged by the supervisor in *Meritor Savings*, serve as proof against employer liability? The Court, in answering this question, focused again on the issue of "unwelcomeness," despite the fact that Vinson admitted to 40 to 50 acts of intercourse with her supervisor. "The correct inquiry is whether respondent by her conduct indicated that the alleged sexual advances were unwelcome, not whether her actual participation was voluntary." *Meritor*, at 68. *But see Trautvetter v. Quick*, 916 F.2d 1140 (7th Cir. 1990), where the court ruled that a teacher's complaint that her principal had violated her rights under Title VII by allegedly pressuring her into a sexual relationship brought no liability to the school district because the relationship was voluntary and consensual and teacher refused several board offers of transfer to other schools.

3. In its analysis, the *Meritor Savings* Court established two types of sexual harassment employment claims. Hostile environment complaints involve the creation of an intimidating or hostile working environment by supervisors or other employees; quid pro quo claims occur where a supervisor makes sexual demands of a subordinate in return for being hired, receiving a salary increase, a promotion or any other benefit of employment. In both kinds of claims the Court looked to the original intent of Title VII and guidelines produced under the

Equal Employment Opportunity Commission announcing, "Title VII is not limited to economic or tangible discrimination" and "[EEOC guidelines prohibit sexual harassment in any form]." Is the Court's decision as sweeping as it appears? Is all workplace conduct that may be described as "sexual harassment" actionable under Title VII or the EEOC?

As Title VII is not limited to economic or tangible discrimination, recovery under Title VII is not limited to tangible, pecuniary losses. The EEOC Decision No. 915-002 in 1992 gives us guidance on the compensatory and punitive damages available under the Civil Rights Act of 1991. Initially, the amount of recovery is limited, based on the size of the employer, ranging from $50,000 for employers of 15 to 100 employees to $300,000 for employers with more than 500 employees. These damage caps apply to each aggrieved party, even if an individual or the EEOC is pursuing a claim on behalf of more than one person. Pecuniary losses recoverable include expenses for moving, job search, medical treatment, psychiatric treatment, physical therapy, and other quantifiable out-of-pocket expenses. Both past and future pecuniary losses may be recovered. Nonpecuniary losses, such as emotional harm, pain and suffering, inconvenience, and loss of enjoyment of life, are also available under the Civil Rights Act. Awards for emotional harm are available only if a causal connection between the employer's illegal actions and the complaining party's injury is established. Except as against a federal, state, or local government, a government agency, or a political subdivision, punitive damages are available where the employer acted with malice or with reckless indifference to the federally protected rights of an aggrieved individual. *See* Section 102 of the Civil Rights Act of 1991, 105 Stat. 1071, Pub. L. No. 102-166 (Sec. 1981A).

4. Chief Justice Rehnquist's unanimous opinion is at odds with the concurring opinion of Justice Marshall as regards the issue of employer liability. What is the source of this difference of opinion that split the court 5-4? Which opinion has influenced subsequent cases? What is the standard of employer liability in such cases? Does the Chief Justice elaborate on this concern?

5. Should sexual harassment victims be expected to report claims earlier than Vinson did in this case? How important is the *fear* of losing one's job? Vinson testified that she gave in and had intercourse several times and was forcibly raped at other times. The facts of the case also state that she filed a sexual harassment claim only after she was fired for excessive use of sick leave in the calendar year following the last of the sexually harassing events.

6. Is the bank's grievance policy and the failure of Vinson to invoke it important to the decision in this case? Assuming the nondiscrimination policy mentioned sexual harassment, would the fact that the first report had to go to Vinson's supervisor, the perpetrator of the harassment, been enough to waive the report requirement on her part?

7. The decision in *Meritor Savings* did not articulate a framework for determining whose perspective of "sexual harassment" should be used in such cases. The notion has been presented in other cases, however. *See, e.g., Rabidue*

B. HIRING AND DISCHARGE

v. Osceola Refining Co., 805 F.2d 61 (6th Cir. 1986) ("reasonable individual"); *Ellison v. Brady*, 924 F.2d 872 (9th Cir. 1991) ("reasonable person of the victim's sex"). The court in *Brady* allowed that a victim's view requires, among other things, an analysis of the different perspectives of men and women. Conduct that men consider unobjectionable may offend many women. Further, conduct which a reasonable woman (victim) would consider sufficiently severe or pervasive to alter the condition of the employment and create an abusive working environment will be considered.

8. The *Rabidue* court, cited in note 7 above, also articulated the test that plaintiffs must prove for a sexual harassment claim to be actionable under Title VII. To wit:

> [Plaintiff] was subjected to unwelcome sexual harassment in the form of sexual advances, requests for sexual favors, or other verbal or physical conduct of a sexual nature; the harassment complained of was based on sex; the charged sexual harassment had the effect of unreasonably interfering with plaintiff's work performance, and creating an intimidating hostile or offensive environment that seriously affected the psychological well-being of the plaintiff; and there exists respondeat superior liability, *i.e.*, knowledge or constructive knowledge on the part of the employer. *Rabidue*, at 126.

9. *Meritor Savings* speaks broadly to the doctrine that Title VII sexual harassment claims may be brought by men or women, *i.e.*, "[t]he phrase 'terms, conditions or privileges of employment' evinces a 'congressional intent' to strike at the entire spectrum of disparate treatment of men and women." *Meritor*, at 64. The claim, however, is often thought of as being exclusive to women in the workplace. *But see Showalter v. Allison Reed Group, Inc.*, 767 F. Supp. 1205 (D.R.I. 1991), where two male employees established liability for their employer under Title VII for both hostile environment and quid pro quo sexual harassment because of being forced to engage in sexual activities with manager's secretary and by being threatened with the loss of employment if they did not acquiesce to the demands.

10. A number of courts had considered the question as to whether Title IX applied to employment practices in educational institutions. *See, e.g., Dougherty County Sch. Sys. v. Harris*, 662 F.2d 735 (1980); *Romeo Community Schs. v. United States Dept. of Health, Educ. and Welfare*, 600 F.2d 119 (1979); *Junior College of St. Louis v. Califano*, 597 F.2d 119 (1979). The question was answered by the Supreme Court in *North Haven Bd. of Educ. v. Bell*, 456 U.S. 512 (1982), in the affirmative, but the Court left open the issue of the conditions of federal financial assistance to such institutions for Title IX to apply. One important interpretation was rendered in *Grove City College v. Bell*, 465 U.S. 555 (1984), where the Court held, in effect, that for a Title IX employment complaint to be brought, the plaintiff must be employed in the specific program receiving federal assistance. This, for example, could mean that if the employment dispute occurred in an extracurricular activity and the school only received funds in academic areas, no claim would apply. Congress, however, in its passage of the Civil Rights Act of 1991, made it plain that a Title IX suit would affect all of an educational institution's federal funds despite the specific areas receiving the funding.

What of the interplay of Title VII and Title IX? Are there analogous situations such as quid pro quo sexual harassment that would permit expansion of liability to school systems for intentional actions of school employees? Two courts have answered this question in the affirmative. *Lipsett v. University of Puerto Rico*, 864 F.2d 881 (1st Cir. 1988) (holding that the hostile environment theory established in *Meritor Savings* is accepted in the academic setting), and *Moire v. Temple Univ. Sch. of Med.*, 613 F. Supp. 1360 (E.D. Pa. 1985), *aff'd*, 800 F.2d 1136 (1986), stating that Title VII doctrines are equally applicable to Title IX.

Lipsett, for example, is a case where a female student who was also an employee in a medical school brought action against the university based on charges of sexual harassment by superiors. The plaintiff brought causes of action under both Title VII and Title IX because of her dual status. Quoting *Mabry v. State Bd. of Community Colleges and Occupational Educ.*, 813 F.2d 311 (10th Cir. 1987), the court stated it "would regard Title VII as the most appropriate analogue when defining Title IX's substantive standards." *Lipsett*, at 896. The court went on to say that even though Title VII's language excludes educational institutions from its terms, "[Title IX] would remove that exemption and bring those in education under the equal protection provision." *Id.* at 897.

What, then, constitutes employee sexual harassment under Title IX? Similar to decisions involving Title VII, will educational institutions be liable for failing to adopt and communicate procedures against sexual harassment? What are the implications for this merger of statutes for school systems and their employees? Recall the limits for recovery for a successful employee suit under the EEOC Guidelines, *supra*. A successful action under Title IX could result in the loss of federal funding, injunctive relief and monetary damages not limited to those in Title VII.

Cases of Title IX complaints by students can be found in Chapter 4 of this text.

11. The EEOC has indicated that school systems and other employers may be able to rebut claims that they authorized or condoned sexual harassment by developing, widely publicizing and strongly adhering to a policy against such acts. In the *EEOC Guidance Memorandum on Sexual Harassment*, 129 L.R.R.M. 238 (Oct. 24, 1988), the EEOC, interpreting *Meritor Savings*, stated that employers can divest supervisors of apparent authority by implementing policies against sexual harassment and maintaining an effective, publicized complaint procedure. The memorandum stressed that prevention is the best method of avoiding liability, and this is assured when employees are aware of such policies and supervisors are trained in their contents. As regards a hostile environment, the memorandum states, "[w]hen employees know that recourse is available, they

B. HIRING AND DISCHARGE

cannot reasonably believe that a harassing work environment is authorized or condoned by an employer." The memorandum went on to relate, however, that internal personnel policies will not insulate an employer from charges of quid pro quo sexual harassment. "No matter what the employer's policy, the employer is always liable for any supervisory actions that affect the victim's employment status, such as hiring, firing, promotion, or pay."

Case law in this area indicates that an employer's response to incidents of sexual harassment must be reasonably calculated to put an end to the harassment. *Waltman v. International Paper Co.*, 875 F.2d 468 (5th Cir. 1989). However, even prompt investigation of complaints will not automatically exempt an employer from liability. *See Craig v. Y&Y Snacks*, 721 F.2d 77 (3d Cir. 1983). In addition, the absence of specificity in a policy may result in liability. *Yates v. AVCO Corp.*, 819 F.2d 630 (6th Cir. 1987).

12. For a review of research on the problems of sexual harassment in educational institutions, *see* Note, *Civil Rights — Sex Discrimination in Education — Compensatory Damages Available in Title IX Sexual Harassment Claim: Franklin v. Gwinnett County Pub. Schs., 112 S. Ct. 1028 (1992)*, 15 U. Ark. Little Rock L.J. 271 (1993); Note, *Sexual Orientation in the Public Schools*, 102 Harv. L. Rev. 1584 (1989); Ingulli, *Sexual Harassment in Education*, 18 Rutgers L.J. 281 (1987); Schneider, *Sexual Harassment in Higher Education*, 65 Tex. L. Rev. 525 (1987); Note, *The Supreme Court's Recognition of the Hostile Environment in Sexual Harassment Claims*, 20 Akron L. Rev. 575 (1987).

13. For a school-related hostile environment claim, consider *Jew v. University of Iowa*, 749 F. Supp. 946 (S.D. Iowa 1990). The plaintiff, Jew, a female professor of Chinese descent in the University of Iowa College of Medicine, asserted a Title VII sex and race discrimination claim against the university. Her charge stemmed from many years of false rumors, office door cartoons depicting her, bathroom wall graffiti, and indirect and direct comments and insults. These acts were committed, in large part, by Jew's colleagues and superiors, many of whom played a substantial role in her tenure proceedings. All of her superiors, including the Dean of the College, knew about these incidents. The Dean brushed off an early complaint as something "women would have to expect." Jew was later denied tenure by a vote of 5-3, despite strong teaching and research history. Three of the five "no" votes came from perpetrators of the harassment. Using the test in *Meritor* and similar cases, the court ruled in favor of Jew, finding a hostile environment. The court will find a hostile environment if:

(1) the victim belongs to a protected group of plaintiffs;
(2) she was subject to unwelcome sexual harassment;
(3) the harassment was based on sex (in nature, or by gender);
(4) the harassment affected a term, condition, or privilege of employment; and

(5) the employer knew or should have known of the harassment in question and failed to take proper remedial action. *Id.* at 958.

Jew also prevailed on a claim for failure to promote. After Jew stated a case for discrimination, the defendant university failed to show that it had a legitimate nondiscriminatory reason for its denial of tenure. The court found that Jew was qualified for tenure, and ordered that she be tenured effective July, 1984, with back pay.

YATVIN v. MADISON METROPOLITAN SCHOOL DISTRICT
United States Court of Appeals
840 F.2d 412 (7th Cir. 1988)

POSNER, CIRCUIT JUDGE:

Joanne Yatvin, the principal of a public school in Wisconsin, brought suit under Title VII of the Civil Rights Act of 1964, 42 U.S.C. § 2000e, and section 1 of the Civil Rights Act of 1871, now 42 U.S.C. § 1983, against a variety of public agencies and officials, complaining that the denial of two promotions that she sought violated her rights under Title VII and the Fourteenth Amendment. She lost, and appeals.

In 1983 Yatvin had applied for the position of Assistant Superintendent of Instruction for the Madison school district. Three men also applied. A committee interviewed all four but recommended only two (both of them men) to the hiring authority, Donald Hafeman, the superintendent of the school district. He picked Jerry Patterson, prompting Yatvin to file charges of sex discrimination with the relevant state and federal agencies. Shortly afterward she applied for the position of Director of Curriculum and Staff Development for the Madison school district. Again there were four applicants. After being interviewed, all were recommended to Hafeman, who delegated the hiring decision to Patterson, who after interviewing the four applicants chose a woman for the job — but not Yatvin. She claims that she was turned down the first time because she was a woman and the second time in retaliation for her action in filing sex discrimination charges growing out of her first application.

The judge ruled that Yatvin was entitled to a jury trial on her claim that the denial of her first application violated the equal protection clause of the Fourteenth Amendment, but not on her claim of retaliation, for he rejected her argument that retaliation for the filing of sex discrimination charges violates the Constitution rather than just Title VII, which confers no right to a jury trial. Nevertheless the judge submitted both of Yatvin's Title VII claims (sex discrimination for the first turn-down and retaliation for the second) to the jury, but for advice only, not decision. The jury brought in a verdict for the defendants on sex discrimination (both the claim under the equal protection clause and the claim under Title VII), but a verdict for Yatvin on retaliation. The judge then made his own findings of fact and conclusions of law on retaliation; finding no

B. HIRING AND DISCHARGE

retaliation and thus rejecting the jury's advisory verdict, he entered judgment for the defendants on all counts.

When Yatvin applied for the job of Assistant Superintendent of Instruction, the Madison school district had an affirmative action plan which provided that "in cases where the position to be filled is for a job classification where a particular protected group is under-utilized or under-represented, if a member of the under-utilized or under-represented groups is as qualified as the other candidate(s), the member of the under-utilized or underrepresented group shall be offered the position." Yatvin contends that the defendants violated this provision by appointing Patterson, a white male, rather than her, the only female applicant, and that by violating it they discriminated against her on grounds of sex, contrary to the equal protection clause and to Title VII. The argument has two fatal flaws. First, the affirmative action plan was not violated. It awards the job to the applicant from the favored group only in the event of a tie, and there was no tie. The interview committee, composed of five men and three women, ranked Yatvin third out of four and forwarded to Hafeman only the two highest-ranked applicants, who had each received almost twice as many points as Yatvin.

In any event, the breach of a promise to give women favored treatment is not sex discrimination. Sex discrimination is treating a person worse because of her (or his) sex; it is not refusing to discriminate in favor of a person on grounds of her sex. *See Szabo Food Service, Inc. v. Canteen Corp.*, 823 F.2d 1073, 1084 (7th Cir. 1987) (race). The Constitution and Title VII have been held, with exceptions irrelevant here, to permit affirmative action; they do not require it. *See, e.g., Texas Department of Community Affairs v. Burdine*, 450 U.S. 248, 259 (1981). Granted, just as the establishment of a bona fide affirmative action plan might help rebut a claim of sex discrimination, *see Coser v. Moore*, 739 F.2d 746, 751 (2d Cir. 1984), so the violation of such a plan might help support such a claim, *see, e.g., Id.* at 751; *Craik v. Minnesota State University Bd.*, 731 F.2d 465, 472 (8th Cir. 1984); *Chang v. University of Rhode Island*, 606 F.Supp. 1161, 1183-84 (D.R.I.1985). Although we have found no case where such evidence played a significant role, we can imagine one. Suppose that a plan favoring women were adopted in settlement of a sex discrimination case and the defendant refused to follow the plan even though it had honored the commitments made in settlement of all its other cases; an inference of sex discrimination might arise from the violation of the affirmative action plan in those circumstances. Yet even then, the violation of the plan would not be sex discrimination as such. We therefore disagree with the suggestion in *Morman v. John Hancock Mutual Life Ins. Co.*, 672 F.Supp. 993, 995 (E.D.Mich.1987), that if an employer uses an affirmative action plan as a "shield from claims of discrimination, employees arguably protected by the plan can use it as a sword to challenge the propriety of their treatment" — if what this means is that a violation of the plan is a violation of Title VII rather than just possible evidence of such a violation.

And where there is substantial compliance with an affirmative action plan, occasional departures have no evidentiary significance at all. *Cf. Coser v. Moore*, *supra*, 739 F.2d at 751; *Gray v. University of Arkansas*, 658 F.Supp. 709, 726-27 (W.D.Ark.1987). The adoption of such plans would be discouraged if failure to achieve perfect compliance with them were treated as evidence of discrimination. The response in *Morman* to this argument — "then so be it," — is not compelling.

....

The due process clauses of the Fifth and Fourteenth Amendments do not entitle a person to a federal remedy for every breach of contract by a state or federal agency. *See Brown v. Brienen*, 722 F.2d 360, 364 (7th Cir. 1983), and cases cited there; *Jett v. Dallas Independent School District*, 798 F.2d 748, 754 n. 3 (5th Cir. 1986). If they did, every breach of every public contract would be actionable in federal court. What is true is that a property right (or what the Supreme Court considers to be a property right for purposes of the due process clauses of the Fifth and Fourteenth Amendments) often is created by contract. A tenured professor in a public university has a Fourteenth Amendment property right in his job; the right is created by his tenure contract with the university. Thus, unless every breach of every public contract is to be actionable as a violation of constitutional rights, it is necessary to distinguish between "mere" contract rights and property rights created by contracts.

The problem is placed in focus by this court's decision in *Vail v. Board of Education of Paris Union School District No. 95*, 706 F.2d 1435 (7th Cir. 1983), *aff'd* by an equally divided Court without opinion, 466 U.S. 377 (1984). A school district had fired a coach in alleged violation of a one-year implied contract — a job right falling far short of tenure as that term is ordinarily understood. The question whether this job right was a property right divided both this court and (one assumes) the Supreme Court; fortunately we need not revisit it today, as there are two grounds on which to distinguish *Vail*.

The first is that there is no suggestion that the appointment which Yatvin sought was a tenure appointment even in the attenuated sense involved in *Vail*: that is, appointment under a contract as distinguished from employment at will. Had she gotten the appointment and been fired the next day, she could not have complained of a deprivation of property; no more should she be allowed to complain that the failure to appoint her deprived her of property, even if the failure was due to a breach of contract. She claims entitlement to consideration for a job that is itself not property in the constitutional sense; and the interest in being considered for a job is even more attenuated than the interest in the job.

Second, the right conferred by the affirmative action plan was too contingent to count as property, which in the constitutional setting is "what is securely and durably yours under state (or ... federal) law, as distinct from what you hold subject to so many conditions as to make your interest meager, transitory, or uncertain." *Reed v. Village of Shorewood*, 704 F.2d 943, 948 (7th Cir. 1983). The affirmative action "contract" (if that is how we should view it) gave Yatvin merely an enforceable expectation of favorable consideration should she apply for a different job from the one she had and turn out to be as qualified as the most qualified competing applicant. That expectation was too exiguous to count as property under the due process clauses, given the inherent uncertainty whether she could meet the condition (that she be no less qualified than the best of her rivals). *See Bigby v. City of Chicago*, 766 F.2d 1053 (7th Cir. 1985). The plaintiff in *Vail* had a contractual entitlement, short term though it was, to a job. The plaintiff in *Goldberg v. Kelly*, 397 U.S. 254, 261-62 (1970), had an entitlement to welfare benefits contingent only on his satisfying clearly specified criteria of financial need. But the plaintiff in the present case (as in *Bigby*) is complaining about conduct that impaired a noncontractual expectation of a job, since even if the affirmative action plan created a contractual right, it was not a right to the job itself. To count as a deprivation of property under the Constitution, a breach of contract must be a breach of a contractual entitlement to property, not a breach of a contractual entitlement to some extra consideration that will result in a job offer only if some other, highly uncertain condition is satisfied.

....

The very dearth of evidence of discrimination might seem to strengthen rather than weaken her argument that the second rejection — the rejection of her application for the position of Director of Curriculum and Staff Development — was in retaliation for filing sex discrimination charges growing out of the first rejection. For one could argue that the more baseless the charges, the stronger the itch to retaliate against the charging party; the counterargument, however, is that the benefits from retaliating are greater if persons having valid charges can be deterred by the threat of retaliation from filing them. A more important point is that if the charges are truly baseless the employee's action in filing them may itself be a form of misconduct justifying disciplinary measures not rightly deemed retaliatory. *See Rucker v. Higher Educational Aids Board*, 669 F.2d 1179, 1182 (7th Cir. 1982). The employer's objection might be, not to suits for discrimination, but to frivolous suits of any description — to malicious prosecution or abuse of process, in other words; and discipline motivated by such an objection would not be retaliation for the exercise of legal rights. There is no right to harass an employer with frivolous suits, and the employer is not required to tolerate the commission of torts against him by employees. Anyway Yatvin presented no evidence of retaliation, but only a conjecture that since she had implicitly accused Patterson of obtaining a job that rightfully belonged to her he must have harbored resentment against her which caused him to reject her second application.

Thus we have no basis for disturbing the district judge's ruling exonerating the defendants from the charge of retaliation. Nor can we agree with Yatvin that the judge showed disrespect for the institution of trial by jury by rejecting the jury's finding (contrary to his) of retaliation. *Wilson v. City of Aliceville*, 779 F.2d 631, 635-36 (11th Cir. 1986). It was an advisory jury, *see* Fed. R. Civ. P. 39(c); 9 Wright & Miller, Federal Practice and Procedure § 2335 (1971) — a hallowed institution in equity cases (and Title VII cases are equity cases) but one that would cease to exist if an advisory jury's verdict had the same effect as the verdict of a regular jury. It makes no difference that the same jury was an advisory jury on some issues and the trier of fact on others.

Yatvin argues further, however, that retaliation for filing charges of sex discrimination in employment violates not only the antiretaliation provision of Title VII, 42 U.S.C. § 2000e-3(a), which does not entitle a plaintiff to trial by jury, but also the equal protection clause and the First Amendment's free speech and petition clauses, when as in this case the defendants are public agencies and officials, and 42 U.S.C. § 1981 when they are private. If she is right, she was entitled to a jury trial on her retaliation claim, since this part of her suit asks for damages.

The equal protection branch of the argument is weak. Although sex discrimination by state agencies has been held to violate the equal protection clause, retaliating against a person for filing charges of sex discrimination is not the same as discriminating against a person on grounds of sex, *see Tafoya v. Adams*, 816 F.2d 555, 558 and n. 4 (10th Cir. 1987); *Irby v. Sullivan*, 737 F.2d 1418, 1430 n. 22 (5th Cir. 1984) — unless, perhaps, those are the only complainants against whom the employer retaliates, and even in that case the retaliation would only be evidence of discrimination, not discrimination per se. Nor is it plausible that Congress would have wanted to allow a victim of a Title VII violation to bypass the administrative procedures created by the statute (procedures as applicable to retaliation claims as to any other claims under Title VII), and go directly to court, through the illogical expedient of equating discrimination against a person for filing charges of sex discrimination to sex discrimination itself. *Day v. Wayne County Board of Auditors*, 749 F.2d 1199, 1204 (6th Cir. 1984). Suppose a male fellow worker had testified on Yatvin's behalf and had been punished for doing so. It would not be a case of treating him badly because he was a man; his sex would be irrelevant. It is because Yatvin filed sex discrimination charges, not because she is a woman, that she was (on her story) denied the second appointment. The groundlessness of Yatvin's charges of sex discrimination reinforces the distinction. If the defendants retaliated against her because they don't like to be harassed with baseless charges of whatever kind, and whether filed by men or by women, they would not be guilty of sex discrimination merely because in one instance the baseless charges happened to be charges of sex discrimination.

The contention that every act of retaliation against a person who files charges of wrongdoing with a public agency denies freedom of speech or the right to petition for redress of grievances rests on the following syllogism: litigation is a method recognized by the Supreme Court, as in *NAACP v. Button*, 371 U.S. 415, 429-31 (1963), and *In re Primus*, 436 U.S. 412 (1978), for advancing ideas and seeking redress of grievances; retaliation against one who institutes litigation (or its condition precedent in Title VII litigation, the lodging of charges with civil rights agencies) discourages litigation; therefore such retaliation invades a First Amendment right. The weakness is in the first premise, which is stated too broadly. Some litigation seeks to advance political or other ideas; litigation by the NAACP seeking to eliminate public school segregation is an example. And even when litigation has private rather than public objectives, communications designed to acquaint individuals with their legal rights are within the scope of the First Amendment. *See Brotherhood of Railroad Trainmen v. Virginia ex rel. Virginia State Bar,* 377 U.S. 1, 5-6 (1964). But not every legal gesture — not every legal pleading — is protected by the First Amendment. *See Altman v. Hurst,* 734 F.2d 1240, 1243-44 and n. 10 (7th Cir. 1984) *(per curiam); cf. Callaway v. Hafeman,* 832 F.2d 414 (7th Cir. 1987). Remedies against baseless litigation do not violate the First Amendment's right to petition, *Bill Johnson's Restaurants, Inc. v. NLRB,* 461 U.S. 731, 743 (1983); ....

All Yatvin sought by filing charges was to get an appointment as Assistant Superintendent of Instruction in the Madison, Wisconsin school district. She wanted to advance her career, not promote a cause. Sex discrimination is a matter of public concern; obviously debate over it is protected by the First Amendment. But so far as we can tell from the record, Yatvin doesn't want to debate sex discrimination....

....

Everyone exaggerates the importance of his or her own activity and it is therefore natural for lawyers to suppose that every legal pleading, however humble, comes trailing clouds of First Amendment glory. But this is an extreme position and we reject it. The vitality of the marketplace of ideas does not depend on the volume of litigation in the federal courts.

....

Yatvin's First Amendment claim is foreclosed not only by Altman but also because not raised below with sufficient particularity, an especially serious omission if we are correct that the First Amendment status of a lawsuit depends on the particulars of the suit rather than on the bare assertion that every lawsuit (or even just every discrimination suit) is a form of speech or petition encompassed by the amendment. Yatvin did tell the district court that she was challenging the alleged retaliation on Fourteenth Amendment grounds as well as under Title VII, but she neglected to specify the nature of those grounds.... A judge might not guess, merely from being told that the Fourteenth Amendment had been violated by retaliation for filing charges of sex discrimination, that the plaintiff was seeking to enforce rights that arise under the First Amendment and have been held applicable to the states by interpretation of the Fourteenth Amendment. Yatvin did not mention the First Amendment, or freedom of speech or petition, in the district court; it is too late to raise such a claim in this court.

Affirmed.

---

1. Consider the following statement of Posner from *Yatvin*: "In any event, the breach of promise to give women favored treatment is not sex discrimination. Sex discrimination is treating a person worse because of her (or his) sex; it is not refusing to discriminate in favor of a person on grounds of her sex." *Yatvin*, 840 F.2d at 415. Apply this interpretation of the principal Title VII language: It is "an unlawful employment practice for an employer ... to discriminate against any individual with respect to his compensation, terms, conditions, or privileges of employment, because of such individual's race, color, religion, sex, or national origin." 42 U.S.C. § 2000e-2(a)(1). Are they consistent?

2. Sex discrimination cases in employment, of course, are not all based on sexual harassment as we saw in *Meritor* and *Jew*. Sex discrimination cases in education have arisen based on a teacher's lifestyle. In *Cameron v. Board of Educ. of Hillsboro, Ohio*, 795 F. Supp. 228 (S.D. Ohio 1991), the District Court denied a summary judgment for the school in a case involving a female teacher who was artificially inseminated. The court held that the woman's right of privacy extended to becoming pregnant by this means. Similarly, a summary judgment for the school was denied in a case where the school did not hire a male teacher due to "homosexual tendencies". The court held that a classification on the basis of sexual orientation is inherently suspect. *Jantz v. Muci*, 759 F. Supp. 1543 (D. Kan. 1991).

3. If it is a known fact that more high school principals are male and more elementary school principals are female, then is a wage and salary difference between the two discriminatory on the basis of sex? Is it due to greater responsibilities placed on the principals in high schools? Is there another reason? *See Siegel v. Board of Educ. of City Sch. Dist. of New York*, 713 F. Supp. 54 (E.D.N.Y 1989). In *Siegel*, the court held that the school board showed reasons for the wage differential other than sex. The fact that the lower paid job was "traditionally female" was not enough to establish a Title VII violation. The school board showed that a high school principal's job required greater responsibility and effort due to the larger staff and student body, difficulties with supervising adolescents, and larger and more complicated budgets.

5. RELIGION

ANSONIA BOARD OF EDUCATION v. PHILBROOK

Supreme Court of the United States
479 U.S. 60 (1986)

CHIEF JUSTICE REHNQUIST delivered the opinion of the Court:

Petitioner Ansonia Board of Education has employed respondent Ronald Philbrook since 1962 to teach high school business and typing classes in Ansonia, Connecticut. In 1968, Philbrook was baptized into the Worldwide Church of God. The tenets of the church require members to refrain from secular employment during designated holy days, a practice that has caused respondent to miss approximately six schooldays each year. We are asked to determine whether the employer's efforts to adjust respondent's work schedule in light of his beliefs fulfill its obligation under § 701(j) of the Civil Rights Act of 1964, 86 Stat. 103, 42 U.S.C. § 2000e(j), to "reasonably accommodate to an

B. HIRING AND DISCHARGE

employee's ... religious observance or practice without undue hardship on the conduct of the employer's business."[1]

Since the 1967-1968 school year, the school board's collective-bargaining agreements with the Ansonia Federation of Teachers have granted to each teacher 18 days of leave per year for illness, cumulative to 150 and later to 180 days. Accumulated leave may be used for purposes other than illness as specified in the agreement. A teacher may accordingly use five days' leave for a death in the immediate family, one day for attendance at a wedding, three days per year for attendance as an official delegate to a national veterans organization, and the like. With the exception of the agreement covering the 1967-1968 school year, each contract has specifically provided three days' annual leave for observance of mandatory religious holidays, as defined in the contract. Unlike other categories for which leave is permitted, absences for religious holidays are not charged against the teacher's annual or accumulated leave.

The school board has also agreed that teachers may use up to three days of accumulated leave each school year for "necessary personal business." Recent contracts limited permissible personal leave to those uses not otherwise specified in the contract. This limitation dictated, for example, that an employee who wanted more than three leave days to attend the convention of a national veterans organization could not use personal leave to gain extra days for that purpose. Likewise, an employee already absent three days for mandatory religious observances could not later use personal leave for "[a]ny religious activity," or "[a]ny religious observance." Since the 1978-1979 school year, teachers have been allowed to take one of the three personal days without prior approval; use of the remaining two days requires advance approval by the school principal.

The limitations on the use of personal business leave spawned this litigation. Until the 1976-1977 year, Philbrook observed mandatory holy days by using the three days granted in the contract and then taking unauthorized leave. His pay was reduced accordingly. In 1976, however, respondent stopped taking unauthorized leave for religious reasons, and began scheduling required hospital visits on church holy days. He also worked on several holy days. Dissatisfied

---

[1]The reasonable accommodation duty was incorporated into the statute, somewhat awkwardly, in the definition of religion. Title VII's central provisions make it an unlawful employment practice for an employer "to fail or refuse to hire or to discharge any individual, or otherwise to discriminate against any individual with respect to his compensation, terms, conditions, or privileges of employment, because of such individual's ... religion ...," § 703(a)(1), 42 U.S.C. § 2000e-2(a)(1), or "to limit, segregate, or classify his employees ... in any way which would deprive or tend to deprive any individual of employment opportunities or otherwise adversely affect his status as an employee, because of such individual's ... religion...." § 703(a)(2), 42 U.S.C. § 2000e-2(a)(2). Section 701(j), 42 U.S.C. § 2000e(j), was added in 1972 to illuminate the meaning of religious discrimination under the statute. It provides that "[t]he term 'religion' includes all aspects of religious observance and practice, as well as belief, unless an employer demonstrates that he is unable to reasonably accommodate to an employee's or prospective employee's religious observance or practice without undue hardship on the conduct of the employer's business."

with this arrangement, Philbrook repeatedly asked the school board to adopt one of two alternatives. His preferred alternative would allow use of personal business leave for religious observance, effectively giving him three additional days of paid leave for that purpose. Short of this arrangement, respondent suggested that he pay the cost of a substitute and receive full pay for additional days off for religious observances. Petitioner has consistently rejected both proposals.

In 1973 Philbrook filed a complaint with the Connecticut Commission on Human Rights and Opportunities and the Equal Employment Opportunity Commission against the school board and the Ansonia Federation of Teachers. After exhausting the available administrative avenues, he filed a complaint in the United States District Court for the District of Connecticut, alleging that the prohibition on the use of "necessary personal business" leave for religious observance violated §§ 703(a)(1), (2) of Title VII, 42 U.S.C. §§ 2000e-2(a)(1), (2), and seeking both damages and injunctive relief.

After a 2-day trial, the District Court concluded that Philbrook had failed to prove a case of religious discrimination because he had not been placed by the school board in a position of violating his religion or losing his job.

The Court of Appeals for the Second Circuit reversed and remanded for further proceedings. It held that a prima facie case of discrimination is established when an employee shows that

> "(1) he or she has a bona fide religious belief that conflicts with an employment requirement; (2) he or she informed the employer of this belief; (3) he or she was disciplined for failure to comply with the conflicting employment requirement." 757 F.2d 476, 481 (1985), quoting *Turpen v. Missouri-Kansas-Texas R. Co.*, 736 F.2d 1022, 1026 (CA5 1984).

Philbrook established his case, the court held, by showing that he had a sincere religious belief that conflicted with the employer's attendance requirements, that the employer was aware of the belief, and that he suffered a detriment — namely, a loss of pay — from the conflict....

We granted certiorari to consider the important questions of federal law presented by the decision of the Court of Appeals. Specifically, we are asked to address whether the Court of Appeals erred in finding that Philbrook established a prima facie case of religious discrimination and in opining that an employer must accept the employee's preferred accommodation absent proof of undue hardship. We find little support in the statute for the approach adopted by the Court of Appeals, but we agree that the ultimate issue of reasonable accommodation cannot be resolved without further factual inquiry. We accordingly affirm the judgment of the Court of Appeals remanding the case to the District Court for additional findings.

As we noted in our only previous consideration of § 701(j), its language was added to the 1972 amendments on the floor of the Senate with little discussion. *Trans World Airlines, Inc. v. Hardison*, 432 U.S. 63, 74, n. 9 (1977). *See* 118

B. HIRING AND DISCHARGE

Cong.Rec. 705-06 (1972). In *Hardison, supra*, at 84, we determined that an accommodation causes "undue hardship" whenever that accommodation results in "more than a de minimis cost" to the employer. Hardison had been discharged because his religious beliefs would not allow him to work on Saturdays and claimed that this action violated the employer's duty to effect a reasonable accommodation of his beliefs. Because we concluded that each of the suggested accommodations would impose on the employer an undue hardship, we had no occasion to consider the bounds of a prima facie case in the religious accommodation context or whether an employer is required to choose from available accommodations the alternative preferred by the employee. The employer in *Hardison* simply argued that all conceivable accommodations would result in undue hardship, and we agreed.

Petitioner asks us to establish for religious accommodation claims a proof scheme analogous to that developed in other Title VII contexts, delineating the plaintiff's prima facie case and shifting production burdens. See *Texas Dept. of Community Affairs v. Burdine*, 450 U.S. 248, 101 (1981); *McDonnell Douglas Corp. v. Green*, 411 U.S. 792 (1973). But the present case raises no such issue.... We may therefore proceed to the question whether the employer's proposed accommodation of respondent's religious practices comports with the statutory mandate of § 701(j).

In addressing this question, the Court of Appeals assumed that the employer had offered a reasonable accommodation of Philbrook's religious beliefs. This alone, however, was insufficient in that court's view to allow resolution of the dispute. The court observed that the duty to accommodate "cannot be defined without reference to undue hardship." It accordingly determined that the accommodation obligation includes a duty to accept "the proposal the employee prefers unless that accommodation causes undue hardship on the employer's conduct of his business."... Because the District Court had not considered whether Philbrook's proposals would impose undue hardship, the Court of Appeals remanded for further consideration of those proposals.

We find no basis in either the statute or its legislative history for requiring an employer to choose any particular reasonable accommodation. By its very terms the statute directs that any reasonable accommodation by the employer is sufficient to meet its accommodation obligation. The employer violates the statute unless it "demonstrates that [it] is unable to reasonably accommodate ... an employee's ... religious observance or practice without undue hardship on the conduct of the employer's business." 42 U.S.C. § 2000e(j). Thus, where the employer has already reasonably accommodated the employee's religious needs, the statutory inquiry is at an end. The employer need not further show that each of the employee's alternative accommodations would result in undue hardship. As *Hardison* illustrates, the extent of undue hardship on the employer's business is at issue only where the employer claims that it is unable to offer any reasonable accommodation without such hardship. Once the Court of Appeals assumed that the school board had offered to Philbrook a reasonable alternative, it erred by requiring the Board to nonetheless demonstrate the hardship of Philbrook's alternatives.

The legislative history of § 701(j), as we noted in *Hardison, supra*, 432 U.S. at 74-75, and n. 9, is of little help in defining the employer's accommodation obligation. To the extent it provides any indication of congressional intent, however, we think that the history supports our conclusion. Senator Randolph, the sponsor of the amendment that became § 701(j), expressed his hope that accommodation would be made with "flexibility" and "a desire to achieve an adjustment." 118 Cong.Rec. 706 (1972). Consistent with these goals, courts have noted that "bilateral cooperation is appropriate in the search for an acceptable reconciliation of the needs of the employee's religion and the exigencies of the employer's business." *Brener v. Diagnostic Center Hospital*, 671 F.2d 141, 145-46 (CA5 1982). Under the approach articulated by the Court of Appeals, however, the employee is given every incentive to hold out for the most beneficial accommodation, despite the fact that an employer offers a reasonable resolution of the conflict. This approach, we think, conflicts with both the language of the statute and the views that led to its enactment. We accordingly hold that an employer has met its obligation under § 701(j) when it demonstrates that it has offered a reasonable accommodation to the employee.

The remaining issue in the case is whether the school board's leave policy constitutes a reasonable accommodation of Philbrook's religious beliefs. Because both the District Court and the Court of Appeals applied what we hold to be an erroneous view of the law, neither explicitly considered this question. We think that there are insufficient factual findings as to the manner in which the collective-bargaining agreements have been interpreted in order for us to make that judgment initially. We think that the school board policy in this case, requiring respondent to take unpaid leave for holy day observance that exceeded the amount allowed by the collective-bargaining agreement, would generally be a reasonable one. In enacting § 701(j), Congress was understandably motivated by a desire to assure the individual additional opportunity to observe religious practices, but it did not impose a duty on the employer to accommodate at all costs. *Trans World Airlines, Inc. v. Hardison*, 432 U.S. 63 (1977). The provision of unpaid leave eliminates the conflict between employment requirements and religious practices by allowing the individual to observe fully religious holy days and requires him only to give up compensation for a day that he did not in fact work. Generally speaking, "[t]he direct effect of [unpaid leave] is merely a loss of income for the period the employee is not at work; such an exclusion has no direct effect upon either employment opportunities or job status."

But unpaid leave is not a reasonable accommodation when paid leave is provided for all purposes except religious ones. A provision for paid leave "that is part and parcel of the employment relationship may not be doled out in a discriminatory fashion, even if the employer would be free ... not to provide the benefit at all." Such an arrangement would display a discrimination against religious practices that is the antithesis of reasonableness. Whether the policy here violates this teaching turns on factual inquiry into past and present administration of the personal business leave provisions of the collective-bargaining agreement. The school board contends that the necessary personal business category in the agreement, like other leave provisions, defines a limited purpose leave. Philbrook, on the other hand, asserts that the necessary personal leave category is not so limited, operating as an open-ended leave provision that may be used for a wide range of secular purposes in addition to those specifically provided for in the contract, but not for similar religious purposes. We do not think that the record is sufficiently clear on this point for us to make the necessary factual findings, and we therefore affirm the judgment of the Court of Appeals remanding the case to the District Court. The latter court on remand should make the necessary findings as to past and existing practice in the administration of the collective-bargaining agreements.

It is so ordered.

JUSTICE MARSHALL, concurring in part and dissenting in part.
....

---

1. In a similar case heard two years before *Philbrook*, the Tenth Circuit Court of Appeals held that a school district's policy of allowing only two days of paid leave for religious reasons did not discriminate against a Jewish teacher who was required to take unpaid leave to accommodate his religious holidays. *Pinsker v. Joint Dist. No. 28J of Adams and Arapahoe Counties*, 735 F.2d 388 (10th Cir. 1984).

Since the case was remanded for further proceedings on the Title VII claim, the Courts of Appeals in *Philbrook* did not hear Philbrook's First Amendment claim. The *Pinsker* court, on the other hand, did hear the First Amendment argument and held that the "two-day" policy did not infringe on Pinsker's right to free exercise of religion.

2. What would the result in the case have been had Philbrook been dismissed for missing too many school days on account of his religion? In 1980, the federal district court in New Jersey held in favor of plaintiff teacher, also a member of the Worldwide Church of God, and awarded him compensatory damages, reinstatement, and attorney fees after he was dismissed due to an unauthorized two-period absence on one day. *Niederhuber v. Camden County Vocational & Tech. Sch. Dist. Bd. of Educ.*, 495 F. Supp. 273 (D.N.J. 1980). The court held that (1) the plaintiff's absence due to religious reasons was a substantial factor in his dismissal; (2) accommodation of five to ten days per year for religious absences would not constitute an "undue hardship" on the school system; and (3) aside from compensation, reinstatement, and attorney fees, plaintiff was not entitled to punitive damages or recovery for distress, mental suffering and emotional anguish.

See also Wangsness v. Watertown Sch. Dist. No. 14-4 of Codington County, South Dakota, 541 F. Supp. 322 (D.S.D. 1982) (Teacher alleged that he was unlawfully discharged for his religious beliefs. The court held that a prima facie case was established; that the school district failed to make a good-faith effort to accommodate the teacher's religious needs; and that the district failed to show that any reasonable accommodation would have constituted undue hardship on the school system. The court ultimately awarded the teacher back pay and attorney fees, but did not order reinstatement.)

3. Recall *Trans-World Airlines, Inc. v. Hardison*, cited in *Philbrook*. Consider the following alternatives to discharge pointed out by the Court of Appeals and rejected as "undue hardships" by the Supreme Court: (1) reduction of Hardison's work week despite some loss in efficient shop functions, (2) payment of overtime wages to secure a substitute employee, and (3) breach of the seniority provision of the contract, thereby accommodating Hardison's religious practices but at the expense of a fellow employee. What if Hardison had been a school teacher? Could he have been accommodated without undue hardship? Suppose there were sufficient substitute teachers available to cover for him? Suppose the costs for employing the substitute were deducted from his salary? *See Rankins v. Commission on Prof. Comp.*, 24 Cal. 3d 167, 593 P.2d 852, 154 Cal. Rptr. 907 (Cal. 1979), where the court held that failure to accommodate an employee's observance of religious holidays ten school days each year constituted illegal discrimination on the basis of religion, despite the district's contention that his frequent absences had a substantial detrimental effect on the educational program of the district.

4. For a general review of public school teachers' rights with respect to religion, *see* Comment, *Religious Rights of Public School Teachers*, 23 UCLA L. Rev. 763 (1976).

6. DISABILITY

SCHOOL BOARD OF NASSAU COUNTY, FLORIDA v. ARLINE

Supreme Court of the United States
480 U.S. 273 (1987)

JUSTICE BRENNAN delivered the opinion of the Court:

Section 504 of the Rehabilitation Act of 1973, 87 Stat. 394, as amended, 29 U.S.C. § 794 (Act), prohibits a federally funded state program from discriminating against a handicapped individual solely by reason of his or her handicap. This case presents the questions whether a person afflicted with tuberculosis, a contagious disease, may be considered a "handicapped individual" within the meaning of § 504 of the Act, and, if so, whether such an individual is "otherwise qualified" to teach elementary school.

B. HIRING AND DISCHARGE

I

From 1966 until 1979, respondent Gene Arline taught elementary school in Nassau County, Florida. She was discharged in 1979 after suffering a third relapse of tuberculosis within two years. After she was denied relief in state administrative proceedings, she brought suit in federal court, alleging that the school board's decision to dismiss her because of her tuberculosis violated § 504 of the Act.

....

... The District Court held ... that although there was "[n]o question that she suffers a handicap," Arline was nevertheless not "a handicapped person under the terms of that statute." The court found it "difficult ... to conceive that Congress intended contagious diseases to be included within the definition of a handicapped person." The court then went on to state that, "even assuming" that a person with a contagious disease could be deemed a handicapped person, Arline was not "qualified" to teach elementary school.

The Court of Appeals reversed, holding that "persons with contagious diseases are within the coverage of section 504," and that Arline's condition "falls ... neatly within the statutory and regulatory framework" of the Act. The court remanded the case "for further findings as to whether the risks of infection precluded Mrs. Arline from being 'otherwise qualified' for her job and, if so, whether it was possible to make some reasonable accommodation for her in that teaching position" or in some other position. We granted certiorari and now affirm.

II

In enacting and amending the Act, Congress enlisted all programs receiving federal funds in an effort "to share with handicapped Americans the opportunities for an education, transportation, housing, health care, and jobs that other Americans take for granted." 123 Cong.Rec. 13515 (1977) (statement of Sen. Humphrey). To that end, Congress not only increased federal support for vocational rehabilitation, but also addressed the broader problem of discrimination against the handicapped by including § 504, an antidiscrimination provision patterned after Title VI of the Civil Rights Act of 1964. Section 504 of the Rehabilitation Act reads in pertinent part: "No otherwise qualified handicapped individual in the United States, as defined in section 706(7) of this title, shall, solely by reason of his handicap, be excluded from participation in, be denied the benefits of, or be subjected to discrimination under any program or activity receiving Federal financial assistance...." 29 U.S.C. § 794. In 1974 Congress expanded the definition of "handicapped individual" for use in § 504 to read as follows: "[A]ny person who (i) has a physical or mental impairment which substantially limits one or more of such person's major life activities, (ii) has a record of such an impairment, or (iii) is regarded as having such an impairment." 29 U.S.C. § 706(7)(B).

The amended definition reflected Congress' concern with protecting the handicapped against discrimination stemming not only from simple prejudice, but also from "archaic attitudes and laws" and from "the fact that the American people are simply unfamiliar with and insensitive to the difficulties confront[ing] individuals with handicaps." To combat the effects of erroneous but nevertheless prevalent perceptions about the handicapped, Congress expanded the definition of "handicapped individual" so as to preclude discrimination against "[a] person who has a record of, or is regarded as having, an impairment [but who] may at present have no actual incapacity at all." *Southeastern Community College v. Davis*, 442 U.S. 397, 405-406, n. 6 (1979).

In determining whether a particular individual is handicapped as defined by the Act, the regulations promulgated by the Department of Health and Human Services are of significant assistance. As we have previously recognized, these regulations were drafted with the oversight and approval of Congress, they provide "an important source of guidance on the meaning of § 504." The regulations are particularly significant here because they define two critical terms used in the statutory definition of handicapped individual. "Physical impairment" is defined as follows: "[A]ny physiological disorder or condition, cosmetic disfigurement, or anatomical loss affecting one or more of the following body systems: neurological; musculoskeletal; special sense organs; respiratory, including speech organs; cardiovascular; reproductive, digestive, genito-urinary; hemic and lymphatic; skin; and endocrine." 45 CFR § 84.3(j)(2)(i) (1985).

In addition, the regulations define "major life activities" as "functions such as caring for one's self, performing manual tasks, walking, seeing, hearing, speaking, breathing, learning, and working." § 84.3(j)(2)(ii).

III

Within this statutory and regulatory framework, then, we must consider whether Arline can be considered a handicapped individual. According to ... testimony ... Arline suffered tuberculosis "in an acute form in such a degree that it affected her respiratory system," and was hospitalized for this condition. Arline thus had a physical impairment as that term is defined by the regulations, since she had a "physiological disorder or condition ... affecting [her] ... respiratory [system]." 45 CFR § 84.3(j)(2)(i) (1985). This impairment was serious enough to require hospitalization, a fact more than sufficient to establish that one or more of her major life activities were substantially limited by her impairment. Thus, Arline's hospitalization for tuberculosis in 1957 suffices to establish that she has a "record of ... impairment" within the meaning of 29 U.S.C. § 706(7)(B)(ii), and is therefore a handicapped individual.

Petitioners concede that a contagious disease may constitute a handicapping condition to the extent that it leaves a person with "diminished physical or mental capabilities," and concede that Arline's hospitalization for tuberculosis in 1957 demonstrates that she has a record of a physical impairment. Petitioners maintain, however, that Arline's record of impairment is irrelevant in this case,

B. HIRING AND DISCHARGE 677

since the school board dismissed Arline not because of her diminished physical capabilities, but because of the threat that her relapses of tuberculosis posed to the health of others.

We do not agree with petitioners that, in defining a handicapped individual under § 504, the contagious effects of a disease can be meaningfully distinguished from the disease's physical effects on a claimant in a case such as this. Arline's contagiousness and her physical impairment each resulted from the same underlying condition, tuberculosis. It would be unfair to allow an employer to seize upon the distinction between the effects of a disease on others and the effects of a disease on a patient and use that distinction to justify discriminatory treatment.

Nothing in the legislative history of § 504 suggests that Congress intended such a result. That history demonstrates that Congress was as concerned about the effect of an impairment on others as it was about its effect on the individual. Congress extended coverage, in 29 U.S.C. § 706(7)(B)(iii), to those individuals who are simply "regarded as having" a physical or mental impairment. The Senate Report provides as an example of a person who would be covered under this subsection "a person with some kind of visible physical impairment which in fact does not substantially limit that person's functioning." S.Rep. No. 93-1297 at 64. Such an impairment might not diminish a person's physical or mental capabilities, but could nevertheless substantially limit that person's ability to work as a result of the negative reactions of others to the impairment.

Allowing discrimination based on the contagious effects of a physical impairment would be inconsistent with the basic purpose of § 504, which is to ensure that handicapped individuals are not denied jobs or other benefits because of the prejudiced attitudes or the ignorance of others. By amending the definition of "handicapped individual" to include not only those who are actually physically impaired, but also those who are regarded as impaired and who, as a result, are substantially limited in a major life activity, Congress acknowledged that society's accumulated myths and fears about disability and disease are as handicapping as are the physical limitations that flow from actual impairment. Few aspects of a handicap give rise to the same level of public fear and misapprehension as contagiousness. Even those who suffer or have recovered from such noninfectious diseases as epilepsy or cancer have faced discrimination based on the irrational fear that they might be contagious. The Act is carefully structured to replace such reflexive reactions to actual or perceived handicaps with actions based on reasoned and medically sound judgments: the definition of "handicapped individual" is broad, but only those individuals who are both handicapped and otherwise qualified are eligible for relief. The fact that some persons who have contagious diseases may pose a serious health threat to others under certain circumstances does not justify excluding from the coverage of the Act all persons with actual or perceived contagious diseases. Such exclusion would mean that those accused of being contagious would never have the opportunity to have their condition evaluated in light of medical evidence and a determination made as to whether they were "otherwise qualified." Rather, they would be vulnerable to discrimination on the basis of mythology — precisely the type of injury Congress sought to prevent. We conclude that the fact that a person with a record of a physical impairment is also contagious does not suffice to remove that person from coverage under § 504.

IV

The remaining question is whether Arline is otherwise qualified for the job of elementary schoolteacher. To answer this question in most cases, the district court will need to conduct an individualized inquiry and make appropriate findings of fact. Such an inquiry is essential if § 504 is to achieve its goal of protecting handicapped individuals from deprivations based on prejudice, stereotypes, or unfounded fear, while giving appropriate weight to such legitimate concerns of grantees as avoiding exposing others to significant health and safety risks.[16] The basic factors to be considered in conducting this inquiry are well established.[17] In the context of the employment of a person handicapped with a contagious disease, we agree with amicus American Medical Association that this inquiry should include

> [findings of] facts, based on reasonable medical judgments given the state of medical knowledge, about (a) the nature of the risk (how the disease is transmitted), (b) the duration of the risk (how long is the carrier infectious), (c) the severity of the risk (what is the potential harm to third parties) and (d) the probabilities the disease will be transmitted and will cause varying

---

[16] A person who poses a significant risk of communicating an infectious disease to others in the workplace will not be otherwise qualified for his or her job if reasonable accommodation will not eliminate that risk. The Act would not require a school board to place a teacher with active, contagious tuberculosis in a classroom with elementary schoolchildren. Respondent conceded as much at oral argument. Tr. of Oral Arg. 45.

[17] "An otherwise qualified person is one who is able to meet all of a program's requirements in spite of his handicap." *Southeastern Community College v. Davis*, 442 U.S. 397, 406 (1979). In the employment context, an otherwise qualified person is one who can perform "the essential functions" of the job in question. 45 CFR § 84.3(k) (1985). When a handicapped person is not able to perform the essential functions of the job, the court must also consider whether any "reasonable accommodation" by the employer would enable the handicapped person to perform those functions. *Ibid.* Accommodation is not reasonable if it either imposes "undue financial and administrative burdens" on a grantee, *Southeastern Community College v. Davis*, 442 U.S. at 412, or requires "a fundamental alteration in the nature of [the] program," *Id.* at 410. *See* 45 CFR § 84.12(c) (1985) (listing factors to consider in determining whether accommodation would cause undue hardship); 45 CFR pt. 84, Appendix A, p. 315 (1985) ("[W]here reasonable accommodation does not overcome the effects of a person's handicap, or where reasonable accommodation causes undue hardship to the employer, failure to hire or promote the handicapped person will not be considered discrimination"); *Davis, supra*, at 410-13; *Alexander v. Choate*, 469 U.S. at 299-301, and n. 19; *Strathie v. Department of Transportation*, 718 F.2d at 231.

B. HIRING AND DISCHARGE

degrees of harm. Brief for American Medical Association as Amicus Curiae 19.

In making these findings, courts normally should defer to the reasonable medical judgments of public health officials. The next step in the "otherwise-qualified" inquiry is for the court to evaluate, in light of these medical findings, whether the employer could reasonably accommodate the employee under the established standards for that inquiry. *See* n. 17, *supra.*

Because of the paucity of factual findings by the District Court, we, like the Court of Appeals, are unable at this stage of the proceedings to resolve whether Arline is "otherwise qualified" for her job. The District Court made no findings as to the duration and severity of Arline's condition, nor as to the probability that she would transmit the disease. Nor did the court determine whether Arline was contagious at the time she was discharged, or whether the School Board could have reasonably accommodated her. Accordingly, the resolution of whether Arline was otherwise qualified requires further findings of fact.

V

We hold that a person suffering from the contagious disease of tuberculosis can be a handicapped person within the meaning of § 504 of the Rehabilitation Act of 1973, and that respondent Arline is such a person. We remand the case to the District Court to determine whether Arline is otherwise qualified for her position. The judgment of the Court of Appeals is

Affirmed.

....

CHALK v. UNITED STATES DISTRICT COURT CENTRAL DISTRICT OF CALIFORNIA

United States Court of Appeals
840 F.2d 701 (9th Cir. 1988)

POOLE, CIRCUIT JUDGE:

....

Facts and Proceedings Below

Petitioner Chalk has been teaching hearing-impaired students in the Orange County schools for approximately six years. In February 1987, Chalk was hospitalized with pneumocystis carinii pneumonia and was diagnosed as having AIDS. On April 20, after eight weeks of treatment and recuperation, he was found fit for duty and released to return to work by his personal physician, Dr. Andrew Siskind. The Department, however, placed him on administrative leave pending the opinion of Dr. Thomas J. Prendergast, the Director of Epidemiology and Disease Control for the Orange County Health Care Agency. On May 22, Dr. Prendergast informed the Department that "[n]othing in his [Chalk's] role as a teacher should place his students or others in the school at any risk of acquiring HIV infection."

Chalk agreed to remain on administrative leave through the end of the school year in June. On August 5, Chalk and representatives of the Department met to discuss his return to the classroom. The Department offered Chalk an administrative position at the same rate of pay and benefits, with the option of working either at the Department's offices or at his home, and informed him that if he insisted on returning to the classroom, it would file an action for declaratory relief. Chalk refused the offer. On August 6, the Department filed an action in the Orange County Superior Court, and Chalk filed this action in the district court seeking a preliminary and permanent injunction barring the Department from excluding him from classroom duties. By agreement of counsel, the Department has not pursued the state court action; instead, it filed a counterclaim in the district court.

On August 18, Chalk moved for a preliminary injunction ordering the Department to reinstate him to his classroom duties pending trial. At a hearing on September 8, the district court denied the motion. Following the ruling, the Department reassigned Chalk to an administrative position coordinating grant applications and educational materials for the hearing-impaired program. A panel of this court denied Chalk's emergency petition for a writ of mandamus, but granted his alternative motion for an expedited appeal. Chalk then filed an emergency motion for an injunction pending appeal. We heard oral argument on November 10, and on November 18 we issued an order reversing the district court with this fuller statement of our reasons to follow.

. . . .

Chalk bases his claim on section 504 of the Rehabilitation Act of 1973, 29 U.S.C. § 794, as amended (the Act), which provides: "No otherwise qualified individual with handicaps ... shall, solely by reason of his handicap, be excluded from the participation in ... or be subjected to discrimination under any program or activity receiving Federal financial assistance...."

As the district court recognized, the Supreme Court recently held that section 504 is fully applicable to individuals who suffer from contagious diseases. *School Bd. of Nassau County v. Arline*, [480] U.S. [273] (1987)....

In its opinion, the Court addressed the question which is of central importance to this case: under what circumstances may a person handicapped with a contagious disease be "otherwise qualified" within the meaning of section 504? Relying on its earlier opinion in *Southeastern Community College v. Davis*, 442 U.S. 397 (1979), the Court said:

> An otherwise qualified person is one who is able to meet all of a program's requirements in spite of his handicap. In the employment context, an otherwise qualified person is one who can perform "the essential functions" of the job in question. When a handicapped person is not able to perform the essential functions of the job, the court must also consider

B. HIRING AND DISCHARGE

whether any "reasonable accommodation" by the employer would enable the handicapped person to perform those functions. Accommodation is not reasonable if it either imposes "undue financial and administrative burdens" on a grantee, or requires a "fundamental alteration in the nature of [the] program." *Arline,* 107 S.Ct. at 1131 n. 17.

In applying this standard to the facts before it, the Court recognized the difficult circumstances which confront a handicapped person, an employer, and the public in dealing with the possibility of contagion in the workplace. The problem is in reconciling the needs for protection of other persons, continuation of the work mission, and reasonable accommodation — if possible — of the afflicted individual. The Court effected this reconciliation by formulating a standard for determining when a contagious disease would prevent an individual from being "otherwise qualified":

> A person who poses a significant risk of communicating an infectious disease to others in the workplace will not be otherwise qualified for his or her job if reasonable accommodation will not eliminate that risk. The Act would not require a school board to place a teacher with active, contagious tuberculosis in a classroom with elementary school children.

The application of this standard requires, in most cases, an individualized inquiry and appropriate findings of fact, so that "§ 504 [may] achieve its goal of protecting handicapped individuals from deprivations based on prejudice, stereotypes, or unfounded fear, while giving appropriate weight to such legitimate concerns of grantees as avoiding exposing others to significant health and safety risks." Specifically, *Arline* requires a trial court to make findings regarding four factors:

> (a) the nature of the risk (how the disease is transmitted),
> (b) the duration of the risk (how long is the carrier infectious),
> (c) the severity of the risk (what is the potential harm to third parties) and
> (d) the probabilities the disease will be transmitted and will cause varying degrees of harm.

Findings regarding these factors should be based "on reasonable medical judgments given the state of medical knowledge," and courts should give particular deference to the judgments of public health officials.

Chalk submitted in evidence to the district court, and that court accepted, more than 100 articles from prestigious medical journals and the declarations of five experts on AIDS, including two public health officials of Los Angeles County. Those submissions reveal an overwhelming evidentiary consensus of medical and scientific opinion regarding the nature and transmission of AIDS....

Transmission of HIV is known to occur in three ways: (1) through intimate sexual contact with an infected person; (2) through invasive exposure to contaminated blood or certain other bodily fluids; or (3) through perinatal exposure (*i.e.*, from mother to infant). Although HIV has been isolated in several body fluids, epidemiologic evidence has implicated only blood, semen, vaginal secretions, and possibly breast milk in transmission. Extensive and numerous studies have consistently found no apparent risk of HIV infection to individuals exposed through close, non-sexual contact with AIDS patients.

Based on the accumulated body of medical evidence, the Surgeon General of the United States has concluded:

> There is no known risk of non-sexual infection in most of the situations we encounter in our daily lives. We know that family members living with individuals who have the AIDS virus do not become infected except through sexual contact. There is no evidence of transmission (spread) of AIDS virus by everyday contact even though these family members shared food, towels, cups, razors, even toothbrushes, and kissed each other. U.S. Public Health Service, Surgeon General's Report on Acquired Immune Deficiency Syndrome at 13 (1986).

....

The district judge addressed each of the four *Arline* factors in his ruling. He found that the duration of the risk was long and the severity was "catastrophic," but that scientifically established methods of transmission were unlikely to occur and that the probability of harm was minimal....

....

That Chalk demonstrates a strong probability of success on the merits is supported by the three published opinions brought to our attention dealing with AIDS discrimination under section 504. In *Thomas v. Atascadero Unified School Dist.*, 662 F.Supp. 376 (C.D.Cal.1987), the court granted a preliminary injunction prohibiting the school district from excluding a child with AIDS from the classroom, despite the child's involvement in a biting incident. The court found that:

> The overwhelming weight of medical evidence is that the AIDS virus is not transmitted by human bites, even bites that break the skin. Based upon the abundant medical and scientific evidence before the Court, Ryan poses no risk of harm to his classmates and teachers. Any theoretical risk of transmission of the AIDS virus by Ryan in connection with his attendance in regular kindergarten class is so remote that it cannot form the basis for any exclusionary action by the School District. Following the entry of the preliminary injunction, the parties in that case stipulated to the entry of a permanent injunction.

In *Ray v. School Dist. of DeSoto County,* 666 F.Supp. 1524 (M.D.Fla.1987), the court followed *Thomas* and granted a preliminary injunction prohibiting the district from excluding three seropositive brothers from the classroom. The court rejected the "future theoretical harm" of transmission of the AIDS virus in the classroom as unsupported by the weight of medical evidence. Significantly, Dr.

Armentrout was one of two doctors who testified for the defendants in *Ray*, and his opinion was implicitly rejected.

The third case, *District 27 Community School Bd. v. Board of Educ.*, 130 Misc.2d 398, 502 N.Y.S.2d 325 (Sup.Ct.1986), concerned the New York City Board of Education's policy of determining on a case-by-case basis whether the health and development of children with AIDS permitted them to attend school in an unrestricted setting. Two school districts challenged the policy, seeking an injunction prohibiting the Board from admitting any child with AIDS into the classroom. After a five-week trial, the court upheld the policy in an exhaustive opinion. One of the central conclusions was that the transmission of the AIDS virus in the classroom setting was "a mere theoretical possibility" and that exclusion of AIDS victims on that basis would violate section 504.

Plaintiff's position is also supported by *New York State Ass'n of Retarded Children v. Carey*, 612 F.2d 644, 650 (2d Cir. 1979), in which the Second Circuit affirmed a district court ruling that the segregation of carriers of hepatitis B by the New York City Board of Education violated section 504. The court said:

> [T]he Board was unable to demonstrate that the health hazard posed by the hepatitis B carrier children was anything more than a remote possibility. There has never been any definite proof that the disease can be communicated by non-parenteral routes such as saliva. Even assuming there were, the activities that occur in classroom settings were not shown to pose any significant risk that the disease would be transmitted from one child to another.

Chalk presented evidence to the district court here that hepatitis B and AIDS are transmitted in similar ways, but that hepatitis B is transmitted much more easily.

Viewing Chalk's submissions in light of these cases, it is clear that he has amply demonstrated a strong probability of success on the merits. We hold that it was error to require that every theoretical possibility of harm be disproved.

....

Having demonstrated a strong probability of success on the merits, Chalk next had to demonstrate that he was threatened with the possibility of irreparable injury. The district court held that Chalk's proof on this element was insufficient....

We believe this determination was clearly erroneous. In making its finding, the court focused on the monetary loss to Chalk and concluded that he was no worse off than before the reassignment. This approach failed to consider the nature of the alternative work offered Chalk. Chalk's original employment was teaching hearing-impaired children in a small-classroom setting, a job for which he developed special skills beyond those normally required to become a teacher. His closeness to his students and his participation in their lives is a source of tremendous personal satisfaction and joy to him and of benefit to them. The alternative work to which he is now assigned is preparing grant proposals. This job is "distasteful" to Chalk, involves no student contact, and does not utilize his skills, training or experience. Such non-monetary deprivation is a substantial injury which the court was required to consider. *See Finot v. Pasadena City Bd. of Educ.*, 250 Cal.App.2d 189, 202-03, 58 Cal.Rptr. 520, 529 (1967) (teacher's reassignment from classroom duty to home teaching, imposed in retaliation for an exercise of first amendment rights, was a "legally remediable detriment").

....

Congress acknowledged that society's accumulated myths and fears about disability and disease are as handicapping as are the physical limitations that flow from actual impairment. Few aspects of a handicap give rise to the same level of public fear and misapprehension as contagiousness. Even those who suffer or have recovered from such noninfectious diseases as epilepsy or cancer have faced discrimination based on the irrational fear that they might be contagious. The Act is carefully structured to replace such reflexive reactions to actual or perceived handicaps with actions based on reasoned and medically sound judgments.

....

Having demonstrated a strong probability of success on the merits and the possibility of irreparable injury, Chalk has shown all that is necessary for a preliminary injunction to issue. Nonetheless, we will also briefly address the claimed injury on the part of the Department, since "at least a minimal tip in the balance of hardships must be found even when the strongest showing on the merits is made."

Even under the balance of hardships standard, plaintiff's injury outweighs any harm to the defendant. Defendant's asserted injury is based entirely on the risk to others posed by plaintiff's return to the classroom. As discussed above, this theoretical risk is insufficient to overcome plaintiff's probability of success on the merits, and it is likewise insufficient to outweigh the injury which plaintiff is likely to suffer. *See Ray*, 666 F.Supp. at 1535 ("actual, ongoing injury to Plaintiffs ... clearly outweighs the potential harm to others"); *cf. Kling v. County of Los Angeles*, 633 F.2d 876, 880 (9th Cir. 1980) (plaintiff with Crohn's disease denied admission to medical school; denial of preliminary injunction reversed where defendant would suffer no harm pending outcome), on appeal after remand, 769 F.2d 532 (9th Cir.), rev'd on other grounds, 474 U.S. 936 (1985).

In denying the preliminary injunction, the district court concluded that Chalk's injury was outweighed by the fear that his presence in the classroom was likely to produce:

> The plaintiff desires to teach despite all these circumstances [*i.e.*, that the results could be "so disastrous if ... by any chance the risk should prove to have been unjustified"]. Counsel has recognized that he doesn't have a constitutional right to do so. On the other hand, he has a statutory right not to be discriminated against. He has a statutory right to go back to the school if he is otherwise qualified.

But I think I have a right — in fact, an obligation to compare on the one hand the trauma on the plaintiff if he is held out from the school for a period of months until we can have a trial in this action. The trauma on him, on the one hand, with the trauma on the children and parents in being required to submit to what they are likely to conclude is an unacceptable risk.

We recognize that the public interest is one of the traditional equitable criteria which a court should consider in granting injunctive relief. Here, however, there is no evidence of any significant risk to children or others at the school. To allow the court to base its decision on the fear and apprehension of others would frustrate the goals of section 504. "[T]he basic purpose of § 504 [is] to ensure that handicapped individuals are not denied jobs or other benefits because of the prejudiced attitudes or ignorance of others." The Supreme Court recognized in *Arline* that a significant risk of transmission was a legitimate concern which could justify exclusion if the risk could not be eliminated through reasonable accommodation; however, it soundly rejected the argument that exclusion could be justified on the basis of "pernicious mythologies" or "irrational fear."

Nonetheless, we recognize that the parties and the district court will have to deal with the apprehensions of other members of the school community, as well as with the inexorable progress of Chalk's disease. Although the time frame is unpredictable, given the current state of medical knowledge, the course of petitioner's condition is reasonably certain. Chalk's immune system will deteriorate over time, leaving him increasingly susceptible to opportunistic infections. These infections do not cause AIDS, nor do they increase the risk of transmission of the AIDS virus, but some of them may themselves be communicable to others in a classroom setting. The district court is in the best position, guided by qualified medical opinion, to determine what reasonable procedures, such as periodic reports from petitioner's doctors, will best give assurance to the Department, the community and the court that no significant risk of harm will arise in the future from Chalk's continued presence in the classroom.

We conclude that petitioner met all of the requirements necessary to receive a preliminary injunction. We therefore reverse the district court's order and remand this action with direction to enter a preliminary injunction ordering defendants forthwith to restore petitioner to his former duties as a teacher of hearing-impaired children in the Orange County Department of Education. This panel will retain jurisdiction over any subsequent appeal.

Reversed and Remanded.

. . . .

---

1. *Arline* describes an "otherwise qualified" disabled person as "one who is able to meet all of a program's requirements in spite of the handicap," and "reasonable accommodation" as being the responsibility of the employer to provide if the employee could perform the job with some element of aid. Did the Court view these in tandem or see the two requirements as separate, thus obligating an institution to accommodate only a disabled person who has already demonstrated that he/she is otherwise qualified?

2. Prior to the decision in *Arline*, a state supreme court decision used language similar to that of the Court in *Arline* to rule that a "reasonable accommodation" could not be made for a disabled teacher who had uncontrollable discipline problems in the classroom. The court held that the teacher's disability could contribute to problems of safety for his students. *See Clark v. Shoreline Sch. Dist. No. 412*, 720 P.2d 793 (Wash. 1986). Would this case have been decided differently in light of the *Arline* decision?

3. Because of the decision in *Arline*, authors have concluded that AIDS is considered a handicap under *Arline*'s analysis. *See, e.g.,* Wasson, *AIDS Discrimination Under Federal, State and Local Law After* Arline, 15 Fla. St. U. L. Rev. 221 (1987); Note, *AIDS: Does It Qualify as a Handicap Under the Rehabilitation Act of 1973*, 61 Notre Dame L. Rev. 572 (1986); Note, *Employment Discrimination and AIDS: Is AIDS a Handicap Under Section 504 of the Rehabilitation Act?*, 38 U. Fla. L. Rev. 649 (1986). However, did the Court express a decision as regards infectious diseases other than tuberculosis? What of the Court's specific statement about AIDS?

4. Does the decision in *Chalk* mean that school officials, responsible for the health, safety, and welfare of children, must permit those with AIDS to teach because other employment within the school system would not adequately utilize the person's skills? Is this possibly carrying the balance of interests between government and an individual a bit too far?

5. The *Chalk* decision addresses the rights of employees with AIDS. Note, as well, that AIDS has been codified as a disability in the Americans with Disabilities Act (ADA) of 1990, 42 U.S.C. Sec. 12101 *et seq.* at Sec. 12102(2). This, together with the recognition of AIDS under Section 504 of the Rehabilitation Act of 1973 provides for the protection of such persons in the workplace.

6. Students with AIDS or other infectious diseases have also been declared "otherwise qualified" by the courts. *See, e.g., Ray v. School Dist. of DeSoto County*, 666 F. Supp. 1524 (M.D. Fla. 1987) (school district prevented from excluding hemophiliac brothers with AIDS from the classroom); *District 27 Community Sch. Bd. v. Board of Educ.*, 103 Misc. 2d 398, 502 N.Y.S.2d 325 (N.Y. Sup. Ct. 1986) (excluding students with AIDS from public schools constitutes Sec. 504 discrimination); *N.Y. State Ass'n for Retarded Children v. Carey*, 612 F.2d 644 (2d Cir. 1979) (exclusion from school for students with hepatitis B violates Section 504). For other cases involving disabled students and their rights under Section 504 and other federal statutes, *see* Chapter 13.

B. HIRING AND DISCHARGE

7. DUE PROCESS

In the area of teacher discharge, due process protections generally include rights to pre-termination hearings and to review of administrative decisions. Due process requirements assure some sort of reasoned decision-making, forcing each official to articulate the reasons and basis for any decision. It provides a forum for the inferences, or facts from which they are drawn, to be brought into the open, thereby allowing an opportunity for erroneous information to be corrected. Some form of due process also performs an independent function of inherent value by allowing the affected party an opportunity to speak for his own cause.

Important issues include the scope of due process protections and the questions when and to whom they apply. The law establishes due process protections for tenured employees, but as will be seen, the legal status of untenured employees is less certain.

BOARD OF REGENTS v. ROTH
Supreme Court of the United States
408 U.S. 564 (1972)

MR. JUSTICE STEWART delivered the opinion of the Court:

In 1968 the respondent, David Roth, was hired for his first teaching job as assistant professor of political science at Wisconsin State University-Oshkosh. He was hired for a fixed term of one academic year. The notice of his faculty appointment specified that his employment would begin on September 1, 1968, and would end on June 30, 1969. The respondent completed that term. But he was informed that he would not be rehired for the next academic year.

The respondent had no tenure rights to continued employment. Under Wisconsin statutory law a state university teacher can acquire tenure as a "permanent" employee only after four years of year-to-year employment. Having acquired tenure, a teacher is entitled to continued employment "during efficiency and good behavior." A relatively new teacher without tenure, however, is under Wisconsin law entitled to nothing beyond his one-year appointment. There are no statutory or administrative standards defining eligibility for re-employment. State law thus clearly leaves the decision whether to rehire a nontenured teacher for another year to the unfettered discretion of university officials.

The procedural protection afforded a Wisconsin State University teacher before he is separated from the University corresponds to his job security. As a matter of statutory law, a tenured teacher cannot be "discharged except for cause upon written charges" and pursuant to certain procedures. A nontenured teacher, similarly, is protected to some extent *during* his one-year term. Rules promulgated by the Board of Regents provide that a nontenured teacher "dismissed" before the end of the year may have some opportunity for review of the "dismissal." But the Rules provide no real protection for a nontenured teacher who simply is not re-employed for the next year. He must be informed by

February 1 "concerning retention or non-retention for the ensuing year." But "no reason for non-retention need be given. No review or appeal is provided in such case."

In conformance with these Rules, the President of Wisconsin State University-Oshkosh informed the respondent before February 1, 1969, that he would not be rehired for the 1969-1970 academic year. He gave the respondent no reason for the decision and no opportunity to challenge it at any sort of hearing.

The respondent then brought this action in Federal District Court alleging that the decision not to rehire him for the next year infringed his Fourteenth Amendment rights. He attacked the decision both in substance and procedure. First, he alleged that the true reason for the decision was to punish him for certain statements critical of the University administration, and that it therefore violated his right to freedom of speech. Second, he alleged that the failure of University officials to give him notice of any reason for nonretention and an opportunity for a hearing violated his right to procedural due process of law.

The District Court granted summary judgment for the respondent on the procedural issue, ordering the University officials to provide him with reasons and a hearing. The Court of Appeals, with one judge dissenting, affirmed this partial summary judgment. We granted certiorari. 404 U.S. 909. The only question presented to us at this stage in the case is whether the respondent had a constitutional right to a statement of reasons and a hearing on the University's decision not to rehire him for another year. We hold that he did not.

I

The requirements of procedural due process apply only to the deprivation of interests encompassed by the Fourteenth Amendment's protection of liberty and property. When protected interests are implicated, the right to some kind of prior hearing is paramount. But the range of interests protected by procedural due process is not infinite.

The District Court decided that procedural due process guarantees apply in this case by assessing and balancing the weights of the particular interests involved. It concluded that the respondent's interest in re-employment at Wisconsin State University-Oshkosh outweighed the University's interest in denying him re-employment summarily. 310 F. Supp. at 977-79. Undeniably, the respondent's re-employment prospects were of major concern to him — concern that we surely cannot say was insignificant. And a weighing process has long been a part of any determination of the *form* of hearing required in particular situations by procedural due process. But, to determine whether due process requirements apply in the first place, we must look not to the "weight" but to the *nature* of the interest at stake. *See Morrissey v. Brewer, ante,* at 481. We must look to see if the interest is within the Fourteenth Amendment's protection of liberty and property.

"Liberty" and "property" are broad and majestic terms. They are among the "[g]reat [constitutional] concepts ... purposely left to gather meaning from experience.... [T]hey relate to the whole domain of social and economic fact, and the statesmen who founded this Nation knew too well that only a stagnant society remains unchanged." For that reason, the Court has fully and finally rejected the wooden distinction between "rights" and "privileges" that once seemed to govern the applicability of procedural due process rights. The Court has also made clear that the property interests protected by procedural due process extend well beyond actual ownership of real estate, chattels, or money. By the same token, the Court has required due process protection for deprivations of liberty beyond the sort of formal constraints imposed by the criminal process.

Yet, while the Court has eschewed rigid or formalistic limitations on the protection of procedural due process, it has at the same time observed certain boundaries. For the words "liberty" and "property" in the Due Process Clause of the Fourteenth Amendment must be given some meaning.

II

"While this Court has not attempted to define with exactness the liberty ... guaranteed [by the Fourteenth Amendment], the term has received much consideration and some of the included things have been definitely stated. Without doubt, it denotes not merely freedom from bodily restraint but also the right of the individual to contract, to engage in any of the common occupations of life, to acquire useful knowledge, to marry, establish a home and bring up children, to worship God according to the dictates of his own conscience, and generally to enjoy those privileges long recognized ... as essential to the orderly pursuit of happiness by free men." In a Constitution for a free people, there can be no doubt that the meaning of "liberty" must be broad indeed.

There might be cases in which a State refused to reemploy a person under such circumstances that interests in liberty would be implicated. But this is not such a case.

The State, in declining to rehire the respondent, did not make any charge against him that might seriously damage his standing and associations in his community. It did not base the nonrenewal of his contract on a charge, for example, that he had been guilty of dishonesty, or immorality. Had it done so, this would be a different case. For "[w]here a person's good name, reputation, honor, or integrity is at stake because of what the government is doing to him, notice and an opportunity to be heard are essential."... In such a case, due process would accord an opportunity to refute the charge before University officials.[12] In the present case, however, there is no suggestion whatever that the respondent's "good name, reputation, honor, or integrity" is at stake.

---

[12]The purpose of such notice and hearing is to provide the person an opportunity to clear his name. Once a person has cleared his name at a hearing, his employer, of course, may remain free to deny him future employment for other reasons.

Similarly, there is no suggestion that the State, in declining to re-employ the respondent, imposed on him a stigma or other disability that foreclosed his freedom to take advantage of other employment opportunities. The State, for example, did not invoke any regulations to bar the respondent from all other public employment in state universities. Had it done so, this, again, would be a different case. For "[t]o be deprived not only of present government employment but of future opportunity for it certainly is no small injury...." *Joint Anti-Fascist Refugee Committee v. McGrath*, [341 U.S. 123 (1951)] at 185 (JACKSON, J., concurring).... The Court has held, for example, that a State, in regulating eligibility for a type of professional employment, cannot foreclose a range of opportunities "in a manner ... that contravene[s] ... due process," *Schware v. Board of Bar Examiners*, 353 U.S. 232, 238, and, specifically, in a manner that denies the right to a full prior hearing. *Willner v. Committee on Character*, 373 U.S. 96, 103.... In the present case, however, this principle does not come into play.

To be sure, the respondent has alleged that the non-renewal of his contract was based on his exercise of his right to freedom of speech. But this allegation is not now before us. The District Court stayed proceedings on this issue, and the respondent has yet to prove that the decision not to rehire him was, in fact, based on his free speech activities.

Hence, on the record before us, all that clearly appears is that the respondent was not rehired for one year at one university. It stretches the concept too far to suggest that a person is deprived of "liberty" when he simply is not rehired in one job but remains as free as before to seek another.

III

The Fourteenth Amendment's procedural protection of property is a safeguard of the security of interests that a person has already acquired in specific benefits. These interests — property interests — may take many forms.

Thus, the Court has held that a person receiving welfare benefits under statutory and administrative standards defining eligibility for them has an interest in continued receipt of those benefits that is safeguarded by procedural due process. *Goldberg v. Kelly*, 397 U.S. 254. *See Flemming v. Nestor*, 363 U.S. 603, 611. Similarly, in the area of public employment, the Court has held that a public college professor dismissed from an office held under tenure provisions, *Slochower v. Board of Educ.*, 350 U.S. 551, and college professors and staff members dismissed during the terms of their contracts, *Wieman v. Updegraff*, 344 U.S. 183, have interests in continued employment that are safeguarded by due process. Only last year, the Court held that this principle "proscribing summary dismissal from public employment without hearing or inquiry required by due process" also applied to a teacher recently hired without tenure or a formal contract, but nonetheless with a clearly implied promise of continued employment. *Connell v. Higginbotham*, 403 U.S. 207, 208.

Certain attributes of "property" interests protected by procedural due process emerge from these decisions. To have a property interest in a benefit, a person clearly must have more than an abstract need or desire for it. He must have more than a unilateral expectation of it. He must, instead, have a legitimate claim of entitlement to it. It is a purpose of the ancient institution of property to protect those claims upon which people rely in their daily lives, reliance that must not be arbitrarily undermined. It is a purpose of the constitutional right to a hearing to provide an opportunity for a person to vindicate those claims.

Property interests, of course, are not created by the Constitution. Rather, they are created and their dimensions are defined by existing rules or understandings that stem from an independent source such as state law — rules or understandings that secure certain benefits and that support claims of entitlement to those benefits. Thus, the welfare recipients in *Goldberg v. Kelly, supra,* had a claim of entitlement to welfare payments that was grounded in the statute defining eligibility for them. The recipients had not yet shown that they were, in fact, within the statutory terms of eligibility. But we held that they had a right to a hearing at which they might attempt to do so.

Just as the welfare recipients' "property" interest in welfare payments was created and defined by statutory terms, so the respondent's "property" interest in employment at Wisconsin State University-Oshkosh was created and defined by the terms of his appointment. Those terms secured his interest in employment up to June 30, 1969. But the important fact in this case is that they specifically provided that the respondent's employment was to terminate on June 30. They did not provide for contract renewal absent "sufficient cause." Indeed, they made no provision for renewal whatsoever.

Thus, the terms of the respondent's appointment secured absolutely no interest in re-employment for the next year. They supported absolutely no possible claim of entitlement to re-employment. Nor, significantly, was there any state statute or University rule or policy that secured his interest in re-employment or that created any legitimate claim to it. In these circumstances, the respondent surely had an abstract concern in being rehired, but he did not have a *property* interest sufficient to require the University authorities to give him a hearing when they declined to renew his contract of employment.

IV

Our analysis of the respondent's constitutional rights in this case in no way indicates a view that an opportunity for a hearing or a statement of reasons for nonretention would, or would not, be appropriate or wise in public colleges and universities. For it is a written Constitution that we apply. Our role is confined to interpretation of that Constitution.

We must conclude that the summary judgment for the respondent should not have been granted, since the respondent has not shown that he was deprived of liberty or property protected by the Fourteenth Amendment. The judgment of the

Court of Appeals, accordingly, is reversed and the case is remanded for further proceedings consistent with this opinion.

PERRY v. SINDERMANN

Supreme Court of the United States
408 U.S. 593 (1972)

MR. JUSTICE STEWART delivered the opinion of the Court:

From 1959 to 1969 the respondent, Robert Sindermann, was a teacher in the state college system of the State of Texas. After teaching for two years at the University of Texas and for four years at San Antonio Junior College, he became a professor of Government and Social Science at Odessa Junior College in 1965. He was employed at the college for four successive years, under a series of one-year contracts. He was successful enough to be appointed, for a time, the co-chairman of his department.

During the 1968-1969 academic year, however, controversy arose between the respondent and the college administration. The respondent was elected president of the Texas Junior College Teachers Association. In this capacity, he left his teaching duties on several occasions to testify before committees of the Texas Legislature, and he became involved in public disagreements with the policies of the college's Board of Regents. In particular, he aligned himself with a group advocating the elevation of the college to four-year status — a change opposed by the Regents. And, on one occasion, a newspaper advertisement appeared over his name that was highly critical of the Regents.

Finally, in May 1969, the respondent's one-year employment contract terminated and the Board of Regents voted not to offer him a new contract for the next academic year. The Regents issued a press release setting forth allegations of the respondent's insubordination. But they provided him no official statement of the reasons for the nonrenewal of his contract. And they allowed him no opportunity for a hearing to challenge the basis of the nonrenewal.

The respondent then brought this action in Federal District Court. He alleged primarily that the Regents' decision not to rehire him was based on his public criticism of the policies of the college administration and thus infringed his right to freedom of speech. He also alleged that their failure to provide him an opportunity for a hearing violated the Fourteenth Amendment's guarantee of procedural due process. The petitioners — members of the Board of Regents and the president of the college — denied that their decision was made in retaliation for the respondent's public criticism and argued that they had no obligation to provide a hearing. On the basis of these bare pleadings and three brief affidavits filed by the respondent, the District Court granted summary judgment for the petitioners. It concluded that the respondent had "no cause of action against the [petitioners] since his contract of employment terminated May 31, 1969, and Odessa Junior College has not adopted the tenure system."

The Court of Appeals reversed the judgment of the District Court. 430 F.2d 939. First, it held that, despite the respondent's lack of tenure, the nonrenewal

B. HIRING AND DISCHARGE

of his contract would violate the Fourteenth Amendment if it in fact was based on his protected free speech. Since the actual reason for the Regents' decision was "in total dispute" in the pleadings, the court remanded the case for a full hearing on his contested issue of fact. Second, the Court of Appeals held that, despite the respondent's lack of tenure, the failure to allow him an opportunity for a hearing would violate the constitutional guarantee of procedural due process if the respondent could show that he had an "expectancy" of re-employment. It, therefore, ordered that this issue of fact also be aired upon remand. We granted a writ of certiorari, and we have considered this case along with *Board of Regents v. Roth*, ante, p. 564.

I

The first question presented is whether the respondent's lack of a contractual or tenure right to re-employment, taken alone, defeats his claim that the nonrenewal of his contract violated the First and Fourteenth Amendments. We hold that it does not.

For at least a quarter-century, this Court has made clear that even though a person has no "right" to a valuable governmental benefit and even though the government may deny him the benefit for any number of reasons, there are some reasons upon which the government may not rely. It may not deny a benefit to a person on a basis that infringes his constitutionally protected interests — especially, his interest in freedom of speech. For if the government could deny a benefit to a person because of his constitutionally protected speech or associations, his exercise of those freedoms would in effect be penalized and inhibited. This would allow the government to "produce a result which [it] could not command directly." *Speiser v. Randall*, 357 U.S. 513, 526. Such interference with constitutional rights is impermissible.

. . . .

Thus, the respondent's lack of a contractual or tenure "right" to re-employment for the 1969-1970 academic year is immaterial to his free speech claim. Indeed, twice before, this Court has specifically held that the nonrenewal of a nontenured public school teacher's one-year contract may not be predicated on his exercise of First and Fourteenth Amendment rights. *Shelton v. Tucker*, [364 U.S. 479 (1960)]; *Keyishian v. Board of Regents*, [385 U.S. 589 (1967)]. We reaffirm those holdings here.

In this case, of course, the respondent has yet to show that the decision not to renew his contract was, in fact, made in retaliation for his exercise of the constitutional right of free speech. The District Court foreclosed any opportunity to make this showing when it granted summary judgment. Hence, we cannot now hold that the Board of Regents' action was invalid.

But we agree with the Court of Appeals that there is a genuine dispute as to "whether the college refused to renew the teaching contract on an impermissible basis — as a reprisal for the exercise of constitutionally protected rights." 430 F.2d at 943. The respondent has alleged that his nonretention was based on his testimony before legislative committees and his other public statements critical of the Regents' policies. And he has alleged that this public criticism was within the First and Fourteenth Amendments' protection of freedom of speech. Plainly, these allegations present a bona fide constitutional claim. For this Court has held that a teacher's public criticism of his superiors on matters of public concern may be constitutionally protected and may, therefore, be an impermissible basis for termination of his employment. *Pickering v. Board of Education, supra.*

For this reason we hold that the grant of summary judgment against the respondent, without full exploration of this issue, was improper.

II

The respondent's lack of formal contractual or tenure security in continued employment at Odessa Junior College, though irrelevant to his free speech claim, is highly relevant to his procedural due process claim. But it may not be entirely dispositive.

We have held today in *Board of Regents v. Roth, ante,* p. 564, that the Constitution does not require opportunity for a hearing before the nonrenewal of a nontenured teacher's contract, unless he can show that the decision not to rehire him somehow deprived him of an interest in "liberty" or that he had a "property" interest in continued employment, despite the lack of tenure or a formal contract. In *Roth* the teacher had not made a showing on either point to justify summary judgment in his favor.

Similarly, the respondent here has yet to show that he has been deprived of an interest that could invoke procedural due process protection. As in *Roth,* the mere showing that he was not rehired in one particular job, without more, did not amount to a showing of a loss of liberty. Nor did it amount to a showing of a loss of property.

But the respondent's allegations — which we must construe most favorably to the respondent at this stage of the litigation — do raise a genuine issue as to his interest in continued employment at Odessa Junior College. He alleged that this interest, though not secured by a formal contractual tenure provision, was secured by a no less binding understanding fostered by the college administration. In particular, the respondent alleged that the college had a de facto tenure program, and that he had tenure under that program. He claimed that he and others legitimately relied upon an unusual provision that had been in the college's official Faculty Guide for many years:

> *Teacher Tenure*: Odessa College has no tenure system. The Administration of the College wishes the faculty member to feel that he has permanent tenure as long as his teaching services are satisfactory and as long as he displays a cooperative attitude toward his co-workers and his superiors, and as long as he is happy in his work.

Moreover, the respondent claimed legitimate reliance upon guidelines promulgated by the Coordinating Board of the Texas College and University System that provided that a person, like himself, who had been employed as a teacher in the state college and university system for seven years or more has some form of job tenure. Thus, the respondent offered to prove that a teacher with his long period of service at this particular State College had no less a "property" interest in continued employment than a formally tenured teacher at other colleges, and had no less a procedural due process right to a statement of reasons and a hearing before college officials upon their decision not to retain him.

We have made clear in *Roth, supra*, at 571-72, that "property" interests subject to procedural due process protection are not limited by a few rigid, technical forms. Rather, "property" denotes a broad range of interests that are secured by "existing rules or understandings." *Id.* at 577. A person's interest in a benefit is a "property" interest for due process purposes if there are such rules or mutually explicit understandings that support his claim of entitlement to the benefit and that he may invoke at a hearing. *Ibid.*

A written contract with an explicit tenure provision clearly is evidence of a formal understanding that supports a teacher's claim of entitlement to continued employment unless sufficient "cause" is shown. Yet absence of such an explicit contractual provision may not always foreclose the possibility that a teacher has a "property" interest in re-employment. For example, the law of contracts in most, if not all, jurisdictions long has employed a process by which agreements, though not formalized in writing, may be "implied." Corbin on Contracts §§ 561-572A (1960). Explicit contractual provisions may be supplemented by other agreements implied from "the promisor's words and conduct in the light of the surrounding circumstances." *Id.* at § 562. And, "[t]he meaning of [the promisor's] words and acts is found by relating them to the usage of the past." *Ibid.*

A teacher, like the respondent, who has held his position for a number of years, might be able to show from the circumstances of this service — and from other relevant facts — that he has a legitimate claim of entitlement to job tenure. Just as this Court has found there to be a "common law of a particular industry or of a particular plant" that may supplement a collective-bargaining agreement, *Steelworkers v. Warrior & Gulf Co.*, 363 U.S. 574, 579, so there may be an unwritten "common law" in a particular university that certain employees shall have the equivalent of tenure. This is particularly likely in a college or university, like Odessa Junior College, that has no explicit tenure system even for senior members of its faculty, but that nonetheless may have created such a system in practice.

In this case, the respondent has alleged the existence of rules and understandings, promulgated and fostered by state officials, that may justify his legitimate claim of entitlement to continued employment absent "sufficient cause." We disagree with the Court of Appeals insofar as it held that a mere subjective "expectancy" is protected by procedural due process, but we agree that the respondent must be given an opportunity to prove the legitimacy of his claim of such entitlement in light of "the policies and practices of the institution." 430

F.2d at 943. Proof of such a property interest would not, of course, entitle him to reinstatement. But such proof would obligate college officials to grant a hearing at his request, where he could be informed of the grounds for his nonretention and challenge their sufficiency.

Therefore, while we do not wholly agree with the opinion of the Court of Appeals, its judgment remanding this case to the District Court is

Affirmed.

---

1. "A property interest in employment can, of course, be created by ordinance, or by an implied contract. In either case, however, the sufficiency of the claim of entitlement must be decided by reference to state law." *Bishop v. Wood*, 426 U.S. 341, 344 (1975). Careful attention must be given to specific contract language and to governing state law to determine interests created and protected. Contrast *Strongin v. Nyquist*, 44 N.Y.2d 943, 380 N.E.2d 150, 408 N.Y.S.2d 318 (1978), holding that a tenured counselor found guilty of inefficiency, incompetency, and insubordination and dismissed by the board of education was entitled to a review only as to whether that determination was capricious and arbitrary, with *Welch v. Board of Educ.*, 45 Ill. App. 3d 35, 358 N.E.2d 1364 (1977), holding that a tenured teacher dismissed without warning because his conduct was "irremediable" was entitled to review as to whether that determination was against the manifest weight of the evidence.

Consider also *Guerra v. Roma Indep. Sch. Dist.*, 444 F. Supp. 812 (S.D. Texas 1977), holding that plaintiff-teachers who had successfully passed a three-year probationary period during which they served under year-to-year contracts were not entitled to due process protections when they were dismissed at the expiration of those contracts. The *Guerra* court read state law to proscribe tenure and therefore to void any school district policy, express, de facto, or implied, and to defeat any due process claim based on understandings fostered by that policy.

2. Absent specific statutory or contract language creating a property interest, the Supreme Court has noted,

> The federal court is not the appropriate forum in which to review the multitude of personnel decisions that are made daily by public agencies. We must accept the harsh fact that numerous individual mistakes are inevitable in the day-to-day administration of our affairs. The United States Constitution cannot feasibly be construed to require federal judicial review for every such error. In the absence of any claim that the public employer was motivated by a desire to curtail or to penalize the exercise of an employee's constitutionally protected rights, we must presume that official action was regular and, if erroneous, can best be corrected in other ways. The Due Process Clause of the Fourteenth Amendment is not a guarantee against

incorrect or ill-advised personnel decisions. *Bishop v. Wood*, 426 U.S. 341, 349-50 (1975).

3. Does a school employee have a property interest in a particular position? Does he have a constitutional right to due process protections in connection with transfer to another school or transfer from one assignment to another assignment within a school? *See Danno v. Peterson*, 421 F. Supp. 950 (N.D. Ill. 1976) (principal reassigned to teaching); *Frank v. Arapahoe County Sch. Dist.*, 506 P.2d 373 (Colo. App. 1972) (counselor reassigned to teaching); and *Thompson v. Modesto City High Sch. Dist.*, 19 Cal. 3d 620, 566 P.2d 237, 139 Cal. Rptr. 603 (1977) (counselor reassigned to teaching). All three cases look to state law to determine whether the property interest created is merely in employment with the district or whether it is in employment with the district in a specific position.

4. Fundamental to any understanding of due process in the education employment context is that collective bargaining protections, restoration of job opportunities based on a violation of civil rights or reemployment because of a denial of due process, represent exceptions to the general rule of employment in the United States. In fact, the vast majority of employees fall under the "at-will doctrine" meaning that persons can be terminated for good reason, bad reason, or no reason. This, in fact, was the ruling in the recent case of *Castro v. New York City Bd. of Educ.*, 777 F. Supp. 1113 (S.D.N.Y. 1990), where a non-tenured teacher challenged his non-renewal of contract, claiming a pre-termination hearing was required. The court concluded that the teacher served "at will" in his non-tenured status and failed to prove that he was dismissed for a constitutionally impermissible purpose.

5. Due process in employment, of course, carries several components. They include, depending on the deprivation of right, notice, a hearing, names of witnesses, right to disclosure of evidence, right to a decision based on the record, and the right to a fair and impartial hearing. The court in *Syquia v. Board of Educ. of Harpursville Central Sch. Dist.*, 568 N.Y.S.2d 263 (1991), was exorcised over the absence of an impartial hearing in that one of the decision makers received more remuneration than that permitted by state law. The hearings under the state Education Law Section 3020-a called for a three-member panel chosen from a list maintained by the Commissioner of Education — one member chosen by the teacher, one by the associated board of education, and the third agreed upon by the other two. The chairperson of the panel is paid according to the American Arbitration Association; the other two are to be paid up to $50 per day for each day of actual service. All parties conceded that the panel member chosen by the Board was paid an additional $100 per day throughout the pendency, amounting to $5,700. In a colorful opinion, the court found a violation of procedural due process.

> A 3020-a hearing is a fact-finding hearing, not a joust.... A biased decision maker is constitutionally not acceptable.... Call it bias, or lack of due process, or lack of fundamental fairness, it is all the same, and violative of

the American idea of justice.... It is difficult enough, even with due process, to assure that a result is fair and just; without, it is impossible.... Once due process is lost it can never be regained. Not 'all the King's horses and all the King's men' can put it together again. *Id.* at 266-67.

The court did note that bias was not actually proven here. "There is in this case a gnawing feeling that a fair and impartial hearing may not have been had — at least we cannot be sure. A unanimous decision [it was 2-1 against the teacher on insubordination claims] might have left us with a less gnawing feeling. But in this split decision, the vote of panel members [chosen by the Board] was crucial.... Due process ought not to leave one with a gnawing feeling...." *Id.* at 267.

How far do you think the court's reasoning as regards a dollar amount should go? What if the member of the tribunal in question had only been paid one dollar more than prescribed by law? Does the fact that the total amount paid to this person over time amounting to $5,700 give you a "gnawing feeling that a fair and impartial hearing may not have been had?" Does this really suggest that "he who pays the piper calls the tune?" *Id.*

6. It is important to remember that the decision in *Roth* dealt only with procedural due process, and not substantive due process. In *Holthaus v. Board of Educ., Cincinnati Pub. Schs.*, 986 F.2d 1044 (6th Cir. 1993), a teacher's supplemental football coaching contract was terminated after he made a comment containing a racial slur to his team. The derogatory term used by the white coach had been used by an African-American team member in an earlier conversation with the coach. The teacher asserted that rather than simply terminating his employment, the Board discharged him by improperly "charging him with immorality and willful violations of School Board rules, which, if true, would seriously impugn his character, undermine his associations, and damage his ability to seek employment elsewhere as a head coach." *Id.* at 1046. The teacher claimed a substantive due process violation, but relied primarily on *Roth*. The court noted that if the coach were, indeed, stigmatized by the circumstances surrounding his termination, *Roth* would apply only if the coach's procedural due process rights were violated; *i.e.*, if the coach had not been given the opportunity to be heard. The court affirmed the summary judgment for the defendant school board.

Did the plaintiff in *Holthaus* trip a decision against himself by missing the mark on the holding in *Roth*? What of the court's statement that *Roth* only makes clear that one is entitled to due process if "stigma" is found, that the school board was guilty of the claim, but that the plaintiff got all the process he was due? Does this now mean that school boards may escape liability by bringing the good name of employees into question, holding hearings, and then relying on *Roth* for rendering the proper due process?

B. HIRING AND DISCHARGE

7. The termination of educators revolves around many issues, all of which bring the due process doctrine into focus. They include:

1) Incompetence and neglect of duties. Generally, dismissals of this kind are based on patterns of conduct rather than isolated occurrences. *See Smith v. Denver Pub. Sch. Bd.*, 767 F. Supp. 226 (D. Colo. 1991); *Independent Sch. Dist. No. 4 of Harper County v. Orange*, 841 P.2d 1177 (Okla. Ct. App. 1992); *Alabama State Tenure Comm'n v. Birmingham Bd. of Educ.*, 564 So. 2d 980 (Ala. Civ. App. 1990);

2) Moral misconduct. Sexual misconduct with students serves as cause for dismissal. *See Kevin v. Board of Educ., Lamar Sch. Dist., No. RE-2, Prowers County*, 860 P.2d 574 (Colo. Ct. App. 1993); *State v. Parker*, 592 A.2d 228 (N.J. Super. Ct. App. Div. 1991); *Sertik v. School Dist. of Pittsburgh*, 584 A.2d 390 (Pa. Commw. Ct. 1990);

3) The dismissal of educators has also been upheld for sexual activity with other adults in such areas as adultery, homosexuality and cohabitation. *See Rowland v. Mad River Local Sch. Dist*, 730 F.2d 444 (9th Cir. 1984), *cert. denied*, 471 U.S. 1062 (1985); *Johnson v. San Jacinto College*, 498 F. Supp. 555 (Tex. 1980); *Yanzick v. School Dist. No. 23*, 41 P.2d 431 (Mont. 1982);

4) Insubordination is another cause of action with much case law implicated. *See Jackson v. Sobol*, 565 N.Y.S.2d 612 (App. Div. 1991); *Fredrickson v. Denver Pub. Sch. Dist. No.1*, 819 P.2d 1068 (Colo. Ct. App. 1991); *Cooper v. Williamson County Bd. of Educ.*, 803 S.W.2d 200 (Tenn. 1990).

Chapter 10
THE TEACHER AS CITIZEN

The public school teacher has three relationships with the state: 1) that of citizen with sovereign; 2) that of employee with employer; and 3) that of instructor measured against the state's role as educator. The first relationship imposes some restrictions on the teacher — he or she is subject to criminal and civil action for violation of the state's laws; but, restrictions are somewhat limited and individual rights are protected by the laws of our constitutional democracy. In its role as sovereign, the state is required to refrain from interfering with individual rights possessed by its teacher citizens. Similarly, the teacher, as part of the citizenry, is a master of the state, working to promote those changes which he or she believes will serve the interests of society.

Tensions arise when the state in its role as employer, with its objective to efficiently educate the populace, attempts to control its teacher-employees. This is partly due to the existence of fewer strictures on the state under the employment enterprise. At the same time, as employee, he or she is servant to the state, charged with loyalty and obedience in carrying out the mandates of law as it presently exists.

Finally, there are even fewer stringent limitations on the state in its capacity as educator, *i.e.*, when state education officials are engaged in the transmission of knowledge and societal values to students. In these situations, recent case law has determined that actions by government do not raise the same constitutional concerns as those found in the state role as either sovereign or employer. Friction may occur because activities such as exposing students to differing points of view or pedagogical methods, heretofore thought to be protected under the doctrine of academic freedom, may now reasonably be restricted by school officials in achieving the goal of protecting "legitimate pedagogical concerns."

These conflicting roles give rise to the issues in school control over teacher conduct and teacher expression.

A. SCHOOL CONTROL OVER TEACHER EXPRESSION

PICKERING v. BOARD OF EDUCATION
Supreme Court of the United States
391 U.S. 563 (1968)

MR. JUSTICE MARSHALL delivered the opinion of the Court:

Appellant Marvin L. Pickering, a teacher in Township High School District 205, Will County, Illinois, was dismissed from his position by the appellee Board of Education for sending a letter to a local newspaper in connection with a recently proposed tax increase that was critical of the way in which the Board and the district superintendent of schools had handled past proposals to raise new revenue for the schools. Appellant's dismissal resulted from a determination by the Board, after a full hearing, that the publication of the letter was "detrimental to the efficient operation and administration of the schools of the district" and hence, under the relevant Illinois statute, Ill. Rev. Stat., c. 122, § 10-22.4 (1963), that "interests of the school require[d] [his dismissal]."

Appellant's claim that his writing of the letter was protected by the First and Fourteenth Amendments was rejected. Appellant then sought review of the Board's action in the Circuit Court of Will County, which affirmed his dismissal on the ground that the determination that appellant's letter was detrimental to the interests of the school system was supported by substantial evidence and that the interests of the schools overrode appellant's First Amendment rights. On appeal, the Supreme Court of Illinois, two Justices dissenting, affirmed the judgment of the Circuit Court. 36 Ill. 2d 568, 225 N.E.2d 1 (1967). We noted probable jurisdiction of appellant's claim that the Illinois statute permitting his dismissal on the facts of this case was unconstitutional as applied under the First and Fourteenth Amendments. 389 U.S. 925 (1967). For the reasons detailed below we agree that appellant's rights to freedom of speech were violated and we reverse.

I

In February of 1961 the appellee Board of Education asked the voters of the school district to approve a bond issue to raise $4,875,000 to erect two new schools. The proposal was defeated. Then, in December of 1961, the Board submitted another bond proposal to the voters which called for the raising of $5,500,000 to build two new schools. This second proposal passed and the schools were built with the money raised by the bond sales. In May of 1964 a proposed increase in the tax rate to be used for educational purposes was submitted to the voters by the Board and was defeated. Finally, on September 19, 1964, a second proposal to increase the tax rate was submitted by the Board and was likewise defeated. It was in connection with this last proposal of the School Board that appellant wrote the letter to the editor ... that resulted in his dismissal.

Prior to the vote on the second tax increase proposal a variety of articles attributed to the District 205 Teachers' Organization appeared in the local paper. These articles urged passage of the tax increase and stated that failure to pass the increase would result in a decline in the quality of education afforded children in the district's schools. A letter from the superintendent of schools making the same point was published in the paper two days before the election and submitted to the voters in mimeographed form the following day. It was in response to the foregoing material, together with the failure of the tax increase to pass, that appellant submitted the letter in question to the editor of the local paper.

The letter constituted, basically, an attack on the School Board's handling of the 1961 bond issue proposals and its subsequent allocation of financial resources

A. SCHOOL CONTROL OVER TEACHER EXPRESSION

between the schools' educational and athletic programs. It also charged the superintendent of schools with attempting to prevent teachers in the district from opposing or criticizing the proposed bond issue.

The Board dismissed Pickering for writing and publishing the letter. Pursuant to Illinois law, the Board was then required to hold a hearing on the dismissal. At the hearing the Board charged that numerous statements in the letter were false and that the publication of the statements unjustifiably impugned the "motives, honesty, integrity, truthfulness, responsibility and competence" of both the Board and the school administration. The Board also charged that the false statements damaged the professional reputations of its members and of the school administrators, would be disruptive of faculty discipline, and would tend to foment "controversy, conflict and dissension" among teachers, administrators, the Board of Education, and the residents of the district. Testimony was introduced from a variety of witnesses on the truth or falsity of the particular statements in the letter with which the Board took issue. The Board found the statements to be false as charged. No evidence was introduced at any point in the proceedings as to the effect of the publication of the letter on the community as a whole or on the administration of the school system in particular, and no specific findings along these lines were made.

The Illinois courts reviewed the proceedings solely to determine whether the Board's findings were supported by substantial evidence and whether, on the facts as found, the Board could reasonably conclude that appellant's publication of the letter was "detrimental to the best interests of the schools." Pickering's claim that his letter was protected by the First Amendment was rejected on the ground that his acceptance of a teaching position in the public schools obliged him to refrain from making statements about the operation of the schools "which in the absence of such position he would have an undoubted right to engage in." It is not altogether clear whether the Illinois Supreme Court held that the First Amendment had no applicability to appellant's dismissal for writing the letter in question or whether it determined that the particular statements made in the letter were not entitled to First Amendment protection.

In any event, it clearly rejected Pickering's claim that, on the facts of this case, he could not constitutionally be dismissed from his teaching position.

II

To the extent that the Illinois Supreme Court's opinion may be read to suggest that teachers may constitutionally be compelled to relinquish the First Amendment rights they would otherwise enjoy as citizens to comment on matters of public interest in connection with the operation of the public schools in which they work, it proceeds on a premise that has been unequivocally rejected in numerous prior decisions of this Court, *e.g.*, *Wieman v. Updegraff*, 344 U.S. 183 (1952); *Shelton v. Tucker*, 364 U.S. 479 (1960); *Keyishian v. Board of Regents*, 385 U.S. 589 (1967). "[T]he theory that public employment which may be denied altogether may be subjected to any conditions, regardless of how unreasonable, has been uniformly rejected." *Keyishian v. Board of Regents, supra,* at 605-606. At the same time it cannot be gainsaid that the State has interests as an employer in regulating the speech of its employees that differ significantly from those it possesses in connection with regulation of the speech of the citizenry in general. The problem in any case is to arrive at a balance between the interests of the teacher, as a citizen, in commenting upon matters of public concern and the interest of the State, as an employer, in promoting the efficiency of the public services it performs through its employees.

III

The Board contends that "the teacher by virtue of his public employment has a duty of loyalty to support his superiors in attaining the generally accepted goals of education and that, if he must speak out publicly, he should do so factually and accurately, commensurate with his education and experience." Appellant, on the other hand, argues that the test applicable to defamatory statements directed against public officials by persons having no occupational relationship with them, namely, that statements to be legally actionable must be made "with knowledge that [they were] ... false or with reckless disregard of whether [they were] ... false or not," *New York Times Co. v. Sullivan,* 376 U.S. 254, 280 (1964), should also be applied to public statements made by teachers. Because of the enormous variety of fact situations in which critical statements by teachers and other public employees may be thought by their superiors, against whom the statements are directed, to furnish grounds for dismissal, we do not deem it either appropriate or feasible to attempt to lay down a general standard against which all such statements may be judged. However, in the course of evaluating the conflicting claims of First Amendment protection and the need for orderly school administration in the context of this case, we shall indicate some of the general lines along which an analysis of the controlling interests should run.

An examination of the statements in appellant's letter objected to by the Board reveals that they, like the letter as a whole, consist essentially of criticism of the Board's allocation of school funds between educational and athletic programs, and of both the Board's and the superintendent's methods of informing, or preventing the informing of, the district's taxpayers of the real reasons why additional tax revenues were being sought for the schools. The statements are in no way directed towards any person with whom appellant would normally be in contact in the course of his daily work as a teacher. Thus no question of maintaining either discipline by immediate superiors or harmony among coworkers is presented here. Appellant's employment relationships with the Board and, to a somewhat lesser extent, with the superintendent are not the kind of close working relationships for which it can persuasively be claimed that personal loyalty and confidence are necessary to their proper functioning. Accordingly, to the extent that the Board's position here can be taken to suggest that even comments on matters of public concern that are substantially correct

A. SCHOOL CONTROL OVER TEACHER EXPRESSION

may furnish grounds for dismissal if they are sufficiently critical in tone, we unequivocally reject it.[3]

We next consider the statements in appellant's letter which we agree to be false. The Board's original charges included allegations that the publication of the letter damaged the professional reputations of the Board and the superintendent and would foment controversy and conflict among the Board, teachers, administrators, and the residents of the district. However, no evidence to support these allegations was introduced at the hearing. So far as the record reveals, Pickering's letter was greeted by everyone but its main target, the Board, with massive apathy and total disbelief. The Board must, therefore, have decided perhaps by analogy with the law of libel that the statements were per se harmful to the operation of the schools.

However, the only way in which the Board could conclude, absent any evidence of the actual effect of the letter, that the statements contained therein were per se detrimental to the interest of the schools was to equate the Board members' own interests with that of the schools. Certainly an accusation that too much money is being spent on athletics by the administrators of the school system (which is precisely the import of that portion of appellant's letter containing the statements that we have found to be false) cannot reasonably be regarded as per se detrimental to the district's schools. Such an accusation reflects rather a difference of opinion between Pickering and the Board as to the preferable manner of operating the school system, a difference of opinion that clearly concerns an issue of general public interest.

In addition, the fact that particular illustrations of the Board's claimed undesirable emphasis on athletic programs are false would not normally have any necessary impact on the actual operation of the schools, beyond its tendency to anger the Board. For example, Pickering's letter was written after the defeat at the polls of the second proposed tax increase. It could, therefore, have had no effect on the ability of the school district to raise necessary revenue, since there was no showing that there was any proposal to increase taxes pending when the letter was written.

More importantly, the question whether a school system requires additional funds is a matter of legitimate public concern on which the judgment of the school administration, including the School Board, cannot, in a society that leaves such questions to popular vote, be taken as conclusive. On such a question

---

[3]It is possible to conceive of some positions in public employment in which the need for confidentiality is so great that even completely correct public statements might furnish a permissible ground for dismissal. Likewise, positions in public employment in which the relationship between superior and subordinate is of such a personal and intimate nature that certain forms of public criticism of the superior by the subordinate would seriously undermine the effectiveness of the working relationship between them can also be imagined. We intimate no views as to how we would resolve any specific instances of such situations, but merely note that significantly different considerations would be involved in such cases.

free and open debate is vital to informed decision-making by the electorate. Teachers are, as a class, the members of a community most likely to have informed and definite opinions as to how funds allotted to the operation of the schools should be spent. Accordingly, it is essential that they be able to speak out freely on such questions without fear of retaliatory dismissal.

In addition, the amounts expended on athletics which Pickering reported erroneously were matters of public record on which his position as a teacher in the district did not qualify him to speak with any greater authority than any other taxpayer. The Board could easily have rebutted appellant's errors by publishing the accurate figures itself, either via a letter to the same newspaper or otherwise. We are thus not presented with a situation in which a teacher has carelessly made false statements about matters so closely related to the day-to-day operations of the schools that any harmful impact on the public would be difficult to counter because of the teacher's presumed greater access to the real facts. Accordingly, we have no occasion to consider at this time whether under such circumstances a school board could reasonably require that a teacher make substantial efforts to verify the accuracy of his charges before publishing them.[4]

What we do have before us is a case in which a teacher has made erroneous public statements upon issues then currently the subject of public attention, which are critical of his ultimate employer but which are neither shown nor can be presumed to have in any way either impeded the teacher's proper performance of his daily duties in the classroom[5] or to have interfered with the regular operation of the schools generally. In these circumstances we conclude that the interest of the school administration in limiting teachers' opportunities to contribute to public debate is not significantly greater than its interest in limiting a similar contribution by any member of the general public.

IV

The public interest in having free and unhindered debate on matters of public importance — the core value of the Free Speech Clause of the First Amendment — is so great that it has been held that a State cannot authorize the recovery of damages by a public official for defamatory statements directed at him except when such statements are shown to have been made either with knowledge of their falsity or with reckless disregard for their truth or falsity. *New York Times Co. v. Sullivan*, 376 U.S. 254 (1964); *St. Amant v. Thompson*, 390 U.S. 727

---

[4]There is likewise no occasion furnished by this case for consideration of the extent to which teachers can be required by narrowly drawn grievance procedures to submit complaints about the operation of the schools to their superiors for action thereon prior to bringing the complaints before the public.

[5]We also note that this case does not present a situation in which a teacher's public statements are so without foundation as to call into question his fitness to perform his duties in the classroom. In such a case, of course, the statements would merely be evidence of the teacher's general competence, or lack thereof, and not an independent basis for dismissal.

A. SCHOOL CONTROL OVER TEACHER EXPRESSION

(1968). Compare *Linn v. United Plant Guard Workers*, 383 U.S. 53 (1966). The same test has been applied to suits for invasion of privacy based on false statements where a "matter of public interest" is involved. *Time, Inc. v. Hill*, 385 U.S. 374 (1967). It is therefore perfectly clear that, were appellant a member of the general public, the State's power to afford the appellee Board of Education or its members any legal right to sue him for writing the letter at issue here would be limited by the requirement that the letter be judged by the standard laid down in *New York Times*.

This Court has also indicated, in more general terms, that statements by public officials on matters of public concern must be accorded First Amendment protection despite the fact that the statements are directed at their nominal superiors. *Garrison v. Louisiana*, 379 U.S. 64 (1964); *Wood v. Georgia*, 370 U.S. 375 (1962). In *Garrison*, the *New York Times* test was specifically applied to a case involving a criminal defamation conviction stemming from statements made by a district attorney about the judges before whom he regularly appeared.

While criminal sanctions and damage awards have a somewhat different impact on the exercise of the right to freedom of speech from dismissal from employment, it is apparent that the threat of dismissal from public employment is nonetheless a potent means of inhibiting speech. We have already noted our disinclination to make an across-the-board equation of dismissal from public employment for remarks critical of superiors with awarding damages in a libel suit by a public official for similar criticism. However, in a case such as the present one, in which the fact of employment is only tangentially and unsubstantially involved in the subject matter of the public communication made by a teacher, we conclude that it is necessary to regard the teacher as the member of the general public he seeks to be.

In sum, we hold that, in a case such as this, absent proof of false statements knowingly or recklessly made by him, a teacher's exercise of his right to speak on issues of public importance may not furnish the basis for his dismissal from public employment. Since no such showing has been made in this case regarding appellant's letter, his dismissal for writing it cannot be upheld and the judgment of the Illinois Supreme Court must, accordingly, be reversed and the case remanded for further proceedings not inconsistent with this opinion. It is so ordered.

. . . .

---

1. What is the significance of the following facts in *Pickering*?

(a) There was no breach of a confidential relationship since none of the information publicized in Pickering's letter drew upon facts he learned in his position as a teacher.

(b) The issue of board policy *Pickering* attacked was one before the electorate and did not involve employer-employee relationships.

(c) Pickering did not attack any individual with whom he had to work closely as a colleague or subordinate.

(d) The letter did not have a harmful impact on the school board.

Are these facts relevant to the decision? Should they be?

2. Decisions in the First Amendment area convey that while teachers may not use the classroom as a forum to discuss matters irrelevant to the subject matter, an argument can be rendered that the doctrine of academic freedom protects the right of teachers to expose students to citizen views when the state cannot articulate a pedagogical reason for limiting such views. The *Pickering* balancing test is used to make such determinations.

The Fourth Circuit Court of Appeals in *Piver v. Pender County Bd. of Educ.*, 835 F.2d 1076 (4th Cir. 1987), applied the *Pickering* balancing test. In *Piver*, a teacher spoke at a board meeting regarding the tenure of another teacher and discussed this matter with students in class. The court held that the school's interest in preventing turmoil in the school was not sufficient to outweigh the rights and interests of the teacher.

Piver is one of a number of cases where courts have recognized a teacher's right to offer personal views in the classroom, at least where there is no effort to indoctrinate. *See, e.g., Zykan v. Warsaw Community Sch. Corp.*, 631 F.2d 1300 (7th Cir. 1980); *Cary v. Board of Education*, 598 F.2d 535 (10th Cir. 1979); *James v. Board of Educ.*, 461 F.2d 566 (2d Cir. 1972); and *Moore v. Gaston County Bd. of Educ.*, 357 F. Supp. 1037 (W.D.N.C. 1973).

3. The other side of the balancing test in *Pickering*, *i.e.*, the state's role as employer, has also been used by the federal courts to indicate that teachers do not have constitutional rights to teach or not to teach certain subjects based on personal views and where indoctrination is an issue. In *Peloza v. Capistrano Unified Sch. Dist.*, 782 F. Supp. 412 (C.D. Cal. 1992), the court held that a high school biology teacher espousing the creationist view in the classroom was not denied his First Amendment free speech rights when he was required to refrain from such comments and to teach according to a school district curriculum the court conveyed that the *Pickering* balance weighed in favor of the school district in that there was a "compelling interest to teach students ... the basic materials needed to become contributing citizens ... [and such an interest is found in the] ... secular purpose of educating high school students." *Id.* at 418. The court went on to find support for the decision in *Tinker v. Des Moines Indep. Community Dist.*, 393 U.S. 503 (1969) [*supra*, Chapter 6] in that a teacher's First Amendment rights may be limited if "the exercise of those rights materially interferes [with the rights of students]."

The *Peloza* court went to some length to determine that the case involved the First Amendment right of free speech and not of the exercise of religion. The ruling is consistent with a parallel case at the college level (cited by the court in *Peloza*), *Bishop v. Aronov*, 926 F.2d 1066 (11th Cir.), *cert. denied, granted sub nom. Bishop v. Delchamp*, ___ U.S. ___, 112 S. Ct. 294 (1991), where the

A. SCHOOL CONTROL OVER TEACHER EXPRESSION

Eleventh Circuit ruled that university restrictions with respect to classroom conduct issued under its authority to control curriculum do not infringe the free speech rights of professors.

Although the district court in *Peloza* claims to employ the *Pickering* test as regards the state role as employer, doesn't the ruling, using *Bishop*, really involve the role of "educator"? If the school district was only seen as employer, would the *Pickering* balance have really weighed so heavily on the side of the state?

4. What about a school board's interest in maintaining a good working relationship with an outspoken district superintendent? In *Kinsey v. Salado Indep. Sch. Dist.*, 950 F.2d 988 (5th Cir. 1992), the school board suspended superintendent Kinsey after he spoke in support of a particular slate of board of education candidates who were later not elected. The Fifth Circuit reversed itself from an earlier ruling and held that the administrator's First Amendment to free speech and political association were not violated. Although Kinsey's activities were clearly matters of public concern, the very nature of the subject matter disrupted any relationship he had with the school board as, unlike the teacher in *Pickering*, the superintendent had direct fiduciary and important policymaking responsibilities to the board of education.

5. The *Pickering* court held constitutional a teacher's letter to a local newspaper condemning the management of school district tax proposals. Would the court hold similarly for a defense letter published in a school newspaper, written in response to claims of sexual harassment? In *Seemuller v. Fairfax County Sch. Bd.*, 878 F.2d 1578 (1989), the Fourth Circuit decided in favor of the teacher, ruling that sex discrimination is a matter of public concern.

Should the fact that the speech was made in a school paper have turned the court in the other direction? Was this a matter of public concern, as the Fourth Circuit determined, or a personal matter between Seemuller and the claimants? See *Givhan v. Western Line Consol. Sch. Dists.*, 439 U.S. 410 (1979).

MT. HEALTHY CITY SCHOOL BOARD OF EDUCATION v. DOYLE

Supreme Court of the United States
429 U.S. 274 (1977)

REHNQUIST, J. delivered the opinion of the unanimous Court:

Respondent Doyle sued petitioner Mt. Healthy Board of Education in the United States District Court for the Southern District of Ohio. Doyle complained that the Board's refusal to renew his contract in 1971 violated his rights under the First and Fourteenth Amendments to the United States Constitution. After a bench trial the District Court held that Doyle was entitled to reinstatement with backpay. The Court of Appeals for the Sixth Circuit affirmed the judgment, 529 F.2d 524, and we granted the Board's petition for certiorari, 425 U.S. 933, to consider an admixture of jurisdictional and constitutional claims.

IV

Having concluded that respondent's complaint sufficiently pleaded jurisdiction under 28 U.S.C. § 1331, that the Board has failed to preserve the issue whether that complaint stated a claim upon which relief could be granted against the Board, and that the Board is not immune from suit under the Eleventh Amendment, we now proceed to consider the merits of respondent's claim under the First and Fourteenth Amendments.

Doyle was first employed by the Board in 1966. He worked under one-year contracts for the first three years, and under a two-year contract from 1969 to 1971. In 1969 he was elected president of the Teachers' Association, in which position he worked to expand the subjects of direct negotiation between the Association and the Board of Education. During Doyle's one-year term as president of the Association, and during the succeeding year when he served on its executive committee, there was apparently some tension in relations between the Board and the Association.

Beginning early in 1970, Doyle was involved in several incidents not directly connected with his role in the Teachers' Association. In one instance, he engaged in an argument with another teacher which culminated in the other teacher's slapping him. Doyle subsequently refused to accept an apology and insisted upon some punishment for the other teacher. His persistence in the matter resulted in the suspension of both teachers for one day, which was followed by a walkout by a number of other teachers, which in turn resulted in the lifting of the suspensions.

On other occasions, Doyle got into an argument with employees of the school cafeteria over the amount of spaghetti which had been served him; referred to students, in connection with a disciplinary complaint, as "sons of bitches"; and made an obscene gesture to two girls in connection with their failure to obey commands made in his capacity as cafeteria supervisor. Chronologically the last in the series of incidents which respondent was involved in during his employment by the Board was a telephone call by him to a local radio station. It was the Board's consideration of this incident which the court below found to be a violation of the First and Fourteenth Amendments.

In February 1971, the principal circulated to various teachers a memorandum relating to teacher dress and appearance, which was apparently prompted by the view of some in the administration that there was a relationship between teacher appearance and public support for bond issues. Doyle's response to the receipt of the memorandum — on a subject which he apparently understood was to be settled by joint teacher-administration action — was to convey the substance of the memorandum to a disc jockey at WSAI, a Cincinnati radio station, who promptly announced the adoption of the dress code as a news item. Doyle subsequently apologized to the principal, conceding that he should have made some prior communication of his criticism to the school administration.

A. SCHOOL CONTROL OVER TEACHER EXPRESSION 711

Approximately one month later the superintendent made his customary annual recommendations to the Board as to the rehiring of nontenured teachers. He recommended that Doyle not be rehired. The same recommendation was made with respect to nine other teachers in the district, and in all instances, including Doyle's, the recommendation was adopted by the Board. Shortly after being notified of this decision, respondent requested a statement of reasons for the Board's actions. He received a statement citing "a notable lack of tact in handling professional matters which leaves much doubt as to your sincerity in establishing good school relationships." That general statement was followed by references to the radio station incident and to the obscene-gesture incident.[1]

The District Court found that all of these incidents had in fact occurred. It concluded that respondent Doyle's telephone call to the radio station was "clearly protected by the First Amendment," and that because it had played a "substantial part" in the decision of the Board not to renew Doyle's employment, he was entitled to reinstatement with backpay. The District Court did not expressly state what test it was applying in determining that the incident in question involved conduct protected by the First Amendment, but simply held that the communication to the radio station was such conduct. The Court of Appeals affirmed in a brief per curiam opinion. 529 F.2d 524.

Doyle's claims under the First and Fourteenth Amendments are not defeated by the fact that he did not have tenure. Even though he could have been discharged for no reason whatever, and had no constitutional right to a rehearing prior to the decision not to rehire him, *Board of Regents v. Roth*, 408 U.S. 564 (1972), he may nonetheless establish a claim to reinstatement if the decision not to rehire him was made by reason of his exercise of constitutionally protected First Amendment freedoms. *Perry v. Sindermann*, 408 U.S. 593 (1972).

That question of whether speech of a government employee is constitutionally protected expression necessarily entails striking "a balance between the interests of the teacher, as a citizen, in commenting upon matters of public concern and the interest of the State, as an employer, in promoting the efficiency of the public services it performs through its employees." *Pickering v. Board of Education*, 391 U.S. 563, 568 (1968). There is no suggestion by the Board that Doyle

---

[1]"I. You have shown a notable lack of tact in handling professional matters which leaves much doubt as to your sincerity in establishing good school relationships.

"A. You assumed the responsibility to notify W.S.A.I. Radio Station in regards to the suggestion of the Board of Education that teachers establish an appropriate dress code for professional people. This raised much concern not only within this community, but also in neighboring communities.

"B. You used obscene gestures to correct students in a situation in the cafeteria causing considerable concern among those students present.

"Sincerely yours,
"Rex Ralph
"Superintendent"

violated any established policy, or that its reaction to his communication to the radio station was anything more than an ad hoc response to Doyle's action in making the memorandum public. We therefore accept the District Court's finding that the communication was protected by the First and Fourteenth Amendments. We are not, however, entirely in agreement with that court's manner of reasoning from this finding to the conclusion that Doyle is entitled to reinstatement with backpay.

The District Court made the following "conclusions" on this aspect of the case:

> 1) If a non-permissible reason, *e.g.*, exercise of First Amendment rights, played a substantial part in the decision not to renew — even in the face of other permissible grounds — the decision may not stand.
>
> 2) A non-permissible reason did play a substantial part. That is clear from the letter of the Superintendent immediately following the Board's decision, which stated two reasons — the one, the conversation with the radio station clearly protected by the First Amendment. A court may not engage in any limitation of First Amendment rights based on "tact" — that is not to say that the "tactfulness" is irrelevant to other issues in this case.

At the same time, though, it stated that

> [i]n fact, as this Court sees it and finds, both the Board and the Superintendent were faced with a situation in which there did exist in fact reason ... independent of any First Amendment rights or exercise thereof, to not extend tenure.

Since respondent Doyle had no tenure, and there was therefore not even a state-law requirement of "cause" or "reason" before a decision could be made not to renew his employment, it is not clear what the District Court meant by this latter statement. Clearly the Board legally *could* have dismissed respondent had the radio station incident never come to its attention. One plausible meaning of the court's statement is that the Board and the Superintendent not only could, but in fact *would* have reached that decision had not the constitutionally protected incident of the telephone call to the radio station occurred. We are thus brought to the issue whether, even if that were the case, the fact that the protected conduct played a "substantial part" in the actual decision not to renew would necessarily amount to a constitutional violation justifying remedial action. We think that it would not.

A rule of causation which focuses solely on whether protected conduct played a part, "substantial" or otherwise, in a decision not to rehire, could place an employee in a better position as a result of the exercise of constitutionally protected conduct than he would have occupied had he done nothing. The difficulty with the rule enunciated by the District Court is that it would require reinstatement in cases where a dramatic and perhaps abrasive incident is inevitably on the minds of those responsible for the decision to rehire, and does

A. SCHOOL CONTROL OVER TEACHER EXPRESSION 713

indeed play a part in that decision — even if the same decision would have been reached had the incident not occurred. The constitutional principle at stake is sufficiently vindicated if such an employee is placed in no worse a position than if he had not engaged in the conduct. A borderline or marginal candidate should not have the employment question resolved against him because of constitutionally protected conduct. But that same candidate ought not to be able, by engaging in such conduct, to prevent his employer from assessing his performance record and reaching a decision not to rehire on the basis of that record, simply because the protected conduct makes the employer more certain of the correctness of its decision.

This is especially true where, as the District Court observed was the case here, the current decision to rehire will accord "tenure." The long-term consequences of an award of tenure are of great moment both to the employee and to the employer. They are too significant for us to hold that the Board in this case would be precluded, because it considered constitutionally protected conduct in deciding not to rehire Doyle, from attempting to prove to a trier of fact that quite apart from such conduct Doyle's record was such that he would not have been rehired in any event.

In other areas of constitutional law, this Court has found it necessary to formulate a test of causation which distinguishes between a result caused by a constitutional violation and one not so caused. We think those are instructive in formulating the test to be applied here.

In *Lyons v. Oklahoma*, 322 U.S. 596 (1944), the Court held that even though the first confession given by a defendant had been involuntary, the Fourteenth Amendment did not prevent the State from using a second confession obtained 12 hours later if the coercion surrounding the first confession had been sufficiently dissipated as to make the second confession voluntary. In *Wong Sun v. United States*, 371 U.S. 471, 491 (1963), the Court was willing to assume that a defendant's arrest had been unlawful, but held that "the connection between the arrest and the statement [given several days later] had 'become so attenuated as to dissipate the taint.' *Nardone v. United States*, 308 U.S. 338, 341." *Parker v. North Carolina*, 397 U.S. 790, 796 (1970), held that even though a confession be assumed to have been involuntary in the constitutional sense of the word, a guilty plea entered over a month later met the test for the voluntariness of such a plea. The Court in *Parker* relied on the same quoted language from *Nardone*, *supra*, as did the Court in *Wong Sun*, *supra*. While the type of causation on which the taint cases turn may differ somewhat from that which we apply here, those cases do suggest that the proper test to apply in the present context is one which likewise protects against the invasion of constitutional rights without commanding undesirable consequences not necessary to the assurance of those rights.

Initially, in this case, the burden was properly placed upon respondent to show that his conduct was constitutionally protected, and that this conduct was a "substantial factor" — or, to put it in other words, that it was a "motivating factor" in the Board's decision not to rehire him. Respondent having carried that burden, however, the District Court should have gone on to determine whether the Board had shown by a preponderance of the evidence that it would have reached the same decision as to respondent's reemployment even in the absence of the protected conduct.

We cannot tell from the District Court opinion and conclusions, nor from the opinion of the Court of Appeals affirming the judgment of the District Court, what conclusion those courts would have reached had they applied this test. The judgment of the Court of Appeals is therefore vacated, and the case remanded for further proceedings consistent with this opinion.

So ordered.

---

1. Consider the burden placed on the trier of fact under *Mt. Healthy*. It must determine what action the school board would have taken, absent the dismissed teacher's exercise of First Amendment rights. Not only must it decide if a school board member speaks truthfully when he testifies that he would have voted for dismissal even without the incident wherein the teacher exercised free speech, but it must also decide how a school board member would have voted who cannot himself testify to that question with certainty. Is the burden too onerous, or is it one that occasionally arises in other situations and is handled as a matter of course?

2. Despite its difficult causation test, note that the *Mt. Healthy* opinion came from a unanimous Court. Consider alternative tests and suppose that the Court had opined that whenever there were independent grounds for dismissal, the presence of a constitutional violation would not invalidate school board action. Under that test, what would happen to the constitutional protections of any teacher who had made mistakes sufficient to warrant dismissal, but who had not been dismissed? On the other hand, suppose the Court had held that where a board of education had been partially motivated by a teacher's exercise of a constitutional right, its decision would be overturned. Can a teacher in trouble "cover" himself by exercising his constitutional rights in a manner objectionable to the school board?

3. Could the court in *Mt. Healthy* have avoided a difficult causation test by deciding on other grounds? In *Barbre v. Garland Indep. Sch. Dist.*, 475 F. Supp. 687 (N.D. Tex. 1979), the District Court held that even if a teacher aide's speech at a school board meeting was a motivating factor in her non-renewal, her insubordination subsequent to the board meeting was a valid and separate explanation for her non-renewal apart from any of her prior expressions.

4. On at least two other occasions, courts have decided cases based on teacher dress codes and appearance standards. In *East Hartford Educ. Ass'n v. Board of Educ. of East Hartford*, 562 F.2d 838 (2d Cir. 1977), the court upheld a dress code requirement that a teacher wear a necktie; there was no First Amendment

A. SCHOOL CONTROL OVER TEACHER EXPRESSION

violation. In *Domico v. Rapides Parish Sch. Bd.*, 675 F.2d 100 (5th Cir. 1982), a rule which prohibited students from wearing beards was extended to teachers. The Court of Appeals upheld this extension as a reasonable means to further the school board's interest in teacher hygiene, discipline, and authority.

5. If Doyle were a tenured teacher, would the court have held differently? Should tenured public employees in effect be awarded more freedom of expression than untenured employees? Does this seem fair under constitutional principles? Should a different principle apply to tenured and untenured teachers?

The Eleventh Circuit said "no" in *Harden v. Adams*, 841 F.2d 1091 (11th Cir. 1988). In *Harden*, a college-level case, the teacher claimed that his efforts in organizing a campus chapter of a statewide teachers' union, and his assistance in bringing a discrimination suit against the school led the school to fire him. The Court of Appeals affirmed a ruling in favor of the defendant school and held the *Mt. Healthy* standard applied regardless of tenure status.

6. Would it have been more prudent for the superintendent in *Mt. Healthy* not to mention the radio incident in his letter to Doyle? Did the mention of the radio incident shift the burden of proof to the school board to show that it had other reasons for terminating Doyle?

For a further discussion on the burden of proof, *see McGee v. South Pemiscot Sch. Dist. R-V*, 712 F.2d 339 (8th Cir. 1983).

7. *See* Gee, *Constitutional Rights: A View From Mt. Healthy*, in School Law in Contemporary Society (NOLPE 1980).

8. The Supreme Court's decisions in *Pickering* and *Doyle* also influenced the case of *Givhan v. Western Line Consol. Sch. Dist.*, 439 U.S. 410 (1979). The Court ruled that teachers facing dismissal are protected under the First Amendment if their expression is a matter of public concern even if those views are expressed privately rather than publicly. The petitioner in the case had complained in private sessions with her principal about overt racism against African-American public school children in a Mississippi school district undergoing desegregation.

Ultimately, the case was remanded and the Fifth Circuit Court of Appeals in *Ayers v. Western Line Consol. Sch. Dist.*, 691 F.2d 766 (5th Cir. 1982), determined that the teacher was dismissed because she spoke on a matter of public concern (racially discriminatory practices) and that all other non-First Amendment reasons for the teacher's discharge were "afterthoughts or pretextual ...." *Id.* at 766.

9. The trial court in *Givhan* actually entertained two issues: one involving a *Mt. Healthy*-type claim — the employee would have been retained but for a First Amendment-protected criticism and a second described as "a now-abandoned racial-discrimination type claim." Was this second claim founded on Title VII, *i.e.*, employment discrimination? Why was it abandoned? Would such a claim carry more weight in racial issues today due to the passage of the 1991 Civil Rights Act?

10. *Givhan* involved a teacher's dismissal based on privately expressed criticism to a public school official. What of a teacher's expressed criticism in a private school? The Supreme Court in *Rendell-Baker v. Kohn*, 457 U.S. 830 (1982), explored this issue where a vocational education teacher had been dismissed because of a dispute over the role of a combined student-staff council in making employment decisions. A resultant letter to the editor of the local newspaper sparked part of the controversy. The Court held that private school personnel may not have constitutional claims against private schools unless the alleged infringements are "fairly attributable to the state." *Id.* at 831. In order to substantiate the claim that a private entity is a "state actor," the complainant would have to prove that his or her discharge was compelled or influenced by some state regulation and that there is some "symbiotic relationship" between the state and the school. *Id.* at 830.

See also Johnson v. Pinkerton Acad., 861 F.2d 335 (1st Cir. 1988), where a private high school teacher's dismissal was upheld for wearing a beard in violation of school rules. The "symbiotic relationship" standard was again used by the court even though the school participated in a state-operated teacher pension fund and the school advisory committee was composed partly of officials from surrounding communities.

CONNICK v. MYERS

Supreme Court of the United States
461 U.S. 138 (1983)

JUSTICE WHITE delivered the opinion of the Court:

In *Pickering v. Board of Education*, 391 U.S. 563 (1968), we stated that a public employee does not relinquish First Amendment rights to comment on matters of public interest by virtue of government employment. We also recognized that the State's interests as an employer in regulating the speech of its employees "differ significantly from those it possesses in connection with regulation of the speech of the citizenry in general." *Id.* at 568. The problem, we thought, was arriving "at a balance between the interests of the [employee], as a citizen, in commenting upon matters of public concern and the interest of the State, as an employer, in promoting the efficiency of the public services it performs through its employees." *Id.* We return to this problem today and consider whether the First and Fourteenth Amendments prevent the discharge of a state employee for circulating a questionnaire concerning internal office affairs.

I

The respondent, Sheila Myers, was employed as an Assistant District Attorney in New Orleans for five and a half years. She served at the pleasure of petitioner Harry Connick, the District Attorney for Orleans Parish. During this period Myers competently performed her responsibilities of trying criminal cases.

A. SCHOOL CONTROL OVER TEACHER EXPRESSION

In the early part of October, 1980, Myers was informed that she would be transferred to prosecute cases in a different section of the criminal court. Myers was strongly opposed to the proposed transfer and expressed her view to several of her supervisors, including Connick. Despite her objections, on October 6 Myers was notified that she was being transferred. Myers again spoke with Dennis Waldron, one of the first assistant district attorneys, expressing her reluctance to accept the transfer. A number of other office matters were discussed and Myers later testified that, in response to Waldron's suggestion that her concerns were not shared by others in the office, she informed him that she would do some research on the matter.

That night Myers prepared a questionnaire soliciting the views of her fellow staff members concerning office transfer policy, office morale, the need for a grievance committee, the level of confidence in supervisors, and whether employees felt pressured to work in political campaigns. Early the following morning, Myers typed and copied the questionnaire. She also met with Connick who urged her to accept the transfer. She said she would "consider" it. Connick then left the office. Myers then distributed the questionnaire to 15 assistant district attorneys. Shortly after noon, Dennis Waldron learned that Myers was distributing the survey. He immediately phoned Connick and informed him that Myers was creating a "mini-insurrection" within the office. Connick returned to the office and told Myers that she was being terminated because of her refusal to accept the transfer. She was also told that her distribution of the questionnaire was considered an act of insubordination. Connick particularly objected to the question which inquired whether employees "had confidence in and would rely on the word" of various superiors in the office, and to a question concerning pressure to work in political campaigns which he felt would be damaging if discovered by the press.

Myers filed suit under 42 U.S.C. § 1983, contending that her employment was wrongfully terminated because she had exercised her constitutionally-protected right of free speech. The District Court agreed, ordered Myers reinstated, and awarded backpay, damages, and attorney's fees. The District Court found that although Connick informed Myers that she was being fired because of her refusal to accept a transfer, the facts showed that the questionnaire was the real reason for her termination. The court then proceeded to hold that Myers' questionnaire involved matters of public concern and that the state had not "clearly demonstrated" that the survey "substantially interfered" with the operations of the District Attorney's office.

Connick appealed to the United States Court of Appeals for the Fifth Circuit, which affirmed on the basis of the District Court's opinion. Connick then sought review in this Court by way of certiorari, which we granted.

II

For at least 15 years, it has been settled that a state cannot condition public employment on a basis that infringes the employee's constitutionally protected interest in freedom of expression. *Keyishian v. Board of Regents*, 385 U.S. 589, 605-06 (1967); *Pickering v. Board of Education*, 391 U.S. 563 (1968); *Perry v. Sindermann*, 408 U.S. 593, 597 (1972); *Branti v. Finkel*, 445 U.S. 507, 515-16 (1980). Our task, as we defined it in *Pickering*, is to seek "a balance between the interests of the [employee], as a citizen, in commenting upon matters of public concern and the interest of the State, as an employer, in promoting the efficiency of the public services it performs through its employees." 391 U.S. at 568. The District Court, and thus the Court of Appeals as well, misapplied our decision in *Pickering* and consequently, in our view, erred in striking the balance for respondent.

A

The District Court got off on the wrong foot in this case by initially finding that, "[t]aken as a whole, the issues presented in the questionnaire relate to the effective functioning of the District Attorney's Office and are matters of public importance and concern." Connick contends at the outset that no balancing of interests is required in this case because Myers' questionnaire concerned only internal office matters and that such speech is not upon a matter of "public concern," as the term was used in *Pickering*. Although we do not agree that Myers' communication in this case was wholly without First Amendment protection, there is much force to Connick's submission. The repeated emphasis in *Pickering* on the right of a public employee "as a citizen, in commenting upon matters of public concern," was not accidental. This language, reiterated in all of *Pickering*'s progeny, reflects both the historical evolvement of the rights of public employees, and the common sense realization that government offices could not function if every employment decision became a constitutional matter.

....

Pickering, its antecedents and progeny, lead us to conclude that if Myers' questionnaire cannot be fairly characterized as constituting speech on a matter of public concern, it is unnecessary for us to scrutinize the reasons for her discharge. When employee expression cannot be fairly considered as relating to any matter of political, social, or other concern to the community, government officials should enjoy wide latitude in managing their offices, without intrusive oversight by the judiciary in the name of the First Amendment. Perhaps the government employer's dismissal of the worker may not be fair, but ordinary dismissals from government service which violate no fixed tenure or applicable statute or regulation are not subject to judicial review even if the reasons for the dismissal are alleged to be mistaken or unreasonable. *Board of Regents v. Roth*, 408 U.S. 564 (1972); *Perry v. Sindermann*, 408 U.S. 593 (1972); *Bishop v. Wood*, 426 U.S. 341, 349-50 (1976).

We do not suggest, however, that Myers' speech, even if not touching upon a matter of public concern, is totally beyond the protection of the First Amendment. "The First Amendment does not protect speech and assembly only to the extent that it can be characterized as political. 'Great secular causes, with smaller ones, are guarded.'" *United Mine Workers v. Illinois State Bar Association*, 389 U.S. 217, 223 (1967), quoting *Thomas v. Collins*, 323 U.S. 516, 531 (1945). We in no sense suggest that speech on private matters falls into one of the narrow and well-defined classes of expression which carries so little social value, such as obscenity, that the state can prohibit and punish such expression by all persons in its jurisdiction. For example, an employee's false criticism of his employer on grounds not of public concern may be cause for his discharge but would be entitled to the same protection in a libel action accorded an identical statement made by a man on the street. We hold only that when a public employee speaks not as a citizen upon matters of public concern, but instead as an employee upon matters only of personal interest, absent the most unusual circumstances, a federal court is not the appropriate forum in which to review the wisdom of a personnel decision taken by a public agency allegedly in reaction to the employee's behavior. *Cf. Bishop v. Wood*, 426 U.S. 341, 349-50 (1976). Our responsibility is to ensure that citizens are not deprived of fundamental rights by virtue of working for the government; this does not require a grant of immunity for employee grievances not afforded by the First Amendment to those who do not work for the state.

Whether an employee's speech addresses a matter of public concern must be determined by the content, form, and context of a given statement, as revealed by the whole record. In this case, with but one exception, the questions posed by Myers to her coworkers do not fall under the rubric of matters of "public concern." We view the questions pertaining to the confidence and trust that Myers' coworkers possess in various supervisors, the level of office morale, and the need for a grievance committee as mere extensions of Myers' dispute over her transfer to another section of the criminal court. Unlike the dissent, we do not believe these questions are of public import in evaluating the performance of the District Attorney as an elected official. Myers did not seek to inform the public that the District Attorney's office was not discharging its governmental responsibilities in the investigation and prosecution of criminal cases. Nor did Myers seek to bring to light actual or potential wrongdoing or breach of public trust on the part of Connick and others. Indeed, the questionnaire, if released to the public, would convey no information at all other than the fact that a single employee is upset with the status quo. While discipline and morale in the workplace are related to an agency's efficient performance of its duties, the focus of Myers' questions is not to evaluate the performance of the office but rather to gather ammunition for another round of controversy with her superiors. These questions reflect one employee's dissatisfaction with a transfer and an attempt to turn that displeasure into a cause celebre.[8]

---

[8]This is not a case like *Givhan, supra*, where an employee speaks out as a citizen on a matter of general concern, not tied to a personal employment dispute, but arranges to do so privately. Mrs. Givhan's right to protest racial discrimination — a matter inherently of public concern — is not forfeited by her choice of a private forum. 439 U.S. at 415-16. Here, however, a questionnaire

To presume that all matters which transpire within a government office are of public concern would mean that virtually every remark — and certainly every criticism directed at a public official — would plant the seed of a constitutional case. While as a matter of good judgment, public officials should be receptive to constructive criticism offered by their employees, the First Amendment does not require a public office to be run as a roundtable for employee complaints over internal office affairs.

One question in Myers' questionnaire, however, does touch upon a matter of public concern. Question 11 inquires if assistant district attorneys "ever feel pressured to work in political campaigns on behalf of office supported candidates." We have recently noted that official pressure upon employees to work for political candidates not of the worker's own choice constitutes a coercion of belief in violation of fundamental constitutional rights. *Branti v. Finkel*, 445 U.S. 507, 515-516 (1980); *Elrod v. Burns*, 427 U.S. 347 (1976). In addition, there is a demonstrated interest in this country that government service should depend upon meritorious performance rather than political service. *CSC v. Letter Carriers*, 413 U.S. 548 (1973); *United Public Workers v. Mitchell*, 330 U.S. 75 (1947). Given this history, we believe it apparent that the issue of whether assistant district attorneys are pressured to work in political campaigns is a matter of interest to the community upon which it is essential that public employees be able to speak out freely without fear of retaliatory dismissal.

B

Because one of the questions in Myers' survey touched upon a matter of public concern, and contributed to her discharge we must determine whether Connick was justified in discharging Myers. Here the District Court again erred in imposing an unduly onerous burden on the state to justify Myers' discharge. The District Court viewed the issue of whether Myers' speech was upon a matter of "public concern" as a threshold inquiry, after which it became the government's burden to "clearly demonstrate" that the speech involved "substantially interfered" with official responsibilities. Yet *Pickering* unmistakably states, and respondent agrees that the state's burden in justifying a particular discharge varies depending upon the nature of the employee's expression. Although such particularized balancing is difficult, the courts must reach the most appropriate possible balance of the competing interests.

---

not otherwise of public concern does not attain that status because its subject matter could, in different circumstances, have been the topic of a communication to the public that might be of general interest. The dissent's analysis of whether discussions of office morale and discipline could be matters of public concern is beside the point — it does not answer whether this questionnaire is such speech.

A. SCHOOL CONTROL OVER TEACHER EXPRESSION

C

....

We agree with the District Court that there is no demonstration here that the questionnaire impeded Myers' ability to perform her responsibilities. The District Court was also correct to recognize that "it is important to the efficient and successful operation of the District Attorney's office for Assistants to maintain close working relationships with their superiors." Connick's judgment, and apparently also that of his first assistant Dennis Waldron, who characterized Myers' actions as causing a "mini-insurrection", was that Myers' questionnaire was an act of insubordination which interfered with working relationships. When close working relationships are essential to fulfilling public responsibilities, a wide degree of deference to the employer's judgment is appropriate. Furthermore, we do not see the necessity for an employer to allow events to unfold to the extent that the disruption of the office and the destruction of working relationships is manifest before taking action. We caution that a stronger showing may be necessary if the employee's speech more substantially involved matters of public concern.

The District Court rejected Connick's position because "unlike a statement of fact which might be deemed critical of one's superiors, [Myers'] questionnaire was not a statement of fact, but the presentation and solicitation of ideas and opinions," which are entitled to greater constitutional protection because "under the First Amendment there is no such thing as a false idea." This approach, while perhaps relevant in weighing the value of Myers' speech, bears no logical relationship to the issue of whether the questionnaire undermined office relationships. Questions, no less than forcefully stated opinions and facts, carry messages and it requires no unusual insight to conclude that the purpose, if not the likely result, of the questionnaire is to seek to precipitate a vote of no confidence in Connick and his supervisors. Thus, Question 10, which asked whether or not the Assistants had confidence in and relied on the word of five named supervisors, is a statement that carries the clear potential for undermining office relations.

Also relevant is the manner, time, and place in which the questionnaire was distributed. As noted in *Givhan v. Western Line Consolidated School Dist.*, 439 U.S. 410, 415 n.4 (1979),

> Private expression ... may in some situations bring additional factors to the *Pickering* calculus. When a government employee personally confronts his immediate superior, the employing agency's institutional efficiency may be threatened not only by the content of the employee's message but also by the manner, time, and place in which it is delivered.

Here the questionnaire was prepared, and distributed at the office; the manner of distribution required not only Myers to leave her work but for others to do the same in order that the questionnaire be completed. Although some latitude in when official work is performed is to be allowed when professional employees are involved, and Myers did not violate announced office policy, the fact that Myers, unlike *Pickering*, exercised her rights to speech at the office supports Connick's fears that the functioning of his office was endangered.

Finally, the context in which the dispute arose is also significant. This is not a case where an employee, out of purely academic interest, circulated a questionnaire so as to obtain useful research. Myers acknowledges that it is no coincidence that the questionnaire followed upon the heels of the transfer notice. When employee speech concerning office policy arises from an employment dispute concerning the very application of that policy to the speaker, additional weight must be given to the supervisor's view that the employee has threatened the authority of the employer to run the office. Although we accept the District Court's factual finding that Myers' reluctance to accede to the transfer order was not a sufficient cause in itself for her dismissal, and thus does not constitute a sufficient defense under *Mt. Healthy City Board of Ed. v. Doyle*, 429 U.S. 274 (1977), this does not render irrelevant the fact that the questionnaire emerged after a persistent dispute between Myers and Connick and his deputies over office transfer policy.

III

Myers' questionnaire touched upon matters of public concern in only a most limited sense; her survey, in our view, is most accurately characterized as an employee grievance concerning internal office policy. The limited First Amendment interest involved here does not require that Connick tolerate action which he reasonably believed would disrupt the office, undermine his authority, and destroy close working relationships. Myers' discharge therefore did not offend the First Amendment. We reiterate, however, the caveat we expressed in *Pickering, supra*, at 569: "Because of the enormous variety of fact situations in which critical statements by ... public employees may be thought by their superiors ... to furnish grounds for dismissal, we do not deem it either appropriate or feasible to lay down a general standard against which all such statements may be judged."

Reversed.

....

---

1. It is clear, from subsequent cases and other discussions, that *Connick* — although involving a claim by an assistant district attorney — is applicable in a school setting, as well. In fact, together with *Pickering, Connick* has set up a two-step test for speech cases involving public employees:

    a. Does the speech involve a matter of public concern?

A. SCHOOL CONTROL OVER TEACHER EXPRESSION

When employee expression cannot be fairly considered as relating to any other matter of political, social, or other concern to the community, government officials should enjoy wide latitude in managing their offices, without intrusive oversight by the judiciary, in the name of the First Amendment. *Connick*, at 146.

b. If so, then the court must apply the *Pickering* balancing test, weighing the interests of the public employee as a citizen in speech related to a matter of public concern against the interests of the state employer and provider of effective, efficient public service.

2. John M. Ryan, in *Teacher Free Speech in Public Schools: Just When You Thought It was Safe to Teach*, 67 Neb. L. Rev. 695, 697-99, 701-04 (1988), summed up the *Pickering-Connick* test:*

After twenty years, *Pickering* remains the seminal case on the issue of a teacher's first amendment rights....

... [T]he Supreme Court indicated that the task of the Court was to balance the interests of the employee, as a citizen, against the interests of the school board, as employer.

... Factors which would be considered relevant to the determination of whether the teacher's speech was protected included the need for harmony among workers, relational factors between the speaker and his subject, the degree to which the speech addresses matters of public concern, and special knowledge which teachers possess concerning operation of schools, making it essential that teachers be able to 'speak freely' on such topics....

The groundwork for future constitutional analysis had been laid....

....

Along with *Pickering*, *Connick v. Myers* stands as the primary case for consideration of free speech in teacher employment cases....

....

... [T]he analysis invoked by the Court was clearly expanded to two parts: first, was the speech of public concern; second, how do the *Pickering* balancing factors apply?

When addressing the initial public concern prong of the test, the content, form, and context of the speech must be considered....

... [T]he Court made it clear that the public concern inquiry was a threshold issue which the teacher must overcome in order to challenge board action on constitutional grounds. Only after the teacher shows that the expression dealt with matters of public concern does the *Pickering* balancing test become crucial.

....

---

*Copyright © 1988 by the Nebraska Law Review. Reprinted with permission.

... *Connick*'s analytical framework stands today as the accepted analysis of teacher free speech cases. Combined with *Pickering*, *Connick* provides a two-part analysis that places a heavy burden on the teacher seeking to sustain a constitutional claim. First, the teacher must show that the expression at issue pertains to matters of public concern. Second, the *Pickering* balance must reveal that the teacher's interest in speaking outweighs the government's interests as employer. Coupled with the stiff causation requirements outlined in *Mt. Healthy*, these constitutional tests place substantial barriers before a teacher seeking to challenge her dismissal on first amendment grounds.

3. The Supreme Court, in 1987, heard a similar case, *Rankin v. McPherson*, 483 U.S. 378 (1987). *Rankin* involved a clerical employee in a county constable's office who made a private political comment to a co-worker in a room not accessible to the public. The comment, "if they go for him again, I hope they get him," referred to the attempt on President Reagan's life in 1981. In holding for the employee, who had been fired as a result of the comment, the court relied on *Pickering*, *Mt. Healthy*, and *Connick*:

> Considering the statement in context, as *Connick* requires, discloses that it plainly dealt with a public concern. The statement was made in the course of a conversation addressing the policies of the President's administration. It came on the heels of a news bulletin regarding what is certainly a matter of heightened public attention: an attempt on the life of the President. While a statement that amounted to a threat to kill the President would not be protected by the First Amendment, the District Court concluded, and we agree, that McPherson's statement did not amount to a threat punishable under 18 U.S.C. § 871(a) or 18 U.S.C. § 2385, or, indeed, that could be properly criminalized at all. The inappropriate or controversial character of a statement is irrelevant to the question whether it deals with a matter of public concern. "[D]ebate on public issues should be uninhibited, robust, and wide-open, and ... may well include vehement, caustic, and sometimes unpleasantly sharp attacks on government and public officials." *New York Times Co. v. Sullivan*, 376 U.S. 254, 270 (1964)....
>
> Because McPherson's statement addressed a matter of public concern, *Pickering* next requires that we balance McPherson's interest in making her statement against "the interest of the State, as an employer, in promoting the efficiency of the public services it performs through its employees." 391 U.S. at 568. The State bears a burden of justifying the discharge on legitimate grounds. *Connick*, 461 U.S. at 150.
>
> ....
>
> ... While McPherson's statement was made at the workplace, there is no evidence that it interfered with the efficient functioning of the office.... In fact, Constable Rankin testified that the possibility of interference with the functions of the Constable's office had not been a consideration in his

A. SCHOOL CONTROL OVER TEACHER EXPRESSION

discharge of respondent and that he did not even inquire whether the remark had disrupted the work of the office.

Nor was there any danger that McPherson had discredited the office by making her statement in public. McPherson's speech took place in an area to which there was ordinarily no public access; her remark was evidently made in a private conversation with another employee....

....

... Given the function of the agency, McPherson's position in the office, and the nature of her statement, we are not persuaded that Rankin's interest in discharging her outweighed her rights under the First Amendment.

....

4. For other interpretations of *Pickering, Mt. Healthy,* and *Connick, see Roberts v. Van Buren Pub. Schs.*, 773 F.2d 949 (8th Cir. 1985), and *Daniels v. Quinn*, 801 F.2d 687 (4th Cir. 1986).

5. According to Ryan, "Only recently have courts applied the *Pickering-Connick* test in a coherent fashion. The primary source of confusion first arose with respect to the two differing prongs of the test; some courts, even after the decision in *Connick,* combined the *Pickering* and *Connick* tests into a single inquiry, not differentiating the factors that each test uniquely employs." 67 Neb. L. Rev. 695, 706 (1988). *See Hamer v. Brown*, 831 F.2d 1398 (8th Cir. 1987).

6. Does the role or motive of the speaker affect the speaker's free speech protection? With respect to the content, form, and context questions that *Connick* raises, many cases have said "yes." These courts picked up on a key statement in *Connick*: "The repeated emphasis in *Pickering* on the right of the public employee 'as a citizen, in commenting upon matters of public concern,' was not accidental." 461 U.S. at 143.

For example, *see Page v. Delaune*, 837 F.2d 233 (5th Cir. 1988). In *Page*, a Texas A & M University CETA [Comprehensive Employment and Training Act] supervisor of an ex-offender program was fired after her boss overheard a telephone conversation between Page (the fired employee) and another worker. The two discussed their intention to go "over the head" of their supervisor and complain about the manner in which the ex-offender program was managed. After citing the language in *Connick* referring to the citizen-employee dichotomy, the court determined that Page was acting as an employee while speaking in this case. Such a decision to bypass normal communication channels is clearly a personal matter, internal to the program, and not a matter of public concern. *Id.* at 238.

See also Callaway v. Hafeman, 832 F.2d 414 (7th Cir. 1987), involving a woman who claimed she was demoted after making complaints regarding sexual harassment by her supervisor. Ms. Callaway, the employee, made the complaints privately and informally because she did not want to make the allegations a public issue. The District Court dismissed her claim and the Seventh Circuit affirmed. "While the content of Callaway's complaint touched on an issue of public concern generally, she was not attempting to speak out as a citizen concerned with problems facing the school district; instead, she spoke as an employee attempting to resolve her private dilemma." *Id.* at 417.

See also Griffin v. Thomas, 929 F.2d 1210 (7th Cir. 1991). In *Griffin*, an assistant principal in the Chicago public school system sued her principal and the board of education alleging a free speech violation; she claimed retaliation as a consequence of the filing of a union grievance. For a number of years at the same school, the assistant principal had received the highest rating for her work performance. Due to an on-the-job injury, she missed months of work and during that year was granted the next highest rating, an action that brought the dispute in question. This was appealed to the teacher's union where the assistant principal prevailed with a restoration of the highest rating. Within a day of having to restore the rating, the principal re-assigned the plaintiff to lesser administrative duties, and as alleged by the assistant principal, "embarked on a course of harassing retaliatory conduct." *Id.* at 1211. The assistant principal then filed suit. Using *Connick*, the Seventh Circuit upheld the district court ruling that unless the expression in question is a matter of public concern, "it is unnecessary for the courts to scrutinize the reasons of the employer's adverse conduct." *Id.* at 1211. The court, after examining the facts, decided that the purpose in filing the grievance was to deal with a personal disagreement between the administrator and her supervisor, a matter of private and not public concern as the plaintiff complained about her performance evaluation.

7. Finally, Ryan leaves us with a summary and some advice to educators:

> Scholars have been critical of the use of balancing tests in constitutional decision making. Even the Fifth Circuit Court of Appeals has derogated the *Pickering* balancing test, saying that the test "inevitably chills some protected activity." Given the seemingly inherent flaws of the test, it may be wise to consider dropping it altogether, leaving the *Connick* test as the only hurdle that must be cleared to establish a first amendment violation. This would leave teachers free to comment on matters of public concern without fear of retaliatory discharge (assuming, of course, that the statements were not made with actual malice). Thus, the public school teacher would be as free from state sanction as the private citizen.
>
> For now, however, the system remains unpredictable....
>
> ....
>
> The lesson for the educator is simple and short: Until the system changes, there is simply no way to tell whether certain speech will be protected by the Constitution. If a teacher chooses to speak, she should consider not only the content of her expression, but also the form and context in which she speaks. She should seek to minimize any perceived "personal interest" she might have in the subject of communication. All of these may help the teacher clear the public concern issue, making constitutional protection of her statements possible.

A. SCHOOL CONTROL OVER TEACHER EXPRESSION

> ... Above all, the educator should consider the expression's potential impact on his job performance (both for constitutional and educational reasons). If the speech impedes the teacher's ability to perform his assigned duty, it almost certainly will be unprotected.

Ryan, 67 Neb. L. Rev. at 715-16.

MILES v. DENVER PUBLIC SCHOOLS
United States Court of Appeals
944 F.2d 773 (10th Cir. 1991)

TACHA, CIRCUIT JUDGE:

This appeal arose out of an incident in which plaintiff-appellant John Miles, a public high school teacher in Denver, Colorado, was disciplined for statements he made in the classroom. Miles seeks damages and injunctive relief pursuant to 42 U.S.C. § 1983, claiming the defendant school district violated his first amendment free speech rights. The district court granted summary judgment in favor of the school. On appeal, Miles argues the district court erred in granting summary judgment for the defendant because there are genuine issues of material fact to be determined before the first amendment issue can be decided. Miles also asserts his classroom expression is protected by the first amendment and the letter of reprimand unconstitutionally regulates his speech. We exercise jurisdiction under 28 U.S.C. § 1291 and affirm the district court's grant of summary judgment.

I. Background

During a ninth grade government class, Miles stated that the quality of the school had declined since 1967. When a student asked for specific examples, Miles replied that in the past the school did not have so many pop cans lying around and school discipline was better. He also commented, "I don't think in 1967 you would have seen two students making out on the tennis court." This comment referred to an incident that allegedly had occurred the previous day and was the topic of rumor throughout the school. The rumor was that two students were observed having sexual intercourse on the tennis court during lunch hour. Miles had heard the rumor from a colleague who had heard of the incident from two students claiming to have witnessed it. Miles never sought official confirmation of the rumor before repeating it in class.

Miles' comments about the rumor led parents of the alleged participants to complain to the principal. Following meetings with Miles and several other individuals, the principal placed Miles on paid administrative leave for four days. Miles wrote to the principal apologizing for exercising "bad judgment." The principal conducted an investigation and issued a reprimand letter that stated:

After completing the investigation of the alleged incident in your period 3 class on March 30, 1989, I find it necessary to write you this letter of reprimand. The investigation revealed that you displayed poor judgment in your comment "making out" on the tennis court. Informing your students of an alleged incident of one of your tennis players "making out" with a female student on the tennis courts during the lunch period was an inappropriate topic for comment in a classroom setting. In the future you will need to refrain from commenting on any items which might reflect negatively on individual members of our student body.

Eight months after his reinstatement, Miles filed this lawsuit claiming that the imposition of paid administrative leave and placement of the letter of reprimand in his file violated and "chilled" his free speech rights. After discovery, the parties filed cross-motions for summary judgment. The court granted summary judgment in favor of the school and denied Miles' motion.

II. *Discussion*

A. *Standard of Review*

We review summary judgment orders de novo, using the same standards the district court applies. Summary judgment is appropriate "if the pleadings, depositions, answers to interrogatories, and admissions on file, together with the affidavits, if any, show that there is no genuine issue as to any material fact and that the moving party is entitled to a judgment as a matter of law." Fed.R.Civ.P. 56(c).... That both parties have moved for summary judgment does not preclude a finding that a genuine issue of material fact exists.

B. *First Amendment Standard*

In *Mount Healthy City School District Board of Education v. Doyle*, 429 U.S. 274 (1977), the Supreme Court established a test for determining whether an adverse employment decision violates a public employee's first amendment rights. This test requires that an employee show (1) the speech for which he was disciplined was constitutionally protected and (2) the protected speech motivated the adverse employment decision. After an employee has made these showings, the employer has the burden of showing by a preponderance of the evidence that she would have made the same decision absent the protected speech. *Id.* at 287.

In determining whether Miles has satisfied the initial burden of showing his classroom expression is constitutionally protected, we look to the Supreme Court's decision in *Hazelwood School District v. Kuhlmeier*, 484 U.S. 260 (1988). In *Hazelwood*, student contributors to a newspaper published as part of a journalism class contested the principal's deletion of material from the newspaper prior to publication. *Id.* at 261. Although the Court emphasized that "students in the public schools do not 'shed their constitutional rights to freedom of speech or expression at the schoolhouse gate,'" the Court held that educators do not offend the first amendment by exercising editorial control over school-sponsored expression "so long as their actions are reasonably related to legitimate pedagogical concerns." The Court explained that if school facilities have not been opened for "'indiscriminate use by the general public'" and the school is not a public forum, then "school officials may impose reasonable

A. SCHOOL CONTROL OVER TEACHER EXPRESSION

restrictions on the speech of students, teachers, and other members of the school community."

In *Hazelwood*, the Supreme Court determined the extent to which classroom expression is constitutionally protected by first asking whether the school's student newspaper was a public forum. *Id.* at 266-70. Similarly, our first inquiry is whether Miles' ninth-grade classroom is a public forum. As the Supreme Court pointed out in *Hazelwood*, "public schools do not possess all of the attributes of streets, parks, and other traditional public forums that, 'time out of mind, have been used for purposes of assembly, communicating thoughts between citizens, and discussing public questions.'" A podium before a captive audience of public school children is decisively different from a street corner soapbox. The Court in *Hazelwood* explained that a public forum is not created "'by inaction or by permitting limited discourse, but only by intentionally opening a nontraditional forum for public discourse.'" If the creation and operation of a school newspaper as part of a journalism class can be devoid of an intent to open a classroom for public discourse, than an ordinary classroom — such as the one in which Miles taught — is not a public forum. There is no evidence that school authorities intended to open Miles' government class for public discourse. Therefore, we conclude that the school "'reserved the forum for its intended purpose'" of teaching government.

A recent Eleventh Circuit case supports this conclusion. In *Bishop v. Aronov*, 926 F.2d 1066 (11th Cir.1991), the Eleventh Circuit, addressing the extent to which a university may restrict a professor's classroom expression, explained that "[w]hile the [institution] may make its classrooms available for other purposes, we have no doubt that during instructional periods the ... classrooms are 'reserved for other intended purposes,' viz. the teaching of a particular ... course for credit." Based on this analysis, the court in *Bishop* held the university classroom was not a public forum and the university could reasonably restrict a professor's classroom expression.

After determining that the student newspaper in *Hazelwood* was not a public forum, the Court focused on whether the students' expression was school-sponsored speech. The Court distinguished its earlier decision in *Tinker* from the facts at issue in *Hazelwood*. *Tinker* addressed whether the first amendment requires a school to tolerate particular student expression not sponsored by the school. *Hazelwood*, on the other hand, dealt with the authority of school officials "over school-sponsored publications, theatrical productions, and other expressive activities that students, parents, and members of the public might reasonably perceive to bear the imprimatur of the school." We are convinced that if students' expression in a school newspaper bears the imprimatur of the school, then a teacher's expression in the "traditional classroom setting" also bears the imprimatur of the school. *See Id.* Based on the analysis in *Hazelwood*, we conclude Miles' expression during a ninth-grade government class must be treated as school-sponsored expression in a nonpublic forum for first amendment purposes. Accordingly, we will apply the *Hazelwood* standard for evaluating the actions of school officials related to the regulation of school-sponsored speech.

Both in the district court and on appeal, the parties have argued that the issue presented here is controlled by *Pickering v. Board of Education*, 391 U.S. 563 (1968), and its progeny. This line of cases develops a test for balancing the interests of the state as employer in preventing the expression of some statements in the workplace against an employee's interest in making such statements. *See Rankin*, 483 U.S. at 388. In these cases, the courts have recognized that the state's interest as an employer in regulating employees' speech does not differ significantly from interests connected with the regulation of speech outside of the employment context. *Pickering* established a test that first asks whether a public employee's expression addresses a matter of public concern and then balances that employee's interest in making the statement with the interests of the government in "promoting the efficiency of the public services it performs."

Although the *Pickering* test accounts for the state's interests as an employer, it does not address the significant interests of the state as educator. The Court in *Hazelwood* recognized that a state's regulation of speech in a public school setting is often justified by peculiar responsibilities the state bears in providing educational services: "to assure that participants learn whatever lessons the activity is designed to teach, that readers or listeners are not exposed to material that may be inappropriate for their level of maturity, and that the views of the individual speaker are not erroneously attributed to the school." *Hazelwood*, 484 U.S. at 271. These responsibilities warrant application of the standard adopted in *Hazelwood* for reviewing regulation of classroom speech rather than the *Pickering* standard for reviewing regulation of speech in a more general public setting. The concern addressed in *Pickering* — the right of an employee to participate as other citizens in debate on public matters — is simply less forceful when considered "'in light of the special characteristics of the school environment.'" (because classroom environment is *sui generis*, public/private speech distinctions drawn in *Pickering* and progeny fail in context of teacher's classroom speech). Because of the special characteristics of a classroom environment, in applying *Hazelwood* instead of *Pickering* we distinguish between teachers' classroom expression and teachers' expression in other situations that would not reasonably be perceived as school-sponsored.

The primary distinction that could be made between the situation in *Hazelwood* and this case is that *Hazelwood* involved students' expression in a secondary school whereas here we are concerned with a secondary school teacher's classroom expression. In *Roberts [v. Madigan]*, 921 F.2d [1047,] 1056-57, we reviewed a school's regulation of a fifth grade teacher's speech. School officials alleged the teacher's speech caused a violation of the first amendment's Establishment Clause. We held there was no reason to distinguish "between students and teachers where classroom discussion is concerned." 921 F.2d at 1057. As in *Roberts*, we find no reason to distinguish between the classroom discussion of students and teachers in applying *Hazelwood* here. A school's

A. SCHOOL CONTROL OVER TEACHER EXPRESSION

interests in regulating classroom speech — such as "assur[ing] that participants learn whatever lessons the activity is designed to teach" and that students are not "exposed to material that may be inappropriate for their level of maturity" — are implicated regardless of whether that speech comes from a teacher or student.

C. *Application of the Standard*

1. *Legitimate Pedagogical Interests*

In *Hazelwood*, the Court found that the school's decision to excise two pages from the newspaper reasonably protected pedagogical interests. The Court noted that these pedagogical interests included preventing speech that was not sufficiently sensitive to students' privacy interests or that was inappropriate for the maturity level of the adolescent audience. The school here proffers several interests to justify its sanction of Miles' remark. First, the school states an interest in preventing Miles from using his position of authority to confirm an unsubstantiated rumor. The Supreme Court already has recognized a school's interest in disassociating itself from speech the school reasonably considers inappropriate to bear its imprimatur.

Second, the school asserts an interest in ensuring that teacher employees exhibit professionalism and sound judgment.... Clearly, professionalism and sound judgment contribute to the competent performance of a teacher's job. Indeed, as Miles himself reminds us,

> The process of educating our youth for citizenship in public schools is not confined to books, the curriculum, and the civics class; schools must teach by example the shared values of a civilized social order. Consciously or otherwise, teachers ... demonstrate the appropriate form of civil discourse and political expression by their conduct and deportment in and out of class.

Third, the school states an interest in providing an educational atmosphere where teachers do not make statements about students that embarrass those students among their peers. This interest is related to two concerns the Court approved in *Hazelwood*. There, the Court held a school could regulate school-sponsored speech to protect the privacy interests of unnamed but potentially identifiable parties mentioned in the article. 484 U.S. at 274-75. The Court also permitted school officials to prevent the publication of allegations against named parties without giving them a fair chance to refute the allegations.

The interests asserted by the school in this case clearly are legitimate pedagogical interests. Thus, the only remaining question under *Hazelwood* is whether the actions taken by the school are reasonably related to legitimate pedagogical interests.

2. *The Relation of the School's Actions to Pedagogical Interests*

The school in this case put Miles on paid administrative leave during the investigation and placed a letter of reprimand in his file. The brief administrative leave allowed the school to investigate the incident and to disassociate itself from the speech; thus, the leave was directly tied to the interest of avoiding the appearance that the comment was sponsored by the school or in any way reflected the views of the school administration. The letter of reprimand stated only that Miles should refrain from the same kinds of comments as those involved in the incident. The letter was specific in articulating the school's interest: it admonished a teacher to refrain from commenting on items that would reflect negatively on individual members of the student body. That portion of the reprimand — particularly when viewed in the context of the incident for which Miles knew he was being reprimanded — serves the precise legitimate pedagogical interests articulated by the school. We hold that the school acted reasonably under the circumstances of this case where the actions taken were directly related to the school's legitimate pedagogical interests.

....

3. *Immaterial Facts*

Miles argues that factual disputes remain regarding whether he named the student, whether the rumor about the alleged incident was true, whether the incident was generally known in the school, and whether other students knew who the participants were. Miles' argument is without merit. The factual issues Miles raises are not material under the *Hazelwood* standard. *See Hazelwood*, 484 U.S. at 273. Therefore summary judgment is appropriate based on *Anderson v. Liberty Lobby*, 477 U.S. 242 (1986).

D. *Academic Freedom*

Finally, Miles contends the school's actions violate his first amendment academic freedom rights. The Supreme Court has recognized a university's institutional right to academic freedom. *See, e.g., Regents of Univ. of California v. Bakke*, 438 U.S. 265, 311-12 (1978) (citing *Sweezy v. New Hampshire*, 354 U.S. 234, 263 (1957) (FRANKFURTER, J., concurring)). At least one lower court has recognized an individual right to academic freedom under limited circumstances in the university setting. *See Parate v. Isibor*, 868 F.2d 821, 830-31 (6th Cir.1989) (university professor's right of academic freedom not violated because the dean's interference did not cast "pall of orthodoxy" over professor's classroom expression). However, the caselaw does not support Miles' position that a secondary school teacher has a constitutional right to academic freedom. *See Board of Educ., Island Trees Union Free School Dist. No. 26 v. Pico*, 457 U.S. 853, 920 (1982) (REHNQUIST, J., dissenting) (state as educator subject to fewer strictures when regulating speech in primary and secondary schools than university; school officials may determine that particular subject is not suitable for education of secondary school children); *Adams v. Campbell City School Dist.*, 511 F.2d 1242, 1247 (10th Cir.1975) (teacher does not have "unlimited liberty as to structure and content of the courses, at least at the secondary level"); *see also Bishop*, 926 F.2d at 1075 (finding no support for individual academic freedom right of university professor); .... The school's mild restrictions of Miles' classroom expression here simply do not threaten to "cast a pall of orthodoxy over the classroom." *Keyishian v. Board of Regents*, 385 U.S. 589, 603 (1967). We find no merit in the argument that Miles has a constitutional right — based on academic freedom or something else — that protects his substantiation of a rumor in a classroom setting.

III. *Conclusion*

The school has identified legitimate educational interests it sought to protect and has shown that its actions are reasonably related to those interests. Miles has failed to raise a genuine factual dispute on either of these issues. Because Miles has not shown his classroom comments under these particular circumstances were constitutionally protected, we do not reach the other two requirements under *Mount Healthy*.

We affirm.

---

1. What makes this case so different from the others discussed thus far in this chapter? How does the decision here contribute to the courts' dilemma in resolving the tension between the state's responsibility for inculcating values in children and refraining from suppressing the free speech rights of teachers?

2. The court relies quite a bit on *Hazelwood v. Kuhlmeier*, 484 U.S. 260 (1988), *supra*, at Chapter 6. Why? Would more reliance on teacher-based cases have rendered a different result? Is it because the other cases in this chapter deal with expression in teacher-administrator relationships? Did the court pick the result, then the standard? "The concern addressed in *Pickering* — the right of an employee to participate as other citizens in debate on public matters — is simply less forceful when considered 'in light of the special characteristics of the school environment.'" *Miles*, 944 F.2d at 777 (quoting *Hazelwood*, 484 U.S. at 266).

Would Miles have won under the *Pickering-Connick* standard? Applying this standard here, Miles' speech with respect to the alleged activity of the two students on the tennis court would probably not be a matter of public concern, but the current problems and state of affairs of the school likely would be.

The court also mentions *Mt. Healthy*. Under this standard, it is fairly clear that Miles' speech was the motivating factor in the school's decision to suspend him. However, such speech may not be constitutionally protected.

3. Due to the use of *Hazelwood* in the *Miles* case, it would appear that courts now may use a new standard to apply with respect to public school teachers' free speech complaints: In its role as "educator" (as opposed to employer or sovereign), provided school policies address legitimate pedagogical concerns, school boards do not have to support public school teacher expression in the classroom and may even restrict such speech without regard to academic freedom.

What are some of the restrictions engendered by the *Miles* ruling? May teachers be inhibited in their use of certain teaching methods and techniques? May teachers be prohibited from discussing matters in class that are external to the assigned curriculum? Are teachers now required to modify their own values to conform with that of the school, its students, and the surrounding community? May schools disallow teachers from bringing controversial issues into the classroom?

4. The decision in *Miles* recognizes the Supreme Court's grant of academic freedom at the university setting, citing such cases as *Sweezy v. New Hampshire*, 354 U.S. 234 (1957) and *Keyishian v. Board of Regents*, 385 U.S. 589 (1967). *Miles*, 944 F.2d at 779. The court goes on to say that the "caselaw does not support Miles' position that a secondary school teacher has a constitutional right to academic freedom." *Id.* Is the court saying here the university professors are entitled to academic freedom while public school teachers are not?

5. Consider the following excerpt from Gregory A. Clarick, Note, *Public School Teachers and the First Amendment: Protecting the Right to Teach*, 65 N.Y.U. L. Rev. 693, 708, 712-13 (1990):*

> In *Hazelwood Sch. Dist. v. Kuhlmeier*, the Supreme Court re-examined the bounds of first amendment protection afforded to student expression and dramatically expanded school boards' powers to regulate student speech. This re-examination of student speech casts doubt on the propriety of lower courts' use of *Tinker* as a guide to delineate teachers' first amendment rights, and adds new concerns which a court must consider in any such case. That teachers' free speech rights are called into doubt by the *Hazelwood* opinion highlights the need for an independent jurisprudence regarding teachers' in-class rights, one unfettered by thin analogies to the right to public and to students' free speech rights.
>
> ....
>
> In light of lower courts' applications of standards forged to protect students' rights to analyses of regulations limiting teachers' speech *Hazelwood* endangers the protection of teachers' rights to speak freely. Although the *Hazelwood* opinion directly addressed students' rights, the Supreme Court's primary reliance on public forum analysis suggests the possibility that lower courts may find that "school-sponsored, curricular" speech, particularly the in-class speech of employee teachers, occurs in nonpublic forums. *Hazelwood* reveals the meager foundation of courts' prior explications of teacher's in-class rights and the need for the development of a jurisprudence that comprehends teachers' rights independent of analogies to the rights of students.
>
> *Hazelwood* casts doubt on the ongoing legitimacy of the reasoning of the circuit court decisions which gave great weight to Tinker's protection of free

---

*Reprinted with permission.

A. SCHOOL CONTROL OVER TEACHER EXPRESSION 735

speech in schools. For example, even assuming that the court in *James v. Board of Educ.*[130] reasonably analyzed the plaintiff-teacher's rights, the court did not base its analysis on the forum categorization of a classroom. Given the recent prominence of the public forum analysis in the Supreme Court's first amendment jurisprudence generally, and in the *Hazelwood* opinion particularly, any viable legal analysis of a teacher's first amendment rights now must contend directly with public forum doctrine.

6. Are the *Hazelwood* and *Miles* decisions simply a result of a pendulum swinging toward conservatism in the federal courts? Note in the following excerpt the similarity between the majority rulings in these cases and the dissenting opinion of Justice William Rehnquist in *Board of Educ. of Island Trees Union Free Sch. Dist. v. Pico*, 457 U.S. 853 (1982):

[*Pico* was a plurality decision in that it featured seven different opinions. In sum, there was agreement that school officials may not remove school books based on orthodoxy or narrow political purposes or deny students access to ideas to which authorities simply disagree.]

JUSTICE REHNQUIST, with whom THE CHIEF JUSTICE and JUSTICE POWELL join, dissenting.

....

I

....

B

Considerable light is shed on the correct resolution of the constitutional question in this case by examining the role played by petitioners. Had petitioners been the members of a town council, I suppose all would agree that, absent a good deal more than is present in this record, they could not have prohibited the sale of these books by private booksellers within the municipality. But we have also recognized that the government may act in other capacities than as sovereign, and when it does the First Amendment may speak with a different voice:

[I]t cannot be gainsaid that the State has interests as an employer in regulating the speech of its employees that differ significantly from those it possesses in connection with regulation of the speech of the citizenry in general. The problem in any case is to arrive at a balance between the interests of the teacher, as a citizen, in commenting upon matters of concern and the interest of the State, as an employer, in promoting the

---

[130] 461 F.2d 566 (2d Cir. 1972).

efficiency of the public services it performs through its employees. *Pickering v. Board of Education*, 391 U.S. 563, 568 (1968).

By the same token, expressive conduct which may not be prohibited by the State as a sovereign may be proscribed by the State as property owner: "The State, no less than a private owner of property, has power to preserve the property under its control for the use to which it lawfully dedicated." *Adderley v. Florida*, 385 U.S. 39, 47 (1966)(upholding state prohibition of expressive conduct on certain state property).

With these differentiated roles of government in mind, it is helpful to assess the role of government as educator, as compared with the role of government as sovereign. When it acts as an educator, at least the elementary and secondary school level, the government is engaged in inculcating social values and knowledge in relatively impressionable young people.... In this connection I find myself entirely in agreement with the observation of the Court of Appeals for the Seventh Circuit in *Zykan v. Warsaw Community School Corp.*, 631 F.2d 1300, 1305 (7th Cir. 1980), that it is "permissible and appropriate for local boards to make educational decisions based upon their personal, social, political, and moral views." In the very course of administering the many-faced operations of a school district, the mere decision to purchase some books will necessarily preclude the possibility of purchasing others. The decision to teach a particular subject may preclude the possibility of teaching another subject. A decision to replace a teacher because of ineffectiveness may by implication be seen as a disparagement of the subject matter taught. In each of these instances, however, the book or the exposure to the subject matter may be acquired elsewhere. The managers of the school district are not proscribing it as to the citizenry in general, but are simply determining that it will not be included in the curriculum or school library. In short, actions by the government as educator do not raise the same First Amendment concerns as actions by the government as sovereign.

....

II

....

B

... "The importance of public schools in the preparation of individuals for participation as citizens, and in the preservation of the values on which our society rests, has long been recognized by our decisions." *Ambach v. Norwick*, 441 U.S. 68, 76 (1979). Public schools fulfill the vital role of teaching students the basic skills necessary to function in our society, and of "inculcating fundamental values necessary to the maintenance of a democratic political system." *Id.* The idea that such students have a right

A. SCHOOL CONTROL OVER TEACHER EXPRESSION

of access, in the school, to information other than that thought by their educators to be necessary is contrary to the very nature of an inculcative education.

Education consists of the selective presentation and explanation of ideas. The effective acquisition of knowledge depends upon an orderly exposure to relevant information. Nowhere is this more true than in elementary and secondary schools, where, unlike the broad-ranging inquiry available to university student, the courses taught are those thought most relevant to the young students' individual development. Of necessity, elementary and secondary educators must separate the relevant from the irrelevant, the appropriate from the inappropriate. Determining what information not to present to the students is often as important as identifying relevant material. This winnowing process necessarily leaves such information to be discovered by students at another time or in another place, and is fundamentally inconsistent with any constitutionally required eclecticism in public education.

....

As already mentioned, elementary and secondary schools are inculcative in nature. The libraries of such schools serve as supplements to this inculcative role. Unlike university or public libraries, elementary and secondary school libraries are not designed for freewheeling inquiry; they are tailored, as the public school curriculum is tailored, to the teaching of basic skills and ideas....

....

I think the Court will far better serve the cause of First Amendment jurisprudence by candidly recognizing that the role of government as sovereign is subject to more stringent limitations than is the role of government as employer, property owner, or educator. It must also be recognized that the elementary and secondary school system than when operating an institution of higher learning....

7. Does *Hazelwood* authorize the state to entirely prohibit teacher expression of disfavored points of view in the school if school officials reasonably conclude that student exposure to these ideas interferes with the school's obligation of inculcating values? May school officials proselytize students to one side of an issue even if such issues, by their very nature, lend themselves to differing points of view?

In *Romano v. Harrington*, 725 F. Supp. 687 (E.D.N.Y. 1989), the district court interpreted the ruling in *Hazelwood* very narrowly, indicating that school officials "exercise editorial control over what students write for class than what they voluntarily submit to extracurricular ... school funded, [teacher-advised], publications." *Id.* The case involved a teacher, serving as the editor of a student newspaper, who was dismissed for fostering an article in that publication opposing the federalizing of the Martin Luther King holiday. The court indicated that the facts of *Hazelwood* and the present case were substantially different in that the school publication in the former case was part of a class while in the latter it was an extracurricular activity. The court minimized as dictum that passage of *Hazelwood* that has been used to limit the speech of students and faculty in post-*Hazelwood* cases:

> The question whether the First Amendment requires a school to tolerate particular student speech ... is different from the question whether the First Amendment requires a school affirmatively to promote particular student speech. The former question addresses educators' ability to silence a student's personal expression that happens to occur on the school premises. The latter question concerns educators' authority over school-sponsored publications, ... and other expressive activities that students, parents, and members of the public might reasonably perceive to bear the imprimatur of the school. These activities may fairly be characterized as part of the school curriculum, whether or not they occur in a traditional classroom setting, so long as they are supervised by faculty members and designed to impart particular knowledge or skills to student participants and audiences. *Hazelwood* at 569-70.

The court in *Romano* allowed that the above statement was not a clear and precise directive and claimed the difference in facts of the two cases was sufficient enough to decide for the teacher. Specifically, the court used the decision in *Board of Educ. Island Trees v. Pico*, 457 U.S. 853 (1982), to stand for the principle that school hegemony over First Amendment issues is limited to curricular issues and is more attenuated with extracurricular activities.

Did the majority in *Hazelwood* intend for this narrow an interpretation of its decision? Are teachers' and students' First Amendment rights more expansive under *Hazelwood* when expression involves a disfavored view if that expression is extracurricular?

8. Recall another Supreme Court case where the free expression of students was the issue, *Bethel v. Fraser*, 478 U.S. 675 (1986), *supra*, Chapter 6. In *Bethel* the Court held that school officials could ban or punish student speech based on sexual innuendo or vulgarity. Thereafter *Bethel* played a role in the dismissal of a teacher in the Sixth Circuit. In *Fowler v. Board of Educ. of Lincoln County*, 819 F.2d 657 (Sixth Cir. 1987), *cert. denied*, 484 U.S. 986 (1987), a teacher was fired for showing a movie containing explicit sex and vulgar language. In a decision involving two concurring opinions one judge ruled that under *Mt. Healthy*, even despite a free speech right on the part of the teacher, the school board could reasonably exercise the dismissal because of the explicit vulgarity and nudity being openly displayed to impressionable young minds. A second judge, using *Bethel*, held that the teacher had no free speech

A. SCHOOL CONTROL OVER TEACHER EXPRESSION

right protection inasmuch as the teacher was engaged in no instructional activity about the film:

> [T]he focus of our inquiry is whether Fowler's conduct was constitutionally protected.... Among the "special circumstances" which must be considered in defining the scope of First Amendment protection inside the classroom is the "inculca[tion of] fundamental values necessary to the maintenance of a democratic political system." (*Fraser*) ... *Fowler*, at 661. Indeed, the "fundamental values necessary to the maintenance of a democratic political system" disfavor the use of terms of debate highly offensive or highly threatening to others. Nothing in the Constitution prohibits the states from insisting that certain modes of expression are inappropriate and subject to sanctions. The inculcation of these values is truly the work of the schools." (*Fraser*) ... The single most important element of this inculcative process is the teacher. "Consciously or otherwise, teachers ... demonstrate the appropriate form of civil discourse and political expression by their conduct and deportment in and out of class. Inescapably, like parents, they are role models." (*Fraser*) ... In the present case the district court concluded that Mrs. Fowler was entitled to the protection of the First Amendment while acting as a teacher. That a teacher does have First Amendment protection under certain circumstances cannot be denied ... However, I conclude that Fowler's conduct in having the movie shown under the circumstances present here did not constitute expression. *Fowler*, at 662.

For other case law involving vulgarity or sexual explicitness in the classroom *see Planned Parenthood v. Clark County Sch. Dist.*, 941 F.2d 817 (9th Cir. 1991); *Virgil v. School Bd. of Columbia County, Fla.*, 862 F.2d 1517 (11th Cir. 1989); *Seyfried v. Walton*, 668 F.2d 214 (3d Cir. 1981); *Piarowski v. Illinois Community College*, 759 F.2d 625 (7th Cir. 1985); *Krizek v. Board of Educ.*, 713 F. Supp. 1131 (N.D. Ill. 1989); *Bell v. U-32 Bd. of Educ.*, 630 F. Supp. 939 (D. Vt. 1986).

LEVIN v. HARLESTON
United States District Court
770 F. Supp. 895 (S.D.N.Y. 1991)

CONBOY, DISTRICT JUDGE:

This case raises serious constitutional questions that go to the heart of the current national debate on what has come to be denominated as "political correctness"[1] in speech and thought on the campuses of the nation's colleges and universities.

A professor who has had tenure for over sixteen years at one of America's most famous institutions of higher learning, singularly noted for its bracing environment of broad and untrammeled speech, claims that his tenure is in jeopardy, his students drawn away, his classes disrupted, his reputation injured, and his speech chilled as a result of the actions of his college's administrators, who are said to be repelled by his views on affirmative action quotas and the relative intelligence of blacks and whites, and who are said to be, by their actions, seeking to suppress those views.

The college officials say that his views are odious, and rightly denounced, and that although he has committed no act of academic misconduct or discrimination against his students, and although there is no complaint by any of his students against him, they are permitted to structure the class schedule to provide alternative professors to "insulate" and "protect" his present and future students from his views.

Professor Michael Levin has brought this action pursuant to federal civil rights law, 42 U.S.C. § 1983, and the First and Fourteenth Amendments to the United States Constitution.

We conclude that Professor Levin has convincingly established his case, that the defendant college officials have sought to and did punish him in retaliation for and solely because of his expressed ideas, that in so doing they have violated his constitutional rights and the civil rights laws of the United States, and that federal injunctive relief is necessary to secure Professor Levin's rights on the campus of City College of the City University of New York. We will now elaborate upon these findings.

....

Factual Background

Professor Levin's Writings

The writings of Professor Levin that have made him a subject of controversy are three in number. They are a letter to the editor of the New York Times, published January 11, 1987; a book review that appeared in the January/February 1988 issue of an Australian journal called Quadrant; and a January 1990 letter published in the Proceedings of the American Philosophical Association.

The Sunday edition of the New York Times for January 11, 1987, carried a letter to the editor signed by Professor Levin, in which he responded to, and criticized, a Times editorial published on the previous December 28th. He

---

[1]The term is now formally defined as follows: "Marked by a progressive orthodoxy on issues involving race, gender, sexual affinity or ecology." Random House Webster's College Dictionary, 1991. *See also* "Political Correctness: New Bias Test?", by Robert D. McFadden; *New York Times*, May 5, 1991, Section 1, Part 1, Page 32.

A. SCHOOL CONTROL OVER TEACHER EXPRESSION

asserted that the editorial had misunderstood the ethical formulations of the eminent Harvard philosopher John Rawls, and that the citation to Rawls was "obviously an effort to bolster a position reached on nonphilosophical grounds."

....

The full text of Professor Levin's letter in response, under a headline selected by The Times [includes the following].

Howard Beach Turns a Beam on Racial Tensions

....

> You say that the Rawls principle that "No one ought to endorse a social order that he could not accept if he were in the shoes of the most disadvantaged" implies that people ought not to take even rational steps to avoid being victimized by black criminals....
>
> You indirectly try to make these points by proposing the quite incredible idea that it is just as bad to be discriminated against as it is to be robbed or murdered — or, at any rate, that a society in which prejudice is rampant is as bad as one in which violent crime is rampant.
>
> Individual tastes in disaster may differ, but surely the innocent black turned away from a Madison Avenue boutique would not wish to change places with a boutique owner who has just been assaulted. It is unfortunate that innocent blacks must be inconvenienced because of the behavior of guilty blacks, but if we are to play the put-yourself-in-his-shoes game, the innocent black who puts himself in the shoes of the vulnerable boutique owner should just as surely conclude that he would not let himself in under similar circumstances.
>
> It is hard to fathom your sudden concern with the penalized innocent given your steadfast endorsement of affirmative action quotas that invariably penalize whites innocent of discriminating. Is discrimination against innocent whites a tolerable price for insuring jobs for blacks while discriminatory inconvenience for innocent blacks is too high a price for reducing the risk of murder for white store owners?

One year later, in the January/February 1988 issue of Quadrant, an Australian journal published in Sidney, there appeared a book review by Professor Levin of two then current and controversial best-sellers in the United States dealing with education, Cultural Literacy, by E.D. Hirsch and The Closing of the American Mind, by Allan Bloom.

This article, approximately 3500 words in length, is in large measure given over to arguments about cultural transmission of common and historical experience, sweeping claims about intellectual history, and the place of value judgments in a college education. The text of that portion of Professor Levin's article that is germane to the case at hand is as follows:

> [A] cause of the malaise of American education is race, a topic approached but not quite reached by Hirsch and Bloom. Since 1954, staggering energies

have been expended to bring American Negroes into the educational mainstream. Yet they continue to exhibit disproportionately high rates of illiteracy, dropping out, absence from the more prestigious disciplines, and other forms of academic failure. The conventional explanation of this failure is bias in the standards by which students are judged; adjust the standards to eliminate race bias, and all will be well. And adjustments have been made to eliminate any measure on which blacks under-perform, it always being assumed that blacks are on average as intelligent as whites and as capable of passing any fair test in proportionate numbers. But there is now quite solid evidence that this assumption is not correct; the average black is significantly less intelligent than the average white. Therefore, the only adjustments in educational measures that will allow blacks their due number of successes amount to making course-work and tests easier and easier, and this is what has been going on for over thirty years. Conversely, if standards are going to be raised, cultural literacy reasserted and college education given its old depth and focus, the American polity will have to reconcile itself to an embarrassing failure rate for blacks.

. . . .

In January 1990, Professor Levin published the following letter in the American Philosophical Association Proceedings:

The June issue of the Proceedings (Volume 62, Number 5) gives survey data concerning the numbers of blacks and other minorities in philosophy. Unsurprisingly, the proportion of blacks in the discipline is considerably below their proportion of the population.

Unfortunately, such findings in the current climate of opinion generally lead to calls for "affirmative action," *i.e.* preference for blacks, accompanied by mea culpas on the part of whites participating in the activity from which blacks have been found to be excluded. It should therefore be good news that whites are not responsible for this under-representation.

It has been amply confirmed over the last several decades that, on average, blacks are significantly less intelligent than whites. The black mean IQ is slightly more than one standard deviation below the white mean. In more familiar terms, that amounts to a difference of more than 15 points of IQ as measured by such standard tests as the Wechsler Adult Intelligence Scale. Philosophers seem to have fixated at a primitive verificationism about such tests, and regard such tests as measuring nothing beyond themselves. In fact, performance on IQ tests correlates quite well with performance on a large number of independently measurable variables. In a recent survey of the psychometric literature, the National Academy of Science concluded that "in the technically precise meaning of the term, [mental] ability tests have not been proved to be biased against blacks; that is, they predict criterion performance as well for blacks as for whites."

The significance of these findings for our profession (as for the rest of society) is that black representation in a field can be expected, absent any discrimination, to decrease as the intellectual demands of the field increase....

The Classroom Disruptions

As indicated, the relevant facts in this case are in large measure not disputed by the parties. Since the fall of 1984, City College policy has officially and in written regulations prohibited students from engaging in demonstrations that disrupt or obstruct teaching and research activities. Any activity disruptive of classes subjects the group and individual participants to disciplinary proceedings....

On March 23, 1987, shortly after the appearance of his letter in The Times, Professor Levin wrote a letter to the City College Dean of Student Affairs, George D. McDonald, complaining of persons distributing pamphlets outside of one of his classes. A week later, on April 1, 1987, Professor Levin reported to Campus Security Chief Albert Dandridge that documents affixed to his door had been burned. Dandridge filed an "Incident Report", and submitted a copy to Dean McDonald, among others, which stated that Professor Levin "had been the target of demonstrations by the Day Student Government." A week after that, on April 8, 1987, a group of between 10 and 15 persons conducted a loud demonstration outside of one of Professor Levin's classes, disrupting that and other classes and blocking entry into and exit from the classroom.

Dandridge was summoned to the scene by Professor Levin. Dandridge observed one of the demonstrators, whom he later identified as Stephen N. Pearl, a student in the College, push against Security personnel in an apparent effort to inflame the situation and to exhort the other demonstrators to assault the Security officers. Dandridge obtained Pearl's student I.D. card, as well as that of another student demonstrator, Vardon Marshall, and submitted copies of the cards with a report on the demonstration, to Dean McDonald. Dandridge also filed an Incident Report. The following day, on April 9, 1987, Professor Levin wrote a letter, to President Harleston, with copies to Deans McDonald and Sherwin, concerning the same incident and contemporaneous acts of harassment against himself, including an anti-Semitic threat. No one replied to this letter. Dandridge submitted an April 8, 1987 Incident Report to Dean McDonald concerning the threat, which was affixed to the door of Professor Levin's office and stated: "We know where you live you Jewish bastard your time is going to come."

....

Shortly thereafter, on April 13, 1987, Dean McDonald sent a letter to Pearl officially summoning Pearl to his office on April 21 to explain why he should not be subject to disciplinary measures for violating College regulations during the April 8 demonstration. A similar letter was sent to Marshall. Pearl and Marshall did not appear before Dean McDonald as required. Dean McDonald received a letter dated April 20, 1987, signed by "Members of INCAR [International Committee Against Racism] and the City College Community." This letter made counter-charges against College officials and stated: "we will not even consider the charges being raised against Mr. Pearl and Mr. Marshall until the charges against Mr. Dandridge, yourself and the administration are resolved to our satisfaction."

At about this time, President Harleston and Dean McDonald met with Professor Levin. They told him that academic freedom protects student demonstrators, but that the time, place, and manner of demonstrations could be regulated by the College. No commitment was forthcoming from these officials that Professor Levin's classes would proceed unimpeded in the future.

Several months later, on September 2, 1987, Dr. Levin wrote a letter to Dean McDonald and President Harleston complaining that Pearl was distributing leaflets outside of his class in a manner that was in apparent violation of College regulations. Neither Dean McDonald nor President Harleston replied to this letter. No further action was taken by anyone with regard to this incident.

... In April, 1987, between 20 and 50 students were outside the door of his classroom with banners, shouting and impeding Professor Levin's students from entering, and "trying to make noise so that the class couldn't continue". The banners and the shouts denounced Professor Levin as a racist.... According to Professor Levin's testimony, which the Court accepts as credible, the President said, " 'What do you want me to do? There's academic freedom issues here. The students have academic freedom as well, and their academic freedom is protected.' "

....

At the trial, President Harleston denied that he had told Professor Levin that academic freedom protected the student demonstrators. He asserted, however, that he could not recall whether he had done anything "to follow-up the college's investigation of the April, 1987 disruption of Professor Levin's class", and that he could recall nothing about the March, 1990 disruption of Professor Levin's class. When counsel directed his attention to a resolution of the faculty senate calling upon him "to prevent disruption of classes and to discipline those who attempt such disruption", President Harleston was unable to say whether the College Administration had carried out its responsibilities to comply with this resolution. Indeed, when the Court pointed out that the question of the adequacy of the Administration's response to the disruptions of Professor Levin's classes had been put to him in a previous hearing in the case held five months earlier, and asked "[i]n the period of time that has elapsed since then, have you had occasion to review [the record] and satisfy yourself as to whether or not there was an adequate response to these complaints of disruptions in the professor's classroom", President Harleston stated that he had not.

President Harleston further testified that at the aforementioned meeting in his office, which meeting had been convened at Professor Levin's request to stop the disruptions of his class, President Harleston had said: "But, Prof. Levin, you

A. SCHOOL CONTROL OVER TEACHER EXPRESSION

wrote about affirmative action and it's not surprising that the students would want to ask you about it." Amazingly, President Harleston also testified that he could not remember ever getting a detailed account of the disruptions complained of by Professor Levin.

....

The Shadow Sections

After the appearance of his Quadrant book review, Professor Levin was summoned on October 21, 1988, to meet with then Philosophy Department Chairman Martin Tawny and Dean Sherwin. Professor Levin was requested by Chairman Tawny and Dean Sherwin to withdraw from teaching his required introductory Philosophy course, the next class session of which was to meet the following Monday. Among the reasons given by Dean Sherwin and Chairman Tawny for the request were that (1) there might be disruption of the class by demonstrators opposing Professor Levin's recently published views; and (2) some persons in the class might feel uncomfortable being taught by one holding such views. The previous day, the Faculty Senate had passed a resolution condemning his views in the Quadrant article, as expressing "racist prejudices [offensive to] our fundamental notions of human decency."

Following the meeting, Professor Levin agreed to withdraw from this class....

The following semester, Professor Levin resumed teaching his required introductory Philosophy course, and he was assigned to teach this course for the spring semester of 1990. Shortly after the appearance of his American Philosophical Association letter, Dean Sherwin, on February 1, 1990, (without prior notice) sent to Professor Levin's students a letter stating that Professor Levin had "expressed controversial views" and informing them of the availability of a newly opened second section — a "shadow" or "parallel" section — of Professor Levin's required introductory philosophy course to be taught by another instructor. Dean Sherwin also stated in that letter that he was "aware of no evidence suggesting that Professor Levin's views on controversial matters have compromised his performance as an able teacher of Philosophy who is fair in his treatment of students."

The College Philosophy Department Chair, Professor Charles Evans, resisted Dean Sherwin's suggestion that there be additional "shadow sections" for Professor Levin's students, but Dean Sherwin established such a class on his own authority. Professor Evans believed such an action to be immoral and illegal, and an unwarranted interference in the discretionary powers of a department chairman.

No other "shadow" or "parallel" section has ever been created for any course at the College in order to provide students with the opportunity to avoid being taught by a particular instructor.

....

On the issue of establishing the shadow sections to Professor Levin's classes, President Harleston testified that he approved the decision to do so because what is at issue is "whether students are to be held hostage to a particular point of view that by its nature impugns numbers of them, or whether students should have a choice."

....

The Fitness Inquiry

In the Spring of 1990, President Harleston made a second request to the College Faculty Senate that it appoint a faculty Committee to investigate allegations of bias or racism then being made at the College, implicating the writings of Professor Levin....

....

As is apparent, the Committee found that utterances by professors, even outside of class, can have a detrimental impact on the educational process, if they "denigrat[e] the intellectual capacity of groups by virtue of race, ethnicity or gender"; that a teacher's "low expectations frequently have a negative effect on student performance"; that it is "clearly unprofessional and inappropriate for any faculty member to *make it difficult* for a student to fully participate in a class by virtue of the student's race, class, ethnic origins, religion, gender or sexual orientation"; that "faculty have a responsibility to exercise appropriate restraint so as not to belittle a student, to prophesy the likelihood of his/her poor performance, or to, in any manner, undermine the equal educational opportunities of all students"; that existing mechanisms for "disciplining professors who *harass students* are ... frequently ineffective"; that in such circumstances the college "must intervene"; and that "the offering of parallel [shadow] sections" may, accordingly, be needed. (Emphasis added).

It is fair to say, therefore, that the President's Committee has found that Professor Levin's writings constitute unprofessional and inappropriate conduct that harms the educational process at the College, and that the College has properly intervened to protect his students from his views by creating the shadow sections.

....

Legal Analysis

....

B. *Professor Levin's First Amendment Right to Free Expression Was Impermissibly Chilled, Impeded and Abridged*

....

When one must guess what conduct or utterance may lose him his position, one necessarily will 'steer far wider of the unlawful zone ...' For '[t]he threat of sanctions may deter ... almost as potently as the actual application of sanctions.' The danger of that chilling effect upon the exercise of vital First Amendment rights must be guarded against by sensitive tools which clearly inform teachers what is being proscribed. [*Keyishian v. Board of Regents*,] 385 U.S. at 604....

Here, precisely that ambiguity was demonstrated at trial, aggravated in this case by several additional factors. First, the Committee's secret deliberations were predicated upon no announced or promulgated criteria or normative proscriptions. Second, Professor Levin had no way of knowing which of his statements were being reviewed by the Committee; that selection was made by President Harleston, with no notice to Professor Levin. Third, Professor Levin was given no opportunity to appear before the Committee or otherwise to defend those statements. Fourth, even though the Committee concededly made an adverse finding against him in his professional capacity as a tenured faculty member, there is apparently no forum or mechanism for him to challenge this finding. Fifth, though the Committee says it has completed its assigned task, its report invites and indeed recommends further and continuing scrutiny of Professor Levin, albeit in its characteristically elliptical and, we must say, Orwellian double-speak. Sixth, the Committee endorses the continued use of the shadow sections, without any indication of the danger such a procedure poses in real terms to a college teacher's standing in the College and the world at large.

The result is exactly that predicted in *Keyishian*, 385 U.S. at 601. Professor Levin was forced to "stay as far away as possible from utterances or acts which might jeopardize his living" and therefore declined at least twenty invitations to speak or to write about his views during the nine-month period they were under scrutiny by the Committee. As we have found, Professor Levin had objectively reasonable bases to fear for his job during the nine months of deliberations of the Committee, despite having had tenure for sixteen years.... President Harleston himself made no effort during the Committee's deliberations, despite a letter from the Professor's counsel seeking a modification of the Committee's charge, and despite the pendency of this lawsuit alleging a threat to his tenure, to assure Professor Levin that his job was and is not in danger....

Nor is it a risk the Constitution permits the State to impose. In *Pickering v. Board of Education of Township High School Dist. 205*, 391 U.S. 563, (1968), a case involving a teacher who wrote a letter to the editor of a local newspaper criticizing school board revenue policies, Justice Marshall made unmistakably clear that the First Amendment protects teachers against such a risk, holding that "absent proof of false statements knowingly or recklessly made by him, a teacher's exercise of his right to speak on issues of public importance may not furnish the basis for his dismissal from public employment." 391 U.S. at 574. Yet Professor Levin's continued employability (under the "conduct unbecoming" standard) was plainly and exactly what the Committee was charged to evaluate, solely on the basis of his statements on issues of public importance. We note that the state has not shown that Professor Levin's statements were knowingly and recklessly made.

Under the rule thus enunciated in *Pickering*, the threat to Professor Levin's job posed by the Committee was simply illegitimate and not susceptible of justification by claims of other, proper motivation. However, even when we analyze defendants' explanations for their conduct under the authorities which provide guidance on screening constitutionally defective retaliatory actions from defenses based on legitimate state interests, the defenses presented here must fail.

The state must have a compelling state interest in the curtailment of speech when it is the content of that speech which the state aims to interdict. *Police Department v. Mosley*, 408 U.S. 92, 99-101 (1972). In *Mt. Healthy City School Dist. Bd. of Education v. Doyle*, 429 U.S. 274 (1977), the Court established a three-step test to measure the propriety of state action where it is claimed that other interests beyond suppression of the speech itself motivate actions taken against the speaker. Step one requires the plaintiff to show that his conduct was constitutionally protected; step two requires proof by him that such conduct was a "substantial" or "motivating" factor behind the adverse action. If the plaintiff makes this showing, the burden shifts to the state, in step three, to demonstrate by a preponderance of the evidence that the adverse action would have been taken against the plaintiff even in the absence of the protected conduct. *Mt. Healthy*, 429 U.S. at 287.

Here, there is no question that the "conduct" of Professor Levin that provoked all of the actions challenged in this suit was protected expression. President Harleston charged the Committee to examine, and the Committee did examine, only his public writings and statements about his views on the relationship between race and test scores and his objections to affirmative action programs, quintessentially "issues of public importance." *Pickering, supra*, 391 U.S. at 572. Thus, the first *Mt. Healthy* requirement is met. At least as to the portion of the Committee's charge pertaining to him and as to the creation of the shadow sections, there is likewise no dispute on the second step, that Professor Levin's expression of his controversial views was not merely a "substantial" or "motivating" factor, it was the only factor.

Under the *Mt. Healthy* analysis, the burden then shifted at trial to defendants to show that their complained-of actions would have been taken without the protected conduct. This they did not do and could not have done, because the only justification for two of the actions complained of (the Committee investigation of Professor Levin's public statements and the shadow sections) was premised upon the protected expression: the supposed necessity to protect Professor Levin's students from the claimed harm they might suffer if they thought, because of the expression of his views, that he might expect less of them or grade them unfairly. As we have already observed, the defendants adduced no evidence to support this justification at trial.

....

It is, therefore, clear that Professor Levin has prevailed on his First Amendment claim.

C. *Professor Levin Was Improperly Deprived of Fourteenth Amendment Liberty and Property Interests*

....

Professor Levin has been stigmatized professionally by the College, has been warned by the Committee that his speech (as it may relate to unbecoming conduct) should be the subject of continuing scrutiny by the College, and his use of his tenure has been undermined by the policy of the College of inducing his students to abandon him because of his views.

These actions by the defendants, as we have found, have damaged his standing in the academic community, and may foreclose future employment and scholarly opportunities.

It is undisputed that Professor Levin was given no due process opportunity, to know, answer and refute the charges made against him by President Harleston, Dean Sherwin and the Committee. It further bears emphasis that the Committee did not flatly assert that the expression of his views alone, outside of his classroom, did not and does not subject him to a future charge of conduct unbecoming a faculty member, a dischargeable offense, his tenure notwithstanding.

In *Perry v. Sindermann*, [408 U.S. 593 (1972),] the Court expanded upon the teaching of *Roth*, warning that the " 'property' interests subject to procedural due process protection are not limited by a few rigid, technical forms", and do not necessarily even require, or implicate, a contractual tenure provision. Rather, "property" denotes a broad range of interests that are secured by "existing rules or understandings officially promulgated and fostered" by a University. 408 U.S. at 601.... We find, based upon the record, that a longstanding, indeed, historic "understanding," officially promulgated and fostered by the College, has been guaranteed and made an inherent part of tenure at City College, that all teachers, tenured and non-tenured alike, shall be free of thought control outside of the classroom (and indeed, inside the classroom as well) by University or College officials and administrators.

....

This case illuminates the fact, recognized by the Supreme Court, that tenure is more than the right to receive a paycheck. Academic tenure, if it is to have any meaning at all, must encompass the right to pursue scholarship wherever it may lead, the freedom to inquire, to study and to evaluate without the deadening limits of orthodoxy or the corrosive atmosphere of suspicion and distrust warned against in *Sweezy v. State of New Hampshire*, 354 U.S. 234, 250 (1957).

Here, Professor Levin has been stigmatized in a setting where, as the City College Faculty Senate has recognized, his academic freedom has been infringed by administrative interference with his expression of ideas and his class assignments. He has been deprived of the freedom to which he is entitled to write and to speak in the areas of his scholarly interest. He is currently deterred from seeking outside grants to fund research on his "controversial" topics of interest because his grant applications must be reviewed by the defendants in this action. He is currently inhibited from discussing "controversial" topics with his own students, even if they raise them and even if the topics are pedagogically appropriate, because of the threat to his career.

It is, therefore, clear that Professor Levin has prevailed on his Fourteenth Amendment claim.

....

---

1. The administration of City College appealed the district court decision with a result in *Levin v. Harleston*, 966 F.2d 85 (2d Cir. 1992). The district court case is printed in this chapter to demonstrate the pertinent facts as well as the court's sanguine reaction against student demonstrators and in favor of Levin, both absent in the circuit court report. On appeal, the Second Circuit affirmed the lower court's decision that Levin's First Amendment rights were violated under *Mt. Healthy City Sch. Dist. Bd. of Educ. v. Doyle*, 429 U.S. 274 (1977), in that the college failed to introduce any evidence that would suggest that Levin's comments harmed any particular student. Hence, the university could not demonstrate any legitimate educational interest to overcome the plaintiff's free speech rights.

2. Why didn't the courts in this case apply *Hazelwood* as the Tenth Circuit did in *Miles v. Denver Pub. Schs.*? *See also Bishop v. Aronov*, 926 F.2d 1066 (11th Cir. 1991), where the *Hazelwood* decision was used to control the free expression rights of a university professor. What pedagogical concerns should the college have had to win this case: professionalism of its faculty? Fear of being associated with or attributed to the speech?

3. The courts in *Levin* indicate that at least part of the decision turns on the fact that college hegemony over speech is limited to that which takes place in the classroom, a vague reference to *Hazelwood*, although that Supreme Court decision appears nowhere in the lower court text. Levin's expression denigrating African-Americans appeared in a newspaper article, a refereed journal, and an academic journal of proceedings. In academe the position of professor normally involves teaching, research, and service to the university. Some of this effort takes place outside the classroom (such as research) and yet is obviously considered a necessary component of an instructor's vital contribution to whatever institution of higher education to which he or she is attached. Why then is so much attention paid to Levin's remarks in class? Moreover, consider the ruling in *Hazelwood* distinguishing between a school's responsibility to tolerate particular speech and its right not to affirmatively promote it. The rationale for such a distinction is telling, for it seems to run to the heart of the decision in *Levin*. To wit:

> The latter question concerns educator's authority over school sponsored publications ... and other expressive activities that students, parents and

A. SCHOOL CONTROL OVER TEACHER EXPRESSION

members of the public might reasonably perceive to bear the imprimatur of the school. These activities may fairly be characterized as part of the school curriculum, whether or not they occur in the traditional classroom setting.... *Hazelwood* at 271.

4. How important is it that Professor Levin was tenured? Should it make a difference under First Amendment analysis?

This case illuminates the fact, recognized by the Supreme Court, that tenure is more than the right to receive a paycheck. Academic tenure, if it is to have any meaning at all, must encompass the right to pursue scholarship wherever it may lead, the freedom to inquire, to study and to evaluate without the deadening limits of orthodoxy or the corrosive atmosphere of suspicion and distrust warned against in *Sweezy v. New Hampshire*, 354 U.S. 234, 250 (1957).

Levin, 770 F. Supp. at 925. *See also Grimes v. Eastern Illinois Univ.*, 710 F.2d 386, 388 (7th Cir. 1983): "The purpose of tenure is to protect academic freedom — the freedom to teach and write without fear of retribution for expressing heterodox ideas — and it is faculty who engage in teaching and writing"; J. Paretsky, *Judicial Review of Discretionary Grants of Higher Education Tenure*, 83 Educ. L. Rep. 17 (1993): "Academic tenure, defined as a faculty appointment for an indefinite period of time, is accompanied by increased prestige, compensation and freedom."*

Does academic freedom really mean that patently racist ideas and expression thereof are absolutely protected by the First Amendment?

If a non-tenured professor had expressed the same or similar views as Levin, would this case have turned out differently? Should it? *See Omlor v. Cleveland State Univ.*, 45 Ohio St. 3d 187 (1989), where a professor was denied tenure for stating, "I like Dean Smith, he's a good guy for a Jew." The resulting tenure denial was held to lie within administrative discretion as the comments were said to not lie in an area of public concern. *But also see Dube v. State Univ. of New York*, 900 F.2d 587, 597 (2d Cir. 1991), *cert. denied*, 111 S. Ct. 2814 (1991), where a professor of political science was denied tenure because he equated Zionism in Israel, with racism in South Africa, and with Nazism in Germany. The court held that, in fact, tenure was denied because the views of the professor ran counter to those of university officials and community activists and, as such, was a violation of First Amendment rights.

5. "Political Correctness" is defined as "marked by or adhering to a typically progressive orthodoxy on issues involving race, gender, sexual affinity or ecology." Random House Webster's Dictionary 1050 (1991) as quoted in C. Anderson, *Political Correctness on College Campuses: Freedom of Expression v. Doing the Politically Correct Thing*, 46 SMU L. Rev. 171 (1992). Does

---

*Copyright © 1993 by West Publishing Company. Reprinted with permission.

"political correctness", mentioned in the district court's introduction, *Levin* at 897, have any legal validity? Under "political correctness", as defined above, was Levin's conduct and expression "politically incorrect"? Did the court's obvious disdain for "political correctness" influence its decision?

6. As noted, there were three publications attributed to Professor Levin in the facts of the district court case. One of them appeared in the New York Times as a letter to the editor and involved support of a policy of overinclusion in the discrimination of African-Americans involving access to certain stores in New York. To protect whites from possible harm, Levin advocates prejudice against all blacks because of the deeds of a few and countenances this as mere "discriminatory inconvenience":

> Individual tastes in disaster may differ, but surely the innocent black turned away from a Madison Avenue boutique would not wish to change places with a boutique owner who has been assaulted. It is unfortunate that innocent blacks must be inconvenienced because of the behavior of guilty blacks, but if we are to play the put-yourself-in-his-shoes game, the innocent black who puts himself in the shoes of the vulnerable boutique owner should just as surely conclude that he would not let himself in under similar circumstances. *Levin* at 901.

Both the district and circuit courts found no harm by these statements and, hence, no defense of college action to disassociate itself with them, as they were not uttered in class. Are African-Americans harmed by such statements and the resulting actions that derive therefrom? Consider the following remarks of Patricia J. Williams, Associate Professor of Law at the University of Wisconsin, in her book, *The Alchemy of Race and Rights** [hereinafter, *Alchemy*], who had such a personal experience in New York:

> I was shopping in Soho and saw in a store window a sweater that I wanted to buy for my mother. I pressed my round face to the window and my finger to the buzzer, seeking admittance. A narrow-eyed, white teenager, ... glared out, evaluating me for signs that would pit me against the limits of his social understanding. After about five seconds, he mouthed "We're closed" .... It was two Saturdays before Christmas, at one o'clock in the afternoon; there were several white people in the store who appeared to be shopping for things for *their* mothers.
>
> I was enraged.... I am struck by the structure of power that drove me into such a blizzard of rage. There was almost nothing I could do, short of physically intruding upon him, that would humiliate him the way he humiliated me. No words, no gestures, no prejudices of my own would

---

*Reprinted with permission of the publishers, from *The Alchemy of Race and Rights* by Patricia J. Williams, Cambridge, Mass.: Harvard University Press, Copyright © 1991 by the President and Fellows of Harvard College.

make a bit of difference to him.... He had no compassion, no remorse, no reference to me.... He saw me only as one who would take his money and therefore could not conceive that I was there to give him money. *Alchemy* at 45.

....

The violence of my desire to burst into [that store] is probably quite apparent. I often wonder if the violence, the exclusionary hatred, is equally apparent in the repeated urgings that blacks understand ... [being discriminated against] ... by putting themselves in the shoes of white storeowners — that, in effect, blacks look into the mirror of frightened white faces for the reality of their undesirability; and that then blacks would "just as surely conclude that [they] would not let [themselves] in under similar circumstances.... *Alchemy* at 46.

7. What are the possible harms of racist hate speech? Some possible answers are found in M. Matsuda, *Legal Storytelling: Public Response to Racist Speech: Considering the Victim's Story*, 87 Mich. L. Rev. 2320 (1987). Matsuda reports that victims of hate speech suffer both emotional and physical symptoms, from fear, increased heart rate, and nightmares to hypertension, psychosis, and suicide. Further, she notes that victims are affected both personally and professionally, often having to give up school, quit work, stay at home. Overall, in order to avoid receiving hate messages, targets of hate speech may sacrifice all aspects of their own "free" expression. *Id.* at 2336-37.

The court indicates that if some harm could have been shown to Levin's students as a result of facts brought in this case the decision may have been different. Is that a true reading of current interpretations of racist speech activity? Would the holding in *R.A.V. v. St. Paul*, 112 S. Ct. 2358 (1992), compel the Second Circuit to reconsider its statement as to whether actual harm on the part of Levin's students could have rendered a different ruling? In *R.A.V.*, the Supreme Court decided that a city ordinance banning hate expression against certain groups was unconstitutional as it involved content discrimination. As Levin's comments were limited to just the groups the courts mention in *R.A.V.*, does this mean that African-Americans would be without redress under a school policy which sought to protect their rights or the rights of all protected class citizens? The Court in *R.A.V.* held the city ordinance violated the First Amendment as it was underinclusive, not abridging enough speech. Does the decision mean that any anti-discrimination policy must be polyglot, *i.e.*, protect all persons including racist speakers, resulting in no protection for victims of hate speech?

8. Another case involving alleged hate speech by a university professor has been decided by the Second Circuit Court of Appeals. *Harleston v. Jeffries*, 21 F.3d 1238 (2d Cir. 1994), is remarkably like the *Levin* case and has its origin in the same institution with the same college president as defendant.

Leonard Jeffries, professor and Chair of the Department of Black Studies, delivered a controversial speech off campus in which he criticized the public school curriculum as being racist. During the speech he claimed that Jews had a history of contributing to black oppression by participating in the slave trade and conspiring with the Mafia to portray a negative image of African-Americans in film. Because of a public outcry, the university's board of trustees voted to reduce Jeffries' administrative term as chair of the department from three years to one year. Jeffries sued alleging a violation of his First Amendment rights to speak on matters of public concern.

Following the *Pickering, Doyle, Connick* standard, the Second Circuit agreed with the professor, reasoning that public employees have a right to "speak on political or social matters without fear of retribution by the government." At 1241. This is true "even if critical of the very government that employs him ... unless his speech has impaired the efficiency of government operations." *Id.* Hence, there is a balance between the employee's interest in speaking on matters of public concern and the employer's interest in the smooth functioning of government. As in *Doyle*, the employee also had to prove that his speech was a substantial or motivating factor in the decision to fire him. The court ruled that Jeffries' speech was a matter of public concern in that he was criticizing the public school curriculum and that this was a substantial factor in his removal from the departmental chairpersonship. Before the speech, the president of the college had attempted to extend congratulations to Jeffries for a new administrative appointment. After the speech, the plaintiff's competence as an employee had been brought into question. *Id.* at 1242. Accordingly, the court affirmed the district court's decision that Jeffries' First Amendment rights had been violated and reinstated his original administrative appointment.

The college appealed the verdict to the Supreme Court which granted certiorari, *Harleston v. Jeffries*, 115 S. Ct. 502 (mem.) (1994) and remanded the case to the Second Circuit in light of its decision in *Waters v. Churchill*, 511 U.S. ____ , 114 S. Ct. 1878 (1994).

Waters concerned a nurse who made negative remarks about the policies of the hospital where she was employed. The employer claimed she was denigrating the hospital and her superiors, thus negatively affecting the efficient operation of a medical institution. The nurse claimed she was voicing a legitimate public concern in that patient care was at risk. The Court addressed the line of cases from *Pickering* to *Connick* determining that employees may be dismissed if their speech is not a matter of public concern and disrupts the smooth running of the workplace. In a plurality opinion, the Court also introduced a new step in this test, *i.e.*, the development of a good faith employer belief that what the employee said was in fact disruptive and arriving at that belief only after making a reasonable investigation. Hence, when an employer reasonably believes that an employee's speech is disruptive, even if it may not be, firing the employee after reasonable procedures does not violate First Amendment rights. Further, even if an employee's speech dealt with a matter of public concern, this would not bar termination, so long as part of the speech did not address a public concern or did address a public concern, but was nonetheless disruptive. The procedure, then, is not based on what the employee said, but on what the employer reasonably thought was said.

9. Does this "reasonable supervisor" standard, representing the first time the Supreme Court has introduced procedural rights in free expression cases, compromise employee First Amendment protections by placing the determination of what was actually said in the hands of the employer? Does this mean that employees can now be punished for what heretofore was considered fully protected speech? Does such a ruling effectively eliminate the balancing of interests in First Amendment employee claims? What is the precedential source for the Court's reasoning here? What are the implications of such a ruling for the *Jeffries* case now that it has been remanded in light of *Waters* back to the Second Circuit? Are there implications for the *Levin* case as well?

B. SCHOOL CONTROL OF TEACHER CONDUCT

1. OUTSIDE THE SCHOOL

Many school board regulations once proscribed the association of unchaperoned female school teachers with males other than their fathers and brothers. The possible detrimental effects of such associations on the education and moral development of students underlay these strictures.

More recently, state law and school board regulations have prohibited allegedly dangerous political and sexual behaviors. The effect of these behaviors on students is often unascertainable as a question of fact, but because the "gut feeling" in many communities is that they are harmful, courts are faced with determining what rules proscribing those behaviors involve appropriate means to legitimate state ends.

KEYISHIAN v. BOARD OF REGENTS
Supreme Court of the United States
385 U.S. 589 (1967)

MR. JUSTICE BRENNAN delivered the opinion of the Court:

Appellants were members of the faculty of the privately owned and operated University of Buffalo, and became state employees when the University was merged in 1962 into the State University of New York, an institution of higher education owned and operated by the State of New York. As faculty members of the State University their continued employment was conditioned upon their compliance with a New York plan, formulated partly in statutes and partly in administrative regulations, which the State utilizes to prevent the appointment or retention of 'subversive' persons in state employment.

Our Nation is deeply committed to safeguarding academic freedom, which is of transcendent value to all of us and not merely to the teachers concerned. That freedom is therefore a special concern of the First Amendment, which does not tolerate laws that cast a pall of orthodoxy over the classroom. "The vigilant protection of constitutional freedoms nowhere more vital than in the community of American schools." The classroom is peculiarly the "marketplace of ideas." The Nation's future depends upon leaders trained through wide exposure to that robust exchange of ideas which discovers truth "out of a multitude of tongues, (rather) than through any kind of authoritative selection." *United States v. Associated Press, D.C.*, 52 F.Supp. 362, 372. In *Sweezy v. State of New Hampshire*, 354 U.S. 234, 250, we said:

> The essentiality of freedom in the community of American universities is almost self-evident. No one should underestimate the vital role in a democracy that is played by those who guide and train our youth. To impose any strait jacket upon the intellectual leaders in our colleges and universities would imperil the future of our Nation. No field of education is so thoroughly comprehended by man that new discoveries cannot yet be made. Particularly is that true in the social sciences, where few, if any, principles are accepted as absolutes. Scholarship cannot flourish in an atmosphere of suspicion and distrust. Teachers and students must always remain free to inquire, to study and to evaluate, to gain new maturity and understanding; otherwise our civilization will stagnate and die.

We emphasize once again that "[p]recision of regulation must be the touchstone in an area so closely touching our most precious freedoms," *N.A.A.C.P. v. Button*, 371 U.S. 415, 438; "[f]or standards of permissible statutory vagueness are strict in the area of free expression.... Because First Amendment freedoms need breathing space to survive, government may regulate in the area only with narrow specificity." *Id.* at 432-33. New York's complicated and intricate scheme plainly violates that standard. When one must guess what conduct or utterance may lost him his position, one necessarily will "steer far wider of the unlawful zone ...." *Speiser v. Randall*, 357 U.S. 513, 526, ... For "[t]he threat of sanctions may deter ... almost as potently as the actual application of sanctions." *NAACP. v. Button, supra*, 371 U.S. at 433. The danger of that chilling effect upon the exercise of vital First Amendment rights must be guarded against by sensitive tools which clearly inform teachers what is being proscribed. *See Stromberg v. People of State of Board of Public Instruction*, 368 U.S. 278.

The regulatory maze created by New York is wholly lacking in "terms susceptible of objective measurement." *Cramp v. Board of Public Instruction, supra*, at 286. It has the quality of "extraordinary ambiguity" found to be fatal to the oaths considered in *Cramp* and *Baggett v. Bullitt*. "[M]en of common intelligence must necessarily guess at its meaning and differ as to its application ...." *Baggett v. Bullitt, supra*, 377 U.S. at 367. Vagueness of wording is

B. SCHOOL CONTROL OF TEACHER CONDUCT

aggravated by prolixity and profusion of statutes, regulations, and administrative machinery, and by manifold cross-references to interregulated enactments and rules.

We therefore hold that § 3021 of the Education Law and subdivisions 1(a), 1(b) and 3 of § 105 of the Civil Service Law as implemented by the machinery created pursuant to § 3022 of the Education Law are unconstitutional.

....

... In *Elfbrandt v. Russell*, 384 U.S. 11, we said, "Those who join an organization but do not share its unlawful purposes and who do not participate in its unlawful activities surely pose no threat, either as citizens or as public employees." *Id.* at 17. We there struck down a statutorily required oath binding the state employee not to become a member of the Communist Party with knowledge of its unlawful purpose, on threat of discharge and perjury prosecution if the oath were violated. We found that "[a]ny lingering doubt that proscription of mere knowing membership, without any showing of 'specific intent,' would run afoul of the Constitution was set at rest by our decision in *Aptheker v. Secretary of State*, 378 U.S. 500." *Elfbrandt v. Russell, supra*, at 16. In *Aptheker* we held that Party membership, without knowledge of the Party's unlawful purposes and specific intent to further its unlawful aims, could not constitutionally warrant deprivation of the right to travel abroad. As we said in *Schneiderman v. United States*, 320 U.S. 118, 136, "[u]nder our traditions beliefs are personal and not a matter of mere association, and ... men in adhering to a political party or other organization ... do not subscribe unqualifiedly to all of its platforms or asserted principles." "A law which applies to membership without the 'specific intent' to further the illegal aims of the organization infringes unnecessarily on protected freedoms. It rests on the doctrine of 'guilt by association' which has no place here." *Elfbrandt, supra*, at 19. Thus mere Party membership, even with knowledge of the Party's unlawful goals, cannot suffice to justify criminal punishment, *see Scales v. United States*, 367 U.S. 203; *Noto v. United States*, 367 U.S. 290; *Yates v. United States*, 354 U.S. 298; nor may it warrant a finding of moral unfitness justifying disbarment. *Schware v. Board of Bar Examiners*, 353 U.S. 232.

These limitations clearly apply to a provision, like § 105, subd. 1(c), which blankets all state employees, regardless of the "sensitivity" of their positions. But even the Feinberg Law provision, applicable primarily to activities of teachers, who have captive audiences of young minds, are subject to these limitations in favor of freedom of expression and association; the stifling effect on the academic mind from curtailing freedom of association in such manner is manifest, and has been documented in recent studies. *Elfbrandt* and *Aptheker* state the governing standard: legislation which sanctions membership unaccompanied by specific intent to further the unlawful goals of the organization or which is not active membership violates constitutional limitations.

Measured against this standard, both Civil Service Law § 105, subd. 1(c), and Education Law § 3022, subd. 2, sweep overbroadly into association which may not be proscribed. The presumption of disqualification arising from proof of mere membership may be rebutted, but only by (a) a denial of membership, (b) a denial that the organization advocates the overthrow of government by force, or (c) a denial that the teacher has knowledge of such advocacy. *Lederman v. Board of Education*, 276 App. Div. 527, 96 N.Y.S.2d 466, *aff'd*, 301 N.Y. 476, 95 N.E.2d 806. Thus proof of nonactive membership or a showing of the absence of intent to further unlawful aims will not rebut the presumption and defeat dismissal. This is emphasized in official administrative interpretations. For example, it is said in a letter addressed to prospective appointees by the President of the State University, "You will note that ... both the Law and regulations are very specifically directed toward the elimination and nonappointment of 'Communists' from or to our teaching ranks...." The Feinberg Certificate was even more explicit: "Anyone who is a member of the Communist Party or of any organization that advocates the violent overthrow of the Government of the United States or of the State of New York or any political subdivision thereof cannot be employed by the State University." This official administrative interpretation is supported by the legislative preamble to the Feinberg Law, § 1, in which the legislature concludes as a result of its findings that "it is essential that the laws prohibiting persons who are members of subversive groups, such as the communist party and its affiliated organizations, from obtaining or retaining employment in the public schools, be rigorously enforced."

Thus § 105, subd. 1(c), and § 3022, subd. 2, suffer from impermissible "overbreadth." *Elfbrandt v. Russell, supra*, at 19; *Aptheker v. Secretary of State, supra*; *N.A.A.C.P. v. Button, supra*; *Saia v. New York*, 334 U.S. 558; *Schneider v. State*, 308 U.S. 147; *Lovell v. Griffin*, 303 U.S. 444; *cf. Hague v. C.I.O.*, 307 U.S. 496, 515-16; *see generally Dombrowski v. Pfister*, 380 U.S. 479, 486. They seek to bar employment both for association which legitimately may be proscribed and for association which may not be proscribed consistently with First Amendment rights. Where statutes have an overbroad sweep, just as where they are vague, "the hazard of loss or substantial impairment of those precious rights may be critical," *Dombrowski v. Pfister, supra*, at 486, since those covered by the statute are bound to limit their behavior to that which is unquestionably safe. As we said in *Shelton v. Tucker, supra*, at 488, "The breadth of legislative abridgment must be viewed in the light of less drastic means for achieving the same basic purpose."

We therefore hold that Civil Service Law § 105, subd. 1(c), and Education Law § 3022, subd. 2, are invalid insofar as they proscribe mere knowing membership without any showing of specific intent to further the unlawful aims of the Communist Party of the United States or of the State of New York.

The judgment of the District Court is reversed and the case is remanded for further proceedings consistent with this opinion.

Reversed and remanded.

B. SCHOOL CONTROL OF TEACHER CONDUCT

1. Consider a loyalty oath which would require a teacher to swear to the following: (1) "that I am not a member of the Communist Party," (2) "that I have not and will not lend my aid, support, advice, council or influence to the Communist Party," (3) "that I am not a member of any organization or party which believes in or teaches, directly or indirectly, the overthrow of the Government of the United States or of [this state] by force or violence," (4) "that I will support the Constitution of the United States and of [this state]," and (5) "that I do not believe in the overthrow of the Government of the United States or of [this state] by force or violence." *See Connell v. Higgenbotham*, 403 U.S. 207 (1970), upholding three and invalidating two of these clauses. *See also Cole v. Richardson*, 405 U.S. 676 (1972), upholding a Massachusetts statute requiring state employees to swear that they "will oppose the overthrow of the government of the United States of America or of this Commonwealth by force, violence, or by any illegal or unconstitutional method."

2. Many states list immorality as a ground for teacher dismissal. Dismissals under these statutes, although sometimes for criminal offenses, are usually for extra-marital sexual behavior. As the courts have developed a constitutional right to privacy, the challenge to dismissals under these statutes have increased. Where sexual improprieties include students, teacher dismissals are almost always upheld. Where the disapproved behavior is between consenting adults, the issues are more difficult and the results more varied.

3. Immorality as a defense held up in two cases involving openly homosexual public employees. In *Gaylor v. Tacoma School Dist.*, 88 Wash. 2d 286, 559 P.2d 1340, *cert. denied*, 434 U.S. 879 (1977), two issues were discussed: 1) whether substantial evidence existed to prove that Gaylord was guilty of immorality, and 2) whether Gaylord's status as a homosexual impaired his fitness as a teacher. The court upheld his dismissal, citing a State immorality statute and establishing that his teaching was impaired.

See also National Gay Task Force v. Board of Educ. of Oklahoma City, 729 F.2d 1270 (10th Cir. 1984). The Task Force brought suit challenging the constitutionality of a statute which suspended teachers for "public homosexual conduct." The Court of Appeals upheld the constitutionality of the statute, holding that the definition of "public homosexual activity" was not unconstitutionally vague, and that classification based on choice of sexual partners was not subject to strict scrutiny equal protection analysis. Note that the court held that mere advocacy of homosexuality was not unconstitutional.

4. What about contrary political affiliations? In *Saquebo v. Rogue*, 716 F. Supp. 709 (D. Puerto Rico 1989), defendant Puerto Rico Department of Education was granted a summary judgment when the plaintiff Saquebo failed to show that nonrenewal of contract was due to political discrimination. Saquebo was an active member of the New Progressive Party (in favor of Statehood for Puerto Rico). The new employee brought in to replace her was a member of the rival Popular Democratic Party.

For a stronger case on the plaintiff's side, *see Karetnikova v. Trustees of Emerson College*, 725 F. Supp. 73 (D. Mass. 1989), where motion to dismiss First Amendment claims was denied in a case brought by a college professor who claimed she was denied tenure due to her conservative political views, despite her outstanding professorial record.

5. In *Keyishian*, the Court specifically recognized the free expression rights of colleges and universities and the fact that even government awarding of funds could not overcome those rights based on the existence of vagueness and overbreadth doctrines. Has what was thought to be axiomatic in academic circles become attenuated by recent decisions of the Supreme Court? *Rust v. Sullivan*, 500 U.S. 173 (1991), a non-education case on its face, could be seen as just such a decision; relevant excerpts are included herein.

[The case concerned a federal statute providing funding for family planning services, but excluding programs where abortion could be used as such a method. Grantees of the funds challenged the regulations as unconstitutional contending that, among other things, the statute's regulations conditioned the receipt of funds on the weakening of First Amendment rights. They also asserted that the regulations discriminated on the basis of viewpoint, that, too, a First Amendment violation. The Supreme Court upheld the regulations stating that the federal government was free to implement policies in favor of non-abortion related methods of family planning and thus restrict the activities, even the speech activities, of clinics and researchers who receive federal funds.]

Petitioners contend that the regulations violate the First Amendment by impermissibly discriminating based on viewpoint.... The Government can, without violating the Constitution, selectively fund a program to encourage certain activities it believes to be in the public interest, without at the same time funding an alternate program which seeks to deal with the problem in another way. In so doing, the Government has not discriminated on the basis of viewpoint; it has merely chosen to fund one activity to the exclusion of the other.... *Id*. at 192.

....

To hold that the Government unconstitutionally discriminates on the basis of viewpoint when it chooses to fund a program dedicated to advance certain permissible goals, because the program in advancing those goals necessarily discourages alternate goals, would render numerous government programs constitutionally suspect. When Congress established a National Endowment for Democracy to encourage other countries to adopt democratic principles, 22 U.S.C. § 4411(b), it was not constitutionally required to fund a program to encourage competing lines of political philosophy such as Communism and Fascism. Petitioners' assertions ultimately boil down to the position that if the government chooses to subsidize one protected right, it must subsidize analogous counterpart rights. But the Court has soundly rejected that

B. SCHOOL CONTROL OF TEACHER CONDUCT

proposition.... Within far broader limits than petitioners are willing to concede, when the government appropriates public funds to establish a program it is entitled to define the limits of that program.

... [W]e have here not the case of a general law singling out a disfavored group on the basis of speech content, but a case of the Government refusing to fund activities, including speech, which are specifically excluded from the scope of the project funded. *Id.* at 194.

....

Petitioners also contend that the restrictions [in the statute] — related speech contained in the regulations are impermissible because they condition the receipt of a benefit, in this case Title X funding, on the relinquishment of a constitutional right, the right to engage in abortion advocacy and counseling. Relying on *Perry v. Sindermann*, 408 U.S. 593, 597, petitioners argue that "even though the government may deny [a] ... benefit for any number of reasons, there are some reasons upon which the government may not rely. It may not deny a benefit to a person on a basis that infringes his constitutionally protected interests — especially his interest in freedom of speech." *Perry, supra*, 408 U.S. at 597. *Id.* at 195.

Petitioners' reliance on th[is] case ... is unavailing, however, because here the government is not denying a benefit to anyone, but is instead simply insisting that public funds be spent for the purposes for which they were authorized. The Secretary's regulations do not force the Title X grantee to give up abortion-related speech; they merely require that the grantee keep such activities separate and distinct from Title X activities. Title X expressly distinguishes between a Title X grantee and a Title X project. The grantee, which normally is a health care organization, may receive funds from a variety of sources for a variety of purposes. The grantee receives Title X funds, however, for the specific and limited purpose of establishing and operating a Title X project. 42 U.S.C. § 300(a). The regulations govern the scope of the Title X project's activities, and leave the grantee unfettered in its other activities. The Title X grantee can continue to perform abortions, provide abortion-related services, and engage in abortion advocacy; it simply is required to conduct those activities through programs that are separate and independent from the project that receives Title X funds. 42 CFR 59.9 (1989). *Id.* at 196.

In contrast, our "unconstitutional conditions" cases involve situations in which the government has placed a condition on the recipient of the subsidy rather than on a particular program or service, thus effectively prohibiting the recipient from engaging in the protected conduct outside the scope of the federally funded program.... *Id.* at 197.

....

By requiring that the Title X grantee engage in abortion-related activity separately from activity receiving federal funding, Congress has ... not denied it the right to engage in abortion-related activities. Congress has merely refused to fund such activities out of the public fisc, and the Secretary has simply required a certain degree of separation from the Title X project in order to ensure the integrity of the federally funded program.

The same principles apply to petitioners' claim that the regulations abridge the free speech rights of the grantee's staff. Individuals who are voluntarily employed for a Title X project must perform their duties in accordance with the regulation's restrictions on abortion counseling and referral. The employees remain free, however, to pursue abortion-related activities when they are not acting under the auspices of the Title X project. The regulations, which govern solely the scope of the Title X project's activities, do not in any way restrict the activities of those persons acting as private individuals. The employees' freedom of expression is limited during the time that they actually work for the project; but this limitation is a consequence of their decision to accept employment in a project, the scope of which is permissibly restricted by the funding authority.[5] *Id.* at 198-99.

What is the message for teachers in *Rust*? Is it that "government may allocate the public's resources any time the political majority chooses to and it may enforce generally applicable laws regardless of their incidental infringement on constitutionally protected conduct"? *See* C. Freelan, *The Political Process as Final Solution*, 68 Ind. L.J. 525 (1993).*

---

[5]Petitioners also contend that the regulations violate the First Amendment by penalizing speech funded with non-Title X monies. They argue that since Title X requires that grant recipients contribute to the financing of Title X projects through the use of matching funds and grant-related income, the regulation's restrictions on abortion counseling and advocacy penalize the privately funded speech.

We find this argument flawed for several reasons. First, Title X subsidies are just that, subsidies. The recipient is in no way compelled to operate a Title X project; to avoid the force of the regulations, it can simply decline the subsidy. *See Grove City College v. Bell*, 465 U.S. 555, 575 (1984) (petitioner's First Amendment rights not violated because it "may terminate its participation in the [federal] program and thus avoid the requirements of [the federal program]"). By accepting Title X funds, a recipient voluntarily consents to any restrictions placed on any matching funds or grant-related income. Potential grant recipients can choose between accepting Title X funds — subject to the Government's conditions that they provide matching funds and forgo abortion counseling and referral in the Title X project — or declining the subsidy and financing their own unsubsidized program. We have never held that the Government violates the First Amendment simply by offering that choice. Second, the Secretary's regulations apply only to Title X programs. A recipient is therefore able to "limi[t] the use of its federal funds to [Title X] activities.".... It is in no way "barred from using even wholly private funds to finance" its pro-abortion activities outside the Title X program. The regulations are limited to Title X funds; the recipient remains free to use private, non-Title X funds to finance abortion-related activities.

*Copyright 1993 by the Trustees of Indiana University. Reprinted with permission.

B. SCHOOL CONTROL OF TEACHER CONDUCT

Does the case stand for a new phase in academic expression where government may condition the granting of funds on the abandonment or modification of First Amendment rights?

Consider the following: Plaintiffs in *Rust* relied on *Perry v. Sindermann*, 408 U.S. 593 (1972):

> [E]ven though a person has no right to a valuable governmental benefit and even though the government may deny him the benefit for any number of reasons, there are some reasons upon which the government may not rely. It may not deny a benefit to a person on a basis that infringes his constitutionally protected interests — especially, his interest in freedom of speech. To do so would allow the government to produce a result which [it] could not command directly. *Id.* at 597.

What force did *Sindermann* have with the majority in *Rust*? Is the Supreme Court moving away from some of the time-honored traditions of what it calls "unconstitutional conditions" cases? For a cogent analysis of the Court routinely departing from such purported rules against free speech infringement *see* The Honorable John Paul Stevens, *The Freedom of Speech*, 102 Yale L.J. 1293 (1993).

6. Does the Court in *Rust* make a distinction between restrictions on the recipient programs themselves and the persons who work in those programs? Specifically, when is the speaker's speech protected? May protection lie while working on a research project, but speaking at a public forum? Does the content of the speech affect the Court's determination as to restrictions?

7. Is it possible that the decision in *Rust* could directly or indirectly command broad speech restrictions in public schools, or colleges and universities by depriving non-conformists of the public dollar?

8. The decision in *Rust* would appear to give a negative answer to the question of an abridgment of free speech rights of the university. In fact, the majority in that case particularly notes a university exemption, preserving the doctrine of academic freedom and the support of free speech:

> This is not to suggest that funding by the Government, even when coupled with the freedom of the fund recipients to speak outside the scope of the Government-funded project, is invariably sufficient to justify government control over the content of expression. For example, this Court has recognized that the existence of a Government "subsidy," in the form of Government-owned property, does not justify the restriction of speech in areas that have "been traditionally open to the public for expressive activity," .... Similarly, we have recognized that the university is a traditional sphere of free expression so fundamental to the functioning of our society that the Government's ability to control speech within that sphere by means of conditions attached to the expenditure of Government funds is restricted by the vagueness and overbreadth of the First Amendment,

Keyishian v. Board of Regents, 385 U.S. 589....*Rust v. Sullivan*, 500 U.S. at 199-200.

9. However, the Justice Department, using *Rust*, has attempted in one case to contend that the government may place free speech limitations on the grant of federal research funds to universities. In *Board of Trustees of Leland Stanford, Jr. Univ. v. Sullivan*, 773 F. Supp. 472 (D.D.C. 1991), the National Institutes of Health offered the university a contract for clinical testing. That offer was withdrawn when Stanford declined to incorporate a clause in the contract prohibiting the grantee from disclosing findings that could create erroneous conclusions or place the grantor government agency in less than a positive light. Stanford sued alleging a supression of speech as a condition for the grant when all other elements of eligibility had been satisfied. The government contended that *Rust* would place this issue under the "non-subsidy doctrine" (plaintiff is free to exercise its free-speech rights with private funds, but not necessarily public funds; government is free to condition its funding on the basis of reasonable requirements), as this is far from a suppression of rights. *Id.* at 475. The district court ruled for the university indicating the government restriction bound the grantee broadly and not merely based on the work in the research project. *Id.* at 476. The contract clause would inhibit speech as the university researchers could not speak on their work, without permission from the grantor, even if they were then being paid solely by the university. *Id.* In addition, the court applied the "university exceptions clause" in *Rust* (*see* above, note 8) and held a violation of academic freedom as the clause could cause the research not to be published as a way of not risking a violation of the contract. *Id.* at 477.

10. As noted, *Stanford* is the only test case to date applying *Rust* to the academic enterprise. However, from both cases (*Rust* and *Stanford*), it is unclear whether the academic freedom announced in *Keyishian* has remained intact and unchanged. The majority in *Rust* pronounced a violation of free speech rights when government conditions for receipt of the public dollar are vague or overbroad. Does that mean that perspicuous and narrowly-tailored government restrictions on funding would permit a weakening of university free speech?

2. INSIDE THE CLASSROOM

The issues arising from the conflict between public school teachers' rights and responsibilities as citizens and their role as state employees are perhaps most complex in those cases involving teacher performance and behavior in the classroom. Many of these issues already have been dealt with at length. The following case illustrates some of the problems arising from the conflict between teachers' roles as citizen and employee and demonstrates some of the approaches taken by the courts in attempting to balance a school district's need for discretion in the substantive aspect of teacher evaluation and dismissal against the district's duty to follow constitutionally, statutorily and contractually guaranteed procedures.

BRADLEY v. PITTSBURGH BOARD OF EDUCATION

United States Court of Appeals
910 F.2d 1172 (3d Cir. 1990)

SLOVITER, CIRCUIT JUDGE:

I

Plaintiff [Diane Murray,] is an advocate of Learnball, a classroom management technique developed by Dr. Earl Bradley, also a teacher in the Pittsburgh public schools and a co-plaintiff in the district court. Learnball's basic elements, which include a sports format, peer approval, dividing each class into teams, student election of team leaders and an assistant teacher, giving students responsibility for establishing class rules and grading exercises, and imposing a system of rewards such as radio playing and shooting baskets with a foam ball in the classroom, are described in the Learnball Handbook. Murray is the executive director of the Learnball League International, which promotes the use of Learnball. Murray alleges that she has used Learnball in her classroom for over a decade and that the system has been adopted by many teachers.

Defendants were not supportive of Murray or Bradley's use of Learnball. They admonished both to limit their use of the method and Bradley was eventually fired, allegedly for violating orders that he cease using certain techniques associated with Learnball.

Murray filed suit on July 8, 1986, with Bradley as her co-plaintiff, alleging that defendants had harassed her because of her advocacy and use of Learnball and that they required her to limit her use of Learnball although there is no policy concerning general classroom management techniques teachers may use. She seeks compensatory and punitive damages, an injunction against violating her constitutional rights, and attorneys' fees. Defendants' motion to dismiss this suit was denied.

....

On August 26, 1988, just before the start of the following school year, Phillips informed plaintiff that she could not use Learnball at all because he did "not consider Learnball to be benefiting our students." Murray then filed the motion for a preliminary injunction at issue here on September 13, 1988.... The district court denied the motion on September 11, 1989.

II

....

Murray contends that she has a right to academic freedom that encompasses the right to use Learnball. She describes Learnball as "a classroom management system" rather than as communicating any subject content material. She contends that

> because it is not a teaching method and does not interfere in any manner with regulation by the state and school district concerning facts to be taught,

it is mainly a method for Murray to express her positive personality, feelings, and philosophy to her students. In that regard ... Learnball is a political statement on Murray's part.

In this case we do not have to delineate the scope of academic freedom afforded to teachers under the First Amendment rights. *See Tinker v. Des Moines Indep. Community School Dist.*, 393 U.S. 503, 506 (1969) (student armbands in protest against war protected; teachers mentioned in dictum); *Keyishian v. Board of Regents of the Univ. of New York*, 385 U.S. 589, 603 (1967) (striking down loyalty oaths). Some courts have found this right to encompass the right to exercise professional judgment in selecting topics and materials for use in class. *See, e.g., Kingsville Indep. School Dist. v. Cooper*, 611 F.2d 1109 (5th Cir.1980) (dismissal of teacher for discussing racial issues in class violates First Amendment).

However, no court has found that teachers' First Amendment rights extend to choosing their own curriculum or classroom management techniques in contravention of school policy or dictates. *See, e.g., Hetrick v. Martin*, 480 F.2d 705 (6th Cir.) (pedagogical methods in classroom are not a protected form of speech), *cert. denied*, 414 U.S. 1075 (1973); *Adams v. Campbell County School Dist.*, 511 F.2d 1242 (10th Cir.1975) (dismissal of high school teachers for failure to discipline their classes, being too informal, discussing current events at the expense of finishing the curriculum, and playing records in class permissible where dismissal not motivated by teachers' political opinions); *Ahern v. Board of Educ. of Grand Island*, 456 F.2d 399 (8th Cir.1972) (high school teacher discharged for introducing methods very similar to Learnball had no right to use methods or teach certain topics in contravention of school policy).

Although a teacher's out-of-class conduct, including her advocacy of particular teaching methods, is protected, *see Pickering v. Board of Educ.*, 391 U.S. 563, 568 (1968) (dismissal of a teacher for writing a letter to a newspaper criticizing the school violates First Amendment), her in-class conduct is not. *See Clark v. Holmes*, 474 F.2d 928 (7th Cir.1972) (per curiam) (upholding firing of teacher whose biology classes contained too much discussion of sex), *cert. denied*, 411 U.S. 972 (1973).

In this case, it is undisputed that defendants have determined that Learnball is not an appropriate pedagogical method. They are entitled to make this determination. Murray has no right of academic freedom that extends to the choice of Learnball classroom management techniques despite the school's ban or that would render the ban unconstitutional.

However, Murray also argues that defendants have engaged in a pattern of harassment which is "a conscious effort to punish and restrict [her] First Amendment activity outside the classroom by curtailing her activities which symbolize her First Amendment activities inside the classroom." If the evidence sustains this claim, it would show conduct that violates Murray's First Amendment rights because the School District's undisputed right to control the classroom curriculum does not extend to a right to control a teacher's proselytization of teaching methods. *See Pickering*, 391 U.S. at 568. Nor can a teacher suffer retaliation for criticism of school officials outside the classroom. *See Trotman v. Board of Trustees of Lincoln Univ.*, 635 F.2d 216 (3d Cir.1980), *cert. denied*, 451 U.S. 986 (1981).

Moreover, Murray contends that defendants' actions, including banning Learnball, ... were motivated not only by the desire to chill her First Amendment activity but also by the wish to retaliate for the filing of this lawsuit. An action that would otherwise be permissible is unconstitutional if it is taken in retaliation for the exercise of the right of access to the courts. Although most cases concerning retaliation in violation of the right of access to the court have arisen in the prison context, the same principles have been applied in other areas. *See California Motor Transp. Co. v. Trucking Unlimited*, 404 U.S. 508, 510 (1972); *Soranno's Gasco, Inc. v. Morgan*, 874 F.2d 1310 (9th Cir. 1989); *Harrison v. Springdale Water & Sewer Comm'n*, 780 F.2d 1422 (8th Cir. 1986); *Cate v. Oldham*, 707 F.2d 1176 (11th Cir. 1983)....

Murray's final claim is that the ban on Learnball is vague and overbroad in violation of the First Amendment. Murray argues that Learnball includes a wide range of class management techniques, such as writing rules on the blackboard and dividing students into teams, many of which are used by other teachers. She argues that the vague direction puts her at risk of discipline because she does not know which particular activities defendants will consider to be part of Learnball. She claims that Bradley was fired for Learnball behavior such as using a gavel, letting students have access to the grade book, and not giving enough homework, and argues that her behavior is chilled and that it is difficult for her to teach.

Although Murray couches her claim in First Amendment terms, her argument is basically a due process one. We have stated in a different context that a rule that forbids the doing of an act in terms so vague that people of common intelligence must guess as to its meaning and differ as to its application violates due process. *See Aiello v. City of Wilmington*, 623 F.2d 845 (3d Cir. 1980).

Because at least some of Murray's claims are legally viable, if the district court denied the preliminary injunction on the ground that all of her claims were legally defective, it erred as a matter of law. On the other hand, the district court may have concluded that Murray's affidavits failed to make a sufficient showing that the school's actions against her were motivated by her out-of-class advocacy of Learnball, her criticisms of the school, or her filing of a lawsuit.

. . . .

The reasons for requiring the district court to give the required explanation for its decision are self-evident, and particularly applicable in this case. Foremost, as the Court noted in *Mayo* [*v. Lakeland Highlands Canning Co.*], "[s]uch findings are obviously necessary to the intelligent and orderly presentation and proper disposition of an appeal." 309 U.S. [310,] 317 [(1940)]. Further, the existence of findings limits the issues on appeal and is important to the determination of res judicata or collateral estoppel questions that may arise in the future. *See [Professional Plan Examiners v.] LeFante*, 750 F.2d at 289 [(3d Cir. 1984)]. Arguably, factual findings when the court denies a preliminary injunction may serve little purpose when there has been no hearing, but conclusions of law are nonetheless essential and the factual bases on which the conclusions are predicated, whether derived from affidavits or testimony, serve to permit evaluation of the legal conclusions reached by the district court.

....

III

For the reasons set forth above, we will vacate the district court's order denying the preliminary injunction and remand for further proceedings....

---

1. It is true, from *Bradley*, that the school may not punish and restrict a teacher's activities inside the classroom in an effort to punish or restrict his or her activities outside the classroom. But what does this holding do to the limits of activity in the classroom? Refer to note 1 following *Tinker v. Des Moines* in Chapter 6. Should teachers be given more latitude in designing lessons and projects for their students, especially when there is a push for more creative, analytic education rather than the prescriptive approach? Should we not encourage teachers to explore new avenues of learning which may, in effect, encourage expansion in free speech and expression for both students and teachers without causing serious disruption of the operation of schools or substantial infringement of the rights of others?

2. The courts, however expansive as many are, have placed limits on the avenues which teachers take in creating lesson plans. In *Krizek v. Board of Educ. of Cicero-Stickney Twp. High Sch. Dist.*, 713 F. Supp. 1131 (M.D. Ill. 1989), a teacher's contract was not renewed after the teacher showed an R-rated film ("About Last Night") to her class as a modern parallel to Thornton Wilder's "Our Town." The District Court denied the teacher's motion for a preliminary injunction. *See also Fowler v. Board of Educ. of Lincoln County, Kentucky*, 819 F.2d 657 (6th Cir. 1987) and related discussion in Chapter 3.

doctrine announced by this Court in *Plessy v. Ferguson*, 163 U.S. 537. Under that doctrine, equality of treatment is accorded when the races are provided substantially equal facilities, even though these facilities be separate. In the Delaware case, the Supreme Court of Delaware adhered to that doctrine, but ordered that the plaintiffs be admitted to the white schools because of their superiority to the Negro schools.

The plaintiffs contend that segregated public schools are not "equal" and cannot be made "equal," and that hence they are deprived of the equal protection of the laws. Because of the obvious importance of the question presented, the Court took jurisdiction. Argument was heard in the 1952 Term, and reargument was heard this Term on certain questions propounded by the Court.

Reargument was largely devoted to the circumstances surrounding the adoption of the Fourteenth Amendment in 1868. It covered exhaustively consideration of the Amendment in Congress, ratification by the states, then existing practices in racial segregation, and the views of proponents and opponents of the Amendment. This discussion and our own investigation convince us that, although these sources cast some light, it is not enough to resolve the problem with which we are faced. At best, they are inconclusive. The most avid proponents of the post-War Amendments undoubtedly intended them to remove all legal distinctions among "all persons born or naturalized in the United States." Their opponents, just as certainly, were antagonistic to both the letter and the spirit of the Amendments and wished them to have the most limited effect. What others in Congress and the state legislatures had in mind cannot be determined with any degree of certainty.

An additional reason for the inconclusive nature of the Amendment's history, with respect to segregated schools, is the status of public education at that time. In the South, the movement toward free common schools, supported by general taxation, had not yet taken hold. Education of white children was largely in the hands of private groups. Education of Negroes was almost nonexistent, and practically all of the race were illiterate. In fact, any education of Negroes was forbidden by law in some states. Today, in contrast, many Negroes have achieved outstanding success in the arts and sciences as well as in the business and professional world. It is true that public school education at the time of the Amendment had advanced further in the North, but the effect of the Amendment on Northern States was generally ignored in the congressional debates. Even in the North, the conditions of public education did not approximate those existing today. The curriculum was usually rudimentary; ungraded schools were common in rural areas; the school term was but three months a year in many states; and compulsory school attendance was virtually unknown. As a consequence, it is not surprising that there should be so little in the history of the Fourteenth Amendment relating to its intended effect on public education.

In the first cases in this Court construing the Fourteenth Amendment, decided shortly after its adoption, the Court interpreted it as proscribing all state-imposed

Chapter 11
RACIAL SEGREGATION IN THE PUBLIC SCHOOLS

Racial desegregation in the public schools has been widely discussed in many different forums from many different viewpoints: legal doctrine, social science findings, political and social dogmas, popular opinions, etc. The legitimacy of school desegregation is a perennial subject of profound national debate. This chapter views the development of Supreme Court decisions from *Brown v. Board of Educ.* through the most recent cases of *Board of Educ. of Oklahoma City Pub. Schs. v. Dowell* and *Freeman v. Pitts* in an attempt to discover, analyze, and criticize the development of the law in this area. The notes attempt to question why the courts have focused their attention on narrow areas of inquiry such as intent on the part of school boards to discriminate while assiduously refusing to address other unconstitutional sources of school segregation. The notes can also be seen as a broader attempt to relate the issues of racial segregation to other areas of discrimination such as that against disabled students, non-English speakers, women and girls, and persons of different religious persuasions. The dictates of *Brown*, for example, serve as the foundation for many of the cases in special education law and gender discrimination. Moreover, *Brown* and its antecedents have had a profound effect upon cases involving ability grouping as seen in Chapter 12. These pervasive issues, which embody a fundamental clash between values of assimilation on the one hand and pluralism on the other, have, and will continue to engage our attention in this book.

BROWN v. BOARD OF EDUCATION
Supreme Court of the United States
347 U.S. 483 (1954)

Mr. Chief Justice Warren delivered the opinion of the Court:

These cases come to us from the States of Kansas, South Carolina, Virginia, and Delaware. They are premised on different facts and different local conditions, but a common legal question justifies their consideration together in this consolidated opinion.

In each of the cases, minors of the Negro race, through their legal representatives, seek the aid of the courts in obtaining admission to the public schools of their community on a non-segregated basis. In each instance, they had been denied admission to schools attended by white children under laws requiring or permitting segregation according to race. This segregation was alleged to deprive the plaintiffs of the equal protection of the laws under the Fourteenth Amendment. In each of the cases other than the Delaware case, a three-judge federal district court denied relief to the plaintiffs on the so-called "separate but equal"

PART FOUR

EQUAL EDUCATIONAL OPPORTUNITY

discriminations against the Negro race. The doctrine of "separate but equal" did not make its appearance in this Court until 1896 in the case of *Plessy v. Ferguson, supra,* involving not education but transportation. American courts have since labored with the doctrine for over half a century. In this Court, there have been six cases involving the "separate but equal" doctrine in the field of public education. In *Cumming v. County Board of Educ.,* 175 U.S. 528, and *Gong Lum v. Rice,* 275 U.S. 78, the validity of the doctrine itself was not challenged. In more recent cases, all on the graduate school level, inequality was found in that specific benefits enjoyed by white students were denied to Negro students of the same educational qualifications. *Missouri ex rel. Gaines v. Canada,* 305 U.S. 337; *Sipuel v. Oklahoma,* 332 U.S. 631; *Sweatt v. Painter,* 339 U.S. 629; *McLaurin v. Oklahoma State Regents,* 339 U.S. 637. In none of these cases was it necessary to re-examine the doctrine to grant relief to the Negro plaintiff. And in *Sweatt v. Painter, supra,* the Court expressly reserved decision on the question whether *Plessy v. Ferguson* should be held inapplicable to public education.

In the instant cases, that question is directly presented. Here, unlike *Sweatt v. Painter,* there are findings below that the Negro and white schools involved have been equalized, or are being equalized, with respect to buildings, curricula, qualifications and salaries of teachers, and other "tangible" factors. Our decision, therefore, cannot turn on merely a comparison of these tangible factors in the Negro and white schools involved in each of the cases. We must look instead to the effect of segregation itself on public education.

In approaching this problem, we cannot turn the clock back to 1868 when the Amendment was adopted, or even to 1896 when *Plessy v. Ferguson* was written. We must consider public education in the light of its full development and its present place in American life throughout the Nation. Only in this way can it be determined if segregation in public schools deprives these plaintiffs of the equal protection of the laws.

Today, education is perhaps the most important function of state and local governments. Compulsory school attendance laws and the great expenditures for education both demonstrate our recognition of the importance of education to our democratic society. It is required in the performance of our most basic public responsibilities, even service in the armed forces. It is the very foundation of good citizenship. Today it is a principal instrument in awakening the child to cultural values, in preparing him for later professional training, and in helping him to adjust normally to his environment. In these days, it is doubtful that any child may reasonably be expected to succeed in life if he is denied the opportunity of an education. Such an opportunity, where the state has undertaken to provide it, is a right which must be made available to all on equal terms.

We come then to the question presented: Does segregation of children in public schools solely on the basis of race, even though the physical facilities and other "tangible" factors may be equal, deprive the children of the minority group of equal educational opportunities? We believe that it does.

In *Sweatt v. Painter, supra,* in finding that a segregated law school for Negroes could not provide them equal educational opportunities, this Court relied in large part on "those qualities which are incapable of objective measurement but which make for greatness in a law school." In *McLaurin v. Oklahoma State Regents, supra,* the Court, in requiring that a Negro admitted to a white graduate school be treated like all other students, again resorted to intangible considerations: "... his ability to study, to engage in discussions and exchange views with other students, and, in general, to learn his profession." Such considerations apply with added force to children in grade and high schools. To separate them from others of similar age and qualifications solely because of their race generates a feeling of inferiority as to their status in the community that may affect their hearts and minds in a way unlikely ever to be undone. The effect of this separation on their educational opportunities was well stated by a finding in the Kansas case by a court which nevertheless felt compelled to rule against the Negro plaintiffs:

> Segregation of white and colored children in public schools has a detrimental effect upon the colored children. The impact is greater when it has the sanction of the law; for the policy of separating the races is usually interpreted as denoting the inferiority of the negro group. A sense of inferiority affects the motivation of a child to learn. Segregation with the sanction of law, therefore, has a tendency to [retard] the educational and mental development of negro children and to deprive them of some of the benefits they would receive in a racial[ly] integrated school system.[10]

Whatever may have been the extent of psychological knowledge at the [t]ime of *Plessy v. Ferguson,* this finding is amply supported by modern authority.[11] Any language in *Plessy v. Ferguson* contrary to this finding is rejected.

We conclude that in the field of public education the doctrine of "separate but equal" has no place. Separate educational facilities are inherently unequal. Therefore, we hold that the plaintiffs and others similarly situated for whom the actions have been brought are, by reason of the segregation complained of, deprived of the equal protection of the laws guaranteed by the Fourteenth

---

[10]A similar finding was made in the Delaware case: "I conclude from the testimony that in our Delaware society, State-imposed segregation in education itself results in the Negro children, as a class, receiving educational opportunities which are substantially inferior to those available to white children otherwise similarly situated." 87 A.2d 862, 865.

[11]K.B. Clark, Effect of Prejudice and Discrimination on Personality Development (Midcentury White House Conference on Children and Youth, 1950); Witmer and Kotinsky, Personality in the Making (1952), c. VI; Dettscher and Chein, *The Psychological Effects of Enforced Segregation: A Survey of Social Science Opinion,* 26 J. Psychol. 259 (1918); Chein, *What are the Psychological Effects of Segregation Under Conditions of Equal Facilities?,* 3 Int. J. Opinion and Attitude Res. 229 (1949); Braineld, Educational Costs, in Discrimination and National Welfare (MacIver, ed., 1949), 44-48; Frazier, The Negro in the United States (1949), 674-81. And *see generally* Myrdal, An American Dilemma (1944).

Amendment. This disposition makes unnecessary any discussion whether such segregation also violates the Due Process Clause of the Fourteenth Amendment.

Because these are class actions, because of the wide applicability of this decision, and because of the great variety of local conditions, the formulation of decrees in these cases presents problems of considerable complexity. On reargument, the consideration of appropriate relief was necessarily subordinated to the primary question — the constitutionality of segregation in public education. We have now announced that such segregation is a denial of the equal protection of the laws. In order that we may have the full assistance of the parties in formulating decrees, the cases will be restored to the docket, and the parties are requested to present further argument on ... [the appropriate decree]. The Attorney General of the United States is again invited to participate. The Attorneys General of the states requiring or permitting segregation in public education will also be permitted to appear as *amici curiae* upon request to do so by September 15, 1954, and submission of briefs by October 1, 1954.

It is so ordered.

---

1. The following year, in *Brown II*, 349 U.S. 294 (1955), the Court stated that, in effectuating *Brown I*, the district courts

> may consider problems related to administration, arising from the physical condition of the school plant, the school transportation system, personnel, revision of school districts and attendance areas into compact units to achieve a system of determining admission to the public schools on a nonracial basis, and revision of local laws and regulations which may be necessary in solving the foregoing problems. They will also consider the adequacy of any plans the defendants may propose to meet these problems and to effectuate a transition to a racially nondiscriminatory school system.
>
> ... [A]nd the cases are remanded to the District Courts to take such proceedings and enter such orders and decrees consistent with this opinion as are necessary and proper to admit to public schools on a racially nondiscriminatory basis with all deliberate speed the parties to these cases. *Id.* at 300-01.

In 1979 a Topeka, Kansas citizens group succeeded in having *Brown I* reopened for a determination of whether the local school board had complied with the Supreme Court's 25 year-old desegregation order. A federal district court judge allowed the Coalition for Equal and Quality Education to intervene in the case on behalf of several children enrolled in city schools, ruling that although no action had occurred in *Brown* since it was remanded to the district court in 1955, the case was never officially closed.

2. The *rationale* of *Brown* immediately became the subject of extensive debate and legal scholarship. A main problem was the extent to which *Brown* rested on

the social science data as to the "inherent inferiority" of segregated black schools and the infliction of mental harm on blacks by racial segregation. Some argued that the case did in fact rest on such data and that the result would change if different data were presented. See Honnold, *Book Review*, 33 Ind. L.J. 612, 614-15 (1958). On the other hand, others rejected this thesis on the basis that the data were too flimsy to justify the *Brown* results. See Cahn, *Jurisprudence*, 30 N.Y.U. L. Rev. 150 (1955). Under this approach the data as to schools were irrelevant and the case was said to have rested on the per se unconstitutionality of compelled racial segregation. Those who took this view found support in the fact that after *Brown* the Court in summary per curiam opinions struck down other forms of state-compelled segregation in such facilities as beaches, golf courses, public transportation, etc., without any reference to social science data.

3. The unanimous decision in *Brown I* declared that the decision of *Plessy v. Ferguson*, 163 U.S. 537 (1896), was overturned. That case upheld a Louisiana law that required "separate but equal" accommodations for African-American and white railroad passengers. The case also marked the evolution of the separate but equal doctrine that governed the Supreme Court's analysis of racially based Equal Protection challenges until *Brown*.

Plessy is as much known for its dissent by Justice Harlan as its majority opinion. In an almost predictive way, part of his opinion produced the following:

> ... [I]n view of the Constitution, in the eye of the law, there is in this country no superior, dominant, ruling class of citizens. There is no caste here. Our Constitution is color-blind, and neither knows nor tolerates classes among citizens. In respect of civil rights, all citizens are equal before the law. The humblest is the peer of the powerful. The law regards man as man, and takes no account of his surroundings or of his color when his civil rights as guaranteed by the supreme law of the land are involved. It is therefore, to be regretted that this high tribunal, the final expositor of the fundamental law of the land, has reached the enjoyment by citizens of their civil rights solely upon the basis of race.
>
> ... In my opinion, the judgement of this day will, in time, prove to be quite ... pernicious .... *Id*. at 559.

4. The Supreme Court intended that *Brown*'s mandate eliminate single-race schools and lead to integration, but can the decision be read more than one way? Did the Court demand racial balance in schools, or did it simply require relative equality of educational opportunity? See the cases that follow in this chapter for interpretive answers.

5. For a seminal history of the lawsuit in *Brown*, see Richard Kluger, *Simple Justice* (1975).

6. Twenty-five years after the original *Brown* decision, suit was brought again by plaintiffs against the school system with the complaint that vestiges of de jure segregation had not been eliminated. In *Brown v. Board of Educ. Topeka, Shawnee County*, 892 F.2d 851 (1989), the Tenth Circuit Court of Appeals found that the school system had not yet reached unitary status and the current condition of segregation was related to that found in previous years. However, the Supreme Court in 1992 granted a petition of certiorari, vacating the judgment in the case and remanded it to the Tenth Circuit for further consideration in light of the decisions in *Board of Educ. of Oklahoma City Pub. Schs. Indep. Sch. Dist. v. Dowell* and *Freeman v. Pitts, infra.*

GREEN v. COUNTY SCHOOL BOARD

Supreme Court of the United States
391 U.S. 430 (1968)

MR. JUSTICE BRENNAN delivered the opinion of the Court:

The question for decision is whether, under all the circumstances here, respondent School Board's adoption of a "freedom-of-choice" plan which allows a pupil to choose his own public school constitutes adequate compliance with the Board's responsibility "to achieve a system of determining admission to the public schools on a nonracial basis...." *Brown v. Board of Education*, 349 U.S. 294, 300-01 (*Brown II*).

Petitioners brought this action in March 1965 seeking injunctive relief against respondent's continued maintenance of an alleged racially segregated school system. New Kent County is a rural county in Eastern Virginia. About one-half of its population of some 4,500 are Negroes. There is no residential segregation in the county; persons of both races reside throughout. The school system has only two schools, the New Kent school on the east side of the county and the George W. Watkins school on the west side. In a memorandum filed May 17, 1966, the District Court found that the "school system serves approximately 1,300 pupils, of which 740 are Negro and 550 are White. The School Board operates one white combined elementary and high school [New Kent], and one Negro combined elementary and high school [George W. Watkins]. There are no attendance zones. Each school serves the entire county." The record indicates that 21 school buses — 11 serving the Watkins school and 10 serving the New Kent school — travel overlapping routes throughout the county to transport pupils to and from the two schools.

The segregated system was initially established and maintained under the compulsion of Virginia constitutional and statutory provisions mandating racial segregation in public education, Va. Const., Art. IX, § 140 (1902); Va. Code § 22-221 (1950). These provisions were held to violate the Federal Constitution in *Davis v. County School Board of Prince Edward County*, decided with *Brown v. Board of Education*, 347 U.S. 483, 487 (*Brown I*). The respondent School Board continued the segregated operation of the system after the *Brown* decisions, presumably on the authority of several statutes enacted by Virginia in resistance to those decisions. Some of these statutes were held to be unconstitutional on their face or as applied. One statute, the Pupil Placement Act, Va. Code § 22-232.1 *et seq.* (1964), not repealed until 1966, divested local boards of authority to assign children to particular schools and placed that authority in a State Pupil Placement Board. Under that Act children were each year automatically reassigned to the school previously attended unless upon their application the State Board assigned them to another school; students seeking enrollment for the first time were also assigned at the discretion of the State Board. To September 1964, no Negro pupil had applied for admission to the New Kent school under this statute and no white pupil had applied for admission to the Watkins school.

The School Board initially sought dismissal of this suit on the ground that petitioners had failed to apply to the State Board for assignment to New Kent school. However on August 2, 1965, five months after the suit was brought, respondent School Board, in order to remain eligible for federal financial aid, adopted a "freedom-of-choice" plan for desegregating the schools.[2] Under that plan, each pupil, except those entering the first and eighth grades, may annually choose between the New Kent and Watkins schools and pupils not making a choice are assigned to the school previously attended; first and eighth grade pupils must affirmatively choose a school. After the plan was filed the District Court denied petitioners' prayer for an injunction and granted respondent leave to submit an amendment to the plan with respect to employment and assignment of teachers and staff on a racially nondiscriminatory basis. The amendment was duly filed and on June 28, 1966, the District Court approved the "freedom-of-choice" plan as so amended. The Court of Appeals for the Fourth Circuit, *en banc*, 382 F.2d 338, affirmed the District Court's approval of the "freedom-of-choice" provisions of the plan but remanded the case to the District Court for entry of an order regarding faculty "which is much more specific and more comprehensive" and which would incorporate in addition to a "minimal, objective time table" some of the faculty provisions of the decree entered by the

---

[2]Congress, concerned with the lack of progress in school desegregation, included provisions in the Civil Rights Act of 1964 to deal with the problem through various agencies of the Federal Government. 78 Stat. 246, 252, 266, 42 U.S.C. §§ 2000c *et seq.*, 2000d *et seq.*, 2000h-2. In Title VI Congress declared that

No person in the United States shall, on the ground of race, color, or national origin, be excluded from participation in, be denied the benefits of, or be subjected to discrimination under any program or activity receiving Federal financial assistance. 42 U.S.C. § 2000d.

The Department of Health, Education, and Welfare issued regulations covering racial discrimination in federally aided school systems, as directed by 42 U.S.C. § 2000d-1, and in a statement of policies, or "guidelines," the Department's Office of Education established standards according to which school systems in the process of desegregation can remain qualified for federal funds. 45 CFR §§ 80.1-80.13, 181.1-181.76 (1967). "Freedom-of-choice" plans are among those considered acceptable, so long as in operation such a plan proves effective. 45 CFR § 181.54. The regulations provide that a school system "subject to a final order of a court of the United States for the desegregation of such school ... system" with which the system agrees to comply is deemed to be in compliance with the statute and regulations. 45 CFR § 80.4 (c). *See also* 45 CFR § 181.6. *See generally* Dunn, *Title VI, the Guidelines and School Desegregation in the South*, 53 VA. L. REV. 42 (1967); Note, 55 Geo. L. J. 325 (1966); Comment, 77 Yale L. J. 321 (1967).

Court of Appeals for the Fifth Circuit in *United States v. Jefferson County Bd. of Educ.*, 372 F.2d 836, *aff'd en banc*, 380 F.2d 385 (1967). Judges Sobeloff and Winter concurred with the remand on the teacher issue but otherwise disagreed, expressing the view "that the District Court should be directed ... also to set up procedures for periodically evaluating the effectiveness of the [Board's] 'freedom of choice' [plan] in the elimination of other features of a segregated school system." *Bowman v. County School Bd.*, 382 F.2d 326, 330. We granted certiorari, 389 U.S. 1003.

The pattern of separate "white" and "Negro" schools in the New Kent County school system established under compulsion of state laws is precisely the pattern of segregation to which *Brown I* and *Brown II* were particularly addressed, and which *Brown I* declared unconstitutionally denied Negro school children equal protection of the laws. Racial identification of the system's schools was complete, extending not just to the composition of student bodies at the two schools but to every facet of school operations — faculty, staff, transportation, extracurricular activities and facilities. In short, the State, acting through the local school board and school officials, organized and operated a dual system, part "white" and part "Negro."

It was such dual systems that 14 years ago *Brown I* held unconstitutional and a year later *Brown II* held must be abolished; school boards operating such school systems were *required* by *Brown II* "to effectuate a transition to a racially nondiscriminatory school system." 349 U.S. at 301. It is of course true that for the time immediately after *Brown II* the concern was with making an initial break in a long-established pattern of excluding Negro children from schools attended by white children. The principal focus was on obtaining for those Negro children courageous enough to break with tradition a place in the "white" schools. *See, e.g., Cooper v. Aaron*, 358 U.S. 1. Under *Brown II* that immediate goal was only the first step, however. The transition to a unitary, nonracial system of public education was and is the ultimate end to be brought about; it was because of the "complexities arising from the transition to a system of public education freed of racial discrimination" that we provided for "all deliberate speed" in the implementation of the principles of *Brown I*. 349 U.S. at 299-301. Thus we recognized the task would necessarily involve solution of "varied local school problems." *Id.* at 299. In referring to the "personal interest of the plaintiffs in admission to public schools as soon as practicable on a nondiscriminatory basis," we also noted that "[t]o effectuate this interest may call for elimination of a variety of obstacles in making the transition...." *Id.* at 300. Yet we emphasized that the constitutional rights of Negro children required school officials to bear the burden of establishing that additional time to carry out the ruling in an effective manner "is necessary in the public interest and is consistent with good faith compliance at the earliest practicable date." *Ibid....*

It is against this background that 13 years after *Brown II* commanded the abolition of dual systems we must measure the effectiveness of respondent School Board's "freedom-of-choice" plan to achieve that end. The School Board contends that it has fully discharged its obligation by adopting a plan by which every student, regardless of race, may "freely" choose the school he will attend. The Board attempts to cast the issue in its broadest form by arguing that its "freedom-of-choice" plan may be faulted only by reading the Fourteenth Amendment as universally requiring "compulsory integration," a reading it insists the wording of the Amendment will not support. But that argument ignores the thrust of *Brown II*. In the light of the command of that case, what is involved here is the question whether the Board has achieved the "racially nondiscriminatory school system" *Brown II* held must be effectuated in order to remedy the established unconstitutional deficiencies of its segregated system. In the context of the state-imposed segregated pattern of long standing, the fact that in 1965 the Board opened the doors of the former "white" school to Negro children and of the "Negro" school to white children merely begins, not ends, our inquiry whether the Board has taken steps adequate to abolish its dual, segregated system. *Brown II* was a call for the dismantling of well-entrenched dual systems tempered by an awareness that complex and multifaceted problems would arise which would require time and flexibility for a successful resolution. School boards such as the respondent then operating state-compelled dual systems were nevertheless clearly charged with the affirmative duty to take whatever steps might be necessary to convert to a unitary system in which racial discrimination would be eliminated root and branch. *See Cooper v. Aaron*, supra, at 7; *Bradley v. School Board*, 382 U.S. 103; cf. *Watson v. City of Memphis*, 373 U.S. 526. The constitutional rights of Negro school children articulated in *Brown I* permit no less than this; and it was to this end that *Brown II* commanded school boards to bend their efforts.

In determining whether respondent School Board met that command by adopting its "freedom-of-choice" plan, it is relevant that this first step did not come until some 11 years after *Brown I* was decided and 10 years after *Brown II* directed the making of a "prompt and reasonable start." This deliberate perpetuation of the unconstitutional dual system can only have compounded the harm of such a system. Such delays are no longer tolerable, for "the governing constitutional principles no longer bear the imprint of newly enunciated doctrine." *Watson v. City of Memphis*, supra, at 529; see *Bradley v. School Board*, supra; Rogers v. Paul, 382 U.S. 198. Moreover, a plan that at this late date fails to provide meaningful assurance of prompt and effective disestablishment of a dual system is also intolerable. "The time for mere 'deliberate speed' has run out," *Griffin v. County School Board*, 377 U.S. 218, 234; "the context in which we must interpret and apply this language [of *Brown II*] to plans for desegregation has been significantly altered." *Goss v. Board of Education*, 373 U.S. 683, 689. See *Calhoun v. Latimer*, 377 U.S. 263. The burden on a school board today is to come forward with a plan that promises realistically to work, and promises realistically to work *now*.

The obligation of the district court, as it always has been, is to assess the effectiveness of a proposed plan in achieving desegregation. There is no universal answer to complex problems of desegregation; there is obviously no one plan that will do the job in every case. The matter must be assessed in light of the circumstances present and the options available in each instance. It is incumbent upon the school board to establish that its proposed plan promises meaningful and immediate progress toward disestablishing state-imposed segregation. It is incumbent upon the district court to weigh that claim in light of the facts at hand and in light of any alternatives which may be shown as feasible and more promising in their effectiveness. Where the court finds the board to be acting in good faith and the proposed plan to have real prospects for dismantling the state-imposed dual system "at the earliest practicable date," then the plan may be said to provide effective relief. Of course, the availability to the board of other more promising courses of action may indicate a lack of good faith; and at the least it places a heavy burden upon the board to explain its preference for an apparently less effective method. Moreover, whatever plan is adopted will require evaluation in practice, and the court should retain jurisdiction until it is clear that state-imposed segregation has been completely removed. *See* No. 805, *Raney v. Board of Education, post*, at 449.

We do not hold that "freedom of choice" can have no place in such a plan. We do not hold that a "freedom-of-choice" plan might of itself be unconstitutional, although that argument has been urged upon us. Rather, all we decide today is that in desegregating a dual system a plan utilizing "freedom of choice" is not an end in itself. As Judge Sobeloff has put it,

> "Freedom of choice" is not a sacred talisman; it is only a means to a constitutionally required end — the abolition of the system of segregation and its effects. If the means prove effective, it is acceptable, but if it fails to undo segregation, other means must be used to achieve this end. The school officials have the continuing duty to take whatever action may be necessary to create a "unitary, nonracial system." *Bowman v. County School Board*, 382 F.2d 326, 333 (C.A. 4th Cir. 1967) (concurring opinion).

... Although the general experience under "freedom of choice" to date has been such as to indicate its ineffectiveness as a tool of desegregation,[5] there

---

[5] The views of the United States Commission on Civil Rights, which we neither adopt nor refuse to adopt, are as follows:

> Freedom of choice plans, which have tended to perpetuate racially identifiable schools in the Southern and border States, require affirmative action by both Negro and white parents and pupils before such disestablishment can be achieved. There are a number of factors which have prevented such affirmative action by substantial numbers of parents and pupils of both races:
>
> (a) Fear of retaliation and hostility from the white community continue to deter many Negro families from choosing formerly all-white schools;

may well be instances in which it can serve as an effective device. Where it offers real promise of aiding a desegregation program to effectuate conversion of a state-imposed dual system to a unitary, nonracial system there might be no objection to allowing such a device to prove itself in operation. On the other hand, if there are reasonably available other ways, such for illustration as zoning, promising speedier and more effective conversion to a unitary, nonracial school system, "freedom of choice" must be held unacceptable.

The New Kent School Board's "freedom-of-choice" plan cannot be accepted as a sufficient step to "effectuate a transition" to a unitary system. In three years of operation not a single white child has chosen to attend Watkins school and although 115 Negro children enrolled in New Kent school in 1967 (up from 35 in 1965 and 111 in 1966) 85% of the Negro children in the system still attend the all-Negro Watkins school. In other words, the school system remains a dual system. Rather than further the dismantling of the dual system, the plan has operated simply to burden children and their parents with a responsibility which *Brown II* placed squarely on the School Board. The Board must be required to formulate a new plan and, in light of other courses which appear open to the Board, such as zoning, fashion steps which promise realistically to convert promptly to a system without a "white" school and a "Negro" school, but just schools.

The judgment of the Court of Appeals is vacated insofar as it affirmed the District Court and the case is remanded to the District Court for further proceedings consistent with this opinion.

It is so ordered.

1. In *Monroe v. Board of Comm'rs*, 391 U.S. 450 (1968), a companion case to *Green*, the Court struck down a variant of "freedom of choice," commonly

---

(b) During the past school year [1966-1967], as in the previous year, in some areas of the South, Negro families with children attending previously all-white schools under free choice plans were targets of violence, threats of violence and economic reprisal by white persons and Negro children were subjected to harassment by white classmates notwithstanding conscientious efforts by many teachers and principals to prevent such misconduct;

(c) During the past school year, in some areas of the South public officials improperly influenced Negro families to keep their children in Negro schools and excluded Negro children attending formerly all-white schools from official functions;

(d) Poverty deters many Negro families in the South from choosing formerly all-white schools. Some Negro parents are embarrassed to permit their children to attend such schools without suitable clothing. In some districts special fees are assessed for courses which are available only in the white schools;

(e) Improvements in facilities and equipment ... have been instituted in all-Negro schools in some school districts in a manner that tends to discourage Negroes from selecting white schools.

Southern School Desegregation, 1966-1967, at 88 (1967). *See id.* at 45-69; Survey of School Desegregation in the Southern and Border States 1965-1966, at 30-44, 51-52 (U.S. Comm'n on Civil Rights 1966).

referred to as "free transfer." Under this system, students were originally assigned to schools based on geographic zones, but could voluntarily transfer to other schools if there was no room. Transportation was not provided. The Court held that this system was invalid in the case involved on the same grounds as in *Green*: it had not resulted in conversion to a "unitary, nonracial" school system.

2. What do *Green* and *Monroe* mean for the rationale of *Brown*? After these decisions, can *Brown* be said not to rest on the social science data cited in the opinion? If the vice of the compelled segregation is a racial classification that assigns children to a school because of their race, is this not cured by freedom of choice? If the vice is compulsion not to associate with members of another race, is this not also cured by removal of the compulsion under freedom of choice plans? To put it another way, it is clear that a state-mandated scheme that requires whites to swim at pool A and blacks at pool B is unconstitutional, even if the pools were otherwise identical. However, it is clear that if all people could go to either A or B and whites chose to go to A and blacks to B this would be unconstitutional if the pools were otherwise identical. Moreover, even if they were not otherwise identical, would there be a constitutional complaint when there was choice between the two? Finally, even if there is such a constitutional complaint, why would the remedy be compelled integration rather than equalization of the facilities at A and B?

3. If the above analysis is correct, what then is the theoretical difference between southern "de jure" segregation and northern-style "de facto" segregation? Is there a meaningful difference between a southern freedom-of-choice plan that results in racially homogeneous schools and a northern freedom-of-choice or neighborhood school plan that produces the same results?

4. The decision in *Green* partly represents the order of action not taken in either of the two *Brown* cases. Neither *Brown I* nor *Brown II* gave school systems appropriate guidance as how to desegregate. Although the Court held that segregated schools had to proceed with "all deliberate speed" in their desegregation efforts, the pace remained slow up to the decision in *Green*. In fact, many judges, interpreting the "deliberate speed" phrase, emphasized the efforts of blacks transferring to white schools. *See* Read, *Judicial Evolution of the Law of School Integration Since* Brown v. Board of Education, 39 Law and Contemp. Probs. 7, 29-30 (1975).

In *Green* the Court held that a pupil assignment process that did not result in a unitary, non-racial system was invalid. Moreover, expressing an annoyance with the slow pace of desegregation, a directive was issued that the school system immediately come up with a plan featuring what have been commonly referred to as the "*Green* factors": 1) student assignment; 2) faculty and staff assignment; 3) quality of education; 4) physical facilities; 5) transportation; and 6) extracurricular activities. These "factors" were to be used in measuring whether a school district had converted to a unitary system.

5. The Board of Education in *Green* asserted that the only way its freedom of choice plan could be faulted was by an interpretation of the Fourteenth

Amendment which would require "compulsory integration." The Board argued that such a reading was not plausible. While the *Green* Court held against the Board, did it go so far as to require "compulsory integration"? Whether the Court held so or not, what is the effect of this decision on parental choice plans that are so popular today? Does *Brown II* require compulsory integration? Do these decisions go beyond the scope of the Fourteenth Amendment?

6. The *Green* decision effectively eliminated segregated schools in the rural south, but these areas had not historically experienced de facto segregation. But what of the question of segregation caused by residential patterns similar to those found in the North? Were the *"Green* factors" sufficient enough for the federal courts to thereby end segregation?

SWANN v. CHARLOTTE-MECKLENBURG BOARD OF EDUCATION

Supreme Court of the United States
402 U.S. 1 (1971)

MR. CHIEF JUSTICE BURGER delivered the opinion of the Court:

....

This case and those argued with it arose in States having a long history of maintaining two sets of schools in a single school system deliberately operated to carry out a governmental policy to separate pupils in schools solely on the basis of race. That was what *Brown v. Board of Education*, 347 U.S. 483 (1954) (*Brown I*) was all about. These cases present us with the problem of defining in more precise terms than heretofore the scope of the duty of school authorities and district courts in implementing *Brown I* and the mandate to eliminate dual systems and establish unitary systems at once. Meanwhile district courts and courts of appeals have struggled in hundreds of cases with a multitude and variety of problems under this Court's general directive. Understandably, in an area of evolving remedies, those courts had to improvise and experiment without detailed or specific guidelines. This Court, in *Brown I*, appropriately dealt with the large constitutional principles; other federal courts had to grapple with the flinty, intractable realities of day-to-day implementation of those constitutional commands. Their efforts, of necessity, embraced a process of "trial and error," and our effort to formulate guidelines must take into account their experience.

I

The Charlotte-Mecklenburg school system, the 43d largest in the Nation, encompasses the city of Charlotte and surrounding Mecklenburg County, North Carolina. The area is large — 550 square miles — spanning roughly 22 miles east-west and 36 miles north-south. During the 1968-1969 school year the system served more than 84,000 pupils in 107 schools. Approximately 71% of the pupils were found to be white and 29% Negro. As of June 1969 there were approximately 24,000 Negro students in the system, of whom 21,000 attended schools within the city of Charlotte. Two-thirds of those 21,000 — approximately 14,000

Negro students — attended 21 schools which were either totally Negro or more than 99% Negro.

[The district court ordered the school board to adopt a desegregation plan grouping two to three predominatly white suburban schools with one predominantly African-American city school. The plans also called for bussing only black students to formerly all-white schools for grades 1-4 and bussing white students to black schools in grades 5-6.]

In April 1969 the District Court ordered the school board to come forward with a plan for both faculty and student desegregation....

....

II

Nearly 17 years ago this Court held, in explicit terms, that state-imposed segregation by race in public schools denies equal protection of the laws. At no time has the court deviated in the slightest degree from that holding or its constitutional underpinnings....

Over the 16 years since *Brown II*, many difficulties were encountered in implementation of the basic constitutional requirement that the State not discriminate between public school children on the basis of their race. Nothing in our national experience prior to 1955 prepared anyone for dealing with changes and adjustments of the magnitude and complexity encountered since then. Deliberate resistance of some of the Court's mandates has impeded the good-faith efforts of others to bring school systems into compliance. The detail and nature of these dilatory tactics have been noted frequently by this Court and other courts.

By the time the Court considered *Green v. County School Board*, 391 U.S. 430, in 1968, very little progress had been made in many areas where dual school systems had historically been maintained by operation of state laws. In *Green*, the Court was confronted with a record of a freedom-of-choice program that the District Court had found to operate in fact to preserve a dual system more than a decade after *Brown II*. While acknowledging that a freedom-of-choice concept could be a valid remedial measure in some circumstances, its failure to be effective in *Green* required that:

> The burden on a school board today is to come forward with a plan that promises realistically to work ... now ... until it is clear that state-imposed segregation has been completely removed.

This was plain language, yet the 1969 Term of Court brought fresh evidence of the dilatory tactics of many school authorities. *Alexander v. Holmes County Board of Education*, 396 U.S. 19, restated the basic obligation asserted in *Griffin v. School Board*, 377 U.S. 218, 234 (1964), and *Green, supra*, that the remedy must be implemented *forthwith*.

The problems encountered by the district courts and courts of appeals make plain that we should now try to amplify guidelines, however incomplete and imperfect, for the assistance of school authorities and courts. The failure of local authorities to meet their constitutional obligations aggravated the massive problem of converting from the state-enforced discrimination of racially separate school systems. This process has been rendered more difficult by changes since 1954 in the structure and patterns of communities, the growth of student population, movement of families, and other changes, some of which had marked impact on school planning, sometimes neutralizing or negating remedial action before it was fully implemented. Rural areas accustomed for half a century to the consolidated schools systems implemented by bus transportation could make adjustments more readily than metropolitan areas with dense and shifting population, numerous schools, congested and complex traffic patterns.

III

The objective today remains to eliminate from the public schools all vestiges of state-imposed segregation. Segregation was the evil struck down by *Brown I* as contrary to the equal protection guarantees of the Constitution. That was the violation sought to be corrected by the remedial measures of *Brown II*. That was the basis for the holding in *Green* that school authorities are "clearly charged with the affirmative duty to take whatever steps might be necessary to convert to a unitary system in which racial discrimination would be eliminated root and branch." 391 U.S. at 437-438.

If school authorities fail in their affirmative obligations under these holdings, judicial authority may be invoked. Once a right and a violation have been shown, the scope of a district court's equitable powers to remedy past wrongs is broad, for breadth and flexibility are inherent in equitable remedies....

....

In seeking to define even in broad and general terms how far this remedial power extends it is important to remember that judicial powers may be exercised only on the basis of a constitutional violation. Remedial judicial authority does not put judges automatically in the shoes of school authorities whose powers are plenary. Judicial authority enters only when local authority defaults.

School authorities are traditionally charged with broad power to formulate and implement educational policy and might well conclude, for example, that in order to prepare students to live in a pluralistic society each school should have a prescribed ratio of Negro to white students reflecting the proportion for the district as a whole. To do this as an educational policy is within the broad discretionary powers of school authorities; absent a finding of a constitutional violation, however, that would not be within the authority of a federal court. As with any equity case, the nature of the violation determines the scope of the remedy. In default by the school authorities of their obligation to proffer acceptable remedies, a district court has broad power to fashion a remedy that will assure a unitary school system....

IV

We turn now to the problem of defining with more particularity the responsibilities of school authorities in desegregating a state-enforced dual school system in light of the Equal Protection Clause. Although the several related cases before us are primarily concerned with problems of student assignment, it may be helpful to begin with a brief discussion of other aspects of the process.

In *Green*, we pointed out that existing policy and practice with regard to faculty, staff, transportation, extracurricular activities, and facilities were among the most important indicia of a segregated system. 391 U.S. at 435. Independent of student assignment, where it is possible to identify a "white school" or a "Negro school" simply by reference to the racial composition of teachers and staff, the quality of school buildings and equipment, or the organization of sports activities, a prima facie case of violation of substantive constitutional rights under the Equal Protection Clause is shown.

When a system has been dual in these respects, the first remedial responsibility of school authorities is to eliminate invidious racial distinctions. With respect to such matters as transportation, supporting personnel, and extracurricular activities, no more than this may be necessary. Similar corrective action must be taken with regard to the maintenance of buildings and the distribution of equipment. In these areas, normal administrative practice should produce schools of like quality, facilities, and staffs. Something more must be said, however, as to faculty assignment and new school construction.

In the companion *Davis* case, *post*, p. 33, the Mobile school board has argued that the Constitution requires that teachers be assigned on a "color blind" basis. It also argues that the Constitution prohibits district courts from using their equity power to order assignment of teachers to achieve a particular degree of faculty desegregation. We reject that contention.

In *United States v. Montgomery County Board of Education*, 395 U.S. 225 (1969), the District Court set as a goal a plan of faculty assignment in each school with a ratio of white to Negro faculty members substantially the same throughout the system....

The District Court in *Montgomery* then proceeded to set an initial ratio for the whole system of at least two Negro teachers out of each 12 in any given school. The Court of Appeals modified the order by eliminating what it regarded as "fixed mathematical" ratios of faculty and substituted an initial requirement of *"substantially* or *approximately"* a five-to-one ratio....

We reversed the Court of Appeals and restored the District Court's order in its entirety, holding that the order of the District Judge

> was adopted in the spirit of this Court's opinion in *Green* ... in that his plan "promises realistically to work, and promises realistically to work *now."*

The principles of *Montgomery* have been properly followed by the District Court and the Court of Appeals in this case.

The construction of new schools and the closing of old ones are two of the most important functions of local school authorities and also two of the most complex. They must decide questions of location and capacity in light of population growth, finances, land values, site availability, through an almost endless list of factors to be considered. The result of this will be a decision which, when combined with one technique or another of student assignment, will determine the racial composition of the student body in each school in the system. Over the long run, the consequences of the choices will be far reaching. People gravitate toward school facilities, just as schools are located in response to the needs of people. The location of schools may thus influence the patterns of residential development of a metropolitan area and have important impact on composition of inner-city neighborhoods.

In the past, choices in this respect have been used as a potent weapon for creating or maintaining a state-segregated school system. In addition to the classic pattern of building schools specifically intended for Negro or white students, school authorities have sometimes, since *Brown*, closed schools which appeared likely to become racially mixed through changes in neighborhood residential patterns. This was sometimes accompanied by building new schools in the areas of white suburban expansion farthest from Negro population centers in order to maintain the separation of the races with a minimum departure from the formal principles of "neighborhood zoning." Such a policy does more than simply influence the short-run composition of the student body of a new school. It may well promote segregated residential patterns which, when combined with "neighborhood zoning," further lock the school system into the mold of separation of the races. Upon a proper showing a district court may consider this in fashioning a remedy.

In ascertaining the existence of legally imposed school segregation, the existence of a pattern of school construction and abandonment is thus a factor of great weight. In devising remedies where legally imposed segregation has been established, it is the responsibility of local authorities and district courts to see to it that future school construction and abandonment are not used and do not serve to perpetuate or re-establish the dual system. When necessary, district courts should retain jurisdiction to assure that these responsibilities are carried out....

V

The central issue in this case is that of student assignment, and there are essentially four problem areas:

(1) to what extent racial balance or racial quotas may be used as an implement in a remedial order to correct a previously segregated system;

(2) whether every all-Negro and all-white school must be eliminated as an indispensable part of a remedial process of desegregation;

(3) what the limits are, if any, on the rearrangement of school districts and attendance zones, as a remedial measure; and

(4) what the limits are, if any, on the use of transportation facilities to correct state-enforced racial school segregation.

(1) Racial Balances or Racial Quotas

The constant theme and thrust of every holding from *Brown I* to date is that state-enforced separation of races in public schools is discrimination that violates the Equal Protection Clause. The remedy commanded was to dismantle dual school systems.

We are concerned in these cases with the elimination of the discrimination inherent in the dual school systems, not with myriad factors of human existence which can cause discrimination in a multitude of ways on racial, religious, or ethnic grounds. The target of the cases from *Brown I* to the present was the dual school system. The elimination of racial discrimination in public schools is a large task and one that should not be retarded by efforts to achieve broader purposes lying beyond the jurisdiction of school authorities. One vehicle can carry only a limited amount of baggage. It would not serve the important objective of *Brown I* to seek to use school desegregation cases for purposes beyond their scope, although desegregation of schools ultimately will have impact on other forms of discrimination. We do not reach in this case the question whether a showing that school segregation is a consequence of other types of state action, without any discriminatory action by the school authorities, is a constitutional violation requiring remedial action by a school desegregation decree. This case does not present that question and we therefore do not decide it.

Our objective in dealing with the issues presented by these cases is to see that school authorities exclude no pupil of a racial minority from any school, directly or indirectly, on account of race; it does not and cannot embrace all the problems of racial prejudice, even when those problems contribute to disproportionate racial concentrations in some schools.

In this case it is urged that the District Court has imposed a racial balance requirement of 71%-29% on individual schools. The fact that no such objective was actually achieved — and would appear to be impossible — tends to blunt that claim, yet in the opinion and order of the District Court of December 1, 1969, we find that court directing

> that efforts should be made to reach a 71-29 ratio in the various schools so that there will be no basis for contending that one school is racially different from the others ..., [t]hat no school [should] be operated with an all-black or predominantly black student body, [and] [t]hat pupils of all grades [should] be assigned in such a way that as nearly as practicable the various schools at various grade levels have about the same proportion of black and white students.

The District Judge went on to acknowledge that variation "from that norm may be unavoidable." This contains intimations that the "norm" is a fixed mathematical racial balance reflecting the pupil constituency of the system. If we were to read the holding of the District Court to require, as a matter of substantive constitutional right, any particular degree of racial balance or mixing, that approach would be disapproved and we would be obliged to reverse. The constitutional command to desegregate schools does not mean that every school in every community must always reflect the racial composition of the school system as a whole.

....

We see therefore that the use made of mathematical ratios was no more than a starting point in the process of shaping a remedy, rather than an inflexible requirement. From that starting point the District Court proceeded to frame a decree that was within its discretionary powers, as an equitable remedy for the particular circumstances. As we said in *Green*, a school authority's remedial plan or a district court's remedial decree is to be judged by its effectiveness. Awareness of the racial composition of the whole school system is likely to be a useful starting point in shaping a remedy to correct past constitutional violations. In sum, the very limited use made of mathematical ratios was within the equitable remedial discretion of the District Court.

(2) One-race Schools

The record in this case reveals the familiar phenomenon that in metropolitan areas minority groups are often found concentrated in one part of the city. In some circumstances certain schools may remain all or largely of one race until new schools can be provided or neighborhood patterns change. Schools all or predominantly of one race in a district of mixed population will require close scrutiny to determine that school assignments are not part of state-enforced segregation.

In light of the above, it should be clear that the existence of some small number of one-race, or virtually one-race, schools within a district is not in and of itself the mark of a system that still practices segregation by law. The district judge or school authorities should make every effort to achieve the greatest possible degree of actual desegregation and will thus necessarily be concerned with the elimination of one-race schools. No per se rule can adequately embrace all the difficulties of reconciling the competing interests involved; but in a system with a history of segregation the need for remedial criteria of sufficient specificity to assure a school authority's compliance with its constitutional duty warrants a presumption against schools that are substantially disproportionate in their racial composition. Where the school authority's proposed plan for conversion from a dual to a unitary system contemplates the continued existence of some schools that are all or predominantly of one race, they have the burden of showing that such school assignments are genuinely nondiscriminatory. The court should scrutinize such schools, and the burden upon the school authorities will be to satisfy the court that their racial composition is not the result of present or past discriminatory action on their part.

An optional majority-to-minority transfer provision has long been recognized as a useful part of every desegregation plan. Provision for optional transfer of those in the majority racial group of a particular school to other schools where they will be in the minority is an indispensable remedy for those students willing to transfer to other schools in order to lessen the impact on them of the state-imposed stigma of segregation. In order to be effective, such a transfer arrangement must grant the transferring student free transportation and space must be made available in the school to which he desires to move. The court orders in this and the companion *Davis* case now provide such an option.

(3) Remedial Altering of Attendance Zones

The maps submitted in these cases graphically demonstrate that one of the principal tools employed by school planners and by courts to break up the dual school system has been a frank — and sometimes drastic — gerrymandering of school districts and attendance zones. An additional step was pairing, "clustering," or "grouping" of schools with attendance assignments made deliberately to accomplish the transfer of Negro students out of formerly segregated Negro schools and transfer of white students to formerly all-Negro schools. More often than not, these zones are neither compact nor contiguous; indeed they may be on opposite ends of the city. As an interim corrective measure, this cannot be said to be beyond the broad remedial powers of a court.

Absent a constitutional violation there would be no basis for judicially ordering assignment of students on a racial basis. All things being equal, with no history of discrimination, it might well be desirable to assign pupils to schools nearest their homes. But all things are not equal in a system that has been deliberately constructed and maintained to enforce racial segregation. The remedy for such segregation may be administratively awkward, inconvenient, and even bizarre in some situations and may impose burdens on some; but all awkwardness and inconvenience cannot be avoided in the interim period when remedial adjustments are being made to eliminate the dual school systems.

No fixed or even substantially fixed guidelines can be established as to how far a court can go, but it must be recognized that there are limits. The objective is to dismantle the dual school system. "Racially neutral" assignment plans proposed by school authorities to a district court may be inadequate; such plans may fail to counteract the continuing effects of past school segregation resulting from discriminatory location of school sites or distortion of school size in order to achieve or maintain an artificial racial separation. When school authorities present a district court with a "loaded game board," affirmative action in the form of remedial altering of attendance zones is proper to achieve truly nondiscriminatory assignments. In short, an assignment plan is not acceptable simply because it appears to be neutral.

In this area, we must of necessity rely to a large extent, as this Court has for more than 16 years, on the informed judgment of the district courts in the first instance and on courts of appeals.

We hold that the pairing and grouping of noncontiguous school zones is a permissible tool and such action is to be considered in light of the objectives sought....

(4) Transportation of Students

The scope of permissible transportation of students as an implement of a remedial decree has never been defined by this Court and by the very nature of the problem it cannot be defined with precision. No rigid guidelines as to student transportation can be given for application to the infinite variety of problems presented in thousands of situations. Bus transportation has been an integral part of the public education system for years, and was perhaps the single most important factor in the transition from the one-room schoolhouse to the consolidated school. Eighteen million of the Nation's public school children, approximately 39%, were transported to their schools by bus in 1969-1970 in all parts of the country.

The importance of bus transportation as a normal and accepted tool of educational policy is readily discernible in this and the companion case, *Davis, supra*. The Charlotte school authorities did not purport to assign students on the basis of geographically drawn zones until 1965 and then they allowed almost unlimited transfer privileges. The District Court's conclusion that assignment of children to the school nearest their home serving their grade would not produce an effective dismantling of the dual system is supported by the record.

Thus the remedial techniques used in the District Court's order were within that court's power to provide equitable relief; implementation of the decree is well within the capacity of the school authority.

The decree provided that the buses used to implement the plan would operate on direct routes. Students would be picked up at schools near their homes and transported to the schools they were to attend. The trips for elementary school pupils average about seven miles and the District Court found that they would take "not over 35 minutes at the most." This system compares favorably with the transportation plan previously operated in Charlotte under which each day 23,600 students on all grade levels were transported an average of 15 miles one way for an average trip requiring over an hour. In these circumstances, we find no basis for holding that the local school authorities may not be required to employ bus transportation as one tool of school desegregation. Desegregation plans cannot be limited to the walk-in school.

An objection to transportation of students may have validity when the time or distance of travel is so great as to either risk the health of the children or significantly impinge on the educational process. District courts must weigh the soundness of any transportation plan in light of what is said in subdivisions (1), (2), and (3) above. It hardly needs stating that the limits on time of travel will vary with many factors, but probably with none more than the age of the students. The reconciliation of competing values in a desegregation case is, of course, a difficult task with many sensitive facets but fundamentally no more so than remedial measures courts of equity have traditionally employed.

VI

The Court of Appeals, searching for a term to define the equitable remedial power of the district courts, used the term "reasonableness." In *Green, supra*, this Court used the term "feasible" and by implication, "workable," "effective," and "realistic" in the mandate to develop "a plan that promises realistically to work, and ... to work *now*." On the facts of this case, we are unable to conclude that the order of the District Court is not reasonable, feasible and workable. However, in seeking to define the scope of remedial power or the limits on remedial power of courts in an area as sensitive as we deal with here, words are poor instruments to convey the sense of basic fairness inherent in equity. Substance, not semantics, must govern, and we have sought to suggest the nature of limitations without frustrating the appropriate scope of equity.

At some point, these school authorities and others like them should have achieved full compliance with this Court's decision in *Brown I*. The systems would then be "unitary" in the sense required by our decisions in *Green* and *Alexander*.

It does not follow that the communities served by such systems will remain demographically stable, for in a growing, mobile society, few will do so. Neither school authorities nor district courts are constitutionally required to make year-by-year adjustments of the racial composition of student bodies once the affirmative duty to desegregate has been accomplished and racial discrimination through official action is eliminated from the system. This does not mean that federal courts are without power to deal with future problems; but in the absence of a showing that either the school authorities or some other agency of the State has deliberately attempted to fix or alter demographic patterns to affect the racial composition of the schools, further intervention by a district court should not be necessary.

For the reasons herein set forth, the judgment of the Court of Appeals is affirmed as to those parts in which it affirmed the judgment of the District Court. The order of the District Court, dated August 7, 1970, is also affirmed.

It is so ordered.

---

1. Why is the Court so concerned to state that it is not dealing with Northern style de facto segregation? Again, is there a real difference between Northern and Southern style segregation, once it is decided that freedom of choice or neighborhood school policies are not sufficient in the South? How far can one push the argument that, since the South was de jure segregated, compelled racial balance can be required as a remedy even though it is not an independent constitutional command that would be applicable in the North? In this regard, note that many Northern states were de jure segregated at some point in their history prior to 1954. In addition, what of school and other state policies that can be said to have contributed either directly to school desegregation or indirectly through encouraging residential segregation? What is the Court's response to these problems in *Swann*? Finally, should sectional differences in compelled racial balance, a highly volatile and sensitive political area, really be predicated and perpetuated on a remedial theory?

2. One of the major factors in determining whether a school district is properly integrated is to survey the hiring practices of the school district. In *Hazelwood School Dist. v. United States*, 433 U.S. 299 (1977), the United States Supreme Court ruled that in determining whether there had been discrimination in hiring, courts should view the racial composition of a school district's teaching staff and the racial composition of the qualified public school teacher population in the relevant market. In a Title VII action, once a prima facie case has been established by statistical work-force disparities, the employer must be given an opportunity to show that "the claimed discriminatory pattern is a product of pre-Act hiring rather than unlawful post-Act discrimination." Thus, in "pattern or practice" suits there must be a showing of post-Act discrimination. As originally enacted, Title VII of the Civil Rights Act of 1964 applied only to private employers. The Act was expanded to include state and local governmental employers (including school districts) by the Equal Employment Opportunity Act of 1972.

3. David Armor, in his article, *The Evidence on Busing*, Pub. Interest, Summer, 1972, p. 90,* reviewed the findings from busing programs in five cities — White Plains, N.Y., Ann Arbor, Mich., Riverside, Calif., Hartford, Conn., and Boston, Mass. (Metco Program). Armor himself was partly responsible for the research design of the Metco program, and the major part of his conclusions are derived from his study of that program. In two of the studies (Hartford and Boston), the children were bused from inner cities to surrounding suburbs. Armor limited his study to those "aspects of the [integration policy] model that postulate positive effects of school integration for black students, namely, that school integration enhances black achievement, aspirations, self-esteem, race relations, and opportunities for higher education." *Id.* at 96. Armor concluded that four of those five major premises were not supported by the data.

As to the first effect, Armor found that "none of the studies were able to demonstrate conclusively that integration has had an effect on academic achievement as measured by standardized tests," *Id.* at 99. Four of the five

---

*The Public Interest, No. 28 (Summer 1972), pp. 90-126. Copyright 1972 by National Affairs Inc. Reprinted by permission.

studies reviewed showed no significant gains in achievement scores, the other study had mixed results.

Armor also found no evidence to support the premise that integration raised black aspirations. To the contrary, he found a significant decline in the aspirations of bused Metco students, with 14% fewer students desiring a college degree. As to the third effect, Armor found that bused Metco students had a considerably lower academic self concept (based on how bright they rated themselves in comparison to their classmates), though the difference between the bused and control groups diminished after two years in the program. Armor also reported findings from two other cities that "integration doesn't seem to affect the self-esteem measures of minority children in clearly consistent or significant ways," *Id.* at 102.

As regards the prediction that race relations should be improved, Armor found that "the effect of integration programs seems the opposite of that predicted. It appears that integration increases racial identity and solidarity over the short run and, at least in the use of black students, leads to increasing desire for separatism. These effects are observed for a variety of indications: attitudes about integration and black power; attitudes towards whites, and contact with whites." *Id.* at 110.

The only positive result Armor found was the evidence on longterm educational effects. Armor saw what he termed a "channeling effect" whereby a substantially higher percentage of bused black students than segregated black students tend to start college ("even though they may not finish at a higher rate than segregated black students") and to enter "higher quality" institutions. Armor considered this finding only a tentative one, however, as it was based on only two fairly small studies.

Armor suggests three reasons for the failure of the evidence to support the underlying rationales for integration or the apparent findings of earlier research: methodological failures of earlier studies, the "induced" nature of present integration programs, and what he calls the "drastic change" in the racial climate since the *Brown* decision.

> The most noteworthy change, of course, has been in the attitudes of black people. Although the majority of blacks may still endorse the concept of integration many younger black leaders de-emphasize integration as a major goal. Black identity, black control, and black equality are seen as the real issues, and integration is regarded as important only insofar as it advances these primary goals. Some black leaders ... feel that integration might actually defeat attainment of these goals by dispersing the more talented blacks throughout the white community and thereby diluting their power potential. Integration is also seen as having white paternalistic overtones and as the means whereby the white man allays his guilty conscience while ignoring reform on the really important issues. Given these sentiments, school integration programs are seen by blacks not as a fulfillment of the

goal of joining white society but only as a means of obtaining better educational opportunities, which would ultimately lead to a more competitive position in the occupational and economic market. *Id.* at 112-13.

On the basis of the findings, Armor reaches two policy conclusions. One is that massive mandatory busing for purposes of improving student achievement and interracial harmony is not effective and should not be adopted at the time. The other is that *voluntary* integration programs should be continued and positively encouraged by substantial federal and state grants. Such voluntary programs should be encouraged so that those parents and communities who believe in the symbolic and potential (but so far unconfirmed) long run benefits of induced integration will have ample opportunity to send their children to integrated schools. *Id.* at 116.

Even in voluntary school integration programs, however, Armor suggests that "some selectivity might be desirable" so that both black and white students reflect a similar achievement capacity thereby avoiding "potentially frustrating experiences."

4. In a response to the Armor article, Pettigrew, Useem, Normond and Smith in *Busing: A Review of "the Evidence,"* Public Interest, Winter, 1973, p. 88, argued that the Armor study was defective in methodology and exhibited a negative bias by not examining seven busing programs which have reported positive achievement results for black students.

The authors' evaluation of the evidence of achievement effects of busing "points to a more encouraging, if more tentative and complex set of conclusions."

First, the academic achievement of both white and black children is not lowered by the types of racial segregation so far studied. Second, the achievement of white and especially of black children in desegregated schools is generally favorable when some of the following critical conditions are met: equal racial access to the school's resources; classroom not just school desegregation; the initiation of desegregation in the early grades; interracial staffs; substantial rather than token student desegregation; the maintenance of an increase in school services and remedial training and the avoidance of strict ability grouping. *Id.* at 106-07.

The authors also found that the evidence that school desegregation "channels" blacks into greater future opportunities is stronger than presented by Armor. First, they state that the "high drop out rate" stressed by Armor in his two studies was no higher than the national rate for white students in four-year colleges. Secondly, and more importantly, they assert that future benefits are not limited to the college-bound, citing a 1970 study by Robert Crain in which he concluded that "American Negroes who attended integrated public schools have better jobs and higher incomes throughout at least the next three decades of their life." *Id.* at 111.

CH. 11: RACIAL SEGREGATION IN THE PUBLIC SCHOOLS 797

5. The "fixed mathematical formula" determination in *Swann* was also undertaken in *Dayton Bd. of Educ. v. Brinkman*, 433 U.S. 406 (1977), *infra*. A district court had ordered that the racial composition of the schools in the district be brought within 15% of the city's citizen ratio of African-Americans to whites. This was "to be accomplished by a variety of desegregation techniques, including the 'pairing of schools,' the redefinition of attendance zones, and a variety of centralized special programs and 'magnet schools.'" *Id.* at 406. The Supreme Court held that the systemwide remedy ordered was unjustified as the school district's actions did not rise to the level of a constitutional violation. The court reasoned that segregated schools were not in and of themselves against the Fourteenth Amendment absent a showing of "intentionally segregative actions on the part of the Board." *Id.*

6. In the more recent case of *Harris v. Crenshaw County Bd. of Educ.*, 968 F.2d 1090 (11th Cir. 1992), the Eleventh Circuit Court of Appeals permitted the elimination of a high school because of low numbers of students brought on because the school board permitted transfers of white students, who wanted to avoid desegregation, to other high schools in the area. Using *Swann*, the court held that when a school board proposes to close a school facility predominated by students of color, it must adduce evidence sufficient to support the conclusion that its actions were not in fact motivated by racial reasons. Here, the court found that even if the transfers of white students had been reversed, the school board could not have achieved an enrollment in that school sufficient to satisfy its desegregation mandate.

KEYES v. SCHOOL DISTRICT NO. 1

Supreme Court of the United States
413 U.S. 189 (1973)

MR. JUSTICE BRENNAN delivered the opinion of the Court:
This school desegregation case concerns the Denver, Colorado, school system. That system has never been operated under a constitutional or statutory provision that mandated or permitted racial segregation in public education. Rather, the gravamen of this action, brought in June 1969 in the District Court for the District of Colorado by parents of Denver school children, is that respondent School Board alone, by use of various techniques such as the manipulation of student attendance zones, school site selection and a neighborhood school policy, created or maintained racially or ethnically (or both racially and ethnically) segregated schools throughout the school district, entitling petitioners to a decree directing desegregation of the entire school district.

The boundaries of the school district are coterminous with the boundaries of the City and County of Denver. There were in 1969 119 schools with 96,580 pupils in the school system. In early 1969, the respondent School Board adopted three resolutions, Resolutions 1520, 1524, and 1531, designed to desegregate the schools in the Park Hill area in the northeast portion of the city. Following an election which produced a Board majority opposed to the resolutions, the resolutions were rescinded and replaced with a voluntary student transfer program. Petitioners then filed this action, requesting an injunction against the rescission of the resolutions and an order directing that the respondent School Board desegregate and afford equal educational opportunity "for the School District as a whole." The District Court found that by the construction of a new, relatively small elementary school, Barrett, in the middle of the Negro community west of Park Hill, by the gerrymandering of student attendance zones, by the use of so-called "optional zones," and by the excessive use of mobile classroom units, among other things, the respondent School Board had engaged over almost a decade after 1960 in an unconstitutional policy of deliberate racial segregation with respect to the Park Hill schools. The court therefore ordered the Board to desegregate those schools through the implementation of the three rescinded resolutions. 303 F. Supp. 279 (1969); 303 F. Supp. 289 (1969).

Segregation in Denver schools is not limited, however, to the schools in the Park Hill area, and not satisfied with their success in obtaining relief for Park Hill, petitioners pressed their prayer that the District Court order desegregation of all segregated schools in the city of Denver, particularly the heavily segregated schools in the core city area. But that court concluded that its finding of a purposeful and systematic program of racial segregation affecting thousands of students in the Park Hill area did not, in itself, impose on the School Board an affirmative duty to eliminate segregation throughout the school district. Instead, the court fractionated the district and held that petitioners must make a fresh showing of de jure segregation in each area of the city for which they seek relief. Moreover, the District Court held that its finding of intentional segregation in Park Hill was not in any sense material to the question of segregative intent in other areas of the city. Under this restrictive approach, the District Court concluded that petitioners' evidence of intentionally discriminatory School Board action in areas of the district other than Park Hill was insufficient to "dictate the conclusion that this is de jure segregation which calls for an all-out effort to desegregate. It is more like de facto segregation, with respect to which the rule is that the court cannot order desegregation in order to provide a better balance." 313 F. Supp. 61, 73 (1970).

Nevertheless, the District Court went on to hold that the proofs established that the segregated core city schools were educationally inferior to the predominantly "white" or "Anglo" schools in other parts of the district — that is, "separate facilities ... unequal in the quality of education provided." *Id.* at 83. Thus, the court held that, under the doctrine of *Plessy v. Ferguson*, 163 U.S. 537 (1896), respondent School Board constitutionally "must at a minimum ... offer an equal educational opportunity," *ibid.*, and, therefore, although all-out desegregation "could not be decreed, ... the only feasible and constitutionally acceptable program — the only program which furnishes anything approaching substantial equality — is a system of desegregation and integration which provides compensatory education in an integrated environment." 313 F. Supp. 90, 96 (1970). The District Court then formulated a varied remedial plan to that end which was incorporated in the Final Decree.

Respondent School Board appealed, and petitioners cross-appealed, to the Court of Appeals for the Tenth Circuit. That court sustained the District Court's finding that the Board engaged in an unconstitutional policy of deliberate racial segregation with respect to the Park Hill schools and affirmed the Final Decree in that respect. As to the core city schools, however, the Court of Appeals reversed the legal determination of the District Court that those schools were maintained in violation of the Fourteenth Amendment because of the unequal educational opportunity afforded, and therefore set aside so much of the Final Decree as required desegregation and educational improvement programs for those schools. 445 F.2d 990 (1971)....

. . . .

II

In our view, the only other question that requires our decision at this time is ... whether the District Court and the Court of Appeals applied an incorrect legal standard in addressing petitioners' contention that respondent School Board engaged in an unconstitutional policy of deliberate segregation in the core city schools. Our conclusion is that those courts did not apply the correct standard in addressing that contention.

Petitioners apparently concede for the purposes of this case that in the case of a school system like Denver's, where no statutory dual system has ever existed, plaintiffs must prove not only that segregated schooling exists but also that it was brought about or maintained by intentional state action. Petitioners proved that for almost a decade after 1960 respondent School Board had engaged in an unconstitutional policy of deliberate racial segregation in the Park Hill schools. Indeed, the District Court found that "[b]etween 1960 and 1969 the Board's policies with respect to those northeast Denver schools show an undeviating purpose to isolate Negro students" in segregated schools "while preserving the Anglo character of [other] schools." 303 F. Supp. at 294. This finding did not relate to an insubstantial or trivial fragment of the school system. On the contrary, respondent School Board was found guilty of following a deliberate segregation policy at schools attended, in 1969, by 37.69% of Denver's total Negro school population, including one-fourth of the Negro elementary pupils, over two-thirds of the Negro junior high pupils, and over two-fifths of the Negro high school pupils. In addition, there was uncontroverted evidence that teachers and staff had for years been assigned on a minority teacher-to-minority school basis throughout the school system. Respondent argues, however, that a finding of state-imposed segregation as to a substantial portion of the school system can be viewed in isolation from the rest of the district, and that even if state-imposed segregation does exist in a substantial part of the Denver school system, it does not follow that the District Court could predicate on that fact a finding that the entire school system is a dual system. We do not agree. We have never suggested that plaintiffs in school desegregation cases must bear the burden of proving the elements of de jure segregation as to each and every school or each and every student within the school system. Rather, we have held that where plaintiffs prove that a current condition of segregated schooling exists within a school district where a dual system was compelled or authorized by statute at the time of our decision in *Brown v. Board of Educ.*, 347 U.S. 483 (1954) *(Brown I)*, the State automatically assumes an affirmative duty "to effectuate a transition to a racially nondiscriminatory school system." *Brown v. Board of Educ.*, 349 U.S. 294, 301 (1955) *(Brown II), see also Green v. County School Board*, 391 U.S. 430, 437-38 (1968), that is, to eliminate from the public schools within their school system "all vestiges of state-imposed segregation." *Swann v. Charlotte-Mecklenburg Board of Educ.*, 402 U.S. 1, 15 (1971).

This is not a case, however, where a statutory dual system has ever existed. Nevertheless, where plaintiffs prove that the school authorities have carried out a systematic program of segregation affecting a substantial portion of the students, schools, teachers and facilities within the school system, it is only common sense to conclude that there exists a predicate for a finding of the existence of a dual school system. Several considerations support this conclusion. First, it is obvious that a practice of concentrating Negroes in certain schools by structuring attendance zones or designating "feeder" schools on the basis of race has the reciprocal effect of keeping other nearby schools predominantly white. Similarly, the practice of building a school — such as the Barrett Elementary School in this case — to a certain size and in a certain location, "with conscious knowledge that it would be a segregated school," 303 F. Supp. at 285, has a substantial reciprocal effect on the racial composition of other nearby schools. So also, the use of mobile classrooms, the drafting of student transfer policies, the transportation of students, and the assignment of faculty and staff, on racially identifiable bases, have the clear effect of earmarking schools according to their racial composition, and this, in turn, together with the elements of student assignment and school construction, may have a profound reciprocal effect on the racial composition of residential neighborhoods within a metropolitan area, thereby causing further racial concentration within the schools. We recognized this in *Swann*....

In short, common sense dictates the conclusion that racially inspired school board actions have an impact beyond the particular schools that are the subjects of those actions. This is not to say, of course, that there can never be a case in which the geographical structure of or the natural boundaries within a school district may have the effect of dividing the district into separate, identifiable and unrelated units. Such a determination is essentially a question of fact to be resolved by the trial court in the first instance, but such cases must be rare. In the absence of such a determination, proof of state-imposed segregation in a substantial portion of the district will suffice to support a finding by the trial court of the existence of a dual system. Of course, where that finding is made, as in cases involving statutory dual systems, the school authorities have an affirmative duty "to effectuate a transition to a racially nondiscriminatory school system." *Brown II, supra,* at 301. .

....

III

....

Although petitioners had already proved the existence of intentional school segregation in the Park Hill schools, this crucial finding was totally ignored when attention turned to the core city schools. Plainly, a finding of intentional segregation as to a portion of a school system is not devoid of probative value in assessing the school authorities' intent with respect to other parts of the same school system. On the contrary, where, as here, the case involves one school board, a finding of intentional segregation on its part in one portion of a school system is highly relevant to the issue of the board's intent with respect to other segregated schools in the system. This is merely an application of the well-settled evidentiary principle that "the prior doing of other similar acts, whether clearly a part of a scheme or not, is useful as reducing the possibility that the act in question was done with innocent intent." II Wigmore, Evidence 200 (3d ed. 1940).... Similarly, a finding of illicit intent as to a meaningful portion of the item under consideration has substantial probative value on the question of illicit intent as to the remainder....

Applying these principles in the special context of school desegregation cases, we hold that a finding of intentionally segregative school board actions in a meaningful portion of a school system, as in this case, creates a presumption that other segregated schooling within the system is not adventitious. It establishes, in other words, a prima facie case of unlawful segregative design on the part of school authorities, and shifts to those authorities the burden of proving that other segregated schools within the system are not also the result of intentionally segregative actions. This is true even if it is determined that different areas of the school district should be viewed independently of each other because, even in that situation, there is high probability that where school authorities have effectuated an intentionally segregative policy in a meaningful portion of the school system, similar impermissible considerations have motivated their actions in other areas of the system. We emphasize that the differentiating factor between de jure segregation and so-called de facto segregation to which we referred in *Swann* is *purpose* or *intent* to segregate. Where school authorities have been found to have practiced purposeful segregation in part of a school system, they may be expected to oppose system-wide desegregation, as did the respondents in this case, on the ground that their purposefully segregative actions were isolated and individual events, thus leaving plaintiffs with the burden of proving otherwise. But at that point where an intentionally segregative policy is practiced in a meaningful or significant segment of a school system, as in this case, the school authorities cannot be heard to argue that plaintiffs have proved only "isolated and individual" unlawfully segregative actions. In that circumstance, it is both fair and reasonable to require that the school authorities bear the burden of showing that their actions as to other segregated schools within the system were not also motivated by segregative intent.

This burden-shifting principle is not new or novel. There are no hard and fast standards governing the allocation of the burden of proof in every situation. The issue, rather, "is merely a question of policy and fairness based on experience in the different situations." IX Wigmore, Evidence § 2486 (3d ed. 1940). In the context of racial segregation in public education, the courts, including this Court, have recognized a variety of situations in which "fairness" and "policy" require state authorities to bear the burden of explaining actions or conditions which appear to be racially motivated. Thus, in *Swann, supra*, 402 U.S. at 18, we observed that in a system with a "history of segregation," "where it is possible to identify a 'white school' or a 'Negro school' simply by reference to the racial composition of teachers and staff, the quality of school buildings and equipment, or the organization of sport activities, a prima facie case of violation of substantive constitutional rights under the Equal Protection Clause is shown." Again, in a school system with a history of segregation, the discharge of a disproportionately large number of Negro teachers incident to desegregation "thrust[s] upon the School Board the burden of justifying its conduct by clear and convincing evidence." ... Nor is this burden-shifting principle limited to former statutory dual systems.... Indeed, to say that a system has a "history of segregation" is merely to say that a pattern of intentional segregation has been established in the past. Thus, be it a statutory dual system or an allegedly unitary system where a meaningful portion of the system is found to be intentionally segregated, the existence of subsequent or other segregated schooling within the same system justifies a rule imposing on the school authorities the burden of proving that this segregated schooling is not also the result of intentionally segregative acts.

In discharging that burden, it is not enough, or course, that the school authorities rely upon some allegedly logical, racially neutral explanation for their actions. Their burden is to adduce proof sufficient to support a finding that segregative intent was not among the factors that motivated their actions. The courts below attributed much significance to the fact that many of the Board's actions in the core city area antedated our decision in *Brown*. We reject any suggestion that remoteness in time has any relevance to the issue of intent. If the actions of school authorities were to any degree motivated by segregative intent and the segregation resulting from those actions continues to exist, the fact of remoteness in time certainly does not make those actions any less "intentional."

This is not to say, however, that the prima facie case may not be met by evidence supporting a finding that a lesser degree of segregated schooling in the core city area would not have resulted even if the Board had not acted as it did. In *Swann*, we suggested that at some point in time the relationship between past segregative acts and present segregation may become so attenuated as to be incapable of supporting a finding of de jure segregation warranting judicial intervention. 402 U.S. at 31-32. We made it clear, however, that a connection between past segregative acts and present segregation may be present even when not apparent and that close examination is required before concluding that the connection does not exist. Intentional school segregation in the past may have been a factor in creating a natural environment for the growth of further segregation. Thus, if respondent School Board cannot disprove segregative intent, it can rebut the prima facie case only by showing that its past segregative acts did not create or contribute to the current segregated condition of the core city schools.

The respondent School Board invoked at trial its "neighborhood school policy" as explaining racial and ethnic concentrations within the core city schools, arguing that since the core city area population had long been Negro and Hispano, the concentrations were necessarily the result of residential patterns and not of purposefully segregated policies. We have no occasion to consider in this case whether a "neighborhood school policy" of itself will justify racial or ethnic concentrations in the absence of a finding that school authorities have committed acts constituting de jure segregation. It is enough that we hold that the mere assertion of such a policy is not dispositive where, as in this case, the school authorities have been found to have practiced de jure segregation in a meaningful portion of the school system by techniques that indicate that the "neighborhood school" concept has not been maintained free of manipulation....

IV

....

The judgment of the Court of Appeals is modified to vacate instead of reverse the parts of the Final Decree that concern the core city schools, and the case is remanded to the District Court for further proceedings consistent with this opinion.

It is so ordered.

MR. CHIEF JUSTICE BURGER concurs in the result.
MR. JUSTICE WHITE took no part in the decision of this case.
MR. JUSTICE POWELL concurring in part and dissenting in part.

I concur in the remand of this case for further proceedings in the District Court, but on grounds that differ from those relied upon by the Court.

This is the first school desegregation case to reach this Court which involves a major city outside the South. It comes from Denver, Colorado, a city and a State which have not operated public schools under constitutional or statutory provisions which mandated or permitted racial segregation....

....

The situation in Denver is generally comparable to that in other large cities across the country in which there is a substantial minority population and where desegregation has not been ordered by the federal courts. There is segregation in the schools of many of these cities fully as pervasive as that in southern cities prior to the desegregation decrees of the past decade and a half. The focus of the school desegregation problem has now shifted from the South to the country as a whole. Unwilling and footdragging as the process was in most places, substantial progress toward achieving integration has been made in southern States. No comparable progress has been made in many nonsouthern cities with large minority populations primarily because of the de facto/de jure distinction nurtured by the courts and accepted complacently by many of the same voices which denounced the evils of segregated schools in the South. But if our national concern is for those who attend such schools, rather than for perpetuating a legalism rooted in history rather than present reality, we must recognize that the evil of operating separate schools is no less in Denver than in Atlanta.

I

In my view we should abandon a distinction which long since has outlived its time, and formulate constitutional principles of national rather than merely regional application. When *Brown v. Board of Educ.*, 347 U.S. 483, was decided, the distinction between de jure and de facto segregation was consistent with the limited constitutional rationale of that case. The situation confronting the Court, largely confined to the southern States, was officially imposed racial segregation in the schools extending back for many years and usually embodied in constitutional and statutory provisions.

The great contribution of *Brown I* was its holding in unmistakable terms that the Fourteenth Amendment forbids state-compelled or authorized segregation of public schools. Although some of the language was more expansive, the holding in *Brown I* was essentially negative: It was impermissible under the Constitution for the States, or their instrumentalities, to force children to attend segregated schools. The forbidden action was de jure, and the opinion in *Brown I* was construed — for some years and by many courts — as requiring only state neutrality, allowing "freedom of choice" as to schools to be attended so long as the State itself assured that the choice was genuinely free of official restraints.

But the doctrine of *Brown I*, as amplified by *Brown II*, 349 U.S. 294 (1955), did not retain its original meaning. In a series of decisions extending from 1954 to 1971 the concept of state neutrality was transformed into the present constitutional doctrine requiring affirmative state action to desegregate school systems. The keystone case was *Green v. County School Board*, 391 U.S. 430, 438 (1968), where school boards were declared to have "the affirmative duty to take whatever steps might be necessary to convert to a unitary system in which racial discrimination would be eliminated root and branch." The school system before the Court in *Green* was operating in a rural and sparsely settled county where there were no concentrations of white and black populations, no neighborhood school system (there were only two schools in the county), and none of the problems of an urbanized school district. The Court properly identified the freedom of choice program there as a subterfuge, and the language in *Green* imposing an affirmative duty to convert to a unitary system was appropriate on the facts before the Court. There was, however, reason to question to what extent this duty would apply in the vastly different factual setting of a large city with extensive areas of residential segregation, presenting problems and calling for solutions quite different from those in the rural setting of New Kent County, Virginia.

But the doubt as to whether the affirmative duty concept would flower into a new constitutional principle of general application was laid to rest by *Swann v. Board of Education*, 402 U.S. 1 (1971), in which the duty articulated in *Green* was applied to the urban school system of metropolitan Charlotte, North Carolina....

....

Whereas *Brown I* rightly decreed the elimination of state-imposed segregation in that particular section of the country where it did exist, *Swann* imposed obligations on southern school districts to eliminate conditions which are not regionally unique but are similar both in origin and effect to conditions in the rest of the country. As the remedial obligations of *Swann* extend far beyond the elimination of the outgrowth of the state-imposed segregation outlawed in *Brown*, the rationale of *Swann* points inevitably towards a uniform constitutional approach to our national problem of school segregation.

II

The Court's decision today, while adhering to the de jure/de facto distinction, will require the application of the *Green/Swann* doctrine of "affirmative duty" to the Denver School Board despite the absence of any history of state-mandated school segregation. The only evidence of a constitutional violation was found in various decisions of the school board. I concur in the Court's position that the public school authorities are the responsible agency of the State, and that if the affirmative duty doctrine is sound constitutional law for Charlotte, it is equally so for Denver. I would not, however, perpetuate the de jure/de facto distinction nor would I leave to petitioners the initial tortuous effort of identifying "segregative acts" and deducing "segregatory intent." I would hold, quite simply, that where segregated public schools exist within a school district to a substantial degree, there is a prima facie case that the duly constituted public authorities (I will usually refer to them collectively as the "school board") are sufficiently responsible to impose upon them a nationally applicable burden to demonstrate they nevertheless are operating a genuinely integrated school system.

A

The principal reason for abandonment of the de jure/de facto distinction is that, in view of the evolution of the holding in *Brown I* into the affirmative duty doctrine, the distinction no longer can be justified on a principled basis. In decreeing remedial requirements for the Charlotte/Mecklenburg school district, *Swann* dealt with a metropolitan, urbanized area in which the basic causes of segregation were generally similar to those in all sections of the country, and also largely irrelevant to the existence of historic, state-imposed segregation at the time of the *Brown* decision. Further, the extension of the affirmative duty concept to include compulsory student transportation went well beyond the mere remedying of that portion of school segregation for which former state segregation laws were ever responsible. Moreover, as the Court's opinion today abundantly demonstrates, the facts deemed necessary to establish de jure discrimination present problems of subjective intent which the courts cannot fairly resolve.

....

... In the evolutionary process since 1954, decisions of this Court have added a significant gloss to this original right. Although nowhere expressly articulated in these terms, I would now define it as the right, derived from the Equal Protection Clause, to expect that once the State has assumed responsibility for education, local school boards will operate *integrated school systems* within their respective districts. This means that school authorities, consistent with the generally accepted educational goal of attaining quality education for all pupils, must make and implement their customary decisions with a view toward enhancing integrated school opportunities.

The term "integrated school system" presupposes, of course, a total absence of any laws, regulations or policies supportive of the type of "legalized" segregation condemned in *Brown*. A system would be integrated in accord with constitutional standards if the responsible authorities had taken appropriate steps to (i) integrate faculties and administration; (ii) scrupulously assure equality of facilities, instruction and curricula opportunities throughout the district; (iii) utilize their authority to draw attendance zones to promote integration; and (iv) locate new schools, close old ones, and determine the size and grade categories with this same objective in mind. Where school authorities decide to undertake the transportation of students, this also must be with integrative opportunities in mind.

The foregoing prescription is not intended to be either definitive or all-inclusive, but rather an indication of the contour characteristics of an *integrated school system* in which all citizens and pupils may justifiably be confident that racial discrimination is neither practiced nor tolerated. An integrated school system does not mean — and indeed could not mean in view of the residential patterns of most of our major metropolitan areas — that *every school* must in fact be an integrated unit. A school which happens to be all or predominantly white or all or predominantly black is not a "segregated" school in an unconstitutional sense if the system itself is a genuinely integrated one.

Having school boards operate an *integrated school system* provides the best assurance of meeting the constitutional requirement that racial discrimination, subtle or otherwise, will find no place in the decisions of public school officials. Courts judging past school board actions with a view to their *general integrative effect* will be best able to assure an absence of such discrimination while avoiding the murky, subjective judgments inherent in the Court's search for "segregatory intent." Any test resting on so nebulous and elusive an element as a school board's segregatory "intent" provides inadequate assurance that minority children will not be shortchanged in the decisions of those entrusted with the nondiscriminatory operation of our public schools.

Public schools are creatures of the State, and whether the segregation is state-created or state-assisted or merely state-perpetuated should be irrelevant to constitutional principle. The school board exercises pervasive and continuing responsibility over the long range planning as well as the daily operations of the public school system. It sets policies on attendance zones, faculty employment and assignments, school construction, closings and consolidations, and myriad other matters. School board decisions obviously are not the sole cause of segregated school conditions. But if, after such detailed and complete public supervision, substantial school segregation still persists, the presumption is strong that the school board, by its acts or omissions, is in some part responsible. Where state action and supervision are so pervasive and where, after years of such action, segregated schools continue to exist within the district to a substantial degree, this Court is justified in finding a prima facie case of a constitutional violation. The burden then must fall on the school board to demonstrate it is operating an *"integrated school system."*

It makes little sense to fine prima facie violations and the consequent affirmative duty to desegregate solely in those States with state-imposed segregation at the time of the *Brown* decision. The history of state-imposed segregation is more widespread in our country than the de jure/de facto distinction has traditionally cared to recognize.

....

Not only does the de jure/de facto distinction operate inequitably on communities in different sections of the country; more importantly, it disadvantages minority children as well.

....

The Court today does move for the first time toward breaking down past sectional disparities, but it clings tenuously to its distinction. It searches for de jure action in what the Denver School Board has done or failed to do, and even here the Court does not rely upon the results or effects of the Board's conduct but feels compelled to find segregatory intent.

....

I can discern no basis in law or logic for holding that the motivation of school board action is irrelevant in Virginia and controlling in Colorado.... The net result of the Court's language, however, is the application of an *effect* test to the actions of southern school districts and an *intent* test to those in other sections, at least until an initial de jure finding for those districts can be made. Rather than straining to perpetuate any such dual standard, we should hold forthrightly that significant segregated school conditions in whatever section of the country are a prima facie violation of constitutional rights.

B

There is thus no reason as a matter of constitutional principle to adhere to the de jure/de facto distinction in school desegregation cases. In addition, there are reasons of policy and prudent judicial administration which point strongly toward the adoption of a uniform national rule. The litigation heretofore centered in the South already is surfacing in other regions. The decision of the Court today, emphasizing as it does the elusive element of segregatory intent, will invite numerous desegregation suits in which there can be little hope of uniformity of result.

....

MR. JUSTICE REHNQUIST, dissenting:

....

Underlying the Court's entire opinion is its apparent thesis that a district judge is at least permitted to find that if a single attendance zone between two individual schools in the large metropolitan district is found by him to have been "gerrymandered," the school district is guilty of operating a "dual" school system, and is apparently a candidate for what is in practice a federal receivership. Not only the language of the Court in the opinion, but its reliance on the case of *Green v. County School Board*, 391 U.S. 430, 437-38 (1968), indicates that such would be the case. It would therefore presumably be open to the District Court to require, inter alia, that pupils be transported great distances throughout the district to and from schools whose attendance zones have not been gerrymandered. Yet unless the Equal Protection Clause of the Fourteenth Amendment now be held to embody a principle of "taint," found in some primitive legal systems but discarded centuries ago in ours, such a result can only be described as the product of judicial fiat.

Green, supra, represented a marked extension of the principles of *Brown v. Board of Education*....

The drastic extension of *Brown* which *Green* represented was barely, if at all, explicated in the latter opinion. To require that a genuinely "dual" system be disestablished, in the sense that the assignment to a child of a particular school is not made to depend on his race, is one thing. To require that school boards affirmatively undertake to achieve racial mixing in schools where such mixing is not achieved in sufficient degree by neutrally drawn boundary lines is quite obviously something else.

The Court's own language in *Green* makes it unmistakably clear that this significant extension of *Brown*'s prohibition against discrimination, and the conversion of that prohibition into an affirmative duty to integrate, was made in the context of a school system which had for a number of years rigidly excluded Negroes from attending the same schools as were attended by whites. Whatever may be the soundness of that decision in the context of a genuinely "dual" school system, where segregation of the races had once been mandated by law,

I can see no constitutional justification for it in a situation such as that which the record shows to have obtained in Denver....

---

1. Try to define precisely what constitutional right was being asserted by the plaintiffs. Does the majority opinion reject all need to find that present segregation in given schools or groups of schools based on neighborhood school attendance is attributable to past de jure action, if there has been de jure segregation in a not insubstantial portion of a school district not divided by a natural boundary? If not, what is the test for determining this causation? If so, is the rejection of the need to find causation justified by "common sense"? Can the opinion be supported on a doctrine of de jure segregation if there is no need to find causation as to given schools or groups of schools? If not, does it suggest that the *Keyes* result is wrong or that the de facto/de jure distinction should be abandoned and that *Keyes* should be decided as a case of segregation regardless of cause? What perceptions do the three opinions provide on these issues?

See also Kutner, *Keyes v. School District Number One: A Constitutional Right to Equal Educational Opportunity?*, 8 J. of L. and Educ. 1 (1979).

2. Is Justice Rehnquist correct in suggesting that causation is not as great an issue in southern de jure cases because the statutes invalidated by *Brown* precluded all black children from going to school with white children? Do we know that but for the statutes, black children would have gone to school with white children? Does that, in part, depend on demographic patterns at the time of *Brown*? More significantly, can it be said that almost 20 years after *Brown*, school segregation in the south is a result of the invalid statutes? Does *Swann* adequately address that issue?

See generally Note, *Reading the Mind of the School Board: Segregative Intent and the De Facto/De Jure Distinction*, 86 Yale L.J. 317 (1976).

3. Consider carefully what is meant by "segregated" schools. Does the term mean schools that deviate significantly in their racial composition from a racial microcosm of the school district, or does it mean schools that deviate from an optimal "racial balance"? Note that the Denver school system is 66% Anglo, 14% Black and 20% Hispano. How would *Keyes* apply to a school district that is 80% Black?

4. *Keyes* allows that plaintiffs in desegregation cases have the burden of finding "intentionally" segregative school board actions in a meaningful portion of ... [the] ... school system." What is "segregative intent"? Is this concept fully explained? Who are the actors within the school system who must harbor this intent, the institution of the school board or individual school board members? Is the standard to be used by lower courts objective or subjective? Are these questions left unanswered by the *Keyes* decision? Have they been answered by court decisions since *Keyes*?

5. The *Brown* decision held that separation of school children on the basis of race is unconstitutional as it creates a "stigma" in minority school children and "generates a feeling of inferiority as to their status in the community." *Brown* at 494. The *Keyes* decision in tandem establishes that a constitutional violation occurs when: 1) school authorities create or maintain racial segregation in the schools vis-à-vis students, schools, teachers, and facilities within the school system and 2) the actions of school authorities are motivated by segregative intent. These unconstitutional actions have been found recently in the case of *People Who Care v. Rockford Bd. of Educ., Sch. Dist. #205*, 851 F. Supp. 905 (N.D. Ill. 1994), suggesting that intentional segregation in schools is yet very much a litigious issue. The district court found intentional discrimination on the part of the local school board over the course of several years. Specific practices included:

> (1) The tracking of students by race into various educational programs ...;
> (2) The drawing and alteration of school attendance area boundaries in such a way as to create, maintain or increase racial or ethnic segregation of students;
> (3) The maintenance of racially and ethnically segregated branches of schools;
> (4) The failure to design and implement an effective desegregation plan even when ordered to do so by a Federal Court and by [the state board of education];
> (5) The provision of inequitable transportation and access to transportation to students based upon their race and ethnic origin;
> (6) The disproportionate placing of the burdens of desegregation on minority students;
> (7) The disparate placement of facilities and equipment so as to burden minority students and not provide them with an equal educational opportunity;
> (8) The perpetuation of discriminatory conditions in the make-up of the [school board]; and
> (9) The disproportionate burdens placed on minorities in the assignment of special education students. *Id*. at 933.

MILLIKEN v. BRADLEY

Supreme Court of the United States
418 U.S. 717 (1974)

[The action was commenced in 1970 by the respondents, the Detroit Branch of the National Association for the Advancement of Colored People, and individual parents and students. The complaint alleged the Detroit Public School System was segregated on the basis of race and attacked the validity of a statute of the State of Michigan on the ground that it put the state in the position of unconstitutionally interfering with the execution and operation of a voluntary plan for partial high school desegregation adopted by the Detroit Board of Education. The District Court found that acts of the Board of Education, including operation of the school transportation and construction programs, resulted in the creation and perpetuation of school segregation in Detroit. Stating that a desegregation plan involving only Detroit schools would not be effective, the District Court imposed a plan involving suburban districts where segregation had not been shown to exist. The Court of Appeals held the imposition of such an interdistrict remedy was within the equity powers of the District Court.]

MR. CHIEF JUSTICE BURGER delivered the opinion of the Court:

We granted certiorari in these consolidated cases to determine whether a federal court may impose a multi-district, areawide remedy to a single-district de jure segregation problem absent any finding that the other included school districts have failed to operate unitary school systems within their districts, absent any claim or finding that the boundary lines of any affected school district were established with the purpose of fostering racial segregation in public schools, absent any finding that the included districts committed acts which effected segregation within the other districts, and absent a meaningful opportunity for the included neighboring school districts to present evidence or be heard on the propriety of a multidistrict remedy or on the question of constitutional violations by those neighboring districts.

....

Viewing the record as a whole, it seems clear that the District Court and the Court of Appeals shifted the primary focus from a Detroit remedy to the metropolitan area only because of their conclusion that total desegregation of Detroit would not produce the racial balance which they perceived as desirable. Both courts proceeded on an assumption that the Detroit schools could not be truly desegregated — in their view of what constituted desegregation — unless the racial composition of the student body of each school substantially reflected the racial composition of the population of the metropolitan area as a whole. The metropolitan area was then defined as Detroit plus 53 of the outlying school districts....

In *Swann*, which arose in the context of a single independent school district, the Court held:

> If we were to read the holding of the District Court to require, as a matter of substantive constitutional right, any particular degree of racial balance or mixing, that approach would be disapproved and we would be obliged to reverse. 402 U.S. at 24.

The clear import of this language from *Swann* is that desegregation, in the sense of dismantling a dual school system, does not require any particular racial balance in each "school, grade or classroom." ...

Here the District Court's approach to what constituted "actual desegregation" raises the fundamental question, not presented in *Swann*, as to the circumstances in which a federal court may order desegregation relief that embraces more than a single school district. The court's analytical starting point was its conclusion that school district lines are no more than arbitrary lines on a map drawn "for political convenience." Boundary lines may be bridged where there has been a constitutional violation calling for interdistrict relief, but the notion that school district lines may be casually ignored or treated as a mere administrative convenience is contrary to the history of public education in our country. No single tradition in public education is more deeply rooted than local control over the operation of schools; local autonomy has long been thought essential both to the maintenance of community concern and support for public schools and to quality of the educational process.... Thus, in *San Antonio School District v. Rodriguez*, 411 U.S. 1, 50 (1973), we observed that local control over the educational process affords citizens an opportunity to participate in decision-making, permits the structuring of school programs to fit local needs, and encourages "experimentation, innovation, and a healthy competition for educational excellence."

The Michigan educational structure involved in this case, in common with most States, provides for a large measure of local control, and a review of the scope and character of these local powers indicates the extent to which the interdistrict remedy approved by the two courts could disrupt and alter the structure of public education in Michigan. The metropolitan remedy would require, in effect, consolidation of 54 independent school districts historically administered as separate units into a vast new super school district.... Entirely apart from the logistical and other serious problems attending large-scale transportation of students, the consolidation would give rise to an array of other problems in financing and operating this new school system. Some of the more obvious questions would be: What would be the status and authority of the present popularly elected school boards? Would the children of Detroit be within the jurisdiction and operating control of a school board elected by the parents and residents of other districts? What board or boards would levy taxes for school operations in these 54 districts constituting the consolidated metropolitan area? What provisions could be made for assuring substantial equality in tax levies among the 54 districts, if this were deemed requisite? What provisions would be made for financing? Would the validity of long-term bonds be jeopardized unless approved by all of the component districts as well as the State? What body would determine that portion of the curricula now left to the discretion of local school boards? Who would establish attendance zones, purchase school equipment, locate and construct new schools, and indeed attend to all the myriad day-to-day decisions that are necessary to school operations affecting potentially more than three-quarters of a million pupils? ...

It may be suggested that all of these vital operational problems are yet to be resolved by the District Court, and that this is the purpose of the Court of Appeals' proposed remand. But it is obvious from the scope of the interdistrict remedy itself that absent a complete restructuring of the laws of Michigan relating to school districts the District Court will become first, a de facto "legislative authority" to resolve these complex questions, and then the "school superintendent" for the entire area. This is a task which few, if any, judges are qualified to perform and one which would deprive the people of control of schools through their elected representatives.

Of course, no state law is above the Constitution. School district lines and the present laws with respect to local control, are not sacrosanct and if they conflict with the Fourteenth Amendment federal courts have a duty to prescribe appropriate remedies. *See, e.g., Wright v. Council of the City of Emporia*, 407 U.S. 451 (1972); *United States v. Scotland Neck Board of Education*, 407 U.S. 484 (1972) (state or local officials prevented from carving out a new school district from an existing district that was in process of dismantling a dual school system); *cf. Haney v. County Board of Education of Sevier County*, 429 F.2d 364 (CA8 1970) (State contributed to separation of races by drawing of school district lines); *United States v. Texas*, 321 F. Supp. 1043 (E.D. Tex. 1970), *aff'd*, 447 F.2d 441 (CA5 1971), *cert. denied sub nom. Edgar v. United States*, 404 U.S. 1016 (1972) (one or more school districts created and maintained for one race). But our prior holdings have been confined to violations and remedies within a single school district. We therefore turn to address, for the first time, the validity of a remedy mandating cross-district or interdistrict consolidation to remedy a condition of segregation found to exist in only one district.

The controlling principle consistently expounded in our holdings is that the scope of the remedy is determined by the nature and extent of the constitutional violation.... Before the boundaries of separate and autonomous school districts may be set aside by consolidating the separate units for remedial purposes or by imposing a cross-district remedy, it must first be shown that there has been a constitutional violation within one district that produces a significant segregative effect in another district. Specifically, it must be shown that racially discriminatory acts of the state or local school districts, or of a single school district have been a substantial cause of interdistrict segregation. Thus an interdistrict remedy might be in order where the racially discriminatory acts of one or more school districts caused racial segregation in an adjacent district, or where district lines have been deliberately drawn on the basis of race. In such circumstances an interdistrict remedy would be appropriate to eliminate the interdistrict segregation directly caused by the constitutional violation. Conversely, without an interdistrict violation and interdistrict effect, there is no constitutional wrong calling for an interdistrict remedy.

The record before us, voluminous as it is, contains evidence of de jure segregated conditions only in the Detroit schools; indeed, that was the theory on which the litigation was initially based and on which the District Court took evidence.... With no showing of significant violation by the 53 outlying school districts and no evidence of any interdistrict violation or effect, the court went beyond the original theory of the case as framed by the pleadings and mandated a metropolitan area remedy. To approve the remedy ordered by the court would impose on the outlying districts, not shown to have committed any constitutional violation, a wholly impermissible remedy based on a standard not hinted at in *Brown I* and *II* or any holding of this Court.

In dissent, Mr. Justice White and Mr. Justice Marshall undertake to demonstrate that agencies having statewide authority participated in maintaining the dual school system found to exist in Detroit. They are apparently of the view that once such participation is shown, the District Court should have a relatively free hand to reconstruct school districts outside of Detroit in fashioning relief. Our assumption, *arguendo*, ... that state agencies did participate in the maintenance of the Detroit system, should make it clear that it is not on this point that we part company. The difference between us arises instead from established doctrine laid down by our cases.... Disparate treatment of white and Negro students occurred within the Detroit school system, and not elsewhere, and on this record the remedy must be limited to that system....

The constitutional right of the Negro respondents residing in Detroit is to attend a unitary school system in that district. Unless petitioners drew the district lines in a discriminatory fashion, or arranged for white students residing in the Detroit District to attend schools in Oakland and Macomb Counties, they were under no constitutional duty to make provisions for Negro students to do so. The view of the dissenters, that the existence of a dual system in Detroit can be made the basis for a decree requiring cross-district transportation of pupils, cannot be supported on the grounds that it represents merely the devising of a suitably flexible remedy for the violation of rights already established by our prior decisions. It can be supported only by drastic expansion of the constitutional right itself, an expansion without any support in either constitutional principle or precedent.

....

---

1. In his concurring opinion in *Milliken*, Justice Stewart noted:

> The courts [below] were in error for the simple reason that the remedy they thought necessary was not commensurate with the constitutional violation found....
>
> This is not to say, however, that an inter-district remedy of the sort approved by the Court of Appeals would not be proper, or even necessary, in other factual situations. Were it to be shown, for example, that state officials had contributed to the separation of the races by drawing or redrawing school district lines; or by purposeful, racially discriminatory use of state housing or zoning laws, then a decree calling for transfer of pupils across district lines or for restructuring of district lines might well be appropriate.

In a dissent, joined by Justices Douglas, Brennan and Marshall, Justice White stated:

> Regretfully, and for several reasons, I can join neither the Court's judgment nor its opinion. The core of my disagreement is that deliberate acts of segregation and their consequences will go unremedied, not because a remedy would be infeasible or unreasonable in terms of the usual criteria governing school desegregation cases, but because an effective remedy would cause what the Court considers to be undue administrative inconvenience to the State. The result is that the State of Michigan, the entity at which the Fourteenth Amendment is directed, has successfully insulated itself from its duty to provide effective desegregation remedies by vesting sufficient power over its public schools in its local school districts. If this is the case in Michigan, it will be the case in most States.
>
> ....
>
> I am even more mystified how the Court can ignore the legal reality that the constitutional violations, even if occurring locally, were committed by governmental entities for which the State is responsible and that it is the State that must respond to the command of the Fourteenth Amendment. An interdistrict remedy for the infringements that occurred in this case is well within the confines and powers of the State, which is the governmental entity ultimately responsible for desegregating its schools. The Michigan Supreme Court has observed that "[t]he school district is a state agency," and that "[e]ducation in Michigan belongs to the State. It is no part of the local self-government inherent in the township or municipality except so far as the Legislature may choose to make it such. The Constitution has turned the whole subject over to the Legislature...."
>
> ....
>
> Finally, I remain wholly unpersuaded by the Court's assertion that "the remedy is necessarily designed, as all remedies are, to restore the victims of discriminatory conduct to the position they would have occupied in the absence of such conduct." In the first place, under this premise the Court's judgment is itself infirm; for had the Detroit school system not followed an official policy of segregation throughout the 1950's and 1960's, Negroes and whites would have been going to school together. There would have been no, or at least not as many, recognizable Negro schools and not, or at least not as many, white schools, but "just schools," and neither Negroes nor whites would have suffered from the effects of segregated education, with all its shortcomings. Surely the Court's remedy will not restore to the Negro community, stigmatized as it was by the dual school system, what it would have enjoyed over all or most of this period if the remedy is confined to present day Detroit; for the maximum remedy available within that area will leave many of the schools almost totally black, and the system itself will be predominantly black and will become increasingly so. Moreover, when a

State has engaged in acts of official segregation over a lengthy period of time, as in the case before us, it is unrealistic to suppose that the children who were victims of the State's unconstitutional conduct could now be provided the benefits of which they were wrongfully deprived. Nor can the benefits which accrue to school systems in which school children have not been officially segregated, and to the communities supporting such school systems, be fully and immediately restored after a substantial period of unlawful segregation. The education of children of different races in a desegregated environment has unhappily been lost, along with the social, economic, and political advantages which accompany a desegregated school system. It is for these reasons that the Court has consistently followed the course of requiring the effects of past official segregation to be eliminated "root and branch" by imposing, in the present, the duty to provide a remedy which will achieve "the greatest possible degree of actual desegregation, taking into account the practicalities of the situation." It is also for these reasons that once a constitutional violation has been found, the District Judge obligated to provide such a remedy "will thus necessarily be concerned with the elimination of one-race schools." These concerns were properly taken into account by the District Judge in this case. Confining the remedy to the boundaries of the Detroit district is quite unrelated either to the goal of achieving maximum desegregation or to those intensely practical considerations, such as the extent and expense of transportation, that have imposed limits on remedies in cases such as this. The Court's remedy, in the end, is essentially arbitrary and will leave serious violations of the Constitution substantially unremedied.

MR. JUSTICE MARSHALL added, in his dissent:

Under a Detroit-only decree, Detroit's schools will clearly remain racially identifiable in comparison with neighboring schools in the metropolitan community. Schools with 65% and more Negro students will stand in sharp and obvious contrast to schools in neighboring districts with less than 2% Negro enrollment. Negro students will continue to perceive their schools as segregated educational facilities and this perception will only be increased when whites react to a Detroit-only decree by fleeing to the suburbs to avoid integration. School district lines, however innocently drawn, will surely be perceived as fences to separate the races when, under a Detroitonly decree, white parents withdraw their children from the Detroit city schools and move to the suburbs in order to continue them in all-white schools. The message of this action will not escape the Negro children in the city of Detroit. It will be of scant significance to Negro children who have for years been confined by de jure acts of segregation to a growing core of all-Negro schools surrounded by a ring of all-white schools that the new dividing line between the races is the school district boundary.

CH. 11: RACIAL SEGREGATION IN THE PUBLIC SCHOOLS   817

> Nor can it be said that the State is free from any responsibility for the disparity between racial makeup of Detroit and its surrounding suburbs. The State's creation, through de jure acts of segregation, of a growing core of all-Negro schools inevitably acted as a magnet to attract Negroes to the areas served by such schools and to deter them from settling either in other areas of the city or in the suburbs. By the same token, the growing core of all-Negro schools inevitably helped drive whites to other areas of the city or to the suburbs....
>
> ....
>
> The State must also bear part of the blame for the white flight to the suburbs which would be forthcoming from a Detroit-only decree and would render such a remedy ineffective. Having created a system where whites and Negroes were intentionally kept apart so that they could not become accustomed to learning together, the State is responsible for the fact that many whites will react to the dismantling of that segregated system by attempting to flee to the suburbs. Indeed, by limiting the District Court to a Detroit-only remedy and allowing that flight to the suburbs to succeed, the Court today allows the State to profit from its own wrong and to perpetuate for years to come the separation of the races it achieved in the past by purposeful state action.

Which opinions are most consistent with the prior cases? Which with sound constitutional analysis?

After *Milliken* was remanded, the district court promptly ordered submission of a new desegregation plan limited to the confines of the Detroit School System. Following extensive hearings the court, in addition to a plan for student assignment, included in its decree educational components proposed by the Detroit School Board in the areas of reading, in-service teacher training, testing, and counseling. The district court determined that these components were necessary to carry out desegregation and directed that the costs were to be borne by the Detroit School Board and the State. The district court's order was appealed to the United States Supreme Court, which held that in order to eliminate de jure segregation, the ordered implementation of remedial education programs is an appropriate means of eliminating consequences of past constitutional violations and is not an abuse of the district court's broad and flexible equity powers. The Supreme Court also ruled that the Eleventh Amendment does not bar the district court's decree that state officials pay one-half the additional costs attributable to the four educational components since the district court was authorized to provide prospective equitable relief, even though such relief requires the expenditure of money by the State. *Milliken v. Bradley*, 433 U.S. 267 (1977).

2. The cases in this area since *Green* all raise fundamental questions about overriding school board or individual parent choice relating to the values of the neighborhood school, or that of racially homogeneous schools. These issues become ever more acute when the objections to compelled racial balance and the busing necessary to accomplish it are raised by members of the minority groups for whom desegregation is primarily aimed. In *Coppedge v. Franklin County Bd. of Educ.*, 394 F.2d 410 (4th Cir. 1968), the court, pre-*Green*, struck down a North Carolina freedom-of-choice plan over the objection of a group of blacks who attempted to intervene in the proceedings to assert their "right to remain in the familiar surroundings of all-Negro schools." The court did not allow the intervention and summarily disposed of the objection. *See also Norwalk CORE v. Norwalk Bd. of Educ.*, 298 F. Supp. 213 (D. Conn. 1969), *aff'd*, 423 F.2d 121 (2d Cir. 1970), and *Moss v. Stamford Bd. of Educ.*, 356 F. Supp. 675 (D. Conn. 1973), in which black groups lost challenges to Northern school boards' integration plans which bused black children to schools in white neighborhoods disproportionately to busing white children to schools in black neighborhoods.

See generally Bell, *Serving Two Masters: Integration Ideals and Client Interests in School Desegregation Litigation*, 85 Yale L.J. 470 (1976), which includes historical background on Black opposition to Boston school busing plans in *Morgan v. Hennigan*, 379 F. Supp. 410 (D. Mass.), *aff'd sub nom. Morgan v. Kerrigan*, 509 F.2d 580 (1st Cir. 1974), *cert. denied*, 421 U.S. 963 (1975).

Some courts have voiced concern that extensive busing to achieve racial balance may prove detrimental to educational achievement of both black and white students and have appeared to seek what they perceive to be the least disruptive means of achieving racial balance in the schools. *See Evans v. Buchanan*, 447 F. Supp. 982 (D. Del. 1978); *Calhoun v. Cook*, 522 F.2d 717 (5th Cir. 1975); and *Hart v. Community School Bd. of Educ., N.Y. Sch. Dist. #21*, 512 F.2d 37 (2d Cir. 1975). *See generally*, Mays, *Comment: Atlanta — Living with Brown Twenty Years Later*, 3 Black L. J. 184 (1974).

3. The *Milliken* Court stressed the importance of local control in education, a notion that it had articulated two years earlier in *San Antonio Indep. Sch. Dist. v. Rodriguez*, 411 U.S. 1 (1973). The legislation at issue in *Milliken* was found by the Court to abolish local control of schools. Does the Court imply by its holding that it is reasonable to place limitations on the reach of remedial powers of lower courts to fashion desegregation remedies if they inhibit the powers of school boards to maintain local control? Does this theme travel into more recent Supreme Court desegregation decisions? *See Board of Educ. of Oklahoma City Pub. Schs. Indep. Sch. Dist. v. Dowell*, 498 U.S. 237 (1991).

DAYTON BOARD OF EDUCATION v. BRINKMAN
Supreme Court of the United States
433 U.S. 406 (1977)

MR. JUSTICE REHNQUIST delivered the opinion of the Court:

This school desegregation action comes to us after five years and two round trips through the lower federal courts. Those protracted proceedings have been devoted to the formulation of a remedy for actions of the Dayton Board of

Education found to be in violation of the Equal Protection Clause of the Fourteenth Amendment. In the decision now under review, the Court of Appeals for the Sixth Circuit finally approved a plan involving districtwide racial distribution requirements, after rejecting two previous, less sweeping orders by the District Court. The plan required, beginning with the 1976-1977 school year, that the racial distribution of each school in the district be brought within 15% of the 48%-52% black-white population ratio of Dayton. As finally formulated, the plan employed a variety of desegregation techniques, including the "pairing" of schools, the redefinition of attendance zones, and a variety of centralized special programs and "magnet schools." We granted certiorari to consider the propriety of this court-ordered remedy in light of the constitutional violations which were found by the courts below.

Whatever public notice this case has received as it wended its way from the United States District Court for the Southern District of Ohio to this Court has been due to the fact that it represented an effort by minority plaintiffs to obtain relief from alleged unconstitutional segregation of the Dayton public schools said to have resulted from actions by the respondent School Board. While we would by no means discount the importance of this aspect of the case, we think that the case is every bit as important for the issues it raises as to the proper allocation of functions between the district courts and the courts of appeals within the federal judicial system.

Indeed, the importance of the judicial administration aspects of the case are heightened by the presence of the substantive issues on which it turns. The proper observance of the division of functions between the federal trial courts and the federal appellate courts is important in every case. It is especially important in a case such as this where the District Court for the Southern District of Ohio was not simply asked to render judgment in accordance with the law of Ohio in favor of one private party against another; it was asked by the plaintiffs, students in the public school system of a large city, to restructure the administration of that system.

There is no doubt that federal courts have authority to grant appropriate relief of this sort when constitutional violations on the part of school officials are proven. *Keyes v. School District No. 1, Denver, Colorado*, 413 U.S. 189 (1973); *Wright v. Council of City of Emporia*, 407 U.S. 451 (1972); *Swann v. Charlotte-Mecklenburg Board of Education*, 402 U.S. 1 (1971). But our cases have just as firmly recognized that local autonomy of school districts is a vital national tradition. *Milliken v. Bradley*, 418 U.S. 717, 741-42 (1974); *San Antonio School District v. Rodriguez*, 411 U.S. 1, 50 (1973); *Wright v. Council of City of Emporia, supra,* at 469. It is for this reason that the case for displacement of the local authorities by a federal court in a school desegregation case must be satisfactorily established by factual proof and justified by a reasoned statement of legal principles.

The lawsuit was begun in April 1972, and the District Court filed its original decision on February 7, 1973. The District Court first surveyed the past conduct of affairs by the Dayton School Board, and found "isolated but repeated instances of failure by the Dayton School Board to meet the standards of the Ohio law mandating an integrated school system." It cited instances of physical segregation in the schools during the early decades of this century, but concluded that "[b]oth by reason of the substantial time that had elapsed and because these practices have ceased, ... the foregoing will not necessarily be deemed to be evidence of a continuing segregative policy."

The District Court also found that as recently as the 1950s, faculty hiring had not been on a racially neutral basis, but that "by 1963, under a policy designated as one of 'dynamic gradualism,' at least one black teacher had been assigned to all eleven high schools and to 35 of the 66 schools in the entire system." It further found that by 1969 each school in the Dayton system had an integrated teaching staff consisting of at least one black faculty member. The Court's conclusion with respect to faculty hiring was that pursuant to a 1971 agreement with the Department of HEW, "the teaching staff of the Dayton public schools became and still remains substantially integrated."

The District Court noted the Dunbar High School had been established in 1933 as a black high school, taught by black teachers and attended by black pupils. At the time of its creation there were no attendance zones in Dayton and students were permitted liberal transfers, so that attendance at Dunbar was voluntary. The court found that Dunbar continued to exist as a citywide all-black high school until it closed in 1962.

Turning to more recent operations of the Dayton public schools, the District Court found that the "great majority" of the 66 schools were imbalanced and that, with one exception, the Dayton School Board had made no affirmative effort to achieve racial balance within those schools. But the court stated that there was no evidence of racial discrimination in the establishment or alteration of attendance boundaries or in the site selection and construction of new schools and school additions. It considered the use of optional attendance zones with the District, and concluded that in the majority of cases the "optional zones had no racial significance at the time of their creation." It made a somewhat ambiguous finding as to the effect of some of the zones in the past, and concluded that although none of the elementary optional school attendance zones today "have any significant potential effects in terms of increased racial separation," the same cannot be said of the high school optional zones. Two zones in particular, "those between Roosevelt and Colonel White and between Kiser and Colonel White, are by far the largest in the system and have had the most demonstrable racial effects in the past."[10]

The court found no evidence that the District's "freedom of enrollment" policy had "been unfairly operated or that black students [had] been denied transfers because of their race." Finally the court considered action by a newly elected Board on January 3, 1972, rescinding resolutions, passed by the previous Board, which had acknowledged a role played by the Board in the creation of segregative racial patterns and had called for various types of remedial measures. The District Court's ultimate conclusion was that the "racially imbalanced schools, optional attendance zones, and recent Board action... are cumulatively a violation of the Equal Protection Clause."

The District Court's use of the phrase "cumulative violation" is unfortunately not free from ambiguity. Treated most favorably to the respondents, it may be said to represent the District Court's opinion that there were three separate although relatively isolated instances of unconstitutional action on the part of petitioners. Treated most favorably to the petitioners, however, they must be viewed in quite a different light. The finding that the pupil population in the various Dayton schools is not homogeneous, standing by itself, it not a violation of the Fourteenth Amendment in the absence of a showing that this condition resulted from intentionally segregative actions on the part of the Board. *Washington v. Davis*, 426 U.S. 229, 239 (1976). The District Court's finding as to the effect of the optional attendance zones for the three Dayton high schools, assuming that it was a violation under the standards of *Washington v. Davis, supra*, appears to be so only with respect to high school districting. *Swann, supra*, at 15. The District Court's conclusion that the Board's recision of previously adopted school board resolutions was itself a constitutional violation is also of questionable validity.

The Board had not acted to undo operative regulations affecting the assignment of pupils or other aspects of the management of school affairs, but simply repudiated a resolution of a predecessor Board stating that it recognized its own fault in not taking affirmative action at an earlier date. We agree with the Court of Appeals' treatment of this action, wherein the court said:

> The question of whether a rescission of previous Board action is in and of itself a violation of appellants' constitutional rights is inextricably bound up

---

[10]The following information about those zones is contained in an appendix to the District Court opinion:

High Schools	Date of Creation	% black population At date of creation	1972 - 73
Roosevelt/	1951	31.5	100.0
Colonel White	(extended 1958)	0.0	54.6
Kiser/	1962	2.7	9.8
Colonel White		1.1	54.6

with the question of whether the Board was under a constitutional duty to take the action which it initially took. *Cf. Hunter v. Erickson*, 393 U.S. 385 (1960); *Gomillion v. Lightfoot*, 364 U.S. 339 (1960). If the Board was not under such a duty, then the rescission of the initial action in and of itself cannot be a constitutional violation. If the Board was under such a duty, then the rescission becomes a part of the cumulative violation, and it is not necessary to ascertain whether the recision *ipso facto* is an independent violation of the Constitution. 503 F.2d 684, 697.

Judged most favorably to the petitioners, then, the District Court's findings of constitutional violations did not, under our cases, suffice to justify the remedy imposed. Nor is light cast upon the District Court's finding by its repeated use of the phrase "cumulative violation." We realize, of course, that the task of factfinding in a case such as this is a good deal more difficult than is typically the case in a more orthodox lawsuit. Findings as to the motivations of multi-membered public bodies are of necessity difficult, and the question of whether demographic changes resulting in racial concentration occurred from purely neutral public actions or were instead the intended result of actions which appeared neutral on their face but were in fact invidiously discriminatory is not an easy one to resolve.

We think it accurate to say that the District Court's formulation of a remedy on the basis of the three part "cumulative violation" was certainly not based on an unduly cautious understanding of its authority in such a situation. The remedy which it originally propounded in light of these findings of fact including requirements that optional attendance zones be eliminated, and that faculty assignment practices and hiring policies with respect to classified personnel be tailored to achieve representative racial distribution in all schools. The one portion of the remedial plan submitted by the School Board which the District Court refused to accept without change was that which dealt with so-called "freedom of enrollment priorities." The court ordered that, as applied to high schools, new students at each school be chosen at random from those wishing to attend. The Board was required to furnish transportation for all students who chose to attend a high school outside the attendance area of their residence.

Both the plaintiffs and the defendant School Board appealed the order of the District Court to the United States Court of Appeals for the Sixth Circuit. 503 F.2d 684. That court considered at somewhat greater length than had the District Court both the historical instances of alleged racial discrimination by the Dayton School Board and the circumstances surrounding the adoption of the Board's resolutions and the subsequent rescission of those resolutions. This consideration was in a purely descriptive vein: no findings of fact made by the District Court were reversed as having been clearly erroneous, and the Court of Appeals engaged in no factfinding of its own based on evidence adduced before the District Court. The Court of Appeals then focused on the District Court's finding of a three-part "cumulative" constitutional violation consisting of racially

CH. 11: RACIAL SEGREGATION IN THE PUBLIC SCHOOLS 823

imbalanced schools, optional attendance zones, and the rescission of the Board resolutions. It found these to be "amply supported by the evidence."

Plaintiffs in the District Court, respondents here, had cross-appealed from the order of the District Court, contending that the District Court had erred in failing to make further findings tending to show segregative actions on the part of the Dayton School Board, but the Court of Appeals found it unnecessary to pass on these contentions. The Court of Appeals also stated that it was unnecessary to "pass on the question of whether the rescission [of the Board resolutions] by itself was a violation of" constitutional rights. It did discuss at length what it described as "serious questions" as to whether Board conduct relating to staff assignment, school construction, grade structure and reorganization, and transfers and transportation, should have been included within the "cumulative violation" found by the District Court. But it did no more than discuss these questions; it neither upset the factual findings of the District Court nor did it reverse the District Court's conclusions of law.

Thus the Court of Appeals, over and above its historical discussion of the Dayton school situation, dealt with and upheld only the three-part "cumulative violation" found by the District Court. But it nonetheless reversed the District Court's approval of the school board plan as modified by the District Court, because the Court of Appeals concluded that "the remedy ordered ... is inadequate, considering the scope of the cumulative violations." While it did not discuss the specifics of any plan to be adopted on remand, it repeated the admonition that the court's duty is to eliminate "all vestiges of state-imposed school segregation." *Keyes, supra,* at 202; *Swann, supra,* at 15.

Viewing the findings of the District Court as to the three-part "cumulative violation" in the strongest light for the respondents, the Court of Appeals simply had no warrant in our cases for imposing the system wide remedy which it apparently did. There had been no showing that such a remedy was necessary to "eliminate all vestiges of the state-imposed school segregation." It is clear from the findings of the District Court that Dayton is a racially mixed community, and that many of its schools are either predominantly white or predominantly black. This fact without more, of course, does not offend the Constitution. *Spencer v. Kugler,* 404 U.S. 1027 (1972); *Swann, supra,* at 24. The Court of Appeals seems to have viewed the present structure of the Dayton school system as a sort of "fruit of the poisonous tree," since some of the racial imbalance that presently obtains may have resulted in some part from the three instances of segregative action found by the District Court. But instead of tailoring a remedy commensurate to the three specific violations, the Court of Appeals imposed a systemwide remedy going beyond their scope.

. . . .

The duty of both the District Court and of the Court of Appeals in a case such as this, where mandatory segregation by law of the races in the schools has long since ceased, is to first determine whether there was any action in the conduct of the business of the school board which was intended to, and did in fact, discriminate against minority pupils, teachers or staff. *Washington v. Davis, supra.* All parties should be free to introduce such additional testimony and other evidence as the District Court may deem appropriate. If such violations are found, the District Court in the first instance, subject to review by the Court of Appeals, must determine how much incremental segregative effect these violations had on the racial distribution of the Dayton school population as presently constituted, when that distribution is compared to what it would have been in the absence of such constitutional violations. The remedy must be designed to redress that difference, and only if there has been a systemwide impact may there by a systemwide remedy. *Keyes, supra,* at 213.

We realize that this is a difficult task, and that it is much easier for a reviewing court to fault ambiguous phrases such as "cumulative violation" than it is for the finder of fact to make the complex factual determinations in the first instance. Nonetheless, that is what the Constitution and our cases call for, and that is what must be done in this case.

While we have found that the plan implicitly, if not explicitly, imposed by the Court of Appeals was erroneous on the present state of the record, it is undisputed that it has been in effect in the Dayton school system during the present year without creating serious problems. While a school board and a school constituency which attempt to comply with a plan to the best of their ability should not be penalized, we think that the plan finally adopted by the District Court should remain in effect for the coming school year subject to such further orders of the District Court as it may find warranted following the hearings mandated by this opinion.

The judgment of the Court of Appeals is vacated, and the cause is remanded for further proceedings consistent with this opinion.

It is so ordered.

MR. JUSTICE MARSHALL took no part in the consideration or decision of this case. [The concurring opinions of MR. JUSTICE BRENNAN and MR. JUSTICE STEVENS are deleted.]

COLUMBUS BOARD OF EDUCATION v. PENICK

Supreme Court of the United States
443 U.S. 449 (1979)

MR. JUSTICE WHITE delivered the opinion of the Court:

The public schools of Columbus, Ohio, are highly segregated by race. In 1976, over 32% of the 96,000 students in the system were black. About 70% of all students attended schools that were at least 80% black or 80% white. 429 F. Supp. 229, 240 (SD Ohio 1977). Half of the 172 schools were 90% black or 90% white. 583 F.2d 787, 800 (CA6 1978). Fourteen named students in the Columbus school system brought this case on June 21, 1973, against the Columbus Board of Education, the State Board of Education, and the appropriate local and state officials. The second amended complaint, filed on October 24, 1974, charged that the Columbus defendants had pursued and were pursuing a course of conduct having the purpose and effect of causing and perpetuating the segregation in the public schools, contrary to the Fourteenth Amendment. A declaratory judgment to this effect and appropriate injunctive relief were prayed. Trial of the case began a year later, consumed 36 trial days, produced a record containing over 600 exhibits and a transcript in excess of 6,600 pages, and was completed in June 1976. Final arguments were heard in September, and in March 1977 the District Court filed an opinion and order containing its findings of fact and conclusions of law. 429 F. Supp. 229.

The trial court summarized its findings:

> From the evidence adduced at trial, the Court has found earlier in this opinion that the Columbus Public Schools were openly and intentionally segregated on the basis of race when *Brown* [*v. Board of Education (I)*, 347 U.S. 483], was decided in 1954. The Court has found that the Columbus Board of Education never actively set out to dismantle this dual system. The Court has found that until legal action was initiated by the Columbus Area Civil Rights Council, the Columbus Board did not assign teachers and administrators to Columbus schools at random, without regard for the racial composition of the student enrollment at those schools. The Columbus Board even in very recent times ... has approved optional attendance zones, discontiguous attendance areas and boundary changes which have maintained and enhanced racial imbalance in the Columbus Public Schools. The Board, even in very recent times and after promising to do otherwise, has adjured [*sic*] workable suggestions for improving the racial balance of city schools.
>
> Viewed in the context of the segregative optional attendance zones, segregative faculty and administrative hiring and assignments, and other such actions and decisions of the Columbus Board of Education in recent and remote history, it is fair and reasonable to draw an inference of segregative intent from the Board's actions and omission discussed in this opinion. *Id.* at 260-61.

The District Court's ultimate conclusion was that at the time of trial the racial segregation in the Columbus school system "directly resulted from [the Board's] intentional segregative acts and omissions," *id.* at 259, in violation of the Equal Protection Clause of the Fourteenth Amendment. Accordingly, judgment was entered against the local and state defendants enjoining them from continuing to discriminate on the basis of race in operating the Columbus public schools and ordering the submission of a systemwide desegregation plan.

Following decision by this Court in *Dayton Board of Education v. Brinkman (I)*, 433 U.S. 406, in June 1977, and in response to a motion by the Columbus Board, the District Court rejected the argument that *Dayton I* required or permitted any modification of its findings or judgment. It reiterated its conclusion that the Board's "'liability in this case concerns the Columbus School District as a whole,'" Pet. App. 94, quoting 429 F. Supp. at 266, asserting that, although it had "no real interest in any remedy plan which is more sweeping than necessary to correct the constitutional wrongs plaintiffs have suffered," neither would it accept any plan "which fails to take into account the systemwide nature of the liability of the defendants." Pet. App. 95. The Board subsequently presented a plan that complied with the District Court's guidelines and that was embodied in a judgment entered on October 7. The plan was stayed pending appeal to the Court of Appeals.

Based on its own examination of the extensive record, the Court of Appeals affirmed the judgments entered against the local defendants. 583 F.2d 787. The Court of Appeals could not find the District Court's findings of fact clearly erroneous. *Id.* at 789. Indeed, the Court of Appeals examined in detail each set of findings by the District Court and found strong support for them in the record. *Id.* at 798, 804, 805, 814. The Court of Appeals also discussed in detail and found unexceptionable the District Court's understanding and application of the Fourteenth Amendment and the cases construing it.

Implementation of the desegregation plan was stayed pending our disposition of the case. 439 U.S. 1348 (1978) (REHNQUIST, J.). We granted the Board's petition for certiorari, 439 U.S. 1066 (1979), and we now affirm the judgment of the Court of Appeals.

II

The Board earnestly contends that when this case was brought and at the time of trial its operation of a segregated school system was not done with any general or specific racially discriminatory purpose, and that whatever unconstitutional conduct it may have been guilty of in the past such conduct at no time had systemwide segregative impact and surely no remaining systemwide impact at the time of trial. A systemwide remedy was therefore contrary to the teachings of the cases, such as *Dayton I*, that the scope of the constitutional violation measures the scope of the remedy.

We have discovered no reason, however, to disturb the judgment of the Court of Appeals, based on the findings and conclusions of the District Court, that the Board's conduct at the time of trial and before not only was animated by an unconstitutional, segregative purpose, but also had current, segregative impact that was sufficiently systemwide to warrant the remedy order by the District Court.

These ultimate conclusions were rooted in a series of constitutional violations that the District Court found the Board to have committed and that together dictated its judgment and decree. In each instance, the Court of Appeals found the District Court's conclusions to be factually and legally sound.

A

First, although at least since 1888 there had been no statutory requirement or authorization to operate segregated schools, the District Court found that in 1954, when *Brown I* was decided, the Columbus Board was not operating a racially neutral, unitary school system, but was conducting "an enclave of separate, black schools in the near east side of Columbus," and that "[t]he then-existing racial separation was the direct result of cognitive acts or omissions of those school board members and administrators who had originally intentionally caused and later perpetuated the racial isolation...." 429 F. Supp. at 236. Such separateness could not "be said to have been the result of racially neutral official acts." *Ibid.*

Based on its own examination of the record, the Court of Appeals agreed with the District Court in this respect, observing that, "[w]hile the Columbus school system's dual black-white character was not mandated by state law as of 1954, the record certainly shows intentional segregation by the Columbus Board. As of 1954 the Columbus School Board had 'carried out a systematic program of segregation affecting a substantial portion of the students, schools, teachers and facilities within the school system.'" 583 F.2d at 798-99, quoting *Keyes v. School Dist. No. 1*, 413 U.S. 189, 201-02 (1973).

The Board insists that, since segregated schooling was not commanded by state law and since not all schools were wholly black or wholly white in 1954, the District Court was not warranted in finding a dual system. But the District Court found that the "Columbus Public Schools were *officially* segregated by race in 1954," Pet. App. 94 (emphasis added); and in any event, there is no reason to question the finding that as the "direct result of cognitive acts or omissions" the Board maintained "an enclave of separate, black schools on the near east side of Columbus." 429 F. Supp. at 236. Proof of purposeful and effective maintenance of a body of separate black schools in a substantial part of the system itself is prima facie proof of a dual school system and supports a finding to this effect absent sufficient contrary proof by the Board, which was not forthcoming in this case. *Keyes, supra,* at 203.

B

Second, both courts below declared that since the decision in *Brown v. Board of Education (II)*, 349 U.S. 294 (1955), the Columbus Board has been under a continuous constitutional obligation to disestablish its dual school system and that it has failed to discharge this duty. Pet. App. 94; 583 F.2d at 799. Under the Fourteenth Amendment and the cases that have construed it, the Board's duty to dismantle its dual system cannot be gainsaid.

Where a racially discriminatory school system has been found to exist, *Brown II* imposes the duty on local school boards to "effectuate a transition to a racially non-discriminatory school system." 349 U.S. at 301. "*Brown II* was a call for the dismantling of well-entrenched dual systems," and school boards operating such systems were "clearly charged with the affirmative duty to take whatever steps might be necessary to convert to a unitary system in which racial discrimination would be eliminated root and branch." *Green v. County School Board*, 391 U.S. 430, 437-38 (1968). Each instance of a failure or refusal to fulfill this affirmative duty continues the violation of the Fourteenth Amendment.

Dayton I, 433 U.S. at 413-14; *Wright v. Council of City of Emporia*, 407 U.S. 451, 460 (1972); *United States v. Scotland Neck City Board of Education*, 407 U.S. 484 (creation of a new school district in a city that had operated a dual school system but was not yet the subject of court-ordered desegregation).

The *Green* case itself was decided 13 years after *Brown II*. The core of the holding was that the school board involved had not done enough to eradicate the lingering consequences of the dual school system that it had been operating at the time *Brown* was decided. Even though a freedom of choice plan had been adopted, the school system remained essentially a segregated system, with many all-black and many all-white schools. The board's continuing obligation, which had not been satisfied, was "'to come forward with a plan that promises realistically to work ... *now* ... until it is clear that state-imposed segregation has been completely removed.'" *Swann v. Charlotte-Mecklenburg Board of Education*, 402 U.S. 1, 13 (1971), quoting *Green*, *supra*, at 439 (emphasis in original).

As the Chief Justice's opinion for a unanimous Court in *Swann* recognized, *Brown* and *Green* imposed an affirmative duty to desegregate. "If school authorities fail in their affirmative obligations under those holdings, judicial authority may be invoked.... In default by the school authorities of their obligation to proffer acceptable remedies, a district court has broad power to fashion a remedy that will assure a unitary school system." 402 U.S. at 15-16. In *Swann*, it should be recalled, an initial segregation plan had been entered in 1965 and had been affirmed on appeal. But the case was reopened, and in 1969 the school board was required to come forth with a more effective plan. The judgment adopting the ultimate plan was affirmed here in 1971, 16 years after *Brown II*.

In determining whether a dual school system has been disestablished, *Swann* also mandates that matters aside from student assignments must be considered:

> [W]here it is possible to identify a "white school" or a "Negro school" simply by reference to the racial composition of teachers and staff, the quality of school buildings and equipment, or the organization of sports activities, a prima facie case of violation of substantive constitutional rights under the Equal Protection Clause is shown. 402 U.S. at 18.

Further, *Swann* stated that in devising remedies for legally imposed segregation the responsibility of the local authorities and district courts is to ensure that future school construction and abandonment are not used and do not serve to perpetuate or re-establish the dual school system. *Id.* at 20-21. As for student assignments, the Court said:

> No per se rule can adequately embrace all the difficulties of reconciling the competing interests involved; but in a system with a history of segregation the need for remedial criteria of sufficient specificity to assure a school authority's compliance with its constitutional duty warrants a presumption

against schools that are substantially disproportionate in their racial composition. Where the school authority's proposed plan for conversion from a dual to a unitary system contemplates the continued existence of some schools that are all or predominantly of one race, they have the burden of showing that such school assignments are genuinely nondiscriminatory. *Id.* at 26.

The Board's continuing "affirmative duty to disestablish the dual school system" is therefore beyond question, *McDaniel v. Barresi*, 402 U.S. 39, 41 (1971), and it has pointed to nothing in the record persuading us that at the time of trial the dual school system and its effects had been disestablished. The Board does not appear to challenge the finding of the District Court that at the time of trial most blacks were still going to black schools and most whites to white schools. Whatever the Board's current purpose with respect to racially separate education might be, it knowingly continued its failure to eliminate the consequences of its past intentionally segregative policies. The Board "never actively set out to dismantle this dual system." 429 F. Supp. at 260.

C

Third, the District Court not only found that the Board had breached its constitutional duty by failing effectively to eliminate the continuing consequences of its intentional systemwide segregation in 1954, but also found that in the intervening years there had been a series of Board actions and practices that could not "reasonably be explained without reference to racial concerns," *Id.* at 241, and that "intentionally aggravated, rather than alleviated," racial separation in the schools. Pet. App. 94. These matters included the general practice of assigning black teachers only to those schools with substantial black student populations, a practice that was terminated only in 1974 as the result of a conciliation agreement with the Ohio Civil Rights Commission; the intentionally segregative use of optional attendance zones, discontiguous attendance areas, and boundary changes; and the selection of sites for new school construction that had the foreseeable and anticipated effect of maintaining the racial separation of the schools. The court generally noted that "[s]ince the 1954 *Brown* decision, the Columbus defendants or their predecessors were adequately put on notice of the fact that action was required to correct and to prevent the increase in" segregation, yet failed to heed their duty to alleviate racial separation in the schools. 429 F. Supp. at 255.

III

Against this background, we cannot fault the conclusion of the District Court and the Court of Appeals that at the time of trial there was systemwide segregation in the Columbus schools that was the result of recent and remote intentionally segregative actions of the Columbus Board. While appearing not to challenge most of the subsidiary findings of historical fact, Tr. of Oral Arg. at

7, petitioners dispute many of the factual inferences drawn from these facts by the two courts below. On this record, however, there is no apparent reason to disturb the factual findings and conclusions entered by the District Court and strongly affirmed by the Court of Appeals after its own examination of the record.

Nor do we discern that the judgments entered below rested on any misapprehension of the controlling law. It is urged that the courts below failed to heed the requirements of *Keyes, Washington v. Davis*, 426 U.S. 229 (1976), and *Village of Arlington Heights v. Metropolitan Housing Dev. Corp.*, 429 U.S. 252 (1977), that a plaintiff seeking to make out an equal protection violation on the basis of racial discrimination must show purpose. Both courts, it is argued, considered the requirement satisfied if it were shown that disparate impact would be the natural and foreseeable consequence of the practices and policies of the Board, which, it is said, is nothing more than equating impact with intent, contrary to the controlling precedent.

The District court, however, was amply cognizant of the controlling cases. It is understood that to prevail the plaintiffs were required to "'prove not only that segregated schooling exists but also that it was brought about or maintained by intentional state action,'" 429 F. Supp. at 251, quoting *Keyes, supra*, at 198 — that is, that the school officials had "intended to segregate." 429 F. Supp. at 254. *See also* 583 F.2d at 801. The District Court also recognized that under those cases disparate impact and foreseeable consequences, without more, do not establish a constitutional violation. *See, e.g.*, 429 F. Supp. at 251. Nevertheless, the District Court correctly noted that actions having foreseeable and anticipated disparate impact are relevant evidence to prove the ultimate fact, forbidden purpose. Those cases do not forbid "the foreseeable effects standard from being utilized as one of the several kinds of proofs from which an inference of segregative intent may be properly drawn." *Id.* at 255. Adherence to a particular policy or practice, "with full knowledge of the predictable effects of such adherence upon racial imbalance in a school system is one factor among many others which may be considered by a court in determining whether an inference of segregative intent should be drawn." *Ibid.* The District Court thus stayed well within the requirements of *Washington v. Davis* and *Arlington Heights*. *See Personnel Administrator of Massachusetts v. Feeney*, 442 U.S. 256, 279 N. 25 (1979).

It is also urged that the District Court and the Court of Appeals failed to observe the requirements of our recent decision in *Dayton I*, which reiterated the accepted rule that the remedy imposed by a court of equity should be commensurate with the violation ascertained, and held that the remedy for the violations that had then been established in that case should be aimed at rectifying the "incremental segregative effect" of the discriminatory acts identified. In *Dayton I*, only a few apparently isolated discriminatory practices had been found; yet a systemwide remedy had been imposed without proof of a systemwide impact. Here, however, the District Court repeatedly emphasized that it had found purposefully segregative practices with current, systemwide impact. 429 F. Supp. at 252, 259-60, 264, 266; Pet. App. 95; 583 F.2d at 799. And the Court of Appeals, responding to similar arguments, said:

> School board policies of systemwide application necessarily have systemwide impact. 1) The pre-1954 policy of creating an enclave of five schools intentionally designed for black students and known as "black" schools, as found by the District Judge, clearly had a "substantial" — indeed, a systemwide — impact. 2) The post-1954 failure of the Columbus Board to desegregate the school system in spite of many requests and demands to do so, of course, had systemwide impact. 3) So, too, did the Columbus Board's segregative school construction and citing policy as we have detailed it above. 4) So too did it's student assignment policy which, as shown above, produced the large majority of racially identifiable schools as of the school year 1975-1976. 5) The practice of assigning black teachers and administrators only or in large majority to black schools likewise represented a systemwide policy of segregation. This policy served until July 1974 to deprive black students of opportunities for contract with and learning from white teachers, and conversely to deprive white students of similar opportunities to meet, know and learn from black teachers. It also served as discriminatory, systemwide racial identification of schools. 583 F.2d at 814.

Nor do we perceive any misuse of *Keyes*, where we held that purposeful discrimination in a substantial part of a school system furnishes a sufficient basis for an inferential finding of a systemwide discriminatory intent unless otherwise rebutted, and that given the purpose to operate a dual school system one could infer a connection between such a purpose and racial separation in other parts of the school system. There was no undue reliance here on the inferences permitted by *Keyes*, or upon those recognized by *Swann*. Furthermore, the Board was given ample opportunity to counter the evidence of segregative purpose and current, systemwide impact, and the findings of the courts below were against it in both respects. 429 F. Supp. at 260; Pet. App. 95, 102, 105.

Because the District Court and the Court of Appeals committed no prejudicial errors of fact or law, the judgment appealed from must be affirmed.

So ordered.

[The concurring opinions of CHIEF JUSTICE BURGER and JUSTICE STEWART and the dissenting opinion of JUSTICE POWELL are omitted.]

MR. JUSTICE REHNQUIST, with whom MR. JUSTICE POWELL joins, dissenting:

The school desegregation remedy imposed on the Columbus school system by the Court's affirmance of the Court of Appeals is as complete and dramatic a displacement of local authority by the federal judiciary as is possible in our federal system. Pursuant to the District Court's order, 42,000 of the system's

96,000 students are reassigned to new schools. There are like reassignment of teachers, staff, and administrators, reorganization of the grade structure of virtually every elementary school in the system, the closing of 33 schools, and the additional transportation of 37,000 students.

It is difficult to conceive of a more serious supplantation because, as this Court recognized in *Brown v. Board of Education*, 347 U. S. 483, 493 (1954) (*Brown I*), "education is perhaps the most important function of state and local government"; indeed, it is "a vital national tradition." *Dayton Board of Education v. Brinkman*, 433 U.S. 406, 410 (1977) (*Dayton I*); See *Milliken v. Bradley*, 418 U.S. 717, 741-42 (1974); *Wright v. Council of the City of Emporia*, 407 U.S. 451, 469 (1972). That "local autonomy has long been thought essential both to the maintenance of community concern and support for public schools and to quality of the educational process," *Milliken, supra*, does not, of course, place the school system beyond the authority of federal courts as guardians of federal constitutional rights. But the practical and historical importance of the tradition does require that the existence of violations of constitutional rights be carefully and clearly defined before a federal court invades the traditional ambit of local control, and that the subsequent displacement of local authority be limited to that necessary to correct the identified violations. "It is for this reason that the case for displacement of the local authorities by a federal court in a school desegregation case must be satisfactorily established by factual proof and justified by a reasoned statement of legal principles." *Dayton I, supra*, at 410.

I think the District Court and Court of Appeals in this case did not heed this admonition. One can search their opinions in vain for any concrete notion of what a "systemwide violation" consists of or how a trial judge is to go about determining whether such a violation exists or has existed. What logic is evident emasculates the key determinants set down in *Keyes v. School District No. 1*, 413 U.S. 189 (1973), for proving the existence and scope of a violation warranting federal court intervention: discriminatory purpose and a causal relationship between acts motivated by such a purpose and a current condition of segregation in the school system. The lower courts' methodology would all but eliminate the distinction between de facto and de jure segregation and render all school systems captives of a remote and ambiguous past.

Today the Court affirms the Court of Appeals for the Sixth Circuit in this case and *Dayton Board of Education v. Brinkman*, No. 78-627 (*Dayton II*), in opinions so Delphic that lower courts will be hard pressed to fathom their implications for school desegregation litigation. I can only offer two suggestions. The first is that the Court, possibly chastened by the complexity and emotion that accompanies school desegregation cases, wishes to relegate the determination of a violation of the Equal Protection Clause of the Fourteenth Amendment in any plan of pupil assignment, and the formulation of a remedy for its violation, to the judgment of a single District Judge. That judgment should be subject to review under the "clearly erroneous" standard by the appropriate Court of Appeals, in much the same way that actions for an accounting between private partners in a retail shoe business or claimants in an equitable receivership of a failing commercial enterprise are handled. "Discriminatory purpose" and "systemwide violation" are to be treated as talismanic phrases which once invoked, warrant only the most superficial scrutiny by appellate courts.

Such an approach is, however, obviously inconsistent with the *Dayton I* admonition and disparages both this Court's oft-expressed concern for the important role of local autonomy in educational matters and the significance of the constitutional rights involved. It also holds out the disturbing prospect of very different remedies being imposed on similar school systems because of the predilections of individual judges and their good faith but incongruent efforts to make sense of this Court's confused pronouncements today. Concepts such as "discriminatory purpose" and "systemwide violation" present highly mixed questions of law and fact. If District Court discretion is not channelized by a clearly articulated methodology, the entire federal court system will experience the disaffection which accompanies violation of Cicero's maxim not to "lay down one rule in Athens and another rule in Rome."

Yet the only alternative reading of today's opinions, *i.e.*, a literal reading, is even more disquieting. Such a reading would require embracing a novel analytical approach to school segregation in systems without a history of statutorily mandated separation of the races — an approach that would have dramatic consequences for urban school systems in this country. Perhaps the adjective "analytical" is out of place, since the Court's opinions furnish only the most superficial methodology, a framework which if it were to be adopted ought to be examined in a far more thorough and critical manner than is done by the Court's "lick and a promise" opinions today. Given the similar approaches employed by the Court in this case and *Dayton II*, this case suffices for stating what I think are the glaring deficiencies both in the Court's new framework and in its decision to subject the Columbus school system to the District Court's sweeping racial balance remedy.

I

The Court suggests a radical new approach to desegregation cases in systems without a history of statutorily mandated separation of the races: if a district court concludes — employing what in honesty must be characterized as an irrebuttable presumption — that there was a "dual" school system at the time of *Brown I*, 347 U.S. 483 (1954), it must find post-1954 constitutional violations in a school board's failure to take every affirmative step to integrate the system. Put differently, *racial imbalance* at the time the complaint if filed is sufficient to support a systemwide, racial balance school busing remedy if the district court can find *some* evidence of discriminatory purpose prior to 1954, without any inquiry into the causal relationship between those pre-1954 violations and current segregation in the school system.

This logic permeates the findings of the District Court and Court of Appeals, and the latter put it most bluntly.

> [T]he District Judge on review of pre-1954 history found that the Columbus schools were de jure segregated in 1954 and, hence, the Board had a continuing constitutional duty to desegregate the Columbus schools. The pupil assignment figures for 1975-76 demonstrate the District Judge's conclusion that this burden has not been carried. On this basis alone (if there were no other proofs), we believe we would be required to affirm the District Judge's finding of present unconstitutional segregation. *Penick v. Columbus Board of Education*, 583 F.2d 787, 800 (1978).

In *Brinkman v. Gilligan*, 583 F.2d 243, 256 (1978), also affirmed today, this post-1954 "affirmative duty" is characterized a duty "to diffuse black and white students" throughout the system.

The Court in this case apparently endorses that view. For the Court finds that "[e]ach instance of a failure or refusal to fulfill this affirmative duty continues the violation of the Fourteenth Amendment," *ante*, at 8, and the mere fact that at the time of suit "most blacks were still going to black schools and most whites to white schools" establishes current effect.

In order to fully comprehend the dramatic reorientation the Court's opinion thus implies, and its lack of any principled basis, a brief historical review is necessary. In 1954 this Court announced *Brown I* and struck down on equal protection grounds laws requiring or permitting school assignment of children on the basis of race. *See also Bolling v. Sharpe*, 347 U.S. 497 (1954). The question of remedy was reserved for a new round of briefing, and the following Term this Court remanded to the district courts in the five consolidated cases "to take such proceedings and enter such orders and decrees consistent with this opinion as are necessary and proper to admit to public schools on a racially nondiscriminatory basis with all deliberate speed the parties to these cases." *Brown v. Board of Education*, 349 U.S. 294, 301 (1955) (*Brown II*).

The majority concedes that this case does not involve racial assignment of students mandated by state law; Ohio abandoned any "statutory requirement or authorization to operate segregated schools" by 1888. *Ante*, at 5. Yet it was precisely this type of segregation — segregation expressly mandated or permitted by state statute or constitution — that was addressed by *Brown* and the mandate of the *Brown* cases was that "[a]ll provisions of federal, state, or local law requiring or permitting such discrimination must yield" to "the fundamental principal that racial discrimination in public education is unconstitutional." 349 U.S. at 298. The message of *Brown* was simple and resonant because the violation was simple and pervasive.

There were, however, some issues upon which the *Brown* Court was vague. It did not define what it meant by "effectuat[ing] a transition to a racially nondiscriminatory school system," *Id.* at 301, and therefore the next 17 years focused on the question of the appropriate remedy where racial separation had been maintained by operation of state law.

The earliest post-*Brown* school cases in this Court only intimated that "a transition to a racially nondiscriminatory school system" required adoption of a policy of nondiscrimatory admission. It was not until the 1967 Term that this Court indicated that school systems with a history of statutorily or constitutionally mandated separation of the races would have to do more than simply permit black students to attend white schools and vice versa. In that Term the Court had before it "freedom-of-choice" plans put forward as desegregation remedies. The factual context of the lead case, *Green v. County School Board*, 391 U.S. 430 (1968), is a far cry from the complicated urban metropolitan system we confront today. The New Kent County school system consisted of two schools — one black and one white — with a total enrollment of 1,300 pupils. At the time of suit a black student had never attended the white school or a white student the black school.

This court found that the "freedom-of-choice" plan approved by the District Court for the desegregation of the New Kent County schools was inadequate. Noting that the "pattern of separate 'white' and 'Negro' schools in the New Kent County school system established under compulsion of state laws is precisely the pattern of segregation to which *Brown I* and *Brown II* were particular addressed," the Court observed that *Brown II* charged "[s]chool boards such as the respondent then operating state-compelled dual systems ... with the affirmative duty to take whatever steps might be necessary to convert to a unitary system in which racial discrimination would be eliminated root and branch." *Id.* at 435, 437-438. In the three years following court approval of the freedom-of-choice plan in New Kent County, not a single white child had chosen to attend the historically black school, which continued to serve 85% of the county's black schoolchildren. The *Green* Court concluded that a freedom-of-choice plan, in a school system such as this and in the absence of other efforts at desegregation, was not sufficient to provide the remedy mandated by *Brown II*. The court suggested zoning, *i.e.*, some variation of a neighborhood school policy, as a possible alternative remedy.

That brings the history of school desegregation litigation in this Court to the Chief Justice's opinion in *Swann v. Charlotte-Mecklenburg Board of Education*, 402 U.S. 1 (1971), upon which the majority and respondents heavily rely. *Swann* also addressed school systems with a history of statutorily or constitutionally mandated separation of the races; "[t]hat was what *Brown v. Board of Education* was all about." *Id.* at 6. *Swann* was an attempt to define "in more precise terms" the appropriate scope of the *remedy* in cases of that nature. *Ibid.* It simply did not attempt to articulate the manner by which courts were to determine the existence of a *violation* in school systems without a history of segregation imposed by statute or the state constitution. Certainly school systems with such a history were charged by *Brown II* to "effectuate a transition to a racially nondiscriminatory school system." But *Swann* did not speak of the failure to conform to this duty as a "continuing violation." The specific references to an affirmative duty in *Swann* were to the duty of a school board found to have overseen a school system with state-imposed segregation to put forward a plan to remedy that situation. It was in this context that the Court observed that upon "default by the school authorities of their obligation to proffer acceptable remedies, a district court has broad power to fashion a remedy that will assure a unitary school system." *Id.* at 16.

This understanding of the "affirmative duty" was acknowledged in the first case confronting a school system without a history of state-mandated racial assignment, *Keyes v. School District No. 1*, 413 U.S. 189 (1973). There the court observed:

> [W]e have held that where plaintiffs prove that a current condition of segregated schooling exists within a school district where a dual system was compelled or authorized by statute at the time of our decision in *Brown v. Board of Education*, 347 U.S. 483 (1954) (*Brown I*), the State automatically assumes an affirmative duty "to effectuate a transition to a racially nondiscriminatory school system," *Brown v. Board of Education*, 349 U.S. 294, 301 (1955) (*Brown II*), *see also Green v. County School Board*, 391 U.S. 430, 437-438 (1968), that is, to eliminate from the public schools within their school system "all vestiges of state-imposed segregation." *Swann v. Charlotte-Mecklenburg Board of Education*, 402 U.S. 1, 15 (1971). This is not a case, however, where a statutory dual system has ever existed. *Id.* at 200-01.

It was at this juncture that the Court articulated the proposition that has become associated with *Keyes*.

> Nevertheless, where plaintiffs prove that the school authorities have carried out a systematic program of segregation affecting a substantial portion of the students, schools, teachers, and facilities within the school system, it is only common sense to conclude that there exists a predicate for a finding of the existence of a dual school system. *Id.* at 201.

The notion of an "affirmative duty" as acknowledged in *Keyes* is a remedial concept defining the obligation on the school board to come forward with an effective desegregation plan *after* a finding of a dual system. This could not be clearer in *Keyes* itself.

> [P]roof of a state-imposed segregation in a substantial portion of the district will suffice to support a finding by the trial court of the existence of a dual system. Of course, where that finding is made, as in cases involving statutory dual systems, the school authorities have an affirmative duty "to effectuate a transition to a racially nondiscriminatory school system." *Brown II, supra*, at 301. *Id.* at 203.

Indeed, *Keyes* did not discuss the complexion of the Denver school system in 1954 or in any other way intimate the analysis adopted by the Court today. Rather it emphasized that the relevance of past actions was determined by their causal relationship to current racially imbalanced conditions.

Even so brief a history of our school desegregation jurisprudence sheds light on more than one point. As a matter of history, case law, or logic, there is nothing to support the novel proposition that the primary inquiry in school desegregation cases involving systems without a history of statutorily mandated racial assignment is what happened in those systems before 1954. As a matter of history, 1954 makes no more sense as a benchmark — indeed it makes *less* sense — than 1968, 1971 or 1973. Perhaps the latter year has the most to commend it, if one insists on a benchmark, because in *Keyes* this Court first confronted the problem of school segregation in the context of systems without a history of statutorily mandated separation of the races.

As a matter of logic, the majority's decision to turn the year 1954 into a constitutional Rubicon also fails. The analytical underpinnings of the concept of discriminatory purpose have received their still incomplete articulation in the 1970's. It is sophistry to suggest that a school board in Columbus in 1954 could have read *Brown* and gleaned from it a constitutional duty "to diffuse black students throughout the system" or take whatever other action the Court today thinks it should have taken. And not only was the school board to anticipate the state of the law 20 years hence, but also to have a full appreciation for discrete acts or omissions of school boards 20 to 50 years earlier.

Of course, there are always instances where constitutional standards evolve and parties are charged with conforming to the new standards. But I am unaware of a case where the failure to anticipate a change in the law and take remedial steps is labeled an independent constitutional violation. The difference is not simply one of characterization: the Court's decision today enunciates, without analysis or explanation, a new methodology that dramatically departs from *Keyes* by relieving school desegregation plaintiffs from any showing of a causal nexus between intentional segregative actions and the conditions they seek to remedy.

Causality plays a central role in *Keyes* as it does in all equal protection analysis. The *Keyes* Court held that before the burden of production shifts to the school board, the plaintiffs must prove "that the school authorities have carried out a systematic program of segregation *affecting a substantial portion of the students, schools, teachers and facilities within the school system.*" 413 U.S. at 201 (emphasis added). The Court recognized that a trial court might find "that a lesser degree of segregated schooling ... would not have resulted even if the Board had not acted as it did," and "that at some point in time the relationship between past segregative acts and present segregation may become so attenuated as to be incapable of supporting a finding of de jure segregation warranting judicial intervention." *Id.* at 211. The relevance of past acts of the school board was to depend on whether "segregation resulting from those actions continues to exist." *Id.* at 210. That inquiry is not central under the approach approved by the Court today. Henceforth, the question is apparently whether pre-1954 acts contributed in some unspecified manner to segregated conditions that existed in 1954. If the answer is yes, then the only question is whether the school board has exploited all integrative opportunities that presented themselves in the subsequent 25 years. If not, a systemwide remedy is in order, despite the plaintiff's failure to demonstrate a link between those past acts and current racial imbalance.

The Court's use of the term "affirmative duty" implies that integration b[e] the pre-eminent — indeed, the controlling — educational consideration in school board decision[-]making. It takes precedence over other legitimate educational objectives subject to some vague feasibility limitation. That implication is dramatically demonstrated in this case. Both lower courts necessarily gave special significance to the Columbus School Board's post-1954 school construction and citing policies as supporting the systemwide remedy in this case. They did not find — in fact, could not have found — that the citing and construction of schools were racially motivated. As the District Court observed:

> In 1950, pursuant to a request of the then Columbus school superintendent, the Bureau of Educational Research at The Ohio State University began a comprehensive, scientific and objective analysis of the school plant needs of the school system. The Bureau studied and reported on community growth characteristics, educational programs, enrollment projections, the system's plan of organization, the existing plant, and the financial ability of the community to pay for new school facilities. Thereafter, a number of general and specific recommendations were made to the Columbus Board by the Bureau. The recommendations included the size and location of new school sites as well as additions to existing sites. The recommendations were conceived to accommodate the so-called "community or neighborhood school concept." The 1950 concept was related to a distance criteria grounded on walking distance to schools as follows: 3/4 mile for elementary, 1 1/2 miles for junior high and 2 miles for senior high students.
>
> The Board of Education adopted and relied upon the Bureau's recommendations in proposing and encouraging the passage of bond issues in 1951, 1953, 1956, 1959 and 1964. School construction of new facilities and additions to existing structures were accomplished in substantial conformity with the Bureau's periodic studies and recommendations. 429 F. Supp. at 237-38.

Thus the Columbus Board of Education employed the most objective criteria possible in the placement of new schools.

Nevertheless the District Court and Court of Appeals found that conformity with these recommendations was a violation of the Equal Protection Clause because "in some instances the need for school facilities could have been met in a manner having an integrative rather than a segregative effect." *Id.* at 243. By endorsing this logic, the Court, as a result of its finding of an affirmative duty, employs remedy standards to determine the existence of post-1954 violations in school construction and ignores the previously pivotal role of discriminatory purpose.

This unprecedented "affirmative duty" superstructure sits atop a weak foundation — the existence of a "dual" school system in 1954. This finding was predicated on the presence of four predominantly black elementary schools and one predominantly black junior high school on the "near east side of Columbus," a then and now black residential area. The Columbus School Board at that time employed, as it does now, a neighborhood school policy. The specific Board actions that the District Court cited were racial assignment of teachers and gerrymandering along part of the border between two school districts. The Court concludes that these violations involved a substantial part of the Columbus school system in 1954, and invokes *Keyes* for the proposition that the finding of a dual school system follows "absent sufficient contrary proof by the Board, which was not forthcoming in this case."

There are two major difficulties with this use of *Keyes*. First, without any explanation the Court for the first time applies it to define the character of a school system remote in time — here 25 or more years ago — without any examination of the justifications for the *Keyes* burden-shifting principles when those principles are used in this fashion. Their use is a matter of "'policy and fairness,'" 413 U.S. at 209 (quoting Wigmore), and I think the *Keyes* "presumption" scores poorly on both counts when focused on a period beyond memory and often beyond records. What records are available are equally available to both sides. In this case the District Court relied almost exclusively on instances that occurred between 1909 and 1943: undoubtedly beyond the period when many Board members had their experiences with the system as students, let alone as administrators. It is much more difficult for school board authorities to piece together the influences that shaped the racial composition of a district 20, 30, or 40 years ago. The evidence on both sides becomes increasingly anecdotal. Yet the consequences of the School Board's inability to make such a showing only become more dramatic. Here violations with respect to five schools, only three of which exist today, occurring over 30 years ago are the key premise for a systemwide racial balance remedy involving 172 schools — most of which did not exist in 1950.

My second concern about the Court's use of the *Keyes* presumption may render my first concern academic. For as I suggest in Part III below, the Court today endorses views regarding the neighborhood school policy and racially identifiable neighborhoods that essentially makes the *Keyes* presumption irrebuttable.

II

The departure from established doctrines of causation and discriminatory purpose does not end with the lower courts' preoccupation with an "affirmative duty" exhumed from the conduct of past generations to be imposed on the present without regard to the forces that actually shaped the current racial imbalance in the school system. It is also evident in their examination of post-1954 violations, which the Court refers to as "the intentionally segregative use of optional attendance zones, discontiguous attendance areas, and boundary changes." *Ante,* at 10-11.

As a preliminary matter I note that the Court of Appeals observed, I think correctly, that these post-1954 incidents "can properly be classified as isolated in the sense that they do not form any systemwide pattern." 583 F.2d at 805. All the incidents cited, let alone those that can meet a properly applied segregative intent standard, could not serve as the basis for a systemwide racial balance remedy.

In *Washington v. Davis,* 426 U.S. 229 (1976), *Village of Arlington Heights v. Metropolitan Housing Development Corp.,* 429 U.S. 252 (1977), and *Personnel Administrator of Massachusetts v. Feeney,* No. 78-233 (1979), we have emphasized that discriminatory purpose as a motivating factor in governmental action is a critical component of an equal protection violation. Like causation analysis, the discriminatory purpose requirement sensibly seeks to limit court intervention to the rectification of conditions that offend the Constitution — stigma and other harm inflicted by racially motivated governmental action — and prevent unwarranted encroachment on the autonomy of local governments and private individuals which could well result from a less structured approach.

This Court has not precisely defined the manner in which discriminatory purpose is to be proved. Indeed, in light of the varied circumstances in which it might be at issue, simple and precise rules for proving discriminatory purpose could not be drafted. The focus of the inquiry in a case such as this, however, is not very difficult to articulate: Is a desire to separate the races among the reasons for a school board's decision or particular course of action? The burden of proof on this issue is on the plaintiffs. *Washington v. Davis, supra,* at 244-245; *Village of Arlington Heights v. Metropolitan Housing Development Corp., supra,* at 270.

The best evidence on this score would be a contemporaneous explanation of its action by the school board, or other less dramatic evidence of the board's actual purpose, which indicated that one objective was to separate the races. *See Village of Arlington Heights, supra,* at 268. Objective evidence is also probative. Indeed, were it not this case would warrant very little discussion, for all the evidence relied on by the courts below was of an "objective" nature.

But objective evidence must be carefully analyzed for it may otherwise reduce the "discriminatory purpose" requirement to a "discriminatory impact" test by another name. Private and governmental conduct in matters of general importance to the community is notoriously ambiguous, and for objective evidence to carry the day it must be a reliable index of actual motivation for a governmental decision — at least sufficient to meet the plaintiff's burden of proof on purpose or intent. We have only recently emphasized:

> "Discriminatory purpose" ... implies more than intent as volition or intent as awareness of consequences .... It implies that the decisionmaker ... selected or reaffirmed a particular course of action at least in part "because of," not merely "in spite of," its adverse affects upon an identifiable group. *Personnel Administrator of Massachusetts v. Feeney, supra,* at 21-22.

The maintenance of this distinction is important: both to limit federal courts to their constitutional missions and to afford school boards the latitude to make good-faith, color-blind decisions about how best to realize legitimate educational objectives without extensive post-hoc inquiries into whether integration would have been better served — even at the price of other educational objectives — by another decision: a different school site, a different boundary or a different organizational structure. In a school system with racially imbalanced schools, *every* school board action regarding construction, pupil assignment, transportation, annexation and temporary facilities will promote integration, aggravate segregation or maintain segregation. Foreseeability follows from the obviousness of that proposition. Such a tight noose on school board decisionmaking will invariably move government of a school system from the town hall to the courthouse.

The District Court in this case held that it was bound by the standard for segregative intent articulated by the Sixth Circuit Court of Appeals in *Oliver v. Michigan State Board of Education*, 508 F.2d 178, 182 (CA6 1974):

> A presumption of segregative purpose arises when plaintiffs establish that the natural, probable, and foreseeable result of public officials' action or inaction was an increase or perpetuation of public school segregation. The presumption becomes proof unless defendants affirmatively establish that their action or inaction was a consistent and resolute application of racially neutral policies. 429 F. Supp. at 254 n. 3.

This is precisely the type of "impact" trigger for shifting the burden of proof on the intent component of an equal protection violation that we rejected in *Washington v. Davis, supra*. There the Court of Appeals had applied the standards of Title VII to determine whether a qualifying test for police candidates discriminated against blacks in violation of the Equal Protection Clause. According to the Court of Appeals, the plaintiffs were initially required to show disproportionate impact on blacks. That impact was a constitutional violation absent proof by the defendants that the test was "an adequate measure of job performance in addition to being an indicator of probable success in the training program." *Id.* at 237. Put differently, the defendants were to show that the test was the product of a racially neutral policy. This Court reversed, rejecting "the view that proof of discriminatory racial purpose is unnecessary in making out an equal protection violation." *Id.* at 245.

Indeed, reflection indicates that the District Court's test for segregative intent in *Columbus* is logically nothing more than the affirmative duty stated a different way. Under the test a "presumption of segregative purpose arises when plaintiffs establish that the natural, probable, and foreseeable result of public officials' ... inaction was ... perpetuation of public school segregation. The presumption becomes proof unless defendants affirmatively establish that their ... inaction was a consistent and resolute application of racially neutral policies." If that standard were to be applied to the average urban school system in the United States, the implications are obvious. Virtually every urban area in this country has racially and ethnically identifiable neighborhoods, doubtless resulting from a melange of past happenings prompted by economic considerations, private discrimination, discriminatory school assignments, or a desire to reside near people of one's own race or ethnic background. *See Austin Independent School District v. United States*, 429 U.S. 990, 994 (1976) (POWELL, J., concurring). It is likewise true that the most prevalent pupil assignment policy in urban areas is the neighborhood school policy. It follows inexorably that urban areas have a large number of racially identifiable schools.

Certainly public officials' ... inaction ... perpetuates ... public school segregation" in *this* context. School authorities could move to pairing, magnet schools or any other device to integrate the races. The failure to do so is a violation under *Oliver* unless the "inaction was a consistent and resolute application of racially neutral policies." The policy that most school boards will rely on at trial, and the policy which the Columbus School Board in fact did rely on, is the neighborhood school policy. According to the District Court in this case, however, not only is that policy not a defense, but in combination with racially segregated housing patterns, it is itself a factor from which one can infer segregative intent and a factor in this case from which the District Court did infer segregative intent, stating that "[t]hose who rely on it as a defense to unlawful school segregation fail to recognize the high priority of the constitutional right involved." 429 F. Supp. at 258.

But the Constitution does not command that school boards not under an affirmative duty to desegregate follow a policy of "integration über alles." If the Court today endorses that view, and unfortunately one cannot be sure, it has wrought one of the most dramatic results in the history of public education and the Constitution. A duty not to discriminate in the School Board's own actions is converted into a duty to ameliorate or compensate for the discriminatory conduct of other entities and persons.

I reserve judgment only because the Court at points in its opinion seems of the view that the District Court applied a test other than the *Oliver* test for segregative intent, despite the District Court's clear indication to the contrary. 429 F. Supp. at 253-54, n. 3. In fact, in *Dayton II*, at 8-9, n. 9, the Court expressly rejects the *Oliver* test, and in its opinion in this case, *ante*, at 14, indicates that the District Court treated foreseeable effects as only another bit of evidence and finds that not incompatible with this Court's prior cases.

> Those cases do not forbid "the foreseeable effects standard from being utilized as one of the several kinds of proofs from which an inference of segregative intent may be properly drawn." *Id.* at 255. Adherence to a particular policy or practice, "with full knowledge of the predictable effects of such adherence upon racial imbalance in a school system is one factor among many others which may be considered by a court in determining whether an inference of segregative intent should be drawn." *Ibid.*

I have no difficulty with the proposition that foreseeable effects are permissible considerations "as one of the several kinds of proofs" as long as they are not the only type of proof. Use of foreseeable effects in the latter fashion would be clearly inconsistent with *Davis, Arlington Heights,* and *Feeney.* But I do have great difficulty with this Court's taking the above quotations from the District Court out of context and thereby imputing a general test for discriminatory purpose to the District Court from a passage which in fact was part of a discussion of the probativeness of a very special kind of evidence on intent: a neighborhood school policy *simpliciter.* As far as gauging the purpose underlying specific actions in concerned, it is quite clear from its expression and application of the relevant test for intent, that the District Court looked for foreseeability per se.

As such, the District Court's treatment of specific post-1954 conduct reflects the same cavalier approach to causality and purpose that underlies the 1954 affirmative duty. That determination requires no more "omnipotence and omniscience," *ante,* at 6-7, n. 6, than similar determinations in *Dayton I, Davis,* and *Arlington Heights.* The court found violations with respect to three optional attendance zones. The Near-Bexley zone, the only zone discussed by this Court, afforded students the option to attend schools in either one of two bordering districts. The District Court found that the zone gave white students of Bexley the opportunity to avoid attending the predominantly black schools to the east. I do not think that the District Court finding can be said to be clearly erroneous despite the lack of any direct evidence on discriminatory purpose, for the school board did not suggest any educational justification for this zone and none is apparent. But as that court recognized, the zone is of little significance as far as the concurrent state of segregation in the school system is concerned. *"The July 10, 1972, minutes of the State Board of Education ... appear to indicate that in 1972, there were 25 public elementary school students and two public high schools students residing in the optional zone."* 429 F. Supp. at 245 (emphasis added). As of 1975 the zone has been dismantled, and the District Court clearly suggests that it does not have any current effect on the Columbus school system.

Two other optional attendance zones were identified as offensive. One existed for two years, between 1955 and 1957, and permitted students in a predominantly white neighborhood to attend the "white" West Broad Elementary school rather than the predominantly black Highland school. Like the Near-Bexley option, there is no apparent educational justification and, therefore, no grounds to upset the District Court's finding of a violation. This optional zone afforded the District Court an excellent opportunity to probe the effects of a past violation, because in 1957 the optional zone was made a permanent part of the West Broad district. But the District Court made no findings as to the current effect of the past violation nor saw fit to hypothesize how many students might have been affected. It was clearly of the opinion that no such inquiry was necessary.

The final optional attendance zone demonstrates the influence of the "affirmative duty" — whether the 1954 variety or that which follows from *Oliver*. This optional zone was also created in 1955 in roughly the same part of Columbus. It gave some students within Highland's boundaries the option of attending the neighboring West Mound Street Elementary School. Again, the District Court found, this permitted transfer to a "whiter" school. But the District Court also found that there was a legitimate educational objective for creation of the zone: Highland was overcrowded and West Mound was under capacity. The District Court, however, concluded that the School Board's actions were objectionable because "feasible alternatives" were available; that is, other optional attendance zones could have been drawn which would have had "an integrative effect on West Mound." This again suggests a duty on the School Board to select the most integrative alternative.

The second set of post-1954 actions faulted by the District Court were two discontiguous attendance areas. These were situations where students in a defined geographical area were assigned to a school in a zone not contiguous with their neighborhood. One zone was established in 1963 and involved about 70 students. The School Board unsuccessfully argued at trial that the children were sent to the predominantly white Moler Elementary School because the nearest school, the predominantly black Alum Crest Elementary, had no room for them. The District Court indicates that this violative condition existed until 1969, presumably because after that date the discontiguous area had a substantial black population and an integrative effect on the Moler Elementary School. Since the discontiguous area now has an integrative effect, one might ask what is its current segregative effect on the school system? Ironically, under the District Court's reasoning, it would be a violation for the Columbus School Board to now disband the Moler Elementary discontiguous attendance area.

The second discontiguous zone existed from 1957 to 1963 and permitted students on three streets within the Heimandale Elementary district to attend the "whiter" Fornof Elementary School. The Columbus School Board "inherited" this discontiguous attendance arrangement when it annexed the Marion-Franklin District in 1957. Both schools at that time were at or over capacity and when a six classroom addition was made to Heimandale in 1963, the discontiguous zone was terminated and the children assigned to Heimandale. According to the HEW Civil Rights Survey, Heimandale today is a racially balanced school. App. at

747. The District Court made no findings as to the current effect of the Board's five-year retention of the Heimandale-Fornof arrangement.

The last discrete violation discussed by the District Court involved the Innis-Cassady alternative organizational proposals. These proposals involved an area of the Columbus School District that was annexed in 1971. The area had one school, the Cassady Elementary School, which was very overcrowded, and placing another school in the district was a priority for the Columbus School Board in 1972. The District Court did not fault the site chosen for the second school in the old Mifflin District. However, it inferred segregative intent in the School Board's decision to use a K-6 organization in both schools, rather than using K-3 organization in one school and 4-6 organization in the other and thereby drawing students from throughout the district. The District Court found that the latter would have been the more integrative alternative because of residential segregation in the District. At trial the School Board attempted to justify its choice by pointing out that the pairing alternative would have required substantial transportation and a deviation from the standard K-6 organization employed throughout the Columbus school system. The court found "no evidence in this record" that pairing would have necessitated "substantial transportation" and that the Board had on prior occasions used a K-3 structure — apparently a reference to the K-3 primary center for crippled children.

Thus the Innis-Cassady discussion evinces this same affirmative duty to select the more integrative alternative and a consequent shift of the burden of proof to the School Board to prove that the segregative choice was mandated by other legitimate educational concerns. But under *Washington v. Davis*, *supra*, and *Arlington Heights*, *supra*, the burden is on the plaintiffs to show impact and purpose and in a situation where there is "no evidence" in the record to prove or disprove a proffered justification for a School Board decision, the plaintiffs have failed to establish a violation of their constitutional rights.

Secondly, the fact that a School Board has once or twice or three times in the past deviated from a policy does not impugn that policy as a justification for a School Board decision. There is no constitutional requirement of perfect consistency. *Arlington Heights*, *supra*, at 269. The fact that the Columbus School Board currently maintains a K-3 organization for crippled children hardly diminishes the Board's interest in maintaining a standard organizational structure for traditional schools throughout the school district. Rather in *Arlington Heights* we spoke of substantive *departures* from existing policy as casting light on discriminatory purpose, "particularly if the factors usually considered important by the decisionmaker strongly favor a decision contrary to the one reached." *Id.* at 267.

Thus it is clear that with respect to a number of the post-1954 actions that the District Court found to be independent violations, foreseeability was not one kind of evidence, but the whole ball game — whether the District Court thought that result dictated by the *Oliver* test or the post-1954 "affirmative duty" purportedly imposed as a result of pre-1954 conduct. Those findings that could be supported by the concept of discriminatory purpose propounded in *Davis* and *Arlington Heights* were not accompanied by any effort to link those violations with current conditions of segregation in the school system. In sum, it is somewhat misleading for the Court to refer to these actions as in some sense independent of the constitutional duty it suggests that the Columbus Board assumed in 1954. And, in any event, the small number of students involved in these instances could not independently support the sweeping racial balance remedy imposed by the District Court. *Cf. Dayton I*, 433 U.S. 406 (1977).

III

The casualness with which the District Court and Court of Appeals assumed that past actions of the Board had a continuing effect on the school system, and the facility and doctrinal confusion with which they went from these actions to announce a "systemwide violation" undermine the basic limitations on the federal court's authority. If those violations are not the product of a careful inquiry of the impact on the current school system, if they are reaction to taint or atmosphere rather than identifiable conditions that would not exist now "but for" the constitutional violation, there are effectively no limits on the ability of federal courts to supplant local authority. Only two Terms ago, in *Dayton I*, 433 U.S. at 420, we set out the basic line of inquiry that should govern school desegregation litigation:

> The duty of both the District Court and the Court of Appeals in a case such as this, where mandatory segregation by law of the races and the school has long since ceased, is to first determine whether there was any action in the conduct of the business of the school board which was intended to, and did in fact, discriminate against minority pupils, teachers, or staff. *Washington v. Davis, supra*. All parties should be free to introduce such additional testimony and other evidence as the District Court may deem appropriate. If such violations are found, the District Court in the first instance, subject to review by the Court of Appeals, must determine how much incremental segregative effect these violations had on the racial distribution of the Dayton school population as presently constituted, when that distribution is compared to what it would have been if the absence of such constitutional violations. The remedy must be designed to redress that difference, and only if there has been a systemwide impact may there be a systemwide remedy. *Keyes*, 413 U.S. at 213.

See also School District of Omaha v. United States, 433 U.S. 667 (1977); *Brennan v. Armstrong*, 433 U.S. 672 (1977).

The District Court made no attempt to determine the incremental segregative effects of identified violations; given the absence of causality considerations in the court's findings, it was simply not in a position to do so. To distinguish *Dayton I* the majority relies on the District Court's conclusion that its "findings of liability in this case concerns the Columbus school district as a whole." 429

F. Supp. at 266. But incantation is not a substitute for analysis and the District Court's findings and analysis do not support its conclusion.

But the majority's opinion takes on its most delusive air when the Court suggests that the scope of the remedy is the Board's own fault.

> [T]he Board was given ample opportunity to counter the evidence of segregative purpose and current, systemwide impact, and the finding of the courts below were against it in both respects. *Ante*, at 17.

Specifically, the Court is alluding to the Board's purported failure to show that the violation was not systemwide under *Keyes* or that a more limited remedy should have been applied under *Swann*. In fact, the logic of the District Court, apparently endorsed by the Court today, turns the *Swann* and *Keyes* showings into chimeras.

Once a showing is made that the District Court believes satisfies the *Keyes* requirement of purposeful discrimination in a substantial part of the school system, the school board will almost invariably rely on its neighborhood school policy and residential segregation to show that it is not responsible for the existence of certain predominantly black and white schools in other parts of the school system. Under the District Court's reasoning, as I have noted, not only is that evidence not probative on the Board's lack of responsibility, it itself supports an inference of a constitutional violation. In addition, the District Court relied on a general proposition that "there is often a substantial reciprocal effect between the color of the school and the color of the neighborhood it serves" to block any inquiry into whether racially identifiable schools were the product of racially identifiable neighborhoods or whether past discriminatory acts bore a "but for" relationship to current segregative conditions.

> It is not now possible to isolate these factors and draw a picture of what Columbus schools or housing would have looked like today without the other's influence. *I do not believe that such an attempt is required.*
>
> I do not suggest that any reasonable action by the school authorities could have fully cured the evils of residential segregation. The Court could not and would not impose such a duty upon the defendants. I do believe, however, that the Columbus defendants could and should have acted to break the segregative snowball created by their interaction with housing. That is, they could and should have acted with an integrative rather than a segregative influence upon housing; they could and should have been cautious concerning the segregation influences that are exerted upon the schools by housing. They certainly should not have aggravated racial imbalance in the schools by their official actions. 429 F. Supp. at 259 (emphasis added).

But as the District Court recognized, other factors play an important role in determining segregated residential patterns.

> Housing segregation has been caused in part by federal agencies which deal with financing of housing, local housing authorities, financial institutions, developers, landlords, personal preferences of blacks and whites, real estate brokers and salespersons, restrictive covenants, zoning and annexation, and income of blacks as compared to whites. *Ibid.*

The *Swann* Court cautioned that "[t]he elimination of racial discrimination in public schools is a large task and one that should not be retarded by efforts to achieve broader purposes lying beyond the jurisdiction of school authorities. One vehicle can carry only a limited amount of baggage." 402 U.S. at 22. Yet today the School Board is called to task for all the forces beyond their control that shaped residential segregation in Columbus. There is thus no room for *Keyes* or *Swann* rebuttal either with respect to the school system today or that of 30 years ago.

IV

I do not suggest that the inquiry required by *Dayton I* and *Keyes* is a simple one, and reviewing courts must defer to the findings of District Court judges. But appellate courts also must ensure that these judges are asking themselves the right questions: it is clear in the instant case that critical questions regarding causality and purpose were not asked at all. The city of Columbus has changed enormously in the last 25 years and with it the racial character of many neighborhoods. Incidents related here may have been paved over by years of private choice as well as undesirable influences beyond the control of school authorities, influences such as poverty and housing discrimination, both public and private. Expert testimony should play an important role in putting together the demographic history of a city and the role of a school board in it. I do not question that there were constitutional violations on the part of the Columbus School Board in the past, but there are no deterrence or retribution components of the rationale for a school desegregation remedy. The fundamental mission of such remedies is to restore those integrated educational opportunities that would now exist but for purposefully discriminatory school board conduct. Because critically important questions were neither asked nor answered by the lower courts, the record before us simply cannot inform as to whether so sweeping a remedy as that imposed is justified.

At the beginning of this dissent, far too many pages ago, I suggested that the Court's opinion may only communicate a "hands-off" attitude in school desegregation cases and that my concerns should therefore be institutional rather than doctrinal. School desegregation cases, however, will certainly be with this Court as long as any of its current Members, and I doubt the Court can for long, like Pilate, wash its hands of disparate results in cases throughout the country.

It is most unfortunate that the Court chooses not to speak clearly today. *Dayton I* and *Keyes* are not overruled, yet their essential messages are ignored. The Court does not intimate that it has fathomed the full implications of the analysis it has sanctioned — an approach that would certainly make school desegregation litigation a "loaded game board," *Swann, supra,* at 28, but one at which a school board could never win. A school system's only hope of avoiding a judicial receivership would be a voluntary dismantling of its neighborhood school program. If that is the Court's intent today, it has indeed accepted the role of Judge Learned Hand's feared "Platonic Guardians" and intellectual integrity — if not the Constitution or the interests of our beleaguered urban school systems and their students of all races — would be better served by discarding the pretextual distinction between de facto and de jure segregation. Whether the Court's result be reached by the approach of Pilate or Plato, I cannot subscribe to it.

---

1. Following the remand by the Supreme Court of *Dayton Bd. of Educ. v. Brinkman (Dayton I)* to the District Court in 1977, the District Court reviewed the entire record and dismissed the plaintiff's complaint, ruling that the plaintiffs had "failed to prove that acts of intentional segregation over 20 years old had any current incremental segregative effects." The Court of Appeals reversed, however, and the Supreme Court upheld this reversal in *Dayton Bd. of Educ. v. Brinkman (Dayton II)*, 443 U.S. 526 (1979), a case heard in tandem with *Columbus Bd. of Educ. v. Penick*. The Court held there was no basis for disturbing the Court of Appeals finding that at the time of *Brown I* the Dayton Board was intentionally operating a dual system and that given the existence of this dual system in 1954, the board was thereafter under a continuing duty to eradicate the effects of that system. The systemwide nature of the violation furnished prima facie proof that current segregation in the Dayton schools was caused, at least in part, by prior intentionally segregative official acts, the Court stated. Justice Rehnquist, joined by Justice Powell, filed a dissenting opinion in *Dayton II* based on the reasoning set forth in Justice Rehnquist's *Columbus* dissent.

2. Writing for the majority in *Columbus*, Justice White stated that the Court's decision in *Dayton Bd. of Educ. v. Brinkman (I)* did not implicitly or explicitly overrule or limit any aspect of *Swann v. Charlotte-Mecklenburg Bd. of Educ.* and *Keyes v. School Dist. No. 1*. Do you agree with Justice White's appraisal or is there evidence to suggest that *Dayton I*, rather than merely reaffirming the *Swann* and *Keyes* standard, is really creating a new standard for desegregation remedies? In *Dayton I*, the Court stated that in reviewing cases where de jure segregation has long since ceased, the lower courts' first inquiry is to determine whether there had been any action by the local school which was intended to, and did in fact, discriminate. If violations are found, the remedy must be designed to

redress the difference between the degree of segregation which currently exists in the school system and that which would have existed but for the unconstitutional acts of the school board. Would application of this standard to the factual situations in *Swann* and *Keyes* change the Court's decisions in those cases? Is it more or less difficult, under *Dayton I*, for a plaintiff to produce evidence which would allow a court to order massive busing to achieve racial balance? *See* Comment, *From Denver to Dayton: The Evolution of Constitutional Doctrine in Northern School Desegregation Litigation*, 3 U. Dayton L. Rev. 115 (1978).

3. How, if at all, do the Court's decisions in *Columbus* and *Dayton II* alter the *Dayton I* standard? Justice Rehnquist, author of the *Dayton I* opinion, dissented from the majority opinions in both *Columbus* and *Dayton II*, stating these decisions failed to follow the *Dayton I* guidelines. What does Justice Rehnquist perceive as the major differences between *Dayton I* and *Columbus*? Would he agree with the statement in the *Columbus* majority opinion that *Dayton I* merely reiterates the rule that the remedy imposed by a court of equity should commensurate with the violation ascertained or does he perceive the role of *Dayton I* more broadly?

4. Can federal courts order school districts to continually readjust desegregation plans even though the necessary readjustment was brought about by shifting demographies rather than any segregated action on the part of school officials? In *Pasadena Bd. of Educ. v. Spangler*, 427 U.S. 424 (1976), the United States Supreme Court considered that issue and ruled that shifts in the racial makeup of schools which result from changes in the demographic residential patterns due to a normal pattern of people moving into, out of, and around the school system, and not attributable to any segregative action on the part of school officials presents a situation in which neither the school officials nor the district court are required to make year-by-year adjustments in the racial composition of the school so long as the affirmative duty to desegregate has been accomplished and racial discrimination through official action is eliminated.

Since *Dayton I* the Supreme Court has considered the viability of several extensive court-ordered desegregation plans. An example of the Court's treatment of such cases is *School Dist. of Omaha v. United States*, 433 U.S. 667 (1977), in which the Court vacated a Court of Appeals decision affirming a District desegregation plan which included, among other elements, the systemwide transportation of pupils. The case was remanded for reconsideration in light of *Dayton I* and *Arlington Heights v. Metropolitan Housing Dev. Corp.*, 429 U.S. 252 (1977), a housing case, which held that proof of racially discriminatory intent is required to prove a violation of the Equal Protection Clause, and official action having a racially disproportionate impact is not per se unconstitutional.

For additional cases in which the United States Supreme Court has recently dealt with the continuing problems of discrimination, and which are important in the public school context *see Brennan v. Armstrong*, 433 U.S. 672 (1977), in which a District Court order requiring Milwaukee, Wisconsin to develop a desegregation plan was vacated, and the case was remanded for a redetermination of the "incremental segregative effect" resulting from the asserted violations, as required by *Dayton, Arlington Heights*, and *Austin Indep. Sch. Dist. v. United States*, 429 U.S. 990 (1977), which vacated and remanded an order by the Fifth Circuit for a busing plan involving between 32% and 42% of the school population. The lower court was instructed to reconsider the case in light of *Washington v. Davis*, 426 U.S. 229 (1976), an employment discrimination case, which held that an official act which has a racially disproportionate effect is not unconstitutional unless it reflects a racially discriminatory purpose; *Hills v. Gautreaux*, 425 U.S. 284 (1976), a housing case, which distinguished *Milliken v. Bradley, supra*, by holding that a metropolitan remedy was necessary to prevent discriminatory action by HUD and that, unlike *Milliken*, this case involved a governmental entity which had jurisdiction beyond city boundaries; *Buchanan v. Evans*, 423 U.S. 963 (1975), which affirmed a Delaware Federal District Court order enjoining the Delaware State Board of Education from relying on an expired state statute which made the City of Wilmington a separate district so that its high racial minority population was segregated from the adjoining district's system; and *Rizzo v. Goode*, 423 U.S. 362 (1975), which held that a § 1983 action was improper against a mayor and other officials for isolated acts of discrimination by police officers.

5. One response to the Supreme Court's decisions on school desegregation has been the growth of private schools or academies which refuse to admit black students. Should parents be permitted to send their children to segregated private schools if they desire? Is the parents' position stronger if the private school's segregation policy has a basis in religious beliefs? The Supreme Court addressed the question of racially motivated admissions policies at private schools in *Runyon v. McCrary*, which will be discussed in Chapter 16, *infra*.

6. For the first twenty-five years after *Brown I*, the focus in desegregation cases rested on whether there was a violation of the Fourteenth Amendment, and if so, what the proper remedy should be. Since that time, however, the emphasis has shifted to what effects such remedies will have on a school system and how long the courts may hold power over the schools.

In *Crawford v. Board of Educ. of Los Angeles*, 458 U.S. 527 (1982), the Supreme Court decided the fate of a state constitutional amendment repealing the busing remedy imposed on Los Angeles to end segregation. Earlier, a state court had found de jure segregation in violation of both the state and federal constitutions. The California Supreme Court affirmed, but based its decision only on the equal protection clause of the California constitution.

The state court ordered busing as the remedy, but California voters passed an amendment that required busing only when a *federal* court required it. The United States Supreme Court upheld the amendment as non-discriminatory. Once a state decides to do more than the Fourteenth Amendment requires, (*i.e.*, state court ordered busing), there is nothing to stop a state, via a state constitutional amendment, from later receding from that action.

7. When a federal court orders desegregation, who has the responsibility for its payment? Case law in this chapter demonstrates that the state bears an affirmative duty to help fund desegregation orders. *See Penick, Milliken* and *Green*. Moreover, *Missouri v. Jenkins*, 495 U.S. 33 (1990), noted that both the state government and the relevant school district should pay. But in what proportion and by what method? The court-ordered remedy in *Jenkins* was to be funded by the state of Missouri and by the Kansas City Missouri School District (KCMSD), but several state law provisions prevented the local school district from being able to pay its share. The district court earlier ordered KCMSD to raise the money by raising taxes, enjoining the effect of one of the state provisions. The court of appeals affirmed the district court, but said that in the future the district court should refrain from imposing a property tax rate. Instead, the school district should submit a levy to state collection authorities.

The case reaffirmed the vast reach of federal courts when formulating desegregation orders. The Supreme Court held that the district court order imposing a property tax increase violated principles of federal and state comity. However, the Court upheld the court of appeals' modification authorizing KCMSD to submit a levy to the state revenue department sufficient to fund the court's required budget and to enjoin the operation of state laws limiting or reducing the levy below the limit set by the court. In other words, a federal court could order a tax increase to fund a desegregation plan, although the executive and legislative branches of state government would actually have to impose the tax.

8. The case law demonstrates that no bright line exists as to proportionality of desegregation funding contributions. *See, e.g., Jenkins v. Missouri*, 855 F.2d 1295 (8th Cir. 1988); *Little Rock Sch. Dist. v. Pulaski County Special Sch. Dist.*, 839 F.2d 1296 (8th Cir.) *cert. denied, Arkansas State Bd. of Educ. v. Little Rock Sch. Dist.*, 488 U.S. 869 (1988). However, in the cited cases, states have been ordered to pay a minimum of 50% of desegregation costs.

BOARD OF EDUCATION OF OKLAHOMA CITY PUBLIC SCHOOLS v. DOWELL

Supreme Court of the United States
498 U.S. 237 (1991)

CHIEF JUSTICE REHNQUIST delivered the opinion of the Court:

Petitioner Board of Education of Oklahoma City sought dissolution of a decree entered by the District Court imposing a school desegregation plan. The District Court granted relief over the objection of respondents Robert L. Dowell, et al., black students and their parents. The Court of Appeals for the Tenth Circuit reversed, holding that the Board would be entitled to such relief only upon "'[n]othing less than a clear showing of grievous wrong evoked by new and unforeseen conditions....'" 890 F.2d 1483, 1490 (1989). We hold that the Court

CH. 11: RACIAL SEGREGATION IN THE PUBLIC SCHOOLS 853

of Appeals' test is more stringent than is required either by our cases dealing with injunctions or by the Equal Protection Clause of the Fourteenth Amendment.

I

This school desegregation litigation began almost 30 years ago. In 1961, respondents, black students and their parents, sued petitioners, the Board of Education of Oklahoma City (Board), to end de jure segregation in the public schools. In 1963, the District Court found that Oklahoma City had intentionally segregated both schools and housing in the past, and that Oklahoma City was operating a "dual" school system — one that was intentionally segregated by race. *Dowell v. School Board of Oklahoma City Public Schools*, 219 F.Supp. 427 (WD Okla.). In 1965, the District Court found that the School Board's attempt to desegregate by using neighborhood zoning failed to remedy past segregation because residential segregation resulted in one-race schools. *Dowell v. School Board of Oklahoma City Public Schools*, 244 F.Supp. 971, 975 (WD Okla.). Residential segregation had once been state imposed, and it lingered due to discrimination by some realtors and financial institutions. *Ibid.* The District Court found that school segregation had caused some housing segregation. *Id.* at 976-977. In 1972, finding that previous efforts had not been successful at eliminating state imposed segregation, the District Court ordered the Board to adopt the "Finger Plan," *Dowell v. Board of Education of Oklahoma City Public Schools*, 338 F.Supp. 1256, *aff'd,* 465 F.2d 1012 (CA10), *cert. denied,* 409 U.S. 1041 (1972), under which kindergartners would be assigned to neighborhood schools unless their parents opted otherwise; children in grades 1-4 would attend formerly all white schools, and thus black children would be bused to those schools; children in grade five would attend formerly all black schools, and thus white children would be bused to those schools; students in the upper grades would be bused to various areas in order to maintain integrated schools; and in integrated neighborhoods there would be stand-alone schools for all grades.

In 1977, after complying with the desegregation decree for five years, the Board made a "Motion to Close Case." The District Court held in its "Order Terminating Case":

> The Court has concluded that [the Finger Plan] worked and that substantial compliance with the constitutional requirements has been achieved. The School Board, under the oversight of the Court, has operated the Plan properly, and the Court does not foresee that the termination of its jurisdiction will result in the dismantlement of the Plan or any affirmative action by the defendant to undermine the unitary system so slowly and painfully accomplished over the 16 years during which the cause has been pending before this court....
>
> ....
>
> ... This unpublished order was not appealed.

In 1984, the School Board faced demographic changes that led to greater burdens on young black children. As more and more neighborhoods became integrated, more stand-alone schools were established, and young black students had to be bused further from their inner-city homes to outlying white areas. In an effort to alleviate this burden and to increase parental involvement, the Board adopted the Student Reassignment Plan (SRP), which relied on neighborhood assignments for students in grades K-4 beginning in the 1985-1986 school year. Busing continued for students in grades 5-12....

In 1985, respondents filed a "Motion to Reopen the Case," contending that the School District had not achieved "unitary" status and that the SRP was a return to segregation. Under the SRP, 11 of 64 elementary schools would be greater than 90% black, 22 would be greater than 90% white plus other minorities, and 31 would be racially mixed. The District Court refused to reopen the case, holding that its 1977 finding of unitariness was *res judicata* as to those who were then parties to the action, and that the district remained unitary. *Dowell v. Board of Education of Oklahoma City Public Schools*, 606 F.Supp. 1548 (WD Okla.1985). The District Court found that the School Board, administration, faculty, support staff, and student body were integrated, and transportation, extracurricular activities and facilities within the district were equal and nondiscriminatory. Because unitariness had been achieved, the District Court concluded that court-ordered desegregation must end.

The Court of Appeals for the Tenth Circuit reversed, *Dowell v. Board of Education of Oklahoma City Public Schools,* 795 F.2d 1516, *cert. denied,* 479 U.S. 938 (1986). It held that, while the 1977 order finding the district unitary was binding on the parties, nothing in that order indicated that the 1972 injunction itself was terminated. The court reasoned that the finding that the system was unitary merely ended the District Court's active supervision of the case, and because the school district was still subject to the desegregation decree, respondents could challenge the SRP. The case was remanded to determine whether the decree should be lifted or modified.

On remand, the District Court found that demographic changes made the Finger Plan unworkable, that the Board had done nothing for 25 years to promote residential segregation, and that the school district had bused students for more than a decade in good-faith compliance with the court's orders. 677 F.Supp. 1503 (WD Okla.1987). The District Court found that present residential segregation was the result of private decisionmaking and economics, and that it was too attenuated to be a vestige of former school segregation. It also found that the district had maintained its unitary status, and that the neighborhood assignment plan was not designed with discriminatory intent. The court concluded that the previous injunctive decree should be vacated and the school district returned to local control.

The Court of Appeals again reversed, 890 F.2d 1483 (CA10 1989).... Relying on *United States v. Swift & Co.*, 286 U.S. 106 (1932), it held that a desegregation decree remains in effect until a school district can show "grievous wrong evoked by new and unforeseen conditions," 286 U.S. at 119, and "dramatic changes in conditions unforeseen at the time of the decree that ... impose extreme and unexpectedly oppressive hardships on the obligor." 890 F.2d at 1490 (quoting T. Jost, *From Swift to Stotts and Beyond: Modification of Injunctions in the Federal Courts*, 64 Tex.L.Rev. 1101, 1110 (1986)). Given that a number of schools would return to being primarily one-race schools under the SRP, circumstances in Oklahoma City had not changed enough to justify modification of the decree. The Court of Appeals held that, despite the unitary finding, the Board had the "'affirmative duty ... not to take any action that would impede the process of disestablishing the dual system and its effects.'" 890 F.2d at 1504 (quoting *Dayton Bd. of Education v. Brinkman*, 443 U.S. 526, 538 (1979)).

We granted the Board's petition for certiorari to resolve a conflict between the standard laid down by the Court of Appeals in this case and that laid down in *Spangler v. Pasadena City Board of Education*, 611 F.2d 1239 (CA9 1979), and *Riddick v. School Bd. of City of Norfolk*, 784 F.2d 521 (CA4 1986). We now reverse the Court of Appeals.

II

. . . .

The lower courts have been inconsistent in their use of the term "unitary." Some have used it to identify a school district that has completely remedied all vestiges of past discrimination. *See, e.g., United States v. Overton*, 834 F.2d 1171, 1175 (CA5 1987); *Riddick v. School Bd. of City of Norfolk, supra*, at 533-534; *Vaughns v. Board of Education of Prince George's Cty.*, 758 F.2d 983, 988 (CA4 1985). Under that interpretation of the word, a unitary school district is one that has met the mandate of *Brown v. Board of Education*, 349 U.S. 294 (1955), and *Green v. New Kent County School Board*, 391 U.S. 430 (1968). Other courts, however, have used "unitary" to describe any school district that has currently desegregated student assignments, whether or not that status is solely the result of a court-imposed desegregation plan. *See, e.g.*, 890 F.2d at 14. In other words, such a school district could be called unitary and nevertheless still contain vestiges of past discrimination. That there is such confusion is evident in *Georgia State Conference of Branches of NAACP v. Georgia*, 775 F.2d 1403 (CA11 1985), where the Court of Appeals drew a distinction between a "unitary school district" and a district that has achieved "unitary status." The court explained that a school district that has not operated segregated schools as proscribed by *Green v. New Kent County School Board, supra*, and *Swann v. Charlotte-Mecklenburg Bd. of Ed.*, 402 U.S. 1 (1971), "for a period of several years" is unitary, but that a school district cannot be said to have achieved "unitary status" unless it "has eliminated the vestiges of its prior discrimination and has been adjudicated as such through the proper judicial procedures." *Georgia State Conference, supra*, at 1413, n. 12.

We think it is a mistake to treat words such as "dual" and "unitary" as if they were actually found in the Constitution. The constitutional command of the

Fourteenth Amendment is that "[n]o State shall ... deny to any person ... the equal protection of the laws." Courts have used the terms "dual" to denote a school system which has engaged in intentional segregation of students by race, and "unitary" to describe a school system which has been brought into compliance with the command of the Constitution. We are not sure how useful it is to define these terms more precisely, or to create subclasses within them. But there is no doubt that the differences in usage described above do exist. The District Court's 1977 order is unclear with respect to what it meant by unitary and the necessary result of that finding. We therefore decline to overturn the conclusion of the Court of Appeals that while the 1977 order of the District Court did bind the parties as to the unitary character of the district, it did not finally terminate the Oklahoma City school litigation. In *Pasadena City Bd. of Education v. Spangler*, 427 U.S. 424 (1976), we held that a school board is entitled to a rather precise statement of its obligations under a desegregation decree. If such a decree is to be terminated or dissolved, respondents as well as the school board are entitled to a like statement from the court.

III

The Court of Appeals relied upon language from this Court's decision in *United States v. Swift and Co.*, supra, for the proposition that a desegregation decree could not be lifted or modified absent a showing of "grievous wrong evoked by new and unforeseen conditions." *Id.* 286 U.S. at 119.... We hold that its reliance was mistaken.

....

United States v. United Shoe Machinery Corp., 391 U.S. 244 (1968), explained that the language used in *Swift* must be read in the context of the continuing danger of unlawful restraints on trade which the Court had found still existed. *Id.* at 248. "*Swift* teaches ... a decree may be changed upon an appropriate showing, and it holds that it may not be changed ... if the purposes of the litigation as incorporated in the decree ... have not been fully achieved." *Ibid.* (emphasis deleted). In the present case, a finding by the District Court that the Oklahoma City School District was being operated in compliance with the commands of the Equal Protection Clause of the Fourteenth Amendment, and that it was unlikely that the school board would return to its former ways, would be a finding that the purposes of the desegregation litigation had been fully achieved. No additional showing of "grievous wrong evoked by new and unforeseen conditions" is required of the school board.

In *Milliken v. Bradley (Milliken II)*, 433 U.S. 267 (1977), we said:

> [F]ederal-court decrees must directly address and relate to the constitutional violation itself. Because of this inherent limitation upon federal judicial authority, federal-court decrees exceed appropriate limits if they are aimed at eliminating a condition that does not violate the Constitution or does not flow from such a violation.... *Id.* at 282.

From the very first, federal supervision of local school systems was intended as a temporary measure to remedy past discrimination. *Brown* considered the "complexities arising from the transition to a system of public education freed of racial discrimination" in holding that the implementation of desegregation was to proceed "with all deliberate speed." 349 U.S. at 299-301. *Green* also spoke of the "transition to a unitary, nonracial system of public education." 391 U.S. at 436.

Considerations based on the allocation of powers within our federal system, we think, support our view that quoted language from *Swift* does not provide the proper standard to apply to injunctions entered in school desegregation cases. Such decrees, unlike the one in *Swift*, are not intended to operate in perpetuity. Local control over the education of children allows citizens to participate in decisionmaking, and allows innovation so that school programs can fit local needs. *Milliken v. Bradley (Milliken I)*, 418 U.S. 717, 742 (1974); *San Antonio Independent School District v. Rodriguez*, 411 U.S. 1, 50 (1973). The legal justification for displacement of local authority by an injunctive decree in a school desegregation case is a violation of the Constitution by the local authorities. Dissolving a desegregation decree after the local authorities have operated in compliance with it for a reasonable period of time properly recognizes that "necessary concern for the important values of local control of public school systems dictates that a federal court's regulatory control of such systems not extend beyond the time required to remedy the effects of past intentional discrimination. *See Milliken v. Bradley [Milliken II]*, 433 U.S. at 280-82." *Spangler v. Pasadena City Bd. of Education*, 611 F.2d at 1245, n. 5 (KENNEDY, J., concurring).

....

A district court need not accept at face value the profession of a school board which has intentionally discriminated that it will cease to do so in the future. But in deciding whether to modify or dissolve a desegregation decree, a school board's compliance with previous court orders is obviously relevant. In this case the original finding of de jure segregation was entered in 1961, the injunctive decree from which the Board seeks relief was entered in 1972, and the Board complied with the decree in good faith until 1985. Not only do the personnel of school boards change over time, but the same passage of time enables the District Court to observe the good faith of the school board in complying with the decree. The test espoused by the Court of Appeals would condemn a school district, once governed by a board which intentionally discriminated, to judicial tutelage for the indefinite future. Neither the principles governing the entry and dissolution of injunctive decrees, nor the commands of the Equal Protection Clause of the Fourteenth Amendment, require any such Draconian result.

Petitioners urge that we reinstate the decision of the District Court terminating the injunction, but we think that the preferable course is to remand the case to that court so that it may decide, in accordance with this opinion, whether the Board made a sufficient showing of constitutional compliance as of 1985, when the SRP was adopted, to allow the injunction to be dissolved. The District Court should address itself to whether the Board had complied in good faith with the desegregation decree since it was entered, and whether the vestiges of past discrimination had been eliminated to the extent practicable.

In considering whether the vestiges of de jure segregation had been eliminated as far as practicable, the District Court should look not only at student assignments, but "to every facet of school operations — faculty, staff, transportation, extra-curricular activities and facilities." *Green*, 391 U.S. at 435. *See also Swann*, 402 U.S. at 18 ("[E]xisting policy and practice with regard to faculty, staff, transportation, extra-curricular activities, and facilities" are "among the most important indicia of a segregated system").

After the District Court decides whether the Board was entitled to have the decree terminated, it should proceed to decide respondent's challenge to the SRP. A school district which has been released from an injunction imposing a desegregation plan no longer requires court authorization for the promulgation of policies and rules regulating matters such as assignment of students and the like, but it of course remains subject to the mandate of the Equal Protection Clause of the Fourteenth Amendment. If the Board was entitled to have the decree terminated as of 1985, the District Court should then evaluate the Board's decision to implement the SRP under appropriate equal protection principles. *See Washington v. Davis*, 426 U.S. 229 (1976); *Arlington Heights v. Metropolitan Housing Development Corp.*, 429 U.S. 252 (1977).

The judgment of the Court of Appeals is reversed, and the case is remanded to the District Court for further proceedings consistent with this opinion.

It is so ordered.

JUSTICE SOUTER took no part in the consideration or decision of this case.

JUSTICE MARSHALL, with whom JUSTICE BLACKMUN and JUSTICE STEVENS join, dissenting.

Oklahoma gained statehood in 1907. For the next 65 years, the Oklahoma City School Board maintained segregated schools — initially relying on laws requiring dual school systems; thereafter, by exploiting residential segregation that had been created by legally enforced restrictive covenants. In 1972 — 18 years after this Court first found segregated schools unconstitutional — a federal court finally interrupted this cycle, enjoining the Oklahoma City School Board to implement a specific plan for achieving actual desegregation of its schools.

The practical question now before us is whether, 13 years after that injunction was imposed, the same School Board should have been allowed to return many of its elementary schools to their former one-race status. The majority today suggests that 13 years of desegregation was enough. The Court remands the case for further evaluation of whether the purposes of the injunctive decree were achieved sufficient to justify the decree's dissolution. However, the inquiry it commends to the District Court fails to recognize explicitly the threatened reemergence of one-race schools as a relevant "vestige" of de jure segregation.

In my view, the standard for dissolution of a school desegregation decree must reflect the central aim of our school desegregation precedents. In *Brown v. Board of Education*, 347 U.S. 483 (1954) (*Brown I*), a unanimous Court declared that racially "[s]eparate educational facilities are inherently unequal." *Id.* at 495. This holding rested on the Court's recognition that state-sponsored segregation conveys a message of "inferiority as to th[e] status [of Afro-American school children] in the community that may affect their hearts and minds in a way unlikely ever to be undone." *Id.* at 494. Remedying this evil and preventing its recurrence were the motivations animating our requirement that formerly de jure segregated school districts take all feasible steps to eliminate racially identifiable schools. *See Green v. New Kent County School Bd.*, 391 U.S. 430, 442 (1968); *Swann v. Charlotte-Mecklenburg Bd. of Ed.*, 402 U.S. 1, 25-26 (1971).

I believe a desegregation decree cannot be lifted so long as conditions likely to inflict the stigmatic injury condemned in *Brown I* persist and there remain feasible methods of eliminating such conditions. Because the record here shows, and the Court of Appeals found, that feasible steps could be taken to avoid one-race schools, it is clear that the purposes of the decree have not yet been achieved and the Court of Appeals' reinstatement of the decree should be affirmed. I therefore dissent.

....

II

I agree with the majority that the proper standard for determining whether a school desegregation decree should be dissolved is whether the purposes of the desegregation litigation, as incorporated in the decree, have been fully achieved.... *Pasadena City Bd. of Education v. Spangler*, 427 U.S. 424, 436-37 (1976); *id.* at 444 (MARSHALL, J., dissenting) ("We should not compel the District Court to modify its order unless conditions have changed so much that 'dangers, once substantial, have become attenuated to a shadow,'" quoting, *Swift, supra,* 286 U.S. at 119. I strongly disagree with the majority, however, on what must be shown to demonstrate that a decree's purposes have been fully realized. In my view, a standard for dissolution of a desegregation decree must take into account the unique harm associated with a system of racially identifiable schools and must expressly demand the elimination of such schools.

Our pointed focus in *Brown I* upon the stigmatic injury caused by segregated schools explains our unflagging insistence that formerly de jure segregated school districts extinguish all vestiges of school segregation. The concept of stigma also gives us guidance as to what conditions must be eliminated before a decree can be deemed to have served its purpose.

....

Concern with stigmatic injury also explains the Court's requirement that a formerly de jure segregated school district provide its victims with "make whole" relief. In *Milliken v. Bradley*, 418 U.S. 717 (1974) (*Milliken I*), the court concluded that a school desegregation decree must "restore the victims of discriminatory conduct to the position they would have occupied in the absence of such conduct." *Id.* at 746. In order to achieve such "make whole" relief, school systems must redress any effects traceable to former de jure segregation. *See Milliken v. Bradley*, 433 U.S. 267, 281-88 (1977) (*Milliken II*) (upholding remedial education programs and other measures to redress the substandard communication skills of Afro-American students formerly placed in segregated schools). The remedial education upheld in *Milliken II* was needed to help prevent the stamp of inferiority placed upon Afro-American children from becoming a self-perpetuating phenomenon. *See id.* at 287.

Similarly, avoiding reemergence of the harm condemned in *Brown I* accounts for the Court's insistence on remedies that insure lasting integration of formerly segregated systems. Such school districts are required to "make every effort to achieve the greatest possible degree of actual desegregation and [to] be concerned with the elimination of one-race schools." *Swann, supra,* 402 U.S. at 26.... This focus on "achieving and preserving an integrated school system," *Keyes v. School Dist. No. 1*, Denver, Colo., 413 U.S. 189, 251, n. 31 (1973) (POWELL, J., concurring in part and dissenting in part), stems from the recognition that the reemergence of racial separation in such schools may revive the message of racial inferiority implicit in the former policy of state-enforced segregation.

Just as it is central to the standard for evaluating the formation of a desegregation decree, so should the stigmatic injury associated with segregated schools be central to the standard for dissolving a decree. The Court has indicated that "the ultimate end to be brought about" by a desegregation remedy is "a unitary, nonracial system of public education." *Green, supra,* 391 U.S. at 436. We have suggested that this aim is realized once school officials have "eliminate[d] from the public schools all vestiges of state-imposed segregation," *Swann, supra,* 402 U.S. at 15, whether they inhere in the school's "faculty, staff, transportation, extracurricular activities and facilities," *Green, supra,* 391 U.S. at 435, or even in "the community and administration['s] attitudes toward [a] school," *Keyes, supra,* 413 U.S. at 196. Although the Court has never explicitly defined what constitutes a "vestige" of state-enforced segregation, the function that this concept has performed in our jurisprudence suggests that it extends to any condition that is likely to convey the message of inferiority implicit in a policy of segregation. So long as such conditions persist, the purposes of the decree cannot be deemed to have been achieved.

B

....

By focusing heavily on present and future compliance with the Equal Protection Clause, the majority's standard ignores how the stigmatic harm identified in *Brown I* can persist even after the State ceases actively to enforce segregation. It was not enough in *Green*, for example, for the school district to withdraw its own enforcement of segregation, leaving it up to individual children and their families to "choose" which school to attend. For it was clear under the circumstances that these choices would be shaped by and perpetuate the state-created message of racial inferiority associated with the school district's historical involvement in segregation. In sum, our school-desegregation jurisprudence establishes that the effects of past discrimination remain chargeable to the school district regardless of its lack of continued enforcement of segregation, and the remedial decree is required until those effects have been finally eliminated.

III

Applying the standard I have outlined, I would affirm the Court of Appeals' decision ordering the District Court to restore the desegregation decree. For it is clear on this record that removal of the decree will result in a significant number of racially identifiable schools that could be eliminated.

....

It is undisputed that replacing the Finger Plan with a system of neighborhood school assignments for grades K-4 resulted in a system of racially identifiable schools. Under the SRP, over one-half of Oklahoma City's elementary schools now have student bodies that are either 90% Afro-American or 90% non-Afro-American. Because this principal vestige of de jure segregation persists, lifting the decree would clearly be premature at this point....

The majority equivocates on the effect to be given to the reemergence of racially identifiable schools. It instructs the District Court to consider whether those "'most important indicia of a segregated system'" have been eliminated, reciting the facets of segregated school operations identified in *Green* — "'faculty, staff, transportation, extra-curricular activities and facilities.'" And, by rendering "res nova" the issue whether residential segregation in Oklahoma City is a vestige of former school segregation, the majority accepts at least as a theoretical possibility that vestiges may exist beyond those identified in *Green*. Nonetheless, the majority hints that the District Court could ignore the effect of residential segregation in perpetuating racially identifiable schools if the court finds residential segregation to be "the result of private decisionmaking and economics." Finally, the majority warns against the application of a standard that would subject formerly segregated school districts to the "Draconian" fate of "judicial tutelage for the indefinite future." *Ante*, at 638.

This equivocation is completely unsatisfying. First, it is well established that school segregation "may have a profound reciprocal effect on the racial composition of residential neighborhoods." *Keyes*, 413 U.S. at 202; *see also Columbus Bd. of Education*, 443 U.S. [449], 465, n. 13, [(1979)] (acknowledging the evidence "that school segregation is a contributing cause of housing segregation")....

Second, there is no basis for the majority's apparent suggestion that the result should be different if residential segregation is now perpetuated by "private decisionmaking." The District Court's conclusion that the racial identity of the northeast quadrant now subsists because of "personal preference[s]," pays insufficient attention to the roles of the State, local officials, and the Board in creating what are now self- perpetuating patterns of residential segregation. Even more important, it fails to account for the unique role of the School Board in creating "all-Negro" schools clouded by the stigma of segregation — schools to which white parents would not opt to send their children. That such negative "personal preferences" exist should not absolve a school district that played a role in creating such "preferences" from its obligation to desegregate the schools to the maximum extent possible.

....

IV

Consistent with the mandate of *Brown I*, our cases have imposed on school districts an unconditional duty to eliminate any condition that perpetuates the message of racial inferiority inherent in the policy of state-sponsored segregation. The racial identifiability of a district's schools is such a condition. Whether this "vestige" of state-sponsored segregation will persist cannot simply be ignored at the point where a district court is contemplating the dissolution of a desegregation decree. In a district with a history of state-sponsored school segregation, racial separation, in my view, remains inherently unequal.

I dissent.

---

1. Recall the following statement from the decision in *Dowell*:

> A school district which has been released from an injunction imposing a desegregation plan no longer requires court authorization for the promulgation of policies and rules regulating matters such as assignment of students and the like, but it of course remains subject to the mandate of the Fourteenth Amendment. 498 U.S. at 250.

Considering the decision in the case, after a desegregation decree is dissolved, is it possible for a school system to fall into the same pattern of segregation (especially de facto segregation in Northern and Western cities) that will lead to another cycle of *Brown* cases? Is this the criticism that Justice Marshall brought in his dissent?

2. Justice Rehnquist's majority opinion suggests some consistency with the *Brown* decision. However, in formulating the determination for when school districts are found in compliance with desegregation, was *Brown*'s provision of "stigmatic injury" to African-American students considered? Did Marshall's dissent focus on the "stigmatic injury" analysis so important to the unanimous decision in *Brown*?

3. The district court remarked that Oklahoma City's Student Reassignment Plan was not designed with discriminatory intent. Is intent to discriminate a necessary factor in *all* desegregation cases? Is this where de jure and de facto forms of discrimination part ways? Is intent necessary in one area of discrimination and not the other? Do the majority or dissenting opinions in this case address this issue?

4. Supreme Court decisions beginning with *Keyes* have used the "intent to discriminate" doctrine as one step in the determination of unconstitutional action on the part of school boards. But what of the influence of these actions in other areas of discrimination? Have the courts, for example, considered that school board discriminatory decisions correlate with the creation of segregated neighborhoods as families make moving decisions based on the schools in the area? In addition, what of the discriminatory actions of other governmental institutions (local, state, and federal) that might have an effect on what goes on in a school system? For a seminal examination of this latter question *see* Paul Dimond, Beyond Busing: Inside the Challenge to Urban Segregation, 1985.

5. The Court ruled that federal supervision of local school systems was intended as a temporary measure to remedy past discrimination and not to operate in perpetuity. From this, three criteria were established: 1) a school district must demonstrate that it has complied in good faith with desegregation orders; 2) that it is unlikely to return to its former ways and 3) the vestiges of segregation have been eliminated to the extent practicable. Did the majority give much guidance on these criteria for those school districts seeking a determination about reaching unitary status?

As to the latter criterion, is the Court clear on how federal courts will determine what constitutes "vestiges of segregation?" The Court instructed that lower courts could disregard predominant one-race schools when the high percentages were caused by "the result of private decisionmaking and economics." But what of the "vestiges of segregation" caused by previous de jure school segregation and new school polices that could result in resegregation? Did the majority or the dissent give a response to this question?

6. Has *Dowell* placed restrictions on any of the court-fashioned remedies used in previous desegregation cases such as the building of new schools, teacher transfer policies, busing or the like? How does this question impact the Court's emphasis (first found in *Milliken*) on local control of education?

7. The majority stated that this decision was to resolve a conflict between the Ninth Circuit (*Spangler v. Pasadena*, 611 F.2d 1239 (1979)) and the Fourth Circuit (*Riddick v. Norfolk*, 784 F.2d 521 (1986)).

In *Spangler*, the Court of Appeals held that the District Court should have relinquished, after nearly ten years, its continuing jurisdiction over the system's schools. The Circuit Court recognized the Pasadena School Board's present compliance with integration efforts and its official representations that it would continue to engage in affirmative action in support of integration. How much effect did the ten years of a court order have on this decision? The court held that a federal court-ordered remedy to desegregate schools should not be more extensive than is necessary to eliminate the effect of the constitutional violation. The court stated that once the remedy has met its purpose, federal court jurisdiction should terminate. Did the court in *Spangler* establish a time limit? Should there be such a limit on court-ordered desegregation plans?

The *Spangler* court also held that a school system policy favoring neighborhood schools was not synonymous with intent to violate the Constitution. Similarly, the court held that jurisdiction over the schools could not be retained solely on the finding that the school board was not likely to remain in compliance with the Constitution if jurisdiction was terminated. Consider this statement with the *Dowell* quote in Note 1 above. Does *Dowell* overrule or affirm *Spangler*?

In *Riddick*, a class of African-American children brought suit challenging a neighborhood pupil assignment plan absent a busing provision. Pupil assignment was to be based on student residence. The school board had determined that "white flight" occurred because of busing and sought to design a plan that would keep the population in the district and the enrollment of the schools integrated. The district court upheld the plan and the court of appeals affirmed. The latter court, as in *Spangler*, held that it had jurisdiction over the school system until the system became "unitary."

The court of appeals held that the district court's finding that the school system had achieved unitary standing was not clearly erroneous: faculty and staff were fully integrated, three of the seven school board members were African-American, as were the school superintendent and three of his assistants, and the overwhelming majority of students attended racially mixed schools.

The *Riddick* court stated that a school system is under a heavy burden to show that any action it takes serves to maintain a unitary system. One of the complaints in the case was that the school system rescinded its earlier busing plan in favor of the neighborhood pupil assignment plan and that the latter plan was intentionally discriminatory. The court of appeals responded that such a change of plans is not unconstitutional as long as the changes are consistent with the system's affirmative duty to eliminate discrimination. Specifically, the plaintiffs have the duty of showing discriminatory intent once a de jure segregated system has been declared unitary.

Is *Riddick* still good law after *Dowell*?

8. Most desegregation cases state that the jurisdiction of the federal court over the schools will be released once the school system has complied with the court order to desegregate. However, what are the benefits of a desegregation decree that would operate in perpetuity? What are the burdens? Would a decision either way — keeping the decree perpetual or making it temporary — decrease desegregation litigation?

9. It is without question that *Dowell* has had and will continue to have an effect on school desegregation cases — from the operation and dissolution of desegregation decrees to local and federal control over school systems. At the end of a 1992 article responding to *Dowell*, Vacca and Hudgins provide a list of emerging issues that face schools as districts reform and restructure public education before and after desegregation orders.

1. What about the recent move in some communities to establish single-race, and/or single-gender schools; or schools for specific ethnic groups? For example, the creation of separate schools for African-American males; or, the creation of elementary schools in areas of this country where high concentrations of new immigrants from Asia or Latin America need extensive help in language development and other skills. In Virginia, the State Legislature is studying the implementation of new tracking and ability grouping programs — especially for those children who need extensive remedial help so that they can succeed in the mainstream of the public schools. Is there a move back to the old "separate but equal" doctrine?

2. What about the renewed emphasis on parent choice, both intra- and interdistrict? Behaving as consumers, parents, especially where their neighborhood schools are weak, likely will seek schools of excellence for their kids. Will schools, where parents do not have the ability to leave, become isolated enclaves with disproportionate numbers of racial and ethnic populations living in lower socio-economic, deteriorating neighborhoods? Recent census figures show growing populations of Asians and Hispanics in the major cities of this country, and show that more African-American families moved out of the cities and to the suburbs. Where do children with educational disabilities fit in the renewed emphasis on choice? Will there be a return to separate school for these kids?

3. Has the major civil rights movement in education spawned by *Brown I* undergone a metamorphosis and become a movement to gain equal access to quality education for the "have nots" of this country? Are the old desegregation cases of the past reappearing in the form of new cases challenging the fiscal disparities that exist in American public school systems?

Vacca and Hudgins, *The Supreme Court Charts a New Course for School Desegregation in the 1990s: Dowell's Pivotal Position*, 75 Educ. L. Rep. 981 (1992).* Many of these issues are considered and discussed throughout this book. *See* Chapters 2 and 13 in particular.

Is the majority decision in *Dowell* consistent with earlier desegregation cases? What of Marshall's dissenting opinion? Steven I. Locke, in *Board of Education v. Dowell: A Look at the New Phase in Desegregation Law*, 21 Hofstra L. Rev. 537, 558-60 (1992), says that the majority opinion is consistent with *Brown* and its progeny. Despite criticizing Marshall's dissent, he also offers some compromises between the two opinions.**

> The Supreme Court's decision in *Board of Educ. v. Dowell* is not a departure from the previous case law regarding desegregation. It provides

---

*Copyright © 1992 by West Publishing Company. Reprinted with permission.
**Reprinted with permission.

a standard for district courts to review desegregation orders that have been complied with while explicitly recognizing that the district courts have the discretion to deny a school board's motion to lift a desegregation injunction if the court is suspicious of the board's intent. The dissent's opinion is severely flawed in that: (1) it fails to address the context in which *Dowell* exists, specifically in terms of the importance of the local interest in controlling public schools; and (2) it ignores the distinction between de facto and de jure segregation, creating a constitutional remedy where none previously existed. These flaws in the dissent's arguments only serve to further evidence that the majority opinion is in line with preceding cases.

Although Justice Marshall's dissent is contrary to contemporary desegregation law, it should not be summarily dismissed. Rather, it should be read to emphasize the failure of both desegregation remedies and the case law implementing those remedies. Clearly, as we enter the new phase in desegregation law, the injunctions may be lifted but the underlying issues have not been resolved.

Justice Marshall's goals could be achieved in three ways not considered in his opinion: (1) overruling *Keyes* and eliminating the distinction between de jure and de facto desegregation; (2) overruling *Milliken I*, in whole or in part; or (3) limiting *Milliken I* to its facts by recognizing that residential segregation is often a vestige [of] prior discrimination, and creating a rebuttable presumption to this effect.

Overruling *Keyes*, however, is senseless. It would create an unnecessary anomaly in well established case law. Eliminating the distinction between de jure and de facto segregation would not only effectively create a new remedy, it would render *Washington v. Davis*,[180] and the requirement of discriminatory intent a nullity in desegregation law. This departure would not only leave the court to rewrite virtually the entire corpus of the equal protection case law, it is wholly unnecessary.

Even overruling *Milliken I*, in whole or in part is unnecessary, and would cause more inconsistencies in the case law than is warranted. The greatest danger of overruling any part of *Milliken I* is that the decision will directly contradict the basic tenet of constitutional construction: that the scope of the remedy cannot exceed the scope of the violation. Altering this rule could easily have unforeseeable repercussions when applied outside of the desegregation law, allowing courts to fashion remedies without limits.

Limiting *Milliken I* to its facts is the best option. By limiting *Milliken I* to its facts, Justice Marshall's goal could be accomplished while eliminating a host of potential problems. By taking this tack, the Court could explicitly find as a general rule that residential segregation is a vestige of past discrimination, and then create a rebuttable presumption to this effect.

---

[180] 426 U.S. 229 (1976).

Although creating a presumption here may seem to place too high a burden on the school boards, it is really no more than a logical extension of the already existing presumption that present day segregation in schools, often coupled with segregated residential patterns, is presumptively unconstitutional. Additionally, patterns of white flight could then be traced to this de jure segregation and give the Court the power to fashion broader remedies.

Although this option sounds similar to Justice Marshall's dissent in *Dowell*, it is different in one important respect: it does not erase the distinction between de jure and de facto segregation. Rather, it just recasts the case law, decreasing the value of the underlying facts of *Milliken I*, without actually altering any of the rules applied in that case. Additionally, the scope of the remedy would not exceed to scope of the violation. Finding residential segregation to be a vestige of prior segregation would simply increase the scope of the violation. This solution should be especially palatable because it does not bind the lower courts to one specific outcome. It still allows the school boards to show that residential patterns are not vestiges of prior discriminatory intent, but rather a result of personal decisionmaking. If a school board can meet this test, unlike the test posited in Marshall's dissent, then the previously issued injunction may be lifted as it was in *Dowell*.

Given the choices that could be adopted to reach Justice Marshall's goals as set out in his dissent in *Dowell*, the best option is to limit *Milliken I* to its facts and create a rebuttable presumption that residential segregation is a vestige of prior discrimination. This presumption would afford more protection to minority children in school districts where desegregation plans have already been implemented for a protracted period of time, but the effects of segregation are still felt, while leaving well entrenched case law essentially intact.

Maria Perugini, Board of Education of Oklahoma City v. Dowell: *Protection of Local Authority or Disregard for the Purpose of* Brown v. Board of Education?, 41 Cath. U. L. Rev. 779 (1992), renders an alternative interpretation of the *Dowell* decision postulating that it is inconsistent with *Brown* and, moreover, gives lower courts little guidance in determining an appropriate standard for dissolving desegregation decrees. She favors Marshall's dissent in that it enunciates a desegregation standard announced in previous cases.

In *Board of Education of Oklahoma City v. Dowell*, the majority concentrated on the limitation of federal judicial powers and, in the process, lost sight of what desegregation is actually supposed to achieve. The majority's remedy does not guarantee that a segregated school system will no longer exist, especially when the remedy is examined in light of lower court interpretations of *Dowell*'s holding, a recent Supreme Court decision that established a more flexible standard for the lifting of a federal court desegregation decree, and a later Supreme Court ruling that allowed a federal court to incrementally or partially withdraw its supervision and control in a school desegregation case. Justice Marshall's dissent, on the other hand, focused on the purpose of desegregation as enunciated in prior desegregation cases: to eliminate the message of racial inferiority. Justice Marshall retained this aim first in formulating a standard for dissolution of a desegregation decree and second in applying that standard to the facts of *Dowell*.

....

... [The] Court missed an opportunity to guide the lower courts in determining what constitutes an appropriate standard for dissolution of a desegregation remedy. Rather, the Court added to the difficulty the courts have in interpreting the disparate results of prior desegregation cases. By constructing a standard for dissolution of a decree without considering the stigmatic injury of African American children, the Court ignored the purpose of the desegregation precedents. As a result, lower courts have little to guide them in determining what must be shown to demonstrate that a decree's purposes have been fully realized. After *Dowell*, a court can decide that the purposes of a desegregation decree have been achieved if a school district has complied with a decree in the past and probably will comply with the decree in the future, regardless if unenforced "vestiges" of segregation remain. For these reasons, *Dowell*'s ambiguous standard will result in disparate results in the future desegregation cases.

The Court should have decided the case consistently with desegregation precedent and taken into account the stigmatic injury that both state-imposed segregation and the effects of segregation after the state has ceased to enforce it inflict upon African American children. By failing to consider the harm in the message of racial inferiority, the Court encourages an environment in which formerly segregated school systems, culturally conditioned by many years of state-imposed segregation, may be allowed to silently slip back to the tragic injustices of a dual school system.*

Id. at 810, 816.

FREEMAN v. PITTS

Supreme Court of the United States
112 S. Ct. 1430 (1992)

JUSTICE KENNEDY delivered the opinion of the Court:

DeKalb County, Georgia, is a major suburban area of Atlanta. This case involves a court-ordered desegregation decree for the DeKalb County School System (DCSS). DCSS now serves some 73,000 students in kindergarten through

---

*Reprinted with permission from The Catholic University Law Review.

high school and is the 32nd largest elementary and secondary school system in the Nation.

DCSS has been subject to the supervision and jurisdiction of the United States District Court for the Northern District of Georgia since 1969, when it was ordered to dismantle its dual school system. In 1986, petitioners filed a motion for final dismissal. The District Court ruled that DCSS had not achieved unitary status in all respects but had done so in student attendance and three other categories. In its order the District Court relinquished remedial control as to those aspects of the system in which unitary status had been achieved, and retained supervisory authority only for those aspects of the school system in which the district was not in full compliance. The Court of Appeals for the Eleventh Circuit reversed, holding that a district court should retain full remedial authority over a school system until it achieves unitary status in six categories at the same time for several years. We now reverse the judgment of the Clourt of Appeals and remand.... A district court need not retain active control over every aspect of school administration until a school district has demonstrated unitary status in all facets of its system.

I

A

For decades before our decision in *Brown v. Board of Education*, 347 U.S. 483 (1954) (*Brown I*), and our mandate in *Brown v. Board of Education*, 349 U.S. 294, 301 (1955) (*Brown II*), which ordered school districts to desegregate with "all deliberate speed," DCSS was segregated by law. DCSS's initial response to the mandate of *Brown II* was an all too familiar one. Interpreting "all deliberate speed" as giving latitude to delay steps to desegregate, DCSS took no positive action toward desegregation until the 1966-1967 school year, when it did nothing more than adopt a freedom of choice transfer plan. Some black students chose to attend former de jure white schools, but the plan had no significant effect on the former de jure black schools.

In 1968 we decided *Green v. New Kent County School Bd.*, 391 U.S. 430 (1968). We held that adoption of a freedom of choice plan does not, by itself, satisfy a school district's mandatory responsibility to eliminate all vestiges of a dual system. *Green* was a turning point in our law in a further respect. Concerned by more than a decade of inaction, we stated that "'[t]he time for mere "deliberate speed" has run out.'" *Id.* at 438, quoting *Griffin v. Prince Edward County School Bd.*, 377 U.S. 218, 234 (1964). We said that the obligation of school districts once segregated by law was to come forward with a plan that "promises realistically to work, and promises realistically to work *now*." 391 U.S. at 439 (emphasis in original). The case before us requires an understanding and assessment of how DCSS responded to the directives set forth in *Green*.

Within two months of our ruling in *Green*, respondents, who are black school children and their parents, instituted this class action in the United States District Court for the Northern District of Georgia.... The District Court in June 1969 entered a consent order approving the proposed plan, which was to be implemented in the 1969-1970 school year. The order abolished the freedom of choice plan and adopted a neighborhood school attendance plan that had been proposed by the DCSS and accepted by the Department of Health, Education and Welfare subject to a minor modification. Under the plan all of the former de jure black schools were closed and their students were reassigned among the remaining neighborhood schools. The District Court retained jurisdiction.

Between 1969 and 1986 respondents sought only infrequent and limited judicial intervention into the affairs of DCSS. They did not request significant changes in student attendance zones or student assignment policies. In 1976 DCSS was ordered: to expand its Minority-to-Majority (M-to-M) student transfer program, allowing students in a school where they are in the majority race to transfer to a school where they are in the minority; to establish a bi-racial committee to oversee the transfer program and future boundary line changes; and to reassign teachers so that the ratio of black to white teachers in each school would be, in substance, similar to the racial balance in the school population systemwide. From 1977 to 1979 the District Court approved a boundary line change for one elementary school attendance zone and rejected DCSS proposals to restrict the M-to-M transfer program. In 1983 DCSS was ordered to make further adjustments to the M-to-M transfer program.

In 1986 petitioners filed a motion for final dismissal of the litigation. They sought a declaration that DCSS had satisfied its duty to eliminate the dual education system, that is to say a declaration that the school system had achieved unitary status. *Green, supra*, 391 U.S. at 441. The District Court approached the question whether DCSS had achieved unitary status by asking whether DCSS was unitary with respect to each of the factors identified in *Green*. The court considered an additional factor that is not named in *Green*: the quality of education being offered to the white and black student populations.

The District Court found DCSS to be "an innovative school system that has travelled the often long road to unitary status almost to its end," noting that "the court has continually been impressed by the successes of the DCSS and its dedication to providing a quality education for all students within that system." It found that DCSS is a unitary system with regard to student assignments, transportation, physical facilities, and extracurricular activities, and ruled that it would order no further relief in those areas. The District Court stopped short of dismissing the case, however, because it found that DCSS was not unitary in every respect. The court said that vestiges of the dual system remain in the areas of teacher and principal assignments, resource allocation, and quality of education. DCSS was ordered to take measures to address the remaining problems.

B

Proper resolution of any desegregation case turns on a careful assessment of its facts. *Green, supra,* at 439. Here, as in most cases where the issue is the degree of compliance with a school desegregation decree, a critical beginning point is the degree of racial imbalance in the school district, that is to say a comparison of the proportion of majority to minority students in individual schools with the proportions of the races in the district as a whole. This inquiry is fundamental, for under the former de jure regimes racial exclusion was both the means and the end of a policy motivated by disparagement of or hostility towards the disfavored race. In accord with this principle, the District Court began its analysis with an assessment of the current racial mix in the schools throughout DCSS and the explanation for the racial imbalance it found. The respondents did not contend on appeal that the findings of fact were clearly erroneous and the Court of Appeals did not find them to be erroneous. The Court of Appeals did disagree with the conclusion reached by the District Court respecting the need for further supervision of racial balance in student assignments.

In the extensive record that comprises this case, one fact predominates: remarkable changes in the racial composition of the county presented DCSS and the District Court with a student population in 1986 far different from the one they set out to integrate in 1969.... Although the public school population experienced only modest changes between 1969 and 1986 (remaining in the low 70,000's), a striking change occurred in the racial proportions of the student population. The school system that the District Court ordered desegregated in 1969 had 5.6% black students; by 1986 the percentage of black students was 47%.

To compound the difficulty of working with these radical demographic changes, the northern and southern parts of the county experienced much different growth patterns.... In 1970, there were 7,615 nonwhites living in the northern part of DeKalb County and 11,508 nonwhites in the southern part of the county. By 1980, there were 15,365 nonwhites living in the northern part of the county, and 87,583 nonwhites in the southern part.... Between 1975 and 1980 alone, approximately 64,000 black citizens moved into southern DeKalb County, most of them coming from Atlanta. During the same period, approximately 37,000 white citizens moved out of southern DeKalb County to the surrounding counties.

The District Court made findings with respect to the number of nonwhite citizens in the northern and southern parts of the county for the years 1970 and 1980 without making parallel findings with respect to white citizens. Yet a clear picture does emerge. During the relevant period, the black population in the southern portion of the county experienced tremendous growth while the white population did not, and the white population in the northern part of the county experienced tremendous growth while the black population did not.

... As the District Court observed, the demographic shifts have had "an immense effect on the racial compositions of the DeKalb County schools." *Ibid.* From 1976 to 1986, enrollment in elementary schools declined overall by 15%, while black enrollment in elementary schools increased by 86%. During the same period, overall high school enrollment declined by 16%, while black enrollment in high school increased by 119%. These effects were even more pronounced in the southern portion of DeKalb County.

Concerned with racial imbalance in the various schools of the district, respondents presented evidence that during the 1986-1987 school year DCSS had the following features: (1) 47% of the students attending DCSS were black; (2) 50% of the black students attended schools that were over 90% black; (3) 62% of all black students attended schools that had more than 20% more blacks than the systemwide average; (4) 27% of white students attended schools that were more than 90% white; (5) 59% of the white students attended schools that had more than 20% more whites than the systemwide average; (6) of the 22 DCSS high schools, five had student populations that were more than 90% black, while five other schools had student populations that were more than 80% white; and (7) of the 74 elementary schools in DCSS, 18 are over 90% black, while 10 are over 90% white. (The respondents' evidence on these points treated all nonblack students as white. The District Court noted that there was no evidence that nonblack minority students comprised even one percent of DCSS student population.)

Respondents argued in the District Court that this racial imbalance in student assignment was a vestige of the dual system, rather than a product of independent demographic forces. In addition to the statistical evidence that the ratio of black students to white students in individual schools varied to a significant degree from the systemwide average, respondents contended that DCSS had not used all available desegregative tools in order to achieve racial balancing. Respondents pointed to the following alleged shortcomings in DCSS's desegregative efforts: (1) DCSS did not break the county into subdistricts and racially balance each subdistrict; (2) DCSS failed to expend sufficient funds for minority learning opportunities; (3) DCSS did not establish community advisory organizations; (4) DCSS did not make full use of the freedom of choice plan; (5) DCSS did not cluster schools, that is, it did not create schools for separate grade levels which could be used to establish a feeder pattern; (6) DCSS did not institute its magnet school program as early as it might have; and (7) DCSS did not use busing to facilitate urban to suburban exchanges.

According to the District Court, respondents conceded that the 1969 order assigning all students to their neighborhood schools "effectively desegregated DCSS for a period of time" with respect to student assignment. The District Court noted, however, that despite this concession the respondents contended there was an improper imbalance in two schools even in 1969. Respondents made much of the fact that despite the small percentage of blacks in the county in 1969, there were then two schools that contained a majority of black students....

The District Court found the racial imbalance in these schools was not a vestige of the prior de jure system. It observed that both ... schools were de jure white schools before the freedom of choice plan was put in place. It cited expert witness testimony that [one of the two] had become a majority black school as a result of demographic shifts unrelated to the actions of petitioners or their predecessors....

Although the District Court found that DCSS was desegregated for at least a short period under the court-ordered plan of 1969, it did not base its finding that DCSS had achieved unitary status with respect to student assignment on that circumstance alone. Recognizing that "[t]he achievement of unitary status in the area of student assignment cannot be hedged on the attainment of such status for a brief moment," the District Court examined the interaction between DCSS policy and demographic shifts in DeKalb County.

The District Court noted that DCSS had taken specific steps to combat the effects of demographics on the racial mix of the schools. Under the 1969 order, a biracial committee had reviewed all proposed changes in the boundary lines of school attendance zones. Since the original desegregation order, there had been about 170 such changes. It was found that only three had a partial segregative effect....

The District Court also noted that DCSS, on its own initiative, started an M-to-M program in the 1972 school year. The program was a marked success. Participation increased with each passing year, so that in the 1986-1987 school year, 4,500 of the 72,000 students enrolled in DCSS participated. An expert testified that the impact of an M-to-M program goes beyond the number of students transferred because students at the receiving school also obtain integrated learning experiences. The District Court found that about 19% of the students attending DCSS had an integrated learning experience as a result of the M-to-M program.

In addition, in the 1980's, DCSS instituted a magnet school program in schools located in the middle of the county. The magnet school programs included a performing arts program, two science programs, and a foreign language program. There was testimony in the District Court that DCSS also had plans to operate additional magnet programs in occupational education and gifted and talented education, as well as a preschool program and an open campus. By locating these programs in the middle of the county, DCSS sought to attract black students from the southern part of the county and white students from the northern part.

....

In determining whether DCSS has achieved unitary status with respect to student assignment, the District Court saw its task as one of deciding if petitioners "have accomplished maximum practical desegregation of the DCSS or if the DCSS must still do more to fulfill their affirmative constitutional duty." Petitioners and respondents presented conflicting expert testimony about the potential effects that desegregative techniques not deployed might have had upon the racial mix of the schools. The District Court found that petitioners' experts were more reliable, citing their greater familiarity with DCSS, their experience and their standing within the expert community. The District Court made these findings:

> [The actions of DCSS] achieved maximum practical desegregation from 1969 to 1986. The rapid population shifts in DeKalb County were not caused by any action on the part of the DCSS. These demographic shifts were inevitable as the result of suburbanization, that is, work opportunities arising in DeKalb County as well as the City of Atlanta, which attracted blacks to DeKalb; the decline in the number of children born to white families during this period while the number of children born to black families did not decrease; blockbusting of formerly white neighborhoods leading to selling and buying of real estate in the DeKalb area on a highly dynamic basis; and the completion of Interstate 20, which made access from DeKalb County into the City of Atlanta much easier.... There is no evidence that the school system's previous unconstitutional conduct may have contributed to this segregation. This court is convinced that any further actions taken by defendants, while the actions might have made marginal adjustments in the population trends, would not have offset the factors that were described above and the same racial segregation would have occurred at approximately the same speed.

The District Court added:

> [A]bsent massive bussing, which is not considered as a viable option by either the parties or this court, the magnet school program and the M-to-M program, which the defendants voluntarily implemented and to which the defendants obviously are dedicated, are the most effective ways to deal with the effects on student attendance of the residential segregation existing in DeKalb County at this time.

Having found no constitutional violation with respect to student assignment, the District Court next considered the other *Green* factors, beginning with faculty and staff assignments. The District Court first found that DCSS had fulfilled its constitutional obligation with respect to hiring and retaining minority teachers and administrators.... Nevertheless, the District Court found that DCSS had not achieved or maintained a ratio of black to white teachers and administrators in each school to approximate the ratio of black to white teachers and administrators throughout the system. *See Singleton v. Jackson Municipal Separate School Dist.*, 419 F.2d 1211 (CA5 1969), *cert. denied*, 396 U.S. 1032 (1970).... The District Court found that in the 1984-1985 school year, seven schools deviated by more than 10% from the systemwide average of 26.4% minority teachers in elementary schools and 24.9% minority teachers in high schools. The District Court also found that black principals and administrators were over-represented in schools with high percentages of black students and underrepresented in schools with low percentages of black students.

The District Court found the crux of the problem to be that DCSS has relied on the replacement process to attain a racial balance in teachers and other staff and has avoided using mandatory reassignment....

... The court ordered DCSS to devise a plan to achieve compliance with *Singleton*, noting that "[i]t would appear that such compliance will necessitate reassignment of both teachers and principals." With respect to faculty, the District Court noted that meeting *Singleton* would not be difficult, citing petitioners' own estimate that most schools' faculty could conform by moving, at most, two or three teachers.

Addressing the more ineffable category of quality of education, the District Court rejected most of respondents' contentions that there was racial disparity in the provision of certain educational resources (*e.g.*, teachers with advanced degrees, teachers with more experience, library books), contentions made to show that black students were not being given equal educational opportunity. The District Court went further, however, and examined the evidence concerning achievement of black students in DCSS. It cited expert testimony praising the overall educational program in the district, as well as objective evidence of black achievement: black students at DCSS made greater gains on the Iowa Tests of Basic Skills (ITBS) than white students, and black students at DCSS are more successful than black students nationwide on the Scholastic Aptitude Test (SAT). It made the following finding:

> While there will always be something more that the DCSS can do to improve the chances for black students to achieve academic success, the court cannot find, as plaintiffs urge, that the DCSS has been negligent in its duties to implement programs to assist black students. The DCSS is a very innovative school system. It has implemented a number of programs to enrich the lives and enhance the academic potential of all students, both blacks and whites. Many remedial programs are targeted in the majority black schools. Programs have been implemented to involve the parents and offset negative socio-economic factors. If the DCSS has failed in any way in this regard, it is not because the school system has been negligent in its duties.

Despite its finding that there was no intentional violation, the District Court found that DCSS had not achieved unitary status with respect to quality of education because teachers in schools with disproportionately high percentages of white students tended to be better educated and have more experience than their counterparts in schools with disproportionately high percentages of black students, and because per pupil expenditures in majority white schools exceeded per pupil expenditures in majority black schools. From these findings, the District Court ordered DCSS to equalize spending and remedy the other problems.

The final *Green* factors considered by the District Court were: (1) physical facilities, (2) transportation, and (3) extracurricular activities. The District Court noted that although respondents expressed some concerns about the use of portable classrooms in schools in the southern portion of the county, they in effect conceded that DCSS has achieved unitary status with respect to physical facilities.

In accordance with its factfinding, the District Court held that it would order no further relief in the areas of student assignment, transportation, physical facilities and extracurricular activities. The District Court, however, did order DCSS to establish a system to balance teacher and principal assignments and to equalize per pupil expenditures throughout DCSS. Having found that blacks were represented on the school board and throughout DCSS administration, the District Court abolished the biracial committee as no longer necessary.

Both parties appealed to the United States Court of Appeals for the Eleventh Circuit. The Court of Appeals affirmed the District Court's ultimate conclusion that DCSS has not yet achieved unitary status, but reversed the District Court's ruling that DCSS has no further duties in the area of student assignment. The Court of Appeals held that the District Court erred by considering the six *Green* factors as separate categories.... We granted certiorari.

II

Two principal questions are presented. The first is whether a district court may relinquish its supervision and control over those aspects of a school system in which there has been compliance with a desegregation decree if other aspects of the system remain in noncompliance. As we answer this question in the affirmative, the second question is whether the Court of Appeals erred in reversing the District Court's order providing for incremental withdrawal of supervision in all the circumstances of this case.

A

The duty and responsibility of a school district once segregated by law is to take all steps necessary to eliminate the vestiges of the unconstitutional de jure system. This is required in order to insure that the principal wrong of the de jure system, the injuries and stigma inflicted upon the race disfavored by the violation, is no longer present. This was the rationale and the objective of *Brown I* and *Brown II*. In *Brown I* we said: "to separate [black students] from others of similar age and qualifications solely because of their race generates a feeling of inferiority as to their status in the community that may affect their hearts and minds in a way unlikely ever to be undone." 347 U.S. at 494....

The objective of *Brown I* was made more specific by our holding in *Green* that the duty of a former de jure district is to "take whatever steps might be necessary to convert to a unitary system in which racial discrimination would be eliminated root and branch." 391 U.S. at 437-438. We also identified various parts of the school system which, in addition to student attendance patterns, must be free from racial discrimination before the mandate of *Brown* is met: faculty, staff, transportation, extracurricular activities and facilities. 391 U.S. at 435. The *Green* factors are a measure of the racial identifiability of schools in a system that is not in compliance with *Brown*, and we instructed the District Courts to fashion remedies that address all these components of elementary and secondary school systems.

The concept of unitariness has been a helpful one in defining the scope of the district courts' authority, for it conveys the central idea that a school district that was once a dual system must be examined in all of its facets, both when a remedy is ordered and in the later phases of desegregation when the question is whether the district courts' remedial control ought to be modified, lessened, or withdrawn. But, as we explained last term in *Board of Education of Oklahoma City v. Dowell*, 498 U.S. ___, ___, 111 S.Ct. 630, 636 (1991), the term "unitary" is not a precise concept:

> [I]t is a mistake to treat words such as "dual" and "unitary" as if they were actually found in the Constitution.... Courts have used the term "dual" to denote a school system which has engaged in intentional segregation of students by race, and "unitary" to describe a school system which has been brought into compliance with the command of the Constitution. We are not sure how useful it is to define these terms more precisely, or to create subclasses within them.

It follows that we must be cautious not to attribute to the term a utility it does not have. The term "unitary" does not confine the discretion and authority of the District Court in a way that departs from traditional equitable principles.

That the term "unitary" does not have fixed meaning or content is not inconsistent with the principles that control the exercise of equitable power. The essence of a court's equity power lies in its inherent capacity to adjust remedies in a feasible and practical way to eliminate the conditions or redress the injuries caused by unlawful action. Equitable remedies must be flexible if these underlying principles are to be enforced with fairness and precision. In this respect, as we observed in *Swann*, "a school desegregation case does not differ fundamentally from other cases involving the framing of equitable remedies to repair the denial of a constitutional right. The task is to correct, by a balancing of the individual and collective interest, the condition that offends the Constitution." *Swann, supra*, 402 U.S. at 15-16. The requirement of a unitary school system must be implemented according to this prescription.

Our application of these guiding principles in *Pasadena City Bd. of Education v. Spangler*, 427 U.S. 424 (1976), is instructive. There we held that a District Court exceeded its remedial authority in requiring annual readjustment of school attendance zones in the Pasadena school district when changes in the racial makeup of the schools were caused by demographic shifts "not attributed to any segregative acts on the part of the [school district]." *Id.* at 436. In so holding we said:

> It may well be that petitioners have not yet totally achieved the unitary system contemplated by ... *Swann*.... But that does not undercut the force of the principle underlying the quoted language from *Swann*. In this case the District Court approved a plan designed to obtain racial neutrality in the attendance of students at Pasadena's public schools. No one disputes that the initial implementation of this plan accomplished that objective. That being the case, the District Court was not entitled to require the [Pasadena Unified School District] to rearrange its attendance zones each year so as to ensure that the racial mix desired by the court was maintained in perpetuity. For having once implemented a racially neutral attendance pattern in order to remedy the perceived constitutional violations on the part of the defendants, the District Court had fully performed its function of providing the appropriate remedy for previous racially discriminatory attendance patterns. *Ibid. See also id.* at 438, n. 5.
>
> ....

Today, we make explicit the rationale that was central in *Spangler*. A federal court in a school desegregation case has the discretion to order an incremental or partial withdrawal of its supervision and control. This discretion derives both from the constitutional authority which justified its intervention in the first instance and its ultimate objectives in formulating the decree.... In construing the remedial authority of the district courts, we have been guided by the principles that "judicial powers may be exercised only on the basis of a constitutional violation," and that "the nature of the violation determines the scope of the remedy." *Swann*, 402 U.S. at 16....

We have said that the court's end purpose must be to remedy the violation and in addition to restore state and local authorities to the control of a school system that is operating in compliance with the Constitution. *Milliken v. Bradley*, 433 U.S. 267, 280-281 (1977).... Partial relinquishment of judicial control, where justified by the facts of the case, can be an important and significant step in fulfilling the district court's duty to return the operations and control of schools to local authorities. In *Dowell*, we emphasized that federal judicial supervision of local school systems was intended as a "temporary measure." 498 U.S. at ____, 111 S.Ct. at 636. Although this temporary measure has lasted decades, the ultimate objective has not changed — to return school districts to the control of local authorities. Just as a court has the obligation at the outset of a desegregation decree to structure a plan so that all available resources of the court are directed to comprehensive supervision of its decree, so too must a court provide an orderly means for withdrawing from control when it is shown that the school district has attained the requisite degree of compliance. A transition phase in which control is relinquished in a gradual way is an appropriate means to this end.

As we have long observed, "local autonomy of school districts is a vital national tradition." *Dayton Board of Education v. Brinkman*, 433 U.S. 406, 410 (1977) (*Dayton I*). Returning schools to the control of local authorities at the earliest practicable date is essential to restore their true accountability in our governmental system. When the school district and all state entities participating with it in operating the schools make decisions in the absence of judicial supervision, they can be held accountable to the citizenry, to the political process, and to the courts in the ordinary course. As we discuss below, one of the prerequisites to relinquishment of control in whole or in part is that a school district has demonstrated its commitment to a course of action that gives full respect to the equal protection guarantees of the Constitution. Yet it must be acknowledged that the potential for discrimination and racial hostility is still present in our country, and its manifestations may emerge in new and subtle forms after the effects of de jure desegregation have been eliminated. It is the duty of the State and its subdivisions to ensure that such forces do not shape or control the policies of its school systems. Where control lies, so too does responsibility.

We hold that, in the course of supervising desegregation plans, federal courts have the authority to relinquish supervision and control of school districts in incremental stages, before full compliance has been achieved in every area of school operations. While retaining jurisdiction over the case, the court may determine that it will not order further remedies in areas where the school district is in compliance with the decree. That is to say, upon a finding that a school system subject to a court-supervised desegregation plan is in compliance in some but not all areas, the court in appropriate cases may return control to the school system in those areas where compliance has been achieved, limiting further judicial supervision to operations that are not yet in full compliance with the court decree. In particular, the district court may determine that it will not order further remedies in the area of student assignments where racial imbalance is not traceable, in a proximate way, to constitutional violations.

A court's discretion to order the incremental withdrawal of its supervision in a school desegregation case must be exercised in a manner consistent with the purposes and objectives of its equitable power. Among the factors which must inform the sound discretion of the court in ordering partial withdrawal are the following: whether there has been full and satisfactory compliance with the decree in those aspects of the system where supervision is to be withdrawn; whether retention of judicial control is necessary or practicable to achieve compliance with the decree in other facets of the school system; and whether the school district has demonstrated, to the public and to the parents and students of the once disfavored race, its good-faith commitment to the whole of the court's decree and to those provisions of the law and the constitution that were the predicate for judicial intervention in the first instance.

In considering these factors a court should give particular attention to the school system's record of compliance. A school system is better positioned to demonstrate its good-faith commitment to a constitutional course of action when its policies form a consistent pattern of lawful conduct directed to eliminating earlier violations. And with the passage of time the degree to which racial imbalances continue to represent vestiges of a constitutional violation may diminish, and the practicability and efficacy of various remedies can be evaluated with more precision.

These are the premises that guided our formulation in *Dowell* of the duties of a district court during the final phases of a desegregation case: "The District Court should address itself to whether the Board had complied in good faith with the desegregation decree since it was entered, and whether the vestiges of past discrimination had been eliminated to the extent practicable." 498 U.S. at ___, 111 S.Ct. at 638.

B

We reach now the question whether the Court of Appeals erred in prohibiting the District Court from returning to DCSS partial control over some of its affairs. We decide that the Court of Appeals did err in holding that, as a matter of law, the District Court had no discretion to permit DCSS to regain control over student assignment, transportation, physical facilities, and extracurricular activities, while retaining court supervision over the areas of faculty and administrative assignments and the quality of education, where full compliance had not been demonstrated.

It was an appropriate exercise of its discretion for the District Court to address the elements of a unitary system discussed in *Green*, to inquire whether other elements ought to be identified, and to determine whether minority students were being disadvantaged in ways that required the formulation of new and further remedies to insure full compliance with the court's decree.... By withdrawing control over areas where judicial supervision is no longer needed, a district court can concentrate both its own resources and those of the school district on the areas where the effects of de jure discrimination have not been eliminated and further action is necessary in order to provide real and tangible relief to minority students.

....

The Court of Appeals was mistaken in ruling that our opinion in *Swann* requires "awkward," "inconvenient" and "even bizarre" measures to achieve racial balance in student assignments in the late phases of carrying out a decree, when the imbalance is attributable neither to the prior de jure system nor to a later violation by the school district but rather to independent demographic forces. In *Swann* we undertook to discuss the objectives of a comprehensive desegregation plan and the powers and techniques available to a district court in designing it at the outset. We confirmed that racial balance in school assignments was a necessary part of the remedy in the circumstances there presented. In the case before us the District Court designed a comprehensive plan for desegregation of DCSS in 1969, one that included racial balance in student assignments.

The desegregation decree was designed to achieve maximum practicable desegregation. Its central remedy was the closing of black schools and the reassignment of pupils to neighborhood schools, with attendance zones that achieved racial balance. The plan accomplished its objective in the first year of operation, before dramatic demographic changes altered residential patterns. For the entire 17-year period the respondents raised no substantial objection to the basic student assignment system, as the parties and the District Court concentrated on other mechanisms to eliminate the de jure taint.

That there was racial imbalance in student attendance zones was not tantamount to a showing that the school district was in noncompliance with the decree or with its duties under the law. Racial balance is not to be achieved for its own sake. It is to be pursued when racial imbalance has been caused by a constitutional violation. Once the racial imbalance due to the de jure violation has been remedied, the school district is under no duty to remedy imbalance that is caused by demographic factors. *Swann*, 402 U.S. at 31-32.... If the unlawful de jure policy of a school system has been the cause of the racial imbalance in student attendance, that condition must be remedied. The school district bears the burden of showing that any current imbalance is not traceable, in a proximate way, to the prior violation.

The findings of the District Court that the population changes which occurred in DeKalb County were not caused by the policies of the school district, but rather by independent factors, are consistent with the mobility that is a distinct characteristic of our society. In one year (from 1987 to 1988) over 40 million Americans, or 17.6 percent of the total population, moved households. U.S. Dept. of Commerce, Bureau of Census, Statistical Abstract of the United States, p. 19, Table 25 (111th ed. 1991). Over a third of those people moved to a different county, and over six million migrated between States. *Ibid.* In such a society it is inevitable that the demographic makeup of school districts, based as they are on political subdivisions such as counties and municipalities, may undergo rapid change.

The effect of changing residential patterns on the racial composition of schools though not always fortunate is somewhat predictable. Studies show a high correlation between residential segregation and school segregation. Wilson & Taeuber, Residential and School Segregation: Some Tests of Their Association, in Demography and Ethnic Groups 57-58 (F. Bean & W. Frisbie eds. 1978). The District Court in this case heard evidence tending to show that racially stable neighborhoods are not likely to emerge because whites prefer a racial mix of 80% white and 20% black, while blacks prefer a 50%-50% mix.

Where resegregation is a product not of state action but of private choices, it does not have constitutional implications. It is beyond the authority and beyond the practical ability of the federal courts to try to counteract these kinds of continuous and massive demographic shifts. To attempt such results would require ongoing and never-ending supervision by the courts of school districts simply because they were once de jure segregated. Residential housing choices, and their attendant effects on the racial composition of schools, present an ever-changing pattern, one difficult to address through judicial remedies.

In one sense of the term, vestiges of past segregation by state decree do remain in our society and in our schools. Past wrongs to the black race, wrongs committed by the State and in its name, are a stubborn fact of history. And stubborn facts of history linger and persist. But though we cannot escape our history, neither must we overstate its consequences in fixing legal responsibilities. The vestiges of segregation that are the concern of the law in a school case may be subtle and intangible but nonetheless they must be so real that they have a causal link to the de jure violation being remedied. It is simply not always the case that demographic forces causing population change bear any real and substantial relation to a de jure violation. And the law need not proceed on that premise.

As the de jure violation becomes more remote in time and these demographic changes intervene, it becomes less likely that a current racial imbalance in a school district is a vestige of the prior de jure system. The causal link between current conditions and the prior violation is even more attenuated if the school district has demonstrated its good faith. In light of its finding that the demographic changes in DeKalb County are unrelated to the prior violation, the District Court was correct to entertain the suggestion that DCSS had no duty to achieve systemwide racial balance in the student population. It was appropriate for the District Court to examine the reasons for the racial imbalance before ordering an impractical, and no doubt massive, expenditure of funds to achieve racial balance after 17 years of efforts to implement the comprehensive plan in a district where there were fundamental changes in demographics, changes not attributable to the former de jure regime or any later actions by school officials. The District Court's determination to order instead the expenditure of scarce resources in areas such as the quality of education, where full compliance had not yet been achieved, underscores the uses of discretion in framing equitable remedies.

To say, as did the Court of Appeals, that a school district must meet all six *Green* factors before the trial court can declare the system unitary and relinquish its control over school attendance zones, and to hold further that racial balancing by all necessary means is required in the interim, is simply to vindicate a legal phrase. The law is not so formalistic. A proper rule must be based on the necessity to find a feasible remedy that insures systemwide compliance with the court decree and that is directed to curing the effects of the specific violation.

We next consider whether retention of judicial control over student attendance is necessary or practicable to achieve compliance in other facets of the school system. Racial balancing in elementary and secondary school student assignments may be a legitimate remedial device to correct other fundamental inequities that were themselves caused by the constitutional violation. We have long recognized that the *Green* factors may be related or interdependent. Two or more *Green* factors may be intertwined or synergistic in their relation, so that a constitutional violation in one area cannot be eliminated unless the judicial remedy addresses other matters as well. We have observed, for example, that student segregation and faculty segregation are often related problems. *See Dayton Board of Education v. Brinkman*, 443 U.S. 526, 536 (1979) (*Dayton II*) ("'[P]urposeful segregation of faculty by race was inextricably tied to racially motivated student assignment practices'").... As a consequence, a continuing violation in one area may need to be addressed by remedies in another....

There was no showing that racial balancing was an appropriate mechanism to cure other deficiencies in this case. It is true that the school district was not in compliance with respect to faculty assignments, but the record does not show that student reassignments would be a feasible or practicable way to remedy this defect. To the contrary, the District Court suggests that DCSS could solve the faculty assignment problem by reassigning a few teachers per school. The District Court, not having our analysis before it, did not have the opportunity to make specific findings and conclusions on this aspect of the case, however. Further proceedings are appropriate for this purpose.

The requirement that the school district show its good faith commitment to the entirety of a desegregation plan so that parents, students and the public have assurance against further injuries or stigma also should be a subject for more specific findings. We stated in *Dowell* that the good-faith compliance of the district with the court order over a reasonable period of time is a factor to be considered in deciding whether or not jurisdiction could be relinquished. *Dowell*, 498 U.S. at ___, 111 S.Ct. at 638 ("The District Court should address itself to whether the Board had complied in good faith with the desegregation decree since it was entered, and whether the vestiges of past discrimination had been eliminated to the extent practicable"). A history of good-faith compliance is evidence that any current racial imbalance is not the product of a new de jure violation, and enables the district court to accept the school board's representation that it has accepted the principle of racial equality and will not suffer intentional discrimination in the future. *See Morgan v. Nucci*, 831 F.2d at 321 ("A finding of good faith ... reduces the possibility that a school system's compliance with court orders is but a temporary constitutional ritual").

When a school district has not demonstrated good faith under a comprehensive plan to remedy ongoing violations, we have without hesitation approved comprehensive and continued district court supervision. *See Columbus Bd. of Education v. Penick*, 443 U.S. 449, 461 (1979) (predicating liability in part on the finding that the school board "'never actively set out to dismantle [the] dual system,'" *Penick v. Columbus Bd. of Education*, 429 F.Supp. 229, 260 (SD Ohio 1977)); *Dayton II, supra*, 443 U.S. at 534 (adopting Court of Appeals holding that the "intentionally segregative impact of various practices since 1954 ... were of systemwide import and an appropriate basis for a systemwide remedy").

In contrast to the circumstances in *Penick* and *Brinkman*, the District Court in this case stated that throughout the period of judicial supervision it has been impressed by the successes DCSS has achieved and its dedication to providing a quality education for all students, and that DCSS "has travelled the often long road to unitary status almost to its end." With respect to those areas where compliance had not been achieved, the District Court did not find that DCSS had acted in bad faith or engaged in further acts of discrimination since the desegregation plan went into effect. This, though, may not be the equivalent of a finding that the school district has an affirmative commitment to comply in good faith with the entirety of a desegregation plan, and further proceedings are appropriate for this purpose as well.

The judgment is reversed and the case is remanded to the Court of Appeals. It should determine what issues are open for its further consideration in light of the previous briefs and arguments of the parties and in light of the principles set forth in this opinion. Thereupon it should order further proceedings as necessary or order an appropriate remand to the District Court.

Each party is to bear its own costs.

It is so ordered.

JUSTICE THOMAS took no part in the consideration or decision of this case.

JUSTICE SCALIA, concurring:

....

Our decision will be of great assistance to the citizens of DeKalb County, who for the first time since 1969 will be able to run their own public schools, at least so far as student assignments are concerned. It will have little effect, however, upon the many other school districts throughout the country that are still being supervised by federal judges, since it turns upon the extraordinarily rare circumstance of a finding that no portion of the current racial imbalance is a remnant of prior de jure discrimination. While it is perfectly appropriate for the Court to decide this case on that narrow basis, we must resolve — if not today, then soon — what is to be done in the vast majority of other districts, where, though our cases continue to profess that judicial oversight of school operations is a temporary expedient, democratic processes remain suspended, with no prospect of restoration, 38 years after *Brown v. Board of Education*, 347 U.S. 483 (1954) (*Brown I*).

Almost a quarter-century ago, in *Green v. School Bd., New Kent County*, 391 U.S. 430, 437-38 (1968), this Court held that school systems which had been enforcing de jure segregation at the time of *Brown I* had not merely an obligation to assign students and resources on a race-neutral basis but also an "affirmative duty" to "desegregate," that is, to achieve insofar as practicable racial balance in their schools. This holding has become such a part of our legal fabric that there is a tendency, reflected in the Court of Appeals opinion in this case, to speak as though the Constitution requires such racial balancing. Of course it does not: The Equal Protection Clause reaches only those racial imbalances shown to be intentionally caused by the State. As the Court reaffirms today, if "desegregation" (*i.e.*, racial balancing) were properly to be ordered in the present case, it would be not because the extant racial imbalance in the DCSS public schools offends the Constitution, but rather because that imbalance is a "lingering effect" of the pre-1969 de jure segregation that offended the Constitution. For all our talk about "unitary status," "release from judicial supervision," and "affirmative duty to desegregate," the sole question in school desegregation cases (absent an allegation that current policies are intentionally discriminatory) is one of remedies for past violations.

....

Since parents and school boards typically want children to attend schools in their own neighborhood, "[t]he principal cause of racial and ethnic imbalance in ... public schools across the country — North and South — is the imbalance in residential patterns." *Austin Independent School Dist. v. United States*, 429 U.S. 990, 994 (1976) (POWELL, J., concurring). That imbalance in residential patterns, in turn, "doubtless result[s] from a melange of past happenings prompted by economic considerations, private discrimination, discriminatory school assignments, or a desire to reside near people of one's own race or ethnic background." *Columbus Bd. of Education v. Penick*, 443 U.S. 449, 512 (1979) (REHNQUIST, J., dissenting); *see also Pasadena City Bd. of Education v. Spangler*, 427 U.S. 424, 435-37 (1976). Consequently, residential segregation "is a national, not a southern phenomenon" which exists "'regardless of the character of local laws and policies, and regardless of the extent of other forms of segregation or discrimination.'" *Keyes v. School Dist. No. 1, Denver, Colo.*, 413 U.S. 189, 223, and n. 9 (1973) (POWELL, J., concurring in part and dissenting in part), quoting K. Taueber, *Negroes In Cities* (1965).

Racially imbalanced schools are hence the product of a blend of public and private actions, and any assessment that they would not be segregated, or would not be as segregated, in the absence of a particular one of those factors is guesswork. It is similarly guesswork, of course, to say that they would be segregated, or would be as segregated, in the absence of one of those factors. Only in rare cases such as this one and *Spangler*, *see* 427 U.S. at 435-37 where the racial imbalance had been temporarily corrected after the abandonment of de jure segregation, can it be asserted with any degree of confidence that the past discrimination is no longer playing a proximate role. Thus, allocation of the burden of proof foreordains the result in almost all of the "vestige of past discrimination" cases. If, as is normally the case under our Equal Protection jurisprudence (and in the law generally), we require the plaintiffs to establish the asserted facts entitling them to relief — that the racial imbalance they wish corrected is at least in part the vestige of an old de jure system — the plaintiffs will almost always lose. Conversely, if we alter our normal approach and require the school authorities to establish the negative — that the imbalance is not attributable to their past discrimination — the plaintiffs will almost always win. *See Penick*, *supra*, 443 U.S. at 471 (STEWART, J., concurring in result).

Since neither of these alternatives is entirely palatable, an observer unfamiliar with the history surrounding this issue might suggest that we avoid the problem by requiring only that the school authorities establish a regime in which parents are free to disregard neighborhood-school assignment, and to send their children (with transportation paid) to whichever school they choose. So long as there is free choice, he would say, there is no reason to require that the schools be made identical. The constitutional right is equal racial access to schools, not access to racially equal schools; whatever racial imbalances such a free-choice system might produce would be the product of private forces....

But we ultimately charted a different course with respect to public elementary and secondary schools. We concluded in *Green* that a "freedom of choice" plan was not necessarily sufficient, 391 U.S. at 439-40 and later applied this conclusion to all jurisdictions with a history of intentional segregation:

> "Racially neutral assignment plans proposed by school authorities to a district court may be inadequate; such plans may fail to counteract the continuing effects of past school segregation resulting from discriminatory location of school sites or distortion of school size in order to achieve or maintain an artificial racial separation. When school authorities present a district court with a "loaded game board," affirmative action in the form of remedial altering of attendance zones is proper to achieve truly nondiscriminatory assignments." *Swann v. Charlotte-Mecklenburg Bd. of Education*, 402 U.S. 1, 28 (1971).

Thus began judicial recognition of an "affirmative duty" to desegregate, *id.* at 15; *Green*, 391 U.S. at 437-38, achieved by allocating the burden of negating causality to the defendant....

....

At some time, we must acknowledge that it has become absurd to assume, without any further proof, that violations of the Constitution dating from the days when Lyndon Johnson was President, or earlier, continue to have an appreciable effect upon current operation of schools. We are close to that time. While we must continue to prohibit, without qualification, all racial discrimination in the operation of public schools, and to afford remedies that eliminate not only the discrimination but its identified consequences, we should consider laying aside the extraordinary, and increasingly counterfactual, presumption of *Green*. We must soon revert to the ordinary principles of our law, of our democratic heritage, and of our educational tradition: that plaintiffs alleging Equal Protection violations must prove intent and causation and not merely the existence of racial disparity, *see ... Washington v. Davis*, 426 U.S. 229, 245 (1976); that public schooling, even in the South, should be controlled by locally elected authorities acting in conjunction with parents, *see, e.g., Dowell, supra*, 498 U.S. at ____, 111 S.Ct. at ____; *Dayton I, supra*, 433 U.S. at 410; *Milliken I, supra*, 418 U.S. at 741-742; and that it is "desirable" to permit pupils to attend "schools nearest their homes," *Swann, supra*, 402 U.S. at 28.

JUSTICE SOUTER, concurring:

... I write separately only to explain my understanding of the enquiry required by a district court applying the principle we set out today.

We recognize that although demographic changes influencing the composition of a school's student population may well have no causal link to prior de jure segregation, judicial control of student assignments may still be necessary to remedy persisting vestiges of the unconstitutional dual system, such as remaining imbalance in faculty assignments.... This is, however, only one of several possible causal relationships between or among unconstitutional acts of school segregation and various *Green*-type factors. I think it is worth mentioning at least two others: the dual school system itself as a cause of the demographic shifts with which the district court is faced when considering a partial relinquishment of supervision, and a *Green*-type factor other than student assignments as a possible cause of imbalanced student assignment patterns in the future.

The first would occur when demographic change toward segregated residential patterns is itself caused by past school segregation and the patterns of thinking that segregation creates. Such demographic change is not an independent, supervening cause of racial imbalance in the student body, and we have said before that when demographic change is not independent of efforts to segregate, the causal relationship may be considered in fashioning a school desegregation remedy. *See Swann v. Charlotte-Mecklenburg Bd. of Education*, 402 U.S. 1, 21 (1971). Racial imbalance in student assignments caused by demographic change is not insulated from federal judicial oversight where the demographic change is itself caused in this way, and before deciding to relinquish supervision and control over student assignments, a district court should make findings on the presence or absence of this relationship.

The second and related causal relationship would occur after the district court has relinquished supervision over a remedied aspect of the school system, when future imbalance in that remedied *Green*-type factor (here, student assignments) would be caused by remaining vestiges of the dual system. Even after attaining compliance as to student composition, other factors such as racial composition of the faculty, quality of the physical plant, or per-pupil expenditures may leave schools racially identifiable.... In such a case, the vestige of discrimination in one factor will act as an incubator for resegregation in others. Before a district court ends its supervision of student assignments, then, it should make a finding that there is no immediate threat of unremedied *Green*-type factors causing population or student enrollment changes that in turn may imbalance student composition in this way. And, because the district court retains jurisdiction over the case, it should of course reassert control over student assignments if it finds that this does happen.

JUSTICE BLACKMUN, with whom JUSTICE STEVENS and JUSTICE O'CONNOR join, concurring in the judgment:

It is almost 38 years since this Court decided *Brown v. Board of Education*, 347 U.S. 483 (1954). In those 38 years the students in DeKalb County, Ga., never have attended a desegregated school system even for one day. The majority of "black" students never have attended a school that was not disproportionately black. Ignoring this glaring dual character of the DeKalb County School System (DCSS), part "white" and part "black," the District Court relinquished control over student assignments, finding that the school district had achieved "unitary status" in that aspect of the system. No doubt frustrated by the continued existence of duality, the Court of Appeals ordered the school district to take extraordinary measures to correct all manifestations of this racial imbalance. Both decisions, in my view, were in error, and I therefore concur in the Court's decision to vacate the judgment and remand the case.

I also am in agreement with what I consider to be the holdings of the Court. I agree that in some circumstances the District Court need not interfere with a particular portion of the school system, even while, in my view, it must retain jurisdiction over the entire system until all vestiges of state-imposed segregation have been eliminated. I also agree that whether the District Court must order DCSS to balance student assignments depends on whether the current imbalance is traceable to unlawful state policy and on whether such an order is necessary to fashion an effective remedy. Finally, I agree that the good faith of the school board is relevant to these inquiries.

I write separately for two purposes. First, I wish to be precise about my understanding of what it means for the District Court in this case to retain jurisdiction while relinquishing "supervision and control" over a subpart of a school system under a desegregation decree. Second, I write to elaborate on factors the District Court should consider in determining whether racial imbalance is traceable to board actions and to indicate where, in my view, it failed to apply these standards.

I

... [T]he Court in the past has required and decides again today that even if the school system ceases to discriminate with respect to one of the *Green*-type factors, "the [district] court should retain jurisdiction until it is clear that state-imposed segregation has been completely removed." *Green v. New Kent County School Board*, 391 U.S. 430, 439 (1968); *Raney v. Board of Education*, 391 U.S. 443, 449 (1968).

That the District Court's jurisdiction should continue until the school board demonstrates full compliance with the Constitution follows from the reasonable skepticism that underlies judicial supervision in the first instance. This Court noted in *Dowell*: "A district court need not accept at face value the profession of a school board which has intentionally discriminated that it will cease to do so in the future." 498 U.S. at ___, 111 S.Ct. at 637. It makes little sense, it seems to me, for the court to disarm itself by renouncing jurisdiction in one aspect of a school system, while violations of the Equal Protection Clause persist in other aspects of the same system. *Cf. Keyes v. School Dist. No. 1, Denver, Colo.*, 413 U.S. 189, 207 (1973). It would seem especially misguided to place unqualified reliance on the school board's promises in this case, because the two areas of the school system the District Court found still in violation of the Constitution — expenditures and teacher assignments — are two of the *Green* factors over which DCSS exercises the greatest control.

The obligations of a district court and a school district under its jurisdiction have been clearly articulated in the Court's many desegregation cases. Until the desegregation decree is dissolved under the standards set forth in *Dowell*, the school board continues to have "the affirmative duty to take whatever steps might be necessary to convert to a unitary system in which racial discrimination would be eliminated root and branch." *Green*, 391 U.S. at 437-38. The duty remains enforceable by the district court without any new proof of a constitutional violation, and the school district has the burden of proving that its actions are eradicating the effects of the former de jure regime. *See Dayton Board of Education v. Brinkman*, 443 U.S. 526, 537 (1979); *Keyes*, 413 U.S. at 208-211; *Swann v. Charlotte-Mecklenburg Board of Education*, 402 U.S. 1, 26 (1971); *Green*, 391 U.S. at 439.

Contrary to the Court of Appeals' conclusion, however, retaining jurisdiction does not obligate the district court in all circumstances to maintain active supervision and control, continually ordering reassignment of students. The "duty" of the district court is to guarantee that the school district "eliminate[s] the discriminatory effects of the past as well as to bar like discrimination in the future." *Green*, 391 U.S. at 438, n. 4. This obligation requires the court to review school-board actions to ensure that each one "will further rather than delay conversion to a unitary, nonracial nondiscriminatory school system." *Monroe v. Board of Comm'rs*, 391 U.S. 450, 459 (1968). But this obligation does not always require the district court to order new, affirmative action simply because of racial imbalance in student assignment.

Whether a district court must maintain active supervision over student assignment, and order new remedial actions depends on two factors. As the Court discusses, the district court must order changes in student assignment if it "is necessary or practicable to achieve compliance in other facets of the school system." The district court also must order affirmative action in school attendance if the school district's conduct was a "contributing cause" of the racially identifiable schools. *Columbus Board of Education v. Penick*, 443 U.S. 449, 465, n. 13 (1979); *see also Keyes*, 413 U.S. at 211 and n. 17 (the school board must prove that its conduct "did not create or contribute to" the racial identifiability of schools or that racially identifiable schools are "in no way the result of" school board action)....

II

A

DCSS claims that it need not remedy the segregation in DeKalb County schools because it was caused by demographic changes for which DCSS has no responsibility. It is not enough, however, for DCSS to establish that demographics exacerbated the problem; it must prove that its own policies did not contribute. Such contribution can occur in at least two ways: DCSS may have contributed to the demographic changes themselves, or it may have contributed directly to the racial imbalance in the schools.

....

School systems can identify a school as "black" or "white" in a variety of ways; choosing to enroll a racially identifiable student population is only the most obvious. The Court has noted: "[T]he use of mobile classrooms, the drafting of student transfer policies, the transportation of students, and the assignment of faculty and staff, on racially identifiable bases, have the clear effect of earmarking schools according to their racial composition." *Keyes*, 413 U.S. at 202. Because of the various methods for identifying schools by race, even if a school district manages to desegregate student assignments at one point, its failure to remedy the constitutional violation in its entirety may result in resegregation, as neighborhoods respond to the racially identifiable schools. Regardless of the particular way in which the school district has encouraged residential segregation, this Court's decisions require that the school district remedy the effect that such segregation has had on the school system.

In addition to exploring the school district's influence on residential segregation, the District Court here should examine whether school board actions might have contributed to school segregation. Actions taken by a school district can aggravate or eliminate school segregation independent of residential segregation. School board policies concerning placement of new schools and closure of old schools and programs such as magnet classrooms and majority-to-minority (M-to-M) transfer policies affect the racial composition of the schools. *See Swann*, 402 U.S. at 20-21, 26-27. A school district's failure to adopt policies that effectively desegregate its schools continues the violation of the Fourteenth Amendment. *See Columbus Board of Education*, 443 U.S. at 458-59; *Dayton Board of Education*, 443 U.S. at 538. The Court many times has noted that a school district is not responsible for all of society's ills, but it bears full responsibility for schools that have never been desegregated. *See, e.g., Swann, supra.*

B

The District Court's opinion suggests that it did not examine DCSS' actions in light of the foregoing principles. The court did note that the migration farther into the suburbs was accelerated by "white flight" from black schools and the "blockbusting" of former white neighborhoods. It did not examine, however, whether DCSS might have encouraged that flight by assigning faculty and principals so as to identify some schools as intended respectively for black students or white students. Nor did the court consider how the placement of schools, the attendance zone boundaries, or the use of mobile classrooms might have affected residential movement. The court, in my view, failed to consider the many ways DCSS may have contributed to the demographic shifts.

Nor did the District Court correctly analyze whether DCSS' past actions had contributed to the school segregation independent of residential segregation. The court did not require DCSS to bear the "heavy burden" of showing that student assignment policies — policies that continued the effects of the dual system — served important and legitimate ends. *See Dayton Board of Education*, 443 U.S. at 538; *Swann*, 402 U.S. at 26. Indeed, the District Court said flatly that it would "not dwell on what might have been," but would inquire only as to "what else should be done now." But this Court's decisions require the District Court to "dwell on what might have been." In particular, they require the court to examine the past to determine whether the current racial imbalance in the schools is attributable in part to the former de jure segregated regime or any later actions by school officials.

As the Court describes, the District Court placed great emphasis on its conclusion that DCSS, in response to the court order, had desegregated student assignment in 1969. DCSS' very first action taken in response to the court decree, however, was to shape attendance zones to result in two schools that were more than 50% black, despite a district-wide black student population of less than 6%. Within a year, another school became majority black, followed by 4 others within the next 2 years. Despite the existence of these schools, the District Court found that DCSS effectively had desegregated for a short period of time with respect to student assignment. The District Court justified this finding by linking the school segregation exclusively to residential segregation existing prior to the court order.

But residential segregation that existed prior to the desegregation decree cannot provide an excuse. It is not enough that DCSS adopt race-neutral policies in response to a court desegregation decree. Instead, DCSS is obligated to "counteract the continuing effects of past school segregation." *Swann*, 402 U.S. at 28. Accordingly, the school district did not meet its affirmative duty simply by adopting a neighborhood-school plan, when already existing residential segregation inevitably perpetuated the dual system. *See Davis v. School Comm'rs of Mobile County*, 402 U.S. 33, 37 (1971); *Swann*, 402 U.S. at 25-28, 30.

Virtually all the demographic changes that DCSS claims caused the school segregation occurred after 1975. Of particular relevance to the causation inquiry, then, are DCSS' actions prior to 1975; failures during that period to implement the 1969 decree render the school district's contentions that its noncompliance is due simply to demographic changes less plausible.

A review of the record suggests that from 1969 until 1975, DCSS failed to desegregate its schools. During that period, the number of students attending racially identifiable schools actually increased, and increased more quickly than the increase in black students. By 1975, 73% of black elementary students and 56% of black high school students were attending majority black schools, although the percentages of black students in the district population were just 20% and 13%, respectively.

Of the 13 new elementary schools DCSS opened between 1969 and 1975, six had a total of four black students in 1975. One of the two high schools DCSS opened had no black students at all. The only other measure taken by DCSS during the 1969-1975 period was to adopt the M-to-M transfer program in 1972. Due, however, to limitations imposed by school district administrators — including a failure to provide transportation, "unnecessary red tape," and limits on available transfer schools — only one-tenth of 1% of the students were participating in the transfer program as of the 1975-1976 school year.

....

Thus, in 1976, before most of the demographic changes, the District Court found that DCSS had not complied with the 1969 order to eliminate the vestiges of its former de jure school system. Indeed, the 1976 order found that DCSS had contributed to the growing racial imbalance of its schools. Given these determinations in 1976, the District Court, at a minimum, should have required DCSS to prove that, but for the demographic changes between 1976 and 1985, its actions would have been sufficient to "convert promptly to a system without a 'white' school and a 'Negro' school, but just schools." *Green*, 391 U.S. at 442. The available evidence suggests that this would be a difficult burden for DCSS to meet.

DCSS has undertaken only limited remedial actions since the 1976 court order. The number of students participating in the M-to-M program has expanded somewhat, comprising about 6% of the current student population. The district also has adopted magnet programs, but they involve fewer than 1% of the system's students. Doubtless DCSS could have started and expanded its magnet and M-to-M programs more promptly; it could have built and closed schools with a view toward promoting integration of both schools and neighborhoods; redrawn attendance zones; integrated its faculty and administrators; and spent its funds equally. But it did not. DCSS must prove that the measures it actually implemented satisfy its obligation to eliminate the vestiges of de jure segregation originally discovered in 1969, and still found to exist in 1976.

III

....

... I would remand for the Court of Appeals to review, under the foregoing principles, the District Court's finding that DCSS has met its burden of proving the racially identifiable schools are in no way the result of past segregative action.

1. The majority opinion in *Freeman* professes some similarity to the decision in *Brown I* in stating that school districts must eliminate a segregated system

CH. 11: RACIAL SEGREGATION IN THE PUBLIC SCHOOLS 893

because leaving it intact would insure that racial stigma would remain. *Freeman*, at 1443. *Brown*'s dictate to eliminate this stigma was to order judiciary control over what school officials were reluctant to do until a "unitary system" was achieved. How, then, does the partial fulfillment rule of *Freeman* comport with the "unitary" order of *Brown*? Was the majority here simply reaching for support that did not exist?

What of *Freeman*'s similarity to other desegregation decisions? Consider the following Comment:

> ....
>
> Through the enactment of the Thirteenth Amendment, Congress abolished slavery in 1865, thus freeing thousands of African-Americans from the brutal chains which had bound them since the mid-fifteenth century. By the time the Fourteenth Amendment was passed in 1868, Congress had theoretically included African-American citizens in the American ideology "that all men are created equal, that they are endowed by their creator with certain unalienable Rights, that among these are life, liberty and the pursuit of happiness." As history has proved, however, the inhumanity of racial discrimination was not eliminated with the passage of the Fourteenth Amendment. When the Supreme Court held that "separate but equal" was the law of the land in *Plessy v. Ferguson*, African-Americans were forced to live, learn, work and socialize in an America that was characteristically "separate and unequal."
>
> *Plessy v. Ferguson* remained intact until 1954 when the Supreme Court again tackled the issue of racial discrimination in public education. With its landmark holding in *Brown v. Board of Education*, the Court declared that "in the field of public education the doctrine of 'separate but equal' has no place." Unfortunately, the promises of *Brown* remain largely unfulfilled today. Countless public educational systems in the United States remain segregated, despite the emphasis the Court placed on education as a means for employment opportunity and social mobility:
>
>> Today, education is perhaps the most important function of state and local governments. Compulsory school attendance laws and the great expenditures for education both demonstrate our recognition of the importance of education to our democratic society. It is required in the performance of our most basic public responsibilities, even service in the armed forces. It is the very foundation of good citizenship. Today it is a principal instrument in awakening the child to cultural values, in preparing him for later professional training, and in helping him to adjust normally to his environment. In these days, it is doubtful that any child may reasonably be expected to succeed in life if he is denied the opportunity of an education. Such an opportunity, where the state has undertaken to provide it, is a right which must be made available to all on equal terms. *Brown v. Bd. of Ed.*, 347 U.S. 483, 495 (1954).

Employment opportunity and social mobility in today's expanding global economy require training and education. If African-Americans and other racial minorities are to achieve the American Dream, educational equality must remain at the forefront of national policy. As one well-respected African-American educator has stated, African-American high school students, particularly those in America's inner cities, often have no idea that a quality education is available to them. Once youngsters are exposed to the opportunities that a quality education can provide, their lives have been and can continue to be dramatically altered for the better.

....

For public school systems across the country, *Freeman* will provide local officials with the opportunity to take control of their schools back from the federal courts. In loosening the grip of judicial control over school desegregation matters, the Court essentially disregarded *Brown*'s promise. The Court cannot hope for equal educational opportunity for all Americans if it continues to ignore the destructiveness of racism.

Now that this nation has a new President in Bill Clinton, a Democrat, civil rights activists are hopeful that a compromise can be forged between the holding in cases like *Freeman* and the reasoning of *Brown I*. In many cases, the federal courts should defer to school district decisions, but only if equal educational opportunity and integration are not jeopardized. A court's determination of unitariness does not give school districts unrestricted license to vitiate prior desegregation efforts, just short of violating the Equal Protection Clause.

For most Americans, the road to increased employment opportunity and social mobility is clearly defined by a quality education, one that cannot be hampered by substandard learning facilities or resources. Government policy-makers, school officials and concerned citizens must realize that to make America work, equal education opportunity for all must never again take a back seat. In this regard, school board decisions should remain unimpaired with two notable exceptions. First, the federal courts should impose mandatory hearings whenever a school board proposes a new reassignment plan. The school district's pre-unitary, court-ordered directives must be scrutinized and evaluated against all categories to insure furtherance of integration and equal opportunity. Second, a mandatory public hearing should be conducted after each official U.S. Census to evaluate the cumulative effect of school board decisions in relation to demographic change.

Although these measures would require the courts to assume a quasi-regulatory function, the end result would substantially reduce the amount of litigation and would further enhance the public's trust in desegregation measures. Recurrent evaluation of school board decisions would also address the concerns of racial minorities, while simultaneously strengthening the credibility of school board decisions.

The federal government and the courts must realize that effective desegregative efforts require vigilance and patience. Those with the responsibility for determining the course our public schools will take must now be willing to make the difficult decisions necessary to achieve an integrated school system. Frank H. Stubbs, III, Freeman v. Pitts: *A Rethinking of Public School Desegregation*, 27 U. Rich. L. Rev. 399 (1993).*

2. Four justices (Blackmun, Stevens, O'Connor, and Souter) disagreed with the majority's finding that residential housing patterns have no correlation to school segregation. Inasmuch as the major issue in *Freeman* dealt with housing and schools, what guidance does this ruling give lower courts as well as school systems experiencing similar problems?

3. Federal judicial supervision of local school systems is intended as a "temporary measure," *Freeman* (quoting *Dowell*), and control is to be restored to local authorities once a certain degree of compliance with a desegregation decree has been attained. *Freeman* states that the *temporary* measure is the desegregation decree and the *ultimate* goal is to give power back to local authorities. Where does the Court derive such a ruling?

What if a school district does not work to alter its segregated system — either in whole or in part — for much longer than DCSS did in *Freeman*? Once federal judicial supervision has been lifted, is there anything keeping such supervision from returning especially if new claims are filed, asserting new or further constitutional violations? Is there a length of time following "requisite compliance" that a system must remain in compliance?

In effect, are the federal courts' eyes watching over previously segregated school systems, regardless of the degree of compliance with a desegregation order? Does the *Freeman* Court say anything about this? Recall the following:

> [I]t must be acknowledged that the potential for discrimination and racial hostility is still present in our country, and its manifestations may emerge in new and subtle forms after the effects of de jure segregation have been eliminated. It is the duty of the State and its subdivisions to ensure that such forces do not shape or control the policies of its school systems. Where the control lies, so does the responsibility. *Freeman*, at 1445.

Recall also: "[T]he good-faith compliance of the district with the court order over a reasonable period of time is a factor to be considered in deciding whether or not jurisdiction could be relinquished." *Id.* at 1449. How long is reasonable and what guidance does this give to school districts under desegregation orders?

---

*Copyright © 1993 by the University of Richmond Law Review. Reprinted with permission.

4. The Court also prescribed the conditions under which racial imbalance would influence a desegregation decree:

> That there was racial imbalance in student attendance zones was not tantamount to a showing that the district was in noncompliance with the decree or with its duties under the law. Racial balance is not to be achieved for its own sake. It is to be pursued when racial imbalance has been caused by a constitutional violation. *Id.*, at 1447.

What effect does this declaration have on the future of desegregation cases? What does the Court mean by "racial imbalance caused by a constitutional violation?" Applying this statement to cases like *Keyes* and *Penick, supra,* what would be a constitutional cause in school districts accused of de facto segregation?

5. Does the *Freeman* decision establish a built-in conflict that might require more litigation to cure? Consider that JUSTICE KENNEDY states that the decision is designed to correct constitutional violations (met with court-ordered desegregation) and to restore hegemony over schools to local authorities. If local authorities aided in perpetuating segregation as so well demonstrated in most of the cases in this chapter, does the decision represent a paradox?

6. *Brown* sought to eliminate the "stigma" of minority status partially perpetuated by segregated schools. The *Freeman* Court also stated this as a goal. By way of alternative argument, does the remedy of desegregation perpetuate such a "stigma"? Consider this Comment:

> . . . .
>
> Supreme Court opinions, like *Brown v. Board of Education* ("*Brown I*"), reveal their consequences and yield their secrets only through the perspective of time and the evolution of American society. The Supreme Court candidly recognized this point seventeen years after that opinion. Almost two generations have passed since the Court decided *Brown I*. That passage of time allows us to put into perspective a reexamination of the Supreme Court's opinions regarding de jure segregation of public schools.
>
> Reexamination is particularly appropriate at this time. In the last two terms, the Supreme Court has issued two major opinions — *Board of Education of Oklahoma City v. Dowell* and *Freeman v. Pitts* — addressing de jure segregation of public schools. With these opinions, the Court entered the final phase of its efforts to eradicate the vestiges of de jure segregation from American public education. In this phase the Supreme Court has turned its attention to defining what a school system must accomplish to free itself from federal court supervision. This phase will herald the end of an epic chapter in American legal history.
>
> The Supreme Court has approved a number of means to remedy the harm resulting from de jure segregation, with desegregation as the principal means. Yet the Court has never supplied a satisfactory justification for the remedies it has approved. Now that the Court may be ready to close this

chapter in its legal history, we may possess all of the Court's insight into its analysis of the harm of de jure segregation and the purposes of its remedies. At this stage, Court-ordered remedies for de jure segregation, including desegregation, are an accomplished fact. Therefore, I do not take a position on whether the remedies ordered for de jure segregation were the most appropriate ones. Rather, I seek to demonstrate the new harm that flows from the Court's ideological framework which justified these remedies.

In *Freeman*, the Court noted that a school system eliminates the vestiges of an unconstitutional de jure system when the injuries and stigma inflicted upon the disfavored race are no longer present. This statement captures the contradictory nature of the Supreme Court's de jure segregation jurisprudence: on the one hand, the Court suggests the harm is an amorphous stigma; and, on the other, the Court suggests the harm is tangible. I will argue that the Supreme Court's de jure segregation jurisprudence is generally consistent with these two notions about the harms resulting from de jure segregation. When, as the Court has done, these two distinct notions are put together, then the remedies for de jure segregation replicate the very disease they should have been intended to cure.

More recently, Supreme Court cases addressing issues in public education have embraced the notion that public schools are cultural institutions engaged in socializing America's children. As a result, the objectives of public education are the inculcation of fundamental American values. In this Article, I will argue that the results, not the rationale, of the Court's opinions addressing de jure segregation are consistent with recognizing the importance of the socializing process of public schools. Viewing de jure segregation from this perspective, its principal harm is stigmatic. In the public education context, this stigmatic harm functions differently than it does in any other area because the state is engaged in socializing students. De jure segregated public schools are inculcating a belief — the inferiority of African-Americans — to students that is inconsistent with the values enshrined by the Constitution. The remedial purpose for the inculcation of "the invidious value" should be directed towards its elimination. Consequently, the primary beneficiary of these remedies is either the socializing process of public schools or all public school students, not only African-American school children.

The Court's ideological framework in this area, however, leads to a different conclusion about both the harm resulting from de jure segregation and its remedial purpose. The Court's ideological framework proceeds from an assumption that racial isolation retarded the intellectual and psychological development of only African-Americans. Thus, the purpose of de jure segregation remedies is to rectify some manifested deficiency of African-American students.

Both the Court's interpretations of the harm of de jure segregation and its resulting remedial purpose make the Supreme Court's de jure segregation jurisprudence suspect. On the one hand, the harm of de jure segregation is inculcating the notion of black inferiority to public school children. Yet, on the other hand, the reason that remedies are necessary is because segregation actually retarded the development of African-Americans, thus making them inferior to Caucasians. As a result, remedies for de jure segregation are based upon an assumption of African-American inferiority — the same assumption that pervaded the constitutional violation of de jure segregation. Just as past segregation distorted the socializing process of public schools, remedies for de jure segregation have done and are doing the same because of the Court's analysis of de jure segregation of public schools.

. . . .

Viewing the harm of de jure segregation as invidious value inculcation sees the harm resulting from de jure segregation as a corruption of the socializing process of public schools. This position is based not so much upon an assumption that de jure segregation of public schools left a lasting impact on African-Americans, but rather, that de jure segregation left a lasting impact on the socializing process of public schools. By viewing remedies for de jure segregation as a remedy to the distortion in the value transmission process of public schools, the meaning attached to desegregation is as a corrective measure to eliminate the inculcation of an invidious value.

If the Court firmly establishes that the harm of de jure segregation was its impact only on the socializing process of public schools, it would amount to the Court declaring that African-Americans are equal to their Caucasian counterparts. The Court would value African-Americans for what they are, rather than attempting to make them something they cannot become. Thus, the Court would not be suggesting that African-Americans reject their racial culture as deviant in order to succeed in public schools. Instead, society would assume that ethnic diversity is a positive element, because it enriches a nation and increases the ways in which its citizens can perceive and solve personal and public problems. It recognizes that both races can learn from interracial contact.

One could raise a legitimate question: Why should the Court now consider articulating an ideological framework for remedies for de jure segregation that differs from the one it has previously employed? Although, one might agree that the Court should have been more careful with its wording in the past, given the Court's opinions in *Dowell* and *Freeman*, shouldn't this entire area be put in the Supreme Court's collective past?

The Court's de jure segregation termination opinions will raise a considerable number of issues that will have to be resolved. Of particular importance will be the issue regarding funding inequalities between black and white schools that are the result of private decision making. The Court's current framework may force those who do not wish to eliminate court supervision to disparage African-Americans further, in an effort to maintain that supervision. Thus, in the process of terminating court supervision, negative messages about African-Americans are likely to be repeated.

In addition to redeeming its ideological framework, the Court could also have a salutary effect on America's public education. The effort to reform America's public schools is far from complete. Given the increasing numbers of racial minority students in public schools, and public school's poor success with effectively educating students, the need for continued educational reform is obvious. While the appropriate educational reformers should be professional educators not federal judges, the role which the Supreme Court could perform is to establish an ideological framework that would directly focus the need for educational reform on the socializing process of public schools. By providing the theoretical underpinnings, the Court could function as a catalyst for educational reform without attempting to determine what the proper solutions should be.

Explaining the harm of de jure segregation in the context of the value inculcating function of public schools will provide the theoretical underpinnings to release the reformist efforts of educators to develop and implement programs directed at bias in the educational process. While it may not be completely clear to lawyers and judges how educators will respond, it might suggest the beginnings of a restructured American educational program.

This new ideological framework could provide educators with a needed mandate to reconsider the secondary level of invidious value inculcation. Not all educators have been unaware of the fact that the traditional educational program undervalues the contribution of minorities. Some educators are in the process of rethinking the very foundations of school curricula by focusing on culturally pluralistic content, perspectives, and experiences. Their particular aim and focus is to allow all students to achieve academic excellence without jeopardizing personal identities or cultural integrity, thereby fulfilling the Fourteenth Amendment's moral imperative of an egalitarian society. The precise parameters of these revisions of public education should be left to educators to work out in succeeding years. But at least the Supreme Court will have provided an intellectual framework that will act as a catalyst in directing educator's energies in that direction. Kevin Brown, *Has the Supreme Court Allowed the Cure for De Jure Segregation to Replicate the Disease?*, 78 Cornell L. Rev. 1 (1992).*

7. Pundits, especially those in the media, evaluating the enterprise of desegregation, have attempted to establish by the rulings in *Freeman* and *Dowell*

---

*Copyright © 1992 by Cornell University. All rights reserved. Reprinted with permission from Fred B. Rothman & Co., and Cornell University.

that court supervision is almost finished. Legal scholars have also questioned the future of court-ordered desegregation given these decisions as with the following:

DAYTON, DESEGREGATION: IS THE COURT PREPARING TO SAY IT IS FINISHED?, 84 Educ. L. Rep. 897 (1993)*

In a 1986 article on public school desegregation, Paul Gewirtz stated that "at some point — perhaps in words that could connote either triumph or despair — the court will come to say: it is finished." The Supreme Court's recent decisions in *Board of Educ. v. Dowell* and *Freeman v. Pitts* suggest that this point may be rapidly approaching. This article provides a brief history of the Court's pivotal decisions on public school desegregation, reviews the Court's decisions in *Board of Educ. v. Dowell* and *Freeman v. Pitts*, and provides an analysis of *Freeman* and its effect on public school desegregation law.

A Brief History of Desegregation

The Supreme Court's involvement in public school desegregation began in 1954 in *Brown v. Board of Education* (*Brown I*). In *Brown I* the Court overturned the separate but equal doctrine, but postponed consideration of the appropriate remedies for racially segregated public schools. One year later in *Brown v. Board of Education* (*Brown II*), the Court ordered defendant schools to "make a prompt and reasonable start toward full compliance" with the Court's decision in *Brown I*, and to pursue desegregation of public schools with "all deliberate speed." However, it became apparent that public school desegregation would be a protracted process. Opposition to public school desegregation was extensive. In the following years the Court addressed only a small number of the many cases of non-compliance with its desegregation mandate.

In the late 1960's the Court became more assertive, holding that schools must do more than merely refrain from additional constitutional violations. The Court in *Green v. County Board* held that segregated schools had an affirmative duty to create unitary schools and to eliminate the vestiges of past racial discrimination "root and branch." To define the school's desegregation duties more specifically the Court in *Green* pointed out student assignments, faculty, staff, transportation, extracurricular activities, and facilities (the *Green* factors) as among the important indicia of a racially segregated school.

In the 1970's the Court addressed racial segregation in states without official segregation statutes. The Court distinguished between de jure segregation resulting from state action, and de facto segregation resulting from private choices. The Court noted that since only de jure segregation involved intentional state action to segregate, that only de jure segregation was constitutionally actionable. *Milliken v. Bradley*, involving Detroit area schools, may have marked

---

*Reprinted with permission. Copyright © 1993 by West Publishing Company.

the beginning of the end of the Supreme Court's support for expansion of desegregation remedies. In *Milliken*, the Court overturned an interdistrict remedy for segregation because of the failure of the plaintiffs to establish that intentional acts of the state were a substantial cause of the interdistrict segregation. The Court became increasingly hesitant to approve expansive remedies, and Court action on desegregation decreased substantially during the 1980's. Desegregation regained prominence on the Court's docket in the 1990's in *Board of Education v. Dowell* and *Freeman v. Pitts*.

Board of Education v. Dowell

In its 1991 decision in *Board of Education v. Dowell*, the Court addressed the proper standards for declaring a formerly segregated school system unitary. A federal district court had declared the Oklahoma City school system unitary in 1977. In 1985, plaintiffs attempted to reopen the case based on racial resegregation in the school system. In response, the Oklahoma City Board of Education sought an end to federal judicial oversight of the district's schools. The district court ruled in favor of the school, finding that present residential segregation resulted from private choices and economics, and that any alleged linkage to former segregation was too remote to justify a new constitutional remedy. The district court concluded that the 1977 declaration of unitary status was res judicata, and the school system remained unitary.

However, the Supreme Court in *Dowell* ruled that the 1977 declaration of unitary status by the district court was too ambiguous. The Court held that plaintiffs were entitled to an unambiguous statement by the district court before a declaration of unitary status could bar future action. Regarding continued supervision by federal courts, the Court stated that federal supervision of local schools was not intended to operate in perpetuity. The Court declared that: "From the very first, federal supervision of local school systems was intended as a temporary measure to remedy past discrimination." Ultimately, control must be returned to local school districts. The Court held that the school need only establish that it had been "operating in compliance with the commands of the Equal Protection Clause of the Fourteenth Amendment, and that it was unlikely that the school board would return to its former ways." Such a showing would demonstrate "that the purposes of the desegregation litigation had been fully achieved." The school can meet its burden by demonstrating good faith compliance with the district court's order, and that vestiges of former segregation had been eliminated "to the extent practicable." In considering whether vestiges of segregation have been eliminated to the extent practicable, the Court explained that district courts should consider the *Green* factors to determine whether unitary status had been achieved. However, the Court did not clarify whether the indicia of unitary status identified in *Green* may be satisfied incrementally, or whether these factors must all be satisfied concurrently before a school may be released from judicial supervision and control.

Freeman v. Pitts

In 1992, *Freeman v. Pitts* presented the Supreme Court with the issue of whether a district court may incrementally terminate judicial supervision of a school system before full compliance with a desegregation order has been achieved, or whether all relevant areas must be satisfied concurrently before termination of judicial oversight. In *Freeman*, the Dekalb County School system was seeking final dismissal of federal judicial supervision that had begun in 1969. The district court ruled that the school had achieved unitary status in student assignments and three other areas, but not in all relevant areas. The district court released Dekalb County Schools from judicial control in those areas which had been found unitary. The court of appeals reversed, holding that a district court should retain full judicial control until the formerly segregated school system achieves unitary status in all areas concurrently for several years.

The Supreme Court reversed the decision of the court of appeals. The Court restated its pronouncement in *Dowell* that judicial supervision was intended only as a temporary measure, and that the ultimate objective was to return control to local authorities. The Court held that federal courts may relinquish control of school systems incrementally before full compliance with the mandates of desegregation had been achieved. District courts may decide not to order further remedies in student assignments despite racial imbalances where racial imbalances are not proximately traceable to constitutional violations. The court stated that: "racial balance is not to be achieved for its own sake" and "where resegregation is a product not of state action but of private choices, it does not have constitutional implications."

Although the Court restated its approval of the *Green* factors as an appropriate basis for evaluating progress toward unitary status, the Court noted that the *Green* factors need not be a rigid framework. District courts may exercise their discretion to determine whether other factors, such as the quality of education, should also be considered to evaluate progress toward unitary status. The Court reemphasized its statement in *Dowell* that federal courts should consider good-faith compliance and whether vestiges of prior segregation had been eliminated to the extent practicable.

An Analysis of Freeman v. Pitts

Freeman v. Pitts provides a current snapshot of the Court's position on public school desegregation. Following the Court's decision in *Freeman*, one commentator stated that "it appeared that a more conservative court was beating a retreat from its earlier activist role in pursuing fully integrated schools." But a close examination of the Court's decision in *Freeman* shows that although the Court is moving away from active federal judicial involvement in public school desegregation, not all Justices are moving in unison.

Eight justices participated in the decision in *Freeman v. Pitts*. Although all eight justices were not in full agreement regarding the proper judicial role in desegregation, it is significant to note that no justice in *Freeman* was advocating an increase in federal judicial involvement. The polarity dividing the justices in *Freeman* was between reducing and maintaining judicial involvement. All eight justices concurred with the judgement to reverse and remand, but only five justices joined Justice Kennedy's majority opinion. Justice Scalia filed a concurrence. Justice Souter filed a concurrence, and Justice Blackmun filed a concurrence that was joined by Justices Stevens and O'Connor. All eight justices agreed that: incremental relinquishment of supervision and control in desegregation cases was permissible; the school's good faith compliance was an important consideration before relinquishing judicial supervision and control; and the remedy should be limited to alleviating the initial constitutional violation. At this point, differences outnumber agreements among the justices. The tone and substance of Justice Blackmun's concurrence more closely resembles a dissent than a concurrence.

> Although a significant victory for defendant schools, Justice Kennedy's majority opinion in *Freeman v. Pitts* may also provide some hope for plaintiffs in future public school desegregation litigation. Some elements of the majority opinion seem to confirm the Court's retreat from federal judicial involvement in desegregation, yet other elements may demonstrate a degree of continued commitment to desegregation efforts by the Court.

Among the elements that seem to confirm the Court's retreat from federal judicial involvement in desegregation is the Court's approval of incremental relinquishment of judicial supervision and control. This holding makes it easier for schools to be released from federal judicial oversight in desegregation cases generally, and much easier regarding a particular factor such as student assignments. After *Freeman*, schools can be released regarding student assignments even though other areas of these schools' programs are not in compliance. The Court stated that "the district court may determine that it will not order further remedies in the area of student assignments where racial imbalance is not traceable, in a proximate way, to constitutional violations." If a district court relinquishes supervision and control over student assignments, the court still retains jurisdiction over the case generally, but there is some disagreement among the justices regarding whether a released issue is then res judicata. However, in deciding whether an earlier determination of unitary status barred future actions by the plaintiffs, the Court in *Board of Education v. Dowell* stated that "a school board is entitled to a rather precise statement of its obligations under a desegregation decree. If such a decree is to be terminated or dissolved, [plaintiffs] as well as the school are entitled to a like statement from the court." Based on the Court's statement in *Dowell*, it seems that a district court should at least be clear about its intention to bar future action regarding student assignments or other issues released from judicial supervision and control.

Other factors also seem to confirm the Court's retreat from federal judicial involvement in desegregation. In *Freeman*, the Court agreed that remedies must be limited to alleviating the initial constitutional violation. Remedies cannot be justified by de facto segregation alone and should not exceed the scope of the de jure violation despite de facto segregation. *Freeman* reaffirms the significance of the distinction between de jure and de facto segregation. Further, the Court stated that remoteness in time reduces the likelihood of a finding of de jure causation for segregation. The Court also recognized limited resources as a legitimate consideration in exercising judicial discretion in desegregation cases.

Parts of Justice Kennedy's majority opinion in *Freeman v. Pitts* reflect a degree of continued commitment to desegregation efforts, and may be beneficial to plaintiffs in future desegregation cases. For example, the Court in *Freeman* ruled narrowly making its ruling turn upon a finding that no portion of the current racial imbalance is a remnant of prior de jure segregation. In his concurring opinion Justice Scalia argued for a broader ruling, and wanted to end federal judicial oversight and restore local control sooner rather than later, arguing that: "Though our cases profess that judicial oversight of school operations is a temporary expedient, democratic processes remain suspended, with no prospect of restoration, 38 years after *Brown*." However, Justice Kennedy's narrower ruling prevailed, meaning that *Freeman* applies to student assignments only where schools can establish a finding of no racial imbalance caused by de jure segregation. The Court approved of assigning the defendant schools the burden of proving that any current racial imbalance is not traceable in any proximate way to prior de jure segregation, retaining a significant advantage for plaintiffs in public school desegregation cases. As Justice Scalia noted, the "allocation of the burden of proof foreordains the result in almost all of the 'vestige of past discrimination' cases." Justice Scalia would instead "revert to ordinary principles of law" and allocate the burden of proof to the plaintiffs.

The Court also approved a discretionary expansion of the *Green* factors in *Freeman*. According to the Court, the *Green* factors need not be a rigid framework and could include discretionary factors such as the quality of education. Presumably, if district courts include discretionary factors in addition to the *Green* factors, it becomes more difficult for schools to establish full compliance with desegregation mandates.

Finally, the Court set out a mandatory checklist that district courts must follow prior to partial withdrawal, but kept the court's decision to allow partial withdrawal discretionary even where a school system is in compliance with some but not all areas of the desegregation mandate. To exercise discretionary withdrawal the court must consider: whether there is full and satisfactory compliance in the area to be withdrawn; the possibility of interconnectedness between the withdrawn area and areas not yet in compliance; and good faith commitment to the whole of the court's decree and the constitutional mandate.

Conclusion

Although it appears that the Court's desegregation efforts are diminishing, it is still too soon to announce the death of public school desegregation. The Court's decision in *Freeman v. Pitts* was a significant loss for public school desegregation plaintiffs, but of a lessor magnitude than if Justice Scalia's views rather than Justice Kennedy's views had prevailed in *Freeman*. Further, although federal courts will likely continue to reduce judicial involvement in public school desegregation, public schools could choose to encourage racial desegregation for educational reasons even without judicial involvement.

An examination of *Freeman v. Pitts*, shows a Court moving away from active federal judicial involvement in public school desegregation efforts, but not in unison. The Court's decisions on public school desegregation illuminate the continuing debate among the justices regarding the proper scope of federal judicial involvement in desegregation. These cases reflect the historical waxing and waning of support among the justices for active judicial intervention in public school desegregation.

Notable progress has been made since *Brown v. Board of Education*. In addition to advancing the interests of African-American children in public schools, *Brown* opened the door for others to challenge inequities based on race, nationality, gender, age, poverty, and handicapping conditions. However, despite this progress significant work remains undone in efforts to desegregate public schools. The Court's decisions in *Dowell* and *Freeman* may indicate that the time is near when "in words that could connote either triumph or despair — the court will come to say: it is finished." If we measure success as genuine racial desegregation, an assessment of the current status of public schools reveals continuing racial segregation and indicates that it may likely be despair that marks the Court's conclusion of desegregation efforts.

Chapter 12

ABILITY GROUPING AND BILINGUAL EDUCATION

A. ABILITY GROUPING AND TRACKING

HOBSON v. HANSEN
United States Court of Appeals
269 F. Supp. 401 (D.D.C. 1967), *aff'd in part and appeal dismissed in part sub nom. Smuck v. Hobson,* 408 F.2d 175 (D.C. Cir. 1969)

[This case involved a multi-faceted attack on the racial and economic patterns of the Washington, D.C. school system. The excerpts below are from the District Court's treatment of the "track system."]

WRIGHT, CIRCUIT JUDGE.*

. . . .

Findings of Fact

. . . .

IV. *The Track System*

... The District of Columbia school system employs a form of ability grouping commonly known as the track system, by which students at the elementary and secondary level are placed in tracks or curriculum levels according to the school's assessment of each student's ability to learn. Plaintiffs have alleged that the track system — either by intent or by effect — unconstitutionally discriminates against the Negro and the poor. In support of this claim they — and the defendants in meeting it — have introduced a massive array of testimonial and documentary evidence. The court will first turn its attention to the beginnings of the track system before moving on to a discussion of the evidence concerning the present-day operation of ability grouping in the District.

A. *Origin*

The track system was approved for introduction into the Washington school system by the Board of Education in 1956, just two years after the desegregation

---

*Sitting by designation pursuant to 28 U.S.C. § 291 (c). [All the district judges disqualified themselves from sitting on this case, as the District Court was then the governmental body which appointed the D.C. School Bd. — Editor.]

decision in *Bolling v. Sharpe*, [347 U.S. 497 (1954)]. As Superintendent Hansen has conceded, "to describe the origin of the four-track system without reference to desegregation in the District of Columbia Public Schools would be to bypass one of the most significant causes of its being. Desegregation was a precipitant of the four-track development in the District's high schools...." Plaintiffs, citing this concession and certain observable segregatory effects of the track system, have claimed that the principal motivation behind the system was and is to resegregate the races in violation of the *Bolling* decision. Defendants have denied this, arguing that the track system is and always has been a legitimate pedagogical method of providing maximum educational opportunity for children of widely ranging ability levels; and that any racial effect is but an innocent and unavoidable coincidence of ability grouping.

....

On May 17, 1954, the day *Bolling v. Sharpe* was handed down, there were 44,897 white students (43%) and 59,963 Negro students (57%) in the District schools. By the following September 73% of the schools were — in varying degree — racially mixed. Until that time no one was aware of the overall achievement level of the Negro students because achievement scores had not been reported on a city-wide basis in the old Division II (Negro) schools. However, soon after integration Dr. Hansen, then Assistant Superintendent in charge of senior high schools, began to receive "reports of very serious retardation in achievement in the basic skills...." The results of a reading and arithmetic achievement test taken by tenth grade students early in 1955 and for the first time reported on a city-wide basis confirmed the reports: (1) Both reading and arithmetic scores ranged from second to beyond twelfth grade; (2) nearly 25% of the students were at or below sixth grade level in reading, and 44% were at or below sixth grade level in arithmetic. The low achievers were predominantly from the Division II schools. It was the discovery of this large number of academically retarded Negro children in the school system that led to the institution of the track system.

....

The court does not, however, rest its decision on a finding of intended racial discrimination. Apart from such intentional aspects, the effects of the track system must be held to be a violation of plaintiffs' constitutional rights. (*See* Opinion of Law.) As the evidence in this case makes painfully clear, ability grouping as presently practiced in the District of Columbia school system is a denial of equal educational opportunity to the poor and a majority of the Negroes attending school in the nation's capital, a denial that contravenes not only the guarantees of the Fifth Amendment but also the fundamental premise of the track system itself. What follows, then, is a discussion of that evidence — an examination of the track system: in theory and in reality.

B. Track Theory

....

Purpose and philosophy. Dr. Hansen believes that the comprehensive high school (and the school system generally) must be systematically organized and structured to provide differing levels of education for students with widely differing levels of academic ability. This is the purpose of the track system.... Dr. Hansen has ... identified as the two objectives on which the track system is founded: "(1) The realization of the doctrine of equality of education and (2) The attainment of quality education."

Student types. Within the student body Dr. Hansen sees generally four types of students: the intellectually gifted, the above-average, the average, and the retarded. He assumes that each of these types of students has a maximum level of academic capability and, most importantly, that that level of ability can be accurately ascertained. The duty of the school is to identify these students and provide a curriculum commensurate with their respective abilities. Dr. Hansen contends that the traditional school curriculum — including the usual two-level method of ability grouping — does a disservice to those at either end of the ability spectrum.

....

Fundamental assumptions. To summarize, the track system's approach is twofold. The separate curriculum levels are for some the maximum education their abilities permit them to achieve. For others, a track is supposed to be a temporary assignment during which a student's special problems are identified and remedied in whatever way possible. The express assumptions of this approach are three: *First*, a child's maximum educational potential can and will be accurately ascertained. *Second*, tracking will enhance the prospects for correcting a child's remediable educational deficiencies. *Third*, tracking must be flexible as so to provide an individually tailored education for students who cannot be pigeon-holed in a single curriculum.

C. The Tracks

1. Honors

Purpose. The Honors Track is for the gifted student, its purpose being to provide him with an enriched, accelerated curriculum and to stimulate scholarship by placing him with similarly gifted students.

....

2. Regular

Purpose. This is a college preparatory track, found only at the senior high school level. It "provides the hard-core of academic offerings normally required for college entrance." According to Dr. Hansen, it merely continues the advanced curriculum found in all high schools having a two-level curriculum sequence (*i.e.*, college preparatory and terminal), although he suggests embodying it in a track level tends to enhance its prestige and effectiveness in stimulating scholarship.

....

3. *General*

Purpose. At the elementary and junior high school levels the General curriculum serves the bulk of the students, excepting only those considered bright enough for Honors or slow enough for Special Academic.

At the senior high school level, however, the nature of the General Track becomes more specific. It is expressly a curriculum "designed to serve students of normal intelligence levels who plan to go to work immediately upon graduation."

....

4. *Special Academic (Basic)*

Purpose. The Special Academic Track is for those students who have been variously described as "slow learners," "retarded," "academically retarded," "retarded slow learners," or "stupid." Its purposes are to provide a useful education for students whose limited abilities prevent them from successfully participating in the normal curriculum; and to give remedial instruction in the basic subjects — especially reading and arithmetic — to those students who can eventually qualify for upgrading to the General curriculum.

Criteria. In general, the criteria for Special Academic Track placement are inability to keep up with the normal curriculum, emotionally disturbed behavior, an IQ of 75 or below, and substandard performance on achievement tests.

....

Structure. Elementary school children may be placed in the Special Academic Track as early as the first grade, although most wind up there after an attempt at the normal first and perhaps second grade curriculum. Some schools place all Special Academic children in one class, so that youngsters ranging from first to sixth grade age levels may be taught in the same classroom; actually, the age spread may be even greater since Special Academic students who do not progress academically to a point where they can be promoted into the junior high school level remain in elementary school until they pass their thirteenth birthday. Other schools divide the track into two groups, the primary Special Academic (grade levels one through three) and the intermediate Special Academic (grade levels four through six), thus reducing the age spread.

....

A major distinction of the Special Academic Track is that classes are to be kept relatively small, the usual pupil-teacher ratio being about 18 or 20 to one. This is to enable more individualized attention than is possible in a larger class.

Dr. Hansen has indicated that teachers in the Special Academic Track need to be specially prepared to deal with the special problems that characterize slow learners. The great majority of those teaching in the Special Academic Track,

A. ABILITY GROUPING AND TRACKING

however, either have had no formal training in special education or have had very little. About half of the teachers are nontenure, or temporary.

Curriculum. The Special Academic curriculum at the elementary and junior high school level can be characterized as a highly simplified, slower-paced version of the standard curriculum.

....

5. *Junior Primary*

The Junior Primary is an ability-grouped class intermediate between kindergarten and first grade. Its purpose is to bring children up to a level of readiness for normal first grade instruction, the usual problem being inadequate preparation in reading-readiness skills.

....

A decision as to whether a child requires Junior Primary placement is based on his score on a standard aptitude test and the teacher's judgment. For those students who have not had kindergarten, however, the test score would have to be the controlling factor since the child would not have had any prior contact with the school and thus would not be known to a teacher.

....

D. *Track Distribution*

....

Plaintiffs have relied strongly on the empirical evidence regarding the distribution of students to prove how the effect of the track system is to discriminate against the lower class and the Negro students, who constitute a majority of the student population in the District public schools. Defendants have acknowledged that enrollment in the tracks is related to the socio-economic status of a student, but they deny that any racial bias is operating. The court will review the evidence on both counts.

1. *Socio-economic and racial patterns*

....

a. *Socio-economic correlation.* Defendants have admitted that, as a general rule, the per cent of students in a given track will correspond to the income level of the neighborhood served by that school. The higher the median income level, the greater the per cent of students who will be found in the higher tracks. This general proposition has its exceptions. However, the exceptions fall within the middle-range schools where small variations can produce pronounced differences in relative position.

....

b. *Racial correlation.* Defendants have gone to some pains to establish that everything about a student's education under the track system can be explained by nonracial considerations. However, as even a hurried glance at the data ... makes plain, for a majority of District schools and school children race and economics are intertwined: when one talks of poverty or low income levels one inevitably talks mostly about the Negro. This is evidenced by the most recent census data for the District of Columbia (1960) which shows the median annual income level to be $5,993 for all families; but for white families the median is $7,692 whereas for Negro families it is $4,800. At least 50% of the Negro population can therefore be placed within a poverty range.

....

c. *Racial distribution within track levels.* Perhaps the most striking illustration of why it is impossible to accept defendants' argument that a student's race is irrelevant to the kind of education he obtains is to be found when one examines the evidence concerning the racial breakdown of the enrollment in the Special Academic or Basic Track, the only track for which defendants maintain records according to race. As a general rule, in those schools with a significant number of both white and Negro students a higher proportion of the Negroes will go into the Special Academic Track than will the white students.

....

Thus, at both the elementary and junior high school levels the per cent of Negroes enrolled in the lowest track exceeds their proportionate representation in the total student body; conversely, the white enrollment in the Special Academic Track is significantly lower than the proportion of whites in the total school enrollment.

....

Clearly, then, race cannot be considered irrelevant in the operation of the track system. Even if the effects of tracking are not racially motivated, the Negro student nonetheless is affected.

2. Effects of the distribution pattern

The data ... reveal the two important effects of the track system. First, tracking tends to separate students from one another according to socio-economic and racial status, albeit in the name of ability grouping. Second, the students attending the lower income predominantly Negro schools — a majority of District school children — typically are confined to the educational limits of the Special Academic or General Track.

a. *Class separation.* The track system is by definition a separative device, ostensibly according to students' ability levels. However, the practical effect of such a system is also to group students largely according to their socio-economic status and, to a lesser but observable degree, to their racial status.

....

The reason for the track system's separative effect (and concomitant cushioning effect as well) inheres largely in the placement methods used in the District, pupils being programmed on the strength of their performances in class and on standardized aptitude tests, both of which criteria are heavily — and, as it turns out, unfairly — weighted against the disadvantaged student. (*See* Section F, *infra.*) Moreover, as will be seen shortly, once a student is separated it tends to

A. ABILITY GROUPING AND TRACKING

be both permanent and complete at least insofar as classroom contacts are concerned.

b. *Availability of Honors programs.* As observed earlier, because of the socio-economic and racial correlations the poorer Negro students for the most part receive the limited offerings of the General and Special Academic Tracks. But more than that, there is a total absence of any Honors programs at a substantial number of schools — almost all of them having predominantly Negro enrollments.

Defendants' explanation for this absence — at least with respect to the elementary schools — is that there are not enough students with the apparent aptitude for advanced work enrolled in the individual schools to warrant organizing an Honors program. For those students who do show Honors potential, the usual option given them is to transfer — at their own expense — to the closest school offering an Honors course. As a practical matter, the burden is such that many parents are forced to leave their children in their neighborhood school and the gifted Negro student stays in the General Track. Presumably these children are at some disadvantage when they move on to junior high school and begin to compete with the more fortunate students — black or white — whose schools were able to provide them with the advanced course work.

....

E. *Flexibility in Pupil Programming*

....

Despite the uncertainties as to the complete accuracy of these statistics, as noted, even the data most favorable to defendants — the 1963-64 figures for senior high schools — show only 264, or 15%, of the students in the slowest track being reassigned upward. Thus, at least 85% of those assigned to the Special Academic Track — and it appears that something over 90% is more typical — remain at the lowest achievement level. Although it cannot be said that an assignment to the Special Academic Track inevitably is permanent, neither can it be said that the chances of progressing into a more challenging curriculum are very high.

Plaintiffs have charged that this lack of movement is attributable to a complex of causes: the simplified curriculum, coupled with the absence of variety in the students' levels of ability, does not stimulate the Special Academic student; remedial training is inadequate; Special Academic teachers are not formally trained for special educational problems; teachers underestimate the potential of their students and therefore undereducate them. None of these reasons can be either isolated or proved with absolute certainty. Nonetheless, there is substantial evidence — examined in Section F, *infra* — that the cause of limited upgrading in the Special Academic Track lies more with faults to be found in the system than with the innate disabilities of the students. And certainly the results — which Dr. Hansen himself has said are an important measure of success — do not support the thesis that tracking is flexible.

To summarize, the pattern observed with respect to upgrading from the Special Academic Track is repeated in all track levels. Movement between tracks borders on the nonexistent.

....

2. *Movement Between Tracks: Cross-Tracking*

....

In practice cross-tracking of the sort described is confined to the senior high level, there being structural reasons why elementary and junior high pupils do not really "cross-track." And, as will be seen, even at the senior high school level cross-tracking proves to be the exception, not the rule.

....

c. *Senior high schools.* A senior high school student is not permitted to cross-track to a higher level — the only direction really at issue here — unless he is "eligible" or "qualified" and has obtained his principal's permission. A student is qualified if, in the judgment of his teacher and principal — based on scholastic performance, aptitude and achievement test scores, IQ, attitude, and mental and physical condition — he can successfully undertake the more advanced subject matter.

Two other preconditions qualify freedom to cross-track. First, in order to graduate from a track the student must complete all the required courses for that track level either in subjects taught at that level or in acceptable substitutes from a higher level. Electives, therefore, are subject to some limitations. Second a student obviously cannot take an advanced course unless he has taken the prerequisite courses for that subject. Thus, for example, in order for a General Track student to be prepared to take trigonometry or calculus in the twelfth grade (taught only in the Regular and Honors Tracks), he would have to begin electing Regular Track algebra at least by the tenth grade. Consequently, while it may be theoretically possible for a General Track pupil to elect an advanced sequence of Regular Track courses, that election must begin early enough in his high school career or he will for all practical purposes be foreclosed. And, according to School Board President Dr. Haynes, lack of preparation is in fact a major inhibition to cross-tracking.

It is and always has been school policy to permit cross-tracking. Nonetheless, a study in 1959 by the League of Women Voters of the District of Columbia revealed that school principals were not uniform in allowing cross-tracking. "'We found that some schools administer the program with a great deal of flexibility; others permit virtually none.'" Although Dr. Hansen in 1964 implied that uniformity had by then been achieved, the evidence in this case suggests otherwise.

F. *Causes of Discrimination and the Collapse of Track Theory*

... Here the focus will be on the major institutional shortcomings that not only thrust the disadvantaged student into the lower tracks but tend to keep him there once placed. The first area of concern is the lack of kindergartens and Honors programs in certain schools; the second relates to remedial and compensatory programs for the disadvantaged and educationally handicapped student; and the third, and most important, involves the whole of the placement and testings process by which the school system decides who gets what kind of education.

1. *Kindergartens and Honors Tracks*

[The court determined that students of color had little access to kindergarten programs and even less to honors classes than their white counterparts.]

2. *Remedial and compensatory education*

One purpose of the track system is to facilitate remedial education for students who are temporarily handicapped in basic academic skills. In addition, the school system has recognized that it must provide a substantial number of its students with special compensatory education programs for there to be any real hope of their becoming qualified for the more advanced tracks. There is substantial evidence, however, that neither the remedial nor the compensatory education programs presently in existence are adequate; rather the disadvantaged student consigned to the lower track tends simply to get the lesser education, not the push to a higher level of achievement.

....

3. *Placement and testing*

What emerges as the most important single aspect of the track system is the process by which the school system goes about sorting students into the different tracks. This importance stems from the fact that the fundamental premise of the sorting process is the keystone of the whole track system: that school personnel can with reasonable accuracy ascertain the maximum potential of each student and fix the content and pace of his education accordingly. If this premise proves false, the theory of the track system collapses, and with it any justification for consigning the disadvantaged student to a second-best education.

Plaintiffs' contention is that the sorting process is based largely on information about a student obtained from testing, specifically standardized tests of achievement and scholastic aptitude. The issues plaintiffs raise with regard to testing and placement are two: First, tests are not given often enough, with the result that a few test scores have an enormous influence on a child's academic career. Second, the tests which are used, and which are of such critical importance to the child, are wholly inappropriate for making predictions about the academic potential of disadvantaged Negro children, the tests being inherently inaccurate insofar as the majority of District schoolchildren is concerned. Both of these circumstances, plaintiffs allege, lead to artificial and erroneous separation of students according to status, and result in the undereducation of the poor and the Negro.

Defendants dispute all of plaintiffs' points. First, they say, tests are but one factor in deciding where to place a student. Second, tests are given often enough where needed. Third, the tests used are appropriate and do give valid results for placement purposes. The first two points of contention can be readily disposed of; it is the third point that raises the most difficult questions.

a. *Fundamentals of track placement.*

....

Those charged with making the decision as to what curriculum best fits the individual student are the student's teacher, his principal, the school counselor, and in special cases the staff of the Department of Public Personnel Services — especially a clinical psychologist. As a practical matter, the burden of the placement decision rests with the teacher. The teacher is the one who, through daily contact with the student, presumably knows him best. Equally important, it is the teacher who gives the grades and records the comments that go into making up the student's "paper image," which follows him through school as a part of his file; and it is the teacher who, in the day-to-day teacher-pupil relationship, greatly influences how the student acts and how well he succeeds in school.

To set the approximate boundaries of the respective tracks, the school system has issued fairly specific criteria to guide the teacher and others in making placement decisions. Those criteria include a number of elements: grades, classroom performance, maturity, emotional stability, physical condition, attitude — and performance on standard achievement and scholastic aptitude tests.

....

Throughout, defendants have tried to play down the importance of tests in the placement process. They have not, however, been wholly consistent in this, nor do the facts permit such a conclusion. The court does accept the general proposition that tests are but one factor in programming students; but it also finds that testing looms as a most important consideration in making track assignments. There are several reasons for this finding.

First, as a review of the official criteria makes obvious, there is a heavy emphasis on achievement and aptitude test scores, including IQ levels.

Second, and more importantly, the proper operation of the track system practically demands reliance on test scores. For one thing, classes are designed to serve students of similar achievement or ability levels, and this requires uniformity in the standards by which students are selected for placement in particular classes. For example, if teachers have different concepts of what constitutes "above average," placement decisions will vary accordingly and the homogeneity of the classes will be undermined. Thus, as defendants have said, a "distinct advantage of the standardized achievement test exists in the fact that it measures the performance of each pupil against a single scale so that the academic growth of a child may be accurately measured." But the most critical aspect of the track system that elevates the importance of testing is the necessity of predicting a student's maximum educational potential. It is in aiding the educator, especially the teacher, to discharge this awesome responsibility that tests become "indispensable for optimum and accurate placement within various pupil ability groupings." It escapes the court, therefore, how defendants can possibly suggest that tests do not have a decisive influence on pupil programming decisions.

b. *Frequency of testing.*

....

A student tested only according to the mandatory schedule will take a total of six aptitude tests of various kinds and five achievement tests of various kinds. Four of the six aptitude tests and three of the five achievement tests are given in elementary school, and one of each at both the junior and the senior high levels. Under such a program a student may go as many as three years without undergoing new tests (sixth grade to ninth grade; ninth grade to 11th grade), so that his most recent test scores may be as much as three years old.

There is a distinct possibility that students are not seriously reevaluated for upgrading except when the time for mandatory testing comes around; moreover, any evaluations in the interim would be based on what might in a year's time become stale data. This would tend to account for the relatively limited amount of upgrading and cross-tracking found to exist. While there is insufficient evidence of a clear causal relationship of this sort, the inflexibility of tracking is an indisputable fact. This, at least, does create substantial doubt as to the sufficiency of the testing schedule, although the lack of evidence precludes an ultimate finding in this regard.

c. *The use and misuse of tests.*

The court now turns to the crucial issue posed by plaintiffs' attack on defendants' use of tests: whether it is possible to ascertain with at least reasonable accuracy the maximum educational potential of certain kinds of schoolchildren. This question goes to the very foundation of the track system since, as was seen in Section B, *supra,* one of the fundamental premises of track theory is that students' potential can be determined. On this premise rests the practice of separating students into homogeneous ability groups; and most importantly, on this premise rests the sole justification for a student's being *permanently* assigned to lower track classes where the instructional pace and content have been scaled down to serve students of supposedly limited abilities. That is, according to track theory, those who remain in a lower curriculum remain *because they are achieving at their maximum level of ability.* They are not admitted to — or are at least discouraged from seeking admission to — a higher instructional level because the school system has determined that they cannot "usefully" and "successfully" rise above their present level. The evidence that defendants are in no position to make such judgments about the learning capacity of a majority of District schoolchildren is persuasive. Because of the importance of testing to the process of evaluating and programming students, the evidence has focused primarily on tests. However, necessarily bound up in the question of testing is the larger problem of the whole evaluation process — how the school goes about deciding who gets what kind of education. Plaintiffs' attack strikes at the heart of this process.

Briefly, plaintiffs make two contentions. First, they allege that for technical reasons the tests being used in the District cannot provide meaningful or accurate information about the learning capacity of a majority of District schoolchildren. Second, largely because of misleading test scores these children are being misjudged and, as a result, undereducated. Although both arguments have a common basis in the technical aspects of testing, they raise somewhat separate questions. The following discussion will therefor begin with a review of the evidence concerning tests in general before turning to the specifics of plaintiffs' arguments.

(1) *Test structure*

(a) *The nature of scholastic aptitude tests*

There are essentially two types of tests used in educational evaluation, achievement tests and scholastic aptitude tests. An achievement test is designed primarily to measure a student's level of attainment in a given subject, such as history, science, literature, and so on. The test presumes the student has been instructed in the subject matter; it seeks to find out how well he has learned that subject. Although achievement test scores play an important role in placement decisions, their use has not been seriously questioned by plaintiffs except to the extent the test scores tend to reinforce already erroneous decisions. Consequently, the discussion here will center on aptitude tests.

A *scholastic aptitude* test is specifically designed to predict how a student will achieve in the future in an academic curriculum. It does this by testing certain skills which have come to be identified as having a high correlation with scholastic achievement. Once a student's present proficiency in these skills is ascertained, an inference is drawn as to how well he can be expected to do in the future.

....

Whether a test is verbal or nonverbal, the skills being measured are *not* innate or inherited traits. They are learned, acquired through experience. It used to be the prevailing theory that aptitude tests — or "intelligence" tests as they are often called, although the term is obviously misleading — do measure some stable, predetermined intellectual process that can be isolated and called intelligence. Today, modern experts in educational testing and psychology have rejected this concept as false. Indeed, the best that can be said about intelligence insofar as testing is concerned is that it is whatever the test measures. In plain words, this means that aptitude tests can only test a student's present level of learning in certain skills and from that infer his capability to learn further.

A. ABILITY GROUPING AND TRACKING

Of utmost importance is the fact that, to demonstrate the ability to learn, a student must have had the opportunity to learn those skills relied upon for prediction. In other words, an aptitude test is necessarily measuring a student's background, his environment. It is a test of his cumulative experiences in his home, his community and his school. Each of these social institutions has a separate influence on his development; one may compensate for the failings of the others, or all may act in concert and reinforce each other — for good or for ill.

(b) *Causes of low test scores*

A low aptitude test score may mean that a student is innately limited in intellectual ability. On the other hand, there may be other explanations possible that have nothing to do with native intelligence. Some of those reasons are pertinent here.

As the discussion in the preceding section indicated, one of the important factors that could account for a low test score is the student's *environment*. If a student has had little or no opportunity to acquire and develop the requisite verbal or nonverbal skills, he obviously cannot score well on the tests.

Another source of variation is the student's *emotional or psychological condition* when he takes the test. He may have a poor attitude toward the test or the testing situation, generally characterized as apathy. This may be due to lack of motivation; or it may be a defensive reaction caused by worry or fear — what has been called "test anxiety."

....

(c) *Test standardization*

A standardized test is one for which a norm or average score has been established so that subsequently obtained scores can be comparatively evaluated. A test is standardized on a selected group of students whose scores are distributed to obtain a median; the median then becomes the norm for that test. Usually the standard is a national one, in the sense that the test publisher seeks to recreate in the norming group a representative cross-section of American schools. Tests may also be standardized on a local basis so as to enable comparisons between students from the same community. All the group aptitude tests used in the District are nationally standardized.

....

The norming group of students is selected according to certain factors. The principal ones are socio-economic and cultural status, as defined by the median annual income and average amount of schooling of the adults in the students' community. Other factors considered are region and school size. Race is not a controlled factor. Given the demography of the total population, the standardizing group will be predominantly white and middle class. Defendants' expert, Dr. Lennon, estimated that at least 60% of the group would fall into this category; the breakdown of the remaining 40 or less per cent was not given.

(2) *Testing the Disadvantaged Child*

Having touched generally upon the technical aspects of scholastic aptitude testing, it is now possible to give attention to plaintiffs specific arguments. At base they are focusing on an area of educational testing that has been given close attention only in recent years: the testing of the disadvantaged child.

....

Although the term "disadvantaged" is by nature imprecise, a working definition adopted for purposes of discussing educational problems is commonly based on two factors: the child's socio-economic status, as measured by the family's annual income; and his cultural status, as measured by the number of years of schooling attained by his parents. Both of these factors have been identified as having a high correlation with achievement both in school and in society generally, since they tend to reflect the kinds of background more or less conducive to developing scholastic-type skills. There are also indications that racial factors may well have some separate bearing on whether a child can be considered disadvantaged.

As was noted in Section D, *supra*, a substantial portion of the District's Negro schoolchildren can be characterized as disadvantaged.

....

Opinion of Law

....

VI. *The Track System*

....

At the outset it should be made clear that what is at issue here is not whether defendants are entitled to provide different kinds of students with different kinds of education. Although the equal protection clause is, of course, concerned with classifications which result in disparity of treatment, not all classifications resulting in disparity are unconstitutional. If classification is reasonably related to the purposes of the governmental activity involved and is rationally carried out, the fact that persons are thereby treated differently does not necessarily offend.

Ability grouping is by definition a classification intended to discriminate among students, the basis of that discrimination being a student's capacity to learn.[206] Different kinds of educational opportunities are thus made available to students of differing abilities. Whatever may be said of the concept of ability

---

[206]"Capacity to learn" — rather than "ability" — is a more precise description of the trait looked to in ability grouping. Although present ability is one element considered, the concept of ability grouping is to provide students with an education designed to help them realize their maximum potential — *i.e.*, to progress as fast and as far as possible according to their innate capacity to learn.

A. ABILITY GROUPING AND TRACKING

grouping in general, it has been assumed here that such grouping can be reasonably related to the purposes of public education. Plaintiffs have eschewed taking any position to the contrary. Rather the substance of plaintiffs' complaint is that in practice, if not by design, the track system — as administered in the District of Columbia public schools — has become a system of discrimination founded on socio-economic and racial status rather than ability, resulting in the under[-]education of many District students.

As the court's findings have shown, the track system is undeniably an extreme form of ability grouping. Students are early in elementary school sorted into homogeneous groups or tracks (and often into subgroups within a track), thereby being physically separated into different classrooms. Not only is there homogeneity, in terms of supposed levels of ability — the intended result — but as a practical matter there is a distinct sameness in terms of socio-economic status as well. More importantly, each track offers a substantially different kind of education, both in pace of learning and in scope of subject matter.... For a student locked into one of the lower tracks, physical separation from those in other tracks is of course complete insofar as classroom relationships are concerned; and the limits on his academic progress, and ultimately the kind of life work he can hope to attain after graduation, are set by the orientation of the lower curricula. Thus those in the lower tracks are, for the most part, molded for various levels of vocational assignments; those in the upper tracks, on the other hand, are given the opportunity to prepare for the higher ranking jobs and, most significantly, for college.

In theory, since tracking is supposed to be kept flexible, relatively few students should actually ever be locked into a single track or curriculum. Yet, in violation of one of its principal tenets, the track system is not flexible at all. Not only are assignments permanent for 90% or more of the students but the vast majority do not even take courses outside their own curriculum. Moreover, another significant failure to implement track theory — and in major part responsible for the inflexibility just noted — is the lack of adequate remedial and compensatory education programs for the students assigned to or left in the lower tracks because of cultural handicaps. Although one of the express reasons for placing such students in these tracks is to facilitate remediation, little is being done to accomplish the task. Consequently, the lower track student, rather than obtaining an enriched educational experience, gets what is essentially a limited or watered-down curriculum.

These are, then, the significant features of the track system: separation of students into rigid curricula, which entails both physical segregation and a disparity of educational opportunity; and, for those consigned to the lower tracks, opportunities decidedly inferior to those available in the higher tracks. A precipitating cause of the constitutional inquiry in this case is the fact that those who are being consigned to the lower tracks are the poor and the Negroes, whereas the upper tracks are the provinces of the more affluent and the whites. Defendants have not, and indeed could not have, denied that the pattern of grouping correlates remarkably with a student's status, although defendants would have it that the equation is to be stated in terms of income, not race. However, as discussed elsewhere, to focus solely on economics is to oversimplify the matter in the District of Columbia where so many of the poor are in fact the Negroes. And even if race could be ruled out, which it cannot, defendants surely "can no more discriminate on account of poverty than an account of religion, race, or color." *Griffin v. People of State of Illinois*, 351 U.S. 12, 17 (1951). As noted before, the law has a special concern for minority groups for whom the judicial branch of government is often the only hope of redressing their legitimate grievances; and a court will not treat lightly a showing that educational opportunities are being allocated according to a pattern that has unmistakable signs of invidious discrimination. Defendants, therefore, have a weighty burden of explaining why the poor and the Negro should be those who populate the lower ranks of the track system.

Since by definition the basis of the track system is to classify students according to their ability to learn, the only explanation defendants can legitimately give for the pattern of classification found in the District schools is that it does reflect students' abilities. If the discriminations being made are founded on anything other than that, then the whole premise of tracking collapses and with it any justification for relegating certain students to curricula designed for those of limited abilities. While government may classify persons and thereby effect disparities in treatment, those included within or excluded from the respective classes should be those for whom the inclusion or exclusion is appropriate; otherwise the classification risks becoming wholly irrational and thus unconstitutionally discriminatory. It is in this regard that the track system is fatally defective, because for many students placement is based on traits other than those on which the classification purports to be based.

The evidence shows that the method by which track assignments are made depends essentially on standardized aptitude tests which, although given on a system-wide basis, are completely inappropriate for use with a large segment of the student body. Because these tests are standardized primarily on and are relevant to a white middle class group of students, they produce inaccurate and misleading test scores when given to lower class and Negro students. As a result, rather than being classified according to ability to learn, these students are in reality being classified according to their socio-economic or racial status, or — more precisely — according to environmental and psychological factors which have nothing to do with innate ability.

Compounding and reinforcing the inaccuracies inherent in test measurements are a host of circumstances which further obscure the true abilities of the poor and the Negro. For example, teachers acting under false assumptions because of low test scores will treat the disadvantaged student in such a way as to make him conform to their low expectations; this acting out process — the self-fulfilling prophecy — makes it appear that the false assumptions were correct, and the student's real talent is wasted. Moreover, almost cynically, many Negro students are either denied or have limited access to the very kinds of programs the track system makes a virtual necessity: kindergartens; Honors programs for the fast-developing Negro student; and remedial and compensatory education programs that will bring the disadvantaged student back into the mainstream of education. Lacking these facilities, the student continues hampered by his cultural handicaps and continues to appear to be of lower ability than he really is. Finally, the track system as an institution cannot escape blame for the error in placements, for it is tracking that places such an emphasis on defining ability, elevating its importance to the point where the whole of a student's education and future are made to turn on his facility in demonstrating his qualifications for the higher levels of opportunity. Aside from the fact that this makes the consequences of misjudgments so much the worse, it also tends to alienate the disadvantaged student who feels unequal to the task of competing in an ethnocentric school system dominated by white middle class values; and alienated students inevitably do not reveal their true abilities — either in school or on tests.

All of these circumstances, and more, destroy the rationality of the class structure that characterizes the track system. Rather than reflecting classifications according to ability, track assignments are for many students placements based on status. Being, therefore, in violation of its own premise, the track system amounts to an unlawful discrimination against those students whose educational opportunities are being limited on the erroneous assumption that they are capable of accepting no more.

Remedy

....

As to the remedy with respect to the track system, the track system simply must be abolished. In practice, if not in concept, it discriminates against the disadvantaged child, particularly the Negro. Designed in 1955 as a means of protecting the school system against the ill effects of integrating with white children the Negro victims of de jure separate but unequal education, it has survived to stigmatize the disadvantaged child of whatever race relegated to its lower tracks — from which tracks the possibility of switching upward, because of the absence of compensatory education, is remote.

Even in concept the track system is undemocratic and discriminatory. Its creator admits it is designed to prepare some children for white-collar, and other children for blue-collar, jobs. Considering the tests used to determine which children should receive the blue-collar special, and which the white, the danger of children completing their education wearing the wrong collar is far too great for this democracy to tolerate. Moreover, any system of ability grouping which, through failure to include and implement the concept of compensatory education for the disadvantaged child or otherwise, fails in fact to bring the great majority of children into the mainstream of public education denies the children excluded equal educational opportunity and thus encounters the constitutional bar.

1. After the Board of Education decided not to appeal the decision of *Hobson v. Hansen*, and after Hansen's resignation from his post as Superintendent and the election of a new D.C. Board of Education to replace the prior appointed Board, an appeal by Hansen, an individual board member (Smuck), and a group of parents seeking to intervene under Rule 24(a) of the F.R.C.P. was brought before the Court of Appeals for the District of Columbia sitting *en banc*. The Court held that only the parents, whose asserted interest was in preserving the freedom of the Board of Education to exercise the broadest discretion constitutionally permissible in deciding upon educational policies, had standing to appeal. The Board's decision not to appeal lent a "quality of artificiality" to the proceedings, the court noted. The court's opinion discussed only the specific orders of the district court and read each of these orders very narrowly. On this basis, the Court of Appeals held that the appellants had no standing to appeal the order abolishing *the track system in existence at the time of the district court order*, which the court stated operated contrary to its own alleged goals. The court held that the district court ruling did not interpose any barrier which a genuinely concerned Board could find limiting its choice of options, since the Board would not look to options that rendered an advance in educational quality and equality impossible. "This Court's ruling is consistent with ... the realistic and understandable concerns of the parents that there be adequate scope for ability groupings.... The Court made it clear, and in any event this Court's opinion makes it clear, that the decree permits full scope for such ability grouping.... The District Court's decree must be taken to refer to the 'track system' as it existed at the time of the decree." *Smuck v. Hobson*, 408 F.2d 189 (D.C. Cir. 1969). A dissenting opinion centered on the concept that the action of the district court in this case is properly in the province of the legislature and the executive, but not the courts. *Id.* at 192-94.

2. Consider carefully the scope of Judge Wright's opinion. Did he invalidate all ability grouping or "tracking" in Washington, D.C.? If not, what type of system would he find constitutional? Consider the significance of each of the following attributes Judge Wright saw in the teaching system before him: use of "culture biased" I.Q. and aptitude tests that do not measure "innate capacity to learn"; little upward mobility among tracks; inadequate educational offerings in the lower tracks; a disproportionate number of black and poor children in the lower tracks. On which of these, or which combination of these does the opinion rest?

3. Arthur Jensen, in *How Much Can We Boost I.Q. and Scholastic Achievement*, 39 Harv. Educ. Rev. 1 (Winter 1969), suggests that there are racial and social class differences in patterns of abilities and that there are probably genetic as well as environmental factors involved in these differences. Jensen's findings have figured prominently in the proof of the heritability of intelligence. He has argued vigorously not only that individual differences in I.Q. are largely inherited, but also that differences between blacks and whites are possibly determined by genetic dissimilarity in the races. Jensen has repeated his position,

especially to education audiences, most recently in Jensen, *Compensatory Education and the Theory of Intelligence*, 66 Phi Delta Kappan 554 (1985). Part of Jensen's argument is that since intelligence is so closely tied to race, compensatory education programs to improve minority student education will have little to no effect. Jensen's views have been influential in circles extending beyond the classroom. His interpretations of intelligence differences based on race have been presented before committees of the United States Congress as regards both schooling and welfare policies.

Jensen's findings at the time were countered by other learned authorities: Bersoff, *Regarding Psychologists Testily: Legal Regulation of Psychological Assessment in the Public Schools*, 39 Md. L. Rev. 27 (1979); Perney, Hyde and Machock, *Black Intelligence: A Re-Evaluation*, 46 J. Negro Educ. 450 (1977); Robinson, *"If You're So Rich, You Must Be Smart: Some Thoughts on Status, Race and I.Q."* in The Fallacy of I.Q., at 18 (C. Sennal ed. 1973); Labov, *"Academic Ignorance and Black Intelligence,"* 229 Atlantic Monthly 59 (June 1972); Light and Smith, *Models of Intelligence: A Methodological Inquiry*, 39 Harv. Educ. Rev. 489 (Summer, 1969).

In 1974 Jensen's findings were brought into some disrepute by Leon Kamin in *The Politics of I.Q.* (1974). Kamin writes that heritability data of fraudulent origin were resurrected by Jensen and served as the major source of his research. Kamin describes Jensen's resulting thesis as "a rare moment of high comedy in the heritability literature." *Id.* at 43.

4. "Tracking" as applied in *Hobson* refers to the practice of separating students into different classes (within the same school) based on some type of ability assessment usually in the form of standardized achievement tests. Professor Jeanne C. Oakes comments on the practice in the following terms:

> How can it be legal for schools to treat some students so much better than others? Isn't it likely that there are some violations of fundamental rights embedded in the processes we have been looking at? Considering what we know about how tracking affects the kind of education ... students get, it is difficult not to question the legality of the process. Tracking can be easily thought of as a barrier to educational equality because it so clearly limits the access some students have to certain school experiences. Viewed in this way, tracking is a likely target for a court challenge on constitutional grounds. Nevertheless, constitutional issues are sticky ones.... [R]egardless of how clear the injustices of tracking appear to be, the question of its legality is as unclear today as was that of many racially discriminatory practices prior to the 1950's.
>
> ....
>
> [However,] several characteristics and effects of tracking ... may be susceptible to legal action in relation to the provision of equal educational opportunity.... [T]hese are: the separation of students resulting in disproportionate placements of poor and minority students in low groups; the reduced

educational quality in low groups; the limited access low groups have to higher education or some occupations; the relative permanence of ability classifications and inflexibility of grouping systems; the stigmatization of low-track students; and the misclassification of students resulting from inappropriate or haphazard classification processes.

Oakes, Keeping Track: How Schools Structure Inequality, Yale University Press, 172, 177 (Yale University Press 1985).*

Are Oakes' concerns, written years after the decision in *Hobson*, synonymous with those of Judge Wright? Oakes comments on the permanence of ability groupings and the inflexibility of the system. Inasmuch as this serves as a stark reality in Wright's reasoning, does this suggest that *Hobson*, still touted as the best known and most important ruling on tracking, has had little effect on actual practice by educators?

Oakes' comments are countered in other studies with the argument that ability sorting is not the problem; instead its use must be better regulated. Two authors state in a California study that school officials make assignments based on courses, teachers, and ability data of students. Yet, this information is often not reevaluated and parents are not regularly informed of the assignments. The researchers surmise that if this procedure was regulated, ability grouping may in fact have a benefit. Friedman and Sugarman, *School Sorting and Disclosure: Disclosure to Families as a School Reform Strategy. Part I.: Existing Practices and the Social Interests in School Information Disclosure*, 17 J. Law and Educ. 53 (1988).

5. Part of the plaintiffs' argument in *Hobson* is that the tests used in ability sorting were unfair and weighted in favor of white students. There were instances, however, where the test results were incorrect and hundreds of black pupils were misclassified to the lower strata tracks. Are there constitutional causes of action that could be brought by plaintiffs so as to be removed to a more appropriate classification? Is there room for such a claim following Judge Wright's decision?

6. Consider also the validity of Judge Wright's findings as to the inadequacy of educational offerings in the lower tracks. On what was the determination based? Do these findings depend on pedagogical expertise? If not, what do they depend on? What of the pedagogical expertise of judges?

The following argument which has been set forth against judges attempting to assess educational issues such as the quality of an educational offering should be considered:

> Judges are not particularly equipped to assume such a role, and, equally important, they are less equipped than those whose judgments they would be called upon to review. Teachers and school administrators have that sort

---

*Copyright © 1985 by Yale University Press. Reprinted with permission.

A. ABILITY GROUPING AND TRACKING

of professional training and experience in education which judges boast of in the field of criminal procedure. Even the laymen who sit on boards of education and make the ultimate policy judgments can be assumed to acquire, through their on-going attention to the problems of the school system, a degree of specialized competence that the generalists of the bench, occupied with a wider range of concerns, cannot hope to match. The decisions of school boards claim not only the respect courts customarily give to judgments of popularly elected legislators but, in addition, the deference normally accorded the determinations of specialized administrative agencies in a position, as courts are not, to deal with particular issues as elements in a comprehensive regulatory scheme. It is true that in the education of disadvantaged youngsters, experts of all stripes — behavioral scientists, curriculum planners, classroom teachers — have fallen short of the mark. And there is intense controversy among knowledgeable authorities as to the proper goals, methods, organizational forms, and governing structures for the public schools. But no amount of dissonance and fallibility on the part of those entrusted with responsibility for the schools recommends turning those vexing problems over to judicial overseers who have fewer qualifications for solving them, perceive them only from a distance, can act upon them only intermittently, have no opportunity to retrieve their mistakes and, above all, are not accountable to the public for the consequences of their decisions. Goodman, *De Facto School Segregation: A Constitutional and Empirical Analysis*, 60 Cal. L. Rev. 275, 361-62 (1972).*

On the other hand, can judges avoid such determinations if they are to perform their function? Note the following statement by which Judge Wright concluded his opinion in *Hobson*:

> It is regrettable, of course, that in deciding this case this court must act in an area so alien to its expertise. It would be far better indeed for these great social and political problems to be resolved in the political arena by other branches of government. But these are social and political problems which seem at times to defy such resolution. In such situations, under our system, the judiciary must bear a hand and accept its responsibility to assist in the solution where constitutional rights hang in the balance.

Oakes, *supra* note 4, as an educator, comprehends the dilemma relative to the expertise of federal judges —

> [A court's] reluctance ... is based on more than a wish not to infringe on educators' areas of special competence. Important too is the court's awareness of how difficult it would be to frame a remedy to harms ensuing

---

*Copyright © 1972 by Professor Frank Goodman and the University of California Press. Reprinted with permission.

from day-to-day schooling practices. Beyond the development of suitable remedies, the degree of court intervention in the administration of schools that could be required to ensure that such remedies were carried out is undoubtedly repugnant to most justices ... Oakes at 190.

— and allows a response in 1985 strikingly similar to Wright in 1967:

The difficulties are real and the court's reluctance to face them directly is understanable. Yet the fundamental issues — students' rights to equal protection of the laws and due process being violated by the processes and effects of tracking — cannot be ignored. It seems imperative that the issue be confronted in the spirit of the mandate in *Brown*:

Where a state has undertaken to provide a benefit to the people, such as public education, the benefits must be provided on equal terms to all the people unless the state can demonstrate a compelling reason for doing otherwise. *Id.*

7. What is the relevance of the racial and economic class "segregation" that resulted from tracking in Washington, D.C.? Is such separation by race per se a violation of the Equal Protection Clause or is there a need for an inadventitious link to past practice of de jure segregation? Consider the following cases.

McNEAL v. TATE COUNTY SCHOOL DISTRICT

United States Court of Appeals
508 F.2d 1017 (5th Cir. 1975)

CLARK, CIRCUIT JUDGE:

The Tate County School system enrolls 3,519 students (2,152 black; 1,367 white) in five schools. Upon court-ordered abolition of freedom of choice in August 1970, the system elected to make pupil assignments to schools in the system based upon residence in one of three zones for elementary and junior high school students, and upon residence in one of two zones for high school students. However, the district also retained a ten-year-old classroom assignment plan for elementary and junior high school students which can best be described as faculty-predicted ability grouping. In this system the teacher evaluates the pupil's past performance and recommends the next year's assignment to the principal, who makes the final decision. Entering first grade students are placed into sections (classrooms) based upon whether they have attended the public preschool program. During the school year students are moved within the sections of their grade if their performance indicates that they were better or worse than initially predicted. High school classes are formed on the basis of student requests following a 'first-come, first-served' formula.

The result of this student assignment program has been to produce one to four all-black sections in every elementary (1-6) grade and a few all-white sections in the advanced grades. Because this effect violated the court's initial order

A. ABILITY GROUPING AND TRACKING

enjoining the maintenance of segregated classrooms, the plaintiffs-appellants sought to hold district officials in contempt and to secure further relief barring segregated classrooms and requiring that the racial ratio in each classroom reflect the ratio in the respective grade.

The following findings were made by the district court. The system was unitary in faculty and staff assignments, transportation and extra curricular activities. The district technically had failed to comply with the earlier order barring segregated classrooms, but should be excused because of a change in the law evidenced by the Supreme Court's allowance of all-black schools in the metropolitan systems of Richmond, Detroit and Memphis. A number of the all-black classrooms were taught by black teachers. Pupil assignments were not based on any specific tests but rather upon a grading of each child's actual performance. It might well be that the segregated classrooms exist 'because the black child has not had the advantages which the white child has had.' School authorities, who were honestly endeavoring to operate a unitary system affording the very best education possible, were in a better position than the court to determine how their schools should be operated. The court could suggest nothing which would result in better schools for the district — the only alternative being to abandon the present plan and require assignments based on race so as to create a classwide racial balance in each section, which would be educationally detrimental.

The court erred in determining that the approach to be taken in adjudging the constitutional permissibility of segregated classrooms had been changed by the recent decisions involving the segregating effects of metropolitan housing patterns upon some school populations in large urban districts. The situations are not comparable. Not only must the attendance zones in such urban areas initially be drawn with racial neutrality, but also the parents of students in those zones retain the right to relocate their residence and students in segregated schools must be granted the right to transfer to schools in which their race is in the minority. On the other hand, segregation caused by ability grouping is fixed. Notwithstanding the fact that tract assignments are made without regard to race, children who have been the victims of educational discrimination in the dual systems of the past may find themselves resegregated in any school in the district solely because they still wear a badge of their old deprivation — underachievement.

An analysis of today's issue should begin with articulation of the basic rule that classrooms which are segregated by race are proscribed regardless of the degree of overall schoolwide desegregation achieved.... The district court finds no breach of this postulate in Tate County because it concludes that individual ability, not race, is the criterion for assignment.

The law of this circuit which bears on ability grouping of students began with dicta. The first decisional mention of student assignments based on a testing of their ability came in a brief ruling in our *en banc* holding in *Singleton v. Jackson Municipal Separate School District*, 419 F.2d 1211, 1219 (1969), in particular regard to the Marshall County and Holly Springs School Districts. There we barred the use of testing for school, as opposed to classroom, assignment of pupils in these words:

> We pretermit a discussion of the validity per se of a plan based on testing except to hold that testing cannot be employed in any event until unitary school systems have been established.

Then came the per curiam decision in *Lemon v. Bossier Parish School Board*, 444 F.2d 1400, 1401 (5th Cir. 1971), which while again refusing to make a per se rule on the validity of student placement into one of two schools based on ability disclosed by testing, stated:

> In *Singleton* we made it clear that regardless of the innate validity of testing, it could not be used until a school district had been established as a unitary system. We think at a minimum this means that the district in question must have for several years operated as a unitary system.

The first consideration of the use of testing as a basis for classroom assignment came in *Moses v. Washington Parish School Board*, 456 F.2d 1285 (5th Cir. 1972), where the school district was making classroom assignments based upon scores on standardized tests. The result was lower sections which were all-black. The district court found this ability grouping to be violative of equal protection particularly in the slower sections which, in an ironic sort of self-fulfilling prophecy, were taught less and learned less. This court's brief order of affirmance found that substantial evidence supported the district court's determination that ability grouping tended to perpetuate segregated classrooms within Bossier Parish's otherwise desegregated system.

From these holdings, we synthesize the rule for this case to be that the court must assay the present district plan of student assignment which results in racial segregation with a punctilious care, to see that it does not result in perpetuating the effects of past discrimination. Ability grouping, like any other non-racial method of student assignment, is not constitutionally forbidden. Certainly educators are in a better position than courts to appreciate the educational advantages or disadvantages of such a system in a particular school or district. School districts ought to be, and are, free to use such grouping whenever it does not have a racially discriminatory effect. If it does cause segregation, whether in classrooms or in schools, ability grouping may nevertheless be permitted in an otherwise unitary system if the school district can demonstrate that its assignment method is not based on the present results of past segregation or will remedy such results through better educational opportunities.

In the case at bar the fact that such classroom groupings were used in each of the dual systems produced by freedom-of-choice cannot be made a justification for continuation of the practice in zonally integrated schools. In fact, the lack of educational equality would predictably cause students from the inferior system to immediately be resegregated within the lower classroom sections. Many of the segregated black students in this system have never been allowed to attend a unitary school system except under such ability groupings. The testing rationale of both *Singleton* and *Lemon* would bar the use of this method of assignment until the district has operated as a unitary system without such assignments for a sufficient period of time to assure that the underachievement achievement of the slower groups is not due to yesterday's educational disparities. Such a bar period may be lifted when the district can show that steps taken to bring disadvantaged students to peer status have ended the educational disadvantages caused by prior segregation.

The district court was in error in assuming that its only alternative to approving ability grouping was to command racial balance in every classroom. If the school district cannot substantiate its present system, it may choose any racially neutral method of classroom assignment it considers educationally sound. That method should be approved by the district court unless its effect is racial segregation or is substantially adverse to the quality of education available to some of the district's children....

Since Tate County's system results in substantial racial segregation in its classrooms, the defendant school district should be afforded an opportunity to meet the burden of proof established here. In the alternative, the district must submit some other plan of student assignment not based upon race or ability grouping. The district court may then proceed to hold such hearings as it deems necessary to permit interested parties and affected parents to respond. The court's order approving such a plan, as submitted or modified, should be entered no later than May 1, 1975, to become effective with the commencement of the September 1975 school year. The judgment appealed from is reversed and the cause is remanded for further proceedings not inconsistent with this opinion.

Reversed and remanded.

QUARLES v. OXFORD MUNICIPAL SEPARATE SCHOOL DISTRICT

United States Court of Appeals
868 F.2d 750 (5th Cir.), *rehearing denied* (1989)

REAVLEY, CIRCUIT JUDGE:

Appellants, the class of black parents and students of the Oxford, Mississippi community, appeal from the district court's judgment which dissolved all injunctive orders entered against the Oxford Municipal Separate School District ("Oxford") and dismissed the nineteen year old school desegregation suit. They argue on appeal that the district court erred not only in dissolving the existing injunctive orders, but also in refusing to grant additional injunctive relief. We affirm....

I. *Background*

This school desegregation case began in July 1969 when appellants complained that schools in Oxford, Mississippi had not desegregated effectively. Oxford's board of trustees took immediate steps to remedy the situation and in January

1970 submitted a desegregation plan to the district court. By order dated January 8, 1970, and with the consent of appellants, the court adopted Oxford's plan in large part, thereby commanding Oxford to "begin immediately to operate a unitary school system." The district court retained jurisdiction to ensure proper implementation of its order and, in addition, required periodic reporting.

In the years since this order was entered, there has been only one issue raised dealing directly with desegregation. In 1972, appellants requested that the district court order Oxford to provide free busing for students. After a fully litigated hearing on the issue, the district court denied appellants' request. In so doing, the court noted that

> [s]tudent activities and functions, administration, staff and all classrooms are and have been since February 1970 fully integrated; one-race schools have been altogether eliminated and are a thing of the past.
>
> ....
>
> Oxford does not have a history of resistance to court integration orders or for devising assignment plans that promise much but achieve little. On the contrary, as a result of a single order entered by this court, the school district did away with every vestige of the dual school system, and it did so within no more than two weeks' time. The evidence unmistakably shows that Oxford was successful to an astonishing degree in putting an instant end to its de jure dual schools and fully realizing unitary schools....

Since the busing issue was addressed in 1972, appellants have filed five complaints against the Oxford school system. The complaints have involved, for the most part, school disciplinary matters; only one was pursued and finally adjudicated in appellants' favor.

In 1982, a complaint was filed against Oxford with the Office of Civil Rights ("OCR") for alleged violations of Title VI of the 1964 Civil Rights Act, 42 U.S.C. § 2000d *et seq.* Following an investigation, the OCR made recommendations in areas in which it felt complaint was justified, which Oxford followed. The OCR has conducted no further investigation.

> ....
>
> [The Court then considered appellants' complaint against the school system in four areas: 1) ability grouping; 2) discipline; 3) employment; and 4) one-race-programs and extra-curricular activities. The edited portion only addresses ability grouping.]

A. *Achievement grouping*

Appellants argue that Oxford's grouping system discriminates against black students on the basis of race in violation of the Fourteenth Amendment, Title VI of the Civil Rights Act of 1964, and state law.

Achievement or ability grouping has been recognized by both courts and educators as an acceptable and commonly used instruction method.... Still, plaintiffs may challenge the school district's assignment practices by demonstrat-

A. ABILITY GROUPING AND TRACKING

ing that such practices have the effect of perpetuating or reestablishing a dual school system. Once evidence of a significant segregative effect resulting from the use of achievement grouping is introduced, a school system may justify its continued use by demonstrating that its practices (1) are not based on the present results of past discrimination or (2) will remedy such present results through better educational opportunities. [*McNeal v. Tate County School Dist.*, 508 F.2d 1017, 1019-20 (5th Cir. 1975).][3]

Oxford's limited form of achievement grouping, which was reviewed, modified and approved by the OCR in 1981-82, is strikingly similar to that which was accepted by the court in *Montgomery v. Starkville Municipal Separate School Dist.*, 665 F.Supp. 487, 495-502 (N.D.Miss.1987), *aff'd*, 854 F.2d 127 (5th Cir. 1988). Basically, only students in the third through the eighth grades are grouped in the traditional sense. Beginning in the third grade, students are placed in groups (high, middle, low) for instruction in language arts and mathematics based on Stanford Achievement Test ("SAT") scores in those respective areas. Thus, a student's placement in mathematics is unrelated to his or her placement in language arts. With the exception of language arts and mathematics, students in grades three through eight are grouped heterogeneously in classrooms where gender and race are balanced.

At the high school level there is no achievement grouping per se. There are, however, advanced placement, or accelerated, courses offered, most of which are racially identifiable as white. Appellants insist that these classes are predominantly white as a result of racial discrimination. Based on the evidence, we disagree. At the hearing, the high school's guidance director testified that, although the state department of education has a cut-off for entrance into the accelerated program, Oxford does not impose that requirement. Therefore, all classes, including the accelerated classes, truly are open to all students. Under these circumstances, the fact that more white students than black students are enrolled in the accelerated classes cannot be attributed to racial discrimination.

It is undisputed that, in those grades in which grouping does occur, there is a high concentration of white students in the upper level groups and of black students in the lower level groups. However, the evidence Oxford presented on this issue led the district court to conclude that "neither the present grouping

---

[3]The applicable standards under Title VI are substantially similar to those outlined above. *See Georgia State Conference of Branches of NAACP v. Georgia*, 775 F.2d 1403, 1417 (11th Cir. 1985). To make out a disparate impact claim under Title VI, the plaintiff first must show by a preponderance of the evidence that a facially neutral practice has a racially disproportionate effect; the burden then shifts to the defendant to provide a substantial legitimate justification for its practice. The plaintiff may ultimately prevail by proffering an equally effective alternative practice which results in less racial disproportionality or proof that the legitimate practices are a pretext for discrimination. *See generally McDonnell Douglas Corp. v. Green*, 411 U.S. 792 (1973). Because the same rationale underlies our conclusion that appellants failed to meet their burden under both the Fourteenth Amendment and Title VI, we do not discuss them separately.

system nor the present disparate impact, however minimal that might be, is causally related to the former segregated system." Dr. Thomas Saterfiel, Deputy Superintendent of Education for the State of Mississippi, and Dr. Thomas Payne, Dean of the School of Education at the University of Mississippi, both testified that the achievement grouping system Oxford employs is educationally sound, both in theory and in practice. Oxford's students, both black and white, consistently rank among the highest in the state in terms of composite scores on the American College Test ("ACT") and the Basic Skills Assessment Program ("BSAP").

Further, expert testimony established that Oxford's students are not locked into place, or tracked, in the grouping system. Oxford's achievement grouping plan provides several opportunities for movement among achievement levels during the school year. Students may be moved on the basis of their scores on the SAT, which is given once a year. In addition, however, in recognition of the fact that all students do not perform as test scores predict, a student may be moved into another level after the initial placement if the child's teachers agree that it is in the best interest of the child and if exceptional progress or lack of progress indicates that movement may be proper. For the same reason, the policy provides that a parent may make written request for a student transfer into a higher level after conferring with the student's teacher and principal. This system appears to be working. After considering all of the evidence, the district court determined that there is an "impressive" degree of movement among achievement levels by black students as well as by white students.

Appellants contend, however, that better student assignment methods exist which involve less segregative impact. They offered the testimony of Dr. Jeanne Oakes, who testified that alternative methods of instruction exist which might produce better results and at the same time reduce the segregative impact. The district court discounted Dr. Oakes' testimony, as it was entitled to do, since "she had never visited the Oxford school system and had no knowledge of the way in which it functioned within the district." In fact, Dr. Oakes stated that she could not offer an opinion as to the achievement grouping practices of the Oxford school district because she did not have all of the necessary evidence upon which to base an opinion. Also, there was testimony from Oxford's expert, Dr. Thomas Payne, that the alternative methods advocated by Dr. Oakes were still in the experimental stages.

Educators have long debated the advantages and disadvantages of placing students in classrooms with others perceived to have similar abilities; "nevertheless, it is educators, rather than courts, who are in a better position ultimately to resolve the question whether such a practice is, on the whole, more beneficial than detrimental to the students involved."... The district court, after careful study, determined that Oxford's achievement grouping system "is neither intended nor does it have the effect of having significant racial impact upon the

A. ABILITY GROUPING AND TRACKING

makeup of the classrooms in the various schools of the system." Based on the record before us, we cannot conclude that these findings are clearly erroneous.

....

---

1. The *McNeal* decision was one of several in the South that during the 1970s declared ability grouping unconstitutional if enacted as a way to forestall the requirements of judicially ordered desegregation. *See, e.g., United States v. Gadsden County Sch. Dist.*, 572 F.2d 1049 (1978); *Lemon v. Bossier Parish Sch. Bd.*, 444 F.2d 1400 (5th Cir. 1971); *United States v. Tunica County Sch. Dist.*, 421 F.2d 1236 (5th Cir. 1970).

However, the decision in *McNeal* declared neither tracking nor ability grouping per se unconstitutional. Instead the court settled on a test designed to determine if past school segregation caused low-track placements of African-American students:

> If it does cause segregation, whether in classrooms or in schools, ability grouping may nevertheless be permitted in an otherwise unitary system if the school district can demonstrate that its assignment method is not based on the present results of past segregation or will remedy such results through better educational opportunities. *McNeal*, at 1020.

By placing such emphasis on whether the school system has achieved unitary status, is the court here ignoring the fact that racial inequality and class groupings may be remnants of the previously segregated system? Is the court establishing an artificial threshold of equal educational opportunity trusting that school evaluation strategies will be fair and ignoring the manifestations of the assessment?

2. Court decisions authorizing the separation of African-Americans and whites in schools based on theories of innate ability have some symbiosis with desegregation complaints. The *Brown* Court, for example, states that the "separate but equal" doctrine articulated in *Plessy v. Ferguson* actually had its origin in *Roberts v. City of Boston*, 59 Mass. (5 Cush.) 198 (1850). (*See Brown*). *Roberts* rejected a state-based equal protection challenge to Boston's segregated school system indicating that equality was apparent, in that black and white children received the same quality of instruction from teachers of equal salary. The court relied on a theory of school administrative prerogative that has since become replete in such cases that "[school boards have] plenary authority ... to arrange, classify and distribute pupils, in such a manner as they think best adapted to their general proficiency and welfare." *Id.* at 208. Finding solace in this ruling, a later court held that school segregation was permissible because of "a natural distinction between the races" and legislation fostering these distinctions could not be unconstitutional. *People ex rel. King v. Gallagher*, 93 N.Y. 438, 450 (1883).

In *Roberts*, the noted abolitionist Charles Sumner represented the black school children and their parents. In language quite similar to the argument, the Supreme Court used in *Brown* in 1954 to end segregated schools ("[segregation] generates a feeling of inferiority [in black students] as to their status in the community that may affect their hearts and minds in a way unlikely ever to be undone." *Brown*, at 494) Sumner argued that separating students on the basis of race "create[s] a feeling of degradation in the blacks, and of prejudice ... in the whites." *Roberts*, at 204.

School segregation in Boston was eliminated in 1855 owing partly to the determined efforts of black parents who initiated a number of complaints and law suits after *Roberts*. For a rendition of Boston's 18th and 19th century desegregation problems, including the activity of black parents, *see* Schulz, *The Culture Factory: Boston Public Schools, 1789-1860* (1973).

3. What are the arguments for interpreting *Brown* to mean that schools may segregate students by ability, but not by race? Could it be that ability groupings are perceived as objective and neutral and racial classifications capricious and arbitrary? Does *McNeal* make such an argument?

4. The *Quarles* court, under the *McNeal* test, *infra*, upheld "tracking" and ability grouping even with a finding of disparate impact on African-American students. Does this mean that such courts are more willing now to perceive racial discrimination as being tied to unitary status and disparate results as a reflection of differences based on ability? Does the court here reason that disparate racial impact is a function of nonracial factors thus permitting the issue to be left to the expert educators?

5. If there is disparate impact on minority students because of school separation of students, plaintiffs may bring a claim under Title VI which prohibits discrimination on the basis of race. The *Quarles* court referred to *NAACP v. Georgia*, 775 F.2d 1403 (11th Cir. 1985), in finding no Title VI violation in that "all students within the [school] system, including blacks as well as whites, are benefited educationally by [ability grouping]." *Quarles*, at 755. Does this mean that courts will require plaintiffs who bring complaints of "tracking" under Title VI to show intentional discrimination as well as a violation of equal protection?

6. The *Quarles* court states that at the high school level there is no ability grouping even though there is a gifted program predominated by white students. *Id.* at 754. What is the court's rationale for such a ruling? Is it rested in any legal theory or doctrine? Is the court here basing its findings completely on the testimony of educational experts? If so, has it considered the possibility that even good faith efforts at ability grouping could be inherently biased?

7. The court completely discounted the testimony of Jeanne Oaks, expert for the plaintiffs, who is quoted in notes following *Hobson*, *supra*. Is the court simply surmising that ability grouping is a technical or scientific issue being hotly debated by the experts or has it taken a side in the issue, only tangentially considering the evidence, so as to arrive at a particular outcome?

A. ABILITY GROUPING AND TRACKING

8. The Supreme Court in *Brown* stated that classifications based on race must be subject to the strict scrutiny test whereby officials are ordered to produce compelling reasons for their decisions. What tests are used by the courts in *McNeal* and *Quarles*?

9. Does ability grouping simply separate students because of existing abilities and compensatory needs or does it relegate students to certain placements because of the accident of racial or social class? Are these arguments entertained by the courts in *McNeal* and *Quarles*?

10. Ability grouping is supported by a number of reasons, some having to do with the avoidance of desegregation as in *McNeal* and *Hobson*, but also because of external challenges to the nation's knowledge and information supremacy. This was an argument put forth in the 1950's because of the scientific threat by the Soviet Union. At that time, America's schools were prompted to segregate "gifted" from other students particularly in science and mathematics. *See* Bettleheim, *Sputnik and Segregation: Should the Gifted Be Educated Separately?*, 26 Commentary 322 (1958). Also, the 1980's began a period of protracted efforts to address perceived shortcomings in American education. Major studies strongly hinted at ability grouping because the Nation's schools were facing "a rising tide of mediocrity." *See* National Comm'n on Excellence in Education United States Dep't of Education, A Nation at Risk: The Imperative for Educational Reform, A Report to the Nation and the Secretary of Education 5 (1983). *See* Christine Shea, et al., The New Servants of Power: A Critique of the 1980's Reform Movement (1989) (surveying the educational reform movements of the 1970's and 1980's and arguing that the reform movements have not reconciled the inequalities suffered by women and minorities).

Is there a built-in conflict between equality of opportunity and the nation's desire for excellence in education? If so, are courts the best place to determine which will receive the greater share of resources?

11. In *Hobson, supra,* Judge Wright finds inadequacy in the educational offerings at the lower tracks. Curiously, the *Quarles* court found no such discrepancy and even allowed that placing students in varied tracks offers a benefit to all. Do the holdings in either *Hobson* or *Quarles* speak to the efficacy of ability grouping?

John Goodlad does speak to this issue in A Place Called School (1984). In his study, Goodlad reports that the effects of ability grouping, the teaching practice in tracked classes, and the behaviors and social relationships among students in these classes differ from conventional wisdom which traditionally reports the educational benefits of ability grouping. The negative effects of ability grouping may include lower self-esteem, higher drop-out rates, more discipline problems, and higher delinquency among students placed in lower tracks. Additionally, a disproportionate number of these students are racial and ethnic minorities and children from lower socioeconomic classes.

Although more research focuses on the effects of tracking, Goodlad states that more attention should be paid to the teaching that occurs in tracked classrooms.

Goodlad reports that teachers in high track classes spend more time on instruction and cognitive development, while teachers in lower tracks spend more time on rote learning and application of skills. In addition, the behaviors these teachers encourage differ greatly among tracked classes. Teachers in high tracks encourage independent thinking, self-direction, creativity, critical thinking, and active involvement in the learning process. Their counterparts in lower tracks encourage more conforming behavior such as working quietly, punctuality, and cooperation.

Lastly, regarding social relationships among students, Goodlad reports higher peer esteem and friendliness among students in higher tracks, as well as an overall feeling that the teachers care about them. The report for students in lower tracked classes was directly contrary.

Could students argue under an equal protection analysis, that by its very nature, ability grouping makes for disparate treatment in classes based on the Goodlad study? Would the argument be somewhat attenuated based on the idea that the difference in treatment results from teachers' natural inclination to expect the best from those identified as "high track" while expecting less from those in the "low track"? Can the requirement of "intent to discriminate" be derived from such teacher expectations? Should courts engage in seeking data from such high profile studies as the one quoted here even if not presented by either side in the conflict? What would be the response of the *Hobson*, *McNeal*, or *Quarles* courts to such data on each of their decisions?

12. Intentional discrimination and disparate treatment of African-American and Hispanic-American students was found in *People Who Care v. Rockford Bd. of Educ. Sch. Dist. #205*, 851 F. Supp. 905 (N.D. Ill. 1994), *supra* Chapter 11. A federal district court held in 1994 that the second largest school district in the State of Illinois had intentionally segregated students for years even in the wake of lawsuits and court orders. The activities of school officials included the separation of minority and white students by school. It was the area of tracking and ability grouping, however, that garnered the ire of the court. Specifically, "it was the policy of the [Rockford, Illinois, School District] to use tracking to intentionally segregate white students from minority students." within the same school. *Id.* at 921. This was accomplished by assigning minority students to the lower tracks in consistently disproportionate numbers and placing black students who qualified for high tracks in low tracks. The court described the practices as "incredibly insensitive [and astonishing] ... labeling the students by color-coding them for all of the student body to see." *Id.* The record was replete with evidence of white students who scored below the national mean on achievement tests who were put in the mostly white high track classes. Concomitantly, there were minority students who scored in the 99th percentile of these tests and who, incredibly, were still relegated to the lower tracks. The activities of the school officials were said to establish a rigid system of ability grouping with no intent to ameliorate disparities and which were designed to give minority students no hope of ever advancing to the higher levels of achievement.

LARRY P. v. RILES
United States Court of Appeals
793 F.2d 969 (9th Cir. 1984)

POOLE, CIRCUIT JUDGE:

The State Superintendent of Public Instruction appeals a decision holding that IQ tests used by the California school system to place children into special classes for the educable mentally retarded (E.M.R.) violated federal statutes and the equal protection clauses of the United States and California Constitutions. The district court enjoined the use of non-validated IQ tests, and ordered the state to develop plans to eliminate the disproportionate enrollment of black children in E.M.R. classes. We affirm on the statutory grounds and reverse on the federal and state constitutional issues.

....

The district court permanently enjoined the defendants from utilizing any standardized IQ test for the identification of black E.M.R. children or their placement into E.M.R. classes, without securing prior approval of the court. The court ordered the defendants to direct each school district to re-evaluate every black child currently identified as an E.M.R. pupil without using standardized intelligence tests.

Further, the defendants were "ordered to monitor and eliminate disproportionate placement of black children in California's E.M.R. classes." The district court specifically ordered the defendants to obtain an annual report from each school district on the racial proportions of E.M.R. classes, to prepare a statewide report, and to direct each school district with a black E.M.R. pupil enrollment one standard deviation above the district rate of white E.M.R. pupil enrollment to prepare a plan to correct the imbalance. The defendants were ordered to bring to the attention of the court any district imbalance if the disparity in excess of one standard deviation existed after three years.

....

In the mid-60's California created programs for several categories of students with educational problems. The "educable mentally retarded" (E.M.R.) program was for schoolchildren of retarded intellectual development who are considered incapable of being educated through the regular educational program, but who could benefit from special educational facilities to make them economically useful and socially adjusted. The "trainable mentally retarded" (T.M.R.) category was for children with more severe retardation than educable mentally retarded....

The E.M.R. classes are for children who are considered "incapable of learning in the regular classes," and the E.M.R. curriculum "is not designed to help students learn the skills necessary to return to the regular instructional program." The E.M.R. classes are designed only to teach social adjustment and economic usefulness. "The [E.M.R.] classes are conceived of as 'dead-end classes,'" and a misplacement in E.M.R. causes a stigma and irreparable injury to the student.

From 1968 until trial in 1977, black children have been significantly overrepresented in E.M.R. classes. For example, in 1968-69, black children were about 9% of the state school population, yet accounted for 27% of the E.M.R. population.

"These apparent overenrollments could not be the result of chance. For example, there is less than a one in a million chance that the overenrollment of black children and the underenrollment of non-black children in the E.M.R. classes in 1976-77 would have resulted under a color-blind system." To explain this overenrollment, the defendants proffered a theory that there is a higher incidence of mental retardation among the black population. The district court found that this theory fails to account for the problem, because even "if it is assumed that black children have a 50 percent greater incidence of this type of mental retardation, there is still less than a one in 100,000 chance that the enrollment could be so skewed towards black children.... [Further,] the disproportionate E.M.R. enrollment of black children is not duplicated in the classes for the so-called 'trainable mentally retarded' children."

....

... In 1969 "the [State] Department [of Education (SDE)] proposed and the State Board of Education adopted, an addition to the California Administrative Code requiring that approved IQ tests be used as part of the E.M.R. placement process."... The district court found that the SDE moved extremely quickly and unsystematically to select those IQ tests for the mandatory list. The district court further found that the person who oversaw this selection was not an expert in IQ testing, and that the SDE did not expressly consider or investigate the problems concerning the disproportionate enrollment of minorities or the cultural bias of IQ tests despite its awareness of these problems. In addition, the SDE contacted no independent testing experts regarding the compilation of the list, and ignored requests from field personnel to take more time to select tests. The court concluded that "by relying on the most commonly used tests, [the Department] opted to perpetuate any discriminatory effects of those tests."

....

The district court found that the requirement of parental consent for E.M.R. placement does not overcome any deficiencies caused by bias in the placement process, because "that consent is rarely withheld, particularly by minorities, since the mystique of teacher authority and IQ scores tends to overwhelm parents."

Since the moratorium on IQ testing in 1975, the total percentage of black children in E.M.R. classes has not changed substantially. The district court, however, examined the data concerning new E.M.R. placements, which were made without IQ tests, and found that uncontradicted expert testimony showed that the four percent drop in the placement of black children into E.M.R. classes is not likely to have occurred by chance.

On the average, black children score fifteen points, or one standard deviation, below white children on standardized intelligence tests. Thus, utilizing the premoratorium criteria used by California for E.M.R. placement, "approximately

A. ABILITY GROUPING AND TRACKING

two percent of the total population fall below the two standard deviation cut-off, while about 15 percent of black children fall below that level."

The court found that "the tests were never designed to eliminate cultural biases against black children; it was assumed in effect that black children were less 'intelligent' than whites.... The tests were standardized and developed on an all-white population, and naturally their scientific validity is questionable for culturally different groups." Since the 1920's it has been generally known that black persons perform less well than white persons on the standardized intelligence tests. IQ tests had been standardized so that they yielded no bias because of sex. For example, when sample tests yielded different scores for boys and girls, the testing experts assumed such differences were unacceptable and modified the tests so that the curve in the standardization sample for boys and girls was identical. No such modifications on racial grounds has ever been tried by the testing companies. The district court noted that "the experts have from the beginning been willing to tolerate or even encourage tests that portray minorities, especially blacks, as intellectually inferior."

The district court analyzed and rejected the defendants' arguments advanced at trial that would explain the test score differences, which theorized that the lower scores for blacks were the result of actual, relevant differences between black and white children. The first argument is the genetic argument, which states that natural selection has resulted in black persons having a "gene pool" with lower intelligence than whites. The district court found the assumptions underlying the genetic argument highly suspect, and in any event that the defendants "were unwilling to admit any reliance on [this theory] for policy-making purposes."

The second theory is the socioeconomic argument, which theorizes that because of blacks' lower socioeconomic status, they are at a greater risk for all kinds of diseases due to malnutrition and poor medical attention. The district court found that the facts did not support this theory, since it did not explain why more severe mental retardation, *e.g.*, that consistent with placement into classes for the trainable mentally retarded children, does not occur in greater proportions among blacks and poorer sections of the population.

The district court found that the appellants failed to show that the IQ tests were validated for blacks with respect to the characteristics consistent with E.M.R. status and placement in E.M.R. classes, *i.e.*, that the defendants failed to establish that the IQ tests were accurate predictors that black elementary schoolchildren who scored less than 70 were indeed mentally retarded.

The district court found that alternatives to IQ testing for E.M.R. placement have been in effect since the state moratorium on IQ testing in 1975. These procedures, in which schools take more time and care with their assessments for E.M.R. classification and rely more on observational data, are less discriminatory than under the IQ-centered standard.

The district court found that defendants were guilty of intentional discrimination in the use of the IQ tests for E.M.R. placement. The court based this determination on the facts that the historical background of the IQ tests shows cultural bias; the adoption of the mandatory IQ testing requirement in 1969 was riddled with procedural and substantive irregularities, in which no outside sources were consulted by the State Board and the question of bias was never considered, even though the officials were well aware of the bias and disproportionate placement problems caused by the IQ tests (this problem having been addressed in a legislative resolution); the defendants' "complete failure to ascertain or attempt to ascertain the validity of the tests for minority children;" and the failure of the state to investigate and act on legal requirements to report significant variances in racial and ethnic composition in E.M.R. classes. The court noted that "the SDE's actions revealed a complacent acceptance of those disproportions, and that complacency was evidently built on easy but unsubstantiated assumptions about the incidence of retardation or at least low intelligence among black children."

....

VI. *Rehabilitation Act*

` ....

... [T]he Education For All Handicapped Children Act specifically requires that tests and evaluation procedures be free of racial and cultural bias. Both the EAHCA and the Rehabilitation Act require that the tests used for evaluation be validated for the specific purpose for which they are used, and that placement not be based upon a single criterion but on a variety of sources....

Appellant argues that the IQ tests were validated for the specific purposes for which they are used. Appellant analogizes to Title VII cases, notably *Washington v. Davis*, 426 U.S. 229 (1976), for the proposition that tests that are valid predictors of future performance can be utilized even if they have a discriminatory impact. There are two problems with appellant's proposition. First, the employment context is quite different from the educational situation. As the district court stated, "[i]f tests can predict that a person is going to be a poor employee, the employer can legitimately deny that person a job, but if tests suggest that a young child is probably going to be a poor student, the school cannot on that basis alone deny that child the opportunity to improve and develop the academic skills necessary to success in our society."... Assigning a student to an E.M.R. class denies that child the opportunity to develop the necessary academic skills, since E.M.R. classes do not teach academic subjects and are essentially a dead-end academic track. Second, and more important, the question for predictive validity in schools is not whether the standardized intelligence tests predict future school performance generally, as appellant argues, but whether the tests predict specifically that black elementary schoolchildren (as opposed to white elementary schoolchildren) who score at or below 70 on the IQ tests are mentally retarded and incapable of learning the regular school curriculum. In this case, the appellant would have to have shown that the tests are a proven tool to determine which students have characteristics consistent with E.M.R. status and

A. ABILITY GROUPING AND TRACKING

placement in E.M.R. classes, *i.e.*, "whose mental capabilities make it impossible for them to profit from the regular educational programs" even with remedial instruction. The regulations place the burden of showing such validation on the defendants.

The district court found that defendants failed to show that the tests were validated for placing black students with scores of 70 or less in E.M.R. classes. The district court noted that very few studies had examined the difference of IQ predictability for black as compared to white populations, and that those studies which had examined this problem found the tests much less valid for blacks than for whites. Further, the district court found that, even assuming the tests were validated for placement of white schoolchildren in E.M.R. classes, such validation for blacks had been generally assumed but not established. For example, the tests had been adjusted to eliminate differences in the average scores between the sexes, but such adjustment was never made to adjust the scores to be equal for black and white children. The court found that the reason for this was a basic assumption of a lower level of intelligence in blacks than in whites. The fact that early test developers indeed made this assumption is borne out by the literature and testimony at trial. In addition, no studies have been made, either by the defendants or the testing companies, to investigate the reasons for the one standard deviation difference in test scores between the races or to determine whether test redesign could eliminate any bias. There was expert testimony that a much larger percentage of black than white children had been misplaced in E.M.R. classes. Based on the evidence in the record, the district court finding that the appellant had not established validation of the test is not clearly erroneous.

The district court also found that the appellant did not utilize the variety of information required by statute and regulation to make E.M.R. placements, but relied primarily on the IQ test. This finding also is not clearly erroneous. Testimony showed that school records lacked sufficient evidence of educational history, adaptive behavior, social and cultural background or health history for these factors to have been utilized in placement.

....

VII. *Title VI*

Title VI of the Civil Rights Act of 1964, 42 U.S.C. § 2000d, provides that:

> No person in the United States shall, on the ground of race, color, or national origin, be excluded from participation in, be denied the benefits of, or be subjected to discrimination under any program or activity receiving federal financial assistance.

Regulations issued under this statutory mandate require that recipients of federal funding may not

> utilize criteria or methods of administration which have the effect of subjecting individuals to discrimination because of their race, color, or national origin, or have the effect of defeating or substantially impairing accomplishment of the objectives of the program as respect individuals of a particular race, color, or national origin. 34 C.F.R. 100.3(b)(2), originally adopted as 45 C.F.R. § 80.3(b)(2).

In *Guardians Association v. Civil Service Commission of City of New York*, 463 U.S. 582 (1983), a majority of the Court held that a violation of Title VI required proof of discriminatory intent. A different majority held, however, that proof of discriminatory effect suffices to establish liability when the suit is brought to enforce regulations issued pursuant to the statute rather than the statute itself.

The appellees relied on the regulations issued pursuant to Title VI. *Larry P., [by his Guardian ad Litem, Lucille P., et al. v. Wilson Riles, Superintendent of Public Instruction for the State of California, et al.]*, 495 F.Supp. at 965. The lower court held that the placement mechanisms for E.M.R. classes operated with a discriminatory effect in violation of the regulations and HEW's "interpretative guidelines". *Id.* In light of appellees' reliance on the regulations, we find it appropriate to apply a discriminatory effect analysis.

A prima facie case is demonstrated by showing that the tests have a discriminatory impact on black schoolchildren. *Board of Education of New York v. Harris*, 444 U.S. 130, 151 (1979). Once a plaintiff has established a prima facie case, the burden then shifts to the defendant to demonstrate that the requirement which caused the disproportionate impact was required by educational necessity....

Appellees clearly demonstrated the discriminatory impact of the challenged tests. It is undisputed that black children as a whole scored ten points lower than white children on the tests, and that the percentage of black children in E.M.R. classes was much higher than for whites. As discussed previously, these test scores were used to place black schoolchildren in E.M.R. classes and to remove them from the regular educational program. The burden therefore shifted to the defendants to demonstrate that the IQ tests which resulted in the disproportionate placement of black children were required by educational necessity.

Appellant argues first that E.M.R. classes are a benefit for, rather than adverse discrimination against, black children, implying that appellees did not even establish a prima facie case. However, the district court found that improper placement in E.M.R. classes has a definite adverse effect, in that E.M.R. classes are dead-end classes which de-emphasize academic skills and stigmatize children improperly placed in them. *Larry P.*, 495 F.Supp. at 941-42. Even appellant's witnesses testified that it would be extremely improper for a non-mentally retarded child to be placed in an E.M.R. classroom. Though the E.M.R. class might be a benefit for those students who are educable mentally retarded, it is clearly damaging to a non-retarded student to be placed in those classes. The district court's finding is not clearly erroneous, and thus appellees established a prima facie case of a Title VI violation based upon discriminatory effect.

Appellant next argues that even if the impact is adverse, it is not caused by discriminatory criteria (the IQ tests), but by other nondiscriminatory factors: (1) placement is based on a variety of information and evaluation tools that are non-discriminatory, and not solely on the IQ tests; (2) the tests are validated for black schoolchildren, and therefore accurately reflect mental retardation in black children; and (3) blacks have a higher percentage of mental retardation than whites.

Appellant's first two arguments have been discussed in VI, *supra*, and are unavailing. Appellant's third argument is that the disproportionate number of black children in E.M.R. classes is based on a higher incidence of mental retardation in blacks than in whites that is due to poor nutrition and poor medical care brought on by the lower socioeconomic status of blacks. This argument also fails. Appellees showed, and the district court made a finding, that "the overrepresentation of black children in E.M.R. classes cannot be explained away solely on the grounds of the generally lower socio-economic status of black children and their parents." *Id.* at 956. The district court specifically found the testimony of appellant's experts in support of this argument failed to explain why more severe mental retardation does not occur in greater proportions among the poorer sections of the population. In addition, there was testimony from other experts that poor nutrition or medical care during early life does not affect later performance on IQ scores, unless it is a severe malnutrition of a type that is rare in this country. This finding of the district court has not been shown to be clearly erroneous.

....

VIII. *Equal Protection Violation*

We have previously held that a violation of Title VI is sustained under the "discriminatory effect" analysis when dealing with the placement mechanisms for E.M.R. classes, partially in the light of the Supreme Court's decision in *Guardians Association*. We cannot, however, sustain the finding of a violation by Superintendent Riles of the equal protection clause of the fourteenth amendment on the theory that the pervasiveness of discriminatory effect can, without more, be equated with the discriminatory intent required by *Washington v. Davis*. Accordingly, we reject these facts of the trial court and reverse the conclusions that the Superintendent was guilty of intentional discrimination under the fourteenth amendment.

....

X. *Remedy*

The district court, in addition to enjoining the use of nonvalidated intelligence tests and requiring re-evaluation of every current black E.M.R. pupil, ordered the defendants to require every school district that had a racial disproportion in E.M.R. classes to devise a three-year remedial plan, and to bring to the court's attention any disparities that persist at the end of this period....

Appellant argues that, since appellees' challenge was solely to the use of IQ tests, the only remedy within the power of the court was the elimination of the tests. Appellees' prayer for relief, however, included a request for an injunction against defendants from retaining any black children presently enrolled in E.M.R. classes who are not mentally retarded, and to place these students in regular classrooms. Since the court found that black students had been improperly placed in E.M.R. classes, it is clearly within its power to correct this error.

Appellant next contends that the court's order to eliminate the disproportionate enrollment requires an impermissible quota. The district court's order, though, does not impose any quota on future E.M.R. placements. Even with respect to eliminating present disproportionate enrollment, the district court allowed an error leeway of one standard deviation. Further, the district court does not require that students properly placed in an E.M.R. class be removed. The court only required that any disproportion in excess of one standard deviation after three years be brought to the court's attention. If the school district can show, utilizing properly validated procedures complying with applicable statutes, that the black students in the E.M.R. classes properly belong there, there would be no need to eliminate the remaining disproportion. Since there are no fixed numerical requirements, the district court's order is not an impermissible quota. *See Regents of the University of California v. Bakke*, 438 U.S. 265 (1978).

....

PARENTS IN ACTION ON SPECIAL EDUCATION (PASE) v. HANNON

United States District Court
506 F. Supp. 831 (N.D. Ill., E.D. 1980)

GRADY, DISTRICT JUDGE:

This case presents the question whether standard intelligence tests administered by the Chicago Board of Education are culturally biased against black children. The action is brought on behalf of all black children who have been or will be placed in special classes for the educable mentally handicapped ("EMH") in the Chicago school system. The defendants are the Chicago Board of Education and its officers responsible for administration of the relevant programs. The named plaintiffs are two black children who were placed in EMH classes after achieving low scores on standard intelligence tests.

....

There are 483,209 children enrolled in the Chicago public school system. Of those, 299,590, or 62 per cent, are black. For the 1978-79 school year, 13,225 children were enrolled in EMH classes. Of these, 10,833, or 82 per cent, were black. Of the 106,581 white children enrolled in the system, 1,404 were attending EMH classes. Three and 7/10 per cent of all black students enrolled in the system are in EMH, whereas only 1.3 per cent of the white students are in EMH.

The EMH curriculum is designed for the child who cannot benefit from the regular curriculum. It is designed for children who learn slowly, who have short attention spans, slow reaction time and difficulty retaining material in both the short term and the long term. The curriculum also recognizes the difficulty an EMH child has in seeing similarities and differences, in learning by implication, in generalizing and in thinking abstractly. The curriculum thus involves much repetition and concrete teaching. Subjects are taught for short periods of time, in recognition of the children's short attention spans. The subject matter of the EMH courses is oriented toward socialization, language skills and vocational training. Academic subjects are taught, but on an elementary level and with the objective of helping the child become economically independent. The assumption of the EMH curriculum is that the child will not go on to college, and, in fact, children who graduate from EMH programs in the Chicago school system are given special diplomas which do not qualify them for college entrance.

....

The Assessment Process

Defendants' system for the identification and placement of mentally handicapped children, which is spelled out in manuals and printed regulations, involves several levels of investigation. It is important to understand that an IQ test is not the first level, nor is an IQ score the catalyst for the assessment process. The first level of investigation is the classroom. Unless the child is having difficulty with his studies in the classroom, the question of EMH placement will never arise and there is no occasion for an IQ test. Individually administered IQ tests of the kind involved in this case have never been given routinely in the Chicago school system, and the former practice of giving group-administered general intelligence tests to all students was discontinued some years ago.

If the classroom teacher has reason to believe the child has an educational handicap, the matter is taken up with the school principal. The teacher prepares a written report concerning the child, using a prescribed form. The principal then convenes a screening conference. The participants are the principal, the classroom teacher, a parent of the child and any other appropriate persons.

The screening committee makes a recommendation to the principal as to whether a case study should be requested for the child. If the principal determines on the basis of this recommendation that a case study is warranted, the matter is referred to the Special Education Bureau for the development of an appropriate case study program.

Various professional personnel then determine what areas of evaluation are appropriate for the child. On the basis of this determination, the child is examined by persons in the appropriate disciplines. This may involve a medical examination, a psychiatric examination, a psychological assessment or reference to a social worker or a speech therapist.

When the case study evaluation has been completed, the principal convenes a multidisciplinary staff conference. The members of this staff include a representative of the special education program, all of the professionals who evaluated the child, the school principal, and the parents of the child. The purpose of this multidisciplinary staff meeting is to determine whether the child should be placed in a special education program, and if so, what program it should be. The report of the staff conference is in writing. Each participant must sign it and indicate whether he or she concurs in the recommendation.

No child can be placed in an EMH class unless the placement is recommended by a psychologist who has evaluated the child. While the conference can decline an EMH placement recommended by the psychologist, it cannot make such a placement without the psychologist's recommendation.

If either the child or his parents on the one hand or the school officials on the other are dissatisfied with the decision, they may request further hearings on the matter. Placement of the child is stayed pending the hearing, which is conducted by an impartial hearing officer assigned from another school district by the State Department of Education. Ultimately, the matter is subject to administrative review in the courts of Illinois.

The evaluation and placement process is not carried out hastily. There are more children in need of placement than there are available seats in the EMH classrooms. Sometimes the decision is against placement even though the parent desires it. A motive for unnecessary placement is nonexistent, since the cost to the local system of administering the program far exceeds the state and federal aid received for it. The total cost of the Chicago special education program exceeds by 50 million dollars per year the state and federal funds received to support it.

Plaintiffs claim that, despite the various steps involved in EMH placement, the placement decision is really made primarily on the basis of the child's IQ score. They argue that the IQ score has a "hypnotic effect" on the participants in the multidisciplinary staffing, so that a child with an IQ of less than 80 stands a high chance of being put in an EMH class on that basis alone. Several of plaintiffs' witnesses so testified. Plaintiffs complain that social workers are not used often enough and that there is insufficient investigation of the child's family situation and his adaptive behavior outside the school environment.

....

In the circumstances of this case, where defendants have shown that IQ scores are only one factor which enters into the EMH assessment and that a low IQ score frequently does not result in such placement, I believe the burden of showing an absence of racial bias in the tests does not rest on the defendants.

....

It is unfortunately true that, despite what I believe are sincere efforts on the part of the defendants to avoid erroneous placements, some children are placed

A. ABILITY GROUPING AND TRACKING 949

in EMH classes who should not be there. Small but significant numbers of EMH students are constantly being moved out of EMH classes back into the regular curriculum. Some of these transfers are due to the fact that the child has progressed in the EMH class and is ready for a greater challenge. In other instances, however, the child is transferred because it is belatedly discovered that he should not have been there in the first place.

These erroneous placements have not been shown to be due to racial bias in the IQ tests. The situations of the two named plaintiffs illustrate this failure of proof. These two black children, Barbara B. and Angela J., were each evaluated as being mentally retarded and were transferred out of their regular classes to EMH classes. Each child was evaluated by a school psychologist and achieved a low score on one of the WISC tests or the Stanford-Binet.

....

The Larry P. Case

This is not a case of first impression. The exact issue of racial bias in the WISC, WISC-R and Stanford-Binet tests has been decided by Judge Robert F. Peckham of the United States District Court for the Northern District of California in the case of *Larry P., by his Guardian ad Litem, Lucille P., et al. v. Wilson Riles, Superintendent of Public Instruction for the State of California, et al.*, 495 F.Supp. 926 (1979). Plaintiffs rely upon that decision heavily, since Judge Peckham held that the tests are culturally biased against black children. Judge Peckham heard a number of the same witnesses who testified here, including Professors Kamin, Albee and Williams and Dr. Gloria Powell. He found their testimony persuasive. Judge Peckham's lengthy and scholarly opinion is largely devoted to the question of what legal consequences flow from a finding of racial bias in the tests. There is relatively little analysis of the threshold question of whether test bias in fact exists, and Judge Peckham even remarked that the cultural bias of the tests "... is hardly disputed in this litigation.... "I find reference to specific test items on only one page of the opinion....

As is by now obvious, the witnesses and the arguments which persuaded Judge Peckham have not persuaded me. Moreover, I believe the issue in the case cannot properly be analyzed without a detailed examination of the items on the tests. It is clear that this was not undertaken in the *Larry P.* case.

Conclusion

I have found one item on the Stanford-Binet and a total of eight items on the WISC and WISC-R to be culturally biased against black children, or at least sufficiently suspect that their use is in my view inappropriate. These few items do not render the tests unfair and would not significantly affect the score of an individual taking the test. The evidence fails to show that any additional test items are racially or culturally unfair or suspect.

I believe and today hold that the WISC, WISC-R and Stanford-Binet tests, when used in conjunction with the statutorily mandated "(other criteria) for determining an appropriate educational program for a child", do not discriminate against black children in the Chicago public schools. Defendants are complying with that statutory mandate.

Intelligent administration of the IQ tests by qualified psychologists, followed by the evaluation procedures defendants use, should rarely result in the misassessment of a child of normal intelligence as one who is mentally retarded. There is no evidence in this record that such misassessments as do occur are the result of racial bias in test items or in any other aspect of the assessment process currently in use in the Chicago public school system.

I find the issues in favor of the defendants and against the plaintiffs. The Clerk is directed to enter judgment for the defendants.

---

1. Refer back to *Hobson v. Hansen* where the court disapproved of the use of I.Q. tests for educational tracking. Drawing on the rationale in *Brown* relating to the development of a negative self-concept due to segregation, Judge Wright states that one ground for disallowing such tests is the "stigma" forced on African-American students of being intellectually inferior caused by a feeling of worthlessness and despair. Does the court in *Larry P.* draw on similar kinds of sociological findings to enjoin the use of I.Q. tests? Is the ruling of *Larry P.* broader than that of *Hobson* in that it disallows EMR placements for all students while *Hobson* targets only black students? What would be the constitutional arguments for white students claiming discrimination in I.Q. testing?

2. Is it the I.Q. test, the way it is administered, or the use of its results that the *Larry P.* court finds an irrational means of identifying children in need of EMR classes? Is it all three? Thomas F. Shea, in *An Educational Perspective of the Legality of Intelligence Testing and Ability Grouping*, 6 J. L. and Educ. 137 (1977), rendered an analysis of the district court decision which is applicable to that given by the Ninth Circuit. He suggests that while the original decision was correct, the reasoning used to determine the issues was improper. Shea distinguishes among genotype, phenotype, and operative intelligence and asserts why the court's failure to recognize this distinction led to a misunderstanding of the real issues in the case.

> Genotype intelligence is the innate genetic potential of an individual, while the phenotype intelligence is the result of environmental factors interacting with and modifying the genetic construct to produce the actual person....
>
> ....
>
> Operative intelligence is the actual behavior of the individual as measured by intelligence tests....
>
> ....
>
> ... The court clearly did not understand the distinction between genotype, phenotype and operative intelligence. Apparently the court conceived

intelligence as meaning genotype intelligence, and ignored the other two meanings.

The problem with having adopted a strictly genotype meaning of intelligence without considering the others is that the court then assumed that intelligence tests were being used to measure genotype intelligence. As has been stated earlier, intelligence tests are generally not good indicators of genotype intelligence. Indeed, the court found that the intelligence tests did not measure this type of intelligence satisfactorily. This should not have been the issue in the case. The issue should have been whether the method of intelligence testing used by the school satisfactorily measured genotype or phenotype intelligence, for it is on the basis of these two types of intelligence that children should be placed in ability grouping programs. Instead, the court jousted at windmills, probably because of the failure of counsel to understand and to raise the correct issues.

Since the decision of court was correct, it might seem that the fact that the reasoning process of the court was incorrect is of little direct importance, but this is not true. The court stated that the school could have ability grouping programs based on classification according to intelligence tests.[78] Since the court apparently adopted a genotype definition of intelligence, this means that the school can group children according to genotype intelligence but implies that the school cannot group children according to operative or phenotype intelligence. Translated, it means the schools can conduct continuing ability grouping but not compensatory ability grouping.

It follows that the children will be unable to receive compensatory education, enabling them to develop as high a phenotype intelligence as they have genotype intelligence. Instead, they will be placed in classrooms along with others who have high genotype intelligence, many of whom also have high phenotype intelligence. As a result, the high genotype-low phenotype children will not be able to compete effectively with the high genotype-high phenotype children.[80] The discouragement and feelings of failure that could result have been discussed earlier.

3. Why didn't the *Larry P.* court accept the argument that I.Q. tests should be used for classifying purposes since they are the best means available for assessing the potential of students? Are I.Q. tests more objective than teacher evaluations,

---

[78]The court stated that children may be grouped according to their ability to learn, implying phenotype intelligence, and the children could not be placed in educable mentally retarded classes based primarily on the I.Q. tests that were used. 343 F. Supp. at 1314-15.

[80]An innately unintelligent child cannot benefit from compensatory education to make him more intelligent. Of course, just because a court says that the children are innately unintelligent does not make them so and they may still benefit from compensatory education. However, the schools may be less ready, or feel less compelled to provide compensatory education where such a court opinion exists.

which have long been viewed as subject to influences of teacher prejudice, particularly in terms of cultural bias and social class? Note the following comment by David Kirp on the use of standardized tests for ability grouping:

> These tests are at least nominally objective, and do not directly depend on such concededly irrelevant factors as teacher prejudice and social class. They are also decent predictors of subsequent school success, better able to estimate performance than school grades or teacher recommendations or parental pressure. Aptitude tests do measure with considerable accuracy the adaptability of a given student to the school's expectations.

Kirp, *Schools as Sorters: The Constitutional and Policy Implications of Student Classification*, 121 U. Pa. L. Rev. 705, 755 (1973).*

4. If the educational structure is designed to teach students to perform white middle-class tasks, why isn't a "culturally biased test" measuring ability to perform these tasks an appropriate method of grouping students? Consider Kirp again:

> Tests do indicate something about a student's capacity to perform. They do not reveal, but merely remind, that non-middle class and minority children fare badly in schools as they are presently organized.
>
> To abolish the tests, while ignoring the fact that different students (and different classes of students) perform differently is about as sensible as the ancient Greek practice of slaying the messenger who brings bad news. In that light, it is sobering but instructive to recognize that minority children do poorly even on so-called culture-free tests, which supposedly do not reward middle-class bias. *Id.* at 758.

More recent law review literature counters the position of Professor Kirp. Connor and Vargyas in *The Legal Implications of Gender Bias in Standardized Testing*, 7 Berkeley Women's L.J. 13 (1992), cite the 1990 report of the National Commission on Testing and Public Policy which shows that test scores of minority students are significantly affected when the tests' content is oriented toward the dominant culture in society. *See also* Taylor and Lee, *Standardized Tests and African-American Children: Communication and Language Issues*, 38 Negro Educ. Rev. 67 (1987).

Did the arguments of Professor Kirp anticipate the decision in *Hannon*? Did the *Hannon* court find that there were questions on the aptitude tests that were culturally biased? If so, what was the judicial response?

Is it possible for an aptitude test to be culture-free? What of the background of the creator of the test? Will this influence any attempt at objectivity?

5. The *Hobson* court relies on socioeconomic data from expert testimony to determine that intelligence tests do not accurately reflect the possible achievement

---

*Copyright © 1973 by The University of Pennsylvania Law Review. Reprinted with permission.

of black students because of impoverished background. The *Larry P.* and *Hannon* cases contain similar arguments, but the courts arrived at differing results. Why did the *Larry P.* court dismiss the school board's argument of lower intelligence scores for blacks being due to poor neighborhoods and poor family educational backgrounds, while the *Hannon* court saw such variables as being very influential to test outcomes? Can the differences be explained by citing separate theories in each case? If one were to accept the idea that socioeconomic background is inextricably tied to test results, then why would the remedy be placing students in special classes? Would this kind of separation tend to perpetuate class differences? What are possible compensatory activities for addressing this problem other than EMR placement?

6. What is the actual prominence of intelligence test scores as to special education placement in *Larry P.* and *Hansen*? Would the court in *Larry P.* have been more likely to rule in favor of the school district had other criteria been used such as course exams or team teacher evaluation to make the placement?

7. Each of the cases discusses the responsibility for proving the veracity of the tests for ability sorting. Who has the burden and when, if ever, does it shift? Is disparate impact analysis part of the reasoning of each court? What of the Fourteenth Amendment arguments?

8. The charge of bias in testing, of course, is not limited to race. *See, e.g., Sharif v. New York State Educ. Dept.*, 709 F. Supp. 345 (S.D.N.Y. 1989), *supra* Chapter 4, where female plaintiffs prevailed under Title IX on the charge that SAT tests were culturally biased against females and resulted in gender discrimination as to the awarding of state scholarships in New York.

9. What if a school district engaged in ability grouping on the basis of language and national origin? Would this mean that a school district that had historically engaged in discrimination would have to overcome allegations of "intent" to segregate if the language group also had the dual status of minority group? Could the school system be accused of discrimination in ability grouping if the practices result in the language minority children being placed in low ability sections? *See Castaneda v. Pickard*, 648 F.2d 989 (5th Cir. 1981) (*Castaneda I*), *infra* and *Castaneda v. Pickard*, 781 F.2d 456 (5th Cir. 1986), (*Castaneda II*).

B. BILINGUAL EDUCATION

The "right" of students from non-English speaking homes to receive bilingual education in the public schools has become a major legal issue in recent years. During the nineteenth century, there were numerous bilingual programs in the United States, though often in immigrant-established private schools. After World War I, as exemplified by the statutes involved in the *Pierce* and *Meyer* decisions, *supra*, a hostile attitude toward immigrant groups and their languages resulted in requirements that all courses be taught in English, in both public and private schools. Note the Supreme Court's treatment of Section 1 of the statute in *Meyer*, *supra*, Chapter 2. Immigrants were to be Americanized by being forced to speak and learn only in English. In addition, little or no special English language training was provided in the public schools for children from non-English speaking homes.

The situation began to change in 1964 when a significant experiment in bilingual instruction began in Coral Gables, Florida, as a response to a sudden influx of Cuban students. In the next few years, other programs were started in Texas, California, Arizona, Massachusetts, New Mexico, New Jersey, and the Virgin Islands. *See* the Fleischmann Report at 33-34.

Federal agencies demonstrated attention to discrimination based on language and culture in the 1960's. The then United States Department of Health, Education and Welfare (HEW) provided guidelines requiring that "[s]chool districts [be] responsible for assuring that students of a particular race, color or national origin are not denied the opportunity to obtain the education generally obtained by other students in the system [and must] rectify the language deficiency of national origin minority children in order to open the instruction to those students [with] linguistic deficiencies." 33 Fed. Reg. 4955 (1968). HEW clarified the guidelines by requiring:

> Where ability to speak and understand the English language excludes national origin minority children from effective participation in the education program offered by a school district, the district must take affirmative steps to rectify the language deficiency in order to open its instructional program to these students. 33 Fed. Reg. 11595 (1970).

The import of this regulation was codified by Congress in the Equal Educational Opportunities Act of 1974 requiring affirmative action by a school district in overcoming language barriers that impede a student's equal participation. Support by the United States Office of Education for bilingual/bicultural education in some form has carried over from HEW where during the Bush administration the Secretary of the United States Office of Education advocated support for language instruction to meet deficiencies.

Both before and after the start of government action, case law has gone in divergent directions concerning the rights of language minorities and how such rights are to be enforced in school districts. The following case law features the ongoing debate.

LAU v. NICHOLS

Supreme Court of the United States
414 U.S. 563 (1974)

MR. JUSTICE DOUGLAS delivered the opinion of the Court:

The San Francisco California school system was integrated in 1971 as a result of a federal court decree, 339 F. Supp. 1315. *See Lee v. Johnson*, 404 U.S. 1215. The District Court found that there are 2,856 students of Chinese ancestry

B. BILINGUAL EDUCATION

in the school system who do not speak English. Of those who have that language deficiency, about 1,000 are given supplemental courses in the English language.[1] About 1,800 however do not receive that instruction.

This class suit brought by non-English speaking Chinese students against officials responsible for the operation of the San Francisco Unified School District seeks relief against the unequal educational opportunities which are alleged to violate the Fourteenth Amendment. No specific remedy is urged upon us. Teaching English to the students of Chinese ancestry who do not speak the language is one choice. Giving instructions to this group in Chinese is another. There may be others. Petitioner asks only that the Board of Education be directed to apply its expertise to the problem and rectify the situation.

The District Court denied relief. The Court of Appeals affirmed, holding that there was no violation of the Equal Protection Clause of the Fourteenth Amendment nor of § 601 of the Civil Rights Act of 1964, which excludes from participation in federal financial assistance, recipients of aid which discriminate against racial groups, 483 F.2d 791....

The Court of Appeals reasoned that "every student brings to the starting line of his educational career different advantages and disadvantages caused in part by social, economic and cultural background, created and continued completely apart from any contribution by the school system," 483 F.2d at 797. Yet in our view the case may not be so easily decided. This is a public school system of California and § 71 of the California Education Code states that "English shall be the basic language of instruction in all schools." That section permits a school district to determine "when and under what circumstances instruction may be given bilingually." That section also states as "the policy of the state" to insure "the mastery of English by all pupils in the schools." And bilingual instruction is authorized "to the extent that it does not interfere with the systematic, sequential, and regular instruction of all pupils in the English language."

Moreover § 8573 of the Education Code provides that no pupil shall receive a diploma of graduation from grade 12 who has not met the standards of proficiency in "English," as well as other prescribed subjects. Moreover by § 12101 of the Education Code children between the ages of six and 16 years are (with exceptions not material here) "subject to compulsory full-time education."

Under these state-imposed standards there is no equality of treatment merely by providing students with the same facilities, text books, teachers, and curriculum; for students who do not understand English are effectively foreclosed from any meaningful education.

---

[1] A report adopted by the Human Rights Commission of San Francisco and submitted to the Court by respondent after oral argument shows that, as of April 1973, there were 3,457 Chinese students in the school system who spoke little or no English. The document further showed 2,136 students enrolled in Chinese special instruction classes, but at least 429 of the enrollees were not Chinese but were included for ethnic balance. Thus, as of April, 1973, no more than 1,707 of the 3,457 Chinese students needing special English instruction were receiving it.

Basic English skills are at the very core of what these public schools teach. Imposition of a requirement that, before a child can effectively participate in the educational program, he must already have acquired those basic skills is to make a mockery of public education. We know that those who do not understand English are certain to find their classroom experiences wholly incomprehensible and in no way meaningful.

We do not reach the Equal Protection Clause argument which has been advanced but rely solely on § 601 of the Civil Rights Act of 1964, 42 U.S.C. § 2000d, to reverse the Court of Appeals.

That section bans discrimination based "on the ground of race, color, or national origin," in "any program or activity receiving Federal financial assistance." The school district involved in this litigation receives large amounts of federal financial assistance. HEW, which has authority to promulgate regulations prohibiting discrimination in federally assisted school systems, 42 U.S.C. § 2000d, in 1968 issued one guideline that "school systems are responsible for assuring that students of a particular race, color, or national origin are not denied the opportunity to obtain the education generally obtained by other students in the system." 33 CFR § 4955. In 1970 HEW made the guidelines more specific, requiring school districts that were federally funded "to rectify the language deficiency in order to open" the instruction to students who had "linguistic deficiencies," 35 Fed. Reg. 11595.

By § 602 of the Act HEW is authorized to issue rules, regulations, and orders to make sure that recipients of federal aid under its jurisdiction conduct any federal financed projects consistently with § 601. HEW's regulations specify, 45 CFR § 80.3(b)(1), that the recipients may not:

> Provide any service, financial aid, or other benefit to an individual which is different, or is provided in a different manner, from that provided to others under the program;
>
> ....
>
> Restrict an individual in any way in the enjoyment of any advantage or privilege enjoyed by others receiving any service, financial aid, or other benefit under the program; ....

Discrimination among students on account of race or national origin that is prohibited includes "discrimination in the availability or use of any academic ... or other facilities of the grantee or other recipient." *Id.* 80.5(b).

Discrimination is barred which has that effect even though no purposeful design is present: a recipient "may not ... utilize criteria or methods of administration which have the effect of subjecting individuals to discrimination" or has "the effect of defeating or substantially impairing accomplishment of the objectives of the program as respect individuals of a particular race, color, or national origin." *Id.* 80.3(b)(2).

It seems obvious that the Chinese-speaking minority receives less benefits than the English-speaking majority from respondents' school system which denies

B. BILINGUAL EDUCATION

them a meaningful opportunity to participate in the educational program — all earmarks of the discrimination banned by the Regulations. In 1970 HEW issued clarifying guidelines (35 Fed. Reg. 11595) which include the following:

> Where inability to speak and understand the English language excludes national origin-minority group children from effective participation in the educational program offered by a school district, the district must take affirmative steps to rectify the language deficiency in order to open its instructional program to these students.
>
> Any ability grouping or tracking system employed by the school system to deal with the special language skill needs of national origin-minority group children must be designed to meet such language skill needs as soon as possible and must not operate as an educational deadend or permanent track.

Respondent school district contractually agreed to "comply with title VI of the Civil Rights Act of 1964 ... and all requirements imposed by or pursuant to the Regulations" of HEW (45 CFR Pt. 80) which are "issued pursuant to that title ..." and also immediately to "take any measures necessary to effectuate this agreement." The Federal Government has power to fix the terms on which its money allotments to the States shall be disbursed....

We accordingly reverse the judgment of the Court of Appeals and remand the case for the fashioning of appropriate relief.

Reversed.

....

MR. JUSTICE BLACKMUN, with whom THE CHIEF JUSTICE joins, concurring in the result.

I join MR. JUSTICE STEWART'S opinion and thus I, too, concur in the result. Against the possibility that the Court's judgment may be interpreted too broadly, I stress the fact that the children with whom we are concerned here number about 1800. This is a very substantial group that is being deprived of any meaningful schooling because they cannot understand the language of the classroom. We may only guess as to why they have had no exposure to English in their preschool years. Earlier generations of American ethnic groups have overcome the language barrier by earnest parental endeavor or by the hard fact of being pushed out of the family or community nest and into the realities of broader experience.

I merely wish to make plain that when, in another case, we are concerned with a very few youngsters, or with just a single child who speaks only German or Polish or Spanish or any language other than English, I would not regard today's decision, or the separate concurrence, as conclusive upon the issue whether the statute and the guideline require the funded school district to provide special instruction. For me, numbers are at the heart of this case and my concurrence is to be understood accordingly.

CASTANEDA v. PICKARD

United States Court of Appeals
648 F.2d 989 (5th Cir. 1981)

RANDALL, CIRCUIT JUDGE:

Plaintiffs, Mexican-American children and their parents who represent a class of others similarly situated, instituted this action against the Raymondville, Texas Independent School District (RISD) alleging that the district engaged in policies and practices of racial discrimination against Mexican-Americans which deprived the plaintiffs and their class of rights secured to them by the Fourteenth Amendment and 42 U.S.C. § 1983 (1976), Title VI of the Civil Rights Act of 1964, 42 U.S.C. § 2000d *et seq.* (1976), and the Equal Educational Opportunities Act of 1974, 20 U.S.C. § 1701 *et seq.* (1976). Specifically, plaintiffs charged that the school district unlawfully discriminated against them by using an ability grouping system for classroom assignments which was based on racially and ethnically discriminatory criteria and resulted in impermissible classroom segregation, by discriminating against Mexican-Americans in the hiring and promotion of faculty and administrators, and by failing to implement adequate bilingual education to overcome the linguistic barriers that impede the plaintiffs' equal participation in the educational program of the district....

... [T]he district court entered judgment in favor of the defendants based upon its determination that the policies and practices of the RISD, in the areas of hiring and promotion of faculty and administrators, ability grouping of students, and bilingual education did not violate any constitutional or statutory rights of the plaintiff class. From that judgment, the plaintiffs have brought this appeal in which they claim the district court erred in numerous matters of fact and law.

....

Before we turn to consider the specific factual and legal issues raised by the plaintiffs in their appeal of the district court's judgment, we think it helpful to outline some of the basic demographic characteristics of the Raymondville school district. Raymondville is located in Willacy County, Texas. Willacy County is in the Rio Grande Valley; by conservative estimate based on census data, 77% of the population of the county is Mexican-American and almost all of the remaining 23% is "Anglo." The student population of RISD is about 85% Mexican-American.

Willacy County ranks 248th out of the 254 Texas counties in average family income. Approximately one-third of the population of Raymondville is composed of migrant farm workers. Three-quarters of the students in the Raymondville schools qualify for the federally funded free school lunch program. The district's assessed property valuation places it among the lowest ten percent of all Texas counties in its per capita student expenditures.

....

... [S]chool systems are free to employ ability grouping, even when such a policy has a segregative effect, so long, of course, as such a practice is genuinely

B. BILINGUAL EDUCATION

motivated by educational concerns and not discriminatory motives. However, in school districts which have a past history of unlawful discrimination and are in the process of converting to a unitary school system, or have only recently completed such a conversion, ability grouping is subject to much closer judicial scrutiny....

....

RISD currently operates a bilingual education program for all students in kindergarten through third grade. The language ability of each student entering the Raymondville program is assessed when he or she enters school. The language dominance test currently employed by the district is approved for this purpose by the TEA. The program of bilingual instruction offered students in the Raymondville schools has been developed with the assistance of expert consultants retained by the TEA and employs a group of materials developed by a regional educational center operated by the TEA. The articulated goal of the program is to teach students fundamental reading and writing skills in both Spanish and English by the end of third grade.

Although the program's emphasis is on the development of language skills in the two languages, other cognitive and substantive areas are addressed, *e.g.*, mathematics skills are taught and tested in Spanish as well as English during these years. All of the teachers employed in the bilingual education program of the district have met the minimum state requirements to teach bilingual classes. However, only about half of these teachers are Mexican-American and native Spanish speakers; the other teachers in the program have been certified to teach bilingual classes following a 100 hour course designed by TEA to give them a limited Spanish vocabulary (700 words) and an understanding of the theory and methods employed in bilingual programs. Teachers in the bilingual program are assisted by classroom aides, most of whom are fluent in Spanish.

RISD does not offer a formal program of bilingual education after the third grade. In grades 4 and 5, although classroom instruction is only in English, Spanish speaking teacher aides are used to assist students having language difficulties which may impair their ability to participate in classroom activities. For students in grades 4-12 having limited English proficiency or academic deficiencies in other areas, the RISD provides assistance in the form of a learning center operated at each school. This center provides a diagnostic/prescriptive program in which students' particular academic deficiencies, whether in language or other areas, are identified and addressed by special remedial programs. Approximately 1,000 of the district's students, almost one-third of the total enrollment, receive special assistance through small classes provided by these learning centers. The district also makes English as a Second Language classes and special tutoring in English available to all students in all grades; this program is especially designed to meet the needs of limited English speaking students who move into the district in grades above 3.

Plaintiffs claim that the bilingual education and language remediation programs offered by the Raymondville schools are educationally deficient and unsound and that RISD's failure to alter and improve these programs places the district in violation of Title VI and the Equal Educational Opportunities Act. The plaintiffs claim that the RISD programs fail to comport with the requirements of the "*Lau* Guidelines" promulgated in 1975 by the Department of Health, Education and Welfare. Specifically, plaintiffs contend that the articulated goal of the Raymondville program to teach limited English speaking children to read and write in both English and Spanish at grade level is improper because it overemphasizes the development of English language skills to the detriment of the child's overall cognitive development. Under the *Lau* Guidelines, plaintiffs argue, "pressing English on the child is not the first goal of language remediation." Plaintiffs criticize not only the premise and purpose of the RISD language programs but also particular aspects of the implementation of the program. Specifically, plaintiffs take issue with the tests the district employs to identify and assess limited English speaking children and the qualifications of the teachers and staff involved in the district's language remediation program. Plaintiffs contend that in both of these areas RISD falls short of standards established by the *Lau* Guidelines and thus has fallen out of compliance with Title VI and the EEOA.

We agree with the district court that RISD's program does not violate Title VI. Much of the plaintiffs' argument with regard to Title VI is based upon the premise that the *Lau* Guidelines are administrative regulations applicable to the RISD and thus should be given great weight by us in assessing the legal sufficiency of the district's programs. This premise is, however, flawed....

. . . .

Following the Supreme Court's decision in *Lau*, HEW developed the *Lau* Guidelines as a suggested compliance plan for school districts which, as a result of *Lau*, were in violation of Title VI because they failed to provide any English language assistance to students having limited English proficiency. Clearly, Raymondville is not culpable of such a failure. Under these circumstances, the fact that Raymondville provides (and long has provided) a program of language remediation which differs in some respects from these guidelines is, as the opinion of the Reviewing Authority for the OCR noted, "not in itself sufficient to rule that program unlawful in the first instance."

. . . .

We must confess to serious doubts not only about the relevance of the *Lau* Guidelines to this case but also about the continuing vitality of the rationale of the Supreme Court's opinion in *Lau v. Nichols* which gave rise to those guidelines. *Lau* was written prior to *Washington v. Davis*, in which the Court held that a discriminatory purpose, and not simply a disparate impact, must be shown to establish a violation of the Equal Protection Clause, and *University of California Regents v. Bakke*, in which, as we have already noted, a majority of the court interpreted Title VI to be coextensive with the Equal Protection Clause. Justice Brennan's opinion (in which Justices White, Marshall and Blackmun joined) in *Bakke* explicitly acknowledged that these developments raised serious questions about the vitality of *Lau*.

B. BILINGUAL EDUCATION

....

Although the Supreme Court in *Bakke* did not expressly overrule *Lau*, as we noted above, we understand the clear import of *Bakke* to be that Title VI, like the Equal Protection Clause, is violated only by conduct animated by an intent to discriminate and not by conduct which, although benignly motivated, has a differential impact on persons of different races. Whatever the deficiencies of the RISD's program of language remediation may be, we do not think it can seriously be asserted that this program was intended or designed to discriminate against Mexican-American students in the district....

Plaintiffs, however, do not base their legal challenge to the district's language program solely on Title VI. They also claim that the district's current program is unlawful under § 1703(f) of the EEOA which makes it unlawful for an educational agency to fail to take "appropriate action to overcome language barriers that impede equal participation by its students in its instructional programs." As we noted above in dissecting the meaning of § 1703(d) of the EEOA, we have very little legislative history from which to glean the Congressional intent behind the EEOA's provisions. Thus, as we did in examining § 1703(d), we shall adhere closely to the plain language of § 1703(f) in defining the meaning of this provision. Unlike subsections (a) and (e) of § 1703, § 1703(f) does not contain language that explicitly incorporates an intent requirement nor, like § 1703(d) which we construed above, does this subsection employ words such as "discrimination" whose legal definition has been understood to incorporate an intent requirement. Although we have not previously explicitly considered this question, in *Morales v. Shannon*, we assumed that the failure of an educational agency to undertake appropriate efforts to remedy the language deficiencies of its students, regardless of whether such a failure is motivated by an intent to discriminate against those students, would violate § 1703(f) and we think that such a construction of that subsection is most consistent with the plain meaning of the language employed in § 1703(f). Thus, although serious doubts exist about the continuing vitality of *Lau v. Nichols* as a judicial interpretation of the requirements of Title VI or the Fourteenth Amendment, the essential holding of *Lau*, *i.e.*, that schools are not free to ignore the need of limited English speaking children for language assistance to enable them to participate in the instructional program of the district, has now been legislated by Congress, acting pursuant to its power to enforce the Fourteenth Amendment, in § 1703(f). The difficult question presented by plaintiffs' challenge to the current language remediation programs in RISD is really whether Congress in enacting § 1703(f) intended to go beyond the essential requirement of *Lau*, that the schools do something, and impose, through the use of the term "appropriate action" a more specific obligation on state and local educational authorities.

....

We note that although Congress enacted both the Bilingual Education Act and the EEOA as part of the 1974 amendments to the Elementary and Secondary Education Act, Congress, in describing the remedial obligation it sought to impose on the states in the EEOA, did not specify that a state must provide a program of "bilingual education" to all limited English speaking students. We think Congress' use of the less specific term, "appropriate action," rather than "bilingual education," indicates that Congress intended to leave state and local educational authorities a substantial amount of latitude in choosing the programs and techniques they would use to meet their obligations under the EEOA. However, by including an obligation to address the problem of language barriers in the EEOA and granting limited English speaking students a private right of action to enforce that obligation in § 1706, Congress also must have intended to insure that schools made a genuine and good faith effort, consistent with local circumstances and resources, to remedy the language deficiencies of their students and deliberately placed on federal courts the difficult responsibility of determining whether that obligation had been met.

Congress has provided us with almost no guidance, in the form of text or legislative history, to assist us in determining whether a school district's language remediation efforts are "appropriate." Thus we find ourselves confronted with a type of task which federal courts are ill-equipped to perform and which we are often criticized for undertaking prescribing substantive standards and policies for institutions whose governance is properly reserved to other levels and branches of our government (*i.e.*, state and local educational agencies) which are better able to assimilate and assess the knowledge of professionals in the field. Confronted, reluctantly, with this type of task in this case, we have attempted to devise a mode of analysis which will permit ourselves and the lower courts to fulfill the responsibility Congress has assigned to us without unduly substituting our educational values and theories for the educational and political decisions reserved to state or local school authorities or the expert knowledge of educators.

In a case such as this one in which the appropriateness of a particular school system's language remediation program is challenged ... we believe that the responsibility of the federal court is threefold. First, the court must examine carefully the evidence the record contains concerning the soundness of the educational theory or principles upon which the challenged program is based. This, of course, is not to be done with any eye toward discerning the relative merits of sound but competing bodies of expert educational opinion, for choosing between sound but competing theories is properly left to the educators and public officials charged with responsibility for directing the educational policy of a school system. The state of the art in the area of language remediation may well be such that respected authorities legitimately differ as to the best type of educational program for limited English speaking students and we do not believe that Congress in enacting § 1703(f) intended to make the resolution of these differences the province of federal courts. The court's responsibility, insofar as educational theory is concerned, is only to ascertain that a school system is pursing a program informed by an educational theory recognized as sound by some experts in the field or, at least, deemed a legitimate experimental strategy.

B. BILINGUAL EDUCATION

The court's second inquiry would be whether the programs and practices actually used by a school system are reasonably calculated to implement effectively the educational theory adopted by the school. We do not believe that it may fairly be said that a school system is taking appropriate action to remedy language barriers if, despite the adoption of a promising theory, the system fails to follow through with practices, resources and personnel necessary to transform the theory into reality.

Finally, a determination that a school system has adopted a sound program for alleviating the language barriers impeding the educational progress of some of its students and made bona fide efforts to make the program work does not necessarily end the court's inquiry into the appropriateness of the system's actions. If a school's program, although premised on a legitimate educational theory and implemented through the use of adequate techniques, fails, after being employed for a period of time sufficient to give the plan a legitimate trial, to produce results indicating that the language barriers confronting students are actually being overcome, that program may, at that point, no longer constitute appropriate action as far as that school is concerned. We do not believe Congress intended that under § 1703(f) a school would be free to persist in a policy which, although it may have been "appropriate" when adopted, in the sense that there were sound expectations for success and bona fide efforts to make the program work, has, in practice, proved a failure.

. . . .

In this case, the plaintiffs' challenge to the appropriateness of the RISD's efforts to overcome the language barriers of its students does not rest on an argument over the soundness of the educational policy being pursued by the district, but rather on the alleged inadequacy of the program actually implemented by the district. Plaintiffs contend that in three areas essential to the adequacy of a bilingual program curriculum, staff and testing Raymondville falls short. Plaintiffs contend that although RISD purports to offer a bilingual education program in grades K-3, the district's curriculum actually overemphasizes the development of reading and writing skills in English to the detriment of education in other areas such as mathematics and science, and that, as a result, children whose first language was Spanish emerge from the bilingual education program behind their classmates in these other areas....

Even if we accept this allegation as true, however, we do not think that a school system which provides limited English speaking students with a curriculum, during the early part of their school career, which has, as its primary objective, the development of literacy in English, has failed to fulfill its obligations under § 1703(f), even if the result of such a program is an interim sacrifice of learning in other areas during this period. The language of § 1703(f) speaks in terms of taking action "to overcome language barriers" which impede the "equal participation" of limited English speaking children in the regular instructional program. We believe the statute clearly contemplates that provision of a program placing primary emphasis on the development of English language skills would constitute "appropriate action."

Limited English speaking students entering school face a task not encountered by students who are already proficient in English. Since the number of hours in any school day is limited, some of the time which limited English speaking children will spend learning English may be devoted to other subjects by students who entered school already proficient in English. In order to be able ultimately to participate equally with the students who entered school with an English language background, the limited English speaking students will have to acquire both English language proficiency comparable to that of the average native speakers and to recoup any deficits which they may incur in other areas of the curriculum as a result of this extra expenditure of time on English language development. We understand § 1703(f) to impose on educational agencies not only an obligation to overcome the direct obstacle to learning which the language barrier itself poses, but also a duty to provide limited English speaking ability students with assistance in other areas of the curriculum where their equal participation may be impaired because of deficits incurred during participation in an agency's language remediation program. If no remedial action is taken to overcome the academic deficits that limited English speaking students may incur during a period of intensive language training, then the language barrier, although itself remedied, might, nevertheless, pose a lingering and indirect impediment to these students' equal participation in the regular instructional program. We also believe, however, that § 1703(f) leaves schools free to determine whether they wish to discharge these obligations simultaneously, by implementing a program designed to keep limited English speaking students at grade level in other areas of the curriculum by providing instruction in their native language at the same time that an English language development effort is pursued, or to address these problems in sequence, by focusing first on the development of English language skills and then later providing students with compensatory and supplemental education to remedy deficiencies in other areas which they may develop during this period. In short, § 1703(f) leaves schools free to determine the sequence and manner in which limited English speaking students tackle this dual challenge so long as the schools design programs which are reasonably calculated to enable these students to attain parity of participation in the standard instructional program within a reasonable length of time after they enter the school system. Therefore, we disagree with plaintiffs' assertion that a school system which chooses to focus first on English language development and later provides students with an intensive remedial program to help them catch up in other areas of the curriculum has failed to fulfill its statutory obligation under § 1703(f).

... [W]e are more troubled by the plaintiffs' allegations that the district's implementation of the program has been severely deficient in the area of preparing its teachers for bilingual education. Although the plaintiffs raised this issue below and introduced evidence addressed to it, the district court made no

B. BILINGUAL EDUCATION

findings on the adequacy of the teacher training program employed by RISD. We begin by noting that any school district that chooses to fulfill its obligations under § 1703 by means of a bilingual education program has undertaken a responsibility to provide teachers who are able competently to teach in such a program. The record in this case indicates that some of the teachers employed in the RISD bilingual program have a very limited command of Spanish, despite completion of the TEA course....

The record in this case thus raises serious doubts about the actual language competency of the teachers employed in bilingual classrooms by RISD and about the degree to which the district is making a genuine effort to assess and improve the qualifications of its bilingual teachers. As in any educational program, qualified teachers are a critical component of the success of a language remediation program. A bilingual education program, however sound in theory, is clearly unlikely to have a significant impact on the language barriers confronting limited English speaking school children, if the teachers charged with day-to-day responsibility for educating these children are termed "qualified" despite the fact that they operate in the classroom under their own unremedied language disability. The use of Spanish speaking aides may be an appropriate interim measure, but such aides cannot, RISD acknowledges, take the place of qualified bilingual teachers. The record in this case strongly suggests that the efforts RISD has made to overcome the language barriers confronting many of the teachers assigned to the bilingual education program are inadequate. On this record, we think a finding to the contrary would be clearly erroneous. Nor can there be any question that deficiencies in the in-service training of teachers for bilingual classrooms seriously undermine the promise of the district's bilingual education program. Until deficiencies in this aspect of the program's implementation are remedied, we do not think RISD can be deemed to be taking "appropriate action" to overcome the language disabilities of its students. Although we certainly hope and expect that RISD will attempt to hire teachers who are already qualified to teach in a bilingual classroom as positions become available, we are by no means suggesting that teachers already employed by the district should be replaced or that the district is limited to hiring only teachers who are already qualified to teach in a bilingual program. We are requiring only that RISD undertake further measures to improve the ability of any teacher, whether now or hereafter employed, to teach effectively in a bilingual classroom.

....

The third specific area in which plaintiffs claim that RISD programs are seriously deficient is in the testing and evaluation of students having limited English proficiency....

... Plaintiffs, contend, RISD apparently does not deny, and we agree that proper testing and evaluation is essential in determining the progress of students involved in a bilingual program and ultimately, in evaluating the program itself. In their brief, plaintiffs contend that RISD's testing program is inadequate because the limited English speaking students in the bilingual program are not tested in their own language to determine their progress in areas of the curriculum other than English language literacy skills. Although during the bilingual program Spanish speaking students receive much of their instruction in these other areas in the Spanish language, the achievement level of these students is tested, in part, by the use of standardized English language achievement tests. No standardized Spanish language tests are used. Plaintiffs contend that testing the achievement levels of children, who are admittedly not yet literate in English and are receiving instruction in another language, through the use of an English language achievement test, does not meaningfully assess their achievement, any more than it does their ability, a contention with which we can scarcely disagree.

Valid testing of students' progress in these areas is, we believe, essential to measure the adequacy of a language remediation program. The progress of limited English speaking students in these other areas of the curriculum must be measured by means of a standardized test in their own language because no other device is adequate to determine their progress vis-à-vis that of their English speaking counterparts. Although, as we acknowledged above, we do not believe these students must necessarily be continuously maintained at grade level in other areas of instruction during the period in which they are mastering English, these students cannot be permitted to incur irreparable academic deficits during this period. Only by measuring the actual progress of students in these areas during the language remediation program can it be determined that such irremediable deficiencies are not being incurred....

Finally plaintiffs contend that test results indicate that the limited English speaking students who participate in the district's bilingual education program do not reach a parity of achievement with students who entered school already proficient in English at any time throughout the elementary grades and that since the district's language program has failed to establish such parity, it cannot be deemed "appropriate action" under § 1703(f). Although this question was raised at the district court level, no findings were made on this claim. While under some circumstances it may be proper for a court to examine the achievement scores of students involved in a language remediation program in order to determine whether this group appears on the whole to attain parity of participation with other students, we do not think that such an inquiry is, as yet, appropriate with regard to RISD. Such an inquiry may become proper after the inadequacies in the implementation of the RISD's program, which we have identified, have been corrected and the program has operated with the benefit of these improvements for a period of time sufficient to expect meaningful results.

To summarize, we affirm the district court's conclusion that RISD's bilingual education program is not violative of Title VI; however, we reverse the district court's judgment with respect to the other issues presented on appeal and we remand these issues for further proceedings not inconsistent with this opinion....

B. BILINGUAL EDUCATION

1. How is a court to choose among these and other possible alternatives? Should the court's order depend upon the relief requested by the petitioning group; upon pedagogical views of the effectiveness of particular techniques; upon the presence of de jure or de facto segregation; upon the assumption of government agency supervision and review in the course of providing funds to the schools involved; or upon a statutory rather than a constitutional basis? Would the implementation of a more extensive ESL program by San Francisco have satisfied the Supreme Court's opinion in *Lau*? Does the answer to this question depend on the view of the federal agency responsible for discrimination in education?

2. If the separation approaches are followed, would the resulting segregation of minority students be desirable or even permissible? Consider again in this regard, *Hobson v. Hansen, supra*, where ability grouping was found to be a denial of equal educational opportunity. Would it make a difference if the bilingual education program was completely voluntary and of limited duration?

3. Even if one assumes the desirability of non-English speaking students learning English, is it clear that bilingual instruction is the only means of accomplishing this? What of the experience of other ethnic groups where, at least according to folklore, the first generation was simply placed into English-speaking schools and learned by the "sink or swim" method? Is it clear that this does not work as a method of teaching English? Is Justice Blackmun referring to this phenomenon in his concurring opinion in *Lau*?

It may be argued that this method may have "worked" for earlier immigrant groups but at the expense of the destruction of their original ethnic culture. If this is the argument for bilingual education, what is its constitutional foundation? Is it a right to "equal educational opportunity"? Can it be argued that language or cultural preservation for non-English speaking citizens is an element of "equal educational opportunity"? Could such a constitutional right be limited to language groups as distinguished from racial, ethnic, or, indeed, religious groups? Consider carefully the goals of the different bilingual programs and directives contained in this section. Are they all the same? If not, how do they differ? Is the argument for cultural preservation ultimately similar to the one for community control?

4. *Lau* aligns discrimination on the basis of national origin with language indicating that if one is proscribed then so is the other. The court allowed that some affirmative action must be taken by school districts to arrest deficiencies caused by such prejudice. However, was the Court remiss in not establishing a bright line for what it called "effective or equal participation?" Subsequent courts have grappled with this question with differing results.

In *Serna v. Portales Municipal Schs.*, 499 F.2d 1147 (10th Cir. 1974), a bilingual/bicultural education program was ordered where the court was said, based on *Lau*, to have the legal prerogative to order such equitable relief if the goal is to foster equal educational opportunity for all students. However, the same court one year later ruled that there is no constitutional right to bilingual/bicultural education. The court stated that this was an option for school districts to remedy past discrimination in language, but on the facts of this case, was no substitute for remedies addressing desegregation. *Keyes v. School Dist. No. 1, Denver, Colo.*, 521 F.2d 465 (10th Cir. 1975).

The Ninth Circuit has also held that no constitutional or federal statutory right exists to bilingual/bicultural education or instructors with expertise in that area. The court based its decision on an analysis of the Equal Protection clause, Title VI of the Civil Rights Act of 1964, and the Equal Educational Opportunity Act of 1974. *Guadalupe Org., Inc. v. Tempe Elem. Sch. Dist. No. 3*, 587 F.2d 1022 (9th Cir. 1978).

5. The Supreme Court decision in *Lau* overturned a decision of the Ninth Circuit Court of Appeals, *Lau v. Nichols*, 483 F.2d 791 (9th Cir. 1973) (the same court that decided *Tempe* above). Justice Stewart, in his concurring opinion in *Lau* speaks to the nation's "changing social and linguistical patterns," a multicultural phenomenon to which the school district had failed to respond. Did this statement start, or better said, contribute to the assimilation versus pluralism debate among educators? What of such positions in the court? Consider the following from the decision in *Tempe*:

> Our analysis returns us to the foundations of organized society as manifested by the nation-state. We commence by recognizing that the existence of the nation-state rests ultimately on the consent of the people. The scope of this fundamental compact may be extensive or limited. Its breadth fixes the effective limits of government by the nation-state.
>
> Linguistic and cultural diversity within the nation-state, whatever may be its advantages from time to time, can restrict the scope of the fundamental compact. Diversity limits unity. Effective action by the nation-state rises to its peak of strength only when it is in response to aspirations unreservedly shared by each constituent culture and language group. As affection which a culture or group bears toward a particular aspiration abates, and as the scope of sharing diminishes, the strength of the nation-state's government wanes.
>
> Syncretism retards, and sometimes even reverses, the shrinkage of the compact caused by linguistic and cultural diversity. But it would be incautious to strengthen diversity in language and culture repeatedly trusting only in syncretic processes to preserve the social compact. In the language of eighteenth century philosophy, the century in which our Constitution was written, the social compact depends on the force of benevolence which springs naturally from the hearts of all men but which attenuates as it crosses linguistic and cultural lines. Multiple linguistic and cultural centers impede both the egress of each center's own and the ingress of all others. Benevolence, moreover, spends much of its force within each center and, to reinforce affection toward insiders, hostility toward outsiders develops.

The fundamental nature of these tendencies makes clear that their scope varies from generation to generation and is fixed by the political process in its highest sense. The Constitution, aside from guaranteeing to individuals certain basic rights, privileges, powers and immunities, does not speak to such matters; it merely evidences a compact whose scope and strength cannot be mandated by the courts but must be determined by the people acting upon the urging of their hearts. The decision of the [school district] to provide a predominantly monocultural and monolingual educational system was a rational response to a quintessentially "legitimate" state interest. 587 F.2d at 1027.

The court allows that the decision for such a judgment is political, and best left to the will of the people. Is this a new conception of the purpose of individual rights in the United States Constitution? Does the issue turn on whether students have a right to education in the first place? If such a right exists because states have chosen to create a system of public education, is it restricted to "monocultural and monolingual education?" If not, is a bilingual or multicultural education only so constitutionally required until a student becomes proficient in the majority culture or the predominant language? Is this what the courts mean by "equal educational opportunity"?

The court's analysis suggests that unity within the nation can only be achieved without diversity. Can a reverse argument be made that such unity is increased with diversity because society develops structures that include and are consistent with other cultures, behaviors and learning styles? Could it also be said that national unity is enhanced when students are encouraged to develop positive attitudes toward different racial, ethnic, religious, and linguistic groups?

James A. Banks, the noted multicultural educator in Teaching Strategies for Ethnic Studies (1991),* fosters a view inapposite to Judge Sneed in *Tempe* that diversity, in fact, integrates well with national unity:

> Ethnic and cultural diversity is ... an opportunity. It can enrich a society by providing novel ways to view events and situations, to solve problems, and to view our relationship with the environment and its creatures.
>
> ....
>
> The challenge to Western societies and their schools is to try to shape a modernized, national culture that has selected aspects of traditional cultures co-existing in some kind of delicate balance with a modernized, postindustrial society. In the past, in their singular quest for modernity and a technocratic society, the Western nation-states tried to eradicate traditional cultures and thus alienated individuals and groups from their first cultures and linguistic origins. This approach to shaping a unified nation-state has created anomie and alienation and has deprived individuals and groups of

---

*Copyright © 1991 by James A. Banks. Reprinted with permission.

some of the most important ways in which people satisfy their needs for symbolic meaning and community. It has also resulted in the political and cultural oppression of some racial and ethnic groups within society and has consequently caused them to focus on their particular needs and goals rather than on the overarching goals of the nation-state. Western nation-states will be able to create societies with overarching goals that are shared by diverse groups only when these groups feel that they have a real stake and place in their nation-states and that their states mirror their own concerns, values and ethos. A multicultural curriculum, which reflects the cultures, values and goals of the groups within a nation, will contribute significantly to the development of a healthy nationalism and national identity. Banks, at 7-8.

6. The *Tempe* court also features a footnote discussing the *Lau* decision and its possible modification by the later decided case of *Regents of the Univ. of California v. Bakke*, 438 U.S. 265 (1978). *Lau* was the Supreme Court's first major Title VI case and under this federal statute the Court held that school districts cannot give preferential treatment to some students simply because they represent the English-speaking majority. However, *Bakke* stated that: "In view of the clear legislative intent, Title VI must be held to proscribe only those racial classifications that would violate the Equal Protection Clause or the Fifth Amendment." *Bakke* at 281. Does *Bakke* bring into question the continuing vitality of *Lau* inasmuch as the *Lau* Court limited its decision to a Title VI analysis?

7. *Castaneda*, decided by the Fifth Circuit, follows *Tempe* in questioning the continued vitality of *Lau*. Does the court give a sound rationale for insisting that Title VI, like the Equal Protection Clause, require a demonstration of intentional discrimination as well as disparate impact?

8. *Castaneda* also relates that schools have much discretion in choosing the kind of English proficiency program to implement: "[S]chools [are] free to determine the sequence and manner in which limited English speaking students tackle this challenge so long as the schools design programs which are reasonably calculated to enable these students to attain parity of participation in the standard instructional program within a reasonable length of time after they enter the school system." *Castaneda*, at 1011. Are there no guidelines for school officials in this area? What of statutory language requiring school systems to take appropriate action to overcome language deficiencies? Can Title VI be interpreted to require the court to evaluate the programs, methods, and techniques used in the schools for these purposes? Is it proper for the courts to endeavor into such areas of school board control?

9. The court permits a program that is "bridge-building" in its approach, *i.e.*, developed so that students can move from the home language environment to proficiency in English. Suppose little movement takes place with the school board plan. What is the remedy for the students and their parents if all programs are left to the discretion of school officials? Does it matter that the court has stated

B. BILINGUAL EDUCATION 971

that the appropriateness of any school program here must be based on recognized educational theory and principles, designed to implement these theories and principles and demonstrable of result?

10. The debate over discrimination in language, culture, and the schools has also been carried on in research. *See* Lawson, *The Child Seated Next to Me: The Continuing Quest for Equal Educational Opportunity*, 16 T. Marshall L. Rev. 35 (1990); Note, *Teaching Inequality: The Problem of Public School Tracking*, 102 Harv. L. Rev. 1318 (1989); Moran, *The Politics of Discretion: Federal Intervention in Bilingual Education*, 73 Cal. L. Rev. 1249 (1988).

11. Does *Lau* or *Castaneda* apply to African-American children who speak and understand "Ebonics" or the black-English dialect? Does the question of *Lau's* application to this situation depend on the view of federal education agencies?

MARTIN LUTHER KING JR. ELEMENTARY SCHOOL CHILDREN v. ANN ARBOR SCHOOL DISTRICT

United States District Court
473 F. Supp. 1371 (E.D. Mich. 1979)

Memorandum Opinion and Order

JOINER, DISTRICT JUDGE: — The issue before this court is whether the defendant School Board has violated Section 1703(f) of Title 20 of the United States Code as its actions relate to the 11 black children who are plaintiffs in this case and who are students in the Martin Luther King Junior Elementary School.... It is alleged that the children speak a version of "black English," "black vernacular" or "black dialect" as their home and community language that impedes their equal participation in the instructional programs, and that the school has not taken appropriate action to overcome the barrier.

....

The problem in this case revolves around the ability of the school system, King School in particular, to teach the reading of standard English to children who, it is alleged, speak "black English" as a matter of course at home and in their home community (the Green Road Housing Development).

This case is not an effort on the part of the plaintiffs to require that they be taught "black English" or that their instruction throughout their schooling be in "black English," or that a dual language program be provided. In this respect, it is different from the facts in *Cintron v. Brentwood Union Free School District*, 455 F. Supp. 57 (E.D.N.Y. 1978). It is a straightforward effort to require the court to intervene on the children's behalf to require the defendant School District Board to take appropriate action to teach them to read in the standard English of the school, the commercial world, the arts, science and professions. This action is a cry for judicial help in opening the doors to the establishment....

I

Report on Current State of Knowledge

The court heard from a number of distinguished and renowned researchers and professionals who told the court about their research and discoveries involving "black English" and how it impacts on the teaching of standard English. They also informed the court on the results of other research relied on by professionals and expressed their opinions. Information about this area of education and linguistics is being uncovered as rapidly as research projects are reaching maturity. The court believes that the research results and the opinions of the researchers and professionals are better received as evidence in the case, on the record and subject to cross-examination, then simply by reading the reports and giving consideration to what appears in those reports as was done in *Brown v. Board of Education*, 347 U.S. 483 (1954). The knowledge produced by the various research projects forms a background basis against which the actions of the School District Board and the teachers in this case can be tested. The research product does permit inferences to be drawn but it must be remembered that this case is a case against one school board for its actions and it must be judged for its actions alone. "[S]chools are not fungible and the fact that some or even most may practice discrimination does not warrant blanket condemnation." *Norwood v. Harrison*, 413 U.S. 455, 471 (1973). The following is a brief summary of some of the research reported as it relates to the problems before the court.

Language Barrier

All of the distinguished researchers and professionals testified as to the existence of a language system, which is a part of the English language but different in significant respects from the standard English used in the school setting, the commercial world, the world of the arts and science, among the professions and in government. It is and has been used at some time by 80% of the black people of this country and has as its genesis the transactional or pidgin language of the slaves, which after a generation or two became a Creole language. Since then it has constantly been refined and brought closer to the standard English as blacks have been brought closer to the mainstream of society. It still flourishes in areas where there are concentrations of black people. It contains aspects of Southern dialect and is used largely by black people in their casual conversation and informal talk....

....

Impediments to Equal Participation in the Instructional Program

A child who does not learn to read is impeded in equal participation in the educational programs. Such a child cannot fully participate in the educational programs which to a significant degree require the student to acquire knowledge from the written word. Reading of all kinds is a major method by which modern society passes on its information and culture among its members and to its children. It is the way in which society conveys its commands and gives direction to its members.

The research evidence supports the theory that the learning of reading can be hurt by teachers who reject students because of the "mistakes" or "errors" made in oral speech by "black English" speaking children who are learning standard English. This comes about because "black English" is commonly thought of as an inferior method of speech and those who use this system may be thought of as "dumb" or "inferior." The child who comes to school using the "black English" system of communication and who is taught that this is wrong loses a sense of values related to mother and close friends and siblings and may rebel at efforts by his teachers to teach reading in a different language.

. . . .

The language of "black English" has been shown to be a distinct, definable version of English, different from standard English of the school and the general world of communications. It has definite language patterns, syntax, grammar and history.

In some communities and among some people in this country, it is the customary mode of oral, informal communication.

A significant number of blacks in the United States use or have used some version of "black English" in oral communications. Many of them incorporate one or more aspects of "black English" in their more formal talk.

"Black English" is not a language used by the mainstream of society — black or white. It is not an acceptable method of communication in the educational world, in the commercial community, in the community of the arts and science, or among professionals. It is largely a system that is used in casual and informal communication among the poor and lesser educated.

The instruction in standard English of children who use "black English" at home by insensitive teachers who treat the children's language system as inferior can cause a barrier to learning to read and use standard English. The language is not as discriminating in its use of sounds as is standard English and much of its grammar is simpler. There are fewer reading models in the life of a child who uses "black English."

II

Application of the Current State of Knowledge to the Children in This Case and King School

Language Barrier

The plaintiff children use a version of "black English" in their informal conversations in their homes.... It is the accepted way of speaking in that environment. Their mothers sometimes use a version of "black English" in speaking with the children in the home setting, but can speak standard English. The mothers testified clearly in standard English and a number of letters written by one or more of them appear in the record and show that they can use standard English effectively.

The teachers in King School had no difficulty in understanding the students or their parents in the school setting and the children could understand the teachers and other children in that setting. In other words, so far as understanding is concerned in the school setting, although there was initially a type of language difference, there was no barrier to understanding caused by the language.

There seems to be no problem existing in this case relating to communication between the children and their teachers or between the children and other children in the school. The answers given by plaintiffs to interrogatories posed by defendants confirm this finding.

Although the evidence in this case indicates that the plaintiffs at times speak "black English" at home, they also to a greater or lesser degree depending on age speak and understand standard English in school and in the home.

If a barrier exists because of the language used by the children in this case, it exists not because the teachers and students cannot understand each other, but because in the process of attempting to teach the students how to speak standard English the students are made somehow to feel inferior and are thereby turned off from the learning process.

There is no direct evidence that any of the teachers in this case has treated the home language of the children as inferior, but it is clear to the court that although some of the teachers rebel at calling the home language "black English" they are acutely aware of it. Each teacher, the court believes, makes his or her own assessment of the language system used by the student in the home environment and attempts to use all of his or her skills to teach the student to read and speak standard English. The teachers do not, however, admit to taking that system into account in helping the student read standard English.

....

The facts in this case indicate, however, that these children have not developed reading skills and the failure to develop these skills impedes equal participation in the instructional program.

....

The court cannot find that the defendant School Board has taken steps (1) to help the teachers understand the problem; (2) to help provide them with knowledge about the children's use of a "black English" language system; and (3) to suggest ways and means of using that knowledge in teaching the students to read.

III

Application of Law to Facts

....

The failure of the defendant Board to provide leadership and help for its teachers in learning about the existence of "black English" as a home and

B. BILINGUAL EDUCATION

community language of many black students and to suggest to those same teachers ways and means of using that knowledge in teaching the black children code switching skills in connection with reading standard English is not rational in light of existing knowledge on the subject.

Section 1706 of Title 20 provides that an individual who has been "denied an equal educational opportunity" (as defined in § 1703) may "institute a civil action ... for such relief as may be appropriate."

Although this statute is a direct congressional mandate to the federal courts to become involved in matters of this kind, this statute makes it clear that discretion is given to the judge to determine what is "appropriate." Accordingly, this court finds it appropriate to require the defendant Board to take steps to help its teachers to recognize the home language of the students and to use that knowledge in their attempts to teach reading skills in standard English. It is the intention of this court that the method of using the students' home language in teaching reading of standard English meet the test of reasonableness and rationality in light of knowledge on the subject. It is not the intention of this court to tell educators how to educate, but only to see that this defendant carries out an obligation imposed by law to help the teachers use existing knowledge as this may bear on appropriate action to overcome language barriers.

The other two factors particularly identified as creating difficulty in learning to read standard English are not the appropriate subject for court order. The court does not believe the language difference between "black English" and standard English to be a language barrier in and of itself. The court cannot deal with the reading role model problem. In one sense it is a cultural, economic and social problem and not a language problem and thus is beyond the issues in this action. In the other sense its remedies involve pedagogical judgments that are for the educators and not for the courts.

....

Counsel for the defendant is directed to submit to this court within thirty (30) days a proposed plan *defining the exact steps to be taken* (1) to help the teachers of the plaintiff children at King School to identify children speaking "black English" and the language spoken as a home or community language, and (2) to use that knowledge in teaching such students how to read standard English. The plan must embrace within its terms the elementary school teachers of the plaintiff children at Martin Luther King Junior Elementary School. If the defendant chooses, however, it may submit a broader plan for the court's consideration, *e.g.*, one embracing other elementary schools.

So ordered.

[The portion of the opinion dealing with the submission of the proposed plan has been omitted.]

The court here restricts plaintiff's claim to the right to equal educational opportunity under the Equal Educational Opportunities Act of 1974. How does the court establish a right under the act to be instructed in a "dialect"? Is the denial of the school district toward an equal opportunity predicated on the student's race, background, language or all three? Does one speak "Ebonics" or "black English" because of one's African heritage? If so, is the case restricted on the basis of its facts to only such children? What are the similarities and differences between this case and *Castaneda*?

Chapter 13
THE EDUCATION OF EXCEPTIONAL CHILDREN

Special Education

For at least the last one-hundred years, reactions and interactions between the legal and educational communities have shaped the educational process for physically or mentally disabled public school students. Historically, these persons have been subjected to discrimination involving segregation into separate educational institutions or classrooms, exclusion from other aspects of society, and the absence of or ineffective provision for needs and services. The issue undertaken by the legislative, executive and judicial branches of government is whether the disabled child has a right to education, and if so, whether the right embraces a program of special education.

This was partially answered in the 1970's when two court decisions, *Pennsylvania Ass'n for Retarded Children (PARC) v. Pennsylvania*, 334 F. Supp. 1257 (E.D. Pa. 1971), and *Mills v. Board of Educ.*, 348 F. Supp. (D.D.C. 1972), articulated and essentially established the disabled child's right to a free appropriate public education. In *PARC* an association for disabled students' rights sued the Commonwealth of Pennsylvania on behalf of mentally handicapped children who were either excluded from public schools, misassigned to special education programs or assigned to programs of doubtful merit. The case became a legal landmark in the battle for equal rights of disabled students. The court in *PARC* recognized a procedural right to an impartial hearing that allowed parents of disabled children to contest a school's classification of the child or the school's placement decision. The *Mills* court went further than *PARC* by extending the right of a free public education to all disabled children, including the mentally handicapped, emotionally disturbed, physically handicapped and children with behavioral problems caused by a disability. Further, the *Mills* court held that the District of Columbia Board of Education had specifically violated the due process rights of disabled children by denying them a publicly supported education.

As a direct response to these cases, Congress promulgated federal statutes so as to codify such rights. They include the Education for All Handicapped Children's Act (EAHCA) which in the late 1980's was amended and renamed the Individuals with Disabilities Education Act (IDEA), 20 U.S.C. § 1400 *et seq.*, and its implementing regulations, 34 C.F.R. § 300.1 *et seq.*, and Section 504 of the Rehabilitation Act of 1973, 29 U.S.C. Sec. 706(8), *et seq.* and its implementing regulations, 34 C.F.R. § 104.1 *et seq.* These two statutes must be considered by those involved with the education of children with disabilities because they serve as the legal structures for determining the most appropriate education for such persons. In 1990 Congress also passed the Americans with Disabilities Act (ADA), 42 U.S.C. § 1201 *et seq.* This too must be considered by educators as evidenced in Wenkart, *The Americans with Disabilities Act and its Impact on Public Education,* 82 Educ. L. Rep. 291 (1993) at the end of the chapter.

The fundamental premise of IDEA is that every child with a disability is entitled to a free appropriate public education (FAPE). A FAPE encompasses special education and related services provided in the least restrictive environment. The provisions of the IDEA set out extensive procedural requirements that center around the development by the school or school system of an individualized education program (IEP) for each child with a disability. For an overview of the basic tenets of IDEA, and the case law interpreting it, *see* Daniel and Coriell, *Traversing the Sisyphean Trails of the Education for All Handicapped Children's Act: An Overview,* 28 Ohio N.U. L. Rev. 571 (1992).

Section 504 covers all programs receiving federal assistance and, unlike IDEA, is not limited to discrimination for public school students; there are employment provisions as well. However, United States Department of Education regulations implementing Section 504 contain procedural and substantive obligations that are binding on school districts and state education departments receiving federal funds.

The ADA, like Section 504, is a broad statute covering not only education and employment, but transportation as well. Like IDEA and Section 504, the ADA mandates that schools must provide and administer programs for disabled populations in an appropriate and integrated environment.

Gifted and Talented Children

Unlike the federal statutory protection provided for children with disabilities, there is no current provision requiring the states to render a free appropriate education for gifted and talented students. Federal legislation for the protection of this group of approximately 3 million students was promulgated in the past by Congress particularly with the advent of the Soviet launching of Sputnik. Congress passed acts allocating funds in this area in 1969 with the Gifted and Talented Children's Education Assistance Act and in 1974 created the Office of Gifted and Talented as an element of the U.S. Bureau of Education for the Handicapped. However, this office was abolished by the Reagan Administration with budget cutbacks in the early 1980's. In 1993 the United States Department of Education reported its first study of gifted and talented education in twenty years. The report stated that this country needs to improve its ranking among other developed nations of the world. Recently, however, this effort as well fell to federal budget cuts with the announcement that the National Research Center on Gifted and Talented Education would be eliminated.

This then has left support and funding for gifted education primarily to the states. Zirkel and Stevens, *The Law Concerning Public Education of Gifted Students,* 36 Educ. L. Rep. 353 (1986), have reported that approximately 90% of the states have some legislation supporting gifted and talented education, but on a very wide continuum between "mandatory" and "permissive." This dichotomy has prompted parents to seek protection for their "gifted" children in the courts where suits have been based on state statutes in this area or on the more general federal provisions of due process or equal protection. For the most part judges have demonstrated a willingness to rule on this issue only with the existence of some established state policy.

A. ELIGIBILITY

TIMOTHY W. v. ROCHESTER, NEW HAMPSHIRE SCHOOL DISTRICT

United States Court of Appeals
875 F.2d 954 (1st Cir. 1989)

BOWNES, CIRCUIT JUDGE:

Plaintiff-appellant Timothy W. appeals an order of the district court which held that under the Education for All Handicapped Children Act, a handicapped child is not eligible for special education if he cannot benefit from that education, and that Timothy W., a severely retarded and multiply handicapped child was not eligible under that standard. We reverse.

I. Background

Timothy W. was born two months prematurely on December 8, 1975 with severe respiratory problems, and shortly thereafter experienced an intracranial hemorrhage, subdural effusions, seizures, hydrocephalus, and meningitis. As a result, Timothy is multiply handicapped and profoundly mentally retarded. He suffers from complex developmental disabilities, spastic quadriplegia, cerebral palsy, seizure disorder and cortical blindness. His mother attempted to obtain appropriate services for him, and while he did receive some services from the Rochester Child Development Center, he did not receive any educational program from the Rochester School District when he became of school age.

On February 19, 1980, the Rochester School District convened a meeting to decide if Timothy was considered educationally handicapped under the state and federal statutes, thereby entitling him to special education and related services. ... In a meeting on March 7, 1980, the school district decided that Timothy was not educationally handicapped — that since his handicap was so severe he was not "capable of benefitting" from an education, and therefore was not entitled to one. During 1981 and 1982, the school district did not provide Timothy with any educational program.

In May, 1982, the New Hampshire Department of Education reviewed the Rochester School District's special education programs and made a finding of non-compliance, stating that the school district was not allowed to use "capable of benefitting" as a criterion for eligibility.... The school district, however, continued its refusal to provide Timothy with any educational program or services.

In response to a letter from Timothy's attorney, on January 17, 1984, the school district's placement team met.... The placement team recommended that Timothy be placed at the Child Development Center so that he could be provided with a special education program. The Rochester School Board, however, refused to authorize the placement team's recommendation to provide educational services for Timothy, contending that it still needed more information. The school district's request to have Timothy be given a neurological evaluation, including a CAT Scan, was refused by his mother.

On April 24, 1984, Timothy filed a complaint with the New Hampshire Department of Education requesting that he be placed in an educational program immediately. On October 9, 1984, the Department of Education issued an order requiring the school district to place him, within five days, in an educational program, until the appeals process on the issue of whether Timothy was educationally handicapped was completed. The school district, however, refused to make any such educational placement. On October 31, 1984, the school district filed an appeal of the order. There was also a meeting on November 8, 1984, in which the Rochester School Board reviewed Timothy's case and concluded he was not eligible for special education.

On November 17, 1984, Timothy filed a complaint in the United States District Court, pursuant to 42 U.S.C. § 1983, alleging that his rights under the Education for All Handicapped Children Act (20 U.S.C. § 1400 *et seq.*), the corresponding New Hampshire state law (RSA 186-C), § 504 of the Rehabilitation Act of 1973 (29 U.S.C. § 794), and the equal protection and due process clauses of the United States and New Hampshire Constitutions, had been violated by the Rochester School District. The complaint sought preliminary and permanent injunctions directing the school district to provide him with special education, and $175,000 in damages.

A hearing was held in the district court on December 21, 1984. Timothy's mother testified that he hears somewhat, sees bright light, smiles when happy, cries when sad, listens to television and music, and responds to touching and talking. Lynn Miller, who had been providing physical therapy to Timothy for over a year, testified that Timothy responded to movement, touch, music, and other sounds, and that his educational needs included postural drainage, range of motion, sensory stimulation of all kinds, correct positioning, proper sitting equipment, and work with his head control. Mariane Riggio, an expert in services for severely handicapped deaf-blind children, testified that Timothy was severely retarded but that he had definite light perception and could differentiate between sounds. She concluded that Timothy would be harmed if he was not given the benefit of an educational program. Dr. William Schofield, an expert in special education for the severely handicapped, testified that he had evaluated Timothy and that his educational needs included occupational therapy, development of some kind of communication program, a toileting program, a feeding program, and tactile stimulation discrimination which might be the basis for a communication process. Dr. Patricia Andrews, a developmental pediatrician, was

A. ELIGIBILITY

the only person who testified that Timothy did not have educational needs and could not benefit from education. Her only contact with Timothy had been during an evaluation when he was two months old. While she testified that Timothy was profoundly mentally retarded and that an X-ray study of his brain showed he had virtually no cortex present, she also stated that such a study alone could not predict how much functioning was going to develop. On January 3, 1985, the district court denied Timothy's motion for a preliminary injunction, and on January 8, stated it would abstain on the damage claim pending exhaustion of the state administrative procedures.

....

In September, 1986, Timothy again requested a special education program. In October, 1986, the school district continued to refuse to provide him with such a program, claiming it still needed more information. Various evaluations were done at the behest of the school district. On December 30, 1985, Dr. Cecilia Pinto-Lord, a neurologist, had given Timothy a negative prognosis for learning, but did indicate he had some awareness of his environment; on October 10, 1986, Dr. Pinto-Lord stated that acquisition of new skills by Timothy was very unlikely. On May 19, 1986, Mary-Margaret Windsor, an occupational therapist, conducted an occupational therapy evaluation and concluded that Timothy might respond to an oral-motor program, and that without consistent management strategies there was great potential for increased deformities and contractures (a condition of fixed high resistance to passive stretch of a muscle). A psychological evaluation conducted by Dr. John Morse, a psychologist, on June 23, 1986, concluded that Timothy demonstrates behavioral awareness of strangers, recognizes familiar voices, positively responds to handling by a familiar person, recognizes familiar sounds, and demonstrates a selective response to sound. He recommended physical and occupational therapy, and cognitive programming efforts to continue in the areas of consistently responding to sound, anticipating feeding, and operating an electronic device to operate a sound source. And on January 9, 1987, Ruth Keans, a physical therapist at the Child Development Center, performed a physical therapy evaluation and concluded that she did not see any voluntary movements, but that Timothy did respond to his mother's voice. She recommended physical therapy.

The school district, on January 12, 1987, arranged another diagnostic placement at the Rochester Child Development Center. A report of March 13, 1987 by Dr. Schofield, an expert in special education for the severely handicapped, indicated that Timothy was aware of his environment, could locate to different sounds made by a busy box, and that he attempted to reach for the box himself. He recommended the establishment of specific teaching/learning strategies for Timothy....

On May 20, 1987, the district court found that Timothy had not exhausted his state administrative remedies before the New Hampshire Department of Education, and precluded pretrial discovery until this had been done. On September 15, 1987, the hearing officer in the administrative hearings ruled that

Timothy's capacity to benefit was not a legally permissible standard for determining his eligibility to receive a public education, and that the Rochester School District must provide him with an education. The Rochester School District, on November 12, 1987, appealed this decision to the United States District Court by filing a counterclaim, and on March 29, 1988, moved for summary judgment. Timothy filed a cross motion for summary judgment.

... Timothy's experts ... testified that Timothy would benefit from a special educational program including physical and occupational therapy, with emphasis on functional skills. The school district ... testified that Timothy had shown no progress. The district court relied heavily on another school district witness, Dr. Patricia Andrews, a developmental pediatrician, who testified that Timothy probably does not have the capacity to learn educational skills and activities....

... The court then reviewed the materials, reports and testimony and found that "Timothy W. is not capable of benefitting from special education.... As a result, the defendant [school district] is not obligated to provide special education under either EAHCA [the federal statute] or RSA 186-C [the New Hampshire statute]." Timothy W. has appealed this order....

....

II. *The Language of the Act*

A. *The Plain Meaning of the Act Mandates a Public Education for All Handicapped Children*

The Education for All Handicapped Children Act, [hereinafter the Act], 20 U.S.C. §§ 1400 *et seq.*, was enacted in 1975 to ensure that handicapped children receive an education which is appropriate to their unique needs. In assessing the plain meaning of the Act, we first look to its title: The Education for *All* Handicapped Children Act. (Emphasis added).... In directly addressing the educability of handicapped children, Congress found that "developments in the training of teachers and in diagnostic and instructional procedures and methods have advanced to the point that, given appropriate funding, State and local educational agencies can and will provide effective special education and related services to meet the needs of handicapped children." The Act's stated purpose was "to assure that all handicapped children have available to them ... a free appropriate public education which emphasizes special education and related services designed to meet their unique needs, ... [and] to assist states and localities to provide for the education of all handicapped children...."

The Act's mandatory provisions require that for a state to qualify for financial assistance, it must have "in effect a policy that assures all handicapped children the right to a free appropriate education." The state must also assure that "all children residing in the State who are handicapped, regardless of the severity of

A. ELIGIBILITY

their handicap, and who are in need of special education and related services are identified, located, and evaluated...." The Act further requires a state to:

> establish ... priorities for providing a free appropriate public education to all handicapped children, ... first with respect to handicapped children who are not receiving an education, and second with respect to handicapped children, within each disability, with the most severe handicaps who are receiving an inadequate education....

Thus, not only are severely handicapped children not excluded from the Act, but the most severely handicapped are actually given priority under the Act.

....

The language of the Act could not be more unequivocal. The statute is permeated with the words "all handicapped children" whenever it refers to the target population. It never speaks of any exceptions for severely handicapped children.... Nor is there any language whatsoever which requires as a prerequisite to being covered by the Act, that a handicapped child must demonstrate that he or she will "benefit" from the educational program. Rather, the Act speaks of the state's responsibility to design a special education and related services program that will meet the unique "needs" of all handicapped children. The language of the Act in its entirety makes clear that a "zero-reject" policy is at the core of the Act, and that no child, regardless of the severity of his or her handicap, is to ever again be subjected to the deplorable state of affairs which existed at the time of the Act's passage, in which millions of handicapped children received inadequate education or none at all. In summary, the Act mandates an appropriate public education for all handicapped children, regardless of the level of achievement that such children might attain.

B. *Timothy W.: A Handicapped Child Entitled to An Appropriate Education*

Given that the Act's language mandates that all handicapped children are entitled to a free appropriate education, we must next inquire if Timothy W. is a handicapped child, and if he is, what constitutes an appropriate education to meet his unique needs.

(1) *Handicapped children:* The implementing regulations define handicapped children as "being mentally retarded, hard of hearing, deaf, speech impaired, visually handicapped, seriously emotionally disturbed, orthopedically impaired, other health impaired, deaf-blind, multi-handicapped, or as having specific learning disabilities, who because of those impairments need special education and related services." ...

There is no question that Timothy W. fits within the Act's definition of a handicapped child: he is multiply handicapped and profoundly mentally retarded. He has been described as suffering from severe spasticity, cerebral palsy, brain damage, joint contractures, cortical blindness, is not ambulatory, and is quadriplegic.

(2) *Appropriate public education:* The Act and the implementing regulations define a "free appropriate public education" to mean "special education and related services which are provided at public expense ... [and] are provided in conformity with an individualized education program."

(a) "Special education" means "specially designed instruction, at no cost to the parent, to meet the unique needs of a handicapped child, including classroom instruction, instruction in physical education, home instruction, and instruction in hospitals and institutions." It is of significance that the Act explicitly provides for education of children who are so severely handicapped as to require hospitalization or institutionalization. Timothy W.'s handicaps do not require such extreme measures, as he can be educated at home....

(b) "Related services" means "transportation and such developmental, corrective, and other supportive services as are required to assist a handicapped child to benefit from special education, and includes speech pathology and audiology, psychological services, physical and occupational therapy, recreation...." ... Furthermore, the "comment" to these implementing regulations notes that "the list of related services is not exhaustive and may include other developmental, corrective, or supportive services ... if they are required to assist a handicapped child to benefit from special education."

(c) An "individualized education program" is a written plan developed by the local educational agency in conjunction with the parents and teacher, which provides "specially designed instruction to meet the unique needs" of the handicapped child. Such a program is to be periodically reviewed, and if appropriate, revised.

The record shows that Timothy W. is a severely handicapped and profoundly retarded child in need of special education and related services. Much of the expert testimony was to the effect that he is aware of his surrounding environment, makes or attempts to make purposeful movements, responds to tactile stimulation, responds to his mother's voice and touch, recognizes familiar voices, responds to noises, and parts his lips when spoon fed. The record contains testimony that Timothy W.'s needs include sensory stimulation, physical therapy, improved head control, socialization, consistency in responding to sound sources, and partial participation in eating. The educational consultants who drafted Timothy's individualized education program recommended that Timothy's special education program should include goals and objectives in the areas of motor control, communication, socialization, daily living skills, and recreation. The special education and related services that have been recommended to meet Timothy W.'s needs fit well within the statutory and regulatory definitions of the Act.

We conclude that the Act's language dictates the holding that Timothy W. is a handicapped child who is in need of special education and related services because of his handicaps. He must, therefore, according to the Act, be provided with such an educational program. There is nothing in the Act's language which even remotely supports the district court's conclusion that "under [the Act], an

A. ELIGIBILITY

initial determination as to a child's ability to benefit from special education, must be made in order for a handicapped child to qualify for education under the Act." The language of the Act is directly to the contrary: a school district has a duty to provide an educational program for every handicapped child in the district, regardless of the severity of the handicap.

---

1. Although the Court in *Timothy W.* seemingly could have stopped with its discussion of the EAHCA's language and plain meaning, it considered the Act's legislative history and prior case law to determine that coverage has nothing to do with the severity of the disability.

2. The Court in *Timothy W.* notes that EAHCA is "permeated with the words 'all handicapped children' whenever it refers to the target population." One of the most important amendments to the statute in 1990 with its renaming to IDEA is that the "child" comes first, *before* the "handicap." Now, the target audience is "children with disabilities." Why is the change so important? Does this "zero reject" principle cover all disabled children needing education services including those with communicable diseases?

3. The decision in *Timothy W.* and provisions in IDEA fully explain that no disabled child may be rejected for educational services because of too severe a handicap. But the court in *Timothy W.* also noted that the child in question was capable of receiving some level of instruction as he was field sensitive and was "stimulated by his environment." Therefore, what would a court's decision be in a case where the severely disabled student was not effected by his environment and did not respond to stimuli?

4. What are the limits of the IDEA's definition of "children with disabilities"? Sec. 1401(a)(16) defines such a term as:

> children with mental retardation, hearing impairments, visual impairments, including blindness, serious emotional disturbance, orthopedic impairments, autism, traumatic brain injury, other health impairments or specific learning disabilities; ... who, by reason thereof, need special education and related services.

State and federal administrative codes define each of these disabilities. *See, e.g.*, 34 C.F.R. § 300, *et seq.*, and Ohio Administrative Code (O.A.C.) 3301-51-01 and 3301-51-05. Each definition helps to clarify the language of the respective statute and gives examples of the types of disabilities covered. For example, orthopedic disabilities include club foot, spina bifida, absence of some member (*e.g.*, an arm), polio, muscular dystrophy and cerebral palsy. 34 C.F.R. § 300.7(B)(7); O.A.C. 3301-51-04.

How "serious" does an emotional disturbance have to be for a child to be eligible for special education services? The last portion of the definition of "children with disabilities" may help answer the question. Disability alone does not guarantee services under IDEA. *See Doe v. Board of Educ. of Connecticut*, 753 F. Supp. 65 (D. Conn. 1990). Despite emotional and behavioral problems, student was held "not handicapped" under EAHCA (predecessor to IDEA) because the child's difficulties did not adversely affect his educational performance. Note also that in *Doe* parents had the burden of proving eligibility because of their request for the due process hearing.

5. When does eligibility under IDEA begin and end? Under Sec. 1412(2)(B), children ages three to twenty-one, inclusive, are covered. This provision qualifies that coverage, though: "... the requirements of this clause shall not be applied in any state if the application of such requirements would be inconsistent with State law or practice, or the order of any court, respecting public education within such age groups in the state." *Id.*

How is this provision applied to a student who has not yet reached age 21, but has graduated from high school? *See O'Donniley v. Metropolitan Pub. Schs.*, 919 F.2d 141 (6th Cir. 1990). The court in that case ruled that through her valid individualized education program, the student received a free, appropriate public education in accordance with the Act and was not entitled to further education past graduation from high school as this was consistent with state law.

May a state promulgate regulations restricting special education to students age 18 through 21? An Indiana state court said "no," if the affected students have not yet graduated and the state law was produced in order to reduce the rights of such students after the fact. *See Evans v. Tuttle*, 613 N.E.2d 854 (Ind. Ct. App. 1993).

6. What if the child is disabled, and is entitled to services under IDEA, but the school fails to identify the disability? In *Zellman v. Kenston Bd. of Educ.*, 71 Ohio App. 3d 287, 593 N.E.2d 392 (Geauga County 1991), the court dismissed parents' negligence claim, noting that the state statute requiring school officials to identify handicapped students did not expressly impose liability on the officials for negligently failing to identify such students. Is this an educational malpractice claim in disguise? *See B.M. v. State of Montana*, 200 Mont. 58, 649 P.2d 425 (1982) (Chapter 2), where the state was held not to be immune from liability as school authorities owed disabled student a duty of reasonable care in testing her and placing her in an appropriate special education program. Moreover, schools have an affirmative responsibility of identifying and locating qualified disabled students who are not receiving an appropriate education. Reg. 34 C.F.R. § 300.128(a)(1). This "child find" provision is also included in Section 504 of the Rehabilitation Act of 1973. Reg. 34 C.F.R. § 104.32(a).

7. Under Section 504, qualified disabled students are ones of the same age as nondisabled students for whom services are provided by the school district. Disabled persons, under Section 504, are those who have "a physical or mental impairment which substantially limits one or more major life activities, has a record of such an impairment or is regarded as having such an impairment." 34 C.F.R. § 104.3(j). Like IDEA, conditions primarily the result of cultural, environmental or economic factors may not be considered handicapping

A. ELIGIBILITY

conditions under Section 504. Students with a physical or mental disability are eligible if the disability causes a substantial limitation such as learning. Specifically, a mental or physical handicap must be associated with the substantial limitation that is not primarily the result of cultural, economic or environmental factors.

The first prong of the Section 504 eligibility statement is fairly clear. A student with an impairment who carries the requisite age qualifications and where the impairment effects a major life activity like "learning" is protected despite negative action on the part of school officials. But does this mean that those who fall under the other two prongs, "a record of impairment" or "regarded as having an impairment" are also so protected? This issue was the subject of an executive opinion of the Office of Civil Rights (OCR), the executive agency under the United States Office of Education, responsible for hearing claims under Section 504. *See Clarification of 'record of' and 'regarded as' in the Definition of Handicap under Section 504*, (OCR, August, 1992). OCR determined that protection under the latter two prongs requires some negative action by state or local school officials in order for the student to qualify. Specifically, officials must take some discriminatory action that results in a negative effect upon some major life activity. The mere fact that a student has a record of or is regarded as having a disability is not enough to trigger Section 504 protection. This means that it is inaccurate for school personnel to interpret Section 504 to mean that simply because a person is regarded as having a handicap this in turn warrants protection. The proper inquiry is whether these opinions would give a person reason to believe that a student, because of proof of actual handicap, may need the required aids and services.

8. Also, unlike IDEA, it is possible that a child's disability may prevent eligibility in particular circumstances. This was found in *Eva N. and Timothy H. v. Brock*, 943 F.2d 51 (6th Cir. 1991). Here, school children brought several causes of action, including a violation of Section 504, against the admission criteria of a state school for the visually disabled. The admission criteria excluded children who required extensive medical care or who were not able to care for themselves. Even though the plaintiffs prevailed, the court held that Section 504 will not support the invalidation of eligibility criteria on its face. Categorical exclusions based on disability are not permitted under Section 504, "but the presence or absence of a particular handicap may well be relevant in determining whether a child could benefit from placement [at a particular school]. The criteria may well be utilized as one means of determining whether placement at [a] school constitutes an appropriate education." *Id.* at 53.

Compare this decision to that of *Timothy W.* What are the similarities and differences, if any? Could any differences be based on the fact that IDEA and Section 504 are federal statutes promulgated by Congress for alternate reasons even though the populations affected may be similar?

B. FREE APPROPRIATE PUBLIC EDUCATION

BOARD OF EDUCATION OF HENDRICK HUDSON CENTRAL SCHOOL DISTRICT v. ROWLEY

Supreme Court of the United States
458 U.S. 176 (1982)

JUSTICE REHNQUIST delivered the opinion of the Court:

....

I

The Education of the Handicapped Act (Act) provides federal money to assist state and local agencies in educating handicapped children, and conditions such funding upon a State's compliance with extensive goals and procedures. The Act represents an ambitious federal effort to promote the education of handicapped children, and was passed in response to Congress' perception that a majority of handicapped children in the United States "were either totally excluded from schools or [were] sitting idly in regular classrooms awaiting the time when they were old enough to 'drop out'." ...

....

In order to qualify for federal financial assistance under the Act, a State must demonstrate that it "has in effect a policy that assures all handicapped children the right to a free appropriate public education." That policy must be reflected in a state plan submitted to and approved by the Secretary of Education which describes in detail the goals, programs, and timetables under which the State intends to educate handicapped children within its borders. States receiving money under the Act must provide education to the handicapped by priority, first "to handicapped children who are not receiving an education" and second "to handicapped children ... with the most severe handicaps who are receiving an inadequate education," § 1412(3), and "to the maximum extent appropriate" must educate handicapped children "with children who are not handicapped."

....

The "free appropriate public education" required by the Act is tailored to the unique needs of the handicapped child by means of an "individualized educational program" (IEP). The IEP, which is prepared at a meeting between a qualified representative of the local educational agency, the child's teacher, the child's parents or guardian, and, where appropriate, the child....

....

In addition to the state plan and the IEP already described, the Act imposes extensive procedural requirements upon States receiving federal funds under its provisions.... § 1415(e)(2).

....

II

This case arose in connection with the education of Amy Rowley, a deaf

B. FREE APPROPRIATE PUBLIC EDUCATION

student at the Furnace Woods School in the Hendrick Hudson Central School District, Peekskill, N.Y. Amy has minimal residual hearing and is an excellent lipreader. During the year before she began attending Furnace Woods, a meeting between her parents and school administrators resulted in a decision to place her in a regular kindergarten class in order to determine what supplemental services would be necessary to her education. Several members of the school administration prepared for Amy's arrival by attending a course in sign-language interpretation, and a teletype machine was installed in the principal's office to facilitate communication with her parents who are also deaf. At the end of the trial period it was determined that Amy should remain in the kindergarten class, but that she should be provided with an FM hearing aid which would amplify words spoken into a wireless receiver by the teacher or fellow students during certain classroom activities. Amy successfully completed her kindergarten year.

As required by the Act, an IEP was prepared for Amy during the fall of her first-grade year. The IEP provided that Amy should be educated in a regular classroom at Furnace Woods, should continue to use the FM hearing aid, and should receive instruction from a tutor for the deaf for one hour each day and from a speech therapist for three hours each week. The Rowleys agreed with parts of the IEP, but insisted that Amy also be provided a qualified sign-language interpreter in all her academic classes in lieu of the assistance proposed in other parts of the IEP. Such an interpreter had been placed in Amy's kindergarten class for a 2-week experimental period, but the interpreter had reported that Amy did not need his services at that time. The school administrators likewise concluded that Amy did not need such an interpreter in her first-grade classroom. They reached this conclusion after consulting the school district's Committee on the Handicapped, which had received expert evidence from Amy's parents on the importance of a sign-language interpreter, received testimony from Amy's teacher and other persons familiar with her academic and social progress, and visited a class for the deaf.

When their request for an interpreter was denied, the Rowleys demanded and received a hearing before an independent examiner. After receiving evidence from both sides, the examiner agreed with the administrators' determination that an interpreter was not necessary because "Amy was achieving educationally, academically, and socially" without such assistance. The examiner's decision was affirmed on appeal by the New York Commissioner of Education on the basis of substantial evidence in the record. Pursuant to the Act's provision for judicial review, the Rowleys then brought an action in the United States District Court for the Southern District of New York, claiming that the administrators' denial of the sign-language interpreter constituted a denial of the "free appropriate public education" guaranteed by the Act.

The District Court found that Amy "is a remarkably well-adjusted child" who interacts and communicates well with her classmates and has "developed an extraordinary rapport" with her teachers. It also found that "she performs better than the average child in her class and is advancing easily from grade to grade," but "that she understands considerably less of what goes on in class than she could if she were not deaf" and thus "is not learning as much, or performing as well academically, as she would without her handicap." This disparity between Amy's achievement and her potential led the court to decide that she was not receiving a "free appropriate public education," which the court defined as "an opportunity to achieve [her] full potential commensurate with the opportunity provided to other children." According to the District Court, such a standard "requires that the potential of the handicapped child be measured and compared to his or her performance, and that the resulting differential or 'shortfall' be compared to the shortfall experienced by nonhandicapped children."...

A divided panel of the United States Court of Appeals for the Second Circuit affirmed....

....

III

A

This is the first case in which this Court has been called upon to interpret any provision of the Act.... "[T]he Act itself does not define 'appropriate education'," but leaves "to the courts and the hearing officers" the responsibility of "giv[ing] content to the requirement of an 'appropriate education.'"...

We are loath to conclude that Congress failed to offer any assistance in defining the meaning of the principal substantive phrase used in the Act. It is beyond dispute that, contrary to the conclusions of the courts below, the Act does expressly define "free appropriate public education":

> "The term 'free appropriate public education' means special education and related services which (A) have been provided at public expense, under public supervision and direction, and without charge, (B) meet the standards of the State educational agency, (C) include an appropriate preschool, elementary, or secondary school education in the State involved, and (D) are provided in conformity with the individualized education program required under section 1414(a)(5) of this title." § 1401(18) (emphasis added).

"Special education," as referred to in this definition, means "specially designed instruction, at no cost to parents or guardians, to meet the unique needs of a handicapped child, including classroom instruction, instruction in physical education, home instruction, and instruction in hospitals and institutions." "Related services" are defined as "transportation, and such developmental, corrective, and other supportive services ... as may be required to assist a handicapped child to benefit from special education."

Like many statutory definitions, this one tends toward the cryptic rather than the comprehensive, but that is scarcely a reason for abandoning the quest for legislative intent. Whether or not the definition is a "functional" one, as respondents contend it is not, it is the principal tool which Congress has given

B. FREE APPROPRIATE PUBLIC EDUCATION

us for parsing the critical phrase of the Act. We think more must be made of it than either respondents or the United States seems willing to admit.

According to the definitions contained in the Act, a "free appropriate public education" consists of educational instruction specially designed to meet the unique needs of the handicapped child, supported by such services as are necessary to permit the child "to benefit" from the instruction. Almost as a checklist for adequacy under the Act, the definition also requires that such instruction and services be provided at public expense and under public supervision, meet the State's educational standards, approximate the grade levels used in the State's regular education, and comport with the child's IEP. Thus, if personalized instruction is being provided with sufficient supportive services to permit the child to benefit from the instruction, and the other items on the definitional checklist are satisfied, the child is receiving a "free appropriate public education" as defined by the Act.

....

Noticeably absent from the language of the statute is any substantive standard prescribing the level of education to be accorded handicapped children. Certainly the language of the statute contains no requirement like the one imposed by the lower courts — that States maximize the potential of handicapped children "commensurate with the opportunity provided to other children."...

B

(i)

....

... By passing the Act, Congress sought primarily to make public education available to handicapped children. But in seeking to provide such access to public education, Congress did not impose upon the States any greater substantive educational standard than would be necessary to make such access meaningful.... Thus, the intent of the Act was more to open the door of public education to handicapped children on appropriate terms than to guarantee any particular level of education once inside.

....

Mills and *PARC* both held that handicapped children must be given access to an adequate, publicly supported education. Neither case purports to require any particular substantive level of education. Rather, like the language of the Act, the cases set forth extensive procedures to be followed in formulating personalized educational programs for handicapped children. The fact that both *PARC* and *Mills* are discussed at length in the legislative Reports suggests that the principles which they established are the principles which, to a significant extent, guided the drafters of the Act. Indeed, immediately after discussing these cases the Senate Report describes the 1974 statute as having "incorporated the major principles of the right to education cases."...

(ii)

Respondents contend that "the goal of the Act is to provide each handicapped child with an equal educational opportunity." Brief for Respondents 35. We think, however, that the requirement that a State provide specialized educational services to handicapped children generates no additional requirement that the services so provided be sufficient to maximize each child's potential "commensurate with the opportunity provided other children."...

The educational opportunities provided by our public school systems undoubtedly differ from student to student, depending upon a myriad of factors that might affect a particular student's ability to assimilate information presented in the classroom. The requirement that States provide "equal" educational opportunities would thus seem to present an entirely unworkable standard requiring impossible measurements and comparisons. Similarly, furnishing handicapped children with only such services as are available to nonhandicapped children would in all probability fall short of the statutory requirement of "free appropriate public education"; to require, on the other hand, the furnishing of every special service necessary to maximize each handicapped child's potential is, we think, further than Congress intended to go. Thus to speak in terms of "equal" services in one instance gives less than what is required by the Act and in another instance more. The theme of the Act is "free appropriate public education," a phrase which is too complex to be captured by the word "equal" whether one is speaking of opportunities or services.

The legislative conception of the requirements of equal protection was undoubtedly informed by the two District Court decisions referred to above. But cases such as *Mills* and *PARC* held simply that handicapped children may not be excluded entirely from public education....

... The right of access to free public education enunciated by these cases is significantly different from any notion of absolute equality of opportunity regardless of [the child's] capacity. To the extent that Congress might have looked further than these cases which are mentioned in the legislative history, at the time of enactment of the Act this Court had held at least twice that the Equal Protection Clause of the Fourteenth Amendment does not require States to expend equal financial resources on the education of each child....

In explaining the need for federal legislation, the House Report noted that "no congressional legislation has required a precise guarantee for handicapped children, *i.e.* a basic floor of opportunity that would bring into compliance all school districts with the constitutional right of equal protection with respect to handicapped children." H.R.Rep. at 14. Assuming that the Act was designed to fill the need identified in the House Report — that is, to provide a "basic floor of opportunity" consistent with equal protection — neither the Act nor its history persuasively demonstrates that Congress thought that equal protection required anything more than equal access. Therefore, Congress' desire to provide

B. FREE APPROPRIATE PUBLIC EDUCATION

specialized educational services, even in furtherance of "equality," cannot be read as imposing any particular substantive educational standard upon the States.

The District Court and the Court of Appeals thus erred when they held that the Act requires New York to maximize the potential of each handicapped child commensurate with the opportunity provided nonhandicapped children. Desirable though that goal might be, it is not the standard that Congress imposed upon States which receive funding under the Act. Rather, Congress sought primarily to identify and evaluate handicapped children, and to provide them with access to a free public education.

(iii)

Implicit in the congressional purpose of providing access to a "free appropriate public education" is the requirement that the education to which access is provided be sufficient to confer some educational benefit upon the handicapped child. It would do little good for Congress to spend millions of dollars in providing access to a public education only to have the handicapped child receive no benefit from that education. The statutory definition of "free appropriate public education," in addition to requiring that States provide each child with "specially designed instruction," expressly requires the provision of "such ... supportive services ... as may be required to assist a handicapped child to benefit from special education." § 1401(17). We therefore conclude that the "basic floor of opportunity" provided by the Act consists of access to specialized instruction and related services which are individually designed to provide educational benefit to the handicapped child.

The determination of when handicapped children are receiving sufficient educational benefits to satisfy the requirements of the Act presents a more difficult problem. The Act requires participating States to educate a wide spectrum of handicapped children, from the marginally hearing-impaired to the profoundly retarded and palsied. It is clear that the benefits obtainable by children at one end of the spectrum will differ dramatically from those obtainable by children at the other end, with infinite variations in between. One child may have little difficulty competing successfully in an academic setting with nonhandicapped children while another child may encounter great difficulty in acquiring even the most basic of self-maintenance skills. We do not attempt today to establish any one test for determining the adequacy of educational benefits conferred upon all children covered by the Act. Because in this case we are presented with a handicapped child who is receiving substantial specialized instruction and related services, and who is performing above average in the regular classrooms of a public school system, we confine our analysis to that situation.

C

When the language of the Act and its legislative history are considered together, the requirements imposed by Congress become tolerably clear. Insofar as a State is required to provide a handicapped child with a "free appropriate public education," we hold that it satisfies this requirement by providing personalized instruction with sufficient support services to permit the child to benefit educationally from that instruction. Such instruction and services must be provided at public expense, must meet the State's educational standards, must approximate the grade levels used in the State's regular education, and must comport with the child's IEP. In addition, the IEP, and therefore the personalized instruction, should be formulated in accordance with the requirements of the Act and, if the child is being educated in the regular classrooms of the public education system, should be reasonably calculated to enable the child to achieve passing marks and advance from grade to grade.

....

[In Part IV of the opinion, the majority discusses the role of the courts in cases like this one. In suits brought under the IDEA's judicial review provisions, a court must first determine whether the state has complied with statutory procedures, and must then determine whether the individualized program developed through such procedures is reasonably calculated to enable the child to receive educational benefits. If those requirements are met, then the state has complied with the obligations imposed by Congress and the court can require no more. The majority also noted that the courts must be careful not to impose their own views or preferable education methods on the states.]

VI

... [W]e conclude that the Court of Appeals erred in affirming the decision of the District Court. Neither the District Court nor the Court of Appeals found that petitioners had failed to comply with the procedures of the Act, and the findings of neither court would support a conclusion that Amy's educational program failed to comply with the substantive requirements of the Act. On the contrary, the District Court found that the "evidence firmly establishes that Amy is receiving an 'adequate' education, since she performs better than the average child in her class and is advancing easily from grade to grade." 483 F.Supp. at 534. In light of this finding, and of the fact that Amy was receiving personalized instruction and related services calculated by the Furnace Woods school administrators to meet her educational needs, the lower courts should not have concluded that the Act requires the provision of a sign-language interpreter. Accordingly, the decision of the Court of Appeals is reversed, and the case is remanded for further proceedings consistent with this opinion.

So ordered.

B. FREE APPROPRIATE PUBLIC EDUCATION

1. "Implicit in the congressional purpose of providing access to a 'free appropriate public education' is the requirement that the education to which access is provided be sufficient to confer some educational benefit upon the handicapped child." *Rowley*, at 200. The Court indicates that there must be "some benefit." But what is that benefit? Moreover are school systems required to produce some benefit or to prepare programs that are merely designed or calculated to produce some benefit?

2. What is your interpretation of an "equal educational opportunity?" Should school districts be required to maximize the potential of each child with a disability despite the holding in this case? What is the "equal educational opportunity" for non-disabled students? Is it safe to say that the potential of each non-disabled student is maximized on a daily basis with typical, conventional education programs? If so, does this fact require a more generous holding than the majority presents in *Rowley*?

3. "Assuming that the Act was designed to fill the need identified in the House Report — that is, to provide a basic 'floor of opportunity' consistent with equal protection — neither the Act nor its history persuasively demonstrates that Congress thought that equal protection required anything more than equal access." *Rowley*, at 200. After *Rowley*, is the "floor" actually a "ceiling"? See *JSK v. Hendry County Sch. Bd.*, 941 F.2d 1563 (11th Cir. 1991). While interpreting the "some benefit" standard of *Rowley*, the court ruled that it must only determine whether the child has received the "basic floor of opportunity."

4. The Supreme Court holds that the state is not required to maximize the educational potential and benefits of disabled children. What is the minimum requirement? In addition to *Rowley*, consider the following case.

POLK v. CENTRAL SUSQUEHANNA INTERMEDIATE UNIT 16

United States Court of Appeals
853 F.2d 171 (3d Cir. 1988)

BECKER, CIRCUIT JUDGE:

....

II. *Facts and Procedural History*

Christopher Polk is severely developmentally disabled. At the age of seven months he contracted encephalopathy, a disease of the brain similar to cerebral palsy. He is also mentally retarded. Although Christopher is fourteen years old, he has the functional and mental capacity of a toddler. All parties agree that he requires "related services" in order to learn. He receives special education from defendants, the Central Susquehanna Intermediate Unit # 16 (the IU) and Central Columbia Area School District (the school district). Placed in a class for the mentally handicapped, Christopher has a full-time personal classroom aide. His education consists of learning basic life skills such as feeding himself, dressing himself, and using the toilet. He has mastered sitting and kneeling, is learning to stand independently, and is showing some potential for ambulation. Christopher is working on basic concepts such as "behind," "in," "on," and "under," and the identification of shapes, coins, and colors. Although he is cooperative, Christopher finds such learning difficult because he has a short attention span.

Although the record is not clear on this point, until 1980, the defendants apparently provided Christopher with direct physical therapy from a licensed physical therapist. Since that time, however, under a newer, so-called consultative model, Christopher no longer receives direct physical therapy from a physical therapist. Instead, a physical therapist (one of two hired by the IU) comes once a month to train Christopher's teacher in how to integrate physical therapy with Christopher's education. Although the therapist may lay hands on Christopher in demonstrating to the teacher the correct approach, he or she does not provide any therapy to Christopher directly, but uses such interaction to teach the teacher. Plaintiffs do not object to the consultative method per se, but argue that, to meet Christopher's individual needs, the consultative method must be supplemented by direct ("hands on") physical therapy.

In support of this position, plaintiffs adduced evidence that direct physical therapy from a licensed physical therapist has significantly expanded Christopher's physical capacities. In the summer of 1985, Christopher received two weeks of intensive physical therapy from a licensed physical therapist at Shriner's Hospital in Philadelphia. According to Christopher's parents, this brief treatment produced dramatic improvements in Christopher's physical capabilities. A doctor at Shriner's prescribed that Christopher receive at least one hour a week of direct physical therapy. Because the defendants were unwilling to provide direct physical therapy as part of Christopher's special education program, the Polks hired a licensed physical therapist, Nancy Brown, to work with Christopher at home. At the time of the hearing, she was seeing Christopher twice a week.

Plaintiffs acknowledge that the school program has benefited Christopher to some degree, but argue that his educational program is not appropriate because it is not individually tailored to his specific needs, as the EHA requires. Moreover, throughout all of the administrative and judicial proceedings that we now describe, plaintiffs have maintained that to comply with the EHA the defendants must provide, as part of Christopher's "free appropriate public education," one session a week with a licensed physical therapist.

....

Plaintiffs present two arguments on appeal. First, they submit that the defendants violated EHA's procedural requirements because Christopher's program is not truly individualized. Plaintiffs rely, in this regard, on the defendants' failure to provide direct ("hands on") physical therapy from a licensed physical therapist to any of the children in the intermediate unit (a fact they learned during Christopher's due process hearing before the state examiner). This failure, they contend, is evidence that the defendants have an inflexible rule prohibiting direct therapy and that such a rigid rule conflicts with the EHA's mandate of providing individualized education. Plaintiffs argue that genuine

B. FREE APPROPRIATE PUBLIC EDUCATION

questions of material fact exist as to the defendants' willingness to provide direct physical therapy under any circumstances, and that such disputes preclude summary judgment.

Second, plaintiffs assert that Christopher's education is inadequate to meet his unique needs. They claim that the district court found Christopher's education appropriate only because it applied an erroneous legal standard in judging the educational benefit of Christopher's program.

III. *Role of Physical Therapy in Providing a Free Appropriate Public Education Under the EHA*

For some handicapped children, the related services provided by the EHA serve as important facilitators of classroom learning....

For children like Christopher with severe disabilities, related services serve a dual purpose. First, because these children have extensive physical difficulties that often interfere with development in other areas, physical therapy is an essential prerequisite to education. For example, development of motor abilities is often the first step in overall educational development....

Second, the physical therapy itself may form the core of a severely disabled child's special education. This court has recognized that "[t]he educational program of a handicapped child, particularly a severely and profoundly handicapped child ... is very different from that of a non-handicapped child. The program may consist largely of 'related services' such as physical, occupational, or speech therapy." In Christopher's case, physical therapy is not merely a conduit to his education but constitutes, in and of itself, a major portion of his special education, teaching him basic skills such as toileting, feeding, ambulation, etc.

IV. *The Plaintiffs' Procedural Claim (That Christopher's Educational Plan Was Not Individualized)*

... [T]he plaintiffs have offered to prove that the defendants never genuinely considered Christopher's unique needs because of a rigid policy of providing only consultative physical therapy. They adduced evidence during cross examination at the state administrative hearing that none of the 65 children in defendants' intermediate unit whose IEPs call for physical therapy actually receive direct physical therapy. The plaintiffs also contend that, since the adoption of the consultative model, this rigid policy has precluded the defendants from recognizing Christopher's individual needs in violation of the EHA....

The defendants respond that it is, and always has been, their position that direct therapy would be provided, if needed. The therapist who consults monthly with Christopher's teacher testified before the Department of Education hearing examiner that she would provide therapy treatment directly if she determined that such therapy were appropriate. The previous physical therapy consultant and the administrator of the IU similarly claimed in testimony before the hearing examiner that direct physical therapy would be provided, if needed, but that such a case has never arisen for Christopher nor for any other student in the Unit.

....

In our view, a rigid rule under which defendants refuse even to consider providing physical therapy, ... would conflict with Christopher's procedural right to an individualized program. Drawing all reasonable inferences in favor of the non-moving party, ... we believe that a genuine dispute exists over whether the defendants would consider, under any circumstances, offering direct physical therapy, and that this dispute is over material facts, precluding summary judgment. Concomitantly, we believe that plaintiffs should be given an opportunity to continue their discovery into this question because the existence of a rigid rule prohibiting such therapy would violate the EHA. Therefore, we will reverse and remand the district court's decision for inquiry into whether defendants possess a rigid policy prohibiting the provision of direct physical therapy to children in the IU.

V. *Plaintiffs' Substantive Claim (That the Court Misapplied the Legal Standard for Evaluating Appropriate Education)*

A. *The Supreme Court's Opinion in Rowley*

We begin our discussion of the substantive protections of the EHA with the Supreme Court's opinion in *Board of Education v. Rowley*, 458 U.S. 176 (1982), because the parties' arguments are so closely tied to that case; only in the context of *Rowley* can we intelligently present the parties' contentions and the district court's opinion.

....

... Adverting to the legislative history, the Court concluded that "the intent of the Act was more to open the door of public education to handicapped children on appropriate terms than to guarantee any particular level of education once inside."

Although the tenor of the *Rowley* opinion reflects the Court's reluctance to involve the courts in substantive determinations of appropriate education and its emphasis on the procedural protection of the IEP process, it is clear that the Court was not espousing an entirely toothless standard of substantive review. Rather, the *Rowley* Court described the level of benefit conferred by the Act as "meaningful." ...

After noting the deference due to states on questions of education and the theme of access rather than a guarantee of any particular standard of benefit, the Court acknowledged that:

> Implicit in the congressional purpose of providing access to a "free appropriate public education" is the requirement that the education to which access is provided be sufficient to confer some educational benefit upon the handicapped child. It would do little good for Congress to spend millions of dollars in providing access to a public education only to have the handi-

B. FREE APPROPRIATE PUBLIC EDUCATION

> capped child receive no benefit from that education.... We therefore conclude that the "basic floor of opportunity" provided by the Act consists of access to specialized instruction and related services which are individually designed to provide educational benefit to the handicapped child.

The preceding quotation demonstrates that the Supreme Court in *Rowley* did not abdicate responsibility for monitoring the substantive quality of education under the EHA. Instead, it held that the education must "provide educational benefit." The Court thus recognized that the substantive, independent judicial review envisioned by the EHA was not a hollow gesture....

Finally, it is important to note that, notwithstanding *Rowley*'s broad language, the Court indicated that its holding might not cover every case brought under the EHA. Indeed, *Rowley* was an avowedly narrow opinion that relied significantly on the fact that Amy Rowley progressed successfully from grade to grade in a "mainstreamed" classroom. The Court self-consciously limited its opinion to the facts before it:

> We do not attempt today to establish any one test for determining the adequacy of educational benefits conferred upon all children covered by the Act. Because in this case we are presented with a handicapped child who is receiving substantial specialized instruction and related services, and who is performing above average in the regular classrooms of a public school system, we confine our analysis to that situation.

... In the case sub judice, however, the question of how much benefit is sufficient to be "meaningful" is inescapable. Therefore we must examine the Act's notion of "benefit" and apply a standard that is faithful to congressional intent and consistent with *Rowley*.

B. *EHA Requires More than a De Minimis Benefit*

We hold that the EHA calls for more than a trivial educational benefit. That holding rests on the Act and its legislative history as well as interpretation of *Rowley*.

1

The opinion of the district court, anchored to the "some benefit" language of *Rowley* explained its holding as follows:

> The fact that Christopher would advance more quickly with intensive therapy rather than the therapy he now receives does not make the School District's program for Christopher defective. Programs need only render some benefit; they need not maximize potential.... The Supreme Court has determined that the Act is primarily a procedural statute and does not impose a substantive duty on the state to provide a student with other than some educational benefits. Increased muscle tone may well fall outside of

the scope of the requirement that Christopher receive some educational benefits from the program in which he is enrolled....

Plaintiffs argue on appeal that the district court applied the wrong standard in measuring the educational benefit of Christopher's program and that the case should be remanded for further proceedings consistent with the correct standard, one that requires more than a de minimis benefit. Defendants rejoin that Rowley's announcement of a "some benefit" test precludes judicial inquiry into the substantive education conferred by the Act, so long as the handicapped child receives any benefit at all. Noting that Christopher's parents acknowledge that he derives some benefit from his education, defendants submit that the inquiry is over and that the district court's summary judgment must be affirmed.

....

2

....

[W]e observe, as did the majority in *Rowley*, that a key concern of and primary justification for the EHA lay in the important goal of fostering self-sufficiency in handicapped children.... The EHA's sponsors stressed the importance of teaching skills that would foster personal independence for two reasons. First, they advocated dignity for handicapped children. Second, they stressed the long-term financial savings of early education and assistance for handicapped children....

Implicit in the legislative history's emphasis on self-sufficiency is the notion that states must provide some sort of meaningful education — more than mere access to the schoolhouse door. We acknowledge that self-sufficiency cannot serve as a substantive standard by which to measure the appropriateness of a child's education under the Act. Indeed, Christopher Polk is not likely ever to attain this coveted status, no matter how excellent his educational program. Instead, we infer that the emphasis on self-sufficiency indicates in some respect the quantum of benefits the legislators anticipated: they must have envisioned that significant learning would transpire in the special education classroom — enough so that citizens who would otherwise become burdens on the state would be transformed into productive members of society. Therefore, the heavy emphasis in the legislative history on self-sufficiency as one goal of education, where possible, suggests that the "benefit" conferred by the EHA and interpreted by *Rowley* must be more than de minimis.

We believe that the teaching of *Rowley* is not to the contrary. As discussed above, the *Rowley* Court described the education that must be provided under the EHA as "meaningful." The use of the term "meaningful" indicates that the Court expected more than de minimis benefit....

However, to the extent that dicta in *Rowley* might be read to imply that courts should not become involved in the substantive aspects of the EHA, we find *Rowley* distinguishable from the case sub judice.... *Rowley* specifically limited itself to the facts before it, involving a hearing-impaired child advancing from grade to grade in a "mainstreamed" classroom....

Additionally, *Rowley* is distinguishable from the case sub judice because of the type of services requested. Unlike the services of a full-time interpreter (which arguably may be deemed extraordinary assistance), physical therapy ... is an integral part of what Congress intended by "appropriate education" as defined in EHA, and it is an essential part of Christopher's education....

Finally, because of the severity of Christopher's disabilities and their qualitative difference from those of Amy Rowley, it is difficult to apply *Rowley* here. Christopher's progress cannot be measured by advancement in grade or acquisition of academic skill. His needs are drastically different, but no less important. Indeed, the needs of children like Christopher were paramount in the eyes of the EHA sponsors. The EHA provides that the most severely handicapped children be served first. That Christopher may never achieve the goals set in a traditional classroom does not undermine the fact that his brand of education (training in basic life skills) is an essential part of EHA's mandate. Therefore, although we believe the holding in *Rowley* is compatible with our holding in this case, to the extent that dicta in the opinion tend to undermine our substantive standard, we find the *Rowley* case distinguishable.

....

... [W]hen the Supreme Court said "some benefit" in *Rowley*, it did not mean "some" as opposed to "none." Rather, "some" connotes an amount of benefit greater than mere trivial advancement.

....

C. *Under the Correct Standard Must Summary Judgment Nevertheless Be Affirmed?*

....

We recognize the difficulty of measuring levels of benefit in severely handicapped children. Obviously, the question whether benefit is de minimis must be gauged in relation to the child's potential. However, we believe that the extent of the factual dispute concerning the level of benefit Christopher received from his educational program precludes summary judgment under the standard that we announce today. The judgment of the district court will therefore be reversed and the case remanded for further proceedings consistent with this opinion.

---

1. Though perhaps unlikely, one interpretation of the provision of special education and related services to children like *Polk* is that it represents too large a cost for schools to bear for the little benefit derived. What does the court mean, then, by requiring more than a de minimis benefit? Can more than a de minimis benefit be conveyed upon this student? For some students can there be more than trivial progress made, *i.e.*, can there be more than the prevention of regression?

2. Section 504 also contains a requirement for a free appropriate public education (FAPE), but unlike, IDEA, the school system may develop the criteria for providing the requisite services. 34 C.F.R. § 104.33. The regulations also state that one means of meeting the guidelines is to develop a FAPE in accordance with the dictates of IDEA. 34 C.F.R. § 104.33(b)(2). This procedure was used in *Girard (Pa.) Sch. Dist.*, 18 IDELR 1048 (1992). Parents claimed discrimination against their child as his regular teachers were not among those developing his Individualized Education Program, a required element of a free appropriate public education under IDEA. The school was found out of compliance as Section 504 indicates that this is only one method of establishing a FAPE. However, doing this exceeds the requirement of Section 504; but, the higher standard is to be used for court evaluation if the school district has elected to follow the standard in this fashion.

3. In *Rogers v. Bennett*, 873 F.2d 1387 (11th Cir. 1989) a federal appeals court held that there are differences between IDEA and Section 504 in the responsibilities of funding a free appropriate public education (FAPE):

> [IDEA requires] that states devote extra resources to meeting the needs of handicapped individuals. Significantly, Section 504 only prevents discrimination against the handicapped; unlike [IDEA], it does not require that states devote extra resources to meeting the needs of handicapped individuals ... To implement the provisions of Section 504, the [U.S.] Department of Education ... prohibit[s] state and local officials from discriminating against the handicapped in the provision of a free and appropriate public education to school age children [in comparison to non-handicapped children]. *Id.* at 1390.

The decision suggests that Section 504's central purpose is to assure disabled students of even-handed treatment, while IDEA, requiring school districts to put forth extra funding, renders something more to students who qualify. Is this an accurate explanation of the purposes of these laws? *See* an executive opinion by the Office of Civil Rights indicating that a Section 504 student, who is not IDEA eligible, is to receive special education services with state (not federal) funds if needed to deliver a FAPE. 18 IDELR 229 (OCR 1991).

C. INDIVIDUALIZED EDUCATION PROGRAM

DOE v. DEFENDANT I
United States Court of Appeals
898 F.2d 1186 (6th Cir. 1990)

KENNEDY, CIRCUIT JUDGE:

John Doe, a minor, appeals the District Court's judgment upholding an Administrative Law Judge's (ALJ) ruling that his parents are not entitled to reimbursement under the Education for All Handicapped Children Act (EAHCA or Act), 20 U.S.C. § 1400 *et seq.*, for expenses incurred while he was enrolled at a private junior high school. Appellant claimed that because appellee, a public local education agency within the meaning of the EAHCA, failed to provide him with a necessary individualized educational program (IEP) to accommodate his learning disability, he was forced to enroll in a private school where his educational needs could be met. He claims the appellee school district is therefore required to pay the cost of his private education as well as the cost of the tutoring he received while attending the public school.

It is undisputed that appellant is handicapped within the meaning of the EAHCA. He suffers primarily from a "dysgraphic disorder," which means he is unable to communicate effectively in writing. His verbal-conceptual skills are average or slightly above average. His learning disability is well-documented by several psychological test results obtained from April 1980 through December 1986.

... Appellant entered the fourth grade at a public elementary school on October 29, 1983 and attended that school without incident for three years. After completing his elementary education, a multi-disciplinary team (M-Team) met to determine the best education strategy for appellant upon his entry into junior high school. It recommended that in junior high school, appellant "be served on a consultative basis by the Resource teacher. [His] total program needs modification because of his difficulty in motor skills. Written tasks are very difficult for [him]; therefore, cutbacks in assignments may be needed."

Appellant began junior high school in the 1986-87 academic year. At the request of appellant's father, consultation work was suspended until the end of the first six-week marking period so the school's special education teacher could determine how well appellant performed on his own. At the end of that period, appellant received an "F" in English and "D's" in math, science, art, and social studies. Appellant was also punished several times by in-school suspension during this period for failing to complete assignments and for being late for class....

The teacher contacted appellant's father a second time by letter of November 5, 1986 and asked him how he wished her to work with appellant. At that time, the second six-week period had expired and the third was about to begin.

On November 7, 1986, another M-Team meeting was held. At that meeting, appellant's parents and educators at the school developed an individualized educational program. One component of the IEP was that the "parents would arrange for a tutor to work with [appellant] during school hours outside of his academic classes." The parents enrolled appellant at a private, for-profit tutorial service, rather than use the volunteer tutors which appellee said it would provide. The IEP also stipulated that appellant's parents would have appellant retested. Although the school officials appeared willing to provide this service, appellant's father refused to allow them to perform the retesting. The IEP did not indicate who had financial responsibility for the required tutoring or retesting.

Appellant was billed for his enrollment at the private tutorial service at a rate of $170 per week. On December 3, 1986, appellee denied appellant's requests for reimbursement of this bill, claiming that it offered a "free appropriate public education" (FAPE) as required by the EAHCA by offering volunteer tutors and to retest appellant at no charge. Appellant's parents subsequently withdrew him from the public school and placed him in a private school. Doe's parents requested and were granted a due process hearing at which they sought reimbursement for the costs of tutoring, tuition at the private school, and testing. On June 17, 1987, the hearing officer found that appellee complied with the EAHCA by providing Doe with a FAPE and that his parents therefore were not entitled to reimbursement. Appellant sought review of that decision in federal district court. The District Court upheld the ALJ and granted appellee's motion for summary judgment on the grounds that appellee provided Doe a free appropriate public education by offering volunteer tutors. Appellant then brought this timely appeal.

....

... In determining whether the state has complied with the Act's procedures, a court must not only "satisfy itself that the State has adopted the state plan, policies, and assurances required by the Act, but also to determine that the State has created an IEP for the child in question which conforms to the requirements of § 1401(19)." An essential element of a FAPE is an appropriate IEP....

Appellant argues that the school failed to comply with the Act because it did not develop an IEP according to the Act's requirements and that the educational alternatives it offered appellant were not sufficient to enable him to receive any educational benefit. Appellant first claims that there was no IEP in place when he began the school year, which is in violation of 34 C.F.R. § 300.342 (1987). However, appellant's contention misreads the requirements of section 300.342.... This regulation merely requires that where it is determined that special educational services are necessary, an IEP must be in place at the beginning of the school year. However, it can only be implemented after the meeting required by section 300.343, which in this case did not occur until November 7, 1986. Although an M-Team meeting was held on May 28, 1986 regarding appellant's junior high school placement, appellant's father specifically requested through November that there be no intervention while his son began his attendance at junior high school so the parents could see how well appellant could do on his own.

C. INDIVIDUALIZED EDUCATION PROGRAM

Appellant also argues that the IEP issued after the November meeting was insufficient because it did not state his present levels of educational performance and because it failed to state appropriate objective criteria for determining whether his instructional objectives were being met. Under the EAHCA, an IEP must be a written statement which includes:

> (A) a statement of the present levels of educational performance of [the] child, (B) a statement of annual goals, including short-term instructional objectives, (C) a statement of the specific educational services to be provided to [the] child, and the extent to which [the] child will be able to participate in regular educational programs, (D) the projected date for initiation and anticipated duration of such services, and (E) appropriate objective criteria and evaluation procedures and schedules for determining, on at least an annual basis, whether instructional objectives are being achieved. 20 U.S.C. § 1401(19).

Although the Supreme Court has said that reviewing courts should be loath to second-guess the efficacy of a state educational program, we are compelled to examine whether the IEP was developed pursuant to the statutory requirements. In doing this, we must see whether the IEP at issue "conforms with the requirements of § 1401(19)."

....

Appellant's IEP contains no reference to his present educational performance as required by section 1401(19)(A). Nor does it include any "objective criteria and evaluation procedures and schedules for determining, at least on an annual basis, whether instructional objectives are being achieved" in violation of section 1401(19)(E). However, to say that these technical deviations from section 1401(19) render appellant's IEP invalid is to exalt form over substance. It is undisputed that appellant's most recent grades were known by both the parents and the school officials. Moreover, because he was to be given instruction in the regular classroom, he would be graded according to the normal criteria used in the class. Only his method of instruction would be different. Thus, the parents and administrators had all of the information required by section 1401(19), even though it was not contained within the four corners of the IEP.

Recognizing that *Rowley* holds that the adequacy of an IEP is to be judged by whether it was produced in conformity with the requirements of section 1401(19), the Court's continued emphasis on the procedural safeguards afforded to parents convinces us that the Court was referring to the process by which the IEP is produced, rather than the myriad of technical items that must be included in the written document....

Adequate parental involvement and participation in formulating an IEP, not adherence to the laundry list of items given in section 1401(19), appear to be the Court's primary concern in requiring that procedures be strictly followed.

We therefore agree with appellee that because appellant's parents were allowed to participate fully in the development of his November 7, 1986 IEP, the procedural requirements of the EAHCA were met even though two items were omitted from the document. We underscore the fact that the information absent from the IEP was nonetheless known to all the parties.

The second portion of the *Rowley* test — that the IEP be "reasonably calculated to enable the child to receive educational benefits" — was also met. Appellant claims that he received D's and an F in his last graded semester at the public school, evidencing the fact that the IEP was not adequate to provide him with any educational benefit. We disagree. While it is true that "[w]hen the handicapped child is being educated in the regular classrooms of a public school system, the achievement of passing marks and advancement from grade to grade will be one important factor in determining educational benefit," 458 U.S. at 207 n. 28, we cannot conclude that appellant's poor grades indicate the inadequacies of the IEP. Appellant received those grades before development of the IEP at the November 7 M-Team meeting. Appellant's parents at that time accepted that IEP as valid and adequate. The ALJ found that the school was sincere in its desire to help appellant and noted that appellant's own expert said the IEP had "some great ideas." Although willing to implement the IEP, the teachers were "frustrated in this endeavor by the frequent absences of the child and by the lack of coordination due to the restrictions placed by the parents on communicating with the tutor." In short, the IEP was never given a chance to succeed. Appellant has the burden of proving by a preponderance of the evidence that the IEP was inadequate.... We agree with the ALJ and the District Court that appellant's IEP was calculated to allow him to receive educational benefit from the instruction.

We turn then to whether appellant's parents are entitled to reimbursement for the cost of tutoring, tuition at private school, and testing. With regard to reimbursement for the private school tuition, the Supreme Court said:

> If the courts ultimately determine that the IEP proposed by the school officials was appropriate, the parents would be barred from obtaining reimbursement for any interim period in which their child's placement violated § 1415(e)(3). *Burlington* [*School Committee v. Massachusetts Dept. of Educ.*], 471 U.S. at 374.

Because we have determined that appellant's IEP was appropriate, he is not entitled to reimbursement for the cost of private schooling. Appellant's parents removed him from the free public school and placed him in a private institution at their own peril. They are responsible for the cost of doing so.

We similarly hold that Doe's parents are responsible for the cost of the private tutoring he received while in public school....

... The school district chose to provide tutoring services through its own resources, which the parents rejected. The parents' desire to use a private service, rather than a public one, does not establish a duty on the part of the

C. INDIVIDUALIZED EDUCATION PROGRAM

school to pay for it, since the choice of how services are to be provided rests initially with the school. There is no showing that the tutoring offered by appellee was inadequate. Therefore, appellant is not entitled to reimbursement.

Accordingly, the judgment of the District Court is Affirmed.

---

1. Does it appear in this case that the court is turning to the procedural requirements of IDEA to avoid the substantive features of the Individualized Education Program (IEP)? Is an IEP or FAPE that is procedurally perfect necessarily appropriate for this child? Does this (or should this) procedural satisfaction depend on parental involvement with the IEP team? Does (or should) substantive provisions depend on procedural requirements? Should bargaining power, clout and expertise on the IEP panel be factors in determining the sufficiency of IEP meetings, and ultimately, the IEP's themselves? Should educators be comfortable with a decision that a perfectly conducted IEP conference equals an adequate IEP? Is such a question synonymous with the court's decision in this case?

2. The IEP team may be made up of school officials, teachers, parents, and other persons qualified to be make educational decisions and interpret evaluation results. Is an otherwise valid IEP invalid if the student's teachers are not present? What about the teachers from the private school in which the parents unilaterally placed the child? The answer to the second question may be found in *Girard (Pa.) Sch. Dist.*, 18 IDELR 1048, *supra*, where the absence of the teacher was considered a violation of IDEA.

3. May IEP members be replaced at the request of the student's parents? *See Norma P. v. Pelham Sch. Dist.*, 19 IDELR 938 (1993). Even though the IEP was ruled appropriate, an Administrative Law Judge held that its members could be replaced due to a breakdown in trust. The parents appealed a denial of compensatory damages. During the pendency of the appeal, a new IEP was developed without the parents being present (they chose not to attend, but did not disagree with the proposed placement). May schools continue to develop IEP's during the pendency of the litigation? The court answered in the affirmative as failure to conduct a required annual IEP conference would violate IDEA. Students are guaranteed a continuous education under the Act based on the most recent IEP.

4. Which party, according to the court in *Doe*, has the burden of demonstrating the adequacy of the IEP? Does the answer depend on who raises the claim? In addition to *Doe*, consider the following case.

LASCARI v. BOARD OF EDUCATION OF RAMAPO INDIAN HILLS REGIONAL HIGH SCHOOL DISTRICT

Supreme Court of New Jersey
116 N.J. 30, 560 A.2d 1180 (1989)

POLLOCK, J:

In May 1981 Anthony and Geraldine Lascari went to the Ramapo-Indian Hills Regional High School (Ramapo) to discuss why their son, John, could not read and what could be done about it. Eight years later they are still waiting for an answer. After conferences with school officials, an administrative hearing in the Department of Education, two trials in the Law Division, and three appeals in the Appellate Division, John's right to an education remains unresolved. In the interim, John has attained his majority and completed his education.

Our purpose in this opinion is to bring this matter to a close and to provide sufficient guidance so that in the future parents, children, and school boards can decide more equitably and efficiently the rights of handicapped children to a public school education. Toward that end, we conclude that the school district has the burden of proving that it is providing an appropriate education to the child. We conclude further that the district did not satisfy that burden in this case, and that Mr. and Mrs. Lascari are entitled from the Board of Education of Ramapo-Indian Hills Regional High School District (the board or the district) to reimbursement for John's tuition, but not for his room and board, at a residential school.

....

II

John attended kindergarten through eighth grade in the Franklin Lake School District. In the second grade, he was classified as "neurologically impaired," and in the seventh and eighth grades he was placed in a class for the "perceptually impaired." He was graduated from grade school in June 1980.

In anticipation of his enrollment at Ramapo, John was evaluated by a child-study team consisting of a learning-disability specialist, a social worker, and a psychologist. He was also examined by a pediatric neurologist. These examinations revealed that John suffered from "a neurologic dysfunction in the form of a marked dyslexia [with] associated difficulties in auditory perceptual skills," and from "low self-esteem." Although tests revealed his I.Q. was 126, John read at second-grade level and felt "segregated" from other students because he had been placed in the perceptually-impaired program.

After discussing the matter with Mr. and Mrs. Lascari, Ramapo designed an IEP, which had five goals: (1) to continue a phonetic-linguistic reading program to strengthen skills; (2) to develop math skills to include all areas necessary for practical math; (3) to develop a language arts program; (4) to build self-esteem and self-worth; and (5) to develop vocational skills.

Pursuant to the IEP, in September 1980 John entered Ramapo's program for the perceptually impaired. A special education teacher taught him reading,

C. INDIVIDUALIZED EDUCATION PROGRAM

mathematics, and language arts. His shop and physical-education classes were with non-handicapped children.

Towards the end of the school year, on May 12, 1981, Mr. and Mrs. Lascari met with Ramapo officials to review John's IEP for 1981-82. As a result of that meeting, Ramapo agreed to provide John with a more intensive reading and writing program, to eliminate a vocational training program, and to "integrate" John as much as possible with the other students. Because of their continuing concern that John was not receiving sufficient academic instruction, the Lascaris refused to agree to the proposed IEP for 1981-82. Through an attorney, Mr. and Mrs. Lascari requested a review of his 1981-82 IEP. Underlying the request was their concern that John still read at a second-grade level and that he had not received proper training to overcome his dyslexia.

Tests conducted in January, May, and June 1981 revealed that John's progress in the 1980-81 school year was insignificant. Essentially, the tests showed that he still read at a second-grade level and that his mathematics skills were at a fourth-grade level.

At a meeting on August 18, 1981, the Lascaris told Ramapo's Director of Special Services that they were contemplating enrolling John at the Landmark School, a private school in Massachusetts that specializes in teaching children with severe dyslexia. The parties disagree on the critical issue whether Mr. Lascari asked whether Ramapo would pay for John's expenses at Landmark.

On September 9, 1981, the Lascaris requested a due-process hearing, in which they sought reimbursement for tuition and residential costs at Landmark. Ramapo wrote to the Lascaris advising them that it believed its IEP was appropriate for John and confirming that John was enrolled at Landmark. On September 18, 1981, John started school at Landmark.

....

... [A] classification officer determined on April 6, 1983, that Ramapo's IEP failed to specify clearly the educational goals and objectives for John as well as the manner of measuring his progress. The classification officer found that the evaluations of John's progress by the Ramapo teachers and psychologists were deficient because they were subjective. Objective test scores indicated that John had failed to progress in word recognition, spelling, or mathematics. The officer found further that the five goals set forth in the 1980-81 IEP were incapable of objective measurement and that Ramapo probably had not intended John's mastery of those goals. Although the 1981-82 IEP was more specific, the officer found that it, too, was flawed.

Based on these findings, the officer concluded that "[n]either [IEP] complies fully with [state law] in that current educational performance is not indicated, no rationale for placement is stated, no statement as to how the placement is the least restrictive environment is made, and the instructional guide for each falls short of requirements." Although he found fault with the district, the officer also criticized the actions taken by the Lascaris.

As to them, he found that they "acted unilaterally and without undue pressure to place [John] in the Landmark School." The classification officer determined that there was no indication that John required placement at a residential facility.

....

The net result of the classification officer's decision was that the Lascaris' request for reimbursement for tuition and residential expenses at Landmark was denied.

... [T]he Lascaris appealed the classification officer's decision to the Superior Court, Chancery Division. After reviewing the administrative record, the court, in an unreported opinion, found that "the education system from the time this child entered school was just pushing him along." In effect, John had been "warehoused" since the second grade....

....

Consequently, the court held that Ramapo had failed to design an appropriate IEP for John, and that his parents should be reimbursed for the tuition but not for his room and board at Landmark....

Ramapo appealed to the Appellate Division and the Lascaris cross-appealed, seeking reimbursement for John's residential expenses. The Appellate Division vacated the Chancery Division's order and remanded the matter for a new trial on the record. In remanding, the Appellate Division stated:

> Our review of this matter has satisfied us that the judge did not make findings sufficient to impose liability on defendant for the placement of John at Landmark....
>
> ....
>
> The Appellate Division has stated that the trial court did not consider what would be the least restrictive environment for John. This Court had before it a proposed program by the School District which had, in its opinion, been established as a failure. No other alternatives were suggested by the School District which is presumed to have expertise. By inference, the Appellate Division requires the plaintiff to establish that there are other less restrictive environments than the boarding school which other experts had recommended for their son.

The Lascaris appealed to the Appellate Division, which affirmed the dismissal of their complaint. We granted certification....

III

As indicated, the State and federal statutory and regulatory schemes outline a district's obligation to educate handicapped children. Nowhere, however, do the statutes or regulations address the basic issue before us, the allocation of the burden of persuasion or proof. The Appellate Division assumed that the burden rested on the parents to prove the inappropriateness of a placement and of an IEP. Consequently, that court concluded that to be entitled to reimbursement, the parents must show that a district would be unable to provide an appropriate

C. INDIVIDUALIZED EDUCATION PROGRAM

education and that the selected residential facility offers the least restrictive environment. The court also suggested that parents select one of the least-expensive private alternatives.

....

In cases in which the district has sought to change a child's placement, some courts have allocated the burden of proof to the district. That allocation is supported by the view that when a child is currently learning in a placement that was jointly developed by the district and the parents, the party attacking the program should show why it is inappropriate.... In placing the burden on the district when it attacks the IEP, those courts have also relied on the statutory preference for maintaining the status quo when the child is receiving an appropriate education. Although we agree with the results of those cases, we are not certain that the courts would have placed the burden of proof on the party seeking to change the IEP if that party had been the parents rather than the school district. We need not, however, dwell on that point. The reason is that we believe it is more consistent with the State and federal scheme to place the burden on the school district not only when it seeks to change the IEP, but also when the parents seek the change.

Various considerations lead us to that conclusion. Underlying the State and federal regulations is an abiding concern for the welfare of handicapped children and their parents. Consistent with that concern, the basic obligation to provide a handicapped child with a free, appropriate education is placed on the local school district. It is the district that must identify handicapped children and then formulate and implement their IEPs. Finally, the regulatory scheme vests handicapped children and their parents with numerous procedural safeguards. Those safeguards include the right to counsel and to the advice of experts; to present evidence and cross-examine witnesses; to "have the child who is the subject of the hearing present"; and to a public hearing.... Like those procedural safeguards, the allocation of the burden of proof protects the rights of handicapped children to an appropriate education.

Our result is also consistent with the proposition that the burdens of persuasion and of production should be placed on the party better able to meet those burdens.... The school board, with its recourse to the child-study team and other experts, has ready access to the expertise needed to formulate an IEP. Through the child-study team, the board generally has extensive records pertaining to a handicapped child. The board is also conversant with the federal and State laws dictating what the district must provide to handicapped children in order to comply with the EAHCA.... By contrast, parents may lack the expertise needed to formulate an appropriate education for their child.

Although the posture of the district in the present case is that of a defendant, the nature of the proceedings suggests that it is not asking too much to require it to carry the burden of proof. These matters are initiated as administrative proceedings and reviewed by a court sitting without a jury. Consequently, the allocation of the burden of proof may not be as important to trial strategy as it would be in other proceedings, such as a jury trial.... To conclude, we believe the obligation of parents at the due-process hearing should be merely to place in issue the appropriateness of the IEP. The school board should then bear the burden of proving that the IEP was appropriate. In reaching that result, we have sought to implement the intent of the statutory and regulatory schemes.

We also conclude that in determining whether an IEP was appropriate, the focus should be on the IEP actually offered and not on one that the school board could have provided if it had been so inclined. Consistent with that proposition which was in effect at the time of the Lascaris' due-process hearing, excused a school district from responsibility for the cost of private school placement if the district "offered" a free, appropriate education, not if it "could offer" such an education.... In short, a school board that has failed to meet its obligation to provide an appropriate education should not escape liability by showing that it could have done so.

A remaining question is the standard to be applied in determining whether an IEP is appropriate. Federal law requires that the education offered to a handicapped child must be "sufficient to confer some educational benefit." Although the federal government furnishes a basic floor of educational opportunity, states may construct a higher ceiling. Accordingly, the 1978 regulations expressly required school districts to provide an education "according to how the pupil can best achieve success in learning ..." (the "best achieve success-in-learning" standard)....

... Because the board did not challenge the Appellate Division's use of the "best achieve success-in-learning" standard, we need not decide if the lower federal standard applies retroactively in the Lascaris' case.

....

IV

Turning to the facts of this case, the classification officer found that the district erred by "providing a program incapable of being evaluated for appropriateness." The officer concluded, however, that the district's offered program "was not demonstrated as improper, only as nonspecific in its written aspirations and evaluation of effectiveness." In contrast, the trial court found that the district failed to provide an appropriate education through 1980-81 and that the proposal for 1981-82 was also inappropriate. We agree.

As previously indicated, the purpose of the IEP is to guide teachers and to insure that the child receives the necessary education. Without an adequately drafted IEP, it would be difficult, if not impossible, to measure a child's progress, a measurement that is necessary to determine changes to be made in the next IEP. Furthermore, an IEP that is incapable of review denies parents the opportunity to help shape their child's education and hinders their ability to assure that their child will receive the education to which he or she is entitled.

Consequently, the shortcomings that rendered John's program incapable of review also rendered it inappropriate. As the classification officer found, "[w]hat

C. INDIVIDUALIZED EDUCATION PROGRAM

it [sic] is not clear from the IEP or testimony are the specific goals and objectives either the child study team or the teacher had for [John]. Equally unclear is how any goals or progress was to be measured or decided." The officer continued:

> All teacher remarks are found to be subjectively based.... [T]he goals and objectives of the IEP for 1980-81 and the proposed plan for 1981-82 were so vague that they were meaningless.
>
> ....
>
> Neither document complies fully with [state law] in that current educational performance is not indicated, no rationale for placement is stated, no statement as to how the placement is the least restrictive environment is made, and the instructional guide for each falls short of requirements.

For its part, the trial court found that John had been "warehoused" and that the district had failed to provide sufficiently individualized instruction in academic subjects. Based on the inadequacies as found by the classification officer and the trial court, we likewise conclude that the district failed to provide an education that would help John best achieve success in learning.

V

The determination that the district failed to provide John with an appropriate IEP leads to the question of the Lascaris' right to reimbursement for the cost of their son's private education. That right to reimbursement is grounded in the statutory grant of power to state and federal courts to "grant such relief as the court determines appropriate." As interpreted by the United States Supreme Court, that statute entitles parents to reimbursement for the cost of private schooling during the pendency of any proceedings if it is later determined that the education offered by the district was inappropriate. Otherwise, parents would be forced to choose between an inappropriate, free public education or providing their child with an appropriate education at their own expense....

... Although it has not defined the showing parents must make to obtain reimbursement for the cost of private schooling, the United States Supreme Court has stated that if parents "pay for what they consider to be the appropriate placement," it "would be an empty victory to have a court tell them several years later that they were right but that these expenditures could not in a proper case be reimbursed by the school officials." That statement is consistent with the goals and purposes of the federal and State schemes for the education of handicapped children. Thus, if the board fails to meet its burden of establishing the appropriateness of its program and if the parents demonstrate that they have acted in good faith, the district should be liable for the cost of the private school placement of a handicapped child.

Here, the district contends that the Lascaris should not be reimbursed for the cost of John's schooling at Landmark because it did not provide him with an education in the least restrictive environment. The major premise underlying that contention is that parents are not entitled to any reimbursement if they send their child to a boarding school unless residential placement is necessary for the education of their child. If residential placement is not necessary, so the argument proceeds, it does not provide an education in the least restrictive environment and is, therefore, inappropriate. With specific reference to this case, the district contends that it was not necessary for John to attend an out-of-state boarding school.

We are sensitive to the possibility that parents may select a private school that affords their child an education that is more elaborate than is required. Conceivably, parents might select a boarding school even though a day program would furnish their child with an appropriate education. It would be anomalous, however, to recognize the parents' right to reimbursement, but to deny completely that right merely because they selected a school that furnished an education beyond that which the district is obliged to offer. It would also be anomalous to deny parents the right to reimbursement when the district failed to provide their child with an appropriate education and the only school that the parents could find was a boarding school. Hence, we reject the district's argument that the Lascaris are necessarily precluded from all reimbursement because they did not select the least restrictive environment for the education of their child.

Because the reviewing court may grant "appropriate" relief ... its award can be informed by equitable considerations. Several courts have held that it is appropriate to balance the equities in determining whether to grant full or partial reimbursement for the cost of private schooling.... We agree.

In balancing the equities, the court or the ALJ may consider whether the private placement selected was the least restrictive alternative. For some children, placement in a boarding school may be the least restrictive alternative. Parents who find an education for their child in a boarding school need not be barred from any reimbursement merely because their child did not require residential placement. Their right to reimbursement may, however, be limited. Unnecessary placement in a boarding school may decrease the amount of reimbursement, but it need not preclude partial reimbursement if the school meets the child's educational needs.

Consistent with the preceding analysis, we conclude that the Lascaris are entitled to reimbursement for the cost of tuition, but not for room and board at Landmark. At no time has the board questioned the academic program offered by Landmark. In fact, the board sought to establish the appropriateness of its own program by proving that it was similar to the Landmark program. As explained above, we reject the board's argument that Landmark, as an out-of-state residential school, did not offer the least restrictive environment. Because the district's program was inappropriate, the Lascaris were forced to find alternative private schooling for their son. Confronted with this stressful decision, they did their best. We should not ask for more.

C. INDIVIDUALIZED EDUCATION PROGRAM

1. Is the *Lascari* opinion consistent with that in *Doe, supra*? Is *Lascari* an "exercise in cooperative federalism?"

2. Recall that even though John Lascari's IQ was 126, he was reading at the second grade level upon entering high school. This fact may indicate that tests alone should not be the determining factors as regards special education needs. The record of the student's experience stated that he felt "segregated" because he had been placed in special education programs since grade school. Is there something to the claim that special education programs may actually harm a student who is legitimately thought to require them?

3. The student in *Lascari* was described as being "perceptually impaired." The EAHCA (or IDEA) does not define this term. What is the court's definition?

4. Part V of the *Lascari* opinion presents a good discussion of remedies for when school districts fail to provide a disabled student with a FAPE or adequate IEP. For further discussion, *see* the "Remedies" section of this chapter.

5. In *Babb v. Knox County Sch. Sys.*, 965 F.2d 104 (6th Cir. 1992), the parents of an emotionally disturbed child brought suit against their public school district for reimbursement of expenses incurred in placing their child in a private residential program specially designed for emotionally disturbed children. The court held that the parents were entitled to reimbursement, including costs for psychological care and related services, since the school failed to fully examine the child's academic, emotional, and psychological profile.

The court in *Babb* looked at only two options for the student when it determined the appropriateness of his IEP: 1) enrolling him in a private placement as his parents did; and 2) keeping him in the original public school placement as the Tennessee school district had done. How far reaching is the court's analysis in the case? Will parents be able to enroll students in expensive private institutions or schools and then receive reimbursement when they know with near certainty that *their* placement represents the "least restrictive environment" for their child? Does this application of *Babb* depend solely on the school's failure to develop and offer an adequate IEP? How important or pronounced must the school's inaction be for reimbursement to be granted?

6. Section 504 does not require the creation of an IEP. However, regulations state that such a plan may be developed in accordance with IDEA provisions as one means of satisfying the Section 504 requirement of a free appropriate public education. 34 C.F.R. § 104.33(b)(2). Moreover, there is a tacit requirement of some kind of plan in that placement procedures must be developed for Section 504 students, and similar to IDEA, this must be accomplished by a committee knowledgeable about the student including teachers, and other professional personnel within the school. 34 C.F.R. § 104.35(c)(3).

D. EXTENDED SCHOOL YEAR PROGRAMS

CORDREY v. EUCKERT
United States Court of Appeals
917 F.2d 1460 (6th Cir. 1990)

ENGEL, SENIOR CIRCUIT JUDGE:

Plaintiff Chance Cordrey, a minor, is a handicapped child within the meaning of The Education For All Handicapped Children Act ("the Act"). With his parents he appeals a judgment entered in the district court in favor of the defendants, the Evergreen Local School District, the Evergreen School Board and several School Board officials (collectively, "Evergreen"). The Cordreys claimed that by failing to provide Chance with an extended school year (ESY) program,[1] Evergreen has denied him a "free appropriate public education" in violation of the Act. The appeal presents several issues, including whether and under what circumstances parents may be deemed to have waived a procedural right under the Act, and the proper standard by which a court should review a denial of an ESY to a handicapped child. We ultimately hold that the parents here did waive certain procedural rights under the Act, and that the district court did not err as a matter of law or fact in ruling that Evergreen was not obligated to provide Chance with an ESY.

I

Chance, now fifteen years old, is handicapped by severe developmental delays following an autistic pattern. His maladaptive autistic behaviors include self-stimulation, self-abusiveness, non-attending behaviors, and social withdrawal. His communication skills consist of four manual signs, and he can work independently for only three to five minutes at best. An individualized educational program (IEP), required under the Act, was formulated for Chance for the 1981-82 school year, and he was placed in a multihandicapped class in a Toledo public school. This class did not operate during the summer. In 1982, the Cordreys enrolled Chance in a summer education program operated by the Toledo Autistic Society (TAS), a non-profit private agency. In May 1984, after two summers of the private program, the Cordreys requested Evergreen to pay for Chance's program as part of his IEP. Without convening a meeting to review Chance's IEP as provided by the Act, the Evergreen Board of Education decided that Chance should receive an ESY at a summer program run by the Fulton County Board of Mental Retardation and Developmental Disabilities.

In November 1985, an IEP meeting was held, but the Cordreys and Evergreen were unable to reach an agreement regarding summer services for Chance. Instead, in May 1986, the parties negotiated a process to address the ESY issue during the 1986-87 school year. Pursuant to the agreement, the parties selected

---

[1]An ESY is an organized program beyond the regular 180 day school year.

D. EXTENDED SCHOOL YEAR PROGRAMS

Dr. Mark Pittner, a clinical psychologist, to evaluate Chance. Dr. Pittner completed the evaluation in April 1987. He concluded that Chance would benefit from an ESY program, and faced an "unacceptable" and "untenable" risk of regression without one. Dr. Pittner also stated, however, that it was impossible to assess empirically or psychometrically whether an ESY program was necessary for Chance since he had been enrolled in a summer program for the previous several years.

On May 5, 1987, the Cordreys met with the Superintendent of Evergreen schools, a Fulton County Board psychologist, a psychology intern and counsel for the parties. Neither Dr. Pittner nor Chance's teacher, Judy Jasco, attended. Based on Dr. Pittner's evaluation, the parties agreed that Chance should be enrolled in an ESY program in the coming summer. While Evergreen suggested that Chance should be placed in the county program, the Cordreys strongly favored the TAS program. Furthermore, Evergreen refused to place an ESY program on Chance's IEP unless the Cordreys agreed to exclude the program from the "stay put" provision of the Act, 20 U.S.C. § 1415(e)(3). This section provides that a handicapped child's placement may not be changed while a hearing or suit challenging an IEP is pending. Rejecting this condition, the Cordreys countered that the IEP meeting was improperly constituted under the Act because Chance's teacher was absent. Evergreen responded that the meeting was not an IEP meeting but only a preliminary discussion of Dr. Pittner's report, and offered to hold a formal IEP meeting at a later date with Chance's teacher in attendance. The Cordreys refused the offer. The meeting then ended without agreement between the parties.

Several days later, on May 11, the Cordreys requested an impartial due process hearing pursuant to the Act to challenge the lack of an ESY in Chance's IEP. Following a hearing in December 1987, the impartial hearing officer concluded that Chance should receive ESY services, and that these could be provided through the county program. On appeal the state-level reviewing officer reversed, concluding that the Cordreys had failed to demonstrate that Chance needed an ESY. The Cordreys then began the present suit in federal district court, where they further alleged that Evergreen had discriminated against Chance on the basis of his handicap. On December 8, 1988, the district court held that Evergreen had not violated the procedural mandates of the Act and that the Cordreys had failed to prove that Chance would suffer significant regression of skills without a summer program. The court did not directly address the discrimination claim.

On appeal, the Cordreys argue that Evergreen violated the procedural requirements of the Act as well as its "stay-put" provision. They also contend that Evergreen's failure to provide an ESY to Chance denied him a "free appropriate public education" under the Act, and that the district court further erred in placing the burden of proof on this issue on the Cordreys. Last, they renew their discrimination claim.

II

The Act requires any state that receives funding thereunder to provide all handicapped children with a "free appropriate public education," 20 U.S.C. § 1412(1), "regardless of the severity of their handicap." § 1412(2)(C). A "free appropriate public education" is one which is designed to meet the unique needs of the child, by means of an "individualized education program" (IEP). §§ 1401(a)(16), (18). The Act and corresponding federal and state regulations detail the procedures by which an IEP is to be developed and revised by the parents, the school district and the teacher. If dissatisfied with any matter relating to the child's evaluation or educational placement, the parents may seek an impartial due process hearing to resolve the matter, with appeal to the state educational agency. Thereafter, "[a]ny party aggrieved by the findings and decision" of the state administrative hearing may bring a civil action in a federal district court. § 1415(e)(2).

In *Hendrick Hudson Bd. of Education v. Rowley*, 458 U.S. 176 (1982), the Supreme Court ... [concluded] that "adequate compliance with the procedures prescribed would in most cases assure much if not all of what Congress wished in the way of substantive content of an IEP." "[A] court's inquiry in suits brought under § 1415(e)(2) is twofold. First, has the state complied with the procedures set forth in the Act? And second, is the individualized educational program developed through the Act's procedures reasonably calculated to enable the child to receive educational benefits?" *Rowley* thus "requir[es] adherence to the procedural demands of the Act, while giving utmost deference to specific educational decisions once it is determined that they stem from the procedures outlined in the Act."

III

We now consider various procedural issues under the first prong of the *Rowley* inquiry.

[The Court in Part III-A held that the Cordreys waived their right to a properly constituted IEP meeting by knowingly and voluntarily refusing Evergreen's offer to schedule a full IEP meeting. The waiver occurred at the May 5, 1987, meeting which Chance's teacher missed. The court in Part III-B considered Cordey's allegations of procedural violations by Evergreen. The Court of Appeals found that (1) Evergreen did not make a placement decision for Chance at the May 5, 1987 meeting, upholding the trial court's finding; (2) Evergreen's failure to document the parents' refusal to attend a reconvened IEP meeting was inconsequential, because the Cordreys rejected an offer to reconvene; and (3) Evergreen did not violate the stay-put provision of the EHA by refusing to maintain Chance in a private summer program, because the school district never formally decided to include an ESY in Chance's IEP.

D. EXTENDED SCHOOL YEAR PROGRAMS

The Court then stated that the provision of an ESY is a substantive issue, and turned to that discussion.]

....

IV

....

B. *Burden of proof*

This circuit has recently joined the Fifth Circuit in holding that the party challenging the terms of an IEP should bear the burden of proving that the educational placement established by the IEP is not appropriate. Under this rule, Chance and his parents would bear the burden of proof since they seek to add ESY services to his IEP.

....

C. *The standard for whether an ESY is necessary to a "free appropriate public education"*

... After a thorough analysis of the Act and its legislative history, the [Supreme] Court set forth the statutory definition by holding that a "free appropriate public education" "consists of access to specialized instruction and related services which are individually designed to provide educational benefit to the handicapped child." However, the Court explicitly declined "to establish any one test for determining the adequacy of educational benefits conferred upon all children covered by the Act." Instead, the opinion in *Rowley* limited its substantive review to the facts of that case.... The facts here are considerably more challenging.

In the context of the severely handicapped, a district court in this circuit has held that a child is entitled to an extended school year if it would be not merely "beneficial but ... a necessary component of an appropriate education for [the child]." *Rettig v. Kent City School Dist.*, 539 F.Supp. 768, 778 (N.D.Ohio 1981), *aff'd in part*, vacated in part on other grounds, 720 F.2d 463 (6th Cir. 1983). More specifically, an ESY "would be appropriate if it would prevent significant regression of skills or knowledge retained by [the child] so as to seriously affect his progress toward self-sufficiency." Under this standard, the district court in *Rettig* held that an ESY was not necessary because the child regressed at the beginning of the regular school year even after attending a summer program and at various times throughout the year. 539 F.Supp. at 779. On appeal, this court briefly affirmed this aspect of the district court's decision by stating that a summer program was "not necessary to permit [the child] to benefit from his instruction."

The district court in the present case cited and followed the standard of the district court in *Rettig* in determining that Chance would benefit from but did not need an ESY. The court explained that "[t]here is no evidence that Chance would suffer significant regression of skills or knowledge without a summer program." The Cordreys and *amici* attack this holding and the underlying standard on a variety of fronts and propose other standards allegedly more faithful to their statutory source. To resolve this issue, we turn to *Rettig*.

Both parties and all *amici* agree that under the standard in *Rettig*, a child must prove his need for an ESY empirically, based on evidence of prior regression and slow recoupment without summer programming. As we have observed, the Cordreys and *amici* object that this standard is too narrow and unfair. Such a standard, they argue, works particularly harsh results where parents have provided an extended school year to their child on their own. These parents would be forced either to allow their child to regress without an ESY (thus empirically proving his need for one) or to provide on their own what they believe their child needs to make reasonable progress and is entitled to by the Act. The Third Circuit has condemned this "Hobson's choice" by rejecting, in dicta, the rule that a child must first show regression in order to demonstrate need. *Polk v. Central Susquehanna Intermediate Unit 16*, 853 F.2d 171, 184 (3d Cir. 1988).

Evergreen's responses are twofold. First, absent hard empirical proof, a finding that a child needs an ESY could be based only on generalized statements regarding children afflicted with such a handicap. As all the experts testifying in this case agree, regression and recoupment patterns vary greatly among similarly handicapped children. Accordingly, to provide an ESY on such generalized rationale is to ignore the Supreme Court's emphasis in *Rowley* that an IEP must be based on an individualized assessment of the child. Second, Evergreen continues, unless hard empirical data are required, parents can force a school district to provide an ESY by providing one for their child independently and thereby preventing the district from later showing that the child will not regress without it.

How "hard" the evidence of regression must be has apparently never been directly addressed by a court or administrative review board. In *Rettig*, the only decision from this circuit addressing whether a child was entitled to an ESY, the child participated in summer educational programs for most if not all of the several previous summers, including the one immediately preceding the lawsuit. As in the present case, there was thus little if any evidence of the child's prior regression absent an ESY. *See Rettig*, 539 F.Supp. at 774-75. Had the district court in *Rettig* or this court on appeal concluded that a child's entitlement to an ESY depended on proof of actual prior regression, it would have been easy for either to have simply said so. Neither did. Also, at least one other circuit apparently has allowed less-than-definitive proof of regression under a standard quite similar to that in *Rettig*. *See Alamo Heights Indep. School District v. State Bd. of Education*, 790 F.2d 1153, 1156-58 (5th Cir. 1986) (affirming the judgment below that a child who had received an ESY privately for several years was entitled to an ESY under the Act)....

The advantages of a "hard empirical proof" rule are obvious. It is clearer and simpler to apply than reliance on conflicting non-empirical expert opinion. It

D. EXTENDED SCHOOL YEAR PROGRAMS

gives parents an incentive to raise and resolve the issue of whether an ESY is necessary before they independently provide one to the child, when the child's regression and recoupment without an ESY can be assessed. At the same time, a policy based upon discouraging parents from structuring a child's summer months solely to gain proof of need for an ESY seems at best unfair. It seems equally unfair to penalize a child previously enrolled in private summer programs but whose situation later deteriorates so that he now might qualify for a publicly-funded ESY....

Further, Evergreen's fear that it could be boxed in by parents who present the district with ESY programming as a *fait accompli* seems exaggerated. While it is true that the district would be denied its best case against an ESY, in such a case it may still rely and, as the ultimate holding in this case illustrates, prevail on the basis of expert testimony and overall proof. Finally, the concern of the Cordreys and *amici* that a regression/recoupment standard, strictly defined, would stray too far from its statutory source and take on a life of its own has some merit. Professional opinions not based solely on empirical observations are less precise, to be sure, but they may in a proper case be as faithful or even more faithful to the Act's general substantive requirement of "some educational benefit" to the child.

In conclusion, then, the regression standard in *Rettig* and like cases is best interpreted not to require absolutely that a child demonstrate that he has regressed in the past to the serious detriment of his educational progress in order to prove his need for a summer program. Instead, where there is no such empirical data available, need may be proven by expert opinion, based upon a professional individual assessment.

Once the content of a proper regression standard as stated in *Rettig* is clarified, the alternatives proposed by the appellants and amici lose their persuasive force. One such standard is cited from the literature in the special education field, in which the regression/recoupment standard is widely questioned or rejected. Allegedly more professionally sound, this alternative standard inquires whether an ESY is "critical to ongoing student progress." The authors of this paper advise that need for an ESY should focus not on ill-defined terms such as regression and recoupment, but instead on measurement of explicit criteria that affect a student's ability to maintain his progress towards his IEP goals. Appellants advance a similar alternative from ESY guidelines recently issued by the Ohio Department of Education. The guidelines do not specifically mention regression or recoupment and instead would have the IEP team consider whether the child "is failing, or is likely to fail, to achieve short-term instructional objectives on the IEP due to interruption of instruction between school years." However, if the existing regression-based standard for ESY is defined loosely to allow for individualized expert opinion and not just empirical predictions based on actual prior regression, the standard would seem flexible enough to accommodate such refinements in professional understanding of when a child needs an ESY. The focus of *Rettig* is clearly on the child's educational "progress," *Rettig*, 539 F.Supp. at 779, and "benefit." The ESY standard should be open to developments in special education science, but not bound to any particular one.

The Cordreys also propose that the *Rettig* regression standard should be broadened to the multi-factored inquiry articulated by a federal district court in an unpublished decision in *Lee v. Thompson*, Educ.Handicapped L.Rptr. 554:429 (D.Haw.1983). There it was held that factors relevant to whether an ESY is proper include the nature and severity of the handicap; the areas of learning crucial to progress towards self-sufficiency; and the extent of regression and the rate of recoupment following an interruption in programming. Again, however, since the regression/recoupment standard in *Rettig* is not limited to empirical proof, the analysis suggested by *Lee* does not differ significantly.

Beyond the verbal formulation of a substantive standard for ESY entitlement, the actual dispute in this case seems to center on a more fundamental issue: what is the role of an ESY within a "free appropriate public education" under the Act? Evergreen believes that the purpose of ESY programming is to allow the student to maintain the progress achieved during the regular school year. The Cordreys and *amici*, on the other hand, endorse the broader view of the court in *Lee*: ESY is no mere "backstop" to a regular school year, but should be "regarded as one additional means of providing a handicapped child with specialized instruction in accordance with his [IEP]."

....

We conclude therefore that it is best to hold that the regression standard for an ESY in *Rettig*, as we have interpreted it here, is consistent with the Act and with *Rowley*. Worthy as the goal of providing unlimited services to handicapped children may be, courts must apply the Act as it was written and is interpreted by the Supreme Court....

D. *Applying the ESY standard in this case*

... The factual questions here are Chance's tendency to regress, prior regression, ability to recoup lost skills, and progress toward his educational goals. The legal question is whether these facts meet the standard of significant skill losses of such degree and duration so as seriously to impede his progress toward his educational goals.

In this case, the district court found, as Chance's teacher's testified, that he lost some skills during the week or over a weekend, and that it was not uncommon for other non-handicapped children to lose skills over the summer vacation. The court also cited testimony by the Fulton County Board of Education psychologist that Chance suffered regression throughout the school year, such as after a weekend or Christmas vacation, and that in her opinion, Chance did not need an ESY. The court also noted Dr. Pittner's report, which states that Chance might regress in his behavior with as well as without an ESY,

D. EXTENDED SCHOOL YEAR PROGRAMS

but that his risk of regression without an ESY would be unacceptable. From these findings, the district court concluded:

> There is no evidence that Chance would suffer significant regression of skills or knowledge without a summer program. This child lost skills throughout the school year. Thus, an ESY program would be beneficial for Chance, but it is not necessary to prevent significant regression of his progress toward self-sufficiency.

The Cordreys challenge this conclusion by citing other evidence in the record regarding Chance's prior experiences of regression and slow, if any, progress with regard to certain skills and behavior affecting these skills. They emphasize that Evergreen had agreed with the Cordreys to settle whether Chance should receive an ESY by having Dr. Pittner examine Chance and recommend whether an ESY was appropriate. Since Evergreen did not specify any criteria for his recommendation, the Cordreys claim, Evergreen may not now reject it. For its part, Evergreen attacks the soundness of Dr. Pittner's report, objecting particularly that he failed to utilize available comparative empirical data to assess Chance's educational progress; that he discussed only Chance's capacity to regress and not to recoup; and that he failed to consult school psychologists familiar with Chance. Evergreen cites evidence which indicates that over the month-long interruption in programming between his private ESY program and the regular school year, Chance retained some skills and lost but adequately recouped others. Evergreen also reiterates that in the opinion of the school psychologists, Chance has been progressing toward his IEP goals at a rate expected for his potential, which is admittedly slow. In response, the Cordreys dispute whether the available empirical data were meaningful and defend the soundness of Dr. Pittner's study.

Thus, the testimony regarding to what degree Chance would regress without a summer program was directly conflicting. The district court concluded from this that there was "no evidence that Chance would suffer significant regression" without an ESY. If by this conclusion the court required that his "need" for an ESY be proven purely by empirical evidence, we would be inclined to remand for further evaluation of the facts against the standard articulated here. Yet we do not believe that the district court's view was so narrow.

The better interpretation of the district court's conclusion is that because Chance regressed throughout the regular school year, the evidence did not show that his further summer regression would be relatively significant. Thus, an ESY would benefit him, but would not be necessary to preserve the benefits he was already receiving from his regular school year programming despite his continual regression. This conclusion draws support from the court's findings of fact and the record. Since Dr. Pittner's report did not address Chance's capacity for recoupment, the district court could legitimately rely on Chance's prior recoupment patterns and on the opinions of the school psychologists long familiar with Chance that his progress, slow as it is, does not depend on his privately-provided ESY programming. ([I]n the face of expert disagreement over whether the child would regress significantly without an ESY, the district court's finding in the affirmative was clearly supported even if not compelled by the record). We therefore affirm the district court's conclusion that Chance is not entitled to an ESY under the Act.

Although Evergreen contends that it is not obliged to provide Chance with a summer program, it has nevertheless provided one or related assistance by reimbursing the Cordreys for their 1985 and 1986 costs and by directly assuming those costs in 1987-1989. This service, however, was provided under the explicit understanding that the summer program was not part of Chance's IEP and hence not subject to the stay-put provision. As we have noted earlier, to the extent the facts of Chance's development and condition were such as to prompt Evergreen to furnish him with an ESY, it was error for the school district to have offered to provide it within his IEP only by exacting from his parents their agreement to exclude it from the protection of the stay-put provision. On the other hand, since we have upheld the trial court's finding under the particular facts here that Evergreen was not legally bound to provide him an ESY, its decision to move beyond the strict obligations of the statutory scheme can only be viewed as laudable and we see nothing in the Act or this decision to prevent it.

. . . .

Affirmed.

---

1. One of the earliest ESY cases under the Handicapped Childrens' Act was *Battle v. Commonwealth of Pennsylvania*, 629 F.2d 269 (3d Cir. 1980). The issue in *Battle*, cited by the Court in *Cordrey*, was whether the state's 180-day limit rule was constitutional as applied to disabled persons. Because a FAPE and IEP must meet the individual needs of the child, the Court held the 180-day rule invalid.

2. Recall the *Cordrey* court's brief discussion of *Rettig v. Kent City Sch. Dist.*, 539 F. Supp. 768 (N.D. Ohio 1981). Despite the "significant regression" standard adopted, that court found that no ESY was required under the facts because significant regression occurred even with the ESY. *Id.* at 779. Do you agree with the principle that no ESY should be provided if regression will occur anyway?

3. *Rettig* held that a child must provide evidence of prior regression and slow recoupment without summer programming. Are there any other factors to consider? What are they? Could the result in *Cordrey* have been different under this or another expanded ESY test? Recall and consider J. Engel's cite and analogy to *Lee v. Thompson*, Educ. Handicapped L. Rep. 554:429 (D. Haw. 1983). *See also Johnson*, presented after these notes.

4. The *Cordrey* court cites to *Polk v. Central Susquehanna Intermediate Unit 16*, 853 F.2d 171 (3d Cir. 1988), presented in Section B of this chapter. Dicta

D. EXTENDED SCHOOL YEAR PROGRAMS

in *Polk* stated that a child must first show regression before allowance of an ESY. What are the pros and cons of such a principle? Which side do you think should be favored? Is there much to a school district's claim that summer tuition payments, for example, are a waste, if the child would not show regression or slow recoupment *without* the summer program? How long does a child have to go without an ESY in order to show regression or slow recoupment? (One year? Two years?) How long did the *Cordrey* case last from inception to finale? How can we balance the school district and state burdens of unnecessary programs and expenditures with the best needs of the child without destroying too many years of the child's young life? What did the *Cordrey* court say about this?

5. Are you comfortable with the statement that "an ESY would be beneficial, but not necessary"? Consider this in context with *Cordrey, Rowley, Polk*, and the other cases we've discussed so far in this chapter.

6. What information should be considered as a basis for entitlement to a free ESY program under IDEA? In *Johnson v. Independent Sch. Dist. No. 4 of Bixby*, 921 F.2d 1022 (10th Cir. 1990), the Court of Appeals reversed the school district's summary judgment, originally granted based on regression-recoupment testimony, in favor of a broader standard:

> While it would be easier for those involved in administrative review under the Act to have one and only one criterion for evaluations the appropriateness of a handicapped child's IEP, the handicapping impediments which for individualization of the child's education program in the first place also mandate an individualized approach to review of the child's IEP.
>
> ....
>
> However, the regression-recoupment analysis is not the only measure used to determine the necessity of structured summer programs. In addition to the degree of regression and the time necessary for recoupment, courts have considered ... the degree of impairment and the ability of the child's parents to provide the educational structure at home, the child's rate of progress, his or her behavioral and physical problems, the availability of alternative resources, the ability of the child to interact with non-handicapped children, the areas of the child's curriculum which needs continuous attention, and the child's vocational needs. *Id.* at 1027

Which case — *Cordrey* or *Johnson* — do you think more properly considers and weighs the interests of the parties in context with the EHA (now IDEA) and its purposes? Do you think the *Johnson* standard is too broad, and will lead to abuse of the Act and harm to the school systems? How do the principles presented in *Rowley* (Section B of this chapter) counteract this?

E. LEAST RESTRICTIVE ENVIRONMENT

DANIEL R.R. v. STATE BOARD OF EDUCATION

United States Court of Appeals
874 F.2d 1036 (5th Cir. 1989)

GEE, CIRCUIT JUDGE:

Plaintiffs in this action, a handicapped boy and his parents, urge that a local school district failed to comply with the Education of the Handicapped Act. Specifically, they maintain that a school district's refusal to place the child in a class with nonhandicapped students violates the Act. The district court disagreed and, after a careful review of the record, we affirm the district court.

I. *Background*

A. *General*

... Before passage of the Act, as the Supreme Court has noted, many handicapped children suffered under one of two equally ineffective approaches to their educational needs: either they were excluded entirely from public education or they were deposited in regular education classrooms with no assistance, left to fend for themselves in an environment inappropriate for their needs....

The Act is largely procedural. It mandates a "free appropriate public education" for each handicapped child and sets forth procedures designed to ensure that each child's education meets that requirement. School officials are required to determine the appropriate placement for each child and must develop an Individualized Educational Plan (IEP) that tailors the child's education to his individual needs. The child's parents are involved at all stages of the process. In addition, the Act requires that handicapped children be educated in regular education classrooms, with nonhandicapped students — as opposed to special education classrooms with handicapped students only — to the greatest extent appropriate. Educating a handicapped child in a regular education classroom with nonhandicapped children is familiarly known as "mainstreaming," and the mainstreaming requirement is the source of the controversy between the parties before us today.

B. *Particular*

Daniel R. is a six year old boy who was enrolled, at the time this case arose, in the El Paso Independent School District (EPISD). A victim of Downs Syndrome, Daniel is mentally retarded and speech impaired. By September 1987, Daniel's developmental age was between two and three years and his communication skills were slightly less than those of a two year old.

In 1985, Daniel's parents, Mr. and Mrs. R., enrolled him in EPISD's Early Childhood Program, a half-day program devoted entirely to special education. Daniel completed one academic year in the Early Childhood Program. Before the

E. LEAST RESTRICTIVE ENVIRONMENT 1027

1986-87 school year began, Mrs. R. requested a new placement that would provide association with nonhandicapped children. Mrs. R. wanted EPISD to place Daniel in Pre-kindergarten — a half-day, regular education class. Mrs. R. conferred with Joan Norton, the Pre-kindergarten instructor, proposing that Daniel attend the half-day Pre-kindergarten class in addition to the half-day Early Childhood class. As a result, EPISD's Admission, Review and Dismissal (ARD) Committee met and designated the combined regular and special education program as Daniel's placement.

This soon proved unwise, and not long into the school year Mrs. Norton began to have reservations about Daniel's presence in her class. Daniel did not participate without constant, individual attention from the teacher or her aide, and failed to master any of the skills Mrs. Norton was trying to teach her students. Modifying the Pre-kindergarten curriculum and her teaching methods sufficiently to reach Daniel would have required Mrs. Norton to modify the curriculum almost beyond recognition. In November 1986, the ARD Committee met again, concluded that Pre-kindergarten was inappropriate for Daniel, and decided to change Daniel's placement. Under the new placement, Daniel would attend only the special education, Early Childhood class; would eat lunch in the school cafeteria, with nonhandicapped children, three days a week if his mother was present to supervise him; and would have contact with nonhandicapped students during recess. Believing that the ARD had improperly shut the door to regular education for Daniel, Mr. and Mrs. R. exercised their right to a review of the ARD Committee's decision.

As the EHA requires, Mr. and Mrs. R. appealed to a hearing officer who upheld the ARD Committee's decision. After a hearing which consumed five days of testimony and produced over 2500 pages of transcript, the hearing officer concluded that Daniel could not participate in the Pre-kindergarten class without constant attention from the instructor because the curriculum was beyond his abilities. In addition, the hearing officer found, Daniel was receiving little educational benefit from Pre-kindergarten and was disrupting the class — not in the ordinary sense of the term, but in the sense that his needs absorbed most of the teacher's time and diverted too much of her attention away from the rest of the class. Finally, the instructor would have to downgrade 90 to 100 percent of the Pre-kindergarten curriculum to bring it to a level that Daniel could master. Thus, the hearing officer concluded, the regular education, Pre-kindergarten class was not the appropriate placement for Daniel.

Dissatisfied with the hearing officer's decision, Mr. and Mrs. R. proceeded to the next level of review by filing this action in the district court. Although the EHA permits the parties to supplement the administrative record, Daniel's representatives declined to do so; and the court conducted its de novo review on the basis of the administrative record alone. The district court decided the case on cross motions for summary judgment. Relying primarily on Daniel's inability to receive an educational benefit in regular education, the district court affirmed the hearing officer's decision.

Mr. and Mrs. R. again appeal....

....

IV. *Substantive Violations*

A. *Mainstreaming Under the EHA*

The cornerstone of the EHA is the "free appropriate public education." ... The Act defines a free appropriate public education in broad, general terms without dictating substantive educational policy or mandating specific educational methods. In *Rowley*, the Supreme Court fleshed out the Act's skeletal definition of its principal term: "a 'free appropriate public education' consists of educational instruction specially designed to meet the unique needs of the handicapped child, supported by such services as are necessary to permit the child 'to benefit' from the instruction." *Rowley*, 458 U.S. at 188-89. The Court's interpretation of the Act's language does not, however, add substance to the Act's vague terms; instruction specially designed to meet each student's unique needs is as imprecise a directive as the language actually found in the Act.

The imprecise nature of the EHA's mandate does not reflect legislative omission. Rather, it reflects two deliberate legislative decisions. Congress chose to leave the selection of educational policy and methods where they traditionally have resided — with state and local school officials. In addition, Congress's goal was to bring handicapped children into the public school system and to provide them with an education tailored to meet their particular needs. Such needs span the spectrum of mental and physical handicaps, with no two children necessarily suffering the same condition or requiring the same services or education. Schools must retain significant flexibility in educational planning if they truly are to address each child's needs....

In contrast to the EHA's vague mandate for a free appropriate public education lies one very specific directive prescribing the educational environment for handicapped children. Each state must establish

> procedures to assure that, to the maximum extent appropriate, handicapped children ... are educated with children who are not handicapped, and that special education, separate schooling or other removal of handicapped children from the regular educational environment occurs only when the nature or severity of the handicap is such that education in regular classes with the use of supplementary aids and services cannot be achieved satisfactorily....

With this provision, Congress created a strong preference in favor of mainstreaming.

By creating a statutory preference for mainstreaming, Congress also created a tension between two provisions of the Act. School districts must both seek to mainstream handicapped children and, at the same time, must tailor each child's educational placement and program to his special needs. Regular classes,

E. LEAST RESTRICTIVE ENVIRONMENT 1029

however, will not provide an education that accounts for each child's particular needs in every case. The nature or severity of some children's handicaps is such that only special education can address their needs. For these children, mainstreaming does not provide an education designed to meet their unique needs and, thus, does not provide a free appropriate public education....

... Thus, the EHA allows school officials to remove a handicapped child from regular education or to provide special education if they cannot educate the child satisfactorily in the regular classroom. Even when school officials can mainstream the child, they need not provide for an exclusively mainstreamed environment; the Act requires school officials to mainstream each child only to the maximum extent appropriate. In short, the Act's mandate for a free appropriate public education qualifies and limits its mandate for education in the regular classroom. Schools must provide a free appropriate public education and must do so, to the maximum extent appropriate, in regular education classrooms. But when education in a regular classroom cannot meet the handicapped child's unique needs, the presumption in favor of mainstreaming is overcome and the school need not place the child in regular education. The Act does not, however, provide any substantive standards for striking the proper balance between its requirement for mainstreaming and its mandate for a free appropriate public education.

B. *Determining Compliance With the Mainstreaming Requirement*

Determining the contours of the mainstreaming requirement is a question of first impression for us. In the seminal interpretation of the EHA, the Supreme Court posited a two-part test for determining whether a school has provided a free appropriate public education: "First, has the State complied with the procedures set forth in the Act. And second, is the individualized educational program developed through the Act's procedures reasonably calculated to enable the child to receive educational benefits." Despite the attractive ease of this two part inquiry, it is not the appropriate tool for determining whether a school district has met its mainstreaming obligations.... Faced with the same issue we face today, both the Sixth and the Eighth Circuit concluded that the *Rowley* test was not intended to decide mainstreaming issues. *A.W.*, 813 F.2d at 163; *Roncker*, 700 F.2d at 1063. Moreover, both Circuits noted that the *Rowley* Court's analysis is ill suited for evaluating compliance with the mainstreaming requirement. *A.W.*, 813 F.2d at 163; *Roncker*, 700 F.2d at 1062. As the Eighth Circuit explained, the *Rowley* test assumes that the state has met all of the requirements of the Act, including the mainstreaming requirement. *A.W.*, 813 F.2d at 163 n. 7. The *Rowley* test thus assumes the answer to the question presented in a mainstreaming case....

Although we have not yet developed a standard for evaluating mainstreaming questions, we decline to adopt the approach that other circuits have taken. In *Roncker*, visiting the same question which we address today, the Sixth Circuit devised its own test to determine when and to what extent a handicapped child must be mainstreamed. According to the *Roncker* court,

> [t]he proper inquiry is whether a proposed placement is appropriate under the Act.... In a case where the segregated facility is considered superior, the court should determine whether the services which make that placement superior could be feasibly provided in a non-segregated setting. If they can, the placement in the segregated school would be inappropriate under the Act. *Roncker*, 700 F.2d at 1063; *accord A.W.*, 813 F.2d at 163.

We respectfully decline to follow the Sixth Circuit's analysis. Certainly, the *Roncker* test accounts for factors that are important in any mainstreaming case. We believe, however, that the test necessitates too intrusive an inquiry into the educational policy choices that Congress deliberately left to state and local school officials. Whether a particular service feasibly can be provided in a regular or special education setting is an administrative determination that state and local school officials are far better qualified and situated than are we to make. Moreover, the test makes little reference to the language of the EHA. Yet, as we shall see, we believe that the language of the Act itself provides a workable test for determining whether a state has complied with the Act's mainstreaming requirement.

Nor do we find the district court's approach to the issue the proper tool for analyzing the mainstreaming obligation. Relying primarily on whether Daniel could receive an educational benefit from regular education, the district court held that the special education class was the appropriate placement for Daniel. According to the court, "some children, even aided by supplemental aids and services in a regular education classroom, will never receive an educational benefit that approximates the level of skill and comprehension acquisition of nonhandicapped children." In these cases, regular education does not provide the child an appropriate education and the presumption in favor of mainstreaming is overcome. As no aspect of the Pre-kindergarten curriculum was within Daniel's reach, EPISD was not required to mainstream him. Given the nature and severity of Daniel's handicap at the time EPISD placed him, we agree with the district court's conclusion that EPISD was not required to mainstream Daniel. We disagree, however, with the court's analysis of the mainstreaming issue, finding it troublesome for two reasons: first, as a prerequisite to mainstreaming, the court would require handicapped children to learn at approximately the same level as their nonhandicapped classmates. Second, the court places too much emphasis on the handicapped student's ability to achieve an educational benefit.

First, requiring as a prerequisite to mainstreaming that the handicapped child be able to learn at approximately the same level as his nonhandicapped classmates fails to take into account the principles that the Supreme Court announced in *Rowley*. Our public school system tolerates a wide range of differing learning abilities; at the same time, it provides educational opportunities that do not necessarily account for all of those different capacities to learn. As the *Rowley*

E. LEAST RESTRICTIVE ENVIRONMENT

Court noted, "[t]he educational opportunities provided by our public school systems undoubtedly differ from student to student, depending upon a myriad of factors that might affect a particular student's ability to assimilate information presented in the classroom."

With the EHA, Congress extended the states' tolerance of educational differences to include tolerance of many handicapped children. States must accept in their public schools children whose abilities and needs differ from those of the average student....

... The *Rowley* court rejected the notion that the EHA requires states to provide handicapped children with educational opportunities that are equal to those provided to nonhandicapped students. Thus, the Court recognized that the Act draws handicapped children into the regular education environment but, in the nature of things, cannot always offer them the same educational opportunities that regular education offers nonhandicapped children. States must tolerate educational differences; they need not perform the impossible: erase those differences by taking steps to equalize educational opportunities. As a result, the Act accepts the notion that handicapped students will participate in regular education but that some of them will not benefit as much as nonhandicapped students will. The Act requires states to tolerate a wide range of educational abilities in their schools and, specifically, in regular education — the EHA's preferred educational environment. Given the tolerance embodied in the EHA, we cannot predicate access to regular education on a child's ability to perform on par with nonhandicapped children.

We recognize that some handicapped children may not be able to master as much of the regular education curriculum as their nonhandicapped classmates. This does not mean, however, that those handicapped children are not receiving any benefit from regular education. Nor does it mean that they are not receiving all of the benefit that their handicapping condition will permit. If the child's individual needs make mainstreaming appropriate, we cannot deny the child access to regular education simply because his educational achievement lags behind that of his classmates.

Second, the district court placed too much emphasis on educational benefits. Certainly, whether a child will benefit educationally from regular education is relevant and important to our analysis. Congress's primary purpose in enacting the EHA was to provide access to education for handicapped children. Implicit in Congress's purpose to provide access is a purpose to provide meaningful access, access that is sufficient to confer some educational benefit on the child. Thus, the decision whether to mainstream a child must include an inquiry into whether the student will gain any educational benefit from regular education. Our analysis cannot stop here, however, for educational benefits are not mainstreaming's only virtue. Rather, mainstreaming may have benefits in and of itself. For example, the language and behavior models available from nonhandicapped children may be essential or helpful to the handicapped child's development. In other words, although a handicapped child may not be able to absorb all of the regular education curriculum, he may benefit from nonacademic experiences in the regular education environment....

Ultimately, our task is to balance competing requirements of the EHA's dual mandate: a free appropriate public education that is provided, to the maximum extent appropriate, in the regular education classroom. As we begin our task we must keep in mind that Congress left the choice of educational policies and methods where it properly belongs — in the hands of state and local school officials. Our task is not to second-guess state and local policy decisions; rather, it is the narrow one of determining whether state and local school officials have complied with the Act. Adhering to the language of the EHA, we discern a two part test for determining compliance with the mainstreaming requirement. First, we ask whether education in the regular classroom, with the use of supplemental aids and services, can be achieved satisfactorily for a given child. If it cannot and the school intends to provide special education or to remove the child from regular education, we ask, second, whether the school has mainstreamed the child to the maximum extent appropriate. A variety of factors will inform each stage of our inquiry; the factors that we consider today do not constitute an exhaustive list of factors relevant to the mainstreaming issue. Moreover, no single factor is dispositive in all cases. Rather, our analysis is an individualized, fact-specific inquiry that requires us to examine carefully the nature and severity of the child's handicapping condition, his needs and abilities, and the schools' response to the child's needs.

In this case, several factors assist the first stage of our inquiry, whether EPISD can achieve education in the regular classroom satisfactorily. At the outset, we must examine whether the state has taken steps to accommodate the handicapped child in regular education. The Act requires states to provide supplementary aids and services and to modify the regular education program when they mainstream handicapped children. If the state has made no effort to take such accommodating steps, our inquiry ends, for the state is in violation of the Act's express mandate to supplement and modify regular education. If the state is providing supplementary aids and services and is modifying its regular education program, we must examine whether its efforts are sufficient. The Act does not permit states to make mere token gestures to accommodate handicapped students; its requirement for modifying and supplementing regular education is broad. Indeed, Texas expressly requires its local school districts to modify their regular education program when necessary to accommodate a handicapped child.

Although broad, the requirement is not limitless. States need not provide every conceivable supplementary aid or service to assist the child. Furthermore, the Act does not require regular education instructors to devote all or most of their time to one handicapped child or to modify the regular education program beyond recognition. If a regular education instructor must devote all of her time to one handicapped child, she will be acting as a special education teacher in a regular education classroom. Moreover, she will be focusing her attentions on one child to the detriment of her entire class, including, perhaps, other, equally deserving,

E. LEAST RESTRICTIVE ENVIRONMENT

handicapped children who also may require extra attention. Likewise, mainstreaming would be pointless if we forced instructors to modify the regular education curriculum to the extent that the handicapped child is not required to learn any of the skills normally taught in regular education. The child would be receiving special education instruction in the regular education classroom; the only advantage to such an arrangement would be that the child is sitting next to a nonhandicapped student.

Next, we examine whether the child will receive an educational benefit from regular education. This inquiry necessarily will focus on the student's ability to grasp the essential elements of the regular education curriculum. Thus, we must pay close attention to the nature and severity of the child's handicap as well as to the curriculum and goals of the regular education class. For example, if the goal of a particular program is enhancing the child's development, as opposed to teaching him specific subjects such as reading or mathematics, our inquiry must focus on the child's ability to benefit from the developmental lessons, not exclusively on his potential for learning to read. We reiterate, however, that academic achievement is not the only purpose of mainstreaming. Integrating a handicapped child into a nonhandicapped environment may be beneficial in and of itself. Thus, our inquiry must extend beyond the educational benefits that the child may receive in regular education.

We also must examine the child's overall educational experience in the mainstreamed environment, balancing the benefits of regular and special education for each individual child. For example, a child may be able to absorb only a minimal amount of the regular education program, but may benefit enormously from the language models that his nonhandicapped peers provide for him. In such a case, the benefit that the child receives from mainstreaming may tip the balance in favor of mainstreaming, even if the child cannot flourish academically. On the other hand, placing a child in regular education may be detrimental to the child. In such a case, mainstreaming would not provide an education that is attuned to the child's unique needs and would not be required under the Act. Indeed, mainstreaming a child who will suffer from the experience would violate the Act's mandate for a free appropriate public education.

Finally, we ask what effect the handicapped child's presence has on the regular classroom environment and, thus, on the education that the other students are receiving. A handicapped child's placement in regular education may prove troublesome for two reasons. First, the handicapped child may, as a result of his handicap, engage in disruptive behavior. "'[W]here a handicapped child is so disruptive in a regular classroom that the education of other students is significantly impaired, the needs of the handicapped child cannot be met in that environment. Therefore regular placement would not be appropriate to his or her needs.'" Second, the child may require so much of the instructor's attention that the instructor will have to ignore the other student's needs in order to tend to the handicapped child. The Act and its regulations mandate that the school provide supplementary aids and services in the regular education classroom. A teaching assistant or an aide may minimize the burden on the teacher. If, however, the handicapped child requires so much of the teacher or the aide's time that the rest of the class suffers, then the balance will tip in favor of placing the child in special education.

If we determine that education in the regular classroom cannot be achieved satisfactorily, we next ask whether the child has been mainstreamed to the maximum extent appropriate. The EHA and its regulations do not contemplate an all-or-nothing educational system in which handicapped children attend either regular or special education. Rather, the Act and its regulations require schools to offer a continuum of services. Thus, the school must take intermediate steps where appropriate, such as placing the child in regular education for some academic classes and in special education for others, mainstreaming the child for nonacademic classes only, or providing interaction with nonhandicapped children during lunch and recess. The appropriate mix will vary from child to child and, it may be hoped, from school year to school year as the child develops. If the school officials have provided the maximum appropriate exposure to non-handicapped students, they have fulfilled their obligation under the EHA.

C. *EPISD's Compliance with the Mainstreaming Requirement*

After a careful review of the voluminous administrative record, we must agree with the trial court that EPISD's decision to remove Daniel from regular education does not run afoul of the EHA's preference for mainstreaming. Accounting for all of the factors we have identified today, we find that EPISD cannot educate Daniel satisfactorily in the regular education classroom. Furthermore, EPISD has taken creative steps to provide Daniel as much access to nonhandicapped students as it can, while providing him an education that is tailored to his unique needs. Thus, EPISD has mainstreamed Daniel to the maximum extent appropriate.

EPISD cannot educate Daniel satisfactorily in the regular education classroom; each of the factors we identified today counsels against placing Daniel in regular education. First, EPISD took steps to modify the Pre-kindergarten program and to provide supplementary aids and services for Daniel — all of which constitute a sufficient effort.... The Pre-kindergarten teacher made genuine and creative efforts to reach Daniel, devoting a substantial — indeed, a disproportionate — amount of her time to him and modifying the class curriculum to meet his abilities.... Such an effort would modify the curriculum beyond recognition, an effort which we will not require in the name of mainstreaming.

Second, Daniel receives little, if any, educational benefit in Pre-kindergarten.... Daniel's handicap has slowed his development so that he is not yet ready to learn the developmental skills offered in Pre-kindergarten. Daniel does not participate in class activities; he cannot master most or all of the lessons taught in the class. Very simply, Pre-kindergarten offers Daniel nothing but an opportunity to associate with nonhandicapped students.

E. LEAST RESTRICTIVE ENVIRONMENT

Third, Daniel's overall educational experience has not been entirely beneficial. As we explained, Daniel can grasp little of the Pre-kindergarten curriculum; the only value of regular education for Daniel is the interaction which he has with nonhandicapped students. Daniel asserts that the opportunity for interaction, alone, is a sufficient ground for mainstreaming him. When we balance the benefits of regular education against those of special education, we cannot agree that the opportunity for Daniel to interact with nonhandicapped students is a sufficient ground for mainstreaming him. Regular education not only offers Daniel little in the way of academic or other benefits, it also may be harming him. When Daniel was placed in Pre-kindergarten, he attended school for a full day; both Pre-kindergarten and Early Childhood were half-day classes. The experts who testified before the hearing officer indicated that the full day program is too strenuous for a child with Daniel's condition.... Special education, on the other hand, is an educational environment in which Daniel is making progress. Balancing the benefits of a program that is only marginally beneficial and is somewhat detrimental against the benefits of a program that is clearly beneficial, we must agree that the beneficial program provides the more appropriate placement.

Finally, we agree that Daniel's presence in regular Pre-kindergarten is unfair to the rest of the class....

Alone, each of the factors that we have reviewed suggests that EPISD cannot educate Daniel satisfactorily in the regular education classroom. Together, they clearly tip the balance in favor of placing Daniel in special education. Thus, we turn to the next phase of our inquiry and conclude that EPISD has mainstreamed Daniel to the maximum extent appropriate. Finding that a placement that allocates Daniel's time equally between regular and special education is not appropriate, EPISD has taken the intermediate step of mainstreaming Daniel for lunch and recess. This opportunity for association with nonhandicapped students is not as extensive as Daniel's parents would like. It is, however, an appropriate step that may help to prepare Daniel for regular education in the future. As education in the regular classroom, with the use of supplementary aids and services cannot be achieved satisfactorily, and as EPISD has placed Daniel with nonhandicapped students to the maximum extent appropriate, we affirm the district court.

....

SACRAMENTO CITY UNIFIED SCHOOL DISTRICT BOARD OF EDUCATION v. HOLLAND

United States Court of Appeals
14 F.3d 1398 (9th Cir. 1994)

Facts and Prior Proceedings

....

Rachel Holland is now 11 years old and is mentally retarded. She was tested with an I.Q. of 44. She attended a variety of special education programs in the

District from 1985-89. Her parents sought to increase the time Rachel spent in a regular classroom, and in the fall of 1989, they requested that Rachel be placed full-time in a regular classroom for the 1989-90 school year. The District rejected their request and proposed a placement that would have divided Rachel's time between a special education class for academic subjects and a regular class for non-academic activities such as art, music, lunch, and recess. The district court found that this plan would have required moving Rachel at least six times each day between the two classrooms. The Hollands instead enrolled Rachel in a regular kindergarten class at the Shalom School, a private school. Rachel remained at the Shalom School in regular classes and at the time the district court rendered its opinion was in the second grade.

The Hollands and the District were able to agree on an Individualized Education Program ("IEP") for Rachel. Although the IEP is required to be reviewed annually because of the dispute between the parties, Rachel's IEP has not been reviewed since January 1990.

The Hollands appealed the District's placement decision to a state hearing officer.... They maintained that Rachel best learned social and academic skills in a regular classroom and would not benefit from being in a special education class. The District contended Rachel was too severely disabled to benefit from full-time placement in a regular class. The hearing officer concluded that the District had failed to make an adequate effort to educate Rachel in a regular class pursuant to the IDEA. The officer found that (1) Rachel had benefitted from her regular kindergarten class — that she was motivated to learn and learned by imitation and modeling; (2) Rachel was not disruptive in a regular classroom; and (3) the District had overstated the cost of putting Rachel in regular education — that the cost would not be so great that it weighed against placing her in a regular classroom. The hearing officer ordered the District to place Rachel in a regular classroom with support services, including a special education consultant and a part-time aide.

The District appealed this determination to the district court.... The court affirmed the decision of the hearing officer that Rachel should be placed full-time in a regular classroom. In considering whether the District proposed an appropriate placement for Rachel, the district court examined the following factors: (1) the educational benefits available to Rachel in a regular classroom, supplemented with appropriate aids and services, as compared with the educational benefits of a special education classroom; (2) the non-academic benefits of interaction with children who were not disabled; (3) the effect of Rachel's presence on the teacher and other children in the classroom; and (4) the cost of mainstreaming Rachel in a regular classroom.

1. *Educational Benefits*

The district court found the first factor, educational benefits to Rachel, weighed in favor of placing her in a regular classroom. Each side presented expert testimony which is summarized in the margin. The court noted that the

E. LEAST RESTRICTIVE ENVIRONMENT

District's evidence focused on Rachel's limitations but did not establish that the educational opportunities available through special education were better or equal to those available in a regular classroom. Moreover, the court found that the testimony of the Hollands' experts was more credible because they had more background in evaluating children with disabilities placed in regular classrooms and that they had a greater opportunity to observe Rachel over an extended period of time in normal circumstances. The district court also gave great weight to the testimony of Rachel's current teacher, Nina Crone, whom the court found to be an experienced, skillful teacher. Ms. Crone stated that Rachel was a full member of the class and participated in all activities. Ms. Crone testified that Rachel was making progress on her IEP goals: She was learning one-to-one correspondence in counting, was able to recite the English and Hebrew alphabets, and was improving her communication abilities and sentence lengths.

The district court found that Rachel received substantial benefits in regular education and that all of her IEP goals could be implemented in a regular classroom with some modification to the curriculum and with the assistance of a part-time aide.

2. Non-academic Benefits

The district court next found that the second factor, non-academic benefits to Rachel, also weighed in favor of placing her in a regular classroom. The court noted that the Hollands' evidence indicated that Rachel had developed her social and communications skills as well as her self-confidence from placement in a regular class, while the District's evidence tended to show that Rachel was not learning from exposure to other children and that she was isolated from her classmates. The court concluded that the differing evaluations in large part reflected the predisposition of the evaluators. The court found the testimony of Rachel's mother and her current teacher to be the most credible. These witnesses testified regarding Rachel's excitement about school, learning, and her new friendships and Rachel's improved self-confidence.

3. Effect on the Teacher and Children in the Regular Class

The district court next addressed the issue of whether Rachel had a detrimental effect on others in her regular classroom. The court looked at two aspects: (1) whether there was detriment because the child was disruptive, distracting or unruly, and (2) whether the child would take up so much of the teacher's time that the other students would suffer from lack of attention. The witnesses of both parties agreed that Rachel followed directions and was well-behaved and not a distraction in class. The court found the most germane evidence on the second aspect came from Rachel's second grade teacher, Nina Crone, who testified that Rachel did not interfere with her ability to teach the other children and in the future would require only a part-time aide. Accordingly, the district court determined that the third factor, the effect of Rachel's presence on the teacher and other children in the classroom weighed in favor of placing her in a regular classroom.

4. *Cost*

Finally, the district court found that the District had not offered any persuasive or credible evidence to support its claim that educating Rachel in a regular classroom with appropriate services would be significantly more expensive than educating her in the District's proposed setting.

The District contended that it would cost $109,000 to educate Rachel full-time in a regular classroom. This figure was based on the cost of providing a full-time aide for Rachel plus an estimated $80,000 for school-wide sensitivity training. The court found that the District did not establish that such training was necessary. Further, the court noted that even if such training were necessary, there was evidence from the California Department of Education that the training could be had at no cost. Moreover, the court found it would be inappropriate to assign the total cost of the training to Rachel when other children with disabilities would benefit.

In addition, the court concluded that the evidence did not suggest that Rachel required a full-time aide. In addition, the court found that the District should have compared the cost of placing Rachel in a special class of approximately 12 students with a full-time special education teacher and two full-time aides and the cost of placing her in a regular class with a part-time aide. The District provided no evidence of this cost comparison.

The court also was not persuaded by the District's argument that it would lose significant funding if Rachel did not spend at least 51% of her time in a special education class. The court noted that a witness from the California Department of Education testified that waivers were available if a school district sought to adopt a program that did not fit neatly within the funding guidelines. The District had not applied for a waiver.

By inflating the cost estimates and failing to address the true comparison, the District did not meet its burden of proving that regular placement would burden the District's funds or adversely affect services available to other children. Therefore, the court found that the cost factor did not weigh against mainstreaming Rachel.

The district court concluded that the appropriate placement for Rachel was full-time in a regular second grade classroom with some supplemental services and affirmed the decision of the hearing officer.

IV

Discussion

....

B. *Mainstreaming Requirements of the IDEA*

1. *The Statute*

The IDEA provides that each state must establish:

> [P]rocedures to assure that, to the maximum extent appropriate, children with disabilities ... are educated with children who are not disabled, and that special classes, separate schooling, or other removal of children with disabilities from the regular educational environment occurs only when the nature or severity of the disability is such that education in regular classes with the use of supplementary aids and services cannot be achieved satisfactorily....

This provision sets forth Congress's preference for educating children with disabilities in regular classrooms with their peers....

....

3. *Test for Determining Compliance with the IDEA's Mainstreaming Requirement*

....

... [T]he district court relied ... on ... a four-factor balancing test in which the court considered (1) the educational benefits of placement full-time in a regular class; (2) the non-academic benefits of such placement; (3) the effect Rachel had on the teacher and children in the regular class; and (4) the costs of mainstreaming Rachel. This analysis directly addresses the issue of the appropriate placement for a child with disabilities.... Accordingly, we approve and adopt the test employed by the district court.

4. *The District's Contentions on Appeal*

The District strenuously disagrees with the district court's findings that Rachel was receiving academic and non-academic benefits in a regular class and did not have a detrimental effect on the teacher or other students. It argues that the court's findings were contrary to the evidence of the state Diagnostic Center and that the court should not have been persuaded by the testimony of Rachel's teacher, particularly her testimony that Rachel would need only a part-time aide in the future. The district court, however, conducted a full evidentiary hearing and made a thorough analysis. The court found the Hollands' evidence to be more persuasive. Moreover, the court asked Rachel's teacher extensive questions regarding Rachel's need for a part-time aide. We will not disturb the findings of the district court.

The District is also not persuasive on the issue of cost. The District now claims that it will lose up to $190,764 in state special education funding if Rachel is not enrolled in a special education class at least 51% of the day. However, the District has not sought a waiver pursuant to California Education Code § 56101. This section provides that (1) any school district may request a waiver of any provision of the Education Code if the waiver is necessary or beneficial to the student's IEP, and (2) the Board may grant the waiver when failure to do so would hinder compliance with federal mandates for a free appropriate education for children with disabilities....

Finally, the District ... argues that Rachel must receive her academic and functional curriculum in special education from a specially credentialed teacher....

More importantly, the District's proposition that Rachel must be taught by a special education teacher runs directly counter to the congressional preference that children with disabilities be educated in regular classes with children who are not disabled.

We affirm the judgment of the district court. While we cannot determine what the appropriate placement is for Rachel at the present time, we hold that the determination of the present and future appropriate placement for Rachel should be based on the principles set forth in this opinion and the opinion of the district court.

Affirmed.

---

1. Portions of the IDEA stipulate that disabled students must be educated in the "least restrictive environment." The cases in this section feature varying themes on that issue. Listed below are portions of IDEA's statute and regulations relative to the requirement. Also listed is a portion of the decision from *Board of Educ., Hendrick Hudson Central Sch. Dist. v. Rowley*, 458 U.S. 176 (1982), that brings the LRE requirement into focus.

> ... [T]o the maximum extent appropriate, handicapped children ... are educated with children who are not handicapped, and that special education, separate schooling or other removal of handicapped children from the regular educational environment occurs only when the nature or severity of the handicap is such that education in regular classes with the use of supplemental aids and services cannot be achieved. 20 U.S.C. Sec. 1412(5)(B).
>
> (a) Each public agency shall ensure that a continuum of alternative placements is available to meet the needs of children with disabilities for special education and related services.

E. LEAST RESTRICTIVE ENVIRONMENT

(b) The continuum required under paragraph (a) of this section must:

(1) Include the alternative placements [of instruction in regular classes, special classes, special schools, home instruction and instruction in hospitals and institutions] and

(2) Make provision for supplementary services [*e.g.*, resource room or itinerant instruction] to be provided in conjunction with regular class placement. 34 C.F.R. Sec. 300.551.

[The school district must assure the right of a] free appropriate public education tailored to the unique needs of the handicapped child by means of an Individualized Education Program ... reasonably calculated to enable the child to [receive educational benefits.] *Rowley*, at 177.

Is there an inherent conflict in the actions of Congress in promulgating the IDEA? There is the promotion of integration of disabled and non-disabled students in that *all* students begin in regular classrooms. Disabled students would not be removed unless it can be shown that with supplementary aids and services, a student "cannot achieve satisfactorily." But the regulations also state that there must be a "continuum of alternative placements," based on the needs of the child, that include "special classes, special schools, home instruction and instruction in hospitals and institutions." Does this mean that the integrating purpose of the statute and rules is significantly qualified? Does the case law in this section support such a notion?

2. The terms "least restrictive environment," "mainstreaming" and "inclusion" are all used in reference to integrating disabled students with non-disabled students in regular classrooms. May the terms be used interchangeably or do each of them actually refer to different practices? If one term represents an extension or replacement of the other, are disabled students being better served under the newer emphasis? If so, are non-disabled students being underserved as a consequence?

3. The court in *Daniel R.R.* followed a separate two-part test. Educators must determine: 1) Whether the student can receive some educational benefit from placement in a regular classroom, with or without supplemental aids and services; and, if not, 2) whether the school has integrated the child to the maximum extent appropriate. This test is followed by several other circuits. The Court of Appeals for the Sixth Circuit, in *Roncker v. Walter*, 700 F.2d 1058 (6th Cir. 1983), adopted a different test for determining the appropriateness of the proposed placement of a child with a disability.

Under *Roncker*, courts are to: 1) compare the benefits of both an education in the regular classroom and those of a segregated special education classroom — and then determine if the services that make a segregated classroom superior could be provided in the regular classroom. This test has been followed by the Fourth, Sixth and Eighth federal appeals circuits.

Can the two tests be reconciled? Which offers the greatest possible benefit to disabled students? Which permits the school district to best provide such a benefit? What are the reasons from the *Daniel R.R.* court for rejecting the test as espoused in *Roncker*?

4. *Roncker* provides that disabled students should be placed with other students who are roughly of the same age and development abilities. Can such a stipulation be found in the IDEA or any of its regulations? Does such reasoning correlate with any of the other cases in this section?

5. Compare *Roncker*'s emphasis on integrating disabled students into regular classroom's with *Rowley*'s focus on "appropriateness". Does *Roncker* expand educators' minimal duty to provide access to an "educational benefit" (as seen in *Rowley*) to a more open ended commitment to provide educational services so that such children can survive and be educated in regular classrooms? Does this transform educators' duty from a negative one — do not separate if at all possible — to an affirmative one — integrate with supplementary aids and services? Does this suggest that the *Rowley* standard of "appropriateness" has no bearing on considerations of "least restrictive environment"? Does this accurately describe the Congress' intent in the overall promulgation of IDEA? What are the implications for such a change in the day to day operations of schools?

6. In determining the placement and the development of an IEP for a child with a disability, what range of services and placements must be considered? What factors should contribute to the determination? Often, schools and parents will disagree with respect to only two proposed placements. For example, the school may suggest that the child be placed in a self-contained classroom in one school, while the parents may resist and argue to keep their child in the neighborhood school. In *Greer v. Rome City Sch. Dist.*, 950 F.2d 688 (11th Cir. 1991), the court considered several factors in its determination that education in a regular classroom setting, with supplemental aids and services, could be achieved satisfactorily for a child with Down's Syndrome. There was a middle ground between regular classroom education and a segregated setting in another building. Similar to the court in *Daniel R.R.*, the court in *Greer* considered the educational and non-educational benefits of the two proposed environments, and the effect of the child's presence in the regular classroom setting and on the non-disabled children.

Greer followed the *Daniel R.R.* test and also introduced cost as a factor. In considering the first prong of *Daniel R.R.*, the *Greer* court expanded on the issue of educational benefits in a regular classroom ruling that there must be a demonstration of "significantly more progress" if the student is assigned to a special education placement. Also, the *Greer* court maintained that there must be such disruption by the disabled student that it would "significantly impair" other children's education. The introduction of cost continued the same stringent kind of test — the cost of educating a disabled child in a regular classroom is not to be considered unless it would be so great as to significantly impact the education

E. LEAST RESTRICTIVE ENVIRONMENT

of other children. Does this decision mean that under no circumstances will school personnel be able to first provide a special education placement, even if this represents the "least restrictive environment" and even if it carries the imprimatur of the parents or guardians? Does this decision, along with *Daniel R.R.*, change the responsibility of school officials from a two-dimensional process, *i.e.*, special education or regular education, to one of a myriad of choices for special education students only one of which is a special education placement?

Is the cost discussion in *Greer* consistent with that of other such cases? Does the cost discussion serve as a determining factor in considerations of overall appropriateness? Consider *Clevenger v. Oak Ridge Sch. Bd.*, 744 F.2d 514 (6th Cir. 1984). Here, the school district and parents disagreed over two different alternative institutional placements for an emotionally disturbed student. Ultimately the Sixth Circuit Court of Appeals ruled that only one of the placements, the one proposed by the parents, was appropriate under the "least restrictive education" mandate. "Cost" influenced the decision of the school board in its placement decision. The court acknowledged cost as a factor, but ruled that such consideration is only relevant when all the alternative placements are appropriate. As in this case, where only one of the two institutional placements was appropriate, cost was not a permissible factor.

7. *Daniel R.R.* indicates that certain factors must be considered when determining if a disabled child can receive some educational benefit for placement in a regular class. They include academic benefit, non-academic benefit, class disruption and curriculum modification. The *Greer* court introduced cost as a factor, but reasoned that merely incurring additional expenses for placing a child in a regular classroom would not be sufficient for a more restrictive alternative. The *Holland* court used each of these factors except "curriculum modification" unless the amount of modification would result in the development of separate divisions in one classroom or the disabled student is deprived of a sense of belonging in the room. Why this break after virtually following every other element of the *Daniel R.R.* test? Has the *Holland* court reasoned that Congress simply meant for such students to be in regular classes irrespective of need or disability? Has that court concluded that any placement must be in a regular class? Could it be argued that such a decision is in fact contrary to Congress' intent?

8. When answering the first question under the *Daniel R.R.* test, some attention should be paid to the efforts taken by the school district in its determination of the appropriateness of the child's placement. The Third Circuit, in *Oberti v. Board of Educ. of Clementon Sch. Dist.*, 995 F.2d 1204 (3d Cir. 1993), adopted the burden under the first prong, in that the school failed to show that the child (with Down's Syndrome) could not be educated satisfactorily in a regular classroom with supplemental aids and services. The court placed the burden on the schools to show that, even with aids and services, placement in a regular classroom is inappropriate. Under *Oberti*, the burden of proof in LRE cases falls on the school, regardless of which party brought the action. According to the court, the presumption in favor of mainstreaming (under IDEA) would be turned on its head if parents had to prove their child worthy of inclusion.

Does *Oberti* correctly interpret the obligations of school officials under the "least restrictive environment" provision of IDEA? Does this case represent a new trend in judicial activism in favor of special education students? The court held that school districts have an affirmative obligation of placing such students in regular classrooms with the use of supplementary aids and services "before exploring other alternatives." This places the burden on schools to maximize a student's educational, integrative activities. Compare this ruling to that of *Rowley* where such maximization as to academic prowess was declared outside the realm of Congress' intent. Are these two decisions categorically different?

The *Oberti* court held that IDEA requires the redistribution of school district resources (and possible increase) so as to better accommodate disabled students in regular classrooms. This means, among other things, modifying the curriculum to accommodate a broader audience. Is the court stating that "inclusion" is a right for such students? What source serves to buttress such a position? Would the decision in *San Antonio Indep. Sch. Dist. v. Rodriguez*, 411 U.S. 1 (1973), Chapter 14, serve as a counter position?

The district court decision in *Oberti*, 801 F. Supp. 1392 (D.N.J. 1992), also found the school in violation of Section 504 of the Rehabilitation Act of 1973 due to a failure to provide a "reasonable accommodation" through an integrated education in a regular classroom and because the student was excluded from such a classroom solely because of his disability. The Third Circuit declined to reach the question of whether Section 504 supports relief as it would have been superfluous to the result. The district court analysis is important, however, for it points to a perhaps unanticipated convergence of the statutes. Section 504 states:

> No otherwise qualified individual with handicaps ... shall, solely by reason of his or her handicap, be excluded from participation in, be denied the benefits of, or be subjected to discrimination under any program or activity receiving Federal financial assistance.... 29 U.S.C. Sec. 794(a).

The district court declared that the student qualified under Section 504 in that he was a handicapped individual, that he was "otherwise qualified" in that he met the age requirement for public school and that he was excluded because of his handicap. The school could only escape liability by demonstrating an "undue burden." At this point in the court's analysis the components of IDEA and Section 504 coincide in that the court relates that Section 504 places limits on an "educational necessity" defense because a school's financial burden is secondary to the requirement of "least restrictive environment." Is this an accurate assessment by the court? The opportunity for students under Section 504 to participate in an educational program must be equal and as effective as that of non-disabled students. The comment section of 34 C.F.R 104.4(B)(2) of Section

504's regulations states that "equally effective" translates to equivalent, but not identical. Therefore, disabled students cannot be separated into other classes unless "necessary," and if necessary, the educational opportunities must be the same. Is such an assessment synonymous to the "least restrictive" requirement of IDEA as the court surmises here?

F. RELATED SERVICES

IRVING INDEPENDENT SCHOOL DISTRICT v. TATRO

United States Supreme Court
468 U.S. 883 (1984)

CHIEF JUSTICE BURGER delivered the opinion of the Court:

We granted certiorari to determine whether the Education of the Handicapped Act or the Rehabilitation Act of 1973 requires a school district to provide a handicapped child with clean intermittent catheterization during school hours.

I

Amber Tatro is an 8-year-old girl born with a defect known as spina bifida. As a result, she suffers from orthopedic and speech impairments and a neurogenic bladder, which prevents her from emptying her bladder voluntarily. Consequently, she must be catheterized every three or four hours to avoid injury to her kidneys. In accordance with accepted medical practice, clean intermittent catheterization (CIC), a procedure involving the insertion of a catheter into the urethra to drain the bladder, has been prescribed. The procedure is a simple one that may be performed in a few minutes by a layperson with less than an hour's training. Amber's parents, babysitter, and teenage brother are all qualified to administer CIC, and Amber soon will be able to perform this procedure herself.

In 1979 petitioner Irving Independent School District agreed to provide special education for Amber, who was then three and one-half years old. In consultation with her parents, who are respondents here, petitioner developed an individualized education program for Amber under the requirements of the Education of the Handicapped Act.... The individualized education program provided that Amber would attend early childhood development classes and receive special services such as physical and occupational therapy. That program, however, made no provision for school personnel to administer CIC.

Respondents unsuccessfully pursued administrative remedies to secure CIC services for Amber during school hours. In October 1979 respondents brought the present action in District Court against petitioner, the State Board of Education, and others. They sought an injunction ordering petitioner to provide Amber with CIC and sought damages and attorney's fees.... [R]espondents invoked the Education of the Handicapped Act. Because Texas received funding under that statute, petitioner was required to provide Amber with a "free appropriate public education," which is defined to include "related services," § 1401(18). Respondents argued that CIC is one such "related service." ...

....

II

This case poses two separate issues. The first is whether the Education of the Handicapped Act requires petitioner to provide CIC services to Amber. The second is whether § 504 of the Rehabilitation Act creates such an obligation. We first turn to the claim presented under the Education of the Handicapped Act.

States receiving funds under the Act are obliged to satisfy certain conditions. A primary condition is that the state implement a policy "that assures all handicapped children the right to a free appropriate public education." ...

A "free appropriate public education" is explicitly defined as "special education and related services." The term "special education" means

> "specially designed instruction, at no cost to parents or guardians, to meet the unique needs of a handicapped child, including classroom instruction, instruction in physical education, home instruction, and instruction in hospitals and institutions."

"Related services" are defined as

> "transportation, and such developmental, corrective, and other supportive services (including speech pathology and audiology, psychological services, physical and occupational therapy, recreation, and medical and counseling services, except that such medical services shall be for diagnostic and evaluation purposes only) as may be required to assist a handicapped child to benefit from special education, and includes the early identification and assessment of handicapping conditions in children."

The issue in this case is whether CIC is a "related service" that petitioner is obliged to provide to Amber. We must answer two questions: first, whether CIC is a "supportive servic[e] ... required to assist a handicapped child to benefit from special education"; and second, whether CIC is excluded from this definition as a "medical servic[e]" serving purposes other than diagnosis or evaluation.

A

The Court of Appeals was clearly correct in holding that CIC is a "supportive servic[e] ... required to assist a handicapped child to benefit from special education." It is clear on this record that, without having CIC services available during the school day, Amber cannot attend school and thereby "benefit from special education." CIC services therefore fall squarely within the definition of a "supportive service."

As we have stated before, "Congress sought primarily to make public education available to handicapped children" and "to make such access meaningful." A service that enables a handicapped child to remain at school during the day is an important means of providing the child with the meaningful

F. RELATED SERVICES

access to education that Congress envisioned. The Act makes specific provisions for services, like transportation, for example, that do no more than enable a child to be physically present in class; and the Act specifically authorizes grants for schools to alter buildings and equipment to make them accessible to the handicapped. Services like CIC that permit a child to remain at school during the day are no less related to the effort to educate than are services that enable the child to reach, enter, or exit the school.

....

B

We also agree with the Court of Appeals that provision of CIC is not a "medical servic[e]," which a school is required to provide only for purposes of diagnosis or evaluation. We begin with the regulations of the Department of Education, which are entitled to deference. The regulations define "related services" for handicapped children to include "school health services," which are defined in turn as "services provided by a qualified school nurse or other qualified person." "Medical services" are defined as "services provided by a licensed physician." Thus, the Secretary has determined that the services of a school nurse otherwise qualifying as a "related service" are not subject to exclusion as a "medical service," but that the services of a physician are excludable as such.

This definition of "medical services" is a reasonable interpretation of congressional intent. Although Congress devoted little discussion to the "medical services" exclusion, the Secretary could reasonably have concluded that it was designed to spare schools from an obligation to provide a service that might well prove unduly expensive and beyond the range of their competence....

Congress plainly required schools to hire various specially trained personnel to help handicapped children, such as "trained occupational therapists, speech therapists, psychologists, social workers and other appropriately trained personnel." School nurses have long been a part of the educational system, and the Secretary could therefore reasonably conclude that school nursing services are not the sort of burden that Congress intended to exclude as a "medical service."...

Petitioner's contrary interpretation of the "medical services" exclusion is unconvincing. In petitioner's view, CIC is a "medical service," even though it may be provided by a nurse or trained layperson; that conclusion rests on its reading of Texas law that confines CIC to uses in accordance with a physician's prescription and under a physician's ultimate supervision. Aside from conflicting with the Secretary's reasonable interpretation of congressional intent, however, such a rule would be anomalous. Nurses in petitioner's school district are authorized to dispense oral medications and administer emergency injections in accordance with a physician's prescription. This kind of service for nonhandicapped children is difficult to distinguish from the provision of CIC to the handicapped....

To keep in perspective the obligation to provide services that relate to both the health and educational needs of handicapped students, we note several limitations that should minimize the burden petitioner fears. First, to be entitled to related services, a child must be handicapped so as to require special education....

Second, only those services necessary to aid a handicapped child to benefit from special education must be provided, regardless how easily a school nurse or layperson could furnish them. For example, if a particular medication or treatment may appropriately be administered to a handicapped child other than during the school day, a school is not required to provide nursing services to administer it.

Third, the regulations state that school nursing services must be provided only if they can be performed by a nurse or other qualified person, not if they must be performed by a physician. It bears mentioning that here not even the services of a nurse are required; as is conceded, a layperson with minimal training is qualified to provide CIC.

....

We conclude that provision of CIC to Amber is not subject to exclusion as a "medical service," and we affirm the Court of Appeals' holding that CIC is a "related service" under the Education of the Handicapped Act.

....

It is so ordered.

[Dissenting opinions omitted.]

---

1. *Tatro* upheld an order requiring an unusual health service to be performed by school personnel so as to enable a student to be educated in a regular setting. To which of the separate cases under "least restrictive environment", *supra*, *Roncker v. Walter* or *Daniel R.R.*, is this decision most compatible? Also, did the Court even consider the counter-argument inherent in the *Rowley* case, *i.e.*, that the child could have obtained "some benefit" by receiving the related service at home and going to the school one-half day or by having a homebound placement?

2. Part III of *Tatro* discusses very briefly the application of Section 504 to the situation in this case. Because relief was granted under EAHCA (IDEA), the Court held that Section 504 was inapplicable. From this decision, then, can we assume that there are cases where 504 will apply (*i.e.*, when no relief under IDEA is available)?

3. Consider also the following excerpt from Daniel and Coriell, *Traversing the Sisyphean Trails of the Education for All Handicapped Children's Act: An Overview*, 18 Ohio N.U. L. Rev. 571 (1992).*

---

*Copyright © 1992 by the Ohio Northern University Law Review. Reprinted with permission.

F. RELATED SERVICES

Citing the high cost of health care as a major limitation, the *Tatro* Court limited medical services under the EAHCA to those for diagnostic and evaluative purposes only. The Ninth Circuit Court of Appeals, in *Hawaii Department of Education v. Katherine D.*, 727 F.2d 809 (9th Cir. 1983), ruled that related services encompassed having an individual available who was capable of reinserting a tracheotomy tube in the event that it became dislodged.

In *Detsel v. Board of Education*, 637 F. Supp. 1022 (N.D.N.Y. 1986), the district court applied the *Tatro* test finding that meaningful access to education must be extended to all handicapped children, but medical services which would incur great expense are not covered by the EAHCA. The student in *Detsel* required constant monitoring to keep her lungs clear. In order to administer this type of medical care, a person must have sufficient knowledge and skill in performing cardiopulmonary resuscitation. The court found that constant care of this nature failed the second prong of the *Tatro* test because of its complexity and the fact that a trained health care professional must perform the procedure. Another district court, applying the *Tatro* test, reached a similar result.

The holding in *Detsel* ... disallowing extensive health services that closely resemble medical services even if not administered by a physician [was] not followed in *Macomb County Intermediate Sch. Dist. v. Joshua S.*, 715 F. Supp. 824 (E.D. Mich. 1989). Cost was a factor in each of the above cases, and it was this that the *Joshua S.* court decried as being inconsistent under the holding in *Tatro*. The court looked to the legislative history of the EAHCA and its regulations and found they were devoid of any statement about a state's liberty to decide whether a related service was medical or supportive on the basis of cost. In fact, the court went on to say that, cost notwithstanding, a finding of whether a service is subject to a medical exclusion is exclusively based on whether it is provided by a licensed physician. Presumably then, under *Joshua S.*, if a needed service can be provided by a nurse or other health personnel, no matter what the cost, it does not fall within the medical services exclusion.

Hence, a major area of ambiguity remaining after *Tatro* and its progeny is which medical services exceed the first prong of the test to the extent that the financial cost is so great that it cannot feasibly be met by school districts. Most likely, this area will remain unclear until Congress clarifies the ambiguity in the EAHCA's language.

4. The "medical services" exclusion under "related services" could be very important. The *Tatro* Court created a two part test to determine whether the service qualifies under IDEA: 1) the service must assist a disabled child in benefiting from special education; and 2) the service must not be a medical service exclusive of diagnosis or evaluation. The question the Court entertains then is whether the service is necessary for education purposes or solely a response to medical needs separate from the learning enterprise. To satisfy the test, the Court sought to determine if the service had to be performed by a licensed physician. If so, the service went beyond the requisite boundaries of diagnosis and evaluation and was said not to be covered by IDEA. If the service could be provided by a school nurse or layperson, then it is considered a "related service."

The *Tatro* test has been challenged in *Clovis Unified Sch. Dist. v. California Office of Admin. Hearings*, 903 F.2d 635 (9th Cir. 1990). *Clovis* concerned the question of whether placement in a psychiatric hospital represents a "related service." The student performed adequately in the classroom, but because of a severe emotional condition was placed unilaterally by her parents in a private acute health care facility. The school system recommended two state approved publicly supported facilities, but the parents rejected both proposals.

The Ninth Circuit considered the question whether placement in the private facility constituted a related service requiring an obligation for the school district under IDEA. In deciding the question, the court rejected *Tatro*'s two-part test as too intrusive because of IDEA's exclusion of medical services. The court reasoned that under *Tatro* all medical services could be considered "related services" if they assist a student to receive an education. Moreover, the court also rejected the implication in *Tatro*, that if a medical service could be provided by a school nurse or layperson, then it is a "related service." The court, instead, announced its "necessity" test, *i.e.*, whether the service was for educational purposes or whether it was for medical disabilities distinguishable from the learning process.

Application of this test resulted in finding that the services provided by the private facility were medical and outside of the protection of IDEA. The court reasoned that the student's hospitalization was caused by an acute "medical" crisis. The program in the private hospital was created entirely by medical staff, not school personnel. No educational services were provided by the hospital; instead, the students educational needs were addressed by a tutor paid for by the public school district.

Has *Clovis* interpreted the "related services" provision too narrowly? Does the decision really ignore the precedent established in *Tatro* or is it that cost ($150,000 per year for the private facility) had an overwhelming impact on the decision? Is there any compatibility between the two cases?

5. One of the most necessary related services provided by IDEA is transportation. However, the need for transportation services, according to some, must be related to the disability. For example, if parents place their hearing-impaired child in a private school for the deaf on their own initiative, the court may hold that the transportation is not related to the disability, and may disallow recovery of transportation costs. *McNair v. Oak Hills Local Sch. Dist.*, 872 F.2d 153 (6th Cir. 1989).

F. RELATED SERVICES

The McNairs want Oak Hills to provide transportation for Kelly to and from St. Rita's as a related service under the EHA. They will succeed only if they establish that which § 1400(c) requires:

(1) that the child is handicapped;
(2) that transportation is a related service;
(3) that the related service is designed to meet the unique needs of the child caused by the handicap; and
(4) the school district must be responsible under the EHA and its regulations for providing the related services under the particular circumstances of the case at hand.

In the instant case, the parties have stipulated that Kelly is handicapped under the EHA because of her hearing impairment. The second requirement is also satisfied, as the service at issue in this case is transportation to and from school, and this is by statute made a related service under the EHA. 20 U.S.C. § 1401(17); *Irving Indep. Sch. Dist. v. Tatro*, 468 U.S. 883, 891 (1984). The third requirement of the statute, the showing that the related services are "designed to meet ... unique needs" of the child is not met in this case. The parties have stipulated that Kelly's handicap does not require any special transportation needs, therefore, she could utilize the same transportation service as a non-handicapped child. The need for transportation, although a related service, is no more unique to Kelly because she is deaf than it would be if she were not deaf. Since the statute specifically requires a relationship between the related service and the unique needs of the child, the third requirement under the EHA has not been satisfied, and the Act does not require Oak Hills to provide Kelly with transportation to St. Rita's.

It is argued that *Tatro* holds to the contrary. *Tatro* does not counsel against this analysis as claimed by plaintiffs at oral argument. In *Tatro*, the question was whether clean intermittent catheterization (CIC) was a related service as defined in the EHA. This involved an analysis of 20 U.S.C. § 1401(17), the EHA definition of related services, which under our analysis is step two of a four-step approach.... The issue in this case is not whether transportation is a related service, but the requirement of its relationship to "unique needs." ...

The court is not reaching any determination as to whether a school district in a situation similar to the instant one would have to provide the related service to the child if it was designed to meet that child's unique needs. In other words, because the third requirement set out above was not satisfied, the court reaches no conclusion as to the final requirement. We leave that for another court on another day. All we hold today is that when a child is voluntarily placed in a private school, a public school district need not provide a related service to that child under the EHA if that particular service is not designed to meet the unique needs of the child. *Id.* at 156-57.

What are the implications of the *McNair* decision? If the student had to go to the private school due to her disability (via the IEP), would transportation be provided under the IDEA, even though the student's actual disability does not require special transportation? How does the court avoid this problem?

6. If an extended school year (ESY) is required due to the unique needs of the child, is the school obligated to provide related services, such as transportation, as well? *See Alamo Heights Indep. Sch. Dist. v. State Bd. of Educ.*, 790 F.2d 1153 (5th Cir. 1986).

G. IDEA AND THE ESTABLISHMENT CLAUSE

ZOBREST v. CATALINA FOOTHILLS SCHOOL DISTRICT

Supreme Court of the United States
113 S. Ct. 2462 (1993)

CHIEF JUSTICE REHNQUIST delivered the opinion of the Court:

Petitioner James Zobrest, who has been deaf since birth, asked respondent school district to provide a sign-language interpreter to accompany him to classes at a Roman Catholic high school in Tucson, Arizona, pursuant to the Individuals with Disabilities Education Act (IDEA) and its Arizona counterpart....

James Zobrest attended grades one through five in a school for the deaf, and grades six through eight in a public school operated by respondent. While he attended public school, respondent furnished him with a sign-language interpreter. For religious reasons, James' parents (also petitioners here) enrolled him for the ninth grade in Salpointe Catholic High School, a sectarian institution.

When petitioners requested that respondent supply James with an interpreter at Salpointe, respondent referred the matter to the County Attorney, who concluded that providing an interpreter on the school's premises would violate the United States Constitution.... [T]he question next was referred to the Arizona Attorney General, who concurred in the County Attorney's opinion.... Respondent accordingly declined to provide the requested interpreter.

Petitioners then instituted this action in the United States District Court for the District of Arizona.... Petitioners asserted that the IDEA and the Free Exercise Clause of the First Amendment require respondent to provide James with an interpreter at Salpointe, and that the Establishment Clause does not bar such relief. The complaint sought a preliminary injunction and "such other and further relief as the Court deems just and proper." The District Court denied petitioners' request for a preliminary injunction, finding that the provision of an interpreter at Salpointe would likely offend the Establishment Clause....

The Court of Appeals affirmed by a divided vote applying the three-part test announced in *Lemon v. Kurtzman*, 403 U.S. 602, 613 (1971). It first found that the IDEA has a clear secular purpose: "'to assist States and Localities to provide for the education of all handicapped children.'" Turning to the second prong of the *Lemon* inquiry, though, the Court of Appeals determined that the IDEA, if applied as petitioners proposed, would have the primary effect of advancing

G. IDEA AND THE ESTABLISHMENT CLAUSE

religion and thus would run afoul of the Establishment Clause. "By placing its employee in the sectarian school," the Court of Appeals reasoned, "the government would create the appearance that it was a 'joint sponsor' of the school's activities." We granted certiorari, and now reverse.

... Respondent first argues that 34 CFR § 76.532(a)(1), a regulation promulgated under the IDEA, precludes it from using federal funds to provide an interpreter to James at Salpointe.... In the alternative, respondent claims that even if there is no affirmative bar to the relief, it is not required by statute or regulation to furnish interpreters to students at sectarian schools....

It is a familiar principle of our jurisprudence that federal courts will not pass on the constitutionality of an Act of Congress if a construction of the Act is fairly possible by which the constitutional question can be avoided. *See, e.g., United States v. Locke*, 471 U.S. 84, 92 (1985), and cases cited therein. In *Locke* ... we said that such an appeal "brings before this Court not merely the constitutional question decided below, but the entire case." "The entire case," we explained, "includes nonconstitutional questions actually decided by the lower court as well as nonconstitutional grounds presented to, but not passed on, by the lower court." Therefore, in that case, we turned "first to the nonconstitutional questions pressed below."

Here, in contrast to *Locke*, and other cases applying the prudential rule of avoiding constitutional questions, only First Amendment questions were pressed in the Court of Appeals.... Respondent did not urge any statutory grounds for affirmance upon the Court of Appeals, and thus the Court of Appeals decided only the federal constitutional claims raised by petitioners....

Given this posture of the case, we think the prudential rule of avoiding constitutional questions has no application. The fact that there may be buried in the record a nonconstitutional ground for decision is not by itself enough to invoke this rule.... We therefore turn to the merits of the constitutional claim.

We have never said that "religious institutions are disabled by the First Amendment from participating in publicly sponsored social welfare programs." For if the Establishment Clause did bar religious groups from receiving general government benefits, then "a church could not be protected by the police and fire departments, or have its public sidewalk kept in repair." Given that a contrary rule would lead to such absurd results, we have consistently held that government programs that neutrally provide benefits to a broad class of citizens defined without reference to religion are not readily subject to an Establishment Clause challenge just because sectarian institutions may also receive an attenuated financial benefit. Nowhere have we stated this principle more clearly than in *Mueller v. Allen*, 463 U.S. 388 (1983), and *Witters v. Washington Dept. of Services for Blind*, 474 U.S. 481 (1986), two cases dealing specifically with government programs offering general educational assistance.

In *Mueller*, we rejected an Establishment Clause challenge to a Minnesota law allowing taxpayers to deduct certain educational expenses in computing their state income tax, even though the vast majority of those deductions (perhaps over

90%) went to parents whose children attended sectarian schools. *See* 463 U.S. at 401.... Two factors, aside from States' traditionally broad taxing authority, informed our decision.... We noted that the law "permits all parents — whether their children attend public school or private — to deduct their children's educational expenses." We also pointed out that under Minnesota's scheme, public funds become available to sectarian schools "only as a result of numerous private choices of individual parents of school-age children," thus distinguishing *Mueller* from our other cases involving "the direct transmission of assistance from the State to the schools themselves."

Witters was premised on virtually identical reasoning. In that case, we upheld against an Establishment Clause challenge the State of Washington's extension of vocational assistance, as part of a general state program, to a blind person studying at a private Christian college to become a pastor, missionary, or youth director. Looking at the statute as a whole, we observed that "[a]ny aid provided under Washington's program that ultimately flows to religious institutions does so only as a result of the genuinely independent and private choices of aid recipients."...

That same reasoning applies with equal force here. The service at issue in this case is part of a general government program that distributes benefits neutrally to any child qualifying as "handicapped" under the IDEA, without regard to the "sectarian-nonsectarian, or public-nonpublic nature" of the school the child attends. By according parents freedom to select a school of their choice, the statute ensures that a government-paid interpreter will be present in a sectarian school only as a result of the private decision of individual parents. In other words, because the IDEA creates no financial incentive for parents to choose a sectarian school, an interpreter's presence there cannot be attributed to state decision-making.... When the government offers a neutral service on the premises of a sectarian school as part of a general program that "is in no way skewed towards religion," it follows under our prior decisions that provision of that service does not offend the Establishment Clause. Indeed, this is an even easier case than *Mueller* and *Witters* in the sense that, under the IDEA, no funds traceable to the government ever find their way into sectarian schools' coffers. The only indirect economic benefit a sectarian school might receive by dint of the IDEA is the handicapped child's tuition — and that is, of course, assuming that the school makes a profit on each student; that, without an IDEA interpreter, the child would have gone to school elsewhere; and that the school, then, would have been unable to fill that child's spot.

Respondent contends, however, that this case differs from *Mueller* and *Witters*, in that petitioners seek to have a public employee physically present in a sectarian school to assist in James' religious education. In light of this distinction, respondent argues that this case more closely resembles *Meek v. Pittenger*, 421 U.S. 349 (1975), and *School Dist. of Grand Rapids v. Ball*, 473 U.S. 373 (1985). In *Meek*, we struck down a statute that, *inter alia*, provided "massive aid" to private schools — more than 75% of which were church related —

through a direct loan of teaching material and equipment. The material and equipment covered by the statute included maps, charts, and tape recorders. *Id.* at 355. According to respondent, if the government could not place a tape recorder in a sectarian school in *Meek*, then it surely cannot place an interpreter in *Salpointe*.... *Ball* similarly involved two public programs that provided services on private school premises; there, public employees taught classes to students in private school classrooms. We found that those programs likewise violated the Constitution, relying largely on *Meek*. According to respondent, if the government could not provide educational services on the premises of sectarian schools in *Meek* and *Ball*, then it surely cannot provide James with an interpreter on the premises of *Salpointe*.

Respondent's reliance on *Meek* and *Ball* is misplaced for two reasons. First, the programs in *Meek* and *Ball* — through direct grants of government aid — relieved sectarian schools of costs they otherwise would have borne in educating their students. *Salpointe* is not relieved of an expense that it otherwise would have assumed in educating its students. And, as we noted above, any attenuated financial benefit that parochial schools do ultimately receive from the IDEA is attributable to "the private choices of individual parents." Handicapped children, not sectarian schools, are the primary beneficiaries of the IDEA; to the extent sectarian schools benefit at all from the IDEA, they are only incidental beneficiaries. Thus, the function of the IDEA is hardly " 'to provide desired financial support for nonpublic, sectarian institutions'."

Second, the task of a sign-language interpreter seems to us quite different from that of a teacher or guidance counselor. Notwithstanding the Court of Appeals' intimations to the contrary the Establishment Clause lays down no absolute bar to the placing of a public employee in a sectarian school.... Nothing in this record suggests that a sign-language interpreter would do more than accurately interpret whatever material is presented to the class as a whole. In fact, ethical guidelines require interpreters to "transmit everything that is said in exactly the same way it was intended." James' parents have chosen of their own free will to place him in a pervasively sectarian environment. The sign-language interpreter they have requested will neither add to nor subtract from that environment, and hence the provision of such assistance is not barred by the Establishment Clause.

The IDEA creates a neutral government program dispensing aid not to schools but to individual handicapped children. If a handicapped child chooses to enroll in a sectarian school, we hold that the Establishment Clause does not prevent the school district from furnishing him with a sign-language interpreter there in order to facilitate his education. The judgment of the Court of Appeals is therefore

Reversed.

1. The *Zobrest* Court held that the Establishment Clause does not bar the provision of a sign-language interpreter via government funds? What are the implications of such a ruling? Does it mean that such services are not mandated by IDEA, only that there is no constitutional bar? Does it mean that school systems do or do not have an obligation for supplying such services each time a parent desires for a child to go to a sectarian school?

2. How does the *Zobrest* decision impact the issue of school choice? For a rendition of "choice" and the Establishment Clause, *see* Daniel, *A Comprehensive Analysis of Educational Choice: Can the Polemic of Legal Problems Be Overcome*, 43 DePaul L. Rev. 1 (1993).

The Court stated that the recipients of the benefits derived were the parents, not the sectarian school. The provision of an interpreter allowed the student to attend a private school of his family's choice, and the choice should not be denied due to his disability. What if the disability required a special classroom and those special classes were not offered in the sectarian school? Would the Court have any further position here?

3. Does this decision relieve the private school or the parents of necessary costs they would have to have incurred anyway? How does the Court deal with this question?

4. Recall the statement of the Ninth Circuit Court of Appeals that the presence of a state-sponsored interpreter would send the message that the government is endorsing a religion and the religious school's activities. The Supreme Court rejected this determination. Consider the lower court's position with respect to free speech in order to avoid the impression that the school was sponsoring its content. Are the two arguments from the same Amendment incompatible? What is the Supreme Court's response to such reasoning?

5. Will the decision in this case expand the scope of special education and related services that have to be supplied by states and their local school districts? Inasmuch as the federal government only pays a fraction of what it costs to educate a special education student, does *Zobrest* bring a cost consideration into the "related services" arena that coincides with the *Clovis* decision, *supra*?

6. The school district did not have a high school. For future reference, could school districts with high schools argue that a free education should be provided in the public schools and that disabled students, like the one in this case, have no right to a sectarian education as long as "some benefit," inclusive of the requisite "related services" can be provided?

7. The Supreme Court has recently decided another case involving disabled students and the Establishment Clause. *See Board of Educ. of Kiryas Joel Village Sch. Dist. v. Grumet*, 114 S. Ct. 2481 (1994), *infra* Chapter 15.

H. THE "STAY-PUT" PROVISION

HONIG v. DOE
Supreme Court of the United States
484 U.S. 305 (1988)

JUSTICE BRENNAN delivered the opinion of the Court:

As a condition of federal financial assistance, the Education of the Handicapped Act requires States to ensure a "free appropriate public education" for all disabled children within their jurisdictions. In aid of this goal, the Act establishes a comprehensive system of procedural safeguards designed to ensure parental participation in decisions concerning the education of their disabled children and to provide administrative and judicial review of any decisions with which those parents disagree. Among these safeguards is the so-called "stay-put" provision, which directs that a disabled child "shall remain in [his or her] then current educational placement" pending completion of any review proceedings, unless the parents and state or local educational agencies otherwise agree. 20 U.S.C. § 1415(e)(3). Today we must decide whether, in the face of this statutory proscription, state or local school authorities may nevertheless unilaterally exclude disabled children from the classroom for dangerous or disruptive conduct growing out of their disabilities....

I

In the Education of the Handicapped Act (EHA or the Act), 84 Stat. 175, as amended, 20 U.S.C. § 1400 *et seq.*, Congress sought "to assure that all handicapped children have available to them ... a free appropriate public education which emphasizes special education and related services designed to meet their unique needs, [and] to assure that the rights of handicapped children and their parents or guardians are protected." § 1400(c). When the law was passed in 1975 ... congressional studies revealed that better than half of the Nation's 8 million disabled children were not receiving appropriate educational services. § 1400(b)(3).... Among the most poorly served of disabled students were emotionally disturbed children: Congressional statistics revealed that for the school year immediately preceding passage of the Act, the educational needs of 82 percent of all children with emotional disabilities went unmet. *See* S.Rep. No. 94-168, p. 8 (1975), U.S.Code Cong. & Admin.News 1975, p. 1425 (hereinafter *S.Rep.*).

....

... [T]he EHA confers upon disabled students an enforceable substantive right to public education in participating States and conditions federal financial assistance upon a State's compliance with the substantive and procedural goals of the Act....

The primary vehicle for implementing these congressional goals is the "individualized educational program" (IEP), which the EHA mandates for each disabled child....

... [T]he Act establishes various procedural safeguards that guarantee parents both an opportunity for meaningful input into all decisions affecting their child's education and the right to seek review of any decisions they think inappropriate....

... The "stay-put" provision at issue in this case governs the placement of a child while these often lengthy review procedures run their course. It directs that:

> During the pendency of any proceedings conducted pursuant to [§ 1415], unless the State or local educational agency and the parents or guardian otherwise agree, the child shall remain in the then current educational placement of such child.... § 1415(e)(3).

The present dispute grows out of the efforts of certain officials of the San Francisco Unified School District (SFUSD) to expel two emotionally disturbed children from school indefinitely for violent and disruptive conduct related to their disabilities. In November 1980, respondent John Doe assaulted another student at the Louise Lombard School, a developmental center for disabled children. Doe's April 1980 IEP identified him as a socially and physically awkward 17-year-old who experienced considerable difficulty controlling his impulses and anger. Among the goals set out in his IEP was "[i]mprovement in [his] ability to relate to [his] peers [and to] cope with frustrating situations without resorting to aggressive acts." App. 17. Frustrating situations, however, were an unfortunately prominent feature of Doe's school career: physical abnormalities, speech difficulties, and poor grooming habits had made him the target of teasing and ridicule as early as the first grade, *id.* at 23; his 1980 IEP reflected his continuing difficulties with peers, noting that his social skills had deteriorated and that he could tolerate only minor frustration before exploding.

On November 6, 1980, Doe responded to the taunts of a fellow student in precisely the explosive manner anticipated by his IEP: he choked the student with sufficient force to leave abrasions on the child's neck, and kicked out a school window while being escorted to the principal's office afterwards. Doe admitted his misconduct and the school subsequently suspended him for five days. Thereafter, his principal referred the matter to the SFUSD Student Placement Committee (SPC or Committee) with the recommendation that Doe be expelled. On the day the suspension was to end, the SPC notified Doe's mother that it was proposing to exclude her child permanently from SFUSD and was therefore extending his suspension until such time as the expulsion proceedings were completed. The Committee further advised her that she was entitled to attend the November 25 hearing at which it planned to discuss the proposed expulsion.

After unsuccessfully protesting these actions by letter, Doe brought this suit against a host of local school officials and the State Superintendent of Public Instructions. Alleging that the suspension and proposed expulsion violated the EHA, he sought a temporary restraining order canceling the SPC hearing and requiring school officials to convene an IEP meeting....

H. THE "STAY-PUT" PROVISION

Respondent Jack Smith was identified as an emotionally disturbed child by the time he entered the second grade in 1976. School records prepared that year indicated that he was unable "to control verbal or physical outburst[s]" and exhibited a "[s]evere disturbance in relationships with peers and adults." Further evaluations subsequently revealed that he had been physically and emotionally abused as an infant and young child and that, despite above average intelligence, he experienced academic and social difficulties as a result of extreme hyperactivity and low self-esteem. Of particular concern was Smith's propensity for verbal hostility; one evaluator noted that the child reacted to stress by "attempt[ing] to cover his feelings of low self worth through aggressive behavior[,] ... primarily verbal provocations."

Based on these evaluations, SFUSD placed Smith in a learning center for emotionally disturbed children. His grandparents, however, believed that his needs would be better served in the public school setting and, in September 1979, the school district acceded to their requests and enrolled him at A.P. Giannini Middle School. His February 1980 IEP recommended placement in a Learning Disability Group, stressing the need for close supervision and a highly structured environment. *Id.* at 111. Like earlier evaluations, the February 1980 IEP noted that Smith was easily distracted, impulsive, and anxious; it therefore proposed a half-day schedule and suggested that the placement be undertaken on a trial basis.

At the beginning of the next school year, Smith was assigned to a full-day program; almost immediately thereafter he began misbehaving. School officials met twice with his grandparents in October 1980 to discuss returning him to a half-day program; although the grandparents agreed to the reduction, they apparently were never apprised of their right to challenge the decision through EHA procedures. The school officials also warned them that if the child continued his disruptive behavior — which included stealing, extorting money from fellow students, and making sexual comments to female classmates — they would seek to expel him. On November 14, they made good on this threat, suspending Smith for five days after he made further lewd comments. His principal referred the matter to the SPC, which recommended exclusion from SFUSD. As it did in John Doe's case, the Committee scheduled a hearing and extended the suspension indefinitely pending a final disposition in the matter. On November 28, Smith's counsel protested these actions on grounds essentially identical to those raised by Doe, and the SPC agreed to cancel the hearing and to return Smith to a half-day program at A.P. Giannini or to provide home tutoring. Smith's grandparents chose the latter option and the school began home instruction on December 10; on January 6, 1981, an IEP team convened to discuss alternative placements.

After learning of Doe's action, Smith sought and obtained leave to intervene in the suit....

II

....

Respondent John Doe is now 24 years old and, accordingly, is no longer entitled to the protections and benefits of the EHA, which limits eligibility to disabled children between the ages of 3 and 21. It is clear, therefore, that whatever rights to state educational services he may yet have as a ward of the State the Act would not govern the State's provision of those services, and thus the case is moot as to him. Respondent Jack Smith, however, is currently 20 and has not yet completed high school. Although at present he is not faced with any proposed expulsion or suspension proceedings, and indeed no longer even resides within the SFUSD, he remains a resident of California and is entitled to a "free appropriate public education" within that State. His claims under the EHA, therefore, are not moot if the conduct he originally complained of is "'capable of repetition, yet evading review.'" Given Smith's continued eligibility for educational services under the EHA, the nature of his disability, and petitioner's insistence that all local school districts retain residual authority to exclude disabled children for dangerous conduct, we have little difficulty concluding that there is a "reasonable expectation," that Smith would once again be subjected to a unilateral "change in placement" for conduct growing out of his disabilities were it not for the statewide injunctive relief issued below.

....

III

The language of § 1415(e)(3) is unequivocal. It states plainly that during the pendency of any proceedings initiated under the Act, unless the state or local educational agency and the parents or guardian of a disabled child otherwise agree, "the child shall remain in the then current educational placement." Faced with this clear directive, petitioner asks us to read a "dangerousness" exception into the stay-put provision on the basis of either of two essentially inconsistent assumptions: first, that Congress thought the residual authority of school officials to exclude dangerous students from the classroom too obvious for comment; or second, that Congress inadvertently failed to provide such authority and this Court must therefore remedy the oversight. Because we cannot accept either premise, we decline petitioner's invitation to rewrite the statute.

Petitioner's arguments proceed, he suggests, from a simple, commonsense proposition: Congress could not have intended the stay-put provision to be read literally, for such a construction leads to the clearly unintended, and untenable, result that school districts must return violent or dangerous students to school while the often lengthy EHA proceedings run their course. We think it clear, however, that Congress very much meant to strip schools of the unilateral authority they had traditionally employed to exclude disabled students, particularly emotionally disturbed students, from school. In so doing, Congress did not leave school administrators powerless to deal with dangerous students; it did,

H. THE "STAY-PUT" PROVISION

however, deny school officials their former right to "self-help," and directed that in the future the removal of disabled students could be accomplished only with the permission of the parents or, as a last resort, the courts.

... Congress passed the EHA after finding that school systems across the country had excluded one out of every eight disabled children from classes. In drafting the law, Congress was largely guided by the recent decisions in *Mills v. Board of Education of District of Columbia*, 348 F.Supp. 866 (1972), and PARC, 343 F.Supp. 279 (1972), both of which involved the exclusion of hard-to-handle disabled students. *Mills* in particular demonstrated the extent to which schools used disciplinary measures to bar children from the classroom. There, school officials had labeled four of the seven minor plaintiffs "behavioral problems," and had excluded them from classes without providing any alternative education to them or any notice to their parents. After finding that this practice was not limited to the named plaintiffs but affected in one way or another an estimated class of 12,000 to 18,000 disabled students the District Court enjoined future exclusions, suspensions, or expulsions "on grounds of discipline."

Congress attacked such exclusionary practices in a variety of ways. It required participating States to educate all disabled children, regardless of the severity of their disabilities, 20 U.S.C. § 1412(2)(C), and included within the definition of "handicapped" those children with serious emotional disturbances. It further provided for meaningful parental participation in all aspects of a child's educational placement, and barred schools, through the stay-put provision, from changing that placement over the parent's objection until all review proceedings were completed. Recognizing that those proceedings might prove long and tedious, the Act's drafters did not intend § 1415(e)(3) to operate inflexibly and they therefore allowed for interim placements where parents and school officials are able to agree on one. Conspicuously absent from § 1415(e)(3), however, is any emergency exception for dangerous students. This absence is all the more telling in light of the injunctive decree issued in PARC, which permitted school officials unilaterally to remove students in "'extraordinary circumstances.'" Given the lack of any similar exception in *Mills*, and the close attention Congress devoted to these "landmark" decisions we can only conclude that the omission was intentional; we are therefore not at liberty to engraft onto the statute an exception Congress chose not to create.

Our conclusion that § 1415(e)(3) means what it says does not leave educators hamstrung. The Department of Education has observed that, "[w]hile the [child's] placement may not be changed [during any complaint proceeding], this does not preclude the agency from using its normal procedures for dealing with children who are endangering themselves or others." Such procedures may include the use of study carrels, timeouts, detention, or the restriction of privileges. More drastically, where a student poses an immediate threat to the safety of others, officials may temporarily suspend him or her for up to 10 schooldays. This authority, which respondent in no way disputes, not only ensures that school administrators can protect the safety of others by promptly removing the most dangerous of students, it also provides a "cooling down" period during which officials can initiate IEP review and seek to persuade the child's parents to agree to an interim placement. And in those cases in which the parents of a truly dangerous child adamantly refuse to permit any change in placement, the 10-day respite gives school officials an opportunity to invoke the aid of the courts under § 1415(e)(2), which empowers courts to grant any appropriate relief.

Petitioner contends, however, that the availability of judicial relief is more illusory than real, because a party seeking review under § 1415(e)(2) must exhaust time-consuming administrative remedies, and because under the Court of Appeals' construction of § 1415(e)(3), courts are as bound by the stay-put provision's "automatic injunction," as are schools. It is true that judicial review is normally not available under § 1415(e)(2) until all administrative proceedings are completed, but as we have previously noted, parents may bypass the administrative process where exhaustion would be futile or inadequate. Nor do we think that § 1415(e)(3) operates to limit the equitable powers of district courts such that they cannot, in appropriate cases, temporarily enjoin a dangerous disabled child from attending school. As the EHA's legislative history makes clear, one of the evils Congress sought to remedy was the unilateral exclusion of disabled children by schools, not courts, and one of the purposes of § 1415(e)(3), therefore, was "to prevent school officials from removing a child from the regular public school classroom over the parents' objection pending completion of the review proceedings." The stay-put provision in no way purports to limit or pre-empt the authority conferred on courts by § 1415(e)(2); indeed, it says nothing whatever about judicial power.

In short, then, we believe that school officials are entitled to seek injunctive relief under § 1415(e)(2) in appropriate cases. In any such action, § 1415(e)(3) effectively creates a presumption in favor of the child's current educational placement which school officials can overcome only by showing that maintaining the child in his or her current placement is substantially likely to result in injury either to himself or herself, or to others. In the present case, we are satisfied that the District Court, in enjoining the state and local defendants from indefinitely suspending respondent or otherwise unilaterally altering his then current placement, properly balanced respondent's interest in receiving a free appropriate public education in accordance with the procedures and requirements of the EHA against the interests of the state and local school officials in maintaining a safe learning environment for all their students.

. . . .

Affirmed.

H. THE "STAY-PUT" PROVISION

1. The Court in *Honig* holds that the language and the legislative history of IDEA are clear. There is no evidence of an intent to provide an exception allowing for long-term suspensions or expulsions of a student with a disability if the misbehavior requiring disciplinary action is a manifestation of the child's disability — not even if the activity is "dangerous." What are the advantages and disadvantages of keeping a "dangerous" student in school during the pendency of review proceedings?

Does this decision aid school personnel with the discipline of disabled students? Is the argument by the Court that schools are being helped because all students are being treated equally and some will no longer be discriminated against because of a handicap? Does the decision, in fact, give disabled students an extra benefit over their non-disabled peers?

2. As far-reaching as the decision in *Honig* seems to be, should there be any exceptions that would allow a school to take disciplinary action beyond time-outs, detentions and short-term suspensions? A district court in Texas capitalized on such an exception. In *Jorstad v. Texas City Indep. Sch. Dist.*, 752 F. Supp. 231 (S.D. Tex. 1990), the court held that a school district was permitted to seek injunctive relief to change a placement from a regular school room to a resource center in the school or to home instruction. The exception is limited though. The student in *Jorstad* suffered from a psychotic disorder resulting in frequent tantrums that threatened his safety and the safety of others. If decided today, would the situations involving the students in *Honig* qualify for the *Jorstad* exception?

3. Section 504 of the Rehabilitation Act of 1973 also has a "stay put" provision. This is best exhibited in *OCR Staff Memorandum*, 307 EHLR 5 (OCR 1988). According to this executive opinion, expulsion or long-term suspension from school is a "change of placement" for a disabled student qualifying under Section 504 and consistent with *Honig v. Doe*, a school district must evaluate such students before a change of placement can take place. The memorandum specifically states that school districts may not change a student's placement if there is a nexus between the disability and the disciplinary action without a re-evaluation and an opportunity for due process procedures. These would include notice, an opportunity for the examination of records, an impartial hearing (with participation by parents or guardians and opportunity for legal counsel) [34 C.F.R. § 104.36].

The memorandum defines a change of placement for Section 504 as "exclusion ... for an indefinite period or for more than 10 consecutive days." The definition also incorporates "serial" suspensions, *i.e.*, "a series of suspensions ... less than 10 days in duration, that creates a pattern of exclusions." This definition would not include short suspensions which in the aggregate amount to 10 days or less. It would include dismissals which would, when joined, add up to 10 or more days.

OCR states that "[a]mong the factors that should be considered in determining whether a series of suspensions has resulted in a 'significant change of placement' are the length of the suspension, the proximity of the suspensions to one another and the total amount of time the child is excluded from school."

In a subsequent memorandum, 16 EHLR 491 (1989), OCR states that a Section 504 student, expelled for conduct unrelated to his disability, is not entitled to a continuation of educational services during the dismissal. Note, however, that this policy does not apply to the Fifth or Sixth Circuit Courts of Appeal. The Fifth is governed by the decision in *S-1 v. Turlington*, 635 F.2d 342 (5th Cir. 1981), holding that a school expulsion was a change of placement under the IDEA and Section 504 and that a complete cessation of educational services during the dismissal period is unauthorized even if the infraction is unrelated to the disability. This decision was also adopted by the Sixth Circuit in *Kaelin v. Grubbs*, 682 F.2d 595 (6th Cir. 1982).

A third OCR memorandum, 17 IDELR 609 (OCR 1992), explains an Americans with Disabilities Act (ADA) amendment to Section 504, 29 U.S.C. § 706(8)(C)(iv), concerning school discipline related to drug and alcohol violations. If a student violates the school's drug or alcohol code by being in possession of illegal drugs or alcohol or is using drugs or alcohol, the school may take the same disciplinary action it would take with any student without reference to the due process procedures contained in Section 504, that is without the use of a "causal relationship conference," re-evaluation or access to an impartial hearing. This feature does not apply to IDEA.

4. Consider this scenario: A very large percentage of students being referred for special education placement are students of color. The United States Office of Civil Rights considers this a problem and establishes as a priority the removal of a number of these students from the special education ranks. This, then, removes the veneer of due process protection since so many of these students are also accused of disciplinary infractions. Is the OCR action a case of disparate treatment? Is this a Hobbesian choice for minority students — a special education label or the absence of disability protection for disciplinary problems? *See* the *OCR Strategic Plan*, October, 1993.

METROPOLITAN SCHOOL DISTRICT OF WAYNE TOWNSHIP, MARION COUNTY, INDIANA v. DAVILA

United States Court of Appeals
969 F.2d 485 (7th Cir. 1992)

BAUER, CHIEF JUDGE:

In this appeal, Robert Davila on behalf of the United States Department of Education challenges the district court's grant of summary judgment in favor of the Metropolitan School District of Wayne Township and the plaintiff class. The district court held that a letter purporting to interpret part B of the Individuals with Disabilities Education Act, 20 U.S.C. §§ 1411-20 ("the IDEA-B" or "the Act"), was a legislative ruling subject to the notice and comment procedures of the Administrative Procedure Act, 5 U.S.C. § 553 ("APA"). We reverse, and

H. THE "STAY-PUT" PROVISION

remand for entry of summary judgment in favor of Davila and the Department of Education.

I

The IDEA-B provides federal funding to states to support the education of disabled children. In order to qualify for funds, a state must establish a policy assuring a free appropriate education ("FAPE") to all disabled children. Most states distribute the federal monies to local educational agencies that provide services to eligible children. The Office of Special Education and Rehabilitative Services of the United States Department of Education ("OSERS") administers the Act. The rule at issue here was announced by OSERS in a letter written by Davila, the Assistant Secretary for Special Education and Rehabilitative Services, in response to an inquiry from Frank E. New, the Director of Special Education for the Ohio Department of Education.

New asked whether the IDEA requires states to provide educational services to disabled children who are expelled or suspended for an extended period for reasons unrelated to their disability. In his letter, Davila stated that OSERS interpreted the IDEA to require states to continue services in these circumstances....

The School District for Wayne Township sued the Secretary on behalf of itself and all similarly situated providers of educational services. The School District asserts that OSERS' position places a large financial burden on school districts, and that the districts are entitled to notice of the proposed rule and the opportunity to comment. Both parties filed motions for summary judgment. The district court agreed with the School District that OSERS' position is a legislative rule subject to the notice and comment requirements of the APA. The district court acknowledged that "the issue is whether ... the New Letter is a 'legislative rule' requiring notice and comment under the APA, or ... merely an 'interpretive rule' exempt from the APA's requirements."

The court applied a three-factor test to determine that the position taken in the letter is "substantive," and therefore subject to the notice and comment requirements of § 553 of the APA and to the restrictions of 20 U.S.C. § 1417(b), the section of the IDEA delegating law-making authority to the Department of Education.... These factors were: "(1) it imposes a new and mandatory duty upon all school districts in the United States, (2) the new duty is not expressly required by EHA [now IDEA], and (3) contrary to the New Letter itself it is not required by *Honig v. Doe*, 484 U.S. 305 (1988)."

We believe the district court used "substantive" as a synonym for "legislative." This usage appears in several other district court opinions, most notably in the one upon which the district court relied to develop its three-factor test.... For these reasons, we believe the district court here also used the terms interchangeably.

The district court interpreted this language to require that any rules the Department proposed under the Act be published in the Federal Register. Based upon its holding that the position announced in Davila's letter to New is "substantive" (legislative), and its reading of § 1417(b), the court concluded that the rule is invalid because OSERS failed to follow the notice and comment procedures of the APA. We find the use of the term "substantive" in this context misleading; an interpretation which explains the meaning of the statute can be just as "substantive" as a legislative rule. We prefer the interpretive/legislative terminology because it avoids any potential confusion.

II

....

In this case, we believe Davila and the Department of Education are entitled to judgment as a matter of law. The APA does not require administrative agencies to follow notice and comment procedures in all situations. Section 553(b)(3)(A) specifically excludes "interpretive rules, general statements of policy, or rules of agency organization, procedure, or practice," from the notice and comment procedures. Based upon our review of Davila's letter and controlling authority, we conclude that the letter announced OSERS' construction of the IDEA, and hence is an interpretive rule that does not trigger the APA's notice and comment requirements.

....

Here, Secretary Davila's letter purports to be an interpretation of the IDEA. Davila based the OSERS' interpretation upon the Supreme Court's decision in *Honig v. Doe*, 484 U.S. 305 (1988), and other cases interpreting IDEA, the language of both the statute and an implementing regulation and the legislative history of the Act. These are the classic tools a reviewing body, be it court or agency, relies upon to determine the meaning of a statute. Thus, the first factor in our analysis, and an "important" one according to the governing authority, weighs in favor of a determination that the rule is interpretive.

Under the more general inquiry, we must determine whether the rule merely states what OSERS thinks the statute means, or creates new law, rights, or duties. We note that a new position does not necessarily make a rule legislative rather than interpretive.

The district court held that the letter announced a "change in long standing policy of OSERS without a corresponding change in the underlying statute or regulations." This holding is factually incorrect and, in this case, legally irrelevant. There is nothing in the record to indicate that OSERS' position is a change in policy — in fact, it appears that the question of whether schools that expel disabled students for reasons unrelated to their disability must continue to provide services, had not been considered before May 1989. In May, a Maryland education official raised the question, and OSERS responded in an unpublished letter that states must continue to provide some form of services. *See* Appellants'

H. THE "STAY-PUT" PROVISION

Brief at 7. Because there was no published policy, Frank New asked OSERS about the issue when it arose in Ohio.

The School District points to a Memorandum issued by the Office of Special Education Programs (a division of OSERS), to support its argument that the agency's position is a change in policy. The Memorandum lists and answers questions about the Act posed by state special education directors. The School District asserts that the following question and answer state a policy contrary to that announced in the letter to Frank New:

> Q. What are the issues and requirements related to suspension and expulsion?
> A. This is a complex area in which we are currently better able to articulate the issues than the answers. It is also relevant that the Supreme Court has decided to hear a case involving suspension and expulsion. Supreme Court review was requested by Superintendent Honig of California, and will take place some time after October 1, 1987. OSEP's position is that a suspension or expulsion of more than ten days' duration constitutes a change in placement which would trigger the procedures and protections of the EHA-B.... Some courts looking at the discipline issue under both EHA-B and Section 504 [of the Rehabilitation Act of 1973] have said that, when the misbehavior is unrelated to the handicapping condition, the child can be disciplined without regard to the fact that the child has a handicap. This is of interest because the basis for this under the EHA-B is not entirely clear. While this may deserve further thought, OSEP will not apply a rule or guideline contrary to this in the absence of a generally applicable statement distributed in advance to the states.

But this response only discusses whether a school can suspend or expel a disabled student (for reasons unrelated to his disability), not whether some educational services must be provided once the student is expelled. As counsel for the Department pointed out at oral argument, until recently it was unclear whether disabled children could be disciplined at all under the Act. *Honig v. Doe* resolved this question in the affirmative. The Memorandum does not support the position that the letter announced a change in longstanding agency policy.

In this case, the treatment of children expelled for reasons unrelated to their disabilities has never arisen....

....

... [A]n agency's change in its reading of a statute does not necessarily make the rule announcing the change legislative. That rules "may have altered administrative duties or other hardships does not make them substantive [legislative]." Further ... the issue here is a new one, and the agency's ruling does not constitute a change in policy.

The rule announced in Davila's letter satisfies the general test of an interpretive rule. It relies upon the language of the statute and its legislative history to determine "that Congress did not intend for educational services to cease for children with handicaps who were removed from schools as a result of behavioral problems." ....

....

Simply because an agency has the power to enact legislative rules does not mean that it has exercised that power.... [A]ll agencies with power to administer statutes also have the authority to interpret them. If the mere delegation of rule-making authority meant all subsequent agency determinations were legislative, and had to meet the notice and comment requirements of the APA, agency functioning would be hamstrung. The ability to issue interpretive rules "preserve[s] agency flexibility" and "allow[s] agencies to explain ambiguous terms in legislative enactments without having to undertake cumbersome proceedings." ...

The second factor the School District relied upon at oral argument similarly is flawed. All rules which interpret the underlying statute must be binding because they set forth what the agency believes is congressional intent. Could an agency announce, "We think Congress intended this when it enacted this statute, but you don't have to do it."? Courts are not bound by an agency's interpretation, as we have discussed, but parties regulated by the statute certainly are....

Further, ... "a rule affecting rights and obligations is [not] *ipso facto* legislative." ... Davila's letter simply explained what the statute already requires.

Prevailing authority rejects the proposition that a rule that has substantial impact is necessarily legislative.... The district court relied in part upon this rationale to find that Davila's letter announced a legislative rule. "[T]he impact of a rule has no bearing on whether it is legislative or interpretative; interpretative rules may have a substantial impact on the rights of individuals." The district court's reliance upon this rationale thus is misplaced.

The district court also found Davila's interpretation of the IDEA was a legislative rule because it found that continuing services are "not expressly required" by the Act. But this rationale again implicitly rejects OSERS' inherent authority to interpret its governing statute. If the IDEA expressly required services to continue after expulsion, there would be no need for OSERS to interpret congressional intent on the subject.

The district court's final reason for holding that OSERS' interpretation of the IDEA was a legislative rather than interpretive rule also misconceives the governing test. The court did not approve of the agency's interpretation of *Honig v. Doe*.

....

In other words, because the district court disagreed with OSERS' interpretation of *Honig* and the statute, the interpretation must be legislative, and thus in violation of the APA. The School District also raises this argument on appeal — because *Honig* does not dictate OSERS' interpretation, that 'interpretation' must be legislative. *Honig* did not reach this issue — it noted that students could be suspended for behavior related to their disability that poses an immediate threat to others. But OSERS' letter did not contend that *Honig* resolved the issue. The district court seems to hold that because *Honig* did not offer the interpretation adopted by OSERS, the interpretation must be legislative. This reasoning is in error. Simply because a reviewing court disagrees with an agency interpretation does not render it legislative. An agency has "inherent authority to issue interpretive rules informing the public of the ... standards it intends to apply in exercising its discretion." Further, the School District has only challenged the OSERS' authority to issue its interpretation, not the interpretation itself. Of course, if the school district were entirely happy with OSERS' reading of IDEA-B, this case would not be before us. Nevertheless, a reviewing court's disagreement with the substance of an agency's interpretive rule does not render the interpretive rule legislative.

Finally, we do not believe that the provision of the IDEA that delegates rulemaking authority to the Department of Education, 20 U.S.C. § 1417(b), requires OSERS to promulgate its interpretation of the Act through notice and comment. This section was designed to ensure that the rules necessary to implement the Act would be in place early enough to allow states to fulfill their statutory obligations by the effective date of the Act. Moreover, as we have discussed, a grant of legislative authority (and the agency's exercise of that authority) does not remove the agency's inherent authority to issue interpretive rules. The School District fundamentally misapprehends § 1417(b), as well as the agency's inherent rulemaking authority. This delegation authorizes legislative rulemaking, it does not revoke interpretive authority.

III

For the foregoing reasons, the decision of the district court is *Reversed*, and the case is *Remanded* for entry of summary judgment in favor of Davila and the Department of Education.

---

1. What is the consequence of this decision? Do school systems in all federal circuits now have to provide an education for disabled students who are expelled for behavior unrelated to their disabilities? Is the decision limited to the Seventh Circuit Court of Appeals? How does this decision comport with IDEA or Section 504? Is the decision consistent with that in *Honig*?

2. How are the decisions in both *Honig* and *Davila* effected by the newly promulgated Improving America's Schools Act of 1994, Pub. L. No. 103-382, 108 Stat. 3518? The law provides that:

> [E]ach state receiving Federal funds ... shall have in effect a state law requiring local educational agencies to expel from school for a period of not less than one year a student who is determined to have brought a weapon to a school under the jurisdiction of local educational agencies in that state, except that such State law shall allow the chief administering officer of such

local educational agency to modify such expulsion requirement for a student on a case-by-case basis. § 14601(b)(1).

Definition — For the purpose of this section, the term 'weapon' means a firearm. § 14601(b)(4).

The law specifically amends the Individuals with Disabilities Education Act relative to students who bring weapons to school:

> [I]f the proceedings ... involve a child with a disability who is determined to have brought a weapon to school ... then the child may be placed in an interim alternative education setting, in accordance with State law, for not more than 45 days. § 314(1)(B)(i).
>
> If a parent or guardian of a [disabled] child requests a due process hearing ... then the child shall remain in the alternative educational setting ... during the pendency of any proceedings ... unless the parents and local educational agency agree otherwise. § 314(1)(B)(iii).

3. Does this Act make a distinction between students who demonstrate a nexus between infraction and disability and those who don't? If not, can both sets of students be expelled for up to 45 days? Would this override the decisions in both *Honig* and *Davila* as well as the policies of the Office of Special Education Programs? How does the Act comport with the decision of *Turlington* and *Kaelin* mentioned in the previous notes? Incidently, has the Congress or any of the courts effectively defined when a disability and an infraction are related?

4. Can this Act be interpreted to mean that if the parents request a due process hearing claiming an inappropriate nexus decision by the other IEP team members the "stay put" provision of IDEA will not force a return to the original placement as in *Honig*? Is this a nullification of "stay put" based on parental objection to "alternative placement"? Does this remove the balance of parent-school official interests to one of school discretion in such circumstances?

5. What of dangerous weapons other than guns? Are states prevented from expelling disabled students for these offenses, even if not mandated by this Act?

6. Does the Act apply to only IDEA, or does it apply to disabled students covered under Section 504 and ADA as well?

I. REMEDIES

SCHOOL COMMITTEE OF THE TOWN OF BURLINGTON, MASSACHUSETTS v. DEPARTMENT OF EDUCATION OF MASSACHUSETTS

Supreme Court of the United States
471 U.S. 359 (1985)

JUSTICE REHNQUIST delivered the opinion of the Court:
The Education of the Handicapped Act (Act) requires participating state and local educational agencies "to assure that handicapped children and their parents

I. REMEDIES

or guardians are guaranteed procedural safeguards with respect to the provision of free appropriate public education" to such handicapped children. These procedures include the right of the parents to participate in the development of an "individualized education program" (IEP) for the child and to challenge in administrative and court proceedings a proposed IEP with which they disagree. Where as in the present case review of a contested IEP takes years to run its course — years critical to the child's development — important practical questions arise concerning interim placement of the child and financial responsibility for that placement. This case requires us to address some of those questions.

Michael Panico, the son of respondent Robert Panico, was a first grader in the public school system of petitioner Town of Burlington, Mass., when he began experiencing serious difficulties in school. It later became evident that he had "specific learning disabilities" and thus was "handicapped" within the meaning of the Act. This entitled him to receive at public expense specially designed instruction to meet his unique needs, as well as related transportation. The negotiations and other proceedings between the Town and the Panicos, thus far spanning more than eight years, are too involved to relate in full detail; the following are the parts relevant to the issues on which we granted certiorari.

In the spring of 1979, Michael attended the third grade of the Memorial School, a public school in Burlington, Mass., under an IEP calling for individual tutoring by a reading specialist for one hour a day and individual and group counselling. Michael's continued poor performance and the fact that Memorial School was not equipped to handle his needs led to much discussion between his parents and Town school officials about his difficulties and his future schooling. Apparently the course of these discussions did not run smoothly; the upshot was that the Panicos and the Town agreed that Michael was generally of above average to superior intelligence, but had special educational needs calling for a placement in a school other than Memorial. They disagreed over the source and exact nature of Michael's learning difficulties, the Town believing the source to be emotional and the parents believing it to be neurological.

In late June, the Town presented the Panicos with a proposed IEP for Michael for the 1979-1980 academic year. It called for placing Michael in a highly structured class of six children with special academic and social needs, located at another Town public school, the Pine Glen School. On July 3, Michael's father rejected the proposed IEP and sought review ... by respondent Massachusetts Department of Education's Bureau of Special Education Appeals (BSEA). A hearing was initially scheduled for August 8, but was apparently postponed in favor of a mediation session on August 17. The mediation efforts proved unsuccessful.

Meanwhile the Panicos received the results of the latest expert evaluation of Michael by specialists at Massachusetts General Hospital, who opined that Michael's "emotional difficulties are secondary to a rather severe learning disorder characterized by perceptual difficulties" and recommended "a highly specialized setting for children with learning handicaps ... such as the Carroll School," a state-approved private school for special education located in Lincoln. Believing that the Town's proposed placement of Michael at the Pine Glen School was inappropriate in light of Michael's needs, Mr. Panico enrolled Michael in the Carroll School in mid-August at his own expense, and Michael started there in September.

The BSEA held several hearings during the fall of 1979, and in January 1980 the hearing officer decided that the Town's proposed placement at the Pine Glen School was inappropriate and that the Carroll School was "the least restrictive adequate program within the record" for Michael's educational needs. The hearing officer ordered the Town to pay for Michael's tuition and transportation to the Carroll School for the 1979-1980 school year, including reimbursing the Panicos for their expenditures on these items for the school year to date.

The Town sought judicial review of the State's administrative decision in the United States District Court for the District of Massachusetts ... naming Mr. Panico and the State Department of Education as defendants. In November 1980, the District Court granted summary judgment against the Town.... The Court of Appeals vacated the judgment....

In the meantime, the Town had refused to comply with the BSEA order, the District Court had denied a stay of that order, and the Panicos and the State had moved for preliminary injunctive relief. The State also had threatened outside of the judicial proceedings to freeze all of the Town's special education assistance unless it complied with the BSEA order. Apparently in response to this threat, the Town agreed in February 1981 to pay for Michael's Carroll School placement and related transportation for the 1980-1981 term, none of which had yet been paid, and to continue paying for these expenses until the case was decided. But the Town persisted in refusing to reimburse Mr. Panico for the expenses of the 1979-1980 school year. When the Court of Appeals disposed of the state claim, it also held that under this status quo none of the parties could show irreparable injury and thus none was entitled to a preliminary injunction. The court reasoned that the Town had not shown that Mr. Panico would not be able to repay the tuition and related costs borne by the Town if he ultimately lost on the merits, and Mr. Panico had not shown that he would be irreparably harmed if not reimbursed immediately for past payments which might ultimately be determined to be the Town's responsibility.

On remand, the District Court entered an extensive pretrial order on the Town's federal claim. In denying the Town summary judgment, it ruled that 20 U.S.C. § 1415(e)(3) did not bar reimbursement despite the Town's insistence that the Panicos violated that provision by changing Michael's placement to the Carroll School during the pendency of the administrative proceedings. The court reasoned that § 1415(e)(3) concerned the physical placement of the child and not the right to tuition reimbursement or to procedural review of a contested IEP. The court also dealt with the problem that no IEP had been developed for the 1980-1981 or 1981-1982 school years. It held that its power under § 1415(e)(2)

I. REMEDIES

to grant "appropriate" relief upon reviewing the contested IEP for the 1979-1980 school year included the power to grant relief for subsequent school years despite the lack of IEPs for those years. In this connection, however, the court interpreted the statute to place the burden of proof on the Town to upset the BSEA decision that the IEP was inappropriate for 1979-1980 and on the Panicos and the State to show that the relief for subsequent terms was appropriate.

After a 4-day trial, the District Court in August 1982 overturned the BSEA decision, holding that the appropriate 1979-1980 placement for Michael was the one proposed by the Town in the IEP and that the parents had failed to show that this placement would not also have been appropriate for subsequent years. Accordingly, the court concluded that the Town was "not responsible for the cost of Michael's education at the Carroll School for the academic years 1979-80 through 1981-82."

....

... We granted certiorari only to consider the following two issues: whether the potential relief available under § 1415(e)(2) includes reimbursement to parents for private school tuition and related expenses, and whether § 1415(e)(3) bars such reimbursement to parents who reject a proposed IEP and place a child in a private school without the consent of local school authorities....

....

The modus operandi of [IDEA] is the already mentioned "individualized educational program." The IEP is in brief a comprehensive statement of the educational needs of a handicapped child and the specially designed instruction and related services to be employed to meet those needs. § 1401(19). The IEP is to be developed jointly by a school official qualified in special education, the child's teacher, the parents or guardian, and, where appropriate, the child. In several places, the Act emphasizes the participation of the parents in developing the child's educational program and assessing its effectiveness.

Apparently recognizing that this cooperative approach would not always produce a consensus between the school officials and the parents, and that in any disputes the school officials would have a natural advantage, Congress incorporated an elaborate set of what it labeled "procedural safeguards" to insure the full participation of the parents and proper resolution of substantive disagreements. Section 1415(b) entitles the parents "to examine all relevant records with respect to the identification, evaluation, and educational placement of the child," to obtain an independent educational evaluation of the child, to notice of any decision to initiate or change the identification, evaluation, or educational placement of the child, and to present complaints with respect to any of the above. The parents are further entitled to "an impartial due process hearing," which in the instant case was the BSEA hearing, to resolve their complaints.

The Act also provides for judicial review in state or federal court to "[a]ny party aggrieved by the findings and decision" made after the due process hearing. The Act confers on the reviewing court the following authority:

> [T]he court shall receive the records of the administrative proceedings, shall hear additional evidence at the request of a party, and, basing its decision on the preponderance of the evidence, shall grant such relief as the court determines is appropriate. § 1415(e)(2).

The first question on which we granted certiorari requires us to decide whether this grant of authority includes the power to order school authorities to reimburse parents for their expenditures on private special education for a child if the court ultimately determines that such placement, rather than a proposed IEP, is proper under the Act.

We conclude that the Act authorizes such reimbursement. The statute directs the court to "grant such relief as [it] determines is appropriate." The ordinary meaning of these words confers broad discretion on the court. The type of relief is not further specified, except that it must be "appropriate." Absent other reference, the only possible interpretation is that the relief is to be "appropriate" in light of the purpose of the Act. As already noted, this is principally to provide handicapped children with "a free appropriate public education which emphasizes special education and related services designed to meet their unique needs." The Act contemplates that such education will be provided where possible in regular public schools, with the child participating as much as possible in the same activities as nonhandicapped children, but the Act also provides for placement in private schools at public expense where this is not possible. In a case where a court determines that a private placement desired by the parents was proper under the Act and that an IEP calling for placement in a public school was inappropriate, it seems clear beyond cavil that "appropriate" relief would include a prospective injunction directing the school officials to develop and implement at public expense an IEP placing the child in a private school.

... As this case so vividly demonstrates ... the review process is ponderous. A final judicial decision on the merits of an IEP will in most instances come a year or more after the school term covered by that IEP has passed. In the meantime, the parents who disagree with the proposed IEP are faced with a choice: go along with the IEP to the detriment of their child if it turns out to be inappropriate or pay for what they consider to be the appropriate placement. If they choose the latter course, which conscientious parents who have adequate means and who are reasonably confident of their assessment normally would, it would be an empty victory to have a court tell them several years later that they were right but that these expenditures could not in a proper case be reimbursed by the school officials. If that were the case, the child's right to a free appropriate public education, the parents' right to participate fully in developing a proper IEP, and all of the procedural safeguards would be less than complete. Because Congress undoubtedly did not intend this result, we are confident that by empowering the court to grant "appropriate" relief Congress meant to include retroactive reimbursement to parents as an available remedy in a proper case.

In this Court, the Town repeatedly characterizes reimbursement as "damages," but that simply is not the case. Reimbursement merely requires the Town to belatedly pay expenses that it should have paid all along and would have borne in the first instance had it developed a proper IEP....

Regardless of the availability of reimbursement as a form of relief in a proper case, the Town maintains that the Panicos have waived any right they otherwise might have to reimbursement because they violated § 1415(e)(3), which provides:

> During the pendency of any proceedings conducted pursuant to [§ 1415], unless the State or local educational agency and the parents or guardian otherwise agree, the child shall remain in the then current educational placement of such child....

We need not resolve the academic question of what Michael's "then current educational placement" was in the summer of 1979, when both the Town and the parents had agreed that a new school was in order. For the purposes of our decision, we assume that the Pine Glen School, proposed in the IEP, was Michael's current placement and, therefore, that the Panicos did "change" his placement after they had rejected the IEP and had set the administrative review in motion. In so doing, the Panicos contravened the conditional command of § 1415(e)(3) that "the child shall remain in the then current educational placement."

....

We do not agree with the Town that a parental violation of § 1415(e)(3) constitutes a waiver of reimbursement. The provision says nothing about financial responsibility, waiver, or parental right to reimbursement at the conclusion of judicial proceedings. Moreover, if the provision is interpreted to cut off parental rights to reimbursement, the principal purpose of the Act will in many cases be defeated in the same way as if reimbursement were never available. As in this case, parents will often notice a child's learning difficulties while the child is in a regular public school program. If the school officials disagree with the need for special education or the adequacy of the public school's program to meet the child's needs, it is unlikely they will agree to an interim private school placement while the review process runs its course. Thus, under the Town's reading of § 1415(e)(3), the parents are forced to leave the child in what may turn out to be an inappropriate educational placement or to obtain the appropriate placement only by sacrificing any claim for reimbursement. The Act was intended to give handicapped children both an appropriate education and a free one; it should not be interpreted to defeat one or the other of those objectives.

....

We think at least one purpose of § 1415(e)(3) was to prevent school officials from removing a child from the regular public school classroom over the parents' objection pending completion of the review proceedings.... Congress was concerned about the apparently widespread practice of relegating handicapped children to private institutions or warehousing them in special classes. We also note that § 1415(e)(3) is located in a section detailing procedural safeguards which are largely for the benefit of the parents and the child.

This is not to say that § 1415(e)(3) has no effect on parents. While we doubt that this provision would authorize a court to order parents to leave their child in a particular placement, we think it operates in such a way that parents who unilaterally change their child's placement during the pendency of review proceedings, without the consent of state or local school officials, do so at their own financial risk. If the courts ultimately determine that the IEP proposed by the school officials was appropriate, the parents would be barred from obtaining reimbursement for any interim period in which their child's placement violated § 1415(e)(3)....

....

Affirmed.

---

1. In November, 1993, the United States Supreme Court granted reimbursement to the parents of a twenty-three-year-old college student who, while in high school, was placed in a private school at her parents' initative. *Florence County Sch. Dist. Four v. Carter*, 114 S. Ct. 361 (1993). The parents had challenged the IEP developed at their public school (the IEP was eventually deemed inappropriate). But rather than keep the child in her then-present placement during the pendency of the claim, the parents unilaterally withdrew her and placed her in a private school for children with learning disabilities. The Court held for the parents and the child, despite the fact that the private school did not meet all of the requirements under Sec. 1401(a) (18) — "free appropriate public education." The deficiences of the private school were that it employed some non-state-certified faculty members, and that it did not develop IEPs. However, the Court held that these requirements — that the school comply with the standards of the State Educational Agency — do not apply to *parental* placements:

> [T]o read the Sec. 1401(a) (18) requirements as applying to parental placements would effectively eliminate the right of unilateral withdrawal recognized in *Burlington*. Moreover, IDEA was intended to ensure that children with disabilities receive an education that is both appropriate and free.... To read the provisions of Sec. 1401(a) (18) to bar reimbursement in the circumstances of this case would defeat this statutory purpose.

Do you agree that Section 1401(a)(18) of the IDEA is inapplicable to parental unilateral placements while very applicable to school placement decisions? Note that, based on the dictates of IDEA, parents are to be included in the development of the IEP, which is designed to comply with the FAPE provision. Under the Court's analysis, could parents place their child in a private school before

I. REMEDIES

dealing with the public school and then be reimbursed for expenses? After all, the requirements of the stated IDEA section do not apply to parents.

2. The Federal District Court in New Jersey echoed the decision in *Burlington* in *B.G. v. Crawford Bd. of Educ.*, 702 F. Supp. 1158 (D.N.J. 1988). The parents of a disabled child requested reimbursement for private school expenses after they unilaterally removed the student from the public school during pendency of proceedings. As in *Burlington*, if the ultimate placement is deemed proper, then reimbursement has a much better chance of being granted. The *B.G.* court held that appropriateness should be determined by balancing the equities case-by-case. In *B.G.* the parents gave no notice of the change in placement and did not discuss the issue with the IEP team. Reimbursement was denied. Is this a correct ruling under IDEA? What if the parents' placement had been properly arranged?

In contrast, *see Jefferson County v. Breen*, 853 F.2d 853 (11th Cir. 1988). The school district was required to fund the education of a disabled student for two years past his 21st birthday due to the district's failure to provide an appropriate education during the pendency of proceedings. According to the court, reimbursement expenses must be paid (even past the statutory age limit) because they represent expenses that the school should have paid all along. Are these compensatory or punitive damages to the school?

For more on punitive damages and the availability of monetary awards to parents under Section 504 for the school's failure to evaluate the disabilities of children, consider the following case.

JOHN AND KATHRYN G. v. BOARD OF EDUCATION OF MOUNT VERNON PUBLIC SCHOOLS

United States District Court
18 IDLER 1026 (S.D.N.Y. 1992)

GERARD L. GOETTEL, DISTRICT JUDGE:

....

George G. attended a Mount Vernon public school during 1985 to 1990. According to the complaint, from the outset, he experienced difficulties in school and his first-grade teacher notified his parents that George was easily distracted in class and had difficulty following directions. It is claimed that Mrs. G., George's mother, took him to the pediatrician who found no medical problems and this information was relayed to George's teacher.

George's difficulties allegedly continued during second grade and third grade. The second grade teacher noted that George had difficulty completing assignments and lagged in many areas. George's third grade teacher observed his continuing problems and called Mrs. G., expressing her concerns about his learning problems. She requested permission to refer him to a school psychologist for testing and it was granted.

George was then allegedly tested in January 1988 by defendant Linda Kalos, who is a psychologist for the Mount Vernon Public Schools. It is claimed that she stated in a report dated February 12, 1988 that George had weak short-term auditory memory and trouble with grapho-motor tasks and recommended that he receive assistance from a speech pathologist, continued remediation in academic subjects and support to bolster his self-esteem. Allegedly, this report was not given to George's parents nor his teacher. Mrs. G. claims that she was informed by Ms. Kalos that nothing was wrong with George and that if he continued to have problems, then Mrs. G. should arrange outside private counseling.

The complaint asserts that George never received any of the services recommended in Ms. Kalos' report. He purportedly continued to experience difficulty in his school work during fourth grade and, additionally, began to exhibit behavioral problems at home. Plaintiffs also claim that George suffered hair loss, a condition associated with stress, and thus required medical attention. His grades declined greatly in fourth grade and he was ranked as below grade level in reading during that year. Mr. and Mrs. G. claim that the school began to provide George with tutoring in reading three times a week outside of the classroom setting although they were not consulted.

Mrs. G. claims that she contacted the principal of George's school, defendant Thomas Pesce, and asked him for assistance. He arranged a meeting with Ms. Kalos, George's regular teacher and his reading teacher. Ms. Kalos allegedly again stated her belief that there was nothing wrong with George.

According to the complaint, George's fourth grade teacher referred him to the speech therapist because his actions suggested to her that he could not hear or understand her all the time. George's parents were never informed of this referral. A hearing test proved negative but still nothing was done to ascertain what was causing George's apparent listening problem. The teacher attempted to address George's needs through lightening his work load but he was still having problems.

In fifth grade, it is asserted that George's grades continued to decline and his behavior further deteriorated. Mrs. G. took George for testing outside the school district at the suggestion of his fifth grade teacher. Testing at the College of New Rochelle during February through April 1990 supposedly revealed that George had serious learning disabilities. Mr. and Mrs. G. allegedly were counseled for the first time by evaluators from the college about their rights under federal and state law, as established by the Individuals with Disabilities Education Act ("IDEA"), 20 U.S.C. § 1400 *et seq.*, and Article 89 of the N.Y Education Law, and told about the District Committee for Special Education ("CSE").

It is claimed that after a confrontation between Mrs. G. and Ms. Kalos, Ms. Kalos finally arranged a formal referral to the CSE. George was evaluated by the committee in the spring of 1990. Allegedly, he was identified as suffering from impaired auditory processing and auditory and visual short-term memory, as well as emotional and social problems stemming from his learning disabilities. Intensive work with a learning disability specialist was recommended as well as speech therapy and individual counseling. Mr. and Mrs. G. believed the individualized education program was not appropriate and challenged it at an

I. REMEDIES

impartial hearing held pursuant to 20 U.S.C. § 1415(b)(2). The impartial hearing officer ("IHO") upheld the program and they appealed to the New York State Education Department. Again, the placement decision was upheld. George is now educated in a private school for children with handicapping conditions.

In this action, the plaintiffs do not challenge the appropriateness of the educational placement recommended by the CSE and affirmed by the IHO. Instead, the gravamen of the complaint is that the failure of Ms. Kalos to inform George's parents about his problems, her failure to refer George to the CSE, and her failure to inform any other school personnel about his problems resulted in George's suffering severe emotional and mental distress and damage to his development. Plaintiffs claim that these failures, along with the failure of the other school authorities to take any action concerning George, constituted a violation of their rights secured by the Rehabilitation, Comprehensive Services, and Developmental Disabilities Act of 1978, 29 U.S.C. § 794, the IDEA, the Civil Rights Act of 1871, 42 U.S.C. § 1983, and the fourteenth amendment to the United States Constitution.

Defendants now move to dismiss the complaint, asserting ... that the complaint fails to state a claim upon which relief can be granted.

....

Failure to State a Claim Upon Which Relief Can Be Granted

Defendants contend that the plaintiffs' claims are nothing more than educational malpractice claims garbed in federal statutory clothing because plaintiffs are not challenging the substance of the placement recommended by the CSE. Instead, plaintiffs seek money damages for the injuries allegedly caused by the school district's purported failure to identify and address George's learning problems as required by federal law. New York does not recognize claims for educational malpractice. However, the facts alleged here do state federal claims.

Section 504 of the Rehabilitation Act provides that "[n]o otherwise qualified individual with handicaps in the United States shall, solely by reason of her or his handicap, be excluded from the participation in, be denied the benefits of, or be subjected to discrimination under any program or activity receiving Federal financial assistance." In order to receive federal funds, states are required to assure that they provide a free appropriate public education to all handicapped students within the state. New York, through its education laws, makes these assurances. Learning disabilities are a handicap protected by the Rehabilitation Act.

Plaintiffs' complaint is that the Mount Vernon Board of Education failed to identify George as a handicapped student by relying solely on Ms. Kalos' recommendations rather than having George referred to the CSE when his learning problems were suspected in violation of regulations promulgated pursuant to the IDEA and the Rehabilitation Act.... They also allege that George was denied a "free appropriate public education," and that his parents were not afforded procedural protection also in violation of the Rehabilitation Act.

To state a claim under the Rehabilitation Act, the complaint must allege that 1) the plaintiff is a handicapped person, 2) that plaintiff is qualified for participation in the program, 3) that plaintiff has been denied the benefits of the program solely because of his handicap and 4) that the relevant program is receiving federal assistance. In the context of education of handicapped children, in order to avoid the court's substitution of its own judgment for educational decisions made by state officials, plaintiffs must show bad faith or gross misjudgment by the officials.

In asserting that George is learning disabled, the first prong has been satisfied for the purposes of this motion. 45 C.F.R. Pt. 84, App. A. In addition, it cannot be disputed that George was entitled to a free, appropriate public education nor that the Mount Vernon Board of Education runs a program receiving federal assistance. As the complaint alleges that George was qualified for participation in special education prior to his identification in fifth grade as learning disabled, the second prong of this test has been satisfied. Our attention is focused, therefore, on the plaintiffs' suggestion that George was denied access to appropriate education by virtue of his handicap.

Plaintiffs posit that George was denied access to appropriate public education through a Mount Vernon Board of Education policy which vested all responsibility for making references to the CSE in the school psychologist. Only upon a determination by the psychologist that the child had a handicapping condition would a reference be made to CSE. Thus, if the psychologist erred in or delayed its evaluation for whatever reason, a necessary reference may not be made. According to the complaint, a Site Visit Report compiled by the New York State Education Department in April 1988 criticized this practice as violating federal and state regulations which required that a child be directly referred to a CSE upon suspicion of a handicapping condition because it imposed a layer of evaluation not required by law. The report also stated that the method of obtaining consents for evaluation by the psychologist were improper and that parents were not accorded full due process rights.

The complaint alleges that despite this criticism the Board of Education persisted in its practice. Thus, plaintiffs claim that George should have been referred to the CSE in 1988 after tests were administered by the school psychologist and that they should have been advised about the existence of the CSE. It is this practice that plaintiffs assert deprived George of his right to a free, appropriate education.

Although defendants may not have intended to discriminate against George through their abrogation of federal and state regulations, under the Rehabilitation Act, the failure to provide access by the handicapped to federally funded programs available to non-handicapped persons may nonetheless constitute discrimination under that statute. Plaintiffs must, though, show that the denial of access resulted from bad faith or gross misjudgment before they can prevail on their claim under the Rehabilitation Act. In addition, the school district, because it receives federal funds, is not permitted to provide benefits or services in a manner that limits or has the effect of limiting the participation of qualified handicapped persons.... As the state recognized in its Site report, the reliance on one psychologist rather than a group of individuals to determine whether a child is handicapped has the potential to limit the participation of a handicapped child in special education if he or she is misdiagnosed. If this practice was developed in order to impede the access of handicapped children to special education, an intent to discriminate may be inferred. We conclude, therefore, that a violation of the Rehabilitation Act has been stated.

Far less discussion is necessary to establish the sufficiency of the plaintiffs' claim under 42 U.S.C. § 1983. The Second Circuit recognized in *Quackenbush v. Johnson City School District*, 716 F.2d 141, 148 (2d. Cir. 1983), *cert. denied*, 465 U.S. 1071 (1984), that a person denied the safeguards of the EHA (later amended to become the IDEA) had a right of action under § 1983. In that case, the plaintiff alleged that her son was placed in a regular kindergarten class even though the school should have known that he was a handicapped child in need of special education services. She was told by school officials to wait until the following year and her son repeated kindergarten, again in a regular class. The mother had the child evaluated and he was diagnosed as learning disabled. This report was sent to the school's committee on the handicapped but no action was taken. The court allowed the action seeking compensatory damages to go forward on the grounds that the school allegedly had a policy intended to reduce the expense of special educational services by preventing handicapped children from gaining access to the procedural safeguards guaranteed by the EHA.

Here, the delay in referring George to the CSE, if truly unjustified, may, as in *Quackenbush*, have denied his access to the procedural safeguards of the IDEA. The complaint does not assert the basis for the school district's action but at the pleading stage, this omission is not fatal. Therefore, we will allow this claim to stand. We emphasize, however, that a violation of the IDEA which did not prevent George's access to that Act's procedural safeguards would not be actionable under § 1983.

Finally, we must address the defendants' argument that the plaintiffs cannot collect the monetary damages they are seeking under the Rehabilitation Act. It is clear that plaintiffs can collect monetary damages under § 1983 should they prove their case. However, whether the remedies available under the Rehabilitation Act encompass the compensatory and punitive damages sought by plaintiffs is not a question that has been definitively resolved....

Unlike § 1983 which is a general remedial statute, the Rehabilitation Act confers specific rights on handicapped individuals. The statute does not specifically provide for compensatory damages but is instead oriented towards fashioning equitable remedies. 29 U.S.C. § 794a. As remediation of discrimination is the intention of the Rehabilitation Act, we see no need to limit the remedies available to the plaintiffs to merely the equitable remedies provided by the IDEA as argued by the defendants. But, there is a question as to whether monetary damages are available under the Rehabilitation Act. Wee see no need to resolve the question at this time as the suit will be proceeding, in any case, under § 1983. We will not in passing the in *Franklin v. Gwinnett County Public Schools*, ___ U.S. ___, 112 S.Ct. 1028 (1992), the Supreme Court held that monetary damages are available under Title IX of the Education Amendments of 1972, 20 U.S.C. §§ 1681-1688, although not specifically authorized by the statute. Additionally, back pay, as a retroactive remedy, is available under the Rehabilitation Act. Moreover, where money damages are the only means of compensating a victim of past discrimination, that remedy must be available to plaintiff.

Conclusion

Defendants' motion to dismiss was denied....

---

1. As demonstrated in *John and Kathryn G.*, courts are ruling that students can recover both compensatory and punitive damages in special education suits. Much of the impetus for this movement derives from the decision in *Franklin v. Gwinnett County Pub. Schs.*, 112 S. Ct. 1028 (1992), *supra* Chapter 4, permitting monetary relief for sexual abuse of a student under Title IX. The Supreme Court held that absent a clear determination by the Congress, federal courts have the authority to award appropriate relief in a cognizable cause of action under a federal statute. As noted in Chapter 4, *Franklin* provides relief under other federal statutes as such laws follow the same pattern. This includes Section 504 and thus the decision in *John and Kathryn G.*

2. In *Doe v. Withers*, 20 IDELR 422 (W. Va. Cir. Ct. 1993), a jury in the state of West Virginia awarded $15,000 in compensatory and punitive damages in a Section 504 suit brought against a public school teacher for refusing to accommodate or follow a student's IEP.

J. THE AMERICANS WITH DISABILITIES ACT

WENKART, THE AMERICANS WITH DISABILITIES ACT AND ITS IMPACT ON PUBLIC EDUCATION, 82 Educ. L. Rep. 291 (1993).*

Numerous articles and commentary have been written about the Americans with Disabilities Act (hereinafter "ADA" or the "Act").[1] However, very few articles have been written about the ADA's impact on public education.

The ADA was signed into law on July 26, 1990. It is a comprehensive statutory scheme designed to prohibit discrimination against the handicapped in a wide range of activities conducted by both public and private entities.

---

*Copyright © 1993 by West Publishing Company. Reprinted with permission.
[1] Public Law 101-336, 42 U.S.C. Sections 12101-12213.

It is expected that the Act will have its greatest impact in the private sector, since the provisions of the ADA are patterned after the provisions of Section 504 of the Rehabilitation Act of 1973, which prohibits discrimination against the handicapped by agencies receiving federal financial assistance.

However, in several respects the ADA will impact public education. The main impact will be in the employment area. School districts, as well as all other education employers covered by the Act, will have to reasonably accommodate disabled individuals and make modifications to the nonessential functions of their programs. In addition, school districts will be prohibited from making medical inquiries or requiring medical examinations prior to an offer of employment. It does not appear that the passage of the ADA will affect the requirements to provide elementary and secondary students with disabilities a free appropriate public education under the Individuals with Disabilities Education Act (IDEA).

II. *Employment*

Title I outlines the provisions of the Act with regard to employment.[9]

The term "qualified individual with a disability" is defined as an individual with a disability who, with or without reasonable accommodation, can perform the essential functions of the employment position that such individual holds or desires.[10] ...

The Act defines the term "reasonable accommodation" to include making existing facilities used by employees readily accessible to and usable by individuals with disabilities, job restructuring, part-time or modified work schedules, reassignment to a vacant position, acquisition or modification of equipment or devices, appropriate adjustment or modifications of examinations, training materials or policies, the provision of qualified readers or interpreters, and other similar accommodations for individuals with disabilities.[12]

Under the ADA, an employer is not required to provide reasonable accommodation to a qualified individual with a disability if it would be an undue hardship.[13]

---

[9]42 U.S.C. Sections 12111, *et seq.*

[10]42 U.S.C. Section 12111(8).

[12]42 U.S.C. Section 12111(9). This definition is virtually identical to the definition of reasonable accommodation under Section 504. *See* 34 C.F.R. Part 104, Appendix A, p. 489 (1988).

[13]The term "undue hardship" means an action requiring significant difficulty or expense when considering the following factors:

1. The nature and cost of the accommodation needed under the Act;
2. The overall financial resources of the facility or facilities involved in the provision of the reasonable accommodation;
3. The number of persons employed at such facility;

In addition, the Act prohibits an employer from discriminating against a qualified individual with a disability because of the disability of such individual in regard to job application procedures, hiring, advancement, discharge, compensation, job training, or other terms and conditions and privileges of employment.[14]

. . . .

VI. *Free Appropriate Public Education Under the ADA*

While the ADA prohibits discrimination against the disabled, it does not specifically guarantee the right to a free appropriate public education. Section 504 also prohibits discrimination against the disabled, but does not explicitly guarantee the right to a free appropriate public education.[53] Therefore, the case law interpreting Section 504 will, most likely, provide guidance to future courts in interpreting the provisions of the ADA.

In *Timms v. Metropolitan School District*,[54] the Court of Appeals stated:

> We agree with the Eighth Circuit, however, that the Rehabilitation Act is broader than the EAHCA [now IDEA] in the range of federally funded activities it reaches but narrower in the kind of actions it regulates.... As *Monahan* notes.... Section 504 is prohibitory, forbidding exclusion from federally-funded programs on the basis of the handicap, rather than mandatory, creating affirmative obligations. *See Southeastern Community College v. Davis....* The EAHCA, by contrast, because of its focus on appropriate education, imposes affirmative duties regarding the content of the programs that must be provided to the handicapped. Because Section 504 forbids exclusion from programs rather than prescribing the

---

4. The effect on expenses and resources, or the impact otherwise of such accommodation upon the operation of the facility;

5. The overall financial resources of the covered entity;

6. The overall size of the business of a covered entity with respect to the number of its employees;

7. The number, type and location of its facilities;

8. The type of operation or operations of the covered entity, including the composition, structure and functions of the work force of such entity; and

9. The geographic separateness, administrative, or fiscal relationship of the facility or facilities in question to the covered entity.

[14] 42 U.S.C. Section 12112(a).

[53] *See Smith v. Robinson*, 468 U.S. 992 [82 Educ. L. Rep. [148]] (1984). While Section 504 does not guarantee the right to a free appropriate public education, the regulations promulgated under Section 504 to address the issue. *See* 34 C.F.R. Section 104.33.

[54] 722 F.2d 1310 [15 Educ. L. Rep. [102]] (7th Cir. 1983).

program's content, it reaches grosser kinds of misconduct than the EAHCA.[55]

In *Smith v. Robinson*, the United Supreme Court concluded that Congress intended the IDEA to be the exclusive avenue through which a plaintiff may assert an equal protection claim to a publicly financed special education.[56] The Supreme Court noted that Section 504 and the IDEA are substantive statutes and while the IDEA guarantees a right to a free appropriate public education, Section 504 simply prohibits discrimination on the basis of handicap. The court, in discussing the difference between Section 504 and the IDEA, stated:

> ... [A]lthough both statutes begin with an equal protection premise that handicapped children must be given access to public education, it does not follow that the affirmative requirements imposed by the two statutes are the same. The significant difference between the two, as applied to special education claims, is that the substantive and procedural rights assumed to be guaranteed by both statutes are specifically required only by the EHA....
> There is no suggestion that Section 504 adds anything to petitioners' substantive rights to a free appropriate public education. The only elements added by section 504 are the possibility of circumventing EHA administrative procedure and going straight to court with a Section 504 claim, the possibility of a damage award in cases where no such award is available under the EHA, and attorneys' fees.
>
> ....

Drawing an analogy to the ADA, had Congress intended the ADA to guarantee a disabled child's right to a free appropriate public education, it would have enacted specific language in the ADA guaranteeing the right to a free appropriate public education. Congress' silence on the issue in light of the United States Supreme Court's decision in *Smith v. Robinson*, indicates that Congress intended the IDEA to be the main vehicle for enforcing the right to a free appropriate education and intended that the ADA would reach grosser forms of discrimination against the disabled in the same manner as Section 504.

VII. *Conclusion*

....

Neither the language of the ADA, nor the legislative history of the ADA, addresses the issue of a free appropriate public education. Therefore, it is unlikely the Congress intended to guarantee a free appropriate public

---

[55] *Id.* at 1317-18.
[56] *Id.* 468 U.S. at 1011-12.

education to students under the ADA. It appears that Congress believed that the right to a free appropriate public education is adequately protected under the IDEA.

Thus, it appears that the major impact of the ADA on public education will be in public education's role as an employer. The role of job descriptions in determining the essential functions of a job will increase in importance when attempting to determine whether the employer has attempted to reasonably accommodate the disability of the employee. In addition, the scope of medical examinations and inquiries to all employees will be limited to job related inquiries consistent with business necessity and may only be made after an offer of employment has been made.

It remains to be seen whether public education will be impacted in other areas. As new issues are raised and litigated, public education may be impacted in ways not previously anticipated.

K. GIFTED AND TALENTED STUDENTS

CENTENNIAL SCHOOL DISTRICT v. COMMONWEALTH DEPARTMENT OF EDUCATION

Supreme Court of Pennsylvania
517 Pa. 540, 539 A.2d 785 (1988)

FLAHERTY, JUSTICE:

The issue in this case is whether the Public School Code and regulations promulgated by the Department of Education require school districts to provide an individualized program of education for mentally gifted students, or whether school districts may lawfully elect to provide only generalized education programs for such students.

In 1981 Centennial School District (the school district) devised an individualized education program (IEP) for an exceptional student, Terry Auspitz, which recommended that Terry be included in the district's program for mentally gifted students. This program (an "enrichment" program) added certain materials to the regular curriculum, but did not attempt to provide accelerated instruction in particular academic areas. Terry's parents agreed that their son should participate in the enrichment program, but they asserted that the enrichment program was insufficient to address Terry's need for accelerated instruction in reading and mathematics. Because the parents and the school district could not agree on the IEP, the parents requested a due process hearing....

The hearing officer concluded that Terry was a mentally gifted student whose academic abilities were advanced beyond his chronological age and that Terry required placement in an age-appropriate setting because his social and emotional development were not advanced beyond that typical of his chronological age. Further, he determined that Terry should be given specialized instruction in

K. GIFTED AND TALENTED STUDENTS

mathematics and reading in addition to inclusion in the "enrichment" program provided by the district. The hearing officer wrote:

> Within the Commonwealth of Pennsylvania, mentally gifted students are considered to be educationally exceptional and therefore entitled to an individually prescribed educational program appropriate to their unique educational needs. The fact that most school districts meet this obligation by providing a part-time program of educational enrichment does not mean that such programming is appropriate for all mentally gifted students. In order to provide an appropriate program for an individual student, that student's IEP must be developed based on his current educational levels and needs regardless of administrative considerations. Further, unlike other educationally exceptional students, mentally gifted students may receive their education within the regular and/or special education programs of the school; this determination is to be based on the student's individual needs and IEP as well.
>
> In the case of Terry, his current educational program is neither appropriate nor adequate in terms of his intellectual potential and levels of academic achievement reflected by considerable evaluation. His inconsistent classroom performance and distracting behaviors can be viewed as indications of boredom and cries for attention from a child whose intellectual development has far exceeded his emotional social [sic] development. In meeting his educational needs, this imbalance must be remembered. Therefore, as much of his educational program as possible should be provided in age-appropriate normalized settings. Although this will undoubtedly present administrative and instructional difficulties and challenges to the school staff, it is consistent with both Terry's needs and the legal mandate for education within the least restrictive environment.

On March 2, 1983, the school district filed exceptions to the hearing officer's decision with the Secretary of Education. In affirming the hearing officer, the Secretary wrote:

> Simply because PDE has approved the district's program of enrichment for gifted students does not relieve the district of its duty ... to provide Terry with an appropriate academic education. Furthermore, the fact that PDE approves a district's special education program does not mean that the program is necessarily appropriate for all students within a particular exceptionality or that individual modifications may not be necessary to meet individual needs....
>
> A regular program with special instruction in accordance with a child's IEP specifying enrichment could be appropriate for certain exceptional children, however, such a gifted enrichment program without advanced instruction in reading and math is not appropriate for Terry.... Moreover,

the district is specifically responsible for developing educational programs appropriate for the needs of each child, not of all children generally....

... The school district appealed this order to Commonwealth Court, which on January 31, 1986, affirmed the decision of the Secretary. Commonwealth Court stated that each school district is required to identify exceptional children and to develop an appropriate program of education suited to each child's individual needs. The court also observed that the Secretary of Education is responsible for determining what educational program is suited for each individual child....

We granted allocatur to determine whether the Secretary and Commonwealth Court exceeded the mandate of the Public School Code in requiring the school district to provide a gifted student with an individualized program of instruction which goes beyond that provided by the district's "enrichment" program.

The School Code defines "exceptional children" as follows:

> (1) The term "exceptional children" shall mean children of school age who deviate from the average in physical, mental, emotional or social characteristics to such an extent that they require special educational facilities or services and shall include all children in detention homes.

In 1973, the State Board of Education published its first proposed regulations on the subject of special education[:]

> The provisions of this Chapter shall provide for the comprehensive education and special training necessary for pupils who are:
>
> (1) mentally impaired;
> (2) physically impaired; or
> (3) gifted and talented.
>
> ....

In general, the School Code requires special treatment for exceptional students:

> (1) *Standards for Proper Education and Training of Exceptional Children.* The State Board of Education shall adopt and prescribe standards and regulations for the proper education and training of all exceptional children by school districts or counties singly or jointly....
>
> (2) *Plans for Education and Training Exceptional Children.* Each intermediate unit, cooperatively with other intermediate units and with school districts shall prepare and submit to the Superintendent of Public Instruction, on or before the first day of August ... for his approval or disapproval, plans for the proper education and training of all exceptional children in accordance with the standards and regulations adopted by the State Board of Education. Plans as provided for in this section shall be subject to revision from time to time as conditions warrant, subject to the approval of the Superintendent of Public Instruction.

K. GIFTED AND TALENTED STUDENTS

In sum, [the school code] requires that the State Board of Education promulgate standards and regulations for the education of all exceptional children, and that each intermediate unit and each school district within those units cooperate to prepare a plan for the education of all exceptional children, subject to the approval of the Superintendent of Public Instruction. In response to this statutory mandate, the State Board of Education has prescribed the following pertinent definitions and regulations:

Definitions.

(iv) *Mentally gifted.* — Outstanding intellectual and creative ability the development of which requires special activities or services not ordinarily provided in the regular program. Persons shall be assigned to a program for the gifted when they have an IQ of 130 or higher. A limited number of persons with IQ scores lower than 130 may be admitted to gifted programs when other educational criteria in the profile of the person strongly indicate gifted ability.

Individualized Education Program.

The Individualized Education Program for each person assigned to special education programs or services shall include:

(1) A statement of the present level of educational performance of the person.

(2) A statement of annual goals which describes the expected behaviors to be achieved through the implementation of the Individualized Education Program of the person.

(3) A statement of short-term instructional objectives.

(4) A statement of specific educational services to be provided to the child, including a description of special education and related services required to meet the unique needs of the child, a special instructional media and materials to be provided, and the type of physical education program in which the child will participate.

(5) A description of the extent to which the child will be able to participate in regular education programs.

(6) The projected date for initiation and the anticipated duration of services.

(7) Appropriate objective criteria, evaluation procedures and schedules for determining, on at least an annual basis, whether the instructional objectives are being achieved. [22 Pa.Code] § 13.1.

Definitions.

The following words and terms, when used in this chapter, have the following meanings, unless the context clearly indicates otherwise:

....

Appropriate program — A program of education or training for exceptional school-aged persons which meets their individual needs as agreed to by a parent, school district or intermediate unit personnel; or as ordered by a hearing officer; or upon appeal as ordered by the Secretary of Education.

Exceptional persons — Persons of school-age who deviate from the average in physical, mental, emotional or social characteristics to such an extent that they require special educational programs, facilities or services and shall include school-aged persons in detention homes and State schools and hospitals.

(i) ....

(ii) *Gifted and talented school-aged persons* — Those who, in accordance with criteria prescribed in standards developed by the Secretary of Education, have outstanding intellectual or creative ability, the development of which requires special activities or services not ordinarily provided to regular children by local educational agencies.

....

Special education — A basic education program adjusted to meet the educational needs of exceptional persons.

These regulatory provisions can be fairly summarized as requiring that mentally gifted students be provided with a plan of individualized instruction (an "appropriate program") designed to meet "the unique needs of the child."

At the root of this case is the school district's concern about costs. The district asks whether it is required to become a Harvard or a Princeton for those who have IQ's over 130, and the School Boards Association, arguing as amicus curiae, asserts that a "subjective standard" will lead to "bankruptcy of the public school system." Both the district and the association assert that what is required of school districts is only that they provide an approved program for exceptional children which "to some degree" addresses the needs of exceptional children. They argue that the district's "enrichment" program, which has been approved by the Secretary, is all they are required to provide. The "enrichment" program, which consists of materials added to the regular curriculum available to exceptional students, augments the regular curriculum, but does not attempt to address the needs of individual students.

Our response to these claims need go no further than reference to the Public School Code and the regulations. It is plain that ... the Code requires that the State Board of Education "adopt and prescribe standards and regulations for the proper education ... of all exceptional children," and it is equally plain that [the Code] requires the school districts to participate in the planning of educational programs for these children, in accordance with the Superintendent's standards and regulations and subject to his approval. It is also abundantly clear that the State Board has promulgated standards and regulations which require the production of an individualized education program for each exceptional child, including "gifted and talented" children, as defined by the General Assembly.

In light of this, the district's claim that individualized planning and education for gifted exceptional children is not required is unfounded. The district's related

K. GIFTED AND TALENTED STUDENTS

claim that its ... approved plan, which consists of "enrichment" of the regular curriculum, is all that it is required to do with respect to gifted students, is equally unfounded. The General Assembly has authorized the State Board of Education to define and regulate special education for exceptional children in Pennsylvania. This the State Board has done, and it has done it in such a way as to require individualized, as well as group planning and education of exceptional children. The district is correct in recognizing that it is required to formulate a plan ... to educate exceptional youngsters, that this plan must be approved by the Secretary, and that the plan may be general in nature, as is the district's "enrichment" program. But it does not follow from the school district's completion of this threshold requirement that it is excused from completing the other requirements found in the regulations concerning exceptional children.

Among these other requirements are that the school district identify all children who may be in need of special education programs or services; that the district evaluate such students; that the district prepare an individualized education program for each child assigned to the special education program; that the district conduct a conference with the parent concerning the IEP; that the IEP be developed jointly by parents and school personnel, and if parents disagree with the program, they may request a hearing before a hearing officer, who will issue an opinion and order defining the assignment, program and services to be provided the child.

Since the State Board of Education has been mandated to promulgate regulations concerning the "proper education and training of all exceptional children," and since these regulations have been duly promulgated and instruct the school districts as indicated above, it is difficult to understand the school district's claim that the districts are required to do no more than provide the generalized "enrichment" programs mentioned earlier.

It is true that the School Code itself does not identify individualized education programs and does not speak, as do the regulations, of the unique needs of each exceptional child. That is to be expected, for when the General Assembly delegated to the State Board of Education the duty of providing the details of "proper education and training of all exceptional children," ... it had no need to be more specific.

The district argues, however, that even if the State Board is empowered to promulgate regulations, these particular regulations exceed its authority. This argument also is without merit. The General Assembly required the State Board to promulgate regulations concerning the proper education and training of exceptional children. That is exactly what these regulations treat, and they are not, therefore, beyond the authority granted by the General Assembly.

Finally, with respect to cost, we not only sympathize, but agree with the district and the Pennsylvania School Boards Association that the district's responsibility is not without limits. The instruction to be offered need not "maximize" the student's ability to benefit from an individualized program. However, the idea that the school district's obligation is limited is not new and does not compel the district's conclusions in this case.... After observing that a senior high curriculum must offer three years of mathematics acceptable for college admission, that it may offer advanced placement courses, and may allow part-time college enrollment, the Secretary wrote:

> Although gifted exceptional students are entitled to a program of special education which will address the student's individual needs, the district's responsibility to provide such is not without bounds.... Accordingly, Scott is entitled to a basic education program adjusted to meet his needs. The curriculum of this program is to be adapted from the regular basic education curriculum. In this regard, the district witnesses testified on the hearing record that Scott had exhausted the district's curricular offerings in mathematics.... In other words, we may assume that Scott has exhausted the district's curricular mathematics offerings in both regular and special education and has completed the mathematics courses required for graduation. Yet, Scott's parents wish him to be provided with more.
>
> We can find neither legal nor factual basis for this....

The rule which we extrapolate and endorse from this well-reasoned opinion of the Secretary is that a school district may not be required to become a Harvard or a Princeton to all who have IQ's over 130. We agree that "gifted" students are entitled to special programs as a group to bring their talents to as complete a fruition as our facilities allow. We do not, however, construe the legislation as authorizing individual tutors or exclusive individual programs outside or beyond the district's existing, regular and special education curricular offerings.

Because we can find no legal basis to determine that the Secretary has exceeded his authority in promulgating regulations pertinent to this case and because the regulations clearly require that school districts create individualized educational plans for exceptional students (which may or may not involve accelerated instruction) as well as create a general plan to educate exceptional students, we affirm the order of Commonwealth Court.

Affirmed.

---

1. The judiciary in *Centennial* had a vehicle by which to accept the case and intervene on behalf of the student; the state of Pennsylvania had passed a statute recognizing gifted and talented students and this had been promulgated in tandem with legislation for disabled students. Thus, all exceptional students were entitled to the same due process protections and school districts were required to provide each one an individualized program. How many states have this kind of legislation supporting an individualized education program for gifted students? *See* Zirkel and Stevens, *The Law Concerning Public Education for Gifted Students*, 34 Educ. L. Rep. 353 (1986).

K. GIFTED AND TALENTED STUDENTS 1093

2. While the court dismissed the school district defense that individualized instruction for gifted students would force them to "become a Harvard or a Princeton," note that school districts do not have to "maximize a student's potential." That is, the districts do not have to prepare programs in addition to current offerings to accommodate a student. Is this ruling consistent with the cases cited earlier in the chapter involving "Free Appropriate Public Education" or FAPE?

3. For a description of the *Centennial* case *see* Marquardt and Karnes, *The Courts and Gifted Education*, 50 Educ. L. Rep. 9 (1989).

Chapter 14
FINANCING PUBLIC EDUCATION

During the last twenty-five years, a growing awareness of the inadequacies and inequalities in public school funding has caused a nationwide conflict over public school funding systems. Reformers seeking a fundamental change in the methods of school finance have sponsored litigation that in some states has upheld the state constitutionality of funding provisions; disputes in other states have resulted in such funding being declared unconstitutional.

For those who believe that the amount of money expended on a child's education can affect educational achievement, one focus of the movement to achieve equal educational opportunity has been to seek court-ordered equalization of funding so that all public school districts within a state receive approximate amounts of money per pupil per year (per-pupil expenditures). This strategy is, in essence, a constitutional challenge to the state's decision to fund public schools partially through local property tax revenue raised by each school district, though the state recognizes that the amount of money school districts can raise varies with the value of the property within the district. School reform plaintiffs contend that the use of this financing system causes significant and unconstitutional differences in the amount spent per child on education between property-rich and property-poor school districts.

In seeking court-ordered school finance reform, the proponents' key premise is that disparity in school funding denies students in property-poor school districts educational opportunities substantially equal to those enjoyed by other students. Initially, plaintiffs argued that a funding system that produces significant financial disparities in per-pupil expenditures among a state's districts should be declared unconstitutional because it violates the equal protection clause of the Fourteenth Amendment of the U.S. Constitution by discriminating against children in poor areas of the state. Plaintiffs have also pursued the equal protection argument at the state level, alleging that this type of funding disparity violates their respective state equal protection clauses as well.

Another basis on which finance litigation has been pursued relies on the education provision in the state's constitution that authorizes the legislature to establish a state public school system. The actual wording of these establishment provisions varies from state to state. Generally, however, provisions specify that the legislature must maintain a school system with certain characteristics such as "efficiency", "thoroughness" or "uniformity". Plaintiffs in such cases argue that a school finance system that results in significant funding disparities lacks one or more of these qualities. Because the federal judiciary effectively removed itself and the U.S. Constitution from the fray, as seen in *San Antonio Indep. Sch. Dist. v. Rodriguez*, 411 U.S. 1 (1973), *infra*, plaintiffs have been forced to turn to state courts for the changes sought. This chapter will feature *Rodriguez* and recent heralded state court decisions that have rejected property tax-based school funding as violative of the education clauses of state constitutions.

SAN ANTONIO INDEPENDENT SCHOOL DISTRICT v. RODRIGUEZ
Supreme Court of the United States
411 U.S. 1 (1973)

MR. JUSTICE POWELL delivered the opinion of the Court:

This suit attacking the Texas system of financing public education was initiated by Mexican-American parents whose children attend the elementary and secondary schools in the Edgewood Independent School District, an urban school district in San Antonio, Texas. They brought a class action on behalf of school children throughout the State who are members of minority groups or who are poor and reside in school districts having a low property tax base. Named as defendants were the State Board of Education, the Commissioner of Education, the State Attorney General, and the Bexar County (San Antonio) Board of Trustees. The complaint was filed in the summer of 1968 and a three-judge court was impaneled in January 1969. In December 1971 the panel rendered its judgment in a per curiam opinion holding the Texas school finance system unconstitutional under the Equal Protection Clause of the Fourteenth Amendment. The State appealed, and we noted probable jurisdiction to consider the far-reaching constitutional questions presented. For the reasons stated in this opinion, we reverse the decision of the District Court.

I

The first Texas State Constitution, promulgated upon Texas' entry into the Union in 1845, provided for the establishment of a system of free schools. Early in its history, Texas adopted a dual approach to the financing of its schools, relying on mutual participation by the local school districts and the State....

Until recent times, Texas was a predominantly rural state and its population and property wealth were spread relatively evenly across the State. Sizeable differences in the value of assessable property between local school districts became increasingly evident as the State became more industrialized and as rural-to-urban population shifts became more pronounced. The location of commercial and industrial property began to play a significant role in determining the amount of tax resources available to each school district. These growing disparities in population and taxable property between districts were responsible in part for increasingly notable differences in levels of local expenditure for education.

Recognizing the need for increased state funding to help offset disparities in local spending and to meet Texas' changing educational requirements, the state legislature in the late 1940's undertook a thorough evaluation of public education with an eye toward major reform. In 1947, an 18-member committee, composed of educators and legislators was appointed to explore alternative systems in other States and to propose a funding scheme that would guarantee a minimum or basic educational offering to each child and that would help overcome interdistrict disparities in taxable resources. The Committee's efforts led to the passage of the Gilmer-Aikin bills, named for the Committee's co-chairmen, establishing the Texas Minimum Foundation School Program. Today, this Program accounts for approximately half of the total educational expenditures in Texas.

The Program calls for state and local contributions to a fund earmarked specifically for teacher salaries, operating expenses, and transportation costs. The State, supplying funds from its general revenues, finances approximately 80% of the Program, and the school districts are responsible — as a unit — for providing the remaining 20%. The districts' share, known as the Local Fund Assignment, is apportioned among the school districts under a formula designed to reflect each district's relative taxpaying ability....

The design of this complex system was twofold. First, it was an attempt to assure that the Foundation Program would have an equalizing influence on expenditure levels between school districts by placing the heaviest burden on the school districts most capable of paying. Second, the Program's architects sought to establish a Local Fund Assignment that would force every school district to contribute to the education of its children but that would not by itself exhaust any district's resources. Today every school district does impose a property tax from which it derives locally expendable funds in excess of the amount necessary to satisfy its Local Fund Assignment under the Foundation Program.

....

The school district in which appellees reside, the Edgewood Independent School District, has been compared throughout this litigation with the Alamo Heights Independent School District. This comparison between the least and most affluent districts in the San Antonio area serves to illustrate the manner in which the dual system of finance operates and to indicate the extent to which substantial disparities exist despite the State's impressive progress in recent years. Edgewood is one of seven public school districts in the metropolitan area. Approximately 22,000 students are enrolled in its 25 elementary and secondary schools. The district is situated in the core-city sector of San Antonio in a residential neighborhood that has little commercial or industrial property. The residents are predominantly of Mexican-American descent: approximately 90% of the student population is Mexican-American and over 6% is Negro. The average assessed property value per pupil is $5,960 — the lowest in the metropolitan area — and the median family income ($4,686) is also the lowest. At an equalized tax rate of $1.05 per $100 of assessed property — the highest in the metropolitan area — the district contributed $26 to the education of each child for the 1967-1968 school year above its Local Fund Assignment for the Minimum Foundation Program. The Foundation Program contributed $222 per pupil for a state-local total of $248. Federal funds added another $108 for a total of $356 per pupil.

Alamo Heights is the most affluent school district in San Antonio. Its six schools, housing approximately 5,000 students, are situated in a residential community quite unlike the Edgewood District. The school population is predominantly "Anglo," having only 18% Mexican-Americans and less than 1% Negroes. The assessed property value per pupil exceeds $49,000, and the median family income is $8,001. In 1967-1968 the local tax rate of $.85 per $100 of valuation yielded $333 per pupil over and above its contribution to the Foundation Program. Coupled with the $225 provided from that Program, the district was able to supply $558 per student. Supplemented by a $36 per-pupil grant from federal sources, Alamo Heights spent $594 per pupil.

....

Despite these recent increases, substantial interdistrict disparities in school expenditures found by the District Court to prevail in San Antonio and in varying degrees throughout the State still exist. And it was these disparities, largely attributable to differences in the amounts of money collected through local property taxation, that led the District Court to conclude that Texas' dual system of public school financing violated the Equal Protection Clause....

Texas virtually concedes that its historically rooted dual system of financing education could not withstand the strict judicial scrutiny that this Court has found appropriate in reviewing legislative judgments that interfere with fundamental constitutional rights or that involve suspect classifications. If, as previous decisions have indicated, strict scrutiny means that the State's system is not entitled to the usual presumption of validity, that the State rather than the complainants must carry a "heavy burden of justification," that the State must demonstrate that its educational system has been structured with "precision," and is "tailored" narrowly to serve legitimate objectives and that it has selected the "less drastic means" for effectuating its objectives, the Texas financing system and its counterpart in virtually every other State will not pass muster. The State candidly admits that "[n]o one familiar with the Texas system would contend that it has yet achieved perfection." Apart from its concession that educational financing in Texas has "defects" and "imperfections," the State defends the system's rationality with vigor and disputes the District Court's finding that it lacks a "reasonable basis."

This, then, establishes the framework for our analysis. We must decide, first, whether the Texas system of financing public education operates to the disadvantage of some suspect class or impinges upon a fundamental right explicitly or implicitly protected by the Constitution, thereby requiring strict judicial scrutiny. If so, the judgment of the District Court should be affirmed. If not, the Texas scheme must still be examined to determine whether it rationally furthers some legitimate, articulated state purpose and therefore does not constitute an invidious discrimination in violation of the Equal Protection Clause of the Fourteenth Amendment.

II

....

A

The wealth discrimination discovered by the District Court in this case, and by several other courts that have recently struck down school-financing laws in other States, is quite unlike any of the forms of wealth discrimination heretofore reviewed by this Court. Rather than focusing on the unique features of the alleged discrimination, the courts in these cases have virtually assumed their findings of a suspect classification through a simplistic process of analysis: since, under the traditional systems of financing public schools, some poorer people receive less expensive educations than other more affluent people, these systems discriminate on the basis of wealth. This approach largely ignores the hard threshold questions, including whether it makes a difference for purposes of consideration under the Constitution that the class of disadvantaged "poor" cannot be identified or defined in customary equal protection terms, and whether the relative — rather than absolute — nature of the asserted deprivation is of significant consequence. Before a State's laws and the justifications for the classifications they create are subjected to strict judicial scrutiny, we think these threshold considerations must be analyzed more closely than they were in the court below.

The case comes to us with no definitive description of the classifying facts or delineation of the disfavored class. Examination of the District Court's opinion and of appellees' complaint, briefs, and contentions at oral argument suggests, however, at least three ways in which the discrimination claimed here might be described. The Texas system of school financing might be regarded as discriminating (1) against "poor" persons whose incomes fall below some identifiable level of poverty or who might be characterized as functionally "indigent," or (2) against those who are relatively poorer than others, or (3) against all those who, irrespective of their personal incomes, happen to reside in relatively poorer school districts. Our task must be to ascertain whether, in fact, the Texas system has been shown to discriminate on any of these possible bases and, if so, whether the resulting classification may be regarded as suspect.

The precedents of this Court provide the proper starting point. The individuals, or groups of individuals, who constituted the class discriminated against in our prior cases shared two distinguishing characteristics: because of their impecunity they were completely unable to pay for some desired benefit, and as a consequence, they sustained an absolute deprivation of a meaningful opportunity to enjoy that benefit....

Only appellees' first possible basis for describing the class disadvantaged by the Texas school-financing system — discrimination against a class of definably "poor" persons — might arguably meet the criteria established in these prior cases. Even a cursory examination, however, demonstrates that neither of the two distinguishing characteristics of wealth classifications can be found here. First, in support of their charge that the system discriminates against the "poor," appellees have made no effort to demonstrate that it operates to the peculiar disadvantage of any class fairly definable as indigent, or as composed of persons whose incomes are beneath any designated poverty level. Indeed, there is reason to believe that the poorest families are not necessarily clustered in the poorest property districts. A recent and exhaustive study of school districts in Connecticut concluded that "[i]t is clearly incorrect ... to contend that the "poor' live in 'poor' districts.... Thus, the major factual assumption of *Serrano [v. Priest (Serrano I)*, 5 Cal.3d 584, 487 P.2d 1241, 96 Cal.Rptr. 601 (1971)] — that the educational financing system discriminates against the 'poor' — is simply false in Connecticut." Defining "poor" families as those below the Bureau of the Census "poverty level," the Connecticut study found, not surprisingly, that the poor were clustered around commercial and industrial areas — those same areas that provide the most attractive sources of property tax income for school districts. Whether a similar pattern would be discovered in Texas is not known, but there is no basis on the record in this case for assuming that the poorest people — defined by reference to any level of absolute impecunity — are concentrated in the poorest districts.

Second, neither appellees nor the District Court addressed the fact that, unlike each of the foregoing cases, lack of personal resources has not occasioned an absolute deprivation of the desired benefit. The argument here is not that the children in districts having relatively low assessable property values are receiving no public education; rather, it is that they are receiving a poorer quality education than that available to children in districts having more assessable wealth. Apart from the unsettled and disputed question whether the quality of education may be determined by the amount of money expended for it, a sufficient answer to appellees' argument is that, at least where wealth is involved, the Equal Protection Clause does not require absolute equality or precisely equal advantages. Nor, indeed, in view of the infinite variables affecting the educational process, can any system assure equal quality of education except in the most relative sense. Texas asserts that the Minimum Foundation Program provides an "adequate" education for all children in the State. By providing 12 years of free public-school education, and by assuring teachers, books, transportation, and operating funds, the Texas Legislature has endeavored to "guarantee, for the welfare of the state as a whole, that all people shall have at least an adequate program of education. This is what is meant by 'A Minimum Foundation Program of Education.'" The State repeatedly asserted in its briefs in this Court that it has fulfilled this desire and that it now assures "every child in every

CH. 14 FINANCING PUBLIC EDUCATION 1101

school district an adequate education." No proof was offered at trial persuasively discrediting or refuting the State's assertion.

For these two reasons — the absence of any evidence that the financing system discriminates against any definable category of "poor" people or that it results in the absolute deprivation of education — the disadvantaged class is not susceptible of identification in traditional terms.

As suggested above, appellees and the District Court may have embraced a second or third approach, the second of which might be characterized as a theory of relative or comparative discrimination based on family income. Appellees sought to prove that a direct correlation exists between the wealth of families within each district and the expenditures therein for education. That is, along a continuum, the poorer the family the lower the dollar amount of education received by the family's children.

. . . .

This brings us, then, to the third way in which the classification scheme might be defined — *district* wealth discrimination. Since the only correlation indicated by the evidence is between district property wealth and expenditures, it may be argued that discrimination might be found without regard to the individual income characteristics of district residents. Assuming a perfect correlation between district property wealth and expenditures from top to bottom, the disadvantaged class might be viewed as encompassing every child in every district except the district that has the most assessable wealth and spends the most on education. Alternatively, as suggested in Mr. Justice Marshall's dissenting opinion, the class might be defined more restrictively to include children in districts with assessable property which falls below the statewide average, or median, or below some other artificially defined level.

However described, it is clear that appellees' suit asks this Court to extend its most exacting scrutiny to review a system that allegedly discriminates against a large, diverse, and amorphous class, unified only by the common factor of residence in districts that happen to have less taxable wealth than other districts. The system of alleged discrimination and the class it defines have none of the traditional indicia of suspectness: the class is not saddled with such disabilities, or subjected to such a history of purposeful unequal treatment, or relegated to such a position of political powerlessness as to command extraordinary protection from the majoritarian political process.

We thus conclude that the Texas system does not operate to the peculiar disadvantage of any suspect class. But in recognition of the fact that this Court has never heretofore held that wealth discrimination alone provides an adequate basis for invoking strict scrutiny, appellees have not relied solely on this contention. They also assert that the State's system impermissibly interferes with the exercise of a "fundamental" right and that accordingly the prior decisions of this Court require the application of the strict standard of judicial review. *Graham v. Richardson*, 403 U.S. 365, 375-376 (1971); *Kramer v. Union School District*, 395 U.S. 621 (1969); *Shapiro v. Thompson*, 394 U.S. 618 (1969). It is this question — whether education is a fundamental right, in the sense that it is among the rights and liberties protected by the Constitution — which has so consumed the attention of courts and commentators in recent years.

B

....

Nothing this Court holds today in any way detracts from our historic dedication to public education. We are in complete agreement with the conclusion of the three-judge panel below that "the grave significance of education both to the individual and to our society" cannot be doubted. But the importance of a service performed by the State does not determine whether it must be regarded as fundamental for purposes of examination under the Equal Protection Clause....

....

... It is not the province of this Court to create substantive constitutional rights in the name of guaranteeing equal protection of the laws. Thus, the key to discovering whether education is "fundamental" is not to be found in comparisons of the relative societal significance of education as opposed to subsistence or housing. Nor is it to be found by weighing whether education is as important as the right to travel. Rather, the answer lies in assessing whether there is a right to education explicitly or implicitly guaranteed by the Constitution.

Education, of course, is not among the rights afforded explicit protection under our Federal Constitution. Nor do we find any basis for saying it is implicitly so protected. As we have said, the undisputed importance of education will not alone cause this Court to depart from the usual standard for reviewing a State's social and economic legislation. It is appellees' contention, however, that education is distinguishable from other services and benefits provided by the State because it bears a peculiarly close relationship to other rights and liberties accorded protection under the Constitution. Specifically, they insist that education is itself a fundamental personal right because it is essential to the effective exercise of First Amendment freedoms and to intelligent utilization of the right to vote. In asserting a nexus between speech and education, appellees urge that the right to speak is meaningless unless the speaker is capable of articulating his thoughts intelligently and persuasively. The "marketplace of ideas" is an empty forum for those lacking basic communicative tools. Likewise, they argue that the corollary right to receive information becomes little more than a hollow privilege when the recipient has not been taught to read, assimilate, and utilize available knowledge.

A similar line of reasoning is pursued with respect to the right to vote. Exercise of the franchise, it is contended, cannot be divorced from the educational foundation of the voter. The electoral process, if reality is to conform to the democratic ideal, depends on an informed electorate: a voter cannot cast his ballot intelligently unless his reading skills and thought processes have been adequately developed.

We need not dispute any of these propositions. The Court has long afforded zealous protection against unjustifiable governmental interference with the individual's rights to speak and to vote. Yet we have never presumed to possess either the ability or the authority to guarantee to the citizenry the most *effective* speech or the most *informed* electoral choice. That these may be desirable goals of a system of freedom of expression and of a representative form of government is not to be doubted. These are indeed goals to be pursued by a people whose thoughts and beliefs are freed from governmental interference. But they are not values to be implemented by judicial intrusion into otherwise legitimate state activities.

Even if it were conceded that some identifiable quantum of education is a constitutionally protected prerequisite to the meaningful exercise of either right, we have no indication that the present levels of educational expenditure in Texas provide an education that falls short. Whatever merit appellees' argument might have if a State's financing system occasioned an absolute denial of educational opportunities to any of its children, that argument provides no basis for finding an interference with fundamental rights where only relative differences in spending levels are involved and where — as is true in the present case — no charge fairly could be made that the system fails to provide each child with an opportunity to acquire the basic minimal skills necessary for the enjoyment of the rights of speech and of full participation in the political process.

. . . .

We need not rest our decision, however, solely on the inappropriateness of the strict-scrutiny test. A century of Supreme Court adjudication under the Equal Protection Clause affirmatively supports the application of the traditional standard of review, which requires only that the State's system be shown to bear some rational relationship to legitimate state purposes. This case represents far more than a challenge to the manner in which Texas provides for the education of its children. We have here nothing less than a direct attack on the way in which Texas has chosen to raise and disburse state and local tax revenues. We are asked to condemn the State's judgment in conferring on political subdivisions the power to tax local property to supply revenues for local interests. In so doing, appellees would have the Court intrude in an area in which it has traditionally deferred to state legislatures.

Thus, we stand on familiar ground when we continue to acknowledge that the Justices of this Court lack both the expertise and the familiarity with local problems so necessary to the making of wise decisions with respect to the raising and disposition of public revenues. Yet, we are urged to direct the States either to alter drastically the present system or to throw out the property tax altogether in favor of some other form of taxation. No scheme of taxation, whether the tax is imposed on property, income, or purchases of goods and services, has yet been devised which is free of all discriminatory impact. In such a complex arena in which no perfect alternatives exist, the Court does well not to impose too rigorous a standard of scrutiny lest all local fiscal schemes become subjects of criticism under the Equal Protection Clause.

In addition to matters of fiscal policy, this case also involves the most persistent and difficult questions of educational policy, another area in which this Court's lack of specialized knowledge and experience counsels against premature interference with the informed judgments made at the state and local levels. Education, perhaps even more than welfare assistance, presents a myriad of "intractable economic, social, and even philosophical problems." The very complexity of the problems of financing and managing a statewide public school system suggest that "there will be more than one constitutionally permissible method of solving them," and that, within the limits of rationality, "the legislature's efforts to tackle the problems" should be entitled to respect....

It must be remembered, also, that every claim arising under the Equal Protection Clause has implications for the relationship between national and state power under our federal system. Questions of federalism are always inherent in the process of determining whether a State's laws are to be accorded the traditional presumption of constitutionality, or are to be subjected instead to rigorous judicial scrutiny. While "[t]he maintenance of the principles of federalism is a foremost consideration in interpreting any of the pertinent constitutional provisions under which this Court examines state action," it would be difficult to imagine a case having a greater potential impact on our federal system than the one now before us, in which we are urged to abrogate systems of financing public education presently in existence in virtually every State.

The foregoing considerations buttress our conclusion that Texas' system of public school finance is an inappropriate candidate for strict judicial scrutiny. These same considerations are relevant to the determination whether that system, with its conceded imperfections, nevertheless bears some rational relationship to a legitimate state purpose. It is to this question that we next turn our attention.

III

....

The Texas system of school finance is responsive to these two forces. While assuring a basic education for every child in the State, it permits and encourages a large measure of participation in and control of each district's schools at the local level. In an era that has witnessed a consistent trend toward centralization of the functions of government, local sharing of responsibility for public education has survived. The merit of local control was recognized last Term in both the majority and dissenting opinions in *Wright v. Council of the City of Emporia*, 407 U.S. 451 (1972). MR. JUSTICE STEWART stated there that "[d]irect control over decisions vitally affecting the education of one's children is a need that is strongly felt in our society." *Id.* at 469. The Chief Justice, in his dissent, agreed that "[l]ocal control is not only vital to continued public support of the schools, but it is of overriding importance from an educational standpoint as well." *Id.* at 478.

The persistence of attachment to government at the lowest level where education is concerned reflects the depth of commitment of its supporters. In part, local control means ... the freedom to devote more money to the education of one's children. Equally important, however, is the opportunity it offers for participation in the decision[-]making process that determines how those local tax dollars will be spent. Each locality is free to tailor local programs to local needs. Pluralism also affords some opportunity for experimentation, innovation, and a healthy competition for educational excellence. An analogy to the Nation-State relationship in our federal system seems uniquely appropriate. Mr. Justice Brandeis identified as one of the peculiar strengths of our form of government each State's freedom to "serve as a laboratory; and try novel social and economic experiments." No area of social concern stands to profit more from a multiplicity of viewpoints and from a diversity of approaches than does public education.

... Appellees suggest that local control could be preserved and promoted under other financing systems that resulted in more equality in educational expenditures. While it is no doubt true that reliance on local property taxation for school revenues provides less freedom of choice with respect to expenditures for some districts than for others, the existence of "some inequality" in the manner in which the State's rationale is achieved is not alone a sufficient basis for striking down the entire system. It may not be condemned simply because it imperfectly effectuates the State's goals. Nor must the financing system fail because, as appellees suggest, other methods of satisfying the State's interest, which occasion "less drastic" disparities in expenditures, might be conceived. Only where state action impinges on the exercise of fundamental constitutional rights or liberties must it be found to have chosen the least restrictive alternative.... The people of Texas may be justified in believing that other systems of school financing, which place more of the financial responsibility in the hands of the State, will result in a comparable lessening of desired local autonomy....

Appellees further urge that the Texas system is unconstitutionally arbitrary because it allows the availability of local taxable resources to turn on "happenstance." ... But any scheme of local taxation — indeed the very existence of identifiable local governmental units — requires the establishment of jurisdictional boundaries that are inevitably arbitrary. It is equally inevitable that some localities are going to be blessed with more taxable assets than others....

Moreover, if local taxation for local expenditures were an unconstitutional method of providing for education then it might be an equally impermissible means of providing other necessary services customarily financed largely from local property taxes, including local police and fire protection, public health and hospitals, and public utility facilities of various kinds. We perceive no justification for such a severe denigration of local property taxation and control as would follow from appellees' contentions. It has simply never been within the constitutional prerogative of this Court to nullify statewide measures for financing public services merely because the burdens or benefits thereof fall unevenly depending upon the relative wealth of the political subdivisions in which citizens live.

In sum, to the extent that the Texas system of school financing results in unequal expenditures between children who happen to reside in different districts, we cannot say that such disparities are the product of a system that is so irrational as to be invidiously discriminatory. Texas has acknowledged its shortcomings and has persistently endeavored — not without some success — to ameliorate the differences in levels of expenditures without sacrificing the benefits of local participation. The Texas plan is not the result of hurried, ill-conceived legislation. It certainly is not the product of purposeful discrimination against any group or class. On the contrary, it is rooted in decades of experience in Texas and elsewhere, and in major part is the product of responsible studies by qualified people. In giving substance to the presumption of validity to which the Texas system is entitled ... it is important to remember that at every stage of its development it has constituted a "rough accommodation" of interests in an effort to arrive at practical and workable solutions. One also must remember that the system here challenged is not peculiar to Texas or to any other State. In its essential characteristics, the Texas plan for financing public education reflects what many educators for a half century have thought was an enlightened approach to a problem for which there is no perfect solution. We are unwilling to assume for ourselves a level of wisdom superior to that of legislators, scholars, and educational authorities in 50 States, especially where the alternatives proposed are only recently conceived and nowhere yet tested. The constitutional standard under the Equal Protection Clause is whether the challenged state action rationally furthers a legitimate state purpose or interest. We hold that the Texas plan abundantly satisfies this standard.

IV

....

The complexity of these problems is demonstrated by the lack of consensus with respect to whether it may be said with any assurance that the poor, the racial minorities, or the children in overburdened core-city school districts would be benefited by abrogation of traditional modes of financing education. Unless there is to be a substantial increase in state expenditures on education across the board — an event the likelihood of which is open to considerable question — these groups stand to realize gains in terms of increased per-pupil expenditures only if they reside in districts that presently spend at relatively low levels, *i.e.*, in those districts that would benefit from the redistribution of existing resources. Yet, recent studies have indicated that the poorest families are not invariably clustered in the most impecunious school districts. Nor does it now appear that there is any more than a random chance that racial minorities are concentrated in property-poor districts. Additionally, several research projects have concluded that any financing alternative designed to achieve a greater equality of expenditures is likely to lead to higher taxation and lower educational expenditures in the major urban centers, a result that would exacerbate rather than ameliorate existing conditions in those areas.

These practical considerations, of course, play no role in the adjudication of the constitutional issues presented here. But they serve to highlight the wisdom of the traditional limitations on this Court's function. The consideration and initiation of fundamental reforms with respect to state taxation and education are matters reserved for the legislative processes of the various States, and we do no violence to the values of federalism and separation of powers by staying our hand. We hardly need add that this Court's action today is not to be viewed as placing its judicial imprimatur on the status quo. The need is apparent for reform in tax systems which may well have relied too long and too heavily on the local property tax. And certainly innovative thinking as to public education, its methods, and its funding is necessary to assure both a higher level of quality and greater uniformity of opportunity. These matters merit the continued attention of the scholars who already have contributed much by their challenges. But the ultimate solutions must come from the lawmakers and from the democratic pressures of those who elect them.

Reversed.

[The concurring opinion of JUSTICE STEWART and the dissenting opinions of JUSTICES BRENNAN, WHITE, AND MARSHALL are omitted.]

---

1. How significant to the majority decision in *Rodriguez* is the conclusion that no correlation has been shown between "poor" (low tax base) school districts and poor people? Should the decision turn on the judgment of the justices as to the affidavit submitted to the district court in this case? The data seem incontrovertible that on a national level there is no correlation between poor people and poor school districts. But assume that in a given state there is such a correlation, perhaps because of large numbers of rural poor. Could *Rodriguez* be distinguished in such a state? Should the results of constitutional attacks on basically similar financing systems vary on the basis of judges' analysis of difficult statistical determinations concerning the correlation discussed in this note?

2. The Court cites to *Serrano v. Priest (Serrano I)*, 5 Cal. 3d 584, 487 P.2d 1241, 96 Cal. Rptr. 601 (1971), a California Supreme Court decision which was the first state high court ruling to recognize constitutional violations resulting from local property tax-based funding of public schools. The plaintiffs in *Serrano I* argued that a financing system that causes disparities in expenditures among districts ultimately results in disparities in the quality of educational opportunities in those districts. Using the Supreme Court's "strict scrutiny" test for measuring legislative acts against the Equal Protection Clause of the Fourteenth Amendment, the *Serrano I* court ruled that no compelling state interest was served by a funding system that seemed to further such disparities. Hence, the court concluded that the funding system violated both the Fourteenth Amendment Equal Protection Clause and the California State Constitution's equal guaranty provision. This rationale established the foundation upon which future litigants challenged public education financing systems on federal equal protection and state guaranty grounds. The viability of such challenges, however, was abruptly terminated with the Supreme Court *Rodriguez* decision.

Unlike *Serrano*, the Court did not apply a "strict scrutiny" analysis. What level did the Court apply and why? Does it appear that all that is necessary in such suits is that there be a small attempt on the part of school districts to "do good"?

3. Should it make any difference that the children of the poorer districts are not absolutely deprived of an education if the education they do receive is so much inferior to that of other students? What is the Court's response to the argument that the quality of education is dependent on wealth?

4. The Court claims that it lacks the expertise and familiarity with local problems necessary to make wise decisions with respect to the raising and disposition of public funds. Yet it urges the states to alter drastically the present system of funding, or in the alternative, to implement a new system. Did the Court claim a similar lack of expertise and familiarity in the desegregation cases (Chapter 11)? If not, what stopped the Court here from finding a fundamental right in the Constitution while it was able to find segregation unconstitutional and to direct school systems to develop desegregation plans?

5. Although *Rodriguez* has apparently ended for the moment the battle to invalidate current school financing systems by use of Federal Constitutional powers, litigation is still continuing in state courts based on state constitutional provisions. Two weeks after the *Rodriguez* decision, the New Jersey Supreme Court considered a challenge to that state's financing system.

ROBINSON v. CAHILL

Supreme Court of New Jersey
62 N.J. 473, 303 A.2d 273, *cert. denied*, 414 U.S. 976 (1973)

The opinion of the Court was delivered by WEINTRAUB, C.J.:

[Portions of the Court's opinion reviewing the trial court's determination that the existing school finance system violated the equal protection mandates of the Federal and State Constitutions are omitted. The Court rejected the trial court's reasoning, holding that *Rodriguez* barred application of the Federal Constitution and refusing to base its decision on the State equal protection clause because "the equal protection clause may be unmanageable if it is called upon to supply categorical answers in the vast area of human needs, choosing those which must be met and a single basis upon which the State must act." The Court then considered the financing system in light of the New Jersey constitutional provision that "the legislature shall provide for the maintenance and support of a thorough and efficient system of free public schools for the instruction of all the children in this state between the ages of five and eighteen."]

In the light of the foregoing, it cannot be said the 1875 amendments [to the New Jersey Constitution quoted above] were intended to insure statewide equality among taxpayers. But we do not doubt that an equal educational opportunity for children was precisely in mind. The mandate that there be maintained and supported "a thorough and efficient system of free public schools for the instruction of all the children in the State between the ages of five and eighteen years" can have no other import. Whether the State acts directly or imposes the role upon local government, the end product must be what the Constitution commands. A system of instruction in any district of the State which is not thorough and efficient falls short of the constitutional command. Whatever the reason for the violation, the obligation is the State's to rectify it. If local government fails, the State government must compel it to act, and if the local government cannot carry the burden, the State must itself meet its continuing obligation.... The trial court found the constitutional demand had not been met and did so on the basis of discrepancies in dollar input per pupil. We agree. We deal with the problem in those terms because dollar input is plainly relevant and because we have been shown no other viable criterion for measuring compliance with the constitutional mandate. The constitutional mandate could not be said to be satisfied unless we were to suppose the unlikely proposition that the lowest level of dollar performance happens to coincide with the constitutional mandate and that all efforts beyond the lowest level are attributable to local decisions to do more than the State was obliged to do.

Surely the existing statutory system is not visibly geared to the mandate that there be "a thorough and efficient system of free public schools for the instruction of all the children in this state between the ages of five and eighteen years." Indeed the State has never spelled out the content of the educational opportunity the Constitution requires. Without some such prescription, it is even more difficult to understand how the tax burden can be left to local initiative with any hope that statewide equality of educational opportunity will emerge. The 1871 statute embraced a statewide tax because it was found that local taxation could not be expected to yield equal educational opportunity. Since then the State has returned the tax burden to local school districts to the point where at the time of the trial the State was meeting but 28% of the current operating expenses. There is no more evidence today than there was a hundred years ago that this approach will succeed.

On its face the statutory scheme has no apparent relation to the mandate for equal educational opportunity. The trial court's opinion discusses the existing scheme at length, and we need but summarize it. As the trial court pointed out, we are in a period of transition from one plan to another with respect to the current operating budget. The new plan, contained in the "State School Incentive Equalization Aid Law" (L. 1970, ch. 234), herein the "1970 Act," is but partially funded, and at the moment serves only to accomplish a modification of the plan it would one day supersede.

The plan which the 1970 Act would ultimately replace establishes a foundation program of $400 per pupil. N.J.S.A. 18A:58-3 as it existed when the 1970 Act was enacted. We are told that when that dollar figure was set, it was believed to be the average per pupil cost of providing elementary and secondary education. The figure is now grossly outdated. At any rate, that statute provides for State aid consisting of the difference between $400 per pupil and the sum per pupil raised by a local tax of 101/2 mills per dollar of equalized valuation of taxable property within the school district. There is a minimum guaranty of $75 per pupil, and by other provisions the State adds an additional $25 per pupil throughout the State and $27 per pupil in the major cities.

Under that program the State contributes about 28% of the statewide current operating costs, the balance being raised by local tax except for a small federal contribution. The 1970 Act is expected when fully funded to raise the State's share to 40% which, when that Act was adopted, was said to be the national average of State aid.

The 1970 Act provides for State aid on the basis of "weighted pupils." The weighting is intended to reflect different costs of educating classes of pupils. Thus, to mention some of the categories, a child in kindergarten is weighted at .75, a child in elementary school at 1 and a high school student at 1.3 plus .75 units for each "AFDC" child (a child on welfare). The 1970 Act further provides that the amount of State aid per resident weighted pupil will depend on whether the school district is a "nonoperating district" (does not itself operate schools), a "basic district," a "limited district," an "intermediate district," a "precomprehensive district" or a "comprehensive district." The 1970 Act would assure "minimum support aid" which would depend upon the classification of the districts, the figure ranging from $110 per weighted pupil in a "basic district" to $160 per weighted pupil in a "comprehensive district." We understand the criteria for these districts have not yet been established or enacted into law, and that all operating districts are for the moment deemed to be "basic districts."

In addition the 1970 Act contemplates "incentive equalization aid." As we understand the program, it provides for additional State aid with respect to the "net operating budget," which, roughly, is the amount of the current expense budget after deducting certain income including the "minimum support aid" described in the paragraph above. The net operating budget is thus the net sum which would remain to be raised by local taxation, and the "incentive equalization aid" is payable with respect to that net sum. Again the amount of that aid is geared to the standing of each district in the scale mentioned above ranging from a "basic district" to a "comprehensive district." For the purpose of calculating the "incentive equalization aid" a "school district guaranteed valuation" is found for the district by multiplying the number of residents weighted pupils by a valuation per pupil ranging from not less than $30,000 in a "basic district" to not less than $45,000 in a "comprehensive district." If the "school district guaranteed valuation" is less than the equalized valuation of the district, no incentive equalization aid will be paid; and if the guaranteed valuation is more than the equalized valuation, then the "net operating budget" is divided by the "guaranteed valuation," and the resulting rate is applied to so much of the guaranteed valuation as exceeds the equalized valuation, to obtain the amount of the incentive equalization aid.

As we have said, the 1970 Act is not fully funded. As of the time of trial, the State aid consisted of the aid under the pre-1970 statutes plus 20% of the difference between that sum and the sum which the 1970 Act would yield if fully funded. Again, since the criteria for the classification of operating districts from "basic" to "comprehensive" have not been established, all districts are deemed to be "basic" for the computation. We note, too, that under the 1970 Act there is a save-harmless provision assuring each district without regard to its wealth that the 1970 Act will not reduce its aid.

We have outlined the formula of the 1970 Act to show that it is not demonstrably designed to guarantee that local effort plus the State aid will yield to all the pupils in the State that level of educational opportunity which the 1875 amendment mandates. We see no basis for a finding that the 1970 Act, even if fully funded, would satisfy the constitutional obligation of the State.

. . . .

We repeat that if the State chooses to assign its obligation under the 1875 amendment to local government, the State must do so by a plan which will fulfill the State's continuing obligation. To that end the State must define in some discernible way the educational obligation and must *compel* the local school districts to raise the money necessary to provide that opportunity. The State has never spelled out the content of the constitutionally mandated educational opportunity. Nor has the State *required* the school districts to raise moneys needed to achieve that unstated standard. Nor is the State aid program designed to compensate for local failures to reach that level. It must be evident that our present scheme is a patchy product reflecting provincial contests rather than a plan sensitive only to the constitutional mandate.

We have discussed the existing scene in terms of the current operating expenses. The State's obligation includes as well the capital expenditures without which the required educational opportunity could not be provided.

Upon the record before us, it may be doubted that the thorough and efficient system of schools required by the 1875 amendment can realistically be met by reliance upon local taxation. The discordant correlations between the educational needs of the school districts and their respective tax bases suggest any such effort would likely fail....

Although we have dealt with the constitutional problem in terms of dollar input per pupil, we should not be understood to mean that the State may not recognize differences in area costs, or a need for additional dollar input to equip classes of disadvantaged children for the educational opportunity. Nor do we say that if the

State assumes the cost of providing the constitutionally mandated education, it may not authorize local government to go further and to tax to that further end, provided that such authorization does not become a device for diluting the State's mandated responsibility.

The present system being unconstitutional, we come to the subject of remedies. We agree with the trial court that relief must be prospective. The judiciary cannot unravel the fiscal skein. Obligations incurred must not be impaired. And since government must go on, and some period of time will be needed to establish another statutory system, obligations hereafter incurred pursuant to existing statutes will be valid in accordance with the terms of the statutes. In other respects we desire the further views of the parties as to the content of the judgment, including argument as to whether the judiciary may, as the trial court did with respect to the "minimum support aid" and the save-harmless provision of the 1970 Act, 118 N.J. Super. at 280-81, 287 A.2d 187, order the moneys appropriated by the Legislature to implement the 1970 Act shall be distributed upon terms other than the legislated ones. A short date for argument will be fixed.

....

---

1. Is it clear whether the court in *Robinson* is requiring an adequate minimum education for all children or some form of equality? Might a theory of "minimum" education itself lead to equality of educational expenditures? Consider, in this regard, Justice Marshall's statement: "It should be obvious that the political process ... is to some degree competitive. It is, thus of little benefit to an individual from a property-poor district to have 'enough' education if those around him have more than enough." Must the "minimum" required for one individual be determined in relation to what his competitor, or future competitor, is receiving? Or is this thesis susceptible to the same challenges asserted in *Rodriguez* as to whether funding beyond a certain point leads to the acquisition of skills which are necessary for competition in the political process or labor market? Can the circle be avoided without establishing specific standards? Is there a feasible judicial method of determining the minimum once equality is rejected as the standard? The court in *Robinson* does not specify precisely what kind of financing scheme will be required in New Jersey, although it is clear that districts will be allowed to raise local taxes beyond the amount provided by the state. Is the court's allowance for local taxation consistent with its interpretation of the state constitution as mandating "equality of educational opportunity," once the court has accepted a correlation between expenditures and quality of education? Or is the answer again that such a correlation exists only up to a certain point?

2. Both *Robinson* and *Rodriguez* used equal protection analyses to determine if students had been denied an appropriate education. They, of course, arrived at differing results. What, if anything, sets *Robinson* apart? Was it because the New Jersey court looked at the importance of the right instead of determining first that there be a fundamental interest?

Not all state courts followed the *Robinson* decision. For example, the Georgia Supreme Court in *McDaniel v. Thomas*, 285 S.E.2d 156 (Ga. 1981), explained that while it was not bound to make the same determination under its own constitution "the fact that education is not a 'fundamental' right under the United States Constitution provides some guidance for the states." *Id.* at 160. In *McDaniel* plaintiffs alleged that the education funding system violated both the state equal protection clause and the state education clause which required an "adequate education." The court found that despite funding disparities, under the *Rodriguez* analysis, the system bore some rational relationship to the legitimate state purpose of providing basic education to the state's public school students.

3. The New Jersey Supreme Court's failure in *Robinson* to define equal educational opportunity or to mandate a specific type of financing system led to problems with implementation of the *Robinson I* decision.

In *Robinson II*, 63 N.J. 196, 306 A.2d 65 (1973), the court directed the state legislature to enact a new school finance statute compatible with *Robinson I* by Dec. 31, 1974. The court withheld a ruling on the question of whether it could order "distribution of appropriated monies toward a constitutional objective" if the required legislation was not forthcoming. A measure creating a new state income tax to fund a revised school finance system was rejected by the legislature in 1974 and in *Robinson III*, 67 N.J. 35, 335 A.2d 6 (1975), the court extended the deadline for compliance, permitting school districts to operate under the existing statutory finance plan for the 1975-76 school year. In May, 1975, the court issued a provisional order to become effective in the 1976-77 school year in the event the legislature continued to fail to act. *Robinson IV*, 69 N.J. 133, 351 A.2d 713, *cert. denied*, 423 U.S. 913 (1975). Two days before the deadline announced in *Robinson IV* the legislature approved the Public School Education Act of 1975. In *Robinson V*, 69 N.J. 449, 335 A.2d 129 (1976), the court upheld the constitutionality of the Act, provided that it was fully funded. The legislature was unable to agree on a means of funding the Act, however, and in *Robinson VI* the court, stating "the existing unconstitutional system of financing the schools into yet another school year cannot be tolerated," enjoined the expenditure of any funds for support of the public schools after July 1, 1976. *Robinson VI*, 70 N.J. 155, 358 A.2d 457 (1976). The legislature responded to the threat of possible school closings by enacting an income tax bill on July 8, 1976, to provide full funding for the Act. The court ordered the injunction dissolved on July 9, 1976, *Robinson VII*, 79 N.J. 464, 360 A.2d 400 (1976).

4. *Robinson v. Cahill* was followed by numerous other state court suits challenging the validity of school financing systems. In *Serrano v. Priest* (*Serrano II*), 18 Cal. 3d 728, 557 P.2d 929, 135 Cal. Rptr. 345, *cert. denied*, 432 U.S. 907 (1977), the California Supreme Court, while recognizing that *Rodriguez* undercut the *Serrano I* ruling of 1971 held that the state's school

finance system violated the California Constitution's equal protection provisions and ordered the state to comply with fair funding standards by 1980. The complaint continued in *Serrano v. Priest (Serrano III)*, 200 Cal. App. 3d 897, 22 Cal. Rptr. 584 (Cal. Ct. App. 2d Dist. 1986), where the court ruled that there was sufficient evidence that the public school financing system had reduced wealth-related disparities to insignificance and that the remaining differences between school districts were justified by legitimate state interests.

Similarly, in *Horton v. Meskill*, 172 Conn. 615, 376 A.2d 359 (1977), the Connecticut Supreme Court relied on the equal protection provisions of that state constitution in finding the state school financing system unconstitutional. Elementary and secondary education is a fundamental right in Connecticut and thus any infringement of that right is subject to strict judicial scrutiny, the court held. *See also Dupree v. Alma Sch. Dist. No. 80*, 651 S.W.2d 90 (Ark. 1988); *Tennessee Small Sch. Sys. v. McWherter*, 851 S.W.2d 139 (Tenn. 1993); *Washakie County Sch. Dist. No. 1 v. Herschler*, 606 P.2d 310 (Wyo. 1980), cert. denied, 449 U.S. 824 (1980); *Board of Educ. v. Nyquist*, 94 Misc. 2d 466, 408 N.Y.S.2d 606 (1978); *Board of Educ. v. Walter*, 58 Ohio St. 2d 368, 390 N.E.2d 813 (1979), cert. denied, 444 U.S. 1015 (1980); *Buse v. Smith*, 74 Wis. 2d 550, 247 N.W.2d 141 (1976); *Milliken v. Green*, 390 Mich. 389, 212 N.W.2d 711 (1973); *Thompson v. Engelking*, 96 Idaho 793, 537 P.2d 635 (1975); *Olsen v. State*, 276 Or. 9, 554 P.2d 139 (1976); *Shofstall v. Hollins*, 110 Ariz. 88, 515 P.2d 590 (1973); *Seattle Sch. Dist. No. 1 v. State*, 90 Wash. 2d 476, 585 P.2d 71 (1978).

See also Hubsch, *The Emerging Right to Education Under State Constitutional Law*, 65 Temp. L. Rev. 1325 (1992). The article contains an appendix that lists all the states and the education clauses of their respective constitutions. As you read the cases in this chapter, notice how each court interprets the constitution at hand and consider how it would deal with different language.

5. Most financing schemes which have been offered as alternatives to the present taxing scheme allow for local supplementation or local choice as to the rate of tax, as with district power equalizing. District power equalizing allows for differential expenditures among school districts, while removing the effect of differential tax bases. Local districts are free to tax as high as they like, only they are assured a fixed rate of revenues per level of taxation, regardless of their property base. Assuming a correlation between expenditures and quality of education, should disparities in educational quality which turn on the extent to which a child's district or his parents value education be more readily tolerated than choices based on district wealth? Is the focus of such a scheme protective of the taxpayer rather than the child?

6. *Robinson* was the first of many state-level court cases to look closely at the education clauses in state constitutions. In most of the cases, the court, and subsequently the state, considered alternative sources for school funds. For a discussion of relatively recent developments, consider the remaining cases in this chapter and the following excerpt:

STUBBS, AFTER RODRIGUEZ: RECENT DEVELOPMENTS IN SCHOOL FINANCE REFORM, 44 Tax Law. 313 (1990)*

I. *Introduction*

....

... In 1973, in the seminal case of *San Antonio Independent School District v. Rodriguez*, the Supreme Court declared that the United States Constitution offered no protection for students from the property-poor districts.

Since *Rodriguez*, school finance suits have been filed in state courts in an attempt to test protection under state constitutions. Subsequently, despite an apparent weakening by the Supreme Court of some aspects of its 1973 decision, this trend has continued. Across the nation, students, parents, educators and property owners have filed suits to limit the role of property taxes as a source of funding for schools. These state constitution-based challenges have met with only mixed success. Recently, however, the courts have handed plaintiffs a string of dramatic victories, stirring new interest in the issue across the nation.

....

III. *The Basic Legal Theories and the Early Decisions*

A. *Overview*

The legal framework now surrounding school finance issues has evolved dramatically over the past twenty years. Four decisions from the early 1970's have laid much of the groundwork for subsequent school finance litigation.[25]...

These four cases established the two fundamental theories under which all subsequent suits have challenged school finance systems. The first theory employs an equal protection analysis of the financing scheme. The second theory utilizes state constitution education provisions.

....

Under the second approach, state constitution education provisions, where present, expressly delineate the state's duty to provide a public school system. These provisions provide two toeholds for challenges to school finance not available in the federal courts: (1) they may elevate the status of education to a fundamental right subject to strict scrutiny under equal protection analysis, or (2)

---

*Copyright © 1990 by A. Thomas Stubbs and the American Bar Association. Reprinted with permission.

[25] *Serrano v. Priest*, 487 P.2d 1241 (Cal. 1971) [hereinafter *Serrano I*]; *Serrano v. Priest*, 557 P.2d 929 (Cal. 1976), *cert. denied*, 432 U.S. 907 (1977) [hereinafter *Serrano II*]; *San Antonio Independent School District v. Rodriguez*, 411 U.S. 1 (1973); *Robinson v. Cahill*, 303 A.2d 273 (N.J. 1973), *cert. denied*, 423 U.S. 813 (1975) [hereinafter *Robinson I*].

the language of the education provision itself may provide a cause of action for plaintiffs. The strength of the provision's language may determine how useful it is to a plaintiff....

B. *Equal Protection Analysis: The Federal Approach and State-Based Alternatives*

Laws analyzed under the federal approach will be subject to either strict, intermediate, or minimum scrutiny. Strict scrutiny is applied when a law employs a suspect classification or infringes on a fundamental interest....

If a law is subject to strict scrutiny, the law will be struck down unless the state demonstrates that an overriding or compelling goal is at stake and that a less drastic alternative to the discriminatory classification is unavailable. Few laws survive strict scrutiny.

If a law neither employs a suspect classification nor infringes on a fundamental interest, then "minimum scrutiny" is applied. This is the test customarily applied to social and economic legislation. Under this standard, the question is whether the "system, with its conceded imperfections, nevertheless bears some rational relationship to a legitimate state purpose."[39] That is, laws subject to minimum scrutiny will be upheld so long as the state can show that a "rational relationship" exists between the classification and the goal. Most laws are upheld when subject only to minimum scrutiny.

Minimum scrutiny applies even if the law has a disproportionately adverse impact on a suspect class so long as on its face the law's classification is not based on a suspect trait. Wealth is an example of a such a facially neutral trait that generates non-neutral impacts in effect. This is particularly noteworthy since wealth classifications are the subject of many school finance cases.

....

Two years prior to *Rodriguez*, the California Supreme Court came to the opposite conclusion in *Serrano I* when it applied an equal protection analysis to the California school finance scheme.[50] Grounding its opinion in both the California and the federal equal protection clauses, the court found that the California school finance laws created a suspect, wealth-based classification and that education was a fundamental right. The California court felt that local control of education was not a sufficiently compelling justification for the discrimination and that less offensive alternatives could be employed to achieve local control.

Serrano I did not conclusively dispose of the matter, however. The court merely found the allegations of the plaintiffs' complaint legally sufficient and returned the cause to the trial court for further proceedings. By the time those further proceedings wound their way back to the California Supreme Court in

---

[39] 411 U.S. at 44.
[50] 487 P.2d 1241.

Serrano II, the U.S. Supreme Court had handed down *Rodriguez*. The California court's reliance on the federal equal protection clause was rendered inoperative by *Rodriguez*. As a result, the equal protection rationale used in *Serrano II* was grounded solely in the California constitution's equal protection provisions.[54] Applying the federal approach to the California constitution, the court held that (1) "discrimination in educational opportunity on the basis of district wealth involves a suspect classification," and (2) "education is a fundamental interest."[55]

Just weeks after the U.S. Supreme Court outlined the federal approach in *Rodriguez*, the New Jersey Supreme Court faced virtually the same issue in *Robinson I*. Yet, despite the authority behind the approach taken in *Rodriguez*, the state court expressly eschewed the federal framework and developed an approach of its own.

The state court acknowledged that classifications might reasonably be devised and used to analyze a statute. However, the court declared that it did "not find helpful the concept of a 'fundamental' right" because "[n]o one has successfully defined the term for this purpose."[56] Whether a state law abridged a fundamental right (however defined) or infringed on the rights of a suspect class, the two-tiered federal analysis imposed a "[m]echanical approach"[57] where the state court felt a more subtle balancing was appropriate. The court stated, "Ultimately, a court must weigh the nature of the restraint or the denial against the apparent public justification, and decide whether the State action is arbitrary."[58] The New Jersey Supreme Court thus felt that equal protection analysis basically amounted to a balancing of interests and that it should be explicitly framed as such.

While the New Jersey Supreme Court exercised its right to frame the equal protection analysis as it felt most useful, the court ultimately decided against resting its decision on equal protection grounds. The court found that the "equal protection clause may be unmanageable if it is called upon to supply categorical answers in the vast area of human needs, choosing those which must be met and a single basis upon which the State must act."[59] Instead, the New Jersey court relied on the education provision in its constitution.

C. *State Constitution Education Clause Analysis*

Education clauses provide two toeholds for challenges to school finance laws. First, these provisions may elevate the status of education to that of a fundamen-

---

[54] 557 P.2d at 949-51.
[55] *Id.*
[56] 303 A.2d at 282.
[57] *Id.*
[58] *Id.*
[59] *Id.* at 283.

tal right. States that employ a version of equal protection analysis that incorporates the concept of fundamental rights may then apply strict scrutiny to the funding laws. Alternatively, these provisions may define the state's responsibilities for establishing a school system. Plaintiffs may then challenge the school funding laws on the grounds that they do not comport with the mandate of the state constitution's education provisions.

Robinson I considered the New Jersey constitution's education clause in the context of both of these toeholds. As discussed previously, the court did not find the fundamental interest aspect of the equal protection analysis to be useful. Instead, the court focused on the nature of the obligation the education provision directly imposed on the state. The New Jersey constitution charged the state with providing a "thorough and efficient" school system. The court ruled that the state had failed to discharge this obligation in light of the wide disparities in funding among the school districts and the lack of any other state-imposed standard to measure educational attainment.

However, the last two years have yielded four dramatic decisions.[65] Each decision ruled that the state's school funding program was unconstitutional under the specifics of the state constitution; each decision was grounded in the unique specifications of a state constitution's education clause. Individually, the decisions are important on a local level. Taken collectively and coupled with the legislative responses, these decisions may represent a fundamental change in the school finance litigation scene.

....

ABBOTT v. BURKE

Supreme Court of New Jersey
119 N.J. 287, 575 A.2d 359 (1990)

WILENTZ, C.J.:

We again face the question of the constitutionality of our school system. We are asked in this case to rule that the Public School Education Act of 1975, L. 1975, [New Jersey] (the Act) violates our Constitution's thorough and efficient clause. We find that under the present system the evidence compels but one conclusion: the poorer the district and the greater its need, the less the money available, and the worse the education. That system is neither thorough nor efficient. We hold the Act unconstitutional as applied to poorer urban school districts. Education has failed there, for both the students and the State. We hold that the Act must be amended to assure funding of education in poorer urban districts at the level of property-rich districts; that such funding cannot be allowed to depend on the ability of local school districts to tax; that such funding

---

[65]*Helena Elementary School Dist. No. 1 v. State*, 769 P.2d 684 (Mont.1989); *Rose v. Council for Better Educ., Inc.*, 790 S.W.2d 186 (Ky.1989); *Edgewood Indep. School Dist. v. Kirby*, 777 S.W.2d 391 (Tex.1989); *Abbott v. Burke*, 575 A.2d 359 (N.J.1990).

must be guaranteed and mandated by the State; and that the level of funding must also be adequate to provide for the special educational needs of these poorer urban districts in order to redress their extreme disadvantages.

....

On this record we find a constitutional deficiency only in the poorer urban districts, and our remedy is limited to those districts. We leave unaffected the disparity in substantive education and funding found in other districts throughout the state, although that disparity too may some day become a matter of constitutional dimension....

....

I. Description of the Issue

Predictably flowing from our decision in *Robinson v. Cahill*, 69 N.J. 449, 355 A.2d 129 (1976) (*Robinson V*), the issue now before us is whether the Act, declared facially constitutional, is constitutional as applied....

....

II. The Constitutional Provision

....

The initial construction of the thorough and efficient clause was permeated by the concept of equality....

What that equality meant, while not precisely defined, was indicated in several ways. First, in deciding that the statute then in place was unconstitutional as not affording a thorough and efficient education, we relied solely on the disparity of funding, *i.e.*, on the fact that the dollars spent on education per pupil varied from one district to another (from below $700 per pupil to over $1,500 per pupil, *Robinson V, supra*, 69 N.J. at 480 n. 4, 355 A.2d 129)....

Rather than on equality, our decision was based on the proposition that the Constitution required a certain level of education, that which equates with thorough and efficient; it is that level that all must attain; that is the only equality required by the Constitution. Embedded in our observation that if the lowest level of expenditures per pupil constituted a thorough and efficient education, then the constitutional mandate would be met was the clear implication that no matter how many districts were spending well beyond that level, the system would be constitutional. Second, we noted that the State, while assigning the obligation to local government to afford a thorough and efficient education, had never defined "in some discernible way the educational obligation," "the content of the constitutionally mandated educational opportunity"; it was "an unstated standard." *Id.* at 519, 303 A.2d 273. Again, the clear import is not of a constitutional mandate governing expenditures per pupil, equal or otherwise, but a requirement of a specific substantive level of education. Equality of expenditures per pupil could not have been constitutionally mandated when we recognized the right of districts to spend more to address students' special needs (the "need for additional dollar input to equip classes of disadvantaged children for the educational opportunity") and disclaimed any intent to deprive the State of the power to "authorize local government to go further" than "the constitutionally mandated education" and "to tax to that further end." *Id.* at 520, 303 A.2d 273. Our only condition was that such excess "not become a device for diluting the State's mandated responsibility." *Ibid.*

Our decision in *Robinson I* was necessarily general because of the narrow record in that case, consisting primarily of dollar per pupil information and related socioeconomic data. Although general, however, our holding in *Robinson I* was clear and formed the basis for our holding in *Robinson V*: a thorough and efficient education requires a certain level of educational opportunity, a minimum level, that will equip the student to become "a citizen and ... a competitor in the labor market." *Robinson I, supra*, 62 N.J. at 515, 303 A.2d 273....

. . . .

The change of focus from the dollar disparity in *Robinson I* to substantive educational content in *Robinson V* is clear; it was the main theme underlying the Court's determination that the Act was constitutional. Noting at the outset that for the first time we had before us a statute that defined the constitutional obligation, provided for its implementation through both state and local administration, required that implementation to be monitored, directed the State to compel compliance where that monitoring revealed deficiencies, and provided a funding mechanism to achieve the constitutional goal, we observed that the state's school-aid provisions "must be considered, not in comparative isolation, but as part of the whole proposal formulated by the Legislature." *Robinson V* ....

. . . .

With that as background, *Abbott v. Burke*, testing the Act as applied, came before us first in a procedural controversy and now in full substance.... When we first viewed the apparent scope of the factual controversy in *Abbott I, supra*, 100 N.J. 269, 495 A.2d 376, as it bore on the issue of appropriate forum, we found it necessary to underline the basic holdings of the *Robinson v. Cahill* cases, including explicitly the power of local districts to spend beyond what was required for a thorough and efficient education, subject to the limitation that "such authorization does not become a device for diluting the State's mandated responsibility," *Abbott I, supra*, 100 N.J. at 291, 495 A.2d 376 (quoting *Robinson I, supra*, 62 N.J. at 520, 303 A.2d 273). We also recognized the revision of *Robinson I* effected in *Robinson V* that the Court has "been constantly mindful that money is only one of a number of elements that must be studied in giving definition and content to the constitutional promise of a thorough and efficient education." *Abbott I, supra*, 100 N.J. at 292, 495 A.2d 376 (quoting *Robinson V, supra*, 69 N.J. at 455, 355 A.2d 129). But we gave, in view of the issues about to be projected, a new potential gloss to the constitutional obligation. For instance, in the context of plaintiffs' claim that the disparities in dollar expenditure disproportionately affected disadvantaged students, we recognized that the State not only had the power to spend in excess of the norm in view of the presumed greater needs of such students, but that it might be required to do so. *Id.* at 291-93, 495 A.2d 376. Our application of the constitutional standard first presented in *Robinson I* ... reflects the context of the present case.

> [T]he thorough and efficient education issues call for proofs that, after comparing the education received by children in property-poor districts to that offered in property-rich districts, it appears that the disadvantaged children will not be able to compete in, and contribute to, the society entered by the relatively advantaged children. [*Abbott I, supra,* 100 N.J. at 296, 495 A.2d 376.]

....

Thus, while leaving the door open to the numerous factual and legal contentions of the parties, we reiterated the constitutional mandate as it had developed through *Robinson V.* But we added a new element of considerable relevance to this case. We said, in effect, that the requirement of a thorough and efficient education to provide "that educational opportunity which is needed in the contemporary setting to equip a child for his role as a citizen and as a competitor in the labor market," *Robinson I* meant that poorer disadvantaged students must be given a chance to be able to compete with relatively advantaged students. The Act and its system of education have failed in that respect, and it is that failure that we address in this case.

....

IV.

Facts and Conclusions

....

A. *The Funding Scheme*

....

The Act gives poorer districts — poor in terms of property valuation per pupil — taxing power to raise more money for school purposes than what a school district with the average property valuation and no equalization aid could raise. Putting aside for the moment the impact of "municipal overburden" (a condition in many poorer districts where the cost of local government — police, firefighters, other municipal employees, road maintenance, garbage collection, etc. — is so high that the municipality and the school district are reluctant to increase taxes for any purpose, including education), equalization aid attempts to obliterate the enormous disparity between rich and poor for school tax purposes; it creates, instead of rich and poor districts, two different classes: those districts with a guaranteed tax base — almost two-thirds of the districts in the state — and those with a tax base in excess of the guaranteed tax base of $223,100, running from $223,667 to $7.8 million and clustering at $300,000 (1984-85 figures)....

B. *Educational Funding Disparities*

... [T]he funding and spending disparities referred to in *Robinson I* are worse now than they were before adoption of the Act. They have done so. Prior to the Act, in 1971-72, the spread between the lowest and highest spending districts was $700 per pupil to $1,500 per pupil, a difference of $800. *Robinson V, supra*.... This difference of $800 per pupil reflects the range between the absolute highest spending districts and the absolute lowest.... In 1975-76, the year immediately prior to the Act, districts at the fifth percentile spent $1,076, while districts at the ninety-fifth spent $1,974, a difference of $898. For a few years after the Act was funded, the disparity diminished, but thereafter it generally increased to the point where in 1984-85 districts at the fifth percentile spent $2,687, while districts at the ninety-fifth percentile spent $4,755, a disparity of $2,068 per pupil. The disparity in expenditures is significant even when adjusted for inflation — in 1975-dollars, the disparity grew from $898 per pupil in 1975-76 to $1,135 per pupil in 1984-85.

The impact of this disparity, solely in dollar terms, is that on the average, in 1984-85, a group of richer districts with 189,484 students spend 40% more per pupil than a group of poorer districts with 355,612 students; one provides an education worth $4,029 per pupil, the other, $2,861....

That disadvantage in expenditures per pupil is clearly related to all of the other aspects of poverty that define poorer urban districts and their youth. Although the statistical relationships are the subject of considerable dispute, we conclude that generally they show that the poorer the district — measured by equalized valuation per pupil, or by other indicators of poverty — the less the per pupil expenditure; the poorer and more urban the district, the heavier its municipal property tax, the greater the school tax burden; whatever the measure of disadvantage, need, and poverty — the greater it is, the less there is to spend.

....

For most districts, plaintiffs have failed to prove substantively that a thorough and efficient education does not exist. Furthermore, their proofs of expenditure disparity in those districts are not sufficient to overcome the deference owed to the conclusions of the Commissioner and the Board. Given the State's attempt to achieve thorough and efficient education, we doubt that any showing of expenditure disparity in the absence of some independent evidence of substantive failure would warrant a conclusion that a thorough and efficient education does not exist. But expenditure disparity does play a role, an important one, in our conclusion that the constitutional level has not been achieved in the poorer urban districts. This disparity has multiple relevance: to the extent educational quality is deemed related to dollar expenditures, it tends to prove inadequate quality of education in the poorer districts, unless we were to assume that the substantial differential in expenditures is attributable to an education in the richer districts far beyond anything that thorough and efficient demands; it indicates even more strongly the probability that the poorer districts' students will be unable to compete in the society entered by the richer districts' students; and by its consistency over the years, it suggests that the system as it now operates is unable to correct this.

....

We have decided this case on the premise that the children of poorer urban districts are as capable as all others; that their deficiencies stem from their socioeconomic status; and that through effective education and changes in that socioeconomic status, they can perform as well as others. Our constitutional mandate does not allow us to consign poorer children permanently to an inferior education on the theory that they cannot afford a better one or that they would not benefit from it.

....

We note the obvious: the State may be correct in its contention that measured against the entire spectrum of districts in the state, the disparities and their relationships are not sufficient to condemn the system, because they exist significantly only when the extremes are compared. That gives little comfort to those students confined to the poorest districts, and they number in the hundreds of thousands (in 1984-85 there were 280,081 resident students in the twenty-nine poorer urban districts, about 25% of the entire public school population). Their deprivation is real, of constitutional magnitude, and not blunted in the least by the State's statistical analysis.

C. *Substantive Educational Opportunity: The Administration of the Act by the Commissioner and the Board*

....

For the overwhelming number of districts, all we know about the substantive education is that the Act commands it, reports are produced, monitoring takes place, and the Commissioner has certified most districts as providing a thorough and efficient education; we have no evidence that they are not. While we know of expenditure disparity, we have no reason to believe the actual funding level in most districts is below that needed to achieve a thorough and efficient education. On this record plaintiffs have not shown that a thorough and efficient education does not indeed exist right now in the overwhelming number of districts in this state. Under those circumstances our State Constitution does not require that this entire system be scrapped and replaced by another at enormous expense based solely on expenditure disparities. We do not imply anything about the importance of such disparities when considered as a matter of policy. As noted at the outset of this opinion, our decision does not deal with optimum educational policy, but with constitutional compliance.

We are unable to conclude that most districts are failing to deliver the educational opportunity required by our State Constitution. There are various elements to that conclusion. In a narrow procedural sense, it reflects our belief that the burden is on the plaintiffs to show that a thorough and efficient education is not being delivered; it represents our conclusion that when the State, through the Legislature and its administrative agency, has conscientiously attempted to achieve a level of education and the State's agency says it has been achieved, some deference must be accorded to that determination. It further embodies our conclusion that all of these factors are sufficient evidence to preclude a finding of constitutional deprivation based solely on expenditure disparity. Most of all it reflects our firmly held belief that before this Court concludes that there is a constitutional failure despite the legally-authorized certification of the Commissioner to the contrary, the Board's conclusion to the contrary, and the Legislature's efforts to achieve it, the proofs must be compelling. Before this Court voids the statute, overrules the Board and the Commissioner, and orders the Legislature to provide a new system, the constitutional failure must be clear. As to most districts of the state, it is not. But as to some — the poorer urban districts — it is glaringly clear.

. . . .

"Municipal overburden" is the excessive tax levy some municipalities must impose to meet governmental needs other than education. It is a common characteristic in poorer urban districts, a product of their relatively low property values against which the local tax is assessed and their high level of governmental need. The governmental need includes the entire range of goods and services made available to citizens: police and fire protection, road maintenance, social services, water, sewer, garbage disposal, and similar services. Although the condition is not precisely defined, it is usually thought of as a tax rate well above the average.

. . . .

We do not pass on the legal contentions of the Commissioner in this respect. Our conclusion concerning municipal overburden is that it effectively prevents districts from raising substantially more money for education. It is a factual conclusion. It is based on the record history of the failure of any effort, whether through the actions of a school district or the Board or Commissioner, legal or otherwise, through the more than ten year period that the Act has been in effect, to achieve substantially increased local funding through school tax increases. That factual finding is one of the bases for our conclusion that the funding mechanism of the Act will never achieve a thorough and efficient education because it relies so heavily on a local property base already over-taxed to exhaustion.

D. *The Quality of Education in the Poorer Urban Districts*

The primary basis for our decision is the constitutional failure of education in poorer urban districts. The record demonstrates beyond debate that a thorough and efficient education does not exist there. Our conclusion that the constitutional mandate has not been satisfied is based both on the absolute level of education in those districts and the comparison with education in affluent suburban districts.

Plaintiffs' proofs of the significantly inferior quality of education in poorer urban districts are persuasive. While exceptions exist, at the extremes — and its strength is limited to the extremes — the comparison between the education offered to students in poorer urban districts with that offered in the richer districts is impressive.... The State's objections were of various kinds: it noted that the comparisons were largely limited to the extremes, the richest against the poorest, the very best against the very worst; evidence was lacking in most cases that would warrant a reliable comparative conclusion. Furthermore, the State claims that the adequacy of the education that was being afforded in poorer districts was not acknowledged. The State's basic objection is that the various circumstantial measures, such as course offerings, experience and education of the staff, and pupil/staff ratio cannot be considered reliable indicators of the quality of education.

....

We note initially that there was little direct proof of substantive education, such as course offerings, for the overwhelming number of districts in the state. On this record, most of the state's districts — except the poorer urban ones — may be offering an education in full compliance with the constitutional mandate.

However, the level of education offered to students in some of the poorer urban districts is tragically inadequate. Many opportunities offered to students in richer suburban districts are denied to them. For instance, exposure to computers is necessary to acquire skills to compete in the workplace. In South Orange/Maplewood school district, kindergartners are introduced to computers; children learn word processing in elementary school; middle school students are offered beginning computer programming; and high school students are offered advanced courses in several programming languages or project-oriented independent studies. Each South Orange/Maplewood school has a computer lab.

By contrast, many poorer urban districts cannot offer such variety of computer science courses. While Princeton has one computer per eight children, East Orange has one computer per forty-three children, and Camden has one computer per fifty-eight children. Camden can offer formal computer instruction to only 3.4% of its students. In many poorer urban districts, computers are purchased with federal or state categorical funds for use in remedial education programs. Paterson offers no computer education other than computer-assisted basic skills programs. Further, many of these districts do not have sufficient space to accommodate computer labs. In Jersey City, computer classes are being taught in storage closets.

Science education is deficient in some poorer urban districts. Princeton has seven laboratories in its high school, each with built-in equipment. South Brunswick elementary and middle schools stress hands-on, investigative science programs. However, many poorer urban districts offer science classes in labs built in the 1920's and 1930's, where sinks do not work, equipment such as microscopes is not available, supplies for chemistry or biology classes are insufficient, and hands-on investigative techniques cannot be taught. In Jersey City and Irvington, middle school science classes are taught without provision for laboratory experience. In East Orange middle schools, teachers wheel a science cart into a three-foot-by-six-foot science area for instruction. The area contains a sink, but no water, gas, or electrical lines.

The disparity in foreign-language programs is dramatic. Montclair's students begin instruction in French or Spanish at the pre-school level. In Princeton's middle school, fifth grade students must take a half-year of French and a half-year of Spanish. Most sixth graders continue with one of these languages. Many begin a second language in the ninth grade, where four-year programs in German, Italian, Russian, and Latin are offered. French and Spanish are offered on two tracks, one for students who began instruction in middle school and the other for those who begin in the ninth grade. Advanced placement courses are available. In contrast, many of the poorer urban schools do not offer upper level foreign language courses, and only begin instruction in high school. Jersey City starts its foreign language program in the ninth grade; Paterson begins it at the tenth grade. Most Jersey City high schools offer only two languages; both of Paterson's high schools offer only Spanish and French, although the two Paterson high schools share one German teacher and one Latin teacher.

Music programs are vastly superior in some richer suburban districts. South Brunswick offers music classes starting in kindergarten; Montclair begins with pre-schoolers. Millburn and South Brunswick offer their middle school students a music curriculum that includes courses such as guitar, electronic-piano laboratory, and music composition on synthesizers. Princeton offers several performing groups, including bands, choruses, and small ensembles. However, Camden and Paterson do not offer a music course until the fourth grade; only introductory level music courses are offered in high school. In 1981, Camden eliminated all its elementary school music teachers and provided "helpers" to assist in teaching music. Many poorer urban school districts have inadequate space for instrumental music lessons, bands, and choruses. In one elementary school in Jersey City, instrumental music lessons are provided in the back of the lunchroom. At lunchtime, the class moves to an area in the school's basement.

Art programs in some poorer urban districts suffer compared to programs in richer suburban districts. In Montclair, the art program begins at the pre-school level; there is an art teacher in every elementary school; every school has at least one art room; and the district has purchased a variety of art equipment, such as a kiln for ceramic artwork. In contrast, art programs in some poorer urban districts are sparse. There are no art classrooms in East Orange elementary schools, and art teachers, who must travel from class to class, are limited in the forms of art they can teach. Jersey City has an excellent art program for gifted children; however, the regular art program can now accommodate only 30% of the district's students.

In South Brunswick school district, the industrial-arts program includes an automotive shop, a woodworking shop, a metal shop, a graphics shop, and a greenhouse for a horticultural course. The vocational education program has a computer drafting laboratory and a graphics laboratory with a darkroom. In Camden, state-of-the-art equipment is not purchased; the old equipment in the classrooms is not maintained or repaired. There have even been problems heating the industrial-arts wing of the school.

Physical education programs in some poorer urban districts are deficient. While many richer suburban school districts have flourishing gymnastics, swimming, basketball, baseball, soccer, lacrosse, field hockey, tennis, and golf teams, with fields, courts, pools, lockers, showers, and gymnasiums, some poorer urban districts cannot offer students such activities. In East Orange High School there are no such sports facilities; the track team practices in the second floor hallway. All of Irvington's elementary schools have no outdoor play space; some of the playgrounds had been converted to faculty parking lots. In a middle school in Paterson, fifth- and sixth-graders play basketball in a room with such a low ceiling that the net is placed at the level appropriate for third-graders.

Many of these poorer urban districts are burdened with teaching basic skills to an overwhelming number of students. They are essentially "basic skills districts." In 1985, 53% of Camden's children received remedial education; in East Orange, 41%; in Irvington, 30%. By contrast, only 4% of the students in Millburn school district received remedial education.

....

Thorough and efficient means more than teaching the skills needed to compete in the labor market, as critically important as that may be. It means being able to fulfill one's role as a citizen, a role that encompasses far more than merely registering to vote. It means the ability to participate fully in society, in the life of one's community, the ability to appreciate music, art, and literature, and the ability to share all of that with friends. As plaintiffs point out in so many ways, and tellingly, if these courses are not integral to a thorough and efficient education, why do the richer districts invariably offer them? The disparity is dramatic. Alongside these basic-skills districts are school systems offering the broadest range of courses, instruction in numerous languages, sophisticated mathematics, arts, and sciences at a high level, fully equipped laboratories, hands-on computer experience, everything parents seriously concerned for their children's future would want, and everything a child needs....

The State contends that the education currently offered in these poorer urban districts is tailored to the students' present need, that these students simply cannot now benefit from the kind of vastly superior course offerings found in the richer districts. No one claims here, however, that students unable to attain a level of reading, writing, or expression even approaching the expectations of their grade, pupils who, according to plaintiffs, are two years behind others on the first day they enter school, would be able to take full advantage of the richness of course offerings found in the wealthier suburbs. The State's conclusion is that basic skills are what they need first, intensive training in basic skills. We note, however, that these poorer districts offer curricula denuded not only of advanced academic courses but of virtually every subject that ties a child, particularly a child with academic problems, to school — of art, music, drama, athletics, even, to a very substantial degree, of science and social studies....

....

Equally, if not more important, the State's argument ignores the substantial number of children in these districts, from the average to the gifted, who can benefit from more advanced academic offerings. Since little else is available in these districts, they too are limited to basic skills.

....

... [A]lthough the incremental showing is far from dramatic, teacher ratios, experience, and education consistently improve as the districts' property wealth, per pupil expenditure, socioeconomic status or other similar factor improves. For instance, when districts are ranked by socioeconomic status (SES), the percentage of teachers with advanced degrees rises from 29% in the lower SES districts to 52% in the higher; teachers' average experience rises from 12 years in the lower SES districts to 15 years in the higher; and the ratio of teachers to pupils rises from 61 to 68 teachers per 1,000 students. There are exceptions, numerous when considered alone, but not significant enough to rebut the truth of the generality.... We are satisfied ... that these indicators support the conclusion that the absolute quality of education in the poorer urban districts is deficient.

....

E. *The Quality of Students' Needs in the Poorer Urban Districts*

This record shows that the educational needs of students in poorer urban districts vastly exceed those of others, especially those from richer districts. The difference is monumental, no matter how it is measured. Those needs go beyond educational needs, they include food, clothing and shelter, and extend to lack of close family and community ties and support, and lack of helpful role models. They include the needs that arise from a life led in an environment of violence, poverty, and despair. Urban youth are often isolated from the mainstream of society. Education forms only a small part of their home life, sometimes no part of their school life, and the dropout is almost the norm. There are exceptions, fortunately, but substantial numbers of urban students fit this pattern. The goal is to motivate them, to wipe out their disadvantages as much as a school district can, and to give them an educational opportunity that will enable them to use their innate ability.

....

The dropout rate in these poorer urban districts is further testimony both to their failure and to the students' needs. The "unofficial" dropout rate (1984-85) for some urban high schools can be as high as 47%. A district cannot deliver a thorough and efficient education to a dropout. For a multitude of tragic reasons, these students lack the most basic requirement for achieving a thorough and efficient education — the will to learn. That characteristic is assumed, accepted, a given, in richer suburban districts.

The record evidence of the quality of education in poorer urban districts and the desperate needs of their students clearly indicates that a significantly different approach to education is required if these districts and their students are to

CH. 14 FINANCING PUBLIC EDUCATION 1129

succeed.... While opinions concerning the methods, approaches, and techniques differ concerning their effectiveness, their advantages and disadvantages, there is solid agreement on the basic proposition that conventional education is totally inadequate to address the special problems of the urban poor. Something quite different is needed, something that deals not only with reading, writing, and arithmetic, but with the environment that shapes these students' lives and determines their educational needs.

Obviously, we are no more able to identify what these disadvantaged students need in concrete educational terms than are the experts. What they don't need is more disadvantage, in the form of a school district that does not even approach the funding level that supports advantaged students. They need more, and the law entitles them to more.

Many students in poorer urban districts do not have books at home. These students obviously need adequate libraries and media centers....

Alternative education programs for students identified as potential dropouts are suggested as necessary to motivate a substantial number of students in poorer urban districts. Several richer suburban districts provide individualized tutoring and vocational education to students in need of alternative education. However, in Jersey City, several alternative education programs were eliminated, and only a program for students in legal trouble is provided....

Other methods have been suggested for these poorer urban districts. For instance, an intensive pre-school and all-day kindergarten enrichment program to reverse the educational disadvantage these children start out with; recruitment of parents to join parent participation programs and become involved with the schools and their schoolchildren. It seems agreed that local boards of education, administrators, and teachers organizations — all must join in this partnership for the benefit of these children if education in poorer urban districts is to succeed.

....

We realize our remedy here may fail to achieve the constitutional object, that no amount of money may be able to erase the impact of the socioeconomic factors that define and cause these pupils' disadvantages. We realize that perhaps nothing short of substantial social and economic change affecting housing, employment, child care, taxation, welfare will make the difference for these students; and that this kind of change is far beyond the power or responsibility of school districts. We have concluded, however, that even if not a cure, money will help, and that these students are constitutionally entitled to that help.

If the claim is that additional funding will not enable the poorer urban districts to satisfy the thorough and efficient test, the constitutional answer is that they are entitled to pass or fail with at least the same amount of money as their competitors.

If the claim is that these students simply cannot make it, the constitutional answer is, give them a chance. The Constitution does not tell them that since more money will not help, we will give them less; that because their needs cannot be fully met, they will not be met at all. It does not tell them they will get the minimum, because that is all they can benefit from. Like other states, we undoubtedly have some "uneducable" students, but in New Jersey there is no such thing as an uneducable district, not under our Constitution.

All of the money that supports education is public money, local money no less than state money. It is authorized and controlled, in terms of source, amount, distribution, and use, by the State. The students of Newark and Trenton are no less citizens than their friends in Millburn and Princeton. They are entitled to be treated equally, to begin at the same starting line. Today the disadvantaged are doubly mistreated: first, by the accident of their environment and, second, by the disadvantage added by an inadequate education. The State has compounded the wrong and must right it.

F. *Impact of the Level of Funding on the Quality of Education*

....

We deal here with questions of educational theory debated over the years, and now debated by experts of the very highest order. These issues have come to the fore not just in this case but throughout the nation, with states struggling as we are here in New Jersey to find an answer to urban problems, especially urban education. Studies of the most sophisticated design, pilot projects, reams after reams of case histories of schools, districts, and students, learned treatises, books, television programs — all directed at the same question: what produces good education in urban schools? The only thing universally agreed on is that those schools are failing. After that, controversy abounds. Our observation, simplistic perhaps, that "money is only one of a number of elements [involved in education]," *Robinson V, supra*, 69 N.J. at 455, 355 A.2d 129, still represents most of what one can profitably glean from this controversy for the purposes of this litigation. More concretely, while we are unable to conclude from this record that the State is clearly wrong, we would not strip all notions of equal and adequate funding from the constitutional obligation unless we were convinced that the State was clearly right.

The results of all of this research, while promising and constructive, are inconclusive, at least on the underlying issue before us. It shows beyond doubt that money alone has not worked. It shows promising success in many different approaches emphasizing techniques, relationships, social forces, motivation, approaches often quite different from conventional instruction. But it does not show that money makes no difference. What it strongly suggests is that money can be used more effectively than it is being used today....

....

We therefore adhere to the conventional wisdom that money is one of the many factors that counts. Staff ratios, breadth of course offerings, teacher experience and qualifications, and availability of equipment make a real difference in educational opportunity. We do not mean that money guarantees a thorough and efficient education, nor that, given the approach recommended by the Commissioner, a lower spending district with an effective schools program will not do better than a higher spending district without it. All we mean is that if "effective schools" is a desirable approach, it should be superimposed on a structure that starts out equal. There is nothing in this modern school of thought that suggests it will not work because it is applied to an urban district that has adequate and equal funding.

One aspect of the State's claims that the deficiencies in education are not related either to expenditures per pupil or to property wealth is that they are related to mismanagement in certain districts. The State's claim is that there has been incompetence, politics, and worse in the operation of some urban districts.

While mismanagement has undoubtedly occurred, we agree with the ALJ that it has not been a significant factor in the general failure to achieve a thorough and efficient education in poorer urban districts. It is not just Jersey City that has failed; students in all of the poorer urban districts simply do not receive the quality of education they need to equip them as citizens and competitors in the market, especially when compared to the education given in the affluent suburbs. No amount of administrative skill will redress this deficiency and disparity — and its cause is not mismanagement.

....

V. *Findings*

From this record we find that certain poorer urban districts do not provide a thorough and efficient education to their students. The Constitution is being violated. These students in poorer urban districts have not been able to participate fully as citizens and workers in our society. They have not been able to achieve any level of equality in that society with their peers from the affluent suburban districts. We find the constitutional failure clear, severe, extensive, and of long duration. We cannot find on this record, however, that there is any constitutional violation in the other districts.

We find that in order to provide a thorough and efficient education in these poorer urban districts, the State must assure that their educational expenditures per pupil are substantially equivalent to those of the more affluent suburban districts, and that, in addition, their special disadvantages must be addressed.

We find that the constitutional deficiency is a product of the Act as applied to these poorer urban districts; that the Board and the Commissioner cannot, even at full funding, achieve a thorough and efficient education in these districts under the present Act.

We find that the changes in the Act proposed by the Board and the Commissioner, and the new regulations adopted, will not achieve a thorough and efficient education in the foreseeable future in these poorer urban districts.

....

VI. *Remedy*

The Act must be amended, or new legislation passed, so as to assure that poorer urban districts' educational funding is substantially equal to that of property-rich districts. "Assure" means that such funding cannot depend on the budgeting and taxing decisions of local school boards. Funding must be certain, every year. The level of funding must also be adequate to provide for the special educational needs of these poorer urban districts and address their extreme disadvantages.

We leave it to the Legislature, the Board, and the Commissioner to determine which districts are "poorer urban districts." ... The assured funding per pupil should be substantially equivalent to that spent in those districts providing the kind of education these students need, funding that approximates the average net current expense budget of school districts in DFGs I and J. In addition, provision will be made, presumably similar to categorical aid, for the special educational needs of these districts in order to redress their disadvantages. Such provision will necessarily depend upon the legislative judgment, informed by the Board and Commissioner.

....

The funding mechanism is for the Legislature to decide. However, it cannot depend on how much a poorer urban school district is willing to tax.

... We do not claim that this is the ideal solution, but given the fundamental limits on judicial power, on this record we cannot justify a sliding scale that attempts to tailor the remedy to the varying conditions of the many districts. The record convinces us of a failure of a thorough and efficient education only in the poorer urban districts. We have no right to extend the remedy any further, nor to legislatively smooth out the remedy because of considerations of fairness unrelated to the constitutional command....

....

The Legislature may devise any remedy, including one that completely revamps the present system, in terms of funding, organization, and management, so long as it achieves a thorough and efficient education as defined herein for poorer urban districts. It may phase in that new system and phase out the old. It may choose, for instance, to equalize expenditures per pupil for all districts in the state at any level that it believes will achieve a thorough and efficient education, and that level need not necessarily be today's average of the affluent suburban districts. The most significant aspect of that average today is not its absolute level, but its disparity with the average of the ... poorer urban districts....

....

We have not attempted to address disparity of spending as such. To the extent that the State allows the richer suburban districts to continue to increase that disparity, it will, by our remedy, be required to increase the funding of the poorer urban districts. We limit our remedy at this point to increasing funding where we find a deficiency. We do not require equalized funding statewide. We are satisfied, however, that whatever degree of statewide equality the Legislature may wish to achieve, or may find it feasible to achieve, it cannot constitutionally do so for these poorer urban districts simply by raising the guaranteed tax base under the present formula. These districts, even assuming the most generous GTB increase, will not be willing or able to fund what is required for a thorough and efficient education. Their need to conserve their tax dollars, their need not to increase their total tax rate, will inevitably persuade them not to spend more but to tax less.

We recognize that the factors that determine our decision can change. The only constant is the definition of a thorough and efficient education — one that will equip all of the students of this state to perform their roles as citizens and competitors in the same society.

....

VII. *Conclusion*

....

This record proves what all suspect: that if the children of poorer districts went to school today in richer ones, educationally they would be a lot better off. Everything in this record confirms what we know: they need that advantage much more than the other children. And what everyone knows is that — as children — the only reason they do not get that advantage is that they were born in a poor district. For while we have underlined the impact of the constitutional deficiency on our state, its impact on these children is far more important. They face, through no fault of their own, a life of poverty and isolation that most of us cannot begin to understand or appreciate.

We reverse the Board's decision. The Act is unconstitutional as applied to poorer urban districts.

....

---

1. The *Abbott* court speaks of providing a "minimum level of education"; does this adequately describe the court's decision given that the court requires a level of education for all students in the state sufficiently close to that of the more affluent school districts? Is this minimum level or substantial equality of education inasmuch as the court prescribes a level of state funding for poor districts concomitant with the increase of spending with wealthy districts?

2. Does this case articulate a new standard of educational attainment in school districts: preparation of graduates to work and live as active, informed citizens in a world populated by graduates of superior school systems? Does the court define the necessary investment to achieve this standard predicated on what the best suburban schools do?

3. The *Abbott* decision focused, in part, on the acute problems of urban areas which consume funds that might otherwise be used for education. The court then ruled that a reordering of priorities must occur within the state legislature to substantially improve the level of educational provision for the poorer school districts.

Courts in other states with similar problems have not always been as sympathetic to the plight of urban school districts. In *Board of Educ. v. Nyquist*, 453 N.Y.S.2d 643 (1982), the New York Supreme Court held that "municipal overburden" was not a violation of equal protection, and the state was not required to compensate urban school districts for their financial burden with additional state aid. Also, in *Hornbeck v. Somerset County Bd. of Educ.*, 458 A.2d 758 (Md. 1983), the Maryland Supreme Court upheld the school finance system under a rational basis review without special consideration of the urban problems of the City of Baltimore.

4. The New Jersey state constitution's education clause reads as follows: "The Legislature shall provide for the maintenance and support of a thorough and efficient system of free public schools." N.J. Const. Art. VIII, Sec. 4(1). The *Abbott* court, after deciding what is meant by "thorough and efficient," held that the funding system in New Jersey did not meet this standard.

The Ohio Constitution provides: "The General Assembly shall make such provisions, by taxation, or otherwise, as, with the income arising from the school trust fund, will secure a *thorough* and efficient system of common schools throughout the state." Ohio Const. Art. VI, Sec. 2. Ohio is one of the states to experience new litigation in finance reform. (*See DeRolphe v. State of Ohio*, No. 22042 (Ct. Comm. Pleas, Perry County, Ohio 1994)). Previously, the Ohio legislature had its "thorough and efficient" clause challenged in *Board of Educ. of Sch. Dist. of Cincinnati v. Walter*, 58 Ohio St. 2d 368, 390 N.E.2d 813 (1979). The Ohio Supreme Court, at that time, recognized funding disparities, yet found the financing constitutional. Does *Abbott*, with its decision, contain the foundation for a new wave of successful constitutional challenges? Why such a difference in the interpretation of "thorough and efficient" between the two states? With respect to the "thorough and efficient" language of the Ohio Constitution the *Walter* court said:

> The plaintiffs, as cross-appellants, seek to reverse the decision of the Court of Appeals sustaining the defendants' third assignment of error before that court, which read: "The trial court erred by determining that R.C. 3317.022, R.C. 3317.023(A), (B) and (C), R.C. 3317.53(A) and (B), R.C. 3317.02(E) and Section 30 of the amended substitute Senate Bill 221 violate the 'thorough and efficient system' clause of Article VI, Section 2 of the Ohio Constitution."

In sustaining that assignment of error, the Court of Appeals stated:

> The court (of common pleas) .... overstepped its power in deciding that the finance system for public schools adopted by the General Assembly represents an 'abdication' by the Assembly of its duty under Article VI, Section 2 of the Ohio Constitution. Although exceptions have been judicially recognized, the general rule of noninterference enjoys widespread acceptance; that is, the courts have no power to enforce the

CH. 14 FINANCING PUBLIC EDUCATION 1135

mandates of the constitution which are directed at the legislative branch of the government or to control the work of the lawmakers.

Plaintiffs argue that ... Section 2 of Article VI of the Ohio Constitution ... does not grant the General Assembly the exclusive authority to determine the criteria against which the exercise of that power is to be measured. They contend further that it does not disqualify the judiciary from adjudicating whether the General Assembly's attempt to formulate a plan for financing elementary and secondary education comports with the constitutional duty which devolves upon it.

The defendants, however, maintain that the issue presented here is a "political question" and, therefore, this court should refrain from addressing it. To do so, they argue, would require this court to exercise powers constitutionally committed to a coordinate branch of government.

....

We find that the issue concerning legislation passed by the General Assembly pursuant to Section 2 of Article VI of the Ohio Constitution presents a justiciable controversy....

However, we agree with that portion of the Court of Appeals' opinion, which states: "Because this constitutional grant reenforces the ordinary discretion reposed in the General Assembly in its enactment of legislation, the judicial department of this state should exercise great circumspection before declaring public school legislation unconstitutional as a violation of Article VI, Section 2."

....

To state that the General Assembly must be granted wide discretion and that it is not the function of this court to question the wisdom of the statutes, is not to say that the General Assembly's discretion in this area is absolute. In *Miller v. Korns* (1923), 107 Ohio St. 287, 140 N.E. 773, the court was confronted with a constitutional challenge to a statute authorizing funds raised by property taxation within one school district to be used to finance schools in other districts within the county. The court passed upon the constitutionality of the legislation, which was clearly related to the powers and duties of the General Assembly under Section 2, Article VI of the Ohio Constitution and upheld the statute as constitutional.

In *Miller v. Korns, supra*, at pages 297-98, 140 N.E. at 776, the court made a statement concerning the "Thorough and Efficient Clause" which is highly pertinent to the case at bar:

....

> This declaration is made by the people of the state. It calls for the upbuilding of a system of schools throughout the state, and the attainment of efficiency and thoroughness in that system is thus expressly made a purpose, not local, not municipal, but state-wide.

With this very state purpose in view, regarding the problem as a state-wide problem, the sovereign people made it mandatory upon the General Assembly to secure not merely a system of common schools, but a system thorough and efficient throughout the state.

A thorough system could not mean one in which part or any number of the school districts of the state were starved for funds. An efficient system could not mean one in which part of any number of the school districts of the state lacked teachers, buildings, or equipment.

In the attainment of the purpose of establishing an efficient and thorough system of schools throughout the state it was easily conceivable that the greatest expense might arise in the poorest districts; that portions of great cities, teeming with life, would be able to contribute relatively little in taxes for the support of schools, which are the main hope for enlightening these districts, while districts underpopulated with children might represent such taxation value that their school needs would be relatively over supplied.

This court, therefore, intimated in *Miller v. Korns, supra*, that the wide discretion granted to the General Assembly is not without limits. For example, in a situation in which a school district was receiving so little local and state revenue that the students were effectively being deprived of educational opportunity, such a system would clearly not be thorough and efficient.

We find, however, that the General Assembly has not so abused its broad discretion in enacting the present system of financing public education as to render the statutes in question unconstitutional....

The fact that a better financing system could be devised which would be more efficient or more thorough is not material.

DeRolphe, in a state lower court decision, has overruled *Walter*. Like *Abbott*, the court articulates a standard of educational attainment: "the state must provide a system of education with a common basis that will allow students to be educated at similar levels and provide students with similar opportunities for growth and educational benefits." *DeRolphe*, at 4. The court went on to rule that unlike the decision in *Walter* (and other cases in this chapter) education is a fundamental right under the State Constitution and, as such, the state funding system is unconstitutional.

As in *Abbott*, the court spent considerable time focusing on the world of the twenty-first century and the need for students to experience an education that is commensurate. It was under such an analysis that education was deemed to be a fundamental right. The court determined that the country in the 1990's is in a global economy, and a "high tech world," concerns not addressed by the *Walter* court in 1979. The court also spoke of the use of state-mandated proficiency tests and the fact that Ohio ranks 48th of 50 states as to the disparity in funding between the wealthiest and poorest districts in the state. *Id.* at 8. These, too, were not at issue in the previous case. Since education was not viewed as a static measure and since the legislative history of the education clause of the Constitution was read by the court as guaranteeing a certain level of opportunity to education based on a high level of advancement, the legislation was subject to strict judicial scrutiny and could be upheld only upon a showing of a compelling state interest. *Id.* at 9-10.

The court then allowed that state legislative history defined "thorough" as intended to mean "complete, absolute and exact," while efficient was intended to mean "effective and working well." *Id.* at 4. Each of these, for the court, translated into a state obligation to create an equal opportunity to "educational excellence" for all students. *Id.*

Like other cases in this chapter, *DeRolphe* is but one episode in a program of protracted litigation. Like the decision in *Walter*, state officials have already appealed the ruling to an appellate court.

5. In *Abbott*, the State Commissioner of Education concluded that the New Jersey Constitution did not require equal expenditures per pupil, but rather required a minimum substantive level of education as defined in the Public School Education Act. Compare the Commissioner's response to the United States Supreme Court's decision in *Board of Educ. v. Rowley*, 458 U.S. 176 (1982), presented in Chapter 13, which held that the Education for All Handicapped Children's Act (EAHCA) (now Individuals with Disabilities Education Act (IDEA)) did not require the state to maximize the potential of each disabled child commensurate with the opportunity provided non-disabled children.

Does the *Rowley* decision make the Commissioner's opinion more acceptable? What was the New Jersey Supreme Court's response to such a position?

6. Under the analysis in *Abbott*, how would claims by residents of poor, rural districts fare — especially those in DFGs A and B, set aside by the *Abbott* case?

7. The New Jersey Legislature responded quickly to the lengthy *Abbott* opinion. A. Thomas Stubbs, in *After Rodriguez: Recent Developments in School Finance Reform*, 44 Tax Law. 313 (1990), *supra*, summarizes the resulting legislation and its impact:

> The response to *Abbott II* was swift. Less than one month after the decision was rendered, the legislature passed the Quality Education Act of 1990 (1990 Act) and the governor signed it into law. Of the $2.8 billion in new taxes raised by this "package" approximately $1 billion were targeted to poorer school districts, bringing total state education aid to $4.5 billion. The 1990 Act was approved over the strong protests of the teachers' union and Republican legislators.
>
> The new money comes from reductions in various spending programs, including education aid to wealthy school districts, as well as increases in personal income and sales taxes....

The 1990 Act establishes a new system for distributing State aid to school districts. Included in this new system is a requirement that a minimum amount, called the "foundation level," be spent on each student. Local districts will be required to contribute some money towards this foundation level, with the state paying the balance.

Pursuant to the mandate of *Abbott II*, the 1990 Act targets thirty poorer urban districts for special relief. These "special needs" districts will receive 5% extra aid. Also pursuant to *Abbott II*, the 1990 Act will eliminate minimum aid for 148 wealthy districts. In addition, responsibility for school employees' pensions will be shifted from the state to the local districts, with state aid going only to districts that qualify for foundation aid.

The new law also will limit growth in the budgets of wealthy school districts. The wealthiest of these districts will be allowed to grow only as fast as average income grows in New Jersey, a rate known as "PCI."[208]

The 1990 Act was passed in the face of some large obstacles including hostile public reaction. Most importantly, New Jersey's state government was running a deficit of $1.6 billion. The new revenues needed to close that gap alone could have posed a politically formidable challenge. In addition, New Jersey already ranked first in the nation in per pupil expenditures, so the statewide pressure for increasing school assistance was not overwhelming. Finally, the teachers' union — normally a staunch Democratic ally — and the Republicans made clear their intentions to use the tax increase and education reform votes against Democratic incumbents.

HELENA ELEMENTARY SCHOOL DISTRICT NO. 1 v. STATE OF MONTANA

Supreme Court of Montana
236 Mont. 44, 769 P.2d 684 (1989)

WEBER, JUSTICE:

In this action for declaratory judgment, plaintiffs challenge the constitutionality of the 1985-86 method of funding public elementary and secondary schools in the State of Montana....

....

In the 1985-86 school year, there were 545 school districts in Montana with a total student enrollment of 153,869. These included 382 elementary and 163 secondary districts. Nearly 45% of Montana schools have enrollments of less than 100 students.

... In addition to the General Fund, each school district uses up to nine other types of budgeted funds. These include transportation funds, teacher retirement funds, debt service funds, and building reserve funds. Some of these depend upon voted levies and all are primarily funded on a district or county level.

---

[208] "PCI" stands for per capita personal income....

CH. 14 FINANCING PUBLIC EDUCATION 1139

School districts also have nonbudgeted funds including food service, traffic education, rental funds, sick leave reserves, block grants, building funds, endowment funds, and interlocal agreement funds. Expenditures from these nonbudgeted funds may only be made from cash on hand.

The General Fund, which provides 70% of school funding in Montana, includes several components. In 1949, the Montana Legislature enacted the Montana School Foundation Program. Under that program, every two years the legislature sets "Maximum General Fund Budget Without a Vote" (MGFBWV) schedules for elementary and secondary school districts in the state. Eighty per cent of the MGFBWV is funded by county and state equalization revenues. These equalization revenues are derived from levies of 45 mills on all taxable property in each county and state aid from such sources as earmarked revenues, surplus county Foundation Program revenue, and direct legislative appropriations.

The remaining 20% of the funding of MGFBWV is through permissive mill levies of up to 6 mills for elementary districts and 4 mills for high school districts. These levies are made without a vote. If the school district is unable to obtain the MGFBWV level through permissive levies and other specified nonlevy revenue, state permissive equalization revenues are used to make up the difference.

The evidence shows that, in 1985-86, most school districts adopted budgets in excess of the MGFBWV. They utilized a third stage of funding under which monies were obtained primarily from property tax levies voted by each school district. Other revenues which were used in this third level of funding included vehicle taxes, interest income, tuition income, and federal "874" funds. By 1985-86, 35% of all General Fund budgets were obtained from this level of funding. In contrast, in 1950, the Foundation Program furnished 81.2% of all general fund revenues in Montana, leaving less than 20% of revenues to be obtained by local levies and other sources.

Plaintiffs presented voluminous evidence to support their theory that the system of funding public education in Montana is unconstitutional. The evidence established great differences in the wealth of the various school districts and, more significantly, established disparities of spending per pupil as high as 8 to 1 in comparisons between similarly-sized school districts. We affirm the following unchallenged findings of the District Court:

> 214. Several Plaintiff witnesses had experience either as teachers or administrators in other Montana districts, including some relatively wealthier districts. Mr. Walt Piipo, for example, currently Superintendent at Drummond, was previously Superintendent for Geraldine schools. The two school districts are very close in size, at both the elementary and high school levels. Geraldine's taxable valuation, however, is more than twice that of Drummond's. The tax efforts for the elementary schools are comparable, while Geraldine levies more General Fund mills than does Drummond at the high school level. Consequently, Geraldine spends

approximately $1,000 more per ANB than Drummond at the elementary level, and over $2,000 more per ANB at the high school level. Approximately 40% of Geraldine's General Fund revenues derive from the voted levy, while at Drummond, the voted levy supplies approximately 15% of General Fund revenue. This illustrates the fact that wealthier districts are able to rely to a greater extent on the voted levy to generate revenues for the General Fund.

215. Mr. Piipo testified unequivocally that Geraldine schools have advantages, and offer opportunities, which Drummond schools cannot afford. Geraldine has much greater budget flexibility to address educational needs and goals than does Drummond. Mr. Piipo testified that there is no question that the educational opportunities afforded students in Drummond could be improved if the district had the same amount of money as Geraldine.

216. The fact that spending disparities result in unequal educational opportunities was established more systematically by Plaintiffs' experts Dr. Ron Mattson, Mary Pace, and Dr. John Picton. Each of these individuals has many years' experience in Montana public education. They comprised a "Study Team" which was commissioned by the Plaintiffs to do a comparative study of several pairs of school districts in the State. They compared three pairs of elementary districts, and three pairs of secondary districts. Schools in each pair were of similar size, with one spending considerably more per pupil than the other. In addition to analyzing the budget data for each of these districts, members of the Study Team visited all 12 districts to observe the schools first hand, and to conduct interviews with administrators and teachers.

217. The Study Team identified clear differences between the schools in each of the pairs. They found that the better funded schools tended to offer more enriched and expanded curricula than those offered in the schools with less money. The richer schools were also better equipped in the areas of textbooks, instructional equipment, audio-visual instructional materials, and consumable supplies. With respect to buildings and facilities, the districts with more money were better able to maintain their facilities than were the poorer districts. The Study Team concluded:

* Availability of funds clearly affect the extent and quality of the educational opportunities.
* There is a positive correlation between the level of school funding and the level of educational opportunity.
* The better funded districts have a greater flexibility in the reallocation of resources to programs where there is a need.
* The differences in spending between the better funded and underfunded districts are clearly invested in educationally related programs.

* All 12 school districts in this study exhibited a responsible and judicious use of their financial resources.

R. Mattson, M. Pace, and J. Picton, Does Money Make a Difference in the Quality of Education in the Montana Schools?

218. Intervenor-Plaintiff MEA commissioned a study similar to that conducted by Plaintiffs' Study Team. Dr. Gary Gray, an assistant professor in Eastern Montana College's School of Education, studied educational opportunities in a number of high and low spending school districts in Montana. His methodology differed from that of the Plaintiffs' Study Team, but he arrived at essentially the same conclusions. Dr. Gray used an extensive checklist of indicators to compare educational opportunities among school districts within two expenditure classifications, a low expenditure category, and high expenditure category.

219. Dr. Gray concluded that there are substantial differences in educational opportunities among Montana school districts, which are manifested significantly between the high versus low expenditure categories which he studied....

220. In the specialty areas of physical education, music, and art, the wealthier schools offered more opportunities. Gifted and Talented Programs were much stronger in the high expenditure districts. Consistent with the situation in many Plaintiff districts, Dr. Gray found that many of the low expenditure districts could not even afford to offer a Gifted and Talented Program.

221. With respect to computers, he found significant differences, with the high expenditure districts having more and better computers and computer labs. He also found significant differences between the two expenditure categories for library and media center services, with the high expenditure districts having larger and newer book collections, larger periodical collections, larger reference collections, larger audio-visual collections, and better special collections.

222. With respect to facilities, high expenditure districts reported that they have not had to defer necessary maintenance or work projects due to a lack of funds, as have low expenditure districts.

223. Wealthier districts also offer a wider range of extracurricular activities to students than low expenditure districts.

224. In sum, the comparative evidence establishes that spending differences among similarly sized school districts in the State result in unequal educational opportunities for students. Furthermore, the comparative evidence verifies the fact that the deficiencies and problems identified by Plaintiff witnesses are part of a consistent pattern in lower-spending districts, and that such deficiencies and problems are not consistently found in relatively higher spending districts. [footnotes and citations to exhibits omitted].

The problems were compounded by the adoption of Initiative 105 in the November 1986 general election. In 1987 the Legislature adopted Senate Bill 71. *See* §§ 15-10-401, -402, -411, and -412, MCA. The District Court correctly found that the net effect was to freeze property tax levies at 1986 levels, which resulted in the locking in of any disparities and inequities.

Federal "874" funding is not presently included in the State's computations for the funding of schools. However, plaintiffs' experts did include "874" funds in some of their studies comparing the wealth of various school districts. Intervenor-defendant *Hays-Lodge Pole Elementary School Dist., et al.*, (*Hays-Lodge Pole*) is an association of Montana public schools which receive "874" funds by reason of the attendance of Indian students on and around the 7 federal treaty reservations in Montana. *Hays-Lodge Pole* argued that "874" funds should remain outside of the State's budgetary process.

The District Court concluded that education is a fundamental right under Montana's Constitution. It concluded that, under the 1985-86 system of funding public elementary and secondary schools, disparities in per pupil spending among schools as a result of disparities in local property wealth do not even pass the rational basis test of equal protection analysis. It concluded that the concept of local control is not related to the spending disparities now present. It further concluded that the State's budgetary difficulties do not constitute a legal defense to these inequalities.

The court also concluded that the Montana School Accreditation standards do not define the constitutional right to education. It concluded that the treatment of federal "874" funding for schools with Indian enrollment exacerbates the inequalities present in the school finance system. The court ordered that the present system of school funding may remain in effect until October 1, 1989, and retained jurisdiction, but left to the Legislature the task of fashioning a constitutional funding system.

The State of Montana and defendants Holje, Ward, and Frederich appeal the District Court's determination that the present system of school funding is unconstitutional.... *Hays-Lodge Pole* raises five allegations of error in the District Court's ruling that federal "874" funding should be considered for purposes of equalization....

I

Does Montana's system of funding the public schools violate the education article, Art. X, of the Montana Constitution?

Art. X, Sec. 1, Mont. Const., provides:

> (1) It is the goal of the people to establish a system of education which will develop the full educational potential of each person. Equality of educational opportunity is guaranteed to each person of the state.

(2) The state recognizes the distinct and unique cultural heritage of the American Indians and is committed in its educational goals to the preservation of their cultural integrity.

(3) The legislature shall provide a basic system of free quality public elementary and secondary schools. The legislature may provide such other educational institutions, public libraries, and educational programs as it deems desirable. It shall fund and distribute in an equitable manner to the school districts the state's share of the cost of the basic elementary and secondary school system.

By referring to the discussions in the transcript of the 1972 Montana Constitutional Convention, the State contends the provision in subsection (1) that "[e]quality of educational opportunity is guaranteed to each person," is an aspirational goal only. We disagree with that contention. In interpreting the Constitution, as in statutory construction, this Court must first look to the plain meaning of the words used. *State ex rel. Cashmore v. Anderson* (1972), 160 Mont. 175, 184, 500 P.2d 921, 926. In the first sentence of Art. X, Sec. 1(1), the framers of the Constitution clearly stated the "goal" of the people to establish a system of education which will develop the full educational potential of each person. In the next sentence, the framers did not use the term "goal." Instead they stated that equality of educational opportunity "is guaranteed" to each person of the state. As we review our Constitution, we do not find any other instance in which the Constitution "guarantees" a particular right. We conclude that the plain meaning of the second sentence of subsection (1) is that each person is guaranteed equality of educational opportunity. The plain meaning of that sentence is clear and unambiguous.

The State argues that the last sentence of subsection (3) limits the Legislature's duty in connection with the guarantee of equal educational opportunity. It points out that Foundation Program funds are conceded by all parties to have been distributed in an equitable manner, and then suggests that because the State has distributed such funds in an equitable manner as required under the last sentence of subsection (3), the Legislature has met its constitutional obligations as required under Art. X, Sec. 1.

Art. X, Sec. 1(3), Mont. Const., requires that the Legislature shall provide a basic system of free quality education, that it may provide various types of educational institutions and programs, and that the state's share of the cost of the basic system shall be distributed in an equitable manner. There is nothing in the plain wording of subsection (3) to suggest that the clear statement of the obligations on the part of the Legislature in some manner was intended to be a limitation on the guarantee of equal educational opportunity contained in subsection (1). The guarantee provision of subsection (1) is not limited to any one branch of government.... We specifically conclude that the guarantee of equality of educational opportunity applies to each person of the State of

Montana, and is binding upon all branches of government whether at the state, local, or school district level....

The evidence presented at the trial of this case clearly and unequivocally established large differences, unrelated to "educationally relevant factors," in per pupil spending among the various school districts of Montana. The evidence also demonstrated that the wealthier school districts are not funding frills or unnecessary educational expenses. Plaintiffs' expert witnesses testified that discrepancies in spending as large as the ones present in Montana translate, in their opinions, into unequal educational opportunities. There was also unrebutted testimony that Foundation Program funding falls short of even meeting the costs of complying with Montana's minimum accreditation standards.

The State attempted to present an argument at trial that equality of educational opportunity is more appropriately measured by output, that is, by analysis of the success of students from the different school districts, rather than by input of dollars. The District Court concluded that the State had failed to submit convincing evidence on the output theory of measurement. We agree with that conclusion on the basis of this record. The District Court found similarly unpersuasive the argument that statewide fiscal difficulties in the last few years somehow excuse the disparities in the spending per pupil in the various school districts. We agree with the District Court that such fiscal difficulties in no way justify perpetuating inequities.

The State also argued that the Constitutional directive of local control of school districts, Art. X, Sec. 8, Mont. Const., requires that spending disparities among the districts be allowed to exist. That section provides: "School district trustees. The supervision and control of schools in each school district shall be vested in a board of trustees to be elected as provided by law." While Section 8 does establish that the supervision and control of schools shall be vested in the board of trustees, there is no specific reference to the concept of spending disparities. Further, as made especially apparent after the passage of Initiative 105, the spending disparities among Montana's school districts cannot be described as the result of local control. In fact, as the District Court correctly found, the present system of funding may be said to deny to poorer school districts a significant level of local control, because they have fewer options due to fewer resources. We conclude that Art. X, Sec. 8, Mont. Const., does not allow the type of spending disparities outlined in the above quoted findings of fact.

In 1972, when our Constitutional Convention met, approximately 65% of General Fund revenues were funded through the Foundation Program. Con. Con. Tr. 2157. The transcript of the debate on Art. X, Sec. 1(3), Mont. Const., clearly expresses the delegates' concern with that level of funding. *See* for example, Con. Con. Tr. 1981-86, 2152-59.

We conclude that as a result of the failure to adequately fund the Foundation Program, forcing an excessive reliance on permissive and voted levies, the State has failed to provide a system of quality public education granting to each student the equality of educational opportunity guaranteed under Art. X, Sec. 1, Mont.

Const. We specifically affirm that portion of the District Court's Conclusion of Law 17 which holds that the spending disparities among the State's school districts translate into a denial of equality of educational opportunity. We hold that the 1985-86 system of funding public elementary and secondary schools in Montana is in violation of Article X, Section 1 of the Montana Constitution.

In analyzing school funding under an equal protection analysis pursuant to the provisions of Art. II, Sec. 4, Mont. Const., the District Court concluded that education is a fundamental right and also made numerous and extensive findings of fact and adopted a number of conclusions of law. Because we have concluded that the school funding system is unconstitutional under Art. X, Sec. 1, Mont. Const., we do not find it necessary to consider the equal protection issue. We therefore make no decision with regard to the findings of fact and conclusions of law relating to the equal protection of the laws analysis of the District Court, and in particular do not rule upon the determination by the District Court that education is a fundamental right.

....

III

Did the District Court err in its findings and conclusions relating to consideration in the equalization process of federal "874" funding?

Public Law 81-874 ("874") was enacted by the United States Congress in 1950. It provides federal payments to school districts which serve children who reside on or whose parents are employed on federal property, including Indian lands, or who have a parent on active duty in the military.

Hays-Lodge Pole asserts that, contrary to the District Court's finding, Public Law 81-874 has as one of its purposes assisting with the special problems in Indian education and is not only a federal effort to replace lost tax revenue resulting from the federal presence. It argues also that the court's finding that, in some districts, "874" funding has been used as tax relief is irrelevant and shows only the State's neglect of the special needs of Indian children. It contends that "874" funding is closely tied to the need on and near Indian reservations for additional school funding because of the extraordinary educational difficulties present-language barriers, poverty, unemployment, and cultural differences. It maintains that any inequity present in "874" districts will vanish when the Montana funding system is equalized without consideration of "874" funding and that the history of neglect of Indian education justifies judicial protection of the benefits provided by "874" funding. Hays-Lodge Pole argues that the District Court erred in ruling that the Legislature may consider "874" funding in equalization.

This issue is resolved by the federal statutory requirement that the United States Secretary of Education must approve of Montana's equalization plan before "874" funding may be taken into account. 20 U.S.C.A. § 240(d) (Supp.1988). The District Court recognized this requirement in its finding no. 235, and found that Montana's system had not secured that federal approval. We specifically affirm the District Court's Conclusions No. 20:

> 20. A state may factor P.L. 81-874 revenue into its school finance equalization system only if the system meets the federal definition of an equalized program, subject to the determination of the Secretary of Education. [*See Gwinn Area Community Schools v. State of Michigan*, 741 F.2d 840 (6th Cir. 1984).] Montana presently does not and may not factor P.L. 81-874 revenue into the Foundation Program equalization formula, because Montana's system does not meet the federal definition of an equalized program.

....

TURNAGE, C.J., and HARRISON, SHEEHY, GULBRANDSON, HUNT and MCDONOUGH, JJ., concur.

....

---

1. Like the decision in *Abbott*, the *Helena* decision circumvented the question of whether education is a fundamental right and, instead, focused on the education clause of the State Constitution ruling that it guaranteed equality of educational opportunity. What is the difference between the two cases as it relates to factual findings? Is there a difference between the basic urban inadequacy as found in *Abbott* and rural inadequacy as pronounced in *Helena* as regards an equal opportunity?

2. "The State attempted to present an argument at trial that equality of educational opportunity is more appropriately measured by output, that is, by analysis of the success of the students from the different school districts, rather than by input of dollars." *Helena*, at 54.

Is there something to this output-based measurement of educational opportunity? Is there a danger that, even if such a method is effective, it waits too long in the lives of school children to determine if school districts are providing equal adequate educational opportunities? Recall also the brief discussion of the New Jersey proficiency tests and the results among school districts.

3. The *Helena* court held that the constitutional directive of local control for school districts does not permit spending disparities between school districts that adversely affect the constitutional guarantee of equal educational opportunity. How does the court justify such a decision? Compare this to the holding in *Abbott*; are the analyses as relative to spending disparities parallel? If not, is the difference between the two cases primarily based on state constitutional language?

EDGEWOOD INDEPENDENT SCHOOL DISTRICT v. KIRBY

Supreme Court of Texas
777 S.W.2d 391 (1989)

MAUZY, JUSTICE:

At issue is the constitutionality of the Texas system for financing the education of public school children. Edgewood Independent School District, sixty-seven other school districts, and numerous individual school children and parents filed suit seeking a declaration that the Texas school financing system violates the Texas Constitution. The trial court rendered judgment to that effect and declared that the system violates the Texas Constitution, article I, section 3, article I, section 19, and article VII, section 1. By a 2-1 vote, the court of appeals reversed that judgment and declared the system constitutional. We reverse the judgment of the court of appeals and, with modification, affirm that of the trial court.

The basic facts of this cause are not in dispute. The only question is whether those facts describe a public school financing system that meets the requirements of the Constitution. As summarized and excerpted, the facts are as follows.

There are approximately three million public school children in Texas. The legislature finances the education of these children through a combination of revenues supplied by the state itself and revenues supplied by local school districts which are governmental subdivisions of the state. Of total education costs, the state provides about forty-two percent, school districts provide about fifty percent, and the remainder comes from various other sources including federal funds. School districts derive revenues from local ad valorem property taxes, and the state raises funds from a variety of sources including the sales tax and various severance and excise taxes.

There are glaring disparities in the abilities of the various school districts to raise revenues from property taxes because taxable property wealth varies greatly from district to district. The wealthiest district has over $14,000,000 of property wealth per student, while the poorest has approximately $20,000; this disparity reflects a 700 to 1 ratio. The 300,000 students in the lowest-wealth schools have less than 3% of the state's property wealth to support their education while the 300,000 students in the highest-wealth schools have over 25% of the state's property wealth; thus the 300,000 students in the wealthiest districts have more than eight times the property value to support their education as the 300,000 students in the poorest districts. The average property wealth in the 100 wealthiest districts is more than twenty times greater than the average property wealth in the 100 poorest districts. Edgewood I.S.D. has $38,854 in property wealth per student; Alamo Heights I.S.D., in the same county, has $570,109 in property wealth per student.

The state has tried for many years to lessen the disparities through various efforts to supplement the poorer districts. Through the Foundation School Program, the state currently attempts to ensure that each district has sufficient funds to provide its students with at least a basic education. *See* Tex.Educ.Code § 16.002. Under this program, state aid is distributed to the various districts according to a complex formula such that property-poor districts receive more state aid than do property-rich districts. However, the Foundation School Program does not cover even the cost of meeting the state-mandated minimum requirements. Most importantly, there are no Foundation School Program allotments for school facilities or for debt service. The basic allotment and the transportation allotment understate actual costs, and the career ladder salary supplement for teachers is underfunded. For these reasons and more, almost all school districts spend additional local funds. Low-wealth districts use a significantly greater proportion of their local funds to pay the debt service on construction bonds while high-wealth districts are able to use their funds to pay for a wide array of enrichment programs.

Because of the disparities in district property wealth, spending per student varies widely, ranging from $2,112 to $19,333. Under the existing system, an average of $2,000 more per year is spent on each of the 150,000 students in the wealthiest districts than is spent on the 150,000 students in the poorest districts.

The lower expenditures in the property-poor districts are not the result of lack of tax effort. Generally, the property-rich districts can tax low and spend high while the property-poor districts must tax high merely to spend low. In 1985-86, local tax rates ranged from $.09 to $1.55 per $100 valuation. The 100 poorest districts had an average tax rate of 74.5 cents and spent an average of $2,978 per student. The 100 wealthiest districts had an average tax rate of 47 cents and spent an average of $7,233 per student.... Many districts have become tax havens. The existing funding system permits "budget balanced districts" which, at minimal tax rates, can still spend above the statewide average; if forced to tax at just average tax rates, these districts would generate additional revenues of more than $200,000,000 annually for public education.

Property-poor districts are trapped in a cycle of poverty from which there is no opportunity to free themselves. Because of their inadequate tax base, they must tax at significantly higher rates in order to meet minimum requirements for accreditation; yet their educational programs are typically inferior. The location of new industry and development is strongly influenced by tax rates and the quality of local schools. Thus, the property-poor districts with their high tax rates and inferior schools are unable to attract new industry or development and so have little opportunity to improve their tax base.

The amount of money spent on a student's education has a real and meaningful impact on the educational opportunity offered that student. High-wealth districts are able to provide for their students broader educational experiences including more extensive curricula, more up-to-date technological equipment, better libraries and library personnel, teacher aides, counseling services, lower student-teacher ratios, better facilities, parental involvement programs, and drop-out prevention programs. They are also better able to attract and retain experienced teachers and administrators.

The differences in the quality of educational programs offered are dramatic. For example, San Elizario I.S.D. offers no foreign language, no pre-kindergarten program, no chemistry, no physics, no calculus, and no college preparatory or honors program. It also offers virtually no extra-curricular activities such as band, debate, or football. At the time of trial, one-third of Texas school districts did not even meet the state-mandated standards for maximum class size. The great majority of these are low-wealth districts. In many instances, wealthy and poor districts are found contiguous to one another within the same county.

Based on these facts, the trial court concluded that the school financing system violates the Texas Constitution's equal rights guarantee of article I, section 3, the due course of law guarantee of article I, section 19, and the "efficiency" mandate of article VII, section 1. The court of appeals reversed. We reverse the judgment of the court of appeals and, with modification, affirm the judgment of the trial court.

Article VII, section 1 of the Texas Constitution provides:

> A general diffusion of knowledge being essential to the preservation of the liberties and rights of the people, it shall be the duty of the Legislature of the State to establish and make suitable provision for the support and maintenance of an efficient system of public free schools.

....

The State argues that, as used in article VII, section 1, the word "efficient" was intended to suggest a simple and inexpensive system. Under the Reconstruction Constitution of 1869, the people had been subjected to a militaristic school system with the state exercising absolute authority over the training of children. *See* Tex. Const. art. VII, § 1, interp. commentary (Vernon 1955). Thus, the State contends that delegates to the 1875 Constitutional Convention deliberately inserted into this provision the word "efficient" in order to prevent the establishment of another Reconstruction-style, highly centralized school system.

While there is some evidence that many delegates wanted an economical school system, there is no persuasive evidence that the delegates used the term "efficient" to achieve that end. *See* Journal of the Constitutional Convention of the State of Texas 136 (Oct. 8, 1875); S. McKay, Debates in the Texas Constitutional Convention of 1875, 107, 217, 350-351 (1930). It must be recognized that the Constitution requires an "efficient," not an "economical," "inexpensive," or "cheap" system. The language of the Constitution must be presumed to have been carefully selected. *Leander Indep. School Dist. v. Cedar Park Water Supply Corp.*, 479 S.W.2d 908 (Tex.1972); *Cramer v. Sheppard*, 140 Tex. 271, 167 S.W.2d 147 (Tex.1943). The framers used the term "economical" elsewhere[2] and could have done so here had they so intended.

---

[2] ... Tex. Const. art. III, § 48 (1876, repealed 1969).

There is no reason to think that "efficient" meant anything different in 1875 from what it now means. "Efficient" conveys the meaning of effective or productive of results and connotes the use of resources so as to produce results with little waste; this meaning does not appear to have changed over time.... One dictionary used by the framers defined efficient as follows:

> Causing effects; producing results; actively operative; not inactive, slack or incapable; characterized by energetic and useful activity.... N. Webster, An American Dictionary of the English Language 430 (1864)....

Considering "the general spirit of the times and the prevailing sentiments of the people," it is apparent from the historical record that those who drafted and ratified article VII, section 1 never contemplated the possibility that such gross inequalities could exist within an "efficient" system.... At the Constitutional Convention of 1875, delegates spoke at length on the importance of education for all the people of this state, rich and poor alike. The chair of the education committee, speaking on behalf of the majority of the committee, declared:

> [Education] must be classed among the abstract rights, based on apparent natural justice, which we individually concede to the State, for the general welfare, when we enter into a great compact as a commonwealth. I boldly assert that it is for the general welfare of all, rich and poor, male and female, that the means of a common school education should, if possible, be placed within the reach of every child in the State. S. McKay, Debates in the Texas Constitutional Convention of 1875, 198 (1930).

Other delegates recognized the importance of a diffusion of knowledge among the masses not only for the preservation of democracy, but for the prevention of crime and for the growth of the economy. *See, e.g., id.* at 199-200, 216-217, 335.

....

If our state's population had grown at the same rate in each district and if the taxable wealth in each district had also grown at the same rate, efficiency could probably have been maintained within the structure of the present system. That did not happen. Wealth, in its many forms, has not appeared with geographic symmetry. The economic development of the state has not been uniform. Some cities have grown dramatically, while their sister communities have remained static or have shrunk. Formulas that once fit have been knocked askew. Although local conditions vary, the constitutionally imposed state responsibility for an efficient education system is the same for all citizens regardless of where they live.

We conclude that, in mandating "efficiency," the constitutional framers and ratifiers did not intend a system with such vast disparities as now exist. Instead, they stated clearly that the purpose of an efficient system was to provide for a "*general* diffusion of knowledge." (Emphasis added.) The present system, by contrast, provides not for a diffusion that is general, but for one that is limited and unbalanced. The resultant inequalities are thus directly contrary to the constitutional vision of efficiency.

The State argues that the 1883 constitutional amendment of article VII, section 3 expressly authorizes the present financing system. However, we conclude that this provision was intended not to preclude an efficient system but to serve as a vehicle for injecting more money into an efficient system. James E. Hill, a legislator and supporter of the 1883 amendment, argued:

> If [article VII, section 1] means anything, and is to be enforced, then additional power must be granted to obtain the means "to support and maintain" an efficient system of public free schools. What is such a system, then? is the question. I have examined the laws of the older States of this Union, especially those noted for efficient free schools, and not one is supported alone by State aid, but that aid is supplemented always by local taxation.... *Galveston Daily News*, August 10, 1883, at 3, col. 9 (interview with Hon. James E. Hill).

....

In the context of article VII, section 1, the legislature has expressed its understanding of the term "efficient" for a long time even though it has never given the term full effect. Sixty years ago, the legislature enacted the Rural Aid Appropriations Act with the express purpose of "equalizing the educational opportunities afforded by the State...." 1929 Tex. Gen. Laws, ch. 14 at 252 (3rd called session). Again, in creating the Gilmer-Aikin Committee to study school finance, the legislature indicated an awareness of this obligation when it spoke of "the foresight and evident intention of the founders of our State and the framers of our State Constitution to provide equal educational advantages for all." Tex.H.Con.Res. 48, 50th Leg. (1948). Moreover, section 16.001 of the legislatively enacted Education Code expresses the state's policy that "a thorough and efficient system be provided ... so that each student ... shall have access to programs and services ... that are substantially equal to those available to any similar student, notwithstanding varying economic factors." Not only the legislature, but also this court has previously recognized the implicit link that the Texas Constitution establishes between efficiency and equality....

By statutory directives, the legislature has attempted through the years to reduce disparities and improve the system. There have been good faith efforts on the part of many public officials, and some progress has been made. However, as the undisputed facts of this case make painfully clear, the reality is that the constitutional mandate has not been met.

The legislature's recent efforts have focused primarily on increasing the state's contributions. More money allocated under the present system would reduce some of the existing disparities between districts but would at best only postpone the reform that is necessary to make the system efficient. A band-aid will not suffice; the system itself must be changed.

We hold that the state's school financing system is neither financially efficient nor efficient in the sense of providing for a "general diffusion of knowledge" statewide, and therefore that it violates article VII, section 1 of the Texas Constitution. Efficiency does not require a per capita distribution, but it also does not allow concentrations of resources in property-rich school districts that are taxing low when property-poor districts that are taxing high cannot generate sufficient revenues to meet even minimum standards. There must be a direct and close correlation between a district's tax effort and the educational resources available to it; in other words, districts must have substantially equal access to similar revenues per pupil at similar levels of tax effort. Children who live in poor districts and children who live in rich districts must be afforded a substantially equal opportunity to have access to educational funds. Certainly, this much is required if the state is to educate its populace efficiently and provide for a general diffusion of knowledge statewide.

Under article VII, section 1, the obligation is the legislature's to provide for an efficient system. In setting appropriations, the legislature must establish priorities according to constitutional mandate; equalizing educational opportunity cannot be relegated to an "if funds are left over" basis. We recognize that there are and always will be strong public interests competing for available state funds. However, the legislature's responsibility to support public education is different because it is constitutionally imposed. Whether the legislature acts directly or enlists local government to help meet its obligation, the end product must still be what the constitution commands — i.e. an efficient system of public free schools throughout the state. *See Lee v. Leonard Indep. School Dist.*, 24 S.W.2d 449, 450 (Tex.Civ.App. — Texarkana 1930, *writ ref'd*). This does not mean that the state may not recognize differences in area costs or in costs associated with providing an equalized educational opportunity to atypical students or disadvantaged students. Nor does it mean that local communities would be precluded from supplementing an efficient system established by the legislature; however any local enrichment must derive solely from local tax effort.

Some have argued that reform in school finance will eliminate local control, but this argument has no merit. An efficient system does not preclude the ability of communities to exercise local control over the education of their children. It requires only that the funds available for education be distributed equitably and evenly. An efficient system will actually allow for more local control, not less. It will provide property-poor districts with economic alternatives that are not now available to them. Only if alternatives are indeed available can a community exercise the control of making choices.

. . . .

Although we have ruled the school financing system to be unconstitutional, we do not now instruct the legislature as to the specifics of the legislation it should enact; nor do we order it to raise taxes. The legislature has primary responsibility to decide how best to achieve an efficient system. We decide only the nature of the constitutional mandate and whether that mandate has been met. Because we hold that the mandate of efficiency has not been met, we reverse the judgment of the court of appeals. The legislature is duty-bound to provide for an efficient system of education, and only if the legislature fulfills that duty can we launch this great state into a strong economic future with educational opportunity for all.

Because of the enormity of the task now facing the legislature and because we want to avoid any sudden disruption in the educational processes, we modify the trial court's judgment so as to stay the effect of its injunction until May 1, 1990. However, let there be no misunderstanding. A remedy is long overdue. The legislature must take immediate action. We reverse the judgment of the court of appeals and affirm the trial court's judgment as modified.

---

1. When *Edgewood* came to the attention of the Texas Supreme Court, the case revealed a classic pattern of revenue disparities between property-rich and property-poor school districts. District spending per pupil ranged from about $2,000 per pupil to almost $20,000 per pupil. Involved in these disparities were the Alamo Heights Independent School District and the Edgewood Independent School District, the same as those featured in *Rodriguez*. Why did the *Edgewood* court not cite to or even mention *Rodriguez*? Were the approaches toward funding different? Were the legal issues that far afield?

2. Compare *Edgewood* to *Abbott v. Burke*, *supra* this chapter. Are there differences between "efficient" as in *Edgewood* and "thorough and efficient" as in *Abbott*? Does the court see a difference? What of the Texas legislature?

3. The Texas Constitution requires a system that will allow for a "general diffusion of knowledge" statewide. Do the remedies in the cases and notes presented in this chapter cause or require richer districts to do with less or offer lesser quality in an effort to equalize educational opportunity across the state? Does this mean that the property-rich districts should be willing to settle for less so that all students get an equal opportunity? How does the court in *Edgewood* respond to these concerns?

4. The "education clause" of the Texas Constitution was important to the decision in *Edgewood*. The court examined the intent of the framers and decided that this was to provide for equality of opportunity between school districts, not to simply supply a minimum level of education as the state had argued. However, the court did not demand the elimination of inadequately financed school programs. Instead, it placed on the state legislature the more limited requirement that poor and rich districts have "equal opportunity to have access to educational funds." In the jargon of school finance, this requires the state to establish a "district power equalization program," otherwise known as a guaranteed valuation plan, under which equal tax rates must yield equal local expenditures per student. State subsidies make up shortfalls and are obviously higher in poor districts. In fact, under such a system, rich districts may not be entitled to any state subsidy. Did the court mandate how the tax-base equalization plan must be

put into effect? Was the court, no matter the answer, playing a quasi-legislative role?

5. This case represents a typically protracted example of school funding legislation. It is noteworthy because of the continued points of contention inspired by the great differences of opinion about the meaning of "efficient." The legislature responded to the State Supreme Court ruling by passing Senate Bill One, 1990 Tex. Gen. Laws 1 (codified in Sections of Tex. Educ. Code Ann. Secs. 16.001-16.403 (West 1991). The bill established a three-tiered school financing arrangement. In the lower tier, districts would levy a uniform property tax rate to support a kind of minimum standard school program. If the state-mandated uniform property tax rate did not generate enough money to support the minimum program, the state would provide the difference between the local yield and the total district cost. The second tier is a power-equalized stratum between the uniform tax rate for the minimum program and a maximum equalized school tax rate. Within the second tier all districts would receive the same dollars per student for each penny increase in the local tax rate. The third tier is unequalized, without state subsidy, and with no upper limit of expenditures.

The state supreme court was not impressed and declared that the bill had failed to accomplish the mandate from its earlier decision of equalization, *i.e.*, "although [the] statute provided guaranteed revenue per student per each cent of local tax effort over specified minimum, [the] statute remained unconstitutional for failure to remedy major causes of wide opportunity gaps between rich and poor school districts." *Edgewood Indep. Sch. Dist. v. Kirby*, 804 S.W.2d 491 (Tex. 1991). The court also ruled that although the state's school finance system was unconstitutional, future plaintiffs could not challenge the system in order to avoid paying taxes.

The "challenge" portion of the State Supreme Court holding became the subject of a case brought in Federal District Court, *Smith v. Travis County Educ. Dist.*, 791 F. Supp. 1170 (W.D. Tex. 1992). Texas taxpayers, contrary to the State Supreme Court ruling, brought action challenging the court's refusal to provide a remedy to taxpayers who paid property taxes under a system found unconstitutional. The District Court, citing precedent in other cases, determined that the State Supreme Court decision was a deliberate statement of law and it was incumbent for the Federal Court to exercise judicial restraint when reviewing such an action; hence, it chose not to expand or restrict the rulings of the State Court. The court finalized its opinion by citing alternative means in state court that the plaintiffs could pursue.

ROSE v. COUNCIL FOR BETTER EDUCATION, INC.

Supreme Court of Kentucky
790 S.W.2d 186 (1989)

STEPHENS, CHIEF JUSTICE:

The issue we decide on this appeal is whether the Kentucky General Assembly has complied with its constitutional mandate to "provide an efficient system of common schools throughout the state."[1]

In deciding that it has not, we intend no criticism of the substantial efforts made by the present General Assembly and by its predecessors, nor do we intend to substitute our judicial authority for the authority and discretion of the General Assembly. We are, rather, exercising our constitutional duty in declaring that, when we consider the evidence in the record, and when we apply the constitutional requirement of Section 183 to that evidence, it is crystal clear that the General Assembly has fallen short of its duty to enact legislation to provide for an efficient system of common schools throughout the state. In a word, the present system of common schools in Kentucky is not an "efficient" one in our view of the clear mandate of Section 183. The common school system in Kentucky is constitutionally deficient.

In reaching this decision, we are ever mindful of the immeasurable worth of education to our state and its citizens, especially to its young people. The framers of our constitution intended that each and every child in this state should receive a proper and an adequate education, to be provided for by the General Assembly. This opinion dutifully applies the constitutional test of Section 183 to the existing system of common schools. We do no more, nor may we do any less.

....

I. *Procedural History*

This declaratory judgment action was filed in the Franklin Circuit Court by multiple plaintiffs, including the Council for Better Education, Inc. a non-profit Kentucky corporation whose membership consists of sixty-six local school districts in the state. Also joining as plaintiffs were the Boards of Education of the Dayton and Harlan Independent School Districts and the school districts of Elliott, Knox, McCreary, Morgan and Wolfe Counties. Twenty-two public school students from McCreary, Wolfe, Morgan and Elliott Counties and Harlan and Dayton Independent School districts were also named, suing, respectively, by and through their parents as next friends.

....

The defendants named in the complaint were the Governor, the Superintendent of Public Instruction, the State Treasurer, the President Pro Tempore of the Senate, the Speaker of the House of Representatives and the State Board of Education and its individual members.

---

[1] Ky. Const. Sec. 183.

The complaint included allegations that the system of school financing provided for by the General Assembly is inadequate; places too much emphasis on local school board resources; and results in inadequacies, inequities and inequalities throughout the state so as to result in an inefficient system of common school education in violation of Kentucky Constitution, Sections 1, 3 and 183 and the equal protection clause and the due process of law clause of the 14th Amendment to the United States Constitution. Additionally the complaint maintains the entire system is not efficient under the mandate of Section 183.

The relief sought by the plaintiffs was a declaration of rights to the effect that the system be declared unconstitutional; that the funding of schools also be determined to be unconstitutional and inadequate; that the defendant, Superintendent of Public Instruction be enjoined from further implementing said school statutes; that a mandamus be issued, directing the Governor to recommend to the General Assembly the enactment of appropriate legislation which would be in compliance with the aforementioned constitutional provisions; that a mandamus be issued, directing the President Pro Tempore of the Senate and the Speaker of the House of Representatives to place before the General Assembly appropriate legislation which is constitutionally valid; and that a mandamus be issued, directing the General Assembly to provide for an "equitable and adequate funding program for all school children so as to establish an 'efficient system of common schools.'"

The answers filed by the various defendants were basically identical. It was pled that the complaint failed to state a claim against any of the defendants; that the court had no jurisdiction because the subject matter is purely a "political" one; that all school boards should have been joined as parties defendants; that all members of the General Assembly (1986) should also have been joined as parties defendant; that all the plaintiffs lacked standing to bring the action; that, specifically, the plaintiff Council for Better Education, Inc., had no legal authority to sue; that the plaintiff school boards similarly had no legal authority to sue; that the class action was improper; and as would be expected, the defendants denied all of the alleged constitutional violations and the facts underlying such alleged violations.

The defendants also filed a self-styled "affirmative defense" claiming that education reform laws passed by the General Assembly at a special session in 1985 and various budget changes and other educational laws passed by the General Assembly at its 1986 regular session inferentially corrected the situation alleged in the complaint. Reference was also made to past legislative efforts of the General Assembly in the education field, presumably to further demonstrate the General Assembly's compliance with its constitutional mandate.

....

The case was tried by the court without the intervention of a jury. Evidence was presented by deposition, along with oral testimony and much documentary evidence. The trial court ... found Kentucky's common school finance system to

CH. 14 FINANCING PUBLIC EDUCATION 1157

be unconstitutional and discriminatory and held that the General Assembly had not produced an efficient system of common schools throughout the state....

A notice of appeal was timely filed by the present appellants, John A. Rose, President Pro Tempore of the Senate of Kentucky and Donald J. Blandford, Speaker of the House of Representatives of Kentucky.

Upon a motion properly made, we transferred the appeal to this Court.

II. *Analysis of Trial Court's Findings of Fact Conclusions of Law and Judgment*

Following the trial of this case, the circuit judge, in three separate documents, prepared extensive findings of fact, conclusions of law and judgment(s)....

Document Number I

....

The trial judge identified four issues before him: (1) The necessity for defining the phrase "an efficient system of common schools" as contained in Section 183 of the Kentucky Constitution; (2) Whether education is a "fundamental right" under our Constitution; (3) Whether Kentucky's current method of financing its common schools violates Section 183, and (4) Whether students in the so-called "poor" school districts are denied equal protection of the laws.

"Efficient," in the Kentucky constitutional sense was defined as a system which required "substantial uniformity, substantial equality of financial resources and substantial equal educational opportunity for all students." Efficient was also interpreted to require that the educational system must be adequate, uniform and unitary.

Because of the language of Section 183, the trial court ruled that education, indeed, is a fundamental right in Kentucky.

In ruling on the issue of whether Kentucky's method of school financing violates Section 183 and underpinning the point with extensive findings of fact, the trial court declared that students in property poor school districts are offered a minimal level of educational opportunities, which is inferior to those offered to students in more affluent districts. Such "invidious" discrimination, based on the place of a student's residence, was determined to be unconstitutional. The trial court ruled that the school finance system violates the equal protection guarantees of Section 1 and 3 of the Kentucky Constitution.

....

In this open ended document, the Court ruled the school finance system unconstitutional, but gave few guidelines, or criteria, to guide the General Assembly in any action it might take to rectify the constitutional failure. The work of the Committee, if adopted by the Court, was to serve as a guidepost in this murky area.

Document Number II

On June 7, 1988, the trial court, in this document, appointed the members of the "select committee." Apparently fearing he would improperly delegate some of his judicial authority by the creation of this committee, the trial judge emphasized that its role would be "advisory only" to him. But he noted that the report would be of "immense benefit" to him in preparing his final judgment. The Committee was ordered to complete its work by September 15, 1988.

Modifying or explaining part of document # I, the court emphatically stated that there is "no judicial intent to merely redivide the funds now available to the common school districts." Moreover, he emphasized that funds should not be taken away (presumably by the General Assembly) from any school district to increase the funding level of more impoverished districts. It is a fair inference from this statement that the trial court was strongly suggesting that additional revenues were needed to make the system "efficient."

....

Document Number III

This final order entered on October 14, 1988, and, cumulated with the first two documents, constitutes the subject matter of this appeal.

....

In his additional Findings of Fact, the judge modified his previous definition of an "efficient" system of schools. It is a "... tax supported, coordinated organization, which provides a free, adequate education to all students throughout the state, regardless of geographical location or local fiscal resources." He opined that an efficient system (of schools) must have "substantial" uniformity.

Ever broadening the definition and setting non-instructional standards, the trial court required an efficient school system to provide sufficient physical facilities, teachers, support personnel, and instructional materials to enhance the educational process. An adequate school system must also include careful and comprehensive supervision at all levels to monitor personnel performance and minimize waste. If and where waste and mismanagement exist, including but not limited to improper nepotism, favoritism, and misallocation of school monies, they must be eliminated, through state intervention if necessary. The General Assembly has all the power necessary to guarantee that the resources provided by Kentucky taxpayers for schools are spent wisely.

The trial court thus, with a very broad brush, included in its constitutional definition of "efficient" goals to be met by an education and requirements as to school financing, curriculum, personnel, accessibility to all children, physical facilities, instructional materials and management of the schools.

Moreover, the trial court made it clear that the duty — the absolute, unequivocal duty — to provide this system is solely the responsibility of the General Assembly. The court reiterated that its judicial power did not extend to

CH. 14 FINANCING PUBLIC EDUCATION 1159

specifying to the General Assembly the methods by which to implement and maintain this efficient system of education.

Addressing again the question of financing this massive task, the trial court stated directly what had been implied previously, that "substantial additional monies" will have to be raised to provide this constitutional school system. The court suggested three possible ways of financing: 1) increasing existing taxes, 2) levying new taxes, or 3) reallocating existing funds. Since a major reallocation of funds would "cripple" other government functions, the trial court postulated that the imposition of new taxes appeared to be the only viable alternative.

....

In the "judgment," the trial judge retained continuing jurisdiction over the subject matter for the purpose of enforcing the judgment....

With this lengthy and dramatic series of documents, the Franklin Circuit Court brought into sharp focus a problem that many dedicated citizens of the Commonwealth have "wrestled" with for many years. It placed the sole responsibility for the establishment and maintenance of an efficient system on the General Assembly. It defined "efficient" in an multi-faceted manner, and directed that all these criteria are not only relevant, but are essential, if the development of a constitutionally valid system of common schools is to be had.

The trial court examined the evidence and declared that the present school system was unconstitutional.

On appeal, this Court must now review the basis for the trial court's ruling.

III. *Contentions of the Parties*

The two remaining defendants, now appellants before this Court, raise numerous issues on appeal. They allege that the Council for Better Education, Inc., does not have either the legal authority or the standing to maintain this action; ... that the complaint does not state a "cognizable claim" against the two named legislators; that the trial court erred in finding that the system of common schools provided by the General Assembly is not efficient; ... that the trial court's definition and standards set for an efficient school system are at variance with Section 183; that the trial court's strong reliance on foreign cases was inappropriate; that the trial court erred in declaring that the school system violates the 14th Amendment of the U.S. Constitution....

Appellees, predictably, defend the trial court's action.

....

IV. *School Financing in Kentucky — Past and Present*

....

... [I]n an attempt to equalize inequities in the educational efforts and abilities to encourage more financial input and effort by local school districts, the General Assembly enacted the so-called Minimum Foundation Program [hereinafter MFP]. To qualify as a participant in this program, a district was required to levy a minimum real property tax of $1.10 per $100 of assessed value in the district.

The maximum tax was set at $1.50 per $100.00 of assessed value (1 1/2% of the total assessed value of the real property in the district). Most districts levied the maximum rates, because the assessed values were very low. The assessments ranged from 33 1/3% of the fair cash value of the property to as low as 12 1/2% of that value. The median statewide assessment rate was 27%.

As a result of this law and diverse local assessments of fair cash value, a lawsuit was filed directly attacking this legislation and the problem of built-in disparity in local school tax levies. Our Court's predecessor, the Court of Appeals, in the case of *Russman v. Luckett, Ky.*, 391 S.W.2d 694 (1965), declared that Section 172 of the Kentucky Constitution requires property to be assessed at 100% of its fair cash value. The mandate of the Court directed the Revenue Cabinet to see that all property in the Commonwealth was so assessed.

The ink was barely dry on this opinion, when, pursuant to a call for a special session by the Governor, the General Assembly enacted H.B. 1, known pleasantly as the "rollback law." Its effect was to countermand and negate the effect of *Russman*....

. . . .

The story continues. At its regular session in 1972, the General Assembly redefined the terms "net assessment growth" to include not only new property, but also the difference in the assessed valuation of all property subject to tax in the previous year, thus boosting total revenues by the tax on property value inflation.

In 1976, the handling of revenue took another turn. The General Assembly transferred the levy and collection of the required local tax effort to the State, to be included as part of the receipts of the General Fund. To provide funds which would help equalize, to some extent, the disparities in local financial effort, the General Assembly, also in 1976 passed the so-called Power Equalization Program [hereinafter PEP].

. . . .

As can be seen, the state's contribution to the local school programs (the so-called common schools) arises primarily from the MFP and the PEP. It is essential to a decision in this case to give a brief summary of each of these legislative acts.

To qualify as a participant in the MFP, a local school district must operate and pay its teachers for 185 days per school year, and it must actually operate its school(s) the same number of days. The State Superintendent of Public Instruction allots the classroom units to each district, the number of which depends on the average daily attendance in each grade. Each district receives a grant of money from the MFP based on the number of classroom units assigned to it. The funds may be used for teachers' salaries, current expenses, capital outlay and transportation of students.

The state also provides financial resources to local school districts through the PEP. Each year, the Kentucky Department of Revenue determines the equalized fair cash value of all taxable property in each local school district. That data is

CH. 14 FINANCING PUBLIC EDUCATION 1161

certified to the Superintendent of Public Instruction. The Superintendent determines annually the maximum tax rate that the PEP fund will equalize and then applies an equal rate to all districts. In order for a local district to receive funds, each local school district must levy a minimum equivalent tax rate of 25 cents per $100 of valuation, or the maximum rate supported by the PEP, whichever is greater. The "minimum equivalent tax rate" is defined as the quotient derived from dividing the districts' previous year's income from tax levies by the total assessed property valuation plus the assessment for motor vehicles.

As pointed out by the trial court, the mandated underlying tax rate has been so low that the results have been that only a fraction of the 25 cents local tax is actually equalized through the PEP.

If one were to summarize the history of school funding in Kentucky, one might well say that every forward step taken to provide funds to local districts and to equalize money spent for the poor districts has been countered by one backward step.

It is certainly true that the General Assembly, over the years, has made substantial efforts to infuse money into the system to improve and equalize the educational efforts in the common schools of Kentucky. What we must decide, based solely on the evidence in the record as tested by the Kentucky Constitution, Section 183, is whether the trial court was correct in declaring that those efforts have failed to create an efficient system of common schools in this Commonwealth.

V. *The Evidence*

....

... The overall effect of appellants' evidence is a virtual concession that Kentucky's system of common schools is underfunded and inadequate; is fraught with inequalities and inequities throughout the 177 local school districts; is ranked nationally in the lower 20-25% in virtually every category that is used to evaluate educational performance; and is not uniform among the districts in educational opportunities. When one considers the evidence presented by the appellants, there is little or no evidence to even begin to negate that of the appellees....

In spite of the Minimum Foundation Program and the Power Equalization Program, there are wide variations in financial resources and dispositions thereof which result in unequal educational opportunities throughout Kentucky. The local districts have large variances in taxable property per student. Even a total elimination of all mismanagement and waste in local school districts would not correct the situation as it now exists. A substantial difference in the curricula offered in the poorer districts contrasts with that of the richer districts, particularly in the areas of foreign language, science, mathematics, music and art.

The achievement test scores in the poorer districts are lower than those in the richer districts and expert opinion clearly established that there is a correlation between those scores and the wealth of the district. Student-teacher ratios are higher in the poorer districts. Moreover, although Kentucky's per capita income is low, it makes an even lower per capita effort to support the common schools.

....

That Kentucky's overall effort and resulting achievement in the area of primary and secondary education are comparatively low, nationally, is not in dispute. Thirty-five percent of our adult population are high school drop-outs. Eighty percent of Kentucky's local school districts are identified as being "poor," in terms of taxable property. The other twenty percent remain under the national average. Thirty percent of our local school districts are "functionally bankrupt."

Evidence relative to educational performance was introduced by appellees to make a comparison of Kentucky with its neighbors — Ohio, Indiana, Illinois, Missouri, Tennessee, Virginia, and West Virginia. It also ranked Kentucky, nationally in the same areas.

In the area of per pupil expenditures, Kentucky ranks 6th among the 8 states and ranks 40th, nationally. With respect to the average annual salary of instructional staff, Kentucky again ranks 6th among its neighbors and 37th nationally. In the area of classroom teacher compensation, Kentucky is 7th and 37th. Our classroom teacher average salary is 84.68% of the national average and our per pupil expenditure is 78.20% of the national average.

When one considers the use of property taxes as a percent of sources of school revenue, Kentucky is 7th among our neighboring states and 43rd nationally. The national average is 30.1% while Kentucky's rate is 18.2%. If any more evidence is needed to show the inadequacy of our overall effort, consider that only 68.2% of ninth grade students eventually graduate from high school in Kentucky. That ranks us 7th among our eight adjacent sister states. Among the 6 of our neighboring states that use the ACT scholastic achievement test, our high school graduates average score is 18.1, which ranks us 4th. Kentucky's ratio of pupil-teacher is 19.2, which ranks us 7th in this region. In spite of the appellants' claim, at both the trial level and on appeal, that appellees' statistics are not current, all the above figures are based on a 1986 study, which was published in 1987.

....

With this background of Kentucky's overall effort with regard to education and its comparison to other states in the area, and nationally, we proceed to examine the trial court's finding relative to inequity and lack of uniformity in the overabundance of local school districts. We will discuss the educational opportunities offered and then address the disparity in financial effort and support.

Educational Effort

The numerous witnesses that testified before the trial court are recognized experts in the field of primary and secondary education. They have advanced college degrees, they have taught school, they have been school administrators, they have been participants at a local or state level in Kentucky's education system, and they have performed in-depth studies of Kentucky's system. Without exception, they testified that there is great disparity in the poor and the more affluent school districts with regard to classroom teachers' pay; provision of basic educational materials; student-teacher ratio; curriculum; quality of basic management; size, adequacy and condition of school physical plants; and per year expenditure per student. Kentucky's children, simply because of their place of residence, are offered a virtual hodgepodge of educational opportunities. The quality of education in the poorer local school districts is substantially less in most, if not all, of the above categories.

....

Summarizing appellants' argument, and without intending to give it short shrift, it is contended that over the years the General Assembly has continually enacted such programs as the MFP, the PEP, and other progressive programs during recent sessions of the General Assembly. Moreover, uncontroverted evidence is adduced to show that the overall amount of money appropriated for local schools has increased by a substantial amount. The argument seems to be to the effect that "we have done our best." However, it is significant that all the experts were keenly aware of the legislative history, including substantive legislation and increased funding and yet, all of them stated that inequalities still exist, and indeed have been exacerbated by some of the legislation. Appellants conceded, the trial court found and we concur that in spite of legislative efforts, the total local and state effort in education in Kentucky's primary and secondary education is inadequate and is lacking in uniformity. It is discriminatory as to the children served in 80% of our local school districts.

Financial Effort

Uniform testimony of the expert witnesses at trial, corroborated by data, showed a definite correlation between the money spent per child on education and the quality of the education received. As we have previously stated in our discussion of the history of Kentucky's school finances, our system does not require a minimum local effort. The MFP, being based on average daily attendance, certainly infuses more money into each local district, but is not designed to correct problems of inequality and lack of uniformity between local school districts. The experts stated that the PEP, although a good idea, was and is underfunded.

The disparity in per pupil expenditure by the local school boards runs in the thousands of dollars per year. Moreover, between the extreme high allocation and the extreme low allocation lies a wide range of annual per pupil expenditures. In theory (and perhaps in actual practice) there could be 177 different per pupil expenditures, thus leading to 177 different educational efforts. The financing effort of local school districts is, figuratively speaking, a jigsaw puzzle.

....

VI. *Do the Local School Boards and the Council for Better Education,*[13] *Inc. Have the Legal Authority to Sue the Legislators and Do They Have the Standing to Maintain the Action?*

....

In considering these issues, we note again that the Council is a non-profit corporation, consisting of sixty-six local school districts. It is a separate, legally constituted authority, formed under the laws of Kentucky. The several local county and independent school districts are also formed under Kentucky statutes.

Legal Authority

The main thrust of appellants' argument is that the local boards of education, being creatures of the state, cannot sue it. Even though the Council is a non-profit corporation it is claimed that because the Council's members are all local boards of education, the Council, whose corporate veil is pierced by some strained logic, is also a servant who cannot challenge the master. We disagree.

In creating the local boards of education, the General Assembly endowed them with broad and specific powers to enable them to execute their statutory mission. "Each board of education shall have general control and management of the public schools in its district...." KRS 160.290(1). It is empowered to promote public education and "the education and the general health and welfare of pupils." *Id.* "... Each board of education shall be a body politic and corporate with perpetual succession. It may sue and be sued; and do all things necessary to accomplish the purposes for which it is created...." KRS 160.160 This corporate body politic is specifically granted the power to do "all things necessary " to carry out its duties and responsibilities, including exercising its right to sue and be sued. Nowhere in the statutes can one find a restriction on the right of the local boards to sue. The General Assembly has not stated that it cannot be sued by local boards. The subject matter of this lawsuit is whether the General Assembly has complied with its constitutional duty to provide an "efficient" system of common schools in Kentucky. Who is better qualified, who is more knowledgeable, who is more duty-bound, than the local school boards to raise the question? If the General Assembly is not adequately meeting its responsibility, how can the local boards meet theirs?

It is sterile logic that says that the local school boards cannot sue their masters, the General Assembly (or the Commonwealth), especially when one considers the statutory grants of authority cited above.

---

[13]Hereinafter referred to as Council.

CH. 14 FINANCING PUBLIC EDUCATION 1165

....

Even if we had not reached this conclusion as to the individual county and local independent school districts, it is beyond cavil that the Council, being an independent, legally separate, properly formed non-profit corporation, has the legal authority to sue the General Assembly. We are cited no authority, and can find none, that would enable us to pierce the corporate veil and legally cut off the rights of the individual corporate members.

Standing

Appellants next argue that the Council and the local school boards have no standing to join in this lawsuit.

In order to have standing to sue, a plaintiff need only have a real and substantial interest in the subject matter of the litigation, as opposed to a mere expectancy. *Winn v. First Bank of Irvington*, Ky.App., 581 S.W.2d 21, 23 (1978)....

....

The Council and the local school boards as plaintiffs in this case are statutorily obligated to promote public education for their respective constituents — the students in their school districts. The local districts are part and parcel of a system of common schools created by the General Assembly, which purports to be constitutionally efficient. If the system is not efficient, the local school board's duty is to make every effort to remedy that situation. Included in that responsibility is the filing of this lawsuit. The local school board and the Council have a judicially recognizable interest in a system of efficient common schools, and we so recognize and declare.

....

IX. *Does the Complaint State a Claim Against the Two Legislator-Appellants?*

The remaining appellants in this action are State Senator John A. Rose, who is President Pro Tempore of the Senate, and Representative Donald J. Blandford, who is Speaker of the House of Representatives.

Appellants argue that the declaratory judgment is a nullity against them. They claim that all 138 members of the Kentucky General Assembly would have to be joined as parties-defendant for the relief granted to be valid.

The premises for this argument are as follows: that the essence of the trial court's decision is that the financing of the system of common schools by the General Assembly is inadequate; and it is the entire General Assembly which will be required to raise more money for the system. Additionally, appellants maintain that since the General Assembly is not a corporate body, and since the appellants are not authorized to accept service for the entire membership, the court is not empowered in this action to direct the General Assembly to take any action. Lastly, appellants contend that the trial court's retention of continuing supervision through an "open-end" type of jurisdiction will lead to the court improperly attempting to direct the actions of the General Assembly.

....

... [W]e believe that the appellants do not correctly interpret the trial court's judgment, and moreover, we believe that the General Assembly, as a legislative body, is properly before this Court.

To begin with, the issue decided by the trial court, is that the system of common schools of the Commonwealth is not efficient, and is not constitutionally valid. The trial court set out numerous standards by which an "efficient system" can be judged. We do the same. The trial court emphasized and re-emphasized, in its three documents, that it was not directing the General Assembly to enact specific legislation and that it was not directing the General Assembly to raise taxes. We do the same.

....

We do not agree that, in order to bring the Kentucky General Assembly within the jurisdiction of a court, a plaintiff must effect service upon all of the individual members thereof. While we have no Kentucky authority directly on point, we do recognize a line of cases holding that members of lesser administrative and legislative bodies must be named individually as parties-defendant in order to invoke a trial court's jurisdiction. [*See*] *Lewis v. Board of Councilmen of Frankfort*, 305 Ky. 509, 204 S.W.2d 813 (1947), for example....

While it is certainly true that the named appellants in the instant case cannot, by themselves, enact any legislation, they can defend the constitutionality of an act or acts. They have done so in this case....

The two appellants in this case are the elected leaders of the House of Representatives and the Senate.... Those defendants are the presiding officers and are representative of their respective legislative bodies. They are named in their official capacities as President Pro Tempore of the Kentucky Senate and Speaker of the Kentucky House of Representatives, respectively. While the legislative leaders are not named as official representatives of the General Assembly in the caption of the complaint, as they should have been, it is clear from the statement of parties contained within the complaint that appellants were in fact named in a representative capacity that is sufficient to indicate the capacity in which they were being sued. *See Beverly v. Highfield*, 307 Ky. 179, 209 S.W.2d 739, 741 (1948).

....

... This case of major statewide importance has been tried and practiced vigorously by all parties and was decided on the merits by the trial court. We will not now initiate useless circuity of action by requiring the cumbersome process of serving all members of the General Assembly....

X. *What Is an "Efficient System of Common Schools"?*

In a few simple, but direct words, the framers of our present Constitution, set forth the will of the people with regard to the importance of providing public education in the Commonwealth. "General Assembly to provide for school system — The General Assembly shall, by appropriate legislation, provide for an efficient system of common schools throughout the State." Ky. Const. Sec. 183.

Several conclusions readily appear from a reading of this section. First, it is the obligation, the sole obligation, of the General Assembly to provide for a system of common schools in Kentucky. The obligation to so provide is clear and unequivocal and is, in effect, a constitutional mandate. Next, the school system must be provided throughout the entire state, with no area (or its children) being omitted. The creation, implementation and maintenance of the school system must be achieved by appropriate legislation. Finally, the system must be an efficient one.

It is, of course, the last "conclusion" that gives us pause and requires study and analysis. What, indeed, is the meaning of the word "efficient" as used in Section 183?

The Constitutional Debates

A brief sojourn into the Constitutional debates will give some idea — a contemporaneous view — of the depth of the delegates' intention when Section 183 was drafted and eventually made its way into the organic law of this state. It will provide a background for our definition of "efficient."

Comments of Delegate Beckner on the report which led to the selection of the language in Section 183 reflect the framers' cognizance of the importance of education and, emphasized that the educational system in Kentucky must be improved....

. . . .

It serves no purpose to further lengthen this opinion with more verbiage from the Constitutional debates. Delegate Beckner ... told ... fellow delegates and [has] told us, what this section means.

> — The providing of public education through a system of common schools by the General Assembly is the most "vital question" presented to them.
> — Education of children must not be minimized to the "slightest degree."
> — Education must be provided to the children of the rich and poor alike.
> — Education of children is essential to the prosperity of our state.
> — Education of children should be supervised by the State.
> — There must be a constant and continuing effort to make our schools more efficient.
> — We must not finance our schools in a *de minimis* fashion.
> — All schools and children stand upon one level in their entitlement to equal state support.

This Court, in defining efficiency must, at least in part, be guided by these clearly expressed purposes. The framers of Section 183 emphasized that education is essential to the welfare of the citizens of the Commonwealth. By this animus to Section 183, we recognize that education is a fundamental right in Kentucky.

Legal Precedents in Kentucky

[The court presented several Kentucky State cases decided throughout the past 100 years which focused, at least in part, on Section 183 and the congressional duty to provide an efficient system of education. The cases were then summarized as follows.]

As can be seen, this Court, since the adoption of the present Constitution, has, in reflecting on Section 183, drawn several conclusions: 1) The General Assembly is mandated, is duty bound, to create and maintain a system of common schools — throughout the state. 2) The expressed purpose of providing such service is vital and critical to the well being of the state. 3) The system of common schools must be efficient. 4) The system of common schools must be free. 5) The system of common schools must provide equal educational opportunities for all students in the Commonwealth. 6) The state must control and administer the system. 7) The system must be, if not uniform, "substantially uniform," with respect to the state as a whole. 8) The system must be equal to and for all students.

....

Appellants argue and cite several cases to support their position, that the General Assembly has sole and exclusive authority to determine whether the system of common schools is constitutionally "efficient" and that a Court may not substitute its judgment for that of the General Assembly.

In *Prowse v. Board of Education for Christian County*, 134 Ky. 365, 120 S.W. 307 (1909), the constitutionality of an act requiring the fiscal court to enact a tax previously set by the board of education for local school operation was upheld. We said, in light of Section 183:

> What system will be most efficient is for the judgment of the General Assembly.... In a matter like this, resting within the discretion of the General Assembly, the Court will not substitute its judgment for the judgment of the General Assembly and it will not interfere with the action of the legislature, unless a palpable effort to evade the mandate of the Constitution should appear. 120 S.W. at 308.

....

In this context, we review the question before us. The ultimate issue is whether the system of common schools in the Commonwealth established by the General Assembly, with respect to the mandate of Section 183, is in compliance with the constitution. Specifically, we are asked — based solely on the evidence in the record before us — if the present system of common schools in Kentucky is "efficient" in the constitutional sense. It is our sworn duty, to decide such questions when they are before us by applying the constitution. The duty of the judiciary in Kentucky was so determined when the citizens of Kentucky enacted the social compact called the Constitution and in it provided for the existence of a third equal branch of government, the judiciary.

....

We believe that what these several cases cited as controlling by appellants mean is that great weight should be given to the decision of the General Assembly. We believe they mean that the presumption of constitutionality is substantial. We believe that they mean that legislative discretion — in this specific matter of common schools — is to be given great weight and, we do so in this decision. We do not question the wisdom of the General Assembly's decision, only its failure to comply with its constitutional mandate. In so doing, we give deference and weight to the General Assembly's enactments; however, we find them constitutionally deficient.

....

Other Authority

In our sister and adjoining state of West Virginia, the state Constitution requires that "The legislature shall provide, by general law, for a thorough and efficient system of free schools." W.Va. Const., Art. XII, Sec. 1. In the landmark case of *Pauley v. Kelly*, 162 W.Va. 672, 255 S.E.2d 859 (1979), the West Virginia Supreme Court faced a lawsuit similar to the one before us. The trial court found that one county's school system was inadequate, in comparison with four other local systems. Although the West Virginia Supreme Court remanded the case for further evidentiary hearings it courageously spoke out in defining the "thorough and efficient" clause of Section 1 of its constitution.

....

Following an analysis of the admitted plethora of legal precedent, the West Virginia Supreme Court adopted a definition of "thorough and efficient."

> "We may now define a thorough and efficient system of schools: It develops, as best the state of education expertise allows, the minds, bodies and social morality of its charges to prepare them for useful and happy occupations, recreation and citizenship, and does so economically." *Id.* at 877.

The court continued by recognizing areas in which each child educated in the system should develop to full capacity: 1) literacy; 2) mathematical ability; 3) knowledge of government sufficient to equip the individual to make informed choices as a citizen; 4) self-knowledge sufficient to intelligently choose life work; 5) vocational or advanced academic training; 6) recreational pursuits; 7) creative interests; 8) social ethics. Support services, such as good physical facilities and instructional resources, and state and local monitoring for waste and incompetency were considered to be implicit in the definition of "a thorough and efficient system." *Id.*

We cite *Pauley*, and quote from it at some length to show that Courts may, should and have involved themselves in defining the standards of a constitutionally mandated educational system.

....

Opinions of Experts

....

The primary expert for the appellees was a local school superintendent who felt that an efficient system is one which is operated as best as can be with the money that was provided. We reject such a definition which could result in a system of common schools, efficient only in the uniformly deplorable conditions it provides throughout the state.

In summary the experts in this case believed that an "efficient" system of common schools should have several elements: 1) The system is the sole responsibility of the General Assembly. 2) The tax effort should be evenly spread. 3) The system must provide the necessary resources throughout the state — they must be uniform. 4) The system must provide an adequate education. 5) The system must be properly managed.

Definition of "Efficient"

We now hone in on the heart of this litigation. In defining "efficient," we use all the tools that are made available to us. In spite of any protestations to the contrary, we do not engage in judicial legislating. We do not make policy. We do not substitute our judgment for that of the General Assembly. We simply take the plain directive of the Constitution, and, armed with its purpose, we decide what our General Assembly must achieve in complying with its solemn constitutional duty.

Any system of common schools must be created and maintained with the premise that education is absolutely vital to the present and to the future of our Commonwealth....

The sole responsibility for providing the system of common schools is that of our General Assembly. It is a duty — it is a constitutional mandate placed by the people on the 138 members of that body who represent those selfsame people.

The General Assembly must not only establish the system, but it must monitor it on a continuing basis so that it will always be maintained in a constitutional manner. The General Assembly must carefully supervise it, so that there is no waste, no duplication, no mismanagement, at any level.

The system of common schools must be adequately funded to achieve its goals. The system of common schools must be substantially uniform throughout the state. Each child, every child, in this Commonwealth must be provided with an equal opportunity to have an adequate education. Equality is the key word here. The children of the poor and the children of the rich, the children who live in the poor districts and the children who live in the rich districts must be given the

CH. 14 FINANCING PUBLIC EDUCATION 1171

same opportunity and access to an adequate education. This obligation cannot be shifted to local counties and local school districts.

As we have indicated, Section 183 requires the General Assembly to establish a system of common schools that provides an equal opportunity for children to have an adequate education. In no way does this constitutional requirement act as a limitation on the General Assembly's power to create local school entities and to grant to those entities the authority to supplement the state system. Therefore, if the General Assembly decides to establish local school entities, it may also empower them to enact local revenue initiatives to supplement the uniform, equal educational effort that the General Assembly must provide. This includes not only revenue measures similar to the special taxes previously discussed, but also the power to assess local ad valorem taxes on real property and personal property at a rate over and above that set by the General Assembly to fund the statewide system of common schools. Such local efforts may not be used by the General Assembly as a substitute for providing an adequate, equal and substantially uniform educational system throughout this state.

Having declared the system of common schools to be constitutionally deficient, we have directed the General Assembly to recreate and redesign a new system that will comply with the standards we have set out. Such system will guarantee to all children the opportunity for an adequate education, through a state system. To allow local citizens and taxpayers to make a supplementary effort in no way reduces or negates the minimum quality of education required in the statewide system.

We do not instruct the General Assembly to enact any specific legislation. We do not direct the members of the General Assembly to raise taxes. It is their decision how best to achieve efficiency. We only decide the nature of the constitutional mandate. We only determine the intent of the framers. Carrying-out that intent is the duty of the General Assembly.

A child's right to an adequate education is a fundamental one under our Constitution. The General Assembly must protect and advance that right. We concur with the trial court that an efficient system of education must have as its goal to provide each and every child with at least the seven following capacities: (i) sufficient oral and written communication skills to enable students to function in a complex and rapidly changing civilization; (ii) sufficient knowledge of economic, social, and political systems to enable the student to make informed choices; (iii) sufficient understanding of governmental processes to enable the student to understand the issues that affect his or her community, state, and nation; (iv) sufficient self-knowledge and knowledge of his or her mental and physical wellness; (v) sufficient grounding in the arts to enable each student to appreciate his or her cultural and historical heritage; (vi) sufficient training or preparation for advanced training in either academic or vocational fields so as to enable each child to choose and pursue life work intelligently; and (vii) sufficient levels of academic or vocational skills to enable public school students to compete favorably with their counterparts in surrounding states, in academics or in the job market.

The essential, and minimal, characteristics of an "efficient" system of common schools, may be summarized as follows:

> 1) The establishment, maintenance and funding of common schools in Kentucky is the sole responsibility of the General Assembly.
> 2) Common schools shall be free to all.
> 3) Common schools shall be available to all Kentucky children.
> 4) Common schools shall be substantially uniform throughout the state.
> 5) Common schools shall provide equal educational opportunities to all Kentucky children, regardless of place of residence or economic circumstances.
> 6) Common schools shall be monitored by the General Assembly to assure that they are operated with no waste, no duplication, no mismanagement, and with no political influence.
> 7) The premise for the existence of common schools is that all children in Kentucky have a constitutional right to an adequate education.
> 8) The General Assembly shall provide funding which is sufficient to provide each child in Kentucky an adequate education.
> 9) An adequate education is one which has as its goal the development of the seven capacities recited previously.

XI. *Is the Present System "Efficient"?*

We have described, *infra*, in some detail, the present system of common schools. We have noted the overall inadequacy of our system of education, when compared to national standards and to the standards of our adjacent states. We have recognized the great disparity that exists in educational opportunities throughout the state. We have noted the great disparity and inadequacy of financial effort throughout the state.

In spite of the past and present efforts of the General Assembly, Kentucky's present system of common schools falls short of the mark of the constitutional mandate of "efficient." When one juxtaposes the standards of efficiency as derived from our Constitution, the cases decided thereunder, the persuasive authority from our sister states and the opinion of experts, with the virtually unchallenged evidence in the record, no other decision is possible.

XII. *Did the Trial Court's Judgment Violate the Separation of Powers Provision of the Kentucky Constitution?*

....

It is argued that the trial court directed the General Assembly to enact specific legislation and to raise taxes and that such is a violation of the separation of powers. We do not agree that that is what the judgment of the trial court does. The trial judge did define "efficient," he did declare that a common school

CH. 14 FINANCING PUBLIC EDUCATION 1173

education is a fundamental constitutional right in this state, and he did say that any educational system to be "efficient," must have certain characteristics. He commented on the possible methods of financing the system of common schools in Kentucky and did, of course, opine that additional money would be required. This later conclusion was based on an abundance of virtually uncontested and unchallenged evidence in this record.

. . . .

Our job is to determine the constitutional validity of the system of common schools within the meaning of the Kentucky Constitution, Section 183. We have done so. We have declared the system of common schools to be unconstitutional. It is now up to the General Assembly to re-create, and re-establish a system of common schools within this state which will be in compliance with the Constitution. We have no doubt they will proceed with their duty.

. . . .

We reverse the decision of the trial court with respect to the requirement that the General Assembly, or any of the defendants in the trial court, further report to the trial court.

. . . .

Summary/Conclusion

. . . .

Lest there be any doubt, the result of our decision is that Kentucky's entire system of common schools is unconstitutional. There is no allegation that only part of the common school system is invalid, and we find no such circumstance. This decision applies to the entire sweep of the system — all its parts and parcels. This decision applies to the statutes creating, implementing and financing the system and to all regulations, etc., pertaining thereto. This decision covers the creation of local school districts, school boards, and the Kentucky Department of Education to the Minimum Foundation Program and Power Equalization Program. It covers school construction and maintenance, teacher certification — the whole gamut of the common school system in Kentucky.

. . . .

Since we have, by this decision, declared the system of common schools in Kentucky to be unconstitutional, Section 183 places an absolute duty on the General Assembly to re-create, re-establish a new system of common schools in the Commonwealth. As we have said, the premise of this opinion is that education is a basic, fundamental constitutional right that is available to all children within this Commonwealth. The General Assembly should begin with the same premise as it goes about its duty. The system, as we have said, must be efficient, and the criteria we have set out are binding on the General Assembly as it develops Kentucky's new system of common schools.

....

COMBS, GANT, LAMBERT AND WINTERSHEIMER, JJ., concur.
GANT AND WINTERSHEIMER, JJ., file separate concurring opinions.
LEIBSON AND VANCE, JJ., file separate dissenting opinions.

....

---

1. Unlike any of the other cases cited in this chapter, the court in *Rose* compares outcome-based measurement of Kentucky school children with that of a national average rather than employing an intra-state analysis. Hence, underfunding has a national as well as local structure to contend with. What is the purpose of such a position; is the problem to be overcome one of equality or equity? Is it possible that the incremental benefit based on a national norm may result in the status quo of educational opportunity within the state?

2. According to the court, the State Constitution, Section 183, requires the General Assembly to establish a system of public schools that provides equal educational opportunity for all the state's children. In defining an efficient system of education, the Kentucky Supreme Court accepted the trial court's statement that an efficient system must seek to provide each child with facility in six areas including: 1) oral and written communication; 2) economic, social and political systems; 3) governmental processes; 4) self-knowledge; 5) arts; and 6) vocational training. Ultimately, the public school system should produce graduates with sufficient academic and vocational skills to compete with anyone in any academic or employment setting. The court continues and states that individual districts may also enact local revenue initiatives to supplement this uniform, equal opportunity effort. Is the responsibility for promulgating and implementing such a system that of the judiciary or the legislature? Has the court overstepped its bounds here?

3. This decision declares the financing system of public schools in Kentucky unconstitutional and commands that a new system be created. It also outlines the skills to be learned by students from such a new system. Does this case, and others like it, portend a trend in judicial activism where the opinions of judges supplant the work of the legislature as well as school officials?

4. The Kentucky General Assembly responded to the State Supreme Court decision by enacting the Kentucky Education Reform Act of 1990, 1990 Ky. Rev. Stat. & R. Serv. 476 (Baldwin) (codified as amended in scattered sections of Ky. Rev. Stat. Ann. (Baldwin 1990).

With respect to state/local financing of education, the Reform Act's provisions are simple and straightforward. It guarantees a base funding level for each student in each district. Sec. 97(1). A local tax contribution in partial support of the guaranteed sum is mandatory, equal to $0.30 of $100 of assessed valuation in the district. Sec. 105(12)(a). If a school board fails to provide this minimum level of local support, the school board members are subject to removal from office. Sec. 105(12)(b). The school board can increase the guaranteed sum by fifteen percent under a state-subsidized guaranteed allocation plan. Sec. 107(1). Subject to the vote of the citizens of the district, the school board may increase expenditures per student at forty-five percent above the basic support level.

The Reform Act also provides for raising standards of quality in Kentucky's schools and for protecting children deemed to be "at risk." The State Board of Education must develop a statewide assessment program, including performance-based testing, to judge the relative success of individual schools in meeting the court's criteria. Sec. 4(1). The legislature will reward schools that show improved student performance over a two-year period with salary increases for teachers and staff. Sec. 5(1). If a school's percentage of successful students does not increase, the school must develop a school improvement plan. Sec. 5(3). If a school's percentage of successful students declines by more than five percent, the school is officially "in crisis." Sec. 5(5). Outside experts assigned to assist the school then have power to dismiss or transfer personnel. Sec. 5(5)(d). In addition, the Act allows students to transfer from a school "in crisis" to a successful school even if they must cross district lines to do so. Sec. 5(5)(c).

The Reform Act sets maximum class sizes, mandates school-based decision making, and provides state funds for new programs in the professional development of teachers and administrators. The state has pledged to explore the effective use of educational technology, and as a first step, will use competitive bidding and negotiation to secure the lowest prices for teachers who wish to purchase personal computers. Sec. 23(1). In short, the Reform Act embraces a substantial number of provisions intended to enhance the quality of schooling.

5. The latter four cases in this chapter were the first since *Robinson* to rely exclusively on the education clause of their respective state constitution's to find the system of funding schools unconstitutional. With the notes on other recently decided cases, *see DeRolphe v. State of Ohio*, quoted in the notes following *Abbott*, a new round of litigation may be in the offing. Such a prospect is demonstrated in the following commentary.

THRO, THE ROLE OF LANGUAGE OF THE STATE EDUCATION CLAUSES IN SCHOOL FINANCE LITIGATION, 79 Educ. L. Rep. 19 (1993)*

Introduction

Every state constitution, except that of Mississippi, has a provision which, at a minimum, mandates that some sort of system of free public education be

---

*Copyright © 1993 by West Publishing Company. Reprinted with permission.

maintained. Prior to 1973, these state education clauses were effectively insignificant. In that year, however, the New Jersey Supreme Court, in *Robinson v. Cahill*, declared the State's school finance system to be unconstitutional and relied exclusively on the state education clause. Inspired in part by the New Jersey decision, litigants have brought state constitutional challenges to the educational finance system in more than half of the states. All of these school finance litigation cases have alleged a violation of the state education clause[4] and the state equal protection clause.

... Indeed, prior to 1989, only two cases, Robinson and *Seattle School District Number 1 v. State*,[8] relied exclusively on the education clauses to invalidate the finance system. Consequently, prior to 1989, one was forced to conclude that, the state equal protection clauses, not the education clauses, offered the best prospects for a plaintiffs' victory in a school finance case.

In 1989, however, the supreme courts of Montana, Kentucky, and Texas, invalidated their respective school finance systems relying exclusively on the state education clause. By doing so, these courts significantly altered the nature of school finance litigation. Recent litigation in New Jersey, Oregon,[18] and, to a lesser extent, Tennessee,[19] confirms this suggestion. Instead of emphasizing the state equal protection clauses and equality of per pupil expenditures ("equality suits") ... these decisions focused on the state education clause and the quality of education delivered ("quality suits"). The finance systems were struck down not because some districts have more money than others and all districts must have the same amount, but because the quality of the poorest schools is below the constitutionally mandated norm and the finance system must be changed in order to bring the schools up to that norm. Moreover, since exclusive reliance on the education clauses has fewer implications for other areas of the law such as the provision of social services, this shift from emphasis on the equal protection clauses to emphasis on the state education clauses appeared to make a plaintiffs' victory more likely.

With this increased emphasis on the state education clauses in school finance reform cases, the subtle differences in language, which previously appeared to be nothing more than a point of curiosity, suddenly becomes potentially important....

---

[4]*But see Dupree v. Alma School Dist. No. 30*, 279 Ark. 340, 651 S.W.2d 90 (1983); *Washakie County School Dist. No. 1 v. Herschler*, 606 P.2d 310 (Wyo.1980); *Pauley v. Kelly*, 162 W.Va. 672, 255 S.E.2d 859 (1979); *Horton v. Meskill*, 172 Conn. 615, 376 A.2d 359 (1977); *Serrano v. Priest (II)*, 18 Cal.3d 728, 135 Cal.Rptr. 345, 557 P.2d 929 (1976) (All cases interpreting only the state equality guarantee clause).

[8]90 Wash.2d 476, 585 P.2d 71 (1978).

[18]*Coalition for Equitable School Funding v. State*, 311 Or. 300, 811 P.2d 116 [67 Educ. L. Rep. [1311]] (1991)....

[19]*Tennessee Small School Systems v. McWherter*, No. 01-A-91111-CH-00433, 1992 WL 119824 (Tenn.App. Jun. 5, 1992).

CH. 14 FINANCING PUBLIC EDUCATION 1177

....

I. *The Differences in Education Clauses*

The seventeen clauses which merely mandate a system of free public schools constitute Category I. A typical example of a Category I clause is Tennessee's which provides:

> The General Assembly shall provide for the maintenance, support and eligibility standards of a system of free public schools.
>
> Unlike the clauses in the other categories, there is no mention of any sort of standard of quality for the schools. Presumably, as long as the state legislature does not abolish the public school system, there can be no violation of the education clause.

In contrast, Category II consists of twenty-two education clauses which impose some minimum standard of quality, usually thorough and/or efficient, that the statewide system of public schools must reach. A typical example is the Pennsylvania Education clause which provides:

> The General Assembly shall provide for the maintenance and support of a thorough and efficient system of public education to serve the needs of the Commonwealth.
>
> When evaluating such a mandate in the context of a public school finance reform case, the state court determines whether the standard of "thorough and/or efficient" means that all local school systems must be funded on a substantially equal basis.

Similarly, the six Category III education clauses go beyond simply mandating the establishment of a school system. However, these clauses are distinguished from the Category I and Category II by both a "stronger and more specific educational mandate," such as "all means," and a "purposive preamble." A typical example of both the purposive preamble and the stronger and more specific educational mandate is provided by the education clause of the California Constitution which reads:

> A general diffusion of knowledge and intelligence being essential to the preservation of the rights and liberties of the people [purposive preamble], the Legislature shall encourage by all suitable means [stronger mandate] and the promotion of intellectual, scientific, moral, and agricultural improvement.

....

Finally, Category IV consists of four clauses which make education an important, if not the most important, duty of the state. Category IV is probably most clearly exemplified by the education clause of Washington which provides that education is "the paramount duty of the state to make ample provision for the education of all children residing within its borders without distinction or preference on account of race, color, or sex."[38] A second example is the Georgia education clause which reads, "[t]he provision of an adequate education for the citizens shall be a primary obligation of the State of Georgia, the expense of which shall be provided for by taxation."[39]

II. *Analysis of the Language of Education Clauses*

....

First, not surprisingly, the language of Category I education clauses has proven to be useless for achieving school finance reform.[42] For example, in *Fair School Finance Council, Inc. v. State*,[43] the Oklahoma Supreme Court, confining its inquiry to the language of the education provisions,[44] held that the education clauses "merely mandate that the legislature maintain a system of free public schools. They (the education clauses) do not on their face guarantee equal expenditures per pupil." ...

Second, the approaches to the language of the education clauses in Category II are far more diverse than the approaches applied to Category I. For example, the Ohio Supreme Court focused on an absolute deprivation standard and held that the state's thorough and efficient standard[51] was met because no "school district was receiving so little local and state revenue that the students were being (absolutely) deprived of educational opportunity."[52] In contrast, in *Lujan v. Colorado State Board of Education*,[53] the Colorado Supreme Court apparently emphasized equality of opportunity at the local, rather than state, level and concluded that the state education clause's mandate of thorough and uniform[54] "is satisfied if thorough and uniform educational opportunities are available in each school district".[55]

---

[38]Wash. Const. art. IX, § 1 (emphasis added)....

[39]Ga. Const. art. VIII, § 1, para. 1 (emphasis added). This is supplemented by Ga. Const. art. VIII, § 8, para. 1 ("(t)he General Assembly shall by taxation provide for an adequate education for the citizens of Georgia."). *See also* Ill. Const. art. X, § 1; Mich. Const. art. VIII, §§ 1, 2 (both provisions make education a "primary" duty).

[42]Indeed, only one Category I state, Connecticut, has declared its system unconstitutional and that decision was based solely on the equality guarantee clause. *Horton v. Meskill*, 172 Conn. 615, 376 A.2d 359 (1977).

[43]746 P.2d 1135 [43 Educ. L. Rep. [805]] (Okla.1987)

[44]Okla. Const. art. XIII, § 1 ("The legislature shall establish and maintain a system of free public schools wherein all the children of the State may be educated.")

[51]Ohio Const. art. VI, sec. 2 ("(t)he General Assembly shall make such provisions ... as ... will secure a thorough and efficient system of common schools throughout the state.")

[52]*Board of Education of the City School District of the City of Cincinnati v. Walter*, 58 Ohio St.2d 368, 387, 390 N.E.2d 813 (1979)....

[53]649 P.2d 1005 [6 Educ. L. Rep. [191]] (Colo.1982) (*en banc*).

[54]Colo. Const. art. IX, § 2.

[55]649 P.2d at 1025.

....

Third, although they appear to confer a higher standard than the Category II clauses because of their purposive preambles and stronger educational mandates, the Category III education clauses have never been explicitly interpreted. In the only Category III state to experience school finance reform litigation at the state supreme court level, California, the decision was based on the state equal protection clause.[60]

Fourth, state courts also have never explicitly interpreted the language of the Category IV provisions. Although there were supreme court cases in Georgia,[61] Illinois,[62] and Washington,[63] all of the decisions employed a historical analysis, were based on the protection clause, or ignored the language.

III. *A Hypothesis of the Role of Language Differences*

This section of the Article suggests that courts should look to the plain language of the education clause and that this one factor should be largely determinative of the outcome.[65] Thus, if two states had nearly identical funding disparities, nearly identical school systems in terms of quality, but very different education clauses in terms of language, it would be perfectly logical to say that one state's system was unconstitutional and that the other was constitutional simply because of the differences in constitutional language.

....

Utilization of this plain language hypothesis will have several effects. First, eliminating varying state interpretations, will make school finance litigation far more predictable and more rational. Litigants will be able to assess their chances simply by looking at the state education clause. Second, plaintiffs' victories in Category I states will become virtually impossible. The mere mandate that a public school system be established will be insufficient to win a quality suit or to establish education as a fundamental right in an equality suit. Third and similarly, the plaintiffs' prospects will be severely diminished in Category II states and, to a lesser extent, in Category III states. It will be extremely difficult to argue that the quality standard requires finance reform or that education is a fundamental right because so many other states appear to require more. Fourth and conversely, the plaintiffs' prospects will be substantially increased in the five Category IV states. After all, the plaintiffs will be able to assert that their state

---

[60]*See Serrano v. Priest (Serrano II)*, 18 Cal.3d 728, 135 Cal.Rptr. 345, 557 P.2d 929, (1976) cert. denied, 432 U.S. 907 (1977).

[61]*McDaniel v. Thomas*, 248 Ga. 632, 285 S.E.2d 156 [1 Educ. L. Rep. [982]] (1981).

[62]*Blase v. State*, 55 Ill.2d 94, 302 N.E.2d 46 (1973).

[63][*Seattle Sch. Dist. No. 1 v. State*,] 90 Wash.2d 476, 585 P.2d 71 (1978).

[65]Of course, language will not be totally determinative. For example, it is possible, indeed probable, that two courts will define "thorough" in different ways. Moreover, even if "thorough" were defined exactly the same way, no two school finance systems are exactly alike. Thus, subtle differences in the system could be determinative.

requires more than virtually every other state. Fifth, the practice of "horizontal federalism" where state courts look to decisions of other states interpreting similarly worded state constitutional provisions will be encouraged. This will promote the development of an independent body of state constitutional law. Sixth and similarly, the potential threat to state court legitimacy posed when two states interpret identical provisions in totally different ways would be substantially diminished.

Conclusion

When interpreting the meaning of an education clause in a school finance case, courts should always begin with an historical analysis and/or an examination of prior judicial interpretations of the provision. In some instances, particularly if the constitution is relatively new, the historical evidence will give clear guidance. In others, there will be a definitive judicial interpretation. However, in most instances, the history will be inconclusive and there will be no precedent. In such a situation, courts must have something to guide their analysis.

When there is no conclusive history or precedent to guide the Court, that something should be the specific language of the education clause.... Although ... subtle language differences have largely been ignored over the past two decades, language should be a decisive factor in those school finance cases whenever history and precedent are inconclusive. By looking at language and comparing the text to provisions in other states, one can determine the level of duty, relative to other States, imposed on a particular state legislature and can also gain insight into whether education may be a fundamental right. Consequently, school finance litigation, which previously has been totally unpredictable, could become more predictable and, more importantly, the legitimacy of both state courts and state constitutional law could be enhanced.

---

1. Footnote 42 of Thro's article states that only one of the Category I states — whose Constitutions merely mandate establishment of a system of free public schools — has declared its system unconstitutional. *See Horton v. Meskill*, 172 Conn. 615, 376 A.2d 359 (1977) (This decision was based solely on the equality guarantee clause). Thro suggests that plaintiffs in Category I states will most often lose under an analysis of such state constitutional language. An exception to this rule may be *Opinion of the Justices No. 338*, 624 So. 2d 107 (Ala. 1993). In that case, an Alabama State Senate Resolution requested an advisory opinion as to whether the State legislature was required to comply with a circuit court order to provide school children with substantially equitable and adequate educational opportunities. The Supreme Court of Alabama held the legislature to this requirement, unless and until the order was modified or reversed by a higher court:

> The executive and legislative branches of the State have broad powers and responsibilities in the area of public education, but the powers of each branch of government are bounded by the mandates and restraints of the constitution of the State of Alabama. This principle of separation of powers of government that is now included in the Alabama constitution was first decided in the famous case of *Marbury v. Madison*, 5 U.S. (1 Cranch) 137 (1803). It is the province and duty of the judicial branch of government to interpret the constitution and to say what the law is, and an order issued by a court of competent jurisdiction that interprets the constitution is binding upon the Legislature unless the order is stayed or overturned by a higher court.
>
> Under the provisions of Amendment 328, Section 6.04, "[t]he circuit court shall exercise general jurisdiction in all cases except as may otherwise be provided by law." Included within the general jurisdiction of the circuit court is the power to decide whether the actions of the executive or legislative branches are consistent with the requirements of the fundamental law of the people — their constitution. In short, the circuit court has the power, and indeed the duty, when requested to do so in cases involving justiciable controversies, to interpret the constitution, and its interpretation, unless changed by a competent court having the power to overturn it, must be accepted and followed. *See* 21 C.J.S. Courts § 3, pp. 11-12 (1940).
>
> Your inquiry, as we understand it, is whether the Legislature is required to follow the order of the Circuit Court of Montgomery County in the consolidated cases referenced above. Our answer, based upon the principles set out herein, is yes. *Id.* at 110.

2. Another case which is an exception to the trend today in declaring state education funding plans unconstitutional is *Skeen v. State*, 505 N.W.2d 299 (Minn. 1993). A fundamental right to education had already been found in the State of Minnesota; the *Skeen* decision held that the current funding system satisfied that right. The Court also held that: (1) supplemental revenue and debt service levy funding provisions were adequately addressed by the legislature and any disparities did not violate the State Constitution; and (2) education finance system did not violate the Constitution, which requires a "general and uniform" system of public schools.

3. The Wisconsin Constitution's education clause is as follows: "The Legislature shall provide by law for the establishment of district schools which shall be as nearly uniform as practicable." Wis. Const., art X, #3. The State legislature of Wisconsin had passed a law creating the Milwaukee Parental Choice Program of public funding to permit children from low-income families to attend non-sectarian private schools. School administration organizations and civil rights organizations challenged the constitutionality of the statute. The State Supreme Court upheld the statute, noting that it complied with the State Constitution requiring the uniform system. *Davis v. Grover*, 480 N.W.2d 460 (1992).

PART FIVE

CHURCH-STATE RELATIONS

Chapter 15

THE RELIGION CLAUSES AND PUBLIC EDUCATION

A. RELIGION AND THE PUBLIC SCHOOL CURRICULUM

1. BIBLE READING AND PRAYER

SCHOOL DISTRICT OF ABINGTON TOWNSHIP v. SCHEMPP
Supreme Court of the United States
374 U.S. 203 (1963)

MR. JUSTICE CLARK delivered the opinion of the Court:

Once again we are called upon to consider the scope of the provision of the First Amendment to the United States Constitution which declares that "Congress shall make no law respecting an establishment of religion, or prohibiting the free exercise thereof...." These companion cases present the issues in the context of state action requiring that schools begin each day with readings from the Bible. While raising the basic questions under slightly different factual situations, the cases permit of joint treatment. In light of the history of the First Amendment and of our cases interpreting and applying its requirements, we hold that the practices at issue and the laws requiring them are unconstitutional under the Establishment Clause, as applied to the States through the Fourteenth Amendment.

I

... The Commonwealth of Pennsylvania by law ... requires that "At least ten verses from the Holy Bible shall be read, without comment, at the opening of each public school on each school day. Any child shall be excused from such Bible reading, or attending such Bible reading, upon the written request of his parent or guardian." The Schempp family, husband and wife and two of their three children, brought suit to enjoin enforcement of the statute.... A three-judge statutory District Court for the Eastern District of Pennsylvania held that the statute was violative of the Establishment clause of the First Amendment as applied to the States by the Due Process Clause of the Fourteenth Amendment and directed that appropriate injunctive relief issue....

The appellees Edward Lewis Schempp, his wife Sidney, and their children, Roger and Donna, are of the Unitarian faith and are members of the Unitarian Church in Germantown, Philadelphia, Pennsylvania, where they, as well as another son, Ellory, regularly attend religious services....

On each school day at the Abington Senior High School between 8:15 and 8:30 a.m., while the pupils are attending their home rooms or advisory sections, opening exercises are conducted pursuant to the statute.

....

At the first trial Edward Schempp and the children testified as to specific religious doctrines purveyed by a literal reading of the Bible "which were contrary to the religious beliefs which they held and to their familial teaching." The children testified that all of the doctrines to which they referred were read to them at various times as part of the exercises. Edward Schempp testified at the second trial that he had considered having Roger and Donna excused from attendance at the exercises but decided against it for several reasons, including his belief that the children's relationships with their teachers and classmates would be adversely affected.[3]

....

... In 1905 the Board of School Commissioners of Baltimore City adopted a rule.... The rule provided for the holding of opening exercises in the schools of the city, consisting primarily of the "reading, without comment, of a chapter in the Holy Bible and/or the use of the Lord's Prayer." The petitioners, Mrs. Madalyn Murray and her son, William J. Murray III, are both professed atheists. Following unsuccessful attempts to have the respondent school board rescind the rule, this suit was filed for mandamus to compel its rescission and cancellation. It was alleged that William was a student in a public school of the city and Mrs. Murray, his mother, was a taxpayer therein; that it was the practice under the rule to have a reading on each school morning from the King James version of the Bible; that at petitioners' insistence the rule was amended to permit children to be excused from the exercise on request of the parent and that William had been excused pursuant thereto; that nevertheless the rule as amended was in violation of the petitioners' rights "to freedom of religion under the First and Fourteenth Amendments" and in violation of "the principle of separation between church and state, contained therein...." The petition particularized the

---

[3] ... Edward Schempp, the children's father, testified that after careful consideration he had decided that he should not have Roger or Donna excused from attendance at these morning ceremonies. Among his reasons were the following. He said that he thought his children would be "labeled as 'odd balls'" before their teachers and classmates every school day; that children, like Roger's and Donna's classmates, were liable "to lump all particular religious difference[s] or religious objections [together] as "atheism" and that today the word "atheism" is often connected with "atheistic communism" and has "very bad" connotations, such as "un-American" or "anti-Red", with overtones of possible immorality. Mr. Schempp pointed out that due to the events of the morning exercises following in rapid succession, the Bible reading, the Lord's Prayer, the Flag Salute, and the announcements, excusing his children from the Bible reading would mean that probably they would miss hearing the announcements so important to children. He testified also that if Roger and Donna were excused from Bible reading they would have to stand in the hall outside their "homeroom" and that this carried with it the imputation of punishment for bad conduct. 201 F. Supp. at 818.

A. RELIGION AND THE PUBLIC SCHOOL CURRICULUM 1187

petitioners' atheistic beliefs and stated that the rule, as practiced, violated their rights

> in that it threatens their religious liberty by placing a premium on belief as against non-belief and subjects their freedom of conscience to the rule of the majority; it pronounces belief in God as the source of all moral and spiritual values, equating these values with religious values, and thereby renders sinister, alien and suspect the beliefs and ideals of your Petitioners, promoting doubt and question of their morality, good citizenship and good faith.

The respondents demurred and the trial court, recognizing that the demurrer admitted all facts well pleaded, sustained it without leave to amend. The Maryland Court of Appeals affirmed, the majority of four justices holding the exercise not in violation of the First and Fourteenth Amendments, with three justices dissenting.

....

V

The wholesome "neutrality" of which this Court's cases speak thus stems from a recognition of the teachings of history that powerful sects or groups might bring about a fusion of governmental and religious functions or a concert or dependency of one upon the other to the end that official support of the State or Federal Government would be placed behind the tenets of one or of all orthodoxies. This the Establishment Clause prohibits. And a further reason for neutrality is found in the Free Exercise Clause, which recognizes the value of religious training, teaching and observance and, more particularly, the right of every person to freely choose his own course with reference thereto, free of any compulsion from the state. This the Free Exercise Clause guarantees. Thus, as we have seen, the two clauses may overlap. As we have indicated, the Establishment Clause has been directly considered by this Court eight times in the past score of years and, with only one Justice dissenting on the point, it has consistently held that the clause withdrew all legislative power respecting religious belief or the expression thereof. The test may be stated as follows: what are the purpose and the primary effect of the enactment? If either is the advancement or inhibition of religion then the enactment exceeds the scope of legislative power as circumscribed by the Constitution. That is to say that to withstand the strictures of the Establishment Clause there must be a secular legislative purpose and a primary effect that neither advances nor inhibits religion.

....

Applying the Establishment Clause principles to the cases at bar we find that the States are requiring the selection and reading at the opening of the school day of verses from the Holy Bible and the recitation of the Lord's Prayer by the students in unison. These exercises are prescribed as part of the curricular activities of students who are required by law to attend school. They are held in the school buildings under the supervision and with the participation of teachers employed in those schools. None of these factors, other than compulsory school attendance, was present in the program upheld in *Zorach v. Clauson*, [343 U.S. 306 (1952)]. The trial court in No. 142 has found that such an opening exercise is a religious ceremony and was intended by the State to be so. We agree with the trial court's finding as to the religious character of the exercises. Given that finding, the exercises and the law requiring them are in violation of the Establishment Clause.

....

It is insisted that unless these religious exercises are permitted a "religion of secularism" is established in the schools. We agree of course that the State may not establish a "religion of secularism" in the sense of affirmatively opposing or showing hostility to religion, thus "preferring those who believe in no religion over those who do believe." *Zorach v. Clauson, supra*, 343 U.S. at 314. We do not agree, however, that this decision in any sense has that effect. In addition, it might well be said that one's education is not complete without a study of comparative religion or the history of religion and its relationship to the advancement of civilization. It certainly may be said that the Bible is worthy of study for its literary and historic qualities. Nothing we have said here indicates that such study of the Bible or of religion, when presented objectively as part of a secular program of education, may not be effected consistently with the First Amendment. But the exercises here do not fall into those categories. They are religious exercises, required by the States in violation of the command of the First Amendment that the Government maintain strict neutrality, neither aiding nor opposing religion.

Finally, we cannot accept that the concept of neutrality, which does not permit a State to require a religious exercise even with the consent of the majority of those affected, collides with the majority's right to free exercise of religion. While the Free Exercise Clause clearly prohibits the use of state action to deny the rights of free exercise to *anyone*, it has never meant that a majority could use the machinery of the State to practice its beliefs. Such a contention was effectively answered by Mr. Justice Jackson for the Court in *West Virginia Bd. of Educ. v. Barnette*, 319 U.S. 624, 638 (1943):

> The very purpose of a Bill of Rights was to withdraw certain subjects from the vicissitudes of political controversy, to place them beyond the reach of majorities and officials and to establish them as legal principles to be applied by the courts. One's right to ... freedom of worship ... and other fundamental rights may not be submitted to vote; they depend on the outcome of no elections.

The place of religion in our society is an exalted one, achieved through a long tradition of reliance on the home, the church and the inviolable citadel of the individual heart and mind. We have come to recognize through bitter experience

A. RELIGION AND THE PUBLIC SCHOOL CURRICULUM 1189

that it is not within the power of government to invade that citadel, whether its purpose or effect be to aid or oppose, to advance or retard. In the relationship between man and religion, the State is firmly committed to a position of neutrality. Though the application of that rule requires interpretation of a delicate sort, the rule itself is clearly and concisely stated in the words of the First Amendment. Applying that rule to the facts of these cases, we affirm the judgment in No. 142. In No. 119, the judgment is reversed and the cause remanded to the Maryland Court of Appeals for further proceedings consistent with this opinion.

It is so ordered.

. . . .

---

1. Notice that the state's argument in *Schempp* that Bible reading was constitutional since objecting students did not have to remain in class was answered by the Court by citing *Engel v. Vitale*, 370 U.S. 421 (1962), which had held unconstitutional New York state's program of daily classroom invocation of God's blessings as prescribed in prayer promulgated by the New York Board of Regents (the State Board of Education). The citation in *Schempp* is apparently to the following language of *Engel*:

> There can be no doubt that New York's state prayer program officially establishes the religious beliefs embodied in the Regents' prayer. The respondents' argument to the contrary which is largely based upon the contention that the Regents' prayer is "non-denominational" and the fact that the program, as modified and approved by state courts, does not require all pupils to recite the prayer but permits those who wish to do so to remain silent or be excused from the room, ignores the essential nature of the program's constitutional defects. Neither the fact that the prayer may be denominationally neutral nor the fact that its observance on the part of the students is voluntary can serve to free it from the limitations of the Establishment Clause, as it might from the Free Exercise Clause, of the First Amendment, both of which are operative against the States by virtue of the Fourteenth Amendment. Although these two clauses may in certain instances overlap, they forbid two quite different kinds of governmental encroachment upon religious freedom. The Establishment Clause, unlike the Free Exercise Clause, does not depend upon any showing of direct governmental compulsion and is violated by the enactment of laws which establish an official religion whether those laws operate directly to coerce nonobserving individuals or not. *Id.* at 430.

2. Although the Court does not seem to rely on it in *Schempp*, in the summary of the testimony in footnotes, the Court repeats the father's testimony as to the ill effects he thought it would have on his children to have them excused from

Bible reading. If one accepts the father's predictions as correct, would this be a basis for invalidating Bible reading even though objecting students are exempted? In other words, is there coercion operating against a student exercising his option not to participate, and if so, is this a basis for holding Bible reading unconstitutional?

3. In his concurrence in the *Schempp* case, Justice Brennan discusses this issue. 374 U.S. at 288-91:

> Thus the short, and to be sufficient, answer is that the availability of excusal or exemption simply has no relevance to the establishment question, if it is once found that these practices are essentially religious exercises designed at least in part to achieve religious aims through the use of public school facilities during the school day.
>
> The more difficult question, however, is whether the availability of excusal for the dissenting child serves to refute challenges to these practices under the Free Exercise Clause. While it is enough to decide these cases to dispose of the establishment questions, questions of free exercise are so inextricably interwoven into the history and present status of these practices as to justify disposition of this second aspect of the excusal issue. The answer is that the excusal procedure itself necessarily operates in such a way as to infringe the rights of free exercise of those children who wish to be excused. We have held in *Barnette* ... that a State may [not] require ... public school students ... to profess beliefs offensive to religious principles. By the same token the state could not constitutionally require a student to profess publicly his disbelief as the prerequisite to the exercise of his constitutional right of abstention.... [B]y requiring what is tantamount in the eyes of teachers and schoolmates to a profession of disbelief, or at least of nonconformity, the procedure may well deter those children who do not wish to participate for any reason based upon the dictates of conscience from exercising an indisputably constitutional right to be excused. Thus the excusal provision in its operation subjects them to a cruel dilemma. In consequence, even devout children may well avoid claiming their right and simply continue to participate in exercises distasteful to them because of an understandable reluctance to be stigmatized as atheists or nonconformists simply on the basis of their request.
>
> ....

What does Justice Brennan mean by his citation to *Barnette*? Is he implying that, in his view, recitation of the Pledge of Allegiance in public schools is unconstitutional, even with an exemption for objectors, because it forces individuals to label themselves as objectors and in so doing violates the rights of objectors? In addition to this argument, Justice Brennan also rests heavily on the analytically different argument that children will be deterred from exempting themselves because of peer group and other pressures. If this is a basis for the result in *Schempp*, is there reason to believe that the pressures on those who

A. RELIGION AND THE PUBLIC SCHOOL CURRICULUM

object to the flag salute are less or different than on those who object to Bible reading? Is there reason to believe that the former are better able to resist these pressures than the latter? *See* discussion of *Barnette* in Part C of this chapter.

4. In his dissent in *Schempp*, Justice Stewart states that the case "turns on the question of coercion," that is, students being coerced into not exempting themselves. In his view, however, the record is not sufficient to determine this, as it contains only the "subjective prophecy" of a parent. Justice Stewart would, therefore, remand the case for determination of this issue. He does not, however, state how it could be determined. Would the plaintiffs have to prove that specific students were, indeed, coerced? Could social science literature or experts be presented to show that the situation is "inherently" coercive?

WALLACE v. JAFFREE
Supreme Court of the United States
472 U.S. 38 (1985)

JUSTICE STEVENS delivered the opinion of the Court:

At an early stage of this litigation, the constitutionality of three Alabama statutes was questioned: (1) § 16-1-20, enacted in 1978, which authorized a 1-minute period of silence in all public schools "for meditation"; (2) § 16-1-20.1, enacted in 1981, which authorized a period of silence "for meditation or voluntary prayer";[2] and (3) § 16-1-20.2, enacted in 1982, which authorized teachers to lead "willing students" in a prescribed prayer to "Almighty God ... the Creator and Supreme Judge of the world."

At the preliminary-injunction stage of this case, the District Court distinguished § 16-1-20 from the other two statutes. It then held that there was "nothing wrong" with § 16-1-20, but that §§ 16-1-20.1 and 16-1-20.2 were both invalid because the sole purpose of both was "an effort on the part of the State of Alabama to encourage a religious activity." After the trial on the merits, the District Court did not change its interpretation of these two statutes, but held that they were constitutional because, in its opinion, Alabama has the power to establish a state religion if it chooses to do so.

The Court of Appeals agreed with the District Court's initial interpretation of the purpose of both § 16-1-20.1 and § 16-1-20.2, and held them both unconstitutional. We have already affirmed the Court of Appeals' holding with respect to § 16-1-20.2. Moreover, appellees have not questioned the holding that § 16-1-20 is valid. Thus, the narrow question for decision is whether § 16-1-20.1, which authorizes a period of silence for "meditation or voluntary prayer," is a law

---

[2]Alabama Code § 16-1-20.1 (Supp.1984) provides:

At the commencement of the first class of each day in all grades in all public schools the teacher in charge of the room in which each class is held may announce that a period of silence not to exceed one minute in duration shall be observed for meditation or voluntary prayer, and during any such period no other activities shall be engaged in.

respecting the establishment of religion within the meaning of the First Amendment.

I

Appellee Ishmael Jaffree is a resident of Mobile County, Alabama. On May 28, 1982, he filed a complaint on behalf of three of his minor children; two of them were second-grade students and the third was then in kindergarten. The complaint named members of the Mobile County School Board, various school officials, and the minor plaintiffs' three teachers as defendants. The complaint alleged that the appellees brought the action "seeking principally a declaratory judgment and an injunction restraining the Defendants and each of them from maintaining or allowing the maintenance of regular religious prayer services or other forms of religious observances in the Mobile County Public Schools in violation of the First Amendment as made applicable to states by the Fourteenth Amendment to the United States Constitution." The complaint further alleged that two of the children had been subjected to various acts of religious indoctrination "from the beginning of the school year in September, 1981"; that the defendant teachers had "on a daily basis" led their classes in saying certain prayers in unison; that the minor children were exposed to ostracism from their peer group class members if they did not participate; and that Ishmael Jaffree had repeatedly but unsuccessfully requested that the devotional services be stopped.

....

In November 1982, the District Court held a 4-day trial on the merits. The evidence related primarily to the 1981-1982 academic year — the year after the enactment of § 16-1-20.1 and prior to the enactment of § 16-1-20.2. The District Court found that during that academic year each of the minor plaintiffs' teachers had led classes in prayer activities, even after being informed of appellees' objections to these activities.

....

The Court of Appeals consolidated the two cases; not surprisingly, it reversed.... The Court of Appeals ... held that the teachers' religious activities violated the Establishment Clause of the First Amendment. With respect to § 16-1-20.1 and § 16-1-20.2, the Court of Appeals stated that "both statutes advance and encourage religious activities." The Court of Appeals then quoted with approval the District Court's finding that § 16-1-20.1, and § 16-1-20.2, were efforts "'to encourage a religious activity. Even though these statutes are permissive in form, it is nevertheless state involvement respecting an establishment of religion.'" Thus, the Court of Appeals concluded that both statutes were "specifically the type which the Supreme Court addressed in *Engel* [*v. Vitale*, 370 U.S. 421].

A. RELIGION AND THE PUBLIC SCHOOL CURRICULUM

II

Our unanimous affirmance of the Court of Appeals' judgment concerning § 16-1-20.2 makes it unnecessary to comment at length on the District Court's remarkable conclusion that the Federal Constitution imposes no obstacle to Alabama's establishment of a state religion. Before analyzing the precise issue that is presented to us, it is nevertheless appropriate to recall how firmly embedded in our constitutional jurisprudence is the proposition that the several States have no greater power to restrain the individual freedoms protected by the First Amendment than does the Congress of the United States.

As is plain from its text, the First Amendment was adopted to curtail the power of Congress to interfere with the individual's freedom to believe, to worship, and to express himself in accordance with the dictates of his own conscience. Until the Fourteenth Amendment was added to the Constitution, the First Amendment's restraints on the exercise of federal power simply did not apply to the States. But when the Constitution was amended to prohibit any State from depriving any person of liberty without due process of law, that Amendment imposed the same substantive limitations on the States' power to legislate that the First Amendment had always imposed on the Congress' power. This Court has confirmed and endorsed this elementary proposition of law time and time again.

....

... As JUSTICE JACKSON eloquently stated in *West Virginia Board of Education v. Barnette*, 319 U.S. 624, 642 (1943):

> "If there is any fixed star in our constitutional constellation, it is that no official, high or petty, can prescribe what shall be orthodox in politics, nationalism, religion, or other matters of opinion or force citizens to confess by word or act their faith therein."

The State of Alabama, no less than the Congress of the United States, must respect that basic truth.

III

When the Court has been called upon to construe the breadth of the Establishment Clause, it has examined the criteria developed over a period of many years. Thus, in *Lemon v. Kurtzman*, we wrote:

> "Every analysis in this area must begin with consideration of the cumulative criteria developed by the Court over many years. Three such tests may be gleaned from our cases. First, the statute must have a secular legislative purpose; second, its principal or primary effect must be one that neither advances nor inhibits religion, *Board of Education v. Allen*, 392 U.S. 236 (1968); finally, the statute must not foster 'an excessive government entanglement with religion.'"

It is the first of these three criteria that is most plainly implicated by this case. As the District Court correctly recognized, no consideration of the second or third criteria is necessary if a statute does not have a clearly secular purpose. For even though a statute that is motivated in part by a religious purpose may satisfy the first criterion, *see, e.g., Abington School District v. Schempp*, 374 U.S. 203 (1963), the First Amendment requires that a statute must be invalidated if it is entirely motivated by a purpose to advance religion.

In applying the purpose test, it is appropriate to ask "whether government's actual purpose is to endorse or disapprove of religion."[42] In this case, the answer to that question is dispositive. For the record not only provides us with an unambiguous affirmative answer, but it also reveals that the enactment of § 16-1-20.1 was not motivated by any clearly secular purpose — indeed, the statute had no secular purpose.

IV

The sponsor of the bill that became § 16-1-20.1, Senator Donald Holmes, inserted into the legislative record — apparently without dissent — a statement indicating that the legislation was an "effort to return voluntary prayer" to the public schools. Later Senator Holmes confirmed this purpose before the District Court. In response to the question whether he had any purpose for the legislation other than returning voluntary prayer to public schools, he stated: "No, I did not have no other purpose in mind." The State did not present evidence of any secular purpose.

....

The legislative intent to return prayer to the public schools is, of course, quite different from merely protecting every student's right to engage in voluntary prayer during an appropriate moment of silence during the schoolday. The 1978 statute already protected that right, containing nothing that prevented any student from engaging in voluntary prayer during a silent minute of meditation. Appellants have not identified any secular purpose that was not fully served by § 16-1-20 before the enactment of § 16-1-20.1. Thus, only two conclusions are consistent with the text of § 16-1-20.1: (1) the statute was enacted to convey a message of state endorsement and promotion of prayer; or (2) the statute was enacted for no purpose. No one suggests that the statute was nothing but a meaningless or irrational act.

... The legislature enacted § 16-1-20.1, despite the existence of § 16-1-20 for the sole purpose of expressing the State's endorsement of prayer activities for one minute at the beginning of each schoolday. The addition of "or voluntary

---

[42]*Lynch v. Donnelly*, 465 U.S. [668] at 690 (O'Connor, J., concurring) ("The purpose prong of the *Lemon* test asks whether government's actual purpose is to endorse or disapprove of religion. The effect prong asks whether, irrespective of government's actual purpose, the practice under review in fact conveys a message of endorsement or disapproval. An affirmative answer to either question should render the challenged practice invalid").

A. RELIGION AND THE PUBLIC SCHOOL CURRICULUM

prayer" indicates that the State intended to characterize prayer as a favored practice. Such an endorsement is not consistent with the established principle that the government must pursue a course of complete neutrality toward religion.

The importance of that principle does not permit us to treat this as an inconsequential case involving nothing more than a few words of symbolic speech on behalf of the political majority. For whenever the State itself speaks on a religious subject, one of the questions that we must ask is "whether the government intends to convey a message of endorsement or disapproval of religion." The well-supported concurrent findings of the District Court and the Court of Appeals — that § 16-1-20.1 was intended to convey a message of state approval of prayer activities in the public schools — make it unnecessary, and indeed inappropriate, to evaluate the practical significance of the addition of the words "or voluntary prayer" to the statute. Keeping in mind, as we must, "both the fundamental place held by the Establishment Clause in our constitutional scheme and the myriad, subtle ways in which Establishment Clause values can be eroded," we conclude that § 16-1-20.1 violates the First Amendment.

The judgment of the Court of Appeals is affirmed.

It is so ordered.

....

JUSTICE O'CONNOR, concurring in the judgment:

... I agree with the judgment of the Court that, in light of the findings of the courts below and the history of its enactment, § 16-1-20.1 of the Alabama Code violates the Establishment Clause of the First Amendment. In my view, there can be little doubt that the purpose and likely effect of this subsequent enactment is to endorse and sponsor voluntary prayer in the public schools. I write separately to identify the peculiar features of the Alabama law that render it invalid, and to explain why moment of silence laws in other States do not necessarily manifest the same infirmity. I also write to explain why neither history nor the Free Exercise Clause of the First Amendment validates the Alabama law struck down by the Court today.

I

....

... I ... believe ... that the standards announced in *Lemon* should be reexamined and refined in order to make them more useful in achieving the underlying purpose of the First Amendment. We must strive to do more than erect a constitutional "signpost,"... to be followed or ignored in a particular case as our predilections may dictate. Instead, our goal should be "to frame a principle for constitutional adjudication that is not only grounded in the history and language of the first amendment, but one that is also capable of consistent application to the relevant problems." This is a refinement of the *Lemon* test with this goal in mind. *Lynch v. Donnelly*, 465 U.S. at 687-689 (concurring opinion).

The *Lynch* concurrence suggested that the religious liberty protected by the Establishment Clause is infringed when the government makes adherence to religion relevant to a person's standing in the political community. Direct government action endorsing religion or a particular religious practice is invalid under this approach because it "sends a message to nonadherents that they are outsiders, not full members of the political community, and an accompanying message to adherents that they are insiders, favored members of the political community." *Id.* at 688. Under this view, *Lemon*'s inquiry as to the purpose and effect of a statute requires courts to examine whether government's purpose is to endorse religion and whether the statute actually conveys a message of endorsement. The endorsement test is useful because of the analytic content it gives to the *Lemon*-mandated inquiry into legislative purpose and effect. In this country, church and state must necessarily operate within the same community. Because of this coexistence, it is inevitable that the secular interests of government and the religious interests of various sects and their adherents will frequently intersect, conflict, and combine. A statute that ostensibly promotes a secular interest often has an incidental or even a primary effect of helping or hindering a sectarian belief. Chaos would ensue if every such statute were invalid under the Establishment Clause. For example, the State could not criminalize murder for fear that it would thereby promote the Biblical command against killing. The task for the Court is to sort out those statutes and government practices whose purpose and effect go against the grain of religious liberty protected by the First Amendment.

The endorsement test does not preclude government from acknowledging religion or from taking religion into account in making law and policy. It does preclude government from conveying or attempting to convey a message that religion or a particular religious belief is favored or preferred. Such an endorsement infringes the religious liberty of the nonadherent, for "[w]hen the power, prestige and financial support of government is placed behind a particular religious belief, the indirect coercive pressure upon religious minorities to conform to the prevailing officially approved religion is plain." *Engel v. Vitale, supra*, 370 U.S. at 431. At issue today is whether state moment of silence statutes in general, and Alabama's moment of silence statute in particular, embody an impermissible endorsement of prayer in public schools.

A

Twenty-five states permit or require public school teachers to have students observe a moment of silence in their classrooms. A few statutes provide that the moment of silence is for the purpose of meditation alone. *See* Ariz.Rev.Stat.Ann. § 15-522 (1984); Conn.Gen.Stat. § 10-16a (1983); R.I.Gen.Laws § 16-12-3.1 (1981). The typical statute, however, calls for a moment of silence at the beginning of the schoolday during which students may meditate, pray, or reflect on the activities of the day.

A. RELIGION AND THE PUBLIC SCHOOL CURRICULUM

The *Engel* and *Abington* decisions are not dispositive on the constitutionality of moment of silence laws. In those cases, public school teachers and students led their classes in devotional exercises.... Under all of these statutes, a student who did not share the religious beliefs expressed in the course of the exercise was left with the choice of participating, thereby compromising the nonadherent's beliefs, or withdrawing, thereby calling attention to his or her nonconformity. The decisions acknowledged the coercion implicit under the statutory schemes, *see Engel*, [370 U.S.] at 431, but they expressly turned only on the fact that the government was sponsoring a manifestly religious exercise.

A state-sponsored moment of silence in the public schools is different from state-sponsored vocal prayer or Bible reading. First, a moment of silence is not inherently religious. Silence, unlike prayer or Bible reading, need not be associated with a religious exercise. Second, a pupil who participates in a moment of silence need not compromise his or her beliefs. During a moment of silence, a student who objects to prayer is left to his or her own thoughts, and is not compelled to listen to the prayers or thoughts of others. For these simple reasons, a moment of silence statute does not stand or fall under the Establishment Clause according to how the Court regards vocal prayer or Bible reading....

By mandating a moment of silence, a State does not necessarily endorse any activity that might occur during the period.... Even if a statute specifies that a student may choose to pray silently during a quiet moment, the State has not thereby encouraged prayer over other specified alternatives. Nonetheless, it is also possible that a moment of silence statute, either as drafted or as actually implemented, could effectively favor the child who prays over the child who does not. For example, the message of endorsement would seem inescapable if the teacher exhorts children to use the designated time to pray. Similarly, the face of the statute or its legislative history may clearly establish that it seeks to encourage or promote voluntary prayer over other alternatives, rather than merely provide a quiet moment that may be dedicated to prayer by those so inclined. The crucial question is whether the State has conveyed or attempted to convey the message that children should use the moment of silence for prayer. This question cannot be answered in the abstract, but instead requires courts to examine the history, language, and administration of a particular statute to determine whether it operates as an endorsement of religion. *Lynch*, 465 U.S. at 694 (concurring opinion) ("Every government practice must be judged in its unique circumstances to determine whether it constitutes an endorsement or disapproval of religion").

Before reviewing Alabama's moment of silence law to determine whether it endorses prayer, some general observations on the proper scope of the inquiry are in order. First, the inquiry into the purpose of the legislature in enacting a moment of silence law should be deferential and limited. In determining whether the government intends a moment of silence statute to convey a message of endorsement or disapproval of religion, a court has no license to psychoanalyze the legislators. If a legislature expresses a plausible secular purpose for a moment of silence statute in either the text or the legislative history, or if the statute disclaims an intent to encourage prayer over alternatives during a moment of silence, then courts should generally defer to that stated intent....

Justice Rehnquist suggests that this sort of deferential inquiry into legislative purpose "means little," because "it only requires the legislature to express any secular purpose and omit all sectarian references." It is not a trivial matter, however, to require that the legislature manifest a secular purpose and omit all sectarian endorsements from its laws. That requirement is precisely tailored to the Establishment Clause's purpose of assuring that government not intentionally endorse religion or a religious practice. It is of course possible that a legislature will enunciate a sham secular purpose for a statute. I have little doubt that our courts are capable of distinguishing a sham secular purpose from a sincere one, or that the *Lemon* inquiry into the effect of an enactment would help decide those close cases where the validity of an expressed secular purpose is in doubt. While the secular purpose requirement alone may rarely be determinative in striking down a statute, it nevertheless serves an important function. It reminds government that when it acts it should do so without endorsing a particular religious belief or practice that all citizens do not share. In this sense the secular purpose requirement is squarely based in the text of the Establishment Clause it helps to enforce.

Second, the *Lynch* concurrence suggested that the effect of a moment of silence law is not entirely a question of fact:

> "[W]hether a government activity communicates endorsement of religion is not a question of simple historical fact. Although evidentiary submissions may help answer it, the question is, like the question whether racial or sex-based classifications communicate an invidious message, in large part a legal question to be answered on the basis of judicial interpretation of social facts." 465 U.S. at 693-94.

The relevant issue is whether an objective observer, acquainted with the text, legislative history, and implementation of the statute, would perceive it as a state endorsement of prayer in public schools. *Cf. Bose Corp. v. Consumers Union of United States, Inc.*, 466 U.S. 485, 517-518, n. 1 (1984) (REHNQUIST, J., dissenting).... A moment of silence law that is clearly drafted and implemented so as to permit prayer, meditation, and reflection within the prescribed period, without endorsing one alternative over the others, should pass this test.

B

The analysis above suggests that moment of silence laws in many States should pass Establishment Clause scrutiny because they do not favor the child who chooses to pray during a moment of silence over the child who chooses to meditate or reflect. Alabama Code § 16-1-20.1 (Supp.1984) does not stand on the same footing. However deferentially one examines its text and legislative history, however objectively one views the message attempted to be conveyed to

A. RELIGION AND THE PUBLIC SCHOOL CURRICULUM

the public, the conclusion is unavoidable that the purpose of the statute is to endorse prayer in public schools. I accordingly agree with the Court of Appeals, 705 F.2d 1526, 1535 (1983), that the Alabama statute has a purpose which is in violation of the Establishment Clause, and cannot be upheld.

....

JUSTICE REHNQUIST, dissenting:

Thirty-eight years ago this Court, in *Everson v. Board of Education*, 330 U.S. 1, 16 (1947), summarized its exegesis of Establishment Clause doctrine thus: "In the words of [Thomas] Jefferson, the clause against establishment of religion by law was intended to erect 'a wall of separation between church and State.' *Reynolds v. United States*, [98 U.S. 145, 164, 25 L. Ed. 244 (1879)]."

....

It is impossible to build sound constitutional doctrine upon a mistaken understanding of constitutional history, but unfortunately the Establishment Clause has been expressly freighted with Jefferson's misleading metaphor for nearly 40 years....

... But when we turn to the record of the proceedings in the First Congress leading up to the adoption of the Establishment Clause of the Constitution, including [James] Madison's significant contributions thereto, we see a far different picture of its purpose than the highly simplified "wall of separation between church and State."

....

The language Madison proposed for what ultimately became the Religion Clauses of the First Amendment was this:

> The civil rights of none shall be abridged on account of religious belief or worship, nor shall any national religion be established, nor shall the full and equal rights of conscience be in any manner, or on any pretext, infringed. *Id.* at 434.

....

... James Madison was undoubtedly the most important architect among the Members of the House of the Amendments which became the Bill of Rights, but it was James Madison speaking as an advocate of sensible legislative compromise, not as an advocate of incorporating the Virginia Statute of Religious Liberty into the United States Constitution. During the ratification debate in the Virginia Convention, Madison had actually opposed the idea of any Bill of Rights. His sponsorship of the Amendments in the House was obviously not that of a zealous believer in the necessity of the Religion Clauses, but of one who felt it might do some good, could do no harm, and would satisfy those who had ratified the Constitution on the condition that Congress propose a Bill of Rights. His original language "nor shall any national religion be established" obviously does not conform to the "wall of separation" between church and State idea which latter-day commentators have ascribed to him. His explanation on the floor of the meaning of his language — "that Congress should not establish a religion, and enforce the legal observation of it by law" is of the same ilk....

It seems indisputable from these glimpses of Madison's thinking, as reflected by actions on the floor of the House in 1789, that he saw the Amendment as designed to prohibit the establishment of a national religion, and perhaps to prevent discrimination among sects. He did not see it as requiring neutrality on the part of government between religion and irreligion. Thus the Court's opinion in *Everson* — while correct in bracketing Madison and Jefferson together in their exertions in their home State leading to the enactment of the Virginia Statute of Religious Liberty — is totally incorrect in suggesting that Madison carried these views onto the floor of the United States House of Representatives when he proposed the language which would ultimately become the Bill of Rights.

The repetition of this error in the Court's opinion in *Illinois ex rel. McCollum v. Board of Education*, 333 U.S. 203 (1948), and, *inter alia*, *Engel v. Vitale*, 370 U.S. 421 (1962), does not make it any sounder historically. Finally, in *Abington School District v. Schempp*, 374 U.S. 203, 214 (1963), the Court made the truly remarkable statement that "the views of Madison and Jefferson, preceded by Roger Williams, came to be incorporated not only in the Federal Constitution but likewise in those of most of our States." On the basis of what evidence we have, this statement is demonstrably incorrect as a matter of history. And its repetition in varying forms in succeeding opinions of the Court can give it no more authority than it possesses as a matter of fact; *stare decisis* may bind courts as to matters of law, but it cannot bind them as to matters of history.

None of the other Members of Congress who spoke during the [floor debates] expressed the slightest indication that they thought the language before them from the Select Committee, or the evil to be aimed at, would require that the Government be absolutely neutral as between religion and irreligion. The evil to be aimed at, so far as those who spoke were concerned, appears to have been the establishment of a national church, and perhaps the preference of one religious sect over another; but it was definitely not concerned about whether the Government might aid all religions evenhandedly....

The actions of the First Congress, which reenacted the Northwest Ordinance for the governance of the Northwest Territory in 1789, confirm the view that Congress did not mean that the Government should be neutral between religion and irreligion. The House of Representatives took up the Northwest Ordinance on the same day as Madison introduced his proposed amendments which became the Bill of Rights; while at that time the Federal Government was of course not bound by draft amendments to the Constitution which had not yet been proposed by Congress, say nothing of ratified by the States, it seems highly unlikely that the House of Representatives would simultaneously consider proposed amendments to the Constitution and enact an important piece of territorial legislation which conflicted with the intent of those proposals. The Northwest Ordinance, 1 Stat. 50, reenacted the Northwest Ordinance of 1787 and provided that "[r]eligion, morality, and knowledge, being necessary to good government and

A. RELIGION AND THE PUBLIC SCHOOL CURRICULUM

the happiness of mankind, schools and the means of education shall forever be encouraged." *Id.* at 52, n. (a). Land grants for schools in the Northwest Territory were not limited to public schools. It was not until 1845 that Congress limited land grants in the new States and Territories to nonsectarian schools.

On the day after the House of Representatives voted to adopt the form of the First Amendment Religion Clauses which was ultimately proposed and ratified, Representative Elias Boudinot proposed a resolution asking President George Washington to issue a Thanksgiving Day Proclamation. Boudinot said he "could not think of letting the session pass over without offering an opportunity to all the citizens of the United States of joining with one voice, in returning to Almighty God their sincere thanks for the many blessings he had poured down upon them." ...

Boudinot's resolution was carried in the affirmative on September 25, 1789. Boudinot and Sherman, who favored the Thanksgiving Proclamation, voted in favor of the adoption of the proposed amendments to the Constitution, including the Religion Clauses; Tucker, who opposed the Thanksgiving Proclamation, voted against the adoption of the amendments which became the Bill of Rights.

....

As the United States moved from the 18th into the 19th century, Congress appropriated time and again public moneys in support of sectarian Indian education carried on by religious organizations. Typical of these was Jefferson's treaty with the Kaskaskia Indians, which provided annual cash support for the Tribe's Roman Catholic priest and church. It was not until 1897, when aid to sectarian education for Indians had reached $500,000 annually, that Congress decided thereafter to cease appropriating money for education in sectarian schools. This history shows the fallacy of the notion found in *Everson* that "no tax in any amount" may be levied for religious activities in any form.

Joseph Story, a Member of this Court from 1811 to 1845, and during much of that time a professor at the Harvard Law School, published by far the most comprehensive treatise on the United States Constitution that had then appeared. Volume 2 of Story's Commentaries on the Constitution of the United States 630-32 (5th ed. 1891) discussed the meaning of the Establishment Clause of the First Amendment this way:

> Probably at the time of the adoption of the Constitution, and of the amendment to it now under consideration [First Amendment], the general if not the universal sentiment in America was, that Christianity ought to receive encouragement from the State so far as was not incompatible with the private rights of conscience and the freedom of religious worship. An attempt to level all religions, and to make it a matter of state policy to hold all in utter indifference, would have created universal disapprobation, if not universal indignation.

The real object of the [First] [A]mendment was not to countenance, much less to advance, Mahometanism, or Judaism, or infidelity, by prostrating Christianity; but to exclude all rivalry among Christian sects, and to prevent any national ecclesiastical establishment which should give to a hierarchy the exclusive patronage of the national government....

....

It would seem from this evidence that the Establishment Clause of the First Amendment had acquired a well-accepted meaning: it forbade establishment of a national religion, and forbade preference among religious sects or denominations. Indeed, the first American dictionary defined the word "establishment" as "the act of establishing, founding, ratifying or ordaining," such as in "[t]he episcopal form of religion, so called, in England." 1 N. Webster, American Dictionary of the English Language (1st ed. 1828). The Establishment Clause did not require government neutrality between religion and irreligion nor did it prohibit the Federal Government from providing nondiscriminatory aid to religion. There is simply no historical foundation for the proposition that the Framers intended to build the "wall of separation" that was constitutionalized in *Everson*.

....

Whether due to its lack of historical support or its practical unworkability, the *Everson* "wall" has proved all but useless as a guide to sound constitutional adjudication....

... The "wall of separation between church and State" is a metaphor based on bad history, a metaphor which has proved useless as a guide to judging. It should be frankly and explicitly abandoned.

The Court has more recently attempted to add some mortar to *Everson's* wall through the three-part test of *Lemon v. Kurtzman, supra*, 403 U.S. at 614-15, which served at first to offer a more useful test for purposes of the Establishment Clause than did the "wall" metaphor. Generally stated, the *Lemon* test proscribes state action that has a sectarian purpose or effect, or causes an impermissible governmental entanglement with religion.

....

... [T]he *Lemon* test has no more grounding in the history of the First Amendment than does the wall theory upon which it rests. The three-part test represents a determined effort to craft a workable rule from a historically faulty doctrine; but the rule can only be as sound as the doctrine it attempts to service. The three-part test has simply not provided adequate standards for deciding Establishment Clause cases, as this Court has slowly come to realize. Even worse, the *Lemon* test has caused this Court to fracture into unworkable plurality opinions, depending upon how each of the three factors applies to a certain state action....

A. RELIGION AND THE PUBLIC SCHOOL CURRICULUM

The Court strikes down the Alabama statute because the State wished to "characterize prayer as a favored practice." It would come as much of a shock to those who drafted the Bill of Rights as it will to a large number of thoughtful Americans today to learn that the Constitution, as construed by the majority, prohibits the Alabama Legislature from "endorsing" prayer. George Washington himself, at the request of the very Congress which passed the Bill of Rights, proclaimed a day of "public thanksgiving and prayer, to be observed by acknowledging with grateful hearts the many and signal favors of Almighty God." History must judge whether it was the Father of his Country in 1789, or a majority of the Court today, which has strayed from the meaning of the Establishment Clause.

The State surely has a secular interest in regulating the manner in which public schools are conducted. Nothing in the Establishment Clause of the First Amendment, properly understood, prohibits any such generalized "endorsement" of prayer. I would therefore reverse the judgment of the Court of Appeals.

---

1. *Schempp*, *supra*, and *Engel v. Vitale* (referenced in *Schempp*), both decided over thirty years ago, are the immediate precedents for *Jaffree*. However, does *Jaffree* follow the logic of either of those two cases? Though disputed in dissent, *Schempp* maintained that it had taken a "neutral" position on religion reasoning that the Establishment Clause prohibited the reading of the Bible in public school classrooms. Does *Jaffree* follow this line of strict neutrality or does the Court demonstrate a willingness to embrace more of a policy of accommodation in such cases? If the latter, what is the Constitutional support for such a position?

2. *Jaffree* must also be looked upon as a case which contributes to the increasing controversy over the mode of analysis to be used in Establishment Clause claims. The Court pointed to the case of *Lemon v. Kurtzman*, 403 U.S. 602 (1971), which for twenty years had provided the framework for evaluating the constitutionality of religious based cases. *Lemon* concerned efforts by Pennsylvania and Rhode Island to reimburse private sectarian schools for teacher salaries and secular educational services. While holding that the laws violated the Establishment Clause, the *Lemon* Court fashioned a three-pronged test to determine whether such statutes were in accordance with the Constitution. First, the Court held that a statute must have some secular legislative purpose. Second, the principal or primary effect of the statute must be one that neither advances nor inhibits religion. And third, the statute must not foster excessive government entanglement with religion. The Court found that although the legislative intent of the reimbursement plans at issue was not to advance religion, the plans entailed excessive governmental entanglement with religion and thus failed to pass constitutional muster.

Jaffree reiterated the test of *Lemon* never getting past the first prong: "[N]o consideration of the second or third criteria was necessary if the statute did not have a clearly secular purpose." In the midst of the controversy over the *Lemon* test evidenced by the several opinions in *Jaffree*, does the Court give any guidance to school systems for its continued application? Inasmuch as the "purpose" prong was the only one addressed by the Court, is there any hint of how to apply the other two prongs to state statutes featuring "school prayer" or "moments of silence"?

3. The question of *Lemon* test controversy is circumvented by a peculiar paradox in *Jaffree*. While the majority uncritically defended its use, they have at other times been critical of it. For example, Justice Stevens, who wrote the majority opinion, advocated abandonment of *Lemon* in the case of *Wolman v. Walter*, 433 U.S. 229, 265-66 (1977). Perhaps the two most telling opinions, however, are those of Justices O'Connor and Rehnquist, concurring and dissenting, respectively. Justice O'Connor has voiced the position that *Lemon* should be modified. This angle of reasoning first appeared in *Lynch v. Donnelly*, 465 U.S. 668 (1984) (O'Connor, J. concurring). In that case, O'Connor maintained that the Establishment Clause is violated in two situations. The first occurs when government becomes excessively entangled with a religious institution, resulting in some religious groups gaining access to governmental powers not shared by all and possibly leading to a political constituency defined along religious lines. The second, more direct infringement occurs when government endorses or disapproves of a certain religion. In putting forth her thesis, O'Connor sought to clarify the *Lemon* test in order to preserve it. In *Lynch*, she agreed with the majority that the inclusion of a creche in an otherwise secular government Christmas display was not an endorsement of religion, as one religious piece in a holiday display did not send a message to reasonable nonadherents that they are outsiders in government. She stated, "[t]he proper inquiry under ... *Lemon* is whether the government intends to convey a message of endorsement or disapproval of religion." *Lynch* at 691. This refinement of *Lemon*, applied to all prongs of the *Lemon* test is what has come to be referred to as the "endorsement" test.

One of the purposes of the Establishment Clause, according to O'Connor, is to avoid political divisions. Her concurring opinion focused on institutional entanglement and endorsement or disapproval of religion in an attempt to clarify *Lemon*. Justice O'Connor, then, seems to give a more "accomodationist" reading in deciding Establishment Clause issues, particularly those relating to school prayer. This gives a restrictive reading to the neutrality requirement of *Schempp*. Does this mean that the O'Connor thesis would endorse public school students' voluntary prayer in any form as long as it passed the "endorsement" test?

Justice Rehnquist takes issue with the historical interpretation that the Establishment Clause requires absolute government neutrality or a wall of separation between church and state. Is Rehnquist persuasive in his arguments, much of which are based on secondary sources and not case law? How wise is it to spend so much time focusing on Constitutional history to solve present day

A. RELIGION AND THE PUBLIC SCHOOL CURRICULUM

problems? As broad, flexible, and long-lasting as the Constitution and its Amendments are, is it prudent to credit the Framers with so much foresight?

According to Rehnquist, years of mistakes, misrepresentations of history, and the Framers' intentions and reliance on these misrepresentations do not make these errors any more acceptable. With respect to universal acknowledgment of differing views, were the Framers as hypocritical as Rehnquist's dissent makes them out to be? For the purposes of "school prayer" and "moments of silent meditation," both problems of the 20th Century, how should a document drafted in the 18th Century be interpreted?

A concurring opinion in the First Circuit Court of Appeals decision of *Lee v. Weisman*, 908 F.2d 1090 (1st Cir. 1990), had a response:

> [T]he Court has spent considerable time considering and debating the history of the religion clauses, ... each time the results have been inconclusive ... The ground has been trodden so much that it is barren of meaning and persuasive power .... Because of the tangled and often conflicting historical record, it is unlikely that, as an empirical matter, we can ever know the original intention of the authors of the Constitution. Even if we could reconstruct the framers' intent, that would not necessarily be determinative in this case ... An additional facet of the problem with the framers' intent is what was the framers' intention about their intent. Scholars have argued that the original intention of the framers was that their intentions were irrelevant to interpreting the Constitution. *Id.* at 1092-93.

Justices Stevens (the author of the *Jaffree* majority opinion) and O'Connor also expressly rejected the application of Rehnquist's interpretation.

4. The *Jaffree* Court also cites to *Marsh v. Chambers*, 463 U.S. 783 (1983). The case represents a time in which the Court *declined* to apply the *Lemon* test to an Establishment Clause complaint. The Court upheld the practice of the Nebraska Legislature of opening legislative sessions with a prayer led by a minister. The Court justified the practice based on the long tradition behind it and the fact that such practices were common during the time of the framing of the Establishment Clause. Note, however, that the Eleventh Circuit Court of Appeals had occasion to decide if *Marsh* applied to public school prayer in *Jager v. Douglas County Sch. Dist.*, 862 F.2d 824 (11th Cir. 1989). The court declared no parallel with *Marsh*, holding that *Lemon* controlled distinguishing school prayer cases from those involving adults based on the coercion inherent in a school setting.

But see Stein v. Plainwell Community Sch. Dist., 822 F.2d 1406 (6th Cir. 1987), *infra*, which upheld the practice of offering a prayer at graduation on the basis that such prayers are analogous to the prayer at legislative sessions discussed in *Marsh*. The court held, unlike *Jager*, that the tradition and history and non-denominational nature of such prayers insulated them from attack. One of the prayers was given by students and included reference to "Our Heavenly Father"; a second prayer was pronounced by a Christian minister.

5. The majority in *Jaffree* cites *Stone v. Graham*, 449 U.S. 39 (1980), a case that invalidated a state statute requiring the posting of the Ten Commandments on public school classroom walls. *Jaffree*, like *Stone*, asked if the school rule had the purpose or effect of advancing religion and whether there was a fostering of excessive entanglement between government and religion. In *Jaffree* the Court found motive for a violation in both the statute and its sponsor. Which aspect of the *Lemon* test invalidates the motive? Purpose? Effect? Would O'Connor's "endorsement test" require that the motive be the advancement of religion? What if the state were to claim that the motive is religious freedom?

6. There are a number of articles on the "moment of silence" issue. *See, e.g.*, Comment, *And a Child Shall Lead Them: Justice O'Connor, the Principal of Religious Liberty and Its Practical Application*, 8 Pace L. Rev. 249 (1988); Wilkins, *One Moment Please: Private Devotion in the Public Schools*, 2 B.Y.U. J. Pub. L. 8 (1988); Vieira, *School Prayer and the Principle of Uncoerced Listening*, 14 Hastings Const. L.Q. 763 (1987); Choper, *Church, State and The Supreme Court: Current Controversy*, 29 Ariz L. Rev. 551 (1987); Case Note, *Silent Moments in Public Schools: Wallace v. Jaffree*, 54 U. Cin. L. Rev. 1405 (1985); Case Note, *And Now for a Moment of Silence: Wallace v. Jaffree*, 39 U. Miami L. Rev. 935.

7. Amongst the controversy may educators be liable for violations of the Establishment Clause as regards school prayer? *See Steele v. Van Buren Pub. Sch. Dist.*, 845 F.2d 1492 (8th Cir. 1988), where damages were ordered to a student who complained of coerced prayers at band rehearsals and performances; *See also May v. Cooperman*, 790 F.2d 240 (3d Cir. 1985), where attorneys fees were awarded to students and their parents for being subjected to observance of one moment of silence based on state statute declared unconstitutional.

8. Justice O'Connor relates that several states "permit or require public school teachers to have students observe a moment of silence in their classrooms." These laws are divided according to the innocuous promotion of "meditation" and the typical statute fostering "meditation, prayer or reflection." Presumably prayer would not be ruled out with either option, but the second clearly countenances such activity. Following is that portion of the Ohio Revised Code featuring a "moment of silence" in the public schools:

> No board of education shall prohibit a classroom teacher from providing in his classroom reasonable periods of time for programs or meditation upon a moral, philosophical or patriotic theme. No pupil shall be required to participate in such programs or meditations if they are contrary to the religious convictions of the pupil or his parents or guardians. Ohio Rev. Code Ann. § 3313.601 (Anderson 1992).

How would Ohio's "moment of silence" law fare under the *Lemon* test or O'Connor's "endorsement" test? Does it make a difference that, unlike the Alabama law, there is no legislative record that the law had a sectarian purpose? Is it more probable that the statute would pass constitutional muster under the

A. RELIGION AND THE PUBLIC SCHOOL CURRICULUM

Lemon or "endorsement test" in that there is no emphasis on prayer, but merely an accommodation for those who want to pray? Can an argument be sustained that an emphasis on a period of meditation requires long term government supervision that would amount to "excessive government entanglement with religion" and therefore render the law unconstitutional? What of the restrictive requirement that meditation must be "upon a moral, philosophical or patriotic theme" — could this be construed as an abridgment of a student's First Amendment right of freedom of conscience?

Recall *Schempp* and that court's reference that even though students were excused from participating in the school's religious exercises, their parents were concerned with "stigma", the imputation of punishment, as well as the missing of important school announcements if the children were excused from these activities. How did the *Schempp* Court with its emphasis toward strict neutrality evaluate this provision? How would such a clause manage under any of the tests in *Jaffree*?

2. GENERAL RESTRAINTS

LEE v. WEISMAN
Supreme Court of the United States
112 S. Ct. 2649 (1992)

JUSTICE KENNEDY delivered the opinion of the Court:

... The question before us is whether including clerical members who offer prayers as part of the official school graduation ceremony is consistent with the Religion Clauses of the First Amendment, provisions the Fourteenth Amendment makes applicable with full force to the States and their school districts.

I

A

Deborah Weisman graduated from Nathan Bishop Middle School, a public school in Providence, at a formal ceremony in June 1989. She was about 14 years old. For many years it has been the policy of the Providence School Committee and the Superintendent of Schools to permit principals to invite members of the clergy to give invocations and benedictions at middle school and high school graduations. Many, but not all, of the principals elected to include prayers as part of the graduation ceremonies. Acting for himself and his daughter, Deborah's father, Daniel Weisman, objected to any prayers at Deborah's middle school graduation, but to no avail. The school principal, petitioner Robert E. Lee, invited a rabbi to deliver prayers at the graduation exercises for Deborah's class. Rabbi Leslie Gutterman, of the Temple Beth El in Providence, accepted.

It has been the custom of Providence school officials to provide invited clergy with a pamphlet entitled "Guidelines for Civic Occasions," prepared by the

National Conference of Christians and Jews. The Guidelines recommend that public prayers at nonsectarian civic ceremonies be composed with "inclusiveness and sensitivity," though they acknowledge that "[p]rayer of any kind may be inappropriate on some civic occasions." The principal gave Rabbi Gutterman the pamphlet before the graduation and advised him the invocation and benediction should be nonsectarian.

Rabbi Gutterman's prayers were as follows:

Invocation

God of the Free, Hope of the Brave:
For the legacy of America where diversity is celebrated and the rights of minorities are protected, we thank You. May these young men and women grow up to enrich it.

For the liberty of America, we thank You. May these new graduates grow up to guard it.
For the political process of America in which all its citizens may participate, for its court system where all may seek justice we thank You. May those we honor this morning always turn to it in trust.

For the destiny of America we thank You. May the graduates of Nathan Bishop Middle School so live that they might help to share it.
May our aspirations for our country and for these young people, who are our hope for the future, be richly fulfilled. *Amen*

Benediction

O God, we are grateful to You for having endowed us with the capacity for learning which we have celebrated on this joyous commencement.
Happy families give thanks for seeing their children achieve an important milestone. Send Your blessings upon the teachers and administrators who helped prepare them.
The graduates now need strength and guidance for the future, help them to understand that we are not complete with academic knowledge alone. We must each strive to fulfill what You require of us all: To do justly, to love mercy, to walk humbly.
We give thanks to You, Lord, for keeping us alive, sustaining us and allowing us to reach this special, happy occasion. *Amen*

....

The case was submitted on stipulated facts. The District Court held that petitioners' practice of including invocations and benedictions in public school graduations violated the Establishment Clause of the First Amendment, and it enjoined petitioners from continuing the practice. The court applied the three-part Establishment Clause test set forth in *Lemon v. Kurtzman*, 403 U.S. 602 (1971). Under that test, to satisfy the Establishment Clause a governmental practice must

(1) reflect a clearly secular purpose; (2) have a primary effect that neither advances nor inhibits religion; and (3) avoid excessive government entanglement with religion. The District Court held that petitioners' actions violated the second part of the test, and so did not address either the first or the third....

....

II

These dominant facts mark and control the confines of our decision: State officials direct the performance of a formal religious exercise at promotional and graduation ceremonies for secondary schools. Even for those students who object to the religious exercise, their attendance and participation in the state-sponsored religious activity are in a fair and real sense obligatory, though the school district does not require attendance as a condition for receipt of the diploma.

....

The principle that government may accommodate the free exercise of religion does not supersede the fundamental limitations imposed by the Establishment Clause. It is beyond dispute that, at a minimum, the Constitution guarantees that government may not coerce anyone to support or participate in religion or its exercise, or otherwise act in a way which "establishes a [state] religion or religious faith, or tends to do so." *Lynch* [*v. Donnelly*, 465 U.S. 668,] 678. The State's involvement in the school prayers challenged today violates these central principles.

That involvement is as troubling as it is undenied. A school official, the principal, decided that an invocation and a benediction should be given; this is a choice attributable to the State, and from a constitutional perspective it is as if a state statute decreed that the prayers must occur. The principal chose the religious participant, here a rabbi, and that choice is also attributable to the State. The reason for the choice of a rabbi is not disclosed by the record, but the potential for divisiveness over the choice of a particular member of the clergy to conduct the ceremony is apparent.

Divisiveness, of course, can attend any state decision respecting religions, and neither its existence nor its potential necessarily invalidates the State's attempts to accommodate religion in all cases. The potential for divisiveness is of particular relevance here though, because it centers around an overt religious exercise in a secondary school environment where, as we discuss below, subtle coercive pressures exist and where the student had no real alternative which would have allowed her to avoid the fact or appearance of participation.

The State's role did not end with the decision to include a prayer and with the choice of clergyman. Principal Lee provided Rabbi Gutterman with a copy of the "Guidelines for Civic Occasions," and advised him that his prayers should be nonsectarian. Through these means the principal directed and controlled the content of the prayer.... It is a cornerstone principle of our Establishment Clause jurisprudence that "it is no part of the business of government to compose official prayers for any group of the American people to recite as a part of a religious program carried on by government," *Engel v. Vitale*, 370 U.S. 421, 425 (1962), and that is what the school officials attempted to do.

....

We are asked to recognize the existence of a practice of nonsectarian prayer, prayer within the embrace of what is known as the Judeo-Christian tradition, prayer which is more acceptable than one which, for example, makes explicit references to the God of Israel, or to Jesus Christ, or to a patron saint. There may be some support, as an empirical observation, to the statement of the Court of Appeals for the Sixth Circuit, picked up by Judge Campbell's dissent in the Court of Appeals in this case, that there has emerged in this country a civic religion, one which is tolerated when sectarian exercises are not. *Stein [v. Plainwell Community Schools]*, 822 F.2d [1406], 1409; 908 F.2d 1090, 1098-99 (CA1 1990) (Campbell, J., dissenting) (case below); *see also* Note, *Civil Religion and the Establishment Clause*, 95 Yale L.J. 1237 (1986). If common ground can be defined which permits once conflicting faiths to express the shared conviction that there is an ethic and a morality which transcend human invention, the sense of community and purpose sought by all decent societies might be advanced. But though the First Amendment does not allow the government to stifle prayers which aspire to these ends, neither does it permit the government to undertake that task for itself.

....

These concerns have particular application in the case of school officials, whose effort to monitor prayer will be perceived by the students as inducing a participation they might otherwise reject. Though the efforts of the school officials in this case to find common ground appear to have been a good-faith attempt to recognize the common aspects of religions and not the divisive ones, our precedents do not permit school officials to assist in composing prayers as an incident to a formal exercise for their students. *Engel v. Vitale, supra*, 370 U.S. at 425. And these same precedents caution us to measure the idea of a civic religion against the central meaning of the Religion Clauses of the First Amendment, which is that all creeds must be tolerated and none favored. The suggestion that government may establish an official or civic religion as a means of avoiding the establishment of a religion with more specific creeds strikes us as a contradiction that cannot be accepted.

....

The lessons of the First Amendment are as urgent in the modern world as in the 18th Century when it was written. One timeless lesson is that if citizens are subjected to state-sponsored religious exercises, the State disavows its own duty to guard and respect that sphere of inviolable conscience and belief which is the mark of a free people. To compromise that principle today would be to deny our own tradition and forfeit our standing to urge others to secure the protections of that tradition for themselves.

As we have observed before, there are heightened concerns with protecting freedom of conscience from subtle coercive pressure in the elementary and

A. RELIGION AND THE PUBLIC SCHOOL CURRICULUM

secondary public schools. Our decisions in *Engel v. Vitale*, 370 U.S. 421 (1962), and *Abington School District*, [374 U.S. 203 (1963)], recognize, among other things, that prayer exercises in public schools carry a particular risk of indirect coercion....

We need not look beyond the circumstances of this case to see the phenomenon at work. The undeniable fact is that the school district's supervision and control of a high school graduation ceremony places public pressure, as well as peer pressure, on attending students to stand as a group or, at least, maintain respectful silence during the Invocation and Benediction. This pressure, though subtle and indirect, can be as real as any overt compulsion. Of course, in our culture standing or remaining silent can signify adherence to a view or simple respect for the views of others. And no doubt some persons who have no desire to join a prayer have little objection to standing as a sign of respect for those who do. But for the dissenter of high school age, who has a reasonable perception that she is being forced by the State to pray in a manner her conscience will not allow, the injury is no less real. There can be no doubt that for many, if not most, of the students at the graduation, the act of standing or remaining silent was an expression of participation in the Rabbi's prayer. That was the very point of the religious exercise. It is of little comfort to a dissenter, then, to be told that for her the act of standing or remaining in silence signifies mere respect, rather than participation. What matters is that, given our social conventions, a reasonable dissenter in this milieu could believe that the group exercise signified her own participation or approval of it.

....

The injury caused by the government's action, and the reason why Daniel and Deborah Weisman object to it, is that the State, in a school setting, in effect required participation in a religious exercise. It is, we concede, a brief exercise during which the individual can concentrate on joining its message, meditate on her own religion, or let her mind wander. But the embarrassment and the intrusion of the religious exercise cannot be refuted by arguing that these prayers, and similar ones to be said in the future, are of a *de minimis* character. To do so would be an affront to the Rabbi who offered them and to all those for whom the prayers were an essential and profound recognition of divine authority. And for the same reason, we think that the intrusion is greater than the two minutes or so of time consumed for prayers like these. Assuming, as we must, that the prayers were offensive to the student and the parent who now object, the intrusion was both real and, in the context of a secondary school, a violation of the objectors' rights. That the intrusion was in the course of promulgating religion that sought to be civic or nonsectarian rather than pertaining to one sect does not lessen the offense or isolation to the objectors.

There was a stipulation in the District Court that attendance at graduation and promotional ceremonies is voluntary. Petitioners and the United States, as amicus, made this a center point of the case, arguing that the option of not attending the graduation excuses any inducement or coercion in the ceremony itself. The argument lacks all persuasion. Law reaches past formalism. And to say a teenage student has a real choice not to attend her high school graduation is formalistic in the extreme. True, Deborah could elect not to attend commencement without renouncing her diploma; but we shall not allow the case to turn on this point. Everyone knows that in our society and in our culture high school graduation is one of life's most significant occasions. A school rule which excuses attendance is beside the point. Attendance may not be required by official decree, yet it is apparent that a student is not free to absent herself from the graduation exercise in any real sense of the term "voluntary," for absence would require forfeiture of those intangible benefits which have motivated the student through youth and all her high school years. Graduation is a time for family and those closest to the student to celebrate success and express mutual wishes of gratitude and respect, all to the end of impressing upon the young person the role that it is his or her right and duty to assume in the community and all of its diverse parts.

. . . .

The Government's argument gives insufficient recognition to the real conflict of conscience faced by the young student. The essence of the Government's position is that with regard to a civic, social occasion of this importance it is the objector, not the majority, who must take unilateral and private action to avoid compromising religious scruples, here by electing to miss the graduation exercise. This turns conventional First Amendment analysis on its head. It is a tenet of the First Amendment that the State cannot require one of its citizens to forfeit his or her rights and benefits as the price of resisting conformance to state-sponsored religious practice. To say that a student must remain apart from the ceremony at the opening invocation and closing benediction is to risk compelling conformity in an environment analogous to the classroom setting, where we have said the risk of compulsion is especially high. Just as in *Engel v. Vitale*, 370 U.S. at 430, and *Abington School District v. Schempp*, 374 U.S. at 224-225, we found that provisions within the challenged legislation permitting a student to be voluntarily excused from attendance or participation in the daily prayers did not shield those practices from invalidation, the fact that attendance at the graduation ceremonies is voluntary in a legal sense does not save the religious exercise.

. . . .

Our society would be less than true to its heritage if it lacked abiding concern for the values of its young people, and we acknowledge the profound belief of adherents to many faiths that there must be a place in the student's life for precepts of a morality higher even than the law we today enforce. We express no hostility to those aspirations, nor would our oath permit us to do so. A relentless and all-pervasive attempt to exclude religion from every aspect of public life could itself become inconsistent with the Constitution. *See Abington School District, supra* at 306, (GOLDBERG, J., concurring). We recognize that, at graduation time and throughout the course of the educational process, there

A. RELIGION AND THE PUBLIC SCHOOL CURRICULUM

will be instances when religious values, religious practices, and religious persons will have some interaction with the public schools and their students. *See Westside Community Bd. of Ed. v. Mergens*, 496 U.S. 226 (1990). But these matters, often questions of accommodation of religion, are not before us. The sole question presented is whether a religious exercise may be conducted at a graduation ceremony in circumstances where, as we have found, young graduates who object are induced to conform. No holding by this Court suggests that a school can persuade or compel a student to participate in a religious exercise. That is being done here, and it is forbidden by the Establishment Clause of the First Amendment.

For the reasons we have stated, the judgment of the Court of Appeals is

Affirmed.

....

JUSTICE SCALIA, with whom THE CHIEF JUSTICE, JUSTICE WHITE, and JUSTICE THOMAS join, dissenting.

....

The history and tradition of our Nation are replete with public ceremonies featuring prayers of thanksgiving and petition. Illustrations of this point have been amply provided in our prior opinions, *see, e.g., Lynch, supra*, 465 U.S. at 674-78; *Marsh, supra*, 463 U.S. at 786-788; *see also Wallace v. Jaffree*, 472 U.S. 38, 100-03 (1985) (REHNQUIST, J., dissenting); *Engel v. Vitale*, 370 U.S. 421, 446-50, and n. 3 (1962) (STEWART, J., dissenting), but since the Court is so oblivious to our history as to suggest that the Constitution restricts "preservation and transmission of religious beliefs ... to the private sphere," it appears necessary to provide another brief account.

From our Nation's origin, prayer has been a prominent part of governmental ceremonies and proclamations. The Declaration of Independence, the document marking our birth as a separate people, "appeal[ed] to the Supreme Judge of the world for the rectitude of our intentions" and avowed "a firm reliance on the protection of divine Providence." In his first inaugural address, after swearing his oath of office on a Bible, George Washington deliberately made a prayer a part of his first official act as President:

> [I]t would be peculiarly improper to omit in this first official act my fervent supplications to that Almighty Being who rules over the universe, who presides in the councils of nations, and whose providential aids can supply every human defect, that His benediction may consecrate to the liberties and happiness of the people of the United States a Government instituted by themselves for these essential purposes. Inaugural Addresses of the Presidents of the United States 2 (1989).

Such supplications have been a characteristic feature of inaugural addresses ever since....

Our national celebration of Thanksgiving likewise dates back to President Washington....

This tradition of Thanksgiving Proclamations — with their religious theme of prayerful gratitude to God — has been adhered to by almost every President. *Id.* at 675, and nn. 2 and 3; *Wallace v. Jaffree, supra,* at 100-03 (REHNQUIST, J., dissenting).

The other two branches of the Federal Government also have a long-established practice of prayer at public events. As we detailed in *Marsh*, Congressional sessions have opened with a chaplain's prayer ever since the First Congress. 463 U.S. at 787-788. And this Court's own sessions have opened with the invocation "God save the United States and this Honorable Court" since the days of Chief Justice Marshall. 1 C. Warren, *The Supreme Court in United States History* 469 (1922).

In addition to this general tradition of prayer at public ceremonies, there exists a more specific tradition of invocations and benedictions at public-school graduation exercises....

The Court presumably would separate graduation invocations and benedictions from other instances of public "preservation and transmission of religious beliefs" on the ground that they involve "psychological coercion." I find it a sufficient embarrassment that our Establishment Clause jurisprudence regarding holiday displays, *see Allegheny County v. Greater Pittsburgh ACLU*, 492 U.S. 573 (1989), has come to "requir[e] scrutiny more commonly associated with interior decorators than with the judiciary." *American Jewish Congress v. Chicago*, 827 F.2d 120, 129 (Easterbrook, J., dissenting)....

....

The Court declares that students' "attendance and participation in the [invocation and benediction] are in a fair and real sense obligatory." *Ibid.* But what exactly is this "fair and real sense"? According to the Court, students at graduation who want "to avoid the fact or appearance of participation," in the invocation and benediction are psychologically obligated by "public pressure, as well as peer pressure, ... to stand as a group or, at least, maintain respectful silence" during those prayers....

... The Court's notion that a student who simply sits in "respectful silence" during the invocation and benediction (when all others are standing) has somehow joined — or would somehow be perceived as having joined — in the prayers is nothing short of ludicrous. We indeed live in a vulgar age. But surely "our social conventions," *ibid.*, have not coarsened to the point that anyone who does not stand on his chair and shout obscenities can reasonably be deemed to have assented to everything said in his presence. Since the Court does not dispute that students exposed to prayer at graduation ceremonies retain (despite "subtle coercive pressures,") the free will to sit, there is absolutely no basis for the Court's decision. It is fanciful enough to say that "a reasonable dissenter," standing head erect in a class of bowed heads, "could believe that the group exercise signified her own participation or approval of it," *ibid.* It is beyond the absurd to say that she could entertain such a belief while pointedly declining to rise.

....

The opinion manifests that the Court itself has not given careful consideration to its test of psychological coercion. For if it had, how could it observe, with no hint of concern or disapproval, that students stood for the Pledge of Allegiance, which immediately preceded Rabbi Gutterman's invocation? The government can, of course, no more coerce political orthodoxy than religious orthodoxy. *West Virginia Board of Education v. Barnette*, 319 U.S. 624, 642 (1943). Moreover, since the Pledge of Allegiance has been revised since Barnette to include the phrase "under God," recital of the Pledge would appear to raise the same Establishment Clause issue as the invocation and benediction. If students were psychologically coerced to remain standing during the invocation, they must also have been psychologically coerced, moments before, to stand for (and thereby, in the Court's view, take part in or appear to take part in) the Pledge. Must the Pledge therefore be barred from the public schools (both from graduation ceremonies and from the classroom)? In *Barnette* we held that a public-school student could not be compelled to recite the Pledge; we did not even hint that she could not be compelled to observe respectful silence — indeed, even to stand in respectful silence — when those who wished to recite it did so. Logically, that ought to be the next project for the Court's bulldozer.

....

---

1. In *Weisman* the Court introduces another Establishment Clause test for K-12 schools. The "coercion" test was first proposed by Justice Kennedy in *County of Allegheny v. American Civil Liberties Union*, 492 U.S. 573 (1989), in a separate opinion concurring and dissenting in part. He noted that *Lemon* provided the applicable framework for analyzing petitioner's claims, but at the same time he questioned the wisdom of retaining that test. Kennedy suggested that several earlier opinions of the Court would require eliminating all contact between government and religion if they were to be strictly applied. The Establishment Clause, however, granted the government some latitude in recognizing and accommodating religion. To not do so would result in a latent hostility toward religion, to the detriment of religion.

According to Kennedy, the case law on the Establishment Clause reveals two limiting principles: 1) government may not coerce anyone to support or participate in religion and 2) government may not give direct benefits to religion in such a degree that it establishes a de facto religion. Justice Kennedy based the majority opinion in *Weisman* on this analysis. However, rather than rely on the concept of "coercion" as envisioned in cases like *Engel* or *Schempp, supra*, Kennedy introduced the notion of "psychological coercion," *i.e.*, whether the challenged graduation prayers operated to "psychologically coerce" students to participate in a religious exercise. Does the Kennedy approach add clarity to the Court's work on Establishment Clause issues or does it further confuse educators as to how to comport their behavior? The decision focuses some on *Lemon* in that it forbids invocations or benedictions at graduation ceremonies that "create a state-sponsored and state-directed exercise at a public school." The decision, also practically ignores the rest of *Lemon*. The Court also ignores any historical precedent such as that found in *Marsh* for evaluating such complaints. This left Justice Scalia to say in dissent: "[the new standard] suffers the double disability of having no roots whatsoever in our people's historic practice, and being as infinitely expandable as the reasons for psychotherapy itself." *Weisman* (Justice Scalia dissenting).

2. "The school board ... argued that these short prayers and others like them at graduation exercises are of profound meaning to many students and parents throughout this country who consider that due respect and acknowledgment for divine guidance and for the deepest spiritual aspirations of our people ought to be expressed at an event as important in life as a graduation." *Weisman*, at 2653.

Does this indicate that the school board thinks that "majority rules" in determining whether graduation prayers should be presented? Should school officials have authority to place such matters to a vote of tax-payers, parents or students?

3. The Court stated this case did not concern a question of whether, by having the cleric's presentation be non-sectarian, the school made a good-faith attempt to make the prayer acceptable to most people. Does it, hence, make no difference in Establishment Clause disputes whether or not school officials seek to satisfy all or most of its constituents?

4. In cases dealing with invocations and benedictions at public school graduations, should a distinction be made between those delivered by students and those delivered by non-school religious leaders? The majority in *Stein v. Plainwell Community Schools*, 822 F.2d 1406 (6th Cir. 1987), made no such distinction. *Stein* involved similar cases at two schools, one which allowed student volunteers to deliver the controversial addresses, and one which authorized students to choose a local minister or member of the clergy. The defendant school boards argued that the graduation ceremonies were merely annual occasions of a festive and celebratory nature — different from the classroom. Plaintiffs argued, nonetheless, that these were religious exercises directed at public school children. The Court of Appeals for the Sixth Circuit reversed the District Court's ruling and struck down the invocations in these two schools. The Court recognized several aspects of a graduation ceremony which differentiate it from classroom settings and contribute their constitutionality: invocations are traditional at graduations; they are used in courts and legislatures; they pose less opportunity for religious indoctrination and peer pressure than does religious activity in the classroom; and the public nature of graduations (with parents and other family present) acts as a buffer against religious coercion. However, the Court struck down invocations framed in language which says to parents and child: "We do not recognize your relgous beliefs, our beliefs are superior to yours.... They are framed and phrased so that they 'symbolically place the government's seal of approval on the religious view' — the Christian view."

5. The Court in *Stein* cites to an O'Connor concurrence in *Lynch v. Donnelly*:

> [S]uch governmental "acknowledgements" of religion as legislative prayers ..., government declaration of Thanksgiving as a public holiday, printing of "In God We Trust" on coins, and opening court sessions with "God save the United States and this honorable court" ... serve ... the legitimate secular purposes of solemnizing public occasions, expressing confidence in the future, and encouraging the recognition of what is worthy of appreciation in society. 465 U.S. 668, 692-93 (1984) (O'Connor, J., concurring).

Do these governmental actions *truly* serve secular purposes? It is likely true that solemnizing such events as a judge presiding over a court holds a secular purpose. Is the reference to God necessary to solemnize the event? With more secular alternatives, can we require the government to change many of its "religious" traditions?

It is also true that allowing judges and legislators the tradition of invocations and disallowing it for public school students at their graduations is an inconsistent application of the principle of "equal liberty of conscience." But are you convinced that invocations in courts and legislatures are valid applications of this principle to begin with?

JONES v. CLEAR CREEK INDEPENDENT SCHOOL DISTRICT

United States Court of Appeals
977 F.2d 963 (5th Cir. 1992)

REAVLEY, CIRCUIT JUDGE:

In *Jones v. Clear Creek Independent School Dist.*, 930 F.2d 416 (5th Cir. 1991) (*Jones I*), vacated, 505 U.S. ___, 112 S.Ct. 3020 (1992), we held that Clear Creek Independent School District's Resolution[1] permitting public high school seniors to choose student volunteers to deliver nonsectarian, nonproselytizing invocations at their graduation ceremonies does not violate the Constitution's Establishment Clause. In applying the tripartite test of *Lemon v. Kurtzman*, 403 U.S. 602, 612-13 (1971), we reasoned that the Resolution has a secular

---

[1]The Resolution provides:

1. The use of an invocation and/or benediction at high school graduation exercise shall rest within the discretion of the graduating senior class, with the advice and counsel of the senior class principal;
2. The invocation and benediction, if used, shall be given by a student volunteer; and
3. Consistent with the principle of equal liberty of conscience, the invocation and benediction shall be nonsectarian and nonproselytizing in nature.

purpose of solemnization, that the Resolution's primary effect is to impress upon graduation attendees the profound social significance of the occasion rather than advance or endorse religion, and that Clear Creek does not excessively entangle itself with religion by proscribing sectarianism and proselytization without prescribing any form of invocation.

Then, in *Lee v. Weisman*, 505 U.S. ___, 112 S.Ct. 2649 (1992), the Supreme Court held that a public-school principal acting in accord with the policy of his Providence, Rhode Island school district, violated the Establishment Clause by inviting a local clergy member to deliver a nonsectarian, nonproselytizing invocation at his school's graduation ceremony. The Court reasoned that *Lee*'s actions represent governmental coercion to participate in religious activities, a paradigmatic establishment of religion. The Court then granted certiorari in this case, vacated our judgment, and remanded it to us for further consideration in light of *Lee*. Upon reconsideration, we hold that *Lee* does not render Clear Creek's invocation policy unconstitutional, and again affirm the district court's summary judgment in Clear Creek's favor.

....

... [I]n the time between *Lemon* and *Lee*, the [Supreme] Court has used five tests to determine whether public schools' involvement with religion violates the Establishment Clause. To fully reconsider this case in light of *Lee*, we reanalyze the Resolution under all five tests that the Court has stated are relevant. We address any statements in *Lee* that bear on our analysis in *Jones I* and apply *Lee*'s coercion test for the first time.

A. *Secular Purpose*

Nothing in *Lee* abrogates our conclusion that the Resolution has a secular purpose of solemnization, and thus satisfies *Lemon*'s first requirement. The Resolution represents Clear Creek's judgment that society benefits if people attach importance to graduation. A meaningful graduation ceremony can provide encouragement to finish school and the inspiration and self-assurance necessary to achieve after graduation, which are secular objectives.

The *Lee* Court stated that the Providence school district's solemnization argument would have "considerable force were it not for the constitutional constraints applied to state action...." The Court did not question its members' previous acknowledgements that solemnization is a legitimate secular purpose of ceremonial prayer. *Lynch*, 465 U.S. at 693 (O'CONNOR, J., concurring); *see also Engel v. Vitale*, 370 U.S. 421, 435 n. 21 (1962). Thus, we take the *Lee* Court to agree with our holding in *Jones I* that a law may pass *Lemon*'s secular-purpose test by solemnizing public occasions, yet still be stricken as an unconstitutional establishment under another test mandated by the Court.

B. *Primary Effect*

In *Jones I*, we held that the Resolution's primary effect was to solemnize graduation ceremonies, not to "advance religion" in contravention of *Lemon*'s second requirement. *Lee* calls into question three statements that we made in support of our advancement holding. We stated that graduating high school seniors would be less easily influenced by prayer than would be their junior schoolmates, but the Court held that all students under school supervision would be unduly influenced by a cleric's prayers. We distinguished the graduation setting from the classroom setting because parents and guests are present only at graduation and school officials can pay much greater attention to individual students in the classroom than at graduation, but the Court stated that the two settings are "analogous." We stated that the brevity and infrequency of the permissible prayers under the Resolution tempered any advancement of religion, but the Court rejected a *de minimis* characterization of the brief prayers at issue in *Lee*.

Lee commands that we not rely on these three points in deciding whether the Resolution's primary effect is to advance religion. Yet even without them, we remain convinced that the Resolution's primary effect is to solemnize graduation ceremonies.

The Resolution can only advance religion by increasing religious conviction among graduation attendees, which means attracting new believers or increasing the faith of the faithful. Its requirement that any invocation be nonsectarian and nonproselytizing minimizes any such advancement of religion. The *Lee* Court held that the nonsectarian nature of the prayers there at issue did not change the fact that *Lee* directed graduation attendees to participate in a religious exercise. Nevertheless, the nonsectarian nature of a prayer remains relevant to the extent to which a prayer advances religion.

The fact that *Lemon* only condemns government action that has the primary effect of advancing religion, requires us to compare the Resolution's secular and religious effect. The Resolution may or may not have any religious effect. The students may or may not employ the name of any deity; heads may or may not be bowed; indeed, an invocation may or may not appear on the program. If the students choose a nonproselytizing, nonsectarian prayer, the effect may well marshall attendees' extant religiosity for the secular purpose of solemnization; but no one would likely expect the advancement of religion by the initiation or increase of religious faith through these prayers. The Resolution's primary effect is secular.

C. *Entanglement*

We held in *Jones I* that the Resolution's proscription of sectarianism does not, of itself, excessively entangle government with religion. We know of no authority that holds yearly review of unsolicited material for sectarianism and proselytization to constitute excessive entanglement.... Moreover, nothing in *Lee* abrogates our reading of the Court's entanglement precedent to limit violative entanglement to institutional entanglement. That a rabbi wrote and delivered the prayer at issue in *Lee* makes entanglement analysis relevant to that case, but the Resolution keeps Clear Creek free of all involvement with religious institutions.

D. *Endorsement*

Like *Lemon*'s advancement test, the Court's endorsement analysis focuses on the effect of a challenged governmental action. This is why, perhaps mistakenly, we conflated advancement and endorsement analysis in *Jones I*. Because the Court has never tolerated a government endorsement of religion that is incidental to a primary secular effect, as it has with incidental religious advancements, we will not now compare endorsement to legitimate effects of the Resolution....

From the Court's various pronouncements, we understand government to unconstitutionally endorse religion when a reasonable person would view the challenged government action as a disapproval of her contrary religious choices....

We may compare the Resolution to the facts in two somewhat similar cases where members of the Court discussed endorsement of religion. Both *Lee* concurrences consider invocations directed by *Lee* to be unconstitutional endorsements of religion. On the other hand, a plurality of the Court recently held that a public school does not unconstitutionally endorse religion by permitting a Christian club to meet on school grounds after class and recruit members through the school's newspaper, bulletin boards, public address system, and annual Club Fair, as long as the school accords equal privileges to other noncurriculum-oriented student organizations. *See Board of Educ. of Westside Community Sch. v. Mergens*, 496 U.S. 226, 247-53 (1990).

To compare the Resolution with *Lee* and *Mergens*, we consider exactly what it does. Unlike the policy at issue in *Lee*, it does not mandate a prayer. The Resolution does not even mandate an invocation; it merely permits one if the seniors so choose. Moreover, the students present Clear Creek with their proposed invocation under the Resolution, while in *Lee* the school explained its idea for an invocation to a member of an organized religion and directed him to deliver it. The Resolution is passive compared to the governmental overture toward religion at issue in *Lee*.

Concerning endorsement, the instant case more closely parallels *Mergens* because a graduating high school senior who participates in the decision as to whether her graduation will include an invocation by a fellow student volunteer will understand that any religious references are the result of student, not government, choice. The *Mergens* plurality states the point directly:

> [T]here is a crucial difference between government speech endorsing religion, which the Establishment Clause forbids, and private speech endorsing religion, which the Free Speech and Free Exercise Clauses protect. We think that secondary school students are mature enough and are likely to understand that a school does not endorse or support student speech that it merely permits on a nondiscriminatory basis. 496 U.S. at 250.

In *Jones I*, we recognized that invocations permitted by the Resolution "may" include supplication to a deity. But the Resolution permits invocations free of all

A. RELIGION AND THE PUBLIC SCHOOL CURRICULUM 1221

religious content, and the 1987 student proposal was acceptable to the plaintiff-appellants. The record does not disclose how each senior class chooses whether to include an invocation nor how the student volunteer who delivers the speech is chosen. We can imagine discriminatory methods of implementing the Resolution that would make it a tool for governmental endorsement of religion, but the Resolution itself is constitutional unless there is no way to implement it on a nondiscriminatory basis.

We think that Clear Creek does not unconstitutionally endorse religion if it submits the decision of graduation invocation content, if any, to the majority vote of the senior class. Clear Creek is legitimately concerned with solemnizing its graduation ceremonies, and the Resolution simply permits each senior class to decide how this can best be done. School districts commonly provide similarly secular criteria for the selection of other student graduation speakers, and no court has held that their religious speech at graduation represents government endorsement of religion. After participating in a student determination of what kind of invocation their graduation will contain, we do not believe that students will perceive any more government endorsement of religion from the Resolution than do students in Westside Community schools who are regularly recruited during school hours to join a Christian club. Clear Creek students certainly perceive a less-direct relationship between state and religion under the Resolution than Providence students did before *Lee*. ("[A]t graduation time and throughout the course of the educational process, there will be instances when religious values, religious practices, and religious persons will have some interaction with the public schools and their students.") (citing *Mergens*). We find no unconstitutional endorsement.

E. *Coercion*

Instead of directly considering any of the tests that we have previously discussed, the *Lee* Court invalidated the Providence school district's policy on its evaluation of the coercive effect of *Lee*'s actions. The Court held that *Lee* coerced graduation attendees to join in a formal religious exercise. The Court summarized its entire analysis of the constitutionality of the school policy at issue in *Lee* as follows:

> These dominant facts mark and control the confines of our decision: State officials direct the performance of a formal religious exercise at promotional and graduation ceremonies for secondary schools. Even for those students who object to the religious exercise, their attendance and participation in the state-sponsored religious activity are in a fair and real sense obligatory....
> *Id.*

Thus, *Lee* identifies unconstitutional coercion when (1) the government directs (2) a formal religious exercise (3) in such a way as to oblige the participation of objectors. *See also Mergens*, 496 U.S. at 261 (KENNEDY, J., concurring) ("The inquiry with respect to coercion must be whether the government imposes pressure upon a student to participate in a religious activity.''). Before *Lee*, no one contended that the Resolution coerced participation in prayer at Clear Creek's graduation ceremonies, and we failed to appreciate the need to address this issue from the Court's precedent that we discussed in *Jones I*. Upon considering this case in light of *Lee*'s coercion analysis, we find that the Resolution does not succumb to one, let alone all three, of the elements of unconstitutional coercion, and thus survives the analysis that felled graduation prayer in *Lee*.

1. *Direction*

Throughout *Lee*'s entire coercion analysis, the Court repeatedly stresses the government's direct and complete control over the graduation prayers there at issue as determinative of the establishment question....

The Court deplored three instances of government involvement in graduation prayer in *Lee*, none of which is tolerated, let alone prescribed, by the Resolution. First, the Court found that Lee "decided that an invocation and benediction should be given; this is a choice attributable to the State, and from a constitutional perspective it is as if a state statute decreed that the prayers must occur." The Resolution requires that the state not decide whether an invocation will occur; it respects the graduating class's choice on the matter. The Resolution acknowledges that a school official may offer "advice and counsel" to the senior class in deciding whether to include invocations at graduation, and officials could exploit this clause to impose their will on the students. But, again, in evaluating the Resolution's facial constitutionality, we are only concerned with whether the Resolution necessarily charges government with the decision of whether to include invocations. Unlike the policy at issue in *Lee*, the Resolution does not.

Second, the Court was critical of the fact that "[t]he principal chose the religious participant, here a rabbi, and that choice is also attributable to the State.'' *Id*. In contrast, the Resolution explicitly precludes anyone but a student volunteer from delivering Clear Creek's invocations. Moreover, the Resolution says nothing of government involvement in the selection of the person who delivers any invocation. That the government can remain detached from this selection consistent with the Resolution maintains the Resolution's facial constitutionality.

The Court recognized that Lee completed his control over the invocation at his school's graduation ceremonies when he "provided Rabbi Gutterman with a copy of the 'Guidelines for Civic Occasions,' and advised him that his prayers should be nonsectarian.'' In three respects, Clear Creek exercises significantly less control over the content of invocations at its schools. Clear Creek does not solicit invocations; the Resolution only forbids Clear Creek schools from accepting sectarian or proselytizing invocations. Moreover, because a graduating senior drafts proposed invocations each year under the Resolution, the same person will never repeatedly propose an invocation. Compare *id*. (noting that Lee could refine an official prayer by repeatedly inviting the same clergy member to deliver invocations). Finally, the Resolution imposes two one-word restrictions "nonsectarian and nonproselytizing" which enhance solemnization and minimize advancement of religion, instead of a pamphlet full of invocation suggestions.

We conclude that Clear Creek does not direct prayer presentations at its graduation ceremonies.

2. *Religiosity*

Lee directed [the cleric] to pray, and the Court characterized this as a "formal religious observance." By contrast, the Resolution tolerates nonsectarian, nonproselytizing prayer, but does not require or favor it.

3. *Participation*

The *Lee* Court held that government-mandated prayer at graduation places a constitutionally impermissible amount of psychological pressure upon students to participate in religious exercises. We think that the graduation prayers permitted by the Resolution place less psychological pressure on students than the prayers at issue in *Lee* because all students, after having participated in the decision of whether prayers will be given, are aware that any prayers represent the will of their peers, who are less able to coerce participation than an authority figure from the state or clergy.

We also consider the age of the graduating seniors relevant to the determination of whether prayers under the Resolution can coerce these young people into participating in a religious exercise. *Lee* explains that the state-initiated clergy prayers there at issue have a coercive effect on public-school students regardless of age, but it nowhere compromises the Court's previous recognition that graduating seniors "are less impressionable than younger students." *Mergens*, 496 U.S. at 235-37....

Accordingly, we think that the coercive effect of any prayer permitted by the Resolution is more analogous to the innocuous "God save the United States and this Honorable Court" stated by and to adults than the government-mandated message delivered to young people from religious authority that the Court considered in *Lee*.

None of *Lee*'s three elements of coercive effect exist here. Prayers allowed under the Resolution do not unconstitutionally coerce objectors into participation.

....

The practical result of our decision, viewed in light of *Lee*, is that a majority of students can do what the State acting on its own cannot do to incorporate prayer in public high school graduation ceremonies. In *Lee*, the Court forbade schools from exacting participation in a religious exercise as the price for attending what many consider to be one of life's most important events. This case requires us to consider why so many people attach importance to graduation ceremonies. If they only seek government's recognition of student achievement, diplomas suffice. If they only seek God's recognition, a privately-sponsored baccalaureate will do. But to experience the community's recognition of student achievement, they must attend the public ceremony that other interested community members also hold so dear. By attending graduation to experience and participate in the community's display of support for the graduates, people should not be surprised to find the event affected by community standards. The Constitution requires nothing different.

....

---

1. Should it make a difference in these cases whether the graduation is held on or off school premises?

2. Graduation ceremonies are only one of a number of educational policies and practices that have been examined in light of court decisions regarding the constitutional status of prayer and Bible reading in the public schools. In *Florey v. Sioux Falls Sch. Dist. 49-5*, 464 F. Supp. 911 (D.S.D. 1979), a federal district court ruled that Christmas assemblies do not have to be "absolutely and irrevocably secular" in order to avoid violation of the Establishment Clause. Christmas music with religious content has been assimilated into American culture and has developed an independent secular and artistic significance, the court said, and to prohibit students from performing such music "would give students a truncated view of our culture." Assuming such religious music has been assimilated into our culture, is this indicative of anything other than the numerical preponderance of members of the Christian faith in the United States? How convincing is the court's rationale that failure to allow students to perform religious music at a Christmas assembly will result in a "truncated view of our culture?" *See* Note, *Religious-Holiday Observances in the Public Schools*, 48 N.Y.U. L. Rev. 116 (1973).

3. In addition to ruling on how the religion clauses should be applied to public school activities, the courts also are faced with the necessity of defining religion for First Amendment purposes. In *Malnak v. Yogi*, 592 F.2d 197 (3d Cir. 1979), the Third Circuit held the teaching of the Science of Creative Intelligence-Transcendental Meditation as an elective in a New Jersey public high school constituted establishment of religion in violation of the First Amendment. Although the proponents and practitioners of Transcendental Meditation themselves stated it was not a religion, the court held the primary effect of the teaching of the course was to advance religion and religious concepts. It has been suggested that one approach to the problem of defining religion for First Amendment purposes is to broadly construe the Free Exercise Clause to include anything which is arguably religious and to narrowly construe the Establishment Clause so that it will not encompass anything which is arguably non-religious. L. Tribe, American Constitutional Law, 827-28 (1978). What arguments can be made for and against such analysis? Is there any support for this view in the language of the First Amendment? *See* Note, *Toward a Constitutional Definition of Religion*, 91 Harv. L. Rev. 1056 (1978); Note, *Transcendental Meditation and*

A. RELIGION AND THE PUBLIC SCHOOL CURRICULUM

the Meaning of Religion Under the Establishment Clause, 62 Minn. L. Rev. 887 (1978); Incorvaia, *Teaching Transcendental Meditation in Public Schools: Defining Religion for Establishment Purposes*, 16 San Diego L. Rev. 325 (1979).

4. In the early case of *Miller v. Cooper*, 56 N.M. 355, 244 P.2d 520 (1952), the Supreme Court of New Mexico held the practice of making religious pamphlets provided by one denomination available in the public school classroom to be violative of the separation of church and state, although the pamphlets were not directly given to students and students were not instructed to either take or read them. In 1979, however, the United States Fifth Circuit Court of Appeals sitting *en banc* upheld a district court's refusal to grant declaratory or injunctive relief to parents seeking to invalidate a school board policy which permitted the distribution of religious literature from designated locations on school premises. The majority opinion with regard to the distribution issue prompted a lengthy dissent from five judges who suggested it jeopardized fundamental First Amendment values and permitted "outsiders to influence the theological beliefs of pupils through subtle and unchecked efforts to proselytize." *Meltzer v. Board of Educ. of Orange County*, 577 F.2d 311, *cert. denied*, 99 S. Ct. 872 (1979). The *Meltzer* decision was marked by controversy and confusion regarding the lower court record and the activities complained of making it uncertain whether, or to what extent the circuit court's holding will be extended beyond the particular factual situation involved.

5. Does the *Weisman* decision leave open the possibility of religiously based prayers at graduations? What if student volunteers deliver a nondenominational prayer? What if such a prayer did not mention a deity? What if the ceremony was not a graduation ceremony, but a school-sponsored activity that carried less importance? What if, as suggested by Justice Scalia in his dissent, there was a disclaimer of "psychological coercion" preceding the activity? Does *Jones* effectively answer these questions especially since the Supreme Court denied a writ of certiorari to hear the case?

6. *Jones* uses the *Lemon* "endorsement" and "coercion" tests in its analysis. Which of these, if any, was persuasive or was the Fifth Circuit simply attempting to cover all bases to avoid being overturned? What guidance does this give educators as regards graduation exercises? Should the "age and maturity" of students like that mentioned in the case impact future decisions?

7. Building on the majority decision in *Weisman*, *Jones* would find unconstitutional "psychological coercion" when: a) there is government activity that directs b) a formal religious exercise that c) requires the participation of both those who do and do not want to participate. Does this help to clarify *Weisman*? Does the analysis compliment or counter the *Lemon* and "endorsement" tests?

8. Another Establishment Clause concern is whether schools should or should not teach Creation science instead of or in tandem with evolution. This was addressed in *Edwards v. Aguillard*, 107 S. Ct. 2573 (1987). The case involved a challenge against the Louisiana Balanced Treatment for Creation-Science and Evolution-Science in Public School Instruction Act. The Supreme Court affirmed a decision striking down the statute as serving no secular purpose and promoting particular religious beliefs. The Court held that the Act impermissibly endorses religion by advancing the religious belief that a supernatural being created mankind. The Act's legislative history demonstrated that the term "creation science", as contemplated by the state legislature, embraces religious teaching.

Can academic freedom be considered a secular purpose under such a statute? The *Edwards* Court responded by indicating that such a statute did not enhance the right of teachers to teach what they pleased. Requiring the teaching of evolution with creation science does not give teachers a flexibility that they did not already possess. The Court went on to say that the Act did not further a basic concept of fairness by requiring the teaching of both theories. (In fact the statute required the development of curriculum guides for creation science, but not for evolution, clearly favoring the teaching of creationism).

9. The Equal Access Act, 20 U.S.C. §§ 4071-74, provides that if a public secondary school allows any non-curriculum-related student group to meet during non-instructional hours then all student groups must be granted that privilege irrespective of philosophical or political persuasion. The Act does not apply if schools have limited such participation to curriculum-affiliated student groups only; moreover, all activities must be student initiated.

The Act was tested in *Board of Educ. of Westside Community Schs. v. Mergens*, 496 U.S. 226 (1990), where students sought permission to form a Christian Club and meet on the same terms and conditions as other non-religious student groups. The organization's purposes were to read and discuss the Bible and to pray. School officials denied the request stating that permitting such a club to use school facilities would violate the Establishment Clause. The students brought suit arguing that the school position was a violation of the Equal Access Act.

The Supreme Court ruled in favor of the students using the *Lemon* test. The Court declared there was no conflict between the Act and the Establishment Clause. The Act features a secular purpose in that it prohibits discrimination based on content of speech, whether political, philosophical or religious. In addition, the Act's primary effect was declared to be neutral in that, because secondary students are more mature than elementary school children, they could understand that by allowing after-hours religious activities, the school would not endorse or support a particular kind of student speech. Moreover, students are free to initiate and organize a broad spectrum of clubs which counteracts any possible message of official endorsement of a particular religious belief. Finally, the Act prohibits school personnel from directing, controlling or regularly attending the student meetings, thus precluding undue church-state entanglement.

On the basis of the above, the Court concluded that since other non-curriculum-related groups were permitted to meet during non-instructional time, a limited open forum was created by the school and religiously affiliated student groups were entitled under the Equal Access Act to receive the same privilege since no Establishment Clause violation was found.

A. RELIGION AND THE PUBLIC SCHOOL CURRICULUM

In another "Equal Access" case, *Lamb's Chapel v. Center Moriches Union Free Sch. Dist.*, 113 S. Ct. 2141 (1993), the Supreme Court did not cite to *Mergens* for authority concerning the use of school facilities for sectarian purposes. In *Lamb's Chapel* a unanimous Supreme Court upheld the right of a religious congregation to use public school facilities for a film series after school hours. The film series was based on fundamentalist Christian views about how families in America are being undermined by media influences. Ultimately, the Court ruled that because school access was extended to non- or quasi-religious groups representing similar viewpoints, permission also had to be granted to Lamb's Chapel.

The majority reasoned that the public school is a "non-public forum" and, as such, may: 1) prevent use of its property after school and 2) if access is granted "control ... [of participants] can be based on subject matter and speech identification so long as the distinctions drawn are reasonable in light of the purpose served by the forum and are viewpoint neutral." *Id.* at 2147. The Court noted, however, that the rules for outside access, even though viewpoint neutral, were not applied toward all groups equally. Specifically, while the subject matter of family values was not prohibited, only religious organizations were kept from delivering their message. The majority wrote that school officials violate the First Amendment "when [they] deny access to [religious groups] solely to suppress the point of view [they] espouse ... on an otherwise includible subject." *Id.*

The school district also defended its actions by claiming a purported violation of the Establishment Clause if religious groups were allowed to use the facilities. The Court responded with an analysis based on both the "Endorsement Test" as seen in *Lee v. Weisman* (O'Connor concurring), *supra* and the *Lemon* Test:

> [T]here would have been no realistic danger that the community would think that the District was endorsing religion or any particular creed, and any benefit to religion or the church would have been incidental.
>
> ... [P]ermitting District property to be used to exhibit the film involved in this case would not have been an establishment of religion under the three part test articulated in *Lemon v. Kurtzman* .... The challenged government action has a secular purpose, does not have the purpose or primary effect of advancing or inhibiting religion, and does not foster an excessive entanglement with religion. *Id.* at 2147-48.

The opinion, although more closely aligned with the decision in *Hazelwood v. Kuhlmeier*, *supra* Chapter 6 (although the case is not cited), will probably be best remembered for the caustic exchange between Justice Scalia (concurring opinion) and his scathing diatribe against the continued use of the *Lemon* Test and the flippant response by Justice White, the author of the majority decision:

[Justice Scalia]
As to the Court's invocation of the *Lemon* Test: Like some ghoul in a late night horror movie that repeatedly sits up in his grave and shuffles abroad

after being repeatedly killed and buried, *Lemon* stalks our Establishment Clause jurisprudence once again, frightening the little children and school attorneys of Center Moriches Union Free School District.

The secret of the *Lemon* Test's survival ... is that it is so easy to kill. It is there to scare us ... when we wish it to do so, but we can command it to return to the tomb at will. When we wish to strike down a practice it forbids, we invoke it ...; when we wish to uphold a practice it forbids, we ignore it entirely.... Sometimes we take a middle course, calling its three prongs "no more than helpful signposts" .... Such a docile and useful monster is worth keeping around, at least in a somnolent state; one never knows when one might need him. *Id.* at 2149-50.

[Justice White]
While we are somewhat diverted by Justice Scalia's evening at the cinema ... we return to the reality that there is a proper way to inter an established decision and *Lemon*, however frightening to some, has not been overruled. Justice Scalia apparently was less haunted by the ghosts of the living when he joined ... [recent] opinion[s] [where the *Lemon* Test was invoked]. *Id.* at 2148, footnote 7.

For a rendition of the myriad questions raised by *Lamb's Chapel* about "Equal Access" and the continued use of the *"Lemon* Test," *see* R. Salomone, *Public Forum Doctrine and the Perils of Categorical Thinking: Lessons From Lamb's Chapel*, 24 New Mex. L. Rev. 1 (1994) and D. Schimmel, *Discrimination Against Religious Viewpoints Prohibited in Public Schools: An Analysis of the Lamb's Chapel Decision*, 85 Educ. L. Rep. 387 (1993).

B. RELEASED TIME FOR RELIGIOUS INSTRUCTION

McCOLLUM v. BOARD OF EDUCATION
Supreme Court of the United States
333 U.S. 203 (1948)

MR. JUSTICE BLACK delivered the opinion of the Court:
This case relates to the power of a state to utilize its tax-supported public school system in aid of religious instruction insofar as that power may be restricted by the First and Fourteenth Amendments to the Federal Constitution.

....

... In 1940 interested members of the Jewish, Roman Catholic, and a few of the Protestant faiths formed a voluntary association called the Champaign Council on Religious Education. They obtained permission from the Board of Education to offer classes in religious instruction to public school pupils in grades four to nine inclusive. Classes were made up of pupils whose parents signed printed cards requesting that their children be permitted to attend; they were held weekly, thirty minutes for the lower grades, forty-five minutes for the higher. The council employed the religious teachers at no expense to the school authorities, but the instructors were subject to the approval and supervision of the superintendent of schools. The classes were taught in three separate religious groups by Protestant teachers, Catholic priests, and a Jewish rabbi, although for the past several years there have apparently been no classes instructed in the Jewish religion. Classes were conducted in the regular classrooms of the school building. Students who did not choose to take the religious instruction were not released from public school duties; they were required to leave their classrooms and go to some other place in the school building for pursuit of their secular studies. On the other hand, students who were released from secular study for the religious instructions were required to be present at the religious classes. Reports of their presence or absence were to be made to their secular teachers.

The foregoing facts, without reference to others that appear in the record, show the use of tax-supported property for religious instruction and the close cooperation between the school authorities and the religious council in promoting religious education. The operation of the state's compulsory education system thus assists and is integrated with the program of religious instruction carried on by separate religious sects. Pupils compelled by law to go to school for secular education are released in part from their legal duty upon the condition that they attend the religious classes. This is beyond all question a utilization of the tax-established and tax-supported public school system to aid religious groups to spread their faith. And it falls squarely under the ban of the First Amendment .... "Neither a state nor the Federal Government can set up a church. Neither can pass laws which aid one religion, aid all religions, or prefer one religion over another. Neither can force or influence a person to go to or to remain away from church against his will or force him to profess a belief or disbelief in any religion. No person can be punished for entertaining or professing religious beliefs or disbeliefs, for church attendance or non-attendance. No tax in any amount, large or small can be levied to support any religious activities or institutions, whatever they may be called, or whatever form they may adopt to teach or practice religion. Neither a state nor the Federal Government can, openly or secretly, participate in the affairs of any religious organizations or groups and vice versa. In the words of Jefferson, the clause against establishment of religion by law was intended to erect 'a wall of separation between church and State.'" ...

To hold that a state cannot consistently with the First and Fourteenth Amendments utilize its public school system to aid any or all religious faiths or sects in the dissemination of their doctrines and ideals does not, as counsel urge, manifest a governmental hostility to religion or religious teachings. A manifestation of such hostility would be at war with our national tradition as embodied in the First Amendment's guaranty of the free exercise of religion. For the First Amendment rests upon the premise that both religion and government can best work to achieve their lofty aims if each is left free from the other within its respective sphere.... [T]he First Amendment has erected a wall between Church and State which must be kept high and impregnable.

Here not only are the State's tax-supported public school buildings used for the dissemination of religious doctrines. The State also affords sectarian groups an invaluable aid in that it helps to provide pupils for their religious classes through use of the State's compulsory public school machinery. This is not separation of Church and State.

The cause is reversed and remanded to the State Supreme Court for proceedings not inconsistent with this opinion.

Reversed and remanded.

[The concurring opinions of MR. JUSTICE FRANKFURTER and MR. JUSTICE JACKSON and the dissenting opinion of MR. JUSTICE REED are omitted.]

ZORACH v. CLAUSON

Supreme Court of the United States
343 U.S. 306 (1952)

MR. JUSTICE DOUGLAS delivered the opinion of the Court:

New York City has a program which permits its public schools to release students during the school day so that they may leave the school buildings and school grounds and go to religious centers for religious instruction or devotional exercises. A student is released on written request of his parents. Those not released stay in the classrooms. The churches make weekly reports to the schools, sending a list of children who have been released from public school but who have not reported for religious instruction.

This "released time" program involves neither religious instruction in public school classrooms nor the expenditure of public funds. All costs, including the application blanks, are paid by the religious organizations. The case is therefore unlike *McCollum v. Board of Education*, 333 U.S. 203....

Appellants, who are taxpayers and residents of New York City and whose children attend its public schools, challenge the present law, contending it is in essence not different from the one involved in the *McCollum* case. Their argument, stated elaborately in various ways, reduces itself to this: the weight and influence of the school is put behind a program for religious instruction; public school teachers police it, keeping tab on students who are released; the classroom activities come to a halt while the students who are released for religious instruction are on leave; the school is a crutch on which the churches are leaning for support in their religious training; without the cooperation of the schools this "released time" program, like the one in the *McCollum* case, would be futile and ineffective....

....

It takes obtuse reasoning to inject any issue of the "free exercise" of religion into the present case. No one is forced to go to the religious classroom and no religious exercise or instruction is brought to the classrooms of the public

B. RELEASED TIME FOR RELIGIOUS INSTRUCTION

schools. A student need not take religious instruction. He is left to his own desires as to the manner of time of his religious devotions, if any.

There is a suggestion that the system involves the use of coercion to get public school students into religious classrooms. There is no evidence in the record before us that supports that conclusion. The present record indeed tells us that the school authorities are neutral in this regard and do no more than release students whose parents so request. If in fact coercion were used, if it were established that any one or more teachers were using their office to persuade or force students to take the religious instruction, a wholly different case would be presented. Hence we put aside that claim of coercion both as respects the "free exercise" of religion and "an establishment of religion" within the meaning of the First Amendment.

Moreover, apart from that claim of coercion, we do not see how New York by this type of "released time" program has made a law respecting an establishment of religion within the meaning of the First Amendment. There is much talk of the separation of Church and State in the history of the Bill of Rights and in the decisions clustering around the First Amendment.... There cannot be the slightest doubt that the First Amendment reflects the philosophy that Church and State should be separated. And so far as interference with the "free exercise" of religion and an "establishment" of religion are concerned, the separation must be complete and unequivocal. The First Amendment within the scope of its coverage permits no exception; the prohibition is absolute. The First Amendment, however, does not say that in every and all respects there shall be a separation of Church and State. Rather, it studiously defines the manner, the specific ways, in which there shall be no concert or union or dependency one on the other. That is the common sense of the matter. Otherwise the state and religion would be aliens to each other — hostile, suspicious, and even unfriendly. Churches could not be required to pay even property taxes. Municipalities would not be permitted to render police or fire protection to religious groups. Policemen who helped parishioners into their places of worship would violate the Constitution. Prayers in our legislative halls; the appeals to the Almighty in the messages of the Chief Executive; the proclamations making Thanksgiving Day a holiday; "so help me God" in our courtroom oaths — these and all other references to the Almighty that run through our laws, our public rituals, our ceremonies would be flouting the First Amendment. A fastidious atheist or agnostic could even object to the supplication with which the Court opens each session: "God save the United States and this Honorable Court."

We would have to press the concept of separation of Church and State to these extremes to condemn the present law on constitutional grounds. The nullification of this law would have wide and profound effects. A Catholic student applies to his teacher for permission to leave the school during hours on a Holy Day of Obligation to attend a mass. A Jewish student asks his teacher for permission to be excused for Yom Kippur. A Protestant wants the afternoon off for a family baptismal ceremony. In each case the teacher, in order to make sure the student is not a truant, goes further and requires a report from the priest, the rabbi, or the minister. The teacher in other words cooperates in a religious program to the extent of making it possible for her students to participate in it. Whether she does it occasionally for a few students, regularly for one, or pursuant to a systematized program designed to further the religious needs of all the students does not alter the character of the act.

We are a religious people whose institutions presuppose a Supreme Being. We guarantee the freedom to worship as one chooses. We make room for as wide a variety of beliefs and creeds as the spiritual needs of man deem necessary. We sponsor an attitude on the part of government that shows no partiality to any one group and that lets each flourish according to the zeal of its adherents and the appeal of its dogma. When the state encourages religious instruction or cooperates with religious authorities by adjusting the schedule of public events to sectarian needs, it follows the best of our traditions. For it then respects the religious nature of our people and accommodates the public service to their spiritual needs. To hold that it may not would be to find in the Constitution a requirement that the government show a callous indifference to religious groups. That would be preferring those who believe in no religion over those who do believe. Government may not finance religious groups nor undertake religious instruction nor blend secular and sectarian education nor use secular institutions to force one or some religion on any person. But we find no constitutional requirement which makes it necessary for government to be hostile to religion and to throw its weight against efforts to widen the effective scope of religious influence. The government must be neutral when it comes to competition between sects. It may not thrust any sect on any person. It may not make a religious observance compulsory. It may not coerce anyone to attend church, to observe a religious holiday, or to take religious instruction. But it can close its doors or suspend its operations as to those who want to repair to their religious sanctuary for worship or instruction. No more than that is undertaken here.

. . . .

Affirmed.

MR. JUSTICE BLACK, dissenting:

McCollum ex rel. Illinois v. Board of Education, 333 U.S. 203, held invalid as an "establishment of religion" an Illinois system under which school children, compelled by law to go to public schools, were freed from some hours of required school work on condition that they attend special religious classes held in the school buildings....

I see no significant difference between the invalid Illinois system and that of New York here sustained. Except for the use of the school buildings in Illinois, there is no difference between the systems which I consider even worthy of mention. In the New York program, as in that of Illinois, the school authorities release some of the children on the condition that they attend the religious classes, get reports on whether they attend, and hold the other children in the

B. RELEASED TIME FOR RELIGIOUS INSTRUCTION 1233

school building until the religious hour is over. As we attempted to make categorically clear, the *McCollum* decision would have been the same if the religious classes had not been held in the school buildings. We said:

> Here *not only* are the State's tax-supported public school buildings used for the dissemination of religious doctrines. The State *also* affords sectarian groups an invaluable aid in that it helps to provide pupils for their religious classes through use of the State's compulsory public school machinery. *This* is not separation of Church and State. (Emphasis supplied.) *McCollum v. Board of Education, supra.*

McCollum thus held that Illinois could not constitutionally manipulate the compelled classroom hours of its compulsory school machinery so as to channel children into sectarian classes. Yet that is exactly what the Court holds New York can do.

. . . .

The Court's validation of the New York system rests in part on its statement that Americans are "a religious people whose institutions presuppose a Supreme Being." This was at least as true when the First Amendment was adopted; and it was just as true when eight Justices of this Court invalidated the released time system in McCollum on the premise that a state can no more "aid all religions" than it can aid one.... The First Amendment was ... to insure that no one powerful sect or combination of sects could use political or governmental power to punish dissenters whom they could not convert to their faith. Now as then, it is only by wholly isolating the state from the religious sphere and compelling it to be completely neutral, that the freedom of each and every denomination and of all nonbelievers can be maintained. It is this neutrality the Court abandons today when it treats New York's coercive system as a program which *merely* "encourages religious instruction or cooperates with religious authorities." The abandonment is all the more dangerous to liberty because of the Court's legal exaltation of the orthodox and its derogation of unbelievers.

Under our system of religious freedom, people have gone to their religious sanctuaries not because they feared the law but because they loved their God. The choice of all has been as free as the choice of those who answered the call to worship moved only by the music of the old Sunday morning church bells. The spiritual mind of man has thus been free to believe, disbelieve, or doubt, without repression, great or small, by the heavy hand of government. Statutes authorizing such repression have been stricken. Before today, our judicial opinions have refrained from drawing invidious distinctions between those who believe in no religion and those who do believe. The First Amendment has lost much if the religious follower and the atheist are no longer to be judicially regarded as entitled to equal justice under law.

State help to religion injects political and party prejudices into a holy field. It too often substitutes force for prayer, hate for love, and persecution for persuasion. Government should not be allowed, under cover of the soft euphemism of "cooperation," to steal into the sacred area of religious choice....

MR. JUSTICE JACKSON, dissenting:

This released time program is founded upon a use of the State's power of coercion, which, for me, determines its unconstitutionality. Stripped to its essentials, the plan has two stages: first, that the State compel each student to yield a large part of his time for public secular education; and, second, that some of it be "released" to him on condition that he devote it to sectarian religious purposes.

No one suggests that the Constitution would permit the State directly to require this "released" time to be spent "under the control of a duly constituted religious body." This program accomplishes that forbidden result by indirection. If public education were taking so much of the pupils' time as to injure the public or the students' welfare by encroaching upon their religious opportunity, simply shortening everyone's school day would facilitate voluntary and optional attendance at Church classes. But that suggestion is rejected upon the ground that if they are made free many students will not go to the Church. Hence, they must be deprived of freedom for this period, with Church attendance put to them as one of the two permissible ways of using it.

The greater effectiveness of this system over voluntary attendance after school hours is due to the truant officer who, if the youngster fails to go to the Church school, dogs him back to the public schoolroom. Here schooling is more or less suspended during the "released time" so the nonreligious attendants will not forge ahead of the churchgoing absentees. But it serves as a temporary jail for a pupil who will not go to Church. It takes more subtlety of mind than I possess to deny that this is governmental constraint in support of religion. It is as unconstitutional, in my view, when exerted by indirection as when exercised forthrightly.

As one whose children, as a matter of free choice, have been sent to privately supported Church schools, I may challenge the Court's suggestion that opposition to this plan can only be antireligious, atheistic, or agnostic. My evangelistic brethren confuse an objection to compulsion with an objection to religion. It is possible to hold a faith with enough confidence to believe that what should be rendered to God does not need to be decided and collected by Caesar.

The day that this country ceases to be free for irreligion it will cease to be free for religion — except for the sect that can win political power. The same epithetical jurisprudence used by the Court today to beat down those who oppose pressuring children into some religion can devise as good epithets tomorrow against those who object to pressuring them into a favored religion. And, after all, if we concede to the State power and wisdom to single out "duly constituted religious" bodies as exclusive alternatives for compulsory secular instruction, it would be logical to also uphold the power and wisdom to choose the true faith

B. RELEASED TIME FOR RELIGIOUS INSTRUCTION

among those "duly constituted." We start down a rough road when we begin to mix compulsory public education with compulsory godliness.

A number of Justices just short of a majority of the majority that promulgates today's passionate dialectics joined in answering them in *McCollum ex rel. Illinois v. Board of Education*, 333 U.S. 203. The distinction attempted between that case and this is trivial, almost to the point of cynicism, magnifying its nonessential details and disparaging compulsion which was the underlying reason for invalidity. A reading of the Court's opinion in that case along with its opinion in this case will show such difference of overtones and undertones as to make clear that the *McCollum* case has passed like a storm in a teacup. The wall which the Court was professing to erect between Church and State has become even more warped and twisted than I expected. Today's judgment will be more interesting to students of psychology and of the judicial processes than to students of constitutional law.

---

1. How can the Court's decisions in *McCollum* and *Zorach* be reconciled? Are the facts on which the Court relies in distinguishing the *Zorach* situation made clear?

2. Although questions remain as to what factual aspects of the *Zorach* situation made that program constitutionally permissible, courts in subsequent released time cases appear to be structuring their constitutional analysis largely in terms of whether religious instruction is held on or off campus. In *State ex rel. Holt v. Thompson*, 66 Wis. 2d 659, 225 N.W.2d 678 (1975), the Wisconsin Supreme Court upheld a statutory released time program, stating that "... where neither religious instruction in the public school classrooms nor the expenditure of public funds are involved, there is no conflict with the establishment of religion clause of the first amendment." Similarly, in *Smith v. Smith*, 523 F.2d 121 (4th Cir. 1975), *cert. denied*, 423 U.S. 1073 (1976), the court held the released time program of a Virginia school district to be indistinguishable from *Zorach* and thus constitutionally permissible, although it appeared that public school classes were scheduled to accommodate religious instruction in the Virginia district. "In the instant case the accommodations of the school program to religious training were generous and thorough-going, but the classrooms were not turned over to religious instruction." In *Fisher v. Clackamas County Sch. Dist. 12*, 13 Or. App. 56, 507 P.2d 839 (1973), the Oregon court found shared time and released time programs which featured dual enrollment in both public and private schools to be a form of public aid to a religious institution in violation of the Oregon Constitution, but did not reach the question of whether the programs also were violative of the First Amendment of the Federal Constitution.

3. The Court in *Zorach* appears to be equating the released-time provision with a teacher's allowance of a student to be excused for a day for a religious holiday — *i.e.*, Yom Kippur. Is this an accurate comparison? Is the teacher who "cooperates in a religious program" by letting students miss school for Yom Kippur or a family baptism in the same position as one who allows students to be released for religious instruction?

Consider *Cammack v. Waihee*, 932 F.2d 765 (9th Cir. 1991), in which Hawaii taxpayers challenged a statute which declared Good Friday a legal holiday. The Court of Appeals held that taxpayers had standing to bring such a challenge, but that the statute did not violate the Establishment Clause. Is this another one of those "technical violations" discussed in *Zorach* that courts tend to excuse?

The Ninth Circuit Court of Appeals held that the statute served a secular purpose. In the Court's view, to have more legal holidays, the holiday could not be regarded as an endorsement of religion any more than Sunday closing laws could, and, to the extent that the actual date of the holiday is determined by church calendars, any such entanglement was the kind of "comprehensive" and "enduring" entanglement the First Amendment prohibits.

Do you agree with the Court's reasoning in *Cammack*? What is more "entangled" — the relationship between the legislature and religion, or the relationship between Courts and years of tradition, Constitutional requirements, and "technical" violations?

4. Can public schools award academic credit for participation in religion classes held off-campus as part of a released time program? Consider *Lanner v. Wimmer*, 662 F.2d 1349 (10th Cir. 1981).

In *Lanner*, a school district implemented a permissive released-time program allowing students in grades nine through twelve to enroll in a course, taken off school property, sponsored by a religious organization. At issue were Old Testament and New Testament classes taken at a nearby seminary. Under the program, many students were released one period per day throughout the year, and could receive up to two "elective" credits towards high school graduation. In addition, a public school representative entered the seminary regularly to pick up attendance reports; the school's intercom and bells were used in the seminary; and the seminary had mailboxes in the school. Parents and students challenged the program under the First Amendment Religion Clauses. The court cited *Zorach* and applied the *Lemon* test to several aspects of the program. Initially, it held that off-campus released-time programs do not violate the First Amendment per se. However, having a school representative go into the seminary for attendance reports unconstitutionally entangles the school and seminary. The least entangling administrative alternatives must be elected when a released-time program is instituted. In *Zorach*, the churches made the attendance reports to the schools. Other aspects of the program, such as the length of released time per day, and the use of intercom, bells, and mailboxes, were constitutional.

On the credit issue, the State Board of Education stated that no credit was to be given for courses devoted "mainly to denominational instruction." This statement, however, according to the court, presupposes some amount of monitoring by the school. Such monitoring fails the *Lemon* test. "The trial court, therefore, properly enjoined the practice of granting 'credit' in satisfaction of 'elective' courses insofar as the programs required a judgment as to whether the courses were 'mainly denominational' in content."

C. RELIGIOUS OBJECTIONS TO PUBLIC SCHOOL ACTIVITIES

SMITH v. BOARD OF SCHOOL COMMISSIONERS OF MOBILE COUNTY

United States Court of Appeals
827 F.2d 684 (11th Cir. 1987)

JOHNSON, CIRCUIT JUDGE:

Appellants, Alabama State Board of Education and Wayne Teague ("Board") and Malcolm Howell, et al. ("Defendant-Intervenors") appeal the district court's order enjoining the use in Alabama public schools of forty-four textbooks approved by the Board for inclusion on the State-Adopted Textbook List, the use of which the district court found to be a violation of the establishment clause of the first amendment. We reverse.

I. *Background*

A. *Procedural History*

... In May 1982, Ishmael Jaffree brought an action on behalf of three of his minor children pursuant to 42 U.S.C.A. § 1983 against the Mobile County School Board, various school officials, and three teachers seeking, inter alia, a declaratory judgment that certain classroom prayer activities conducted in the Mobile public school system violated the establishment clause of the first amendment and an injunction against classroom prayer. By his second amended complaint, Jaffree added as defendants the Governor of Alabama and other state officials, including Appellant Board, and challenged three Alabama statutes relevant to the school prayer issue as violative of the establishment clause. Douglas T. Smith and others ("Appellees") filed a motion to intervene in the Jaffree action alleging that an injunction against religious activity in the public schools would violate their right to free exercise of religion, and the district court allowed them to intervene as defendants. Subsequently, Appellees filed a motion entitled "Request for Alternate Relief" in which Appellees requested that, if an injunction were granted in favor of Jaffree, that injunction be enforced "against the religions of secularism, humanism, evolution, materialism, agnosticism, atheism and others" or, alternatively, that Appellees be allowed to produce additional evidence showing that these religions had been established in the Alabama public schools.

... The district court ... dismissed Jaffree's complaint for failure to state a claim upon which relief could be granted. [*Jaffree v. Board of School Commissioners*, 554 F.Supp. 1104; *Jaffree v. James*,] 554 F.Supp. at 1132.

This Court reversed, finding that both the school room prayer activities and sections 16-1-20.1 and 16-1-20.2 violated the establishment clause, and remanded the action to the district court with directions that the district court "award costs to appellant and forthwith issue and enforce an order enjoining the statutes and activities held in this opinion to be unconstitutional." *Jaffree v. Wallace*, 705 F.2d 1526, 1536-37 (11th Cir. 1983). The Supreme Court denied certiorari with regard to the nonstatutory school prayer practices, and affirmed this Court's decision with regard to the statutory provisions. *Wallace v. Jaffree*, 472 U.S. 38 (1985); *Wallace v. Jaffree*, 466 U.S. 924 (1984).

In its opinion denying relief in *Jaffree*, the district court had stated that "[i]f the appellate courts disagree with this Court in its examination of history and conclusion of constitutional interpretation thereof, then this Court will look again at the record in this case and reach conclusions which it is not now forced to reach." *Jaffree*, 554 F.Supp. at 1129. In a footnote, the district court indicated that the issues not reached dealt with (1) the free speech rights of teachers and students who wished to pray in school and (2) the teaching of the religion of secular humanism in the schools. *Id.* at n. 41.[1]... [On remand, the] district court interpreted the position of the Appellees as that "if Christianity is not a permissible subject of the curriculum of the public schools, then neither is any

---

[1] With regard to the secular humanism issue, the district court stated: It was pointed out in the testimony that the curriculum in the public schools of Mobile County is rife with efforts at teaching or encouraging secular humanism — all without opposition from any other ethic — to such an extent that it becomes a brainwashing effort. If this Court is compelled to purge "God is great, God is good, we thank Him for our daily food" from the classroom, then this Court must also purge from the classroom those things that serve to teach that salvation is through one's self rather than through a deity. *Jaffree*, 554 F.Supp. at 1129 n. 41. The district court had expressed similar views on the merits of this issue in its earlier opinion granting a preliminary injunction, which was issued before Appellees had filed their "Request for Alternate Relief": The case law, in the opinion of the Court, has overlooked the totality of what is religion in its consideration when deciding issues under the establishment clause of the Constitution.... It is apparent from a reading of the decision law that the courts acknowledge that Christianity is the religion to be proscribed.... The religions of atheism, materialism, agnosticism, communism and socialism have escaped the scrutiny of the courts throughout the years, and make no mistake these are to the believers religions; they are ardently adhered to and quantitatively advanced in the teachings and literature that is presented to the fertile minds of the students in the various school systems. If the courts are to involve themselves in the proscription of religious activities in the schools, then it appears to this Court that we are going to have to involve ourselves in a whole host of areas, such as censoring, that we have heretofore ignored or overlooked. An example of what the Court heard reflecting on this point is in connection with the claimed use of foul language in literature read by a fourth grader and, though it might seem innocuous to some to condemn the use of the word "Goddamn" as it is used in the writings that are required reading, it can clearly be argued that as to Christianity it is blasphemy and is the establishment of an advancement of humanism, secularism or agnosticism. If the state cannot teach or advance Christianity, how can it teach or advance the Antichrist? *Jaffree*, 544 F.Supp. at 732. In that opinion, the district court stated that "[i]t is common knowledge that miscellaneous doctrines such as evolution, socialism, communism, secularism, humanism, and other concepts are advanced in the public schools." *Id.* at n. 2.

C. RELIGIOUS OBJECTIONS TO PUBLIC SCHOOL ACTIVITIES 1239

other religion, and under the evidence introduced it is incumbent upon this Court to strike down those portions of the curriculum demonstrated to contain other religious teachings." For the purpose of considering this issue, the district court *sua sponte* realigned the parties by making Appellees parties plaintiff, consolidated the cases, and invited the parties to submit briefs in support of their positions and to petition the Court to reopen the record for the presentation of additional evidence. The district court stated that the original plaintiffs could withdraw, if they felt their position had been "fully justified," in which case the district court would consider the attorney's fees question, or could remain in the litigation, in which event the motion for attorney's fees would be denied as premature. The original plaintiffs did withdraw, and Appellees filed a position statement in which they asserted, inter alia, that the curriculum in the Mobile County School System unconstitutionally advanced the religion of Humanism and unconstitutionally inhibited Christianity, and that the exclusion from the curriculum of "the existence, history, contributions and role of Christianity in the United States and the world" violated their constitutional rights of equal protection, teacher and student free speech, the student's right to receive information, and teacher and student free exercise of religion.

The twelve Defendant-Intervenors, who are parents of children currently enrolled, or soon to be enrolled, in the Mobile County School System, filed a motion to intervene as defendants in the action, which was granted by the district court....

A bench trial was held October 6-22, 1986 with regard to Appellees' claims. Appellees' evidence focused on elementary and secondary school textbooks in the areas of history, social studies, and home economics, which were on the Alabama State Approved Textbook List, and which Appellees argued unconstitutionally established the religion of secular humanism. The district court found that use of forty-four of these textbooks violated the establishment clause of the first amendment, and permanently enjoined the use of the textbooks in the Alabama public schools. *Smith v. Board of School Comm'rs*, 655 F.Supp. 939, 988 (S.D.Ala.1987). This appeal followed.

II. *Discussion*

The first amendment provides in pertinent part that "Congress shall make no law respecting an establishment of religion...." The district court found that secular humanism constitutes a religion within the meaning of the first amendment and that the forty-four textbooks at issue in this case both advanced that religion and inhibited theistic faiths in violation of the establishment clause. The Supreme Court has never established a comprehensive test for determining the "delicate question" of what constitutes a religious belief for purposes of the first amendment, and we need not attempt to do so in this case, for we find that, even assuming that secular humanism is a religion for purposes of the establishment clause, Appellees have failed to prove a violation of the establishment clause through the use in the Alabama public schools of the textbooks at issue in this case.

The religion clauses of the first amendment require that states "pursue a course of complete neutrality toward religion." *Jaffree*, 472 U.S. at 60; *accord School Dist. of Abington Township v. Schempp*, 374 U.S. 203, 215 (1963) ("The government is neutral, and, while protecting all, it prefers none, and it disparages none."). The establishment clause, however, has not been interpreted as requiring mechanical invalidation of all government conduct conferring benefit on or giving special recognition to religion, but rather has been seen as erecting a "blurred, indistinct and variable barrier depending on all the circumstances of a particular relationship." *Lynch v. Donnelly*, 465 U.S. 668, 678-79 (1984). The Supreme Court has developed three criteria to serve as guidelines in determining whether this barrier has been breached by challenged government action:

> First, the statute must have a secular legislative purpose; second, its principal or primary effect must be one that neither advances nor inhibits religion; finally, the statute must not foster "an excessive government entanglement with religion." *Lemon v. Kurtzman*, 403 U.S. 602, 612-13 (1971).[3]

....

The parties agree that there is no question of a religious purpose or excessive government entanglement in this case and our review of the record confirms that conclusion. Our inquiry, therefore, must center on the second *Lemon* criterion: whether use of the challenged textbooks had the primary effect of either advancing or inhibiting religion.

"The effect prong [of the *Lemon* test] asks whether, irrespective of government's actual purpose, the practice under review in fact conveys a message of endorsement or disapproval." *Jaffree*, 472 U.S. at 56 n. 42, (quoting *Lynch*, 465 U.S. at 690 (O'CONNOR, J., concurring)). If government identification with religion conveys such a message of government endorsement or disapproval of religion, then "a core purpose of the Establishment Clause is violated." *[School District of Grand Rapids v.] Ball*, 473 U.S. [373,] 389 [(1985)]. In determining the message conveyed by use of the textbooks in this case, we recognize that we must use "particular care" as "many of the citizens perceiving the governmental message are children in their formative years." *Id.* at 390.

The district court found that the home economics, history, and social studies textbooks both advanced secular humanism and inhibited theistic religion. Our review of the record in this case reveals that these conclusions were in error. As

---

[3] Although the *Lemon* test and the establishment clause itself speak in terms of laws regarding establishment of religion, "[t]he reach of the establishment clause is not limited by the lack of statutory authorization." *Jaffree v. Wallace*, 705 F.2d 1526, 1534 (11th Cir. 1983). If state action is present and the activities do not satisfy the *Lemon* criteria, then the activities violate the establishment clause. *Id.*

C. RELIGIOUS OBJECTIONS TO PUBLIC SCHOOL ACTIVITIES

discussed below, use of the challenged textbooks has the primary effect of conveying information that is essentially neutral in its religious content to the school children who utilize the books; none of these books convey a message of governmental approval of secular humanism or governmental disapproval of theism.

A. *Home Economics Textbooks*

The district court found that the home economics textbooks required students to accept as true certain tenets of humanistic psychology, which the district court found to be "a manifestation of humanism." *Smith*, 655 F.Supp. at 987. In particular, the district court found that the books "imply strongly that a person uses the same process in deciding a moral issue that he uses in choosing one pair of shoes over another,"[5] and teach that "the student must determine right and wrong based only on his own experience, feelings and [internal] values" and that "the validity of a moral choice is only to be decided by the student." *Id.* at 986. The district court stated that "[t]he emphasis and overall approach implies, and would cause any reasonable thinking student to infer, that the book is teaching that moral choices are just a matter of preferences, because, as the books say, 'you are the most important person in your life.'" *Id.* The district court stated that "[t]his highly relativistic and individualistic approach constitutes the promotion of a fundamental faith claim" that "assumes that self-actualization is the goal of every human being, that man has no supernatural attributes or component, that there are only temporal and physical consequences for man's actions, and that these results, alone, determine the morality of an action." *Id.* at 986-87. According to the district court, "[t]his belief strikes at the heart of many theistic religions' beliefs that certain actions are in and of themselves immoral, *whatever the consequences*, and that, in addition, actions will have extra-temporal consequences." *Id.* at 987 (emphasis in original). The district court stated that "some religious beliefs are so fundamental that the act of denying them will completely undermine that religion" and "[i]n addition, denial of *that* belief will result in the affirmance of a contrary belief and result in the establishment of an opposing religion." *Id.* (emphasis in original). It concluded that, while the state may teach certain moral values, such as that lying is wrong, "if, in so doing it advances a reason for the rule, the possible different reasons

---

[5]In support of this statement, the district court refers to a passage in one of the home economics textbooks in which the author lists the steps in the decision-making process and states that "[a]s you can see, the steps in decision-making can be applied to something as simple as buying a new pair of shoes" and "can also be applied to more complex decisions such as those which involve religious preferences; education and career choices; the use of alcohol, tobacco and drugs; and sexual habits." F. Parnell, Homemaking Skills for Everyday Living 26 (1984). The book lists the steps in decision-making as (1) Define the problem; (2) Establish your goals; (3) List your goals in order of importance; (4) Look for resources; (5) Study the alternatives; (6) Make a decision; (7) Carry out the decision; (8) Evaluate the results of your decision. *Id.*

must be explained evenhandedly" and "the state may not promote one particular reason over another in the public schools." *Id.*

In order to violate the primary effect prong of the *Lemon* test through advancement of religion, it is not sufficient that the government action merely accommodates religion. The constitution "affirmatively mandates accommodation, not merely tolerance, of all religions, and forbids hostility towards any." *Lynch*, 465 U.S. at 672. Nor is it sufficient that government conduct confers an indirect, remote or incidental benefit on a religion, *Ball*, 473 U.S. at 393, or that its effect merely happens to coincide or harmonize with the tenets of a religion....

... In order for government conduct to constitute an impermissible advancement of religion, the government action must amount to an endorsement of religion. *Lynch*, 465 U.S. at 681. Further, the primary effect of challenged government action must be determined in light of the overall context in which it occurs: "[f]ocus exclusively on the religious component of any activity would inevitably lead to its invalidation under the Establishment Clause." *Id.* at 679-80.

Examination of the contents of these textbooks, including the passages pointed out by Appellees as particularly offensive,[7] in the context of the books as a whole and the undisputedly nonreligious purpose sought to be achieved by their use, reveals that the message conveyed is not one of endorsement of secular humanism or any religion. Rather, the message conveyed is one of a governmental attempt to instill in Alabama public school children such values as independent thought, tolerance of diverse views, self-respect, maturity, self-reliance and logical decision-making. This is an entirely appropriate secular effect. Indeed, one of the major objectives of public education is the "inculcat[ion of] fundamental values necessary to the maintenance of a democratic political system." *Bethel School Dist. No. 403 v. Fraser*, ___ U.S. ___, 106 S.Ct. 3159, 3164, (1986) (quoting *Ambach v. Norwick*, 441 U.S. 68, 77 (1979)) (brackets in original). It is true that the textbooks contain ideas that are consistent with secular humanism; the textbooks also contain ideas consistent with theistic religion. However, as discussed above, mere consistency with religious tenets is insufficient to constitute unconstitutional advancement of religion.

Nor do these textbooks evidence an attitude antagonistic to theistic belief. The message conveyed by these textbooks with regard to theistic religion is one of neutrality: the textbooks neither endorse theistic religion as a system of belief, nor discredit it. Indeed, many of the books specifically acknowledge that religion is one source of moral values and none preclude that possibility. While the Supreme Court has recognized that "the State may not establish a 'religion of secularism' in the sense of affirmatively opposing or showing hostility to religion, thus 'preferring those who believe in no religion over those who do

---

[7]These passages are found in Appendix N of the district court's opinion. *See Smith*, 655 F.Supp. at 999.

believe,'" *Abington*, 374 U.S. at 225, that Court also has made it clear that the neutrality mandated by the establishment clause does not itself equate with hostility towards religion. *See, e.g., id.*; *McCollum v. Board of Ed.*, 333 U.S. 203, 211-12 (1948); *Engel v. Vitale*, 370 U.S. 421, 433-35 (1962)....

It is obvious that Appellees find some of the material in these textbooks offensive. That fact, however, is not sufficient to render use of this material in the public schools a violation of the establishment clause. *See Epperson*, 393 U.S. at 107 (quoting *Joseph Burstyn, Inc. v. Wilson*, 343 U.S. 495, 505 (1952)) ("The state has no legitimate interest in protecting any or all religions from views distasteful to them.").[10] The district court erred in concluding that the challenged home economics books advanced secular humanism and inhibited theistic religion.

B. *History and Social Studies Textbooks*

The district court's conclusion that the history and social studies textbooks violated the establishment clause was based on its finding that these books failed to include a sufficient discussion of the role of religion in history and culture. The district court found that the history books omit certain historical events with religious significance and "uniformly ignore the religious aspect of most American culture." *Smith*, 655 F.Supp. at 985. The district court found that "[r]eligion, where treated at all, is generally represented as a private matter, only influencing American public life at some extraordinary moments," and that "[t]his view of religion is one humanists have been seeking to instill for fifty years." *Id*. The district court concluded that the history books "assist that effort by perpetuating an inaccurate historical picture" and held that the books "lack so many facts as to equal ideological promotion." *Id*. The district court also found that the history books "discriminate against the very concept of religion, and theistic religions in particular, by omissions so serious that a student learning history from them would not be apprised of relevant facts about America's history." *Id*. Use of the social studies books was found unconstitutional because the books failed to integrate religion into the history of American society, ignored the importance of theistic religion as an influence in American society and contained "factual inaccuracies ... so grave as to rise to a constitutional violation." *Id*. at 985-86.

It is clear on the record of this case that, assuming one tenet of secular humanism is to downplay the importance of religion in history and in American society, any benefit to secular humanism from the failure of the challenged history and social studies books to contain references to the religious aspects of certain historical events or to adequately integrate the place of religion in modern

---

[10]Indeed, given the diversity of religious views in this country, if the standard were merely inconsistency with the beliefs of a particular religion there would be very little that could be taught in the public schools....

American society is merely incidental. There is no doubt that these textbooks were chosen for the secular purpose of education in the areas of history and social studies, and we find that the primary effect of the use of these textbooks is consistent with that stated purpose. We do not believe that an objective observer could conclude from the mere omission of certain historical facts regarding religion or the absence of a more thorough discussion of its place in modern American society that the State of Alabama was conveying a message of approval of the religion of secular humanism. Indeed, the message that reasonably would be conveyed to students and others is that the education officials, in the exercise of their discretion over school curriculum, chose to use these particular textbooks because they deemed them more relevant to the curriculum, or better written, or for some other nonreligious reason found them to be best suited to their needs. *Cf. Board of Ed. v. Pico*, 457 U.S. 853, 880 (1982) (BLACKMUN, J., concurring)....

Nor can we agree with the district court's conclusion that the omission of these facts causes the books to "discriminate against the very concept of religion." *Smith*, 655 F.Supp. at 985. Just as use of these books does not convey a message of governmental approval of secular humanism, neither does it convey a message of government disapproval of theistic religions merely by omitting certain historical facts concerning them.

The district court's reliance on *Epperson v. Arkansas*, 393 U.S. 97 (1968), to support its conclusion that omission of certain material regarding religion in this case constituted a first amendment violation is misplaced. *Epperson* involved an Arkansas statute that made it a crime to teach the theory of evolution in the public schools. *Id.* at 98. The Supreme Court found that the law violated the establishment clause under the purpose prong of the *Lemon* test: the state forbade the teaching of evolution because it conflicted with a particular religious doctrine. 393 U.S. at 103....

There is no question in this case that the purpose behind using these particular history and social studies books was purely secular. Selecting a textbook that omits a particular topic for nonreligious reasons is significantly different from requiring the omission of material because it conflicts with a particular religious belief. Further, unlike the situation in *Epperson*, which involved total exclusion of information regarding evolution from the school curriculum, Appellees in this case merely complain that the historical treatment of religion in the challenged textbooks is inadequate. Finally, the record indicates that teachers in Alabama were free to supplement the discussion contained in the textbooks in areas they found inadequate. Thus, unlike the situation in *Epperson* where the State of Arkansas had made an attempt to teach the omitted material a criminal offense, there is no active policy on the part of Alabama that prohibits teaching historical facts about religion. There simply is nothing in this record to indicate that omission of certain facts regarding religion from these textbooks of itself constituted an advancement of secular humanism or an active hostility towards theistic religion prohibited by the establishment clause. While these textbooks may be inadequate from an educational standpoint, the wisdom of an educational policy or its efficiency from an educational point of view is not germane to the constitutional issue of whether that policy violates the establishment clause. *Zorach v. Clauson*, 343 U.S. 306, 310 (1952).

III. *Conclusion*

The home economics, social studies, and history textbooks at issue in this case do not violate the establishment clause of the first amendment....

---

1. What is "secular humanism"? Is this a religion? Has it been "discovered" or developed? Is it a result of attempts by schools and other governmental entities to be neutral and to avoid establishing a religion (or giving the impression of such an establishment)? Consider the following quote from *Smith*:

> [T]he message conveyed is one of a governmental attempt to instill in Alabama public school children such values as independent thought, tolerance of diverse views, self-respect, maturity, self-reliance and logical decision-making. This is an entirely appropriate secular effect. 827 F.2d at 692.

The Court held that the use of textbooks that convey such messages did not advance secular humanism in violation of the Establishment Clause. Could the above quote be considered a good description of secular humanism? If so, would this not mean that the disputed textbooks do, indeed, advance secular humanism?

Whether you call it secular humanism, give it another title, or leave it unnamed, what are the positive effects that could result from using books that present the above themes? On balance, do they outweigh the negatives associated with schools teaching value systems? In many school systems today, it is safe to assume that many children do not come from stable households and are in dire need of positive influences. Should the potential benefits of "secular humanism" for these children be used as an argument for the continued use of materials that contain the related themes? If, someday, secular humanism is expressly declared a religion by the courts (is it in *Smith*?), will we be able to add this to the list of accepted "technical violations"?

2. "The Establishment Clause, however, has not been interpreted as requiring mechanical invalidation of all government conduct conferring benefit on or giving special recognition to religion, but rather has been seen as erecting a 'blurred, indistinct and variable barrier depending on all the circumstances of a particular relationship.'" *Smith*, 827 F.2d at 689 (quoting *Lynch v. Donnelly*, 465 U.S. 668, 678-79). Is the Alabama Board School Commissioners in *Smith* attempting to draw a line avoiding the establishment and endorsement of a particular view while allowing for a neutral one? If so, does the Court give the Board the credit it deserves for their efforts?

3. The court states that in the attempt to downplay particular religions (via the chosen textbooks), any benefit to secular humanism is merely incidental. What if these books were a little more blatant in their presentation of secular humanism, or any (other) religion. Would an argument that the books were chosen for other, secular, academic reasons hold up — even if such argument were as strong as the argument here? In other words, how "incidental" must this religion be, and is there a control on which religions may be presented "incidentally"?

4. Whether religious beliefs should be allowed to outweigh a showing of patriotism and expression of support for the government and American way of life is an issue which arose initially during World War II, a period of great stress and high patriotism. Although the plaintiffs in the following case alleged an unconstitutional denial of religious freedom, the Supreme Court's decision was not directly based on the First Amendment religion clauses. *West Virginia State Board of Educ. v. Barnette* has proved of precedential value in subsequent cases involving religious issues, however, both because of the Court's analysis of the tension between the State's power to condition access to public education and the individual's right to free expression and because of the Court's articulation of the proposition that "no official can prescribe what shall be orthodox in politics, nationalism, religion or other matters of opinion...."

WEST VIRGINIA STATE BOARD OF EDUCATION v. BARNETTE

Supreme Court of the United States
319 U.S. 624 (1943)

MR. JUSTICE JACKSON delivered the opinion of the Court:

Following the decision by this Court on June 3, 1940, in *Minersville School District v. Gobitis*, 310 U.S. 586, 127 A.L.R. 1493, the West Virginia legislature amended its statutes to require all schools therein to conduct courses of instruction in history, civics, and in the Constitutions of the United States and of the State "for the purpose of teaching, fostering and perpetuating the ideals, principles and spirit of Americanism, and increasing the knowledge of the organization and machinery of the government." Appellant Board of Education was directed, with advice of the State Superintendent of Schools, to "prescribe the courses of study covering these subjects" for public schools. The Act made it the duty of private, parochial and denominational schools to prescribe courses of study similar to those required for the public schools.

The Board of Education on January 9, 1942, adopted a resolution containing recitals taken largely from the Court's *Gobitis* opinion and ordering that the salute to the flag become "a regular part of the program of activities in the public schools," that all teachers and pupils "shall be required to participate in the salute honoring the Nation represented by the Flag; provided, however, that refusal to salute the Flag be regarded as an Act of insubordination, and shall be dealt with accordingly." The resolution originally required the "commonly

C. RELIGIOUS OBJECTIONS TO PUBLIC SCHOOL ACTIVITIES 1247

accepted salute to the Flag" which it defined. Objections to the salute as "being too much like Hitler's" were raised by the Parent and Teachers Association, the Boy and Girl Scouts, the Red Cross, and the Federation of Women's Clubs. Some modification appears to have been made in deference to these objections, but no concession was made to Jehovah's Witnesses. What is now required is the "stiff-arm" salute, the saluter to keep the right hand raised with palm turned up while the following is repeated: "I pledge allegiance to the Flag of the United States of America and to the Republic for which it stands; one Nation, indivisible, with liberty and justice for all."

Failure to conform is "insubordination" dealt with by expulsion. Readmission is denied by statute until compliance. Meanwhile the expelled child is "unlawfully absent" and may be proceeded against as a delinquent. His parents or guardians are liable to prosecution, and if convicted are subject to fine not exceeding $50 and jail term not exceeding thirty days.

Appellees, citizens of the United States and of West Virginia, brought suit in the United States District Court for themselves and others similarly situated asking its injunction to restrain enforcement of these laws and regulations against Jehovah's Witnesses. The Witnesses are an unincorporated body teaching that the obligation imposed by law of God is superior to that of laws enacted by temporal government. Their religious beliefs include a literal version of Exodus, Chapter 20, verses 4 and 5, which says: "Thou shalt not make unto thee any graven image, or any likeness of anything that is in heaven above, or that is in the earth beneath, or that is in the water under the earth; thou shalt not bow down thyself to them nor serve them." They consider that the flag is an "image" within this command. For this reason they refuse to salute it.

Children of this faith have been expelled from school and are threatened with exclusion for no other cause. Officials threaten to send them to reformatories maintained for criminally inclined juveniles. Parents of such children have been prosecuted and are threatened with prosecutions for causing delinquency.

. . . .

This case calls upon us to reconsider a precedent decision, as the Court throughout its history often has been required to do. Before turning to the *Gobitis* case, however, it is desirable to notice certain characteristics by which this controversy is distinguished.

The freedom asserted by these appellees does not bring them into collision with rights asserted by any other individual. It is such conflicts which most frequently require intervention of the State to determine where the rights of one end and those of another begin. But the refusal of these persons to participate in the ceremony does not interfere with or deny rights of others to do so. Nor is there any question in this case that their behavior is peaceable and orderly. The sole conflict is between authority and rights of the individual. The State asserts power to condition access to public education on making a prescribed sign and profession and at the same time to coerce attendance by punishing both parent and child. The latter stand on a right of self-determination in matters that touch individual opinion and personal attitude.

....

It is also to be noted that the compulsory flag salute and pledge requires affirmation of a belief and an attitude of mind. It is not clear whether the regulation contemplates that pupils forego any contrary convictions of their own and become unwilling converts to the prescribed ceremony or whether it will be acceptable if they simulate assent by words without belief and by a gesture barren of meaning. It is now a commonplace that censorship or suppression of expression of opinion is tolerated by our Constitution only when the expression presents a clear and present danger of action of a kind the State is empowered to prevent and punish. It would seem that involuntary affirmation could be commanded only on even more immediate and urgent grounds than silence. But here the power of compulsion is invoked without any allegation that remaining passive during a flag salute ritual creates a clear and present danger that would justify an effort even to muffle expression. To sustain the compulsory flag salute we are required to say that a Bill of Rights which guards the individual's right to speak his own mind, left it open to public authorities to compel him to utter what is not in his mind.

Whether the First Amendment to the Constitution will permit officials to order observance of ritual of this nature does not depend upon whether as a voluntary exercise we would think it to be good, bad or merely innocuous. Any credo of nationalism is likely to include what some disapprove or to omit what others think essential, and to give off different overtones as it takes on different accents or interpretations. If official power exists to coerce acceptance of any patriotic creed, what it shall contain cannot be decided by courts, but must be largely discretionary with the ordaining authority, whose power to prescribe would no doubt include power to amend. Hence validity of the asserted power to force an American citizen publicly to profess any statement of belief or to engage in any ceremony of assent to one presents questions of power that must be considered independently of any idea we may have as to the utility of the ceremony in question.

Nor does the issue as we see it turn on one's possession of particular religious views or the sincerity with which they are held. While religion supplies appellees' motive for enduring the discomforts of making the issue in this case, many citizens who do not share these religious views hold such a compulsory rite to infringe constitutional liberty of the individual. It is not necessary to inquire whether non-conformist beliefs will exempt from the duty to salute unless we first find power to make the salute a legal duty.

The *Gobitis* decision, however, *assumed*, as did the argument in that case and in this, that power exists in the State to impose the flag salute discipline upon school children in general. The Court only examined and rejected a claim based on religious beliefs of immunity from an unquestioned general rule. The question which underlies the flag salute controversy is whether such a ceremony so touching matters of opinion and political attitude may be imposed upon the individual by official authority under powers committed to any political organization under our Constitution. We examine rather than assume existence of this power and, against this broader definition of issues in this case, re-examine specific grounds assigned for the *Gobitis* decision.

....

The Fourteenth Amendment, as now applied to the States, protects the citizen against the State itself and all of its creatures — Boards of Education not excepted. These have, of course, important, delicate, and highly discretionary functions, but none that they may not perform within the limits of the Bill of Rights. That they are educating the young for citizenship is reason for scrupulous protection of Constitutional freedoms of the individual, if we are not to strangle the free mind at its source and teach youth to discount important principles of our government as mere platitudes.

....

The very purpose of a Bill of Rights was to withdraw certain subjects from the vicissitudes of political controversy, to place them beyond the reach of majorities and officials and to establish them as legal principles to be applied by the courts. One's right to life, liberty, and property, to free speech, a free press, freedom of worship and assembly, and other fundamental rights may not be submitted to vote; they depend on the outcome of no elections.

....

National unity as an end which officials may foster by persuasion and example is not in question. The problem is whether under our Constitution compulsion as here employed is a permissible means for its achievement.

....

If there is any fixed star in our constitutional constellation, it is that no official, high or petty, can prescribe what shall be orthodox in politics, nationalism, religion, or other matters of opinion or force citizens to confess by word or act their faith therein. If there are any circumstances which permit an exception, they do not now occur to us.

We think the action of the local authorities in compelling the flag salute and pledge transcends constitutional limitations on their power and invades the sphere of intellect and spirit which it is the purpose of the First Amendment to our Constitution to reserve from all official control.

The decision of this Court in *Minersville School District v. Gobitis* and the holdings of those few *per curiam* decisions which preceded and foreshadowed it are overruled, and the judgment enjoining enforcement of the West Virginia Regulation is affirmed.

1. Consider carefully the basis of Justice Jackson's decision in *Barnette*. What constitutional right of the plaintiffs was violated by the mandatory flag salute: their free exercise of religion; their freedom of speech; generalized substantive due process; all of these; none of these?

Is *Barnette* in this regard more like *Meyer* (*see* Chapter 3) and *Pierce* (Chapter 2) or more like *Yoder* (Chapter 2)? Why did Justice Jackson take the approach he did? What approach should have been taken? Would the case have been easier if it were clearly put on religious grounds? Would it have been more or less significant if clearly on religious grounds?

2. Neither in *Schempp* nor *Engel*, discussed earlier in this chapter, does the Court discuss the fact that in *Barnette* all that was required was an exemption for objectors. Should the "establishment" of political orthodoxy in *Barnette* be treated differently in this regard than the "establishment of religion" in *Engel* and *Schempp*? Is it relevant that the First Amendment explicitly prohibits the "establishment of religion" but does not specifically prohibit the "establishment" of a particular political view? Consider again the basis of *Barnette*.

3. Consider the validity of the following distinctions between compelled attendance in a class and a compelled flag salute. Indoctrination in the former is subject to student resistance and opportunity for parents and others to counter-indoctrinate outside school whereas the latter is an irrevocable act which cannot be retracted once committed. Is this distinction persuasive? Could not this irrevocable act be made meaningless as a means of indoctrination of students by being done by them mechanically? If so, does this suggest that the distinction, if any, is not in the effect of the salute as indoctrination but rather in the required act of saluting itself as being constitutionally offensive? If so, is there a distinction between required acts which affect one's political beliefs and those which affect religious beliefs, *i.e.*, those viewed as religious "sins"? Consider again the basis of the *Barnette* opinion.

In addition, can classroom instruction be viewed only as students having to listen to the views expressed by the teacher? What about required student responses in class, such as on tests? Is it constitutionally permissible for a teacher to mark "wrong" a test answer that contradicts the "orthodox" or the teacher's view on social or political issues? If this is constitutionally permissible, what is the difference between marking an unorthodox answer wrong and a compulsory flag salute?

4. Consider the fact that the relief in *Barnette* was limited to excusing objectors from having to salute the flag. If the constitutional defect was political indoctrination, why was the flag salute itself not held unconstitutional and prohibited completely? Might not non-objecting students need even greater protection from indoctrination than those who have the insight and strength to object? Compare the *Schempp* case.

5. The Court in *Barnette* does not consider the impact which parental desires probably had on refusal of a third grader to salute the flag. Instead, Justice Jackson finds that West Virginia has underestimated "the appeal of our institutions to free minds." Does his analysis give appropriate weight to the specific facts of the case and the potential for parental influence?

AGUILAR v. FELTON

Supreme Court of the United States
473 U.S. 402 (1985)

JUSTICE BRENNAN delivered the opinion of the Court:

The City of New York uses federal funds to pay the salaries of public employees who teach in parochial schools. In this companion case to *School District of Grand Rapids v. Ball*, 473 U.S. 373, we determine whether this practice violates the Establishment Clause of the First Amendment.

I

A

The program at issue in this case, originally enacted as Title I of the Elementary and Secondary Education Act of 1965, authorizes the Secretary of Education to distribute financial assistance to local educational institutions to meet the needs of educationally deprived children from low-income families. The funds are to be appropriated in accordance with programs proposed by local educational agencies and approved by state educational agencies....

Since 1966, the City of New York has provided instructional services funded by Title I to parochial school students on the premises of parochial schools. Of those students eligible to receive funds in 1981-1982, 13.2% were enrolled in private schools. Of that group, 84% were enrolled in schools affiliated with the Roman Catholic Archdiocese of New York and the Diocese of Brooklyn and 8% were enrolled in Hebrew day schools. With respect to the religious atmosphere of these schools, the Court of Appeals concluded that "the picture that emerges is of a system in which religious considerations play a key role in the selection of students and teachers, and which has as its substantial purpose the inculcation of religious values."

The programs conducted at these schools include remedial reading, reading skills, remedial mathematics, English as a second language, and guidance services. These programs are carried out by regular employees of the public schools (teachers, guidance counselors, psychologists, psychiatrists, and social workers) who have volunteered to teach in the parochial schools. The amount of time that each professional spends in the parochial school is determined by the number of students in the particular program and the needs of these students.

The City's Bureau of Nonpublic School Reimbursement makes teacher assignments, and the instructors are supervised by field personnel, who attempt to pay at least one unannounced visit per month. The field supervisors, in turn, report to program coordinators, who also pay occasional unannounced supervisory visits to monitor Title I classes in the parochial schools. The professionals involved in the program are directed to avoid involvement with religious activities that are conducted within the private schools and to bar religious materials in their classrooms. All material and equipment used in the programs funded under Title I are supplied by the Government and are used only in those programs. The professional personnel are solely responsible for the selection of the students. Additionally, the professionals are informed that contact with private school personnel should be kept to a minimum. Finally, the administrators of the parochial schools are required to clear the classrooms used by the public school personnel of all religious symbols.

B

....

II

In *School District of Grand Rapids v. Ball*, 473 U.S. 373, the Court has today held unconstitutional under the Establishment Clause two remedial and enhancement programs operated by the Grand Rapids Public School District, in which classes were provided to private school children at public expense in classrooms located in and leased from the local private schools. The New York City programs challenged in this case are very similar to the programs we examined in *Ball*. In both cases, publicly funded instructors teach classes composed exclusively of private school students in private school buildings. In both cases, an overwhelming number of the participating private schools are religiously affiliated. In both cases, the publicly funded programs provide not only professional personnel, but also all materials and supplies necessary for the operation of the programs. Finally, the instructors in both cases are told that they are public school employees under the sole control of the public school system.

Appellants attempt to distinguish this case on the ground that the City of New York, unlike the Grand Rapids Public School District, has adopted a system for monitoring the religious content of publicly funded Title I classes in the religious schools. At best, the supervision in this case would assist in preventing the Title I program from being used, intentionally or unwittingly, to inculcate the religious beliefs of the surrounding parochial school. But appellants' argument fails in any event, because the supervisory system established by the City of New York inevitably results in the excessive entanglement of church and state, an Establishment Clause concern distinct from that addressed by the effects doctrine. Even where state aid to parochial institutions does not have the primary effect of advancing religion, the provision of such aid may nonetheless violate the Establishment Clause owing to the nature of the interaction of church and state in the administration of that aid.

The principle that the state should not become too closely entangled with the church in the administration of assistance is rooted in two concerns. When the state becomes enmeshed with a given denomination in matters of religious significance, the freedom of religious belief of those who are not adherents of that denomination suffers, even when the governmental purpose underlying the involvement is largely secular. In addition, the freedom of even the adherents of the denomination is limited by the governmental intrusion into sacred matters.

C. RELIGIOUS OBJECTIONS TO PUBLIC SCHOOL ACTIVITIES

"[T]he First Amendment rests upon the premise that both religion and government can best work to achieve their lofty aims if each is left free from the other within its respective sphere."

In *Lemon v. Kurtzman*, 403 U.S. 602 (1971), the Court held that the supervision necessary to ensure that teachers in parochial schools were not conveying religious messages to their students would constitute the excessive entanglement of church and state:

> A comprehensive, discriminating, and continuing state surveillance will inevitably be required to ensure that these restrictions are obeyed and the First Amendment otherwise respected. Unlike a book, a teacher cannot be inspected once so as to determine the extent and intent of his or her personal beliefs and subjective acceptance of the limitations imposed by the First Amendment. These prophylactic contacts will involve excessive and enduring entanglement between state and church. *Id.* at 619.

Similarly, in *Meek v. Pittenger*, 421 U.S. 349 (1975), we invalidated a state program that offered, inter alia, guidance, testing, and remedial and therapeutic services performed by public employees on the premises of the parochial schools. *Id.* at 352-53. As in *Lemon*, we observed that though a comprehensive system of supervision might conceivably prevent teachers from having the primary effect of advancing religion, such a system would inevitably lead to an unconstitutional administrative entanglement between church and state.

....

The critical elements of the entanglement proscribed in *Lemon* and *Meek* are thus present in this case. First, as noted above, the aid is provided in a pervasively sectarian environment. Second, because assistance is provided in the form of teachers, ongoing inspection is required to ensure the absence of a religious message.... In short, the scope and duration of New York City's Title I program would require a permanent and pervasive state presence in the sectarian schools receiving aid.

This pervasive monitoring by public authorities in the sectarian schools infringes precisely those Establishment Clause values at the root of the prohibition of excessive entanglement. Agents of the city must visit and inspect the religious school regularly, alert for the subtle or overt presence of religious matter in Title I classes. *Cf. Lemon v. Kurtzman*, 403 U.S. at 619 ("What would appear to some to be essential to good citizenship might well for others border on or constitute instruction in religion"). In addition, the religious school must obey these same agents when they make determinations as to what is and what is not a "religious symbol" and thus off limits in a Title I classroom. In short, the religious school, which has as a primary purpose the advancement and preservation of a particular religion must endure the ongoing presence of state personnel whose primary purpose is to monitor teachers and students in an attempt to guard against the infiltration of religious thought.

The administrative cooperation that is required to maintain the educational program at issue here entangles church and state in still another way that infringes interests at the heart of the Establishment Clause. Administrative personnel of the public and parochial school systems must work together in resolving matters related to schedules, classroom assignments, problems that arise in the implementation of the program, requests for additional services, and the dissemination of information regarding the program. Furthermore, the program necessitates "frequent contacts between the regular and the remedial teachers (or other professionals), in which each side reports on individual student needs, problems encountered, and results achieved." 739 F.2d at 65.

....

III

Despite the well-intentioned efforts taken by the City of New York, the program remains constitutionally flawed owing to the nature of the aid, to the institution receiving the aid, and to the constitutional principles that they implicate — that neither the State nor Federal Government shall promote or hinder a particular faith or faith generally through the advancement of benefits or through the excessive entanglement of church and state in the administration of those benefits.

Affirmed.

---

1. "When the state becomes enmeshed with a given denomination in matters of religious significance, the freedom of religious belief of those who are not adherents of that denomination suffers, even when the governmental purpose underlying the involvement is largely secular." *Aguilar*, 437 U.S. 402, 410-11. Can this be applied to situations like *Smith v. Board of Comm'rs of Mobile County* and the alleged secularly humanistic textbooks? Recall that the underlying governmental purpose was to provide good textbooks and that any religious connection was labeled purely incidental.

2. Is this case decided correctly?

3. In all of our line drawing, where should depiction and recognition of religious, national, and ethnic holidays *within the classrooms* be placed? In *Clever v. Cherry Hill Twp. Bd. of Educ.*, 838 F. Supp. 929 (D.N.J. 1993), the court held that calendars and seasonal displays in classrooms which depicted religious and other holidays did not violate the First Amendment.

C. RELIGIOUS OBJECTIONS TO PUBLIC SCHOOL ACTIVITIES

BOARD OF EDUCATION OF KIRYAS JOEL VILLAGE SCHOOL DISTRICT v. GRUMET

Supreme Court of the United States
114 S. Ct. 2481 (1994)

JUSTICE SOUTER delivered the opinion of the Court with respect to Parts II-B, II-C, and III, concluding that Chapter 748 violates the Establishment Clause:

....

JUSTICE SOUTER delivered the opinion of the Court:

The Village of Kiryas Joel in Orange County, New York, is a religious enclave of Satmar Hasidim, practitioners of a strict form of Judaism. The village fell within the Monroe-Woodbury Central School District until a special state statute passed in 1989 carved out a separate district, following village lines, to serve this distinctive population. 1989 N.Y.Laws, ch. 748. The question is whether the Act creating the separate school district violates the Establishment Clause of the First Amendment, binding on the States through the Fourteenth Amendment. Because this unusual act is tantamount to an allocation of political power on a religious criterion and neither presupposes nor requires governmental impartiality toward religion, we hold that it violates the prohibition against establishment.

I

The Satmar Hasidic sect takes its name from the town near the Hungarian and Romanian border where, in the early years of this century, Grand Rebbe Joel Teitelbaum molded the group into a distinct community. After World War II and the destruction of much of European Jewry, the Grand Rebbe and most of his surviving followers moved to the Williamsburg section of Brooklyn, New York. Then, 20 years ago, the Satmars purchased an approved but undeveloped subdivision in the town of Monroe and began assembling the community that has since become the Village of Kiryas Joel. When a zoning dispute arose in the course of settlement, the Satmars presented the Town Board of Monroe with a petition to form a new village within the town, a right that New York's Village Law gives almost any group of residents who satisfy certain procedural niceties. Neighbors who did not wish to secede with the Satmars objected strenuously, and after arduous negotiations the proposed boundaries of the Village of Kiryas Joel were drawn to include just the 320 acres owned and inhabited entirely by Satmars....

The residents of Kiryas Joel are vigorously religious people who make few concessions to the modern world and go to great lengths to avoid assimilation into it. They interpret the Torah strictly; segregate the sexes outside the home; speak Yiddish as their primary language; eschew television, radio, and English-language publications; and dress in distinctive ways that include headcoverings and special garments for boys and modest dresses for girls. Children are educated in private religious schools, most boys at the United Talmudic Academy where they receive a thorough grounding in the Torah and limited exposure to secular subjects, and most girls at Bais Rochel, an affiliated school with a curriculum designed to prepare girls for their roles as wives and mothers.

These schools do not, however, offer any distinctive services to handicapped children, who are entitled under state and federal law to special education services even when enrolled in private schools.... Starting in 1984 the Monroe-Woodbury Central School District provided such services for the children of Kiryas Joel at an annex to Bais Rochel, but a year later ended that arrangement in response to our decisions in *Aguilar v. Felton*, 473 U.S. 402 (1985), and *School Dist. of Grand Rapids v. Ball*, 473 U.S. 373 (1985). Children from Kiryas Joel who needed special education (including the deaf, the mentally retarded, and others suffering from a range of physical, mental, or emotional disorders) were then forced to attend public schools outside the village, which their families found highly unsatisfactory. Parents of most of these children withdrew them from the Monroe-Woodbury secular schools, citing "the panic, fear and trauma [the children] suffered in leaving their own community and being with people whose ways were so different," and some sought administrative review of the public-school placements.

Monroe-Woodbury, for its part, sought a declaratory judgment in state court that New York law barred the district from providing special education services outside the district's regular public schools. *Id.* at 180, 531 N.Y.S.2d at 892, 527 N.E.2d at 770. The New York Court of Appeals disagreed, holding that state law left Monroe-Woodbury free to establish a separate school in the village because it gives educational authorities broad discretion in fashioning an appropriate program. *Id.* at 186-87, 531 N.Y.S.2d at 895, 527 N.E.2d at 773. The court added, however, that the Satmars' constitutional right to exercise their religion freely did not require a separate school, since the parents had alleged emotional trauma, not inconsistency with religious practice or doctrine, as the reason for seeking separate treatment. *Id.* at 189, 531 N.Y.S.2d at 897, 527 N.E.2d at 775.

By 1989, only one child from Kiryas Joel was attending Monroe-Woodbury's public schools; the village's other handicapped children received privately funded special services or went without. It was then that the New York Legislature passed the statute at issue in this litigation, which provided that the Village of Kiryas Joel "is constituted a separate school district, ... and shall have and enjoy all the powers and duties of a union free school district...." 1989 N.Y.Laws, ch. 748. The statute thus empowered a locally elected board of education to take such action as opening schools and closing them, hiring teachers, prescribing textbooks, establishing disciplinary rules, and raising property taxes to fund operations. In signing the bill into law, Governor Cuomo recognized that the residents of the new school district were "all members of the same religious sect," but said that the bill was "a good faith effort to solve th[e] unique problem" associated with providing special education services to handicapped

C. RELIGIOUS OBJECTIONS TO PUBLIC SCHOOL ACTIVITIES

children in the village. Memorandum filed with Assembly Bill Number 8747 (July 24, 1989), App. 40-41.

Although it enjoys plenary legal authority over the elementary and secondary education of all school-aged children in the village, the Kiryas Joel Village School District currently runs only a special education program for handicapped children. The other village children have stayed in their parochial schools, relying on the new school district only for transportation, remedial education, and health and welfare services. If any child without handicap in Kiryas Joel were to seek a public-school education, the district would pay tuition to send the child into Monroe-Woodbury or another school district nearby. Under like arrangements, several of the neighboring districts send their handicapped Hasidic children into Kiryas Joel, so that two thirds of the full-time students in the village's public school come from outside. In all, the new district serves just over 40 full-time students, and two or three times that many parochial school students on a part-time basis.

....

II

"A proper respect for both the Free Exercise and the Establishment Clauses compels the State to pursue a course of 'neutrality' toward religion," *Committee for Public Ed. & Religious Liberty v. Nyquist*, 413 U.S. 756, 792-93 (1973), favoring neither one religion over others nor religious adherents collectively over nonadherents. Chapter 748, the statute creating the Kiryas Joel Village School District, departs from this constitutional command by delegating the State's discretionary authority over public schools to a group defined by its character as a religious community, in a legal and historical context that gives no assurance that governmental power has been or will be exercised neutrally.

Larkin v. Grendel's Den, Inc., 459 U.S. 116 (1982), provides an instructive comparison with the litigation before us. There, the Court was requested to strike down a Massachusetts statute granting religious bodies veto power over applications for liquor licenses. Under the statute, the governing body of any church, synagogue, or school located within 500 feet of an applicant's premises could, simply by submitting written objection, prevent the Alcohol Beverage Control Commission from issuing a license. In spite of the State's valid interest in protecting churches, schools, and like institutions from "'the hurly-burly' associated with liquor outlets," the Court found that in two respects the statute violated "the wholesome 'neutrality' of which this Court's cases speak," *School Dist. of Abington v. Schempp*, 374 U.S. 203, 222 (1963). The Act brought about a "'fusion of governmental and religious functions'" by delegating "important, discretionary governmental powers" to religious bodies, thus impermissibly entangling government and religion. 459 U.S. at 126, 127. And it lacked "any 'effective means of guaranteeing' that the delegated power '[would] be used exclusively for secular, neutral, and nonideological purposes,'" 459 U.S. at 125; this, along with the "significant symbolic benefit to religion" associated with "the mere appearance of a joint exercise of legislative authority by Church and State," led the Court to conclude that the statute had a "'primary' and 'principal' effect of advancing religion," 459 U.S. at 125-26. Comparable constitutional problems inhere in the statute before us.

A

....

The Establishment Clause problem presented by Chapter 748 is more subtle, but it resembles the issue raised in *Larkin* to the extent that the earlier case teaches that a State may not delegate its civic authority to a group chosen according to a religious criterion. Authority over public schools belongs to the State, and cannot be delegated to a local school district defined by the State in order to grant political control to a religious group. What makes this litigation different from *Larkin* is the delegation here of civic power to the "qualified voters of the village of Kiryas Joel," as distinct from a religious leader, or an institution of religious government like the formally constituted parish council in *Larkin*. In light of the circumstances of this case, however, this distinction turns out to lack constitutional significance.

It is, first, not dispositive that the recipients of state power in this case are a group of religious individuals united by common doctrine, not the group's leaders or officers. Although some school district franchise is common to all voters, the State's manipulation of the franchise for this district limited it to Satmars, giving the sect exclusive control of the political subdivision. In the circumstances of this case, the difference between thus vesting state power in the members of a religious group as such instead of the officers of its sectarian organization is one of form, not substance. It is true that religious people (or groups of religious people) cannot be denied the opportunity to exercise the rights of citizens simply because of their religious affiliations or commitments, for such a disability would violate the right to religious free exercise, which the First Amendment guarantees as certainly as it bars any establishment. That individuals who happen to be religious may hold public office does not mean that a state may deliberately delegate discretionary power to an individual, institution, or community on the ground of religious identity. If New York were to delegate civic authority to "the Grand Rebbe," *Larkin* would obviously require invalidation, and the same is true if New York delegates political authority by reference to religious belief. Where "fusion" is an issue, the difference lies in the distinction between a government's purposeful delegation on the basis of religion and a delegation on principles neutral to religion, to individuals whose religious identities are incidental to their receipt of civic authority.

Of course, Chapter 748 delegates power not by express reference to the religious belief of the Satmar community, but to residents of the "territory of the village of Kiryas Joel." 1989 N.Y.Laws, ch. 748. Thus the second (and arguably more important) distinction between this case and *Larkin* is the identification here of the group to exercise civil authority in terms not expressly religious. But our

C. RELIGIOUS OBJECTIONS TO PUBLIC SCHOOL ACTIVITIES 1259

analysis does not end with the text of the statute at issue, and the context here persuades us that Chapter 748 effectively identifies these recipients of governmental authority by reference to doctrinal adherence, even though it does not do so expressly. We find this to be the better view of the facts because of the way the boundary lines of the school district divide residents according to religious affiliation, under the terms of an unusual and special legislative act.

It is undisputed that those who negotiated the village boundaries when applying the general village incorporation statute drew them so as to exclude all but Satmars, and that the New York Legislature was well aware that the village remained exclusively Satmar in 1989 when it adopted Chapter 748. The significance of this fact to the state legislature is indicated by the further fact that carving out the village school district ran counter to customary districting practices in the State. Indeed, the trend in New York is not toward dividing school districts but toward consolidating them. The thousands of small common school districts laid out in the early 19th century have been combined and recombined, first into union free school districts and then into larger central school districts, until only a tenth as many remain today. Most of these cover several towns, many of them cross county boundaries, and only one remains precisely coterminous with an incorporated village. The object of the State's practice of consolidation is the creation of districts large enough to provide a comprehensive education at affordable cost, which is thought to require at least 500 pupils for a combined junior-senior high school. The Kiryas Joel Village School District, in contrast, has only 13 local, full-time students in all (even including out-of-area and part-time students leaves the number under 200), and in offering only special education and remedial programs it makes no pretense to be a full-service district.

The origin of the district in a special act of the legislature, rather than the State's general laws governing school district reorganization, is likewise anomalous. Although the legislature has established some 20 existing school districts by special act, all but one of these are districts in name only, having been designed to be run by private organizations serving institutionalized children. They have neither tax bases nor student populations of their own but serve children placed by other school districts or public agencies. The one school district petitioners point to that was formed by special act of the legislature to serve a whole community, as this one was, is a district formed for a new town, much larger and more heterogeneous than this village, being built on land that straddled two existing districts. Thus the Kiryas Joel Village School District is exceptional to the point of singularity, as the only district coming to our notice that the legislature carved from a single existing district to serve local residents. Clearly this district "cannot be seen as the fulfillment of [a village's] destiny as an independent governmental entity."...

Because the district's creation ran uniquely counter to state practice, following the lines of a religious community where the customary and neutral principles would not have dictated the same result, we have good reasons to treat this district as the reflection of a religious criterion for identifying the recipients of civil authority. Not even the special needs of the children in this community can explain the legislature's unusual Act, for the State could have responded to the concerns of the Satmar parents without implicating the Establishment Clause, as we explain in some detail further on. We therefore find the legislature's Act to be substantially equivalent to defining a political subdivision and hence the qualification for its franchise by a religious test, resulting in a purposeful and forbidden "fusion of governmental and religious functions." *Larkin v. Grendel's Den*, 459 U.S. at 126 (internal quotation marks and citation omitted).

B

The fact that this school district was created by a special and unusual Act of the legislature also gives reason for concern whether the benefit received by the Satmar community is one that the legislature will provide equally to other religious (and nonreligious) groups. This is the second malady the *Larkin* Court identified in the law before it, the absence of an "effective means of guaranteeing" that governmental power will be and has been neutrally employed. But whereas in *Larkin* it was religious groups the Court thought might exercise civic power to advance the interests of religion (or religious adherents), here the threat to neutrality occurs at an antecedent stage.

The fundamental source of constitutional concern here is that the legislature itself may fail to exercise governmental authority in a religiously neutral way. The anomalously case-specific nature of the legislature's exercise of state authority in creating this district for a religious community leaves the Court without any direct way to review such state action for the purpose of safeguarding a principle at the heart of the Establishment Clause, that government should not prefer one religion to another, or religion to irreligion. *See Wallace v. Jaffree*, 472 U.S. at 52-54; *School Dist. of Abington v. Schempp*, 374 U.S. at 216-17. Because the religious community of Kiryas Joel did not receive its new governmental authority simply as one of many communities eligible for equal treatment under a general law, we have no assurance that the next similarly situated group seeking a school district of its own will receive one .... Nor can the historical context in this case furnish us with any reason to suppose that the Satmars are merely one in a series of communities receiving the benefit of special school district laws. Early on in the development of public education in New York, the State rejected highly localized school districts for New York City when they were promoted as a way to allow separate schooling for Roman Catholic children. And in more recent history, the special Act in this case stands alone.

The general principle that civil power must be exercised in a manner neutral to religion is one the *Larkin* Court recognized, although it did not discuss the specific possibility of legislative favoritism along religious lines because the statute before it delegated state authority to any religious group assembled near the premises of an applicant for a liquor license, as well as to a further category of institutions not identified by religion. But the principle is well grounded in our

C. RELIGIOUS OBJECTIONS TO PUBLIC SCHOOL ACTIVITIES 1261

case law, as we have frequently relied explicitly on the general availability of any benefit provided religious groups or individuals in turning aside Establishment Clause challenges. In *Walz v. Tax Comm'n of New York City*, 397 U.S. 664, 673 (1970), for example, the Court sustained a property tax exemption for religious properties in part because the State had "not singled out one particular church or religious group or even churches as such," but had exempted "a broad class of property owned by nonprofit, quasi-public corporations." Here the benefit flows only to a single sect, but aiding this single, small religious group causes no less a constitutional problem than would follow from aiding a sect with more members or religion as a whole, and we are forced to conclude that the State of New York has violated the Establishment Clause.

C

In finding that Chapter 748 violates the requirement of governmental neutrality by extending the benefit of a special franchise, we do not deny that the Constitution allows the state to accommodate religious needs by alleviating special burdens....

But accommodation is not a principle without limits, and what petitioners seek is an adjustment to the Satmars' religiously grounded preferences that our cases do not countenance. Prior decisions have allowed religious communities and institutions to pursue their own interests free from governmental interference, but we have never hinted that an otherwise unconstitutional delegation of political power to a religious group could be saved as a religious accommodation. Petitioners' proposed accommodation singles out a particular religious sect for special treatment, and whatever the limits of permissible legislative accommodations may be, it is clear that neutrality as among religions must be honored.

This conclusion does not, however, bring the Satmar parents, the Monroe-Woodbury school district, or the State of New York to the end of the road in seeking ways to respond to the parents' concerns. Just as the Court in *Larkin* observed that the State's interest in protecting religious meeting places could be "readily accomplished by other means," 459 U.S. at 124, there are several alternatives here for providing bilingual and bicultural special education to Satmar children. Such services can perfectly well be offered to village children through the Monroe-Woodbury Central School District. Since the Satmars do not claim that separatism is religiously mandated, their children may receive bilingual and bicultural instruction at a public school already run by the Monroe-Woodbury district. Or if the educationally appropriate offering by Monroe-Woodbury should turn out to be a separate program of bilingual and bicultural education at a neutral site near one of the village's parochial schools, this Court has already made it clear that no Establishment Clause difficulty would inhere in such a scheme, administered in accordance with neutral principles that would not necessarily confine special treatment to Satmars.

To be sure, the parties disagree on whether the services Monroe-Woodbury actually provided in the late 1980's were appropriately tailored to the needs of

Satmar children, but this dispute is of only limited relevance to the question whether such services could have been provided, had adjustments been made. As we understand New York law, parents who are dissatisfied with their handicapped child's program have recourse through administrative review proceedings (a process that appears not to have run its course prior to resort to Chapter 748), and if the New York Legislature should remain dissatisfied with the responsiveness of the local school district, it could certainly enact general legislation tightening the mandate to school districts on matters of special education or bilingual and bicultural offerings.

III

JUSTICE CARDOZO once cast the dissenter as "the gladiator making a last stand against the lions." B. Cardozo, Law and Literature 34 (1931). JUSTICE SCALIA's dissent is certainly the work of a gladiator, but he thrusts at lions of his own imagining. We do not disable a religiously homogeneous group from exercising political power conferred on it without regard to religion. Unlike the states of Utah and New Mexico (which were laid out according to traditional political methodologies taking account of lines of latitude and longitude and topographical features[)] the reference line chosen for the Kiryas Joel Village School District was one purposely drawn to separate Satmars from non-Satmars. Nor do we impugn the motives of the New York Legislature, which no doubt intended to accommodate the Satmar community without violating the Establishment Clause; we simply refuse to ignore that the method it chose is one that aids a particular religious community, as such, rather than all groups similarly interested in separate schooling. The dissent protests it is novel to insist "up front" that a statute not tailor its benefits to apply only to one religious group, but if this were so, ... [it] would have turned out differently, (plurality opinion); *id.* at 28 (BLACKMUN, J., concurring in judgment), and language in *Walz v. Tax Comm'n of New York City*, 397 U.S. at 673, and *Bowen v. Kendrick*, 487 U.S. at 608, purporting to rely on the breadth of the statutory schemes would have been mere surplusage. Indeed, under the dissent's theory, if New York were to pass a law providing school buses only for children attending Christian day schools, we would be constrained to uphold the statute against Establishment Clause attack until faced by a request from a non-Christian family for equal treatment under the patently unequal law. *Cf. Everson v. Board of Ed. of Ewing*, 330 U.S. at 17 (upholding school bus service provided all pupils). And to end on the point with which JUSTICE SCALIA begins, the license he takes in suggesting that the Court holds the Satmar sect to be New York's established church, is only one symptom of his inability to accept the fact that this Court has long held that the First Amendment reaches more than classic, 18th century establishments.

Our job, of course would be easier if the dissent's position had prevailed with the Framers and with this Court over the years. An Establishment Clause diminished to the dimensions acceptable to JUSTICE SCALIA could be enforced by a few simple rules, and our docket would never see cases requiring the

C. RELIGIOUS OBJECTIONS TO PUBLIC SCHOOL ACTIVITIES

application of a principle like neutrality toward religion as well as among religious sects. But that would be as blind to history as to precedent, and the difference between JUSTICE SCALIA and the Court accordingly turns on the Court's recognition that the Establishment Clause does comprehend such a principle and obligates courts to exercise the judgment necessary to apply it.

In this case we are clearly constrained to conclude that the statute before us fails the test of neutrality. It delegates a power this Court has said "ranks at the very apex of the function of a State," *Wisconsin v. Yoder*, 406 U.S. 205, 213 (1972), to an electorate defined by common religious belief and practice, in a manner that fails to foreclose religious favoritism. It therefore crosses the line from permissible accommodation to impermissible establishment. The judgment of the Court of Appeals of the State of New York is accordingly

Affirmed.

JUSTICE BLACKMUN, concurring:

... I agree that the New York statute under review violates the Establishment Clause of the First Amendment. I write separately only to note my disagreement with any suggestion that today's decision signals a departure from the principles described in *Lemon v. Kurtzman*, 403 U.S. 602 (1971). The opinion of the Court (and of the plurality with respect to Part II-A) relies upon several decisions, including *Larkin v. Grendel's Den, Inc.*, 459 U.S. 116 (1982), that explicitly rested on the criteria set forth in *Lemon*. Indeed, the two principles on which the opinion bases its conclusion that the legislative act is constitutionally invalid essentially are the second and third *Lemon* criteria. *Larkin*, 459 U.S. at 126-27 (finding "a fusion of governmental and religious functions" under *Lemon*'s "entanglement" prong); (finding a lack of any "effective means of guaranteeing" that governmental power will be neutrally employed under *Lemon*'s "principal or primary effect" prong).

I have no quarrel with the observation of JUSTICE O'CONNOR, that the application of constitutional principles, including those articulated in *Lemon*, must be sensitive to particular contexts. But I remain convinced of the general validity of the basic principles stated in *Lemon*, which have guided this Court's Establishment Clause decisions in over 30 cases. *See Lee v. Weisman*, 505 U.S. ___, ___, n. 4, 112 S.Ct. 2649, 2663, n. 4, (1992) (BLACKMUN, J., concurring).

JUSTICE STEVENS, with whom JUSTICE BLACKMUN and JUSTICE GINSBURG join, concurring.

... By creating a school district that is specifically intended to shield children from contact with others who have "different ways," the State provided official support to cement the attachment of young adherents to a particular faith. It is telling, in this regard, that two thirds of the school's full-time students are Hasidic handicapped children from outside the village; the Kiryas Joel school thus serves a population far wider than the village — one defined less by geography than by religion.

Affirmative state action in aid of segregation of this character is unlike the evenhanded distribution of a public benefit or service, a "release time" program for public school students involving no public premises or funds, or a decision to grant an exemption from a burdensome general rule. It is, I believe, fairly characterized as establishing, rather than merely accommodating, religion. For this reason, as well as the reasons set out in JUSTICE SOUTER's opinion, I am persuaded that the New York law at issue in these cases violates the Establishment Clause of the First Amendment.

JUSTICE O'CONNOR, concurring in part and concurring in the judgment.

I

The question at the heart of this case is: What may the government do, consistently with the Establishment Clause, to accommodate people's religious beliefs? The history of the Satmars in Orange County is especially instructive on this, because they have been involved in at least three accommodation problems, of which this case is only the most recent.

....

II

The three situations ... shed light on an important aspect of accommodation under the First Amendment: Religious needs can be accommodated through laws that are neutral with regard to religion. The Satmars' living arrangements were accommodated by their right — a right shared with all other communities, religious or not, throughout New York — to incorporate themselves as a village. From 1984 to 1985, the Satmar handicapped children's educational needs were accommodated by special education programs like those available to all handicapped children, religious or not. Other examples of such accommodations abound: The Constitution itself, for instance, accommodates the religious desires of those who were opposed to oaths by allowing any officeholder — of any religion, or none — to take either an oath of office or an affirmation....

We have time and again held that the government generally may not treat people differently based on the God or gods they worship, or don't worship. "The clearest command of the Establishment Clause is that one religious denomination cannot be officially preferred over another." *Larson v. Valente*, 456 U.S. 228, 244 (1982)....

This emphasis on equal treatment is, I think, an eminently sound approach. In my view, the Religion Clauses — the Free Exercise Clause, the Establishment Clause, the Religious Test Clause, Art. VI, cl. 3, and the Equal Protection Clause as applied to religion — all speak with one voice on this point: Absent the most unusual circumstances, one's religion ought not affect one's legal rights or duties or benefits. As I have previously noted, "the Establishment Clause is infringed when the government makes adherence to religion relevant to a person's standing in the political community." *Wallace v. Jaffree*, 472 U.S. 38, 69 (1985) (O'CONNOR, J., concurring in judgment).

That the government is acting to accommodate religion should generally not change this analysis. What makes accommodation permissible, even praiseworthy, is not that the government is making life easier for some particular religious group as such. Rather, it is that the government is accommodating a deeply held belief. Accommodations may thus justify treating those who share this belief differently from those who do not; but they do not justify discriminations based on sect....

III

I join Parts I, II-B, II-C, and III of the Court's opinion because I think this law, rather than being a general accommodation, singles out a particular religious group for favorable treatment. The Court's analysis of the history of this law and of the surrounding statutory scheme, persuades me of this.

On its face, this statute benefits one group — the residents of Kiryas Joel. Because this benefit was given to this group based on its religion, it seems proper to treat it as a legislatively drawn religious classification. I realize this is a close question, because the Satmars may be the only group who currently need this particular accommodation. The legislature may well be acting without any favoritism, so that if another group came to ask for a similar district, the group might get it on the same terms as the Satmars. But the nature of the legislative process makes it impossible to be sure of this. A legislature, unlike the judiciary or many administrative decisionmakers, has no obligation to respond to any group's requests. A group petitioning for a law may never get a definite response, or may get a "no" based not on the merits but on the press of other business or the lack of an influential sponsor. Such a legislative refusal to act would not normally be reviewable by a court. Under these circumstances, it seems dangerous to validate what appears to me a clear religious preference.

Our invalidation of this statute in no way means that the Satmars' needs cannot be accommodated. There is nothing improper about a legislative intention to accommodate a religious group, so long as it is implemented through generally applicable legislation. New York may, for instance, allow all villages to operate their own school districts. If it does not want to act so broadly, it may set forth neutral criteria that a village must meet to have a school district of its own; these criteria can then be applied by a state agency, and the decision would then be reviewable by the judiciary. A district created under a generally applicable scheme would be acceptable even though it coincides with a village which was consciously created by its voters as an enclave for their religious group. I do not think the Court's opinion holds the contrary.

I also think there is one other accommodation that would be entirely permissible.... The Religion Clauses prohibit the government from favoring religion, but they provide no warrant for discriminating against religion. All handicapped children are entitled by law to government-funded special education.

If the government provides this education on-site at public schools and at nonsectarian private schools, it is only fair that it provide it on-site at sectarian schools as well.

I thought this to be true in *Aguilar, see* 473 U.S. at 421-31 (O'CONNOR, J., dissenting), and I still believe it today. The Establishment Clause does not demand hostility to religion, religious ideas, religious people, or religious schools. *Cf. Lamb's Chapel v. Center Moriches Union Free School Dist.*, 508 U.S. ___, 113 S.Ct. 2141 (1993). It is the Court's insistence on disfavoring religion in *Aguilar* that led New York to favor it here. The court should, in a proper case, be prepared to reconsider *Aguilar*, in order to bring our Establishment Clause jurisprudence back to what I think is the proper track — government impartiality, not animosity, towards religion.

IV

One aspect of the Court's opinion in this case is worth noting: Like the opinions in two recent cases, *Lee v. Weisman*, 505 U.S. ___, 112 S.Ct. 2649 (1992); *Zobrest v. Catalina Foothills School Dist.*, 509 U.S. ___, 113 S.Ct. 2462 (1993), and the case I think is most relevant to this one, *Larson v. Valente*, 456 U.S. 228 (1982), the Court's opinion does not focus on the Establishment Clause test we set forth in *Lemon v. Kurtzman*, 403 U.S. 602 (1971).

It is always appealing to look for a single test, a Grand Unified Theory that would resolve all the cases that may arise under a particular clause. There is, after all, only one Establishment Clause, one Free Speech Clause, one Fourth Amendment, one Equal Protection Clause.

But the same constitutional principle may operate very differently in different contexts. We have, for instance, no one Free Speech Clause test. We have different tests for content-based speech restrictions, for content-neutral speech restrictions, for restrictions imposed by the government acting as employer, for restrictions in nonpublic fora, and so on. This simply reflects the necessary recognition that the interests relevant to the Free Speech Clause inquiry — personal liberty, an informed citizenry, government efficiency, public order, and so on — are present in different degrees in each context. And setting forth a unitary test for a broad set of cases may sometimes do more harm than good. Any test that must deal with widely disparate situations risks being so vague as to be useless. I suppose one can say that the general test for all free speech cases is "a regulation is valid if the interests asserted by the government are stronger than the interests of the speaker and the listeners," but this would hardly be a serviceable formulation. Similarly, *Lemon* has, with some justification, been criticized on this score.

Moreover, shoehorning new problems into a test that does not reflect the special concerns raised by those problems tends to deform the language of the test. Relatively simple phrases like "primary effect ... that neither advances nor inhibits religion" and "entanglement," acquire more and more complicated definitions which stray ever further from their literal meaning. Distinctions are

C. RELIGIOUS OBJECTIONS TO PUBLIC SCHOOL ACTIVITIES

drawn between statutes whose effect is to advance religion and statutes whose effect is to allow religious organizations to advance religion. Assertions are made that authorizing churches to veto liquor sales in surrounding areas "can be seen as having a 'primary' and 'principal' effect of advancing religion." *Larkin v. Grendel's Den, Inc.*, 459 U.S. 116 (1982). "Entanglement" is discovered in public employers monitoring the performance of public employees — surely a proper enough function — on parochial school premises, and in the public employees cooperating with the school on class scheduling and other administrative details. *Aguilar v. Felton*, 473 U.S. at 413. Alternatives to *Lemon* suffer from a similar failing when they lead us to find "coercive pressure" to pray when a school asks listeners — with no threat of legal sanctions — to stand or remain silent during a graduation prayer. *Lee v. Weisman*, 505 U.S. ___, ___, 112 S.Ct. 2649, 2658 (1992). Some of the results and perhaps even some of the reasoning in these cases may have been right. I joined two of the cases cited above, *Larkin* and *Lee*, and continue to believe they were correctly decided. But I think it is more useful to recognize the relevant concerns in each case on their own terms, rather than trying to squeeze them into language that does not really apply to them.

Finally, another danger to keep in mind is that the bad test may drive out the good. Rather than taking the opportunity to derive narrower, more precise tests from the case law, courts tend to continually try to patch up the broad test, making it more and more amorphous and distorted. This, I am afraid, has happened with *Lemon*.

....

As the Court's opinion today shows, the slide away from *Lemon*'s unitary approach is well under way. A return to *Lemon*, even if possible, would likely be futile, regardless of where one stands on the substantive Establishment Clause questions. I think a less unitary approach provides a better structure for analysis. If each test covers a narrower and more homogeneous area, the tests may be more precise and therefore easier to apply. There may be more opportunity to pay attention to the specific nuances of each area. There might also be, I hope, more consensus on each of the narrow tests than there has been on a broad test. And abandoning the *Lemon* framework need not mean abandoning some of the insights that the test reflected, nor the insights of the cases that applied it.

....

JUSTICE KENNEDY, concurring in the judgment:

The Court's ruling that the Kiryas Joel Village School District violates the Establishment Clause is in my view correct, but my reservations about what the Court's reasoning implies for religious accommodations in general are sufficient to require a separate writing. As the Court recognizes, a legislative accommodation that discriminates among religions may become an establishment of religion. But the Court's opinion can be interpreted to say that an accommodation for a particular religious group is invalid because of the risk that the legislature will not grant the same accommodation to another religious group suffering some similar burden. This rationale seems to me without grounding in our precedents and a needless restriction upon the legislature's ability to respond to the unique problems of a particular religious group. The real vice of the school district, in my estimation, is that New York created it by drawing political boundaries on the basis of religion. I would decide the issue we confront upon this narrower theory, though in accord with many of the Court's general observations about the State's actions in this case.

I

This is not a case in which the government has granted a benefit to a general class of recipients of which religious groups are just one part. *See Zobrest v. Catalina Foothills School Dist.*, 509 U.S. ___, 113 S.Ct. 2462 (1993). It is rather a case in which the government seeks to alleviate a specific burden on the religious practices of a particular religious group. I agree that a religious accommodation demands careful scrutiny to ensure that it does not so burden nonadherents or discriminate against other religions as to become an establishment. I disagree, however, with the suggestion that the Kiryas Joel Village School District contravenes these basic constitutional commands. But for the forbidden manner in which the New York Legislature sought to go about it, the State's attempt to accommodate the special needs of the handicapped Satmar children would have been valid.

....

New York's object in creating the Kiryas Joel Village School District — to accommodate the religious practices of the handicapped Satmar children — is valid.... First, by creating the district, New York sought to alleviate a specific and identifiable burden on the Satmars' religious practice. The Satmars' way of life, which springs out of their strict religious beliefs, conflicts in many respects with mainstream American culture. They do not watch television or listen to radio; they speak Yiddish in their homes and do not read English-language publications; and they have a distinctive hairstyle and dress. Attending the Monroe-Woodbury public schools, where they were exposed to much different ways of life, caused the handicapped Satmar children understandable anxiety and distress. New York was entitled to relieve these significant burdens, even though mainstream public schooling does not conflict with any specific tenet of the Satmars' religious faith....

Second, by creating the district, New York did not impose or increase any burden on non-Satmars, compared to the burden it lifted from the Satmars, that might disqualify the District as a genuine accommodation....

Third, the creation of the school district to alleviate the special burdens born by the handicapped Satmar children cannot be said, for that reason alone, to favor the Satmar religion to the exclusion of any other. "The clearest command of the Establishment Clause," of course, "is that one religious denomination cannot be officially preferred over another." *Larson v. Valente*, 456 U.S. 228,

C. RELIGIOUS OBJECTIONS TO PUBLIC SCHOOL ACTIVITIES

244 (1982). I disagree, however, with the Court's conclusion that the school district breaches this command. The Court insists that religious favoritism is a danger here, because the "anomalously case-specific nature of the legislature's exercise of state authority in creating this district for a religious community leaves the Court without any direct way to review such state action" to ensure interdenominational neutrality. "Because the religious community of Kiryas Joel did not receive its new governmental authority simply as one of many communities eligible for equal treatment under a general law," the Court maintains, "we have no assurance that the next similarly situated group seeking a school district of its own will receive one; ... a legislature's failure to enact a special law is itself unreviewable."

This reasoning reverses the usual presumption that a statute is constitutional and, in essence, adjudges the New York Legislature guilty until it proves itself innocent. No party has adduced any evidence that the legislature has denied another religious community like the Satmars its own school district under analogous circumstances. The legislature, like the judiciary, is sworn to uphold the Constitution, and we have no reason to presume that the New York Legislature would not grant the same accommodation in a similar future case. The fact that New York singled out the Satmars for this special treatment indicates nothing other than the uniqueness of the handicapped Satmar children's plight. It is normal for legislatures to respond to problems as they arise — no less so when the issue is religious accommodation. Most accommodations cover particular religious practices....

....

II

....

This particularity takes on a different cast, however, when the accommodation requires the government to draw political or electoral boundaries. "The principle that government may accommodate the free exercise of religion does not supersede the fundamental limitations imposed by the Establishment Clause," *Lee v. Weisman*, 505 U.S. ___, ___, 112 S.Ct. 2649, 2655 (1992), and in my view one such fundamental limitation is that government may not use religion as a criterion to draw political or electoral lines. Whether or not the purpose is accommodation and whether or not the government provides similar gerrymanders to people of all religious faiths, the Establishment Clause forbids the government to use religion as a line-drawing criterion. In this respect, the Establishment Clause mirrors the Equal Protection Clause. Just as the government may not segregate people on account of their race, so too it may not segregate on the basis of religion. The danger of stigma and stirred animosities is no less acute for religious line-drawing than for racial....

I agree with the Court insofar as it invalidates the school district for being drawn along religious lines. As the plurality observes the New York Legislature knew that everyone within the village was Satmar when it drew the school district along the village lines, and it determined who was to be included in the district by imposing, in effect, a religious test. There is no serious question that the legislature configured the school district, with purpose and precision, along a religious line. This explicit religious gerrymandering violates the First Amendment Establishment Clause.

It is important to recognize the limits of this principle. We do not confront the constitutionality of the Kiryas Joel Village itself, and the formation of the village appears to differ from the formation of the school district in one critical respect. As the Court notes the village was formed pursuant to a religion-neutral self-incorporation scheme. Under New York law, a territory with at least 500 residents and not more than five square miles may be incorporated upon petition by at least 20 percent of the voting residents of that territory or by the owners of more than 50 percent of the territory's real property. N.Y. Village Law §§ 2-200, 2-202 (McKinney 1973 and Supp.1994).... The residents of the town then vote upon the incorporation petition in a special election. N.Y. Village Law § 2-212 (McKinney 1973). By contrast, the Kiryas Joel Village School District was created by state legislation. The State of New York had complete discretion not to enact it. The State thus had a direct hand in accomplishing the religious segregation.

... People who share a common religious belief or lifestyle may live together without sacrificing the basic rights of self-governance that all American citizens enjoy, so long as they do not use those rights to establish their religious faith. Religion flourishes in community, and the Establishment Clause must not be construed as some sort of homogenizing solvent that forces unconventional religious groups to choose between assimilating to mainstream American culture or losing their political rights. There is more than a fine line, however, between the voluntary association that leads to a political community comprised of people who share a common religious faith, and the forced separation that occurs when the government draws explicit political boundaries on the basis of peoples' faith. In creating the Kiryas Joel Village School District, New York crossed that line, and so we must hold the district invalid.

III

This is an unusual case, for it is rare to see a State exert such documented care to carve out territory for people of a particular religious faith. It is also unusual in that the problem to which the Kiryas Joel Village School District was addressed is attributable in no small measure to what I believe were unfortunate rulings by this Court.

Before 1985, the handicapped Satmar children of Kiryas Joel attended the private religious schools within the village that the other Satmar children attended. Because their handicaps were in some cases acute (ranging from mental retardation and deafness to spina bifida and cerebral palsy), the State of New York provided public funds for special education of these children at annexes to the religious schools. Then came the companion cases of *School Dist. of Grand*

C. RELIGIOUS OBJECTIONS TO PUBLIC SCHOOL ACTIVITIES

Rapids v. Ball, 473 U.S. 373 (1985), and *Aguilar v. Felton*, 473 U.S. 402 (1985). In *Grand Rapids*, the Court invalidated a program in which public school teachers would offer supplemental classes at private schools, including religious schools, at the end of the regular school day. And in *Aguilar*, the Court invalidated New York City's use of Title I funding to pay the salaries of public school teachers who taught educationally deprived children of low-income families at parochial schools in the city. After these cases, the Monroe-Woodbury School District suspended its special education program at the Kiryas Joel religious schools, and the Kiryas Joel parents were forced to enroll their handicapped children at the Monroe-Woodbury public schools in order for the children to receive special education. The ensuing difficulties, as the Court recounts led to the creation of the Kiryas Joel Village School District.

The decisions in *Grand Rapids* and *Aguilar* may have been erroneous. In light of the case before us, and in the interest of sound elaboration of constitutional doctrine, it may be necessary for us to reconsider them at a later date. A neutral aid scheme, available to religious and nonreligious alike, is the preferable way to address problems such as the Satmar handicapped children have suffered. *See Witters*, 474 U.S. at 490-92 (POWELL, J., concurring). But for *Grand Rapids* and *Aguilar*, the Satmars would have had no need to seek special accommodations or their own school district. Our decisions led them to choose that unfortunate course, with the deficiencies I have described.

One misjudgment is no excuse, however, for compounding it with another. We must confront this case as it comes before us, without bending rules to free the Satmars from a predicament into which we put them. The Establishment Clause forbids the government to draw political boundaries on the basis of religious faith. For this reason, I concur in the judgment of the Court.

JUSTICE SCALIA, with whom THE CHIEF JUSTICE and JUSTICE THOMAS join, dissenting.

. . . .

I

Unlike most of our Establishment Clause cases involving education, these cases involve no public funding, however slight or indirect, to private religious schools. They do not involve private schools at all. The school under scrutiny is a public school specifically designed to provide a public secular education to handicapped students. The superintendent of the school, who is not Hasidic, is a 20-year veteran of the New York City public school system, with expertise in the area of bilingual, bicultural, special education. The teachers and therapists at the school all live outside the village of Kiryas Joel. While the village's private schools are profoundly religious and strictly segregated by sex, classes at the public school are co-ed and the curriculum secular. The school building has the bland appearance of a public school, unadorned by religious symbols or markings; and the school complies with the laws and regulations governing all other New York State public schools. There is no suggestion, moreover, that this public school has gone too far in making special adjustments to the religious needs of its students. In sum, these cases involve only public aid to a school that is public as can be. The only thing distinctive about the school is that all the students share the same religion.

None of our cases has ever suggested that there is anything wrong with that. In fact, the Court has specifically approved the education of students of a single religion on a neutral site adjacent to a private religious school. *See Wolman v. Walter*, 433 U.S. 229, 247-48 (1977). In that case, the Court rejected the argument that "any program that isolates the sectarian pupils is impermissible," *id.* at 246, and held that, "[t]he fact that a unit on a neutral site on occasion may serve only sectarian pupils does not provoke [constitutional] concerns,".... And just last Term, the Court held that the State could permit public employees to assist students in a Catholic school. *See Zobrest v. Catalina Foothills School Dist.*, 509 U.S. ___, 113 S.Ct. 2462, 2469 (1993) (sign-language translator for deaf student). If a State can furnish services to a group of sectarian students on a neutral site adjacent to a private religious school, or even within such a school, how can there be any defect in educating those same students in a public school? As the Court noted in *Wolman*, the constitutional dangers of establishment arise "from the nature of the institution, not from the nature of the pupils," *Wolman, supra*, 433 U.S. at 248. There is no danger in educating religious students in a public school.

For these very good reasons, JUSTICE SOUTER's opinion does not focus upon the school, but rather upon the school district and the New York Legislature that created it....

....

Contrary to the Court's suggestion ... I do not think that the Establishment Clause prohibits formally established "state" churches and nothing more. I have always believed, and all my opinions are consistent with the view, that the Establishment Clause prohibits the favoring of one religion over others. In this respect, it is the Court that attacks lions of straw. What I attack is the Court's imposition of novel "up front" procedural requirements on state legislatures. Making law (and making exceptions) one case at a time, whether through adjudication or through highly particularized rulemaking or legislation, violates, *ex ante*, no principle of fairness, equal protection, or neutrality, simply because it does not announce in advance how all future cases (and all future exceptions) will be disposed of. If it did, the manner of proceeding of this Court itself would be unconstitutional. It is presumptuous for this Court to impose — out of nowhere — an unheard-of prohibition against proceeding in this manner upon the Legislature of New York State. I never heard of such a principle, nor has anyone else, nor will it ever be heard of again. Unlike what the New York Legislature has done, this is a special rule to govern only the Satmar Hasidim.

C. RELIGIOUS OBJECTIONS TO PUBLIC SCHOOL ACTIVITIES

The Court's decision today is astounding. Chapter 748 involves no public aid to private schools and does not mention religion. In order to invalidate it, the Court casts aside, on the flimsiest of evidence, the strong presumption of validity that attaches to facially neutral laws, and invalidates the present accommodation because it does not trust New York to be as accommodating toward other religions (presumably those less powerful than the Satmar Hasidim) in the future. This is unprecedented — except that it continues, and takes to new extremes, a recent tendency in the opinions of this Court to turn the Establishment Clause into a repealer of our Nation's tradition of religious toleration. I dissent.

---

1. Justice Souter, in his majority opinion, declares the creation of the Kiryas Joel School District by the state unconstitutional because of a usurpation of government power and the discrimination of other religious groups based on the Equal Protection Clause. Has Souter created still another Establishment Clause test to which educators must become familiar or is this simply a different approach to the *Lemon* doctrine as stated in Justice Blackmun's concurrence?

2. Has this case effectively sounded the death knell of *Lemon* as voiced by Justice O'Connor in her concurring opinion? Does this case even comport with *Lemon* or O'Connor's "endorsement" test? What of O'Connor's tacit suggestion that on the basis of the Court's contemporary Establishment Clause approaches even the decision in *Felton* has been brought into question?

3. The opinion cites to *Zobrest v. Catalina Foothills Sch. Dist.*, 113 S. Ct. 2462 (1993), involving the question of whether provision by a public school district of a sign language interpreter in a pervasively sectarian school would violate the Establishment Clause. Hence, the case related to the application of not only the First Amendment, but also regulations promulgated under the Individuals with Disabilities Education Act, 20 U.S.C. Sec. 1400 *et seq*. The Supreme Court, in a 5-4 decision, determined that there was no constitutional bar to a school district supplying such services. *See* Chapter 13 for a full discussion of *Zobrest*.

Justice Kennedy in his concurring opinion distinguishes *Zobrest* from *Grumet* by reasoning that the former case was constitutional because it granted a benefit to a general class of persons where religion was incidental while *Grumet* grants the same benefit because of religion. The benefit in both cases is generally the same — special education services for those students who qualify. Each of these secular services was offered in a sectarian atmosphere. Can the difference in these cases be reasoned on the fact that the State of New York specifically ordered such services to Kiryas Joel students because of their religious affiliation while *Zobrest* simply indicates that there is no "constitutional bar" to such services? Does the decision in the case now mean that public school personnel can reverse themselves and go into the village to offer such services? If so does this contravene the decision in *Felton*?

Chapter 16
ALTERNATIVES TO PUBLIC EDUCATION

At present the most significant alternative to public schooling appears to be the variety of church-sponsored private schools throughout the country. Without these private schools the cost of public education would be substantially higher given the large number of students (approximately 10% of total school enrollment) presently educated in private schools. Because of this public benefit derived from private schooling, the issue of whether public monies can be used to support parochial schooling has been a continuing concern to public and private educators. The following cases and articles explore the present legal parameters of that issue.

MAWDSLEY, EMERGING LEGAL ISSUES IN NONPUBLIC EDUCATION, 83 Educ. L. Rep. 1 (1993)*

Introduction

Nonpublic educational institutions were removed from much of the litigation explosion that dramatically affected public institutions in the post-*Tinker* era. A major reason for this insularity was the immunity of nonpublic educational institutions from the wide range of constitutional rights granted to employees and students at public schools....

....

Although litigation involving nonpublic educational institutions does not come close to reaching the number of cases in the public sector, the kinds of issues now being litigated reflect the uniqueness of nonpublic education. The issues also indicate that litigation may be viewed as an acceptable conflict resolution strategy by both the schools and their parent-clients. Among issues unique to nonpublic institutions, religious schools in particular, are successful claims to public services or funds using a modified child benefit theory and successful resistance to regulatory requirements using a revived method of statutory construction. Along a different avenue of legal discussion, an emerging body of case law reflects litigation involving nonpublic schools, their faculty, and the parents of students, raising concerns about unity and stability within the schools.

....

---

*Copyright © 1993 by West Publishing Company. Reprinted with permission.

Nonpublic Schools and Government

Entitlement to Public Funds or Services

The notion is not new that nonpublic educational institutions should be eligible for state or federal services or funds in recognition of the educative function performed by those schools. However, the provision of such services or funds has frequently been challenged as violative of the establishment clause. Over the past twenty years various legislative efforts to provide services or financial assistance to religious schools generally have not met with success. Such assistance has consistently run afoul of one or more of the parts of the *Lemon v. Kurtzman* tripartite test[9] interpretation of the establishment clause. Under the *Lemon* test services or funds received by the religious school have generally been found to be violations of the establishment clause because the religious school itself was viewed as the primary recipient of the assistance.

To make government assistance to religious schools constitutionally palatable, those advocating such assistance have pressed courts to consider parents and/or students, rather than the schools, as the primary recipients of the assistance. This approach, remarkably similar to the discarded child benefit doctrine of forty-five years ago, has found a receptive audience among several federal justices. Such receptivity is important not only because traditional forms of governmental services and financial assistance may now be available to religious schools, but because vouchers under the rapidly emerging and controversial state programs of educational choice may now pass constitutional muster even if used in religious schools.

. . . .

Conclusion

Nonpublic educational institutions have never been strangers to litigation. In the areas of government aid and regulation, a considerable body of case law has developed over the past forty years. What are now emerging — or more properly, reemerging — are child benefit and statutory construction theories that may give nonpublic schools access to aid, on one hand, but permit them to remain free from government regulation, on the other.

. . . .

Extension of educational choice plans to all nonpublic schools might not have the anticipated effect of increasing enrollments of disadvantaged students in those schools. States may attach conditions to participation in a voucher scheme which the nonpublic schools would find unacceptable, or nonpublic schools may not participate out of concerns about state action and section 1983.

---

[9]403 U.S. 602, 612-13 (1971) ("First [the practice] must have a secular purpose; second, its principal or primary effect must be one that neither advances nor inhibits religion; finally, [it] must not foster 'an excessive governmental entanglement with religion.'")

....

Litigation within the nonpublic schools represents a serious threat to the continuity of such schools. Most nonpublic schools, especially the religious ones, can be likened more to extended families than to arms-length providers of educational services. Introduction into a school of legal confrontation involving a member of that family represents a threat to an image of unity and stability which the school seeks to provide. Efforts by nonpublic schools to control all faculty disputes through internal conflict resolution methods is probably only partially successful. Unhappy faculty members with litigable claims may elect not to sue for reasons that have nothing to do with dispute resolution procedures in the faculty handbook; faculty members may elect to forego litigation out of concern for its divisive effect on parents, students and other faculty colleagues in the school, or from concern that publicity may adversely affect the continuance of the school, and thus threaten the jobs of colleagues. Equally possible, a faculty member may not choose to sue because the school has made an accommodation in some tangible or intangible form, even if the accommodation does not necessarily address the cause of the legal dispute.

....

Lawsuits involving nonpublic schools reflect that we live in a litigious age and that no aspect of society is isolated from the legal system. Emerging legal issues in nonpublic education address whether nonpublic schools are going to be able to meet the needs of a varied student population and whether the schools can continue to thrive as close-knit communities.

....

A. FINANCING PRIVATE SCHOOLS FOR PUBLIC BENEFIT

1. TEXTBOOKS, TRANSPORTATION AND OTHER SPECIAL SERVICES

One of the major ways in which state legislatures have attempted to fund parochial schools is by purchasing textbooks and providing other public services such as bus transportation for such schools.

EVERSON v. BOARD OF EDUCATION

Supreme Court of the United States
330 U.S. 1 (1947)

MR. JUSTICE BLACK delivered the opinion of the Court:

A New Jersey statute authorizes its local school districts to make rules and contracts for the transportation of children to and from schools. The appellee, a township board of education, acting pursuant to this statute, authorized reimbursement to parents of money expended by them for the bus transportation of their children on regular busses operated by the public transportation system.

Part of this money was for the payment of transportation of some children in the community to Catholic parochial schools. These church schools give their students, in addition to secular education, regular religious instruction conforming to the religious tenets and modes of worship of the Catholic Faith. The superintendent of these schools is a Catholic priest.

The appellant, in his capacity as a district taxpayer, filed suit in a state court challenging the right of the Board to reimburse parents of parochial school students. He contended that the statute and the resolution passed pursuant to it violated both the State and the Federal Constitutions....

....

The only contention here is that the state statute and the resolution, insofar as they authorized reimbursement to parents of children attending parochial schools, violate the Federal Constitution in these two respects, which to some extent overlap. *First.* They authorize the State to take by taxation the private property of some and bestow it upon others, to be used for their own private purposes. This, it is alleged. violates the due process clause of the Fourteenth Amendment. *Second.* The statute and the resolution forced inhabitants to pay taxes to help support and maintain schools which are dedicated to, and which regularly teach, the Catholic Faith. This is alleged to be a use of state power to support church schools contrary to the prohibition of the First Amendment which the Fourteenth Amendment made applicable to the states.

First. The due process argument that the state law taxes some people to help others carry out their private purposes is framed in two phases. The first phase is that a state cannot tax A to reimburse B for the cost of transporting his children to church schools. This is said to violate the due process clause because the children are sent to these church schools to satisfy the personal desires of their parents, rather than the public's interest in the general education of all children. This argument, if valid, would apply equally to prohibit state payment for the transportation of children to any non-public school, whether operated by a church or any other non-government individual or group. But, the New Jersey legislature has decided that a public purpose will be served by using tax-raised funds to pay the bus fares of all school children, including those who attend parochial schools. The New Jersey Court of Errors and Appeals has reached the same conclusion. The fact that a state law, passed to satisfy a public need, coincides with the personal desires of the individuals most directly affected is certainly an inadequate reason for us to say that a legislature has erroneously appraised the public need.

... Changing local conditions create new local problems which may lead a state's people and its local authorities to believe that laws authorizing new types of public services are necessary to promote the general well-being of the people. The Fourteenth Amendment did not strip the states of their power to meet problems previously left for individual solution....

It is much too late to argue that legislation intended to facilitate the opportunity of children to get a secular education serves no public purpose. *Cochran v.*

A. FINANCING PRIVATE SCHOOLS FOR PUBLIC BENEFIT

Louisiana State Board of Education, 281 U.S. 370.... The same thing is no less true of legislation to reimburse needy parents, or all parents, for payment of the fares of their children so that they can ride in public busses to and from schools rather than run the risk of traffic and other hazards incident to walking or "hitchhiking." ... Nor does it follow that a law has a private rather than a public purpose because it provides that tax-raised funds will be paid to reimburse individuals on account of money spent by them in a way which furthers a public program.... Subsidies and loans to individuals such as farmers and home-owners, and to privately owned transportation systems, as well as many other kinds of businesses, have been commonplace practices in our state and national history.

Insofar as the second phase of the due process argument may differ from the first, it is by suggesting that taxation for transportation of children to church schools constitutes support of a religion by the State. But if the law is invalid for this reason, it is because it violates the First Amendment's prohibition against the establishment of religion....

This Court has previously recognized that the provisions of the First Amendment, in the drafting and adoption of which Madison and Jefferson played such leading roles, had the same objective and were intended to provide the same protection against governmental intrusion on religious liberty as the Virginia state [Virginia's Bill for Religious Liberty] *Reynolds v. United States, supra*, at 164; *Watson v. Jones*, 13 Wall. 679; *Davis v. Beason*, 133 U.S. 333, 342....

The "establishment of religion" clause of the First Amendment means at least this: Neither a state nor the Federal Government can set up a church. Neither can pass laws which aid one religion, aid all religions, or prefer one religion over another. Neither can force nor influence a person to go to or to remain away from church against his will or force him to profess a belief or disbelief in any religion. No person can be punished for entertaining or professing religious beliefs or disbeliefs, for church attendance or non-attendance. No tax in any amount, large or small, can be levied to support any religious activities or institutions, whatever they may be called, or whatever form they may adopt to teach or practice religion. Neither a state nor the Federal Government can, openly or secretly, participate in the affairs of any religious organizations or groups and *vice versa*. In the words of Jefferson, the clause against establishment of religion by law was intended to erect "a wall of separation between Church and State." *Reynolds v. United States, supra* at 164.

We must consider the New Jersey statute in accordance with the foregoing limitations imposed by the First Amendment. But we must not strike that state statute down if it is within the State's constitutional power even though it approaches the verge of that power.... New Jersey cannot consistently with the "establishment of religion" clause of the First Amendment contribute tax-raised funds to the support of an institution which teaches the tenets and faith of any church. On the other hand, other language of the amendment commands that New Jersey cannot hamper its citizens in the free exercise of their own religion. Consequently, it cannot exclude individual Catholics, Lutherans, Mohammedans,

Baptists, Jews, Methodists, Non-believers, Presbyterians, or the members of any other faith, *because of their faith, or lack of it*, from receiving the benefits of public welfare legislation. While we do not mean to intimate that a state could not provide transportation only to children attending public schools, we must be careful, in protecting the citizens of New Jersey against state-established churches, to be sure that we do not inadvertently prohibit New Jersey from extending its general state law benefits to all its citizens without regard to their religious belief.

Measured by these standards, we cannot say that the First Amendment prohibits New Jersey from spending tax-raised funds to pay the bus fares of parochial school pupils as a part of a general program under which it pays the fares of pupils attending public and other schools. It is undoubtedly true that children are helped to get to church schools. There is even a possibility that some of the children might not be sent to the church schools if the parents were compelled to pay their children's bus fares out of their own pockets when transportation to a public school would have been paid for by the State. The same possibility exists where the state requires a local transit company to provide reduced fares to school children including those attending parochial schools, or where a municipally owned transportation system undertakes to carry all school children free of charge. Moreover, state-paid policemen, detailed to protect children going to and from church schools from the very real hazards of traffic, would serve much the same purpose and accomplish much the same result as state provisions intended to guarantee free transportation of a kind which the state deems to be best for the school children's welfare. And parents might refuse to risk their children to the serious danger of traffic accidents going to and from parochial schools, the approaches to which were not protected by policemen. Similarly, parents might be reluctant to permit their children to attend schools which the state had cut off from such general government services as ordinary police and fire protection, connections for sewage disposal, public highways and sidewalks. Of course, cutting off church schools from these services, so separate and so indisputably marked off from the religious function, would make it far more difficult for the schools to operate. But such is obviously not the purpose of the First Amendment. That Amendment requires the state to be a neutral in its relations with groups of religious believers and non-believers; it does not require the state to be their adversary. State power is no more to be used so as to handicap religions than it is to favor them.

This Court has said that parents may, in the discharge of their duty under state compulsory education laws, send their children to a religious rather than a public school if the school meets the secular educational requirements which the state has power to impose. *See Pierce v. Society of Sisters*, 268 U.S. 510. It appears that these parochial schools meet New Jersey's requirements. The State contributes no money to the schools. It does not support them. Its legislation, as applied, does no more than provide a general program to help parents get their

A. FINANCING PRIVATE SCHOOLS FOR PUBLIC BENEFIT

children, regardless of their religion, safely and expeditiously to and from accredited schools.

The First Amendment has erected a wall between church and state. That wall must be kept high and impregnable. We could not approve the slightest breach. New Jersey has not breached it here.

Affirmed.

MR. JUSTICE JACKSON, dissenting:

I find myself, contrary to first impressions, unable to join in this decision. I have a sympathy, though it is not ideological, with Catholic citizens who are compelled by law to pay taxes for public schools, and also feel constrained by conscience and discipline to support other schools for their own children. Such relief to them as this case involves is not in itself a serious burden to taxpayers and I had assumed it to be as little serious in principle. Study of this case convinces me otherwise. The Court's opinion marshals every argument in favor of state aid and puts the case in its most favorable light, but much of its reasoning confirms my conclusions that there are no good grounds upon which to support the present legislation. In fact, the undertones of the opinion, advocating complete and uncompromising separation of Church from State, seem utterly discordant with its conclusion yielding support to their commingling in educational matters. The case which irresistibly comes to mind as the most fitting precedent is that of Julia who, according to Byron's reports, "whispering 'I will ne'er consent,' — consented."

....

MR. JUSTICE RUTLEDGE, with whom MR. JUSTICE FRANKFURTER, MR. JUSTICE JACKSON and MR. JUSTICE BURTON agree, dissenting:

....

Two great drives are constantly in motion to abridge, in the name of education, the complete division of religion and civil authority which our forefathers made. One is to introduce religious education and observances into the public schools. The other, to obtain public funds for the aid and support of various private religious schools.... In my opinion both avenues were closed by the Constitution. Neither should be opened by this Court. The matter is not one of quantity, to be measured by the amount of money expended. Now as in Madison's day it is one of principle, to keep separate the separate spheres as the First Amendment drew them; to prevent the first experiment upon our liberties; and to keep the question from becoming entangled in corrosive precedents. We should not be less strict to keep strong and untarnished the one side of the shield of religious freedom than we have been of the other.

The judgment should be reversed.

1. The Court in *Everson* countered the plaintiff's Establishment Clause argument by asserting the "... legislation, as applied, does no more than provide a general program to help parents get their children, regardless of their religion, safely and expeditiously to and from accredited schools." 330 U.S. at 18. This "child benefit theory" was first articulated by the Court in *Cochran v. Louisiana State Bd. of Educ.*, 281 U.S. 370 (1930), when a Louisiana statute which appropriated public tax funds for the purchase of free textbooks for children in private as well as public schools was upheld against a challenge that the state was taking private property for a non-public use. The Court held the child and his parents, not the church, were the beneficiaries of the legislation, stating:

> One may scan the acts in vain to ascertain where any money is appropriated for the purchase of school books for the use of any church, private, sectarian or even public school. The appropriations were made for the specific purpose of purchasing school books for the use of the school children of the state, free of cost to them.

See also Board of Educ. v. Allen, 392 U.S. 236 (1967), in which the Court held that a New York law requiring local public school authorities to lend textbooks without charge to both public and private school students did not violate the Establishment or Free Exercise Clauses, in that the financial benefit was to parents and children, not to schools.

2. Although the courts have continued to apply the "child benefit theory" to justify state aid to private schools in a number of cases which have arisen since *Everson*, an opposing line of judicial reasoning also has developed. One of the earliest rejections of the theory by a state court occurred in *Judd v. Board of Educ.*, 278 N.Y. 200, 17 N.E.2d 134 (1938), when the New York Court of Appeals held a state education law authorizing the use of public funds to pay for the transportation of pupils to private schools was violative of the state constitution. While the court based its decision in part on the wording of the state constitutional provision, which forbid both direct and indirect aid to nonpublic schools, it also expressly rejected the argument that the furnishing of transportation was aid to the pupils, and not to the religious schools. The court stated "(f)ree transportation of pupils induces attendance at the school. The purpose of the transportation is to promote the interests of the private school or religious or sectarian institution that controls and directs it." Which view is more realistic, that of the *Everson* court, which saw the child as the beneficiary of free transportation, or that of the court in *Judd*, which believed the school to be the true beneficiary? Consider also the viewpoint expressed by Justice Dimond in his dissenting opinion in *Matthews v. Quinton*, 362 P.2d 932 (1961), in which the majority of the Supreme Court of Alaska held a statute providing for the transportation of children to nonpublic schools at public expense to be in contravention of a state constitutional prohibition of the appropriation of public

A. FINANCING PRIVATE SCHOOLS FOR PUBLIC BENEFIT

funds for the support of nonpublic schools. Dimond, contesting the majority's conclusion that the furnishing at public expense of transportation for a child who attends a nonpublic school constitutes a direct benefit to such school, stated:

> ... I fail to see where there is any benefit when public monies are spent ... solely for the purpose of aiding children in getting to the school. It seems to me that as children are encouraged to attend school and are given assistance in getting there, there will be an increased need and demand for additional school facilities. This, logically, will result in additional cost to the school. Thus, the money spent by the state for transportation of school children cannot really benefit the school. The effect of such transportation, if more children will attend school when transported, will not be advantage and profit, but will be just the opposite — increased costs and expenses.

How is Dimond's definition of "benefit" different from that of the courts in *Cochran* and *Everson*? Is "benefit" too ambiguous a concept on which to judge the constitutionality of legislation, or, in the alternative, is one view of these "benefits" clearly correct?

3. The legislation reviewed and upheld by the court in *Everson* provided the same benefits for both public and private school students. Should legislation which results in different or unequal benefits for one group (public or private) of students be viewed in the same way by the courts? In *Americans United for Separation of Church and State v. Benton*, 413 F. Supp. 955 (S.D. Iowa 1975), a federal district court in Iowa held a state statute which provided for the transportation by local districts of nonpublic school pupils to schools outside the district was violative of the Establishment Clause because it provided special benefits to the nonpublic students. Similarly, in *Members of Jamestown Sch. Comm. v. Schmidt*, 427 F. Supp. 1338 (D.R.I. 1977), a federal district court in Rhode Island held that a state statute providing for the transportation of sectarian school students out of their home districts to regional schools was violative of the Establishment Clause because the same option was not provided for public school students. The court noted that while the statute purported to provide equal transportation benefits to both public and sectarian school children, in practice the statute benefited only the children attending private schools.

The *Schmidt* case traveled through the system a second time. In 1983, the First Circuit Court of Appeals responded to an appeal to a decision striking down the statute which provided transportation to private school students. The Court held that (1) the statute had a constitutional secular purpose; and (2) the statute was not invalid as advancing religion because it provided for transportation of sectarian students beyond school district limits, so long as public and parochial students were eligible for busing to their schools on equal terms and the relative busing costs were roughly proportional. 699 F.2d 1 (1st Cir. 1983).

A slightly different issue and a slightly different result surfaced in Maryland in *McCarthy v. Hornbeck*, 590 F. Supp. 936 (D. Md. 1984). There, the district court held that (1) failure to provide transportation to private, parochial schools did not violate free exercise rights of parents sending their children to those schools, and (2) the pattern of Maryland law, under which some, but not all, counties provide transportation to students attending private schools did not deprive plaintiffs of equal protection.

4. Recall the materials in Chapter 13 regarding related services provided to children with disabilities. Is a school district in violation of the Individuals with Disabilities Education Act (IDEA) for failing to provide transportation from a parochial school to special education classes at a public school? Or is it in violation of the Establishment Clause if it does provide such transportation? *See Felter v. Cape Girardeau Sch. Dist.*, 810 F. Supp. 1062 (E.D. Mo. 1993) (Under IDEA, the student is entitled to the transportation without violating the Establishment Clause of the Federal Constitution or the religion clauses of the Missouri Constitution).

WOLMAN v. WALTER

Supreme Court of the United States
433 U.S. 229 (1977)

MR. JUSTICE BLACKMUN delivered the opinion of the Court (Parts I, V, VI, VII, and VIII), together with an opinion (Parts II, III, and IV), in which THE CHIEF JUSTICE, MR. JUSTICE STEWART, and MR. JUSTICE POWELL joined:

This is still another case presenting the recurrent issue of the limitations imposed by the Establishment Clause of the First Amendment, made applicable to the States by the Fourteenth Amendment, *Meek v. Pittenger*, 421 U.S. 349 (1975) on state aid to pupils in church-related elementary and secondary schools. Appellants are citizens and taxpayers of Ohio. They challenge all but one of the provisions of Ohio Rev. Code § 3317.06 (Supp. 1976) which authorize various forms of aid.... A three-judge court ... held the statute constitutional in all respects.

I

Section 3317.06 was enacted after this Court's May 1975 decision in *Meek v. Pittenger, supra*, and obviously is an attempt to conform to the teachings of that decision.... In broad outline, the statute authorizes the State to provide nonpublic school pupils with books, instructional materials and equipment, standardized testing and scoring, diagnostic services, therapeutic services, and field trip transportation.

The initial biennial appropriation by the Ohio Legislature for implementation of the statute was the sum of $88,800,000. Funds so appropriated are paid to the State's public school districts and are then expended by them. All disbursements made with respect to nonpublic schools have their equivalents in disbursements for public schools, and the amount expended per pupil in nonpublic schools may not exceed the amount expended per pupil in the public schools.

A. FINANCING PRIVATE SCHOOLS FOR PUBLIC BENEFIT

The parties stipulated that during the 1974-1975 school year there were 720 chartered nonpublic schools in Ohio. Of these, all but 29 were sectarian. More than 96% of the nonpublic enrollment attended sectarian schools, and more than 92% attended Catholic schools. It was also stipulated that, if they were called, officials of representative Catholic schools would testify that such schools operate under the general supervision of the Bishop of their Diocese; that most principals are members of a religious order within the Catholic Church; that a little less than one-third of the teachers are members of such religious orders; that "in all probability a majority of the teachers are members of the Catholic faith"; and that many of the rooms and hallways in these schools are decorated with a Christian symbol. All such schools teach the secular subjects required to meet the State's minimum standards. The state-mandated five-hour day is expanded to include, usually, one-half hour of religious instruction. Pupils who are not members of the Catholic faith are not required to attend religion classes or to participate in religious exercises or activities, and no teacher is required to teach religious doctrine as a part of the secular courses taught in the schools.

The parties also stipulated that nonpublic school officials, if called, would testify that none of the schools covered by the statute discriminate in the admission of pupils or in the hiring of teachers on the basis of race, creed, color, or national origin.

. . . .

II

The mode of analysis for Establishment Clause questions is defined by the three-part test that has emerged from the Court's decisions. In order to pass muster, a statute must have a secular legislative purpose, must have a principal or primary effect that neither advances nor inhibits religion, and must not foster an excessive government entanglement with religion.

In the present case we have no difficulty with the first prong of this three-part test. We are satisfied that the challenged statute reflects Ohio's legitimate interest in protecting the health of its youth and in providing a fertile educational environment for all the school children of the State. As is usual in our cases, the analytical difficulty has to do with the effect and entanglement criteria.

We have acknowledged before, and we do so again here, that the wall of separation that must be maintained between church and state "is a blurred, indistinct, and variable barrier depending on all the circumstances of a particular relationship." Nonetheless, the Court's numerous precedents "have become firmly rooted," and now provide substantial guidance. We therefore turn to the task of applying the rules derived from our decisions to the respective provisions of the statute at issue.

III. *Textbooks*

Section 3317.06 authorizes the expenditure of funds:

> (A) To purchase such secular textbooks as have been approved by the superintendent of public instruction for use in public schools in the state and to loan such textbooks to pupils attending nonpublic schools within the district or to their parents. Such loans shall be based upon individual requests submitted by such nonpublic school pupils or parents. Such requests shall be submitted to the local public school district in which the nonpublic school is located. Such individual requests for the loan of textbooks shall, for administrative convenience, be submitted by the nonpublic school pupil or his parent to the nonpublic school which shall prepare and submit collective summaries of the individual requests to the local public school district. As used in this section, "textbook" means any book or book substitute which a pupil uses as a text or text substitute in a particular class or program in the school he regularly attends.

The parties' stipulations reflect operation of the textbook program in accord with the dictates of the statute. In addition, it was stipulated:

> The secular textbooks used in nonpublic schools will be the same as the textbooks used in the public schools of the state. Common suppliers will be used to supply books to both public and nonpublic school pupils.
>
> Textbooks, including book substitutes, provided under this Act shall be limited to books, reusable workbooks, or manuals, whether bound or in looseleaf form, intended for use as a principal source of study material for a given class or a group of students, a copy of which is expected to be available for the individual use of each pupil in such class or group.

This system for the loan of textbooks to individual students bears a striking resemblance to the systems approved in *Board of Education v. Allen*, 392 U.S. 236 (1968), and in *Meek v. Pittenger, supra*....

... [A]ppellants urge that we overrule *Allen* and *Meek*. This we decline to do. Accordingly, we conclude that § 3317.06(A) is constitutional.

IV. *Testing and Scoring*

Section 3317.06 authorizes expenditure of funds:

> (J) To supply for use by pupils attending nonpublic schools within the district such standardized tests and scoring services as are in use in the public schools of the state.

These tests "are used to measure the progress of students in secular subjects." Nonpublic school personnel are not involved in either the drafting or scoring of the tests. The statute does not authorize any payment to nonpublic school personnel for the costs of administering the tests.

A. FINANCING PRIVATE SCHOOLS FOR PUBLIC BENEFIT

In *Levitt v. Committee for Public Education*, 413 U.S. 472 (1973), this Court invalidated a New York statutory scheme for reimbursement of church-sponsored schools for the expenses of teacher-prepared testing. The reasoning behind that decision was straightforward. The system was held unconstitutional because "no means are available, to assure that internally prepared tests are free of religious instruction."

There is no question that the State has a substantial and legitimate interest in insuring that its youth receive an adequate secular education. The State may require that schools that are utilized to fulfill the State's compulsory education requirement meet certain standards of instruction, and may examine both teachers and pupils to ensure that the State's legitimate interest is being fulfilled. *Cf. Pierce v. Society of Sisters*, 268 U.S. 510 (1925). Under the section at issue, the State provides both the schools and the school district with the means of ensuring that the minimum standards are met. The nonpublic school does not control the content of the test or its result. This serves to prevent the use of the test as a part of religious teaching, and thus avoids that kind of direct aid to religion found present in *Levitt*. Similarly, the inability of the school to control the test eliminates the need for the supervision that gives rise to excessive entanglement. We therefore agree with the District Court's conclusion that § 3317.06(J) is constitutional.

V. *Diagnostic Services*

Section 3317.06 authorizes expenditures of funds:

> (D) To provide speech and hearing diagnostic services to pupils attending nonpublic schools within the district. Such service shall be provided in the nonpublic school attended by the pupil receiving the service.
>
> ....
>
> (F) To provide diagnostic psychological services to pupils attending nonpublic schools within the district. Such services shall be provided in the school attended by the pupil receiving the service.

It will be observed that these speech and hearing and psychological diagnostic services are to be provided within the nonpublic school. It is stipulated, however, that the personnel (with the exception of physicians) who perform the services are employees of the local board of education; that physicians may be hired on a contract basis; that the purpose of these services is to determine the pupil's deficiency or need of assistance; and that treatment of any defect so found would take place off the nonpublic school premises.

Appellants assert that the funding of these services is constitutionally impermissible. They argue that the speech and hearing staff might engage in unrestricted conversation with the pupil and, on occasion, might fail to separate religious instruction from secular responsibilities. They further assert that the communication between the psychological diagnostician and the pupil will provide an impermissible opportunity for the intrusion of religious influence.

The District Court found these dangers so insubstantial as not to render the statute unconstitutional. We agree. This Court's decisions contain a common thread to the effect that the provision of health services to all school children — public and nonpublic — does not have the primary effect of aiding religion.... Indeed, appellants recognize this fact in not challenging subsection (E) of the statute that authorizes publicly funded physician, nursing, dental, and optometric services in nonpublic schools. We perceive no basis for drawing a different conclusion with respect to diagnostic speech and hearing services and diagnostic psychological services.

In *Meek* the Court did hold unconstitutional a portion of a Pennsylvania statute at issue there that authorized certain auxiliary services — "remedial and accelerated instruction, guidance counseling and testing, speech and hearing services" — on nonpublic school premises. The Court noted that the teacher or guidance counselor might "fail on occasion to separate religious instruction and the advancement of religious beliefs from his secular educational responsibilities." The Court was of the view that the publicly employed teacher or guidance counselor might depart from religious neutrality because he was "performing important educational services in schools in which education is an integral part of the dominant sectarian mission and in which an atmosphere dedicated to the advancement of religious belief is constantly maintained." The statute was held unconstitutional on entanglement grounds, namely, that in order to insure that the auxiliary teachers and guidance counselors remained neutral, the State would have to engage in continuing surveillance on the school premises. *Id.* at 372. The Court in *Meek* explicitly stated, however, that the provision of diagnostic speech and hearing services by Pennsylvania seemed "to fall within that class of general welfare services for children that may be provided by the State regardless of the incidental benefit that accrues to church-related schools." The provision of such services was invalidated only because it was found unseverable from the unconstitutional portions of the statute.

The reason for considering diagnostic services to be different from teaching or counseling is readily apparent. First, diagnostic services, unlike teaching or counseling, have little or no educational content and are not closely associated with the educational mission of the nonpublic school. Accordingly, any pressure on the public diagnostician to allow the intrusion of sectarian views is greatly reduced. Second, the diagnostician has only limited contact with the child, and that contact involves chiefly the use of objective and professional testing methods to detect students in need of treatment. The nature of the relationship between the diagnostician and the pupil does not provide the same opportunity for the transmission of sectarian views as attends the relationship between teacher and student or that between counselor and student.

We conclude that providing diagnostic services on the nonpublic school premises will not create an impermissible risk of the fostering of ideological views. It follows that there is no need for excessive surveillance, and there will

VI. *Therapeutic Services*

Sections 3317.06(G), (H), (I), and (K) authorize expenditures of funds for certain therapeutic, guidance, and remedial services for students who have been identified as having a need for specialized attention. Personnel providing the services must be employees of the local board of education or under contract with the State Department of Health. The services are to be performed only in public schools, in public centers, or in mobile units located off the nonpublic school premises....

Appellants concede that the provision of remedial, therapeutic, and guidance services in public schools, public centers, or mobile units is constitutional if both public and nonpublic school students are served simultaneously. Their challenge is limited to the situation where a facility is used to service only nonpublic school students....

We recognize that, unlike the diagnostician, the therapist may establish a relationship with the pupil in which there might be opportunities to transmit ideological views. In *Meek* the Court acknowledged the danger that publicly employed personnel who provide services analogous to those at issue here might transmit religious instruction and advance religious beliefs in their activities. But the Court emphasized that this danger arose from the fact that the services were performed in the pervasively sectarian atmosphere of the church-related school. The danger existed there not because the public employee was likely deliberately to subvert his task to the service of religion, but rather because the pressures of the environment might alter his behavior from its normal course. So long as these types of services are offered at truly religiously neutral locations, the danger perceived in *Meek* does not arise.

The fact that a unit on a neutral site on occasion may serve only sectarian pupils does not provoke the same concerns that troubled the Court in *Meek*. The influence on a therapist's behavior that is exerted by the fact that he serves a sectarian pupil is qualitatively different from the influence of the pervasive atmosphere of a religious institution. The dangers perceived in *Meek* arose from the nature of the institution, not from the nature of the pupils.

Accordingly, we hold that providing therapeutic and remedial services at a neutral site off the premises of the nonpublic schools will not have the impermissible effect of advancing religion. Neither will there be any excessive entanglement arising from supervision of public employees to insure that they maintain a neutral stance. It can hardly be said that the supervision of public employees performing public functions on public property creates an excessive entanglement between church and state. Sections 3317.06(G), (H), (I), and (K) are constitutional.

VII. *Instructional Materials and Equipment*

Sections 3317.06(B) and (C) authorize expenditures of funds for the purchase and loan to pupils or their parents upon individual request of instructional materials and instructional equipment of the kind in use in the public schools within the district and which is "incapable of diversion to religious use." Section 3717.06 also provides that the materials and equipment may be stored on the premises of a nonpublic school and that publicly hired personnel who administer the lending program may perform their services upon the nonpublic school premises when necessary "for efficient implementation of the lending program."

Although the exact nature of the material and equipment is not clearly revealed, the parties have stipulated: "It is expected that materials and equipment loaned to pupils or parents under the new law will be similar to such former materials and equipment except that to the extent that the law requires that materials and equipment capable of diversion to religious issues will not be supplied." Equipment provided under the predecessor statute included projectors, tape recorders, record players, maps and globes, science kits, weather forecasting charts, and the like. The District Court found the new statute, as now limited, constitutional because the Court could not distinguish the loan of material and equipment from the textbook provisions upheld in *Meek*.

In *Meek*, however, the Court considered the constitutional validity of a direct loan to nonpublic schools of instructional material and equipment, and, despite the apparent secular nature of the goods, held the loan impermissible. MR. JUSTICE STEWART, in writing for the Court, stated:

> The very purpose of many of those schools is to provide an integrated secular and religious education; the teaching process is, to a large extent, devoted to the inculcation of religious values and belief. Substantial aid to the educational function of such schools, accordingly, necessarily results in aid to the sectarian school enterprise as a whole. "[T]he secular education those schools provide goes hand in hand with the religious mission that is the only reason for the schools' existence. Within the institution, the two are inextricably intertwined."

Thus, even though the loan ostensibly was limited to neutral and secular instructional material and equipment, it inescapably had the primary effect of providing a direct and substantial advancement of the sectarian enterprise.

Appellees seek to avoid *Meek* by emphasizing that it involved a program of direct loans to nonpublic schools. In contrast, the material and equipment at issue under the Ohio statute are loaned to the pupil or his parent. In our view, however, it would exalt form over substance if this distinction were found to justify a result different from that in *Meek*. Before *Meek* was decided by this Court, Ohio authorized the loan of material and equipment directly to the nonpublic schools. Then, in light of *Meek*, the state legislature decided to channel the goods through the parents and pupils. Despite the technical change in legal

A. FINANCING PRIVATE SCHOOLS FOR PUBLIC BENEFIT

bailee, the program in substance is the same as before: the equipment is substantially the same; it will receive the same use by the students; and it may still be stored and distributed on the nonpublic school premises. In view of the impossibility of separating the secular education function from the sectarian, the state aid inevitably flows in part in support of the religious role of the schools.

Indeed, this conclusion is compelled by the Court's prior consideration of an analogous issue in *Committee for Public Education v. Nyquist*, 413 U.S. 756 (1973). There the Court considered, among others, a tuition reimbursement program whereby New York gave low income parents who sent their children to nonpublic schools a direct and unrestricted cash grant of $50 to $100 per child (but no more than 50% of tuition actually paid). The State attempted to justify the program, as Ohio does here, on the basis that the aid flowed to the parents rather than to the church-related schools. The Court observed, however, that, unlike the bus program in *Everson v. Board of Education*, and the book program in *Allen*, there "has been no endeavor 'to guarantee the separation between secular and religious educational functions and to insure that State financial aid supports only the former.'" The Court thus found that the grant program served to establish religion. If a grant in cash to parents is impermissible, we fail to see how a grant in kind of goods furthering the religious enterprise can fare any better. Accordingly, we hold §§ 3317.06(B) and (C) to be unconstitutional.

VIII. *Field Trips*

Section 3317.06 also authorizes expenditures of funds:

> (L) To provide such field trip transportation and services to nonpublic school students as are provided to public school students in the district. School districts may contract with commercial transportation companies for such transportation service if school district busses are unavailable.

The District Court, held this feature to be constitutionally indistinguishable from that with which the Court was concerned in *Everson v. Board of Education*. We do not agree.... [T]he bus fare program in *Everson* passed constitutional muster because the school did not determine how often the pupil traveled between home and school — every child must make one round trip every day — and because the travel was unrelated to any aspect of the curriculum.

The Ohio situation is in sharp contrast. First, the nonpublic school controls the timing of the trips and, within a certain range, their frequency and destinations. Thus, the schools, rather than the children, truly are the recipients of the service and, as this Court has recognized, this fact alone may be sufficient to invalidate the program as impermissible direct aid. Second, although a trip may be to a location that would be of interest to those in public schools, it is the individual teacher who makes a field trip meaningful. The experience begins with the study and discussion of the place to be visited; it continues on location with the teacher pointing out items of interest and stimulating the imagination; and it ends with a discussion of the experience. The field trips are an integral part of the educational experience, and where the teacher works within and for a sectarian institution, an unacceptable risk of fostering of religion is an inevitable byproduct.... Funding of field trips, therefore, must be treated as was the funding of maps and charts in *Meek v. Pittenger, supra,* the funding of buildings and tuition in *Committee for Public Education v. Nyquist, supra,* and the funding of teacher-prepared tests in *Levitt v. Committee for Public Education*; it must be declared an impermissible direct aid to sectarian education.

Moreover, the public school authorities will be unable adequately to insure secular use of the field trip funds without close supervision of the non-public teachers. This would create excessive entanglement....

We hold § 3317.06(L) to be unconstitutional.

IX

In summary, we hold constitutional those portions of the Ohio statute authorizing the State to provide nonpublic school pupils with books, standardized testing and scoring, diagnostic services, and therapeutic and remedial services. We hold unconstitutional those portions relating to instructional materials and equipment and field trip services.

The judgment of the District Court is therefore affirmed in part and reversed in part.

It is so ordered.

THE CHIEF JUSTICE dissents from Parts VII and VIII of the Court's opinion.

... MR. JUSTICE WHITE and MR. JUSTICE REHNQUIST concur in the judgment with respect to textbooks, testing, and scoring, and diagnostic and therapeutic services (Parts III, IV, V and VI of the opinion) and dissent from the judgment with respect to instructional materials and equipment and field trips (Parts VII and VIII of the opinion).

MR. JUSTICE BRENNAN, concurring and dissenting:

I join Parts I, VII, and VIII of the Court's opinion, and the reversal of the District Court's judgment insofar as that judgment upheld the constitutionality of §§ 3317.06(B), (C), and (L).

I dissent however from Parts II, III, IV, V, and VI of the opinion and the affirmance of the District Court's judgment insofar as it sustained the constitutionality of §§ 3317.06(A), (D), (F), (G), (H), (I), (J), and (K). The Court holds that Ohio has managed in these respects to fashion a statute that avoids an effect or entanglement condemned by the Establishment Clause. But "The [First] Amendment nullifies sophisticated as well as simple-minded ..." attempts to avoid its prohibitions, and, in any event, ingenuity in draftsmanship cannot obscure the fact that this subsidy to sectarian schools amounts to $88,800,000 (less now the sums appropriated to finance §§ 3317.06(B) and (C) which today are invalidated) just for the initial biennium. The Court nowhere evaluates this factor in determining the compatibility of the statute with the Establishment Clause, as that Clause requires. Its evaluation, even after deduction of the amount appropriated to finance §§ 3317.06(B) and (C), compels in my view the conclusion that a divisive political potential of unusual magnitude inheres in the Ohio program. This suffices without more to require the conclusion that the Ohio statute in its entirety offends the First Amendment's prohibition against laws "respecting an establishment of religion."

MR. JUSTICE MARSHALL, concurring and dissenting:

I join Parts I, V, VII, and VIII of the Court's opinion. For the reasons stated below, however, I am unable to join the remainder of the Court's opinion or its judgment upholding the constitutionality of §§ 3317.06(A), (G), (H), (I), (J), and (K).

The Court upholds the textbook loan provision, § 3317.06(A), on the precedent of *Board of Education v. Allen*. It also recognizes, however, that there is "a tension" between *Allen* and the reasoning of the Court in *Meek v. Pittenger*. *I would resolve that tension by overruling Allen.* I am now convinced that *Allen* is largely responsible for reducing the "high and impregnable" wall between church and state erected by the First Amendment, to "a blurred, indistinct, and variable barrier," incapable of performing its vital functions of protecting both church and state.

In *Allen*, we upheld a textbook loan program on the assumption that the sectarian school's twin functions of religious instruction and secular education were separable. In *Meek*, we flatly rejected that assumption as a basis for allowing a State to loan secular teaching materials and equipment to such schools.... Thus, although *Meek* upheld a textbook loan program on the strength of *Allen*, is left the rationale of *Allen* undamaged only if there is a constitutionally significant difference between a loan of pedagogical materials directly to a sectarian school and a loan of those materials to students for use in sectarian schools. As the Court convincingly demonstrates there is no such difference.

....

It is, of course, unquestionable that textbooks are central to the educational process. Under the rationale of *Meek*, therefore they should not be provided by the State to sectarian schools because "[s]ubstantial aid to the educational function of such schools ... necessarily results in aid to the sectarian school enterprise as a whole." It is also unquestionable that the cost of textbooks is certain to be substantial. Under the rationale of *Lemon*, therefore, they should not be provided because of the dangers of political "devisiveness on religious lines." I would, accordingly, overrule *Board of Education v. Allen* and hold unconstitutional § 3317.06(A).

By overruling *Allen*, we would free ourselves to draw a line between acceptable and unacceptable forms of aid that would be both capable of consistent application and responsive to the concerns discussed above. That line, I believe, should be placed between general welfare programs that serve children in sectarian schools because the schools happen to be a convenient place to reach the programs' target populations and programs of educational assistance. General welfare programs, in contrast to programs of educational assistance, do not provide "[s]ubstantial aid to the educational function" of schools, whether secular or sectarian, and therefore do not provide the kind of assistance to the religious mission of sectarian schools we found impermissible in *Meek*. Moreover, because general welfare programs do not assist the sectarian functions of denominational schools, there is no reason to expect that political disputes over the merits of those programs will divide the public along religious lines.

In addition to § 3317.06(A), which authorizes the textbook loan program, paragraphs (B), (C), and (L), held unconstitutional by the Court, clearly fall on the wrong side of the constitutional line I propose. Those paragraphs authorize, respectively, the loan of instructional materials and equipment and the provision of transportation for school field trips. There can be no contention that these programs provide anything other than educational assistance.

I also agree with the Court that the services authorized by paragraphs (D), (F) and (G) are constitutionally permissible. Those services are speech and hearing diagnosis, psychological diagnosis, and psychological and speech and hearing therapy. Like the medical, nursing, dental and optometric services authorized by paragraph (E) and not challenged by appellants, these services promote the children's health and well-being, and have only an indirect and remote impact on their educational progress.

The Court upholds paragraphs (H), (I), and (K), which it groups with paragraph (G), under the rubric of "therapeutic services." I cannot agree that the services authorized by these three paragraphs should be treated like the psychological services provided by paragraph (G). Paragraph (H) authorizes the provision of guidance and counseling services ... that would directly support the educational programs of sectarian schools. It is, therefore, in violation of the First Amendment.

Paragraphs (I) and (K) provide remedial services and programs for disabled children ... clearly intended to aid the sectarian schools to improve the performance of their students in the classroom. I would not treat them as if they were programs of physical or psychological therapy.

Finally, the Court upholds paragraph (J), which provides standardized tests and scoring services, on the ground that these tests are clearly non-ideological and that the State has an interest in assuring that the education received by sectarian school students meets minimum standards. I do not question the legitimacy of this interest, and if Ohio required students to obtain specified scores on certain tests before being promoted or graduated, I would agree that it could administer those tests to sectarian school students to ensure that its standards were being met. The record indicates, however, only that the tests "are used to measure the progress of students in secular subjects." It contains no indication that the measurements are taken to assure compliance with state standards rather than for internal administrative purposes of the schools. To the extent that the testing is done to serve the purposes of the sectarian schools rather than the State, I would hold that its provision by the State violates the First Amendment.

A. FINANCING PRIVATE SCHOOLS FOR PUBLIC BENEFIT

MR. JUSTICE POWELL, concurring in part and dissenting in part:

Our decisions in this troubling area draw lines that often must seem arbitrary. No doubt we could achieve greater analytical tidiness if we were to accept the broadest implications of the observation in *Meek v. Pittenger*, that "[s]ubstantial aid to the educational function of [sectarian] schools ... necessarily results in aid to the sectarian enterprise as a whole." If we took that course, it would become impossible to sustain state aid of any kind — even if the aid is wholly secular in character and is supplied to the pupils rather than the institutions. *Meek* itself would have to be overruled, along with *Board of Education v. Allen*, and even perhaps *Everson v. Board of Education*. The persistent desire of a number of States to find proper means of helping sectarian education to survive would be doomed. This Court has not yet thought that such a harsh result is required by the Establishment Clause. Certainly few would consider it in the public interest. Parochial schools, quite apart from their sectarian purpose, have provided an educational alternative for millions of young Americans; they often afford wholesome competition with our public schools; and in some States they relieve substantially the tax burden incident to the operation of public schools. The State has, moreover, a legitimate interest in facilitating education of the highest quality for all children within its boundaries, whatever school their parents have chosen for them.

It is important to keep these issues in perspective. At this point in the 20th century we are quite far removed from the dangers that prompted the Framers to include the Establishment Clause in the Bill of Rights. The risk of significant religious or denominational control over our democratic processes — or even of deep political division along religious lines — is remote, and when viewed against the positive contributions of sectarian schools, any such risk seems entirely tolerable in light of the continuing oversight of this Court. Our decisions have sought to establish principles that preserve the cherished safeguard of the Establishment Clause without resort to blind absolutism. If this endeavor means a loss of some analytical tidiness, then that too is entirely tolerable. Most of the Court's decision today follows in this tradition, and I join Parts I through VI of its opinion.

With respect to Part VII, I concur only in the judgment. I am not persuaded, nor did *Meek* hold, that all loans of secular instructional material and equipment "inescapably [have] the primary effect of providing a direct and substantial advancement of the sectarian enterprise." If that were the case, then *Meek* surely would have overruled *Allen*. Instead the Court re-affirmed *Allen*, thereby necessarily holding that at least some such loans of materials helpful in the educational process are permissible — so long as the aid is incapable of diversion to religious uses, and so long as the materials are lent to the individual students or their parents and not to the sectarian institutions. Here the statute is expressly limited to materials incapable of diversion. Therefore the relevant question is whether the materials are such that they are "furnished for the use of *individual* students and at their request."

The Ohio statute includes some materials such as wall maps, charts and other classroom paraphernalia for which the concept of a loan to individuals is a transparent fiction. A loan of these items is indistinguishable from forbidden "direct aid" to the sectarian institution itself, whoever the technical bailee. Since the provision makes no attempt to separate these instructional materials from others meaningfully lent to individuals, I agree with the Court that it cannot be sustained under our precedents. But I would find no constitutional defect in a properly limited provision lending to the individuals themselves only appropriate instructional materials and equipment similar to that customarily used in public schools.

I dissent as to Part VIII, concerning field trip transportation. The Court writes as though the statute funded the salary of the teacher who takes the students on the outing. In fact only the bus and driver are provided for the limited purpose of physical movement between the school and the secular destination of the field trip. As I find this aid indistinguishable in principle from that upheld in *Everson*, I would sustain the District Court's judgment approving this part of the Ohio statute.

MR. JUSTICE STEVENS, concurring in part and dissenting in part:

The distinction between the religious and secular is a fundamental one. To quote from Clarence Darrow's argument in the *Scopes* case:

> The realm of religion ... is where knowledge leaves off, and where faith begins, and it never has needed the arm of the State for support, and wherever it has received it, it has harmed both the public and the religion that it would pretend to serve.

The line drawn by the Establishment Clause of the First Amendment must also have a fundamental character. It should not differentiate between direct and indirect subsidies, or between instructional materials like globes and maps on the one hand and instructional materials like textbooks on the other. For that reason, rather than the three-part test described in Part II of the Court's opinion, I would adhere to the test enunciated for the Court by MR. JUSTICE BLACK:

> No tax in any amount, large or small, can be levied to support any religious activities or institutions, whatever they may be called, or whatever form they may adopt to teach or practice religion. *Everson v. Board of Education*.

Under that test, a state subsidy of sectarian schools is invalid regardless of the form it takes. The financing of buildings, field trips, instructional materials, educational tests, and school books are all equally invalid. For all give aid to the school's educational mission, which at heart is religious. On the other hand, I am not prepared to exclude the possibility that some parts of the statute before us may be administered in a constitutional manner. The State can plainly provide public health services to children attending nonpublic schools. The diagnostic and therapeutic services described in Parts V and VI of the Court's opinion may fall

A. FINANCING PRIVATE SCHOOLS FOR PUBLIC BENEFIT 1297

into this category. Although I have some misgivings on this point, I am not prepared to hold this part of the statute invalid on its face.

This Court's efforts to improve on the *Everson* test have not proved successful. "Corrosive precedents" have left us without firm principles on which to decide these cases. As this case demonstrates, the States have been encouraged to search for new ways of achieving forbidden ends. What should be a "high and impregnable" wall between church and state, has been reduced to a "blurred, indistinct, and variable barrier" *ante*, at 2599. The result has been, as Clarence Darrow predicted, harm to "both the public and the religion that [this aid] would pretend to serve."

Accordingly, I dissent from Parts II, III and IV of the Court's opinion.

---

1. *Wolman* follows the case of *Meek v. Pittenger*, 421 U.S. 349 (1975), which held unconstitutional a direct loan of educational materials to private school students while upholding the loan of textbooks to individual students in private institutions. After *Meek* was handed down by the United States Supreme Court, and in an obvious attempt to conform to the teaching of that decision, the State of Ohio passed a statute authorizing various forms of aid to nonpublic schools, most of which were sectarian. In *Wolman*, the Supreme Court reviewed the constitutionality of the Ohio statute in an effort to provide further enlightenment on how, and if, sectarian schools can receive public funds.

2. In a 1979 decision the Supreme Court refused to order Ohio officials to recover instructional equipment and materials which were loaned by public school districts to private schools under provisions of the statute held unconstitutional in the 1977 *Wolman* decision. The Court affirmed without opinion the ruling of an Ohio federal district court that the involvement of the courts in the return of the equipment would risk unconstitutional government entanglement with religion. *Wolman v. Walter*, 100 S. Ct. 26 (1979).

The proliferation of opinions in the *Wolman* decision reflects the Court's lack of consensus in applying Establishment Clause analysis to the area of state aid to private schools. It is, therefore, important to see how *Wolman* is being viewed by the lower federal courts to determine whether this lack of consensus has caused further confusion. In *Filler v. Port Washington Union Free Sch. Dist.*, 436 F. Supp. 1231 (E.D.N.Y. 1977), a federal district court in New York delayed its decision on a challenge to a state law which required public school districts to provide a variety of health and welfare services to nonpublic school children until the *Wolman* case was decided. In interpreting the *Wolman* decision, the New York court stated:

> Merely from the fact that there were five separate opinions and two justices refused to join in any of those opinions, it is apparent that different constitutional premises and analytical approaches were applied by the Supreme Court in arriving at its June 24, 1977 judgment. Notwithstanding

the diverse views, in its actual holdings, the Supreme Court split with a relatively solid six to three vote.

As to those parts of the Ohio statute which authorized public funds for textbook loans (Part III of the Blackmun opinion); standardized tests and scoring services (Part IV); speech, hearing, and psychological diagnostic services (Part V); and remedial services, guidance and counselling services, as well as therapeutic psychological and speech and hearing services when provided off the non public school premises (Part VI); the Court agreed by vote of at least six to three that the statute did not offend the first amendment. As to loans of instructional materials and equipment (Part VII) and field trip transportation and services (Part VIII), the court found the statute invalid, voting six to three on the former, and five to four on the latter.

Because they significantly extend the establishment clause mode of analysis for health and welfare services, the criteria expounded in Justice Blackmun's opinion must now be used to determine the constitutional validity of N.Y. Education Law § 912 as last amended in 1974. In Part II of his *Wolman* opinion Justice Blackmun noted:

> The mode of analysis for Establishment Clause questions is defined by the three-part test that has emerged from the Court's decisions. In order to pass muster, a statute must have a secular legislative purpose, must have a principal or primary effect that neither advances nor inhibits religion, and must not foster an excessive government entanglement with religion. [433] U.S. at [235, 236].

As suggested in that opinion, when dealing with services of the health and welfare type, there is no difficulty with the first part of the test, secular legislative purpose. Problems do arise, however, in determining the "effect" and "excessive entanglement" criteria. Dealing with services such as are contemplated by § 912, the majority opinion in *Wolman* drew a distinction between, on the one hand, "therapeutic, guidance, and remedial services," which might be provided at public expense to parochial school students only when they were performed off the non public school premises, and, on the other hand, "diagnostic services" which could be provided to parochial school students even within the parochial school building itself. The Court found a common thread in its decisions "to the effect that the provision of health services to all school children — public and non public — does not have the primary effect of aiding religion." [433] U.S. at [242].

Justice Blackmun pointed out that no challenge was raised in *Wolman* to subsection (E) of the statute which authorized the provision of "physician, nursing, dental and optometric services" to parochial school pupils. Viewing

A. FINANCING PRIVATE SCHOOLS FOR PUBLIC BENEFIT

those services as being clearly constitutional, he concluded with respect to the "diagnostic services":

> We perceive no basis for drawing a different conclusion with respect to diagnostic speech and hearing services and diagnostic psychological services. [433] U.S. at [242].

The "therapeutic services" which the Supreme Court held could be provided to parochial school students only "at a neutral site off the premises of the non public schools", were described in the Ohio statute as including "therapeutic psychological and speech and hearing services", "guidance and counseling services", "remedial services", and "programs for the deaf, blind, emotionally disturbed, crippled, and physically handicapped children". The danger to be avoided, according to the Supreme Court, was that a relationship between "therapist" and pupil might provide opportunities to transmit ideological views. But, *Meek v. Pettinger, supra*, 421 U.S. at 371, stressed that "this danger arose from the fact that the services were performed in the pervasively sectarian atmosphere of the church-related school." The Court concluded that if those types of services were to be offered at truly religiously neutral locations, then the danger perceived in *Meek* would not arise. [433] U.S. at [247].

Thus, the "therapeutic services" of the Ohio statute in *Wolman*, limited as they were to being provided "in the public school, in public centers, or in mobile units located off the non public premises" were held to be constitutional.

In short, *Wolman v. Walter* has added considerable specific content to many of the general principles previously enunciated by the Supreme Court for determining the scope of permissible aid to students attending parochial schools. Within the group of permissible health and welfare services, whether a particular service is "diagnostic" or "therapeutic" determines whether it may be performed on the parochial school premises or only at a religiously neutral site.

The court in *Filler* ultimately held that provisions of the New York statute which authorized the providing of services performed by a physician, dentist, dental hygienist or nurse in a nonpublic school were constitutional. The court further held that although the providing of services by a psychologist or speech correctionist pursuant to the statute was constitutional, such services were to be rendered in a religiously neutral location to the extent that the services might be "therapeutic" or "remedial" as opposed to "diagnostic." *See also Springfield Sch. Dist. v. Pennsylvania Dep't of Educ.*, 397 A.2d 1154 (1979), in which the Pennsylvania Supreme Court held that a state statute requiring school districts to provide free transportation for resident students attending public and private nonprofit schools within 10 miles of the district border did not violate the Establishment Clause. The court noted that one teaching of *Wolman* is that

Everson did not provide blanket approval of school transportation programs, but held the Pennsylvania statute constitutional on the grounds that it did not confer unequal benefits on private school children and did not require continuing surveillance of nonpublic school teachers, as was the case in *Wolman*.

3. The Supreme Court rulings on the issue of state aid to nonpublic schools have been described as "a body of opinion that concededly makes no sense." As Justice Marshall notes in his dissenting opinion to *Wolman*, the Court in *Board of Educ. v. Allen*, 392 U.S. 236 (1967), upheld a textbook loan program on the assumption that the sectarian school's functions of religious instruction and secular education were separable, but rejected that assumption in *Meek v. Pittinger* in forbidding the loan of secular teaching materials and equipment. Why is it permissible to lend books, but impermissible to lend filmstrips? In *Everson*, bus rides to and from nonpublic schools were held to be constitutional but in *Wolman* the providing of transportation to cultural centers as part of a field trip program was viewed as unconstitutional. Is the Supreme Court's reasoning in support of its decision that diagnostic services can be conducted on nonpublic school grounds while therapeutic services cannot persuasive? Are there valid policy considerations underlying the Court's rulings in the state aid cases or, as one commentator has suggested, is the court elevating subtle distinctions to the level of First Amendment commandments?

2. PAYMENT FOR PERSONNEL SALARIES, TUITION, AND OTHER TAX BENEFITS

The "child benefit" theory which was the basis for attempts to use public monies for such things as the purchase of textbooks for parochial schools was extended even further when some legislatures provided tax monies for personnel salaries, tuition reimbursement, and other benefits for nonpublic schools. The United States Supreme Court first dealt with the questions raised by this extension in 1971.

LEMON v. KURTZMAN
Supreme Court of the United States
403 U.S. 602 (1971)

MR. CHIEF JUSTICE BURGER delivered the opinion of the Court:

These two appeals raise questions as to Pennsylvania and Rhode Island statutes providing state aid to church-related elementary and secondary schools. Both statutes are challenged as violative of the Establishment and Free Exercise Clauses of the First Amendment and the Due Process Clause of the Fourteenth Amendment.

A. FINANCING PRIVATE SCHOOLS FOR PUBLIC BENEFIT

I

The Rhode Island Statute

The Rhode Island Salary Supplement Act was enacted in 1969. It rests on the legislative finding that the quality of education available in nonpublic elementary schools has been jeopardized by the rapidly rising salaries needed to attract competent and dedicated teachers. The Act authorizes state officials to supplement the salaries of teachers of secular subjects in nonpublic elementary schools by paying directly to a teacher an amount not in excess of 15% of his current annual salary. As supplemented, however, a nonpublic school teacher's salary cannot exceed the maximum paid to teachers in the State's public schools, and the recipient must be certified by the state board of education in substantially the same manner as public school teachers.

In order to be eligible for the Rhode Island salary supplement, the recipient must teach in a nonpublic school at which the average per-pupil expenditure on secular education is less than the average in the State's public schools during a specified period. Appellant State Commissioner of Education also requires eligible schools to submit financial data. If this information indicates a per-pupil expenditure in excess of the statutory limitation, the records of the school in question must be examined in order to assess how much of the expenditure is attributable to secular education and how much to religious activity.

The Act also requires that teachers eligible for salary supplements must teach only those subjects that are offered in the State's public schools. They must use "only teaching materials which are used in the public schools." Finally, any teacher applying for a salary supplement must first agree in writing "not to teach a course in religion for so long as or during such time as he or she receives any salary supplements" under the Act.

A three-judge federal court ... found that Rhode Island's nonpublic elementary schools accommodated approximately 25% of the State's pupils. About 95% of these pupils attended schools affiliated with the Roman Catholic church. To date some 250 teachers have applied for benefits under the Act. All of them are employed by Roman Catholic schools.

....

The Pennsylvania Statute

Pennsylvania has adopted a program that has some but not all of the features of the Rhode Island program. The Pennsylvania Nonpublic Elementary and Secondary Education Act was passed in 1968 in response to a crisis that the Pennsylvania Legislature found existed in the State's nonpublic schools due to rapidly rising costs. The statute affirmatively reflects the legislative conclusion that the State's educational goals could appropriately be fulfilled by government support of "those purely secular educational objectives achieved through nonpublic education...."

The statute authorizes appellee state Superintendent of Public Instruction to "purchase" specified "secular educational services" from nonpublic schools. Under the "contracts" authorized by the statute, the State directly reimburses nonpublic schools solely for their actual expenditures for teachers' salaries, textbooks, and instructional materials. A school seeking reimbursement must maintain prescribed accounting procedures that identify the "separate" cost of the "secular educational service." These accounts are subject to state audit. The funds for this program were originally derived from a new tax on horse and harness racing, but the Act is now financed by a portion of the state tax on cigarettes.

There are several significant statutory restrictions on state aid. Reimbursement is limited to courses "presented in the curricula of the public schools." It is further limited "solely" to courses in the following "secular" subjects: mathematics, modern foreign languages,[4] physical science, and physical education. Textbooks and instructional materials included in the program must be approved by the state Superintendent of Public Instruction. Finally, the statute prohibits reimbursement for any course that contains "any subject matter expressing religious teaching, or the morals or forms of worship of any sect."

....

II

In *Everson v. Board of Education*, 330 U.S. 1 (1947), this Court upheld a state statute that reimbursed the parents of parochial school children for bus transportation expenses. There Mr. Justice Black, writing for the majority, suggested that the decision carried to "the verge" of forbidden territory under the Religion Clauses. *Id.* at 16. Candor compels acknowledgment, moreover, that we can only dimly perceive the lines of demarcation in this extraordinarily sensitive area of constitutional law.

The language of the Religion Clauses of the First Amendment is at best opaque, particularly when compared with other portions of the Amendment. Its authors did not simply prohibit the establishment of a state church or a state religion, an area history shows they regarded as very important and fraught with great dangers. Instead they commanded that there should be "no law *respecting* an establishment of religion." A law may be one "respecting" the forbidden objective while falling short of its total realization. A law "respecting" the proscribed result, that is, the establishment of religion, is not always easily identifiable as one violative of the Clause. A given law might not *establish* a state religion but nevertheless be one "respecting" that end in the sense of being a step that could lead to such establishment and hence offend the First Amendment.

In the absence of precisely stated constitutional prohibitions, we must draw lines with reference to the three main evils against which the Establishment

---

[4]Latin, Hebrew, and classical Greek are excluded.

A. FINANCING PRIVATE SCHOOLS FOR PUBLIC BENEFIT

Clause was intended to afford protection: "sponsorship, financial support, and active involvement of the sovereign in religious activity." *Walz v. Tax Commission*, 397 U.S. 664, 668 (1970).

Every analysis in this area must begin with consideration of the cumulative criteria developed by the Court over many years. Three such tests may be gleaned from our cases. First, the statute must have a secular legislative purpose; second, its principal or primary effect must be one that neither advances nor inhibits religion, *Board of Education v. Allen*, 392 U.S. 236, 243 (1968); finally, the statute must not foster "an excessive government entanglement with religion." *Walz, supra*, at 674.

Inquiry into the legislative purposes of the Pennsylvania and Rhode Island statutes affords no basis for a conclusion that the legislative intent was to advance religion. On the contrary, the statutes themselves clearly state that they are intended to enhance the quality of the secular education in all schools covered by the compulsory attendance laws. There is no reason to believe the legislatures meant anything else. A State always has a legitimate concern for maintaining minimum standards in all schools it allows to operate. As in *Allen*, we find nothing here that undermines the stated legislative intent; it must therefore be accorded appropriate deference.

In *Allen* the Court acknowledged that secular and religious teachings were not necessarily so intertwined that secular textbooks furnished to students by the State were in fact instrumental in the teaching of religion. 392 U.S. at 248. The legislatures of Rhode Island and Pennsylvania have concluded that secular and religious education are identifiable and separable. In the abstract we have no quarrel with this conclusion.

The two legislatures, however, have also recognized that church-related elementary and secondary schools have a significant religious mission and that a substantial portion of their activities is religiously oriented. They have therefore sought to create statutory restrictions designed to guarantee the separation between secular and religious educational functions and to ensure that State financial aid supports only the former. All these provisions are precautions taken in candid recognition that these programs approached, even if they did not intrude upon, the forbidden areas under the Religion Clauses. We need not decide whether these legislative precautions restrict the principal or primary effect of the programs to the point where they do not offend the Religion Clauses, for we conclude that the cumulative impact of the entire relationship arising under the statutes in each State involves excessive entanglement between government and religion.

III

....

(a) *Rhode Island program*

The District Court made extensive findings on the grave potential for excessive entanglement that inheres in the religious character and purpose of the Roman Catholic elementary schools of Rhode Island, to date the sole beneficiaries of the Rhode Island Salary Supplement Act.

The church schools involved in the program are located close to parish churches. This understandably permits convenient access for religious exercises since instruction in faith and morals is part of the total educational process. The school buildings contain identifying religious symbols such as crosses on the exterior and crucifixes, and religious paintings and statues either in the classrooms or hallways. Although only approximately 30 minutes a day are devoted to direct religious instruction, there are religiously oriented extracurricular activities. Approximately two-thirds of the teachers in these schools are nuns of various religious orders. Their dedicated efforts provide an atmosphere in which religious instruction and religious vocations are natural and proper parts of life in such schools. Indeed, as the District Court found, the role of teaching nuns in enhancing the religious atmosphere has led the parochial school authorities to attempt to maintain a one-to-one ratio between nuns and lay teachers in all schools rather than to permit some to be staffed almost entirely by lay teachers.

On the basis of these findings the District Court concluded that the parochial schools constituted "an integral part of the religious mission of the Catholic Church." The various characteristics of the schools make them "a powerful vehicle for transmitting the Catholic faith to the next generation." This process of inculcating religious doctrine is, of course, enhanced by the impressionable age of the pupils, in primary schools particularly. In short, parochial schools involve substantial religious activity and purpose.

The substantial religious character of these church-related schools gives rise to entangling church-state relationships of the kind the Religion Clauses sought to avoid. Although the District Court found that concern for religious values did not inevitably or necessarily intrude into the content of secular subjects, the considerable religious activities of these schools led the legislature to provide for careful governmental controls and surveillance by state authorities in order to ensure that state aid supports only secular education.

....

... The Rhode Island Legislature has not, and could not, provide state aid on the basis of a mere assumption that secular teachers under religious discipline can avoid conflicts. The State must be certain, given the Religion Clauses, that subsidized teachers do not inculcate religion — indeed the State here has undertaken to do so. To ensure that no trespass occurs, the State has therefore

A. FINANCING PRIVATE SCHOOLS FOR PUBLIC BENEFIT

carefully conditioned its aid with pervasive restrictions. An eligible recipient must teach only those courses that are offered in the public schools and use only those texts and materials that are found in the public schools. In addition the teacher must not engage in teaching any course in religion.

A comprehensive, discriminating, and continuing state surveillance will inevitably be required to ensure that these restrictions are obeyed and the First Amendment otherwise respected. Unlike a book, a teacher cannot be inspected once so as to determine the extent and intent of his or her personal beliefs and subjective acceptance of the limitations imposed by the First Amendment. These prophylactic contacts will involve excessive and enduring entanglement between state and church.

There is another area of entanglement in the Rhode Island program that gives concern. The statute excludes teachers employed by nonpublic schools whose average per-pupil expenditures on secular education equal or exceed the comparable figures for public schools. In the event that the total expenditures of an otherwise eligible school exceed this norm, the program requires the government to examine the school's records in order to determine how much of the total expenditures is attributable to secular education and how much to religious activity. This kind of state inspection and evaluation of the religious content of a religious organization is fraught with the sort of entanglement that the Constitution forbids. It is a relationship pregnant with dangers of excessive government direction of church schools and hence of churches. The Court noted "the hazards of government supporting churches" in *Walz v. Tax Commission, supra,* at 675, and we cannot ignore here the danger that pervasive modern governmental power will ultimately intrude on religion and thus conflict with the Religion Clauses.

(b) *Pennsylvania program*

The Pennsylvania statute also provides state aid to church-related schools for teachers' salaries. The complaint describes an educational system that is very similar to the one existing in Rhode Island. According to the allegations, the church-related elementary and secondary schools are controlled by religious organizations, have the purpose of propagating and promoting a particular religious faith, and conduct their operations to fulfill that purpose. Since this complaint was dismissed for failure to state a claim for relief, we must accept these allegations as true for purposes of our review.

As we noted earlier, the very restrictions and surveillance necessary to ensure that teachers play a strictly nonideological role give rise to entanglements between church and state. The Pennsylvania statute, like that of Rhode Island, fosters this kind of relationship. Reimbursement is not only limited to courses offered in the public schools and materials approved by state officials, but the statute excludes "any subject matter expressing religious teaching, or the morals or forms of worship of any sect." In addition, schools seeking reimbursement must maintain accounting procedures that require the State to establish the cost of the secular as distinguished from the religious instruction.

The Pennsylvania statute, moreover, has the further defect of providing state financial aid directly to the church-related school. This factor distinguishes both *Everson* and *Allen*, for in both those cases the Court was careful to point out that state aid was provided to the student and his parents — not to the church-related school. *Board of Education v. Allen, supra*, at 243-44; *Everson v. Board of Education, supra*, at 18. In *Walz v. Tax Commission, supra*, at 675, the Court warned of the dangers of direct payments to religious organizations:

> Obviously a direct money subsidy would be a relationship pregnant with involvement and, as with most governmental grant programs, could encompass sustained and detailed administrative relationships for enforcement of statutory or administrative standards....

The history of government grants of a continuing cash subsidy indicates that such programs have almost always been accompanied by varying measures of control and surveillance. The government cash grants before us now provide no basis for predicting that comprehensive measures of surveillance and controls will not follow. In particular the government's post-audit power to inspect and evaluate a church-related school's financial records and to determine which expenditures are religious and which are secular creates an intimate and continuing relationship between church and state.

IV

A broader base of entanglement of yet a different character is presented by the divisive political potential of these state programs. In a community where such a large number of pupils are served by church-related schools, it can be assumed that state assistance will entail considerable political activity. Partisans of parochial schools, understandably concerned with rising costs and sincerely dedicated to both the religious and secular educational missions of their schools, will inevitably champion this cause and promote political action to achieve their goals. Those who oppose state aid, whether for constitutional, religious, or fiscal reasons, will inevitably respond and employ all of the usual political campaign techniques to prevail. Candidates will be forced to declare and voters to choose. It would be unrealistic to ignore the fact that many people confronted with issues of this kind will find their votes aligned with their faith.

Ordinarily political debate and division, however vigorous or even partisan, are normal and healthy manifestations of our democratic system of government, but political division along religious lines was one of the principal evils against which the First Amendment was intended to protect....

....

The potential for political divisiveness related to religious belief and practice is aggravated in these two statutory programs by the need for continuing annual appropriations and the likelihood of larger and larger demands as costs and populations grow. The Rhode Island District Court found that the parochial school system's "monumental and deepening financial crisis" would "inescapably" require larger annual appropriations subsidizing greater percentages of the salaries of lay teachers. Although no facts have been developed in this respect in the Pennsylvania case, it appears that such pressures for expanding aid have already required the state legislature to include a portion of the state revenues from cigarette taxes in the program.

V

In *Walz* it was argued that a tax exemption for places of religious worship would prove to be the first step in an inevitable progression leading to the establishment of state churches and state religion. That claim could not stand up against more than 200 years of virtually universal practice imbedded in our colonial experience and continuing into the present.

The progression argument, however, is more persuasive here. We have no long history of state aid to church-related educational institutions comparable to 200 years of tax exemption for churches. Indeed, the state programs before us today represent something of an innovation. We have already noted that modern governmental programs have self-perpetuating and self-expanding propensities. These internal pressures are only enhanced when the schemes involve institutions whose legitimate needs are growing and whose interests have substantial political support. Nor can we fail to see that in constitutional adjudication some steps, which when taken were thought to approach "the verge," have become the platform for yet further steps. A certain momentum develops in constitutional theory and it can be a "downhill thrust" easily set in motion but difficult to retard or stop. Development by momentum is not invariably bad; indeed, it is the way the common law has grown, but it is a force to be recognized and reckoned with. The dangers are increased by the difficulty of perceiving in advance exactly where the "verge" of the precipice lies. As well as constituting an independent evil against which the Religion Clauses were intended to protect, involvement or entanglement between government and religion serves as a warning signal.

Finally, nothing we have said can be construed to disparage the role of church-related elementary and secondary schools in our national life. Their contribution has been and is enormous. Nor do we ignore their economic plight in a period of rising costs and expanding need. Taxpayers generally have been spared vast sums by the maintenance of these educational institutions by religious organizations, largely by the gifts of faithful adherents.

The merit and benefits of these schools, however, are not the issue before us in these cases. The sole question is whether state aid to these schools can be squared with the dictates of the Religion Clauses. Under our system the choice has been made that government is to be entirely excluded from the area of religious instruction and churches excluded from the affairs of government. The Constitution decrees that religion must be a private matter for the individual, the family, and the institutions of private choice, and that while some involvement and entanglement are inevitable, lines must be drawn.

The judgment of the Rhode Island District Court in No. 569 and No. 570 is affirmed. The judgment of the Pennsylvania District Court in No. 89 is reversed, and the case is remanded for further proceedings consistent with this opinion.

....

TILTON v. RICHARDSON

United States Supreme Court
403 U.S. 672 (1971)

MR. CHIEF JUSTICE BURGER announced the judgment of the Court and an opinion in which MR. JUSTICE HARLAN, MR. JUSTICE STEWART, and MR. JUSTICE BLACKMUN join:

This appeal presents important constitutional questions as to federal aid for church-related colleges and universities under Title I of the Higher Education Facilities Act of 1963, 77 Stat. 364, as amended, 20 U.S.C. §§ 711-21 (1964 ed. and Supp. V), which provides construction grants for buildings and facilities used exclusively for secular educational purposes. We must determine first whether the Act authorizes aid to such church-related institutions, and, if so, whether the Act violates either the Establishment or Free Exercise Clauses of the First Amendment.

I

The Higher Education Facilities Act was passed in 1963 in response to a strong nationwide demand for the expansion of college and university facilities to meet the sharply rising number of young people demanding higher education. The Act authorizes federal grants and loans to "institutions of higher education" for the construction of a wide variety of "academic facilities." But § 751 (a)(2) (1964 ed., Supp. V) expressly excludes

> any facility used or to be used for sectarian instruction or as a place for religious worship, or ... any facility which ... is used or to be used primarily in connection with any part of the program of a school or department of divinity....

The Act is administered by the United States Commissioner of Education. He advises colleges and universities applying for funds that under the Act no part of the project may be used for sectarian instruction, religious worship, or the programs of a divinity school. The Commissioner requires applicants to provide assurances that these restrictions will be respected. The United States retains a 20-year interest in any facility constructed with Title I funds. If, during this period, the recipient violates the statutory conditions, the United States is entitled to recover an amount equal to the proportion of its present value that the federal grant bore to the original cost of the facility. During the 20-year period, the

A. FINANCING PRIVATE SCHOOLS FOR PUBLIC BENEFIT

statutory restrictions are enforced by the Office of Education primarily by way of on-site inspections.

[The opinion concludes that the Act does authorize aid to church-related institutions, that it has a valid legislative purpose of aiding higher education and that its "principal or primary" effect does not advance religion, except for the twenty-year limitation on the right of the United States to recover its money if the project is used for religious purposes, which limitation was stricken down. The opinion then goes on to discuss "entanglement."]

....

We next turn to the question of whether excessive entanglements characterize the relationship between government and church under the Act. *Walz v. Tax Comm'n, supra*, at 674-76. Our decision today in *Lemon v. Kurtzman* and *Robinson v. DiCenso* has discussed and applied this independent measure of constitutionality under the Religion Clauses. There we concluded that excessive entanglements between government and religion were fostered by Pennsylvania and Rhode Island statutory programs under which state aid was provided to parochial elementary and secondary schools. Here, however, three factors substantially diminish the extent and the potential danger of the entanglement.

In *DiCenso* the District Court found that the parochial schools in Rhode Island were "an integral part of the religious mission of the Catholic Church." There, the record fully supported the conclusion that the inculcation of religious values was a substantial if not the dominant purpose of the institutions. The Pennsylvania case was decided on the pleadings, and hence we accepted as true the allegations that the parochial schools in that State shared the same characteristics.

Appellants' complaint here contains similar allegations. But they were denied by the answers, and there was extensive evidence introduced on the subject. Although the District Court made no findings with respect to the religious character of the four institutions of higher learning, we are not required to accept the allegations as true under these circumstances, particularly where, as here, appellants themselves do not contend that these four institutions are "sectarian."

There are generally significant differences between the religious aspects of church-related institutions of higher learning and parochial elementary and secondary schools. The "affirmative if not dominant policy" of the instruction in pre-college church schools is "to assure future adherents to a particular faith by having control of their total education at an early age." *Walz v. Tax Comm'n, supra*, at 671. There is substance to the contention that college students are less impressionable and less susceptible to religious indoctrination. Common observation would seem to support that view, and Congress may well have entertained it. The skepticism of the college student is not an inconsiderable barrier to any attempt or tendency to subvert the congressional objectives and limitations. Furthermore, by their very nature, college and postgraduate courses tend to limit the opportunities for sectarian influence by virtue of their own internal disciplines. Many church-related colleges and universities are characterized by a high degree of academic freedom and seek to evoke free and critical responses from their students.

The record here would not support a conclusion that any of these four institutions departed from this general pattern. All four schools are governed by Catholic religious organizations, and the faculties and student bodies at each are predominantly Catholic. Nevertheless, the evidence shows that non-Catholics were admitted as students and given faculty appointments. Not one of these four institutions requires its students to attend religious services. Although all four schools require their students to take theology courses, the parties stipulated that these courses are taught according to the academic requirements of the subject matter and the teacher's concept of professional standards. The parties also stipulated that the courses covered a range of human religious experiences and are not limited to courses about the Roman Catholic religion. The schools introduced evidence that they made no attempt to indoctrinate students or to proselytize. Indeed, some of the required theology courses at Albertus Magnus and Sacred Heart are taught by rabbis. Finally, as we have noted, these four schools subscribe to a well-established set of principles of academic freedom, and nothing in this record shows that these principles are not in fact followed. In short, the evidence shows institutions with admittedly religious functions but whose predominant higher education mission is to provide their students with a secular education.

Since religious indoctrination is not a substantial purpose or activity of these church-related colleges and universities, there is less likelihood than in primary and secondary schools that religion will permeate the area of secular education. This reduces the risk that government aid will in fact serve to support religious activities. Correspondingly, the necessity for intensive government surveillance is diminished and the resulting entanglements between government and religion lessened. Such inspection as may be necessary to ascertain that the facilities are devoted to secular education is minimal and indeed hardly more than the inspections that States impose over all private schools within the reach of compulsory education laws.

The entanglement between church and state is also lessened here by the nonideological character of the aid that the Government provides. Our cases from *Everson* to *Allen* have permitted church-related schools to receive government aid in the form of secular, neutral, or nonideological services, facilities, or materials that are supplied to all students regardless of the affiliation of the school that they attend. In *Lemon* and *DiCenso*, however, the state programs subsidized teachers, either directly or indirectly. Since teachers are not necessarily religiously neutral, greater governmental surveillance would be required to guarantee that state salary aid would not in fact subsidize religious instruction. There we found the resulting entanglement excessive. Here, on the other hand, the Government provides facilities that are themselves religiously neutral. The risks of Government aid to religion and the corresponding need for surveillance are therefore reduced.

A. FINANCING PRIVATE SCHOOLS FOR PUBLIC BENEFIT

Finally, government entanglements with religion are reduced by the circumstance that, unlike the direct and continuing payments under the Pennsylvania program, and all the incidents of regulation and surveillance, the Government aid here is a one-time, single-purpose construction grant. There are no continuing financial relationships or dependencies, no annual audits, and no government analysis of an institution's expenditures on secular as distinguished from religious activities. Inspection as to use is a minimal contact.

No one of these three factors standing alone is necessarily controlling; cumulatively all of them shape a narrow and limited relationship with government which involves fewer and less significant contacts than the two state schemes before us in *Lemon* and *DiCenso*. The relationship therefore has less potential for realizing the substantive evils against which the Religion Clauses were intended to protect.

We think that cumulatively these three factors also substantially lessen the potential for divisive religious fragmentation in the political arena. This conclusion is admittedly difficult to document, but neither have appellants pointed to any continuing religious aggravation on this matter in the political processes. Possibly this can be explained by the character and diversity of the recipient colleges and universities and the absence of any intimate continuing relationship or dependency between government and religiously affiliated institutions. The potential for divisiveness inherent in the essentially local problems of primary and secondary schools is significantly less with respect to a college or university whose student constituency is not local but diverse and widely dispersed.

....

---

1. In *Roemer v. Board of Pub. Works of Maryland*, 426 U.S. 736 (1976), the United States Supreme Court was again asked to police the constitutional boundaries existing between Church and State. In this particular case, a Maryland statute was involved. The statute authorized the payment of state funds to any private institution of higher learning within the State that met certain minimum criteria, and that refrained from rewarding "only seminarian or theological degrees." The aid was in the form of an annual fiscal year subsidy to qualifying colleges and universities, based upon the number of students, excluding those in seminarian or theological academic programs. Among the type of schools receiving aid were four colleges affiliated with the Roman Catholic Church. The state aid to these colleges was challenged as violative of the Establishment Clause of the First Amendment.

Mr. Justice Blackmun, joined by the Chief Justice and Mr. Justice Powell concluded that the Maryland Act does not, under the standards set by *Lemon v. Kurtzman* violate the Establishment Clause. The three justices held that because the colleges are not "pervasively sectarian" that the aid provided under the Maryland statute did not have a primary effect of advancing religion. Mr. Justice

White and Mr. Justice Rehnquist joined in upholding the Maryland statute, concluding that there was no violation of the Establishment Clause where, as with the statute in question, there is a secular legislative purpose and the primary effect of the legislation is neither to advance nor inhibit religion.

Subsequent to *Roemer*, the Supreme Court was again asked to decide the constitutionality of state student assistance programs which also benefit students attending private colleges with religious ties. The tuition grant statutes in North Carolina and Tennessee were upheld by the three-judge federal district court. On appeal, the Supreme Court affirmed the judgments without opinion. *See Smith v. Board of Governors of Univ. of North Carolina*, 429 F. Supp. 871 (W.D.N.C.), *judgment aff'd*, 98 S. Ct. 39 (1977); *Americans United for Separation of Church and State v. Blanton*, 433 F. Supp. 97 (N.D. Tenn.), *judgment aff'd*, 98 S. Ct. 39 (1977).

In the *Smith* case the state program of tuition grants and scholarships was challenged as it applied to Belmont Abbey College (Catholic affiliation) and Pfeiffer College (United Methodist affiliation). In upholding the North Carolina statute, the three-judge district court made the following analysis of the present thrust of the law as applied to these types of cases:

> The criteria for determining the constitutionality of governmental aid to sectarian colleges are set forth in *Lemon v. Kurtzman*, 403 U.S. 602, 612-613 (1971), where they were summarized:
>
> First, the statute must have a secular legislative purpose; second, its principal or primary effect must be one that neither advances nor inhibits religion; ... finally, the statute must not foster "an excessive government entanglement with religion."
>
> Here the plaintiffs concede that North Carolina's three scholarship and tuition assistance programs have a secular legislative purpose. We are left to consider the other two prongs of the test; the primary effect of advancing or inhibiting religion and excessive entanglement of government with religion.
>
> As to the primary effect criterion, it was said in *Hunt v. McNair*, 413 U.S. 734 (1973):
>
> [That] aid normally may be thought to have a primary effect of advancing religion when it flows to an institution in which religion is so pervasive that a substantial portion of its functions are subsumed in the religious mission or when it funds a specifically religious activity in an otherwise substantially secular setting.
>
> More specific guidelines are provided in *Roemer v. Board of Public Works of Maryland*, 426 U.S. 736 (1976), for the colleges here seem indistinguishable from the Catholic colleges involved in *Roemer*.

A. FINANCING PRIVATE SCHOOLS FOR PUBLIC BENEFIT

Maryland established a program of noncategorical grants to the state's private colleges, some of which had religious affiliations. In *Roemer* that program was challenged insofar as it provided grants to four Catholic colleges, the contention being that the colleges were "constitutionally ineligible for this ... aid." A three-judge district court, after finding the facts extensively, concluded the four Catholic colleges were not "pervasively sectarian." The Supreme Court accepted the findings and agreed with the conclusion.

Among the characteristics of the Maryland colleges with which the Supreme Court was concerned in *Roemer* were the following:

(1) Despite their formal affiliation with the Roman Catholic Church, the colleges are "characterized by a high degree of institutional autonomy." 426 U.S. at 755.

(2) The colleges employ Roman Catholic chaplains and hold Roman Catholic religious exercises on campus. Attendance at such is not required. *Id.*

(3) Mandatory religion or theology courses are taught at each of the colleges, primarily by Roman Catholic clerics, but these only supplement a curriculum covering "the spectrum of a liberal arts program." *Id.* at 756.

(4) Some classes are begun with prayer.... There is no "actual college policy" of encouraging the practice. *Id.*

(5) Some instructors wear clerical garb and some classrooms have religious symbols. *Id.*

(6) Apart from the theology department, ... faculty hiring decisions are not made on a religious basis. *Id.* at 757.

(7) The great majority of students at each of the colleges are Roman Catholic, but ... the student bodies "are chosen without regard to religion." *Id.*

As to those characteristics, there appears no material distinction between the Maryland colleges and Belmont Abbey and Pfeiffer College. In all of these schools there was a presence of religion, but each of them is a liberal arts college in which the inculcation of religion is not the primary purpose. Formal religious ties are present, but beyond the minimal requirement of courses in religion or theology, taught as academic exercises, religion is not forced upon the students. Their general liberal arts curricula are not designed to prepare students for service in a religious vocation, and students are neither required to accept a set of religious beliefs nor to practice religious rituals.

Since these colleges are not distinguishable from those with which the Supreme Court dealt in *Roemer*, we conclude that they are not so pervasively religious that their secular activities cannot be separated from their sectarian ones.

It would not be enough that the secular aspects of these institutions may be separated from the sectarian if the state specifically funded religious activities at these colleges. The North Carolina General Assembly not only has not undertaken to do that, it has imposed an express restriction that the funds be used only for secular educational purposes. The plaintiffs, however, question whether this has been observed in practice because both the Board of Governors and the North Carolina Educational Assistance Authority take the position that grants of student aid in the form of scholarships and tuition credits were, themselves, secular purposes so long as the aided student in an eligible college was not in a program of study designed as preparation for a career in a religious vocation.

When these funds are received from the state, the colleges have set them up in separate accounts for scholarship or tuition grants. Once the scholarships are awarded, however, and the scholarship and grant funds are credited to the accounts of the individual students, there is a bookkeeping transfer of the funds from the scholarship and tuition grant accounts to the general funds of the colleges. Since general funds are used to serve sectarian as well as the secular purposes of these colleges, the plaintiffs contend that *Roemer* is uncontrolling here.

This contention of the plaintiffs seems only a variant of the "recurrent argument" that secular aid indirectly but inevitably results in sectarian aid. This was clearly recognized in *Roemer* where it was said:

> The Court has not been blind to the fact that in aiding a religious institution to perform a secular task, the State frees the institution's resources to be put to sectarian ends. 426 U.S. 736.

That fact, nevertheless, was held not to be a basis for invalidating the aid. It is enough that the state does not directly aid the sectarian activities and purposes. Consequential and incidental benefits that flow from state assistance in serving its secular mission are unavoidable, but they do not invalidate the secular aid extended by the state.

The scholarship and tuition grants with which we are concerned primarily benefit the eligible students and their families. It serves the state's secular purpose in assisting a North Carolina resident student to attend a private college of his choice. Since the schools here are not pervasively religious and the students receiving assistance are not preparing for a religious vocation, the grant of tuition and scholarship assistance to them is a secular use.

Of course, the colleges receive a benefit from these funds. Without such funds they might have fewer students, be able to charge less tuition, or be forced to divert other resources to student aid. In either such event, the receipt of these funds may be said to free other college funds for sectarian purposes which, otherwise, might not be available. That, however, is the precise reasoning which the Supreme Court held in *Roemer* was insufficient for First Amendment invalidation of the program.

The plaintiffs seem to concede that if, when the scholarships are awarded and the tuition credits made, the funds were transferred to restricted accounts for clearly defined secular purposes, the plans would be unassailable. Were that done, funds in the general account would be freed for sectarian use, funds which otherwise might not be available for those purposes. There is no difference in result, whether the transfer is to a restricted account or to the general fund.

Since a transfer of these funds to a restricted account would serve no useful practical purpose, it should be avoided, for policing the expenditure of such accounts would involve the state in the operation of the colleges to a greater extent then it now is. North Carolina is now "entangled" in the operation of these colleges only minimally. It requires a minimum number of reports and certificates, and the audits it has conducted have been short and objective. A requirement that the college keep its books on a basis which would disclose the ultimate use of the funds, and the state's auditing those accounts, would be a substantial increase in the state's involvement.

In considering whether Maryland was excessively involved in the operation of the Catholic colleges there, the Court in *Roemer* considered the characteristics and nature of the colleges, the form of the aid, the funding process and the potential for political divisiveness. Particular emphasis was placed upon the first factor.

Since we have determined that Belmont Abbey and Pfeiffer College are not pervasively sectarian, that the aid primarily benefits the students rather than the colleges, and that the funding process requires little state supervision, there is little need for extensive state surveillance of the secular activities being funded. As the Supreme Court noted in *Roemer*, secular activities, in general, may be funded without further inquiry, and we have found that scholarship grants and tuition credits to students are secular in purpose. Hence, we conclude that these programs are not constitutionally deficient because the state does not require bookkeeping disclosing the ultimate expenditure of all of the funds and state supervision of such bookkeeping.

Having concluded that these two colleges are not pervasively sectarian, that the state's purpose in providing the assistance is a secular one and the use of the funds is secular, and that there is no excessive entanglement of the state with religious activities, we conclude that these programs are unassailable under the First Amendment of the Federal Constitution.

2. Is there any way of avoiding the dilemma that unrestricted governmental aid to parochial schools is unconstitutional as it aids religion, whereas restricted aid is unconstitutional on entanglement grounds? Does Justice White suggest a solution?

3. Do you agree with Justice Douglas' statement that "a state system may attempt to mold all students alike according to the views of the dominant group and to discourage the emergence of individual idiosyncracies." Is this mainly a prediction of the conduct of state systems or is it a statement that the Constitution and our societal structure permit state systems to do this? If the latter, is the statement consistent with *Barnette*, *Yoder*, and *Tinker*?

4. If state systems so act and thereby encourage minority groups to educate their own children in order to preserve their identity, why is "equilibrium," in Justice Douglas' view, achieved by government not helping to finance parochial schools, when it is financing the dominant culture public schools? Might not true equilibrium require financing of private schools? Does the Douglas view favor wealthy church groups who can afford to finance their own schools? Further issues concerning *Lemon* will be explored in the following cases and notes.

COMMITTEE FOR PUBLIC EDUCATION v. NYQUIST

Supreme Court of the United States
413 U.S. 756 (1973)

MR. JUSTICE POWELL delivered the opinion of the Court:

This case raises a challenge under the Establishment Clause of the First Amendment to the constitutionality of a recently enacted New York law which provides financial assistance, in several ways, to nonpublic elementary and secondary schools in that State. The case involves an intertwining of societal and constitutional issues of the greatest importance.

....

I

....

The first section of the challenged enactment, entitled "Health and Safety Grants for Nonpublic School Children," provides for direct money grants from the State to "qualifying" nonpublic schools to be used for "maintenance and repair of ... school facilities and equipment to ensure the health, welfare and safety of enrolled pupils." A "qualifying" school is any nonpublic, nonprofit elementary or secondary school which "has been designated during the [immediately preceding] year as serving a high concentration of pupils from low-income families for purposes of Title IV of the Federal Higher Education Act of 1965 (20 U.S.C. § 425)." Such schools are entitled to receive a grant of $30 per pupil per year, or $40 per pupil per year if the facilities are more than 25 years old. Each school is required to submit to the Commissioner of Education an audited statement of its expenditures for maintenance and repair during the preceding year, and its grant may not exceed the total of such expenses. The Commissioner is also required to ascertain the average per-pupil cost for equivalent maintenance and repair services in the public schools, and in

A. FINANCING PRIVATE SCHOOLS FOR PUBLIC BENEFIT 1317

no event may the grant to nonpublic qualifying schools exceed 50% of that figure.

....

The remainder of the challenged legislation — §§ 2 through 5 — is a single package captioned the "Elementary and Secondary Education Opportunity Program." It is composed, essentially, of two parts, a tuition grant program and a tax benefit program. Section 2 establishes a limited plan providing tuition reimbursements to parents of children attending elementary or secondary nonpublic schools. To qualify under this section the parent must have an annual taxable income of less than $5,000. The amount of reimbursement is limited to $50 for each grade school child and $100 for each high school child. Each parent is required, however, to submit to the Commissioner of Education a verified statement containing a receipted tuition bill, and the amount of state reimbursement may not exceed 50% of that figure. No restrictions are imposed on the use of the funds by the reimbursed parents.

This section, like § 1, is prefaced by a series of legislative findings designed to explain the impetus for the State's action. Expressing a dedication to the "vitality of our pluralistic society," the findings state that a "healthy competitive and diverse alternative to public education is not only desirable but indeed vital to a state and nation that have continually reaffirmed the value of individual differences." The findings further emphasize that the right to select among alternative educational systems "is diminished or even denied to children of lower-income families, whose parents, of all groups, have the least options in determining where their children are to be educated." Turning to the public schools, the findings state that any "precipitous decline in the number of nonpublic school pupils would cause a massive increase in public school enrollment and costs," an increase that would "aggravate an already serious fiscal crisis in public education" and would "seriously jeopardize the quality education for all children." Based on these premises, the statute asserts the State's right to relieve the financial burden of parents who send their children to nonpublic schools through this tuition reimbursement program. Repeating the declaration contained in § 1, the findings conclude that "such assistance is clearly secular, neutral and nonideological."

The remainder of the "Elementary and Secondary Education Opportunity Program," contained in §§ 3, 4, and 5 of the challenged law, is designed to provide a form of tax relief to those who fail to qualify for tuition reimbursement. Under these sections parents may subtract from their adjusted gross income for state income tax purposes a designated amount for each dependent for whom they have paid at least $50 in nonpublic school tuition. If the taxpayer's adjusted gross income is less than $9,000 he may subtract $1,000 for each of as many as three dependents. As the taxpayer's income rises, the amount he may subtract diminishes. Thus, if a taxpayer has adjusted gross income of $15,000, he may subtract only $400 per dependent, and if his income is $25,000 or more, no deduction is allowed. The amount of the deduction is not dependent upon how much the taxpayer actually paid for nonpublic school tuition, and is given in addition to any deductions to which the taxpayer may be entitled for other religious or charitable contributions....

....

Although no record was developed in this case, a number of pertinent generalizations may be made about the nonpublic schools which would benefit from these enactments....

... Some 700,000 to 800,000 students, constituting almost 20% of the State's entire elementary and secondary school population, attend over 2,000 nonpublic schools, approximately 85% of which are church-affiliated. And while "all or practically all" of the 280 schools entitled to receive "maintenance and repair" grants "are related to the Roman Catholic Church and teach Catholic religious doctrine to some degree," *id.* at 661, institutions qualifying under the remainder of the statute include a substantial number of Jewish, Lutheran, Episcopal, Seventh Day Adventist, and other church-affiliated schools.

Plaintiffs argued below that because of the substantially religious character of the intended beneficiaries, each of the State's three enactments offended the Establishment Clause. The District Court, in an opinion carefully canvassing this Court's recent precedents, held unanimously that § 1 (maintenance and repair grants) and § 2 (tuition reimbursement grants) were invalid. As to the income tax provisions of §§ 3, 4, and 5, however, a majority of the District Court, over the dissent of Circuit Judge Hays, held that the Establishment Clause had not been violated. Finding the provisions of the law severable, it enjoined permanently any further implementation of §§ 1 and 2 but declared the remainder of the law independently enforceable.

... We affirm the District Court insofar as it struck down §§ 1 and 2 and reverse its determination regarding §§ 3, 4, and 5.

....

Most of the cases coming to this Court raising Establishment Clause questions have involved the relationship between religion and education. Among these religion-education precedents, two general categories of cases may be identified: those dealing with religious activities within the public schools, and those involving public aid in varying forms to sectarian educational institutions. While the New York legislation places this case in the latter category, its resolution requires consideration not only of the several aid-to-sectarian-education cases but also of our other education precedents and of several important noneducation cases. For the now well defined three-part test that has emerged from our decisions is a product of considerations derived from the full sweep of the Establishment Clause cases. Taken together these decisions dictate that to pass muster under the Establishment Clause the law in question, first, must reflect a clearly secular legislative purpose, *e.g., Epperson v. Arkansas*, 393 U.S. 97 (1968), second, must have a primary effect that neither advances nor inhibits religion, *e.g., School District of Abington Township v. Schempp*, 374 U.S. 203 (1963), and, third, must avoid excessive government entanglement with religion,

A. FINANCING PRIVATE SCHOOLS FOR PUBLIC BENEFIT

e.g., Walz v. Tax Comm'n, 397 U.S. 664 (1970). *See Lemon v. Kurtzman,* 403 U.S. 602 (1971), at 612-13; *Tilton v. Richardson,* 403 U.S. 672, 678 (1971).

In applying these criteria to the three distinct forms of aid involved in this case, we need touch only briefly on the requirement of a "secular legislative purpose." As the recitation of legislative purposes appended to New York's law indicates, each measure is adequately supported by legitimate, nonsectarian state interests. We do not question the propriety, and fully secular content, of New York's interest in preserving a healthy and safe educational environment for all of its school children. And we do not doubt — indeed, we fully recognize — the validity of the State's interests in promoting pluralism and diversity among its public and nonpublic schools. Nor do we hesitate to acknowledge the reality of its concern for an already overburdened public school system that might suffer in the event that a significant percentage of children presently attending nonpublic schools should abandon those schools in favor of the public schools.

But the propriety of a legislature's purposes may not immunize from further scrutiny a law which either has a primary effect that advances religion, or which fosters excessive entanglements between Church and State. Accordingly, we must weigh each of the three aid provisions challenged here against these criteria of effect and entanglement.

A

The "maintenance and repair" provisions of § 1 authorize direct payments to nonpublic schools, virtually all of which are Roman Catholic schools in low income areas. The grants, totaling $30 or $40 per pupil depending on the age of the institution, are given largely without restriction on usage. So long as expenditures do not exceed 50% of comparable expenses in the public school system, it is possible for a sectarian elementary or secondary school to finance its entire "maintenance and repair" budget from state tax-raised funds. No attempt is made to restrict payments to those expenditures related to the upkeep of facilities used exclusively for secular purposes, nor do we think it possible within the context of these religion-oriented institutions to impose such restrictions. Nothing in the statute, for instance, bars a qualifying school from paying out of state funds the salary of employees who maintain the school chapel, or the cost of renovating classrooms in which religion is taught, or the cost of heating and lighting those same facilities. Absent appropriate restrictions on expenditures for these and similar purposes, it simply cannot be denied that this section has a primary effect that advances religion in that it subsidizes directly the religious activities of sectarian elementary and secondary schools.

....

B

New York's tuition reimbursement program also fails the "effect" test, for much the same reasons that govern its maintenance and repair grants. The state program is designed to allow direct, unrestricted grants of $50 to $100 per child (but no more than 50% of tuition actually paid) as reimbursement to parents in low-income brackets who send their children to nonpublic schools. To qualify, a parent must have earned less than $5,000 in taxable income and must present a receipted tuition bill from a nonpublic school, the bulk of which are concededly sectarian in orientation.

There can be no question that these grants could not, consistently with the Establishment Clause, be given directly to sectarian schools, since they would suffer from the same deficiency that renders invalid the grants for maintenance and repair. In the absence of an effective means of guaranteeing that the state aid derived from public funds will be used exclusively for secular, neutral, and nonideological purposes, it is clear from our cases that direct aid in whatever form is invalid.... The controlling question here, then, is whether the fact that the grants are delivered to parents rather than schools is of such significance as to compel a contrary result. The State and interventor-appellees rely on *Everson* and *Allen* for their claim that grants to parents, unlike grants to institutions, respect the "wall of separation" required by the Constitution. It is true that in those cases the Court upheld laws that provided benefits to children attending religious schools and to their parents: As noted above, in *Everson* parents were reimbursed for bus fares paid to send children to parochial schools, and in *Allen* textbooks were loaned directly to the children. But those decisions make clear that, far from providing a per se immunity from examination of the substance of the State's program, the fact that aid is disbursed to parents rather than to the schools is only one among many factors to be considered.

In *Everson*, the Court found the bus fare program analogous to the provision of services such as police and fire protection, sewage disposal, highways, and sidewalks for parochial schools. Such services, provided in common to all citizens, are "so separate and so indisputably marked off from the religious function," *id.* at 18, that they may fairly be viewed as reflections of a neutral posture toward religious institutions. *Allen* is founded upon a similar principle. The Court there repeatedly emphasized that upon the record in that case there was no indication that textbooks would be provided for anything other than purely secular courses. "Of course books are different from buses. Most bus rides have no inherent religious significance, while religious books are common. However, the language of [the law under consideration] does not authorize the loan of religious books, and the State claims no right to distribute religious literature.... Absent evidence, we cannot assume that school authorities ... are unable to distinguish between secular and religious books or that they will not honestly discharge their duties under the law."

The tuition grants here are subject to no such restrictions. There has been no endeavor "to guarantee the separation between secular and religious educational functions and to ensure that State financial aid supports only the former." Indeed, it is precisely the function of New York's law to provide assistance to private schools, the great majority of which are sectarian. By reimbursing parents for a portion of their tuition bill, the State seeks to relieve their financial burdens

A. FINANCING PRIVATE SCHOOLS FOR PUBLIC BENEFIT 1321

sufficiently to assure that they continue to have the option to send their children to religion-oriented schools. And while the other purposes for that aid — to perpetuate a pluralistic educational environment and to protect the fiscal integrity of overburdened public schools — are certainly unexceptionable, the effect of the aid is unmistakably to provide desired financial support for nonpublic, sectarian institutions.

....

Although we think it clear, for the reasons above stated, that New York's tuition grant program fares no better under the "effect" test than its maintenance and repair program, in view of the novelty of the question we will address briefly the subsidiary arguments made by the state officials and intervenors in its defense.

First, it has been suggested that it is of controlling significance that New York's program calls for *reimbursement* for tuition already paid rather than for direct contributions which are merely routed through the parents to the schools, in advance of or in lieu of payment by the parents. The parent is not a mere conduit, we are told, but is absolutely free to spend the money he receives in any manner he wishes. There is no element of coercion attached to the reimbursement, and no assurance that the money will eventually end up in the hands of religious schools. The absence of any element of coercion, however, is irrelevant to questions arising under the Establishment Clause. In *School District of Abington Township v. Schempp*, it was contended that Bible recitations in public schools did not violate the Establishment Clause because participation in such exercises was not coerced. The Court rejected that argument, noting that while proof of coercion might provide a basis for a claim under the Free Exercise Clause, it was not a necessary element of any claim under the Establishment Clause.... A similar inquiry governs here: if the grants are offered as an incentive to parents to send their children to sectarian schools by making unrestricted cash payments to them, the Establishment Clause is violated whether or not the actual dollars given eventually find their way into the sectarian institutions. Whether the grant is labeled a reimbursement, a reward or a subsidy, its substantive impact is still the same....

....

[Also], the State argues that its program of tuition grants should survive scrutiny because it is designed to promote the free exercise of religion. The State notes that only "low-income parents" are aided by this law, and without state assistance their right to have their children educated in a religious environment "is diminished or even denied." It is true, of course, that this Court has long recognized and maintained the right to choose nonpublic over public education. It is also true that a state law interfering with a parent's right to have his child educated in a sectarian school would run afoul of the Free Exercise Clause. But this Court repeatedly has recognized that tension inevitably exists between the Free Exercise and the Establishment Clauses, and that it may often not be possible to promote the former without offending the latter. As a result of this tension, our cases require the State to maintain an attitude of "neutrality," neither "advancing" nor "inhibiting" religion. In its attempt to enhance the opportunities of the poor to choose between public and nonpublic education, the State has taken a step which can only be regarded as one "advancing" religion. However great our sympathy, for the burdens experienced by those who must pay public school taxes at the same time that they support other schools because of the constraints of "conscience and discipline," *ibid.*, and notwithstanding the "high social importance" of the State's purposes, neither may justify an eroding of the limitations of the Establishment Clause now firmly implanted.

C

Sections 3, 4, and 5 establish a system for providing income tax benefits to parents of children attending New York's nonpublic schools....

... [A] taxpayer's benefit under these sections is unrelated to, and not reduced by, any deductions to which he may be entitled for charitable contributions to religious institutions.

In practical terms there would appear to be little difference, for purposes of determining whether such aid has the effect of advancing religion, between the tax benefit allowed here and the tuition grant allowed under § 2. The qualifying parent under either program receives the same form of encouragement and reward for sending his children to nonpublic schools. The only difference is that one parent receives an actual cash payment while the other is allowed to reduce by an arbitrary amount the sum he would otherwise be obliged to pay over to the State....

Appellees defend the tax portion of New York's legislative package on two grounds. First, they contend that it is of controlling significance that the grants or credits are directed to the parents rather than to the schools. This is the same argument made in support of the tuition reimbursements and rests on the same reading of the same precedents of this Court, primarily *Everson* and *Allen*. Our treatment of this issue in Part IIB, is applicable here and requires rejection of this claim. Second, appellees place their strongest reliance on *Walz v. Tax Commission*, *supra*, in which New York's property tax exemption for religious organizations was upheld. We think that *Walz* provides no support for appellees' position. Indeed, its rationale plainly compels the conclusion that New York's tax package violates the Establishment Clause.

Tax exemptions for church property enjoyed an apparently universal approval in this country both before and after the adoption of the First Amendment.... We know of no historical precedent for New York's recently promulgated tax relief program. Indeed, it seems clear that tax benefits for parents whose children attend parochial schools are a recent innovation, occasioned by the growing financial plight of such nonpublic institutions and designed, albeit unsuccessfully, to tailor state aid in a manner not incompatible with the recent decisions of this Court.

But historical acceptance without more would not alone have sufficed, as "no one acquires a vested or protected right in violation of the Constitution by long use." It was the reason underlying that long history of tolerance of tax exemptions for religion that proved controlling. A proper respect for both the Free Exercise and the Establishment Clauses compels the State to pursue a course of "neutrality" toward religion. Yet governments have not always pursued such a course, and oppression has taken many forms, one of which has been taxation of religion. Thus, if taxation was regarded as a form of "hostility" toward religion, "exemption constitute[d] a reasonable and balanced attempt to guard against those dangers." Special tax benefits, however, cannot be squared with the principle of neutrality established by the decisions of this Court. To the contrary, insofar as such benefits render assistance to parents who send their children to sectarian schools, their purpose and inevitable effect are to aid and advance those religious institutions.

Apart from its historical foundations, *Waltz* [*sic*] is a product of the same dilemma and inherent tension found in most government-aid-to-religion controversies. To be sure, the exemption of church property from taxation conferred a benefit, albeit an indirect and incidental one. Yet that "aid" was a product not of any purpose to support or to subsidize, but of a fiscal relationship designed to minimize involvement and entanglement between Church and State. "The exemption," the Court emphasized, "tends to complement and reinforce the desired separation insulating each from the other." Furthermore, "[e]limination of the exemption would tend to expand the involvement of government by giving rise to tax valuation of church property, tax liens, tax foreclosures, and the direct confrontations and conflicts that follow in the train of those legal processes." The granting of the tax benefits under the New York statute, unlike the extension of an exemption, would tend to increase rather than limit the involvement between Church and State.

One further difference between tax exemptions for church property and tax benefits for parents should be noted. The exemption challenged in *Walz* was not restricted to a class composed exclusively or even predominantly of religious institutions. Instead the exemption covered all property devoted to religious, educational or charitable purposes. As the parties here must concede, tax reductions authorized by this law flow primarily to the parents of children attending sectarian, nonpublic schools. Without intimating whether this factor alone might have controlling significance in another context in some future case, it should be apparent that in terms of the potential divisiveness of any legislative measure the narrowness of the benefited class would be an important factor.

....

III

Because we have found that the challenged sections have the impermissible effect of advancing religion, we need not consider whether such aid would result in entanglement of the State with religion in the sense of "[a] comprehensive, discriminating, and continuing state surveillance." But the importance of the competing societal interests implicated in this case prompts us to make the further observation that, apart from any specific entanglement of the State in particular religious programs, assistance of the sort here involved carries grave potential for entanglement in the broader sense of continuing political strife over aid to religion.

....

The Court recently addressed this issue specifically and fully in *Lemon v. Kurtzman*. After describing the political activity and bitter differences likely to result from the state programs there involved, the Court said:

> The potential for political divisiveness related to religious belief and practice is aggravated in these two statutory programs by the need for continuing annual appropriations and the likelihood of larger and larger demands as costs and population grow. 403 U.S. at 623.

The language of the Court applies with peculiar force to the New York statute now before us. Section 1 (grants for maintenance) and § 2 (tuition grants) will require continuing annual appropriations. Sections 3, 4, and 5 (income tax relief) will not necessarily require annual re-examination, but the pressure for frequent enlargement of the relief is predictable. All three of these programs start out at modest levels: the maintenance grant is not to exceed $40 per pupil per year in approved schools; the tuition grant provides parents not more than $50 a year for each child in the first eight grades and $100 for each child in the high school grades; and the tax benefit, though more difficult to compute, is equally modest. But we know from long experience with both Federal and State Governments that aid programs of any kind tend to become entrenched, to escalate in cost, and to generate their own aggressive constituencies. And the larger the class of recipients, the greater the pressure for accelerated increases. Moreover, the State itself, concededly anxious to avoid assuming the burden of educating children now in private and parochial schools, has a strong motivation for increasing this aid as public school costs rise and population increases. In this situation, where the underlying issue is the deeply emotional one of Church-State relationships, the potential for serious divisive political consequences needs no elaboration. And while the prospect of such divisiveness may not alone warrant the invalidation of state laws that otherwise survive the careful scrutiny required by the decisions of this Court, it is certainly a "warning signal" not to be ignored.

Our examination of New York's aid provisions, in light of all relevant considerations, compels the judgment that each, as written, has a "primary effect that advances religion" and offends the constitutional prohibition against laws "respecting the establishment of religion." We therefore affirm the three-judge court's holding as to §§ 1 and 2, and reverse as to §§ 3, 4, and 5.

It is so ordered.

MUELLER v. ALLEN

Supreme Court of the United States
463 U.S. 388 (1983)

JUSTICE REHNQUIST delivered the opinion of the Court:

Minnesota allows taxpayers, in computing their state income tax, to deduct certain expenses incurred in providing for the education of their children. Minn.Stat. § 290.09(22). The United States Court of Appeals for the Eighth Circuit held that the Establishment Clause of the First and Fourteenth Amendments was not offended by this arrangement. Because this question was reserved in *Committee for Public Education v. Nyquist*, 413 U.S. 756 (1973), and because of a conflict between the decision of the Court of Appeals for the Eighth Circuit and that of the Court of Appeals for the First Circuit in *Rhode Island Federation of Teachers v. Norberg*, 630 F.2d 855 (CA1 1980), we granted certiorari. We now affirm.

Minnesota, like every other state, provides its citizens with free elementary and secondary schooling. Minn.Stat. §§ 120.06, 120.72. It seems to be agreed that about 820,000 students attended this school system in the most recent school year. During the same year, approximately 91,000 elementary and secondary students attended some 500 privately supported schools located in Minnesota, and about 95% of these students attended schools considering themselves to be sectarian.

Minnesota, by a law originally enacted in 1955 and revised in 1976 and again in 1978, permits state taxpayers to claim a deduction from gross income for certain expenses incurred in educating their children. The deduction is limited to actual expenses incurred for the "tuition, textbooks and transportation" of dependents attending elementary or secondary schools. A deduction may not exceed $500 per dependent in grades K through six and $700 per dependent in grades seven through twelve. Minn.Stat. § 290.09.

Petitioners — certain Minnesota taxpayers — sued in the United States District Court for the District of Minnesota claiming that § 290.09(22) violated the Establishment Clause by providing financial assistance to sectarian institutions. They named as respondents the Commissioner of the Department of Revenue of Minnesota and several parents who took advantage of the tax deduction for expenses incurred in sending their children to parochial schools. The District Court granted respondent's motion for summary judgment, holding that the statute was "neutral on its face and in its application and does not have a primary effect of either advancing or inhibiting religion." 514 F.Supp. 998, 1003 (D.Minn.1981). On appeal, the Court of Appeals affirmed, concluding that the Minnesota statute substantially benefited a "broad class of Minnesota citizens."

Today's case is no exception to our oft-repeated statement that the Establishment Clause presents especially difficult questions of interpretation and application. It is easy enough to quote the few words comprising that clause — "Congress shall make no law respecting an establishment of religion." It is not at all easy, however, to apply this Court's various decisions construing the Clause to governmental programs of financial assistance to sectarian schools and the parents of children attending those schools....

One fixed principle in this field is our consistent rejection of the argument that "any program which in some manner aids an institution with a religious affiliation" violates the Establishment Clause. For example, it is now well-established that a state may reimburse parents for expenses incurred in transporting their children to school, *Everson v. Board of Education*, 330 U.S. 1 (1947), and that it may loan secular textbooks to all schoolchildren within the state, *Board of Education v. Allen*, 392 U.S. 236 (1968).

Notwithstanding the repeated approval given programs such as those in *Allen* and *Everson*, our decisions also have struck down arrangements resembling, in many respects, these forms of assistance. *See, e.g., Lemon v. Kurtzman; Levitt v. Committee for Public Education*, 413 U.S. 472 (1972); *Meek v. Pittenger*, 421 U.S. 349 (1975); *Wolman v. Walter*, 433 U.S. 229, 237-38 (1977). In this case we are asked to decide whether Minnesota's tax deduction bears greater resemblance to those types of assistance to parochial schools we have approved, or to those we have struck down. Petitioners place particular reliance on our decision in *Committee for Public Education v. Nyquist, supra*, where we held invalid a New York statute providing public funds for the maintenance and repair of the physical facilities of private schools and granting thinly disguised "tax benefits," actually amounting to tuition grants, to the parents of children attending private schools. As explained below, we conclude that § 290.09(22) bears less resemblance to the arrangement struck down in *Nyquist* than it does to assistance programs upheld in our prior decisions and those discussed with approval in *Nyquist*.

The general nature of our inquiry in this area has been guided, since the decision in *Lemon v. Kurtzman*, 403 U.S. 602 (1971), by the "three-part" test laid down in that case:

> First, the statute must have a secular legislative purpose; second, its principal or primary effect must be one that neither advances nor inhibits religion ...; finally, the statute must not foster 'an excessive government entanglement with religion.'

While this principle is well settled, our cases have also emphasized that it provides "no more than [a] helpful signpost" in dealing with Establishment Clause challenges. *Hunt v. McNair, supra*, 413 U.S. at 741. With this caveat in mind, we turn to the specific challenges raised against § 290.09(22) under the *Lemon* framework.

Little time need be spent on the question of whether the Minnesota tax deduction has a secular purpose. Under our prior decisions, governmental assistance programs have consistently survived this inquiry even when they have run afoul of other aspects of the *Lemon* framework....

A. FINANCING PRIVATE SCHOOLS FOR PUBLIC BENEFIT

A state's decision to defray the cost of educational expenses incurred by parents — regardless of the type of schools their children attend — evidences a purpose that is both secular and understandable. An educated populace is essential to the political and economic health of any community, and a state's efforts to assist parents in meeting the rising cost of educational expenses plainly serves this secular purpose of ensuring that the state's citizenry is well-educated. Similarly, Minnesota, like other states, could conclude that there is a strong public interest in assuring the continued financial health of private schools, both sectarian and non-sectarian. By educating a substantial number of students such schools relieve public schools of a correspondingly great burden — to the benefit of all taxpayers....

We turn therefore to the more difficult but related question whether the Minnesota statute has "the primary effect of advancing the sectarian aims of the nonpublic schools." ... In concluding that it does not, we find several features of the Minnesota tax deduction particularly significant. First, an essential feature of Minnesota's arrangement is the fact that § 290.09(22) is only one among many deductions — such as those for medical expenses, Minn.Stat. § 290.09(10) and charitable contributions, Minn.Stat. § 290.21 — available under the Minnesota tax laws. Our decisions consistently have recognized that traditionally "[l]egislatures have especially broad latitude in creating classifications and distinctions in tax statutes," *Regan v. Taxation with Representation*, ___ U.S. ___, 103 S.Ct. 1997 (1983), in part because the "familiarity with local conditions" enjoyed by legislators especially enables them to "achieve an equitable distribution of the tax burden." Under our prior decisions, the Minnesota legislature's judgment that a deduction for educational expenses fairly equalizes the tax burden of its citizens and encourages desirable expenditures for educational purposes is entitled to substantial deference.[6]

---

[6]Our decision in *Nyquist* is not to the contrary on this point. We expressed considerable doubt there that the "tax benefits" provided by New York law properly could be regarded as parts of a genuine system of tax laws. Plainly, the outright grants to low-income parents did not take the form of ordinary tax benefits. As to the benefits provided to middle-income parents, the Court said:

> "The amount of the deduction is unrelated to the amount of money actually expended by any parent on tuition, but is calculated on the basis of a formula contained in the statute. The formula is apparently the product of a legislative attempt to assure that each family would receive a carefully estimated net benefit, and that the tax benefit would be comparable to, and compatible with, the tuition grant for lower income families."

Indeed, the question whether a program having the elements of a "genuine tax deduction" would be constitutionally acceptable was expressly reserved in *Nyquist, supra*, 413 U.S. at 790, n. 49. While the economic consequences of the program in *Nyquist* and that in this case may be difficult to distinguish, we have recognized on other occasions that "the form of the [state's assistance to parochial schools must be examined] for the light that it casts on the substance." *Lemon v. Kurtzman, supra*, 403 U.S. at 614. The fact that the Minnesota plan embodies a "genuine tax deduction" is thus of some relevance, especially given the traditional rule of deference accorded legislative classifications in tax statutes.

Other characteristics of § 290.09(22) argue equally strongly for the provision's constitutionality. Most importantly, the deduction is available for educational expenses incurred by all parents, including those whose children attend public schools and those whose children attend non-sectarian private schools or sectarian private schools....

In this respect, as well as others, this case is vitally different from the scheme struck down in *Nyquist*. There, public assistance amounting to tuition grants, was provided only to parents of children in nonpublic schools. This fact had considerable bearing on our decision striking down the New York statute at issue; we explicitly distinguished both *Allen* and *Everson* on the grounds that "In both cases the class of beneficiaries included all schoolchildren, those in public as well as those in private schools." 413 U.S. at 782, n. 38 (emphasis in original). Moreover, we intimated that "public assistance (*e.g.*, scholarships) made available generally without regard to the sectarian-nonsectarian or public-nonpublic nature of the institution benefited," *ibid.*, might not offend the Establishment Clause. We think the tax deduction adopted by Minnesota is more similar to this latter type of program than it is to the arrangement struck down in *Nyquist*. Unlike the assistance at issue in *Nyquist*, § 290.09(22) permits all parents — whether their children attend public school or private — to deduct their children's educational expenses. As *Widmar* and our other decisions indicate, a program, like § 290.09(22), that neutrally provides state assistance to a broad spectrum of citizens is not readily subject to challenge under the Establishment Clause.

... It is true, of course, that financial assistance provided to parents ultimately has an economic effect comparable to that of aid given directly to the schools attended by their children. It is also true, however, that under Minnesota's arrangement public funds become available only as a result of numerous, private choices of individual parents of school-age children.... It is noteworthy that all but one of our recent cases invalidating state aid to parochial schools have involved the direct transmission of assistance from the state to the schools themselves. The exception, of course, was *Nyquist*, which, as discussed previously is distinguishable from this case on other grounds. Where, as here, aid to parochial schools is available only as a result of decisions of individual parents no "imprimatur of State approval," *Widmar*, at 274, can be deemed to have been conferred on any particular religion, or on religion generally.

We find it useful, in the light of the foregoing characteristics of § 290.09(22), to compare the attenuated financial benefits flowing to parochial schools from the section to the evils against which the Establishment Clause was designed to protect. These dangers are well-described by our statement that "what is at stake as a matter of policy [in Establishment Clause cases] is preventing that kind and degree of government involvement in religious life that, as history teaches us, is

A. FINANCING PRIVATE SCHOOLS FOR PUBLIC BENEFIT 1329

apt to lead to strife and frequently strain a political system to the breaking point." ... It is important, however, to "keep these issues in perspective":

> At this point in the 20th century we are quite far removed from the dangers that prompted the Framers to include the Establishment Clause in the Bill of Rights. The risk of significant religious or denominational control over our democratic processes — or even of deep political division along religious lines — is remote, and when viewed against the positive contributions of sectarian schools, and such risk seems entirely tolerable in light of the continuing oversight of this Court.

The Establishment Clause of course extends beyond prohibition of a state church or payment of state funds to one or more churches. We do not think, however, that its prohibition extends to the type of tax deduction established by Minnesota. The historic purposes of the clause simply do not encompass the sort of attenuated financial benefit, ultimately controlled by the private choices of individual parents, that eventually flows to parochial schools from the neutrally available tax benefit at issue in this case.

Petitioners argue that, notwithstanding the facial neutrality of § 290.09(22), in application the statute primarily benefits religious institutions. Petitioners rely, as they did below, on a statistical analysis of the type of persons claiming the tax deduction. They contend that most parents of public school children incur no tuition expenses, *see* Minn.Stat. § 120.06, and that other expenses deductible under § 290.09(22) are negligible in value; moreover, they claim that 96% of the children in private schools in 1978-1979 attended religiously-affiliated institutions. Because of all this, they reason, the bulk of deductions taken under § 290.09(22) will be claimed by parents of children in sectarian schools. Respondents reply that petitioners have failed to consider the impact of deductions for items such as transportation, summer school tuition, tuition paid by parents whose children attended schools outside the school districts in which they resided, rental or purchase costs for a variety of equipment, and tuition for certain types of instruction not ordinarily provided in public schools.

We need not consider these contentions in detail. We would be loath to adopt a rule grounding the constitutionality of a facially neutral law on annual reports reciting the extent to which various classes of private citizens claimed benefits under the law. Such an approach would scarcely provide the certainty that this field stands in need of, nor can we perceive principled standards by which such statistical evidence might be evaluated....

Finally, private educational institutions, and parents paying for their children to attend these schools, make special contributions to the areas in which they operate. "Parochial schools, quite apart from their sectarian purpose, have provided an educational alternative for millions of young Americans; they often afford wholesome competition with our public schools; and in some States they relieve substantially the tax burden incident to the operation of public schools." *Wolman*, at 262 (POWELL, J., concurring and dissenting). If parents of children in private schools choose to take especial advantage of the relief provided by § 290.09(22), it is no doubt due to the fact that they bear a particularly great financial burden in educating their children. More fundamentally, whatever unequal effect may be attributed to the statutory classification can fairly be regarded as a rough return for the benefits, discussed above, provided to the state and all taxpayers by parents sending their children to parochial schools. In the light of all this, we believe it wiser to decline to engage in the type of empirical inquiry into those persons benefited by state law which petitioners urge.

Thus, we hold that the Minnesota tax deduction for educational expenses satisfies the primary effect inquiry of our Establishment Clause cases.

Turning to the third part of the *Lemon* inquiry, we have no difficulty in concluding that the Minnesota statute does not "excessively entangle" the state in religion. The only plausible source of the "comprehensive, discriminating, and continuing state surveillance," 403 U.S. at 619, necessary to run afoul of this standard would lie in the fact that state officials must determine whether particular textbooks qualify for a deduction. In making this decision, state officials must disallow deductions taken from "instructional books and materials used in the teaching of religious tenets, doctrines or worship, the purpose of which is to inculcate such tenets, doctrines or worship." Minn.Stat. § 290.09 (22). Making decisions such as this does not differ substantially from making the types of decisions approved in earlier opinions of this Court. In *Board of Education v. Allen*, 392 U.S. 236 (1968), for example, the Court upheld the loan of secular textbooks to parents or children attending nonpublic schools; though state officials were required to determine whether particular books were or were not secular, the system was held not to violate the Establishment Clause. *See also Wolman v. Walter, supra; Meek v. Pittenger, supra*. The same result follows in this case.

For the foregoing reasons, the judgment of the Court of appeals is

Affirmed.

JUSTICE MARSHALL, with whom JUSTICE BRENNAN, JUSTICE BLACKMUN and JUSTICE STEVENS join, dissenting:

The Establishment Clause of the First Amendment prohibits a State from subsidizing religious education, whether it does so directly or indirectly. In my view, this principle of neutrality forbids not only the tax benefits struck down in *Committee for Public Education v. Nyquist*, 413 U.S. 756 (1973), but any tax benefit, including the tax deduction at issue here, which subsidizes tuition payments to sectarian schools. I also believe that the Establishment Clause prohibits the tax deductions that Minnesota authorizes for the cost of books and other instructional materials used for sectarian purposes.

. . . .

1. "We would be loath to adopt a rule grounding the constitutionality of a facially neutral law on annual reports reciting the extent to which various classes

of private citizens claimed benefits under the law." *Mueller*, 463 U.S. at 401. Compare this to the following statement in *Rhode Island Fed'n of Teachers v. Norberg*, 630 F.2d 855 (1st Cir. 1980):

> The pivotal factor in determining the constitutionality of tax devices affecting religious institutions or religious education has been the breadth of the affected class. In all but one of the cases holding tax credits or deductions for educational expenses unconstitutional, the courts have found that most of the qualifying schools were sectarian. *Norberg*, 630 F.2d at 861.

The *Norberg* court appears to base its decision, holding the financial benefits unconstitutional, on the fact that so many of the benefitted parties attended sectarian schools. *Mueller* says courts should not count numbers. The *Mueller* decision wins the legal debate, due to Supreme Court superiority. Which decision is more logical?

J. Edward Goff, in an article for the Villanova Law Review, questions the Supreme Court's move in rejecting the statistical data. The majority expressed a concern that there exist only dim "lines of demarcation in this extraordinarily sensitive area of constitutional law." *Mueller*, at 393 (quoting *Lemon v. Kurtzman*, 403 U.S. 602, 609). Yet it refused to recognize the data relied on by the taxpayers and the dissenting opinion. See 29 Vill. L. Rev. 505 (1983-1984).

2. Similar thoughts are expressed by Elizabeth Baergen in, *Tuition Tax Deductions and Credits in Light of* Mueller v. Allen, 31 Wayne L. Rev. 157 (1984):*

> *Mueller v. Allen* held that facially neutral income tax deductions for educational expenses are not an unconstitutional infringement of the establishment clause. This Note suggests that tax credit provisions, which could entirely subsidize private sectarian education, should be carefully scrutinized for an unconstitutional legislative purpose. Such an impermissible purpose should be found if the credit is limited to private educational expenses or if the credit gives such an unbalanced benefit to the parents of private schoolchildren that it is clearly intended as a tax incentive to subsidize private, primarily sectarian education. Likewise, a credit limited to private school expenses would suffer an unconstitutional primary effect of advancing religious education, unmitigated by the deference shown by courts to true legislative tax enactments which equitably allocate tax burdens based upon a definition of net income. Moreover, tax credit provisions which are facially neutral but only supply a *de minimis* benefit to parents of public school children should be subject to statistical analysis to determine the true beneficiaries of the program and expose the facial neutrality as a facade. Finally, the Court should not limit its considerations of potential

---

*Copyright © 1984 by Wayne Law Review. Reprinted with permission.

political divisiveness when considering indirect tax benefit provisions. Rather, if a tax measure is truly an effort to fairly and equitably distribute the tax burden, there should be no real potential for political divisiveness.

Thus, if a tax credit for educational expenses is to pass constitutional muster, it should reflect the following characteristics of the Minnesota tax deduction upheld in *Mueller*: first, it must be an effort to distribute the tax burden equitably rather than a tax incentive which subsidizes private, primarily sectarian, education; second, it must neutrally provide benefits to all parents of schoolchildren, public as well as private, and the benefit to public parents must be more than a mere pretext; finally, it must not have a potential for political divisiveness along religious lines.

3. Whether or not you agree with the Court in *Mueller*, is it correct in basing its decision, in part, on the recognition that non-public schools relieve some of the burden on public schools?

4. A recent district court case addressed similar issues. In *Luthens v. Blair*, 788 F. Supp. 1032 (S.D. Iowa 1992), the court upheld a statute granting tax benefits for payment of tuition and purchase of textbooks. The statute was held not to violate the Establishment Clause, the Free Exercise Clause, or the Equal Protection Clause.

5. A unanimous Supreme Court approved another recent case in which state tax dollars were indirectly distributed to a religious organization because of an independent choice by a private citizen. In *Witters v. Department of Services for Blind*, 474 U.S. 481 (1986), the Court held that state moneys could be used to fund the tuition of a Bible college student for training in the ministry, pursuant to a program of vocational assistance for the visually disabled. Similar to the "child benefit theory" first enunciated in *Cochran v. Louisiana State Bd. of Educ.*, 281 U.S. 370 (1930), and repeated in a line of cases in this chapter, including a similar higher education case, *Committee for Pub. Educ. and Religious Liberty v. Nyquist*, 413 U.S. 756 (1973), the Court reiterated that the recipient institution only receives the funds through the conduit student or his or her family. Moreover, the education received is "'made available generally without regard to the sectarian-non-sectarian, or public-non-public nature of the institution benefited,' and is in no way skewed toward religion." *Witters*, at 487, quoting *Nyquist* at 782-83 n. 38. Finally, the Court determined that the program passed constitutional muster because there was no financial incentive for the student to undertake a sectarian education and "nothing in the record indicates that ... any significant portion of the aid expended under the ... program as a whole will end up flowing to religious education." *Witters*, at 488.

6. As noted in Chapter 15, Justices on the current Supreme Court have suggested modifications in the *Lemon* Test or its outright elimination as regards Establishment Clause cases. Justice O'Connor, for example voiced modification of *Lemon* in *Lynch v. Donnelly*, 465 U.S. 668 (1984) (O'Connor, J. concurring), a case concerning the constitutionality of a nativity scene display on public

A. FINANCING PRIVATE SCHOOLS FOR PUBLIC BENEFIT

property during the December holiday season. O'Connor reasoned that a government celebration of Christmas is so common that it is generally not understood to be an endorsement of religion. She went on to explain that the nativity scene, a traditional symbol of the holiday, is commonly displayed with purely secular symbols. *Id.* at 692. Justice O'Connor advocated an "endorsement test," grafted on to the primary or principal effects of *Lemon*, which she contends asks whether the government's actual purpose is to endorse or disapprove of religion. *Id.* at 691. She argued that the strength of this application was that it avoided invalidation of some laws that the Court has upheld even though they may advance or inhibit religion, such as tax exemptions for religious organizations. *Id.*

In another concurring opinion, O'Connor applied her "endorsement test." Like the cases in the current chapter, at issue in *School Dist. of City of Grand Rapids v. Ball*, 473 U.S. 373 (1985), were programs offered by the school district in which parochial school students could attend public school classes during the regular school day ("shared time") or shortly after school ("Community Education"). Justice William Brennan, writing for the Court, applied the "*Lemon* Test" and held that the program had the primary or principal effect of advancing religion. Justice O'Connor, concurring in part, distinguished between a parochial school teacher paid by the state, which could violate the Establishment Clause, and a public school teacher who taught parochial school students, which would not run afoul of the Establishment Clause. *Id.* at 399-400 (O'Connor, J. concurring in part and dissenting in part.)

Recall also Justice Anthony Kennedy's alternative to *Lemon*. In *Lee v. Weisman*, 112 S. Ct. 2649 (1992) (*see* Chapter 15), the Court asked whether a benediction or invocation invoking a deity and delivered by clergy at a public school ceremony had the principal effect of advancing religion in violation of the Establishment Clause. In his majority opinion, Justice Kennedy used his "coercion test." The test holds that it is unconstitutional for public officials to be involved in religious activity that induces students to participate through public or peer pressure. This includes a prohibition against direct pressure as well as indirect or subtle coercion that is psychological or social in origin. *Id.* at 2658-59. The majority in *Weisman* held that inasmuch as graduation is a ceremony that students are subtly obligated to attend, state authorized prayer at graduation coerces some students to compromise their beliefs. *Id.* at 2661.

Readers will find no solace in recent opinions by the Court as regards the Establishment Clause. In *Board of Educ. v. Grumet*, 114 S. Ct. 2481 (1994), presented in Chapter 15, over six different opinions were rendered in a 6-3 decision striking down a New York statute establishing a public school district whose boundaries coincided with a devoutly religious village. The school district was created so as to provide mandated special education services to disabled students who were members of a sect of Hasidic Jews. The sect refused to send its children to the public schools in the area because of its religious beliefs and differences shown through attire, language, customs, etc.

The Court found that the creation of the Kiryas Joel Village School District represented an Establishment Clause violation because of a delegation of government authority to a sectarian group and of the absence of government impartiality toward religion. In doing so Justice Souter, in his plurality opinion, did not cite precisely to the *"Lemon Test"*; Justice Kennedy did speak to the "coercion test," but did not join in Souter's opinion; Justice O'Connor joined the opinion, and, in addition, rendered a concurring opinion using her "endorsement test." Only Justice Blackmun stated that *Grumet* rested exclusively on *Lemon*. In a dissenting opinion Justice Scalia, joined by Chief Justice Rehnquist and Justice Thomas, criticized the veiled use of the *Lemon* test declaring it "utterly meaningless" and used when it is convenient for the Court.

B. PRIVATE SCHOOLS: GOVERNMENT ACTION AND RACIAL SEGREGATION

RUNYON v. McCRARY
Supreme Court of the United States
427 U.S. 160 (1976)

MR. JUSTICE STEWART delivered the opinion of the Court:

The principal issue presented by these consolidated cases is whether a federal law, namely 42 U.S.C. § 1981, prohibits private schools from excluding qualified children solely because they are Negroes.

I

The respondents in No. 75-62, Michael McCrary and Colin Gonzales, are Negro children. By their parents, they filed a class action against the petitioners in No. 75-62, Russell and Katheryne Runyon, who are the proprietors of Bobbe's Private School in Arlington, Va. Their complaint alleged that they had been prevented from attending the school because of the petitioners' policy of denying admission to Negroes, in violation of 42 U.S.C. § 1981 and Title II of the Civil Rights Act of 1964, 78 Stat. 243, 42 U.S.C. § 2000a *et seq*. They sought declaratory and injunctive relief and damages. On the same day Colin Gonzales, the respondent in No. 75-66, filed a similar complaint by his parents against the petitioner in No. 75-66, Fairfax-Brewster School, Inc., located in Fairfax County, Va. The petitioner in No. 75-278, the Southern Independent School Association, sought and was granted permission to intervene as a party defendant in the suit against the Runyons. That organization is a nonprofit association composed of six state private school associations, and represents 395 private schools. It is stipulated that many of these schools deny admission to Negroes.

The suits were consolidated for trial. The findings of the District Court, which were left undisturbed by the Court of Appeals, were as follows. Bobbe's School opened in 1958 and grew from an initial enrollment of five students to 200 in 1972. A day camp was begun in 1967 and has averaged 100 children per year. The Fairfax-Brewster School commenced operations in 1955 and opened a summer day camp in 1956. A total of 223 students were enrolled at the school during the 1972-1973 academic year, and 236 attended the day camp in the summer of 1972. Neither school has ever accepted a Negro child for any of its programs.

In response to a mailed brochure addressed "resident" and an advertisement in the "Yellow Pages" of the telephone directory, Mr. and Mrs. Gonzales telephoned and then visited the Fairfax-Brewster School in May 1969. After the visit, they submitted an application for Colin's admission to the day camp. The school responded with a form letter, which stated that the school was "unable to accommodate [Colin's] application." Mr. Gonzales telephoned the school. Fairfax-Brewster's Chairman of the Board explained that the reason for Colin's rejection was that the school was not integrated. Mr. Gonzales then telephoned Bobbe's School, from which the family had also received in the mail a brochure addressed to "resident." In response to a question concerning that school's admissions policies, he was told that only members of the Caucasian race were accepted. In August 1972, Mrs. McCrary telephoned Bobbe's School in response to an advertisement in the telephone book. She inquired about nursery school facilities for her son, Michael. She also asked if the school was integrated. The answer was no.

Upon these facts, the District Court found that the Fairfax-Brewster School had rejected Colin Gonzales' application on account of his race and that Bobbe's school had denied both children admission on racial grounds. The court held that 42 U.S.C. § 1981 makes illegal the schools' racially discriminatory admissions policies. It therefore enjoined Fairfax-Brewster School and Bobbe's School and the member schools of the Southern Independent School Association from discriminating against applicants for admission on the basis of race. The court awarded compensatory relief to Mr. and Mrs. McCrary, Michael McCrary, and Colin Gonzales. In a previous ruling the court had held that the damages claim of Mr. and Mrs. Gonzales was barred by Virginia's two-year statute of limitations for personal injury actions, "borrowed" for § 1981 suits filed in that State....

The Court of Appeals for the Fourth Circuit, sitting *en banc*, affirmed the District Court's grant of equitable and compensatory relief and its ruling as to the applicable statute of limitations....

....

II

It is worth noting at the outset some of the questions that these cases do not present. They do not present any question of the right of a private social organization to limit its membership on racial or any other grounds. They do not present any question of the right of a private school to limit its student body to boys, to girls, or to adherents of a particular religious faith, since 42 U.S.C. § 1981 is in no way addressed to such categories of selectivity. They do not even present the application of § 1981 to private sectarian schools that practice *racial* exclusion on religious grounds. Rather, these cases present only two basic questions: whether § 1981 prohibits private, commercially operated, nonsectarian schools from denying admission to prospective students because they are Negroes, and, if so, whether that federal law is constitutional as so applied.

A. *Applicability of § 1981*

It is now well established that § 1 of the Civil Rights Act of 1866, 14 Stat. 27, 42 U.S.C. § 1981, prohibits racial discrimination in the making and enforcement of private contracts. *See Johnson v. Railway Express Agency*, 421 U.S. 454, 459-60; *Tillman v. Wheaton-Haven Recreation Assn.*, 410 U.S. 431, 439-40. *Cf. Jones v. Alfred H. Mayer Co.*, 392 U.S. 409, 441-43, n. 78.

In *Jones* the Court held that the portion of § 1 of the Civil Rights Act of 1866 presently codified as 42 U.S.C. § 1982 prohibits racial discrimination in the sale or rental of real or personal property. Relying on the legislative history of § 1, from which both § 1981 and § 1982 derive, the Court concluded that Congress intended to prohibit "all racial discrimination, private and public, in the sale ... of property," 392 U.S. at 437, and that this prohibition was within Congress' power under § 2 of the Thirteenth Amendment "rationally to determine what are the badges and the incidents of slavery, and ... to translate that determination into effective legislation."

As the Court indicated in *Jones*, that holding necessarily implied that the portion of § 1 of the 1866 Act presently codified as 42 U.S.C. § 1981 likewise reaches purely private acts of racial discrimination. The statutory holding in *Jones* private acts of racial discrimination. The statutory holding in *Jones* was that the "[1866] Act was designed to do just what its terms suggest: to prohibit all racial discrimination, whether or not under color of law, with respect to the rights enumerated therein — including the right to purchase or lease property," 392 U.S. at 436. One of the "rights enumerated" in § 1 is "the same right ... to make and enforce contracts ... as is enjoyed by white citizens ...." 14 Stat. 27. Just as in *Jones* a Negro's § 1 right to purchase property on equal terms with whites was violated when a private person refused to sell to the prospective purchaser solely because he was a Negro, so also a Negro's § 1 right to "make and enforce contracts" is violated if a private offeror refuses to extend to a Negro, solely because he is a Negro, the same opportunity to enter into contracts as he extends to white offerees.

The applicability of the holding in *Jones* to § 1981 was confirmed by this Court's decisions in *Tillman v. Wheaton-Haven Recreation Assn.*, *supra*, and *Johnson v. Railway Express Agency, Inc.*, *supra*....

It is apparent that the racial exclusion practiced by the Fairfax-Brewster School and Bobbe's Private School amounts to a classic violation of § 1981. The parents of Colin Gonzales and Michael McCrary sought to enter into contractual relationships with Bobbe's Private School for educational services. Colin Gonzales' parents sought to enter into a similar relationship with the Fairfax-Brewster School. Under those contractual relationships, the schools would have received payments for services rendered, and the prospective students would have received instruction in return for those payments. The educational services of Bobbe's Private School and the Fairfax-Brewster School were advertised and offered to members of the general public. But neither school offered services on an equal basis to white and non-white students....

The petitioning schools and school association argue principally that § 1981 does not reach private acts of racial discrimination. That view is wholly inconsistent with *Jones'* interpretation of the legislative history of § 1 of the Civil Rights Act of 1866, an interpretation that was reaffirmed in *Sullivan v. Little Hunting Park, Inc.*, 396 U.S. 229, and again in *Tillman v. Wheaton-Haven Recreation Assn., supra.* And this consistent interpretation of the law necessarily requires the conclusion that § 1981, like § 1982, reaches private conduct. *See Tillman v. Wheaton-Haven Recreation Assn.*, 410 U.S. at 439-40; *Johnson v. Railway Express Agency*, 421 U.S. at 459-60.

It is noteworthy that Congress in enacting the Equal Employment Opportunity Act of 1972, 86 Stat. 103, as amended, 42 U.S.C. § 2000e *et seq.* (1970 ed., Supp. IV), specifically considered and rejected an amendment that would have repealed the Civil Rights Act of 1866, as interpreted by this Court in *Jones*, insofar as it affords private-sector employees a right of action based on racial discrimination in employment. There could hardly be a clearer indication of congressional agreement with the view that § 1981 does reach private acts of racial discrimination. *Cf. Flood v. Kuhn*, 407 U.S. 258, 269-85; *Joint Industry Board v. United States*, 391 U.S. 224, 228-29. In these circumstances there is no basis for deviating from the well-settled principles of *stare decisis* applicable to this Court's construction of federal statutes.

B. *Constitutionality of § 1981 as Applied*

The question remains whether § 1981, as applied, violates constitutionally protected rights of free association and privacy, or a parent's right to direct the education of his children.

1. *Freedom of Association*

In *NAACP v. Alabama*, 357 U.S. 449, and similar decisions, the Court has recognized a First Amendment right "to engage in association for the advancement of beliefs and ideas...." That right is protected because it promotes and may well be essential to the "[e]ffective advocacy of both public and private points of view, particularly controversial ones" that the First Amendment is designed to foster.

From this principle it may be assumed that parents have a First Amendment right to send their children to educational institutions that promote the belief that racial segregation is desirable, and that the children have an equal right to attend such institutions. But it does not follow that the *practice* of excluding racial minorities from such institutions is also protected by the same principle. As the Court stated in *Norwood v. Harrison*, 413 U.S. 455, "the Constitution ... places no value on discrimination," *id.* at 469, and while "[i]nvidious private discrimination may be characterized as a form of exercising freedom of association protected by the First Amendment ... it has never been accorded affirmative constitutional protections. And even some private discrimination is subject to special remedial legislation in certain circumstances under § 2 of the Thirteenth Amendment; Congress has made such discrimination unlawful in other significant contexts." *Id.* at 470. In any event, as the Court of Appeals noted, "there is no showing that discontinuance of [the] discriminatory admission practices would inhibit in any way the teaching in these schools of any ideas or dogma." 515 F.2d at 1087.

2. *Parental Rights*

In *Meyer v. Nebraska*, 262 U.S. 390, the Court held that the liberty protected by the Due Process Clause of the Fourteenth Amendment includes the right "to acquire useful knowledge, to marry, establish a home and bring up children," *id.* at 399, and, concomitantly, the right to send one's children to a private school that offers specialized training — in that case, instruction in the German language. In *Pierce v. Society of Sisters*, 268 U.S. 510, the Court applied "the doctrine of *Meyer v. Nebraska*," *id.* at 534, to hold unconstitutional an Oregon law requiring the parent, guardian, or other person having custody of a child between 8 and 16 years of age to send that child to public school on pain of criminal liability. The Court thought it "entirely plain that the [statute] unreasonably interferes with the liberty of parents and guardians to direct the upbringing and education of children under their control." *Id.* at 534-35. In *Wisconsin v. Yoder*, 406 U.S. 205, the Court stressed the limited scope of *Pierce*, pointing out that it lent "no support to the contention that parents may replace state educational requirements with their own idiosyncratic views of what knowledge a child needs to be a productive and happy member of society" but rather "held simply that while a State may posit [educational] standards, it may not pre-empt the educational process by requiring children to attend public schools." *Id.* at 239....

It is clear that the present application of § 1981 infringes no parental right recognized in *Meyer, Pierce, Yoder,* or *Norwood*. No challenge is made to the petitioner schools' right to operate or the right of parents to send their children to a particular private school rather than a public school. Nor do these cases involve a challenge to the subject matter which is taught at any private school. Thus, the Fairfax-Brewster School and Bobbe's Private School and members of the intervenor association remain presumptively free to inculate whatever values and standards they deem desirable. *Meyer* and its progeny entitle them to no more.

3. *The Right of Privacy*

The Court has held that in some situations the Constitution confers a right of privacy. *See Roe v. Wade*, 410 U.S. 113, 152-53; *Eisenstadt v. Baird*, 405 U.S.

438, 453; *Stanley v. Georgia*, 394 U.S. 557, 564-65; *Griswold v. Connecticut*, 381 U.S. 479, 484-85.

While the application of § 1981 to the conduct at issue here — a private school's adherence to a racially discriminatory admissions policy — does not represent governmental intrusion into the privacy of the home or a similarly intimate setting, it does implicate parental interests. These interests are related to the procreative rights protected in *Roe v. Wade, supra*, and *Griswold v. Connecticut, supra*. A person's decision whether to bear a child and a parent's decision concerning the manner in which his child is to be educated may fairly be characterized as exercises of familial rights and responsibilities. But it does not follow that because government is largely or even entirely precluded from regulating the child-bearing decision, it is similarly restricted by the Constitution from regulating the implementation of parental decisions concerning a child's education.

The Court has repeatedly stressed that while parents have a constitutional right to send their children to private schools and a constitutional right to select private schools that offer specialized instruction, they have no constitutional right to provide their children with private school education unfettered by reasonable government regulation. *See Wisconsin v. Yoder, supra*, at 213; *Pierce v. Society of Sisters, supra*, at 534; *Meyer v. Nebraska*, 262 U.S. at 402. Indeed, the Court in *Pierce* expressly acknowledged "the power of the State reasonably to regulate all schools, to inspect, supervise and examine them, their teachers and pupils.... "268 U.S. at 534. *See also Prince v. Massachusetts*, 321 U.S. 158, 166.

Section 1981, as applied to the conduct at issue here, constitutes an exercise of federal legislative power under § 2 of the Thirteenth Amendment fully consistent with *Meyer*, *Pierce*, and the cases that followed in their wake. As the Court held in *Jones v. Alfred H. Mayer Co., supra*: "It has never been doubted ... 'that the power vested in Congress to enforce [the Thirteenth Amendment] by appropriate legislation' ... includes the power to enact laws 'direct and primary, operating upon the acts of individuals, whether sanctioned by State legislation or not.'" 392 U.S. at 438. The prohibition of racial discrimination that interferes with the making and enforcement of contracts for private educational services furthers goals closely analogous to those served by § 1981's elimination of racial discrimination in the making of private employment contracts and, more generally, by § 1982's guarantee that "a dollar in the hands of a Negro will purchase the same thing as a dollar in the hands of a white man." *Jones v. Alfred H. Mayer Co., supra*, at 443.

....

For the reasons stated in this opinion, the judgment of the Court of Appeals is in all respects affirmed.

It is so ordered.

MR. JUSTICE WHITE, with whom MR. JUSTICE REHNQUIST joins, dissenting:

We are urged here to extend the meaning and reach of 42 U.S.C. § 1981 so as to establish a general prohibition against a private individual's or institution's refusing to enter into a contract with another person because of that person's race. Section 1981 has been on the books since 1870 and to so hold for the first time would be contrary to the language of the section, to its legislative history, and to the clear dictum of this Court in the *Civil Rights Cases*, 109 U.S. 3, 16-17 (1883), almost contemporaneously with the passage of the statute, that the section reaches only discriminations imposed by state law. The majority's belated discovery of a congressional purpose which escaped this Court only a decade after the statute was passed and which escaped all other federal courts for almost 100 years is singularly unpersuasive. I therefore respectfully dissent.

....

[The concurring opinions of MR. JUSTICE POWELL AND MR. JUSTICE STEVENS are not reproduced.]

---

1. *See also Brumfield v. Dodd*, 405 F. Supp. 338 (E.D. La. 1975), where black students who attended public schools in Louisiana brought a civil rights action against state and local education officials to challenge a state statutory scheme whereby the state provided books, school materials, and funds for student transportation to students attending all-white segregated private schools in Louisiana. The three-judge district court ruled that provision of such services to "... racially segregated schools which serve as a haven to those leaving racially integrated public schools are in violation of rights vested in plaintiffs and their class by the Fourteenth Amendment to the United States Constitution." Similarly, in *Brown v. Dade Christian Schs., Inc.*, 556 F.2d 310 (5th Cir. 1977), *cert. denied*, 434 U.S. 1063 (1978), the Fifth Circuit affirmed the district court's ruling in favor of black parents and their school-age children who brought an action against a private sectarian school, seeking damages and an injunction to prevent the school from barring the children's enrollment solely on the grounds of their race. The court held that the evidence, including the absence of references to school desegregation in written literature stating the church's beliefs, indicated the school's policy of racial segregation was not one adopted in the exercise of religion, but was social or political in nature.

2. *Runyon v. McCrary* was preceded by another decision of the United States Supreme Court which held that a Mississippi state statute authorizing the government purchase of textbooks for private schools with racially discriminatory admissions policies was unconstitutional. In *Norwood v. Harrison*, 413 U.S. 455 (1973), the Court determined that no state may "provide tangible assistance to students attending private schools that are racially discriminatory." Specifically, "[r]acial discrimination in state-operated schools is barred by the Constitution and [ipso facto] ... a state may not induce, encourage or promote private persons to accomplish what is constitutionally forbidden to accomplish."

BOB JONES UNIVERSITY v. UNITED STATES

Supreme Court of the United States
461 U.S. 574 (1983)

CHIEF JUSTICE BURGER delivered the opinion of the Court:

We granted certiorari to decide whether petitioners, nonprofit private schools that prescribe and enforce racially discriminatory admissions standards on the basis of religious doctrine, qualify as tax-exempt organizations under § 501(c)(3) of the Internal Revenue Code of 1954.

I

Until 1970, the Internal Revenue Service granted tax-exempt status to private schools, without regard to their racial admissions policies, under § 501(c)(3) of the Internal Revenue Code, 26 U.S.C. § 501(c)(3), and granted charitable deductions for contributions to such schools under § 170 of the Code, 26 U.S.C. § 170.

On January 12, 1970, a three-judge District Court for the District of Columbia issued a preliminary injunction prohibiting the IRS from according tax-exempt status to private schools in Mississippi that discriminated as to admissions on the basis of race. *Green v. Kennedy*, 309 F.Supp. 1127 (D.D.C.), *app. dismissed sub nom. Cannon v. Green*, 398 U.S. 956 (1970). Thereafter, in July 1970, the IRS concluded that it could "no longer legally justify allowing tax-exempt status [under § 501(c)(3)] to private schools which practice racial discrimination." ... At the same time, the IRS announced that it could not "treat gifts to such schools as charitable deductions for income tax purposes [under § 170]." ...

On June 30, 1971, the three-judge District Court issued its opinion on the merits of the Mississippi challenge. *Green v. Connally*, 330 F.Supp. 1150 (D.D.C.), *aff'd sub nom. Coit v. Green*, 404 U.S. 997 (1971) (*per curiam*). That court approved the IRS' amended construction of the Tax Code. The court also held that racially discriminatory private schools were not entitled to exemption under § 501(c)(3) and that donors were not entitled to deductions for contributions to such schools under § 170. The court permanently enjoined the Commissioner of Internal Revenue from approving tax-exempt status for any school in Mississippi that did not publicly maintain a policy of nondiscrimination.

The revised policy on discrimination was formalized in Revenue Ruling 71-447, 1971-2 Cum.Bull. 230:

> Both the courts and the Internal Revenue Service have long recognized that the statutory requirement of being 'organized and operated exclusively for religious, charitable, ... or educational purposes' was intended to express the basic common law concept [of 'charity'].... All charitable trusts,

educational or otherwise, are subject to the requirement that the purpose of the trust may not be illegal or contrary to public policy.

Based on the "national policy to discourage racial discrimination in education," the IRS ruled that "a private school not having a racially nondiscriminatory policy as to students is not 'charitable' within the common law concepts reflected in sections 170 and 501(c)(3) of the Code."

The application of the IRS construction of these provisions to petitioners, two private schools with racially discriminatory admissions policies, is now before us.

B

No. 81-3, Bob Jones University v. United States

Bob Jones University is a nonprofit corporation located in Greenville, South Carolina. Its purpose is "to conduct an institution of learning ... giving special emphasis to the Christian religion and the ethics revealed in the Holy Scriptures." The corporation operates a school with an enrollment of approximately 5,000 students, from kindergarten through college and graduate school. Bob Jones University is not affiliated with any religious denomination, but is dedicated to the teaching and propagation of its fundamentalist Christian religious beliefs. It is both a religious and educational institution. Its teachers are required to be devout Christians, and all courses at the University are taught according to the Bible. Entering students are screened as to their religious beliefs, and their public and private conduct is strictly regulated by standards promulgated by University authorities.

The sponsors of the University genuinely believe that the Bible forbids interracial dating and marriage. To effectuate these views, Negroes were completely excluded until 1971. From 1971 to May 1975, the University accepted no applications from unmarried Negroes, but did accept applications from Negroes married within their race.

Following the decision of the United States Court of Appeals for the Fourth Circuit in *McCrary v. Runyon*, 515 F.2d 1082 (CA4 1975), *aff'd* 427 U.S. 160 (1976), prohibiting racial exclusion from private schools, the University revised its policy. Since May 29, 1975, the University has permitted unmarried Negroes to enroll; but a disciplinary rule prohibits interracial dating and marriage. That rule reads:

> There is to be no interracial dating
> 1. Students who are partners in an interracial marriage will be expelled.
> 2. Students who are members of or affiliated with any group or organization which holds as one of its goals or advocates interracial marriage will be expelled.
> 3. Students who date outside their own race will be expelled.

4. Students who espouse, promote, or encourage others to violate the University's dating rules and regulations will be expelled.

The University continues to deny admission to applicants engaged in an interracial marriage or known to advocate interracial marriage or dating.

Until 1970, the IRS extended tax-exempt status to Bob Jones University under § 501(c)(3). By the letter of November 30, 1970, that followed the injunction issued in *Green v. Kennedy, supra,* the IRS formally notified the University of the change in IRS policy, and announced its intention to challenge the tax-exempt status of private schools practicing racial discrimination in their admissions policies.

After failing to obtain an assurance of tax exemption through administrative means, the University instituted an action in 1971 seeking to enjoin the IRS from revoking the school's tax-exempt status. That suit culminated in *Bob Jones University v. Simon,* 416 U.S. 725 (1974), in which this Court held that the Anti-Injunction Act of the Internal Revenue Code, 26 U.S.C. § 7421(a), prohibited the University from obtaining judicial review by way of injunctive action before the assessment or collection of any tax.

Thereafter, on April 16, 1975, the IRS notified the University of the proposed revocation of its tax-exempt status. On January 19, 1976, the IRS officially revoked the University's tax-exempt status, effective as of December 1, 1970, the day after the University was formally notified of the change in IRS policy. The University subsequently filed returns under the Federal Unemployment Tax Act for the period from December 1, 1970, to December 31, 1975, and paid a tax totalling $21.00 on one employee for the calendar year of 1975. After its request for a refund was denied, the University instituted the present action, seeking to recover the $21.00 it had paid to the IRS. The Government counter-claimed for unpaid federal unemployment taxes for the taxable years 1971 through 1975, in the amount of $489,675.59, plus interest.

The United States District Court for the District of South Carolina held that revocation of the University's tax-exempt status exceeded the delegated powers of the IRS, was improper under the IRS rulings and procedures, and violated the University's rights under the Religion Clauses of the First Amendment. 468 F.Supp. 890, 907 (D.S.C.1978). The court accordingly ordered the IRS to pay the University the $21.00 refund it claimed and rejected the IRS counterclaim.

The Court of Appeals for the Fourth Circuit, in a divided opinion, reversed. 639 F.2d 147 (CA4 1980). Citing *Green v. Connally, supra,* with approval, the Court of Appeals concluded that § 501(c)(3) must be read against the background of charitable trust law. To be eligible for an exemption under that section, an institution must be "charitable" in the common law sense, and therefore must not be contrary to public policy. In the court's view, Bob Jones University did not meet this requirement, since its "racial policies violated the clearly defined public policy, rooted in our Constitution, condemning racial discrimination and, more specifically, the government policy against subsidizing racial discrimination in education, public or private." *Id.* at 151. The court held that the IRS acted within its statutory authority in revoking the University's tax-exempt status. Finally, the Court of Appeals rejected petitioner's arguments that the revocation of the tax exemption violated the Free Exercise and Establishment Clauses of the First Amendment. The case was remanded to the District Court with instructions to dismiss the University's claim for a refund and to reinstate the Government's counterclaim.

C

No. 81-1, Goldsboro Christian Schools, Inc. v. United States

Goldsboro Christian Schools is a nonprofit corporation located in Goldsboro, North Carolina. Like Bob Jones University, it was established "to conduct an institution of learning ..., giving special emphasis to the Christian religion and the ethics revealed in the Holy scriptures." Articles of Incorporation, P 3(a). The school offers classes from kindergarten through high school, and since at least 1969 has satisfied the State of North Carolina's requirements for secular education in private schools. The school requires its high school students to take Bible-related courses, and begins each class with prayer.

Since its incorporation in 1963, Goldsboro Christian Schools has maintained a racially discriminatory admissions policy based upon its interpretation of the Bible.[6] Goldsboro has for the most part accepted only Caucasians. On occasion, however, the school has accepted children from racially mixed marriages in which one of the parents is Caucasian.

Goldsboro never received a determination by the IRS that it was an organization entitled to tax exemption under § 501(c)(3). Upon audit of Goldsboro's records for the years 1969 through 1972, the IRS determined that Goldsboro was not an organization described in § 501(c)(3), and therefore was required to pay taxes under the Federal Insurance Contribution Act and the Federal Unemployment Tax Act.

Goldsboro paid the IRS $3,459.93 in withholding, social security, and unemployment taxes with respect to one employee for the years 1969 through 1972. Thereafter, Goldsboro filed a suit seeking refund of that payment, claiming that the school had been improperly denied § 501(c)(3) exempt status. The IRS counterclaimed for $160,073.96 in unpaid social security and unemployment taxes for the years 1969 through 1972, including interest and penalties.

The District Court for the Eastern District of North Carolina decided the action on cross-motions for summary judgment. 436 F.Supp. 1314 (E.D.N.C.1977). In addressing the motions for summary judgment, the court assumed that

---

[6] According to the interpretation espoused by *Goldsboro*, race is determined by descendance from one of Noah's three sons — Ham, Shem and Japheth. Based on this interpretation, Orientals and Negroes are Hamitic, Hebrews are Shemitic, and Caucasians are Japhethitic. Cultural or biological mixing of the races is regarded as a violation of God's command.

Goldsboro's racially discriminatory admissions policy was based upon a sincerely held religious belief. The court nevertheless rejected Goldsboro's claim to tax-exempt status under § 501(c)(3), finding that "private schools maintaining racially discriminatory admissions policies violate clearly declared federal policy and, therefore, must be denied the federal tax benefits flowing from qualification under Section 501(c)(3)." *Id.* at 1318. The court also rejected Goldsboro's arguments that denial of tax-exempt status violated the Free Exercise and Establishment Clauses of the First Amendment. Accordingly, the court entered summary judgment for the Government on its counterclaim.

The Court of Appeals for the Fourth Circuit affirmed, 644 F.2d 879 (CA4 1981) (*per curiam*). That court found an "identity for present purposes" between the *Goldsboro* case and the *Bob Jones University* case, which had been decided shortly before by another panel of that court, and affirmed for the reasons set forth in *Bob Jones University*.

We granted certiorari in both cases, 454 U.S. 892 (1981), and we affirm in each.

II

A

In Revenue Ruling 71-447, the IRS formalized the policy first announced in 1970, that § 170 and § 501(c)(3) embrace the common law "charity" concept. Under that view, to qualify for a tax exemption pursuant to § 501(c)(3), an institution must show, first, that it falls within one of the eight categories expressly set forth in that section, and second, that its activity is not contrary to settled public policy.

Section 501(c)(3) provides that "[c]orporations ... organized and operated exclusively for religious, charitable ... or educational purposes" are entitled to tax exemption. Petitioners argue that the plain language of the statute guarantees them tax-exempt status. They emphasize the absence of any language in the statute expressly requiring all exempt organizations to be "charitable" in the common law sense, and they contend that the disjunctive "or" separating the categories in § 501(c)(3) precludes such a reading. Instead, they argue that if an institution falls within one or more of the specified categories it is automatically entitled to exemption, without regard to whether it also qualifies as "charitable."...

It is a well-established canon of statutory construction that a court should go beyond the literal language of a statute if reliance on that language would defeat the plain purpose of the statute....

Section 501(c)(3) therefore must be analyzed and construed within the framework of the Internal Revenue Code and against the background of the Congressional purposes. Such an examination reveals unmistakable evidence that, underlying all relevant parts of the Code, is the intent that entitlement to tax exemption depends on meeting certain common law standards of charity —

namely, that an institution seeking tax-exempt status must serve a public purpose and not be contrary to established public policy.

This "charitable" concept appears explicitly in § 170 of the Code. That section contains a list of organizations virtually identical to that contained in § 501(c)(3). It is apparent that Congress intended that list to have the same meaning in both sections.... On its face, therefore, § 170 reveals that Congress' intention was to provide tax benefits to organizations serving charitable purposes. The form of § 170 simply makes plain what common sense and history tell us: in enacting both § 170 and § 501(c)(3), Congress sought to provide tax benefits to charitable organizations, to encourage the development of private institutions that serve a useful public purpose or supplement or take the place of public institutions of the same kind.

....

When the Government grants exemptions or allows deductions all taxpayers are affected; the very fact of the exemption or deduction for the donor means that other taxpayers can be said to be indirect and vicarious "donors." Charitable exemptions are justified on the basis that the exempt entity confers a public benefit — a benefit which the society or the community may not itself choose or be able to provide, or which supplements and advances the work of public institutions already supported by tax revenues. History buttresses logic to make clear that, to warrant exemption under § 501(c)(3), an institution must fall within a category specified in that section and must demonstrably serve and be in harmony with the public interest. The institution's purpose must not be so at odds with the common community conscience as to undermine any public benefit that might otherwise be conferred.

We are bound to approach these questions with full awareness that determinations of public benefit and public policy are sensitive matters with serious implications for the institutions affected; a declaration that a given institution is not "charitable" should be made only where there can be no doubt that the activity involved is contrary to a fundamental public policy. But there can no longer be any doubt that racial discrimination in education violates deeply and widely accepted views of elementary justice. Prior to 1954, public education in many places still was conducted under the pall of *Plessy v. Ferguson*, 163 U.S. 537 (1896); racial segregation in primary and secondary education prevailed in many parts of the country.... This Court's decision in *Brown v. Board of Education*, 347 U.S. 483 (1954), signalled an end to that era. Over the past quarter of a century, every pronouncement of this Court and myriad Acts of Congress and Executive Orders attest a firm national policy to prohibit racial segregation and discrimination in public education.

An unbroken line of cases following *Brown v. Board of Education* establishes beyond doubt this Court's view that racial discrimination in education violates a most fundamental national public policy, as well as rights of individuals.

B. PRIVATE SCHOOLS: GOV'T ACTION AND RACIAL SEGREGATION

Few social or political issues in our history have been more vigorously debated and more extensively ventilated than the issue of racial discrimination, particularly in education. Given the stress and anguish of the history of efforts to escape from the shackles of the "separate but equal" doctrine of *Plessy v. Ferguson, supra,* it cannot be said that educational institutions that, for whatever reasons, practice racial discrimination, are institutions exercising "beneficial and stabilizing influences in community life," or should be encouraged by having all taxpayers share in their support by way of special tax status.

There can thus be no question that the interpretation of § 170 and § 501(c)(3) announced by the IRS in 1970 was correct. That it may be seen as belated does not undermine its soundness. It would be wholly incompatible with the concepts underlying tax exemption to grant the benefit of tax-exempt status to racially discriminatory educational entities, which "exer[t] a pervasive influence on the entire educational process." Whatever may be the rationale for such private schools' policies, and however sincere the rationale may be, racial discrimination in education is contrary to public policy. Racially discriminatory educational institutions cannot be viewed as conferring a public benefit within the "charitable" concept discussed earlier, or within the Congressional intent underlying § 170 and § 501(c)(3).

....

III

Petitioners contend that, even if the Commissioner's policy is valid as to nonreligious private schools, that policy cannot constitutionally be applied to schools that engage in racial discrimination on the basis of sincerely held religious beliefs. As to such schools, it is argued that the IRS construction of § 170 and § 501(c)(3) violates their free exercise rights under the Religion Clauses of the First Amendment. This contention presents claims not heretofore considered by this Court in precisely this context.

....

On occasion this Court has found certain governmental interests so compelling as to allow even regulations prohibiting religiously based conduct. In *Prince v. Massachusetts,* 321 U.S. 158 (1944), for example, the Court held that neutrally cast child labor laws prohibiting sale of printed materials on public streets could be applied to prohibit children from dispensing religious literature. The Court found no constitutional infirmity in "excluding [Jehovah's Witness children] from doing there what no other children may do." *Id.* at 170.... Denial of tax benefits will inevitably have a substantial impact on the operation of private religious schools, but will not prevent those schools from observing their religious tenets.

The governmental interest at stake here is compelling. As discussed in Part II(B), *supra,* the Government has a fundamental, overriding interest in eradicating racial discrimination in education — discrimination that prevailed, with official approval, for the first 165 years of this Nation's history. That governmental interest substantially outweighs whatever burden denial of tax benefits places on petitioners' exercise of their religious beliefs. The interests asserted by petitioners cannot be accommodated with that compelling governmental interest....

IV

The remaining issue is whether the IRS properly applied its policy to these petitioners. Petitioner Goldsboro Christian Schools admits that it "maintain[s] racially discriminatory policies," ... but seeks to justify those policies on grounds we have fully discussed. The IRS properly denied tax-exempt status to Goldsboro Christian Schools.

Petitioner Bob Jones University, however, contends that it is not racially discriminatory. It emphasizes that it now allows all races to enroll, subject only to its restrictions on the conduct of all students, including its prohibitions of association between men and women of different races, and of interracial marriage. Although a ban on intermarriage or interracial dating applies to all races, decisions of this Court firmly establish that discrimination on the basis of racial affiliation and association is a form of racial discrimination....

The judgments of the Court of Appeals are, accordingly,

Affirmed.

....

[JUSTICE REHNQUIST's dissenting opinion is deleted.]

---

1. The Court spends considerable effort establishing that the actions of the Congress, executive agencies and the judiciary are against tax-exempt status for organizations practicing racial discrimination. However, at no time during this narrative is there information provided for when a public policy is formed or when schools are obligated to conform to it. For private institutions does this mean no bright line for when its policies may foster a denial of tax-exempt status? Moreover, does this case set a precedent for executive agency activity without the express approval of Congress? Does this case confirm an inappropriate broadening of IRS authority? Does Justice Rehnquist address these issues in his dissent?

2. Justice Rehnquist, in a dissent to *Bob Jones* (omitted above), exhibits a "strict constructionist" view of Congressional intent as IRS policy; to wit, Section 501(c)(3) provides for tax exemptions for educational institutions without mentioning racial discrimination. Hence, if the entity is educational, it meets statutory requirements. Does this approach place form over substance when considering Supreme Court interpretation? Would not such a decision as advocated by Rehnquist ignore the precedent of a line of Supreme Court cases that have, in effect, set the public policy at the basis of the holding in *Bob Jones*? Could Rehnquist have cited to *Walz v. Tax Comm'n*, 397 U.S. 664 (1970).

3. *Bob Jones* cites to *Green v. Kennedy*, 309 F. Supp. 1127, *appeal dismissed sub nom. Cannon v. Green*, 398 U.S. 956 (1970), *appeal dismissed sub nom. Coit v. Green*, 400 U.S. 986 (1971), a case in Mississippi that challenged prior Internal Revenue Service (IRS) policy that permitted tax exempt status for private, sectarian organizations despite racially discriminatory policies. Under *Green* a permanent injunction was ordered prohibiting such policies with the provision that, in such cases, public policy against racial discrimination could outweigh religious freedom protected by the First Amendment. The district court stated:

> We are not now called upon to consider the hypothetical inquiry whether tax-exemption or tax-deduction status may be available to a religious school that practices acts of racial restriction because of the requirements of religion. Such a problem may never arise; and if it ever does arise, it will have to be considered in the light of the particular facts and issues presented, and in light of the established rule ... that the law may prohibit an individual from taking certain actions even though his religion commands or prescribes them. *Green*, 309 F. Supp. at 1169.

Following this decision the IRS adopted a policy against such discrimination in private schools. The policy required private schools to publicize admission and matriculation procedures in accordance with the clear federal mandate of no discrimination to be eligible for tax benefits. This had to be accomplished whether or not the discrimination was based on religion.

This case laid the foundation for the decision in *Bob Jones*; in addition plaintiffs in the case following filed a class action seeking to have the standard under *Green*, which was limited to schools in Mississippi, apply to the nation.

ALLEN v. WRIGHT

Supreme Court of the United States
468 U.S. 737 (1984)

JUSTICE O'CONNOR delivered the opinion of the Court:

....

I

The Internal Revenue Service denies tax-exempt status under §§ 501(a) and (c)(3) of the Internal Revenue Code, 26 U.S.C. §§ 501(a) and (c)(3) — and hence eligibility to receive charitable contributions deductible from income taxes under §§ 170(a)(1) and (c)(2) of the Code, 26 U.S.C. §§ 170(a)(1) and (c)(2) — to racially discriminatory private schools. Rev.Rul. 71-447, 1971-2 Cum.Bull. 230.[1] The IRS policy requires that a school applying for tax-exempt status

---

[1] As the Court explained last Term in *Bob Jones University v. United States*, 461 U.S. ____, ____ - ____ (1983), the IRS announced this policy in 1970 and formally adopted it in 1971.

show that it "admits the students of any race to all the rights, privileges, programs, and activities generally accorded or made available to students at that school and that the school does not discriminate on the basis of race in administration of its educational policies, admissions policies, scholarship and loan programs, and athletic and other school-administered programs." *Ibid.* To carry out this policy, the IRS has established guidelines and procedures for determining whether a particular school is in fact racially nondiscriminatory. Rev.Proc. 75-50, 1975-2 Cum.Bull. 587. Failure to comply with the guidelines "will ordinarily result in the proposed revocation of" tax-exempt status.

The guidelines provide that "[a] school must show affirmatively both that it has adopted a racially nondiscriminatory policy as to students that is made known to the general public and that since the adoption of that policy it has operated in a bona fide manner in accordance therewith." The school must state its nondiscrimination policy in its organizational charter, and in all of its brochures, catalogues, and other advertisements to prospective students. The school must make its nondiscrimination policy known to the entire community served by the school and must publicly disavow any contrary representations made on its behalf once it becomes aware of them. The school must have nondiscriminatory policies concerning all programs and facilities, including scholarships and loans, and the school must annually certify, under penalty of perjury, compliance with these requirements.

The IRS rules require a school applying for tax-exempt status to give a breakdown along racial lines of its student body and its faculty and administrative staff, as well as of scholarships and loans awarded. They also require the applicant school to state the year of its organization, and to list "incorporators, founders, board members, and donors of land or buildings," and state whether any of the organizations among these have an objective of maintaining segregated public or private school education. The rules further provide that, once given an exemption, a school must keep specified records to document the extent of compliance with the IRS guidelines. Finally, the rules announce that any information concerning discrimination at a tax-exempt school is officially welcomed.

In 1976 respondents challenged these guidelines and procedures in a suit filed in Federal District Court against the Secretary of the Treasury and the Commissioner of Internal Revenue. The plaintiffs named in the complaint are parents of black children who, at the time the complaint was filed, were attending public

---

Rev.Rul. 71-447, 1971-2 Cum.Bull. 230. This change in prior policy was prompted by litigation over tax exemptions for racially discriminatory private schools in the State of Mississippi, litigation that resulted in the entry of an injunction against the IRS largely if not entirely coextensive with the position the IRS had voluntarily adopted. *Green v. Kennedy*, 309 F.Supp. 1127 (DC), *appeal dism'd sub nom. Cannon v. Green*, 398 U.S. 956 (1970) (entering preliminary injunction); *Green v. Connally*, 330 F.Supp. 1150 (DC), *summarily aff'd sub nom. Coit v. Green*, 404 U.S. 997 (1971) (entering permanent injunction).

schools in seven States in school districts undergoing desegregation. They brought this nationwide class action "on behalf of themselves and their children, and ... on behalf of all other parents of black children attending public school systems undergoing, or which may in the future undergo, desegregation pursuant to court order [or] HEW regulations and guidelines, under state law, or voluntarily." They estimated that the class they seek to represent includes several million persons.

Respondents allege in their complaint that many racially segregated private schools were created or expanded in their communities at the time the public schools were undergoing desegregation. According to the complaint, many such private schools, including 17 schools or school systems identified by name in the complaint (perhaps some 30 schools in all), receive tax exemptions either directly or through the tax-exempt status of "umbrella" organizations that operate or support the schools. Respondents allege that, despite the IRS policy of denying tax-exempt status to racially discriminatory private schools and despite the IRS guidelines and procedures for implementing that policy, some of the tax-exempt racially segregated private schools created or expanded in desegregating districts in fact have racially discriminatory policies. (IRS permits "schools to receive tax exemptions merely on the basis of adopting and certifying — but not implementing — a policy of nondiscrimination");[11] Respondents allege that the IRS grant of tax exemptions to such racially discriminatory schools is unlawful.

---

[11] The complaint generally uses the phrase "racially segregated school" to mean simply that no or few minority students attend the school, irrespective of the school's maintenance of racially discriminatory policies or practices. Although the complaint, on its face, alleges that granting tax-exempt status to any "racially segregated" school in a desegregating public school district is unlawful, App. 39, it is clear that respondents premise their allegation of illegality on discrimination, not on segregation alone.

The nub of respondent's complaint is that current IRS guidelines and procedures are inadequate to detect false certifications of nondiscrimination policies. This allegation would be superfluous if respondents were claiming that racial segregation even without racial discrimination made the grant of tax-exempt status unlawful. Moreover, respondents have noticeably refrained from asserting that the IRS violates the law when it grants a tax exemption to a nondiscriminatory private school that happens to have few minority students. Indeed, respondents' brief in this Court makes a point of noting that their complaint alleges not only segregation but discrimination, and it repeatedly states that the challenged Government conduct is the granting of tax exemptions to racially discriminatory private schools, ("Respondents alleged that the federal petitioners are continuing to grant tax-exempt status to racially discriminatory private schools ..."). Since respondents' entire argument is built on the assertion that their rights are violated by IRS grants of tax-exempt status to some number of unidentified racially discriminatory private schools in desegregating districts, we resolve the ambiguity in respondents' complaint by reading it as making that assertion.

Contrary to Justice Brennan's statement, ... the complaint does not allege that each desegregating district in which they reside contains one or more racially discriminatory private schools unlawfully receiving a tax exemption.

Respondents allege that the challenged Government conduct harms them in two ways. The challenged conduct

> (a) constitutes tangible federal financial aid and other support for racially segregated educational institutions, and
>
> (b) fosters and encourages the organization, operation and expansion of institutions providing racially segregated educational opportunities for white children avoiding attendance in desegregating public school districts and thereby interferes with the efforts of federal courts, HEW and local school authorities to desegregate public school districts which have been operating racially dual school systems.

Thus, respondents do not allege that their children have been the victims of discriminatory exclusion from the schools whose tax exemptions they challenge as unlawful. Indeed, they have not alleged at any stage of this litigation that their children have ever applied or would ever apply to any private school. ("Plaintiffs ... maintain they have no interest whatever in enrolling their children in a private school.") Rather, respondents claim a direct injury from the mere fact of the challenged Government conduct and, as indicated by the restriction of the plaintiff class to parents of children in desegregating school districts, injury to their children's opportunity to receive a desegregated education. The latter injury is traceable to the IRS grant of tax exemptions to racially discriminatory schools, respondents allege, chiefly because contributions to such schools are deductible from income taxes under §§ 170(a)(1) and (c)(2) of the Internal Revenue Code and the "deductions facilitate the raising of funds to organize new schools and expand existing schools in order to accommodate white students avoiding attendance in desegregating public school districts."

Respondents request only prospective relief. They ask for a declaratory judgment that the challenged IRS tax-exemption practices are unlawful. They also ask for an injunction requiring the IRS to deny tax exemptions to a considerably broader class of private schools than the class of racially discriminatory private schools. Under the requested injunction, the IRS would have to deny tax-exempt status to all private schools

> which have insubstantial or nonexistent minority enrollments, which are located in or serve desegregating public school districts, and which either —
>
> (1) were established or expanded at or about the time the public school districts in which they are located or which they serve were desegregating;
>
> (2) have been determined in adversary judicial or administrative proceedings to be racially segregated; or
>
> (3) cannot demonstrate that they do not provide racially segregated educational opportunities for white children avoiding attendance in desegregating public school systems....

Finally, respondents ask for an order directing the IRS to replace its 1975 guidelines with standards consistent with the requested injunction.

In May 1977 the District Court permitted intervention as a defendant by petitioner Allen, the head of one of the private school systems identified in the complaint. Thereafter, progress in the lawsuit was stalled for several years. During this period, the Internal Revenue Service reviewed its challenged policies and proposed new Revenue Procedures to tighten requirements for eligibility for tax-exempt status for private schools. In 1979, however, Congress blocked any strengthening of the IRS guidelines at least until October 1980. The District Court thereupon considered and granted the defendants' motion to dismiss the complaint, concluding that respondents lack standing, that the judicial task proposed by respondents is inappropriately intrusive for a federal court, and that awarding the requested relief would be contrary to the will of Congress expressed in the 1979 ban on strengthening IRS guidelines.

The United States Court of Appeals for the District of Columbia reversed, concluding that respondents have standing to maintain this lawsuit. The court acknowledged that *Simon v. Eastern Kentucky Welfare Rights Org.*, 426 U.S. 26 (1976), "suggests that litigation concerning tax liability is a matter between taxpayer and IRS, with the door barely ajar for third party challenges." 211 U.S.App.D.C. at 239, 656 F.2d at 828. The court concluded, however, that the *Simon* case is inapposite because respondents claim no injury dependent on taxpayers' actions: "[t]hey claim indifference as to the course private schools would take." Instead, the court observed, "[t]he sole injury [respondents] claim is the denigration they suffer as black parents and schoolchildren when their government graces with tax-exempt status educational institutions in their communities that treat members of their race as persons of lesser worth." The court held this denigration injury enough to give respondents standing since it was this injury which supported standing in *Coit v. Green*, 404 U.S. 997 (1971), *summarily aff'g Green v. Connally*, 330 F.Supp. 1150 (DC); *Norwood v. Harrison*, 413 U.S. 455 (1973). The Court of Appeals also held that the 1979 congressional actions were not intended to preclude judicial remedies and that the relief requested by respondents could be fashioned "without large scale judicial intervention in the administrative process," The court accordingly remanded the case to the District Court for further proceedings, enjoining the defendants meanwhile from granting tax-exempt status to any racially discriminatory school....

The Government defendants and defendant-intervenor Allen filed separate petitions for a writ of certiorari in this Court. They both sought review of the Court of Appeals' holding that respondents have standing to bring this lawsuit. We granted certiorari, 462 U.S. ____ (1983), and now reverse.

II

A

Article III of the Constitution confines the federal courts to adjudicating actual "cases" and "controversies." As the Court explained in *Valley Forge Christian*

College v. Americans United for Separation of Church and State, Inc., 454 U.S. 464, 471-76 (1982), the "case or controversy" requirement defines with respect to the Judicial Branch the idea of separation of powers on which the Federal Government is founded. The several doctrines that have grown up to elaborate that requirement are "founded in concern about the proper — and properly limited — role of the courts in a democratic society."

"All of the doctrines that cluster about Article III — not only standing but mootness, ripeness, political question, and the like — relate in part, and in different though overlapping ways, to an idea, which is more than an intuition but less than a rigorous and explicit theory, about the constitutional and prudential limits to the powers of an unelected, unrepresentative judiciary in our kind of government."

The case-or-controversy doctrines state fundamental limits on federal judicial power in our system of government.

The Art. III doctrine that requires a litigant to have "standing" to invoke the power of a federal court is perhaps the most important of these doctrines. "In essence the question of standing is whether the litigant is entitled to have the court decide the merits of the dispute or of particular issues." Standing doctrine embraces several judicially self-imposed limits on the exercise of federal jurisdiction, such as the general prohibition on a litigant's raising another person's legal rights, the rule barring adjudication of generalized grievances more appropriately addressed in the representative branches, and the requirement that a plaintiff's complaint fall within the zone of interests protected by the law invoked. The requirement of standing, however, has a core component derived directly from the Constitution. A plaintiff must allege personal injury fairly traceable to the defendant's allegedly unlawful conduct and likely to be redressed by the requested relief.

Like the prudential component, the constitutional component of standing doctrine incorporates concepts concededly not susceptible of precise definition. The injury alleged must be, for example, "'distinct and palpable,'" and not "abstract" or "conjectural" or "hypothetical." ... The injury must be "fairly" traceable to the challenged action, and relief from the injury must be "likely" to follow from a favorable decision. These terms cannot be defined so as to make application of the constitutional standing requirement a mechanical exercise.

The absence of precise definitions, however, as this Court's extensive body of case law on standing illustrates, hardly leaves courts at sea in applying the law of standing. Like most legal notions, the standing concepts have gained considerable definition from developing case law. In many cases the standing question can be answered chiefly by comparing the allegations of the particular complaint to those made in prior standing cases. More important, the law of Art. III standing is built on a single basic idea — the idea of separation of powers. It is this fact which makes possible the gradual clarification of the law through judicial application. Of course, both federal and state courts have long experience in applying and elaborating in numerous contexts the pervasive and fundamental notion of separation of powers.

Determining standing in a particular case may be facilitated by clarifying principles or even clean rules developed in prior cases. Typically, however, the standing inquiry requires careful judicial examination of a complaint's allegations to ascertain whether the particular plaintiff is entitled to an adjudication of the particular claims asserted. Is the injury too abstract, or otherwise not appropriate, to be considered judicially cognizable? Is the line of causation between the illegal conduct and injury too attenuated? Is the prospect of obtaining relief from the injury as a result of a favorable ruling too speculative? These questions and any others relevant to the standing inquiry must be answered by reference to the Art. III notion that federal courts may exercise power only "in the last resort, and as a necessity," and only when adjudication is "consistent with a system of separated powers and [the dispute is one] traditionally thought to be capable of resolution through the judicial process." ...

B

Respondents allege two injuries in their complaint to support their standing to bring this lawsuit. First, they say that they are harmed directly by the mere fact of Government financial aid to discriminatory private schools. Second, they say that the federal tax exemptions to racially discriminatory private schools in their communities impair their ability to have their public schools desegregated.

....

Because respondents have not clearly disclaimed reliance on either of the injuries described in their complaint, we address both allegations of injury. We conclude that neither suffices to support respondents' standing. The first fails under clear precedents of this Court because it does not constitute judicially cognizable injury. The second fails because the alleged injury is not fairly traceable to the assertedly unlawful conduct of the IRS.

1

Respondents' first claim of injury can be interpreted in two ways. It might be a claim simply to have the Government avoid the violation of law alleged in respondents' complaint. Alternatively, it might be a claim of stigmatic injury, or denigration, suffered by all members of a racial group when the Government discriminates on the basis of race. Under neither interpretation is this claim of injury judicially cognizable.

This Court has repeatedly held that an asserted right to have the Government act in accordance with law is not sufficient, standing alone, to confer jurisdiction on a federal court. In *Schlesinger v. Reservists Committee to Stop the War*, 418 U.S. 208 (1974), for example, the Court rejected a claim of citizen standing to challenge Armed Forces Reserve commissions held by Members of Congress as violating the Incompatibility Clause of Art. I, § 6, cl. 2, of the Constitution. As citizens, the Court held, plaintiffs alleged nothing but "the abstract injury in nonobservance of the Constitution ...." More recently, in *Valley Forge, supra,* we rejected a claim of standing to challenge a Government conveyance of property to a religious institution. Insofar as the plaintiffs relied simply on "'their shared individuated right'" to a Government that made no law respecting an establishment of religion, *id.,* 454 U.S. at 482 (quoting *Americans United v. U.S. Dept. of HEW,* 619 F.2d 252, 261 (CA3 1980)), we held that plaintiffs had not alleged a judicially cognizable injury. "[A]ssertion of a right to a particular kind of Government conduct, which the Government has violated by acting differently, cannot alone satisfy the requirements of Art. III without draining those requirements of meaning." 454 U.S. at 483.... Respondents here have no standing to complain simply that their Government is violating the law.

Neither do they have standing to litigate their claims based on the stigmatizing injury often caused by racial discrimination. There can be no doubt that this sort of noneconomic injury is one of the most serious consequences of discriminatory government action and is sufficient in some circumstances to support standing. Our cases make clear, however, that such injury accords a basis for standing only to "those persons who are personally denied equal treatment" by the challenged discriminatory conduct, *ibid.*

In *Moose Lodge No. 107 v. Irvis,* 407 U.S. 163 (1972), the Court held that the plaintiff had no standing to challenge a club's racially discriminatory membership policies because he had never applied for membership. In *O'Shea v. Littleton,* 414 U.S. 488 (1974), the Court held that the plaintiffs had no standing to challenge racial discrimination in the administration of their city's criminal justice system because they had not alleged that they had been or would likely be subject to the challenged practices.... In each of those cases, the plaintiffs alleged official racial discrimination comparable to that alleged by respondents here. Yet standing was denied in each case because the plaintiffs were not personally subject to the challenged discrimination. Insofar as their first claim of injury is concerned, respondents are in exactly the same position: [T]hey do not allege a stigmatic injury suffered as a direct result of having personally been denied equal treatment.

The consequences of recognizing respondents' standing on the basis of their first claim of injury illustrate why our cases plainly hold that such injury is not judicially cognizable. If the abstract stigmatic injury were cognizable, standing would extend nationwide to all members of the particular racial groups against which the Government was alleged to be discriminating by its grant of a tax exemption to a racially discriminatory school, regardless of the location of that school. All such persons could claim the same sort of abstract stigmatic injury respondents assert in their first claim of injury. A black person in Hawaii could challenge the grant of a tax exemption to a racially discriminatory school in Maine. Recognition of standing in such circumstances would transform the federal courts into "no more than a vehicle for the vindication of the value interests of concerned bystanders." Constitutional limits on the role of the federal courts preclude such a transformation.

2

It is in their complaint's second claim of injury that respondents allege harm to a concrete, personal interest that can support standing in some circumstances. The injury they identify — their children's diminished ability to receive an education in a racially integrated school — is, beyond any doubt, not only judicially cognizable but, as shown by cases from *Brown v. Board of Education* to *Bob Jones University v. United States*, one of the most serious injuries recognized in our legal system. Despite the constitutional importance of curing the injury alleged by respondents, however, the federal judiciary may not redress it unless standing requirements are met. In this case, respondents' second claim of injury cannot support standing because the injury alleged is not fairly traceable to the Government conduct respondents challenge as unlawful.

The illegal conduct challenged by respondents is the IRS's grant of tax exemptions to some racially discriminatory schools. The line of causation between that conduct and desegregation of respondents' schools is attenuated at best. From the perspective of the IRS, the injury to respondents is highly indirect and "results from the independent action of some third party not before the court." As the Court pointed out in *Warth v. Seldin*, 422 U.S. at 505 "the indirectness of the injury ... may make it substantially more difficult to meet the minimum requirement of Article III...."

The diminished ability of respondents' children to receive a desegregated education would be fairly traceable to unlawful IRS grants of tax exemptions only if there were enough racially discriminatory private schools receiving tax exemptions in respondents' communities for withdrawal of those exemptions to make an appreciable difference in public-school integration. Respondents have made no such allegation. It is, first, uncertain how many racially discriminatory private schools are in fact receiving tax exemptions. Moreover, it is entirely speculative, as respondents themselves conceded in the Court of Appeals, whether withdrawal of a tax exemption from any particular school would lead the school to change its policies. It is just as speculative whether any given parent of a child attending such a private school would decide to transfer the child to public school as a result of any changes in educational or financial policy made by the private school once it was threatened with loss of tax-exempt status. It is also pure speculation whether, in a particular community, a large enough number of the numerous relevant school officials and parents would reach decisions that collectively would have a significant impact on the racial composition of the public schools.

The links in the chain of causation between the challenged Government conduct and the asserted injury are far too weak for the chain as a whole to sustain respondents' standing. In *Simon v. Eastern Kentucky Welfare Rights Org.*, *supra*, the Court held that standing to challenge a Government grant of a tax exemption to hospitals could not be founded on the asserted connection between the grant of tax-exempt status and the hospitals' policy concerning the provision of medical services to indigents. The causal connection depended on the decisions hospitals would make in response to withdrawal of tax-exempt status, and those decisions were sufficiently uncertain to break the chain of causation between the plaintiffs' injury and the challenged Government action. The chain of causation is even weaker in this case. It involves numerous third parties (officials of racially discriminatory schools receiving tax exemptions and the parents of children attending such schools) who may not even exist in respondents' communities and whose independent decisions may not collectively have a significant effect on the ability of public-school students to receive a desegregated education.

. . . .

C

The Court of Appeals relied for its contrary conclusion on *Gilmore v. City of Montgomery*, 417 U.S. 556 (1974), on *Norwood v. Harrison*, 413 U.S. 455 (1973), and on *Coit v. Green*, 404 U.S. 997 (1971), *summarily aff'g Green v. Connally*, 330 F.Supp. 1150 (DC). Respondents in this Court, though stressing a different injury from the one emphasized by the Court of Appeals, place principal reliance on those cases as well. None of the cases, however, requires that we find standing in this lawsuit.

In *Gilmore v. City of Montgomery*, the plaintiffs asserted a constitutional right, recognized in an outstanding injunction, to use the city's public parks on a nondiscriminatory basis. They alleged that the city was violating that equal protection right by permitting racially discriminatory private schools and other groups to use the public parks. The Court recognized plaintiffs' standing to challenge this city policy insofar as the policy permitted the exclusive use of the parks by racially discriminatory private schools: the plaintiffs had alleged direct cognizable injury to their right to nondiscriminatory access to the public parks.

Standing in *Gilmore* thus rested on an allegation of direct deprivation of a right to equal use of the parks. Like the plaintiff in *Heckler v. Mathews* — indeed, like the plaintiffs having standing in virtually any equal protection case — the plaintiffs in *Gilmore* alleged that they were personally being denied equal treatment. The *Gilmore Court* did not rest its finding of standing on an abstract denigration injury, and no problem of attenuated causation attended the plaintiffs' claim of injury.

In *Norwood v. Harrison*, *supra*, parents of public school children in Tunica County, Mississippi, filed a statewide class action challenging the State's provision of textbooks to students attending racially discriminatory private schools in the State. The Court held the State's practice unconstitutional because it breached "the State's acknowledged duty to establish a unitary school system." The Court did not expressly address the basis for the plaintiffs' standing.

In *Gilmore*, however, the Court identified the basis for standing in *Norwood*: "The plaintiffs in *Norwood* were parties to a school desegregation order and the relief they sought was directly related to the concrete injury they suffered." 417

B. PRIVATE SCHOOLS: GOV'T ACTION AND RACIAL SEGREGATION 1359

U.S. at 571, n. 10. Through the school-desegregation decree, the plaintiffs had acquired a right to have the State "steer clear" of any perpetuation of the racially dual school system that it had once sponsored. 413 U.S. at 467. The interest acquired was judicially cognizable because it was a personal interest, created by law, in having the State refrain from taking specific actions. The plaintiffs' complaint alleged that the State directly injured that interest by aiding racially discriminatory private schools. Respondents in this lawsuit, of course, have no injunctive rights against the IRS that are allegedly being harmed by the challenged IRS action.

Unlike *Gilmore* and *Norwood*, *Coit v. Green*, cannot easily be seen to have based standing on an injury different in kind from any asserted by respondents here. The plaintiffs in *Coit*, parents of black school children in Mississippi, sued to enjoin the IRS grant of tax exemptions to racially discriminatory private schools in the State. Nevertheless, *Coit* in no way mandates the conclusion that respondents have standing.

First, the decision has little weight as a precedent on the law of standing. This Court's decision in *Coit* was merely a summary affirmance; for that reason alone it could hardly establish principles contrary to those set out in opinions issued after full briefing and argument.... Moreover, when the case reached this Court, the plaintiffs and the IRS were no longer adverse parties; and the ruling that was summarily affirmed, did not include a ruling on the issue of standing, which had been briefly considered in a prior ruling of the District Court. Thus, "the Court's affirmance in *Green* lacks the precedential weight of a case involving a truly adversary controversy."

In any event, the facts in the *Coit* case are sufficiently different from those presented in this lawsuit that the absence of standing here is unaffected by the possible propriety of standing there. In particular, the suit in *Coit* was limited to the public schools of one State. Moreover, the District Court found, based on extensive evidence before it as well as on the findings in *Coffey v. State Educational Finance Comm'n*, 296 F.Supp. 1389 (SD Miss.1969), that large numbers of segregated private schools had been established in the State for the purpose of avoiding a unitary public school system; that the tax exemptions were critically important to the ability of such schools to succeed; and that the connection between the grant of tax exemptions to discriminatory schools and desegregation of the public schools in the particular State was close enough to warrant the conclusion that irreparable injury to the interest in desegregated education was threatened if the tax exemptions continued. What made possible those findings was the fact that, when the Mississippi plaintiffs filed their suit, the IRS had a policy of granting tax exemptions to racially discriminatory private schools; thus, the suit was initially brought, not simply to reform Executive Branch enforcement procedures, but to challenge a fundamental IRS policy decision, which affected numerous identifiable schools in the State of Mississippi.

The limited setting, the history of school desegregation in Mississippi at the time of the *Coit* litigation, the nature of the IRS conduct challenged at the outset of the litigation, and the District Court's particular findings, which were never challenged as clearly erroneous, amply distinguish the *Coit* case from respondents' lawsuit. Thus, we need not consider whether standing was properly found to exist in *Coit*. Whatever the answer to that question, respondents' complaint, which aims at nationwide relief and does not challenge particular identified unlawful IRS actions, alleges no connection between the asserted desegregation injury and the challenged IRS conduct direct enough to overcome the substantial separation-of-powers barriers to a suit seeking an injunction to reform administrative procedures.

III

"The necessity that the plaintiff who seeks to invoke judicial power stand to profit in some personal interest remains an Art. III requirement." Respondents have not met this fundamental requirement. The judgment of the Court of Appeals is accordingly reversed, and the injunction issued by that court is vacated.

It is so ordered.

....

JUSTICE BRENNAN, dissenting:

....

B

....

Viewed in light of the injuries they claim, the respondents have alleged a direct causal relationship between the government action they challenge and the injury they suffer: their inability to receive an education in a racially integrated school is directly and adversely affected by the tax-exempt status granted by the IRS to racially discriminatory schools in their respective school districts. Commonsense alone would recognize that the elimination of tax-exempt status for racially discriminatory private schools would serve to lessen the impact that those institutions have in defeating efforts to desegregate the public schools.

The Court admits that "[t]he diminished ability of respondents' children to receive a desegregated education would be fairly traceable to unlawful IRS grants of tax exemptions ... if there were enough racially discriminatory private schools receiving tax exemptions in respondents' communities for withdrawal of those exemptions to make an appreciable difference in public-school integration," but concludes that "[r]espondents have made no such allegation." With all due respect, the Court has either misread the complaint or is improperly requiring the respondents to prove their case on the merits in order to defeat a motion to dismiss. For example, the respondents specifically refer by name to at least 32 private schools that discriminate on the basis of race and yet continue to benefit illegally from tax-exempt status. Eighteen of those schools — including at least 14 elementary schools, two junior high schools, and one high school — are located in the city of Memphis, Tennessee, which has been the subject of several court orders to desegregate. Similarly, the respondents cite two private schools in Orangeburg, South Carolina that continue to benefit from federal tax exemptions even though they practice race discrimination in school districts that are desegregating pursuant to judicial and administrative orders. At least with respect to these school districts, as well as the others specifically mentioned in the complaint, there can be little doubt that the respondents have identified communities containing "enough racially discriminatory private schools receiving tax exemptions ... to make an appreciable difference in public-school integration."

....

Even accepting the relevance of the Court's distinction, moreover, that distinction goes to the injury suffered by the respective plaintiffs, and not to the causal connection between the harm alleged and the governmental action challenged. *Cf. ante*, at 3328 (conceding that the respondents have alleged constitutionally sufficient harm in these cases). The causal relationship existing in *Norwood* between the alleged harm (*i.e.*, interference with the plaintiffs' injunctive rights to a desegregated school system) and the challenged governmental action (*i.e.*, free textbooks provided to racially discriminatory schools) is indistinguishable from the causal relationship existing in the present cases, unless the Court intends to distinguish the lending of textbooks from the granting of tax-exempt status. The Court's express statement on causation in *Norwood* therefore bears repeating: "the Constitution does not permit the State to aid discrimination even when there is no precise causal relationship between state financial aid to a private school and the continued well-being of that school." 413 U.S. at 465-66.

....

---

1. What is the true holding in this case as regards government accountability and discrimination? Is it that government can only be held accountable when its actions directly injure plaintiffs and not when it facilitates discrimination by private parties?

2. One of the reasons the Court held against respondents in the case was because no direct injury was found since "there were [not] enough racially discriminatory private schools receiving tax exemptions in [their] communities for withdrawal of those exemptions to make an appreciable difference in public-school integration." *Wright*, at 758. Hence, the respondents were required under this analysis to prove not only a government (IRS) impact on desegregation, but that ceasing this activity would have provided the requested remedy. Under a "standing" analysis do plaintiffs have to satisfy this sort of proximate cause for a favorable decision? Is the Court's decision, instead, more attuned to Justice Brennan's criticism in that the respondents are really being asked to prove their case on the merits? Is the Court confusing "standing" with "merit"? Does this mean there is a lack of adequate attention to both?

3. The majority states that its decision in *Wright* is distinguishable from that in *Norwood v. Harrison*. Justice Brennan in his dissent takes issue with this asking whether there isn't some parallel between government support of racially discriminatory schools by supplying textbooks (*Norwood*) and government support of such schools by offering tax exemptions (*Wright*). This criticism goes to the heart of "standing" analysis in that the *Wright* Court determines that plaintiffs must show direct injury from the government activity. Is this the correct form of inquiry or is it as Justice Brennan states that such proximation is unnecessary since the Constitution does not permit a state to promote discrimination, precise causal relationship notwithstanding?

4. In *Bob Jones, supra*, the Court ruled that if a school discriminates on the basis of race, the IRS is prohibited from granting tax exempt status and from allowing donations to such schools that would be tax deductible. Does the *Wright* decision now neuter *Bob Jones* by illustrating that these schools may accomplish such discrimination anyway since few plaintiffs would have standing to challenge government indirect aid to such schools? Does the ruling establish what Justice Brennan called an IRS policy of adopting and certifying [without] implementing non-discrimination? (Justice Brennan, dissenting in *Allen v. Wright*, 468 U.S. at 768).

5. Consider the decisions in *Green*, *Bob Jones* and *Wright* and the following comment from V. Davis Nordin and W. Lloyd Turner, *Tax Exempt Status of Private Schools: Wright, Green and Bob Jones*, 35 Educ. L. Rep. 329, 331 (1986):*

> Thus, three lines of cases [from the cases mentioned above] ... have produced sharply disparate results. At present, three different standards exist determining whether a private school qualifies for tax exemption. They may be summarized as follows:
>
> *If the school admits making any distinction on the basis of race, however minimal, there is an irrebuttable presumption of guilt.*
>
> *If the school denies making any distinction on the basis of race, and is located in Mississippi, there is a rebuttable presumption of guilt and the burden is on the school to prove that it does not discriminate. If the school denies making any distinction on the basis of race and is located outside the state of Mississippi, there is no presumption of guilt; if the school states that it does not discriminate, the IRS will accept this declaration as true.* (authors' emphasis)

---

*Copyright © 1986 by West Publishing Company. Reprinted with permission.

This rule, which has emerged from fifteen years of litigation ... penalizes honesty, rewards duplicity and invites perjury. Congress, when it enacted the Internal Revenue Code, surely did not intend this result.

Do you agree with the authors' assessment of the three cases?

C. EDUCATIONAL CHOICE

Educational choice has emerged as one vehicle for alternatives in education and several states and many individual school districts are considering programs in this area. "Educational choice" has been referred to as a "panacea" for educational reform, yet the term has several definitions (for definitions, *see* Daniel, *A Comprehensive Analysis of Educational Choice: Can the Polemic of Legal Problems Be Overcome?*, 43 DePaul L. Rev. 1, 10-24 (1993)). An examination of the states' individual choice plans indicates little uniformity and much confusion. State legislation has taken many different forms and has resulted in unanticipated problems and other less-than-positive effects on program participants. The articles and cases that follow give an overview of "choice" with pro and con arguments discussing implications for policy makers.

1. PUBLIC SCHOOL PROBLEMS AND CHOICE PROPOSALS

JENCKS, IS THE PUBLIC SCHOOL OBSOLETE?, The Public Interest, 18, 21-27 (Winter 1966)*

It would be politically difficult to equalize opportunity between the slums and the suburbs under the best of circumstances. But not even the better financed slum schools (*e.g.* those in Harlem, on which more money is spent than in most suburbs outside the New York area) achieve results comparable to suburban systems. This in turn makes it even more difficult to raise the necessary money than it would otherwise be. If an extra $20 billion a year would bring slum children up to the academic level of their suburban rivals, some legislators would support the expenditure out of idealism. But many legislators feel — and not without reason — that even if they gave the schools an unlimited budget, the children of the slums would continue to grow up both personally and academically crippled.

These fears may be exaggerated. They certainly ought to be tested empirically before being accepted at face value. The Ford Foundation, for example, instead of sprinkling money around in dozens of different projects and places, ought to try raising school expenditures in one slum area to, say, double the level in nearby suburbs — just to see what would happen. It would, of course, take many years to tell. Children who were more than two or three when the experiment began would already have been scarred, often hopelessly, by the existing system.

---

*The Public Interest (Winter 1966) pp. 18, 21-27. Copyright 1966 by National Affairs Inc. Reprinted by permission.

It would be a generation before the impact of the extra money on today's infants could be fully weighed. But if it turned out that an extra $100 million a year made a dramatic difference in, say, the slums of Washington, D.C., it would become very much easier to get comparable sums from taxpayers in other areas.

Unfortunately, an extra $100 million might not make a dramatic difference in Washington — or in most other places either. Much that has been said and written about slum schools, not only in Washington but in places where race is not an issue, suggests that inadequate funds are only part of their problem. They also have the wrong motives and objectives. Some slum schools seem to be less educational than penal institutions. Their function is more to pacify the young than to teach them. They are ruled by fear, not love, infected by boredom, not curiosity. Such schools should not be given more money; they should be closed.

The roots of the problem go very deep. At times the problem seems to be public control itself. Because the slum school is public, it is accountable to the taxpayer. As in every other public enterprise, this kind of minute accountability to publicity-hungry elected officials leads to timidity among the employees. Public control puts a premium not on achieving a few spectacular successes but on avoiding any spectacular failures. In this respect there is not much difference between education and other fields of public endeavor. Nevertheless, public control over education has achieved a sanctity and respectability which public control over other enterprises has never mustered. Conversely, the ideologists of private enterprise have, with the conspicuous exception of Milton Friedman, been comparatively slow to apply their arguments in behalf of private schools.

Yet public control is not a sufficient explanation of the problems of the slum school, for public control seems to have worked quite well in some suburbs and small towns. The problem seems to be that in the slums public control has been linked to inadequate funds for performing the job assigned. Slum schools have found it difficult to get extra money even when there was reason to believe that the marginal return on this money would be very good. Educators might argue, for example, that doubling expenditures in the slums would treble results. But since we have no good way to measure this, skeptical legislators have been slow to provide extra money. As a result, pay scales in big city school systems have been too low to compete with most other jobs requiring equivalent training, skill, and masochism. And so, in turn, many slum teachers and administrators have comparatively little competence, confidence or commitment.

In city after city this has led to the creation of a system of education whose first axiom is that *everyone*, on every level, is incompetent and irresponsible. From this axiom comes the corollary that everyone must be carefully watched by a superior. The school board has no faith in the central administration, the central administration has no faith in the principals, the principals have no faith in the teachers, and the teachers have no faith in the students. Decision-making is constantly centralized into as few hands as possible rather than being decentralized into as many hands as possible, in the hope of reducing errors to a minimum. Of course such a system also reduces individual initiative to a minimum, but that is a price which a publicly-controlled bureaucracy, whose aim is not profits but survival, usually seems willing to pay. In such a system it seems natural not to give the principal of a school control over his budget, not to give teachers control over their syllabus, and not to give the students control over anything. Distrust is the order of the day, symbolized by the elaborate accounting system, the endless forms to be filled out for the central office, the time clocks and the two-way radios for monitoring classrooms from the front office, the constant tests and elaborate regulations for students.

In such a system everyone gets along by going along with the man over him. Most come to see themselves as play actors. The student tries to dope out what the teacher wants, and gives it to him. Usually all he wants is a reasonable amount of quiet in class and some appearance of docility in doing assignments. The teachers, in turn, try to figure out what the principal wants. That usually means filing grades and attendance records promptly, keeping trouble over discipline to a minimum, and avoiding complaints from parents or students. The principal, in turn, tries to keep the central administration happy (and the administration tries to keep the school board happy) by not sticking his neck out and by damping down "trouble" before it gets "out of hand."

Organizational sclerosis of this kind is extremely difficult to cure. For obvious reasons innovation from the bottom up becomes impossible and unthinkable. But even innovation from the top down is difficult. It is easy to get people to through the *forms* of change, but it is almost impossible to get them to *really* change, because they are frozen into defensive postures based on years of stand-pattism. If the principal tells the teachers he wants them to revamp the curriculum, they immediately begin looking to him — not to their students in the classroom — for cues and clues about what kinds of changes to propose. If the teachers tell the students to think for themselves, the students interpret this as just another move by the teacher to complicate "the game," another frustration in their efforts to "give the teacher what he wants." If the school board tries raising salaries in order to attract new kinds of teachers, it must still assign them to the same old schools, where they are still treated like filing clerks. So the more imaginative and dedicated teachers leave after a year or two for other schools — often in suburbia — which treat them better. In such circumstances more money may just mean more of the same.

A business which becomes afflicted with this kind of disease either goes bankrupt or else creates a monopoly or cartel to protect itself from more dynamic competition. The same is true of school systems. Were it not for their monopoly on educational opportunities for the poor, most big city school systems would probably go out of business. If, for example, the poor were simply given the money that is now spent on their children's education in public schools, and were told they could spend this money in private institutions, private schools would begin to spring up to serve slum children. In due course such schools would probably enroll the great majority of these children. The case of the parochial schools illustrates this point. These schools are seldom really free, but many parents, including some non-Catholics, make considerable sacrifices to send their children to them. In some cases, of course, this is a matter of religious faith. But if one asks parents why they prefer the parochial schools, the answer is often that they think the schooling itself is better than what the public schools in their area offer. Evidence collected by Peter Rossi and Andrew Greeley of the National Opinion Research Center suggests that the parochial schools usually *do* do more for their students than their public competitors, at least judging by the records of their alumni. This seems to be so despite the fact that they have less money, pay lower salaries to lay teachers, have larger classes, older buildings, and fewer amenities of every sort.

There is, of course, considerable reluctance among non-Catholics (and also among anti-clerical Catholics) to admit that the parochial schools might be doing something of value. Most non-Catholics, including myself, have an instinctive distrust of the Church. We have readily accepted the proposition that its schools were "divisive," despite research evidence which shows that aside from their religious practices parochial school graduates have about the same habits and values as Catholics who attend public schools. A similar prejudice clouds efforts to discuss what have traditionally been called "private" schools. Educators have taught us to use "public" as a synonym for "democratic" or just plain "good", and to associate "private" with "elitist" and "inequality." In part this is because when we think of a "public" school we conjure up a small-town or suburban school which is responsible and responsive to those whom it serves; a "private" school, on the other hand, is imagined as a posh country club for the sons of the rich. Yet using this kind of language to describe the "public" schools of Harlem surely obscures as much as it reveals. The Harlem schools are hardly more responsible or responsive to those whom they nominally serve than the typical "private" school. They are "public" only in the legal sense that the Post Office, for example, is "public", *i.e.*, they are tax supported, open to all, ultimately answerable to public officials who have almost no interest in them. Conversely, while it is true that "private" schools have in the past catered mainly to the well-off, this seems to reflect economic necessity more than social prejudice. If the poor were given as much money to spend on education as the rich, there is every reason to assume that the private sector would expand to accommodate them. Indeed, if we were to judge schools by their willingness to subsidize the poor, we would have to say that private schools have shown *more* interest in the poor than public ones. Has any suburban board of education used its own money to provide scholarships for slum children? Most refuse to admit such children even if their way is paid. Many private boards of trustees, on the other hand, have made such efforts, albeit on a small scale.

Private control has several advantages in a school which serves slum children. To begin with, it makes it possible to attack the problem in manageable bites. It is inconceivable that a big city school system can be reformed all at once. Failing that, however, it may be impossible to reform it at all. If, for example, the system is geared to docile teachers who do not want and cannot handle responsibility, how is it to accommodate the enterprising minority to have ideas of their own and want freedom to try them out? The superintendent cannot alter the whole system to deal with a handful of such teachers, even if he wants to. But if he does not alter the system, the better teachers will usually leave — or not come in the first place. Somehow the system must be broken up so that its parts can develop at different paces, in different styles, and even in different directions. Little cells of excellence must be nourished, gradually adding to their own number and excitement. Unusual talent must not be spread so thin over the whole system that no single place achieves the critical mass needed to sustain a chain reaction. Yet this is just what a conventional, centrally controlled system tends to do, for in such a system "special treatment" for a particular school is quickly defined as "favoritism." (This attitude is illustrated in the response of big cities to the offer of federal funds under the new Elementary and Secondary Education Act. Almost nobody wants to concentrate this money in a few places to create really good schools; everyone wants to spread it across the whole system.)

A second virtue of private schools is that they get away from the increasingly irrelevant tradition of neighborhood schools. Every psychologist and sociologist now recognizes that what children learn formally from their teachers is only a small fraction of their overall education. What they learn informally from their classmates is equally or more important. For this reason it is extremely important to expose slum children to classmates who teach them things which will be an asset rather than a liability as they grow older. A school which draws only from the slum itself will not provide this kind of stimulus. Instead, ways must be found to mix slum children with racially and economically different classmates.

In principle, of course, this kind of ethnic and economic mixing ought to be easier within a public system than a private one. But this may not be so in practice. In a publicly controlled system every school is required to follow essentially the same educational policies and practices as every other one. This means that the differences between schools derive largely if not exclusively from the differences in their student bodies. (Ability to hold good administrators and teachers seems to depend largely on this, for example.) So long as the student "mix" is decisive, middle-class parents are understandably reluctant to send their children to school with substantial numbers of lower-class children. White parents feel the same way about schools with large numbers of Negro children. But if the traditions and distinctive identity of a school depend not on the character of the student body but on the special objectives and methods of the staff, middle-class parents who approve of these objectives and methods will often send their children despite the presence of poorer classmates. This is clearest, perhaps, in the parochial schools. It might also be possible in non-sectarian private schools, if these had the money to give poor children scholarships, or if outside groups provided such scholarships to large numbers of children.

Getting rid of the neighborhood school, whether by creating city-wide public schools or private ones, could also have the virtue of providing the poor with a real choice about the kinds of schools their children attend. At present, the neighborhood school must try to be all things to all people in its area. Anything daring is bound to displease somebody, and so must be avoided. But if schools could simply tell those who disliked their methods to look elsewhere, and could look all over a large city for a clientele which wanted a particular brand of education, there would be a better chance both for innovation in the schools and for satisfying the diverse needs of different students. It should be possible, for example, for poor people to send their children to a school which segregates the sexes, or employs the Montessori method, or teaches reading phonetically, or emulates the Summerhill approach. Not everyone wants such things, but *some* do, and they should be able to get them. Given the present outlook of the men who control big city public schools, the only way to make these choices available is probably in the private sector.

In principle there are two ways to develop a larger measure of private initiative and room for maneuver in educating the poor. One would be to provide tuition grants to children who opted out of the public-controlled schools, equal to what would be spent on them if they stayed in. These tuition grants could be used to pay the bills in private schools. There are not, of course, enough private schools today to handle all the potential applicants from the slums, but more would spring up if money were available. But even without tuition grants it should be possible to create much more diversity and decentralization in the schools. School boards could, for example, contract with various groups to manage particular schools in their own system.

A university might be given contract to run a model school system in the slums, as suggested by the Panel on Educational Research and Development of the President's Science Advisory Committee. This is apparently to be tried in New York.

A local business group might also take over the management of a school. (If Litton Industries can run a Job Corps camp, it can surely run a school.)

A group of teachers might incorporate itself to manage a school on contract from the citywide board. This could be done at no expense within the present system, using present personnel and facilities, and it might have appreciable advantages. Suppose, for example, that the New York City Board of Education were to rent its facilities to their present staffs and provide them with a management contract subject to annual review. Ultimate control over the school could be vested in the teachers, who would hire administrators. Hiring and firing teachers, budget-making, programming and so forth would all be decided on the spot. If the school did a poor job — which some surely would — the contract could be terminated. A group of parents, working through an elected board, might also take over a school. This alternative, which should be especially appealing to the New Left and to the prophets of "community action," is perhaps better described as a new kind of public control than as private control.

In effect, it would mean replacing responsibility to the taxpayer-stockholder with responsibility to the consumer — a kind of educational cooperative.

All these alternatives aim at a radical decentralization of both power and responsibility. All would liberate the schools from the dead hand of central administration, from minute accountability to the public for every penny, every minute, and every word. They all recognize that so far as the slum child is concerned, the present system of "socialized education" has failed, and that some kind of new departure, either "capitalist" or "syndicalist," is needed.

Either tuition grants or management contracts to private organizations would, of course, "destroy the public school system as we know it." When one thinks of the remarkable past achievements of public education in America, this may seem a foolish step. But we must not allow the memory of past achievements to blind us to present failures. Nor should we allow the rhetoric of public school men to obscure the issue. It is natural for public servants to complain about private competition, just as private business complains about public competition. But if the terms of the competition are reasonable, there is every reason to suppose that it is healthy. Without it, both public and private enterprises have a way of ossifying. And if, as some fear, the public schools could not survive in open competition with private ones, then perhaps they *should* not survive.

....

FRIEDMAN, CAPITALISM AND FREEDOM, 85-93 (1962)*

The Role of Government in Education

Formal schooling is today paid for and almost entirely administered by government bodies or non-profit institutions. This situation has developed gradually and is now taken so much for granted that little explicit attention is any longer directed to the reasons for the special treatment of schooling even in countries that are predominantly free enterprise in organization and philosophy. The result has been an indiscriminate extension of governmental responsibility.

... [G]overnmental intervention into education can be rationalized on two grounds. The first is the existence of substantial "neighborhood effects," *i.e.*, circumstances under which the action of one individual imposes significant costs on other individuals for which it is not feasible to make him compensate them, or yields significant gains to other individuals for which it is not feasible to make them compensate him — circumstances that make voluntary exchange impossible. The second is the paternalistic concern for children and other irresponsible individuals. Neighborhood effects and paternalism have very different implications for (1) general education for citizenship, and (2) specialized vocational education. The grounds for governmental intervention are widely different in these two areas and justify very different types of action.

---

*Reprinted by permission of the author and the University of Chicago Press.

One further preliminary remark: it is important to distinguish between "schooling" and "education." Not all schooling is education nor all education, schooling. The proper subject of concern is education. The activities of government are mostly limited to schooling.

A stable and democratic society is impossible without a minimum degree of literacy and knowledge on the part of most citizens and without widespread acceptance of some common set of values. Education can contribute to both. In consequence, the gain from the education of a child accrues not only to the child or to his parents but also to other members of the society. The education of my child contributes to your welfare by promoting a stable and democratic society. It is not feasible to identify the particular individuals (or families) benefited and so to charge for the services rendered. There is therefore a significant "neighborhood effect."

What kind of governmental action is justified by this particular neighborhood effect? The most obvious is to require that each child receive a minimum amount of schooling of a specified kind. Such a requirement could be imposed upon the parents without further government action, just as owners of buildings, and frequently of automobiles, are required to adhere to specified standards to protect the safety of others. There is, however, a difference between the two cases. Individuals who cannot pay the costs of meeting the standards required for buildings or automobiles can generally divest themselves of the property by selling it. The requirement can thus generally be enforced without government subsidy. The separation of a child from a parent who cannot pay for the minimum required schooling is clearly inconsistent with our reliance on the family as the basic social unit and our belief in the freedom of the individual. Moreover, it would be very likely to detract from his education for citizenship in a free society.

If the financial burden imposed by such a schooling requirement could readily be met by the great bulk of the families in a community, it might still be both feasible and desirable to require the parents to meet the cost directly. Extreme cases could be handled by special subsidy provisions for needy families. There are many areas in the United States today where these conditions are satisfied. In these areas, it would be highly desirable to impose the costs directly on the parents. This would eliminate the governmental machinery now required to collect tax funds from all residents during the whole of their lives and then pay it back mostly to the same people during the period when their children are in school. It would reduce the likelihood that governments would also administer schools, a matter discussed further below. It would increase the likelihood that the subsidy component of school expenditures would decline as the need for such subsidies declined with increasing general levels of income. If, as now, the government pays for all or most schooling, a rise in income simply leads to a still larger circular flow of funds through the tax mechanism, and an expansion in the role of the government. Finally, but by no means least, imposing the costs on the parents would tend to equalize the social and private costs of having children and so promote a better distribution of families by size.[1]

Differences among families in resources and in number of children, plus the imposition of a standard of schooling involving very sizable costs, make such a policy hardly feasible in many parts of the United States. Both in such areas, and in areas where such a policy would be feasible, government has instead assumed the financial costs of providing schooling. It has paid, not only for the minimum amount of schooling required of all, but also for additional schooling at higher levels available to youngsters but not required of them. One argument for both steps is the "neighborhood effects" discussed above. The costs are paid because this is the only feasible means of enforcing the required minimum. Additional schooling is financed because other people benefit from the schooling of those of greater ability and interest, since this is a way of providing better social and political leadership. The gain from these measures must be balanced against the costs, and there can be much honest difference of judgment about how extensive a subsidy is justified. Most of us, however, would probably conclude that the gains are sufficiently important to justify some government subsidy.

These grounds justify government subsidy of only certain kinds of schooling. To anticipate, they do not justify subsidizing purely vocational training which increases the economic productivity of the student but does not train him for either citizenship or leadership. It is extremely difficult to draw a sharp line between the two types of schooling. Most general schooling adds to the economic value of the student — indeed it is only in modern times and in a few countries that literacy has ceased to have a marketable value. And much vocational training broadens the student's outlook. Yet the distinction is meaningful. Subsidizing the training of veterinarians, beauticians, dentists, and a host of other specialists, as is widely done in the United States in governmentally supported educational institutions, cannot be justified on the same grounds as subsidizing elementary schools or, at a higher level, liberal arts colleges....

The qualitative argument from "neighborhood effects" does not, of course, determine the specific kinds of schooling that should be subsidized or by how much they should be subsidized. The social gain presumably is greatest for the lowest levels of schooling, where there is the nearest approach to unanimity about content, and declines continuously as the level of schooling rises. Even this statement cannot be taken completely for granted. Many governments subsidized universities long before they subsidized lower schools. What forms of education have the greatest social advantage and how much of the community's limited resources should be spent on them must be decided by the judgment of the

---

[1] It is by no means so fantastic as may appear that such a step would noticeably affect the size of families. For example, one explanation of the lower birth rate among higher than among lower socio-economic groups may well be that children are relatively more expensive to the former, thanks in considerable measure to the higher standards of schooling they maintain, the costs of which they bear.

community expressed through its accepted political channels. The aim of this analysis is not to decide these questions for the community but rather to clarify the issues involved in making a choice, in particular whether it is appropriate to make the choice on a communal rather than individual basis.

As we have seen, both the imposition of a minimum required level of schooling and the financing of this schooling by the state can be justified by the "neighborhood effects" of schooling. A third step, namely the actual administration of educational institutions by the government, the "nationalization," as it were, of the bulk of the "education industry" is much more difficult to justify on these, or, so far as I can see, any other, grounds. The desirability of such nationalization has seldom been faced explicitly. Governments have, in the main, financed schooling by paying directly the costs of running educational institutions. Thus this step seemed required by the decision to subsidize schooling. Yet the two steps could readily be separated. Governments could require a minimum level of schooling financed by giving parents vouchers redeemable for a specified maximum sum per child per year if spent on "approved" educational services. Parents would then be free to spend this sum and any additional sum they themselves provided on purchasing educational services from an "approved" institution of their own choice. The educational services could be rendered by private enterprises operated for profit, or by non-profit institutions. The role of the government would be limited to insuring that the schools met certain minimum standards, such as the inclusion of a minimum common content in their programs, much as it now inspects restaurants to insure that they maintain minimum sanitary standards. An excellent example of a program of this sort is the United States educational program for veterans after World War II. Each veteran who qualified was given a maximum sum per year that could be spent at any institution of his choice, provided it met certain minimum standards. A more limited example is the provision in Britain whereby local authorities pay the fees of some students attending non-state schools. Another is the arrangement in France whereby the state pays part of the costs for students attending non-state schools.

One argument for nationalizing schools resting on a "neighborhood effect" is that it might otherwise be impossible to provide the common core of values deemed requisite for social stability. The imposition of minimum standards on privately conducted schools, as suggested above, might not be enough to achieve this result. The issue can be illustrated concretely in terms of schools run by different religious groups. Such schools, it can be argued, will instil sets of values that are inconsistent with one another and with those instilled in non-sectarian schools; in this way, they convert education into a divisive rather than a unifying force.

Carried to its extreme, this argument would call not only for governmentally administered schools, but also for compulsory attendance at such schools. Existing arrangements in the United States and most other Western countries are a halfway house. Governmentally administered schools are available but not

C. EDUCATIONAL CHOICE

compulsory. However, the link between the financing of schooling and its administration places other schools at a disadvantage: they get the benefit of little or none of the governmental funds spent on schooling — a situation that has been the source of much political dispute, particularly in France and at present in the United States. The elimination of this disadvantage might, it is feared, greatly strengthen the parochial schools and so render the problem of achieving a common core of values even more difficult.

Persuasive as this argument is, it is by no means clear that it is valid or that denationalizing schooling would have the effects suggested. On grounds of principle, it conflicts with the preservation of freedom itself. Drawing a line between providing for the common social values required for a stable society, on the one hand, and indoctrination inhibiting freedom of thought and belief, on the other is another of those vague boundaries that is easier to mention than to define.

In terms of effects, denationalizing schooling would widen the range of choice available to parents. If, as at present, parents can send their children to public schools without special payment, very few can or will send them to other schools unless they too are subsidized. Parochial schools are at a disadvantage in not getting any of the public funds devoted to schooling, but they have the compensating advantage of being run by institutions that are willing to subsidize them and can raise funds to do so. There are few other sources of subsidies for private schools. If present public expenditures on schooling were made available to parents regardless of where they send their children, a wide variety of schools would spring up to meet the demand. Parents could express their views about schools directly by withdrawing their children from one school and sending them to another, to a much greater extent than is now possible. In general, they can now take this step only at considerable cost — by sending their children to a private school or by changing their residence. For the rest, they can express their views only through cumbrous political channels. Perhaps a somewhat greater degree of freedom to choose schools could be made available in a governmentally administered system, but it would be difficult to carry this freedom very far in view of the obligation to provide every child with a place. Here, as in other fields, competitive enterprise is likely to be far more efficient in meeting consumer demand than either nationalized enterprises or enterprises run to serve other purposes. The final result may therefore be that parochial schools would decline rather than grow in importance.

A related factor working in the same direction is the understandable reluctance of parents who send their children to parochial schools to increase taxes to finance higher public school expenditures. As a result, those areas where parochial schools are important have great difficulty raising funds for public schools. Insofar as quality is related to expenditure, as to some extent it undoubtedly is, public schools tend to be of lower quality in such areas and hence parochial schools are relatively more attractive.

Another special case of the argument that governmentally conducted schools are necessary for education to be a unifying force is that private schools would tend to exacerbate class distinctions. Given greater freedom about where to send their children, parents of a kind would flock together and so prevent a healthy intermingling of children from decidedly different backgrounds. Whether or not this argument is valid in principle, it is not at all clear that the stated results would follow. Under present arrangements, stratification of residential areas effectively restricts the intermingling of children from decidedly different backgrounds. In addition, parents are not now prevented from sending their children to private schools. Only a highly limited class can or does do so, parochial schools aside, thus producing further stratification.

Indeed, this argument seems to me to point in almost the diametrically opposite direction — toward the denationalizing of schools. Ask yourself in what respect the inhabitant of a low income neighborhood, let alone of a Negro neighborhood in a large city, is most disadvantaged. If he attaches enough importance to, say, a new automobile, he can, by dint of saving, accumulate enough money to buy the same car as a resident of a high income suburb. To do so, he need not move to that suburb. On the contrary, he can get the money partly by economizing on his living quarters. And this goes equally for clothes, or furniture, or books, or what not. But let a poor family in a slum have a gifted child and let it set such high value on his or her schooling that it is willing to scrimp and save for the purpose. Unless it can get special treatment, or scholarship assistance, at one of the very few private schools, the family is in a very difficult position. The "good" public schools are in the high income neighborhoods. The family might be willing to spend something in addition to what it pays in taxes to get better schooling for its child. But it can hardly afford simultaneously to move to the expensive neighborhood.

Our views in these respects are, I believe, still dominated by the small town which had but one school for the poor and rich residents alike. Under such circumstances, public schools may well have equalized opportunities. With the growth of urban and suburban areas, the situation has changed drastically. Our present school system, far from equalizing opportunity, very likely does the opposite. It makes it all the harder for the exceptional few — and it is they who are the hope of the future — to rise above the poverty of their initial state.

Another argument for nationalizing schooling is "technical monopoly." In small communities and rural areas, the number of children may be too small to justify more than one school of reasonable size, so that competition cannot be relied on to protect the interests of parents and children. As in other cases of technical monopoly, the alternatives are unrestricted private monopoly, state-controlled private monopoly, and public operation — a choice among evils. This argument, though clearly valid and significant, has been greatly weakened in recent decades by improvements in transportation and increasing concentration of the population in urban communities.

The arrangement that perhaps comes closest to being justified by these considerations — at least for primary and secondary education — is a combination of public and private schools. Parents who choose to send their children to private schools would be paid a sum equal to the estimated cost of educating a child in a public school, provided that at least this sum was spent on education in an approved school. This arrangement would meet the valid features of the "technical monopoly" argument. It would meet the just complaints of parents that if they send their children to private non-subsidized schools they are required to pay twice for education — once in the form of general taxes and once directly. It would permit competition to develop. The development and improvement of all schools would thus be stimulated. The injection of competition would do much to promote a healthy variety of schools. It would do much, also, to introduce flexibility into school systems. Not least of its benefits would be to make the salaries of school teachers responsive to market forces. It would thereby give public authorities an independent standard against which to judge salary scales and promote a more rapid adjustment to changes in conditions of demand and supply.

....

TANCREDO, THE CASE FOR VOUCHERS, 71 Educ. L. Rep. 593 (1992)*

....

The power and influence of the public education establishment are as great as ever even though it has been discredited by every standard used to gauge its output. The system remains undisturbed by a miserable performance record and almost daily revelations of its inadequacies and excesses.

We need to change the system. We can do it with choice, and I mean the kind of choice that allows parents and students to pick from the widest possible variety of educational opportunities, both public and private. The best way of providing that choice is with education vouchers.

....

Many government schools, as an enterprise, failed long ago; but because the resources flowing into them are not influenced by the degree to which they are unsuccessful, they cannot go out of business.

Americans are increasingly turning to reforms based on parental choice of schools as the best solution to America's education crisis. Support for choice comes from across the political spectrum: Republicans and Democrats, liberals and conservatives, minorities and whites, support choice. The liberal Brookings Institution and the conservative Heritage Foundation have identified it as the most important aspect of reform.

---

*Reprinted with permission from West Publishing Company.

While political support has been growing, a number of legal questions concerning choice remain as serious impediments to wide spread adoption. Perhaps the most significant legal hurdles for any choice plan are federal anti-discrimination requirements and the "establishment" clause of the First Amendment.

Although there is an element of racism in the present debate over education choice plans, it is exhibited by opponents of vouchers who fear that black and brown youngsters, if given the freedom to escape poor urban schools, would flood into white suburban enclaves. It is the economically disadvantaged of the inner city who would most benefit from choice. Choice can, and often does, have the effect of increasing the process of integration and doing so in a manner much less problematic than forced bussing.

Education vouchers which could be used at schools with a religious affiliation will almost certainly face the constitutional challenge of the "*Lemon* test." That is, any plan:

1. Must serve a secular purpose.
2. In its "primary effect" must neither advance nor inhibit religion.
3. Must not foster an "excessive entanglement" between government and religion.

Although it is highly likely that the *Lemon* test will be reviewed and perhaps "liberalized" by the new Court, I believe that voucher legislation could withstand the establishment clause challenge as long as the plan does not discriminate in favor of any religiously affiliated school; and that the vouchers be placed directly in the hands of parents to then be used against tuition costs.

Indeed, as the Heritage Foundation has contended-well crafted choice programs provide more answers to legal problems than they create barriers.

Taking this outside of the legal arena for a moment, I'd like to discuss other implications of vouchers, and to take on the most often heard criticisms. The first being the fallacy of "creaming" which is the idea that choice will siphon off the best and the brightest, so that the inner city public schools will be left with only the poor and otherwise educationally disadvantaged children. Of course, the fact is that today the only group which is not able to escape a rotten school is the poor. There may be transportation problems, but these could be addressed in a variety of ways, including the use of transportation vouchers.

One must also consider the dynamics of a market place. Entrepreneurs go to where demand exists. There is no reason to believe that children would have to travel long distances for better schools. Also, technology has the potential of dramatically changing the present delivery system. Who says tomorrow's schools will be expensive buildings to which children go and in which teachers are placed for seven hours a day? Of course because the development of this technology threatens to reduce the number of NEA protected jobs, research and development in this area proceeds at a snails' pace.

Others charge that competitive schools would be at a disadvantage to non-public schools because the latter are not forced to "play by the same rules." The implication here is that it is impossible to have high quality education exist in any classroom regulated by the state. The fact is, there are some great public schools and some lousy private schools. Without the benefits of free market competition however, there is little, if any, incentive to expand the number of the former or eliminate the latter.

The rules that actually produce a successful school are the same for everyone everywhere. A school succeeds because it (a) maintains high academic standards, (b) maintains a disciplined environment, and (c) presents a challenging curriculum. There is no reason that public schools can't "play by these rules." To do so, however, requires a tremendous amount of effort and commitment by everyone involved. The present system offers educators no incentive to maintain this effort over a long period of time; nor does it present a threat to those unwilling to do so.

Yet another criticism of vouchers arises out of the fear that giving parents the opportunity to choose their childrens' schools would have the effect of balkanizing our society and destroying its democratic ethos.

I suggest, on the contrary, that the greatest threat to this democratic ethos is the radical multicultural curriculum we now see working its way into the public schools. This is an ethnocentric curriculum politicized in the extreme. For the multiculturalists, race and ethnicity have become the one and only lens through which all historical events are examined.

As the distinguished education historian and now U.S. Assistant Secretary of Education for Educational Research and Improvement, Diane Ravitch, has argued, "Afrocentrism and other such curricular changes throw into question the very idea of American public education. When public schools cease to transmit common values and a shared culture — and they are now dangerously close to doing just that — the main argument in support of their exclusive claim to taxpayers' money will have lost its force."

How Parents Can Get What They Want

Most parents want schools to share the responsibility for transmitting the values of honesty, rewards for hard work, and appreciation of our republican system.

The average parent, recognizing economic realities in today's competitive world, would obviously prefer a system that teaches children how to read, write and compute over one in which children spend nearly half their time "getting in touch with their feelings."

But it's not hard to understand why the system has opted for the latter method. Which one of these two education philosophies is more difficult, if not impossible, to grade? Which philosophy makes accountability almost meaningless? Which one would suffer grievously in a free-market atmosphere?

The shift to a fuzzy, unmeasurable curriculum, while no doubt sincere at one level, can be read at a deeper level as a classic blame-avoidance maneuver.

It is apparent that this change in the basic nature of the present system can now only come about when schools are free to respond to majority sentiment, to consumers voting not just with ballots but with attendance decisions and dollars. Of course, moving to this free-market approach to education would in itself send an important message. It would say that we recognize the merits of individualism over the collective, that risk takers are valued, and that monopolies, whether they are private or governmental, have the effect of destroying initiative.

If we are to cure America's ailing public school system we must establish competitive markets and parental choice. As the Brookings Institution researchers Chubb and Moe concluded, the organizational structure of America's school system is the biggest factor contributing to the poor quality of public education in this country. Believing that the "key to quality education is principals who give greater autonomy to teachers" they recommended that parental choice and competitive markets be used to create a "highly competitive school system in which competent principals are rewarded by growing enrollments, while incompetent principals are punished by falling enrollments."

Choice is a powerful instrument, yet we have chosen to bypass it for administrative convenience, job protection, or some other reason totally unrelated to student welfare and achievement. Real improvement, will not occur without providing choice. Choice will not only improve student motivation and performance, but it will also force institutional accountability that for so long we have been trying to achieve through other artificial less effective means.

The reason America so urgently needs education vouchers is that they would give millions of parents the economic ability to make that kind of decisive change on their children's behalf.

DANIEL, A COMPREHENSIVE ANALYSIS OF EDUCATIONAL CHOICE: CAN THE POLEMIC OF LEGAL PROBLEMS BE OVERCOME?, 43 DePaul L. Rev. 1 (1993)*

Introduction

....

School choice, in general terms, is the privilege of parents to select schools for their children, either inside or outside their district of residence, with enabling support provided by their local, state, or national government. The idea of choice rests upon the twin principles of increased competition and the alignment of students with the best possible schools for their needs. The privilege of choice may extend to a public or private school, with parents being subsidized by the

---

*Copyright © 1993 by The DePaul Law Review. Reprinted with permission. Citations from this excerpt have been omitted.

C. EDUCATIONAL CHOICE

government in the form of a voucher or income tax credit. There are a wide range of possible structures for these plans, but "they share the common element of agreement that greater choice is desirable in the US [sic] system of education." ...

....

III. *Arguments for and Against School Choice Plans*

Parental choice, especially when it involves private schools, serves as one of the more hotly debated issues in education today. Until recently, the debate has been highly theoretical due to the absence of empirical studies evaluating both theories and programs. This section of the article will continue some of that theoretical discussion, but it will also note the work of empirical studies conducted to date. Much of the empirical information emanates from analysis of pro-choice reports such as the Chubb and Moe study. To delineate the colloquy, this section will examine parental choice under topics that are prominent among the theorists: school competition, student achievement, equitable concerns regarding low income students, and the right of parents to choose the schools their children attend.

A. *Competition*

The values embodied in economic competition underlie most school choice legislation. As early as 1974, Peter Drucker argued that educational institutions, like other government service institutions, are ineffective due to the way they are funded. According to Drucker, leaders in business recognize that satisfying the customer is the only way to guarantee continued existence and growth of the company. However, others point out that involuntary taxes consistently fund public schools. Regardless of whether they satisfy student needs or perform effectively in the process, public schools still collect a major share of tax dollars to stay in "business." As the argument goes, this type of funding situation, absent choice legislation, results in a "captive audience" regardless of the school's performance or its responsiveness to children and parents.

This latter set of comments also forms the basis of the most widely-quoted work on school choice, *Politics, Markets and America's Schools*, by John Chubb and Terry Moe. These authors believe that schools driven by the market place are more effective than those under public control. They argue that deregulating the public school system will create a highly differentiated set of offerings for students and will lead to greater efficiency, thereby offering a better educational product. They accuse public school systems of being complacent, lethargic, inefficient, and unresponsive to the needs of most students. They argue that only by providing greater choice to parents in a pure market situation involving public and private schools can the quality of education in the United States ever improve.

Using the Chubb and Moe thesis, many state legislatures have enacted educational choice legislation. As a general rule, such states have left intact the ability of educational organizations to use tax dollars to support education. Furthermore, local school authorities have been able to maintain authority to seek additional local tax dollars through referenda. Choice advocates seek a variation of this arrangement by supporting the right of parents to choose a school, inside or outside the district, with public funds supporting the student. The economic theory of supply and demand, therefore, suggests that state funds would continue to enable these school districts to meet consumers' demands. If the state were to adopt a completely free-market approach to educational choice, this theory says, it would force public schools to be more responsive to the needs of parents and students. As a result, schools would provide more desirable educational services. Conversely, schools that did not meet these demands would either have to improve educational programs or go out of business.

Detractors of this competition theory indicate that the experience of business can hardly serve as a model for the public school system to do its job. They state that the work of Chubb and Moe, as well as that of other researchers, provides little in the way of evidence that marketplace justice will improve school processes or increase efficiency. In fact, such detractors indicate that the marketplace is often indifferent to the needs of certain people, particularly low-income groups, because they can be "manipulated through fraud and false advertising." Stated another way, educational choice can never operate as a pure market because the seller of the service gets to choose the students and may charge different prices for services to discriminate on the basis of religion, race, disability, or any other arbitrarily chosen reason.

Detractors of the competition theory also state that markets do not operate naturally, but rather are socially constructed. Moreover, gambling in free markets for profit is one thing, but playing stocks with a child's education is quite another. Hence, the business model is not one for the education of the general public, as its private structures are incongruent with the public challenges.

Indeed, the notion of a pure competitive model in education ignores the fact that it is practically obligatory for every state and local government to provide a system of public education. There will always be students for whom public, non-magnet education is the only alternative. Hence, as a matter of public policy, it would be difficult to create a constitutionally supportable option of closing schools when the government's obligation is to ensure a viable, free educational program to which all students have access. Where inadequate education exists, the state's duty is to improve rather than abandon.

B. *Student Achievement*

At the center of the school choice revolution is the position that competition among schools will not only promote efficiency, but will have the corollary effect of vastly improving student academic achievement. Chubb and Moe, for example, argue that student achievement can be enhanced by the injection of market competition. Market theory drives this attitude, since its basis is the view

C. EDUCATIONAL CHOICE

that public schools have a monopoly on education, and that monopolies are devoid of pressure to operate efficiently. Specifically, Chubb and Moe state that parents should be further empowered, with the help of the state, to choose schools for their children; thus, parents will choose schools of higher academic quality, and this will in turn coerce schools of inferior quality to either provide better service or cease to exist.

Chubb and Moe condemn the current public school enterprise, claiming that current student achievement is a function of school organization and the structure of the school. The public school system has as its foundation the notion of shared governance between the state, the school board, parents, teachers, and other school personnel. Therefore, public schools suffer from bureaucratic control, and this in and of itself inhibits student achievement. Chubb and Moe state that the current system also diminishes school achievement because a democratic system of politics promotes centralized bureaucratic control and inhibits the autonomy of front-line administrators. Market choice, by contrast, is by nature decentralized, and this independence from democratic politics and bureaucracy fosters the development of organizational characteristics necessary for greater student achievement. Such organizational characteristics include varied and up to date academic programs, teacher creativity, high levels of teacher and administrative professionalism, increased discipline, and greater independent thinking on the part of students.

Anyone concerned about the welfare of public education in the United States can not overlook Chubb and Moe's arguments. Whether or not their arguments have merit or persuade legislators, public education is in great peril. If it is true that student achievement is a function of school organization and such public school organization is incapable of promoting this achievement, the door will open for pundits to openly call for the absence of shared governance in schooling and to collapse the boundary between public and private schooling.

Chubb and Moe based their viewpoint on data gathered from two surveys. Using this information, Chubb and Moe determined that school organization is one of four significant variables affecting student achievement, as measured by increases in standardized test scores from the sophomore to the senior year in high school. The other three significant variables were: (1) the student's ability at the sophomore year; (2) the socioeconomic status of the student's family; and (3) the socioeconomic status of the student body. They surmised from this data that well-organized schools with clear academic goals, strong educational leadership, and ambitious programs can make a meaningful difference in student achievement, and that this is comparable in importance to a student's background.

Curiously, the authors did not discuss the correlation between the other variables, such as the student's sophomore year ability, family socioeconomic status, and the socioeconomic status of the student body. Because of this and other inconsistencies, critical analyses of their work began to appear. Early on, John Witte examined the data in The High School and Beyond Survey ("HS &

B''), one of the surveys relied on by Chubb and Moe. Witte surveyed the statistical models, findings, and interpretations as well as the insights derived from that data set. He concluded that studies from it provide no useful information for the debate on school choice because reported differences in achievement between the schools in the set are *de minimis*, and that even these differences could be accounted for by measurement errors.

Henry Levin also examined Chubb and Moe's statistical analysis of the HS & B study. He found that although the Chubb and Moe study was "arcane and incomprehensible to the vast public audience," it nevertheless "succeeded in creating the perception that their conclusions were based on scientific findings." Levin instead postulated that the authors' findings were based on "tendentious reasoning and personal opinion that passed for analysis." Another author, David Hogan, joined Levin in questioning the integrity of the Chubb and Moe research. Hogan stood incredulous that the variables of student ability at the sophomore year, socioeconomic status of the family, and the socioeconomic status of the student body were left out of the analysis relative to student achievement. Hogan saw this as "academic alchemy," since such variables figure so prominently in the work of the authors who created the data set in the first place. Hogan viewed this as a serious conceptual and methodological flaw which undermines the credibility of the position that student achievement is a function of school organization.

Anthony Bryk and Valerie Lee, who used the same HS & B data, concluded that Chubb and Moe took unwarranted liberties in defining key concepts and in creating analytical models that the data did not justify. They postulated that the effect of this activity was to skew the results of the data to a particular outcome. They concluded that this kind of work is intellectually irresponsible, as it supplants a critical, disinterested analysis with a position nurtured by partisan politics.

Finally, the Carnegie Foundation for the Advancement of Teaching completed a 118-page report which surveyed school districts and parents concerning the issue of school choice. Pointing to student achievement, the study demonstrated that the impact of choice programs is ambiguous at best. While there was some small evidence of a correlation in district-wide programs, there was no such connection at the statewide level. Furthermore, although the essence of school choice for most proponents is that competition will stimulate academic programs, the survey offered little evidence of this notion. Of the states with competitive open enrollment legislation, no educational gains were attributable to parental choice.

C. *Race, Class, and Choice*

Supporters of educational choice also argue that it enables children of low-income and minority families to achieve educational equity and opportunities previously denied them because of their economic status. The rationale is that such students are victims of neighborhood schools because they must deal with

C. EDUCATIONAL CHOICE

an intellectually starved curriculum, a disproportionate track, and the stigma of being less-capable learners. Choice proponents suggest that if given innovative choices, parents will elect to leave these neighborhood schools for more effective options. Consequently, the neighborhood schools will be held more accountable.

Chubb and Moe are once again the progenitors of this idea. Through parent choice, low-income parents would have the alternatives wealthy parents have always enjoyed: public, private, secular, or sectarian schools. They propose a voucher system, keyed to parental income, that would prohibit parents from subsidizing the vouchers with "add-on" dollars but enable the state government to uniformly supplement the vouchers through the raising of taxes. These measures answer the concern of those who advocate equalizing the financial footing of all children regardless of socioeconomic status. Far from dispossessing economically disadvantaged families, supporters argue that choice programs would empower these families as never before.

One can hardly deny that the criticism of the public schools in connection with minority and low-income children is absolutely true. Public schools discriminate. In fact, the Supreme Court had to arrest state policies authorizing the separation of black and white children. School administrators and teachers have actually stifled the efforts of poor and minority students to achieve academic parity with other students. Even now the disciplinary procedures in public schools appear to be differentially applied between poor minority and more wealthy white students. The question is whether educational choice has demonstrated any amelioration of this and whether poor families who do not do well in the job and housing markets will become winners in a deregulated education market.

The research of equity advocates, however, seems devoid of any specific evidence that choice will better the situation of minority and low-income students. In fact, the empirical evidence indicates just the opposite. There is little proof that private schools and suburban public schools readily accept minority children from the city even when choice is an option. There is greater evidence that white students are better able to use choice to transfer from integrated urban schools to all-white suburban schools. Moreover, urban choice appears to exacerbate social divisions because middle class students have disproportionate access to the best public schools. In the San Francisco magnet school program, for example, schools resulting in an "unintentional two-tiered school system." Finally, choice legislation is unlikely to give a student enough money to attend a private school of his or her choice. In contrast to the Chubb and Moe proposal, suggested choice programs do not contemplate a voucher for the full cost of private tuition. This would do little to help poor parents because they would be forced to make up the difference out of family funds. Such a proposal seems rather naive, if not disingenuous.

Choice supporters tout the experience of the East Harlem schools in New York City as a successful example of school choice. This is because it was the first such program in the country and because, over the past twenty years, the area has raised itself from being dead last on proficiency tests (compared to the rest of the city) to a level approximating the city-wide average. An understanding of the demographics of the area is important to fully comprehend the magnitude of the accomplishment. There are approximately 14,000 students in the district, 80 percent of whom are eligible for free or reduced lunch programs. Ninety-five percent of the children are either African-American or hispanic. Before reform came to the district, there was a tremendous gang problem, a malaise among the teachers and administrators, and children existed in an atmosphere void of learning. This changed radically with the influx of generous amounts of state and federal money and new administrative leadership. The change, however, may not have helped those students most in need; instead, it put them in a position of competing for the good schools in East Harlem under the rubric of choice. Choice, therefore, became a gate-keeper for school administrators, not parents. School officials used choice to select and admit the most academically gifted of the students. In fact, until recently, these schools had hidden admissions criteria enabling them to choose students long before parents had a chance to apply. This was school choice in Harlem, and using the same criteria as other selective institutions, good students were already in the better schools.

Activities of school personnel notwithstanding, there is some research that suggests a difference in the way parents of varied socioeconomic backgrounds make decisions relative to choice. One study of a choice program in Alum Rock, California, involved tuition vouchers given to parents over a five-year period between 1972 and 1977. The study found that information levels regarding the voucher program were much higher among white parents with higher incomes, and the parents' educational backgrounds proved to be an especially important factor. To wit, these parents were much more likely to use the vouchers and to choose schools that offered the best possible education.

The Alum Rock study highlights the role of information acquisition in educational choice, as well as education and experience in choosing among alternatives. Henry Levin also concludes that in all these respects, low-income minority parents are simply ill-equipped to make the informed decisions that other parents can. Part of the reason is the lack of access to information, and even if information is readily available, the fact remains that these parents suffer the inability to decipher the argot of legislative and administrative jargon. Lévin notes that in a different California choice experiment, even with a substantial effort to inform parents through various media, there was considerably less awareness of choice options among low-income minority parents. A similar pattern was found in the choice program in Milwaukee, where many low-income minority parents had little idea of the names or descriptions of available schools.

Levin raises a further related difficulty concerning choice among low-income minority parents. Choices are made on the basis of the context of one's own experience, and studies have shown that blue-collar parents tend to emphasize obedience to authority in the choice of schools while white-collar families tend to emphasize critical and independent thinking. Extending these findings, this would mean that low-income parents would tend to emphasize highly structured

C. EDUCATIONAL CHOICE

schools stressing discipline and basic skills as opposed to middle and upper class parents, who would push the development of greater freedom in the curriculum based on good communication skills and conceptual learning. The latter type of emphasis coincides with the college preparatory strand of schools. Such an inbred problem, therefore, would likely perpetuate rather than ameliorate class status under choice.

The Carnegie study confirmed this problem, indicating that choice programs work better for the better-educated. Those with the sophistication, the knowledge, and the income were better able to choose the best academic programs in Minnesota and Milwaukee. Low-income students, including those who may be homeless, in the care of under-educated grandparents, in group homes, or have drug problems stand little chance if the choice is left to any but very knowledgeable, culturally sensitive, and committed school personnel. Furthermore, unless regulation of choice programs addresses the needs of the least economically able, such persons will have no real choice.

D. *Parental Rights*

In the choice debate, one of the major points of contention relates to parental rights in influencing a child's education. In fact, this argument has served as one of the foundations for choice programs from the beginning. Choice advocates claim that parents should have the right to choose not only the type of school, but the type of education they want for their children. The most strident proponents of increased family control are usually fundamentalist/evangelical sects and other religious groups. These groups advocate including private schools in the educational choice programs. They promote the idea that parents should have a greater role in selecting the educational programs that serve to shape the values of their children. The notion is that just as parents themselves influence the values and traditions of their children, they should be able to select schools that reinforce these mores. A choice of schools, therefore, is necessary to exercise such a right.

Proponents of this idea include Ruth Randall, former Commissioner of Public Education in Minnesota, who stated that "choice is for everyone." She also stated that although Americans have many choices with regard to most of the fundamentals of life, "The one place ... where [they] have not been able to choose is education for children from the time they start kindergarten through grade 12 unless ... [they] have money to pay for private school or for tuition to a different public school."

The Carnegie report notes that the United States Office of Education under the Bush administration espoused this idea of a "fundamental right" of choice, claiming that assignment to a school based on residence was undemocratic and that choice as a program would improve schools for all strata of society. The official position of the federal government, therefore, followed that of the choice proponents, maintaining that the state had gradually and unjustifiably supplanted parents in shaping the education, beliefs, and values of children.

Contrary to the above positions, the right of parents to influence or effect changes in the education their children receive has never been held to be absolute. States have assumed the responsibility for the education of children by enacting, for example, compulsory attendance laws. Children, however, are not required to attend a public school.

Federal and state courts have consistently upheld the right of the state to regulate education within its borders. In *People v. Turner*, the court rejected a claim that a California statute, which required parents to place their children in either a public school or a private school meeting certain prescribed conditions, deprived parents of their constitutional right to determine how their children should be educated. Similarly, the Supreme Court of Maine upheld the state's compulsory attendance laws and the right of the state to control and regulate education, declaring that "where the state has provided a reasonable procedure whereby [parents] may vindicate their asserted right to educate their children[,] ... they may not ignore the procedure and then appeal to this court claiming that their right has been denied." Also, a New York court upheld the legal authority of the state to impose reasonable educational guidelines requiring parents to educate their children. The court noted that parents have no absolute right to educate their children free from state regulation and that they must observe the reasonable requirements imposed by the state.

The above short legal review exemplifies the rights of parents and the state to make decisions regarding the education of children. Proponents of choice would take this issue further, asking that parents receive special benefits for choosing to place their children in either private or secular schools. Clearly, private and secular schools are an important option for many citizens. Attendance at these institutions is a choice made for various reasons, including religious ones. As a matter of public policy, though, the state's taxpayers should have no obligation to pay for this decision. The state's job is to regulate the nonpublic schools, not to ensure their survival.

....

---

1. What is your opinion of the various options under educational choice? What are the advantages and disadvantages of such programs?

2. Does Daniel make a distinction between choice programs that involve public and private schools, and those programs that exist wholly within on public school system? If so, what is his perception of each?

3. Tancredo seems very pleased that a wide variety of people, Democrats and Republicans, blacks and whites, support educational choice. Are the reasons for such support the same for all these groups? Do the rationales of the supporting groups mentioned by Tancredo amplify the problems raised by Daniel?

4. What is the potential impact of choice programs? Does this depend on whether the program involves both public and private schools? Is it possible that

C. EDUCATIONAL CHOICE

voucher systems could hurt the very population they may be designed to help? Consider the following excerpt from C. Zeigler and N. Lederman, *School Vouchers: Are Urban Students Surrendering Rights for Choice?*, 19 Fordham Urb. L.J. 813 (1992).*

I. *Introduction*

If "excellence" was the education buzzword of the 1980s, "choice" has already established itself as the buzzword for the 1990s.... President Bush's America 2000 Excellence in Education Act to underwrite state and local programs which provide vouchers to enable parents to choose public, private or religious schooling for their children, has moved "school choice" to the forefront of the national education reform agenda. Nowhere is this more prevalent than in urban centers, where the breakdown of the public education system has been the focus of considerable attention and debate.

Supporters argue that choice is an important tool for improving a failing public system of elementary and secondary education by utilizing principles of free market competition to weed out failing schools and improve mediocre ones. Choice, it is said, will increase the diversity of educational programs available to meet the particular needs and interests of students, extend to poor and minority families the opportunity that affluent families now have to avoid poorly run and overcrowded urban schools and increase parental involvement, which is believed to be a significant factor in student achievement. Supporters point to successful school choice programs, like those in East Harlem's District 4, as models for school reform.

The distinction between choice programs wholly within the public system and those which include private and religious schools is often obscured in the debate over school choice. As a result, when school reformers speak about increasing and facilitating choice in schooling decisions, they may be speaking of radically different, and often mutually exclusive, things. Not only does the use of the term choice by supporters of vouchers, evoking as it does the "liberal" side of the abortion rights debate, confuse the ideological landscape, the praise of public models like District 4 in East Harlem as exemplars of choice obscures profound political and educational differences.

In the debate over school choice programs, as in many other public policy debates, semantics shed more heat than light. As the Cheshire Cat said to Alice in Lewis Carroll's *Alice in Wonderland*, words mean what we want them to mean. Likewise, choice means many things to many people. It can mean choice within the public school system for a limited number of students, or for greater numbers or even all students in the form of "magnet schools" or "alternative" schools designed to offer special programming

---

*Copyright © 1992 by the Fordham Urban Law Journal. Reprinted with permission.

to meet particular needs. It can also mean allowing parents and students to opt out of public education altogether by using vouchers to underwrite private and religious education.

To speak of choice in public schooling as pioneered by Anthony Alvarado, community schools superintendent of the East Harlem School District in the 1970s, and the "educational choice" programs endorsed and funded under President Bush's America 2000 Education proposals as part of the same trend, is to mix proverbial apples and oranges. The most obvious difference between them is, of course, the exclusively public nature of the District 4 movement in contrast to the mandated inclusion of private and parochial schools in the choice programs supported by ... [America 2000]. Beyond the First Amendment church-state entanglement concerns that inevitably emerge in this debate are sharply divergent views about the personal and political purposes of schooling, the values each seeks to promote and the nature of parental, student and staff involvement in the process. Thus, while each touts "choice" as a path to "excellence," these educational models define excellence and how to achieve it in radically different ways.

Moreover, the "privatization" of education ... through the use of vouchers would mean the loss of legally defined procedural and participatory rights for students and parents. Furthermore, it would permit schools to exclude those students who are difficult to teach on the theory that other schools will take them. Such forces would facilitate nothing more than the radical and economic segregation which already characterizes private school admissions. For these reasons, the use of vouchers will have a profound and, in our view, adverse impact on the social and political role of schooling which should be at the forefront of the debate ... over school choice.

....

The rights of parents and students which are acknowledged and expected in our public schools are a direct extension of the Jeffersonian ideal of a nation enlightened through education. A voucher system that includes private schools inevitably involves a false choice between these accepted rights and "choice" in schooling. Thus, the challenge in education reform remains in the improvement of public education and not in its abandonment, and in strengthening the ties between schooling and democracy rather than in severing them.

C. EDUCATIONAL CHOICE

2. PARENTAL CHOICE

TEACHERS, INC. v. SMITH
Supreme Court of Wisconsin
480 N.W.2d 460 (1992)

CALLOW, JUSTICE:

This is a review under sec. (Rule) 809.62, Stats., of a decision of the court of appeals, *Davis v. Grover*, 159 Wis.2d 150, 464 N.W.2d 220 (Ct.App.1990). The court of appeals reversed the decision of the Dane county circuit court, Judge Susan R. Steingass, and found that the Milwaukee Parental Choice Program (MPCP) violated art. IV, sec. 18 of the Wisconsin Constitution. The MPCP is a publicly funded program that permits selected children from low-income families to attend nonsectarian private schools at no cost to the student.

The scope of our inquiry is strictly confined to the specific issues raised on this review. We pass no judgment on the wisdom or desirability of the MPCP. The propriety of the program is most appropriately addressed by the legislature, not the judiciary.

Three issues are raised in this review. The first issue concerns whether the MPCP is a private or local bill which was enacted in violation of the procedural requirements mandated by art. IV, sec. 18 of the Wisconsin Constitution. We hold that the MPCP is not a private or local bill and, thus, is not subject to the procedural requirements of Wis. Const. art. IV, sec. 18.

The program was and remains politically controversial. As such, it was greatly debated in legislative committee public hearings and by the entire legislature. It is evident the program was not smuggled through the legislature. The purpose of this experimental legislation is to determine if it is possible to improve, through parental choice, the quality of education in Wisconsin for children of low-income families.[2] Logically, the best location to test the program is in a city such as Milwaukee where the socio-economic disparities and educational problems are particularly great and the potential private educational choices are most abundant.

The second issue concerns whether the MPCP violates art. X, sec. 3 of the Wisconsin Constitution, which requires the establishment of uniform school districts. We hold that the MPCP does not violate art. X, sec. 3 of the Wisconsin Constitution because the participating private schools do not constitute "district schools," even though they receive some public monies to educate students participating in the program.

---

[2]Wisconsin is the first state in the nation to experiment with a parental choice program which involves the use of private schools as an alternative to the public school system. The program is an attempt to identify factors which could improve the quality of education. Clearly, the program is not only of statewide importance but national significance as well because education of our citizens knows no boundaries and other states could benefit from the knowledge resulting from this innovative experiment....

The third issue concerns whether the MPCP violates the public purpose doctrine which requires that public funds be spent only for public purposes. We hold that the MPCP does not violate the public purpose doctrine. We give great weight to legislative determinations of public policy. Sufficient safeguards are included in the program to ensure that participating private schools are under adequate governmental supervision reasonably necessary under the circumstances to attain the public purpose of improving educational quality. Further, the cost of education and the funds available for education are dependent upon the taxpayers' ability to fund an intensive public educational program. The amount of money allocated under this program to participating private schools for the education of a participating student is less than 40 percent of the full cost of educating that same student in the Milwaukee Public School (MPS) system. The total amount of public funds appropriated to fund this experimental program is inconsequential when compared to the total expenditures for public education allocated to schools throughout the state of Wisconsin.

The relevant facts follow. The MPCP, as enacted into law, provides that a kindergarten through twelfth grade (K-12) student who resides in a city of the first class may attend, at no charge to the student, any nonsectarian private school located in the city if the following criteria are met:

(1) the family income does not exceed 175% of the poverty level;
(2) the pupil was enrolled in a public school in the city, was attending a private school under this program, or was not enrolled in school the previous year;
(3) the private school notifies the State Superintendent of its intent to participate in the program by June 30 of the previous school year;
(4) the private school complies with 42 U.S.C. sec. 2000d;[3] and
(5) the private school meets all health and safety laws or codes that apply to public schools. Section 119.23(2)(a), Stats.

Additionally, private schools participating in the program must meet defined performance criteria and submit to financial and performance audits by the state. For each participating student, approximately $2,500 in state educational funding is diverted from the Milwaukee Public Schools (MPS) to the participating private school.

....

In October 1989, the bill that led to the enactment of the Milwaukee Parental Choice Program was introduced by a bipartisan coalition of 47 members of the assembly and nine senate co-sponsors. The bill was referred to the Assembly Committee on Urban Education, which held a public hearing on the proposal. A

---

[3] 42 U.S.C. sec. 2000d states: No person in the United States shall, on the ground of race, color, or national origin, be excluded from participation in, be denied the benefits of, or be subjected to discrimination under any program or activity receiving Federal financial assistance.

C. EDUCATIONAL CHOICE 1391

broad array of persons and organizations, encompassing many of the interests represented in this case, appeared at the public hearing. Based on committee reports and the statements made at the public hearing, the committee recommended an amended version of the bill to the assembly. After considering a number of amendments to the bill, the assembly passed the bill.

The program, as passed by the assembly, was then considered by the senate and referred to the Committee on Educational Financing, Higher Education and Tourism. Subsequently, it was added to the senate budget adjustment bill, a multi-subject bill addressing numerous unrelated topics. The language of this component of the bill was preceded by the title, "Milwaukee Parental Choice Program." Following the addition of a fiscal amendment relating to the program, the entire budget bill was adopted by the senate. The assembly passed the budget bill without again considering the parental choice program. The governor signed the bill, but vetoed a sunset provision included in the program which would have limited the effective period of the program to a five-year time span. Thereafter, the MPCP was enacted into law under ch. 119, Stats., the chapter applicable to the school system in cities of the first class.

Lonzetta Davis, et al. (Davis), representing families of participating students and private schools participating in the program, initiated this action challenging a number of regulatory actions taken by State Superintendent of Public Instruction Herbert Grover (Superintendent Grover). Davis believed Superintendent Grover's actions were designed to frustrate the MPCP and exceeded his authority as State Superintendent.

Felmers O. Chaney, et al. (Chaney), representing various school administration organizations and the National Association for the Advancement of Colored People, intervened, challenging the MPCP on state constitutional grounds; namely, that it violates Wis. Const. art. IV, sec. 18 (private/local legislation clause), Wis. Const. art. X, sec. 3 (uniform district schools clause), and the public purpose doctrine.

The State of Wisconsin, acting on its own behalf, argues that the MPCP is constitutional in all respects.

The circuit court found the MPCP constitutional and that Superintendent Grover's actions exceeded his regulatory authority. Chaney filed an appeal on the constitutional issues with the court of appeals. Superintendent Grover did not appeal the circuit court's decision on the regulatory issues.

The court of appeals reversed the decision of the circuit court and held that the MPCP violated the private/local legislation clause of Wis. Const. art. IV, sec. 18. It did not reach the uniformity clause and public purpose doctrine issues.

No injunction was ever issued against the Milwaukee Parental Choice Program, which continues to operate unaffected by the pending litigation.

The issues presented in this case involve questions of law. On review, this court decides questions of law independently without deference to the decisions of the trial court and court of appeals. We now address each of these issues separately.

I. *The Private/Local Legislation Clause*

Article IV, sec. 18 of the Wisconsin Constitution states:

> No private or local bill which may be passed by the legislature shall embrace more than one subject, and that shall be expressed in the title.

It was adopted as part of the original Wisconsin Constitution of 1848 and has remained unchanged. In previous cases, we have explained that art. IV, sec. 18 has three underlying purposes:

> 1) [T]o encourage the legislature to devote its time to the state at large, its primary responsibility; 2) to avoid the specter of favoritism and discrimination, a potential which is inherent in laws of limited applicability; and 3) to alert the public through its elected representatives to the real nature and subject matter of legislation under consideration.

The requirements of art. IV, sec. 18 are prescribed to ensure accountability of the legislature to the public and to "guard against the danger of legislation, affecting private or local interests, being smuggled through the legislature." *Milwaukee County v. Isenring*, 109 Wis. 9, 23, 85 N.W. 131 (1901). In *Brookfield v. Milwaukee Sewerage*, 144 Wis.2d 896, 426 N.W.2d 591 (1988), we further examined legislative accountability. Section 18 also recognizes the need to avoid "internal logrolling"[7] on the part of the legislature. Multisubject bills by their nature are subject to a greater susceptibility of smuggling and logrolling. They intermingle a variety of unrelated legislation which singly may not have the support of the majority and, thus, tend to reduce accountability to the public. Nevertheless, the fact that a multi-subject bill contains a program such as the MPCP does not necessarily condemn the process in which the program was enacted as unconstitutional.

....

We are aware that time constraints sometimes force legislators to pass a variety of worthy legislation in one multi-subject package. However, multi-subject bills reduce accountability to the public and are very susceptible to the charge of violating the procedural requirements of Wis. Const. art. IV, sec. 18. The legislature could avoid litigatory challenges of this nature by using separate, single subject bills for legislation that is not plainly of statewide concern.

However, we find no evidence in this case that suggests the program was smuggled or logrolled through the legislature without the benefit of deliberate legislative consideration. As mentioned earlier, the MPCP legislation was passed by the assembly as a single subject bill. Even though the senate included the

---

[7]"Logrolling" is the legislative practice of embracing in one bill several distinct matters, none of which could singly obtain the assent of the legislature, and then procuring its passage by a combination of the minorities in favor of each of the separate measures into a majority that will adopt them all. Black's Law Dictionary 942 (6th ed. 1990).

MPCP as part of the budget bill, the budget bill was debated by the senate and the senate specifically amended the MPCP prior to enactment of the budget bill. Clearly, the legislature "intelligently participate[d] in considering" this program. Therefore, under the circumstances of this case, it is proper for us to apply a presumption of constitutionality to the process in which the MPCP was enacted into law....

....

Even though we conclude that there is no indication that the MPCP was smuggled or logrolled through the legislature without due consideration and we apply a presumption of constitutionality to such process, our analysis does not end here. Article IV, sec. 18 specifies certain procedural requirements that must be satisfied if legislation is found to be private or local.... We now turn to the determination of whether the MPCP is private or local legislation.

This court has developed three prongs of analysis for cases involving a challenge to legislation as being private or local. The first prong of analysis involves legislation that is specific on its face as to particular people, places or things that allegedly runs afoul of art. IV, sec. 18. [This prong] explain[s] that "such legislation is private or local within the meaning of sec. 18 and therefore prohibited unless the general subject matter of the provision relates to a state responsibility of statewide dimension and its enactment will have a direct and immediate effect on a specific statewide concern or interest."

The second prong of analysis involves legislation that is not specific on its face, but which involves classifications and allegedly runs afoul of the specific prohibitions of art. IV, sec. 31, which was adopted as an aid in a sec. 18 analysis. Section 31 explains specific areas in which the legislature is prohibited from enacting any special or private laws. The resolution of these cases depends on whether the legislation "falls into the category of matters upon which the legislature is competent to legislate pursuant to sec. 32 notwithstanding the prohibition of sec. 31." *Id.*

The third, and final, prong of analysis involves legislation that is not specific on its face, involves classifications, does not violate the provisions of sec. 31, but allegedly runs afoul of sec. 18. A statute creating a closed classification can be the same as legislation that is specific on its face to a certain locality. In *Brookfield v. Milwaukee Sewage*, 426 N.W.2d. 591 (Wis. 1988), we determined that such cases must be analyzed consistent with the classification concepts developed in cases under art. IV, secs. 31 and 32.

Five primary elements comprise the *Brookfield* test. These elements are as follows:

> First, the classification employed by the legislature must be based on substantial distinctions which make one class really different from another.
>
> Second, the classification adopted must be germane to the purpose of the law.

Third, the classification must not be based on existing circumstances only. Instead, the classification must be subject to being open, such that other cities could join the class.

Fourth, when a law applies to a class, it must apply equally to all members of the class.

[F]ifth, the characteristics of each class should be so far different from those of the other classes so as to reasonably suggest at least the propriety, having regard to the public good, of substantially different legislation.

....

... In the classification legislation context, it is necessary to use the five-factor test to determine exactly what the substance of the legislation is in order to determine whether the procedural requirements of Wis. Const. art. IV, sec. 18 apply....

Notwithstanding the fact that the title of sec. 119.23, Stats., expressly mentions Milwaukee, the text of the MPCP as well as its placement in the statutes suggests that it involves a classification and should be analyzed under *Brookfield* rather than *Milwaukee Brewers*. The MPCP applies to any school district in a city of the first class. It is not limited to Milwaukee because Madison presently meets the population requirement and could become a city of the first class by a simple declaration. While the title of legislation expressly refers to Milwaukee, titles of statutes are not part of the statute itself. We find no reason why this rule should not encompass legislative bills as well. Therefore, the MPCP is similar to the statute in *Brookfield* in that it involves a classification and not expressly a specific person, place or thing. Thus, we are required to apply the *Brookfield* five-factor test to determine whether the MPCP is private or local legislation.

The first element of the *Brookfield* test requires that "the classification employed by the legislature must be based on substantial distinctions which make one class really different from another." The MPCP does not create a new classification, but involves a classification that has consistently been recognized and accepted by this court: namely, cities of the first class. "Cities of the first class" is defined under sec. 62.05, Stats., as cities with a population of 150,000 or more. Presently, Milwaukee is the only city to declare itself a city of the first class in the state of Wisconsin.

In *Brookfield*, we acknowledged that the mere size of a particular city does not necessarily justify treating that city differently than any other city in the state. *Brookfield*, 144 Wis.2d at 916, 426 N.W.2d 591. However, cities of the first class, by virtue of their large population and concentration of poverty, are substantially distinct from other cities. In *Lamasco Realty Co. v. Milwaukee*, 242 Wis. 357, 377, 8 N.W.2d 372 (1943), where the challenged law pertained to cities of the first class, we noted that "the requirements of a metropolitan city like Milwaukee as against the smaller municipal corporations of the state are so obvious that any other result would be opposed to the public welfare." ...

C. EDUCATIONAL CHOICE

School districts located in areas with monumentally oppressive poverty problems as found in first class cities have particular educational problems as well. These problems were recognized also in *Kukor v. Grover*, 148 Wis.2d 469, 482-83, 436 N.W.2d 568 (1989). As demonstrated by dropout rates, welfare statistics, and population data, the Milwaukee Public School District has significantly greater education and poverty problems than any other school district in the state.

Various statistical analyses, while not entirely consistent, dramatically show the need for legislative attention. The dropout rate for the Milwaukee Public Schools is higher than any other area in the state. For example, in the 1988-89 school year, the dropout rate for students in grades 9-12 in the MPS reached 14.4 percent. In contrast, the public school dropout rate for the state at large during the 1988-89 school year was 3.11 percent, with no county, other than Milwaukee County, having a dropout rate of greater than 4.3 percent.

During the 1988-89 fiscal year, Wisconsin spent $2.4 billion, or $499.57 per capita, on public welfare. Wisconsin ranked sixth among all states for welfare-related expenditures. In 1988, over 50 percent of the general public assistance in Wisconsin was spent in Milwaukee County alone and the city of Milwaukee comprises about two-thirds of the population of Milwaukee County. Furthermore, of the $485 million spent in Wisconsin in 1988 for Aid to Families with Dependent Children, $213 million was allocated to Milwaukee County.

The statistical data clearly illustrates that the socioeconomic disparities and the educational problems are greater in the large urban area of Milwaukee than any other part of Wisconsin. By definition, first class cities encompass large urban cities in Wisconsin, such as the city of Milwaukee. Therefore, we find that the classification of first class cities is based on substantial distinctions which make the class really different from all others. The first element of the *Brookfield* test is satisfied.

The second element of the *Brookfield* test requires that "the classification adopted must be germane to the purpose of the law." Both the trial court and the court of appeals concluded that the only reasonable inference to be drawn from the MPCP was that it was an experiment intended to address a perceived problem of inadequate educational opportunities for disadvantaged children. *Davis*, 159 Wis.2d at 164-65, 464 N.W.2d 220. We agree with this conclusion.

Improving the quality of education in Wisconsin is, without a doubt, a matter of statewide importance. It is apparent that on a national scale the educational needs of many students are not being met by the present educational structure and options. Average School Aptitude Test (SAT) scores fell from 978 in 1960 to just 870 in 1980. Nearly 25 percent of public high school students drop out before graduation and the dropout rates for minorities often reach 50 percent. These are some of the highest dropout rates in the western world.

The educational problems that the nation is experiencing are also evident in the Milwaukee Public Schools, where 55-60 percent of MPS students do not graduate from high school or do not graduate in a six-year period of time. A recent report by the Greater Milwaukee Education Trust states that only 40-45 percent of the students who start high school in the MPS graduate in four, five or six years. This completion rate is down from 57 percent in 1984. Of those who do graduate from high school, 36 percent graduate with a "D" average. Students of MPS, in general, score below the national average on the basic skills tests, and minority students score dramatically below the average. The grade point average (GPA) on a scale of 4.0 for MPS students in general is 1.60, whereas the GPA for African-American students in the MPS is just 1.31.

The consequences of school dropouts and inadequate education are shocking. High school dropouts comprise 75 percent of the prison population and 80 percent of the families receiving Aid for Families with Dependent Children. Only 55 percent of the male dropouts under age thirty have jobs and only 20 percent have full-time jobs.

Recently, researchers have attempted to discover the reasons underlying inadequate public instruction. A Brookings Institution study examined data from more than 60,000 students in 1,000 public and private schools to test the relationship between 220 different variables. The study concluded that the three most important factors that affected student achievement were student ability, school organization, and family background. Chubb & Moe, Politics, Markets & America's Schools, 140 (1990). The factor which is most amenable to legislative efforts appears to be school organization....

In response to the conclusions reached by the Brookings Institution study and others, the MPCP was drafted to include two main features to help fulfill the statewide purpose of improving education. The first feature empowers selected low-income parents to choose the educational opportunities that they deem best for their children. Concerned parents have the greatest incentive to see that their children receive the best education possible. Parental choice allows parents to send their children to nonsectarian private schools which, except for the statutory responsibilities of the State Superintendent, are autonomously operated free from the bureaucracy of the public school system. In so providing, the program will engender educational success competition between the public and private educational sectors for students of low-income families.

However, the program is not an abandonment of the public school system. Rather, the MPCP would affect at most only 1 percent of the students in the MPS, giving the program a very small window of opportunity to test the effectiveness of an alternative to the MPS.

Furthermore, the MPCP contains a second feature which not only should benefit the MPS but also the state at large. The second main feature of the MPCP creates an extensive data compilation and reporting process which the state can use to measure the effects of choice and competition in education. The experimental nature of the program is evident from these detailed compilation and reporting requirements.

The experimental nature of the program can also be inferred from the fact that the program, as originally drafted, would have been effective for only a five-year

C. EDUCATIONAL CHOICE

period of time. However, in a partial veto, the governor removed the five-year time limit. It is unclear whether the governor felt that the time limitation was too short or too long. It is apparent, though, that the governor and the legislature directed the gathering of extensive information for the purpose of reacting to this experimental program.

The success of the program is dependent upon the participation of numerous and diverse nonsectarian private schools such that the fate of the program does not rest on the operations of one or a few schools. The record indicates that at least nine private schools in Milwaukee filed an intent to participate in the MPCP when it was first implemented. We assume no other city in Wisconsin offers as many private schools as Milwaukee. The significant availability of private schools is so necessary to a reliable sampling of alternative educational methods that it distinguishes a first class city such as Milwaukee from all other communities. This experiment tests a theory of education. The possible failure in one or more private schools may be the fault of the school rather than the program's concept. Therefore, locating the program in a first class city such as Milwaukee where numerous and diverse private schools exist will enable the legislature to determine which, if any, of the private schools were most effective and why they are particularly successful in their mission of education.

We conclude that the classification of first class cities is germane to the purpose of the law. Clearly, improving the quality of education and educational opportunities in Wisconsin is a matter of statewide importance. The best location to experiment with legislation aimed at improving the quality of education is in a first class city, a large urban area where the socio-economic and educational disparities are greatest and the private educational choices are most abundant. The experimental nature of the MPCP places this case in direct contrast to *Brookfield* where we found no relationship between Milwaukee county's size and the challenged financing scheme. *See Brookfield*, 144 Wis.2d at 920, 426 N.W.2d 591. Therefore, the second element of the *Brookfield* test is satisfied.

The third element of the *Brookfield* test requires that the classification not be based only on existing circumstances. Rather, "the classification must be subject to being open, such that other cities could join the class." Granted, the title of the statute is "Milwaukee Parental Choice Program." However, the statute is located in ch. 119, Stats., which addresses first class city schools and is applicable, by virtue of sec. 119.01, Stats., to cities of the first class. There are two requirements for a city to be of the first class. The city must have a population of at least 150,000 and the city's mayor must make an official proclamation that the city is of the first class. *See* sec. 62.05, Stats.

Presently, Milwaukee, with a population of 628,088, is the only city in Wisconsin which is officially a first class city. However, it is not the only city in Wisconsin which qualifies for such status, nor is the classification limited only to Milwaukee. Madison is large enough to qualify as a city of the first class. Madison has a population of 191,262. If the mayor of Madison officially declares Madison to be a first class city, it will be subject to all legislation affecting cities of the first class, including the parental choice program. Therefore, we conclude that the classification is subject to being open and is not based only on existing circumstances. The third element of the *Brookfield* test is satisfied.

The fourth element of the *Brookfield* test requires that the law be applied equally to all members of the class. As mentioned earlier, there is only one member of the class at the present time. Milwaukee is the only official first class city. However, if Madison or any other qualifying city were to become an official first class city, then there appears nothing to indicate that the benefits and obligations of the MPCP would not equally apply to these additional members. Therefore, we find that the law would apply equally to all cities of the first class. The fourth element of the *Brookfield* test is also satisfied.

The fifth, and final, element of the *Brookfield* test which is applicable to the present case requires that "the characteristics of each class should be so far different from those of the other classes so as to reasonably suggest at least the propriety, having regard to the public good, of substantially different legislation." The satisfaction of this element has already been addressed. *Supra* at 469-470. The immense disparity in the socio-economic conditions and educational problems in the MPS as well as the greatest potential private educational choices in the urban area of Milwaukee create the ideal testing ground for experimental legislation such as the MPCP. Therefore, we find that the MPCP also satisfies the fifth element of the *Brookfield* test.

The MPCP satisfies all elements of the *Brookfield* classification test. Therefore, we hold that the MPCP is not a private or local bill within the meaning of Wis. Const. art. IV, sec. 18 and, thus, not subject to its procedural requirements. We emphasize that the MPCP is not a private or local bill because it satisfies the applicable tests, not because of the amount of legislative consideration afforded to it.

II. *The Uniformity Clause*

Wisconsin Constitution art. X, sec. 3 states:

> The legislature shall provide by law for the establishment of district schools, which shall be as nearly uniform as practicable; and such schools shall be free and without charge for tuition to all children between the ages of 4 and 20 years.

This court has stated on several occasions that the requirement of uniformity "applies to the districts after they are formed, — to the 'character of instruction' given, — rather than to the means by which they are established and their boundaries fixed." *Kukor v. Grover*, 148 Wis.2d 469, 486, 436 N.W.2d 568 (1989). Furthermore, the *Kukor* court concluded that "character of instruction" refers to that of "district schools" and is legislatively regulated by sec. 121.02, Stats.

Chaney argues that the MPCP violates the uniformity clause of Wis. Const. art. X, sec. 3. The thrust of Chaney's argument involves two steps: (1) the participating private schools are "district schools" within the meaning of the uniformity clause; and (2) by offering a "character of instruction" that is different from the one found under the mandate of sec. 121.02, the participating private schools violate the uniformity clause. The key to this argument is whether private schools participating in the MPCP are considered "district schools" for the purposes of the uniformity clause.

In *Comstock v. Jt. School Dist. No. 1*, 65 Wis. 631, 636-37, 27 N.W. 829 (1886), this court held that a statute allowing school districts to determine whether to admit nonresident school children did not violate the uniformity clause. In that case, we declared that "when the legislature has provided for each such child the privileges of a district school, which he or she may freely enjoy, the constitutional requirement in that behalf is complied with." *Id.* at 636-37, 27 N.W. 829. Thereafter, the legislature is free to act as it deems proper.

This sentiment was reiterated in several subsequent cases and most recently in *Kukor*, 148 Wis.2d at 496-97, 436 N.W.2d 568. In *Kukor*, we found that a statutory school finance system did not violate Wis. Const. art. X, sec. 3 because every Wisconsin student has an opportunity to attend a public school with uniform character of instruction.

The MPCP unambiguously refers to nonsectarian private schools. "Private school" is a defined term under sec. 115.001(3r), Stats., and means "an institution with a private educational program that meets all of the criteria under § 118.165(1) or is determined to be a private school by the state superintendent under § 118.167." We assume that the legislature was aware of this statutory meaning and intended to use "private school" in the MPCP as a statutory term of art.

Similar to the legislation in *Kukor*, the MPCP in no way deprives any student the opportunity to attend a public school with a uniform character of education. Even these students participating in the program may withdraw at any time and return to a public school. The uniformity clause clearly was intended to assure certain minimal educational opportunities for the children of Wisconsin. It does not require the legislature to ensure that all of the children in Wisconsin receive a free uniform basic education. Rather, the uniformity clause requires the legislature to provide the opportunity for all children in Wisconsin to receive a free uniform basic education. The legislature has done so. The MPCP merely reflects a legislative desire to do more than that which is constitutionally mandated.

Therefore, we hold that the private schools participating in the MPCP do not constitute "district schools" for purposes of the uniformity clause. The legislature has fulfilled its constitutional duty to provide for the basic education of our children. Their experimental attempts to improve upon that foundation in no way denies any student the opportunity to receive the basic education in the public school system.

III. *The Public Purpose Doctrine*

Chaney also argues that the public purpose doctrine prohibits the legislature from authorizing the expenditure of public funds for the basic education of students to private schools without adequate supervision and controls. Therefore, Chaney concludes that the MPCP violates the public purpose doctrine because the program lacks adequate supervision and controls.

Although the public purpose doctrine is not an express provision of the Wisconsin Constitution, this court has long held that public expenditures may be made only for public purposes. *[Warren v.] Reuter*, 44 Wis.2d ... [201] 211, 170 N.W.2d 790 [1969]. In *Reuter*, we stated, "[w]e need not go into the origin or the validity of the doctrine which commands that public funds can only be used for public purposes. The doctrine is beyond contention." *Id.*

....

No party disputes that education constitutes a valid public purpose, nor that private schools may be employed to further that purpose. Rather, the parties dispute whether the private schools participating in the MPCP are under proper government control and supervision, as required by *Wisconsin Indus. Sch. for Girls v. Clark Co.*, 103 Wis. 651, 668, 79 N.W. 422 (1899).

Chaney and, particularly, Superintendent Grover contend the controls in the MPCP over participating private schools are woefully inadequate and insist that these schools be subject to the stricter requirements of sec. 121.02, Stats. MPCP advocates, on the other hand, believe the statutory controls applicable to private schools coupled with parental involvement suffice to ensure the public purpose is met. The circuit court agreed with the MPCP advocates' contention, as we do.

....

The MPCP specifically allows participating students to attend a "nonsectarian private school." *See* sec. 119.23(2)(a), Stats. "Private school" has an express statutory definition under sec. 115.001(3r), Stats., which requires the institution to meet all of the criteria under secs. 118.165(1) or 118.167, Stats.

Under sec. 118.165, Stats., a private school must:

(1) be organized to primarily provide private or religious-based education;
(2) be privately controlled;
(3) provide at least 875 hours of instruction each school year;
(4) provide a sequentially progressive curriculum of fundamental instructions in reading, language arts, mathematics, social studies, science, and health;
(5) not be operated or instituted for the purpose of avoiding or circumventing compulsory school attendance; and
(6) have pupils return home not less than two months of each year unless the institution is also licensed as a child welfare agency.

Even though private schools are not subject to the same amount of controls which are applicable to public schools, they are subject to a significant amount of regulation which is geared toward providing a sequentially progressive

C. EDUCATIONAL CHOICE

curriculum. This issue is uniquely complicated, however, by the underlying thesis of the MPCP that less bureaucracy coupled with parental choice improves educational quality.

Keenly aware of this potential problem, the legislature included within the MPCP sufficient supervision and control measures. The State Superintendent is required to annually report to the legislature comparing the students participating in the MPCP with students in the MPS. The report includes data on academic achievement, daily attendance, percentage of dropouts, and percentage of pupils suspended and expelled. The State Superintendent is authorized to conduct financial and performance audits on the program, and the Legislative Audit Bureau is mandated to perform financial and performance evaluation. We believe that these detailed reports and evaluations in conjunction with the private school requirements under secs. 118.165(1) and 118.167, Stats., provide sufficient and reasonable control under the circumstances to attain the public purpose to which this legislation is directed.

Control is also fashioned within the MPCP in the form of parental choice. Parents generally know their children better than anyone. The program allows participating parents to chose a school with an environment that matches their child's personality, with a curriculum that matches their child's interest and needs, and with a location that is convenient. If the private school does not meet the parents' expectations, the parents may remove the child from the school and go elsewhere. In this way, parental choice preserves accountability for the best interests of the children.

In *Wisconsin v. Yoder*, 406 U.S. 205 (1972), the United States Supreme Court also recognized the importance and the strong tradition of parental choice in education. Using a balancing of interests test, the *Yoder* Court held that the First and Fourteenth Amendments prevent the state from compelling Amish parents to cause their children to attend formal high school to age sixteen. In so deciding, it stated:

> Providing public schools ranks at the very apex of the function of a State. Yet even this paramount responsibility ... yield[s] to the right of parents to provide an equivalent education in a privately operated system.

Yoder involved the protection of the Religion Clauses, whereas the present case involves purely secular considerations. However, the *Yoder* Court declared that purely secular considerations "may not be interposed as a barrier to reasonable state regulation of education." *Id.* at 215. We have determined in this case that the reporting and private school requirements applicable to the MPCP provide sufficient and reasonable state control under the circumstances.

Further, the cost of education and the funds available for education are dependent upon the taxpayers' ability to fund an intensive public educational program. The amount of money allocated to a private school participating in the MPCP to educate a participating student is less than 40 percent of the full cost of educating that same student in the MPS. Each of the participating private schools is willing to accept the responsibility of educating a child for the $2,500 granted by the state. In contrast, it costs the MPS an average of $6,451 to educate each student. At most, $2.5 million of public funds will be appropriated to fund this experimental legislation. This amount is inconsequential compared to the more than $6.4 billion that is annually expended for public education in Wisconsin. The amount of money to fund the MPCP represents only about four one-hundredths of one percent (.04 percent) of the public money allocated for public education throughout the state. Therefore, we hold that the MPCP does not violate the public purpose doctrine because the MPCP contains sufficient and reasonable controls to attain its public purpose.

We conclude that the Milwaukee Parental Choice Program passes constitutional scrutiny in all issues presented before this court. Accordingly, we reverse the decision of the court of appeals.

The decision of the court of appeals is reversed.

....

1. How dispositive to this case is the fact that the state will save money through the Milwaukee Parental Choice Program — decreasing its expenditure per student from about $6500 to $2500?

2. Do you favor parental choice plans which cover both public and private schools? Could Milwaukee and other large cities in similar situations improve the quality of education by designing a choice plan to operate within its own district? What about inter-district or countywide choice plans involving suburban and rural public schools?

3. How do choice programs affect families with children with disabilities? Consider, for example, the following from J. McKinney, *Special Education and Parental Choice: An Oxymoron in the Making*, 76 Educ. L. Rep. 667 (1992):*

Introduction

Parental choice is a major part of the educational reform and restructuring movement currently consuming the agendas of federal, state and local policy makers. President Bush has called "schools of choice" programs "the single most promising" reform idea and decreed that "further expansion of public-school choice is a national imperative."

Special education students are directly affected by school choice programs.... [P]arental choice programs that occur completely within the context of the public school system ... can be divided into two distinct subcategories: those involving interdistrict or cross-boundary programs and those involving intradistrict plans, including magnet schools and alternative schools. There has been little mention of choice programs and open

---

*Copyright © 1992 by West Publishing Company. Reprinted with permission.

C. EDUCATIONAL CHOICE

enrollment legislation and the effects of these policies on children with disabilities either in the special education or school law related literature....

Two comprehensive federal statutes combine to create substantive and procedural rights and protection for children with disabilities. The two statutory schemes that relate to the education of students with disabilities are the Individuals with Disabilities Education Act (IDEA, formerly EAHCA) and Section 504 of the Rehabilitation Act of 1973. Both of these statutes impose obligations on school districts to provide a free appropriate public education to children with disabilities. When the IDEA and Section 504 are read together, a complimentary set of standards emerges to determine the appropriate education including the educational setting for students with disabilities.

....

... [S]tates that have enacted either interdistrict and/or intradistrict choice programs have not designed the admissions processes nor the funding systems in ways that would eliminate disincentives for school districts to provide educational services to children with disabilities. States need to provide incentives and ensure that school districts do not encounter adverse consequences, such as financial shortfalls when providing necessary services for children with handicaps. States must take steps to eliminate discrimination against children with disabilities that result from inadequate funding systems. Issues related to transportation costs and tuition must be taken into account in the structure and content of choice programs.

When the Nebraska Commissioner of Education turned to the U.S. Department of Education, Office of Special Education and Rehabilitative Services for instructions on how to proceed with special education programs and the choice legislation OSEP responded:

> It is the Department's position that, under interdistrict choice programs, states must ensure that the rights guaranteed to children with handicaps and their parents by EHA-B and Section 504 are not diminished by virtue of a child's participation in the program.

While the Department of Education leaves determinations as to the scope and applicability of choice programs to individual state's discretion, a state parental choice law cannot operate or deny or otherwise impede rights, although it may expand rights, guaranteed by the IDEA and Section 504.

As participants in public school programs built on the alleged value of choice, it is ironic that children with disabilities are being denied the opportunities of choice. The effects of the discrimination are clear. If states do not carefully address and correct the present discriminatory parental choice schemes, choice may become a code word for segregation. As it stands today, parental choice has become an oxymoron for special education students.

4. For more on parental choice, *see* A. Parker, *Public Free Schools: A Constitutional Right to Educational Choice in Texas*, 45 Sw. L.J. 825 (1991); C.L. Cusenbary, *Educational Choice Legislation after* Edgewood v. Kirby*: A Proposal for Clearing the Sectarian Hurdle*, 23 St. Mary's L.J. 269 (1991); and D. Futterman, *School Choice and the Religion Clauses: The Law and Politics of Public Aid to Private Parochial Schools*, 81. Geo. L.J. 711 (1993).

PART SIX

TORTS

Chapter 17
SUPERVISION AND TORT LIABILITY

Where a right is violated, injury ensues and a remedy may be necessitated. It then follows that the necessary remedy must be commensurate with the nature of the injury. The invasion of legal rights creates a judicial duty to fashion a remedy to make good the wrong done. Such is the case when the issues are supervision and liability on the part of school officials and there is a physical or psychological injury to students or other school personnel. Normally, if such injury occurs while a student is under the supervision of the school, and a suit results, it will be in tort.

Under state law a tort is a civil wrong, not in contract, that may be based on intentional acts, strict liability or negligence. Intentional torts are based on malicious or hostile actions of individuals that invade the rights of others with substantial certainty that harm will result. Such torts include assault, battery, intentional infliction of emotional distress, and false imprisonment.

Strict liability, the imposition of liability without regard to fault, places the burden for harm upon the person or entity best able to bear it. In the case of school officials this is a hardly recognized cause of action by the courts as it would burden even those school districts that operate in good faith and without culpability. Moreover, such a tort ignores the intentional harm of third parties and would thus make the school district the insurer of child welfare, despite the actions of others.

Negligence is the tort theory most relied upon by plaintiffs arguing that a school district or its agents should be liable for injury. To establish an institution's negligence, plaintiffs must prove that the school owed a duty of care to students or personnel, that this duty was breached by the defendant, that the breach of duty caused the harm prayed for and the institution's conduct was the direct or proximate cause of the injury. Moreover, under negligence, the extent to which the school district knew, or should have known, that a plaintiff was exposed to a risk of injury has a direct influence on whether a court will find a duty of care or whether such a duty was the proximate cause of the injury alleged. A defendant's knowledge is determined through the concept of "foreseeability" of injury. Specifically, an injury cannot be attributed to the school or its agents if it was not foreseen or could not have been foreseen or reasonably anticipated. This is often determined from the hypothetical point of view of an ordinary, reasonable, and prudent person in the same circumstances as the defendant school official. Liability would ordinarily not be held under negligence if such a person could not foresee a resulting injury from his or her actions. In addition, such liability would not be held if it could not be foreseen that a breach of the school official's breach of duty was the proximate cause of the injury.

Defendants in negligence actions may claim certain defenses against liability. The most common are contributory negligence, comparative negligence, assumption of the risk, and immunity.

"Contributory negligence" is conduct on the part of the one injured that contributes to his or her injuries and that falls below the standard of care required for protection and that represents a substantial factor in the injury. Hence, under this theory, a plaintiff, even if he or she has proven negligence on the part of a defendant, must also show that his or her own conduct was reasonable and comported with acceptable standards of care. Under this standard courts will look at a plaintiff's age and maturity to determine standard of care. It is important to note that if a state has a contributory negligence standard, such negligence is ordinarily an absolute bar to any recovery no matter how slight the negligence of the one injured.

The doctrine of "comparative negligence," adopted by a majority of the states, rejects the severity of contributory negligence up to a point. Instead the theory indicates that liability should be apportioned according to the proportion of fault. So in each instance a finding must be shown as to each party's negligence and damages are reduced or added accordingly. Hence, recovery will not be barred if the plaintiff's negligence is not greater than that of the defendant and will be diminished according to the amount attributable to the plaintiff.

"Assumption of the risk" completely bars a plaintiff's cause of action against another person's negligent act. In asserting such a defense a party must prove that a plaintiff expressly or impliedly consented to take the chance of harm, recognized and understood the risk and voluntarily chose to encounter it. Accordingly, the defendant would be absolved of liability as the issue of foreseeability transfers to the plaintiff. Here again, age, maturity and experience play a role as to whether students will be said to have assumed the risk. Though somewhat rare in school situations, this defense is mostly leveled against athletes, particularly in contact sports such as wrestling or football.

Other defenses may be claimed that have nothing to do with a plaintiff's actions. "Sovereign immunity" prevents a suit against government and some state officials unless statutory consent or waiver of liability has been granted. This means that unless a government consents, officials may be immune from liability. Tied to sovereign immunity is "qualified immunity" where a school official is immune from liability unless his or her acts or omissions were outside the scope of employment and unless the actions or omissions were malicious, reckless or in bad faith.

Finally, it is possible for a school employee to commit negligent acts or to omit an act that should have been performed and to be indemnified by the school district. Indemnification occurs when the school district covers the cost of a suit resulting from a tortious act or omission by a school employee.

Recently, victims of abuse in public schools have sought redress through the federal courts as well. This has been accomplished via 42 U.S.C Section 1983 which provides a federal cause of action to those whose constitutional or other federal rights have been violated by those acting under color of law. To establish a claim under this statute a plaintiff must bring evidence: 1) of a violation of a constitutional or statutory right; and 2) that the violation occurred under the auspices of government-sponsored activity. Allegations brought under this cause of action have mostly involved sexual assaults and other personal harms to students while under the auspices of the school. Section 1983 is often referred to as a "constitutional tort," incorporating constitutional and tort principles, recognizing that persons in school have a right to be free from intrusions of bodily integrity or personal security. Students and teachers have sued public schools under this statute claiming a denial of right because school districts negligently hired or retained abusive teachers or failed to protect them against the injurious actions of school personnel or other students.

A. NEGLIGENCE AND STRICT LIABILITY

ROBERTS v. ROBERTSON COUNTY BOARD OF EDUCATION

Court of Appeals of Tennessee
692 S.W.2d 863 (1985)

KOCH, JUDGE:

....

I

The Facts

Wallace Glenn Roberts, Jr. was a fourteen year old freshman at the Greenbrier High School in 1976. He elected to enroll in the school's Vocational Agriculture I class that was taught by Billy Ross Ballard. Mr. Ballard had taught this class at Greenbrier High School since 1960. There were twenty-three students enrolled in this class when it began in the middle of August, 1976. The class met one hour each day during the school week.

....

This course was taught in a separate modular building in back of the old Greenbrier High School. This building contained a classroom outfitted with tables and chairs, a tool room, two restrooms, Mr. Ballard's office, and an L-shaped shop area. There were a number of entrances to the shop area from the interior rooms and one primary outside entrance separated from the shop area by a hallway running between the tool room, the classroom, and the two restrooms.

Mr. Ballard testified that he taught this course in 1976 in much the same way he had taught it in past years. He did not rely upon a written lesson plan but generally relied upon his memory and his "philosophy on learning the students." In this regard, Mr. Ballard testified that

> I just go historically day to day. After so many years, it just sort of falls in. And there are some old lesson books there, maybe ten, twelve years old.

Every once in a while you will thumb through and pick up where you left off.

Mr. Ballard did not believe that the drill press was a very difficult piece of equipment to use, although he did state that some of its uses were more "delicate" than others. He demonstrated the use of this machine to his students by showing how it could be used to drill holes in metal and then how it could be fitted with a router bit for use in drawing letters and words in wood.

Mr. Ballard also testified that he taught "safety" in each one of his classes, although the record is not clear concerning the exact nature of the instruction Roberts' class received. This instruction took several forms including handouts, films, signs posted in the shop, and shop demonstrations on each piece of equipment. It also appears to have involved general safety rules as well as specific operational rules with regard to each piece of equipment.

While Mr. Ballard could not remember whether he passed out a written sheet of his safety rules to his Vocational Agriculture I class in 1976, he stated that these rules were a matter of general knowledge among his students. Mr. Ballard's three main general safety rules were: (1) that the machinery could not be operated when he was not in the shop;[4] (2) that "horseplay and horsepower don't mix"; and (3) that students should not talk to or distract persons who were working with the machinery. He also stated that there were other general rules with regard to the use of protective eye wear and disconnecting a piece of equipment while it was being adjusted. Students were also told not to try to do anything on a piece of equipment that they had not done before without asking Mr. Ballard first or without his direct supervision.

Mr. Ballard also testified that in addition to these general safety rules, there were a number of specific safety rules with regard to the operation of the drill press that he reviewed with his students when he demonstrated the use of each piece of equipment. A number of these operational rules were also included in a sign posted on the wall near the drill press which contained a list of eight safety precautions.[5]

---

[4]The exact substance of this rule is not free from doubt. The shop students who testified had various understandings of the rule, and Mr. Ballard himself testified of two different versions. At one point, he stated that the machines were not to be used when he was not in the building. At another point, he testified that the machines were not to be used when he was not in the shop area itself. In either case, it was apparently Mr. Ballard's practice to instruct his students to turn off the machines when he did not want them to be used. The students were not instructed that it was their responsibility to keep track of Mr. Ballard's whereabouts.

[5]Three of these posted precautions relevant to this case are:

Safety Precautions

....

2. Before placing the drill or bit in the drill press chuck, check the speed by starting the motor. Then, if necessary, adjust for proper speed. Use a low speen [sic] for large bits,

A. NEGLIGENCE AND STRICT LIABILITY

....

The class in which Roberts and Yount were students received its group instruction in the use of the drill press in late October or early November, 1976. This instruction included a demonstration wherein Mr. Ballard showed students how to drill holes in metal and how to carve letters in wood using a short router bit. Mr. Ballard could not state whether either Roberts or Yount viewed this demonstration and did not testify to any steps he took to make sure that each student attended the demonstration or understood the basic techniques he was teaching. Yount testified, in fact, that he was not directly involved in Mr. Ballard's demonstration of the drill press because he was using the welding equipment at the time in another area of the shop. There is no evidence in this record that this demonstration of the drill press or any other instruction included warnings to the students of the dangers attendant to more complicated uses of the drill press or instructions concerning how students should help each other use the drill press.

On December 17, 1976, the last school day before the Christmas vacation, Yount desired to use the drill press to drill a hole through a fourteen inch, cylindrical piece of wood he was fashioning into a lamp base he intended to give as a Christmas present. Mr. Yount had only seen the drill press used to drill holes in metal and to carve names in wood. The work he wanted to do was not one of the basic uses of the drill press that had been covered in Mr. Ballard's demonstration conducted a month earlier. Yount had never received instruction concerning the use of the drill press to drill holes in larger pieces of wood. Likewise, he had never tried to do this before and had never seen anyone else try to use the drill press in this way. Mr. Ballard testified that this use required a more elaborate setup and that it could be dangerous if the drill press was not set up properly.

Yount talked to Mr. Ballard about what he wanted to do. Mr. Ballard understood from this conversation that Yount was eager to do this work that day because he wanted to take the lamp base home. This job could not be done using the drill bits that the students were accustomed to using. It required a much longer drill bit that Mr. Ballard kept in his desk drawer in his office. Even though the students were not making full use of the shop that day, Mr. Ballard took this special drill bit from his desk drawer and gave it to Yount. While there is some disagreement concerning Mr. Ballard's instructions at this point, Mr. Ballard testified that he instructed Yount to wait before he started to use the drill

---

medium speed for medium-sized bits; and higher speed for small bits and drills.

....

4. Material of a size and shape which might be seized by the turning drill must be clamped securely to the drill press table. When in doubt, ask the instructor for advice.

....

6. Keep hands clear of the line of travel of the bit or drill.

bit because he wanted to be present to supervise the student's work.[7] Yount went into the shop and set up the drill press as best he knew how. He then waited for Mr. Ballard.

Mr. Ballard was not in the shop area at that time, nor did he follow Yount into the shop. He was in another part of the building. He had promised to give his students free soft drinks that day, and at the time Yount was ready to work on his lamp base, Mr. Ballard was near the outside entrance to the shop building where he was moving the soft drink machine into the classroom area. The drill press could not be seen from where Mr. Ballard was located near the outside door.

Yount waited for approximately ten minutes for Mr. Ballard to return to the shop. There were other students using shop machinery during this time. When Mr. Ballard did not come in, Yount asked his classmate, Roberts, to assist him in drilling a hole in the lamp base. Roberts had been helping another classmate use a hand saw, and this was the first time he was aware that Yount desired to use the drill press. He was not aware that Yount had talked with Mr. Ballard about this job and thus, was not aware of any instructions that Mr. Ballard might have given Yount. He was just helping a friend. Roberts had never been instructed or warned concerning the danger of what Yount was doing or the manner in which people could be injured when using a longer drill bit.

At Yount's request to hold the piece of wood while the hole was drilled, Roberts knelt down next to the drill press and held the piece of wood firmly in both hands. His face was approximately ten to twelve inches away from the drill itself. Yount turned on the drill, and in an instant, the long drill bit deflected at an angle of approximately forty-five degrees striking Roberts on the right temple. The drill bit caused a long cut and skull fracture from Roberts' right temple to behind his right ear. He fell back immediately from the machine, and other students came to his aid and carried him to Mr. Ballard's office. Mr. Ballard did not know what had happened until one of the students came to get him. Mr. Ballard and the school principal then transported Roberts to the hospital.

. . . .

Mr. Ballard testified later that Yount had not set up the drill press properly because he had not reduced the drill bit's speed and had not properly clamped the cylindrical piece of wood in place before he started. Mr. Ballard stated that the drill press would have been properly adjusted had he been supervising Yount and that this accident would not have happened had he been in the shop when Yount was working on his lamp base.

---

[7] Yount testified that Mr. Ballard told him "[t]o go ahead and he [Mr. Ballard] would be in in a minute."

II

The Negligence of the School Officials

Roberts alleged in his complaint that his injury was the result of the negligence of his vocational agriculture teacher, the local school administrators, and the county school board. As in all negligence actions, he must prove in order to recover that the defendants had a legally recognized duty to him, that this duty was breached, and that this action or failure to act was the proximate cause of his injury.

....

The trial court in this case determined that Mr. Ballard had a duty "to properly supervise and properly instruct" his students. While we agree with this generalized determination as far as it goes, we find it necessary to define this duty more precisely and to describe carefully the scope of the teacher's standard of care.

Teachers and local school districts are not expected to be insurers of the safety of students while they are at school. Nor are teachers expected in every instance to supervise all the activities of all students at all times. However, most courts having occasion to consider cases involving injuries to students while in shop class have determined that teachers, and through them their local school systems, are required to exercise such care as ordinarily reasonable and prudent persons would exercise under the same or similar circumstances. Thus, the Louisiana Court of Appeal has held:

> The standard of care for school teachers and administrators is that of a reasonable person in such a position acting under similar circumstances....

....

The Tennessee Supreme Court has adopted the reasonable person standard in other cases involving the safety of students. In a case where a high school student was injured when she fell on the steps of a school bus, the Tennessee Supreme Court held the school system to the standard of "reasonable and ordinary care under the circumstances." However, our courts have also recognized that this standard of care can be related directly to the nature of the persons to whom the duty is owed and the circumstances giving rise to the duty. The Tennessee Supreme Court has recognized, for example, that an adult's standard of care to children should be tempered by the recognition of children's youthful impulsiveness and inexperience. Likewise, this Court has recognized that a person who deals with inherently dangerous instrumentalities has a duty to exercise caution commensurate with the dangers involved. Thus, with regard to the duty of care owed by school bus drivers to students placed in their charge, the Tennessee Supreme Court held:

> Reasonable and ordinary care under the circumstances, when one of the circumstances is that the care of a child of tender years is entrusted to the

school bus driver, requires that the driver exercise special care proportionate to the age of the child and its ability, or lack of ability, to care for itself. *Hawkins County v. Davis*, 216 Tenn. 262, 267, 391 S.W.2d 658, 660 (1965).

Based upon these precedents, we find that a high school vocational teacher has the duty to take those precautions that any ordinarily reasonable and prudent person would take to protect his shop students from the unreasonable risk of injury. The extent of these precautions must be determined with reference to the age and inexperience of the students involved, their less than mature judgment with regard to their conduct, and the inherently dangerous nature of the power driven equipment available for their use in the shop. In order to discharge this duty, it is incumbent upon a teacher, at a minimum, to instruct his students in the safe and proper use of the equipment, to warn the students of known dangers, and to supervise the students to the extent necessary for the enforcement of adequate rules of shop safety.

Once the trial court has determined that the defendant was under a duty to protect the plaintiff against the event that did, in fact, occur, then it must be proven that the defendant's actions or failure to act constituted a breach of this duty. This second element of proof in a negligence case usually requires a factual determination that can only be made upon the unique facts of each case.

The final element of proof in a negligence action is the issue of causation. This is the ultimate question. A defendant in a negligence action cannot be found liable unless it has been determined that his conduct was the proximate cause of the plaintiff's injuries. While the proximate cause concept has been described in many ways, the Tennessee Supreme Court has described proximate causation as

> [t]hat act or omission which immediately causes or fails to prevent the injury; an act or omission occurring or concurring with another which, if it had not happened, the injury would not have been inflicted. *Tennessee Trailways, Inc. v. Ervin*, 222 Tenn. 523, 528, 438 S.W.2d 733, 735 (1969).

See also Shouse v. Otis, 224 Tenn. 1, 8, 448 S.W.2d 673, 676 (1969). A defendant's conduct will be regarded as the proximate cause of the plaintiff's injury if it was the "procuring", "efficient", or "predominant" cause of the injury. As long as the defendant's conduct is a substantial factor causing the injury, it need not be the sole cause or even the last act prior to the injury.

. . . .

Foreseeability is also an essential element of the proof of proximate causation. If the injury giving rise to the action could not have been reasonably foreseen or anticipated, then there is no proximate cause. However, this foreseeability requirement is not so strict as to require that a defendant must foresee the exact manner in which an injury takes place. The requirement is met as long as it has been determined that the defendant could foresee, or through the exercise of

A. NEGLIGENCE AND STRICT LIABILITY

reasonable diligence should have foreseen, the general manner in which the injury occurred....

With specific reference to the conduct of teachers, we do not impose upon them the duty to anticipate or foresee the hundreds of unexpected student acts that occur daily in our public schools.... However, like other courts, we have no hesitation in holding a teacher or local school system to the duty of safeguarding students while at school from reasonably foreseeable dangerous conditions including the dangerous acts of fellow students.

Based upon our *de novo* review of this record, we conclude that the evidence supports a finding that Mr. Ballard was negligent and that his failure to furnish adequate instruction and supervision to his vocational agriculture students was the proximate cause of Roberts' injuries. There are four separate aspects of Mr. Ballard's conduct that support this conclusion. First, Mr. Ballard had a practice of permitting inexperienced freshman students to remain in the shop area unsupervised in the presence of fully operational power driven equipment which, if used improperly, could cause serious injury. Second, there is no proof that Mr. Ballard ever instructed his students in the proper techniques for assisting others in operating shop machinery. Third, there is no proof that Mr. Ballard ever gave his students any instruction concerning the ways a drill press could cause injury if it was not used properly. While there is proof that Mr. Ballard demonstrated two of the many ways that a drill press could be used, neither Mr. Ballard nor any of his students testified that any instruction was given concerning the other ways that a drill press, if improperly used, could cause injury. Fourth, Mr. Ballard gave Yount a drill bit knowing that he had never used the drill bit before and that he was eager to use it during that class period.

The evidence supports a conclusion that Mr. Ballard was aware that Yount did not know how to use the longer drill bit properly when he gave it to him and that Mr. Ballard knew that this drill bit could be dangerous if used improperly. Apart from his conceded general recognition that fourteen year old boys have a characteristic impatience and curiosity, Mr. Ballard also had direct knowledge that Yount intended to use the special drill bit at that time because this was his last opportunity to do so before Christmas vacation. Rather than keeping the drill bit and telling Yount that he would come into the shop area to supervise his work, Mr. Ballard gave Yount the instrument that caused Roberts' injury. Providing the drill bit to Yount, knowing at the time that the shop equipment was fully operable, that other students were working in the shop area without supervision, and that Yount was eager to use the drill bit constitutes a breach of Mr. Ballard's duty to supervise his students properly and provides a sufficient basis for a judgment in Roberts' favor.

III

The School Board's Liability in Light of Yount's Conduct

....

While we make no determination with regard to Yount's negligence — an issue still to be decided — we do not find that his actions are independent, intervening causes sufficient in and of themselves to excuse the negligence of Mr. Ballard or the local school system.

We have already noted that a person whose negligent conduct causes a foreseeable injury will not be relieved from liability because of a negligent act of another....

Mr. Ballard candidly conceded that Roberts would not have been injured had he been present in the shop supervising Yount's use of the drill press. We agree. This provides a basis, independent of any consideration of Yount's actions, to hold Mr. Ballard, and thus, the local school board,[13] liable for Roberts' injuries.

[In Part IV of the opinion, the Court held that Roberts' motion for a directed verdict was out of place in a non-jury trial and was thus properly denied.]

....

V

Judgment for Roberts and Assessment of Damages

... [T]he Tennessee Supreme Court has held:

> If, in the judgment of the Court of Appeals, the evidence preponderates against the finding of the trial court the presumption as to its correctness vanishes and the Court of Appeals must enter such judgment as it deems the preponderance of the evidence warrants. *Perry v. Carter*, 188 Tenn. 409, 411-12, 219 S.W.2d 905, 906 (1949).

While this decision was handed down prior to the advent of the Tennessee Rules of Appellate Procedure, the Advisory Commission Comments to these rules make it clear that they were intended to preserve the ability of the Court of Appeals to "grant whatever relief an appellate proceeding requires."

We have reviewed this record. The case was fully tried, and thus, no useful purpose would be served to put the litigants to the time and expense of a new trial. Based upon the proof in the record, we have already determined that Mr. Ballard, and through him the Robertson County Board of Education, was negligent in its instruction and supervision of Yount, Roberts, and their fellow

---

[13]Mr. Ballard, acting in his capacity as a teacher, was an agent of the Robertson County Board of Education. Thus, pursuant to Tenn.Code Ann. § 29-20-205, the County is liable for his negligent acts....

A. NEGLIGENCE AND STRICT LIABILITY

students and thus, that they are liable for the injuries Roberts sustained on December 17, 1976, in his Vocational Agriculture I class.

The issue of damages remains. The record contains evidence that Roberts' family sustained approximately $4,225 in medical bills as a result of this injury. Further, Roberts himself was hospitalized for ten days and experienced moderate pain for some time thereafter. His surgical treatment required that his head be shaved, and thus, for some time after the accident, he was subjected to the ridicule and teasing of his peers. This embarrassment to a fourteen year old boy can be as painful as the injury itself. His treating physician also determined that this injury has caused a permanent weakening of his skull in the area of the injury. While placing no limitation on Roberts' activities, his doctor determined that this injury has resulted in a five percent disability to the body as a whole. Based upon this testimony, we find that an award of $25,000 in damages is warranted.

For the reasons stated herein, the judgment of the trial court is reversed and the case is remanded with directions that a judgment in the amount of $25,000 be entered in favor of Wallace Glenn Roberts, Jr. and against Billy R. Ballard and the Robertson County Board of Education.

....

---

1. What would you have done in Mr. Ballard's place here? Consider footnote 12, edited out of this opinion:

> While the availability or expense of more effective safety procedures does not bear upon the issue of negligence, other courts have noted that other safety procedures are available at minimal cost. *See, e.g., Lawrence v. Grant Parish School Board*, 409 So.2d 1110 (La. 1982). In *Roberts*, for example, Roberts' injury would have been prevented had Mr. Ballard adopted and enforced a rule prohibiting students from being in the shop when he was not present in the shop. The injury would also have been avoided had Mr. Ballard been provided with the central ability to render all machines inoperable while he was not in the shop area.

2. In many cases involving inherently dangerous activities, defendants who are best able to bear the loss or avoid the recurrence of the loss are often held strictly liable. In addition to abnormally dangerous activities (*see* Restatement (Second) of Torts §§ 519-521), strict liability claims may also be asserted when defendant's animals cause injury (Rest. 2d § 504 *et seq.*), or when their defective products do (Rest. 2d § 402A).

Could *Roberts* have asserted a strict liability tort claim? Read the following excerpt from *Fallon v. Indian Trail Sch.*, 500 N.E.2d 101 (Ill. App. 1986). How would *Roberts* be decided under Rest. 2d §§ 519-20?

The plaintiff's amended complaint sought to recover damages for spinal injuries suffered as a result of a trampoline accident which occurred on February 23, 1975. At that time the plaintiff was a sixth-grade student at the school and the defendants ... were physical education teachers....

....

In count I, the plaintiff alleged that the trampoline was an abnormally dangerous instrumentality, and the school district should, therefore, be held accountable under strict tort liability for any injuries due to its use. In count II, the plaintiff charged the school and school district with negligence as a result of a violation of section 10.20.8 of the School Code (Ill. Rev. Stat. 1985, ch. 122, par. 10-20.8) because the trampoline was an abnormally dangerous instrumentality. We must, therefore, decide whether the plaintiff has alleged sufficient facts to support the contention that the trampoline is an abnormally dangerous instrumentality and trampoline usage is an abnormally dangerous activity.

Illinois recognizes strict liability under two theories: unreasonably dangerous defective products (*Suvada v. White Motor Co.* (1965), 32 Ill.2d 612, 621, 210 N.E.2d 182), and the theory which plaintiff alleges is applicable to this case, ultrahazardous activities (*City of Joliet v. Harwood* (1877), 86 Ill. 110). Sections 519 and 520 of the Restatement (Second) of Torts (1981) (Restatement) have formulated a definition of ultrahazardous activities. Under section 519(1) of the Restatement,

> "[o]ne who carries on an abnormally dangerous activity is subject to liability for harm to the person, land or chattels of another resulting from the activity, although he has exercised the utmost care to prevent the harm." (Restatement (Second) of Torts sec. 519(1) (1981).)

Section 520 of the Restatement considers:

> "[E]xistence of a high degree of risk of some harm....; likelihood that the harm that results from it will be great; inability to eliminate the risk by the exercise of reasonable care; extent to which the activity is not a matter of common usage...." Restatement (Second) of Torts sec. 520 (1981).

Illinois has long recognized strict liability for damages caused by engaging in an ultrahazardous activity, although it has never explicitly relied upon the Restatement factors in determining whether a given activity is abnormally dangerous....

The plaintiff concedes that there is no Illinois authority discussing either whether (1) trampoline usage of this sort is an ultrahazardous activity, or (2) the trampoline is an abnormally dangerous instrumentality. Indeed, the trial court, in its written disposition dismissing counts I and II, noted that most of the discussion which related to this subject had to do with such obviously dangerous instrumentalities and activities as blasting, transport of explosives,

A. NEGLIGENCE AND STRICT LIABILITY

maintenance of high electrical current, large animals, and maintenance of water reservoirs. In support of her argument, the plaintiff attached Exhibit A, "Trampoline-Related Quadriplegia: Review of the Literature and Reflections on the American Academy of Pediatrics' Position Statement," a review documenting cervical spine injuries resulting from trampoline-related accidents.

After reviewing Exhibit A, the trial court's disposition, as well as the plaintiff's amended complaint, we believe the trial court was correct in finding that trampoline usage, as alleged in the present case, does not fall within the parameter of an abnormally dangerous activity. We also agree that the trampoline, as a matter of law, is not an abnormally dangerous instrumentality.

Trampolines are widely used in the school systems as well as other centers of gymnastic activity. The injuries that may be caused result not from the trampoline itself but rather from the manner of its use. The terms "ultrahazardous," "abnormally dangerous," or "intrinsically dangerous," as traditionally used, refer to that type of danger which is inherent in the instrumentality itself at all times and do not mean danger which arises from mere casual or collateral negligence of others with respect to it under the particular circumstances. More concisely, it means dangerous in its normal or nondefective state. (*Clark v. City of Chicago* (1980) 88 Ill. App. 3d 760, 763, 43 Ill. Dec. 892, 410 N.E.2d 1025.) We conclude that although its negligent use can be the basis for liability, neither the trampoline itself nor its ordinary use is abnormally dangerous or ultrahazardous. (*Cf. Snow v. Judy* (1968), 96 Ill. App. 2d 420, 423, 239 N.E.2d 327.) Therefore, counts I and II were properly dismissed.

....

3. It may be clear that a drill press, as in *Roberts*, would not fall into a list of obviously dangerous instrumentalities and activities which include "blasting, transport of explosives, maintenance of high electrical current, large animals, and maintenance of water reservoirs." *Fallon*, 500 N.E.2d at 103. But what about Justice Strouse's later classification (in *Fallon*)?

> The terms "ultrahazardous," "abnormally dangerous," or "intrinsically dangerous," as traditionally used, refer to that type of danger which is inherent in the instrumentality itself at all times and do not mean danger which arises from mere casual or collateral negligence of others with respect to it under the particular circumstances. More concisely, it means dangerous in its normal or nondefective state. *Fallon*, 500 N.E.2d at 103.

Would shop class machinery fit here, imposing strict liability on the school district? Or is a negligence claim the only successful claim under *Roberts'* circumstances? *See Barbin v. State*, 506 So. 2d 888 (La. App. 1987). In *Barbin*, a seventh grade student was injured in woodworking class while using a power saw owned by the school. The court held the teacher negligent and the state, as owner of the saw, strictly liable. However, due to the teacher's negligence, the state was indemnified for 80% of its liability.

4. Does a drill press pose an "unreasonable risk of harm" to a child? Apply *Roberts* to the following case.

LEVIE, III v. ORLEANS PARISH SCHOOL BOARD
Court of Appeals of Louisiana
537 So. 2d 351 (4th Cir. 1989)

KLEES, JUDGE:

....

On May 24, 1983, twelve-year-old Jennifer Levie fell and hurt her ankle in the school yard of Hynes Elementary, where she was waiting to meet her cousins, who were Hynes students. The fall occurred when, while walking toward the monkey bars, Jennifer stepped in a hole in the ground and her foot became trapped by the Y-shaped root of a tree which surrounded the hole. Both the hole and the root were covered with grass.

Jennifer was immediately diagnosed as having either strained ligaments or a displaced fracture, and her leg was placed in a cast to her knee. The cast was removed by Dr. Bruce Razza, her orthopedic surgeon, on June 21, 1983, and Jennifer was released. On May 16, 1984, she again consulted Dr. Razza concerning pain in her ankle which had begun about one month after the cast was removed. She also complained of swelling and pain in her knee and occasions when her knee would "lock," causing her to fall. At this point, Dr. Razza determined that Jennifer had a probable torn medial meniscus (torn cartilage) in her right knee, as well as post-traumatic arthritis in her right ankle and knee, all of which were likely to have been caused by her fall in the school yard. Dr. Razza has not recommended surgery, but has treated these problems with medication and heat therapy. As a result of these injuries, Jennifer has had to severely restrict her participation in physical activities, such as sports, dancing, and physical education classes.

Jennifer's parents sued the Orleans Parish School Board claiming it was strictly liable under Civil Code article 2317 for the defective condition of the playground. The case was tried in the district court on December 10, 1987, and the trial judge found in favor of plaintiffs, awarding them $176,000 ($1,000 medical expenses plus $175,000 general damages) for their daughter's injuries. On appeal, the school board contends that the trial judge committed manifest error by finding that the condition of the school yard posed an unreasonable danger to Jennifer Levie and thus holding the board strictly liable....

In order to make out a case under Civil Code article 2317, the injured party must show: (1) that the thing he complains of was in the care or custody of the defendant; (2) the existence of a vice or defect in the thing; and (3) that his injury was caused by the vice or defect. *Loescher v. Parr*, 324 So.2d 441, 449

A. NEGLIGENCE AND STRICT LIABILITY

(La.1975). The school board does not dispute that it had custody of the Hynes school yard nor that Jennifer's injury was caused by a condition of the yard; the issue is whether the school yard was defective.

For a thing to be defective so as to trigger strict liability, it must pose "an unreasonable risk of harm to persons." *Entrevia v. Hood*, 427 So.2d 1146, 1149 (La.1983). Regarding this criterion, the Supreme Court in *Entrevia* stated:

> The unreasonable risk of harm criterion, however is not a simple rule of law which may be applied mechanically to the facts of a case. It is a concept employed by this court to symbolize the judicial process required by the civil code. Since Article 2317 and 2322 state general precepts and not detailed rules for all concrete cases, it becomes the interpreter's duty to decide which risks are encompassed by the codal obligations from the standpoint of justice and social utility. *Id.* at 1149.

Defendant first argues that the hole in the Hynes school yard did not pose an unreasonable risk of harm because it was not visible, and because "[s]tudents had played ... around this tree for years without any reports of injury." In essence, defendant's argument is that the hole did not constitute a defect because it was not discoverable. Unfortunately, under the law as it existed at the time of Jennifer's accident, whether or not the defect is discovered or discoverable is not relevant in determining the existence of strict liability. As the Court stated in *Entrevia v. Hood*, "The owner is absolved from his strict liability neither by his ignorance of the [defective] condition ... nor by circumstances that the defect could not easily be detected." 427 So.2d at 1148. Thus, the inability of the defendant to know or prevent the risk is not a defense in a strict liability case.

Defendant also argues that the condition of the yard did not pose an unreasonable risk of harm because it was caused by a natural phenomenon, the tree, which has aesthetic value and is a desirable thing to have on a school playground. This argument is partially based upon the assumption that the hole had formed naturally, which was not proven or even addressed at trial. Moreover, while we recognize that the determination of what constitutes an unreasonable risk of harm involves a balancing of interests we believe that the risk of injury to a child such as Jennifer Levie greatly outweighs the aesthetic value of this particular tree. Furthermore, it was never shown that the only appropriate remedial measure would be removal of the tree, rather than merely cutting back the offensive root and/or filling in the hole.

In *Landry v. State*, 495 So.2d 1284 (La.1986), the Supreme Court found that a hole immediately adjacent to the Lake Pontchatrain seawall presented an unreasonable risk of harm to the plaintiff, a recreational fisherman who was injured when he tried to avoid stepping in the hole, which was partially obscured by grass. Although the hole was a natural consequence of wave action and erosion, the Court found that the risk of harm it created in this heavily used recreational area outweighed the cost of prevention....

The facts of *Landry* are similar to those of the instant case in several key ways. Like the lakefront, a school playground is a heavily used recreational area. As in *Landry*, there was no showing at trial that the cost of repair would be prohibitive; in fact, the supervisor of grounds for the Orleans Parish school system testified that he inspected the Hynes playground more frequently than most other schools, about three to five times per year, because of the special hazards posed by the large number of trees. He also stated that the employees who mow the grass three times per month are instructed to check for holes and other potentially dangerous conditions so that these may be corrected.

Jennifer Levie testified that the hole into which she stepped was deep enough that the ground came to one inch above her ankle. We find that the hole combined with the tree root posed an unreasonable risk of harm to Jennifer. Under the law, the fact that this condition was not easily discoverable does not absolve the school board. Therefore, the trial court did not commit manifest error by holding defendant strictly liable for Jennifer's injuries.

....

BARRY, JUDGE, dissenting:

....

I disagree with the majority's conclusion that the ground "combined with the tree root posed an unreasonable risk of harm." The record establishes only a minor, very common irregularity in the ground which cannot be described as unreasonable. The tree root was the cause of this alleged accident and it cannot be considered an unreasonable risk of harm.

Finding liability under these facts is tantamount to the School Board becoming the insurer for any ground/tree-related accident in a school yard. Such a holding will encourage the removal of trees from school yards and create liability in other areas used by children.

....

---

1. Do you agree with the majority or the dissent? Is it possible that there will be a flood of litigation against schools after decisions like that in *Levie*? Should the school be required to search for natural conditions such as tree roots in order to avoid liability? Does it make any difference if the school knows about the defects? What did the *Levie* court say about this?

See also Waltz v. Wake County Bd. of Educ., 409 S.E.2d 106 (N.C. App. 1991). In *Waltz*, the court held that the school breached no duty of care to a student who tripped over a tree root on the playground, and thus was not negligent.

> We do not go so far as to say that a school may never be liable for injury resulting from a natural condition. However, school officials simply cannot be expected to protect children from every natural condition they may

A. NEGLIGENCE AND STRICT LIABILITY

encounter on a school yard or playground. Falls and mishaps, though unfortunate, are part of every school child's life and are something that neither teachers nor parents can reasonably be expected to guarantee to prevent. *Id.* at 107-08.

An additional factor noted by the court, though perhaps not dispositive, was that the school had earlier placed sand around the tree whose root caused the injury. The court found that the sand served to mitigate the natural condition of the roots and to cushion the fall.

2. What about artificial playground objects? A greater degree of care is required if a student is to use or come in contact with an inherently dangerous object, or to engage in an activity where it is reasonably foreseeable that an accident or injury may occur. In *Rollins v. Concordia Parish Sch. Bd.*, 465 So. 2d 213 (La. Ct. App. 1985), the court found no evidence sufficient enough to hold a merry-go-round defective. (The court considered the height off the ground, the ring, the handrail, etc.). The *Rollins* court did, however, find that the school was negligent. The school had combined two classes for a recess period, but only used one of the teachers as a playground supervisor. (The other teacher was given a free period.) Because there was another teacher available to supervise the recess, the court found the supervision inadequate and held the school negligent.

EISEL v. BOARD OF EDUCATION OF MONTGOMERY COUNTY

Court of Appeals of Maryland
324 Md. 376, 597 A.2d 447 (1991)

RODOWSKY, JUDGE:

The legal theory advanced by the plaintiff in this wrongful death and survival action is that school counselors have a duty to intervene to attempt to prevent a student's threatened suicide. The specific question presented is whether the duty contended for may be breached by junior high school counselors who fail to inform a parent of suicidal statements attributed to the parent's child by fellow students where, when the counselors sought to discuss the subject, the adolescent denied ever making the statements....

The decedent, Nicole Eisel (Nicole), was a thirteen year old student at Sligo Middle School in Montgomery County. She and another thirteen year old girl consummated an apparent murder-suicide pact on November 8, 1988. Nicole's father, Stephen Eisel (Eisel), brought the instant action. His amended complaint alleges negligence on the part of two counselors at Nicole's school, among others....

....

II

The amended complaint avers that Nicole became involved in satanism, causing her to have an "obsessive interest in death and self-destruction." During the week prior to the suicide, Nicole told several friends and fellow students that she intended to kill herself. Some of these friends reported Nicole's intentions to their school counselor, [Diedre] Morgan, who relayed the information to Nicole's school counselor, [Dorothy] Jones. Morgan and Jones then questioned Nicole about the statements, but Nicole denied making them. Neither Morgan nor Jones notified Nicole's parents or the school administration about Nicole's alleged statements of intent. Information in the record suggests that the other party to the suicide pact shot Nicole before shooting herself. The murder-suicide took place on a school holiday in a public park at some distance from Sligo Middle School. The other party to the pact attended another school.

III

There is no direct Maryland precedent on the issue before us. We have not been cited to, nor have we found, any decision by any other court that deals with the issue of duty on substantially similar facts. Before the circuit court the defendants' argument that the counselors owed no duty to intervene rested largely on language in judicial decisions that defendants say are analogous.

On the issue of duty Eisel argued that, by the School Board's own policy, counselors were required to contact the parents of any child who had expressed suicidal thoughts. Eisel pointed to deposition testimony on that subject by the principal, who said: "If the student is in danger, of course, you take care of that first. Then the next thing you do would be to notify a parent. If the student is in no apparent danger, you will notify the parent."

There appear to be two broad categories of cases in which a person may be held liable for the suicide of another. The first type occurs when the defendant's conduct actually causes the suicide, as when a negligent driver causes head injuries that lead to psychosis. It is not contended here that Nicole's suicide was caused, in that sense, by the defendants' conduct.

The second type of case holds that a special relationship between a defendant and the suicidal person creates a duty to prevent a foreseeable suicide. For instance, many courts have held that a hospital or a prison that has custody over a person who commits suicide may be liable if the suicide was foreseeable. In *State ex rel. Shockey v. Washington Sanitarium & Hosp.*, 223 Md. 554, 557, 165 A.2d 764, 765-66 (1960), we said:

> "[T]here is a duty upon a sanitarium or hospital to exercise such care in looking out for and protecting a patient as the circumstances, including known mental and physical conditions, may reasonably require. Failure to do so may be negligence, and if suicide is a proximate result of the negligence, recovery may be had under the wrongful death statute...."

At least one case has concluded that a professional therapist may be held liable when a patient commits suicide, even if the therapist or the therapist's hospital does not have custody over the patient. *Bellah v. Greenson*, 81 Cal.App.3d 614, 620, 146 Cal.Rptr. 535, 538 (1978); *but see Nally v. Grace Community Church of the Valley*, 47 Cal.3d 278, 295-96, 763 P.2d 948, 958, 253 Cal.Rptr. 97, 107-08 (1988) (limiting *Bellah*), *cert. denied*, 490 U.S. 1007 (1989). Liability against therapists for outpatient suicides is rarely imposed, *e.g.*, *Farwell v. Un*, 902 F.2d 282 (4th Cir. 1990) (applying Maryland law); Comment, *Civil Liability for Causing or Failing to Prevent Suicide*, 12 Loy.L.A.L.Rev. 967, 993 (1979), and some commentators have suggested that liability under these circumstances should never be imposed. *See Id.* at 993 & n. 142.

Recent attempts to extend the duty to prevent suicide beyond custodial or therapist-patient relationships have failed.... [*See, e.g., Nally*, 47 Cal.3d at 299-300, 763 P.2d at 960-961, 253 Cal.Rptr at 110. (Church pastor has no duty to refer a twenty-four year old suicidal counselee to a mental health professional); *McLaughlin v. Sullivan*, 123 N.H. 335, 461 A.2d 123 (1983) (Attorney has no duty to prevent suicide of a client who kills himself twelve hours after incarceration. Attorney had no custody, no control, and no expertise and training necessary to foresee that such a client would commit suicide); and *Bogust v. Iverson*, 10 Wis.2d 129, 102 N.W.2d 228 (1960) (College professor-counselor has no duty to secure psychiatric treatment for the student or to advise her parents of her emotional state. There was no evidence that the counselor was aware of the suicidal tendencies.]

....

A number of factors distinguish the instant matter from those cases finding an absence of any duty, reviewed above, in which the custodial relationship between the suicide victim and the defendant was other than that of hospital and patient or jailer and prisoner. Eisel's claim involves suicide by an adolescent. The negligence relied on is a failure to communicate to the parent the information allegedly possessed by the defendants concerning the child's contemplated suicide, not a failure by the school authorities physically to prevent the suicide by exercising custody and control over Nicole. The theory of Eisel's case is that he could have exercised his custody and control, as parent, over Nicole, had he been warned, and inferentially, that there was nothing known to the counselors about Eisel's relationship with Nicole that would make such a warning unreasonable....

Further, we have recognized

> "the doctrine that the relation of a school vis-à-vis a pupil is analogous to one who stands in *loco parentis*, with the result that a school is under a special duty to exercise reasonable care to protect a pupil from harm, *Segerman v. Jones*, 256 Md. 109, 123-24, 259 A.2d 794, 801 (1969); Restatement (Second) of Torts § 320 at 130 (1965); 2 Harper and James, The Law of Torts § 18.7 at 1058 (1956); Annot., 86 A.L.R.2d 489, 565-68 (1962); Annot., 32 A.L.R.2d 1163, 1178-81 (1953); Annot., 160 A.L.R. 7, 155-56 (1946)." *Lunsford v. Board of Educ.*, 280 Md. 665, 676, 374 A.2d 1162, 1168 (1977).

Finally, the relationship of school counselor and pupil is not devoid of therapeutic overtones. The "Counselor Job Description," published by the Department of Professional Personnel of the Board lists the first two "[p]riorities of the counseling profession" to be:

> "1. Counseling with individuals and groups concerning school adjustment, physical and emotional development, educational planning, and career awareness....
> "2. Identifying students with significant problems and taking steps to provide help for these students."

The defendant Jones has been a counselor in the Montgomery County school system since 1977. She holds an M.A. in guidance and counseling. [She has also completed coursework on crisis intervention and suicide].

Given the peculiar mix of factors presented, it is an open question whether there is a duty to attempt to prevent an adolescent's suicide, by reasonable means, including, in this case, by warning the parent. Therefore, we must analyze whether we should recognize a duty in this case.

IV

A tort duty is "an expression of the sum total of those considerations of policy which lead the law to say that the plaintiff is entitled to protection." *Jacques v. First Nat'l Bank*, 307 Md. 527, 533, 515 A.2d 756, 759 (1986) (quoting Prosser & Keeton on the Law of Torts § 53 at 358 (5th ed. 1984)). "[A]mong the variables to be considered in determining whether a tort duty should be recognized are:

> '[T]he foreseeability of harm to the plaintiff, the degree of certainty that the plaintiff suffered the injury, the closeness of the connection between the defendant's conduct and the injury suffered, the moral blame attached to the defendant's conduct, the policy of preventing future harm, the extent of the burden to the defendant and consequences to the community of imposing a duty to exercise care with resulting liability for breach, and the availability, cost and prevalence of insurance for the risk involved.'" *Village of Cross Keys, Inc. v. United States Gypsum Co.*, 315 Md. 741, 752, 556 A.2d 1126, 1131 (1989) (quoting *Tarasoff v. Regents of Univ. of Calif.*, 17 Cal.3d 425, 434, 551 P.2d 334, 342, 131 Cal.Rptr. 14, 22 (1976)).

A. *Foreseeability and Certainty of Harm*

Foreseeability is the most important variable in the duty calculus, *Ashburn*, 306 Md. at 628, 510 A.2d at 1083, and without it there can be no duty to prevent suicide. Comment, *Civil Liability for Suicide*, 12 Loy.L.A.L.Rev. at 991. Here Nicole's suicide was foreseeable because the defendants allegedly had direct evidence of Nicole's intent to commit suicide. That notice to the defendants

A. NEGLIGENCE AND STRICT LIABILITY

distinguishes this case from *Bogust v. Iverson*, 10 Wis.2d 129, 102 N.W.2d 228, where the counselor had no notice of contemplated suicide.

The degree of certainty that Eisel and Nicole suffered the harm foreseen is one hundred percent.

Nor would reasonable persons necessarily conclude that the harm ceased to be foreseeable because Nicole denied any intent to commit suicide when the counselors undertook to draw out her feelings, particularly in light of the alleged declarations of intent to commit suicide made by Nicole to her classmates. "An adolescent who is thinking of suicide is more likely to share these feelings with a friend than with a teacher or parent or school guidance counselor. But, we all — parents, teachers, administrators, service providers and friends — can learn what the warning signs are and what to do." Jurors, as triers of fact, may well conclude that the quoted point of view is consistent with their own experiences with adolescents....

B. *Policy of Preventing Future Harm*

The General Assembly has made it quite clear that prevention of youth suicide is an important public policy, and that local schools should be at the forefront of the prevention effort. A Youth Suicide Prevention School Programs Act (the Act) was enacted by Chapter 122 of the Acts of 1986, codified as Md.Code (1978, 1989 Repl.Vol.), §§ 7-4A-01 through 7-4A-06 of the Education Article (EA)....

"A statewide Youth Suicide Prevention School Program is essential to address" the problem. § 7-4A-01(1). "County suicide prevention and crisis center agencies along with local education agencies are best suited for developing and implementing programs for statewide youth suicide prevention." § 7-4A-01(5). Section 7-4A-03(a)(1) provides for a statewide Youth Suicide Prevention School Program administered by the State Department of Education in cooperation with, *inter alia*, participating local education agencies. Any program established under the Act "shall ... [t]rain school personnel in individual and school wide strategies for teenage suicide prevention." EA § 7-4A-04(c)(2).

....

Nicole's school had a suicide prevention program prior to her death....

....

There is no indication in the Act that the Legislature intended to create a statutorily based cause of action against school counselors who negligently fail to intervene in a potential suicide. Nevertheless, holding counselors to a common law duty of reasonable care to prevent suicides when they have evidence of a suicidal intent comports with the policy underlying this Act.

C. *Closeness of Connection Between Conduct and Injury*

This factor is the proximate cause element of a negligence action considered on the macroscale of policy....

The defendants say that the law considers suicide to be "a deliberate, intentional and intervening act which precludes a finding that a given defendant is responsible for the harm." Defendants cite *McLaughlin v. Sullivan*, 123 N.H. at 339, 461 A.2d at 125, where the court held that an attorney's alleged malpractice, in not requesting a stay of sentence or bail pending appeal in a criminal case, could not have been the proximate cause of the client's suicide in jail during the first day of confinement following conviction. Here, however, we deal with the relationship between an adolescent and school counselors who allegedly were informed that the adolescent was suicidal. Legally to categorize all suicides by adolescents as knowing and voluntary acts which insulate the death, as a matter of law, from all other acts or omissions which might operate, in fact, as causes of the death is contrary to the policy manifested by the Act. The Act does not view these troubled children as standing independently, to live or die on their own. In a failure to prevent suicide case, Maryland tort law should not treat an adolescent's committing suicide as a superseding cause when the entire premise of the Act is that others, including the schools, have the potential to intervene effectively.

....

D. *Moral Blame*

Moral blame as a factor to be weighed in deciding whether to recognize a legal duty in tort is less than an intent to cause harm. This factor considers the reaction of persons in general to the circumstances. Is it the sense of the community that an obligation exists under the circumstances? Certainly if classmates of Nicole found her lying on the floor of a lavatory, bleeding from slashed wrists, and those students told one or more teachers of the emergency, society would be outraged if the teachers did nothing and Nicole bled to death. Here, the information allegedly received by the counselors involved intent, not a description of physical facts. The distinction does not form a bright line separating duty from the absence of duty. The youth suicide prevention programs provided for by the Act call for awareness of, and response to, emotional warning signs, thus evidencing a community sense that there should be intervention based on emotional indicia of suicide.

E. *Burden on the Defendant*

....

The harm that may result from a school counselor's failure to intervene appropriately when a child threatens suicide is total and irreversible for the child, and severe for the child's family. It may be that the risk of any particular suicide is remote if statistically quantified in relation to all of the reports of suicidal talk that are received by school counselors. We do not know. But the consequence of the risk is so great that even a relatively remote possibility of a suicide may be enough to establish duty. We pointed out in *Jacques v. First Nat'l Bank*, 307 Md. 527, 537, 515 A.2d 756, 761 (1986), that "[a]s the magnitude of the risk increases, the requirement of privity is relaxed — thus justifying the imposition of a duty in favor of a large class of persons where the risk is of death or personal injury." ...

Moreover, when the risk of death to a child is balanced against the burden sought to be imposed on the counselors, the scales tip overwhelmingly in favor of duty. Certainly the physical component of the burden on the counselors was slight. Eisel claims only that a telephone call, communicating information known to the counselors, would have discharged that duty here. We agree.

The counselors argue that there are elements of confidentiality and discretion in their relationships with students that would be destroyed by the imposition of a duty to notify parents of all reports of suicidal statements. Confidentiality does not bar the duty, given that the school policy explicitly disavows confidentiality when suicide is the concern.

The defendants further point out that counselors are required to exercise discretion when dealing with students. Their discretion, however, cannot be boundless when determining whether to treat a student as a potential suicide. Discretion is relevant to whether the standard of conduct has been breached under the circumstances of a given case. Discretion does not create an absolute immunity, which would be the effect of denying any duty.

F. *Community Consequences of Liability — Insurability*

EA § 4-105(d) and Md.Code (1974, 1989 Repl.Vol., 1991 Cum.Supp.), § 5-353(b) of the Courts and Judicial Proceedings Article (CJ) allow a county board of education to "raise the defense of sovereign immunity to any amount claimed above the limit of its insurance policy or, if self-insured or a member of a pool ... above $100,000." The Board participates in the Montgomery County self-insurance program. CJ § 5-353(e) provides that a "county board employee acting within the scope of employment, without malice and gross negligence, is not individually liable for damages resulting from a tortious act or omission for which a limitation of liability is provided ... under subsection (b)." Recognizing the duty contended for by Eisel in this case would not appear to have any substantial adverse impact on this legislative scheme, or on the community at large.

....

---

1. In *Eisel*, school policy explicitly disavowed confidentiality when suicide is concerned. How would the court have proceeded if there had been no such policy? Should confidentiality weigh more heavily in such a case? Should we return to the test balancing risk of death and burden?

2. Is "moral blame," as a factor to consider in determining the existence of a duty of care, a subjective or objective inquiry? How does the *Eisel* court approach moral blame? Put yourself into the situation of the counselors. How would you feel?

3. Are there degrees of foreseeability? Is there a difference between foresight and expectation? In *Anderson v. Shaugnessy*, a student was blinded in one eye after a paintball pistol in the possession of another student discharged. Shaugnessy, the owner of the pistol (he bought it from another student at school), was told by the bus driver on the way home from school to put the pistol away. The court held the school liable for negligence; the school breached its duty of ordinary care to prevent a student's sudden and foreseeable misconduct from injuring another student. The driver knew that Shaugnessy had the pistol; it was clearly foreseeable that someone with a gun (toy or not) might shoot someone with it (intentionally or not).

4. Recall the discussion earlier in the chapter regarding dangerous conditions and dangerous activities (tree roots, woodworking classes, etc.). Such concepts may be applicable in cases involving students and vehicle accidents. In *Joyce v. Simi Valley Unified Sch. Dist.*, 7 Cal. Rptr. 2d 783 (Cal. App. 1992), a junior high school student was struck by a car in a crosswalk at an uncontrolled intersection less than forty feet from school. Joyce had used an open school yard gate to reach the dangerous intersection. The school knew of the danger and of prior accidents and near misses at the intersection; yet, it still encouraged students to use the gate and the intersection. The court found that the open gate was a dangerous condition and held that Joyce sufficiently stated a cause of action.

5. The court in *Tryon v. City of Lowell*, 29 Mass. App. 720, 565 N.E.2d 456 (1990), found that the erection and maintenance of a fence along a railroad route was not a discretionary act on the part of the city. Because the city could anticipate harm as a result of the failure to maintain the fence, the court found that the city and the school owed a duty to an identifiable category of city inhabitants: the school children. Christopher Tryon and many other students had often used a hole in the 23-year-old fence to enter and exit school property. Despite a finding of comparative negligence, Christopher and his parents sued the school and the city successfully after Christopher was struck by a train on the way to school.

6. There is probably no vehicle more recognizable, inside and out, than the school bus. Nearly everyone, young and old, is familiar with the small, cramped seats, the famous yellow exterior, and of course the stop signs, flashing lights, and the "STOP: STATE LAW" stenciled on the back emergency door. Nevertheless, accidents in and around school buses are very common. Automobile and truck drivers must be aware of the buses and their stopping signals, and bus drivers must be aware that children, despite daily routine, are always unpredictable.

In *Yeager v. Morgan*, 429 S.E.2d 61 (W. Va. 1993), Denise Yeager was struck by a car after exiting a school bus. Yeager ran around the back of the bus to cross the street and was hit by the car. Although the bus driver had turned on the safety lights, when the accident occurred, the lights had been turned off. Despite the fact that Yeager admitted that the accident would not have occurred

A. NEGLIGENCE AND STRICT LIABILITY

if she had looked before running into traffic, and that the driver of the car was the person directly responsible, the court held that there were questions of fact with respect to the duty owed by the school and the proximate causation of the accident.

So, what is the duty of care owed by the school bus driver (and the school itself)? The court in *Yurkovich v. Rose*, 68 Wash. App. 643, 847 P.2d 925 (1993), held that school bus drivers, both under common law and statute, owe child passengers "a duty of the highest degree of care consistent with the practical operation of the bus." *Id.* at 648, 847 P.2d at 928. This duty includes the time the student leaves the bus and completes crossing the street (if necessary for the student to reach his or her home). *Id.*

The *Yurkovich* court continued and stated that school buses are a specialized carrier with duties over and above those of a common carrier. The applicable laws do not vary according to the age of the student, his or her familiarity with the surroundings, or other individual factors. *Id.* at 652, 847 P.2d at 930. However, such factors may be used as evidence of contributory or comparative negligence. *Id.*

In *Yurkovich*, the bus driver did not use his stop sign or flashing lights when dropping the student off at dusk, did not keep the student in view until she was safely across the street, and permitted the student to go to the back of the bus before attempting to cross the street. All of these actions were violations of state law. The student was struck and killed in a car accident. The court held that the school did not meet its duty of care. *Id.* at 653, 847 P.2d at 931.

What if there is evidence that drivers ignore the stopping signals anyway? Does this justify the driver's action? According to the court, such evidence is irrelevant and inadmissible on the issue of whether the bus driver is justified in violating the state law requiring the use of the safety signals. *Id.* at 650, 847 P.2d at 929.

Instead of the issue concerning the other drivers' habits, consider the young passengers' habits. For example, a school bus driver is well aware of the male students at the front of the bus who habitually harass the female students as they exit. Instead of stopping the harassment, the driver allows some students to use the rear emergency exit. The school bus pulls into a parking lot, as always, to drop off some passengers. No safety signals need to be activated. Traffic continues as normal. While other passengers are still getting off, one student crosses the highway in the middle of the block, and is killed in an auto accident. Should the bus driver and the school be held liable?

The court in *Nolan v. Bronson*, 460 N.W.2d 284 (Mich. Ct. App. 1990), held that both the driver and the school district could be held liable. The court held that there was a question of fact as to whether the driver could have prevented the actions the students took; and under a motor vehicle exception to sovereign immunity, the court held that the school district could be held liable.

7. The rules and regulations regarding school bus operation are fairly strict as they are. However, there is a special case, often with additional requirements,

when special education children are involved. For example, bus companies may adopt a rule requiring that all children with disabilities be met by a parent upon delivery home from school unless the parent has given written permission for the child to be left alone. In *Martinez v. Moroldo*, 553 N.Y.S.2d 751 (N.Y. App. Div. 1990), the court found that a genuine question of fact existed as to whether the mother of a mentally disabled student had given the bus company permission to drop the student off at home after school without the student having to be met, as required by bus company rule.

8. The cases in this section of the chapter have attempted to define the duty of care that schools owe to students. Is there a line that can be drawn between the school's liability and the individual tortfeasor's (teacher, counselor, bus driver, etc.) liability? What about activities that are not within the scope of the employee's job? Does a school have a duty to protect students from sexual assaults by teachers? The answer may depend on whether the school knows or has reason to know that such an assault may occur. In *Virginia G. v. ABC Unified Sch. Dist.*, 15 Cal. App. 4th 1848, 19 Cal. Rptr. 2d 671 (1993), the court held that the school district does have a duty to protect students from such assaults. However, the court continued and said that the teacher's conduct could not be imputed to the school district. The plaintiff could pursue claims against the school district based on the district's own direct negligence in hiring and supervising the teacher.

In order to bring 42 U.S.C. Sec. 1983 claims against the school in sexual assault cases, however, one court has stated that the school must know or have reason to know of the teacher's misconduct. *See Jones v. Board of Educ. of Sch. Dist. 50, Archuleta and Hinsdale Counties*, 854 P.2d 1386 (Colo. Ct. App. 1993).

Does a school district have a duty of care to protect students against sexual assaults by other students? Should this duty depend on the age of the students? *See Hager v. Bellingham Sch. Dist. No. 501*, 74 Wash. App. 49, 871 P.2d 1106 (1994) (There was a material issue of fact as to whether a fourth-grade student's alleged sexual assaults on a first-grader during recess fell within the ambit of hazards which should have been anticipated by the school district. No summary judgment).

BROWNELL v. LOS ANGELES UNIFIED SCHOOL DISTRICT
Court of Appeals of California
4 Cal. App. 4th 787, 5 Cal. Rptr. 2d 756 (2d Dist., Div. 5, 1992)

BOREN, ASSOCIATE JUSTICE:

The Los Angeles Unified School District (LAUSD) appeals following a $120,000 jury verdict arising from an incident in which a student, Ernest P. Brownell, III, was shot and wounded by gang members. The shooting occurred immediately after school hours and on a public street adjacent to school property. Brownell alleged negligent supervision in that LAUSD personnel had dismissed the students after school without first ascertaining if the street in front of the school was free of any gang members.

....

Facts

After the school day ended on January 28, 1985, Brownell went out the main door of Johnson High School and stood in front of the school on the sidewalk along 42nd Street among a group of 15 to 20 people. He was listening to his Walkman radio and waiting for some friends with whom he was going to walk to a nearby bus stop. Among the group of people was another student, Keesha Pierson, who was herself waiting for some friends with whom she was going to walk home. At trial, Pierson testified as to the ensuing events. After Brownell had stood outside for approximately five minutes, several youths wearing red gang colors associated with the Bloods gang ran or walked quickly across the street and gathered around Brownell. One of the gang members swung at Brownell, causing him to go into the middle of the street where another gang member pulled out a gun and shot him.

....

Brownell, who had never been a member of a gang, was apparently shot because he was mistaken by members of the Bloods for a member of a rival gang, the Crips. Johnson High School is located in an area known as a Crips neighborhood.... The member of the Bloods who shot Brownell, Douglas Smith, was not a student at Johnson High School, and Brownell had never encountered Smith before Smith shot him.

At the time Brownell was shot, he and the other students had been dismissed from school for the day. Mary Maddox, dean and counselor at Johnson High School, and Wilma Manyweather, the principal of the school, were inside the school near the doors passing out bus tickets to the students. They normally gave out the tickets at the school gate, but they did so inside the building that day because it was raining. On the day Brownell was shot, neither Maddox nor Manyweather had heard any rumors or threats to any of the students or detected any other indications of trouble. As Maddox explained, "Usually when something was about to happen [in such a small school] you could feel it all day long, and the kids would be whispering and stuff like that. But I don't recall any of that happening on that day."

Johnson High School had a population of approximately 200 students. The students at Johnson High School were referred there from other high schools where they had had behavior problems, such as inability to get along with other students, truancy, destructiveness in the classroom, and involvement in gang-related activities. The school had no school police or security guards, but had campus aides who could contact the school administrators or school police by walkie-talkie. It was the policy of the school to prohibit the display on campus of gang colors and paraphernalia associated with gangs. During 1985, the year Brownell was shot, the school removed such gang-related items from students on almost a daily basis and also on occasion confiscated weapons from students. There had been no prior shootings at Johnson High School.

Discussion

....

II. *Injury Occurring Off School Premises and After School Hours*

LAUSD contends that it has no duty of care to students going to or from school regarding accidents which occur off school premises. Indeed, as a general principle, "school districts are not legally responsible for accidents that students may suffer once they have been released from school ...." (*Perna v. Conejo Valley Unified School Dist.* (1983) 143 Cal.App.3d 292, 294, 192 Cal.Rptr. 10.) However, as noted in *Perna*, Education Code section 44808 qualifies this principle somewhat and provides, in pertinent part, that no school district "shall be responsible or in any way liable for the conduct or safety of any pupil of the public schools at any time when such pupil is not on school property, unless such district ... [has] specifically assumed such responsibility or liability or has failed to exercise reasonable care under the circumstances." (*See Perna v. Conejo Valley Unified School Dist.*, *supra*, 143 Cal.App.3d at pp. 294, 296, 192 Cal.Rptr. 10.)

In *Hoyem v. Manhattan Beach City Sch. Dist.* (1978) 22 Cal.3d 508, 150 Cal.Rptr. 1, 585 P.2d 851, the court held that school districts have a duty to exercise reasonable care in supervising students during school hours. In *Hoyem*, the complaint alleged that a 10-year-old truant who left school early one day and was injured by a motorcycle at a public intersection sustained injuries proximately caused by the school district's lack of supervision, even though the accident occurred off school premises....

For example, in *Perna v. Conejo Valley Unified School Dist.*, *supra*, 143 Cal.App.3d 292, 192 Cal.Rptr. 10, the court held a cause of action was properly stated for injuries to two students struck by a vehicle as they walked home. The complaint alleged proximate cause imputed to the school district from a teacher who kept the students after school hours and knew or reasonably should have known that a school crossing guard would be gone from the intersection by the time the students arrived to cross it on their way home.

In *Calandri v. Ione Unified School Dist.* (1963) 219 Cal.App.2d 542, 33 Cal.Rptr. 333, a student was injured at home by a toy cannon he built in school as a shop project and alleged that the failure of the teacher to warn of the toy's danger was a proximate cause of the off-campus injury. In reversing a verdict in favor of the school district because of instructional error, the court found that a duty of care was owed and that the claims of negligence and proximate cause were questions of fact for the jury. (*Id.* at pp. 548, 551, 33 Cal.Rptr. 333.) Accordingly, under certain circumstances a school district may be held liable for injuries suffered by a student off school premises and after school hours where

A. NEGLIGENCE AND STRICT LIABILITY

the injury resulted from the school's negligence while the student was on school premises.

III. *Claimed Breach of Duty of Reasonable Care to Adequately Supervise Students*

It is well settled that although a school district is not an insurer of its pupils' safety, school authorities have a duty to supervise the conduct of students on school grounds and to enforce rules and regulations necessary for their protection. The standard of due care imposed on school authorities in exercising their supervisorial responsibilities is that degree of care which a person of ordinary prudence, charged with comparable duties, would exercise under the same circumstances. As the court explained in *Hoyem*, in the context of a student who claimed negligent supervision after he absented himself from the school grounds during school hours and was subsequently injured by a motorist, "We require ordinary care, not fortresses; schools must be reasonably supervised, not truant-proof."

In the present case, we find that the school district exercised due care and, under any view of the evidence, satisfied its supervisorial responsibilities in regard to protecting students from potential gang-related violence. It is a tragic and sad commentary upon our society when an innocent student attending high school is assaulted and shot by gang members upon leaving school premises. Nonetheless, a school cannot and should not be an insurer of the safety of students, particularly after school and off school premises, when it has exercised ordinary prudence and due care appropriate to the circumstances. To paraphrase *Hoyem v. Manhattan Beach City Sch. Dist.*, *supra*, 22 Cal.3d at page 519, 150 Cal.Rptr. 1, 585 P.2d 851, the law requires ordinary care, not fortresses; schools must be reasonably supervised, not impenetrable to all gang-related violence.

LAUSD exercised reasonable and ordinary care and satisfied its duty to supervise adequately students in view of (1) the general precautions the school always took to minimize gang-related problems (*e.g.*, prohibiting wearing gang colors and confiscating weapons), and (2) the absence of any advance indication to school personnel of potential gang violence pertinent to the incident involving Brownell. Although Johnson High School is located in a gang neighborhood and rival gangs attended the school with trouble ensuing on occasion in the school, it does not follow that the school had any duty to supervise to the extent of sending observers outside to scout the neighborhood for gang members off the campus and to wait until, so to speak, "all was clear" before releasing the students.

Imposing such a duty of visual precaution is unwarranted and impractical, as indicated by the very sudden and unexpected nature of the attack upon Brownell. Even if school personnel happened to observe the mere presence of gang members near the school, it would apparently not constitute an unusual or alarming phenomenon, since gang members were present in the school and lived in the neighborhood of the school. We find that school personnel of ordinary prudence under the circumstances described should not be required to engage in such visual precaution, absent either (1) any specific indication of a real and imminent gang-related threat at the particular time and place of the shooting, or (2) prior incidents reflecting not necessarily this identical type of assault but that "the possibility of this type of harm was foreseeable." (*Frances T. v. Village Green Owners Assn.* (1986) 42 Cal.3d 490, 503, 229 Cal.Rptr. 456, 723 P.2d 573.)

....

Our Supreme Court has rejected the legal principle of a rigid foreseeability concept in the context of a duty of care. Rather, as explained in *Frances T. v. Village Green Owners Assn.*, *supra*, 42 Cal.3d 490, 229 Cal.Rptr. 456, 723 P.2d 573, foreseeability is determined in light of all the circumstances and does not require prior identical or even similar events. (*Id.* at p. 503, 229 Cal.Rptr. 456, 723 P.2d 573.) However, the facts must demonstrate the defendant's awareness of the need for the precaution not taken or that such a precaution "could aid in deterring criminal conduct." (*Frances T.*, *supra*, at p. 503, 229 Cal.Rptr. 456, 723 P.2d 573.) The facts in the present case fail to establish LAUSD's awareness of the need for a visual precaution or that such a precaution would have aided in deterring the injury suffered here. LAUSD's duty to protect against the acts of third persons is a duty of reasonable care to protect only against known or reasonably foreseeable risks. Here, LAUSD did not fail to take reasonable precautions against any foreseeable risk and fulfilled its duty of reasonable care.

....

---

1. On January 11, 1983, a thirteen-year-old junior high school student was shot to death during an argument outside on school premises. It was lunch recess. Under school rules, those who ate lunch in school were required to leave the building after finishing lunch. No staff monitors were in the vicinity of the shooting when it occurred. Despite the fact that fewer staff members were outside monitoring student activities than were required by school policy, the Supreme Court of New York, Appellate Division, found insufficient evidence to establish lack of supervision as the proximate cause of death. *Maness v. City of New York*, 607 N.Y.S.2d 325 (1994). The court held that the board of education has a duty to exercise the same degree of care and supervision over students as a reasonably prudent parent would under the same circumstances. However, it also held that a school is not an insurer of its students' safety, and will not be held liable for injuries not proximately related to the absence of supervision. *Id.* at 326.

In both *Brownell* and *Maness* the trial-level juries found for the student-plaintiffs, while both appeals courts reversed. Do you agree with the final results? What do these reversals seem to indicate? Based on these two recent cases, do you think society (at least by way of jury rooms) is trying desperately,

A. NEGLIGENCE AND STRICT LIABILITY

perhaps more desperately than the courts, to put the blame for increased school violence on someone or something identifiable? Do you think these cases demonstrate the proper position of schools with regard to young people and gang violence? Do you think schools should take a more responsible role?

2. Do you believe that the gang shooting in *Brownell* was unforeseeable? How foreseeable do such events have to be? Should a history of similar events in the crime-ridden and gang-populated neighborhood be enough? The *Brownell* court cited, as evidence that the LAUSD met its duty, the "absence of any advance indication to school personnel of potential gang violence pertinent to the incident involving Brownell." This statement indicates that actual knowledge and anticipation of the event is necessary to find causation. Is this standard too stringent today?

3. Consider the following case. When the school year began in August, 1984, third grader Kristy Guhn began to have emotional problems. She was absent from school on several occasions, and left school without permission twice in the first three weeks of the year (one time, brought back by her mother; the other, found at home by a truant officer). The principal of the school discussed the matter with the school psychologist and Kristy's parents and they all agreed to schedule Kristy for counseling. On the day the counseling was to begin, Kristy again left school early. Unfortunately, she was found at home hanging from a window. Kristy had tried to enter her home by standing on two bicycles. She died six days later. *Guhn v. Board of Educ., Clyde-Green Springs Sch. Dist.* (No. S-86-23, Ohio Ct. App., Sandusky County 1987).

A wrongful death, mental anguish and distress claim was met with a successful summary judgment motion. The court held that the consequences of the alleged negligent act (allowing Kristy to leave school and head home, killing herself in an attempt to get inside) were unforeseeable.

> Applying this to the facts of the case *sub judice*, the question is whether the principal could have foreseen or reasonably anticipated that Kristy, would leave school, would go home, would attempt to enter her locked home by placing two bicycles below a window which she would climb upon and that a sill would fall upon her neck as she was attempting to enter the house causing her death. None of these events were foreseeable but rather they were intervening and superseding (*sic*) causes. *Id.* at 2.

Guhn cited to *Person v. Gum*, 7 Ohio App. 3d 307, 455 N.E.2d 713 (1983), in presenting the court's definition of proximate cause:

> For an act to be the proximate cause of an injury, it must appear that the injury was the natural and probable consequence of such act.... To find that an injury was the natural and probable consequence of an act, it must appear that the injury complained of could have been foreseen or reasonably anticipated from the alleged negligent act. *Person*, 7 Ohio App. 3d at 309.

In *Person*, a student (by and through his mother) filed suit against his elementary school alleging that his teacher's negligence proximately caused his injuries when he was struck by a car while on his way home for lunch recess. At trial, the jury found for the child. The decision was reversed on appeal. The Court of Appeals held that the events were too remotely connected with the teacher's conduct.

4. The court in *Guhn* rejected the causation rule which says the defendant need not have foreseen the injury in its precise form in order to be held liable. *Person*, 7 Ohio App. 3d 307 (1983). If the precise form of the injury (death) is not critical to the finding of liability, does Kristy's past activity (absences, leaving early) and the school's awareness of it indicate that the school could have foreseen *some* injury to Kristy or a third party (given insufficient supervision)?

5. Was Kristy's conduct and death foreseeable? Do you agree with the results in *Guhn* and *Person*, presented in Note 3? Judge Wilkowski, dissenting in *Guhn*, did not. "The trial court's view ... ignores that it is foreseeable that a person — adult or child — prudent or imprudent — male or female, when locked out of a house may resort to a possible second avenue of ingress — a window. It happens all the time." *Guhn*, at 8. In fact, in Kristy's case, it likely happened twice during the three weeks prior to her death. Considering the knowledge of the school regarding Kristy's track record, it remains debatable whether the school could have foreseen an injury to Kristy.

Consider the following example. A school board has a policy not to release children to anyone except a parent or guardian. An eleven-year-old child complains of illness. While she is unable to contact her parents, she does reach her uncle, who comes to pick up the child. The child shows no reluctance to leave with the uncle. She is later raped by him. Is the school liable for the girl's injuries? The Tennessee Court of Appeals said no. *See Snider v. Snider*, 855 S.W.2d 588 (1993). Releasing the child to her uncle, under these circumstances was not negligent per se, and the injury to the child was not foreseeable by the school.

6. What impact would an opposite result in *Guhn* have? Would schools virtually have to give up the business of educating to concentrate only on watching and supervising? Does Judge Wilkowski's dissent stretch causation too far?

7. Compare *Maness*, presented in note 1 above, with *Guhn*. The results are similar — the school is not the child's insurer and is not liable for wrongful death. Should the results be the same? Should school officials today be more concerned about and work harder to prevent violence in the schools? Does the existence of more weapons and violence in schools today, especially large urban districts, create a higher level of foreseeability — of injury or death — on the part of the school officials? Is the chain of causation in *Maness* shorter than that in *Guhn*? What about the distance from the school to the scene of the event? Should closeness to the school, regardless how many steps there are in the chain of causation, have an effect on the liability of the school for injury to students during school hours?

A. NEGLIGENCE AND STRICT LIABILITY

MIRAND v. NEW YORK

Court of Appeals of New York
1994 WL 270422 (1994)

CIPARICK, JUSTICE:

This appeal requires us to consider the nature and extent of the tort liability of a school district based on the theory of negligent supervision for injuries caused to plaintiffs by the intentional acts of a fellow student.

....

I

Plaintiffs Virna and Vivia Mirand, sisters, were students at Harry S. Truman High School in the Bronx at the time of the incident giving rise to this action. According to Virna's testimony, on September 20, 1982, she was released from her last class at 2:00 P.M. and went to wait for her sister, whose last class ended at 2:40 P.M., at their usual meeting place. On the way there, Virna accidentally bumped into Donna Webster, another student with whom Virna had not had any previous encounters. Although Virna apologized, Webster, believing the contact to be intentional, cursed Virna and attempted to kick her. Virna blocked the kick and caught Webster's leg. According to Virna, Webster threatened to kill her. At that point a bystander intervened and prevented anything further from occurring.

Virna proceeded to the first floor of the school where by chance she met her sister who was going to her last class. Webster was a student in Vivia's class and Vivia suggested that Virna report the altercation to the security office. Virna proceeded to the security office, which was located on the first floor near the building entrance, and knocked on the door. She received no response. Virna testified that as she was walking down a first-floor hallway she met a woman she knew to be an art teacher but whose name she could not recall. She told the teacher of the altercation with Webster, that Webster had threatened her, and that there was no one in the security office. Virna was not allowed to testify regarding what the art teacher said in response. Virna conceded at this point that, in an examination before trial made six years earlier, she had not mentioned her meeting with the art teacher.

According to Virna, after her encounter with the art teacher, she returned to the security office, where again she knocked on the door and received no response. She then went to the second floor and left the building through the main entrance to wait for her sister on the building veranda where school security officers were sometimes present. None were present on that day. Vivia eventually arrived about a half-hour later and the two proceeded to descend the staircase when they found their path blocked by Webster and two male companions. Although the sisters tried to avoid her, Webster approached Virna and struck her on the elbow and head with a hammer. When Vivia tried to seize the hammer, she was hit in the back by an unknown girl. One of the males with Webster, a nonstudent, later identified as her brother, stabbed Vivia through the wrist with a knife. No security or police officers were present during the incident. The sisters were taken to a hospital. Virna was treated and released. Vivia's hand was operated on and placed in a cast. She spent seven days in the hospital. Since then she has undergone further surgery and hospitalization together with physical therapy. She experiences pain in her injured hand and has limited movement and use of it.

At trial, the evidence concerning general security measures at Truman High School disclosed that in the fall of 1982 there were 13 trained school safety officers assigned to the school. They wore uniforms, carried radios, and operated out of the school's first-floor security office. There was also a first-floor security desk located by the main entrance to which an officer was assigned at all times. The security officers were assigned throughout the building and were expected to cover the building's exits at dismissal time. According to the school's security plan, two to five officers were assigned to the second-floor main entrance at dismissal, although they were not required by the plan to be on the second-floor veranda outside. Teachers were also expected to assist in providing security by using their independent judgment with minor matters and seeking the assistance of other personnel with more serious incidents. At trial, the school's security coordinator could not recall how many fights had occurred at the school during the preceding year nor whether security officers were at their posts at dismissal time on the day in question.

The jury found that defendant Board of Education negligently failed to provide adequate supervision and awarded plaintiff Virna Mirand $50,000 for past pain and suffering, and Vivia Mirand $750,000 for her past and future pain and suffering. Defendant Board moved to set aside the verdict in plaintiffs' favor and to dismiss the complaint. Supreme Court granted the motion and dismissed plaintiffs' complaint, concluding that plaintiffs had not established that defendant Board was on notice of a specific danger, and that there was a failure of proof concerning inadequate supervision and proximate cause.

The Appellate Division reversed the judgment of Supreme Court, denied the motion to set aside the verdict in plaintiffs' favor, and reinstated the verdict....

....

III

Schools are under a duty to adequately supervise the students in their charge and they will be held liable for foreseeable injuries proximately related to the absence of adequate supervision[.] Schools are not insurers of safety, however, for they cannot reasonably be expected to continuously supervise and control all movements and activities of students; therefore, schools are not to be held liable "for every thoughtless or careless act by which one pupil may injure another" The nature of the duty owed was set forth in the seminal case of *Hoose v. Drumm*, 281 N.Y. 54, 57-58, 22 N.E.2d 233: "[A] teacher owes it to his [or her] charges to exercise such care of them as a parent of ordinary prudence would observe in comparable circumstances." The duty owed derives from the simple fact that a school, in assuming physical custody and control over its students, effectively takes the place of parents and guardians.

In determining whether the duty to provide adequate supervision has been breached in the context of injuries caused by the acts of fellow students, it must be established that school authorities had sufficiently specific knowledge or notice of the dangerous conduct which caused injury; that is, that the third-party acts could reasonably have been anticipated. Actual or constructive notice to the school of prior similar conduct is generally required because, obviously, school personnel cannot reasonably be expected to guard against all of the sudden, spontaneous acts that take place among students daily; an injury caused by the impulsive, unanticipated act of a fellow student ordinarily will not give rise to a finding of negligence absent proof of prior conduct that would have put a reasonable person on notice to protect against the injury-causing act.

Even if a breach of the duty of supervision is established, the inquiry is not ended; the question arises whether such negligence was the proximate cause of the injuries sustained. In some cases, the wrongful conduct of a fellow pupil may be considered extraordinary and intervening, thus breaking the causal nexus between a defendant's negligent act or omission and a plaintiff's injury. The test to be applied is whether under all the circumstances the chain of events that followed the negligent act or omission was a normal or foreseeable consequence of the situation created by the school's negligence.

IV

We agree with the Appellate Division that there was sufficient evidence as a matter of law to establish liability for negligent supervision in this case. Considering the evidence in the light most favorable to plaintiffs, the verdict should stand. Based on Virna's testimony, which the jury was entitled to credit, it was not unreasonable for the jury to infer that defendant Board was on notice of an imminent foreseeable danger to Virna. The violent acts which caused plaintiffs' injuries were sparked by a prior altercation and death threat of which defendant, through one of its teachers, was expressly made aware; yet no action was taken to prevent escalation of the incident by the teacher who met Virna and was in a position to assist her. Indeed, no security personnel were even present in the main security office or at key locations throughout the school when Virna sought to report the run-in and Webster's threat.

It was not irrational for the jury to conclude on such evidence that defendant Board was on notice of an imminent danger to Virna and did nothing reasonably calculated to protect her from that danger. Nor can it necessarily be said that this case involved the type of unforeseeable, spontaneous acts of violence for which school districts cannot be held liable.

Supervision of students is obviously needed at dismissal time, when the largest number of students congregate and fights are most likely to occur. Indeed, this is reflected in the high school's security plan, which called for two to five security officers to be positioned at the second-floor main entrance at dismissal.

The uncontradicted testimony revealed that no security officers were present at the second-floor main entrance at the time plaintiffs were assaulted. We stress, however, that defendant's failure to comply with the requirements of its security plan was not the only factor establishing negligence. The jury needed little more than its own common experience to conclude that security or supervisory personnel should have been present at dismissal.

On the issue of proximate cause, we conclude that a rational jury could find that the complete absence of security or supervisory personnel at a time and place when vigilance was absolutely essential constituted the proximate cause of plaintiffs' injuries. Proximate cause is a question of fact for the jury where varying inferences are possible. Proper supervision depends largely on the circumstances surrounding the event.

....

Accordingly, the order of the Appellate Division should be affirmed, with costs.

....

---

1. The Court in *Mirand* held that lack of supervision may be the proximate cause of injuries suffered in a threatened fight (reported to a teacher in advance) at the end of the school day. The court held that supervisory personnel were absolutely essential at dismissal time. Supervision is, of course, also essential at recess, on the playground — especially in cases of repeat attacks by one student or a group of students against another. Future attacks — same time, same place — become more foreseeable by the school teachers and other officials. *Paliska v. St. Anselm Sch.* (No. 93-G-1832, Ohio App., 11th Dist. 1994).

> ... [H]ere, the previous attacks upon appellant by Gromek and his gang were of the exact same kind, nature, and extent as the one giving rise to this action: to wit, tackling from behind. Therefore, since the prior attacks upon appellant were the same as the one in question, appellee should have reasonably anticipated that Gromek and his gang would tackle appellant from behind again if not supervised.

2. That accidents and injuries occur during school sports events can hardly be questioned. Where the liability for such accidents and injuries falls, however, is questioned often. When is it the athlete's liability for making mistakes or assuming the risks? When is it the school's fault for negligent failure to train, to warn of dangers, or to provide safe and effective equipment? The Supreme Court of Nebraska, in *Ohnstad v. Omaha Pub. Sch. Dist. No. 1 of Douglas County*, upheld the trial court's decision that — on the weight of the evidence — it was the student's low, late pole vault plant that proximately caused the severe head injuries and subsequent death of the student. 232 Neb. 788, 442 N.W.2d 859 (1989).

A. NEGLIGENCE AND STRICT LIABILITY

3. The school's duty of care at a track meet may go beyond the actual competition. In *Reddick v. Stanton Pub. Sch. Dist. No. 55*, 1 Neb. C.A. 904 (No. A-90-431 1992), an elementary school student sustained a fractured nose while playing on a mat at a countywide track meet. The girl had finished competing and went to play on the mats used for pole vaulting and high jump (though neither of those events were scheduled at the meet). After doing a flip and sitting up on the edge of the mat, another child came flying at her at an angle and hit her in the face. There were no witnesses.

The court held that the girl's accident and injuries were reasonably foreseeable, and were the natural and probable result of the school district's negligence.

4. "Jean Baker, then a 16-year-old student at Briarcliff Manor High School, sustained injuries ... while participating in a varsity field hockey practice. Ms. Baker ... was struck in the mouth by a field hockey stick swung by a fellow student. All parties acknowledge that Ms. Baker was not wearing a mouth protector at the time of the incident." *Baker v. Briarcliff Sch. Dist.*, 613 N.Y.S.2d 660, 661 (A.D. 2d Dep't 1994). Plaintiff argued that the defendants' school district and school board were negligent in failing to properly supervise the practice, and in allowing students to practice without proper safety equipment, particularly mouth protectors. It was discovered that Baker's coach often allowed the players to practice without mouthpieces. The court found the defendants liable holding that schools have a duty to protect students from unreasonably increased risks of harm.

5. The key in *Baker* to finding a breach of duty by the school may be that the risks must be *unreasonable*. In *La Mountain v. South Colonie Central Sch. Dist.*, 566 N.Y.S.2d 745 (N.Y. App. Div. 1991), a junior varsity soccer player fell when she planted her leg in an attempt to kick. The court held that there was no indication on the record that La Mountain's injuries were the result of any breach of duty by the school district. The court declared that the duty owed to students who voluntarily participate in school athletics is one of ordinary, reasonable care. Schools must protect from unassumed, concealed, or increased risks.

The opinion in *Benitez v. New York City Bd. of Educ.*, 541 N.E.2d 29 (N.Y. 1988), perhaps states it most succinctly: It "was a luckless accident arising from the vigorous, voluntary participation in competitive interscholastic athletics."

6. What is the duty of care a school owes its students in incidents involving involuntarily assumed, unforeseeable risks? In *St. Pierre v. Lombard*, 512 So. 2d 1206 (La. Ct. App. 1987), for example, parents of a student fatally stabbed at a high school football game sued the school board which rented the stadium to the school. The court held the school board not liable in negligence. According to the court, the school board assumed no contractual duty to provide security. In addition, the court found that the school board had no knowledge or reason to know of gang warfare. "Rather, the decedent was stabbed by a third party, who, of course, must bear the *principal* blame for his voluntary act." *Id.* at 1209 (emphasis supplied).

Does the court's reasoning here answer all the questions and right all the wrongs? It is very clear that the assailant should bear the principal criminal blame for his acts. But will this relieve all the injuries suffered by the decedent's family? Which defendants are in a better position to compensate for losses? The criminal defendant or the school board? How much impact should this have?

B. DEFENSES TO NEGLIGENCE AND STRICT LIABILITY

HURLBURT v. NOXON
Supreme Court, Chenango County
149 Misc. 2d 374, 565 N.Y.S.2d 683 (1990)

IRAD S. INGRAHAM, JUSTICE:

Plaintiffs seek damages for personal injuries sustained by the infant Rodney Hurlburt who was involved in an automobile accident occurring after he exited a school bus prior to reaching its summer school destination.

The Plaintiffs and Defendant School District are now before the Court by motion and cross-motion, respectively, seeking summary judgment. Both appeared by counsel for oral argument on November 2, 1990, in Norwich, New York.

Findings of Fact

On August 3, 1989, the infant Plaintiff was to have been transported by the Defendant Bainbridge-Guilford Central School to summer school at Windsor, New York. He boarded the school bus at Bainbridge. The bus stopped en route at Afton, New York, for the purpose of picking up additional students. The infant Plaintiff and several other students exited the bus at Afton in order to ride the rest of the way to Windsor in the car of Defendant Sean Noxon, a fellow student. Noxon was thereupon involved in an accident and Plaintiffs bring this action for Rodney's injuries alleging negligent supervision by the Bainbridge-Guilford Central School District.

The Defendant Bainbridge-Guilford Central School had in effect a policy that no student be allowed to exit the school bus before its destination unless written permission from a parent was presented. No such permission was given by Plaintiffs here. The school bus driver observed the Plaintiff leave the bus and asked "where are you going?" One of the exiting students said "it's okay that we get off." No further colloquy ensued. On several occasions prior to August 3, Plaintiff had exited the bus at the Afton stop and continued to school with Defendant Noxon.

Defendant School District moves for summary judgment, arguing that any negligence on its part was not the proximate cause of injury. Defendant maintains that Plaintiff's own conduct in leaving the school bus, and the negligence of Defendant Noxon were intervening acts which broke the chain of causation. School personnel allegedly had no knowledge of Noxon's reckless driving on this or prior occasions.

Plaintiffs bring a cross-motion for summary judgment in their favor. Plaintiffs focus on duty rather than proximate cause, arguing that Defendant was under a duty to supervise the infant Plaintiff, which did not end when Plaintiff left the bus. Plaintiffs characterize the accident as a foreseeable event, arguing that every case of negligent supervision by definition involves an intervening cause, and the true issue is whether that cause is foreseeable.

Conclusions of Law

The School District acts *in loco parentis* and is responsible for exercising that degree of care that a parent would reasonably provide.... The responsibility of the school commences upon entry of the student to the school bus. It includes proper supervision while the student is in school or on the school bus.... Injuries to students directly following their exit from a school bus are the subject of statutory school responsibility.

Such responsibility does not ordinarily extend beyond the area of control of school authority, however. Where a student injures himself in his home as a result of his culpable conduct committed on school grounds, the school is not responsible. Injuries caused by a student to third parties off school grounds are not the responsibility of the school.

"A school district does not have a duty to protect a high school student from injury arising from the negligence of a fellow student when the incident occurs off school grounds and not at a school sponsored event." *Bushnell v. Lee and Berne-Knox-Westerlo Sch. Dist.*, 125 A.D.2d 859, 510 N.Y.S.2d 488.

The *Bushnell* holding, affirmed by the Appellate Division Third Department on the unpublished opinion of Justice Hughes, involved a fact pattern virtually identical to the instant case. Plaintiff in that case, a 15 year old boy, left the school bus with the driver's knowledge and contrary to school rules. He was thereafter injured while riding with a fellow student who was racing and lost control of the automobile. If any distinction can be drawn, the instant Plaintiff was en route to school and the Bushnell infant was en route from school at the time each left the bus. This distinction is not sufficiently substantive to warrant casting responsibility on the school in this case.

Accordingly it is the conclusion herein that the school owed a duty to Plaintiff while Plaintiff remained in its custody. That duty terminated however at the time that Plaintiff left the school bus in contravention of the school policy. The events occurring thereafter and resulting in the accident and injury to Plaintiff, were not within the control of and cast no liability upon the Defendant School.

Accordingly the Defense motion for summary judgment is granted. The Plaintiff's motion for summary judgment is denied. No costs are assessed.

---

1. The Court notes that the only difference between *Hurlburt* and *Bushnell*, cited in the opinion, is that Hurlburt was on his way *to* school and the plaintiff

in *Bushnell* was coming *from* school. The *Hurlburt* court says that this distinction is "not sufficiently substantive to warrant casting responsibility on the school in this case." Do you agree? Granted, the foreseeability of a subsequent automobile accident may be no different before and after school. But is the school's duty to care for the child's safety higher on the way to school than it is on the way home? Vice versa?

2. How important is it to the decision that the child exited the bus before it reached its designated destination? What does the court in *Hurlburt* say on this matter? *See also State Farm Mut. Auto. Ins. Co. v. Pharr*, 305 Ark. 459, 808 S.W.2d 769 (1991) (Operation of a truck which struck a child was not an efficient intervening cause so as to relieve school district of liability). In *Pharr*, a student, after exiting the bus, went to check the family mailbox before crossing the street to his home. The bus driver had waited a short period of time before turning off the safety lights and proceeding.

3. You may be comfortable with the fact that a school district and a bus driver would be liable in negligence for the injuries of occupants of other vehicles involved in accidents with school buses. But how far should this chain go? What about an automobile occupant who is injured in a fall on the icy road *after* an accident with a school bus? It is true that the occupant would not have broken a leg in the fall had she not been in the earlier accident with the bus. Is the icy road an intervening cause which interrupted the original accident? *See Weese v. Muir*, 188 W. Va. 542, 425 S.E.2d 218 (1992) (Question of fact for the jury).

4. Can a school be held liable in negligent supervision for the injuries suffered by a child who is waiting for a parent after school? In *Sutton v. Duplessis*, 584 So. 2d 362 (La. Ct. App. 1991), Peter Sutton was injured when he ran in front of a car driven by Duplessis, one of the school's teachers. Peter was waiting for his mother to pick him up. He had been waiting in the school office (the school day ended early) until he saw his friend outside. The school secretary was in the office but was not actually watching him. Peter went outside, darted into the street and was hit by Duplessis.

Were Peter's actions foreseeable, thereby holding the school's inadequate supervision as the proximate cause of Peter's injuries? "Under the circumstances, the school authorities should have foreseen that a six-year-old might disobey orders not to leave, especially when he realized that no adult was actually watching him." *Id*. at 366.

What effect did the fact that a teacher was driving the car have on the decision in *Sutton*? The court held that Duplessis was not at fault in the accident. *Id*.

Do you think the *Sutton* court was swayed by the fact that the child stayed in the school office before wandering? Should the result be the same if the child had simply waited outside the whole time? The *Hurlburt* court said that the schools' duty to the student ended when he exited the bus in contravention of school policy. When does a school's duty terminate in a case like *Sutton*, where children are waiting at school for rides?

5. Suits against teachers and schools for failure to supervise are common. But where is the line between a teacher's failure to supervise and a student's intervening and superseding misbehavior drawn? The Supreme Court of Florida in 1982 answered the question by adopting the position that "certain student misbehavior is itself foreseeable and therefore is not an intervening cause which will relieve principals or teachers from liability for supervise." *Rupp v. Bryant*, 417 So. 2d 658, 668 (Fla. 1982). The Florida Court of Appeals recognized this rule in *Roberson v. Duval County Sch. Bd.*, 618 So. 2d 360 (Fla. Ct. App. 1993). In *Roberson*, a seventh grade student suffered a broken jaw when she was hit in the face by another student on the way back to class after lunch. Roberson was led by her teacher, Ms. Bauer, who allegedly had not enforced the "quiet, single-file" rule well enough to prevent Roberson's injury. Roberson testified that she told the assailant twice, in a voice loud enough for Bauer to hear, to stop bothering her.

The court held that "a principal task of supervisors is to anticipate and curb rash student behavior[;] our courts have often held that a failure to prevent injuries caused by the intentional or reckless conduct of the victim or a fellow student may constitute negligence." *Roberson*, 618 So. 2d at 362. Therefore, such misbehavior may not always constitute an intervening cause relieving the school of liability.

6. The best way for injured plaintiffs to ensure success against a school in tort claims is to prove that the conduct of the school (or an agent/employee of the school) is the *direct* cause of the plaintiffs' injuries. In *Patterson v. Meramec Valley R-III Sch. Dist.*, 864 S.W.2d 14 (Mo. Ct. App. 1993), the plaintiff attempted to prove that the dangerous condition of broken asphalt in the street directly caused the student's injuries. However, because the child was hit when another student threw a piece of asphalt, the allegation of direct causation was defeated. As a result, the "dangerous condition" exception to sovereign immunity did not apply and the plaintiff's petition against the school was dismissed. The court relied on *Dale v. Edmonds*, 819 S.W.2d 388 (Mo. Ct. App. 1991), which held that a dangerous condition must itself pose a physical threat to a plaintiff without the intervention of third parties. In *Dale* and *Patterson*, the plaintiffs were hit by "debris" thrown by third parties.

7. While the superseding intentional act of a third party often cuts off the liability of an earlier actor, such acts (and consequences) must be unforeseeable. See *Lockett v. Board of Educ. for Sch. Dist. No. 189*, 555 N.E.2d 1055 (Ill. Ct. App. 1990) (Evidence sufficient to establish foreseeability of danger to student and to show that bus line's negligence was proximate cause of injury; student was hit by flying glass thrown by another student at an open bus window).

In another case of injury by flying glass, the Supreme Court of Alabama held that an elementary school principal and physical education teacher could not be held liable in negligence for injuries suffered when student was cut by glass falling from gymnasium light bulb that was shattered by a ball. Neither had any responsibility for the design or maintenance of lighting fixtures or light bulbs. *See Beasley v. Morton*, 564 So. 2d 45 (Ala. 1990).

8. Can a teacher or a school be held liable for negligent supervision in a case where a child burns himself by spilling hot food at lunch? The Fresno Unified School District argued that such an injury could occur even in the presence of adequate supervision. *Espinosa v. Fresno Unified Sch. Dist.*, 7 Cal. Rptr. 2d 346 (Cal. Ct. App. 1992). However, the court held that such an act by the student was foreseeable, though an intervening cause, especially in light of the fact that school lunchrooms often become boisterous. The court held that whether the school's inadequate supervision was a proximate cause of the injury was a question of the fact for the jury.

9. Generally, defendants are not liable for injuries caused by unforeseeable events and consequences. In *Doe v. Durtschi*, 110 Idaho 466, 716 P.2d 1238 (1986), the Supreme Court of Idaho held that the sexual assault of a student by a teacher was not unforeseeable. Therefore, the concept of the supervening cause was inapplicable. The plaintiffs argued that the school was negligent in hiring and retaining the teacher, whose sexual misconduct was allegedly within the knowledge of the school. The court held that "[t]he fact that the foreseeable danger was from intentional or criminal misconduct is irrelevant; the school district had a statutory duty to make reasonable efforts to protect its students from such danger." *Id.* at 472, 716 P.2d at 1244. For a complete discussion of the avenues students may take in redressing sexual harassment by a teacher, *see* Mawdsley, *Compensation for the Sexually Abused Student*, 84 Educ. L. Rep. 13 (1993).

What about when the intervenor is non-school-related? In *Tinkham v. Groveport-Madison Local Sch. Dist.*, 77 Ohio. App. 3d 242, 602 N.E.2d 256 (1991), a parent and her child brought an action against a taxicab company, school district, and taxicab driver for injuries suffered in the sexual assault of the developmentally disabled plaintiff. The court held that the taxi driver's willful misconduct in sexually abusing the developmentally disabled child whom he was transporting to school constituted an intervening cause of the child's injury. The Board of Education was not accountable.

Two cases in Minnesota were among the first in the nation in which high school students have successfully brought sexual harassment complaints dealing with peer sexual harassment against a school district. *See Minnesota Dep't of Human Rights*, REF: 360 (1991) (Garman, Enforcement Supervisor); *Minnesota Dep't of Human Rights*, REF: 341 (1990) (Lapinsky, Director). For a complete discussion of these two cases and the effects of student versus student sexual harassment, *see* Strauss, *Peer Sexual Harassment of High School Students: A Reasonable Student Standard and an Affirmative Duty Imposed on Educational Institutions*, 10 Law and Ineq. J. 163 (1992).

BRAZELL v. BOARD OF EDUCATION OF NISKAYUNA PUBLIC SCHOOLS

Supreme Court, Appellate Division, Third Department
161 A.D.2d 1086, 557 N.Y.S.2d 645 (1990)

HARVEY, JUSTICE:

....

Plaintiff commenced this personal injury action to recover for damages caused when her teen-aged son Colin stole an oxidizing agent (sodium chlorate) from defendant's science lab during school hours on April 23, 1987. A fire somehow started later that night at plaintiff's home and burned Colin's leg and personal property belonging to plaintiff. As a result, plaintiff basically alleges that defendant negligently supervised and allowed the boy to have access to the dangerous chemical without adequate warnings or precautions. Defendant denied these allegations and raised contributory negligence as a defense. Defendant brought a motion for summary judgment claiming, among other things, that Colin's wrongful act in stealing the chemicals was the sole proximate cause of his injuries. Supreme Court denied defendant's motion and this appeal ensued.

There must be a reversal. In our view, Supreme Court incorrectly denied defendant's motion for summary judgment.... In his testimony, Colin relates that his science class on the day of the accident was conducted from approximately 1:45 P.M. to around 2:30 P.M. An assignment that day was to measure out five grams of sodium chlorate with his lab partner to put aside for an experiment for the next class. After taking the container and measuring the five grams, Colin admitted he took an unspecified extra amount of the chemical and secreted it in his pants pocket so that he could take it home to burn with matches. He claims that he was told by another student that the chemical would burn and sparkle like fire crackers if ignited. Significantly, Colin admits that his teacher specifically told the class to never remove chemicals from the classroom and also that his teacher had gone over the safety procedures in the classroom with him. Once Colin had taken the chemical, he carried it around in his pocket all day until approximately 10:00 P.M. when he was upstairs in his bedroom with two younger cousins. At that time, Colin claimed that the chemical spontaneously ignited in his pocket causing him injuries. Although Colin claimed that there were no matches in his room, this assertion is contradicted by the police report attached to defendant's papers stating that two matchbook pieces were found at the scene.

Based on this and other information, defendant established its entitlement to summary judgment as a matter of law. Plaintiff argues that there are still questions of fact as to how detailed the science teacher's warnings were and how adequate the safety precautions were. Plaintiff points out, based on the teacher's deposition, that the chemical was not kept in a locked desk. However, because the chemical was being used in class that day and Colin received it from the teacher himself for class use, this fact is hardly surprising and raises no inference of negligence. In any event, it is our opinion that even if the science teacher was negligent in any way by reason of being unable to watch some 28 students every minute of the time they were there, Colin's intervening culpable act in intentionally stealing the chemical constituted a superseding force absolving defendant from any liability. It is clear from Colin's own testimony that his conduct, aside from being unforeseeable by others, went beyond mere contributory negligence and rose to such a level of culpability as to replace any negligence on the part of defendant as the legal cause of the accident.

The instant case is distinguishable from *Kush v. City of Buffalo*, 59 N.Y.2d 26, 462 N.Y.S.2d 831, 449 N.E.2d 725, where a school was held liable for the injuries of a small child who found dangerous chemicals that had been stolen earlier by two unsupervised juvenile workers from an unlocked storeroom in the school laboratory. Here, Colin's classroom was supervised, the rules were clear and there is no evidence that anyone knew, other than the teenaged boys themselves, that chemicals were being taken. Although it is conceivable that chemicals left unattended in an unlocked room might be stolen as in *Kush*, in this case the boy surreptitiously stole the chemical while the class was in session. The fact that it was possible to sneak chemicals out of the room without the teacher's knowledge does not make the outcome that occurred in this case a probable one. "In short, a series of new and unexpected causes intervened and had to intervene" before the injuries to Colin, some seven to eight hours after the theft, could occur (*Id.*). Because we perceive no issues of fact requiring resolution at trial, we reverse and grant defendant's motion for summary judgment dismissing the complaint.

Order reversed, on the law, without costs, motion granted, summary judgment awarded to defendant and complaint dismissed.

---

1. How much difference did it make that the fire and burn injuries occurred away from school at Brazell's home? If Brazell's science class met in the morning, and Brazell set the fire outside at lunchtime, would the case have been decided differently? Is the key here precisely where the injury occurred? Or where it didn't occur? Is the key where the initial culpable conduct occurred?

2. *Brazell* held that a school is not liable for damages caused at a student's home which result from culpable conduct committed by the student at school. What about a school's liability for injuries suffered by third parties as a result of a student's culpable conduct committed at school? In *Thompson v. Ange*, 443 N.Y.S.2d 918 (1981), motorists injured in a multiple car accident caused by a student's operation of his car on a public highway in violation of school rules brought a negligence action against the student and his school's authorities to recover for their injuries. The court in *Ange* held that the student's conduct in cases such as this is not the responsibility of the school.

B. DEFENSES TO NEGLIGENCE AND STRICT LIABILITY

3. On October 10, 1972, the plaintiff-appellant, Ronald M. Rixmann, was injured while students were conducting a science class experiment. The class was taught by the defendant, Harold Ammerman.

Ammerman had demonstrated the experiment the previous day. The experiment involved heating a beaker of water and a beaker of alcohol on an electric plate and using these liquids to remove starch from a leaf. Because alcohol is flammable, the students were instructed to have no open flames near the experiment.

The class was divided into two groups for the purpose of conducting the experiment. Ronald, the defendants-respondents, Thomas LeMire and Robert Kieckhoefer, and three other students were in one group. During the course of the experiment, Kieckhoefer used a plastic spoon to pour a small puddle of the heated alcohol onto the table top for the purpose of lighting it with a match. LeMire then set fire to the puddle with a match furnished by Ronald. Eventually, the spoon itself caught fire. Kieckhoefer, in an attempt to extinguish the burning spoon, waved it in the air. He then proceeded to place the spoon in the beaker of water, but in so doing ignited the fumes from the beaker of heated alcohol.

Ammerman, who was at that time with the other group of students, saw the beaker on fire and attempted to extinguish it by placing a notebook over its mouth. The alcohol beaker tipped over, spilling the flaming liquid onto Ronald. He was severely burned. *Rixmann v. Somerset Pub. Schs., St. Croix County*, 266 N.W.2d 326 (Wis. 1978).

The facts in *Rixmann* involve several actors, all of whom contributed to Ronald's injury. In such cases, causation is determined by the "substantial factor" test. Any actor whose actions played a substantial role in bringing about the harm or injury is deemed negligent. All three students admitted that they knew alcohol was highly flammable, and all admitted their roles in setting the puddle of alcohol on fire. The Supreme Court of Wisconsin upheld, therefore, the trial court's finding that all three were negligent as a matter of law. However, the two student defendants, LeMire and Kieckhoefer, asserted that the actions of Ammerman constituted a superseding cause. The Court disagreed. The manner in which Ammerman attempted to extinguish the flames, while perhaps not the most effective, was neither surprising to the students nor extraordinarily negligent. Ultimately, the court stated that it would shock the conscience of the courts to relieve the students of liability for Ronald's injuries.

Generally, before an act can be labelled "superseding," it must first be "intervening." The Restatement (Second) of Torts, § 441(1), defines an "intervening force" as "one which actively operates in producing the harm to another after the actor's negligent act or omission has been committed." This is the case with respect to Ammerman's conduct in *Rixmann*. However, according to the Restatement, a superseding cause is "an act of a third person ... which by its intervention prevents the actor from being liable for harm to another which his antecedent negligence is a substantial factor in bringing about." Restatement (Second) of Torts, § 440. "The fact that an intervening act of a third person

[Ammerman, in *Rixmann*] is negligent in itself or is done in a negligent manner does not make it a superseding cause of harm to another [Ronald] which the actor's [LeMire and Kieckhoefer] negligent conduct is a substantial factor in bringing about, if

> "(a) the actor at the time of his negligent conduct should have realized that a third person might so act, or
>
> "(b) a reasonable man knowing the situation existing when the act of the third person was done would not regard it as highly extraordinary that the third person had so acted, or
>
> "(c) the intervening act is a normal consequence of a situation created by the actor's conduct and the manner in which it is done is not extraordinarily negligent."

Restatement (Second) of Torts, § 447.

JARREAU v. ORLEANS PARISH SCHOOL BOARD

Court of Appeal of Louisiana
600 So. 2d 1389 (4th Cir. 1992)

LANDRIEU, JUDGE:

....

Facts

During the 1986 football season, Darrin Jarreau participated on the Francis T. Nicholls High School team, which was coached by Michael Sims. Although Jarreau had been an All-District running back as a junior in the previous year, his senior season was less productive. Testimony indicated that during a game that season, his wrist was injured when struck by another player's helmet. That injury may have been aggravated in subsequent practice and games, but his coaches did not withhold him from any participation. Allegedly, however, his play was adversely affected by the injury.

At the end of the season and at Jarreau's request, the team trainer, Henry Dunbar, referred him for treatment to Michael Brunet, M.D., a board certified orthopedist at the Tulane Medical Center, who specializes in sports medicine. At the initial exam on December 8, 1986, Dr. Brunet ordered x-rays to confirm his suspicion of a navicular fracture. The x-ray verified a non-union of the fracture as well as cystic changes, indicating that either the fracture occurred through a cyst or the cyst formed because of collapse. According to Dr. Brunet, the cyst, whether pre- or post-fracture, affected the healing. He testified that, if the cystic changes occurred from the non-union, a delay in treatment of the fracture likely exacerbated the injury by extending the period of recovery and limiting the results of treatment.

... In addition to ... two surgeries, treatment involved immobilization by casts for approximately one year total, the use of the bone stimulator, and therapy to regain strength and motion in the wrist. Jarreau was discharged on March 14, 1988. However, Dr. Brunet concluded that this young man had permanent limitations with his wrist movement, which will preclude vigorous manual labor.

After a trial on the merits, the jury decided that both Henry Dunbar and Michael Sims were negligent and their negligence was the legal cause of damages to Darrin R. Jarreau. Accordingly, the jury awarded the plaintiff $50,000 for "past, present, and future pain and suffering, disability, and mental anguish and $12,725 for past medical expenses." The judge likewise concluded that the Orleans Parish School Board was liable to Jarreau for the negligent acts of its employees, as well as for failing to provide adequate training for its coaching staff, and for failing to provide a physician at the football game where plaintiff was injured. She awarded to Jarreau $80,000 in general damages, plus past medical expenses of $12,724.89.

Discussion

....

Cause-In-Fact

The School Board urges us to conclude that the jury and the trial court erred in holding that causation between the defendants' negligent conduct and any damages the plaintiff suffered had been proved. The only medical evidence presented at trial was that of Dr. Michael Brunet, the orthopedic surgeon, who eventually treated Jarreau for his wrist injury. According to his testimony, the delayed treatment probably adversely affected Jarreau's recovery, if the cyst developed after the fracture. And, since the medical expert had no way of knowing whether the cyst caused the fracture or was caused by the trauma, there is certainly a reasonable possibility of a causal connection between the delay in referral and the disabling condition.

... Having established a reasonable possibility that the delay in medical referral extended the term of treatment and resulted in the disability, Jarreau enjoys a presumption of causation.

Duty

The School Board claims that the court erred in holding that Dunbar and Sims had a duty to the plaintiff under general negligence principles to refer him for medical treatment. Based on the difficulty in diagnosing the plaintiff's particular injury, they argue that the court was clearly wrong in finding the two negligent for "failing to recognize that Darrin sustained a fracture."

All persons have a duty to act reasonably under the circumstances. According to La.Civ.Code Ann. art. 2316 (West 1979),

> [e]very person is responsible for the damage he occasions not merely by his act, but by his negligence, his imprudence, or his want of skill.

However the imposition of a legal duty depends on a case by case determination. In determining whether such obligation exists, the court will consider the relationship and circumstances of the parties....

... We agree with appellant that these individuals could not be expected to diagnose the extent of this injury. Indeed, according to the reasonable man standard, they should recognize their limitations in this regard and seek expert medical advice for their players in the face of continuing complaints involving pain and swelling. This responsibility is especially clear in view of the inherent relationship between a coach and his players and the School Board's referral system for medical care through these coaches. Therefore, since this student/athlete presented a persistent medical complaint, we find that Coaches Sims and Dunbar did have a duty to enable Jarreau to access treatment made available to him by the School Board.

Breach

We must consider now whether the duty was breached. The School Board urges us to conclude that, in the absence of expert testimony as to the standard of care of reasonably prudent coaches and/or trainers, a finding of breach is manifestly erroneous. However, the duty of the coaches in this case is that of medical referral, in accordance with established School Board policies, in the face of persistent complaints of pain and swelling. It is a duty which requires no particular expertise and which can be evaluated by the trier of fact without "expert testimony."

The jury decided that the acts or omissions of Sims and Dunbar resulted in an extended period of treatment for this football related injury as well as in a permanent disability. The testimony of the medical expert, while not conclusive, provided evidence to support the jury's determination.

Great deference is given to the findings of the trier of fact, be it jury or judge. Only the factfinder can be aware of the variations in demeanor and tone of voice that contribute to the listener's understanding and belief in what is said. Consequently, when findings are based on credibility, great weight must be given especially to the findings of the trier of fact. As long as there is a reasonable factual basis for the trial court's finding, it will not be disturbed even though the appellate court may recognize that other evaluations and inferences of fact are as reasonable. Therefore, we cannot say that the trial court was clearly wrong.

The School Board also argues that the trial court erred in concluding that it failed to train its coaching staff to diagnose injuries and failed to have a physician present at the game at which plaintiff was initially injured. Since we have decided that the School Board is vicariously liable in this case, we need not address these assignments of error.

Comparative Fault

Having found that the School Board breached a duty to this plaintiff and caused him damages, we now consider whether plaintiff is responsible in whole or in part for the resulting damages. At the time the injury was sustained, plaintiff, as an eighteen year old, had attained the age of majority. He chose to participate in football, a contact sport associated with a degree of pain and injury. After suffering the initial injury and experiencing pain which interfered with his performance on the field, he did not ask to be referred by his coaches for medical care nor did he consult his own physician. Since he hoped to earn a football scholarship to college, he willingly played the remainder of the season. Jarreau, therefore, bears some of the responsibility for the delayed treatment.

Considering all the evidence, we conclude that the trial court was clearly wrong in deciding that Jarreau was without fault in causing the damages that resulted from the delay in treating his football injury. Since we are empowered by La.Code Civ.Proc. art. 2164 to render any judgment which is "just, legal, and proper," we decide that one-third of the fault should be apportioned to Jarreau and that his award from the trial court of $80,000.00 in general damages plus the stipulated past medical expenses of $12,724.89 should be correspondingly reduced to $61,816.91.

....

---

1. Restatement (Second) of Torts § 463 defines contributory negligence as:

> ... conduct on the part of the plaintiff which falls below the standard to which he should conform for his own protection, and which is a legally contributing cause co-operating with the negligence of the defendant in bringing about the plaintiff's harm.

Typically, contributorily negligent plaintiffs do not recover for their injuries and damages. Rest. 2d § 467. However, some states may still allow statutory tort recovery for contributorily negligent claimants, as long as the claimant is a member of the class of people which the statute intends to protect. For example, see *Byrd v. Bossier Parish Sch. Bd.*, 543 So. 2d 35 (La. Ct. App. 1989) (Fourteen year-old student athletic manager was injured while operating power driven machinery. State statute bars minors under 16 from working around such machinery. Despite negligence of student, recovery for damages is not barred).

2. "Contributory negligence is conduct which involves an undue risk of harm to the person who sustains [the harm]." Rest. 2d § 463, comment b. One court in Oklahoma has interpreted contributory negligence to mean that if the claimant has no knowledge of the harm or risk, then he will not be contributorily negligent. See *Lewis v. Dependent Sch. Dist. No. 10*, 808 P.2d 710 (Okla. Ct. App. 1991) (Student could not be found contributorily negligent for participating in the field hockey game unless he knew of the danger posed by that activity and his borderline hemophilia). Is this concept universally applicable? Can you think of any examples of justifiable contributory negligence where the claimant does not know of the danger or risk involved in the activity?

3. Because the results upon application of contributory negligence concepts are so often harsh to legitimately injured plaintiffs (no recovery), some courts have opted for a comparative negligence standard. "Pure" comparative negligence serves not to totally bar recovery, but to reduce a plaintiff's recovery in proportion to his or her fault. Prosser & Keeton, Torts, ch. 11, § 67 (1984). For example, if the jury determined that a plaintiff were 30% negligent, the plaintiff could only recover 70% of his or her damages.

A second type of comparative negligence, "modified" or "partial" comparative negligence, requires that the plaintiff be less than 50% negligent in order to recover anything. Under this theory, if the plaintiff is even 51% negligent, then recovery is barred. Obviously, there are advantages and disadvantages to both systems. Which is more fair? Efficient? Which is more susceptible to questionable percentage allocations?

4. It can be argued that participants in school athletics know the risks, and assume the risks, of their sports. But does this relieve schools of liability? Are there some risks for which the school is still responsible? In *Thomas v. St. Mary's Roman Catholic Church*, 283 N.W.2d 254 (S.D. 1979), an aggressive high school basketball player from a visiting team dove for a ball as it was heading out-of-bounds, tapped it back in, but crashed into a glass wall, shattering it. He suffered severe injuries, permanently restricting the use of his hands and arms. The student sued, alleging a violation of the school's duty to provide a safe place to play basketball. The jury returned a verdict in favor of the student. The Supreme Court affirmed, denying St. Mary's its defenses of contributory negligence and assumption of the risk. Under the facts of the case, it was not possible for the student to fully appreciate and voluntarily assume the danger involved in using the glass, or in crashing into it.

"Testimony disclosed that Thomas did not know the type of glass, did not realize it was breakable, and did not receive any warning concerning the inherent danger of the glass panels so close to the playing floor." *Thomas v. St. Mary's*, 283 N.W.2d at 256. Assume this testimony to be true, and assume that the court found, at least in part, for Thomas. Does it make any difference that Thomas was from the visiting team? What if the home team players knew the type of glass and the inherent danger of the panels' proximity to the playing floor? Would their injuries not be compensated even if the visitors' are?

ARBEGAST v. BOARD OF EDUCATION OF SOUTH NEW BERLIN CENTRAL SCHOOL

Court of Appeals of New York
65 N.Y.2d 161, 480 N.E.2d 365, 490 N.Y.S.2d 751 (1985)

MEYER, JUDGE:

....

I

Plaintiff, a student teacher at the South New Berlin Central School, was injured during a donkey basketball game when the donkey she was riding put its head down and she fell off. The game, sponsored as a fund-raising event for the senior class, was staged under contract by the defendant Buckeye Donkey Ball Company, which provided the donkeys, helmets for each of the players, and an employee who transported and handled the animals, gave instructions to the participants, and acted as referee of the games, in return for which the company received a percentage of the receipts. Two games were played; the first pitted the faculty team against the fire department team and was won by the faculty team; the faculty team then opposed the senior class team in the second game. Plaintiff participated in the first game without mishap, but had a different, larger donkey for the second game than she had had for the first. She spent a good deal of the game walking the donkey around but, at the urging of another faculty member, mounted. Soon thereafter she was thrown over the donkey's head when it put its head down as it stopped, with resultant permanent injury to her left arm.

Plaintiff sued both the Board of Education and defendant Buckeye, but settled her claim against the Board of Education prior to trial. The claimed negligence on the part of Buckeye as particularized was that knowing of the vicious propensities of the donkey, defendant allowed plaintiff to ride without sufficient warning of such propensities, failed to provide adequate supervision and failed to provide adequate safety equipment. Buckeye, in addition to denying negligence on its part, pleaded as separate affirmative defenses assumption of the risk and reduction of damages by reason of plaintiff's culpable conduct. There was evidence that the instructions given by Buckeye's employee to the participants included the statements that the donkeys do buck and put their heads down causing people to fall off and that if injuries happened the participants were at their own risk.

....

The matter is before us by our leave. We conclude that the comparative causation principle enacted by CPLR 1411 applies to a strict liability action involving the vicious propensities of a domesticated animal, and to the implied assumption of risk by a person injured by such an animal, but not to the express assumption of risk by such a person. Although implied assumption of risk, therefore, was under these circumstances a defense in mitigation of damages to be pleaded and proved by defendant rather than an element of plaintiff's cause of action, defendant was entitled to dismissal of the complaint at the end of the plaintiff's case by reason of her admission that she had been informed both of the risk of injury and that "the participants were at their own risk." We, therefore, affirm.

....

III

A

Until the enactment in 1975 of CPLR article 14-A, it was, except in an action for wrongful death, a substantive part of the plaintiff's right to recover in a negligence action that plaintiff prove himself or herself free from negligence contributing in the slightest degree to the occurrence. The theory was that plaintiff's negligence was an intervening cause, which broke the causal connection between the defendant's negligent act and plaintiff's injury.

Assumption of the risk, on the other hand, was predicated not upon plaintiff's intervening act, but upon his or her agreement, express or implied, not to hold defendant responsible for the injury-causing act, negligent though it may have been, which resulted from plaintiff's entering into the activity with knowledge of its danger, or under circumstances from which it could be found that he or she should have had such knowledge. The burden of proving such a contract rested upon defendant, not plaintiff.

....

B

... CPLR article 14-A was enacted in 1975, providing that as to all causes of action accruing on or after September 1, 1975, "the culpable conduct attributable to the claimant or to the decedent, including contributory negligence or assumption of risk, shall not bar recovery, but the amount of damages otherwise recoverable shall be diminished in the proportion which the culpable conduct attributable to the claimant or decedent bears to the culpable conduct which caused the damages" (CPLR 1411), and "shall be an affirmative defense to be pleaded and proved by the party asserting the defense." ...

With respect to "culpable conduct" the Report of the Judicial Conference stated that the phrase was "used instead of 'negligent conduct' because this article will apply to cases where the conduct of one or more of the parties will be found to be not negligent, but will nonetheless be a factor in determining the amount of damages", and that "[t]his article permits the apportionment of damages in cases ... in which the plaintiff's negligence may be the only negligence, but the defendant's conduct is nonetheless 'culpable' and therefore to be considered in determining damages" (1976 Judicial Conference Report, at 240). Culpable conduct, it noted, included not only assumption of the risk and contributory negligence, but also product misuse and the patent danger rule declared in *Campo v. Scofield*, 301 N.Y. 468, 95 N.E.2d 802, and applied in strict liability cases (*Bolm v. Triumph Corp.*, 33 N.Y.2d 151, 350 N.Y.S.2d 644, 305 N.E.2d 769)....

Because the Legislature contemplated that article 14-A would "apply to cases where the conduct of one or more of the parties will be found not negligent" and "in which the plaintiff's negligence may be the only negligence," but also that defendant's culpable conduct would include "conduct giving rise to liability upon a theory of strict liability," it is clear that both the basis of liability asserted against the present defendant and the plaintiff's acts may constitute "culpable conduct" within the meaning of the statute.

C

Thus, what the statute requires comparison of is not negligence but conduct which, for whatever reason, the law deems blameworthy, in order to fix the relationship of each party's conduct to the injury sustained and the damages to be paid by the one and received by the other as recompense for that injury. Comparative causation is, therefore, the more accurate description of the process.... [F]or the statute to operate, plaintiff's conduct must be a cause in fact of his or her injury. When it is, the statute "requires that the culpable conduct attributable to the decedent or claimant be compared with the total culpable conduct which caused the damages."

D

Neither article 14-A nor its legislative history defines "assumption of risk." The common law distinguished between express and implied assumption of risk. Express assumption, which was held to preclude any recovery, resulted from agreement in advance that defendant need not use reasonable care for the benefit of plaintiff and would not be liable for the consequence of conduct that would otherwise be negligent (Prosser, Law of Torts, at 442 [4th ed.]; Schwartz, Comparative Negligence § 9.2; Comparative Negligence Law & Practice § 4.20[1][b][i] [Matthew Bender]; Restatement [Second] of Torts § 496B; Uniform Comparative Fault Act § 1[b], 12 ULA [1985 Cum.Ann.Pocket Part], at 41; Ann., 16 A.L.R.4th 700). Implied assumption was founded not on express contract, but on plaintiff's voluntarily encountering the risk of harm from defendant's conduct with full understanding of the possible harm to himself or herself (Prosser, op. cit., at 445; Schwartz, op. cit. §§ 9.1, 9.3; Comparative Negligence Law & Practice op. cit. § 4.20[1][b][ii]; Restatement [Second] of Torts §§ 496C, 496D, 496E), and according to some authorities required that plaintiff's consent to the risk involved be unreasonable under the circumstances (Schwartz, op. cit. § 9.1, at 157; Comparative Negligence Law & Practice, op. cit., at 4-33-4-34; Uniform Comparative Fault Act § 1[b] and comment; Restatement [Second] of Torts § 496E comment d).

The Legislature is, however, presumed to be aware of the decisional and statute law in existence at the time of an enactment ... and to have abrogated the common law only to the extent that the clear import of the language used in the statute requires.

Here, as noted by Schwartz (*op. cit.* § 9.2, 1981 Cum. Supp., at 74), CPLR 1411 leaves it "unclear whether express assumption of risk is subject to comparison." But, when article 14-A was enacted, it had long been the law that a contractual limitation of liability for negligence or other fault of a party seeking to be relieved of his ordinary responsibility did not violate public policy ... except as specific statutes imposed limitations upon such agreements ... or interdicted them entirely (*see* General Obligations Law, §§ 5-321, 5-322, 5-322.1, 5-323, 5-324, 5-325, 5-326 [all of which were enacted well prior to 1975 except § 5-322.1, which was enacted at the same legislative session as was CPLR art. 14-A]). We conclude, therefore, that CPLR 1411 requires diminishment of damages in the case of an implied assumption of risk but, except as public policy proscribes an agreement limiting liability, does not foreclose a complete defense that by express consent of the injured party no duty exists and, therefore, no recovery may be had. Added support for that conclusion may be found in the decisions of courts of other States.

The existence of such an express assumption of risk by the injured party is a matter of defense upon which the burden of proof will be on the party claiming to have thus been absolved of duty (CPLR 3018[b] and will be a factual issue for the jury, unless there is no real controversy as to the facts.

IV

Here there is evidence from which the jury could have concluded that plaintiff had knowledge of the risk and by participating in the games voluntarily assumed it, and no question that plaintiff's conduct in mounting the donkey from which she was thrown was a cause in fact of her injuries. She would, therefore, have been entitled to a comparative causation charge on implied assumption of the risk had she not conceded that she was told before the games began that "participants are at their own risk." In light of that concession, however, the Trial Judge should have directed a verdict for defendant.

For the foregoing reasons, the order of the Appellate Division should be affirmed, with costs.

....

---

1. What is the effect of the statute applied in *Arbegast*? How is it applied to implied assumption of the risk? To express assumption of the risk?

2. Christy Arbegast expressly assumed the risk of her activity, and therefore could not recover from the defendants for her injuries. Voluntary participation in athletic activity, without prior admission of the dangers involved, is typically merely an implied assumption of the risk. For example, *see Locilento v. John A. Coleman Catholic High Sch.*, 523 N.Y.S.2d 198 (N.Y. App. Div. 1987)

(School's failure to provide students with proper equipment for an intramural football game was the proximate cause of plaintiff's injuries; however, plaintiff's voluntary participation was an implied assumption of the risks, and reduced possible recovery for injuries suffered).

Assumption of the risk is also applicable in cases of failure to supervise. *See Lucas v. Fresno Unified Sch. Dist.*, 18 Cal. Rptr. 2d 79 (Cal. App. 1993) (Doctrine of implied assumption of the risk would not bar the plaintiffs from holding the school district liable for failure to supervise, which proximately caused plaintiff student to be struck in the eye with a dirt clod during recess).

3. The *Arbegast* opinion divides the doctrine of assumption of the risk into two categories — express and implied. The court in *Thomas v. St. Mary's*, 283 N.W.2d 254 (S.D. 1979), in note 4 following *Jarreau, supra*, held that Thomas did not assume the risk that the glass panel would be of ordinary glass, unable to withstand impact. The Restatement (Second) of Torts defines assumption of the risk as either express or implied. *See* Rest. 2d § 469A-F. Express assumption of the risk occurs where the plaintiff agrees in advance that the defendant would not be liable for the consequence of conduct on the part of the defendant that would otherwise be negligent. Implied assumption of the risk occurs when a plaintiff fully understands a risk of harm to himself or his property caused by defendant's conduct, and nevertheless voluntarily chooses to accept that risk. What does the court say about the portions of the paneling that were boarded up rather than glass-covered? Should this be enough, on sight, to imply an assumption of the risk on Thomas' part?

The Supreme Court of Washington, in *Tincani v. Inland Empire Zoological Soc'y*, 124 Wash. 2d 121, 875 P.2d 621 (1994), divides assumption of the risk into four categories: (1) express, (2) implied primary, (3) implied reasonable, and (4) implied unreasonable. *See also Scott v. Pacific West Mt. Resort*, 119 Wash. 2d 645, 655, 695 P.2d 116, *cert. denied*, 474 U.S. 827 (1985).

Implied primary assumption of the risk means that the plaintiff assumes risks that are inherent in and necessary to the particular activity. (Sports-related cases, typically). *Scott*, at 500-01. According to Prosser & Keeton, implied primary assumption of the risk is total bar to recovery. Prosser & Keeton at 497. The Supreme Court of Washington found *Tincani* to be a case of implied unreasonable assumption, and did not bar recovery totally. "[T]he jury may apportion the percentage of fault attributable to each party." *Tincani*, 124 Wash. 2d at 145, 875 P.2d at 634.

4. If a plaintiff attends a baseball or a hockey game, most courts hold that in seeking admission, the plaintiff must be regarded as having chosen to encounter the well-known risk of flying baseballs or hockey pucks. *See Kennedy v. Providence Hockey Club*, 376 A.2d 329 (R.I. 1977).

In the school context, consider *Marlowe v. Rush-Henrietta Central Sch. Dist.*, 561 N.Y.S.2d 934 (N.Y. App. Div. 1990). In *Marlowe*, a 17-year-old student was hit by a thrown bat during a gym class baseball game *voluntarily joined* by the plaintiff. There was no evidence that the player who threw the bat did so intentionally or recklessly. The majority held that the plaintiff assumed the risk that a bat might be thrown. The court dismissed the complaint. Which category of assumption of the risk applies here? Is this consistent with the other New York cases presented? Which of the four *Tincani* categories would apply if *Tincani* were controlling in this jurisdiction?

The dissent in *Marlowe* notes that the bat was thrown 35 feet. Should this make a difference? The dissenters thought so: "A participant in a sporting activity assumes only risks that are known, apparent, or reasonably foreseeable." 561 N.Y.S.2d at 935. The dissent also notes that "Nesmith [the bat thrower] had a history of bat throwing and because of this behavior was referred to by the other players as the 'Dave Winfield' of Roth High School." Which opinion does this statement most benefit? Does it make any difference? Is the dissent trying to say that application of the assumption of the risk varies depending on who is up to bat?

5. Whether you call it "implied assumption of the risk" or "implied primary assumption of the risk," it is generally conceded that participants in sporting activities assume the inherent and obvious dangers of their sport. How should the experience of the player affect the application of assumption of the risk? In *Laboy v. Wallkill Central Sch. Dist.*, 607 N.Y.S.2d 746 (N.Y. App. Div. 1984), a high school student attempting to pole vault at his first interscholastic meet landed feet first on a seam in the mats, separating them and falling to the pavement, injuring his knee. Laboy had been coached in advance and had completed several successful vaults at that meet. Despite this, the court noted that "[a]wareness of the risk assumed must be assessed in light of the skill and experience of the particular plaintiff." *Id.* at 748. *See also Maddox v. City of New York*, 496 N.Y.S.2d 726 (1986) (professional baseball assumed the risk of muddy baseball field). Are we to assume that novice baseball players and track and field athletes do *not* assume such risks as muddy fields and separating landing mats? Nevertheless, the court in *Laboy* reversed the school district's summary judgment.

6. Express assumption of the risk can be compared to exculpatory clauses in contracts. Where the relationship between the plaintiff and defendant arises out of a contract, defendant may attempt to limit or exclude liability in advance by the use of exculpatory provisions. Whether plaintiff is barred or limited by assumption of the risk in these situations depends upon the enforceability of such provisions. *See Barnes v. New Hampshire Karting Ass'n*, 509 A.2d 151 (N.H. 1986).

The Court of Appeals of Tennessee held that a release form signed by the mother of an injured child (severely developmentally disabled child participating in Special Olympics) was effective to relieve the defendant of liability to the mother, but did not waive the rights of the child. *Childress v. Madison County*, 777 S.W.2d 1 (Tenn. App. 1989). Did the release do what it was supposed to?

If the enforceable, exculpatory clauses or releases serve to shift the burden of the risk of injury from the defendant (school) to the plaintiff (student). In *Hohe v. San Diego Unified Sch. Dist.*, 274 Cal. Rptr. 647, 224 Cal. App. 3d 1559 (1990), the California Court of Appeals held that release signed by a parent and a student prior to the student's participation in a school hypnotism show was not void as against public policy (though there remained a question of fact as to the scope of the release). The student volunteered to participate in the show because it would be "fun."

GOPLERUD, LIABILITY OF SCHOOLS AND COACHES: THE CURRENT STATUS OF SOVEREIGN IMMUNITY AND ASSUMPTION OF THE RISK, 39 Drake L. Rev. 759 (1989/1990)*

I. Introduction

John, a seventeen year old high school football superstar, was injured near the end of the third quarter of the last game of the season. John's injuries have rendered him permanently disabled. A few weeks earlier, John had signed a national letter of intent to play football for a Big Ten power-house. Prior to the disabling injury, John was looking forward to a promising athletic and academic career.

John and his family filed suit shortly after the accident, alleging defective manufacturing on the part of the helmet manufacturer. The complaint also alleged that the school system was negligent in supplying the defective helmet, and that the football coach and principal were negligent in allowing John to play in a football game while fatigued. In their answer, the high school and coach claimed that the school district was immune from liability under the theory of sovereign immunity. Moreover, it was asserted that the plaintiff had knowledge of the potential danger involved, and knowingly and voluntarily assumed the risk of injury while competing in a high school football game.

The above situation is becoming commonplace as lawsuits for injuries due to athletic injuries are increasing. Injured athletes have brought lawsuits against school districts,[1] school boards,[2] principals,[3] coaches,[4] referees,[5] and even athletic associations.[6] This explosion of lawsuits is due to the slow erosion of two important doctrines, which served as the wall of defense for public schools and their officials. The doctrines of sovereign immunity and assumption of risk have slowly been chipped away so that the two doctrines are only available in limited situations.

. . . .

---

*Copyright © 1990 by The Drake Law Review. Reprinted with permission.

[1]*Fallon v. Indian Trail Sch.*, 148 Ill. App. 3d 931, 500 N.E.2d 101 (1986)....

[2]*Benitez v. New York City Bd. of Educ.*, 141 A.D.2d 457, 530 N.Y.S.2d 825 (1988)....

[3]*Vargo v. Svitchan*, 100 Mich. App. 809, 301 N.W.2d 1 (1980)....

[4]*Beckett v. Clinton Prairie Sch. Corp.*, 504 N.E.2d 552 (Ind. 1987)....

[5]*Carabba v. Anacortes School Dist.*, 72 Wash. 2d 939, 435 P.2d 936 (1967)....

[6]*Harvey v. Ouachita Parish Sch. Bd.*, 545 So. 2d 1241 (La. Ct. App. 1989).

II. *Theories of Recovery*

....

A. *Negligent Failure to Provide Proper Supervision*

When an injured athlete seeks recovery for injuries suffered in connection with high school athletic events, the issue of liability generally depends upon whether the defendant coach fulfilled the duty of care owed to the injured athlete. The athletic coach's duty is primarily to supervise and train the athletes under his or her supervision. The duty of care owed is that care which a coach of ordinary prudence, charged with the same duties, would exercise under the same or similar circumstances.

....

To minimize risks of liability by schools and coaches, coaches should keep a record of all programs used to teach players proper techniques. Though potentially time consuming, a coach should have a schedule or program organized as to what is being taught in a particular practice.

B. *Negligent Hiring of an Incompetent Coach*

The Restatement (Second) of Agency states that "a person conducting an activity through servants or other agents is subject to liability for harm resulting from his conduct if he is negligent or reckless ... (b) in the employment of improper persons or instrumentalities in work involving risk of harm to others."[17]

When hiring coaches, schools and school districts should prepare a comprehensive job description and complete a thorough background investigation of the applicants being interviewed. Although this entails considerable time on the part of a hiring committee, it is time well spent. Education, certification, training, and continuing education are among the criteria to be considered when selecting new coaches. It has even been suggested that potential coaches and physical education instructors should be required to pass examinations, much like lawyers, and demonstrate their knowledge and abilities in their specialized fields.

C. *Negligently Supplying Defective Athletic Equipment*

Under a theory of negligently supplying defective athletic equipment, an injured student athlete alleges that the high school has breached an affirmative duty to exercise reasonable care in providing equipment that is safe and not defective, and that the school/coach knew or had reason to know of the danger.

....

There are several factors that courts may consider when examining the negligent supply cause of action. These factors can also be used by the schools and coaches to minimize or eliminate the risk of exposure to liability due to the

---

[17]Restatement (Second) of Agency § 213 (1957).

injury of an amateur athlete. Schools and coaches should consider the following procedures. Equipment records may play an important part in the suits filed by injured student athletes. Schools and coaches should keep records and catalogues of all equipment bought and the reasons why the coaches purchased particular products. Also, records should be kept listing comments, recommendations, and representations made by sales representatives about the features and qualities of their products. Finally, records should be maintained of all maintenance and periodic inspections of equipment.

D. *Negligent Care of an Injured Player*

When a student athlete is injured, school personnel, primarily coaches, have a duty to provide reasonable medical care to the injured athlete as soon as possible. The duty that is owed may be breached either by delaying medical care or by negligently moving an injured player.

....

Reasonable care in obtaining medical assistance for an injured athlete means reasonable care under the circumstances. Coaches should have immediate access to medical assistance or access to a telephone with which to obtain such assistance. A physician should be present at all athletic competitions in order to assist if any injuries occur. With the risk of enhanced injury due to delay in receiving proper medical attention, coaches and schools should be instructed to seek medical assistance immediately whenever there is a possibility of severe injury.

In an effort to minimize any exposure to liability for negligent care, schools and coaches should consider the following procedures. Coaches should keep records of any injuries, minor or otherwise, that have occurred. All game films should be retained and statements from witnesses regarding the injuries should be recorded. Many suits are not filed until many years after an injury, and game films should be kept as evidence that due care was provided. Trainers and coaches must be properly trained and knowledgeable about first aid care in case of a serious accident. Records should be kept of the procedures taken when an injury occurs. Additionally, trainers and coaches should continually update their education through seminars and literature regarding new developments in equipment, training, and/or first aid care.

E. *Negligently Allowing an Injured Player to Compete*

A cause of action has been recognized where an injured student athlete can prove that a coach negligently coerced or forced the athlete to participate in a practice or competition while injured, and the athlete sustained further injury.... [I]f a coach had reason to know, or in the exercise of reasonable care should have known, that a student athlete was injured, the coach had an affirmative duty to prevent further injury by refusing to allow the player to compete.

If the student athlete competes while the coach knows that the athlete is fatigued beyond a point of safety, and the athlete is injured, then a cause of action arises. The coach may also be liable if he or she knowingly allows a fatigued athlete to continue to compete despite the enhanced potential for injury.

III. *Sovereign Immunity*

A. *The General Rule*

Under the doctrine of sovereign immunity, the state is generally immune from tort liability. The doctrine can be harsh, in that it can bar an otherwise valid cause of action, unless the state has abrogated the defense either judicially or legislatively.

As a general rule, all public bodies in charge of, or responsible for, the public schools enjoy immunity from tort liability absent specific legislation to the contrary. The immune public bodies include, but are not limited to, school districts, school boards or similar agencies, counties, towns, townships, and municipalities that are in charge of such schools or institutions. These public bodies are immune on the theory that they are merely agents acting in the furtherance of the public educational systems and are agents of the sovereign state.

Courts have also extended this doctrine to immunize people who assist in the functioning of the government. Courts have held that the doctrine of sovereign immunity is worthless if the individuals that make the government function are subject to tort claims.[60]

B. *Theory of Sovereignty*

. . . .

The public school system and the bodies responsible for the administration of the system are immunized from liability by sovereign immunity for several reasons. The school system and administrative bodies act as agents of the sovereign state in their governmental duties and act on behalf of or for the welfare of the state. In addition, school districts and school boards lack the necessary funds with which to pay damages awarded for tort claims.

Public policy considerations also support the application of sovereign immunity to the public school system. Public education benefits everyone and the payment of damages for tort claims should not be diverted from the school system. Several courts have stated that immunity from tort claims on the part of governmental subdivisions (including schools) is a matter of public policy, and as such, any change in the policy towards abrogation of tort immunity is best determined by the legislature and not the courts.

. . . .

---

[60]*Lentz v. Morris*, 236 Va. 78, _____, 372 S.E.2d 608, 610 (1988).

D. The Attack on Sovereign Immunity

Most recently, the constitutionality of the doctrine of sovereign immunity has been attacked, based on due process and equal protection claims.[72] In examining the doctrine, the courts have applied a rational basis test.[73] The courts examine the goals that are to be achieved by the immunity and balance them against the limitation of redress in the courts.[74] The fourteenth amendment's due process clause does not protect potential claimants against all deprivations of life and liberty by the state.[75] The amendment only protects against deprivations without due process of law. This is balanced against the interests of the stated objectives of providing for the maintenance and support of public education of the general citizenry.[77] The fear is that competent people will be discouraged from entering the educational field if they will be subject to suit for their actions in performance of governmental duties.

The same test has been applied to the equal protection claims. The court held in *Stout v. Grand Prairie Independent School District*[80] that the disparate treatment of claimants injured by a teacher's negligence is "rationally related to the legislative goal of ensuring the continued availability of quality public education."[81] The court concluded that any other change in the doctrine is a matter for the legislature and not for the courts to determine.

Another attack on the sovereign immunity that school districts and their related bodies have enjoyed is that any insurance coverage acts as a waiver of immunity.[83] The question arises as to what extent, if any, a local school district waives governmental immunity for tort actions by purchasing general liability insurance coverage. The purchase of liability insurance has typically acted as a waiver only for those injuries specifically covered by the insurance policy.

The statute examined in *Overcash v. Statesville City Board of Education* plainly stated that a waiver exists to the extent that the board "is actually indemnified by insurance for such negligence or tort."[87] The insurance policy involved in *Overcash* had a specific waiver for negligent acts arising out of

---

[72]*Sisson v. Douglas County School Dist.*, 181 Ga. App. 77, ____, 351 S.E.2d 272, 274 (1986); *Wilson v. Gipson*, 753 P.2d 1349, 1353 (Okla. 1988); *Stout v. Grand Prairie Indep. School Dist.*, 733 S.W.2d 290, 295 (Tex.Ct.App. 1987).

[73]*Id.*

[74]*Stout v. Grand Prairie Indep. School Dist.*, 733 S.W.2d 290 (Tex. Ct. App. 1987).

[75]*Sisson v. Douglas County School Dist.*, 181 Ga. App. 77, ____, 351 S.E.2d 272, 275 (1986).

[77]*Stout v. Grand Prairie Indep. School Dist.*, 733 S.W.2d at 294.

[80]*Stout v. Grand Prairie Indep. School Dist.*, 733 S.W.2d 290 (Tex.Ct.App. 1987).

[81]*Id.* at 295.

[83]*Overcash v. Statesville City Bd. of Educ.*, 83 N.C. App. 21, 348 S.E.2d 524 (1986); *Dugger v. Sprouse*, 257 Ga. 778, 364 S.E.2d 275 (1988).

[87]*Id.* at ____, 348 S.E.2d at 528.

athletic events. The court held that the exclusion did not mandate a waiver of the general doctrine of sovereign immunity. Therefore, the school district was still immune from liability for those injuries arising out of athletic events.

IV. *Assumption of the Risk*

A. *Generally*

The doctrine of assumption of the risk is a more recent development in the common law. The doctrine completely bars a plaintiff's cause of action against a defendant's negligent act. In asserting a defense that the plaintiff assumed the risk, the defendant must allege and prove that the plaintiff had knowledge of the danger involved, appreciated its character, and voluntarily accepted the risk involved. The result is that the defendant is relieved of the legal duty owed to the plaintiff. Because there is no duty, the defendant cannot be held liable for negligence.

A subjective standard is used to determine whether the plaintiff assumed the risk. The standard is judged by what a particular plaintiff sees, understands, and appreciates. The subjective awareness of the risk by the injured plaintiff is a question for the jury, and should not be ruled on as a matter of law unless reasonable minds could not come to any other inference. This subjective approach differs from the objective standard employed for determining contributory negligence. If the plaintiff does not fully understand the risk involved in a particular situation by reason of age, experience, intelligence, or information, he will not be found to have assumed the risk. However, under an objective reasonable man standard, a plaintiff may be found contributorily negligent.

The student athlete necessarily assumes the risks that are inherent to the sport. For example, in football, the student athlete necessarily assumes the risk of being hit hard and sustaining bruises and lacerations. But the plaintiff does not assume the risk of another's (*e.g.*, the coach's) negligence or incompetence.

B. *Current Status of Assumption of the Risk*

Courts frequently struggle with the doctrine of assumption of the risk because it leads to harsh results for injured plaintiffs. The doctrine has been narrowed by the courts' interpretation of what risk was assumed and whether it was voluntarily assumed. The doctrine has also been severely limited in its application by the growing use of comparative negligence. Many jurisdictions have either abolished the doctrine entirely or have reserved it for use only when the risk was expressly assumed or preserved by statute.

....

The rise of comparative negligence has also led to the diminished use of the defense of assumption of the risk. This rise in comparative negligence has benefitted the injured plaintiff who otherwise would have no opportunity for recovery if his action was barred by assumption of the risk.

Express assumption of the risk is characterized as a contractual, bargained-for agreement.... Express assumption of the risk involves the plaintiff-athlete voluntarily bargaining to relieve the defendant school or coach of any duty. Thus, if no policy reasons exist, contractual agreements, disclaimers, and waivers will continue to serve as a total bar in comparative negligence cases.... However, express assumption of the risk in high school athletics is rarely recognized. This express assumption occurs when the student athlete or parent sign a waiver or release relieving coaches or schools of any liability.

....

Sports participants impliedly consent to assume those risks that are inherent in the game. This implied consent to the inherent risks of the sport is similar to the express waiver or contractual consent to encounter known risks of a particular activity. Thus, in sports-related injuries, this consent to inherent risks acts as a total bar to plaintiffs' recovery.

Other forms of assumption of the risk may be given various names, such as primary, secondary, reasonable and unreasonable assumptions of the risk. It may be easier to understand the doctrine of assumption of the risk by labeling the risks as either reasonable or unreasonable. Many states that have either judicially or legislatively adopted comparative negligence have abolished the doctrine of assumption of the risk (except for express assumption of the risk). Many courts have merged the type of risk that is unreasonably assumed into contributory negligence. In comparative negligence jurisdictions, this merger results in a recovery that is reduced by the plaintiff's percentage of fault. Thus, the unreasonable assumption of risk is one of many factors considered in the reduction of damages. Courts have described this voluntary but unreasonable assumption of the risk created by the defendant as a form of contributory negligence to be "compared to the negligent conduct of the defendant in allocating relative fault and apportioning damages under the comparative fault scheme."[126]

....

For different situations involving the immunity defense, consider the following cases, and the accompanying notes and articles.

---

[126] *Blair v. Mount Meadows Dev. Corp.*, 291 Or. 293, ____, 630 P.2d 827, 832 (1981)....

C. TORT IMMUNITY

STONEKING v. BRADFORD AREA SCHOOL DISTRICT
United States Court of Appeals
882 F.2d 720 (3d Cir. 1989)

SLOVITER, CIRCUIT JUDGE:

This case is before us on remand from the United States Supreme Court which vacated our judgment and remanded for further consideration in light of *DeShaney v. Winnebago County Department of Social Services*, ___ U.S. ___, 109 S.Ct. 998 (1989). This case was originally heard on the appeal of the individual defendants from the denial by the district court of their motion for summary judgment on the grounds of qualified immunity. We affirmed, rejecting the defendants' contention that they were not alleged to have violated plaintiff's clearly established right. *Stoneking v. Bradford Area School Dist.*, 856 F.2d 594 (3d Cir. 1988) (*Stoneking I*), vacated sub nom. *Smith v. Stoneking*, ___ U.S. ___, 109 S.Ct. 1333 (1989). It is now incumbent upon us to reconsider that decision.

I

Kathleen Stoneking filed suit under 42 U.S.C. § 1983 against the Bradford Area School District, Frederick Smith, the principal of the Bradford Area High School, Richard Miller, the assistant principal, and Frederick Shuey, the superintendent of the School District. Each of the individual defendants was sued in both his individual and official capacity. Stoneking prayed for relief in the form of compensatory and punitive damages against Shuey, Smith, Miller and the School District.

Stoneking's complaint alleged that Edward Wright, a School District employee who was the Band Director at Bradford High, used physical force, threats of reprisal, intimidation and coercion to sexually abuse and harass her and to force her to engage in various sexual acts beginning October 1980, when she was a high school student, and continuing through Stoneking's sophomore, junior and senior years until her graduation in 1983 and thereafter until 1985. Defendants concede that some of these acts occurred in the band room at the high school and on trips for band functions, as well as in Wright's car and in his house while Stoneking babysat or after he gave her a music lesson. Wright was ultimately prosecuted for various sex-related crimes and pled guilty.

Stoneking averred that in 1979, before Wright's actions toward her, another female member of the band informed Smith that Wright had attempted to rape or sexually assault her; that Smith, in his capacity as principal, maintained a personal file on Wright which contained reports of complaints of sexual misconduct by female students in the band program; that Smith announced to Wright a "policy" with respect to his contact with female students under which he was to have no further "one on one" contacts with female band members; that Smith, Miller and Shuey "failed to take any action to protect the health,

C. TORT IMMUNITY

safety and welfare of the female student body" and Stoneking; that Miller and Shuey were also on notice of the complaints of sexual misconduct by Wright and of the policy adopted by Smith under which Wright was to have no one-on-one contact with female band members, or, if Shuey was not aware, it was because of "the defective and deficient policies and customs" of the School District; and that Wright threatened his victims that if they reported his actions they would incur "loss of parental support, the esteem of friends and the dissolution of the school band which had become ... a significant institution to the School District and the community in general."

After discovery in this case and in cases filed by other students who alleged they were also sexually abused by Wright, defendants moved for summary judgment in the actions against them in their individual capacities on the basis of qualified immunity....

The district court denied the defendants' motion for summary judgment, holding that there was evidence from which a jury could conclude that defendants were reckless in their handling of an incident of abuse which had been reported to Smith in 1979, in their failure to investigate other reported incidents involving Wright and other female students, and in their attempts to remedy and/or rectify the problems involving Wright....

On appeal, defendants argued that they were entitled to qualified immunity because they had no clearly established duty to protect Stoneking, and therefore there was no basis upon which a violation of 42 U.S.C. § 1983 could be predicated. We rejected that contention, holding that under the applicable state law a special relationship arose between the school officials and students entrusted to their care, and that the Pennsylvania child abuse reporting and in loco parentis statutes, coupled with the broad common law duty of officials to students, evidenced a desire on the part of the state to provide affirmative protection to students. Defendants now argue that the Supreme Court's decision in *DeShaney* controls our decision and mandates a holding that the school authorities owed no constitutional duty of protection to Stoneking.

In *DeShaney*, the Court held that a minor could not maintain an action against Winnebago County, its Department of Social Services, and various individual employees of the Department for injuries he received at the hands of his father, even though the county caseworker returned DeShaney to the father's custody and allegedly knew or should have known of the risk of violence to him at his father's hands. The Court's analysis was straightforward: it held that "a State's failure to protect an individual against private violence simply does not constitute a violation of the Due Process Clause." 109 S.Ct. at 1004....

The Court held that because there was no constitutional duty on the state to provide its citizens with particular protective services, "the State cannot be held liable under the [Due Process] Clause for injuries that could have been averted had it chosen to provide them." 109 S.Ct. 1004. It distinguished DeShaney's situation from those "limited circumstances [in which] the Constitution imposes upon the State affirmative duties of care and protection with respect to particular individuals." 109 S.Ct. at 1004-05....

In light of the Supreme Court's discussion in *DeShaney* distinguishing between affirmative duties of care and protection imposed by a state on its agents and constitutional duties to protect, we can no longer rely on the statutory and common law duties imposed in Pennsylvania on school officials as the basis of a duty to protect students from harm occurring as a result of a third person.

Arguably, our earlier discussion noting that "students are in what may be viewed as functional custody of the school authorities" during their presence at school because they are required to attend under Pennsylvania law, *see* 856 F.2d at 601 (citing 24 Pa.Stat.Ann. § 13-1327 (Purdon Supp.1988)), is not inconsistent with the *DeShaney* opinion....

... However, we prefer not to rest our decision again on an affirmative duty to protect such students in this situation because the uncertainty of the law in this respect may cause further delay. We are advised that the trial of this case against the School District and the defendants in their official capacities has been held up during the pendency of the appeal by defendants on the denial of their motion for summary judgment on the claims against them in their individual capacities. Therefore, we believe it is more expedient to decide whether plaintiff's claim before us would withstand summary judgment even if we could not rely on the special relationship which the Supreme Court's footnote in *DeShaney* may still leave as a viable basis for liability.

II

The principal distinction between DeShaney's situation and that of Stoneking is that DeShaney's injuries resulted at the hands of a private actor, whereas Stoneking's resulted from the actions of a state employee....

....

It is immaterial for this purpose whether Wright's sexual abuse is viewed as attributable to the state. This consideration would be relevant had Stoneking sued Wright under section 1983, alleging that he acted under color of state law. She did not. Instead, the suit is against the School District and its supervisory officials, and they were incontestably acting under color of state law.

Defendants argue that Stoneking's emphasis on the fact that Wright was an agent and employee of the school district is merely an assertion of "supervisory liability", or respondeat superior, which cannot be a basis of liability. However, this is not a case in which Stoneking alleges that defendants are vicariously liable because of Wright's actions. Instead, she argues defendants are liable because of their own actions in adopting and maintaining a practice, custom or policy of reckless indifference to instances of known or suspected sexual abuse of students by teachers, in concealing complaints of abuse, and in discouraging students' complaints about such conduct. She argues that these practices, customs or policies created a climate which, at a minimum, facilitated sexual abuse of students by teachers in general, and that there was a causal relationship between

C. TORT IMMUNITY

these practices, customs or policies and the repeated sexual assaults against her by Wright. Thus, this is not respondeat superior in another guise, but an assertion of liability against the individual defendants based on theories recognized in a line of Supreme Court cases.

Nothing in *DeShaney* suggests that state officials may escape liability arising from their policies maintained in deliberate indifference to actions taken by their subordinates. As the Supreme Court recently reconfirmed in *City of Canton v. Harris*, ___ U.S. ___, 109 S.Ct. 1197, 1205 (1989), a municipality may be liable under section 1983 where its policymakers made "a deliberate choice to follow a course of action ... from among various alternatives," (quoting *Pembauer v. Cincinnati*, 475 U.S. 469, 483-84 (1986) (plurality op.)), and the policy chosen "reflects deliberate indifference to the constitutional rights of [the city's] inhabitants," 109 S.Ct. at 1206....

This is an independent basis for liability previously pled and preserved by Stoneking which is unrelated to the issue decided in *DeShaney*. Liability of municipal policymakers for policies or customs chosen or recklessly maintained is not dependent upon the existence of a "special relationship" between the municipal officials and the individuals harmed. *See Bordanaro v. McLeod*, 871 F.2d 1151 (1st Cir. 1989), [*cert. denied* 493 U.S. 820 (1989)]....

Thus, to the extent that the Supreme Court's remand of this case in light of *DeShaney* required us to consider whether Stoneking still may maintain a viable section 1983 claim if there is no predicate duty by defendants to protect her, we hold that she may because she has also alleged that defendants, with deliberate indifference to the consequences, established and maintained a policy, practice or custom which directly caused her constitutional harm.

....

IV

The principles applicable to defendants' assertion of qualified immunity have not changed to any significant degree since our opinion in *Stoneking I*. It is the defendants' burden to establish that they are entitled to such immunity. *Ryan v. Burlington County*, 860 F.2d 1199, 1204 n. 9 (3d Cir. 1988), *cert. denied*, ___ U.S. ___, 109 S.Ct. 1745 (1989). The defendants must show that their conduct did "not violate clearly established statutory or constitutional rights of which a reasonable person would have known." *Harlow v. Fitzgerald*, 457 U.S. 800, 818 (1982).

Under the test announced in *Harlow*, reasonableness is measured by an objective standard; arguments that the defendants desired to handle or subjectively believed that they had handled the incidents properly are irrelevant. *Anderson v. Creighton*, 483 U.S. 635, 641 (1987). The defendants are entitled to qualified immunity if reasonable officials in the defendants' position at the relevant time could have believed, in light of clearly established law, that their conduct comported with established legal standards. *See Id.*

It may seem ludicrous to be obliged to consider whether it was "clearly established" that it was impermissible for school teachers and staff to sexually molest students. Nonetheless, we construe the proper inquiry as whether it was established that the students' rights were constitutionally based. Applying this standard, we reiterate the conclusion we reached in *Stoneking I* that the constitutional right Stoneking alleges, to freedom from invasion of her personal security through sexual abuse, was well-established at the time the assaults upon her occurred. The Supreme Court in considering the closely analogous right implicated by corporal punishment in schools, held that "[a]mong the historic liberties ... protected [by the Due Process Clause] was a right to be free from ... unjustified intrusions on personal security." *Ingraham v. Wright*, 430 U.S. 651, 673 & n. 41 (1977)....

A teacher's sexual molestation of a student is an intrusion of the schoolchild's bodily integrity not substantively different for constitutional purposes from corporal punishment by teachers. Reasonable officials would have understood the "contours" of a student's right to bodily integrity, under the Due Process Clause, to encompass a student's right to be free from sexual assaults by his or her teachers. *See Anderson*, 483 U.S. at 639-40 (discussing level of particularity required for definition of clearly established rights).

Since a teacher's sexual molestation of a student could not possibly be deemed an acceptable practice, as some view teacher-inflicted corporal punishment, a student's right to be free from such molestation may be viewed as clearly established even before *Ingraham*. *See Rochin v. California*, 342 U.S. 165, 172 (1952) (substantive due process violation occurs where conduct "shocks the conscience"); *cf. Mitchell v. Forsyth*, 472 U.S. 511, 534 (1985) (right against warrantless security wiretaps was not "clearly established" where many successive administrations employed the practice and considered it constitutional).

We turn then from the issue of the clearly established constitutional right of Stoneking to be free from sexual abuse by school staff to an inquiry into the objective reasonableness of defendants' conduct from late 1980 through at least 1983 when Stoneking was molested by Wright while still a student. *Anderson* teaches us that this inquiry into reasonableness requires examination of the information possessed by the defendants. 483 U.S. at 641. We set forth some of the evidence in the record because the parties now agree that we are not limited to the allegations of the complaint on which our prior opinion was based. *But see Stoneking I*, 856 F.2d at 597-98 nn. 5, 6 & 7.

According to the deposition testimony of Theresa Rodgers, her social studies teacher Richard DeMarte sexually accosted her in late 1977 or early 1978. *See* 667 F.Supp. at 1100 (summarizing *Rodgers* deposition). She immediately reported the incident to Miller and Smith. They responded by warning her that it would be her word against the teacher's and that she should not tell her parents. *Id.* Although Smith told Rodgers that he would "take care" of the problem, DeMarte's personnel file shows no evidence of any disciplinary action

C. TORT IMMUNITY

taken against him; to the contrary, his teaching evaluation showed a perfect score. *Id.*

According to the deposition testimony of Judith Grove Sowers, she was sexually assaulted by Wright in 1979 and reported the incident to Miller and Smith. She claims that Smith told her "it was my [Sowers'] fault. That's why he wanted to clear up the rumors because he wanted the band to get back on their feet again.... He had told me that if the rumors were true ... I could find myself in front of a jury, in front of a judge, telling exactly what happened, that being that I had been drinking [and that I was] at his house voluntarily ... I wouldn't look very good is what he said." *Id.* at 1101 n. 24 (quoting deposition). Miller brought Wright to the office, asked Sowers to repeat her allegation in front of him, and asked Wright if it was true, which Wright denied....

According to the deposition testimony of Sowers' father, who requested a conference with Miller and Sowers about the incident, the defendants attempted to persuade him that no teacher would behave as his daughter alleged. 667 F.Supp. at 1101. Both Sowers and her father testified that she was presented with the option of recanting her story in front of the band or withdrawing from all band activities. Sowers stated that the band was assembled and she was called before it for this purpose, but fled from the room in tears.

As the district court noted, it could be inferred that "the 'forced apology' served as a trump card in the hands of Edward Wright," who could threaten his other victims with similar treatment if they reported his actions, *Id.* at 1101-02, and Stoneking in fact testified that she did not report Wright's assaults because "I knew about Judy Grove and what happened."

Smith's handwritten notes refer to three other incidents in 1981-1982 with respect to sexual harassment by DeMarte, the social studies teacher. In 1981, Lori Tsepelis complained to Miller and Smith that DeMarte had kissed her on the back of the neck several times while she was taking a make-up test.... Ms. Tsepelis' parents also complained. DeMarte admitted one kiss, explaining "that he had kissed her on the cheek as a thank you for her having brought food to him at the radio station on two occasions in November." *Id.* at 74. Smith conceded that when a teacher kisses a student it is generally a sexual advance but Smith and Miller merely arranged that Ms. Tsepelis would, for the remainder of the semester, pick up her homework from DeMarte via Miller and that she would not be scheduled for DeMarte's class in the future. Although Smith told DeMarte "he had not used good judgment in having [Ms. Tsepelis] alone in the room," *Id.* at 93, he placed no discipline report in DeMarte's file.

Two months later, two female students reported to Miller that another student, Lorie Lamberson, was crying in the restroom and when she emerged she told Smith and Miller that she had gone to DeMarte's room with a friend to get a make-up assignment, that he sent her friend away, blindfolded her to demonstrate the sense of touch, and after doing so was down on his hands and knees looking up her dress. The student was so distraught that she was sent to the nurse's office and then told to contact her parents. *Id.* at 99-106.... DeMarte admitted the incident except for the complaint that he had looked up Ms. Lamberson's dress. Nonetheless, Smith's notes continue, "'I also pointed out that it was her word against [DeMarte's] and that Mr. Miller and I would have to judge from that.'" *Id.* at 115. Again, the only action taken was to arrange that the student be scheduled for a different class and no reprimand or other note was placed in DeMarte's file.

The next year, another parent called to complain about DeMarte's relationship with a student because DeMarte had asked the student to sit on his lap at a Halloween party on a social occasion and again no written warning was placed in DeMarte's file.

In sum, there is evidence in the record that between 1978 and 1982 Smith and Miller received at least five complaints about sexual assaults of female students by teachers and staff members; that Shuey was told about some of these complaints; that Smith recorded these and other allegations in a secret file at home rather than in the teachers' personnel files, which a jury could view as active concealment; that the defendants gave such teachers excellent performance evaluations, which a jury could view as communication by the defendants to the teachers that the conduct of which they were accused would not be considered to reflect negatively on them; and that Smith and Miller discouraged and/or intimidated students and parents from pursuing complaints, on one occasion by forcing a student to publicly recant her allegation.

For this purpose, the fact that Stoneking did not complain to the defendants about Wright's molestation of her is not dispositive.... Although Stoneking's failure to complain may be relevant at trial to her credibility or the causation issue for qualified immunity purposes it is sufficient that there is adequate evidence that defendants were on notice of complaints of sexual harassment of students by teachers and staff at the school.

In their brief, defendants correctly state that "[i]n determining whether or not a public official is entitled to a defense of qualified immunity, one must identify legal principles governing analogous factual situations at the time the alleged constitutional violation occurred, and if any existed, determine whether the public officials should have related this established law to the situation before them."

After *Monell* had established that government officials could be held liable for policies and practices which they established and maintained, this court held in two cases in 1981 that public officials in administrative positions with notice of assaultive behavior by their subordinates must not take actions which communicate that they encourage or even condone such behavior. [*Commonwealth v. Porter*, 659 F.2d 306 (3d Cir. 1981), *cert. denied*, 458 U.S. 1121 (1982); *Black v. Stephens*, 662 F.2d 181 (3d Cir. 1981), *cert. denied*, 455 U.S. 1008 (1982)].

....

In sum, although the mere failure of supervisory officials to act or investigate cannot be the basis of liability, *see Chinchello v. Fenton*, 805 F.2d 126, 133-34 (3d Cir. 1986), by at least 1981 when this court's cases in *Porter* and *Black* were decided (both incidentally arising, as this case does, in the Western District of

C. TORT IMMUNITY

Pennsylvania), it was clearly established law that such officials may not with impunity maintain a custom, practice or usage that communicated condonation or authorization of assaultive behavior.

If the testimony of the various complainants is believed, Smith and Miller discouraged and minimized reports of sexual misconduct by teachers. A jury could construe such actions, as plaintiff's expert did, as "encourag[ing] a climate to flourish where innocent girls were victimized." ... Although ... [it] may seem a farfetched possibility, there is enough in this record from Smith and Miller's suggestion to Ms. Lamberson about "framing" DeMarte and their statement that it was "her word against his," as well as from the forced apology by Judy Grove Sowers about her allegations of Wright's sexual harassment, that a jury could reasonably conclude that such discouragement of complaints amounted to a communication of condonation of the teacher's behavior. Thus, Stoneking has asserted a sufficiently tenable theory that there was an "affirmative link," *see Rizzo v. Goode*, 423 U.S. at 371, between her injury and the policies and practices that Smith and Miller employed and affirmative acts they took in furtherance of them to make this a jury issue.

We are cognizant that defendants deny many of these allegations, and assert that they imposed an adequate policy to deal with Stoneking's allegations against Wright by ordering Wright "never to get into a 'one on one' situation with female students again." Whether there was an adequate policy and whether their other defenses have merit will be up to the jury.

On the other hand, we must conclude, in light of our precedent, that Stoneking's claims against Shuey amount to mere "inaction and insensitivity" on his part. We cannot discern from the record any affirmative acts by Shuey on which Stoneking can base a claim of toleration, condonation or encouragement of sexual harassment by teachers which occurred in one of the various schools within his district.

For the foregoing reasons, we conclude that the district court did not err in denying the motion for summary judgment of defendants Smith and Miller on grounds of qualified immunity, but we conclude that Shuey's motion should have been granted.

....

---

1. For further discussion of the legal problems associated with recovery under § 1983, *see* Valente, *School District and Official Liability for Teacher Sexual Abuse of Students Under 42 U.S.C. sec. 1983*, 57 Educ. L. Rep. 645 (1990).

2. The Fifth Circuit Court of Appeals heard a case similar to *Stoneking* in 1992. In *Doe v. Taylor Indep. Sch. Dist.*, 975 F.2d 137 (5th Cir. 1992), a high school student brought a civil rights suit against her teacher, school district, superintendent, and principal, alleging violation of due process and equal protection arising from sexual molestation by her teacher. The Court of Appeals held (1) that there was a constitutional right under the Fourteenth Amendment to be free from sexual molestation by a state-employed school teacher; and (2) superintendent and principal had a duty to protect students from intrusions into bodily integrity and were therefore unprotected by the Qualified Immunity Doctrine.

3. From *Stoneking* and other Third Circuit cases cited by the Court (*Commonwealth v. Porter*, and *Black v. Stephens*), it is clear that schools may not maintain a custom, practice, or usage which indicates that the schools authorize or condone sexual misconduct of teachers with and against students. According to the Tenth Circuit, schools also may not maintain a custom of failure to receive, investigate or act on complaints of violations of students' constitutional rights to be free of sexual abuse at the hands of district employees. *See Gates v. Unified Sch. Dist. No. 449 of Leavenworth County, Kansas*, 996 F.2d 1035 (10th Cir. 1993) (Plaintiff failed to establish a custom of school officials failing to receive or investigate complaints of sexual abuse; and plaintiff failed to establish that the principal had any notice of sexual misconduct by teacher which the principal failed to investigate, or which the principal tacitly authorized).

4. Despite the fact that the abuse came at the hands of a state-employed teacher, the Court in *Stoneking II* chose to approach this case from a theory of deliberate indifference on the part of school officials, rather than a "special relationship" theory. With respect to the claim against the principal and assistant principal, a "special relationship" approach was not necessary. Would it have worked for the claim against the superintendent?

From this, can we say that, despite a duty to protect students from intrusion into bodily integrity, there can be no successful claim against the school and its administrators for sexual abuse through the actions of non-state actors? Which theory could be used? Special relationship? Deliberate indifference stemming from established custom, practice, and lack of action? In *Elliott v. New Miami Bd. of Educ.*, 799 F. Supp. 818 (S.D. Ohio 1992), a student filed a claim under § 1983 alleging a failure of the school to protect against repeated harassment and assaults by classmates. The District Court dismissed the claim, holding that the school district did not have a special relationship with the student giving rise to the duty to protect, and that liability could not be imposed on the school system for its policies, customs, or practices where violative acts were committed by private actors.

Should the degree of notice make a difference? What if the school knows that a certain private actor has the propensity to commit such violative acts and fails to take protective action? *See Dorothy J. v. Little Rock Sch. Dist.*, 794 F. Supp. 1405 (E.D. Ark. 1992). In *Dorothy J.*, the mother of a developmentally disabled student in a high school community-based instruction program brought a civil rights lawsuit against the school district and various state and local officials after her son was allegedly sexually molested and raped by a ward of the Department of Human Services. The Court held that no special or custodial relationship existed between the child and the state actors for the allegedly violative actions committed by a private actor. The Court continued and held that despite knowledge of the attacker's violent propensities, the state defendants and school defendants owed no constitutional duty to protect the student.

For more on the "special relationship" and "deliberate indifference" theories, consider the excerpt from Valente, *Liability for Teacher's Sexual Misconduct with Students — Closing and Opening Vistas*, 74. Ed. Law Rep. 1021 (1992) *infra*.

5. Readers may think, at first, that sovereign immunity relieving school officials of tort liability, is unfair to injured, helpless plaintiffs. However, such immunity does not necessarily give schools carte blanche to operate schools in any manner desirable. Despite sovereign immunity, complaints filed under 42 U.S.C. § 1983 are allowed in sexual assault cases. *Thurmond v. Richmond County Bd. of Educ.*, 207 Ga. App. 437, 428 S.E.2d 392 (1993). In addition, teachers and other school personnel are liable for their own actions as individuals. *See also Burns v. Board of Educ. of the City of Stamford*, presented later in this chapter.

VALENTE, LIABILITY FOR TEACHER'S SEXUAL MISCONDUCT WITH STUDENTS — CLOSING AND OPENING VISTAS, 74 Educ. L. Rep. 1021, et seq. (1992)*

....

I. *Claims Under 42 U.S.C. § 1983 Based upon a General Right of Bodily Integrity*

....

The nascent state of the federal law is illustrated by the recent case of *D.R. v. Middle Bucks Area Vocational Technical School.*[5] .... The Third Circuit Court of Appeals there revisited a crucial liability theory that was first considered, but not resolved, by that Circuit two years ago. The question is whether § 1983 liability for sexual molestation of students at school may be imposed upon school districts and superiors because the school has a "special relationship" to its students, which creates a duty to protect them, at least while at school, from actions that deprive them of their constitutional right to bodily security. Although the few decided cases to date rejected the "special relationship" argument, the *D.R.* decision should command serious attention because that contention is not likely to disappear....

....

The Background Facts In D.R. The case came to the Court of Appeals from the district court's dismissal of amended complaints by several female high school students whose fact allegations, accepted as true for purposes of the appeal, were as follows. Three female high school students at the Middle Bucks

---

*Copyright © 1992 by West Publishing Company. Reprinted with permission.
[5] ___ F.2d ___ (3rd Cir. 1991).

Area Vocational Technical School were physically, verbally, and sexually molested by their male classmates, on a regular basis over a period of several months, in a unisex bathroom and an adjoining darkroom that were part of the school's graphic arts classroom. The assaults took place on an average of two to four times per week from January to May of 1990 and consisted of offensive touching of the girls' breasts and genitalia, sodomization, and forcing them to watch similar acts on other students. During that period, the student teacher in charge of the graphic arts class was or should have been present, and heard or should have heard what was going on. The student teacher experienced difficulty in controlling the class and was allegedly exposed to male student misconduct in the main classroom, including obscene language and gestures, and physical, though not sexual, offensive touching of other females, including herself.

One female student told the Assistant Director of Middle Bucks School of an attempt to force her into the darkroom to engage in sexual conduct, but he took no action to correct the situation. Other school supervisors knew of severe nonsexual misconduct occurring in the graphic arts classroom. On the foregoing assertions, the students sued the Vocational School, the related local school district, the county Intermediate Unit, and individual teachers and officials, as well as the offending male students, under 42 U.S.C. § 1983.

The dismissal of the action against the male students (who were not state actors) was not challenged on appeal. Regarding the other defendants, the district court found that the state compulsory attendance laws created a special custodial relationship between the school defendants and the students, and an affirmative constitutional duty to protect plaintiffs. But it dismissed the amended complaints as failing to allege sufficient knowledge by the school defendants to charge them with reckless indifference to plaintiffs' rights. The Third Circuit later interpreted this curious ruling as a finding that the defendants were entitled to qualified immunity.

The Third Circuit Disposition. The Court of Appeals affirmed dismissal on its threshold finding that the school defendants had no constitutional duty to protect the plaintiffs from peer molestation, because there was no basis to find a special relationship that would support such a duty. "We hold that compulsory attendance laws cannot be viewed as creating a special custodial relationship between schools and students akin to that between a state and its prisoners or those otherwise involuntarily committed."[15]

Referring to the Supreme Court's discussion in *DeShaney* of confinement cases which recognized an affirmative constitutional duty of state officials to protect state-confined prisoners, mental hospital patients, and state-placement of child wards in foster homes, the majority judges in *D.R.* concluded that the special relationship foundation of those cases does not exist in school relationships to students.

---

[15] ___ F.2d at ___.

C. TORT IMMUNITY 1481

....

The court then dispatched the second *D.R.* contention for § 1983 liability, deliberate indifference of the school defendants, with the observation that "section 1983 liability may not be predicated upon a [deliberate indifference] ... theory where private actors committed the underlying violative acts." It found *Stoneking II* inapplicable, because that case presented injury by a state actor, the school band director. The "special relationship" thesis thus took on a second significance, for without it, molestation by a subordinate student rather than a state actor, escaped the charge of "deliberate indifference".

The Chief Judge on the *D.R.* panel, who authored both *Stoneking I* and *Stoneking II*, predictably entered a forceful dissent. Noting the clear case recognition that the plaintiffs had "a constitutional liberty interest in 'safety and freedom from bodily restraint,'"[16] she denied that the *DeShaney* decision covered the *D.R.* setting, and invoked, as more apt, the confinement precedents that extended § 1983 protection to children in foster homes. Stressing the control of the school locus of student injury by state employees, and the compelled attendance (*sic* confinement) of students by law, and the subjection of those students by law to the authority of public school teachers, Chief Judge Sloviter made a strong case for analogizing the plight of the graphic arts students to the involuntary confinement cases, and for rejecting the parental protection rationale that underlay the majority's analogy to the *DeShaney* case. To the end of demonstrating the relevance and persuasiveness of the prison, hospital and foster home cases to *D.R.*, and to buttress its finding of sufficient official restraint and confinement in the *D.R.* circumstances, the dissent further noted that *D.R.* had repeatedly requested, but had been denied by the student teacher, a pass to use a different lavatory other than the unisex lavatory which the male students used to harass the female students. In brief, the dissenter adhered to the "special relationships" analysis of her *Stoneking* opinions.

....

Random Observations....

....

A comparison of *D.R.* with *Stoneking* indicates the treachery of inflexible formal doctrine. *D.R.* is uniquely different from *Stoneking II*. Unlike Stoneking, who apparently was a healthy, normal adolescent, in a common school environment, D.R. presented uncommon facts:

(1) the physical confinement imposed upon D.R. by the school's arrangement of adjoining classroom, darkroom and unisex lavatory (which no student could avoid entering for use) was much more restrictive of student movement, and much more conducive to sexual abuse, than normal school classroom and lavatory settings;

---

[16] ___ F.2d at ___.

(2) D.R. was more like a vulnerable elementary school child than a brassy adolescent. As a transferee from regular school to the vo-tech school, a fact known to her school superiors, she was especially insecure, having no other place to go;

(3) D.R. was placed in a classroom zoo run by an overwhelmed student-teacher — facts which school authorities knew.

In such circumstances, it would not be rash to find a school duty to protect this particular student in this particular environment. One might argue that such a situation reveals no more than negligence, which, however egregious, is not actionable under § 1983, but the combination of the above factors adds up to "confinement," rendering the student unable to take care of herself, and constitutes ground for finding the requisite special relationship.

The need to redress such injuries as were suffered in *D.R.* is manifest, and the prospect for such redress under state tort law is not bright. Since the federal tort law is still in its infancy, there is hope that it will develop to fashion a better balance between the concerns of vulnerable students and of school defendants. We can only await more cases to see whether it will move in that direction.

....

---

1. Is the decision in *D.R.*, as presented by Valente, more dependent on the fact that the court opted not to go with the *Stoneking II* theory of "deliberate indifference" by school authorities (instead of using the "special relationship" doctrine) or by the fact that the perpetrators of the sexual abuse and harassment were students? How would the Third Circuit decide a case with teacher-perpetrators and the "special relationship" theory? What about a case with student-perpetrators and the "deliberate indifference" theory?

2. In addition to 42 U.S.C. Section 1983, students have also brought sexual misconduct claims against school personnel under Title IX of the Educational Amendments of 1972, 20 U.S.C. Sec. 1681. In *Franklin v. Gwinnett County Pub. Schs.*, 112 S. Ct. 1028 (1992) a unanimous United States Supreme Court ruled that a school district was liable for money damages for gender discrimination under Title IX. This case effectively overruled previous decisions that limited entitlement for sexual abuse to injunctive relief.

In *Franklin* a female high school student alleged sexual harassment by a teacher including forcible kissing, and coercive intercourse. Thereafter, a mutual agreement was arranged between the teacher and the school district resulting in the teacher's resignation. No disciplinary action was taken despite the student's complaints, however, and then she sued under Title IX.

Although Title IX does not expressly provide students the right to state a claim for damages for sexual imposition, the case of *Cannon v. University of Chicago*, 441 U.S. 677 (1979) held that such a right is implied. Following this decision, the *Gwinnett* Court stated that where Congress has not been explicit in determining a remedy under statute, all appropriate remedies are deemed to be available including money damages.

See Chapter 4 for the case of *Franklin v. Gwinnett County Schools* and a more extensive explanation of its reach.

DOE v. ESCAMBIA COUNTY SCHOOL BOARD
District Court of Appeal of Florida, First District
599 So. 2d 226 (1992)

ZEHMER, JUDGE:

Raymond Doe and Susan Doe, as parents and natural guardians of Daughter Doe, appeal a summary judgment entered in favor of the Escambia County School Board. The Does sued the School Board for personal injuries to their daughter, alleging that its negligent failure to properly supervise students under its control resulted in Daughter Doe being taken from her school grounds and raped. The summary judgment is based on the trial court's ruling that the level of security of which the Does complain is a discretionary function that subjects the Board to the defense of sovereign immunity. The court further ruled that even if the complaint were aimed at an operational function to which the sovereign immunity defense does not apply, there was no showing that the Board breached any legal duty to supervise Daughter Doe's activities. We reverse.

Briefly, the evidence viewed in a light most favorable to the Does' case established the following. Daughter Doe is an emotionally handicapped and learning disabled student who was attending Woodham High School at the time of this incident. Although she was 14 years old and in ninth grade at that time, she functioned on a third or fourth grade level and was extremely naive and socially immature. On the morning in question, three of the teachers at Woodham High School were aware that Daughter Doe was behaving out of character because she twice changed out of her conservative dress into a mini-skirt. Each time, a teacher compelled her to change back into the dress she initially wore to school. During Daughter Doe's lunch period, a male student took her by the arm, walked her out to the school parking lot, put her in a car, and took her to a house. At the same time, several other male students also left the school by car and went to this house. Daughter Doe was taken into a bedroom where five of the students forced her to have sex with them.

The essence of the Does' cause of action is that the School Board owed Daughter Doe a duty to provide reasonably safe conditions and supervision while she and other students were under the school's control, and that it breached this duty by negligently failing to supervise and control Daughter Doe and the other students under its control so as to prevent their unauthorized departure from the school campus. In ruling on the School Board's motion for summary judgment, the court made the following statement in the appealed order:

> It appears that what Plaintiffs are complaining of is the level of security provided on the school campus. This Court is of the opinion that such

consideration is a discretionary function subject to the defense of sovereign immunity.

The trial court erred in characterizing the plaintiff's cause of action as one for lack of adequate security; the complaint and the evidence of record clearly show that it is for the negligent breach of the school's duty to adequately supervise students under its control.

The School Board and its teachers are under a common law and statutory duty to supervise the activity of students under their care and control, and such duty is operational, not discretionary, and is not protected by sovereign immunity. The scope of that duty is determined from the circumstances involved, the applicable statutes, *e.g.*, §§ 232.25 and 232.257, Fla.Stat. (1989), and the rules and regulations adopted by the Board to implement these statutory provisions. The record contains rules and regulations adopted by the School Board which require that school administrative and teaching personnel provide the required supervision during school hours both in the school building and its appurtenant areas, including the parking lot. Providing inadequate or no supervision at all is a breach of this duty.

....

Recall *Tinkham v. Groveport Madison Local Sch. Dist.*, 602 N.E.2d 256 (Ohio. App. 1991), presented in the notes following *Hurlburt*. In addition to holding that the criminal, intentional sexual assault by the taxicab driver was an intervening cause of the child's injuries, the court also held that sovereign immunity applied to the school district's decision to transport the developmentally disabled child by taxicab. The district's decision in *Tinkham* was declared "discretionary," and was thus protected by sovereign immunity. "This type of decision requiring a high degree of discretion by a government body is precisely the type contemplated under the doctrine of sovereign immunity." *Id.* at 262. The district's decisions, like those in *Doe v. Escambia*, regarding supervision of students were declared "operational," while the provision of security was discretionary. What are the differences?

In a similar case, the Supreme Court of Oregon distinguished between the discretionary decisions regarding number and allocation of security and the operational decisions regarding supervision of students. *Mosley v. Portland Sch. Dist. No. 1J*, 315 Or. 85, 843 P.2d 415 (1992). The plaintiff had been in a fight and argued that the lack of security and the school's failure to break up the fight caused her injuries. The court held that the discretionary decisions on the number and allocation of security personnel immunized the school district from liability. In addition, the court held that while inadequate supervision is not immunized, the plaintiff failed to support this claim with sufficient evidence.

Obviously, the label the courts put on the school district's activity is critical to the determination of liability. The *Escambia* court held that supervision

C. TORT IMMUNITY

decisions were not immune from challenge because such decisions are operational. *But see Doe v. Howell*, 212 Ga. App. 305, 441 S.E.2d 767 (1994) (Second-grade teacher's decision regarding amount of supervision to provide in classroom was "discretionary act," for which the teacher was entitled to qualified immunity when, while classroom was darkened during overhead projector show, one of the teacher's students sexually molested another student).

Worse yet may be the determination of when the rape of a student by students occurred. In *Williams v. Columbus Bd. of Educ.*, 82 Ohio App. 3d 18, 610 N.E.2d 1175 (1992), the court held that the school does not have the duty to provide after-hours protection to students. (Female student stays after school to work on project and is raped by other students).

PARKER v. WYNN

Court of Appeals of Georgia
211 Ga. App. 78, 438 S.E.2d 147 (1993)

BLACKBURN, JUDGE:

On March 8, 1991, the appellant, Christopher Parker, by next friend brought this action against the Harris County School District and James Wynn, alleging that Wynn's negligent supervision of a high school classroom resulted in a permanent injury to Parker's right eye. The trial court eventually granted summary judgment for the School District and Wynn on the basis of sovereign or official immunity, and Parker appeals from that grant of summary judgment for Wynn.

It appears from the record that Wynn was a teacher in charge of a senior physical education class at Harris County High School. On November 18, 1987, written examinations were being administered to senior and freshmen physical education classes in the school gym. As the students reported to the gym, Wynn stood at the doorway instructing them not to change clothing. When the tardy bell rang, Wynn went to his office to retrieve his roll book and the test papers. While he did so, one of the senior students threw pecans at a group of freshmen students, striking Parker's right eye.

Although the action in this case was filed after the 1991 amendment of Art. I, Sec. II, Par. IX of the Georgia Constitution of 1983, the cause of action accrued prior to the effective date of that amendment. Accordingly, the 1991 amendment of that constitutional provision regarding sovereign immunity is inapplicable here, and sovereign immunity could still be waived to the extent of any liability insurance provided. *Curtis v. Bd. of Regents etc. of Ga.*, 262 Ga. 226, 416 S.E.2d 510 (1992); *Thigpen v. McDuffie County Bd. of Ed.*, 255 Ga. 59, 335 S.E.2d 112 (1985).

In moving for summary judgment, the school district established that it had not purchased liability insurance, and for that reason had not waived its sovereign immunity. Wynn, however, was insured under a private liability insurance policy issued to the Professional Association of Georgia Educators. It is undisputed that his alleged negligent supervision of his class constituted a discretionary act performed in the exercise of his official capacity as teacher, involving no wilfulness, malice, or corruption, for which he would enjoy immunity in the absence of a waiver. *See Sisson v. Douglas County School District*, 181 Ga.App. 77, 351 S.E.2d 272 (1986). The sole issue in this appeal thus is whether Wynn's private liability insurance resulted in a waiver of that immunity otherwise available to him. We conclude that it did not.

Prior to the 1991 amendment of Art. I, Sec. II, Par. IX of the Georgia Constitution, the defense of sovereign immunity was waived for tort claims against the State or its departments and agencies to the extent of any liability insurance coverage provided for such claims. However, nothing in that former constitutional provision authorized an individual to waive sovereign immunity for either the State or himself by purchasing private liability insurance covering his acts.

"Immunity from suit is a basic attribute of sovereignty. The sovereignty of the State is supreme, and to maintain that sovereignty the supremacy must also be maintained...." (Citation and punctuation omitted.) The immunity is vested in the sovereign, and assertion or waiver of that defense is the original prerogative of the sovereign, and not the individual. *See, e.g., Martin v. Ga. Dept. of Public Safety*, 257 Ga. 300, 357 S.E.2d 569 (1987), and *Swofford v. Cooper*, 184 Ga.App. 50, 360 S.E.2d 624 (1987), where the immunity defense was unavailable to State officials employed by departments of the State which had waived immunity by purchasing liability insurance.

... In the instant case, there being no waiver of immunity by the school district, this action against Wynn in his official capacity as agent of that entity is likewise barred by official immunity.

Parker contends that shielding Wynn with official immunity obviates his need for any private insurance and thus serves no purpose other than providing a windfall for the private insurance carrier in this case. However, notwithstanding the immunity he enjoys for claims based on his discretionary acts performed in the exercise of his official duties, Wynn remains subject to suit individually for his acts done with wilfulness, malice, or corruption, or for his negligent performance of purely ministerial functions. *Hennessy v. Webb*, 245 Ga. 329, 264 S.E.2d 878 (1980). Inasmuch as Wynn's private insurance protects him from that exposure, finding Wynn immune in this case does not bestow a windfall upon the private insurer.

Judgment affirmed.

....

---

1. What is your definition of a sovereign? Does the concept of "sovereign immunity" include school districts, as they act as agents for the state? For the city/municipality? For both? The plaintiffs in *Farace v. Board of Educ. of*

C. TORT IMMUNITY

Guilford (No. CV91-0239185S, Conn. Super. Ct. 1992), argued that sovereign immunity was inapplicable in its suit against the school board to recover injuries allegedly suffered when two fighting students pushed the plaintiff to the floor. The court held that "The protection afforded by [the doctrine of sovereign immunity] has been extended to agents of state acting in its behalf. A town board of education can be an agent of the state for some purposes and an agent of the municipality for other purposes. A town board of education potentially enjoys immunity ... for acts carried out within its governmental capacity." *Id.*

Because the plaintiff's allegation dealt with the defendant's maintenance of control in the school, the court held that the defendant, for this purpose, was not acting as an agent for the state or for the municipality. Sovereign immunity was inapplicable to bar the claim. However, the court continued and said that the supervision of students in a school is a discretionary concern, immunizing the defendant from liability. Summary judgment for the defendant school board, which has no specific duty to supervise students, was granted.

2. The State of Texas has a statute which waives a school district's sovereign immunity and a teacher's qualified immunity in cases involving the "operation" or "use" of motor vehicles. Does this statute extend to injuries suffered in an auto mechanics class? The Texas Court of Appeals said no. In *Naranjo v. Southwest Indep. Sch. Dist.*, 777 S.W.2d 190 (Tex. App. 1989), the Court held that working on a carburetor in a mechanics class did not constitute use or operation as contemplated by the state; both the teacher and the district were immune from suit.

3. Recall *Hurlburt v. Noxon*, presented earlier in the chapter, which held that the school district's duty of care to a student terminates when that student exits the school bus before the bus reaches its destination. In *Goston v. Hutchison*, 853 S.W.2d 729 (Tex. App. 1993), the court held that the school district and the bus driver were immune from suit involving students who exited the bus prior to its designated stop and were subsequently involved in a car accident.

BURNS v. BOARD OF EDUCATION OF STAMFORD

Supreme Court of Connecticut
228 Conn. 640, 638 A.2d 1 (1994)

PETERS, CHIEF JUSTICE:

The principal issue in this certified appeal is whether a school child may bring an action for the negligent maintenance of public school grounds during school hours because he is one of a foreseeable class of victims and thus qualifies for an exception to the doctrine of governmental immunity. The plaintiffs, David Burns and his mother, Darlene Vrendburgh, as next friend, brought a four count action against the defendants, the superintendent of schools, William R. Papallo, the Stamford board of education and the city of Stamford, after David had been injured in a fall on an icy high school courtyard during school hours. The trial court rendered partial summary judgment in favor of the defendants on all counts sounding in negligence on the grounds that the alleged negligent acts were discretionary in nature and that no exception to the doctrine of governmental immunity encompassed such claims. The plaintiffs appealed that decision of the trial court to the Appellate Court, which affirmed, and we granted certification to appeal to this court. We reverse the judgment of the Appellate Court.

The decision of the Appellate Court recites the pertinent facts and procedural history. "On January 13, 1988, David, a student at West Hill High School in Stamford, was walking across the courtyard en route to his guidance counselor's office when he slipped and fell on a sheet of ice, fracturing his left elbow. The courtyard is the main access between the two buildings that comprise the high school. The area was not sanded or salted and no warnings had been issued to the students as to its condition. School policy under which the school custodians operated called for inspection of the entire area by the head custodian who would order sanding and salting as necessary.

"The gravamen of the fourth count of the complaint is that the defendant superintendent of schools was negligent in failing to ensure that the courtyard was properly salted and sanded and in failing to warn of the icy conditions existing in the courtyard....

"The superintendent's affidavit, filed in conjunction with the motion for summary judgment, indicated that his duties as superintendent did not include the personal inspection of the grounds of the high school or verification that ice and snow conditions had been corrected. He stated that he did not visit the high school, was unaware of the icy conditions and did not instruct or encourage any student to use the courtyard on the day in question.

"The head custodian stated in a deposition that the decision of whether to salt and sand the premises was his to make and was not the superintendent's decision. The defendants filed a motion for partial summary judgment as to the negligence and derivative suit counts, arguing that the superintendent was protected under the doctrine of governmental immunity. The motion was granted." *Burns v. Board of Education*, 30 Conn.App. 594, 596-97, 621 A.2d 1350 (1993).

On the plaintiffs' appeal, the Appellate Court held in relevant part that

> "[b]ecause there was no duty imposed on the superintendent to ensure that the courtyard was sanded and salted, he was not negligent and, therefore, he was entitled to summary judgment.... [E]ven if the superintendent possessed a duty, the duty was discretionary and fell within the ambit of the doctrine of governmental immunity.... Any duty to sand and salt the courtyard in this case would affect, not only David, but every member of the student population at West Hill High School. [Because it] was not apparent that the failure to salt and sand the high school courtyard would be likely to subject David to imminent harm ... the trial court properly determined that the doctrine of governmental immunity applied and that the foreseeable victim exception was inapplicable. Thus, summary judgment was proper." *Id.* at 598-601, 621 A.2d 1350.

C. TORT IMMUNITY

We granted the plaintiffs certification to appeal limited to the following question: "Whether there is a 'foreseeable class of victim' exception to the governmental immunity doctrine which would include students allegedly the victims of improper school maintenance?" We answer this question in the affirmative and, in the circumstances alleged by the pleadings in this case, reverse the judgment of the Appellate Court.

The doctrines that determine the tort liability of municipal employees are well established. Although municipalities are generally immune from liability in tort, municipal employees historically were personally liable for their own tortious conduct. *Evon v. Andrews*, 211 Conn. 501, 505, 559 A.2d 1131 (1989). The doctrine of governmental immunity has provided some exceptions to the general rule of tort liability for municipal employees. "'[A] municipal employee ... has a qualified immunity in the performance of a governmental duty, but he may be liable if he misperforms a ministerial act, as opposed to a discretionary act.... The word "ministerial" refers to a duty which is to be performed in a prescribed manner without the exercise of judgment or discretion....'" *Evon v. Andrews*, *supra*, 211 Conn. at 505, 559 A.2d at 1131.

The plaintiffs acknowledge that any duty owed by the defendant superintendent to the plaintiff child was discretionary in nature. To succeed in their claim of liability, therefore, they must be entitled to recover within one of the exceptions to a municipal employee's qualified immunity for discretionary acts. Our cases recognize three such exceptions:

> "first, where the circumstances make it apparent to the public officer that his or her failure to act would be likely to subject an identifiable person to imminent harm ... second, where a statute specifically provides for a cause of action against a municipality or municipal official for failure to enforce certain laws ... and third, where the alleged acts involve malice, wantonness or intent to injure, rather than negligence." (Citations omitted.) *Id.*

The only exception to the qualified immunity of a municipal employee for discretionary acts that is of relevance to the present case is the exception permitting a tort action in circumstances of perceptible imminent harm to an identifiable person. We have construed this exception to apply not only to identifiable individuals but also to narrowly defined identified classes of foreseeable victims. The plaintiffs contend that the plaintiff school child was a member of a foreseeable class of victims to whom the superintendent owed a special duty of care and, thus, the defense of governmental immunity should not lie. We agree.

The existence of a duty of care, an essential element of negligence, is a matter of law for the court to decide. "A duty to act with reasonable care to prevent harm to a plaintiff which, if violated, may give rise to tort liability is based on a 'special relationship' between the plaintiff and the defendant. *See* W. Prosser, *Torts* § 56 (4th ed. 1971)." "A duty to use care may arise from a contract, from a statute, or from circumstances under which a reasonable person, knowing what he knew or should have known, would anticipate that harm of the general nature of that suffered was likely to result from his act or failure to act." *Calderwood v. Bender*, 189 Conn. 580, 584, 457 A.2d 313 (1983).

"The ultimate test of the existence of a duty to use care is found in the foreseeability that harm may result if it is not exercised...." (Citations omitted; internal quotation marks omitted.) *Frankovitch v. Burton*, 185 Conn. 14, 20-21, 440 A.2d 254 (1981). "Foreseeability" in this context is a flexible concept, and may be supported by reasonable reliance, impeding others who might seek to render aid, statutory duties, property ownership or other factors. Moreover, just as the doctrine of governmental immunity and its exceptions are the product of the policy considerations that aid the law in determining whether the interests of a particular type are entitled to protection; so may evolving expectations of a maturing society change the harm that may reasonably be considered foreseeable.

In delineating the scope of a foreseeable class of victims exception to governmental immunity, our courts have considered numerous criteria, including the imminency of any potential harm, the likelihood that harm will result from a failure to act with reasonable care, and the identifiability of the particular victim. Other courts, in carving out similar exceptions to their respective doctrines of governmental immunity, have also considered whether the legislature specifically designated an identifiable subclass as the intended beneficiaries of certain acts; *see, e.g., Halvorson v. Dahl*, 89 Wash.2d 673, 676, 574 P.2d 1190 (1978); whether the relationship was of a voluntary nature; *McLeod v. Grant County School District*, 42 Wash.2d 316, 319, 255 P.2d 360 (1953); the seriousness of the injury threatened; *Irwin v. Ware, supra*, 392 Mass. at 756, 467 N.E.2d 1292; the duration of the threat of injury; *Id.*; and whether the persons at risk had the opportunity to protect themselves from harm. *Id.*

Applying these factors to the circumstances of this case, we note that statutory and constitutional mandates demonstrate that school children attending public schools during school hours are intended to be the beneficiaries of certain duties of care. Statutes describe the responsibilities of school boards and superintendents to maintain and care for property used for school purposes. The supervisory responsibilities of the superintendent of schools are not automatically abrogated by the designation of a head custodian to undertake immediate responsibility for the salting and sanding of the school campus on any particular day.

Statutes also describe the responsibilities of school children to attend school. The presence of the plaintiff child on the school premises where he was injured was not voluntary. As a fourteen year old at the time of the accident, he was statutorily compelled to attend school and to obey school rules and discipline formulated and enforced pursuant to statute. His corresponding entitlement to a public education has constitutional underpinnings in this state.

The result of this network of statutory and constitutional provisions is that the superintendent of schools bears the responsibility for failing to act to prevent the risk of imminent harm to school children as an identifiable class of beneficiaries of his statutory duty of care. At least during school hours on school days, when

C. TORT IMMUNITY 1491

parents are statutorily compelled to relinquish protective custody of their children to a school board and its employees, the superintendent has the duty to protect the pupils in the board's custody from dangers that may reasonably be anticipated. As a matter of policy, this conclusion comports with our case law that has traditionally recognized that children require special consideration when dangerous conditions are involved.

In this case, the plaintiff school child slipped and fell due to icy conditions on a main accessway of the school campus, during school hours, while the child was compelled by statute to be on those school grounds. Unlike the incident in *Evon v. Andrews*, *supra*, 211 Conn. 501, 559 A.2d 1131, this accident could not have occurred at any time in the future; rather, the danger was limited to the duration of the temporary icy condition in this particularly "treacherous" area of the campus. Further, the potential for harm from a fall on ice was significant and foreseeable. Under these circumstances, we conclude that the plaintiff school child was one of a class of foreseeable victims to whom the superintendent owed a duty of protection in relation to the maintenance and safety of the school grounds, and accordingly governmental immunity is no defense.

....

---

1. Recall, from *Doe v. Escambia*, presented earlier in this chapter, that "[t]he School Board and its teachers are under a common law and statutory duty to supervise the activity of students under their care and control, and such a duty is operational, not discretionary, and is not protected by sovereign immunity." *Doe*, 599 So. 2d 226, 227. In *Burns*, the lower court held that the superintendent's decisions in sanding and salting and keeping the school grounds safe for walking were discretionary and were protected by governmental immunity. The appeals court did not disagree; however, it applied one of the three exceptions to "discretionary act" immunity and denied the superintendent qualified immunity.

2. Typically, discretionary decisions may include both decisions to act and decisions not to act. In *Burns*, the discretionary decision not to sand and salt was superseded by an exception to the immunity rule. In *Alter v. City of Newton*, 35 Mass. App. Ct. 142, 617 N.E.2d 656 (1993), the discretionary decision not to erect a fence separating the athletic fields from the rest of the school grounds was superseded by the government's duty to warn of and minimize the hazards caused by athletic activity on the field (bystander/student was hit by flying lacrosse ball).

A court in Missouri was not as kind. In *Goben v. School Dist. of St. Joseph*, 848 S.W.2d 20 (Mo. Ct. App. 1992), the court held that a student failed to establish the dangerousness exception to sovereign immunity when she tripped over a hurdle placed on a concrete floor in gym class.

See also Stevenson v. City of St. Louis Sch. Dist., 820 S.W.2d 609 (Mo. Ct. App. 1991) (Since stairwell was not physically defective, school district's sovereign tort immunity was not waived in a suit by a student who fell into the stairwell).

3. In *Wood v. Strickland*, 420 U.S. 308 (1975), the Supreme Court considered the doctrine of qualified immunity for public education officials as the result of a Section 1983 suit brought by high school students who alleged that their expulsions violated procedural due process. The Court in *Wood* held that a school board member is not immune from liability under Section 1983 if he knew or reasonably should have known that the action he took would violate the constitutional rights of the student affected, or if he took the action with malicious intention to deprive the student of constitutional rights. The Court held that tradition and public policy required that school board members be qualifiedly immune from suit in that case.

Is tort immunity really a good idea, traditionally and by public policy? Consider the following statement:

> "Implicit in the idea that officials have some immunity — absolute or qualified — for their acts, is a recognition that they may err. The concept of immunity assumes this and goes on to assume that it is better to risk some error and possible injury from such error than not to decide to act at all." *Gay Activists Alliance v. Board of Regents of the Univ. of Oklahoma*, 638 P.2d 1116 (Okla. 1981).

D. DEFAMATION

BREWER v. ROGERS
Court of Appeals of Georgia
211 Ga. App. 343, 439 S.E.2d 77 (1993)

BEASLEY, PRESIDING JUDGE:

Brewer appeals from the grant of summary judgment to State Superintendent of Schools Rogers, Gillett Communications of Atlanta, Inc. d/b/a WAGA-TV 5, and its news reporter Shuler. Brewer sued these parties, plus the State of Georgia, in a number of counts. Relevant to the appeal are claims of libel and defamacast by WAGA and Shuler, slander by Rogers, and false light invasion of privacy by WAGA and Shuler.

The television newscast at issue was aired on November 14, 1989, and was prompted by a then-current investigation of alleged grade changes for a football-playing student at an Athens high school, which WAGA first learned about from a wire service within the two weeks prior to WAGA's newscast. Brewer was the head football coach, and the team was known to be one of the best in the state. The news report of the investigation was given by Shuler and, through his interview, Rogers. It featured Brewer as one involved in the affair and named no one else. Shuler related that fifteen years earlier, in 1974, Brewer and three major gambling kingpins had been arrested when Brewer was assistant football coach at Cobb County's Wheeler High School, in a $7,000,000 sports

D. DEFAMATION

gambling ring which police called "one of the biggest operations in the state," netting $20,000 a month on college and professional sports.

Shuler related that Brewer was charged with commercial gambling, keeping a gambling place, and felony possession of a pound of marijuana, pointing out that Brewer's was the only raided location which yielded drugs. He stated that when Brewer was indicted by the grand jury, he pleaded guilty to the drug charge "and, in a first offender plea arrangement, pleaded no contest to the gambling charges." In return, he reported, a judge "sentenced Brewer to one year of probation and a $1,000 fine and sealed the court records."

Shuler then introduced an interview with State School Superintendent Rogers, conducted a few hours earlier, by reporting that Rogers said his office was not aware of Brewer's criminal record until it was revealed by Eyewitness News. He asked Rogers how these things slip by, and Rogers said he did not know and wished they had not, and that if they had known of it, "of an individual being found guilty of a felony," they would have reported it to the PPC[2] for investigation. Shuler then reported that Rogers advised that when some school systems discover a problem teacher, they avoid controversy by "passin' the trash" on to another school.

Rogers stated that he thought it unacceptable to have individuals involved in activities "like that," particularly any that involve young people, grade changing, morals charges, or anything like that. The newscast continues with Shuler stating that Rogers said he wanted to know what Brewer stated on his application form on the line that asks, "Have you ever been convicted of a felony?" It ends with Shuler stating that Rogers says he will have the state investigate the principals if he catches school systems failing to report "incidents like this one."

Brewer and his wife at the time were arrested on October 21, 1974, for commercial gambling, keeping a gambling place, and violation of the Georgia Controlled Substances Act. The PPC was advised of this shortly thereafter by letter dated October 29 from Cobb's Assistant Superintendent of Schools, which included attachments documenting this. It also advised that Mr. and Mrs. Brewer resigned on October 22 and their resignations were accepted on October 24. The letter shows that a copy was sent to the then State Superintendent of Schools, Nix....

. . . .

The information about Brewer which was related on the newscast was obtained by Shuler on the day of the newscast from the superior court docket book and two news articles from the Marietta Daily Journal. One, undated in the record, apparently appeared a few days after the arrests on October 21 and was primarily about Brewer, although the arrests of others were also included. He and they were described as "bookmakers." The other is dated November 5, four days

---

[2]State of Georgia Professional Practices Commission, a public agency. OCGA § 20-2-790 *et seq.*

after the plea and sentencing, and reports the arrest of the three "kingpins" of the large gambling operation the day before the article. It connected Brewer with the gambling ring and reported on Brewer's pleas and sentences, but it did not mention the first offender treatment.

Shuler testified that the court docket stated that Brewer had been "adjudicated not guilty," and this as well as other portions of the docket sheet were flashed across the screen.

Brewer testified that he disclosed the arrest and discharge to his subsequent employers in various school systems, including the last one in Athens. The superintendent of the Clarke County schools testified that he disclosed it prior to his employment there.

....

2. The count of libel against WAGA and its employee Shuler merges with the count alleging "defamacast" and is constituted of defamation on television. *American Broadcasting etc. v. Simpson*, 106 Ga.App. 230(1), 126 S.E.2d 873 (1962); OCGA § 51-5-10(a). The count alleging slander by Rogers is governed by OCGA § 51-5-4. "Defamation by broadcast includes elements of both libel (OCGA § 51-5-1) and slander (OCGA § 51-5-4)." *S & W Seafoods Co. v. Jacor Broadcasting*, 194 Ga.App. 233, 234(1), 390 S.E.2d 228 (1989).

(a) We cannot say as a matter of law that the statements made were true. As appeared in the public record, if not fully on the docket sheet itself, then in the record of the PPC, Brewer had been discharged without court adjudication of guilt. The law states that "[t]he discharge shall completely exonerate the defendant of any criminal purpose and shall not affect any of his civil rights or liberties; and the defendant shall not be considered to have a criminal conviction." OCGA § 42-8-62(a). As said in *Witcher v. Pender*, 260 Ga. 248, 249, 392 S.E.2d 6 (1990), "[t]his provides the person who successfully completes his probation under the first offender statute protection against the stigma of a criminal record."

As described above, there was also public record evidence of PPC knowledge and action and of Brewer's non-involvement in the widespread gambling operation.

A defamatory statement "may be made in indirect terms or by insinuation, [and] the publication thereof must be construed as a whole." *Thomason v. Times-Journal*, 190 Ga.App. 601, 602(1), 379 S.E.2d 551 (1989). The question is what construction the average viewer would place upon the telecast. See *Macon Tel. Pub. Co. v. Elliott*, 165 Ga.App. 719, 721(1), 302 S.E.2d 692 (1983). "Except where an alleged [publication] is not defamatory as a matter of law, the general rule is that the issue of defamation is a matter of fact to be determined by a jury. [Cit.]" *Id.* at 720, 302 S.E.2d 692.

As in *Pacific & Southern Co. v. Montgomery*, 233 Ga. 175, 177, 180, 210 S.E.2d 714 (1974), "[t]he telecast, the pictures and spoken narrative taken in their entire context, together with the testimony of the plaintiff and the defendant news reporter [and interviewee Rogers, and other evidence in the record],

D. DEFAMATION

convince us that the issue of defamation or no defamation [is] a question of fact for determination by the jury ... In short, whether this telecast was defamatory of the plaintiff on its face, and whether it was true or not pursuant to [the evidence], [are] issues for determination by the jury."

The concept of *falsity vel non* was aired by the United States Supreme Court in *Masson* [*v. New Yorker Magazine*, 111 S.Ct. 2419 (1991)], *supra*. Defamation law "overlooks minor inaccuracies and concentrates upon substantial truth.... a statement is not considered false unless it 'would have a different effect on the mind of the [viewer] from that which the pleaded truth would have produced.'" *Masson, supra* at ___, 111 S.Ct. at 2432-33. The Court concluded that it was a jury question in that case.

(b) If there is falsity, the question arises whether Brewer is a public figure. A mixed question of law and fact, it is one for the court and not the jury to determine.... It is decided on a case-by-case basis.... *Compare Gertz v. Robert Welch, Inc.*, 418 U.S. 323 (1974), which set out that an individual becomes a public figure on one of two alternative bases: "In some instances an individual may achieve such pervasive fame or notoriety that he becomes a public figure for all purposes and in all contexts. More commonly, an individual voluntarily injects himself or is drawn into a particular public controversy and thereby becomes a public figure for a limited range of issues. In either case such persons assume special prominence in the resolution of public questions." *Id.* at 351.

Based on the record, we conclude that the trial court did not err in finding Brewer to be a public figure, for the purposes of this suit.

(c) Because Brewer was a public figure, both at the time of the 1974 episode and also at the time of the 1989 broadcast, actual malice of the truth must be proved. *New York Times Co. v. Sullivan*, 376 U.S. 254 (1964). "A public figure may not recover damages for a defamatory falsehood without clear and convincing proof that the false 'statement was made with "actual malice" — that is, with knowledge that it was false or with reckless disregard of whether it was false or not.'" *Harte-Hanks Communications v. Connaughton*, 491 U.S. 657, 659 (1989).... A better term than "actual malice," wrote the United States Supreme Court in *Masson, supra*, 501 U.S. at ___, 111 S.Ct. at 2430-31, is that the publication must be "with knowledge of falsity or reckless disregard as to truth or falsity." On summary judgment in such cases, the question is "whether a genuine issue of actual malice exists — that is, whether the evidence presented is such that a reasonable jury might find that actual malice had been shown with convincing clarity." *Anderson v. Liberty Lobby*, 477 U.S. 242, 257 (1986).

For First Amendment purposes, "reckless conduct is not measured by whether a reasonably prudent man would have published, or would have investigated before publishing. There must be sufficient evidence to permit the conclusion that the defendant in fact entertained serious doubts as to the truth of his publication. Publishing with such doubts shows reckless disregard for truth or falsity and demonstrates actual malice." *St. Amant v. Thompson*, 390 U.S. 727, 731 (1968).

The Court considered the competing interests and applied the following rationale: "Neither lies nor false communications serve the ends of the First Amendment, and no one suggests their desirability or further proliferation. But to insure the ascertainment and publication of the truth about public affairs, it is essential that the First Amendment protect some erroneous publications as well as true ones." *Id.* at 732.

Assuming the broadcast communicated falsities or a falsity by Shuler or Rogers or both, there is no evidence which would indicate an awareness by either of them of the probable falsity. *Compare Barber, supra,* 194 Ga.App. at 290-91, 390 S.E.2d 234. Brewer's complaint is that they failed to investigate adequately. However, "[f]ailure to investigate does not in itself establish bad faith." *St. Amant, supra,* 390 U.S. at 733, citing *New York Times Co. v. Sullivan, supra,* 376 U.S. at 287-88. There is no evidence which would establish the required degree of reckless disregard with respect to Rogers, other than his apparent failure to investigate at all before he spoke in the televised interview. Shuler's failure to go beyond the court docket sheet or the two 1974 newspaper articles to ascertain the meaning and ramifications of first offender and "adjudicated not guilty," or the actions of the PPC, or the accuracy of the newspaper-alleged tie to a huge gambling operation, or whether Brewer had disclosed the matter to school employers, does not evince actionable reckless disregard....

....

3. Brewer's claims for false light invasion of privacy by Shuler and WAGA likewise do not survive summary judgment, based on the evidence of record.

"Invasion of privacy was first recognized in this state in the landmark case of *Pavesich v. New England Life Insurance Co.*, 122 Ga. 190, 50 S.E. 68 (1904): The right of privacy is embraced within the absolute rights of personal security and personal liberty. Personal security includes the right to exist and the right to the enjoyment of life while existing, ... Personal liberty includes not only freedom from physical restraint, but also the right 'to be let alone,' ..." *Yarbray v. Southern Bell Tel. etc., Co.*, 261 Ga. 703, 704(1), 409 S.E.2d 835 (1991).

Cabaniss v. Hipsley, 114 Ga.App. 367, 370, 151 S.E.2d 496 (1966), divides the tort of invasion of privacy into four types, only one of which is relevant here: "publicity which places the plaintiff in a false light in the public eye."

In a false light case, "'[t]he interest protected is clearly that of reputation, with the same overtones of mental distress as in defamation.'" *Id.* at 375(3), 151 S.E.2d 496. The essential element is that "'the false light in which the other was placed would be highly offensive to a reasonable person.'" *Thomason v. Times-Journal*, 190 Ga.App. 601, 604(4), 379 S.E.2d 551 (1989).

We agree with the trial court that the absence of actual malice in the constitutionally-mandated sense precludes recovery under *Cabaniss, supra*. It was held in *Time, Inc. v. Hill*, 385 U.S. 374 (1967), "that the constitutional protections for speech and press preclude the application of [state law allowing a privacy action] to redress false reports of matters of public interest in the absence of proof that the defendant published the report with knowledge of its

D. DEFAMATION

falsity or in reckless disregard of the truth." *Id.* at 387-88. *See also Rosenbloom v. Metromedia*, 403 U.S. 29, 31 n. 1 (1971).

Judgment affirmed.

....

---

1. How important to the court do you think it was that Brewer's 1974 arrests and court proceedings information were communicated to the PPC and the state superintendent in 1974? Would the decision have been the same if Brewer's prior teaching and these incidents had occurred in another state?

2. It can be argued that Brewer's arrest is newsworthy and is protected upon publication. Is there a time limit (inherent, variable) on newsworthiness? Fifteen years passed from the time of the arrest in Cobb County to the publication on WAGA in Athens. Is this too long? Would this publication conceivably be a public disclosure of a private fact? Or is once public, always public? Can a person be a public figure-coach in one county with respect to some incidents, and a public figure-coach in another county with respect to others?

3. At common law, to prove defamation, a plaintiff must show that the alleged defamatory matter was published to a third party, understood as defamatory to that third party, and harmful to the plaintiff's reputation. *See* Rest. 2d (Torts) § 559.

In *Salek v. Passaic Collegiate Sch.*, 255 N.J. Super. 355, 605 A.2d 276 (1992), a teacher claimed that school yearbook photos of her were defamatory in that they implied that the teacher wished to engage in a sexual relationship with another faculty member. The court held that the pictures did not meet the definition of defamation. There is no libel where the disputed material is susceptible only to a nondefamatory meaning. In the book, the pictures were clearly meant to be parody, satire, humor, or fantasy, did not place the teacher in a false light, and were not highly offensive to the reasonable person.

4. Statements of opinion cannot in themselves be defamatory. *Gertz v. Welch, Inc.*, 418 U.S. 323 (1974). *See, e.g., Moyer v. Amador Valley Joint Union High Sch.*, 225 Cal. App. 3d 720, 275 Cal. Rptr. 494 (1990) (Statement by student that teacher was a babbler, and the worst teacher in school, which was printed in the school newspaper, was not a factual assertion capable of being proved as true or false and was thus not actionable); *but see Milkovich v. News-Herald*, 497 U.S. 1 (1990) (Statements in reporter's column which implied an assertion that high school coach perjured himself in a judicial proceeding was sufficiently factual to be susceptible of being proved true or false and might permit defamation recovery).

FREIER v. INDEPENDENT SCHOOL DISTRICT NO. 197

Court of Appeals of Minnesota
356 N.W.2d 724 (1984)

WOZNIAK, JUDGE:

....

Facts

Duane M. Freier, a gym teacher at Pilot Knob Elementary School, was dismissed from his position in January 1981. The discharge proceeding was brought pursuant to Minn.Stat. § 125.12, subd. 8 (1980). Freier had been accused of improper touching of students and insubordination.

....

The decision and order published, the alleged defamatory writing, recounted the series of events which led to Freier's dismissal. It detailed the letter from the superintendent of schools directing Freier to refrain from touching students and instructing him to use a uniform disciplinary procedure for all of the children in his classes. Also, it stated that Freier had willingly and knowingly disregarded this mandate and had touched fifth grade girls in the upper chest area. Also, it put forth how he had spanked a first grade boy for failing to perform an exercise, knowing the boy had been suffering pain and lameness in his legs.

The decision concluded:

> Based upon Findings of Fact 3, 4 and 5, this Board concludes that Duane M. Freier *willfully and knowingly violated the condition contained in the letter of February 22, 1980*, addressed to him from the Superintendent of Schools, that he "*cease immediately the practice of touching children or having them touch you*, except in those instances where it is necessary as part of the instructional process in physical education or there is a danger of injury to the student that requires action on your part", and he was therefore insubordinate and engaged in conduct unbecoming a teacher which requires his immediate removal from his classroom and other duties; based upon Finding of Fact 5, this Board concludes that Duane M. Freier *willfully and knowingly violated the condition of the letter of February 22, 1980* which admonished him to "use a uniform disciplinary procedure for all of the children you teach", and that he was therefore insubordinate and engaged in conduct unbecoming a teacher which requires his immediate removal from his classroom and other duties; and based upon Finding of Fact 6, this Board concludes that Duane M. Freier engaged in conduct unbecoming a teacher which requires his immediate removal from his classroom and other duties. (Emphasis added.)

All defendants moved for summary judgment, which was granted in favor of some of the board members. Remaining in this litigation as defendants are the school district and the five school board members who voted in favor of discharging Freier.

In their motion, defendants argued that the decision to publish the decision and order discharging Freier was protected by an absolute privilege. The district court disagreed, finding that they were only protected by a qualified privilege, yet certified the question as being important and doubtful. Consequently, the school district and the five individual school board members appeal from an order denying them summary judgment pursuant to Rule 103.03(h) of the Minnesota Rules of Civil Appellate Procedure. We reverse.

....

Analysis

Appellants argue that the publication of their decision to discharge Freier is protected by an absolute privilege grounded in three different contexts.

First, they argue they were entitled to an absolute judicial privilege because the school board was acting as a quasi-judicial tribunal when it reached and published its decision to discharge Freier.

Second, appellants argue they were entitled to an absolute privilege to follow the requirements of law. (The school board and school district were required to make their decision to discharge Freier public pursuant to Minn.Stat. § 125.12, subd. 10 (1980), Minn.Stat. § 123.33, subd. 11 (1980), and the Minnesota Data Practices Act, Minn.Stat. § 15.1692 (1980).)

Finally, appellants argue they were entitled to an absolute official privilege to carry out discretionary functions of public bodies, in accordance with Minnesota case law and Minn.Stat. § 466.03, subd. 6 (1980).

The lower court found that the quasi-judicial nature of a teacher discharge proceeding does not give automatic rise to a grant of absolute immunity, and, consequently, "The question of malice, bad faith or other action by the school board defendants in the instant case are questions to be resolved by the trier of fact."

Further, the court found that appellants failed to comply with all requirements of applicable Minnesota law, while engaged in discharge proceedings, namely:

> 1. The school board chose not to follow the recommended decision of the hearing officer, and
> 2. Appellant's decision was not based upon substantial and competent evidence in the record, thereby forfeiting any cloak of absolute immunity they may have had.

Finally, the court found the publication was not "discretionary" and immunity under Minn.Stat. § 466.03, subd. 6 is not applicable.

I

We hold that a school district and school board members are protected by an absolute privilege to publish a decision to discharge a teacher pursuant to Minn.Stat. § 125.12.

II

This is a case of first impression. It is undisputed that the Minnesota Supreme Court has, in past decisions, characterized teacher discharge proceedings as "quasi-judicial" in nature. However, it has not directly addressed the question of whether the absolute privilege with which it cloaked participants in other quasi-judicial proceedings would be available to a school district and school board members under the circumstances of the instant case.

A. *Application of Minn.Stat. § 125.12*

Minn.Stat. § 125.12, the continuing contract law, guarantees continued employment to Minnesota public school teachers who have completed their probationary period of employment. Once a teacher acquires continuing contract status, the teacher's employment can only be terminated in accordance with the grounds and procedures set forth in Minn.Stat. § 125.12. *See* Minn.Stat. § 125.12, subd. 4 (1982). The current discharge procedures are identical to the 1980 statute governing this decision.

In this case, the school board gave Freier written notice that it proposed to discharge him, effective immediately, under the statute. Also in accordance with the statute, Freier requested a hearing, which was granted by the school board. *See* Minn.Stat. § 125.12, subds. 4, 8.

Once a teacher requests a hearing and the hearing is completed, the school board must issue its written decision and order. According to the statute:

> After the hearing, the board shall issue a written decision and order. Minn.Stat. § 125.12, subd. 10.

It is the publication of this written decision which Freier alleges to have resulted in defamation and emotional distress.

B. *The Absolute Judicial Privilege*

All parties are in agreement that matters of teacher discharge under Section 125.12 are "quasi-judicial" proceedings. At issue is whether the absolute privilege of judicial immunity applies to these quasi-judicial proceedings.

In *Matthis v. Kennedy*, 243 Minn. 219, 67 N.W.2d 413 (1954), the supreme court extended the absolute judicial privilege to quasi-judicial proceedings:

> In judicial proceedings the privilege is not restricted to trials but includes every proceeding of a judicial nature if the hearing is before a competent court or before a tribunal or officer clothed with judicial or even quasi-judicial powers. The general rule in this country is that, with certain

D. DEFAMATION

recognized exceptions, defamatory matter published in the due course of a judicial proceeding is absolutely privileged and will not support a civil action for defamation although made maliciously and with knowledge of its falsehood. It extends to the protection of the judge, the jury, the party or parties, counsel and witnesses. *Id.* at 224, 67 N.W.2d at 417.

In *Jenson v. Olson*, 273 Minn. 390, 141 N.W.2d 488 (1966), the court extended the absolute judicial privilege to a quasi-judicial hearing concerning a city employee's discharge before the Minneapolis Civil Service Commission, a non-elected board.

The *Jenson* court described the characteristics of the quasi-judicial proceeding to which the absolute judicial privilege applies:

> the body has the power to issue subpoenas;
> it can administer oaths;
> it can order the production of books, records, and papers;
> it is required to put its charges in writing, and to provide the charged party with an opportunity to be heard; and
> its determination is reviewable in district court by certiorari. *Id.* at 392-93, 141 N.W.2d 490.

These characteristics are identical with a section 125.12 proceeding. The *Jenson* court further held that whether a tribunal is judicial is not a question of fact, but one of law.

Accordingly, any action taken to discharge a teacher under Minn.Stat. § 125.12 is a quasi-judicial proceeding to which the absolute judicial privilege will apply.

The immunity is total and absolute, and it will apply even if the defamatory statements were made with malice or were known to be false. *See Johnson v. Dirkswager*, 315 N.W.2d 215, 220 (Minn.1982); *Jenson v. Olson*, 273 Minn. at 393, 141 N.W.2d at 490.

In *Johnson v. Dirkswager*, 315 N.W.2d 215 (Minn.1982), the court stated:

> We have held that participants in judicial and legislative proceedings are entitled to an absolute privilege, a grant of total immunity for false and defamatory statements regardless of the nature or intent of the speaker. *Id.* at 220.

Under these principles, the decision and order of the school board is an absolutely privileged communication. Therefore, neither the members of the school board nor the school district itself can be held liable in defamation for any communication contained in the decision.

C. Communications

Communications incidental to judicial proceedings are absolutely privileged. Statements incidental to judicial proceedings, whether defamatory or not, are absolutely privileged. The judicial privilege extends to the tribunal that is responsible for making the decision.

> A judge or other officer performing a judicial function is absolutely privileged to publish defamatory matter in the performance of the function if the publication has some relation to the matter before him. Restatement (2d) of Torts § 585 (1977).

Here, the school board was the tribunal that performed the judicial function.

D. *Absolute Privilege to Follow the Requirements of the Law*

Public bodies have an absolute privilege to follow the requirements of law. It is well established:

> One who is required by law to publish defamatory matter is absolutely privileged to publish it. Restatement (2d) of Torts Section 592A (1977); *Johnson v. Dirkswager*, 315 N.W.2d 215, 223 (Minn.1982).

Once the school board voted to discharge Freier, it was required to publish that decision by three different laws: Minn.Stat. § 125.12, subd. 10, Minn.Stat. § 123.33, subd. 11, and the Minnesota Data Practices Act.

1. Minn.Stat. § 125.12, subd. 10: "After the hearing, the board shall issue a written decision and order." Under Minn.Stat. § 125.12, subd. 10, a school board's decision "shall include findings of fact." Since the decision had to be in writing, appellants are protected by an absolute privilege to follow the requirements of law.

2. Minn.Stat. § 123.33, subd. 11, states:

> The board shall cause its official proceedings to be published once in the official newspaper of the district. Such publication shall be made within 30 days of the meeting at which such proceedings occurred.

It would be illegal for the school board to have kept its decision to discharge Freier a secret from the public.

3. The Minnesota Data Practices Act states in pertinent part:

> [T]he following personnel data on current and former employees of a state agency, ... the status of any complaints or charges against the employee, whether or not the complaint or charge resulted in a disciplinary action; and the final disposition of any disciplinary action and supporting documentation .... Minn.Stat. § 15.1692, subd. 2 (1980). *See* Minn.Stat. § 13.43, subd. 2 (1982).

In the case at hand ...: Freier's claim of defamation is met full force by the need of the public to know what is occurring in the classrooms and by the statutory duty of the school board to report its findings in full to the public; the mode of challenge to the school board's findings was available to plaintiff and was used; he was reinstated with back pay; he was returned to his employment; his compensation can go no further.

E. *The Absolute Official Privilege*

School board members and school districts, like most government officials, are entitled to an absolute official privilege in the exercise of discretionary school district functions. Minn.Stat. § 466.03, subd. 6 (1982). The decision to discharge Freier involved the exercise of a discretionary act on the part of the school board. Because school districts are charged with the duty, in the exercise of their discretion, to carry out this function, appellants enjoy an absolute privilege of immunity from liability.

....

The discretionary act was the school board's actual decision which followed a three-day hearing. Only after discretion was exercised and the decision reached did the school board have to perform the statutorily-mandated "ministerial" act of putting the decision down on paper and making it available to the public.

....

Conclusion

Public policy requires absolute privilege for the public good. School boards have a duty to investigate allegations of an employee's improper behavior toward school children, and they have a duty to initiate discharge proceedings when, in their discretion, the school board members believe such action is appropriate. This issue is especially important when allegations of sexual misconduct with children are involved. This duty is for the benefit of the public and for the school children.

If there is no absolute immunity protecting school board members from liability in defamation for their decision to discharge a teacher, school board members will have a strong incentive to ignore complaints about employees, in order to avoid any risk of exposure to liability. Only the most courageous and the most foolhardy school board members would ever vote in favor of discharge. This would chill the rights of the public, and hamper the ability of a school district to protect its children. The children would then suffer the greatest risk.

It is true that mistakes can be made, and that lay board members might vote in favor of discharge even though the evidence might ultimately be found by the court to be legally insufficient. But teachers already have a remedy through judicial review and reinstatement with back pay. This remedy allows a teacher to clear his name and to be compensated for all economic hardship. Therefore, there is no justification for limiting board members' exposure to a qualified immunity under Minnesota's statutory scheme.

....

Reversed. Summary judgment granted.

---

1. "If there is no absolute immunity protecting school board members from liability in defamation for their decision to discharge a teacher, school board members will have a strong incentive to ignore complaints about employees, in order to avoid any risk of exposure to liability. Only the most courageous and most foolhardy school board members would ever vote in favor of discharge. This would chill the rights of the public, and hamper the ability of a school district to protect its children. The children would then suffer the greatest risk." *Freier*, 356 N.W.2d at 732-33.

It is the constitutional right (*Roth v. Board of Regents*, 408 U.S. 564 (1972)) and the statutory right (*e.g.*, Minn. Stat. § 125.12, subds. 4,8) of teachers to request and receive a hearing upon a school board's proposal of discharge. It is true that teachers also have the opportunity for judicial review, reinstatement, and back pay. But, is this right effectively defeated for some employees, given that publication of the decision to discharge is mandatory under the same statutes (§ 125.12, subd. 10)? After cases like *Freier*, which hold such publications absolutely privileged, would you expect many teachers to waive the hearing in order to avoid publication of embarrassing or humiliating facts?

2. With the discussion of tort immunity and absolute and qualified privilege, readers may think that privileged defendants are free to act as they wish, without worry. This is not entirely true. For example, in *Moss v. Stockard*, 580 A.2d 1011 (D.C. App. 1990), the court denied qualified privilege to the athletic director of a public university who made statements concerning a coach's alleged misappropriation without investigating the matter first to test the truth of the allegations.

Freier involved a school system following state law in publishing a record of its decision and order discharging an employee. The defendants in *Freier* were immune from a defamation suit. Where there is no such law, and a school sends to a discharged teacher a letter detailing the teacher's termination, the school may not avoid liability. *See Disend v. Meadowbrook Sch.*, 33 Mass. App. Ct. 674, 604 N.E.2d 54 (1992).

3. In cases of defamation, without privileged actors or statements, generally there is a presumption of malice; the plaintiff need not prove actual malice in order to recover for damages suffered. However, in privileged situations, the inquiry changes. For example, remarks made by the father of a student at a school board meeting regarding the curriculum and instruction of one of the teachers fell within the qualified privilege (due to the mutual interest of the speaker and listener concerning the matter of public concern). *Nodar v.*

D. DEFAMATION

Galbreath, 462 So. 2d 803 (Fla. 1985). Consequently, express malice was not presumed; and must be proved by the teacher. In *Nodar*, the court held that the speaker was motivated more by the protection of a personal or social interest than by a desire to harm the teacher. Therefore, the statements by the father were not made with express malice.

Similarly, in *McCartney v. Oblates of St. Francis DeSales*, 80 Ohio App. 3d 345, 609 N.E.2d 216 (1992), a teacher was unable to prove actual malice in order to overcome the qualified privilege of the school and school officials in the teacher's defamation suit.

KELLEY v. BONNEY

Supreme Court of Connecticut
221 Conn. 549, 606 A.2d 693 (1992)

CALLAHAN, JUSTICE:

... The plaintiff, John J. Kelley, formerly a teacher at West Side Junior High School in Groton, initiated this action as a result of statements made about him that allegedly impugned his personal and professional integrity. The plaintiff named as defendants Winifred Bonney, the Groton board of education, Mary Keith, Bruce McDermott, Christian Mitchell, Sherrie Neilson, Wendy Sawyer, Paulann H. Sheets and Lenny Winkler. Keith, McDermott, Sheets and Winkler had been members of the Groton board of education; Mitchell had been a student of the plaintiff; Neilson and Sawyer had been parents of students of the plaintiff; and Bonney had been a neighbor of a student of the plaintiff. The plaintiff alleged that each of the individual defendants had maliciously and negligently published defamatory material and intentionally caused him emotional distress. He further alleged that the Groton board of education had breached a contract with him and had recklessly and negligently caused him emotional distress. After the plaintiff had presented his case, the trial court directed verdicts in favor of McDermott, Mitchell and Sawyer. At the close of all the evidence, the jury returned verdicts in favor of Keith, Neilson and Winkler. The jury, however, found Bonney and Sheets liable to the plaintiff in the amount of $10,000. The jury also found the Groton board of education liable for breach of contract and for tortious infliction of emotional distress to the plaintiff, and awarded him $3000 against the board. The plaintiff appealed to the Appellate Court, and Sheets and Bonney cross appealed to the Appellate Court. We transferred the appeals to this court in accordance with Practice Book § 4023. We now reverse that part of the judgment of the trial court that imposes liability upon Bonney and Sheets.

... In March, 1987, a significant number of the plaintiff's students at West Side Junior High School signed a petition setting forth various allegations of his inappropriate conduct in the classroom. The petition included, *inter alia*, allegations that the plaintiff verbally abused his students, touched female students against their will and failed to conduct his classes properly. The students' petition was brought to the attention of the Groton board of education, and the Groton superintendent of schools, Joan Stipetic. Stipetic immediately began an investigation into the students' allegations. On April 3, 1987, following her investigation, Stipetic informed the plaintiff that she planned to recommend that the Groton board of education pursue termination proceedings against him. On the advice of his attorney, rather than contesting the termination proceedings, the plaintiff chose to retire from his teaching position. Sometime during the following two weeks, an agreement was reached between the school board and the plaintiff that, among other things, required that the plaintiff retire and that he be paid a lump sum of $2500. Because it was agreed that the plaintiff would retire, Stipetic did not disclose the findings of her investigation or the details of the agreement.

Following the public announcement that the plaintiff would retire, the local newspapers and the public began to demand an explanation for the administration's actions, and also that the allegations made against the plaintiff be more fully investigated. On May 6, 1987, Stipetic and the board's attorney, Richard O'Connor, attended a meeting of the Groton board of education. O'Connor explained to the board members that, because the plaintiff had communicated his intent to retire and, therefore, would no longer be an employee of the Groton board of education, the board would no longer retain jurisdiction over the plaintiff and should not continue to investigate him. Following publication of the fact that no further investigation would be conducted, there was further outcry by some members of the public who sought to have the matter more thoroughly examined. On May 27, 1987, at a meeting of the Groton board of education, Keith moved to place on the agenda the question of whether the matter involving the plaintiff should be referred to the state board of education for investigation.... Following ... [a] tie vote, Sheets telephoned the state department of education and was told by Mark Stapleton of the office of legal affairs that she, individually, could further pursue this matter by requesting that the state conduct an investigation.

Sheets, Keith, McDermott and Winkler agreed that a request to the state should be made. Accordingly, on May 27, 1987, those four defendants drafted a letter and petition to the state board of education.... Following the submission of the May 27, 1987 petition, commissioner of education Gerald N. Tirozzi notified the petitioners that the state board of education could not act upon the petition unless the petition conformed with the requirements of State Board of Education Regulations § 10-145a-10(b), which provided that such a petition be submitted under oath.

Thereafter, on July 13, 1987, the petitioners submitted a verified petition and complaint to the state board of education. The verified petition and complaint was a more detailed version of the May 27, 1987 petition that had been revised to conform to the regulations. In the verified petition and complaint, Keith, McDermott, Sheets and Winkler requested that the state board of education "investigate the fitness of [the plaintiff] to hold a state teaching certificate and to revoke said certificate if, upon proper determination of the evidence, that revocation is warranted." They further stated that, "[o]n information and belief," there were grounds to revoke the plaintiff's teaching certificate including: (1) the plaintiff "has persistently neglected to perform the duties for which certification was granted"; and (2) the plaintiff is "professionally unfit to perform the duties for which certification was granted." The petitioners asserted as a basis for the request that: (1) the plaintiff conveyed to students the belief that females are mentally and morally inferior to males; (2) he "sexualized" his classroom presentations causing his students to feel anger, embarrassment and fright; (3) he failed to cover the curriculum material for his courses; (4) he failed to set a good example regarding patience, fairness, compassion, and respect for the rights of others without regard to race, sex, religion or nationality; (5) students were "traumatized" by him; (6) he "repeatedly [verbally] abused" students; (7) he committed rough and hurtful batteries on male students; and (8) he touched female students against their will. The petitioners appended to the verified petition and complaint a number of affidavits signed by students and parents describing specific incidents of misconduct.

Despite the support for the defendants' assertions offered by the affidavits, the jury could reasonably have found that the defendants' statements were untrue, and that the defendants knew they were untrue, or acted with reckless disregard of the truth. In addition to sending the material to the state board of education, Sheets forwarded copies of the petition and complaint to the Department of Children and Youth Services (DCYS), the attorney general, and The New London Day newspaper. The jury could also reasonably have found that the plaintiff suffered harm as a result of the publication of the material. The defendants' exoneration therefore depends largely on the validity of their claims of privilege.

I

....

D

The plaintiff ... claims that he introduced sufficient evidence in his case-in-chief for the jury reasonably to conclude that McDermott, Mitchell and Sawyer published nonprivileged, defamatory material concerning his professional and personal integrity. As a result, he claims that verdicts were improperly directed in their favor. We do not agree.

To find that the defendants were liable for defamation or intentional infliction of emotional distress as alleged in the plaintiff's complaint, the jury was required to find that the defendants published false statements that harmed the defendant, and that the defendants were not privileged to do so....

1

The plaintiff claims that the trial court improperly directed verdicts in favor of Mitchell and Sawyer at the conclusion of the plaintiff's case because they published statements that were not absolutely privileged. It is unnecessary for us to address the question of absolute privilege to conclude that the verdicts were properly directed in favor of Mitchell and Sawyer.

... Regarding Mitchell and Sawyer, the record demonstrates that the plaintiff failed in his case-in-chief to offer any evidence to indicate that either defendant published statements concerning the plaintiff.

Concerning Mitchell, the only evidence offered in the plaintiff's case-in-chief was a sworn affidavit and complaint dated July 13, 1987, in which Mitchell described specific examples of inappropriate behavior by the plaintiff. Significantly, this affidavit and complaint were offered through the defendant Winkler, for the limited purpose of demonstrating Winkler's state of mind at the time she submitted the verified petition and complaint to the state board of education. The document was not offered for the substantive purpose of proving that Mitchell made damaging allegations.

Similarly, the evidence offered in the plaintiff's case-in-chief concerning Sawyer was admitted for the limited purpose of showing Winkler's state of mind. Winkler testified that Sawyer had stated that the plaintiff had made racist and sexist comments in the classroom. In response to an objection by the plaintiff, the court ruled that the statements made to Winkler by other people could be considered only for their effect on Winkler's mind. The defendant then introduced two letters written by Sawyer. The first was a letter from Sawyer to Winkler, in which Sawyer specifically described racist and sexist incidents that she claimed had occurred in the plaintiff's classroom. The second was a letter from Sawyer to the principal of West Side Junior High School that made similar accusations against the plaintiff. Both of these letters were introduced solely for the limited purpose of demonstrating Winkler's state of mind.

In view of the limited purpose for the introduction of the evidence described, there was no evidence from which the jury could reasonably have concluded that either Mitchell or Sawyer made defamatory statements about the plaintiff. Accordingly, we conclude that the trial court properly directed verdicts in favor of both Mitchell and Sawyer.

2

In his case-in-chief, the plaintiff elicited the following evidence to prove that McDermott published defamatory material. McDermott testified that he had viewed affidavits of parents and students, and that he had viewed police reports that contained allegations concerning the plaintiff's behavior. Ultimately, McDermott signed the May 27, 1987 petition and the verified petition and complaint to which the affidavits and reports were appended, and sent them to the state board of education to request an investigation of the plaintiff.... The trial court ruled that McDermott's submission of the material to the state board of education was absolutely privileged.

The effect of an absolute privilege in a defamation action is that damages cannot be recovered for a defamatory statement even if it is published falsely and maliciously. *Petyan v. Ellis, supra*, 200 Conn. at 246, 510 A.2d 1337. "'[L]ike the privilege which is generally applied to pertinent statements made in formal judicial proceedings, an absolute privilege also attaches to relevant statements made during administrative proceedings which are "quasijudicial" in nature.'...'" Once it is determined that a proceeding is quasijudicial in nature, the absolute privilege that is granted to statements made in furtherance of it "extends to every step of the proceeding until final disposition." *Id.* at 246, 510 A.2d 1337.

We must first determine whether the proceedings in this case were quasi-judicial in nature. "The judicial proceeding to which [absolute] immunity attaches has not been defined very exactly. It includes any hearing before a tribunal which performs a judicial function, ex parte or otherwise, and whether the hearing is public or not. It includes for example, lunacy, bankruptcy, or naturalization proceedings, and an election contest. It extends also to the proceedings of many administrative officers, such as boards and commissions, so far as they have powers of discretion in applying the law to the facts which are regarded as judicial or quasijudicial, in character." (Internal quotation marks omitted.) *Id.*; W. Prosser & W. Keeton, Torts (5th Ed. 1984) § 114, pp. 818-19.

....

The foregoing clearly demonstrates that the state board of education possessed significant regulatory authority to conduct proceedings of a quasijudicial nature. The detailed procedures, which ensure the reliability of teacher decertification proceedings, and the compelling public policy concern for the protection of school age children persuade us that the decertification proceedings before the state board of education were quasijudicial in nature, and that any statements made as a requisite step in those proceedings were absolutely privileged.

Having concluded that a decertification proceeding before the state board of education is quasijudicial in nature, we must determine whether McDermott's submission of the verified petition and complaint was a step in that proceeding. We have stated that allegations contained within a complaint in a quasijudicial proceeding are absolutely privileged. State Board of Education Regulations § 10-145a-10(b) (now § 10-145a-109[b]) specifically provides that "a request for revocation of a certificate may be made by ... any person or persons with a legitimate interest involved...." Such a request was necessary under the circumstances to initiate the decertification process as contemplated by § 10-145a-10. We conclude, therefore, that any statements made by McDermott in his verified petition and complaint filed pursuant to § 10-145a-10(c) were absolutely privileged and could not provide the basis for liability in a defamation action. Accordingly, the trial court properly directed a verdict in his favor.

II

We next address the cross appeal of Bonney and Sheets, against whom the jury returned a verdict of $10,000. Their cross appeal raises additional issues concerning the scope of absolute privilege in a decertification proceeding. Bonney and Sheets claim that they were entitled to judgments notwithstanding the verdict because any defamatory material they published was absolutely privileged. We agree.

A

Regarding the publication of defamatory material by Bonney, the evidence allowed the jury reasonably to find the following. Bonney drafted a letter to the state board of education that described inappropriate conduct by the plaintiff, and she submitted the letter to Sheets to be forwarded to the state along with the verified petition, complaint and other attachments. Additionally, Bonney telephoned Janice Waller, believing that Waller might have information concerning the plaintiff's conduct. Bonney had telephoned Waller to enlist Waller's support for the verified petition and complaint that was to be submitted to the state board of education. During the conversation with Waller, Bonney stated that her paper girl had been "molested or attacked or something" by the plaintiff. Waller testified that she assumed that Bonney's allegations about the plaintiff were of a sexual nature. There was no further evidence offered to indicate that Bonney had communicated, or had attempted to communicate, her paper girl's allegations to any other potential witnesses, or that Bonney published any other defamatory material.

"[I]n instances where communications are made to alleged potential witnesses, the court must particularly evaluate the factual circumstances peculiar to each case to determine whether application of [absolute] privilege is warranted." *Hoover v. Van Stone*, 540 F.Sup. 1118, 1123 (D.Del.1982)....

... [I]n *Brody v. Montalbano, supra*, 87 Cal.App.3d at 729, 151 Cal.Rptr. 206, the parents of school children, defendants in a defamation action brought by a teacher, filed a formal complaint with the local school board against the teacher. In the complaint, the parents alleged that the teacher had made inappropriate comments to a student and had failed to follow proper procedures following the injury of one of his students. The defendants apparently had discussed the content of their complaint with other parents. The court held:

> "It appears that [absolute] privilege extended to the defendant parents' communications with the [other parents]. To accomplish the purpose of judicial or quasi-judicial proceedings, it is obvious that the parties or persons interested must confer and must marshal their evidence for presentation at the hearing. The right of private parties to combine and make presentations to an official meeting and, as a necessary incident thereto, to prepare materials to be presented is a fundamental adjunct to the right of access to judicial and quasi-judicial proceedings. To make such preparations

and presentations effective, there must be an open channel of communication between the persons interested and the forum, unchilled by the thought of subsequent judicial action against such participants; provided always, of course, that such preliminary meetings, conduct and activities are directed toward the achievement of the objects of the litigation or other proceedings." (Internal quotation marks omitted.) *Id.* at 734, 151 Cal.Rptr. 206.

It is uncontradicted that Bonney's discussion with Waller was conducted for the purpose of marshaling evidence against the plaintiff to be used to support the complaint that was to be submitted to the state board of education. The evidence reveals no communication of a similar nature by Bonney to any other person. Accordingly, given the particular factual circumstances of Bonney's communications, we conclude that the discussion with Waller and her submission of her written complaint to Sheets were absolutely privileged. Therefore, the trial court improperly denied her motion for a judgment notwithstanding the verdict.

B

Regarding Sheets, the jury could reasonably have found the following defamatory publications. Sheets prepared the verified petition and complaint and attached affidavits and forwarded copies of those documents to DCYS, the attorney general and the state board of education. Further, Sheets was requested by an editorial writer for *The New London Day* to provide *The Day* with a copy of the petition and complaint that had been sent to the state board of education. Sheets provided the writer with a copy of the verified petition and complaint, but not with the affidavits of parents and students that had been attached. No evidence was offered to indicate that Sheets published any other statements to *The Day*....

Although we have concluded that the decertification proceedings before the state board of education were quasijudicial in nature, not all communications relating to that topic are necessarily absolutely privileged. "In determining whether an occasion is absolutely privileged, the pivotal factor is frequently to whom the matter is published." *Asay v. Hallmark Cards, Inc.*, 594 F.2d 692, 697 (8th Cir. 1979)....

"Publication to the news media is not ordinarily sufficiently related to a judicial proceeding to constitute a privileged occasion." *Asay v. Hallmark Cards, Inc.*, supra at 697; *Pelagatti v. Cohen*, 370 Pa.Super. 422, 437, 536 A.2d 1337 (1987), *appeal denied*, 519 Pa. 667, 548 A.2d 256 (1988); *Hoover v. Van Stone*, supra.... Publication to the media is ordinarily not privileged because,

"[t]he salutary policy of allowing freedom of communication in judicial proceedings does not warrant or countenance the dissemination and distribution of defamatory accusations outside of the judicial proceeding. No public purpose is served by allowing a person to unqualifiedly make libelous or defamatory statements about another, but rather such person should be called upon to prove the correctness of his allegations or respond in damages. The privilege or immunity granted to defamatory statements in judicial proceedings is a narrow one." *Asay v. Hallmark Cards, Inc., supra.*

Publication to the media of material that the media was independently entitled to view, however, cannot provide a basis for a claim of defamation. *See DeLaurentis v. New Haven, supra,* 265-66, 597 A.2d 807; *Green Acres Trust v. London,* 142 Ariz. 12, 25, 688 P.2d 658 (1983).... The pivotal question here is whether, regardless of the actions of the defendant, the media would have been entitled to access to the complaint. We are aware of no persuasive justification for punishing Sheets for publication to *The Day* of the formal written complaint and petition if *The Day* was independently permitted to view the material.

....

With respect to the plaintiff's status as a public official, evidence was offered indicating that the plaintiff had been a public school science teacher at the West Side Junior High School in Groton for nineteen years. The trial court instructed the jury that the plaintiff, as a teacher, was a public official as a matter of law, and that he could not recover damages unless he was able to demonstrate by clear and convincing proof that the statements made by the defendants were false and made with actual malice. Following that charge, the plaintiff properly took exception.

In an action for defamation, a public official is prohibited from recovering damages for a defamatory falsehood relating to his official conduct unless he proves by clear and convincing evidence that the falsehood was published with "actual malice." *New York Times Co. v. Sullivan,* 376 U.S. 254 (1964); *Brown v. K.N.D. Corporation,* 205 Conn. 8, 10, 529 A.2d 1292 (1987); *Holbrook v. Casazza,* 204 Conn. 336, 342, 528 A.2d 774 (1987), *cert. denied,* 484 U.S. 1006 (1988). The state of mind that constitutes actual malice has been defined as "'with knowledge that it was false or with reckless disregard of whether it was false or not.'" *Brown v. K.N.D. Corporation, supra.*

Although the United States Supreme Court has not definitively resolved the question of "how far down into the lower ranks of government employees the 'public official' designation would extend"; *New York Times Co. v. Sullivan, supra,* 376 U.S. 283 n. 23; it is clear that not all public employees are included within that category. *Hutchinson v. Proxmire,* 443 U.S. 111, 119 n. (1979). The question of whether a school teacher is a public official for defamation purposes is one of first impression in this state.

In determining whether a particular individual holds the status of a public official, courts have remarked on various significant considerations. The United States Supreme Court indicated that the underlying purpose of limiting an individual's ability to protect his reputation was to allow citizens to voice their opinions more freely on matters of public concern. *New York Times Co. v. Sullivan, supra,* 376 U.S. at 270. "[D]ebate on public issues should be uninhibited, robust, and wide-open, and ... may well include vehement, caustic, and sometimes unpleasantly sharp attacks on government and public officials."

Id. "[T]he 'public official' designation applies at the very least to those among the hierarchy of government employees who have, or appear to the public to have, substantial responsibility for or control over the conduct of governmental affairs." *Rosenblatt v. Baer*, 383 U.S. 75, 85 (1966); *Moriarty v. Lippe*, 162 Conn. 371, 378, 294 A.2d 326 (1972). Additionally, it is important to consider whether "a position in government has such apparent importance that the public has an independent interest in the qualifications and performance of the person who holds it, beyond the general public interest in the qualifications and importance of all government employees...." *Rosenblatt v. Baer, supra*, 383 U.S. at 86; *Moriarty v. Lippe, supra*. Further, it has been postulated that public figures require less protection from defamation because they tend to enjoy greater access to the media for purposes of rebutting any defamatory publication.

Taking into account these considerations, we conclude that a public school teacher is a public official for defamation purposes. Robust and wide open debate concerning the conduct of the teachers in the schools of this state is a matter of great public importance. In *Moriarty v. Lippe, supra*, we indicated that a police patrolman is a public official. There we noted that "a patrolman's office, if abused, has great potential for social harm and thus invites independent interest in the qualifications and performance of the person who holds the position." *Id.*, 162 Conn. at 378, 294 A.2d 326. We also stated that the patrolman "has, or appears to the public to have, substantial responsibility for or control over the conduct of government affairs, at least where law enforcement and police functions are concerned...." *Id.* Similarly, teachers' positions, if abused, potentially might cause serious psychological or physical injury to school aged children. Unquestionably, members of society are profoundly interested in the qualifications and performance of the teachers who are responsible for educating and caring for the children in their classrooms. Further, teachers exercise almost unlimited responsibility for the daily implementation of the governmental interest in educating young people. In the classroom, teachers are not mere functionaries. Rather, they conceive and apply both policy and procedure. As a result of that significant public interest, it is also likely that the media would not only provide a teacher about whom allegations have been made with an opportunity to respond, but that the media would encourage comment by the teacher. Therefore, we conclude that the trial court properly instructed the jury that the plaintiff school teacher was a public official for defamation purposes.

. . . .

The judgment is reversed in part and the case is remanded to the trial court with direction to render judgment in favor of Bonney and Sheets.

In this opinion the other Justices concurred.

---

1. Recall from the facts of *Kelley* that Kelley's attorney advised him to retire in lieu of contesting the termination. As a result, Stipetic did not disclose the findings of the investigation. Recall also the disclosure statutes and requirements in *Freier*. Do you think similar publication requirements caused Kelley and his attorney to rethink their course of action and go with retirement instead of challenge? By seeking retirement, was Kelley seeking to avoid the media attention he eventually received anyway?

2. Do you think that teachers are fairly treated by the law with regard to defamation actions? What are their chances of a successful defamation suit? This clearly depends on whether they are regarded as public officials. Public official status was established in the landmark defamation case, *New York Times v. Sullivan*, 376 U.S. 254 (1964). In addition to proving that a statement was made to a third party which damaged the plaintiff's reputation, plaintiffs are required to prove actual malice. That is, the plaintiff must prove that the defamatory statements were made with knowledge of their falsity, or in reckless disregard for the truth. The First Amendment dictates that "debate on public issues ... be uninhibited, robust, and wide-open," including critical attacks on public officials.

However, the *Sullivan* opinion did not specifically define "public official." "We have no occasion here to determine how far down into the lower ranks of government employees the 'public official' designation would extend...." *Id.* at 283, note 23.

Two years later, in *Rosenblatt v. Baer*, the Supreme Court noted two qualifications on the public official status. First, "the 'public official' designation applies at the very least to those among the hierarchy of government employees who have, or appear to the public to have, substantial responsibility for or control of government affairs." 383 U.S. 75, 85 (1966). Second, the Court also recognized government positions that have "such apparent importance that the public has an independent interest in the qualifications and performance of the person who holds it, beyond the general public interest." *Id.*

3. Do you agree that public school teachers are public officials? As matters of public concern, this status may be conceded; but, do teachers have substantial responsibility or control over the conduct of government affairs? How does the court in *Kelley* get around this point? What are government affairs? Even if teachers' government responsibility and control is low, did the *Kelley* court come to the correct conclusion on this matter?

For more on this issue, *see* Bjorklun, *Are Teachers Public Officials for Defamation Purposes?*, 80 Educ. L. Rep. 527 (1993). Bjorklun's article notes that absolute privilege generally extends to school boards — individuals who perform vital governmental functions in judicial, legislative, and executive proceedings, while qualified privilege extends to other school officials and parents.

Bjorklun cites to fifteen lower court opinions between 1974 and 1987 that discuss the status of teachers as public officials. Six cases, most decided in the 1970s, held that teachers were public officials. *See, e.g.*, *Basarich v. Rodeghero*, 24 Ill. App. 3d 889, 321 N.E.2d 739 (1974) (Teachers and coaches sue for libel with respect to publication of statements in newsletters); and *Johnston v.*

D. DEFAMATION

Corinthian T.V. Corp., 583 P.2d 1101 (Okla. 1978)) (Grade school wrestling coach brought suit alleging defamation in news broadcasts).

The other nine held that teachers were not public officials. Most of these nine were decided in the 1980's, and applied the *Rosenblatt* test. Bjorklun noted that seven of the nine held that teachers did not have enough responsibility for or control over governmental affairs. *See, e.g., Milkovich v. News-Herald*, 15 Ohio St. 3d 292, 473 N.E.2d 1191 (1984) (Former high school wrestling coach brought libel suit against newspaper and sports writer); and *Richmond Newspapers v. Lipscomb*, 234 Va. 277, 363 S.E.2d 32 (1987) (Public school teacher sues reporter and newspaper for statements contained in article concerning teacher's performance in classroom). An eighth decision held that the independent interest in the teaching qualifications and performance of a teacher was not sufficient enough to justify designating the teacher a public official. *See Nodar v. Galbreath*, 462 So. 2d 803 (Fla. 1985) (High school English teacher brought slander action against father of student for statements made at a school board meeting). The ninth decision found the teacher to be a private person because he was no longer a teacher at the time of the alleged defamation. *DeLuca v. New York News, Inc.*, 109 Misc. 2d 341, 438 N.Y.S.2d 199 (1981).

Where does *Kelley* fit on the spectrum? Is this decision reflective of a trend, or is it the beginning of a shift back to the earlier cases? *See also Johnson v. Southwestern Newspapers Corp.*, 855 S.W.2d 182 (Tex. Ct. App. 1993) (High school athletic director-football coach brought libel action against newspaper and its sports writer. The court held teacher to be a public official, and found no actual malice on the part of the defendants); and *Palmer v. Bennington Sch. Dist.*, 159 Vt. 31, 615 A.2d 498 (1992) (Principal held to be a public official in counterclaim against school district, but statements were made without actual malice); *but see Ellerbee v. Mills*, 262 Ga. 516, 422 S.E.2d 539 (1992) (Principal *not* a public official in defamation action against teacher).

Consider, finally, Bjorklun's thoughts:*

> The most recent decision on the issue, however is a return to the decisions of the 1970s. In *Kelley v. Bonney*, the Connecticut Supreme Court held that in order to encourage robust discussion about the conduct of public school teachers, they must be considered public officials. They have almost unlimited responsibility for the implementation of the governmental interest in education in their classrooms and the public has a greater than normal interest in their performance of duties because of the potential harm to children if teachers abuse their positions. Thus, teachers meet the *Rosenblatt* criteria and are public officials.
>
> If the *Kelley* decision signals the start of a trend toward returning to the judicial designation of teachers as public officials, teachers' protections

---

*Reprinted with permission from 80 Educ. L. Rep. 527, Copyright © 1993 by West Publishing Company.

against assaults on their reputations will be diminished further. Teachers will probably never be able to secure damages for defamatory statements made within the context of a quasi-judicial school board proceeding, including all statements made by school administrators and parents leading to an investigation of charges against a teacher, because those statements have either absolute or qualified privilege. By extending public official status to teachers, courts will make it even more difficult for teachers to successfully defend their reputations against defamation that occurs outside the quasi-judicial setting.

Public education in recent years has become the focus of much public interest and concern so that teachers can expect close examination in regard to both their personal and professional lives. As Hopkins stated:

> With intense new scrutiny on public education; controversies over the competency of teachers and competency testing; and disputes over sex education, textbooks and other curriculum issues teachers are in the news more and more and, therefore, are more often becoming subjects of news accounts they believe damage their reputations.[41]

There is also evidence that the reluctance to report child abuse, especially abuse of a sexual nature, is fast disappearing. Berglund reported that in Minnesota, the Minnesota Education Association responded to 15 cases involving charges of teacher abuse of children in the 1987-88 school year. That number jumped to 50 in the 1988-89 school year.[42] Nationwide, Hooker investigated state appellate court decisions involving teacher dismissals for improper touching or sexual contact with students from 1968 through 1986. He found that approximately two-thirds of all the reported cases occurred within the last three years of the period.[43] Sorenson found a "steady increase" in the number of reported judicial cases dealing with sexual abuse of students by school personnel from 1987 through 1990.[44]

With growing public awareness of schools and education and the heightened concern for child abuse, it is likely that there will be increased criticism of teachers and an increased number of abuse charges against teachers. It is also likely that at least some of the criticisms will be unwarranted and some of the charges will be untrue. Sorenson criticized state statutes that deny legal counsel at state expense to teachers accused of

---

[41][W. Wat Hopkins, "Teachers as Public Officials in Libel Actions," 47 Educ. L. Rep 350, 354 (1998).]

[42]Judy Berglund, "Child Abuse: Teacher Conduct Under Scrutiny," MEA Advocate, (November, 1989).

[43]Clifford P. Hooker, "Teacher Dismissal for Improper Touching or Sexual Contact With Students," 39 Educ. L. Rep. [941] (Aug. 20, 1987), 941.

[44]Gail Paulus Sorenson, "Sexual Abuse in Schools: Reported Court Cases from 1987-1990," 27 Educational Administration Quarterly 460 (November, 1991), 461.

criminal sexual conduct based on nothing more than the nature of the complaint. Noting that some teachers may be falsely accused, she stated that "... innocent teachers ... simply by pursuing a profession that brings them into contact with children and young adults ..." may be subjecting themselves to potentially serious problems.[45] By designating teachers public officials, it might similarly be argued that innocent teachers will be unable to secure damages for defamation simply because they have pursued a profession that brings them into contact with children and young adults. In posing the question of what protection teachers have in their professional lives against defamatory statements, Nolte observed that "... the cards seem stacked ..." against the teacher.[46] Designating teachers as public officials would seem to stack the cards against the teacher even more.

4. What makes an athletics coach more of a public figure than any other teacher? Is this stereotypical of coaches, or the people who say things about them?

5. Most of our defamation discussion has dealt with suits by teachers and other school officials. This is not to indicate that students are unable to file defamation claims in the school context, as well. In *Rich v. Kentucky Country Day School*, 93 S.W.2d 832 (Ky. Ct. App. 1990), a student and his guardian filed a defamation against his teacher after the teacher wrote in the student's report card that the student was lazy and irresponsible. The Court held in favor of the teacher.

> In a defamation action based on slander *per quod* [not relating to moral turpitude, commission of a crime, or conduct of business, trade, or profession], the plaintiff must ... allege specific damages resulting from the statements made, other than just mental pain, humiliation, disgrace or mortification. If ... plaintiff's prayer is for general damages only, the Complaint does not state a cause of action for slander *per quod. Id.* at 837.

The court found that Rich alleged no specific damages. In addition, the court found that the teacher's statements were mere opinion, qualifiedly privileged, and not "published" within the law of slander or libel. (Only the student had told third parties what the teacher said). *Id.* at 838.

For other privilege cases involving student defamation actions, *see Doe v. McMillan*, 412 U.S. 306 (1973) (Members of the U.S. House of Representatives absolutely privileged in their publication and dissemination of a report which identified several students in a derogatory context, only to the extent that such dissemination and publication served legitimately legislative functions); *Roman v. Appleby*, 558 F. Supp. 449 (High school guidance counselor entitled to

---

[45]*Id.* at 474.

[46][M. Chester Nolte, "Crosses Teachers Bear: The Parental Right to Criticize," 18 Educ. L. Rep 1, 8 (1984).]

qualified immunity under state law with respect to referral of student to county children services and recommendation that the student undergo psychiatric testing); *Kraft v. William Alanson White Psychiatric Found'n*, 498 A.2d 1145 (D.C. App. 1985) (Faculty members had absolute privilege from claim of defamation where student had impliedly consented to evaluations, statements made by faculty members were relevant to the purpose that was object of student's consent, and broadcast of statements was limited to those with legitimate interest in subject matter); and *Morrison v. Mobile County Bd. of Educ.*, 495 So. 2d 1086 (Ala. 1986) (Statements made by school board member in response to charges leveled by student's father concerning student's suspension were a fair response and were thus absolutely privileged).

6. Of course, the tables can be turned. Teachers have filed defamation suits against students after the teachers have received poor evaluations. For example, *see Lester v. Powers*, 596 A.2d 65 (Me. 1991) (Letter which was written by student in connection with tenure review was qualifiedly privileged, and contained only statements of opinion, not within the definition of defamatory statements). *See also Baker v. Lafayette College*, 350 Pa. Super. 68, 504 A.2d 247 (1984) (Professor's consent to publication of evaluations gave college absolute privilege against defamation claims as to those evaluations).

Table of Cases

References are to page numbers. Principal cases and the pages where they appear are in italics.

Abbott v. Burke, 17, *1118,* 1133, 1134, 1136, 1137, 1146, 1153, 1175
Abood v. Detroit Board of Education, 577, 586
Abremski v. Southeastern Sch. Dist., 414
Ackerman v. Rubin, 220
Aguilar v. Felton, 1251, 1254, 1273
Alabama High Sch. Athletic Ass'n v. Medders, 220
Alabama State Tenure Comm'n v. Birmingham Bd. of Educ., 698
Alabama Student Party v. Student Gov't Ass'n of the Univ. of Ala., 352
Alamo Heights Indep. Sch. Dist. v. State Bd. of Educ., 1052
Alexander v. Yale Univ., 163
Allen v. Wright, 1349, 1362, 1363
Alter v. City of Newton, 1491
Ambach v. Norwick, 642
Americans United for Separation of Church and State v. Benton, 1283
Americans United for the Separation of Church and State v. Blanton, 1311
Anderson v. Shaugnessy, 1430
Andrews v. Knowlton, 421
Ansonia Board of Education v. Philbrook, 668, 672, 673
Arbegast v. Board of Education of South New Berlin Central School, 1457, 1460-61
Arkansas Activities Association v. Meyer, 215
Arkansas State Bd. of Educ. v. Little Rock Sch. Dist., 852
Arlington Heights v. Metropolitan Housing Dev. Corp., 850
Armstrong v. Manzo, 85
Augustus v. School Bd., 341
Austin Indep. Sch. Dist. v. United States, 850

Ayers v. Western Line Consol. Sch. Dist., 715

B

B.G. v. Crawford Bd. of Educ., 1077
B.M. v. State of Montana, 19, 22, 23, 986
Babb v. Knox County Sch. Sys., 1015
Bahr v. Jenkins, 448
Baker v. Briarcliff Sch. Dist., 1443
Baker v. Lafayette College, 1518
Baker v. Owen, 537
Banks v. Muncie Community Schs., 341
Barbin v. State, 1419
Barbre v. Garland Indep. Sch. Dist., 714
Barnard v. Inhabitants of Shelburne, 424
Barnes v. New Hampshire Karting Ass'n, 1462
Basarich v. Rodeghero, 1514
Battle v. Commonwealth of Pa., 1024
Bazaar v. Fortune, 352
Beasley v. Morton, 1448
Bell v. U-32 Bd. of Educ., 739
Bellnier v. Lund, 462
Ben-Shalom v. Marsh, 281, 282
Benitez v. New York City Bd. of Educ., 1443
Bennett v. City Sch. Dist. of New Rochelle, 221
Bethel School District No. 403 v. Fraser, 305, *326,* 331, 738
Bishop v. Aronov, 708, 709, 750
Bishop v. Wood, 696
Black Coalition v. Portland Sch. Dist. No. 1, 421
Black v. Stephens, 1478

Board of Curators of the Univ. of Mo. v. Horowitz, 424, 559
Board of Educ. of the Sch. Dist. of the City of Cincinnati v. Walter, 1114, 1134, 1136, 1137
Board of Education of Hendrick Hudson Central School District v. Rowley, 988, 995
Board of Education, Island Trees Union Free School District No. 26 v. Pico, *103*, 735, 738
Board of Education of Kiryas Joel Village School District v. Grumet, 1056, *1255*, 1273, 1333, 1334
Board of Education of Oklahoma City Public Schools v. Dowell, 771, 777, 818, *852*, 862-65, 867, 895, 899
Board of Education of Rogers, Arkansas v. McCluskey, 253
Board of Educ. of the Westside Community Schs. v. Mergens, 1226, 1227
Board of Educ. v. Allen, 1282, 1299
Board of Educ. v. Nyquist, 1114, 1134
Board of Educ. v. School Committee of Quincy, 515
Board of Regents v. Roth, 687, 698
Bob Jones University v. United States, *1341*, 1349, 1362, 1363
Boster v. Philpot, 416, 510
Bowers v. Hardwicke, 280-82
Bowsher v. Snyar, 253
Boyd v. Board of Directors of the McGehee School District No. 17, *334*
Boynton v. Casey, 424
Bradley v. Pittsburgh Board of Education, *765*, 768
Bray v. Lee, 158
Brazell v. Board of Education of Niskayuna Public Schools, *1449*, 1450
Breen v. Kahl, 268
Brennan v. Armstrong, 850
Brewer v. Austin Indep. Sch. Dist., 300, 422
Brewer v. Rogers, *1492*

Brooks v. East Chambers Consol. Indep. Sch. Dist., 495
Brown v. Board of Education, 15, 17, 64, 82, *771*, 775, 776, 783, 784, 795, 809, 810, 849, 851, 862, 865, 867, 892, 896, 935-37, 950
Brown v. Dade Christian Schs., 1340
Brown v. Johnson, 542, 549
Brown v. Woodland Joint Unified Sch. Dist., 133
Brownell v. Los Angeles Unified School District, *1432*, 1436, 1437
Brumfield v. Dodd, 1340
Bucha v. Illinois High Sch. Ass'n, 201
Buchanan v. Evans, 851
Burnham v. West, *455*, 462, 463, 477
Burns v. Board of Education of Stamford, 1479, *1487*, 1491
Buse v. Smith, 1114
Byrd v. Bossier Parish Sch. Bd., 1455
Bystrom v. Fridley High Sch., Indep. Sch. Dist. No. 14, 350, 396

C

Cales v. Howell Public Schools, 441, *444*, 449, 463
Calhoun v. Cook, 818
Callaway v. Hafeman, 725
Cameron v. Board of Educ. of the Hillsboro, Ohio, City Sch. Dist., 286, 667
Cammack v. Waihee, 1236
Cannon v. University of Chicago, *158*, 163, 164, 175, 177, 213, 1482
Cape v. Tennessee Secondary Sch. Athletic Ass'n, 200, 201
Carey v. Piphus, 431, 465, 466
Carnes v. Tennessee Secondary Sch. Athletic Ass'n, 200
Cary v. Board of Educ., 708
Casey County Bd. of Educ. v. Luster, 252
Cashdollar v. Northridge Local Sch. Dist. Bd. of Educ., 421
Cason v. Cook, 448

TABLE OF CASES 1521

Castaneda v. Pickard, 953, *958*, 970, 971, 976
Castro v. New York City Bd. of Educ., 697
Centennial School District v. Commonwealth Department of Education, 1086, 1093
Chalk v. United States District Court Central District of California, 679, 686
Chamberlain v. 101 Realty Co., 656
Chambers v. Omaha Girls Club, 286
Chicago Teachers Union, Local No. 1, AFT, AFL-CIO v. Hudson, 589, 594, 595
Childress v. Madison County, 1462
City of Madison Joint Sch. Dist. No. 8 v. Wisconsin Employment Relations Comm'n, 585, 586
Clark v. Jesuit High Sch., 466
Clark v. Shoreline Sch. Dist. No. 412, 685
Clevenger v. Oak Ridge Sch. Bd., 1043
Clever v. Cherry Hill Township Bd. of Educ., 1254
Clinton v. Nagy, 199
Clovis Unified Sch. Dist. v. California Office of Admin. Hearings, 1050, 1056
Cochran v. Louisiana State Bd. of Educ., 1282, 1283, 1332
Coffman v. Kuehler, 415
Cohen v. Brown Univ., 213
Cole v. Newton Special Mun. Separate Sch. Dist., 414
Cole v. Richardson, 758
Coleman v. Franklin Parish Sch. Bd., 537
Columbus Board of Education v. Penick, 818, *824,* 849, 850, 851, 895
Committee for Public Education v. Nyquist, 1316, 1332
Commonwealth v. Bey, 84
Commonwealth v. Carey, 463
Commonwealth v. Pennsylvania Interscholastic Athletic Ass'n, 199
Commonwealth v. Porter, 1478
Community Affairs v. Burdine, 641
Connell v. Higgenbotham, 758
Connick v. Myers, 716, 722-26, 733, 753, 754
Cooper v. Eugene Sch. Dist. No. 4J, 342
Cooper v. Williamson County Bd. of Educ., 699
Coppedge v. Franklin County Bd. of Educ., 818
Cordrey v. Euckert, 1016, 1024, 1025
Coronado v. State, 468
County of Allegheny v. American Civil Liberties Union, 1215
Craig v. Alabama State University, 638
Craig v. Selma City Sch. Bd., 515
Craig v. Y&Y Snacks, 660
Crawford v. Board of Educ. of Los Angeles, 851
Crews v. McQueen, 549
Crosby v. Holsinger, 339, 341, 376
Cross v. Princeton City Sch. Dist. Bd. of Educ., 300
Cunningham v. Beavers, 548, 549

D

D.S.W. v. Fairbanks North Star Borough Sch. Dist., 22
Dahl v. Secretary of U.S. Navy, 280
Dale v. Edmonds, 1515
Daniel R.R. v. State Board of Education, 1026, 1041-43, 1048
Daniels v. Quinn, 725
Danno v. Peterson, 696
Darby v. Schoo, 423, 514
Darrin v. Gould, 200
Davis v. Grover, 1182
Davis v. Henry, 596, 604
Dayton Board of Education v. Brinkman, 797, *818,* 849, 850
Dayton Christian Schs. v. Ohio Civil Rights Comm'n, 286
DeRolphe v. State of Ohio, 1134, 1136, 1137, 1175
DeRosa v. City of N.Y., 22

Dillon v. Pulaski County Special Sch. Dist., 421
Disend v. Meadowbrook Sch., 1504
District 27 Community Sch. Bd. v. Board of Educ., 686
Dixon v. Alabama State Board of Education, 397, 412, 413
Dodson v. Arkansas Athletic Ass'n, 200, 201
Doe v. Board of Educ. of Montgomery County, 22
Doe v. Board of Educ. of Conn., 986
Doe v. Defendant I, *1003*, 1007, 1015
Doe v. District of Columbia, 214
Doe v. Durtschi, 1448
Doe v. Escambia County School Board, *1483*, 1484, 1485, 1491
Doe v. Howell, 1485
Doe v. McMillan, 1517
Doe v. Renfrow, 476
Doe v. Taylor Indep. Sch. Dist., 1477
Doe v. Withers, 1082
Domico v. Rapides Parish Sch. Bd., 715
Donaldson v. Board of Educ., 264
Donohue v. Copiague Sch. Dist., 18, 22, 23
Dorothy J. v. Little Rock Sch. Dist., 1478
Dougherty County Sch. Sys. v. Harris, 659
Draper v. Columbus Public Schools, *515*
Drayden v. Needville Indep. Sch. Dist., 295
Dronenburg v. Zeck, 281
Dubbs v. Central Intelligence Agency, 281
Dube v. The State Univ. of N.Y., 751
Dupree v. Alma Sch. Dist. No. 80, 1114
Duran v. Nitsche, *362*, 368

E

East Brunswick Bd. of Educ. v. East Brunswick Educ. Ass'n, 604
East Hartford Educ. Ass'n. v. Board of Educ. of East Hartford, 342, 714
Edgewood Independent School District v. Kirby, *1147*, 1153, 1154
Edwards v. Aguillard, 103, 1225, 1226
Edwards v. Rees, *442*, 448
Eisel v. Board of Education of Montgomery County, *1423*, 1429
Ellerbee v. Mills, 1515
Elliot v. Rice, 296
Elliott v. New Miami Board of Education, 1478
Ellison v. Brady, 658
Employment Div., Dep't of Human Resources of Or. v. Smith, 86, 87
Engel v. Vitale, 1189, 1203, 1215, 1250
Epperson v. Arkansas, *96*, 101-03
Equal Employment Opportunity Comm'n v. Atlantic Community Sch. Dist., 616
Espinosa v. Fresno Unified Sch. Dist., 1448
Esteban v. Central Missouri State College, *384*, 391, 392, 413
Eva N. and Timothy H. v. Brock, 987
Evans v. Buchanan, 818
Evans v. Romer, 280
Evans v. Tuttle, 222, 986
Everson v. Board of Education, *1277*, 1281-83, 1299, 1300

F

Fallon v. Indian Trail Sch., 1417, 1419
Farace v. Board of Educ. of Guilford, 1487
Faulkner v. Jones, 186
Favia v. Indiana Univ. of Pa., 213
Fee v. Herndon, *543*, 548, 549
Felter v. Cape Girardeau Sch. Dist., 1284
Filler v. Port Washington Union Free Sch. Dist., 1297, 1299
Fisher v. Burkburnett Indep. Sch. Dist., 559

Fisher v. Clackamas County Sch. Dist. 12, 1235
Fitzpatrick v. Board of Educ., 252
Fleischfresser v. Directors of Sch. Dist. 200, 133
Florence County Sch. Dist. Four v. Carter, 1076
Florey v. Sioux Falls Sch. Dist. 49-5, 1224
Florida High Sch. Activities Ass'n v. Bryant, 220
Flory v. Smith, 249, 252, 253, 261
Foley v. Benedict, 424
Force v. Pierce City R-VI Sch. Dist., 200
Forrest v. School City of Hobart, 514
Fowler v. Board of Education of Lincoln County, Kentucky, 141, 738, 739, 768
Frain v. Baron, 319, 324, 325
Frank v. Arapahoe County Sch. Dist., 696
Franklin v. Gwinnett County Public Schools, 164, 177, 207, 213-215, 295, 660, 1082, 1482, 1483
Franks v. Bowman Transp. Co., 637
Fredrickson v. Denver Pub. Sch. Dist. No.1, 699
Freeman v. Pitts, 771, 777, 868, 892, 894-96, 899
Freidhoff v. Board of Sch. Dirs. of Conemaugh Valley Sch. Dist., 570
Freier v. Independent School District No. 197, 1498, 1504, 1513
Fricke v. Lynch, 275, 279, 280, 282
Fullilove v. Klutznick, 240, 637

G

Garcia v. Miera, 537, 542, 549
Garnett v. Renton Sch. Dist., 369
Garrett v. Board of Education of School District of City of Detroit, 177, 186
Garrett v. Rader, 543
Gates v. Unified Sch. Dist. No. 449 of Leavenworth County, Kansas, 1478
Gaylor v. Tacoma Sch. Dist., 759

Geller v. Markham, 608, 616
Gertz v. Welch, 1497
Gibson v. Florida Bar, 595
Givhan v. Western Line Consol. Sch. Dists., 709, 715, 716
Glover v. Cole, 352
Goben v. School Dist. of St. Joseph, 1492
Goetz v. Ansell, 324
Gonzales v. McEuen, 416, 421, 422
Gordon v. Warren Consol. Bd. of Educ., 299
Gorman v. University of Rhode Island, 422
Goss v. Lopez, 405, 413-16, 421-23, 497, 520, 525, 535, 559
Goston v. Hutchison, 1487
Gott v. Berea College, 424
Graham v. Renbrook Sch., 616
Green v. County School Board, 777, 783, 784, 818, 851
Green v. Kennedy, 1349, 1363
Greenspan v. Antin, 414
Greer v. Rome City Sch. Dist., 1042, 1043
Gregoire v. Centennial Sch. Dist., 369
Griffin v. Thomas, 726
Griggs v. Duke Power Co., 616, 617
Grimes v. Eastern Illinois Univ., 725
Griswold v. Connecticut, 64
Grove City College v. Bell, 175, 659
Grove v. Mead Sch. Dist. No. 354, 135
Grunwald v. San Bernardino Teachers Ass'n, 594, 595
Guardians Ass'n v. Civil Serv. Comm'n, N.Y.C., 240, 295
Guerra v. Roma Indep. Sch. Dist., 696
Guhn v. Board of Educ., Clyde-Green Springs Sch. Dist., 1437, 1438
Guzick v. Drebus, 318
Gwirtz v. Ohio Educ. Ass'n, 595

H

Hager v. Bellingham Sch. Dist. No. 501, 1432
Hailey v. Brooks, 252

Hale v. Pringle, 543
Hamer v. Board of Educ., 263
Harden v. Adams, 715
Harleston v. Jeffries, 753, 754
Harlow v. Fitzgerald, 431
Harper v. Edgewood Board of Education, 272, 279, 280, 282
Harris v. Crenshaw County Bd. of Educ., 797
Harris v. Galilley, 534
Harris v. United States, 468
Harrison v. Sobol, 42, 59
Hart v. Community Sch. Bd. of Educ., 818
Hawkins v. Coleman, 520, 525, 537
Hazelwood Sch. Dist. v. United States, 794
Hazelwood School District v. Kuhlmeier, 116, 317, *342,* 349-52, 376, 733, 735, 737, 738, 750, 1227
Helbig v. City of N.Y., 22
Helena Elementary School District No. 1 v. State of Montana, 1138, 1146
Hemry v. School Bd. of Colorado Springs Sch. Dist., 369
Henson v. University of Ark., 41
High Tech Gays v. Defense Indus. Sec. Clearance Office, 281
Hillman v. Elliott, 414
Hills v. Gautreaux, 851
Hobson v. Hansen, 907, 924-27, 936-38, 950, 952, 953, 967
Hohe v. San Diego Unified Sch. Dist., 1462
Holthaus v. Board of Educ., 698
Honig v. Doe, 305, *1057,* 1063, 1069, 1070
Hoover v. Meiklejohn, 200
Hornbeck v. Somerset County Bd. of Educ., 1134
Horowitz v. Board of Curators of the Univ. of Mo., 416, 424
Horton v. Goose Creek Independent School District, 466, *469,* 476, 477
Horton v. Meskill, 1114, 1180

Hortonville Educ. Ass'n v. Hortonville Joint Sch. Dist. No. 1, 603, 604
Howard v. Colonial Sch. Dist., 505
Hurlburt v. Noxon, 1444-46, 1484, 1487

I

In Interest of Dumas, 465
In re Alexander B., 462
In re Gault, 84
In re Jension, 83
In re William G., 441, 450
In the Matter of P.J., 265
Independent Sch. Dist. No. 4 of Harper County v. Orange, 698
Industrial Union Dep't v. American Petroleum Inst., 252
Ingraham v. Wright, 526, 534-36, 542, 548, 549
Iron Arrow Honor Soc'y v. Heckler, 207
Irving Independent School District v. Tatro, 1045, 1049-1050
Israel v. West Virginia Secondary Schools Activities Commission, 202, 206

J

Jackson v. Sobol, 699
Jager v. Douglas County Sch. Dist., 1205
James v. Board of Educ., 708
Jantz v. Muci, 667
Jarreau v. Orleans Parish School Board, 1452
Jefferson County v. Breen, 1077
Jenkins v. Louisiana Bd. of Educ., 390
Jenkins v. Missouri, 851, 852
Jerabek v. Public Employment Relations Bd., 595
Jersey Shore Area School District v. Jersey Shore Education Ass'n, 564, 570, 604
Jew v. University of Iowa, 660, 667

John and Kathryn G. v. Board of Education of Mount Vernon Public Schools, 1077, 1082
Johnson v. Indep. Sch. Dist. No. 4 of Bixby, 1024, 1025
Johnson v. Pinkerton Academy, 716
Johnson v. San Jancinto College, 699
Johnson v. Southwestern Newspapers Corp., 1515
Johnson v. Transportation Co., 639
Johnston v. Corinthian Television Corp., 1514
Joint Anti-Fascist Refugee Comm. v. McGrath, 412
Jones v. Board of Educ. of Sch. Dist. 50, Archuleta and Hinsdale Counties, 1432
Jones v. Clear Creek Independent School District, 1217, 1225
Jones v. Latexo Indep. Sch. Dist., 463, 476
Jones v. Oklahoma Secondary Sch. Activities Ass'n, 201
Jones v. Wesco Investments, 656
Jorstad v. Texas City Indep. Sch. Dist., 1063
Joyce v. Simi Valley Unified Sch. Dist., 1430
Joyner v. Whiting, 351
JSK v. Hendry County Sch. Bd., 995
Judd v. Board of Educ., 1282
Junior College of St. Louis v. Califano, 659

K

Kadrmas v. Dickinson Pub. Schs., 35-6
Kaelin v. Grubbs, 1064, 1070
Karetnikova v. Trustees of Emerson College, 759
Katchak v. Glasgow Indep. Sch. Sys., 262
Katz v. United States, 282
Katzman v. Cumberland Valley School District, 263, *556,* 559, 560
Kelley v. Bonney, 1505, 1513-15

Kennedy v. Providence Hockey Club, 1461
Keough v. Tate County Bd. of Educ., 421
Kevin v. Board of Educ., Lamar Sch. Dist., No. RE-2, Prowers County, 698
Keyes v. School District No. 1, 797, 809, 810, 849, 862, 895, 968
Keyishian v. Board of Regents, 734, 755, 759, 764
Kinsey v. Salado Indep. Sch. Dist., 709
Kirkland v. Northside Indep. Sch. Dist., 148, 351
Knight v. State of Alabama, 40
Kraft v. William Alanson White Psychiatric Found., 1518
Krizek v. Board of Educ. of Cicero-Stickney Twp. High Sch. Dist. No. 201, 148, 351, 739, 768
Krueth v. Independent School District No. 38, Red Lake, Minnesota, 632, 636, 637, 640, 641
Kuehn v. Renton Sch. Dist. #403, 461

L

La Mountain v. South Colonie Cent. Sch. Dist., 1443
Laboy v. Wallkill Cent. Sch. Dist., 1462
Lamb v. Panhandle Community Unit Sch. Dist. No. 2, 421
Lamb's Chapel v. Center Moriches Union Free Sch. Dist., 369, 1227, 1228
Lampkin v. District of Columbia, 47, 59
Lanner v. Wimmer, 1236
Larry P. v. Riles, 939, 950-53
Lascari v. Board of Education of Ramapo Indian Hills Regional High School District, 1008, 1015
Lau v. Nichols, 954, 967, 968, 970, 971
Lee v. Thompson, 1024
Lee v. Weisman, 342, 368, 369, *1207,* 1215, 1216, 1225, 1227, 1333

Leffel v. Wisconsin Interscholastic Athletic Ass'n, 214
Lehnert v. Ferris Faculty Ass'n, 587
Lemon v. Bossier Parish Sch. Bd., 935
Lemon v. Kurtzman, 1203-07, 1215, 1216, 1225-28, 1236, 1273, *1300*, 1311, 1315, 1331-34
Lester v. Powers, 1518
Levie, III v. Orleans Parish School Board, 1420, 1422
Levin v. Harleston, 739, 749, 750, 751, 753, 754
Lewis v. Dependent Sch. Dist. No. 10, 1455
Lieberman v. University of Chicago, 294
Lippincott v. Lippincott, 85
Lipsett v. University of Puerto Rico, 659
Little Rock Sch. Dist. v. Pulaski County Special Sch. Dist., 852
Lochner v. New York, 64
Locilento v. John A. Coleman Catholic High Sch., 1460
Lockett v. Board of Educ. for Sch. Dist. No. 189, 1447
Long v. Thornton Twp. High Sch. Dist. 205, 526
Lowary v. Lexington Bd. of Educ., 595
Lowe v. Commack Union Free Sch. Dist., 615, 616
Lucas v. Fresno Unified Sch. Dist., 1461
Lujon v. Franklin County Bd. of Educ., 640
Luthens v. Blair, 1332
Lynch v. Donnelly, 1224, 1333

M

M. v. Board of Educ., 423
Mabry v. State Bd. of Community Colleges and Occupational Educ., 659
Maddox v. City of N.Y., 1462
Maness v. City of N.Y., 252, 1436, 1438
Marlowe v. Rush-Henrietta Cent. Sch. Dist., 1461, 1462
Marsh v. Chambers, 1205, 1216
Martens v. District No. 220 Bd. of Educ., 448
Martin Luther King Jr. Elementary School Children v. Ann Arbor School District, 971
Martinez v. Moroldo, 1432
Martinez v. School Dist. No. 60, 462, 463
Matter of Johnson, 505
Matter of Richards, 59
Matthews v. Quinton, 1282
May v. Cooperman, 1206
McCain v. Koch, 55
McCarthy v. Fletcher, 121
McCarthy v. Hornbeck, 1283
McCartney v. Oblates of St. Francis DeSales, 1505
McClain v. Lafayette County Bd. of Educ., 262
McCollum v. Board of Education, 1228, 1235
McDaniel v. Thomas, 1113
McDonnell Douglas Corp. v. Green, 641
McGee v. South Pemiscot Sch. Dist. R-V, 715
McNair v. Oak Hills Local Sch. Dist., 1050, 1052
McNeal v. Tate County School District, 928, 935-38
Meek v. Pittinger, 1297, 1300
Meltzer v. Board of Educ. of Orange County, 1225
Members of Jamestown Sch. Comm. v. Schmidt, 1283
Memphis Comm. Sch. Dist. v. Stachura, 431
Mercer v. Michigan, 102
Meritor Savings Bank, F.S.B. v. Vinson, 648, 656-61, 667
Metropolitan School District of Wayne Township, Marion County, Indiana v. Davila, 1064, 1069, 1070

TABLE OF CASES 1527

Meyer v. State of Nebraska, 34, 64, 83, *91*, 95, 101, 132, 319, 953, 1250
Miles v. Denver Public Schools, 351, 727, 733-35, 750
Milkovich v. News-Herald, 1497, 1515
Miller v. Cooper, 1225
Milliken v. Bradley, *810*, 814, 817, 818, 851, 863
Milliken v. Green, 1114
Mills v. Board of Education, 977
Mills v. Board of Education of the Dist. of Columbia, 414
Mirand v. New York, *1439*, 1442
Mississippi Employment Sec. Comm'n v. McGlothin, 341
Mississippi Univ. for Women v. Hogan, 86
Missouri v. Jenkins, 851
Mistretta v. United States, 253
Mitchell v. Board of Trustees of Oxford Municipal Separate School District, 253, *300*
Mitchell v. Los Angeles Unified Sch. Dist., 595
Moire v. Temple Univ. Sch. of Med., 659
Monell v. Department of Social Servs., 431
Monroe v. Board of Comm'rs, 783
Moore v. Gaston County Bd. of Educ., 708
Morgan v. Hennigan, 818
Morrison v. Mobile County Bd. of Educ., 1518
Morton v. Mancari, 640, 641
Mosley v. Portland Sch. Dist. No. 1J, 1484
Moss v. Stamford Bd. of Educ., 818
Moss v. Stockard, 1504
Moyer v. Amador Valley Joint Union High Sch., 1497
Mozert v. Hawkins County Board of Education, *124*, 132, 133, 135
Mt. Healthy City School Board of Education v. Doyle, *709*, 714, 715, 724, 725, 733, 738, 750, 753, 754
Mueller v. Allen, *1325*, 1331, 1332

Murray v. West Baton Rouge Parish Sch. Bd., 390

N

NAACP v. Georgia, 936
Napolitano v. Trustees of Princeton Univ., 559
Naranjo v. Southwest Indep. Sch. Dist., 1487
Narogon v. Wharton, 281
Nash v. Auburn Univ., 416
National Gay Task Force v. Board of Educ. of Oklahoma City, 759
New Braunfels Independent School District v. Armke, 264, *554*, 559, 560
New Jersey v. T.L.O., 305, *432*, 439, 441, 442, 448, 461, 462, 465, 468, 514
New York State Ass'n for Retarded Children v. Carey, 686
New York Times v. Sullivan, 1514
Newberg v. Board of Public Education, *153*, 156, 157, 185
Newsome v. Batavia Local School District, 415, 422, 423, *510*, 514
Nicholson v. Bd. of Educ., Torrance Unified Sch. Dist., 350
Niederhuber v. Camden County Vocational & Technical Sch. Dist. Bd. of Educ., 673
Nodar v. Galbreath, 1504, 1515
Nolan v. Bronson, 1431
Norma P. v. Pelham Sch. Dist., 1007
North Haven Bd. of Educ. v. Bell, 659
Norwalk CORE v. Norwalk Bd. of Educ., 818
Norwood v. Harrison, 1341, 1362

O

O'Brien v. Board of Educ. of City of N.Y., 604
O'Connor v. Ortega, 442
O'Donniley v. Metropolitan Pub. Schs., 222, 986

O'Halloran v. University of Washington, 494
Oberti v. Board of Educ. of Clementon Sch. Dist., 1043, 1044
Odenheim v. Carlstadt-East Rutherford Regional Sch. Dist., 494
Ohnstad v. Omaha Pub. Sch. Dist. No. 1 of Douglas County, 1442
Olesen v. Board of Education of School District No. 228, 265, 268, 269, 271, 272
Olmstead v. United States, 282
Olsen v. State, 1114
Omlor v. Cleveland State Univ., 751
Orozco v. Sobol, 36, 58, 59
Osterbeck v. State, 549

P

Padula v. Webster, 281
Page v. Delaune, 725
Paliska v. St. Anselm Sch., 1442
Palko v. Connecticut, 282
Palmer v. Bennington Sch. Dist., 1515
Palmer v. Board of Educ. of City of Chicago, 148
Papasan v. Allain, 35, 36
Parducci v. Rutland, 136
Paredes v. Curtis, 413, 415, 416
Parents in Action on Special Education (PASE) v. Hannon, 946, 952, 953
Parker v. Wynn, 1485
Pasadena Bd. of Educ. v. Spangler, 850
Patterson v. Meramec Valley R-III Sch. Dist., 1447
Paul v. McGhee, 536
Peloza v. Capistrano Unified Sch. Dist., 708, 709
Pennsylvania Ass'n for Retarded Children (PARC) v. Pennsylvania, 977
People ex. rel. King. v. Gallagher, 935
People v. Singletary, 448
People Who Care v. Rockford Bd. of Educ. Sch. Dist. #205, 938
Perry v. Sindermann, 692, 762, 763
Person v. Gum, 1437, 1438

Pervis v. LaMarque Indep. Sch. Dist., 421
Peter W. v. San Francisco Unified Sch. Dist., 17-19, 22, 23
Peters v. Moses, 240
Pfeiffer v. Marion Center Area School District, 287, 294-96
Piarowski v. Illinois Community College, 739
Pickering v. Board of Education, 701, 707-09, 715, 722-25, 733, 754
Pierce v. Board of Educ., 19
Pierce v. Society of Sisters of the Holy Names of Jesus and Mary, 34, 61, 64, 65, 82, 83, 86, 953, 1250
Pinsker v. Joint Dist. No. 28J of Adams and Arapahoe Counties, 672, 673
Piver v. Pender County Ct. of Educ., 708
Planned Parenthood of Southern Nevada, Inc. v. Clark County School District, 352
Planned Parenthood v. Clark County Sch. Dist., 739
Plessy v. Ferguson, 636, 776, 935
Plyler v. Doe, 24, 33-36, 58-60
Podberesky v. Kirwan, 241, 247
Poe v. Hamilton, 22
Poling v. Murphy, 350, 369, 376
Polk v. Central Susquehanna Intermediate Unit 16, 995, 1001, 1024, 1025
Pollnow v. Glennon, 500, 505
Ponton v. Newport News Sch. Bd., 286
Prince v. Massachusetts, 82
Princeton Educ. Ass'n v. Princeton Bd. of Educ., 585
Psi Upsilon v. University of Pa., 510
Pyle v. South Hadley School Committee, 332

Q

Quappe v. Endry, 369
Quarles v. Oxford Municipal Separate School District, 931, 936-38

TABLE OF CASES

R

R.A.V. v. St. Paul, 753
Rabidue v. Osceola Refining Co., 658
Rankin v. McPherson, 724
Rankins v. Commission on Prof. Comp., 673
Ray v. School Dist. of DeSoto County, 686
Reddick v. Stanton Pub. Sch. Dist. No. 55, 1443
Regents of the University of California v. Bakke, 223, *224*, 238, 240, 637, 970
Regents of Univ. of Mich. v. Ewing, 424
Reichley by Wall v. North Penn Sch. Dist., 570
Rendell-Baker v. Kohn, 716
Rettig v. Kent City Sch. Dist., 1024
Rhode Island Fed'n of Teachers v. Norberg, 1331
Rhodus v. Dumiller, 536
Rich v. Kentucky Country Day Sch., Inc., 23, 1517
Richards v. Thurston, 269
Richardson v. Braham, 252
Richmond Newspapers v. Lipscomb, 1515
Riddick v. Norfolk, 863, 864
Rivera v. East Otero Sch. Dist., 396
Rixmann v. Somerset Pub. Schs., St. Croix County, 1451
Rizzo v. Goode, 851
Roberson v. Duval County Sch. Bd., 1447
Roberts v. City of Boston, 935, 936
Roberts v. Colorado State Univ., 213
Roberts v. Madigan, 116, 120
Roberts v. Robertson County Board of Education, *1409*, 1417, 1419, 1420
Roberts v. Van Buren Public Schools, 725
Robinson v. Cahill, 16, 17, *1108*, 1112-14
Robinson v. Oak Park and River Forest High Sch., 264
Roe v. Wade, 65, 282
Roemer v. Board of Pub. Works of Md., 1311
Rogers v. Bennett, 1002
Rohraugh v. Elida Bd. of Educ., 262
Rollins v. Concordia Parish Sch. Bd., 1423
Roman v. Appleby, 1504
Romano v. Harrington, 737, 738
Romeo Community Schs. v. United States Dept. of Health, Educ. and Welfare, 659
Roncker v. Walter, 1041, 1042, 1048
Rosa R. v. Connelly, 515
Rose v. Council for Better Education, Inc., *1155*, 1174
Ross v. Creighton Univ., 18
Rowland v. Mad River Local Sch. Dist, 699
Runyon v. McClary, 851, *1334*, 1340
Rupp v. Bryant, 1447
Rust v. Sullivan, 759, 762-764, 1514

S

S-1 v. Turlington, 1064, 1070
S.C. v. State, 465
Sacramento City Unified School District Board of Education v. Holland, *1035*, 1043
Salazar v. Luty, *296*, 299
Salek v. Passaic Collegiate Sch., 1497
Same v. Hill Military Academy, *61*
San Antonio Independent School District v. Rodriguez, 16, 17, 33-36, 818, 1044, *1096*, 1107, 1108, 1112, 1113, 1153
Saquebo v. Rogue, 759
Schaill v. Tippecanoe County School Corporation, 487, 494, 495
Schmerber v. California, 468
School Board of Nassau County, Florida v. Arline, *674*
School Bd. of the County of Prince William, Va. v. Malone, 299

School Committee of the Town of Burlington, Massachusetts v. Department of Education of Massachusetts, 1070, 1077
School Dist. of the City of Grand Rapids v. Ball, 1333
School District of Abington Township v. Schempp, 1185, 1189-91, 1203, 1204, 1207, 1215, 1250
School Dist. of Omaha v. United States, 850
Scoggins v. Board of Educ. of Nashville, 638
Scott v. Pacific West Mt. Resort, 1461
Scoville v. Board of Educ. of Joliet Twp. High Sch. Dist. 204, 318, 350
Seattle Sch. Dist. No. 1 v. State, 1114
Seemuller v. Fairfax County Sch. Bd., 709
Serna v. Portales Mun. Schs., 967
Serrano v. Priest , 1107, 1108, 1113, 1114
Sertik v. School Dist. of Pittsburgh, 699
Seyfried v. Walton, 350, 739
Shamloo v. Mississippi State Bd. of Trustees of Insts. of Higher Learning, 392
Sharif v. New York State Education Department, 164, 175, 177, 214, 953
Sheck v. Baileyville Sch. Comm., 116
Sherman v. Community Consol. Sch. Dist., 325
Sherpell v. Humnoke Sch. Dist. No.5, 265, 397
Shofstall v. Hollins, 1114
Showalter v. Allison Reed Group, 659
Siegel v. Board of Educ. of City Sch. Dist. of N.Y., 667
Sinn v. Daily Nebraskan, 352
Skeen v. State, 1181
Slocum v. Holton Board of Education, 263 550, 559
Slotterback v. Interboro Sch. Dist., 369, 396
Smith v. Board of Governors of the Univ. of N.C., 1311

Smith v. Board of Commissioners of Mobile County, 1237, 1245, 1254
Smith v. Board of Sch. Comm'rs of Ala., 135
Smith v. Denver Pub. Sch. Bd., 698
Smith v. Little Rock School District, 505, 509, 510
Smith v. School City of Hobart, 256, 261-64, 559
Smith v. Smith, 1235
Smith v. St. Tammany Parish Sch. Bd., 340
Smith v. Travis County Educ. Dist., 1154
Smuck v. Hobson, 924
Snider v. Snider, 1438
Soglin v. Kauffman, 381, 390, 391
Spangler v. Pasadena, 863, 864
Springfield Sch. Dist. v. Pennsylvania Dept. of Educ., 1299
Squires v. Sierra Nevada Educ. Found., Inc., 23
St. Mary's Honor Ctr. v. Hicks, 641
St. Pierre v. Lombard, 1443
State ex rel. Holt v. Thompson, 1235
State ex rel. Kelley v. Ferguson, 121, 124
State ex rel. Sheibley v. School Dist., 124
State ex rel. Sherman v. Hyman, 412
State ex rel. Shineman v. Board of Educ., 16
State Farm Mut. Auto. Ins. Co. v. Pharr, 1446
State of Washington v. Slattery, 448, 466, 468
State v. D.T.W., 468
State v. Joseph T., 465
State v. McKinnon, 468
State v. Parker, 698
Steele v. Van Buren Pub. Sch. Dist, 1206
Steffan v. Aspin, 280
Steffan v. Cheney, 281
Stein v. Plainwell Community Sch. Dist., 1205, 1216, 1217

Dist., 1492
Stone v. Graham, 1206
Stoneking v. Bradford Area School District, 1470, 1477-78, 1482
Street v. Cobb County School District, 282, 285, 286
Strickland v. Inlow, 422, 423, 431
Strongin v. Nyquist, 696
Student Alpha ID No. Guja v. School Bd. of Volusia County, 510
Sutton v. Duplessis, 1446
Swann v. Charlotte-Mecklenburg Board of Education, 784, 794, 797, 809, 849
Sweet v. Childs, 526
Sweezy v. New Hampshire, 734
Swentek v. USAir, 656
Syquia v. Board of Educ. of Harpursville Cent. Sch. Dist., 697

T

T.A. O'B v. State, 441
Tanberg v. Weld County Sheriff, 14
Tarter v. Rayback, 449
Teachers, Inc. v. Smith, 1389
Tennessee Small Sch. Sys. v. McWherter, 1114
Texas State Teachers Association v. Garland Independent School District, 571
Thomas v. St. Mary's Roman Catholic Church, 1456, 1461
Thompson v. Ange, 1450
Thompson v. Engelking, 1114
Thompson v. Modesto City High Sch. Dist., 696
Thompson v. Waynesboro Area Sch. Dist., 369
Thrasher v. General Cas. Co. of Wis., 536
Thurmond v. Richmond County Bd. of Educ., 1479
Tilton v. Richardson, 1307
Timothy W. v. Rochester, New Hampshire, School District, *979*, 985, 987

Tincani v. Inland Empire Zoological Soc'y, 1461, 1462
Tinker v. Des Moines Independent Community School District, 132, 269, 305, *307*, 312, 313, 317-19, 324, 325, 331, 342, 350, 352, 549, 576, 708, 768, 1315
Tinkham v. Groveport Madison Local Sch. Dist., 1448, 1484
Torres v. Little Flower Children's Servs., 22
Trachtman v. Anker, 350
Trans-World Airlines, Inc. v. Hardison, 673
Trautvetter v. Quick, 657
Trustees of Univ. of Del. v. Gebelein, 247
Tryon v. City of Lowell, 1432
Turley v. School Dist. of Kansas City, 536

U

United States v. Tunica County Sch. Dist., 935
United Pub. Workers v. Mitchell, 59
United States v. Commonwealth of Virginia, 186
United States v. Gadsden County Sch. Dist., 935
United States v. Place, 477

V

Vaughns v. Board of Educ. of Prince George's County, 638
Vernonia Sch. Dist. v. Acton, 495
Vigars v. Valley Christian Ctr. of Dublin, Cal., 286
Virgil v. School Board of Columbia County, Florida, 116, 120, 739
Vorchheimer v. School Dist. of Philadelphia, 156, 157

W

Wallace v. Ford, 269
Wallace v. Jaffree, 1191, 1203-07
Waltman v. International Paper Co., 660
Waltz v. Wake County Bd. of Educ., 1422
Walz v. Tax Comm'n, 1349
Wangsness v. Watertown Sch. Dist. No. 14-4 of Codington County, 673
Ward v. Flood, 16
Wards Cove Packing Co. v. Atonio, 177, 617
Warren County Bd. of Educ. v. Wilkinson, 559
Washakie County Sch. Dist. #1 v. Herschler, 1114
Washington v. Davis, 851
Waters v. Churchill, 754
Watkins v. United States Army, 281
Wayne County Bd. of Educ. v. Tyre, 415
Webb v. McCullough, 450, 461, 462
Webster v. Doe, 281
Webster v. New Lenox Sch. Dist. No. 122, 148, 351
Weese v. Muir, 1446
Welch v. Board of Educ., 696
West Virginia State Board of Education v. Barnette, 95, 1190, 1191, *1246*, 1250, 1251, 1315
Westchester County v. Rowley, 988, 995, 1025, 1040-42, 1044, 1048, 1137
Widener v. Frye, 449
Wiemerslage v. Maine Township High School District 207, 392, 396
Williams v. Columbus Bd. of Educ., 1485
Williams v. Ellington, 477, 494
Wisconsin v. Yoder, 65, 81-87, 132, 1250, 1315
Wise v. Pea Ridge Sch. Dist., 536, 548
Witters v. Department of Servs. for the Blind, 1332
Wolman v. Walter, 1204, *1284*, 1297-1300
Wood v. Strickland, 261, 263, 264, 422, *425*, 439, 1492
Wort v. Vierling, 296
Wygant v. Jackson Board of Education, 617, 636-41
Wynn v. Board of Educ., 462

Y

Yanzick v. School Dist. No. 23, 699
Yates v. AVCO Corp., 660
Yatvin v. Madison Metropolitan School District, 662, 667
Yeager v. Morgan, 1430
Yellow Springs Exempted Village School District v. Ohio High School Athletic Association, 187, 199, 202, 206, 207
Yurkovich v. Rose, 1431

Z

Zellman v. Kenston Bd. of Educ., 986
Zobrest v. Catalina Foothills School District, 1052, 1056, 1273
Zorach v. Clauson, 1230, 1235, 1236
Zykan v. Warsaw Community Sch. Corp., 708

Index

A

ACADEMIC CREDIT.
Religious classes held off-campus, pp. 1236, 1237.

ACADEMIC FREEDOM.
Instructional materials, pp. 765 to 768.

ACADEMIC OPPORTUNITIES.
Student classification by sex, pp. 153 to 186.

ACADEMIC SANCTIONS, pp. 550 to 560.

ACHIEVEMENT TESTS.
Student ability grouping.
  Generally, pp. 907 to 953.
    See STUDENT ABILITY GROUPING.

ACTIONS.
Private right of action.
  See PRIVATE RIGHT OF ACTION.

ADMINISTRATIVE HEARING RIGHTS, pp. 397 to 431.
Due process, pp. 397 to 425.
School authority liability for failure to provide, pp. 425 to 431.

ADULTERY.
Discharge of teacher.
  Due process issue, p. 699.

AFRICAN AMERICANS.
At-risk urban male academies, pp. 177 to 186.
Racial segregation.
  Generally, pp. 771 to 905.
    See RACIAL SEGREGATION.
Student classification by race, pp. 222 to 247.
  See STUDENT CLASSIFICATION BY RACE.
Student conduct, p. 265.
Teaching in colonial times, p. 6.

AGE.
Student classification by age, pp. 215 to 222.

AGE—Cont'd
Teacher employment relations.
  Hiring and discharge, pp. 608 to 616.

AIDS-INFECTED TEACHERS.
Employment discrimination, pp. 679 to 686.

ALIENS.
Right of universal education, pp. 24 to 36.
Teacher employment discrimination, pp. 642 to 646.

ALTERNATIVE SCHOOL PROGRAMS FOR THE HOMELESS, p. 61.

ALTERNATIVES TO PUBLIC EDUCATION.
Educational choice.
  Parental choice, pp. 1389 to 1404.
  Public school problems and choice proposals, pp. 1363 to 1388.
Private schools.
  See PRIVATE SCHOOLS.

ASSUMPTION OF RISK, pp. 1408, 1457 to 1463, 1468, 1469.

ATHEISM.
Church-state relations, pp. 1185 to 1189.

ATHLETIC PARTICIPATION AND EVENTS.
Assumption of risk, pp. 1457 to 1463, 1468, 1469.
Contributory negligence, pp. 1452 to 1456.
Immunity from liability, pp. 1485, 1486.
Negligence, pp. 1442 to 1444, 1463 to 1466.
Student classification by age, pp. 215 to 222.
Student classification by sex, pp. 187 to 207.

AT-RISK URBAN MALE ACADEMIES, pp. 177 to 186.

AUTOMOBILE SEARCHES, pp. 466 to 469.

B

BAKKE CASE, pp. 224 to 237.

BENEDICTIONS AT GRADUATION CEREMONIES.
Church-state relations, pp. 1207 to 1224.

BIBLE READING AND PRAYER, pp. 1185 to 1228.
Graduation ceremonies.
   Invocations and benedictions, pp. 1207 to 1224.

BILINGUAL EDUCATION, pp. 953 to 976.
Adequacy of language remediation program, pp. 958 to 966.
Federal statutory predicate, pp. 954 to 957.
Home/community language barriers, pp. 971 to 976.
Student ability grouping.
   Generally, pp. 907 to 953.
     See STUDENT ABILITY GROUPING.

BLACK PERSONS.
See AFRICAN AMERICANS.

BOOK BANNING.
High school courses, pp. 116 to 120.
Libraries, pp. 103 to 116.

BURFORD ABSTENTION.
Right of universal education.
   Residence requirements.
     Termination of education for nonresidents, pp. 44, 45.

BURN CASES.
Defenses to negligence, pp. 1449, 1452.

C

CAR SEARCHES, pp. 466 to 469.

CENSORSHIP.
Books banned from high school courses, pp. 116 to 120.
Books banned from libraries, pp. 103 to 116.

CHILDREN WITH DISABILITIES.
Americans with Disabilities Act.
   Impact of Act upon public education, pp. 1082 to 1086.
Bilingual education.
   Generally, pp. 953 to 976.
     See BILINGUAL EDUCATION.
Classification by age, pp. 221, 222.

CHILDREN WITH DISABILITIES
—Cont'd
Homeless children.
   Right to education compared to handicapped children, p. 60.
Special education.
   Generally, pp. 977 to 1086.
     See SPECIAL EDUCATION.
Student ability grouping.
   IQ tests and E.M.R. placement, pp. 939 to 950.

CHOICE BY PARENTS, pp. 1389 to 1404.

CHOICE PROPOSALS AND PUBLIC SCHOOL PROBLEMS, pp. 1363 to 1388.

CHRISTMAS ASSEMBLIES.
Church-state relations, p. 1225.

CHURCH-RELATED COLLEGES AND UNIVERSITIES.
Financing, pp. 1308 to 1316.

CHURCH-STATE RELATIONS.
Bible reading and prayer, pp. 1185 to 1228.
Christmas assemblies, p. 1224.
Compelled public school attendance, pp. 61 to 65.
Compulsory education conflicting with religious beliefs, pp. 65 to 87.
Curriculum, pp. 1224 to 1226.
   Choices by parents, pp. 124 to 136.
   Religious objections, pp. 1237 to 1246.
Equal Access Act, pp. 1226 to 1228.
Excusal from religious practices, pp. 1189, 1190.
Expression of religious viewpoints by students in schools, pp. 362 to 369.
Financing parochial schools for public benefit, pp. 1251 to 1254.
Financing private schools for public benefit generally.
   See FINANCING PRIVATE SCHOOLS FOR PUBLIC BENEFIT.
Flag salute, pp. 1246 to 1250.
General restraints, pp. 1207 to 1228.
Graduation ceremonies.
   Invocations and benedictions, pp. 1207 to 1224.
Home schooling, pp. 65 to 87.
Meditation periods, pp. 1191 to 1207.
Pledge of Allegiance, pp. 1246 to 1260.
Released at time for religious instruction, pp. 1228 to 1237.
Religious holidays, pp. 1235, 1236.

INDEX

CHURCH-STATE RELATIONS
—Cont'd
Religious pamphlets in the classroom, p. 1225.
School districts.
Religiously based, pp. 1255 to 1273.

CITIZENSHIP.
Equal protection.
Alien-teachers, pp. 642 to 646.

CIVILITY IN STUDENT CAMPAIGN SPEECHES, pp. 369 to 376.

COHABITATION.
Discharge of teacher.
Due process issue, p. 699.

COLLECTIVE BARGAINING.
Teacher employment relations, pp. 563 to 608.
"Right" to bargain collectively, pp. 563 to 576.
Employee organization use of public forum, pp. 571 to 576.
Illegal delegation of powers argument, pp. 563, 564.
Injunctive relief pursuant to inherent student inconveniences, pp. 564 to 570.
Sovereignty argument, pp. 563, 564.
Statutory protections, pp. 577 to 608.
Challenging the validity of the "Agency shop," pp. 577 to 585.
Fair share fees, pp. 589 to 596.
Use of service fees, pp. 586 to 588.
Principle of exclusivity, pp. 585, 586.
Right to strike, pp. 596 to 604.
Commentary on public employees' right to strike, pp. 604 to 608.

COLLEGES.
Generally.
See UNIVERSITIES AND COLLEGES.

COLONIAL LAWS, pp. 5, 6.

COMMUNIST PARTY AFFILIATION.
Teacher conduct, pp. 755 to 758.

COMPARATIVE NEGLIGENCE, p. 1408.

COMPULSORY EDUCATION, pp. 61 to 87.
Forced public school attendance, pp. 61 to 65.
Home schooling, pp. 65 to 87.
Religious beliefs and conflict, pp. 65 to 87.

CONSTITUTIONAL LAW.
Cruel and unusual punishment.
Paddling students, pp. 527 to 530.
Equal protection.
See EQUAL PROTECTION.
Establishment clause.
Church-state relations generally.
See CHURCH-STATE RELATIONS.
First amendment.
See FIRST AMENDMENT.
Freedom of association.
Racial segregation in private schools, pp. 1337, 1338.
Freedom of religion.
Church-state relations generally.
See CHURCH-STATE RELATIONS.
Freedom of speech.
See FIRST AMENDMENT.
Privacy, right of.
Racial segregation in private schools, pp. 1338, 1339.
Right of universal education, pp. 16, 17.
State constitution education clauses.
Remedying financial disparity among school districts, pp. 1108 to 1182.

CONTRIBUTORY NEGLIGENCE.
Athletic participation and events, pp. 1452 to 1456.
Overview, p. 1408.
Restatement definition, p. 1455.
School bus accidents, pp. 1444 to 1446.
Student conduct.
Chemical from school science lab wrongfully taken and used at home, pp. 1449, 1450.

CORPORAL PUNISHMENT, pp. 526 to 549.

COURSES OF STUDY, pp. 89 to 149.
See CURRICULUM.

CREATION SCIENCE.
Church-state relations, pp. 1225, 1226.

CROSS DRESSING BY STUDENTS, pp. 272 to 275.

CRUEL AND UNUSUAL PUNISHMENT.
Paddling students, pp. 527 to 530.

CULTURAL DIVERSITY.
Teacher employment relations.
Preferential protection against layoffs, pp. 616 to 642.

CURRICULUM, pp. 89 to 149.
Books banned from courses, pp. 116 to 120.
Books banned from libraries, pp. 103 to 116.

CURRICULUM—Cont'd
Church-state relations, pp. 1224 to 1226.
Constitutional limitations, pp. 91 to 121.
Creation science.
　Church-state relations, pp. 1225, 1226.
English only, pp. 91 to 96.
Foreign languages, pp. 91 to 96.
History and social studies textbooks.
　Religious objections, pp. 1243 to 1245.
Home economics textbooks.
　Religious objections, pp. 1241 to 1243.
Parent control, pp. 121 to 136.
Religious classes held off-campus.
　Academic credit, pp. 1236, 1237.
Religious objections, pp. 1237 to 1246.
State prescribed offerings, pp. 89, 90.
Teacher control, pp. 136 to 149.
Theory of evolution, pp. 96 to 103.
Transcendental meditation.
　Church-state relations, pp. 1224, 1225.

D

DAMAGES.
Gender discrimination, pp. 293 to 295.
Punitive damages.
　See PUNITIVE DAMAGES.
Right of universal education.
　Residence requirements.
　　Termination of education for nonresidents, pp. 46, 47.
Student classification by sex, pp. 207 to 214.

DARWINISM.
Curriculum, pp. 96 to 103.

DEFAMATION, pp. 1492 to 1518.
Actual malice.
　Teacher defamation, pp. 1495, 1496, 1505 to 1518.
Defenses.
　Absolute privilege, pp. 1498 to 1505.
School officials, pp. 1492 to 1497.
School yearbook, p. 1497.
Sexual misconduct by teachers, pp. 1498 to 1504.
Student defamation of teacher, p. 1497.
Teacher defamation, in general.
　Proof of "actual malice," pp. 1495, 1496, 1505 to 1518.

DEFENSES.
Assumption of risk, pp. 1457 to 1463, 1468, 1469.
Contributory negligence.
　See CONTRIBUTORY NEGLIGENCE.

DEFENSES—Cont'd
Defamation.
　Absolute privilege, pp. 1498 to 1505.
Negligence, pp. 1444 to 1469.
　Assumption of risk, pp. 1457 to 1463, 1468, 1469.
　Contributory negligence.
　　See CONTRIBUTORY NEGLIGENCE.
　Independent intervening causes.
　　Burn case in science lab, pp. 1451, 1452.
　Overview, p. 1408.
　School bus accidents, pp. 1444 to 1446.
　Sovereign immunity generally.
　　See SOVEREIGN IMMUNITY.

DISABILITY OF TEACHER.
Persons with infectious diseases, pp. 674 to 686.

DISABLED CHILDREN.
Bilingual education.
　Generally, pp. 953 to 976.
　　See BILINGUAL EDUCATION.
Classification by age, pp. 221, 222.
Right to education by homeless children compared, p. 60.
Special education.
　Amercians with Disabilities Act.
　　Impact of Act upon public education, pp. 1082 to 1086.
　Generally, pp. 977 to 1086.
　　See SPECIAL EDUCATION.
　Student ability grouping.
　　IQ tests and E.M.R. placement, pp. 939 to 950.

DISCIPLINING STUDENTS.
Academic sanctions, pp. 550 to 560.
Corporal punishment, pp. 526 to 549.
Expulsion, pp. 510 to 526, 1492.
Suspension, pp. 500 to 510.

DISCRIMINATORY CLASSIFICATIONS.
Racial segregation.
　Generally, pp. 771 to 905.
　　See RACIAL SEGREGATION.
Student classification by race, pp. 222 to 247.
　See STUDENT CLASSIFICATION BY RACE.
Student classification by sex, pp. 153 to 214.
　See STUDENT CLASSIFICATION BY SEX.

DOG SNIFFING SEARCHES, pp. 469 to 477.

DRESS CODE.
Cross dressing, pp. 272 to 275.
Earrings on boys, pp. 265 to 272.
Restrictions on student clothing, pp. 307 to 312.
Sexually suggestive clothing, pp. 332 to 334.

DRILL PRESSES.
Negligence in shop, pp. 1409 to 1420.

DRUG TESTING STUDENTS, pp. 487 to 495.

DUE PROCESS.
Administrative hearing rights, pp. 397 to 425.
Educational malpractice, pp. 19 to 23.
Teacher employment relations.
　Discharge of teacher.
　　Specific conduct involving due process doctrine, p. 699.
　　When due process requires hearing, pp. 687 to 699.

E

EARRINGS.
Student conduct of boys, pp. 265 to 268.

EDUCATIONAL CHOICE, pp. 1363 to 1404.
Government's role in education, pp. 1369 to 1375.
Parental choice, pp. 1389 to 1404.
Public school problems and choice proposals, pp. 1363 to 1388.
Vouchers for education, pp. 1375 to 1378.

EDUCATIONAL MALPRACTICE.
Generally, pp. 17 to 19.
Placement in special education, pp. 19 to 23.
Private schools, p. 23.

EDUCATIONAL VOUCHERS, pp. 1375 to 1378.

EDUCATION FOR HOMELESS CHILDREN AND YOUTH ACT.
Title VI violations, pp. 47 to 54.

EMANCIPATED MINORS.
School attendance, pp. 282 to 285.

ENGLISH.
Curriculum, pp. 91 to 96.

EQUAL ACCESS ACT.
Church-state relations, pp. 1226 to 1228.

EQUAL EDUCATIONAL OPPORTUNITY.
Bilingual education.
　Generally, pp. 953 to 976.
Gifted and talented students.
　Generally, pp. 1086 to 1093.
Poverty as suspect class warranting equal protection, pp. 1096 to 1108.
Racial segregation.
　Generally, pp. 771 to 905.
　See RACIAL SEGREGATION.
Special education.
　Generally, pp. 977 to 1093.
　See SPECIAL EDUCATION.
State constitutional education clauses.
　Remedying financial disparity among districts, pp. 1108 to 1182.
Student ability grouping.
　Generally, pp. 907 to 953.
　See STUDENT ABILITY GROUPING.

EQUAL PROTECTION.
Age discrimination.
　Teacher employment relations, pp. 608 to 616.
Bilingual education.
　Generally, pp. 953 to 976.
　See BILINGUAL EDUCATION.
Citizenship.
　Alien-teachers, pp. 642 to 646.
　Right of universal education, pp. 24 to 36.
Gender discrimination.
　Teacher employment relations, pp. 646 to 668.
Property-poor districts, pp. 1096 to 1108.
State constitutional education clauses, overview, pp. 116 to 118.
Racial discrimination.
　Teacher employment relations, pp. 616 to 642.
　"Business necessity" test, p. 617.
Racial segregation.
　Generally, pp. 771 to 905.
　See RACIAL SEGREGATION.
Right of universal education.
　Citizenship, pp. 24 to 36.
　Residence requirements.
　　Transportation assistance, p. 54.
Sex discrimination.
　Teacher employment relations, pp. 646 to 668.
Special education.
　Generally, pp. 977 to 1086.
　See SPECIAL EDUCATION.

EQUAL PROTECTION—Cont'd
Student ability grouping.
    Generally, pp. 907 to 953.
        See STUDENT ABILITY GROUPING.

ESTABLISHMENT CLAUSE.
Church-state relations generally.
    See CHURCH-STATE RELATIONS.
Special education, pp. 1052 to 1056.

EVOLUTION.
Church-state relations.
    Evolution-science vs. creation science, pp. 1225, 1226.
Curriculum, pp. 96 to 103.

EXCEPTIONAL STUDENTS.
Gifted and talented students, pp. 978, 979, 1086 to 1093.
Special education.
    Generally, pp. 977 to 1086.
        See SPECIAL EDUCATION.

EXCUSAL FROM SCHOOL FOR RELIGIOUS INSTRUCTION, pp. 1228 to 1237.

EXPULSION OF STUDENTS, pp. 510 to 526, 1492.

EXTENDED SCHOOL YEAR PROGRAMS.
Special education, pp. 1016 to 1025.

EXTRA-CURRICULAR ATHLETICS.
Student classification by sex, pp. 187 to 207.

F

FIELD TRIPS.
Financing private schools for public benefit, pp. 1291, 1292.

FINANCING PRIVATE SCHOOLS FOR PUBLIC BENEFIT.
Colleges and universities, pp. 1308 to 1316.
Field trip transportation, pp. 1291, 1292.
Health services, pp. 1297 to 1300.
Income tax deductions, pp. 1325 to 1332.
Income tax relief, pp. 1316 to 1324.
Maintenance grants, pp. 1316 to 1324.
Teacher salaries, pp. 1300 to 1308.
Textbooks, pp. 1284 to 1297.
    Income tax deductions, pp. 1325 to 1332.
Therapeutic services, pp. 1289, 1297 to 1300.
Transportation, pp. 1277 to 1284.
    Field trip transportation, pp. 1291, 1292.

FINANCING PRIVATE SCHOOLS FOR PUBLIC BENEFIT—Cont'd
Transportation—Cont'd
    Income tax deductions, pp. 1325 to 1332.
Tuition deductions.
    Income taxes, pp. 1325 to 1332.
Tuition grants, pp. 1316 to 1324.

FINANCING PUBLIC EDUCATION, pp. 1095 to 1182.
Equal protection issues.
    Property-poor districts, pp. 1096 to 1108.
Historical development, pp. 3, 4.
Property-poor districts.
    Property-poor districts, pp. 1096 to 1108.
State constitutional education clauses.
    Remedying financial disparity among districts, pp. 1108 to 1182.

FIRST AMENDMENT.
Advertisements in school newspapers, pp. 352 to 361.
Articles in school newspapers, pp. 342 to 352.
Books banned from high school courses, pp. 116 to 120.
Books banned from libraries, pp. 103 to 116.
Civility in student campaign speeches, pp. 369 to 376.
Clothing restrictions on students, pp. 307 to 319.
Earrings on boys, pp. 265 to 268.
Elections by students, pp. 334 to 339.
Evolution as a course of study, p. 99.
Flag burning, p. 325.
Future control of curriculum, pp. 136 to 149.
Lewd speeches at student assemblies, pp. 326 to 332.
Pledge of Allegiance recitals, pp. 319 to 325.
Religious viewpoints of students expressed in school, pp. 362 to 369.
Same sex dating by students, pp. 275 to 281.
School mascots, pp. 339 to 342.
Sexually suggestive colthing, pp. 332 to 334.
Teacher conduct.
    Generally, pp. 755 to 768.
Teacher expression.
    Generally, pp. 701 to 755.
Tinker case, pp. 307 to 319.

FLAG BURNING, p. 325.

INDEX

FLAG SALUTE.
Church-state relations. pp. 1246 to 1250.

FOREIGN LANGUAGES.
Curriculum, pp. 91 to 96.

FREE APPROPRIATE PUBLIC EDUCATION.
Special education, pp. 988 to 1002.
  Reimbursement to parents for private school tuition and related expenses, pp. 1070 to 1077.
  What does it mean.
    Intensive physical therapy, pp. 995 to 1001.
    Sign-language interpreter, pp. 988 to 995.

FREEDOM OF ASSOCIATION.
Racial segregation in private schools, pp. 1337, 1338.

FREEDOM OF RELIGION.
Church-state relations generally.
  See CHURCH-STATE RELATIONS.

FREEDOM OF SPEECH.
See FIRST AMENDMENT.

G

GANGS.
Earrings on boys, pp. 265 to 268.
Shootings on property adjacent to school, pp. 1432 to 1437.

GAYS.
Generally.
  See HOMOSEXUALITY.

GIFTED AND TALENTED STUDENTS, pp. 1086 to 1093.
Federal statutory enactments.
  Abolishment, p. 978.
Special education.
  State educational policy, pp. 978, 979, 1086 to 1093.
Student ability grouping.
  Generally, pp. 907 to 953.
  See STUDENT ABILITY GROUPING.

GOVERNMENTAL TORT IMMUNITY.
See TORT IMMUNITY.

GOVERNMENT'S ROLE IN EDUCATION, pp. 1369 to 1375.

GRADUATION CEREMONIES.
Prayer during, pp. 1207 to 1224.

H

HEALTH SERVICES.
Financing private schools for public benefit, pp. 1297 to 1300.

HEARINGS.
Administrative hearing rights, pp. 387 to 431.
Due process, pp. 397 to 431.
Liability of school authorities for failure to provide, pp. 425 to 431.

HIGH SCHOOLS, SINGLE SEX.
Student classifications, pp. 153 to 158.

HISTORICAL DEVELOPMENT, pp. 3 to 14.
Federal government and educational policy, p. 14.
Fiscal structure, pp. 13, 14.
Generally, pp. 3 to 5.
Georgia colonial records, p. 6.
Jefferson, notes on Virginia, pp. 6 to 8.
Jefferson's letter to N. Burwell and K. Padover, pp. 9 to 11.
Massachusetts colonial laws and statutes, pp. 5, 6.
Right of universal education, pp. 15 to 17.
School districts, p. 11.
State education agencies and intermediate units, pp. 12, 13.

HISTORY TEXTBOOKS.
Religious objections, pp. 1243 to 1245.

HOLDIAYS.
Religious holidays.
  Church-state relations, pp. 1235, 1236.

HOME ECONOMICS TEXTBOOKS.
Religious objections, pp. 1241 to 1243.

HOMELESS CHILDREN.
Right of universal education.
  Civil rights violations, pp. 47 to 54.
  Injunctions, pp. 36 to 41.
  Termination of education for nonresidents, pp. 42 to 47.

HOME SCHOOLING, pp. 65 to 87.

HOMOSEXUALITY.
Cross dressing by students, pp. 272 to 275.
Student conduct of extracurricular activities, pp. 275 to 281.
Teacher conduct, p. 759.
  Due process issue, p. 699.

I

IMMUNITY FROM LIABILITY.
Athletic participation and events, pp. 1485, 1486.
Searches and seizures.
   Individualized suspicion, p. 460.
What is a "sovereign," pp. 1486, 1487.

IMMUNITY FROM TORT LIABILITY, pp. 1470 to 1492.
See TORT IMMUNITY.

INCOME TAX DEDUCTIONS.
Financing private schools for public benefit, pp. 1325 to 1332.

INCOME TAX RELIEF.
Financing private schools for public benefit, pp. 1316 to 1324.

INCOMPETENCE OF TEACHER.
Discharge of teacher.
   Due process issue, p. 699.

INDIVIDUALIZED EDUCATION PROGRAM.
Special education, pp. 1003 to 1015.
   Adequacy of IEP.
      Allowance of reimbursement for private instruction, pp. 1008 to 1015.
      Disallowance of reimbursement for private instruction, pp. 1003 to 1007.

INSTRUCTIONAL MATERIALS.
Academic freedom, pp. 765 to 768.

INTEGRATION.
Racial segregation.
   Generally, pp. 771 to 905.
      See RACIAL SEGREGATION.
Student classification by race, pp. 222 to 247.
   See STUDENT CLASSIFICATION BY RACE.

INTENTIONAL ACTS OF FELLOW STUDENTS.
Defenses to negligence actions against school districts, pp. 1447, 1448.
Negligent supervision, pp. 1439 to 1442.

INTENTIONAL BREACH OF DUTY.
Educational liability theories, p. 19.

INTENTIONAL MISREPRESENTATION.
Educational liability theories, pp. 18, 19.

INVASION OF PRIVACY.
Defamation suit by school official, p. 1496.

INVOCATIONS AT GRADUATION CEREMONIES.
Church-state relations, pp. 1207 to 1224.

IQ TESTS.
Student ability grouping, pp. 907 to 953.
   See STUDENT ABILITY GROUPING.

J

JEWELRY.
Earrings on boys, pp. 265 to 268.

L

LEAST RESTRICTIVE ENVIRONMENT.
Special education, pp. 1026 to 1045.

LEMON TEST.
Financing private schools for public benefit, pp. 1300 to 1308.
   Modificaitons or elimination, pp. 1332 to 1334.

LESBIANS.
Generally.
   See HOMOSEXUALITY.

LEWD STUDENT SPEECHES, pp. 326 to 332.

LIBEL AND SLANDER, pp. 1492 to 1518.
See DEFAMATION.

LIBRARIES.
Book banning, pp. 103 to 116.

LOCKER SEARCHES, pp. 463 to 466.

LOYALTY OATHS.
Teacher conduct, p. 759.

M

MAINSTREAMING.
Special education, pp. 1026 to 1045.

MAINTENANCE GRANTS.
Financing private schools for public benefit, pp. 1316 to 1324.

MALPRACTICE.
Educational malpractice.
   See EDUCATIONAL MALPRACTICE.

MARYLAND.
Curriculum.
   Requirements of state and localities, p. 90.

MASCOTS OF SCHOOLS, pp. 339 to 342.

MASSACHUSETTS COLONIAL LAWS AND STATUTES, pp. 5, 6.

MCKINNEY HOMELESS ASSISTANCE ACT.
Title VI violations, pp. 47 to 54.

MEDITATION PERIODS.
Church-state relations, pp. 1191 to 1207.

METAL SHOP.
Negligence, pp. 1409 to 1420.

MINISTRY TRAINING.
Tuition grants, p. 1332.

MINORITY STUDENTS.
Racial segregation.
   Generally, pp. 771 to 905.
   See RACIAL SEGREGATION.
Student classification by race, pp. 222 to 247.
   See STUDENT CLASSIFICATION BY RACE.

MISREPRESENTATION.
Educational liability theories, pp. 18, 19.

MOMENTS OF SILENCE.
Church-state relations, pp. 1191 to 1207.

MORAL MISCONDUCT OF TEACHER.
Discharge of teacher.
   Due process issue, p. 699.

MOTOR VEHICLE SEARCHES, pp. 466 to 469.

MUSLIMS.
Compulsory school attendance on Fridays, p. 84.

N

NEGLIGENCE.
Assumption of risk, pp. 1457 to 1463, 1468, 1469.
Defenses, pp. 1444 to 1469.
   Assumption of risk, pp. 1457 to 1463, 1468, 1469.
   Contributory negligence.
     See CONTRIBUTORY NEGLIGENCE.
   Independent intervening causes, pp. 1444 to 1448.
     Burn case in science lab, pp. 1451, 1452.
Overview, p. 1408.
School bus accidents, pp. 1444 to 1446.
Sovereign immunity generally.
   See SOVEREIGN IMMUNITY.
Educational malpractice.
   See EDUCATIONAL MALPRACTICE.

NEGLIGENCE—Cont'd
Foreseeability.
   Foresight vs. expectation, p. 1430.
   Students with emotional problems, pp. 1437, 1438.
   Suicide, pp. 1423 to 1429.
Gang-related violence.
   Shootings on property adjacent to school, pp. 1432 to 1437.
Intentional acts of a fellow student.
   Defenses to negligence actions against school districts, pp. 1447, 1448.
   Negligent supervision, pp. 1439 to 1442.
Overview, p. 1407.
School bus accidents.
   Defenses, pp. 1444 to 1446.
School counselors.
   Student suicide, pp. 1423 to 1429.
Shop classes, pp. 1409 to 1420.
Sovereign immunity.
   See SOVEREIGN IMMUNITY.
Sport participation and events, pp. 1442 to 1444, 1463 to 1466.
   Assumption of risk, pp. 1457 to 1463, 1468, 1469.
   Contributory negligence, pp. 1452 to 1456.

NEGLIGENT MISREPRESENTATION.
Educational liability theories, pp. 18, 19.

NEW YORK.
Right of universal education.
   Residence requirements.
     State plans and constitution, pp. 55 to 58.

O

OLD DELUDER SATAN ACT, pp. 5, 6.

P

PADDLING STUDENTS, pp. 526 to 549.

PARENTAL CHOICE LEGISLATION.
Private schools, pp. 1389 to 1404.

PAROCHIAL SCHOOLS.
Financing private schools for public benefit, pp. 1251 to 1254.
See PRIVATE SCHOOLS.

PAROCHIAL SCHOOLS—Cont'd
Income tax deductions.
    Financing for public benefit, pp. 1325 to 1332.
Income tax relief, pp. 1316 to 1324.
Maintenance grants, pp. 1316 to 1324.
Private schools generally.
    See PRIVATE SCHOOLS.
Released time for religious instruction, pp. 1228 to 1237.
Tuition grants, pp. 1316 to 1324.

PLAYGROUND CONDITIONS.
Sovereign immunity, pp. 1487 to 1491.
Strict liability, pp. 1420 to 1423.

PLEDGE OF ALLEGIANCE.
Church-state relations, pp. 1246 to 1260.
Reciting by students, pp. 319 to 325.

POLITICALLY CORRECT SPEECH.
Teacher expression, pp. 739 to 755.

POLITICAL PARTY AFFILIATIONS.
Teacher conduct, pp. 755 to 760.

PRAYER AND BIBLE READING, pp. 1185 to 1228.
Graduation ceremonies.
    Invocations and benedictions, pp. 1207 to 1224.

PREFERENTIAL PROTECTION AGAINST LAYOFFS.
Teacher employment relations, pp. 616 to 642.

PRIVACY, INVASION OF.
Defamation suit by school official, p. 1496.

PRIVACY, RIGHT OF.
Racial segregation in private schools, pp. 1338, 1339.

PRIVATE COLLEGES.
Financing, pp. 1308 to 1316.
Tax-exempt status.
    Racially segregated colleges, pp. 1341 to 1349.

PRIVATE RIGHT OF ACTION.
Educational malpractice, pp. 17, 18.
Student classification by sex, pp. 158 to 164.
    Damages, pp. 207 to 214.

PRIVATE SCHOOLS.
Compulsory public school attendance, pp. 61 to 65.
Educational malpractice, p. 23.
Financing for public benefit.
    Health and therapeutic services, pp. 1289, 1297 to 1300.

PRIVATE SCHOOLS—Cont'd
Financing for public benefit—Cont'd
    Income tax deductions, pp. 1325 to 1332.
    Income tax relief, pp. 1316 to 1324.
    Maintenance grants, pp. 1316 to 1324.
    Parochial schools, pp. 1251 to 1254.
    Teacher salaries, pp. 1300 to 1308.
    Textbooks, pp. 1284 to 1297.
    Transportation of students, pp. 1277 to 1284.
        Field trip transportation, pp. 1291, 1292.
    Tuition grants, pp. 1316 to 1324.
Home schooling, pp. 65 to 87.
Parochial schools.
    Financing for public benefit, pp. 1251 to 1254.
Parental choice legislation, pp. 1389 to 1404.
Racial segregation, pp. 1334 to 1363.
Tax-exempt status.
    Racially segregated schools, pp. 1341 to 1363.

PROPERTY-POOR DISTRICTS.
Equal protection, pp. 1096 to 1108.
State constitutional education clauses.
    Remedying financial disparity among districts, pp. 1108 to 1182.

PUBLIC SCHOOLS.
Compulsory attendance, pp. 61 to 65.
Home schooling, pp. 65 to 87.

PUBLIC SECTOR BARGAINING.
Teacher employment relations, pp. 563 to 608.
    "Right" to bargain collectively, pp. 563 to 576.
    Statutory protections, pp. 577 to 608.

PULLMAN ABSTENTION.
Right of universal education.
    Residence requirements.
        Termination of education for nonresidents, pp. 44, 45.

PUNITIVE DAMAGES.
Right of universal education.
    Residence requirements, pp. 46, 47, 59.
Searches and seizures.
    Individualized suspicion, p. 461.
Student classification by sex, p. 215.

INDEX

R

RACIAL DISCRIMINATION.
Teacher employment relations.
  Preferential protection against layoffs, pp. 616 to 642.
    "Business necessity" test, p. 617.

RACIAL QUOTAS.
Student classification by race generally, pp. 222 to 247.
  See STUDENT CLASSIFICATION BY RACE.

RACIAL SEGREGATION, pp. 771 to 905.
Abolishment of "separate but equal" doctrine, pp. 771 to 777.
"Cumulative violation" theory, pp. 818 to 824.
"Fixed mathematical formula" determination, pp. 784 to 797.
"Freedom-of-choice" plan, pp. 777 to 784.
"Free transfer" system, pp. 782, 783.
Inference of "segregative intent," pp. 824 to 852.
Multi-district remedy to single-district problem, pp. 810 to 818.
"Neighborhood school policy" concept, pp. 797 to 803.
Private schools, pp. 1334 to 1363.
Relief from court-ordered school desegregation plans.
  Commentary on court's finished business, pp. 900 to 905.
  Federal district court relinquishment of authority, pp. 868 to 892.
  Standard of proof, pp. 852 to 868.
Separate but equal doctrine.
  Abolishment, pp. 771 to 777.
Student ability grouping.
  Dual school system, pp. 928 to 931.
  Impact of "track system" on racial and economic patterns, pp. 907 to 928.
  IQ tests and E.M.R. placement.
    Culturally-biased test against minority children, pp. 946 to 950.
    Disproportionate placement of minority children, pp. 939 to 946.
  Unitary school system, pp. 931 to 935.

RAPE.
See SEXUAL MISCONDUCT...

RELEASED TIME FOR RELIGIOUS INSTRUCTION, pp. 1228 to 1237.

RELIGION.
Church-state relations.
  See CHURCH-STATE RELATIONS.
Teacher employment relations.
  Hiring and discharge, pp. 668 to 674.

RELIGIOUS HOLIDAYS.
Church-state relations, pp. 1235, 1236.

RELIGIOUS PAMPHLETS IN THE CLASSROOM.
Church-state relations, p. 1225.

RELIGIOUS SECULARISM, p. 1188.

REVERSE DISCRIMINATION.
Student classification by race, p. 241.

RIGHT OF UNIVERSAL EDUCATION, pp. 15 to 61.
Accountability, pp. 17 to 23.
Citizenship, pp. 24 to 36.
Historical development, pp. 15 to 17.
Residence requirements.
  Civil rights violations, pp. 47 to 54.
  Emancipated minors, pp. 282 to 285.
  Injunctions, pp. 36 to 41.
  State plans and constitutions, pp. 55 to 58.
  Termination of education for nonresidents, pp. 42 to 37.

RIGHT TO ADMINISTRATIVE HEARING, pp. 397 to 431.
Due process, pp. 397 to 425.
School authority liability for failure to provide, pp. 425 to 431.

S

SAT.
See SCHOLASTIC APPTITUDE TESTS.

SCHOLARSHIPS.
Student classification by race, pp. 241 to 247.
Student classification by sex, pp. 164 to 177.

SCHOLASTIC APTITUDE TESTS.
Student ability grouping.
  Generally, pp. 907 to 953.
    See STUDENT ABILITY GROUPING.
Student classification by sex, pp. 164 to 177.

SCHOOL BUS ACCIDENTS.
Defenses to negligence, pp. 1444 to 1446.

SCHOOL BUS DRIVERS.
Duty of care, pp. 1430 to 1432.
  Defenses to negligence, pp. 1444 to 1446.

SCHOOL BUSES.
Transportation generally.
  See TRANSPORTATION.

SCHOOL CHOICE.
Compelled public school attendance, pp. 61 to 65.

SCHOOL COUNSELORS.
Negligence.
  Student suicide, pp. 1423 to 1429.

SCHOOL DISTRICTS.
Historical development, p. 11.
Religiously based school districts, pp. 1255 to 1273.

SCHOOL NEWSPAPER ADVERTISEMENTS, pp. 352 to 361.

SCHOOL NEWSPAPER ARTICLES, pp. 342 to 352.

SCHOOL YEARBOOK.
Defamation, p. 1497.

SEARCHES AND SEIZURES, pp. 431 to 495.
Automobile searches, pp. 466 to 469.
Drug testing students, pp. 487 to 495.
Generally, pp. 431 to 442.
Individualized suspicion, pp. 450 to 463.
Locker searches, pp. 463 to 466.
Reasonable suspicion, pp. 442 to 450.
"Sniff searches," pp. 469 to 477.
Strip searches, pp. 477 to 486.

SECULAR HUMANISM.
Religious objections to public school activities, pp. 1237 to 1246.

SEPARATION OF CHURCH AND STATE.
Church-state relations generally.
  See CHURCH-STATE RELATIONS.

SEX DISCRIMINATION.
Equal protection.
  Teacher employment relations, pp. 646 to 668.
Student classification by sex, pp. 153 to 214.
  See STUDENT CLASSIFICATION BY SEX.
Student conduct.
  Ineligibility for high school awards, pp. 287 to 296.

SEXUAL HARASSMENT.
Teacher employment relations, pp. 648 to 662.
Tort liability, p. 1448.

SEXUALLY SUGGESTIVE CLOTHING, pp. 332 to 334.

SEXUAL MISCONDUCT BY FELLOW STUDENTS.
Sovereign immunity, pp. 1479 to 1482.
  Conduct off school premises, pp. 1483 to 1485.
Student conduct, p. 265.

SEXUAL MISCONDUCT BY SCHOOL PERSONNEL, p. 1482.

SEXUAL MISCONDUCT BY TEACHERS.
Defamation, pp. 1498 to 1504.
Discharge of teacher, p. 699.
Sovereign immunity, pp. 1470 to 1479.

SHOOTING STUDENTS ON PROPERTY ADJACENT TO SCHOOL.
Negligence actions, pp. 1432 to 1437.

SHOP CLASSES.
Negligence, pp. 1409 to 1420.

SINGLE SEX HIGH SCHOOLS.
Student classifications, pp. 153 to 158.

SINGLE SEX URBAN MALE ACADEMIES, pp. 177 to 186.

SLANDER AND LIBEL, pp. 1492 to 1518.
See DEFAMATION.

SNIFF SEARCHES, pp. 469 to 477.

SOCIAL STUDIES TEXTBOOKS.
Religious objections, pp. 1243 to 1245.

SOVEREIGN IMMUNITY, pp. 1470 to 1492.
Attack on, pp. 1467, 1468.
Defamation suits, pp. 1498 to 1505.
Educational malpractice, p. 21.
Expulsion of students, p. 1492.
General rule, p. 1466.
Overview, p. 1408.
Playground conditions, pp. 1487 to 1491.
Right of universal education.
  Residency requirements.
    Termination of education for nonresidents, pp. 45, 46.
Sexual misconduct by fellow students, pp. 1479 to 1482.
  Conduct off school premises, pp. 1483 to 1485.
Sexual misconduct by teachers, pp. 1470 to 1479.
Sport participation or events, pp. 1485, 1486.
Theory of sovereignty, p. 1466.
What constitutes a "sovereign," pp. 1486, 1487.

SPECIAL EDUCATION.

Americans with Disabilities Act.
  Impact of Act upon public education, pp. 1082 to 1086.
Bilingual education.
  Generally, pp. 953 to 976.
    See BILINGUAL EDUCATION.
Educational malpractice, pp. 19 to 23.
Eligibility for special education, pp. 979 to 987.
Establishment clause, pp. 1052 to 1056.
Extended school year programs, pp. 1016 to 1025.
Free appropriate public education, pp. 988 to 1002.
  Reimbursement to parents for private school tuition and related expenses, pp. 1070 to 1077.
  What does it mean.
    Intensive physical therapy, pp. 995 to 1001.
    Sign-language interpreter, pp. 988 to 995.
Individualized education program, pp. 1003 to 1015.
  Adequacy of IEP.
    Allowance of reimbursement for private instruction, pp. 1008 to 1015.
    Disallowance of reimbursement for private instruction, pp. 1003 to 1007.
Least restrictive environment, pp. 1026 to 1045.
Mainstreaming, pp. 1026 to 1045.
Paddling students, pp. 543 to 549.
Related services, pp. 1045 to 1052.
  "Medical services" exclusion, pp. 1045 to 1048.
  Two-part test, pp. 1049, 1050.
  Transportation services, pp. 1050 to 1052.
School bus drivers.
  Duty of care, pp. 1431, 1432.
Statutory violation of right to special education.
  Recovery of compensatory and punitive damages, pp. 1077 to 1082.
  Reimbursement of expenditures for private special education, pp. 1070 to 1077.
"Stay-put" provision, pp. 1057 to 1070.
  Dangerous students, pp. 1057 to 1063.
  Lengthy expulsion or suspension of students, pp. 1064 to 1070.

SPECIAL EDUCATION—Cont'd

Student ability grouping.
  IQ tests and E.M.R. placement, pp. 939 to 950.
    See STUDENT ABILITY GROUPING.
Student classification by age, pp. 220, 221.

SPORT PARTICIPATION AND EVENTS.

Assumption of risk, pp. 1457 to 1463, 1468, 1469.
Contributory negligence, pp. 1452 to 1456.
Immunity from liability, pp. 1452 to 1456.
Negligence, pp. 1442 to 1444, 1463 to 1466.
Student classification by age, pp. 215 to 222.
Student classification by sex, pp. 187 to 207.

STANDARDIZED TESTS.

Student ability grouping.
  Generally, pp. 907 to 953.
    See STUDENT ABILITY GROUPING.
Student classification by sex, pp. 164 to 177.

STATE DEPARTMENTS AND AGENCIES.

Curriculum, p. 90.
Historical development, pp. 12, 13.

STAY-PUT PROVISION.

Special education, pp. 1057 to 1070.
  Dangerous students, pp. 1057 to 1063.
  Lengthy expulsion or suspension of students, pp. 1064 to 1070.

STRICT LIABILITY.

Defenses to negligence and strict liability, pp. 1444 to 1469.
Overview, p. 1407.
Playground conditions, pp. 1420 to 1423.

STRIP SEARCHES, pp. 477 to 486.

STUDENT ABILITY GROUPING, pp. 907 to 953.

Bilingual education.
  Generally, pp. 953 to 976.
    See BILINGUAL EDUCATION.
Dual school system, pp. 928 to 931.
Impact of "tract system" on racial and economic patterns, pp. 907 to 928.

STUDENT ABILITY GROUPING —Cont'd
IQ tests and E.M.R. placement, pp. 939 to 950.
   Culturally-biased test against minority children, pp. 946 to 950.
   Disproportionate placement of minority children, pp. 939 to 946.
Unitary school system, pp. 931 to 935.

STUDENT ATHLETICS.
See SPORT PARTICIPATION AND EVENTS.

STUDENT CLASSIFICATION BY AGE, pp. 215 to 222.

STUDENT CLASSIFICATION BY RACE, pp. 222 to 247.
Admissions, pp. 222 to 241.
Scholarships, pp. 241 to 247.

STUDENT CLASSIFICATION BY SEX, pp. 153 to 215.
Academic opportunities, pp. 153 to 186.
Athletics, pp. 187 to 207.
At-risk urban male schools only, pp. 177 to 186.
Graduate school admissions, pp. 158 to 164.
Remedies, pp. 207 to 215.
Single sex high schools, pp. 153 to 158.
Standardized tests, pp. 164 to 177.

STUDENT CONDUCT.
Academic sanctions, pp. 550 to 560.
Administrative hearing right, pp. 397 to 431.
   Due process, pp. 397 to 425.
   School authority liability for failure to provide, pp. 425 to 431.
Contributory negligence.
   Chemical from school science lab wrongfully taken and used at home, pp. 1449, 1450.
Corporal punishment, pp. 526 to 549.
Cross dressing, pp. 272 to 275.
Disciplinary hearing procedures, pp. 297, 298.
Earrings on boys, pp. 265 to 268.
Emancipated minors, pp. 282 to 285.
High school award eligibility, pp. 287 to 296.
Reasonableness of school rules.
   Student conduct.
      Judicial review of school regulations, pp. 253 to 255.
Relationship between offense and punishment, pp. 256 to 261.
Rule vagueness, pp. 381 to 397.
Same sex dating, pp. 275 to 281.

STUDENT CONDUCT—Cont'd
Searches and seizures, pp. 431 to 495.
   Automobile searches, pp. 466 to 469.
   Drug testing students, pp. 487 to 495.
   Generally, pp. 431 to 442.
   Individualized suspicion, pp. 450 to 463.
   Locker searches, pp. 463 to 466.
   Reasonable suspicion, pp. 442 to 450.
   "Sniff searches," pp. 469 to 477.
   Strip searches, pp. 477 to 486.
State actors, pp. 298, 299.
Texas expulsion standard, p. 298.
Weapons possession, pp. 300 to 305.

STUDENT DEFAMATION OF TEACHER, p. 1497.

STUDENT DISCIPLINE.
Academic sanctions, pp. 550 to 560.
Corporal punishment, pp. 526 to 549.
Expulsion, pp. 510 to 526, 1492.
Suspension of students, pp. 500 to 510.

STUDENT DRUG TESTING, pp. 487 to 495.

STUDENT ELECTIONS, pp. 334 to 339.

STUDENT EXPRESSION, pp. 307 to 380.
Advertisements in school newspapers, pp. 352 to 361.
Articles in school newspapers, pp. 342 to 352.
Civility in campaign speeches, pp. 369 to 376.
Elections by students, pp. 334 to 339.
Lewd speeches and assemblies, pp. 326 to 332.
Reciting the Pledge of Allegiance, pp. 319 to 326.
Religious viewpoints, pp. 362 to 369.
Restrictions generally, pp. 376 to 380.
School mascots, pp. 339 to 342.
Sexually suggestive clothing, pp. 332 to 334.
Tinker case, pp. 307 to 319.

STUDENT EXPULSION, pp. 510 to 526, 1492.

STUDENT SEXUAL MOLESTATION BY OTHER STUDENTS.
Sovereign immunity, pp. 1479 to 1482.
   Conduct off school premises, pp. 1483 to 1485.

STUDENT SEXUAL MOLESTATION BY SCHOOL PERSONNEL, p. 1482.

STUDENT SEXUAL MOLESTATION BY TEACHERS.
Defamation, pp. 1498 to 1504.
Discharge of teacher, p. 699.
Sovereign immunity, pp. 1470 to 1479.

STUDENT SPORTS.
See SPORT PARTICIPATION AND EVENTS.

STUDENT SUICIDE.
Negligence of school counselors, pp. 1423 to 1429.

STUDENT SUSPENSION, pp. 500 to 510.

STUDENTS WITH EMOTIONAL PROBLEMS.
Suicide, pp. 1423 to 1429.
Wrongful death actions, pp. 1437, 1438.

STUDENT TRANSPORTATION.
See TRANSPORATION.

SUSPENSION OF STUDENTS, pp. 500 to 510.

T

TALENTED STUDENTS.
Generally, pp. 1086 to 1093.
See GIFTED AND TALENTED STUDENTS.

TAX-EXEMPT STATUS.
Private schools.
Racially segregated schools, pp. 1341 to 1363.

TEACHER CONDUCT, pp. 755 to 768.
Communist party affiliation, pp. 755 to 758.
Inside the classroom, pp. 764 to 768.
Instructional materials, pp. 765 to 768.
Loyalty oaths, p. 759.
Outside the school, pp. 755 to 764.
Political party affiliations, pp. 755 to 760.

TEACHER DEFAMATION BY STUDENT, p. 1497.
Proof of "actual malice," pp. 1495, 1496, 1505 to 1518.

TEACHER EMPLOYMENT RELATIONS.
Age.
Hiring and discharge, pp. 608 to 616.
Citizenship.
Hiring and discharge, pp. 642 to 646.

TEACHER EMPLOYMENT RELATIONS—Cont'd
Collective bargaining, pp. 563 to 608.
"Right" to bargain collectively, pp. 563 to 576.
Employee organization use of public forum, pp. 571 to 576.
Illegal delegation of powers argument, pp. 563, 564.
Injunctive relief pursuant to inherent student inconveniences, pp. 564 to 570.
Sovereignty argument, pp. 563, 564.
Statutory protections, pp. 577 to 608.
Challenging the validity of the "Agency shop," pp. 577 to 585.
Fair share fees, pp. 589 to 596.
Use of service fees, pp. 586 to 588.
Principle of exclusivity, pp. 585, 586.
Right to strike, pp. 596 to 604.
Commentary on public employees' right to strike, pp. 604 to 608.
Disability.
Hiring and discharge, pp. 674 to 686.
Persons with infectious diseases, pp. 674 to 686.
Discharge of teacher.
Due process issue, p. 699.
Teacher conduct, pp. 755 to 768.
Teacher expression, pp. 701 to 755.
Due process.
Discharge of teacher.
Specific conduct involving due process doctrine, p. 699.
When due process requires hearing, pp. 687 to 699.
Gender.
Hiring and discharge, pp. 646 to 668.
Race.
Hiring and discharge, pp. 616 to 642.
Religion.
Hiring and discharge, pp. 668 to 674.
Sexual harassment, pp. 648 to 662.
Teacher conduct.
School control over teacher conduct, pp. 755 to 768.
Teacher expression.
School control over teacher expression, pp. 701 to 755.
Teacher salaries, pp. 1300 to 1308.
Unmarried pregnant teachers, p. 286.

TEACHER EXPRESSION, pp. 701 to 755.
Dress codes and appearance standards, pp. 714, 715.
Employee questionnarie, pp. 716 to 722.

TEACHER EXPRESSION—Cont'd
Letter to local newspaper, pp. 701 to 709.
"Politically correct" speech, pp. 739 to 755.
Repeating defamatory rumors, pp. 727 to 733.
Telephone call to radio station, pp. 709 to 714.
Vulgarity or sexual explicitness in the classroom, pp. 738, 739.

TEACHER SALARIES.
Financing public schools for public benefit, pp. 1300 to 1308.

TEACHERS WITH INFECTIOUS DISEASES.
Americans with Disabilities Act.
    Employment discrimination, pp. 674 to 686.

TEXAS.
Student expulsions, p. 298.

TEXTBOOKS.
Curriculum generally.
    See CURRICULUM.
Financing private schools for public benefit, pp. 1284 to 1297.
    Income tax deductions, pp. 1325 to 1332.
Religious objections, pp. 1237 to 1246.

THERAPEUTIC SERVICES.
Financing private schools for public benefit, pp. 1289, 1297 to 1300.

TINKER CASE, pp. 307 to 319.

TORT ACTIONS, pp. 1407 to 1469.
Defamation, pp. 1492 to 1518.
    See DEFAMATION.
Educational malpractice.
    See EDUCATIONAL MALPRACTICE.
Negligence.
    See NEGLIGENCE.
Strict liability.
    See STRICT LIABILITY.

TORT IMMUNITY, pp. 1470 to 1492.
Athletic participation and events, pp. 1485, 1486.
Defamation suits, pp. 1498 to 1505.
Expulsion of students, p. 1492.
Playground conditions, pp. 1487 to 1491.
Sexual misconduct by fellow students, pp. 1479 to 1482.
    Conduct off school premises, pp. 1483 to 1485.
Sexual misconduct by teachers, pp. 1470 to 1479.

TORT IMMUNITY—Cont'd
Sovereign immunity.
    Attack on, pp. 1467, 1468.
    General rule, p. 1466.
    Theory of sovereignty, p. 1466.
What constitutes a "sovereign," pp. 1486, 1487.

TRACK SYSTEM.
Student ability grouping.
    Generally, pp. 907 to 953.
    See STUDENT ABILITY GROUPING.

TRANSPORTATION.
Financing private schools for public benefit, pp. 1277 to 1284.
    Field trip transportation, pp. 1291, 1292.
    Income tax deductions, pp. 1325 to 1332.
School bus drivers' duty of care, pp. 1430, 1431.
    Special education children, pp. 1431, 1432.

TUITION DEDUCTIONS.
Financing private schools for public benefit.
    Income taxes, pp. 1325 to 1332.

TUITION GRANTS.
Financing private schools for public benefit, pp. 1316 to 1324.
Ministry training, p. 1332.

U

UNITED STATES.
Financing public education.
    Historical development, pp. 13, 14.
Historical development of educational policy, p. 14.

UNIVERSITIES AND COLLEGES.
Admissions.
    Student classification by race, pp. 222 to 241.
Educational malpractice, p. 18.
Financing church-related institutions, pp. 1308 to 1316.
Law enforcement.
    On-campus investigations and interrogations, pp. 299, 300.
Rule vagueness, pp. 381 to 392.
Scholarships.
    Student classification by race, pp. 241 to 247.

UNIVERSITIES AND COLLEGES
—Cont'd

Student classification by sex.
   Graduate school admissions, pp. 158 to 164.

Tax-exempt status of private colleges.
   When racially segregated, pp. 1341 to 1349.

V

VOUCHERS FOR EDUCATION, pp. 1375 to 1378.

W

WEAPONS.
Student possession on campus, pp. 300 to 305.

WOOD SHOP.
Negligence, pp. 1409 to 1420.

Y

YEARBOOK.
Defamation of teacher, p. 1497.